Educators
Resource
Directory

2015/16
Eleventh Edition

Educators
Resource
Directory

- Associations & Organizations
- Professional Development
- Consultants
- Financial Resources
- Conferences & Trade Shows
- Opportunities Abroad
- National & State Statistics

ELMHURST COLLEGE LIBRARY

A SEDGWICK PRESS Book

Grey House Publishing

PUBLISHER: Leslie Mackenzie
EDITOR: Richard Gottlieb
EDITORIAL DIRECTOR: Laura Mars

PRODUCTION MANAGER: Kristen Thatcher
MARKETING DIRECTOR: Jessica Moody

Grey House Publishing, Inc.
4919 Route 22
Amenia, NY 12501
518.789.8700
FAX 518.789.0545
www.greyhouse.com
e-mail: books@greyhouse.com

First edition published 1994
Eleventh edition published 2015
Printed in Canada

ISBN: 978-1-61925-549-4 softcover
ISSN: 1549-7224

Table of Contents

Introduction

This eleventh edition of *Educators Resource Directory* is a comprehensive resource designed to provide educators, administrators, and other education professionals access to a unique combination of educational resources and educational statistics and rankings.

Listings in *Educators Resource Directory* include associations, publications, trade shows, workshops and training programs designed not only to help educators advance professionally, but also to give them the resources they need to help their students, their schools, and their state meet educational standards. It provides tools for classroom and career management, and resources that truly make a difference in job, school, and student performance.

Listings in this comprehensive volume are thoughtfully organized in 13 chapters and 76 subchapters, making information significantly easier to access than the unfocused data available online or the scattered in dozens of different sources. Statistics and rankings are designed to help states, school districts, and individual educators better understand their educational environment, crucial to making informed decisions on careers, curriculum and funding.

Praise for previous edition:

"... an important reference source overflowing with information educators may use for their own improvement or as an aid for winning a ... Race to the Top grant. ... The glossary is handy and the indexes are accurate. All school, public and academic libraries need an up to date education directory ... and this is a worthy choice."

American Reference Books Annual

"... This handy tool, appropriate for larger public and academic libraries as well as school districts, will be highly valuable to those writing education grants ... "

Library Journal

SECTION ONE: RESOURCES

Educators Resource Directory includes 6,408 listings in **Section One.** All records have been reviewed for currency, and we have added more than 140 NEW listings. This section includes 7,956 key contact names, 4,506 fax numbers, 3,718 e-mail addresses, and 5,199 web sites, and is categorized as follows, for easy research:

Associations & Organizations disseminate information, host seminars, provide educational literature and promote study councils. This chapter organizes associations into 16 distinct categories from *Administration* to *Technology.*

The chapter on **Conferences & Trade Shows** lists everything from large conventions of classroom resources and equipment suppliers to small, specialized conferences that target rural education and specific teaching challenges. Events are listed regionally.

Consultants give information on educational consulting services, including curriculum-building guidance, school district organizations, and facility format.

Teaching Opportunities Abroad include not only U.S. government schools, but also American schools overseas. The chapter is organized geographically by region, and provides contact information, grade level and enrollment numbers.

Details on 626 grants, foundations and scholarships can be found in **Financial Resources**. Learn how to obtain funds for individual professional advancement, schools, programs, students, and education districts and communities.

The **Professional Development** listings include *Associations, Awards, Conferences* and *Training Materials.*

Publications list directories, magazines and journals, divided into 16 subjects. Find where to publish research findings, which testing materials best suit your needs, how to incorporate technology into your classroom, and where to find innovative classroom supplies.

Publishers include educational publishers of textbooks, testing resources and specific curriculums.

Research results on general learning and training issues, and data on specific subjects, like *Gifted & Talented, Educational Media* and *Scientific Learning*, is easy to find from the **Research Centers** profiled in this edition.

The chapter on **School Supplies** focuses on the latest in *Classroom Technology, Scientific Equipment, Furniture* and *Sports & Playground Equipment*.

Software, Hardware & Internet Resources include 16 subchapters from *Administration* to *Technology in Education* that provide easy access to everything from educational computer programs to web sites with information on classroom resources for every level and subject.

Testing Resources include resources for written materials and web sites in six categories: *Elementary Education, Language Arts, Mathematics, Music & Art, Reading* and *Secondary Education.*

SECTION TWO: STATISTICS, RANKINGS & GLOSSARY

Section Two includes 236 tables and charts in 24 total categories. From elementary to post-secondary levels, these statistics and rankings include data not only on the American educational system, but also on Canadian and international education.

The main categories are *Educational Attainment *Elementary & Secondary Education *Federal Programs *International Comparisons *Libraries & Educational Technology *Opinions on Education *Outcomes of Education *Post-secondary Education *Canadian Education. Specific topics include degrees, enrollment, completions, dropouts, faculty, revenues, expenditures, and student behavior. Many tables offer state-by-state rankings.

Using the most current data available, this section helps to complete the picture for educators making career development decisions, for school administrators interested in comparing fiscal health and educational scores, and for anyone doing educational research.

Following the statistics and rankings is a **Glossary** with over 100 education terms from Accountability to Vocational.

SECTION THREE: INDEXES

Entry & Publisher Name Index – alphabetical list of both entry names and the companies that publish the listed material. Publishers and parent organizations are boldfaced.

Geographic Index – state-by-state listing of all entries.

Subject Index – organized by core subjects plus Special Education and Technology.

Educators Resource Directory 2015/16 is also available for subscription via Grey House OnLine Database. Subscribers can do customized searches that instantly locate needed information. Visit http://gold.greyhouse.com or call 800-562-2139 to set up a free trial.

General

ASPIRA Association
1444 I Street NW
Suite 800
Washington, DC 20005-6543
202-835-3600
Fax: 202-835-3613
E-mail: info@aspira.org
http://www.aspira.org
Founded in 1961 the ASPIRA Association promotes the empowerment of the Puerto Rican and Latino community by developing and nurturing the leadership, intellectual, and cultural potential of its youth so that they may contribute their skills and dedication to the fullest development of the Puerto Rican and Latino community everywhere.
Founded: 1961

Ronald Blackburn-Moreno, President/CEO
John Villamil-Casanova, EVP & CIO

2 Advance Program for Young Scholars
ADVANCE Program
NSU Box 5671
Natchitoches, LA 71497
318-357-4500
Fax: 318-357-4547
E-mail: palmerh@nsula.edu
http://advance.nsula.edu
From chemistry to history, from foreign languages to ecology, the program offers a broad spectrum of academic opportunities to the qualified 12-17 year old student.

David Wood PhD, Director
Harriette Palmer, Assistant Director

3 Alliance for Parental Involvement in Education
PO Box 59
East Chatham, NY 12060-59
518-392-6900
E-mail: info@allpie.org
http://www.allpie.org
Seeks to nurture parents' natural teaching abilities and offer tools and resources, public, private and home in becoming active participants in the education of their children.

Katharine Houk, Executive Director

4 American Academy of Pediatrics
141 NW Point Boulevard
Elk Grove Village, IL 60007-1098
847-434-4000
800-433-9016
Fax: 847-434-8000
E-mail: kidsdoc@aap.org
http://www.aap.org
Committed to the attainment of optimal physical, mental and social health for all infants, children, adolescents and young adults.

James M. Perrin, MD, FAAP, President
Errol R Alden, MD, FAAP, Executive Director

5 American Association for Vocational Instructional Materials (AAVIM)
220 Smithonia Road
Winterville, GA 30683-1418
706-742-5355
800-228-4689
Fax: 706-742-7005
E-mail: sales@aavim.com
http://www.aavim.com

Develops, produces and distributes quality instructional materials for career education instructors, students, and administrators.
Founded: 1949

Gary Farmer, Director
Vicki J Eaton, Art Director/Production Coor

6 American Council for Drug Education
50 Jay Street
Brooklyn, NY 11201
718-222-6641
888-671-9392
Fax: 212-595-2553
E-mail: bgillam@phoenixhouse.org
http://www.phoenixhouse.org
Distributes packaged information about drugs and the consequences of their use and identifies effective community programs to address the drug problem in the country.
Founded: 1977

William F Current, Executive Director

7 American Council of Trustees and Alumni
1726 M Street NW
Suite 802
Washington, DC 20036
202-467-6787
E-mail: info@goacta.org
http://www.goacta.org
An independent, non-profit organization committed to academic freedom, excellence, and accountability at America's colleges and universities. Works with alumni, donors, trustees, and education leaders across the United States to support liberal arts education, uphold high academic standards, safeguard the free exchange of ideas on campus, and ensure that the next generation receives a philosophically rich, high-quality college education at an affordable price.
Founded: 1995

8 American Council on Education (ACE)
1 Dupont Circle NW
Washington, DC 20036
202-939-9300
Fax: 202-833-4730
E-mail: comments@ace.nche.edu
http://www.acenet.edu
Represents accredited degree-granting colleges and universities directly and through national and regional higher education associations. Seeks to advance education and serves as an advocate for adult education.

James H. Mullen Jr., Chair
Renu Khator, Vice Chair / Chair-elect

9 American Council on Rural Special Education (ACRES)
West Virginia University
509 Allen Hall
PO Box 6122
Morgantown, WV 26506-6122
304-293-3450
888-866-3822
E-mail: acres-sped@mail.wvu.edu
http://acres-sped.org
The organization is comprised of special educators, general educators, related service providers, administrators, teacher trainers, researchers, and parents committed to the enhancement of services to students and individuals living in rural America.
Founded: 1981

Robert Pennington, Chair
Ginevra Courtade, Chair Elect

10 American Driver and Traffic Safety Education Association (ADTSEA)
Highway Safety Services
1434 Trim Tree Road
Indiana, PA 15701
724-801-8246
877-485-7172
Fax: 724-349-5042
E-mail: office@adtsea.org
http://www.adtsea.org
The purpose of the American Driver and Traffic Safety Education Association is to promote quality traffic safety education by publishing policies and guidelines. ADTSEA conducts conferences, workshops, seminars and consultative services and educational materials.

Cathy Broderick, President
Brett Robinson, Executive Director

11 American Federation of Teachers
555 New Jersey Avenue NW
Washington, DC 20001
202-879-4400
Fax: 202-879-4556
E-mail: online@aft.org
http://www.aft.org
The AFT is a union of professionals that champions fairness, democracy, economic opportunity and high quality public education, healthcare and public services for our students, their families and our communities. The AFT is committed to advancing these principles through the work that their members do.
Founded: 1916

Randi Weingarten, President
Lorreta Johnson, Secretary/ Treasurer

12 American Montessori Society
116 East 16th Street
New York, NY 10003
212-358-1250
Fax: 212-358-1256
E-mail: ams@amshq.org
http://www.amshq.org
Provides the leadership and inspiration to make Montessori a significant voice in education.ÿ The Society advocates quality Montessori education, strengthens members through its services, and champions Montessori principles to the greater community.
Founded: 1960

Joyce S. Pickering, President
Dane L. Peters, Vice President

13 American School Health Association
7918 Jones Branch Drive
Suite 300
McLean, VA 22102
703-506-7675
Fax: 703-506-3266
E-mail: info@ashaweb.org
http://www.ashaweb.org
A nonprofit organization founded to protect and improve the health and well-being of children and youth by supporting comprehensive, preschool-12 school health programs.

Linda Morse, RN, MA, CHES, President
Holly Hunt, MA, President-Elect

14 American Society for Engineering Education
1818 N Street NW
Suite 600
Washington, DC 20036-2479
202-331-3500
Fax: 202-265-8504
E-mail: aseeexec@asee.org
http://www.asee.org

1

A nonprofit organization of individuals and institutions committed to furthering education in engineering and engineering technology.

Founded: 1893

Norman Fortenberry, Executive Director
Keith Mounts, Chief Information Officer

15   Association For Childhood Education International
1101 16th St NW
Suite 300
Washington, DC 20036
202-372-9986
800-423-3563
Fax: 202-372-9989
http://www.acei.org
To promote and support in the global community the optimal education, development, and well-being of children, from birth through early adolescence, and to influence the professional growth of educators and the efforts of others who are committed to the needs of children in a changing society.

Debora Wisneski, President

16   Association Montessori International
526 King St
Ste. 203
Alexandria, VA 22314
703-746-9919
800-872-2643
E-mail: montessori@amiusa.org
http://amiusa.org
AMI/USA represents the Association Montessori International in the United States, bringing the principles of Dr. Montessori to the education of children. Founded in 1929, AMI maintains the integrity of Dr. Montessori's approach and life's work.

Founded: 1929

Bonnie Beste, Executive Director

17   Association for Business Communication (ABC)
Virginia Tech
181 Turner St., NW
Blacksburg, VA 24061
540-231-8460
E-mail: abcoffice@businesscommunication.org
http://www.businesscommunication.org
Committed to fostering excellence in business communication scholarship, research, education, and practice.

Founded: 1936

Dr. Jim Dubinsky, Executive Director
Marilyn Buerkens, Office Manager

18   Association for Community-Based Education
1806 Vernon Street NW
Washington, DC 20009-1217
202-462-6333
Offers technical assistance on planning, management and program development for community-based education. Further education through discussion groups, forums, panel lectures, as well, study and research.

Christofer Zachariadis, Executive Director

19   Association for Disabled Students
University of Oklahoma
Disability Resource Center
620 Elm Avenue, Suite 166
Norman, OK 73019-2093

405-325-3852
Fax: 405-325-4491
E-mail: drc@ou.edu
http://www.ou.edu/drc/home.html
Also known as ADS, this student organization provides a forum for support, regular meetings, and social and recreational activities. ADS sponsors Disability Awareness Week each October and Disability Arts Week the first week of April. ADS also sponsors a wheelchair basketball team, affiliated with the Intercollegiate Wheelchair Division of the National Wheelchair Basketball Association. The team competes nationally.

Chelle' Guttery, Ph.D., Director

20   Association for Environmental and Outdoor Education (AEOE)
15555 Sanborn Rd
Saratoga, CA 90507
714-838-8990
714-474-1377
E-mail: helen@aeoe.org
http://www.aeoe.org
The Association for Environmental and Outdoor Education supports and inspires educators in their quest for the knowledge, skills, and attitudes essential to help all learners understand, appreciate and care for their environment.

Founded: 1954

Reed Schneider, President
Helen M De La Maza, Membership Coordinator

21   Association for Gender Equity Leadership in Education
317 S. Division St., PM #54
Ann Arbor, MI 48104
734-769-2456
Fax: 734-769-2456
E-mail: businessmgr@agele.org
http://www.agele.org
A national organization for gender equity specialists and educators. Individuals and organizations committed to reducing sex role stereotyping for females and males. Services include an annual national training conference, a quarterly newsletter and a membership directory. Members may join task forces dealing with equity related topics such as computer/technology issues, early childhood, male issues, sexual harassment prevention, sexual orientation and vocational issues.

Marta Larson, Business Manager
Keith Eccarius, Communications Manager

22   Association for Integrative Studies
School of Interdisciplinary Studies
Miami University
501 E. High Street
Oxford, OH 45056-3653
513-529-2213
Fax: 513-529-5849
E-mail: aisorg@miamioh.edu
http://www.units.muohio.edu/aisorg
The Association for Integrative Studies is an interdisciplinary professional organization founded in 1979 to promote the interchange of ideas among scholars and administrators in all of the arts and sciences on intellectual and organizational issues related to furthering integrative studies. Incorporated as a non-profit educational association in the State of Ohio, it has an international membership.

Founded: 1979

Bill Newell, Executive Director
Rick Szostak, President

23   Association for Middle Level Education
4151 Executive Parkway
Suite 300
Westerville, OH 43081
614-895-4730
800-528-6672
Fax: 614-895-4750
E-mail: info@amle.org
http://www.amle.org
AMLE has been a voice for those committed to the educational and developmental needs of young adolescents. AMLE is the only national education association dedicated exclusively to those in middle level grades.

Ashley Smith, Jr., President
Kathleen McCaffrey, President-Elect

24   Association for Play Therapy
3198 Willow Avenue
Suite 110
Clovis, CA 93612
559-294-2128
Fax: 559-294-2129
E-mail: info@a4pt.org
http://www.a4pt.org
Founded in 1982 APT promotes the value of play, play therapy and credentialed play therapists by advancing the psychosocial development and mental health of all people and sponsoring and supporting those programs, services and related activities that promote public understanding of play therapy.

Founded: 1982

Kathryn Lebby, President/ CEO
Jodi Crane, Secretary of the Board

25   Association for Supervision & Curriculum Development (ASCD)
1703 N Beauregard Street
Alexandria, VA 22311-1714
703-578-9600
800-933-2723
Fax: 703-575-5400
E-mail: member@ascd.org
http://www.ascd.org
A membership organization that develops programs, products, and services essential to the way educators learn, teach, and lead.

Founded: 1943

Nancy Gibson, President
Judy Seltz, Executive Director

26   Association of American Educators
27405 Puerta Real
Suite 230
Mission Viejo, CA 92691
949-595-7979
800-704-7799
Fax: 949-595-7970
http://www.aaeteachers.org
Provides professional benefits and services to educators, including liability insurance, scholarships and grants, and professional resources.

Gary Beckner, Executive Director

27   Association of Boarding Schools
1 North Pack Square
Suite 301
Asheville, NC 28801
828-258-5354
Fax: 828-258-6428
E-mail: tabs@schools.com
http://www.schools.com
A marketing consortium founded in 1975 of 300 boarding schools that seeks to increase the applicant pool of member schools by increasing public awareness of benefits and advantages of boarding school education. TABS is a resource for educators seeking training, research, guidance and sup-

port on all issues pertaining to the residential school experience.

Founded: 1975

Steve Banks, Director of Operations
Peter Upham, Executive Director

28 Association of Mathematics Teacher Educators
c/o Meredith College
3800 Hillsborough Street
Raleigh, NC 27607
919-760-8240
Fax: 919-760-8763
E-mail: arbaugh@psu.edu
http://amte.net
AMTE is the largest professional organization devoted to the improvement of mathematics teacher education - it includes over 1,000 members supporting the preservice education and professional development of K-12 teachers of mathematics.

Founded: 1991

Fran Arbaugh, President
Dr. Timothy M. Hendrix, Executive Director

29 Association of State Supervisors of Mathematics
E-mail: diana.suddreth@schools.utah.gov
http://www.assm.us
The Association of State Supervisors of Mathematics is an organization whose members provide supervising and/or consulting services in the area of mathematics as a staff member of the education agency of any state in the United States of America, the District of Columbia, possessions of the United States of America, territory of the United States, US Department of Defense, Canadian Province, or Bermuda.

Diana Suddreth, President
Robin Hill, Vice President for Program

30 Association of Teacher Educators
PO Box 793
Manassas, VA 20113
703-659-1708
Fax: 703-595-4792
E-mail: info@ate1.org
http://www.ate1.org
The mission of the Association of Teacher Educators is to improve the effectiveness of teacher education through leadership in the development of quality programs to prepare teachers, by analyzing issues and practices relating to professional development, and by providing opportunities for the personal and professional growth of Association members.

Founded: 1920

Linda Houser, President-Elect
Emma Savage-Davis, President

31 Attention Deficit Disorder Association
PO Box 103
Denver, PA 17517
800-939-1019
Fax: 800-939-1019
E-mail: info@add.org
http://www.add.org
ADDA, provides information, resources and networking opportunities to help adults with Attention Deficit/Hyperactivity Disorder (AD/HD) lead better lives.

Evelyn Polk Green, MS.Ed, President
Linda Roggli, PCC, VP

32 Awards and Recognition Association
4700 W Lake Avenue
Glenview, IL 60025
847-375-4800
800-344-2148
Fax: 888-374-7257
E-mail: info@ara.org
http://www.ara.org
The purpose of ARA is to advance the capabilities and growth of businesses whose primary focus is the manufacture, distribution or sales of awards and recognition goods and services. ARA is the essential component for success in the awards and recognition business.

B J Bailey Jr, President
Guy Barone, President-Elect

33 Better Chance
240 W 35th Street
Floor 6
New York, NY 10001-2506
646-346-1310
800-562-7865
Fax: 646-346-1311
http://www.abetterchance.org
Our mission is to substantially increase the number of well-educated young people of color who are capable of assuming positions of responsibility and leadership in American society.

Founded: 1963

Sandra E Timmons, President
Chantal Stevens, National Director

34 CHADD: Children & Adults with Attention Deficit/Hyperactivity Disorder
4601 Presidents Drive
Suite 300
Lanham, MD 20706
301-306-7070
800-233-4050
Fax: 301-306-7090
E-mail: help@chadd.org
http://www.chadd.org
National nonprofit organization which offers advocacy, information and support for patients and parents of children with attention deficit disorders. Maintains support groups, provides a forum for continuing education about ADHD, and maintains a national resource center for information about ADD.

April Gower, Chief Operating Officer
Michael MacKay, President

35 Cable in the Classroom
25 Massachusetts Avenue NW
Suite 100
Washington, DC 20001
202-222-2300
Fax: 202-222-2336
E-mail: webmaster@ncta.com
http://www.ciconline.org
Promotes visionary, sensible, responsible and effective use of cable's broadband technology and services and content in learning and teaching. Represents the cable industry's commitment to education by showcasing a variety if cable initiatives in education.

Frank Gallagher, Executive Director
Helen Dimsdale, Deputy Executive Director

36 Center for Civic Education
5115 Douglas Fir Road
Suite J
Calabasas, CA 91302
818-591-9321
800-350-4223
Fax: 818-591-9330
E-mail: cce@civiced.org
http://www.civiced.org
Non-profit, nonpartisan educational corporation dedicated to fostering the development

of informed, responsible participation in civic life by citizens committed to values and principles fundamental to American constitutional democracy.

Charles N. Quigley, Executive Director
Margaret Stimmann Branson, Associate Director

37 Center for Lifelong Learning
American Council on Education
One Dupont Circle NW
Washington, DC 20036-1193
202-939-9300
E-mail: lifelong_learning@acenet.edu
http://www.acenet.edu
ACE's Center for Lifelong Learning (CLLL) has led the national movement to recognize and promote adult learner programs in higher education.

James H. Mullen Jr., Chair
Renu Khator, Vice Chair/ Chair-elect

38 Center for Parent Information and Resources
c/o Statewide Parent Advocacy Netwo
35 Halsey St., Fourth Floor
Newark, NJ 07102
202-884-8200
800-695-0285
Fax: 202-884-8441
E-mail: malizo@spannj.org
http://www.parentcenterhub.org
The center that provides information to the nation on disabilities in children and youth; programs and services for infants, children, and youth with disabilities; IDEA, the nation's special education law; No Child Left Behind, the nation's general education law; and research-based information on effective practices for children with disabilities.

Lisa K☐pper, Product Dev Coordinator
Debra Jennings, Project Director

39 Center on Education Policy
2129 G Street, NW.
1st Floor
Washington, DC 20052
202-994-9050
Fax: 202-994-8859
E-mail: cep-dc@cep-dc.org
http://www.cep-dc.org
Understand the role of public education in a democracy and the need to improve the academic quality of public schools. Help citizens make sense of the conflicting make sense of conflicting perceptions about publlic education and create the conditions that will lead to better public schools.

Maria Voles Ferguson, Executive Director
Diane Stark Rentner, Deputy Director

40 Center on Human Policy
805 S Crouse Avenue
101 Hoople Building
Syracuse, NY 13244-2280
315-443-3851
800-894-0826
Fax: 315-443-4338
E-mail: staylo01@syr.edu
http://disabilitystudies.syr.edu
Promotes its mission of inclusion by developing and sponsoring academic programs and courses, conferences and publications, research and training programs, and public education and advocacy efforts on behalf of, and with, people with disabilities.

Founded: 1971

Steven J Taylor, Co-Director
Arlene S Kanter, Co-Director

41 Citizens for Educational Freedom
498 Woods Mill Road
Manchester, MO 63011-4144
636-686-7101
Fax: 636-686-7173
E-mail:
citedfree@educational-freedom.org
http://www.educational-freedom.org
Secures legal recognition for the right of parents to direct and control the education of their children; secures freedom of choice in education of their children, including an alternative to the government-established school system.

Founded: 1959

Mae Duggan, President/CEF
Herman Kriegshauser, Executive Director

42 Civic Practices Network
Brandeis University
60 Turner Street
Waltham, MA 02154
617-736-4890
Fax: 617-736-4891
E-mail: cpn@cpn.org
http://www.cpn.org
Collaborative and nonpartisan project dedicated to bring practical tools for public problem solving into communities and institutional settings across America.

Carmen Sirianni, Co-Editor
Lewis Friedland, Co-Editor

43 Constitutional Rights Foundation
601 S Kingsley Drive
Los Angeles, CA 90005
213-487-5590
Fax: 213-386-0459
E-mail: crf@crf-usa.org
http://www.crf-usa.org
Seeks to instill in our nation's youth a deeper understanding of citizenship through values expressed in our Constitution and its Bill of Rights, and educate them to become active and responsible participants in our society. Dedicated to assuring our country's future by investing in our youth today.

Marshall Croddy, President
Keri Doggett, Director of Program Dev

44 Council for Advancement & Support of Education
1307 New York Avenue NW
Suite 1000
Washington, DC 20005-4701
202-328-2273
Fax: 202-387-4973
E-mail: membersupportcenter@case.org
http://www.case.org
An international membership association that advances and supports educational institutions by providing knowledge, standards, advocacy and training designed to strengthen the combined efforts of alumni relations, communications, fundraising, marketing and allied professionals. CASE helps members raise funds for campus projects, produce recruitment materials, market their institutions to prospective students, diversify the profession and foster public support of education.

Founded: 1974

John Lippincott, President
Donald Falkenstein, VP, Business & Finance

45 Council for Christian Colleges and Universities
321 Eighth Street NE
Washington, DC 20002

202-546-8713
http://www.cccu.org
To advance the cause of Christ-centered higher education and to help our institutions transform lives by faithfully relating scholarship and service to biblical truth.

Founded: 1976

46 Council for Exceptional Children
2900 Crystal Drive
Suite 1000
Arlington, VA 22202-3557
703-620-3660
888-232-7733
Fax: 703-264-9494
E-mail: service@cec.sped.org
http://www.cec.sped.org
The Council for Exceptional Children works to improve the educational success of individuals with disabilities and/or gifts and talents.

Founded: 1922

James P. Heiden, President
Alexander T. Graham, Executive Director

47 Council for the Accreditation of Educator Preparation
1140 19th Street, N.W.
Suite 400
Washington, DC 20036
202-223-0077
Fax: 202-296-6620
E-mail: caep@CAEPnet.org
http://www.CAEPnet.org
Professional accrediting organization for schools, colleges and departments of education and alternative educator preparation providers in the United States.

James G. Cibulka, President
Stevie Chepko, Sr. VP Accreditation

48 Council of Graduate Schools
1 Dupont Circle NW
Suite 230
Washington, DC 20036-1173
202-223-3791
Fax: 202-331-7157
E-mail: general_inquiries@cgs.nche.edu
http://www.cgsnet.org
CGS has been the national voice for the graduate dean community. The only national organization in the United States that is dedicated solely to the advancement of graduate education and research. This is accomplished through advocacy in policy, innovative research and the development and dissemination of the best practices.

Patricia McAllister, VP Government Relations
Belle Woods, Manager External Affairs

49 Council of Independent Colleges
One Dupont Circle NW
Suite 320
Washington, DC 20036-1142
202-466-7230
Fax: 202-466-7238
E-mail: cic@cic.nche.edu
http://www.cic.edu
The major national organization that focuses on providing services to leaders of independent colleges and universities as well as conferences, seminars, and other programs that help institutions to improve the quality of education, administrative and financial performance, and institutional visibility.

Founded: 1956

50 Council on Postsecondary Accreditation
1 Dupont Circle NW
Suite 230
Washington, DC 20036-1173
202-223-3791
Fax: 202-331-7157
E-mail: general_inquiries@cgs.nche.edu
http://www.cgsnet.org
Has been the national voice for the graduate dean community. The only national organization in the United States that is dedicated solely to the advancement of graduate education and research.

Patricia McAllister, VP Government Relations
Belle Woods, Manager External Affairs

51 Crittenton Women's Union
Crittenton Women's Union
One Washington Mall
3rd Floor
Boston, MA 02108
617-259-2900
Fax: 617-247-8826
E-mail: info@liveworkthrive.org
http://www.liveworkthrive.org
Crittenton Women's Union transforms the course of low-income women's lives so that they can attain economic independence and create better futures for themselves and their families.

Elisabeth D. Babcock, MCRP, Ph.D, President/CEO
Heidi Brooks, Chair

52 Disability Rights Education & Defense Fund
3075 Adeline Street
Suite 210
Berkeley, CA 94703
510-644-2555
800-348-4232
Fax: 510-841-8645
E-mail: info@dredf.org
http://www.dredf.org
The mission of the Disability Rights Education and Defense Fund is to advance the civil and human rights of people with disabilities through legal advocacy, training, education, and public policy and legislative development.

Founded: 1979

Claudia Center, President/ Chair
Ann Cupolo Freeman, Secretary/ Treasurer

53 Drug Information & Strategy Clearinghouse
3109 Lubbock Ave
Fort Worth, TX 76109
800-955-2232
Provides housing officials, residents and community leaders with information and assistance on drug abuse prevention and trafficking control techniques.

Nancy Kay, Director

54 EF Educational Tours
8 Education Street
Cambridge, MA 02141-1883
800-637-8222
Fax: 617-619-1803
http://www.eftours.com
EF Educational Tours helps educators like you enrich what you teach in the classroom with international group travel. Your students actually learn it by living it by experiencing the world's very best historic, cultural and natural sights.

Founded: 1965

Martha H Doyle, President
Amy Connolly, Director of Customer Service

55 ERIC - Education Resources Information Center
655 15th Street NW
Suite 500
Washington, DC 20005
800-538-3742
http://www.eric.ed.gov/
The ERIC mission is to provide a comprehensive, easy-to-use, searchable, Internet-based bibliographic and full-text database of education research and information that also meets the requirements of the Education Sciences Reform Act of 2002.

Founded: 1964

Arthuree Wright, Interim Library Director
Alvin Walker, Jr, Product Development Manager

56 ERIC Clearinghouse on Assessment & Evaluation
University of Maryland
1129 Shriver Laboratory
College Park, MD 20742-5701
301-405-7449
800-464-3742
Fax: 301-405-8134
E-mail: feedback3@ericae.net
http://www.ericae.net
Disseminates education information on topics pertaining to tests and other measurement devices, research design and methodology.

Lawrence M Rudner, Director
Carol Boston, Associate Director

57 ERIC Clearinghouse on Rural Education & Small Schools
Edvantia
PO Box 1348
Charleston, WV 25325-1348
304-347-0400
800-624-9120
Fax: 304-347-0487
E-mail: info@edvantia.org
http://www.edvantia.org
Works in partnership with clients to provide workable solutions to issues facing education today. Services grounded in research and best practices and delivered by social scientists, former teachers, administrators and state evaluation leaders.

Doris Redfield, Ph.d, President

58 Easter Seals Communications
Easter Seals
233 South Wacker Drive
Suite 2400
Chicago, IL 60606
312-726-6200
800-221-6827
Fax: 312-726-1494
E-mail: info@easter-seals.org
http://www.easterseals.com
Easter Seals provides exceptional services, education, outreach, and advocacy so that people living with autism and other disabilities can live, learn, work and play in our communities.

Founded: 1934

Rick Davidson, Chairman
Ralph F. Boyd, Jr, Treasurer

59 Education Commission of the States
700 Broadway
#810
Denver, CO 80203-3442
303-299-3600
Fax: 303-296-8332
E-mail: ecs@ecs.org
http://www.ecs.org
To help states develop effective policy and practice for public education by providing data, research, analysis and leadership; and

by facilitating collaboration, the exchange of ideas among the states and long-range strategic thinking

Jeremy Anderson, President
Brian Sandoval, Chairman

60 Education Development Center
43 Foundry Avenue
Waltham, MA 02453-8313
617-969-7100
Fax: 617-969-5979
E-mail: contact@edc.org
http://www.edc.org
EDC designs, delivers and evaluates programs addressing some of the world's challenges in education, health and economic opportunity. working with the public-sector and private partners, EDC uses the power of people and systems to improve education, health promotion and care, workforce preparation, communications technologies and civic engagement. Services include research, training, educational materials and strategy.

Founded: 1958

Luther S. Luedtke, President
Stephen Anzalone, Vice President

61 Education Extension
Oklahoma State University-Stillwater
327 Willard
Stillwater, OK 74078-4034
405-744-6254
800-765-8933
Fax: 405-744-7713
E-mail: education.outreach@okstate.edu
http://education.okstate.edu
The school counseling specialization prepares students to work as school counselors in public schools, serving students, teachers, and parents.

Dr Pamela Fry, Dean
Dr C Robert Davis, Associate Dean

62 Education Industry Association
1839 Batten Hollow Road
Vienna, VA 22182
709-938-2429
800-252-3280
Fax: 703-242-1479
E-mail: spines@educationindustry.org
http://www.educationindustry.org
To promote increased public support for the education industry in order to improve educational opportunities and outcomes for all students.

Steven Pines, Executive Director
Robert Lytle, Board President

63 Education Writers Association
3516 Connecticut Avenue NW
Washington, DC 20008
202-452-9830
http://www.ewa.org
As the professional organization of members of the media who cover education at all levels, EWA has worked for more than 65 years to help journalists get the story right. Today, EWA has more than 3,000 members benefiting from our high-quality programs, training, information, support, and recognition.

Caroline W. Hendrie, Executive Director
Lori Crouch, Assistant Director

64 Education, Training and Research Associates
100 Enterprise Way
Suite G300
Scotts Valley, CA 95066
831-438-4060
800-620-8884
Fax: 831-438-4284
http://www.etr.org

To maximize the physical, social and emotional health of all individuals, families and communities by advancing the work of health, education and social service providers through high-quality research, publications, information resources and programs.

Dan McCormick, MHA, BS, CEO
David Kitchen, MBA, Chief Financial Officer

65 Educational Equity Concepts
Educational Equity Center at FHI 360
71 5th Avenue
6th Floor
New York, NY 10003
212-243-1110
Fax: 212-627-0407
E-mail: eec@fhi360.org
http://www.edequity.org
EEC develops programs and materials that promote bias-free learning in school and after school. We provide professional development, consulting services and community partnerships. Our goal is to eliminate inequities based on gender, race/ethnicity, disability and level of family income.

Merle Froschl, Co-Founder/Co-Director
Linda Colⁱn, Program Manager

66 Educational Register
Vincent-Curtis
PO Box 724
Falmouth, MA 02541-0724
508-457-6473
Fax: 508-457-6499
E-mail: register@vincentcurtis.com
http://www.theeducationalregister.com
Hundreds of illustrated announcements describing a variety of private boarding schools and resident summer programs in the United States, Canada and Europe, together with articles by school heads and camp directors of interest to parents of students 10-18.

Founded: 1941

Stanford B Vincent, Editor

67 Equity Clearinghouse
Mid-Continent Regional Educational Laboratory
4601 DTC Boulevard
Suite 500
Denver, CO 80237-2596
303-337-0990
Fax: 303-337-3005
http://www.mcrel.org
Researchers and education consultants work together to provide educators with research-based, practical guidance on the issues and challenges facing k-16 education. Data analyses, scientific studies, field-tested products and services and reports, articles, books and tools are all crated and delivered to help with challenges facing education today.

Founded: 1966

Bryan Goodwin, President
C. Patrick Woods, Chair

68 Excelencia in Education
1717 N Street NW
2nd Floor
Washington, DC 20036
202-785-7350
Fax: 202-785-7351
http://www.edexcelencia.org
Aims to accelerate higher education success for Latino students by providing data-driven analysis of the educational status of Latino students and by promoting education policies and institutional practices that support their academic achievement.

69 FHI 360
359 Blackwell Street
Suite 200
Durham, NC 27701
919-544-7040
Fax: 919-544-7261
E-mail: web@aed.org
http://www.aed.org
Assists schools, colleges and other educational institutions of developing countries in researching, planning, designing, implementing and evaluating development programs. In the US, manages the Center for Youth Development and Policy Research (disadvantaged youth), Disabilities Studies and Services Center (clearinghouse on special education and children with disabilities), National Institute for Work and Learning (school-to-work transition), and schools and Community Services Department.

Founded: 1961

Patrick C. Fine, Med, CEO
Rasika Padmaperuma, CPA, Acting CFO

70 Facing History & Ourselves
16 Hurd Road
Brookline, MA 02445-6919
617-232-1595
800-856-9039
Fax: 617-232-0281
E-mail: info@facing.org
http://www.facinghistory.org
Facing History is an international nonprofit that helps teachers and students link the past to moral choices they face today.

Founded: 1976

Roger Brooks, President/ CEO
Anne Burt, Chief Communications Officer

71 Family Centered Learning Alternatives (FCLA)
Context Institute
PO Box 946
Langley, WA 98260
360-221-6044
Fax: 360-221-6045
http://www.context.org
Supports parents' right to choose the educational environment best suited for their children's needs and to promote homeschooling as a legal nationwide learning alternative.

Founded: 1979

Eric Stewart, Founder/Director
Debra Stewart, Founder/Director

72 Foundation for Student Communication
Princeton University
48 University Place
Princeton, NJ 8544
609-258-1111
Fax: 609-258-1222
http://www.businesstoday.org
Student subscribers and conference participants who promote communication among students and business persons.

Founded: 1968

Jonathan Hastings, President
Daniel Toro, Director of Finance

73 Friends Council on Education
1507 Cherry Street
Philadelphia, PA 19102
215-241-7245
Fax: 215-241-7299
E-mail: Info@friendscouncil.org
http://www.friendscouncil.org

A national organization of Friends schools, which assists teachers, students and families by providing publications and programs supporting Friends values in the classroom and in the life of the school community.

Founded: 1931

Drew Smith, Executive Director
Betsy Torg, Director, Dev & Comm

74 Gifted Child Society
190 Rock Road
Glen Rock, NJ 07452-1736
201-444-6530
Fax: 201-444-9099
E-mail: admin@gifted.org
http://www.giftedchildsociety.com
Educational enrichment and support services specifically designed for gifted children. Assistance to parents in raising gifted children to full and productive adulthood. Professional training to encourage educators to meet the special needs of those children and a greater effort to win public recognition and acceptance of these special needs.

Founded: 1957

Gina G Riggs, Executive Director

75 Girls Incorporated
120 Wall Street
New York, NY 10005-3902
212-509-2000
Fax: 212-509-8708
E-mail: communications@girlsinc.org
http://www.girlsinc.org
A national nonprofit youth organization dedicated to inspiring all girls to be strong, smart, and bold. Informal education programs encorage girls to master physical, intellectual and emotional challenges.

Founded: 1864

Judy Vredenburgh, President/CEO
Ellen Stafford-Sigg, Chairman

76 Global Exploration for Educators Organization
2945 Morris Rd
Ardmore, PA 19003
877-600-0105
http://www.geeo.org
A non-profit organization dedicated to encouraging and assisting as many teachers as possible to travel abroad and then share their experiences with their students upon their return to the classroom.

Jesse Weisz, Founder/Executive Director

77 HEATH Resource Center at the National Youth Transitions Center
George Washington University
HEATH Resource Center
2134 G Street N.W.
Washington, DC 20052-0001
202-973-0904
800-544-3284
Fax: 202-994-3365
E-mail: askheath@gwu.edu
http://www.HEATH.gwu.edu
The HEATH Resource Center has served as a national clearinghouse on postsecondary education for individuals with disabilities, managed by the George Washington University Graduate School of Education and Human Development. Now the HSC Foundation has partnered with the George Washington University to expand the content of this resource and to designate it as

the official site of The HSC Foundation's National Youth Transitions Center.

Founded: 2000

Reina Guartico, Principal Investigator
Jessica Queener, Project Director

78 Independent Schools Association of the Southwest (ISAS)
Energy Square
505 N Big Spring Street
Suite 406
Midland, TX 79701
432-684-9550
800-688-5007
Fax: 432-684-9401
E-mail: rdurham@isasw.org
http://www.isasw.org
Independent Schools Association of the Southwest (ISAS) is a voluntary membership association of private schools. The membership of ISAS consists of 84 schools located in Arizona, Kansas, Louisiana, Mexico, New Mexico, Oklahoma and Texas enrolling over 38,000 students. A central purpose of ISAS is to encourage, support and develop the highest standard for independent schools of the region and to recognize by formal accreditation those schools in which these standards are maintained.

Founded: 1955

Rhonda Durham, Executive Director
Jananne McLaughlin, Accreditation Director

79 Institute for Educational Leadership
4301 Connecticut Ave. NW
Suite 100
Washington, DC 20008
202-822-8405
Fax: 202-872-4050
E-mail: iel@IEL.ORG
http://www.iel.org
To build the capacity of individuals and communities to work together - across policies, programs and sectors, to prepare all children and youth for post-secondary education, careers and citizenship

Founded: 1964

Martin J Blank, President/CEO
Aimee Rogstad Guidera, Founder/ Executive Director

80 InterAction - American Council for Voluntary International Action
1400 16th Street, NW
Suite 210
Washington, DC 20036
202-667-8227
Fax: 202-667-8236
E-mail: ia@interaction.org
http://www.interaction.org/
Using its collective voice Interaction hopes to shape important policy decisions on relief and long term development issues including foreign assistance, the environment, women, health, education and agriculture.

Sam Worthington, President/CEO
Mark Lotwis, VP, Policy & Gov Relations

81 International Association of Educators for World Peace
2013 Orba Drive NE
Huntsville, AL 35811-2414
256-534-5501
Fax: 256-536-1018
E-mail: info@iaewp.org
http://www.iaewp.org
To contribute to the improvement of man's ability to live at peace, to educate world citizens for peaceful co-existence and cooperation so that all people may have free access to the achievement of science and civilization. Belief that international

understanding and world peace can be attained through education.

Dr Charles Mercieca, President
Dr Surya Nath Prasad, Executive Vice President

82 International Society for Technology in Education
1530 Wilson Boulevard
Suite 730
Arlington, VA 22209
703-348-4784
800-336-5191
Fax: 703-348-6459
E-mail: iste@iste.org
http://www.iste.org
Providing leadership and service to improve teaching and learning by advancing the effective use of technology in education.

Brian Lewis, MA, CAE, CEO
Craig Thibaudeau, Chief External Relations

83 Jewish Education Council
Jewish Federation Greater Seattle
2031 Third Avenue
Seattle, WA 98121-2412
206-443-5400
Fax: 206-770-6363
E-mail: info@jewishinseattle.org
http://www.jewishinseattle.org
Works to ensure a vibrant Jewish cimmunity that is connected locally, in Israel and worldwide.

Liat Zaidenberg, Education Services Director
Keith Dvorchik, President/ CEO

84 Jewish Education Service of North America
JESNA
247 West 37th Street
5th Floor
New York, NY 10018
212-284-6950
Fax: 212-284-6951
E-mail: info@jesna.org
http://www.jesna.org
Ensure that Jewish education is the best that it can be in all of its variety. JESNA's role is to strengthen communities and their educational offerings by providing tested solutions, leveraging partnerships, promoting synergies, and building the connections that strengthen us all.

Cass Gottlieb, Chiair
Mandell L Berman, Honorary Chair

85 Jewish Educators Assembly
Broadway and Locust Avenue
PO Box 413
Cedarhurst, NY 11516
516-569-2537
Fax: 516-295-9039
E-mail: jewisheducators@aol.com
http://www.jewisheducators.org
Promotes excellence among educators committed to Conservative Jewish education by advancing professionalism, encouraging leadership, pursuing lifelong learning and building community. Serve educators in their efforts to strengthen the Conservative Movement and inspire greater Jewish learning. JEA will be the leading advocate for the welfare of the Jewish educator and for the best practices in Jewish education.

Michael Schatz, President
Edward Edelstein, Executive Director

86 John Dewey Society for the Study of Education & Culture
1801 NW 11th Road
Gainesville, FL 32605-5323

352-378-7365
http://www.johndeweysociety.org
Founded in 1935, John Dewey's commitment to the use of critical and reflective intelligence in the search for solutions to crucial problems in education and culture.

Founded: 1935

Kathleen Knight Abowitz, President
Kyle Greenwalt, Secretary/Treasurer

87 Learning Disabilities Association of America (LDA)
Learning Disabilities Association of America
4156 Library Road
Pittsburgh, PA 15234-1349
412-341-1515
888-300-6710
Fax: 412-344-0224
E-mail: info@ldaamerica.org
http://www.ldanatl.org
(LDA) is a national network, with 14, 00 national state and local members individuals with learning disabilities, their families and the professionals who work with them. LDA is dedicated to identifying causes and promoting prevention of learning disabilities and to enhancing the quality of life for all individuals with learning disabilities and their families by encouraging effectiveidentification, interventions, fostering research and protecting their rights under the law.

Founded: 1963

Patricia Latham, President
B J Wiemer, VP

88 Lutheran Education Association
7400 Augusta Street
River Forest, IL 60305
708-209-3343
Fax: 708-209-3458
E-mail: lea@lea.org
http://www.lea.org
Seeks to spark ideas, thoughts and practices among Lutherans. The Lutheran Education Association links, equips and affirms educators and workers in ministry for the purpose of building up the body of Christ.

Dr Jonathan Laabs, Ed.D., Executive Director
Kathy Slupik, Executive Assistant

89 MATRIX: A Parent Network and Resource Center
94 Galli Drive
Suite C
Novato, CA 94949
415-884-3535
800-578-2592
Fax: 415-884-3555
E-mail: info@matrixparnets.org
http://www.matrixparents.org
Matrix provides training and information to parents of children of any age with all disabilities-physical, cognitive, emotional and learning. The Matrix network consists of parent training and info centers, family empowerment centers and family resource centers.

Founded: 1983

Nora Thompson, Executive Director
Joanne Ferris, Development Director

90 Mathematics Common Core Coalition

http://www.nctm.org/standards/mathcommoncore
The Common Core State Standards (CCSS) are a set of academic standards in mathematics and English language arts/literacy (ELA)

developed under the direction of the Council of Chief State School Officers (CCSSO) and the National Governors Association (NGA).

91 Music Teachers National Association
441 Vine Street
Suite 3100
Cincinnati, OH 45202-3004
513-421-1420
888-512-5278
Fax: 513-421-2503
E-mail: mtnanet@mtna.org
http://www.mtna.org
Advance the value of music study and music making to society while supporting the careers and professionalism of teachers of music. MTNA provides a collective voice for teachers worldwide and powerful alliance for music teaching professionals.

Gary Ingle, Executive Director
Benjamin D. Caton, President

92 National Academy of Education
500 5th Street, NW
Washington, DC 20001-9580
202-334-2341
Fax: 202-334-2350
E-mail: info@naeducation.org
http://www.naeducation.org
Advances quality education research and its use in policy formation and practice. Offers professional development fellowship programs as well.

Founded: 1965

Michael Feuer, President
James Pellegrino, VP

93 National Alliance for Safe Schools
PO Box 335
Slanesville, WV 25444-0335
304-496-8100
888-510-6500
Fax: 304-496-8105
E-mail: nass@frontiernet.net
http://www.safeschools.org
Founded in 1977 NASS a non-profit corporation, ascribes to the belief that schools need to take back control and identify what the local issues are that may be causing fear and anxiety on the part of the students and staff. Once local issues have been identified, school administrators, working with students, teachers, parents and support staff, are able to effect change.

Peter D Blauvelt, CEO/President

94 National Association For Gifted Children
1331 H St NW
Suite 1001
Washington, DC 20005
202-785-4268
Fax: 202-785-4248
E-mail: nagc@nagc.org
http://www.nagc.org
Organization of parents, teachers, educators, other professionals, and community leaders who unite to address the unique needs of children and youth with demonstrated gifts and talents as well as those children who may be able to develop their talent potential with appropriate educational experiences.

Nancy Green, Executive Director
Paula Olszewski-Kubilius, President

95 National Association for Asian and Pacific American Education
PO Box 3471
Palos Verdes Peninsula, CA 90274
818-677-6853
Fax: 818-366-2714

E-mail: naapae@naapae.net
http://www.naapae.net
Objectives are to enhance awareness of multicultural studies in the United States as well as to promote the inclusion of Asian and Pacific American culture and history into the school curriculum. In addition to these, NAAPAE looks to maintain a network of educators and community members to share information and resources, support research on Asian and Pacific American educational needs and encourage Asian and Pacific Americans to aim for leadership roles.

Founded: 1977

John N Tsuchida, President
Betty Jeung, Vice President

96 National Association for Developmental Education (NADE)

170 Kinnelon Road
Ste. 33
Kinnelon, NJ 07405
877-233-9455
Fax: 623-792-5747
E-mail: office@nade.net
http://www.nade.net
Seeks to improve the theory and practice of developmental educationat all levels of the educational spectrum, the professional capabilities of developmental educators and the design of programs to prepare developmental educators.

Taunya Paul, M.S., President
Marguerite MacDonald, M.H.S., Vice President

97 National Association for Legal Support of Alternative Schools (NALSAS)

PO Box 2823
Santa Fe, NM 87504-2823
505-474-0300
E-mail: nalsas@msn.com
http://www.nalsas.org/
It was originally designed to help interested persons/organizations locate/evaluate/create viable alternatives to traditional schooling approaches including home study.

Founded: 1973

Ed Nagel, CEO

98 National Association for Year-Round Education

PO Box 711386
San Diego, CA 92171-1386
619-276-5296
Fax: 858-571-5754
E-mail: info@nayre.org
http://www.NAYRE.org
Founded in 1972 NAYRE fosters and disseminates information about year-round education as a way to improve educational programs.

Dr. Charles Ballinger, Executive Director Emeritus
Sam Pepper, Executive Director

99 National Association of Catholic School Teachers

1700 Sansom Street
Suite 903
Philadelphia, PA 19103
215-665-0993
800-996-2278
Fax: 215-568-8270
E-mail: Rita@NACST.com
http://www.nacst.com

Unifies, advises and assists Catholic school teachers in matters of collective bargaining.

Founded: 1978

Rita C Schwartz, President
William Blumstein, Executive Vice President

100 National Association of Federally Impacted Schools

Hall of the States
444 N Capitol Street NW
Suite 419
Washington, DC 20001-1512
202-624-5455
Fax: 202-624-5468
E-mail: bryan@nafisdc.org
http://www.nafisdc.org
NAFIS is a corporation of school districts through the country organized primarily to educate Congress on Impact Aid. The association works to ensure that the needs of federally connected children are met with adequate federal funds.

Terry Smith, Vice President
Rick Carson, President

101 National Association of Secondary School Principals

1904 Association Drive
Reston, VA 20191-1537
703-860-0200
866-647-7253
Fax: 703-476-5432
E-mail: nhs@nassp.org
http://www.nassp.org
NASSP promotes excellence in middle level and high school leadership through research based professional development, resources, and advocacy so that every student can be prepared for postsecondary learning opportunities and be workforce ready.

Founded: 1916

JoAnn Bartoletti, Executive Director
G. A. Buie, President

102 National Association of Special Education Teac

1250 Connecticut Avenue, N.W.
Suite 200
Washington, DC 20036
800-754-4421
Fax: 800-754-4421
E-mail: contactus@naset.org
http://www.naset.org
TheÿNational Association of Special Education Teachers (NASET)ÿis the only national membership organization dedicated solely to meeting the needs of special education teachers and those preparing for the field of special education teaching.

Dr. Roger Pierangelo, Co-Executive Director
Dr. George Giuliani, Co-Executive Director

103 National Association of State Boards of Education

333 John Carlyle Street
Suite #530
Alexandria, VA 22314
703-684-4000
800-368-5023
Fax: 703-836-2313
E-mail: boards@nasbe.org
http://www.nasbe.org
NASBE works to strengthen state leadership in educational policymaking, promote excellence in the education of all students, advocate equality of access to educational

opportunity, and assure continued citizen support for public education.

Founded: 1958

Jane Coff, President
Kristen Amundson, Executive Director

104 National Association of Student Councils (NASC)

1904 Association Drive
Reston, VA 20191
703-860-0200
866-647-7253
Fax: 703-476-5432
E-mail: nasc@nasc.us
http://www.nasc.us
Promote student participation within school and its community, encourage development of new student councils, assist in student councils becoming more effective, assist state associations of student councils, provide leadership training for council members and advisors, encourage and support healthy living for young poeple.

Founded: 1931

Scott D Thompson, Executive Officer

105 National Association of Trade & Industrial Instructors

Canadian Valley Vo Tech
6505 East Highway 66
El Reno, OK 73036-579
405-262-2629
Fax: 405-422-2354
Founded in 1965 the National Association of Trade and Industrial Instructors seeks to improve communication among members and to support the needs of classroom teachers.

Carol McNish, President
Greg Winters, Superintendent

106 National Board for Professional Teaching Standards

11827 Tech Com
Suite 200
San Antonio, TX 78233
888-780-7805
Fax: 888-811-3514
http://www.nbpts.org
Formed to advance the quality of teaching and learning by developing professional standards for accomplished teaching, creating a voluntary system to certify teachers who meet those standards and integration certified teachers into educational reform efforts.

Founded: 1987

107 National Catholic Educational Association

1005 N Glebe Rd
Suite 525
Arlington, VA 22201
800-711-6232
Fax: 703-243-0025
E-mail: nceaadmin@ncea.org
http://www.ncea.org
Rooted in the Gospel of Jesus Christ, the National Catholic Educational Association (NCEA) is a professional membership organization that provides leadership, direction and service to fulfill the evangelizing, catechizing and teaching mission of the Church.

Robert R. Bimonte, FSC, President
Patrick Lofton, Executive Vice President

108 National Center For School Engagement

450 Lincoln St
Suite 100
Denver, CO 80203
303-837-8466
E-mail: info@schoolengagement.org
http://www.schoolengagement.org

Provides training and technical assistance, research and evaluation to school districts, law enforcement agencies, courts, as well as state and federal agencies.

Ken Seeley, Founder/CEO

09 National Center for Learning Disabilities
32 Laight Street
Second Floor
New York, NY 10013
212-545-7510
888-575-7373
Fax: 212-545-9665
E-mail: ncld@ncld.org
http://www.ncld.org
The National Center for Learning Disabilities (NCLD) works to ensure that the nation's 15 million children, adolescents and adults with learning disabilities have every opportunity to succeed in school, work and life.

Frederic M Poses, Chairman of the Board
James H Wendorf, Executive Director

10 National Coalition for Parent Involvement in Education (NCPIE)
1201 16th Street NW
Suite 317
Washington, DC 20036
202-289-6790
Fax: 202-289-6791
E-mail: ferguson@ncpie.org
http://www.ncpie.org/
National Coalition for Parent Involvement in Education (NCPIE) advocates the involvement of parents and families in their children's education, and to foster relationships between home, school, and community to enhance the education of all our nation's young people.
Founded: 1980

Sue Ferguson, Chairperson
Hilda Crespo, Vice President

11 National Coalition of Alternative Community Schools
1129 Gault Drive
Ypsilanti, MI 48198
734-483-7040
888-771-9171
Fax: 734-482-7436
E-mail: ncacs2@earthlink.net
http://www.ncacs.org
Our mission is to unite and organize a grassroots movement of learners and learning communities dedicated to participant control, liberation from all forms of oppression, and the pursuit of freedom.

Terri Wheeler, Treasurer

12 National Coalition of Independent Scholars
PO Box 120182
San Antonio, TX 78212
E-mail: Info@NCIS.org
http://www.ncis.org
Provide information for the creation of local organizations of independent scholars
Founded: 1989

Mona Berman, President
Janet Wasserman, Secretary

13 National Commission for Cooperative Education
WACE
Suite 125
600 Suffolk Street
Lowell, MA 01854
Fax: 978-934-4084
E-mail: Marty_Ford@uml.edu
http://www.waceinc.org

Organization linking higher institutions, employers and public authorities through research, programs, and services designed to advance learning where education and work experience are linked.
Founded: 1962

Dr Paul J Stonely, CEO
Marty Ford, Director

114 National Consortium for Academics and Sports
University of Central Florida
PO Box 161400
Orlando, FL 32816-1400
407-823-4770
Fax: 407-823-3542
E-mail: rlapchick@bus.ucf.edu
http://www.ncasports.org
To create a better society by focusing on educational attainment and using the power and appeal of sport to positively affect social change.
Founded: 1985

Dr Richard Lapchick, President/Founder
Keith L Lee, VP/ COO

115 National Council for Black Studies
National Council for Black Studies
University of Cincinnati
Africana Studies Department, Box 210370
Cincinnati, OH 45221-0370
513-556-0785
E-mail: info@ncbsonline.org
http://www.ncbsonline.org
Promote academic excellence and social responsibility in the discipline of Africana/Black Studies through the production and dissemination of knowledge, professional development and training, and advocacy for social change and social justice.
Founded: 1975

Georgene Bess Montgomery, President
Amilcar Shabazz, Vice President

116 National Council for Science and the Environment
1101 17th Street NW
Suite 250
Washington, DC 20036
202-530-5810
Fax: 202-628-4311
E-mail: ncse@ncseonline.org
http://www.ncseonline.org
Improve the scientific basis of environmental decision making through an accurate understanding of the underlying science, its meaning and limitations, and the potential consequences of their action or inaction.
Founded: 1990

David Blockstein, Ph.D., Senior Scientist
Peter Saundry, Ph.D., Executive Director

117 National Council of Higher Education
National Education Association (NEA)
1201 16th Street NW
Room 410
Washington, DC 20036-3290
202-833-4000
Fax: 202-822-7974
E-mail: nche@nea.org
http://www.nea.org
Our mission is to advocate for education professionals and to unite our members and the nation to fulfill the promise of public education to prepare every student to succeed in a diverse and interdependent world

Lily Eskelsen García, President
Becky Pringle, VP

118 National Council of Supervisors of Mathematics
6000 E Evans Ave
Ste 3-205
Denver, CO 80222-5423
303-758-9611
Fax: 303-758-9616
E-mail: office@mathedleadership.org
http://www.mathedleadership.org/index.html
The National Council of Supervisors of Mathematics (NCSM) is a mathematics leadership organization for educational leaders that provides professional learning opportunities necessary to support and sustain improved student achievement.

Valerie L. Mills, President
Mike Hall, eNews Editor

119 National Council of Urban Education Associations
National Education Association (NEA)
1201 16th Street NW
Washington, DC 20036-3290
202-833-4000
Fax: 202-822-7974
E-mail: ncuea@nea.org
http://www.nea.org
NCUEA is a caucus of local affiliates of the National Education Association (NEA), which is dedicated to strengthening member advocacy and making the NEA more responsive to member needs. Promote and advance high quality Public Education is urban schools by empowering and supporting local associations, leaders and members.

Lily Eskelsen García, President
Becky Pringle, VP

120 National Council on Measurement in Education
2424 American Lane
Suite 3800
Madison, WI 53704
608-443-2487
Fax: 608-443-2474
E-mail: plovelace@ncme.org
http://www.ncme.org
NCME is a professional organization for individuals involved in assessment, evaluation, testing, and other aspects of educational measurement

Lauress Wise, President
Richard J. Patz, VP/ President-elect

121 National Council on Rehabilitation Education (NCRE)
1099 E. Champlain Drive
Suite A, PMB #137
Fresno, CA 93720
559-906-0787
Fax: 559-412-2550
E-mail: info@ncre.org
http://www.ncre.org
A professional organization of educators dedicated to quality services for persons with disabilities through education and research.

J. Chad Duncan, Ph.D., CRC, CPO, President
Noel?? Estrada-Hernndez, 1st Vice-President

122 National Council on Student Development (NCSD)
2851 S. Parker Rd.
Suite 560
Aurora, CO 80014
866-972-0717
Fax: 303-755-7363
E-mail: ncsd@ncsdonline.org
http://www.ncsdonline.org

NCSD is to promote knowledge, expertise and professional development opportunities; support decision-making based on empirical and ethical principles, and demonstrate a commitment to the personal and professional advancement of student development professionals through advocacy and education.

Nicole Singleton, Executive Director
Tyjaun Lee, President

123 National Education Association
1201 16th Street NW
Washington, DC 20036-3290
202-833-4000
Fax: 202-822-7974
E-mail: ncuea@nea.org
http://www.nea.org
Advocate for education professionals in the effort to prepare every student to succeed in a diverse world.

Lily Eskelsen Garc¡a, President
Becky Pringle, VP

124 National Education Association Student Program
National Education Association (NEA)
1201 16th Street NW
Washington, DC 20036-3290
202-833-4000
Fax: 202-822-7974
E-mail: ncuea@nea.org
http://www.nea.org
Strive to promote community partnerships; foster leadership through pre-professional opportunities and peer mentoring; promote membership among diverse populations, provide networking support; supplement formal teacher-education training, promote the national accreditation of teacher-education training; recruit and retain pre-professional members and maintain a presence at all NEA conferences.

Lily Eskelsen Garc¡a, President
Becky Pringle, VP

125 National Education Association-Retired
National Education Association (NEA)
1201 16th Street NW
Washington, DC 20036-3290
202-833-4000
Fax: 202-822-7974
http://www.nea.org/retired
NEA-Retired exists to meet the needs of retired education employees.

Lily Eskelsen Garc¡a, President
Becky Pringle, Vice President

126 National Education Policy Institute
National Alliance of Black School Educators
310 Pennsylvania Avenue
Washington, DC 20003
202-608-6310
800-221-2654
Fax: 202-608-6319
E-mail: info@nabse.org
http://www.nabse.org
NABSE is the nation's premiere non-profit organization devoted to furthering the academic success for the nation's children - particularly children of African descent. NABSE is dedicated to improving both the educational experiences and accomplishments of African American youth through the development and use of instructional and motivational methods that increase

levels of inspiration, attendance and overall achievement.

Bernard Hamilton, Ed.D., President/ Interim Exe Dir
Doreen E. Barrett, Ph.D., Treasurer

127 National Lekotek Center
2001 N Clybourn
1st Floor
Chicago, IL 60614
773-528-5766
800-366-7529
Fax: 773-537-2992
E-mail: lekotek@lekotek.org
http://www.lekotek.org
Therapeutic toy lending library and play education for children ages 0-8 with disabilities. Lekotek uses interactive play experiences and the learning that results to promote the inclusion of children with special needs into family and community life.

Joanna Horsnail, Chair
Steve Gilson, Treasurer

128 National Organization on Disability
77 Water Street
Suite 204
New York, NY 10005
646-505-1191
Fax: 646-505-1184
E-mail: info@nod.org
http://www.nod.org
Expands the participation and contribution of America's 54 million men, women and children with disabilities in all aspects of life. By raising disability awareness through programs and information, together we can work toward closing the participation gaps.

Founded: 1982

Carol Glazer, President
Thomas J. Ridge, Chairman

129 National Rural Education Association
Purdue University
Beering Hall of Liberal Arts & Ed
100 N University St
W Lafayette, IN 47907
765-494-0086
Fax: 765-496-1228
E-mail: jehill@purdue.edu
http://www.nrea.net
Organization of rural school administrators, teachers, board members, regional service agency personnel, researchers, business and industry representatives and others interested in maintaining the vitality of rural school systems across the country.

Founded: 1907

Dr. John Hill, Executive Director
Dr. Sandra G. Watkins, Ph.D., President

130 National School Boards Association
1680 Duke Street
Alexandria, VA 22314-3455
703-838-6722
Fax: 703-683-7590
E-mail: info@nsba.org
http://www.nsba.org
Not-for-profit Federation of state associations of school boards across the United States. Its mission is to foster excellence and equity in public education through school board leadership.

Thomas J. Gentzel, Executive Director
Anne M. Byrne, President

131 National School Public Relations Association
15948 Derwood Road
Rockville, MD 20855
301-519-0496
Fax: 301-519-0494
E-mail: nspra@nspra.org
http://www.nspra.org
Advance education through responsible public relations and communication that leads to success for all students. This can be accomplished by developing and providing a variety of diverse projects, services and professional development ideas to our members as well as to other education leaders interested in improving their communication efforts.

Rich Bagin, APR, Executive Director
Karen H. Kleinz, APR, Associate Director

132 National Society for Experiential Education
19 Mantua Road
Mt. Royal, NJ 08061
856-423-3427
Fax: 856-423-3420
E-mail: nsee.@talley.com
http://www.nsee.org
National Society for Experiential Education (NSEE) is a nonprofit membership association of educators, businesses, and community leaders. NSEE also serves as a national resource center for the development and improvement of experiential education programs nationwide.

Founded: 1971

Jim Colbert, President
Gregg Lorenz, VP

133 National Society for the Study of Education (NSSE)
University of Illinois at Chicago
525 W 120th Street
New York, NY 10027
312-996-4529
773-702-7748
Fax: 773-702-9756
E-mail: nsse@uic.edu
http://www.nsse-chicago.org/
The National Society for the Study of Education (NSSE) is an organization of education scholars, professional educators, and policy makers dedicated to the improvement of education research, policy, and practice. NSSE's mission is to advance the study and practice of education by providing accessible scholarship and promoting informed discourse about the challenges and opportunities of education in a democratic society.

Founded: 2008

David Hansen, Board of Directors
Deborah Loewenberg Ball, Board of Directors

134 National Student Exchange
4656 W Jefferson Boulevard
Suite 140
Fort Wayne, IN 46804
260-436-2634
Fax: 260-436-5676
E-mail: bworley@nse2.org
http://www.nse.org
The National Student Exchange (NSE) is a program for undergraduate exchange within the United States and Canada. Instead of crossing oceans, NSE students cross state, regional, provincial, and cultural borders. NSE students gain insight into the historical and cultural makeup of different regions, improve their communication skills with individuals from different backgrounds and prepare themselves to live and work in a culturally diverse society.

Founded: 1968

Bette Worley, President
Wendel Wickland, Vice President

135 National Telemedia Council
517 N Segoe Rd
Suite 210
Madison, WI 53703
608-274-3107
Fax: 608-257-7714
E-mail: ntc@danenet.wicip.org
http://www.danenet.org
Offers on-site technical support, technical training and technical planning and consulting services. DANEnet is dedicated to helping Dane County non-profits find and use quality information technology that efficiently serves their mission.

Founded: 1953

Eric Howland, Director
John Jordan, Community Outreach

136 National Women's Student Coalition (NWSC)
United States Student Association
1211 Connecticut Avenue NW
Suite 406
Washington, DC 20036
202-640-6570
Fax: 202-223-4005
E-mail: ussa@usstudents.org
http://www.usstudents.org
National Women's Student Coalition (NWSC), an affiliate of the United States Student Association, provides a space for women of different economic backgrounds, races, sexual orientations, religions and abilities to come together and strategize ways to increase campus safety, diversity, fight against bias related violence and build women's leadership.

Maxwell John Love, President
Alexandra Flores-Quilty, VP

137 National Women's Studies Association
National Women's Studies Association
11 E. Mount Royal Avenue
Suite 110
Baltimore, MD 21202
410-528-0355
Fax: 410-528-0357
E-mail: nwsaoffice@nwsa.org
http://www.nwsa.org
The National Women's Studies Association shows the ways in which women's studies are vital to education; demonstrate the contributions of feminist scholarship; and to promote relationships between scholarship, teaching and civic engagement in understandings of culture and society.

Founded: 1977

Allison Kimmich, Executive Director
Vivian M. May, President

138 Native American Homeschool Association
474 Brush Creek Road
Fries, VA 24330
540-636-1020
Fax: 540-636-1464
http://www.expage.com/page/nahomeschool 2
Association of Native American homeschoolers.

Misty Dawn Thomas Ruff, Tribal Chairwoman

139 New England School Development Council
28 Lord Rd
#210
Marlborough, MA 01752
508-481-9444
Fax: 508-481-5655
http://www.nesdec.org

Helps schools achieve and maintain high performing status through education management tools.

140 North American Association for Environmental Education (NAAEE)
2000 P Street NW
Suite 540
Washington, DC 20036
202-419-0412
Fax: 202-419-0415
E-mail: info@naaee.net
http://www.naaee.net
Teaches children and adults how to learn about and investigate their environment and to make intelligent, informed decisions about how they can take care of it.

October

Judy Braus, Executive Director
Christiane Maertens, Deputy Director

141 North American Association of Educational Negotiators
PO Box 1068
Salem, OR 97308
519-503-0098
Fax: 503-588-2813
E-mail: execdir@naen.org
http://www.naen.org
Improves the knowledge and performance of K-12 school district, community college, and university, management negotiators by advancing their professional status, providing a forum for effective communication, and encourage information exchanges among educational negotiators.

Tim Alexander, President
Justin Petrarca, President-Elect

142 North American Students of Cooperation
330 S. Wells St
Suite 618-F
Chicago, IL 60606
773-404-2667
Fax: 331-223-9727
E-mail: info@nasco.coop
http://www.nasco.coop
Organizes and educates affordable group equity co-ops and their members for the purpose of promoting a community oriented cooperative movement.

Founded: 1946

Tom Pierson, Executive Director
Jim Jones, Sr Director of Development

143 Northwest Commission on Colleges and Universities
1910 University Drive
Boise, ID 83725
208-426-1000
Fax: 208-334-3228
E-mail: sclemens@boisestate.edu
http://www.boisestate.edu
Assure educational quality, enhance institutional effectiveness, and foster continuous improvement of colleges and universities in the Northwest region through analytical institutional self-assessment and critical peer review based upon evaluation criteria that are objectively and equitably applied to institutions with diverse missions, characteristics and cultures.

Bob Kustra, President
Martin Schimpf, Provost/ VP, Academic Affair

144 Odyssey of the Mind
Creative Competitions, Inc.
406 Ganttown Road
Sewell, NJ 08080

856-256-2797
Fax: 856-256-2798
E-mail: info@odysseyofthemind.com
http://www.odysseyofthemind.com
An international educational program that provides creative problem-solving opportunities for students from kindergarten through college. With creativity and imaginative paths to problem solving, students learn skills that will provide them with the ability to solve problems for a lifetime.

Samuel Micklus, Founder

145 PACER Center
8161 Normandale Boulevard
Bloomington, MN 55437
952-838-9000
888-248-0822
Fax: 952-838-0199
E-mail: pacer@pacer.org
http://www.pacer.org
Founded in 1976 PACER a coalition of organizations founded on the concept of Parents Helping Parents. PACER strives to improve and expand opportunities that enhance the quality of life for children and young adults with disabilities and their families. Helps parents become informed and effective representatives for their children in early childhood, school-age and vocational settings through agencies and appropriate service.

Founded: 1977

Paula F Goldberg, Executive Director
Alison Bakken, Board Vice-President

146 Parents, Let's Unite for Kids
516 N 32nd Street
Billings, MT 59101-6003
406-255-0540
800-222-7585
Fax: 406-255-0523
E-mail: info@pluk.org
http://www.pluk.org
Parent's Let's Unite for Kids unites parents, professionals, families and friends of children with special needs to support one another, and share information for the benefit of their children.

Founded: 1984

William J O'Connor II, President
Dave Rye, Vice President

147 Partnership for the Assessment of Readiness for College and Careers
202-748-8100
E-mail: Questions@PARCConline.Org
http://www.parcconline.org
The Partnership for Assessment of Readiness for College and Careers is a consortium of states working together to develop a set of assessments that measure whether students are on track to be successful in college and their careers. These high quality, computer-based K-12 assessments in mathematics and English language arts/literacy give teachers, schools, students and parents better information about whether students are on track in their learning and for success after high school.

Laura McGiffert Slover, Chief Executive Officer
David Connerty-Marin, Director of Communications

148 Peace & Justice Studies Association
1421 37th Street NW
Suite 130, Poulton Hall
Washington, DC 20057
928-350-2008
E-mail: randall@peacejusticestudies.org
http://www.peacejusticestudies.org

Bring together academics, K-12 teachers and grassroots activists to explore alternatives to violence and share visions and strategies for peacebuilding, social justice and social change. PJSA also serves as a professional association for scholars in the filed of peace and conflict resolution studies and is the North-American affiliate of the International Peace Research Association.

Founded: 2001

Randall Amster, Executive Director
Cris E. Toffolo, Co-Chair

149 Public Relations Student Society of America

33 Maiden Lane
11th Floor
New York, NY 10038-5150
212-460-1474
Fax: 212-995-0757
E-mail: prssa@prsa.org
http://www.prssa.org
The PRSSA is the foremost organization for students interested in public relations and communications. We seek to advance the public relations profession by nurturing generations of future professionals. We advocate rigorous academic standards for public relations education, the highest ethical principles and diversity in the profession.

Heather Harder, National President
Jeneen Garcia, VP, Education

150 Religious Education Association (REA)

PO Box 200392
Evans, CO 80620-0392
765-225-8836
Fax: 970-351-1269
E-mail: reaapprre@msn.com
http://www.religiouseducation.net
Creates opportunities for exploring and advancing the interconnected practices of scholarship, research, teaching, and leadership in faith communities, academic institutions, and the wider world community.

Founded: 1903

Dr Lucinda Huffaker, REA Executive Secretary
Siebren Miedema, President

151 SMARTER Balanced Assessment Consortium

http://www.smarterbalanced.org
Smarter Balancedÿis a public agency supported by 18 states and one territory. Through the work of thousands of educators, Smarter Balanced created an on-line assessment system aligned to theÿCommon Core State Standards (CCSS), as well as tools for educators to improve teaching and learning. Smarter Balanced is housed at UCLA's Graduate School of Education & Information Studies (GSE&IS).

Joe Willhoft, Ph.D., Executive Director
Tony Alpert, Chief Operating Officer

152 STEM Education Coalition

700 North One Lafayette Center
1120 20th Street NW
Washington, DC 20036
202-223-1187
Fax: 202-973-8211
http://www.stemedcoalition.org
Works to raise awareness in congress, the administration, and other organizations about the critical role that STEM education plays in enabling the U.S to remain the economic and technological leader of the global marketplace of the 21st century.

James Brown, Executive Director

153 Sexuality Information & Education Council of the US

90 John Street
Suite 704
New York, NY 10038
212-819-9770
Fax: 212-819-9776
E-mail: mrodriguez@siecus.org
http://www.siecus.org
SIECUS promotes sexuality education for people of all ages, protect sexual rights, and expand access to sexual health services. SIECUS trains educators, advocates for the sound public policies related to sexuality, and provides information and resources on a host of sexuality topics.

Monica Rodriguez, President/CEO
Jason I. Osher, COO

154 Society for the Advancement of Excellence in Education (SAEE)

1889 Springfield Road
Suite 225
Kelowna, BC V1Y-5V5
250-717-1163
Fax: 250-717-1134
E-mail: info@saee.ca
http://www.saee.ca/
Provides non-partisan education research and information to policy-makers, education partners and the public. Our purpose is to encourage higher performance throughout Canada's public education system.

Founded: 1996

Elizabeth Bredberg, Research Director
Mame McCrea Silva, General Manager

155 Solution Tree

555 North Morton Street
Bloomington, IN 47404
812-336-7700
800-733-6786
Fax: 812-336-7790
E-mail: info@solution-tree.com
http://www.solution-tree.com
Strive to be the premier provider of books, videos, multimedia resources, and professional development opportunities designed to help educators throughout the United States and Canada realize continuous school improvement and connect with youth at risk.

Founded: 1998

Paul Breda, Representative
Amy Purdy, Representative

156 Southeastern Library Association

PO Box 950
Rex, GA 30273
678-466-4334
Fax: 678-466-4349
E-mail: gordonbaker@clayton.edu
http://selaonline.org
A unifying force strong enough to influence legislation and to attract foundation and federal funds for regional library projects. This has resulted in two regional library surveys, the adoption of school library standards, the establishment of state library agencies and the position state school library supervisor; the founding of library schools; the sponsoring of a variety of informative workshops and the publication of significant regional research.

Camille McCutcheon, President
Linda Harris, President-Elect

157 Summit Vision

5640 Lynx Drive
Westerville, OH 43081
614-403-3891
Fax: 614-895-8326
E-mail: tmcbane@wideopenwest.com
http://www.summit-vision.com
Summit Vision believes that through the use of adventure and experiential learning tools, people have the opportunity to reach their full potential—both individually and as part of a larger team.

Founded: 1997

Trey McBane, President
Larissa Kopestonsky, VP

158 Teach Plus

374 Congress St
Suite 502
Boston, MA 02210
617-428-0700
E-mail: info@teachplus.org
http://www.teachplus.org
To improve the outcomes for urban children by ensuring that a greater proportion of students have access to effective, experienced teachers.

159 Utah Library Association (ULA)

PO Box 708155
Sandy, UT 84070-8155
801-200-3129
E-mail: anna.neatrour@gmail.com
http://ula.org
The mission of the Utah Library Association is to serve the professional development and educational needs of its members and to provide leadership and direction in developing and improving library and information services in the state. The Association also initiates and supports legislation promoting library development and monitors legislation that might threaten Utah libraries and librarians.

Andy Spackman, President
Barbara Hopkins, Executive Director

160 Wilderness Education Association

2150 N 107th St.
Suite 205
Seattle, WA 98133
206-209-5275
800-572-3015
Fax: 206-367-8777
E-mail: nationaloffice@weainfo.org
http://www.weainfo.org
The Wilderness Education Association is a not-for-profit organization whose purpose is to educate the general public and outdoor leaders in the appropriate use of wildlands and protected areas by developing and implementing educational curricula, programs and by forming strategic alliances with federal land management agencies, conservation groups and all organizations that benefit from wildlands and feel that the existence of wildlands is important to the quality of life

Founded: 1977

Ricky Haro, President
Rose Verbos, Secretary/Treasurer

161 World Trade Centers Association

120 Broadway
Suite 3350
New York, NY 10271
212-432-2626
800-937-8886
E-mail: info@wtca.org
http://www.wtca.org
Fosters a global Trade Center Network that enhances the brand and promotes prosperity through trade and investment.

Founded: 1970

Ghazi Abu Nahl, Chairman
Bella Heule, President

Administration

162 American Association of Collegiate Registrars & Admissions Officers
1 Dupont Circle NW
Suite 520
Washington, DC 20036
202-293-9161
Fax: 202-872-8857
E-mail: reillym@aacrao.org
http://www.aacrao.org
Promotes higher education and furthers the professional development of members working in admissions, enrollment management, financial aid, institutional research, records and registration.

Brad Myers, President
Nicole Rovig, VP, Information Technology

163 American Association of School Administrators
1615 Duke Street
Alexandria, VA 22314
703-528-0700
Fax: 703-841-1543
E-mail: Info@aasa.org
http://www.aasa.org
The mission of the American Association of School Administrators is to support and develop effective school system leaders who are dedicated to the highest quality public education for all children

Founded: 1865

Daniel A Domenech, Executive Director
Chuck Woodruff, Chief Operating Officer

164 American Association of University Administrators
214 Meadville Street
Edinboro, PA 16412
814-460-6498
Fax: 814-732-2623
E-mail: dking@aaua.org
http://www.aaua.org
The mission of the American Association of University Administrators is to develop and advance superior standards for the profession of higher education administration.

Founded: 1970

Dan L. King, Ed.D., President

165 American Education Finance Association (AEFA)
258 Norman Hall
PO Box 117049
Gainesville, FL 32611-7049
352-392-2391
Fax: 303-670-8986
E-mail: AEFA@coe.ufl.edu
http://www.afajof.org
Promotes understanding of means by which resources are generated, distributed and used to enhance human learning.

Founded: 1976

Sheridan Titman, President
Robert Stambaugh, President-Elect

166 Association of Arts Administration Educators
188 Hanford Street
Columbus, OH 43206
312-469-0795
E-mail: info@artsadministration.org
http://www.artsadministration.org
The Association of Arts Administration Educators (AAAE) is an international organization incorporated as a nonprofit institution within the United States. Its mission is to represent college and university graduate and undergraduate programs in arts administra-tion, encompassing training in the management of visual, performing, literary, media, cultural and arts service organizations.

Founded: 1975

Alan Salzenstein, President
Ellen Rosewall, Vice-President

167 Association of College Administration Professionals
PO Box 1389
Staunton, VA 24402
540-885-1873
Fax: 540-885-6133
E-mail: acap@cfw.com
http://acap.webstarts.com
The Association of College Administration Professionals was started in 1995 to provide services to all college and university administrators, regardless of their positions.

Founded: 1995

168 Association of School Business Officials International
ASBO International Annual Meetings and Exhibits
11401 N Shore Drive
Reston, VA 20190-4232
703-478-0405
866-682-2729
Fax: 703-708-7060
E-mail: asboreq@asbointl.org
http://www.asbointl.org
Provide programs and services to promote the highest standards of school business management practices, professional growth, and the effective use of educational resources.

Founded: 1910

John D Musso, Executive Director
Ronald A. Skinner, Deputy Executive Director

169 Association of University Programs in Health Administration
2000 14th Street N
Suite 780
Arlington, VA 22201
703-894-0940
Fax: 703-894-0941
E-mail: aupha@aupha.org
http://www.aupha.org
The Association of University Programs in Health Administration (AUPHA) is a global network of colleges, universities, faculty, individuals and organizations dedicated to the improvement of healthcare delivery through excellence in healthcare management and policy education.

Gerald Glandon, PhD, President/ CEO
Lucinda Flowers, Senior Director of Education

170 Council for the Advancement of Standards in Higher Education
One Dupont Circle, NW
Suite 300
Washington, DC 20036
202-862-1400
Fax: 202-296-3286
E-mail: executive_director@cas.edu
http://www.cas.edu
Founded in 1979, the Council for the Advancement of Standards in Higher Education (CAS) is the pre-eminent force for promoting standards in student affairs, student services, and student development programs. CAS creates and delivers dynamic, credible standards, guidelines, and Self-Assessment Guides that are designed to lead to a host of quality programs and services.

Founded: 1979

Deborah Garrett, President
Douglas Lange, Secretary

171 Council of Chief State School Officers
1 Massachusetts Avenue NW
Suite 700
Washington, DC 20001-1431
202-336-7000
Fax: 202-408-8072
E-mail: communications@ccsso.org
http://www.ccsso.org
Envision a system of schooling in each state that ensures high standards of performance and prepares each child to succeed as a productive member of a democratic society.

June Atkinson, President
Lillian Lowery, President Elect

172 Council of Higher Education Management Associations
NACUBO, 1110 Vermont Ave, NW
Suite 800
Washington, DC 20005-3593
202-861-2584
Fax: 202-449-1246
E-mail: rroberson@nacubo.org
http://www.chemanet.org
The Council of Higher Education Management Associations (CHEMA) is an informal voluntary assembly of management-oriented higher education associations in the United States and Canada. By sharing information, comparing experiences, and working collectively on projects of shared interest, CHEMA members maximize their resources and create substantial benefits for the colleges and universities they represent.

Founded: 1971

173 Heads Network (The)
23490 Caraway Lakes Drive
Bonita Springs, FL 34135-8441
239-947-4323
Fax: 239-390-3245
E-mail: napsg@mac.com
http://www.napsg.org
Provides forum for school leaders to learn from each other in the interest of the education of girls and young women.

Founded: 1920

Bruce W Galbraith, Executive Director
Elizabeth Speers, President

174 Independent Schools Association of the Central States
55 West Wacker
Suite 701
Chicago, IL 60601
312-750-1190
Fax: 312-750-1193
E-mail: info@isacs.org
http://www.isacs.org
The purpose of ISACS is to promote the development of strong learning communities characterized by high achievements, social responsibility, and independence of governance, programs and policies.

1165 pages

Claudia Daggett, President
Jacob Isaac, Program Services Manager

175 NASPA - Student Affairs Administrators in Higher Education
111 K Street, NE
10th Floor
Washington, DC 20002

202-265-7500
Fax: 202-898-5737
E-mail: office@naspa.org
http://www.naspa.org
NASPA is the leading voice for student affairs administration, policy, and practice, and affirms the commitment of the student affairs profession to educating the whole student and integrating student life and learning. With more than 12,000 members at 1,400 campuses, and representing 29 countries, NASPA is the foremost professional association for student affairs administrators, faculty, and graduate and undergraduate students.

Founded: 1919

Kevin Kruger, President
Amy Shopkorn, VP, Operations

176   National Association for Supervision and Curriculum Development (ASCD)
1703 N Beauregard Street
Alexandria, VA 22311-1714
703-578-9600
800-933-2723
Fax: 703-575-5400
E-mail: member@ascd.org
http://www.ascd.org
A membership organization that develops programs, products, and services essential to the way educators learn, teach, and lead.

Founded: 1943

Kathy Clayton, Executive Director
Debra Hill, President

177   National Association of Elementary School Principals
1615 Duke Street
Alexandria, VA 22314-3483
703-684-3345
800-386-2377
Fax: 703-549-5568
E-mail: naesp@naesp.org
http://www.naesp.org
Advocate for support principals need to achieve the highest results for children, families and communities.

Founded: 1921

Gail Connelly, Executive Director
Ernest Mannino, CEO

178   National Association of Gifted Children
1331 H Street NW
Suite 1001
Washington, DC 20005
202-785-4268
Fax: 202-785-4248
E-mail: nagc@nagc.org
http://www.nagc.org
NAGC supports and engages in research and development, staff development, advocacy, communication, and collaboration with other organizations and agencies who strive to improve the quality of education for all students.

Tracy L. Cross, President
Andrew Bassett, Director of Finance & Admin

179   National Association of Private Special Education Centers
601 Pennsylvania Avenue, NW
Suite 900 - South Building
Washington, DC 20004
202-434-8225
Fax: 202-434-8224
E-mail: napsec@aol.com
http://www.napsec.org

Provides funding for educational, research and charitable activities, and special projects for NAPSEC and/or other related and similar organizations.

Founded: 1971

Sherry Kolbe, Executive Director

180   National Association of Secondary School Principals
1904 Association Drive
Reston, VA 20191-1537
703-860-0200
800-253-7746
Fax: 703-476-5432
E-mail: nhs@nassp.org
http://www.nassp.org
To promote excellence in school leadership and to provide members with a wide variety of programs and services to assist them in administration, supervision, curriculum planning, and effective staff development.

JoAnn D. Bartoletti, Executive Director
Denise Greene-Wilkinson, President

181   National Association of State Directors of Special Education
225 Reinekers Lane
Suite 420
Alexandria, VA 22314
703-519-3800
Fax: 703-519-3808
E-mail: nasdse@nasdse.org
http://www.nasdse.org
A nonprofit corporation that promotes and supports education programs for students with disabilities in the United States and outlying areas.

Founded: 1938

Frank Podobnik, President
Bill East, Executive Director

182   National Association of Student Financial Aid Administrators
1101 Connecticut Avenue NW
Suite 1100
Washington, DC 20036-4303
202-785-0453
Fax: 202-785-1487
E-mail: Web@NASFAA.org
http://www.nasfaa.org
A nonprofit corporation of postsecondary institutions, individuals, agencies and students interested in promoting the effective administration of student financial aid in the United States.

Justin Draeger, President/CEO
Ron Day, National Chair

183   National Association of Student Personnel Administrators
111 K Street NE
10th Floor
Washington, DC 20002
202-265-7500
E-mail: office@naspa.org
http://www.naspa.org
The leading association for the advancement, health, and sustainability of the student affairs profession. Our work provides high-quality professional development, advocacy, and research for 14,000 members in all 50 states, 25 countries, and 8 U.S. territories.

Founded: 1919

Kevin Kruger, President
Amy Shopkorn, VP, Operations

184   National Center for the Improvement of Educational Assessment
31 Mount Vernon Street
Dover, NH 3820
603-516-7900
Fax: 603-516-7910
http://www.nciea.org
The Center for Assessment, short for The National Center for the Improvement of Educational Assessment, Inc. (NCIEA), was founded to address the changes currently underway in assessment and accountability in the United States. The Center's mission is to contribute to improved student achievement through enhanced practices in educational assessment and accountability.

Richard Hill, Founder
Brian Gong, Executive Director

185   National Center on Educational Outcomes
University of Minnesota, 207 Pattee
150 Pillsbury Dr. SE
Minneapolis, MN 55455
612-626-1530
Fax: 612-624-0879
E-mail: nceo@umn.edu
http://www.cehd.umn.edu/nceo/default.html
The National Center on Educational Outcomes (NCEO) was established in 1990 to provide national leadership in designing and building educational assessments and accountability systems that appropriately monitor educational results for all students, including students with disabilities and English Language Learners (ELLs).

Founded: 1990

Martha Thurlow, Ph.D., Director
Deb Albus, Research Fellow

186   National Council for Accreditation of Teacher Education
1140 19th Street
Suite 400
Washington, DC 20036
202-223-0077
Fax: 202-296-6620
E-mail: caep@caepnet.org
http://www.ncate.org
CAEP advances excellent educator preparation through evidence-based accreditation that assures quality and supports continuous improvement to strengthen P-12 student learning.

Founded: 1954

James G. Cibulka, President
Emerson J. Elliott, Director, Special Projects

187   National Council of State Directors of Adult Education
444 N Capitol Street, NW
Suite 422
Washington, DC 20001
202-624-5250
Fax: 202-624-1497
E-mail: dc2@ncsdae.org
http://www.ncsdae.org
to attend to legislative needs and concerns, to work with other adult education organizations, to exchange ideas and solve common problems, and to establish and maintain a nationwide communication network regarding national policy and legislative issues.

Founded: 1967

Reecie Stagnolia, Chairman
Dr Lennox McLendon, Executive Director

188   National Data Bank for Disabled Student Services
University of Maryland
Room 0126, Shoemaker Building
College Park, MD 20742
301-314-7682
301-314-7682

Fax: 301-405-0813
http://www.inform.umd.edu
Provides assessment of statistics related to services, staff, budget and other components of disabled student services programs across the country.

Vivian S Boyd, Director
Jo Ann Hutchinson, Assistant Director, DSS

89   National Institute for School and Workplace Safety
257 Plaza Drive
Suite B
Oviedo, FL 32765-6457
407-366-4878
Fax: 407-977-1210
http://www.nisws.com
Believes that every school and workplace must implement school and workplace safety standards. Committed to enhance school and workplace safety and to increase awareness of school and workplace safety issues.

Steven Burhoe, CEO

90   National Orientation Directors Association
2829 University Avenue
Suite 415
Minneapolis, MN 55414
612-301-6632
866-521-6632
Fax: 612-624-2628
E-mail: noda@umn.edu
http://www.nodaweb.org
The mission of NODA is to provide education, leadership and professional development in the fields of college student orientation, transition and retention.

Rick Sparks, President
Stephen Matthews, Secretary/Treasurer

91   National Policy Board for Educational Administration
University Council for Educational
The University of Texas at Austin, 1 Uni
Austin, TX 78712

http://www.npbea.org
The National Policy Board for Educational Administration is a national consortium of major stakeholders in educational leadership and policy. The purpose of the Board is to provide a forum for collaborative actions by organizations interested in the advancement of school and school-system leadership.

Gene Wilhoit, Chair
Michelle Young, Treasurer

92   National School Safety Center
141 Duesenberg Drive
Suite 7B
Westlake Village, CA 91362-3815
805-373-9977
Fax: 805-373-9277
E-mail: info@schoolsafety.us
http://www.schoolsafety.us
Serves as an advocate for safe, secure and peaceful schools worldwide and as a catalyst for the prevention of school crime and violence.
Founded: 1984

Ronald D Stephens, Executive Director
June Lane Arnette, Associate Director

93   Psychological Corporation
19500 Bulverde Road
San Antonio, TX 78259
210-339-8190
800-627-7271
Fax: 800-232-1223
http://www.pearsonassess.com

Our mission is to improve teaching and learning. We help student, families, educators, and professionals use assessment, research, and innovative technologies to promote learning and personal development, advance academic achievement, and transform educational communities.

Doug Kubash, President/CEO
Karamjeet Singh, SVP/Chief Technology Officer

Early Childhood Education

194   Association for Early Learning Leaders
8000 Centre Park Drive
Ste. 170
Austin, TX 78754
800-537-1118
E-mail: info@earlylearningleaders.org
http://www.earlylearningleaders.org
The Association for Early Learning Leaders, formerly known as the National Association of Child Care Professionals is a 501(c)(3) nonprofit organization committed to excellence by promoting leadership development and enhancing program quality through the National Accreditation Commission's standards. Since 1984, Early Learning Leaders have been serving childcare directors, owners and administrators.
Founded: 1984

Mary S. Hornbeck, President
Colleen Tracy Haddad, Executive Director

195   Association to Benefit Children
419 East 86th Street
New York, NY 10028
212-845-3821
Fax: 212-426-9488
E-mail: info@a-b-c.org
http://www.a-b-c.org
Association to Benefit Children (ABC)ÿis dedicated to bringing joy and warmth to disadvantaged children and their families through compassionate, sustainable, comprehensive and integrated services, designed to permanently break the cycles of abuse, neglect, sickness and homelessness.

Gretchen Buchenholz, President
Michael Lewis, Vice President

196   Building Blocks For Literacy
183 Talcott Rd
Suite 101
Willston, VT 05495-9209
802-878-2332
http://www.buildingblocksforliteracy.org
Promotes early literacy skills for children in child care and preschool environments.
Founded: 1997

197   Child Care Aware of America
1515 North Courthouse Road
11th Floor
Arlington, VA 22201
800-424-2246
E-mail: news@usa.childcareaware.org
http://www.childcareaware.org
Child Care Aware(c) is the nation's most respected hub of information for parents and child care providers. A program of Child Care Aware(R) of America, Child Care Aware(R) helps families learn more about the elements of quality child care and how to locate programs in their communities. Child Care Aware(R) also provides child care providers with access to resources for their child care programs.

198   Child Care Information Exchange
Exchange Press, Inc.
17725 NE 65th Street
B-275
Redmond, WA 98052
425-883-9394
800-221-2864
Fax: 425-861-9386
E-mail: infor@ChildCareExchange.com
http://www.ccie.com
Exchange has promoted the exchange of ideas among leaders in early childhood programs worldwide through its magazine, books, training products, training seminars, and international conferences.

Bonnie Neugebauer, Editor in Chief
Debra Hartzell, Advertising

199   Child Development Resources
P.O. Box 280
Norge, VA 23127
757-566-3300
Fax: 757-566-8977
http://www.cdr.org
CDR is a comprehensive resource for physicians, teachers, and parents-in fact, for anyone who has a question about an infant or toddler-throughout the Historic Triangle.
Founded: 1966

A. Vaughn Poller, Chair
Eddie Robinson, Vice-Chair

200   Children's Place Association (The)
700 N. Sacramento Blvd.
Suite 300
Chicago, IL 60612
312-733-9954
Fax: 312-243-7653
http://childrens-place.org
The Children's Place Association transforms the lives of children in the very worst circumstances - those confronting illness and extreme poverty. We help them overcome challenges so they can lead their best lives.
Founded: 1991

Cathy Krieger, LCSW, MA, MBA, President/ CEO
Curt Schubert, Chief Financial Officer

201   Dimensions of Early Childhood
Southern Early Childhood Association
PO Box 55930
Little Rock, AR 72215-5930
501-221-1648
800-305-7322
Fax: 501-227-5297
E-mail: info@southernearlychildhood.org
http://www.southernearlychildhood.org
Southern Early Childhood Association has brought together preschool, kindergarten, and primary teachers and administrators, caregivers, program directors, and individuals working with and for families, to promote quality care and education for young children.

Nancy Jane Chesire, President
Kathy Attaway, President-Elect

202   Division for Early Childhood
The Council for Exceptional Children
27 Fort Missoula Road
Suite 2
Missoula, MT 59804
406-543-0872
Fax: 406-543-0887
E-mail: dec@dec-sped.org
http://www.dec-sped.org
The Division for Early Childhood promotes policies and advances evidence-based practices that support families and enhance the optimal development of young children who

have or are at risk for developmental delays and disabilities.

Sarah Mulligan, Executive Director
Cynthia Wood, Associate Executive Director

203 Education Advisory Group

6239 Woodlawn Avenue North
Seattle, WA 98810
206-323-1838
Fax: 206-267-1325
http://www.eagstrategies.com
Specializes in matching children with learning environments. Helps families identify concerns and establish priorities about their child's education.

204 HighScope Educational Research Foundation

600 North River Street
Ypsilanti, MI 48198-2898
800-587-5639
Fax: 734-485-0704
E-mail: info@highscope.org
http://www.highscope.org
HighScope Educational Research Foundation is an independent nonprofit research, development, training, and public outreach organization with headquarters in Ypsilanti, Michigan. HighScope's mission is toÿlift lives through education.ÿWe envision a world in which all educational settings useactive participatory learningÿso everyone has a chance to succeed in life and contribute to society.

Founded: 1970

Cheryl Polk, PhD, President
Steven Schwartz, Chief Financial Officer

205 Military Child Education Coalition

909 Mountain Lion Circle
Harker Heights, TX 76548
254-953-1923
Fax: 254-953-1925
http://www.militarychild.org
The work of the Military Child Education Coalition (MCEC) is focused on ensuring quality educational opportunities for all military children affected by mobility, family separation, and transition. A 501(c)(3) non-profit, world-wide organization, the MCEC performs research, develops resources, conducts professional institutes and conferences, and develops and publishes resources for all constituencies.

Mary M. Keller, Ed.D., President/ CEO
Daryl McLauchlin, Chief Technology Officer

206 National AfterSchool Association

2961A Hunter Mill Road
#626
Oakton, VA 22124
E-mail: info@naaweb.org
http://naaweb.org
NAA is the membership association for professionals who work with children and youth in diverse school and community-based settings to provide a wide variety of extended learning opportunities and care during out-of-school hours. Our members include afterschool program directors, coordinators, sponsors, front-line staff, school leaders, principals, teachers, paraprofessionals, board of education members, non-profit leaders, advocates, community leaders, policymakers, researchers, and more.

Barbara Roth, Chair
Vincent LaFontan, Vice Chair

207 National Association for Family Child Care

1743 W. Alexander Street
Salt Lake City, UT 84119
801-886-2322
801-88 -AFCC
Fax: 801-886-2325
E-mail: edaniels@nafcc-mail.org
http://www.nafcc.org
The National Association for Family Child Care (NAFCC) is a 501(c)(3) non-profit membershipÿ association.ÿ NAFCC represents professional providers throughout the United States and in some cases on US Military bases located internationally.ÿ NAFCC is dedicated to promoting quality child care by strengthening the profession of family child care.

Patricia Dischler, President
Eva Daniels, Executive Director

208 National Association for the Education of Homeless Children and Youth

P.O. Box 26274
Minneapolis, MN 55426
866-862-2562
Fax: 763-545-9499
E-mail: info@naehcy.org
http://www.naehcy.org
NAEHCY is the only professional organization specifically dedicated to meeting the educational needs of children and youth experiencing homelessness. We provide professional development, resources, and training support for anyone and everyone interested in supporting the academic success of children and youth challenged by homelessness.

Founded: 1989

Dana Scott, President
Barbara Duffield, Director of Policy/Programs

209 National Association of Early Childhood Specialists in State Departments of Education

E-mail: information@naecs-sde.org
http://www.naecs-sde.org
NAECS-SDE (National Association of Early Childhood Specialists in State Departments of Education) is a national organization for state education agency staff members with major responsibilities in the field of early childhood education. The Association promotes high-quality services to young children and their families through improvement of instruction, curriculum, and administration of programs.

Founded: 1972

Deborah Adams, President
John Pruette, Vice President

210 National Child Care Association

325 G Street NW
Suite 500
Washington, DC 20005
800-543-7161
E-mail: president@nccanet.org
http://www.nccanet.org
NCCA in conjunction with our members will work to generate information based upon our years of experience of best practice to deliver the highest quality along with what is most practical for our members.

Founded: 1987

211 National Early Childhood Technical Assistance Center

ECTA Center
517 S Greensboro Street
Carrboro, NC 27510
919-962-2001
919-843-3269
Fax: 919-966-7463
E-mail: ectacenter@unc.edu
http://www.nectac.org
NECTAC is the national early childhood technical assistance center supported by the U.S. Department of Education's Office of Special Education Programs.

Lynne Kahn, Director
Joan Danaher, Associate Director

212 National Educational Systems (NES)

6333 De Zavala
Suite 106
San Antonio, TX 78249
800-231-4380
Fax: 210-699-4674
E-mail: info@shopnes.com
http://www.shopnes.com
NES is committed to providing quality materials to its customers and prides itself on the friendly customer service that is readily available.

Lupe Garza, Owner
Diana Garza, Owner

213 National Head Start Association

1651 Prince Street
Alexandria, VA 22314
703-739-0875
866-677-8724
Fax: 703-739-0878
http://www.nhsa.org
The National Head Start Association is a private not-for-profit membership organization dedicated exclusively to meeting the needs of Head Start children and their families.

Ron Herndon, Chairman
Linda Broyles, Vice- Chairperson

214 National Institute for Early Education Research

73 Easton Avenue
New Brunswick, NJ 08901-1879
848-932-4350
http://www.nieer.org
Conducts and communicates research to support high-quality, effective early childhood education for all young children.

Jen Fitzgerald, Public Information Officer

215 Professional Association for Childhood Education

436 14th St.
Suite 205
Oakland, CA 94612
415-749-6851
800-924-2460
Fax: 415-397-7223
E-mail: info@pacenet.org
http://www.pacenet.org
The Professional Association for Childhood Education (PACE) is a non-profit, California statewide organization established in 1955 to advance the profession of childhood education. PACE members operate in excess of 1,000 centers, serving more than 55,000 children in California. PACE members make a significant difference for educators, families, and children, ultimately affecting our future.

Founded: 1955

Gina Ayllon, Executive Director
Estela Alvarez, Events/ Education Director

Elementary Education

216   Center for Play Therapy
University of North Texas
1400 Highland Street
Room 14
Denton, TX 76203-0829
940-565-3864
Fax: 940-565-4461
E-mail: cpt@unt.edu
http://www.centerforplaytherapy.com
Encourages the unique development and emotional growth of children through the process of play therapy, a dynamic interpersonal relationship between a child and a therapist trained in play therapy procedures. Provides training, research, publications, counseling services and acts as a clearinghouse for literature in the field.

Sue Bratton, Director
Garry Landreth, Founder

217   Clearinghouse on Early Education and Parenting (CEEP)
University of Illinois at Urbana-Champaign
51 Gerty Drive
Champaign, IL 61820-7469
217-333-1386
877-275-3227
Fax: 212-244-7732
E-mail: ecap@illinois.edu
http://ecap.crc.illinois.edu
The Clearinghouse on Early Education and Parenting (CEEP) is part of the Early Childhood and Parenting (ECAP) Collaborative at the University of Illinois at Urbana-Champaign. CEEP provides publications and information to the worldwide early childhood and parenting communities on topics relating to the physiological, psychological and cultural development of children from birth through early adolescence.

Lilian G Katz Ph.D, Co-Director
Bernard Cesarone, Assitant Director Pub &Tech

218   National Association for the Education of Young Children
1313 L Street, NW
Suite 500
Washington, DC 20005-4101
202-232-8777
800-424-2460
Fax: 202-328-1846
E-mail: naeyc@naeyc.org
http://www.naeyc.org
Supports those interested in serving and acting on behalf of the needs and rights of the education of young children.

Jarlean Daniel, Executive Director
Adele B Robinson, Deputy Executive Director

219   Tribeca Learning Center-PS 150
334 Greenwich Street
New York, NY 10013
212-732-4392
Fax: 212-766-5895
E-mail: Info@ps150.net
http://www.ps150.net
Tribeca Learning Center, PS 150 opened in 1987 as a public school that encourages student-centered learning and family involvement fostering the optimal development and learning of every child and reaffirming the pivotal role of the elementary school. The school offers specialized classes in art, music, dance, technology and library as well as daily classroom activities which encourage the integration of a child's academic development, emotional-social growth, and the arts.

Brian Fingeret, President
Laura Cohen, Coordinator

220   Voyager Expanded Learning
Cambium Learning Group
17855 Dallas Parkway
Suite 400
Dallas, TX 75287
214-932-3213
888-899-1995
Fax: 888-589-0085
E-mail: jnowakowski@voyagerlearning.com
http://www.voyagerlearning.com
Voyager Expanded Learning is a leading provider of in-school core reading programs, reading and math intervention programs, and professional development programs for school districts throughout the United States

Founded: 1994

David Cappellucci, President
Ron Klausner, CEO

Employment

221   English Language Fellow Program
Center for Intercultural Development Center
3300 Whitehaven Street
Suite 1000
Washington, DC 20007
202-687-2608
Fax: 202-687-2555
E-mail: elf@georgetown.edu
http://www.elfellowprogram.org
The English Language Fellow Program provides American professional expertise in teaching English as a foreign language by sending American experts on ten-month fellowships to overseas academic institutions to improve foreign teachers' and students' access to diverse perspectives on a broad variety of issues, giving foreign teachers and students information enabling them to better understand and convey concepts about American values, democratic representative government, and free enterprise.

Magdalena Potocka, Director
Katherine Alisa Mustter, Program Officer

222   Graphic Arts Education & Research Foundation
1899 Preston White Drive
Reston, VA 20191
703-264-7200
866-381-9839
Fax: 703-620-3165
E-mail: gaerf@npes.org
http://www.gaerf.org
To advance knowledge and education in the field of graphic communications by supporting programs that prepare the workforce of the future. 1

James H. Mayes, Chairman
Ralph J. Nappi, President

223   Graphic Arts Technical Foundation
200 Deer Run Road
Sewickley, PA 15143
412-741-6860
800-910-4283
Fax: 412-741-2311
E-mail: printing@printing.org
http://www.gain.net
Deliver products and services that enhance the growth, efficiency, and profitability of its members and the industry through: Advocacy, ÿ Education, ÿ Research, and Technical information

Denna Hower, Marketing Coordinator
Mary Garnett, Executive Vice President

224   Health Occupations Students of America
6021 Morriss Road
Suite 111
Flower Mound, TX 75028
972-874-0062
800-321-4672
Fax: 972-874-0063
E-mail: hosa@hosa.org
http://www.hosa.org
Provides health occupations educators with a student organization used to recruit and develop a competent and motivated work force for the health care field.

David Kelly, National President
Jim Koeninger, Executive Director

225   Mountain Pacific Association of Colleges and Employers
16 Santa Ana Place
Walnut Creek, CA 94598
925-934-3877
Fax: 925-906-0922
E-mail: info@mpace.org
http://www.mpace.org
The Mountain-Pacific Association of Colleges and Employers, Inc. is committed to attaining a pluralistic, diverse membership, and providing access to all programs and resources to individuals regardless of race, color, national origin, religion, gender, age, sexual orientation, veteran status, disability, or appearance

Deborah Dobbs, Executive Director
Patty Bishop, President

226   NPES: Association for Suppliers of Printing, Publishing & Converting Technologies
1899 Preston White Drive
Reston, VA 20191
703-264-7200
Fax: 703-620-0994
E-mail: npes@npes.org
http://www.npes.org
A US trade association representing more than 400 companies that manufacture and distribute equipment, software and supplies used across the workflow of nearly every printing, publishing and converting process.

Ralph J Nappi, President
William K Smythe Jr, Vice President

227   National Association of Colleges and Employers
62 Highland Avenue
Bethlehem, PA 18017
610-868-1421
E-mail: customer_service@naceweb.org
http://www.naceweb.org
The National Association of Colleges and Employers connects campus recruiting and career services professionals, and provides best practices, trends, research, professional development, and conferences.

Founded: 1956

Sam Ratcliffe, President
Manuel Perez, Vice President, College

228   National Association of Professional Employer Organizations
707 North Saint Asaph Street
Alexandria, VA 22314
703-836-0466
Fax: 703-836-0976

E-mail: info@napeo.org
http://www.napeo.org
The National Association of Professional Employer Organizations (NAPEO) is the largest trade association for professional employer organizations (PEOs) nationwide.ÿNAPEO provides robust member resources, vital networking and referrals, hard-hitting education, and effective public relations and marketing support.ÿNAPEO advocates for the interests of its PEO members at all levels of government.

Founded: 1984

Pat Cleary, President/ CEO
Melissa Viscovich, CAE, Senior Vice President/ COO

229 National Business Education Association

1914 Association Drive
Reston, VA 20191-1596
703-860-8300
Fax: 703-620-4483
E-mail: nbea@nbea.org
http://www.nbea.org
NBEA is committed to the advancement of the professional interest and competence of its members and provides programs and services that enhance members' professional growth and development.

Ramona Schoenrock, President
Janet M. Treichel, Executive Director

230 National Student Employment Association

9600 Escarpment Blvd.
Suite 745 PMB 11
Austin, TX 78749
512-423-1417
Fax: 972-767-5131
E-mail: nsea@nsea.info
http://www.nsea.info
The National Student Employment Association is an organization of several hundred professionals involved with programs for college students who work. Membership is open to anyone with an interest in administering student employment or hiring students. NSEA supports and promotes student employment through research, publications, professional development opportunities, and the open exchange of information.

Desiree F Noah, President
Joan Gamble, Vice President

231 Windsor Mountain International

One World Way
Windsor, NH 03244
603-478-3066
800-862-7760
Fax: 603-478-5260
E-mail: mail@WindsorMountain.org
http://www.windsormountain.org/
Windsor Mountain International was founded in 1961, as Interlocken International Camp, hosting young people from more than 60 countries through international youth travel programs where students learn by doing, thereby enriching their lives with lasting friendships, new skills, self discovery, and increased environmental and cross-cultural awareness.

Kerry Labovitz, Director
Jake Labovitz, Owner/Director

232 Women's International League for Peace & Freedom

U.S. Section
11 Arlington Street
Boston, MA 02116

617-266-0999
Fax: 617-266-1688
http://www.wilpf.org
Works to create an environment of political, economic, social and psychological freedom for all members of the human community, so that true peace can be enjoyed by all.

Tanya Henderson, National Director
Laura Roskos, President

Guidance & Counseling

233 American Association of Sex Educators, Counselors & Therapists (AASECT)

1444 I Street NW
Suite 700
Washington, DC 20005
202-449-1099
Fax: 202-216-9646
E-mail: info@aasect.org
http://www.aasect.org
Interest in promoting understanding of human sexuality and healthy sexual behavior.

Founded: 1967

Dee Ann Walker, Executive Director
Dr Patricia Schiller, Founder

234 American College Counseling Association

E-mail: tknappgr@scad.edu
http://www.collegecounseling.org
The American College Counseling Association is made up of diverse mental health professionals from the fields of counseling, psychology, and social work. Our common theme is working within higher education settings.

Tamara Knapp-Grosz, President
Ky Heinlen, PhD, LPCC-S, Secretary

235 American College Personnel Association

One Dupont Circle, NW
Suite 300
Washington, DC 20036
202-835-2272
Fax: 202-296-3286
E-mail: info@acpa.nche.edu
http://www.myacpa.org
Founded in 1994 during the presidency of Charles Schroeder, the purpose of the ACPA Educational Leadership Foundation (501c3 non-profit organization) is to enhance the student affairs profession and to generate and disseminate knowledge of college students at all levels within higher education (Article Three of the Articles of Incorporation).

Cindi Love, Ed.D., Executive Director
Marguerite Comfort, Team Lead, Entity Engagement

236 American Counseling Association

5999 Stevenson Avenue
Alexandria, VA 22304-3302
800-347-6647
Fax: 800-473-2329
E-mail: membership@counseling.org
http://www.counseling.org
A not-for-profit, professional and educational organization that is dedicated to the growth and enhancement of the counseling profession.

Brad Erford, ACA President

237 American School Counselor Association

1101 King Street
Suite 625
Alexandria, VA 22314
703-683-2722
800-306-4722
Fax: 703-683-1619
E-mail: asca@schoolcounselor.org
http://www.schoolcounselor.org
Supports school counselors' efforts to help students focus on academic, personal/social and career development so they achieve success in school and are prepared to lead fulfilling lives as responsible members of society.

Richard Wong, Executive Director
Jill Cook, Assistant Director

238 American School Counselors Association

1101 King Street
Suite 310
Alexandria, VA 22314
703-683-ASCA
800-306-4722
Fax: 703-997-7572
E-mail: asca@schoolcounselor.org
http://www.schoolcounselor.org
The American School Counselor Association (ASCA) supports school counselors' efforts to help students focus on academic, career and social/emotional development so they achieve success in school and are prepared to lead fulfilling lives as responsible members of society.

Richard Wong, Ed.D., CAE, Executive Director
Jill Cook, Assistant Director

239 Association for Addicted Professionals

1521 Hillary Street
New Orleans, LA 70118-4007
504-286-5000
Sustains an information network of substance abuse/chemical dependency training programs in higher education.

Thomas Lief, Director

240 Association for Financial Counseling and Planning Education

1940 Duke Street
Suite 200
Alexandria, VA 22314
703-684-4484
Fax: 703-684-4485
E-mail: rwiggins@afcpe.org
http://www.afcpe.org
AFCPE is the Association for Financial Counseling and Planning Education. We're a nonprofit, professional organization dedicated to educating, training, and certifying financial counselors and educators.

Michael Gutter, President
Rebecca Wiggins, Executive Director

241 Association for University and College Counseling Center Directors

http://www.aucccd.org
The mission of the Association for University and College Counseling Center Directors (AUCCCD) is to assist college/university directors in providing effective leadership and management of their centers, in accord with the professional principles and standards with special attention to issues of diversity and multiculturalism.

Founded: 1950

Elizabeth Gong-Guy, Ph.D., President
Charles Davidshofer, Ph.D., Treasurer

242 Association of Educational Therapists

7044 S. 13th Street
Oak Creek, WI 53154
414-908-4949
Fax: 414-768-8001

E-mail: aet@aetonline.org
http://www.aetonline.org
Founded in 1979 the Association of Educational Therapists establishes professional standards and defines roles, responsibilities and ethics of educational therapists; studies techniques, technologies, philosophies and research related to educational therapy; represents/defines educational therapy to the community, school and professional group; provides opportunities for continued professional growth.

Jeanette Rivera, President
Alice Pulliam, President-Elect

243 Council for Accreditation of Counseling and Related Educational Programs
1001 North Fairfax Street
Suite 510
Alexandria, VA 22314
703-535-5990
Fax: 703-739-6209
http://www.cacrep.org
The vision of CACREP is to provide leadership and to promote excellence in professional preparation through the accreditation of counseling and related educational programs.ÿAs an accrediting body, CACREP is committed to the development of standards and procedures that reflect the needs of a dynamic, diverse, and complex society.
Founded: 1981

Sylvia Fernandez, Chair
Thomas Davis, Vice Chair

244 ERIC/CASS Virtual Libraries: Online Resources for Parents, Teachers, and Counselors
Computer Sciences Corporation
655 15th Street SW
Suite 500
Washington, DC 20005
800-538-3742
http://www.eric.ed.gov
Collects and disseminates information on counseling, guidance and student services. (ERIC/CASS) serves counseling and student professionals as well as parents who have an interest in personal and social factors that affect learning and development. ERIC/CASS has developed virtual libraries to provide online access to full-text documents on topics within its scope.

Robert Boruch, Chairman
John Collins, ERIC Steering Committee

245 Higher Education Consultants Association
http://www.hecaonline.org
The Higher Education Consultants Association (HECA) is the premiere professional organization for consultants who focus exclusively on helping high school students realize their full potential, especially the transition from secondary schools to undergraduate and graduate programs.
Founded: 1997

Eric Delehoy, President

246 International Association of Counseling Services
101 S Whiting Street
Suite 211
Alexandria, VA 22304-3415
703-823-9840
Fax: 703-823-9843
E-mail: iacsinc@earthlink.net
http://www.iacsinc.org
IACS is committed to furthering the visibility of the counseling profession and improving

its quality. IACS has evolved standards that define professional quality and has established criteria for accreditation which reflect these standards.

Nancy E Roncketti, Executive Officer
Rattana Thanagosol, Administrative Assistant

247 National Association of School Psychologists
4340 E West Highway
Suite 402
Bethesda, MD 20814
301-657-0270
866-331-6277
Fax: 301-657-0275
E-mail: center@naspweb.org
http://www.nasponline.org
Founded in 1977 the National Association of School Psychologists is a professional association representing over 22,000 school psychologists and related professionals.

Laura Benson, COO
Susan Gorin, Executive Director

International

248 Academic Travel Abroad
1920 N Street NW
Suite 200
Washington, DC 20036
202-785-9000
800-556-7896
Fax: 202-342-0317
E-mail: epawlowski@academic-travel.com
http://www.academic-travel.com
Create unparalleled, educational travel programs to satisfy curious travelers.
Founded: 1950

David Parry, Chairman
Kate Simpson, President

249 Academy for International School Heads
110 Breeds Hill Road
Unit 2
Hyannis, MA 2601
508-790-1748
Fax: 508-576-9490
E-mail: office@academyish.org
http://www.academyish.org
The Academy for International School Heads was established in 1999 by current and former international school heads and several international organizations serving schools around the world to provide a professional 'community'. Members collaborate, offer advice and support, share best practice and define areas of advocacy.
Founded: 1999

Bambi Betts, CEO
Robert Landau, President

250 Alberta Association of Recreation Facility Personnel
Box 100
Cochrane, AB T4C-1A4
403-851-7626
888-253-7544
Fax: 403-851-9181
E-mail: office@aarfp.com
http://www.aarfp.com
A provincial organization dedicated to providing excellence in training and professional development for individuals involved in the operation of recreation facilities.
Founded: 1978

Aaron Singh, President
Kim Snell, Executive Director

251 Alberta Council on Admissions and Transfer
10155-102 Street
11th Floor
Edmonton, AB T5J-4L5
780-422-9021
800-232-7215
Fax: 780-422-3688
E-mail: acat@gov.ab.ca
http://www.acat.gov.ab.ca
Responsible for developing policies, guidelines and procedures designed to facilitate transfer agreements among post-secondary programs.
Founded: 1974

Ron Woodward, Chairman
Marg Leathem, Director

252 American Councils For International Education
1828 L Street N.W.
Suite 1200
Washington, DC 20036
202-833-7522
Fax: 202-833-7523
E-mail: info@americancouncils.org
http://www.americancouncils.org
American Councils for International Educationÿis a premier, international non-profit creating educational opportunities that prepare individuals and institutions to succeed in an increasingly interconnected world. Through academic exchanges, overseas language immersion, and educational development programs, American Councils designs and administers innovative programs that broaden individual perspectives, increase knowledge, and deepen understanding.
Founded: 1974

Dr. Dan E. Davidson, President
Dr. David Patton, Executive Vice President

253 American Friends Service Committee
Human Resources
1501 Cherry Street
Philadelphia, PA 19102-1429
215-241-7000
Fax: 215-241-7275
E-mail: afscinfo@afsc.org
http://www.afsc.org
The American Friends Service Committee carries out service, development, social justice, and peace programs throughout the world. Founded by Quakers in 1917 to provide conscientious objectors with an opportunity to aid civilian war victims, AFSC's work attracts the support and partnership of people of many races, religions, and cultures.

Arlene Kelly, Presiding Clerk
Phil Lord, Assistant Clerk

254 American Schools Association of Central America, Columbia-Caribbean and Mexico
1209 San Dario Ave
Suite 92-96
Laredo, TX 78040
011 52 81 83384454
E-mail: skeller@tri-association.org
http://www.tri-association.org
Works with over 60 schools to improve the quality of teaching and learning, provide avenue for communication between schools, facilitate cooperation with national, state, local and non-governmental and more in the field of international education.

Sonia Keller, Executive Director
Paul Williams, President

255 Aprovecho Research Center
80574 Hazelton Rd.
PO Box 1175
Cottage Grove, OR 97424
541-942-8198
E-mail: aprovecho.mail@gmail.com
http://www.aprovecho.org
A non-profit organization whose purpose is To research, develop, and disseminate technological solutions for meeting the basic human needs of low income and impoverished people and communities in third world countries, in order to help relieve their suffering, improve their health, enhance their safety, and reduce their adverse impacts on their environment.

Jeremy Roth, Director
Rosemary Kirincic, Outreach Coordinator

256 Associated Schools Project Network
UNESCO
7 Place de Fontenoy
Paris, France 75352
33(0)1 45 68 10 00
Fax: 331-43067925
E-mail: aspnet@unesco.org
http://www.unesco.org
Network of committed schools engaged in fostering and delivering quality education, in pursuit of peace, liberty, justice and human development, in order to meet the pressing educational needs of children and young people throughout the world.

Livia Saldari, International Coordinator
Fouzia Belhami, Program Specialist

257 Association for Asian Studies
Association For Asian Studies, Inc.
825 Victors Way
Suite 310
Ann Arbor, MI 48108
734-665-2490
Fax: 734-665-3801
E-mail: mpaschal@asian-studies.org
http://www.asian-studies.org
Founded in 1941 the Association for Asian Studies seeks through publications, meetings, and seminars to facilitate contact and an exchange of information among scholars to increase their understanding of East, South, and Southeast Asia.

Michael Paschal, Executive Director
Bob Snow, Director of Development

258 Association for Canadian Education Resources
Unit 44, Flamewood Drive
Mississauga, ON L4Y-3P5
905-275-7685
Fax: 905-275-9420
E-mail: acerinfo@rogers.com
http://www.acer-acre.org
Initiate and facilitate development, production and promotion of Canadian materials to meet the needs of today's learners especially those monitoring changes in forest biodiversity.

Alice Casselman, President
Irene Katkov, Chairman

259 Association for Canadian Studies in the US
1740 Massachusetts Ave NW
Nitze 516
Washington, DC 20036
202-775-9007
Fax: 202-775-0061
E-mail: info@acsus.org
http://www.acsus.org

Committed to raising awareness and understanding of Canada and the bilateral relationship.

Myrna Delson-Karan, President
Nadine Fabbi, Secretary

260 Association for Studies in International Education

http://www.asie.org
The Association for Studies in International Education (ASIE) is a group of organizations whose mission is to encourage serious research and publications dealing with international education and academic mobility, to stimulate interest in such work (both in the international education community and in academic circles in general), and to develop and promote ways to disseminate this work in cost-effective and accessible formats.

Hanneke Teekens, Chair
Hans de Wit, Editor

261 Association of Advancement of International Education
Nova Southeastern University
11501 N. Military Trail
Palm Beach Gardens, FL 33410-6507
561-805-2193
Fax: 561-805-2187
E-mail: g.aaie@nova.edu
http://www.aaie.org
AAIE is a dynamic global community that provides a forum for the exchange of ideas and research concerning development in the field of international education, and school leadership and advance international education through participation with educational institutions and associations worldwide.

Founded: 1966

Elsa Lamb, Executive Director
Randy Ward, Office Assistant

262 Association of American International Colleges & Universities
PO Box 21021
Pylea, Thessaloniki
Greece 555-10
33-4-42-23-39-35
Fax: 33-4-42-21-11-38
E-mail: rjackson@act.edu
http://www.aaicu.org
Encourages collaboration and the sharing of information and resources among schools which share many issues in common.

Founded: 1971

Panos Vlachos, President

263 Association of American Schools of Brazil
Conjunto E, Lotes 34/37
SGAS 605
Brasilia, DF, Brazil 70200-650
55 (61) 3442 9700
Fax: 55 (61) 3442 9729
E-mail: cjohnson@eabdf.br
http://www.eabdf.br
Provides a US accredited, pre-K through grade 12 program based on a comprehensive college preparatory curriculum taught in English to students of all nationalities.

Elizabeth Lopez, Principal
Michael Ellis, Board President

264 Association of American Schools of Central America
American School of Tequciqalpa
c/o United States Embassy
Tequciqalpa, M.D.C., Honduras
504-239-3333
Fax: 504-239-6162
E-mail: ccorrales@amschool.org
http://www.aascaonline.net
Provides opportunities for school communities to participate in activities to develop their full potential, social responsibility and global citizenship.

Linda Niehaus, President
Maria Motz, President (Principal's)

265 Association of American Schools of South America
1911 NW 150 Ave
Suite 101
Pembroke Pines, FL 33028
954-436-4034
Fax: 954-436-4092
E-mail: ppoore@aassa.com
http://www.aassa.com
Provide and promote programs and services to member schools to enhance the quality of American International Education. As an organization, AASSA values service leadership, quality and effectiveness.

Paul Joslin, President
Paul Poore, Executive Director

266 Association of British Schools in Spain
c/o Urbanizacion Los Pinos
S-N 18690, Almunecar, Granada
Spain
34-958-639-003
Fax: 34-958-639-003
E-mail: info@nabss.org
http://www.nabss.org
Defends members' interests, maintain the quality of British education in Spain, and support school development.

Donat Morgan, President
Roger Deign, VP

267 Association of Christian Schools International
731 Chapel Hills Drive
PO Box 65130
Colorado Springs, CO 80920-5130
719-528-6906
800-367-0798
Fax: 719-531-0631
E-mail: membership@acsi.org
http://www.acsi.org
Promotes Christian education and provides training and resources to Christian schools and educators. Strengthen Christian school and equip educators worldwide as they prepare students academically, spiritually and culturally.

Brian S Simmons, President

268 Association of International Education Administrators
Duke University, Box 90404, 107 Fra
2204 Erwin Rd.
Durham, NC 27708-402
919-668-1928
Fax: 919-684-8749
E-mail: aiea@duke.edu
http://www.aieaworld.org
The Association of International Education Administrators (AIEA), a membership organization formed in November 1982, is composed of institutional leaders engaged in advancing the international dimensions of higher education.

Founded: 1982

Dr. Darla K. Deardorff, Executive Director
Dafina Blacksher Diabate, Assistant Director

69 Association of International Educators (NAFSA)
1307 New York Avenue NW
8th Floor
Washington, DC 20005-4701
202-737-3699
Fax: 202-737-3657
E-mail: inbox@nafsa.org
http://www.nafsa.org
Serves international educators and their institutions and organizations by setting standards of good practice, providing training and professional development opportunities, providing networking opportunities, and advocating for international education.

Marlene Johnson, Executive Director/CEO
Victor C Johnson, Senior Advisor Public Policy

70 Association of International Schools in Africa
Peponi Road
P O Box 14103, Nairobi
Kenya 00800
254 (20) 2697442
Fax: 254 (20) 418 0596
E-mail: info@aisa.or.ke
http://www.aisa.or.ke
Facilitates communications, cooperation, and professional growth among member schools. Promotes intercultural understanding and friendships as well as facilitating collaboration between its members, host country schools, and other regional and professional groups.

Peter Bateman, Executive Director
John Roberts, Chairperson

71 Atlantic Provinces Special Education Authority
5940 S Street
Halifax, Nova Scotia
Canada B3H-1S6
902-424-8500
Fax: 902-424-0543
E-mail: apsea@apsea.ca
http://www.apsea.ca
Provide quality services and supports, in collaboration with our partners, to meet the educational needs of children and youth from birth to 21 who are blind/visually impaired(BVI) and/or deaf/hard of hearing(DHH).

Bertram Tulk, Superintendent

72 British American Educational Foundation
520 Summit Avenue
Oradell, NJ 07649
201-261-4438
http://www.baef.org
Founded by a group of American alumni of British schools, the BAEF is a non-profit charitable foundation governed by a Board of Directors, comprised primarily of alumni, and a President.

Laurel Zimmermann, Executive Director
Denise Bryan, Founder

73 CARE
151 Ellis Street NE
Atlanta, GA 30303-2400
404-681-2552
800-422-7385
Fax: 404-589-2651
E-mail: managemyaccount@care.org
http://www.care.org
CARE is a leading humanitarian organization fighting global poverty
Founded: 1945

Helene D Gayle, President/CEO
W Bowman Cutter, Chair

274 Canadian Association of Communicators in Education
2900 Don Reid Drive
Ottawa, ON K1H-1E1
E-mail: khamilton@qesba.qc.ca
http://www.cace-acace.org
Promote and contribute to the development of professional communication services in the Canadian education sector.
Founded: 1984

Kim Hamilton, President
Maxeen Jolin, VP

275 Canadian Association of Independent Schools
2 Ridley Road
PO Box 3013
St. Cathatines, ON L2R-7C3
905-684-5658
Fax: 905-684-5057
E-mail: execasst@cesi.edu
http://cais.ca
Explore and pursue exemplary leadership, training, research and international standards of educational excellence.

Anne-Marie Kee, Executive Director

276 Canadian Council for the Advancement of Education
4 Cataraqui Street
Suite 310
Kingston, ON K7K-1Z7
613-531-9213
Fax: 613-531-0626
E-mail: admin@ccaecanada.org
http://www.ccaecanada.org
The Canadian Council for the Advancement of Education (CCAE) fosters excellence in Canadian education by providing bilingual programs and services to professionals in institutional advancement.

Melana Soroka, President
Mark Hazlett, Executive Director

277 Canadian Memorial Chiropractic College
6100 Leslie Street
Toronto, ON M2H-3J1
416-482-2340
800-463-2923
Fax: 416-646-1114
E-mail: communications@cmcc.ca
http://www.cmcc.ca
CMCC is a registered organization in chiropractic education and research dedicated to delivering world class chiropractic education, research and patient care.
Founded: 1945

Jean A Moss, President

278 Canadian Society for the Study of Education
260 Dalhousie Street
Suite 204 Ottawa, Ontario
Canada K1N-7E4
613-241-0018
Fax: 613-241-0019
E-mail: csse-scee@csse.ca
http://www.csse-scee.ca
To promote the advancement of Canadian research and scholarship in education. In order to fulfill its mandate
Founded: 1972

Fernand Gervais, President
Marc-Andre Ethier, VP

279 Catholic Medical Mission Board
10 W 17th Street
New York, NY 10011-5765

212-242-7757
800-678-5659
Fax: 212-645-1485
E-mail: info@cmmb.org
http://www.cmmb.org
To provide quality healthcare programs and services, without discrimination, to people in need around the world.
Founded: 1912

Bruce Wilkinson, President/CEO
Michael Doring Connelly, Chairman

280 Central and Eastern European Schools Association
American International School of Zagreb
Vocarska 106
Zagreb 10000
Croatia
+385-1-460-9935
Fax: +385-1-460-9936
E-mail: office@ceesa.org
http://www.ceesa.org
A collaborative community of international schools which enhances school effectiveness and inspires student learning and development.

Kathey Stetson, Executive Director
David Ottaviano, Chmn, Executive Committee

281 Commonwealth of Learning
1055 W Hastings Street
Suite 1200
Vancouver, BC V6E-2E9
604-775-8200
Fax: 604-775-8210
E-mail: info@col.org
http://www.col.org
An intergovernmental organization created by Commonwealth Heads of Government to encourage the development and sharing of open learning/distance education knowledge, resources and technologies.
Founded: 2001

Asha S. Kanwar, President/CEO
Vis Naidoo, VP

282 Communicating for America
112 E Lincoln Avenue
PO Box 677
Fergus Falls, MN 56537
218-739-3241
800-432-3276
Fax: 218-739-3832
E-mail: memberbenefits@cain.org
http://www.communicatingforamerica.org
Promotes agriculture, protects business and farmland ownership and creates education opportunities with international exchange programs.

Wayne Nelson, President
Milt Smedsrud, Chairman/CEO

283 Comparative and International Education Society
19 Mantua Road
Mt. Royal, NY 8061
856-423-3629
E-mail: secretariat@cies.us
http://www.cies.us
The Comparative and International Education Society (CIES), Inc., was founded in 1956 to foster cross-cultural understanding, scholarship, academic achievement and societal development through the international study of educational ideas, systems, and practices. The Society's members include nearly

2500 academics, practitioners, and students from around the world.

Founded: 1956

Karen Mundy, President
Mark Bray, Vice-President

284 Concern-America Volunteers

2015 N Broadway Avenue
PO Box 1790
Santa Ana, CA 92706-1790
714-953-8575
800-266-2376
Fax: 714-953-1242
E-mail: concamerinc@earthlink.net
http://www.concernamerica.org
Train local populations in health, education, agriculture and/or environmental health enabling them to build local, functional and social systems meeting basic needs

Founded: 1972

John Straw, Executive Director
Denis Garvey, Director of Development

285 Cordell Hull Foundation for International Education

501 Fifth Avenue
Third Floor
New York, NY 10017
212-300-2138
Fax: 646-349-3455
E-mail: cordellhull@aol.com
http://www.cordellhull.org
Offers programs to improve relations between the United States and other countries, primarily through educational and cultural exchange.

Marianne Mason, Executive Director

286 Council of British International Schools

St. Mary's University College
Strawberry Hill
Twickenham, UK TW1-4SX
44(0) 208 240 4142
Fax: 44(0) 208 240 4255
E-mail: executive.director@cobis.org.uk
http://www.cobis.org.uk
COBIS is a Membership Association of British Schools of quality and is a member of the Independent Schools Council (ISC) of the United Kingdom.

Trevor Rowell, Chairman
Colin Bell, Executive Director

287 Council of Education Facility Planners-International

11445 E. Via Linda
Suite 2-440
Scottsdale, AZ 85259
480-391-0840
Fax: 480-391-0940
E-mail: contact@cefpi.org
http://www.cefpi.org
Advocacy and education of general public; resource for planning effective educational facilities; research/information showing link between students success and educational facility/design—- improving the places where children learn.

Irene Nigaglioni, Chairman
David M. Waggoner, Vice-Chair

288 Council of Ministers of Education, Canada

95 St Clair Avenue W
Suite 1106
Toronto, Ontario, Canada M4V-1N6
416-962-8100
Fax: 416-962-2800

E-mail: information@cmec.ca
http://www.cmec.ca
CMEC provides leadership in education at the pan-Canadian and international levels and contributes to the fulfillment of the constitutional responsibility for education conferred on provinces and territories.

Jean-Gilles Pelletier, Administration Director
Andrew Parkin, Director General

289 Council on Foreign Relations

The Harold Pratt House
58 E 68th Street
New York, NY 10065
212-434-9400
Fax: 212-434-9800
http://www.cfr.org
Resource for its members, government officials, business executives, journalists, educators and students, civic and religious leaders, and other interested citizens to help them better understand the world and foreign policy choices facing the United States and other countries.

Richard Haass, President
Jeffrey Reinke, Chief of Staff

290 Council on Hemispheric Affairs

1250 Connecticut Avenue NW
Suite 1C
Washington, DC 20036
202-223-4975
888-922-9261
Fax: 202-223-4979
E-mail: coha@coha.org
http://www.coha.org
Promotes the common interests of the hemisphere , raise the visibility of regional affairs and increase the importance of the inter-American relationship, as well as encourage the formulation of rational and constructive US policies towards Latin America.

Founded: 1975

Larry Birns, Director

291 Council on International Educational Exchange

Educational Exchange
300 Fore St.
Portland, ME 4104
207-553-4000
Fax: 207-553-4299
E-mail: contact@ciee.org
http://www.ciee.org
A nonprofit, nongovernmental organization, CIEE is theÿworld leader in international education and exchange. For more than 65 years CIEE has helped thousands of people gain the knowledge and skills necessary to live and work in a globally interdependent and culturally diverse world by offering the most comprehensive, relevant, and valuable exchange programs available.

Dr. James P. Pellow, President/ CEO
Jorge Barroso, Chief Information Officer

292 Council on Islamic Education

10055 Slater Avenue
Suite 250
Fountain Valley, CA 92708
714-839-2929
Fax: 714-839-2714
E-mail: info@cie.org
http://www.cie.org
CIE is formally comprised of Muslim academic scholars of religion, history, political science, cultural studies, communications, education, and other fields, along with a full-time professional

staff with expertise on matters related to U.S. education, civics, politics, the media, faith communities and other components of American society and the institutional system.

Founded: 1990

Shabbir Mansuri, Founding Director
Munir A Shaikh, Executive Director

293 Cultural Vistas

440 Park Avenue S
2nd Floor
New York, NY 10016
212-497-3500
Fax: 212-497-3535
E-mail: info@culturalvistas.org
http://www.culturalvistas.org
Cultural Vistas is committed to its mission to enrich minds, advance global skills, build careers and connect lives through international exchange.

Robert Fenstermacher, President & CEO
Linda Boughton, CFO & Senior VP

294 East Asia Regional Council of Overseas Schools

Barangay Mamplasan
Binan, Laguna
Philippines 4024
+63 (02) 697-9170
Fax: +63 (49) 511-4694
E-mail: info@earcos.org
http://www.earcos.org
Inspires adult and student learning through its leadership and service and fosters intercultural understanding, global citizenship and exceptional educational practices within our learning community,

Tim Carr, President
Dick Krajczar, Executive Director

295 Global Learning

22 Mary Ann Drive
Brick, NJ 08723
732-281-8929
Fax: 723-528-1027
E-mail: globallearningnj@comcast.net
http://www.globallearningnj.org/
A non-profit educational organization that translates the world's growing interdependence into educational activities for teachers, students, librarians, and educational systems, from elementary school through college and in community settings

Jeffrey L Brown, Executive Director
Paula Gotsch, Associate Director

296 Institute of Cultural Affairs

4750 N Sheridan Road
Chicago, IL 60640
773-769-6363
800-742-4032
Fax: 773-944-1582
E-mail: Chicago@ica-usa.org
http://www.ica-usa.org/
Releasing the capacity for positive, sustainable futures.

Founded: 1962

Terry Bergda, CEO

297 Institute of International Education

809 United Nations Plaza
New York, NY 10017-3580
212-883-8200
Fax: 212-984-5452
http://www.iie.org
Advance international education and access to education worldwide. Manages scholarship, training, exchange & leadership programs.

Allan Goodman, President/CEO
Rajika Bhandari, VP Research & Evaluation

298 International Association Of Medical Science Educators
3327B US Route 60 E
Huntington, WV 25705
304-522-1270
Fax: 304-523-9701
http://www.iamse.org
To advance medical education through faculty development and to ensure that the teaching and learning of medicine continues t o be firmly grounded in science.
Founded: 1988

299 International Association for Continuing Education & Training
1760 Old Meadow Road
Suite 500
McLean, VA 22102
703-506-3275
Fax: 703-506-3266
E-mail: info@iacet.org
http://www.iacet.org
Promote and enhance quality in continuing education and training through research, education and the development and continuous improvement of criteria, principles and standards.

Michael Todd Shinholster, President
Kristopher Newbauer, President-Elect

300 International Association for the Exchange of Students for Technical Experience
440 Park Avenue South
2nd Floor
New York, NY 10016-3519
212-497-3530
Fax: 212-997-3584
E-mail: iaeste@culturalvistas.org
http://www.iaesteunitedstates.org
Operate a practical training exchange program between members in order to enhance technical and professional development. Promote international understanding and goodwill amongst students, academic institutions, employers and the wider community.

Gina Del Tito, Associate Program Manager
Katerina Holubova, Senior Program Director

301 International Association of Students in Economics & Business Management (AIESC)
11 Hanover Square
Suite 1700
New York, NY 10005
212-757-3774
Fax: 212-757-4062
E-mail: info@aiesecus.org
http://www.aiesecus.org/
Agency offering international internships, experience leadership and participate in a global learning environment. Offers young people the opportunity to be global citizens, to change the world and get experience and skills that matter today.
Founded: 1956

Cole Wirpels, President
Lucia Trochez, VP Communications

302 International Baccalaureate American Global Centre
7501 Wisconsin Ave
Suite 200 W
Bethesda, MD 20814
301-202-3000
Fax: 301-202-3033
E-mail: ibid@ibo.org
http://www.ibo.org
Aims to develop inquiring, knowledgeable and caring young people who help to create a better and more peaceful world through intercultural understanding and respect.

Carol Bellamy, Chair
Jeffrey Beard, Director General

303 International Baccalaureate Organization
Route des Morillons 15
Grand-Saconnex, Geneve
Switzerland CH-1218
+41 22 309 2540
Fax: +44 22 791 0277
E-mail: ibhq@ibo.org
http://www.ibo.org
The International Baccalaureate (IB) aims to develop inquiring, knowledgeable and caring young people who help create a better and more peaceful world through intercultural understanding and respect.

Jeffrey Beard, Director General
Carol Bellamy, Chair

304 International Education Council
1101 Vermont Avenue, N.W
Suite 400
Washington, DC 20005
202-289-3900
E-mail: contact@internationaleducationcouncil.org
http://www.internationaleducationcouncil.org
International Education Council (IEC) is a non-profit association based in Washington D.C. IEC closely tracks the issues and policies affecting international education, specifically those dealing with student financial aid. IEC seeks to communicate with and influence policy maker decisions regarding U.S. financial aid programs on behalf of its members, the international colleges and universities enrolling U.S. students.

Harrison Wadsworth, Executive Director

305 International Education Exchange Council
San Francisco State University
1600 Holloway Avenue, CVC-C
San Francisco, CA 94132
415-338-1293
E-mail: ieec@mail.sfsu.edu
http://www.sfsuieec.com
The International Education Exchange Council maintains a goal of encouraging international education, student exchange, and study abroad at San Francisco State University, and a sharing of cultures between international and domestic students at SF State.

306 International Education and Resource Network
E-mail: ec@iearn.org
http://www.iearn.org
iEARNÿis a non-profit organization made up of over 30,000 schools and youth organizations in more than 140 countries.ÿiEARNÿempowers teachers and young people to work together online using the Internet and other new communications technologies. Over 2,000,000 students each day are engaged in collaborative project work worldwide.
Founded: 1988

Lisa Jobson, Coordinator
Daniel Rosenblum, Coordinator

307 International Graphic Arts Education Association (IGAEA)
1899 Preston White Drive
Reston, VA 26191

http://www.igaea.org

The International Graphic Arts Education Association (IGAEA) is an association of educators in partnership with industry, dedicated to sharing theories, principles, techniques and processes relating to graphic communications and imaging technology.

Michael Williams, President
Tom Loch, President-Elect

308 International Physicians for the Prevention of Nuclear War
66-70 Union Square
#204
Somerville, MA 02143-1024
617-440-1733
Fax: 617-440-1734
E-mail: ippnwbos@ippnw.org
http://www.ippnw.org
Federation of national medical organizations in 62 countries representing doctors, medical students, health workers and concerned citizens whose goal is creating a more peaceful and secure world freed from the threat of nuclear annihilation.

Michael Christ, Executive Director
Douglas Kline, Director of Administration

309 International Research and Exchanges Board (IREX)
IREX
2121 K Street NW
Suite 700
Washington, DC 20037
202-628-8188
Fax: 202-628-8189
E-mail: irex@irex.org
http://www.irex.org
Promotes positive lasting change globally. Enable local individuals and institutions to build key elements of a vibrant society: quality education; independent media; and strong communities.

W Robert Pearson, President
Joyce Warner, VP/ Chief of Staff

310 International Schools Services
15 Roszel Road
PO Box 5910
Princeton, NJ 08543
609-452-0990
Fax: 609-452-2690
E-mail: iss@iss.edu
http://www.iss.edu
Advance the quality of international education for children across the globe by providing comprehensive, world-class services and solutions for learning communities and corporations throughout the world.

Roger Hove, President
Kristin Evins, CFO

311 International Society For Technology In Education
1710 Rhode Island Ave NW
Suite 900
Washington, DC 20036
866-654-4777
Fax: 202-861-0888
http://www.iste.org
Improving learning and teaching by advancing the effective use of technology in PK-12 and teacher education.

312 International Society for Business Education
US Chapter
1914 Association Drive
Reston, VA 20191-1596
703-860-8300
Fax: 703-620-4483
E-mail: mrbsherry@comcast.net
http://www.isbeusa.org

Form an interactive exchange among individuals at national and international levels to assist with the development of the globalization process as it applies to Business Education.

Marilyn Sherry, President
Lee Kantin, President-Elect

313 International Studies Association (ISA)

University of Arizona
324 Social Sciences
Tucson, AZ 85721
520-621-7715
Fax: 520-621-5780
E-mail: isa@isanet.org
http://www.isanet.org
Promote research and education in international affairs and to give American scholars and practitioners interested in international studies a regional base for developing and sharing research.

Founded: 1959

Thomas J Volgy, Executive Director
Lyn Brabant, Director of Administration

314 Mediterranean Association of International Schools (MAIS)

Apartado 80
Madrid
Spain 28080
34-91-740-1900
Fax: 34-91-357-2678
E-mail: info@amerschmad.org
http://www.mais-web.org
Improve quality of education in member schools: promote professional development of faculty, administrators and school board members, effect communication and interchange and create international understanding.

Founded: 1981

Sister Anne M Hill, President
Saara Tatem, VP

315 National Registration Center for Study Abroad

PO Box 1393
Milwaukee, WI 53201-1393
414-278-0631
Fax: 414-271-8884
E-mail: study@nrcsa.com
http://www.nrcsa.com
Improve international understanding through educational exchanges. NRCSA welcomes participants of all ages, nationalities, and occupations.

Founded: 1968

Mike Wittig, General Manager

316 Near East-South Asia Council of Overseas Schools (NESA)

Gravias 6 Aghia Paraskevi
Athens, Greece 15342
+30 210 600-9821
Fax: +30 210 600-9928
E-mail: nesa@nesacenter.org
http://www.nesacenter.org
Maximize student learning by facilitating sustainable and systemic school improvement based on the best practices of American and international education.

David J Chojnacki, Executive Director
Kevin Schafer, President

317 Ontario Business Education Partnership

170 Louisa Steert
Kitchener, ON N2H 5
519-208-5966
888-672-7996
Fax: 519-208-5919
E-mail: sherryl@obep.on.ca
http://www.obep.ca
Facilitate a network among government-supported and private sector partners enabling informed relationships between industry and educators, effective communication of government programs and shaping of new policy and well-supported experiential learning opportunities in Ontario communities.

Founded: 1999

Sherryl Petricevic, Executive Director
Jeremy Hill, Co-Chair

318 Ontario Operative Education Association

35 Reynar Drive
Quispamsis, NB E2G-1J9
Fax: 506-849-8375
E-mail: OCEA@Rogers.com
http://www.ocea.on.ca
Promote the development of Cooperative Education, Work Experience, School-Work Transition and OYAP Programs and to assist in the professional growth of members.

Donna Thomson, President
Donna Flasza, VP

319 Operation Crossroads Africa

PO Box 5570
New York, NY 10027
212-289-1949
Fax: 212-289-2526
E-mail: oca@igc.org
http://www.operationcrossroadsafrica.org
Promote understanding of Africa and the African Diaspora based on the belief that one can truly enter another culture only by living and working in it. Operation Crossraods Africa is a cross cultural exchange program.

Founded: 1958

James Robinson Ph.D, Founder
Willis Logan, President

320 Opportunities Industrialization Centers International (OIC)

1500 Walnut St
Suite 1304
Philadelphia, PA 19102-3295
215-842-0220
Fax: 215-842-2276
E-mail: info@oici.org
http://www.oici.org
OIC International provides individuals with the education, skills and confidence they need to help themselves, their households and their communities.

Crispian Kirk, President/CEO
Edmund D Cooke Jr, Chair of the Board

321 People to People International

911 Main Street
Suite 2110
Kansas City, MO 64105
816-531-4701
Fax: 816-561-7502
E-mail: ptpi@ptpi.org
http://www.ptpi.org
Enhance international understanding and friendship through educational, cultural and humanitarian activities involving the exchange of ideas and experiences directly among peoples of different countries and diverse cultures.

Mary Eisenhower, President/CEO
Mark Stansberry, Chairman

322 Phi Delta Kappa International

320 W. Eighth Street
Suite 216
Bloomington, IN 47404
812-339-1156
800-766-1156
Fax: 812-339-0018
E-mail: memberservices@pdkintl.org
http://www.pdkintl.org
One of largest education associations in the world with members dedicated to improving education. Hundreds of chapters give members the opportunity to network with like-minded educators.

Kathleen Andreson, President
William J Bushaw, Executive Director

323 School Milk Foundation of New Foundland and Labrador

27 Sagona Avenue
Mount Pearl
Canada, NL A1N-4P8
709-364-2776
Fax: 709-364-8364
E-mail: info@schoolmilkfdn.nf.net
http://www.schoolmilk.nl.ca
Foundation promoting consumption of milk amongst school aged children—- part of giving children a healthy active lifestyle.

Founded: 1991

324 Teach Overseas

International Schools Services
15 Roszel Road
PO Box 5910
Princeton, NJ 8543
609-452-0990
Fax: 609-452-2690
E-mail: iss@iss.edu
http://www.iss.edu/
Placed over 17,000 K-12 teachers and administrators in overseas schools since 1955. Most candidates attend US-based International Recruitment Centers where ISS candidates interview with overseas school heads seeking new staff.

Kristin Evins, CFO
Roger Hove, President

325 Teachers of English to Speakers of Other Languages

1925 Ballenger Ave
Suite 550
Alexandria, VA 22314-6820
703-836-0774
888-547-3369
Fax: 703-836-7864
E-mail: info@tesol.org
http://www.tesol.org
TESOL is an international professional organization whose mission is to ensure excellence in English language to speakers of other languages.

Suzanne Panferov, President
Deena Boraie, President-Elect

326 United Nations Development Program

One United Nations Plaza
New York, NY 10017-3515
212-906-5000
Fax: 212-906-5001
E-mail: ohr.recruitment.hq@undp.org
http://www.undp.org
Help countries rebuild and share solutions to achieve poverty reduction, democratic governance, crisis prevention and recovery, environment and energy for sustainable development. Help developing countries attract and use aid effectively.

Helen Clark, Administrator
Rebecca Grynspan, Associate Administrator

327 Visions in Action

2710 Ontario Road NW
Washington, DC 20009-2154

301-944-3370
Fax: 202-588-9344
E-mail: visions@visionsinaction.org
http://www.visionsinaction.org
Visions in Action is committed to achieving social and economic justice in the developing world through grassroots programs and communities of self-reliant volunteers

Shaun Skelton PhD, Director
Samuel Bong, Int'l Exchange Prog. Mgr.

328 World Association of Publishers, Manufacturers & Distributors
Worlddidac
Bollwerk 21, PO Box 8866 CH-3001
Bern
Switzerland
+41 31 311 76 82
Fax: +41 31 312 17 44
E-mail: info@worlddidac.org
http://www.worlddidac.org
Global trade association for companies providing products for education and training at all levels.

Beat Jost, Director General
Kateryna Schuetz, Project Manager

329 World Learning
1 Kipling Rd
PO Box 676
Brattleboro, VT 05302
800-257-7751
Fax: 802-258-3508
E-mail: info@worldlearning.org
http://www.worldlearning.org
A non-profit organization that empowers people and strengthens institutions through education, exchange, and development programs.

Language Arts

330 Academic Language Therapy Association
14070 Proton Road
Suite 100, LB 9
Dallas, TX 75244
972-233-9107
Fax: 972-490-4219
E-mail: office@altaread.org
http://www.altaread.org
The Academic Language Therapy Associationr (ALTA) is a non-profit national professional organization incorporated in 1986 for the purpose of establishing, maintaining, and promoting standards of education, practice and professional conduct for Certified Academic Language Therapists. Academic Language Therapy is an educational, structured, comprehensive, phonetic, multisensory approach for the remediation of dyslexia and/or written-language disorders.
Founded: 1985

Marilyn Mathis, President
Christine Bedenbaugh, Secretary

331 American Association of Teachers of French
Southern Illinois University
Mailcode 4510
Carbondale, IL 62901-4510
618-453-5731
Fax: 618-453-5733
E-mail: abrate@siu.edu
http://www.frenchteachers.org
Founded in 1927, AATF is the largest national association of French teachers in the world with nearly 10,000 members.

Jayne Abrate, Executive Director
Mary Helen Kashuba, President

332 American Comparative Literature Association
E-mail: info@acla.org
http://www.acla.org
TheÿAmerican Comparative Literature Association, founded in 1960, is the principal learned society in the United States for scholars whose work involves several literatures and cultures as well as the premises of cross-cultural literary study itself.
Founded: 1960

Andy Anderson, Administrative Assistant

333 American Council on Education in Journalism and Mass Communication (ACEJMC)
University of Kansas
Stauffer Flint Hall
1435 Jayhawk Blvd
Lawrence, KS 66045-7575
785-864-3973
Fax: 785-864-5225
E-mail: sshaw@ku.edu
http://www2.ku.edu/~acejmc
The Accrediting Council on Education in Journalism and Mass Communications, or ACEJMC, is responsible for the evaluation of professional journalism and mass communications programs in colleges and universities. These programs offer education to prepare students for careers in advertising, newspaper or magazine journalism, photo journalism, public relations, radio and television broadcasting and related fields.

Susanne Shaw, Executive Director
Peter Bhatia, President

334 American Council on the Teaching of Foreign Languages
1001 N Fairfax Street
Suite 200
Alexandria, VA 22314
703-894-2900
Fax: 703-894-2905
E-mail: headquarters@actfl.org
http://www.actfl.org
National organization dedicated to the improvement and expansion of the teaching and learning of all languages at all levels of instruction.

Toni Theisen, President
Mary Lynn Redmond, President-Elect

335 American Speech-Language-Hearing Association
2200 Research Boulevard
Rockville, MD 20852-3289
301-296-5700
800-498-2071
Fax: 301-296-8580
E-mail: actioncenter@asha.org
http://www.asha.org
Support speech-language pathologists, audiologists and speech, language and hearing scientists. Advocate for persons with communication and related disorders, advancing communication science, promote effective human communication.

Patricia A. Prelock, President
Elizabeth S. McCrea, President Elect

336 Association of Schools of Journalism and Mass Communication (ASJMC)
234 Outlet Pointe Boulevard
Columbia, SC 29210-5667
803-798-0271
Fax: 803-772-3509
E-mail: aejmchq@aol.com
http://www.asjmc.org
ASJMC works to support the purposes of schools of journalism and mass communication in order to encourage high standards in administration, raise professional standards and promote public understanding.
Jennifer McGill, Executive Director
Peggy Kuhr, President

337 Center for Applied Linguistics (CAL)
4646 40th Street NW
Washington, DC 20016-1859
202-362-0700
Fax: 202-362-3740
E-mail: info@cal.org
http://www.cal.org
Working to improve communication through better understanding of language and culture. CAL's staff of researchers and educators conduct research, design and develop instructional materials and language tests, provide technical assistance and professional development, conduct needs assessments and program evaluations, and disseminate information and resources related to language and culture.

JoAnn Crandall, Chair
Guadalupe Vald,s, Vice Chair

338 Children's Literature Assembly
E-mail:
info@childrensliteratureassembly.org
http://www.childrensliteratureassembly.org
The Children's Literature Assembly of theÿNational Council of Teachers of Englishÿadvocates the centrality of literature for teaching children. We believe every teacher needs a wide and extensive knowledge base of books published for children and young adults.

James Stiles, President
Trish Bandre, Vice-President

339 Children's Literature Association
1301 W. 22nd Street
Suite 202
Oak Brook, IL 60523
630-571-4520
Fax: 708-876-5598
E-mail: info@childlitassn.org
http://www.childlitassn.org
The Children's Literature Association (ChLA) is a non-profit association of scholars, critics, professors, students, librarians, teachers and institutions dedicated to the academic study of literature for children. For our members, children's literature includes books, films, and other media created for, or adopted by, children and young adults around the world, past, present, and future.

Kara Keeling, President
Annette Wannamaker, VP/President-Elect

340 ERIC Clearinghouse on Languages and Linguistics
Eric Program c/o CSC
655 15th Street NW
Suite 500
Washington, DC 20005
202-362-0700
800-538-3742
Fax: 202-362-3740
E-mail: ericpub@csc.com
http://www.eric.ed.gov
Promotes and improves the teaching and learning of languages, Identifies and solves problems related to language and culture.

John Collins, Steering Committee
Mark Constas, Steering Committee

341 International Dyslexia Association (IDA)
40 York Road
4th Floor
Baltimore, MD 21204-2044

410-296-0232
800-222-3123
Fax: 410-321-5069
E-mail: info@interdys.org
http://www.interdys.org/
The International Dyslexia Association (IDA) is a scientific and educational organization dedicated to the study and treatment of the learning disability dyslexia as well as related language based differences.

Lee Grossman, Executive Director
Eric Q Tridas, President

342   Journalism Education Association
Kansas State University
103 Kedzie Hall
Manhattan, KS 66506-1505
785-532-5532
866-532-5532
Fax: 785-532-5563
E-mail: jea@spub.ksu.edu
http://www.jea.org
Among JEA's 2,100 members are journalism teachers and publications advisers, media professionals, press associations, adviser organizations, libraries, yearbook companies, newspapers, radio stations and departments of journalism.

Mark Newton, President
Sarah Nichols, Vice President

343   Modern Language Association
26 Broadway
3rd floor
New York, NY 10004-1789
646-576-5000
Fax: 646-458-0030
E-mail: bookorders@mla.org
http://www.mla.org
Founded in 1883, the Modern Language Association of America provides opportunities for its members to share their scholarly findings and teaching experiences with colleagues and to discuss trends in the academy.

Founded: 1883

Rosemary G. Feal, Executive Director
Terrence Callaghan, Director of Admin/ Finance

344   National Association for Bilingual Education
NABE Marketplace
8701 Georgia Ave
Suite 700
Silver Spring, MD 20910
240-450-3700
Fax: 240-450-3799
E-mail: nabe@nabe.org
http://www.nabe.org
Advocate for our nation's Bilingual and English Language Learners and families and to cultivate a multilingual multicultural society by supporting and promoting policy, programs, pedagogy, research and professional development that yield academic success, value native language, lead to English proficiency and respect cultural and linguistic diversity.

Eudes Budhi, President
Santiago V. Wood, Ed.D, National Executive Director

345   National Association for Poetry Therapy
E-mail: naptadmin@poetrytherapy.org
http://www.poetrytherapy.org
The National Association for Poetry Therapy is an energetic, world-wide community of poets, writers, journalkeepers, helping professionals, health care professionals, educators, and lovers of words who recog-

nize and appreciate the healing power of language.

Alma Maria Rolfs, LICSW, PTR, President
Barbara Kreisberg, VP, Conference

346   National Council of Teachers of English
1111 W Kenyon Road
Urbana, IL 61801-1096
217-328-3870
877-369-6283
Fax: 217-328-9645
E-mail: public_info@ncte.org
http://www.ncte.org
Promotes the development of literacy, the use of language to construct personal and public worlds and to achieve full participation in society, through the learning and teaching of English and the related arts and sciences of language.

Sandy Hayes, President
Ernest Morrell, President-Elect

347   National Federation of Modern Language Teachers Association (NFMLTA)
c/o University of Wisconsin-Madison
460 Pierce Street
Monterey, CA 93940
831-647-6510
Fax: 831-647-6514
E-mail: mlj@miis.edu
http://mlj.miis.edu//nfmlta.htm
The purposes of the National Federation of Modern Language Teachers Associations (NFMLTA) are the expansion, promotion, and improvement of the teaching of languages, literatures, and cultures throughout the United States, by a variety of activities including but not limited to the publication of The Modern Language Journal.

Carol Klee, President
Aleidine Moeller, VP

348   National Network for Early Language Learning (NELL)
PO Box 75003
Oklahoma City, OK 73147
405-604-0041
Fax: 405-604-0491
E-mail: nnell@wfu.edu
http://www.nnell.org
Provide leadership to advocate for and support successful early language learning and teaching.

Nadine Jacobsen-McLean, Vice President
Rita Oleksak, President

349   National Research Center on English Learning and Achievement
School of Education
University of Albany
1400 Washington Avenue
Albany, NY 12222-100
518-442-4985
Fax: 518-442-4953
E-mail:
educationdean@uamail.albany.edu
http://www.albany.edu
Conduct research dedicated to gaining knowledge to improve students' English and literacy achievement.

Janet I Angelis, Associate Director
Judith A. Langer, Co-Director

350   ReadWriteThink
800 Barksdale Road
P.O. Box 8139
Newark, DE 19714-8139

http://www.readwritethink.org
At ReadWriteThink, their mission is to provide educators, parents, and afterschool professionals with access to the highest quality practices in reading and language arts instruction by offering the very best in free materials.

351   Sigma Tau Delta
Northern Illinois University
Department of English
Northern Illinois University
DeKalb, IL 60115-2867
815-981-9974
E-mail: sigmatd@niu.edu
http://www.english.org
Main purpose is to confer distinction upon students of the English language and literature in undergraduate, graduate and professional studies. Sigma Tau Dalta also recognizes the accomplishments of professional writers who have contributed to the fields of language and literature.

Gloria Hochstein, President-Elect
Sarah Dangelantonio, President

352   Teachers & Writers Collaborative
520 Eighth Avenue
Suite 2020
New York, NY 10018-3306
212-691-6590
888-266-5789
Fax: 212-675-0171
E-mail: info@twc.org
http://www.twc.org
Educate the imagination by offering innovative creative writing programs for students and teachers and by providing a variety of publications and resources to support learning through the literary arts.

Amy Swauger, Director
Jade Triton, Director of Operations

Library Services

353   American Association of Law Libraries
105 W. Adams Street
Suite 3300
Chicago, IL 60603-6225
312-939-4764
Fax: 312-431-1097
http://www.aallnet.org
The American Association of Law Libraries was founded in 1906 to promote and enhance the value of law libraries to the legal and public communities, to foster the profession of law librarianship, and to provide leadership in the field of legal information.

Kate Hagan, Executive Director
Pamela Reisinger, Director of Meetings

354   American Indian Library Association
E-mail: ailawebsite@gmail.com
http://ailanet.org
AILA was founded in 1979 in conjunction with the White House Pre-Conference on Indian Library and Information Services on or near Reservations. At the time, there was increasing awareness that library services for Native Americans were inadequate. Individuals as well as the government began to organize to remedy the situation.

Founded: 1979

Zora Sampson, President
Paulita Aguilar, VP/ President-Elect

355   American Library Association (ALA)
50 E Huron
Chicago, IL 60611-2795
312-944-6780
800-545-2433

Fax: 312-440-9374
E-mail: ala@ala.org
http://www.ala.org
Created to provide leadership for the development, promotion and improvement of library and information services and the profession of librarianship in order to enhance learning and ensure access for all.

Molly Raphael, President-Elect
James G Neal, Treasurer

56 American Theological Library Association
300 South Wacker Drive
Suite 2100
Chicago, IL 60606-6701
312-454-5100
888-665-2852
Fax: 312-454-5505
E-mail: atla@atla.com
http://www.atla.com
The American Theological Library Associationÿ(ATLA) is a professional association providing support of theological and religious studies libraries and librarians. ATLA produces a prestigious line of electronic resources to support the scholarly study of religion and theology.

Founded: 1946

Brenda Bailey-Hainer, Executive Director
Gillian Harrison Cain, Director of Member Programs

57 Art Libraries Society of North America
7044 South 13th Street
Oak Creek, WI 53154
414-908-4954
800-817-0621
E-mail: customercare@arlisna.org
http://www.arlisna.org
ARLIS/NAÿis a dynamic organization of over 1,000 individuals devoted to fostering excellence in art and design librarianship and image management.

Founded: 1972

Carole Ann Fabian, President
Kristen Regina, VP/ President-Elect

58 Asian American Curriculum Project (AACP)
529 E Third Avenue
San Mateo, CA 94401
650-375-8286
800-874-2242
Fax: 650-375-8797
E-mail: aacpinc@asianamericanbooks.com
http://www.asianamericanbooks.com
Educate the public about the great diversity of the Asian American experience, through the books we distribute; fostering cultural awareness and to educate Asian Americans about their own heritage, instilling a sense of pride. AACP believes that the knowledge which comes from the use of appropriate materials can accomplish these goals.

Florence M Hongo, President
Shizue Yoshina, Vice President

59 Asian Pacific American Librarians Association
PO Box 677593
Orlando, FL 32867-7593
E-mail: ebosch@bgsu.edu
http://www.apalaweb.org
APALA, and AALC before it, were organized and founded by librarians of diverse Asian and Pacific ancestries committed to working together toward a common goal:ÿto create an organization that would address the needs of Asian Pacific American librarians and those

who serve Asian Pacific American communities.

Founded: 1980

Eileen K. Bosch, President
Buenaventura Basco, Executive Director

360 Association for Library & Information Science Education
65 E Wacker Place
Suite 1900
Chicago, IL 60601-7246
312-795-0996
Fax: 312-419-8950
E-mail: contact@alise.org
http://www.alise.org
Promotes innovation and excellence in research, teaching and service for educators and scholars in Library and Information Science and cognate disciplines internationally through leadership, collaboration, advocacy and dissemination of research.

January

Melissa Gross, President
Kathleen Combs, Executive Director

361 Association for Library and Information Scienc
2150 N 107th St
Suite 205
Seattle, WA 98133
206-209-5267
Fax: 206-367-8777
E-mail: office@alise.org
http://www.alise.org
ALISE (Association for Library and Information Science Education) is a non-profit organization that serves as the intellectual home of university faculty in graduate programs in library and information science in North America. Its mission is to promote innovation and excellence in research, teaching, and service for educators and scholars in Library and Information Science and cognate disciplines internationally through leadership, collaboration, advocacy, and dissemination of research.

Clara Chu, President
Andrew Estep, Executive Director

362 Association of Research Libraries
21 Dupont Circle NW
Suite 800
Washington, DC 20036
202-296-2296
Fax: 202-872-0884
E-mail: webmgr@arl.org
http://www.arl.org
The Association of Research Libraries (ARL) is a nonprofit organization ofÿ124 research librariesÿat comprehensive, research institutions in the US and Canada that share similar research missions, aspirations, and achievements.

Founded: 1932

Deborah Jakubs, President
Elliott Shore, Executive Director

363 Black Caucus of the American Library Association
P.O. Box 5837
Chicago, IL 60680

http://www.bcala.org
The Black Caucus of the American Library Association serves as an advocate for the development, promotion, and improvement of library services and resources to the nation's African American community; and provides leadership for the recruitment and profes-

sional development of African American librarians.

Kelvin A. Watson, President
Denyvetta Davis, President-Elect

364 Center for Research Libraries
6050 S. Kenwood Avenue
Chicago, IL 60637-2804
773-955-4545
800-621-6044
Fax: 773-955-4339
E-mail: falba@crl.edu
http://www.crl.edu
The Center for Research Libraries (CRL) is an international consortium of university, college, and independent research libraries. Founded in 1949, CRL supports original research and inspired teaching in the humanities, sciences, and social sciences by preserving and making available to scholars a wealth of rare and uncommon primary source materials from all world regions.

Founded: 1949

Bernard F. Reilly, President
Toni Kibort, Director of Human Resources

365 Council on Library Technical Assistants (COLT)
900 University Avenue
Riverside, CA 92521
951-872-1012
E-mail: lowen@ucr.edu
http://colt.ucr.edu
An international organization which works to address the issues and concerns of library support staff personnel. The issues cover areas such as technical education, continuing education, certification, job description uniformity and goals of gaining recognition and respect for the professional work done.

Founded: 1967

Jackie Hite, President
Chris Egan, VP

366 Institute of Museum and Library Services
1800 M Street NW
9th Floor
Washington, DC 20036-5802
202-653-4657
Fax: 202-653-4600
E-mail: nweiss@imls.gov
http://www.imls.gov
The mission of IMLS is to inspire libraries and museums to advance innovation, lifelong learning, and cultural and civic engagement. We provide leadership through research, policy development, and grant making.

Nancy E. Weiss, General Counsel
Michael D. Jerger, Chief Operating Office

367 International Association of School Librarianship
65 E. Wasker Place
Suite 1900
Chicago, IL 60601-7246
Fax: 312-419-8950
E-mail: iasl@mlahq.org
http://www.iasl-online.org
Provides an international forum for those people interested in promoting effective school library media programs as viable instruments in the educational process. Also provides guidance and advice for the development of school library programs and the school library profession.

Dr Diljit Singh, President
Lorense Das, VP: Association Operations

368 Literary Research Association
7044 S 13th St
Oak Creek, WI 53154
414-908-4924
Fax: 414-768-8001
http://www.literaryresearchassociation.org
A community of scholars dedicated to promoting research that enriches the knowledge, understanding, and development of lifespan literacies in a multicultural and multilingual world.
Founded: 1950

Robert Jimenez, President
Betsy Purcell, Association Manager

369 Pro LiBRA Associates Inc.
436 Springfield Avenue
Summit, NJ 07901-2618
908-918-0077
800-262-0070
Fax: 908-918-0977
E-mail: staffing@prolibra.com
http://www.prolibra.com
PRO LiBRA Associates Inc., is a library service company providing experienced personnel who are specialists in all facets of library service and maintenance to corporations, public entities and individuals. Pro LiBRA has been actively involved staffing libraries and information centers.

Margaret Bennett, Owner/President

370 The American Philatelic Society
100 Match Factory Place
Bellefonte, PA 16823-1367
814-933-3803
Fax: 814-933-6128
E-mail: webmaster@stamps.org
http://stamps.org
With nearlyÿ32,000 membersÿin more than 110 countries, the APS is the largest, non-profit organization for stamp collectors in the world. Founded in 1886, the APS serves collectors, educators, postal historians, and the general public by providing a wide variety of programs and services.

Stephen Reinhard, President
Rick Banks, Controller

Mathematics

371 American Institute of Mathematics
600 E. Brokaw Road
San Jose, CA 95112
408-350-2088
E-mail: conrey@aimath.org
http://www.aimath.org
To advance mathematical knowledge through collaboration, to broaden participation in the mathematical endeavor, and to increase the awareness of the contributions of the mathematical sciences to society.
Founded: 1994

Brian Conrey, Director
Estelle Basor, Deputy Director

372 American Mathematical Association of Two-Year Colleges
Southwest Tennessee Community Colle
5983 Macon Cove
Memphis, TN 38134
901-333-6243
Fax: 901-333-6251
E-mail: amatyc@amatyc.org
http://www.amatyc.org
The American Mathematical Association of Two-Year Colleges was founded in 1974. It is the only organization exclusively devoted to providing a national forum for the improvement of mathematics instruction in the first two years of college. AMATYC has approximately 1,800 individual members, including more than 150 institutional members in the United States and Canada.ÿ
Founded: 1974

Nancy J. Sattler, President
Wanda L. Garner, Executive Director

373 Association for Symbolic Logic
Box 742, Vassar College
124 Raymond Avenue
Poughkeepsie, NY 12604
845-437-7080
Fax: 845-437-7830
E-mail: asl@vassar.edu
http://www.aslonline.org
The Association for Symbolic Logic is an international organization supporting research and critical studies in logic. Its primary function is to provide an effective forum for the presentation, publication, and critical discussion of scholarly work in this area of inquiry.
Founded: 1936

Alasdair Urquhart, President
Ulrich Kohlenbach, Vice-President

374 Association for Women in Mathematics
11240 Waples Mill Road
Suite 200
Fairfax, VA 22030
703-934-0163
Fax: 703-359-7562
E-mail: awm@awm-math.org
http://sites.google.com/site/awmmath/
The purpose of the Association for Women in Mathematics is to encourage women and girls to study and to have active careers in the mathematical sciences, and to promote equal opportunity and the equal treatment of women and girls in the mathematical sciences.
Founded: 1971

Ruth Charney, President
Magnhild Lien, Executive Director

375 Association of Mathematics Teacher Educators
c/o Meredith College
3800 Hillsborough Street
Raleigh, NC 27607
919-760-8240
Fax: 919-760-8763
E-mail: arbaugh@psu.edu
http://amte.net
AMTE is the largest professional organization devoted to the improvement of mathematics teacher education - it includes over 1,000 members supporting the preservice education and professional development of K-12 teachers of mathematics.ÿMembersÿinclude professors, researchers, teacher-leaders, school mathematics coordinators, policy experts, graduate students, and others.
Founded: 1991

Fran Arbaugh, President
Tim Hendrix, Executive Director

376 Eisenhower National Clearinghouse for Mathematics and Science Education
1275 Kinnear Road
Columbus, OH 43212
614-378-4567
800-471-1045
Fax: 614-523-0883
E-mail: info@goENC.com
http://www.goenc.org
Provides excellent resources for professional development programs and for district curriculum coordinators. We can help by providing carefully selected online resources to support effective teaching and learning in K-12 math and science.

Len Simutis, President

377 Institute for Operations Research and the Management Sciences
5521 Research Park Drive
Suite 200 (On the campus of University o
Catonsville, MD 21228
443-757-3500
800-446-3676
Fax: 443-757-3515
E-mail: informs@informs.org
http://www.informs.org
The Institute for Operations Research and the Management Sciences (INFORMS)ÿis the largest society in the world for professionals in the field of operations research (O.R.), management science, andÿanalytics.

L. Robin Keller, President
Melissa Moore, Executive Director

378 Mathematical Association of America (MAA)
1529 18th Street NW
Washington, DC 20036-1358
202-387-5200
800-741-9415
Fax: 202-265-2384
E-mail: maahq@maa.org
http://www.maa.org
Advance the mathematical science, especially at the collegiate level by encouraging effective curriculum and teaching, supporting research, foster scholarship, professional growth and cooperation among professional and students and promote general understanding of mathematics.

Paul Zorn, President
Bob Devaney, President-Elect

379 National Academy of Sciences
500 Fifth Street, NW
Washington, DC 20001
202-334-2000
E-mail: mlcarter@nas.edu
http://www.nasonline.org
The National Academy of Sciences (NAS) is a private, nonprofit organization of the country's leading researchers. The NAS recognizes and promotes outstanding science through election to membership; publication in its journal, PNAS; and its awards, programs, and special activities. Through the National Research Council, the NAS provides objective, science-based advice on critical issues affecting the nation.
Founded: 1863

Ralph J. Cicerone, President
Diane Griffin, Vice President

380 National Council of Supervisors of Mathematics
6000 E Evans Ave
Ste 3-205
Denver, CO 80222-5423
303-758-9611
Fax: 303-758-9616
E-mail: office@mathedleadership.org
http://www.mathedleadership.org
The National Council of Supervisors of Mathematics (NCSM) is a mathematics leadership organization for educational leaders that provides professional learning opportunities necessary to support and sustain improved student achievement.

Cheryl Avalos, Affiliate Chair
Valerie L. Mills, President

381 National Council of Teachers of Mathematics
1906 Association Drive
Reston, VA 20191-1502
703-620-9840
800-235-7566
Fax: 703-476-2970
E-mail: nctm@nctm.org
http://www.nctm.org
The National Council of Teachers of Mathematics is a public voice of mathematics education, providing vision, leadership and professional development to support teachers in ensuring equitable mathematics learning of the highest quality for all students.

Linda M. Gojak, President
Kichoon Yang, Executive Director

382 Society for Industrial and Applied Mathematics
3600 Market Street
6th Floor
Philadelphia, PA 19104-2688
215-382-9800
800-447-SIAM
Fax: 215-386-7999
E-mail: membership@siam.org
http://www.siam.org
Our mission is to build cooperation between mathematics and the worlds of science and technology through our publications, research, and community.

Founded: 1951

L. Pamela Cook, President
Rachel Levy, Vice President for Education

383 Society of Actuaries
888-697-3900
E-mail: customerservice@soa.org
http://www.soa.org
The Society of Actuaries (SOA) is the largest professional organization dedicated to serving 24,000 actuarial members and the public in the United States, Canada and worldwide. The SOA's vision is for actuaries to be the leading professionals in the measurement and management of risk.

Founded: 1889

Errol Cramer, FSA, MAAA, President
R. Thomas Herget, Vice-President

384 The Society for Mathematical Biology
c/o Renee Fister
Department of Mathematics and Statistics
Murray, KY 42071
270-809-2491
E-mail: adler@math.utah.edu
http://www.smb.org
The Society for Mathematical Biology promotes the development and dissemination of research at the interface between the mathematical and biological sciences through its meetings, awards, and publications. The Society serves a diverse community of researchers and educators in academia, industry, and in government agencies throughout the world.

Fred Adler, President
Amina Eladdadi, Secretary

Music & Art

385 American Art Therapy Association, Inc.
National Office American Art Therapy Association
4875 Eisenhower Avenue
Suite 240
Alexandria, VA 22304

700-548-5860
888-290-0878
Fax: 703-783-8468
E-mail: info@arttherapy.org
http://www.arttherapy.org
Organization of professional dedicated to the belief that making art is healing and life enhancing.

Mercedes ter Maat, Ph.D, President
Susan Corrigan, Executive Director

386 American Dance Therapy Association
10632 Little Patuxent Parkway
Suite 108
Columbia, MD 21044-3273
410-997-4040
Fax: 410-997-4048
E-mail: info@adta.org
http://www.adta.org
Establish, maintain and support the highest standards of professional identity and competence among dance/movement therapists by promoting education, training, practice and research. Provides avenues of communication among dance/movement therapists and those working in related fields and increases public awareness of dance/movement therapy.

Sharon Goodill, President
Judy Wager, VP

387 American Guild of Music
PO Box 599
Warren, MI 48090
248-686-1975
http://www.americanguild.org
The American Guild of Music, a multi-national organization whose mission is to advance the study of music and to foster interest in, promote and advance the artistic, educational, recreational and commercial position of music of all kinds.

388 American Musicological Society
6010 College Station
Brunswick, ME 04011-8451
207-798-4243
877-679-7648
Fax: 207-798-4254
E-mail: ams@ams-net.org
http://www.ams-net.org
A non-profit organization to advance research in the various fields of music as a branch of learning and scholarship.

Robert Judd, Executive Director
Al Hipkins, Office Manager

389 Arts Education Partnership
One Massachusetts Avenue NW
Suite 700
Washington, DC 20001-1431
202-326-8693
http://www.aep-arts.org
Dedicated to securing a high-quality arts education for every young person in America.

Founded: 1995

Sandra Ruppert, Director

390 Association for Public Art
1528 Walnut Street
Suite 1000
Philadelphia, PA 19102-3627
215-546-7550
Fax: 215-546-2363
E-mail: apa@associationforpublicart.org
http://associationforpublicart.org
The Association for Public Art (aPA, formerly the Fairmount Park Art Association) is the nation's first private, nonprofit organization dedicated to integrating public art and urban planning. Founded in 1872, the Associ-

ation commissions, preserves, promotes and interprets public art in Philadelphia.

Founded: 1872

Barbara B. Aronson, President
Suzanne Sheehan Becker, Vice President

391 Civic Music Association
900 Mulberry Street
Suite 203
Des Moines, IA 50309
515-280-4020
Fax: 515-286-4080
E-mail: calla@civicmusic.org
http://civicmusic.org
The Civic Music Association exists to engage, enrich and educate the central Iowa community through provocative, world-class musical performances by legends and rising stars.

Founded: 1925

Jeff Kane, President
Peter Stevenson, Executive Director

392 College Art Association
50 Broadway
21st Floor
New York, NY 10004
212-691-1051
Fax: 212-627-2381
E-mail: nyoffice@collegeart.org
http://www.collegeart.org
The College Art Association (CAA), as the preeminent international leadership organization in the visual arts, promotes these arts and their understanding through advocacy, intellectual engagement, and a commitment to the diversity of practices and practitioners.

Linda Downs, Executive Director/ CEO
Teresa Lopez, Chief Financial Officer

393 Country Music Association
1 Music Cir S
Nashville, TN 37203
E-mail: donations@cmaworld.com
http://www.cmaworld.com
Heighten the awareness of Country Music and support its on-going growth by recognizing excellence in the genre, serving as a repository for critical and timely information and communication, while providing a forum for industry leadership dialogue toward its goals.

Sarah Trahern, Chief Executive Officer
Mechalle Myers, Executive Assistant

394 Future Music Oregon
School of Music
1225 University of Oregon
Eugene, OR 97403-1225
541-346-5652
Fax: 541-346-0723
E-mail: stolet@uoregon.edu
http://pages.uoregon.edu/fmo/home
Educational Institute dedicated to the exploration of sound and its creation, and to new forms of musical and new media performance and to the innovative use of computers and other recent technologies to create expressive music and media composition.

Jeffrey Stolet, Director
Brad Foley, Dean, School of Music/Dance

395 International Technology and Engineering Educators Association (ITEEA)
1914 Association Drive
Suite 201
Reston, VA 20191
703-860-2100
Fax: 703-860-0353

E-mail: iteea@iteea.org
http://www.iteea.org
Advance technological capabilities for all
people and to nurture and promote the professionalism of those engaged in these pursuits. Meet professional needs and
interests of its members as well as improve
public understanding of technology, innovation, design and engineering.

William F. Bertrand, President
Steven A. Barbato, Executive Director

396 International Thespian Society
Educational Theatre Association
2343 Auburn Avenue
Cincinnati, OH 45219-2815
513-421-3900
Fax: 513-421-7077
E-mail: info@schooltheatre.org
http://www.schooltheatre.org
Shaping lives through theatre education-
honoring student achievement, supporting
educators and influencing public opinion.
Thespian troupes serve students in grades
nine through twelve, and Junior Thespian
troupes serve students in grades six
through eight.
Founded: 1929

Julie Woffington, Executive Director
Jim Flanagan, Director of Operations

**397 Kennedy Center Alliance for Arts
Education**
John F Kennedy Center for the
Performing Arts
PO Box 101510
Arlington, VA 22210
202-416-8817
800-444-1324
Fax: 202-416-8802
E-mail: kcaaen@kennedy-center.org
http://www.kennedy-center.org/education
/kcaaen
Advance the quality of education through
the inclusion of the arts in K-12 curriculum. The Kennedy Center supports the
growth and development of the network
and the efforts of participating State Alliances through staff consultation, professional development and other resources.

Nancy Welch w/Andrea Greene, Author
Michael Kaiser, President
David M Rubenstein, Chairman

**398 National Art Education
Association**
1806 Robert Fulton Drive
Suite 300
Reston, VA 20191-1590
703-860-8000
800-299-8321
Fax: 703-860-2960
E-mail: info@arteducators.org
http://www.arteducators.org
Advance visual arts education to fulfill hu-
man potential and promote global under-
standing.
Founded: 1947

Deborah B. Reeve, Ed.D, Executive
Director
Dr Robert Sabol, President

**399 National Association for Music
Education**
1806 Robert Fulton Drive
Reston, VA 20191
703-860-4000
800-336-3768
Fax: 703-860-1531
E-mail: mbrserv@menc.org
http://www.nafme.org

The MENC serves millions of students
through activities from pre-school and up
and works to ensure every student has access to comprehensive, well-balanced, and
high quality music instruction taught by
qualified teachers.
72 pages
ISSN: 0027-4321

Michael Butera, Executive Director/CEO
Mike Blakeslee, Deputy Exec Dir/COO

**400 National Association of Schools of
Music (NASM)**
11250 Roger Bacon Drive
Suite 21
Reston, VA 20190-5248
703-437-0700
Fax: 703-437-6312
E-mail: info@arts-accredit.org
http://nasm.arts-accredit.org/
NASM is an organization of schools, conservatories, colleges and universities, with
approximately 638 accredited members. It
establishes national standards for undergraduate and graduate degrees and other
credentials.
Founded: 1924

Samual Hope, Executive Director
Karen P. Moynahan, Associate Director

**401 National Dance Education
Organization**
8609 Second Ave
Suite 203 B
Silver Spring, MD 20910
301-585-2880
Fax: 301-585-2888
http://www.ndeo.org
Affords every citizen equal access and opportunity to quality dance arts education
regardless of gender, age, race or culture,
socio-economic status, ability or interest.
Founded: 1998

402 National Endowment For The Arts
1100 Pennsylvania Ave
Washington, DC 20506
202-682-5400
http://www.nea.gov
To advance artistic excellence, creativity,
and innovation for the benefit of individuals and communities.

Joan Shigekawa, Acting Chairman

**403 National Guild of Community
Schools of the Arts**
National Guild for Community Arts
Education
520 8th Avenue
Suite 302
New York, NY 10018
212-268-3337
Fax: 212-268-3995
E-mail:
jonathanherman@nationalguild.org
http://www.nationalguild.org
Supports and advances access to lifelong
learning opportunities in the arts. Foster
the creation and development of community arts education organizations by providing research and information resources,
professional development networking opportunities and funding and by advocating
on behalf of the field.

Jonathan Herman, Executive Director
Kenneth Cole, Associate Director

**404 National Institute of Art and
Disabilities**
551 23rd Street
Richmond, CA 94804-1626

510-620-0290
Fax: 510-620-0326
E-mail: gallery@niadart.org
http://www.niadart.org
NIAD is an innovative visual arts center assisting
adults with developmental and other physical disabilities.

Deborah Dyer, Executive Director
Brian Stechshschulte, Gallery Director

405 The Americana Music Association
The Factory at Franklin
PO Box 628
Franklin, TN 37065
615-386-6936
Fax: 615-386-6937
E-mail: danna@americanamusic.org
http://americanamusic.org
The Americana Music Association is a profes-
sional trade organization whose mission is to ad-
vocate for the authentic voice of American Roots
Music around the world.
Founded: 1999

Jed Hilly, Executive Director
Danna Strong, Director of Operations

Physical Education

**406 American Alliance for Health, Physical
Education, Recreation and
Dance(AAHPERD)**
1900 Association Drive
Reston, VA 20191-1598
703-476-3400
800-213-7193
Fax: 703-476-9527
E-mail: info@aahperd.org
http://www.aahperd.org
Promote and support leadership, research, education and best practices in the professions that support creative, healthy and active lifestyles.

E Paul Roetert, CEO
Irene Cucina, President

407 American Canoe Association
503 Sophia Street
Ste 100
Fredericksburg, VA 22401
540-907-4460
Fax: 888-229-3792
http://www.americancanoe.org
Founded in 1880, The American Canoe Association (ACA) is a national nonprofit organization
serving the broader paddling public by providing
education related to all aspects of paddling; stew-
ardship support to help protect paddling environments; and sanctioning of programs and events to
promote paddlesport competition, exploration
and recreation.
Founded: 1880

Anne Maleady, President
Jim Virgin, Vice President

**408 International Council for Health,
Physical Education and Recreation**
1900 Association Drive
Reston, VA 20191-1598
703-476-3462
Fax: 703-476-9527
E-mail: ichper@aahperd.org
http://www.ichpersd.org
ICHPERúSD is committed to fostering the es-
sence of education in HPERSD fields through international understanding and goodwill,
safeguarding peace, freedom, and respect for human dignity. ICHPERúSD is committed to promoting quality HPERSD programs, professional
standards, scholarly pursuits, research, and exchanges of knowledge among its constituent

members, as well as other concerned professionals and institutions.

Dr Adel M. Elnashar, President
Dr Magda Al-Shazly, Secretary General

409 National Alliance for Youth Sports
2050 Vista Parkway
West Palm Beach, FL 33411
561-684-1141
800-688-5437
Fax: 561-684-2546
E-mail: nays@nays.org
http://www.nays.org
The National Alliance for Youth Sports (NAYS) is America's leading advocate for positive and safe sports for children. NAYS provides programs, services and a variety of resources for volunteer coaches, administrators, officials and parents of young athletes to help ensure that everyone's experience is memorable for all the right reasons.

Founded: 1993

Fred Engh, President/ CEO
John Engh, Chief Operating Officer

410 National Association for Girls and Women in Sports
1900 Association Drive
Reston, VA 20191-1598
703-476-3453
800-213-7193
Fax: 703-476-4566
E-mail: nagws@aahperd.org
http://www.aahperd.org/nagws
Develop and deliver equitable and quality sport opportunities for all girls and women through relevant research, advocacy, leadership development, educational strategies and programming in a manner that promotes social justice and change.

Lynda Ransdell, President
Heidi Parker, VP

411 National Association for Kinesiology in Higher Education
E-mail: steven.estes@mtsu.edu
http://www.nakhe.org
The mission of NAKHE is to foster leadership in kinesiology administration and policy as it relates to teaching,ÿscholarship and service in higher education.

Steve Estes, President
Mark G. Urtel, Vice President

412 National Association of Academic Advisors for Athletics
240 Jeter Drive
300 Case Academic Center
Raleigh, NC 27695-9007
919-513-1007
Fax: 919-513-0541
E-mail: info@nfoura.org
http://www.nfoura.org
Aim is to promote academic achievement and personal development among student athletes.

Bart Byrd, President
Jim Pignataro, President-Elect

413 National Association of Sport and Physical Education
1900 Association Dr
Reston, VA 20191
703-476-3410
800-213-7193
Fax: 703-476-8316
E-mail: naspe@aahperd.org
http://www.aahperd.org/naspe
To enhance knowledge, improve professional practice, and increase support for high

quality physical education, sport, and physical activity programs.

Mary Jo Sariscsany, President
Steve Mitchell, President Elect

414 National Athletic Trainers' Association
2952 Stemmons Freeway
Suite 200
Dallas, TX 75247-6196
214-637-6282
Fax: 214-637-2206
E-mail: webmaster@nata.org
http://www.nata.org
Enhance the quality of health care provided by certified athletic trainers and to advance the athletic training profession.

Jim Thornton, President
Eve Becker-Doyle, Executive Director

415 National Collegiate Athletic Association
700 W. Washington Street
P.O. Box 6222
Indianapolis, IN 46206-6222
317-917-6222
Fax: 317-917-6888
http://www.ncaa.org
The National Collegiate Athletic Association is a membership-driven organization dedicated to safeguarding the well-being of student-athletes and equipping them with the skills to succeed on the playing field, in the classroom and throughout life.

Mark Emmert, President

416 President's Council on Fitness, Sports & Nutrition
President's Council on Fitness, Sports & Nutrition
Tower Bldg
1101 Wootton Pkwy, Suite 560
Rockville, MD 20852
202-276-9567
Fax: 202-276-9860
E-mail: fitness@hhs.gov
http://www.fitness.gov
Promotes programs motivating people to make healthy lifestyle choices including good nutrition and regular physical activity in order to lead active, healthy lives.

Shellie Pfohl, Executive Director
Shannon Foster, Communications/Public Aff

417 Society of Health and Physical Educators
1900 Association Drive
Reston, VA 20191
703-476-3400
800-213-7193
Fax: 703-476-9527
E-mail: board@shapeamerica.org
http://www.shapeamerica.org
SHAPE America is the largest organization of professionals involved in school-based health, physical education and physical activity, who are dedicated to teaching and promoting active, healthy lifestyles.

Dolly D. Lambdin, President
E. Paul Roetert, Chief Executive Officer

418 Sporting Goods Manufacturers Association
8505 Fenton Street
Suite 211
Silver Spring, MD 20910
301-495-6321
Fax: 301-495-6322
E-mail: mmay@sgma.com

Boosts amateur sports and physical education at all levels.

Mike May, Executive Director

Reading

419 Clearinghouse on Reading, English & Communication
ERIC Program
c/o CSC 655 15th St NW
Suite 500
Washington, DC 20005
202-362-0700
800-538-3742
Fax: 202-362-3740
E-mail: ericpub@csc.com
http://www.eric.ed.gov
Provide a comprehensive, easy to use, searchable, internet based bibliographic and full text database of education research and information that also meets the requirements of the Education Sciences Reform Act of 2002.

John Collins
Mark Constas

420 College Reading & Learning Association
7044 S. 13th Street
Oak Creek, WI 53154
414-908-4961
E-mail: customercare@crla.net
http://crla.net
CRLA (formerly WCRLA) is a group of student-oriented professionals active in the fields of reading, learning assistance, developmental education, tutoring, and mentoring at the college/adult level. CRLA is inherently diverse in membership. CRLA's most vital function and overall purpose is to provide a forum for the interchange of ideas, methods, and information to improve student learning and to facilitate the professional growth of its members.

Rosemarie Woodruff, President
Kathy Stein, Secretary

421 International Reading Association
International Reading Association
800 Barksdale Road
PO Box 8139
Newark, DE 19714-8139
302-731-1600
800-336-7323
Fax: 302-731-1057
E-mail: customerservice@reading.org
http://www.reading.org
Promote reading by continuously advancing the quality of literacy instruction and research worldwide.

Carrice C. Cummins, President
Marcie Craig, Executive Director

422 National Center for ESL Literacy Education
CAELA Newtwork
c/o Center for Applied Linguistics
4646 40th Street NW, Suite 200
Washington, DC 20016-1859
202-362-0700
Fax: 202-363-7204
E-mail: caelntwork@cal.org
http://www.cal.org/
Improve communication through better understanding of language and culture by promoting the teaching & learning of languages, solving problems related to language and culture, resource for information about language

and conducting research on issues related to language and culture.

Donna Christian, President
Joy Kreeft Peyton, Vice President

423 National Contact Hotline

Contact Center, Inc.
PO Box 81826
Lincoln, NE 68501-1826
800-228-8813
A 25-year-old information and referral agency, to help individuals with literacy problems. Maintains a database of over 7,000 literacy programs across the country and the 7-day hotline.

424 National Summer Learning Association

575 South Charles Street
Suite 310
Baltimore, MD 21201
410-856-1370
Fax: 410-856-1146
http://www.summerlearning.org
The National Summer Learning Association (NSLA) is the only national nonprofit exclusively focused on closing the achievement gap through high-quality summer learning for all children and youth.

Founded: 1992

Pam Franco, Chief Financial Officer
Jody Libit, Director of Operations

425 Organization of Teacher Educators in Literacy

E-mail: akeneman@nl.edu
http://oter.coedu.usf.edu
The purpose of the organization is to facilitate communication among its membership.

Ayn Keneman, President
Karen Bates, Treasurer

426 ProLiteracy Worldwide

104 Marcellus Street
Syracuse, NY 13204
315-422-9121
888-528-2224
Fax: 315-422-6369
E-mail: info@proliteracy.org
http://www.proliteracy.org
ProLiteracy champions the power of literacy to improve the lives of adults and their families creating a world where everyone can read, write and use technology to lead healthy, productive and fulfilling lives.

Kevin Morgan, Interim President/CEO
Nikki Zollar, Secretary

427 Reach Out and Read

56 Roland Street
Suite 100D
Boston, MA 2129-1243
617-455-0600
Fax: 617-455-0601
E-mail: info@reachoutandread.org
http://www.reachoutandread.org
Reach Out and Read prepares America's youngest children to succeed in school by partnering with doctors to prescribe books and encourage families to read together.

Steven Dow, Co-Chair
Linda Fayne Levinson, Co-Chair

428 Reading Education Association

1800 N. 12th St.
Reading, PA 19604
610-374-7101
Fax: 610-374-3173
E-mail: office@readingea.com
http://readingea.com

To promote the general welfare of educators and students; to protect the interests and defend the rights of our members; to foster professional zeal; to advance the educational atmosphere; and to promote professional relationships and respect between the Association, administration, and the community.

Mitch Hettinger, President
Priscilla Knight, Office Manager

429 Reading Recovery Council of North America

500 W Wilson Bridge Road
Suite 250
Worthington, OH 43085-5218
614-310-7323
Fax: 614-310-7345
E-mail: jjohnson@readingrecovery.org
http://www.readingrecovery.org
We prevent literacy failure by supporting specialized and continuous professional development that results in strong teaching to improve student achievement.

Jady Johnson, Executive Director
Linda Wilson, Executive Assistant

430 Reading to Kids

1600 Sawtelle Boulevard
Suite 210
Los Angeles, CA 90025
310-479-7455
Fax: 310-479-7435
E-mail: info@readingtokids.org
http://readingtokids.org
Reading to Kidsŷis a grassroots organization dedicated to inspiring underserved children with a love of reading, thereby enriching their lives and opportunities for future success.

Founded: 1999

Charlie Orchard, Managing Director
Alexandra Babiarz, Literacy Coordinator

431 Women's National Book Association

PO Box 237
FDR Station
New York, NY 10150
E-mail: info@wnba-books.org
http://www.wnba-books.org
The Women's National Book Association is a national organization of women and men who work with and value books. WNBA exists to promote reading and to support the role of women in the community of the book.

Founded: 1917

Carin Siegfried, President
Shannon Janeczek, Secretary

Secondary Education

432 American Association for Adult and Continuing

10111 Martin Luther King, Jr. Hwy
Suite 200C
Bowie, MD 20720
301-459-6261
Fax: 301-459-6241
E-mail: office@aaace.org
http://www.aaace.org
The mission of the American Association for Adult and Continuing Education (AAACE) is to provide leadership for the field of adult and continuing education by expanding opportunities for adult growth and development; unifying adult educators; fostering the development and dissemination of theory, research,

information, and best practices; promoting identity and standards for the profession; and advocating relevant public policy and social change initiatives.

Founded: 1982

Jean Fleming, President
Cle Anderson, Association Manager

433 American Association for Colleges of Teacher E

1307 New York Ave., NW
Suite 300
Washington, DC 20005
202-293-2450
Fax: 202-293-2450
E-mail: aacte@aacte.org
http://www.aacte.org
AACTE leads the field in advocating for and building capacity for high-quality educator preparation programs in a dynamic landscape.

Sharon P. Robinson, President/ CEO
Jerry Wirth, COO/ CFO

434 American Driver & Traffic Safety Education Association (ADTSEA)

National Education Association (NEA)
Indiana University of Pennsylvania
1434 Trim Tree Road
Indiana, PA 15701
724-801-8246
877-485-7172
Fax: 724-349-5042
E-mail: office@adtsea.org
http://www.adtsea.org
Develop and promote a level of excellence among driver education professionals in the delivery of instruction to the novice driver; thus equipping the novice driver with skills for driving in today's challenging highway transportation system.

Connie Sessoms, Jr., President
Stan Henderson, President-Elect

435 Association for Institutional Research

Association for Institutional Research
1435 E Piedmont Drive
Suite 211
Tallahassee, FL 32308
850-385-4155
Fax: 850-385-5180
E-mail: air@airweb.org
http://www.airweb.org
Provides educational resources, best practices and professional development opportunities for more than 4,000 members.

Randy Swing, Ph.D., Executive Director
Donna Carlsen, Membership Coordinator

436 Association for Middle Level Education

4151 Executive Parkway
Suite 300
Westerville, OH 43081
614-895-4730
800-528-6672
Fax: 614-895-4750
E-mail: info@amle.org
http://www.amle.org
AMLE has been a voice for those committed to the educational and developmental needs of young adolescents. AMLE is the only national education association dedicated exclusively to those in the middle level grades.

Jeff La Roux, President
William D. Waidelich, Ed.D., Executive Director

437 Association for Supervision and Curriculum Development

1703 N. Beauregard St.
Alexandria, VA 22311-1714
703-578-9600
800-933-2723

Fax: 703-575-5400
http://www.ascd.org
Founded in 1943, ASCD (doing business as the Association for Supervision and Curriculum Development) is the global leader in developing and delivering innovative programs, products, and services that empower educators to support the success of each learner.

Founded: 1943

Marge Scherer, Editor in Chief
Amy Azzam, Senior Associate Editor

38 Close-Up Foundation
1330 Braddock Place
Suite 400
Alexandria, VA 22314
703-706-3300
800-336-5479
Fax: 703-706-0001
E-mail: info@closeup.org
http://www.closeup.org
Informs, inspires and empowers young people to exercise their rights and accept the responsibilities of citizens in a democracy.

Joel Jankowsky, Chairman, Board of Directors
Timothy S Davis, President/CEO

39 College Board
The College Board National Office
45 Columbus Avenue
New York, NY 10023-6917
212-713-8000
Fax: 212-713-8282
E-mail: store.help@collegeboard.org
http://www.collegeboard.com
The College Board seeks to ensure all students are prepared to succeeed in college, helps students connect with and complete a college education and is a leading advocate and resource for excellence and equity in education.

David Coleman, President
Herb Elish, COO

40 National Alliance for Secondary Education and Transition
University of Minnesota
6 Pattee Hall, 150 Pillsbury Drive SE
Minneapolis, MN 55455
612-624-2097
E-mail: ncset@umn.edu
http://www.nasetalliance.org
The National Alliance for Secondary Education and Transition (NASET) is a national voluntary coalition of more than 40 organizations and advocacy groups representing special education, general education, career and technical education, youth development, multicultural perspectives, and parents.

Founded: 2003

41 National Business Education Association
1914 Association Drive
Reston, VA 20191-1596
703-860-8300
Fax: 703-620-4483
E-mail: nbea@nbea.org
http://www.nbea.org
NBEA is committed to the advancement of the professional interest and competence of its members and provides programs and services that enhance members' professional growth and development.

Ramona Schoenrock, President
Marlene T. Stout, President-Elect

42 National Parent Teacher Association
1250 N. Pitt Street
Alexandria, VA 22314

703-518-1200
800-307-4782
Fax: 703-836-0942
E-mail: info@pta.org
http://www.pta.org
The overall purpose of PTA is to make every child's potential a reality by engaging and empowering families and communities to advocate for all children.

Founded: 1897

Otha Thornton, President
Joanne Dunne, Interim Executive Director

Science

443 Academy of Applied Science
24 Warren Street
Concord, NH 03301
603-228-4530
Fax: 603-228-4730
E-mail: admin@aas-world.org
http://www.aas-world.org
Promotes interest of youth in the applied science, disseminate results of scientific research and studies. Nationally recognized resource center offering enrichment programs for children and professional development for teachers and administrators.

Sheldon Apsell, Chairman
Joanne Hayes-Rines, Vice-President

444 American Association for the Advancement of Science
1200 New York Ave NW
Washington, DC
202-326-6400
http://www.aaas.org
The American Association for the Advancement of Science is an international non-profit organization dedicated to advancing science for the benefit of all people.

Founded: 1848

Phillip A. Sharp, Chair
Gerald Fink, President

445 American Association of Physics Teachers
One Physics Ellipse
College Park, MD 20740-3845
301-209-3311
Fax: 301-209-0845
http://www.aapt.org
To enhance the understanding and appreciation of physics through teaching.

Founded: 1930

Beth Cunningham, Executive Officer

446 American Dairy Science Association
1800 S. Oak Street
Suite 100
Champaign, IL 61820-6974
217-356-5146
Fax: 217-398-4119
E-mail: ADSA@assochq.org
http://www.adsa.org
The American Dairy Science Association provides leadership in scientific and technical support to improve and grow the global dairy industry through generation, dissemination, and exchange of information and services.

Founded: 1906

Peter Studney, MBA, CAE, Executive Director
Vicki Paden, Administrative Assistant

447 American Medical Student Association
45610 Woodland Road
Suite 300
Sterling, VA 20166
703-620-6600
Fax: 703-620-6445
http://www.amsa.org
The American Medical Student Association (AMSA), with a half-century history of medical student activism, is the oldest and largest independent association of physicians-in-training in the United States.

Founded: 1950

Britani Kessler, DO, President
Joshua Caulfield, Executive Director

448 American Society for Clinical Laboratory Science
1861 International Drive
Suite 200
McLean, VA 22102
571-748-3770
E-mail: ascls@ascls.org
http://www.ascls.org
The mission of ASCLS is to make a positive impact in health care through leadership that will assure excellence in the practice of laboratory medicine.

Founded: 1936

449 American Society of Nephrology
1510 H Street, NW
Suite 800
Washington, DC 20005
202-640-4660
Fax: 202-637-9793
E-mail: email@asn-online.org
http://www.asn-online.org
The American Society of Nephrology (ASN) leads the fight against kidney disease by educating health professionals, sharing new knowledge, advancing research, and advocating the highest quality care for patients.

Jonathan Himmelfarb, MD, FASN, President
John R. Sedor, MD, FASN, Secretary-Treasurer

450 Association for Advancement of Computing in Education (AACE)
PO Box 1545
Chesapeake, VA 23327-1545
757-366-5606
Fax: 703-997-8760
E-mail: info@aace.org
http://www.aace.org
An international, not-for-profit educational organization advancing information technology in education and e-learning research, development, learning and its practical application.

Gary H Marks Ph.D, Executive Director

451 Association for Information Science and Technology
8555 16th Street
Suite 850
Silver Spring, MD 20910
301-495-0900
Fax: 301-495-0810
E-mail: asis@asis.org
http://www.asis.org
The Association for Information Science and Technology (ASIS&T) is the only professional association that bridges the gap between information science practice and research. For over 75 years, ASIS&T has been leading the search for new and better

theories, techniques, and technologies to improve access to information.

Founded: 1937

Dr. Sandra G. Hirsh, President
Dr. Vicki L. Gregory, Treasurer

452 Association for Science Teacher Education
9324 27th Avenue
Eau Claire, WI 54703
715-838-0893
Fax: 715-838-0893
E-mail:
ExecutiveDirector@TheASTE.org
http://theaste.org
Promotes leadership and support for professionals involved in the education and development of teachers of science at all levels. ASTE advances practice and policy through scholarship, collaboration and innovation in science teacher education across the world.

John Tillotson, President
Robert Hollon, Executive Director

453 Association of Science-Technology Centers
1025 Vermont Avenue NW
Suite 500
Washington, DC 20005-6310
202-783-7200
Fax: 202-783-7207
E-mail: info@astc.org
http://www.astc.org
The Association of Science-Technology Centers (ASTC) is an organization of science centers and museums dedicated to furthering the public understanding of science among increasingly diverse audiences. ASTC encourages excellence and innovation in informal science learning by serving and linking its members worldwide and advancing their common goals.

Bryce Seidl, President
Nohora Hoyos, Executive Director

454 California Biomedical Research Association
PO Box 19340
Sacramento, CA 95819-0340
916-558-1515
Fax: 916-558-1523
E-mail: info@ca-biomed.org
http://www.ca-biomed.org
To promote and protect the continued advancement of human and animal health through biomedical research, teaching, and testing

Michael B. Ballinger, Chair
Boris Predovich, President and CEO

455 Energy Education Group(Educators for the Environment)
The California Study, Inc.
664 Hilary Drive
Tiburon, CA 94920
415-435-4574
Fax: 415-435-7737
E-mail: energyforkeeps@aol.com
http://www.energyforkeeps.org
Provides information about where our electricity comes from and how energy choices affect our lives, our environment and future generations.

Marilyn Nemzer, Executive Director
Deborah Page, Lead Writer

456 Entomological Society of America
3 Park Place
Suite 307
Annapolis, MD 21401-3722
301-731-4535
Fax: 301-731-4538
E-mail: esa@entsoc.org
http://www.entsoc.org
The Entomological Society of America (ESA) is the largest organization in the world serving the professional and scientific needs of entomologists and individuals in related disciplines.ÿ

Founded: 1889

David Gammel, Executive Director
Chris Stelzig, Director of Certification

457 Geothermal Education Office
664 Hilary Drive
Tiburon, CA 94920
Fax: 415-435-7737
E-mail: 24hrcleanpower@gmail.com
http://www.geothermal.marin.org
To promote public understanding about geothermal resources and its importance in providing clean sustainable energy while protecting our environment.

Marlyn L Nemzer, Executive Director

458 History of Science Society
University of Notre Dame
440 Geddes Hall
Notre Dame, IN 46556
574-631-1194
Fax: 574-631-1533
E-mail: Info@hssonline.org
http://www.hssonline.org
Foster interest in the history of science and its social and cultural relations.

Founded: 1924

Robert J Malone, Executive Director
Greg Macklem, Society Coordinator

459 Institute for Earth Education
Cedar Cove
PO Box 115
Greenville, WV 24945
304-832-6404
Fax: 304-832-6077
E-mail: info@ieetree.org
http://www.eartheducation.org
An international network of individuals and organizations committed tot developing a serious educational response to the environmental problems of the earth.

Steve Van Matre, Chairman
David Dodson, Office Coordinator

460 National Association for Research in Science Teaching (NARST)
12100 Sunset Hills Road
Suite 130
Reston, VA 20190-3221
703-234-4138
Fax: 703-435-4390
E-mail: info@narst.org
http://www.narst.org
NARST is a worldwide organization of professionals committed to the improvement of science teaching and learning through research. NARST promotes research in science education and the communication of knowledge generated by the research. The ultimate goal of NARST is to help all learners achieve science literacy.

William C Kyle JR, Executive Director
Sharon Lynch, President

461 National Association of Biology Teachers
1313 Dolley Madison Boulevard
Suite 402
McLean, VA 22101
703-264-9696
888-501-6227
Fax: 703-790-2672
E-mail: office@nabt.org
http://www.nabt.org
Empowers educators to provide the best possible biology and life science education for all students.

Mark Little, President
Jaclyn Reeves-Pepin, Executive Director

462 National Association of Geoscience Teachers
200 Division St
Suite 210
Northfield, MN 55057
507-222-5634
Fax: 507-222-5175
http://www.nagt.org
Works to foster improvement in the teaching of the earth sciences at all levels of formal and informal instruction, to emphasize the cultural significance of the earth sciences and to disseminate knowledge in this field to the general public..

Cathryn Manduca, Executive Director

463 National Center for Science Education
420 40th Street
Suite 2
Oakland, CA 94609-2688
510-601-7203
800-290-6006
Fax: 510-601-7204
E-mail: info@ncse.com
http://www.ncse.com
Provides information and resources for schools, parents and concerned citizens working to keep evolution and climate science in public school education. We educate the press and the public about the scientific and educational aspects of controversies surrounding the teaching of evolution and climate change and supply needed information and advice to defend good science education at local, state and national levels.

ISSN: 1064-2358

Eugenie C Scott, Executive Director

464 National Earth Science Teachers Association
PO Box 20854
Boulder, CO 80308-3854

http://www.nestanet.org
To facilitate and advance excellence in Earth and space science education.

Founded: 1983

Missy Holzer, President
Roberta Johnson, Executive Director

465 National Institute for Science Education
1025 W Johnson Street
Suite 753
Madison, WI 53706-1706
608-263-4200
E-mail: uw-wcer@education.wis.edu
http://www.wcer.wisc.edu/nise
A partnership of the University of Wisconsin-Madison and the National Center for Improving Science Education, Washington, DC, with funding from the National Science Foundation. Strives to strengthen the nation's science enterprise by helping to extend science, mathematics, engineering and technology literacy to all students.

Andrew C Porter, Director
Norman Webb, Associate Director

466 **National Science Teachers Association**
1840 Wilson Boulevard
Arlington, VA 22201-3000
703-243-7100
800-782-6782
Fax: 703-243-7177
E-mail: pubinfo@nsta.org
http://www.nsta.org
A member-driven organization that publish books and journals for science teachers from kindergarten through college. Provide ways for science teachers to connect with one another, inform congress and the public on questions affecting science literacy and a well educated work force.

Dr. Karen L. Ostlund, President
Bill Badders, President-Elect

467 **School Science and Mathematics Association**
245 Willard
Stillwater, OK 74078
405-744-8018
http://www.ssma.org
Promotes research, scholarship, and practice that improves school science and mathematics and advances the integration of science and mathematics.
Founded: 1901

468 **Science Service**
1719 N Street NW
Washington, DC 20036-2888
202-785-2255
Fax: 202-785-1243
E-mail: webmaster@societyforscience.org
http://www.societyforscience.org
Society for Science & the Public (SSP) is a nonprofit 501(c) (3) organization dedicated to the public engagement in scientific research and education. Promote the understanding and appreciation of science and the vital role it plays in human advancement: to inform, educate, inspire.

Elizabeth Marincola, President/Publisher
H Robert Horvitz, Chair

469 **Soil Science Society of America**
5585 Guilford Rd.
Madison, WI 53711-5801
608-273-8085
Fax: 608-273-2081
E-mail: certification@soils.org
http://www.soils.org
TheÿSoil Science Society of America (SSSA)ÿis a progressive international scientific society that fosters the transfer of knowledge and practices to sustain global soils.
Founded: 1936

Carolyn G. Olson, President
Ellen G.M. Bergfeld, Chief Executive Officer

Social Studies

470 **African-American Institute**
42nd Floor Chanin Building
380 Lexington Avenue
New York, NY 10168-4298
212-949-5666
Fax: 212-682-6174
E-mail: aainy@aaionline.org
http://www.aaionline.org
Promote enlightened engagement between Africa and America through education, training and dialogue.

Amini Kajunju, President/CEO
Kofi A Appenteng, Co-Founder/Chair

471 **American Association for History and Computing**
http://www.theaahc.org
The American Association for History and Computing (AAHC) is dedicated to the reasonable and productive marriage of history and computer technology.ÿ

472 **American Association of Geographers**
1710 16th Street NW
Washington, DC 20009-3198
202-234-1450
Fax: 202-234-2744
E-mail: gaia@aag.org
http://www.aag.org
The Association of American Geographers (AAG) is a nonprofit scientific and educational society founded in 1904.
Founded: 1904

Mona Domosh, President
Sarah Witham Bednarz, Vice President

473 **American Geographical Society**
32 Court Street
Brooklyn Heights, NY 11201
917-847-9773
Fax: 917-677-8328
E-mail: ags@amergeog.org
http://www.amergeog.org
The American Geographical Society (AGS) advances and promotes geography in business, government, science, and education. Our goal is to enhance the nation's geographic literacy so as to engender sound public policy, national security, and human well-being worldwide.ÿ
Founded: 1851

John E. Gould, Chairman
Jerome E. Dobson, President

474 **American Political Science Association**
1527 New Hampshire Ave NW
Washington, DC 20036-1206
202-483-2512
Fax: 202-483-2657
E-mail: apsa@apsanet.org
http://www.apsanet.org
Founded in 1903, the American Political Science Association is the leading professional organization for the study of political science and serves more than 13,000 members in more than 80 countries.
Founded: 1903

Rodney E. Hero, President
Steven Rathgeb Smith, Executive Director

475 **Association Of American Geographers**
1710 16th St NW
Washington, DC 20009-3198
202-234-1450
Fax: 202-234-2744
E-mail: gaia@aag.org
http://www.aag.org
A non-profit scientific and educational society that contributes to the advancement of geography.
Founded: 1904

476 **Center for Education Studies**
American Textbook Council
1150 Park Ave
12th Floor
New York, NY 10128-599
212-289-5177
http://www.historytextbooks.org
The council reviews history textbooks and other educational materials. It is dedicated to improving the social studies curriculum and civic education in the nation's elementary and high schools.
Founded: 1989

Gilbert T Sewall, Director
Stapley W Emberling, Assistant Director

477 **Council for Economic Education**
122 East 42nd Street
Suite 2600
New York, NY 10168
212-730-7007
Fax: 212-730-1793
E-mail:
customerservice@councilforeconed.org
http://www.councilforeconed.org
The Council for Economic Education (CEE) is the leading organization in the United States that focuses on the economic and financial education of students from kindergarten through high school-and we have been doing so for over 65 years.

Nan J. Morrison, President/ CEO
Sally Wood, COO/ CFO

478 **Council for Indian Education**
1240 Burlington Avenue
Billings, MT 59102-4224
406-248-3465
Fax: 406-248-1297
E-mail: cie@cie-mt.org
http://www.cie-mt.org
A non-profit corporation that publishes books sold to elementary schools. The council only publishes material that accurately interprets Native American life, culture and ideals to educate Native American readers on their background and history, and to help other readers gain a better understanding of Native Americans.

Hap Gilliland, President/Editor

479 **Council of State Social Studies Specialists**
E-mail: dgifford@ksde.org
http://cs4.socialstudies.org/home
The Council of State Social Studies Specialists was founded in 1965 with the primary goal of providing a vehicle for the exchange of ideas among the various states.

Don Gifford, President
Kris McDaniel, Chair

480 **ERIC Clearinghouse for Social Studies Education**
Indiana University, Social Studies Dev. Center
2805 E Tenth Street
Suite 140
Bloomington, IN 47408-2698
812-855-3838
800-266-3815
Fax: 812-855-0455
E-mail: ericso@indian.edu
http://www.servicelearning.org
The primary mission of the CSSIE is to improve education in the social studies (history, geography, economics, civics, anthropology, and the social sciences) in elementary and secondary schools. A secondary mission of the CSSIE is to meet professional development needs of the international community of educators through in-service training, content seminars, and curriculum workshops in all curriculum areas.

Dr Terrance Mason, Director
Jane E Henson, Associate Director

481 **Foundation for Teaching Economics**
260 Russell Blvd
Suite B
Davis, CA 95616

530-757-4630
Fax: 530-757-4636
E-mail: information@fte.org
http://www.fte.org
Introduces young individuals to an economic way of thinking.

Roger Ream, President
Ken Leonard, Associate VP

482   National Council for Geographic Education
1145 17th St NW
Room 7620
Washington, DC 20036
202-862-8683
E-mail: ncge@ncge.org
http://www.ncge.org
To enhance the status and quality of geography teaching and learning.

Founded: 1915

483   National Council for the Social Studies
8555 Sixteenth Street
Suite 500
Silver Spring, MD 20910
301-588-1800
800-683-0812
Fax: 301-588-2049
E-mail: sgriffin@ncss.org
http://www.socialstudies.org
Social studies educators teach students the content knowledge, intellectual skills, and civic values they need for college, career and civic life. The National Council for the Social Studies provides leadership, service and support for all social studies educators.

Founded: 1921

Susan Griffin, Executive Director
Michael Simpson, Publications Director

484   National Council on Public History
127 Cavanaugh Hall-IUPUI
425 University Blvd
Indianapolis, IN 46202
317-274-2716
Fax: 317-278-5230
E-mail: ncph@iupui.edu
http://www.ncph.org
NCPH inspires public engagement with the past and serves the needs of practitioners in putting history to work in the world by building community among historians, expanding professional skills and tools, fostering critical reflection on historical practice, and publicly advocating for history and historians.

Founded: 1980

Patrick Moore, President
Alexandra Lord, Vice President

485   New England History Teachers Association
Bentley University
Waltham, MA 02452-4705
617-646-0557
E-mail: info@nehta.org
http://www.nehta.org
NEHTA provides teachers, students and academics opportunities to engage in meaningful conversations about the teaching and learning of history and its related disciplines.

Founded: 1897

Edward Dorgan, President
Stephen Armstrong, Vice President

486   North American Association for Environmental Education
2000 P Street NW
Suite 540
Washington, DC 20036
202-419-0412
Fax: 202-419-0415
E-mail: communicator@naaee.org
http://www.naaee.org
Advances environmental education and supports environmental educators in Canada, the United States and Mexico.

October

Michael A. Marzolla, President

487   Oral History Association
Georgia State University
PO Box 4117
Atlanta, GA 30302-4117
404-413-5751
Fax: 404-413-6384
E-mail: oha@gsu.edu
http://www.oralhistory.org
OHA engages with policy makers, educators, and others to help foster best practices and encourage support for oral history and oral historians.

Stephen Sloan, President
Cliff Kuhn, Executive Director

488   Society for History Education
PO Box 1578
Borrego Springs, CA 92004
760-767-5938
562-985-8703
Fax: 760-767-5938
E-mail:
conniegeorge@thehistoryteacher,org
http://www.csulb.edu/~histeach/ AND
www.thehistoryteacher.org/
Serves as a network for those interested in history and its importance in the classroom.

Connie George, General Manager
Troy Johnson, Board of Directors President

489   Street Law, Inc.
1010 Wayne Avenue
Suite 870
Silver Spring, MD 20910
301-589-1130
Fax: 301-589-1131
E-mail: clearinghouse@streetlaw.org
http://www.streetlaw.org
Street Law develops classroom and grassroots programs that educate students and communities about law, democracy, and human rights.

Founded: 1972

Lee Arbetman, Executive Director
Jos, A. Ar,valo, Chief Financial Officer

490   Western History Association
University of Alaska Fairbanks
Department of History
605 Gruening
Fairbanks, AK 99775-6460
907-474-6508
E-mail:
westernhistoryassociation@gmail.com
http://www.westernhistoryassociation.wil dapricot.org
The Western History Association promotes the study and teaching of the North American West as both a frontier and a region.

Founded: 1961

Donald Worster, President
Margaret Connel-Szasz, President-Elect

491   What So Proudly We Hail
1730 M Street, N.W.
Suite 905
Washington, DC 20036
202-499-5267
E-mail: cheryl@whatsoproudlywehail.org
http://www.whatsoproudlywehail.org
Created by distinguished teacher-scholars Amy Kass and Leon Kass, the What So Proudly We Hail literary-based e-curriculum is a rich source of materials compiled to aid in the classroom instruction of American history, civics, social studies, and language arts.

492   World History Association
Meserve Hall, Northeastern Universi
360 Huntington Avenue
Boston, MA 2130
617-373-6818
Fax: 617-373-2661
E-mail: info@thewha.org
http://www.thewha.org
The WHA is the foremost organization for the promotion of world history through the encouragement of teaching, research, and publication.

Founded: 1982

Technology in Education

493   Agency for Instructional Technology
1800 N StoneLake Drive
Bloomington, IN 47404
812-339-2203
800-457-4509
Fax: 812-333-4218
E-mail: info@ait.net
http://www.ait.net
Provides services and products to enhance student learning. AIT is one of the largest providers of instructional TV programs and other educational media in North America.

Founded: 1962

Robert E. Yocum Jr., President/CEO
Ruth Blankenbaker, Vice Chair

494   Alliance for Technology Access Conference
Alliance for Technology Access
1119 Old Hunboldt Road
Jackson, TN 38301
731-554-5282
Fax: 731-554-5283
E-mail: ATAinfo@ATAccess.org
http://www.ataccess.org
Increases the use of technology by children and adults with disabilities and functional limitations. Encourages and facilitates the empowerment of people with disabilities to participate fully in their communities through public education, information and referral, capacity building in community organizations and advocacy/policy efforts.

James Allison, President
Bob Van der Linde, VP

495   American Distance Education Consortium
http://www.adec.edu
ADEC is a non-profit distance education consortium composed of approximately 20 state universities and land-grant colleges.

Ian Tebbett, President/ CEO
Dave King, Chair

496   Association for Career and Technical Education
1410 King Street
Alexandria, VA 22314
703-683-3111
800-826-9972
Fax: 703-683-7424

E-mail: acte@acteonline.org
http://www.acteonline.org
The Association for Career and Technical Education is dedicated to the advancement of education that prepares youth and adults for careers.

Founded: 1926

Karen Mason, President
Doug Major, President-Elect

497 Association for Educational Communications & Technology
PO Box 2447
1800 Stonelake Drive
Bloomington, IN 47402-2447
812-335-7675
877-677-2328
Fax: 812-335-7678
E-mail: aect@aect.org
http://www.aect.org
Provides leadership in educational communications and technology by linking a wide range of professionals holding a common interest in the use of educational technology and its application learning process.

Mark Childress, President
Dr. Phillip Harris, Executive Director

498 Association for the Advancement of Computing in Education
P.O. Box 719
Waynesville, NC 28786
Fax: 828-246-9557
E-mail: info@aace.org
http://www.aace.org
The Association for the Advancement of Computing in Education (AACE), founded in 1981, is an international, not-for-profit, educational organization with the mission of advancing Information Technology in Education and E-Learning research, development, learning, and its practical application.

Founded: 1981

499 Center for Children and Technology
96 Morton Street
7th Fl
New York, NY 10014
212-807-4200
Fax: 212-633-8804
http://cct.edc.org
The Center for Children and Technology (CCT) began as the educational research and development division of Bank Street College in New York City. As one of the first education technology research-and-development organizations, CCT recognized early on that digital technologies would change people's understanding of the world in crucial and complex—but unpredictable—ways.

Founded: 1980

Shelley Pasnik, Director/ Vice President
Katherine Culp, Director of Research

500 Center for Educational Leadership & Technology
65 West Boston Post Road
Suite 200
Marlborough, MA 1752
508-624-4474
Fax: 508-624-6565
E-mail: info@celtcorp.com
http://www.celtcorp.com
The Center for Educational Leadership and Technology (CELT) is one of the largest and most comprehensive providers of research, planning, and implementation services for public/private schools, education service agencies, departments of education, institutions of higher education, national education

associations, and major education foundations.

John Phillipo, Chairman/ CEO
Richard Rozzelle, President/ CIO

501 Center for Educational Technologies
316 Washington Avenue
Wheeling, WV 26003-6243
304-243-2388
800-624-6992
Fax: 304-243-2497
E-mail: webmaster@cet.edu
http://www.cet.edu
The Center for Educational Technologies is an internationally recognized education facility that houses cutting edge educational technology such as rooms wired for distance learning, videoconferencing, multimedia development for the web and much more.

Charles Wood, Executive Director
Laurie Ruberg, Associate Director

502 Center for Implementing Technology in Educatio
American Institutes for Research
1000 Thomas Jefferson Street, N.W.
Washington, DC 20007
202-403-6869
E-mail: cited@air.org
http://www.cited.org
CITEdÿidentifies evidence-based practices for integrating instructional technology toÿsupportÿthe achievement of all students.

Nancy Safer, Co-Principal Investigator
Mary Thorngren, Deputy Director

503 Computer Using Educators, Inc (CUE)
877 Ygnacio Valley Road
Suite 200
Walnut Creek, CA 94596
925-478-3460
Fax: 925-934-6799
E-mail: cueinc@cue.org
http://www.cue.org
Provides leadership and support to advance student achievement in the educational technology community.

Mike Lawrence, Executive Director
Marisol Valles, Director of Operations

504 Consortium for School Networking
1025 Vermont Avenue NW
Suite 1010
Washington, DC 20005-3007
202-861-2676
866-267-8747
Fax: 202-393-2011
E-mail: info@cosn.org
http://www.cosn.org
CoSN is committed to providing the leadership, community and advocacy tools essential for the success of school district technology leaders. CoSN empowers educational leaders to leverage technology to realize engaging learning environments.

Keith Krueger, CEO
Irene Spero, COO

505 Consortium of College and University Media Centers
306 North Union Street
Indiana University
Bloomington, IN 47405-3888
812-855-6049
E-mail: ccumc@ccumc.org
http://www.ccumc.org
The mission of CCUMC is to provide leadership and a forum for information exchange to the providers of media content, academic technology, and support for quality teaching

and learning at institutions of higher education.

Sue Clabaugh, President
Brenda White, Secretary

506 EDUCAUSE
282 Century Place
Suite 5000
Louisville, CO 80027
303-449-4430
Fax: 303-440-0461
E-mail: info@educause.edu
http://www.educause.edu
A nonprofit association whose mission is to advance higher education by promoting the intelligent use of information technology.

Malcolm Brown, Director
Diana G Oblinger, President and CEO

507 Educational Technology Center

360 Huntington Avenue
215 Snell Library
Boston, MA 02115
617-373-2350
Fax: 617-373-3768
E-mail: teaching@neu.edu
http://www.edtech.neu.edu
The exploration, development and dissemination of technology to enhance teaching, learning and research goals. The Center is also an agent of change, helping to formulate policy on technology-supported teaching and learning

Dr. Laurie Poklop, Associate Director
Audrey Aduama, Assistant Director

508 Instructional Technology Council
426 C Street, NE
Washington, DC 20002-5839
202-293-3110
Fax: 202-293-3132
E-mail: cmullins@itcnetwork.org
http://www.itcnetwork.org
ITC'sÿmissionÿis toÿprovide exceptional leadership and professional development in higher education to its network of eLearning practitioners by advocating, collaborating, researching, and sharing exemplary, innovative practices and potential in educational technologies.

Founded: 1977

Loraine Schmitt, Chair
Carol Spalding, Ed.D., Treasurer

509 International Society for Technology in Education
1710 Rhode Island Ave NW
Suite 900
Washington, DC 20036
202-861-7777
866-654-4777
Fax: 202-861-0888
E-mail: iste@iste.org
http://www.iste.org
Providing leadership and service to improve teaching and learning by advancing the effective use of technology in PK-12 and teacher education.

Kecia Ray, Ed.D., President-Elect
Holly Jobe, President

510 MarcoPolo
WorldCom Foundation
One Verizon Way
Basking Ridge, NJ 07920
509-374-1951
800-360-7955
Fax: 908-630-2660
E-mail: oposewa@edumedia.com
http://www.marcopolo-education.org

A non-profit consortium of premier national and international education organizations and the MCI Foundation dedicated to providing high quality internet and professional development to teachers and students throughout the United States.

Oksana Posewa, Project Manager
Della Cronin, Prog Officer
Communications

511 National Association of Media and Technology Centers
PO Box 9844
Cedar Rapids, IA 52409
319-654-0608
Fax: 319-654-0609
http://www.namtc.org
Committed to promoting leadership among its membership through networking, advocacy, and support activities that will enhance the equitable access to media, technology, and information services to educational communities.

Denise Grasso, President
SIly Lindtren, President-Elect

512 National Center for Technology Innovation
1000 Thomas Jefferson St, NW
Washington, DC 20007
202-403-5323
Fax: 202-403-5001
E-mail: ncti@air.org
http://www.nationaltechcenter.org
The National Center for Technology Innovation (NCTI) advances learning opportunities for individuals with disabilities by fostering technology innovation. Specifically, we help researchers, product developers, manufacturers and publishers to create and commercialize products of value to students with special needs.

Tracy Gray, Director
Heidi Silver-Pacuilla, Deputy Director

513 National Center for Technology Planning
P. O. Box 2393
Tupelo, MS 38803
662-844-9630
Fax: 662-844-9630
http://www.nctp.com
The National Center for Technology Planning (NCTP) is a clearinghouse for the exchange of many types of information related to technology planning.ÿ

Dr. Larry S. Anderson, Founder/Director

514 National Coalition for Technology in Education and Training
E-mail: whitney@jbernsteinstrategy.com
http://www.nctet.org
The National Coalition for Technology in Education and Training (NCTET) is a non-partisan organization that examines and supports the use of technology to improve education and training in America.
Founded: 1993

515 National Institute on Disability and Rehabilitation Research
U.S. Department of Education
400 Maryland Avenue SW
Washington, DC 20202-2572
202-245-7640
800-872-5327
Fax: 202-245-7323
E-mail: nidrr-mailbox@ed.gov
http://www.ed.gov/about/offices/list/oser
s/nidrr
Generates new knowledge and promotes its effective use to improve the abilities of people with disabilities to perform activities of their choice in the community, and also to expand society's capacity to provide full opportunities accommodations for its citizens.
Founded: 1978

Arne Duncan, Secretary of Education
Leonard L Haynes III, Executive Director

516 Online Learning Consortium
PO Box 1238
Newburyport, MA 1950-8238
617-716-1414
E-mail: info@onlinelearning-c.org
http://onlinelearningconsortium.org
The Online Learning Consortium (OLC) is the leading professional organization devoted to advancing quality online learning by providing professional development, instruction, best practice publications and guidance to educators, online learning professionals and organizations around the world. OLC is a key factor in the transformation of the e-Education field.
Founded: 1992

Joel Hartman, President
Marie Cini, Vice President

517 State Educational Technology Directors Association
P.O. Box 10
Glen Burnie, MD 21060
202-715-6636
http://www.setda.org
The State Educational Technology Directors Association (SETDA) is a 501(c)3 not-for-profit membership association launched by state education agency leaders in 2001 to serve, support and represent their emerging interests and needs with respect to the use of technology for teaching, learning, and school operations.

Douglas Levin, Executive Director
Dr. Geoffrey H. Fletcher, Deputy Executive Director

518 Technology & Media Division
The Council for Exceptional Children
2900 Crystal Drive
Suite 1000
Arlington, VA 22202-3557
703-620-3660
888-232-7733
Fax: 703-264-9494
E-mail: contactus@tamcec.org
http://www.tamcec.org
The purpose of TAM is to support educational participation and improved results for individuals with disabilities and diverse learning needs through the selection, acquisition, and use of technology.

Joel Mittler, President

519 Technology Student Association
1914 Association Drive
Reston, VA 20191-1540
703-860-9000
888-860-9010
Fax: 703-758-4852
E-mail: general@tsaweb.org
http://www.tsaweb.org
Leadership and opportunities in technology, innovation, design and engineering. Members apply STEM concepts through co-curricular programs.

Kevin Terronez, President
Matthew Strinden, President-Elect

520 Technology and Children
International Technology Education Association
1914 Association Drive
Suite 201
Reston, VA 20191-1539
703-860-2100
Fax: 703-860-0353
E-mail: iteea@iteea.org
http://www.iteea.org
To advance technological capabilities for all people and to nurture and promote the professionalism of those engaged in these pursuits.ÿ ITEA seeks to meet the professional needs and interests of members as well as to improve public understanding of technology, innovation, design, and engineering education and its contributions.

Steven A. Barbato, Executive Director
William F. Bertrand, President

521 Telemetrics
6 Leighton Place
Mahwah, NJ 07430-3198
201-848-9818
Fax: 201-848-9819
E-mail: info@telemetricsinc.com
http://www.telemetricsinc.com
offers a comprehensive line of camera robotics and control systems for broadcast, industrial, educational and military applications.
Founded: 1950

Anthony C Cuomo, President
Jim Wolfe, Sales Manager

522 Twenty First Century Teachers Network: The McGuffey Project
888 17th Street NW
12th Floor
Washington, DC 20006
202-429-0572
Fax: 202-296-2962
E-mail: info@mcguffey.org
http://www.21ct.org/
A nationwide, non-profit initiative of the McGuffey Project, dedicated to assisting K-2 teachers learn, use and effectively integrate technology in the curriculum for improved student learning.

Wade D Sayer, Project Director, Director Program Development

523 United States Distance Learning Association
76 Canal Street
Suite 400
Boston, MA 2114
617-399-1770
800-275-5162
Fax: 617-399-1771
E-mail: info@usdla.org
http://www.usdla.org
The United States Distance Learning Association was the first nonprofit Distance Learning association in the United States to support Distance Learning research, development and praxis across the complete arena of education, training and communications.

Marilyn Gardner, Ph.D., J.D., Director, BD
Patricia Marcelonis, Executive Assistant

524 V-LINC
V-LINC
2301 Argonne Drive
Baltimore, MD 21218
410-554-9134
800-772-7372
Fax: 410-261-2907
E-mail: info@linc.org
http://www.v-linc.org
V-LINC was created out of a merger between Learning Independence through computers and Volunteers for Medical Engineering. V-LINC's focus is on improving the independence and qual-

ity of life for individuals with disabilities. Provides innovative technology solutions and training that assist individuals in their home, community and workplace.

Founded: 2010

Theo Pinette, Executive Director
John Walker, Project Coordinator

25 Western Cooperative for Educational Telecommunications
3035 Center Green Drive
Suite 200
Boulder, CO 80301-2204
303-541-0231
Fax: 303-541-0291
E-mail: wcetinfo@wiche.edu
http://wcet.wiche.edu
WICHE Cooperative for Educational Technologies (WCET) accelerates the adoption of effective practices and policies, advancing excellence in technology-enhanced teaching and learning in higher education.

Founded: 1989

Mike Abbiatti, Executive Director
Sherri Artz Gilbert, Manager, Operations

26 eLearning Guild
120 Stony Point Rd.
Suite 125
Santa Rosa, CA 95401
707-566-8990
Fax: 707-566-8963
E-mail: service@elearningguild.com
http://www.elearningguild.com
The eLearning Guildÿis the oldest and most trusted source of information, networking, and community for eLearning professionals.

Alabama

27 Alabama Business Education Association
A&M University
School of Business
PO Box 429
Normal, AL 35762
256-372-4799
Fax: 256-851-5568
E-mail: karzetta@bellsouth.net
http://www.alabamabusinessed.org
A professional association for business and marketing educators at the secondary and post-secondary levels.

Karzetta Bester, President
Emma Fault, President-Elect

28 Alabama Commission on Higher Education
PO Box 302000
Montgomery, AL 36130-2000
334-242-1998
800-960-7773
Fax: 334-242-0268
E-mail: deborah.nettles@ache.alabama.gov
http://www.ache.alabama.gov
Provides information on the state's education programs, college and universities, financial aid assistance programs, grants, scholarships, continuing education programs, and career opportunities.

29 Alabama Education Association
422 Dexter Avenue
Montgomery, AL 36104-3743
334-834-9790
800-392-5839
Fax: 334-262-8377
E-mail: myaea@alaedu.org
http://www.myaea.org

Serves as an advocate for Alabama teachers and leads in the advancement of equitable and quality public education.

Dorothy Strickland, President
Dr. Henry Mabry, Executive Secretary

530 Alabama Library Association
9154 Eastchase Parkway
Suite 418
Montgomery, AL 36117
334-414-0113
877-563-5146
Fax: 334-265-1281
E-mail: admin@allanet.org
http://www.allanet.org
Non-profit corporation formed to encourage and promote the welfare of libraries and professional interests of librarians in Alabama. Provides leadership for the development, advocacy and improvement of library and information services and to promote the profession of librarianship, in order to enhance learning and ensure access to information for all.

Emily Tish, President
Jeff Simpson, President-Elect

531 Alabama Public Library Service
6030 Monticello Dr
Montgomery, AL 36130
334-213-3900
800-723-8459
Fax: 334-213-3993
E-mail: vcarr@apls.state.al.us
http://www.statelibrary.alabama.gov

532 Alabama State Council on the Arts
201 Monroe St
Suite 110
Montgomery, AL 36104
334-240-4076
800-548-2546
Fax: 334-240-3269
E-mail: staff@arts.alabama.gov
http://www.arts.state.al.us
Promotes high-quality education in the arts.

533 Alabama State Education for Homeless Children and Youth
Gordon Persons Building, Room 5348
PO Box 302101
Montgomery, AL 36130-3901
334-242-8199
888-725-9321
Fax: 334-242-0496
E-mail: bthompson@alsde.edu
http://www.alsde.edu/html/home.asp
Ensures that all homeless children and youth have equal access to the same free, appropriate public education.

Alaska

534 Alaska Association of School Librarians
PO Box 101085
Anchorage, AK 99510-1085
907-269-6569
800-776-6566
Fax: 907-269-6580
E-mail: association@akasl.org
http://www.akasl.org
Advances a high standard for the school librarian profession and the library information program in the schools of Alaska.

Nicole Roohi, President
Wendy Stout, President-Elect

535 Alaska Commission on Postsecondary Education
PO Box 110505
Juneau, AK 99811-0505
907-465-2962
800-441-2962
Fax: 907-465-5316
E-mail: customer_service@acpe.state.ak.us
http://www.acpe.alaska.gov
Provides information on the state's education programs, colleges and universities, financial aid assistance programs, grants, scholarships, continuing education programs, and career opportunities.

536 Alaska Library Association
PO Box 81084
Fairbanks, AK 99708
907-459-1020
Fax: 907-459-1024
E-mail: webdeveloper@akla.org
http://www.akla.org
Provides leadership and advocacy for the educational and political concerns of the library community in Alaska. Encourages cooperation among libraries and related groups, safeguards intellectual freedom, and promotes access to information for all Alaskans.

Linda Wynne, President
Stacey Glaser, President-Elect

537 Alaska State Council on the Arts
411 West Fourth Ave
Suite 1E
Anchorage, AK 99501-2343
907-269-6610
888-278-7424
Fax: 907-269-6601
E-mail: gina.brown@alaska.gov
http://www.eed.state.ak.us/aksca
Promotes high-quality education in the arts.

538 Alaska State Education for Homeless Children and Youth
801 West 10th St, Suite 200
PO Box 110500
Juneau, AK 99811-0500
907-465-3826
877-854-5437
Fax: 907-465-2989
E-mail: eed.webmaster@alaska.gov
http://www.eed.state.ak.us/tls/titleX/home.s
html
Ensures that all homeless children and youth have equal access to the same free, appropriate public education.

Arizona

539 Arizona Commission for Postsecondary Education
2020 North Central Ave
Suite 650
Phoenix, AZ 85004-4503
602-258-2435
Fax: 602-258-2483
E-mail: acpe@highered.gov
http://www.azhighered.gov
Provides information on the state's education programs, colleges and universities, financial aid assistance programs, grants, scholarships, continuing education programs, and career opportunities.

540 Arizona Commission on the Arts
471 West Roosevelt St
Phoenix, AZ 85003-1326
602-771-6501
Fax: 602-256-0282
E-mail: info@azarts.gov
http://www.azarts.gov
Promotes high-quality education in the arts.

541 Arizona Library Association
1030 E Baseline Road
Suite 105-1025
Tempe, AZ 85283
480-609-3999
Fax: 480-609-3939
E-mail: admin@azla.org
http://www.azla.org
Promotes library service and librarianship in libraries of all types in the state of Arizona.

Debbie Hanson, Executive Director

542 Arizona School Boards Association
2100 N Central Avenue
Suite 200
Phoenix, AZ 85004-1441
602-254-1100
800-238-4701
Fax: 602-254-1177
http://www.azsba.org
Promotes community volunteer governance of public education and continuous improvement of student success by providing training, leadership and assistance to public school governing boards.ÿ

Randy Schiller, President
Dr. Timothy Ogle, Executive Director

543 Arizona State Education for Homeless Children and Youth
1535 West Jefferson St
Bin 14
Phoenix, AZ 85007
602-542-4963
800-352-4558
Fax: 602-542-5175
E-mail: frank.migali@azed.gov
http://www.azed.gov/schooleffectiveness/specialpops/homeless
Ensures that all homeless children and youth have equal access to the same free, appropriate public education.

544 Arizona State Library, Archives, and Public Records
1700 West Washington
Suite 200
Phoenix, AZ 85007
602-926-4035
800-228-4710
Fax: 602-256-7983
E-mail: services@lib.az.us
http://www.lib.az.us

Arkansas

545 Arkansas Arts Council
323 Center St
1500 Tower Building
Little Rock, AR 72201-2606
501-324-9766
Fax: 501-324-9207
E-mail: info@arkansasarts.com
http://www.arkansasarts.com
Promotes high-quality education in the arts.

546 Arkansas Business Education Association
Bryant Junior High School
201 Sullivan
Bryant, AR 72022
501-847-5620
Fax: 501-847-5627
E-mail: keliason@nettleschools.net
http://www.abea.us
A professional association comprised of business and marketing educators involved at the secondary and post-secondary levels. Promotes quality education in all phases of business and to encourage professional growth and cooperative interaction among all individuals involved in this sector of education.

Michael Lentz, President
Tammy Ward, President-Elect

547 Arkansas Department of Higher Education
114 East Capitol
Little Rock, AR 72201-3818
501-371-2000
Fax: 501-371-2001
E-mail: rickj@adhe.edu
http://www.adhe.edu
Provides information on the state's education programs, colleges and universities, financial aid assistance programs, grants, scholarships, continuing education programs, and career opportunities.

548 Arkansas Education Association
1500 W 4th Street
Little Rock, AR 72201
501-375-4611
800-632-0624
Fax: 501-375-4620
E-mail: ldimond@nea.org
http://www.aeaonline.org
Advocates for education professionals and unites members and the state to fulfill the promise of public education to prepare every student to succeed in a diverse and interdependent world.

Donna Morey, President
Brenda Robinson, VP

549 Arkansas Library Association
PO Box 958
Benton, AR 72018-0958
501-860-7585
Fax: 501-778-4014
E-mail: arlib2@sbcglobal.net
http://www.arlib.org
Furthers the professional development of all library staff members, fosters communication and cooperation among librarians, trustees and friends of libraries; increases the visibility of libraries among the general public and funding agencies; to serve as an advocate for librarians and libraries.

Founded: 1911

Lynda Hampel, Executive Administrator
Patricia Miller, President

550 Arkansas State Education for Homeless Children and Youth
Four Capitol Mall, Arch Ford Bldg
Room 305-B
Little Rock, AR 72201-1071
501-682-4847
Fax: 501-682-3372
E-mail: cindy.hogue@arkansas.gov
http://www.askansased.org
Ensures that all homeless children and youth have equal acces to the same free, appropriate public education.

California

551 California Arts Council
1300 I St
Suite 930
Sacramento, CA 95814
916-322-6555
800-201-6201
Fax: 916-322-6575
E-mail: dgolling@cac.ca.gov
http://www.cac.ca.gov
Promotes high-quality education in the arts.

552 California Association for Bilingual Education
16033 E San Bernadino Rd
Covina, CA 91722-3900
626-814-4441
Fax: 626-814-4640
http://www.bilingualeducation.org

553 California Business Education Association
PO Box 2591
Walnut Creek, CA 94595
925-295-1104
Fax: 925-295-1104
E-mail: cbeaquestions@cbeaonline.org
http://www.cbeaonline.org
The prime mission of CBEA is to recognize, encourage, and promote excellence in business disciplines. Also, it is to collaborate with other disciplines and other groups dedicated to this mission.

Irina Weisblat, President
Lisa Natwick, Secretary

554 California Classical Association-Northern Section
San Francisco State University
Department of Classics
San Francisco, CA 94132
415-253-2267
Fax: 415-338-2514
E-mail: ccanorth@yahoo.com
http://www.ccanorth.org
Funds support programs to enrich and promote Classical Studies.

Founded: 1969

Mary McCarty, President
Holly Coty, VP

555 California Foundation for Agriculture in the Classroom
2300 River Plaza Drive
Sacramento, CA 95833
916-561-5625
800-700-2482
Fax: 916-561-5697
E-mail: info@learnaboutag.org
http://www.LearnAboutAg.org
Our mission is to increase awareness and understanding of agriculture among California's educators and students. Our vision is an appreciation of agriculture by all.

Judy Culbertson, Executive Director
Mindy DeRohan, Communications Coordinator

556 California Library Association
2471 Flores St
San Mateo, CA 94403
650-376-0886
Fax: 650-539-2341
E-mail: info@cla-net.org
http://www.cla-net.org
Provides leadership for the development, promotion, and improvement of library services, librarianship, and the library community. A resource for learning about new ideas and technology.

Derek Wolfgram, President
Rosario Garza, Executive Director

557 California Reading Association
638 Camino De Los Mares
Suite H130/476
San Clemente, CA 92673
714-435-1983
Fax: 714-435-0269
E-mail: kathy@californiareads.org
http://www.californiareads.org
CRA is an independent, self-governing organization dedicated to increasing literacy in California.

Kathy Belanger, Administrative Director
Lynn Gurnee, President

558 California School Library Association
6444 E. Spring Street
#237
Long Beach, CA 90815-1553
888-655-8480
Fax: 888-655-8480
E-mail: info@csla.net
http://www.csla.net
Advocates, educates and collaborates to ensure the all California students and educators are effective users of ideas and information.
Jane Lofton, President

559 California State Homeless Education
1430 N St
Suite 4401
Sacramento, CA 95814
916-319-0383
866-856-8214
Fax: 916-319-0126
E-mail: lwheeler@cde.ca.gov
http://www.cde.ca.gov/sp/hs
Ensures that all homeless children and youth have equal access to the same free, appropriate public education.

560 California Student Aid Commission
PO Box 419027
Rancho Cordova, CA 95741-9027
916-526-7590
888-224-7268
Fax: 916-526-8004
E-mail: studentsupport@csac.ca.gov
http://www.csac.ca.gov
Provides information on the state's education programs, college and universities, financial aid assistance programs, grants, scholarships, continuing education programs, and career opportunities.

561 California Teachers Association
1705 Murchison Drive
Burlingame, CA 94010
650-697-1400
Fax: 650-552-5002
E-mail: webmaster@cta.org
http://www.cta.org
Protects and promotes the well-being of California teachers by improving the conditions of teaching and learning and advancing the cause of universal education.
Dean E. Vogel, President
Eric Heins, Vice President

562 Northern California Comprehensive Assistance Center
730 Harrison Street
San Francisco, CA 94107
415-565-3000
877-493-7833
Fax: 415-565-3012
E-mail: plloyd@wested.com
http://www.wested.org
WestEd's Assessment and Standards Development Services program has helped shape effective statewide assessment and accountability systems nationwide. Works with education and other communities to promote excellence, achieve equity, and improve learning for children, youth and adults.
Sri Ananda, Chief Program Officer
Glen Harvey, Chief Executive Officer

563 WestEd
730 Harrison Street
San Francisco, CA 94107-1242
415-565-3000
877-493-7833
Fax: 415-565-3012
E-mail: dtorres@wested.org
http://www.WestEd.org

A research, development and service agency, works with education and other communities to promote excellence, achieve equity, and improve learning for children, youth and adults. WestEd has offices in Georgia, Arizona, Vermont, Illinois and Washington DC as well.
Danny Torres, Publications Manager
Glen H. Harvey, CEO

Colorado

564 Colorado Association of Libraries
3030 W 81st Ave
Westminster, CO 80031
303-463-6400
Fax: 303-458-0002
E-mail: cal@cal-webs.org
http://www.cal-webs.org
The Colorado Association of Libraries (CAL) is the common bond, voice, and power for the library community. Advocate for quality library services, support access to information and foster the professional development.
Stephen Sweeney, President
Kari May, VP/President-Elect

565 Colorado Business Educators
Prairie High School
300 Thomas
Box 82
New Rayemr, CO 80742
970-437-5386
Fax: 970-437-5732
E-mail: jean.sykes@mcclave.k12.co.us
http://www.cbeweb.org
Supports business educators in Colorado with curriculum material and career networking.
Lucinda Carpenter, President
Rebecca Diggs, Secretary

566 Colorado Community College & Occupational Education System
9101 E Lowry Boulevard
Denver, CO 80230-6011
303-620-4000
Fax: 303-620-4030
E-mail: marybeth.noble@cccs.edu
http://www.cccs.edu
The Colorado Community College System comprises the state's largest system of higher education serving more than 117,000 students annually. Provides an accessible, responsive learning environment that facilitates the achievement of educational, professional and personal goals.
Nancy McCallin, President
Claire Kuhns, Executive Asst to President

567 Colorado Council on the Arts
1625 Broadway
Suite 2700
Denver, CO 80202
303-892-3802
Fax: 303-892-3848
E-mail: jeanette.albert@state.co.us
http://www.coloarts.org
Promotes high-quality education in the arts.

568 Colorado Department of Higher Education
1560 Broadway
Suite 1600
Denver, CO 80202
303-866-2723
Fax: 303-866-4266
E-mail: executivedirector@dhe.state.co.us
http://www.highered.colorado.gov

Provides information on the state's education programs, colleges and universities, financial aid assistance programs, grants, scholarships, continuing education programs, and career opportunities.

569 Colorado Education Association
1500 Grant Street
Denver, CO 80203-1800
303-837-1500
800-332-5939
Fax: 303-837-9006
http://www.coloradoea.org
The Colorado Education Association is a voluntary membership organization of 38,000 K-12 teachers and education support professionals; higher education faculty and support professionals; retired educators; and students preparing to become teachers.
Kerrie Dallman, President
Amie Baca-Oehlert, Vice President

570 Colorado State Education for Homeless Children and Youth
201 East Colfax Ave
Room 306 E
Denver, CO 80203-1799
303-866-6930
Fax: 303-866-6785
E-mail: scott_d@cde.state.co.us
http://www.cde.state.co.us/cdeprevention/homeless_index.htm
Ensures that all homeless children and youth have equal opportunity to the same free, appropriate public education.

Connecticut

571 Connecticut Business & Industry Association (CBIA)
350 Church Street
Hartford, CT 06103-1126
860-244-1900
Fax: 860-278-8562
E-mail: bellj@cbia.com
http://www.cbia.com
Serves as an advocate for the general business and industry community in Connecticut. Promotes a business climate that is globally competitive, encourages communication and cooperation among businesses, government, the private sector and general public.
Jim Bell, Business Consulting Director
Joe Budd, Media/Public Relations

572 Connecticut Commission on Culture and Tourism
1 Constitution Plaza
Hartford, CT 06103
860-256-2800
Fax: 860-256-2811
E-mail: leigh.johnson@ct.gov
http://www.cultureandtourism.org/cct/site/default.asp
Promotes high-quality education in the arts.

573 Connecticut Department of Higher Education
61 Woodland St
Hartford, CT 06105-2326
860-947-1800
Fax: 860-947-1310
E-mail: lnegro@ctdhe.org
http://www.ctdhe.org
Provides information on the state's education programs, colleges and universities, financial aid assistance programs, grants, scholarships, continuing education programs, and career opportunities.

574 Connecticut Education Association (CEA)
Capitol Place
21 Oak Street
Suite 500
Hartford, CT 06106-8001
860-525-5641
800-842-4316
Fax: 860-725-6323
E-mail: johny@cea.org
http://www.cea.org
CEA advocates for teachers and public education, lobbying legislators for the resources public schools need and campaigning for high standards for teachers and students.

Mark Waxenberg, Executive Director
Linette Branham, Dir. Policy/Pro. Practice

575 Connecticut Educational Media Association
21 Oak Street
Suite 500
Hartford, CT 06106
860-525-5641
800-842-4316
Fax: 860-725-6323
http://www.cea.org
Professional association of Connecticut school library media specialist.

Shelia Cohen, President
Jeff Leake, Vice President

576 Connecticut State Education for Homeless Children and Youth
25 Industrial Park Rd
Middletown, CT 06457
860-807-2058
Fax: 860-807-2127
E-mail: louis.tallarita@ct.gov
http://www.sde.ct.gov
Ensures that all homeless children and youth have equal access to the same free, appropriate public education.

Delaware

577 Delaware Business Education Association
Delcastle High School
140 Brennen Drive
Newwark, DE 19713
302-454-2164
E-mail: rhuddj@christina.k12.de.us
Fosters business education in the state of Delaware.

Jennifer Rhudd, President
Lisa Stoner, Membership Director

578 Delaware Division of Libraries
121 Duke Of York St
Dover, DE 19901
302-739-4748
800-282-8696
Fax: 302-739-8436
E-mail: sonja.brown@state.de.us
http://www.state.lib.de.us

579 Delaware Division of the Arts
820 North French St
Wilmington, DE 19801
302-577-8278
302-577-6561
E-mail: delarts@state.de.us
http://www.artsdel.org
Promotes high-quality education in the arts.

580 Delaware Higher Education Commission
820 North French St
Wilmington, DE 19801
302-577-5240
800-292-7935
Fax: 302-577-6765
E-mail: dhec@doe.k12.de.us
http://www.doe.k12.de.us/dehc
Provides information on the state's education programs, colleges and universities, financial aid assistance programs, grants, scholarships, continuing education programs, and career opportunities.

581 Delaware Library Association
PO Box 816
Dover, DE 19903-816
816-531-2468
Fax: 302-831-1631
E-mail: danbradbury@gossagesager.com
http://www2.lib.udel.edu/dla
Promotes the profession of librarianship and provides library information and media services to the people of Delaware through a unified library community.

Terri Jones, President
Christine Payne, VP/Conference Planning Chair

582 Delaware State Education Association
136 East Water Street
Dover, DE 19901-3630
302-734-5834
866-734-5834
Fax: 392-674-8499
E-mail: pamela.nichols@dsea.org
http://www.dsea.org/
The Delaware State Education Association is a union of public school employees that advocates for the rights and interests of its members and outstanding public education for all students.

Frederika Jenner, President
Mike Hoffman, VP

583 Delaware State Education for Homeless Children and Youth
401 Federal St
Suite 2
Dover, DE 19901
302-735-4273
Fax: 301-739-4483
Ensures that all homeless children and youth have equal access to the same free, appropriate public education.

District of Columbia

584 American Council on Education Library & Information Service
American Council on Education
1 Dupont Circle NW
Suite 1B-20
Washington, DC 20036-1193
202-939-9300
Fax: 202-833-4730
E-mail: comments@ace.nche.edu
http://www.acenet.edu
The council seeks to provide leadership and a unifying voice on key higher education issues and to influence public policy through advocacy, research, and program initiatives.

Jospeh Aoun, Chair
Diana Natalicio, Vice Chair/Chair-elect

585 Associates for Renewal in Education (ARE)
Brenda Strong Nixon Community Complex
45 P Street NW
Brenda Strong Nixon Community Complex
Washington, DC 20001-1133
202-483-9424
Fax: 202-667-5299
E-mail: info@areinc.org
http://www.areinc.org
A multi project agency working to improve the quality of life and education of the young people of the District of Columbia, with an emphasis on youth-at risk and under served populations.

Dayna Nokes, President/CEO
Evie Saunders Davis, Deputy Finance/HR

586 District Of Columbia Commission on the Arts and Humanities
1371 Harvard St NW
Washington, DC 20009
202-724-5613
Fax: 202-724-4493
E-mail: carolyn.parker@dc.gov
http://www.dcarts.dc.gov
Promotes high-quality education in the arts.

587 District of Columbia Library Association
Benjamin Franklin Station
PO Box 14177
Washington, DC 20044
202-872-1112
E-mail: April.King@dc.gov
http://www.dcla.org
Provides library services to the residents of D.C. and represents the region at the Council of the American Library Association, promoting general and joint enterprises with the American Library Association and other library groups.

Jacqueline Protka, President
Amanda Wilson, VP/President-Elect

588 District of Columbia Office of the State Superintendent of Education
441 Fourth St NW
Suite 350 North
Washington, DC 20001
202-727-6436
877-485-6751
Fax: 202-727-2834
E-mail: osse@dc.gov
http://www.osse.dc.gov
Provides information on the state's education programs, colleges and universities, financial aid assistance programs, grants, scholarships, continuing education programs, and career opportunities.

Florida

589 Florida Arts
500 South Bronough St
Tallahassee, FL 32399-0250
850-245-6470
Fax: 850-245-6497
E-mail: info@florida-arts.org
http://www.florida-arts.org
Promotes high-quality education in the arts.

590 Florida Association for Media in Education
16350 Bruce B. Downs Blvd
#46545
Tampa, FL 33647
813-380-5673
Fax: 850-531-8344
E-mail: floriaeducators@gmail.com
http://www.floridamedia.org
FAME advocates for every student in Florida to be involved in and have open access to a quality

school library media program administered by a highly competent, certified library media specialist. FAME is a collaborative, responsive, dynamic network for Florida library media professionals.

Cora P. Dunkley, Ph.D, President
Lou Greco, VP

591 Florida Business Technology Education Association
c/o Palm Beach County School District
3310 Forest Hill Boulevard
C-225
West Palm Beach, FL 33406
561-434-7395
E-mail: sslarsen@bellsouth.net
http://www.fbtea.org
Fosters business education in the state of Florida.

Connie Myrick, President
Sue Larsen, Treasurer

592 Florida Education Association
213 South Adams Street
Tallahassee, FL 32301
850-201-2800
888-807-8007
Fax: 850-222-1840
http://www.feaweb.org
Advocates the right to a free, quality public education for all. Advances professional growth, development and status of all who serve the students in Florida's public schools. Engages members and communities to ensure that all students learn and succeed in a diverse world.

Andy Ford, President
Joanne McCall, Vice President

593 Florida Library Association (FLA)
164 NW Madison Street
Suite 104
Lake City, FL
386-438-5795
850-322-5005
Fax: 386-438-5796
E-mail: fla.admin@comcast.net
http://www.flalib.org
The Florida Library Association (FLA) develops programs and undertakes activities to earn it a leadership position for all areas of librarianship. FLA provides opportunities for librarians and support staff in Florida to advance their skills so that they can maintain their effectiveness in the new information age.

Faye C Roberts, Executive Director
Ruth O'Donnell, Conference Manager

594 Florida State Office Of Student Financial Assistance
1940 North Monroe St
Suite 70
Tallahassee, FL 32303-4759
850-410-5180
888-827-2004
Fax: 850-487-1809
E-mail: theresa.antworth@fldoe.org
http://www.floridastudentfinancialaid.org
Provides information on the state's education programs, colleges and universities, financial aid assistance programs, grants, scholarships, continuing education programs, and career opportunities.

Georgia

595 Georgia Association of Educators
100 Crescent Center Parkway
Suite 500
Tucker, GA 30084
678-837-1118
800-282-7142
Fax: 678-837-1100
http://www.gae2.org
The Georgia Association of Educators is a professional organization for public education professionals.

Christopher Turner, Executive Director
Sid Chapman, VP

596 Georgia Business Education Association (GBEA)
Perry High School
1307 N Avenue
Perry, VA 31069
478-988-6315
E-mail: lary.debra@newton.k12.ga.us
http://www.georgiagbea.org/
Serves individuals and groups involved in instruction, administration, research and dissemination of information for/about business at all instructional levels.

Dwionne Freeman, President
Renee Waters, President Elect

597 Georgia Council for the Arts
260 14th St NW
Suite 401
Atlanta, GA 30318-5360
404-685-2787
Fax: 404-685-2788
E-mail: gaarts@gaarts.org
http://www.gaarts.org
Promotes high-quality education in the arts.

598 Georgia Library Association
PO Box 793
Rex, GA 30273
678-466-4334
800-999-8558
Fax: 678-466-4349
E-mail: karamullen@clayton.edu
http://gla.georgialibraries.org
Provides support and encouragement for libraries to advance the educational, cultural, and economic life of the state.

Diana Very, President
Susan Morris, VP

599 Georgia Parents & Teachers Association
114 Baker Street NE
Atlanta, GA 30308-3366
404-659-0214
800-782-8632
Fax: 404-525-0210
E-mail: gapta@bellsouth.net
http://www.georgiapta.org
A powerful voice for children, families and communities advocating for the education, engagement and empowerment of every child in the state of Georgia.

Donna Kosicki, President
Rita Erves, President Elect

600 Georgia Public Library Service
1800 Century Plaza
Suite 150
Atlanta, GA 30345-4304
404-235-7200
Fax: 404-235-7201
http://www.georgialibraries.org

601 Georgia State Education for Homeless Children and Youth
205 Jesse Hill Jr Drive SE
1866 Twin Towers East
Atlanta, GA 30334
404-656-2004
Fax: 404-657-1534
E-mail: jjohnson@doe.k12.ga.us
Ensures that all homeless children and youth have equal access to the same free, appropriate public education.

602 Georgia Student Finance Commission
2082 East Exchange Place
Tucker, GA 30084
770-724-9000
800-505-4732
Fax: 770-724-9089
E-mail: gsfcinfo@gsfc.org
http://www.gsfc.org
Provides information on the state's education programs, colleges and universities, financial aid assistance programs, grants, scholarships, continuing education programs, and career opportunities.

603 Southeastern Library Association
PO Box 950
Rex, GA 30273
678-466-4334
Fax: 678-466-4349
E-mail: karamullen@clayton.edu
http://selaonline.org
A unifying force strong enough to influence legislation and to attract foundation and federal funds for regional library projects.

Michael Seigler, President
Gordon N. Baker, President-Elect

Hawaii

604 Hawaii Business Education Association
Leeward Community College
Normadeene Musick
96-045 Ala Ike
Pearl City, HI 96782-3393
808-455-0206
Fax: 808-453-6735
E-mail: president@hbea.org
http://www.hbea.org
HBEA is devoted exclusively to serving individuals and groups engaged in instruction, administration, research, and dissemination of information for and about business and technology. Hosts conferences and other professional improvement opportunities.

Jean Hara, President
Angeline Nelson, VP

605 Hawaii Education Association (HEA)
1953 S. Beretania St.
Suite 5C
Honolulu, HI 96826
808-949-6657
866-653-9372
Fax: 808-944-2032
E-mail: hea.office@heaed.com
http://www.heaed.com
Strengthens and supports quality education for all through the enrichment and growth of future, current and retired educators as well as through acknowledgment of their contribution to the community.

June Motokawa, President
Ron Toma, VP

606 Hawaii Library Association
PO Box 4441
Honolulu, HI 96812-4441

808-292-2068
Fax: 808-956-5968
E-mail:
hawaii.library.association@gmail.com
http://www.hlaweb.org
Promotes library service and librarianship
in Hawaii in cooperation and affiliation
with the American Library Association and
other groups having allied objectives.

Christine Pawliuk, President
Christina Abelardo, VP/President-Elect

607 Hawaii State Education for Homeless Children and Youth
595 Pepeekeo St
Building H Room 1
Honolulu, HI 96825
808-394-1384
866-927-9095
Fax: 808-394-1388
http://www.doe.k12.hi.us/programs/index
.htm
Ensures that all homeless children and
youth have equal access to the same free,
appropriate public education.

608 Hawaii State Foundation on Culture and the Arts
250 South Hotel St
Honolulu, HI 96813
808-586-0300
Fax: 808-586-0308
http://www.hawaii.gov/sfca
Promotes high-quality education in the
arts.

609 Hawaii State Postsecondary Education Commission
2444 Dole St
Room 209
Honolulu, HI 96822-2302
808-956-8213
Fax: 808-956-5158
E-mail: bor@hawaii.edu
http://www.hawaii.edu/offices/bor
Provides information on the state's education programs, colleges and universities,
financial aid assistance programs, grants,
scholarships, continuing education programs, and career opportunities.

610 Hawaii State Teachers Association (HSTA)
1200 Ala Kapuna Street
Honolulu, HI 96819
808-833-2711
Fax: 808-839-7106
E-mail: info@hsta.org
http://www.hsta.org
Supports the professional roles of teachers,
advocates for teachers' interests, and assures quality education for Hawaii's youth.

Wil Okabe, President
Alvin Nagasako, Executive Director

Idaho

611 Idaho Commission for Libraries
325 West State St
Boise, ID 83702
208-334-2150
800-458-3271
Fax: 208-334-4016
http://www.libraries.idaho.gov

612 Idaho Commission on the Arts
2410 N Old Penitentiary Rd
PO Box 83720
Boise, ID 83720-0008
208-334-2119
800-278-3863

Fax: 208-334-2488
E-mail: info@arts.idaho.gov
http://www.arts.idaho.gov
Promotes high-quality education in the
arts.

613 Idaho Education Association
620 N 6th Street
PO Box 2638
Boise, ID 83701
208-344-1341
800-727-9922
Fax: 208-336-6967
E-mail: info@idahoea.org
http://www.idahoea.org
Advocates the professional and personal
well-being of its members and the vision of
excellence in public education.

Rick Jones, VP
Penni Cyr, President

614 Idaho Library Association
PO Box 8533
Moscow, ID 83843-1033
208-334-2150
Fax: 208-334-4016
http://www.idaholibraries.org
Supports the library community in Idaho
and encourages both students and professionals to engage with the services that libraries offer.

Gena Marker, President
Karen Yother, VP/President-Elect

615 Idaho State Homeless Education Program Office
650 West State
PO Box 83720
Boise, ID 83720-0027
208-332-6978
800-432-4601
Fax: 208-334-2228
http://www.sde.state.id.us/homeless/defa
ult.asp
Ensures that all homeless children and
youth have equal access to the same free,
appropriate public education.

Illinois

616 Illinois Affiliation of Private Schools for Exceptional Children
Lawrence Hall Youth Services
4833 N Francisco Avenue
Chicago, IL 60625-3640
773-769-3500
http://www.iapsec.org
A non-profit organization consisting of
private schools serving Illinois children
with exceptional needs and works to maintain the quality of special education made
available to special needs students.

Ken Carwell, President
Sol Rappaport, Secretary

617 Illinois Art Council
100 W Randolph St
Chicago, IL 60601
312-814-6750
800-237-6994
Fax: 312-814-1471
E-mail: iac.info@illinois.gov
http://www.state.il.us/agency/iac
Promotes high-quality education in the
arts.

618 Illinois Association of School Administrators
2648 Beechler Court
Springfield, IL 62703-7305

217-753-2213
Fax: 217-753-2240
http://www.iasaedu.org

619 Illinois Association of School Business Officials
Northern Illinois University
108 Carroll Avenue
DeKalb, IL 60115
815-753-1276
Fax: 815-516-0184
E-mail: grizaffigi@vvsd.org
http://www.iasbo.org
Provides its members and stakeholders a comprehensive range of professional development activities and services through networking and
participation.

Mark E. Staehlin, President
Michael A Jacoby, Executive Director

620 Illinois Business Education Association (IBEA)
8536 E Jackson Street
Du Quoin, IL 62832-4078
Fax: 618-542-5528
E-mail: president@ibea.org
http://www.ibea.org
Promoting the profession and providing the environment and encouragement to improve professional endeavors

Ethel Holladay, Executive Director
Jodee Werkheiser, President

621 Illinois Citizens' Education Council
100 East Edwards Street
Springfield, IL 62704-1999
217-544-0706
Fax: 217-333-2736
Association of 120,000 members composed of Illinois elementary and secondary teachers, higher
education faculty and staff, educational support
professionals, retired educators, and college students preparing to become teachers.

Anne Davis, President
Ken Swanson, Vice President

622 Illinois Education Association
100 E Edwards Street
Springfield, IL 62704-1999
217-544-0706
800-252-8076
Fax: 217-544-7383
http://www.ieanea.org
Represents public, academic, and special libraries
as well as librarians, library assistants, trustees,
students and library vendors. Promotes excellence and equity in public education and acts as
the advocacy organization for all public education
employees.

Cinda Klickna, President
Kathi Griffen, Vice President

623 Illinois Homeless Education Program
100 N First St
Springfield, IL 62777-0001
217-557-7323
800-215-6379
http://www.isbe.state.il.us/homeless/default.htm
Ensures that all homeless children and youth have
equal access to the same free, appropriate public
education.

624 Illinois Library Association
33 W Grand Avenue
Suite 401
Chicago, IL 60654-6799
312-644-1896
Fax: 312-644-1899
E-mail: ila@ila.org
http://www.ila.org
The Illinois Library Association is the voice for
Illinois libraries and the millions who depend on
them. Provides leadership for the development,

promotion and improvement of library services in Illinois and for the library community in order to enhance learning and ensure access to information for all.

Pamela Van Kirk, President
Stu Erickson, Executive Director

25 Illinois School Library Media Association
PO Box 598
Canton, IL 61520
309-649-0911
Fax: 309-649-0916
E-mail: islma@islma.org
http://www.islma.org
Promotes student interaction, and continuing education of school library media specialists, and collaboration among parents, community members, teachers and administrators as they prepare students for life-long learning.

Christine Graves, President
Debra Turner, President-Elect

26 Illinois Student Assistance Commission
1755 Lake Cook Rd
Deerfield, IL 60015-5209
847-948-8500
800-899-4722
Fax: 847-831-8549
E-mail: collegezone@isac.org
http://www.collegezone.com
Provides information on the state's education programs, colleges and universities, financial aid assistance programs, grants, scholarships, continuing education programs, and career opportunities.

Indiana

27 Indiana Arts Commission
150 W Market St
Indianapolis, IN 46204-2211
317-232-1268
Fax: 317-232-5595
E-mail: indianaartscommission@iac.in.gov
http://www.in.gov/arts
Promotes high-quality education in the arts.

28 Indiana Association of School Business Officials
1 N Capital Avenue
Suite 1215
Indianapolis, IN 46204-2095
765-639-3586
Fax: 317-639-4360
E-mail: dcosterison@indiana-asbo.org
http://www.indiana-asbo.org
The Indiana Association of School Business Officials is a professional organization which strives for the promotion and union of those individuals involved in school business affairs such as finance, accounting, purchasing, maintenance and operations, human resources, facilities and grounds, food service, technology, and transportation.

Lynn Kwilasz, President
Steve Sonntag, VP

29 Indiana Business Education Association
8103 E. Highway 36
Box 180
Avon, IN 46123
765-653-3149
Fax: 317-232-9121
E-mail: gvalenti@usi.edu
http://ind-ibea.org
Promotes business education as a central component to essential life skills, career and

workplace preparation and life-long learning.

John Dawson, President
Scott Truelove, VP

630 Indiana Commission for Higher Education
101 W Ohio St
Suite 550
Indianapolis, IN 46204-1984
317-464-4400
Fax: 317-464-4410
http://www.che.in.gov
Provides information on the state's education programs, colleges and universities, financial aid assistance programs, grants, scholarships, continuing education programs, and career opportunities.

631 Indiana Library Federation
941 E 86th Street
Suite 260
Indianapolis, IN 46240
317-257-2040
Fax: 317-257-1389
E-mail: askus@ilfonline.org
http://www.ilfonline.org
Fosters the professional growth of its members and promotes all libraries in Indiana.

Robin Crumrin, President
Marcia Au, President-Elect

632 Indiana State Teachers Association
150 W Market Street
Suite 900
Indianapolis, IN 46204
317-263-3400
800-382-4037
Fax: 317-655-3700
http://www.ista-in.org
Provides the resources necessary to enable local affiliates to effectively advocate for members, children and for public education.

Nathan Schnellenberger, President
Teresa Meredith, Vice President

Iowa

633 Iowa Arts Council
600 E Locust
Des Moines, IA 50319-0290
515-281-5773
Fax: 515-242-6498
http://www.iowaartscouncil.org
Promotes high-quality education in the arts.

634 Iowa Business Education Association
Highway 150 S
PO Box 400
Calmar, IA 52132-400
515-471-8005
Fax: 563-562-4363
E-mail: rselwood@mchsi.com
http://www.ibeaonline.org
Works to discover and serve the needs of business education in Iowa.

Patrick Geer, President
Crystal Combs, President-Elect

635 Iowa College Student Aid Commission
200 10th St
4th Floor
Des Moines, IA 50309
515-725-3400
800-383-4222
Fax: 515-725-3401
E-mail: info@iowacollegeaid.org
http://www.iowacollegeaid.org

Provides information on the state's education programs, colleges and universities, financial aid assistance programs, grants, scholarships, continuing education programs, and career opportunities.

636 Iowa Library Association
525 SW 5th Street
Suite A
Des Moines, IA 50309
515-282-8192
800-452-5507
Fax: 515-282-9117
http://www.iowalibraryassociation.org
The Iowa Library Association advocates for quality library services for all Iowans and provides leadership, education and support for members.

Lorraine Borowski, President
Mary Heinzman, VP/President-Elect

637 Iowa State Education Association
777 Third Street
Des Moines, IA 50309
515-471-8000
800-445-9358
E-mail: ISEAnews@isea.org
http://www.isea.org
Designed to promote and support quality education.

Tammy Wawro, President
Mary Jane Cobb, Executive Director

638 Iowa State Education for Homeless Children and Youth
400 E 14th St
Des Moines, IA 50319-0146
515-281-3999
Fax: 515-242-6025
http://www.iowa.gov/educate
Ensures that all homeless children and youth have equal access to the same free, appropriate public education.

Kansas

639 Educating Homeless Children and Youth
120 SE 10th Ave
Topeka, KS 66612-1182
785-296-6714
Fax: 785-296-5867
http://www.ksde.org
Ensures that all homeless children and youth have equal access to the same free, appropriate public education.

640 Kansas Arts Commission
700 SW Jackson
Suite 1004
Topeka, KS 66603-3774
785-296-3335
866-433-0688
Fax: 785-296-4989
E-mail: kac@arts.ks.gov
http://www.arts.state.ks.us

641 Kansas Association of School Librarians
8517 W Nothridge
Wichita, KS 67205

http://kasl.typepad.com/kasl
Association of school librarians in the state of Kansas.

Judy Eller, Executive Secretary
Cindy Pfeiffer, President

45

642 Kansas Board of Regents
1000 SW Jackson St
Suite 520
Topeka, KS 66612-1368
785-296-3421
Fax: 785-296-0983
http://www.kansasregents.org

643 Kansas Business Education Association
Fory Hays State University
600 Park Street
Hays, KS 67601
785-628-4019
Fax: 785-628-5398
http://www.ksbea.org
Fosters business education in the state of Kansas.
Founded: 1949
Jean Anna Sellers, Contact
Gina Stanley, President

644 Kansas Education Association
715 SW 10th Avenue
Topeka, KS 66612-1686
785-232-8271
Fax: 785-232-6012
E-mail: KNEAnews@knea.org
http://www.knea.org
Empowers its members to promote quality public schools, strengthen the teaching profession, and improve the well-being of members.
Founded: 1862
Blake West, President
Sherri Yourdon, Vice President

645 Kansas Library Association
1020 SW Washburn
Topeka, KS 66604
785-580-4518
Fax: 785-580-4595
E-mail: kansaslibraryassociation@yahoo.com
http://www.kansaslibraryassociation.org
KLA develops a legislative push card, tracks legislation and keeps association members and the library community at large informed on the status of bills related to library issues
Laura Loveless, President
Denise Smith, First Vice President

Kentucky

646 Kentucky Arts Council
500 Mero St
21st Floor, Capital Plaza Tower
Frankfort, KY 40601-1987
502-564-3757
888-833-2787
Fax: 502-564-2839
E-mail: kyarts@ky.gov
http://www.artscouncil.ky.gov
The Kentucky Arts Council is the state government agency responsible for developing and promoting support for the arts in Kentucky. The agency creates opportunities for people to find value in the arts, participate in the arts and benefit from the arts through programs, grants and services.
Lori Meadows, Executive Director
Chris Cathers, Program Branch Manager

647 Kentucky Department for Libraries and Archives
300 Coffee Tree Rd
Frankfort, KY 40601
502-564-8300
800-928-7000

Fax: 502-564-5773
http://www.kdla.ky.gov

648 Kentucky Education for Homeless Children and Youth
500 Mero St
Frankfort, KY 40601
502-564-3141
Fax: 502-564-8149
http://www.education.ky.gov/kde/default.htm

649 Kentucky Higher Education Assistance Authority
PO Box 798
Frankfort, KY 40602-0798
502-696-7200
800-928-8926
Fax: 502-696-7496
E-mail: inquiries@kheaa.com
http://www.kheaa.com

650 Kentucky Library Association
1501 Twilight Trail
Frankfort, KY 40601
502-223-5322
Fax: 502-223-4937
E-mail: info@kylibasn.org
http://www.kylibasn.org
Holds a conference in October and publishes a journal.
Kim Goff, Associate Director
John Underwood, Executive Secretary

651 Kentucky School Media Association
Scott County School
1080 Cardinal Drive
Georgetown, KY 40324
E-mail: mroberts@scott.k12.ky.us
http://www.kysma.org
Promotes the use of media in schools.
Tara Griffith, President
Fred Tilsleyÿ, Secretary

652 Mountain-Plains Business Education Association(M-PBEA)
Newcastle High School
4771 West Scott Road
Beatrice, NE 68310
307-746-2713
E-mail: tlandenb@gmail.com
http://www.mpbea.org
The Mountain-Plains Business Education Association (M-PBEA) is an affiliate of the National Business Education Association (NBEA), a professional organization serving individuals and groups engaged in instruction, administration, research, and dissemination of information for and about business. M-PBEA is comprised of the following states and provinces: Colorado, Kansas, Manitoba, Nebraska, New Mexico, North Dakota, Oklahoma, Saskatchewan, South Dakota, Texas, and Wyoming.
Sheryl Piening Keller, President
Connie Lindell, Kansas State Representative

Louisiana

653 Louisiana Association of Business Educators
Alfred M Barbe High School
2200 W McNeese Street
Lake Charles, LA 70615
337-478-3628
Fax: 337-474-6782
E-mail: spiening@southeast.edu
http://www.laabe.org

Foster business education in the state of Louisiana.
Marilyn Gastineau, President
Joseph Lane Jr, Vice President

654 Louisiana Association of Educators
8322 One Calais Avenue
Baton Rouge, LA 70821
225-343-9243
800-256-4523
Fax: 225-343-9272
E-mail: joyce.haynes@lae
http://www.lae.org
Dedicated to improving the education profession and the quality of education. Affiliated with National Education Association.
Joyce Haynes, President
Bruce Hunt, Executive Director

655 Louisiana Association of School Business Officials (LASBO)
PO Box 1029
Gonzales, LA 70707-1029
225-644-0619
Fax: 225-644-0122
E-mail: cctripp@eatel.net
http://www.lasbo.org/
To promote excellence and professional ethical standards in the practice of public school business finance by educating and training our membership in the most efficient and economic methods of conducting our business affairs
Founded: 1993
Tami Austin, President-elect
Juanita Duke, President

656 Louisiana Division of the Arts
1051 N Third St
PO Box 44247
Baton Rouge, LA 70804-4247
225-342-8180
Fax: 225-342-8173
http://www.crt.state.la.us/arts

657 Louisiana Education for Homeless Children and Youth
PO Box 94064
Baton Rouge, LA 70804
225-342-3031
877-453-2721
http://www.doe.state.la.us/lde/eia/1315.html

658 Louisiana Library Association
8550 United Plaza Boulevard
Suite 1001
Baton Rouge, LA 70809
225-922-4642
877-550-7890
Fax: 225-408-4422
E-mail: office@llaonline.org
http://www.llaonline.org
Holds a conference in March and publishes a journal.
Founded: 1925
Beth Paskoff, Registration
Melissa Elrod, Chair

659 Louisiana Office of Student Financial Assistance
PO Box 91202
Baton Rouge, LA 70821-9202
225-922-1012
800-259-5626
Fax: 225-922-0790
E-mail: custserv@osfa.la.gov
http://www.osfa.la.gov

Maine

660 Education for Homeless Children and Youth
State House Station #23
Augusta, ME 04333-0023
207-624-6637
Fax: 207-624-6624
http://www.state.me.us/education/tdae

661 Maine Arts Commission
State House Station #25
Augusta, ME 04333-0025
207-287-2724
Fax: 207-287-2725
E-mail: mainearts.info@maine.gov
http://www.mainearts.maine.gov

662 Maine Association of School Libraries
PO Box 634
Augusta, ME 04333
207-287-5620
Fax: 207-287-5624
E-mail: MASL@gwi.net
http://www.maslibraries.org
Dedicated to total involvement between Library Media Specialists, support staff and students.

Eileen Broderick, President
Joyce Lucas, Secretary

663 Maine Library Association
PO Box 634
Augusta, ME 04332-634
207-623-8428
Fax: 207-626-5947
E-mail: MASL@gwi.net
http://mainelibraries.org/home.php
is to promote and enhance the value of libraries and librarianship, to foster cooperation among those who work in and for libraries, and to provide leadership in ensuring that information is accessible to all citizens via their libraries

Eileen Broderick, President
Joan Kiszely, Executive Secretary

Maryland

664 Division of Library Development and Services
200 W Baltimore St
Baltimore, MD 21201-2595
410-767-0435
Fax: 410-333-2507

665 Maryland Educational Media Organization
PO Box 21127
Baltimore, MD 21228

http://www.tcps.md.us
Brings students and information regarding educational media together.

Dorothy D'Ascanio, President
Patricia Goff, Secretary

666 Maryland Higher Education Commission
839 Bestgate Rd
Annapolis, MS 21401-3013
410-260-4500
800-974-0203
Fax: 410-260-3200
http://www.mhec.state.md.us

667 Maryland Library Association
1401 Hollins Street
Baltimore, MD 21223
410-947-5090
Fax: 410-947-5089
E-mail: mla@mdlib.org
http://www.mdlib.org
Maryland Library Association provides leadership for those who are committed to libraries by providing opportunities for professional development and communication and by advocating principles and issues related to librarianship and library service.

Margaret Carty, Executive Director
Kate Monagan, Executive Assistant

668 Maryland State Arts Council
175 W Ostend
Baltimore, MD 21230
410-767-6555
Fax: 410-333-1062
http://www.msac.org

669 Maryland State Teachers Association
140 Main Street
Annapolis, MD 21401-2003
410-263-6600
800-448-6782
Fax: 410-263-3605
E-mail: feedback@mseanea.org
http://www.mstanea.org/
Organization representing 60,000 Maryland teachers, support professionals, retired educators, school administers, higher education faculty, and future educators.

Clara B Floyd, President
Betty Weller, VP

Massachusetts

670 Board of Library Commissioners
98 N Washington St
Suite 401
Boston, MA 02114
617-725-1860
800-952-7403
Fax: 617-725-0140
http://www.mblc.state.ma.us

671 Massachusetts Business Educators Association
Amherst Regional High School
21 Mattoon Street
Amherst, MA 01002
413-549-9700
Fax: 413-549-9704
E-mail: www.ma-mbea.org
Fosters business education in the state of Massachusetts.

Mary Ann Shea, Contact

672 Massachusetts Cultural Council
10 St James Ave
Boston, MA 02116-3803
617-727-3668
800-232-0960
Fax: 617-727-0044
E-mail: mcc@art.state.ma.us
http://www.massculturalcouncil.org

673 Massachusetts Department of Higher Education
One Ashburton Place
Boston, MA 02108-1696
617-994-6950
Fax: 617-727-6397
http://www.mass.edu

674 Massachusetts Library Association
PO Box 535
Bedford, MA 01730

781-275-7729
Fax: 781-998-0393
E-mail: mlaoffice@masslib.org
http://www.masslib.org
The mission of the Government Relations Advisory Board is to represent the interests of all libraries to the state legislature on behalf of the citizens of the Commonwealth

Elizabeth Hacala, VP/President elect
Dinah O'Brien, President

675 Massachusetts Teachers Association
20 Ashburton Place
Boston, MA 02108-2727
617-878-8000
800-392-6175
Fax: 617-742-7046
E-mail: awass@massteacher.org
http://www.massteacher.org
The MTA is a union, dedicated to improving the workplace and the quality of life for all education employees and to protecting their hard-won rights. MTA and local affiliates are highly democratic organizations in which members' views and concerns are vital to the development of policies and programs.

Anne Wass, President
Paul Toner, Vice President

676 New England Library Association
55 North Main Street
Unit 49
Belchertown, MA 01007
413-813-5254
E-mail: rscheier@gmail.com
http://www.nelib.org
Provides educational and leadership opportunities for library staff in support of improved library services for the people of New England.

Deborah Kelsey, President
Deb Hoadley, Vice President

677 Office for the Education of Homeless Children and Youth
75 Pleasant St
Malden, MA 02148-4906
781-338-6330
Fax: 781-338-3090
http://www.doe.mass.edu

Michigan

678 Education for Homeless Children and Youth
608 W Allegan St
PO Box 30008
Lansing, MI 48909
517-241-1162
Fax: 517-241-0247
http://www.michigan.gov/homeless

679 Michigan Association for Media in Education
1407 Rensen Street
Suite 3
Lansing, MI 48910
517-394-2808
Fax: 517-394-2096
E-mail: mame@mame.gen.mi.us
http://www.mame.gen.mi.us
Michigan Association for Media in Education is an independent, professional association of library media specialists dedicated to educational, literary and technological excellence in library / media services in Michigan's schools.

Roger Ashley, Executive Director
Diane Nye, Media Spectrum

680 Michigan Association of School Administrators
1001 Centennial Way
Suite 300
Lansing, MI 48917-9279
517-327-5910
Fax: 517-327-0779
E-mail: jscofield@gomasa.org
http://www.gomasa.org/
Professional organization serving superintendents and their first line of assistants.

Dan Pappas, Associate Executive Director
Jon Tomlanovich, Associate Executive Director

681 Michigan Council for Arts and Cultural Affairs
702 W Kalamazoo St
PO Box 30705
Lansing, MI 48909-8205
517-241-4011
Fax: 517-241-3979
E-mail: artsinfo@michigan.gov
http://www.michigan.gov/arts

682 Michigan Education Association
1216 Kendale Boulevard
PO Box 2573
East Lansing, MI 48826-2573
517-332-6551
800-292-1934
Fax: 517-337-5598
E-mail: webmaster@mea.org
http://www.mea.org/
A self-governing education association, representing more than 157,000 teaches, faculty, and education support staff throughout the state.

Iris Salters, President
Steven Cook, Vice President

683 Michigan Elementary & Middle School Principals Association
1980 N College Road
Mason, MI 48854
517-694-8955
800-227-0824
Fax: 517-694-8945
E-mail: bob@memspa.org
http://www.memspa.org
Professional organization serving elementary and middle level principals as they deliver quality educational experiences to the students of Michigan by providing leadership, legislative advocacy, professional development and guidance.

Paul Liabenow, Executive Director
Rob Kauffman, President

684 Michigan Library Association
1407 Rensen Street
Suite 2
Lansing, MI 48910
517-394-2774
Fax: 517-394-2675
E-mail: mla@mlcnet.org
http://www.mla.lib.mi.us
The Michigan Library Association is a professional organization dedicated to the support of its members, to the advancement of librarianship, and to the promotion of quality library service for all Michigan citizens.

Kathy Irwin, President
Larry Neal, President-Elect

685 Student Financial Services Bureau
430 W Allegan
PO Box 30047
Lansing, MI 48909-7547
800-642-5626
Fax: 571-241-0155
http://www.michigan.gov/studentaid

Minnesota

686 Education Minnesota
41 Sherburne Avenue
St. Paul, MN 55103-2196
651-227-9541
800-652-9073
Fax: 651-292-4802
http://www.educationminnesota.org
Education Minnesota is the largest advocate for public education in the state. Our 70,000 members work at all levels from pre-kindergarten through post-secondary, at public schools, state residential schools and college campuses.

Thomas A Dooher, President
Paul Mueller, Vice President

687 Minnesota Business Educators
2620 Eleventh Avenue NW
Rochester, MN 55901-7722
507-282-7079
Fax: 507-282-4925
E-mail: rhmeyer@rconnect.com
http://www.mbei-online.org
To keep abreast with the state legislature and with issues related to business education

Mary Flesberg, Past President
Cindy Drahos, President

688 Minnesota Congress of Parents, Teachers & Students/Minnesota PTA
1667 Snelling Avenue
N Suite 111
Saint Paul, MN 55108
651-999-7320
800-672-0993
Fax: 651-999-7321
E-mail: mnptaofc@mnpta.org
http://www.mnpta.org
Minnesota PTA, an affiliate of the National PTA, extends the concept of a volunteer organization engaged in educating parents and teachers on issues affecting children and youth. It supports public education and the welfare of children.

Founded: 1922

Rosie Loeffler Kemp, President
Bonnie Beery, Secretary

689 Minnesota Library Association
1821 University Avenue West
Suite S256
Saint Paul, MN 55104
651-999-5343
877-867-0982
Fax: 651-917-1835
E-mail: mlaoffice@mnlibraryassociation.org
http://www.mnlibraryassociation.org
MLA meets the interests of its members by facilitating educational opportunities, supporting strong ethical standards, and fostering connections between the library community and various constituencies. MLA organizes an annual multi-day fall conference that features approximately 70 programs planned and sponsored by divisions, sections, round tables and committees.

Founded: 1891

Anna Hulseberg, Treasurer
Carla Urban, President

690 Minnesota School Boards Association
1900 W Jefferson Avenue
Saint Peter, MN 56082-3015
507-934-2450
800-324-4459
Fax: 507-931-1515
E-mail: gabbott@mnmsba.org
http://www.mnsba.org
The purpose of the Association is to support, promote and enhance the work of public school boards.

Walter Hautala, President
Greg Abbott, MSBA Dir. of Communications

691 Office of Higher Education
1450 Energy Park Dr
Suite 350
St Paul, MN 55108-5227
651-259-3901
800-657-3866
Fax: 651-642-0597
http://www.ohe.state.mn.us

692 State Arts Board
400 Sibley St
Suite 200
Saint Paul, MN 55101-1928
651-215-1600
800-866-2787
Fax: 651-215-1602
http://www.arts.state.mn.us

Mississippi

693 Education for Homeless Children and Youth
359 North West St
PO Box 771
Jackson, MS 39205-0771
601-359-3499
Fax: 601-359-2587
http://www.mde.k12.ms.us/acad/is/homeless.htm

694 Mississippi Advocate for Education
775 N State Street
Jackson, MS 39202-3086
601-354-4463
800-530-7998
Fax: 601-352-7054
E-mail: mmarks@nea.org
http://www.maetoday.nea.org
The Mississippi Association of Educators advocates great public schools for every child by empowering members, providing services and promoting parental/community environment.

Kevin F Gilbert, President
Seyed Darbandi, Vice President

695 Mississippi Arts Commission
501 North West St
Suite 1101A
Jackson, MS 39201
601-359-6030
Fax: 601-359-6008
http://www.arts.state.ms.us

696 Mississippi Business Education Association
Itawamba Community College
2176 S Eason Boulevard
Tupelo, MS 38801
662-620-5001
Fax: 601-982-5801
E-mail: acbrown@nmsd.k12.ms.us
http://www.ms-mbea.org
To establish and maintain active state leadership in promotion of all types of business and technology education

Aimee Brown, President
Judith Hurtt, President-Elect

697 Mississippi Institutions of Higher Learning
3825 Ridgewood Rd
Jackson, MS 39211-6453
601-432-6623
800-327-2980
Fax: 601-432-6972
http://www.ihl.state.ms.us

698 Mississippi Library Association
PO Box 13687
Jackson, MS 39236-3687
601-981-4586
Fax: 601-981-4501
E-mail: info@misslib.org
http://www.misslib.org
Provides professional leadership for the development, promotion, and the improvement of library and information services and the profession of librarianship in order to enhance learning and ensure access to information for all.

Founded: 1909

Patsy C. Brewer, President
Molly McManus, Vice-President

699 Mississippi Library Commission
3881 Eastwood Dr
Jackson, MS 39211
601-432-4111
800-647-7542
Fax: 601-432-4478
E-mail: mslib@mlc.lib.ms.us
http://www.mlc.lib.ms.us

Missouri

700 Education for Homeless Children and Youth
PO Box 480
Jefferson City, MO 65102
573-526-3232
Fax: 573-526-6698

701 Missouri Arts Council
815 Olive St
Suite 16
Saint Louis, MO 63101-1503
314-340-6845
866-407-4752
Fax: 314-340-7215
E-mail: moarts@ded.mo.gov
http://www.missouriartscouncil.org

702 Missouri Association of Elementary School Principals
3550 Amazonas Drive
Jefferson City, MO 65109
573-638-2692
Fax: 573-556-6270
E-mail: maesp@mcsa.org
http://www.mcsa.org
MAESP is a statewide professional association that has grown to include over 1,000 school administrators. The services provided by MAESP to its membership have also increased as members have identified and approved long-range plans incorporating key services.

Matthew Martz, President
Connie Browning, President-Elect

703 Missouri Association of Secondary School Principals
2409 W Ash Street
Columbia, MO 65203-45
573-445-5071
Fax: 573-445-6416
E-mail: massp@moassp.org
http://www.moassp.org

The mission of the Missouri Association of Secondary School Principals is to improve secondary education through positive leadership and the enhancement of student performance. In pursuing the mission of MASSP, the Association shall be involved in providing information and leadership; encouraging research and service; promoting high educational standards; focusing attention on state educational issues; providing for the general welfare of principals; and working with other organizations.

Ron Helms, President
Jenny Swanson, Secretary

704 Missouri Congress of Parents & Teachers/Missouri PTA
2101 Burlington Street
Columbia, MO 65203
573-445-4161
800-328-7330
Fax: 573-445-4163
E-mail: kimw@mopta.org
http://www.mopta.org
A powerful voice for all children, a relevant resource for all families and communities and a strong advocate for the education and well-being of every child.

Mary Oyler, President
Kim Weber, Vice President and Director

705 Missouri Department of Higher Education
3515 Amazonas Dr
Jefferson City, MO 65109
573-751-2361
800-473-6757
Fax: 573-751-6635
E-mail: info@dhe.mo.gov
http://www.dhe.mo.gov

706 Missouri Library Association
3212-A Lemone Industrial Boulevard
Columbia, MO 65201-45
573-449-4627
Fax: 573-449-4655
E-mail: mla001@more.net
http://www.molib.org
A non-profit, educational organization operating to promote library service, the profession of librarianship, and cooperation among all types of libraries and organizations concerned with library service in Missouri.

Founded: 1900

Kimberlee Ried, President
Margaret Booker, Executive Director

707 Missouri National Education Association
1810 E Elm Street
Jefferson City, MO 65101-4174
573-634-3202
Fax: 573-634-5646
http://www.mnea.org
The Missouri National Education Association is an advocate for public schools, public school students and public school employees

November annual
1,500 attendees

Ben Simmons, Executive Director
Chris Guinther, President

708 Missouri State Teachers Association
PO Box 458
407 S Sixth Street
Columbia, MO 65205-4201
573-442-3127
800-392-0532
Fax: 573-443-5079
E-mail: membercare@msta.org
http://www.msta.org

A grassroots organization made up of local community teachers associations in each school district.

Tami Pasley, Board of Directors
Russell Smithson, Vice President

709 North Central Business Education Association (NCBEA)
Mineral Area College
803 Rambling Brook Circle
Elgin, IL 60124
573-243-9513
Fax: 573-243-9524
E-mail: satbfl@aol.com
http://www.ncbea.com
The objectives of this Association are to improve the relationship in business education at the state, regional, and national levels; to promote the professional growth of those in business education; to promote better business education through whatever means seem desirable; and to offer assistance and service to state associations within the region.

Kim Schultz, President
Susan Elwood, Secretary

Montana

710 Education for Homeless Children and Youth
1300 11th Ave
PO Box 202501
Helena, MT 59620-2501
406-444-2036
Fax: 406-444-3924
http://www.opi.state.mt.us/homeless

711 Montana Arts Council
830 N Warren St
PO Box 202201
Helena, MT 59620-2201
406-444-6430
800-282-3092
Fax: 406-444-6548
http://www.art.mt.gov

712 Montana Association of County School Superintendents
1134 Butte Avenue
Helena, MT 59601
406-442-2510
http://www.sammt.org/macss
Organization of school superintendents.

Darrell Rud, Executive Director
Julia Sykes, Associate Director

713 Montana Association of School Librarians (MASL)
PO Box 2107
Jefferson City, MO 65109
573-893-4155
Fax: 573-635-2858
E-mail: masl_org@earthlink.net
http://www.maslonline.org/
Montana Association of School Librarians/MASL is a professional organization for library media specialists who work in Missouri schools.

Linda Weatherspoon, President
Sandy Roth, Treasurer

714 Montana Library Association
PO Box 1352
Belgrade, MT 59714-3126
406-579-3121
Fax: 406-243-2060
http://www.mtlib.org

Holds a conference in April and publishes a journal.

Debra Kramer, Executive
Della Dubbe, President

715 Western Business and Information Technology Educators (WBITE)
Hardin High School
720 N Terry
Hardin, MT 59034
406-665-6300
Fax: 406-665-1909
E-mail: odellj@hardin.k12.mt.us
http://www.nbea.org/aboutrda.html
Western Business and Information Technology Educators, an affiliate of the National Business Education Association seeks to share educational experiences preparing individuals to excel as consumers, workers, and citizens in our economic systems. WBITE is comprised of Alaska, Alberta, American Samoa, Arizona, British Columbia, California, Guam, Hawaii, Idaho, Montana, Nevada, Northern Marianas Islands, Northwest Territories, Oregon, Utah, Yukon and Washington.

Julie O'Dell, President
Roy Kamida, Treasurer

Nebraska

716 Education for Homeless Children and Youth
301 Centennial Mall S
PO Box 94987
Lincoln, NE 68509
402-471-2968
Fax: 402-471-0117
http://www.nde.state.ne.us

717 Nebraska Arts Council
1004 Farnam St
Omaha, NE 68102
402-595-2122
800-341-4067
Fax: 402-595-2334
http://www.nebraskaartscouncil.org

718 Nebraska Library Association
1402 N Jackson
Lexington, NE 68850
402-826-2636
Fax: 402-471-6244
E-mail: nebraskalibraries@gmail.com
http://www.nebraskalibraries.org
The Nebraska Library Association supports and promotes all libraries, library media centers and library services in the state.

Pam Bohmfalk, President
Scott Childers, Vice President

719 Nebraska Library Commission
1200 N Street
Suite 120
Lincoln, NE 68508-2023
402-471-2045
800-307-2665
Fax: 402-471-2083
http://www.nlc.nebraska.gov

720 Nebraska State Business Education Association
Wayne State College
1111 Main Street-Gardner Hall 206F
Wayne, NE 68787
402-375-7255
E-mail: paarnes1@wsc.edu
http://www.nsbea.org

Foster business education in the state of Nebraska.

Patricia Arneson, Contact
Janelle Stansberry, President

721 Nebraska State Education Association
605 S 14th Street
Suite 200
Lincoln, NE 68508
402-475-7611
800-742-0047
Fax: 402-475-2630
http://www.nsea.org
NSEA is a member-directed union of professional educators and education support professionals dedicated to providing quality public education for the students of Nebraska.

Mark Shively, Director
Leann Widhalm, Director

Nevada

722 Education for Homeless Children and Youth
700 E Fifth St
Carson City, NV 89701-5096
775-687-9235
Fax: 775-687-9250
http://www.nde.doe.nv.gov/si.htm

723 Nevada Arts Council
716 N Carson St
Suite A
Carson City, NV 89701
775-687-6680
Fax: 775-687-6688
http://www.nevadaculture.org

724 Nevada Library Association
West Charleston Library
Clark County Library District
Las Vegas, NV 89030
702-507-3941
Fax: 702-649-2576
E-mail: rjdebuff@hotmail.com
http://www.nevadalibraries.org
The purpose of NLA shall be to promote library service of the highest quality for all present and potential users of libraries in Nevada.

Founded: 1946

Jeanette Hammons, President
Robbie DeBuff, Executive Secretary

725 Nevada State Education Association
1890 Donald Street
Reno, NV 89502
775-828-6732
800-232-6732
Fax: 775-828-6745
http://www.nsea-nv.org
Advocate the professional rights and economic security of its members, while also serving as the prominent voice for excellence in public education in Nevada.

Terry Hickman, Executive Director
Lynn Warne, President

New Hampshire

726 Education for Homeless Children and Youth
101 Pleasant St
Concord, NH 03301-3860

603-271-3840
Fax: 603-271-2760

727 New Hampshire Business Education Association
Newfound Regional High School
2500 N River Road
Manchester, NH 3106
603-926-3395
Fax: 603-926-5418
E-mail: mmatarazzo@rivier.edu
http://www.nhbea.org
Fosters business education in the state of New Hampshire.

Karen Hvizda, President
Maria Matarazzo, Business Administration Dir

728 New Hampshire Education Association
60 Connolly Parkway
Suite 103
Concord, NH 00654-2425
603-224-7751
866-556-3264
Fax: 603-224-2648
http://www.neanh.org
To strengthen and support public education and to serve our members' professional, political, economic and advocacy needs.

Rhonda Wesolowski, President
Jim Sweeny, Executive Director

729 New Hampshire Library Association
LGC, PO Box 617
Concord, NH 03302-617
603-641-4123
Fax: 603-641-4124
E-mail: annie.donahue@unh.edu
http://www.nhlibrarians.org
advance the interests of its members through advocacy on library issues and increasing public awareness of library service; to support the professional development of its members; to foster communication and encourage the exchange of ideas among its members; and to promote participation in the association and its sections.

Annie Donahue, Conference Committee
Steven Butzel, President

730 New Hampshire Postsecondary Education Commission
3 Barrell Court
Suite 300
Concord, NH 03301-8543
603-271-2555
Fax: 603-271-2696
http://www.state.nh.us/postsecondary

731 State Council of the Arts
Two 1/2 Beacon St
Suite 225
Concord, NH 03301
603-271-2789
Fax: 603-271-3584
http://www.nh.gov/nharts

New Jersey

732 Education for Homeless Children and Youth
PO Box 500
Trenton, NJ 08625-0500
609-984-4974
Fax: 609-292-1211
http://www.state.nj.us/education

733 Educational Media Association of New Jersey
PO Box 610
Trenton, NJ 08607

609-394-8032
Fax: 609-394-8164
http://www.emanj.org
Promotes the use of media in education.
Sue Henis, President

34 Higher Education Student Assistance Authority
4 Quakerbridge Plaza
PO Box 540
Trenton, NJ 08625-0540
609-588-3226
800-792-8670
Fax: 609-588-7389
http://www.hesaa.org

35 New Jersey Education Association (NJEA)
180 W State Street
Trenton, NJ 08607-1211
609-599-4561
800-359-6049
Fax: 609-392-6321
E-mail: lmaher@njea.org
http://www.njea.org
The mission of the New Jersey Education Association is to advance and protect the rights, benefits, and interests of members, and promote a quality system of public education for all students.

Joyce Powell, President
Stephen K Wollmer, Director of Communications

36 New Jersey Library Association
PO Box 1534
Trenton, NJ 08607
609-394-8032
Fax: 609-394-8164
E-mail: ptumulty@njla.org
http://www.njla.org
Advocates for advancement of library services for the residents of New Jersey; provides continuing education and networking opportunities for librarians; supports principles of intellectual freedom and promotes access to library materials for all.

Patricia A Tumulty, Executive Director
Susan Rice, Office Manager

37 New Jersey School-Age Care Coalition
231 North Avenue West
Westfield, NJ 07090
908-789-0259
Fax: 908-789-4237
http://www.njsacc.org

38 New Jersey State Council on the Arts
225 W State St
Trenton, NJ 08625-0306
609-292-6130
Fax: 609-989-1440
http://www.njartscouncil.org

39 New Jersey State Department of Education Resource Center
PO Box 500
Trenton, NJ 08625-500
609-292-4469
http://www.state.nj.us/education
Provide leadership to prepare all students for their role as citizens and for the career opportunities of the 21st century.

Josephine Hernandez, President
Arcelio Aponte, Vice President

New Mexico

740 Mountain Plains Business Education Association(M-PBEA)
c/o Newcastle High School
4771 West Scott Road
Beatrice, NE 68310
307-746-2713
E-mail: tlandenb@gmail.com
http://www.mpbea.org
The Mountain-Plains Business Education Association (M-PBEA), an affiliate of the National Business Education Association (NBEA), is a professional organization serving individuals and groups engaged in instruction, administration, research, and dissemination of information for and about business. M-PBEA is comprised of the following states and provinces: Colorado, Kansas, Manitoba, Nebraska, New Mexico, North Dakota, Oklahoma, Saskatchewan, South Dakota, Texas, and Wyoming.

Sheryl Piening Keller, President
DeLayne Havlovic, M-PBEA Treasurer

741 National Education Association of New Mexico
2007 Botulph
Santa Fe, NM 87505
505-982-1916
Fax: 505-982-6719
http://www.nea-nm.org
The NEA-NM and its affiliates will be the recognized advocate for students, public education, and public education employees in New Mexico.

Eduardo Holg un, Political Affairs Specialist
Sharon Morgan, President

742 New Mexico Arts
PO Box 1450
Santa Fe, NM 87504-1450
505-827-6490
800-879-4278
Fax: 505-827-6043
http://www.nmarts.org

743 New Mexico Higher Education Department
1068 Cerrillos Rd
Santa Fe, NM 87505-1650
505-476-8400
800-279-9777
Fax: 505-476-8453
http://www.hed.state.nm.us

744 New Mexico Library Association (NMLA)
PO Box 26074
Albuquerque, NM 87125
505-400-7309
Fax: 505-891-5171
E-mail: admin@nmla.org
http://www.nmla.org/
The New Mexico Library Association is a non-profit organization dedicated to the support and promotion of libraries and the development of library personnel through education and the exchange of ideas to enrich the lives of all New Mexicans.

Cassandra Osterloh, President
Lorie Christian, Administrator

New York

745 Business Teachers Association of New York State
5260 Rogers Road
Apt A-5
Hamburg, NY 14075
315-369-6133
Fax: 315-369-6216
E-mail: President@btanys.org
http://www.btanys.org
The Business Teachers Association of New York State provides networking, support, and professional growth opportunities for its members to effectively educate today's students for tomorrow's global economy.

Sharon L Keller, Secretary/Awards Director
Susan Hall, President

746 Education for Homeless Children and Youth
151 W 30th Street
New York, NY 10001
800-388-2014
Fax: 212-807-6872
http://www.nysteachs.org

747 New York Library Association (NYLA)
6021 State Farm Road
Albany, NY 12210-1802
518-432-6952
800-252-6952
Fax: 518-427-1697
E-mail: info@nyla.org
http://www.nyla.org/
The Association was the first state-wide organization of librarians in the United States.

Michael J Borges, Executive Director
Johanna Geiger, Deputy Director

748 New York State Council on the Arts
175 Varick St
New York, NY 10014
212-627-4455
Fax: 212-620-5911
http://www.nysca.org

749 New York State Higher Education Services Corporation
99 Washington Ave
Albany, NY 12255
518-473-1574
888-697-4371
Fax: 518-474-2839
http://www.hesc.org

750 New York State United Teachers (NYSUT)
800 Troy-Schenectady Road
Latham, NY 12210-2455
518-213-6000
800-342-9810
Fax: 518-213-6409
E-mail: mediarel@nysutmail.org
http://www.nysut.org/cps/rde/xchg/nysut/hs
.xsl/index.htm
Through a representative democratic structure, New York State United Teachers improves the professional, economic and personal lives of our members and their families, strengthens the institutions in which they work, and furthers the cause of social justice through the trade union movement.

Richard C Iannuzzi, President
Linda Stanczik, Regional Staff Director

North Carolina

751 Homeless Education Program
PO Box 5367
Greensboro, NC 27435
336-315-7491
Fax: 336-315-7457
http://www.serve.org/hepnc

752 North Carolina Arts Council
109 E Jones St
Paleigh, NC 27601
919-807-6502
Fax: 919-807-6532
http://www.ncarts.org

753 North Carolina Association for Career and Technical Education
PO Box G
Catawba, NC 28609-5159
828-241-3910
Fax: 919-782-8096
E-mail: tony.bello@gmail.com
http://www.actenc.org
Act as a central agency in keeping the people of the state informed of the mission, scope, needs, quality, importance, and contributions of career and technical education .

Paul Heiderpiem, Author
Scot Whitfield, President
Tom H Jones, Executive Director

754 North Carolina Association of Educators (NCAE)
700 S Salisbury Street
Raleigh, NC 27601
919-832-3000
800-662-7924
Fax: 919-829-1626
E-mail: colleen.borst@ncae.org
http://www.ncae.org
NCAE's mission is to advocate for members and students, to enhance the education profession, and to advance public education.

Colleen Borst, Executive Director
Kevin Spragley, Associate Executive Director

755 North Carolina Business Education Association(NCBEA)
King's College
700 E Stonewall Street
Suite 400
Charlotte, NC 28202
980-343-2738
Fax: 704-348-2029
E-mail: bpetersen@kingscollegecharlotte.edu
http://www.ncbea.org
NCBEA seeks to promote and improve the quality of business education at all levels through membership activities and meetings and through cooperation with public and private educational agencies and institutions with related professional organizations and with business and industry.

Becky Petersen, Executive Director
Cindi Sweeney, President Elect

756 North Carolina Department of Public Instruction (DPI)
301 N Wilmington Street
Education Building, Suite 5540
Raleigh, NC 27601
919-807-3952
Fax: 919-807-3826
E-mail: information@dpi.state.nc.us
http://www.ncpublicschools.org

The North Carolina Department of Public Instruction (DPI) is the agency charged with implementing the State's public school laws and the State Board of Education's policies and procedures governing pre-kindergarten through 12th grade public education. DPI develops the Standard Course of Study which describes the subjects and course content that should be taught in North Carolina public schools and develops the assessments and accountability model used to evaluate school and district success.

Melissa E Bartlett, Executive Director
Peter Asmar, Chief Information Officer

757 North Carolina Library Association (NCLA)
1841 Capital Blvd
Raleigh, NC 27604
919-839-6252
Fax: 919-839-6253
E-mail: nclaonline@ibiblio.org
http://www.nclaonline.org
An affiliate of the American Library Association and the Southeastern Library Association, the North Carolina Library Association (NCLA) is a statewide organization concerned with the total library community in North Carolina. NCLA's purpose is to promote libraries, library and information services, librarianship, intellectual freedom and literacy. Holds conferences in September and October and publishes a journal.

Sherwin Rice, VP/President elect
Wanda Brown, President

758 North Carolina State Education Assistance Authority
PO Box 13663
Research Triangle Park, NC 27709-3663
919-549-8614
866-866-2362
Fax: 919-549-8481
http://www.cfnc.org

North Dakota

759 Education for Homeless Children and Youth
600 E Boulevard Ave
Bismarck, ND 58505-0440
701-328-4646
888-605-1951
Fax: 701-328-4770

760 North Dakota Council on the Arts
1600 E Century Ave
Bismarck, ND 58503-0649
701-328-7590
Fax: 701-328-7595
http://www.nd.gov/arts

761 North Dakota Education Association (NDEA)
301 N 4th Street
Bismarck, ND 58501-5005
701-223-0450
Fax: 701-224-8535
E-mail: Dakota.draper@ndea.org
http://nd.nea.org/
Since 1887, the North Dakota Education Association has been advocating on behalf of North Dakota students and their teachers. NDEA's mission is to improve the political climate and economic conditions for public education and the status of teaching professionals and educational employees, in addition to promoting educational excellence, innovation, and equal opportunity in

working toward the elimination of all forms of discrimination.

Dakota Draper, President
Mark Berntson, Vice President

762 North Dakota Library Association
604 East Boulevard Avenue
Bismarck, ND 58502-1595
701-328-3495
Fax: 701-231-7138
E-mail: alpeterson@nd.gov
http://www.ndla.info
The North Dakota Library Association is concerned with the needs and rights of all citizens of North Dakota to have free access to library collections of sufficient scope and quality to provide the means for fruitful inquiry.

ISSN: 0882-4746
150 attendees and 25 exhibits

Cathy Langemo, Executive Secretary
Phyllis Ann K Bratton, President

Ohio

763 Education for Homeless Children and Youth
25 S Front St
Mail Stop 404
Columbus, OH 43215
614-466-4161
877-644-6338
Fax: 514-752-1622

764 Ohio Arts Council
727 E Main St
Columbus, OH 43205-1796
614-466-2613
888-243-8622
Fax: 614-466-4479
http://www.oac.state.oh.us

765 Ohio Association of School Business Officials
8050 North High Street
Suite 170
Columbus, OH 43235
614-431-9116
800-64 -2726
Fax: 614-431-9137
http://www.oasbo-ohio.org
The Ohio Association of School Business Officials is a not-for-profit educational management organization dedicated to learning, utilizing and sharing the best methods and technology of school business administration.

David A Varda, Executive Director
Mark Pepera, Treasurer

766 Ohio Association of Secondary School Administrators
8050 N High Street
Suite 180
Columbus, OH 43235-6484
614-430-8311
Fax: 614-430-8315
http://www.oassa.org
The Ohio Association of Secondary School Administrators is dedicated to the adnocacy and welfare of its members. Our mission is to provide high standards of leadership through professional development, political astuteness, legislative influence, positive public relations and collaboration with related organization.

Craig S Kupferberg, President
James J Harbuck, Executive Director

'67 Ohio Library Council
1105 Schrock Road
Suite 440
Columbus, OH 43229-1174
614-410-8092
Fax: 614-410-8098
E-mail: olc@olc.org
http://www.olc.org
The Ohio Library Council is the State wide professional association which represents the interests of Ohio's public libraries as well as their trustess, friends and staff. The OLC is governed by a Board of Directors composed of three library employees with an MLIS degree, three library trustees currently serving on library boards, and seven a- 1 arge members.

Margaret Danziger, President
Douglas Evans, Executive Director

68 Ohio Technology Education Association (OTEA)
c/o State Supervisor
25 South Front Street
Room 509
Edison, OH 43320
419-946-2071
Fax: 614-995-5568
E-mail: william_s@treca.org
http://www.otea.info/
The mission of the Ohio Technology Education Association (OTEA) is to promote technological literacy for all Ohio students; provide leadership in curriculum and professional development; inform governmental and educational decision makers on technological literacy issues; advocate society wide the understanding of technological literacy and why it is vital; and form and maintain alliances with the business and industrial community.

Richard A Dieffenderfer Ph.D, State Supervisor
Timothy N Tryon, Executive Director

Oklahoma

69 Education for Homeless Children and Youth
2500 N Lincoln Blvd
Oklahoma City, OK 73105
405-521-2846
Fax: 405-521-2998
http://www.sde.ok.us

70 Oklahoma Arts Council
PO Box 52001-2001
Oklahoma City, OK 73152-2001
405-521-2931
Fax: 405-521-6418
http://www.arts.ok.gov

71 Oklahoma Department of Libraries
200 NE 18th St
Oklahoma City, OK 73105
405-521-2502
800-522-8116
Fax: 405-525-7804
http://www.odl.state.ok.us

72 Oklahoma Education Association (OEA)
323 East Madison Avenue
PO 18485
Oklahoma City, OK 73154
402-528-7785
800-522-8091
Fax: 405-524-0350
E-mail: lodom@okea.org
http://www.okea.org

The Oklahoma Education Association (OEA) supports public education as the cornerstone of a democratic society in that education employees, parents, community leaders and elected officials should work together to promote quality education. OEA has 40,000 members, comprised of public school teachers, coaches, counselors, and administrators; nurses, librarians, custodians, cafeteria workers, bus drivers, secretaries; retired teachers; and education majors at Oklahoma colleges and universities.

Roy Bishop, President
Lela Odom, Executive Director

773 Oklahoma Library Association (OLA)
P.O. Box 6550
Edmond, OK 73013
405-525-5100
Fax: 405-525-5103
E-mail: kboies@sbcglobal.net
http://www.oklibs.org
The Oklahoma Library Association works to strengthen the quality of libraries, library services and librarianship in Oklahoma. Members of OLA work in public, school, academic and special libraries of all sizes. Members include professional, paraprofessional and clerical library staff, library trustees, Friends, students, volunteers, vendors of library products and services and many others. Holds a conference in April and publishes a journal.

Sarah Robbins, President
Leslie Langley, Marketing/Communications

Oregon

774 AFT-Oregon (American Federation of Teachers-Oregon)
7035 SW Hampton Street
Tigard, OR 97223-8313
503-595-3880
Fax: 503-595-3887
E-mail: AFTOregon@aft-oregon.org
http://or.aft.org/
Charted in 1952, AFT-Oregon, a state affiliate of the American Federation of Teachers, AFL-CIO, is a non-profit organization representing some 11,000 Oregon workers in K-12, community college and higher education in faculty and classified positions; and child care workers, in both public and private sectors. AFT-Oregon, in coalition with other unions and community groups, advocates for quality education and health care for all Oregonians, and gives working people a voice in our state's capitol.

Mark Schwebke, President
Richard Schwarz, Executive VP

775 Homeless Education Program
255 Capitol St NE
Salem, OR 97310-0203
503-947-5781
Fax: 503-378-5156
http://www.ode.state.or.us/go/homelessed

776 Oregon Arts Commission
775 Summer St NE
Salem, OR 97301-1284
503-986-0082
Fax: 503-986-0082
http://www.oregonartcommission.org

777 Oregon Association of Student Councils (OASC)
707 13th Street SE
Suite 100
Salem, OR 97301-4035

503-480-7206
Fax: 503-581-9840
E-mail: sara@oasc.org
http://www.oasc.org
The Oregon Association of Student Councils (OASC) is a non-profit member association, serving middle and high schools throughout the state. It provides leadership development to both students and advisors and is sponsored by the Confederation of Oregon School Administrators.

Sara S Nilles, Program Director

778 Oregon Education Association (OEA)
6900 SW Atlanta Street
Portland, OR 97223
503-684-3300
800-858-5505
Fax: 503-684-8063
E-mail: larry.wolf@oregoned.org
http://www.oregoned.org
The mission of the Oregon Education Association (OEA) is to assure quality public education for every student in Oregon by providing a strong, positive voice for school employees. OEA's school funding priority, established in December 2002, seeks to restore stable and adequate funding for Oregon's schools and community colleges so that all Oregon students have access to a quality public education.

Larry Wolf, President
Jerry Caruthers, Executive Director

779 Oregon Educational Media Association
PO Box 277
Terrebonne, OR 97760
503-625-7820
E-mail: j23hayden@aol.com
http://www.oema.net
To provide progressive leadership to ensure that Oregon students and educators are effective users of ideas and information, and to pursue excellence in school library media programs by advocating information literacy for all student, supporting reading instruction and enjoyment of literature, supporting the highest levels of library media services in schools, strengthening member professionalism through communications and educational opportunities and promoting visibility in education, governme

Jim Hayden, Executive Director
Merrie Olson, President

780 Oregon Library Association (OLA)
P.O. Box 3067
La Grande, OR 97850-2042
503-370-7019
Fax: 503-587-8063
E-mail: ola@olaweb.org
http://www.olaweb.org
The mission of the Oregon Library Association is to promote and advance library service through public and professional education and cooperation. Holds a conference in March and publishes two journals.

Mary Ginnane, President
Connie A Cohoon, Vice President

781 Oregon Student Assistance Commission
1500 Valley River Dr
Suite 100
Eugene, OR 97401
541-687-7400
800-452-8807
Fax: 541-687-7414
http://www.osac.state.or.us

Pennsylvania

782 Office of Postsecondary Higher Education
333 Market St
Harrisburg, PA 17126-0333
717-787-5041
Fax: 717-772-3622
http://www.pdehighered.state.pa.us/higher/site/default.asp

783 Pennsylvania Council on the Arts
215 Finance Building
Harrisburg, PA 17120
717-787-6883
Fax: 717-783-2538
http://www.pacouncilonthearts.org

784 Pennsylvania Library Association (PaLA)
220 Cumberland Parkway
Suite 10
Mechanicsburg, PA 17055
717-766-7663
800-622-3308
Fax: 717-766-5440
E-mail: glenn@palibraries.org
http://www.palibraries.org
The Pennsylvania Library Association (PaLA) is a professional non-profit organization with strong volunteer leadership, dedicated to the support of its members, to the advancement of librarianship, and to the improvement and promotion of quality library service for citizens of the Commonwealth.

Glenn Miller, Executive Director
Mary O Garm, President

785 Pennsylvania School Librarians Association
9 Saint James Avenue
Somerville, MA 02144
617-628-4451
http://www.psla.org
Provides school librarians/media specialists with educational opportunities and current information through publications, workshops, seminars and conferences

Marg Foster, Secretary
Nancy S Latanision, President

786 Pennsylvania State Education Association (PSEA)
400 N 3rd Street
PO Box 1724
Harrisburg, PA 17105-1724
717-255-7000
800-944-7732
Fax: 717-255-7124
E-mail: cdumaresq@psea.org
http://www.psea.org
PSEA's mission is to advocate for quality public education and our members through collective action. PSEA is a member-driven organization, headed by elected officers, an executive director and a board of directors.

James P Testerman, President
John F Springer, Executive Director

Rhode Island

787 Higher Education Assistance Authority
560 Jefferson Blvd
Suite 100
Warwick, RI 02886-1304
401-736-1100
800-922-9855
Fax: 401-732-3541
http://www.riheaa.org

788 National Education Association Rhode Island (NEARI)
99 Bald Hill Road
Cranston, RI 02920
401-463-9630
Fax: 401-463-5337
E-mail: RWalsh@nea.org
http://www.neari.org/matriarch/default.asp
The NEA Rhode Island is both a union and a professional organization.

Robert A Walsh Jr, Executive Director
Vincent P Santaniello, Deputy Executive Director

789 Rhode Island Association of School Business Officials
600 Mount Pleasant Avenue
Building #16, RIC
Providence, RI 02908
401-272-9811
Fax: 401-272-9834
http://www.riasp.org
Is an umbrella association serving elementary, middle level, and high school leaders from all across Rhode Island. Affiliated with both the National Association of Elementary School Principals (NAESP) and the National Association of Secondary School Principals (NASSP)

Norma Cole, President
Arlene Miguel, Secretary

790 Rhode Island Educational Media Association
6946 Camp Avenue
Suite 402
North Kingstown, RI 02852
401-398-7500
Fax: 401-886-0855
E-mail: www@ride.ri.net
http://www.ri.net
RINET provides complete Internet solutions for organizations that serve children, such as schools, libraries, municipalities, as well as high quality technology programs and services in support of K-12 teaching, learning and administration
Founded: 1999

Mike Mello, Membership Chairman
Sharon Hussey, Executive Director

791 Rhode Island Library Association
PO Box 6765
Providence, RI 02940
401-943-9080
Fax: 401-946-5079
E-mail: book_n@yahoo.com
http://www.rilibraryassoc.org
The Rhode Island Library Association is a profesional association of Librarians, Library Staff, Trustees, and Library supporters whose purpose is to promote the profession of librarianship and to improve the visibility, accessibility, responsiveness and effectiveness of library and information services throughout Rhode Island.

Christopher Laroux, President
Laura Marlane, Vice President

792 State Council on the Arts
One Capitol Hill
Providence, RI 02908
401-222-3880
Fax: 401-222-3018
http://www.arts.ri.gov

South Carolina

793 Education for Homeless Children and Youth
1429 Senate St
Suite 1114-E
Columbia, SC 29201
803-734-3215
Fax: 803-734-3043
http://www.ed.sc.gov/

794 South Carolina Arts Commission
1800 Gervais St
Columbia, SC 29201
803-734-8696
Fax: 803-734-8526
http://www.state.sc.us/arts

795 South Carolina Commission on Higher Education
1333 Main St
Suite 200
Columbia, SC 29201
803-737-2260
877-349-7183
Fax: 803-737-2297
http://www.che.sc.gov

796 South Carolina Education Association (SCEA)
421 Zimalcrest Drive
Columbia, SC 29210
803-772-6553
800-422-7232
Fax: 803-772-0922
E-mail: help@thescea.org
http://www.thescea.org/
Professional association for educators in South Carolina.

Aaron Wallace, Executive Director
Carolyn Randolph, Assistant Executive Director

797 South Carolina Library Association
PO Box 1763
Columbia, SC 29202
803-252-1087
Fax: 803-252-0589
E-mail: scla@capconsc.com
http://www.scla.org
Informs members of issues and to provide training and networking opportunities.

Libby Young, President
Rayburne Turner, Vice President

South Dakota

798 Education for Homeless Children and Youth
700 Governors Dr
Pierre, SD 57501
605-773-6400
Fax: 605-773-3782

799 Mountain Plains Library Association (MPLA)
14293 West Center Drive
Lakewood, CO 80228
303-985-7795
E-mail: mpla_execsecretary@operamail.com
http://www.mpla.us
The Mountain Plains Library Association (MPLA) is a twelve state association of librarians, library paraprofessionals and friends of libraries in Arizona, Colorado, Kansas, Montana, Nebraska, Nevada, New Mexico, North Dakota, Oklahoma, South Dakota, Utah and Wyoming. Its purpose is to promote the development of librarians and libraries by providing significant educational and networking opportunities. Holds

conferences in September, October and November. Also publishes a newsletter.

Judy Zelenski, Interim Executive Secretary
Dan Chaney, MPLA Webmaster

800 South Dakota Arts Council
711 E Wells Ave
Pierre, SD 57501-3369
605-773-3301
800-952-3625
Fax: 605-773-5657
http://www.artscouncil.sd.gov

801 South Dakota Education Association (SDEA)
441 E Capitol Avenue
Pierre, SD 57501
605-224-9263
800-529-0090
Fax: 605-224-5810
E-mail: Bryce.Healy@sdea.org
http://www.sdea.org/
The South Dakota Education Association/SDEA advocates new directions for public education, providing professional services that benefit students, schools and the public.

Bryce Healy, Executive Director
Paul McCorkle, CFO/CIO

802 South Dakota Library Association
28363 472nd Ave
Worthing, SD 57707
605-343-3750
E-mail: bkstand@rap.midco.net
http://www.sdlibraryassociation.org
The SD Library Association strives to promote library service of the highest quality for present and potential SD library users; to provide opportunities for professional involvement of all persons engaged in any phase of librarianship within the state; and to further the professional development of SD librarians, trustees, and library employees.

Jan Brue Enright, President
Laura Olson, Secretary/Treasurer

Tennessee

803 Education for Homeless Children and Youth
710 James Robertson Parkway
Nashville, TN 37243-0379
615-532-6309
Fax: 615-253-5706

804 Tennessee Arts Commission
401 Charlotte Ave
Nasville, TN 37243-0780
615-532-5934
Fax: 615-741-8559
http://www.arts.state.tn.us

805 Tennessee Association of Secondary School Principals (TASSP)
2671 Bebe Branch Lane
Knoxville, TN 37928
423-309-6187
866-737-2777
Fax: 865-687-2341
E-mail: tassp@bellsouth.net

The mission of the Tennessee Association of Secondary School Principals is: to promote professional standards of practice for secondary school administrators; provide high quality professional development experiences for rural, urban, and suburban administrators, statewide, based on their common and unique professional development needs; and advocate on behalf of secondary adminis-

trators in their efforts to provide high quality education for all students.

Dana Finch, President
Tommy Everette, Executive Director

806 Tennessee Higher Education Commission
404 James Robertson Parkway
Suite 1900
Nashville, TN 37243-0830
615-741-3605
Fax: 615-741-6230
http://www.state.tn.us/thec

807 Tennessee Library Association
PO Box 241074
Memphis, TN 38124-1074
901-485-6952
Fax: 615-269-1807
E-mail: arhuggins1@comcast.net
http://www.tnla.org
Promote the establishment, maintenance, and support of adequate library services for all people of the state.

Annelle R Huggins, Executive Director
Dinah Harris, President

808 Tennessee School Boards Association
525 Brick Church Park Drive
Nashville, TN 37207
615-815-3900
800-448-6465
Fax: 615-815-3911
E-mail: webadmin@tsba.net
http://www.tsba.net
The mission of the Tennessee School Boards Association is to assist school boards in effectively governing school districts.
Founded: 1953

Tammy Grissom, Executive Director
David Pickler, President

Texas

809 Texas Association of Secondary School Principals (TASSP)
1833 S IH-35
Austin, TX 78741
512-443-2100
Fax: 512-442-3343
E-mail: aarguello@tassp.org
UELLO@TASSP.ORG
HTTP://WWW.TASSP.ORG/
TASSP provides proactive leadership to systemically change schools into learning communities in which all students and other participants achieve their full potential as life long learners in a diverse and changing society.

Bob Alvey, President
Tom Leyden, Associate Executive Director

810 Texas Commission on the Arts
PO Box 13406
Austin, TX 78711-3406
512-463-5535
800-252-9415
Fax: 512-475-2699
http://www.arts.state.tx.us

811 Texas Higher Education Coordinating Board
PO Box 12788
Austin, TX 78711-2788
512-427-6101
800-242-3062
Fax: 512-427-6127
http://www.thecb.state.tx.us

812 Texas Homeless Education Office
2901 N IH35
Austin, TX 78722
512-475-8765
800-446-3142
Fax: 512-471-6193

813 Texas Library Association (TLA)
3355 Bee Cave Road
Suite 401
Austin, TX 78746-6763
512-328-1518
800-580-2852
Fax: 512-328-8852
E-mail: tla@txla.org
http://www.txla.org
The Texas Library Association is a professional organization that promotes librarianship and library service in Texas. Through legislative advocacy, continuing education events, and networking channels, TLA offers members opportunities for service to the profession as well as for personal growth.

Patricia H Smith, Executive Director
Gloria Meraz, Communications Director

Utah

814 Education for Homeless Children and Youth
250 East 500 S
PO Box 144200
Salt Lake City, UT 84114-4200
801-538-7975
Fax: 801-538-7991
http://www.schools.utah.gov

815 Utah Arts Council
617 East South Temple
Salt Lake City, UT 84102
801-320-9794
Fax: 801-533-3210
http://www.arts.utah.gov

816 Utah Education Association (UEA)
875 E 5180 S
Murray, UT 84107-5299
801-266-4461
800-594-8996
Fax: 801-265-2249
E-mail: mark.mickelsen@utea.org
http://www.utea.org
The mission of the Utah Education Association (UEA) is to advance the cause of public education in partnership with others: strengthen the teaching profession, promote quality schools for Utah's children, and advocate the well-being of members.

Kim Campbell, President
Mark Mickelsen, Executive Director

817 Utah State Library Division
250 North 1950 W
Suite A
Salt Lake City, UT 84116-7901
801-715-6777
800-433-1479
Fax: 801-715-6767
http://www.library.utah.gov

818 Utah System of Higher Education
60 South 400 W
Salt Lake City, UT 84101-1284
801-321-7103
Fax: 801-321-7156
http://www.utahsbr.edu

Vermont

819 Education for Homeless Children and Youth
120 State St
Montpelier, VT 05620-2501
802-828-5148
Fax: 802-828-0573
http://www.education.vermont.gov/new/html/pgm_homeless.html

820 Vermont Arts Council
136 State St
Montpelier, VT 05633-6001
802-828-3778
Fax: 802-828-3363
http://www.vermontartscouncil.org

821 Vermont Department of Libraries
109 State St
Montpelier, VT 05609-0601
802-828-3261
Fax: 802-828-2199
http://www.libraries.vermont.gov

822 Vermont Library Association
PO Box 803
Burlington, VT 05402
802-388-3845
Fax: 802-388-4367
E-mail: vlaorg@sover.net
http://www.vermontlibraries.org
The Vermont Library Association is an educational Organization working to develop, promote, and improve library and information services and librarianship in the state of Vermont.

Judah S Hamer, President
David Clark, Chapter Councilor

823 Vermont National Education Association (VTNEA)
10 Wheelock Street
Montpelier, VT 05602-3737
802-223-6375
800-649-6375
Fax: 802-223-1253
E-mail: vtnea@together.net
http://www.vtnea.org/
The Vermont National Education Association is a voluntary organization of 11,000 Vermont teachers and education support professionals, their purpose being to make sure that members have a satisfying work environment where they are acknowledged for the work they perform and where the work they perform helps students do their best.

Joel D Cook, Executive Director
Darren M Allen, Communications Director

824 Vermont Student Assistance Corporation
10 East Allen St
PO Box 2000
Winooski, VT 05404-2601

http://www.vsac.org

825 Volunteers for Peace
7 Kilburn Street
Suite 316
Burlington, VT 05401
802-540-3060
E-mail: vfp@vfp.org
http://www.vfp.org
Volunteers for Peace promotes intercultural education, service learning and community development, so that people from diverse backgrounds can work together.

Megan Brook, Executive Director
Scott Simpson, President

Virginia

826 Action Alliance for Virginia's Children and Youth
701 E Franklin Street
Suite 807
Richmond, VA 23219
804-649-0184
Fax: 804-649-0161
E-mail: info@vakids.org
http://www.vakids.org
Nonprofit and non-partisan, Voices for Virginia's Children is a persistent voice of reason in advocating for better lives and futures for children. The Commonwealth's only statewide multi-issue organization advocating for children and youth, Voices promotes sound, far-reaching program and policy solutions, focusing on early care and education, health care, family economic success, and foster care and adoption.

James V Duty, Chairman
John R Morgan, Executive Director

827 Division of Student Leadership Services
701 East Franklin Streetÿ
Richmond, VA 23288-0001
804-285-2829
Fax: 804-285-1379
http://www.vaprincipals.org
Organization that sponsors the Virginia Student Councils Association; the Virginia Association of Honor Societies; and the Virginia Association of Student Activity Advisers.

Dr. Randy Barrack, President

828 Eastern Business Education Association (EBEA)
1914 Association Drive
Reston, VA 20191-1596
703-860-8300
Fax: 703-620-4483
E-mail: nbea@nbea.org
http://www.nbea.org
NBEA is committed to the advancement of the professional interest and competence of its members and provides programs and services that enhance members' professional growth and development.

Sharon Fisher-Larson, President
Janet M Treichel, Executive Director

829 Education for Homeless Children and Youth
PO Box 8795
Williamsburg, VA 23187-8795
757-221-4002
877-455-3412
Fax: 757-221-5300
http://www.wm.edu/hope

830 Organization of Virginia Homeschoolers
PO Box 5131
Charlottesville, VA 22905
866-513-6173
Fax: 804-946-2263
E-mail: info@vahomeschoolers.org
http://www.vahomeschoolers.org
The Organization of Virginia Homeschoolers' most effective action is screening legislation for potential impact on homeschoolers. We pay attention to a large list of topics: home instruction statute, tutor provision, religious exemption provision, driver training, truancy, curfews, tax credits, and more.

Parrish Mort, President
Kenneth L Payne, Executive Director

831 Southern Association of Colleges & Schools
Virginia Secondary & Middle School Committee
PO Box 7007
Radford, VA 24142-7007
540-831-5399
Fax: 540-831-6309
E-mail: mdalderm@runet.edu
http://www.sacs.org
Public and private school accreditation organization. 12,000 member schools in 11 southern state regions. 430 middle and secondary SACS member schools in Virginia.

Dr. Emmett Sufflebarger, President
Lanny Holsinger, President-Elect

832 State Council of Higher Education for Virginia
101 North 14th St
Richmond, VA 23219
804-225-2600
Fax: 804-225-2604
http://www.schev.edu

833 Virginia Alliance for Arts Education
PO Box 70232
Richmond, VA 23255-0232
804-740-7865
Fax: 804-828-2335
http://www.socialarchive.iath.virginia.edu
To promote aesthetic and creative art education for the development of the individual at all levels in the commonwealth of Virginia. To assist teachers in improving the quality of art education. To organize and conduct panels, forums, lectures, and tours for art educators and the general public on art and art instruction. To keep the public informed of the arts through whatever means are available.

Founded: 1974

Margaret Edwards, Division Director

834 Virginia Association for Health, Physical Education, Recreation & Dance
817 W Franklin Street
Box 842037
Richmond, VA 23284-2037
800-918-9899
Fax: 800-918-9899
http://www.vahperd.org
VAHPERD is a professional association of educators that advocate quality programs in health, physical education, recreation, dance and sport. The association seeks to facilitate the professional growth and educational practices and legislation that will impact the profession.

Judith Clark, President

835 Virginia Association for Supervision and Curriculum Development
33074 Clay Street
Hopewell, VA 23860
804-458-9554
E-mail: vascd1@verizon.net
http://www.vaascd.org/
VASCD is an organization committed to excellence in education by providing programs and services that promote quality instruction for lifelong learning.

Linda Hyslop, Executive Director
Judy Lam, Administrative Coordinator

36 Virginia Association for the Education ofthe Gifted
PO Box 26212
Richmond, VA 23260-6212
804-355-5945
Fax: 804-355-5137
E-mail: vagifted@comcast.net
http://www.vagifted.org
The Virginia Association for the Gifted supports research in gifted education and advocates specialized preparation for educators of the gifted. The association disseminates information, maintains a statewide network of communication, and cooperates with organizations and agencies to improve the quality of education in the Commonwealth of Virginia.

Liz Nelson, Executive Director

37 Virginia Association of Elementary School Principals
1805 Chantilly Street
Richmond, VA 23230
804-355-6791
Fax: 804-355-1196
E-mail: info@vaesp.org
http://www.vaesp.org
Nonprofit professional association advocating for public education and equal educational opportunities. Promotes leadership of school administrators, principals as educational leaders, and provides professional development opportunities.

Thomas L Shortt, Executive Director
Jeanne Grady, Operations Director

38 Virginia Association of Independent Specialized Education Facilities
6802 Paragon Place
Suite 525
Richmond, VA 23230
804-282-3592
Fax: 804-282-3596
E-mail: info@vais.org
http://www.vais.org
The Virginia Association of Independent Schools is a service organization that promotes educational, ethical and professional excellence. Through its school evaluation/accreditation program, attention to professional development and insistence on integrity, the Association safeguards the interests of its member schools.

Kimberly E Failon, Director Professional Develo
Sally K Boese, Executive Director

39 Virginia Association of Independent Schools
6802 Paragon Place
Suite 525
Richmond, VA 23230
804-282-3592
Fax: 804-282-3596
E-mail: info@vais.org
http://www.vais.org
The Virginia Association of Independent Schools is a service organization that promotes educational, ethical and professional excellence. Through its school evaluation/accreditation program, attention to professional development and insistence on integrity, the Association safeguards the interests of its member schools.

Kimberly E Failon, Director Professional Develo
Sally K Boese, Executive Director

40 Virginia Association of School Superintendents
1805 Chantilly Street
PO Box 400265
Richmond, VA ÿ2323-4265

804- 5-2
Fax: 434-982-2942
http://vass.edschool.virginia.edu/
The Virginia Association of School Superintendents (VASS) is a professional organization dedicated to the mission of providing leadership and advocacy for public school education throughout the Commonwealth of Virginia.

J Andrew Stamp, Associate Executive Director
Alfred R Butler IV, Executive Director

841 Virginia Association of School Business Officials
Williamsburg-James City County Public Schools
PO Box 8783
Williamsburg, VA 23187-8783
757-253-6748
Fax: 757-253-0173
http://www.vasbo.org/
The mission of the Virginia Association of School Business Officials is to promote the highest standards of school business practices for its membership through professional development, continuing education, networking, and legislative impact.

David C Papenfuse, Division Director

842 Virginia Association of School Personnel Administrators
800 E City Hall Avenue
Norfolk, VA 23510-2723
757-340-1217
Fax: 757-340-1889
E-mail: president@vaspa.org
http://www.vaspa.org/
The Virginia Association of School Personnel Administrators helps personnel/human resources professionals improve their administrative skills and grow extensively in their profession.

Eddid P Antoine II, Division Director
Barbara Warren Jones, President

843 Virginia Commission for the Arts
223 Governor St
Richmond, VA 23219-2010
804-225-3132
Fax: 804-225-4327
http://www.arts.virigina.gov

844 Virginia Congress of Parents & Teachers
1027 Wilmer Avenue
Richmond, VA 23227-2419
804-264-1234
866-482-497
Fax: 804-264-4014
E-mail: info@vapta.org
http://www.vapta.org
The Virginia Congress of Parents and Teachers, better known as the Virginia PTA is a volunteer child advocacy association working for ALL children and youth in the Commonwealth of Virginia.

Melissa S Nehrbass, President
Eugene A Goldberg, Executive Director

845 Virginia Consortium of Administrators for Education of the Gifted
RR 5 Box 680
Farmville, VA 23901-9011
804-225-2884
Fax: 814-692-3163
http://www.vagifted.org
Catherine Cottrell, Division Director

846 Virginia Council for Private Education
1901 Huguenot Road
Suite 301
Richmond, VA 23235
804-423-6435
Fax: 804-423-6436
E-mail: jwebster@vcpe.org
http://www.vcpe.org
The Virginia Council for Private Education (VCPE) oversees accreditation of nonpublic preschool, elementary and secondary schools in the Commonwealth.

George McVey, President
Joanne L Webster, Vice President

847 Virginia Council of Administrators of Special Education
Franklin County Public Schools
25 Bernard Road
Rocky Mount, VA 24151
703-493-0280
Fax: 540-483-5806
E-mail: kkirst@k12albemarle.org
http://www.vcase.org
The Virginia Council of Administrators of Special Education is a professional organization that promotes professional leadership through the provision of collegial support and current information on recommended instructional practices as well as local, state and national trends in Special Education for professionals who serve students with disabilities in order to improve the quality and delivery of special education services in Virginia's public Schools

Dr. Sheila Bailey, President
Wyllys VanDerwerker, President-Elect

848 Virginia Council of Teachers of Mathematics
1033 Backwoods Road
Virginia Beach, VA 23455-6617
757-671-7316
E-mail: gnelson@vctm.org.
http://www.vctm.org/
The purpose of the Virginia Council of Teachers of Mathematics is to stimulate an active interest in mathematics, to provide an interchange of ideas in the teaching of mathematics, to promote the improvement of mathematics education in Virginia, to provide leadership in the professional development of teachers, to provide resources for teachers and to facilitate cooperation among mathematics organizations at the local, state and national levels

Ellen Smith Hook, Division Director
Ian Shenk, President

849 Virginia Council on Economic Education
301 W Main Street
Box 844000
Richmond, VA 23284-4000
804-828-1627
Fax: 804-828-7215
E-mail: shfinley@vcu.edu
http://www.vcee.org
Goal is for students to understand our economy and develop the life-long decision-making skills they need to be effective, informed citizens, consumers, savers, investors, producers and employees.

Yvonne Toms Allmond, Senior Vice President
Sallie Garrett, Contact

850 Virginia Education Association
116 S 3rd Street
Richmond, VA 23219

804-648-5801
800-552-9554
Fax: 804-775-8379
E-mail: kboitnott@veanea.org
http://www.veanea.org/
VEA is a statewide community of more than 60,000 teachers and school support professionals working for the betterment of public education in the Commonwealth. First organized in 1863, VEA has consistently advocated for quality instruction and curriculum, adequate funding, and excellent working conditions for Virginia public employees.

Robert Whitehead, Executive Director
Kitty Boitnott, President

851 Virginia Educational Media Association
PO Box 2743
Fairfax, VA 22031-2743
703-764-0719
Fax: 703-272-3643
E-mail: jremler@pen.k12.va.us
http://www.vema.gan.va.us
Aim is to promote literacy, information access and evaluation, love of literature, effective use of technology, collaboration in the teaching and learning process, intellectual freedom, professional growth, instructional leadership and lifelong learning.

Jean Remler, Executive Director
Terri Britt, President

852 Virginia Educational Research Association
3354 Taleen Court
Annandale, VA 22003-1161
703-698-1325
Fax: 703-698-0587
E-mail: mpowell@ctb.com
http://www.va-edresearch.org
The mission of the Educational Research Service is to improve the education of children and youth by providing educators and the public with timely and reliable research and information.

Dr. Edith Carter, Assistant Professor
Michaeline M Powell, President

853 Virginia High School League
1642 State Farm Boulevard
Charlottesville, VA 22911-8609
434-977-8475
Fax: 434-977-5943
E-mail: ktillry@vhsl.org
http://www.vhsl.org
The Virginia High School League is an alliance of Virginia's public high schools that promotes education, leadership, sportsmanship, character and citizenship for students by establishing and maintaining high standards for school activities and competitions.

Craig Barbrow, President
Susan Bechtol, Chairman

854 Virginia Library Association
PO Box 56312
Virginia Beach, VA 23503-0277
757-583-0041
Fax: 757-583-5041
E-mail: lhahne@coastalnet.com
http://www.vla.org
The Virginia Library Association is a statewide organization whose purpose is to develop, promote, and improve library and information services and the profession of librarianship in order to advance literacy and learning and to ensure access to information in the Commonwealth of Virginia.

Linda Hahne, Executive Director

855 Virginia Middle School Association
11138 Marsh Road
Bealeton, VA 22712-9360
703-439-3207
Fax: 540-439-2051
http://www.vmsa.org/
Lisa Norris, President
Virginia Jones, President Elect

856 Virginia School Boards Association
200 Hansen Road
Charlottesville, VA 22911
434-295-8722
800-446-8722
Fax: 434-295-8785
http://www.vsba.org
The Virginia School Boards Association is a voluntary, nonpartisan association whose primary mission is the advancement of education through the unique American tradition of local citizen control of, and accountability for, the Commonwealth's public schools.

Gina Patterson, Assistant Executive Director
Frank E Barham, Executive Director

857 Virginia Student Councils Association
4909 Cutshaw Avenue
Richmond, VA 23230
804-355-2777
Fax: 804-285-1379
E-mail: rbarrack@vassp.org
http://www.vassp.org/vsca.html
Assist school principals and assistant principals in providing leadership to their schools and communities for the purpose of improving the education of Virginia's youth.

Randy D Barrack, Executive Director
Lawrence W Lenz, President

858 Virginia Vocational Association
10259 Lakeridge Square Court
Suite G
Ashland, VA 23005-8159
804-365-4556
Jean Holbrook, President
Kathy Williams, Executive Director

Washington

859 Education for Homeless Children and Youth
600 Washington St SE
PO Boc 47200
Olympia, WA 98504-7200
360-725-6050
Fax: 360-664-3575
http://www.k12.wa.us/homelessed/default.aspx

860 Washington Education Association
32032 Weyerhaeuser Way S
PO Box 9100
Federal Way, WA 98063-9100
253-941-6700
Fax: 253-946-4735
http://www.washingtonea.org
The mission of the Washington Education Association is to advance the professional interests of its members in order to make public education the best it can be for students, staff and communities

Mary Lindquist, President
Mike Ragan, VP

861 Washington Library Association
23607 Highway 99
Suite 2-C
Edmonds, WA 98026
425-967-0739
Fax: 425-771-9588
E-mail: info@wla.org
http://http://wla.org/
Washington's citizens rely upon libraries to further their education, enhance their skills in the work place, fully function in today's global society, and enrich and enjoy their daily lives. The Washington Library Association, with a membership of over 1300 individuals and 39 institutions, provides the leadership needed to develop, improve, and promote library services to all Washington residents

ISSN: 8756-4173

Becky Shaddox, Executive Director
Kristin Crowe, Executive Director

862 Washington State Arts Commission
PO Box 42675
Olympia, WA 98504-2675
360-753-3860
Fax: 360-586-5351
http://www.arts.wa.gov

863 Washington State Higher Education Coordinating Board
917 Lakeridge Way
PO Box 43430
Olympia, WA 98504-3430
360-753-7800
Fax: 360-753-7808
http://www.hecb.wa.gov

West Virginia

864 Commission of the Arts
199 Kanawha Blvd E
Charleston, WV 25305-0300
604-558-0240
Fax: 304-558-3560
http://www.wvculture.org

865 Education for Homeless Children and Youth
1900 Kanawha Blvd E
Charleston, WV 25305-0330
304-558-8833
Fax: 304-558-5042
http://www.wvde.state.wv.us/institutional

866 Edvantia
1031 Quarrier Street
PO Box 1348
Charleston, WV 25325-1348
304-347-0400
800-624-9120
Fax: 304-347-0487
E-mail: info@edvantia.org
http://www.edvantia.org
Edvantia is a nonprofit corporation committed to helping client-partners improve education and meet federal and state mandates. Schools, districts, and state education agencies-as well as publishers and service providers-rely on Edvantia's core capabilities in research, evaluation, professional development, and technical assistance to help them succeed.

Nancy Balow, Author
Patricia Hammer, Director of Communications
Carolyn Luzader, Communications Specialist

867 West Virginia Education Association
1558 Quarrier Street
Charleston, WV 25311-2497
304-346-5315
800-642-8261

Fax: 304-346-4325
http://www.wvea.org
We are education employees like you who care deeply about children and public education. We help employees throughout the state face the demands of their profession
Dale Lee, President
Wayne Spangler, Vice President

68 West Virginia Higher Education Policy Commission
1018 Kanawha Blvd E
Suite 700
Charleston, WV 25301
304-558-0699
Fax: 304-558-1011
http://www.hepc.wvnet.edu

69 West Virginia Library Association
PO Box 5221
Charleston, WV 25361
304-558-2045
Fax: 304-558-2044
E-mail: webmaster@wvla.org
http://www.wvla.org
The West Virginia Library Association (WVLA) was established in 1914 to promote library service and librarianship in West Virginia. Since then, WVLA has offered leadership in the development and expansion of library services of all types
Myra Ziegler, President
Olivia L Bravo, Chairperson

70 West Virginia Library Commission
1900 Kanawha Blvd E
Charleston, WV 25305-0620
304-558-2041
800-642-9021
Fax: 304-558-2044
http://www.librarycommission.lib.wv.us

Wisconsin

71 Division for Libraries, Technology, and Community Learning
125 S Webster St
PO Box 7841
Madison, WI 53707-7841
608-266-2205
800-441-4563
Fax: 608-266-8770
http://www.dpi.wi.gov/dltcl

72 Education for Homeless Children and Youth Program
125 S Webster St
PO Box 7841
Madison, WI 53707-7841
608-261-6322
800-441-4563
Fax: 607-267-0364
http://www.dpi.wi.gov/homeless

73 Wisconsin Arts Board
101 E Wilson St
Madison, WI 53702
608-266-0190
Fax: 608-267-0380
http://www.artsboard.wisconsin.gov

74 Wisconsin Education Association Council
33 Nob Hill Drive
PO Box 8003
Madison, WI 53708-8003
608-276-7711
800-362-8034
Fax: 608-276-8203
E-mail: AskOnWEAC@weac.org.
http://www.weac.org

To fulfill the promise of a democratic society, the mission of the Wisconsin Education Association Council is to promote respect and support for quality public education and to provide for the professional and personal growth and economic welfare of members.
Mary Bell, President
Dan Burkhalter, Executive Director

875 Wisconsin Educational Media Association
PO Box 206
Boscobel, WI 53809
608-375-6020
E-mail: wemtamanager@hughes.net
http://www.wemaonline.org
Providing programs and services that enhance the professional growth of all members
Courtney Rounds, Association Manager
Jo Ann Carr, President

876 Wisconsin Higher Educational Aids Board
131 W Wilson St
Suite 902
Madison, WI 53703
608-267-2206
Fax: 607-267-2808
http://www.heab.state.wi.us

877 Wisconsin Library Association
4610 South Biltmore Lane
Suite A1
Madison, WI 53718-8345
608-245-3640
Fax: 608-245-3646
E-mail: wla@scls.lib.wi.us
http://www.wla.lib.wi.us/
WLA brings together and supports people from all types of libraries to advocate and work for the improvement and development of library and information services for all of Wisconsin
Pat Chevis, President
Lisa Strand, Executive Director

Wyoming

878 Education for Homeless Children and Youth
2300 Capitol Ave
Cheyenne, WY 82002-0050
307-777-5315
Fax: 307-777-7633
http://www.k12.wy.us/fp.asp

879 Wyoming Arts Council
2320 Capitol Ave
Cheyenne, WY 82002
307-777-7742
Fax: 307-777-5499
http://www.wyoarts.state.wy.us

880 Wyoming Education Association
115 E 22nd Street
Suite 1
Cheyenne, WY 82001-3795
307-634-7991
Fax: 800-778-8161
E-mail: mkruse@nea.org
http://www.wyoea.org
Advance public education at all levels by creating equitable educational opportunity for all learners, promoting the highest quality standards for the profession, and expanding the rights and furthering the interests of educational personnel.
Kathryn Valido, President
Craig Williams, Vice President

881 Wyoming Library Association
PO Box 1387
Cheyenne, WY 82003-1387
307-632-7622
Fax: 307-638-3469
E-mail: grottski@aol.com
http://www.wyla.org
Promotes library service and profession of librarianship in Wyoming.
Cynthia Twing, President
Laura Grott, Executive Secretary

882 Wyoming School Boards Association
2323 Pioneer Avenue
Cheyenne, WY 82001-3274
307-634-1112
Fax: 307-634-1114
E-mail: wsba@wsba-wy.org
http://www.wsba-wy.org
The official voice of local school boards.
Gregg Blikre, President
Mike Eathorne, President-Elect

International

883 ACSI Teachers' Convention
Assocation of Christian Schools
International
731 Chapel Hills Drive
PO Box 65130
Colorado Springs, CO 80920
719-528-6906
800-367-0798
Fax: 791-531-0716
E-mail: exhibitors@acsi.org
http://www.acsi.org
Educational convention for administrators, school board members, and early childhood educators that encourages staff and volunteer development throughout the year.

50000 attendees

Brian S. Simmons, President
Janet Stump, Public Relations

884 AISA School Leaders' Retreat and Educators Conference
Association of International Schools in Africa
Peponi Road
PO Box 14103, Nairobi
Kenya 00800
254-20-2697442
Fax: 254-20-4183272
E-mail: info@aisa.or.ke
http://www.aisa.or.ke
Facilitates communications, cooperation, and professional growth among member schools. Promotes intercultural understanding and friendships as well as facilitating collaboration between its members, host country schools, and other regional and professional groups.

Annual/October

Peter Bateman, Executive Director

885 Association for Childhood Education International Bi-Annual Conference
Assn for Childhood Educational International
1101 16th St. N.W.
Suite 300
Washington, DC 20036
202-372-9986
800-423-3563
Fax: 202-372-9989
E-mail: headquarters@acei.org
http://www.acei.org
Symposium focusing on education for bi-lingual and culturally diverse children, international issues and offers over 200 workshops.

April
50 booths with 1000 attendees

Debora Wisneski, President
Carrie Whaley, President Elect

886 Association for Experiential Education Annual Conference
3775 Iris Avenue
Suite 4
Boulder, CO 80301-2043
303-440-8844
866-522-8337
Fax: 303-440-9581
E-mail: membership@aee.org
http://www.aee.org
Annual international and regional conference dedicated to promoting, defining, developing, and applying the theories and practices of experiential education.

November
1,200 attendees

Mary Breunig, President
Leslie Stevens, Office Manager

887 CIEE Annual Conference
Council on International Educational Exchange
300 Fore Street
Portland, ME 04101
207-553-7600
800-407-8839
Fax: 207-553-7699
E-mail: conference@ciee.org
http://www.ciee.org
Open to study-abroad advisors, administrators, faculty and other international education professionals. The conference is an opportunity to share ideas, keep up with developments in the field, and meet with colleagues from around the world.

November

888 Center for Critical Thinking and Moral Critique Annual International
Po Box196
Tomales, CA 94971
707-878-9100
800-833-3645
Fax: 707-878-9111
E-mail: cct@criticalthinking.org
http://www.criticalthinking.org
Over 1,200 educators participate to discuss critical thinking and educational change.

March, July

Dr Linda Elder, President

889 Council for Advancement and Support of Education
1307 New York Avenue NW
Suite 1000
Washington, DC 20005-4701
202-328-2273
Fax: 202-387-4973
E-mail: conferences@case.org
http://www.case.org
Offers numerous opportunities in the United States, Canada, Mexico, mainland Europe, and the United Kingdom to network with colleagues.

Fall/Winter

John Lippincott, President
Richard Salatiello, Sr Conference Program Coord.

890 Council for Learning Disabilities International Conference
1184 Antioch Road
Box 405
Overland Park, KS 66210
913-491-1011
Fax: 913-491-1012
E-mail: cldinfo@cldinternational.org
http://www.cldinternational.org
Intensive interaction with and among professional educators and top LD researchers. Concise, informative and interesting forums on topics from effective instruction to self-reliance are presented by well-known professionals from across the country and around the world.

October
35 booths with 800 attendees

Diane Bryant, Conference Contact
Judy Voress, Conference Contact

891 Council of British Independent Schools in the European Communities Annual Conference
St. Mary's University Palace
Strawberry Hill
Twickenham, UK TW1-4SX
44(0) 208 240 4142
Fax: 44(0) 208 240 4255
E-mail: excecutive.director@cobis.org.uk
http://www.cobis.org.uk
Conference for members of senior management educational teams.

May
75 attendees and 20 exhibits

Colin Bell, Executive Director
Suzanne Howarth, Membership

892 European Council of International Schools
146 Buckingham Palace Road
Fourth Floor
London, UK SW1W-9TR
+44 0 20 7824 7040
Fax: +44 0 20 7824 7041
E-mail: ecis@ecis.org
http://www.ecis.org
Support professional development, curriculum and instruction, leadership and good governance in international schools located in Europe and around the world.

April, November

Michelle Clue, Conference Coordinator
Jean Vahey, Executive Director

893 Hort School: Conference of the Association of American Schools
International School of Panama
P.O. Box 0819-02588
Panama City
507-293-3000
Fax: 507-266-7808
E-mail: isp@isp.edu.pa
http://www.isp.edu.pa
Educates and inspires our students to reach their full potential and contribute to the world by providing an exemplary English language education enriched by our multicultural community.

October
600 attendees and 35 exhibits

Rajiv Bhat, Director
Terry McCoy, President

894 International Association of Teachers of English as a Foreign Language
Darwin College
University of Kent
Canterbury, Kent, UK CT2-7NY
44-1227-824430
Fax: 44-1227-824431
E-mail: generalenquires@iatefl.org
http://www.iatefl.org
Plenary sessions by eminent practitioners, a large number of workshops, talks and round tables given by other speakers, an ELT Resources Exhibition and Pre-Conference Events organized by Special Interest Groups.

April
80 booths with 1500 attendees

Alison Medland, Conference Organizer
Glenda Smart, Executive Director

895 International Awards Market
Awards and Recognition Association
4700 W Lake Avenue
Glenview, IL 60025
847-375-4800
800-344-2148
Fax: 888-374-7257
E-mail: info@ara.org
http://www.ara.org

Providing outstanding business and educational opportunities for both retailers and suppliers. Retailers can view the latest industry products, take advantage of special show offers and benefit from a full educational program.

Feb, March, Nov
200 booths with 6,000 attendees

Lori Warren, President

896 International Conference

World Association for Symphonic Bands & Ensembles
1037 Mill Street
San Luis Obispo, CA 93401
805-541-8000
Fax: 805-543-9498
E-mail: admin@wasbe2005.com
http://www.wasbe.org
WASBE is a nonprofit, international association open to individuals, institutions, and industries interested in symphonic bands and wind ensembles. Dedicated to enhancing the quality of the wind band throughout the world and exposing its members to new worlds of repertoire, musical culture, people and places.

Every 2 years

Bert Aalders, President

897 International Congress for School Effectiveness & Improvement

International Congress Secretariat
86 Ellison Road
Springwood
Australia NSW-2777
61 2 4751 7974
Fax: 61 2 4751 7974
E-mail: admin@icsei.net
http://www.icsei.net
The purpose of building and using an expanded base for advancing research, practice and policy in the area of school effectiveness and improvement. The Congress offers the opportunity to exchange information and networking for the educational community.

January
500 attendees

Dr. Lorna Earl, President
Dr. Alma Harris, President Elect

98 International Dyslexia Association Annual Conference

40 York Road
4th Floor
Baltimore, MD 21204-2044
410-296-0232
800-ABC-D123
Fax: 410-321-5069
E-mail: info@interdys.org
http://www.interdys.org
Provide the most comprehensive range of information and services that address the full scope of dyslexia and related difficulties in learning to read and write.

November
3000 attendees

Darnella Parks, Conference Manager
Kristen Penczek, Conference Director

99 International Exhibit

National Institute for Staff & Organizational Dev.
University of Texas
1912 Speedway, Stop D5600
Austin, TX 78712-1607
512-471-7545
Fax: 512-471-9426
E-mail: membership@nisod.oeg
http://www.nisod.org

The largest international conference to focus specifically on the celebration of teaching, learning, and leadership excellence.

May
1500 attendees

Sheryl Powell, Conference Director

900 International Listening Association Annual Convention

International Listening Association
Box 164
Belle Plaine, MN 56011
952-594-5697
Convention topics cover broad spectrum of listening practice and research. Papers, panels, courses, practice and workshops can be found at the convention in effort to network, spread research and new practices in effetcive listening training,

June

Dr. Nanette Johnson-Curiskis, Executive Director
Debra Worthington, Convention Planner

901 International Multicultural Institute (IMCI) Annual Conference

International Multicultural Institute
595 6th Street
Brooklyn, NY 11215
718-832-8625
http://www.imciglobal.org
Brings together practitioners from across the country and around the world to explore diversity and multiculturalism in both personal and professional contexts. Leaders from academia, business, and government present the latest thinking and action on diversity issues to conference participants.

June

Nancy J. Di Dia, Executive Director
Margaret Regan, President

902 International Reading Association Annual Convention

800 Barksdale Road
PO Box 8139
Newark, DE 19714-8139
302-731-1600
800-336-7323
Fax: 302-731-1057
E-mail: customerservice@reading.org
http://www.reading.org
Contains exhibitors involved in various lectures and workshops dealing with illiteracy, literature and some library science courses.

May
800 booths with 13M attendees

Carrice C. Cummins, President
Marcie Craig Post, Executive Director

903 International Technology Education Association Conference

1914 Association Drive
Suite 201
Reston, VA 20191-1539
703-860-2100
Fax: 703-860-0353
E-mail: iteea@iteea.org
http://www.iteea.org
Provides teachers with new and exciting ideas for educating students of all grade levels. The conference gives educators an opportunity for better understanding of the constant changes that take place in technology education.

varies
150 booths with 2,200+ attendees

Ken Starkman, Program Chair
Christine Maggio, Exhibit Opportunities

904 International Trombone Festival

International Trombone Association
PO Box 441
Coppell, TX 75019
888-684-2361
Fax: 888-684-2362
E-mail: jon@trombonefestival.net
http://www.trombone.net
Annual festival giving trombonists the opportunity to meet and share with other trombonists for performances, lectures, exhibits, competitions and more.

June

John Drew, President
Jon Bohls, Festivals Director

905 Learning Disabilities Association of America International Conference

4156 Library Road
Pittsburgh, PA 15234-1349
412-341-1515
Fax: 412-344-0224
E-mail: info@ldaamerica.org
http://www.ldanatl.org
The largest meeting on learning disabilities (LD) in the world. Disabled, parents, various educators and administrators. The conference follows a general theme set by LDAA.

Febuary
95 booths with 2600 attendees and 300 exhibits

Mary Clare Reynolds, Executive Director

National

906 AAUW National Convention

American Association of University Women
1111 16th Street NW
Washington, DC 20036
202-785-7700
800-326-2289
Fax: 202-872-1425
E-mail: convention@aauw.org
http://www.aauw.org
The nation's leading voice promoting education and equity for women and girls. Speakers, panels and workshops allow for networking with other AAUW members and explore opportunities to further empower women.

Katie Broendel, Media/PR Manager
Christy Jones, Membership Director

907 ASCD Annual Conference & Exhibit Show

1703 N Beauregard Street
Alexandria, VA 22311-1714
703-578-9600
800-933-2723
Fax: 703-575-5400
E-mail: member@ascd.org
http://www.ascd.org
Explore the big ideas in education today, or examine new developments in your content area or grade level. Stretch your professional development learning into new areas, or pick an issue you care about most and examine it in depth.

March
12000 attendees

Barbara Gleason, Public Information Director
Christy Guilfoyle, Public Relations Specialist

908 AZLA Conference

Arizona Library Association
1030 E Baseline Road
Suite 105-1025
Tempe, AZ 85283

480-609-3999
Fax: 480-998-7838
E-mail: admin@azla.org
http://www.azla.org
Advance the education advantages of the state through libraries, and to promote general interest in library extension (traveling libraries). Sometimes conference is a joint venture between two libraries(2014 held by AZLA and MPLA libraries).

November
90+ booths with 2,000 attendees

Rene Tanner, Conference Planning

909 AdvancED

National Study of School Evaluation
9115 Westside Parkway
Alpharetta, GA 30009-4958
678-392-2285
888-413-3669
Fax: 847-995-9088
E-mail: contactus@advanc-ed.org
http://www.advanc-ed.org
Annual international summit held in Washington, DC. Share research on best educational practices, research based products. Research helps shape educational policy and strengthen learning practices worldwide.

November

Dr. Mark A Elgart, President/CEO

910 American Association for Employment in Education Annual Conference

American Association for Employment in Education
947 E. Johnstown Rd.
#170
Gahanna, OH 43230
614-485-1111
800-678-6010
Fax: 360-244-7802
E-mail: aaee@osu.edu
http://www.aaee.org
Disseminate information on the educational marketplace, and job search process. Promote ethical standards and practices in the employment process. Promote dialogue and cooperation among institutions which prepare educators and institutions which provide employment opportunities.

November
20 booths with 150-200 attendees

Doug Peden, Executive Director
Diana Sanchez, Nat'l Conference Prog. Chair

911 American Association of Colleges for Teacher Ed Annual Meeting and Exhibits

1307 New York Avenue NW
Suite 300
Washington, DC 20005-4701
202-293-2450
Fax: 202-457-8095
E-mail: aacte@aacte.org
http://www.aacte.org
Learning event for educator preparation professionals. Oppportunities for networking, advancing understanding of new concepts and theories, hear new research and discover innovative practices and programs.

Feb
75 booths with 2400 attendees

Sharon P Robinson, President/CEO
Gail M. Bozeman, VP Meetings and Events

912 American Association of French Teachers Conference

American Association of French Teachers
Mailcode 4510
Southern Illinois University
Carbondale, IL 62901-4510
618-453-5731
Fax: 618-453-5733
E-mail: aatf@frenchteachers.org
http://www.frenchteachers.org/convention
Conventions regularly occur in French-speaking areas. Representing the French language in North America and to encourage the dissemination, both in the schools and in the general public, of knowledge concerning all aspects of the culture and civilization of France and the French-speaking world.

July
1100 attendees

Dr Jayne Abrate, Executive Director

913 American Association of Physics Teachers National Meeting

One Physics Ellipse
College Park, MD 20740-3311
301-209-3311
Fax: 301-209-0845
E-mail: aapt-meet@aapt.org
http://www.aapt.org
Gives members the opportunity to network, discuss innovations in teaching methods and share the results of research about teaching and learning.

summer & winter

Tiffany Hayes, Director of Conferences
Cerena Cantrell, Associate Program Director

914 American Association of School Administrators National Conference on Education

1615 Duke Street
Alexandria, VA 22314
703-528-0700
Fax: 703-841-1543
E-mail: info@aasa.org
http://www.aasa.org
For school administrators to hear education leaders, exhibits, vendors for public education and network with others sharing practices and learning new ways in education. Support and develop effective school system leaders dedicated to the highest quality public education for all children.

Daniel Domenech, Executive Director
Christopher Daw, Director of Conferences

915 American Association of School Librarians National Conference

American Library Association
50 E Huron Street
Chicago, IL 60611
312-280-4382
800-545-2433
Fax: 312-280-5276
E-mail: aasl@ala.org
http://www.ala.org/aasl
An open conference holding seminars, workshops and tours of local libraries and facilities.

October
3,000 attendees

Julie Walker, Executive Director
Melissa Jacobsen, Professional Development Mgr

916 American Association of Sexuality Educators, Counselors & Therapists Conference

1444 I Street NW
Suite 700
Washington, DC 20005-1960
202-449-1099
Fax: 202-216-9646
E-mail: aasect@aasect.org
http://www.aasect.org
Facilitate productive discussions about identity and human sexuality; encourage interdisciplinary, intergenerational and cross-cultural collaboration and networking of current sexual health topics; provide opportunities for developing and refining skills in sexuality education, therapy, counseling and research

06/20-06/24
50 booths with 400-500 attendees

Dee Ann Walker, Executive Director
Carey Roth Bayer, Conference Co Chair

917 American Camp Association National Conference

American Camp Association
5000 State Road 67 N
Martinsville, IN 46151-7902
765-342-8456
800-428-2267
Fax: 765-342-2065
E-mail: conference@ACAcamps.org
http://www.acacamps.org
Largest national camp conference hosted in the United States. Focuses on professional development, networking and commerce.

February
175 booths with 1500 attendees

Peg Smith, CEO
Kim Bruno, Marketing Manager

918 American Council on Education Annual Meeting

American Council on Education
1 Dupont Circle NW
Washington, DC 20036-1110
202-939-9300
Fax: 202-833-4760
E-mail: annualmeeting@ace.nche.edu
http://www.acenet.edu
Brings together higher education leaders form all sectors. The ACE Annual Meeting is seen as the go-to event to network with colleagues, hear about emerging trends from national thought leaders and learn about new approaches to campus challenges.

March
74 booths

Stephanie Marshall, Meeting Services Director
Wendy Bresler, Program Planning

919 American Council on the Teaching of Foreign Languages Annual Conference

101 N Fairfax Street
Suite 200
Alexandria, VA 22314
703-894-2900
Fax: 703-894-2905
E-mail: morehouse@actfl.org
http://www.actfl.org
More than 600 professional development opportunities, including pre and post convention workshops and sessions focused on all aspects of teachiing and learning languages and cultures.

November
250 booths with 6,000+ attendees

Julia Richardson, Convention Coordinator
Marty Abbott, Executive Director

20 American Counseling Association Annual Conference & Expo
American Counseling Association
5999 Stevenson Avenue
Alexandria, VA 22304-3302
703-823-9800
800-347-6647
Fax: 703-823-0252
E-mail: rhayes@counseling.org
http://www.counseling.org
Education sessions, speakers, mental health training and time and space for networking with other professionals in the mental health field.

March
4000 attendees

Robin Hayes, Convention & Meeting Contact
Theresa Holmes, Convention & Meeting Contact

21 American Educational Research Association Annual Meeting
1430 K Street
Suite 1200
Washington, DC 20005-3078
202-238-3200
Fax: 202-238-3250
E-mail: annualmtg@aera.net
http://www.aera.net
Talks, courses, papers submissions related to the meeting theme and education research as a whole.

April
120 booths with 12M attendees

Felice J Levine, Executive Director
Laurie Cipriano, CMO, Director

22 American Indian Science & Engineering Society Annual Conference
AISES
PO Box 9828
Albuquerque, NM 87119-9828
505-765-1052
Fax: 505-765-5608
E-mail: info@aises.org
http://www.aises.org
Provides an opportunity for networking, educational workshops, a career fair, showcase academic research and study and how to bridge the waysbewtween tradition and STEM.

November
3000 attendees

Chris Echohawk, Vice Chair
Dr. Mary Jo Ondrechen, Chair

23 American Library Association (ALA) Annual Conference
American Library Association
50 E Huron
Chicago, IL 60611
312-944-6780
800-545-2433
Fax: 312-440-9374
E-mail: ala@ala.org
http://www.ala.org
Programs, updates, conversations about key issues like digital content, e-books, technology in libraries, books, leadership, literacy advocacy, community engagement and library marketing. Also a great way to network with other librarians and libraries.

June/January
20000+ attendees

Alicia Babcock, Conference Services
Keith Fiels, Executive Director

924 American Mathematical Society
American Mathematical Society
201 Charles Street
Providence, RI 02904-2294
401-455-4000
800-321-4267
Fax: 401-331-3842
E-mail: meet@ams.org
http://www.ams.org
Advance mathematical achievement, encouraging research and provide communication necessary to progress in the field. Preserve, supplement and utilize the results of the research of mathematicians throughout the world.

January

Dr. Donald McClure, Executive Director
Penny Pina, Director Meetings/Conference

925 American Montessori Society Conference
116 East 16th St
New York, NY 10003
212-358-1250
Fax: 212-358-1256
E-mail: ams@amshq.org
http://www.amshq.org
Promotes quality Montessori education for all children from birth to 18 years of age. Conference participants share knowledge and research and strengthen bonds while creating new networks.

May
75 booths with 1000 attendees

Kathy Roemer, President
Joyce S. Pickering, Vice President

926 American Psychological Association Annual Conference
750 1st Street NE
Washington, DC 20002-4242
202-336-5500
800-374-2721
Fax: 202-336-6123
E-mail: convention@apa.org
http://www.apa.org
A national conference attended by psychologists from around the world. The conference has workshops, lectures, discussions, roundtables and symposiums.

August

13,000 attendees

Donald N Bersoff, Ph.D, JD, President

927 American Public Health Association Annual Meeting
American Public Health Association
800 I Street NW
Washington, DC 20001-3710
202-777-2742
Fax: 202-777-2534
E-mail: anna.keller@apha.org
http://www.apha.org
The premier platform to share successes and failures, discover exceptional best practices and learn from expert colleagues and the latest research in the field.

November
650 booths with 13000 attendees

Georges C. Benjamin, Executive Director
James E. Dale, CoA Chair

928 American School Health Association's National School Conference
4340 East West Highway
Suite 403
Bethesda, MD 20814-5960
301-652-8072
Fax: 301-652-8077

E-mail: info@ashaweb.org
http://www.ashaweb.org
Attendees include school nurses, health educators, health counselors, physicians and students. During the five-day conference, presentations are made by ASHA members, government officials and health education professionals.

October
40 booths with 700 attendees

Linda Morse, President
Julie Greenfield, Mkting/Conferences Director

929 American Speech-Language-Hearing Association Annual Convention
ASHA
2200 Research Blvd.
Rockville, MD 20850-3289
301-296-5700
800-638-8255
Fax: 301-296-8580
E-mail: convention@asha.org
http://www.asha.org
A scientific and professional conference of speech-language pathology, audiology and other professionals. Opportunity to learn about latest evidence based research , enhance clinical skills, improve technique and gain new tools and resources to advance career.

Annual
November
400 booths with 12,000 attendees

Arlene A Pietranton, CEO
Patricia A. Prelock, President

930 American Technical Education Association Annual Conference
American Technical Education Association
Dunwoody College of Technology
818 Dunwoody Blvd.
Minneapolis, MN 55403
612-381-3315
E-mail: info@ateaonline.org
http://www.ateaonline.org
Administrators/directors and faculty of various technical institutes, junior colleges, universities and colleges. Topics cover all aspects of computer assisted instruction, distance education and technical education. Professional development opportunity for all involved in postsecondary technical education.

March
35 booths with 700 attendees and 75 exhibits

Dr. Sandra Krebsbach, Executive Director
DeeAnn Bilben, Administrative Assistant

931 Annual Effective Schools Conference
7227 North 16th Street
Suite 190
Phoenix, AZ 85020
866-626-7556
Fax: 888-756-7628
E-mail: now@4aplus.com
http://www.effectiveschoolsconference2013.com
Latest research and methods for creating successful educational environments where all students can reach their academic potential. Gain valuable hands-on experience, learn proven implementation strategies and hear from some of the greatest minds in the field.

March

Amber Countiss
Annie Hanks

932 Annual NCEA Convention & Exposition
National Catholic Educational Association
1005 North Glebe Road
Suite 525
Arlington, VA 22201-3852
571-257-0010
800-711-6232
Fax: 703-243-0025
E-mail: nceaadmin@ncea.org
http://www.ncea.org
Attendees represent all aspects of Catholic and faith based education from pre-school to universities, to local parishes and more. Provides development sessions, departmental meetings, special events in order to gain knowledge and network with fellow colleagues.

Annually
April

Regina M. Haney, Executive Director
Amy Durkin, Convention/Events

933 Association for Behavior Analysis Annual Convention
Association for Behavior Analysis
550 W. Centre Ave.
Portage, MI 49024-5364
269-492-9310
Fax: 269-492-9316
E-mail: convention@abainternational.org
http://www.abainternational.org
Psychologists, psychology faculty and students, counselors and social workers are among the attendees of this conference offering over 25 exhibitors. The conference is research and education oriented.

43 booths

Maria E Malott, PhD, CEO

934 Association for Behavioral and Cognitive Therapies Annual Convention
305 7th Avenue
16th Floor
New York, NY 10001-6008
212-647-1890
Fax: 212-647-1865
E-mail: mebrown@abct.org
http://www.abct.org
Provide participants with clinical knowledge of specific issues or new research in the field, networking possibilities, clinical roundtable, panel discussions on training and symposia of the presentation of data or research.

November
2,000 attendees

Mary Ellen Brown, Education/Mtg Services Dir.
Mary Jane Eimer, Executive Director

935 Association for Education Finance and Policy
6703 Madison Creek
Columbia, MO 65203
573-814-9878
Fax: 314-256-2831
E-mail: info@aefpweb.org
http://www.aefpweb.org
The conference theme changes yearly; this year the focus is education renewal and reform and the fact that domestic policy and global economic competition challenge our education system. The conference will present, discuss and evaluate the latest research on education topics and current reforms and policy directions.

March
3000 attendees

Deborah Cunningham, President
Angela M. Hull, Executive Director

936 Association for Education in Journalism and Mass Communication Convention
AEJMC
234 Outlet Pointe Boulevard
Suite A
Columbia, SC 29210-5667
803-798-0271
Fax: 803-772-3509
http://www.aejmc.org
Featuring the latest in technology as well as special sessions on teaching, research and public service in the various components of journalism and mass communication — from advertising and public relations to radio and television journalism to media management and newspapers.

August
1,500 attendees

Fred Williams, Convention Manager
Jennifer McGill, Executive Director

937 Association for Persons with Severe Handicaps Annual Conference
1001 Connecticut Ave NW
Suite 235
Washington, DC 20036
202-540-9020
Fax: 202-540-9019
E-mail: info@tash.org
http://www.tash.org
Provides a forum for individuals with disabilities, families, researchers, educators, scholars, and others to create dialogue around creating action for social and systems reform.

December
2,500 attendees

Barbara Trader, Executive Director

938 Association for Play Therapy Conference
Association for Play Therapy
3198 Willow Avenue
Suite 110
Clovis, CA 93612
559-294-2128
Fax: 559-294-2129
E-mail: info@a4pt.org
http://www.a4pt.org
Major interdisciplinary event for mental health professionals wishing to earn continuing education credit for licensure or credentialing, network with popular authors, speakers and vendors and enjoy extra curricular activities with peers.

October
1000 attendees

Kathryn Lebby, Events Coordinator
Bill Burns, Executive Director

939 Association for Science Teacher Education Annual Meeting
The Association For Science Teacher Education
5040 Haley Center
Auburn, AL 36849
972-690-2496
E-mail: executivedirector@theaste.org
http://www.theaste.com
Offers programs in science, mathematics and environmental education with a wide variety of teachers and professors attending.

January

Kathy Cabe Trundle, President
Bob Hollon, Executive Director

940 Association for the Advancement of International Education
Nova Southeastern University
11501 N. Military Trail
Palm Beach Gardens, FL 33418
561-805-2193
Fax: 561-805-2187
E-mail: g.nicoll@nove.edu
http://www.aaie.org
Provides the organizational leadership to initiate and promote an understanding of the need for and the support of American/International education.

February
70 booths with 550 attendees

Elleana Austin, Administrative Assistant
Elsa Lamb, Executive Director

941 Association for the Education of Gifted Underachieving Students Conference
6 Wildwood Street
Burlington, MA 01803
651-962-5385
E-mail: aegusquestions@gmail.com
http://www.aegus1.org
Attended by teachers, professors, administrators and social workers, this conference deals with cultural awareness and education of the disabled and gifted students.

April

Lois Baldwin, President
Terry Neu, Vice President

942 Association for the Study of Higher Education Annual Meeting
University Of Nevada
4505 S. Maryland Parkway
453068
Las Vegas, NV 89154-3068
702-895-2737
Fax: 702-895-4269
E-mail: ashe@unlv.edu
http://www.ashe.ws
Promotes collaboration among its members and others engaged in the study of higher education; as a community of scholarly practice and as practicing scholars and educators.

November

Kim Nehls, Executive Director
Christal Allen, Conference Coordinator

943 Association of American Colleges & Universities Annual Meeting
Association of American Colleges & Universities
1818 R Street NW
Washington, DC 20009-1604
202-387-3760
Fax: 202-265-9532
http://www.aacu.org
Bringing together college educators from across institutional types, disciplines, and departments. Providing participants with innovative ideas and practices, and shaping the direction of their educational reform efforts.

January
1,200 attendees

Carol Geary, President

944 Association of Community College Trustees Conference
1233 20th Street NW
Suite 301
Washington, DC 20036-2907

202-775-4667
Fax: 202-223-1297
E-mail: acctinfo@acct.org
http://www.acct.org
Exists to develop effective lay governing board leadership to strengthen the capacity of community colleges to achieve their missions on behalf of their communities.

1500+ attendees

J. Noah Brown, President/CEO
Lila Farmer, Conference Logistics Coord.

945 Association of Science-Technology Centers Incorporated Conference
Association of Science-Technology Centers Incorp.
1025 Vermont Avenue NW
Suite 500
Washington, DC 20005-3516
202-783-7200
Fax: 202-783-7207
E-mail: conference@astc.org
http://www.astc.org
An organization of science centers and museums dedicated to furthering the public understanding of science. ASTC encourages excellence and innovation in informal science learning by serving and linking its members worldwide and advancing the common goals.

October
165 booths with 1600 attendees

David Corson, Mgr. Conference/Exhibit Hall
Nina Humes, Meetings/Conference Coord.

946 CHADD: Children & Adults with Attention Deficit/Hyperactivity Disorder
CHADD
8181 Professional Place
Suite 150
Landover, MD 20785
301-306-7070
800-233-4050
Fax: 301-306-7090
http://www.chadd.org
National non-profit organization which offers advocacy, information and support for patients and parents of children with attention deficit disorders. Maintains support groups, provides a forum for continuing education about ADHD, and maintains a national resource center for information about ADD.

October
60 booths with 1,500 attendees

Marsha Bokman, Mtgs/Events Director

947 Center for Appalachian Studies Annual Conference
Appalachian Studies Center
One John Marshall Drive
Huntington, WV 25755-0918
304-696-2904
E-mail: mthomas@marshall.edu
http://www.appalachianstudies.org
Central theme each year about some facet of Appalachia- communities, landscapes, evoulution of their work together-history, etc.

March

Katherine Ledford, Conference Chair
Mary Thomas, Executive Director

948 Center on Disabilities Conference
Students with Disabilities Resources
1811 Nordhoff
Bayramian Hall 110
Northridge, CA 91330-8264

818-677-1200
E-mail: conference@csun.edu
http://www.csun.edu/cod
Provides a setting for researchers, practitioners, exhibitors, end users, speakers and participants to share knowledge and best practices in the field of assistive technology.

March
130 booths with 4800 attendees

Wayne Fernades, Mktg/Events Manager
Sandy Plotin, Managing Director

949 Choristers Guild's National Festival & Directors' Conference
Choristers Guild
12404 Park Central Drive
Suite 100
Dallas, TX 75251-1802
469-398-3606
800-246-7478
Fax: 469-398-3611
E-mail: conferences@mailcg.org
http://www.choristersguild.org
Enables leaders to nurture the spiritual and musical growth of children and youth.

June

Jim Rindelaub, Director
Eve Hehn, Conferences

950 Closing the Gap
526 Main Street
PO Box 68
Henderson, MN 56044-0068
507-248-3294
Fax: 507-248-3810
E-mail: info@closingthegap.com
http://www.closingthegap.com
Conference themes change yearly. Always focus on technology and howit changes—primarily with assistive technology.

October
150+ booths with 2400 attendees

Jan Latzke, Conference Registration
Connie Kneip, VP/General Manager

951 Conference for Advancement of Mathematics Teaching
Texas Education Agency
PO Box 200669
Austin, TX 78720-0669
512-335-2268
Fax: 512-335-8517
E-mail: camt@camtonline.org
http://www.camtonline.org
Exhibits educational materials useful to mathematics teachers; education of the use of technology on the classroom and effective use of manipulative materials in the classroom.

July
175 booths with 7.5M-8M attendees

Joyce Polanco, Program Chair

952 Council for Exceptional Children Annual Convention
The Council for Exceptional Children
2900 Crystal Drive
Suite 1000
Arlington, VA 22202-3557
703-620-3660
888-232-7733
Fax: 703-264-1637
E-mail: service@cec.sped.org
http://www.cec.sped.org
Largest professional organization dedicated to improving educational results of individuals with disabilities and the gifted. 50,000 members. Educational sessions, endless opportunities to network with others working with children and learn about new and pend-

ing legislation and explore cutting edge products and services.

April
437 booths with 7000 attendees and 299 exhibits

Christy A. Chambers, President
Mikki Garcia, Executive Director

953 EDUCAUSE Annual Convention
282 Century Place
Suite 5000
Louisville, KY 80027
303-449-4430
Fax: 303-440-0461
E-mail: info@educause.edu
http://www.educause.edu
Provides opportunity for educators to network with colleagues and learn form each other by sharing experience, ideas and information through presentations and sessions.

October
4,000+ attendees and 180 exhibits

Diana Oblinger, President
Beverly Williams, Conference Director

954 Education Market Association
8380 Colesville Road
Silver Spring, MD 20910
301-495-0240
800-395-5550
Fax: 301-495-3330
E-mail: awatts@nssea.org
http://www.edmarket.org
Lists 1,500 member dealers and manufacturers representatives for school supplies, equipment and instructional materials.

March
1200 booths with 5,000 attendees and 700 exhibits

Adrienne Dayton, VP of Marketing/Communicatio
Jim McGarry, President/ CEO

955 Educational Publishing Summit
Association of Educational Publishers
300 Martin Luther King Blvd.
Suite 200
Wilmington, DE 19801
302-295-8350
Fax: 302-656-2918
E-mail: mail@aepweb.org
http://www.aepweb.org
Presents a range of informative and practical sessions that address all issues relating to the development and distribution of high-quality learning resources.

June

Charlene F Gaynor, CEO
JoAnn McDevitt, VP Sales/Mrktg/Business Dev.

956 Educational Theatre Association Conference
Educational Theatre Association
2343 Auburn Avenue
Cincinnati, OH 45219-2815
513-421-3900
Fax: 513-421-7077
E-mail: mpeitz@edta.org
http://www.edta.org
Supports the association's mission by supporting educators through networking opportunities, educational workshops, speakers and resources that can enrich students' educational experience.

September
2,400 attendees

Julie Woffington, Executive Director
Gloria McIntyre, President

957 Foundation for Critical Thinking Regional Workshop & Conference
Foundation for Critical Thinking
PO Box 196
Tomales, CA 94971
707-878-9100
800-833-3645
Fax: 707-878-9111
E-mail: cct@criticalthinking.org
http://www.criticalthinking.org
Investigates and reports on the value and use of analytical thinking programs and curriculum in the classroom.

July

Dr Linda Elder, President

958 Gifted Child Society Conference
190 Rock Road
Glen Rock, NJ 07452-1736
201-444-6530
Fax: 201-444-9099
E-mail: admin@gifted.org
http://www.gifted.org
Provides educational enrichment and support for gifted children through national advocacy and various programs.

September
250 attendees

Janet L Chen, Executive Director

959 INFOCOMM Tradeshow
InfoComm International
11242 Waples Mill Road
Suite 200
Fairfax, VA 22030
703-273-7200
800-659-7469
Fax: 703-273-5924
E-mail: inief@chiefmfg.com
http://www.infocommshow.org
Designed for professionals in the audiovisual, information communications and system integration industries. Attendees can explore audiovisual products and services from the industry's leading manufacturers, and there are educational seminars, workshops and labs taught with a focus on technology, trends and the best practices in the country.

June

David Labuskes, Executive Director
Jason McGraw, Sr. VP Expositions

960 Independent Education Consultants Association Conference
3251 Old Lee Highway
Suite 510
Fairfax, VA 22030-1504
703-591-4850
800-888-4322
Fax: 703-591-4860
E-mail: info@IECAonline.com
http://www.IECAonline.com
Attended by consultants, school, college and program admissions officers, administrators and staff and related service companies. Workshops and discussions led by leaders in their fields including specialists in educational trends, college admissions and boarding school issues, adolescent development, learning differences and emotional disorders and treatments.

Spring & Fall
400 booths with 800 attendees

Mark H Sklarow, Executive Director
Rachel King, Conference Manager

961 International Performance Improvement Conference
International Society for Performance
PO Box 13035
Silver Spring, MD 20910
301-587-8570
Fax: 301-587-8573
E-mail: info@ispi.org
http://www.ispi.org
Provides educational opportunities with sessions in multiple formats across multiple tracks, keynote presentations, networking opportunities with other performance minded professionals across the spectrum of performance improvement disciplines.

April
60 booths with 1500 attendees

Ellen Kaplan, Conference Manager

962 Iteachk
Staff Development for Educators
10 Sharon Road
PO Box 577
Peterborough, NH 03458
603-924-9621
800-462-1478
Fax: 800-337-9929
http://www.sde.com
Explore new technology engaging teachers and students, new games and tools for students, meet and learn from nation's top kindergarten experts, use strategies right away and network with others.

Jim Grant, Executive Director/Founder
Terra Tarango, President

963 Journalism Education Association
Kansas State University
103 Kedzie Hall
Manhattan, KS 66506-1505
785-532-5532
866-532-5532
Fax: 785-532-5563
E-mail: lindarp@ksu.edu
http://www.jea.org/
An organization of about 2,300 journalism teachers and advisers, offers two national teacher-student conventions a year, quarterly newsletter and magazines, bookstore and national certification program. This association serves as a leader in scholastic press freedom and media curriculum.

Mark Newton, President
Sarah Nichols, Vice President

964 Lutheran Education Association National Administrators Conference
Lutheran Education Association
7400 Augusta Street
River Forest, IL 60305
708-209-3343
Fax: 708-209-3458
E-mail: lea@lea.org
http://www.lea.org
Presentations devoted to positive partnerships—parish partnerships, public/government, community, international— that will serve will in the future.

Cheryl Ehlers, Conference Chair
Jonathan C Laabs, Executive Director

965 MEMSPA Annual State Conference
Michigan Elementary & Middle School Principals Association
1980 N. College Road
Mason, MI 48854
517-694-8955
800-227-0824
Fax: 517-694-8945

E-mail: bob@memspa.org
http://www.memspa.org
Professional association for elementary & middle level principals.

Annual/December

Paul Liabenow, Executive Director
Rob Kauffman, President

966 Modern Language Association Annual Conference
26 Broadway
3rd Floor
New York, NY 10004-1789
646-576-5000
Fax: 646-458-0030
E-mail: convention@mla.org
http://www.mla.org
Opportunity for memberes to share scholarly findings and teaching experience and discuss trends in the academy.

January
2000+ attendees

Rosemary G. Feal, Executive Director

967 Music Teachers Association National Conference
Music Teachers National Association
441 Vine Street
Suite 3100
Cincinnati, OH 45202-3004
513-421-1420
888-512-5278
Fax: 513-421-2503
E-mail: mtnanet@mtna.org
http://www.mtna.org
Supports and supplies music teachers with information on development and training.

March
160 booths with 2000 attendees

Brian Shepard, Deputy Executive Director
Gary L. Ingle, Executive Director/CEO

968 NAAEE Annual Conference
North American Assoc for Environmental Education
2000 P Street NW
Suite 540
Washington, DC 20036
202-419-0412
Fax: 212-419-0415
E-mail: info@naaee.net
http://www.naaee.net
Promotes environmental education in the classroom and public, shares the latest research and information.

October
1000+ attendees

Judy Braus, Executive Director
Lori Mann, Conference Manager

969 NAFSA: National Association of International Educators
1307 New York Ave. NW
8th Floor
Washington, DC 20005-4701
202-737-3699
800-836-4994
Fax: 202-737-3657
E-mail: inbox@nafsa.org
http://www. nafsa.org
Annual meeting of professionals in the field of international education, for training workshops, educational sessions, networking opportunities and special events.

May
150 booths with 8,500 attendees

Marlene M. Johnson, Executive Director/CEO
Chris Seamens, Conference Program, Coord.

970 NASDSE National Conference
National Association of State Directors of
Special
Education
225 Reinekers Lane, Suite 420
Alexandria, VA 22314
703-519-3800
Fax: 703-519-3808
E-mail: nasdse@nasdse.org
http://www.nasdse.org
Multiple presentations, Annual business
meeting for state directors and networking
opportunities.

Colleen Riley, President
Bill East, Executive Director

971 NASPA Annual Conference
NASPA-Student Affairs Administrators in
Higher
Education
111 K Street NE, 10th Floor
Washington, DC 20002
202-265-7500
Fax: 202-898-5737
E-mail: office@naspa.org
http://www.naspa.org
Exchange ideas with peers, earn continuing
education credits, build new partnerships
with vendors, gain tools and ideas and remain
current on issues.
Annual/March
5000 attendees

Kevin Kruger, President
Arlene Kidwell, Sr. Director of Meetings

972 NELA Annual Conference
New England Library Association
55 North Main Street
Unit 49
Belchertown, MA 01007
413-813-5254
Fax: 603-654-3526
E-mail: rscheier@gmail.com
http://www.nelib.org
Bringing together librarians from New England in a forum to educate and network about
moving libraries into the 21st century.
600 attendees

Robert Scheier, Association Administrator
Mary Ann Rupert, Conference Manager

973 NJLA Spring Conference
New Jersey Library Association
PO Box 1534
Trenton, NJ 08607
609-394-8032
Fax: 609-394-8164
E-mail: ptumulty@njla.org
http://www.njla.org
1139 attendees

Patricia A Tumulty, Executive Director
Susan Rice, Office Manager

974 NSTA Annual Conference
National Science Teachers Association
1840 Wilson Boulevard
Arlington, VA 22201-3000
703-243-7100
888-400-6782
Fax: 703-243-7177
E-mail: conferences@nsta.org
http://www.nsta.org
To promote excellence and innovation in science teaching and learning for all. Discover
strategies for improving science teaching and
learning, engage in professional discussions,
receive the latest information of science edu-

cation and network with colleagues from
across the country and the globe.
April
Dr. Karen L. Ostlund, President
Dr. Gerald F. Wheeler, Interim Executive
Director

**975 National Academy Foundation
NEXT**
National Academy Foundation
218 West 40th Street
5th Floor
New York, NY 10018
212-635-2400
Fax: 212-635-2409
http://www.naf.org
Formerly the Institute for Staff Development,
NEXT is a professional learning experience
that will ignite innovation and spread effective practices across
July
JD Hoye, President
David Moore, Sr. VP Programs

**976 National Alliance of Black School
Educators Conference**
310 Pennsylvania Avenue SE
Washington, DC 20003-3819
202-608-6310
800-221-2654
Fax: 202-608-6319
E-mail: info@nabse.org
http://www.nabse.org
Teachers, principals, specialists, superintendents, school board members and higher education personnel. Educational workshops,
plenary sessions, informative presentations,
public forums, networking and fellowship.
November
300 booths with 6,000 attendees

Quentin R Lawson, Executive Director
Ed Potillo, Conference Director

**977 National Art Education Association
Annual Convention**
National Art Education Association
1806 Robert Fulton Drive
Suite 300
Reston, VA 20191-1590
703-860-8000
Fax: 703-860-2960
E-mail: info@arteducators.org
http://www.arteducators.org
Provides substantive professional development services that include the advancement
of knowledge in all sessions, events and activities for the purpose of improving visual
arts instruction in American schools.
March
171 booths with 5,000 attendees

Kathy Duse, Conference Manager
Deborah B. Reeve, Executive Director

**978 National Association for Bilingual
Education**
8701 Georgia Avenue
Suite 700
Silver Spring, MD 20910-4018
240-450-3700
Fax: 240-450-3799
E-mail: nabe@nabe.org
http://www.nabe.org
Contains publishers and Fortune 500 companies displaying educational materials and
multi-media products. Educational materials, products and services for use in linguisti-

cally and culturally diverse learning
environments.
March
350 booths with 2,000+ attendees

Dr. Santiago Wood, Executive Director
Nilda Aguirre, Conference Coordinator

**979 National Association for College
Admission Counseling Conference**
Nat'l Association for College Admission
Counseling
1050 N Highland Street
Suite 400
Arlington, VA 22201-2818
703-836-2222
800-822-6285
Fax: 703-243-9375
E-mail: info@nacacnet.org
http://www.nacacnet.org
Membership association offering information to counselors and guidance professionals working in the college admissions office.
September
142 booths with 4,000 attendees

Joyce E. Smith, CEO
Bethany Blue Chirico, Director of
Conference/Mtgs

**980 National Association for Girls and
Women in Sports Yearly Conference**
1900 Association Drive
Reston, VA 20191-1598
703-476-3543
800-213-7193
Fax: 703-476-4566
E-mail: nagws@aahperd.org
http://www.aahperd.org/nagws
An association providing information for
girls and women in sports.
March/April
280 booths with 6,000 attendees

Lynda Ransdell, President
Sandra K. Sims, VP of
Programs/Convention

**981 National Association for
Multicultural Education**
NAME National Office
2100 M Street
Suite 170-245
Washington, DC 20037
202-628-6263
Fax: 202-628-6264
E-mail: name@nameorg.org
http://www.nameorg.org
Opportunity to build networks, confront
challenges and renews sense of possibility
and hope in making schools and societies a
better place through community advocacy
and multicultural education.

Bette Tate Beaver, Executive Director

**982 National Association of Biology
Teachers Conference**
1313 Dolley Madison Blvd.
Suite 402
McLean, VA 22101
703-264-9696
888-501-6228
Fax: 703-790-2672
E-mail: office@nabt.org
http://www.nabt.org
Speakers, hands-on workshops, informative
sessions teaching biology in the 21st century.
November
140 booths with 1,700 attendees

Jaclyn Reeves-Pepin, Executive Director
Matthew D. Wells, Conference Committee

983 National Association of Elementary School Principals Conference
1615 Duke Street
Alexandria, VA 22314-3406
703-684-3345
800-386-2377
Fax: 703-549-5568
E-mail: naesp@naesp.org
http://www.naesp.org
Products and services in the educational market shopping area. Industry leaders offer solutions on areas such as teacher recruitment and retention, integration of the new common core standards, leading school change and improving student learning and running the best possible building- from the cafeteria to the parking lot.

April
300 booths

Gail Connelly, Executive Director
Deborah Young, Director, Convention/Mtgs.

984 National Association of Independent Schools Conference
National Association of Independent Schools
1129 20th Street NW
Suite 800
Washington, DC 20036-3425
202-973-9700
Fax: 888-316-3862
E-mail: annualconference@nais.org
http://www.nais.org
New ways to cultivate leadership in independent schools- for administrators, faculty and students- with workshops and speakers.

February/March
166 booths with 4000 attendees

Patrick Bassett, President
Amy Ahart, Director Annual Conference

985 National Association of Private Schools for Exceptional Children Conference
1522 K Street NW
Suite 1032
Washington, DC 20005-1211
202-408-3338
Fax: 202-408-3340
E-mail: napsec@aol.com
http://www.napsec.com
This in an annual conference that is held for administrators/directors/principals and private school educators.

January
300 attendees and 8 exhibits

Sherry L. Kolbe, Executive Director/CEO

986 National Association of School Psychologists Annual Convention
4340 EW Highway
Suite 402
Bethesda, MD 20814
301-657-0270
866-331-6277
Fax: 301-657-0275
E-mail: convention@naspweb.org
http://www.nasponline.org
Gathering of school psychologists and related professionals, offering workshops, seminars, symposia, papers, presentations and exhibits on topics from solutions for individual children to answers to your most difficult professional challenges and find

ways to be a more efficient and effective practitioner.

April
100 booths with 4000 attendees

Susan Gorin, Executive Director
Marcia Harvey, Manager, Conventions

987 National Association of State Directors of Teacher Education and Certification Conference
1629 K Street NW
Suite 300
Washington, DC 20006
202-204-2208
Fax: 202-204-2210
E-mail: nasdtec@attbi.com
NASDTEC is the National Association of State Directors of Teacher Education and Certification. It is the organization that represents professional standards boards and commissions and state departments of education in all 50 states.

June

Phillip S. Rogers, Executive Director

988 National Association of Student Financial Aid Administrators
1101 Connecticut Avenue NW
Suite 1100
Washington, DC 20036-4303
202-785-0453
Fax: 202-785-1487
http://www.nasfaa.org
Provides valuable, up-to-date information on the student aid programs from financial aid veterans. Unique training and professional development opportunity that will equip student aid professionals with the tools to better serve students and families. Also receive individual guidance from the U.S. Department of Education and learn about product and software innovations.

July
July
105 booths with 3,000 attendees

Barbara Kay Gordon, Conference Contact
Justin Draeger, President

989 National Black Child Development Institute Annual Conference
1313 L Street NW
Suite 110
Washington, DC 20005-4110
202-833-2220
800-556-2234
Fax: 202-833-8222
E-mail: moreinfo@ndcdi.orh
http://www.nbcdi.org
Educators and professionals in early care and education; elementary and secondary education and administration; child welfare and youth development; research; and local, state and federal policy convene to gain knowledge and acquire skills needed to ensure a quality future for all children and youth.

October

Felicia DeHaney, Pd.D, President/CEO
Keami Harris, Director of Programs

990 National Coalition for Aviation and Space Education
Omni Rosen Hotel
Orlando, FL
334-953-5095
E-mail: mail@ncase.info
http://www.ncase.info
Provides educators with the tools that make classroom learning fun.

April

991 National Coalition of Alternative Community Schools
PO Box 1451
Ann Arbor, MI 48106
505-474-4312
888-771-9171
E-mail: office@ncacs.org
http://www.ncacs.org
Students, parents and teachers come together to learn how to teach and learn from one another. Workshops, networking

April

Kristin Lamoureux, Contact

992 National Coalition of ESEA Title 1 Parents
310 Pennsylvania Ave. SE
3rd Floor
Washington, DC 20003
205-923-7955
Fax: 205-925-5403
E-mail: ethomas@nctic1p.org
http://www.nctic1p.org
Annual In-Service Professional Development conference on current education laws, legislation and educational issues with the assistance of the Department of Education.

October

Ernestine Thomas, President

993 National Conference on Student Services
Magna Publications
2718 Dryden Drive
Madison, WI 53704
608-246-3590
800-206-4805
Fax: 608-246-3597
E-mail: carriej@magnapubs.com
http://www.magnapubs.com
Build strong foundation as a student leader, secure leadership skills and experience a possibly life-changing event.

April
35 booths with 500 attendees

Susan Liimata, Conference Manager
Catherine Stover, Managing Editor

994 National Council of Higher Education
National Education Association (NEA)
1201 16th Street NW
Washington, DC 20036-3290
202-833-4000
Fax: 202-822-7974
E-mail: nche@nea.org
http://www.nea.org
Assessing a 20 year journey of the academy.

February, March
400 attendees

Lily Eskelsen Garc¡a, President
Becky Pringle, Vice President

995 National Council on Alcoholism & Drug Abuse
9355 Olive Boulevard
St. Louis, MO 63132
314-962-3456
Fax: 314-968-7394
E-mail: info@ncada-stl.org
http://www.ncada-stl.org
A not-for-profit community health agency serving the metropolitan St. Louis area, provides educational materials on substance abuse and addiction, information and referral services, prevention and intervention.

Jim Murphy, President
Jenny Armbruster, Director, Community Services

96 National Dropout Prevention Center/Network Conference
205 Martin Street
Clemson, SC 29631-1555
864-656-2599
800-443-6392
Fax: 864-656-0136
E-mail: ndpc@clemson.edu
http://www.dropoutprevention.com
Concentrating on programs and services for educators and counselors who deal with at-risk students.

October
100 booths with 1000 attendees

Dr. Sandy Addis, Interim Director
Dr. Loujeania Williams Bost, Director

97 National Education Association-Retired
National Education Association (NEA)
1201 16th Street NW
Washington, DC 20036-3290
202-833-4000
Fax: 202-822-7974
http://www.nea.org/retired
Serves as a resource in the maintenance of quality public education, promotes improved services and legislation for seniors, provides training for members and serves as a vehicle for local input to the National Education Association.

150 attendees

Lily Eskelsen García, President
Becky Pringle, Vice President

98 National Guild of Community Arts Education
520 8th Avenue
Suite 302, 3rd Floor
New York, NY 10018
212-268-3337
Fax: 212-268-3995
E-mail: info@natguild.org
http://www.nationalguild.org
The National Guild of Community Schools of the Arts fosters and promotes the creation and growth of high-quality arts education in communities across the country. The Guild provides community arts organizations with multiple levels of support, including training, advocacy, information resources, and high-profile leadership in arts education.

November
15 booths with 300 attendees and 15 exhibits

Jonathan Herman, Executive Director
Heather Ikemire, Director

99 National Head Start Association Annual Conference
1651 Prince Street
Alexandria, VA 22314-2818
703-739-0875
866-677-8724
Fax: 703-739-0878
http://www.nhsa.org
Seeks to advance program development, policy and promote training of the Head Start program professionals.

May

Vanessa Rich, Chairman
Alvin Jones, Vice-Chairperson

000 National In-Service Conference
National Association for Music Education (NAFME)
1806 Robert Fulton Drive
Reston, VA 20191-4348
703-860-4000
800-336-3768
Fax: 703-860-1531
http://www.musiced.nafme.org

Opportunities to network with peers from across the United States, professional development sessions giving tools and techniques for use in classrooms, receptions and keynote speakers.

April

Michael A. Butera, Executive Director/CEO

1001 National Institute for School and Workplace Safety Conference
160 International Parkway
Suite 250
Heathrow, FL 32746
407-804-8310
Fax: 407-804-8306
http://www.nisws.com/
Believes that every school and workplace must implement school and workplace safety standards.

April
80 attendees

Wolfgang Halbig, CEO/Manager

1002 National Parent-Teacher Association Annual Convention & Exhibition
501 South College Street
Charlotte, NC 28202
703-518-1234
E-mail: nptameetings@pta.org
http://www.pta.org
Addresses parent-teacher involvement in education. Includes lectures, workshops and seminars for parents and professionals.

June

1003 National Reading Styles Institute Conference
PO Box 737
Syosset, NY 11791-3933
512-224-4555
800-331-3117
Fax: 516-921-5591
E-mail: readingstyle@nrsi.com
http://www.nrsi.com
This conference addresses reading instruction and the problems of illiteracy.

July

Juliet Carbo, Conference Contact

1004 National Rural Education Annual Convention
National Rural Education Association
230 Education
Colorado State University
Fort Collins, CO 80523-0001
970-491-1101
Fax: 970-491-1317
http://www.nrea.net
Exchanges ideas, practices and better ways to enhance rural educational school systems.

October
30 booths with 400 attendees

Joseph T Newlin, PhD, Conference Contact

1005 National Rural Education Association Annual Convention
National Rural Education Association
820 Van Vleet Oval
Room 227
Norman, OK 73019
Fax: 405-325-7959
E-mail: bmooney@ou.edu
http://www.nrea.net
The NREA will be the leading national organization providing services which enhance

educational opportunities for rural schools and their communities.

October
35 booths with 400 attendees

Bob Mooneyham, Executive Director

1006 National School Boards Annual Conference
1680 Duke Street
Alexandria, VA 22314-3493
703-838-6722
Fax: 703-683-7590
E-mail: info@nsba.org
http://www.nsba.org
The nation's largest policy and training conference for local education officials on national and federal issues affecting public schools in the U.S.

March
7,000 attendees and 300 exhibits

Sandra Folks, Conferences Manager
Karen Miller, Director, Exhibits

1007 National School Conference Institute
11202 N 24th Street
Suite 103
Phoenix, AZ 85029
602-371-8655
888-399-8745
Fax: 602-371-8790
http://www.nscinet.com
Our purpose is to increase every student's opportunity for academic success.

1008 National Society for Experiential Education Conference
National Society for Experiential Education
19 Mantua Road
Mt. Royal, NJ 08061
856-423-3427
Fax: 856-423-3420
E-mail: nsee@talley.com
http://www.nsee.org
To foster the effective use of experience as an integral part of education, in order to empower learners and promote the common good.

October
600-700 attendees

Jim Colbert, President
Gregg Lorenz, Vice President

1009 National Student Assistance Conference
1270 Rakin Drive
Suite F
Troy, MI 48033-2843
800-453-7733
Fax: 800-499-5718
Learn to maintain and improve safe, drug free schools, student assistance programs. Develop skills to implement the Principles of Effectiveness. Choose from workshops and skill building sessions.

1010 National Women's History Project Annual Conference
730 Second Street #469
PO Box 469
Santa Rosa, CA 95402
707-636-2888
Fax: 707-636-2909
E-mail: nwhp1980@gmail.com
http://www.nwhp.org

Posters, reference books, curriculum materials and biographies of American women in all subjects for grades K-12.

July
72 attendees

Molly Murphy MacGregor, Executive Director/ Chair
Shona Rocco, Financial Manager

1011 Natural Learning Institute Seminar

54385 Pine Crest Ave
Idyllwild, CA 92549
951-691-0139
Fax: 951-659-0242
http://www.naturallearninginstitute.org

Linda Hargan, President

1012 Neag Center for Gifted Education and Talent Development Conference

University of Connecticut
2131 Hillside Road
Unit 3007
Storrs, CT 06269-3007
860-486-4826
Fax: 860-486-2900
http://www.gifted.uconn.edu
Provides educators with research based practical strategies for engagement and enrichment learning for all students, as well as meeting the needs of gifted and talented students.

Annual

JoAnn Easton, Confratute

1013 New Learning Technologies

Society for Applied Learning Technology
50 Culpeper Street
Warrenton, VA 20186
540-347-0055
800-457-6812
Fax: 540-349-3169
E-mail: info@lti.org
http://www.salt.org
To provide a comprehensive overview of the latest in research, design, and development in order to furnish attendees information on systems that are applicable to their organizations.

1014 New Learning Technologies Conference

Society for Applied Learning Technology
50 Culpeper Street
Warrenton, VA 20186
540-347-0055
800-457-6812
Fax: 540-349-3169
E-mail: info@lti.org
http://www.salt.org
For over 30 years the Society has sponsored conferences which are educational in nature and bring together senior professionals from government, industry, academia and the military to present the latest developments in the field of learning and training technologies.

August
20 booths with 400 attendees

Raymond G Fox, President

1015 North American Montessori Teachers' Association

13693 Butternnut Road
Burton, OH 44021
440-834-4011
Fax: 440-834-4016
E-mail: staff@montessori-namta.org
http://www.montessori-namta.org/

Professional organization for Montessori teachers and administrators. Services include The NAMTA Journal and other publications, videos and slide shows. Conferences in January and March.

David J Kahn, Executive Director

1016 Parents as Teachers National Center Conference

2228 Ball Drive
Saint Louis, MO 63146
314-432-4330
Fax: 314-432-8963
E-mail: patnc@patnc.org
http://www.patnc.org
An international early childhood parent education and family support program designed to enhance child development and school achievement through parent education accessible to all families. Serves families throughout pregnancy and until their child enters kindergarten, usually age 5.

April-May
40 booths with 1400+ attendees

Susan S Stepleton, President/CEO
Cheryl Dyle-Palmer, Director Operations

1017 Retention in Education Today for All Indigenous Nations

ConferencePROS
University of Oklahoma
1639 Cross Center Drive, Suite 101
Norman, OK 73072
405-325-3760
800-203-5494
Fax: 405-325-7075
E-mail: lasmith@ou.edu
http://www.conferencepros.com
National conference designed to discuss and share retention strategies for indigenous students.

Laurie Smith, Manager/ Projects Director
Richard Feinberg, Media Specialist Manager

1018 SERVE Conference

SERVE
5900 Summit Avenue, #201
Browns Summit, NC 27214
336-315-7400
800-755-3277
Fax: 336-315-7457
E-mail: jsanders@serve.org
http://www.serve.org
The Regional Educational Laboratories are educational research and development organizations supported by contracts with the US Education Department, National Institute for Education Sciences. Specialty area: Expanded Learning Opportunities.

October-November

Elliott Wolf, Director of Operations
Greg LeePow, Technical Systems Director

1019 STEMtech Conference

League for Innovation in the Community College
4505 East Chandler Boulevard
Suite 250
Phoenix, AZ 85048
480-705-8200
Fax: 480-705-8201
E-mail: harris@league.org
http://www.league.org
Emphasizes student success in science, technology, engineering and mathematices (STEM) at all levels.

October
3,000 attendees

Robin Piccilliri, Meeting Planner

1020 School Equipment Show

830 Colesville Road
Suite 250
Silver Spring, MD 20910-3297
301-495-0240
800-395-5550
Fax: 301-495-3330
E-mail: customerservice@nnsea.org
http://www.nnsea.org
Annual show featuring exhibits from manufacturers of school equipment such as bleachers, classroom furniture, lockers, playground and athletic equipment, computer hardware, software, etc.

February

Elizabeth Bradley, Conference Contact

1021 Sexual Assault and Harassment on Campus Conference

c/o Sexual Conference
PO Box 1338
Holmes Beach, FL 34218-1338
800-537-4903
http://www.ed.mtu.edu
Topics include gender based hate crime, sexual assault investigators, generational legacy of rape, innovations in the military, sexual harassment in K-12, updates on date-rape drugs and many more. Hosted by the Hyatt Orlando Hotel in Kissimmee, Florida.

Karen McLaughlin, Conference Co-Chair
Alan McEvoy, Conference Co-Chair

1022 Society for Research in Child Development Conference

2950 S. State St.
Suite 401
Ann Arbor, MI 48104
734-926-0600
Fax: 734-926-0601
E-mail: communications@srcd.org
http://www.srcd.org
Working to further research in the area of child development and education.

March/April
40 booths

Barbara Kahn, Conference Contact

1023 Teacher Link: An Interactive National Teleconference

Center for the Study of Small/Rural Schools
555 E Constitution Street
Room 138
Norman, OK 73072-7820
405-325-1450
Fax: 405-325-7075
E-mail: jcsimmons@ou.edu
http://cssrs.ou.edu
Prevention Series

Spring
5 booths with 100 attendees

Jan C Simmons, Program Director

1024 Teachers of English to Speakers of Other Languages Convention and Exhibit

1925 Ballenger Avenue
Suite 550
Alexandria, VA 22314-6820
703-836-0774
888-547-3369
Fax: 703-836-6447
E-mail: info@tesol.org
http://www.tesol.org
Leading worldwide professional development opportunity. Simulating program of presentations sponsored by nineteen interest sections, a half-dozen caucus groups and TESOL's advocacy

division as well as sessions invited especially for their relevance to our work and our students.

March
245 booths with 8000 attendees

Rita Gainer, Executive Assistant
Rosa Aronson, Executive Director

025 Teaching for Intelligence Conference

SkyLight
2626 S Clearbrook Drive
Arlington Heights, IL 60005
847-290-6600
800-348-4474
Fax: 877-260-2530
E-mail: info@irisskylight.com
http://www.irisskylight.com
Focuses on student achievement, brain-based learning and multiple intelligences.

April

026 Technology & Learning Schooltech Exposition & Conference

212-615-6030
http://www.SchoolTechExpo.com
Over 150 targeted sessions specifically designed for all education professionals: technology directors, teachers, principals, superintendents and district administrators.

027 Technology Student Conference

Technology Student Association
1914 Association Drive
Reston, VA 20191-1538
703-860-9000
Fax: 703-758-4852
http://www.tsawww.org
Devoted to the needs of technology education students and supported by educators, parents, and business leaders who believe in the need for a technologically literate society.

June
2,500 attendees

Rosanne White, Conference Manager

028 Technology in 21st Century Schools

National Conference Institute
PO Box 37527
Phoenix, AZ 85069-7527
602-371-8655
Fax: 602-371-8790
http://www.nscinet.com
Conference will cover managing the Internet, literacy skills, Web Site designs, short and long term planning, creating curriculum, and staff development. Being held at the Boston Park Plaza Hotel in Boston, Massachusetts.

July

Alan November

029 Technology, Reading & Learning Difficulties Conference

International Reading Association
19 Calvert Court
Piedmont, CA 94611
510-594-1249
888-594-1249
Fax: 510-594-1838
http://www.trld.com
Focuses on ways to use technology for reading, learning difficulties, staff development, adult literacy, and more.

January

030 Training of Trainers Seminar

Active Parenting Publishers
1220 Kennestone Circle
Suite 130
Marietta, GA 30066-6022
770-429-0565
800-825-0060
Fax: 770-429-0334
E-mail: cservice@activeparenting.com
http://www.activeparenting.com
Delivers quality education programs for parents, children and teachers to schools, hospitals, social services organizations, churches and the corporate market.

Michael H. Popkin, Ph.D., Founder/President
Micole Mason, Training Coordinator

1031 U.S. Conference on Adult Literacy (USCAL)

Proliteracy
104 Marcellus Street
Syracuse, NY 13204
315-422-9121
888-528-2224
Fax: 315-422-6369
E-mail: infor@proliteracy.org
http://www.proliteracy.org
Bring together adult literacy advocates and educators to share new ideas, learn from leading thinkers and inspire one another.

November
50 booths with 1,000 attendees

Robyn Smith, Conference/Events Coord.
David Harvey, President

1032 USC Summer Superintendents' Conference

University of Southern California, School of Ed.
Waite Philips Hall, Room 901
Los Angeles, CA 90089-0031
213-740-2182
Fax: 213-749-2707
E-mail: lpicus@bcf.usc.edu
http://www.usc.edu/dept/CREF/SSC.html
A select group of educational leaders nationwide engaged in reform practices offer discussions with nationally renowned speakers; tour innovative schools; and network with colleagues from the United States, Great Britain and Australia.

Lawrence O Picus, Conference Director
Carolyn Bryant, Conference Coordinator

Northeast

1033 Clonlara School Annual Conference Home Educators

Clonlara Home Based Education Programs
1289 Jewett Street
Ann Arbor, MI 48104-6201
734-769-4511
Fax: 734-769-9629
E-mail: info@clonlara.org
http://www.clonlara.org
Clonlara School is committed to illuminating educational rights and freedoms through our actions and deep dedication to human rights and dignity.

June
300 attendees

Terri Wheeler, Associate Director

1034 Connecticut Library Association

234 Court St.
Middletown, CT 06457
860-346-2444
Fax: 860-344-9199
E-mail: cla@ctlibrarians.org
http://ctlibraryassociation.org/index.php?by passCookie=1

Holds a conference in April and publishes a journal.

April
1000 attendees and 100 exhibits

Dawn La Valle, President
Beth A Crowley, VP/ President Elect

1035 Hoosier Science Teachers Association Annual Meeting

5007 W 14th Street
Indianapolis, IN 46224-6503
317-244-7238
Fax: 317-486-4838
Papers, workshops, demonstrations and presentations in each area of science.

February
78 booths

Edward Frazer, Conference Contact

1036 Illinois Library Association Conference

Illinois Library Association
33 W Grand Avenue
Suite 301
Chicago, IL 60654-6799
312-644-1896
Fax: 312-644-1899
E-mail: ila@ila.org
http://www.ila.org
More than 70 program sessions, exploring nearly every facet of library services, from building projects and professional recruitment to storytelling and the latest revisions of AACR2.

September
2,400+ attendees

Cyndi Robinson, Conference Manager
Bob Doyle, Executive Director

1037 Illinois Vocational Association Conference

230 Broadway
Suite 150
Springfield, IL 62701-1138
217-585-9430
Fax: 217-544-0208
E-mail: iva@eosinc.com
Equipment and supplies, publications, teaching aids, computers and food services.

February
75 booths with 600 attendees

Karen Riddle, Conference Contact

1038 National Association of Student Financial Aid Administrators

1101 Connecticut Avenue NW
Suite 1100
Washington, DC 20036-4303
202-785-0453
Fax: 202-785-1487
http://www.nasfaa.org
Exists to promote the professional preparation, effectiveness, and mutual support of persons involved in student financial aid administration.

May
40 booths

Justin Draeger, President
Eileen O'Leary, Chair

1039 New Jersey School Boards Association Annual Meeting

413 W State Street
PO Box 909
Trenton, NJ 08605-0909
609-695-7600
888-886-5722
Fax: 609-695-0413
http://www.njsba.org

School/office supplies, furniture, equipment, counseling services and more.

October
630 booths with 9,000 attendees

Wendy L. Wilson, Conference Contact

1040 New York State Council of Student Superintendents Forum

111 Washington Avenue
Suite 104
Albany, NY 12210-2210
518-449-1063
Fax: 518-426-2229
Offers educational products and related services.

February
12 booths

Dr. Claire Brown, Conference Contact

1041 Northeast Regional Christian Schools International Association

P.O. Box 65130
Colorado Springs, CO 80962-5130
717-285-3022
800-367-0798
Fax: 719-531-0716
E-mail: customerservices@acsi.org
http://www.acsi.org
40 booths.

November

Dr. Dan Egeler, President

1042 Ohio Library Council Trade Show

35 E Gay Street
Suite 305
Columbus, OH 43215-3138
614-221-9057
Fax: 614-221-6234
Exhibits will offer products and services for library administrators and professionals.

May

Lori Hensley, Exhibits Manager

1043 Ohio School Boards Association Capital Conference & Trade Show

Greater Columbus Convention Center
400 N. High St.
Columbus, OH 43215
614-891-6466
http://conference.ohioschoolboards.org
Provides school officials from Ohio an opportunity to gain information about products, equipment, materials and services.

November
425 booths

Richard Lewis, Conference Contact

1044 Satellites and Education Conference

189 Schmucker Science Center
W Chester University
West Chester, PA 19383
610-436-1000
Fax: 610-436-2790
http://www.sated.org/eceos
The Satellite Educators Association was established in 1988 as a professional society to promote the innovative use of satellite technology in education and disseminate information nationally to all members.

March
15 booths with 200 attendees

Nancy McIntyre, Director

1045 UNI Overseas Recruiting Fair

University of Northern Iowa Career Services
102 Gilchrist Hall
Cedar Falls, IA 50614-0390
319-273-2083
Fax: 319-273-6998
E-mail: overseas.placement@uni.edu
http://www.uni.edu/placement/overseas
About 160 recruiters from 120 schools in 80 countries recruit at this fair for certified K-12 educators.

February

Tracy Roling, Coordinator

1046 Wisconsin Vocational Association Conference

44 E Mifflin Street
Suite 104
Madison, WI 53703-2800
608-283-2595
Fax: 608-283-2589
Trade and industry vendor equipment and book publishers.

April
50 booths

Linda Stemper, Conference Contact

Northwest

1047 Montana High School Association Conference

1 S Dakota Street
Helena, MT 59601-5111
406-442-6010
School athletic merchandise.

January
15 booths

Dan Freund, Conference Contact

1048 Nebraska School Boards Association Annual Conference

140 S 16th Street
Lincoln, NE 68508-1805
402-475-4951
Fax: 402-475-4961
60 booths exhibiting products and services directed at the public school market.

November
60 booths

Burma Kroger, Conference Contact

1049 North Dakota Vocational Educational Planning Conference

State Capitol
600 East Boulevard Avenue, Dept. 270
Bismarck, ND 58505-610
701-328-3180
Fax: 701-328-1255
E-mail: cte@nd.gov
http://www.nd.gov/cte/

August
30 booths

Ernest Breznay, Conference Contact

1050 Pacific Northwest Library Association

Boise Public Library
715 Capitol Boulevard
Boise, ID 83702
208-384-4026
Fax: 208-384-4156
E-mail: sprice@pobox.ci.boise.id.us
http://www.pnla.org

Oldest regional library association in the United States and the only binational association in North America.

Honore Bray, President
Gwendolyn Haley, First VP/President-Elect

1051 WA-ACTE Career and Technical Exhibition for Career and Technical Education

Washington Association for Career & Tech Education
PO Box 315
Olympia, WA 98507-0315
360-786-9286
Fax: 360-357-1491
E-mail: wa-acte@wa-acte.org
http://www.wa-acte.org

August
40 booths with 1,000 attendees

Tim Knue, Executive Director
Tess Alviso, Executive Assistant

Southeast

1052 Association for Continuing Higher Education Conference

Trident Technical College
PO Box 118067
Charleston, SC 29423-8067
843-722-5546
Fax: 843-574-6470
15 tabletops.

October

Dr. Wayne Whelan, Executive VP

1053 Center for Play Therapy Summer Institute

425 S. Welch St., Complex 2
Denton, TX 76203
940-565-3864
Fax: 940-565-4461
E-mail: cpt@unt.edu
http://www.centerforplaytherapy.com
Encourage the unique development and emotional growth of children through the process of play therapy, a dynamic interpersonal relationship between a child and a therapist trained in play therapy procedures. The therapist provides the child with selected play materials and facilitates a safe relationship to express feelings, thoughts, experiences and behaviors through play, the child's natural medium of communication.

July
500 attendees

Garry Landreth PhD, Founder/ Director Emeritus
Sue Bratton, Director

1054 Missouri Library Association Conference

1306 Business 63 S
Suite B
Columbia, MO 65201
573-449-4627
Fax: 573-449-4655
E-mail: jmccartn@mail.more.net
http://molib.org/conference
The mission of the Missouri Library Network Corporation (MLNC) is to organize and deliver to its member libraries and other contracting entities OCLC-based information services, related electronic services and content, and training in the management and use of information.

October
75 booths with 400 attendees

Dan Brower, Conference coordinator
Kelly Fann, Conference coordinator

055 National Youth-At-Risk Conference
Georgia Southern University
1332 Southern Drive
Statesboro, GA 30458
912-478-4636
Fax: 912-681-0306
http://academics.georgiasouthern.edu
Stresses education and development for professionals working with at-risk students.

February

Sybil Fickle, Conference Contact

056 Technology and Learning Conference
National School Boards Association
1680 Duke Street
Alexandria, VA 22314
703-838-6722
Fax: 703-683-7590
E-mail: info@nsba.org
http://www.nsba.org
This conference offers programs, equipment, services, and ideas. It will be held at the Dallas Convention Center.

Southwest

057 CBEA State Conference
Westin Hotel
400 West Broadway
San Diego, CA 92109
925-295-1104
E-mail: cbeaquestions@cbeaonline.org
http://www.cbeaonline.org
Annual conference featuring computer workshops, information sessions, speakers, exhibitions, tours and more.

11/15-11/17 2013
200 attendees

Susan White, Office Manager

058 Children's Literature Festival
Department of Library Science
Sam Houston State University
PO Box 2236
Huntsville, TX 77341-2236
936-294-1614
Fax: 936-294-3780
This annual event is sponsored by the Department of Library Science at Sam Houston State University.

059 Colorado Library Association Conference
12011 Tejon Street
Suite 700
Westminister, CO 80234
303-463-6400
Fax: 303-458-0002
E-mail: cal@cal-webs.org
http://www.cal-webs.org

October
60 booths with 450 attendees

Kari May, President
Dinah Kress, Secretary

060 Phoenix Learning Resources Conference
12 W 31st Street
New York, NY 10001-4415
212-629-3887
800-221-1274
Fax: 212-629-5648
Supplemental and remedial reading and language arts programs for early childhood, K-12, and adult literacy programs.

Alexander Burke, President
John Rothermich, Executive VP

1061 Southwest Association College and University Housing Officers
624 W. University Drive
Suite 418
Denton, TX 76204
936-294-1812
Fax: 936-294-1920
E-mail: swacuho@gmail.com
http://www.swacuho.org
Products and services for college and university housing.

Febuary/March
45 booths

Diane Brittingham, President

1062 Texas Classroom Teachers Association Conference
PO Box 1489
Austin, TX 78767-1489
512-477-9415
Fax: 512-469-9527
http://www.tcta.org
Educational materials, fundraising and jewelry.

February
150 booths

Jan Lanfear, Conference Contact

1063 Texas Library Association Conference
3355 Bee Cave Road
Suite 401
Austin, TX 78746-6763
512-328-1518
800-580-2852
Fax: 512-328-8852
E-mail: pats@txla.org
http://www.txla.org
Established in 1902 to promote and improve library services in Texas.

March
750 booths with 6,000 attendees

Sharon Amastae, President
Patricia H. Smith, Executive Director

1064 Texas Vocational Home Economics Teachers Association Conference
3737 Executive Center Drive
Suite 210
Austin, TX 78731-1633
512-794-8370

July/August

Terry Green, Conference Contact

1065 Western History Association Annual Meeting
605 Gruening Bldg.
University of Alaska Fairbanks
Fairbanks, AK 99775
505-277-5234
Fax: 505-277-6023
E-mail: westernhistoryassociation@gmail.com
http://www.westernhistoryassociation.wildapricot.org
Exhibits by book sellers.

October
45 booths

Paul Hutton, Conference Contact

General

1066 Accuracy Temporary Services Incorporated
20674 Hall Road
Clinton Township, MI 48038
248-399-0220
800-297-2119
Fax: 586-465-9481
E-mail:
info@atsprojectsuccessworks.com
http://atsprojectsuccess.com
Educational consultant for public and private schools.

Howard Weaver, President

1067 Add Vantage Learning Incorporated
6805 Route 202
New Hope, PA 18938
800-230-2213
Fax: 215-579-8391
http://http://www.vantagelearning.com/
Management and educational consultant for the general public.

Jim Pepitone, Chairman

1068 Advance Infant Development Program
2232 D Street
Suite 203
LaVerne, CA 91750-5409
909-593-3935
Fax: 909-593-7969
Business and educational consultant for general trade.

Diane Hinds, President
Jeanine Coleman, Executive Director

1069 American International Schools
2203 Franklin Road SW
Roanoak, VA 24014-1109
852-233-3812
Fax: 852-233-5276
E-mail: asisadmin@ais.edu.hk
American International School is pledged to preparing students to contribute to an increasingly international and interdependent world. AIS strives to provide an atmosphere conducive to building interpersonal relationships and global awareness. AIS is committed to working closely with students and families to attain academic excellence and to inspire the growth of well-rounded individuals.

Andrew Hurst, President
Lewis C Smith Jr, Executive VP

1070 Area Cooperative Educational Services
350 State Street
North Haven, CT 06473
203-498-6800
Fax: 203-498-6817
E-mail: acesinfo@aces.org
http://www.aces.org
ACES is the regional educational service center for twenty-five school districts in south central Connecticut.

Erika Forte, Assistant Executive Director
Thomas M. Danehy Ed.D., Executive Director

1071 Aspira of Penna
2726 N 6th Street
Philadelphia, PA 19133-2714
215-229-1226
Educational consultant for educational institutions.

Oscar Cardona, President

1072 Association for Refining Cross-Cultured International
Japanese American Cultural Center
244 S San Pedro Street
Suite 505
Los Angeles, CA 90012
213-620-0696
Fax: 213-620-0930
E-mail: support@eryugaku.org
http://www.arcint.com
Educational consultants for international studies.

Chiey Nomura, Director

1073 Association of Christian Schools International
PO Box 69103
Colorado Springs, CO 80962-3509
719-528-6906
800-367-0798
Fax: 719-531-0631
E-mail: customerservices@acsi.org
http://www.acsi.org
Educational consultant for Christian Schools.

Dr. Dan Egeler, President

1074 Basics Plus
921 Aris Avenue
Suite C
Metairie, LA 70005-2200
504-832-5111
Fax: 504-832-5110
Educational consultants.

Scott Green, President

1075 Beacon Education Management
112 Turnpike Road
Suite 107
Westborough, MA 01581
508-836-4461
800-789-1258
Fax: 508-836-2604
http://www.beaconedu.com
A K-12, education services company that offers contracted management services to public schools and charter school boards. Currently operating 27 charter schools in Massachusetts, Michigan, Missouri and North Carolina.

1076 Beverly Celotta
13517 Haddonfield Lane
Gaitherburg, MD 20878
301-330-8803
E-mail: bev@celotta.net
http://www.celotta.net
Provides psychological and educational services to organizations that serve children and parents.

1077 Bluegrass Regional Recycling Corporation
540 Recycle Drive
Richmond, KY 40475
859-626-9117
Fax: 859-233-7787
E-mail: thebrrc@qx.net
http://www.thebrrc.com
Consultants for educational, training, and services for governments and school systems.

Douglas Castle, Chairman

1078 CPM Educational Program
1233 Noonan Drive
Sacramento, CA 95822-2569
916-446-9936
Fax: 916-444-5263
E-mail: lorraynegraham@cpm.org
http://www.cpm.org

Educational and training consultants for school districts.

Karen Wootton, Executive Director
Paul Chmelik, Director

1079 Caldwell Flores Winters
2187 Newcastle Avenue
Suite 201
Cardiff, CA 92007-1848
760-634-4239
800-273-4239
Fax: 760-436-7357
E-mail: cfw@cfwinc.com
http://http://www.cfwinc.com/index.html
Offers educational counsel to school districts.

Ernesto Flores, President
Scott Gaudineer, AIA, Program Executive

1080 Career Evaluation Systems
1024 N Oakley Boulevard
Suite 4
Chicago, IL 60622-3586
773-772-9595
800-448-7552
Fax: 773-772-5010
Testing instruments for vocational evaluation.

1081 Carnegie Foundation for the Advancement of Teaching
51 Vista Lane
Stanford, CA 94305
650-566-5100
Fax: 650-326-0278
E-mail: publications@carnegiefoundation.org
http://www.carnegiefoundation.org/
Educational consultant for the educational field.

Tom Payzant, Chair
Anthony S Bryk, President

1082 Carney Sandoe & Associates
44 Bromfield Street
Boston, MA 02108-4608
617-542-0260
800-225-7986
Fax: 617-542-9400
http://www.carneysandoe.com/
Educational consultant for private schools.

James H Carney, Chairman/President
Jonathan Ball, Managinf Associate

1083 Carter/Tardola Associates
419 Pleasant Street
Suite 307
Beloit, WI 53511
608-365-3163
Fax: 608-365-5961
E-mail: tardola@tucm.net
http://http://www.carter-tardola.com/
Evaluates program, administration, staff, resource and time organization, and utilization of resources. Proposal development, language skills development, diversity training.

Betty Tardola, Educational Consultant

1084 Center for Educational Innovation
28 West 44th Street
Suite 300
New York, NY 10036-6600
212-302-8800
Fax: 212-302-0088
E-mail: info@the-cei.org
http://www.the-cei.org
Educational consultant for private and commercial accounts.

Seymour Fliegel, President
John Falco, Vice President

1085 Center for Professional Development & Services
1525 Wilson Blvd
Suite 705
Arlington, VA 22209-0789
812-339-1156
800-766-1156
Fax: 812-339-0018
E-mail: membersevices@pdkintl.org
http://www.pdkintl.org
Examines school district curriculum management system. Determines how effectively a school district designs and delivers its curriculum.

Patricia Williams, Chair
Douglas Christensen, Vice Chair

1086 Center for Resource Management
1861 E. Beaumont Circle
Salt Lake City, UT 84121
801-509-5308
Fax: 603-427-6983
E-mail: info@crm.org
http://www.crm.org
Employment, human resources, educational, development, training, computer software, organizational and management consultants for Human Service Agencies and Educational Institutions/ Schools.

Paul Parker, President
Colleen Parker, VP/ Office Manager

1087 Child Like Consulting Limited
700 E Rambling Drive
Wellington, FL 33414-5010
561-798-5847
800-487-6725
Fax: 866-468-4555
Training in literacy, music, classroom and learning center management.

1088 Children's Educational Opportunity Foundation
P.O Box 59
South Glastonbury, CT 06073
860-430-2756
855-326-4935
Fax: 479-273-9362
Educational consultant for institutions.

Mark R. Rousseau, President
Mary Jane Sullivan, Executive Director

1089 Childs Consulting Associates
514 Lakeside Drive
P O Box 550
Mackinaw City, MI 49701
231-436-4099
Fax: 231-436-4101
E-mail: info@childs.com
http://www.childs.com
Educational, schools and technology consultants for schools, banking and automotive industries.

John W Childs, President
Sheryl Childs, Executive Assistant

1090 Classroom
245 Fifth Avenue
Room 1901
New York, NY 10016-8728
212-545-8400
800-258-0640
Fax: 212-481-7178
http://www.classroominc.org
Technology based curriculum and teacher professional development for middle school and high school use.

Lewis W Bernard, Chairman
Lisa Holton, President

1091 Coalition of Essential Schools
482 Congress Street
Suite 500A
Portland, ME 04101
401-426-9638
Fax: 510-433-1455
E-mail: info@essentialschools.org
http://essentialschools.org
The Coalition of Essential Schools (CES) is a leading comprehensive school reform organization, fundamentally changing the way people think about teaching and learning and transforming American education.

Hudi Podolsky, Executive Director

1092 College Bound
17316 Edwards Road
Suite 180
Cerritos, CA 90703
562-860-2127
Fax: 562-407-2131
E-mail: info@collegeboundca.org
http://www.collegeboundca.org
Educational consultants.

Janice Criddle, Chair
Denise McLeod, Vice Chair

1093 College Entrance Examination Board
45 Columbus Avenue
New York, NY 10023-6917
212-713-8000
E-mail: emonts@umich.edu
http://www.collegeboard.com
Educational, research, testing and financial consultant for learning institutions and students.

David Coleman, President
Jeremy Singer, Chief Operating Officer

1094 Community Connections
1865 W Broad Street
Suite C
Athens, GA 30606
706-353-1313
800-924-5085
Fax: 706-353-1375
E-mail: info@communityconnection211.org
http://www.communityconnection211.org
Educational consultant for the general public.

Ashley Harp, President
Julia Weckbeck, Vice President

1095 Community Foundation for Jewish Education
30 S Wells-216
Chicago, IL 60606
312-673-3270
Fax: 312-913-1763
http://www.cfje.org
Educational consultant for the general public and schools.

Howard Swibel, President

1096 Connecting Link
387 Coopers Pond Drive
Suite 1
Lawrenceville, GA 30044-5231
770-979-5804
Fax: 770-931-6831
Business and educational consultants for teachers.

Dr. Bernard F Cleveland, President

1097 Conover Company
4 Brookwood Court
Appleton, WI 54914-8618
920-231-4667
800-933-1933
Fax: 800-933-1943
E-mail: sales@conovercompany.com
http://www.conovercompany.com
Training and setting up workplace literacy programs; emotional intelligence assessment and skill enhancement; functional literacy software, career exploration and assessment software

Rebecca Schmitz, Member

1098 Consortium on Reading Excellence
1300 Clay Street
Suite 600
Oakland, CA 94612-1923
888-249-6165
Fax: 510-540-4242
E-mail: orders@corelearn.com
http://www.corelearn.com
Educational consultant for public and private schools.

Bill Honig, President
Linda Diamond, CEO

1099 Continuous Learning Group Limited Liability Company
500 Cherrington Parkway
Suite 350
Pittsburgh, PA 15108
412-269-7240
Fax: 412-269-7247
E-mail: info@clg.com
http://www.clg.com
Educational consultants.

Steve Jacobs, Non-Executive Chairman
Vikesh Mahendroo, President & CEO

1100 Corporate Design Foundation
20 Park Plaza
Suite 400
Boston, MA 02116-4303
617-566-7676
E-mail: admin@cdf.org
http://www.cdf.org
Educational consultant for universities and colleges.

Peter G Lawrence, Chairman

1101 Corporate University Enterprise
909 North Washington Street
Suite 310
Alexandria, VA 22314
703-848-0070
866-848-1675
Fax: 703-848-0071
E-mail: info@cuenterprise.com
http://www.cuenterprise.com
Corporate University Enterprise, Inc. is and educational consulting firm designed to bring a strategic approach to workforce education in both private and public organizations. The company was incorporated in 1998 and has since served clients throughout the United States, Europe, and Asia.

Teresa Sayasithsena, Vice President
Karen Barley, President

1102 Council for Aid to Education
215 Lexington Avenue
Floor 16
New York, NY 10016-1599
212-661-5800
Fax: 212-661-9766
http://www.cae.org
Non-profit educational consultant for government and commercial concerns.

Roger W Benjamin, President
James Hundley, Executive Vice President

1103 Council on Occupational Education
7840 Roswell Road
Suite 325
Atlanta, GA 30350-1903

770-396-3898
800-917-2081
Fax: 770-396-3790
E-mail: bowmanh@council.org
http://www.council.org
Managerial and educational consultant for post secondary technical education institutions.

Al Salazar, Chair
James Spruel, Vice Chair

1104 Creative Learning Consultants
1990 Market Road
Marion, IL 62959-1906
800-729-5137
Fax: 800-844-0455
E-mail: info@piecesoflearning.com
http://www.piecesoflearning.com
Educational consulting for school districts, teachers, book stores and parents.

Stanley Balsamo, Secretary/Treasurer
Kathy Balsamo, President

1105 Creative Learning Systems
2065 S Escondido Blvd
Suite 108
Escondido, CA 92025
800-458-2880
Fax: 858-592-7055
E-mail:
info@creativelearningsystems.com
http://www.creativelearningsystems.com
Educational consulting firm.

Matt Dickstein, Chief Executive Officer

1106 Dawson Education Cooperative
711 Clinton Street
Suite 201
Arkadelphia, AR 71923-5921
870-246-3077
Fax: 870-246-5892
E-mail: rds@dawson.dsc.k12.ar.us
http://www.dawson.dsc.k12.ar.us
Educational consulting group.

Nathan Gills, President
Ron Wright, Director

1107 Dawson Education Service Cooperative
711 Clinton Street
Suite 201
Arkadelphia, AR 71923-5921
870-246-3077
Fax: 870-246-5892
http://www.dawson.dsc.k12.ar.us
Educational and organizational consultants for school districts

Ron Wright, Director
Beth Neel, Assisstant Director

1108 Designs for Learning
2233 University Ave W
Suite 450
St. Paul, MN 55114-1634
651-645-0200
Fax: 651-645-0240
E-mail: dalley@designlearn.net
http://www.designlearn.net
Educational consultants for primary schools and the private sector.

David Alley, Chair
Pamela Meade, President

1109 Direct Instructional Support Systems
535 Lakeview Plaza Blvd.
Suite B
Worthington, OH 43085-4146
614-846-8946
Fax: 614-846-1794

Educational consultant for public and private agencies.

Gary Moore, President

1110 Dr. Anthony A Cacossa
4300 N Charles Street
Apartment 9B
Baltimore, MD 21218-1052
410-889-1806
Fax: 410-889-1806
Assists schools in marketing academic programs that offer internship opportunities.

1111 EPIE Institute: Educational Products Information Exchange Institute
103 West Montauk Highway
PO Box 590
Hampton Bays, NY 11946-4006
631-728-9100
E-mail: kkomoski@epie.org
http://www.epie.org
Curriculum development, training and evaluation of education products.

1112 EPPA Consulting
1116 Comanche Trail
Georgetown, KY 40324-1071
502-863-6053
Fax: 502-867-0157
E-mail: eppa@juno.com
Strategic and operational planning.

Theo R Leverenz, PhD, Contact, Owner

1113 East Bay Educational Collaborative
317 Market Street
Warren, RI 02885
401-245-4998
Fax: 401-245-9332
E-mail: Karen.corr@ebecri.org
http://www.ebecri.org
Business and educational consultant for member school districts.

Kathryn Crowley, Chair
Gerald Kowalczyk, Executive Director

1114 East Central Educational Service Center
1601 Indiana Avenue
Connersville, IN 47331
765-825-1247
Fax: 765-825-2532
E-mail: harrison@ecesc.k12.in.us
http://www.ecesc.k12.in.us
Educational services for school districts in East Central Indiana.

William J Harrison, Executive Director

1115 Edge Learning Institute
4807 Rockside Rd.
Ste. 720
Z, OH 44131-3320
216-674-1085
888-892-0300
Fax: 216-674-8204
E-mail: info@legacycultures.com
http://legacycultures.com
Educational consultants for the general public, commercial concerns, government agencies and school districts.

Paul Meshanko, President & CEO
Todd Costello, VP Business Operations

1116 Edison Schools
485 Lexington Avenue
2nd Floor
New York, NY 10017
212-419-1600
Fax: 212-419-1746
E-mail: information@edisonlearning.com
http://www.edisonschools.com

The country's largest private manager of public schools. Implemented its design in 79 public schools, including 36 charter schools, which it operates under management contracts with local school districts and charter school boards.

Jeff Wahl, President, CEO

1117 Education Concepts
9861 Strausser Street
Canal Fulton, OH 44614
330-497-1055
Fax: 330-966-8000
E-mail: info@ed-concepts.com
http://www.ed-concepts.com
Professional development programs for early childhood educators.

1118 Education Data
1305 E Waterman
Witchata, KS 67211
800-248-4135
Expertise in organizational needs assessments.

1119 Education Development Center
43 Foundry Avenue
Waltham, MA 02453-8313
617-969-7100
Fax: 617-969-5979
E-mail: contact@edc.org
http://www.edc.org
Developing programs in science, mathematics, reading, writing, health and special education.

1120 Education Management Consulting LLC
49 Coryell Street
Lambertville, NJ 08530
609-397-8989
800-291-0199
Fax: 609-397-1999
E-mail: edragan@edmgt.com
http://www.edmgt.com
Consultation for schools on special education and administration consultation for lawyers working on education and school related issues.

Dr. Edward F Dragan, President

1121 Educational Consultants of Oxford
10431 Highway 51 S
Courtland, MS 38620
601-563-8954
All areas of educational information services, tutoring, scholarship information, and non-traditional and overseas training.

1122 Educational Credential Evaluators
101 W. Pleasant St. Suite 200
PO Box 514070
Milwaukee, WI 53212-3963
414-289-3400
Fax: 414-289-3411
E-mail: eval@ece.org
http://www.ece.org
Evaluates foreign educational credentials.

James Frey, President
Margit Schatzman, VP

1123 Educational Data Service
236 Midland Avenue
Saddle Brook, NJ 07663-4604
973-340-8800
Fax: 973-340-0078
http://www.ed-data.com
Educational and school consulting for Boards of Education.

Gil Wohl, President
Alan Wohl, Chairman

1124 Educational Information & Resource Center
900 Hollydell Drive
Sewell, NJ 08080
856-582-7000
Fax: 856-582-4206

E-mail: info@eirc.org
http://www.eirc.org
Programs and consulting services for schools, on many topics from teaching techniques to technical assistance.

Rena Alpert, Board of Director
Jack Hill, Board of Director

125 Educational Resources
8910 W 62nd Terrace
Shawnee Mission, KS 66202-2814
651-592-3688
Fax: 651-690-2188
E-mail: info@eduresources.org
http://www.eduresources.org
Educational consulting for colleges.

Dr. Steven L. Derfler, Director
Karen Harrison, VP

126 Educational Services Company
3535 East 96th Street
Suite 126
Indianapolis, IN 46240-1754
317-818-3535
888-351-3535
Fax: 317-818-3533
E-mail: info@educationalservicesco.com
http://www.educationalservicesco.com
Educational and management consulting for primary and secondary schools.

Douglas Cassman, President
William McMaster, Secretary

127 Educational Specialties
9923 S Wood Street
Chicago, IL 60643-1809
773-445-1000
Fax: 773-445-5574
http://www.educationalspecialties.com
Educational consultant for schools.

Elois W Steward, President

128 Educational Systems for the Future
11415 Georgetown Circle
Tampa, FL 33625-1560
813-814-1192
Fax: 813-814-1193
E-mail: info@esf-protainer.com
http://www.esf-protainer.com
Development of teaching skills, training needs analysis, and training management.

Dr. Mary Sullivan Esseff, President & Director
Dr. Peter J Esseff, Vice President

129 Educational Technology Design Consultants
100 Allentown Parkway
Suite 110
Allen, TX 75002
972-727-1234
Fax: 972-727-1491
http://www.etdc.com/html/about_us.html
Developing system design for virtual campus control and support.

130 Educational Testing Service
1800 K Street, NW,
Suite 900
Washington, DC 20006-0001
202-659-0616
Fax: 202-659-8075
E-mail: etsinfo@ets.org
http://www.ets.org
Educational and professional consulting for schools.

Kurt M. Landgraf, President
Sharon Robison, COO, Senior VP

1131 Edusystems Export
820 Wisconsin Street
Walworth, WI 53184-9765
262-275-5761
Fax: 262-275-2009
E-mail: sales@edusystems.com;admin@edusystems.com
Expertise in educational systems.

1132 Effective Schools Products
PO Box 1337
Okemos, MI 48805-5983
517-349-8841
800-827-8041
Fax: 517-349-8852
E-mail: staff@effectiveschools.com
http://www.effectiveschools.com
Publishing consultants for schools, teachers, directors of planning and others in this field.

Ruth Lezotte, PhD, President
Dr. Carmen Granto, Superintendent

1133 Effective Training Solutions
93 Linden Street
Oakland, CA 94607-1447
510-834-1901
800-949-5035
Fax: 510-834-1905
E-mail: boris@trainingsuccess.com
http://www.trainingsuccess.com
Design and implementation of training strategies. Proficiency training-performance improvement training.

Ingrid Gudenas, CEO

1134 Efficacy Institute
182 Felton Street
Waltham, MA 02453-4134
781-547-6060
Fax: 781-547-6077
E-mail: info@efficacy.org
http://www.efficacy.org
Non-profit, educational consultants for educational and community service institutions.

Dr Jeff Howard, Chair
Barbara M. Logan, Vice President

1135 Emerging Technology Consultants
216 Heritage Lane
New Brighton, MN 55112
651-639-3973
Fax: 651-639-3973
Serves as a connection between technology producers and the education and training industries.

Richard Pollak, Chief Executive Officer
Rubyanna Pollak, President

1136 Epistemological Engineering
5269 Miles Avenue
Oakland, CA 94618-1044
510-653-3377
866-341-3377
Fax: 866-879-7797
E-mail: publications@eeps.com
http://www.eeps.com
Educational consultants.

Tim Erickson, President

1137 Examiner Corporation
600 Marshall Avenue
Suite 100
St. Paul, MN 55102-1723
651-451-7360
800-395-6840
Fax: 651-451-6563
E-mail: examine@xmn.com
http://www.xmn.com

Educational and certification evaluation instruments.

Gary C Brown, President
Michelle Smith, Sales and Marketing

1138 Excell Education Centers
3807 Wilshire Boulevard
Los Angeles, CA 90010-3101
213-386-1953
Educational and planning consultants.

Raymond Hahl, Owner

1139 FPMI Communications
707 Fiber Street NW
Huntsville, AL 35801-5833
256-539-1850
Fax: 256-539-0911
http://www.fmpi.com
Educational management consulting.

1140 First District Resa
201 West Lee Street
P.O. Box 780
Brooklet, GA 30415
912-842-5000
Fax: 912-842-5161
E-mail: wmyers@fdresa.org
http://www.fdresa.org
Educational consultants for the general public and commercial concerns.

Dr. Whit Myers, Executive Director
Donna Mangrum, Chief Financial Officer

1141 Foundation for Educational Innovation
401 M Street SW
2nd Floor, Suite 1
Washington, DC 20024-2610
202-554-7400
Fax: 202-554-7401
Educational consultant for educational/school systems.

Archie Prioleau, President

1142 George Dehne & Associates
33 Main Street
Suite F
Old Saybrook, CT 06475
843-971-9088
860-388-3958
Fax: 843-971-7759
E-mail: george@dehne.com
http://www.dehne.com
Educational and business consultants for commercial concerns and colleges.

George Dehne, President
Christopher Topher Small, Executive Vice President

1143 Health Outreach Project
825 Cascade Avenue
Atlanta, GA 30331-8362
404-755-6700
Educational consultants.

Sandra McDonald, President

1144 Higher Education Consortium
2233 University Avenue W
Suite 210
St. Paul, MN 55114
651-287-3300
Fax: 651-659-9421
E-mail: hecua@hecua.org
http://www.hecua.org
Educational consultants.

Jenny Keyser, Executive Director
Patrick Mulvihill, Director of Operations

1145 Highlands Program
PO Box 76168
Atlanta, GA 30358-3915

404-497-0835
Educational consultants for educational institutions, corporations and consumers.

Don Hutcheson, President

1146 Howard Greene Associates
60 Post Road West
Westport, CT 06880-4208
203-226-4257
Fax: 203-226-5595
E-mail:
counseling@howardgreeneassociates.com

http://www.greenesguides.com
Educational consultants for school systems and individuals.

Howard R Greene, President & Founder
Ginger F.C. Miller, Director

1147 Huntley Pascoe
19125 N Creek Parkway
Bothel, WA 98011-8035
425-485-0900
Fax: 425-487-1825
Educational consultant for architects, utility companies, computer facilities, school districts and hospitals.

Roger Huntley, President

1148 Ingraham Dancu Associates
121 Bald Cypress Court
Pawleys Island, SC 29585
843-235-8709
Fax: 843-235-3422
E-mail: dedancu@ingrahamdancu.com
http://www.ingrahamdancu.com
Development planning for educational and industrial clients.

Daniel E. Dancu, PhD, President

1149 Innovative Learning Group
514 East Fourth Street
Royal Oak, MI 48067
248-544-1568
Fax: 248-544-2159
http://www.innovativelg.com
Educational consultants for schools and the general public.

Lisa Toenniges, Owner/ CEO

1150 Innovative Programming Systems
9001poplar Bridge Road
Bloomington, MN 55437
612-835-1290
Development of instructional and training programs.

1151 Insight
12 S 6th Street
Suite 510
Minneapolis, MN 55402-1510
612-338-5777
Educational consultants for commercial concerns.

Mark Kovatch, President

1152 Institute for Academic Excellence
901 Deming Way
Suite 301
Madison, WI 53717-1964
608-664-0965
Fax: 608-664-382
Educational consultants for K-12 schools.

John Hickey, Chairman

1153 Institute for Development of Educational Activities
259 Regency Ridge
Dayton, OH 45459
937-434-6969
Fax: 937-434-5203

E-mail: ideadayton@aol.com
http://www.idea.com
Assistance for administrators and teachers of elementary and secondary schools.

1154 Institute for Global Ethics
10 East Doty St.,
Suite 825
Madison, WI 53703
207-594-3969
888-607-0883
Fax: 207-236-6614
E-mail: ethics@globalethics.org
http://www.globalethics.org
Educational consultants for the general public, corporations and educators.

David F. Hurwitt, Chairman
Anthony J. Gray, President & CEO

1155 Interface Network
321 SW 4th Avenue
Suite 502
Portland, OR 97204-2323
503-222-2702
Fax: 503-222-7503
E-mail: www.daggettt.com
http://info@leaderEd.com
Educational consultant for the United States Department of Education, businesses, school districts and other governmental agencies.

1156 International Center for Leadership in Education
1587 Route 146
Rexford, NY 12148
518-399-2776
Fax: 518-399-7607
E-mail: info@leadered.com
http://www.leadered.com
Educational consultants for educational institutions, governments and commercial concerns.

Willard R Daggett, Chairman
Susan A. Gendron, President

1157 International Schools Association
1033 Diego Drive South
BOCA RATON, FL 33428
561-883-3854
39-011-645-967
Fax: 561-483-2004
Fax: 39-011-643-298
E-mail: info@isaschools.org
http://www.isaschools.org
Provides advisory and consultative services to its international and internationally minded member schools, as well as to other organizations in the field of education, such as UNESCO. The Association promotes innovations in international education, conducts conferences and workshops and publishes various educational materials.

Luis Martinez-Zorzo, Chairman
Freida Pilus, Vice Chairman

1158 J&Kalb Associates
300 Pelham Road
Suite 5K
New Rochelle, NY 10805
914-636-6154
Consulting experience to school districts.

1159 JBS International
5515 Security Lane
Suite 800
North Bethesda, MD 20852-5007
301-495-1080
Fax: 650-348-0260
E-mail: info@jbsinternational.com
http://www.jbsinternational.com

Educational, data, market analysis, statistical and research consultants for US Government Agencies.

Jerri Shaw, Co-CEO/ President
Gail Bassin, Co-CEO/ CFO

1160 JCB/Early Childhood Education Consultant Service
813 Woodchuck Place
Bear, DE 19701
302-836-8505
Program design and cross-cultural staff development through seminars.

1161 JJ Jones Consultants
1206 Harrison Avenue
Oxford, MS 38655-3904
662-234-6755
Educational consultant for high school and college students.

JJ Jones, Owner

1162 JP Associates Incorporated
131 Foster Avenue
Valley Stream, NY 11580-4726
516-561-7803
Fax: 516-561-4066
Educational consultant for schools.

Jane Dinapoli, President

1163 Janet Hart Heinicke
1302 W Boston Avenue
Indianola, IA 50125
515-961-8933
Fax: 515-961-8903
E-mail: heinicke@simpson.edu
Development of new programs and maintenance strategies.

1164 Jewish Learning Venture
7607 Old York Road
Melrose Park, PA 19027-3010
215-320-036
Fax: 215-635-8946
E-mail: info@jewishlearningventure.org
http://jewishlearningventure.org
Educational consultants.

Rabbi Philip Warmflash, Executive Director
Elana Rivel, Associate Director

1165 Jobs for California Graduates
2525 O Street
Merced, CA 95340-3634
209-385-8466
Educational consultants for high school students.

Obie Obrien, Director

1166 John McLaughlin Company
1524 S Summit Avenue
Sioux Falls, SD 57105
605-332-4900
Fax: 605-339-1662
http://www.mclaughlincompany.com
Advises companies regarding private-sector activities in K-12 and higher education.

John Laughlin, Owner

1167 Johnson & Johnson Associates
3970 Chain Bridge Road
Fairfax, VA 22030-3316
703-359-5969
800-899-6363
Fax: 703-359-5971
E-mail: info@jjaconsultants.com
http://www.jjaconsultants.com
Educational consultants for governmental agencies and commercial concerns.

Dr. Johnson Edosomwan, President/CEO

168 Joseph & Edna Josephson Institute
9841 Airport Blvd.
Suite 300
Los Angeles, CA 90045-6621
310-846-4800
800-711-2670
Fax: 310-846-4858
http://charactercounts.org
Educational consultant for organizations, government, businesses and the general public.

Scott Raecker, Chairman
Robert Holmes, Vice Chairman

169 Kaludis Consulting Group
1050 Connecticut Avenue NW
10th Floor
Washington, DC 20036
202-772-3120
Fax: 202-331-1428
E-mail: info@kaludisconsulting.com
http://www.kaludisconsulting.com
Educational consultants for colleges and universities.

George Kaludis, President/Chairman
Barry M Cohen, Senior Vice President

170 Kentucky Association of School Administrators
152 Consumer Lane
Suite 154
Frankfort, KY 40601-8489
502-875-3411
800-928-kasa
Fax: 502-875-4634
E-mail: webmaster@kasa.com
http://www.kasa.org
Educational consultant for school administrators.

Lu S. Young, President
Barry Lee, President-elect

171 Kleiner & Associates
8636 SE 75th Place
Mercer Island, WA 98040-5235
206-236-0608
Educational consultants for public and private institutions.

Charles Kleiner, Owner

172 Lawrence A Heller Associates
324 Freeport Road
Pittsburgh, PA 15238-3422
412-820-0670
Fax: 412-820-0669
Development and implementation of educational programs.

173 Leona Group
7878 N. 16th St
Suite 150
Phoenix, AZ 85020
602-953-2933
Fax: 602-953-0831
http://www.leonagroup.com
Currently manages more than 40 school sites in Michigan, Arizona, Ohio and Indiana

Wieland Wettstein, Chairman
Dr. Bill Coats, CEO

174 Linkage
200 Wheeler Road
3rd Floor South Tower
Burlington, MA 01803-7305
781-402-5555
Fax: 781-402-5556
E-mail: info@linkageinc.com
http://www.linkageinc.com

Linkage, Inc. is a global organizational development company that specializes in leadership development.

Phil Harkins, Executive Chairman
Harley Ostis, President & CEO

1175 Logical Systems
605 East 1st Street
Suite 101
Rome, GA 30161-3109
706-234-9896
Fax: 706-290-0998
http://www.logsysinc.com
Educational consultants for school districts.

Francis Ranwez, President

1176 Los Angeles Educational Alliance for Restructuring Now
445 S Figueroa Street
Los Angeles, CA 90071
323-255-3276
Fax: 213-626-5830
E-mail: asant@ccf-la.org
Educational consulting for school systems.

Mary Chambers, Vice President
Michael Roos, President

1177 Louisiana Children's Research Center for Development & Learning
1 Galleria Blvd.
Suite 903
Metairie, LA 70001-3036
504-840-9786
Fax: 504-840-9968
E-mail: learn@cdl.org
http://www.cdl.org
Educational consultants for the general public.

Frank Williams, Chairman
Gregory N. Rattler, Vice Chairman

1178 MK & Company
132 Bronte Street
San Francisco, CA 94110
415-826-5923
Program development and project management for educational products, services and organizations.

1179 MPR Associates
3040 East Cornwallis Road
Post Office Box 12194
Research Triangle Park, NC 27709-2194
510-849-4942
Fax: 510-849-0794
E-mail: info@mprinc.com
http://www.mprinc.com
Educational consultants for governmental, educational and commercial concerns including law firms.

Gary Hoachlander, President

1180 Magi Educational Services Incorporated
7-11 Broadway
Suite 402
White Plains, NY 10601-3546
914-682-1861
Fax: 914-682-1760
E-mail: info@westchesterinst.com
http://www.westchesterinst.org
Educational consultant for educational institutions.

Dr. Ronald Szczypkowski, President

1181 Management Concepts
8230 Leesburg Pike
Suite 800
Tysons Corner, VA 22182-2639
703-790-9595
888-545-8571

Fax: 703-790-1371
E-mail: info@managementconcepts.com
http://www.managementconcepts.com
Educational consultants for commercial and governmental concerns.

Stephen L. Maier, President
Thomas F. Dungan lll, CEO

1182 Management Simulations
55 E Monroe
Chicago, IL 60093-1250
312-477-7200
877-477-8787
E-mail: welcome@capsim.com
http://www.capsim.com
Educational consultants for commercial concerns and universities.

Daniel Smith, President
Shridhar Sampath, General Manager

1183 Marketing Education Resource Center
1375 King Avenue
PO Box 12279
Columbus, OH 43212-2220
614-486-6708
800-448-0398
Fax: 614-486-1819
http://www.mbaresearch.org
Educational, development and curriculum consulting for high schools and post secondary schools.

Trey Michael, Chair
James R Gleason Ph.D., President, CEO

1184 Maryland Educational Opportunity Center
2305 N. Charles St.
Suite 101
Baltimore, MD 21218
410-728-3400
888-245-2774
Fax: 410-523-6340
E-mail: edhoward@meoconline.com
http://www.meoconline.com
Consultant services for educational institutions.

Ellen Howard, Executive Director
Lynn Drummond, Associate Director

1185 Maryland Elco Incorporated Educational Funding Company
4740 Chevy Chase Drive
Chevy Chase, MD 20815-6461
301-654-8677
Fax: 301-654-7750
E-mail: info@efconline.com
http://www.efconline.com
Educational, accounting and billing consultants for service and vocational schools and businesses.

Nicholas Cokinos, Chairman
John Cokinos, President

1186 Mason Associates
142 N Mountain Avenue
Montclair, NJ 07042
201-744-9143
Educational services for independent secondary schools, colleges and universities.

1187 Matrix Media Distribution
28310 Roadside Drive
Suite 237
Agoura, CA 91301-4951
818-865-3470
Educational consultant for the educational market.

Paul Luttrell, President

1188 McKenzie Group
1100 17th Street NW
Suite 1100
Washington, DC 20036-4638
202-466-1111
Fax: 202-466-3363
Educational consultant for commercial
concerns and government.

Floretta D McKenzie, President

1189 Measurement
423 Morris Street
Durham, NC 27701-2128
919-683-2413
Fax: 919-425-7726
http://www.measurementinc.com
Educational, research, testing and printing
consultant for schools, state governments
and private businesses.

Dr. Henry H Scherich, President
Dr. Michael B Bunch, Senior Vice
President

**1190 Measurement Learning
Consultants**
80920 Highway 10
Tolovana Park, OR 97145
503-436-1464
Business, educational, testing and development consultants for the general public
and commercial concerns such as schools.

Albert G Bennyworth, Partner

1191 Merrimack Education Center
101 Mill Road
Chelmsford, MA 01824-4844
978-256-3985
Fax: 978-937-5585
http://www.mec.edu
Educational consultant for educational facilities.

John Barranco, Executive Director

1192 Michigan Education Council
40440 Palmer Road
Canton, MI 48188-2034
734-729-1000
Fax: 734-729-1004
Educational consultant for individuals.

Dawud Tauhidi, Director

1193 Midas Consulting Group
4600 S Syracuse Street
Suite 900
Denver, CO 80237
303-256-6500
Fax: 866-790-9500
E-mail: info@midasconsultinggroup.com
http://www.midasconsultinggroup.com
Educational consultant for schools, universities, training centers and government
agencies.

Michael Blimes, Executive Consultant

1194 Miller, Cook & Associates
1606 Bellview Avenue
Suite 1
Roanoke, VA 24014-4923
540-345-4393
800-591-1141
Fax: 239-394-2652
E-mail: info@millercook.com
http://www.millercook.com
Educational consultants for colleges and
universities.

William B Miller, President
Catherine R. Cook, Chief Executive
Officer

1195 Model Classroom
4095 173rd Place SW
Bellvue, WA 98008-5929
425-746-0331
Educational consultant for school districts,
commercial concerns and the Department
of Education.

Cheryl Avena, Owner

1196 Modern Educational Systems
15 Limestone Terrace
Ridgefield, CT 06877-2621
203-431-4144
Educational consultant for schools.

Edward T McCormick, President

1197 Modern Red Schoolhouse Institute
1901 21st Avenue
South Nashville, TN 37212-1502
615-320-8804
888-275-6774
Fax: 615-320-5366
E-mail: info@mrsh.com
http://www.mrsh.com
Educational consultant for school districts.

Sally B Kilgore, President

**1198 Montana School Boards
Association**
863 Great Northern Blvd.
Suite 301
Helena, MT 59601-5156
406-442-2180
Fax: 406-442-2194
E-mail: cwilson@mtsba.org
http://www.mtsba.org
Training, educational and school districts
consultant for school boards.

Charles Wilson, President
Lance Melton, Executive Director

1199 Montgomery Intermediate Unit 23
1605 West Main Street
Suite B
Norristown, PA 19403-3268
610-539-8550
Fax: 610-539-5073
E-mail: webmaster@mciu.org
http://www.mciu.org
Educational consultants for professional
associations, groups and student organizations.

Marc Lieberson, President

1200 Moore Express
865 Pancheri Drive
Idaho Falls, ID 83402
208-523-6276
Educational consultant for public school
districts, state and local governments and
commercial concerns.

Lawry Wilde, President

1201 Mosaica Education
45 Broadway
17th Floor
New York, NY 10006
212-232-0305
Fax: 212-232-0309
E-mail: partner@mosaicaeducation.com
http://www.mosaicaeducation.com
Manages public schools either under contract with local school districts or funded
directly by states under charter school laws
that permit private management.

Gene Eidelman, President
Michael J Connelly, Chief Executive
Officer

1202 Multicorp
1912 Avenue K
Suite 210
Plano, TX 75074-5960
972-551-8899
Computer and educational consultant.

Fred Sammet, Chairman

**1203 National Center on Education & the
Economy**
2121 K Street NW
Suite 700
Washington, DC 20037-4507
202-379-1800
Fax: 202-293-1560
E-mail: info@ncee.org
http://www.ncee.org
Educational consultant for schools.

Marc S Tucker, President
Betsy Brown Ruzzi, Vice President

1204 National Evaluation Systems
30 Gatehouse Road
PO Box 226
Amherst, MA 01004
Fax: 413-256-8221
Educational testing, test development, and assess-
ment for education agencies.

1205 National Heritage Academies
3850 Broadmoor Avenue SE
Suite 201
Grand Rapids, MI 49512
877-223-6402
Fax: 616-575-6801
E-mail: info@heritageacademies.com
http://www.nhaschools.com
Manages 22 charter academies (K-8) in Michigan
and North Carolina.

2007, Author
Harry Hurlburt, President, CEO
Todd McKee, Chief Academic Officer

1206 National Reading Styles Institute
PO Box 737
Syosset, NY 11791
516-921-5500
800-331-3117
Fax: 516-921-5591
E-mail: readingstyle@nrsi.com
http://www.nrsi.com
Educational consultants for schools and educa-
tors.

Marie Carbo, Executive Director

**1207 National School Safety and Security
Services**
PO Box 110123
Cleveland, OH 44111
216-251-3067
E-mail: ken@schoolsecurity.org
http://www.schoolsecurity.org
National consulting firm specializing in school
security and crisis preparedness training, security
assessments, and related safety consulting for
K-12 schools, law enforcement, and other youth
safety providers.

Kenneth S Trump, President/CEO
Dr. Asia Jones, Director

1208 Noel/Levitz Centers
2350 Oakdale Blvd.
Coralville, IA 52241-9581
319-626-8380
800-876-1117
Fax: 319-626-8388
E-mail: ContactUs@noellevitz.com
http://www.noellevitz.com
Educational consultant for colleges and universities.

Tom Williams, President/CEO

209 Ome Resa
2230 Sunset Boulevard
Steubenville, OH 43952-1349
740-283-2050
Fax: 740-283-1500
E-mail: angie.underwood@omeresa.net
http://www.omeresa.net
Educational consultants for school districts.

Dave Hire, Chair
John Wilson, Vice Chair

210 Oosting & Associates
200 Seaboard Lane
Franklin, TN 37067-8237
615-771-7706
Fax: 615-771-7810
Educational consultants for colleges and universities.

Dr. Kenneth Oosting, President

211 Pamela Joy
1049 Whipple Avenue
Suite A
Redwood City, CA 94062-1414
650-368-9968
Fax: 650-368-2794
Educational consultants for schools.

Pamela Joy, Owner

212 Parsifal Systems
155 N Craig Street
Pittsburgh, PA 15213
412-682-8080
Fax: 412-682-6291
Educational consultants for commercial concerns and schools.

Marcia Morton, President

213 Paul H Rosendahl, PHD
240 Mohouli Street
Hilo, HI 96720-2445
808-935-5233
Fax: 808-961-6998
Science, archaeology, historical, resources and management consultant for developers, government agencies, educational institutions, groups and individuals.

Paul H Rosendahl, Owner

214 Perfect PC Technologies
15012 Red Hill Avenue
Tustin, CA 92780-6524
714-258-0800
Computer consultants for commercial concerns, schools and institutions.

Neil Lin, President

215 Performa
124 N Broadway
De Pere, WI 54115
920-336-9929
Fax: 920-336-2899
E-mail: jeffk@performaic.com
http://www.performainc.com
Planning and facility consultants for higher education, manufacturing and government agencies.

Doug Page, President
Jeff Kanzelberger, CEO

216 Poetry Alive!
70 Woodfin Place
Suite WW4C
Asheville, NC 28801
828-255-7636
800-476-8172
Fax: 828-232-1045
E-mail: poetry@poetryalive.com
http://www.poetryalive.com

Educational consultants for commercial concerns and school systems.

Bob Falls, President

1217 Post Secondary Educational Assistance
500 Century Park South
Suite 200
Birmingham, AL 35226-3920
205-930-4930
Fax: 205-930-4905
E-mail: mystudentloanassistance
http://mystudentloanassistance.com
Educational consultant for commercial concerns.

Kenneth Horne, President

1218 Prevention Service
7614 Morningstar Avenue
Harrisburg, PA 17112-4226
717-651-9510
Educational consultant for corporations, private health clubs, school districts and other organizations.

Mark Everest, President

1219 Princeton Review
2315 Broadway
2nd Floor
New York, NY 10024-4332
212-874-8282
888-955-4600
Fax: 212-874-0775
http://www.princetonreview.com
Educational consultants for commercial concerns.

John Katzman, President

1220 Priority Computer Services
6561 Lonewolf Drive
Suite 110
South Bend, IN 46628
574-236-5979
866-661-9049
E-mail: priority@pcserv-inc.com
http://www.prioritycomputer.biz
Computer consultant for commercial education.

Ben Hahaj, President

1221 Prism Computer Corporation
2 Park Plaza
Suite 1060
Irvine, CA 92614-8520
800-774-7622
Fax: 949-553-6559
Educational consultant for manufacturers, government agencies and colleges.

Micheal A Ellis, President

1222 Professional Computer Systems
849 SE Greenville Avenue
Winchester, IN 47394-8441
765-584-2288
Fax: 765-584-1283
http://www.pcswin.com
Computer consultants for businesses, schools and municipalities.

Steve Barnes, President

1223 Professional Development Institute
280 S County Road
Suite 427
Longwood, FL 32750-5468
407-834-5224
Educational consultants for US Department of Transportation and commercial concerns.

Elsom Eldridge, Jr, President

1224 Profiles
507 Highland Avenue
Iowa City, IA 52240-4516
319-354-7600
Fax: 319-354-6813
Educational consultants for school districts and commercial concerns.

Douglas Paul, President

1225 Pyramid Educational Consultants
13 Garfield Way
Newark, DE 19713
302-368-2515
888-732-7462
Fax: 302-368-2516
E-mail: pyramid@pecs.com
http://www.pecsusa.com
Educational consultant for general trade, historical commissions and other public bodies.

Andrew Bondy, President
Lori A Frost, Vice President

1226 Quality Education Development
41 Central Park West
New York, NY 10023
212-724-3335
800-724-2215
Fax: 212-724-4913
E-mail: info@qedconsulting.com
Structures courses that promote knowledge and understanding through interactive learning, and communication programs.

1227 Quantum Performance Group
5050 Rushmore Road
Palmyra, NY 14522-9414
315-986-9200
Educational consultant for commercial concerns, including schools.

Dr. Mark Blazey, President

1228 Rebus
4111 Jackson Road
Ann Arbor, MI 48103-1827
734-668-4870
Fax: 734-913-4750
Educational consultant for schools and school districts.

Linda Borgsdorf, President

1229 Records Consultants
10826 Gulfdale Street
San Antonio, TX 78216-3607
210-366-4127
Fax: 210-366-0776
Educational consultant for school districts and municipalities.

Lang Glotfelty, President

1230 Regional Learning Service of Central New York
770 James Street Office
Syracuse, NY 13203-1644
315-446-0500
Fax: 315-446-5869
Educational consultants for commercial concerns.

Rebecca Livengood, Executive Director

1231 Reinventing Your School Board
Aspen Group International,Inc
PO Box 260301
Highlands Ranch, CO 80163-0301
303-478-0125
Fax: 208-248-6084

Linda Dawson, Contact
Dr. Randy Quinn, Contact

1232 Relearning by Design
447 Forcina Hall
PO Box 7718
Ewing, NJ 08628-0718
609-771-2921
Fax: 609-637-5130
E-mail: info@relearning.org
http://www.relearning.org
Grant Wiggins, Author/Editor
Jacquelyn Nance, Chair

1233 Research Assessment Management
816 Camarillo Springs Road
Camarillo, CA 93012-9441
805-987-5538
Fax: 805-987-2868
Educational consultants for governmental
agencies and commercial concerns.
Adrienne McCollum, PhD, President

1234 Robert E Nelson Associates
120 Oak Brook Center
Suite 208
Oak Brook, IL 60523
630-954-5585
Fax: 630-954-5606
Consulting for private colleges, universities and secondary schools.

1235 Rookey Associates
1740 Little York Xing
Little York, NY 13087
607-749-2325
Educational consultant for school districts,
public utility companies and the government.
Ernest J Rookey, President

1236 Root Learning
810 W S Boundary Street
Perrysburg, OH 43551-5200
419-874-0077
Fax: 419-874-4801
Business, educational, employment consultant for commercial concerns.
Randall Root, Chairman/CEO

1237 School Management Study Group
1649 Lone Peoh Drive
Salt Lake City, UT 84117
801-277-3725
Fax: 801-277-4547
Organization seeking to promote improvement of schools and to involve educators in
critical school problems.
Donald Thomas, President
Dale Holden, Associate

1238 SchoolMatch by Public Priority Systems
2200 Lane Woods Drive
Columbus, OH 43221
973-831-1757
http://schoolmatch.com
An educational consultant for private and
public schools.
William L. Bainbridge, Ph.D., FACFE,
President/ CEO

1239 Sensa of New Jersey
110 Mohawk Trail
Wayne, NJ 07470-5030
973-831-1757
An educational consultant for private and
public schools.
John Pinto, President

1240 Shirley Handy
4151 Wild Lilac Drive
Turlock, CA 95382-8308

209-668-4142
Fax: 209-668-1855
E-mail: info@n-e-n.com
http://www.n-e-n.com
Educational consultants for school districts and teachers.
Shirley Handy, Owner

1241 Sidney Kreppel
704 E Benita Boulevard
Vestal, NY 13850-2629
607-754-6870
Educational consultants.
Sidney Kreppel, Owner

1242 Solutions Skills
545 E Tennessee Street
Tallahassee, FL 32308-4981
850-681-6543
Fax: 850-681-6543
http://www.solutionsskills.com
Business and educational consultants for
state and governments, educational, medical and legal publishing companies.
Randall Vickers, President

1243 Special Education Service Agency
3501 Denali Street
Suite 101
Anchorage, AK 99503-1068
907-563-8284
877-890-9269
Fax: 907-562-0545
E-mail: sesa@sesa.org
http://www.sesa.org
Educational consultant for school districts.
Nancy Nagarkar, Executive Director
Laraine Adams, Secretary

1244 Sports Management Group
918 Parker Street
Suite A-13
Berkeley, CA 94710
510-849-3090
Fax: 510-849-3094
E-mail: tsmq@sportsmqmt.com
http://www.sportsmgnt.com
Educational consulting for universities.
Lauren Livingston, President

1245 Stewart Howe Alumni Service of New York
3109 N Triphammer Road
Lansing, NY 14882
607-533-9200
Fax: 607-533-9218
E-mail: programs@stewarthowe.com
http://www.stewarthowe.com
Educational consultants for college organizations.
Peter McChesney, Director
Mike Duesing, Managing Partner

1246 Strategies for Educational Change
11 Whitby Court
Mount Holly, NJ 08060
609-261-1702
E-mail: barbd@prodigy.net
Development of programs for youths at
risk.

1247 Success for All Foundation
300 E. Joppa Road
Suite 500
Baltimore, MD 21286
410-616-2300
800-548-4998
Fax: 410-324-4444
E-mail: sfainfo@successforall.net
http://www.successforall.net

A not-for-profit organization dedicated to the development, evaluation and dissemination of
proven reform models for preschool, elementary
and middle schools.
Nancy Madden, Ph.D., CEO

1248 Teachers Curriculum Institute
P.O. Box 1327
Rancho Cordova, CA 95741
916-366-3686
800-497-6138
Fax: 800-343-6828
E-mail: infor@teachtci.com
http://www.teachtci.com
Educational consultant for schools and teachers.
Bert Bower, President/ CEO
Amy Larson, Chief Operating Officer

1249 Teachers Service Association
1107 E Lincoln Avenue
Orange, CA 92865-1939
714-282-6342
Educational consultants for schools and teachers.
Richard Ghysels, Secretary Treasurer

1250 Tech Ed Services
One World Trade Center
8th Floor
Long Beach, CA 90831
562-869-1913
800-832-4411
Fax: 562-869-5673
E-mail: info@techedservices.com
http://techedservices.com
Computer, planning and training consultant for
k-12 educators and adult educators.
Patricia K Sanford, President/ CEO
Brenna Terrones, TES Senior Specialist

1251 Technical Education Research Centers
2067 Massachusetts Avenue
Cambridge, MA 02140-1340
617-873-9600
Fax: 617-873-9601
E-mail: contactus@terc.edu
http://www.terc.edu
Educational consultant for the National Science
Foundation and the Department of Education.
Arthur Nelson, Founder
George E. Hein, Chairman

1252 Tesseract Group
18 W 27th Street
11th Floor
New York, NY 10001
212-481-8304
Fax: 212-481-8306
E-mail: info@tesseractllc.com
http://tesseractllc.com
An integrated education management company,
serving private and public charter elementary,
middle and high schools in six states.
Erica Payne, Founder

1253 Timothy Anderson Dovetail Consulting
936 Nantasket Avenue
Hull, MA 02045-1453
781-925-3078
Fax: 781-925-9830
Educational consultant for businesses.
Eric Anderson, Owner

1254 University Research
7200 Wisconsin Avenue
Suite 600
Bethesda, MD 20814-4811
301-654-8338
Fax: 301-941-8427
http://www.urc-chs.com

Educational consultants for the federal government along with other government and private sectors.

Barbara N. Turner, President

255 University of Georgia-Instructional Technology

630 Aderhold Hall
Athens, GA 30602
706-542-4110
Fax: 706-542-4240
E-mail: coeinfo@uga.edu
http://www.coe.uga.edu
Instructional design and development.

Aurthur M. Horne, Dean
Pedro R Portes, Professor

256 Uplinc

48 Capital Drive
West Springfield, MA 01089
413-693-0700
E-mail: sales@uplinc.com
http://www.uplinc.com
Computer consultants for commercial, general public and educational concerns.

Ron Marino, President

257 William A Ewing & Company

505 S Main Street
Suite 700
Orange, CA 92868
714-245-1850
Fax: 714-456-1755
E-mail: ewingo@aol.com
http://www.members.aol.com/ewingo
Expertise in compensation and classification.

258 Wisconsin Technical College System Foundation

1 Foundation Circle
Waunakee, WI 53597-8914
608-849-2400
Fax: 608-849-2468
E-mail: foundation@wtcsf.tec.wi.us
http://www.wtcsf.tec.wi.us
Educational consultant for educational institutions and businesses.

Loren Brumm, Executive Director

Africa

1259 Alexandra House School
King George V Avenue
Floreal
Mauritius
230-696-4108
Fax: 230-696-4108
E-mail:
admin@alexandrahouseschool.com
http://www.alexandrahouseschool.com
A private English Primary day school in Mauritius for boys and girls between 4 and 11 years of age. Cater for approximately 100 children and provide a British curriculum with a strong international flavour.

M Wrenn-Beejadhur, Principal

1260 American International School-Dhaka
United Nations Road Baridhara
Dhaka
Bangladesh
880-2-882-2414
Fax: 880-2-883-3175
E-mail: info@ais-dhaka.net
http://www.ais-dhaka.net
Provides a program based on American educational principles to students from an international community, creates an academic and social environment that challenges students to achieve their potential, become life-long learners and contribute to changing global society.

Kyra Buchko, President
Diane Lindsey, Vice President

1261 American International School-Johannesburg
Private Bag X 4
Bryanston 2021
Republic of South Africa
011 464 1505
Fax: 27-11-464-1327
E-mail: info@aisj-jhb.com
http://www.aisj-jhb.com
Serves a diverse community of students from around the world and provides a challenging education emphasizing academic excellence through a collaborative partnership with families and staff. Our program inspires and prepares the students to become responsible world citizens with a passion for life long learning.

Andy Page-Smith, Director
Ellinor Parkes, Admissions Coordinator

1262 American International School-Zambia
PO Box 31617
Lusaka
Zambia
260-211-260509 (10
Fax: 260-211-260-538
E-mail: SpecialPerson@aislusaka.org
http://www.aislusaka.org
Committed to being a leading IB World School, offering a balanced, academically rigorous and internationally recognized college preparatory education and seeks to enable its students to become successful, lifelong learners, as well as humane, self-directed, confident and well-rounded individuals.

Chris Mulind, Director
Jim Anderson, Secondary Principal

1263 American School of Kinshasa
Unit 31550
APO AE
09828
243-884-6619
Fax: 243-884-1161
E-mail: irene.epp@gmail.com
http://www.tasok.cd
rawing on the strengths of a committed and culturally diverse community, The American School of Kinshasa aims to provide a high quality American primary and secondary education for English speaking students living in the Democratic Republic of Congo

Irene Epp, Superintendent
Fiona M Merali, Business Manager

1264 American School-Tangier
Rue Christophe Colomb
Tangier 9000
Morocco
212-39 93 98 27/28
Fax: 212-39 94 75 35
E-mail: ast@tangeroise.net.ma
http://http://www.theamericanschooloftangier.com/
An independent, coeducational day and boarding school which offers an educational program from prekindergarten through grade 12 for students of all nationalities.

Brian Horvath, Head of School

1265 American School-Yaounde
BP 7475
Yaounde
Cameroon
237-2223-0421
Fax: 237-2223-6011
E-mail: school@asoy.org
http://asoy.org
Ensures that all students achieve high academic success, demonstrate critical thinking skills, and become responsible and compassionate, global citizens prepared for their next stage in life; as gained through an enriched, American curriculum and offered in a challenging, secure, and diverse environment.

Paul Sheppard, School Director

1266 Arundel School
28 Arundel School Road
PO Box MP 91 Mount Pleasant
Harere, Zimbabwe
263-4-335654/7
Fax: 263 4 335671 / 304
E-mail: head@arundel.ac.zw
http://http://www.arundel.ac.zw/
Gives all students the opportunity to reach their full potential, both in and out of the classroom. This is achieved through an active educational program, which encompasses the search for excellence in the fields of academic endeavour, culture, sports and personal development.

G Alcock, Principal

1267 Arusha International School
PO Box 733
Moshi, Kilimanjaro
Tanzania
255-27-275-5004
Fax: 255-27-275-2877
E-mail: director@ismoshi.net
http://www.ismoshi.org
Offers a fully accredited, academically rigorous international education for students of ages three to nineteen years old.

Barry Sutherland, CEO
Bob Woods, Director

1268 Asmara International Community School
117-19 Street, #6
PO Box 4941, Asmara
Eritrea
291-1-161-705
Fax: 291-1-161-705
E-mail: johnston@gmail.com
http://www.aicsasmara.com
Grade levels pre K-12.

Paul Johnston, Director

1269 Banda School
PO Box 24722
Nairobi
Kenya 00502
254-20-8891220/260
Fax: 254-20-8890004
E-mail: bandaschool@swiftkenya.com
http://www.bandaschool.com
Meet the educational needs of children living in and around Nairobi whose parents required a Preparatory School education for their children but who did not wish them to go to boarding school overseas.

Michael D Dickson, Headmaster
W Rutter, Deputy Head

1270 Bishop Mackenzie International Schools
PO Box 102
Lilongwe
Malawi
265-1-756-364
Fax: 265-1-751-374
E-mail: info@bmismw.com
http://bmis.ecis.org
The mission of the school is to prepare students to become responsible, self-reliant, contributing and productive citizens of our ever-changing world.

Peter Todd, Director
Janette Johnson, Primary Head Teacher

1271 Braeburn High School
Kisongo Campus
Gitanga Road
PO Box 45112 GPO Nairobi
Kenya 00100
254-20-5018000
Fax: 254-20-3872310
E-mail: andy.hill@braeburn.ac.ke
http://www.braeburn.com
This is a co-educational international boarding school following the British National Curriculum (University of Cambridge International General Certificate of Secondary Education Examinations IGCSE), with boarding options.

R E Diaper, Principal
Mr. Terry L. K. Childs, CEO

1272 Braeburn School
Gitanga Road
PO Box 45112 GPO Nairobi
Kenya 00100
254-722 68557
Fax: 254-2-572310
E-mail: scott.webber@braeburn.ac.ke
http://www.braeburn.com
This school caters to close to 600 children from 61 different countries.

R E Diaper, Principal
Mr. Terry L. K. Childs, CEO

1273 British International School Cairo
km 38, Cairo-Alex Desert Road
Beverly Hills, 6th of October
Egypt, EG
202-3859-2000
Fax: 202-3859-1720
E-mail: info@bisc.edu.eg
http://www.bisc.edu.eg

The School was established in 1976 to provide a balanced and challenging education based on British principles and curricula to meet the needs of the children of the expatriate British and Anglo-Egyptian communities; children from the Commonwealth and other countries with educational systems based upon British standards; children of the English-speaking Egyptian community and other nationalities tied to British-type schooling.

Simon O'Grady, Assistant
Ahmed Ezz, Principal

274 British School-Lom
BP 20050
Lome
Togo
228-222-606
Fax: 228-222-498
E-mail: admin@bsl.tg
http://www.bsl.tg
We value not only academic success but encourage talent of all kinds, whether in academic studies, art, drama, music or games; and that we take the position that the pupil who is kind and helpful, who has a positive attitude to school life and fellow pupils, is considered every bit as worthwhile as the brilliant scholar, artist or athlete.

275 British School-Lom,
228-226-46-06
Fax: 228-226-49-89
This school offers an English based curriculum for 120 day students and 95 boarding students (110 boys; 105 girls), ages 4-18. The school is an independent, co-educational day and boarding school. External exams from the University of London and Cambridge-UK plus International Baccalaureate (IB) is offered. Applications needed to teach include science, pre-school, French, math, social sciences, administration, Spanish, reading, German, English and physical education.

276 British Yeoward School
Parque Taoro
Tenerife
Spain, ES 38400
00-34-922-384685
Fax: 00-34-922-37-35-65
E-mail: office@yeowardschool.org
http://www.yeowardschool.org
The International British Yeoward School provides a high quality British education for children of all ages in an open, multi-cultural environment; allowing each child to achieve their full potential in a positive learning community

Karen Hernandez, Head of Primary Grades
Alan Halstead, Head of School

277 Broadhurst Primary School
Private Bag BR 114 Broadhurst
Garborone
Botswana, BW
267-3971-221
Fax: 267-307987
E-mail: broadhurst@info.bw
http://www.info.bw
To create, together with the family, a caring environment of learning and experience, in which children may develop their potential to the full, may acquire the knowledge and skills to equip them for living, may experience the best that the human spirit has achieved, may develop respect for themselves, for other people and the world around them and have the courage to make a difference to future

Rehana Khan, Head Teacher
Michael Eisen, Deputy Headteacher

1278 Brookhouse Preparatory School
PO Box 24987- 00502
Nairobi
Kenya
254-20-2430260
Fax: 254-20-891641
E-mail: info@brookhouse.ac.ke
http://http://www.brookhouse.ac.ke/index.asp
Provides education in general computer literacy.

Eric Mulind, School Coordinator

1279 Cairo American College
PO Box 39
Maadi 11431
Cairo, EG 11431
20-2-755-5505
Fax: 20-2-2519-6584
E-mail: support@cacegypt.org
http://www.cacegypt.org
Cairo American College is a world class learning environment that affirms the voice, passions and talents of students and inspires them to use their hearts and minds as global citizens.

Nivine Captan-Amr, Board Chair
Elizabeth Bredin, Secretary

1280 Casablanca American School
Route de la Mecque,Lotissement Ougo
Casablanca, Morocco 20150
212-22-214-115
Fax: 212-22-212-488
E-mail: cas@cas.ac.ma
http://www.cas.ac.ma
To offer the best possible U.S. and international university preparatory education program, curriculum and instruction for its students.

Simohamed Erroussafi, President
Karima Abisourour, Vice President

1281 Cavina School
PO Box 43090
Nairobi
Kenya
254-2-3866011
Fax: 254-2-3866676
E-mail: cavina@iconnect.co.ke
http://www.cavina.ac.ke
Cavina aims to develop many qualities in the children who come through her gates - academic excellence, an inquiring mind, a sense of moral and social responsibility, and most of all a recognition of their relationship with their Creator who has revealed Himself through His son Jesus.

Massie Bloofield, Headmaster/Managing Director

1282 Dakar Academy
BP 3189 Route des Peres Maristes
Dakar, Senegal
West Africa
221-33-832-06-82
Fax: 221-33-832-17-21
E-mail: office@dakar-academy.org
http://www.dakar-academy.org
Dakar Academy exists to partner in the advancement of the Kingdom of God through serving missionary families by providing education services for their children

Charlie Campbell, Chairman
Joseph Rosa, Director

1283 Greensteds School
Private Bag
Nakuru
Kenya
254 50 50770
Fax: 254 50 50775

E-mail: office@greenstedsschool.com
http://http://www.greenstedsschool.com/
An international school for boys and girls.
MP Bentley, Headmaster

1284 Harare International School
66 Pendennis Road
Mount Pleasant
Harare, Zimbabwe
(263 4) 870514/5
Fax: 263-4-883-371
E-mail: his@his.ac.zw
http://www.his-zim.com
Grade levels prekindergarten through twelfth, with enrollment of 376.

Marcel Gerrmann, Board Chair
Shannon Brauchli, Vice Chair

1285 Hillcrest Secondary School
PO Box 24819
Nairobi
Kenya 00502
254-20-882-222
Fax: 254-20-882-350
E-mail: admin@hillcrest.ac.ke
http://www.hillcrest.ac.ke/secondary/
Mixed boarding school.

Christopher Drew, Head Teacher

1286 International Community School-Addis Ababa
PO Box 70282
Addis Adaba
Ethiopia
251-11-3-711-544
Fax: 251-11-371-0722
E-mail: info@icsaddis.edu.et
http://http://www.icsaddis.edu.et/
An independent, coeducational day school which offers an educational program from prekindergarten through grade 12 for students of all nationalities.

Jim Laney, Director

1287 International School-Kenya
PO Box 14103
Nairobi
Kenya 00800
254-20-418-3622
Fax: 254-20-418-3272
E-mail: info@isk.ac.ke
http://www.isk.ac.ke
Students from many backgrounds go to this school, which prepares them for successful transitions to other schools and universities around the world, offering both a North American Hogh School Diploma as well as the International Baccalaureate Diploma to its graduates.

John Roberts, Director
Jodi Lake, Curriculum Coordinator

1288 International School-Moshi
PO Box 733
Moshi, Kilimanjaro
Tanzania
255-27-275-5004
Fax: 255-27-275-2877
E-mail: school@ismoshi.org
http://www.ismoshi.org
The school inspires individuals to be lifelong learners in a global community.

Bob Woods, Director of ISM
Keiron White, Head, Moshi Campus

1289 International School-Tanganyika
United Nations Road
PO Box 2651, Dar es Salaam
Tanzania
255-22-2151817/8
Fax: 255-22-2152077

E-mail: ist@raha.com
http://www.istafrica.com
IST aspires to provide an outstanding international education. We value and respect cultural diversity and embrace the people and natural environment of Tanzania. Within this safe, secure and caring community students reach their full potential as citizens of the world.

David Shawver, Director
Nazir Thawer, General Manager

1290 John F Kennedy International School
CH-3792 Saanen
Switzerland
41-033-744-1372
Fax: 41- 033-744-8982
E-mail: lovell@jfk.ch
http://www.jfk.ch
Boarding day school for boys and girls aged 5-14 years.

William Lovell, Co-Director
Sandra Lovell, Co-Director

1291 Kabira International School
PO Box 34249
Kampala
Uganda
256-0414-530-472
Fax: 256-0414-543-444
E-mail: office@kisu.com
http://www.kabiraschool.com
Grade levels Pre-K through 8, school year - September - July

Emma Whitney, Admissions
Elaine Whelen, Principal

1292 Kestrel Manor School
Ring Road Westlands
PO Box 14489, Nairobi
Kenya 00200
254-20-3740-311
E-mail: info@kestrelmanorschool.com
http://www.kestrelmanorschool.com
Coeducational school for children Kindergarten through secondary schooling.

1293 Khartoum American School
PO Box 699
Khartoum
Sudan
249-15-577-0105
Fax: 249-183-512044
E-mail: kas@krtams.org
http://www.krtams.org
An independent, coeducational day school which offers an educational program from prekindergarten through grade 12 for students of all nationalities.

Gregory Hughes, Superintendent
Brad Waugh, Principal

1294 Kigali International School
Caisse Sociale Estates, Gaculiro
BP 6558
Kigali, Rwanda
250-0783307282
Fax: 250-72128
E-mail: office.kics@gmail.com
http://www.kicsrw.org
Non-profit, co-educational day school

Bryan Hixson, Chairman
Mark Thiessen, Vice Chairman

1295 Kingsgate English Medium Primary School
Box 169
Mafeteng, 900 Lesotho
Africa
Kingsgate is the only non-denominational primary school in the district. The curriculum is English-based offered to a total of 460 day students (240 boys; 220 girls), PreK-7. Overseas teachers are welcome with the length of stay being one year, with housing provided. Applications needed to teach include pre-school and reading.

M Makhothe, Principal

1296 Kisumu International School
PO Box 1276
Kisumu
Kenya
254-35-21678
E-mail: admin@kis.co.ke
http://www.kisumu.braeburn.com
This school is located on the shores of Lake Victoria and offers a unique education to students of all nationalities and cultural backgrounds. The total enrollment of the school is 35 day students, in grades K-7. The school does participate in the teacher exchange programs, with the length of stay being two years with housing provided by the school. Applications needed to teach include science, preschool, math, social sciences, English and physical education.

Neena Sharma, Principal

1297 Lincoln Community School
American Embassy Accra
N126/21 Dedeibaa Street
Abelemkpe, Accra
Ghana, West Africa
233 30 277 4018
Fax: 233 302 78 09 85
E-mail: headofschool@lincoln.edu.gh
http://www.lincoln.edu.gh
is committed to inspiring students to achieve the highest standards of intellectual and personal development through a stimulating and comprehensive program.

Dennis Larkin, Head of School
Sanjay Rughani Tanzanian, President

1298 Lincoln International School of Uganda
PO Box 4200
Kampala
Uganda
256-41-4200374/8/9
Fax: 256-41-200303
E-mail: dtodd@isumail.ac.ug
http://www.lincoln.ac.ug
Grade levels Pre-K through 12, school year August - June

Daniel Todd, Dean of Studied/Admission
Jim Campbell, Chairman

1299 Maru A Pula School
Plot 4725
Maruapula Way
Botswana 00045
267-391-2953
Fax: 267-397-3338
E-mail: principal.map@gmail.com
http://www.maruapula.org/
Maru-a-Pula is a dynamic, world-class school rooted in Botswana. We offer a rigorous curriculum that prepares students for entry to highly selective universities and to pursue challenging careers. Through programmes emphasizing self-discipline and community service, each student learns personal and social responsibility.

Andrew S Taylor, Principal

1300 Mombasa Academy
PO Box 86487
Mombasa
Kenya, KE
254-11-471629
Fax: 254-11-221484
E-mail: msaacademy@swiftmombasa.com
http://www.msaacademy.com
Our aim is to help our pupils to reach their true potential. Within the academic and extra-curricular frameworks, staff offer pupils considerable personal support; warm and productive working relations are a distinguishing feature of our community and are instrumental in helping each girl and boy on the road towards maturity and self-fulfillment

Kishor Joshi, Headmaster
FJ Bentley, Founder

1301 Northside Primary School
PO Box 897
Gaborone
Botswana
267-395-2440
Fax: 267-395-3573
E-mail: administration@northsideschool.net
http://www.northsideschool.net
In Gaborone, Botswana, Northside Primary School provides education in English and serves the needs of primary school children of all nationalities.

Mandy Watson, Headteacher

1302 Nsansa School
PO Box 70322
Ndola
Zambia
26-2-611753
Fax: 26-2-618465
This school offers an English curriculum to 185 day students (96 boys; 124 girls), in grades K-7. Length of stay for overseas teachers is one year with housing provided. Student/teacher ratio is 20:1.

Nel Mather, Principal

1303 Peterhouse
Private Bag 3741
Marondera
Zimbabwe
263 (0)279 - 22200
Fax: 263 (0)279 - 24200
E-mail: peterhouse@peterhouse.co.zw
http://www.peterhouse.org
This Anglican school offers an English based curriculum for 19 day students and 790 boarding students (535 boys; 255 girls), in Form I-Form VI. The school is willing to participate in a teacher exchange program with the length of stay being one year, with housing provided. Applications needed to teach include science, math, and physical education.

JB Calderwood, Rector

1304 Rabat American School
1 Bis Rue Emir Ibn Abdelkade
Agdal, Rabat
Morocco 10000
212-537-671-476
Fax: 212-537-670
Fax: 212-537-670-963
E-mail: info@ras.ma
http://www.ras.ma
We provide our students with a breadth of experiences which encourage them to realize their full potential and allow them to acquire the knowledge, skills, character, and confidence to contribute positively and responsibly to an ever-changing, interconnected world.

Paul W Johnson, Director

1305 Rift Valley Academy
PO Box 80
Kijabe, 00220
Kenya
254-20-3246-249
Fax: 254-20-3246-111

E-mail: rva@rva.org
http://www.rva.org
RVA is a Christian boarding school located in central Kenya. The academy, a branch of Africa Inland Mission International, exists to provide a quality education in a nurturing environment for the children of missionaries serving in Africa.

Roy E Entwistle, Principal
Tim Cook, Superintendent

306 Rosslyn Academy
PO Box 14146
Nairobi
Kenya 00800
254-20-263-5294
Fax: 254-20-263-5281
E-mail: info@rosslynacademy.com
http://www.rosslynacademy.com
The purpose of Rosslyn Academy is to provide a K-12 North American and Christian-oriented educational program for children of missionaries. Rosslyn also welcomes children from privately sponsored families who are in sympathy with the philosophy of the school.

Phil Dow, Superintendent
Don McGavran, Director of Operations

307 Sandford English Community School
PO Box 30056 MA
Addis Ababa
Ethiopia
251-11-123-38-92
Fax: 251-11-123-3728
E-mail: admission@sandfordschool.org
http://www.sandfordschool.org
A co-educational, non-boarding, nursery to pre University institution. Its committed to providing a standard of education that is accepted within Ethiopia and by the international community.

Jon D P Lane, Head of Primary School
Tsegaye Kassa, Senior Manager

308 Schutz American School
51 Schutz Street
PO Box 1000
Alexandria, Egypt 21111
(20) (3) 576-2205
Fax: (20) (3) 576-0229
E-mail: jlujan@schutzschool.org.eg
http://www.schutzschool.org.eg
A single campus houses PreK-3 through grade twelve in two main classroom buildings and an auditorium/ classroom complex, as well as the administrative center, dining room, resident staff housing, clinic, art room, computer labs, libraries and snack bar. Sports facilities on the campus include basketball, volleyball, tennis and football courts, a half-size grass soccer pitch, and a swimming pool and weight training room.

Dr Joyce Lujan, Head of School
Nathan Walker, Upper School Principal

309 Sifundzani School
PO Box A286, Swazi Plaza
Mbabane
Swaziland
268-404-2465
Fax: 268-404-0320
E-mail: sifundzani@realnet.co.sz
A coeducational day school which offers an educational program from grades 1 through 10 for students of all nationalities.

Ella Magongo, Principal

310 Sir Harry Johnston Primary School
Kalimbuka Road
Zomba PO Box 52
Malawi

265-1525280
Fax: 265 888202374
E-mail: admin@shjzomba.com
http://www.shjzomba.com
Una Barras-Hargan, Headteacher

1311 St. Barnabas College
34 Langeberg Avenue Bostmont Johann
PO Box 88188 Newclare
South Africa 02112
011-27-474-2055
Fax: 011-27-474-2249
E-mail: theronn@stbarnabas.co.za
http://www.stbarnabas.co.za
St Barnabas College is a co-educational secondary school in Johannesburg. It is well known as a centre of excellence. The school's mission is to provide quality secondary education to young people, the main criterion for admission being intellectual potential and the motivation to succeed.

Glynn Blignaut, Headmaster
Faizel Panker, Deputy Headmaster

1312 St. Mary's School
Rhapta Road, PO Box 40580- 00100
Nairobi
Kenya
254-020-4444569
Fax: 254-020-4446191
E-mail: info@stmarys.ac.ke
http://www.stmarys.ac.ke
We are a Catholic Private School committed to our international character in the provision of a spiritual, intellectual and physical education. We aim at developing the gifts of the young in an atmosphere which encourages the ethos of self-expression and mutual respect with a view to their facing the future responsibly, with confidence and courage.

John Awiti, Head of School
Rosemary Abuodha Omogo, Deputy Principal

1313 St. Paul's College
St. Paul's United Theological College
Po Private Bag
Limuru
Kenya 00217
254 - 20 - 2020505
Fax: 254-66-73033
E-mail:
assistantregistrar@stpaulslimuru.ac.ke
http://www.stpaulslimuru.ac.ke/
The school prepares men and women for ministry in the Christian Church and present day society.

Samuel Kobia, Chancellor
Joseph Galgalo, Vice Chancellor

1314 Tigoni Girls Academy
Box 10
Limuru
Kenya
This Academy is a small, closely knit community of individuals from different cultures in which physical, emotional, creative and intellectual development is fortified in all aspects of daily life. Total enrollment is 40 boarding students, ages 11-16. Applications from overseas include science, math, social sciences, French, Spanish and English. Length of stay for overseas teachers is 2 years with housing provided. The Academy is affiliated with the Church of England.

Duncan Kelly, Principal

1315 Waterford-Kamhlaba United World College
PO Box 52
Mbabane
Swaziland

011-268-422-0866
Fax: 011-268-422-0088
E-mail: admissions@waterford.sz
http://www.waterford.sz/index.php
This school offers a curriculum based in English for 181 day students and 295 boarding (251 boys; 226 girls), in grades 6-12. Overseas teachers length of stay is three years with housing provided. Applications needed to teach include math, English, and physical education.

Laurence Nodder, Principal
Bruce Wells, Deputy Principal

1316 Westwood International School
PO Box 2446
Gabarone
Botswana
011-267-390-6736
Fax: 011-267-390-6734
E-mail: westwood-admissions@info.bw
http://www.westwoodis.com
Westwood International School shall provide students with a quality international education that shall effectively prepare them for access to tertiary study and the world of work, and enable them to confidently meet future challenges as life long learners

Phyllis Hildebrandt, Principal
Michael Francis, Director

1317 Windhoek International School
Private Bag
Windhoek
Namibia 16007
264-61-241-783
Fax: 264-61-243-127
E-mail: k.jarman@wis.edu.na
http://www.wis.edu.na
The Windhoek International School prepares its students to be inquiring, knowledgeable and caring participants in the global arena through an international curriculum of the highest standard. WIS embraces the diversity of its students from the international community and Namibia, in an atmosphere of mutual respect, tolerance and educational enrichment for all

Catherine O'Connor-Smith, Secretary
Neville Field, Chairperson

Asia, Pacific Rim & Australia

1318 Aiyura International Primary School
PO Box 407
Ukarumpa Papua
New Guinea
Perry Bradford, Principal

1319 Ake Panya International School
158/1 Moo 3 Hangdong-Samoeng Road
Banpong, Hangdong, Chiang Mai 50230
Thailand
66-53-36-5303
Fax: 66-53-365-304
E-mail: akepanya@cm.ksc.co.th
http://www.akepanya.co.th
Grade levels 1-12, school year August - June
Barry Sutherland, Headmaster
Holly Shaw, Director of Studies

1320 Alotau International Primary School
PO Box 154
Alotau, Milne Bay Province
Papua New Guinea
675-641-1078
Fax: 675-641-1627

E-mail: alotauis@iea.ac.pg
http://www.iea.ac.pg
Lucy Kula, Principal

1321 Amelia Earhart Intermediate School

Unit 5166
APO AP 96368
Okinawa
011-81-611-734-132
Fax: 011-81-611-734-720
E-mail: aeis_okinawa@pac.dodea.edu
http://www.earhart-is.pac.dodea.edu
Success in Education is a Partnership in Responsibility characterized by the opportunities and the guidance necessary to motivate learners, the desire and ability to be successful in human interactions, to access and process information, and to accept personal responsibility for all decisions made throughout one's lifetime.

Deborah Carlson, Principal

1322 American International School-Dhaka

P.O. Box: 6106
Gulshan, Dhaka 1212
Bangladesh
880-2-882-2452
Fax: 880-2-882-3175
E-mail: info@ais-dhaka.net
http://www.ais-dhaka.net
Provides a program based on American educational principles to students from an international community, creates an academic and social environment that challenges students to achieve their potential, become life-long learners and contribute to changing global society.

Richard Boerner, Superintendent
Kyra Buchko, President

1323 American International School-Guangzhou

No 3 Yan Yu Street S
Ersha Island, Yuexiu District
Guangzhou PR China 51010
86-20-8735-3392
Fax: 86-20-8735-3339
E-mail: admissions@aisgz.org
http://http://www.aisgz.org/
Prepares students for entrance into the very best universities in the world is enhanced by being in the cultural center of Guangzhou and Southern China.

Joseph Stucker, Director
Katherine Farrell, Chair

1324 American School-Bombay

SF 2 G Block
Bandra Kurla Complex
Mumbai 400 0
91 22 6772 7272ÿ
Fax: 91 22 6252 6666
E-mail: admissions@asbindia.org
http://www.asbindia.org
ASB delivers a dynamic educational program that encourages each student to achieve her or his highest potential. While ASB is a U.S. style school, the Indian setting and multi-national community, representing over 51 countries, brings children who have varied experiences together to learn in a rich and unique environment

Paul M Fochtman, Superintendent

1325 American School-Guangzhou (China)

Number 3 Yan Yu Street S
Ersha Island, Yuexiu District
Guangzhou, China 51010

8620-8735-3393
Fax: 8620-8735-3339
E-mail: admissions@aisgz.org
http://http://www.aisgz.org/
An independent, coeducational day school which offers an educational program from kindergarten through grade 12

Joseph Stucker, Director
Paul Wood, Principal

1326 American School-Japan

1-1 Nomizu 1
Chofu-shi, Tokyo
Japan 182-0
0422-34-5300
Fax: 0422-34-5303
E-mail: info@asij.ac.jp
http://www.asij.ac.jp
The American School in Japan is a private, coeducational day school which offers an educational program from nursery through grade 12 for students of all nationalities, but it primarily serves the American community living in the Tokyo area. The school was founded in 1902. The school year comprises 2 semesters extending from September to January and January to June.

Ed Ladd, Headmaster

1327 Aoba International School

2-10-34 Aobadai
Meguro-Ku, Tokyo
Japan 153-0-42
03-3461-1442
Fax: 81-3-3463-9873
E-mail: meguro@aobajapan.jp
http://www.aobaonline.jp
A co-educational school located on campuses in Meguro and Suginami. Over 550 students are enrolled in classes from pre-kindergarten to grade nine.

Neal Dilk, Head of School
Chiharu Uemura, VP

1328 Ashgabat International School

Berzengi, Ata Turk Street
Ashgabat
Turkmenistan
386-12-007870
Fax: 386-12-007871
E-mail: ashgabat@qsi.org
http://tkm.qsi.org
Offers high quality education in the English language for elementary students from three years through thirteen years of age.

Brad Goth, Director

1329 Bali International School

PO Box 3259
Denpasar
Bali, Indonesia
62-361-288-770
Fax: 62-361-285-103
E-mail: admin@baliis.net
http://www.baliinternationalschool.com
Provides educational excellence in a supportive, secure environment, preparing students to thrive and succeed as responsible citizens in a changing world. Offers the three IB Programs (PYP, MYP and DP) and is accredited by WASC.

Chris Akin, Director
Russell McGrath, PS-12 Assistant Principal

1330 Bandung Alliance International School

Jalan Bujanggamanik Kav 2
Kota Baru Parahyangan
Bandung, Indonesia 40553
62-22-8681-3949
Fax: 62-22-8681-3953

E-mail: info@baisedu.org
http://www.baisedu.org
BAIS operates as a private non-profit school to serve the international community. BAIS provides quality education in the traditions of classic, conservative ethics and values.

Pete Simano, Director
Charity Lamertha, Elementary Principal

1331 Bandung International School

Jl Suria Sumantri No 61
Bandung
West Java, Indonesia 40164
62-22-201-4995
Fax: 62-22-201-2688
E-mail: bisadmin@poboxes.com
http://www.bisdragons.com
At Bandung International Scholl, it is our vision to be a preeminent school providing world class secular education in the English language to the children of expatriates and others while maintaining strong links with the Indonesian community

Henri Behelmans, Head of School
Mark Holland, Chair

1332 Bangalore International School

Geddalahalli, Hennur Bagalur Road
Kothanur Post
Bangalore, India 560 0
91-802-846-5060
Fax: 91-802-846-5059
E-mail: info@bisedu.co.in
http://www.bangaloreinternationalschool.com
Provides internationally recognized standards of education with an India ethos and enable students to fulfill their potential in a culturally rich atmosphere.

Anuradha Monga, Principal

1333 Bangkok Patana School

643 Lasalle road Sukhumvit 105 Bang
Bangkok, Thailand 10260
6602-398-0200
Fax: 6602-399-3179
E-mail: reception@patana.ac.th
http://www.patana.ac.th
We are an academically directed school, focussed on our commitment to offer all of our students the best intellectual and physical preparation for higher education.

Tej Bunnag, Chairman
Kulvadee Siribhadra, Director

1334 Beijing BISS International School

No 17, Area 4 An Zhen Xi Li
Chaoyang District, Beijing
China 10002
86-10-6443-3151
Fax: 86-10-6443-3156
E-mail: Admissions@biss.com.cn
http://www.biss.com.cn
To educate and empower our students to attain personal excellence and positively impact the world.

Chan Ching Oi, CEO
Ettie Zilber, Head of School

1335 Bob Hope Primary School

Unit 5166
APO AP 96368-5166
Okinawa, Japan 96368-5166
11-81-611-734-0093
Fax: 11-81-98-934-6806
E-mail: bhps.okinawa@pac.dodea.edu
http://www.bob-hope-ps.pac.dodea.edu
The Bob Hope Primary School community is committed to teaching basic skills using developmentally appropriate strategies.

Jim Journey, Principal
Luldes Giraud, Vice Principal

336 Bogor Expatriate School
PO Box 258
Jalan Papandayan 7, Bogor 16151
Indonesia
62-251-324360
Fax: 62-251-328512
Mission is to provide opportunities to foster positive attitudes towards learning.

Chris Rawlins, Head of School
Lance Kelly, Principal

337 Bontang International School
15 Roszel Road
Po Box 5910
Princeton, NJ 08543
62-548551176
E-mail: iss@iss.edu
An international school with an English/Japanese based curriculum for twenty day students (6 boys; 14 girls), grades PreK-8. Student/teacher ration 5:1.

Roger Hove, Executive Vice President

338 Brent International School-Manila
Brentville Subdivision
Mamplasan, Bian, Laguna
Philippines 04024
63 (049) 511-4330
Fax: 632-633-8420
E-mail: webmaster@brent.edu.ph
http://www.brent.edu.ph
Brent Schools, in a Christian ecumenical environment in the Philippines, are committed to develop individual students as responsible global citizens and leaders in their respective communities, with a multicultural and international perspective, and equipped for entry to colleges and universities throughout the world.

Dick B Robbins, Headmaster
Jeffrey W Hammett, Deputy Headmaster

339 Brent School
Brent Road
PO Box 35, Baguio City
Philippines 02600
63 (074) 442-3628
Fax: 63 (074) 442-2260
E-mail: webmaster@brent.edu.ph
http://www.brentschoolbaguio.com
Brent Schools, in a Christian ecumenical environment in the Philippines, are committed to develop individual students as responsible global citizens and leaders in their respective communities, with a multicultural and international perspective, and equipped for entry to colleges and universities throughout the world.

Dick B Robbins, Headmaster
Ursula Banga-an Daoey, Deputy Head

340 British International School
Bintayo Jaya Sektor IX JI
Raya Jomabang Ciledug Pondok Aren
Jakarta, ID 15227
62-21-745-1670
Fax: 62-21-745-1671
E-mail: enquiries@bis.or.id
http://www.bis.or.id
The new premises and facilities enable the school to excel further in the range of opportunities and experiences that can be offered to its students.

Christian Barkei, Principal
Brian Dallamore, Chairman

341 British School Manila
36th Street University Park Forth B
Fort Bonifacio Global City
Taguig, PH
63 2 860 4800
Fax: 63 2 860 4900
E-mail:
admissions@britishschoolmanila.org
http://www.britishschoolmanila.org
The British School Manila will deliver the highest standard of education in the Philippines for British children and for English speaking children of other nationalities The British School Manila provides outstanding education for English speaking children of all nationalities aged 3-18, based on an adapted form of the National Curriculum of England, and the I.B. Diploma

Chris Mantz, Head of School
Glenn Hardy, Head of Primary School

1342 British School-Muscat
PO Box 1907
Ruwi
Oman 00112
00968ÿ24600842ÿ
Fax: 00968 24601062
E-mail: admin@britishschoolmuscat.com
http://www.britishschoolmuscat.com
The Vision of the British School-Muscat is to offer the highest quality British education to children of wide ranging abilities and nationalities. It values cultural diversity and provides a caring, innovative and stimulating environment, realizing the full potential and celebrating the success of every student. The School's curriculum will also develop the child as a whole person, provide them with learning-to-learn skills and will prepare them to lead a successful life in an inter-cultural wor

Kai Vacher, Principal
Deirdre Selway, Registrar

1343 Calcutta International School Society
18 Lee Road
Calcutta 700 020
India

http://www.calcuttais.edu.in
This school offers an English-based curriculum to 480 day students (230 boys; 250 girls), grades Nursery-12. CIS follows GCE London Curriculum. The cultures represented by the student body include expatriates, NRIs, local children. The student body is mainly Indians. Highly qualified individuals offering excellent results. The school is willing to participate in a teacher exchange program with the length of stay being 1-2 years, with no housing provided.

N Chatterjee, Principal
L Chaturvedi, Faculty Head

1344 Caltex American School
CPI Rumbal
Pekanbaru, Sumatra Riau
Indonesia
62-765-995-501
Fax: 62-765-996-321
Grade level preK through 8.

Daniel Hovde, Superintendent

1345 Camberwell Grammar School
55 Mout Albert Road
Canterbury 3126, Victoria
Australia
61 3 9835 1777
Fax: 61 3 9836 0752
E-mail: registrar@cgs.vic.edu.au
http://http://www.cgs.vic.edu.au/index.asp
Independent boys school.

CF Black, Principal

1346 Canadian Academy
4-1 Koyo Cho Naka
Higashinada-Ku, Kobe
Japan 658-0-32
81-78-857-0100
Fax: 81-78-857-3250
E-mail: hdmstr@canacad.ac.jp
http://www.canacad.ac.jp/canacad/welcome.html
Canadian Academy inspires students to inquire, reflect, and choose to compassionately impact the world throughout their lives.

Fred Wesson, Headmaster
Charles Kite, Assistant Headmaster

1347 Canadian School-India
14/1 Kodigehalli Main Road
Sahakar Nagar, Bangalore 560 092
India
91-80-343-8414
Fax: 91-80-343-6488
E-mail: csib@vsnl.com
http://www.canschoolindia.org
Grade levels K-13, school year August - June

T Alf Mallin, Principal

1348 Canberra Grammar School
40 Monaro Crescent
Red Hill
Australia ACT 2
02-6260-9700
Fax: 02-6260-9701
E-mail: headmaster@cgs.act.edu.au
http://www.cgs.act.edu.au
To develop a cultured man, ready for today's world and the future, balanced in intellectual, spiritual, emotional and physical aspects, with a love of learning and a willingness to serve fellow students and the wider community

Justin Garrick, Headmaster
Alan Ball, Head of Senior School

1349 Carmel School-Hong Kong
10 Borrett Road
Mid-Levels
Hong Kong
852-2964-1600
Fax: 852-2813-4121
E-mail: admin@carmel.edu.hk
http://www.carmel.edu.hk
Carmel School is committed to providing children living in Hong Kong with the highest international standard of secular and Jewish education. Through small classes and individual attention, the school offers a supportive environment that develops students' confidence, imagination and skills, in both academic and social spheres.

Edwin Epstein, Head of School
Kaisha Chow, Operations Director

1350 Casa Montessori Internationale
17 Palm Avenue Forbes Park Makati
Etro Manila D-3117
Philippines
Pre-nursery, nursery and kindergarten classes.

Carina Lebron, Principal

1351 Cebu International School
Banilad Road
PO Box 735, Cebu City 6000
Philippines
(63 32)ÿ401-1900
Fax: (63 32) 401-1904
E-mail: deidref@cis.edu.ph
http://http://www.cis.edu.ph/main.aspx
The primary aim of Cebu International School is to develop well-balanced global citizens who are intelligent, dynamic, respectful of universal moral values within a

multicultural environment, and able to cope responsibly in an ever-changing interdependent world.

Deidre Fischer, Superintendent
Jenny Basa, Dean of Student Services

1352 Central Java Inter-Mission School

Jl Nakula Sadewa Raya Number 55
Salatiga, Jateng
Indonesia 50722
62-298-311673
Fax: 62-298-321609
E-mail: office@mountainviewics.org
http://www.mountainviewics.org
Primary intent of the school is that all students be thoroughly exposed to Scripture and that they find and sustain a vital relationship to Jesus Christ through Holy Spirit.

Willliam J Webb III, Superintendent
Kirk Thornton, Assistant Superintendent

1353 Central Primary School

Winston Churchill Avenue
Port Vila
Republic of Vanuatu
678-23122
Fax: 678-22526
E-mail: central@vanuatu.com.vu
http://www.central.herts.sch.uk
Meet the needs of children from most countries and to provide an equivalent level of education for local children in an 'English as a First Language' context.

John Path, Chairman
John Lee Solomon, PEO

1354 Chiang Mai International School

PO Box 38
13 Chetupon Road
Thailand, TH 50000
665-324-2027
Fax: 665-324-2455
E-mail: info@cmis.ac.th
http://www.cmis.ac.th
Encourage the development of students' abilities in critical, analytical, and independent thinking, demonstrated in fluent oral and written communication.

Lance Potter, Principal
Sinturong Pannavalee, Director

1355 Chinese International School

1 Hau Yuen Path
Braemar Hill, Hong Kong
China
852-2510-7288
Fax: 852-2510-7488
E-mail: cis_info@cis.edu.hk
http://www.cis.edu.hk
Committed to the achievement of academic excellence and is characterized and enriched by its dual-language program in Chinese and English.

Theodore S Faunce, Headmaster
Li Bin, Deputy Head of School

1356 Chittagong Grammar School

Sarson Valley, 448/B Joynagar,
Chiottagong
Bangladesh
88-031-632900
E-mail: cgslower@hotmail.com
http://www.chittagonggrammarschool.com
Dedicated to the total growth and development of each student. Provides the students a broad, challenging and sound education to enable children to achieve the highest standards of which they are capable.

Afran Sanchita, Teacher
Akther Sharmin, Teacher

1357 Colombo International School

28, Gregory's Road
Colombo 7
Sri Lanka
94-11-269-7587
Fax: 94-11-269-9592
E-mail: management@cis.lk
http://www.cis.lk
English medium co-educational day school with separate Infant, Junior and Secondary sections.

M.J. Chappell, Principal
Armyne Wirasinha, Chairman

1358 Concordia International School-Shanghai

999 Mingyue Road, Jinqiao, Pudong
Shanghai
201206, China
86-21-5899-0380
Fax: 86-21-5899-1685
E-mail: admissions@ciss.com.cn
http://www.ciss.com.cn
Concordia's vision to offer academic excellence in a faith-based, caring community finds its roots in the 150-year educational tradition of the Lutheran Church-Missouri Synod.

James Koerschen, Head of School
Carol Ann Tonn-Bourg, Director of Admissions

1359 Cummings Elementary School

Unit 5039
APO AP
Japan 96319-5039
81-3117-66-2226
Fax: 81-3117-62-5110
E-mail: pcumming@pac.dodea.edu
http://www.cummings-es.pac.dodea.edu
We, the community of Cummings Elementary School, are committed to guiding our students to become successful learners and responsible citizens in an ever-changing world

Scott Sterry, Principal

1360 Dalat School

11200 Penang
Tanjung Bunga
Malaysia
60-4-899-2105
Fax: 60-4-890-2141
E-mail: info@dalat.org
http://www.dalat.org
The mission of Dalat International School is to prepare young people to live fully for God in a rapidly changing world by enabling them to understand, evaluate, and reconcile that world with the foundation of God's unchanging values.

Karl Steinkamp, Director
Fred Colburn, High School Principal

1361 Dover Court Prep School

Dover Road
Singapore, 139644
Singapore
65-67757664
Fax: 65-67774165
E-mail: admin@dover.edu.sg
http://www.dovercourt.org
To teach goals of the learning process, which is facilitated through encouraging pupils to pose and solve problems, take risks, demonstrate responsible attitudes and behaviour, adopt a critical and self-evaluative approach to their work.

Maureen Roach, Director
Catherine Alliott, Chief Executive Officer

1362 Ela Beach International School

PO Box 1137
Boroko
Papua New Guinea
675-325-2183
Fax: 675-325-7925
E-mail: bmackinlay@temis.iea.ac.pg
This school consists of 262 boys and 222 girl day students in PreK-Grade 6. The length of stay for overseas teachers is three years with housing provided. School enrollment is made up of 260 PNG children, 224 non PNG children, overseas and PNG staff team teaching in mixed age group classrooms.

Bruce E Mackinlay, Principal

1363 Elsternwick Campus-Wesley College

577 Street Kilda Road
Melbourne
Australia 03004
61-3-8102-6100
Fax: 61 3 8102 6054
E-mail: stkildaroad@wesleycollege.net
http://www.wesleycollege.net
Wesley College is a coeducational school of the Uniting Church which has enriched the lives of thousands of young people, since it opened on 18 January 1866 as a boy's boarding school. In its 140 year history, it has experienced the influence of 14 principals, each of whom has in turn, enriched the life of the College.

Jack Moshakis, Executive Director
Helen Drennen, Principal

1364 Faisalabad Grammar School

Kohinoor Nagar
Faisalabad 728593
Pakistan

http://www.fgschools.edu.pk
This Islamic school offers a curriculum taught in both English and Urdu to 2,000 day students (1,000 boys; 1,000 girls), in Junior Nursery up to eighteen years of age. The school runs 50% of classes in Matriculation Streams Local, and 50% in 'O' and 'A' level University of Cambridge UK examinations. Applications needed to teach include science, math, English and computers, with the length of stay for overseas teachers being one year.

RY Saigol Sarfraz, Principal
N Akhtar, VP

1365 Faith Academy

MCPO Box 2016
Makati City
Philippines 00706
11-632-248-5000
Fax: 63-2-658-0026
E-mail: vanguard@faith.edu.ph
http://www.faith.edu.ph
Faith Academy envisions expanding children's educational delivery options to meet the needs of the missions enterprise throughout Asia.

Tom Hardeman, Superintendent
Mike Hause, Deputy Superindentent

1366 French International School

165 Blue Pool
Happy Valley, SAR, Hong Kong
China
852-257-76217
Fax: 852-257-79658
E-mail: lfi@lfis.edu.hk
http://www.fis.edu.hk
To provide, together with families, a nurturing, culturally diverse community that inspires our young people to realize their true potential as confident, independent learners and responsible global citizens with moral values and integrity.

Francis Cauet, Headmaster
Samuel Hureau, Administrator

367 Fukuoka International School
3-18-50 Momochi
Sawara-ku, Fukuoka
Japan 00814-6
81-92-841-7601
Fax: 81-92-841-7602
E-mail: adminfis@fka.att.ne.jp
http://www.fis.ed.jp
To create a dynamic learning environment in which students can be educated in high international academic standards. We strive to be a model of unity in diversity in which the individual is respected in each student is challenged at his/her own level.

Linda Gush, Head of School
Daniel Habel, Dean of Students

368 Garden International School
16 Jalan Kiara 3, Off Jalan Bukit K
Kuala Lumpur
Malaysia 50480
011-60-3-6209-6888
Fax: 011-60-3-6201-2468
E-mail: admissions@gardenschool.edu.my
http://www.gardenschool.edu.my
Grade levels Pre-K through eleventh.

Simon Mann, Principal
Dato' Loy Teik Ngan, Chairman

369 Geelong Grammar School-Glamorgan
14 Douglas Street
Toorak, Victoria
Australia 03142
011-61-3-9829-1444
Fax: 011-61-3-9826-2829
E-mail: toorakcampus@ggs.vic.edu.au
http://www.ggs.vic.edu.au
Geelong Grammar School offers an exceptional Australian education. Our students are girls and boys who see the richness of the world through confident eyes.

Lisa Marchetti, Fundraising Coordinator
Stephen Meek, Principal

370 German Swiss International School
11 Guildford Road, The Peak
Hong Kong
China
011-852-2849-6216
Fax: 011-852-2849-6347
E-mail: gsis@gsis.edu.hk
http://www.gsis.edu.hk
Encourage and foster the talents of our students - as well-rounded individuals, responsible team members and open-minded citizens of the 21st century.

Hans PeterÿNaef, COO
Jens-Peter Green, Principal

371 Glenunga International High School
99 L'Estrange Street
Glenuga
South Australia 05064
011-61-8-8379-5629
Fax: 011-61-8-8338-2518
E-mail: glenunga@gihs.sa.edu.au
http://www.gihs.sa.edu.au
Grade levels 8-12.

Wendy Johnson, Principal
Jeremy Cogan, Deputy Principal

372 Good Hope School-Kowloon
303 Clear Water Bay Road
Kowloon
Hong Kong
011-852- 2321-0250
Fax: 011-852- 2324-8242
E-mail: goodhope@ghs.edu.hk
http://www.ghs.edu.hk

Provides equal opportunities to develop their moral, intellectual, physical, social, emotional and artistic aspects of life.

Pauline Yuen, Supervisor
Paul Chow, Principal

1373 Goroka International School
PO Box 845
Goroka EHP
Papua New Guinea
011-675-732-1452
Fax: 011-675-732-2146
E-mail: gorokais@online.net.pg
http://www.iea.ac.pg
Provide education of a high academic standard from early childhood to grade 12

James M Masa, Principal

1374 Hebron School-Lushington Hall
Lushington Hall, Ootacamund
Tamil Nadu
India 64300
11-91-42-3244-2372
Fax: 11-91-42-3244-1295
E-mail: admin@hebronooty.org
http://www.hebronooty.org
Independent, international Christian school.

Mark Noonan, Principal

1375 Hillcrest International School
PO Box 249
Sentani 99352
Papua, Indonesia
011-62-967-591460
Fax: 011-62-967-592673
E-mail: director@hismk.org
http://www.hismk.org
HIS is a Christian international school. Teachers must raise their own support, normally with a mission. Enrollment consists of 97 day students and 24 boarding (53 boys; 68 girls), in grades K-12.

Margaret Hartzler, Director
Ryan Kennedy, Director

1376 Hiroshima International School
3-49-1 Kurakake
Asakita-Ku
Hiroshima, Japan 739-1
011-81-82-843-4111
Fax: 011-81-82-843-6399
E-mail: info@hiroshima-is.ac.jp
http://www.hiroshima-is.ac.jp
The Hiroshima International School is an independent, coeducational day school which offers educational programs from preschool through grade 12. The school year comprises 2 semesters extending from early September to mid-June.

Peter MacKenzie, Principal

1377 Hokkaido International School
1-55, 5-Jo, 19-Chome
Hirahishi, Toyohira-Ku
Sapporo, Japan 062-0
011-81-11-816-5000
Fax: 011-81-11-816-2500
E-mail: his@his.ac.jp
http://www.his.ac.jp
A private, coeducational day and boarding school which offers an America-style education from preschool through grade 12.

Michael Branson, Headmaster
Eri Kashiwabara, Business Manager

1378 Hong Kong International School
1 Red Hill Road
Tai Tam, Hong Kong
Republic of China
011-852-3149-7000
Fax: 011-852-2813-8740

E-mail: Advancement@hkis.edu.hkÿ
http://www.hkis.edu.hk
The Hong Kong International School is a private, Christian, coeducational day school which offers an educational program from pre-primary through grade 12 for students of all nationalities and religious backgrounds. The school year comprises 2 semesters extending approximately from August 19 to January 16 and from January 19 to June 12.

Doug Werth, Chair
David Condon, Head of School

1379 Ikego Elementary School
PSC 474 Box 300
FPO, AP
Japan 96351-300
011-81-46-806-8320
Fax: 011-81-46-806-8324
E-mail: principal_ikegoes@pac.dodea.edu
http://www.ikego-es.pac.dodea.edu
Provides developmentally-appropriate learning experiences that teaches, problem solving, critical thinking, make responsible choices.

Scott Finlay, Principal

1380 International Christian School
1 On Muk Lane
Shek Mun
N.T. Hong Kong
011-852-3920 0010
Fax: 011-852-2336-6114
E-mail: ics@ics.edu.hk
http://www.ics.edu.hk
International Christian School is an exceptional school for a number of reasons. Every ICS graduate has enrolled in a college or university somewhere in the world.

Jack Young, Board Chair
Noel Chu, Executive Assistant

1381 International Community School
1225 The Parkland Road
Khwaeng Bangna, Khet Bangna Bangkok
Thailand 10260
011-66-2-338-0777
Fax: 011-66-2-338-0778
E-mail: info@icsbangkok.com
http://www.icsbangkok.com
Based on the Bible, in partnership with parents, we teach the whole student to know and apply wisdom for the good of our world and the glory of God.

Darren Gentry, Headmaster
Gary Opfer, High School Principal

1382 International School Manila
University Parkway
Fort Bonifacio Global City, Taguig
Philippines 01634
011-63-2-840-8400
Fax: 011-63-2-840-8405
E-mail: superintendent@ismanila.com
http://www.ismanila.com
International School Manila is an independent international school whose structure, traditions and style emanate from the United States and whose curriculum and methodology reflect the best in worldwide educational research and practice. Our school is diverse and dynamic, and our students have the highest aspirations for their education and future lives.

William Brown, High School Principal
David Toze, Superintendent

1383 International School of the Sacred Heart
4-3-1 Hiroo, Shibuya-ku
Tokyo
Japan 150-0

011-81-3-3400-3951
Fax: 011-81-3-3400-3496
E-mail: info@issh.ac.jp
http://www.issh.ac.jp
ISSH is a multicultural Catholic school that warmly welcomes students and families from many faiths. The Pre-Kindergarten and Kindergarten classes for 3, 4 and 5 year olds are for boys and girls, while grades 1-12 are for girls only.

Yvonne Hayes, Headmistress
Charmaine Young, High School Principal

1384 International School-Bangkok
39/7 Soi Nichada Thani,Samakee Road
Nonthaburi
Thailand 11120
011-66-2-963-5800
Fax: 011-66-2-583-5432
E-mail: daladk@isb.ac.th
http://www.isb.ac.th
Our Vision states that our students will make extraordinary academic progress. They become smart about their own learning processes, understanding what does and does not work for them as learners.

Dr Bill Gerritz, Head of School
Dr Ugo Costessi, Deputy Head of School/CFO

1385 International School-Beijing
10 An Hua Street
Shunyi District,,Beijing
China 10131
86-10-8046-2345
Fax: 86-10-8046-2001
E-mail: isb-info@isb.bj.edu.cn
http://www.isb.bj.edu.cn
Educate and inspire students to reach their unique potential and contribute positively to society by providing a world class education enriched by diversity and the Chinese culture.

Thomas Hawkins, Head of School
Rodney Fagg, High School Principal

1386 International School-Eastern Seaboard
PO Box 6
Banglamung, Chonburi
Thailand 20150
(6638) 372 591
Fax: (6638) 372 950
E-mail: ise@ise.ac.th
http://www.ise.ac.th
Prepare an international student population for higher education and lifelong learning by emphasizing higher level thinking skills, effective communication, global responsibilities, and personal wellness within a cooperative and supportive school community.

Robert Brewitt, Superintendent
Heather Naro, Elementary Principal

1387 International School-Fiji
PO Box 10828
Laucala Beach Estate, Suva
Fiji Islands
11-679-3393-560
Fax: 11-679-3340-017
E-mail: info@international.school.fj
http://www.international.school.fj
An independent co-educational day school offering pre-school, primary and secondary education and offers excellent education and a caring and nurturing environment for young people. The curriculum includes International Baccalaureate (Primary Years Programme, Middle Years Programme, Diploma Programme), University of Cambridge - International General Certificate of Secondary Education

and the Australian Capital Territory Year 12 Certificate and University Admissions Index (UAI).
Dianne Korare, Principal
Sera Brown, Registrar

1388 International School-Ho Chi Minh City
16 Vo Truong Toan St
An Phu Ward, District 2, Ho Ci Minh City
Vietnam
84-8-898-9100
Fax: 84 (8) 3 519-4110
E-mail: admissions@ishcmc.edu.vn
http://www.ishcmc.com
The school provides and teaches the students about intellectual, emotional, social, creative, linguistic, cultural, moral, aesthetic and physical needs of each students. The school seeks to involve parents in the education of their children through regular communication.

Sean O'Maonaigh, Headmaster
Chris Byrne, Admissions/Marketing

1389 International School-Kuala Lumpur
PO Box 12645
Kuala Lumpur
Malaysia 50784
603-4259-5600
Fax: 603-4257-9044
E-mail: iskl@iskl.edu.my
http://www.iskl.edu.my
Offers its students a superior education to prepare them to be responsible world citizens who think creatively, reason critically, communicate effectively and learn enthusiastically throughout life.

Paul Chmelik, Headmaster
Amina O'Kane, Admissions Director

1390 International School-Lae
PO Box 2130
Lae, Morobe
Papua New Guinea 00411
011-675-479-1425
Fax: 011-675-472-3485
E-mail: mail@tisol.iea.ac.pg
http://www.tisol.ac.pg
Offers high quality education, from ages 18 months to grade 8. The curriculum prepares students for national and international success.

Neal Mather, Principal

1391 International School-Manila
Univiersty Parkway
Fort Bonifacio, Taguig City
Philippines 01634
632-840-8488
Fax: 632-840-8489
E-mail: superintendent@ismanila.com
http://www.ismanila.org
An independent international school whose structure, traditions and style emanate from the United States. It aims to build a community of reflective learners who are passionate, caring and responsible contributors to the world in which we live.

Ray Dempsey, President
David Toze, Superintendent

1392 International School-Penang-Uplands
Jalan Sungai Satu
Batu Feringgi, Penang
Malaysia 11100
011-604-8819-777
Fax: 011-604-8819-778

E-mail: info@uplands.org
http://www.uplands.org
Uplands aims to provide excellent international education for students of all nationalities in a challenging multi-cultural environment. It favours methods of teaching which foster the joys of learning, discovery and enquiry, aiming to nurture students into thinking, learning, caring and striving to meet the needs of a better world.

John Horsfall, Acting Principal
M R Chandran, Chair

1393 International School-Phnom Penh, Cambodia
146 Norodom Boulevard
PO Box 138, Phnom Penh
Cambodia
855-23-213-103
Fax: 855-23-213-104
E-mail: ispp@ispp.edu.kh
http://www.ispp.edu.kh
ISPP empowers students, in a caring international environment, to achieve their potential by pursuing personal and academic excellence, and to grow as responsible global citizens who celebrate diversity.

Barry Sutherland, Director
Laura Watson, Chairperson

1394 International School-Phnom Penh-Cambodia
146 Norodom Boulevard
PO Box 138, Phnom Penh
Cambodia
855-23-213-103
Fax: 855-23-361-002
E-mail: ispp@ispp.edu.kh
http://www.ispp.edu.kh
ISPP empowers students, in a caring international environment, to achieve their potential by pursuing personal and academic excellence, and to grow as responsible global citizens who celebrate diversity.

Barry Sutherland, Director
Laura Watson, Chairperson

1395 International School-Pusan
798 Nae-ri, Gijang-eup
Gijang-gun, Busan 619-902
South Korea
82 51 742-3332
Fax: 82 51 742 3375
E-mail: enquiries@bifskorea.org
http://www.isbusan.org
The school possess a caring, family-like ethos, giving the children a high level of self-confidence and esteem, and teaching them tolerance and respect for other cultures.

Stephen Palmer, Principal
Thomas Walker, Chairman

1396 International School-Singapore
25 Paterson Road
Singapore 23851
(65) 6235 5844
Fax: (65) 6732 5701
E-mail: admissions@iss.edu.sg
http://www.iss.edu.sg
ISS mission is to provide a multicultural educational environment for our students in which they achieve academic success, personal growth and become socially responsible and active global citizens with an appreciation of learning as a life-long process.

Mak Lai Ying, Principal
Anthony Race, Headmaster

1397 International School-Ulaanbaatar
Four Seasons Garden, Khan-Uul Distr
1st Khoroo, PO Box 36/10
Ulaanbaatar, Mongolia 17032

976-70160010
Fax: 976-70160012
E-mail:
administration@isumongolia.edu.mn
http://www.isumongolia.edu.mn
The International School of Ulaanbaatar seeks to offer the best educational system possible, based on an international curriculum.

Gregory Rayl, Director
Tuul Arildii, Deputy Director

398 Island School
20 Borrett Road
Mid Levels
Hong Kong
852-2524-7135
Fax: 852-2840-1673
E-mail: school@mail.island.edu.hk
http://www.island.edu.hk
An international, co-educational, comprehensive school, providing secondary education for children of all nations who can benefit from an education through the medium of English.

Pinder Wong, Council Chairman
Chris Binge, Principal

399 Ivanhoe Grammar School
PO Box 91
The Ridgeway, Ivanhoe, Victoria
Australia 03079
61 3 9490 1877
Fax: 61 3 9497 4060
E-mail: info@ivanhoe.com.au
http://www.igs.vic.edu.au
Our mission is to be a community of learning that develops in students the skills and values that will prepare them for the challenges and responsibilities of adult citizenship.

Roderick D Fraser, Principal
Andrew Sloane, Head of School

400 JN Darby Elementary School
PSC 485 Box 99
FPO, AP
Japan 96321
011-81-956-50-8800
Fax: 011-81-956-50-8804
E-mail: Darby_ES@pac.dodea.edu
http://http://www.darby-es.pac.dodea.edu/
The Darby Community promotes academic and social excellence so all students can become positive contributors to society.

Joy Jaramillo, Principal

401 Jakarta International School
PO Box 1078/JKS
Jakarta 12010
Indonesia
(62-21) 750-3644
Fax: 62-21-765-7852
E-mail: parentnet@jisedu.org
http://jisedu.org
JIS is a place where people from almost 60 countries come together to share ideas, experiences and values.

Tim Carr, Head of School

402 Japan International School
7-5-1 Hikarigaoka
Shibuya-Ku, Tokyo 168-0081
Japan
81-3-3335-6620
Fax: 81-3-3332-6930
E-mail: hikarigaoka@aobajapan.jp
http://http://www.aobaonline.jp/
Student of all nationalities, and religions are welcome.

Charles S Barton, Headmaster

1403 John McGlashan College
2 Pilkington Street
Maori Hill, Dunedin
New Zealand
03-467-6620
Fax: 03-467-6622
http://www.mcglashan.school.nz
ohn McGlashan College is an integrated, Year 7-13, secondary school for boys. The roll comprises approximately 380 dayboys from Dunedin city and its surrounds and 110 boarders, most of whom come from rural Otago and Southland. In addition, up to 20 international students are enrolled each year

K Michael Corkery, Principal
Neil Garry, Deputy Principal

1404 Kansai Christian School
282-2 Oaza Misato, Heguri-cho, Ikom
Nara Ken 636-0904
Japan
0745-45-6422
Fax: 011-81-745-45-6422
E-mail: office@kansaichristianschool.com
http://www.kansaichristianschool.com
Kansai Christian School was established in 1970 to provide a general education in a Christian environment for children of the evangelical missionary community

Albert Greeff, Principal

1405 Kaohsiung American School
35 Sheng Li Road
Tzuo-Ying District (813)
Taiwan
886-7-583-0112
Fax: 886-7-582-4536
E-mail: dchang@kas.kh.edu.tw
http://www.kas.kh.edu.tw
Kaohsiung American School (KAS) is a private, non-profit Pre-K - 12 institution with 330 students offering college preparatory programs leading to a U.S. high school diploma. It is located in Kaohsiung, a city of 1.5 million in southwestern Taiwan.

Tom Farrell, Superintendent
Deborah Taylor, Assistant Director

1406 Kellett School
2 Wah Lok Path
Wah Fu, Pokfulam
Hong Kong
852-2551-8234
Fax: 852-2875-0262
E-mail: admissions@kellettschool.com
http://www.kellettschool.com
Kellett School is an independent non-for-profit school catering to the English-speaking children living in Hong Kong. The school is operated by Kellett School Association Limited through a Board of Governors; seven of whom are parents, elected by the Association, and the remaining three are ex-officio members. All parents become members of the Association.

Ann McDonald, Principal

1407 Kilmore International School
40 White Street
Kilmore, Victoria
Australia 03764
61-357-822-211
Fax: 61-357-822-525
E-mail: info@kilmore.vic.edu.au
http://www.kilmore.vic.edu.au
The Kilmore International School is an independent, non-denominational, co-educational boarding and day school for academically motivated students undertaking their secondary education (Years 7-12 inclusive).

John Settle, Principal

1408 Kinabalu International School
PO Box 12080
88822 Kota Kinabalu, Sabah
Malaysia
608-822-4526
Fax: 608-824-4203
E-mail: kismy@streamyx.com
http://www.kis.edu.my
This school offers an English-based curriculum for 100 day students (50 boys; 50 girls), ages 3-13 years.

1973 pages

Stuart McLay, Principal
Elis Ho, Office Manager

1409 King George V School
2 Tin Kwong Road
Homantin, Kowloon
Hong Kong
852-2711-3029
Fax: 852-2760-7116
E-mail: office@kgv.edu.hk
http://www.kgv.edu.hk
Non selective secondary school which provides a broad.

Ed Wickins, Principal
Richard Bradford, Vice Principal

1410 Kitakyushu International School
Yahata Higashi-ku, Takami 2,
Shinnittetsu, Shijo, Kitakyushu
Japan
81-93-652-0682
This school offers an English based curriculum for 8 day students (2 boys; 6 girls), in kindergarten through elementary. The school is always looking for dedicated and qualified teachers to teach children and adults in school and preschool (especially female teachers). Applications needed include preschool and English.

Ann Ratnayake, Principal

1411 Kodaikanal International School
Seven Roads Junction, PO Box 25
Kodaikanal, Tamil Nadu
India 624 1-0101
91-4542-247-500
Fax: 91-4542-241-109
E-mail: contact@Kis.in
http://www.kis.in
Kodaikanal Internationa lSchool is an autonomous residential school with a broad college-oriented curriculum, serving young people from a wide diversity of cultures. The School's academic program is intentionally set within a community life based on the life and teaching of Jesus Christ and devoted to service in India and the whole human community.

Geoffrey Fisher, Principal
Gregg Faddegon, Vice Principal

1412 Kooralbyn International School
Shop 1, 29 Wellington Bundock Drive
Kooralbyn QLD 4285
Australia
61-7-5544-6111
Fax: 61-7-5544-6702
E-mail: info@kooralbyn.com
http://www.tkis.qld.edu.au
Aims to provide students with a broad liberal education.

Geoff Mills, Principal

1413 Kowloon Junior School
20 Perth Street
Ho Man Tin, Kowloon
Hong Kong
852-2714-5279
Fax: 852 2760 4438

E-mail: office@kjs.edu.hk
http://www.kjs.edu.hk
Primary students learn English, math, science, technology, history, geography, art, music and physical education.

Mark Cripps, Principal
Deborah Graham, ESF Representative

1414 Kyoto International School
Kitatawara-cho,Nakadachiuri-sagaru
Yoshiyamachi-Dori, Kamigyo-ku, Kyoto
Japan 00602-8247
81-75-451-1022
Fax: 81-75-451-1023
E-mail:
kis@kyotointernationalschool.org
http://www.kyoto-is.org
Independent day school, offering education from Preschool level through to Middle School

Annette Levy, Head of School
Amanda Gillis-Furutaku, Board Chair

1415 Lahore American School
American Consulate General Lahore
15 Upper Mall, Canal Bank
Lahore
Pakistan 54000
92-42-576-2406
Fax: 92-42-571-1901
E-mail: las@las.edu.pk
http://www.las.edu.pk
An independent, coeducational day school which offers an educational program from nursery through grade 12 for students of all nationalities.

Kathryn Cochran, Superintendent
Imran Aslam, Board Chair

1416 Lanna International School Thailand
300 Grandview Moo 10
Chiang-Mai to Hang Dong, T Mae-hea, A. M
Thailand 50100
66-53-806-231
Fax: 66-53-271-159
E-mail: head@lannaist.ac.th
http://www.lannaist.ac.th
t is the goal of Lanna International School to prepare its students to be responsible world citizens who demonstrate a commitment to life-long learning and the application of that learning to the improvement of self, and local and global communities.

Roy Lewis, Head of School
Ajarn Kannika, School Director

1417 Lincoln School
PO Box 2673
Rabi Bhawan, Kathmandu
Nepal
977-1-4270482
Fax: 977-142-7268
Fax: 977-1-4272685
E-mail: info@lsnepal.com.np
http://www.lsnepal.com
is an independent, international school in Kathmandu, Nepal with an American Curriculum

Allan Bredy, Director
Craig Baker, Principal

1418 Malacca Expatriate School
2443-C Jalan Batang Tiga
Tanjung Kling, Melaka
Malaysia 76400
011-60-6-315-4970
Fax: 011-60-6-315-4970
E-mail: sossb@pd.jaring.my
http://www.meschool.virtualave.net

Mission is provide a high standard of learning. The students benefit from a high level of individual attention because of their low student to teacher ratio.

Susheila Samuel, Principal

1419 Marist Brothers International School
1-2-1 Chimori-cho
Suma-ku, Kobe
Japan 654-0
011-81-787-326266
Fax: 011-81-787-326268
E-mail: enquiries@marist.ac.jp
http://www.marist.ac.jp
The philosophy of MBIS is designed to awaken students to the realities of life and to prepare them for the future. school aims to give to each student a well-rounded education incorporating the academic, moral, social and physical aspects of life.

Ed Fitzgerald, Principal
Geraldo de Couto, Vice Principal

1420 Matthew C Perry Elementary School
PSC 561 Box 1874
FPO Iwakuni 96310 0019
Japan
011-81-827-79-3447
Fax: 011-81-827-79-6490
E-mail: principal.perryes@pac.dodea.edu
http://www.perry-es.pac.dodea.edu/
Committed to promoting student achievement in a positive safe environment. It provides a quality education for every student based on the needs of each child.

Shelia Cary, Principal
Christopher Racek, Asst. Principal

1421 Matthew C Perry Middle & High School
PSC 561 Box 1874
FPO Iwakuni 96310 1874
Japan
011-81-827-79-5449
Fax: 011-81-827-79-4600
E-mail: principal.perryhs@pac.dodea.edu
http://www.perry-es.pac.dodea.edu/
Morgan Nugent, Principal
Robert Funk, Assistant Principal

1422 Mentone Boys Grammar School
63 Venice Street
Mentone, Victoria
Australia 03194
011-61-3-9584-4211
Fax: 011-61-3-9581-3290
E-mail: enquiry@mentonegrammar.net
http://www.mentonegrammar.net
We are a school for boys and girls providing a flexible and sensitive approach which considers what boys and girls need at various stages of their development.

Mal Cater, Principal
Simon Appel, Chairman

1423 Mercedes College
540 Fullarton Road
Springfield 5062
South Australia
011-61-8-8372-3200
Fax: 011-61-8-8379-9540
E-mail:
info@mercedes.adl.catholic.edu.au
http://www.mercedes.adl.catholic.edu.au/index.cfm
Mercedes College, in Adelaide, South Australia, is a Reception to Year 12 Catholic

co-educational school in the Mercy tradition.

Peter Daw, Principal
Steve Bowley, Business Manager

1424 Methodist Ladies College
207 Barkers Road Kew
Victoria 3101
Australia
011-61-3-9274-6333
Fax: 011-61-3-9819-2345
E-mail: college@mlc.vic.edu.au
http://www.mlc.vic.edu.au
This college prepares its students for the world of tomorrow by liberating their talents through challenge, enrichment, and opportunity in a supportive Christian environment. Committed to technology and to student initiated learning so each girl from year five onward works with her personal computer to understand the present and shape the future. Total enrollment: 2,135 day students; 105 boarding. Grade range K-12. The school is willing to participate in a teacher exchange program.

Rosa Swtorelli, Principal
Louise Adler, Chairperson

1425 Minsk International School
DOS/Administrative Officer
7010 Minsk Place
Washington, DC 20521-7010
375-172-343-035
Fax: 375-172-343-035
E-mail: mis@open.by
http://www.minsk.qsischool.org
An independent, coeducational day school which offers an educational program from kindergarten through grade 8 for students of all nationalities. Enrollment 11.

Stanley Harrison Orr, Director

1426 Moreguina International Primary School
PO Box 438
Konedobu Papua
New Guinea

Wayne Coleman, Principal

1427 Morrison Christian Academy
136-1 Shui Nan Road
Taichung 40679
Taiwan, TW 40679
11-886-4-2297-3927
Fax: 11-886-4-2292-1174
E-mail: mcgillt@mca.org.tw
http://www.mca.org.tw
Morrison Academy exists to meet the educational needs of the children of missionaries throughout Taiwan, helping fulfill Christ's commission to go into all the world. Morrison seeks to provide a Christ-centered school culture where all students, from missionary and non-missionary families, experience a Biblically-integrated quality education. Therefore, Morrison structures learning so that students may develop the knowledge, discernment, and ability to dynamically impact their world as Christian

Tim McGill, Superintendent
Matt Strange, Director of Curriculum

1428 Mount Hagen International School
PO Box 945
Mount Hagen
Papua New Guinea
675-542-1964
Fax: 675-542-1840
E-mail: mhis@online.net.pg
http://www.iea.ac.pg
It is envisaged that students enrolled at the Mount Hagen International School will always remain encouraged by their schooling. They will earn an education of International standard, their learning will be contextualized within Papua New Guinea

culture, and they will learn how to become productive members of their community

Bruce Imatana, Principal

429 Mt Zaagham International School
PT Freeport
Tembagapura W Papua
Indonesia
62 901 407876
Fax: 62 901 403170
E-mail: joecuthbertson@efmi.com
http://mzis.org
Grade levels Pre-K through 98, school year September - June. Two campuses Tembagapura and Kuala Kencana

Barney Latham, Superintendent
Richard Ledger, Principal

430 Murray International School
PO Box 1137
Boroko
Papua New Guinea
675-325-2183
Fax: 675-325-7925
E-mail: ssavage@temis.iea.ac.pg
http://www.elamurray.ac.pg
Non-profit, private, co-educational day school that provides quality international standard education for the expatriate and local community in Port Moresby.

Suzanne Savage, Principal
Marlene Filippi, Deputy Principal

431 Murree Christian School
Jhika Gali, Murree Hills
Punjab
Pakistan 47180
0092-513-410321
Fax: 0092-513-411668
E-mail: mcs@mcs.org.pk
http://www.mcs.org.pk
This school offers an English-based curriculum for 20 day students and 140 boarding students (75 boys; 85 girls), in grades K-12. Murree Christian School educates the children of missionaries from 14 different countries working in Pakistan and the region. Living allowances rather than salaries are awarded. Overseas teacher stay is two years with housing provided by the school.

Phil Billing, Director
Linda Fisher, HS Faculty Head

432 Mussoorie International School
Srinagar Estate, Mussoorie 248179
Uttarakhand
India
91-135-2632007
Fax: 91-135-2631160
E-mail: misadmission@gmail.com
http://www.misindia.net
One of the leading residential educational institutions for girls and is recognized for its progressive education with a definite account on India culture and traditions.

HK Rawal, Principal
A. Ghosh, Headmaster

433 Nagoya International School
2686 Minamihara, Nakashidami
Moriyama-ku, Nagoya, 463-0002
Japan
81-52-736-2025
Fax: 81-52-736-3883
E-mail: info@nis.ac.jp
http://www.nagoyais.jp
Envisions a school community devoted to developing the skills, attitudes, and values that allow students to realize their full potential, lead lives of purpose, and become responsible, global citizens.

Rob Risch, Headmaster

1434 Narrabundah College
Jerrabomberra Avenue
Narrabundah, ACT 2604
Australia
61-2-6205-6999
Fax: 61-2-6205-6969
E-mail: laura.beacroft@cbit.net.au
http://www.narrabundahc.act.edu.au
This college is a government college for years 11 and 12 students - the final two years of secondary education. It offers a challenging curriculum in a caring environment and meets the needs of an international community.

Steve Kyburz, Head of School
Laura Beacroft, Board Chair

1435 New International School of Thailand
36 Sukhumvit Soi 15
Bangkok, TH 10110
66-2651-2065
Fax: 66-2253-3800
E-mail: nist@nist.ac.th
http://www.nist.ac.th
Co-educational, day school, IBO World School

Simon Leslie, Headmaster
Adrian Watts, Deputy Head

1436 Nile C Kinnick High School
PSC 473 Box 95
FPO, AP
96349-95
011-81-46816-7392
Fax: 011-81-46-816-7278
E-mail: Kinnick_Principal@pac.dodea.edu
http://www.kinnick-hs.pac.dodea.edu
The mission of Nile C. Kinnick High School is to challenge students to maximize potential in order to prepare them to be responsible and productive citizens in an ever-changing world.

Lorenzo Brown, Principal

1437 Nishimachi International School
2-14-7 Moto Azabu
Minato-ku Tokyo
Japan 106-0-46
81-3-3451-5520
Fax: 81-3-3456-0197
E-mail: info@nishimachi.org
http://www.nishimachi.ac.jp
Offers a dual-language, multicultural program ro 430 student k-9.

Terence Christian, Headmaster

1438 Okinawa Christian School International
1835 Zakimi, Yomitan-son
Okinawa 904-0301
Japan
81-098-958-3000
800-446-6423
Fax: 81-098-958-6279
E-mail: info@ocsi.org
http://www.ocsi.org
Provides a major educational support base for the international community living on Okinawa.

Rich Barnett, Contact
Randel J Hadley, Superintendent

1439 Osaka International School
4-4-16 Onohara Nishi
Mino-shi, Osaka, 562-0032
Japan
81-72-727-5050
Fax: 81-72-727-5055
E-mail: addmissions@senri.ed.jp
http://www.senri.ed.jp

OIS is an English-language-based, preK-12 grade coeducational college-preparatory school.

John Searle, Head of School

1440 Osaka YMCA International High School
6-7-34 Benten Minato-ku
Osaka 552-0007
Japan
06-4395-1002
Fax: 06-4395-1004
E-mail: general-inquiry@oyis.org
http://www.oyis.org
OYIS strives to be a leading provider of international education for the citizens and residents of Osaka and its environs.

John Murphy, Principal

1441 Osan American High School
Unit 2037
APO AP 96278-0005
Korea
011-82-31-661-9076
Fax: 011-82-31-661-9121
E-mail: PRINCIPAL.OSANHS@pac.dodea.edu
http://www.osan-hs.pac.dodea.edu
Provides student with successful, productive and rewarding educational experiences.

Timothy Erickson, Principal
Truly Schramm, Assistant Principal

1442 Osan Elementary School
Unit 2037
APO, AP 96278-2037
Korea
011-82-31-661-6912
Fax: 011-82-31-661-5733
E-mail: david.petree.pac.dodea.edu
http://www.osan-es.pac.dodea.edu
Provides quality and challenging educational opportunities for all students to become critical thinkers, life-long learners, and productive citizens in a global society.

Mia Plourde, Secretary
David Petree, Principal

1443 Overseas Children's School
PO Box 9, Pelawatte
Battaramulla
Sri Lanka
94 11 2784920-2
Fax: 94-11-2784999
E-mail: admin@osc.lk
http://www.osc.lk
OSC develops the whole person as a responsible learner striving for personal excellence within a culturally diverse school

Areta Williams, Head of School
Jerry Huxtable, Chair

1444 Overseas Family School
25 F Paterson Road
Singapore 23851
65-6738-0211
Fax: 65-6733-8825
E-mail: executive_director@ofs.edu.sg
http://www.ofs.edu.sg
To focus on the individual needs of every student and to provide a supportive atmosphere designed to help students achieve personal academic goals.

David Perry, Chairman
Irene Wong, Executive Director

1445 Overseas School of Colombo
Pelawatte
PO Box 9, Battaranmulla
Sri Lanka
94 11 2784920-2
Fax: 94 11 2784999

E-mail: admin@osc.lk
http://www.osc.lk
OSC develops the whole person as a responsible learner striving for personal excellence within a culturally diverse school.

Areta Williams, Head of School
Jerry Huxtable, Chair

1446 Pacific Harbour International School

PO Box 50
Pacific Harbour, Deuba
Fiji Islands
679-450-0005
Fax: 679-450-566
http://www.isbi.com

Janet Tuni, Principal

1447 Pasir Ridge International

Unocal-po Box 3-tampines S
Balikpapan 9152
Singapore
62-542-543-474
Fax: 62-542-767-126
E-mail: prschool@bpp.mega.net.id
http://pasirridgeinternationalschool.com
Grade levels preK through 8.

Kathryn Carter-Golden PhD, Principal

1448 Peak School

20 Plunketts Road
The Peak
Hong Kong
852-2849 7211
Fax: 852-2849 7151
E-mail: office@peakschool.net
http://www.ps.edu.hk
Helping promote a better understanding of Americans on the part of the peoples served

Annette Ainsworth, Principal/Secretary
Bill Garnett, Vice Principal

1449 Phuket International Preparatory School

115/15 Moo 7 Thepkasattri Road
Thepkasattri, Thalang, Phuket 83110
Thailand
66 (0)76 336 000
Fax: 66 (0)76 336 081
E-mail:
info@phuketinternationalacademy.com
http://http://www.phuketinternationalaca
demy.com

Agnes Hebler, Principal

1450 Popondetta International School

PO Box 10
Popondetta, Papua
New Guinea

Michael Whitting, Principal

1451 Prahram Campus-Wesley College

577 St Kilda Road-Prahran
Melbourne
Australia
61 3 8102 6100
Fax: 61 3 8102 6054
E-mail: stkildaroad@wesleycollege.net
http://http://www.wesleycollege.net

AB Conabere, Principal

1452 Pusan American School

Do DOS
Pusan 96259
South Korea
82-51-801-7528
Fax: 82-51-803-1729
E-mail: pas@pac.odedodea.edu

Alexia Venglek, Principal

1453 Pusan Elementary & High School

Unit 15625
APO AP 96259-0005, Pusan
Korea
82-52-801-7528
Fax: 82-51-803-1729

1454 QSI International School-Phuket

Box 432 A Muang
Phuket 83000
Thailand
66-076-354-077
Fax: 66-76-354077
E-mail: phuket@qsi.org
http://www.qsi.org
To keep this urge to learn alive in every child in QSI schools. Our schools are established to provide in the English language a quality education for students in the cities we serve.

Khun Janrita Hnobnorb, Administrative Coordinator
Alan Siporin, Director

1455 QSI International School-Zhuhai

No. 168 Anning Road
Xianzhou District
Zuhai, China 51900
86-756-815-6134
Fax: 86-756-8189021
E-mail: zhuhai@qsi.org
http://http://www.qsi.org/zhu_home/cont
act.htm
To keep this urge to learn alive in every child in QSI schools. Our schools are established to provide in the English language a quality education for students in the cities we serve.

Matthew Farwell, Director

1456 Quarry Bay School

6 Hau Yuen Path Braemar Hill
North Point, Hong Kong
China
852 2566 4242ÿ
Fax: 852 2887 9849
E-mail: debra.gardiner@qbs.edu.hk
http://www.qbs.edu.hk
Our aim is to encourage in our children the enjoyment of learning by providing activities both in and outside the classroom which help to develop confident, happy and successful individuals.

Mina Dunstan, Principal

1457 Rabaul International School

PO Box 855
Rabaul Enbp, Papua
New Guinea
675-982-8770
Fax: 675-982-8770
http://www.iea.ac.pg

Ian Smith, Principal

1458 Richard E Byrd Elementary School

PSC 472 Box 12
FPO
Japan, AP 96348-12
011-81-45-281-4815
Fax: 011-81-45-281-4870
http://www.byrd-es.pac.dodea.edu
Richard E. . Byrd envisions a school unbound by traditional school concepts of time, location and age requirements. Byrd Elementary School will provide all students with vast opportunities for learning and civic involvement

Gwen Baxter-Oakley, Principal

1459 Robert D Edgren High School

Unit 5040
APO
Japan, AP 96319-5040
011-81-176-77-4377
Fax: 011-81-176-77-4959
E-mail: principal_*edgren_hs@pac.dodea.edu
http://www.edgren-hs.pac.dodea.edu
Committed to helping students develop academically, socially, physically and emotionally in a global community.

Gerogia Watters, Principal

1460 Ruamrudee International School

6 Ramkamhaeng 184 Road
Minburi, Bangkok
Thailand 10510
66-2-518-0320
Fax: 66-2-518-0334
E-mail: info@rism.ac.th
http://www.rism.ac.th/risweb
Grade levels K-12, school year August - June

Fr. Leo Travis, Director
Dave Parsons HS Principal

1461 Saigon South International School

Tan Phong Ward
Ho Chi Minh City
Vietnam
(84-8) 5413-0901
Fax: (84-8) 5413-0902
E-mail: info@ssis.edu.vn
http://www.ssischool.org
Saigon South International School is a college preparatory school committed to the intellectual and personal development of each student in preparation for a purposeful life as a global citizen.

Robert Crowther, Headmaster
Charles Barton, Head of School

1462 Sancta Maria International School

41 Karasawa Minami-ku
Yokohama
Japan

Sr Mary Elizabeth Doll, Principal

1463 School at Tembagapura

PO Box 616 Cairns
Queensland 4870
Australia

Bruce Goforth, Principal

1464 Scots PGC College

60 Oxenham Street
Warwick, QLD
Australia 04370
61 7 4666 9811
Fax: 61 7 4666 9812
E-mail: postbox@scotspgc.qld.edu.au
http://www.scotspgc.qld.edu.au
Our philosophy of schooling rests squarely on the belief that a true education encourages young people to question and explore, to develop a strong sense of personal identity, to strive to achieve one's best, and to value the act of serving without losing one's desire to lead.

Michael Harding, Principal
Nigel Grant, Director of Learning

1465 Seisen International School

12-15 Yoga 1-chome
Setagaya-Ku, Tokyo
Japan 158-0-97
03-3704-2661
Fax: 033701-1033
E-mail: sisinfo@seisen.com
http://www.seisen.com
Seisen International School seeks to provide a happy, stable and secure environment in which students are prepared through teaching and exam-

ple, to live in a world of tremendous challenge and rapid change.

Concesa Martin, Headmistress

466 Semarang International School
Asad Ave-Mohammedpur
Semarang, Central Java
Indonesia 50254
62-24-8311-424
Fax: 62-24-8311-994
E-mail: info@semarangis.or.id
http://www.semarangis.or.id
Offer Semarang 's international community high quality and affordable education based on the International Baccalaureate Organization's Primary Years Programme, (PYP) philosophy. Provide an educational and motivational base from which each pupil may take his or her place with confidence in any school in any country in the medium of English.

Barry Burns, Principal

467 Seoul Academy
988-5, Daechi-dong
Kangamku Seoul
Korea 135-2
82-02-554-1690
Fax: 82-2-562-0451
E-mail: sais5541690@hanmail.net
http://http://www.seoulacademy.net/
Grade levels pre-K through eighth.

Thomas O'Connor, Director

468 Seoul British School
55 Yonhi Dong Sudaemun Ku
Seoul
Korea
822-330-3100
http://www.seoulforeign.org

Richard Schlueter, Principal

469 Seoul Elementary School
Unit 15549
APO, AP
Korea 96205-5549
011-82-2-7916-4613
Fax: 011-82-2-793-6925
E-mail: principal.seoules@pac.dodea.edu
http://www.seoul-es.pac.dodea.edu
Provides standards based instruction in a safe learning environment which fosters independent thinking and respects cultural diversity through collaboration among staff, students, parents and community

Catherine Yurica, Principal

470 Seoul Foreign School
55 Yonhi-Dong Sodaemun-Gu
Seoul
Korea 120-8-113
82-2-330-3100
Fax: 82-2-335-1857
E-mail: sfsoffice@seoulforeign.org
http://www.sfs.or.kr
As has been true throughout our history, Seoul Foreign School is committed to academic excellence. Our rigorous college preparatory curriculum - which includes the International Baccalaureate diploma program - and our dynamic learning environment challenge students to achieve their full intellectual potential. Equally, we cherish Christian values which encourage our students to develop strong character, live and work with integrity, and accept responsibility for themselves and others.

John Engstrom, Head of School
Barry Benger, Director Human Resources

1471 Seoul High School
Unit 15549
APO, AP
South Korea 96205-5549
011+82-2-7918-5261
Fax: 011+82-2-7918-8822
http://www.seoul-hs.pac.dodea.edu
Seoul American High School is located on Yongsan Army Base in the center of Seoul, Korea. The school complex is comprised of eight buildings containing over 60 classrooms and special purpose rooms.

Richard Schlueter, Principal

1472 Shanghai American School
258 Jin Feng Lu
Huacao Town, Minhang Dist. Shanghai
China 20110
86-21-6221-1445
Fax: 86-21-6221-1269
E-mail: admission@saschina.org
http://www.saschina.org
Shanghai American School, in partnership with parents, fosters the development of each student's personal potential through a balance of the academic, physical, social, emotional and ethical aspects of life. SAS provides a challenging American core curriculum with an international perspective that inspires a passion for learning and intellectual vitality.

Kerry Jacobson, Superintendent
Andrew Torris, Deputy Superintendent

1473 Shatin College
3 Lai Wo Lane
Sha Tin
Hong Kong
852 26991811
Fax: 852 26950592
E-mail: info@shatincollege.edu.hk
http://www.shatincollege.edu.hk
Independent, coeducational, secondary school within the English Schools Foundation

David Cottam, Principal
Grahame Carder, Chairman

1474 Shatin Junior College
3A Lai Wo Lane
Fo Tan, New Terretories
Hong Kong
852 2692 2721
Fax: 852 2602 5572
E-mail: info@sjs.esf.edu.hk
http://http://www.sjs.edu.hk/
At Sha Tin Junior School we aim to provide a secure and happy environment in which a child can develop their academic, social and physical potential to the full.

Perry Tunesi, Principal

1475 Shirley Lanham Elementary School
PSC 477 Box 38
FPO AP
Japan 96306-5
011-81-467-63-3664
Fax: 011-81-467-63-4476
E-mail: Principal.lanhames@pac.dodea.edu
http://www.lanham-es.pac.dodea.edu
We are preparing all students to be responsible, positive contributors within a diverse, global community.

Dave Russell, Principal

1476 Singapore American School
40 Woodlands Street 41
Singapore 73854
65-6363-3403
Fax: 65-6363-3408
E-mail: communications@sas.edu.sg
http://www.sas.edu.sg

The Singapore American School is committed to providing each student an exemplary American educational experience with an international perspective.

Brent Mutsch, Superintendent

1477 Sollars Elementary School
Unit 5041
APO, AP
Japan 96319-5041
011-81-176-77-3933
Fax: 011-81-176-77-3873
E-mail:
PRINCIPAL.SOLLARSES@pac.dodea.edu
http://www.sollars-es.pac.dodea.edu

Dana Chandler, Principal

1478 South Island School
50 Nam Fung Road
Aberdeen
Hong Kong
852-255- 931
Fax: 852-255- 881
E-mail: sis@mail.sis.edu.hk
http://www.sis.edu.hk
School Aims to develop students' confidence, self-esteem and a range of positive values and personal qualities and to produce enthusiastic, active, independent and lifelong learners.

Graham Silverthorne, Principal
Roberta Kam, Admission

1479 St. Andrews International School-Bangkok
Pridi Banomyong 20/1
Sukhumvit Soi 71, Prakanong, Bangkok
Thailand 10110
(+66) 23 81 23 87-
Fax: (+66) 23 91 52 27
E-mail: info@standrews.ac.th
http://http://www.standrews.ac.th/
Our mission is to provide an inclusive, international education in a happy, supportive and stimulating environment, where all the needs of the individual learner are met and students are inspired to achieve their full potential enabling them to become responsible global citizens

Paul Schofield, Head of School
Jamsai Anuvongchareon, Director

1480 St. Christopher's School
10 Nunn Road
Penang
Malaysia 10350
604-226-3589
Fax: 604-226-4340
E-mail: principal@scips.org.my
http://www.scips.org.my
St. Christopher's International Primary School of Penang, caters for expatriates' and also Malaysian children. It is located in one of the most sought after residential areas on the island of Penang Malaysia.

John G Jones, Principal

1481 St. John's International School
Ladprao
Bangkok
Thailand 10900
662-513-8575
Fax: +66 2 513 5273
E-mail: sjiadmin@stjohn.ac.th
http://www.international.stjohn.ac.th
A holistic British style school preparing students of all nationalities to become life long learners and effective communicators in the global community.

Chainarong Monthienvic, Principal

1482 St. Joseph International School
5-16-10 Shibamata, Katsushika-ku
Tokyo
Japan 125-0
035-694-4550
E-mail: schray@stjoseph-k.org
http://www.stjoseph-k.org
Coeducational day/boarding school, pre-
school through grade 12.

James Mueller, Principal
Thomas Schray, Head Teacher

1483 St. Joseph's International Primary School
177 Currie Street
Nambour
New Guinea
54 -19 -22
http://www.stjosephsnambour.qld.edu.au

Barbara D'Arbon, Principal

1484 St. Mark's College
46 Pennington Terrace
North Adelaide
Australia, SA 05006
08-8334-5600
Fax: 08-8267-4694
E-mail: stmarks@stmarkscollege.com.au
http://www.stmarkscollege.com.au
Grade levels Pre-K through 12, school year
March - December

Rose Alwyn, Headmaster
James Raw, Dean

1485 St. Mary's International School
1-6-19 Seta Setagaya-ku
Tokyo
Japan 158-8
813-370- 341
Fax: 813-370- 195
E-mail: michelj@smis.ac.jp
http://www.smis.ac.jp
St. Mary's is committed to educating boys
to be lifelong learners of good character
who demonstrate academic, physical, artistic, and moral excellence, respect for religious and cultural beliefs, and
responsibility as international citizens.

Michel Jutras, Headmaster
Br Lawrence G Lambert, Elementary
School Principal

1486 St. Maur International School
83 Yamate-cho Naka-ku
Yokohama
Japan 231-8
81-45-641-5751
Fax: 81-45-641-6688
E-mail: office@stmaur.ac.jp
http://www.stmaur.ac.jp
he basic objective of Saint Maur International School is to provide a Pre-school, Elementary and Secondary education for
international students residing in Japan, by
using the English language as the primary
medium of instruction. An international
student is defined as a student whose life
experiences span more than one cultural di-
mension. From this basic goal stem specific objectives which fall into three
conceptual categories: spiritual, cultural,
and academic.

Jeanette K Thomas, Head of School
Richard B Rucci, Coordinating Principal

1487 St. Michael's International School
17-2 Nakayamate-dori 3-chome
Chuo-ku, Kobe-shi 650-0004
Japan
81-78-231-8885
Fax: 81-78-231-8899

E-mail: head@smis.org
http://www.smis.org
Provides a distinctive Primary education
within a positive culture of academic excellence and caring family community.

Aileen Pardon, Principal
Paul Grisewood, Head of School

1488 St. Stephen's International School
998 Viphavadi Rangsit Road
Lad Yao, Chatuchak, Bangkok
Thailand 10900
66-2-5130270
Fax: 66-2-9303307
E-mail: info@sis.edu
http://www.sis.edu
To encourage all students in their studies,
personal life and in all their interactions to
strive for excellence on their journey to becoming effective and compassionate citizens and leaders. Our goal is to nurture a
culture and a community of learners creating a unique East meets West environment .

Richard A Ralphs, School Director
Gary Rodbard, Principal

1489 St. Xavier's Greenherald School
Asad Ave-Mohammedpur
Dhaka 1207
Bangladesh

Mary Imelda, Principal

1490 Stearley Heights Elementary School
Unit 5166
APO Kadena 96368 5166
Okinawa 36368
001-81-611-694-452
Fax: 001-81- 98-934-681
E-mail:
Stearley-Heights.Principal@pac.dodea.ed
u
http://http://www.stearley-es.pac.dodea.e
du

Thomas Godbold, Principal

1491 Sullivans Elementary School
PSC 473, Box 96
Yokosuka 96349 0096
Japan
011-81-468-16-7336
Fax: 011-81-468-16-7865
E-mail:
principal_*sullivan_es@pac.dodea.edu
http://http://www.sullivans-es.pac.dodea.
edu

Walter Wilhoit, Principal

1492 Surabaya International School
CitraRaya International Village
Citra Raya, Lakarsantri
Tromol Pos 2/SBDK, Surabaya
Indonesia 60225
62-31-741-4300
Fax: 62-31-741-4334
E-mail: sisadmin@sisedu.net
http://www.sisedu.net
The Surabaya International School Community is committed to developing the social, emotional, physical, creative, and
intellectual abilities necessary for its students to become reasoning, responsible,
contributing, successful members of our
global community.

Larry Jones, Superintendent
Christopher Burke, Chairperson

1493 TEDA International School-Tianjin
Number 72 Third Avenue Teda
Tianjin, CN 30045

86 -2 6-2261
Fax: 86 -2 6-0018
E-mail: Principal@tedainternationalschool.net
http://www.tedainternationalschool.net
provide outstanding education to the students of
all nationalities.

Nick Bowley, Director
Joseph Azmeh, Headmaster

1494 Tabubil International School
PO Box 408 Tabubil
Tabubil
Papua New Guinea
675-548-9233
Fax: 675-542-9641
E-mail: tabis@online.net.pg
http://www.tis.ac.pg
To provides a high quality international school
education catering to the varied needs of
Tabubil's multicultural mining community. The
school employs a well motivated and productive
staff, with good working conditions and a high de-
gree of community involvement

SE Walker, Principal

1495 Taegu Elementary & High School
Unit 15623
APO Taegu 96218 0005
Korea

Leon Rivers, Principal

1496 Taipei American School
800 Chung Shan N Road Section 6
Taipei
Taiwan 11152
886-2-287-39900
Fax: 886-2-287-31641
E-mail: admissions@tas.edu.tw
http://www.tas.edu.tw
Our mission is to inspire each student to be a confident, creative, caring and moral individual prepared to adapt and succeed anywhere in a rapidly
changing world. We provide an American-based
education with a global perspective that results in
a love of learning, academic excellence, a balanced life, and service to others.

Sharon D Hennessy, Superintendent
Ira B Weislow, Business Manager

1497 Tanglin Trust Schools
95 Portsdown Road
Singapore 13929
65-67780711
Fax: 65-67775862
E-mail: admissions@tts.edu.sg
http://www.tts.edu.sg
Our vision is to be the premier school, providing
the highest quality learning experiences for 3 to
18 year olds, and cultivating strong relationships
in an environment where the individual is important. Our students enjoy a rich and stimulating
all-round education which prepares them thoroughly for life in a rapidly-changing and
competitive world.

Ronald Stones, Head of School
Peter Derby-Crook, CEO

1498 Thai-Chinese International School
101/177 Moo 7 Soi Mooban Bangpleeni
Prasertsin Road Bangplee Yai
Samutprakarn, TH 10540
66-2-260-8202
E-mail: tcis@schoolmail.com
http://www.tcis.ac.th
provide an education which allows each student to
develop his/her full being in all areas of human development, academic, physical, emotional, spiritual and social, to interact as critical and
compassionate thinkers, and to become a responsible member of our global society.

499 Timbertop Campus
Timbertop PB-Mansfield
Victoria 3722
Australia
61 3 5733 6777
Fax: 61 3 5777 5772
E-mail: timbertop@ggs.vic.edu.au
http://http://www.ggs.vic.edu.au/Contact.as
px

Stephen Meek, Principal

500 Traill Preparatory School
34-36 S01
18 Ramkhamheng Road, Huamark Bangkok
Thailand
660-271- 877
Fax: 660-271- 854
http://www.traillschool.ac.th

AM Traill, Principal

501 Ukarumpa High School
PO Box 406
Ukarumpa Via Lae, Papua
New Guinea
675-737-4498
Fax: 675-737-4618
http://www.ukarumpainternationalschool.or
g

Steve Walker, Principal

**502 United Nations International
School-Hanoi**
Phu Thuong Ward Lac Long Quan Road
Tay Ho District
Veitnam, VN
(84 4) 3758 1551
Fax: (84 4) 3758 1542
E-mail: info@unishanoi.org
http://www.unishanoi.org
A private, nonprofit, English language,
coeducational day school which offers an ed-
ucational program from prekindergarten
through grade 12 for the expatriate commu-
nity of Hanoi.

Chip Barder, Head of School

503 United World College-SE Asia
1207 Dover Road
PO Box 15, Singapore 9111
Singapore 13965
65 6775 5344
Fax: 65 6778 5846
E-mail: info@uwcsea.edu.sg
http://www.uwcsea.edu.sg
The United World College Movement makes
education a force to unite people, nations and
cultures for peace and a sustainable future.
We educate individuals to take responsibility
for shaping a better world

Julian Whiteley, Head of College
Geraint Jones, Assistant Head of College

504 University Vacancies in Australia
Australian Vice-Chancellors' Committee
GPO Box 1142
Canberra City
Australia
61-02-6285-8200
Fax: 60-02-6285-8211
E-mail:
contact@universitiesaustralia.edu.au
Universities Australia was established on 22
May 2007 as the industry peak body repre-
senting the university sector.

G Withers, Chief Executive Officer
P Rodely, Committee Executive Officer

505 Vientiane International School
PO Box 3180
Phonesavanh Road, Saphanthong Tai Villag
Lao PDR

856 21 486001
Fax: 856 21 486009
E-mail: contact@vislao.com
http://www.vislao.com/
Vientiane International School (VIS) is an independent, non-profit day school offering a
quality international-standard curriculum
from Preschool (3 year olds) through Grade
12 (18 year olds).

Greg Smith, Director

1506 Wellesley College
PO Box 41037
Eastbourne, Lower Hutt 5047, Wellington
New Zealand
64 -56 -03
Fax: 64 -56 -28
E-mail: office@wellesley.school.nz
http://www.wellesley.school.nz
Wellesley is a full independent primary day
school for boys from Year 0 (aged five) to
Year 8.

Warren Owen, Principal
Charlotte Gendall, Board member

1507 Wesley International School
Kotak Pos 275
Malang, East Java
Indonesia 65101
62-341-586410
Fax: 62-341-586413
E-mail: wesley@wesleyinterschool.org
http://www.wesleyinterschool.org
Our mission at Wesley International School
is to provide students with a Christ-centered
education: one that inspires them to live a
Godly life, that instills a biblical worldview,
and produces academic excellence-an education that will prepare our students to impact
and bless their world with knowledge,
insight, action and love

Paul Richardson, HS Principal
Jonathan Heath, Director

1508 Western Academy of Beijing
PO Box 8547
10 Lai Guang Ying dong Lu, Beijing 10010
China
86-10-8456-4155
Fax: 86 10 6433-3974
E-mail: wabinfo@wab.edu
http://www.wab.edu
The Western Academy of Beijing offers a
challenging and caring, community based educational environment in which students are
active participants in the learning process

Robert Landau, Director
Karen O'Connell, Deputy Chair

**1509 Wewak International Primary
School**
PO Box 354
Wewak Esp, Papua
New Guinea

Darian Sullavan, Principal

1510 Woodstock School
Mussoorie
Uttarakhand
India 24817
91-135-632-610
Fax: 91-135-632-885
E-mail: mail@woodstock.ac.in
http://www.woodstock.ac.in
Woodstock aims to develop responsible
global citizens and leaders by providing a
world-class international education, rooted
in its Christian heritage and values, for a diverse group of students, especially from fam-

ilies in Christian or public service, in an
Indian Himalayan environment

David Laurenson, Principal
Thomas Chandy, President

1511 Xiamen International School
262 Xingbei San Lu, Xinglin
Jimei, Xiamen, Fujian
China
86-592-625-6581
Fax: 86-592-625-6584
E-mail: askxis@xischina.com
http://www.xischina.com
Develops confident, knowledgeable students
who enjoy life-long learning, demonstrate
global awareness and contribute compassionately to the world around them.

Paul Raschke, Headmaster
Yuan Yuan Deng, Vice Chairman

**1512 Yew Chung Shanghai International
School**
18 W Rong Hua Road, Gubei New Area
Shanghai
China 20110
(8621) 6219 5910
Fax: (8621) 6219 0675
E-mail: enquiry@ycef.com
http://www.ycis-sh.com
Provide an all-round education that nurtures
the whole person - spiritual, academic, physical, social and emotional that includes relationships with others.

Andrew Mellor, Co-Principal
Julie Zheng, Co-Principal

1513 Yogyakarta International School
P.O. Box 1175
Yogyakarta 55011, Jalan Cendrawasih No.1
Indonesia
62-274-625965
Fax: 62-274-625966
E-mail: board@ yis-edu.org
http://http://www.yis-edu.org/
Operates as a not for profit social foundation
and is overseen by a School Board made up of
both parents and non-parents.

Chris Scott, Principal

1514 Yokohama International School
258 Yamate-cho Naka-ku
Yokohama
Japan 231-0
81-45-622-0084
Fax: 81-45-621-0379
E-mail: yis@yis.ac.jp
http://www.yis.ac.jp
Provides the highest-quality, balanced education to internationally minded students in
an inquiring and supportive environment.

Simon Taylor, Headmaster
John Inge, Chairman

1515 Yokota East Elementary School
DoDDS P J YE Unit 5072
APO, Yokota 96328 5072
Japan 96328
81-3117-55-5503
Fax: 81-3117-55-5502
E-mail: principal.mendel@pac.dodea.edu
http://http://www.mendel-es.pac.dodea.edu
Yokota East Elementary School is located on
Yokota Air Force Base near Tokyo, Japan.
There are approximately 900 students grades
K-6.

Hattie Phipps, Principal

1516 Yokota High School
DoDDS P J YH Unit 5072
APO AP
Japan 96328-5072

011-81-3117-55-701
Fax: 011-81-3117-55-722
E-mail:
principal_*yokotahs@pac.dodea.edu
http://www.yokota-hs.pac.dodea.edu
Yokota High School, working in partnership with the family and local community, provides a safe, academically-inspiring environment in which all students will develop to their maximum potential as life-long learners and responsible participants in an ever-changing global society.

Darrell Mood, Principal

1517 Yokota West Elementary School
DoDDS P J YW Unit 5072
APO AP
Japan 96328-5072
011-81-3117-55-761
Fax: 011-81-3117-55-573
E-mail:
principal_*yokota_west_es@pac.dodea.e
du
http://www.ywes.pac.dodea.edu

Sharon Carter, Principal

1518 Yonggwang Foreign School
Ceii Site Office
PO Box 9, Yonggwang-Kun 513-880
Korea

Eleanor Jones, Principal

1519 Zama Junior High & High School
USA Garrison, Camp Zama
APO, Honshu 96343 0005
Japan

Samuel Menniti, Principal

1520 Zukeran Elementary School
Unit 35017
FPO AP
Japan 96379-5017
011-81-611-7452576
Fax: 011-81-098-892-795
E-mail:
Zukeran.Principal@pac.dodea.edu
http://www.zukeran-es.pac.dodea.edu
Zukeran Elementary School shares the vision of creating a community of learners actively engaged in the pursuit of the knowledge, skills and experiences necessary to empower all children to meet the challenges of the 21st century.

Cindy Templeton, Principal
Roger Reade, Assistant Principal

Central & South America

1521 Academia Cotopaxi American International School
De las Higuerillas y Alondras
Quito
Ecuador
593-2-246-7411
Fax: 593-2-244-5195
E-mail: info@cotopaxi.k12.ec
http://www.cotopaxi.k12.ec
Premier English-language school from early childhood through secondary school.

Kurt Kywi, President
Robert Moss, Vice President

1522 American Cooperative School
Lawton 20
Paramaribo
Suriname
597-49-9461
Fax: 597-498-853

E-mail: acs_suriname@sil.org
http://www.acslp.org
A private, coeducational day school which offers an educational program from prekindergarten through grade 12 for students of all nationalities.

Frank Martens, Administrator

1523 American Elementary & High School
Caixa Postal 7432
01064-970, Sao Paulo
Brazil
55-11-3842-2499
Fax: 55-11-3842-9358
E-mail: graded@eagle.aegsp.br
A private, coeducational day school which offers a full college-preparatory educational program from preschool through grade 12 for students of all nationalities.

Dr Gunther Brandt, Principal

1524 American International School-Bolivia
Casilla 5309
Cochabamba
Bolivia
591-4-428-8577
Fax: 591-4-428-8576
E-mail: administracion@aisb.edu.bo
http://www.aisb.edu.bo
The American International School of Bolivia was founded in 1993 as an international, non-governmental, co-educational day school. The AIS/B educational system covers from Early Childhood education up to the IB program in grades 11 and 12 for students representing all nationalities and socio-economical levels.

Dr Silke Marina Scholer, Director General
Tatiana Jimenez BA, Chief Administrator

1525 American International School-Lincoln Buenos Aires
Andres Ferreyra 4073
B1637 AOS La Lucila, Buenos Aires
Argentina
(54)(11) 4851-1700
Fax: 54-11-479-02117
E-mail: pacha_c@lincoln.edu.ar
http://www.lincoln.edu.ar
Provides education based on United States accredited curriculum in an environment of academic excellence that develops ethical, responsible and globally conscious world citizens.

Phil T Joslin, Superintendent

1526 American School
PO Box (01) 35
El Salvador
503-26-38-330
Fax: 503-26-38-385
E-mail: recruiting@amschool.edu.sv
http://www.amschool.edu.sv
Founded in 1946 and is an independent, international, coeducational, college-preparatory institution

Yolanda de Lopez, Director of Admissions

1527 American School Foundation AC
Bondojito 215
Colonia Las Americas
Mexico City, Mexico 01120
52-55-5227-4900
Fax: 52-55-5273-4357
E-mail: asf@asf.edu.mx
http://www.asf.edu.mx
is an academically rigorous, international, university preparatory school, which of-

fers students from diverse backgrounds the best of American independent education

Julie Hellmund, Director

1528 American School Foundation-Guadalajara
Colomos 2100, Coronel Providencia
Guadalajara, Jalisco
Mexico 44640
52 (33) 3648-0299
Fax: 52-33-3817-3356
E-mail: asfg@asfg.mx
http://www.asfg.mx
Educating students in a bilingual, bicultural and secular environment to be purposeful learners, critical and creative thinkers, effective communicators and community contributors, based on a foundation of honor, freedom and commitment

David McGrath, Principal
Jabet Heinze, Superintendent

1529 American School Foundation-Monterrey
Ave. Ignacio Morones Prieto No. 150
Col. San Isidro, Santa Catarina, N.L.
Nuevo Leon, Mexico 66190
(52)-81-5000-4400
Fax: (52)-81-5000-4428
E-mail: jeff.keller@asfm.edu.mx
http://www.asfm.edu.mx
A private, nonprofit, coeducational day school which offers an educational program from nursery through grade 12 for students of all nationalities.

Dr. Jeffrey Keller, Superintendent

1530 American School-Belo Horizonte
Avenida Deputado Cristovan Chiaradia 120
Caixa Postal 1701
Bairro Buritis, Belo Horizonte 30575-440
Brazil
55-31-378-6700
Fax: 55-31-378-6878
E-mail: eabh@eabh.com.br
http://www.eabh.com.
A coeducational, private day school which offers an educational program from prekindergarten through grade 12 for students of all nationalities.

Sid Stewart, Principal

1531 American School-Brasilia
SGAS 605
Bloco E, Lotes 34/37
Brasilia,DF,Brazil 70200-650
55 (61) 3442-9700
Fax: 55 (61) 3442-9729
E-mail: kpuzic@eabdf.br
http://www.eabdf.br
A private, coeducational day school which offers an educational program from prekindergarten through grade 12 for students of all nationalities

Barry Dequanne, Headmaster
Beth Lopez, Lower School Principal

1532 American School-Campinas
Rua Cajamar, 35 - Jardim Alto da Ba
Campinas- SP
Brazil 13090
55 19 2102-1000
Fax: 55 19 2102-1016
http://http://www.escolaamericanadecampinas.com.br/?contact

Steve Herrara, Superintendent

1533 American School-Durango
Francisw Sarabia #416 Pte
Durango 34000
Mexico
(618) 813-36-36
Fax: (618) 811-28-39
E-mail: colegio_americano@cadurango.edu.mx
http://http://www.cadurango.edu.mx

Dr Jorge O Nelson, Principal

534 American School-Guatemala
11 Calle 1579 Zona 15 Vista Hermosa
Guatemala
Guatemala
502-690-
Fax: 502-698-
E-mail: director@cag.edu.gt
http://www.cag.edu.gt
is to educate independent, critical-thinking, responsible, bilingual individuals prepared to meet the challenges of the future

Robert Gronniger, General Director
Edward Langlais, High School Principal

535 American School-Guayaquil
PO Box 3304
Guayaquill
Ecuador
593-4-255-503
Fax: 593-4-250-453
E-mail: dir_asg@gye.satnet.net
http://www.americanschool.edu.ec
Grade levels K-12, school year April - January

Francisco Andrade, Interim General Director
Patricia Ayala de Coronel, HS Principal

536 American School-Laguna Verde
Veracruz, Mexico

Maurice H Blum, Principal

537 American School-Lima
Apartado 18-0977
Lima 18
Peru
51-14-35-0890
Fax: 51 1 619-9301
E-mail: fdr@amersol.edu.pe
http://www.amersol.edu.pe/fdr/
is to empower our students to pursue their passion for learning, lead lives of integrity and create socially responsible solutions.

Caron Kluznik, Superintendent

538 American School-Pachuca
Valle de Anahuac S/N Valle de San J
ZC: 42083 Pachuca de Soto Hidalgo
Mexico
01-771 713 9608
Fax: 52-771-85077
E-mail: admisiones@americana.edu.mx
http://http://www.americana.edu.mx/
Grade levels prekindergarten through ninth.

Nic,foro Ramirez, General Director

539 American School-Puebla
Apartado 665
Puebla
Mexico

http://http://www.cap.edu.mx/english/
Dr Arthur W Chaffee, Principal

540 American School-Puerto Vallarta
PO Box 2-280
Puerto Vallarta, Jalisco 48300
Mexico
52 322-221-1525
Fax: (52) 322-226-7677
E-mail: Info@aspv.edu.mx
http://http://www.aspv.edu.mx
Gerald Selitzer, Director

541 American School-Recife
408 Se Souza Street
Boa Viagem
Brazil 51030-60
55 81 3341.4716
Fax: 55-81-341-0142

E-mail: info@ear.com.br
http://www.ear.com.br
A private, coeducational day school which offers an instructional program from prekindergarten through grade 12 for students of all nationalities.

George Takacks, Superintendent

1542 American School-Tampico
Hidalgo # 100
Tancol, Tampico
Mexico
52-12-272-081
Fax: 52-12-280-080
E-mail: racevedo@ats.edu.mx
http://www.ats.edu.mx
Grade levels N through tenth.

Emma deSalazar, Headmaster

1543 American School-Torreon
Paseo del Algodn y Boulevard Carlo
Fracc Los Viedos Torren, Coahuila
Mexico 27019
871ÿ222 51 00 TO 0
Fax: 871 733 26 68
E-mail: cat@cat.mx
http://www.cat.mx
A prestigious center of academic excellence dedicated to creating life-long learners and ethical leaders in a global and changing world.

Makhlouf Ouyed, Director General
Martha Martinez, Business Manager

1544 Anglo American School
PO Box 3188-1000
San Jose
Costa Rica
506-279-2626
Fax: 506-279-7894
E-mail: angloam@racsa.co.cr
http://www.aas.ru
Grade levels Pre-K through 6, school year February - November

Virginia Hine Barrantes, Principal

1545 Anglo Colombian School
Apaptado Aereo 253393
Bogota
Colombia

http://www.anglocolombiano.edu.co
David Toze, Principal

1546 Anglo-American School
Calle 37
Avenida Central, 1000 San Jose
Costa Rica
495-231-447
E-mail: angloam@sd.racsa.co.cr
http://www.aas.ru

Virginia Hine, Principal

1547 Antofagasta International School
Avda. Jaime Guzman Errazurz #04300
Antofagasta
Chile
56 - 55 - 694900
Fax: 56 - 55 - 694912
E-mail: ais@ais.cl
http://www.ais.cl
A Pre-Kindergarten through 12th grade educational institution that is dedicated to offering a challenging, English-based curriculum to its students.

Carlos Ignacio Figueroa Ahumada, Principal
Carlos Arturo Calussen Calvo, Chairman

1548 Asociacion Colegio Granadino
AA 2138
Manizales, Caldas
Colombia
57-68-745-774
Fax: 57-68-746-066
E-mail: granadino@emtelsa.multi.net.co
http://www.granadino.edu.co
Grade levels Pre-K through 12, school year August - June

Gonzalo Arango, General Director

1549 Asociacion Escuelas Lincoln
Andres Ferreyra 4073
B1636 AOS La Lucila, Buenos Aires
Argentina
(54)(11) 4851-1700
Fax: 54-11-4790-2117
E-mail: joslin_p@lincoln.edu.ar
http://www.lincoln.edu.ar
Provide an education based on United States accredited curriculum

Phil Joslin, Superintendent
Claudia Pacha, Admissions

1550 Balboa Elementary School
Unit 9025
APO Balboa 34002
Panama
818-241-1801
http://www.gusd.net

Susan Beattie, Principal

1551 Balboa High School
Unit 9025
APO Balboa 34002
Panama
818-241-1801
http://www.gusd.net

Ernest Holland, Principal

1552 Barker College
91 Pacific Highway
Hornsby
NSW, Australia 02077
612-984- 83
Fax: 02 -4 6-3
E-mail: reception@barker.nsw.edu.au
http://www.barker.nsw.edu.au
That Barker College be, and be recognized as, a leading Australian Christian independent school, which provides a broadly-based education and encourages young people to strive to fulfil their potential, and which is acknowledged as a centre of excellence in pastoral care and in teaching and learning

Jimmy Cappanera, Principal
Roderic Kefford, Headmaster

1553 Belgrano Day School
Juramento 3035
Ciudad de Buenos Aires
Argentina c1428
54 -1 -81
Fax: 54 -1 -786
E-mail: rrpp@bdsnet.com.ar
http://www.bds.edu.ar
We cooperate with the family to offer bilingual education quality for the training of future leaders and citizens of the world committed to the common good, free, responsible, creative and respectful of diversity and dissent.

Maria Matilde V Green, President
Carol Halle, Faculty Head

1554 Bilingue School Isaac Newton
Chihuahua, Mexico

Lauya Gonzalez Valenzula, Principal

1555 British American School
AA 4368
Barranquilla
Colombia 28277
704-341-3236
http://britishschoolofcharlotte.org
Rafael Ortegon Rocha, Principal

1556 British School-Costa Rica
PO Box 8184-1000
San Jose
Costa Rica 02232-7833
50 - 2 -0 0
Fax: 50 - 2 -2 7
E-mail: britsch@racsa.co.cr
http://http://www.thebritishschoolofcosta
rica.com/
David John Lloyd, Principal

1557 British School-Rio de Janeiro
R Real Grandeza 99
Botafogo, Rio de Janeiro
Brazil, BR 22281-30
55(21) 2539-2717
Fax: 55(21) 2244-5591
E-mail: edu@britishschool.g12.br
http://www.britishschool.g12.br
The British School aims to develop responsible, well-informed, open-minded, confident and caring individuals by providing an educational community within which all pupils are motivated to realize their full potential through a challenging British-based education in a non-discriminatory and bi-cultural environment
Paul Wiseman, Director
Adam Reid, Chairman

1558 British School-Venezuela
Sector 8 and Sector 12
Panchkula
India 13410
91-172-5028556
E-mail: tbs@thebritishschool.org
http://www.thebritishschool.org
aims to provide education with global standards. This will not only make students studying in the school eligible for higher education in the institutions across the world but also give NRI's settled abroad, an opportunity to send their children to such schools to have a better idea of the social system back home.
TBS Panchkula, Principal
U Sethi, Board Member

1559 Buenos Aires International Christian Academy
Red de Escuelas Mundiales Cristiana
Av Libertador General San Mart-n 2170
Buenos Aires, AR 01646
5411 4549 1300
Fax: 5411 4549 1300
E-mail: info@baica.com
http://www.baica.com
Our school is unique in that we are home to both Argentineans and the expat community.
Andy Simon, Principal
Robert Newman, Director

1560 Caribbean International School
Box 1594
Cristobal Colon
Panama
507-445-0933
http://cis.edu.pa
Anderson, Principal

1561 Centro Cultural Brazil-Elementary School
Rua Jorge Tibirica 5
11100 Santos, Sao Paulo
Brazil
Newton Antonio Martin, Principal

1562 Cochabamba Cooperative School
Casilla 1395
Cochabamba
Bolivia 01395
591-42-987-61
Fax: 591-42-329-06
E-mail: Cwieburg@ccs.edu.bo
http://www.ccs.edu.bo
President
Provide attendees
Carl Wieburg, Director
Jos Leonis, Manager

1563 Colegio Abraham Lincoln
Calle 170, # 51A-81
SedePrimaria Avenue Calle 170 #65-31
Columbia
571-676-7360
http://www.abrahamlincoln.edu.co
Promoting human development within a humanistic philosophy and pruricultural.
Amparo Rueda, Director

1564 Colegio Alberto Einstein
PO Box 5018
Av. Diego V squez de Cepeda N77-157
Quito, Ecuador
(593-2)2477-901
Fax: 2470-144
E-mail: einstein@einstein.k12.ec
http://http://www.einstein.k12.ec/home-e.
html
Benjamin Tobar, Principal
Raquel Katzkowicz, General Director

1565 Colegio Americano De Guayaquil
Juan Tanca Marengo Avenue PO Box 33
Guayaquil
Ecuador
593-4-255-03
Fax: 593-4-250-453
E-mail: info@colegioamericano.edu.ec
http://www.colegioamericano.edu.ec
Provide an education with the highest standards of quality, thus contributing to the improvement of our society.
Stanley Whitman, Principal
Francisco Andrade, Association President

1566 Colegio Anglo Colombiano
Avenida 19 # 152A-48
Bogota
, DC
571-259-5700
E-mail:
admissions@anglocolombiano.edu.co
http://www.anglocolombiano.edu.co
Our purpose is to educate human beings with open minds, real social awareness and the power of critical thinking.
David Toze, Principal
Catherine Cushnan, Admission

1567 Colegio Bilingue Juan Enrigue
Pestalozzi AC
Veracruz
Mexico
Michael S Garber, Principal

1568 Colegio Bolivar
Calle 5 Number 122-21 V-a Pance
Cali
Colombia

(57-2) 684 8600
Fax: 57-2-555-2041
E-mail: cbinfo@colegiobolivar.edu.co
http://www.colegiobolivar.edu.co
Colegio Bolivar is an educational community whose mission is to educate its students in a bilingual, democratic environment to be autonomous, and to demonstrate a spirit of inquiry and collaboration, a commitment to excellence, and the highest aspirations for the welfare of both the individual and society.
Joseph Nagy, Director
Richard Martin, Dean of Students

1569 Colegio Columbo Britanico
Apartado Aereo 5774
Cali
Colombia

http://www.colombobritanico.edu.co
Ian Watson, Principal

1570 Colegio Gran Bretana
Carrera 51 #215-20
Bogota
Colombia
57-1-676-0391
Fax: 57-1-676-0426
E-mail: admissions@cgb.edu.co
http://http://www.cgb.edu.co/
Grade levels N-10, school year August-June
Daryl Barker, Director
David Simpson, Deputy Director

1571 Colegio Granadino
AA 2138 Manizales
Colombia
57-6-874-57-74
Fax: 57-6-874-60-66
E-mail: granadino@emtelsa.multi.net.com
http://www.granadino.edu.co
Early Childhood, Elementary, Middle School and High School
Gonzalo Arango, Principal
Robert Sims, Director

1572 Colegio Interamericano de la Montana
Boulevard La Montana
Finca El Socorro, Zona 16
Guatemala, GT 01016
502 2200.2990
Fax: 502-3-641-779
http://www.interamericano.edu.gt
The mission of Colegio Interamericano is to prepare its students for life and for studies anywhere in the world, by orienting them towards being responsible members of society.
Dr Michael Farr, General Director
Griselda de Amezquita, Head of Human Resources

1573 Colegio Jorge Washington
Zona Norte, Anillo Vial Km.12
Cartagena
Colombia, CO
57-5-673 5505
Fax: 57-5-665-6447
E-mail: director@cojowa.edu.co
http://cojowa.edu.co
The mission of the George Washington School is to form bilingual and bicultural citizens who possess high ethical values and commitment to the search for academic excellence and success in life.
Pete Nonnenkamp, Director
Maritza Garcia, Assistant Director

1574 Colegio Karl C Parrish
Kilometer 2 Antigua Via a Puerto Co
Barranquilla
Colombia, CO 52962

57-5-359-8929
Fax: 57-5-359-8828
E-mail: mail@kcparrish.edu.co
http://www.kcparrish.edu.co
strives to provide an environment that results in students displaying personal integrity and character in their relationships both within and outside the school.

Laura Horbal Rebolledo, Director
Hectalina Donado, Elementary School Principal

575 Colegio Montelibano
AA 6823 Cerromatoso
Montelibano, Bogota
Colombia

Francisco Cajiao, Principal

576 Colegio Nueva Granada
Carrera 2 Este Number 70-20
Bogota
Colombia, CO
57-1-2123511
Fax: 57-1-211-3720
E-mail: sngrana@COL1.telecom.com.co
http://www.cng.edu
Prepare tomorrow's leaders by educating the mind, nurturing the spirit, and strengthening the body.

Barry McCombs PhD, Director
Michael Adams, Deputy Director

577 Colegio Peterson SC
Apartado Postal 10-900
DF 11000
Mexico
52-5-81-30-11-4
Fax: 52-5-81-31-38-5
E-mail: kapm@mail.internet.com.mx
http://www.peterson.edu

Marvin Peterson, Principal

578 Colegio San Marcus
61 Ourense
Buenas Aires
Argentina 32004
988-247-4
Fax: 988- 39-5
E-mail: csmarcos@csmarcos.com
http://www.csmarcos.com
Collegio San Marcos was established in 1988, when it began its first year of dentures, being recognized by the Galician regional government, as accredited Vocational Training Second Grade, under the Order of May 20 1.988 of the Department of Education and University (DOG num.110 June 1988).

Susana Raffo, Principal

579 Colegio Ward
Hector Coucheiro 599
1706 DF Sarmiento, Ramos Mejia
Buenos Aires, Argentina
541- 46-8 03
E-mail: info@ward.edu.ar
http://www.ward.edu.ar

Ruben Carlos Urcola, Principal
Daniel Campagna, Director

580 Costa Rica Academy
Apartado Postal 4941
San Jose 1000
Costa Rica
506-239-03-76
Fax: 506-239-06-25
A private, coeducational school which offers an educational program from prekindergarten through grade 12 for students of all nationalities.

William D Rose, BS, Med, Principal

1581 Cotopaxi Academy
PO Box 17-11-6510
Quito
Ecuador
593-2-246-7411
Fax: 593-2-244-5195
E-mail: info@cotopaxi.k12.ec
http://www.cotopaxi.k12.ec
Premier English-language early childhood through secondary school in Ecuador. The internationally recognized program is aggressively sought out by all National and International parents who truly want to join a partnership to provide the very best education possible for their children.

Eddie Wexler, Principal
Kurt Kywi, President

1582 Country Day School
Apartado 1139 - 1250
Escazu
Costa Rica
(506) 2289 - 0919
Fax: (506) 2228 - 2076
E-mail: gloria_doll@cds.ed.cr
http://www.cds.ed.cr
CDS is an American School serving an international population. Accredited by the Middle States Association of Colleges and Schools in the United States, and by the Costa Rican Ministry of Education

Gloria Doll, Director
Maria Fernanda Cardona, Admissions Coordinator

1583 Crandon Institute
Casilla Correo 445
Montevideo
Uruguay
248- 33-5
http://www.crandon.edu.uy
This school offers a curriculum taught in Spanish for 2,000 day students (700 boys; 1,300 girls), in high school through junior college level (home economics, commercial). The school, affiliated with the Methodist church, employs 300 teachers.

Marcos Rocchietti, Principal

1584 Curundu Elementary School
Unit 0925
APO Curundu 34002 0005
Panama

Clifford Drexler, Principal

1585 Curundu Junior High School
Unit 0925
APO Curundu 34002 0005
Panama

Charles Renno, Principal

1586 Edron Academy-Calz Al Desierto
Desierto de los Leones 5578
Mexico City 01740
Mexico
5-585-30-49
Fax: 5-585-28-46
http://www.edron.edu.

Richard Gilby Travers, Principal

1587 El Abra School
Phelps Dodge Corporation
Calama
Chile
56-55-313-600
Fax: 56-55-315-182
E-mail: elabraschool@hotmail.com
Grade levels K-11, school year August - June

Margaret Maclean, Head of School

1588 English School
AA 51284
Bogota
Colombia

Leonard Mabe, Principal

1589 Escola Americana do Rio de Janeiro
Estrada Da Gavea 132
Rio de Janeiro
Brazil 22451-263
(916) 458-5932
Fax: 55-21-259-4722
E-mail: americanrio@ax.apc.org
http://www.earj.com.br
Escola Americana motivates engaged learners to become independent critical thinkers in a multicultural community.

Dr Dennis Klumpp, Principal
Caren Addis, Director of Admissions

1590 Escola Maria Imaculada
Rua Vig rio Joao de Pontes, 537, Ch
Sao Paulo
Brazil 04748
551- 2-01 7
Fax: 551- 55-1 77
http://http://www.chapelschool.com/

Gerald Gates, Principal

1591 Escuela Anaco
Avenue Jose Antonio Anzoategui, KM
Anaco
Venezuela
58 -82 -22 2
E-mail: director@ESCUELAANACO.COM
http://princeton.iss.edu
Offers a United States High School Diploma with a full schooling program from Day Care through Grade 12. Also have on-line courses to enhance our program. Uses the best of the educational standards of the states of California, New York, and Virginia.

Francene Conte, Principal
Bill Kralovec, Director

1592 Escuela Bilingue Santa Barbara
Apartado 342-El Marchito
San Pedro Sila
Honduras
504-659-3053
Fax: 504-659-3059
E-mail: mochitoschool@breakwater.hn
http://princeton.iss.edu
Grade levels preK through 8.

John P Leddy, Principal

1593 Escuela Bilingue Valle De Sula
Apartado 735
San Pedro Sula
Honduras

Carole A Black, Principal

1594 Escuela International Sampedrana
Col Gracias A Dios 500 mts W Hospit
San Pedro Sula
Honduras
504-566-2722
Fax: 504-566-1458
E-mail: eperez@seishn.com
http://www.seishn.org
EIS seeks to be the premier school in the city of San Pedro Sula, the country of Honduras and region of Central America through the use of best teaching practices with the goal of reaching all of its students.

Gregorg E Werner, Principal
Ronald Vair, Superintendent

1595 Escuela Las Palmas
Apartdo 6-2637
Panama

797-530-
http://www.cmpuentealto.cl
Aleida Molina, Principal

1596 Foreign Students School
Avenue Station B
#6617-6615 Esquina 70
Miramar Havana City, Cuba

Gillian P Greenwood, Principal

1597 Fort Clayton Elementary School
2000 Park Place Avenue
APO, Fort Clayton 34004 0005
Panama, TX
817-814-5400
http://www.lilybclayton.org

Barbara Seni, Principal

1598 Fort Kobbe Elementary School
Unit 0714
APO, Fort Kobbe 34001 0005
Panama

Dr Vinita Swenty, Principal

1599 Fundacion Colegio Americano de Quito
Manuel Benigno Cueva N80 - 190 Urba
PO Box 17-01-157, Carcel,n, Quito
Ecuador, DC
(593) 2 3976 300
Fax: 593-2-472-972
E-mail: dirgeneral@fcaq.k12.ec
http://www.fcaq.k12.ec
Grade levels Pre-K through 12, school year
September - June.

Susan Barbara, Director General

1600 George Washington School
Apartado Aereo 2899
Cartagena
Colombia
57-5-665-3396
Fax: 57-5-665-6447
A private, coeducational day school which
offers and educational program from
prekindergarten through grade 12 for stu-
dents of all nationalities.

Steven Fields, Principal

1601 Grange School
Casilla 218
Correo 12, Santiago
Chile
(56) 2- 5981500?
Fax: 56-2-227-1204
E-mail: admissions@grange.cl
http://www.grange.cl
Places great importance on the idea of 'fair
play', a concept with connotations of
sportsmanship, rule obedience, and
honesty

Mike Freeman, Headmaster
Carolina Varela, Deputy Headmaster

1602 Greengates School
Avenue Circumbalacion Pte 102
Baliones De San Mateo, Naucalpah
Edo de Mexico, Mexico 53200
52-55-5373-0088
Fax: 52-55-5373-0765
E-mail: sarav@greengates.edu.mx
http://www.greengates.edu.mx
Grade levels prekindergarten through
twelfth.

Susan E Mayer, Principal

1603 Howard Elementary School
805 Long Hollow Pike
Gallatin
Panama, TN 37066

615-452-3025
http://www.hes.sumnerschools.org
Jean Lamb, Principal

1604 Inst Tecnologico De Estudios
Apartado Postal 28B
Chihuahua
Mexico
528- 83-8 20
http://www.itesm.edu
Hector Chavrez Barron, Principal

1605 International Preparatory School
PO Box 20015-LC
Santiago
Chile
56-2-321-5800
Fax: 56-2-321-5821
E-mail: info@tipschool.com
http://www.internationalpreparatoryschool.com
Grade levels Pre-K through 12, school year
March - December

Lesley Easton-Allen, Headmistress
Pamela Thomson, Curriculum
Coordinator

1606 International School Nido de Aguilas
Avenida El Rodeo 14200
Santiago
Chile
(562) 339-8105
Fax: 56-2-216-7603
E-mail: abattistoni@nido.cl
http://www.nido.cl
The International School Nido de Aguilas
is committed to offering each student excellence in the pursuit of academic
achievement in preparation for attendance
at a US, Chilean or other international university, all within the framework of a challenging US-based, English-language
curriculum. We encourage open-mindedness, global diversity, environmental
awareness, community service and the development of leadership skills, including
integrity, responsibility and
self-discipline.

Dr Don Bergman, Headmaster
Jared Harris, HS Principal

1607 International School-Curitiba
Av Dr Eug^nio Bertolli
3900 Santa Felicidade, Curitiba, Paran~
Brazil 18241
413-525-7400
Fax: 413-525-7499
E-mail: isc@iscbrazil.com~
http://www.iscbrazil.com
It is a private, nonprofit, self-governed
school that serves students and families
from our local and international community; offers a U.S. based curriculum in English with American, Brazilian and
International Baccalaureate diplomas;
commits to academic and personal excellence and prepares students for universities
around the world.

Elizabeth Mello, Principal 1-12
Bill Pearson, Superintendent

1608 International School-La Paz
CC1075870 Villa Dolores
La Paz, Cordoba
Argentina
LH Sullivan, Principal

1609 International School-Panama
PO Box 0819-02588
El Dorado
Panama

(507) 293-3000
Fax: 507-266-7808
E-mail: isp@isp.edu.pa
http://www.isp.edu.pa
A private, coeducational day school which offers
an educational program from prekindergarten
through grade 12 for students of all nationalities.

Rajiv Bhatt, Director
Jania Jacob, Business Manager

1610 Karl C Parrish School
Km 2 Antigua via a Puerto
Barranquilla
Colombia
(57-5) 3598929
Fax: 57-5-3598828
E-mail: mail@kcparrish.edu.co
http://www.kcparrish.edu.co
Karl C. Parrish is a private, non-sectarian,
non-profit elementary and secondary school that
is open to children of all nationalities.

Laura H Rebolledo, Director

1611 Liceo Pino Verde
Vereda Los Planes kilometro 5
V¡a Cerritos Entrada 16, El Tigre
Colombia
963-379368
E-mail: info@liceopinoverde.edu.co
http://www.liceopinoverde.edu.co
This school teaches English as a second language;
builds strong human values; develops logical
thinking skills and prepares students for the world
of technology and communication. Enrollment
consists of 110 day students (57 boys; 53 girls, in
grades PK-12. Overseas teachers are welcome to
apply with the length of stay being two years, with
housing provided. Applications needed to teach
include science, math and English.

Luz Stella Rios Patino, Principal

1612 Limon School
P.O. Box 249
847 F Avenue
Limon, CO 80828
719-775-2350
Fax: 719-775-9052
http://limonbadgers.com
strive to provide a safe environment and develop
responsible and productive citizens who have the
knowledge and skills to seize their chosen opportunities

Chris Selle, Principal

1613 Lincoln International Academy
PO Box 52-7444
Miami, FL 33152
1 (305) 395-4825ÿ
E-mail: lincoln@lincoln.edu.ni
http://www.lincoln.edu.ni
instilling in them solid Christian and human vir-
tues as taught by the Catholic faith, challenging
them to reach their full intellectual capacity and
achieve a high integral academic excellence in order to face the challenges of today's world. providing them with English instruction while
preserving our Hispanic-Nicaraguan culture.

Henningston Hammond, Operation Manager
Adolfo Gonzalez, General Director

1614 Mackay School
Vicuna Mackenna 700
Renaca
Chile
563-223- 660
Fax: 563-223- 667
http://www.mackay.cl

Nigel William Blackbur, Principal

615 Marian Baker School
Apartado 4269
San Jose
Costa Rica 01000
560-273-3426
Fax: 506-273-4609
E-mail: mbschool@sol.racsa.co.cr
http://www.mbs.ed.cr/
Marian Baker School (MBS) is an International English speaking school educating preschool through high school students.

Linda Niehaus, Director
Bonnie Heigold, Business Manager

616 Marymount School
1026 Fifth Avenue
Barranquilla
Colombia, NY 10028
212-744-4486
Fax: 212-744-0163
http://www.marymountnyc.org

Dr. Kathleen Cunniffe, Principal

617 Metropolitan School
7281 Sarah Avenue
Maplewood, MO 63143
314-644-0850
E-mail: nsmith@metroschool.org
The School is dedicated to providing a highly individualized educational experience for middle and senior high school students whose potential has not been recognized and/or meaningfully challenged in traditional school settings.

Judi Thomas, Head of School

618 Modern American School
Cerro del Hombre 18
Col. Romero de Terreros
Mexico
565-476-
http://www.modernamerican.edu.mx
To provide our students with the educational elements which will promote the optimum development of the intellect, instill social awareness and emotional sensitivity, encourage artistic creativity, and emphasize physical well-being, aiming for excellence toward future success

619 Northlands Day School
Roma 1210
1636 Olivos, Buenos Aires
Argentina
541-147-1 84
Fax: 541- 47-1 84
http://www.northlands.org.ar/
This bilingual day school for girls offers modern facilities, sports, etc. on a spacious campus. Languages spoken include English and Spanish and total enrollment is 1,100 students, ranging in grade from K1-12. Overseas teachers are accepted, with the length of stay being 2-6 years with housing provided.

Susan Brooke Jackson, MA, Principal

620 Our Lady of Mercy School
Rua Visconde de Caravelas
48, Botafogo, Rio de Janeiro
Brazil
336-722-7204
http://www.ourladyofmercyschool.org
Our Lady of Mercy School is an American Catholic English speaking school whose main purpose is to educate the whole student towards global understanding.

Charles Lyndaker, Superintendent

621 Pan American Christian Academy
1730 Link Road
04829-310 Sao Paulo
Brazil

480.471.5339
Fax: 55-11-59289591
E-mail: info@paca.com.br
http://www.paca.com.br
American international school located in the city of Sao Paulo, working with 350 students from different parts of the world with an American-style pre-school through high school education. Since 1960, we've served the local and international community of Sao Paulo.

Micheal Epp, Superintendent

1622 Pan American School-Bahia
Caixa Postal 231
Salvador
Brazil, SA 40901-970
55-71-3368-8400
Fax: 55-71-3368-8441
E-mail: info@escolapanamericana.com
http://www.escolapanamericana.com
A private, coeducational day school which offers a program from preschool through grade 12 for students of all nationalities.

Mary Jo Heatherington, PhD,
Superintendent

1623 Pan American School-Costa Rica
Apartado 474
Monterrey
Costa Rica, NL 64000
(81) 83-42-07-78
Fax: (81) 83-40-27-49
E-mail: dadmission@pas.edu.mx
http://www.pas.edu.mx
Offer excellent educational programs in English that foster the integral development of students.

Robert Arpee, Director

1624 Pan American School-Monterrey
Hidalgo 656 Pte
Apartado Postal 474, Monterrey 64000
Mexico
(81) 83-42-07-78
http://www.pas.edu.mx
This school offers an English curriculum for 1,393 day students and 100 boarding students (709 boys; 684 girls), grades preschool through nine. The school is willing to participate in a teacher exchange program with the length of stay being one year. Applications needed to teach include science, preschool, math, reading, English, and physical education.

Tobert L Arpee, Principal
Lenor Arpee, Faculty Head

1625 Pan American School-Porto Alegre
Rua Joao Paetzel 440
91 330 Porto Alegre
Brazil
555- 33-4 58
http://www.panamerican.com.br
Jennifer Sughrue, Principal

1626 Panama Canal College
Unit 0925
APO Balboa 34002 0005
Panama

http://www.educationusapanama.wetpaint.com

1627 Prescott Anglo American School
PO Box 1036
Arequipa
Peru

http://www.prescott.edu.pe

This school offers a Spanish/English curriculum for 1,050 day students (450 boys; 600 girls) in grades K-12. Students are taught English three hours a day, so they can reach an intermediate level in grade 9, and high intermediate in grades 11-12.

Jorge Pachecot, Principal

1628 Redland School
272 Military Road
Cremorne
Chile, NS 02090
612-990- 313
Fax: 612-990- 322
http://www.redlands.nsw.edu.au
This school offers an English/Spanish curriculum to 820 day students (420 boys; 400 girls), in grades PreK-12. The student body is mostly Chilean and 90% of the teachers are Chilean. However, overseas teachers are welcome, with the applications being pre-school and English.

Richard Collingwood-Selby, Principal

1629 Reydon School for Girls
5178 Cruz Chica
Sierras de Cordoba, Cordoba
Argentina

NJ Milman, Principal

1630 Saint George's School
Carrera 92 No 156-88, Suba
Bogota
Colombia
057-168- 917
E-mail: sanjorge@sgs.edu.co
http://www.sgs.edu.co

Mary De Acosta, Principal

1631 Santa Cruz Cooperative School
Barrio Las Palmas Calle Barcelona #
Casilla 753 Santa Cruz
Bolivia
(591) (3) 353-0808
Fax: (591) (3) 352-6993
E-mail: william.j.mckelligott@gmail.com
http://www.sccs.edu.bo
College preparatory school equipping students with the necessary skills and values to be citizens and leaders for the 21st century. Preparing students to become productive citizens, leaders and life-long learners.

William J McKelligott, Director General
Hugo Paz, Board Director

1632 Santa Margarita School
22062 Antonio Parkwayÿÿ Rancho Santa
Surco, Lima
Peru, CA 92688
949-766-6000
http://www.smhs.org

Guillermo Descalzi, Principal

1633 St. Albans College
110 Clearwater Road
Lynnwood Glen Pretoria
South Africa
271-234- 122
Fax: 271-236- 191
E-mail: robertr@stalbanscollege.com
http://www.stalbanscollege.com
St Alban's College is a learning community of boys, staff and parents. We are forward looking, committed to quality and service, and we pursue innovative strategies and encourage personal responsibility in the interest of all-round development of the boy as he journeys towards manhood.

Tom Hamilton, Headmaster
Carlos Palermo, Faculty Director

1634 St. Andrew's Scots School
Rosales 2809
Olivos
Argentina 01636
54-114-799-8318
Fax: 54-114-799-8318
E-mail:
admissions@sanandres.esc.edu.ar
http://www.sanandres.esc.edu.ar
St. Andrew's Scots School aims to graduate responsible citizens committed to serving Argentina and contributing to its equitable development through a well-balanced, bilingual education which meets high international standards and fosters a joy for learning.

Gabriel Rshaid, Headmaster
Ana Repila, Admissions Director

1635 St. Catherine's School
Carbajal 3250
1426 Capital Federal, Buenos Aires
Argentina
54-114-552-4353
Fax: 54-114-554-4113
E-mail: stcath@ciudad.com.ar
http://www.redeseducacion.com.ar
Pre-K through 12, school year March-December

Mabel Manzitti, Principal

1636 St. George's College
Guido 800 CP
Quilmes, Buenos Aires
Argentina 01878
(5411) 4254-8237
Fax: 54-11-425-30030
E-mail: info@stgeorge.com.ar
http://www.stgeorge.com.ar
Our mission is to provide students of varying abilities and backgrounds between the ages of 3 - 18 with a bilingual, fully integrated education of the highest calibre in order that they may develop their potential to the full in an appropriately resourced co-educational environment which nurtures individual development, independent thinking and the highest moral standards.

Derek Pringle, Headmaster
Peter Ashton, Deputy Headmaster

1637 St. Hilda's College
Cowley Place Oxford
OX4 1DY
England
44-1865-276884
Fax: 44-1865-276816
E-mail: college.office@st-hildas.ox.ac.uk
http://www.st-hildas.ox.ac.uk
To promote the education of women within Oxford University and the tradition of excellence in women's education which it pioneered.

Sheila Forbes, Principal
Lucia Nixon, Senior Tutor

1638 St. John School
Casilla 284
Concepcion
Chile

http://www.sjs.org
St. John School is a bilingual school that caters to children from PK through grade twelve. The student body includes 1,170 day students (580 boys and 590 girls). The school does participate in teacher exchange programs with the length of stay for teachers being two years. The languages spoken include Spanish and English and the student/teacher ratio is 10:1.

Chris Pugh, Principal

1639 St. Margaret's British School-Girls
Calle Saint Margaret
150 Lomas de Montemar
Chile
451-00 -
E-mail: admissions@stmargarets.cl
http://www.stmargarets.cl
St. Margarets objective is to protect in its pupil its motto: Recte Fac Nec Time (Do Right , Fear not) This implies assigning value to great ideals, acting fairly and courteously, having sound judgement, enriched understanding, a discipline manner and making responsible use of their freedom.

Margery Byrne, Principal
Avril Cooper, Headmistress

1640 St. Paul's School
325 Pleasant Street
Concord, NH 03301-2591
603-229-4600
http://www.sps.edu
St. Paul's School is a fully residential academic community that pursues the highest ideals of scholarship. We strive to challenge our students intellectually and morally - to nurture a love for learning and a commitment to engage as servant leaders in a complex world.

Richardo Pons, Principal
William R Matthews, Jr, Rector

1641 St. Pauls School
1600 St Paul's Drive
Clearwater, FL 33764
727-536-2756
Fax: 727-531-2276
http://www.st.pauls.edu
To educate and inspire young minds in a challenging and nurturing community of learning.

AH Thurn, Principal
Angel W Kytle, Head of the School

1642 St. Peter's School
Pacheco 715
1640 Martinez, Buenos Aires
Argentina

http://www.st.peterspanchgani.org

Joy Headland, Principal

1643 Teaching Opportunities in Latin America for US Citizens
Organization of American States
17th & Constitution Avenue NW
Washington, DC 20036
202-458-3000
Fax: 202-458-3967
http://www.st.peterspanchgani.org
Supports teaching abroad opportunities.

1644 The American School Foundation of Monterrey
Ave. Ignacio Morones Prieto No. 150
Santa Catarina, N.L., C.P.
Mexico, MX 66190
(52)-81-5000-4400
Fax: (52)-81-5000-4428
E-mail:
jeff.keller@missouri.asfm.edu.mx
http://www.asfm.edu.mx
providing the type of learning environment which will prepare its students to successfully assume their role in the international community during the current millennium.

Jeff Keller, Superintendent
Jeff Farrington, Principal

1645 Uruguayan American School
Av Saldon de Rodriguez
Montevideo
Uruguay 11500-3360
598-2-600-7681
Fax: 598-2-606-1935
E-mail: MSchramm@uas.edu.uy
http://www.uas.edu.uy
Uruguayan American School is to provide, together with the family, a balanced college preparatory education. UAS integrates a US style curriculum with Uruguayan studies to equip our national and international students to be successful in a diverse, ever changing world

Mike Schramm, Director
Cecilia Burgueo, UP Coordinator

1646 William T Sampson
Elementary & High School
PSC 1005 Box 49
FPO, Guantanamo Bay 09593 0005
Cuba

Eastern Europe

1647 American Academy Larnaca
Gregory Afxentious Avenue
PO Box 40112, Larnaca
Cyprus 06301
357-248-5400
Fax: 357-246-1046
E-mail: info@academy.ac.cy
http://www.academy.ac.cy
Non-profit making school that is supported by an active multi-functional operation to achieve its core purpose: pre-school to University entrance education of the highest standard. It is a private, selective, co-educational, independent school, registered under the Private Schools' Law, 1971, of the Republic of Cyprus and uniquely, is run by its own graduates.

Doros Neocleous, Principal
Tom Widdows, Director

1648 American College-Sofia
PO Box 873
Sofia
Bulgaria 01000
(359-2) 434 10 08
Fax: (359-2) 434 10 09
E-mail: acs@acs.bg
http://www.acs.bg
The primary mission is to educate Bulgarian youth, it embraces qualified students of all nationalities, races and faiths in the belief that a wide variety of students will enrich educational opportunities for all.

Paul Johnson, President
Maria Angelova, Deputy Director

1649 American International School-Bucharest
Sos Pipera-Tunari 196
Voluntari Jud Ilfov 077190
Romania
40-21-2044300
Fax: 40-21-2044306
E-mail: office@aisb.ro
http://www.aisb.ro
The American International School of Bucharest is a multicultural and international learning community, located in Romania. English is the principal language of instruction.

David Ottaviano Ed D, Director
Tamara Shreve, Elementary Principal

1650 American International School-Budapest
PO Box 53
Budapest
Hungary 01525

36 26 556 000
Fax: 36 26 556 003
E-mail: admissions@nk.aisb.hu
http://www.aisb.hu
The American International School of Budapest (AISB) is a private and independent co-educational day school governed by a Board of Directors elected and appointed from the parent community. Established in 1973 by the United States Embassy to serve United States Government employees' dependents, AISB currently serves the needs of a rapidly expanding international population, including children of the local and expatriate business and diplomatic communities.

Ray Holliday Bersegeay, School Director
Larry Kinde, Chairman

651 American International School-Cyprus
PO Box 23847, 11 Kassos Street
1086 Nisocia
Cyprus
357-22-316345
Fax: 357-22-316549
E-mail: aisc@aisc.ac.cy
http://www.aisc.ac.cy
Founded in 1987, a private, coeducational, college preparatory day school providing a first class American and international university preparatory education within the Cyprus local community that incorporates a Greek as a First Language program for our Cypriot students.

Michelle Kleiss, Director
Terry Wolfson, Principal

652 American International School-Krakow
Lusina ul. sw. Floriana 57
30-698 Krakow
Poland
48 12 270-1409
Fax: 48 12 270-1409
E-mail: director@iskonline.org
http://www.aisk.kompit.com.pl
Affiliated with the American School of Warsaw, AISK is an independent, coeducational day school which offers an educational program from preschool through grade 8 for students of all nationalities.

Ellen Deitsch Stern, Director

653 American International School-Vienna
Salmannsdorfer Strasse 47
A-1190 Vienna
Austria
43-1-40-132-0
Fax: 43-1-40-132-5
E-mail: info@ais.at
http://www.ais.at
Provide a culture of educational excellence, a nurturing environment, and an atmosphere of open communication and aims to prepare a diverse student body for higher education; to inspire the youth to realize their potential; to foster life-long learning, tolerance, personal integrity, and democratic values; and to prepare students to become responsible adults, with respect for different cultures and beliefs.

Carol Kluznik, Director
Gail McMillan, HS Principal

654 American School of Bucharest
Sos Pipera-Tunari 196
Voluntari Jud Ilfov
Romania 07719
40-21-2044300
Fax: 40-21-2044306
E-mail: office@aisb.ro
http://www.aisb.ro

An independent, international, coeducational day school which offers an educational program from prekindergarten through grade 12 for students of all nationalities.

David Ottaviano, Director
Jeri Guthrie Corn, Chair

1655 Asuncion Christian Academy
Avenida Santisimo Sacramento
1181 Casilla 1562
Asuncion, Paraguay-1209
011-595-21-607-378
Fax: 011-595-21-604-855
E-mail: aca@aca.edu.py
http://http://www.acaknights.org/
Asuncion Christian Academy believes that the best education to prepare a student for adult life is an education based upon the truth of God's Word and having a growing and personal relationship with Jesus Christ.

Bethany Abreu, Director

1656 Falcon School
PO Box 23640
Nicosia
Cyprus 01685
357 22 424781
Fax: 357 22 313764
E-mail: falconschool@cytanet.com.cy
http://http://www.falconschool.ac.cy/default.asp?id=261
Nikolas Michael Ieride, Principal

1657 Gimnazija Bezigrad
Periceva ulica 4
PO Box 2504
Ljubljana 01001-1001
Fax: 010-044-
E-mail: info@gimb.org
http://www.gimb.org
Assistance to parents in raising gifted children to full and productive adulthood

Cyril Dominko, Principal
Janez Sustersic, Director

1658 International Elementary School-Estonia
Juhkentali 18
Tallinn
Estonia 10132
372-666-4380
Fax: 372-666-4383
E-mail: office@ise.edu.ee
http://www.ise.edu.ee
Provide high-quality, international education; maximize personal potential; develop life-long learners who appreciate diversity; foster active, compassionate world citizens

Don Fitzmahan, Director
Terje Akke, PYP Coordinator

1659 International School-Belgrade
Temisvarska 19
Belgrade
Serbia 11040
381 11 206-9999
Fax: 381 11 206-9940
E-mail: isb@isb.rs
http://www.isb.rs/main/?pgid=263
An independent, coeducational day school which offers an educational program from kindergarten through grade 8 for students of all nationalities.

Dr. Eric Sands, Director
Sanja Ilic, Admissions Director

1660 International School-Budapest
P.O. Box 53
Budapest
Hungary 01525

36 26 556 000
Fax: 36 26 556 003
E-mail: admissions@aisb.hu
http://http://www.aisb.hu/DOCS/1/contact.html
Grade levels N-8, school year August - June

Ray Holliday-Bersegeay, Director

1661 International School-Estonia
Juhkentali 18
Tallinn
Estonia 10132
372-666-4380
Fax: 372-666-4383
E-mail: office@ise.edu.ee
http://www.ise.edu.ee
Provides high-quality, international education, maximize personal potential, develop life-long learners who appreciate diversity and foster active, compassionate world citizens.

Don Fitzmahan, Terje
Akke PYP Coordinator

1662 International School-Latvia
Viestura iela 6a
Jurmala
Latvia LV 20
(+371) 6775 5146
Fax: (+371) 6775 5009
E-mail: merliha@isl.edu.lv
http://www.isl.edu.lv
Offers English-language, academically challenging programmes designed to develop life-long learners who are critical, creative and open-minded thinkers prepared and motivated to meet the diverse challenges of an ever-changing environment; act with integrity and responsibility locally and globally to transform their world in positive ways and appreciate and respect human diversity.

Larry Molacek, Director
Kevin Reimer, Deputy Director

1663 International School-Paphos
100 Aristotelous Savva Avenue
PO Box 62018, Paphos
Cyprus 08025
26 821700ÿ
Fax: 26 942541
E-mail: info@isop-ed.org
http://www.isop-ed.org
The school caters for the needs of children from Kindergarten to Year 13. Its mission is to serve each and every one of the pupils as part of our school family and as an individual.

Litsa Olympiou, Headmistress

1664 International School-Prague
Nebusicka 700
164 00 Prague 6
Czech Republic
420 2 2038 4111
Fax: 420-2-2038-4555
E-mail: ispmail@isp.cz
http://www.isp.cz
Educates students to be responsible, productive, ethical and healthy citizens with the ability to think creatively, reason critically, and communicate effectively through a variety of educational philosophies and methods, combining the best methodology and practices from a variety of national systems with an international perspective.

Rajiv Bhatt, Director
Barry Freckmann, Business Manager

1665 International Teachers Service
47 Papakyriazi Street
Larissa, Greece
41-253856
Fax: 41-251022

A recruitment service for teachers of English in Greece. Must have a BA/BS in education preferably English and/or EFL training or past experience in EFL and be a native speaker of English.

Fani Karatzou

1666 Kiev International School

3A Svyatoshinsky Provuluk
Kyiv
Ukraine 03115
380-44-452-2792
Fax: 380-44-452-2998
E-mail: kiev@qsi.org
http://www.qsi.org
Kyiv International School, a private non-profit institution

Scott D'Alterio, Director
David Pera, Director Instruction

1667 Limassol Grammar-Junior School

10 Manoli Kalomiri & Theklas Lisiot
PO Box 51340
Limassol, Cyprus 03504
357-257-7933
Fax: 357-257-7818
E-mail: junior@grammarschool.com.cy
http://www.grammarschool.com.cy/servic es.htm
The primary goal of the Grammar School is to provide its students with a solidly grounded liberal education. Thus, it seeks to encourage the intellectual, spiritual, and physical development of its students.

EWP Foley, Principal
Demetris Gregoriou, Director

1668 Logos School of English Education

33-35 Yialousa Street
PO Box 51075 Limassol
Cyprus 03501
357-25336061
Fax: 357-25335578
E-mail: Principal@Logos.ac.cy
http://www.logos.ac.cy

Gary Love, Principal

1669 Magyar British International School

H-1519 Budapest
PO Box 219, Budapest
Hungary
361-466-9794
http://www.bisb.hu

Mary E Pazsit, Principal

1670 Melkonian Educational Institute

PO Box 1907
Nicosia
Cyprus

http://www.englishschool.ac.cy/?link=co ntact.php
An Armenian boarding school with high academic standards.

S Bedikan, Principal

1671 Private English Junior School

P.O Box 23575
Nicosia
Cyprus 01684
357-22 -9930
Fax: 357-22 -9930
E-mail: info@englishschool.ac.cy
http://www.englishschool.ac.cy/?link=co ntact.php

Vassos Hajierou, BA, Principal

1672 QSI International School-Bratislava

Karloveska 64
Bratislava
Slovak Republic 842-2
421-2-6542-2844
Fax: 421-2-6541-1646
E-mail: bratislava@qsi.org
http://www.qsi.org
To keep this urge to learn alive in every child in QSI schools. Our schools are established to provide in the English language a quality education for students in the cities we serve.

Britt Brantley, Director

1673 QSI International School-Ljubljana

Dolgi most 6A
1000 Ljubljana
Solvenia
386-1-2441750
Fax: 386-1-2441754
E-mail: ljubljana@qsi.org
http://www.qsi.org
To keep this urge to learn alive in every child in QSI schools. Our schools are established to provide in the English language a quality education for students in the cities we serve.

Jay Loftin, Director

1674 QSI International School-Tbilisi

Village Zurgovani
Tbilisi
Republic of Georgia
995-32-53767
Fax: 995-32-322607
E-mail: tbilisi@qsi.org
http://www.qsi.org
To keep this urge to learn alive in every child in QSI schools. Our schools are established to provide in the English language a quality education for students in the cities we serve.

James Rehberg, Director

1675 QSI International School-Yerevan

PO Box 82, Ashtarok Highway
Yerevan
Republic of Armenia 37501
374-10-349130
Fax: 374-10-397599
E-mail: yerevan@qsi.org
http://www.qsi.org/arm_home
To keep this urge to learn alive in every child in QSI schools. Our schools are established to provide in the English language a quality education for students in the cities we serve.

Douglas Shippert, Director

Middle East

1676 ACI & SEV Elementary School

Inonu Caddesi No 476
Goztepe, Izmir
Turkey 35290
90-232-285-3401
Fax: 90-232-246-1674
E-mail: channa@aci.k12.tr
http://www.aci.k12.tr
Contribute to the growth of individuals who combine self-confidence with a firm sense of personal, social, and environmental responsibility. Enable students to be strong bilinguals in English and Turkish, well-educated adults, lifelong learners, and efficient communicators, who have developed skills, accountability, and atti-

tudes for leading a fulfilling life and for serving their country and humanity.

Charles C Hanna, Director
Anet Gomel, Turkish First Vice Principal

1677 Abdul Hamid Sharaf School

PO Box 6008
Amman
Jordan 11118
962-615-2418
Fax: 962-651-2462
E-mail: ahss@go.com.jo
http://www.ahss.edu.jo
A private, coeducational, K-12 day school serving the needs of a diverse group of students, international and local. Languages of instruction for the basic subjects are Arabic and English.

Sue Dahdah, Director

1678 Abquaiq Academy

PO Box 31677
Al-Khobar
Saudi Arabia 31952
966-3 5-6 04
Fax: 966-3 5-6 23
E-mail: abqaiq@isgdh.org
The sole purpose of the school is for serving the educational needs of children from expatriate families.

Vineeta Dambal, Administrator/Principal

1679 Al Ain English Speaking School

PO Box 17939
Al Ain
United Arab Emirates
00971-3-7678636
Fax: 00971-3-767-1973
E-mail: school@aaess.sch.ae
http://www.aaess.org
Al Ain English Speaking School is a member of the Association of British Schools in the Middle East and the Incorporated Association of Preparatory Schools (UK). The basic curriculum is that of the National Curriculum of England.

Peter Hodge, Principal

1680 Al Bayan Bilingual School

PO Box 24472
Safat 13105
Kuwait
965 2227 - 5000
Fax: 965 2227 - 5002
E-mail: bbsjadm@bbs.edu.kw
http://www.bbs.edu.kw
A non-profit Arabic-English university preparatory educational institution, which fosters an environment for students to develop the intellectual qualities, ethical values, and positive attitudes required for effective participation and leadership in the overall development of Kuwait and the rapidly changing world.

Brian L McCauley, Director

1681 Al Khubairat Community School

PO Box 4001
Abu Dhabi
United Arab Emirates
971-244- 228
Fax: 971-244-6819
E-mail: principal@britishschool.sch.ae
http://www.britishschool.sch.ae
British curriculum school for children aged 3 to 18.It is a non-profit school administered by a Board consisting of parent representatives and nominees of the British Ambassador.

Paul Coackley, Principal

1682 Al Rabeeh School

PO Box 41807
Abu Dhabi
United Arab Emirates

971 2 4482856
Fax: 971 2 4482854
http://www.alrabeeh.sch.ae/
HJ Kadri, Principal

683 Al-Nouri English School
PO Box 46901
Fahaheel
Kuwait
PD Oldfield, Principal

684 Al-Worood School
PO Box 46673
Abu Dhabi
United Arab Emirates
971-2-444-7655
Fax: 971-2-444-9732
E-mail: alworood@emirates.net.ae
http://http://www.alwarood.sch.ae/alworoo
d/StaticContentDetails.asp
Grade levels N-12, school year September -
June

Ahmed Osman, Academic Principal
Abdulla Al Nuwais, President

685 American Collegiate Institute
Inonu Caddesi #476 Goztepe
Izmir
Turkey 35290
90-232-285-3401
Fax: 90-232-246-4128
E-mail: channa@aci.k12.tr
http://www.aci.k12.tr
Offers a 1 + 4 year academic program. Students enter the school based upon a competitive national high-school entrance exam
needing to improve their English language
skills go into the intensive English one-year
preparatory program before entering the
school's rigorous four-year educational
program.

Charles C Hanna, Director
Anet Gomel, First Vice Principal

686 American Community School
Rue de Paris, Jel El Bahr
PO Box 11-8129, Riad El Solh
Beirut, Lebanon 01107-2260
961-1-374-370
Fax: 961-1-366-050
E-mail: gdamon@acs.edu.lb
http://www.acs.edu.lb
Founded in 1905, an independent, non-profit,
non-sectarian, pre-K-12 coeducational day
school.

George Damon, Headmaster
David Warren, Deputy Headmaster

687 American Community School-Abu Dhabi
PO Box 42114
Abu Dhabi
United Arab Emirates
971-2-681-5115
Fax: 971-2-681-6006
E-mail: acs@acs.sch.ae
http://www.acs.sch.ae
The mission is to empower and inspire all stu-
dents to define and shape their futures, pur-
sue their dreams and contribute to society.

Dr George Robinson, Superintendent
Waheeda Al Tamimi, Administrative
Assistant

688 American Community School-Beirut
Rue de Paris, Jel El Bahr
PO Box 11-8129, Riad El Solh
Beirut, Lebanon 01107-2260
961-1-374-370
Fax: 961-1-366-050
E-mail: gdamon@acs.edu.lb
http://www.acs.edu.lb

Founded in 1905, an independent, non-profit,
non-sectarian, pre-K-12 coeducational day
school. It draws students from both the Leba-
nese and international communities in Lebanon and embraces diversity in race, gender,
religion, national origin and economic
background.

Dr George Robinson, Superintendent
David Warren, Deputy Headmaster

1689 American International School
PO Box 22090
Doha
Qatar
974-445-0150
Fax: 974-445-0157
E-mail: info@asd.edu.qa
http://http://www.asd.edu.qa/
The American School of Doha is an independent, U.S. accredited, college preparatory
school, committed to provide the highest
standard of educational excellence, through
an enriched American curriculum.

Deborah Welch, Director
Michael Shahen, High School Principal

1690 American International School-Abu Dhabi
PO Box 5992
Abu Dhabi
United Arab Emirates
971-2-444-4333
Fax: 971-2-444-4005
E-mail: admissions@aisa.sch.ae
http://www.aisa.sch.ae
Founded in 1995 to serve the needs of the local and expatriate residents of Abu Dhabi
who want their children to pursue both American and International Baccalaureate curricula in an international setting.

Gareth Jones, Director
Abdulla Al-Hashly, Chairman

1691 American International School-Israel
PO Box 484, 65 Hashomron St
Even Yehuda
Israel 40500
972-9-890-1000
Fax: 972-9-890-1001
E-mail: aisrael@wbais.org
http://http://www.wbais.org/~joomla/index.
php?option=com_frontpage&
An independent, coeducational day school
which offers an educational program from
kindergarten through grade 12 for students of
all nationalities.

Richard Detwiler, Principal

1692 American International School-Kuwait
PO Box 3267
Salmiya
Kuwait 22033
(965) 22255155
Fax: (965) 22255156
E-mail: director@aiskuwait.org
http://www.aiskuwait.org
Grade levels kindergarten through twelfth.

Samera Al Rayes, Owner/Director
Noreen Hawley, Superintendent

1693 American International School-Muscat
PO Box 584
Azaiba Postal Code 130
Sultanate of Oman
968 24 595 180
Fax: 968 24 503 815
E-mail: taism@omantel.net.com
http://www.taism.com

Pursues academic excellence for students in
the international community through an
American-based education that develops ethical, responsible, and globally conscious
life-long learners.

Kevin Schafer, Director
Keith Boniface, High School Principal

1694 American International School-Riyadh
PO Box 990
Riyadh
Saudi Arabia 11421
966-1-491-4270
Fax: 966-1-491-7101
E-mail: registration@ais-r.edu.sa
http://www.aisr.org
As a school committed to excellence, we will
educate and inspire our students to be responsible, productive and ethical world citizens
with the skills and passion to think creatively,
reason critically, communicate effectively
and learn continuously. We will accomplish
this in an American educational environment
characterized by high measurable standards
and a clearly defined, appropriately interrelated college preparatory curriculum, implemented by a superior staff in partnership with
parents a

Dr. Dennis Larkin, Superintendent

1695 American School-Doha
PO Box 22090
Doha
Qatar
974-4459-1500
Fax: 974-4459-1570
E-mail: dwelch@asd.edu.ga
http://www.asd.edu.qa/pages/sitepage.cfm?
page=32659
is an independent, U.S. accredited, college
preparatory school, committed to provide the
highest standard of educational excellence,
through an enriched American curriculum

Deborah Welch, Director
Colin Boudreau, High School Principal

1696 American School-Kuwait
PO Box 6735
Hawalli
Kuwait 32040
965-266-4341
Fax: 965-265-0438
E-mail: ask@ask.edu.kw
http://www.ask.edu.kw
It is a privately owned, independent
coeducational day school which offers a gen-
eral academic curriculum for students of all
nationalities

Bernard Mitchell, Superintendent
Fawsi Hasan, Arabic Studies Principal

1697 American-British Academy
PO Box 372
Medinat Al Sultan Qaboos
Sultanate of Oman PC 11
968-24603646
Fax: 968-24603544
E-mail: admin@abaoman.edu.om
http://www.abaoman.edu.om
Provides an international education of the
highest quality to enable students to be confi-
dent, responsible, caring life-long learners.

Mona Nashman-Smith, Superintendent
Rod Harding, Director of Operations

1698 Amman Baccalaureate School
PO Box 441
Sweileh Amman
Jordan 11910
962-6-541-1191/7
Fax: 962-6-541-2603

E-mail: info@abs.edu.jo
http://www.abs.edu.jo
A coeducational and non-profit school which caters to students aged 3-18 years that offers an academically rigorous programme, enriched by extensive co-curricular activities, that culminates in the International Baccalaureate Diploma or Certificates.

Stuart Bryan, Principal
Robert Jones, Vice-Principal

1699 Anglican International School-Jerusalem
82 Rechov Haneviim
PO Box 191 Jerusalem
Israel 91001
972-2-567-7200
Fax: 972-2-538-474
E-mail: hoskino@aisj.co.il
http://www.aisj.co.il
An internationally accredited, pre-Kindergarten to Grade 12 [ages 3-18] school. It creates student-focused academic and educational environment which aspires to achieve excellence.

Owen Hoskin, Director
Matthew Dufty, Deputy Principal

1700 Ankara Elementary & High School
PSC 89 Unit 7010
APO, Ankara 09822 7010
Turkey
011-90-312-287-253
Fax: 011-90-312-285-179
E-mail:
AnkaraEHS.Principal@eu.dodea.edu
http://http://www.anka-ehs.eu.dodea.edu/
Kathleen Reiss, Principal
Rosie Uluer, Assistant Principal

1701 Arab Unity School
PO Box 10563
Rashidiya, Dubai
United Arab Emirates
971-4-886-226
Fax: 971 4 2886321
E-mail: auschool@amirates.net.ae
http://www.arabunityschool.com/aus/home.htm
Provide an equal opportunity, to all students, to develop their intellectual faculties and to awaken their latent, creative talents, irrespective of their ethnic background.

Zainab A Taher, Founder Director

1702 Baghdad International School
PO Box 571
Baghdad
Iraq
Amen A Rihani, Principal

1703 Bahrain Bayan School
PO Box 32411
Isa Town
Bahrain
973-682-227
Fax: 973-780-019
E-mail: bayanschool@bayan.edu.bh
http://www.bayanschool.edu.bh
A bilingual, coeducational, college preparatory school with an international curriculum and faculty. It aims to preserve the tenets of Arabic /Islamic values, to assist students to a depth of cross-cultural knowledge and to promote the global perspective necessary for future world citizens.

Dr Nakhle Wehbe, Director General
Gilbert Daoura, Operations Manager

1704 Bahrain Elementary & High School
Psc 451 Box 690
FPO Bahrain
Bahrain 09834-5200
973 1772-7828
Fax: 973 1772-8583
http://http://www.bahr-ehs.eu.dodea.edu/
Grade levels K-12.

Gail Anderson, Principal

1705 Bahrain School
PO Box 934
Juffair
Bahrain
973 1772-7828
Fax: 973 1772-8583
E-mail:
BahrainEHS.Principal@eu.dodea.edu
http://www.bahr-ehs.eu.dodea.edu/
To provide a safe environment in which our students are challenged to their maximum potential as responsible members of a multi-cultural society.

Gail Anderson, Principal
Laura Bleck, Assistant Principal

1706 Bilkent University Preparatory School-Bilkent International School
East Campus
Bilkent Ankara
Turkey 06800
90 312 290 53 61
Fax: 90 312 266 49 63
E-mail: school@bups.bilkent.edu.tr
http://www.bupsbis.bilkent.edu.tr
BUPS serves the educational needs of selected Turkish students while BIS serves the needs of selected international students in the Ankara area.

James Swetz, Director
Dan Keller, Associate Director

1707 Bishop's School
PO Box 2001
Amman
Jordan
962-6-653668
This Episcopal boy's school, founded in 1936, teaches both the Jordanian Curricula and the London University General Certification of Education Curriculum. Total enrollment is 855 day students in grades 1-12. Length of stay for teachers is one year with no housing provided. Languages spoken are English and Arabic.

Najib F Elfarr, Principal
Jamil Ismair, Faculty Head

1708 British Aircraft Corp School
PO Box 3843
Riyadh
Saudi Arabia
MR Pound, Principal

1709 British Embassy Study Group
Sehit Ersan Caddesi 46A, 06680
Cankaya Ankara
Turkey 06680
90 (312) 468 6563
Fax: 90 (312) 468 6239
E-mail: admin@besg.org
http://www.besg.org
BESG is a co-educational primary school with 135 children aged between 3 and 11, representing nearly 26 countries. We are known as a friendly and caring British school, which values a holistic approach to education

Dawn Akyurek, Head Teacher
Katie Vincent, Deputy Head Teacher

1710 British International School-Istanbul
Dilhayat Sokak No:18 Etiler
Istanbul
Turkey, TR
90 (0) 212 257 51
Fax: 90-0-212-257 53 33
E-mail: registrar2@bis.k12.tr
http://www.bis.k12.tr
The British International School Istanbul (BISI) provides a wide range of educational choices for international families. We are a private, coeducational school providing British-style international education for 520 students of 40 nationalities between the ages of 2r and 18.

Graham Pheby, Principal
Roger Short, Governor of the School

1711 Cairo American College
PO Box 39
Maadi 11431
Cairo, EG 11431
(20-2) 2755-5507
Fax: 20-2-519-6584
E-mail: support@cacegypt.org
http://www.cacegypt.org
Cairo American College is a world class learning environment that affirms the voice, passions and talents of students and inspires them to use their hearts and minds as global citizens.

Nivine Captan-Amr, Board Chair
Elizabeth Bredin, Secretary

1712 Cambridge High School
PO Box 60835
Dubai
United Arab Emirates
971 - 4 282 4646
Fax: 971 - 4 282 4109
E-mail: cambridge@cis-dxb.ae
http://www.gemscis-garhoud.com
David Mcaughlin, Principal
Nigel Cropley, Vice Principal

1713 Continental School (Sais British)
PO Box 6453
Jeddah 21442
Saudi Arabia
966-269-9001
Fax: 966-269-9194
E-mail: conti@conti.sch.sa
http://www.continentalschool.com
Inspire in students a love of learning using a child centered, British style of education. Strive for excellence, recognizing, celebrating and encouraging a spirit of internationalism.

Bruce Gamwell, Director
Marina Alibhai, Registrar

1714 Dhahran Academy International School Group
PO Box 31677
Al Khobar 31952
Saudi Arabia 31952
966-3-330-0555
Fax: 966-3-330-2450
E-mail: info@isgdh.org
http://www.isgdh.org
Grades preSchool-11, enrollment 994.

Norma Hudson, Superintendent

1715 Dhahran Central School
PO Box 31677
Dhahran 31311
Saudi Arabia 31952
966-3-330-0555
Fax: 966-3-330-2450
E-mail: info@isgdh.org
http://www.isgdh.org
Norma Hudson, Principal

716 Dhahran Hills School
PO Box 31677
Dhahran 31311
Saudi Arabia 31952
966-3-330-0555
Fax: 966-3-330-2450
E-mail: info@isgdh.org
http://www.isgdh.org
Norma Hudson, Principal

717 Doha College-English Speaking
PO Box 7660
Doha Qatar
Arabian Gulf
974-806-770
Fax: 974-806-311
E-mail: dess@dess.org
http://www.dess.org
An independent, coeducational day school which offers an educational program from children of all nationalities from kindergarten through grade12.
E Goodwin, Principal
Emad Turkman, Chairman

718 Doha English Speaking School
PO Box 7660
Doha
Qatar
(974) 44592750
Fax: ÿ(974) 44592761
E-mail: dess@dess.org
http://www.dess.org
Create a happy, secure, stimulating and supportive learning environment
Emad Turkman, Chairman
Eddie Liptrot, Head Teacher

719 Doha Independent School
PO Box 5404
Doha Qatar
Arabian Gulf

http://www.dohaacademy.net
SJ Williams, Principal

720 Emirates International School
PO Box 6446
Dubai
United Arab Emirates
971-4-348-9804
Fax: 971-4-348-2813
E-mail: mail@eischools.ae
http://www.eischools.ae
We offer a broad international education, in English, designed for local and expatriate students, that promotes excellence in all academic activities. It is our mission to enhance the educational, social and physical development of our students encouraging them to think analytically and creatively in preparation for the next stage of their education.
Daryle Russell, EdD, Headmaster
Jason Kirwin, HS Principal

721 English School-Fahaheel
PO Box 7209
Fahaheel
Kuwait 64003
096-023-1010
Fax: 096-023-1054
E-mail: esf@skee.com
http://www.skee.com
The English School Fahaheel recognizes the need for all students to be made aware of the demands placed upon them for Further Education and the world of work.
Ibrahim J Shuhaiber, Chairman
John J MacGregor, Principal

1722 English School-Kuwait
PO Box 379
Safat
Kuwait 13004
965-256-7205
Fax: 965-256-7147
http://www.tes.edu.kw
The English School was founded in 1953 under the auspices of the British Embassy and is the longest established school in Kuwait catering for the expatriate community. The School operates as a not-for-profit independent co-educational establishment providing the highest standards in education for children of Pre-Preparatory and Preparatory School age.
William James Strath, Principal
Richard Davis, Chair

1723 English Speaking School
PO Box 2002
Dubai
United Arab Emirates
974-445- 275
Fax: 974-445- 276
E-mail: dess@dessdubai.com
http://www.dessdxb.com
The school opened in 1963 in the upstairs room of a villa where expatriate workers were housed. There was one class which was taught by parents and a British Officer called Flight Lieutenant F. Loughman.
Bernadette McCarty, Principal
David Hammond, Headteacher

1724 Enka Okullari-Enka Schools
Sadi Gulcelik Spor Sitesi
Istinye, Istanbul
Turkey 34460
90-212-276-05-4547
Fax: 90-212-286-59-3035
E-mail: mailbox@enkaschools.com
http://www.princeton.iss.edu
Enka Schools provide an international education for our students. We have a well qualified and passionate group of teachers from Turkey and overseas. Most of our students are Turkish while some of them have international backgrounds.
Darlene Fisher, Director
Ayten Yilmaz, Preschool Principal

1725 Gulf English School
PO Box 2440
Doha
Qatar
974-445-8 77
Fax: 974-448-1 25
E-mail: info@gulfenglishschool.com
http://www.gulfenglishschool.com
Provide a positive and stimulating environment which facilitates individual learning, encourages experimentation, and develops critical thinking and problem solving skills. We must enable each student to achieve his or her best in the pursuit of academic excellence, and give them the confidence to be independent thinkers, able to assume responsibility and leadership and to take their place in the wider world
Paul Andrews, Principal
Tim Brosnan, Faculty Head

1726 Habara School
PO Box 26510
Bahrain
973-172- 173
http://www.ameinfo.com
PM Wrench, Principal

1727 IBN Khuldoon National School
Po Box 20511
Manama
Bahrain
973-16-687-073
Fax: 973-17-689-028
E-mail: info@ikns.edu.bh
http://www.ikns.edu.bh
This IBN school is a private, fee paying, non-profit, coeducational, accredited middle states school. The curriculum offered to the 1,210 day students (630 boys and 580 girls) in grades K-12, is English/Arabic. The school is willing to participate in a teacher exchange program with the applications needed being science, math, social sciences, pre-school and English.
Kamal Abdel-Nour, President
Ghada R Bou Zeineddine, Principal

1728 Incirlik Elementary School
Unit 7180 Box 270
APO AE 09824
Turkey
011-90-322-316-310
Fax: 011-90-322-332-757
E-mail:
IncirlikEHS.Principal@eu.dodea.edu
http://http://www.inci-ehs.eu.dodea.edu/
Mary Davis, Principal

1729 Incirlik High School
Unit 7180 Box 270
APO AE 09824
Turkey
011-90-322-316-310
Fax: 011-90-322-332-757
E-mail:
IncirlikEHS.Principal@eu.dodea.edu
http://http://www.inci-ehs.eu.dodea.edu/
Dr. Donald Torrey, Principal

1730 Infant School-House #45
Khalil Kando Gardens Road, 5651
Manama
Bahrain
Maria Stiles, Principal

1731 International Community School
PO Box 2002
Amman
Jordan 11181
962-6 5-2 10
Fax: 962-6 5-2 71
E-mail: office@ics-amman.edu.jo
http://www.ics-amman.edu.jo
Ours is a school where people matter. ~We want good results for each student, according to his or her own abilities in the classroom, in sport , music, drama or art.
John Light, Principal
Sue Hill, Primary Head

1732 International School of Choueifat
PO Box 7212
Abu Dhabi
United Arab Emirates
971-2-446-1444
Fax: 971-2-446-1048
E-mail: iscad@sabis.net
http://www.iscad-sabis.net
Over the last 27 years hundreds of students have graduated from The International Schools of Choueifat in the region and then graduated from top universities in the world. In the UK, these universities include Oxford, Cambridge, LSE, Bristol, Edinburgh, Bath, Birmingham, Liverpool, The Imperial College of Science and Technology and all other Colleges of London University.
Marilyn Abu-Esber, Director

1733 Istanbul International Community School
Karaagac Mahallesi, G 72 Sokak No:1
Buyukcekmece , Istanbul
Turkey 34866
90-212-857-8264
Fax: 90-212-857-8270
E-mail: jlewis@iics.k12.tr
http://www.iics.k12.tr
Through its challenging curriculum and strong staff-student relationships, IICS provides a caring environment that inspires each student to excel and to be inquisitive, creative, compassionate, balanced and internationally-minded.
Peter Welch, Headmaster
Sean Murphy, Primary Principal

1734 Izmir Elementary & High School
PSC 88
APO, Izmir 09821 0005
Turkey
Terry Emerson, Principal

1735 Jeddah Preparatory School
British Consulate, Box 6316
Jeddah 21442 Saudi Arabia
265-235-
Fax: 065-183-
E-mail: registrar@jpgs.org
http://http://www.jpgs.org/
John GF Parsons, Principal

1736 Jubail British Academy
PO Box 10059 Madinat Al Jubail
Jubail 31961
Saudi Arabia
966.3.341.7550
Fax: 966.3.341.6990
E-mail: mmcdougall@isgdh.org
http://http://www.isg-jubail.org/
Norman Edwards, Principal

1737 Jumeirah English Speaking School
PO Box 24942, Dubai
United Arab Emirates
971-4-394-5515
Fax: 971-4-394-3531
E-mail: jess@jess.sch.ae
http://http://www.jess.sch.ae/Home.aspx
CA Branson, Headmaster
RD Stokoe, Director

1738 King Faisal School
PO Box 94558, Riyadh 11614
Saudia Arabia
966-1-482-0802
Fax: 966-1-482-1521
E-mail: kfs@kfs.sch.sa
http://www.kfs.sch.sa/English/adefault.aspx
Grade levels preK-12, enrollment 600.
Mohammed Al-Humood, Director General

1739 Koc School
PK 60-Tuzla
Istanbul
Turkey 34941
(90)216 585 6200
Fax: 90-216-304-1048
E-mail: info@kocschool.k12.tr
http://www.kocschool.k12.tr
The goal of KoO School is to be respected nationally and internationally as a model K-12 school, offering an educational program of the highest academic and ethical standards.
Suna Kirac, Chairman

1740 Kuwait English School
PO Box 8640
Salmiya 22057
Kuwait
256-552-
Fax: 256-293-
E-mail: keschool@kes.edu.kw
http://http://www.kes.edu.kw/?page_id=69
Craig Halsall, Principal

1741 Mohammed Ali Othman School
PO Box 5713
Taiz Yeman
Arab Republic
967-422-3671
Fax: 967-4 2-1495
http://www.maoschoolyemen.com.ye
Mohammed Ali Othman School is a well established school which has been running for over thirty years. At present it has around a thousand students from the Foundation Stage through to Year 12
Abdulla Ahmad, Principal
Fowzia Abdo Saeed, Deputy Head

1742 Nadeen Nursery & Infant School
PO Box 26367
Adliya
Bahrain
973-177- 888
Fax: 973-177- 888
E-mail: info@nadeenschool.com
http://www.nadeenschool.info/
Nadeen School is dedicated to providing a caring, nurturing, and stimulating environment in which all children can learn and thrive. All of our students are treated with respect, care, and with the utmost sensitivity to their individual needs and requirements.
Pauline Puri, Principal

1743 New English School
PO Box 6156
Hawalli
Kuwait, KW 32036
[00965] 25318060
Fax: [00965] 25319924
E-mail: admin@neskt.com
http://www.neskt.com
Private, co-educational day-school to offer a British style curriculum from Kindergarten to 'A' level.
Tareq S Rajab, Founder

1744 Pakistan International School-Peshawar
23 Sahibzada Abdual Qayyum Road
University Town
Peshawar
92-441-4428
Fax: 92-441-7272
http://www.isbi.com
An independent, coeducaional day school which offers an educational program from prekindergarten through grade 8 and supervised correspondence study for the high school grades for all expatriate nationalities.
Angela Coleridge, Principal

1745 Rahmaniah-Taif-Acad International School
American Consulate General, Dhahran
District Saudi Arabia
03 -30 -555
Fax: 03 -30 -450
http://www.isgdh.org
Dean May, Principal

1746 Ras Al Khaimah English Speaking School
PO Box 975
Ras Al Khaimah
United Arab Emirates
971-7-362-441
Fax: 971-7-362-445
http://www.rakess.net
Roy Burrows, Principal

1747 Ras Tanura School
PO Box 6140
Ras Tanura
Saudi Arabia 31311
067-367-
E-mail: david.weston@aramco.com
http://www.saudiaramco.com
David Weston, Principal

1748 Sanaa International School
PO Box 2002
Sanaa
Yemen
967-1-370192
Fax: 967-1-370-193
E-mail: qsi-sanaa@qsi.org
http://www.qsi.org/yem_home/yem_home.htm
Sanaa International School, a non-profit institution that opened in September 1971 offers a high quality education in the English language for pre-school, elementary, and secondary students. The Campus is located on 34 acres on the outskirts of Sanaa constructed and entered in September 1978.
Mr. Philip Weirich, Director

1749 Saudi Arabian International British School
PO Box 85769
Riyadh
Saudi Arabia 11612
966- 12-8 23
Fax: 966- 12-8 23
E-mail: principal@britishschoolriyadh.com
http://www.britishschoolriyadh.com
Improve standards of teaching, learning and citizenship within a safe and secure environment. Our Mission Statement and School Improvement Plan provide the direction for the future development of our pupils and the continuous improvement of our school.
Peter Wiles, Acting Principal
Terry Sayce, Chairman

1750 Saudi Arabian International School-Dhahran
SAIS-DD, Box 677
Dhahran International Airport
Dhahran 31932, Saudi Arabia
996-3-330-0555
Fax: 966-3-330-0555
E-mail: brent_mutsch%sais@macexpress.org
http://http://www.isgdh.org/
Dr. Leo Ruberto, Principal

1751 Saudi Arabian International School-Riyadh
PO Box 990
Riyadh
Kingdom of Saudi Arabia 11421
966-1-491-4270
Fax: 966-1-491-7101
E-mail: registration@ais-r.edu.sa
http://www.aisr.org
Educate and inspire our students to be responsible, productive and ethical world citizens with the skills and passion to think creatively, reason critically, communicate effectively and learn continuously. We will accomplish this in an American educational environment characterized by high measurable standards and a clearly defined, appropriately interrelated college preparatory cur-

riculum, implemented by a superior staff in partnership with parents and community.

Daryle Russell, EdD, Principal
Brian Matthews, Superintendent

752 Saudia-Saudi Arabian International School
PO Box 167, CC 100
Jeddah 21231
Saudi Arabia

http://www.saudigazette.com

John Hazelton, Principal

753 Sharjah English School
PO Box 1600
Sharjah
United Arab Emirates
971-655- 930
Fax: 971- 55- 930
E-mail: seschool@emirates.net.ae
http://www.seschool.ae
Not for profit school. It is self-supporting and financed by fees paid by parents for the education of their children.

David Throp, Principal
Jenefer Race, Primary Headteacher

754 Sharjah Public School
PO Box 6125, Sharjah
United Arab Emirates
971-652- 124
http://www.sharjahpublicschool.ae

Nazim Khan, Principal

755 St. Mary's Catholic High School
PO Box 52232
Dubai
United Arab Emirates
009-104-3370
Fax: 009-104-3368
E-mail: maryscol@emirates.net.ae
http://www.stmarysdubai.com
St. Mary's Catholic High School is reputed for its high standards in academic work and also in the standards of discipline which we try to inspire in the children.

Sr Anne Marie Quigg, Principal
U D'Souza, Vice Principal

756 Sultan's School
PO Box 665
Seeb
Sultanate of Oman 00121
968-24 -367
Fax: 968-24 -362
E-mail: admissions@sultansschool.org
http://www.sultansschool.org
The Sultan's School is a co-educational school offering a bilingual Arabic-English education from early childhood to pre-university.

Anthony J Cashin, Principal

757 Sunshine School
2 Dutcher Avenue
Pawling, NY 12564
845-855-9238
Fax: 845-855-0222
http://sunshineschool-pawling.org
Our goal is to provide a quality pre-school education for young children. We do this by addressing both the social and the intellectual development of the child.

David Brinded, Principal

758 Tarsus American College and SEV Primary
Cengiz Topel Cd Caminur Mah 201 Sk
Tarsus/Mersin
Turkey 33440

90-324-613-5402
Fax: 90-324-624-6347
E-mail: info@tac.k12.tr
http://www.tac.k12.tr
The mission of Tarsus American Schools is to contribute to the growth of individuals who combine self-confidence with a firm sense of personal and social responsibility.

Bernard Mitchell, PhD, Superintendent
Jale Sever, Primary School Principal

1759 Universal American School
PO Box 17035
Khalidiya
Kuwait 72451
965-562-0297/561
Fax: 965-562-5343
E-mail: uas@qualitynet.net
http://www.uas.edu.kw
The Universal American School is a private, college-preparatory, N-12 school serving a multinational student body from the diverse populations residing in Kuwait

Nora Al-Ghanim, Administrative Director
Mike Church, Assistant Principal

1760 Uskudar American Academy
Vakif Sokak Number 1
Baglarbasi Istanbul
Turkey, TR
90-216-310-6823
Fax: 90-216-333-1818
E-mail: wshepard@uaa.k12.tr
http://www.uaa.k12.tr
The mission of SEV/ABH Schools is to contribute to the growth of individuals who combine self-confidence with a firm sense of personal, social, and environmental responsibility. We aim to enable our students to be strong bilinguals in English and Turkish, well-educated adults, lifelong learners, and efficient communicators, who have developed skills, accountability, and attitudes for leading a fulfilling life and for serving their country and humanity

Whitman Shepard, Director
Dilek Yakar, Primary Principal

1761 Walworth Barbour American International School in Israel
65 Hashomron Street
PO Box 484
Israel 40500
972-9-961-8100
Fax: 972-9-961-8111
E-mail: aisrael@wbais.org
http://www.american.hasharon.k12.il
Through a rigorous and dynamic American international curriculum, AIS, a private secular school in Israel, inspires each student to cultivate a respect for diversity, develop a passion for life-long learning, achieve academic potential, assume leadership, contribute actively to society, and resolve conflict through dialogue and understanding

Robert A Sills, Superintendent
John Chere, Chairman

Western Europe

1762 AC Montessori Kids
Route De Renipont 4
Lasne B-1380
Belgium
32-2-633-6652
Fax: 32-2-633-6652
E-mail: info@acmontessorikids.com
http://www.acmontessorikids.com

A bilingual English/French Montessori School for children aged 18 months - 12 years.

Laurence Randoux, Director
Mark Ciepers, Director

1763 AFCENT Elementary & High School
Unit 21606
APO AE 09703
Brunssum, Netherlands

http://www.afcent.org

1764 Abbotsholme School
Rocester (Uttoxeter, Staffordshire)
ST14 5BS
England
01889-590217
Fax: 01889-590001
E-mail: admissions@abbotsholme.co.uk
http://www.abbotsholme.com
This interdenominational school offers an English-based curriculum for 78 day students and 166 boarding (152 boys; 92 girls), in grades 7-13.

Darrell J Farrant, MA, FRSA, Principal
Steve Fairclough, Head

1765 Academy-English Prep School
Apartado 1300 Palma D Mallorca
525 W 17th Street Bloomington
Spain, IN 47404
812-333-2882
Fax: 812-339-2253
http://www.theprepschool.info

CA Walker, Principal

1766 Ackworth School, Ackworth
Pontefract, West Yorkshire
England WF7 7
0977-611401
E-mail: admissions@ackworthschool.com
http://www.ackworthschool.com
This school offers an English-based curriculum to 264 day students and 111 boarding students (180 boys; 195 girls), ages 11-18 years of age.

Peter J Simpson, Head
Jeffrey Swales, Deputy Head, Curriculum

1767 Alconbury Elementary School
Unit 5570 Box 60
APO AE 09470
Great Britain
011-44-1480-843620
Fax: 011-44-1480-843172
E-mail:
AlconburyES.Principal@eu.dodea.edu
http://www.alco-es.eu.dodea.edu
To provide a safe and productive learning environment in which all students reach their fullest potential by developing knowledge and skills.

Teddy Emerson, Principal

1768 Alconbury High School
Unit 5570 Box 60
APO AE 09470
Great Britain
441- 80-4 36
Fax: 441- 80-4 31
http://www.alco-hs.eu.dodea.edu
To develop healthy, adaptable, independently thinking, and socially responsible members of the global community.

Teddy Emerson, Principal
Lance Posey, Assistant Principal

1769 Alexander M Patch Elementary School
Unit 30401
APO AE 09107
Germany
071- 68- 520
Fax: 071- 68- 713
http://www.patch-es.eu.dodea.edu
Provide a standards-based curriculum that develops lifelong learners and promotes highest student achievement in partnership with our community.

Robert Allen, Principal
Ronald Lathrop, Assistant. Principal

1770 Alexander M Patch High School
Unit 30401
APO AE 09107-0401
Germany
071- 68- 520
Fax: 071- 68- 713
http://www.patch-es.eu.dodea.edu
Prepares all students to exceed challenging academic standards, know how to learn, communicate effectively, and make responsible decisions so that they can be continuous learners and productive citizens in a diverse society.

Robert Allen, Principal
Ronald Lathrop, Assistant. Principal

1771 Alfred T Mahan Elementary School
PSC 1003 Box 48
FPO Keflavik 09728
Iceland

Jan Long, Principal

1772 Alfred T Mahan High School
PSC 1003 Box 52
FPO Keflavik 09728 0352
Iceland

M Deatherage, Principal

1773 Amberg Elementary School
CMR 414
APO, Amberg 09173 0005
Germany

Letcher Connell, Principal

1774 Ambrit Rome International School
Via Filippo Tajani, 50
Rome, Italy 00149
39-06-559-5305
Fax: 39-06-559-5309
E-mail: ambrit@ambrit-rome.com
http://www.ambrit-rome.com
Grade levels Pre-K through 8, school year September - June

Bernard C Mullane, Director
Loretta Nanini, Admissions Director

1775 American College-Greece
6 Gravias Street
Aghia Paraskevi
Athens, Greece GR-15
30-1-600-9800
Fax: 30-1-600-9811
E-mail: info@acg.edu
http://www.acg.edu
Founded in 1875, combining the best of American education with the intellectual and cultural heritage of Greece, provide a unique foundation for international educational excellence.

David G Horner, President
Nicholas Jiavaras, Executive Vice President

1776 American Community School-Cobham
Heywood, Portsmouth Road
Cobham, Surrey
United Kingdom KT11
44-1932-869-744
Fax: 44-1932-869-789
E-mail: hayoub@acs-england.co.uk
http://www.acs-england.co.uk
Promotes a high standard of scholarship, responsibility, and citizenship in a supportive, international community.

Tom Lehman, Head of School
Heidi Ayoub, Dean of Admissions

1777 American Community School-Egham
Woodlee London Road (A30)
Egham, Surrey
United Kingdom TW20
44-1784-430-611
Fax: 44-1784-430-626
E-mail: jlove@acs-england.co.uk
http://www.acs-england.co.uk
Promotes high standards of scholarship, responsibility and citizenship in a supportive, international community

Julia Love, Dean of Admissions
Moyra Hadley, Head of School

1778 American Community School-Hillingdon
108 Vine Lane
Hillingdon, Middlesex
United Kingdom UB10
44-189-581-3734
Fax: 44-189-581-0634
E-mail: HillingdonAdmissions@acs-england.co.uk
http://www.acs-england.co.uk
Foundes in 1978, has endeavoured to provide a quality education for a multi-national community in the London area.

Ginger Apple, Head of School
Rudianne Soltis, Dean of Admissions

1779 American Community Schools
108 Vine Court
Hillingdon, Uxbridge, Middlesex
UB100BE
England
44-189-581-3734
Fax: 44-189-581-0634
E-mail: hmulkey@acs-england.co.uk
http://www.acs-england.co.uk
This school serves the needs of the international business families in Greater London. Programs are nonsectarian, coeducational day schools with lower, middle and high school divisions offering coordinate college preparatory curricula from pre-kindergarten through grade twelve.

Paul Berg, Headmaster

1780 American Community Schools-Athens
129 Aghias Paraskevis Avenue and Ka
Halandri, Athens
Greece 15343
301-639-3200
Fax: 301-639-0051
E-mail: gialamas@acs.gr
http://www.acs.gr
Provides a student-centered environment where individuals excel academically and develop intellectually, socially and ethically to thrive as healthy, responsible members of global society.

Stefanos Gialamas, President
Steve Kakaris, Business Manager

1781 American Embassy School-Reykjavik
Lngul nu 8
210 Gardab'r
Iceland
354-590-3106
Fax: 354-590-3110
E-mail: isi@internationalschool.is
http://www.internationalschool.is
The International School of Iceland (ISI) is a private elementary school housed in an Icelandic public school, Sjÿlandssk›li. The school offers an international educational program to children in grades 1-7.

Berta Faber, Headmistress
Hanna Hilmarsdottir, Assistant Headmistress

1782 American International School-Carinthia
Friesacher Strasse 3 Audio ICC
A-9330 Althofen
Austria

http://www.cic-network.at

Ron Presswood, Principal

1783 American International School-Florence
Villa le Tavernule - via del Carota
Bagno a Ripoli, Florence
Italy, VA 50012
39-055-646-1007
Fax: 39-055-644-226
E-mail: admin.tav@isfitaly.org
http://www.isfitaly.org
Business Manager
Provide attendees

Christopher Maggio, Head of School
Marie Jos , Manzini

1784 American International School-Genoa
Via Quarto 13-C
Genoa
Italy 16148
39-010-386-528
Fax: 39-010-398-700
E-mail: info@aisge.it
http://www.aisge.it
Provides students of internationally- minded families with a high quality education in the English language, from Pre-School through to the 12th Grade.

Sheldon Friedman, Director
Raffaele Boccardo, President

1785 American International School-Lisbon
Rua Antonio Dos Reis, 95
Linho, 2710-301 Sintra
Portugal
351-21-923-98-00
Fax: 351-21-923-98-26
E-mail: tesc0893@mail.telepac.pt
http://www.ecis.org/aislisbon/index.html
An independent, coeducational day school which offers an educational program from early childhood through grade 12 for student of all nationalities.

Blannie M Curtis, Director

1786 American International School-Rotterdam
Verhulstlaan 21
3055 WJ Rotterdam
Netherlands
31-10-422-5351
Fax: 31-10-422-4075
E-mail: queries@aisr.nl
http://www.aisr.nl
Provides a comprehensive program of learning, with well-qualified and experienced faculty who

prepare students Pre-School through Grade 12 for the ever-changing world in which we live.

Brian Atkins, Director
Anne-Marie Blitz, Elementary Principal

787 American International School-Salzburg

Moosstrasse 106
Salzburg A-5020
Austria
43-662-824-617
Fax: 43-662-824-555
E-mail: office@ais.salzburg.at
http://www.ais-salzburg.at
A boarding and day school committed to the college-preparatory education of conscientious young men and women. The academic and boarding programs nurture the students' intellectual growth and artistic potential, as well as their social, physical, and personal development.

Paul McLean, Headmaster
Felicia Gundringer, Admissions Coordinator

788 American International School-Vienna

Salmannsdorfer Strasse 47
A-1190 Vienna
Austria
43-1-401-320
Fax: 43-1-401-325
E-mail: info@ais.at
http://www.ais.at
Provide a culture of educational excellence, a nurturing environment, and an atmosphere of open communication and aims to prepare a diverse student body for higher education; to inspire the youth to realize their potential; to foster life-long learning, tolerance, personal integrity, and democratic values; and to prepare students to become responsible adults, with respect for different cultures and beliefs.

Ellen Stern, Director
Dr Greg Moncada, HS Principal

789 American Overseas School-Rome

Via Cassia 811
Rome, IT 00189
39-06-3326-4841
Fax: 39-06-3326-2608
E-mail: aosr@aosr.org
http://www.aosr.org
An independent, coeducational day school for students of all nationalities in prekindergarten through grade 13 and offers a boarding program for select students in grades 9-12.

Beth Kempler, Head of School

790 American School of the Hague

Rijksstraatweg 200
2241 BX Wassenaar
The Netherlands
31-70-512-1060
Fax: 31-70-511-2400
E-mail: info@ash.nl
http://www.ash.nl
educates students to excel in critical inquiry, creative thinking, clear communication, and commitment to others.

Paul De Minico, Superintendent
Douglas Buckley, Chair

791 American School-Barcelona

Jaume Balmes 7
Esplugues de Llobregat
Spain 08950
34-93-371-4016
Fax: 34-93-473-4787

E-mail: info@a-s-b.com
http://www.a-s-b.com
fully develop each student's unique potential by providing a high quality American/Spanish curriculum in an English-language based, respectful and diverse environment

Nancy Boyd, Elementary School Principal
Bill Volckok, Secondary School Principal

1792 American School-Bilbao

Soparda Bidea 10
Berang (Bizkaia)
Spain 48640
34-94-668-0860
Fax: 34-94-668-0452
E-mail: asob@asob.es
http://www.asob.es/en
s a private, non-profit, International School, Offers students an American-style educational programme taught in English. The curriculum has an international focus and leads to the American High School Diploma

Roger West, Director

1793 American School-Las Palmas

Carretera de los Hoyos, Km 1.7
Las Palmas de Gran Canaria
Las Palmas, Spain 35017
34-928-430-023
Fax: 34-928-430-017
E-mail: info@dns.aslp.org
http://www.aslp.org
Supports students in becoming life long learners in the tradition of American education

Linnah Sanab, Director
Conchita Neyra, Assistant Director

1794 American School-London

One Waverly Place
London
United Kingdom NW8 0
44-207-449-1200
Fax: 44-207-449-1350
E-mail: admissions@asl.org
http://www.asl.org
is to develop the intellect and character of each student by providing an outstanding American education with a global perspective.

Jodi Coats, Dean of Admissions

1795 American School-Madrid

Apartado 80
Madrid
Spain 28080
34-91-740-1900
Fax: 34-91-357-2678
E-mail: info@asmadrid.org
http://www.amerschmad.org
Grade levels Pre-K through 12, school year September - June

Robert Thompson, Director
William O'Hale, Headmaster

1796 American School-Milan

Via K Marx 14
Noverasco di Opera, Milan
Italy 20090
39-02-530-001
Fax: 39-02-576-06274
E-mail: director@asmilan.org
http://www.asmilan.org
s to provide a fulfilling educational environment where learners can discover and develop their capacities and achieve personal excellence.

Alen P Austen, Director
Samer Khoury, High School Principal

1797 American School-Paris

41, rue Pasteur
Saint Cloud
France 92210
33-1-411-28282
Fax: 33-1-460-22390
E-mail: webteam@asparis.fr
http://www.asparis.org
We develop lifelong learners with an international focus who use their social, thinking and problem-solving skills to contribute constructively to a changing global society

Pilar Cabeza de Vaca, Headmistress
Jack Davis, Head of the School

1798 American School-Valencia

Avenida Sierra Calderona 29
Urb Los Monasterios, Puzol
Spain 46530
34-96-140-5412
Fax: 34-96-140-5039
E-mail: asvalencia@asvalencia.org
http://www.asvalencia.org
An international, private, bilingual, university-preparatory school that provides a broad and balanced curriculum in a safe and positive learning environment that encourages students to seek challenges.

Saara Tatem, Director
Ildefonso Segura, Financial Director

1799 American School-the Hague

Rijksstraatweg 200
BX Wassenaar
Netherlands 02241
31-70-514-0113
Fax: 31-70-511-2400
E-mail: info@ash.nl
http://www.ash.nl
Educates students to excel in critical inquiry, creative thinking, clear communication, and commitment to others.

Rick Spradling, Director

1800 Anatolia College

PO Box 21021
Pylea Thessaloniki
Greece 55510
30-31-398-201
Fax: 30-31-327-500
E-mail: admissions@act.edu
http://www.anatolia.edu.gr
Offers undergraduate and graduate programs of study characterized by reasoned and open inquiry, acquisition of the breadth and depth of knowledge associated with traditional university curricula, and achievement of the highest possible standards in student-centered teaching and faculty scholarship, with emphasis on individual growth.

Richard L Jackson, President
Panayiotis Kanellis, Executive Vice President

1801 Anglo-American School-Moscow

American Embassy
Itainen Puistotie 14
Finland 00140
7-095-231-4488
Fax: 7-095-231-4477
E-mail: director@aas.ru
http://www.aas.ru
An international learning community where students, teachers and parents demand excellence and engagement from one another.

Drew Alexander, Director
Nicolette Kirk, Admissions Officer

1802 Anglo-American School-St. Petersburg
c/o American Embassy
Itainen Puistotie 14, Box L, Helsinki
Finland
7-812-320-8925
Fax: 7-812-320-8926
E-mail: nastia.smirnova@aas.ru
http://www.aas.ru/stpetersburg
An international learning community where students, teachers and parents demand excellence and engagement from one another.

Ronald Gleason, Principal
Ellen D Stren, Director

1803 Ansbach Elementary School
Unit 28614 APO AE 09177
Germany
011-49 -802
Fax: 011-46 -802
E-mail:
AnsbachES.Principal@eu.odedodea.edu
http://www.ansb-es.eu.dodea.edu
Provides many excellent opportunities to encouage and support all students intellectual, physical, social, emotional and creative developments and prepare them to meet the challengges of a dynamic and diverse world community.

Essie Grant, Principal

1804 Ansbach High School
Unit 28614
APO AE 09177
Germany
49-9802-223
Fax: 49-9802-1496
E-mail:
AnsbachHS.Principal@eu.dodea.edu
http://www.ansb-hs.eu.dodea.edu
A public school serving the children of American Army units.

Jennifer Rowland, Principal

1805 Antwerp International School
Veltwijcklaan 180
2180 Ekeren-Antwerpen
Belgium
32-3-543-9300
Fax: 32-3-541-8201
E-mail: ais@ais-antwerp.be
http://www.ais-antwerp.be
Educates young people to be responsible, caring, and productive members of a democratic society in a global community, and to prepare them for continued education. It promotes integrity, self-realization, mutual respect and understanding in a multi-cultural environment of students and teachers.

Alun Cooper, Headmaster

1806 Argonner Elementary School
Unit 20193 Box 0015
APO, Hanau 09165 0015
Germany
Christine Holsten, Principal

1807 Athens College
420 Madison Avenue
New York, NY 10017
212-697-7071
Fax: 212-697-7093
E-mail: trustees@athenscollege.org
http://www.athenscollege.org
The mission of Athens College is to provide, by international standards, the highest quality education to the most deserving candidates and to cultivate in its students those habits of mind, body, and spirit necessary for responsible citizenship in GReece and the world; moral courage, intellectual discipline, compassion, and an unswerving devotion to justice and truth. Our goal is to instill in our students, by teaching and by example, a strong sense of measure.

Walter McCanny Eggleston, Principal
Dr Nicholas G Bacopoulos, President

1808 Aviano Elementary School
Unit 6210 Box 180
APO, AE 09604-0180
Italy
011-39-0434-660921
E-mail: avianoes.principal@eu.dodea.edu
http://www.avia-es.eu.dodea.edu
Lillian Hiyama, Principal
Phyllis Fuglaar, Assistant Principal

1809 Aviano High School
Unit 6210 Box 180
APO, AE 09604-0180
Italy
632-567-
Fax: 390- 34-6 09
E-mail:
avianohs.principal@eu.dodea.edu
http://www.avia-hs.eu.dodea.edu
Debra K Johnson, Principal

1810 BEPS 2 Limal International School
23 Avenue Franklin Roosevelt
Brussels
Belgium 01050
32-10-417-227
Fax: 32-2-687-2968
E-mail: info@beps.com
http://www.beps.com
The schools share a common philosophy and approach to education. An average class size of 16 allows for a high level of individual attention in a caring and supportive environment.

Charles A Gellar, Head
Henny de Waal, Headmistress

1811 Babenhausen Elementary School
CMR 426 Unit 20219
APO, Babenhausen 09089 0005
Germany
Ida Rhodes, Principal

1812 Bad Kissingen Elementary School
CMR 464
APO, Bad Kissingen 09226 0005
Germany
Beatrice McWaters, Principal

1813 Bad Kreuznach Elementary School
CMR 441
APO, Bad Kreuznach 09525 0005
Germany
Peter Grenier, Principal

1814 Bad Kreuznach High School
Unit 24324
APO, Bad Krueznach 09252 0005
Germany
Jennifer Beckwith, Principal

1815 Bad Nauheim Elementary School
Unit 21103
APO, Bad Nauheim 09074 0005
Germany
Raymond Burkard, Principal

1816 Badminton School
Westbury-on-Trym, Bristol
BS9 3BA
England
0272-623141
E-mail: admissions@badminton.bristol.sch.uk
http://www.badminton.bristol.sch.uk
The school combines excellent facilities and teaching standards with a friendly atmosphere and a strong emphasis on pastoral care. Badminton is also focused on ensuring that girls realise their potential so that they can be capable of achieving whatever they want to be when they leave school.

Jan Scarrow, Headmistress

1817 Bamberg Elementary School
USAG Bamberg, Unit 27539
APO AE 09139
Germany
469-761-
Fax: 095- 31-15
E-mail: BambergES.Principal@eu.dodea.edu
http://www.bamb-es.eu.dodea.edu
John G Rhyne, Principal

1818 Bamberg High School
Unit 27539
APO AE 09139
Germany
469-088-
E-mail: BambergHS.Principal@eu.dodea.edu
http://www.bamb-hs.eu.dodea.edu/
Preparing all students to achieve success and personal fulfillment in a dynamic global environment.

Dominick Calabria, Principal
Richard Jimenez, Assistant Principal

1819 Barrow Hills School
Roke Lane
Witley, Godalming
Surrey, England GU8 5
01428-683639
Fax: 01428-683639
E-mail: sec@barrowhills.org.uk
http://www.barrowhills.org.uk
Michael Connolly, Headmaster

1820 Baumholder High School
Unit 23816 Box 30
APO, AE 09034-0034
Germany
011-49 -783
Fax: 011-49 -783
E-mail: BaumholderHS.Principal@eu.dodea.edu
http://www.baum-hs.eu.dodea.edu
Danny Robinson, Principal
Patrick McDonald, Assistant Principal

1821 Bavarian International School
Haputstrasse 1
Schloss Haimbausen
Haimhausen, Germany 85778
49-8133-9170
Fax: 49-8133-917-135
E-mail: k.lippacher@bis-school.com
http://www.bis-school.com
Inspiring young minds and challenging young individuals to achieve their intellectual and personal potential within a caring international environment

Bryan Nixon, Director

1822 Bedales School
Church Road Steep
Petersfield Hampshire
England, UK GU32
01730-300100
Fax: 01730-300500
E-mail: admin@bedales.org.uk
http://www.bedales.org.uk
Keith Budge, Headmaster
Leo Winkley, Deputy Head

823 Bedford School
De Parys Avenue Bedford
England, UK MK40
44-0-1234-362200
Fax: 44-0-1234-362283
E-mail: info@bedfordschool.org.uk
http://www.bedfordschool.org.uk
We pride ourselves on the pursuit of excellence, on encouraging boys to develop their talent, discover new interests and prepare for the world beyond school.

John Moule, Head Master

824 Bedgebury School
Goudhurst
Cranbrook
Kent TN17
0580-211954
E-mail: bedgebury@bell-centres.com
http://www.bedgeburyschool.co.uk
Our goal at Bell Bedgebury is a simple one - to offer all our students the best possible preparation for their future educational careers.

Eric Squires, Headmaster
David Morse, Principal

825 Belgium Antwerp International School
Veltwijcklaan 180
Ekeren-Antwerp
Belgium 02180
32-3-543-9300
Fax: 32-3-541-8201
E-mail: ais@ais-antwerp.be
http://www.ais-antwerp.be
The school is concerned with the student's social, physical, emotional and intellectual development. It is committed to excellence and to providing the best possible opportunities for growth for each student.

Alun Cooper, Headmaster
Matthew Cox, Elementary School Principal

826 Benjamin Franklin International School
Martorell i Pena 9
Barcelona
Spain 08017
34-93-434-2380
Fax: 34-93-417-3633
E-mail: bfranklin@bfis.org
http://www.bfis.org
We view education as an opportunity for children to live fully and become global citizens able to build a more humane world.

David Penberg, Director
James Duval, Elementary Principal

827 Berlin International School
Lentzeallee 8/14
Berlin
Germany 14195
49-30-790-00370
Fax: 49-30-3790-00370
E-mail: office@berlin-international-school.de
http://www.berlin-international-school.de
Berlin International School is a private, non-profit, non-denominational day school offering student-centered learning to international and local students from pre-school through university entrance preparation.

Hubert Keulers, Acting Director
Michael Cunningham, Principal

828 Berlin Potsdam International School
Am Hochwald 30, Haus 2
14 532 Kleinmachnow
Germany
49-332-086-760
Fax: 49-332-086-7612

E-mail: office@bpis.de
http://www.bpis.de
Grade levels N-12, school year August - June

Stephen Middlebrook, Director

1829 Bitburg Elementary School
52 MSG/CCSE-B Unit 3820 Box 45
APO, AE
Germany 09126-45
119-661-
Fax: 119- 61-
E-mail: BitburgES.Principal@eu.dodea.edu
http://www.bitb-es.eu.dodea.edu

Joseph Lovett, Principal

1830 Bitburg High School
52 MSG/CCSH-B Unit 3820 Box 50
APO, AE
Germany 09126-50
065-692-
Fax: 065- 90-0
E-mail: webmaster@eu.dodea.edu
http://www.bitb-hs.eu.dodea.edu

David W Carlisle, Principal
Jennifer Remoy, Assistant Principal

1831 Bitburg Middle School
52 MSG/CCSM-B Unit 3820 Box 55
APO, AE
Germany 09126
561-946-3200
Fax: 065-611-2091
E-mail: webmaster@eu.dodea.edu
http://www.bitb-ms.eu.dodea.edu

Douglas Carlson, Principal

1832 Bjorn's International School
Gartnerivej 5
Copenhagen
Denmark 02100
453-929-2937
Fax: 453-929-1938
E-mail: kontoret.101152@skolekom.dk
http://www.b-i-s.dk

Lea Kroghly, Principal

1833 Black Forest Academy
Postfach 1109
Kandern
Germany 79396
49-7626-91610
Fax: 49-7626-8821
http://www.bfacademy.com
Black Forest Academy's vision is globally-minded Christians changing their world for Christ.

George Durance, Principal
Tim Shuman, Director

1834 Bloxham School
Bloxham
Banbury
Oxfordshire, UK OX15
01295-720206
Fax: 01295-721897
E-mail: registar@bloxhamschool.com
http://www.bloxhamschool.com
As the largest group of Church of England Schools in the UK, Woodard was established in 1847 and today is known for providing academic excellence and an unrivalled supportive environment where individuals can flourish.

Mark Allbrook, Headmaster
B Hurst, Chairman

1835 Blue Coat School
Birmingham Street
Walsall
West Midlands, UK WS1 2

0121-456-3966
E-mail:
postbox@blue-coat-s.walsall.sch.uk
http://www.bluecoatschool.org

Brian Bissell, Principal
Ken Yeates, Headteacher

1836 Boeblingen Elementary School
Unit 30401
APO
AE 09107
070-1 1-2715
Fax: 070-1 2-1368
http://www.stut-esb.eu.dodea.edu
To inspire curiosity and ambition for life-long learning in every student.

Dale Moore, Principal
Toufy Haddad, Assistant Principal

1837 Bonn International School
Martin-Luther-King Strasse 14
Bonn
Germany 53175
49-228-308-540
Fax: 49-228-308-5420
E-mail: admin@bis.bonn.org
http://www.bis.bonn.org
The mission of Bonn International School is to inspire and empower students, aged 3-19, to become balanced, responsible global citizens who are successful, independent thinkers with a passion for learning.

Peter Murphy, Director
Diane Lewthwaite, Secondary School Principal

1838 Bordeaux International School
252 rue Jadaique
Bordeaux
France 33000
33-557-870-211
Fax: 33-556-790-047
E-mail: bis@bordeaux-school.com
http://www.bordeaux-school.com
Conveniently located in the centre of historic Bordeaux, the school is purpose-built around a secure, enclosed and partially covered courtyard, which provides a space for pupils across the school to socialise with each other.

Christine Cussac, Head Teacher

1839 Brillantmont International School
16, avenue Charles-Secretan
Lausanne
Switzerland, CH 01005
41-21-310-0400
Fax: 41-21-320-8417
E-mail: info@brillantmont.ch
http://www.brillantmont.ch
Brillantmont International School houses some 100 boarding boys and girls and about 50 day students.

Philippe Pasche, Director
Geraldine Boland, Deputy Director

1840 British Council School-Madrid
Prado de Somosaguas
Pozuelo de Alarcon
Madrid, UK 28223
34-91-337-3500
Fax: 34-91-337-3573
E-mail:
general.enquiries@britishcouncil.org
http://www.britishcouncil.org
The British Council School is one of the leading bilingual, bi-cultural schools in the world, offering the very best of British and Spanish education. The school is divided into three departments (Early Years, Primary and

Secondary) and offers education from children aged three to eighteen years old.

Jack Cushman, Principal
Norman Roddom, Head of School

1841 British Kindergarten
Ctra Del La Coruna Km 17
Las Rozas, 28230 Madrid
Spain

http://www.britishnursery.com
Mary Jane Maybury, Principal

1842 British Primary School
Stationsstraat 3 Vossem
Tervuren, BE 03080
32-2-767-3098
Fax: 32-2-767-0351
E-mail: info@stpaulsbps.com
http://www.britishprimary.com
Our aim at St Paul's is to provide 'The Best Possible Start in Life '. We offer a secure, nurturing and truly caring environment for children, whether settling into a new country or going to school for the first time.

Katie Tyrie, Headteacher
Bruce Guy, Financial Manager

1843 British Primary School-Stockholm
Vossem
182 68 Djursholm
Sweden
468-755-2375
http://www.britishinternationalprimarysc hool.se

Gaye Elliot, Principal

1844 British School-Amsterdam
Anthonie van Dijckstraat 1
Amsterdam, ME 01077
31-20-347-1111
Fax: 31-20-347-1222
http://www.britishschoolofamsterdam.nl
Our school is commited to providing the best possible eduction for our students. This is achieved in a calm, friendly, purposeful learning environment. Our strong and experieced team of teaching professionals are supported with excellent resources and facilities.

John Light, Principal
K McCarthy, Chairman

1845 British School-Bern
Hintere Dorfgasse 20
Gumligen
Switzerland 03073
41-31-951-2358
Fax: 41-31-951-1710
E-mail: britishschool@bluewin.ch
http://www.britishschool.ch
We aim to provide a high quality programme for children of all abilities that promotes the social, emotional, cognitive, moral, physical and aesthetic development of each child

Enid Potts, Head Teacher/Administrator
Joe Quinn, Support Staff

1846 British School-Brussels
Leuvensesteenweg 19
Tervuren
Belgium, BE 03080
322-767-4700
Fax: 322-767-8070
E-mail: reception@britishschool.be
http://www.britishschool.be
The British School of Brussels, situated 30 minutes from the city centre on a beautiful campus, offers a British education to International families in the heart of Europe,

with pupils from some 70 nationalities on roll.

Roland Chant, Principal
Brenda Despontin, Principal

1847 British School-Netherlands
Wheatfields
Tarwekamp 3
Netherlands 02592
071-616958
Fax: 071-617144
E-mail: foundation@britishschool.nl
http://www.britishschool.nl
BSN provides the opportunity of becoming part of a student community defined by an ethos of mutual understanding and cultural harmony. We have high expectations of our students, so whilst appreciating the difference in the ability and achievement of individual children within the classroom, we expect the same high level of behaviour from all. Good behaviour, manners and a respect for teachers and other adults are everyday expectations of our students.

Martin Coles, Principal
Nigel Collins, Assistant Principal

1848 British School-Oslo
PO Box 7531, Skillebekk 0205
Oslo 2
Norway

Margaret Stark, Principal

1849 British School-Paris
21B Lavant Street
Petersfield
Hampshire GU32-3EL
01-34-80-45-94
Fax: 01-39-76-12-69
E-mail: ecis@ecis.org
http://www.ecis.org
The European Council of International Schools (ECIS) is a collaborative network promoting the ideals and best practice of international education.

Pilar Cabeza de Vaca, Executive Director
Mary Langford de Donoso, Deputy Executive Director

1850 Bromsgrove School
Worcester Road
Bromsgrove
Worcestershire B61-7DU
44-0-1527-579679
Fax: 44-0-1527-576177
E-mail: headmaster@bromsgrove-school.co.uk
http://www.bromsgrove-school.co.uk
This school offers an English curriculum to 840 day students and 350 boarding (700 boys; 490 girls), ages 3 to 18. The curriculum is English based but french, german and Spanish are also taught. Teachers from overseas are welcome with the length of stay being 1-2 years. Applications needed to teach include science, French, math, Spanish, reading, German, English and physical education.

Chris Edwards, Headmaster
John Rogers, Foundation Director

1851 Brooke House College
Market Harborough Leicestershire
Leicestershire
England LE16-7AU
44-0-1852-462452
Fax: 44-0-1858-462487
E-mail: enquiries@brookehouse.com
http://www.brookehouse.com
Brooke House College is a co-educational, international boarding college, specialising in preparing students from all over the

globe, and from Britain, for entrance to the most prestigious universities to which they can aspire in both the U.K. and U.S.A

K Anderton, Academic Tutor
A Burditt, Diploma Personal Assistant

1852 Brussels American School
Unit 8100 Box 13
APO AE 09714-9998
Belgium, BE
320-271-9552
Fax: 302-717-9577
E-mail: BrusselsEHS.Principal@eu.dodea.edu
http://www.brus-ehs.eu.dodea.edu
Brussels American School (BAS) serves students in Kindergarten through Grade 12. The elementary section of the school consists of Kindergarten through Grade 5. It is housed in one of the four major buildings and has a playground and special learning facilities. Grades 6-8 serve as transitional grades between the elementary and secondary programs; students attend classes in both the elementary and high school buildings

Walter G Seely, Principal
Cheryl A Aeillo, Assistant Principal

1853 Brussels English Primary School
23 Avenue Franklin Roosevelt
Brussels
Belgium 01050
62-010-41-72-27
Fax: 62-010-40-10-43
E-mail: info@beps.com
http://www.beps.com
Offering the Primary Years Programme, a prestigious programme supported by many international schools around the world (ages 3 to 11).

Henny de Waal, Head of School
Dominique Floridor, Secretary

1854 Bryanston School
Blandford
Dorset
UK DT11-0PX
0258-452411
E-mail: development@bryanston.co.uk
http://www.bryanston.co.uk
Bryanston they are those which encourage independence, individuality, and thinking, as well as being able to learn from living in a loving community which fast becomes, and remains, a family

Paul Speakman, Treasurer
Robert Ware, Chair

1855 Buckswood Grange International School
Broomham Hall Rye Road Guestling
Nr Hastings E Suxxex
England TN35-4LT
44-182-574-7000
Fax: 44-182-576-5010
E-mail: achieve@buckswood.co.uk
http://www.buckswood.co.uk
A multinational boarding school for British and foreign students which combines the British curriculum with specialist EFL tution and close attention to social skills in an international environment.

Michael Reiser, Principal
David Walker, Marketing Manager

1856 Butzbach Elementary School
CMR 452 Box 5500
APO, Butzbach 09045 0005
Germany

Carl Ford, Principal

1857 Byron Elementary School
202 New Dunbar Road
Byron, GA 31008
478-956-5020
Fax: 478-956-5910

E-mail: dmartin@peachschools.org
http://bes.peachschools.org
Our teachers are dedicated, hard working educators who are life learners themselves. An enriched, standards-based instruction is provided through collegial partnerships and staff development. Teachers continue to refine their instructional skills through book study discussions, grade level meetings, and attending various workshops.

Martin Dannelly, Principal
Dennis Teresia, Assistant Principal

858 CIV International School-Sophia Antipolis

BP 97, 190 rue Frederic Mistral
Sophia Antipolis 06902
France
33-4-929-65224
Fax: 33-4-936-52215
E-mail: secretary@civissa.org
http://www.civissa.org
Grade levels 1-12, school year September-June

Andrew Derry, Head of Section

859 Calpe College International School

Cta de Cadiz Km 171
29670 Malaga
Spain
95-278-1479
Fax: 95-278-9416
E-mail: info@calpeactivanet.es
http://www.calpeschool.com

Luis Proetta, Principal

860 Campion School

PO Box 67484
Pallini GR-15302
Greece
301-813-5901
Fax: 301-813-6492
E-mail: dbaker@hol.gr
http://www.campionschool.in

Dennis MacKinnon, Principal

861 Canadian College Italy-The Renaissance School

59 Macamo Courte
Maple, Ontario
Canada L6A-1G1
905-508-7108
800-422-0548
Fax: 905-508-5480
E-mail: cciren@rogers.com
http://www.ccilanciano.com
A unique source of highest-quality English-language education, preparing students for university entrance in the U.S.A., U.K., Canada and Europe, become one of the pre-eminent high school boarding schools in Europe. Graduates from CCI's founding years earned acceptances, and a variety of scholarships

862 Cascais International School

Rua Das Faias, Lt 7 Torre
2750 Cascais
Portugal

http://www.icsc.pt
An international nursery school, founded in 1996, that caters to children ages 1-6 years on a fulltime or part-time basis. The first language of the school is English and Portuguese is the second. Many other languages are spoken throughout the school. Offers an individual approach, flexible hours and transport. Total enrollment is 75 day students (45 boys; 30 girls).

Evan Lerven Sixma, Principal

1863 Castelli Elementary School

Via Dei Laghi, 8.60
Ligetta Di Marinus, Ag, 00047 Marina
Italy
39-06-9366-1311
Fax: 39-06-9366-1311
http://www.castelli-international.it

Diana Jaworska, Principal

1864 Castelli International School

Via Degli Scozzesi
13-Grottaferrata
Rome, Italy
39-06-943-15779
Fax: 39-06-943-15779
E-mail: maryac@castelli-international.it
http://www.castelli-international.it/
To provide a stimulating educational environment for international families living south of Rome and in the Castelli Romani area. CIS believes that the children, being naturally curious, are eager to learn, and that they learn best through inquiry, experience, and trial and error

Marianne Palladino, BA, MA, PhD, Director of Studies

1865 Casterton School

Kirkby Lonsdale, Via Carnforth
Lancashire, United Kingdom LA6-2SG
052-42-71202
E-mail: admissions@castertonschool.co.uk
http://www.castertonschool.co.uk
One of the most established academic girls boarding and day schools in the UK, with a national and international reputation.

P McLaughlin, Headmaster
G A Sykes, Deputy Head

1866 Caxton College

Ctra De Barcelona S/N 46530
Puzol Valencia
Spain
34-96-146-4500
Fax: 34-96142-0930
E-mail: caxton@caxtoncollege.com
http://www.caxtoncollege.com
Aim to provide pupils with the skills necessary to form independent opinions enabling them to make personal decisions in response to situations which will arise in their lives.

Amparo Gil, Principal
Marta Gil, Vice Principal

1867 Center Academy

92 St John's Hill Battersea
London SW11 1SH
England
071-821-5760
http://www.centeracademy.com
To provide students with a learning environment that facilitates the development of self-confidence, motivation, and academic skills, and gives students the opportunity to achieve success in life.

Robert Detweiler, Principal
Mack R Hicks, Founder and Chairman

1868 Centre International De Valbonne

Civ-bp 097 06902 Sophia
Antipolis Cedex
France
33-4-929-652-24
Fax: 33-4-936-522-15
E-mail: greta.antipolis languages @ ac-nice.fr
http://www.civfrance.com

Ian Hill, Principal

1869 Charters-Ancaster School

Penland Road, Bexhill on Sea
TN40 2JQ
England
0424-730499
Boarding girls ages eleven to eighteen; day school for boys three to eight and girls three-eighteen.

K Lewis, MA, Headmaster

1870 Children's House

Kornbergvegen 23-4050 Sola
Stavanger
Norway

http://www.hr.umich.edu

Christine Grov, Principal

1871 Cite Scolaire International De Lyon

2 Place De Montreal
69007 Lyon
France
33-04-78-69-60-06
Fax: 33-04-78-69-60-36
E-mail: csi-lyon-gerland@ac-lyon.fr
http://www.csilyon.fr
Grade levels 1-12.

Donna Galiana, Director

1872 Cobham Hall

Cobham (Nr Gravesend, Kent)
DA12 3BL
England, UK
0474-82-3371
E-mail: enquiries@cobhamhall.com
http://www.cobhamhall.com
Encouraged and supported to make the most of your talents, whether these are academic, musical, sporting ... or as yet undiscovered!

Paul Mitchel, Headmaster
C Sykes, Chairman

1873 Colegio Ecole

Santa Rosa 12
Lugo Llanera
Asturias 33690
985- 77-8
E-mail: ecole1@colegioecole.com
http://www.colegioecole.com

Patrick Wilson, Principal

1874 Colegio International-Meres

Apartado 107
33080 Oviedo, Asturias
Spain
985-792-427
Fax: 985-794-582
http://www.colegiomeres.com

Belen Orejas Fernandez, Principal

1875 Colegio International-Vilamoura

Apt 856, 8125 Vilamoura
Loule Algarve
Portugal

http://www.civ.com

Lawrence James, Principal

1876 College Du Leman International School

74 Route De Sauverny
CH-1290 Versoix, Geneva
Switzerland
41-22-775-5555
Fax: 41-22-775-5559
E-mail: admissions@cdl.ch
http://www.cdl.ch
Grade levels include N-13 with an enrollment of 1700.

Francis Clivaz, General Director
Cedric Chaffois, Director of Admission

119

1877 College International-Fontainebleau
48 Rue Guerin 77300
Fontainebleau
France
01-64-22-11-77
Fax: 01-64-23-43-17
E-mail:
glenyskennedy@compuserve.com
http://www.fontainebleau.fr

Mrs. G Kennedy, Principal

1878 College Lycee Cevenol International
43400 Le Chambon sur Lignon
France
04-71-59-72-52
Fax: 04-71-65-87-38
E-mail: contact@lecevenol.org
http://www.lecevenol.org
he CollSge Lyc,e International C,venol (a
private establishment under a contract of
state sponsorship since 1971) today welcomes boarders and day students of local,
regional, national and international
origins.

Christiane Minssen, Principal
Robert Lassey, Headmaster

1879 Copenhagen International School
Hellerupvej 22-26
2900 Hellerup
Denmark
45-39-463-300
Fax: 45-39-612-230
E-mail: cis@cisdk.dk
http://www.cis-edu.dk
Develop the potential of each student in a
stimulating environment of cultural diversity, academic excellence and mutual
respect.

Peter Wellby, Director
Simon Watson, Senior School Principal

1880 Croughton High School
Unit 5485 Box 15
APO Croughton, 09494 0005
Great Britain

Dr. Charles Recesso, Principal

1881 Danube International School
Josef Gall-Gassee 2
1020 Vienna
Austria
00-43-1-720-3110
Fax: 43-1-720-3110-40
E-mail: info@ danubeschool.at
http://www.danubeschool.at
DIS started off life in 1992 in
Schrutkagasse in the 13th District. The
school had another name, then - 'Pawen International Community School' that now
houses a Rudolf Steiner school

Peter Harding, Director
Sabine Biber-Brussmann, Registrar

1882 Darmstadt Elementary School
CMR 431
APO, Darmstadt 09175 0005
Germany

Sherry Templeton, Principal

1883 Darmstadt Junior High School
CMR 431
APO, Darmstadt 09175 0005
Germany

Daniel Basarich, Principal

1884 De Blijberg
Graaf Florisstraat 56
Rotterdam
Netherlands 3032C
010-448-2266
Fax: 010-448-2270
E-mail:
deblijberg_international@hotmail.com
http://www.blijberg.nl

Barbera Everaars, Director
Bart Loman, Director

1885 Dean Close School
Lansdown Road
Cheltenham
England GL51
0242-522640
E-mail: squirrels@deanclose.org.uk
http://www.deanclose.co.uk
Aim to provide a rich variety of opportunities that will enable your son or daughter to
develop in confidence and independance
within our happy and caring community.

Sue Bennett, Headmistress
Anthony R Barchand, Faculty Head

1886 Dexheim Elementary School
Unit 24027
APO, Dexheim 09110 0005
Germany

Gary Waltner, Principal

1887 Downside School
Stratton-on-the-Fosse, Bath (Avon)
Radstock Bath
England, UK BA3
0761-232-206
E-mail: admin@downside.co.uk
http://www.downside.co.uk
Downside is an independent Catholic
co-educational boarding school for pupils
aged 9 to 18.

Dom Leo Maidlow Davis, Head Master
AR Hobbs, Deputy Head Master

1888 Dresden International School
Annenstr 9
D-01067 Dresden
Germany
49-351-3400428
Fax: 49-351-3400430
E-mail: dis@dredsen-is.de
http://www.dresden-is.de
Committed to the aim of continuous im-
provement, which has been such a feature
of the school since it opened in 1996.

Chrissie Sorenson, Director
Steve Ellis, Secondary School Principal

1889 ECC International School
Jacob Jordaensstraat 85-87
2018 Antwerp
Belgium

Dr. X Nieberding, Principal

1890 Ecole Active Bilingue
70 rue du Theatre
Paris
France 75015
01-44-37-00-80
Fax: 01-45-79-06-66
E-mail: info@eabjm.net
http://www.eabjm.org
An associated UNESCO school, EABJM is
also contractually part of the French national education system. The high school
prepares students for the French Baccalaureate, the French Baccalaureate with Option Internationale, or the International
Baccalaureate. An official testing site for
the SAT, EABJM is also accredited by the
College Entrance Examination Board and

the Cambridge University Local Examination
Syndicate.

Danielle Monod, Principal

1891 Ecole Active Bilingue Jeannine Manuel
70 rue du Theatre
75015 Paris
France 75015
45-44-37-00-80
Fax: 01-45-79-06-66
E-mail: info@eabjm.net
http://www.eabjm.com
Grade levels k-12.

Elizabeth Zeboulon, Directrice

1892 Ecole D'Humanite
CH-6085 Hasliberg-Goldern
Switzerland
41-33-972-9292
Fax: 41-33-972-9211
E-mail: us.office@ecole.ch
http://www.ecole.ch
150 boys and girls, aged 6 to 20 and faculty live in
small family-style groups. International, inter-ra-
cial student body. Main language is German, with
special classes for beginners.

Kathleen Hennessy, Interim Director
Arsheles Curturils, Director

1893 Ecole Des Roches & Fleuris
3961 Bluche
Valais
Switzerland

Marcel Clivez, Principal

1894 Ecole Lemania
Chemin de Preville 3
CP500 1001 Lausanne
Switzerland
41-0-21-320-15-01
Fax: 41-0-21-312-67-00
E-mail: info@lemania.com
http://www.lemania.com
This international college represents over 65 nationalities offering French and English intensive
courses, summer programs, American academic
studies at graduate and undergraduate levels,
sports and cultural activities, and accommodation
in boarding school. Total enrollment: 800 day students; 100 boarding (450 boys; 450 girls), in
grades 1-10.

M JP du Pasquier, Principal

1895 Ecole Nouvelle Preparatoire
Route Du Lac 22, Ch-1094
Paudex
Switzerland

Marc Desmet, Principal

1896 Ecole Nouvelle de la Suisse Romande
Ch de Rovereaz 20, CP-161
CH-1000 Lausanne 12
Switzerland
41-21-654-65-00
Fax: 41-21-654-65-05
E-mail: info@ensr.ch
http://www.ensr.ch
The mission of the school is to prepare its students

Isabel Matos, Director Administrative/Fina
Beth Krasna, President

1897 Edinburgh American School
29 Chester Street
Edinburgh EH37EN
Scotland
013-155- 460
Fax: 013-162- 499
http://www.edinburghacademy.org.uk

AW Morris, Principal

898 Edradour School
Edradour House - Pitlochry
Perthshire PH165JW,
Scotland

JPA Romanes, Principal

899 El Plantio International School Valencia
Urbanizacion El Plantio
Calle 233, N36, La Canada, Paterna
Spain
96-132-14-10
Fax: 96-132-18-41
E-mail: plantiointernational@retemail.es
http://www.plantiointernational.com
To educate young people who can adapt to their environment and therefore our objective is based on providing our students with the necessary skills to enable a better knowledge of the modern world and maximising the ability to communicate in an ever-changing and broadening society.

Anthony C Nelson, Principal

900 Ellerslie School
Abbey Road, Malvern
WR14 3HF
England
0684-575701
http://www.ellerslie.school.nz

Elizabeth M Baker, BA, Headmaster

901 English Junior School
Lilla Danska Vagen 1
412 74 Gothenburg
Sweden
31-401819

Patricia Gabrielsson, Principal

902 English Kindergarten
Valenjanpolku 2
05880 Hyvinkaa
Finland

http://www.theenglishkindergarten.co.in

Riva Rentto, Principal

903 English Montessori School
C/ de la Salle S/N
Aravaca, Madrid
Spain 28023
91-357-26-67
Fax: 91-307-15-43
E-mail: t.e.m.s@teleline.es
http://englishmontessorischool.com
Each year of school up to and including Year 10 at The English Montessori School is validated with the Spanish Educational System. The importance of this is that a students entering or leaving the school can transfer to the equivalent level in any other school.

Elaine Fitzpatrick, Headmistress
Milagros Alonso, Director

904 English School-Helsinki
Mantytie 14
Helinski
Finland 00270
358-9-477-1123
Fax: 358-9-477-1980
E-mail: english.school@edu.hel.fi
http://www.eschool.edu.hel.fi
The English School is a private, national language school based on Christian values. The Ministry of Education has placed a special responsibility on the school to familiarize the students with Finnish and English languages as well as the culture of Finnish and Anglo-Saxon language areas.

Erkki Lehto, Principal
Riitta Volanen, Secretary

1905 English School-Los Olivos
Avda Pino Panera 25, 46110 Godella
Valencia
Spain 46110
96-363-99-38
Fax: 96-364-48-63
http://www.school-losolivos.es

Jane Rodriguez, Principal

1906 European Business & Management School
Frederik de Merodestraat, 12-16
Antwerp
Belgium 02600
323-218-8182
Fax: 323-218-5868
E-mail: info@ebms.edu
http://www.ebms.edu
Once a year, European Business and Management School organizes a cross-cultural business tour, providing our students with another opportunity to strengthen their competencies in global thinking in international business.

Luc Van Meli, Director

1907 European School Culham
Thame Lane, Abingdon
Oxfordshire
Great Britain OX14
44 -235-5226
Fax: 44 -235-5546
E-mail: esculham@eursc.org
http://www.esculham.net
Educated side by side, untroubled from infancy by divisive prejudices, acquainted with all that is great and good in different cultures, it will be borne in upon them as they mature that they belong together.

T Hyem, Principal
Simon Sharron, Head

1908 European School-Brussels I
Avenue Du Vert Chasseur 46
Brussels
Belgium 01180
02-374-58-44
E-mail: kari.kivinen@eursc.org
http://www.eeb1.org
The European Schools fulfil a task that national schools are unable to fulfil: to teach pupils from different countries in their respective mother tongues and to instil in them the cultural values of their home country room a European perspective.

J Marshall, Principal
Kari Kivinen, Director

1909 European School-Italy
Via Montello 118
21100 Varese
Italy
32 -297-5990
http://www.ec.europa.eu

Jorg Hoffman, Principal

1910 Evangelical Christian Academy
Calle La Manda 47
Camarma de Esteruelas, Madrid
Spain 28816
34-91-741-2900
Fax: 34-91-320-8606
E-mail: secretary@ecaspain.com
http://www.ecaspain.com
The vision drives every facet of ECA's existence. ECA offers a challenging, college preparatory curriculum in an American-based system. Students at ECA study Bible each year, and a Christian worldview is

integrated into every aspect of the curriculum.

Beth Hornish, Principal
Scot Musser, Business Manager

1911 Feltwell Elementary School
CCSE/F Unit 5185 Box 315
APO AE
Great Britain 09461-5315
011-44 -842
Fax: 018-2 8-7931
E-mail: feltwell.attendance@eu.dodea.edu
http://www.felt-es.eu.dodea.edu
School where teachers, parents, and community share the responsibility for each child's learning.

Tom LaRue, Principal

1912 Frankfurt International School
An der Waldlust 15
Oberursel
Germany 61440
49-6171-2020
Fax: 49-6171-202384
E-mail: admissions@fis.edu
http://www.fis.edu
To be the leading culturally diverse and family-oriented international school with English as the principal language of instruction. We inspire young individuals to develop their intellect, creativity and character to grow into adaptable, socially responsible global citizens by ensuring a dynamic, 21st-century, inquiry-driven education of the highest standard.

Jutta Kuehne, Director
Mark Ulfers, Head of School

1913 Frederiksborg Gymnasium
Carlsbergvej 15
3400 Hillerod
Denmark
800-055-7314
Fax: 482- 07-1
E-mail: post@frborg-gymhf.dk
http://www.frborg-gymhf.dk

Peter Kuhlman, Principal

1914 Friends School
Saffron Walden, Essex
England CB11
0642-722141
E-mail: admissions@friends.org.uk
http://www.friends.org.uk
Friends' School strives to be a unique community where the potential and talent of each individual is realised within a friendly and challenging environment based on Quaker principles.

Graham Wigley, Head

1915 Gaeta Elementary & Middle School
PSC Box 811
FPO Gaeta 09609 0005
Italy

Dr. Robert Kirkpatrick, Principal

1916 Garmisch Elementary School
Unit 24511
APO AE, Garmisch
Germany 09053
440-261-
Fax: 088-176-949
E-mail:
GarmischEMS.Webmaster@eu.dodea.edu
http://www.garm-es.eu.dodea.edu
To provide a challenging curriculum in an atmosphere respectful of individual needs and cultural diversity. All students will learn the

academic and social skills necessary for their future success.

Debbie Strong, Principal

1917 Geilenkirchen Elementary School
Unit 8045
APO AE, Geilenkirchen 09104 0005
Germany 09104
024-1 9- 308
Fax: 024-1 9- 308
E-mail:
GeilenkirchenES.Webmaster@eu.dodea.edu
http://www.geil-es.eu.dodea.edu/
Educating our students to be responsible, productive and ethical citizens with the skills to think creatively, reason critically, communicate effectively and learn continuously.

James V Dierendonck, Principal

1918 Gelnhausen Elementary School
CMR 465
APO, Gelnhausen 09076 0005
Germany

Jim Harrison, Principal

1919 Geneva English School
36 Route de Malagny
1294 Genthod
Switzerland
41-22-755-18-55
Fax: 41-22-779-14-29
E-mail: admin@genevaenglishschool.ch
http://www.geneva-english-school.ch
A private, nonprofit primary school that is owned and managed by an association which is composed of parents whose children attend the school. The main objective of the school is to offer education on British lines for children of primary school age living in or near Geneva, and to prepare them for secondary education in any English-speaking school.

Denis Unsworth, Principal
Gareth Davies, Headmaster

1920 Giessen Elementary School
414th BSB GSN, Unit 20911
APO, Giessen 09169 0005
Germany
496-414-6265
496-414-8333
http://www.aoshs.org

Mary Ann Burkard, Principal

1921 Giessen High School
414th BSB GSB, Unit 20911
APO, Giessen 09169 0005
Germany
496-414-6266
http://www.aoshs.org

Gordon Gartner, Principal

1922 Grafenwoehr Elementary School
Unit 28127
APO AE
Germany 09114-8127
964-183-7133
Fax: 964- 32-4ÿ
E-mail:
GrafenwoehrES.Principal@eu.dodea.edu
http://www.graf-es.eu.dodea.edu
To maintain a meaningful partnership with the community through which physical well being, cognitive growth, and emotional support are provided to all learners.

Crystal Bailey, Principal
David Eldredge, Assistant Principal

1923 Greenwood Garden School
Via Vito Sinisi 5
Rome
Italy
39-06-332-66703
Fax: 39-06-332-66703
E-mail: greenwoodgarden@libero.it
http://www.greenwoodgardenschool.com
An international pre-school and kindergarten for children aging from 2-6 with teaching being done in English by mother-tongue educators experienced with young children

Donna Seibert, Directress

1924 Gstaad International School
Ahorn
Gstaad
Switzerland CH-37
41-33-744-2373
Fax: 41-33-744-3578
E-mail: gis@gstaad.ch
http://www.gstaadschool.ch
The school's mission includes the building of endurance and stamina in both academics and sports, as well as stimulating personal achievement by teaching the values of respect, gratitude, humour and real caring for others. Students are continually presented with challenges and the opportunities to achieve where perhaps before they thought impossible.

Alain Souperbiet, Director

1925 Haagsche School Vereeniging
Nassaulaan 26
Den Haag-2514
003-170-363
E-mail: info@hsvdenhaag.nl
http://www.hsvdenhaag.nl

HM Jongeling, Principal
Lorraine Dean, Director

1926 Hainerberg Elementary School
Unit 29647 Box 0086
APO AE, Wiesbaden
Germany 09096-86
337-516-
Fax: 011-49 -11 7
E-mail:
Wiesbadenes.principal@eu.dodea.edu
http://www.wies-esh.eu.dodea.edu
Provide exemplary educational programs that inspire and prepare all students for success in a global environment.

Maren James, Principal

1927 Halvorsen Tunner Elementary and Middle School
Unit 7565
APO, Rhein Main 09050 0005
Germany

Julie Gaski, Principal

1928 Hanau High School
Unit 20235
APO, Hanau 09165 0005
Germany

Allen Davenport, Principal

1929 Hanau Middle School
Unit 20193
APO, Hanau 09165 0016
Germany

Robert Sennett, Principal

1930 Harrow School
5 High Street
Harrow on the Hill
England HA1 3
01-423-2366
E-mail: harrow@harrowschool.org.uk
http://www.harrowschool.org.uk

Barnaby Lenon, Headmaster

1931 Hatherop Castle School
Hatherop, Cirencester
England GL7 3
028-575-206
http://www.hatheropcastle.com

Paul Easterbrook, Headmaster

1932 Heidelberg High School
Unit 29237
APO AE
Germany 09102
370-800-
Fax: 062-213- 587
http://www.heid-hs.eu.dodea.edu

Kevin J Brewer, Principal

1933 Heidelberg Middle School
Unit 29237
APO AE
Germany 09102
221-338-9310
http://www.heid-ms.eu.dodea.edu

Donald Johnson, Principal

1934 Hellenic College-London
67 Pont Street
London SWIX OBD
England
0171-581-5044
Fax: 0171-589-9055
E-mail: hellenic@rmplc.co.uk
http://www.rmplc.co.uk/eduweb/sites/hellenic

James Wardrobe, Principal

1935 Hellenic-American Education Foundation Athens College-Psychico College
15 Stefanou Delta
Psychico
Greece 154 5
30-1-671-2771
Fax: 30-1-674-8156
E-mail: info@haef.gr
http://www.haef.gr
Grade levels 1-12, school year September - June

David William Rupp, President

1936 Helsingin Suomalainen
Isonnevantie 8
Helsinki, Finland 00320
358- 47-1
http://www.syk.fi
Helsingin Suomalainen Yhteiskoulu (SYK) is an independent coeducational, which prepares its students either for the national matriculation exam or the International Baccalaureate, both of which give a student general university entry qualifications.

Anja-Liisa Alanko, Principal

1937 Het Nederlands Lyceum
Wijndaelerduin 1
Hague, Netherlands 02554
070-338-4567
Fax: 070-328-2049
E-mail: primary@ishthehague.nl
http://www.ishthehague.nl
Offers young people of all nationalities between the ages of 4 and 18 top quality international education in a caring environment, which aim for academic success and encourage sporting and creative abilities in a community based on honesty, fairness, open-mindedness and tolerance.

Graeme Scott, Principal Primary School

938 Het Rijnlands Lyceum
Appollolaan 1 2341 BA
Oegstgeest
Netherlands
31-3771-5155640
E-mail:
administratie@rijnlandslyceum-rlo.nl
http://www.rlo.nl
Lyceum is a state subsidized school with an international department offering IBMYP and IB. Offers an English/Dutch spoken curriculum to 1,190 day students and 60 boarding (650 boys; 600 girls), in grades 6 through 12. Student/teacher ratio is 15:1, and the school is willing to participate in a teacher exchange program, however, housing will not be provided by the school.

Drs LE Timmerman, Principal

939 Hillhouse Montessori School
Avenida Alfonso Xiii 30 Y 34
Madrid 2
Spain

http://www.houseonthehill.com.sg

Judy Amick, Principal

940 Hohenfels Elementary School
Unit 28214
APO AE
Germany 09173
466-400-ÿ
Fax: 094-2 8-32
http://www.hohe-es.eu.dodea.edu

Olaf Zwicker, Principal

941 Hohenfels High School
CMR 414
APO, AE
Germany 09173
094-2 -9096
Fax: 094-2 8- 316
http://www.hohe-hs.eu.dodea.edu

Daniel J Mendoza, Principal

942 Holmwood House
Chitts Hill, Lexden
Colchester, Essex
England CO3 9
44-0-1904-626183
Fax: 44-0-1904-670899
E-mail: hst@holmwood.essex.sch.uk
http://www.holmwood.essex.sch.uk
Holmwood House is an independent coeducational day and boarding preparatory school. The total enrollment of the school is 310 day students and 50 boarding students (240 boys and 120 girls), ages 4 1/2 to 13 1/2.

Alexander Mitchell, Headmaster

943 Hvitfeldtska Gymnasiet
Rektorsgatan 2, SE-411 33
Goteborg
Sweden
46-31-367-0623
Fax: 46-31-367-0602
E-mail: agneta.santesson@educ.goteborg.se
http://www.hvitfeldt.educ.goteborg.se
State school, founded 1647, offers the International Baccalaureate curriculum to a total enrollment of 90 girls and 90 boys, in grades 10-12.

Christen Holmstrom, Principal
Agneta Santesson, Deputy Headmaster

944 Illesheim Elementary and Middle School
CMR 416 Box J
APO, Hohenfels 09140 0005
Germany

49-9841-8408
Fax: 49-9841-8987

Donald J Ness, Principal

1945 Independent Bonn International School
Tulpenbaumweg 42
Bonn 53177
Germany
49-228-32-31-66
Fax: 49-228-32-39-58
E-mail: ibis@ibis-school.com
http://www.ibis-school.com
IBIS is an international primary school.

Irene Bolik, Headteacher

1946 Independent Schools Information Service
Grosveror Gardens House 35-37
Frosvernor Gardens, London SW1W 0BS
England
020-77981575
Fax: 020-77981561
E-mail: national@isis.org.uk
http://www.isis.org.uk
Provides information on 1400 elementary and secondary schools in the United Kingdom and Ireland.

David J Woodhead

1947 Innsbruck International High School
Schonger, Austria A-6141
0-5225-4201
Fax: 0-5225-4202
An accredited coeducational boarding and day school. The school offers an American college preparatory high school curriculum for grades 9-12.

Gunther Wenko, Director
John E Wenrick, Headmaster

1948 Institut Alpin Le Vieux Chalet
1837 Chateau D'oex
Switzerland
212-338-9743
Fax: 212-949-7534
http://www.christusrex.org

Jean Bach, Principal

1949 Institut Auf Dem Rosenberg
Hohenweg 60-9000 St Gallen
Switzerland
417- 27-0777
Fax: 417- 27- 982
E-mail: info@instrosenberg.ch
http://www.instrosenberg.ch

Felicitas Scharli, Principal

1950 Institut Chateau Beau-Cedre
57 Av De Chillion
CH-1820 Territet Montreux
Switzerland
41-21-963-5341
Fax: 41-21-963-4783
E-mail: info@monterosaschool.com
This Institut is an exclusive boarding and finishing international school for girls. American high school with a general culture section for 30 boarding students in grades 9 through twelve. Languages spoken include French and English and the student/teacher ratio is 1:6.

Pierre Gay, Principal

1951 Institut Le Champ Des Pesses
1618 Chatel-st-denis
Montreux
Switzerland

PL Racloz, Principal

1952 Institut Le Rosey
Chateau du Rosey
1180 Rolle
Switzerland
41-21-822-5500
Fax: 41-21-822-5555
E-mail: rosey@rosey.ch
http://www.rosey.ch
Le Rosey's philosophy is inspired by what Harvard educationalist Howard Gardner has called multiple intelligences: its aim is to develop all Roseans' talents through academic, sporting and artistic programs.

Philippe Gudin, General Director
Michael Gray, Headmaster

1953 Institut Montana Bugerbug-American Schools
Zugerberg
CH 6300 Zug
Switzerland
41-41-711-1722
Fax: 41-41-711-5465
E-mail: kob@montana.zug.ch
http://www.montana.zug.ch
Grade levels include 7-13 with a total enrollment of 111.

Daniel Fredez, Director

1954 Institut Monte Rosa
57, Ave de Chillon,
CH-1820 Territet/Montreux
Switzerland
021-963-5341
Fax: 021-963-4783
E-mail: info@monterosa.ch
http://www.monterosa.ch

Bernhard Gademann, BS, MS, Principal

1955 Inter-Community School
Strubenacher 3 Postfach
Zumikon
Switzerland 08126
41-1-919-8300
Fax: 41-1-919-8320
http://www.icsz.ch
The Inter-Community School is committed to providing a supportive and enabling learning environment in which all members of the community are challenged to achieve their individual potential, encouraged to pursue their passions, and expected to fulfil their responsibilities

Michael Matthews, Head of School
Martin Hall, Secondary Principal

1956 International Academy
Via di Grottarossa 295
00189 Rome
Italy
39-340-731-4195
E-mail: info@internationalacademy.in
http://www.internationalacademy.in

Joan Bafaloukas Bulgarini, Principal

1957 International College Spain
C/Vereda Norte 3
La Moraleja, Madrid
Spain 28109
34-91-650-2398
Fax: 34-91-650-1035
E-mail: admissions@icsmadrid.org
http://www.icsmadrid.com
The philosophy of the school is to provide students with a high quality international education which places a strong emphasis on fostering respect for the world's nations and cultures.

Terry Hedger, Director
Hubert Keulers, Head of Primary School

1958 International Management Institute
Garden Square Building, Block-C Laa
Antwerp
Belgium 02610
32-3-21-85-431
Fax: 32-3-21-85-868
E-mail: info@timi.edu
http://www.timi.edu
Our vision is to empower our students in terms of all the faculties required to pursue a career in the competitive globalized world. The focus of our curriculum is to enhance the learning perspective through customized modules and simulation exercises from globally renowned academicians and professionals.

Luc Van Mele, Director

1959 International Preparatory School
Rua Do Boror 12 Carcavelos
2775 Parede
Portugal
56-2-321-5800
Fax: 56-2-321-5821
E-mail: info@tipschool.com
http://www.tipschool.com

1960 International School Beverweerd
Beverweerdseweg 60, 3985 RE
Werkhoven
Netherlands
03437-1341
Fax: 03437-2079
http://www.isbeverweerd.nl

Ray Kern, BA, MA, Principal

1961 International School-Aberdeen
296 N Deeside Road
Milltimber, Aberdeen
Scotland, UK AB13
44-1224-732267
Fax: 44-1224-735648
E-mail: admin@isa.aberdeen.sch.uk
http://www.isa.aberdeen.sch.uk
The International School of Aberdeen (ISA) is an independent, non-profit school (K-12) that delivers excellence in education. We do this through a safe and caring learning environment where students are challenged to reach their maximum potential through academic success and personal growth, becoming socially responsible and active global citizens.

Daniel A Hovde PhD, Director
Don Newbury, Elementary Principal

1962 International School-Algarve
Apartado 80 Porches 8400
Lagoa Algarve
Portugal

http://www.algarveschool.com

Peter Maddison, Principal

1963 International School-Amsterdam
PO Box 920
AX Amstelveen
The Netherlands 01180
31-20-347-1111
Fax: 31-20-347-1222
E-mail: info@isa.nl
http://www.isa.nl
The International School of Amsterdam (ISA) was founded in 1964 to serve the educational needs of the children of the international community living in and around Amsterdam. ISA is a nonsectarian, non-profit coeducational day school, enrolling students in Pre-School through Grade 12 (from 3 to 18 years of age).
Dr Edward Greene, Director
Sarah Grace, Head of Lower School

1964 International School-Basel
Fleischbachstrasse 2
4153 Reinach BL
Switzerland
41-61-426-96-26
Fax: 41-61-426-96-25
http://www.isbasel.ch
mission of the International School Basel is to provide an international education to the highest recognized academic standards

Geoff Tomlinson, Principal

1965 International School-Bergen
Vilhelm Bjerknesvei 15
Bergen
Norway 05081
47-55-30-63-30
Fax: 47-55-30-63-31
E-mail: post@isob.no
http://www.isb.gs.hl.no
Provide an education for the children of expatriate oil company personnel in Bergen and to attract further corporate investment in the Bergen area.

June Murison, Director

1966 International School-Berne
170 Mattenstrasse
Gumligen
Switzerland 03073
41-31-951-2358
Fax: 41-31-951-1710
E-mail: office@isberne.ch
http://www.isberne.ch
Creative learning community for students from all over the world, within the framework of the three International Baccalaureate Programmes, guided by ISBerne teachers and staff, students aged 3 - 18 have the opportunity to become open-minded, principled, knowledgeable, confident life-long learners and multilingual citizens of the world, who respect themselves and others.

Kevin Page, Director
Cory Etchberger, Chair

1967 International School-Brussels
Kattenberg 19
Brussels 1170
Belguim
32-2-661-4211
Fax: 32-2-661-4200
E-mail: admissions@isb.be
http://www.isb.be
Offers a challenging, inclusive international education designed to give every student opportunities for success within and beyond our school.

Kevin Bartlett, Director
Andrei Teixeira, Chairman

1968 International School-Cartagena
Manga Club Cp 30385 Cartagena
Los Belones Murcia
Spain
34-68-175000
E-mail: isc@sendanet.es
http://www.cartagenainternationalschool.com

Robert Risch, Principal

1969 International School-Curacao
PO Box 3090
Koninginnelaan Emmastad, Curacao
Netherlands Antilles
599-9-737-3633
Fax: 599-90737-3142
E-mail: iscmec@attglobal.net
http://www.isc.an
Offers a rigorous academic program in order to prepare students planning to pursue higher learning at colleges and universities around the world. The School's curriculum includes International Baccalaureate (IB) coursework that allows students the opportunity to receive the IB Diploma.

Margie Elhage, Director
Rene Romer, President

1970 International School-Dusseldorf
Niederrheinstrasse 336
Dusseldorf
Germany 40489
49-211-94066-799
Fax: 49-211-4080-744
E-mail: nmcw@isdedu.de
http://www.isdedu.eu
Provide the students of the International School of D□sseldorf with the best possible program of academic and personal development in a challenging and supportive environment.

Neil A McWilliam, Director
Michael Coffey, Senior School Principal

1971 International School-Eerde
Kasteellaan 1
PJ Ommen
The Netherlands 07731
031-0529-451452
Fax: 031-0529-456377
E-mail: info@eerde.nl
http://www.eerde.nl
Offers numerous programmes tailored to the individual needs of each student, including children with learning difficulties and dyslexia, as well as highly gifted children. Eerde carefully monitors the personal, academic, athletic and creative development of each individual student ages 4 to 19.

Herman Voogd, Principal

1972 International School-Friuli
Via Delle Grazie 1/A
Pordenone 33170
Italy

http://www.udineis.org

Susan Clarke, Principal

1973 International School-Geneva
62 route de Chene
Geneva
Switzerland CH-12
41-22-787-2400
Fax: 41-22-787-2410
E-mail: administration@ecolint.ch
http://www.ecolint.ch
Aims to provide a distinctive high quality international education that prepares pupils for membership of a world community based on mutual understanding, tolerance and shared humanitarian values.

Nicholas Tate, Director General
John Douglas, Director

1974 International School-Hamburg
Holmbrook 20
Hamburg
Germany 22605
49-40-883-1101
Fax: 49-40-1881-1405
E-mail: info@ishamburg.org
http://www.international-school-hamburg.de
A co-educational day school enrolling students from Primary 1 (age 3) to Grade 12. The school was founded in 1957 as the first international school in Germany.

Peter Gittin, Headmaster
Nick Ronai, Junior School Director

975 International School-Hannover Region
Bruchmeisterstrasse 6
Hannover
Germany D-301
49-511-27041650
Fax: 49-511-557934
E-mail: adminoffice@is-hr.de
http://www.is-hr.de
Provides a high quality, balanced educational program in the English language for children of internationally-minded families.Offer a dynamic environment where each student is challenged and supported to become a dedicated learner for life and a contributing member of the local and global community.

Patricia Baier, Director
Steffen Stegeman, Business Manager

976 International School-Helsinki
Selkamerenkatu 11
Helsinki
Finland 00180
358-9-686-6160
Fax: 358-9-685-6699
E-mail: mainoffice@ish.edu.hel.fi
http://www.ish.edu.hel.fi
Office Manager
Provide attendees
Bob Woods, Headmaster
Therese Thibault, Director

977 International School-Iita
PMB 5320
Ibadan
Nigeria CR9 3
E-mail: iita@cgiar.org
http://www.iita.org
Provide a comprehensive, international curriculum in an environment which promotes confidence, caring and understanding, and prepares our students for successful learning here and in schools around the world.

Neil Jackson, Principal

978 International School-Lausanne
Chemin de la Grangette 2
Le Mont-sur-Lausanne
Switzerland CH -
41-21-728-1733
Fax: 41-21-728-7868
E-mail: info@isl.ch
http://www.isl.ch
The school is committed to excellence in education, it strives to fulfill the unique potential of each student in a supportive and challenging holistic learning environment that prepares the student for continuing education and an active and responsible role in a multicultural world.

Lyn Cheetham, Director
John Ivett, Assistant Director

979 International School-Le Chaperon Rouge
3963 Crans Sur Sierre
Crans/Montana
Switzerland
41-27-4812-500
Fax: 41-27-4812-502
http://www.chaperonrouge.ch

Prosper Bagnoud, Principal

980 International School-London
139 Gunnersbury Avenue
London
England W3 8L
44-20-8992-5823
Fax: 44-20-8993-7012
E-mail: mail@ISLondon.com
http://www.islondon.com

Aims to maximize the achievement of its students throughout the curriculum and in personal and social fields. Drawing on the rich variety of cultures represented at the school, ISL aims to develop in each student a global outlook which seeks to understand and appreciate the attitudes and values of others.

Amin Makarem, Director
Sergio Pawel, Deputy Head, Curriculum

1981 International School-Lyon
80 chemin du Grand Roule
Ste-Foy-LSs-Lyon
France F-691
47 -86 -190
Fax: 47 -86 -198
E-mail: info@islyon.org
http://www.islyon.org
The school's curriculum is based on the programmes and pedagogy of the International Baccalaureate Organization which aims to develop in the students the skills, values and knowledge that will help them to become responsible citizens in an increasingly interconnected world.

Donna Philip, Director
Michael Ford, Curriculum Coordinator

1982 International School-Naples
Viale della Liberazione, 1
Bagnoli, Napoli 80125
Italy
39-081-721-2037
Fax: 39-081-570-0248
E-mail: info@isnaples.it
http://www.isnaples.it
Provide a nurturing environment where students can grow intellectually, socially, psychologically and physically. Through a dedicated partnership of parents and educators, we strive to prepare our students to become productive, global citizens of the twenty-first century.

Josephine Sessa, Principal
Patricia Montesano, Vice Principal

1983 International School-Nice
15 Avenue Claude Debussy
Nice
France 06200
33-493-210-400
Fax: 33-493-216-911
E-mail: robert.silvetz@cote-azur.cci.fr
http://www.isn-nice.org
The school offers Pre-Kindergarten through grade 12 instruction and college preparatory education and provides an intellectually challenging programme of studies which aims to promote analytic understanding with an integrated view of the various academic disciplines and to encourage creativity and self-expression. Serves both the international community and local families who wish to offer their children an education in English, which is both international and versatile.

Wylie Michael, Director

1984 International School-Paris
6 Rue Beethoven
Paris
France 75016
33-1-422-40954
Fax: 33-1-452-71593
E-mail: info@isparis.edu
http://www.isparis.edu
ISP create a challenging and motivating English-speaking environment where students and staff from around the world use the programs of the International Baccalaureate Organisation and work in harmony to develop

every student's full intellectual and human potential.

Audrey Peverelli, Headmaster
Catherine Hard, Head of Admissions

1985 International School-Sotogrande
Apartado 15
Sotogrande San Roque Cadiz
Spain 11310
34-956-79-59-02
Fax: 34-956-79-48-16
E-mail: director@sis.ac
http://www.sis.ac
Our school is a learning organisation with a passion for learning. Learning is a complex process and it is vitally important that our teachers know how pupils learn best and that they create exciting opportunities for learning to take place.

Geroge O'Brien, Headmaster
Christopher TJ Charleson, Head of School

1986 International School-Stavanger
Treskeveien 3
Hafrsfjord
Norway 04043
47-51-559-100
Fax: 47-51-552-962
E-mail: LDuevel@isstavanger.no
http://www.isstavanger.no
The International School of Stavanger is dedicated to providing its students with an English language education in a supportive, academically stimulating, and multi-cultural environment.

Linda Duevel, PhD, Director
Gareth Jones, High School Principal

1987 International School-Stockholm
Johannesgatan 18
Stockholm SE-111 38
Sweden
46-8-412-4000
Fax: 46-8-412-4001
E-mail: admin@intsch.se
http://www.intsch.se
SIS vision is to enable students to learn, develop, grow, and fulfill their potential in an international environment, which is student-centered, safe, nurturing and rich with opportunities to learn.

Chris Mockrish, Principal
Richard Mast, Director

1988 International School-Stuttgart
Sigmaringer Street 257
Stuttgart
Germany 70597
49-7-11-76-9600-0
Fax: 49-7-11-76-9600-0
E-mail: iss@issev.de
http://www.international-school-stuttgart.de

The International School of Stuttgart provides students of internationally-minded families with a high quality, English language education.

Timothy Kelley, Director
Sarah Kupke, Head of School

1989 International School-Trieste
Via Conconello 16 Opicina
Trieste Friuli - Venezia Giulia
Italy 34151
39-040-211-452
Fax: 39-040-213-122
E-mail: istrieste@interbusiness.it
http://www.istrieste.org
It is our mission to provide students from the international and local community with a broad, balanced education using English

both in curricular and extra-curricular life of the school.

Peter Metzger, Principal
Jim Pastore, Director

1990 International School-Turin

Vicolo Tiziano 10
Moncalieri
Italy 10024
391- 45-9
Fax: 39 -11 -43 2
E-mail: info@acat-ist.it
http://www.acat-ist.it
The school's goal is to create self-motivated, independent learners who strive for excellence. The school community feels that this is best achieved in an environment which fosters trust and respect between the educational staff and the student body, demands accountability and team-work, while inspiring a general sense of well-being and self-confidence.

George Selby, BA, MA, Principal

1991 International School-Venice

Via Terraglio 30
Mestre, Venice
Italy 30174
04 -98 -711
Fax: 04 -98 -001
E-mail: info@isvenice.com
http://www.isvenice.com
The fundamental aim of The International School of Venice is to give its pupils a bilingual education and an intellectual education based on tolerance, open-mindedness and an acceptance of diversity.

John Millerchip, Principal

1992 International School-Zug

Walterswil
Baar 6340
Switzerland
41-41-768-1188
Fax: 41-41-768-1189
E-mail: office@isoz.ch
http://www.iszl.ch
Grade levels include preK-8 with a total enrollment of 354.

Martin Latter, Head of School

1993 International Schule-Berlin, Potsdam

Seestrasse 45
14467 Potsdam
Germany
49-332-086-760
Fax: 49-332-086-7612
E-mail: office@isbp.p.bb.schule.de
http://www.shuttle.de/p/isbp
This school offers an English curriculum to 157 day students (87 boys and 64 girls) in grades PreK-12. Applications needed to teach include science, pre-school, math, social sciences, reading, English and physical education.

Matthias Truper, Principal

1994 International Secondary School-Eindhoven

Venetiestraat 43
RM Eindhoven
Netherlands 05632
040-413600
E-mail: isse@issehv.nl
http://www.issehv.nl
By striving for excellence in education and by engaging with the international community, the ISSE seeks to be an asset to Eindhoven and the Noord-Brabant region.

JM Westerhout, Principal
M Watts, Acting Head of School

1995 Internationale Schule Frankfurt-Rhein-Main

Strasse zur Internationalen Schule
Frankfurt
Germany 65931
49-69-954-3190
Fax: 49-69-954-31920
E-mail: isf@sabis.net
http://www.isf-net.de
ISF Internationale Schule-Rhein-Main, as a member of the SABISr School Network, is academically oriented without being highly selective.

Angus Slesser, School Director
Carl Bistany, Managing Director

1996 Interskolen

Engtoften 22
8260 Viby J
Denmark
45-8611-4560
Fax: 45-8614-9670
E-mail: adm@interskolen.dk
http://www.interskolen.dk
Coeducational day program for ages five to seventeen.

Tommy Schou Christesen, Principal

1997 John F Kennedy International School

CH-3792 Saanen
Switzerland 03792
41-33-744-1372
Fax: 41-33-744-8982
E-mail: lovell@jfk.ch
http://www.jfk.ch
Boarding day school for boys and girls aged 5-14 years.

William Lovell, Co-Director
Sandra Lovell, Co-Director

1998 John F Kennedy School-Berlin

Teltower Damm 87-93
Berlin
Germany 14167
49-30-6321-5711
Fax: 49-30-6321-6377
E-mail: jfks-el-adm@t-online.de
http://www.jfks.de
The John F. Kennedy School is a bilingual, bicultural German-American tuition-free public school.

Herr Ulrich Schurmann, Managing Principal
HR Roth, German Principal

1999 Joppenhof/Jeanne D'arc Clg

PO Box 4050, 6202 Rb Maastricht
Netherlands
47 -77 -000
http://www.paguro.net

L Spronck, Principal

2000 Kaiserslautern Elementary School

Unit 3240 Box 425
APO
Germany, AE 09021
080- -520
063- 99-46
Fax: 063- 58-06
http://www.kais-es.eu.dodea.edu

Bariett Prince, Principal

2001 Kaiserslautern High School

Unit 3240 Box 425
APO
Germany, AE 09021
801- 1-20
063- 99-47
Fax: 063- 99-46
http://www.kais-hs.eu.dodea.edu

Bariett Prince, Principal
Richard Nicholson, Assistant Principal

2002 Kaiserslautern Middle School

Unit 3240 Box 425
APO
Germany, AE 09021
802- 1-20
063- 99-48
Fax: 063- 99-25
http://www.kais-ms.eu.dodea.edu

Bariett Prince, Principal
Marion Sutton, Assistant Principal

2003 Kendale Primary International School

Via Gradoli 86, Via Cassia Km 10300
00189 Rome
Italy
39-06-332-676-08
Fax: 39-06-332-676-08
E-mail: kendale@diesis.com
http://www.diesis.com/kendale

Veronica Said Tani, Principal

2004 Kensington School

Carrer Dels Cavallers 31-33 Pedralb
Barcelona
Spain 08034
930-345-
Fax: 938-006-
E-mail: info@kensingtonschoolbcn.com
http://www.kensingtonschoolbcn.com

EP Giles, Principal

2005 King Fahad Academy

Bromyard Avenue, Acton
London
United Kingdom W3-7HD9
020-7259-3350
E-mail: academy@thekfa.org.uk
http://www.thekfa.org.uk
The idea for the establishment of an academy that caters for the educational needs of the Saudi Arabian, Arab and Muslim communities in the UK took its genesis in the creation of the King Fahad Academy in London in 1985 AD/1405 H

Dr. Ibtissam Al-Bassam, Dean
Mohammed Bin Na Al Saud, Chairman

2006 King's College

Paseo de los Andes, 35
Soto De Viuelas, Madrid
Spain
91-803-48-00
Fax: 91-803-65-57
E-mail: info@kingscollege.es
http://www.kingscollege.es
to sustain and develop an educational environment in which all students are able to fulfil their maximum potential, both as individuals and as members of a community.

CA Clark, Principal
David Johnson, Headmaster

2007 Kitzingen Elementary School

Unit 26124
APO, Kitzingen 09031 0005
Germany

Fred Paesel, Principal

008 Kleine Brogel Elementary School
701 MUNSS
Unit 8150, APO AE
Belgium 09719
001-179-2527
Fax: 001-179-0091
E-mail: terry.emerson@eu.dodea.edu
http://www.kbro-es.eu.dodea.edu

Terry Emerson, Principal

009 La Chataigneraie International School
Geneva La Chataigneraie, 1297
1208 Geneva
Switzerland
122-787-2400
http://www.ecolint.ch

Michael Lee, Principal

010 La Maddalena Elementary School
PSC 816 Box 1755
FPO, La Maddalena, Sardinia 09612 0005
Italy
907-897- 820
http://www.aoshs.org

Janice Barber, Principal

011 Lajes Elementary School
Unit 7725
APO AE
Portugal 09720
351-295-5741
Fax: 011-351-295
http://www.laje-ehs.eu.dodea.edu/index.htm

Mary Waller, Principal

012 Lajes High School
Unit 7725
APO AE
Portugal 09720
351-295-5741
Fax: 351-295-5425
http://www.laje-hs.eu.dodea.edu/main1.htm

Virginia Briggs, Principal

013 Lakenheath Elementary School
Unit 5185 Box 40
APO AE
Great Britain 09464-8540
016-805-3072
Fax: 016-8 5-3943
http://www.lake-es.eu.dodea.edu/index.htm
Lakenheath Elementary School serves the US Military overseas as part of the Department of Defense Dependent Schools

Charles Yahres, Principal
Rhonda Bennett, Assistant Principal

014 Lakenheath High School
Unit 5185 Box 45
APO AE
Great Britain 09461-8545
044- 01- 852
Fax: 044- 01- 853
E-mail:
lakenheathhs.attendance@eu.dodea.edu
http://www.lake-hs.eu.dodea.edu
Lakenheath High School (LHS) serves three U.S. Air Force bases located in the East Anglia region of England; about 1.5 hours drive northeast of London. LHS is coeducational.

Kent Worford, Principal
Barbara Lee, Assistant Principal

015 Lakenheath Middle School
Unit 5185 Box 55
APO AE
Great Britain 09461-8555

011-44 -638
Fax: 226-737-
E-mail:
LakenheathMS.Principal@eu.dodea.edu
http://www.lake-ms.eu.dodea.edu

Mary Zimmerman-Bayer, Principal
D J LaFon, Assistant Principal

2016 Lancing College
Lancing, West Sussex
BN15 0RW
England
0273-452213
Fax: 01273-464720
E-mail: admissions@lancing.org.uk
http://www.lancingcollege.co.uk
One of Britain's leading independent schools for boys and girls aged 13 to 18

Jonathan W J Gillespie, Headmaster
Harry Brunjes, Chairman

2017 Landstuhl Elementary and Middle School
CMR 402
APO AE
Germany 09180-402
637-192-6508
Fax: 637-192-6514
E-mail:
LandstuhlEMS.Principal@eu.dodea.edu
http://www.lans-ems.eu.dodea.edu

Susan Ransom, Principal
Stephen Austin, Assistant Principal

2018 Leighton Park School
Shinfield Road
Reading RG2 7DH
England
4-118-987-9600
Fax: 44-118-987-9625
E-mail: info@leightonpark.com
http://www.leightonpark.com
Life at Leighton Park reflects the school's Quaker foundation and is influenced by Quaker thinking and practice. We seek to create a community of tolerance and understanding within which a balance between discipline, especially self-discipline, freedom and exploration is maintained.

John Dunston, Headmaster
Elizabeth Thomas, Deputy Head

2019 Leipzig International School
Konneritzstrasse 47
Leipzig
Germany 04229
49-341-421-0574
Fax: 49-341-421-2154
E-mail: admin@intschool-leipzig.com
http://www.intschool-leipzig.com
The Leipzig International School provides a quality education conducted primarily in English for children of all nationalities and cultures living in the Leipzig region. We seek to give all students the opportunity to discover and develop their intellectual, creative, social and physical potential to the full.

Michael Webster, Headmaster
Clemens Gerteiser, Commercial Editor

2020 Lennen Bilingual School
65 Quai d'Orsay
Paris
France 75007
01-47-05-66-55
Fax: 01-47-05-17-18
http://www.lennenbilingual.com
This school teaches a curriculum in English and French to 120 day students. The school is willing to participate in a teacher exchange program with the length of stay being one year, with no housing provided by the school.

Bilingual education is offered in the pre-school and grade school (until Grade 3).

Michelle Lennen, Principal

2021 Leys School
The Leys School
Cambridge CB2 7AD
England
44-1223-508-900
Fax: 44-1223-505-333
E-mail: office@theleys.net
http://www.theleys.cambs.sch.uk
The Leys is one of England's premier independent schools.

Mark Slater, Headmaster

2022 Leysin American School
1854 Leysin
Switzerland
41-24-493-3777
Fax: 41-24-493-3790
E-mail: admissions@las.ch
http://www.las.ch
At the core of Leysin American School is a guiding set of principles and beliefs that set the highest standards for our efforts every day.

Steven Oh, Executive Director
Vladimir Kuskovski, Headmaster

2023 Livorno Elementary School
Unit 31301 Box 65
APO, Livorno 09613 0005
Italy

http://www.livo-ems.eu.dodea.edu

Dr. Robert Kethcart, Principal

2024 Livorno High School
Unit 31301 Box 65
APO, Livorno 09613 0005
Italy, AE 09613-5

http://www.livo-ems.eu.dodea.edu

Dr. Frank Calvano, Principal

2025 London Central High School
PSC 821 Box 119
APO, High Wycombe 09421 0005
Great Britain, AE 09421-5

http://www.londoncentral.org

Dr. Charles Recesso, Principal

2026 Lorentz International School
Groningensingel 1245, 6835HZ
Arnhem
Netherlands
31-26-320-0110
Fax: 31-26-320-0113

Jan M Meens, Principal

2027 Lusitania International College Foundation
Apartado 328
8600 Lagos
Portugal

Krisine Byrne, Principal

2028 Lyce International-American Section
BP 230, rue du Fer A Cheval
St Germain-En-Laye, 78104 Cedex
France
033-051-7485
Fax: 139-100-914
E-mail: american.lycee@wanadoo.fr
http://lycee-intl-american.org
pursues this mission through a rigorous and rewarding American curriculum which culminates in the French Baccalaureate with In-

ternational Option, as well as through a broad and enriching co-curricular program including such activities as drama, community service, sports and student publications.

Sean Lynch, Director
Beth Heudebourg, President

2029 Lycee Francais De Belgique
9 Avenue Du Lycee Francais
1180 Brussels
Belgium
02-374-58-78
http://www.lyceefrancais-jmonnet.be
Jean-Claude Giudicelli, Principal

2030 Lyc,e International-American Section
33-1-345-17485
Fax: 33-1-308-70049
Grade levels Pre-K through 12, school year September - June

2031 Malvern College
College Road, Malvern
Worcestershire WR14 3DF
England
01684-581-500
E-mail: inquiry@malcol.org
http://www.malcol.org
Roy de C Chapman, MA, Headmaster

2032 Mannheim Elementary School
Unit 29938
APO AE
09086
380-4705
Fax: 0621-723-905
E-mail: esmannattend@eu.dodea.edu
http://www.mann-es.eu.dodea.edu
Dr. Ardelle Hamilton PhD, Principal
Dr. Ellen Minette, Assistant Principal

2033 Mannheim High School
Unit 29939
APO AE
09267
380-409-
Fax: 062- 73-901
E-mail: MannheimHS.Principal@eu.dodea.edu
http://www.mann-hs.eu.dodea.edu
is to equip all students to be conscientiously contributing citizens through a challenging curriculum and effective instruction
Sharon O'Donnell, Principal

2034 Margaret Danyers College
N Downs Road, Cheadle Hulme
Cheadle SK8 5HA
England
061-485-4372
Harry Tomlinson, BA, MA, MS, Headmaster

2035 Mark Twain Elementary School
Unit 29237
APO, Heidelberg 09102 0005
Germany 80909

http://www.mtwain.k12.ca.us
Joseph Newbury, Principal

2036 Marymount International School-Rome
Via di Villa Lauchli 180
00191 Rome
Italy
33-1-462-41051
Fax: 33-1-463-70750

E-mail: marymount@marymountrome.org
http://www.marymountrome.org/
Marymount International School provides an education based on Christian values. Marymount is dedicated to fostering individual dignity in an atmosphere of love and respect in which students, faculty, staff and parents work and pray together.
Anne Marie Clancy, Headmistress

2037 Marymount International School-United Kingdom
George Road
Kingston upon Thames, Surrey, KT2 7PE
Surrey , United Kingdom KT2 7
44-20-8949-0571
Fax: 44-20-8336-2485
E-mail: admissions@marymount.kingston.sch.uk
http://www.marymountlondon.com/home.php
Marymount London is a vibrant and dynamic learning community where all are respected and encouraged to contribute,committed to developing individuals.
Cathleen Fagan, Headmistress

2038 Mattlidens Gymnasium
Mattliden 1
02230 Esbo
Finland
09 -16 -30 5
Fax: 09 -16 -30 5
E-mail: gun-maj.roiha@esbo.fi
http://www.mattliden.fi/gym/
Mattlidens Gymnasium is a coeducational Swedish-speaking upper secondary school
Tom Ginman, Headmaster

2039 Mayenne English School
Chateau les Courges 53420
Chailland
France
J Braillard, Principal

2040 Menwith Hill Estates & Middle School
PSC 45 Unit 8435
APO, High Wycombe 09468 0005
Great Britain
142-377-7778
Fax: 142-377-0236
http://www.mhil-ehs.eu.dodea.edu
Dr. Arnold Watland, Principal

2041 Millfield School
Butleigh Road Street
Somerset
England BA16-0YD
145-844-2291
E-mail: office@millfieldschool.com
http://www.millfieldschool.com
With its outstanding facilities, a staff:pupil ratio of 1:7.5, an extraordinary range of academic courses and the unrivalled strength of its extra-curricular programme, Millfield strives to achieve all these aims. It also seeks to move with the times whilst maintaining the important traditions of good manners, discipline and respect for others
Craig Considine, Headmaster
Adrian E White, Chairman of the Governors

2042 Monkton Combe School
Church Lane
Monkton Combe, Bath
England BA2-7HG

01225-721102
Fax: 01225-721208
E-mail: reception@monkton.org.uk
http://www.monktoncombeschool.com
Boarding and day school for girls and boys ages two to nineteen.
Chris Stafford, Headmaster
Richard Backhouse, Principal

2043 Monti Parioli English School
Via Monti Parioli 50
00197 Rome
Italy
Lynette Surtees, Principal

2044 Mougins School
615 Avenue Drive, Maurice Donat
BP 401, 06251 Mougins Cedex
France
33-4-93-90-15-47
Fax: 33-4-93-75-31-40
E-mail: information@mougins-school.com
http://www.mougins-school.com
The School has a capacity of 460 students, large enough to provide a stimulating environment and small enough to retain a caring family atmosphere. With thirty-five nationalities the School is culturally rich and its philosophy is designed to encourage pupils to develop morally, emotionally, culturally, intellectually and physically
Brian G Hickmore, Headmaster
Jane Hart, Deputy Head

2045 Mountainview School
Bosch 35-6331 Hunenberg
Switzerland
Brenda Moors, Principal

2046 Munich International School
Schloss Buchhof
Starnberg
Germany 82319
49-8151-366-100
Fax: 49-8151-366-109
E-mail: admissions@mis-munich.de
http://www.mis-munich.de
MIS caters for the physical, social, emotional and educational development of its children by providing a student-centred, inquiry-based learning environment which fosters an appreciation in its students of their cultural heritage and the cultural richness of the global community.
Mary Sepalla, Head of School
Maha Kattoura, Chairman

2047 Naples Elementary School
PSC 808 Box 39
FPO, AE
Italy 09618
011-39 -8108
Fax: 011-39 -8108
E-mail: NaplesES.Principal@eu.dodea.edu
http://www.napl-es.eu.dodea.edu
Dr. Jacqueline Hulbert, Principal

2048 Naples High School
PSC 808 Box 15
FPO, AE
Italy 09618
011-39 -8108
Fax: 011-39 -8108
E-mail: NaplesHS.Principal@eu.dodea.edu
http://www.napl-hs.eu.dodea.edu
Students will be prepared to be critical thinkers, effective communicators, and accountable members in a global society.
Carl Albrecht, Principal

049 Neubruecke Elementary School
Unit 23825
APO, Neubruecke 09034 0005
Germany

Margaret Hoffman-Otto, Principal

050 Neuchatel Junior College
44 Victoria Street
Suite 1310
Toronto, ON M5C-1Y2
038-25-27-00
800-263-2923
Fax: 038-24-42-59
E-mail: info@neuchatel.org
http://www.njc.ch
To provide students a rigorous university preparatory programme in a culturally rich and multi-lingual European setting where learning through educational travel, engagement with world affairs and service to others fosters personal growth and leadership.

Norman Southward, Principal
Dayle Leishman, Director

051 New School Rome
Via Della Camilluccia 669
Roma
Italy 00135
39-329-4269
E-mail: info@newschoolrome.com
http://www.newschoolrome.com
The School is a non-profit making organisation run by the Academic Council (all staff and seven student representatives) which also elects the headteacher, and by the Executive Council (three elected teachers and four elected parents).

Josette Fusco, Head Teacher
Richard Lydiker, Executive Chairman

052 Newton College
Av Ricardo El as Aparicio 240
La Molina
Lima-Peru, PE
511-479-0460
Fax: 511-479-0430
E-mail: college@newton.edu.pe
http://www.newton.edu.pe
Newton College is an Anglo-Peruvian, co-educational, bilingual, day school for students aged 2 to 18.

David Few, Principal

053 Norra Reals Gymnasium
Roslagsgatan 1
Stockholm
Sweden 113 5
087-420-
Fax: 087-328-
E-mail:
infonorrareal@utbildning.stockholm.se
http://www.norrareal.stockholm.se
Offers two preparatory study programs: the science and social science.

Per Engback, Principal
Maria Sellberg, Assistant Principal

054 Numont School
C/ Parma 16
Madrid
Spain 28043
349-130-0243
Fax: 349-759-
E-mail: numont@telefonica.net
http://eoficina.e.telefonica.net
Provide a warm, happy and challenging atmosphere where children can derive pleasure from learning and achieving their personal goals. The emphasis is on the individual, so that all of the children, regardless of strengths and weaknesses, colour, creed or

sex, feel valued and able to reach their full potential.

Margaret Ann Swanson, Principal

2055 Oak House School
Sant Pere Claver 12-18
Barcelona
Spain 08017
349-325- 402
Fax: 349-325- 402
E-mail: sec@oakhouseschool.com
http://www.oakhouseschool.com
The training of students both personal and social is one of the main objectives of the educational work.

Teresa Armadans, Director of Finance
VicenØ Orobitg, Information Technology

2056 Oakham School
Chapel Close
Market Place
Oakham,Rutland, UK LE15
44-0-1572-758758
Fax: 44-0-1572-758595
E-mail: registrar@oakham.rutland.sch.uk
http://www.oakham.rutland.sch.uk
A pioneer of full co-education, a boarding and day school for boys and girls aged 10 to 18 years that has become widely known for developing new ideas and making them work to the benefit of all Oakham's pupils.

Joseph AF Spence, Headmaster
Jon Wills, Registrar

2057 Oporto British School
Rua Da Cerca 326/338
PORTO
Portugal 4150-
226-666-
E-mail: school@obs.edu.pt
http://www.obs.edu.pt
As the oldest British School in Continental Europe, the Oporto British School is committed to providing a high quality international education for its students.

Mark Rogers, Principal
David Butcher, Headmaster

2058 Oslo American School
Gml Ringeriksv 53, 1340 Bekkestua
Oslo
Norway 05507

http://www.oasalumni.org

James Mcneil, Principal

2059 Panterra American School
Via Ventre D'oca 41, Fontanella
Pescara 65131
Italy

http://www.panamterra.com

Virginia Simpson, Principal

2060 Paris American Academy
277 Rue Street Jacques
Paris
France 75005
001-449-
Fax: 01 -4 4- 99
http://www.parisamericanacademy.edu
To create and maintain a system of higher education that contributes to the transformation of students into

Peter Carman, President/Executive Director
Jean-Michel Ageron-Blanc, General Director

2061 Patrick Henry Elementary School
Unit 29237
APO, Heidelberg
Germany, AE 09102
388-905-
Fax: 062-1 7-5 49
E-mail:
PatrickHenryES.Principal@eu.dodea.edu
http://www.heid-esp.eu.dodea.edu
To educate all children by providing a nurturing environment and standards-based curriculum dedicated to meeting he diverse needs of every child.

Russ Claus, Principal
Marie Granger, Assistant Principal

2062 Perse School
Hills Road
Cambridge CB2 8QF
England
0223-248127
E-mail: office@perse.co.uk
http://www.perse.co.uk
Edward Elliott, Head of Politics
Dan Cross, Deputy Head

2063 Pinewood Schools of Thessaloniki
PO Box 21001
555 10 Pilea
Greece
30-31-301-221
Fax: 30-31-323-196
E-mail: pinewood@spark.net.gr
http://www.pinepeaceschool.k12.vi
Independent, coeducational schools which offer an educational program from prekindergarten through grade 12 and boarding facilities from grade 7 though grade 12 for students of all nationalities. The school year comprises 2 semesters extending from September to January and from January to June.

Peter B Baiter, Director

2064 Pordenone Elementary School
PSC 1
Aviano
Italy
39-0434-28462
Fax: 39-0434-28761

D Jean Waddell, Principal

2065 Priory School
West Bank, Dorking
Surrey RH4 3DG
England
130-688-7337
Fax: 130-688-8715
E-mail:
enquiries@staff.priorycofe.surrey.sch.uk
http://www.priorycofe.surrey.sch.uk
To provide an educational environment which encourages pupils to become confident, competent, self-reliant and happy members of society, fully prepared for adult life and the world of work

A C Sohatski, Headteacher
M Pinchin, Senior Deputy Headteacher

2066 Queen Elizabeth School
Queen's Road, Barnet
Hertfordshire
England, UK EN5 4
020-844-0464
Fax: 020-844-0750
E-mail: enquiries@qebarnet.co.uk
http://www.qebarnet.co.uk
To produce boys who are confident, able and responsible.

John Marincowitz, Headmaster

2067 Queens College the English School
Juan De Saridakis 64
Palma de Malorca
Spain
809-393-2153
http://www.qc.cuny.edu
This Methodist affiliated school offers an English-based curriculum to a total of 1,200 female students, grades K1-12. The school does recruit from overseas, offering three year contracts with housing provided for one week at the beginning of the contract, while they find accommodations. Applications needed to teach include science, pre-school, French, math, Spanish, English and physical education.

Philip Cash, Principal

2068 Rainbow Elementary School
Unit 28614 Box 0040
APO, Ansbach 09177 0005
Germany
407-320-8450
http://www.rainbow.scps.k12.fl.us

Thomas Murdock, Principal

2069 Ramstein Elementary School
Unit 3240 Box 430
APO AE
Germany 09094
067-014-0 39
Fax: 067- 15- 835
http://www.rams-es.eu.dodea.edu
To provide a quality education for eligible minor dipendents of DoD military and civilian personnel stationed overseas.

Kathy Downs, Principal

2070 Ramstein High School
Unit 3240 Box 445
APO AE
Germany 09094-445
067-1 4-6095
Fax: 067-1 4-9 86
http://www.rams-hs.eu.dodea.edu
To provide a varied and challenging curriculum that will allow students to be life-long learners and responsible participants in a global community.

Greg Hatch, Principal

2071 Ramstein Intermediate School
Unit 3240 Box 600
APO AE
Germany 09094-600
067-1 4-6023
Fax: 067-1 5-238
http://www.rams-is.eu.dodea.edu
To provide an educational environment designed to maximize the potential of all Students.

Stanley B Caldwell, Principal

2072 Ramstein Junior High School
86 SPTG CCSI R, Unit 3240 Box 455
APO, Ramstein 09094 0005
Germany

Richard Snell, Principal

2073 Rathdown School
Upper Glenageary Road Glenageary
Co Dublin
Ireland
01-853133
E-mail: admin@rathdownschool.ie
http://www.rathdownschool.ie/contact_us
.php
Our aim is to offer a high-quality, modern, challenging and liberal education. In an inclusive and friendly environment, Rathdown School hopes to foster a love of learning which will enable each student to

develop her own unique potential. Our purpose is to support and promote the student's academic, cultural, sporting, creative, musical and spiritual capabilities.

Barbara Ennis, Principal

2074 Rikkyo School in England
Guildford Road, Rudgwick, W Sussex
RH12 3BE
Great Britain
014-3 8-2107
Fax: 014-3 8-2535
E-mail: eikoku@rikkyo.w-sussex.sch.uk
http://www.rikkyo.co.uk

M Usuki, Principal

2075 Riverside School
Walterswil
6340 Baar
Switzerland
41-41-724-5690
Fax: 41-41-724-5692
E-mail: office.zug@iszl.ch
http://www.iszl.ch
The International School of Zug and Luzern (ISZL) provides a high quality Pre-School to Grade 12 international education to day students resident in the Cantons of central Switzerland.

Dominic Currer, Director
Elaine Tomlinson, Headmaster

2076 Robinson Barracks Elementary School
Unit 30401
APO
Germany, AE 09107
491-119-
Fax: 071- 85- 473
E-mail:
RobinsonBarracksES.Principal@eu.dode
a.edu
http://www.rbar-es.eu.dodea.edu
The Robinson Barrack's school community provides a respectful environment where all members learn to recognize their strengths and gain confidence to become lifelong learners and leaders in an ever-changing world.

Shirley Sheck, Principal

2077 Rome International School
Via Panama 25
00198 Rome
Italy
039-06 -4482
Fax: 039-06 -4482
E-mail:
office@romeinternationalschool.it
http://www.romeinternationalschool.it
Provides a nurturing environment, in which children of all nationalities and faiths can explore and respect their own and each other's cultural and religious heritage.

Patricia Martin-Smith, Principal Primary School
Ivano Boragine, Managing Director

2078 Rosall School
Fleetwood
Lancashire
United Kingdom FY7 8
012- 37- 420
Fax: 012- 37- 205
E-mail:
enquiries@rossallcorporation.co.uk
http://www.rossall.co.uk
Providing a unique educational experience we offer a wide ranging choice of curriculums underpinned by a commitment to academic excellence.

RDW Rhodes, Principal
GSH Penelley, Faculty Head

2079 Rosemead
East Street, Littlehampton
BN17 6AL
England
0903-716065

J Bevis, BA, Headmaster

2080 Rota Elementary School
PSC 819 Box 19
FPO AE 09645 0019
Spain
345-624-
Fax: 011-34 -56 8
E-mail: rotaes.principal@eu.dodea.edu
http://www.rota-es.eu.dodea.edu
Provides a standards-based educational program, which creates lifelong learners and responsible citizens.

Charles Callahan, Principal

2081 Rota High School
PSC 819 Box 63
FPO AE 09645 0005
Spain
345-624-
Fax: 011-34 -56 8
E-mail: RotaHS.Principal@eu.dodea.edu
http://www.rota-hs.eu.dodea.edu

Lynne Michael, Principal

2082 Roudybush Foreign Service School
Place des Arcades, Sauveterre de Rouergue (Averyon)
France
This European school prepares men for the foreign service.

Franklin Roudybush, AB, MA, Headmaster

2083 Rugby School
Rugby, Warwickshire
United Kingdom CV22
44-178-854-3465
Fax: 44-178-856-9124
E-mail: enquiries@rugbyschool.net
http://www.rugbyschool.net
Rugby School is an educational community whose philosophy embraces the challenges of academic excellence, spiritual awareness, responsibility and leadership, friendships and relationships and participation in a wide variety of activities

Patrick Derham, Headmaster
SK Fletcher, Deputy Head

2084 Runnymede College School
Calle Salvia 30
28109 La Moraleja, Madrid
Spain
34-91-650-8302
Fax: 34-91-650-8236
E-mail: office@runnymede-college.com
http://www.runnymede-college.com
Provides an all-round, academic, liberal humanist education to all students regardless of their sex, race, religion or nationality. There is no religious instruction.

Frank M Powell, Headmaster
FJ Murphy, Deputy Head

2085 Rygaards International School
Bernstorffsvej 54, DK-2900
Hellerup
Denmark
45-39-62-10-53
Fax: 45-39-62-10-81

E-mail: admin@rygaards.com
http://www.rygaards.com
Rygaards School is a private, Christian/Catholic, co-educational establishment. It is recognised by and subject to, Danish law and receives a subsidy from the Danish State.

Mathias Jepsen, Principal
Charles Dalton, Headmaster

2086 Salzburg International Preparatory School
Moosstrasse 106
A-5020 Salzburg
Austria
662-844485
Fax: 662-847711
http://www.ais-salzburg.a
A coeducational boarding school offering an American college preparatory high school curriculum for grades 7 to 12 as well as a post graduate course.

2087 Schiller Academy
51-55 Waterloo Road
London, SE1 8TX
United Kingdom
44-207-928-1372
Fax: 44-207-928-8089
E-mail: office@schiller-academy.org.uk
http://www.schiller-academy.org.uk
Grade levels 9-12, school year August - June

George Selby, Headmaster
Renee Miller, Director Studies

2088 Schools of England, Wales, Scotland & Ireland
J. Burrow & Company
Imperial House, Lypiatt Road
Cheltenham 50201
England

2089 Schweinfurt American Elementary School
CMR 457
AP, AE
Germany 09033
09721-81893
Fax: 09721-803905
E-mail:
schweinfurtes.principal@eu.dodea.edu
http://www.schw-es.eu.dodea.edu
The mission of Schweinfurt Elementary School is to help all students become respectful, responsible citizens and life-long learners.

Wilma Holt, Principal
Beverly Erdmann, Assistant Principal

2090 Schweinfurt Middle School
CMR 457
AP, AE
Germany 09033-5
354-681-1800
Fax: 097-1 8-363
E-mail:
SchweinfurtMS.Principal@eu.dodea.edu
http://www.schw-ms.eu.dodea.edu
Schweinfurt Middle School will engage all students in meaningful experiences that develop 21st Century Skills, preparing them to be successful and responsible citizens in a technological, global society.

Dr George P Carpenter, Principal

2091 Sembach Elementary School
Unit 4240 Box 325
APO, AE
Germany 09136
063- 67-0
Fax: 063-271-
E-mail:

SembachES.Principal@eu.dodea.edu
http://www.semb-es.eu.dodea.edu
Monica Harvey, Principal

2092 Sembach Middle School
Unit 4240 Box 320
APO, AE
Germany 09136
063- 67-0
Fax: 063-271-
E-mail:
SembachMS.Principal@eu.dodea.edu
http://www.semb-ms.eu.dodea.edu
Bonnie B Hannan, Principal

2093 Sevenoaks School
Sevenoaks
Kent TN13 1HU
England
44 -017-245
Fax: 44 -017-245
E-mail: enq@sevenoaksschool.org
http://www.sevenoaksschool.org
Sevenoaks School is an independent, co-educational boarding and day school, set in 100 acres in the heart of Southeast England. Half an hour from Central London, and half an hour from Gatwick International Airport, we are situated on the edge of Sevenoaks, overlooking the 15th century deer park of the Knole Estate.

Katy Ricks, Head of School
Tony Evans, Chairman

2094 Sevilla Elementary & Junior High School
496 ABS DODDS Unit 6585
APO Moron AB 09643 0005
Spain

Robert Ludwig, Principal

2095 Shape Elementary School
Unit 21420
APO, AE
Belgium 09705
011-32 -5044
Fax: 011-32 -31
E-mail: ShapeES.Principal@eu.dodea.edu
http://www.shap-es.eu.dodea.edu
It is the mission of SHAPE Elementary School to educate all students in an integrated, multi-cultural environment to become productive thinkers, to achieve their maximum physical and mental potential, and to be literate, responsible members of a global society through excellence in teaching and learning.

Charlene Leister, Principal
Miles Shea, Assistant Principal

2096 Shape High School
Unit 21420
APO, AE
Belgium 09705
011-32 -5044
Fax: 011-32 -31
E-mail: david.tran@eu.dodea.edu
http://www.shap-hs.eu.dodea.edu

David Tran, Principal
Arlena Ray, Assistant Principal

2097 Shape International School
Avenue de Reijkjavik 717
SHAPE
Belgium 07010
65-44-52-83
http://www.nato.int/shape/community/school.htm

Performs the operational duties previously undertaken by Allied Command Europe and Allied Command Atlantic

Jacques Laurent, Principal

2098 Sidcot School
Winscombe
N Somerset BS25 1PD
England
44-193-484-3102
Fax: 44-193-484-4181
E-mail: addmissions@sidcot.org.uk
http://www.sidcot.org.uk
This friendly school with an international enrollment of 277 day students and 149 boarding students (255 boys; 171 girls), in grades K-12, is set in over one hundred acres of Somerset countryside. The school offers an English-based curriculum and the student/teacher ratio is 10:1.

John Walmsley, Headteacher
Ross Wallis, Head of Art

2099 Sierra Bernia School
La Caneta s/n
Alfaz del Pi Alicante
Spain 03580
96-687-51-49
Fax: 96-687-36-33
E-mail: duncan@ctv.es
http://sierraberniaschool.com/news.php
Forefront of modern education. Combining both traditional and innovative methods of teaching made possible by the wealth and immense knowledge base of its fully qualified teaching body

Duncan Allan, Owner/Director
Iain Macinnes, Headteacher

2100 Sigonella Elementary & High School
PSC 824 Box 2630
FPO Signoella, Sicily 09627 2630
Italy
624-440-
http://www.sigo-es.eu.dodea.edu/

Dr. Peter Price, Principal

2101 Sigtunaskolan Humanistiska Laroverket
Manfred Bjorkquists Alle 6
Box 508, Sigtuna
Sweden 19328
46-8-592-57100
Fax: 46-8-592-57250
E-mail: info@sshl.se
http://www.sshl.se
Grade levels include 7-12 with an enrollment of 543.

Kent Edberg, Principal
Rune Svaninger, Director

2102 Sir James Henderson School
Via Pisani Dossi 16
Milano
Italy 20134
39-02-264-13310
Fax: 39-02-264-13515
E-mail: sirjames@bbs.infosquare.it
http://www.sjhschool.com
To ensure that its diverse student body grows to its full potential as independent learners in a caring British and international community, uniting the best of British educational tradition with the values, practices and beliefs of the International Baccalaureate

Stephen Anson, Principal
Jim Noble, Chairman

2103 Skagerak Gymnas
PO Box 1545-Veloy
3206 Sandefjord
Norway

473-345-6500
http://www.skagerak.org
Elisabeth Norr, Principal

2104 Smith Elementary School
Unit 23814 Box 30
APO, AE
Germany 09034-3814
067-783-5693
Fax: 067-783-8874
E-mail:
SmithES.Principal@eu.dodea.edu
http://www.baum-ess.eu.dodea.edu
Kent Bassett, Principal

2105 Southlands English School
Via Teleclide 40
Casalapalocco, Rome
Italy 00124
39 -605-5039
Fax: 06 -091-7192
http://www.southlands.it
Our aim is to give you a flavour of the quality educational experience available at Southlands and encourage you to visit the school so you can see for yourself the happy, successful community that Southlands nurtures.

Deryck M Wilson, Principal

2106 Spangdahlem Elementary School
52 MSG/CCSE S, Unit 3640 Box 50
APO, AE
Germany 09126-4050
065-056- 688
Fax: 065-056- 710
E-mail:
SpnagdahlemES.Principal@eu.dodea.edu
http://www.spang-es.eu.dodea.edu
Richard R Alix, Principal

2107 Spangdahlem Middle School
52 CSG CCSM, Unit 3640 Box 45
APO, AE
Germany 09126-4045
065-506- 725
Fax: 065-506-0279
E-mail:
SpangdahlemMS.Principal@eu.dodea.edu
http://www.spang-ms.eu.dodea.edu
Spangdahlem Middle School promotes high achievement and lifelong learning for all students through positive interactions and standards-based educational program.

Joseph Malloy, Principal

2108 Sportfield Elementary School
Unit 20193 Box 0014
APO, Hanau
Germany, AE 09165-14
John O'Reilly, Jr, Principal

2109 St. Andrew's College
19 Carillon Avenue
Newtown NSW
Australia 02042
02-9626-1999
E-mail:
principalassist@standrewscollege.edu.au
http://www.standrewscollege.edu.au
St Andrew's is proud of its reputation as a leading academic institution, fostering leaders within the community and moulding the leaders of tomorrow. The College places emphasis on academic and intellectual development and excellence as core to the development of the individual.

Wayne Erickson, Principal
Donna Wiemann, Development Manager

2110 St. Anne's School
Jarama 9
Madrid 2
Spain

http://www.stannes.edu.in

Margaret Raines, Principal

2111 St. Anthony's International College
Camino de Coin km 53.5
Mijas-Costa, Malaga
Spain 29649
00 -09 -247
Fax: 00 -09 -046
E-mail: info@stanthonyscollege.com
http://www.stanthonyscollege.com
The school with its friendly, family atmosphere provides opportunities for our students to achieve their best. Trying not to cater just for high achievers we endeavour, through a broad and balanced education, to find courses for all abilities.

2112 St. Catherine's British School
PO Box 51019
Kifissia 145 10 Athens
Greece
301- 8-97
Fax: 301- 8-64
E-mail: administrator@stcatherines.gr
http://www.stcatherines.gr
The school endeavors to foster a love of learning through a well taught, appropriately challenging, clearly defined and balanced curriculum. Our aim is to fully develop intellectual, social, physical and creative potential, giving students the foundatin to develop into sensitive, informed, and capable global citizens of the future.

Michael Toman, Principal
R Morton, Headmaster & CEO

2113 St. Christopher School
Barrington Road, Letchworth
Hertfordshire SG6 3JZ
England
0462-679301
Fax: 0462-481578
E-mail: school.admin@stchris.co.uk
http://www.stchris.co.uk
St Christopher has a distinctive ethos, based on the development of each child's individuality whilst teaching a sense of responsibility towards others, towards the School and towards the local and global community.

Richard Palmer, Head of School
Emma-Kate Henry, Deputy Head of St Christophe

2114 St. Clare's Oxford
139 Banbury Road
Oxford OX2 7AL
England
44-186-555-2031
Fax: 44-186-551-3359
E-mail: admissions@stclares.ac.uk
http://www.stclares.ac.uk
St. Clare's welcomes students and staff of all nationalities and cultures who will benefit from, and contribute to, our learning community. Living and studying together, we learn from one another. We are enriched and challenged by a diversity of views and ideas.

Paula Holloway, Principal
Tom Walsh, Vice Principal

2115 St. David's School
Justin Hall, Beckenham Road
West Wickham BR4 0QS
England

01784-252494
Fax: 01784-252494
E-mail: office@stdavidsschool.com
http://www.sdsw.org
Boarding school for girls ages nine to eighteen; day school for girls ages four to eighteen.

Judith G Osborne, BA, Headmaster

2116 St. Dominic's International School
Outeiro de Polima-Arneiro
2785-816 Sao Domingos da Rana
Portugal
351-21-448-0550
351-214-5505
Fax: 351-21-444-3027
E-mail: school@dominics-int.org
http://www.dominics-int.org
Our school mission is to offer an international education of the highest calibre enriched and enlivened by the Dominican tradition of study and education; promoting the development of each student's potential: physical, emotional, social, intellectual, moral and spiritual.

Maria do Rosýri Empis, Principal
Manuel Lucas, President of Supervision

2117 St. Dominic's Sixth Form College
Mount Park Avenue Harrow on the Hil
Middlesex HA1 3HX
England
020-84228084
208-422-3759
Fax: 020-8422-3759
E-mail: stdoms@stdoms.ac.uk
http://www.stdoms.ac.uk
St. Dominic's is a Roman Catholic Sixth Form College committed to the pesonal and spiritual growth of all its members based on Christian values, academic excellence and high quality pastoral care.

Patrick Harty, Principal

2118 St. Georges English School
Via Cassia Km 16
La Storta Rome
Italy 00123
06-3790141
Fax: 06-3792490
E-mail: Secretary@stgeorge.school.it
http://www.stgeorge.school.it
To develop the individual talents of young people and teach them to relate the experience of the classroom to the realities of the world outside.

Martyn Hales, Principal

2119 St. Georges School
Vila Goncalve, Quinta Loureiras
2750 Cascais
Portugal
112-602-4645
http://www.sgs.edu.in
MPB Hoare, Principal

2120 St. Georges School-Switzerland
Chemin de St Georges 19
Clarens Montreux
Switzerland 01815
21-964-34-11
Fax: 21-964-49-32
E-mail: office@st-georges.ch
http://www.st-georges.ch
St. George's School encourages students to lift their eyes and recognise positive qualities within themselves and others and to nurture a caring and dynamic attitude in today's demanding world.

Dr Ilya V Eigenbrot, Principal
Francis Kahn, President of Directors

2121 St. Gerard's School
Thornhill Road, Bray Co Wicklow
Republic of Ireland

353-001-2821
Fax: 353-001-2821
E-mail: info@stgerards.ie
http://www.stgerards.ie
To provide an opportunity for each student to realise his or her potential in all areas: academic, moral, personal, physical, social, spiritual and sporting.

Tom Geraghty, Headmaster
Victor Drummy, Deputy Principal

122 St. Helen's School

Eastbury Road Northwood, Middlesex
England HA6-3AS
09274-28511
Fax: 0923-835824
E-mail: enquiries@sthn.co.uk
http://www.sthn.co.uk
We aim to give every pupil an academic, innovative and stimulating education, developing her intellectual, creative and physical talents to the full. We provide a friendly, supportive and well-ordered environment in which every girl is treated as an individual and where integrity, personal responsibility and respect for others are highly valued.

YA Burne, Principal

123 St. John's International School

Dreve Richelle 146
Waterloo
Belguim 01410
32-2-352-0610
Fax: 32-2-352-0630
E-mail: contact@stjohns.be
http://www.stjohns.be
we exist to provide an English-speaking education that emphasizes Christian values, encourages academic excellence and stimulates social development within a culturally diverse environment. St. John's is also a caring environment where students are encouraged to reach their full potential, prepared to think globally, with a commitment to justice and challenged to act responsibly in a consistently changing society.

Joseph Doenges, Director
Judith Hoskins, Director Admissions

124 St. Mary's School

Rhapta Road, PO Box 40580- 00100
Nairobi
Kenya
0990-23721
E-mail: info@stmarys.ac.ke
http://www.stmarys.ac.ke
We are a Catholic Private School committed to our international character in the provision of a spiritual, intellectual and physical education. We aim at developing the gifts of the young in an atmosphere which encourages the ethos of self-expression and mutual respect with a view to their facing the future responsibly, with confidence and courage.

M Mark Orchard, IBVM, BA, Principal

125 St. Michael's School

Otford Court
Otford TN14 5SA
England
095-92-2137
http://www.stmichaels-otford.co.uk

Keith Crombie, Headmaster

126 St. Stephen's School

Via Aventina 3
Rome
Italy 00153
39-06-575-0605
Fax: 39-06-574-1941

E-mail: ststephens@ststephens-rome.com
http://www.ststephens-rome.com

Philip Allen, Headmaster
Lesley Murphey, Head of the School

2127 Stavenger British School

Gauselbakken 107
4032 Gausel
Norway
475-195-0250
http://www.biss.no

Zelma Roisli, Principal

2128 Stover School

Newton Abbot
Devon
England TQ12
0626-54505
351-214-5505
E-mail: mail@stover.co.uk
http://www.stover.co.uk

Susan Bradley, Principal

2129 Stowe School

Stowe
Buckingham
England MK18
44-1280-818000
351-214-5505
Fax: 44-1280-818181
E-mail: enquiries@stowe.co.uk
http://www.stowe.co.uk
Our vision for Stowe, a co-educational independent boarding and day school in the heart of the English countryside, is of a school that delivers the highest academic and cultural achievement; and a school that continues to foster the development of Stoics who are as original and individual as their school.

Anthony Wallersteiner, Headmaster
GM Hornby, Faculty Head

2130 Summerfield School SRL

Via Tito Poggi 21 Divino Amore
00134 Rome
Italy

http://www.summerfields.co.in

Vivien Franceschini, Principal

2131 Summerhill School

Westward Ho
Leiston, Suffolk
England IP16
0728-830540
E-mail: zoe@summerhillschool.co.uk
http://www.summerhillschool.co.uk
A S Neill's Summerhill School, a co-educational boarding school in Suffolk, England, is the original alternative 'free' school. Founded in 1921, it continues to be an influential model for progressive, democratic education around the world.

Zoe Readhead, Principal

2132 Sunny View School

C/ Teruel No 32, Cerro del Toril
Torremolinos Malaga
Spain 29620
345-283-
Fax: 345-272-
E-mail: sunny@acade.es
http://www.sunnyviewschool.com
Sunny View is a privately owned day school, which accepts students of all nationalities from the age of 3 years to 18 years. It is a long-established International School.

Jane Barbadillo, Principal
David McConnell, HS Principal

2133 Sutton Park School

St Fintan's Road
Sutton, Dublin 13
Ireland
353-1-832-2940
Fax: 353-1-832-5929
E-mail: info@sps.ie
http://www.suttonparkschool.com
Sutton Park School aims to provide its pupils with an educational environment that is intellectually, physically and culturally challenging, so that they can grow into balanced, mature and confident adults.

Laurence J Finnegan, Chief Executive
Michael Moretta, Head of School

2134 Sutton Valence School

Maidstone
Kent
England ME17
0622-842281
E-mail: enquiries@svs.org.uk
http://www.svs.org.uk
Our aim today is to give our girls and boys an excellent all round education in an atmosphere of togetherness and trust, where day and boarding pupils benefit from the same supportive ethos.

Joe Davies, Headmaster
Kathy Webster, Admissions Officer

2135 Swans School

Capricho s/n
Marbella, Malaga
Spain 29600
95 -77 -248
Fax: 95 -77 -431
E-mail: info@swansschool.net
http://www.swansschool.net
Swans' motto is Constancy and Truth.

TJ Swan, Principal
Nick Lee, Head Teacher

2136 TASIS Hellenic International School

PO Box 51051
Kifissia Gr-145 10
Greece
30-1-623-3888
Fax: 30-1-623-3160
E-mail: info@tasis.edu.gr
http://www.tasis.com
Grade levels Pre-K through 12, school year September - June

Basile Daskalakis, President

2137 TASIS The American School in England

Coldharbour Lane
Thorpe, Surrey, TW20 8TE
England
44-1932-565-252
Fax: 44-1932-564-644
E-mail: ukadmissions@tasis.com
http://www.tasis.com
Grade levels Pre-K through 12, school year August - June

Barry Breen, Headmaster

2138 Taunus International Montessori School

Altkonigstrasse 1 6370
Oberursel
Germany
496-171-9133
http://www.tims-frankfurt.com

Kathleen Hauer, Principal

2139 Teach in Great Britain

5 Netherhall Gardens
London, NW3, England

http://www.teachaway.com

2140 Thessaloniki International High School & Pinewood Elementary School
PO Box 21001
555 10 Pilea, Thessaloniki
Greece
30-31-301-221
Fax: 30-31-323-196
E-mail: pinewood@spark.net.gr
http://www.users.otenet.gr/~pinewood
Grades preK-12, enrollment 256.

Peter B Baiter, Director

2141 Thomas Jefferson School
4100 South Lindbergh Boulevard
Saint Louis
Missouri, MO 63127
314-843-4151
http://www.tjs.org
The mission of Thomas Jefferson School is to give its students the strongest possible academic background, responsibility for their own learning, a concern for other people, and the resources to live happily as adults and become active contributors to society

William C Rowe, Head of School
Susan S Stepleton, Chair, Board of Trustees

2142 United Nations Nursery School
40 Rue Pierre Guerin
75016 Paris
France
33-1-452-72024
Fax: 33-1-428-87146
http://www.unns.net
Pre-K and kindergarten levels.

Brigitte Weill, Directrice

2143 United World College-Adriatic
Via Treste 29
Duino (TS)
Italy 34011
39 -40 -7391
Fax: 39 -40 -7392
http://www.uwcad.it
The United World Colleges offer students of all races and creeds the opportunity of developing international understanding through programmes which combine high quality academic study and activities which encourage

DB Sutcliffe, Principal
David Sutcliffe, Headmaster

2144 United World College-Atlantic
St Donats Castle Llantwit
Major S Glamorgan
United Kingdom
441- 46-9 90
http://www.atlanticcollege.org
a sense of adventure and social responsibility

Colin Jenkins, Principal

2145 Vajont Elementary School
PSC 1
Aviano
Italy
427-701553

Nick Suida, Principal

2146 Verdala International School
Fort Pembroke
Pembroke, STJ 14
Malta

356-332-361
Fax: 356-372-387
E-mail: vis@maltanet.net
http://www.verdala.org
An independent, coeducational day and boarding school which offers an educational program from play school through grade 12 for students of all nationalities.

Adam Pleasance, Headmaster
Charles Zerafa, Business Manager

2147 Verona Elementary School
1011 Lee Highway
Verona, VA 24482
540-248-0141
Fax: 540-248-0562
http://www.augusta.k12.va.us/veronaes/site/default.asp

Marguerite McDonald, Principal

2148 Vicenza Elementary School
Unit 31401 Box 11
APO, Vicenza
Italy 09630-5
011-390-444
Fax: 011-39 -444
E-mail: VicenzaES.Principal@eu.dodea.edu
http://www.vice-es.eu.dodea.edu/index.htm
Increase student achievement, we are committed to improving our children's ability to communicate in writing across all curricular areas, and to reason mathematically.

Martha Parsons, Principal

2149 Vicenza High School
Unit 31401 Box 11
APO, Vicenza
Italy 09630
011-390-444
Fax: 011-39 -444
E-mail: VicenzaHS.Principal@eu.dodea.edu
http://www.vice-hs.eu.dodea.edu/

Lauri Kenney, Principal
Chris Beane, Assistant Principal

2150 Vicenza International School
Viale Trento 141
Vicenza 36100
Italy
39-0444-288-475
Fax: 39-0444-963-633
E-mail: vix-ib@vip.it
Grade levels 11-13, school year September - June

Dionigio Tanello, PhD, Director

2151 Vienna Christian School
Wagramerstrasse 175
Panthgasse 6A
Wien, Austria A-122
43-1-25122-501
351-214-5505
E-mail: office@vcs-austria.org
http://www.viennachristianschool.org/
VCS is an international school with a United States-based curriculum.

Ken Norman, Director
Nancy L Deibert, Athletic Director/PE

2152 Vienna International School
Strasse der Menschenrechte 1
Vienna, Austria 01220
43-1-203-5595
Fax: 43-1-203-0366
E-mail: visinfo@vis.ac.at
http://www.vis.ac.at
To serve the children of the United Nations and diplomatic community in Vienna. It is

also open to children of the international business community and of Austrian families.

James S Walbran, Director
Neil Tomalin, Head Primary School

2153 Vilseck Elementary School
Unit 28040
APO, Vilseck
Germany 09112-14
011-490-662
Fax: 011-490-662
E-mail: VilseckES.Principal@eu.dodea.edu
http://www.vils-es.eu.dodea.edu/
Vilseck Elementary School prepares students for lifelong learning within a safe, nurturing environment. Honoring the uniqueness of our military community, we foster respect for all people and for cultural diversity

Hammack, Principal, Assistant Principal

2154 Vilseck High School
Unit 20841
APO, Vilseck
Germany 09112-5
011-490-662
Fax: 011-490-662
E-mail: Duane.Werner@eu.dodea.edu
http://www.vils-hs.eu.dodea.edu/
VHS is home to approximately 520 students, grades 9-12, who have the opportunity to participate in Engaged Learning projects in academic areas. They have a wide range of choices in elective areas to include art, band, chorus, German, Spanish, home economics and technical education.

Duane Werner, Principal

2155 Violen School, International Department
Violenstraat 3, 1214
CJ Hilversum
Netherlands
035-621-6053
http://www.ipsviolen.nl
This school offers an enrollment of 240 day students (125 boys and 115 girls), in grades K through 6. The primary education is in the English language for international mobile families, set up and supported by the Dutch government.

Atse R Spoor, Principal

2156 Vogelweh Elementary School
Unit 3240 Box 435
APO
Germany, AE 09021
011-49 -3109
Fax: 011-49 -3105
http://www.voge-es.eu.dodea.edu
Vogelweh Elementary School is committed to creating an environment that supports lifelong learning in order for students to be successful in a global society.

Donna E Donaldson, Principal
Janie Page, Assistant Principal

2157 Volkel Elementary School
752 MUNSS Unit 6790
APO, Volkel 09717 5018
Netherlands

http://www.aoshs.org

Claudia Holtzclaw, Principal

2158 Westwing School
Kyneton House
Thornbury BS122JZ
England
0454-412311
http://westwing.dvusd.org

Marjorie Crane, MA, Headmaster

159 Wetzel Elementary School
Unit 23815
APO, Baumholder 09034 0005
Germany

http://www.baum-esw.eu.dodea.edu
Robert Richards, Principal

160 Wiesbaden Middle School
Unit 29647
APO, AE
Germany 09096
011-049- 110
Fax: 011-049- 110
E-mail:
wiesbadenMS.Webmaster@eu.dodea.edu
http://www.wies-ms.eu.dodea.edu
The entire WMS community strives to provide a positive school climate through which all students can mature socially, academically and physically, while developing a life-long love of learning.

Alexia Venglik, Principal

161 Wolfert Van Borselen
Bredewater 24, Postbus 501
2700 AM Zoetermeer
Netherlands
E-mail: info@owinsp.nl
http://http://www.wolfert.nl/
Gilles Schuilenburg, Principal

162 Worksop College
Worksop, Nottinghamshire
S80 3AP
England
0909-472391
E-mail:
enquiries@worksopcollege.notts.sch.uk
http://http://www.worksopcollege.notts.sch.uk/
Worksop College was founded as St Cuthbert's School in 1890 by Nathaniel Woodard. As a parish priest working in London in the 1840s Woodard was dismayed by the ignorance of the middle classes and believed that there was a need for something comparable to the National School's Christian schools for the poor in order to serve the needs of the trade classes.

Roy Collard, Headmaster

163 Worms Elementary School
CMR 455
APO, Worms 09058 0005
Germany
011-490-662
http://www.wikimapia.org
Charles Raglan, Principal

164 Wuerzburg Elementary School
CMR 475 Box 6
APO, Wuerzburg 09244 6627
Germany
011-490-662
http://www.wikimapia.org
Dee Ann Edwards, Principal

165 Wuerzburg High School
CMR 475 Box 8
APO, Wuerzburg 09036 0005
Germany
011-490-662
http://www.wikimapia.org
Robert Kubarek, Principal

166 Wuerzburg Middle School
CMR 475 Box 7
APO, Wuerzburg 09036 0005
Germany

011-490-662
http://www.wikimapia.org
Karen Kroon, Principal

2167 Zurich International School
Steinacherstrasse 140
8820 Wadenswill
Switzerland
41-43-833-2222
Fax: 41-43-833-2223
E-mail: zis@zis.ch
http://www.zis.ch
Zurich International School is a co-educational international day school in the Zurich area for students aged 3 to 18 and is fully accredited by both the Council of International Schools and the New England Association of Schools and Colleges and is an IB World School.

Peter C Mott, Director
Jennifer Saxe, Director Development

West Indies & Carribean

2168 American School-Santo Domingo
Apartado 20212
Santo Domingo
Dominican Republic
809-565-7946
809-549-5841
E-mail: info@assd.edu.do
http://www.assd.edu.do
The American School of Santo Domingo provides all students with quality educational opportunities to make life long learners while fostering moral values and physical development.

Lourdes Tomas, School Director

2169 Aquinas College
1607 Robinson Road SE
Grand Rapids, MI 49506-1799
616-632-8900
http://www.aquinas.edu
Emphasizes career preparation with a focus on leadership and service to others.

Vincent Ferguson, Principal

2170 Belair School
43 Decarteret Road
Mandeville
Jamaica
1-876-962-2168
Fax: 1-876-962-3396
E-mail: admissions@belairschool.com
http://www.belairschool.com
The Belair School seeks to promote the academic, social and emotional development of students and a value system of integrity through an integrated curriculum, so that students will become self-assured and responsible citizens.

Sylvan Shields, Director

2171 Bermuda High School
19 Richmond Road
Pembroke
Bermuda HM 08
1-441-295-6153
Fax: 1-441-295-2754
E-mail: info@bhs.bm
http://www.bhs.bm
This girls school offers an English-based curriculum for 620 total day students in grades 1-12.

Martina Harris, Primary Head
Jennifer Howarth, Primary Assistant

2172 Bermuda Institute-SDA
234 Middle Road
Southampton
Bermuda SN BX
441-238-1566
http://www.bermudainstitute.bm
The Bermuda Institute family exists to show children Jesus, nurture their love for Him and others, teach them to think, and empower them to serve.

Lois Tucker, Principal
Kathleen Allers, Elementary Vice Principal

2173 Bishop Anstey Junior School
Ariapita Road
Port of Spain
Trinidad and Tobago
868-624-1177
E-mail: admin@bishopansteyjunior.edu.tt
http://www.bishopansteyjunior.edu.tt
To stimulate learning within the spiritual, academic, social , cultural and sporting disciplines aimed at developing rounded individuals, within an environment that allows the flexibility to cope with the challenges of the changing education landscape.

Grace Campbell, Principal

2174 Capitol Christian School
C-11 #3 Urb Real Santo Domingo
Dominican Republic
916-856-5630
Fax: 916-856-5609
http://www.ccscougars.org
Stacy Lee Blossom, Principal

2175 Ecole Flamboyant
PO Box 1744-A Schweitzer Hosp
Port-au-Prince
Haiti
509-381-141/2
Fax: 509-381-141
E-mail: has-pap@acn.com
William Dunn, Principal

2176 International School-Aruba
Wayaca 238 A
Aruba
Dutch Caribbean
297-845-365
Fax: 297-847-341
E-mail: info@isaruba.com
http://www.isaruba.com
A nonprofit, coeducational English-speaking day school serving students from prekindergarten to grade 12.

Paul D Sibley, Headmaster
Mary B Sibley, Academic Dean/Counselor

2177 International School-Curacao
PO Box 3090
Koninginnelaan Emmastad, Curacao
Netherlands Antilles
5-999-737-3633
Fax: 5-999-737-3142
E-mail: iscmec@attglobal.net
http://www.isc.an
Offers a rigorous academic program in order to prepare students planning to pursue higher learning at colleges and universities around the world. The School's curriculum includes International Baccalaureate (IB) coursework that allows students the opportunity to receive the IB Diploma.

Margie Elhage PhD, Director
Rene Romer, President

2178 International School-West Indies
PO Box 278 Leeward
Providenciales
British West Indies

Alison Hodges, Principal

2179 Kingsway Academy
PO Box N-4378
Nassau
Bahamas
242-324-6887
Fax: 242-393-6917
http://www.kingswayacademy.com
Kingsway Academy endeavours to provide children with a sound education that is thoroughly Christian in its outlook and practices - Training Children in the King's Way .

Carol Harrison, Principal

2180 Mount Saint Agnes Academy
PO Box HM 1004
Hamilton HMDX
Bermuda
441-292-4134
Fax: 441-295-7265
E-mail: msaoffice@msa.bm
http://www.msa.bm
The Mission of Mount Saint Agnes Academy is to provide quality education in a caring, Christian environment. Belief in Christ and fidelity to the Roman Catholic Church form the foundation upon which all academic learning and social interaction take place. To this end we make a strong commitment to recognize each child as an individual and to help him/her to develop according to his/her own potential in order to become a responsible member of the community

Sue Moench, Principal
Margaret DiGiacomo, Assistant Principal

2181 Queens College
PO Box N7127
Nassau
Bahamas
242-393-1666
Fax: 242-393-3248
E-mail: info@qchenceforth.com
http://www.qchenceforth.com
Our interests lie not only in academic excellence but also in raising well-rounded, courteous, spiritually grounded global citizens.

Andrea Gibson, Principal

2182 Saltus Cavendish School
PO Box DV 209
Devonshire DV BX
Bermuda
441-236-3215
Fax: 441-292-0438
E-mail: head.cavendish@saltus.bm
http://www.saltus.bm
Saltus Grammar School is a co-educational, independent day school of excellent reputation. It is the premier independent school in Bermuda and is well known in the international community.

Susan Furr, Headteacher
Stephanie Queary, Secretary

2183 St. Andrew's School
16 Valleton Avenue
Marraval Trinidad West Indies
Trinidad and Tobago
868-622-2630
Fax: 868-628-1857
E-mail: principal@standrews.edu.tt
http://www.standrews.edu.tt

St. Andrew's is a progressive school that produces a caring, confident and responsible child. St. Andrew's also supports the development of social and moral values that allow the child to appreciate and respect diversity.

Sandra Farinha, Principal
Paula Moses, Vice Principal

2184 St. Anne's Parish School
PO Box SS6256
Nassau
Bahamas
868-622-2631
Fax: 868-628-1858
http://www.standrewsindia.com

Rev. Patrick Adderley, Principal

2185 St. John's College
PO Box N4858
Nassau
Bahamas
868-622-2632
Fax: 868-628-1859
http://www.standrewsindia.com

Arlene Ferguson, Principal

2186 St. Paul's Methodist College
PO Box F897
Freeport
Grand Bahamas
814-237-2163
http://stpaulsc.org

Annette Poitier, Principal

2187 Sunland Lutheran School
PO Box F2469
Freeport
Bahamas

http://www.sunlandbaptistacademy.org

J Pinder, Principal

2188 Tapion School
PO Box 511 La Toc
Castries, St Lucia
West Indies
758-452-2902
Fax: 758-453-0582
E-mail: tapionsch@candw.lc
http://tapionschool.com
The Tapion School will endeavour to produce individuals who would be empowered to meet the demands of a changing society.

Laurena Primus, Principal
Margaret Francois, Administration Officer

U.S. Branches

2189 Aisha Mohammed International School
Washington, DC 20521-1

http://www.joh.cam.ac.uk

Daryl Barker, Principal

2190 Albania Tirana International School
DOS/Administrative Officer
9510 Tirana Place
Washington, DC 20521-9510
355-436-5239
E-mail: qsialb@albaniaonline.net
http://www1.qsi.org/alb
Provides a quality education in the English language for expatriates living in Tirana

and Albanian citizens who want their children to be educated in English.

Scott D'Alterio, Director
Sotiraq Trebicka, Administrative Coordinator

2191 Alexander Muss High School Israel
78 Randall Avenue
Rockville Centre, NY 11570
212-472-9300
800-327-5980
Fax: 212-472-9301
E-mail: info@amiie.org
http://amiie.org
Provide a superior Israel education experience to learners of all ages in Israel and within communities throughout North America and abroad. The Institute promotes, builds and strengthens lifelong bonds between Jews and Israel through education, experiences and understanding.

Gideon Shavit, CEO
Chaim Fischgrund, Headmaster

2192 Almaty International School
DOS/Administrative Officer
7030 Almaty Place
Washington, DC 20521-7030
E-mail: director@ais.almaty.kz
http://www.state.gov/www/about_state/schools/oalmaty.html
Grades preK-12, enrollment 169.

Robert B Draper, Director

2193 American School
Col Lomas del Guijarro Avenue Repœb
Tegucigalpa
Honduras 02134
504-239-3333
Fax: 504-239-6162
E-mail: eagurcia@amschool.org
http://www.amschool.org
Provides a student-centered, enriching, college-preparatory education that emphasizes social responsibility in a safe, bicultural, and disciplined learning environment.

Liliana F Jenkins, Superintendent
David Mendoza, Business Administrator

2194 American Cooperative School
Calle 10 y Pasaje Kantutas, Calacot
c/o American Embassy, La Paz, Bolivia
La Paz, Bolivia
519-2-792-302
Fax: 591-2-797-218
E-mail: acs@acslp.org
http://www.acslp.org
Offers college prepatory North American education that enables our graduates to enter the best universities in the United States, Canada, Europe and Latin America.

Matthew Kirby, Superintendent
Robert Boni, Chair

2195 American Cooperative School of Tunis
6360 Tunis Place
Washington, DC 20521-6360
216-71-760-905
Fax: 216-71-761-412
E-mail: acst@acst.intl.tn
http://www.acst.net

Dennis Sheehan, Superintendent

2196 American Embassy School
Department of State/AES
9000 New Delhi Place
Washington, DC 20521-9000
91-11-611-7140
Fax: 91-11-687-3320
E-mail: aesindia@aes.ac.in
http://www.serve.com/aesndi

Grade levels Pre-K through 12, school year August - May

Rob Mochrish, PhD, Director

197 American Embassy School of New Delhi

Chandragupta Marg
Chanakyapuri, New Delhi
India 11002
91-11-611-7140
Fax: 91-11-687-3320
E-mail: aesindia@del2.vsnl.net.in
http://aes.ac.in/splash.php
Serves students from the United States and other nations. It provides a quality American education that enables students to be inspired learners and responsible global citizens through the collaboration of a dedicated faculty and a supportive community.

Dr Robert Hetzel, Director
Linda McGinnis, Secretary, AES School Board

198 American International School of Nouakchott

DOS/Administrative Officer
2430 Nouakchott Place
Washington, DC 20521-2430
222-2-52967
Fax: 222-2-52967
E-mail: aisnsahara@yahoo.com
http://www.aisn.mr
At the American International School of Nouakchott, a partnership of educators and parents is committed to providing our culturally diverse students a safe, nurturing and respectful learning environment. We promote academic achievement through a curriculum founded on an American educational philosophy.

Sharon Orlins PhD, Director

199 American International School-Abuja

DOS/Administrative Officer
8300 Abuja Place
Washington, DC 20521-8300
234-9-413-4464
Fax: 234-9-413-4464
E-mail: info@aisabuja.com
http://www.aisabuja.com
Provide a quality education, utilizing an American curriculum for students of all nationalities from preschool through 12th grade.

Amy Uzoewulu, Director
Peter Williams, Primary Principal

200 American International School-Bamako

DOS/Administrative Officer
2050 Bamako Place
Washington, DC 20189-2050
223-222-4738
Fax: 223-222-0853
E-mail: aisb@aisbmali.org
http://www.aisbmali.org
An independent, coeducational day school which offers an educational program from prekindergarten through grade 10. Supervised study using the University of Nebraska High School correspondence courses for grades 12 may also be arranged.

David Henry, Director
Rob Van Doeselaar, Chairman

201 American International School-Chennai

100 Feet Road
Taramani
Chennai 00600-113
91-44-499-0881
Fax: 91-44-466-0636
E-mail: HeadofSchool@aisch.org
http://www.aisch.org
Embraces international diversity and strives to provide an academically challenging environment in order to foster intellectual curiosity and a sense of responsibility in our students. To fully educate the whole person, we are committed to cultivating lifelong learners and balanced, service-oriented citizens, who are thereby prepared to positively contribute in a globally competitive world.

Barry Clough, Head of School
Dr James R Fellabaum, High School Principal

2202 American International School-Costa Rica

Interlink 249
PO Box 02-5635
Miami, FL 33102
506-229-3256
Fax: 506-223-9062
E-mail: ais@aiscr.com
http://www.aiscr.com
A private, non-profit school that was founded in 1970 under the name of Costa Rica Academy. AIS serves approximately 200 students from pre-school through 12th grade.

Austin Briggs Jr, Headmaster
Neli Santiago, Principal

2203 American International School-Freetown

Department of State/MGT
2160 Freetown Place
Washington, DC 20521-2160
232-22-232-480
Fax: 232-22-225-471
E-mail: aisfinfo@yahoo.com
http://www.aisfreetown.websiteanimal.com
A private, non-profit, PreK-8th grade school providing an American curriculum to a multinational community in Freetown, Sierra Leone.

Ndye Njie, Director
Nielette Gordon, Administrative Assistant

2204 American International School-Kingston

1a Olivier Road
Kingston 8
Jamaica
876-977-3625
Fax: 876-977-3625
E-mail: aiskoff@cwjamaica.com
http://www.aisk.com
A non-profit, non-sectarian, private day school funded by tuition income receiving small annual grants from the U.S. Government through it Office of Overseas Schools.

Sean Goudie, Director
Anna Wallace, Lower School Coordinator

2205 American International School-Lesotho

DOS/Administrative Officer
2340 Maseru Place
Washington, DC 20521-2340
266-322-987
Fax: 266-311-963
E-mail: aisl@lesoff.co.za
http://www.aisl.lesoff.co.za
An independent, coeducational day school which offers an American education from preschool through grade 8. The school was founded in 1991 to serve the needs of the American community and other students seeking an English-language education.

Harvey Cohen, Principal

2206 American International School-Libreville

2270 Libreville Place
Washington, DC 20521-2270
241-76-20-03
Fax: 241-74-55-07
E-mail: aisl@internetgabon.com
http://www.aisa.or.ke

Paul Sicard, Director

2207 American International School-Lome

DOS/Administrative Officer
2300 Lome Place
Washington, DC 20521-2300
E-mail: aisl@cafe.tg
http://www.aisa.or.ke
Established in 1967 as a private, coeducational day school offering an educational program to students of all nationalities in pre-kindergarten through grade 8.

Clover Afokpa, Director
Warace Tchamsi, Administrative Assistant

2208 American International School-Lusaka

PO Box 31617
Lusaka
Zambia
260-1-260-509
Fax: 260-1-260-538
E-mail: SpecialPerson@aislusaka.org
http://www.aislusaka.org
Committed to being a leading IB World School, offering a balanced, academically rigorous and internationally recognized college preparatory education.

Chris Muller, Director
Shirley Mee, Business Manager

2209 American International School-Mozambique

DOS/Administrative Officer
2330 Maputo Place
Washington, DC 20521-2330
258-1-49-1994
Fax: 258-1-49-0596
E-mail: aism@aism-moz.com
http://www.aisa.or.ke

Don Reeser, Director

2210 American International School-N'Djamena

DOS/Administrative Officer
2410 N'Djamena Place
Washington, DC 20521-2410
235-52-2103
Fax: 235-51-5654
E-mail: aisn@intent.td
http://www.aisa.or.ke

Gay Mickle, Director

2211 American International School-Nouakchott

2430 Nouakchott Place
Washington, DC 20521-2430
222-2-52967
Fax: 222-2-52967
E-mail: aisnsahara@yahoo.com
http://www.aisn.mr
Committed to provide culturally diverse students a safe, nurturing and respectful learning environment and promotes academic achievement through a curriculum founded on an American educational philosophy.

Sharon Orlins PhD, Director

2212 American Nicaraguan School

c/o American Embassy
Unit No 2710 Box 7, APO AA 34021
Washington, DC 20521-3240

505-278-0029
Fax: 505-267-3088
E-mail: info@ans.edu.ni
http://www.ans.edu.ni
A private, nonsectarian coeducaitonal day school which offers an educaional program from prekindergarten through grade 12 for students of all nationalities.

Fredy Ramirez, Elementary School Principal
Joseph Azmeh, Secondary Principal

2213 American Samoa Department of Education
Pago Pago
American Samoa 96799
011-684-633-5237
Fax: 011-684-633-5733
http://www.doe.as
Is to ensure student success by providing high quality teaching and learning opportunities to all our children

Sili K Sataua

2214 American School Honduras
American Embassy Tegucigalpa
Department of State
Washington, DC 20521-3480
504-239-333
Fax: 504-239-6162
E-mail:
admin_assistant@asamadagascar.org
http://www.amschool.org
A private, coeducational day school which offers an educational program from nursery through grade 12 for students of all nationalities.

James Szoka, Principal

2215 American School-Algiers
American Embassy Algiers
Washington, DC 20520-1
202-265-2800
Fax: 202-667-2174
Richard Gillogly, Principal

2216 American School-Antananarivo
2040 Antananarivo Place
Dulles, VA 20189-2040
261-20-22-420-39
Fax: 261-20-22-345-39
E-mail: miasaadm@gmail.com
http://www.asamadagascar.org
As the only English language institution in Madagascar offering a K-12 diploma program, we challenge our students to actively engage with the exceptional educational opportunities that are available to them in our school.

Jay Long, Director

2217 American School-Asuncion
Avenida Esapaa 1175
PO Box 10093
Asuncion, Paraguay
595-21-600-476
Fax: 595-21-603-518
E-mail: asagator@asa.edu.py
http://www.asa.edu.py
A bilingual learning community of International and Paraguayan families, is to prepare responsible proactive world citizens in a student-centered, caring environment through a college preparatory program that adheres to the highest U.S. and Paraguayan standards of excellence

Dennis Klumpp, Director
David Warken, Elementary Principal

2218 American School-Dschang
Washington, DC 20521-1
Jane French, Principal

2219 American School-Guatemala
11 Calle 1579 Zona 1511 calle 15-79
Guatemala
Guatemala
502-236- 079
Fax: 502-236- 833
E-mail: director@cag.edu.gt
http://www.cag.edu.gt
The school's goal is to educate independent, critical-thinking, responsible, bilingual individuals prepared to meet the challenges of the future.

Tracy Berry-Lazo, General Director
Fabio Corvaglia, High School Principal

2220 American School-Niamey
DOS/Administrative Officer
2420 Niamey Place
Dulles, VA 20189-2420
227-723-942
Fax: 227-723-457
E-mail: asniger@intnet.ne
http://www.geocities.com/asniamey
A coeducational day school offering an educational program from prekindergarten through grade 9, and 10-12 correspondence.

Deborah M Robinson, Director

2221 American School-Port Gentil
1100 Louisiana Street
Suite 2500
Houston, TX 77002-5215
Keith Marriott, Principal

2222 American School-Tegucigalpa
Coronel Lomas del Guijarro
Avenue Repœblica Dominicana Calle
Costa
Tegucigalpa, Honduras
504-239-3333
Fax: 504-239-6162
http://www.amschool.org
Provides a Student Centered, enriching, college-preparatory education that emphasizes social responsibility in a safe, bicultural, and disciplined learning enviroment

James Shepherd, Principal
Liliana Jerkins, Superintendent

2223 American School-Warsaw
Ul Warszawska 202
Konstancin-Jeziorna
Poland 05520
48-22-651-9611
Fax: 48-22-642-1506
E-mail: admissions@asw.waw.pl
http://www.asw.waw.pl
Offers a rigorous, supportive and balanced PK-12 program in English for the international community of Warsaw that is driven by a strong commitment to prepare students for lives as responsible world citizens

Tony Gerlicz, Director
Rebecca Brown, Finance/Operations Director

2224 American School-Yaounde
BP 7475
Yaounde
Cameroon
234-223-0421
Fax: 237-223-6011
E-mail: school@asoy.org
http://asoy.org

Ensures that all students achieve high academic success, demonstrate critical thinking skills, and become responsible and compassionate, global citizens prepared for their next stage in life; as gained through an enriched, American curriculum and offered in a challenging, secure, and diverse environment.

Nanci Shaw, School Director

2225 American-Nicaraguan School
Frente al Club Lomas de Monserrat
PO Box 2670, Managua
Nicaragua
505-2-782-565
Fax: 505-2-673-088
E-mail: elementary@ans.edu.ni
http://www.ans.edu.ni
Provides its multicultural student community with a US-accredited college preparatory program, based on democratic and universal values, that develops critical thinkers and ethical individuals capable of realizing their leadership potential by making meaningful contributions to society.

Stan Key, Director General
Roberto Cardenal, Director of Finance

2226 Amoco Galeota School
PO Box 4381
Houston, TX 77210-4381
Barbara Punch, Principal

2227 Andersen Elementary & Middle School
Unit 14057
APO, Mariana Islands 96543 4057
Guam

http://www.extranet.guam.pac.dodea.edu

2228 Anzoategui International School
PO Box 020010, M-42
Jet Cargo International
Miami, FL 33102-10
58-82-22683
Fax: 58-82-22683
E-mail: aishead@telcel.net.ve
http://www.anaco.net
Grade levels Pre-K through 12, school year August - June

Jorge Nelson EdD, Superintendent

2229 Armenia QSI International School-Yerevan
DOS/Administrative Officer
7020 Yerevan Place
Washington, DC 20521-7020
374-1-391-030
Fax: 374-1-151-438
E-mail: qsiy@arminco.com
http://www.qsi.org
An independent, coeducational day school which offers an educational program from preschool (3-4 years) through grade 12 for students of all nationalities. Enrollment 45.

Arthur W Hudson, Director

2230 Atlanta International School
2890 N Fulton Drive NE
Atlanta, GA 30305-3155
404-841-3840
Fax: 404-841-3873
E-mail: info@aischool.org
http://www.aischool.org
Continuing to develop and deserve a worldwide reputation as an exemplary center of teaching and learning, a school that achieves and sets, within the framework of the International Baccalaureate.Maintaining an optimal size composition of faculty and students so that opportunities for individual learning, mutual understanding, and community feeling are maximized.

Robert Brindley, Headmaster
Charlotte Smith, Executive Assistant

231 Awty International School
7455 Awty School Lane
Houston, TX 77055-7222
713-686-4850
Fax: 713-686-4956
E-mail: admissions@awty.org
http://www.awty.org
Grade level prekindergarten through twelfth, with total enrollment of 900 students.

David Watson, Headmaster
John Ransom, Chairman

232 Azerbaijan Baku International School
Darnagul Qasabasi Street Ajami Nakc
Block 3097
Baku, Azerbaijan 01108
994-12-90-63-52
Fax: 994-12-90-63-51
E-mail: baku@qsi.org
http://www.qsi.org
the primary purpose of the school is to meet the needs of the children in Baku who require this type of education with a view to continuing their education in their home countries with a minimum of adjustment problems.

Scott Root, Director
Arthur W Hudson, Director

233 Baku International School
Darnagul Qasabasi Street Ajami Nakc
Block 3097
Baku, Azerbaijan, AZ 01108
994-12-656352
Fax: 991-12-4105951
E-mail: baku@qsi.org
http://www.qsi.org
the primary purpose of the school is to meet the needs of the children in Baku who require this type of education with a view to continuing their education in their home countries with a minimum of adjustment problems.

Scott Root, Director
Arthur W Hudson, Director

234 Ball Brothers Foundation
222 S Mulberry Street
Muncie, IN 47305
765-741-5500
Fax: 765-741-5518
E-mail: info@ballfdn.org
http://www.ballfdn.org
The Foundation's primary focus is Muncie and East Central Indiana. The Foundation has been a philanthropic leader, serving as initiator, convener, and catalyst among donors and nonprofit organizations. Within Muncie, the Foundation seeks to forge active partnerships with effective nonprofit agencies by providing consultation and financial support to promote their success.

Jud Fisher, Executive Director/ COO
John W Fisher, Chairman & President

235 Banjul American Embassy School
2070 Banjul Place
Dulles, VA 20189-2070
220-495-920
Fax: 220-497-181
E-mail: baes@qanet.gm
http://www.baes.gm
The school demonstrates U.S. education abroad to a multi-ethnic, multi-cultural, diverse student body and otherwise increases mutual understanding through its emphasis on an American-based curriculum, use of American textbooks and supplemental materials, and its teaching staff, of whom four are American nationals trained in American universities.

Dianne Zemichael, Director
Leah Moore, Administrative Secretary

2236 Bingham Academy Ethiopia
SIM International
PO Box 4937
Addis Ababa, Ethiopia
East Africa
251-11 -791
Fax: 251-11 -791
E-mail: director@binghamacademy.net
http://www.binghamacademy.net
The purpose of Bingham Academy is to provide high quality, culturally sensitive education, within a Christian environment, which challenges each student to impact the world for God's glory.

Murray Overton, Director

2237 Bishkek International School
14A Tynystanova Street
Bishkek
Kyrgyzstan 72005
996-312-66-35-03
Fax: 996-312-66-35-03
E-mail: bishkek@qsi.org
http://www.qsi.org
The primary purpose of the school is to meet the needs of the children in Bishkek who require this type of education with a view to continuing their education in their home countries with a minimum of adjustment problems.

MaryKay Gudkova, Director

2238 Bosnia-Herzegovina QSI International School Sarajevo
Omladinska #12
Vogosca-Saravejo
Bosnia & Herzegovina 71320
387-33-434-756
Fax: 387-33-434-756
E-mail: saravejo@qsi.org
http://www.qsi.org
The primary purpose of the school is to meet the needs of the expatriate children living in Sarajevo who require this type of education.

Jay Hamric, Director
Arthur W Hudson, Director

2239 Bratislava American International School
American Embassy Bratislava
Karloveska 64
Bratislava
Slovak Republic 842-2
421-7-722-844
Fax: 721-7-722-844
E-mail: bratislava@qsi.org
http://www.qsi.sk
The primary purpose of the school is to meet the needs of the children in Bratislava who require this type of education with a view to continuing their education in their home countries with a minimum of adjustment problems.

Ronald Adams, Principal
Matthew Lake, Director

2240 Bulgaria Anglo-American School-Sofia
DOS/Administrative Officer
5740 Sophia Place
Washington, DC 20521-5740
359-2-974-4575
Fax: 359-2-974-4483
E-mail: aasregist@infotel.bg
http://www.geocities.com/angloamericanschool

An independent, coeducational day school which offers an educational program from prekindergarten through grade 8 for students of all nationalities. The school year comprises 2 semesters extending from August to December and from January to June. Enrollment 140.

Brian M Garton, Director
Arthur W Hudson, Director

2241 Burma International School Yangon
DOS/Administrative Officer
4250 Rangoon Place
Washington, DC 20521-4250
95-1-512-793/795
Fax: 95-1-525-020
E-mail: ISYDIRECTOR@mptmail.net.mm
http://www.internationalschoolyangon.org
Grades PK-12, enrollment 331.

Merry Wade, Director

2242 Burns Family Foundation
410 N Michigan Avenue
Room 1600
Chicago, IL 60611-4213
Offers support in secondary school education, higher education and youth services.

2243 Caribbean American School
5 Gates Court
Cranbury, NJ 08512-2926
509-257-7961
http://www.isbi.com

Ernestine Rochelle, Principal
Ernestine Roche Robinson, Director

2244 Caribbean-American School
PO Box 407139
Lynx Air
Ft Lauderdale, FL 33340-7139
509-257-7961
http://www.isbi.com
Grade levels Pre-K through 12, school year September - June

Ernestine Roche Robinson, Director
Ernestine Rochelle, Principal

2245 Chinese American International School
150 Oak Street
San Francisco, CA 94102
415-865-6000
Fax: 415-865-6089
E-mail: caishead@aol.com
http://www.cais.org
Educates students for academic excellence, moral character and international perspective through immersion in American and Chinese culture and language.

Andrew W Corcoran, Executive Director

2246 Colegio Albania
PO Box 25573
Miami, FL 33102-5573

Eric Spindler, Principal

2247 Colegio Corazon de Maria
Ferrer y Ferrer-Santiago Igles
San Juan
Puerto Rico

M Cyril Stauss, Principal

2248 Colegio De Parvulos
263 Calle San Sebastian
San Juan 00901-1205
Puerto Rico

Maria Dolores Vice, Principal

2249 Colegio Del Buen Pastor
Camino Alejandrino Km 3.4
Rio Piedras 00927
Puerto Rico

http://www.colegiobuenpastor.com
Adria M Borges, Principal

2250 Colegio Del Sagrado Corazon
Obispado Final Urb La Alhambra
Ponce 00731
Puerto Rico
556- 14-2
http://www.sagradocorazon.edu.co
Joan G Dedapena, Principal

2251 Colegio Espiritu Santo
Box 191715 San Juan
Puerto Rico 00019-1715
787-754-0555
Fax: 754-715-
E-mail: admision@colespiritusanto.com
http://www.colespiritusanto.com
Carmen Jovet, Principal

2252 Colegio Inmaculada
Carr Militar 2 Km 49.6
Manati 00674
Puerto Rico

http://www.colegioinmaculada.es
Sor Nichlasa Maderea, Principal

2253 Colegio Inmaculada Concepcion
2 Calle Isabela
Guayanilla 00656-1703
Puerto Rico

http://www.colegioinmaculada.es
Sor Alejandrina Torres, Principal

2254 Colegio Internacional-Carabobo
VLN 1010
PO Box 025685
Miami, FL 33102-5685
58-41-421-807
Fax: 58-41-426-510
E-mail: admin@cic-valencia.org.ve
http://www.cic-valencia.org.ve
To develop young men and women of character through an international college-preparatory program, in English, based on high intellectual and moral standards

Frank Anderson, Superintendent
Joe Walker, Director

2255 Colegio Internacional-Caracas
PAKMAIL 6030
PO Box 025323
Miami, FL 33102-5304
58-2-945-0444
Fax: 58-2-945-0533
E-mail: cic@cic-caracas.org
http://www.cic-caracas.org
Colegio Internacional de Caracas is an English-medium, Pre-Nursery to Grade 12 school dedicated to the intellectual and personal development of each student in a caring and supportive environment. CIC offers a challenging program to prepare an international student body to excel in a variety of the world's finest schools and universities.

Alan Benson, Superintendent
Carmen Sweeting, Director of Academics

2256 Colegio Internacional-Puerto La Cruz
11010 NW 30th Street
Suite 104
Miami, FL 33172-5032

58-281-277-6051
Fax: 58-281-274-1134
E-mail: ciplc@telcel.net.ve
http://www.ciplc.net
Inspiring students to learn and serve by cultivating each student's full potential as an effective communicator, problem solver, and contributing global citizen.

Mike Martell, Superintendent
Frank Capuccio, Administrative Assistant

2257 Colegio La Inmaculada
1711 Ave Ponce De Leon
San Juan 00909-1905
Puerto Rico
787-754-0555
Fax: 754-715-
http://www.colegioinmaculada.es
Sor Teresa Del Rio, Principal

2258 Colegio La Milagrosa
107 Calle De Diego
San Juan 00925-3303
Puerto Rico
787-754-0555
Fax: 754-715-
http://www.colegioinmaculada.es
Maria Flores, Principal

2259 Colegio Lourdes
Box 190847
San Juan, PR 00919-847
787-767-6106
Fax: 787-767-5282
E-mail: clourdes@coqui.net
http://www.colegiolourdes.net
Forming strong Christian faith and critical, able to make a commitment within the society and the church that is open to the realities and needs of his time, able to integrate into an attitude of service in a democratic society, as understand and explain the Preamble to the Constitution of Puerto Rico.

Paz Asiain, Director
Thalia Lopez, Principal

2260 Colegio Madre Cabrini
1564 Calle Encarnacion
San Juan 00920-4739
Puerto Rico
787-792-6180
http://www.madrecabrini.com.b
Anne Marie Gavin, Principal

2261 Colegio Maria Auxiliadora
PO Box 797
Carolina 00986-0797
Puerto Rico
787-792-6181
http://www.auxiliadora.ne
Leles Rodriguez, Principal

2262 Colegio Marista
Final Santa Ana Alt Torrimar
Guaynabo 00969
Puerto Rico

http://www.marista.org.br
Hilario Martinez, Principal

2263 Colegio Marista El Salvador
PO Box 462
Manati 00674-0462
Puerto Rico

http://www.marista.org.br
Hnio Efrain Romo, Principal

2264 Colegio Mater Salvatoris
RR 3 Box 3080
San Juan 00926-9601
Puerto Rico
821- 99- 963
Fax: 821- 99- 973
http://www.matersalvatoris.org
Maria Luisa Benito, Principal

2265 Colegio Notre Dame Nivel
PO Box 967
Caguas 00726-0967
Puerto Rico

Francisca Suarez, Principal

2266 Colegio Nuestra Senora de La Caridad
PO Box 1164
Caparra Heigh 00920
Puerto Rico

http://www.colegiosdepr.com
Madre Esperanza Sanchez, Principal

2267 Colegio Nuestra Senora de La Merced
PO Box 4048
San Juan 00936-4048
Puerto Rico

http://www.colegiolamercedpr.com
Ivette Lopez, Principal

2268 Colegio Nuestra Senora de Lourdes
1050 Demetrio Odaly-Country Club
Rio Piedras 00924
Puerto Rico

Rita Manzano, Principal

2269 Colegio Nuestra Senora de Valvanera
53 Calle Jose I Quinton # 53
Coamo 00769-3108
Puerto Rico

Cruz Victor Colon, Principal

2270 Colegio Nuestra Senora del Carmen
RR 2, Box 9KK, Carr Trujillo Alt
Rio Piedras 00721
Puerto Rico

Candida Arrieta, Principal

2271 Colegio Nuestra Senora del Pilar
PO Box 387
Canovanas 00729-0387
Puerto Rico

Sor Leonilda Mallo, Principal

2272 Colegio Nuestra Senora del Rosario
Aa7 Calle 5
Bayamon 00959-3719
Puerto Rico
341-425-9781
http://www.maristasrosario.com
Theresita Miranda, Principal

2273 Colegio Nuestra Sra del Rosario
PO Box 1334
Ciales 00638-0414
Puerto Rico
787-871-1318
Fax: 787-871-5797
http://www.maristasrosario.com
Parrochial School - Prekindergarten to 9th grade.

Angel Mendoza, Principal
Padre Gabriel M Jorres, Director

2274 Colegio Padre Berrios
PO Box 7717
San Juan 00916-7717
Puerto Rico

http://www.colegiopadreberrios.webs.com
Sor Enedina Santos, Principal

275 Colegio Parroquial San Jose
PO Box 7718
San Juan 00916-7718
Puerto Rico 00644

http://www.colegiopadreberrios.webs.com
Sor Enedina Santos, Principal

276 Colegio Ponceno
PO Box 7718
San Juan 00916-7718
Puerto Rico 00644
809-848-2525
http://www.colegiopadreberrios.webs.com
Sor Enedina Santos, Principal

277 Colegio Puertorriqueno de Ninas
Calle Turquessa 208
Golden Gate
Guaynabo, PR 00968
787-782-2618
Fax: 787-782-8370
E-mail: Info@cpnpr.org
http://www.cpnpr.org
Ivette Nÿter, School Director
Millie Suau, Principal

278 Colegio Reina de Los Angeles
M-19 Calle Frontera
San Juan, PR 00926
787-761-7455
Fax: 787-761-7440
E-mail: info@reinaangeles.org
http://www.reinaangeles.org
Train Students education with a focus on physical, moral, intellectual, religious and social development within a framework of faith.
Victorina Ortega, Principal
Juana F Gomez, Director

279 Colegio Rosa Bell
Calle Oviedo Number 42
Torrimar-Guaynabo, PR 00966
787-781-4240
Fax: 787-792-5415
E-mail: exalumno@rosabell.com
http://rosabell.wordpress.com
The purpose of a good education is to maximize the capabilities of the individual: intellectually, socially, emotionally and physically.
Rose Rodriquez, Director
Miguel Arzola-Barris, Executive Director

280 Colegio Sacred Heart
Palma Real Urb, Univ Gardens
San Juan 00927
Puerto Rico
Paul Marie, CSB, Principal

281 Colegio Sagrada Familia
7 Hostos
Ponce
Puerto Rico 00731

http://www.safa.edu.uy
Sor Pilar Becerra, Principal

282 Colegio Sagrados Corazones
A Esmeralda Urb, Ponce De Leon
Guaynabo 00969
Puerto Rico

http://home.coqui.net/sagrado
Ana Arce de Marrer, Principal

2283 Colegio San Agustin
PO Box 4263
Bayamon 00958-1263
Puerto Rico

http://csa.edu.ph
Georgina Ortiz, Principal

2284 Colegio San Antonio
PO Box 21350
San Juan 00928-1350
Puerto Rico
809-764-0090
http://www.colegio-san-antonio.org
Rev. Paul S Brodie, Principal

2285 Colegio San Antonio Abad
PO Box 729
Humacao 00792-0729
Puerto Rico
809-764-0090
http://www.colegio-san-antonio.org
Padre Eduardo Torrella, Principal

2286 Colegio San Benito
PO Box 728
Humacao 00792-0728
Puerto Rico

http://www.csb.cl
Hermana Carmen Davila, Principal

2287 Colegio San Conrado (K-12)
PO Box 7111
Ponce 00732-7111
Puerto Rico
Fax: 787-841-7303
E-mail: sanconrado@pucpr.edu
Sister Nildred Rodriguez, Principal
Sister Wilma de Echevarria, Assistant Principal

2288 Colegio San Felipe
566 Ave San Luis # 673
Arecibo 00612-3600
Puerto Rico
809-878-3532
http://www.colegiosanfelipe.edu.mx
Veronica Oravec, Principal

2289 Colegio San Francisco De Asis
PO Box 789
Barranquitas
Puerto Rico 00794
787-857-2123
Fax: 787-857-2123
E-mail: info@csfabarranquitas.com
http://www.csfabarranquitas.com
Founded in August 7, 1985
Hermana Maria Carbonell, Principal
Carlos Colon-Bernadi, Director

2290 Colegio San Gabriel
Gpo Box 347
San Juan 00936
Puerto Rico

http://www.sangabriel.cl
Sor Antonia Garatachea, Principal

2291 Colegio San Ignacio de Loyola
Urb Santa Mar a, 1940 Calle Saœco
San Juan
Puerto Rico 00927
787-765-3814
Fax: 787-758-4145
http://www.sanignacio.org
Dr Luis O Pino, Principal
Mario Alberto Torres, President

2292 Colegio San Jose
PO Box 21300
San Juan
Puerto Rico 00928-1300
787-751-8177
Fax: 787-767-7146
E-mail: sanjose@csj-rpi.org
http://www.csj-rpi.org
Bro Francisco T Gonzalez, Principal
Sra Elaine Torrens, Vice Principal

2293 Colegio San Juan Bautista
PO Box E
Orocovis 00720
Puerto Rico
787-751-8177
Fax: 787-767-7146
http://www.colegiosanjuanbautista.com
Sor Maria Antonia Miya, Principal

2294 Colegio San Juan Bosco
PO Box 14367
San Juan 00916-4367
Puerto Rico

http://www.sanjuanboscosalamanca.eu
Rev. P Jose Luis Gomez, Principal

2295 Colegio San Luis Rey
43 Final SE, Urb Reparto Metro
San Juan 00921
Puerto Rico

Rosario Maria, Principal

2296 Colegio San Miguel
GPO Box 1714
San Juan 00936
Puerto Rico

http://www.sanluisrey.edu.co
Elvira Gonzalez, Principal

2297 Colegio San Rafael
PO Box 301
Quebradillas 00678-0301
Puerto Rico

http://www.maristas.com.a

2298 Colegio San Vicente Ferrer
PO Box 455
Catano 00963-0455
Puerto Rico

Maria Soledad Colon, Principal

2299 Colegio San Vicente de Paul
Calle Bolivar 709, Parada 24
San Juan
Puerto Rico 00909
787-727-4273
Fax: 787-728-2263
http://www.csvp-sj.org
Dra Isabel C Machado, Principal
P Evaristo Oliveras, Director

2300 Colegio Santa Clara
Via 14-2JL-456 Villa Fontana
Carolina 00983
Puerto Rico

http://www.colegiostaclara.com
Elsie Mujica, Principal

2301 Colegio Santa Cruz
PO Box 235
Trujillo Alto 00977-0235
Puerto Rico
113-024-5197
http://www.santacruz.g12.br
Maria Ramon Santiago, Principal

2302 Colegio Santa Gema
PO Box 1705
Carolina 00984-1705
Puerto Rico
491-711-5093
http://www.colegio-santagema.es
Lilia Luna De Anaya, Principal

2303 Colegio Santa Rita
Calle 9, Apartado 1557
Bayamon 00958
Puerto Rico

http://www.colegiosantarita.com.br
Elba N Villalba, Principal

2304 Colegio Santa Rosa
Calle Marti, 15 Esquina Maceo
Bayamon 00961
Puerto Rico

http://www.colegiosantarosa-pa.com.br
Ana Josefa Colon, Principal

2305 Colegio Santa Teresita
342 Victoria
Ponce 00731
Puerto Rico
015-278-1202
http://www.santateresita.edu.pe
Mary Terence, Principal

2306 Colegio Santiago Apostol
Calle 23 Bloque 23 #17, Urb Sierra
Bayamon
Puerto Rico 00961
787-786- 917
Fax: 787-269-3965
E-mail:
colegiosantiagoapostol@onlinkpr.net
http://www.colegiosantiagoapostol.net
Hilda Velazquez, Principal

2307 Colegio Santisimo Rosario
PO Box 26
Yauco 00698-0026
Puerto Rico
Judith Negron, Principal

2308 Colegio Santo Domingo
192 Calle Comerio
Bayamon 00959-5358
Puerto Rico

http://www.colegiosantodomingo.edu.do
Pura Huyke, Principal

2309 Colegio Santo Nino de Praga
PO Box 25
Penuelas 00624-0025
Puerto Rico
Aminta Santos, Principal

2310 Colegio Santos Angeles Custod
3 Sicilia Urb, San Jose
San Juan 00923
Puerto Rico

http://www.angelescustodios.com
Roberto Rivera, Principal

2311 Colegio de La Salle
PO Box 518
Bayamon 00960-0518
Puerto Rico

http://www.colsalle.edu.co
Wilfredo Perez De, Principal

2312 Commandant Gade Special Education School
St. Thomas, Virgin Islands 00801
Miss Jeanne Richards, Principal

2313 Community United Methodist School
PO Box 681
Frederiksted 00841-0681
Virgin Islands
Marva Oneal, Principal

2314 Country Day
RR 1 Box 6199
Kingshill, VI 00850
340-778-1974
Fax: 340-779-3331
E-mail: bsinfield@stxcountryday.com
http://www.stxcountryday.com
An independent, multicultural, college preparatory educational community set on a 34-acre tropical campus.
William Sinfield, Headmaster
Mariska Nurse, Dean of Guidance

2315 Croatia American International School-Zagreb
Vocarska 106
10 000 Zagreb
Croatia-5080
385-1-4680-133
Fax: 385-1-4680-171
E-mail: asz@asz.hr
http://www.aisz.hr
Grades K-8, enrollment 112.
Robin Heslip, Director

2316 Dallas International School
6039 Churchill Way
Dallas, TX 75230
972-991-6379
Fax: 972-991-6608
E-mail: rwkdis@metronet.com
http://www.dallasinternationalschool.org
DIS students will have the skills to continue their studies at universities in the United States or abroad and launch a professional career which will take advantage of all the opportunities created by globalization
Mea Ahlberg, Director of Admissions
MylSne Dumont, Middle School Coordinator

2317 Dominican Child Development Center
PO Box 5668
Agana
Guam 96910
617-477-7228
Fax: 671-472-4782
Kindergarten and nursery school.
Lednor Flores, Principal

2318 Dorado Academy
Urb Dorado del Mar Calle Madre Perl
Dorado
Puerto Rico 00646
787-796-2180
Fax: 787-796-7398
E-mail: mescabi@doradoacademy.org
http://www.doradoacademy.org
Its objective is to provide to all students an education that reflects the school's philosophy. The teachers strive to implement by instruction the school's philosophy and meet instructional goals and objectives.
Liutma Caballero, Principal
Nancy Escabi, Headmaster

2319 Dwight School
291 Central Park W
New York, NY 10024
212-724-7524
Fax: 212-724-2539
E-mail: admissions@dwight.edu
http://www.dwight.edu
Dwight's rigorous IB program and world-class faculty prepare a future generation of well-educated and ethical global leaders who will seek to create an environment of equality and respect for all human beings.
Marina Bernstein, Director Admissions
Alyson Waldman, Associate Director

2320 Educare
4235 Reserve Road
Unit 202
Lexington, KY 40514
859-396-7087
Fax: 859-201-1064
E-mail: mnaidu@educare.org
http://www.educare.org
To inspire children to achieve their very best; to educate children in character and leadership by drawing out their hidden character traits and leadership qualities.
Sara Connell, Principal

2321 Episcopal Cathedral School
PO Box 13305
Santurce
Puerto Rico 00908-3305
787-721-5478
Fax: 787-724-6668
E-mail: esc@gocougars.com
http://www.gocougars.com
Founded in 1946.
Gary J DeHope, Director

2322 Escole Tout Petit
PO Box 1248
San Juan 00902
Puerto Rico
Vivian Aviles, Principal

2323 Escuela Beata Imelda
PO Box 804
Guanica 00653-0804
Puerto Rico
P Salvador Barber, Principal

2324 Escuela Bella Vista
Avenido Cecilio Acosta Calle 67 Ent
Maracaibo
Venezuela
58-61-966-696
Fax: 58-61-969-417
E-mail: ebvnet@ebv.org.ve
http://www.ebv.org.ve
At EBV we offer an internationally enriched accredited U.S. program that prepares our students to participate actively, independently, cooperatively, and effectively in a multicultural, multilingual world. It is our commitment to educate each student to his/her maximum potential.
Steve Sibley, Superintendent
Todd Zukewich, High School Principal

2325 Escuela Campo Alegre
8424 NW 56th Street
Suite CCS 00007
Miami, FL 33166
58-2-993-3230
Fax: 58-2-993-0219
E-mail: info@eca.com.ve
http://www.eca.com.ve
ECA seeks to inspire its students toward the highest standards and expectations through a stimulat-

ing and comprehensive program of intellectual and personal development.

Bambi Betts, Director
Phil Redwine, Principal

326 Escuela Campo Alegre-Venezuela
8424 NW 56th Street
Suite CCS00007
Miami, FL 33166
58-2-993-7135
Fax: 58-2-993-0219
E-mail: info@eca.com.ve
http://www.eca.com.ve
A private, coeducational day school offering a program for students from prekindergarten through grade 12.

Phil Redwine, Principal

327 Escuela Caribe Vista School
8424 NW 56th Street
Suite CCS00007
Miami, FL 33166
765-668-4009
E-mail: info@eca.com.ve
http://www.eca.com.ve

Phil Redwine, Principal

328 Escuela Las Morochas
Apartado Postal # 235
Ciudad Ojeda, Estado Zulia
Venezuela
58-265-6315-539
Fax: 58-265-6315-539
E-mail: jtrudeau@escuelalasmorochas.com
http://www.escuela-lasmorochas.com
Escuela Las Morochas is an English medium international school that offers a challenging U.S. education that encourages students to be life-long learners and responsible global citizens.

Jeff Trudeau, Director
Zulay Marcano, Assistant Secretary

329 Escuela Nuestra Senora Del Carmen
PO Box 116, Playa De Ponce
Ponce 00731
Puerto Rico 00731
266-282-
Fax: 266-253-
http://www.colegionuestrasradelcarmen.edu

Paquita Alvarado, Principal

330 Escuela Superior Catolica
PO Box 4245
Bayamon 00958-1245
Puerto Rico

Eledis Diaz, Principal

331 Evangelical School for the Deaf
HC-01 Buzon 7111
Luquillo
Puerto Rico 00773-9602
787-889-3488
866-928-2836
E-mail: esdluquillo@gmail.com
http://www.esdluquillo.com
We believe that it is the obligation of the saved to witness by life and by words to the truths of Scripture, and to seek to proclaim the Gospel to all mankind.

Pamela Eadie, Principal
Hector Saroza, President

332 Fajardo Academy
55 Calle Federico Garcia
PO Box 1146, Fajardo 00648
Puerto Rico
809-863-1001
http://fajardoacademy.org

Miguel A Rivera, BA, MA, MEd, Principal

2333 Freewill Baptist School
PO Box 6265
Christiansted 00823-6265
Virgin Islands

http://www.freewillschool.com
Joe Postlewaite, Principal

2334 French-American International School
150 Oak Street
San Francisco, CA 94102
415-558-2000
Fax: 415-558-2024
E-mail: fais@fais-ihs.org
http://www.fais-ihs.org
Grade levels preK-12, with total student enrollment of 813.

Jane Camblin, Head of School

2335 George D Robinson School
5 Nairn Condado
Santurce 00907
Puerto Rico
845-344-2292
http://www.orangeahrc.org

Daniel W Sheehan, Principal

2336 Georgetown American School
3170 Georgetown Place
Washington, DC 20521-3170
592-225-1595
Fax: 592-226-1459
E-mail: admin@amschoolguyana.net
http://www.geocities.com/Athens/Atlantis/6811

Thurston Riehl, Director

2337 Georgia QSI International School-Tbilisi
Village Zurgovani
Tbilisi
Republic of Georgia
995-32-982909
Fax: 995-32-322-607
E-mail: tbilisi@qsi.org
http://www.qsi.org/grg_home
A private non-profit organization, organizes and operates schools of excellence, identifies quality educators for these schools, and provides educational consulting services

Scott D'Alterio, Director
David Pera, Director Instruction

2338 Glynn Christian School
Club 6, Christian Hill
St Croix, Kingshill 00851
Virgin Islands
340-778-1932
http://www.virginislandsdailynews.com

Muriel Francis, Principal

2339 Good Hope School-St. Croix
Estate Good Hope Frederiksted
St Croix 00840
Virgin Islands
340-778-1932
http://www.virginislandsdailynews.com

Tanya L Nichols, Principal

2340 Good Shepherd School
PO Box 1069
St Croix, Kingshill 00851
Virgin Islands 00851
340-772-2280
Fax: 340-772-1021
http://www.virginislandsdailynews.com

Mary Ellen Mcencil, Director
Susan P Eversley, Assistant Director

2341 Grace Baptist Academy
7815 Shallowford Road
Chattanooga, TN 37421
423-892-8223
Fax: 423-892-1194
E-mail: jmccurdy@gracechatt.org
http://www.gracechatt.org

Helen Yasper, Principal

2342 Guam Adventist Academy
1200 Aguilar Road
Yoa
Guam 96915
617-789-1515
Fax: 617-789-3547
E-mail: Office@GAAsda.org
http://www.gaasda.org
Learn about God and His character through Bible study, aided by the study of nature and E.G. White's writings. Develop a personal friendship with Jesus Christ

John N Youngberg, Principal
Dori Talon, Accountant

2343 Guam Department of Education
PSC 455 Box 192
FPO, Mariana Islands 96540 1192
Guam 96915-1054
011-671-475-0457
Fax: 011-671-472-5003
http://www.gdoe.net
Develop a personal friendship with Jesus Christ

Rosie R Tainatongo, Director

2344 Guam High School
PSC 455 Box 192
FPO, Mariana Islands 96540 1192
Guam 96915-1054
671-475-0462
Fax: 671-472-5003
http://www.gdoe.net

Rosie R Tainatongo, Director

2345 Guam S Elementary & Middle School
PSC 455 Box 192
FPO, Mariana Islands 96540 1192
Guam 96915-1054
671-475-0462
Fax: 671-472-5003
http://www.gdoe.net

Rosie R Tainatongo, Director

2346 Guamani School
PO Box 3000
Guayama
Puerto Rico 00785
787-864-6880
Fax: 787-866-4947
E-mail: edelgado@guamani.com
http://www.guamani.com
A private non-profit, co-educational, non-sectarian school committed in offering an English-based academic college preparatory program geared in preparing students to become knowledgeable and responsible individuals for today's changing society.

Eduardo Delgado, Director
Pedro A Dominguez, Administrator

2347 Harvest Christian Academy
PO Box 23189
Barrigada
Guam 96921
671-477-6341
Fax: 671-477-7136
http://www.harvestministries.net

Harvest Christian Academy is a K-12th grade school. It is a ministry of Harvest Baptist Church.

John McGraw, Principal

2348 Hogar Colegio La Milagrosa
Ave Cotto 987 Barrio Cotto
Arecibo 00612
Puerto Rico 00612
787-878-0341
http://www.hogarcolegiolamilagrosa.com

Sor Trinidad Ibizarry, Principal

2349 India American Embassy School-New Delhi
Chandragupta Marg Chanakyapuri
New Delhi
India 11002
91-11-611-7140
Fax: 91-11-687-3320
E-mail: aesindia@aes.ac.in
http://aes.ac.in
The American Embassy School serves students from the United States and other nations. It provides a quality American education that enables students to be inspired learners and responsible global citizens through the collaboration of a dedicated faculty and a supportive community.

Bob Hetzel, Director

2350 India American International School-Bombay
6240 Mumbai Place
Dulles, VA 20189
91-22-652-1837
Fax: 91-22-652-1838
E-mail: personnel@asbindia.org
http://www.asbindia.org
We inspire all of our students to continuous inquiry, empowering them with the skills, courage, optimism, and integrity to pursue their dreams and enhance the lives of others.

Paul M Fochtman, Superintendent
Julie A Cox, Elementary School Principal

2351 Inter-American Academy
Suite 8227
6964 NW 50th Street
Miami, FL 33166-5632
593-4-871-790
Fax: 593-4-873-358
E-mail: bgoforth@acig.k12.ec
http://www.acig.k12.ec

Dr. Bruce Goforth, Executive Director

2352 International Community School-Abidjan
DOS/Administrative Officer
2010 Abidjan Place
Washington, DC 20521-2010
225-22-47-11-52
Fax: 225-22-47-19-96
E-mail: rmockrish@icsa.ac.ci
http://www.icsa.ac.ci
American style curriculum from kindergarten through grade 12 for children of all nationalities.

Rob Mockrish, Director

2353 International High School-Yangon
4250 Rangoon Place
Department of State
Washington, DC 20521-4250
95-1-512-793
Fax: 95-1-525-020
E-mail: isydirector@mptmail.net.mm

http://www.internationalschoolyangon.org

Merry Wade, Director

2354 International School of Port-of-Spain
#POS 1369 1601 NW 97th Avenue
PO Box 025307
Miami, FL 33102-5307
868-632-4591
Fax: 868-632-4595
E-mail: elarson@isps.edu.tt
http://www.isps.edu.tt
ISPS will provide an outstanding educational programme for both international and resident families who want their children to pursue higher education.

Eric Larson, Director
John Horsfall, High School Principal

2355 International School-Conakry
2110 Conakry Place
Washington, DC 20521-2110
224-12-661-535
Fax: 224-41-15-22
E-mail: isc@biasy.net
http://www.iscguinea.org
A private, coeducational school offering an educational program from pre-kindergarten through grade 12 for children from expatriate and host country families. Develop pupils' academic knowledge; learning, thinking, social, and communication skills; international attitudes; and appreciation for cultural diversity.

Greg Hughes, Director
Robert Merritt, Management Officer

2356 International School-Dakar
BP 5136
Dakar
Senegal
221-033- 250
Fax: 221-033- 250
E-mail: admin_isd@orange.sn
http://www.isd.sn
An independent English-medium international school, which offers, in a nurturing environment, a rigorous, US-based, PK-12 curriculum enriched to reflect the needs and diversity of its international student body and faculty.

Wayne Rutherford, Director

2357 International School-Grenada
Washington, DC 20521-1

http://www.international-schoolfriends.com

Mary Delaney Dunn, Principal

2358 International School-Havana
Department of State
18 Street, 315 and 5th Avenue
Miramar, Havana City
Cuba 10600
053- 02- 281
Fax: 530-020-2740
E-mail: office@ish.co.cu
http://www.ishav.org
The school offer high quality education to the children of the expatriate community in Cuba. Serves and can admit students who have a foreign (non-Cuban) citizenship, and are temporarily living in Cuba with their parent(s) or guardian(s), and as such form part of the diplomatic or expatriate non-diplomatic community in the country.

Ian Morris, Principal
Richard Fluit, Head, Secondary School

2359 International School-Islamabad
H-9/1, PO Box 1124
Islamabad
Pakistan 44000
92-51-434-950
Fax: 92-51-440-193
E-mail: school@isoi.edu.pk
http://www.isoi.edu.pk
Offers an American- based curriculum to students of over 29 nationalities.

Rose C Puffer, Superintendent

2360 International School-Ouagadougou
s/c Ambassade des, Etats Unis
01 BP35, Ouagadougou
Burkina Faso
226-36-21-43
Fax: 226-36-22-28
E-mail: iso@iso.bf
http://www.iso.bf
ISO strives to cultivate a student's intellect and character in an English-speaking environment, offering strong academic programs and promoting cultural understanding.

Larry Ethier, Director
Kim Overton, Curriculum Coordinator

2361 International School-Port of Spain
1601 NW 97th Avenue
PO Box 025307
Miami, FL 33102-5307
868-633-4777
Fax: 868-632-4595
E-mail: elarson@isps.edu.tt
http://www.isps.edu.tt
Provides a college preparatory, holistic education for children in grades pre-kindergarten through grade 12, providing them with the skills, knowledge, and values necessary to be productive individuals in an interdependent world.

Eric Larson, Director
Jackie Fung-Kee-Fung, Admission Director/PR

2362 International School-Sfax
Brit Gas 1100 Louisiana
Houston, TX 77002

Sidney Norris, Principal

2363 International School-Yangon
20 Shwe Taungyar
Bahan Township, Yangon
Myanmar-1
512-93 -
Fax: 95 - 52-020
E-mail: director@isy.net.mm
http://www.isy.net.mm
We inspire students with a challenging, international education, based on an American curriculum, in a nurturing learning environment that promotes responbibility and respect. We aim to develop socially engaged, self-motivated, creative, compassionate individuals who will be a force for positive change in their communities and the world.

DJ Condon, Middle/High School Principal
Dennis MacKinnon, Director

2364 Izmir American Institute
Friends-850 Third Avenue
18th Floor
New York, NY 10022
232-355-0555
http://www.aci.k12.tr

Richard Curtis, Principal

2365 John F Kennedy School-Queretaro
Sabinos #272, Jurica
Queretaro
Mexico 76100
442-218-0075
Fax: 442-218-1784

E-mail: admissions@jfk.edu.mx
http://www.jfk.edu.mx
The American School of Queretaro, is to provide the whole individual an opportunity for high quality U.S. type, bilingual education that recognizes individual talents and encourages lifelong learning

Dr. Francisco Galicia, Principal
Mirtha Stappung, General Director

366 Jordan American Community School
PO Box 310, Dahiat Al-Amir Rashid
Amman 11831
Jordan
962-6-581-3944
Fax: 962-6-582-3357
E-mail: school@acsamman.edu.jo
http://www.acsamman.edu.jo
ACS is fully accredited K-12 by the Middle States Association of Colleges and Schools and is a member in good standing of NESA, the Near East South Asia Association of Overseas Schools

Dr. Gray Duckett, Superintendent

367 Karachi American Society School
American Consulate General Karachi
610 Karachi Place
Washington, DC 20521-6150
92-21-453-909619
Fax: 92-21-453-7305
http://www.kas.edu.pk

David Holmer, Principal

368 Kongeus Grade School
44-46 Gade
St Thomas 00802
Virgin Islands 00802

Veronica Miller, Principal

369 Lincoln International School-Kampala
Co of State
Washington, DC 20521-1

Margaret Bell, Principal

370 Lincoln School
Lincoln School 565-20
PO Box 025331
Miami, FL 33102-5331
506-224- 660
Fax: 506-224- 670
E-mail: director@ns.lincoln.ed.cr
http://www.lincoln.ed.cr
offer an integrated education, using English as the primary language of instruction, to motivate a continuing search for excellence and stimulate students to fully develop their potential to become responsible, enterprising, creative, open-minded citizens with solid ethical values, committed to democracy, and capable of being successful in a multicultural, global society.

Charles Prince, Principal

371 Lincoln-Marti Schools
2700 SW 8 Street
Miami, FL 33135
305-643-4888
877-874-1999
Fax: 305-649-2767
E-mail: info@lincoln-marti.com
http://www.lincolnmarti.com
Lincoln-Mart is an institution dedicated to educating the future of our community, both academically and socially.

Demitrio Perez, President

2372 Little People's Learning Center
9605 SE 7th Street
Vancouver, WA 98664
360-892-7570
E-mail: info@lplc.net
http://www.lplc.net/home.html

Daphne Maynard, Principal
Becky Dolan, Director

2373 Little School House
47 Kongens Gade
St Thomas 00802
Virgin Islands
416-303-7282
http://www.littleschoolhouse.ca

Carol Struiell, Principal

2374 Luanda International School
Rua da Talatona Caixa 1566
Barrio da Talatona Luanda Sul Samba
Republica de Angola
244-2-44-3416
Fax: 244-2-44-3416
E-mail: officesec@lisluanda.com
http://www.lisluanda.com
offers a balanced, academically challenging, English language education to the international community of Luanda, designed to develop individuals who are both independent learners and international citizens.

Anthony Baron, Director
Di Atkinson, Senior Administrator

2375 Lutheran Parish School
#1 Lille Taarne Gade
Charlotte Aml 00802
Puerto Rico 00802

Nancy Gotwalt, Principal

2376 Manor School
236 La Grande Princesse
Christiansted, VI 00820-4449
340-718-1448
Fax: 340-718-3651
E-mail: jgadd@manorschoolstx.com
http://www.manorschoolstx.com
is dedicated to personal and academic growth in an extended-family environment. We promote academic confidence, creativity, community involvement and citizenship, a sense of respon-sibility, and positive decision-making. We strive to ensure that our graduates are person-ally and academically prepared to succeed in their future endeavors.

Judith C Gadd, Headmistress
Hanley Hamed, Office Manager

2377 Maranatha Christian Academy
9201 75th Avenue N
Brooklyn Park, MN 55428
612- 58- 285
Fax: 763-315-7294
E-mail: info@mca.lwcc.org
http://www.maranathachristianacademy.org
is to offer a pre-kindergarten through 12th grade traditional classroom education providing a quality educational experience, which encourages and enables students to mature spiritually, intellectually, physically, emotionally, and socially in accordanc

Rev. Gary Sprunger, Principal
Brian Sullivan, Chief Administrator

2378 Martin De Porress Academy
621 Elmont Road
Elmont, NY 11003
516-502-2840
Fax: 516-502-2841
E-mail: sfagin@mdp.org
http://www.mdp.org/
The Martin De Porress Academy program provides academic instruction based upon

the NY State Learning Standards as well as hands on experiences in business enterprises, performing arts, home improvement skills, life skills, culinary arts, maintenance services and community services.

Raymond R Blixt, Executive Director
Philip E Chance, Assistant Executive Director

2379 Montessori House of Children
572 Dunholme Way
Suite 103
Sunnyvale, CA 94086
408-749-1602
http://www.sunnyvalemontessori.com
Our program is based on the premise that every child is an individual with his own needs and abilities. All children need affection and friendliness. They require affirmation, encouragement and understanding

William Myers, Principal
Priya Medelberg, Founder-Director

2380 Moravian School
4313 Green Pond Road
Bethlehem
Virgin Islands
610-868-4744
http://www.moravianacademy.org
This Moravian affiliated school offers a curriculum based in English for 200 day students (96 boys; 104 girls), in grades K-6. The school is willing to participate in a teacher exchange program, with the length of stay being one year, with housing provided. Applications include science, Spanish and computer skills.

Condon L Joseph, Principal

2381 Morrocoy International
MUN 4051
PO Box 025352
Miami, FL 33102-5352
58-286-9520016
Fax: 58-286-9521861
E-mail: kempenich@telcel.net.ve
http://www.geocities.com/minaspov
Grade levels Pre-K through 10, school year August - June

Michael Kempenich, Headmaster

2382 Mount Carmel Elementary School
PO Box 7830
Agat 96928 0830
Guam-b830
256-852-7187
Fax: 256-852-0039
http://www.vrml.k12.la.us/mc
This Catholic school offers an English (primary) curriculum for 206 day students (100 boys; 106 girls), in Kinder 4 - 8th grade. Overseas teachers are accepted, with the length of stay being one year. Applications needed to teach include reading, English and counseling/counselor.

Bernadette Quintanilla, Sr, SSND, Principal
Augustin Gumataotao, Administrator

2383 Nazarene Christian School
385 Hazel Mill Road
Asheville, NC 28806
828-252-9713
E-mail:
ncsoffice@ashevillefirstnazarene.org
http://www.ashevillefirstnazarene.org
The Nazarene International Center provides support services to more than 1.2 million members worshiping in more than 11,800 churches in the United States, Canada, and 135 other world areas

Peggy Neighbors, Administrator

2384 Nepal Lincoln School
Kathmandu (LS)
Department of State
Washington, DC 20521-6190
977-1-270-482
Fax: 977-1-272-685
E-mail: info@lsnepal.com.np
http://www.lsnepal.com
Lincoln School is an independent, international school in Kathmandu, Nepal with an American Curriculum. We are committed to nurture of the individual student, excellence in all spheres of achievement, pursuit of personal responsibility, appreciation of diversity, and love of learning

Allan Bredy, Director
Craig Baker, Principal

2385 Northern Mariana Islands Department of Education
PO Box 501370 CK
Siapan, MP 96950
011-670-664-3720
Fax: 011-670-664-3798
http://www.cnmipss.org

Rita Hocog Inos, Commissioner

2386 Notre Dame High School
480 S San Miguel Street
Talofofo
Guam 96930-4699
671-789-1676
http://www.ndhs.org
Notre Dame is a co-educational, year-round high school run by the School Sisters of Notre Dame. This Roman Catholic affiliated school offers a curriculum in English for 191 day students and 9 boarding (32 boys; 168 girls), in grades 9-12. Student/teacher ratio is 10:1, and the applications needed to teach include science, math, social sciences, and English.

Regina Paulino, SSND, Principal

2387 Nuestra Senora de La Altagracia
672 Calle Felipe Gutierrez #672
San Juan 00924-2225
Puerto Rico

2388 Nuestra Senora de La Providencia
PO Box 11610
San Juan 00922-1610
Puerto Rico

2389 Okinawa Christian School
1835 Zakimi
Yomitan, Okinawa
Japan 904-0
098-958-3000
Fax: 098-958-6279
E-mail: info@ocsi.org
http://www.ocsi.org
A non-denominational mission whose purpose is to partner with families of the international community of Okinawa by offering an excellent Christian education in the English language.

Paul Gieschen, Principal

2390 Open Classroom
PO Box 4046
St Thomas 00803
Virgin Islands 00803
805-904-5931
805-289-1817
Fax: 852- 54- 133
http://www.openclassroom.stanford.edu

Janie Lang, Principal

2391 Osaka International School
4-16 Onohar Nishi 4-Chome
Mino, Osaki, 562-0032
Japan
072-727-5050
Fax: 072-727-5055
E-mail: addmissions@senri.ed.jp
http://www.senri.ed.jp
OIS is an english-language-based, preK-12 grade coeducational college-preparatory school.

John Searle, Head of School

2392 Palache Bilingual School
PO Box 1832
Arecibo 00613-1832
Puerto Rico

Rev. David Valez, Principal

2393 Peace Corp
1111 20th Street NW
Washington, DC 20526
202-692-1470
800-424-8580
Fax: 202-692-1897
E-mail: psa@peacecorps.gov
http://www.peacecorps.gov
Helping the people of interested countries in meeting their need for trained men and women. Helping promote a better understanding of Americans on the part of the peoples served

2394 Pine Peace School
PO Box 1657
St John, VI 00831
340-776-6595
E-mail: pinepeace@viaccess.net
http://www.pinepeaceschool.k12.vi
An independent, non-profit, English language school that serves students without regard to sex, race, religion, or nationality.

Beth Knight, Headmistress

2395 Ponce Baptist Academy
72 Calle 1 Belgica
Ponce 00731
Puerto Rico

Vivian Medina, Principal

2396 Prophecy Elementary School
PO Box 10497
APO St Thomas 00801-3497
Virgin Islands 00801
340-775-7223
Fax: 340-714-5354
E-mail: pai@prophecyacademy.org
http://www.prophecyacademy.net
Church of God of Prophecy Academy, Inc. offers a Christian atmosphere which develops the physical, spiritual, intellectual and the social skills of every student. Our primary purpose is to help train students while teaching them the Christian way of life.

Anne E Bramble-Johnson, Principal
VeronaCeleste Hutchinson, Secretary/Office Manager

2397 Puerto Rico Department of Education
PO Box 190759
San Juan
Puerto Rico 00919-759
787-759-2000
http://www.de.gobierno.pr

Cesar A Rey-Hernandez, Secretary

2398 QSI International School-Chisinau
18 Anton Crihan Street
Chisinau
Moldova 20521-7080
373-24-2366
E-mail: chisinau@qsi.org
http://www.qsi.org
To keep this urge to learn alive in every child in QSI schools. Our schools are established to provide in the English language a quality education for students in the cities we serve.

Sandra Smith, Director

2399 QSI International School-Skopje
Inlindenska BB, Reon 55
1000 Skopje
Macedonia 20521-7120
389-91-367-678
Fax: 389-91-362-250
E-mail: skopje@qsi.org
http://www.qsi.org
To keep this urge to learn alive in every child in QSI schools. Our schools are established to provide in the English language a quality education for students in the cities we serve.

Robert Tower, Director
Aleksandar Kostadinovski, Finance Manager

2400 QSI International School-Vladivostok
DOS/Administrative Officer
5880 Vladivostok Place
Washington, DC 20521-5880
7-4232-321-292
Fax: 7-4232-313-684
E-mail: qsiisv@fastmail.vladivostok.ru
http://www.qsi.org
Grades preK-9, enrollment 18.

Harold M Strom Jr, Director

2401 Rainbow Development Center
PO Box 7618
Christiansted 00823-7618
Virgin Islands
408-215-1386
http://www.rainbowccc.com

Gloria Henry, Principal

2402 Rainbow Learning Institute
PO Box 75
Christiansted 00821-0075
Virgin Islands
408-215-1386
http://www.rainbowccc.com

Alda Lockhart, Principal

2403 Rainbow School
PO Box 422
Charlotte Aml 00801
Virgin Islands
408-215-1386
http://www.rainbowccc.com

Louise Thomas, Principal

2404 Robinson School
5 Nairn Street Condado
San Juan 00907
Puerto Rico 00907
1-787-728-6767
Fax: 1-787-727-7736
E-mail: robinson_school@hotmail.com
http://www.robinsonschool.org
The Heart of Educational Excellence. Robinson offers its students a solid foundation for their future academic and career pursuits.

Giberto Quintana, Executive Director
Hugh Andrews, President

2405 Roosevelt Roads Elementary School
PO Box 420132
Roosevelt Roads 00742-0132
Puerto Rico
787-865-3073
Fax: 787-865-4891
http://www.netdial.caribe.net

406 Roosevelt Roads Middle & High School
PO Box 420131
Roosevelt Roads 00742-0131
Puerto Rico
787-865-4000
Fax: 787-865-4893
E-mail: wjames@caribe.net
http://www.antilles.odedodea.edu

Waynna James, Principal

407 Saint Anthony School
529 Chalan San Antonio
Tamuning
Guam 96913
671-647-1140
Fax: 471-649-7130
http://stanthonyschoolguam.org/index.php
A Catholic co-educational elementary school in the Archdiocese of Agana, exists to educate the whole person by providing a rich integrated curriculum served by enabling adults.

Doris San Agustin, Principal
Elizabeth E San Nicolas, Vice-Principal

408 Saint Eheresas Elementary School
2701 Indian Mound Trail
Coral Gables
American Samoa, ÿF
305-446-1738
Fax: 305-446-2877
http://www.cotlf.org

Sister Katherine, Principal

409 Saint Francis Elementary School
2701 Indian Mound Trail
Coral Gables
American Samoa, ÿF
305-446-1738
Fax: 305-446-2877
http://www.cotlf.org

Sister Gaynor Ana, Principal

410 Saint John's School
911 N Marine Corps Drive
Tumon Bay 96913
Guam
671-646-8080
Fax: 617-649-6791
E-mail: info@stjohns.edu.gu
http://www.stjohns.edu.gu
St. John's students on average score in the top 20% on national scholastic achievement tests in all academic subjects in all grades K-12, a tangible result of an integrated academic program supported by a dedicated faculty, many with advanced degrees in their respective areas of instruction

Glenn Chapin, Headmaster
Imelda D Santos, Dean of Students

411 Saint John's School, Puerto Rico
1454-66 Ashford Avenue
San Juan 00907
Puerto Rico
787-728-5343
Fax: 787-268-1454
http://www.sjspr.org/home.aspx
Saint John's School is a college preparatory, nonsectarian, coeducational day school founded in 1915. The school, located in a residential area of the Condado, has an enrollment of approximately 750 students from preschool to grade twelve. 84% come from Hispanic backgrounds, 8% percent from diverse backgrounds and 8% from the continental United States. With the exception of Spanish and French classes, instruction is in English.

Louis R Christiansen, Principal
Barry Farnham, Headmaster

2412 Saints Peter & Paul High School
900 High Street
Easton, MD
410-822-2275
Fax: 410-822-1767
E-mail: jnemeth@ssppeaston.org
http://www.ssppeaston.org/schools/high_school
Saints Peter and Paul High School is a parochial, Catholic, college preparatory,

James Nemeth, Principal
Carolyn Hayman, Administrative Assistant

2413 Samoa Baptist Academy
Tafuna
Pago Pago 96799
American Samoa

Janice Yerton, Principal

2414 San Carlos & Bishop McManus High School
PO Box Loo 9, Yumet
Aguadilla 00605
Puerto Rico
504-246-5121
E-mail: questions@bishopmcmanus.ws
http://www.bishopmcmanus.ws

Nydia U Nieves, Principal

2415 San Vincente Elementary School
San Vincente School Drive
Soledad
Puerto Rico 96913
671-734-4242
http://www.soledad.monterey.k12.ca
This campus is on five acres of outside Barrigada Village. The average enrollment of 460 students consists of 234 boys and 226 girls in grades PreK-8. SVS holds a Certificate of Accreditation from the Western Association of Schools and Colleges until 1998. Length of stay for overseas teachers is two years, with housing provided. Applications needed to teach include English and physical education.

Adrian Cristobal, Principal
Tarcisia Sablan SSND, Faculty Head

2416 Santa Barbara School
274A W Santa Barbara Avenue
Dededo
Guam 96929
671-632-5578
Fax: 671-632-1414
http://www.santabarbaraschool.org
To ensure that each student is given the opportunity to realize his or her full potential according to God's design by recognizing and affirming the gifts of each child.

Sr Jeanette Mar Pangelinan, Principal
Sr Maria Rosari Gaite, Vice Principal

2417 Santiago Christian School
PO Box 5600
Santiago
Dominican Republic, FL 33310-5600
809-570-6140
http://www.santiagochristianschool.org

Lloyd Haglund, Principal

2418 School of the Good Shepherd
1069 Kinghill
St Croix 00851
Virgin Islands 00851

http://www.goodshepherdtvm.org

Linda Navarro, Principal

2419 Seventh Day Adventist
PO Box 7909
St Thomas 00801-0909
Virgin Islands

Josiah Maynard, Principal

2420 Shekou International School
Jing Shan Villas, Nan Hai Road Shek
Guangdong Province
China 51806
86-755-2669-3669
Fax: 86-755-2667-4099
E-mail: sis@sis.org.cn
http://www.sis.org.cn
Shekou International School follows a rigorous college preparatory US style curriculum and is dedicated to meeting the outcomes of the Expected Student Learning Results.

Robert Dunseth, Director
Jennifer Lees, Curriculum Coordinator

2421 Slovak Republic QSI International School of Bratislava
Karloveska 64
Bratislava
Slovak Republic 84220
421-2-6541-1636
Fax: 421-2-6541-1646
E-mail: bratislava@qsi.org
http://www.qsi.sk
THE PRIMARY PURPOSE of the school is to meet the needs of the children in Bratislava who require this type of education with a view to continuing their education in their home countries with a minimum of adjustment problems.

Ronald Adams, Principal
Matthew Lake, Director

2422 Slovenia QSI International School-Ljubljana
Dolgi Most 6A
Ljubljana
Slovenia 01000
386-1-439-6300
Fax: 386-1-439-6305
E-mail: bratislava@qsi.org
http://www.qsi.org/sln_home
THE PRIMARY PURPOSE of the school is to meet the needs of the children in Ljubljana who require this type of education with a view to continuing their education in their home countries with a minimum of adjustment problems.

Ronald Adams, Principal
Matthew Lake, Director

2423 South Pacific Academy
PO Box 520
Pago Pago 96799 0520
American Samoa
644-237-4072
http://www.spa.ac.nz

Tina Senrud, Principal

2424 Southern Peru Staff Schools-Peru
180 Maiden Lane
New York, NY 10038-4925

http://www.isbi.com

John Dansdill, Principal

2425 St. Croix Christian Academy
26-28 Golden Rock, Christiansted, S
PO Box 716
Virgin Islands, US 00821
340-718-4974
Fax: 340-718-6768
E-mail: stccacademy@vipowernet.net
http://www.stcroixchristianacademy.com

The mission of the school is to foster knowledge of God and to give the children a solid academic foundation, along with effective Christian training.

Linus Gittens, Principal

2426 St. Croix Country Day School
Rt-01, Box 6199
Kingshill
Virgin Islands, US 00850
1-340-778-1974
Fax: 1-340-779-3331
E-mail: bsinfield@stxcountryday.com
http://www.stxcountryday.com
It is dedicated to providing students with an enriched and challenging education, encouraging them to love learning, grow as individuals and be prepared for a productive and responsible future.

Bill Sinfield, Headmaster
Susan Gibbons, Business Manager

2427 St. Croix Moravian School
PO Box 117
St Thomas 00801
Virgin Islands

http://www.aavirginislands.org
Condon L Joseph, Principal

2428 St. Croix SDA School
PO Box 930
Kingshill 00851-0930
Virgin Islands

http://www.stcroixsdaschool.org
Peter Archer, Principal

2429 St. Joseph High School
PO Box 517
Frederiksted 00841-0517
Virgin Islands

Kevin Marin, Principal

2430 St. Patrick School
PO Box 988
Frderiksted 00841-0988
Virgin Islands

http://www.spsasansol.com
Juliette Clarke, Principal

2431 St. Peter & Paul Elementary School
PO Box 1706
St Thomas 00803
Virgin Islands

http://www.sppschool.org
Annamay Komment, Principal

2432 Sunbeam
36 Hospital Ground
St Thomas 00803
Virgin Islands
202-427-2383
Fax: 202-426-0308
http://www.sunbeaminfo.com
Ione Leonard, Principal

2433 Syria Damascus Community School
6110 Damascus Place
Dulles, VA 20189-6110
963-11-333-0331
Fax: 963-11-332-1457
E-mail: dcs-dam@net.sy
http://www.dcssyria.org
An independent, coeducational day school which offers an American educational pro-

gram from preschool through grade 12 for students of all nationalities.

John Gates, Director
Maura Connelly, Chairman

2434 Tashkent International School
7117 Tashkent Place
Dulles, VA 20189-7110
998-71-191-9671
Fax: 998-71-120-6621
E-mail: office@tashschool.org
http://www.tashschool.org
To provide a high academic standard of education, educating students to become ethical, responsible, productive citizens of the world with the skills to think creatively, reason critically, and to communicate effectively

John Thomas, Director

2435 Teaching in Austria
Austrian Institute
11 E 52nd Street
New York, NY 10022-5301
212-579-5165

2436 Temple Christian School
PO Box 3009
Agana 96910
Guam 96910

Rev. Ray Fagan, Principal

2437 Tirana International School-Albania
Kutia Postare
Tirana
Albania, DC 01527-9510
355-4-365-239
Fax: 335-4-227-734
E-mail: tirana@qsi.org
http://www.qsi.org
The school's educational philosophy, which includes a personalized approach to instruction, leads to teaching for mastery.

Ronald Adams, Principal
Matthew Lake, Director

2438 Trinity Christian School
1231 East Pleasant Run Road
Yiga 96929 0343
Cedar Hill, TX 75104
972-291-2505
Fax: 972-291-4739
http://www.trinitychristianschool.com
Being a Christian school means we assist parents in fulfilling their divine responsibility to thoroughly train each child to obey God in every area of life and make him or her a true disciple of Jesus Christ. Our program is designed to challenge and educate students of good moral character who are in the middle to upper range of academic ability

Kathleen L Watts, Superintendent
Rhonda Parker, Executive Assistant

2439 Turkmenistan Ashgabat International School
Box 2002
7070 Ashgabat Place
Washington, DC 20521-7070
967-1-234-437
Fax: 967-1-234-438
E-mail: director@ais.cat.glasnet.ru
Grades K-11, enrollment 75.

Scott Root, Director

2440 Ukraine Kiev International School-An American Institution
EOS/Administrative Officer
5850 Kiev Place
Washington, DC 20521-5850
380-44-452-2792
Fax: 380-44-452-2998
E-mail: kisukr@sovamua.com
http://www.kis.net.ua
An independent, coeducational day school which offers an educational program from prekindergarten through high school for students of all nationalities.

E Michael Tewalthomas, Director

2441 United Nations International School
24-50 FDR Drive
New York, NY 10010-4046
212-684-7400
Fax: 212-685-5023
E-mail: admissions@unis.org
http://www.unis.org
The United Nations International School provides an international education that emphasizes academic excellence within a caring community for kindergarten through twelfth grade students from families of the United Nations, as well as from other families seeking a similar education for their children

Kenneth Wrye, EdD, Executive Director
Satya Nandan, Chairperson

2442 University del Sagrado Corazon
PO Box 12383
San Juan
Puerto Rico 00914-383
787-728-1515
http://www.sagrado.edu

2443 Uruguayan American School
Av Saldœn de Rodriguez
Montevideo
Uruguay, DC 11500-3360
598-2-600-7681
Fax: 598-2-600-1935
E-mail: info@uas.edu.uyuy
http://www.uas.edu.uy
Uruguayan American School is to provide, together with the family, a balanced college preparatory education. UAS integrates a US style curriculum with Uruguayan studies to equip our national and international students to be successful in a diverse, ever changing world

Thomas Oden, Director
Cecilia Burgueo, UP Coordinator

2444 Uruguayan American School-Montevideo
Av Saldœn de Rodriguez
Montevideo
Uruguay, DC 11500-3360
598-2-600-7681
Fax: 598-2-606-1935
E-mail: info@uas.edu.uyuy
http://www.uas.edu.uy
Uruguayan American School is to provide, together with the family, a balanced college preparatory education. UAS integrates a US style curriculum with Uruguayan studies to equip our national and international students to be successful in a diverse, ever changing world

Thomas Oden, Director
Cecilia Burgueo, UP Coordinator

2445 Uzbekistan Tashkent International School
38 Sarikul Street
Tashkent, Uzbekistan 10000
998-71-191-9671
Fax: 998-71-120-6621
E-mail: office@tashschool.org
http://www.tashschool.org

Tashkent International School (TIS), an IB World School, is a private, not for profit, independent, co-educational day school governed by a Board of Directors elected and appointed from the parent community. TIS offers an American based international curriculum from Kindergarten - grade 12. TIS is an IB World School offering: the full International Baccalaureate Diploma in grades 11 - 12, the Primary Years Program for Kindergarten - grade 5, and is a candidate school for the Middle Years Program

Kevin Glass, Director
John Zohrab, Treasurer

446 Venezuela Colegio Internacional-Carabobo
PO Box 025685
Miami, FL 33102-5685
58-41-426-551
Fax: 58-41-426-510
E-mail: admin@cic-valencia.org.ve
http://www.cic-valencia.org.ve
Colegio Internacional de Carabobo (CIC) is a school dedicated to the development of the whole child. Our teachers are innovative, skilled, and dedicated. Creativity and self-esteem are essential qualities for students to develop as they ascend the academic ladder.

Frank Anderson, Superintendent
Joe Walker, Director

447 Venezuela Escuela Campo Alegre
8424 NW 56th Street
Suite CCS 00007
Miami, FL 33166
58-2-993-7135
Fax: 58-2-993-0219
E-mail: info@eca.com.ve
http://www.eca.com.ve
Escuela Campo Alegre is a private non-profit English language school, designed primarily to serve the needs of the children from ages 3-18 of its shareholding members.

Jean K Vahey, Superintendent

448 Venezuela International School-Caracas
Pakmail 6030
PO Box 025304
Miami, FL 33102-5304
58-2-945-0422
Fax: 58-2-945-0533
E-mail: cic@cic-caracas.org
http://www.cic-caracus.org
Colegio Internacional de Caracas is an English-medium, Pre-Nursery to Grade 12 school dedicated to the intellectual and personal development of each student in a caring and supportive environment.

Alan Benson, Superintendent

449 Virgin Island Montessori School
6936 Vessup Lane
Saint Thomas, VI 00802
340-775-6360
Fax: 340-775-3080
E-mail: info@vimontessori.com
http://www.vimontessori.com/
Virgin Islands Montessori School and International Academy offers a unique environment and learning experience to over 200 students from two years of age through High School

Shournagh Mcweeney, Administrator
Michael Bornn, President

450 Virgin Islands Department of Education
44-46 Kongens Gade
Saint Thomas, Virgin Islands 00802
340-774-2810
Fax: 340-774-7153
http://www.doe.vi/
The mission of the Department of Education is to provide the Territory's students with an education that makes them competitive with their peers in the rest of the Caribbean, the United States, and the World; take advantage of our uniqueness of being geographically Caribbean and politically American; integrate all discipline; and educate the whole child.

LaVerne Terry, Commissioner
Donna Frett-Gregory, Assistant Commissioner

2451 Washington International School
3100 Macomb Street NW
Washington, DC 20008-3324
202-243-1800
Fax: 202-243-1802
E-mail: admissions@wis.edu
http://www.wis.edu
Washington International School (WIS) is a coeducational day school offering 890 students a challenging curriculum and rich language program from Pre-Kindergarten through Grade 12

Clayton W. Lewis, Head of School
Sandra Bourne, Middle School Principal

2452 We Care Child Development Center
PO Box 818
Christiansted 00821-0818
Virgin Islands

http://www.utexas.edu
Pauline Canton, Principal

2453 Wesleyan Academy
PO Box 1489
Guaynabo
Puerto Rico 00970-1489
787-008-
Fax: 787-790-0730
http://www.wesleyanacademy.org
We are a nonprofit, private, coeducational, English Christian school providing a Pre-Pre Kinder through Twelfth grade college preparatory education.

Jack Mann, Principal

2454 Yakistan International School-Karachi
DOS/Administrative Officer
6150 Karachi Place
Washington, DC 20521-6150
92-21-453-9096
Fax: 92-21-454-7305
E-mail: ameschl@cyber.net.pk
http://www.isk.edu.pk
Grades N-12, enrollment 338.

Glen Shapin, Superintendent

2455 Zion Academy
7629 199th Street SW
Lynnwood, WA 98036
425-640-3311
E-mail: info@zionacademy.com
http://www.zionacademy.com
Zion Academy is a fully accredited private school. Consists of students that wish to work at home and desire complete oversight and administrative services.

Evelyn Williams, Principal
Marigene Lindsey, Founder and Headmaster

International

2456 Center for Strategic & International Studies
1800 K Street NW
Suite 400
Washington, DC 20006-2202
202-887-0200
Fax: 202-775-3199
E-mail: books@csis.org
http://www.csis.org
Provides strategic insights and policy solutions to decisionmakers in government, international institutions, the private sector, and civil society. A bipartisan, nonprofit organization headquartered in Washington, DC, CSIS conducts research and analysis and develops policy initiatives that look into the future and anticipate change.

John J Hamre, President/CEO
Sam Nunn, Cochairman & CEO

2457 Council for International Exchange of Scholars
3007 Tilden Street NW
Suite 5-L
Washington, DC 20008-3009
202-686-4000
Fax: 202-362-3442
E-mail: apprequest@cies.iie.org
http://www.cies.org
Helped administer the Fulbright Scholar Program on behalf of the United States Department of State, Bureau of Educational and Cultural Affairs.

Michael A Brintnall, Executive Director
Judy Pehrson, Director External Relations

2458 Defense Language Institute-English Language Branch
US Civil Service Commission, San Antonio Area
2235 Andrews Avenue
Lackland, TX 78236-5514
210-671-3783
Fax: 210-671-5362
http://www.dlielc.org
The DLIELC is a Department of Defense (DOD) agency responsible for the management and operation of the Defense English Language Program (DELP) to train international military and civilian personnel to speak and teach English, manage the English as a second language program for the US military

2459 Education Information Services which Employ Americans
Education Information Services
PO Box 620662
Newton, MA 02462-662
781-433-0125
Fax: 781-237-2842
http://www.alis.alberta.ca
Devoted to helping Americans who wish to teach in American overseas schools and International Schools in which English is the primary teaching language. Supports those wishing to teach English as a second language. Publish papers covering every country in the world, list of recruiting fairs, internships, volunteers, jobs, summer overseas jobs.

Frederic B Viaux, President

2460 Educational Information Services
PO Box 662
Newtown Lower Falls, MA 02162
617-964-4555
http://www.fulbright.jp
Offers information on employment opportunities including books, periodicals and more

for the teaching professional who wishes to teach in American overseas schools, international schools, language (ESL) schools, and Department of Defense Dependencies Schools (DODDS).

Frederick B Viaux, President
Michelle V Curtin, Editor

2461 Educational Placement Sources-US
Education Information Services/Instant Alert
PO Box 620662
Newton, MA 02462-662
617-433-0125
Lists 100 organizations in the United States that find positions for teachers, educational administrators, counselors and other professionals. Listings are classified by type, listed alphabetically and offer all contact information.

4 pages Annual
FB Viaux, President

2462 Educational Staffing Program
International Schools Services
15 Roszel Road
PO Box 5910
Princeton, NJ 08543
609-452-0990
Fax: 609-452-2690
E-mail: edustaffing@iss.edu
http://www.iss.edu/edustaff/edstaffingprog.html
The Educational Staffing Program has placed almost 15,000 K-12 teachers and administrators in overseas schools since 1955. Most candidates obtain their overseas teaching positions by attending our US-based International Recruitment Center where ISS candidates have the potential to interview with overseas school heads seeking new staff. You must be an active ISS candidate to attend an IRC. Applicants must have a bachelor's degree and two years of current relevant experience.

2463 European Council of International Schools
21B Lavant Street
Petersfield, Hampshire GU3 23EL
United Kingdom GU32
44-0-1730-268244
Fax: 44-0-1730-267914
E-mail: ecis@ecis.org
http://www.ecis.org
The European Council of International Schools (ECIS) is a collaborative network promoting the ideals and best practice of international education.

T Michael Maybury, Executive Secretary
Pilar Cabeza de Vaca, CEO

2464 FRS National Teacher Agency
PO Box 298
Seymour, TN 37865-298
865-577-8143
http://www.ffiec.gov
Offers employment options to educators in the United States and abroad.

2465 Foreign Faculty and Administrative Openings
Education Information Services
PO Box 620662
Newton, MA 02462-662
617-433-0125
150 specific openings in administration, counseling, library and other professional positions for American teachers in American schools overseas and in international

schools in which teaching language is English.

15 pages Every 6 Weeks
FB Viaux, Coordinating Education

2466 Fulbright Teacher Exchange
600 Maryland Avenue SouthWest
Suite 320
Washington, DC 20024-2520
202-314-3520
800-726-0479
Fax: 202-479-6806
E-mail: fulbright@grad.usda.gov
http://www.fulbrightexchanges.org
An organization that offers opportunities for two-year college faculty and secondary school teachers who would like to exchange with teachers in Eastern or Western Europe, Latin America, Australia, Africa, and Canada. To qualify, teachers must be US citizens, have three years full-time teaching experience and be employed in a full-time academic position.

2467 International Educators Cooperative
212 Alcott Road
East Falmouth, MA 02536-6803
508-540-8173
Fax: 508-540-8173
http://www.icemenlo.com
In addition to year round recruitment, International Educators Cooperative hosts Recruitment Centers in the United States each year.

Dr. Lou Fuccillo, Director

2468 National Association of Teachers' Agencies
National Association of Teachers' Agencies
799 Kings Highway
Fairfield, CT 06432
203-333-0611
Fax: 203-334-7224
E-mail: fairfieldteachers@snet.net
http://www.jobsforteachers.com
Provides placement services for those seeking professional positions at all levels of teaching/administration/support services worldwide.

Mark King, Secretary/Treasurer

2469 National Council of Independent Schools' Associations
1129ÿ20th Street
PO Box 324
Australia
06-282-3488
Fax: 06-282-2926
http://www.nais.org
Services include career placement.

Fergus Thomson, President

2470 Overseas Employment Opportunities for Educators
Department of Defense, Office of Dependent Schools
2461 Eisenhower Avenue
Alexandria, VA 22331-3000
703-325-0867
This publication tells about teaching jobs in 250 schools operated for children of US military and civilian personnel stationed overseas. Applicants usually must qualify in two subject areas.

2471 Recruiting Fairs for Overseas Teaching
Education Information Services/Instant Alert
PO Box 620662
Newton, MA 02462-662
781-433-0125
Fax: 781-237-2842
Recruiting fairs and sponsors in the US and elsewhere for American educators who wish to teach outside of the United States.

FB Viaux, Coordinating Education

2472 UNI Overseas Recruiting Fair
University of Northern Iowa
102 Gilchrist Hall
Cedar Falls, IA 50614-390
319-273-2083
Fax: 319-273-6998
E-mail: overseas.placement@uni.edu
http://www.uni.edu/placement/overseas
UNI is home to the oldest international recruitment event in the world. The event began in 1976 after the UNI Career Services staff and several school headmasters recognized the need for more efficient and cost-effective recruitment techniques. It became readily apparent that UNI was meeting a need for school recruiters and interested educators all over the globe. In addition to inventing the international recruitment fair, UNI developed fact sheets, credential files, vacancy listings, referral

February

Brian Atkins, Advisory Board
Susan Barba, Advisory Board

2473 WorldTeach
Center for International Development
79 John F Kennedy Street
Box 122
Cambridge, MA 02138
617-495-5527
800-483-2240
Fax: 617-495-1599
E-mail: info@worldteach.org
http://www.worldteach.org
WorldTeach is a non-profit, non-governmental organization that provides opportunities for individuals to make a meaningful contribution to international education by living and working as volunteer teachers in developing countries

Laurie Roberts Belton, Executive Director
Eric Weiss, Program Manager

Alabama

474 Auburn University at Montgomery Library
PO Box 244023
Montgomery, AL 36124-4023
334-244-3649
Fax: 334-244-3720
http://www.aumnicat.aum.edu
Member of The Foundation Center network, maintaining a collection of private foundation tax returns which provide information on the scope of grants dispensed by that particular foundation.
R Best, Dean Administration
T Bailey, ILL/ Reference

475 Benjamin & Roberta Russell Educational and Charitable Foundation
PO Box 272
Alexander City, AL 35010-0272
256-329-4224
http://www.non-profit-organizations.findthebest.com
Offers giving in the areas of higher and public education, youth programs and a hospital.
James D Nabors, Executive Director

476 Birmingham Public Library
Government Documents
2100 Park Place
Birmingham, AL 35203-2794
205-226-3600
Fax: 205-226-3729
http://www.bplonline.org/resources/subjects/gov/deault
Member of The Foundation Center network, maintaining a collection of private foundation tax returns which provide information on the scope of grants dispensed by that particular foundation.

477 Carolina Lawson Ivey Memorial Foundation
PO Box 340
Smiths, AL 36877-0340
334-826-5760
Scholarships are offered to college juniors and seniors who are pursuing careers of teaching social studies in middle or secondary grades. The grants are also offered to teachers in Alabama and west Georgia for curriculum planning and development, in-service training, the development of instructional materials for use in elementary and secondary schools, and other projects that focus on the cultural approach method of teaching.

478 Huntsville Public Library
915 Monroe Street SW
Huntsville, AL 35801-5007
256-532-5940
http://www.hpl.lib.al.us/
Member of The Foundation Center network, maintaining a collection of private foundation tax returns which provide information on the scope of grants dispensed by that particular foundation.
Donna B Schremser, Library Director

479 JL Bedsole Foundation
PO Box 1137
Mobile, AL 36633-1137
251-432-3369
Fax: 251-432-1134
http://www.jlbedsolefoundation.org
The foundation's primary interest is the support of educational institutions within the state of Alabama and civic and economic development which is limited to the geographical area of Southwest Alabama. The arts, social service and health programs receive limited grants. Organizations or projects outside of the State of Alabama are not considered for funding by the Foundation.
Mabel B Ward, Executive Director
Scott A Morton, Assistant Director

2480 Mildred Weedon Blount Educational and Charitable Foundation
PO Box 607
Tallassee, AL 36078-0007
334-283-4931
http://www.schoolsoup.com
Support for Catholic schools, public schools and a scholarship fund for secondary school students.
Arnold B Dopson, Executive Director

2481 Mitchell Foundation
PO Box 1126
Mobile, AL 36633
251-432-1711
Fax: 334-432-1712
http://www.cgmf.org
Places an emphasis on secondary and higher education, social services programs, youth agencies, and aid for the handicapped.
Augustine Meaher, Executive Director
Marilu Hastings, Director

2482 University of South Alabama
307 University Boulevard
Mobile, AL 36688-0002
251-460-7025
Fax: 251-460-7636
http://www.library.southalabama.edu
Richard Wood, Dean of Libraries

Alaska

2483 University of Alaska-Anchorage Library
3211 Providence Drive
Anchorage, AK 99508-8000
907-786-1848
Fax: 907-786-6050
http://www.lib.uaa.alaska.edu
Member of The Foundation Center network, maintaining a collection of private foundation tax returns which provide information on the scope of grants dispensed by that particular foundation.
Stephen J Rollins, Dean of Library

Arizona

2484 Arizona Department of Education
1535 W Jefferson Street
Phoenix, AZ 85007
602-542-5393
800-352-4558
Fax: 602-542-5440
http://www.ade.state.az.us
Implements procedures that ensure the proper allocation, distribution, and expenditure of all federal and state funds administerd by the department. The following links to our web pages contain information pertaining to educational grants funded from the state or federal programs.
Tom Horne, Superintendent

2485 Arizona Governor's Committee on Employment of People with Disabilities
Samaritan Rehabilitation Institute
1012 E Willetta Street
Phoenix, AZ 85006-3047
602-239-4762
Fax: 602-239-5256
Jim Bruzewski, Executive Director

2486 Education Services
Arizona Department of Education
1535 W Jefferson Street
Phoenix, AZ 85007-3280
602-364-1961
Fax: 602-542-5440
http://www.ade.state.az.us/edservices
Provides quality services and resources to schools, parent groups, government agencies, and community groups to enable them to achieve their goals.
Lillie Sly, Associate Superintendent

2487 Evo-Ora Foundation
2525 E Broadway Boulevard
Suite 111
Tucson, AZ 85716-5398
Giving is primarily aimed at education, especially Catholic high schools and universities.

2488 Flinn Foundation
1802 N Central Avenue
Suite 2300
Phoenix, AZ 85012-2513
602-744-6800
Fax: 602-744-6815
E-mail: info@flinn.org
http://www.flinn.org
Supports nonprofit organizations in the state of Arizona for programs in health care, as well as an annual awards competition for Arizona's principal arts institutions and a college scholarship program for Arizona high school graduates. Scholarship provides expenses for four years, two summers of study-related travel abroad and other benefits.
John W Murphy, Executive Director

2489 Phoenix Public Library
Business & Sciences Department
12 E McDowell Road
Phoenix, AZ 85004-1627
602-262-4636
Fax: 602-261-8836
http://www.phxlib.org
Member of The Foundation Center network, maintaining a collection of private foundation tax returns which provide information on the scope of grants dispensed by that particular foundation.

2490 Special Programs
721 Broadway
12th Floor
New York, NY 10003
212-998-1800
E-mail: tisch.special.info@nyu.edu
http://www.specialprograms.tisch.nyu.edu
Tom Horne, Superintendent

2491 Support Services
Arizona Department of Education
1535 W Jefferson Street
Phoenix, AZ 85007-3280
602-542-5393
Fax: 602-542-5440
Rachel Arroyo, School Finance

2492 Vocational Technological Education
Arizona Department of Education
1535 W Jefferson Street
Phoenix, AZ 85007-3280
602-542-5393
Fax: 602-542-5440
Tom Horne, Superintendent

Arkansas

2493 Charles A Frueauff Foundation
200 River Market Avenue
Suite 100
Little Rock, AR 72201-3848
501-324-2233
http://www.frueauff.org
Will review proposals from private four-year colleges and universities.
David Frueauff, President
Sue Frueauff, Chief Administrative Officer

2494 Northwest Arkansas Community College
Borham Library
One College Drive
Bentonville, AR 72904-7397
479-636-9222
800-995-6922
http://www.nwacc.edu
Member of The Foundation Center network, maintaining a collection of private foundation tax returns which provide information on the scope of grants dispensed by that particular foundation.
Daniel Shewmaker, Secretary
Ric Clifford, Chairman

2495 Roy and Christine Sturgis Charitable and Educational Trust
PO Box 92
Malvern, AR 72104-0092
501-337-5109
Giving is offered to Baptist and Methodist organizations, including schools, churches and higher and secondary education.
Katie Speer, Executive Director

2496 The Jones Center For Families
922 East Emma Avenue
Springdale, AR 72765
479-756-8090
http://www.thejonescenter.net
Focuses funds on education, medical resources and religious organizations in Arkansas.
HG Frost Jr, Executive Director
Grace Donoho, Director Of Education

2497 Walton Family Foundation
125 W Central Avenue
Room 217 Po Box 2030
Bentonville, AR 72712-5248
479-464-1570
Fax: 479-464-1580
http://www.wffhome.com
Offers giving for systemic reform of primary education (K-12) and early childhood development.
Stewart T Springfield, Executive Director

2498 William C & Theodosia Murphy Nolan Foundation
200 N Jefferson Avenue
Suite 308
El Dorado, AR 71730-5853
870-863-7118
Fax: 870-863-6528
Supports education and the arts (historic preservation, arts centers) as well as religious welfare and youth organizations in Northern Louisiana and Southern Arkansas.
William C Nolan, Executive Director

2499 Winthrop Rockefeller Foundation
225 East Markham Street
Suite 200
Little Rock, AR 72201-3999
501-376-6854
Fax: 501-374-4797
E-mail: webfeedback@wrfoundation.org
http://www.wrfoundation.org
Dedicated to improving the quality of life and education in Arkansas. Grants go to schools that work to involve teachers and parents in making decisions; to universities and local schools to strengthen both levels of education; and for projects that promote stakeholder participation in the development of educational policy.
Sherece Y West, President
Jackie Cox-New, Sr Program Officer

California

2500 Ahmanson Foundation
9215 Wilshire Boulevard
Beverly Hills, CA 90210-5538
310-278-0770
E-mail: info@theahmansonfoundation.org
http://www.theahmasonfoundation.org
Concentrates mainly on education, health and social services in Southern California.
Lee E Walcott, Executive Director
William H Ahmanson, President

2501 Alice Tweed Tuohy Foundation
205 E Carrillo Street
Suite 219
Santa Barbara, CA 93101-7186
805-962-6430
Priority consideration is given to applications from organizations serving: young people; education; selected areas of interest in health care and medicine; and community affairs.
Harris W Seed, President
Eleanor Van Cott, Executive VP

2502 Arrillaga Foundation
2560 Mission College Boulevard
Suite 101
Santa Clara, CA 95054-1217
408-980-0130
Fax: 408-988-4893
Giving is aimed at secondary schools and higher education in the state of California.
John Arrillaga, Executive Director

2503 Atkinson Foundation
1720 So.Amphlett Blvd
Suite 100
San Mateo, CA 94402-2710
650-357-1101
E-mail: atkinfdn@aol.com
http://www.atkinsonfdn.org
Provides opportunities for people in San Mateo County, California to reach their highest potential and to improve the quality of their lives and to assist educational institutions and supporting organizations with the implementation of effective programs that reach and serve their target populations.
Elizabeth H Curtis, Administrator

2504 BankAmerica Foundation
Bank of America Center
PO Box 37000
San Francisco, CA 94137-0001
800-678-2632
Fax: 818-507-4023
E-mail: banknote@bankamerica.com
http://www.bankamerica.com
Fields of interest include arts/cultural programs, higher education, community development and general federated giving programs.
Elizabeth Nachbaur, Program Director

2505 Bechtel Group Corporate Giving Program
Po Box 193965
San Francisco, CA 94119-3965
415-768-5974
Offers support for higher education and programs related to engineering and construction, math and science in grades K-12 and general charitable programs.
Kathryn M Bandarrae, Executive Director

2506 Bernard Osher Foundation
One Ferry Building
Suite 255
San Francisco, CA 94111
415-861-5587
Fax: 415-677-5868
E-mail: nagle@osherfoundation.org
http://www.osherfoundation.org
Funds in the arts, post-secondary education and environmental education on San Francisco and Alameda Counties.
Patricia Nagle, Sr VP
Jeanie Hirokane, Corporate Secretary and Exec

2507 Boys-Viva Supermarkets Foundation
955 Carrillo Drive
Suite 103
Los Angeles, CA 90048-5400
Wide range of support for education of school-aged children, especially the at-risk population, tutoring, and social opportunities.
Fred Snowden, Executive Director

2508 California Community Foundation
221 S Figueroa Street
Suite 400
Los Angeles, CA 90012-1638
213-413-4130
Fax: 213-383-2046
http://www.calfund.org
Improving human condition through nonprofit agencies in Los Angeles County. Integral parts of eligible proposals are, hosting conferences, incurring debt, individuals, sectarian purposes or regranting.
Judy Spiegel, Sr VP of Programs
Antonia Hernandez, President/CEO

2509 Carrie Estelle Doheny Foundation
707 Wilshire Boulevard
Suite 4960
Los Angeles, CA 90017-2659
213-488-1122
Fax: 213-488-1544
http://www.dohenyfoundation.org
This foundation funds a myriad of organizations ranging from the education and medicine field to public health and science areas.
Robert A Smith III, Executive Director

2510 Dan Murphy Foundation
PO Box 711267
Los Angeles, CA 90071-9767

213-623-3120
Fax: 213-623-1421
Funds Roman Catholic institutions, with a primary interest in religious orders and schools.

Daniel J Donohue, Executive Director

2511 David & Lucile Packard Foundation
343 Second Street
Los Altos Hills, CA 94022-3643
650-948-7658
Fax: 650-941-3151
http://www.packard.org
Concentrates on four categories: education, the arts, conservation and child health. Also allocates funds to companies interested in public improvement and public policy.

Colburn S Wilbur, Executive Director

2512 Evelyn & Walter Haas Jr Fund
114 Sansome Street
Suite 600
San Francisco, CA 94104
415-856-1400
Fax: 415-856-1500
http://www.haasjr.org
Interested in strengthening neighborhoods, communities, and human services. Funds mainly in San Francisco Bay Area.

Ira Hirschfield, President
Clayton Juan, Grants Administrator

2513 Foundation Center-San Francisco
312 Sutter Street
Suite 606
San Francisco, CA 94108-4314
415-397-0902
Fax: 415-397-7670
http://www.fdncenter.org
One of five Foundation Centers nationwide, the Foundation Center - San Francisco is a library which collects information on private foundations, corporate philanthropy, nonprofit management, fundraising and other topics of interest to nonprofit organization representatives.

Melissa A Berman, President & CEO
John Colborn, Vice President

2514 Foundations Focus
Marin Community Foundation
5 Hamilton Landing
Suite 200
Novato, CA 94949
415-464-2500
Fax: 415-464-2555
http://www.marincf.org
Grants support projects that benefit residents of Marin County, CA.

Don Jen, Program Officer/Education
Thomas Peters, President/CEO

2515 Francis H Clougherty Charitable Trust
500 Newport Center Drive
Suite 910
Newport Beach, CA 92660-7009
Offers grants in the areas of elementary, secondary school and higher education in Southern California.

2516 Freitas Foundation
C/O Fiduciary Resources
874 Fourth St
Suite D
San Rafael, CA 94901-3246
Offers giving in the areas of elementary and secondary education, as well as theological education.

Margaret Boyden, Executive Director

2517 Fritz B Burns Foundation
4001 W Alameda Avenue
Suite 201
Burbank, CA 91505-4338
818-840-8802
Fax: 818-840-0468
Grants are primarily focused on education, hospitals and medical research organizations.

Joseph E Rawlinson, Executive Director

2518 George Frederick Jewett Foundation
235 Montgomery Street
Suite 612
San Francisco, CA 94104-2915
415-421-1351
Fax: 415-421-1351
Concerns itself mainly with voluntary, nonprofit organizations that promote human welfare.

2519 Grant & Resource Center of Northern California
2280 Benton Drive, Building C
Suite A
Redding, CA 96003
530-244-1219
Fax: 530-244-0905
E-mail: library@grcnc.org
Member of The Foundation Center network, maintaining a collection of private foundation tax returns which provide information on the scope of grants dispensed by that particular foundation.

2520 Greenville Foundation
PO Box 4667
Scottsdale, AZ 85261-4667
707-938-9377
Fax: 707-939-9311
This foundation focuses its support on education, the environment and human rights. The main focus of the educational grants lie within the areas of elementary, secondary and higher education.

Virginia Hubbell, Executive Director
Virginia Hubbell, Administrator

2521 HN & Frances C Berger Foundation
PO Box 3064
Arcadia, CA 91006
626-447-3351
http://www.hnberger.org
Provides scholarships and endowments to colleges and universities.

Ronald M Auen, President/CEO
Christopher M McGuire, Vice President of Programs

2522 Henry J Kaiser Family Foundation
Quadrus
2400 Sand Hill Road
Menlo Park, CA 94025-6941
650-854-9400
Fax: 650-854-4800
http://www.kff.org
Concentrates on health care, minority groups and South Africa.

Drew Altman, President/CEO
Susan V Berresford, Former President

2523 Hon Foundation
25200 La Paz Road
Suite 210
Laguna Hills, CA 92653-5110
949-586-4400
Offers giving in the areas of elementary, secondary and higher education in the states of Hawaii and California.

2524 Hugh & Hazel Darling Foundation
520 S Grand Avenue
7th Floor
Los Angeles, CA 90071-2645
213-683-5200
Fax: 213-627-7795
Supports education in California with special emphasis on legal education; no grants to individuals; grants only to 501(c)(3) organizations.

Richard L Stack, Trustee

2525 Ingraham Memorial Fund
C/O Emrys J. Ross
301 E Colorado Boulevard
Suite 900
Pasadena, CA 91101-1916
626-796-9123
Offers giving in the areas of elementary, secondary and higher education, as well as theological education in Claremont and Pasadena, California.

2526 James G Boswell Foundation
101 W Walnut Street
Pasadena, CA 91103-3636
626-583-3000
Fax: 626-583-3090
Funds hospitals, pre-college private schools, public broadcasting and youth organizations.

James G Boswell II, Chairman
Sherman Railsback, EVP/COO

2527 James Irvine Foundation
575 Market Street
Suite 3400
San Francisco, CA 94105-1017
415-777-2244
Fax: 415-777-0869
http://www.irvine.org
Giving is primarily aimed at the areas of education, youth and health.

James E Canales, President/CEO
Kristin Nelson, Executive Assistant

2528 James S Copley Foundation
7776 Ivanhoe Avenue #1530
La Jolla, CA 92037-4520
858-454-0411
Fax: 858-729-7629
Support is offered for higher and secondary education, child development, cultural programs and community services.

Anita A Baumgardner, Executive Director

2529 John Jewett & H Chandler Garland Foundation
PO Box 550
Pasadena, CA 91102-0550
Support given primarily for secondary and higher education, social services and cultural and historical programs.

GE Morrow, Executive Director

2530 Joseph Drown Foundation
1999 Avenue of the Stars
Suite 2330
Los Angeles, CA 90067-4611
310-277-4488
Fax: 310-277-4573
http://www.jdrown.org
The Foundation's goal is to assist individuals in becoming successful, self-sustaining, contributing citizens. The foundation is interested in programs that break down any barrier that prevents a person from continuing to grow and learn.

Norman Obrow, Executive Director

2531 Jules & Doris Stein Foundation
PO Box 30
Beverly Hills, CA 90213-0030
213-276-2101
Supports charitable organizations.

2532 Julio R Gallo Foundation
PO Box 1130
Modesto, CA 95353-1130
209-579-3373
Offers grants and support to secondary schools and higher education universities.

Sam Gallo, Chairman

2533 Kenneth T & Eileen L Norris Foundation
11 Golden Shore Street
Suite 450
Long Beach, CA 90802-4214
562-435-8444
Fax: 562-436-0584
E-mail: grants@ktn.org
http://www.norrisfoundation.org
Funding categories include medical, education/science, youth, cultural and community.

Ronald Barnes, Executive Director

2534 Koret Foundation
33 New Montgomery Street
Suite 1090
San Francisco, CA 94105-4526
415-882-7740
Fax: 415-882-7775
E-mail: sandyedwards@koretfoundation.org
http://www.koretfoundation.org
Funding includes; public policy and selected programs in K-12 public education, higher education, youth programs, Jewish studies at colleges and universities, and Jewish education. The geographical area for grant-making is the San Francisco Bay area.

Tad Taube, President
Susan Koret, Board Chair

2535 Lane Family Charitable Trust
500 Almer Road
Apartment 301
Burlingame, CA 94010-3966
Offers giving in the areas of secondary schools and higher education facilities in California.

Ralph Lane, Trustee
Joan Lane, Trustee

2536 Levi Strauss Foundation
1155 Battery Street
Floor 7
San Francisco, CA 94111-1230
415-501-6000
Fax: 415-501-7112
http://www.levistrauss.com
Grants are made in four areas: AIDS prevention and care; economic empowerment; youth empowerment; and social justice. Grants are limited to communities where Levi Strauss and Company has plants or customer service centers.

Theresa Fay-Buslillos, Executive Director

2537 Louise M Davies Foundation
180 Montgomery St
Suite 1616
San Francisco, CA 94104-4235
Offers giving in the areas of elementary, secondary and higher education, as well as scholarship funding for California students.

Donald Crawford Jr, Executive Director

2538 Lowell Berry Foundation
3685 Mount Diablo Boulevard
Suite 269
Lafayette, CA 94549
925-284-4427
Fax: 925-284-4332
http://www.lowellberryfoundation.org
Assists Christian ministry at local church levels.

Debbie Coombe, Office Manager
Larry R Langdon, President

2539 Luke B Hancock Foundation
360 Bryant Street
Palo Alto, CA 94301-1409
650-321-5536
Fax: 650-321-0697
E-mail: lhancock@lukebhancock.org
http://www.fdcenter.org/grantmaker/hancock
Provides funding for programs which promote the well being of children and youth. Priority is given to programs which address the needs of youth who are at risk of school failure. Additional funding is provided for early childhood development, music education and homeless families.

Ruth M Ramel, Executive Director

2540 Margaret E Oser Foundation
1911 Lyon Court
Santa Rosa, CA 95403-0974
949-553-4202
Offers grants in the areas of elementary and secondary and higher education, which will benefit women.

Carl Mitchell, Executive Director

2541 Marin Community Foundation
5 Hamilton Landing
Suite 200
Novato, CA 94949-1736
415-461-3333
Fax: 415-464-2555
http://www.marincf.org
Established as a nonprofit public benefit corporation to engage in educational and philanthropic activities in Marin County, California.

Thomas Peterson, President&CEO
Julie Absey, Vice President

2542 Mary A Crocker Trust
233 Post Street
Floor 2
San Francisco, CA 94108-5003
415-982-0138
Fax: 415-982-0141
E-mail: staff@mactrust.org
http://www.mactrust.org
Giving is aimed at precollegiate education, as well as conservation and environmental programs.

Barbaree Jernigan, Executive Director

2543 Maurice Amado Foundation
3940 Laurel Canyon Boulevard
Suite 809
Studio City, CA 91604
818-980-9190
Fax: 818-980-9190
E-mail: pkaizer@mauriceamadofdn.org
http://www.mauri
Concentrates on the Jewish heritage.

Pam Kaizer, Executive Director

2544 McConnell Foundation
PO Box 492050
800 Shasta View Drive
Redding, CA 96003

530-226-6200
Fax: 530-226-6210
http://www.mcconnellfoundation.org
Interested in cultural, community and health care related projects.

Ana Diaz, Program Assistant

2545 McKesson Foundation
1 Post Street
San Francisco, CA 94104-5203
415-983-8300
http://www.mckesson.com/foundation.html
Giving is primarily to programs for junior high school students and for emergency services such as food and shelter.

Marcia M Argyris, Executive Director

2546 Milken Family Foundation
C/O Foundations of the Milken Families
1250 4th Street
Floor 6
Santa Monica, CA 90401-1353
310-570-4800
Fax: 310-570-4801
http://www.mff.org
Offers support to the educational community to reward educational innovators, stimulate creativity among students, involve parents and other citizens in the school system, and help disadvantaged youth.

Dr. Julius Lesner, Executive Director
Lowell Milken, Chairman & Co Founder

2547 Miranda Lux Foundation
57 Post Street
Suite 510
San Francisco, CA 94104-5020
415-981-2966
E-mail: admin@mirandalux.org
http://www.mirandalux.org
Offers support to promising proposals for pre-school through junior college programs in the fields of pre-vocational and vocational education and training.

Kenneth Blum, Executive Director

2548 Northern California Grantmakers
625 Market Street
3rd Floor
San Francisco, CA 94105
415-777-4111
Fax: 415-777-1714
E-mail: ncg@ncg.org
http://www.ncg.org
Northern California Grantmakers is an association of foundations, corporate contributions programs and other private grantmakers. Its mission is to jpromote the well being of people and their communities in balance with a healthy environment by the thoughtful and creative use of private wealth and resources for the public benefit. To this end, NCG works to enhance the effectiveness of philanthropy, including nonprofit organizations, government, business, media, academia and the public at large.

Colin Lacon, President

2549 Pacific Telesis Group Corporate Giving Program
130 Kearny Street
San Francisco, CA 94108-4818
415-394-3000
Primary areas of interest include K-12 education reform, education of minorities, women and disabled individuals in the math, science, engineering, education and MBA fields; and specific K-12 issues such as dropouts, information technology and parent involvement.

Jere A Jacobs, Executive Director

550 Peninsula Community Foundation
11742 Jefferson Avenue
Suite 350
Newport News, VA 23606-3049
757-327-0862
Fax: 757-327-0865
http://www.pcfvirginia.org
Serving a population from Daly City to
Mountain View, the foundations focus is on
children and youth, adult services, programs
serving homeless families and children, prevention of homelessness and civic and public
benefit grants.

Sterling K Speirn, Executive Director
Gregory F Lawson, President

551 Peter Norton Family Foundation
225 Arizona Avenue
Floor 2
Santa Monica, CA 90401-1243
310-576-7700
Fax: 310-576-7701
Offers giving in the areas of early childhood
education, elementary school education,
higher education, childrens services and
AIDS research.

Anne Etheridge, ED, Executive Director

552 RCM Capital Management Charitable Fund
4 Embarcadero Center
Suite 2900
San Francisco, CA 94111-4189
415-954-5474
Fax: 415-954-8200
http://www.rcm.com
Giving is offered in many areas including
youth development, early childhood education and elementary education.

Jami Weinman, Executive Director

553 Ralph M Parsons Foundation
888 West Sixth Street
Suite 700
Los Angeles, CA 90017-5600
213-362-7600
Fax: 213-482-8878
http://www.rmpf.org
Giving is focused on higher and pre-collegiate education, with an emphasis on engineering, technology, and science; social
impact programs serving families, children
and the elderly; health programs targeting
underserved populations; civic and cultural
programs.

Wendy G Hoppe, Executive Director
Walter B Rose, Vice Chairman

554 Riordan Foundation
PO Box 491190
Los Angeles, CA 90049-3110
310-472-2020
Fax: 310-472-1414
E-mail: contact@riordanfoundation.org
http://www.riordanfoundation.org
Priorities of the foundation include early
childhood literacy, youth programs, leadership programs, job training, direct medical
services to young children, and cyclical, targeted mini-grants. When determining levels
of support, priority is always given to programs which impact young children.

Jessica Flores, President
Jaime Kalenik, Program Coordinator

555 Royal Barney Hogan Foundation
PMB 220,3000 S.Hulen
Ste 124
Forth Worth, TX
E-mail:
RoyalHoganFoundation@yahoo.com
http://www.royalhoganfoundation.org

Offers grants specifically for secondary education in the state of California.

Jacque Hogan, President/Treasurer
Robert L Towery, Secretary/Chief
Executive Of

2556 SH Cowell Foundation
595 Market Street
Suite 950
San Francisco, CA 94105-4303
415-397-0285
Fax: 415-986-6786
http://www.shcowell.org
Offers support for educational programs, including pre-school and primary public educational programs.

JD Erickson, Executive Director
Anna Alpers, President

2557 Sacramento Regional Foundation
555 Capitol Mall
Suite 550
Sacramento, CA 95814-4502
916-492-6510
Fax: 916-492-6515
http://www.sacregfoundation.org
Primary interests of this foundation include
the arts, humanities and education.

Stephen F Boutin, President
Janice Gow Pettey, CEO

2558 San Diego Foundation
2508 Historic Decatur Rd
Suite 200
San Diego, CA 92106-2434
619-235-2300
Fax: 619-239-1710
E-mail: info@sdfoundation.org
http://www.sdfoundation.org
Offers grants in the areas of social services
with emphasis on children and families, education and health for San Diego County.

Robert A Kelly, President/CEO
Rebecca Reichmann, VP Programs

2559 San Francisco Foundation
225 Bush Street
Suite 500
San Francisco, CA 94104-4224
415-733-8500
Fax: 415-477-2783
E-mail: rec@sff.org
http://www.sff.org
Addresses community needs in the areas of
community health, education, arts and culture, neighborhood revitalization, and environmental justice. Works to support families
and communities to help children and youth
succeed in school and provide opportunities
for them to become confident, caring and
contributing adults.

Sandra R Hernandez MD, CEO
Sara Ying Kelley, Director Public Affairs

2560 Santa Barbara Foundation
1111 Chapala Street
Suite 200
Santa Barbara, CA 93101-2780
805-963-1873
Fax: 805-966-2345
http://www.sbfoundation.org
Offers a student aid program with no inter-
est-1/2 loan and 1/2 scholarship. Funding
limited to long-term Santa Barbara County
residents.

Claudia Armann, Program Officer
Peter MacDougall, Chairman

2561 Sega Youth Education & Health Foundation
255 Shoreline Drive
Suite 200
Redwood City, CA 94065-1428
Offers support only to organizations that address and promote youth education and
health issues.

Trizia Carpenter, Executive Director

2562 Sidney Stern Memorial Trust
PO Box 893
Pacific Palisades, CA 90272-0893
310-459-2117
E-mail: info@sidneysternmemorialtrust.org
http://www.sidneysternmemorialtrust.org
Funding offered includes education, commu-
nity action groups, the arts and the disabled.

2563 Sol & Clara Kest Family Foundation
5150 Overland Avenue
Culver City, CA 90230-4914
213-204-2050
Offers support for Jewish organizations in
the areas of education.

Sol Kest, Executive Director

2564 Szekely Family Foundation
3232 Dove Street
San Diego, CA 92103
619-295-2372
Offers giving in the areas of early childhood
education, child development, elementary
education, higher education, and adult and
continuing education.

Deborah Szekely, Executive Director

2565 Thomas & Dorothy Leavey Foundation
10100 Santa Monica Boulevard
Suite 610
Los Angeles, CA 90067
310-551-9936
Focus is placed on college scholarships, medical research, youth groups and programs,
and secondary and higher education
purposes.

J Thomas McCarthy, Executive Director

2566 Times Mirror Foundation
202 West First Street
Los Angeles, CA 90012
213-237-3945
Fax: 213-237-2116
http://www.timesmirrorfoundation.org
Giving is largely for higher education purposes including liberal arts and business education.

Cassandra Malry, Executive Director

2567 Timken-Sturgis Foundation
7421 Eads Avenue
La Jolla, CA 92037-5037
619-454-2252
Offers support for education in Southern California and Nevada.

Joannie Barrancotto, Executive Director

2568 Toyota USA Foundation
19001 S Western Avenue
Torrance, CA 90501-1106
310-715-7486
800-331-4331
Fax: 310-468-7814
E-mail: b_pauli@toyota
http://www.toyota.com/foundation
Supports K-12 education programs, with
strong emphasis on math and science.

William Pauli, National Manager

2569 Turst Funds Incorporated
100 Broadway Street
Floor 3
San Francisco, CA 94111-1404
415-434-3323
Offers grants for Catholic Schools, including elementary and secondary education, in the San Francisco Bay Area.

James T Healy, President

2570 Ventura County Community Foundation
Funding & Information Resource Center
4001 Mission Oaks Blvd
Suite 150
Camarillo, CA 93012-8504
805-988-0196
Fax: 805-484-2700
E-mail: vccf@vccf.org
http://www.vccf.org
Member of The Foundation Center network, maintaining a collection of private foundation tax returns which provide information on the scope of grants dispensed by that particular foundation.

Gary E Erickson, President/CEO
Virginia Weber, Program Officer

2571 WM Keck Foundation
550 S Hope Street
Suite 2500
Los Angeles, CA 90071
213-680-3833
Fax: 213-614-0934
E-mail: info@wmkeck.org
http://www.wmkeck.org
The Foundation also gives some consideration, limited to Southern California, for the support of arts and culture, civic and community services, health care and precollegiate education. The foundation's grant-making is focused primarily on pioneering research efforts in the areas of science, engineering and medical research, and on higher education, including liberal arts.

Dorothy Fleisher, Program Director
Allison Keller, Executive Director and Chief

2572 Walter & Elise Haas Fund
1 Lombard Street
Suite 305
San Francisco, CA 94111-1130
415-398-4474
Fax: 415-986-4779
http://www.haassr.org
Supports education, arts, environment, human services, humanities and public affairs; is especially in projects which have a wide impact within their respective fields through enhancing public education and access to information, serving a central organizing role, addressing public policy, demonstrating creative approaches toward meeting human needs, or supporting the work of a major institution in the field.

Pamela H David, Executive Director
Peter E Hass Jr, President

2573 Walter S Johnson Foundation
1660 Bush Street
Suite 300
San Francisco, CA 94025-3447
415-561-6540
Fax: 415-561-6477
http://www.wsjf.org
Giving is centered on education in public schools and social service agencies concerned with the quality of public education

in Northern California and Washoe County, Nevada.

Pancho Chang, Executive Director

2574 Wayne & Gladys Valley Foundation
1939 Harrison Street
Suite 510
Oakland, CA 94612-3535
510-466-6060
Fax: 510-466-6067
Supports four areas: education, medical research, community services and special projects.

Michael D Desler, Executive Director

2575 Weingart Foundation
1055 W 7th Street
Suite 3200
Los Angeles, CA 90017-2509
213-688-7799
Fax: 213-688-1515
http://www.weingartfnd.org
Offers support for community services including a student loan program.

William C Allen, Chairman & CEO
Fred J Ali, President/Chief Adm. Officer

2576 Wells Fargo Foundation
550 California Street
7th Floor MAC A0112-073
San Francisco, CA 94104
415-396-5830
Fax: 415-975-6260
http://www.wellsfargo.com
Offers support for elementary school education, secondary school education and community development.

Tim Hanlon, Executive Director

2577 Wilbur D May Foundation
C/O Brookhill Corporation
2716 Ocean Park Boulevard
Suite 2011
Santa Monica, CA 90405
Gives to youth organizations and hospitals.

2578 William & Flora Hewlett Foundation
2121 Sand Hill Road
Menlo Park, CA 94025-3448
650-234-4500
Fax: 650-234-4501
http://www.hewlett.org
The Hewlett Foundation concentrates its resources on the performing arts, education, population issues, environmental issues, conflict resolution and family and community development. Grants in the education program, specifically the elementary and secondary education part of it, are limited to K-12 areas in California programs, with primary emphasis on public schools in the San Francisco Bay area. The program favors schools, school districts and universities.

Larry Kramer, President
Walter B Hewlett, Chairman

2579 William C Bannerman Foundation
9255 Sunset Boulevard
Suite 400
West Hollywood, CA 90069
310-273-9933
Fax: 310-273-9931
Offers grants in the fields of elementary school, secondary schools, education, human services and youth programs K-12 in Los Angeles County, Adult Education and Vocational Training.

Elliot Ponchick, President

2580 Y&H Soda Foundation
1635 School Street
Moraga, CA 94556
925-631-1133
Fax: 925-631-0248
E-mail: jNM@silcom.com
http://www.yhsodafoundation.org
Offers support in the areas of early childhood education, child development, elementary education and vocational and higher education.

Bob Uyeki, Executive Director

2581 Zellerbach Family Fund
575 Market Street
Suite 2950
San Francisco, CA 94105-4318
415-421-2629
Fax: 415-421-6713
http://www.zellerbachfamilyfoundation.org
Provides funds to nonprofit organizations in the San Francisco Bay area.

Cindy Rambo, Executive Director
Linda Avidan, Program Director

Colorado

2582 Adolph Coors Foundation
4100 East Mississippi Avenue
Suite 1850
Denver, CO 80246
303-388-1636
Fax: 303-388-1684
http://www.adolphcoors.org
Giving is primarily offered for programs with an emphasis on education, human services, youth and health.

Sally W Rippey, Executive Director
Jeanne L Bistranin, Program Officers

2583 Boettcher Foundation
600 17th Street
Suite 2210
Denver, CO 80202-5422
303-534-1937
800-323-9640
http://www.boettcherfoundation.org
Offers grants to educational institutions, with an emphasis on scholarships and fellowships.

Timothy W Schultz, President/Executive Director

2584 Denver Foundation
55 Madison Street
8th Floor
Denver, CO 80206
303-300-1790
Fax: 303-300-6547
http://www.denverfoundation.org
The Foundation serves as the steward and the administrator of the endowment, charged with investing its earned income in programs that meet the community's growing and changing needs. The Foundation has a solid history of supporting a broad array of community efforts. Grants are awarded to nonprofit organizations that touch nearly every meaningful artistic, cultural, civic, educational, human service and health interest of metro Denver's citizens.

David Miller, President/CEO
Betsy Mangone, VP Philanthropic Services

2585 El Pomar Foundation
10 Lake Circle
Colorado Springs, CO 80906-4201
719-633-7733
800-554-7711
Fax: 719-577-5702
http://www.elpomar.org
Founded in 1937, the philosophy of this foundation is simply to help foster a climate for excel-

lence in Colorado's third sector, the nonprofit community, as well as the foundation's own responsibility to improve the quality of life for all residents of Colorado. The foundation gives grants to the arts and humanities, civic and community, education, health, human services, and youth in community service.

William J Hybl, Executive Director

586 Gates Foundation
500 Fifth Avenue North
Seattle, WA 98109
206-709-3100
E-mail: info@gatesfoundation.org
http://www.gatesfoundation.org
The purpose of this foundation is to aid, assist, encourage, initiate, or carry on activities that will promote the health, well-being, security and broad education of all people. Because of a deep concern for and confidence in the future of Colorado, the foundation will invest primarily in institutions and programs that will enhance the quality of life for those who live and work in the state.

Thomas C Stokes, Executive Director

587 Ruth & Vernon Taylor Foundation
518 17th Street
Suite 1670
Denver, CO 80202
303-893-5284
Fax: 303-893-8263
Offers support for education, the arts, human services and conservation.

Friday A Green, Executive Director

588 US West Foundation
915 Memorial Drive
Manitowoc, WI 54220
920-684-6110
Fax: 920-684-7381
E-mail: info@westfoundation.us
http://www.westfoundation.us
Grants are given in the areas of health and human services, including programs for youth, early childhood, elementary, secondary, higher and other.

Janet Rash, Executive Director
Thomas Bare, President

Connecticut

589 Aetna Foundation
151 Farmington Avenue
Hartford, CT 06156-0001
860-273-0123
Fax: 860-273-4764
http://www.aetna.com/foundation/
Aetna gives grants in various areas that improve the community and its citizens. Certain areas include; children's health, education for at-risk students, and community initiatives. Geographic emphasis is placed on organizations and initiatives in Aetna's Greater Hartford headquarters communities; organizations in select communities across the country where Aetna has a significant local presence; and national organizations that can influence state, local or federal policies and programs.

Marilda L Gandara, President
Dave Wilmont, Executive Assistant

590 Community Foundation of Greater New Haven
70 Audubon Street
New Haven, CT 06510-1248
203-777-2386
Fax: 203-787-6584

E-mail: contactus@cfgnh.org
http://www.cfgnh.org
Offers a wide variety of giving with an emphasis on social services, youth services, AIDS research and education.

William W Ginsberg, President/CEO
Ronda Maddox, Administrative Assistant

2591 Connecticut Mutual Financial Services
140 Garden Street
Hartford, CT 06154-0200
860-987-6500
Giving is aimed at education, primarily higher education, equal opportunity programs and social services.

Astrida R Olds, Executive Director

2592 Hartford Foundation for Public Giving
10 Columbus Boulevard
8th Floor
Hartford, CT 06106-2693
860-548-1888
Fax: 860-524-8346
E-mail: hpfg@hpfg.org
http://www.hfpg.org
Offers grants for demonstration programs and capital purposes with emphasis on educational institutions, social services and cultural programs.

Michael R Bangser, Executive Director
Edward Forand Jr, Chairman

2593 Loctite Corporate Contributions Program
Hartford Square North
10 Columbus Boulevard
5th Floor
Hartford, CT 06106-1976
860-571-5100
Fax: 860-571-5430
Offers support in various fields of interest including funding for educational programs for inner city youths in grades K-12.

Kiren Cooley, Corporate Contributions

2594 Louis Calder Foundation
125 Elm Street
New Canaan, CT 06840
203-966-8925
Fax: 203-966-5785
http://www.louiscalderfdn.org
Offers support to organizations who promote education, health and welfare of children and youth in New York City.

Holly Nuechterlein, Program Manager

2595 Sherman Fairchild Foundation
71 Arch Street
Greenwich, CT 06830-6544
203-661-9360
Fax: 203-661-9360
Offers grants in higher education, fine arts and cultural institutions.

Patricia A Lydon, Executive Director

2596 Smart Family Foundation
74 Pin Oak Lane
Wilton, CT 06897-1329
203-834-0400
Fax: 203-834-0412
The foundation is interested in educational projects that focus on primary and secondary school children.

Raymond Smart, Executive Director

2597 Worthington Family Foundation
P.O Box 4311
Traverse City, MI 49685

203-255-9400
http://www.worthington-family-foundation.
org
Offers grants in the areas of elementary school education and secondary school education in Connecticut.

Worthington Johnson, Executive Director
Ruth Worthington, President

Delaware

2598 Crystal Trust
Po Box 39
Montchanin, DE 19710-0039
302-651-0533
Grants are awarded for higher and secondary education and social and family services.

Stephen C Doberstein, Executive Director

2599 HW Buckner Charitable Residuary Trust
JP Morgan Services
PO Box 8714
Wilmington, DE 19899-8714
302-633-1900
Focuses giving on educational and cultural organizations in New York, Rhode Island and Massachusetts.

2600 Longwood Foundation
100 W 10th Street
Suite 1109
Wilmington, DE 19801-1694
302-654-2477
Fax: 302-654-2323
Limited grants are offered to educational institutions and cultural programs.

David D Wakefield, Executive Director

District of Columbia

2601 Abe Wouk Foundation
3255 N Street NW
Washington, DC 20007-2845
Offers grants in elementary, secondary education and federated giving programs.

Herman Wouk, Executive Director

2602 Eugene & Agnes E Meyer Foundation
1250 Connecticut Avenue
Suite 800
Washington, DC 20036-2215
202-483-8294
Fax: 202-328-6850
http://www.meyerfoundation.org
Offers grants in the areas of development and housing, education and community services, arts and humanities, law and justice, health and mental health.

Julie L Rogers, President
Barbara Krumsiek, Chairman

2603 Foundation Center-District of Columbia
1627 K Street NW
3rd Floor
Washington, DC 20006-1708
202-331-1400
Fax: 202-331-1739
http://www.fdncenter.org/washington/index
.jhtml
Member of The Foundation Center network, maintaining a collection of private foundation tax returns which provide information on the scope of grants dispensed to nonprofit organizations by those particular foundations.

2604 Foundation for the National Capitol Region
1201 15th Street NW
Suite 420
Washington, DC 20005
202-955-5890
Fax: 202-955-8084
http://www.cfncr.org
Grants are focused on organization strengthening and regional collaboration. The Foundation wishes to foster collaborations that identify, address, and increase awareness of regional issues, as well as help strengthen the region's existing non-profit organizations to improve their financial stability. The Foundation welcomes requests from organizations serving the Greater Washington area that are tax-exempt under Section 501(c)(3) of the Internal Revenue Code.

Terry Lee Freeman, President

2605 Gilbert & Jaylee Mead Family Foundation
2700 Virginia Avenue NW #701
Washington, DC 20037-1908
202-338-0208
Offers support for education (K-12), the performing arts and community service programs for Washington, DC, Montgomery County, Maryland, and Geneva, Switzerland.

Linda Smith, Executive Director

2606 Hitachi Foundation
1509 22nd Street NW
Washington, DC 20037-1073
202-457-0588
Fax: 202-296-1098
http://www.hitachi.org
The majority of projects supported by the foundation: promote collaboration across sectors and among institutions, organizations and individuals; reflect multi-or-interdisciplinary perspectives; respect and value diversity of thought, action, and ethnicity. Grants are given in the areas of community development, education, global citizenship and program related investments.

Barbara Dyer, President/CEO

2607 Morris & Gwendolyn Cafritz Foundation
1825 K Street NW
Suite 1400
Washington, DC 20006-1202
202-223-3100
Fax: 202-296-7567
http://www.cafritzfoundation.org
Gives grants to organizations in the metropolitan area, focusing on arts, humanities and scholarships.

Sara Cofrin, Program Assistant
Michael Bigley, Program Officer

2608 Public Welfare Foundation
1200 U Street NW
Washington, DC 20009-4443
202-965-1800
Fax: 202-265-8851
E-mail: info@publicwelfare.org
http://www.publicwelfare.org
Offers grants to grass roots organizations in the US and abroad with emphasis on the environment and education.

Larry Kressley, Executive Director
Teresa Langston, Director Of Programs

2609 Washington Post Company Educational Foundation
1150 15th Street NW
Washington, DC 20071-0002
202-334-6000
Offers support for pre-college and higher education including student scholarships and awards for academic excellence.

Eric Grant, Director Contributions

Florida

2610 Applebaum Foundation
1111 Biscaynees Boulevard
Tower 3, Room 853
North Miami, FL 33181
Offers an emphasis on higher education.

2611 Benedict Foundation for Independent Schools
607 Lantana Lane
Vero Beach, FL 32963-2315

http://www.thebenedictfoundation.org
Support is offered primarily for independent secondary schools that have been members of the National Association of Independent Schools for ten consecutive years.

Nancy H Benedict, Executive Director
Davis M Benedict, Vice President & Director

2612 Chatlos Foundation
PO Box 915048
Longwood, FL 32791-5048
407-862-5077
Fax: 407-862-0708
http://www.chatlos.org
Bible colleges and seminaries, liberal arts colleges, vocation and domestic education, medical education; children, elderly, disabled and learning disabled. The Foundation is non-receptive to primary or secondary education, the arts, medical research, individual churches. No direct scholarship support to individuals.

William J Chatlos, Executive Director

2613 Citibank of Florida Corporate Giving Program
8750 Doral Boulevard
7th Floor
Miami, FL 33718
305-599-5775
Fax: 305-599-5520
Offers support for K-12 education for at-risk children. Funding is also available through the program for housing and community development in the state of Florida.

Susan Yarosz, Executive Director

2614 Dade Community Foundation
200 S Biscayne Boulevard
Suite 505
Miami, FL 33131-2343
305-371-2711
Fax: 305-371-5342
http://www.dadecommunityfoundation.org
Offers support for projects in the fields of education, arts and culture.

Ruth Shack, Executive Director

2615 Innovating Worthy Projects Foundation
Lakeview Corporate Center
4045 Sheridan Avenue
Miami, FL 33140-2904

305-861-5352
Fax: 305-868-4293
E-mail: info@IWPF.org
http://www.iwpf.org
Offers grants and support for education in the areas of childhood education and elementary education.

Dr. Irving Packer, Executive Director

2616 Jacksonville Public Library
Business, Science & Documents
303 N Laura St
Jacksonville, FL 32202-3374
904-630-2665
Fax: 904-630-2431
http://www.jpl.coj.net
Member of The Foundation Center network, maintaining a collection of private foundation tax returns which provide information on the scope of grants dispensed by that particular foundation.

Gretchen Mitchell, Business/Science Department

2617 Jessie Ball duPont Fund
One Independent Drive
Suite 1400
Jacksonville, FL 32202-5011
904-353-0890
800-252-3452
Fax: 904-353-3870
E-mail: smagill@dupontfund.org
http://www.dupontfund.org
Grants limited to those institutions to which the donor contributed personally during the five year period ending December 31, 1964. Among the 325 institutions eligible to recieve funds are higher and secondary education intitutions, cultural and historic preservation programs, social services organizations, hospitals, health agencies, churches and church-related organizations and youth agencies.

Dr. Sherry P Magill, President
JoAnn Bennett, Director Administration

2618 Joseph & Rae Gann Charitable Foundation
10185 Collins Avenue
Apartment 317
Bal Harbour, FL 33154-1606
Offers support in the areas of elementary, secondary and theological education.

2619 Orlando Public Library-Orange County Library System
Social Sciences Department
101 E Central Boulivard
Orlando, FL 32801-2471
407-835-7323
Fax: 407-835-7646
E-mail: ajacobe@ocls.lib.fl.us
http://www.ocls.lib.fl.us
Member of The Foundation Center network, maintaining a collection on microfiche of Florida private foundation tax returns which provide information on the scope of grants dispensed by that particular foundation. Other available resources include directories of foundations, guide to funding, and materials on successful grant acquisition. FC Search Foundation Center CD Rom.

Angela C Jacobe, Head Social Science Dpt

2620 Peter D & Eleanore Kleist Foundation
12734 Kenwood Lane
Suite 89
Fort Myers, FL 33907-5638
Support is given to secondary school education and higher education.

Peter D Kleist, Executive Director

2621 Robert G Friedman Foundation
76 Isla Bahia Drive
Fort Lauderdale, FL 33316-2331

Giving is offered to elementary and high schools, with minor support to indigent individuals and charitable activities.

Robert G Friedman, Executive Director

622 Southwest Florida Community Foundation
8771 College Parkway
Suite 201
Fort Myers, FL 33919
239-274-5900
Fax: 239-274-5930
E-mail: swflcfo@earthlink.net
http://www.floridacommunity.com
Offers grants and support in the areas of education, higher education, children and youth services and general charitable giving to Lee, Charlotte, Hendry, Glades, and Collier Counties, Florida.

Paul B Flynn, Executive Director
Carol McLaughlin, Program Director

623 Student Help and Assistance Program to Education
C/O Michael Bienes
141 Bay Colony Drive
Fort Lauderdale, FL 33308-2024
Offers grants and support in the areas of elementary and secondary education, music and dance.

624 Thomas & Irene Kirbo Charitable Trust
550 Water St
Suite 1327
Jacksonville, FL 32202-5113
904-354-7212
Favors smaller colleges in Florida and Georgia.

Murray Jenks, Executive Director

625 Thompson Publishing Group
PO Box 26185
Tampa, FL 33623
800-876-0226
http://www.thompson.com or www.grantsandfunding.com
Assists education administrators and grant seekers in successful fundraising in the public and private sectors.

Joel M Drucker, Executive Director

Georgia

626 Atlanta-Fulton Public Library
Foundation Collection/Ivan Allen Department
1 Margaret Mitchell Square NW
Atlanta, GA 30303-1089
404-730-1700
Fax: 404-730-1990
http://www.af.public.lib.ga.us.org
Member of The Foundation Center network, maintaining a collection of private foundation tax returns which provide information on the scope of grants dispensed by that particular foundation.

627 BellSouth Foundation
C/O BellSouth Corporation
1155 Peachtree Street NE
Sutie 7H08
Atlanta, GA 30309-3600
404-249-2396
Fax: 404-249-5696
http://www.bellsouthfoundation.org

The foundation's purpose is to improve education in the South and to address the problem of the inadequate schooling in the region.

Mary D Boehm, President
Beverly Fleming, Administrative Assistant

2628 Bradley Foundation
1241 North Franklin Place
Milwaukee, WI 53202-2901
414-291-9915
Fax: 414-291-9991
http://www.bradleyfdn.org
Focuses on higher educational facilities, elementary and secondary education, human services and federated giving programs.

Terry Considine, Chairman

2629 Callaway Foundation
209 W Broome Street
#790
Lagrange, GA 30241-3101
706-884-7348
Fax: 706-884-0201
http://www.callawayfoundation.org
Offers giving in the areas of elementary, higher and secondary education, including libraries and community giving.

JT Gresham, Executive Director

2630 Coca-Cola Foundation
Po Box 1734
Atlanta, GA 30301
404-676-2568
Fax: 404-676-8804
http://www.thecoca-colacompany.com
Committed to serving communities through education. The foundation supports programs for early childhood education, elementary and secondary schools, public and private colleges and universities, teacher training, adult learning and global education programs, among others.

Donald R Greene, Executive Director

2631 J Bulow Campbell Foundation
3050 Peachtree Road
Suite 270
Atlanta, GA 30305
404-658-9066
Fax: 404-659-4802
http://www.jbcf.org
The purpose of this foundation is to offer grants and support to privately supported education, human welfare, youth services and the arts in the state of Georgia.

John W Stephenson, Executive Director

2632 JK Gholston Trust
C/O NationsBank of Georgia
PO Box 992
Athens, GA 30603-0992
706-357-6271
Support is offered to elementary school and higher education facilities in the Comer, Georgia area.

Janey M Cooley, Executive Director

2633 John & Mary Franklin Foundation
C/O Bank South N.A.
PO Box 4956
Atlanta, GA 30302
404-521-7397
Offers grants in secondary school/education, higher education and youth services.

Virlyn Moore Sr, Executive Director

2634 John H & Wilhelmina D Harland Charitable Foundation
2 Piedmont Center NE
Suite 710
Atlanta, GA 30305-1502

404-264-9912
Fax: 404-266-8834
E-mail: info@harlandfoundation.org
http://www.harlandfoundation.org
Children and higher education.

Jane G Hardesty, Executive Director
Gail G Byers, Grants Manager

2635 Joseph B Whitehead Foundation
191 Peachtree Street NE
Suite 3540
Atlanta, GA 30303-2916
404-522-6755
Fax: 404-522-7026
E-mail: fdns@woodruff.org
http://www.jbwhitehead.org
Offers grants in education, cultural programs, the arts and civic affairs.

Charles H McTier, Executive Director
James B William, Chairman

2636 Lettie Pate Evans Foundation
191 Peachtree Street NE
Suite 3540
Atlanta, GA 30303-2916
404-522-6755
Fax: 404-522-7026
E-mail: fdns@woodruff.org
http://www.lpevans.org
Offers grants in the areas of higher education, and support for educational and cultural institutions.

Charles H McTier, Executive Director
James B William, Chairman

2637 McCamish Foundation
1 Buckhead Loop NE #3060
Atlanta, GA 30326-1528

http://www.mccamish.com
Offers grants for conservation and educational institutions.

2638 Metropolitan Atlanta Community Foundation
50 Hurt Plaza
Suite 449
Atlanta, GA 30303
404-688-5525
Fax: 404-688-3060
http://www.atlcf.org
This foundation was organized for the administration of funds placed in trust for the purposes of improving education, community development and civic health of the 19-county metropolitan area of Atlanta.

Winsome Hawkins Sr, Executive Director
Alicia Phillip, President

2639 Mill Creek Foundation
4400 Braselton Hwy
Hoschton, GA 30548-0190
478-237-0101
Fax: 478-237-6187
http://www.mccef.org
The foundation's primary interests are educational programs in all levels of study in Emanuel County, Georgia.

James H Morgan, Executive Director

2640 Mills Bee Lane Memorial Foundation
Nations Bank of Georgia
PO Box 9626
Savannah, GA 31412-9626
Offers support in various areas of education, including higher, secondary, and elementary.

2641 Peyton Anderson Foundation
577 Mulberry Street
Suite 830
Macon, GA 31201

478-743-5359
Fax: 912-742-5201
E-mail: grants@pafdn.org
http://www.peytonanderson.org
Supports organizations and programs that center on elementary education, higher education, adult education, literacy and basic skills and youth services, in Bibb County, Georgia only.

Juanita T Jordan, Executive Director
Karen Lambert, President

2642 Rich Foundation
11 Piedmont Avenue NE
Atlanta, GA 30303
404-262-2266
Funds are allocated to social services, health, the arts and education.

Anne Berg, Executive Director

2643 Robert & Polly Dunn Foundation
PO Box 723194
Atlanta, GA 31139-0194
404-816-2883
Fax: 404-237-2150
Offers support in the areas of child development, education, higher education, and children and youth services.

Karen C Wilbanks, Executive Director

2644 Sapelo Foundation
1712 Ellis Street
2nd Floor
Brunswick, GA 31520
912-265-0520
Fax: 912-265-1888
E-mail:
sapelofoundation@mindspring.com
http://www.sapelofoundation.org
The Sapelo Foundation's scholarship program, The Richard Reynolds Scholarship Program offers college scholarships only to students who are legal residents of McIntosh County, Georgia.

Phyllis Bowen, Executive Director

2645 Tull Charitable Foundation
50 Hurt Plaza SE
Suite 1245
Atlanta, GA 30303-2916
404-659-7079
http://www.tullfoundation.org
Offers support to secondary schools, elementary schools and higher education facilities in the state of Georgia.

Barbara Cleveland, Executive Director

2646 Warren P & Ava F Sewell Foundation
PO Box 645
Bremen, GA 30110-0645
Offers support in elementary school, secondary school education and religion.

Jack Worley, Executive Director

Hawaii

2647 Barbara Cox Anthony Foundation
1132 Bishop Street #120
Honolulu, HI 96813-2807
Offers support to secondary schools, higher education, and human service organizations in Hawaii.

Barner Anthony, Executive Director

2648 Cooke Foundation
827 Fort Street Mall
Honolulu, HI 96813

808-537-6333
888-731-3863
Fax: 808-521-6286
E-mail: foundations@hcf-hawaii.org
http://www.hawaiicommunityfoundation.org
The environment, the arts, education and social services are the priority areas for this foundation.

Lisa Schiff, Private Foundation Service
Samuel Cooke, President & Trustee

2649 Harold KL Castle Foundation
1197 Auloa Road
Kailua, HI 96734-2835
808-263-7073
Fax: 808-261-6918
http://www.castlefoundation.org
Grants are given in the area of education, community and cultural/community affairs.

Terrence R George, Executive Director
H Mitchell D'Olier, President

2650 Hawaiian Electric Industries Charitable Foundation
PO Box 730
Honolulu, HI 96808-0730
808-532-5862
http://www.hei.com/heicf/heicf.html
Offers support for education, including higher education, business education, educational associations and secondary schools.

Scott Shirai, Executive Director
Robert F Clark, President

2651 James & Abigail Campbell Foundation
1001 Kamokila Boulevard
Kapolei, HI 96707-2014
808-674-3167
Fax: 808-674-3349
E-mail: keolal@jamescampbell.com
http://www.campbellfamilyfoundation.org
Offers support in education for schools and educational programs related to literacy or job training in Hawaii.

Theresia McMurdo, Public Relations
D. Keola Lloyd, Grants Manager

2652 Oceanic Cablevision Foundation
200 Akamainui Street
Mililani, HI 96789-3999
808-625-8359
Offers support in a variety of areas with an emphasis on education, especially early childhood and cultural programs.

Kit Beuret, Executive Director

2653 Samuel N & Mary Castle Foundation
733 Bishop Street
Suite 1275
Honolulu, HI 96813-2912
808-522-1101
Fax: 808-522-1103
E-mail: acastle@aloha.net
http://www.fdncenter.org
Funding is offered in the areas of education, human services and the arts for the state of Hawaii.

Annually

Al Castle, Executive Director

2654 University of Hawaii
Hamilton Library
2550 The Mall
Honolulu, HI 96822-2233

808-956-7214
Fax: 808-956-5968
http://www.libweb.hawaii.edu/uhmlib
Member of The Foundation Center network, maintaining a collection of private foundation tax returns which provide information on the scope of grants dispensed by that particular foundation.

Idaho

2655 Boise Public Library
715 S Capitol Boulevard
Boise, ID 83702-7115
208-384-4076
http://www.boisepubliclibrary.org
Member of The Foundation Center network, maintaining a collection of private foundation tax returns which provide information on the scope of grants dispensed by that particular foundation.

2656 Claude R & Ethel B Whittenberger Foundation
PO Box 1073
Caldwell, ID 83606-1073
208-459-0091
E-mail: whittfnd@cableone.net
http://www.whittenberger.org
Offers support for youth and children in higher and secondary education.

William J Rankin, Executive Director

2657 Walter & Leona Dufresne Foundation
1150 W State Street
Boise, ID 83702-5327
Offers support in the areas of secondary school education and higher education.

Royce Chigbrow, Executive Director

Illinois

2658 Ameritech Foundation
30 S Wacker Drive
Floor 34
Chicago, IL 60606-7487
312-750-5223
Fax: 312-207-1098
http://www.ntlf.com
A foundation that offers grants to elementary school/education, secondary school/education and higher education.

Michael E Kuhlin, Executive Director

2659 Carus Corporate Contributions Program
315 5th Street
Peru, IL 61354-2859
815-223-1500
Offers support for higher, secondary, elementary and early childhood education.

Robert J Wilmot, Executive Director

2660 Chauncey & Marion Deering McCormick Foundation
410 N Michigan Avenue
Suite 590
Chicago, IL 60611-4220
312-644-6720
Preschool education, journalism and the improvement of socio-economic condition of Metropolitan Chicago are the main areas of giving for this foundation.

Charles E Schroeder, Executive Director

2661 Chicago Community Trust
225 North Michigan Avenue
Suite 2200
Chicago, IL 60601-1088

312-616-8000
Fax: 312-616-7955
E-mail: sandy@cct.org
http://www.cct.org
A community foundation that offers support for general operating projects and specific programs and projects in areas including child development, education and higher education.

Sandy Chears, Grants Manager
Terry Mazany, President

662 Coleman Foundation
651 West Washington Boulevard
Suite 306
Chicago, IL 60661-2515
312-902-7120
Fax: 312-902-7124
E-mail: info@colemanfoundation.org
http://www.colemanfoundation.org
A nonprofit, private foundation established in the state of Illinois in 1951. Major areas of support include health, educational, cultural, scientific and social programs. Grants generally focus on organizations within the Midwest and particularly within the state of Illinois and the Chicago Metropolitan area. No grants are made for programs outside of the United States. Ongoing support is not available, continuing programs must indicate how they will be sustained in the future.

Rosa Janus, Program Manager
Michael W Hennessy, President/CEO

663 Dellora A & Lester J Norris Foundation
PO Box 4325
Saint Charles, IL 60174-9075
630-377-4111
Education, health and social services are the main concerns of this foundation, with Illinois, Colorado and Florida being their priority.

Eugene W Butler, Executive Director

664 Dillon Foundation
PO Box 454
Boulder, MT 59632-0537
406-980-1588
E-mail: info@dillonfoundation.org
http://www.dillonfoundation.org
Offers support for educational purposes, including higher education and community services.

Peter W Dillon, Executive Director

665 Dr. Scholl Foundation
1033 Skokie Boulevard
Suite 230
Northbrook, IL 60062
847-559-7430
http://www.drschollfoundation.com
Applications for grants are considered in the following areas: private education at all levels including elementary, secondary schools, colleges and universities and medical and nursing institutions; general charitable organizations and programs, including grants to hospitals and programs for children, developmentally disabled and senior citizens; civic, cultural, social services, health care, economic and religious activities.

Pamela Scholl, Executive Director

666 Evanston Public Library
1703 Orrington Avenue
Evanston, IL 60201-3886
847-866-0300
Fax: 847-866-0313
http://www.evanston.lib.il.us
Member of The Foundation Center network, maintaining a collection of private founda-

tion tax returns which provide information on the scope of grants dispensed by that particular foundation.

Neal J Ney, Director

2667 Farny R Wurlitzer Foundation
PO Box 418
Sycamore, IL 60178-0418
Offers support in the areas of education, including programs for minorities, early childhood, elementary and secondary institutions, music education and organizations.

William A Rolfing, Executive Director

2668 Grover Hermann Foundation
1000 Hill Grove
Suite 200
Western Springs, IL 60558-6306
708-246-8331
Focus of giving is on higher education and private schooling activities.

Paul K Rhoads, Executive Director

2669 Joyce Foundation
70 W Madison Street
Suite 2750
Chicago, IL 60602
312-782-2464
Fax: 312-782-4160
E-mail: info@joycefdn.org
http://www.joycefdn.org
Based in Chicago with assets of $1 billion, the Joyce foundation supports efforts to strengthen public policies in ways that improve the quality of life in the Great Lakes region. Last year the foundation made nearly $17 million in grants to groups working to improve public education in Chicago, Cleveland, Detroit and Milwaukee.

Ellen Alberding, President

2670 Lloyd A Fry Foundation
120 S Lasalle Street
Suite 1950
Chicago, IL 60603-3419
312-580-0310
Fax: 312-580-0980
http://www.fryfoundation.org
The foundation primarily supports education, higher education, the performing arts, and social service organizations.

Unmi Song, Executive Director

2671 Northern Trust Company Charitable Trust
Community Affairs Division
50 S Lasalle Street
Chicago, IL 60603-1006
312-630-6000
http://www.ntrs.com
Offers grants in the areas of community development, education and early childhood education.

Marjorie W Lundy, Executive Director

2672 Palmer Foundation
734 15th Street NW
Suite 600
Washington, DC 20005
202-595-1020
Fax: 202-833-5540
E-mail: admin@thepalmerfoundation.org
http://www.thepalmerfoundation.org
Offers grants in elementary and secondary education, as well as youth services and Protestant churches.

2673 Philip H Corboy Foundation
33 N Dearborn Street
Chicago, IL 60602-2502

312-346-3191
http://www.corboydemetrio.com
Offers grants in the areas of elementary, secondary, law school education and health care.

2674 Polk Brothers Foundation
20 W Kinzie Street
Suite 1100
Chicago, IL 60610-4600
312-527-4684
Fax: 312-527-4681
http://www.polkbrosfdn.org
Offers grants for new or ongoing programs to organizations whose work is based in the areas of education, social services and health care.

Nikki W Stein, Executive Director
Shiela A Robinson, Grants Administrator

2675 Prince Charitable Trust
303 West Madison Street
Suite 1900
Chicago, IL 60606-7407
312-419-8700
Fax: 312-419-8558
http://www.fdncenter.org/grantmaker/prince/chicago.html
Offers support for cultural programs, public school programming and social service organizations.

Benna B Wilde, Managing Director
Sharon L Robison, Grants Manager

2676 Regenstein Foundation
8600 W Bryn Mawr Avenue
Suite 705N
Chicago, IL 60631-3579
773-693-6464
Fax: 773-693-2480
Offers grants for educational and general charitable institutions within the metropolitan Chicago area and the state of Illinois.

Joseph Regenstein Jr, Executive Director

2677 Richard H Driehaus Foundation
333 N Michigan Avenue
Suite 510
Chicago, IL 60601-1604
312-641-5772
Fax: 312-641-5736
http://www.driehausfoundation.org
Offers support in elementary, secondary and higher education in the state of Illinois.

Susan Fischer, Executive Director
Peter Handler, Program Director

2678 Robert R McCormick Tribune Foundation
435 N Michigan Avenue
Suite 770
Chicago, IL 60611-4066
312-222-3512
Fax: 312-222-3523
http://www.rrmtf.org
Offers contributions for private higher education and rehabilitation services.

Nicholas Goodban, Senior VP/Philanthropy
Richard A Behrenhausen, President/CEO

2679 Sears-Roebuck Foundation
Sears Tower
Department 903-BSC 51-02
Chicago, IL 60684
312-875-8337
The foundation focuses its giving primarily on projects that address education and volunteerism.

Paula A Banke, Executive Director

2680 Spencer Foundation
875 N Michigan Avenue
Suite 3930
Chicago, IL 60611-1803
312-337-7000
Fax: 312-337-0282
http://www.spencer.org
Supports research aimed at the practice of understanding and expanding knowledge in the area of education.

Michael McPherson, President

2681 Sulzer Family Foundation
1940 W Irving Park Road
Chicago, IL 60613-2437
312-321-4700
Offers giving for education, including higher, secondary, elementary and adult education in the areas of Chicago, Illinois.

John J Hoellen, Executive Director

2682 United Airlines Foundation
1800 Massachusetts Avenue
Suite 400
Washington, DC 20036-0919
847-952-5714
http://www.unfoundation.org
Offers a wide variety of support programs with an emphasis on education and educational reform.

Eileen Younglove, Executive Director
Timothy E Wirth, President

2683 Valenti Charitable Foundation
Valenti Builders
PO Box 2534
Rancho Santa Fe, CA 92067-3311
858-759-9239
Fax: 858-759-1319
E-mail: Irene@valentifoundation.org
http://www.valentifoundation.org
Offers support in elementary education, secondary school education, higher education and children and youth services.

Valenti Sr Trustee, Executive Director

Indiana

2684 Allen County Public Library
900 Library Plaza
Fort Wayne, IN 46802-3699
260-421-1200
Fax: 260-421-1386
http://www.acpl.lib.in.us
Member of The Foundation Center network, maintaining a collection of private foundation tax returns which provide information on the scope of grants dispensed by that particular foundation.

2685 Arvin Foundation
1 Noblitt Plaza #3000
Columbus, IN 47201-6079
812-379-3207
Fax: 812-379-3688
Giving is offered primarily to primary, secondary and higher education and technical training.

E Fred Meyer, Executive Director

2686 Clowes Fund
320 N Meridian Street Suite 316
The Chamber of Commerce Building
Indianapolis, IN 46204-1722
800-943-7209
Fax: 800-943-7286
http://www.clowesfund.org

Offers giving for higher and secondary education; the performing arts; marine biology and social service organizations.

Elizabeth Casselman, Executive Director
Alexander W Clowes, President

2687 Dekko Foundation
PO Box 548
Kendallville, IN 46755-0548
260-347-1278
Fax: 260-347-7103
Offers support for all levels of education and human service organizations.

Linda Speakman, Executive Director

2688 Eli Lilly & Company Corporate Contribution Program
Lilly Corporate Center D.C. 1627
Indianapolis, IN 46285
317-276-2000
Offers support in the areas of secondary school/education, higher education and health care programs.

Thomas King, President

2689 Foellinger Foundation
520 E Berry Street
Fort Wayne, IN 46802-2002
260-422-2900
Fax: 260-422-9436
E-mail: info@foellinger.org
http://www.foellinger.org
Giving is aimed at higher education and other secondary and elementary projects, community programs and social service organizations.

Harry V Owen, Executive Director

2690 Indianapolis Foundation
615 N Alabama Street
Suite 119
Indianapolis, IN 46204-1498
317-634-2423
Fax: 317-684-0943
http://www.indyfund.org
Offers support in the areas of education and neighborhood services.

Kenneth Gladish, Executive Director

2691 John W Anderson Foundation
402 Wall Street
Valparaiso, IN 46383-2562
219-462-4611
Fax: 219-531-8954
Offers grants in the areas of higher education, youth programs, human services, and arts and humanities. Grants are limited primarily to Northwest Indian organizations.

William Vinovich, Vice Chairman/Trustee

2692 Lilly Endowment
2801 N Meridian Street
Indianapolis, IN 46208-0068
317-924-5471
Fax: 317-926-4431
http://www.lillyendowment.org
Supports the causes of religion, education and community development. Although the Endowment supports efforts of national significance, especially in the field of religion, it is primarily committed to its hometown, Indianapolis, and home state, Indiana.

Sue Ellen Walker, Communications Associate

2693 Moore Foundation
1661 Page Mill Road
Palo Alto, CA 94304-2158

317-848-2013
Fax: 317-571-0744
E-mail: info@moore.org
http://www.moore.org
Offers support in elementary school and secondary school education, higher education, business school education and youth services in Indiana.

Eileen C Ryan, Executive Director
Gordon Moore, Chairman

2694 W Brooks Fortune Foundation
7933 Beaumont Green W Drive
Indianapolis, IN 46250-1652
317-842-1303
Support is limited to education-related programs in Indiana.

William Brooks Fortune, Executive Director

Iowa

2695 Cedar Rapids Public Library
Funding Information Center
500 1st Street SE
Cedar Rapids, IA 52401-2095
319-398-5123
Fax: 319-398-0476
http://www.crlibrary.org
Member of The Foundation Center network, maintaining a collection of private foundation tax returns which provide information on the scope of grants dispensed by that particular foundation.

Tamara Glise, Public Services Manager
Eileen C Ryan, Executive Director

2696 RJ McElroy Trust
425 Cedar Street
Suite 312
Waterloo, IA 50701
312
http://www.mcelroytrust.org
The trust funds grants to educational youth programs in the northeast quarter of Iowa. The trust guidelines do not include grants to individuals.

Linda L Klinger, Executive Director

Kansas

2697 Mary Jo Williams Charitable Trust
PO Box 660075
Dallas, TX 75266-0075
866-866-7509
Offers support in the areas of early childhood education, higher education, and children and youth services.

Michael E Collins, Executive Director

2698 Sprint Foundation
2330 Shawnee Mission Parkway
Westwood, KS 66205-2090
913-624-3343
http://www.sprint.com
Offers grants in a variety of areas with an emphasis on education, including business education, secondary education and higher education.

Don G Forsythe, Executive Director

2699 Wichita Public Library
223 S Main Street
Wichita, KS 67202-3795
316-261-8500
Fax: 316-262-4540
http://www.wichita.lib.ks.us
Member of The Foundation Center network, maintaining a collection of private foundation tax returns which provide information on the scope of grants dispensed by that particular foundation.

Kentucky

700 Ashland Incorporated Foundation
50 E River Center Boulevard
Covington, KY 41012
859-815-3630
Fax: 859-815-4496
http://www.ashland.com
Offers support to educational organizations, colleges and universities, as well as giving an employee matching gift program to higher education and community funding.

James O'Brien, CEO

701 Gheens Foundation
401 W Main Street
Suite 705
Louisville, KY 40202
502-584-4650
Fax: 502-584-4652
http://www.gheensfoundation.org
The foundation's support is aimed at higher and secondary education, ongoing teacher education, and social service agencies.

James N Davis, Executive Director
William G Duncan, Secretary

702 James Graham Brown Foundation
4350 Brownsboro Road
Suite 200
Louisville, KY 40207
502-896-2440
Fax: 502-896-1774
E-mail: info@jgbf.org
http://www.jgbf.org
Offers grants in the areas of higher education and social services.

Mason Rummel, Executive Director
Dodie L McKenzie, Program Officer

703 Louisville Free Public Library
301 York Street
Louisville, KY 40203-2257
502-574-1611
Fax: 502-574-1657
http://www.lfpl.org
Member of The Foundation Center network, maintaining a collection of private foundation tax returns which provide information on the scope of grants dispensed by that particular foundation.

704 Margaret Hall Foundation
6685 Walnutwood Circle
Baltimore, MD 21212-1727
443-708-3548
http://www.margarethallfoundation.org
Awards grants and scholarships to private, nonprofit secondary schools for innovative programming.

Helen R Burg, Executive Director

705 VV Cooke Foundation Corporation
220 Mount Mercy Drive
Pewee Valley, KY 40056-9068
502-241-0303
Offers support in education and youth services with an emphasis on Baptist church and school support.

John B Gray, Executive Director

Louisiana

706 Baton Rouge Area Foundation
402 N 4th Street
Baton Rouge, LA 70802
225-387-6126
877-387-6126
Fax: 225-387-6153
http://www.braf.org
Offers grants in the area of elementary and secondary education and health.

John G Davies, President

2707 Booth-Bricker Fund
826 Union Street
Suite 300
New Orleans, LA 70112-1421
504-581-2430
Fax: 504-566-4785
Does not have a formal grant procedure or grant application form; nor does it publish an annual report. The Booth-Bricker Fund makes contributions for the purposes of promoting, developing and fostering religious, charitable, scientific, literary or educational programs, primarily in the state of Louisiana. It does not make contributions to individuals.

Gray S Parker, Chairman

2708 East Baton Rouge Parish Library
Centroplex Branch Grants Collection
7711 Goodwood Boulevard
Baton Rouge, LA 70806
225-231-3750
http://www.ebrpl.com
Member of The Foundation Center network, maintaining a collection of private foundation tax returns which provide information on the scope of grants dispensed by that particular foundation.

2709 Fred B & Ruth B Zigler Foundation
Zigler Foundation
PO Box 986
Zigler Building
Jennings, LA 70546-0986
337-824-2413
Fax: 337-824-2414
E-mail: frizler@bellsouth.net
http://www.ziglerfoundation.org
Offers support to higher, secondary and primary education.

Julie G Berry, President
Marie Romero, Secretary

2710 New Orleans Public Library
Business & Science Division
219 Loyola Avenue
New Orleans, LA 70112-2044
504-529-7323
Fax: 504-596-2609
http://www.nutrias.org
Member of The Foundation Center network, maintaining a collection of private foundation tax returns which provide information on the scope of grants dispensed by that particular foundation.

2711 Shreve Memorial Library
424 Texas Street
Shreveport, LA 71101-5452
318-226-5897
Fax: 318-226-4780
E-mail: webmaster@shreve-lib.org
http://www.shreve-lib.org
Member of The Foundation Center network, maintaining a collection of private Louisiana foundation tax returns which provide information on the scope of grants dispensed by that particular foundation.

Carlos Colon, Reference Supervisor

Maine

2712 Clarence E Mulford Trust
PO Box 290
Fryeburg, ME 04037-0290
207-935-2061
Fax: 207-935-3939
Offers grants to charitable, educational and scientific organizations for the purpose of improving education.

David R Hastings II, Executive Director

2713 Harold Alfond Trust
C/O Dexter Shoe Company
Two Monument Square
Portland, ME 04101-0353
207-828-7999
E-mail: info@haroldalfoundation.org
http://www.haroldalfondfoundation.org
Grants are offered to secondary and higher education in Maine and Maryland.

Keith Burden, Executive Director

Maryland

2714 Abell Foundation
111 S Calvert Street
Suite 2300
Baltimore, MD 21202-6182
410-547-1300
Fax: 410-539-6579
E-mail: abell@abell.org
http://www.abell.org
The foundation supports education with an emphasis on public education, including early childhood and elementary, research, and minority education.

Robert C Embry Jr, Executive Director
Ellen Mullan, Controller

2715 Aegon USA
1111 N Charles Street
Baltimore, MD 21201-5505
410-576-4571
Fax: 410-347-8685
http://www.aegonins.com
Offers grants in elementary school, secondary school, higher education and medical school education.

Larry G Brown, Executive Director

2716 Clarence Manger & Audrey Cordero Plitt Trust
C/O First National Bank of Maryland
25 S Charles St
Baltimore, MD 21201-3330
410-566-0914
Offers grants to educational institutions for student loans and scholarships.

Mary M Kirgan, Executive Director

2717 Clark-Winchcole Foundation
Air Rights Building
3 Bethesda Metro Center
Suite 550
Bethesda, MD 20814
301-654-3607
Fax: 301-654-3140
Offers grants in the areas of higher education and social service agencies.

Laura E Philips, Executive Director

2718 Commonwealth Foundation
9737 Colesville Road
Suite 800
Silver Spring, MD 20910
301-495-4400
Offers grants in the areas of early childhood education, child development, elementary schools, secondary schools and youth services.

Barbara Bainum, Executive Director

2719 Dresher Foundation
4940 Campbell Boulevard
Suite 110
Baltimore, MD 21236
410-933-0384
E-mail: web@jdgraphicdesign.com
http://www.jdgraphicdesign.com/dresher/dresherfoundation/
Offers giving in the areas of elementary school, early childhood education, meals on wheels, and food distribution.

2720 Edward E Ford Foundation
66 Pearl Street
Suite 322
Portland, ME 04101
207-774-2346
Fax: 207-774-2348
E-mail: office@eeford.org
http://www.eeford.org
Offers giving to secondary schools and private education in the US and its protectorates.

Robert Hallett, Executive Director

2721 Enoch Pratt Free Library
Social Science & History Department
400 Cathedral Street
Baltimore, MD 21201-4484
301-396-5430
http://www.pratt.lib.md.us
Member of The Foundation Center network, maintaining a collection of private foundation tax returns which provide information on the scope of grants dispensed by that particular foundation.

2722 France-Merrick Foundation
The Exchange
2 Hamill Rd,Quadrangle East
Suite 302
Baltimore, MD 21210-2139
410-464-2004
Fax: 410-832-5704
E-mail: rschaefer@france-merrickfdn-org
Offers giving in the areas of public education, private and higher education, health, social services and cultural activities.

Frederick W Lafferty, Executive Director

2723 Grayce B Kerr Fund
117 Bay Street
Easton, MD 21601-2769
410-822-6652
Fax: 410-822-4546
E-mail: office@gbkf.org
http://www.gbkf.org
The major area of interest to the fund is education, including higher, elementary and early childhood education for the state of Maryland with focus on the Eastern Shore Counties.

Margaret van den Berg, Administrative Assistant
John R Valliant, President

2724 Henry & Ruth Blaustein Rosenberg Foundation
Blaustein Building
10 East Baltimore Street
Suite 1111
Baltimore, MD 21202
410-347-7201
Fax: 410-347-7210
E-mail: info@blaufund.org
http://www.blaufund.org
Offers grants in the areas of secondary and higher education.

Betsy F Ringel, Executive Director
Henry A Rosenberg Jr, President

2725 James M Johnston Trust for Charitable and Educational Purposes
2 Wisconsin Circle
Suite 600
Chevy Chase, MD 20815-7003
301-907-0135
Grants are given to higher and secondary educational institutions located in Washington, DC and North Carolina.

Julie Sanders, Executive Director

2726 John W Kluge Foundation
15004 Sunflower CT
Rockville, MD 20853-0174
301-929-9340
Offers grants in higher education and secondary education.

2727 Marion I & Henry J Knott Foundation
3904 Hickory Avenue
Baltimore, MD 21211-1834
410-235-7068
Fax: 410-889-2577
E-mail: info@knottfoundation.org
http://www.knottfoundation.org
Grantmaking limited to private nonsectarian schools and Catholic schools geographically located within the Archdiocese of Baltimore, Maryland.

Greg Cantori, Executive Director

2728 Robert G & Anne M Merrick Foundation
The Exchange
1122 Kenilworth Drive
Suite 118
Baltimore, MD 21204-2142
410-832-5700
Fax: 410-832-5704
Offers grants for public education, higher education and social services.

Frederick W Lafferty, Executive Director

Massachusetts

2729 Associated Grantmakers of Massachusetts
55 Court Street
Suite 520
Boston, MA 02108-4304
617-426-2606
Fax: 617-426-2849
http://www.agmconnect.org
Member of The Foundation Center network, maintaining a collection of private foundation tax returns which provide information on the scope of grants dispensed by that particular foundation.

Ron Ancrum, President
Martha Moore, Director Center Philanthropy

2730 Boston Foundation
75 Arlington Street
10th Floor
Boston, MA 02116-4407
617-338-1700
Fax: 617-338-1604
http://www.tbf.org
Supports local educational, social and housing programs and institutions.

Paul Grogan, President

2731 Boston Globe Foundation II
135 Morrissey Boulevard
Boston, MA 02107

617-929-2895
Fax: 617-929-7889
http://www.bostonglobe.com/community/foundation/partner.stm
The foundation's highest priority is community based agencies which understand, represent and are part of the following populations; children and youth with disabilities, children and youth with AIDS, refugees, low-birth weight babies, pregnant and nursing mothers and incarcerated youth.

Suzanne W Maas, Executive Director
Leah P Bailey

2732 Boston Public Library
Social Sciences Reference
700 Boylston Street
Boston, MA 02116-2813
617-536-5400
http://www.bpl.org
Member of The Foundation Center network, maintaining a collection of private foundation tax returns which provide information on the scope of grants dispensed by that particular foundation.

Bernard Margolis, President

2733 Dean Foundation for Little Children
C/O Boston Safe Deposit & Trust Company
PO Box 185
Pittsburgh, PA 15230-0185
Giving is centered on little children age twelve and under for the care and relief of destitute children. Provides support for preschools, day care, summer camps and other programs.

Nancy Criscitiello, Executive Director

2734 Hyams Foundation
50 Federal Street
Floor 9
Boston, MA 02110-2210
617-426-5600
Fax: 617-426-5696
http://www.hyamsfoundation.org
The foundation seeks to promote understanding and appreciation of diversity, including race, ethnicity, gender, sexual orientation, age, physical ability, class and religion. The foundation's primary objective is to meet the needs of low-income and other underserved populations, striving to address the causes of those needs, whenever possible. Foundation supports low-income communities in their efforts to identify their own problems, solve these problems and improve people's lives.

Elizabeth B Smith, Executive Director
Angela Brown, Director of Programs

2735 Irene E & George A Davis Foundation
C/O Ann T Keiser
1 Monarch Place
Suite 1450
Springfield, MA 01144-1300
413-734-8336
Fax: 413-734-7845
E-mail: info@davisfdn.org
http://www.davisfdn.org
Education and social service organizations and programs in Western Massachusetts are the primary concern of this foundation.

Mary E Walachy, Executive Director

2736 James G Martin Memorial Trust
122 Pond Street
Jamaica Plain, MA 02130-2714
Giving is centered on elementary education and higher education in Massachusetts.

Ms Martin, Executive Director

2737 Jessie B Cox Charitable Trust
Grants Management Association
60 State Street
Boston, MA 02109-1899

617-227-7940
Fax: 617-227-0781
http://www.hemenwaybarnes.com/selectsrv/jbcox/cox.html
This trust makes grants for projects which will address important social issues in the trust's fields of interest and for which adequate funding from other sources cannot be obtained. The trust funds projects in New England in the areas of health, education and the environment. The trustees look to support special projects which will assist the applicants to achieve their long-range organizational goals.

Michaelle Larkins, Executive Director
Susan M Fish, Grants Administrator

738 LG Balfour Foundation
Fleet Bank of Massachusetts
75 State Street
Boston, MA 02109-1775
617-346-4000
Offers support for scholarships and innovative projects designed to eliminate barriers and improve access to education for all potentially qualified students.

Kerry Herliney, Executive Director

739 Little Family Foundation
33 Broad Street
Suite 10
Boston, MA 02109-4216
617-723-6771
Fax: 617-723-7107
Offers scholarships at various business schools and Junior Achievement programs in secondary schools.

Arthur D Little, Executive Director

740 Rogers Family Foundation
10 Clay Street
Suite 200
Oakland, CA 94067-4501
510-899-7918
Fax: 978-685-1588
http://www.rogersfoundation.org
Offers support in the areas of secondary and higher education in the Lawrence, Massachusetts area.

Kathleen Rogers, President
Nicole Taylor, Secretary/Treasurer

741 State Street Foundation
225 Franklin Street
12th Floor
Boston, MA 02110
617-664-1937
http://www.statestreet.com
Offers grants to organizations that help improve the quality of life in the greater Boston area. Interest includes human services, public and secondary education, vocational education, and arts and culture programs.

Madison Thompson, Executive Director

742 Sudbury Foundation
326 Concord Road
Sudbury, MA 01776-1843
978-443-0849
Fax: 978-579-9536
http://www.sudburyfoundation.org
Offers college scholarships to local high school seniors who meet eligibility criteria.

Marilyn Martino, Executive Director
Tricia Brunner, Grants Administrator

743 Trustees of the Ayer Home
PO Box 1865
Lowell, MA 01853-1865
978-452-5914
Fax: 978-452-5914

Funding (greater Lowell, MA only) educational programs (RLF, SMARTS). Primary interests are women and children.

D Donahue, Assistant Treasurer

2744 Weld Foundation
Peter Loring/Janice Palumbo
Loring, Wolcott & Coolidge
30 Congress Street
Boston, MA 02110-2409
617-523-6531
Fax: 617-523-6535
Grants are offered in the areas of elementary, secondary and higher education in Massachusetts.

2745 Western Massachusetts Funding Resource Center
65 Elliot Street
Springfield, MA 01105-1713
413-732-3175
Fax: 413-452-0618
http://www.diospringfield.org/wmfrc.html
Member of The Foundation Center network, maintaining a collection of private foundation tax returns which provide information on the scope of grants dispensed by that particular foundation.

Kathleen Dowd, Director
Jean Los, Administrative Assistant

2746 William E Schrafft & Bertha E Schrafft Charitable Trust
77 Summer Street
Boston, MA 02110
617-457-7327
http://www.schrafftcharitable.org
Giving is primarily allocated to educational programs in the Boston metropolitan area.

Arthur H Parker, Trustee
Lavinia B Chase, Trustee

2747 Woodstock Corporation
Woodstock Corporation
27 School Street
Suite 200
Boston, MA 02108-2301
617-227-0600
Fax: 617-523-0229
E-mail: info@woodstockcorp.com
http://www.woodstockcorp.com
Offers support in the area of secondary school education in the state of Massachusetts.

2748 Worcester Public Library
Grants Resource Center
3 Salem Square
Worcester, MA 01608
508-799-1655
Fax: 508-799-1652
http://www.worcpublib.org
Member of The Foundation Center network, maintaining a collection of private foundation tax returns which provide information on the scope of grants dispensed by that particular foundation.

J Peck, Director Grants Resource

Michigan

2749 Alex & Marie Manoogian Foundation
21001 Van Born Road
Taylor, MI 48180-1340
313-274-7400
Fax: 313-792-6657

Supports higher and secondary education, cultural programs and human service organizations.

Alex Manoogian, Executive Director

2750 Charles Stewart Mott Foundation
Office of Proposal Entry
503 S Saginaw Street
Suite 1200
Flint, MI 48502-1851
810-238-5651
800-645-1766
Fax: 810-237-4857
E-mail: infocenter@mott.org
http://www.mott.org
Grants are given to nonprofit organizations with an emphasis on programs of volunteerism, at-risk youth, environmental protection, economic development and education.

2751 Chrysler Corporate Giving Program
12000 Chrysler Drive
Detroit, MI 48288-0001
810-576-5741
Offers support for education, especially secondary education and leadership development.

Lynn A Feldhouse, Executive Director

2752 Community Foundation for Southeastern Michigan
333 W Fort Street
Suite 2010
Detroit, MI 48226-3134
313-961-6675
Fax: 313-961-2886
E-mail: cfsem@cfsem.orq
http://www.cfsem.org
Supports projects in the areas of education, culture and social services.

Mariam C Noland, President

2753 Community Foundation of Greater Flint
500 South Saginaw Street
Flint, MI 48502-2013
810-767-8270
Fax: 810-767-0496
E-mail: cfgf@cfgf.org
http://www.cfgf.org
A community foundation that makes grants to benefit residents of Genesee County, Michigan. Areas of interest include: arts, education, environment, community services and health and social services.

Kathi Horton, President
Evan M Albert, VP Program

2754 Cronin Foundation
203 E Michigan Avenue
Marshall, MI 49068-1545
616-781-9851
Fax: 616-781-2070
Offers support to expand educational, social and cultural needs of the community within the Marshall, Michigan school district.

Joseph E Schroeder, Executive Director

2755 Detroit Edison Foundation
2000 2nd Avenue
Room 1046
Detroit, MI 48226-1279
313-235-9271
Fax: 313-237-9271
http://www.my.dteenergy.com
Offers support for all levels of education, and local community social services and cultural organizations in Southeast Michigan.

Katharine W Hunt, Executive Director

2756 Ford Motor Company Fund
One American Road
PO Box 1899
Dearborn, MI 48126-2798
888-313-0102
Fax: 313-337-6680
http://www.ford.com
Ford Motor Company Fund continues the legacy of Henry Ford's commitment to innovative education at all levels. We remain dedicated to creating and enriching educational opportunities, especially in the areas of science, engineering, math and business, while promoting diversity in education.

Sandra E Ulsh, President
Jim Graham, Manager Education Programs

2757 Frey Foundation
40 Pearl Street NW
Suite 1100
Grand Rapids, MI 49503-3023
616-451-0303
Fax: 616-451-8481
http://www.freyfdn.org
Awards grants and supports the needs of children in their early years, support for environmental education and protection of our natural resources.

Milton W Rohwer, President
Teresa J Crawford, Grants Manager

2758 General Motors Foundation
PO Box 33170
Detroit, MI 48232-5170
313-556-4260
http://www.gm.com/company/gmability/philanthropy
Offers support for higher education, cultural programs and civic affairs.

Ronald L Theis, Executive Director

2759 Grand Rapids Foundation
185 Oakes St SW
Grand Rapids, MI 49503
616-454-1751
Fax: 616-454-6455
E-mail: grfound@grfoundation.org
http://www.grfoundation.org
A community foundation established in 1922. The foundation actively serves the people of Kent County by administering funds it receives and by making philanthropic grants to non-profit organizations in response to community needs. Various educational scholarships are offered on the basis of a competitive process which considers academic achievement, extracurricular activities, a statement of one's own personal aspirations and educational goals, and financial need. Kent County Residency required.

Ruth Bishop, Program Associate-Education
Diana Sieger, President

2760 Harry A & Margaret D Towsley Foundation
3055 Plymouth Road
Suite 200
Ann Arbor, MI 48105-3208
312-662-6777
Areas of support include pre-school education, social services, and continuing education.

Margaret Ann Riecker, Executive Director

2761 Henry Ford Centennial Library
Adult Services
16301 Michigan Avenue
Dearborn, MI 48126-2792
313-943-2330
Fax: 313-943-3063
http://www.dearborn.lib.mi.us/aboutus/adult.htm
Member of The Foundation Center network, maintaining a collection of private foundation tax returns which provide information on the scope of grants dispensed by that particular foundation.

2762 Herbert H & Grace A Dow Foundation
1018 W Main Street
Midland, MI 48640-4292
989-631-3699
Fax: 989-631-0675
http://www.hhdowfdn.org
Limited to organizations within Michigan. Has charter goals to improve the educational, religious, economic and cultural lives of Michigan's people.

Margaret Ann Riescker, President
Elysa M Rogers, Assistant VP

2763 Herrick Foundation
150 W Jefferson Avenue
Suite 2500
Detroit, MI 48226-4415
313-496-7585
Offers grants to colleges and universities, health agencies and social service organizations.

Dolores de Galleford, Executive Director

2764 Kresge Foundation
3215 W Big Beaver Road
Troy, MI 48084
248-643-9630
Fax: 313-643-0588
http://www.kresge.org
Giving is aimed at areas of interest including arts and humanities, social services and public policy.

John E Marshall III, Executive Director
Sandra McAlister Ambrozy, Senior Program Officer

2765 Malpass Foundation
PO Box 1206
East Jordan, MI 49727-1206
Offers giving in the areas of education and community development.

William J Lorne, Executive Director

2766 McGregor Fund
333 W Fort Street
Suite 2090
Detroit, MI 48226-3134
313-963-3495
Fax: 313-963-3512
E-mail: info@mcgregorfund.org
http://www.mcgregorfund.org
Social services, health and education grants awarded to organizations located in Ohio, primarily the Detroit area.

C David Campbell, President
Kate Levin Markel, Program Officer

2767 Michigan State University Libraries
Social Sciences/Humanities
366 W Circle Drive
East Lansing, MI 48824
517-353-8700
Fax: 517-432-3532
http://www.lib.msu.edu
Member of The Foundation Center network, maintaining a collection of private foundation tax returns which provide information on the scope of grants dispensed by that particular foundation.

2768 Richard & Helen DeVos Foundation
190 Muncie NW
Suite 500
Grand Rapids, MI 49503
616-454-4114
Fax: 616-454-4654
Strong geographical preference to Western Michigan. Funding includes Christian education, cultural, community, education (not an individual basis) and government services. Donations are also made on a national level to organizations based in Washington, DC.

Stephanie Roy, Executive Director

2769 Rollin M Gerstacker Foundation
PO Box 1945
Midland, MI 48641-1945
989-631-6097
Fax: 517-832-8842
E-mail: lanphear@concentric.net
http://www.tamu.edu/baum/gerstack.html
Primary purpose of this foundation is to carry on, indefinitely, financial aid to charities concentrated in the states of Michigan and Ohio. Grants are given in the areas of community support, schools, education, social services, music and the arts, youth activities, health care and research, churches and other areas.

Carl A Gerstacker, Executive Director

2770 Steelcase Foundation
PO Box 1967, CH-4E
Grand Rapids, MI 49501-1967
616-246-4695
Fax: 616-475-2200
E-mail: sbroman@steelcse.com
http://www.steelcase.com
Offers support for human services and education, to improve the quality of life for children, the elderly and the disabled in the areas where there are manufacturing plants.

Susan Broman, Executive Director

2771 Wayne State University
Purdy-Kresge Library
5265 Cass Avenue
Detroit, MI 48202-3930
313-577-6424
http://www.lib.wayne.edu
Member of The Foundation Center network, maintaining a collection of private foundation tax returns which provide information on the scope of grants dispensed by that particular foundation.

2772 Whirlpool Foundation
2000 N M 63
MD 3106
Benton Harbor, MI 49022-2692
269-923-5584
Fax: 269-925-0154
http://www.whirlpoolcorp.com
Giving centers on learning, cultural diversity, adult education, and scholarships for children of corporation employees.

Ddaniel Hopp, President & Chairman
Pamela Silcox, Operations Manager

Minnesota

2773 Andersen Foundation
Andersen Corporation
100 4th Avenue N
Bayport, MN 55003-1058
651-264-5150
Fax: 651-264-5537
Grants are given in the areas of higher education, health, youth and the arts in Minnesota.

774 Bush Foundation
E-900 First National Bank Building
332 Minnesota Street
Saint Paul, MN 55101-1314
651-227-0891
Fax: 651-297-6485
http://www.bushfoundation.org
The foundation is predominantly a regional grantmaking foundation, with broad interests in education, human services, health, arts and humanities and in the development of leadership.

Anita M Pampusch, President
John Archabal, Senior Program Officer

775 Cargill Foundation
PO Box 9300
Minneapolis, MN 55440-9300
952-742-4311
Fax: 612-742-7224
http://www.cargill.com
Offers grants in the areas of education, health, human service organizations, arts and cultural programs and social service agencies.

Audrey Tulberg, Executive Director

776 Charles & Ellora Alliss Educational Foundation
800 Nicollet Mall
Minneapolis, MN 55402-1314
612-303-4411
Fax: 651-244-0860
E-mail: allissfoundation@usbank.com
http://www.allissfoundation.org
The foundation is organized exclusively for support of the education of young people, up to and including the period of postgraduate study. As a matter of policy, the foundation generally has limited its program to universities and colleges located in Minnesota. Grants are made to such institutions in support of undergraduate scholarship programs administered by their student aid offices. The foundation makes no direct grants to individuals.

John Bultena, Executive Director
Anita M Pampusch, Board of Trustee

777 Duluth Public Library
520 W Superior Street
Duluth, MN 55802-1578
218-723-3802
Fax: 218-723-3815
http://www.duluth.lib.mn.us
Member of The Foundation Center network, maintaining a collection of private foundation tax returns which provide information on the scope of grants dispensed by that particular foundation.

Elizabeth Kelly, Library Director

778 FR Bigelow Foundation
Center 55th Street East
Suite 600
St. Paul, MN 55101-1797
651-224-5463
800-875-6167
Fax: 651-224-8123
E-mail: info@frbiquelow.org
http://www.frbigelow.org
Offers support in early childhood education, elementary and secondary education, higher and adult education and human services.

Richard B Heydinger, Chair
Carleen K Rhodes, Secretary

779 First Bank System Foundation
PO Box 522
Minneapolis, MN 55480-0522
612-973-2440

Offers support for public elementary and secondary education, arts and cultural programs.

Cheryl L Rantala, Executive Director

2780 Hiawatha Education Foundation
360 Vila Street
Winona, MN 55987-1500
507-453-5550
Giving is centered on Catholic high schools and colleges, as well as awarding scholarships to college-bound high school graduates.

Robert Kierlin, Executive Director

2781 IA O'Shaughnessy Foundation
2001 Killebrew Drive
Suite 120
Bloomington, MN 55425-0704
952-698-0959
Fax: 952-698-0959
http://www.iaoshaughessyfdn.org
Giving is centered on cultural programs, secondary and higher education, human services and medical programs.

John Bultena, Executive Director
John F O'Shaughnessy, President

2782 Marbrook Foundation
730 2nd Avenue
Suite 1300
Minneapolis, MN 55402
612-752-1783
Fax: 612-752-1780
E-mail: jhara@marbrookfoundation.org
http://www.marbrookfoundation.org
Offers grants in the areas of the environment, the arts, social empowerment, spiritual endeavors, basic human needs and health.
Annual Report

Julie S Hara, Executive Director

2783 Medtronic Foundation
7000 Central Avenue NE
Minneapolis, MN 55432-3576
763-514-4000
800-328-2518
Fax: 763-514-8410
http://www.medtronic.com
Offers grants in the areas of education (especially at the pre-college level), community funding and social services.

Penny Hunt, Executive Director

2784 Minneapolis Foundation
800 Ids Center 80 S 8th Street
Minneapolis, MN 55402
612-672-3878
Fax: 612-672-3846
E-mail: mplsfoundation.org
http://www.minneapolisfoundation.org
The foundation strives to strengthen the community for the benefit of all citizens. Grants are awarded for the purposes of achieving this goal in the areas of early childhood education, child development, and education.

Karen Kelley-Ariwoola, VP Community Philanthropy

2785 Minneapolis Public Library
Music, Art, Sociology & Humanities
250 S Marquette
Minneapolis, MN 55401-2188
612-630-6000
Fax: 612-630-6220
http://www.mplib.org
Member of The Foundation Center network, maintaining a collection of private foundation tax returns which provide information on the scope of grants dispensed by that particular foundation.

Katherine G Hadle, Director

2786 Otto Bremer Foundation
445 Minnesota Street
Suite 2250
Saint Paul, MN 55101-2135
651-227-8036
888-291-1123
Fax: 651-312-3665
http://www.ottobremer.org
Offers support for post-secondary education, human services and community affairs.

John Kostishack, Executive Director
Karen Starr, Senior Program Officer

2787 Saint Paul Foundation
55 Fifth Street East
Suite 600
St. Paul, MN 55101-1797
651-224-5463
800-875-6167
Fax: 651-224-8123
E-mail: info@saintpaulfoundation.org
http://www.saintpaulfoundation.org
Offers support for educational, charitable and cultural purposes of a public nature.

Carleen K Rhodes, President
Mindy K Molumby, Grants Administrator

2788 TCF Foundation
Code EXO-02-C
200 Lake Street
East Wayzata, MN 55391-1693
952-745-2757
Fax: 612-661-8554
http://www.tcfexpress.com
Giving is primarily for education through grants and employee matching gifts, including secondary schools, higher education and organizations that increase public knowledge.

Neil I Whitehouse, Executive Director

Mississippi

2789 Foundation for the Mid South
134 East Amite Street
Jackson, MS 39201
601-355-8167
Fax: 601-355-6499
http://www.fndmidsouth.org
Makes grants in the area of education, as well as economic development and families and children.

George Penick, Executive Director
Kay Kelly Arnold, Vice Chairman

2790 Jackson-Hinds Library System
300 N State Street
Jackson, MS 39201-1705
601-968-5811
E-mail: reference@jhlibrary.com
http://www.jhlibrary.com
Member of The Foundation Center network, maintaining a collection of private foundation tax returns which provide information on the scope of grants dispensed by that particular foundation.

Carolyn McCallum, Executive Director

2791 Mississippi Power Foundation
PO Box 4079
Gulfport, MS 39502-4079
228-864-1211
http://www.mississippipower.com
The foundation is dedicated to the improvement and enhancement of education in Mississippi from kindergarten to twelfth grade.

Huntley Biggs, Executive Director

2792 Phil Hardin Foundation
2750 North Park Drive
Meridian, MS 39305-5800
601-483-4282
Fax: 601-483-5665
E-mail: info@philhardin.org
http://www.philhardin.org
Offers giving in Mississippi for schools and educational institutions and programs.

C Thompson Wacaster, Executive Director

Missouri

2793 Ameren Corporation Charitable Trust
Ameren Corporation
PO Box 66149
MC 100
Saint Louis, MO 63166-6149
314-554-2789
877-426-3736
Fax: 314-554-2888
E-mail: sbell@ameren.com
http://www.ameren.com
Offers giving in the areas of education, environment, youth and seniors; giving restricted to nonprofits located in Ameren service area in Missouri and Illinois.

Annually

Susan M Bell, Sr Community Relations
Otis Cowan, Community Relations Manger

2794 Clearinghouse for Midcontinent Foundations
University of Missouri
5110 Cherry Street
Suite 310
Kansas City, MO 64110-2426
816-253-1176
Fax: 816-235-5727
Member of The Foundation Center network, maintaining a collection of private foundation tax returns which provide information on the scope of grants dispensed by that particular foundation.

2795 Danforth Foundation
205 E Butterfield Road
Suite 410
Elmhurst, IL 60126-2733
630-501-1235
Fax: 314-588-0035
E-mail: meboozell@danforthfoundation.com
http://www.danforthfoundation.com
This foundation is aimed at enhancing human life through activities which emphasize the theme of improvement in teaching and learning. Serves the pre-collegiate education through grantmaking and program activities.

Dr. Bruce J Anderson, President

2796 Enid & Crosby Kemper Foundation
C/O UMB Bank, N.A.
PO Box 419692
Kansas City, MO 64141-6692
816-860-7711
Fax: 816-860-5690
Giving is primarily allocated to organizations and programs focusing on educational and cultural needs.

Stephen J Campbell, Executive Director

2797 Hall Family Foundation
Charitable & Crown Investment - 323
PO Box 419580
Kansas City, MO 64141-6580
816-274-8516
Fax: 816-274-8547
http://www.hallfamilyfoundation.org
Offers grants in the areas of all levels of education, performing and visual arts, community development, and children, youth and families.

William S Berkley, President & CEO
David A Warm, Executive Director

2798 James S McDonnell Foundation
1034 S Brentwood Boulevard
Suite 1850
Saint Louis, MO 63117-1284
314-721-1532
Fax: 314-721-7421
http://www.jsmf.org
Foundation Program, Cognitive Studies for Educational Practice, funding available through competition in broadly announced requests for proposals. Program grant guidelines are announced in 3 year cycles.

John T Bruer, President
Cheryl A Washington, Grants Manager

2799 Kansas City Public Library
14 West 10th Street
Kansas City, MO 64105
816-701-3400
Fax: 816-701-3401
http://www.kclibrary.org
Member of The Foundation Center network, maintaining a collection of private foundation tax returns which provide information on the scope of grants dispensed by that particular foundation.

Jonathan Kemper, President
David Mayta, Vice President

2800 Mary Ranken Jordan & Ettie A Jordan Charitable Foundation
Mercantile Bank
PO Box 387
Saint Louis, MO 63166-0387
314-231-7626
Giving is limited to charitable institutions with an emphasis on secondary education and cultural programs, as well as higher education and social services.

Fred Arnold, Executive Director

2801 McDonnell Douglas Foundation
PO Box 419692
M S 10203
Kansas City, MO 64141-6692
314-234-0360
Fax: 314-232-7654
Offers various grants with an emphasis on higher and other education and community funding.

AM Bailey, Executive Director

2802 Monsanto Fund
800 N Lindbergh Boulevard
Saint Louis, MO 63167-0001
314-694-1000
Fax: 314-694-7658
E-mail: monsanto.fund@monsanto.com
http://www.monsanto.com/monsanto/about_us/monsanto_fund
Giving is offered primarily in the area of education, specifically science and math.

Deborah J Patterson, President

Montana

2803 Eastern Montana College Library
Special Collections-Grants
1500 N 30th Street
Billings, MT 59101-0245
406-657-1662
800-565-6782
Fax: 406-657-2037
http://www.msubillings.edu/library
Member of The Foundation Center network, maintaining a collection of private foundation tax returns which provide information on the scope of grants dispensed by that particular foundation.

Joan Bares, Grants Manager

2804 Montana State Library
Library Services
1500 University Drive
Billings, MT 59101-4542
406-657-2011
800-565-6782
Fax: 406-444-5612
http://www.msl.state.mt.us/
Member of The Foundation Center network, maintaining a collection of private foundation tax returns which provide information on the scope of grants dispensed by that particular foundation.

Barbara Duke, Administrative Assistant

Nebraska

2805 Dr. CC & Mabel L Criss Memorial Foundation
US Bank
PO Box 64713
Saint Paul, MN 55614-0713
800-441-2117
Fax: 402-348-6666
Offers support for educational and scientific purposes, including higher education.

2806 Thomas D Buckley Trust
PO Box 647
Chappell, NE 69129-0647
308-874-2212
Fax: 308-874-3491
Offers giving in the areas of education, health care and youth and religion. Grants awarded in Chappell, NE, community and surrounding area.

Connie Loos, Secretary

2807 W Dale Clark Library
Social Sciences Department
215 S 15th Street
Omaha, NE 68102-1601
402-444-4826
Fax: 402-444-4504
http://www.omahapubliclibrary.org
Member of The Foundation Center network, maintaining a collection of private foundation tax returns which provide information on the scope of grants dispensed by that particular foundation.

Angela Green-Garland, President
Arun K Agarwal, Vice President

Nevada

2808 Conrad N Hilton Foundation
30440 Agoura Road
Agoura Hills, CA 91301-1988
818-851-3700
Fax: 775-323-4150
http://www.hiltonfoundation.org
Founded in 1944 as a Trust, this foundation is dedicated to fulfilling and expanding Conrad Hilton's philanthropic vision by carrying out grantmaking

activities. The foundation's giving is focused primarily in two areas: the alleviation of human suffering, particularly among disadvantaged children; and the human services works of the Catholic Sisters through a separate entity as described under Major Projects (supportive housing, disabled, education and prevention of domestic violence).

Donald H Hubbs, Executive Director
Steven M Hilton, President

809 Cord Foundation
E.L. Cord Foundation Center For Learning Literacy
1664 N Virginia Street
Reno, NV 89557-0208
775-784-4951
Fax: 775-784-4758
http://www.unr.edu/cll
Offers support for secondary and higher education, including youth organizations and cultural programs.

Donald Bear, Director/Professor

810 Donald W Reynolds Foundation
1701 Village Center Circle
Las Vegas, NV 89134-6303
702-804-6000
Fax: 702-804-6099
E-mail: generalquestions@dwrf.org
http://www.dwreynolds.org
Devotes funds to further the cause of free press and journalism education.

Fred Smith, Chairman
Wes Smith, Vice-Chairman

811 EL Wiegand Foundation
Wiegand Center
165 W Liberty Street
Reno, NV 89501-1915
775-333-0310
Fax: 775-333-0314
Offers grants in of culture and the arts, organizations, health and medical institutions, with an emphasis on Roman Catholic organizations.

Kristen A Avansino, Executive Director

812 Las Vegas-Clark County
Library District
7060 W Windmill Lane
Las Vegas, NV 89113-2030
702-382-5280
Fax: 702-382-5491
http://www.lvccld.org
Member of The Foundation Center network, maintaining a collection of private foundation tax returns which provide information on the scope of grants dispensed by that particular foundation.

Daniel L Walters, Executive Director
Kelly Benavidez, Chairman

813 Washoe County Library
301 S Center Street
Reno, NV 89501-2102
775-327-8300
Fax: 775-327-8341
http://www.washoe.lib.nv.us/
Member of The Foundation Center network, maintaining a collection of private foundation tax returns which provide information on the scope of grants dispensed by that particular foundation.

Fred Lokken, Chairman

New Hampshire

2814 Lincolnshire
Liberty Lane
Hampton, NH 03842
Giving is primarily for secondary school education, business school education and recreation.

William Coffey, Executive Director

2815 New Hampshire Charitable Foundation
37 Pleasant Street
Concord, NH 03301-4005
603-225-6641
Fax: 603-225-1700
E-mail: info@nhcf.org
http://www.nhcf.org
Offers grants for charitable and educational purposes including college scholarships, existing charitable organizations, child welfare, community services, health and social services and new programs that emphasize programs rather than capital needs.

Racheal Stuart, VP Program

2816 Plymouth State College
Herbert H. Lamson Library
17 High Street
Plymouth, NH 03264-1595
603-535-2258
Fax: 603-535-2445
http://www.plymouth.edu/psc/library
Member of The Foundation Center network, maintaining a collection of private foundation tax returns which provide information on the scope of grants dispensed by that particular foundation.

New Jersey

2817 Community Foundation of New Jersey
Knox Hill Road
PO Box 338
Morristown, NJ 07963-0338
973-267-5533
Fax: 973-267-2903
E-mail: cfnj@bellatlantic.net
http://www.cfnj.org
Offers support for programs that offer a path of solution of community problems in the areas of education, leadership development and human services.

Hans Dekker, President

2818 Fund for New Jersey
Kilmer Square
One Palmer Square East
Suite 303
Princeton, NJ 08542-1242
609-356-0241
Fax: 732-220-8654
http://www.fundfornj.org
Offers grants on projects which provide the basis of action in education, AIDS research, minorities/immigrants, public policy and community development.

Mark M Murphy, Executive Director
Kiki Jamieson, President

2819 Hoechst Celanese Foundation
Route 202-206 N
PO Box 2500
Somerville, NJ 08876
908-522-7500
Fax: 908-598-4424

Provides support for education, particularly in the sciences.

Lewis F Alpaugh, Executive Director

2820 Honeywell Foundation
101 Columbia Road
Morristown, NJ 07962-4658
973-455-2000
877-841-2840
Fax: 973-455-4807
http://www.honeywell.com/about/foundation.html
Offers support for education, including fellowship and scholarship aid to colleges.

2821 Hyde & Watson Foundation
31-F Mountain Boulevard
Warren, NJ 07059-1454
908-753-3700
Fax: 908-753-0004
E-mail: hydeandwatson@yahoo.com
http://www.fdncenter.org/grantmaker/hydeandwatson
Support of capital projects of lasting value which tend to increase quality, capacity, or efficiency of a grantee's programs or services, such as purchase or relocation of facilities, capital equipment, instructive materials development, and certain medical research areas. Broad fields include health, education, religion, social services, arts, and humanities. Geographic areas served include the New York City Metropolitan region and primarily Essex, Union, and Morris Counties in New Jersey.

Hunter W Corbin, President

2822 Mary Owen Borden Memorial Foundation
160 Hodge Road
Princeton, NJ 08540-3014
609-924-3637
Fax: 609-252-9472
E-mail: tborden@ibm.net
http://www.fdncenter.org/grantmaker/borden/index.htm
Offers grants in the areas of childhood education, child development, education, conservation and health and human services.

Thomas Borden, Executive Director

2823 Merck Company Foundation
1 Merck Drive #100
Whitehouse Station, NJ 08889-0100
908-423-2042
http://www.merck.com
Offers support of education, primarily medical through community programs, grants and matching gift programs for colleges and secondary education.

John R Taylor, Executive Director
Kenneth C Fraizer, Chairman,President& CEO

2824 Prudential Foundation
Prudential Plaza
751 Broad Street
Floor 15
Newark, NJ 07102-3714
973-802-4791
http://www.prudential.com
Focus is on children and youth for services that can better their lives. Grants are made in the areas of education, health and human services, community and urban development, business and civic affairs, culture and the arts. Emphasis is placed on programs that serve the city of Newark and the surrounding New Jersey urban centers, programs in cities where The Prudential has a substantial pres-

ence and national programs that further the company's objectives.

Barbara L Halaburda, Executive Director

2825 Turrell Fund
21 Van Vleck Street
Montclair, NJ 07042-2358
973-783-9358
Fax: 973-783-9283
E-mail: turrell@turrellfund.org
http://www.fdncenter.org/grantmaker/turrell
Offers grants to organizations and agencies that are dedicated to the care of children and youth under twelve years of age, with an emphasis on education, early childhood education, delinquency prevention and child and youth services.

E Belvin Williams, Executive Director

2826 Victoria Foundation
31 Mulberry Street
5th Floor
Newark, NJ 07102
973-792-9200
Fax: 793-792-1300
E-mail: cmcfarvic@aol.com
http://www.victoriafoundation.org
Grants are limited to Newark, New Jersey in the following areas: elementary and secondary education, after school enrichment programs, teacher training and academic enrichment.

Catherine M McFarland, Executive Officer
Nancy K Zimmerman, Senior Program Officer

2827 Warner-Lambert Charitable Foundation
201 Tabor Road
Morris Plains, NJ 07950-2614
212-573-2323
Fax: 212-573-7851
Grants are given in the areas of education, health care, culture and the arts. Supports higher institutions of learning which concentrate on pharmacy, medicine, dentistry, the sciences and mathematics. Current support is aimed at the higher levels of education, but the foundation has begun to place more of its attention on the growing needs that impact elementary and secondary training.

Evelyn Self, Community Affairs
Richard Keelty, VP Investor Affair

2828 Wilf Family Foundation
820 Morris Tpke
Short Hills, NJ 07078-2619
973-467-5000
Awards grants in the areas of Jewish higher education and religion.

Joseph Wilf, Executive Director

New Mexico

2829 Dale J Bellamah Foundation
PO Box 36600
Albuquerque, NM 87176-6600
858-756-1154
Fax: 858-756-3856
Offers grants for higher education including military academies, hospitals and social service organizations.

AF Potenziani, Executive Director

2830 New Mexico State Library
Information Services
1209 Camino Carlos Rey
Santa Fe, NM 87507
505-476-9700
Fax: 505-476-9701
http://www.stlib.state.nm.us
Member of The Foundation Center network, maintaining a collection of private foundation tax returns which provide information on the scope of grants dispensed by that particular foundation.

2831 RD & Joan Dale Hubbard Foundation
PO Box 1679
Ruidoso Downs, NM 88346-1679
505-378-4142
Giving is offered in the areas of childhood education, elementary, secondary and higher education as well as other cultural programs.

Jim Stoddard, Executive Director

New York

2832 Achelis Foundation
767 3rd Avenue
4th Floor
New York, NY 10017-2023
212-644-0322
Fax: 212-759-6510
E-mail: main@achelis-bodman-fnds.org
http://www.fdncenter.org/grantmaker/achelis-bodman
Grants include biomedical research at Rockefeller University, rebuilding the Hayden Planetarium at the American Museum of Natural History, support for the arts and culture, the charter school movement, youth organizations, and special efforts to curb father absence and strengthen family life with awards.

Russell P Pennoyer, President
Joseph S Dolan, Executive Director

2833 Adrian & Jessie Archbold Charitable Trust
401 East 60th Street
New York, NY 10022
212-371-1152
Eastern United States educational institutions and health care service organizations are the main recipients of the Trust.

Myra Mahon, Executive Director

2834 Alfred P Sloan Foundation
630 5th Avenue
Suite 2550
New York, NY 10111-0100
212-649-1649
Fax: 212-757-5117
http://www.sloan.org
A nonprofit foundation offering Sloan Research Fellowships which are awarded in chemistry, computer science, economics, mathematics, neuroscience and physics. These are competitive grants given to young faculty members with high research potential on the recommendation of department heads and other senior scientists.

Ralph E Gomory, President

2835 Altman Foundation
521 5th Avenue
35th Floor
New York, NY 10175
212-682-0970
E-mail: info@altman.org
http://www.altmanfoundation.org

In education, the Altman Foundation supports programs that identify, sponsor and tutor talented disadvantaged youngsters and help them to obtain educations in non-public and independent schools. The Foundation awards grants only in New York State with an almost-exclusive focus on the five boroughs of New York City. The Foundation does not award grants or scholarships to individuals.

Karen L Rosa, VP/Executive Director

2836 Ambrose Monell Foundation
C/O Fulton, Duncombe & Rowe
1 Rockefeller Plaza
Room 301
New York, NY 10020-2002
212-586-0700
Fax: 212-245-1863
E-mail: info@monellvetlesen.org
http://www.monellvetlesen.org
Broad range of allocation including education, social service, cultural organizations and the environment.

Ambrose K Monell, Executive Director
George Rowe, President, Treasurer and Dire

2837 American Express Foundation
American Express Company
World Financial Center
New York, NY 10285
212-640-5661
http://www.home3.americanexpress.com/corp/philanthropy/contacts.asp
The foundation's giving focuses on three areas including community service, education and employment.

Mary Beth Salerno, Executive Director
Angela Woods, Philanthropic Program

2838 Andrew W Mellon Foundation
140 E 62nd Street
New York, NY 10065-8187
212-838-8400
Fax: 212-888-4172
http://www.mellon.org
Offers grants in the areas of higher education, cultural affairs and public affairs.

W.Taylor Revely, President
Lewis W Bernard, Chairman

2839 Arnold Bernhard Foundation
220 E 42nd Street
Floor 6
New York, NY 10017-5806
212-907-1500
Offers funding in the areas of education with the emphasis placed on college and universities as well as college preparatory schools.

Jean B Buttner, Executive Director

2840 Atran Foundation
23-25 East 21st Street
3rd Floor
New York, NY 10010
212-505-9677
Offers grants and funding to nonprofit educational and religious organizations.

2841 Beatrice P Delany Charitable Trust
The Chase Manhattan Bank
1211 Avenue of the Americas
34th Floor
New York, NY 10036
212-935-9935
Giving is offered for education, especially higher education and religion.

John HF Enteman, Executive Director

2842 Bodman Foundation
767 3rd Avenue
4th Floor
New York, NY 10017-2023

212-644-0322
Fax: 212-759-6510
E-mail: main@achelis-bodman-fnds.org
http://www.achelis-bodman-fnds.org
Grants include biomedical research at Rockefeller University, building the Congo Gorilla Forest Education Center at the Bronx Zoo through the Wildlife Conservation Society, rebuilding of the Hayden Planetarium for Science and Technology at the American Museum of Natural History, support for Symphony Space, the charter school movement, youth organizations, and the Rutgers University Foundation.

John N Irwin III, Chairman
John B Krieger, Executive Director

2843 Bristol-Myers Squibb Foundation
345 Park Avenue
Floor 43
New York, NY 10154-0004
212-546-4331
http://www.bms.com
Offers support for elementary and secondary school, math and science education reform, civic affairs and health care.

Cindy Johnson, Executive Director
Lamberto Andreotti, Chief Executive Officer

2844 Buffalo & Erie County Public Library
History Department
Lafayette Square
Buffalo, NY 14203
716-858-8900
Fax: 716-858-6211
http://www.buffalolib.org/libraries/central
Member of The Foundation Center network, maintaining a collection of private foundation tax returns which provide information on the scope of grants dispensed by that particular foundation.

Michael C Mahaney, Director

2845 Caleb C & Julia W Dula Educational & Charitable Foundation
C/O Chemical Bank
112 S Hanley RD
St Louis, MO 63105-3418
212-270-9066
Offers grants to charities with an emphasis on secondary and higher education.

G Price-Fitch, Executive Director

2846 Capital Cities-ABC Corporate Giving Program
77 W 66th St
New York, NY 10023-6201
212-456-7498
Fax: 212-456-7909
Offers support in adult education, literary and basic skills, reading, and AIDS research.

Bernadette Longford Williams, Executive Director

2847 Carl & Lily Pforzheimer Foundation
950 Third Ave
30th Floor
New York, NY 10022-2705
212-764-0655
Offers support primarily for higher and secondary education, cultural programs, public administration, and health care.

Carl H Pforzheimer III, Executive Director

2848 Carnegie Corporation of New York
437 Madison Avenue
New York, NY 10022-7001

212-374-3200
Fax: 212-754-4073
http://www.carnegie.org
The foundation has several program goals including education and healthy development of children and youth, including early childhood health and education, early adolescence educational achievement, science education and education reform.

Janet L Robinson, President
Kurt L Schmoke, Vice-Chairman

2849 Chase Manhattan Corporation Philanthropy Department
1 Chase Manhattan Plaza
Floor 9
New York, NY 10005-1401
212-552-7087
Offers support to various organizations to enhance the well-being of the communities Chase Manahattan serves. Grants are awarded in the areas of education, youth services, community and economic development, homeless, library science, health care and housing development.

Steven Gelston, Executive Director

2850 Christian A Johnson Endeavor Foundation
1060 Park Avenue
New York, NY 10128-1008
212-534-6620
http://www.csuohio.edu/uored/funding/johnson.htm
Offers support to private institutions of higher education at the baccalaureate level and on educational outreach programs.

Wilmot H Kidd, Executive Director

2851 Cleveland H Dodge Foundation
420 Lexington Avenue
Suite 2331
New York, NY 10170-3292
212-972-2800
Fax: 212-972-1049
http://www.chdodgefoundation.org
Bestows funding for nonprofit organizations aimed at improving higher education and youth organizations.

William D Rueckert, President
Bayard Dodge, Vice-President

2852 Cowles Charitable Trust
P.O Box 219
Rumson, NJ 07760
732-936-9826
http://www1.mville.edu/Grants/GrantDescriptionPages/Cowles.htm
Funding for higher education and cultural organizations.

Gardner Cowles, President

2853 Daisy Marquis Jones Foundation
1600 S Avenue
Suite 250
Rochester, NY 14620-3921
585-461-4950
Fax: 585-461-9752
E-mail: mail@dmjf.org
http://www.dmjf.org
Offers grants for nonprofit organizations focusing on improving the lives of children, youth and the elderly, in Monroe and Yates counties in New York State.

Donald W Whitney, President
Marless A Honan, Administrative Assistant

2854 DeWitt Wallace-Reader's Digest Fund
5 Penn Plaza
7th Floor
New York, NY 10001-9301
212-251-9700
Fax: 212-679-6990
http://www.wallacefoundation.org
The mission of this foundation is to invest in programs and projects that enhance the quality of educational and career development opportunities for all school-age youth.

M Christine De Vita, President

2855 Edna McConnell Clark Foundation
415 Madison Avenue
10th Floor
New York, NY 10017
212-551-9100
Fax: 212-421-9325
http://www.emcf.org
Supports select youth, serving organizations working with children 9-24 during the non-school hours.

Michael Bailin, President

2856 Edward John Noble Foundation
32 E 57th Street
Floor 19
New York, NY 10022-2513
212-759-4212
Fax: 212-888-4531
Offers grants to major cultural organizations in New York City, especially for arts educational programs and management training internships.

June Noble Larkin, Chairman

2857 Edward W Hazen Foundation
333 Seventh Avenue
14 th Floor
New York, NY 10001
212-889-3034
Fax: 212-889-3039
E-mail: hazen@hazenfoundation.org
http://www.hazenfoundation.org
The foundation focuses giving on public education and youth development in the area of public education.

Lori Bezahler, President
Sonia Jarvis, Chairman

2858 Edwin Gould Foundation for Children
126 East 31st Street
New York, NY 10016
212-251-0907
Fax: 212-982-6886
Supports projects that promote the welfare and education of children. Interests lies in early childhood education, higher education, children and youth services and family services.

Michael W Osheowitz, Executive Director

2859 Elaine E & Frank T Powers Jr Foundation
81 Skunks Misery Road
Locust Valley, NY 11560-1306
Offers support in the areas of secondary and higher education as well as youth services.

2860 Elmer & Mamdouha Bobst Foundation
Elmer Holmes Bobst Library, NYU
70 Washington Square S
New York, NY 10012-1019
212-998-2440
Fax: 212-995-4070
Offers grants and funding in the areas of youth, community development and the arts.

2861 Equitable Foundation
3rd Floor Champaca II Building
162 L.P Leviste Street, Salcedo Village
Makati City 10019-6018
E-mail: mail@equitablefoundation.com
http://www.equitablefoundation.com
Offers grants in the areas of secondary
school education, arts, community services, art and cultural programs, and higher
education.

Kathleen A Carlson, Executive Director
Darlene Ramos, Administrative Assistant

2862 Ford Foundation
320 E 43rd Street
New York, NY 10017-4890
212-573-5000
Fax: 212-351-3677
E-mail: offsec@fordfound.rog
http://www.fordfound.org
Offers grants to advance public well-being
and educational opportunities. Grants are
given in the areas of education, secondary
school/education, early childhood education, development services, human services, citizenship, academics and more.

Barron M Tenny, Secretary
Luis Ubinas, President

**2863 Frances & Benjamin Benenson
Foundation**
C/O Door County Community Foundation
P.O. Box 802
Sturgeon Bay, WI 54235-1006
920-746-1786
Fax: 212-755-0021
http://www.benensoncapital.com
Offers grants in elementary/secondary ed-
ucation, higher education and human
services.

Cynthia Green Colin, Executive Director

2864 George F Baker Trust
C/O JPMorgan Chase Bank
N.A Philanthropic Services
270 Park Avenue
New York, NY 10017
212-473-1587
Fax: 212-464-2305
E-mail:
jonathan.q.horowitz@jpmchase.com
Offers giving in the areas of higher and sec-
ondary education, social services, civic af-
fairs and international affairs.

Monica J Neal, Vice President

2865 George Link Jr Foundation
10 Rockefeller Plaza
16th Floor
New York, NY 10020
212-713-7654
Fax: 212-645-4055
Giving is primarily centered on higher education, secondary school/education and
medical research.

Eve Weiss, Executive Director

**2866 Gladys & Roland Harriman
Foundation**
51 Madison Avenue
30 th Floor
New York, NY 10010-1202
212-489-7700
Fax: 212-581-9541
E-mail: hlfl@hluce.org
Giving is centered on education and sup-
port for youth and social service agencies.

Michael Gilligan, President
Margaret B Fitzgerald, Chairman

2867 Gladys Brooks Foundation
1055 Franklin Avenue
Garden City, NY 11530
212-943-3217
http://www.gladysbrooksfoundation.org
The purpose of this foundation is to provide for the intellectual, moral and physical welfare of the people of this country by
establishing and supporting nonprofit libraries, educational institutions, hospitals
and clinics. In the area of education, grant
applications will be considered generally
for (a) educational endowments to fund
scholarships based solely on leadership
and academic ability of the student; (b)
endowments to support salaries of
educators.

Harman Hawkins, Chairman
Robert E Hill, Executive Director

2868 Green Fund
14 E 60th Street
Suite 702
New York, NY 10022-1006
212-755-2445
Fax: 212-755-0021
Offers grants in the area of higher and sec-
ondary education.

Cynthia Green Colin, Executive Director

2869 Hagedorn Fund
C/O JPMorgan Private Bank
Private Foundation Services
270 Park Avenue, 16th floor
New York, NY 10017
212-473-1587
Fax: 212-464-2304
E-mail: g.horowitz@jpmorgan.com
http://fdnweb.org
Offers support for higher and secondary
education, youth agencies and social ser-
vice agencies.

Jonathan Horowitz, Program Officer

2870 Hasbro Children's Foundation
10 Rockefeller Plaza
16th Floor
New York, NY 10020
212-713-7654
888-836-7025
Fax: 212-645-4055
http://www.hasbro.org
Offers support to improve the quality of
life for children. Areas of interest include
education, AIDS research, literacy, special
education, and youth services.

Eve Weiss, Executive Director

2871 Henry Luce Foundation
51 Madison Avenue, 30th Floor
New York, NY 10010
212-489-7700
Fax: 212-581-9541
E-mail: hlfl@hluce.org
http://www.hluce.org
Offers grants for specific programs and
projects in the areas of higher education
and scholarship, social sciences at private
colleges and universities, American arts
and public affairs.

Michael Gilligan, President
Ellen Holtzman, Program Director

2872 Herman Goldman Foundation
61 Broadway
Floor 18
New York, NY 10006-2701
212-797-9090
Fax: 212-797-9161
This foundation offers grants in the areas
of social, legal and organizational approaches to aid for deprived or handicapped people; education for new or improved
counseling for effective pre-school, vocational,
and paraprofessional training; and the arts.

Richard K Baron, Executive Director

2873 Hess Foundation
1185 Avenue of the Americas
New York, NY 10036-2601
212-997-8500
Fax: 212-536-8390
E-mail: webmaster@hess.com
http://www.hess.com
Offers grants that focus on higher education, performing arts, and welfare organizations.

Leon Hess, Executive Director

2874 Horace W Goldsmith Foundation
375 Park Avenue
Suite 1602
New York, NY 10152-1699
212-319-8700
800-319-2881
Fax: 212-319-2881
Offers giving and support for education, higher
education, cultural programs and museums.

James C Slaughter, Executive Director

2875 IBM Corporate Support Program
Old Orchard Road
Armonk, NY 10504
914-765-1900
The mission of this fund is to improve the areas
and the communities that IBM operates in. Grants
are awarded in various areas including early
childhood education, elementary education, secondary education, business school/education, and
engineering school/education.

Stanley Litow, Executive Director

2876 JI Foundation
C/O Patterson, Belknap, Webb & Tyler
1133 Avenue of the Americas
New York, NY 10036
212-336-2000
Offers grants in the areas of elementary education, higher education, and general charitable
giving.

2877 JP Morgan Charitable Trust
60 Wall Street
Floor 46
New York, NY 10005-2836
212-648-9673
Offers support in the area of education, housing,
economic development, advocacy and international affairs.

Roberta Ruocco, Executive Director

2878 Joukowsky Family Foundation
410 Park Avenue
Suite 1610
New York, NY 10022-4407
212-355-3151
Fax: 212-355-3147
http://www.joukowsky.org
Giving is focused on higher and secondary education.

Nina J Koprulu, Director/President
Emily R Kessler, Executive Director

2879 Julia R & Estelle L Foundation
1 HSBC Center
Suite 3650
Buffalo, NY 14203-1217
716-856-9490
Fax: 716-856-9493
E-mail: info@oisheifdt.com
http://www.oisheifdt.org

This fund offers grants in the areas of higher and secondary education, medical research, social services and support agencies.

Thomas E Baker, President
James M Wadsworth, Chairman

880 Leon Lowenstein Foundation
575 Madison Avenue
New York, NY 10022-3613
212-605-0444
Fax: 212-688-0134
Support is given for New York City public education and medical research.

John F Van Gorder, Executive Director

881 Levittown Public Library
1 Bluegrass Lane
Levittown, NY 11756-1292
516-579-8585
Fax: 516-735-3168
http://www.nassaulibrary.org/levtown/
Member of The Foundation Center network, maintaining a collection of private foundation tax returns which provide information on the scope of grants dispensed by that particular foundation.

Margaret Santer, President

882 Louis & Anne Abrons Foundation
C/O First Manhattan Company
437 Madison Avenue
New York, NY 10022-7001
212-756-3376
Fax: 212-832-6698
Offers support in the areas of education, improvement programs, environmental and cultural projects.

Richard Abrons, Executive Director

883 Margaret L Wendt Foundation
40 Fountain Plaza
Suite 277
Buffalo, NY 14202-2200
716-855-2146
Fax: 716-855-2149
Offers various grants with an emphasis on education, the arts and social services in Buffalo and Western New York.

Robert J Kresse, Executive Director

884 McGraw-Hill Foundation
1221 Avenue of the Americas
Room 2917
New York, NY 10020
212-512-6113
800-442-9685
http://www.mcgraw-hillresearchfoundation.org
Offers support to educational organizations in the areas of company operations or to national organizations.

Susan A Wallman, Executive Director

885 New York Foundation
10 East 34th Street
10 th Floor
New York, NY 10016-2996
212-594-8009
Fax: 212-594-5918
E-mail: webmaster@nyf.org
http://www.nyf.org
Provides support for the implementation of programs that offer support for the quality of life including educational services, health organizations, centers and services, civil rights, public policy, research and more.

Maria Mottola, Executive Director
Melissa Hall, Operations Manager

2886 Palisades Educational Foundation
C/O Gibney, Anthony & Flaherty
665 5th Avenue
Floor 2
New York, NY 10022-5305
Offers support for secondary and higher education in New York, New Jersey and Connecticut.

Ralph F Anthony, Executive Director

2887 Robert Sterling Clark Foundation
135 E 64th Street
New York, NY 10065-7307
212-288-8900
Fax: 212-288-1033
E-mail: rscf@rsclark.org
http://www.rsclark.org
For more than 15 years, this foundation has provided support to New York City's cultural community. During this time, the Foundation has tried to structure a grants program so that it is flexible and meets the needs of the institutions and organizations. Grants are given in the areas of cultural institutions, arts advocacy, family planning services and supporting new initiatives in the area of arts and education.

Margaret C Ayers, President
James A Smith, Chairman

2888 Rochester Public Library
Business, Economics & Law
115 S Avenue
Rochester, NY 14604-1896
585-428-8045
Fax: 585-428-8353
http://www.rochester.lib.ny.us/central
Member of The Foundation Center network, maintaining a collection of private foundation tax returns which provide information on the scope of grants dispensed by that particular foundation.

Emeterio M Otero, President

2889 Ronald S Lauder Foundation
Rykestrasse 53
10405 Berlin
Berlin 10153-0023
212-572-6966
http://www.lauderfoundation.com
Offers giving in the areas of elementary/secondary education, human services and religion.

Marjorie S Federbush, Executive Director
Ronald S Lauder, Chairman & President

2890 SH & Helen R Scheuer Family Foundation
350 5th Avenue
Suite 3410
New York, NY 10118-0110
212-947-9009
Fax: 212-947-9770
Offers support in the areas of higher education, welfare funding and cultural programs.

2891 Samuel & May Rudin Foundation
345 Park Avenue
New York, NY 10154-0004
212-407-2544
Fax: 212-407-2540
Offers support for higher education, social services, religious welfare agencies, hospitals and cultural programs.

Susan H Rapaport, Executive Director

2892 Seth Sprague Educational and Charitable Foundation
C/O U.S. Trust Company of New York
114 W 47th Street
New York, NY 10036-1510

212-852-3683
Fax: 212-852-3377
Offers support in the areas of education, culture, the arts, human services, community development and government/public administration.

Maureen Augusciak, Executive Director

2893 Starr Foundation
399 Park Avenue
17th Floor
New York, NY 10022-0002
212-909-3600
Fax: 212-750-3536
http://www.fdncenter.org/grantmaker/starr
Support is given for educational projects with an emphasis on higher education, including scholarships under specific programs.

Ta Chun Hsu, Executive Director
Florence A Davis, President

2894 Tiger Foundation
101 Park Avenue
47th Floor
New York, NY 10178-0002
212-984-2565
Fax: 212-949-9778
E-mail: info@tigerfoundation.org
http://www.tigerfoundation.org
Support is given primarily for early childhood education, youth programs and job training.

Phoebe Boyer, Executive Director

2895 Tisch Foundation
667 Madison Avenue
New York, NY 10021-8029
212-545-2000
Support is given in the area of education, especially higher education, and includes institutions in Israel and research-related programs.

Laurence A Tisch, Executive Director

2896 Travelers Group
388 Greenwich Street
New York, NY 10013-2375
212-816-8000
Fax: 212-816-5944
The main purpose of this foundation is to support public education, offering grants in the communities that the company serves.

Dee Topol, Executive Director

2897 White Plains Public Library
100 Martine Avenue
White Plains, NY 10601-2599
914-422-1400
Fax: 914-422-1462
http://www.whiteplainslibrary.org
Member of The Foundation Center network, maintaining a collection of private foundation tax returns which provide information on the scope of grants dispensed by that particular foundation.

2898 William Randolph Hearst Foundation
300 West 57th Street
26th Floor
New York, NY 10019-3741
212-649-3750
Fax: 212-586-1917
E-mail: heart.ny@hearstfdn.org
http://www.hearstfdn.org
Offers support to programs that aid priority-level and minority groups, educational programs especially private secondary and

higher education, health systems and cultural programs.

Paul ""Dino"" Dinovitz, Executive Director

Ligia Cravo, Senior Program Officer

2899 William T Grant Foundation
570 Lexington Avenue
Floor 18
New York, NY 10022-6837
212-752-0071
Fax: 212-752-1398
E-mail: info@wtgrantfdn.org
http://www.wtgrantfoundation.org
The goal of the foundation is to help create a society that values people and helps them to reach their potenial. The Foundation is interested in environmentally friendly approaches

Edward Seidman, Senior VP Programs
Robert Granger, President

North Carolina

2900 AE Finley Foundation
P.O. Box 98266
Raleigh, NC 27624-8266
919-782-0565
Fax: 919-782-6978
E-mail: lesa@aeffinc.org
http://www.aefinleyfoundationinc.org
Private foundation contributing and supporting to charitable, scientific, literary, religious and educational organizations. It endeavors to contribute to soundly managed and operated qualifying organizations which fundamentally give service with a broad scope and impact, aid all kinds of people and contribute materially to the general welfare.

Robert C Brown, Executive Director

2901 Cannon Foundation
PO Box 548
Concord, NC 28026-0548
704-786-8216
Fax: 704-785-2052
E-mail: info@cannonfoundation.org
http://www.thecannonfoundationinc.org
Offers support for higher and secondary education, cultural programs, and grants to social service and youth agencies.

Frank Davis, Executive Director
William C Cannon Jr, President

2902 Dickson Foundation
301 S Tryon Street
Suite 1800
Charlotte, NC 28202
704-372-5404
Fax: 704-372-6409
Main focus is on areas of education & healthcare. Considers funding programs in the Southeast.

Susan Patterson, Secretary/Treasurer

2903 Duke Endowment
100 N Tryon Street
Suite 3500
Charlotte, NC 28202-4012
704-376-0291
Fax: 704-376-9336
http://www.dukeendowment.org
Support is given to higher education, children and youth services, churches and hospitals.

Eugene W Cochrane Jr, Executive Director
Minor M Shaw, Chairman

2904 First Union University
Two 1st Union Center
Charlotte, NC 28288
704-374-6868
Fax: 704-374-4147
Offers support for higher education and special programs for public elementary and secondary schools.

Ann D Thomas, Executive Director

2905 Foundation for the Carolinas
220 N Tryon Street
Charlotte, NC 28202
704-973-4500
800-973-7244
Fax: 704-376-1243
http://www.fftc.org
Offers support for education, the arts and health in North Carolina and South Carolina.

Ron Carter, President/CEO
Catherine P Bessant, Chairman

2906 Kathleen Price and Joseph M Bryan Family Foundation
3101 N Elm Street
Greensboro, NC 27408-3184
336-288-5455
Grants are primarily offered in the fields of higher, secondary, and early childhood education.

William Massey, Executive Director

2907 Mary Reynolds Babcock Foundation
2920 Reynolda Road
Winston Salem, NC 27106-4618
336-748-9222
Fax: 336-777-0095
http://www.mrbf.org
This foundation traditionally provides funds to programs in education, social services, the environment, the arts and citizen participation in the development of public policy. The foundation prefers to fund programs of two kinds: those particularly sensitive to the changing and emerging needs of society and those addressing society's oldest needs in new and imaginative ways.

Gayle W Dorman, Executive Director
Sandra H Mikush, Assitant Director

2908 Non-Profit Resource Center/Pack Memorial Library
Learning Resources Center
67 Haywood Street
Asheville, NC 28801-4897
828-254-4960
Fax: 828-251-2258
Cooperating collection of the Foundation Center. Other resources for non-profit organizations are also available.

Ed Sheary, Library Director

2909 State Library of North Carolina
Government & Business Services
109 E Jones Street
Raleigh, NC 27601-2806
919-807-7450
Fax: 919-733-5679
http://www.statelibrary.dcr.state.nc.us
Member of The Foundation Center network, maintaining a collection of private foundation tax returns which provide information on the scope of grants dispensed by that particular foundation.

2910 William R Kenan Jr Charitable Trust
Kenan Center
PO Box 3858
Chapel Hill, NC 27515-3858

919-962-0343
Fax: 919-962-3331
The focus of this foundation is on education, primarily at private institutions in the US. The emphasis now is on national literacy and the importance of early childhood education. Grants have just established an institute for the arts and an institute for engineering, technology and science. No grants are given to individuals for scholarships, for research or other special projects or for medical, public health or social welfare projects. This Trust does not accept unsolicited requests.

William C Friday, Executive Director

2911 Winston-Salem Foundation
860 W 5th Street
Winston Salem, NC 27101-2506
336-725-2382
Fax: 336-727-0581
http://www.wsfoundation.org
Educational grants and loans to residents of Forsyth County, North Carolina in most areas.

Scott Wierman, President
Donna Rader, VP Grants & Programs

2912 Z Smith Reynolds Foundation
102 West Third Street
Suite 1110
Winston Salem, NC 27101-3940
336-725-7541
800-443-8319
Fax: 336-725-6069
http://www.zsr.org
Grants are limited to the state of North Carolina. General purpose foundation provides for their current priorities including community economic development, women's issues, minority issues, environment and pre-collegiate education. No grants are given to individuals.

Thomas W Ross, Executive Director

North Dakota

2913 Myra Foundation
PO Box 13536
Grand Forks, ND 58208-3536
701-775-9420
E-mail: jbotsford@myrafoundation.org
http://www.myrafoundation.org
Offers grants in the areas of secondary school, and higher education to residents of Grand Forks County, North Dakota.

Edward C Gillig, Executive Director

2914 Tom & Frances Leach Foundation
1720 Burnt Boat Drive
PO Box 1136
Bismarck, ND 58502-1136
701-255-0479
http://www.leachfoundation.org
Offers grants in the areas of higher and other education in North Dakota.

Clement C Weber, Executive Director

Ohio

2915 Akron Community Foundation
345 W Cedar Street
Akron, OH 44307-2407
330-376-8522
Fax: 330-376-0202
E-mail: acf_fund@ix.netcom.com
http://www.akroncommunityfdn.org

The foundation receives donations to permanent endowment and makes grants to qualified nonprofit organizations within Summit County, Ohio.

Jody Bacon, President

916 American Foundation Corporation
720 National City Bank Building
Cleveland, OH 44114
216-241-6664
Fax: 216-241-6693
Offers support in the areas of higher and secondary education, the arts and community funds.

Maria G Muth, Executive Director

917 Burton D Morgan Foundation
22 Aurora Street
Hudson, OH 44236-1500
330-655-1660
Fax: 330-655-1673
E-mail: admin@bdmorganfdn.org
http://www.bdmorganfdn.org
The foundation's present areas of interest include economics, education, mental health and organizations principally located in Northeast Ohio. No grants are made to individuals and few grants are made to social service organizations.

Deborah D Hoover, President
Denise M Griggs, Chief Financial Officer

918 Dayton Foundation
500 Kettering Tower
Dayton, OH 45423-1395
937-222-0410
Fax: 937-222-0636
E-mail: info@daytonfoundation.org
http://www.daytonfoundation.org
Educational and community service grants.

Michael M Parks, President
Ellen S Ireland, Vice-Chairman

919 Eva L & Joseph M Bruening Foundation
1422 Euclid Avenue
Suite 966
Cleveland, OH 44115-1952
216-621-2632
Fax: 216-621-8198
http://www.fmscleveland.com/bruening
Support is offered in the fields of education, early childhood education, education fund-raising, higher education, youth services and health agencies.

Janet E Narten, Executive Director
Karen Noster, Chairman

920 GAR Foundation
Andrew Jackson House
277 East Mill Street
Akron, OH 44308-1828
330-576-2926
800-686-2825
Fax: 330-437-2843
E-mail: info@garfdn.org
http://www.garfdn.org
Established in 1967 as a charitable trust, the foundation offers grants to organizations located primarily in Akron, Ohio area or, secondarily, in Northeastern Ohio or elsewhere in the United States at the discretion of the Distribution Committee. Grants for research projects of educational or scientific institutions, capital improvement projects, or matching campaigns are the priorities of this foundation.

Richard A Chenoweth, Executive Director
Robert W Briggs, Co-Trustee

2921 George Gund Foundation
1845 Guildhall Building
45 Prospect Avenue
West Cleveland, OH 44115
216-241-3114
Fax: 216-241-6560
E-mail: info@gundfdn.org
http://www.gundfdn.org
The primary interest of this foundation is in educational projects, with an emphasis on inventive movements in teaching and learning, and on increasing educational opportunities for the disadvantaged.

David Abbott, Executive Director
Marcia Egbert, Senior Program Officer

2922 Hoover Foundation
101 E Maple Street
North Canton, OH 44720-2517
330-499-9499
Fax: 330-497-5065
Offers grants for elementary education, secondary and higher education and youth agencies.

LR Hoover, Executive Director
Annette Bravard, Vice President of Marketing

2923 Kettering Fund
1480 Kettering Tower
Dayton, OH 45423-1001
937-228-1021
888-719-1185
http://www.cfketteringfamilies.com
Support is offered for social and educational studies and research as well as community development and cultural programs.

Judith M Thompson, Executive Director

2924 Kulas Foundation
Tower City Center
50 Public Square
Suite 600
Cleveland, OH 44113-2267
216-623-4770
Fax: 216-623-4773
http://www.fdncenter.org/grantmaker/kulas/
A major general interest foundation, but with an emphasis on music. Giving is limited to Cuyahoga County and its surrounding area. Provides support to musical educational programs at Baldwin Wallace College, Case Western Reserve University and Cleveland Institute of Music. Also provides tickets to cultural programs to students in 16 colleges and universities in the area. The Foundation does not provide grants or loans to individuals. Support is geared to local primary and secondary schools.

Nancy W McCann, President/Treasurer

2925 Louise H & David S Ingalls Foundation
20600 Chagrin Boulevard
Suite 301
Shaker Heights, OH 44122-5334
216-921-6000
Offers support to organizations whose primary interest in the improvement of the educational, physical and mental condition of humanity throughout the world. Grants are given in secondary, elementary, and educational research.

Jane W Watson, Executive Director

2926 Louise Taft Semple Foundation
425 Walnut Street
Suite 1800
Cincinnati, OH 45202-3948
513-381-2838
Fax: 513-381-0205

Support is offered in the areas of secondary school/education, higher education, human services and health care organizations.

Dudley S Taft, Executive Director

2927 Martha Holden Jennings Foundation
Advisory & Distribution Committee Office
1228 Euclid Avenue
Suite 710
Cleveland, OH 44115-1831
216-589-5700
Fax: 216-589-5730
http://www.mhjf.org
The purpose of this foundation is to foster the development of young people to the maximum possible extent through improving the quality of teaching in secular elementary and secondary schools.

William T Hiller, Executive Director
Kathy L Kooyman, Grants Manager

2928 Mead Corporation Foundation
Courthouse Plz NE
Dayton, OH 45463-0001
937-495-3883
Fax: 937-495-4103
Grants are given to elementary, secondary, higher and minority education.

Ronald F Budzik, Executive Director

2929 Nord Family Foundation
747 Milan Avenue
Amherst, OH 44001
440-984-3939
Fax: 440-984-3934
http://www.nordff.org
Offers support for a variety of programs, including giving for early childhood, secondary, and higher education, social services, cultural affairs and civic activities.

David R Ashenhurst, Executive Director

2930 Ohio Bell Telephone Contribution Program
45 Erieview Plaza
Room 870
Cleveland, OH 44114-1814
216-822-4445
800-257-0902
Offers support of elementary school/education, secondary school/education, higher education, literacy and basic skills.

William W Boag Jr, Executive Director

2931 Ohio State Library Foundation Center
Kent H. Smith Library
1480 West Lane Avenue
Columbus, OH 43221-2001
614-292-2141
Member of The Foundation Center network, maintaining a collection of private foundation tax returns which provide information on the scope of grants dispensed by that particular foundation.

John B Gerlach, Chairman & CEO
Martin Murrer, Vice-Chairman

2932 Owens-Corning Foundation
PO Box 1688
Toledo, OH 43603-1688
419-248-8000
Fax: 419-325-4273
Offers support for education, including religious schools and science and technology programs.

Emerson J Ross, Executive Director

2933 Procter & Gamble Fund
200 West Fourth Street
Cincinnati, OH 45202-2775

513-241-2880
Fax: 513-983-8250
E-mail: info@gcfdn.org
http://www.gcfdn.org
Always considers the interests of the company's employees helping in the community, the arts, improving of schools and universities and to meet the needs of the less-fortunate neighbors. Some donations into the education program include grants to the United Negro College Fund, The National Hispanic Scholarship Fund, The Leadership Conference on Civil Rights Education Fund and more than 600 colleges and universities.

RL Wehling, President
G Talbot, VP

2934 Public Library of Cincinnati

Grants Resource Center
800 Vine Street #Library
Cincinnati, OH 45202-2009
513-369-6900
Fax: 513-665-3384
http://www.cincinnatilibrary.org
Member of The Foundation Center network, maintaining a collection of private foundation tax returns which provide information on the scope of grants dispensed by that particular foundation.

Kimber L Fender, Director

2935 Thomas J Emery Memorial

Frost & Jacobs
201 E 5th Street
Suite 2500
Cincinnati, OH 45202-4113
513-621-3124
Offers support in secondary school/education, higher education, health care, human services and arts/cultural programs.

Henry W Hobson Jr, Executive Director

2936 Timken Foundation of Canton

200 Market Avenue N
Suite 210
Canton, OH 44702-1622
330-452-1144
Fax: 330-455-1752
Offers support to promote the broad civic betterment including the areas of education, conservation and recreation. Grants restricted to caption projects only.

Don D Dickes, Secretary
Nancy Kuvdsen

2937 Wolfe Associates

34 S 3rd Street
Columbus, OH 43215-4201
614-461-5220
Fax: 614-469-6126
The foundation supports those organizations whose programs educate the individual and cultivate the individual's ability to participate in and contribute to the community or which enhance the quality of life which the community can offer to its citizens. The foundation has six general program areas in which it focuses its support: health and medicine, religion, education, culture, community service and environment.

AK Pierce Jr, Executive Director

Oklahoma

2938 Grace & Franklin Bernsen Foundation

15 W 6th Street
Suite 1308
Tulsa, OK 74119-5407
918-584-4711
Fax: 918-584-4713
E-mail: gfbersen@aol.com
http://www.bernsen.org
The foundation is limited by its policies to support of nonprofit organizations within the metropolitan area of Tulsa. The foundation discourages applications for general support or reduction of debt or for continuing or additional support for the same programs, although a single grant may cover several years. No grant is made to individuals or for the benefit of specific individuals and the applications must be received before the twelfth of each month.

John Strong Jr, Trustee

2939 Mervin Bovaird Foundation

100 W 5th Street
Suite 800
Tulsa, OK 74103-4291
918-583-1777
Fax: 918-592-5809
Awards scholarships to the University of Tulsa. Recipients are selected by Tulsa Area high schools and by Tulsa Junior College. No individual grants are made.

R Casey Cooper, President

2940 Oklahoma City University

Dulaney Brown Library
2501 N Blackwelder Avenue
Oklahoma City, OK 73106-1493
405-521-5000
Fax: 405-521-5291
http://www.okcu.edu
Member of The Foundation Center network, maintaining a collection of private foundation tax returns which provide information on the scope of grants dispensed by that particular foundation.

Victoria Swinney, Director

2941 Public Service Company of Oklahoma Corporate Giving Program

212 E 6th Street #201
Tulsa, OK 74119-1295
918-586-0420
http://www.psoklahoma
Offers support in the areas of elementary, secondary and higher education.

Mary Polfer, Executive Director

2942 Samuel Roberts Noble Foundation

2510 Sam Noble Parkway
Ardmore, OK 73401-2180
580-223-5810
Fax: 580-224-6380
http://www.noble.org
Offers support in the areas of higher education, agricultural research, human services and educational grants for health research pertaining to degenerative diseases, cancer and for health delivery systems.

Michael A Cawley, Executive Director
Emily Bynum, Administrative Assistant

Oregon

2943 Collins Foundation

1618 SW 1st Avenue
Suite 305
Portland, OR 97201-5708
503-227-7171
Fax: 503-295-3794
http://www.collinsfoundation.org
Offers general support with an emphasis on higher education, hospices and health agencies, youth programs and arts and culture.

Cynthia G Adams, Executive Vice President
Cindy Knowles, Director Of Programs

2944 Ford Family Foundation

1600 NW Stewart Parkway
Roseburg, OR 97471-1957
541-957-5574
Fax: 541-957-5720
E-mail: info@tfff.org
http://www.tfff.org
Giving is centered on education, youth organizations and human service programs in Oregon and Siskiyou County in California.

Bart Howard, Director Scholarship Program
Sarah Reeve, Scholarship Program Officer

2945 Meyer Memorial Trust

425 NW 10th Avenue
Suite 400
Portland, OR 97209
503-228-5512
Fax: 503-228-5840
E-mail: mmt@mmt.org
http://www.mmt.org
The Trust operates three different funding programs, all of which are restricted primarily to Oregon: 1) a broad-based General Purpose program that provides funds for education, arts, and humanities, health, social welfare, community development, and other activities; 2) a Small Grants program that provides up to $12,000 for small projects in the general purpose categories; and 3) the Support for Teacher Initiatives program, which provides grants of up to $7,000- to teachers.

Doug Stamm, Executive Director
Cathie Glennon, Executive Assistant

2946 Multnomah County Library

Government Documents
801 SW 10th Avenue
Portland, OR 97205-2597
503-988-5123
Fax: 503-988-8014
http://www.multcolib.org
Member of The Foundation Center network, maintaining a collection of private foundation tax returns which provide information on the scope of grants dispensed by that particular foundation.

2947 Oregon Community Foundation

1221 SW Yamhill
Suite 100
Portland, OR 97205
503-227-6846
Fax: 503-274-7771
http://www.ocfl.org
The purpose of this foundation is to improve the cultural, educational and social needs in all levels of society throughout the state of Oregon.

Gregory A Chaille, Executive Director

2948 Tektronix Foundation

PO Box 1000
Wilsonville, OR 97070-1000
503-627-7111
http://www.tek.com

Offers support for education, especially science, math and engineering, and some limited art grants.

Jill Kirk, Executive Director

Pennsylvania

949 Alcoa Foundation
201 Isabella Street
Pittsburgh, PA 15212-5858
412-553-4545
Fax: 412-553-4498
http://www.alcoa.com
Grants are given for education, arts and cultural programs.

F Worth Hobbs, Executive Director

950 Annenberg Foundation
St. David's Center
2000 Avenue of the Stars
Suite 1000 S
Los Angeles, CA 90067-5293
310-209-4560
Fax: 310-209-1631
E-mail: info@annenbergfoundation.org
http://www.annenbergfoundation.org
Primary support is given to childhood and K-12 education.

Dr. Gail C Levin Sr, Executive Director
Wallis Annenberg, Chairman

951 Arcadia Foundation
105 E Logan Street
Norristown, PA 19401-3058
215-275-8460
http://www.arcadiafoundation.org
Gives only in Eastern Pennsylvania, no personal scholarships, accepts proposals only between June 1-August 15. These will be considered for the following calendar year. Proposal has to be no more than 2 pages long and longer submissions will be discarded. Must have a copy of the IRS tax-identified letter with no other enclosures.

Marilyn Lee Steinbright, Executive Director

952 Audrey Hillman Fisher Foundation
2000 Grant Building
Pittsburgh, PA 15219
412-338-3466
Fax: 412-338-3463
Offers support for secondary school/education, higher education, rehabilitation, science and engineering.

Ronald W Wertz, Executive Director

953 Bayer Corporation
100 Bayer Court
Pittsburgh, PA 15205
412-777-2000
Fax: 412-777-3468
http://www.bayerus.com/about/community/
Support is given primarily in education, especially science programs, chemistry and the arts.

Rebecca Lucore, Executive Director

54 Buhl Foundation
650 Smithfield Street
Pittsburgh, PA 15222-1207
412-566-2711
Fax: 412-566-2714
E-mail: buhl@buhlfoundation.org
http://www.buhlfoundation.org
Grants are given to colleges and universities, secondary schools and educational associations, community educational and training programs, and other community programs of-

fering health and education to the community. Grants are not made for building funds, overhead costs, accumulated deficits, ordinary operating budgets, general fund-raising campaigns, loans, scholarships and fellowships, other foundations, nationally funded organized groups or individuals.

Dr. Doreen Boyce, President

2955 Connelly Foundation
One Tower Bridge
Suite 1450
West Conshohocken, PA 19428-2873
610-834-3222
Fax: 610-834-0866
http://www.connellyfdn.org
Offers support for education, health, human service, culture and civic programs to nonprofit organizations located in the city of Philadelphia and the greater Delaware Valley region.

Victoria K Flaville, VP Administration
Josephine C Mandeville, President/CEO

2956 Eden Hall Foundation
Pittsburgh Office And Research Park
600 Grant Street
Suite 3232
Pittsburgh, PA 15219
412-642-6697
Fax: 412-642-6698
http://www.edenhallfdn.org
This foundation offers support for higher education, social welfare and the improvement of conditions of the poor and needy.

Sylvia V Fields, Program Director
George C Greer, Chairman/President

2957 Erie County Library System
160 E Front Street
Erie, PA 16507-1554
814-451-6927
Fax: 814-451-6969
http://www.ecls.lib.pa.us
Member of The Foundation Center network, maintaining a collection of private foundation tax returns which provide information on the scope of grants dispensed by that particular foundation.

2958 Foundation Center-Carnegie Library of Pittsburgh
Foundation Collection
4400 Forbes Avenue
Pittsburgh, PA 15213-4080
412-622-6277
Fax: 412-454-7001
E-mail: foundati@carnegielibrary.org
http://www.clpgh.org/clp/Foundation
Member of the Foundation Center network, of cooperating collections; providing current, factual information about grants and grantmaking organizations, and other aspects of philanthropy to the local nonprofit community.

Jim Lutton, Manager
Herb Elish, Director

2959 HJ Heinz Company Foundation
PO Box 57
Pittsburgh, PA 15230-0057
412-456-5772
Fax: 412-456-7859
E-mail: heinz.foundation@hjheinz.com
http://www.heinz.com/jsp/foundation.jsp
Offers support for higher education, employee matching gifts, social service agencies and cultural programs.

Loretta M Oken, Executive Director

2960 John McShain Charities
540 N 17th Street
Philadelphia, PA 19130-3988
215-564-2322
Offers support for higher and secondary education, Roman Catholic church support and social welfare.

Mary McShain, Executive Director

2961 Mary Hillman Jennings Foundation
625 Stanwix Street
Apt 2203
Pittsburgh, PA 15222-1408
412-434-5606
Fax: 412-434-5907
Offers grants to schools, youth agencies, and hospitals and health associations.

Paul Euwer Jr, Executive Director

2962 McCune Foundation
750 Six PPG Place
Pittsburgh, PA 15222
412-644-8779
Fax: 412-644-8059
http://www.mccune-db.mccune.org
The foundation provides support to independent higher education and human services.

Henry S Beukema, Executive Director

2963 Pew Charitable Trusts
One Commerce Square
2005 Market Street
Suite 1700
Philadelphia, PA 19103-7077
215-575-9050
Fax: 215-575-4939
E-mail: info@pewtrusts.org
http://www.pewtrusts.com
Offers support for education (including theology), arts culture, as well as public policy and religion.

Rebecca W Rimel, Executive Director
Robert H Campbell, Board of Director

2964 Richard King Mellon Foundation
One Mellon Bank Center
500 Grant Street
Suite 4106
Pittsburgh, PA 15219-2502
412-392-2800
Fax: 412-392-2837
http://www.fdncenter.org/grantmaker/rkmellon/
Offers local grant programs with an emphasis on education, social services and the environment.

Seward Prosser Mellon, Trustee/President
Bruce King Mell Henderson, President

2965 Rockwell International Corporation Trust
625 Liberty Avenue
Pittsburgh, PA 15222-3110
414-212-5200
Fax: 414-212-5201
Offers support in the areas of K-12 math and science education, and higher education in the field of engineering and science.

William R Fitz, Executive Director

2966 Samuel S Fels Fund
1528 Walnut Street
Suite 1002
Philadelphia, PA 19102-5308
215-731-9455
Fax: 215-731-9457
http://www.samfels.org
Offers grants in continuing support that help prevent, lessen or resolve contemporary social problems including education, arts/cul-

tural programs, and community development.

Helen Cunningham, Executive Director
Robin N Culmer, Office Administrator

2967 Sarah Scaife Foundation
Three Mellon Bank Center
301 Grant Street
Suite 3900
Pittsburgh, PA 15219-6401
412-392-2900
http://www.scaife.com
Offers grants in the areas of education and community development.

Joanne B Beyer, Executive Director
Michael W Gleba, Executive Vice President

2968 Shore Fund
C/O Melton Bank N.A.
PO Box 185
Pittsburgh, PA 15230-0185
412-234-4695
Fax: 412-234-3551
Although the foundation appreciates funding opportunities within the field of education, most grants given out have been to schools with which the foundation's trustees have been personally involved.

Helen M Collins, Executive Director

2969 Stackpole-Hall Foundation
44 S Saint Marys Street
Saint Marys, PA 15857-1667
814-834-1845
Fax: 814-834-1869
E-mail: stackpolehall@windstream.net
http://www.stackpolehall.org
Offers support for higher education and secondary education, literacy and vocational projects, social services, arts and cultural programs, and community development.

William C Conrad, Executive Director

2970 United States Steel Foundation
600 Grant Street
Suite 639
Pittsburgh, PA 15219-2800
412-433-5237
Fax: 412-433-2792
http://www.psc.uss.com/usxfound
Grants are awarded for capital development, special projects or operating needs. Support is limited to organizations within the United States, with preference to those in the US Steel Corporation's operating areas. US Steel does not award grants for religious purposes. Additionally, grants are not awarded for conferences, seminars or symposia, travel, publication of papers, books or magazines, or production of films, videotapes or other audiovisual materials.

Craig D Mallick, General Manager
Pamela E DiNardo, Program Administrator

2971 William Penn Foundation
2 Logan Square11th Floor
100 North 18th Street
Philadelphia, PA 19103-2757
215-988-1830
Fax: 215-988-1823
E-mail: grants@williampennfoundation.org
http://www.williampennfoundation.org
The foundation supports culture, environment, human development, including programs for youth and elderly, education,

including early childhood, secondary, elementary and higher.

Kathryn J Engebretson, President
Bergen Bruce, Director of Finance and Admi

Rhode Island

2972 Champlin Foundations
2000 Chapel View Boulevard
Suite 350
Cranston, RI 02920
401-944-9200
Fax: 401-944-9299
E-mail: champlinfons@worldnet.att.net
http://www.fdncenter.org/grantmaker/champlin
Offers giving in the areas of higher, secondary and other education. Exclusively in Rhode Island.

David A King, Executive Director
Jonathan K Farnum, Distribution Committee Membe

2973 Providence Public Library
Reference Department
150 Empire Street
Providence, RI 02903-3219
401-455-8000
http://www.provlib.org
Member of The Foundation Center network, maintaining a collection of private foundation tax returns which provide information on the scope of grants dispensed by that particular foundation.

Dale Thompson, Director
Robert K Taylor, Chairman

2974 Rhode Island Foundation
One Union Station
Providence, RI 02903-4630
401-274-4564
Fax: 401-331-8085
http://www.rifoundation.org
Promotes charitable activities which tend to improve the living conditions and well-being of the residents of Rhode Island.

Ned Handy, President
David M Hirsch, Chairman

South Carolina

2975 Charleston County Library
68 Calhoun Street
Charleston, SC 29401
843-805-6930
Fax: 843-727-3741
http://www.ccpl.org
Member of The Foundation Center network, maintaining a collection of private foundation tax returns which provide information on the scope of grants dispensed by that particular foundation.

Janet Segal, Chairperson
Harlan Greene, Chairperson

2976 South Carolina State Library
1500 Senate Street
Columbia, SC 29201-3815
803-734-8666
Fax: 803-734-8676
http://www.state.sc.us/scsl/
Member of The Foundation Center network, maintaining a collection of private foundation tax returns which provide in-

formation on the scope of grants dispensed by that particular foundation.

James B Johnson Jr, Director

South Dakota

2977 South Dakota Community Foundation
1714 North Lincoln Ave
Box 296
Pierre, SD 57501-3159
605-224-1025
800-888-1842
Fax: 605-224-5364
http://www.sdcommunityfoundation.org
The mission of the foundation is to promote philanthropy, receive and administer charitable gifts and invest in a wide range of programs promoting the social and economic well being of the people of the South Dakota. Grants given in South Dakota only.

Bob Sutton, President
Stephanie Judson, Administrative Vice Presiden

2978 South Dakota State Library
Reference Department
800 Governors Drive
Pierre, SD 57501-2294
605-773-5070
Fax: 605-773-4950
http://www.sdstatelibrary.com
Member of The Foundation Center network, maintaining a collection of private foundation tax returns which provide information on the scope of grants dispensed by that particular foundation.

Tennesse

2979 Benwood Foundation
736 Market Street
Suite 1600
Chattanooga, TN 37402-4803
423-267-4311
Fax: 423-267-9049
http://www.benwood.org
The general purpose of this foundation is to support such religious, charitable, scientific, literary and educational activities as will promote the advancement of mankind in any part of the United States of America. It should be recognized by all prospective grantees that while the foundation is not limited to the Chattanooga, Tennessee area, the bulk of the grants are made to organizations in the immediate area.

Jean R McDaniel, Executive Director
Sarah Morgan, President

2980 Christy-Houston Foundation
1296 Dow Street
Murfreesboro, TN 37130-2413
615-898-1140
Fax: 615-895-9524
Offers grants for education, arts, culture and health care to residents and organizations of Rutherford County, Tennessee.

James R Arnhart, Executive Director

2981 Frist Foundation
3100 West End Avenue
Suite 1200
Nashville, TN 37203
615-292-3868
Fax: 615-292-5843
http://www.fristfoundation.org
Broad general-purposed charitable foundation whose grants are restricted primarily to Nashville.

Peter F Bird Jr, President/CEO
Thomas F Frist Jr, Chairman

982 JR Hyde Foundation
17 West Pontotoc Ave
Suite 200
Memphis, TN 38103-0084
901-685-3400
Fax: 901-683-7478
E-mail: info@hydefoundation.org
http://www.hydefoundation.org
Offers grants for higher education, including scholarships for the children of Malone and Hyde employees, community funds, secondary education and youth services.

JR Hyde III, Executive Director

983 Lyndhurst Foundation
517 E 5th Street
Chattanooga, TN 37403-1826
423-756-0767
Fax: 423-756-0770
http://www.lyndhurstfoundation.org
Support local arts and culture and downtown revitalzation efforts in Chattanooga. Support the protection and enhancement of the natural environment of the Southern Appalachian Region. Support the elementary and secondary public schools in Chattanooga.

Jack E Murrah, President

984 Nashville Public Library
Business Information Division
615 Church Street
Nashville, TN 37219
615-862-5800
http://www.library.nashville.org
Member of The Foundation Center network, maintaining a collection of private foundation tax returns which provide information on the scope of grants dispensed by that particular foundation.

Keith B Simmons, Board Chair

985 Plough Foundation
6410 Poplar Avenue
Suite 710
Memphis, TN 38119-5736
901-761-9180
Fax: 901-761-6186
Offers grants for community projects, including a community fund, early childhood and elementary education, social service agencies and the arts.

Noris R Haynes Jr, Executive Director

986 RJ Maclellan Charitable Trust
Provident Building
Suite 501
Chattanooga, TN 37402
423-755-1366
Supports higher and theological education, social services and youth programs.

Hugh O Maclellan Jr, Executive Director

Texas

987 Albert & Ethel Herzstein Charitable Foundation
6131 Westview Drive
Houston, TX 77055-5421
713-681-7868
Fax: 713-681-3652
http://www.herzsteinfoundation.org
Concentrates support on temples and medical research with grants offered to medical schools.

L Michael Hajtman, President
Nathan H Topek, Chairman

2988 Burlington Northern Foundation
3800 Continental Plaza
777 Main Street
Fort Worth, TX 76102
817-352-6425
Fax: 817-352-7924
The major channel of philanthropy for Burlington Northern and its subsidiaries. The foundation administers a consistent contribution program in recognition of the company's opportunity to support and improve the general welfare and quality of life in communities it serves.

Beverly Edwards, President
Becky Blankenship, Grant Administrator

2989 Burnett Foundation
801 Cherry Street
Suite 1400
Fort Worth, TX 76102-6814
817-877-3344
Fax: 817-338-0448
Focus is on Fort Worth and Santa Fe, NM, seeking to be a positive force in the community, supporting the energy and creativity that exist in the nonprofit sector, and building capacity in organizations and people in the fields of education, health, community affairs, human services and arts and humanities.

Thomas F Beech, Executive Director

2990 Cooper Industries Foundation
PO Box 4446
Houston, TX 77210-4446
713-209-8400
Fax: 713-209-8982
E-mail: evans@cooperindustries.com
http://www.cooperindustries.com
The policy of this foundation is to carry out the responsibilities of corporate citizenship, by supporting nonprofit organizations in areas where employees are located, which best serve the educational, health, welfare, civic, cultural and social needs of the foundation's communities. All gifts are consistent with the company's objectives to enhance the quality of life and to honor the principles and freedoms that have enabled the company to prosper and grow. Average Grant: $5,000.

Victoria Guennewig, President
Jennifer L Evans, Secretary

2991 Corpus Christi State University
Library-Reference Department
805 Comanche
Corpus Christi, TX 78401
361-880-7000
Fax: 361-880-7005
http://www.library.ci.corpus-christi.tx.us
Member of The Foundation Center network, maintaining a collection of private foundation tax returns which provide information on the scope of grants dispensed by that particular foundation.

Denise Landry

2992 Cullen Foundation
601 Jefferson Street
Floor 40
Houston, TX 77002-7900
713-651-8837
Fax: 713-651-2374
http://www.cullenfdn.org
Supports educational, medical purposes, community funds and conservation.

Alan M Stewart, Executive Director
Sue A Alexander, Grants Administrator

2993 Dallas Public Library
Urban Information
1515 Young Street
Dallas, TX 75201-5499
214-670-1400
Fax: 214-670-1451
http://www.dallaslibrary.org
Member of The Foundation Center network, maintaining a collection of private foundation tax returns which provide information on the scope of grants dispensed by that particular foundation.

2994 El Paso Community Foundation
333 North Oregon St
2nd Floor
El Paso, TX 79901
915-533-4020
Fax: 915-532-0716
http://www.epcf.org
Grants to 501(c)(3) organizations in the El Paso geographic area. Fields of interest are arts and humanities, education, environment, health and disabilities, human services and civic benefits. No grants to individuals are offered.

Janice Windle, President
Virginia Martinez, Executive VP

2995 Ellwood Foundation
PO Box 52482
Houston, TX 77052-2482
713-739-0763
Scholarships for social services and education.

H Wayne Hightower, Executive Director

2996 Eugene McDermott Foundation
1155 Union Circle
Suite 311580
Denton, TX 76203-5017
940-369-5200
Fax: 940-369-5248
http://www.tshaonline.org
Offers support primarily for higher and secondary education, health, cultural programs, and general community interests.

Eugene McDermott, Executive Director
Laurie E Jasinski, Research Editor

2997 Ewing Halsell Foundation
711 Navarro Street
Suite 535
San Antonio, TX 78205-1786
210-223-2649
Fax: 210-271-9089
http://www.ewinghalsell.org
Offers grants in the areas of art and cultural programs, education, medical research, human services and youth services.

Jackie Moczygemba

2998 Exxon Education Foundation
5959 Las Colinas Boulevard
Irving, TX 75039-2298
972-444-1106
Fax: 972-444-1405
http://www.exxon.mobile.com
Grants are given in the areas of environment, education, public information and policy research, united appeals and federated drives, health, civic and community service organizations, minority and women-oriented service organizations, arts, museums and historical associations. In the education area grants are awarded to mathematics education programs, elementary and secondary school improvement programs, undergraduate general education programs, research, training and support programs.

EF Ahnert, Executive Director

2999 Fondren Foundation
7 TCT 37
PO Box 2558
Houston, TX 77252
713-236-4403
Provides support in various areas of interest with an emphasis on higher and secondary education, social services and cultural organizations.

Melanie Scioneaus, Executive Director

3000 George Foundation
310 Morton Street
PMB Suite C
Richmond, TX 77469-3135
281-342-6109
Fax: 281-341-7635
http://www.thegeorgefoundation.org
Offers giving for religious, educational, charitable or scientific purposes.

Roland Adamson, Executive Director
Sandra Thompson, Chief Financial Officer

3001 Gordon & Mary Cain Foundation
8 E Greenway Plaza
Suite 702
Houston, TX 77046-0892
713-960-9283
Fax: 713-877-1824
The foundation is not limited to education but does contribute a large amount to that area. For a company to apply for a grant they must offer a statement of purpose or a summary of the project needing funding; budget with balance sheet, fund balance, distribution of funds, audited statement and number of employees; latest copy of IRS tax-exempt status letter 501(c)(3); current projects needing funding with amounts needed for entire project and the amount of the grant being requested.

James D Weaver, Executive Director

3002 Haggar Foundation
6113 Lemmon Avenue
Dallas, TX 75209-5715
214-352-8481
Fax: 214-956-4446
Offers support in various areas with an emphasis on higher and secondary education, including a program for children of company employees.

Mary Vaughan Rumble, Executive Director

3003 Hobby Foundation
2131 San Felipe Street
Houston, TX 77019-5620
713-521-4694
Fax: 713-521-3950
Offers grants to educational facilities in the state of Texas.

Oveta Culp Hobby, Executive Director

3004 Houston Endowment
600 Travis Street
Suite 6400
Houston, TX 77002-3000
713-238-8100
Fax: 713-238-8101
E-mail: info@houstonendowment.org
http://www.houstonendowment.org
Offers support for charitable, religious or educational organizations.

H Joe Nelson III, Executive Director
Ann B Stern, President

3005 Houston Public Library
Bibliographic Information Center
500 McKinney Street
Houston, TX 77002-2534

832-238-9640
Fax: 832-393-1383
http://www.hpl.lib.tx.us/hpl/hplhome
Member of The Foundation Center network, maintaining a collection of private foundation tax returns which provide information on the scope of grants dispensed by that particular foundation.

3006 James R Dougherty Jr Foundation
PO Box 640
Beeville, TX 78104-0640
361-358-3560
Fax: 361-358-9693
Offers support for Roman Catholic church-related industries including education, higher, secondary and other education.

Hugh Grove Jr, Executive Director

3007 Leland Fikes Foundation
3050 Lincoln Plaza
500 N Akard
Dallas, TX 75201
214-754-0144
Fax: 214-855-1245
Giving is focused on education, youth services, family planning, public interest and cultural programs.

Nancy Solana, Executive Director

3008 MD Anderson Foundation
1515 Holcombe Blvd
Houston, TX 77030-2558
713-658-2316
http://www.mdanderson.org
The purpose of this foundation is to improve lives in the areas of health care, education, human service, youth and research.

John W Lowrie, Executive Director

3009 Meadows Foundation
3003 Swiss Avenue
Wilson Historic Block
Dallas, TX 75204-6049
214-826-9431
800-826-9431
Fax: 214-824-0642
E-mail: besterline@mfi.org
http://www.mfi.org
Support is given in the area of arts and culture, civic and public affairs , education, health, including mental health, and human services.

Bruce Esterline, VP Grants
Carol Stabler, Director Communications

3010 Moody Foundation
2302 Post Office Street
Suite 704
Galveston, TX 77550-1994
409-797-1500
Fax: 409-763-5564
E-mail: info@moodyf.org
http://www.moodyf.org
Provides major support for two foundation-initiated projects: the Transitional Learning Center, a residential rehabilitation and research facility for the treatment of traumatic brain injury, and Moody Gardens, a world-class education and recreation complex that includes a 1-acre enclosed rainforest, the area's largest aquarium, a space museum, IMAX theater, and the Moody Hospitality Institute.

Peter M Moore, Grants Director
Robert L Moody, Sr.Chiarman

3011 Paul & Mary Haas Foundation
PO Box 2928
Corpus Christi, TX 78403-2928
361-887-6955

Offers scholastic grants to graduating high school seniors from Corpus Christi, Texas. The student must have above average grades and ability to prove financial need. The Foundation asks that the senior contact them in the Fall of his/her senior year in order to begin the in-house application process. The grant is a maximum of $1,500 per semester and is renewable for a total of eight semesters if the student maintains a 3.0 GPA. The student may attend college or university of his choice.

Karen Wesson, Executive Director

3012 Perot Foundation
12377 Merit Drive
Suite 1700
Dallas, TX 75251-2239
972-788-3000
Fax: 972-788-3091
Educational grants, medical research funding and grantmaking for the arts and cultural organizations.

Bette Perot, Executive Director

3013 RW Fair Foundation
PO Box 689
Tyler, TX 75710-0689
903-592-3811
Grants are given for secondary and higher education, church-related programs and legal education.

Wilton H Fair, Executive Director

3014 Sid W Richardson Foundation
309 Main Street
Fort Worth, TX 76102-4006
817-336-0494
Fax: 817-332-2176
E-mail: www.sidrichardson.org
http://www.sidrichardson.org
This foundation was established for the purpose of supporting organizations that serve the people of Texas. Grants are given in the areas of education, health, the arts and human services.

Valleau Wilkie Jr, Executive Director

3015 Strake Foundation
712 Main Street
Suite 3300
Houston, TX 77002-3210
713-546-2400
Fax: 713-216-2401
Foundation gives primarily in Texas in the areas of operating budgets, continuing support, annual campaigns, special projects, research, matching funds and general purposes.

George W Strake Jr, Executive Director

3016 Trull Foundation
404 4th Street
Palacios, TX 77465-4812
361-972-5241
Fax: 361-972-1109
E-mail: trullfdn@ncnet.net
http://www.trullfoundation.org
1. A concern for the needs of the Palacios, Matagorda county are, where the foundation has its roots. Local health care, the senior center, and other local projects were considered and supported. 2. A concern for children and families. Grants are given to direct and channel lives away from child abuse, neglect from hunger and poverty. 3. A concern for those persons and families devastated by the effects of substance abuse.

Gail Purvis, Executive Director
Lucja White, Administrative Assistant

Utah

3017 Marriner S Eccles Foundation
79 S Main Street
Salt Lake City, UT 84111-1901
801-246-5155
General support for Utah's human services, education and the arts programs.

Erma E Hogan, Executive Director

3018 Ruth Eleanor Bamberger and John Ernest Bamberger Memorial Foundation
136 S Main Street
Salt Lake City, UT 84101-1690
801-364-2045
Fax: 801-322-5284
E-mail:
bambergermemfdn@qwestoffice.net
http://www.ruthandjohnbambergermemorial
fdn.org
Offers support for secondary education, especially undergraduate scholarships for student nurses and for schools.

William H Olwell, Executive Director

3019 Salt Lake City Public Library
210 East 400 south
Salt Lake City, UT 84111-3280
801-524-8200
Fax: 801-524-8272
http://www.slcpl.lib.ut.us
Member of The Foundation Center network, maintaining a collection of private foundation tax returns which provide information on the scope of grants dispensed by that particular foundation.

Dana Tumtowsky, Comm Relations Coordinator
Nancy Tessman, Director

Vermont

3020 Vermont Community Foundation
PO Box 30
Three Court Street
Middlebury, VT 05753-0030
802-388-3355
Fax: 802-388-3398
http://www.vermontcf.org
Offers support for the arts and education, the environment, preservation of the community, public affairs and more for the betterment of Vermont.

David F Finney, President/CEO
John Killacky, Executive Director

3021 Vermont Department of Libraries
Reference Services
109 State Street
Montpelier, VT 05609-0001
802-828-3268
Fax: 802-828-2199
http://www.dol.state.vt.us
Member of The Foundation Center network, maintaining a collection of private foundation tax returns which provide information on the scope of grants dispensed by that particular foundation.

3022 William T & Marie J Henderson Foundation
PO Box 600
Stowe, VT 05672-0600
Offers grants in the areas of elementary and secondary education.

William T Henderson, Executive Director

Virginia

3023 Beazley Foundation
3720 Brighton Street
Portsmouth, VA 23707-3902
757-393-1605
Fax: 757-393-4708
E-mail: info@beazleyfoundation.org
http://www.beazleyfoundation.org
The purpose of this foundation to further the causes of charity, education and religion. Offers support for higher, secondary and medical education, youth agencies, community agencies and development.

Judge Richard S Bray, President
Donna M Russell, Associate Director

3024 Flagler Foundation
PO Box 644
Richmond, VA 23205
804-648-5033
Offers support for secondary and higher education, cultural programs and restoration.

Lawrence Lewis Jr, Executive Director

3025 Hampton Public Library
22 Lincoln Street
Hampton, VA 23669-4200
757-727-6315
Fax: 757-728-3037
E-mail: council@hampton.gov
http://www.hampton.va.us
Member of The Foundation Center network, maintaining a collection of private foundation tax returns which provide information on the scope of grants dispensed by that particular foundation.

Molly Joseph Ward, Mayor
George E Wallace, Vice Mayor

3026 Jeffress Memorial Trust
Bank Of America Private Bank
Po Box 8795
Williamsburg, VA 23187-8795
804-788-3698
Fax: 804-788-2700
http://www.wm.edu/grants/opps/jeffress.ht
m
Funds research in higher education.

Richard B Brandt, Advisor

3027 Kentland Foundation
267 Kentlands Boulevard
Gaithesrsburg, MD 20878-5442
301-926-6636
E-mail: info@kentlands.org
http://www.kentlands.org
Focuses on civic affairs organizations and education.

Helene Walker, Executive Director

3028 Longview Foundation for Education in World Affairs/International Understanding
1069 West Broad Street
Suite 801
Falls Church, VA 22046
301-681-0899
Fax: 301-681-0925
E-mail: globaled@longviewfdn.org
http://www.longviewfdn.org
Offers grants and scholarships with an emphasis on pre-collegiate education, primarily elementary education, and also supports teacher education.

Betsy Devlin-Foltz, Director
Stevenson McIlvaine, President

3029 Richmond Public Library
Business, Science & Technology Department
3100 Ellwood Avenue
Richmond, VA 23221-2193
804-646-1139
Fax: 804-646-4757
http://www.richmondpubliclibrary.org
Member of The Foundation Center network, maintaining a collection of private foundation tax returns which provide information on the scope of grants dispensed by that particular foundation.

Peter Blake, Chairman
Brenda Drew, Vice-Chairman

3030 Virginia Foundation for Educational Leadership
2204 Recreation Drive
Virginia Beach, VA 23456-6178
757-430-2412
Fax: 757-430-3247

George E McGovern, Division Director

Washington

3031 Comstock Foundation
3010 Gull Road
Kalamazoo, MI 49048
269-250-8900
Fax: 269-250-8901
http://www.comstockps.org
The Foundation contributes only to 501(c)(3) organizations, limited to Spokane County and its environs. In the field of general education, Comstock Foundation favors grants only to private institutions of higher learning, and no grants are made to individuals.

Horton Herman, Trustee
Charles M Leslie, Trustee

3032 Foster Foundation
13 Central Way
Kirland, WA 98033
206-726-1815
E-mail: info@thefosterfoundation.org
http://www.thefosterfoundation.org
Offers support in art, culture, higher education, adult education, literacy and basic reading, health care and children and youth services.

Jill Goodsell, Executive Director

3033 MJ Murdock Charitable Trust
703 Broadway Street
Suite 701
Vancouver, WA 98660-3308
360-694-8415
Fax: 360-694-1819
http://www.murdock-trust.org
Offers support primarily for special projects of private organizations in the areas of education, higher education, human services and program development.

John Van Zytveld, Senior Program Director

3034 Seattle Foundation
1200 5th Avenue
Suite 1300
Seattle, WA 98101-3151
206-622-2294
Fax: 206-622-7673
http://www.seattlefoundation.org
A community foundation that facilitates charitable giving; administers charitable funds, trusts and bequests; and distributes grants to non-profit organizations that are making a positive difference in our community. Grants are awarded to organizations working in areas that include social service, children and

youth, civic, culture, elderly, conservation, education and health/rehabilitation.

Phyllis J Campbell, President/CEO
Molly Stearns, Senior Vice President

3035 Seattle Public Library
Science, Social Science
1000 4th Avenue
Seattle, WA 98104-1109
206-386-4636
Fax: 206-386-4634
http://www.spl.org
Member of The Foundation Center network, maintaining a collection of private foundation tax returns which provide information on the scope of grants dispensed by that particular foundation.

3036 Spokane Public Library
Funding Information Center
906 West Main Street
Spokane, WA 99201-0903
509-444-5300
Fax: 509-444-5365
http://www.spokanelibrary.org
Member of The Foundation Center network, maintaining a collection of private foundation tax returns which provide information on the scope of grants dispensed by that particular foundation.

Pat Partovi, Director

West Virginia

3037 Clay Foundation
1426 Kanawha Boulevard E
Charleston, WV 25301-3084
304-344-8656
Fax: 304-344-3805
Private charitable foundation making grants for health, education and programs for the aging or disadvantaged children.

Charles M Avampao, Executive Director

3038 Kanawha County Public Library
123 Capitol Street
Charleston, WV 25301-2686
304-343-4646
Fax: 304-348-6530
http://www.kanawha.lib.wv.us
Member of The Foundation Center network, maintaining a collection of private foundation tax returns which provide information on the scope of grants dispensed by that particular foundation.

Michael Albert, President
Elizabeth O Lord, First Vice President

3039 Phyllis A Beneke Scholarship Fund
Security National Bank & Trust Company
PO Box 511
Wheeling, WV 26003-0064
Offers support and scholarships for secondary education.

GP Schramm Sr, Executive Director

Wisconsin

3040 Faye McBeath Foundation
101 W Pleasant Street
Suite 210
Milwaukee, WI 53212-3157
414-272-2626
Fax: 414-272-6235
E-mail: info@fayemcbeath.org
http://www.fayemcbeath.org
The purpose of the foundation is to provide Wisconsin people the best in education,

child welfare, homes and care for the elderly and research in civics and government.

Scott E Gelzer, Executive Director
Aileen Mayer, Executive Assistant

3041 Lynde & Harry Bradley Foundation
1241 N Franklin Place
Milwaukee, WI 53202-2901
414-291-9915
Fax: 414-291-9991
http://www.bradleyfdn.org
The Foundation encourages projects that focus on cultivating a renewed, healthier and more vigorous sense of citizenship among the American people, and among peoples of all nations, as well. Grants are awarded to organizations and institutions exempt from federal taxation under Section 501(c)(3) and publicly supported under section 509(a), favor projects which are not normally financed by public tax funds, consider requests from religious organizations and institutions as well.

Michael W Grebe, President/CEO
Terry Considine, Chairman

3042 Marquette University Memorial Library
1355 West Wisconsin Avenue
Milwaukee, WI 53233-2287
414-288-7556
Fax: 414-288-5324
http://www.marquette.edu/library/
Member of The Foundation Center network, maintaining a collection of private foundation tax returns which provide information on the scope of grants dispensed by that particular foundation.

3043 Siebert Lutheran Foundation
300 N Corporate Dr
Suite 200
Brookfield, WI 53045-1392
262-754-9160
Fax: 262-754-9162
E-mail: contactus@siebertfoundation.org
http://www.siebertfoundation.org
Offers support in elementary and secondary, higher education and early childhood education.

Ronald D Jones, President
Deborah Engel, Administrative Assistant

3044 University of Wisconsin-Madison
Memorial Library
728 State Street
Madison, WI 53706-1418
608-262-3242
Fax: 608-262-8569
E-mail: grantsinfo@library.wisc.edu
http://www.grants.library.wisc.edu
Member of The Foundation Center network, maintaining a collection of private foundation tax returns which provide information on the scope of grants dispensed by that particular foundation.

Wyoming

3045 Natrona County Public Library
307 E 2nd Street
Casper, WY 82601-2598
307-237-4935
Fax: 307-266-3734
http://www.library.natrona.net
Member of The Foundation Center network, maintaining a collection of private foundation tax returns which provide in-

formation on the scope of grants dispensed by that particular foundation.

Grants, Federal & Private

3046 American Honda Foundation
PO Box 2205
Torrance, CA 90509-2205
310-781-4090
Fax: 310-781-4270
http://www.hondacorporate.com/community
Offers support for national organizations whose areas of interest include youth and scientific education. Grants reach private elementary, secondary, higher, vocational and scientific education.

Kathryn A Carey, Manager

3047 Awards for University Administrators and Librarians
Association of Commonwealth Universities
John Foster House
36 Gordon Square
London WC1H OPF, England
171 3878572
Fax: 171 3872655
E-mail: pubinfo@acu.ac.uk;
acusales@acu.ac.uk
Lists approximately 40 sources of financial assistance for administrative and library staff for universities worldwide. Includes name, address, phone, fax, tenure place and length, amount of aid, requirements for eligibility and application procedure, and frequency and number of grants available.

40 pages Biennial
ISSN: 0964-2714

Moira Hunter, Editor

3048 Awards for University Teachers and Research Workers
Association of Commonwealth Universities
36 Gordon Square
London
WC1H OPF, England
44-20-7380-6700
Fax: 44-20-7387-2655
E-mail: info@devry.edu
http://www.devry.edu
Lists approximately 740 awards open to university teachers and research workers in one country for research, study visits or teaching at a university in another country. Offers fellowships, visiting professorships and lectureships and travel grants.

364 pages Biennial
ISSN: 0964-2706

3049 Educational Foundation of America
55 Walls Drive
Fairfield, CT 06824-3515
203-226-6498
Fax: 203-227-0424
http://www.efaw.org
Funds projects in arts, education and programs benefiting Native Americans.

Diane M Allison, Executive Director
Lynn P Babicka, President

3050 Foundation Center
79 5th Avenue
Floor 8
New York, NY 10003-3076
212-620-4230
Fax: 212-807-3677
http://www.fdncenter.org
A national service organization which disseminates information on private giving through public service programs, publications, and through a national network of library reference collections for free public use. Over 100 network members

have sets of private foundation information returns, and the New York, Washington, DC, Cleveland and San Francisco reference collections operated by the Foundation offer a wide variety of services and collections of information on foundations and grants.

Cheryl Loe, Director Of Communications
Laura Cascio, Fulfillment Management

3051 GTE Foundation
PO Box 152257
Irving, TX 75015-2257
972-507-5434
Fax: 972-615-4310
http://www.gte.com
The emphasis of giving for the foundation is on higher education in math, science and technology. It also sponsors scholarships and supports community funds and social service agencies that emphasize literacy training.

Maureen Gorman, VP

3052 George I Alden Trust
370 Main Street
Worcester, MA 01608-1714
508-459-8005
Fax: 508-459-8305
E-mail: trustees@aldentrust.org
http://www.aldentrust.org
Gives to higher education organizations and facilities with an emphasis on scholarship endowments.

Francis H Dewey III, Executive Director
Warner S Fletcher, Chairman

3053 Gershowitz Grant and Evaluation Services
505 Merle Hay Tower
Des Moines, IA 50310
515-270-1718
Fax: 515-270-8325
E-mail: gershowitz@netins.net
To give schools an edge in funding their technology programs

Michael V Gershowitz, PhD
Steve Panyan, PhD

3054 Grants and Contracts Service
Department of Education/Regional Office Building
7th & D Streets
Suite 3124
Washington, DC 20202-0001
202-401-2000
Fax: 202-260-7225
To support improvements in teaching and learning and to help meet special needs of schools and students in elementary and secondary education

Gary J Rasmussen, Director

3055 Grantsmanship Center
PO Box 17220
Los Angeles, CA 90017-0220
213-482-9860
Fax: 213-482-9863
E-mail: norton@tgci.com
http://www.tgci.com
The world's oldest and largest training organization for the nonprofit sector. Since it was founded in 1972, the has trained trains more than 75,000 staff members of public and private agencies; training provided includes grantsmanship, program management and fundraising. Center also produces publications on grantsmanship, fundraising, planning, management and personnel issues for nonprofit agencies.

Norton Kiritz, President

3056 John S & James L Knight Foundation
Wachovia Financial Center
Suite 3300
200south Biscayne Boulevard
Miami, FL 33131-2349
305-908-2600
Fax: 305-908-2698
E-mail: web@knightfoundation.org
http://www.knightfdn.org
The foundation makes national grants in journalism, education and the field of arts and culture. It also supports organizations in communities where the Knight brothers were involved in publishing newspapers but is wholly separate from and independent of those newspapers.

James D Spaniolo, Executive Director

3057 National Academy of Education
500 Fifth Street NW
Washington, DC 20001
212-998-9035
Fax: 212-995-4435
E-mail: info@naeducation.org
http://www.naeducation.org
Offers the Spencer Postdoctoral Fellowship which is designed to promote scholarship in the United States and abroad on matters relevant to the improvement of education in all its forms.

Debbie Leong-Childs, Executive Director

3058 National Science Foundation
4201 Wilson Boulevard
Arlington, VA 22230
703-292-5111
Fax: 703-292-9184
http://www.nsf.gov
Offers grants, workshops and curricula for all grade levels.

Arden L Bement Jr, Director

3059 Trust to Reach Education Excellence
1904 Association Drive
Reston, VA 20191-1537
703-860-0200
800-253-7746
Fax: 703-476-5432
E-mail: tree@principals.org
http://www.tree.principals.org
Founded to make grants to educators and students who would ordinarily not have access to outstanding NASSP programs, such as camps, programs and workshops on leadership, technology and school reform.

Dr. Anne Miller, Executive Director

3060 Union Carbide Foundation
39 Old Ridgebury Road
Danbury, CT 06817-0001
203-794-6945
Fax: 203-794-7031
http://www.unioncarbide.com
Offers grants in the areas of elementary and secondary education, with an emphasis on systemic reform; higher education with a focus on science and engineering; and environmental protection awareness.

Nancy W Deibler, Executive Director

3061 United States Institute of Peace
2301 Constitution Avenue
Washington, DC 20037
202-457-1700
Fax: 202-429-6063
http://www.usip.org
Includes grants, fellowships, a National Peace Essay Contest for high school students and teacher training institutes.

Richard H Solomon, President
Judy Ansley, Board of Director

3062 United States-Japan Foundation
145 E 32nd Street
Floor 12
New York, NY 10016-6055
212-481-8753
Fax: 212-481-8762
E-mail: info@us-jf.org
http://www.us-jf.org
A nonprofit, philanthropic organization with the principal mission of promoting a greater mutual knowledge between United States and Japan and to contribute to a strengthened understanding of important public policy issues of interest to both countries. Currently the focus is on precollegiate education, policy studies, and communications and public opinion.

3063 Westinghouse Foundation
Westinghouse Electric Corporation
Po Box 355
ECE 575C
Pittsburgh, PA 15230-0355
412-374-6824
Fax: 412-642-4874
http://www.westinghousenuclear.com
Makes charitable contributions to community priorities primarily where Westinghouse has a presence. Areas of emphasis include: education, health and welfare, culture and the arts and civic and social grants. Support for education is central to Westinghouse's contributions program, particularly higher education in the areas of engineering, applied science and business. Also encourages educational programs that strengthen public schools through enhanced student learning opportunities.

G Reynolds Clark, Executive Director

3064 Xerox Foundation
800 Long Ridge Road #1600
Stamford, CT 06902-1227
203-968-3445
http://www.xerox.com
Offers giving in the areas of higher education to prepare qualified men and women for careers in business, government and education.

Joseph M Cahalan, Executive Director

Fundraising

3065 A&L Fund Raising
29 Carriage Drive
South Windsor, CT 06074-1140
860-242-2476
800-286-7247
http://www.alstudentservices.com
Offers many successful fundraising programs including Christmas gifts, designer gift wraps from Ashley Taylor and Geoffrey Boehm chocolates. A&L sells only the highest quality items at affordable prices with great service to schools and organizations.

Anita Brown

3066 A+ Enterprises
1426 Route 33
Hamilton Square, NJ 08690-1704
609-587-1765
800-321-1765
A promotional corporation offering a variety of fundraising programs for schools and educational institutions, ranging from Christmas campaigns to chocolates, as well as magnets and gift campaigns.

3067 Aid for Education
CD Publications
8204 Fenton Street
Sliver Spring, MD 20910

301-588-6380
800-666-6380
Fax: 301-588-0519
E-mail: afe@cdpublications.com
http://www.cdpublications.com
18 pages Newsletter
ISSN: 1058-1324
Frank Kimko, Editor

3068 All Sports
21 Round Hill Road
Wethersfield, CT 06109
860-721-0273
800-829-0273
Fax: 860-257-9609
E-mail: shirts2graduationshirts.com
http://www.graduationshirts.com
Fundraising and school promotion company offering crew sweatshirts, hoods, tees, jackets, caps, gymwear and specialty signature shirts for graduating classes.
Wally Schultz, Owner

3069 Art to Remember
5535 Macy Drive
Indianapolis, IN 46235
317-826-0870
800-895-8777
Fax: 317-823-2822
E-mail: brackney@arttoremember.com
http://www.arttoremember.com
Raises funds for art departments and special school programs.

3070 Childrens Youth Funding Report
CD Publications
8204 Fenton Street
Sliver Spring, MD 20910
301-588-6380
800-666-6380
Fax: 301-588-6385
E-mail: cye@cdpublications.com
http://www.cdpublications.com
Detailed coverage of federal and private grant opportunities and legislative initiatives effecting childrens programs in such areas as child welfare, education healthcare.
18 pages Monthly
Steve Albright, Editor

3071 Dutch Mill Bulbs
PO Box 407
Hershey, PA 17033-0407
717-868-3120
800-533-8824
Fax: 800-556-0539
E-mail: info@dutchmillbulbs.com
http://www.dutchmillbulbs.com
Spring and Fall fundraising with flower bulbs program.
Jeffrey E Ellenberger, President

3072 E-S Sports Screenprint Specialists
47 Jackson Street
Holyoke, MA 01040-5512
413-534-5634
800-833-3171
Fax: 413-538-8648
Scholastic Spirit Division offers screenprinted T-shirts, sweatshirts, shorts and apparel. This program offers schools and organizations an easy way to increase school spirit with no risk, no minimum orders and prompt delivery.
Aaron Porchelli, Division Director

3073 Fundraising USA
1395 State Route 23
Butler, NJ 07405-1736
973-283-1946
800-428-6178
Fundraiser offering a variety of programs for schools and organizations including Walk-A-Thons. This program is fast becoming the most popular way for schools to raise money. The walks are designed to take place at your own school, and children are not responsible for collecting any money. Fundraising USA collects all donations through the mail.

3074 Gold Medal Products
10700 Medallion Drive
Cincinnati, OH 45241-4807
513-769-7676
800-543-0862
Fax: 513-769-8500
E-mail: info@gmpopcorn.com
http://www.gmpopcorn.copm
Offers a full line of fundraising products popcorn poppers and supplies and programs including candy, clothing and sports programs for schools and colleges.
Chris Petroff
Dan Kroeger, President

3075 Human-i-Tees
400 Columbus Avenue
Valhalla, NY 10595-1335
800-275-2638
Fax: 914-745-1799
http://www.humanitees.com
Environmental T-shirt fundraisers that provide large profits while raising environmental awareness for thousands of school, youth and service organizations across the country.

3076 Hummel Sweets
PO Box 232
Forestville, MD 20747
800-998-8115
Offer fundraising programs with 45% to 50% profit.

3077 M&M Mars Fundraising
800 High Street
Hackettstown, NJ 07840-1552
908-852-1000
Fax: 908-850-2734
Offers America's favorite candies for fundraising programs throughout the year.

3078 QSP
Subsidiary of the Reader's Digest Association
PO Box 2003
Ridgefield, CT 06877-0903
203-756-3022
800-667-2536
Fax: 800-844-3568
E-mail: customerservice@qsp.ca
http://www.qsp.ca
For twenty-seven years, this fundraiser has helped students raise more than $900,000,000 for extracurricular programs and projects that are essential to a meaningful, well-rounded education. With QSP programs, students earn money to fund worthwhile projects and learn about the business world at the same time. QSP offers various fundraising programs including: Family Reading Programs; The Music Package; Delightful Edibles; and The Parade of Gifts.
Robert L Metivier, Sales Manager

3079 Sally Foster Gift Wrap
PO Box 539
Duncan, SC 29334-0539
800-552-5875
Fax: 800-343-0809
http://www.sallyfoster.com
Fundraiser offers gift wrap packages to schools. Offers high quality merchandise,

including the heaviest papers and foils available. This proven two-week program is quick, easy and profitable offering your school or organization the opportunity to raise thousands of dollars to buy computers, books, athletic equipment and more. Organizations and schools keep 50% of all the profits, and there are no up-front costs or risks.
Mark Metcalfe, Sr VP

3080 School Identifications
Chas. E. Petrie Comapny
PO Box 527
Woodburn, OR 97071-0012
503-982-0757
800-772-0798
Fax: 503-981-3038
E-mail: info@schoolidents.com
http://www.schoolidents.com
An easy fundraising project for schools, offering school identification cards and tags for students.

3081 School Memories Collection
Fundcraft Publishing
PO Box 340
Collierville, TN 38027
901-853-7070
800-853-1363
Fax: 901-853-6196
E-mail: info@fundcraft.com
http://www.schoolmemories.com
Memory books with games and activities.
Chris Bradley, Marketing Director

3082 Sports Shoes & Apparel
3 Moulton Drive
Londonderry, NH 03053-4061
603-437-7844
800-537-7844
Fax: 603-437-2300
Offers customized sweatshirts, T-shirts and beach towels at group discount, with several complete fund raising programs being available as well. Beach towels for fundraising.
Bill McMahon, Regional Manager

3083 Steve Wronker's Funny Business
39 Boswell Road
W Hartford, CT 06107-3708
860-233-6716
800-929-swfb
Fax: 860-561-8910
http://www.swfb.net/swfb.htm
Comedy and educational magic shows available for preschool and elementary school aged children. Award winning programs such as The Magic of Books and Magic from Around the World are available for any size audience. For middle schools and high schools, comedy hypnosis is a perfect venue for entertainment as a fundraising program, for high school after-prom parties, graduation parties, or just for an evening's entertainment.
Steve Wronker

3084 T-Shirt People/Wearhouse
10722 Hanna Street
Beltsville, MD 20705-2123
301-937-4843
800-638-7070
Fax: 301-937-2916
http://www.t-shirtpeople.com
Fundraiser offering customized T-shirts to boost school spirit, raise funds, instill school pride and save money.

3085 Troll Book Fairs
100 Corporate Drive
Mahwah, NJ 07430-2041
201-529-4000
Fax: 201-529-8282
A profit-making program designed to introduce children to the wonderful world of books.

3086 Union Pen Company
166 Wallins Corner Road
Amsterdam, NY 12010
800-203-9917
Fax: 800-688-4877
E-mail: unionpen@aol.com
http://www.unionpen.com
This company offers advertising gifts including customized pens and key chains that will increase confidence, school spirit and community goodwill in education. Group discounts are available.

Matt Roberts, General Manager
Morton Tenny, President

3087 www.positivepins.com
802 E 6th Streetve
PO Box 52528
Tulsa, OK 74152
918-587-2405
800-282-0085
Fax: 918-382-0906
E-mail: pinrus@aol.com
http://www.thepinman-pins.com
Fundraising organization used by educational organizations. Designer and manufacturer of lapel pins used for employee service, appreciation, volunteer recognition, donor incentives and recognition, public relations and spirit.

Bern L Gentry, President
Michelle Anderson, VP

Scholarships & Financial Aid

3088 AFL-CIO Guide to Union Sponsored Scholarships, Awards & Student Aid
AFL-CIO
1100 1st St NE
Suite 850
Washington, DC 20002-4104
202-637-5000
E-mail: info@unionprivelege.org
http://www.unionplus.org
Lists international and national unions, local unions, state federations and labor councils offering scholarships, awards or financial aid to students.

100 pages Annual

3089 American-Scandinavian Foundation
58 Park Avenue at 38th Street
New York, NY 10016
212-779-3587
E-mail: info@amscan.org
http://www.amscan.org
The Foundation provides information, scholarships and grants on the study programs in Scandinavia.

Edward P. Gallagher, President
Steven B. Peri, Deputy Chairman

3090 Arts Scholarships
Jewish Foundation for Education of Women
430 Park Ave
Suite 3A
Highland Park, IL 60035-1827
212-288-3931
Fax: 212-288-5798
E-mail: fdnscholar@aol.com
http://www.scholarships.com
These scholarships are being offered at the Julliard School, Tisch School, of the Arts at New York University, and the Manhattan School of Music to qualified students enrolled in their programs. Faculty members will select recipients.

Marge Goldwater, Executive Director

3091 CUNY Teacher Incentive Program
Jewish Foundation for Education of Women
135 E 64th Street
New York, NY 10019-1827
212-288-3931
Fax: 212-288-5798
E-mail: fdnscholar@aol.com
http://www.jfew.org
Provide stipends to CUNY graduates who are studying for a master's degree in education and interested in a teaching career in the New York City public school system. Contact the office of the Vice Chancellor for Academic Affairs at CUNY for further information.

Marge Goldwater, Executive Director

3092 College Board
45 Columbus Avenue
New York, NY 10023-6917
212-713-8000
Fax: 212-713-8282
http://www.collegeboard.org
The College Board is a national, nonprofit membership association that supports educational transitions through programs and services in assessment, guidance, admission, placement, financial aid, and educational reform.

David Coleman, President

3093 Dissertation Fellowships in the Humanities
Jewish Foundation for Education of Women
135 E 64th Street
New York, NY 10065-1827
212-288-3931
Fax: 212-288-5798
E-mail: fdnscholar@aol.com
http://www.jfew.org
A small number of fellowships will be awarded through the CUNY Graduate Center to qualified applicants.

Marge Goldwater, Executive Director

3094 George & Mary Kremer Foundation
1100 5th Avenue S
Suite 411
Naples, FL 34102-7415
941-261-2367
Fax: 941-261-1494
http://www.kremerfoundation.com
Provides scholarship funding for needy children in elementary Catholic schools throughout the Continental United States.

Mary Anderson Goddard, Director
Sister MT Ballrach, Assistant Director

3095 Intel Science Talent Search Scolarship
1719 N Street NW
Washington, DC 20036-2888
202-785-2255
Fax: 202-785-1243
E-mail: sciedu@sciserv.org
http://www.sciserv.org
Offers a variety of services to teachers and students, including Intel Science Talent Search Scholarship competition, science fairs and publications.

3096 Jewish Foundation for Education of Women
Jewish Foundation for Education of Women
135 E 64th Street
New York, NY 10019-1827
212-288-3931
Fax: 212-288-5798
E-mail: fdnscholar@aol.com
http://www.jfew.org
The Jewish Foundation for Education of Women is a private, nonsectarian foundation providing scholarships to women for higher education in the New York City area. A vari-

ety of specific programs are available. Most programs are administered collaboratively with area schools and organizations; the Foundation's mission is to help women of all ages attain the education and training needed to make them productive, economically independent members of the community.

Marge Goldwater, Executive Director
Sharon L Weinberg, Chairman

3097 Octameron Associates
P.O Box 2748
Alexandria, VA 22301-0748
703-836-5480
Fax: 703-836-5650
E-mail: info@octameron.com
http://www.octameron.com
Octameron is a publishing and consulting firm with over 25 years experience in financial aid and admissions.

Anna Leider, Publisher

3098 Scholarship America
One Scholarship Way
Saint Peter, MN 56082-1556
507-931-1682
800-537-4180
Fax: 507-931-9250
E-mail: dsnatoff@aol.com
http://www.dollarsforscholars.org
Provides community volunteers with the tools and support to create, develop and sustain legally constituted community-based scholarship foundations. Over 15,000 volunteers are active on 760 Dollars for Scholars chapter boards and committees throughout the United States. In addition, 20,000 high school youth and community residents are active in fund-raising events and academic support programs. Since the late 1950's, over 155,000 students have received Dollars for Scholars scholarships.

David Bach, VP
Susan Ponwith, President&CEO

3099 Scholarships in the Health Professions
Jewish Foundation for Education of Women
135 E 64th Street
New York, NY 10021
212-288-3931
Fax: 212-288-5798
E-mail: fdnscholar@aol.com
http://www.jfew.org
Provides scholarships to emigres from the former Soviet Union who are studying medicine, dentistry, nursing, pharmacy, OT, PT, dental hygiene, and physician assistanceship.

Marge Goldwater, Executive Director

Federal Listings

3100 Accounting & Financial Management Services
U.S. Department of Education
400 Maryland Avenue, SW
Washington, DC 20202-0001
800-872-5327
Fax: 202-401-0207
http://www2.ed.gov

Arne Duncan, Secretary of Education
Emma Vadehra, Chief of Staff

3101 Assistance to States Division
U.S. Department of Education
400 Maryland Avenue, SW
Washington, DC 20202
202-401-2000
800-872-5327
Fax: 202-260-7225
http://www2.ed.gov

Arne Duncan, Secretary of Education
Emma Vadehra, Chief of Staff

3102 Brody Professional Development
Brody Communications Ltd.
115 West Avenue
Suite 114
Jenkintown, PA 19046
215-886-1688
Fax: 215-886-1699
E-mail: info@brodypro.com
http://www.brodypro.com
Brody offers tailored training programs, executive coaching and presentations in the areas of communication skills and professional development.

Miryam Roddy, Manager of Maximum Exposure

3103 Compensatory Education Program
US Department of Education
400 Maryland Avenue SW
Washington, DC 20202
202-401-2000
800-872-5327
Fax: 202-260-7764
http://www.ed.gov

Emma Vadehra, Chief of Staff
Richard Culatta, Director, Education Tech

3104 Elementary Secondary Bilingual & Research Branch
U.S. Department of Education
400 Maryland Avenue, SW
Suite 3653
Washington, DC 20202
202-401-0113
800-872-5327
Fax: 202-260-7225
http://www2.ed.gov

Arne Duncan, Secretary of Education
Emma Vadehra, Chief of Staff

3105 Elementary, Secondary & Vocational Analysis
U.S. Department of Education
400 Maryland Avenue SW
3043 Main Building
Washington, DC 20202-0001
202-401-0318
800-872-5327
Fax: 202-260-7225
http://www2.ed.gov

Arne Duncan, Secretary of Education
Emma Vadehra, Chief of Staff

3106 Management Services
U.S. Department of Education
400 Maryland Avenue SW
Washington, DC 20202-0001
202-401-0500
800-872-5327
Fax: 202-260-7225
http://www2.ed.gov

Arne Duncan, Secretary of Education
Emma Vadehra, Chief of Staff

3107 National Center for Education Statistics
1990 K Street NW
8th & 9th Floors
Washington, DC 20006
202-502-7300
Fax: 202-502-7466
http://www.nces.ed.gov

Sean P. Jack Buckley, Commissioner

3108 National Council on Disability
1331 F Street NW
Suite 850
Washington, DC 20004-1107
202-272-2004
Fax: 202-272-2022
E-mail: ncd@ncd.gov
http://www.ncd.gov/
An independent federal agency comprised of 15 members appointed by the President and confirmed by the Senate.

Jonathan M. Young, Ph.D., Chairman
Aaron Bishop, Executive Director

3109 National Institute of Child Health and Human Development
Bldg.31, Room 2A32, MSC 2425
31 Center Drive
Bethesda, MD 20892-2425
800-370-2943
Fax: 866-760-5947
E-mail: NICHDInformationResourceCenter@mail.nih.gov
http://www.nichd.nih.gov
Develops research to solve problems in the physical and mental evolution of development. Including some of the most emotionally draining disorders, learning disabilities, behavioral disabilities, birth defects and infant mortality. Acts as a clearinghouse of materials, information and referrals and more.

Ellie Brown Hochman, Administrative Officer
Brenda Hanning, Program Management Officer

3110 National Library of Education
U.S. Department of Education
400 Maryland Avenue, SW
Washington, DC 20202
202-401-2000
800-872-5327
Fax: 202-401-0547
E-mail: library@ed.gov
http://www.ed.gov

Emma Vadehra, Chief of Staff
Richard Culatta, Director, Education Tech

3111 National Trust for Historic Preservation: Office of Education Initiatives
The Watergate Office Building
2600 Virginia Avenue, Suite 1000
Washington, DC 20037
202-588-6000
800-944-6847
Fax: 202-588-6038

E-mail: info@savingplaces.org
http://www.nationaltrust.org
Teaching with Historic Places, a program offered by the National Park Service's National Register of Historic Places, and the National Trust for Historic Preservation Press.

Stephanie Meeks, President & CEO
Tabitha Almquist, Chief of Staff

3112 No Child Left Behind
U.S. Department of Education
400 Maryland Avenue, SW
Washington, DC 20202
202-401-2000
800-872-5327
Fax: 202-401-0689
http://www.ed.gov
Provides education standards and incentives for states in adopting academic standards that prepare students to succeed in college and the workplace.

Emma Vadehra, Chief of Staff
Richard Culatta, Director, Education Tech

3113 Office for Civil Rights
U.S. Department of Education
400 Maryland Avenue SW
Lyndon Baines Johnson Dept of Ed Bldg.
Washington, DC 20202-1100
202-401-2000
800-872-5327
Fax: 202-453-6012
E-mail: ocr@ed.gov
http://www.ed.gov

Emma Vadehra, Chief of Staff
Richard Culatta, Director, Education Tech

3114 Office of Bilingual Education and Minority Languages Affairs
U.S. Department of Education
400 Maryland Avenue SW
Washington, DC 20202-6510
202-401-2000
800-872-5327
Fax: 202-260-7225
E-mail: askncbe@ncbe.gwu.edu
http://www.ed.gov

Emma Vadehra, Chief of Staff
Richard Culatta, Director, Education Tech

3115 Office of Elementary & Secondary Education
U.S. Department of Education
400 Maryland Avenue SW
Washington, DC 20202
202-401-2000
800-872-5327
Fax: 202-205-0310
E-mail: oese@ed.gov
http://www.ed.gov

Emma Vadehra, Chief of Staff
Richard Culatta, Director, Education Tech

3116 Office of Indian Education
U.S. Department of Education
400 Maryland Avenue SW
LBJ Building, 3E205
Washington, DC 20202-6335
202-401-2000
800-872-5327
Fax: 202-260-7779
E-mail: indian.education@ed.gov
http://www.ed.gov

Emma Vadehra, Chief of Staff
Richard Culatta, Director, Education Tech

3117 Office of Legislation & Congressional Affairs
U.S. Department of Education
400 Maryland Avenue SW
Washington, DC 20202-3100

202-401-2000
800-872-5327
Fax: 202-401-1438
E-mail: olca@ed.gov
http://www.ed.gov

Emma Vadehra, Chief of Staff
Richard Culatta, Director, Education Tech

118 Office of Migrant Education
U.S. Department of Education
400 Maryland Avenue SW
Room 3E317 FOB-6
Washington, DC 20202-6135
202-401-2000
800-872-5327
Fax: 202-205-0089
http://www.ed.gov

Emma Vadehra, Chief of Staff
Richard Culatta, Director, Education Tech

119 Office of Overseas Schools
US Department of State
Room H328, SA-1
Washington, DC 20522-0132
202-261-8200
Fax: 202-261-8224
E-mail: OverseasSchools@state.gov
http://www.state.gov
Maintains detailed information on 190 overseas elementary and secondary schools which receive some assistance from the US Department of State. These schools provide an American-type education which prepares students for schools, colleges and universities in the United States.

Dr. Keith D Miller, Director

120 Office of Planning, Evaluation and Policy Development
U.S. Department of Education
400 Maryland Avenue SW
Suite 4022
Washington, DC 20201-0001
202-401-2000
800-872-5327
Fax: 202-260-7225
E-mail: judy.wurtzel.ed.gov
http://www.ed.gov

Emma Vadehra, Chief of Staff
Richard Culatta, Director, Education Tech

121 Office of Special Education Programs
Department of Education/3086 Mary E. Switzer Bldg.
600 Independence Avenue SW
Washington, DC 20202-2570
202-205-5507
Fax: 202-260-7225
E-mail: thomas_hehir@ed.gov
http://www.ed.gov./offices/osers/idea/index.htm

Thomas Hehir, Director

122 Office of Student Financial Assistance Programs
U.S. Department of Education
400 Maryland Avenue SW
Washington, DC 20202-0001
202-401-2000
800-872-5327
http://www.ed.gov

Emma Vadehra, Chief of Staff
Richard Culatta, Director, Education Tech

123 Planning & Evaluation Service
U.S. Department of Education
400 Maryland Avenue, SW
Washington, DC 20202
202-401-2000
800-872-5327

Fax: 202-260-7225
http://www.ed.gov

Emma Vadehra, Chief of Staff
Richard Culatta, Director, Education Tech

3124 Rehabilitation Services Administration
U.S. Department of Education
400 Maryland Avenue SW
Washington, DC 20202-2800
202-401-2000
800-872-5327
Fax: 202-260-7225
E-mail: rsa.ed.gov
http://www.ed.gov

Emma Vadehra, Chief of Staff
Richard Culatta, Director, Education Tech

3125 Research to Practice Division
U.S. Department of Education
Ofc of Special Ed/Rehabilitative Sv
400 Maryland Avenue SW
Washington, DC 20202-7100
202-401-2000
800-872-5327
http://www.ed.gov

Emma Vadehra, Chief of Staff
Richard Culatta, Director, Education Tech

3126 School Assistance Division
U.S. Department of Education
400 Maryland Avenue, SW
Washington, DC 20202-2141
202-260-2270
800-872-5327
Fax: 202-260-7225
http://www2.ed.gov

Arne Duncan, Secretary of Education
Emma Vadehra, Chief of Staff

3127 School Improvement Grants
U.S. Department Of Education
400 Maryland Avenue SW
Washington, DC 20202
202-401-2000
800-872-5327
http://www.ed.gov

Emma Vadehra, Chief of Staff
Richard Culatta, Director, Education Tech

3128 School Improvement Programs-Equity and Educational Excellence Division
U.S. Department of Education
400 Maryland Avenue, SW
Washington, DC 20202-2141
202-260-3693
800-872-5327
Fax: 202-260-7225
http://www2.ed.gov

Arne Duncan, Secretary of Education
Emma Vadehra, Chief of Staff

3129 School Improvement Programs-Safe and Drug Free Schools
Office of Safe and Drug Free Schools
400 Maryland Avenue, SW
Washington, DC 20202
202-245-7896
800-872-5327
Fax: 202-485-0013
E-mail: osdfs.safeschl@ed.gov
http://www.ed.gov
Works to promote safe schools that are free from drug abuse and violence.

Arne Duncan, Secretary of Education
Emma Vadehra, Chief of Staff

3130 US Department of Defense Dependents Schools
2461 Eisenhower Avenue
Alexandria, VA 22331-3000
571-325-0867

Marilyn Witcher

3131 US Department of Education
400 Maryland Avenue SW
Washington, DC 20202
800-872-5327
Fax: 202-401-0689
E-mail: customerservice@inet.ed.gov
http://www.ed.gov
Ensures equal access to education and promotes educational excellence for all Americans.

Arne Duncan, Secretary of Education
Emma Vadehra, Chief of Staff

3132 Vocational & Adult Education
U.S. Department of Education
400 Maryland Avenue, SW
Washington, DC 20202
202-205-5451
800-872-5327
Fax: 202-260-7225
http://www2.ed.gov

Arne Duncan, Secretary of Education
Emma Vadehra, Chief of Staff

3133 Washington DC Department of Education
825 N Capitol Street NE
Suite 900
Washington, DC 20202-4210
202-442-5885
Fax: 202-442-5026

Paul L Varce, Superintendent

Alabama

3134 Alabama State Department of Education
50 N Ripley Street
PO Box 302101
Montgomery, AL 36104
334-242-9700
E-mail: astarks@alsde.edu
http://www.alsde.edu
Mission is to provide a state system of education which is committed to academic excellence and which provides education of the highest quality to all Alabama students, preparing them for the 21st century. For certification information contact the Alabama certification office at 334-242-9977.

Dr. Joseph B Morton, State Superintendent of Ed.
Dr. Craig Pouncey, Deputy State Superintendent

3135 General Counsel
Alabama Department of Education
50 N Ripley Street
PO Box 302101
Montgomery, AL 36130-0624
334-242-9700
E-mail: studor@alsde.edu
http://www.alsde.edu
Provides legal counsel to the State Superintendent of Education, State Board of Education and State Department of Education.

Larry Craven, General Counsel
Juliana Teixeira Dean, Associate General Counsel

3136 Instructional Services
Alabama Department of Education
50 N Ripley Street
P.O. Box 302101?
Montgomery, AL 36104
334-242-9700
Fax: 334-242-9708
http://www.alsde.edu

Charlie G Williams, Assistant
Superintendent

3137 Professional Services
Alabama Department of Education
50 N Ripley Street
P.O. Box 302101?
Montgomery, AL 36104
334-242-9700
Fax: 334-242-9708
http://www.alsde.edu

Eddie R Johnson, Assistant
Superintendent

3138 Rehabilitation Services
Alabama Department of Rehabilitation
Services
602 S. Lawrence St.
Montgomery, AL 36104
334-293-7500
800-441-7607
Fax: 334-293-7383
http://www.rehab.alabama.gov
State agency that provides and services and
assistance to Alabama's children and
adults with disabilities and their families.

Steve Shrivers, Commissioner

3139 Special Education Services
Alabama Department of Education
50 N Ripley Street
P.O. Box 302101?
Montgomery, AL 36104
334-242-9700
Fax: 334-242-9192
http://www.alsde.edu

Bill East, Division Director

3140 Student Instructional Services
Alabama Department of Education
50 N Ripley Street
P.O. Box 302101?
Montgomery, AL 36104
334-242-9700
Fax: 334-242-9708
http://www.alsde.edu

Martha V Beckett, Assistant
Superintendent

3141 Superintendent
Alabama Department of Education
50 N Ripley Street
P.O. Box 302101?
Montgomery, AL 36104
334-242-9700
Fax: 334-242-9708
http://www.alsde.edu

Ed Richardson, Superintendent

3142 Vocational Education
Alabama Department of Education
50 N Ripley Street
P.O. Box 302101?
Montgomery, AL 36104
334-242-9700
Fax: 334-353-8861
http://www.alsde.edu

Stephen B Franks, Division Director

Alaska

3143 Alaska Commission on Postsecondary Education
PO Box 110510
Juneau, AK 99811-0510
907-465-2962
800-441-2962
Fax: 907-465-5316
E-mail: ACPE@alaska.gov
http://www.akadvantage.alaska.gov
This state agency coordinates administration of state-funded educational financial
assistance for students and their families.
This agency is also responsible for licensing and regulating postsecondary institutions to operate in Alaska.

Diane Barrans, Executive Director
Kenneth Dodson, Dir. Information
Support Svc

3144 Alaska Department of Education Administrative Services
801 W 10th Street
Suite 200
Juneau, AK 99801-1894
907-465-2802
Fax: 907-465-4156
For certification information visit
www.eed.state.ak.us/TeacherCertification
/ or contact 907-465-2831.

Shirley J Halloway, Commissioner

3145 Alaska Department of Education & Early Development
801 W 10th Street, Suite 200
PO Box 110500
Juneau, AK 99811-500
907-465-2800
Fax: 907-465-4156
E-mail: eed.webmaster@alaska.gov
http://www.educ.state.ak.us

Gerald Covey, Commissioner

3146 Libraries, Archives & Museums
PO Box 110571
333 Willoughby Avenue
Juneau, AK 99811-0571
907-465-2910
Fax: 907-465-2151
E-mail: eed.webmaster@alaska.gov
http://www.lam.alaska.gov
Summer reading programs

Linda Thibodeau, Director
Bob Banghart, Chief Curator

3147 School Finance & Data Management
Alaska Department of Education & Early
Development
801 W 10th Street, Suite 200
PO Box 110500
Juneau, AK 99811-0500
907-465-2800
Fax: 907-465-4156
E-mail: eed.webmaster@alaska.gov
http://www.eed.state.ak.us
Public school funding programs

Cynthia Curran, Director
Paul Prussing, Deputy Director

3148 Teaching And Learning Support Program
Alaska Department of Education & Early
Development
801 W 10th Street, Suite 200
PO Box 110500
Juneau, AK 99811-0500
907-465-2800
Fax: 907-465-4156

E-mail: eed.webmaster@alaska.gov
http://www.eed.state.ak.us
To improve students performance as well as the
administering of a variety of federal, state and private programs that provide support to school district staff across the state.

Cynthia Curran, Director
Paul Prussing, Deputy Director

3149 Vocational Rehabilitation
Alaska Department of Labor & Workforce
Development
801 W 10th Street
Suite A
Juneau, AK 99801-1894
907-465-2814
800-478-2815
Fax: 907-465-2856
E-mail: dawn.duval@alaska.gov
http://www.labor.state.ak.us
Helping individuals with disabilities to find em-
ployment

Cheryl Walsh, Director
John Cannon, Chairperson

Arkansas

3150 Arkansas Department of Education
4 Capitol Mall
Room 403-A
Little Rock, AR 72201-1071
501-682-4475
E-mail: virginia.hill@arkansas.gov
http://www.arkansased.org
Mission is to provide the highest quality leadership, service, and support to school districts and
schools in order that they may provide equitable,
quality education for all to ensure that all public
schools comply with the standards.

Samuel Ledbetter, Chair
Abby Cress, Administrative Analyst

3151 Arkansas Department of Education: Special Education
4 Capitol Mall
Room 403-A
Little Rock, AR 72201-1071
501-682-4475
E-mail: virginia.hill@arkansas.gov
http://www.arkansased.org

Samuel Ledbetter, Chair
Abby Cress, Administrative Analyst

3152 Federal Programs
Arkansas Department of Education
4 Capitol Mall
Room 403-A
Little Rock, AR 72201-1011
501-682-4475
E-mail: virginia.hill@arkansas.gov
http://www.arkansased.org

Samuel Ledbetter, Chair
Abby Cress, Administrative Analyst

California

3153 California Department of Education
1430 N Street
Sacramento, CA 95814-5901
916-319-0800
Fax: 916-657-4975
E-mail: EHughes@cde.ca.gov.
http://www.cde.ca.gov
Works to encourage the highest achievement for
students by defining the knowledge, concepts and

skills that students should aquire in each grade level.

Tom Torlakson, St Superintendent Public Ins
Richard Zeiger, Chief Deputy Superintendent

4154 California Department of Education's Educational Resources Catalog

CDE Press Sales
1430 N Street
Suite 3207
Sacramento, CA 95814-5901
916-319-0800
800-995-4099
Fax: 916-323-0823
E-mail: EHughes@cde.ca.gov.
http://www.cde.ca.gov
Offers new techniques and fresh perspectives in handbooks, guides, videos and more.

Tom Torlakson, St Superintendent Public Ins

4155 California Department of Special Education

1430 N Street
Sacramento, CA 95814-5901
913-319-0800
Fax: 916-327-3516
E-mail: EHughes@cde.ca.gov
http://www.cde.ca.gov/sp/se
Resources and information that serve the unique needs of persons with disabilities by helping them to meet or exceed high standards of achievement in both academic and nonacademic skills.

Tom Torlakson, St Superintendent Public Ins

4156 Curriculum & Instructional Leadership Branch

California Department of Education
1430 N Street
Sacramento, CA 95814-5901
916-319-0800
E-mail: EHughes@cde.ca.gov.
http://www.cde.ca.gov
Works to improve students academic achievements

Tom Torlakson, St Superintendent Public Ins

4157 Region 9: Education Department

San Diego COE
6401 Linda Vista Road
Suite 321
North San Diego, CA 92111
858-569-5304
E-mail: dbrashear@sdcoe.net
Part of a statewide system of school support established to meet state and federal requirements, the support system works within county offices offering intensive and sustained assistance to local schools and educational agencies receiving Title I funds, helping to increase the opportunity for all student's to meet the state academic content standards.

David Brashear, Director

4158 Specialized Programs Branch

California Department of Education
1430 N Street
Sacramento, CA 95814-5901
916-319-0800
E-mail: EHughes@cde.ca.gov.
http://www.cde.ca.gov

Works to ensure that all children have the opportunity to obtain high-quality education.

Tom Torlakson, St Superintendent Public Ins
Mary Payne, District/School Improvement

Colorado

3159 Colorado Department of Education

201 E Colfax Avenue
Denver, CO 80203-1799
303-866-6600
Fax: 303-866-6938
http://www.cde.state.co.us
For certification information visit www.cde.state.co.us/index_license.htm or contact 303-866-6628.

William T Moloney, Commissioner

3160 Educator Licensing Unit

Colorado Department of Education
201 E Colfax Avenue
Denver, CO 80203-1704
303-866-6628
Fax: 303-866-6866
Licensing applications for educators, career and technical education. Issues educators licenses, reviews content, induction/professional development and disciplinary actions

Ed Almon, Educator Licensing

3161 Office of Federal Program Administration

Colorado Department of Education
1560 Broadway
Suite 1450
Denver, CO 80202-5149
303-866-6600
Fax: 303-866-6637
Administers funds under the elementary and secondary education act as well as a variety of other state and federal competitive awards and grants with the main goal to help all students to reach proficiency in English language arts, mathematics and reading.

Patrick Chapman, Executive Director
Lynn Bamberry, Director

3162 State Library

Colorado Department of Education
201 E Colfax Avenue
Room 309
Denver, CO 80203-1704
303-866-6900
Fax: 303-866-6940
http://www.cde.state.co.us
Provides leadership and expertise in library related activities and policies and provides assistance to public and academic schools.

Eugene Hainer, Assistant Commissioner
Sharon Morris, Director

3163 Supplemental Educational Services

Colorado Department of Education
1560 Broadway
Suite 1450
Denver, CO 80202
303-866-6600
Fax: 303-866-6637
E-mail: medler_l@cde.state.co.us
http://www.cde.state.co.us
SES offers tutoring outside the regular school day that is designed to increase the academic achievement in reading/mathematics and language arts to low-income students in low-income schools

Patrick Chapman, Executive Director
Lisa Medler, Title IIA Coordinator

Connecticut

3164 Connecticut Early Childhood Unit

Connecticut State Department of Education
165 Capital Avenue
Hartford, CT 06106
860-713-6740
Fax: 860-713-7018
E-mail: www.sde.ct.gov
Offers programs for children, infants and toddlers with disabilities.

Steven Adamowski, Superintendent

3165 Connecticut Governor's Committee on Employment of the Handicapped

Labor Department Building
200 Constitution Ave. NW
Washington, DC 20210
860-263-6774
866-4 U-A DO
Fax: 860-263-6039
http://www.dol.gov

3166 Connecticut State Department of Education

165 Capitol Avenue
Hartford, CT 06106
860-713-6543
Fax: 860-722-8502
http://www.sde.ct.gov

Steven Adamowski, Superintendent

3167 Education Programs & Services

Connecticut Department of Education
25 Industrial Park Road
Middletown, CT 06457-1520
860-807-2005
Fax: 860-635-7125

Theodore S Sergi, Division Director

3168 Finance & Grants Department

Connecticut State Department of Education
Grants Management
165 Capitol Avenue
Hartford, CT 06106
860-713-0466
Fax: 860-713-7046
http://www.sde.ct.gov

Eugene Croce, Manager
Candace Madison, Secretary

3169 Office of State Coordinator of Vocational Education for Disabled Students

Vocational Prgs. for the Disabled & Disadvantaged
PO Box 2219
Hartford, CT 06145
860-807-2001
Fax: 860-807-2196

3170 Teaching & Learning Division

Connecticut State Department of Education
165 Capital Avenue
Hartford, CT 06106-1659
860-713-6740
Fax: 860-713-7018
E-mail: ciquest@ct.gov
http://www.sde.ct.gov

George Coleman, Acting Commissioner

3171 Vocational-Technical School Systems

Connecticut Technical High School System
25 Industrial Park Road
Middletown, CT 06457-1520
800-822-6832
Fax: 860-807-2196

E-mail: cthsinternet@ct.gov
http://www.cttech.org

Patricia Ciccone, Superintendent
Robert Lombardi, Assistant

Delaware

3172 Assessments & Accountability Branch Delaware Department of Education
The Townsend Building
401 Federal Street, Suite 2
Dover, DE 19901-3639
302-735-4000
Fax: 302-739-4654
http://www.doe.k12.de.us

Mark T. Murphy, Secretary of Education
Mary Kate McLaughlin, Chief of Staff

3173 Delaware Department of Education
The Townsend Building
401 Federal Street, Suite 2
Dover, DE 19901-3639
302-735-4000
Fax: 302-739-4654
E-mail: dedoe@doe.k12.de.us
http://www.doe.k12.de.us
Our mission is to promote the highest quality education for every Delaware student by providing visionary leadership and superior service.

Mark T. Murphy, Secretary of Education
Mary Kate McLaughlin, Chief of Staff

3174 Delaware Department of Education: Administrative Services
The Townsend Building
401 Federal Street, Suite 2
Dover, DE 19901-3639
302-735-4000
Fax: 302-739-4654
E-mail: dedoe@doe.k12.de.us
http://www.doe.k12.de.us

Mark T. Murphy, Secretary of Education
Mary Kate McLaughlin, Chief of Staff

3175 Improvement & Assistance Branch Delaware Department of Education
The Townsend Building
401 Federal Street, Suite 2
Dover, DE 19901-3639
302-735-4000
Fax: 302-739-4654
E-mail: dedoe@doe.k12.de.us
http://www.doe.k12.de.us

Mark T. Murphy, Secretary of Education
Mary Kate McLaughlin, Chief of Staff

District of Columbia

3176 DC Office of Special Education
District of Columbia Public Schools
441 4th Street, NW, 700S
Washington, DC 20001
202-727-0252
Fax: 202-727-9385
E-mail: ocp@dc.gov
http://www.ocp.dc.gov

Nancy Hapeman, Interim Director
Yinka Alao, Chief of Staff

3177 District of Columbia Department of Education
441 4th Street, NW, 700S
Washington, DC 20001
202-727-0252
Fax: 202-727-9385
E-mail: ocp@dc.gov
http://www.ocp.dc.gov

Nancy Hapeman, Interim Director
Yinka Alao, Chief of Staff

Florida

3178 Florida Department of Education
Turlington Building Suite 1514
325 West Gaines Street
Tallahassee, FL 32399
850-245-0505
Fax: 850-245-9667
E-mail: commissioner@fldoe.org
http://www.fldoe.org
Offers information on community colleges, vocational education, public schools, human resources, financial assistance, adult education and more.

Pam Stewart, Commissioner/Fl. Dept of Ed
Kathy Hebda, Chief of Staff

Georgia

3179 Georgia Department of Education
2054 Twin Towers East
205 Jesse Hill Jr. Drive SE
Atlanta, GA 30334
404-656-2800
800-311-3627
Fax: 404-651-6867
E-mail: askdoe@doe.k12.ga.us
http://www.gadoe.org
Among many other features, this organization offers agriculture education, federal programs, Leadership Development Academy, school and community nutrition progams, Spanish language and cultural program, technology/career (vocational) education and more.

Richard Woods, Superintendent
Sue Goodman, Manager

Hawaii

3180 Career & Technical Education Center
University of Hawaii
Lunalilo Portable 1
Lower Campus Road
Honolulu, HI 96822-2489
808-956-7461
Fax: 808-956-9096
E-mail: hicte@hawaii.edu
http://www.hawaii.edu/cte

Angela Meixell, Interim Director
Sherilyn Lau, Education Specialist

3181 Hawaii Department of Education
1390 Miller Street
PO Box 2360
Honolulu, HI 96813
808-586-3230
Fax: 808-586-3234
E-mail: doe_info@notes.k12.hi.us
http://www.hawaiipublicschools.org

Kathryn Matayoshi, Superintendent
Ronn Nozoe, Deputy Superintendent

3182 Information & Telecommunications Services Branch
Hawaii Department of Education
1390 Miller St., Room 417
PO Box 2360
Honolulu, HI 96813
808-586-3230
Fax: 808-586-3234
E-mail: doe_info@notes.k12.hi.us
http://www.hawaiipublicschools.org

Kathryn Matayoshi, Superintendent
Ronn Nozoe, Deputy Superintendent

3183 Office of Curriculum, Instruction and Student Support
Hawaii Department of Education
Queen Liliuokalani Bldg, Rm 316
1390 Miller St,
Honolulu, HI 96813
808-586-3446
Fax: 808-586-3429
E-mail: doe_info@notes.k12.hi.us
http://www.ociss.k12.hi.us

Kathryn Matayoshi, Superintendent
Leila Hayashida, Acting Assis Superintendent

3184 Special Education Department
Hawaii Department of Education
1390 Miller Street
Ofc Curriculum/Instruction/Student Supp.
Honolulu, HI 96813
808-586-3230
Fax: 808-586-3234
E-mail: doe_info@notes.k12.hi.us
http://www.hawaiipublicschools.org

Kathryn Matayoshi, Superintendent
Ronn Nozoe, Deputy Superintendent

3185 State Public Library System
Hawaii State Public Library System
478 South King Street
Honolulu, HI 96813-2901
808-586-3617
Fax: 808-586-3314
http://hawaii.sdp.sirsi.net

Richard P. Burns, State Librarian

Idaho

3186 Idaho State Department of Education
650 West State Street
PO Box 83720
Boise, ID 83720-0027
208-332-6800
800-432-4601
Fax: 208-334-2228
E-mail: infosuperintendent@sde.idaho.gov
http://www.sde.idaho.gov

Tom Luna, Superintendent
Sherri Ybarra, Superintendent

3187 Special Education Division
Idaho State Department of Education
650 W. State Street
PO Box 83720
Boise, ID 83720-0027
208-332-6806
Fax: 208-334-2228
E-mail: infosuperintendent@sde.idaho.gov
http://www.sde.idaho.gov
Committed to empower people with disabilities with appropriate resources to make informed choices about their futures.

Sherri Ybarra, Superintendent
Casandra Myers, Administrative Assistant

Illinois

188 Educator & School Development
Illinois Department of Education
100 N. 1st Street
Springfield, IL 62777
217-782-4321
866-262-6663
http://www.isbe.state.il.us

Dr. Christopher Koch, State Superintendent
Gery J. Chico, Board Chair

189 Educator Certification
Illinois Department of Education
100 N. 1st Street
Springfield, IL 62777
217-782-4321
866-262-6663
http://www.isbe.state.il.us

Dr. Christopher Koch, State Superintendent
Gery J. Chico, Board Chair

190 Finance & Support Services
Illinois Department of Education
100 N. 1st Street
Springfield, IL 62777
217-782-4321
866-262-6663
E-mail: finance@isbe.net
http://www.isbe.state.il.us

Dr. Christopher Koch, State Superintendent
Gery J. Chico, Board Chair

191 Illinois Department of Education
100 N 1st Street
Springfield, IL 62777
217-782-4321
866-262-6663
http://www.isbe.state.il.us

Dr. Christopher Koch, State Superintendent
Gery J. Chico, Board Chair

192 School Finance
Illinois State Department of Education
100 N. 1st Street
Springfield, IL 62777
217-782-4321
866-262-6663
E-mail: finance@isbe.net
http://www.isbe.state.il.us

Dr. Christopher Koch, State Superintendent
Gery J. Chico, Board Chair

193 School Improvement & Assessment Services
Illinois State Board of Education
100 N 1st Street
Springfield, IL 62777
217-782-4321
866-262-6663
http://www.isbe.state.il.us

Chris Koch, Superintendent
Gery J. Chico, Board Chair

194 Special Education
Illinois State Board of Education
100 N 1st Street
Springfield, IL 62777
217-782-4321
866-262-6663
http://www.isbe.state.il.us

Dr. Christopher Koch, State Superintendent
Gery J. Chico, Board Chair

Indiana

3195 Center for School Assessment & Research
Indiana Department of Education
South Tower, Suite 600
115 W. Washington Street
Indianapolis, IN 46204-2203
317-232-6610
Fax: 317-232-8004
E-mail: webmaster@doe.in.gov
http://www.doe.in.gov

Glenda Ritz, Superintendent

3196 Community Relations & Special Populations
Indiana Department of Education
South Tower, Suite 600
115 W. Washington Street
Indianapolis, IN 46204-2203
317-232-6610
Fax: 317-232-8004
E-mail: webmaster@doe.in.gov
http://www.doe.in.gov

Glenda Ritz, Superintendent

3197 External Affairs
Indiana Department of Education
South Tower, Suite 600
115 W. Washington Street
Indianapolis, IN 46204-2203
317-232-6610
Fax: 317-232-8004
E-mail: webmaster@doe.in.gov
http://www.doe.in.gov

Glenda Ritz, Superintendent

3198 Indiana Department of Education
South Tower, Suite 600
115 W. Washington Street
Indianapolis, IN 46204-2798
317-232-6610
Fax: 317-232-8004
E-mail: webmaster@doe.in.gov
http://www.doe.in.gov
For certification information visit
www.in.gov/psb or contact 866-542-3672.

Glenda Ritz, Superintendent

3199 Office of Legal Affairs
Indiana Department of Education
South Tower, Suite 600
115 W. Washington Street
Indianapolis, IN 46204-2203
317-232-6610
Fax: 317-232-8004
E-mail: webmaster@doe.in.gov
http://www.doe.in.gov

Glenda Ritz, Superintendent

3200 Office of School Financial Management
Indiana Department of Education
South Tower, Suite 600
115 W. Washington Street
Indianapolis, IN 46204-2203
317-232-6610
Fax: 317-232-8004
E-mail: webmaster@doe.in.gov
http://www.doe.in.gov

Glenda Ritz, Superintendent

3201 Office of the Deputy Superintendent
Indiana Department of Education
South Tower, Suite 600
115 W. Washington Street
Indianapolis, IN 46204-2203
317-232-6610
Fax: 317-232-8004

E-mail: webmaster@doe.in.gov
http://www.doe.in.gov

Glenda Ritz, Superintendent

3202 School Improvement & Performance Center
Indiana Department of Education
South Tower, Suite 600
115 W. Washington Street
Indianapolis, IN 46204-2203
317-232-6610
Fax: 317-232-8004
E-mail: webmaster@doe.in.gov
http://www.doe.in.gov

Glenda Ritz, Superintendent

Iowa

3203 Community Colleges Division
Iowa Department of Education
400 E. 14th Street
Des Moines, IA 50319-0146
515-281-5294
Fax: 515-281-5988
http://www.educateiowa.gov

Brad Buck, Director
Jeremy Varner, Administrator

3204 Division of Library Services
Iowa Department of Education
400 E. 14th Street
Des Moines, IA 50319-0146
515-281-5294
Fax: 515-281-5988
http://www.educateiowa.gov

Brad Buck, Director
Jeremy Varner, Administrator

3205 Educational Services for Children & Families
Iowa Department of Education
400 E. 14th Street
Des Moines, IA 50319-0146
515-281-5294
Fax: 515-281-5988
http://www.educateiowa.gov

Brad Buck, Director
Jeremy Varner, Administrator

3206 Elementary & Secondary Education
Iowa Department of Education
400 E. 14th Street
Des Moines, IA 50319-0146
515-281-5294
Fax: 515-281-5988
http://www.educateiowa.gov
Strives for higher levels of learning and achievement for students in public elementary and secondary schools

Brad Buck, Director
Jeremy Varner, Administrator

3207 Financial & Information Services
Iowa Department of Education
400 E. 14th Street
Des Moines, IA 50319-0146
515-281-5294
Fax: 515-242-5988
E-mail: lee.tack@ed.state.ia.us
http://www.educateiowa.gov

Brad Buck, Director
Jeremy Varner, Administrator

3208 Iowa Department of Education
Iowa Department of Education
400 E. 14th Street
Des Moines, IA 50319-0146

515-281-5294
Fax: 515-281-5988
E-mail: webmaster@ed.state.ia.us
http://www.educateiowa.gov
Serves the students of Iowa by providing leadership and resources for schools, area education agencies and community colleges. For certification information visit www.state.ia.us/boee or contact 515-281-3245.

Brad Buck, Director
Jeremy Varner, Administrator

3209 Iowa Public Television
Iowa Department of Education
400 E. 14th Street
Des Moines, IA 50319-0146
515-281-5294
Fax: 515-281-5988
http://www.educateiowa.gov

Brad Buck, Director
Jeremy Varner, Administrator

3210 Vocational Rehabilitation Services
Iowa Department of Education
400 E. 14th Street
Des Moines, IA 50319-0146
515-281-5294
Fax: 515-281-5988
http://www.educateiowa.gov

Brad Buck, Director
Jeremy Varner, Administrator

Kansas

3211 Kansas Department of Education
Kansas State Department of Education
900 SW Jackson Street
Topeka, KS 66612-1212
785-296-3201
Fax: 785-796-7933
E-mail: contact@ksde.org
http://www.ksde.org

Dr. Diane DeBacker, Commissioner of Education
Brad Neuenswander, Interim Commissioner

3212 Office of the Commissioner
Kansas State Department of Education
900 SW Jackson Street
Topeka, KS 66612-1212
785-296-3201
Fax: 785-296-7933
E-mail: contact@ksde.org
http://www.ksde.org

Dr. Diane DeBacker, Commissioner of Education
Brad Neuenswander, Interim Commissioner

3213 Special Education Services Department
Kansas State Department of Education
900 SW Jackson Street
Topeka, KS 66612-1212
785-296-3201
Fax: 785-296-7933
E-mail: contact@ksde.org
http://www.ksde.org

Dr. Diane DeBacker, Commissioner of Education
Brad Neuenswander, Interim Commissioner

3214 Teacher Education & Licensure
Kansas State Department of Education
900 SW Jackson Street
Topeka, KS 66612-1212

785-296-3201
Fax: 785-296-7933
E-mail: contact@ksde.org
http://www.ksde.org

Dr. Diane DeBacher, Commissioner of Education
Brad Neuenswander, Interim Commissioner

Kentucky

3215 Communications Services
Kentucky Department of Education
500 Mero Street
Frankfort, KY 40601-1957
502-564-4770
E-mail: andrew.liaupsin@education.ky.gov
http://www.education.ky.gov

Terry Holliday, Ph.D, Commissioner of Education
Rebecca Blessing, General Counsel

3216 Curriculum, Assessment & Accountability Council
Kentucky Department of Education
??Capital Plaza Tower
500 Mero St.
Frankfort, KY 40601-1957
502-564-4770
Fax: 502-564-7749
E-mail: rebecca.blessing@education.ky.gov
http://education.ky.gov/Pages/default.aspx

Terry Holliday, Ph.D, Commissioner of Education
Rebecca Blessing, General Counsel

3217 Education Technology Office
Kentucky Department of Education
500 Mero Street
16th Floor CPT
Frankfort, KY 40601-1957
502-564-4770
E-mail: rebecca.blessing@education.ky.gov
http://education.ky.gov/Pages/default.aspx

Terry Holliday, Ph.D, Commissioner of Education
Rebecca Blessing, General Counsel

3218 Kentucky Department of Education
Kentucky Department of Education
500 Mero Street
Capital Plaza Tower
Frankfort, KY 40601-1957
502-564-4770
Fax: 502-564-5680
E-mail: rebecca.blessing@education.ky.gov
http://education.ky.gov/Pages/default.aspx
For certification information visit www.kyepsb.net or contact 502-573-4606.
Terry Holliday PhD, Commissioner of Education
Rebecca Blessing, General Counsel

3219 Regional Services Centers
Kentucky Department of Education
500 Mero Street
18th Floor CPT
Frankfort, KY 40601-1957
502-564-4770
E-mail: rebecca.blessing@education.ky.gov

http://education.ky.gov/Pages/default.aspx
Terry Holliday, Ph.D, Commissioner of Education
Rebecca Blessing, General Counsel

3220 Special Education Services
Kentucky Department of Education
500 Mero Street
8th Floor
Frankfort, KY 40601-1957
502-564-4770
Fax: 502-564-6721
E-mail: rebecca.blessing@education.ky.gov
http://education.ky.gov/Pages/default.aspx

Terry Holliday, Ph.D, Commissioner of Education
Rebecca Blessing, General Counsel

3221 Teacher Education & Certification
Kentucky Department of Education
500 Mero Street
17th Floor
Frankfort, KY 40601-1957
502-564-4770
E-mail: rebecca.blessing@education.ky.gov
http://education.ky.gov/Pages/default.aspx

Terry Holliday, Ph.D, Commissioner of Education
Rebecca Blessing, General Counsel

Louisiana

3222 Academic Programs Office
Louisiana Department of Education
1201 North Third Streetÿ
PO Box 94064
Baton Rouge, LA 70804-9064
877-453-2721
Fax: 225-342-0193
E-mail: customerservice@la.gov
http://www.louisianabelieves.com

Paul Pastorek, State Superintendent of Educ
Rene Greer, Director, Public Affairs

3223 Louisiana Department of Education
1201 North Third Streetÿ
PO Box 94064
Baton Rouge, LA 70804-9064
504-342-3607
877-453-2721
Fax: 225-342-0193
http://www.louisianabelieves.com
Provides leadership and enacts policies that result in improved academic achievement and responsible citizenship for all students. For certification information visit www.louisianaschools.net or contact 225-342-3490.

Cecil J Picard, Superintendent

3224 Management & Finance Office
Louisana State Department of Education
1201 North Third Streetÿ
PO Box 94064
Baton Rouge, LA 70804-9064
225-342-3617
877-453-2721
Fax: 225-219-7538
E-mail: mlangley@doe.state.la.us
http://www.louisianabelieves.com

Marlyn J Langley, Deputy Superintendent

3225 Office of Educator Support
Louisiana Department of Education
1201 North Third Streetÿ
PO Box 94064
Baton Rouge, LA 70804-9064
877-453-2721
Fax: 225-342-0193

E-mail: customerservice@la.gov
http://www.louisianabelieves.com
Paul Pastorek, State Superintendent of
Educ
Karen Burke, Acting Asst. Superintendent

226 Special Education Services
Louisiana Department of Education
1201 North Third Streetÿ
PO Box 94064
Baton Rouge, LA 70804-9064
877-453-2721
Fax: 225-342-0193
E-mail: customerservice@la.gov
http://www.louisianabelieves.com
Paul Pastorek, State Superintendent of
Educ
Rene Greer, Director, Public Affairs

**227 Standards, Assessments &
Accountability**
Louisiana Department of Education
1201 North Third Streetÿ
PO Box 94064
Baton Rouge, LA 70804-9064
877-453-2721
Fax: 225-342-3600
E-mail: customerservice@la.gov
http://www.louisianabelieves.com
Paul Pastorek, State Superintendent of
Educ
Scott Norton, Assistant Superintendent

Maine

**228 Administrator and Teacher
Certification**
Maine Department of Education
Certification Office
23 State House Station
Augusta, ME 04333-0023
207-624-6600
Fax: 207-624-6700
E-mail: commish.doe@maine.gov
http://www.maine.gov
Jim Rier, Commissioner
Charlene Tucker, Team Coordinator

229 Adult Education
Maine Department of Education
23 State House Station
Augusta, ME 04333-0023
207-624-6600
Fax: 207-624-6700
E-mail: commish.doe@maine.gov
http://www.maine.gov
Jim Rier, Commissioner
Charlene Tucker, Team Coordinator

230 Maine Department of Education
23 State House Station
Augusta, ME 04333-0023
207-624-6600
Fax: 207-624-6700
E-mail: commish.doe@maine.gov
http://www.maine.gov
Jim Rier, Commissioner
Charlene Tucker, Team Coordinator

Maryland

231 Career & Technology Education
Maryland State Department of Education
200 W Baltimore Street
Baltimore, MD 21201-2595
410-767-0100
888-246-0016

Fax: 410-333-2099
E-mail: pmikos@msde.state.md.us
http://www.marylandpublicschools.org
Pat Mikos, Program Manager
Kimberlee Schultz, Public Affair Officer

3232 Certification & Accreditation
Maryland State Department of Education
200 W. Baltimore Street
Baltimore, MD 21201-2595
410-767-0100
888-246-0016
http://www.marylandpublicschools.org
Nancy S. Grasmick, St Superintendent of
Schools
Kimberlee Schultz, Public Affair Officer

3233 Instruction Division
Maryland State Department of Education
200 W Baltimore Street
Baltimore, MD 21201-2595
410-767-0100
888-246-0016
http://www.marylandpublicschools.org
Mary Cary, Assistant Superintendent
Kimberlee Schultz, Public Affair Officer

3234 Library Development & Services
Maryland State Department of Education
200 West Baltimore Street
Baltimore, MD 21201-2595
410-767-0100
888-246-0016
E-mail: www.marylandpublicschools.org
http://www.marylandpublicschools.org
Irene Padilla, Asst St Superintendent Lib.
Kimberlee Schultz, Public Affair Officer

3235 Maryland Department of Education
Maryland State Department of Education
200 W Baltimore Street
Baltimore, MD 21201-2595
410-767-0100
888-246-0016
Fax: 410-333-6033
http://www.marylandpublicschools.org
Mission of MSDE is to provide leadership,
support, and accountability for effective systems of public education, library services and
rehabilitation services. For certification information visit www.certifica-
tion.msde.state.md.us or contact
410-767-0412.
Nancy S Grasmick, Superintendent
Kimberlee Schultz, Public Affair Officer

**3236 Office of Special Education and
Rehabilitative Services**
U.S. Department of Education
400 Maryland Avenue SW
Washington, DC 20202-7100
202-245-7459
http://www.ed.gov
Melody Musgrove, Director
Bill Wolf, Acting Deputy Director

**3237 Special Education/Early Intervention
Services Division**
Maryland State Department of Education
200 W Baltimore Street
9th Floor
Baltimore, MD 21201-2595
410-767-0100
888-246-0016
Fax: 410-333-8165
http://www.marylandpublicschools.org
Nancy S. Grasmick, St Superintendent of
Schools
Kimberlee Schultz, Public Affair Officer

Massachusetts

**3238 Massachusetts Department of
Education**
75 Pleasant Streetÿ
Malden, MA 02148-4906
781-338-3000
Fax: 781-338-3770
E-mail: boe@doe.mass.edu
http://www.doe.mass.edu
David P Driscoll, Commissioner

**3239 Massachusetts Department of
Educational Improvement**
75 Pleasant Streetÿ
Malden, MA 02148-4906
781-388-3300
Fax: 781-338-3770
E-mail: boe@doe.mass.edu
http://www.doe.mass.edu
Andrea Perrault, Division Director

3240 Region 1: Education Department
J.W. McCormick Post Office & Courthouse
540 McCormick Courthouse
Boston, MA 02109-4557
617-223-9317
Fax: 617-223-9324
Michael Sentance

Michigan

3241 Administrative Services Office
Michigan Department of Education
608 W Allegan Street
Lansing, MI 48933-1524
517-373-3324
877-932-6424
Fax: 517-335-4565
http://www.michigan.gov
Rick Snyder, Governor

3242 Adult Extended Learning Office
Michigan Department of Education
608 W Allegan Street
Lansing, MI 48933-1524
517-373-3324
877-932-6424
Fax: 517-335-4565
http://www.michigan.gov
Rick Snyder, Governor

3243 Career & Technical Education
Michigan Department of Education
608 W Allegan Street
Lansing, MI 48933-1524
517-373-3324
877-932-6424
Fax: 517-373-8776
http://www.michigan.gov
Rick Snyder, Governor

**3244 Higher Education Management
Office**
Michigan Department of Education
608 W Allegan Street
Lansing, MI 48933-1524
517-373-3324
877-932-6424
Fax: 517-373-2759
http://www.michigan.gov
Rick Snyder, Governor

3245 Instructional Programs
Michigan Department of Education
608 W Allegan Street
Lansing, MI 48933-1524

517-373-3324
877-932-6424
Fax: 517-335-4565
http://www.michigan.gov

Rick Snyder, Governor

3246 Michigan Department of Education

Michigan Department of Education
608 W Allegan Street
PO Box 30008
Lansing, MI 48909
517-373-3324
877-932-6424
Fax: 517-335-4565
E-mail: MDEweb@michigan.gov
http://www.michigan.gov/mde

Rick Snyder, Governor

3247 Office of School Management

Michigan Department of Education
608 W Allegan Street
Lansing, MI 48933-1524
517-373-3324
877-932-6424
Fax: 517-335-4565
http://www.michigan.gov

Rick Snyder, Governor

3248 Office of the Superintendent

Michigan Department of Education
608 W Allegan Street
Lansing, MI 48933-1524
517-373-3324
877-932-6424
Fax: 517-335-4565
http://www.michigan.gov

Rick Snyder, Governor

3249 Postsecondary Services

Michigan Department of Education
608 W Allegan Street
Lansing, MI 48909
517-373-3324
877-932-6424
Fax: 517-335-4565
http://www.michigan.gov

Rick Snyder, Governor

3250 School Program Quality

Michigan Department of Education
608 W Allegan Street
Lansing, MI 48933-1524
517-373-3324
877-932-6424
Fax: 517-373-4565
http://www.michigan.gov

Rick Snyder, Governor

3251 Special Education

Michigan Department of Education
608 W Allegan Street
Lansing, MI 48933-1524
517-373-3324
877-932-6424
Fax: 581-733-5456
http://www.michigan.gov

Rick Snyder, Governor

3252 Student Financial Assistance

Michigan Department of Education
608 W Allegan Street
Lansing, MI 48933-1524
517-373-3324
877-932-6424
Fax: 517-335-4565
http://www.michigan.gov

Rick Snyder, Governor

3253 Teacher & Administrative Preparation

Michigan Department of Education
608 W Allegan Street
Lansing, MI 48933-1524
514-373-3324
877-932-6424
Fax: 517-335-4565
http://www.michigan.gov

Rick Snyder, Governor

Minnesota

3254 Data & Technology

Minnesota Department of Education
1500 Highway 36 West
Roseville, MN 55113-2233
651-582-8200
E-mail: mde.commissioner@state.mn.us
http://education.state.mn.us/mde

Brenda Cassellius, Commissioner
Charlene Briner, Chief of Staff

3255 Data Management

Minnesota Department of Education
1500 Highway 36 West
Roseville, MN 55113
651-582-8200
Fax: 651-582-8873
E-mail: mde.commissioner@state.mn.us
http://education.state.mn.us/mde

Brenda Cassellius, Commissioner
Charlene Briner, Chief of Staff

3256 Education Funding

Minnesota Department of Education
1500 Highway 36 West
Roseville, MN 55113-2233
651-582-8200
E-mail: mde.commissioner@state.mn.us
http://education.state.mn.us/mde

Brenda Cassellius, Commissioner
Charlene Briner, Chief of Staff

3257 Financial Conditions & Aids Payment

Minnesota Department of Education
1500 Highway 36 West
Roseville, MN 55113-2233
651-582-8200
E-mail: mde.commissioner@state.mn.us
http://education.state.mn.us/mde

Brenda Cassellius, Commissioner
Charlene Briner, Chief of Staff

3258 Government Relations

Minnesota Department of Education
1500 Highway 36 West
Roseville, MN 55113-2233
651-582-8200
E-mail: mde.commissioner@state.mn.us
http://education.state.mn.us/mde

Brenda Cassellius, Commissioner
Charlene Briner, Chief of Staff

3259 Human Resources Office

Minnesota Department of Education
1500 Highway 36 West
Roseville, MN 55113-2233
651-582-8200
E-mail: mde.commissioner@state.mn.us
http://education.state.mn.us/mde

Brenda Cassellius, Commissioner
Charlene Briner, Chief of Staff

3260 Minnesota Department of Children, Families & Learning

Minnesota Department of Education
1500 Highway 36 W
Roseville, MN 55113-4266
651-582-8200
Fax: 651-582-8724
E-mail: mde.commissioner@state.mn.us
http://education.state.mn.us/mde
Works to help communities to measurably improve the well-being of children through programs that focus on education, community services, prevention, and the preparation of young people for the world of work. All department efforts emphasize the achievement of positive results for children and their families.

Brenda Cassellius, Commissioner
Charlene Briner, Chief of Staff

3261 Minnesota Department of Education

Minnesota Department of Education
1500 Highway 36 W
Roseville, MN 55113-4266
651-582-8200
Fax: 651-582-8724
E-mail: mde.commissioner@state.mn.us
http://www.education.state.mn.us

Brenda Cassellius, Commissioner
Charlene Briner, Chief of Staff

3262 Residential Schools

Minnesota Department of Education
1500 Highway 36 West
Roseville, MN 55113-2233
651-582-8200
E-mail: mde.commissioner@state.mn.us
http://education.state.mn.us/mde

Brenda Cassellius, Commissioner
Charlene Briner, Chief of Staff

Mississippi

3263 Community Outreach Services

Mississippi Department of Education
PO Box 771
Jackson, MS 39205-0771
601-359-3513
Fax: 601-359-3033
http://www.mde.k12.ms.us

Sarah Beard, Division Director

3264 Educational Innovations

Mississippi Department of Education
PO Box 771
Jackson, MS 39205-0771
601-359-3513
Fax: 601-359-2587
http://www.mde.k12.ms.us

David Robinson, Division Director

3265 External Relations

Mississippi Department of Education
PO Box 771
372 Central High Building
Jackson, MS 39205-0771
601-359-3513
Fax: 601-359-3033
http://www.mde.k12.ms.us

Andrew P Mullins, Division Director

3266 Management Information Systems

Mississippi Department of Education
PO Box 771
Jackson, MS 39205-0771
601-359-3513
Fax: 601-359-3033
http://www.mde.k12.ms.us

Rusty Purvis, Division Director

267 Mississippi Department of Education
Mississippi Department of Education
359 NW Street
PO Box 771
Jackson, MS 39205-0771
601-359-3513
Fax: 601-359-3242
http://www.mde.k12.ms.us

Dr.Henry Johnson, Superintendent

268 Mississippi Employment Security Commission
Mississippi Department of Education
PO Box 771
Jackson, MS 39205-0771
601-359-3513
Fax: 601-961-7405
http://www.mde.k12.ms.us

269 Office of Accountability
Mississippi Department of Education
PO Box 771
Jackson, MS 39205-0771
601-359-3513
Fax: 601-359-1748
http://www.mde.k12.ms.us

Judy Rhodes, Division Director

270 Vocational Technical Education
Mississippi Department of Education
359 NW Street
PO Box 771
Jackson, MS 39205-0771
601-359-3513
Fax: 601-359-3989
http://www.mde.k12.ms.us

Samuel McGee, Division Director

Missouri

271 Deputy Commissioner
Missouri Department of Education
205 Jefferson Street
PO Box 480 Floor 6
Jefferson City, MO 65101-0480
573-751-4212
Fax: 573-751-1179
http://dese.mo.gov

Margie Vandeven, Commissioner

272 Division of Instruction
Missouri Department of Education
205 Jefferson Street
Floor 6
Jefferson City, MO 65101-0480
573-751-4212
Fax: 573-751-8613
http://dese.mo.gov

Margie Vandeven, Commissioner

273 Missouri Department of Education
Missouri Department of Education
205 Jefferson Street, 6th Floor
PO Box 480
Jefferson City, MO 65101-0480
573-751-4212
Fax: 573-751-8613
E-mail: pubinfo@mail.dese.state.mo.us
http://dese.mo.gov
A team of dedicated individuals working for the continuous improvement of education and services for all citizens. We believe that we can make a positive difference in the quality of life for all Missourians by providing exceptional service to students, educators, schools and citizens.

Margie Vandeven, Commissioner

3274 Region 7: Education Department
Missouri Department of Education
10220 NW Executive Hills Boulevard
Kansas City, MO 64153-2312
816-891-7972
Fax: 816-891-7972
http://dese.mo.gov

Margie Vandeven, Commissioner

3275 Special Education Division
Missouri Department of Education
205 Jefferson Street
PO Box 480 Floor 6
Jefferson City, MO 65101-0480
573-751-4212
Fax: 573-751-8613
E-mail: communications@dese.mo.gov
http://dese.mo.gov

Margie Vandeven, Commissioner

3276 Urban & Teacher Education
Missouri Department of Education
205 Jefferson Street
Floor 6
Jefferson City, MO 65101-0480
573-751-4212
Fax: 573-751-8613
E-mail: communications@dese.mo.gov
http://dese.mo.gov

Margie Vandeven, Commissioner

3277 Vocational & Adult Education
Missouri Department of Education
205 Jefferson Street, 5th Floor
PO Box 480
Jefferson City, MO 65101-0480
573-751-4212
Fax: 573-751-8613
E-mail: communications@dese.mo.gov
http://dese.mo.gov

Margie Vandeven, Commissioner

3278 Vocational Rehabilitation
Missouri Department of Education
205 Jefferson Street
PO Box 480
Jefferson City, MO 65101-0480
573-751-4212
Fax: 573-751-8613
E-mail: communications@dese.mo.gov
http://dese.mo.gov

Margie Vandeven, Commissioner

Montana

3279 Accreditation & Curriculum Services Department
Montana Department of Education
106 State Capitol
PO Box 200113
Helena, MT 59620-113
406-444-2511
Fax: 406-444-2701
http://mt.gov/education

Steve Bullock, Governor

3280 Division of Information-Technology Support
Montana Department of Education
106 State Capitol
PO Box 200113
Helena, MT 59620-113
406-444-2511
Fax: 406-444-2701
http://mt.gov/education

Steve Bullock, Governor

3281 Montana Department of Education
Montana Department of Education
1227 11th Avenue
PO Box 200113
Helena, MT 59620-113
406-444-2511
Fax: 406-444-2701
http://mt.gov/education
For certification information visit www.opi.state.mt.us or contact 406-444-3150.

Steve Bullock, Governor

3282 Operations Department
Montana Department of Education
106 State Capitol
PO Box 200113
Helena, MT 59620-113
406-444-2511
Fax: 406-444-2701
http://mt.gov/education

Steve Bullock, Governor

Nebraska

3283 Administrative Services Office
Nebraska Department of Education
301 Centennial Mall S
Lincoln, NE 68508-2529
402-471-2295
Fax: 402-471-6351
http://www.education.ne.gov
To provide quality services and support in the areas of finance human resource management continuous quality improvement, office/building services,and technical assistant.

Mike Stefkovich, Division Director

3284 Division of Education Services
Nebraska Department of Education
301 Centennial Mall S
Lincoln, NE 68508-2529
402-471-2783
Fax: 402-471-0117
http://www.education.ne.gov

Marge Harouff, Division Director

3285 Nebraska Department of Education
Nebraska Department of Education
301 Centennial Mall S
PO Box 94987
Lincoln, NE 68509-4987
402-471-5020
Fax: 402-471-4433
http://www.education.ne.gov

Douglas D Christensen, Commissioner

3286 Rehabilitation Services Division
Nebraska Department of Education
301 Centennial Mall S 6th Floor
PO Box 94987
Lincoln, NE 68509-2529
402-471-3649
877-637-3422
Fax: 402-471-0788
http://www.education.ne.gov

Frank C Lloyd, Director

Nevada

3287 Administrative & Financial Services
Nevada Department of Education
700 E. Fifth Street
Carson City, NV 89701-4204
775-687-9200
888-590-6726

Fax: 775-687-9101
http://www.doe.nv.gov
Dale A.R. Erquiaga, Superintendent
Steve Canavero, Ph.D., Deputy
Superintendent

3288 Instructional Services Division
Nevada Department of Education
700 E. Fifth Street
Carson City, NV 89701-4204
775-687-9200
Fax: 775-687-9101
http://www.doe.nv.gov
Dale A.R. Erquiaga, Superintendent
Steve Canavero, Ph.D., Deputy
Superintendent

3289 Nevada Department of Education
700 E 5th Street
Carson City, NV 89701-5096
775-687-9200
Fax: 775-687-9101
http://www.doe.nv.gov
Mission is to lead Nevada's citizens in accomplishing lifelong learning and educational excellence.
Dale A.R. Erquiaga, Superintendent
Steve Canavero, Ph.D., Deputy
Superintendent

New Hampshire

3290 Information Services
New Hampshire Department of Education
101 Pleasent Street
Concord, NH 03301-3860
603-271-3494
Fax: 603-271-1953
http://www.education.nh.gov
New Hampshire schools enrollment, financial, assessment information.
Virginia M. Barry, Commissioner
Paul K. Leather, Deputy Commissioner

3291 New Hampshire Department of Education
New Hampshire Department of Education
101 Pleasant Street
State Office Park S
Concord, NH 03301-3860
603-271-3494
800-339-9900
Fax: 603-271-1953
E-mail: llovering@ed.state.nh.us
http://www.education.nh.gov
Mission is to provide educational leadership and services which promote equal educational opportunities and quality practices and programs than enable New Hampshire residents to become fully productive members of society.
Virginia M. Barry, Commissioner
Paul K. Leather, Deputy Commissioner

3292 New Hampshire Division of Instructional Services
New Hampshire Department of Education
101 Pleasant Street
Concord, NH 03301-3860
603-271-3494
Fax: 603-271-1953
http://www.education.nh.gov
Virginia M. Barry, Commissioner
Paul K. Leather, Deputy Commissioner

3293 Standards & Certification Division
New Hampshire Department of Education
101 Pleasant St
Concord, NH 03301-3860

603-271-3494
Fax: 603-271-1953
http://www.education.nh.gov
Virginia M. Barry, Commissioner
Paul K. Leather, Deputy Commissioner

New Jersey

3294 New Jersey Department of Education
New Jersey Department of Education
100 Riverview Plaza
PO Box 500
Trenton, NJ 08625-0500
609-292-4450
877-900-6960
Fax: 609-777-4099
http://www.state.nj.us/education
Develops and implements policies that address the major education issues in New Jersey. The State Board will engage in an effort to ensure that all children receive a quality public education that prepares them to succeed as responsible, productive citizens in a global society.
David C. Hespe, Commissioner
Bari Anhalt Erlichson, Chief
Performance Officer

3295 New Jersey Department of Education: Finance
New Jersey Department of Education
100 Riverview Plaza
PO Box 500
Trenton, NJ 08625-0500
609-292-4421
877-900-6960
Fax: 609-292-6794
http://www.state.nj.us/education
David C. Hespe, Commissioner
Bari Anhalt Erlichson, Chief
Performance Officer

3296 New Jersey Division of Special Education
New Jersey Department of Education
100 Riverview Plaza
PO Box 500
Trenton, NJ 08625-0500
609-292-0147
877-900-6960
Fax: 609-984-8422
http://www.state.nj.us/education
David C. Hespe, Commissioner
Bari Anhalt Erlichson, Chief
Performance Officer

3297 New Jersey State Library
New Jersey Department of Education
PO Box 520
Trenton, NJ 08625-0500
609-292-6200
877-900-6960
Fax: 609-292-2746
E-mail: nblake@njstatelib.org
http://www.state.nj.us/education
David C. Hespe, Commissioner
Bari Anhalt Erlichson, Chief
Performance Officer

3298 Professional Development & Licensing
New Jersey Department of Education
PO Box 500
Trenton, NJ 08625-0500
609-292-2070
877-900-6960

Fax: 609-292-3768
http://www.state.nj.us/education
David C. Hespe, Commissioner
Bari Anhalt Erlichson, Chief Performance
Officer

3299 Urban & Field Services
New Jersey Department of Education
100 Riverview Plaza
PO Box 520
Trenton, NJ 08625-0500
609-292-4442
877-900-6960
Fax: 609-292-3830
http://www.state.nj.us/education
David C. Hespe, Commissioner
Bari Anhalt Erlichson, Chief Performance
Officer

New Mexico

3300 Agency Support
New Mexico Department of Education
300 Don Gaspar
Education Building
Santa Fe, NM 87501-2786
505-827-5800
http://ped.state.nm.us/ped
Tres Giron, Division Director

3301 Learning Services
New Mexico Department of Education
300 Don Gaspar
Education Building
Santa Fe, NM 87501
505-827-5800
Fax: 505-827-6689
http://ped.state.nm.us/ped
Albert Zamora, Division Director

3302 New Mexico Department of Education
New Mexico Department of Education
300 Don Gaspar
Education Building
Santa Fe, NM 87501-2786
505-827-5800
Fax: 505-827-6520
http://ped.state.nm.us/ped
Michael J Davis, Superintendent

3303 New Mexico Department of School-Transportation & Support Services
New Mexico Department of Education
300 Don Gaspar
Education Building
Santa Fe, NM 87501
505-827-5800
http://ped.state.nm.us/ped
Susan Brown, Division Director

3304 School Management Accountability
New Mexico Department of Education
300 Don Gaspar
Education Building
Santa Fe, NM 87501
505-827-5800
Fax: 505-827-6689
http://ped.state.nm.us/ped
Michael J Davis, Division Director

3305 Vocational Education
New Mexico Department of Education
300 Don Gaspar
Education Building
Santa Fe, NM 87501

505-827-5800
http://ped.state.nm.us/ped
Tom Trujillo, Division Director

New York

306 Cultural Education
New York Department of Education
89 Washington Avenue
Albany, NY 12234
518-474-3852
Fax: 518-474-2718
E-mail: SiteSupport@mail.nysed.gov
http://www.nysed.gov
Carole F Huxley, Division Director

307 Elementary, Middle & Secondary Education
New York Department of Education
89 Washington Avenue
Albany, NY 12234-0001
518-474-3852
Fax: 518-474-2718
E-mail: SiteSupport@mail.nysed.gov
http://www.nysed.gov
James Kadamus, Deputy

308 Higher & Professional Education
New York Department of Education
89 Washington Avenue
Albany, NY 12234-0001
518-474-3852
Fax: 518-474-2718
E-mail: SiteSupport@mail.nysed.gov
http://www.nysed.gov
Johanna Duncan-Poitier, Deputy
Commissioner

309 New York Department of Education
New York Department of Education
89 Washington Avenue
Albany, NY 12234
518-474-3852
Fax: 518-473-4909
E-mail: SiteSupport@mail.nysed.gov
http://www.nysed.gov
Richard P Mills, President

310 Professional Responsibility Office
New York Department of Education
89 Washington Avenue
Albany, NY 12234-2643
518-474-3852
Fax: 518-485-9361
E-mail: SiteSupport@mail.nysed.gov
http://www.nysed.gov

311 Region 2: Education Department
New York Department of Education
89 Washington Avenue
Albany, NY 12234
518-474-3852
Fax: 212-264-4427
E-mail: SiteSupport@mail.nysed.gov
http://www.nysed.gov

312 Vocational & Educational Services for Disabled
New York Department of Education
89 Washington Avenue
Albany, NY 12234
518-474-3852
800-272-5448
Fax: 518-457-4562
E-mail: SiteSupport@mail.nysed.gov
http://www.nysed.gov
David Segalla, Regional Coordinator

North Carolina

3313 Auxiliary Services
North Carolina Department of Education
301 N Wilmington Street
Raleigh, NC 27601-2825
919-807-3300
Fax: 919-733-5279
http://www.ncpublicschools.org
Charles Weaver, Division Director

3314 Financial & Personnel Services
North Carolina Department of Education
301 N Wilmington Street
Raleigh, NC 27601-2825
919-807-3300
http://www.ncpublicschools.org
James O Barber, Division Director

3315 North Carolina Department of Education
North Carolina Department of Education
301 N Wilmington Street
Raleigh, NC 27601-2825
919-807-3300
Fax: 919-807-3279
http://www.ncpublicschools.org
Bob R Etheridge, Division Director

3316 North Carolina Department of Instructional Services
North Carolina Department of Education
301 N Wilmington Street
Raleigh, NC 27601-2825
919-807-3300
Fax: 919-807-3279
http://www.ncpublicschools.org
Henry Johnson, Division Director

3317 Staff Development & Technical Assistance
North Carolina Department of Education
301 N Wilmington Street
Raleigh, NC 27601-2825
919-807-3300
http://www.ncpublicschools.org
Nancy Davis, Division Director

North Dakota

3318 North Dakota Department of Education
North Dakota Department of Education
600 E Boulevard Avenue
Dept. 201
Bismarck, ND 58505-0440
701-328-2260
Fax: 701-328-2461
E-mail: dpi@nd.gov
http://www.dpi.state.nd.us
Wayne G Sanstead, Superintendent
Kirsten Baesler, State Superintendent

3319 North Dakota Department of Public Instruction Division
North Dakota Department of Education
600 E Boulevard Avenue
Dept. 201
Bismarck, ND 58505-0440
701-328-2260
Fax: 701-328-2461
E-mail: dpi@nd.gov
http://www.dpi.state.nd.us
Kirsten Baesler, State Superintendent

3320 North Dakota State Board for Vocational & Technical Education
North Dakota Department of Education
600 E Boulevard Avenue
Dept. 201
Bismarck, ND 58505-0440
701-328-2260
Fax: 701-328-2461
E-mail: dpi@nd.gov
http://www.dpi.state.nd.us
Kirsten Baesler, State Superintendent
Reuben Guenthner, Division Director

3321 Study & State Film Library
North Dakota Department of Education
600 E Boulevard Avenue
Dept. 201
Bismarck, ND 58505-0440
701-328-2260
E-mail: dpi@nd.gov
http://www.dpi.state.nd.us
Kirsten Baesler, State Superintendent
Robert Stone, Division Director

Ohio

3322 Blind School
Ohio Department of Education
25 S Front Street
Columbus, OH 43215-4131
614-466-3641
877-644-6338
Fax: 614-752-1713
E-mail: contact.center@education.ohio.gov
http://education.ohio.gov
Richard A. Ross, Superintendent
Tom Gunlock, President

3323 Curriculum, Instruction & Professional Development
Ohio Department of Education
25 S Front Street
Columbus, OH 43215-4131
614-466-2761
877-644-6338
Fax: 704-992-5168
E-mail: contact.center@education.ohio.gov
http://education.ohio.gov
Richard A. Ross, Superintendent
Tom Gunlock, President

3324 Early Childhood Education
Ohio Department of Education
25 S Front Street
Columbus, OH 43215-4131
614-466-0224
877-644-6338
Fax: 614-728-2338
E-mail: contact.center@education.ohio.gov
http://education.ohio.gov
Richard A. Ross, Superintendent
Tom Gunlock, President

3325 Federal Assistance
Ohio Department of Education
25 S Front Street
Columbus, OH 43215-4131
614-466-4161
877-644-6338
Fax: 704-992-5168
E-mail: contact.center@education.ohio.gov
http://education.ohio.gov
Richard A. Ross, Superintendent
Tom Gunlock, President

3326 Ohio Department of Education
Ohio Department of Education
25 S Front Street
7th Floor
Columbus, OH 43215-4183
614-466-7578
877-644-6338
Fax: 614-728-4781
E-mail:
contact.center@education.ohio.gov
http://education.ohio.gov
Works in partnership with school districts
to assure high achievements for all learners, promote a safe and orderly learning environment, provide leadership, support,
and build capacity, and provide support to
school districts particularly those who
need it most.

Richard A. Ross, Superitendent
Tom Gunlock, President

3327 Personnel Services
Ohio Department of Education
25 S Front Street
Columbus, OH 43215-4131
614-466-3763
877-644-6338
Fax: 704-992-5168
E-mail:
contact.center@education.ohio.gov
http://education.ohio.gov

Richard A. Ross, Superitendent
Tom Gunlock, President

3328 School Finance
Ohio Department of Education
25 S Front Street
Columbus, OH 43215-4183
614-466-6266
877-644-6338
Fax: 704-992-5168
E-mail:
contact.center@education.ohio.gov
http://education.ohio.gov

Richard A. Ross, Superitendent
Tom Gunlock, President

3329 School Food Service
Ohio Department of Education
25 S Front Street
Columbus, OH 43215-4131
614-466-2945
877-644-6338
Fax: 704-992-5168
E-mail:
contact.center@education.ohio.gov
http://education.ohio.gov

Richard A. Ross, Superitendent
Tom Gunlock, President

3330 School for the Deaf
Ohio Department of Education
25 S Front Street
Columbus, OH 43215-4131
614-466-3641
877-644-6338
Fax: 704-992-5168
E-mail:
contact.center@education.ohio.gov
http://education.ohio.gov

Richard A. Ross, Superitendent
Tom Gunlock, President

3331 Special Education
Ohio Department of Education
25 S Front Street
Worthington, OH 43085
614-466-2650
877-644-6338
Fax: 704-992-5168
E-mail:

contact.center@education.ohio.gov
http://education.ohio.gov

Richard A. Ross, Superintendent
Tom Gunlock, President

3332 Student Development
Ohio Department of Education
25 S Front Street
Columbus, OH 43215-4131
614-466-3641
877-644-6338
Fax: 704-992-5168
E-mail:
contact.center@education.ohio.gov
http://education.ohio.gov

Richard A. Ross, Superintendent
Tom Gunlock, President

3333 Teacher Education & Certification
Ohio Department of Education
25 S Front Street
Columbus, OH 43215-4131
614-466-3430
877-644-6338
Fax: 704-992-5168
E-mail:
contact.center@education.ohio.gov
http://education.ohio.gov

Richard A. Ross, Superintendent
Tom Gunlock, President

3334 Vocational & Career Education
Ohio Department of Education
25 S Front Street
Columbus, OH 43215-4131
614-466-3430
877-644-6338
Fax: 704-992-5168
E-mail:
contact.center@education.ohio.gov
http://education.ohio.gov

Richard A. Ross, Superintendent
Tom Gunlock, President

Oklahoma

**3335 Accreditation & Standards
Division**
Oklahoma State Department of Education
2500 N Lincoln Boulevard
Oklahoma City, OK 73105-4599
405-521-3301
Fax: 405-521-6205
E-mail: sdeservicedesk@sde.ok.gov
http://www.ok.gov/sde

Joy Hofmeister, Superintendent
Liz Young, Executive Assistant

**3336 Federal/Special/Collaboration
Services**
Oklahoma State Department of Education
2500 N Lincoln Boulevard
Oklahoma City, OK 73105-4599
405-521-3301
Fax: 405-521-6205
E-mail: sdeservicedesk@sde.ok.gov
http://www.ok.gov/sde

Joy Hofmeister, Superintendent
Liz Young, Executive Assistant

**3337 Oklahoma Department of Career
and Technology Education**
Oklahoma Department of Career and
Technology Educa
1500 W 7th Avenue
Stillwater, OK 74074-4398
405-377-2000
Fax: 405-743-5541

E-mail: Paula.Bowles@careertech.ok.gov
http://www.okcareertech.org

Roy Peters Jr, Division Director
Paula Bowles, Chief Comm Officer/ CMO

3338 Oklahoma Department of Education
Oklahoma State Department of Education
2500 N Lincoln Boulevard
Hodge Education Building
Oklahoma City, OK 73105-4599
405-521-3301
Fax: 405-521-6205
E-mail: sdeservicedesk@sde.ok.gov
http://www.ok.gov/sde

Joy Hofmeister, Superintendent
Liz Young, Executive Assistant

**3339 Oklahoma Department of Education;
Financial Services**
Oklahoma State Department of Education
2500 N Lincoln Boulevard
Oklahoma City, OK 73105-4599
405-521-3301
Fax: 405-521-6205
E-mail: sdeservicedesk@sde.ok.gov
http://www.ok.gov/sde

Joy Hofmeister, Superintendent
Liz Young, Executive Assistant

3340 Professional Services
Oklahoma State Department of Education
2500 N Lincoln Boulevard
Oklahoma City, OK 73105-4599
405-521-3301
Fax: 405-521-6205
E-mail: sdeservicedesk@sde.ok.gov
http://www.ok.gov/sde

Joy Hofmeister, Superintendent
Liz Young, Executive Assistant

3341 School Improvement
Oklahoma State Department of Education
2500 N Lincoln Boulevard
Oklahoma City, OK 73105-4599
405-521-3301
Fax: 405-521-6205
E-mail: sdeservicedesk@sde.ok.gov
http://www.ok.gov/sde

Joy Hofmeister, Superintendent
Liz Young, Executive Assistant

Oregon

3342 Assessment & Evaluation
Oregon Department of Education
255 Capitol Street NE
Salem, OR 97310-0203
503-378-3600
Fax: 503-378-5156
E-mail: ode.frontdesk@ode.state.or.us
http://www.ode.state.or.us

Rob Saxton, Deputy Superintendent

3343 Community College Services
Oregon Department of Education
225 Capitol Street NE
Salem, OR 97310-1341
503-378-3600
Fax: 503-378-5156
E-mail: ode.frontdesk@ode.state.or.us
http://www.ode.state.or.us

Rob Saxton, Deputy Superintendent

3344 Compensatory Education Office
Oregon Department of Education
225 Capitol Street NE
Salem, OR 97310-1341
503-378-3569
Fax: 503-378-5156

E-mail: ode.frontdesk@ode.state.or.us
http://www.ode.state.or.us

Rob Saxton, Deputy Superintendent

345 Deputy Superintendent Office
Oregon Department of Education
225 Capitol Street NE
Salem, OR 97310-1341
503-378-3573
Fax: 503-378-5156
E-mail: ode.frontdesk@ode.state.or.us
http://www.ode.state.or.us

Rob Saxton, Deputy Superintendent

346 Early Childhood Council
Oregon Department of Education
225 Capitol Street NE
Salem, OR 97310-1341
503-378-5585
Fax: 503-378-5156
E-mail: ode.frontdesk@ode.state.or.us
http://www.ode.state.or.us

Rob Saxton, Deputy Superintendent

347 Government Relations
Oregon Department of Education
225 Capitol Street NE
Salem, OR 97310-1341
503-378-8549
Fax: 503-378-5156
E-mail: ode.frontdesk@ode.state.or.us
http://www.ode.state.or.us

Rob Saxton, Deputy Superintendent

348 Management Services
Oregon Department of Education
225 Capitol Street NE
Salem, OR 97310-1341
503-378-8549
Fax: 503-378-5156
E-mail: ode.frontdesk@ode.state.or.us
http://www.ode.state.or.us

Rob Saxton, Deputy Superintendent

349 Office of Field, Curriculum & Instruction Services
Oregon Department of Education
225 Capitol Street NE
Salem, OR 97310-1341
503-378-8004
Fax: 503-378-5156
E-mail: ode.frontdesk@ode.state.or.us
http://www.ode.state.or.us

Rob Saxton, Deputy Superintendent

350 Oregon Department of Education
Oregon Department of Education
225 Capitol Street NE
Salem, OR 97310-0203
503-378-3569
Fax: 503-378-5156
E-mail: ode.frontdesk@ode.state.or.us
http://www.ode.state.or.us

Rob Saxton, Deputy Superintendent

351 Professional Technical Education
Oregon Department of Education
225 Capitol Street NE
Salem, OR 97310-1341
503-378-3584
Fax: 503-378-5156
E-mail: ode.frontdesk@ode.state.or.us
http://www.ode.state.or.us

Rob Saxton, Deputy Superintendent

352 Special Education
Oregon Department of Education
225 Capitol Street NE
Salem, OR 97310-1341

503-378-3600
Fax: 503-378-5156
E-mail: ode.frontdesk@ode.state.or.us
http://www.ode.state.or.us

Rob Saxton, Deputy Superintendent

3353 Student Services Office
Oregon Department of Education
225 Capitol Street NE
Salem, OR 97310-1341
503-378-5585
Fax: 503-378-5156
E-mail: ode.frontdesk@ode.state.or.us
http://www.ode.state.or.us

Rob Saxton, Deputy Superintendent

3354 Twenty First Century Schools Council
Oregon Department of Education
225 Capitol Street NE
Salem, OR 97310-1341
503-378-3600
Fax: 503-378-5156
E-mail: ode.frontdesk@ode.state.or.us
http://www.ode.state.or.us

Rob Saxton, Deputy Superintendent

Pennsylvania

3355 Chief Counsel
Pennsylvania Department of Education
333 Market Street
Harrisburg, PA 17126-2210
717-783-6788
Fax: 717-783-0347
http://www.education.state.pa.us

Carolyn Dumaresq, Acting Secretary

3356 Chief of Staff Office
Pennsylvania Department of Education
333 Market Street
Harrisburg, PA 17126-2210
717-783-6788
Fax: 717-787-7222
http://www.education.state.pa.us

Carolyn Dumaresq, Acting Secretary

3357 Higher Education/Postsecondary Office
Pennsylvania Department of Education
333 Market Street
Harrisburg, PA 17126-2210
717-783-6788
Fax: 717-783-0583
http://www.education.state.pa.us

Carolyn Dumaresq, Acting Secretary

3358 Office of Elementary and Secondary Education
Pennsylvania Department of Education
333 Market Street
5th Floor
Harrisburg, PA 17126
717-783-6788
Fax: 717-783-6802
E-mail: dhaines@state.pa.us
http://www.education.state.pa.us

Carolyn Dumaresq, Acting Secretary

3359 Office of the Comptroller
Pennsylvania Department of Education
333 Market Street
Harrisburg, PA 17126-2210
717-783-6788
Fax: 717-787-3593
http://www.education.state.pa.us

Carolyn Dumaresq, Acting Secretary

3360 Pennsylvania Department of Education
Pennsylvania Department of Education
333 Market Street
Harrisburg, PA 17126
717-783-6788
Fax: 717-787-7222
http://www.education.state.pa.us

Carolyn Dumaresq, Acting Secretary

3361 Region 3: Education Department
Pennsylvania Department of Education
333 Market Street
Harrisburg, PA 17126-3309
717-783-6788
http://www.education.state.pa.us

Carolyn Dumaresq, Acting Secretary

Rhode Island

3362 Career & Technical Education
Rhode Island Department of Education
255 Westminster Street
Providence, RI 02903-3414
401-222-4600
Fax: 401-222-2537
http://www.ride.ri.gov

Deborah Gist, Commissioner
Andy Andrade, Commissioner Support

3363 Equity & Access Office
Rhode Island Department of Education
255 Westminster Street
Providence, RI 02903-3414
401-222-4600
Fax: 401-222-2537
http://www.ride.ri.gov

Deborah Gist, Commissioner
Andy Andrade, Commissioner Support

3364 Human Resource Development
Rhode Island Department of Education
255 Westminster Street
Providence, RI 02903-3414
401-222-4600
Fax: 401-222-2537
http://www.ride.ri.gov

Deborah Gist, Commissioner
Andy Andrade, Commissioner Support

3365 Instruction Office
Rhode Island Department of Education
255 Westminster Street
Providence, RI 02903-3414
401-222-4600
Fax: 401-222-2537
http://www.ride.ri.gov

Deborah Gist, Commissioner
Andy Andrade, Commissioner Support

3366 Office of Finance
Rhode Island Department of Education
255 Westminster Street
Providence, RI 02903-3414
401-222-4600
Fax: 401-222-2537
http://www.ride.ri.gov

Deborah Gist, Commissioner
Andy Andrade, Commissioner Support

3367 Outcomes & Assessment Office
Rhode Island Department of Education
255 Westminster Street
Providence, RI 02903-3414

401-222-4600
Fax: 401-222-2537
http://www.ride.ri.gov
Deborah Gist, Commissioner
Andy Andrade, Commissioner Support

3368 Resource Development
Rhode Island Department of Education
255 Westminster Street
Providence, RI 02903-3414
401-222-4600
Fax: 401-222-6033
http://www.ride.ri.gov
Deborah Gist, Commissioner
Andy Andrade, Commissioner Support

3369 Rhode Island Department of Education
Rhode Island Department of Education
255 Westminster Street
Providence, RI 02903
401-222-4600
Fax: 401-222-6178
E-mail: ride0001@ride.ri.net
http://www.ride.ri.gov
Goal of all our work is to improve student performance and help all students meet or exceed a high level of performance. Standards, instruction, and assessment intertwine to provide a system that ensures a strong education for our students.
Deborah Gist, Commissioner
Andy Andrade, Commissioner Support

3370 School Food Services Administration
Rhode Island Department of Education
255 Westminster Street
Providence, RI 02903-3414
401-222-4600
Fax: 401-222-3080
http://www.ride.ri.gov
Deborah Gist, Commissioner
Andy Andrade, Commissioner Support

3371 Special Needs Office
Rhode Island Department of Education
255 Westminster Street
Providence, RI 02903-3414
401-456-9331
Fax: 401-456-8699
http://www.ride.ri.gov
Deborah Gist, Commissioner
Andy Andrade, Commissioner Support

3372 Teacher Education & Certification Office
Rhode Island Department of Education
255 Westminster Street
Providence, RI 02903-3414
401-222-4600
Fax: 401-222-2048
http://www.ride.ri.gov
Deborah Gist, Commissioner
Andy Andrade, Commissioner Support

South Carolina

3373 Budgets & Planning
South Carolina Department of Education
1429 Senate Street
Suite 950
Columbia, SC 29201-3730
803-734-8500
Fax: 803-734-0645
E-mail: SCSuptED@ed.sc.gov
http://ed.sc.gov
Molly Spearman, Superintendent

3374 Communications Services
South Carolina Department of Education
1429 Senate Street
Columbia, SC 29201-3730
803-734-8500
Fax: 803-734-3389
E-mail: SCSuptED@ed.sc.gov
http://ed.sc.gov
Molly Spearman, Superintendent

3375 General Counsel
South Carolina Department of Education
1429 Senate Street
Columbia, SC 29201-3730
803-734-8500
Fax: 803-734-4384
E-mail: SCSuptED@ed.sc.gov
http://ed.sc.gov
Molly Spearman, Superintendent

3376 Internal Administration
South Carolina Department of Education
1429 Senate Street
Columbia, SC 29201-3730
803-734-8500
Fax: 803-734-6225
E-mail: SCSuptED@ed.sc.gov
http://ed.sc.gov
Molly Spearman, Superintendent

3377 Policy & Planning
South Carolina Department of Education
1429 Senate Street
Columbia, SC 29201-3730
803-734-8500
Fax: 803-734-8624
E-mail: SCSuptED@ed.sc.gov
http://ed.sc.gov
Molly Spearman, Superintendent

3378 South Carolina Department of Education
South Carolina Department of Education
1429 Senate Street
Columbia, SC 29201
803-734-8500
Fax: 803-734-3389
E-mail: SCSuptED@ed.sc.gov
http://ed.sc.gov
Provides leadership and services to ensure a system of public education in which all students become educated, responsible, and contributing citizens. For certification information visit www.myscschools.com or contact 803-734-5280.
Molly Spearman, Superintendent

3379 Support Services
South Carolina Department of Education
1429 Senate Street
Columbia, SC 29201-3730
803-734-8500
Fax: 803-734-8254
E-mail: SCSuptED@ed.sc.gov
http://ed.sc.gov
Molly Spearman, Superitendent

South Dakota

3380 Finance & Management
South Dakota Department of Education
800 Governors Drive
Pierre, SD 57501-2291
605-773-3248
Fax: 605-773-6139
http://doe.sd.gov
Stacy Krusemark, Division Director

3381 Services for Education
South Dakota Department of Education
800 Governors Drive
Pierre, SD 57501-2291
605-773-4699
Fax: 605-773-3782
http://doe.sd.gov
Donlynn Rice, Division Director

3382 South Dakota Department of Education & Cultural Affairs
South Dakota Department of Education
800 Governors Drive
Pierre, SD 57501-2291
605-773-2291
Fax: 605-773-6139
E-mail: ray.christensen@state.sd.us
http://doe.sd.gov
Advocates for education, facilitate the delivery of statewide educational and cultural services, and promote efficient, appropriate, and quality educational opportunities for all persons residing in South Dakota.
Ray Christensen, Secretary
Patrick Keating, Division Director

3383 South Dakota State Historical Society
South Dakota Dept of Education & Cultural Affairs
800 Governors Drive
Pierre, SD 57501-2291
605-773-3458
Fax: 605-773-6041
E-mail: jay.vogt@state.sd.us
http://doe.sd.gov
Program areas: Archaeology, archives, historic preservation, museum, research, and publishing
Jay D Vogt, History Manager

3384 Special Education Office
South Dakota Department of Education
800 Governors Drive
Pierre, SD 57501-2291
605-773-3678
Fax: 605-773-3782
http://doe.sd.gov
Michelle Powers, Division Director

Tennessee

3385 Special Education
Tennessee Department of Education
710 James Robertson Parkway
6th Floor
Nashville, TN 37243-5158
615-741-2851
Fax: 615-532-9412
http://www.tn.gov
Kevin S. Huffman, Commissioner
Kathleen Airhart, Deputy Commissioner

3386 Teaching and Learning
Tennessee Department of Education
710 James Robertson Parkway
5th Floor
Nashville, TN 37243-5158
615-532-6195
Fax: 615-741-1837
E-mail: wprotoe@mail.state.tn.us
http://www.tn.gov
Kevin S. Huffman, Commissioner
Kathleen Airhart, Deputy Commissioner

3387 Tennessee Department of Education
Tennessee Department of Education
710 James Robertson Parkway
6th Floor
Nashville, TN 37243-5158

615-741-2731
Fax: 615-741-6236
E-mail: jwalters@mail.state.tn.us
http://www.tn.gov

Kevin S. Huffman, Commissioner
Kathleen Airhart, Deputy Commissioner

388 Vocational Education
Tennessee Department of Education
710 James Robertson Parkway
4th Floor
Nashville, TN 37243-5158
615-532-2800
Fax: 615-532-8226
http://www.tn.gov

Kevin S. Huffman, Commissioner
Kathleen Airhart, Deputy Commissioner

Texas

389 Accountability Reporting and Research
Texas Education Agency
1701 N. Congress Avenue
WBT Building Room 3-111
Austin, TX 78701-1494
512-463-9734
Fax: 512-463-9838
E-mail: ccloudt@tmail.tea.state.tx.us
http://tea.texas.gov

Rick Perry, Commissioner

390 Chief Counsel
Texas Department of Education
1701 N. Congress Avenue
Austin, TX 78701-1402
512-463-9734
Fax: 512-463-9838
http://tea.texas.gov

Rick Perry, Commissioner

391 Continuing Education
Texas Education Agency
1701 N. Congress Avenue
Austin, TX 78701-1402
512-463-9734
Fax: 512-463-9838
E-mail: wtillian@tea.state.tx.us
http://tea.texas.gov

Rick Perry, Commissioner

392 Curriculum Development & Textbooks
Texas Department of Education
1701 N. Congress Avenue
Austin, TX 78701-1402
512-463-9734
Fax: 512-463-9838
http://tea.texas.gov

Rick Perry, Commissioner

393 Curriculum, Assessment & Professional Development
Texas Department of Education
1701 N. Congress Avenue
Austin, TX 78701-1402
512-463-9734
Fax: 512-463-9838
http://tea.texas.gov

Rick Perry, Commissioner

394 Curriculum, Assessment and Technology
Texas Department of Education
1701 N. Congress Avenue
Austin, TX 78701-1402
512-463-9734
Fax: 512-463-9838

E-mail: asmisko@tea.tetn.net
http://tea.texas.gov

Rick Perry, Commissioner

3395 Education of Special Populations & Adults
Texas Department of Education
1701 N. Congress Avenue
Austin, TX 78701-1402
512-463-9734
Fax: 512-463-9838
http://tea.texas.gov

Rick Perry, Commissioner

3396 Field Services
Texas Department of Education
1701 N. Congress Avenue
Austin, TX 78701-1402
512-463-9734
Fax: 512-463-9838
http://tea.texas.gov

Rick Perry, Commissioner

3397 Internal Operations
Texas Department of Education
1701 N. Congress Avenue
Austin, TX 78701-1402
512-463-9734
Fax: 512-463-9838
http://tea.texas.gov

Rick Perry, Commissioner

3398 Operations & School Support
Texas Department of Education
1701 N. Congress Avenue
Austin, TX 78701-1494
512-463-9734
Fax: 512-463-9838
http://tea.texas.gov

Rick Perry, Commissioner

3399 Permanent School Fund
Texas Department of Education
1701 N. Congress Avenue
Room 5-120
Austin, TX 78701-1402
512-463-9734
Fax: 512-463-9838
http://tea.texas.gov

Rick Perry, Commissioner

3400 Region 6: Education Department
Texas Department of Education
1200 Main Tower
Dallas, TX 75202-4325
512-463-9734
Fax: 512-463-9838
http://tea.texas.gov

Rick Perry, Commissioner

3401 Texas Department of Education
Texas Department of Education
1701 N Congress Avenue
William B Travis Building
Austin, TX 78701-1494
512-463-9734
Fax: 512-463-9838
http://tea.texas.gov

Rick Perry, Commissioner

Utah

3402 Applied Technology Education Services
Utah Department of Education
250 E 500 S
PO Box 144200
Salt Lake City, UT 84111-3204

801-538-7840
Fax: 801-538-7868
E-mail: rbrems@usoe.kiz.ut.us
http://www.schools.utah.gov
State agency for career and technical education.

Rod Brems, Associate Superintendent
Mark Peterson, Director

3403 Instructional Services Division
Utah Department of Education
250 E 500 S
PO Box 144200
Salt Lake City, UT 84111-3204
801-538-7515
Fax: 801-538-7768
http://www.schools.utah.gov

Jerry P Peterson, Division Director
Mark Peterson, Director

3404 Schools for the Deaf & Blind
Utah Department of Education
250 E 500 S
PO Box 144200
Salt Lake City, UT 84111-3204
801-629-4700
Fax: 801-629-4896
http://www.schools.utah.gov

Wayne Glaus, Division Director
Mark Peterson, Director

3405 Utah Office of Education
Utah Department of Education
250 E 500 South
PO Box 144200
Salt Lake City, UT 84111-3204
801-538-7510
Fax: 801-538-7768
http://www.schools.utah.gov

Steven O Laing, Superintendent
Mark Peterson, Director

3406 Utah Office of Education; Agency Services Division
Utah Department of Education
250 E 500 S
PO Box 144200
Salt Lake City, UT 84114-4200
801-538-7500
Fax: 801-538-7768
http://www.schools.utah.gov

Patrick Ogden, Associate Superintendent
Mark Peterson, Director

Vermont

3407 Career & Lifelong Learning
Vermont Department of Education
120 State Street
Montpelier, VT 05620-0001
802-479-1030
Fax: 802-828-3146
E-mail: AOE.EdInfo@state.vt.us
http://education.vermont.gov

Rebecca Holcombe, Secretary
John Fischer, Deputy Secretary

3408 Core Services
Vermont Department of Education
120 State Street
Montpelier, VT 05620-0001
802-479-1030
Fax: 802-828-3140
E-mail: AOE.EdInfo@state.vt.us
http://education.vermont.gov

Rebecca Holcombe, Secretary
John Fischer, Deputy Secretary

3409 Family & School Support
Vermont Department of Education
120 State Street
Montpelier, VT 05620-0001
802-479-1030
Fax: 802-828-3140
E-mail: AOE.EdInfo@state.vt.us
http://education.vermont.gov

Rebecca Holcombe, Secretary
John Fischer, Deputy Secretary

3410 Financial Management Team
Vermont Department of Education
120 State Street
Montpelier, VT 05620-0001
802-479-1030
Fax: 802-828-3140
E-mail: AOE.EdInfo@state.vt.us
http://education.vermont.gov

Rebecca Holcombe, Secretary
John Fischer, Deputy Secretary

3411 School Development & Information
Vermont Department of Education
120 State Street
Montpelier, VT 05620-0001
802-479-1030
Fax: 802-828-3140
E-mail: AOE.EdInfo@state.vt.us
http://education.vermont.gov

Rebecca Holcombe, Secretary
John Fischer, Deputy Secretary

3412 Teaching & Learning
Vermont Department of Education
120 State Street
Montpelier, VT 05620-0001
802-479-1030
Fax: 802-828-3140
E-mail: AOE.EdInfo@state.vt.us
http://education.vermont.gov

Rebecca Holcombe, Secretary
John Fischer, Deputy Secretary

3413 Vermont Department of Education
Vermont Department of Education
120 State Street
Montpelier, VT 05620-0001
802-479-1030
Fax: 802-828-3140
E-mail: AOE.EdInfo@state.vt.us
http://education.vermont.gov
For certification information visit
www.pen.k12.va.us or contact
804-225-2022.

Rebecca Holcombe, Secretary
John Fischer, Deputy Secretary

3414 Vermont Special Education
Vermont Department of Education
120 State Street
Montpelier, VT 05620-0001
802-479-1030
E-mail: AOE.EdInfo@state.vt.us
http://education.vermont.gov

Rebecca Holcombe, Secretary
John Fischer, Deputy Secretary

Virginia

3415 Administrative Services
Virginia Department of Education
14th & Franklin Streets
PO Box 2120
Richmond, VA 23218

804-225-3252
Fax: 804-786-5828
http://www.doe.virginia.gov

Steven R. Staples, Superintendent

3416 Policy, Assessment, Research & Information Systems
Virginia Department of Education
101 N 4th Street
PO Box 2120
Richmond, VA 23218-2120
804-225-2102
800-292-3820
Fax: 804-371-8978
E-mail: charris@pen.k12.va.us
http://www.doe.virginia.gov

Steven R. Staples, Superitendent

3417 Student Services
Virginia Department of Education
14th & Franklin Streets
PO Box 2120
Richmond, VA 23218
804-225-2757
Fax: 804-786-5828
http://www.doe.virginia.gov

Steven R. Staples, Superintendent

3418 Virginia Centers for Community Education
Virginia Department of Education
101 N 4th Street
PO Box 2120
Richmond, VA 23218-2120
804-225-2293
Fax: 804-786-5828
http://www.doe.virginia.gov

Steven R. Staples, Superintendent

3419 Virginia Department of Education
Virginia Department of Education
James Monroe Building
101 N 14th Street
Richmond, VA 23219
804-225-2023
800-292-3820
Fax: 804-371-2099
E-mail: rlayman@pen.k12.va.us
http://www.doe.virginia.gov

Steven R. Staples, Superintendent

Washington

3420 Region 10: Education Department
US Department of Education
915 2nd Avenue
Room 3362
Seattle, WA 98174-1001
206-220-7800
Fax: 202-220-7806
http://www.ed.gov

3421 Washington Department of Education
Washington State Board of Education
600 Washington Street SE
P.O. Box 47206
Olympia, WA 98504-7200
360-725-6025
Fax: 360-753-6712
E-mail: sbe@k12.wa.us
http://www.sbe.wa.gov

Theresa Bergeson, Superintendent
Isabelÿ Munoz-Colon, Chair

3422 Washington Department of Education; Instruction Program
Washington State Board of Education
600 Washington Street SE
P.O. Box 47206
Olympia, WA 98504-7200
360-725-6025
Fax: 360-586-0247
E-mail: sbe@k12.wa.us
http://www.sbe.wa.gov

John Pearson, Division Director
Isabelÿ Munoz-Colon, Chair

3423 Washington Department of Education; Commission on Student Learning Administration
Washington State Board of Education
600 Washington Street SE
P.O. Box 47206
Olympia, WA 98504-7200
360-725-6025
Fax: 360-664-3028
E-mail: sbe@k12.wa.us
http://www.sbe.wa.gov

Terry Bergeson, Division Director
Isabelÿ Munoz-Colon, Chair

3424 Washington Department of Education; Executive Services
Washington State Board of Education
600 Washington Street SE
P.O. Box 47206
Olympia, WA 98504-7200
360-725-6025
Fax: 360-753-6754
E-mail: sbe@k12.wa.us
http://www.sbe.wa.gov

Ken Kanikeberg, Division Director
Isabelÿ Munoz-Colon, Chair

3425 Washington Department of Education; School Business & Administrative Services
Washington State Board of Education
600 Washington Street SE
P.O. Box 47206
Olympia, WA 98504-7200
360-725-6025
E-mail: sbe@k12.wa.us
http://www.sbe.wa.gov

David Moberly, Division Director
Isabelÿ Munoz-Colon, Chair

West Virginia

3426 Division of Administrative Services
West Virginia Department of Education
1900 Kanawha Boulevard E
Building 6
Charleston, WV 25305-0009
304-558-2441
Fax: 304-558-8867
http://www.wvde.state.wv.us

Carolyn Arrington, Division Director

3427 Research, Accountability & Professional
West Virginia Department of Education
1900 Kanawha Boulevard E
Building 6
Charleston, WV 25305-0009
304-558-3762
Fax: 304-558-8867
http://www.wvde.state.wv.us

William J Luff Jr, Division Director

428 Student Services & Instructional Services
West Virginia Department of Education
1900 Kanawha Boulevard E
Building 6
Charleston, WV 25305-0009
304-558-2691
Fax: 304-558-8867
http://wvde.state.wv.us

Keith Smith, Division Director

429 Technical & Adult Education Services
West Virginia Department of Education
1900 Kanawha Boulevard E
Building 6
Charleston, WV 25305-0009
304-558-2346
Fax: 304-558-8867
http://www.wvde.state.wv.us

Adam Sponaugle, Division Director

430 West Virginia Department of Education
West Virginia Department of Education
1900 Kanawha Boulevard E
Building 6, Room B-358
Charleston, WV 25305-0330
304-558-2681
Fax: 304-558-0048
http://www.wvde.state.wv.us
The constitutional mission is to provide supervision of the K-12 education system.

David Stewart, Superintendent
Audrey Horne, President

Wisconsin

431 Division for Learning Support: Equity & Advocacy
Wisconsin Department of Education
125 S Webster Street
PO Box 7841
Madison, WI 53707-7841
608-266-3390
800-441-4563
Fax: 608-267-3746
http://dpi.wi.gov

Tony Evers, Superintendent
Carolyn Stanford-Taylor, Division Director

432 Instructional Services Division
Wisconsin Department of Education
125 S Webster Street
PO Box 7841
Madison, WI 53707-7841
608-266-3390
800-441-4563
Fax: 608-267-3746
http://dpi.wi.gov

Tony Evers, Superintendent
Pauline Nikolay, Division Director

433 Library Services Division
Wisconsin Department of Education
2109 S. Stoughton Road
PO Box 7841
Madison, WI 53707-7841
608-266-3390
800-441-4563
Fax: 608-267-3746
http://dpi.wi.gov

Tony Evers, Superintendent
William Wilson, Division Director

3434 School Financial Resources & Management
Wisconsin Department of Education
125 S Webster Street
PO Box 7841
Madison, WI 53707-7841
608-266-3390
800-441-4563
Fax: 608-267-3746
http://dpi.wi.gov

Tony Evers, Superintendent
Bambi Statz, Division Director

3435 Wisconsin College System Technical
Wisconsin Department of Education
125 S Webster Street
PO Box 7841
Madison, WI 53707-7841
608-266-3390
800-441-4563
Fax: 608-266-1285
E-mail: wtcsb@board.tec.wi.us
http://dpi.wi.gov

Tony Evers, Superintendent
Richard Carpenter, President

3436 Wisconsin Department of Public Instruction
Wisconsin Department of Education
125 S Webster Street
PO Box 7841
Madison, WI 53707-7841
608-266-3390
800-441-4563
Fax: 608-266-5188
E-mail: statesuperintendent@dpi.wi.gov
http://www.dpi.wi.gov

Tony Evers, Superintendent
Mike Thompson, Deputy State Superintendent

Wyoming

3437 Accounting, Personnel & School Finance Unit
Wyoming Department of Education
2300 Capitol Avenue
Hathaway Building, 2nd Floor
Cheyenne, WY 82002-2060
307-777-7675
Fax: 307-777-6234
http://edu.wyoming.gov

Ron Micheli, Chairman
Barry Nimmo, Division Director

3438 Applied Data & Technology Unit
Wyoming Department of Education
2300 Capitol Avenue
Hathaway Building, 2nd Floor
Cheyenne, WY 82002-2060
307-777-7675
Fax: 307-777-6234
http://edu.wyoming.gov

Ron Micheli, Chairman
Steven King, Division Director

3439 Services for Individuals with Hearing Loss
Wyoming Department of Education
2300 Capitol Avenue
Hathaway Building, 2nd Floor
Cheyenne, WY 82002-2060
307-777-7675
Fax: 307-777-6234
http://edu.wyoming.gov

Ron Micheli, Chairman
Tim Sanger, Division Director

3440 Support Programs & Quality Results Division
Wyoming Department of Education
2300 Capitol Avenue
Hathaway Building, 2nd Floor
Cheyenne, WY 82002-2060
307-777-7675
Fax: 307-777-6234
http://edu.wyoming.gov

Ron Micheli, Chairman
Dr. Alan Sheinker, Division Director

3441 Wyoming Department of Education
Wyoming Department of Education
2300 Capitol Avenue
Hathaway Building, 2nd Floor
Cheyenne, WY 82002-2060
307-777-7675
Fax: 307-777-6234
http://edu.wyoming.gov

Dr.Trent Blankenship, Superintendent
Ron Micheli, Chairman

Associations

3442 Agency for Instructional Technology
Agency for Instructional Technology
8111 N. Lee Paul Road
Box A
Bloomington, IN 47404-7916
812-339-2203
800-457-4509
Fax: 812-333-4218
E-mail: info@ait.net
http://www.ait.net
AIT's mission is to be the premier provider of services and products to enhance student learning. A nonprofit organization and is one of the largest providers of instructional TV programs in North America.

Robert E. Yocum, President and CEO
Cynthia M. Mosca, Director

3443 American Association for Higher Education & Accreditation
2020 Pennsylvania Avenue NW
#975
Washington, DC 20006
202-293-6440
Fax: 877-510-4240
E-mail: admin@aahea.org
http://www.aahea.org
The individual membership organization that promotes the changes higher education must make to ensure its effectiveness in a complex, interconnected world. The association equips individuals and institutions committed to such changes with the knowledge they need to bring those changes about.

Jose Luis Gomez, President
Ken Rabac, International Director

3444 American Association of Colleges for Teacher Education
1307 New York Avenue NW
Suite 300
Washington, DC 20005
202-293-2450
Fax: 202-457-8095
E-mail: aacte@aacte.org
http://www.aacte.org
A national alliance of educator preparation programs dedicated to the highest quality professional development of teachers and school leaders in order to enhance PK-12 student learning.

Sharon P Robinson, President/CEO
Jerry Wirth, Chief Operating Officer

3445 American Educational Research Association
1430 K Street NW
Suite 1200
Washington, DC 20005
202-238-3200
Fax: 202-238-3250
E-mail: flevine@aera.net
http://www.aera.net
Supports improvement of the educational process through the encouragement of scholarly inquiry related to education, the dissemination of research results, and their practical application. Holds a conference and publishes books, videos, and magazines.

Joyce E. King, President
Felice J Levine PhD, Executive Director

3446 American Educational Studies Association
Department of Education
235 Morton Hall
Huntsville, AL 35899
330-972-7111
http://www.educationalstudies.org
An international learned society for students, teachers, research scholars, and administrators who are interested in the foundations of education. A society primarily comprised of college and university professors who teach and research in the field of education utilizing one or more of the liberal arts disciplines of philosophy, history, politics, sociology, anthropology, or economics as well as comparative/international and cultural studies.

Audrey Thompson, President
Susan Laird, Vice President

3447 American Foundation for Negro Affairs
117 S 17th Street
Suite 1200
Philadelphia, PA 19103-5011
215-854-1470
Fax: 215-854-1487
Offers a model for educational programs preparing minority students for professional careers.

Samuel L Evans, President

3448 American Society for Training and Development Information Center
1640 King Street
Box 1443
Alexandria, VA 22313-1443
703-683-8100
800-628-2783
Fax: 703-683-8103
E-mail: customercare@astd.org
http://www.td.org
Dedicated to workplace learning and performance professionals. Members come from more than 100 countries and connect locally in more than 130 U.S. chapters and with more than 30 international partners.

Charles Fred, Chair
Tony Bingham, President and CEO

3449 Association of Teacher Educators
11350 Random Hills Rd.
Suite 800, PMB 6
Fairfax, VA 22030-2407
703-659-1708
Fax: 703-595-4792
E-mail: info@ate1.org
http://www.ate1.org
The mission of the Association of Teacher Educators is to improve the effectiveness of teacher education through leadership in the development of quality programs to prepare teachers, by analyzing issues and practices relating to professional development, and by providing opportunities for the personal and professional growth of Association members.

Emma Savage-Davis, President
Sandy Brownscombe, Board Representative

3450 Center for Rural Studies
University of Vermont
206 Morrill Hall
146 University Place
Burlington, VT 05405
802-656-3021
Fax: 802-656-1423
E-mail: crs@uvm.edu
http://www.uvm.edu/crs

A nonprofit, fee-for-service research and resource center that works with people and communities to address social, economic, and resource-based challenges. CRS supports the research and teaching missions of the university through its work in applied research, community outreach, program evaluation, and consulting services.

Fred Schmidt, Founder/Director Emeritus
Jane Kolodinsky, Director

3451 Committee on Continuing Education for School Personnel
Kean College of New Jersey
Academic Services
Union, NJ 07083
908-737-5326
Fax: 908-737-5845
Develops activities for professional and personal growth among teachers and educators.

George Sisko, Director

3452 Council for Learning Disabilities
11184 Antioch Road
PO Box 405
Overland Park, KS 66210
913-491-1011
Fax: 913-491-1012
E-mail: CLDInfo@ie-events.com
http://www.cldinternational.org
An international organization that promotes evidence-based teaching, collaboration, research, leadership, and advocacy. Comprised of professionals who represent diverse disciplines and are committed to enhancing the education and quality of life for individuals with learning disabilities and others who experience challenges in learning.

Silvana Watson, President
Mary Beth Calhoon, Vice President

3453 Council of Administrators of Special Education
Osigian Office Centre
101 Katelyn Circle, Suite E
Warner Robins, GA 31088
478-333-6892
Fax: 478-333-2453
E-mail: lpurcell@casecec.org
http://www.casecec.org
An international professional educational organization which is affiliated with the Council for Exceptional Children (CEC) whose members are dedicated to the enhancement of the worth, dignity, potential, and uniqueness of each individual in society.

Dr. Mary Lynn Boscardin, President
Julie Bost, Secretary

3454 Distance Education & Training Council
1601 18th Street NW
Suite 2
Washington, DC 20009
202-234-5100
Fax: 202-332-1386
E-mail: info@deac.org
http://www.deac.org
A voluntary, non-governmental, educational organization that was founded to promote sound educational standards and ethical business practices within the correspondence field.

Leah K. Matthews, Executive Director
Sally R. Welch, Associate Director

3455 ERIC Clearinghouse on Teaching and Teacher Education
American Association of Colleges for Teacher Ed.
1307 New York Avenue NW
Suite 300
Washington, DC 20005-4701
202-293-2450
Fax: 202-457-8095

E-mail: aacte@aacte.org
http://www.aacte.org
To promote the learning of all PK-12 students through high-quality, evidence-based preparation and continuing education for all school personnel.

Mary Dilworth, Director
Deborah Newby, Associate Director

456 Educational Leadership Institute
4301 Connecticut Ave NW
Suite 100
Washington, DC 20008
202-822-8405
Fax: 202-822-8405
E-mail: iel@iel.org
http://www.iel.org
A non-profit, nonpartisan organization that envisions a society that uses its resources effectively to achieve better futures for all children and youth. IEL's mission continues to be to build the capacity of individuals and organizations in education and related fields to work together, across policies, programs and sectors.

S. Decker Anstrom, Chair
June Atkinson, Superintendent

457 International Council on Education for Teaching
National-Louis University
1000 Capitol Drive
Wheeling, IL 60090
847-947-5881
Fax: 847-947-5881
E-mail: contact@icet4u.org
http://icet4u.org
An international association of policy and decision-makers in education, government and business dedicated to global development through education. ICET provides programs and services that give its members access to a worldwide resource base of organizations, programs, specialized consultative services and research and training opportunities at the university level.

Maria Assuncao Flores, Chairman
James O'Meara, President

458 National Association of State Directors of Teacher Education & Certification
1629 K Street, NW
Suite 300
Washington, DC 20006
202-204-2208
Fax: 202-204-2210
E-mail: rje@nasdtec.com
http://www.nasdtec.org
The organization that represents professional standards boards and commissions and state departments of education in all 50 states, the District of Columbia, the Department of Defense Education Activity, the U.S. Territories, Alberta, British Columbia, and Ontario that are responsible for the preparation, licensure, and discipline of educational personnel.

D. T. Magee, President
Elisabeth Keller, Vice President

459 National Center for Community Education
1017 Avon Street
Flint, MI 48503-2797
810-238-0463
800-811-1105
Fax: 810-238-9211
E-mail: info@nccenet.org
http://www.nccenet.org
It is the mission of the National Center for Community Education to promote commu-

nity and educational change emphasizing community schools by providing state-of-the-art leadership development, training and technical assistance.

Maxine Murray, Operations Director
Marion Baldwin, Chief Administrator

3460 National Middle School Association
4151 Executive Parkway
Suite 300
Westerville, OH 43081
614-895-4730
800-528-6672
Fax: 614-895-4750
E-mail: info@amle.org
http://www.amle.org
NMSA has been a voice for those committed to the educational and developmental needs of young adolescents. NMSA is the only national education association dedicated exclusively to those in the middle level grades.

Ashley Smith, President
William D. Waidelich, EdD, Executive Director

3461 National Staff Development Council
504 S Locust Street
Oxford, OH 45056
513-523-6029
800-727-7288
Fax: 513-523-0638
E-mail: office@learningforward.org
http://learningforward.org
The largest non-profit professional association committed to ensuring success for all students through staff development and school improvement. The purpose of the NSDC is that every educator engages in effective professional learning every day so every student achieves.

Deborah Renee Jackson, President
Scott Laurence, Superintendent

3462 National Women's Studies Association
11 E Mount Royal Ave
Suite 100
Baltimore, MD 21202
410-528-0355
Fax: 410-528-0357
E-mail: nwsaoffice@nwsa.org
http://www.nwsa.org
A professional organization dedicated to leading the field of women's studies and gender studies, as well as its teaching, learning, research and service wherever they be found.

Vivian M. May, President
Nana Osei-Kofi, Vice President

3463 Recruiting New Teachers
385 Concord Avenue
Suite 103
Belmont, MA 02478-3037
617-489-6000
800-45 -EACH
Fax: 617-489-6005
E-mail: rnt@rnt.org
http://www.rnt.org/channels/clearinghouse
Conducts public service advertising campaign encouraging people to consider teaching careers.

Mildred Hudson, CEO

3464 Search Associates
PO Box 636
Dallas, PA 18612-636
570-696-4600
Fax: 570-696-9500
E-mail: SearchCentralHQ@cs.com
http://www.search-associates.com
Each year Search Associates places over 1,500 teachers, administrators and interns in

international schools throughout the world, making us the largest of the International School placement organizations. However, it is our personalized approach to the schools and candidates we serve which we would most like to emphasize.

John Magagna, Founding Director
Robert Barlas, Senior Associate

Awards & Honors

3465 Apple Education Grants
Apple Computer
1 Infinite Loop
Cupertino, CA 95014
408-996-1010
800-800-2775
Fax: 512-919-2992
http://www.apple.com
Awarded each year to teams of K-12 educators working on educational technology plans. Potential awardees find innovative uses of technology in the classroom and come from schools that would otherwise have limited access to technology.

3466 Bayer/NSF Award for Community Innovation
105 Terry Drive
Suite 120
Newtown, PA 18940
215-579-8590
800-291-6020
Fax: 215-579-8589
E-mail: success@edumedia.com
A community-based science and technology competition to give all sixth, seventh and eighth-graders a hands-on experience with real-world problems using the scientific method.

Stephanie Hallman, Program Manager
Stacey Gall, Competition Coordinator

3467 Excellence in Teaching Cabinet Grant
Curriculm Associates
PO Box 2001
North Billerica, MA 01862
800-225-0248
Fax: 800-366-1158
Awarded to educators who wish to implement unique educational projects. Potential awardees propose projects using a variety of teaching tools, including technology and print.

3468 Magna Awards
American School Board Journal
1680 Duke Street
Alexandria, VA 22314
703-838-6722
http://www.asbj.com
A national recognition program co-sponsored by American School Board Journal, the National School Boards Association, and Sodexo School Services that honors school board best practices and innovative programs that advance student learning.

Thomas J Gentzel, Publisher
Kathleen Vail, Managing Editor

3469 NSTA Fellow Award
National Science Teachers Association
1840 Wilson Boulevard
Arlington, VA 22201
703-243-7100
Fax: 703-243-7177
http://www.nsta.org
This award recognizes NSTA members who have made extraordinary contributions to science education through personal commit-

ment to education, specifically science teaching or science; educational endeavors and original work that position recipients as exemplary leaders in their field; significant contributions to the profession that reflect dedication to NSTA as well the entire educational community.

Dr. Julianaÿ Texley, President
David L. Evans, Executive Director

3470 NSTA Legacy Award

National Science Teachers Association
1840 Wilson Boulevard
Arlington, VA 22201
703-243-7100
Fax: 703-243-7177
http://www.nsta.org
This NSTA award posthumously recognizes long-standing members of NSTA for significant lifelong service to NSTA and contributions to science education.

Dr. Julianaÿ Texley, President
David L. Evans, Executive Director

3471 National Teachers Hall of Fame

National Teachers Hall of Fame
1200 Commercial
Box 4017
Emporia, KS 66801
620-341-5660
800-968-3224
Fax: 620-341-5912
E-mail: hallfame@emporia.edu
http://www.nthf.org
The mission of The National Teachers Hall of Fame is to recognize and honor exceptional career teachers, encourage excellence in teaching, and preserve the rich heritage of the teaching profession in the United States.

Roberts T Jones, President
Dr Anne L Bryant, Executive Director

3472 Presidential Awards for Excellence in Mathematics and Science Teaching

National Science Foundation
4201 Wilson Boulevard
Arlington, VA 22230
703-292-8620
Fax: 703-292-9044
E-mail: msaul@nsf.gov
http://www.ehr.nsf.gov
This award is the nation's highest commendation for K-12 math and science teachers. Approximately 108 teachers are recognized annually with this prestigious award.

Mark Saul, Director

3473 Senior Researcher Award

Music Education Research Council
Deptartment of Music
138 Fine Arts Center
Columbia, MO 65211
573-884-1604
Fax: 573-884-7444
For recognition of a significant scholarly achievement maintained over a period of years.

3474 Toyota Tapestry Grants for Teachers

National Science Teachers Association
1840 Wilson Boulevard
Arlington, VA 22201
703-243-7100
Fax: 703-243-7177
http://www.nsta.org

Awards 50 grants of up to $10,000 each to K-12 teachers of science in the fields of environmental science education.

Dr. Julianaÿ Texley, President
David L. Evans, Executive Director

Conferences

3475 AASA National Conference on Education

American Association of School Administrators
1615 Duke Street
Suite 700
Alexandria, VA 22314-1730
703-528-0700
Fax: 703-841-1543
E-mail: info@aasa.org
http://www.aasa.org
Where America's school leaders go for a vision of the future in public education; to explore new thinking, new products, new services and new technologies.

February

Daniel A Domenech, Executive Director
Christopher Daw, Meetings Director

3476 ACE Fellows Program

American Council on Education
One Dupont Circle NW
Washington, DC 20036-1193
202-939-9300
E-mail: fellows@ace.nche.edu
http://www.acenet.edu
The nation's premier higher education leadership development program in preparing senior leaders to serve American colleges and universities. Enables participants to immerse themselves in the culture, policies, and decision-making processes of another institution.

Jim Sirianni, Director
Deborahÿ IngramÿAllen, Program Coordinator

3477 AFT Convention

American Federation of Teachers
AFL-CIO
555 New Jersey Avenue NW
Washington, DC 20001
202-879-4400
E-mail: online@aft.org
http://www.aft.org
The AFT represents one million teachers, school support staff, higher education faculty and staff, health care professionals, and state and municipal employees. AFT is an affiliated international union of the AFL-CIO.

Randi Weingarten, President
Mary Cathryn Ricker, Executive Vice President

3478 Alaska Department of Education Bilingual& Bicultural Education Conference

University of Alaska, Conference & Special Events
117 Eielson Building
Fairbanks, AK 99775-7680
907-474-7436
Fax: 907-474-6586
http://www.uaf.edu/anla/contact-us/
Stresses the importance of literacy and multicultural education for Alaskan educators.

February

Gary Holton, Director

3479 American Association of Collegiate Registrars & Admissions Officers

American Assoc of Collegiate Registrars/Admissions
1 Dupont Circle NW
Suite 520
Washington, DC 20036
202-293-9161
Fax: 202-872-8857
E-mail: meetings@aacrao.org
http://www.aacrao.org
Provides the opportunity to reflect on where the association has been, where it currently stands, and what we can do to lead our colleagues, our students, and our institutions into the future.

March

Brad Myers, President
Nicole Rovig, Vice President

3480 American Society for Training & Development International Conference & Exposition

American Society for Training & Development
1640 King Street
Box 1443
Alexandria, VA 22314-1443
703-683-8100
800-628-2783
Fax: 703-683-8103
E-mail: customercare@td.org
http://www.td.org
This premier event for workplace learning and performance professionals welcomes attendees from more than 70 countries. The conference features 200+ educational sessions from industry leading experts, and a world-class EXPO filled with the latest products and services available from top suppliers.

Annual/May

Charles Fred, Chair
Tony Bingham, President/CEO

3481 Annual Building Championship Schools Conference

Center for Peak Performing Schools
2021 Clubhouse Drive
Greeley, CO 80634
970-339-9277
Interested in curriculum development and instructional assessment. Members include administrators at all levels of education.

February

3482 Annual New England Kindergarten Conference

Lesley University
29 Everett Street
Cambridge, MA 02138
617-349-8544
800-999-1959
Fax: 617-349-8125
E-mail: hr@lesley.edu
http://www.lesley.edu
Committed to active learning, scholarly research, critical inquiry, and diverse forms of artistic practice through close mentoring relationships among students, faculty, and practitioners in the field

November
1000 attendees

Mary Mindess, Conference Coordinator
Kari Nygaard, Conference Manager

3483 Annual State Convention of Association of Texas Professional Educators

Association of Texas Professional Educators
305 E Huntland Drive
Suite 300
Austin, TX 78752
800-777-2873
Fax: 512-467-2203

E-mail: info@atpe.org
http://www.atpe.org
A member-owned, member-governed professional association with more than 112,000 members leading educators' association in the state and the largest independent association for public school educators in the nation.

March
100 booths with 1,300 attendees

Richard Wiggins, President
Cory Colby, Vice President

484 Association for Educational Communications & Technology Annual Convention
Assoc for Educational Communications & Technology
320 W. 8th St.ÿ
Suite 101
Bloomington, IN 47404-3745
812-335-7675
Fax: 812-335-7678
E-mail: aect@aect.org
http://www.aect.org
Provide leadership in educational communications and technology by linking a wide range of professionals holding a common interest in the use of educational technology and its application learning process.

November

Stephen Harmon, President
Ellen Hoffman, Executive Secretary

485 Association for Library & Information Science Education Annual Conference
ALISE
2150 N 107th St
Suite 205
Seattle, WA 98133-7246
206-209-5267
Fax: 206-367-8777
E-mail: office@alise.org
http://www.alise.org
Promotes excellence in education for library and information sciences as a means of increasing library services.

January

Clara Chu, President
Samantha K. Hastings, Vice President

486 Association of Teacher Educators Annual Meeting
Association of Teacher Educators
PO Box 793
Manassas, VA 20113
703-659-1708
Fax: 703-595-4792
E-mail: info@ate1.org
http://www.ate1.org

February

Emma Savage-Davis, President
David A Ritchey, Executive Director

487 CASE Annual Convention
Colorado Association of School Executives
4101 S Bannock Street
Englewood, CO 80110-4606
303-762-8762
Fax: 303-762-8697
E-mail: case@co-case.org
http://www.co-case.org

July

Bruce Caughey, Executive Director
Melissa Gibson, Director

3488 CCAE/COABE National Conference
California Council for Adult Education
19332 Peachtree Lane
PO Box 978
Los Alamitos, CA 90720
626-825-9363
888-542-2231
Fax: 866-941-5129
E-mail: membership@ccaestate.org
http://www.ccaestate.org

April
1200 attendees

Lariann Torrez, President
Adriana Sanchez-Aldana, Executive Director

3489 CSBA Education Conference & Trade Show
California School Boards Association
3100 Beacon Boulevard
West Sacramento, CA 95691
800-266-3382
Fax: 916-371-3407
E-mail: dfernandes@csba.org
http://www.csba.org
Premier continuing education program - delivering practical solutions to help governance teams from districts and county offices of education improve student learning and achievement.

Annual/December
200 booths

Jesus Holguin, President
Sherri Reusche, Vice President

3490 California Kindergarten Conference and PreConference Institute
California Kindergarten Association
1014 Chippendale Way
Roseville, CA 95661
916-780-5331
Fax: 916-780-5330
E-mail: cka@ckanet.org
http://www.ckanet.org
The original conference for teachers by teachers.

January
120 booths with 2,000 attendees and 100 exhibits

Ada Hand, President
Debra Weller, President

3491 Careers Conference
University of Wisconsin-Madison
Center on Education & Work
1025 W Johnson Street, Room 964
Madison, WI 53706-1796
608-265-6700
800-862-1071
Fax: 608-262-3063
E-mail: cewmail@cew.wisc.edu
http://www.cew.wisc.edu
Designed to serve everyone and anyone who is involved with career development, careers education, and related fields. This national conference presents learning opportunities at all levels, from a basic introduction for those starting out. to the very latest practices, strategies, and resources for those who are advanced in the field.

Annual/Januaray
40 booths with 1500 attendees

Carol Edds, Conference Manager
Ross Benbow, Staff

3492 Center for Play Therapy Fall Conference
University of North Texas
425 S. Welch St.
Complex 2
Denton, TX 76203-0829

940-565-3864
Fax: 940-565-4461
E-mail: cpt@unt.edu
http://cpt.unt.edu
Features a one day workshop led by a recognized authority in the field of play therapy. This workshop enables professionals in the field of mental health to broaden their knowledge and clinical skills in play therapy.

Annual/October
350 attendees

Sue Bratton, Director
Alyssa Swan, Staff

3493 Central States Conference on the Teaching of Foreign Languages
Central States Conference on the Teaching
7141A Ida Red Road
PO Box 251
Egg Harbor, WI 54209-0251
414-405-4645
Fax: 920-868-1682
E-mail: csctfl@aol.com
http://www.csctfl.org
Includes approximately 140 workshops and sessions presented by world language teachers at all levels of instruction. Serves Arkansas, Colorado, Illinois, Indiana, Iowa, Kansas, Kentucky, Michigan, Minnesota, Missouri, Nebraska, North Dakota, Ohio, Oklahoma, South Dakota, Tennessee and Wisconsin.

Annual/March

Vickie Scow, Chair
Mary Goodwin, Vice Chair

3494 Chicago Principals Association Education Conference
221 N Lasalle Street
Suite 3316
Chicago, IL 60601-1505
312-263-7767
Fax: 312-263-2012
Educational or fund raising products including copy machines, computers, book companies, etc.

February

Beverly Tunney, Conference Coordinator

3495 Classroom Connect
6277 Sea Harbor Drive
Orlando, FL 32887
800-638-1639
888-801-8299
Fax: 650-351-5300
E-mail: help@classroom.com
http://www.classroom.com
A leading provider of professional development programs and online instructional content for K-12 education.

October

Jim Bowler, President
Melinda Cook, Vice President Sales

3496 Florida Elementary School Principals Association Conference
206 S Monroe Street
Suite B
Tallahassee, FL 32301-1801
800-593-3626
Fax: 850-224-3892
Exhibitors from fundraisers to computer companies.

November
50 booths

Lisa Begue, Conference Coordinator

3497 Florida School Administrators Association Summer Conference
Florida Association of School Administrators
206B S. Monroe St.
Tallahassee, FL 32301
850-224-3626
800-593-3626
Fax: 850-224-3892
http://www.fasa.net
Exhibits include computer software, textbooks and school supplies, fundraising companies, schoolyear book and ring companies, video and audio companies, furniture suppliers and other school related products.

Annual/July

Bob Jones, President
Mark Shanoff, President

3498 Florida Vocational Association Conference
1420 N Paul Russell Road
Tallahassee, FL 32301-4835
850-878-6860
Fax: 850-878-5476
Curriculum materials, industrial equipment and supplies, computer hardware and software, medical equipment and other materials utilized by vocational educators.

July
150 booths

Donna Harper, Conference Coordinator

3499 Foundation for Critical Thinking Annual Conference
PO Box 196
Tomales, CA 94971
707-878-9100
800-833-3645
Fax: 707-878-9111
E-mail: cct@criticalthinking.org
http://www.criticalthinking.org
Provides a unique opportunity to improve understanding of critical thinking, as well as one's ability to foster it in the classroom and other aspects in work/life.

July-August
1200 attendees

Dr. Richard Paul, Fellow
Dr. Linda Elder, Fellow

3500 IASB Convention
Iowa Association of School Boards
6000 Grand Avenue
Des Moines, IA 50312-1417
515-288-1991
800-795-4272
Fax: 515-243-4992
http://www.ia-sb.org
IASB is an organization of elected school board members dedicated to assisting school boards in achieving their goal of excellence and equity in public education.

Annual/November

LouAnn Gvist, Convention Director
Veronica Stalker, Interim Executive Director

3501 IASB Joint Annual Conference
Illinois Association of School Boards
2921 Baker Drive
Springfield, IL 62703-5929
217-528-9688
http://www.iasb.com
Recognized as one of the nation's largest state education conferences, the event was open to local school board members, superintendents and secretaries, school administrators, state and regional educators and officials, school attorneys, university professors, exhibitors, and guests.

November
235 booths with 9500+ attendees

Roger L. Eddy, Executive Director
Ben Schwarm, Deputy Executive Director

3502 IASSIST Annual Conference
Int'l Assoc for Social Science Info Service & Tech
405 Hilgard Avenue
Attn: Wendy Treadwell
Los Angeles, CA 90095-9000
612-624-4389
Fax: 612-626-9353
E-mail: melanie@essex.ac.uk
http://www.iassistdata.org
IASSIST is an international organization of professionals working with information technology and data services to support research and teaching in the social sciences. Its 300 members work in a variety of settings, including data archives, statistical agencies, research centers, libraries, academic departments, government departments, and non-profit organizations.

May-June

Bill Block, President
Tuomas J. Alatera, Vice President

3503 ISBA/IAPSS Annual Conference
Indiana School Board Association
1 N Capitol Avenue
Suite 1215
Indianapolis, IN 46204-2225
317-639-0330
Fax: 317-639-3591
E-mail: mwagers@isba-ind.org
http://www.isba-ind.org
Jointy sponsored by the Indiana School Boards Association and Indiana Association of Public School Superintendents. A comprehensive program, designed by the ISBA and IAPPS, that brings the latest information and some of the most informed experts on current topics in education.

Fall

Sally Krouse, President
Bill Wilson, Vice President

3504 Illinois Assistant Principals Conference
Illinois Principals Association
2940 Baker Drive
Springfield, IL 62703
217-525-1383
Fax: 217-525-7264
E-mail: support@ilprincipals.org
http://www.il-ilprincipals.org
Where assistant principals and deans attend annually to hear outstanding educational leaders; participate in educational sessions and to network with colleagues across the state

Annual/February
120 booths with 200 attendees

Jason Leahy, Executive Director
Jean Smith, Professional Development Dir

3505 Illinois Resource Center Conference of Teachers of Linguistically Diverse Students
Illinois Resource Center
2626 Clearbrook Drive
Arlington Heights, IL 60005-4626
224-366-8555
Fax: 847-649-0551
http://www.thecenterweb.org/irc/

A conference that caters to those educators involved with teaching multi-licensed pupils.

March

3506 Iowa Council Teachers of Math Conference
Iowa Council of Teachers of Mathematics
1712 55th Street
Des Moines, IA 50310-1548
515-242-7846
http://www.iowamath.org
Math teachers conference.

Annual/February
48 booths

Megan Balong, President
Maureen Busta, Executive Secretary

3507 Iowa Reading Association Conference
Iowa Reading Association
512 Lynn Avenue
Ames, IA 50014-7320
712-754-3636
E-mail: jneal@jefferson0scranton.k12.ia.us
http://www.iowareading.org
Nationally prominent speakers, published authors, and experienced instructors will anchor the conference, sharing current research and creative reading strategies.

Annual/April

Deb Mortensen, President
Nancy White, Conference Chair

3508 KSBA Annual Conference
Kentucky School Boards Association
260 Democrat Drive
Frankfort, KY 40601
800-372-2962
Fax: 502-695-5451
http://www.ksba.org

February

Allen Kennedy, President
Mike Armstrong, Executive Director

3509 Kansas School Boards Association Conference
1420 SW Arrowhead Road
Topeka, KS 66604-4024
785-273-3600
800-432-2471
Fax: 785-273-7580
E-mail: ahartzell@kasb.org
http://www.kasb.org
Wide variety of school district vendors and contacts for products and services.

December
70 booths

Dennis Depew, President
Frank Henderson, President-Elect

3510 Kentucky School Superintendents Association Meeting
152 Consumer Lane
Frankfort, KY 40601
502-875-3411
800-928-5272
Fax: 502-875-4634
E-mail: webmaster@kasa.org
http://www.kasa.org
KASA is dedicated to serving school administrators throughout Kentucky through advocacy, professional development, research and leadership.

June
36 booths

Dr. Roland Haun, Conference Contact
Wayne Young, Executive Director

3511 LSBA Convention
Louisiana School Boards Association
7912 Summa Avenue
Baton Rouge, LA 70809

225-769-3191
877-664-5722
Fax: 225-769-6108
http://www.lsba.com
Annual/March

John Smith, President
Russ Wise, Vice President

512 Lilly Conference on College Teaching

Miami University
317 Laws Hall
551 East High St.
Oxford, OH 45056
513-529-9266
Fax: 513-529-9984
E-mail: lillycon@miamioh.edu
http://www.units.muohio.edu/lillycon
One of the nation's most renowned conferences presenting the scholarship of teaching and learning. Teacher-scholars from across the U.S. and internationally gather to share innovative pedagogies and discuss questions, challenges, and insights about teaching and learning.

Annual/November
660 attendees

Melody Barton, Administrative Associate
Milton Cox, Conference Director

513 MASB Annual Fall Conference

Michigan Association of School Boards
1001 Centennial Way
Suite 400
Lansing, MI 48917-8249
517-327-5900
Fax: 517-327-0775
E-mail: info@masb.org
http://www.masb.org
The premier leadership event that features nationally acclaimed speakers addressing current education topics.

October
110 booths with 500 attendees and 110 exhibits

Kathy Hayes, Executive Director
Nanette Pearson, Chief Financial Officer

514 MESPA Spring Conference

Massachusetts Elementary School Principals Assoc
28 Lord Road
Suite 125
Marlborough, MA 01752
508-624-0500
Fax: 508-485-9965
E-mail: mespa@mespa.org
http://www.mespa.org
Features nationally-known speakers, numerous workshops on relevant topics, awards presentation, and an outstanding exhibition of school-related vendors.

Annual/May
100 booths

Jennifer Chapin, President
Kirk Downing, Vice President

515 MNEA Fall Conference

Missouri National Education Association
1810 E Elm Street
Jefferson City, MO 65101
573-634-3202
800-392-0236
Fax: 573-634-5646
E-mail: chris.guinther@mnea.org
http://www.mnea.org

Free and open to the public. Includes workshops, exhibits and features a keynote address presented by Diane Ravitch
Annual/November
95 booths with 1,500 attendees

Charles Smith, President
Brent Fullington, Vice President

3516 MSBA Annual Conference

Missouri School Boards Association
2100 I-70 Drive SW
Columbia, MO 65203
800-221-6722
Fax: 573-445-9981
E-mail: info@msbanet.org
http://www.msbanet.org
September/October
125 booths

Dr Carter Ward, Executive Director
Jaime Fessler, Conference/Events Manager

3517 Maine Principals Association Conference

50 Industrial Drive
PO Box 2468
Augusta, ME 04330-2468
207-622-0217
Fax: 207-622-1513
E-mail: mpa@mpa.cc
http://www.mpa.cc
To assure a quality education for all students, promote the principalship

April

Barbara Proko, Conference Contact
Mary Martin, President

3518 Massachusetts School Boards Association Meeting

One Mckinley Square
Boston, MA 02109-1650
617-523-8454
800-392-6023
http://www.masc.org
May
100 booths

Capt. Edward Bryant, NCCC, Conference Contact
Glen Koocher, Executive Director

3519 Michigan Association of Elementary and Middle School Principals Conference

1980 N College Road
Mason, MI 48854
517-694-8955
Fax: 517-694-8945
http://www.memspa.org
Exhibits offer books, fundraisers, camps, insurance groups and non-profit organizations.

October
100 booths

William Hays, Jr, Conference Contact

3520 Michigan Science Teachers Association Annual Conference

Michigan Science Teachers Association
1390 Eisenhower Place
Ann Arbor, MI 48108
734-973-0433
Fax: 734-677-3287
E-mail: cchopp@kamsc.k12.mi.us
http://www.msta-mich.org
A conference that aims to supply science teachers with information and research.

February

Charles Bucienski, President
Robby Cramer, Executive Director

3521 Mid-South Educational Research Association Annual Meeting

Louisiana State University, School of Dentistry
1100 Florida Avenue
#223
New Orleans, LA 70119-2714
504-619-8700
Fax: 504-619-8740
http://www.dtm10.cep.msstate.edu/
Focuses on assessment and involvement in education by releasing research and statistics.

November

Diana Gardiner PhD, Conference Contact

3522 Middle States Council for the Social Studies Annual Regional Conference

P.O Box 1196
Savona, NY 14879
717-865-2117
http://www.mscssonline.org
Seeks to develop and implement new curriculum into the social studies area.

April

Dan Sidelnick, Conference Contact
Rebecca Herndon, President

3523 Minnesota Leadership Annual Conference

Minnesota School Boards Association
1900 W Jefferson Avenue
Saint Peter, MN 56082-3015
507-934-2450
800-324-4459
Fax: 507-931-1515
E-mail: gabbott@mnmsba.org
http://www.mnmsba.org
The purpose of the Association is to support, promote and enhance the work of public school boards

January
200+ booths with 2,000+ attendees

Kevin Donovan, President
Kirk Schneidawind, Executive Director

3524 Minnesota School Administrators Association

1884 Como Avenue
Saint Paul, MN 55108-2715
651-645-6272
866-444-5251
Fax: 651-645-7518
E-mail: members@mnasa.org
http://www.mnasa.org
MASA's Educational Leaderswill establish the statewide agenda for children, serve as the preeminent voice for public education and empower members through quality services and support.

October
70 booths

Gary Amoroso, Executive Director
Mia Urick, Director of Communications

3525 Minnesota School Boards Association Annual Meeting

1900 W Jefferson Street
Saint Peter, MN 56082-3015
507-934-2450
800-324-4459
Fax: 507-931-1515
http://www.mnmsba.org
School supplies and services as diverse as buses and architectural services.

January
190 booths

Mike Torkelson, Conference Contact
Kent Thiesse, President

3526 Missouri State Teachers Association Conference

PO Box 458
Columbia, MO 65205-458
573-442-3127
800-392-0532
Fax: 573-443-5079
E-mail: membercare@msta.org
http://www.msta.org
Educational materials.

November
280 booths

Kent King, Conference Contact

3527 Montana Association of Elementary School Principals Conference

1134 Butte Avenue
Helena, MT 59601-5178
406-442-2510
Fax: 406-442-2518

January/Febuary
20 booths

Loran Frazier, Conference Contact

3528 NAAEE Annual Conference

North American Assoc for Environmental Education
2000 P Street NW
Suite 540
Washington, DC 20036
202-419-0412
Fax: 202-419-0415
E-mail: communicator@naaee.org
http://www.naaee.org

October

Jose Marcos-Iga, President
Judy Braus, Executive Director

3529 NCASA Annual Conference

North Carolina Association of School Administrator
333 Fayetteville Street
Suite 1410
Raleigh, NC 27601
919-828-1426
Fax: 919-828-6099
E-mail: info@ncasa.net
http://www.ncasa.net
Delivers a powerful agenda packed with essential training and sessions led by key education leaders and political insiders in the state and nation.

March-April
40 booths

Rodney Shotwell, President
Katherine Joyce, Executive Director

3530 NCTM Annual Meeting & Exposition

National Council of Teachers of Mathematics
1906 Association Drive
Reston, VA 20191-1502
703-620-9840
800-235-7566
Fax: 703-476-2970
E-mail: nctm@nctm.org
http://www.nctm.org
Covers topics like differentiated instruction, common core standards, intervention, technology and more

April
650 booths with 18M attendees

Diane J. Briars, President
Bob Doucette, Executive Director

3531 NELMS Annual Conference

New England League of Middle Schools
120 Water Street
Suite 403
North Andover, MA 01983
978-557-9311
Fax: 978-557-9312
E-mail: nelms@nelms.org
http://www.nelms.org

April
160+ booths with 3800+ attendees

Esther Asbell, Chair
Brenda Needham, Executive Director

3532 NMSA Annual Education Conference & Exhibit

National Middle School Association
4151 Executive Parkway
Suite 300
Westerville, OH 43016
614-895-4730
800-528-6672
Fax: 614-895-4750
E-mail: info@amle.org
http://www.amle.org
Provides information, tools, and encouragement necessary to provide a high-quality education for every young adolescent.

November

Ashley Smith, President
William D. Waidelich, EdD, Executive Director

3533 NSBA Annual Confernce & Exposition

National School Boards Association
1680 Duke Street
Alexandria, VA 22314
703-838-6722
Fax: 703-683-7590
E-mail: info@nsba.org
http://www.nsba.org
The largest national gathering of elected officials and offers an impressive collection of professional development opportunities for school board members and other education leaders. Offers a great opportunity to improve leadership skills and learn what is happening in public education.

April
550 booths

Anne M. Byrne, President
Miranda A. Beard, Secretary-Treasurer

3534 NSTA National Conference

National Science Teachers Association
1840 Wilson Boulevard
Arlington, VA 22201
703-243-7100
Fax: 703-243-7177
E-mail: conferences@nsta.org
http://www.nsta.org

March

Dr. Julianaÿ Texley, President
David L. Evans, Executive Director

3535 NYSSBA Annual Convention & Expo

New York School Board Association
24 Century Hill Drive
Suite 200
Latham, NY 12210-2125
518-783-0200
Fax: 518-783-0211
E-mail: info@nyssba.org
http://www.nyssba.org
Join your fellow school board colleagues from all corners of the state for an unsurpassed opportunity to learn, network with peers, and hear about the latest products

and services impacting education at this all-important event.

October

Lynne L. Lenhardt, President
Timothy G. Kremer, Executive Director

3536 National Association of Secondary School Principals Annual Convention and Exposition

1904 Association Drive
Reston, VA 20191-1537
703-860-0200
800-253-7746
Fax: 703-476-5432
E-mail: membership@principals.org
http://www.nassp.org
Offers workshops for principals on leadership training, student personnel services, and how to deal with at-risk students. Convention highlights include more than 200 educational sessions, special interest forums and luncheons and spotlights on the latest education products and services.

Phoenix
March
290 booths

Gayle Mercer, Conference Contact

3537 National Association of State Boards of Education Conference

National Association of State Boards of Education
333 John Carlyle Street
Suite 530
Alexandria, VA 22314
703-684-4000
Fax: 703-836-2313
E-mail: boards@nasbe.org
http://www.nasbe.org
Aims are to study problems of mutual interest and concern, improve communication among state boards, and exchange and collect information concerning all aspects of education.

October
24 booths with 150 attendees

Jane Goff, President
Kristen Amundson, Executive Director

3538 National Career Development Association Conference

National Career Development Association
305 N Beech Circle
Broken Arrow, OK 74012
918-663-7060
866-367-6232
Fax: 918-663-7058
E-mail: webeditor@ncda.org
http://www.ncda.org

Mark Danaher, President
Deneen Pennington, Executive Director

3539 National Conference on Education

American Association of School Administrators
1615 Duke Street
Suite 700
Alexandria, VA 22314-1730
703-528-0700
E-mail: info@aasa.org
http://www.aasa.org
Rich with content about the issues and challenges in public education. Take this opportunity to hear recognized speakers discuss solutions, beest practices, challenges and more.

Annual/February

Molly O'Neill, Meetings Manager

3540 National Conference on Standards and Assessment

National School Conference Institute
Riviera Hotel
Las Vegas, NV 89101

602-371-8655
Fax: 602-371-8790
http://www.nscinet.com
Two pre-conference workshops: The five most important things that educators need to know when using information for continuous program improvement, and The key to sustained leadership effectiveness. Conference will also hold over 60 breakout sessions.
April
Bill Daggett
Bob Marzano

541 National Council for Geographic Education Annual Meeting
National Council for Geographic Education
1101 14ÿStreet, NW
Suite 350
Washington, DC 20005-5647
202-216-0942
Fax: 202-618-6249
http://www.ncge.org
Where geography educators from across the country and around the world meet to exchange ideas, research, resources, and best practices in geogrpahy education.
October
45 booths with 800 attendees
Eric J. Fournier, Chair
Susan E. Hume, President

542 National Council for History Education Conference
National Council for History Education
13940 Cedar Road
Suite 393
University Heights, OH 44118
240-696-6600
Fax: 240-523-0245
E-mail: nche@nche.net
http://www.nche.net
bring school and university people together to tackle all the issues that concern them—from curricular design, K to Ph.D., through state, local, and university standards and requirements, teacher education, certification, and professional development, to the implications of the assessment movement, of new technologies, and of school re-structuring.
March-April
750 attendees and 75 exhibits
Dale Steiner, Chairman
Justin Jakovac, Executive Director

543 National Council for Social Studies Annual Conference
National Council for the Social Studies
8555 Sixteenth Street
Suite 500
Silver Spring, MD 20910
301-588-1800
800-683-0812
Fax: 301-588-2049
E-mail: sgriffin@ncss.org
http://www.socialstudies.org
Provides new ideas, resources, techniques, and skills that will pay off in the classroom, school, district, and invigorate your career. Features more than 400 sessions, workshops, poster presentations, clinics, tours, speakers and panels, and social events.
December
Michelle Herczog, President
Peggy Jackson, Vice President

544 National Council of English Teachers Conference
National Council of Teachers of English
1111 W Kenyon Road
Urbana, IL 61801-1096

217-328-3870
877-369-6283
Fax: 217-328-9645
E-mail: public_info@ncte.org
http://www.ncte.org
Annual/November
Keith Gilyard, Program Chair

3545 National Education Association Annual Meeting
National Education Association (NEA)
1201 16th Street NW
Washington, DC 20036-3290
202-833-4000
Fax: 202-822-7974
E-mail: ncuea@nea.org
http://www.nea.org
A general conference that addresses all facets and concerns of the educator.
July
Gloria Durgin, Conference Contact
Dennis Van Roekel, President

3546 National Educational Computing Conference
Washington State Convention & Trade Center
Walter E Washington Convention Cent
Washington, DC 20001
800-336-5191
Fax: 206-694-5399
E-mail: neccinfo@iste.org
http://www.center.uoregon.edu/ISTE
NECC has been the premier forum in which to learn, exchange, and survey the field of educational technology.
June
417 booths with 12,500 attendees
Dr Heidi Rogers, First Executive Director
Trina Davis, President

3547 National Occupational Information Coordinating Committee Conference
2100 M Street NW
Suite 156
Washington, DC 20037-1207
202-653-7680
Focuses on policy, social issues and social services addressing career development and occupational information.
August
Mary Susan Vickers, Conference Contact

3548 New Mexico School Boards Association Conference
New Mexico School Boards Association
300 Galisteo Street
Suite 204
Santa Fe, NM 87501
505-983-5041
Fax: 505-983-2450
E-mail: nmsba@nmsba.org
http://www.nmsba.org
The New Mexico School Boards Association aspires to be recognized as the premier source of development and support for local boards of education in New Mexico.
February
20 booths
Joe Guillen, Executive Director
Elizabeth Egelhoff, Programs Director

3549 New York School Superintendents Association Annual Meeting
111 Washington Avenue
Suite 404
Albany, NY 12210-2210
518-449-1063
Fax: 518-426-2229

Provides leadership and membership services through a professional organization of school superintendents.
October
50 booths
Dr. Claire Brown, Conference Contact

3550 New York Science Teachers Association Annual Meeting
2449 Union Boulevard
Apartment 20B
Islip, NY 11751-3117
516-783-5432
Fax: 516-783-5432
Education related publications, equipment, supplies and services.
November
110 booths
Harold Miller, Conference Contact

3551 New York State United Teachers Conference
159 Wolf Road
Albany, NY 12205-1106
518-213-6000
Fax: 518-213-6415
http://www.nysut.org
February
40 booths
Anthony Bifaro, Conference Contact

3552 New York Teachers Math Association Conference
92 Governor Drive
Scotia, NY 12302-4802
518-399-0149
October-November
50 booths
Phil Reynolds, Conference Contact

3553 North Carolina Association for Career and Technical Education Conference
Association for Career and Technical Education
1410 King Street
Alexandria, VA 22314
703-683-3311
800-826-9972
Fax: 703-683-7424
http://www.acteonline.org
July
110 booths with 3000 + attendees
Sarah Heath, President
Katrina Plese, Finance Chair

3554 North Central Association Annual Meeting
North Central Association Commission on Accred.
9115 Westside Parkway
Alpharetta, GA 30009-1008
866-837-2229
800-525-9517
Fax: 480-773-6901
E-mail: denz@ncacasi.org
http://www.ncacasi.org
Founded in 1895, NCA CASI accredits over 8,500 public and private schools in 19 states, the Navajo Nation, and the Department of Defense Schools. NCA CASI is an accreditation division of AdvancED.
April
30 booths with 1,800 attendees
William Fisher, CEO
Jay Cummings, Dean, College of Education,

3555 North Central Conference on Summer Sessions Conference

North Central Conference on Summer Sessions
University of Wisconsin
410 S 3rd Street
River Falls, WI 54022
715-425-3851
Fax: 715-425-3785
http://www.nccss.org
This conference attracts a wide variety range of attendees, from faculty, admissions personnel, registrars, business office and marketing representatives, and a wide variety of academic and student affairs administrators with responsibility for overseeing or direecting some aspect of their institution's summer session activities.

Annual/March

Molly Berger, President
Diane Dingfelder, President-Elect

3556 Northeast Conference on the Teaching of Foreign Languages

Northeast Conference at Dickinson College
PO Box 1773
Carlisle, PA 17013-2896
717-243-5121
800-644-1773
Fax: 717-245-1976
E-mail: nectfl@dickinson.edu
http://www.nectfl.org
NECTFL aspires to serve the diverse community of language professionals through responsive leadership in its outreach activities and its annual conference.

April
160 booths with 2500 attendees

Rebecca Kline, Executive Director
Susan M Shaffer, Associate Executive Director

3557 Northeast Teachers Foreign Language Conference

Northeast Conference at Dickinson College
PO Box 1773
Carlisle, PA 17013-2896
717-243-5121
800-644-1773
Fax: 802-654-2595
E-mail: nectfl@dickinson.edu
http://www.nectfl.org
Foreign language textbooks, supplementary materials, audio equipment, computer software, travel abroad program materials and other related teaching aids and publications.

April
130 booths

Rebecca Kline, Executive Director

3558 Northwest Association of Schools & Colleges Annual Meeting

1910 University Drive
Boise, ID 83725-1060
208-426-1000
Fax: 208-334-3228
http://www.boisestate.edu
The university offers more than 190 fields of interest. Undergraduate, graduate and technical programs are available in seven colleges: Arts and Sciences, Business and Economics, Education, Engineering, Graduate Studies, Health Sciences, and Social Sciences and Public Affairs. Students can also study abroad and participate in one of the largest internship programs in the Northwest.

December
120 attendees

Bob Kustra, President
Martin Schimpf, Vice President for Academic

3559 Northwest Regional Educational Laboratory Conference

101 SW Main Street
Suite 500
Portland, OR 97204-3213
503-275-9500
800-547-6339
Fax: 503-275-0660
E-mail: info@nwrel.org
http://www.nwrel.org
The mission of the Northwest Regional Educational Laboratory (NWREL) is to improve learning by building capacity in schools, families, and communities through applied research and development

October/November

Jeffrey Weldon, Chairperson
Steve Bradshaw, Vice Chairperson

3560 Ohio Business Teachers Association

Wright State University, Lake Campus
2350 Westbelt Drive
Colcumbus, OH 43228-2921
419-586-0337
Fax: 419-586-0368
E-mail: MCWhite@itt-tech.edu
http://www.obta-ohio.org
Promote among educators the desire to find better techniques and methods in an effort to improve instruction in the field of business so that the students are well prepared to take their place in the business world.

October
40 booths

Daniel McCarthy, President
Stella Hull, Treasurer

3561 Ohio Public School Employees Association Convention

6805 Oak Creek Drive
Columbus, OH 43229
614-890-4770
800-786-2773
Fax: 614-890-3540
http://www.oapse.org
Committed in developing the most effective programs in the labor movement today.

May
15 booths

Joseph P Rugola, Executive Director
JoAnn Johntony, State President

3562 Ohio Secondary School Administrators Association Conference

Ohio Association of Secondary School Administrator
8050 N High Street
Suite 180
Columbus, OH 43235-6484
614-430-8311
Fax: 614-430-8315
http://www.oassa.org
Offers school secretaries the opportunity to network with colleagues while gaining valuable information that will add to their performance. Current administrators, representatives from the business community, OASSA legal counsel, and fellow secretaries combine to update these valuable employees.

April
42 booths

Kenneth C. Baker, Executive Director
John Richard, Associate Executive Director

3563 Oklahoma School Boards Association & School Administrators Conference

2801 N Lincoln Boulevard
Suite 125
Oklahoma City, OK 73105-4223
405-528-3571
888-528-3571
Fax: 405-528-5695
http://www.ossba.org
The mission of the Oklahoma State School Boards Association shall be to offer services to safeguard,represent and improve public education.The Association shall represent the interests of public school boards before the legislature; provide training programs for school board members; provide school system services; and provide to the individual school board members a variety of other services and information that will improve the quality of educational leadership for each school district in Okla

August
195 booths

Joann Yandell, Conference Contact
Beth Schieber, President

3564 Oregon School Boards Association Annual Convention

Oregon School Boards Association
1201 Court Street NE
Suite 400
Salem, OR 97301
503-588-2800
800-578-6722
Fax: 503-588-2813
E-mail: info@osba.org
http://www.osba.org
To improve student achievement through advocacy, leadership and services to Oregon public school boards.

November

Betsy Miller-Jones, Executive Director
Jim Green, Deputy Executive Director

3565 PDK International Conference

Int'l Honor and Professional Assoc in Education
PO Box 7888
Bloomington, IN 47407-7888
812-339-1156
800-766-1156
Fax: 812-339-0018
E-mail: plt@pdkintl.org
http://www.pilambda.org
Conference on Innovations in Teaching and Learning was selected because of its relevance to educators everywhere as new and effective educational practices continue to emerge. Includes interactive sessions, research presentations, and networking events.

Annual/February
400 attendees

Dan Brown, Executive Director
Bill Bushaw, Chief Executive Officer

3566 PSBA School Board Secretaries and Affiliates Conference

Pennsylvania School Boards Association
400 Bent Creek Blvd.
PO Box 2042
Mechanicsburg, PA 17050-1873
717-506-2450
800-932-0588
Fax: 717-506-2451
E-mail: trustinfo@psba.org
http://www.psba.org

To promote excellence in school board governance through leadership, service and advocacy for public education.

October
140 booths

William S. LaCoff, President
Mark B. Miller, Vice President

567 Pacific Northwest Council on Languages Annual Conference

5290 University of Oregon
Eugene, OR 97403
541-346-5699
Fax: 541-346-6303
E-mail: pncfl@uoregon.edu
http://www.pncfl.org
The Pacific Northwest Council for Languages unites, serves, and supports all world language educators in Alaska, Idaho, Montana, Oregon, Washington, and Wyoming.

April

Brenda Gaver, President
Laura Kiolet, Executive Director

568 Pennsylvania Council for the Social Studies Conference

Pennsylvania Council for the Social Studies
1212 Smallman Street
Senator John Heinz Regional Histiry Cnt
Pittsburgh, PA 15222-4200
717-238-8768
E-mail: JKEARNEY@CBSD.ORG
http://www.pcssonline.org
The PCSS promotes quality Social Studies education from kindergarten to higher learning by advocating the Social Studies at all levels of education in Pennsylvania.

October
50 booths with 500 attendees

David Trevaskis, President elect
Don Imler, Executive Secretary

569 Pennsylvania Science Teachers Association

Center for Science & Technology Education
PO Box 330
Shippenville, PA 16254-330
814-782-6301
http://www.pascience.org
Work towards the advancement, improvement, and coordination of science education in all areas of science at all educational levels.

December
70 booths

Don Kine, President
Kathleen Jones, Vice President

570 Principals' Center Spring Institute Conference

Harvard Graduate School of Education
6 Appian Way
#336
Cambridge, MA 02138-3704
617-495-1825
Fax: 617-495-5900
http://www.gse.harvard.edu
Administrative professionals get together to discuss issues, policy and procedures.

April

Nindy Leroy, Conference Contact

571 Restructuring Curriculum Conference

National School Conference Institute
PO Box 35099
Phoenix, AZ 85069-5099
602-674-8990

Presents research, studies, and new information relevant to curriculum development.

January

3572 SAI Annual Conference

School Administrators of Iowa
12199 Stratford Drive
Clive, IA 50325
515-267-1115
Fax: 515-267-1066
E-mail: dsmith@sai-iowa.org
http://www.sai-iowa.org

August

Deron Durflinger, President
Paul Wenger, Vice President

3573 SchoolTech Forum

Miller Freeman
600 Harrison Street
San Francisco, CA 94109
415-947-6657
Fax: 415-947-6015
National forum for educational technology professional development and exhibits, devoted to intensive instruction by today's leading practitioners, eye-opening special events, unparalleled networking opportunities, and exposure to products and services.

3574 South Carolina Library Association Conference

South Carolina Library Association
PO Box 1763
Columbia, SC 29202
803-252-1087
Fax: 803-252-0589
E-mail: scla@capconsc.com
http://www.scla.org

Annual/October
125 booths with 350 attendees

Crystal Johnson, President
John Kennerly, 1st Vice President

3575 Southern Association Colleges & Schools

1866 Southern Lane
Decatur, GA 30033-4097
404-679-4500
Fax: 404-679-4556
http://www.sacs.org
Exhibits publications, data and word processing equipment, school photography, charter bus services and more.

December
50 booths with 3700 attendees

Dr. James Rogers, Chief Academic Officer

3576 Southern Early Childhood Annual Convention

Southern Early Childhood Association
1123 S. University Ave.
Suite 255
Little Rock, AR 72204-5930
501-221-1648
800-305-7322
Fax: 501-227-5297
E-mail: info@southernearlychildhood.org
http://www.southernearlychildhood.org
Southern Early Childhood Association has brought together preschool, kindergarten, and primary teachers and administrators, caregivers, program directors, and individuals working with and for families, to promote quality care and education for young children.

January
2,500 attendees

Janie Humphries, President
Glenda Bean, Executive Director

3577 Superintendents Work Conference

Teachers College, Columbia University
525 W 120th Street
PO Box 179
New York, NY 10027-6696
212-678-7449
Fax: 212-678-3682
E-mail: swc@tc.columbia.edu
http://www.superintendentsworkconference.com
Offers practicing school superintendents a unique opportunity for professional growth in stimulating surroundings.

July
60 attendees

Thomas Sobol, Conference Chair
Gibran Matdalany, Associate Chair

3578 TASA/TASB Convention

Texas Association of School Boards
PO Box 400
Austin, TX 78767-0400
512-467-0222
800-580-8272
Fax: 512-467-3554
E-mail: tasb@tasb.org
http://www.tasb.org
Offers school board members and school administrators the opportunity to earn almost 17 hours of continuing education credit, hear outstnading keynote speakers, explore a tradeshow with hundreds of exhibitors, and network with more than 6,000 public school officials.

September-October

James B Crow, Executive Director
Grover Campbell, Associate Executive Director

3579 Teachers Association in Instruction Conference

150 W Market Street
Indianapolis, IN 46204-2806
317-634-1515
Exhibits a wide variety of teaching materials and information from Grades K-12.

October
150 booths

Barbara Stainbrook, Conference Contact

3580 Tennessee School Boards Association Conference

525 Brick Church Park Drive
Nashville, TN 37207-2884
615-815-3900
800-448-6465
Fax: 615-815-3911
E-mail: webadmin@tsba.net
http://www.tsba.net
The mission of the Tennessee School Boards Associationis to assisst school boards in effectively governing school districts.

November
60 booths with 1,000 attendees

Tammy Grissom, Executive Director
David Pickler, President

3581 Texas Middle School Association Conference

Texas Middle School Association
PO Box 152499
Austin, TX 78715-2499
512-468-1168
888-529-8672
Fax: 512-462-0991
E-mail: tmsa2@austin.rr.com
http://www.tmsanet.org
To promote the implementation of student-centered programs and highly effective practices by providing vision, knowledge, and resources which meet the unique individ-

ual needs of adolescents in an ever-changing society.

February

Thad Spears, President
Cecil Floyd, Executive Director

3582 Texas State Teachers Association

316 W 12th Street
Austin, TX 78701-1815
877-275-8782
Fax: 512-476-9555
http://www.tsta.org
The Texas State Teachers Association will unite, organize and empower public education advocates to shape public education in Texas thus providing a quality public school for every child

April
120 booths

Carla Bond, Conference Contact
Rita Haecker, President

3583 Training & Presentations

Chief Manufacturing, Inc.
6436 City West Parkway
Eden Prairie, MN 55344-4839
612-894-6280
800-582-6480
Fax: 877-894-6918
E-mail: chief@chiefmfg.com
http://www.chiefmfg.com
Providing top quality mounting solutions for projectors, monitors, and flat panel TVs. Committed to responding to industry needs in Commercial, Residential and Workstation/IT markets, Chief is dedicated to producing solutions that packed with form, function, and flexibility

Chicago, Illinois
February

Kris Murray, Director Customer Service/Pr
Yvette Danz, Manager Customer Service

3584 UPCEA Annual Conference

University Professional/Continuing Education Assoc
One Dupont Circle
Suite 615
Washington, DC 20036
202-659-3130
Fax: 202-785-0374
E-mail: nkats@upcea.edu
http://www.upcea.edu
The largest single gathering of higher education professionals who develop, implement, and promote professional and continuing education and online learning in North America.

April
70 booths with 1,000 attendees

Robert Hansen, CEO/Executive Director
Lori Derkay, Chief Operating Officer

3585 USA Kansas Annual Convention

United School Administrators of Kansas
515 S Kansas Avenue
Suite 201
Topeka, KS 66603
785-232-6566
Fax: 785-232-9776
E-mail: usaoffice@usa-ks.org
http://www.usakansas.org
Offers quality professional development opportunities for education administrators and leaders. During the convention, administrators are able to participate in professional workshops or learning clusters.

180 booths

Cheryl Semmel, Executive Director

3586 VAIS Conference

Virginia Association of Independent Schools
6802 Paragon Place
Suite 525
Richmond, VA 23230
804-282-3592
Fax: 804-282-3596
E-mail: info@vais.org
http://www.vais.org
The Virginia Association of Independent Schools is a service organization that promotes educational, ethical and professional excellence. Through its school evaluation/accreditation program, attention to professional development and insistence on integrity, the Association safeguards the interests of its member schools.

November
1,500 attendees

Henry D. Berg, President
Betsy Hunroe, Executive Director

3587 Virginia ASCD Conference

Virginia ASCD
2516 Old Lynchburg Rd
North Garden, VA 22959
434-293-3290
E-mail: vascded@gmail.com
http://vaascd.org
Dedicated to advancing excellence in Teaching, Learning and Leadership.

December
30 booths with 600 attendees

Daniel Smith, President
Laurie McCullough, Executive Director

3588 Virginia Association of Elementary School Principals Conference

Virginia Assoc of Elementary School Principals
1805 Chantilly Street
Richmond, VA 23230
804-355-6791
Fax: 804-355-1196
E-mail: info@vaesp.org
http://www.vaesp.org
Nonprofit professional association advocating for public education and equal educational opportunities. Promotes leadership of school administrators, principal as educational leaders, and provides professional development opportunities.

50 booths with 300 attendees

Shane Wolfe, President
Jim Baldwin, Executive Director

3589 Virginia School Boards Association Conference

Virginia School Boards Association
200 Hansen Road
Charlottesville, VA 22911
434-295-8722
800-446-8722
Fax: 434-295-8785
http://www.vsba.org
A voluntary, self-supporting and nonpartisan organization that promotes quality education through its services for local school boards. Provides member boards with services, training, and advocacy so that they may exercise effective leadership in public school governance on behalf of public education for all the children of the Commonwealth.

Annual/November

Juandiego R. Wade, President
Gina G Patterson, Executive Director

3590 Wisconsin Association of School Boards Annual Conference

Wisconsin Association of School Boards
122 W Washington Avenue
Suite 400
Madison, WI 53703-2761
608-257-2622
Fax: 608-257-8386
E-mail: info@wasb.org
http://www.wasb.org
The WASB provides background and support for elected school leaders as they do the difficult work of democracy: weighing and balancing the unique values of their communities.

January
370 booths with 3,000 attendees

John Ashley, Executive Director
Patti Welch, Administrative Assistant

3591 Wisconsin Association of School District Administrators Conference

Wisconsin Assoc of School District Administrators
4797 Hayes Road
Suite 201
Madison, WI 53704
608-242-1090
Fax: 608-242-1290
E-mail: mturner@wasda.org
http://www.wasda.org
The premiere collaborative leadership association, serves superintendents by providing professional support and expanding their capacity to be effective, innovative leaders.

Annual/May
70 booths

Kristine Gilmore, President
Jon Bales, Executive Director

3592 Wisconsin School Administrators Association Conference

Association of Wisconsin School Administrators
4797 Hayes Road
Suite 103
Madison, WI 53704
608-241-0300
Fax: 608-249-4973
E-mail: patricia@awsa.org
http://www.awsa.org
The Association of Wisconsin School Administrators exists to coordinate the collective interests and needs of school administrators and to enhance their professional growth and competency for the purpose of improving the quality of educational opportunities for the youth of Wisconsin

October
60 booths

Jim Lynch, Executive Director
Kelly Meyers, Associate Executive Director

Directories & Handbooks

3593 American Association of Colleges for Teacher Education-Directory

American Association of Colleges for Teacher Ed.
1307 New York Avenue NW
Suite 300
Washington, DC 20005
202-293-2450
Fax: 202-457-8095
E-mail: aacte@aacte.org
http://www.aacte.org

Promote the learning of all PK-12 students through high-quality, evidence-based preparation and continuing education for all school personnel.

144 pages Annual
ISSN: 0516-9313

Sharon P Robinson, President/CEO
Jeannette Knight-Mills, Associate Director Executive

594 American Society for Training/Development-Training Video

American Society for Training & Development
1640 King Street
Box 1443
Alexandria, VA 22313-1443
703-683-8100
800-628-2783
Fax: 703-683-8103
E-mail: customercare@astd.org
http://www.astd.org
Serves as the educational society for persons engaged in training and development of business, industry, education and government personnel.

Tony Bingham, President/CEO
Cindy Huggett, Chair

595 Appropriate Inclusion and Paraprofessionals

National Education Association (NEA)
1201 16th Street NW
Washington, DC 20036-3290
202-833-4000
Fax: 202-822-7974
E-mail: ncuea@nea.org
http://www.nea.org
A book offering information on mainstreaming disabled students and the work of paraprofessionals in the education process.

10 pages

Dennis Van Roekel, President
Lily Eskelsen, Vice President

596 Assessing Student Performance: Exploring the Purpose and Limits of Testing

Jossey-Bass/Pfeiffer
989 Market Street
San Francisco, CA 94103-1741
415-433-1740
Fax: 415-433-0499
E-mail: info@wiley.com
http://www.josseybass.com
Clarifies the limits of testing in an assessment system. Analyzes problematic practices in test design and formats that prevent students from explaining their answers by showing that assessment is more than testing and intellectual performance is more than right answers.

336 pages Softcover
ISBN: 0-7879-5047-5

597 Association for Continuing Higher Education Directory

1700 Asp Avenue
Norman, OK 73072-6400
405-329-0249
800-807-2243
Fax: 405-325-7196
E-mail: admin@acheinc.org
http://www.acheinc.org
Dedicated to promoting lifelong learning and excellence in continuing higher education. Encourage professional development, research and exchange of information for its

members and continuing higher education as a means of enhancing and improving society.

102 pages Annual/March
10 booths with 250 attendees

James P Pappas, Executive VP
Rick E Osborn, President

3598 BBX Teacher Clearinghouse

175 Norwood Road
Silver Spring, MD 20905
301-628-9776
Fax: 301-989-9606
E-mail: CEO@BBXOnline.com
http://www.teachersclearinghouse.com
BBX's Teacher Clearinghouse is a comprehensive resume databank where elementary and secondary school teachers, administrators, and education majors can post their resumes at no charge for review by subscribing school districts. Subscribers are public and private schools with an interest in receiving applications from, and importantly, a commitment to hiring, members of the African American/Black communities.

J R Moore, Administrator

3599 Before the School Bell Rings

Phi Delta Kappa Educational Foundation
320 W Eight Street
Suite 216
Bloomington, IN 47404
812-339-1156
800-766-1156
Fax: 812-339-0018
E-mail: memberservices@pdkintl.org
http://www.pdkintl.org
Early childhood teachers and administrators, childcare providers and parents will enjoy and learn from this practical, insightful book.

84 pages Paperback
ISBN: 0-87367-476-6

Carol B Hillman, Author
George Kersey, Executive Director
Donovan R Walling, Editor, Special Publications

3600 Beyond Tracking: Finding Success in Inclusive Schools

Phi Delta Kappa Educational Foundation
PO Box 7888
Bloomington, IN 47407-7888
812-339-1156
800-766-1156
Fax: 812-339-0018
E-mail: memberservices@pdkintl.org
http://www.pdkintl.org
Research data, practical ideas and reports from educators involved in untracking schools make this an authoritative and useful collection of important articles.

293 pages Hardcover
ISBN: 0-87367-470-7

Harbison Pool and Jane A Page, Author
George Kersey, Executive Director
Donovan R Walling, Dir Publications/Research

3601 Book of Metaphors, Volume II

AEE and Kendall/Hunt Publishing Company
4050 Westmark Drive
P.O Box 1840
Dubuque, IA 52004-1840
563-589-1000
800-228-0810
Fax: 800-772-9165
E-mail: orders@kendallhunt.com
http://www.kendallhunt.com
A compilation of presentations designed to enhance learning for those participating in adventure-based programs. Practitioners

share how they prepare experiences for presentations.

256 pages Paperback
ISBN: 0-7872-0306-8

AEE, Author
Karen Berger, Customer Service Assistant

3602 Brief Legal Guide for the Independent Teacher

441 Vine Street
Suite 505
Cincinnati, OH 45202-2811
Offering insights into the most common legal issues faced by independent music teachers.

28 pages

3603 Building Life Options: School-Community Collaborations

Academy for Educational Development
1255 23rd Street NW
Washington, DC 20037-1125
202-884-8800
Fax: 202-884-8400
A handbook for family life educators on how to prevent pregnancy in the middle grades.

3604 Closing the Achievement Gap

Master Teacher
Leadership Lane
PO Box 1207
Manhattan, KS 66505-1207
785-539-0555
800-669-9633
Fax: 800-669-1132
http://www.masterteacher.com
A complete step-by-step approach to building a system that narrows the gap between student potenial and student performance—between success and failure.

162 pages
ISBN: 0-914607-73-1

Kristy Meeks, Author

3605 Coming Up Short? Practices of Teacher Educators Committed to Character

Character Education Partnership
1025 Connecticut Avenue NW
Suite 1011
Washington, DC 20036
202-296-7743
800-988-8081
Fax: 202-296-7779
E-mail: rsipos@character.org
http://www.character.org
Nonprofit, nonpartisan, nonsectarian coalition of organizations and individuals committed to fostering effective character education in our nation's K-12 schools.

Henry Huffman, Author
Rebecca Sipos, Director Communications
Anne Bryant, Executive Director

3606 Competency-Based Framework for Professional Development of Certified Health Specialists

Nat'l Health Education Credentialing
1541 Alta Drive
Suite 303
Whitehall, PA 18052-5642
484-223-0770
888-624-3248
Fax: 800-813-0727
http://www.nchec.org
Aims to help the health education profession provide the leadership necessary for improving health in a rapidly changing, culturally pluralistic and technologically complex society. Provides universities, professional organizations, and accreditation a common basis of skills for the development, assessment,

and improvement of professional preparation for health educators.

Linda Lysoby, Executive Director
Melissa Rehrig, Communication Director

3607 Contracting Out: Strategies for Fighting Back
National Education Association (NEA)
1201 16th Street NW
Washington, DC 20036-3290
202-833-4000
Fax: 202-822-7974
E-mail: ncuea@nea.org
http://www.nea.org
The voice of education professionals. Advocate for education professionals

John I Wilson, Executive Director
Dennis Van Roekel, President

3608 Directory of Curriculum Materials Centers
PO Box 399
Addison, IL 60101-0399
630-833-5300
877-850-2300
Fax: 630-833-5303
E-mail: info@telusys.net
http://www.telusys.com
Listing of over 275 centers that have collections of curriculum materials to aid in elementary and secondary teaching preparation.

200 pages

Jackie Bedell, Supervisor
Ruth Miller, Supervisor

3609 Distance Learning Directory
Virginia A Ostendorf
PO Box 2896
Littleton, CO 80161-2896
303-797-3131
Fax: 303-797-3524
E-mail: ostendorf@vaostendorf.com
Comprehensive list of distance learning practitioners and vendors. Each listing includes names, addresses, e-mail, fax and phones, credits awarded, program content, peripherals and technologies used, class configurations and more. Includes a lists of vendors offering descriptions of distance learning products, services and programming.

308 pages Annual

Virginia A Ostendorf, President
Ronald Ostendorf, VP

3610 Education Index
H.W. Wilson Company
950 University Avenue
Bronx, NY 10452-4224
718-588-8400
800-367-6770
Fax: 718-590-1617
E-mail: rsky@hwwilson.com
http://www.hwwilson.com
Contains more than 456,000 citations to articles, interviews, editorials and letters, reviews of books, educational films, and software for approximately 427 English-language periodicals, monographs and yearbooks in the field of education. Available electronically on the Web with index, abstracts and full text versions.

Monthly

Roseward Sky, Assistant Manager/Marketing
Harold Regan, President

3611 Educational Administration Resource Centre Database
3-300 Edmonton Clinic Health Academy
11405-87 Ave
Edmonton, AB G1C9
780-492-0560
Fax: 780-492-0364
E-mail: school.publichealth@ualberta.ca
http://www.publichealth.ualberta.ca
Over 3,650 bibliographic descriptions of the Centre's collection of educational administration print and audiovisual materials.

Laing Lory, Interim Dean

3612 Ethical Issues in Experiential Education
AEE and Kendall/Hunt Publishing Company
4050 Westmark Drive
Dubuque, IA 52002-2624
319-589-1000
800-228-0810
Fax: 800-772-9165
http://www.kendallhunt.com
An examination of ethical issues in the field of adventure programming and experiential education. Topics include ethical theory, informed consent, sexual issues, student rights, environmental concerns and programming practices.

144 pages
ISBN: 0-7872-93083

Karen Berger, Customer Service Assistant

3613 Finishing Strong: Your Personal Mentoring & Planning Guide for the Last 60 Days of Teaching
Master Teacher
Leadership Lane
PO Box 1207
Manhattan, KS 66505-1207
785-539-0555
800-669-9633
Fax: 800-669-1132
http://www.masterteacher.com
In this book we've selected from the 32 years of The Master Teacher, the writings we know you would most like your teachers to have to support that last 60 days of the school year.

132 pages
ISBN: 1-58992-095-3

Robert L De Bruyn, Author

3614 How to Plan and Develop a Career Center
Center on Education and Work
1025 W Johnson Street
Room 964
Madison, WI 53706-1796
608-265-6700
800-862-1071
Fax: 608-262-3063
E-mail: cewmail@education.wisc.edu
http://www.cew.wisc.edu
High school, postsecondary, adult, and virtual career centers-a comprehensive blueprint that covers all the bases.

3615 How to Raise Test Scores
Skylight Professional Development
1900 E Lake Avenue
Glenview, IL 60025
847-657-7450
800-348-4474
Fax: 847-486-3183
E-mail: info@skylightedu.com
http://www.skylightedu.com

Addresses the teaching and learning process at its most basic and important level-the classroom.

30 pages Softcover
ISBN: 1575171635

Robin Fogarty, Author

3616 Inclusion: The Next Step DVD
Master Teacher
Leadership Lane
PO Box 1207
Manhattan, KS 66505-1207
785-539-0555
800-669-9633
Fax: 800-669-1132
http://www.masterteacher.com
Offers practical help for regular classroom teachers and special education teachers in meeting the challenges of inclusion.

225 pages
ISBN: 0-914607-69-3

Wendy Dover, Author

3617 Law of Teacher Evaluation: A Self-Assessment Handbook
Phi Delta Kappa Educational Foundation
PO Box 7888
Bloomington, IN 47407-7888
812-339-1156
800-766-1156
Fax: 812-339-0018
http://www.pdkintl.org
This handy guidebook provides a concise, authoritative overview of US state statutes, regulations and guidelines regarding the performance evaluation of educators.

51 pages Paperback
ISBN: 0-87367-488-X

Perry A. Zirkel, Author
DR Walling, Director Publications/Resear

3618 Learning for Life
1329 W Walnut Hill Lane
PO Box 152225
Irving, TX 75015-2225
972-580-2433
855-806-9992
Fax: 972-580-2137
E-mail: exploring@lflmail.org
http://www.learning-for-life.org
Learning for Life is designed to support schools and other youth-serving organizations in their efforts toward preparing youth to successfully handle the complexities of today's society and to enhance their self-confidence, motivation, and self-worth.

Diane E Thornton, National Director
William Taylor, Director of Criminal Justice

3619 Lesson Plans for the Substitue Teacher: Elementary Edition
Master Teacher
Po Box 1207
Manhattan, KS 66505-1207
785-539-0555
800-669-9633
Fax: 800-669-1132
http://www.masterteacher.com
Gives you more than 100 lessons developed and tested by teachers across the curriculum and at all grade levels.

145 pages
ISBN: 1-58992-107-0

Robert L DeBruyn, Author

3620 Libraries Unlimited
PO Box 1911
Santa Barbara, CA 93116-1911
800-368-6868
800-225-5800
Fax: 805-968-1911

E-mail: CustomerService@abc-clio.com
http://www.lu.com
Publisher of resource books written by educators for educators. The books offer innovative ideas, practical lessons, and classroom-tested activities in the areas of math, science, social studies, whole language literature and library connections.

Debby LaBoon, Manager of Authors/Workshops

3621 Life Skills Training
711 Westchester Avenue
White Plains, NY 10604
914-421-2525
800-293-4969
Fax: 914-421-2007
E-mail: lstinfo@nhpamail.com
http://www.LifeSkillsTraining.com
Botvin LifeSkills Training (LST) is a research-validated substance abuse prevention program proven to reduce the risks of alcohol, tobacco, drug abuse, and violence by targeting the major social and psychological factors that promote the initiation of substance use and other risky behaviors.

Gilbert J Botvin, Developer

3622 List of Regional, Professional & Specialized Accrediting Association
Educational Information Services
PO Box 662
Newton Lower Falls, MA 02162
617-964-4555
A list of those associations involved in accreditation for the education fields.

3623 MacMillan Guide to Correspondence Study
MacMillan Publishing Company
1633 Broadway
New York, NY 10019
212-512-2000
Fax: 800-835-3202
Listing of 175 colleges, accredited trade, technical and vocational schools that offer home study courses.

500 pages

3624 Middle Grades Education in an Era of Reform
Academy for Educational Development
1255 23rd Street NW
Washington, DC 20037-1125
202-884-8800
Fax: 202-884-8400
Reviews middle-grades educational reform policies and practices.

3625 Middle School Teachers Guide to FREE Curriculum Materials
Educators Progress Service
214 Center Street
Randolph, WI 53956-1408
920-326-3126
888-951-4469
Fax: 920-326-3127
E-mail: epsinc@centurytel.net
http://www.freeteachingaids.com
Lists and describes free supplementary teaching aids for the middle school and junior high level.

290 pages Annual
ISBN: 87708-401-7

Kathy Nehmer, President

3626 NASDTEC Knowledge Base
1629 K Street NW
Suite 300
Washington, DC 20006
202-204-2208
Fax: 202-204-2210

E-mail: rje@nasdtec.com
http://www.nasdtec.org
It is the organization that represents professional standards boards and commissions and state departments of education in all 50 states, the District of Columbia, the Department of Defense Education Activity, the U.S. Territories, Alberta, British Columbia, and Ontario that are responsible for the preparation, licensure, and discipline of educational personnel.

Annually
ISBN: 0-9708628-3-0

Phillip Rogers, Executive Director

3627 Orators & Philosophers: A History of the Idea of Liberal Education
College Board Publications
45 Columbus Avenue
New York, NY 10023-6992
212-713-8165
800-323-7155
Fax: 212-713-8143
E-mail: aces@info.collegeboard.org
http://www.collegeboard.org
A cogent study of the historical evolution of the idea of liberal education. Clearly and forcefully argued, the book portrays this evolution as a struggle between two contending points of view, one oratorical and the other philosophical.

308 pages

Bruce A Kimball, Author
David Coleman, President

3628 Parent Training Resources
PACER Center
8161 Normandale Boulevard
Bloomington, MN 55437
952-838-0190
800-537-2237
Fax: 952-838-0199
E-mail: pacer@pacer.org
http://www.pacer.org
A Minnesota nonprofit, tax-exempt organization that provides information, training, and assistance to parents of children and young adults with all disabilities; physical, learning, cognitive, emotional, and health

130 pages

Paula F Goldberg, Executive Director
Mary Schrock, Chief Operating and Developm

3629 Personal Planner and Training Guide for the Paraprofessional
Master Teacher
Po Box 1207
Manhattan, KS 66505-1207
785-539-0555
800-669-9633
Fax: 800-669-1132
http://www.masterteacher.com
Includes numerous forms which allow each para to keep track of vital information he or she will need in working with specific teachers and their special students.

128 pages
ISBN: 0-914607-39-1

Wendy Dover, Author

3630 Practical Handbook for Assessing Learning Outcomes in Continuing Education
International Association for Continuing Education
1760 Old Meadow Road
Suite 500
McLean, VA 22102

703-506-3275
Fax: 703-506-3266
http://www.iacet.org
Innovative guide offers readers a series of steps to help select an assessment plan which will work for any organization.

Michael Todd Shinholster, President
Kristopher Newbauer, President-Elect

3631 Principles of Good Practice in Continuing Education
International Association for Continuing Education
1760 Old Meadow Road
Suite 500
McLean, VA 22102
703-506-3275
Fax: 703-506-3266
http://www.iacet.org
Principles from many sources for the field of continuing education, placing a pervasive emphasis on learning outcomes for the individual learner.

Michael Todd Shinholster, President
Kristopher Newbauer, President-Elect

3632 Professional Learning Communities at Work
National Educational Service
65 West Shore Drive
Enfield, CT 06082
860-763-2609
800-733-6786
Fax: 812-336-7790
E-mail: nes@nesonline.com
http://www.nesonline.com
This publication provides specific, practical, how-to information on the best practices in use in schools through the US and Canada for curriculum development, teacher preparation, school leadership, professional development programs, school-parent partnerships, assessment practices and much more.

3633 Programs for Preparing Individuals for Careers in Special Education
The Council for Exceptional Children
1920 Association Drive
Reston, VA 20191-1545
703-620-3660
800-232-7323
Fax: 703-264-1637
This directory offers over 600 colleges and universities with programs in special education. Information includes institution name, address, contact person, telephone, fax, Internet, accreditation status, size of faculty, level of program, and areas of specialty.

256 pages

3634 Quality School Teacher
National Professional Resources
25 South Regent Street
Port Chester, NY 10573-8295
914-937-8897
800-453-7461
Fax: 914-937-8879
E-mail: service@nprinc.com
http://www.nprinc.com
Provides the specifics that classroom teachers are asking for as they begin the move to quality schools. It is written for educators who are trying to give up the old system of boss-managing, and to create classrooms that produce quality work.

144 pages
ISBN: 0060-952857

William Glasser, Author
Robert Hanson, President
Helene Hanson, VP

3635 Requirements for Certification of Teachers & Counselors
University of Chicago Press
5801 S Ellis Avenue
Floor 4
Chicago, IL 60637-5418
312-702-7700
800-621-2736
Fax: 800-621-8476
A list of state and local departments of education for requirements including teachers, counselors, librarians, and administrators for elementary and secondary schools.

256 pages Annual
ISBN: 0-226-42850-8

Elizabeth Kaye, Author
John Tryneski, Coordinating Education

3636 Research for Better Schools Publications
123 South Broad Street
Philadelphia, PA 19109-2471
215-568-6150
Fax: 215-568-7260
E-mail: info@rbs.org
http://www.rbs.org
RBS is a private, nonprofit educational organization funded primarily through grants and contracts from the U.S. Department of Education, the National Science Foundation, Mid-Atlantic state departments of education, institutions of higher education, foundations, and school districts.

Dr. Keith M Kershner, Executive Director
Rev. John F Bloh, President

3637 Resources for Teaching Middle School Science
National Academy Press
901 D Street SW
Suite 704B
Washington, DC 20024-403
202-633-2966
Fax: 202-287-7309
E-mail: shulers@si.edu
http://www.nsrconline.org
The NSRC is an intermediary organization that bridges research on how children learn with best practices for the classroom.

496 pages

National Science Resources Center, Author
Sally Goetz Shuler, Executive Director
Tanya Miller, Executive Assistant

3638 Restructuring in the Classroom: Teaching, Learning, and School Organization
Jossey-Bass/Pfeiffer
989 Market Street
San Francisco, CA 94103-1741
415-433-1740
Fax: 415-433-0499
http://www.josseybass.com
Teaching, learning and school organization.

288 pages Hardcover
ISBN: 0-7879-0239-X

Riched Elmore, Penelope Peterson & Sara McCarthey, Author

3639 Revolution Revisited: Effective Schools and Systemic Reform
Phi Delta Kappa Educational Foundation
320 W Eight Street
Suite 216
Bloomington, IN 47404-3800
812-339-1156
800-766-1156

Fax: 812-339-0018
E-mail: memberservices@pdkintl.org
http://www.pdkintl.org
The authors examine the Effective Schools movement of the past quarter century as a school reform philosophy and renewal process for today and for the coming years.

132 pages Paperback
ISBN: 0-873674-83-9

BO Taylor and P Bullard, Author
Donovan R Walling, Director Publications/Resear
Kathleen Andreson, President

3640 Seminar Information Service
250 El Camino Real
Suite 112
Tustin, CA 92780-4469
714-508-0340
877-736-4636
Fax: 714-734-8027
E-mail: info@seminarinformation.com
http://www.seminarinformation.com
In 1981, Catherine Bellizzi and Mona Piontkowski founded Seminar Information Service, Inc. (SIS). Their idea was to fill a void - thousands of seminars were taking place, but there wasn't any one central source to tell someone where and when they were being held.

1,000 pages Annual

Mona Pointkowski, Co-Founder
Catherine Bellizzi, Co-Founder

3641 Service-Learning and Character Education: One Plus One is More Than Two
Character Education Partnership
1025 Connecticut Avenue NW
Suite 1011
Washington, DC 20036
202-296-7743
800-988-8081
Fax: 202-296-7779
E-mail: jmazzola@character.org
http://www.character.org
Leading the nation in helping schools develop people of good character for a just and compassionate society.

Rebecca Sipos, Director Communications
Joe Mazzola, Executive Director

3642 Teacher Created Resources
Teacher Created Resources
6421 Industry Way
Westminster, CA 92683-3652
888-343-4335
800-662-4321
Fax: 800-525-1524
E-mail: custserv@teachercreated.com
http://www.teachercreated.com
We publish quality resource books at the early childhood, elementary, and middle school levels. Our books cover all aspects of the curriculum—language arts, social studies, math, science, technology, and the arts.

Ina Levin, Managing Editor
Karen Goldfluss, Managing Editor

3643 Teachers as Educators of Character: Are the Nations Schools of Education Coming Up Short?
Character Education Partnership
1025 Connecticut Avenue NW
Suite 1011
Washington, DC 20036
202-296-7743
800-988-8081
Fax: 202-296-7779
E-mail: rsipos@character.org
http://www.character.org

Leading the nation in helping schools develop people of good character for a just and compassionate society.

Henry Huffman, Author
Rebecca Sipos, Director Communications
Joseph W Mazzola, Executive Director

3644 Teachers as Leaders
Phi Delta Kappa Educational Foundation
PO Box 7888
Bloomington, IN 47407-7888
812-339-1156
800-766-1156
Fax: 812-339-0018
http://www.pdkintl.org
Examines teacher recruitment, retention, professional development and leadership. The central theme of these twenty essays is excellence in education and how to achieve it.

320 pages Hardcover
ISBN: 0-873674-68-5

Donovan R Walling, Author
Donovan R Walling, Director Publications/Resear

3645 Teachers in Publishing
Pike Publishing Company
221 Town Center W
Suite 112
Santa Maria, CA 93458-5083
Editorial, research, sales, consulting, in office positions or travel to learn teachers' needs and instruct new texts.

3646 Teaching About Islam & Muslims in the Public School Classroom
9300 Gardenia Avenue
#B3
Fountain Valley, CA 92708-2253
714-839-2929
Fax: 714-839-2714

117 pages
ISBN: 1-930109-008

Susan Douglas, Author
Shabbir Mansuri, Founding Director

3647 Teaching as the Learning Profession: Handbookof Policy and Practice
Jossey-Bass/Pfeiffer
989 Market Street
San Francisco, CA 94103-1741
415-433-1740
Fax: 415-433-0499
Provides the best essays about the status of teaching, and the contributing writers are among the best thinkers in education today.

426 pages Hardcover

Linda Darling-Hammond, Editor
Gary Sykes, Editor

3648 Teaching for Results
Master Teacher
Leadership Lane
PO Box 1207
Manhattan, KS 66505-1207
800-669-9633
Fax: 800-669-1132
http://www.masterteacher.com
An easy-to-implement powerful method for helping to ensure sucess in the classroom.

45 pages
ISBN: 1-58992-120-8

3649 Their Best Selves: Building Character Education and Service Learning Together
Character Education Partnership
1025 Connecticut Avenue NW
Suite 1011
Washington, DC 20036

202-296-7743
800-988-8081
Fax: 202-296-7779
E-mail: rsipos@character.org
http://www.character.org
Character Education Partnership (CEP) is one of the world's premier character education organizations. It is recognized as a leader in the field and a foremost advocate for developing young people of good character and civic virtue.

Joseph Mazzola, Executive Director
David W Fisher, Chairman

3650 Theory of Experiential Education
AEE and Kendall/Hunt Publishing Company
4050 Westmark Drive
PO Box 1840
Dubuque, IA 52004-2624
319-589-1000
800-228-0810
Fax: 563-589-1253
http://www.kendallhunt.com
This groundbreaking resource looks at the theoretical foundations of experiential education from philosophical, historical, psychological, social and ethical perspectives.

496 pages
ISBN: 0-7872-0262-2
AEE, Author
Karen Berger, Customer Service Assistant

3651 Time to Teach, Time to Learn: Changing the Pace of School
1615 Duke Street
Alexandria, VA 22314
703-528-0700
800-360-6332
Fax: 413-774-1129
E-mail: info@aasa.org
Giving students the chance to learn and their teachers the chance to teach.

322 pages Softcover
Chip Wood, Author

3652 Top Quality School Process (TQSP)
National School Services
390 Holbrook Drive
Wheeling, IL 60090-5812
847-541-2768
800-262-4511
Fax: 847-541-2553
A customized School Improvement Program that incorporates input from all stakeholders in the educational process to establish baseline data, implement a continuous process of school improvement, and select quality programs for professional development.

3653 US Department of Education: Office of Educational Research & Improvement
National Library of Education
555 New Jersey Avenue NW
Washington, DC 20208-5573
202-219-2230
Fax: 202-219-2030
http://www2.ed.gov/pubs/TeachersGuide/oeri.html
Offers a variety of publications for professional development. The list of sources includes statistical reports, topical reports and effective programs, schools and practices.

John Blake, Reference/Information
Nancy Cavanaugh, Collection Development

3654 Understanding and Relating To Parents Professionally
Master Teacher
Leadership Lane
PO Box 1207
Manhattan, KS 66505-1207
800-669-9633
Fax: 800-669-1132
http://www.masterteacher.com
From one man with a mission to over sixty employees and growing, The MASTER Teacher has developed and matured. We will continue to provide educators with cutting-edge professional development solutions as we advance into the future.

70 pages
ISBN: 0-914607-65-0
Robert L DeBruyn, Author

3655 Welcome to Teaching and our Schools
Master Teacher
Leadership Lane
PO Box 1207
Manhattan, KS 66505-1207
800-669-9633
800-669-9633
Fax: 800-669-1132
http://www.masterteacher.com
Sets the stage for teachers so that they can have an enthusiastic and successful year in the classroom.

50 pages
ISBN: 0-914607-49-9
Robert L DeBryon, Author

3656 World Exchange Program Directory
Center for U.N. Studies, GPO Box 2786
Ramna
Dacca 1000, Bangladesh
Offers listings, by geographical location, of exchange programs available to United States and abroad students. Listings include all contact information, schedules, fields and levels of study and bilingual information.

Biennial

3657 You Can Handle Them All
Master Teacher
Leadership Lane
PO Box 1207
Manhattan, KS 66505-1207
800-669-9633
Fax: 800-669-1132
http://www.masterteacher.com
Encyclopedia of student misbehaviors offering answers that work. one hundred seventeen student misbehaviors are covered.

320 pages
ISBN: 0-914607-04-9
Robert L DeBruyn, Author

3658 Your Personal Mentoring & Planning Guide forthe First 60 Days of Teaching
Master Teacher
Leadership Lane
PO Box 1207
Manhattan, KS 66505-1207
800-669-9633
Fax: 800-669-1132
http://www.masterteacher.com
In this book we've selected from 32 years of The Master Teacher, the writings we know you would most like your teachers to have to support the first 60 days of the school year.

116 pages
ISBN: 1-58992-056-2

Periodicals

3659 AACTE Briefs
American Association of Colleges for Teacher Ed.
1307 New York Avenue NW
Suite 300
Washington, DC 20005-4701
202-293-2450
Fax: 202-457-8095
E-mail: aacte@aacte.org
http://www.aacte.org
To promote the learning of all PK-12 students through high-quality, evidence-based preparation.

4-12 pages Monthly
ISSN: 0731-602x
Kristin McCabe, Publications Specialist/Edit
Aimee J Hall, Meetings Coordinator

3660 ATEA Journal
American Technical Education Association
Dunwoody College of Technology
818 Dunwoody Blvd
Minneapolis, MN 55043
612-381-3315
Fax: 701-671-2260
E-mail: skrebsbach@dunwoody.edu
http://www.ateaonline.org
To be recognized as the preeminent international organization dedicated to the professional growth and development of postsecondary educators and industrial trainers. Provide leadership in assessing the needs of targeted technology initiatives and providing an array of professional growth and development opportunities to meet or exceed the expectation of institutional and individual members.

32 pages Quarterly
ISSN: 0889-6488
Sandra Krebsbach, Executive Director
DeeAnn Bilben, Administrative Assistant

3661 Action in Teacher Education
University of Georgia, College of Education
820 Van Vleet Oval
Rome 100
Norman, OK 73019
405-325-1081
Fax: 706-542-4277
E-mail: educationinformation@ou.edu
http://www.ou.edu/action
The official publication of the Association of Teacher Educators, serving as a forum for the exchange of information and ideas related to the improvement of teacher education at all levels.

Quarterly
John J Chiodo, Editor
Laura Bolf-Beliveau, Editor

3662 American Educational Research Journal
Columbia University Teachers College
PO Box 51
New York, NY 10027
212-678-3498
Fax: 212-678-4048
http://www.aer.sagepub.com
Publishes research articles that explore the processes and outcomes of teaching, learning, and human development at all educational levels and in both formal and informal settings.

Quarterly
Lois Weis, Editor
Philip Altbach, Associate Editor

3663 American Educator
American Federation of Teachers
555 New Jersey Avenue NW
Washington, DC 20001-2029
202-879-4420
E-mail: amered@aft.org
http://www.aft.org/pubs-reports/american
_educator/index.htm
Professional journal of the American Federation of Teachers, is a quarterly magazine published for classroom teachers and other education professionals from preschool through university

Quarterly

Elizabeth McPike, Editor
Mary Kearney, Advertising/Sales

3664 Arts Management in Community Institutions: Summer Training
National Guild of Community Schools of the Arts
520 8th Avenue
Suite 302
New York, NY 10018
212-268-3337
Fax: 212-268-3995
E-mail: info@natguild.org
http://www.nationalguild.org
Advances high-quality, community arts education so all people may participate in the arts according to their interests and abilities. Support the creation and development of community arts education organizations by providing research and information resources, professional development and networking opportunities, advocacy, and high-profile leadership.

June

Jonathan Herman, Executive Director
Kenneth T Cole, Associate Director

3665 Balance Sheet
ITP South-Western Publishing
5101 Madison Road
Cincinnati, OH 45227-1427
513-271-8811
800-824-5179
Fax: 800-487-8488
Informational publication for high school accounting educators. Articles contain information about innovations in teaching accounting, producing an extensive line of educational texts and software for K-postsecondary markets.

2x Year

Larry Qualls, Editor
Carol Bross-McMahon, Coordinating Editor

3666 Better Teaching
The Parent Institute
PO Box 7474
Fairfax Station, VA 22039-7474
703-323-9170
800-756-5525
Fax: 703-323-9173
http://www.parent-institute.com
Newsletter for teachers (grades 1-12) that offers tips and techniques to improve student learning.

Monthly
ISSN: 1061-1495

John Wherry, President

3667 C/S Newsletter
Center for Instructional Services
Purdue University
W. Lafayette, IN 47907
317-494-9454

Contains descriptions of CIS services and articles about instructional techniques.

4 pages 7x Year

Vickie Lojek

3668 Curriculum Brief
International Technology Education Association
1914 Association Drive
Reston, VA 20191-1538
703-860-2100
Fax: 703-860-0353
Seeks to advance technological literacy through professional development activities and publications.

4x Year

Kendall Starkweather, Executive Director

3669 Education & Treatment of Children
Pressley Ridge School
PO Box 6295
Morgantown, WV 26506-3016
304-293-8400
Fax: 304-293-6585
E-mail: fdowney@wvu.edu
http://www.educationandtreatmentofchild
ren.net
A journal devoted to the dissemination of information concerning the development and improvement of services for children and youth. Its primary criterion for publication is that the material be of direct value to educators and other child care professionals in improving their teaching/training effectiveness. Various types of material are appropriate for publication including originial experimental research, experimental replications, adaptations of previously reported research and reviews.

Quarterly

Bernie Fabry, Managing Editor
Daniel E Hursh, Senior Editor

3670 Educational Placement Sources-US
Education Information Services/Instant Alert
PO Box 620662
Newton, MA 2462-662
617-433-0125
Lists 100 organizations in the United States that find positions for teachers, educational administrators, counselors and other professionals. Listings are classified by type, listed alphabetically and offers all contact information.

4 pages Annual

FB Viaux, President

3671 Exceptional Child Education Resources
The Council for Exceptional Children
2900 Crystal Drive
Suite 1000
Arlington, VA 22202-3557
703-620-3660
888-232-7733
Fax: 703-264-1637
E-mail: askeric@ericir.syr.edu
http://www.cec.sped.org
A quarterly abstract journal that helps teachers stay abreast of the book, nonprint media, and journal literature in special and gifted education.

Quarterly
ISSN: 0160-4309

Robin D. Brewer, President
Alexander T. Graham, Executive Director

3672 Extensions - Newsletter of the High/Scope Curriculum
High/Scope Educational Research Foundation
600 N River Street
Ypsilanti, MI 48198-2898
734-485-2000
800-587-5639
Fax: 734-485-0704
E-mail: info@highscope.org
http://www.highscope.org
Teacher guide for users of the High/Scope curriculum. Articles on classroom strategies, training techniques, problem-solving ideas, and news from the field. Also includes updated training data.

8 pages BiMonthly
ISSN: 0892-5135

Cheryl Polk, President
Steven Schwartz, Chief Financial Officer

3673 Guild Notes Bi-Monthly Newswletter
National Guild of Community Schools of the Arts
520 8th Avenue
Suite 302, 3rd Floor
New York, NY 10018
212-268-3337
Fax: 212-268-3995
E-mail: info@natguild.org
http://www.nationalguild.org

Bi-Monthly

Terry Hueneke, Chairman
Jonathan Herman, Executive Director

3674 Infocus: A Newsletter of the University Continuing Education Association
University Continuing Education Association
1 Dupont Circle NW
Suite 615
Washington, DC 20036-1134
202-659-3130
Fax: 202-785-0374
E-mail: kjkohl@ucea.edu
http://www.upcea.edu
Reports on higher education activities, federal legislation and government agencies, innovative programming at institutions across the country; member institutions; trends in continuing and part-time education; resources; professional development opportunities within the field; and changes in member personnel.

12-20 pages Monthly

Roger Whitaker, President
Robert Hansen, Chief Executive Officer

3675 Innovator
Alumni Association of the University of Michigan
200 Fletcher St.
Ann Arbor, MI 48109-1007
734-764-0394
800-874-4764
Fax: 734-615-3151
E-mail: m.alumni@umich.edu
http://alumni.umich.edu
For professional educators and alumni of University of Michigan's School of Education.

20 pages Quarterly

Eric Warden, Contact

3676 International Journal of Instructional Media
Westwood Press
149 Goose Lane
Tolland, CT 6084-3822
860-875-5484
E-mail: PLSleeman@aol.com
http://www.adprima.com/ijim.htm

A professional journal directly responsive to the need for precise information on the application of media to your instructional and training needs.

Quarterly

Dr Phillip J Sleeman, Executive Editor
Dr Bruce R Ledford, Associate Editor

677 Intervention in School and Clinic
Pro-Ed., Inc.
8700 Shoal Creek Boulevard
Austin, TX 78757-6897
512-451-3246
800-897-3202
Fax: 800-397-7633
E-mail: general@proedinc.com
http://www.proedinc.com
The hands-on how-to resource for teachers and clinicians working with students (especially LD and BD) for whom minor curiculum and environmental medications are ineffective.

64 pages 5x Year Magazine
ISSN: 1053-4512

Judith K Voress, Periodicals Director
Brenda Smith Myles, Editor

678 Journal of Classroom Interaction
University of Houston-University Park
4800 Calhoun Rd
University of Houston
Houston, TX 77204-5026
713-743-2255
Fax: 713-743-8664
E-mail: jci@bayou.uh.edu
http://www.uh.edu
The Journal is a semi-annual publication devoted to empirical investigations and theoretical papers dealing with observation techniques, research on student and teacher behavior, and other issues relevant to the domain of classroom interaction.

Bi-Annually

Renu Khator, Chancellor
Paula Myrick Short, Vice Chancellor

679 Journal of Economic Education
Heldref Publications
1319 18th Street NW
Washington, DC 20036-1802
202-296-6267
800-365-9753
Fax: 202-296-5149
http://www.indiana.edu/~econed/index.html
The Journal of Economic Education offers original articles on innovations in and evaluations of teaching techniques, materials, and programs in economics

Quarterly

William E Becker, Executive Editor

680 Journal of Experiential Education
Association for Experiental Education
1435 Yarmouth Ave
Suite 104
Boulder, CO 80304-2043
303-440-8844
866-522-8337
Fax: 303-440-9581
E-mail: webmaster@aee.org
http://www.aee.org
Association for Experiential Education develops and promotes experiential education. The association is committed to supporting professional development, theoretical advancement and the evaluation of experiential education worldwide.

64 pages 3x Year
ISSN: 1053-8259

Maurie Lung, President
Marin Burton, Secretary

3681 Journal on Excellence in College Teaching
Miami University
Miami University
Oxford, OH 45056
513-529-9265
Fax: 531-529-9264
E-mail: wentzegw@muohio.edu
http://celt.muohio.edu/ject
A peer-reviewed journal published by and for faculty at colleges and universities to increase student learning through effective teaching, interest in and enthusiasm for the profession of teaching, and communication among faculty about their classroom experiences. The Journal provides a scholarly forum for faculty to share proven, innovative pedagogies and thoughtful, inspirational insights about teaching.

Journal 3x/Yr
ISSN: 1052-4800

Gregg Wentzell, Author
Gregg Wentzell, Managing Editor
Milton D. Cox, Editor-in-Chief

3682 Journalism Education Association
Kansas State University
105 Kedzie Hall
Manhattan, KS 66506-1505
785-532-5532
866-532-5532
Fax: 785-532-5563
E-mail: staff@jea.org
http://www.jea.org
Among JEA's 2,100 members are journalism teachers and publications advisers, media professionals, press associations, adviser organizations, libraries, yearbook companies, newspapers, radio stations and departments of journalism.

April & November
25-30 booths with 4700 attendees

Mark Newton, President
Sarah Nichols, Vice President

3683 NCRTL Special Report
National Center for Research on Teacher Education
Michigan State University
East Lansing, MI 48824
517-355-9302
E-mail: floden@msu.edu
http://ncrtl.msu.edu
Membership news and updates.

Robert E. Floden, Contact

3684 NCSIE Inservice
National Council of States on Inservice Education
Syracuse University
402 Huntington Hall
Syracuse, NY 13244
315-443-1870
Fax: 315-443-9082
Professional development, staff development and inservice education.

20 pages Quarterly
James Collins

3685 On The Go! for the Educational Office Professional
Master Teacher
One Leadership Lane
PO Box 1207
Manhattan, KS 66502-1207
800-669-9633
Fax: 800-669-1132
http://www.masterteacher.com

Positive, practical, and successful insights and techniques to help you manage and work with your support staff.

1 pages Monthly Newsletter

Tracey H DeBruyn, Executive Editor

3686 On-The-Go For Educational Office Professionals
Master Teacher
One Leadership Lane
PO Box 1207
Manhattan, KS 66502-1207
785-539-0555
800-669-9633
Fax: 800-669-1132
http://www.masterteacher.com
The publication that provides you with great articles to complete your in-house newsletters and newsletters to parents, without fear of copyright violations.

1 pages Monthly Newsletter

Erica Parkinson, Executive Editor

3687 Paraeducator's Guide to Instructional & Curricular Modifications
Master Teacher
One Leadership Lane
PO Box 1207
Manhattan, KS 66502-1207
800-669-9633
Fax: 800-669-1132
http://www.masterteacher.com
An indispensible tool your paras can use to understand, plan for and carry out appropriate modification for students with all types of special needs.

100 pages
ISBN: 0-914607-88-X

Wendy Dover, Author

3688 Pennsylvania Education
Pennsylvania Department of Education
333 Market Street
Harrisburg, PA 17126-2210
717-783-6788
Fax: 717-783-8230
E-mail: ra-edwebmaster@pa.gov
http://www.pde.state.pa.us
The mission of the Pennsylvania Department of Education is to assist the General Assembly, the Governor, the Secretary of Education and Pennsylvania educators in providing for the maintenance and support of a thorough and efficient system of education.

8-10 pages 8x Year

Gary Tuma, Press Secretary
Beth Boyer, Information Specialist

3689 Performance Improvement Journal
International Society for Performance
PO Box 13035
Suite 260
Silver Spring, MD 20910-2753
301-587-8570
Fax: 301-587-8573
E-mail: info@ispi.org
http://www.ispi.org
To develop and recognize the proficiency of its members and advocate the use of Human Performance Technology.

48 pages Monthly
ISSN: 1090-8811

Mary Ellen Kassotakis, President
Rhonda Buckley, Interim Executive Director

3690 Preventing School Failure
Heldref Publications
325 Chestnut Streetÿ
Suite 800
Philadelphia, PA 19106-1802
215-625-8900
800-354-1420
Fax: 202-296-5149
E-mail:
customer.service@taylorandfrancis.com
http://www.heldref.org
The journal for educators and parents seeking strategies to promote the success of students who have learning and behavior problems. It includes practical examples of programs and practices that help children and youth in schools, clinics, correctional institutions, and other settings. Articles are written by educators and concern teaching children with various kinds of special needs.

48 pages Quarterly
ISSN: 1045-988X

Mary O'Donnell, Managing Editor

3691 Prevention Researcher
Integrated Research
333 South Hope Street
Floor 48
Los Angeles, CA 90071
541-683-9278
800-929-2955
Fax: 541-683-2621
E-mail: orders@TPRonline.org
http://globalsportsdevelopment.org
A quarterly journal that uses a straightforward and easy-to-read approach to present the most current research and developments in adolescent behavioral research. In addition to cutting-edge, evidence-based research it also examines exemplary prevention programs and strategies that can help youth workers see which of today's best practices are most successful.

24 pages Magazine/Quarterly
ISSN: 1086-4385

Melanie Raffle, Vice President of Operations
Brooke Lusk, Director of Communication

3692 Progressive Teacher
Progressive Publishing Company
2678 Henry Street
Augusta, GA 30904-4656
770-868-1691
Offers new information and updates for the improvement and development of higher education.

Quarterly
ISSN: 0033-0825

MS Adcock

3693 Retaining Great Teachers
Master Teacher
One Leadership Lane
PO Box 1207
Manhattan, KS 66502-1207
800-669-9633
Fax: 800-669-1132
http://www.masterteacher.com
The Retaining Great Teachers Book is a systemic approach for attracting, mentoring, supporting, and retaining new and veteran teacher.

85 pages
ISBN: 1-58992-097-X

Michael J Lovett PhD, Author

3694 Rural Educator-Journal for Rural and Small Schools
National Rural Education Association
Colorado State University
Fort Collins, CO 80523-1588
970-491-6444
Fax: 970-491-1317
E-mail: presofc@lamar.colostate.edu
http://www.colostate.edu
Official journal of the NREA. A nationally recognized publication that features timely and informative articles written by leading rural educators from all levels of education. All NREA members are encouraged to submit research articles and items of general information for publication.

40 pages Quarterly Magazine
ISSN: 0273-446X

Anthony A Frank, President
Joseph T Newlin, Editor

3695 TED Newsletter
The Council for Exceptional Children
1920 Association Drive
Reston, VA 20191-1545
703-620-3660
888-232-7733
Fax: 703-264-9494
http://www.tedcec.org
Newsletter of the Teacher Education Division offering information about TED activities, upcoming events, current trends and practices, state and national legislation, recently published materials and practical information of interest to persons involved in the preparation and continuing professional development of effective professionals in special education and related service fields.

3x Year

Mary Anne Prater, President
Marcia Rock, Vice President

3696 TESOL Journal: A Journal of Teaching and Classroom Research
Teachers of English to Speakers of Other Languages
1925 Ballenger Avenue
Suite 550
Alexandria, VA 22314-6820
703-836-0774
Fax: 703-836-7864
E-mail: info@tesol.org
http://www.tesol.org
TESOL's mission is to develop the expertise of its members and others involved in teaching English to speakers of other languages to help them foster communication in diverse settings. The association advances standards for professional preparation and employment, continuing education, and student programs, produces programs, services, and products, and promotes advocacy to further the profession. TESOL has 91 affiliates worldwide.

50 pages Quarterly

Yilin Sun, President
Rosa Aronson, Executive Director

3697 Teacher Education Reports
Feistritzer Publishing
4401-A Connecticut Avenue NW
#212
Washington, DC 20008-2302
202-822-8280
Fax: 202-822-8284
http://www.ncei.com
Covers the field of teacher education for elementary and secondary schools, including pre-service preparation, in-service training and professional development, related federal programs, legislation and funding.

8 pages BiWeekly

David T Chester, Editor

3698 Teacher Education and Special Education
The Council for Exceptional Children
1920 Association Drive
Reston, VA 20191-1545
703-620-3660
Fax: 352-392-7159
http://eric.ed.gov
Contains information on current research, exemplary practices, timely issues, legislation, book reviews, and new programs and materials relative to the preparation and continuing professional development of effective professionals in special education and related service fields.

Quarterly

Vivian Correa, Editor

3699 Teacher Magazine
6935 Arlington Road
Suite 100
Bethesda, MD 20814-5233
301-280-3100
800-346-1834
Fax: 301-280-3250
E-mail: webeditors@epe.org
http://www.edweek.org
Our primary mission is to help raise the level of awareness and understanding among professionals and the public of important issues in American education.

Kevin Bushweller, Executive Editor
Gregory Chronister, Executive Editor

3700 Teacher's Guide to Classroom Management
Economics Press
12 Daniel Road
Fairfield, NJ 7004-2507
973-227-1224
http://www.marketingconsultants.cc
Bulletins showing teachers how to solve problems and avoid problematic situations.

BiWeekly

Alan Yohalem, President

3701 Teachers in Touch
ISM Independent School Management
1316 N Union Street
Wilmington, DE 19806-2594
302-656-4944
800-955-4944
Fax: 302-656-0647
E-mail: smedina@isminc.com
http://isminc.com
Faculty professional development publication with strategies for career satisfaction, good teaching practices and stress-reducing techniques. The forum for professional sharing for private-independent school educators.

4 pages 5x Year

Rozanne S Elliott, Publisher
Kelly Rawlings, Editor

3702 Teaching Education
University of South Carolina, College of Education
Wardlaw College
Room 231
Columbia, SC 29208-1
803-777-6301
Fax: 803-777-3068
http://www.ashe.ws

Focuses on the actual profession of teaching and new methodology by which to learn.

2x Year

Laura Perna, President
James T. Sears, PhD, Editor

703 Techniques-Connecting Education and Careers
Association for Career and Technical Education
1410 King Street
Alexandria, VA 22314-2749
703-683-3111
800-826-9972
Fax: 703-683-7424
E-mail: sackley@acteonline.org
http://www.acteonline.org
To provide leadership in developing an educated, prepared, adaptable and competitive workforce.

Newsletter/Magazine

Peter Magnuson, Director of Programs/Communi
Jan Bray, Executive Director

704 Technology Integration for Teachers
Master Teacher
One Leadership Lane
Po Box 1207
Manhattan, KS 66502-1207
785-539-0555
800-669-9633
Fax: 800-669-1132
http://www.masterteacher.com
The publication that provides teachers with innovative strategies for integratinjg technology into the classroom.

Monthly Newsletter

Brad Roberts, Executive Editor

705 The Board
Master Teacher
One Leadership Lane
Po Box 1207
Manhattan, KS 66502-1207
785-539-0555
800-669-9633
Fax: 800-669-1132
http://www.masterteacher.com
A complete program of in-service training for school board members.

Robert DeBruyn, Executive Editor

706 The Professor In The Classroom
Master Teacher
One Leadership Lane
PO Box 1207
Manhattan, KS 66502-1207
785-539-0555
800-669-9633
Fax: 800-669-1132
http://www.masterteacher.com
From one man with a mission to over sixty employees and growing, The MASTER Teacher has developed and matured. We will continue to provide educators with cutting-edge professional development solutions as we advance into the future.

1 pages Semi-Monthly

Robert DeBruyn, Author

707 Today's Catholic Teacher
2621 Dryden Road
Suite 300
Dayton, OH 45439
937-293-1415
800-523-4625
Fax: 937-293-1310
E-mail: service@peterli.com
http://www.catholicteacher.com

Today's Catholic Teacher magazine is written for you, a teacher in a Catholic school. Each issue is filled with information that will help you succeed in the classroom

72 pages Bimonthly
ISSN: 0040-8441

Cullen Schippe, President/ Publisher
Chris Orsborne, VP/ COO

3708 Training Research Journal: The Science and Practice of Training
Educational Technology Publications
700 Paliside Avenue
Englewood Cliffs, NJ 7632
Fax: 201-871-4009
E-mail: contactÿ@mcweadon.com
http://mcweadon.com
Peer-reviewed publication, published once yearly by Educational Technology Publications, is now in its fourth volume. Provides a high-quality, peer-reviewed forum for theoretical and empirical work relevant to training.

Annually

Badrul H. Khan, Founder
Kelee Plagis, Advisor

Software, Hardware & Internet Resources

3709 Analog & Digital Peripherals
PO Box 499
Troy, OH 45373-3585
937-339-2241
800-758-1041
Fax: 937-339-0070
E-mail: info@adpi.com
http://www.adpi.com
Established in 1978 to provide OEM manufacturers and end users with practical solutions in data logging, storage, and retrieval as well as program loading and back-up.

Lyle Ellicott

3710 E-Z Grader Software
E-Z Grader Company
PO Box 23608
Chagrin Falls, OH 44023
800-432-4018
Fax: 800-689-2772
E-mail: ezgrader@voyager.net
http://www.ezgrader.com
Electronic guidebook designed by teachers for teachers.

3711 K12jobs.Com
PO Box 210811
West Palm Beach, FL 33421
E-mail: beth@k12jobs.com
http://k12jobs.com
To provide schools with an efficient and cost-effective recruiting tool, providing service and opportunities to institutions and job seekers alike.

Also: K-12jobs.Com

Beth Jones, CSR & General Information

3712 KidsCare Childcare Management Software
770 Cochituate Road
Framingham, MA 1701-4672
508-875-3451
Sells software programs to education professionals involved in childcare to aid their development and understanding.

3713 Mental Edge
Learning ShortCuts
PO Box 382367
Germantown, TN 38183-2367
901-218-8163
Fax: 309-406-5358
E-mail: feedback@learningshortcuts.com
http://www.learningshortcuts.com
The Mental Edge is specifically designed to facilitate review and reinforcement. It is the quickest, easiest, and most thorough way to bring the things that have been learned back to mind in preparation for any testing scenario.

3714 The Center For The Future of Teaching and Learning
Center for the Future of Teaching & Learning
730 Harrison Street
Suite 220
San Francisco, CA 94170
415-565-3000
877-493-7833
Fax: 415-565-3012
E-mail: info@cftl.org
http://www.cftl.org
A not-for-profit organization dedicated to strengthening teacher development policy and practice.

Margaret Gaston, President/Executive Director
Tacy C. Ashby, Vice President

3715 www.aasa.org
American Association of School Administrators
1615 Duke Street
Suite 700
Alexandria, VA 22314-1730
703-528-0700
Fax: 703-841-1543
E-mail: info@aasa.org
http://www.aasa.org
Supports and develops effective school system leaders who are dedicated to the highest quality public education for all children.

Randall H Collins, President
Mark T Bielang, President-Elect

3716 www.classbuilder.Com
Class Builder
Free teachers toolbox! Grade book, Create tests, Reports, Lessons, Distance Learning Courseware, and more.

Internet Only Access

Edhelper.Com, Author

3717 www.ed.gov/free
Federal Resources for Educational Excellence
202-401-1444
E-mail: tech@ed.gov
Teaching and learning resources from Federal Agencies

Richard Culatta, Director
Bernadette Adams, Senior Policy Advisor

3718 www.eduverse.com
Leading Internet e-Knowledge software developer building core technologies for powering international distance education.

3719 www.freeteachingaids.com
Free Teaching Aids.com
214 Center Street
Beaver Dam, WI 53956
920-210-3684
888-951-4469
E-mail: info@monumentalhosting.com
Guides for finding free resources for teachers.

3720 www.gsn.org
Global SchoolNet Foundation
270 N. El Camino Real
Suitte 395
Encinitas, CA 92024
760-635-0001
Fax: 760-635-0003
E-mail: helper2009@globalschoolnet.org
Collaborative projects, communication
tools and professional development.
Yvonne Marie Andres, President
John St. Clair, Vice President

**3721 www.imagescape.com/helpweb/ww
w/oneweb.html**
An Overview of the World Wide Web
E-mail: webmaster@imagescape.com

3722 www.learningpage.com
1840 E River Road
Suite 320
Tucson, AZ 85718
E-mail: learningpage@learningpage.com.
LearningPage provides a huge collection
of professionally produced instructional
materials you can download and print.

3723 www.mmhschool.com
McGraw Hill School Division
220 E Danieldale Road
Desoto, TX 75115
800-442-9685
Fax: 972-228-1982
Dedicated to educating children and to
helping educational professionals by providing the highest quality materials and
services.
John Predmore, Privacy Official

3724 www.nprinc.com
National Professional Resources
25 S Regent Street
Port Chester, NY 10573
914-937-8879
800-453-7461
Fax: 914-937-9327
E-mail: service@nprinc.com
Produces videos/DVDs and publishes
books on the most significant and current
topical areas in the educational arena. New
to this product line are laminated reference
guides that provide a succinct summary of
the topic being addressed.
Robert M. Hanson, Founder/ President
Helene Hanson, Vice President

3725 www.onlinelearning.net
OnlineLearning.net
12975 Coral Tree Place
Los Angeles, CA 90066
800-669-9011
E-mail:
customerservice@laureate-inc.com
Source for teacher education online.
Susan Ko, Vice President

3726 www.pagestarworld.com
Pagestar
E-mail: orders@pagestarworld.com
Software products that are specifically designed for teachers. Over 600 electronic
forms that are commonly used by teachers
for planning, administering, delivering
and assessing student learning.

3727 www.pbs.org
PBS TeacherSource
2100 Crystal Drive
Arlington, VA 22202

Offers all Americans the opportunity to
explore new ideas and new worlds
through television and online content.
Jonathan Barzilay, Chief Operating
Officer

3728 www.pbs.org/uti/quicktips.html
QuickTips
2100 Crystal Drive
Arlington, VA 22202
On understanding and using the Internet,
you'll find tips on navigating the Web.
Jonathan Barzilay, Chief Operating
Officer

3729 www.rhlschool.com
RHL School
E-mail: webmaster@rhlschool.net
Free ready to use quality worksheets for
teaching, reinforcement,and review.

**3730 www.sanjuan.edu/select/structures.
html**
San Juan Select - Structures
E-mail: info@sanjuan.edu
A Web site that examines various ways to
structure and facilitate student projects using Internet capabilities. Each suggestion
is accompanied by a specific example of
how that structure can be or is being used
on the Internet.
San Juan, Contact

3731 www.schoolrenaissance.com
School Renaissance Model
2911 Peach Street
PO Box 8036
Wisconsin Rapids, WI 54495-8036
715-424-3636
800-338-4204
Fax: 715-424-4242
E-mail: answers@renlearn.com
Advance technology for essential practice.
Makes the practice component of reading,
math, and writing curriculum more person-
alized and effective.
John J. Luynch, CEO
Mary T. Minch, VP/ CFO

3732 www.teachingjobs.com
The Teachers Employment Network
510-653-1521
E-mail: info@teachingjobs.com
Leading resource for education employ-
ment.

3733 www.usajobs.opm.gov/b1c.htm
Overseas Employment Info- Teachers
US Office of Personnel Management
1900 E Street, NW
Washington, DC 20415-1000
202-606-1800
Covers eligibility, position categories and
special requirements, application procedures, program information and entitle-
ment, housing, living/working conditions,
shipment of household goods, and complete application forms and guidance.
Katherine Archuleta, Director
Earl L. Gay, Senior Advisor

3734 www.webworkshops.com
Web Work Shops
A series of on-line courses, designed to
prepare teachers to integrate both the
Internet and classroom computer applica-
tions into daily lessons.

Training Materials

**3735 At-Risk Students: Identification and
Assistance Strategies**
Center for the Study of Small/Rural Schools
555 E Constitution Street
Room 138
Norman, OK 73072-7820
405-325-1450
Fax: 405-325-7075
E-mail: jcsimmons@ou.edu
http://cssrs.ou.edu
The Center for the Study of Small/Rural Schools
is a cooperative effort between the University of
Oklahoma's Colleges of Education and Continu-
ing Education. Endorsed by the National Rural
Education Association as one of its five recog-
nized rural education research
Video
Jan C Simmons, Program Director

**3736 Character Education: Making a
Difference**
Character Education Partnership
1634 I Street NW
Suite 550
Washington, DC 20036
202-296-7743
800-988-8081
Fax: 202-296-7779
E-mail: information@character.org
http://www.character.org
Leading the nation in helping schools develop
people of good character for a just and compas-
sionate society.
Becky Sipos, President/ CEO
Sheril Morgan, Director

**3737 Character Education: Restoring Respect
& Responsibility in our Schools**
Master Teacher
One Leadership Lane
Po Box 1207
Manhattan, KS 66502-1207
785-539-0555
800-669-9633
Fax: 800-669-1132
http://www.masterteacher.com
Provides a comprehensive model for character ed-
ucation in our nations schools. Specific classroom
stategies as well as school wide approaches are
outlines in a clear and compelling fashion.
Thomas Lickona PhD, Author

3738 Cisco Educational Archives
University of North Carolina at Chapel Hill
170 W Tasman Drive
Po Box 1207
San Jose, CA 95134-3455
408-526-4000
800-553-6387
http://www.cisco.com
Focus on business operations, product innovation
and design, and customer solutions. We develop
products with minimal environmental impact and
extend our technology to reduce environmental
footprints globally.
John T Chambers, Chairman / CEO
Frank Calderoni, Executive VP/CFO

**3739 Classroom Teacher's Guide for Working
with Paraeducators Video Set**
Master Teacher
One Leadership Lane
PO Box 1207
Manhattan, KS 66502-1207
785-539-0555
800-669-9633
Fax: 800-669-1132
http://www.masterteacher.com

Covers a range of nuts-and-bolts topics including why the job duties of paras have changed so much over the years, what a classroom teacher needs to know to get started working effectively with a para. Useful tips for managing another adult, and how para factor into the planning process.

Wendy Dover, Author

740 Clinical Play Therapy Videos: Child-Centered Developmental & Relationship Play Therapy
University of North Texas
425 S. Welch St.
Complex 2
Denton, TX 76203-829
940-565-3864
Fax: 940-565-4461
E-mail: cpt@unt.edu
http://cpt.unt.edu
Encourage the unique development and emotional growth of children through the process of play therapy, a dynamic interpersonal relationship between a child and a therapist trained in play therapy procedures.

Garry Landreth PhD, Founder
Sue Bratton PhD, Director

41 Conferencing with Students & Parents Video Series
Master Teacher
One Leadership Lane
PO Box 1207
Manhattan, KS 66502-1207
800-669-9633
800-669-9633
Fax: 800-669-1132
http://www.masterteacher.com
Will help teachers turn both formal and informal conferences with students and parents into opportunities for student success.

Robert L DeBruyn, Author/Publisher

42 Conflict Resolution Strategies in Schools
Center for the Study of Small/Rural Schools
555 E Constitution Street
Room 138
Norman, OK 73072-7820
405-325-1450
Fax: 405-325-7075
E-mail: jcsimmons@ou.edu
http://cssrs.ou.edu
Series IV
Video
Jan C Simmons, Program Director

43 Conover Company
4 Brookwood Court
Appleton, WI 54914-8618
800-933-1933
Fax: 800-933-1943
E-mail: sales@conovercompany.com
http://www.conovercompany.com
Developing training programs for industry. Provide off-the-shelf as well as custom sales and marketing, training, presentation, and application programs that connect learning to the workplace

Rebecca Schmitz, Member

44 Cooperative Learning Strategies
Center for the Study of Small/Rural Schools
555 E Constitution Street
Room 138
Norman, OK 73072-7820
405-325-1450
Fax: 405-325-7075
E-mail: jcsimmons@ou.edu
http://cssrs.ou.edu

Series I
Video
Jan C Simmons, Program Director

3745 Creating Schools of Character Video Series
Master Teacher
One Leadership Lane
PO Box 1207
Manhattan, KS 66502-1207
785-539-0555
800-669-9633
Fax: 800-669-1132
http://www.masterteacher.com
Visit a Blue Ribbon School of excellence and hear staff and others discuss how to create or improve a whole school character education program.

ISBN: 0-914607-90-1

3746 Crisis Management in Schools
Center for the Study of Small/Rural Schools
555 E Constitution Street
Room 138
Norman, OK 73072-7820
405-325-1450
Fax: 405-325-7075
E-mail: jcsimmons@ou.edu
http://cssrs.ou.edu
Series IV
Video
Jan C Simmons, Program Director

3747 Critical Thinking Video Set
Master Teacher
One Leadership Lane
PO Box 1207
Manhattan, KS 66502-1207
785-539-0555
800-669-9633
Fax: 800-669-1132
http://www.masterteacher.com
Will help teachers challange students to think in a new way. Research shows that when we engage students in critical and creative though, retention increases tremendously.

ISBN: 1-58992-079-1

3748 Curriculum Alignment: Improving Student Learning
Center for the Study of Small/Rural Schools
555 E Constitution Street
Room 138
Norman, OK 73072-7820
405-325-1450
Fax: 405-325-7075
E-mail: jcsimmons@ou.edu
http://cssrs.ou.edu
Series I
Video
Jan C Simmons, Program Director

3749 Datacad
20 Tower Lane
P.O. Box 815
Simsbury, CT 6070
860-217-0490
800-394-2231
Fax: 860-217-1866
E-mail: info@datacad.com
http://www.datacad.com
DATACAD's product development, sales, and marketing activities are managed at the corporate headquarters in Avon, Connecticut

Mark F Madura, President/CEO
David A Giessleman, Senior Vice President and CT

3750 Discipline Techniques you can Master in a Minute Video Series
Master Teacher
One Leadership Lane
PO Box 1207
Manhattan, KS 66502-1207
800-669-9633
Fax: 800-669-1132
http://www.masterteacher.com
he MASTER Teacher provides essential solutions to meet the professional development needs of educators at all levels-from the paraeducator to the superintendent. For over 30 years, we have provided practical strategies to inspire, enrich, and motivate educators.

ISBN: 1-58992-040-6

Robert L DeBruyn, Founder

3751 Educational Productions Inc
7101 Wisconsin Avenue
Suite 700
Bethesda, MD 20814
800-950-4949
800-637-3652
Fax: 301-634-0826
E-mail: custserv@edpro.com
http://teachingstrategies.com
To increase the skills and understanding of the adults who work with, teach and care for young children.

Linda Freedman, President
Rae Latham, Vice-President

3752 Eleven Principals of Effective Character Education
Master Teacher
One Leadership Lane
PO Box 1207
Manhattan, KS 66502-1207
800-669-9633
Fax: 800-669-1132
http://www.masterteacher.com
Takes you to schools in Maryland, New York, and Missouri, where quality character education programs are being implemented by skilled and resourceful staff.

ISBN: 1-887943-13-7

Thomas Lickona PhD, Author

3753 Eleven Principles of Effective Character Education
Character Education Partnership
1634 I Street NW
Suite 550
Washington, DC 20036
202-296-7743
800-988-8081
Fax: 202-296-7779
E-mail: information@character.org
http://www.character.org
Leading the nation in helping schools develop people of good character for a just and compassionate society.

Becky Sipos, President/ CEO
Sheril Morgan, Director

3754 Eye on Education
7625 Empire Drive
Florence, KY 41042-2919
888-299-5350
800-634-7064
Fax: 914-833-0761
E-mail: orders@taylorandfrancis.com
http://www.routledge.com
Books on performance-based learning and assessment.

3755 Great Classroom Management Series DVD
Master Teacher
One Leadership Lane
PO Box 1207
Manhattan, KS 66502-1207
800-669-9633
Fax: 800-669-1132
http://www.masterteacher.com
Effestive classroom management is getting more difficult everday. teachers face increasing demands and expectations in ebery aspect of their jobs.

ISBN: 0-914607-90-1

3756 Great Classroom Management Video Series VHS
Master Teacher
One Leadership Lane
PO Box 1207
Manhattan, KS 66502-1207
800-669-9633
Fax: 800-669-1132
http://www.masterteacher.com
Effective classroom management is getting more difficult everyday. teachers face increasing demands and expectations in everyday. Teachers face increasing demands and expectations in every aspect of their jobs.

ISBN: 1-58992-121-6

3757 Handling Chronically Disruptive Students at Risk Video Series
Master Teacher
One Leadership Lane
PO Box 1207
Manhattan, KS 66502-1207
800-669-9633
Fax: 800-669-1132
http://www.masterteacher.com
Implement and utlize a CARE couscil, develop and individual Action plan, strategies for enhancing individual action plan.

ISBN: 1-58992-031-7

3758 Hearlihy & Company
Po Box 1708
Pittsburg, KS 66762-1747
866-622-1003
Fax: 800-443-2260
E-mail: orders@hearlihy.com
http://www.hearlihy.com
Training and installation for schools purchasing modular labratories.

Kevin Bolte, Contact

3759 Improving Parent/Educator Relationships
Center for the Study of Small/Rural Schools
555 E Constitution Street
Room 138
Norman, OK 73072-7820
405-325-1450
Fax: 405-325-7075
E-mail: jcsimmons@ou.edu
http://cssrs.ou.edu
Series I
Video

Jan C Simmons, Program Director

3760 Improving Student Thinking in the Content Area
Center for the Study of Small/Rural Schools
555 E Constitution Street
Room 138
Norman, OK 73072-7820
405-325-1450
Fax: 405-325-7075
E-mail: jcsimmons@ou.edu
http://cssrs.ou.edu
Series II
Video

Jan C Simmons, Program Director

3761 Inclusion: The Next Step the Video Series
Master Teacher
One Leadership Lane
PO Box 1207
Manhattan, KS 66502-1207
800-669-9633
Fax: 800-669-1132
http://www.masterteacher.com
Will help you propel your inclusion efforts to a new level of success giving you the necessary insights and stategies for building consensus; weighing your program, curriculum, and instructional options.

ISBN: 1-58992-012-0

Wendy Dover, Author

3762 Integrating Technology into the Curriculum Video Series
Master Teacher
One Leadership Lane
PO Box 1207
Manhattan, KS 66502-1207
800-669-9633
Fax: 800-669-1132
http://www.masterteacher.com
Gives teachers the tools and strategies they need to make information technology work for then and for students while empowering then to teach the skills necessary for students to be productive in a technology driven world.

ISBN: 1-58992-007-Y

3763 International Clearinghouse for the Advancement of Science Teaching
University of Maryland
Benjamin Building
Room 226
College Park, MD 20742-1100
301-405-1000
Fax: 301-314-9055
http://www.umd.edu
Provides curriculum information about science and mathematics teaching.

Wallace D. Loh, President
Mary Ann Rankin, Vice President

3764 Lesson Plans and Modifications for Inclusionand Collaborative Classrooms
Master Teacher
One Leadership Lane
PO Box 1207
Manhattan, KS 66502-1207
800-669-9633
Fax: 800-669-1132
http://www.masterteacher.com
Discover specific strategies lesson plans and activity modifications to enhance

learning for all students in the inclusive classroom.

ISBN: 1-58992-022-8

3765 Managing Students Without Coercion
Center for the Study of Small/Rural Schools
555 E Constitution Street
Room 138
Norman, OK 73072-7820
405-325-1450
Fax: 405-325-7075
E-mail: jcsimmons@ou.edu
http://cssrs.ou.edu
Series II
Video

Jan C Simmons, Program Director

3766 Mentoring Teachers to Mastery Video Series
Master Teacher
One Leadership Lane
PO Box 1207
Manhattan, KS 66502-1207
800-669-9633
Fax: 800-669-1132
http://www.masterteacher.com
The MASTER Teacher's e-learning solutions provide cost-effective, subscription-based systems that help meet educators' time demands and continuous learning needs.

ISBN: 1-58992-001-5

3767 Motivating Students in the Classroom Video Series
Master Teacher
One Leadership Lane
PO Box 1207
Manhattan, KS 66502-1207
800-669-9633
Fax: 800-669-1132
http://www.masterteacher.com
The MASTER Teacher has developed and matured. We will continue to provide educators with cutting-edge professional development solutions as we advance into the future

ISBN: 1-58992-074-0

3768 Multicultural Education: Teaching to Diversity
Center for the Study of Small/Rural Schools
555 E Constitution Street
Room 138
Norman, OK 73072-7820
405-325-1450
Fax: 405-325-7075
E-mail: jcsimmons@ou.edu
http://cssrs.ou.edu
Series II
Video

Jan C Simmons, Program Director

3769 Outcome-Based Education: Making it Work
Center for the Study of Small/Rural Schools
555 E Constitution Street
Room 138
Norman, OK 73072-7820
405-325-1450
Fax: 405-325-7075
E-mail: jcsimmons@ou.edu
http://cssrs.ou.edu
Series III
Video

Jan C Simmons, Program Director

770 Overview of Prevention: A Social Change Model
Center for the Study of Small/Rural Schools
555 E Constitution Street
Room 138
Norman, OK 73072-7820
405-325-1450
Fax: 405-325-7075
E-mail: jcsimmons@ou.edu
http://cssrs.ou.edu
Prevention Series

Video

Jan C Simmons, Program Director

771 Quality School
Center for the Study of Small/Rural Schools
555 E Constitution Street
Room 138
Norman, OK 73072-7820
405-325-1450
Fax: 405-325-7075
E-mail: jcsimmons@ou.edu
http://cssrs.ou.edu
Series II

Video

Jan C Simmons, Program Director

772 SAP Today
Performance Resource Press
1270 Rankin Drive
Suite F
Troy, MI 48083-2843
800-453-7733
Fax: 800-499-5718
Overview offers the basics of student assistance.

773 School-Wide Strategies for Retaining Great Teachers Video Series
Master Teacher
One Leadership Lane
PO Box 1207
Manhattan, KS 66502-1207
800-669-9633
Fax: 800-669-1132
http://www.masterteacher.com
You will hear proven strategies for supporting new teachers through all those typical expirences that cansabatage their efforts and cause them to leave your district or even abandon teaching all together.

ISBN: 1-58992-098-8

774 Site-Based Management
Center for the Study of Small/Rural Schools
555 E Constitution Street
Room 138
Norman, OK 73072-7820
405-325-1450
Fax: 405-325-7075
E-mail: jcsimmons@ou.edu
http://cssrs.ou.edu
Series III

Video

Jan C Simmons, Program Director

775 Strategic Planning for Outcome-Based Education
Center for the Study of Small/Rural Schools
555 E Constitution Street
Room 138
Norman, OK 73072-7820
405-325-1450
Fax: 405-325-7075
E-mail: jcsimmons@ou.edu
http://cssrs.ou.edu
Series II

Video

Jan C Simmons, Program Director

3776 Strengthening the Family: An Overview of a Holistic Family Wellness Model
Center for the Study of Small/Rural Schools
555 E Constitution Street
Room 138
Norman, OK 73072-7820
405-325-1450
Fax: 405-325-7075
E-mail: jcsimmons@ou.edu
http://cssrs.ou.edu
Prevention Series

Video

Jan C Simmons, Program Director

3777 Students-at-Risk Video Series
Master Teacher
One Leadership Lane
PO Box 1207
Manhattan, KS 66502-1207
800-669-9633
Fax: 800-669-1132
http://www.masterteacher.com
Gives you specific stategies for reaching those students who are giving up.

ISBN: 1-58992-060-0

Mildred Odom Bradley, Author

3778 Superintendent/School Board Relationships
Center for the Study of Small/Rural Schools
555 E Constitution Street
Room 138
Norman, OK 73072-7820
405-325-1450
Fax: 405-325-7075
E-mail: jcsimmons@ou.edu
http://cssrs.ou.edu
Series I

Video

Jan C Simmons, Program Director

3779 TQM: Implementing Quality Management in Your School
Center for the Study of Small/Rural Schools
555 E Constitution Street
Room 138
Norman, OK 73072-7820
405-325-1450
Fax: 405-325-7075
E-mail: jcsimmons@ou.edu
http://cssrs.ou.edu
Series III

Video

Jan C Simmons, Program Director

3780 Teachers as Heros
Center for the Study of Small/Rural Schools
555 E Constitution Street
Room 138
Norman, OK 73072-7820
405-325-1450
Fax: 405-325-7075
E-mail: jcsimmons@ou.edu
http://cssrs.ou.edu
Series IV

Video

Jan C Simmons, Program Director

3781 Teaching for Intelligent Behavior
Center for the Study of Small/Rural Schools
555 E Constitution Street
Room 138
Norman, OK 73072-7820
405-325-1450
Fax: 405-325-7075
E-mail: jcsimmons@ou.edu
http://cssrs.ou.edu

Series IV

Video

Jan C Simmons, Program Director

3782 The Master Teacher
Master Teacher
One Leadership Lane
PO Box 1207
Manhattan, KS 66502-1207
800-669-9633
Fax: 800-669-1132
http://www.masterteacher.com
From one man with a mission to over sixty employees and growing, The MASTER Teacher has developed and matured. We will continue to provide educators with cutting-edge professional development solutions as we advance into the future.

2 pages Weekly

3783 Training Video Series for the Substitute Teacher
Master Teacher
One Leadership Lane
PO Box 1207
Manhattan, KS 66502-1207
800-669-9633
Fax: 800-669-1132
http://www.masterteacher.com
From one man with a mission to over sixty employees and growing, The MASTER Teacher has developed and matured. We will continue to provide educators with cutting-edge professional development solutions as we advance into the future.

ISBN: 0-914607-95-2

3784 Voices in the Hall: High School Principals at Work
Phi Delta Kappa Educational Foundation
320 W. Eighth Street
Suite 216
Bloomington, IN 47404-3800
812-339-1156
800-766-1156
Fax: 812-339-0018
E-mail: memberservices@pdkintl.org
http://www.pdkintl.org
The mission of Phi Delta Kappa International is to promote high-quality education, in particular publicly supported education, as essential to the development and maintenance of a democratic way of life. This mission is accomplished through leadership, research, and service in education

William E Webster, Author
Dan Brown, Executive Director
Bill Bushaw, Chief Executive Officer

3785 Wavelength
4753 N Broadway
Suite 818
Chicago, IL 60640
773-784-1012
877-528-47 2
Fax: 773-784-1079
E-mail: info@wavelengthinc.com
http://www.wavelengthinc.com
Wavelength offers a fresh perspective on the key challenges in education today. Our programs are founded on the tenet that humor heals and enlightens. Of course, we also realized that by focusing our humor on education, we'd never run out of material

3786 You Can Handle Them All Discipline Video Series
Master Teacher
One Leadership Lane
PO Box 1207
Manhattan, KS 66502-1207

800-669-9633
Fax: 800-669-1132
http://www.masterteacher.com
Based upon the best selling books You Can Handle Them All and BEfore you can Discipline by Robert L Debruyn. It contains the vital professional foundations that must underpin and solid philosophy of discipline.

ISBN: 1-58992-035-X
Robert L DeBruyn, Author

Workshops & Programs

3787 ACE Fellows Program
American Council on Education
1 Dupont Circle NW
Washington, DC 20036-1193
202-939-9300
Fax: 202-785-8056
E-mail: comments@ace.nche.edu
http://www.acenet.edu
Provides comprehensive leadership development for senior faculty and administrators of universities and colleges. Offers mentor-intern relationships programs. Special institutional grants available for candidates from community colleges, tribal colleges and private historical black universities and colleges.

James H. Mullen, Chairman
Renu Khator, Vice Chair

3788 ART New England Summer Workshops
Massachusetts College of Art and De
621 Huntington Avenue
Boston, MA 2115-5801
617-879-7175
E-mail: Nancy.Mccarthy@massart.edu
http://ane.massart.edu
Offers painting, drawing, photography, jewelry making, sculpting, computer imaging and ceramics.

Nancy McCarthy, Administrator

3789 Annual Conductor's Institute of South Carolina
University of South Carolina
School of Music
Columbia, SC 29208
803-777-7500
Fax: 803-777-9774
E-mail: charl@mailbox.sc.edu
http://www.conductorsinstitute.com
Since its inception, more than 600 conductors have traveled to Columbia to study with guest conductors and composers. Academic credit is available.

Donald Portnoy, Director

3790 Annual Summer Institute for Secondary Teachers
Rock and Roll Hall of Fame
E-mail: soehler@rockhall.org
http://www.rockhall.com/programs/institute.asp
The institute provides teachers with the knowledge and tools needed to bring popular music into the curriculum. The program includes a rock and roll history survey; guest speakers; discussions and workshops.

June

Susan Oehler, Education Programs Manager

3791 Ball State University
2000 W University Avenue
Muncie, IN 47306
765-289-1241
800-382-8540
E-mail: askus@bsu.edu
http://cms.bsu.edu
At Ball State, we're more than just educators-we're educational entrepreneurs. Combining top-flight talent with the top-notch resources Ball State has to offer, our students and faculty inject endless energy and creativity into what they teach and how they learn. The result-a university The Princeton Review calls one of the best in the Midwest.

Rick Hall, Chairman
Frank Hancock, Vice Chair

3792 Bryant and Stratton College
1259 Central Avenue
Albany, NY 12205-142
518-437-1802
Fax: 716-821-9343
E-mail: rpferrell@bryantstratton.edu
http://www.bryantstratton.edu
For 150 years, Bryant & Stratton College has been helping students develop meaningful career skills in a concise, contemporary and effective manner - providing graduates with the marketable job skills they need to succeed in an increasingly competitive marketplace

Bryant H Prentice, Chairman of the Board
David J Ament, Managing Partner

3793 Center for Educational Leadership Trinity University
Trinity University
One Trinity Place
San Antonio, TX 78212-7200
210-999-7207
Fax: 210-999-8164
E-mail: admissions@trinity.edu
http://new.trinity.edu
Offers three Masters degree programs for Arts, Teaching, Psychology and School Administration. The school also offers summer institutes and training programs for educators and administrators. Also see information regarding the Master of Education: School Administration at http://carme.cs.trinity.edu/education/graduate/medschoolleadership.htm

Paul Kelleher, Chairman
Sonia L Mireles, Senior Secretary

3794 Center for Global Education
Augsbury College
2211 Riverside Avenue
Minneapolis, MN 55454-1350
612-330-1000
800-299-8889
Fax: 612-330-1695
E-mail: globaled@augsburg.edu
http://www.augsburg.edu/global
To provide cross-cultural educational opportunities in order to foster critical analysis of local and global conditions so that personal and systemic change takes place leading to a more just and sustainable world.

Orval Gingerich, Associate Dean
Regina McGoff, Associate Director

3795 Center for Image Processing in Education
1155 15TH STREET NW
SUITE 700
Washington, DC 20005-3750
202-721-9200
800-322-9884

Fax: 202-721-9250
E-mail: kRISR@evisual.org
http://www.cipe.com
CIPE promotes computer-aided visualization as a tool for inquiry-based learning. In support of that mission, it develops instructional materials and conducts workshops that use digital image analysis and geographic information systems technologies as platforms for teaching about science, mathematics, and technology.

Greg Lebedev, Chair
Karen Karrigan, Vice Chair

3796 Center for Learning Connections
Edmonds Community College
20000 68th Ave West
Lynnwood, WA 98036-9800
425-640-1463
Fax: 425-640-1826
E-mail: peter.schmidt@edcc.edu
http://www.learningconnections.org
The mission of the Center for Learning Connections is to prepare learners to manage change and create successful futures.

Peter Schmidt, Executive Director
Cal Crow, Program Director

3797 Center for Occupational Research & Development
4901 Bosque Blvd.
2nd Floor
Waco, TX 76710
254-772-8756
800-231-3015
Fax: 254-776-2306
E-mail: twarner@cord.org
http://www.cord.org
The Center for Occupational Research and Development (CORD) is a national nonprofit organization dedicated to leading change in education

Richard Hinckley, President/ CEO
Ann-Claire Anderson, Assistant Vice President

3798 Center for Play Therapy
University of North Texas
425 S. Welch St.
Complex 2
Denton, TX 76203-829
940-565-3864
Fax: 940-565-4461
E-mail: cpt@unt.edu
http://cpt.unt.edu
Encourages the unique development and emotional growth of children through the process of play therapy, a dynamic interpersonal relationship between a child and a therapist trained in play therapy procedures. Provides training, research, publications, counseling services and acts as a clearinghouse for literature in the field.

Sue Bratton, Director
Alyssa Swan, Staff

3799 Classroom Connect
6277 Sea Harbor Drive
Orlando, FL 32887
800-638-1639
888-801-8299
Fax: 650-351-5300
E-mail: support@classroom.tv
http://www.classroom.tv
A leading provider of professional development programs and online instructional content for K-12 education.

October

Eduardo Abeliuk, Founder
Nicolas Velasco, Operations

3800 College of the Ozarks
1 Industrial Place
PO Box 17
Point Lookout, MO 65726

417-334-6411
800-222-0525
Fax: 417-335-2618
E-mail: webmaster@cofo.edu
http://www.cofo.edu
The College of the Ozarks began as a dream. In 1905, young Presbyterian missionary James Forsythe was assigned to serve the region that encompassed Sparta, Mansfield, and Forsyth, Missouri

Jerry C Davis, President

3801 Connect
Synergy Learning
116 Birge Street
PO Box 60
Brattleboro, VT 5302-60
802-257-2629
800-769-6199
Fax: 802-254-5233
E-mail: info@synergylearning.org
http://www.synergylearning.org
To engage in publishing and professional development for educators, pre-K through middle school

28 pages
ISSN: 1041-682X

Casey Murrow, Executive Director
Susan Hathaway, Circulation Manager

3802 Critical Issues in Urban Special Education: The Implications of Whole-School Change
Harvard Graduate School of Education
Appian Way
Fifth Floor
Cambridge, MA 2138
617-495-3572
800-545-1849
Fax: 617-496-8051
E-mail: webeditor@gse.harvard.edu
http://www.gse.harvard.edu/~ppe
A one-week summer seminar that examines the implications of whole-school change on students with disabilities, policy, procedure, and practice. The program will clarify competing agendas, illuminate various models, and identify unified approaches to ensuring measurable benefits to all children.

Genet Jeanjean, Program Coordinator
Al Written, Interim Director

3803 Critical and Creative Thinking in the Classroom
National Center for Teaching Thinking
1703 N. Beauregard St.
Suite 8
Alexandria, VA 22311
703-578-9600
800-933-2723
Fax: 703-575-5400
http://www.ascd.org
A unique summer program of courses for K-12 teachers, curriculum developers, staff-development specialists, school/district administrators, teacher educators and college faculty.

Nancy Gibson, President
Marie Adair, Executive Director

3804 Curriculum Center - Office of Educational Services
Southern Illinois University Carbondale
1263 Lincoln Drive
Suite 114
Carbondale, IL 62901-6899
618-453-2121
Fax: 217-786-3020
E-mail: oesiscc@siu.edu
http://coas.siu.edu

Programs in vocational areas, career awareness, career development, integration, technology, tech preparation.

Mickey A.ÿ Latour, Dean

3805 Darryl L Sink & Associates
1 Cielo Vista Place
Suite 101
Monterey, CA 93940
831-649-8384
800-650-7465
Fax: 831-649-3914
E-mail: jane@dsink.com
http://www.dsink.com
DSA encourages customers to evaluate such adult learning strategies as cognitive apprenticeship, problem-based learning, goal-based scenarios, and real world authentic learning activities as the cornerstones of efficient, effective, and appealing learning experiences.

3806 DeVry University
One Tower Lane
Oakbrook Terrace, IL 60181
602-216-7700
866-338-7937
Fax: 602-943-4108
http://www.devry.edu
Subjects include communications, computer technology, electronics, graphic communications, and training and development.

Peter Anderson, Chief Strategist
Richard L Ehrlickman, Executive Vice President

3807 Delmar Thomson Learning
10650 Toebben Drive
Independence, KY 41051
518-464-3500
800-354-9706
Fax: 518-464-7000
E-mail: info@delmar.com
http://solutions.cengage.com/brands/Delmar/
Subjects include welding, HVAC-R, electrical, electronics, automotive, CADD and drafting, construction, blueprint reading, and fire science.

Josef Blumenfeld, Senior Vice President
Lindsay Stanley, Senior Director

3808 Depco
689 S. Hwy. 69
PO Box 178
Pittsburg, KS 66762
620-231-0019
800-767-1062
Fax: 620-231-0024
E-mail: tcoon@depcollc.com
http://www.depcollc.com
DEPCO (Dependable Education Products Company) was introduced as a manufacturers' representative organization, which represented manufacturers of vocational education products

3809 Eastern Illinois University School of Technology
1014 Klehm Hall
600 Lincoln Avenue
Charleston, IL 61920-3099
217-581-3226
Fax: 217-581-6607
http://www.eiu.edu/tech/
Subjects include manufacturing, construction, electronics, graphic communications, training and development.

Austin Cheney, Chair
Rendong Bai, Associate Professor

3810 Edison Welding Institute
EWI
1250 Arthur E Adams Drive
Columbus, OH 43221-3585
614-688-5000
Fax: 614-688-5001
E-mail: info@ewi.org
http://www.ewi.org
The NJC's mission is to enhance the life-cycle affordability and mission capability of critical Navy weapon systems through the implementation of materials joining technology

Richard Rogovin, Chair
Henry Cialone, President/ CEO

3811 Educational Summit
The Principals' Center
20 Nassau Street
Suite 211
Princeton, NJ 8542-4509
609-497-1907
Fax: 609-497-1927
An educational summit held in August for school principals to explore, debate and design new models for schooling in America with implications for choice, charters and the community.

3812 Effective Strategies for School Reform
Harvard Graduate School of Education
Appian Way
5th Floor
Cambridge, MA 2138
617-495-3572
800-545-1849
Fax: 617-496-8051
E-mail: webeditor@gse.harvard.edu
http://www.gse.harvard.edu/~ppe
To enrich the professional practice of individuals and institutions worldwide that share our commitment to improving education.

Rosanne Boyle, Program Coordinator
Jennifer Stine, Managing Director/Profession

3813 Electronics Industries Alliance/CEA
2500 Wilson Boulevard
Arlington, VA 22201-3834
703-907-7670
Fax: 703-907-7968
http://www.CEMAweb.org
Electronics workshops.

3814 Elementary Education Professional Development School
Pennsylvania State University
228 Chambers Building
Pennsylvania State University
University Park, PA 16802
814-865-0488
E-mail: n78@psu.edu
http://www.ed.psu.edu
The first goal is to enhance the educational experiences of all children. The second goal focuses on ensuring high quality field experiences for new teachers.

David H. Monk, Dean
Greg J. Kelly, Associate Dean

3815 Emco Maier Corporation
46850 Magellan Drive
Unit 160
Novi, MI 48377-2448
248-313-2700
Fax: 248-313-2701
E-mail: info@emcomaier-usa.com
http://www.emco-world.us
The EMCO success story began in 1947 with the production of conventional lathes. In the years to follow, EMCO repeatedly impressed

the market with extraordinary, innovative solutions.

Josh Dack, Sales Manager
Karen Fahy, Sales/Marketing Coordinator

3816 Energy Concepts

1001 Cottonwood Drive NEÿ
PO Box 628
Willmar, MN 56201
320-235-9079
800-621-1247
Fax: 847-837-8171
E-mail: info@energyconceptsinc.com
http://www.energyconceptsinc.com
Subjects include material science technology, principles of technology year I&II.

3817 Fastech

1750 Westfield Drive
Findlay, OH 45840
419-425-2233
Fax: 419-425-9431
E-mail: info@fastechinc.net
http://www.fastechinc.net
Subjects include mastercam training, and FMMT CD's.

Roger J. Darr, President

3818 Festo Corporation

395 Moreland Road
PO Box 18023
Hauppauge, NY 11788
631-435-0800
Fax: 631-435-8026
E-mail: customer.service@us.festo.com
http://www.festo-usa.com
Subjects include fluid power, PLC, industrial automation.

Fred Zieram, Sales Manager
Petra Milks, Product Coordinator

3819 Foundation for Critical Thinking

PO Box 196
Tomales, CA 94971
707-878-9100
800-833-3645
Fax: 707-878-9111
E-mail: cct@criticalthinking.org
http://www.criticalthinking.org
The work of the Foundation is to integrate the Center's research and theoretical developments, and to create events and resources designed to help educators improve their instruction. Materials developed through the Foundation for Critical Thinking include books, thinker's guides, videos, and other teaching and learning resources.

Dr Richard Paul, Fellow
Dr Linda Elder, Fellow

3820 Four State Regional Technology Conference

Pittsburg State University
College of Technology
1701 S Broadway
Pittsburg, KS 66762
620-235-7000
800-854-7488
Fax: 620-235-4343
E-mail: tbaldwin@pittstate.edu
http://www.pittstate.edu
Subjects include educational technology and technology management.

November
30 booths with 250 attendees

Tom Baldwin, Dean, College of Technology
Steve Scott, President

3821 Graduate Programs for Professional Educators

North Central Association of Colleges & Schools
Walden University
155 5th Avenue S
Minneaoplis, MN 55401
800-444-6795
Fax: 941-498-4266
E-mail: request@waldenu.edu
http://www.northcentralassociation.org
Both the MS and PhD in Education allow study from home or work. The Master of Science in Education serves classroom teachers and the PhD in education serves the advanced learning needs of educators from a wide range that serves practice fields and levels.

Benny Gooden, President
David Ho, Vice President

3822 Grand Canyon University College of Education

3300 W Camelback Road
Phoenix, AZ 85017-3030
602-639-7500
800-800-9776
Fax: 312-263-7462
E-mail: cmosby@gcu.edu
http://www.gcu.edu
Prepares learners to become global citizens, critical thinkers, effective communicators, and responsible leaders by providing an academically challenging, values-based curriculum from the context of our Christian heritage.

Brain Mueler, President/ CEO
Stan Meyer, Chief Operating Officer

3823 Harvard Institute for School Leadership

Harvard Graduate School of Education
Appian Way
Fifth Floor
Cambridge, MA 2138
617-495-3572
800-545-1849
Fax: 617-496-8051
E-mail: webeditor@gse.harvard.edu
http://www.gse.harvard.edu/ppe
An intensive residential program for leadership teams from school districts. Participants will gain new perspectives on the processes and goals of school reform and practical skills for leading change in their districts.

July

3824 Harvard Seminar for Superintendents

Harvard Graduate School of Education
Appian Way
Fifth Floor
Cambridge, MA 2138
617-495-3572
800-545-1849
Fax: 617-496-8051
E-mail: webeditor@gse.harvard.edu
http://www.gse.harvard.edu/ppe
Veteran superintendents from around the country participate in a week of intellectually stimulating conversations with Harvard faculty and networking with colleagues. Topics discussed include the arts, science, social science, and current events.

July

Julia Bean, Program Assistant

3825 Hobart Institute of Welding Technology

400 Trade Square East
Troy, OH 45373
800-332-9448
Fax: 937-332-9550
E-mail: info@welding.orgÿ
http://www.welding.org
Preparation course for CWI/CWE exams. Instructor course devoted to welding theory and hand-son practice.

Elmer Swank, Contact

3826 Indiana University-Purdue University of Indianapolis, IUPUI

Department of Construction Technology
420 University Blvd.
ET 209
Indianapolis, IN 46202-5160
317-274-5555
Fax: 317-274-4567
E-mail: askiu@iu.edu
http://www.iupui.edu
Subjects include architectural technology, civil engineering technology, construction technology, interior design.

Charles R. Bantz, Chancellor
Nasser H. Paydar, Executive Vice Chancellor

3827 Industrial Training Institute

3385 Wheeling Road
Lancaster, OH 43130
740-687-5262
800-638-4180
Fax: 740-687-5262
E-mail: drbillstevens1@msn.com
http://www.dvdcoach.com
Subjects include basic electricity, motors, controls, PLC's, NEC and process control; custom designed training and consulting.

3828 Institute of Higher Education

General Board of Higher Education & Ministry/UMC
1001 19th Avenue S
P. O. ÿBox 340007
Nashville, TN 37203-7
615-340-7400
Fax: 615-340-7379
E-mail: scu@gbhem.org
http://www.gbhem.org/highed.html
An annual seminar for administrators and faculty of United Methodist-related educational institutions addressing current themes related to the college's mission.

June
125 attendees

James E. Dorff, President
Lanther Marie Mills, Vice President

3829 International Curriculum Management Audit Center

Phi Delta Kappa International
320 W Eight Street
Suite 216
Bloomington, IN 47404
812-339-1156
800-766-1156
Fax: 812-339-0018
E-mail: memberservices@pdkintl.org
http://www.pdkintl.org
The mission of Phi Delta Kappa International is to promote high-quality education, in particular publicly supported education, as essential to the development and maintenance of a democratic way of life. This mission is accomplished through leadership, research, and service in education.

William Bushaw, Executive Director
Diana Daugherty, Administrative Assistant

830 International Graduate School
Berne University
35 Center Street
Suite 18
Wolfeboro Falls, NH 03896-1080
603-569-8648
866-755-5557
Fax: 603-569-4052
E-mail: berne@berne.edu
http://www.berne.edu
Doctoral Degrees in one to two years, Specialist Diplomas in six to twelve months in: business, education (all specialties), government, health services, international relations, psychology, religion, social work and human services.

831 International Workshops
187 Aqua View Road
Cedarburg, WI 53012
262-377-7062
Fax: 262-377-7096
E-mail: thintz@internationalworkshops.org
http://www.internationalworkshops.org
International Workshops creates an international community of artists and teachers in a site that combines touristic and cultural interest.
400 attendees
Tori Hintz, Manager
Gerald F Fischbach, Director

32 Island Drafting & Technical Institute
128 Broadway
Amityville, NY 11701-2704
631-691-8733
Fax: 631-691-8738
E-mail: info@idti.edu
http://www.idti.edu
Our aim is to graduate students well-trained and technically qualified so that they may enter their chosen field or continue their education at the baccalaureate or higher level.
John G Diliberto, VP

33 Janice Borla Vocal Jazz Camp
N Central College, Music Department
30 N Brainard Street
Naperville, IL 60540
630-416-3911
Fax: 630-416-6249
E-mail: jborla@aol.com
http://www.janiceborlavocaljazzcamp.org
The camp's mission is to enable jazz vocalists to develop and enhance their individual performing skills and musical creativity, regardless of prior experience level, by studying with and attending performances of professional artists actively engaged in the field of jazz performance.
Janice Borla, Director
Jay Clayton, Faculty

34 Jefferson State Community College
2601 Carson Road
Birmingham, AL 35215
205-853-1200
800-239-5900
Fax: 205-856-8572
E-mail: workforcedev@jeffstateonline.com
http://www.jeffstateonline.com
Certificate and degree programs in automated manufacturing, electromechanical systems, industrial maintenance, and CAD.

35 July in Rensselaer
St Joseph's College, Graduate Dept
PO Box 984
Rensselaer, IN 47978
219-866-6352
Fax: 219-866-6102
E-mail: jamesc@saintjoe.edu

Solo, ensemble, liturgy, accompanying, history, improvisation, private lessons, technique, repertoire, sight reading, workshops, theory and sacred choral music.
Rev. James Challancin, Director

3836 K'nex Education Division
2990 Bergey Road
PO Box 700
Hatfield, PA 19440
888-ABC-KNEX
Fax: 215-996-4222
E-mail: abcknex@knex.com
http://www.knexeducation.com
Introductory, set specific, regional and design your own professional development programs offered for any/all K-12 technology, math and science sets.

3837 Kaleidoscope
Consulting Psychologists Press
3803 E Bayshore Road
Palo Alto, CA 94303-4300
800-624-1765
Fax: 650-969-8608
An institute for educators that develops insights into teaching styles and learning styles; administers and interprets the Myers-Briggs Type Indicator (personality inventory); learn new techniques to help children understand and value their unique qualities; create and deliver lessons that enlighten all students and more.
July

3838 Kent State University
375 Terrace Drive
Van Deusen Hall
Kent, OH 44242
330-672-2892
Fax: 330-672-2894
E-mail: lepps@kent.edu
http://www.tech.kent.edu
Subjects include aeronautics, electronics, manufacturing engineering, computer technology, and automotive engineering technology.
Verna Fitzsimmons, Interim Dean
Isaac Richmond Nettey, Associate Dean

3839 Kentucky State University
400 East Main Street
Frankfort, KY 40601
502-597-6000
Fax: 502-227-6236
E-mail: webadmin@kysu.edu
http://www.kysu.edu
Associates in applied science in drafting and design technology and applied science in electronics technology.
Mary Evans Sias, President
Stephen Mason, Executive Assistant to the P

3840 Kodaly Teaching Certification Program
DePaul University, School of Music
804 West Belden Avenue
Chicago, IL 60614
773-325-4355
Fax: 773-325-7263
Music education, pedagogy and workshops.
Robert Krueger, Director Operations

3841 Lab Volt Systems
1710 State Highway 34
Farmingdale, NJ 07727
732-938-2000
800-522-2658
Fax: 732-774-8573
E-mail: us@labvolt.com
http://www.labvolt.com

Global leader in the design and manufacture of hands-on training laboratories for public education, industry, and the military.
Eric Maynard, Contact

3842 Leadership and the New Technologies
Harvard Graduate School of Education
44 Brattle Street
Fifth Floor
Cambridge, MA 02138
800-545-1849
800-545-1849
Fax: 617-496-8051
E-mail: ppe@gse.harvard.edu
http://www.gse.harvard.edu/~ppe
Programs designed to help teams of school leaders anticipate the far-reaching impacts that new technologies can have on students, teachers, curriculum, and communication. Participants make long-term plans for the use of technology in their schools and districts and learn how to take advantage of federal and state technology initiatives.
July
Ann Doyle, Program Coordinator

3843 Learning & The Enneagram
National Enneagram Institute at Milton Academy
230 Atherton Street
Milton, MA 02186-2424
617-898-1798
Fax: 617-898-1712
An educational enterprise dedicated to guiding individuals and organizations in the most responsible and effective format for their needs. Programs include exploration of what every educator needs to know; why we learn in the way we do; and how we teach.
July
Regina Pyle, Coordinator

3844 Learning Materials Workshop
58 Henry Street
Burlington, VT 05401
800-693-7164
Fax: 802-862-8399
E-mail: info@learningmaterialswork.com
http://www.learningmaterialswork.com
Learning Materials Workshop Blocks are learning tools in the hands of young children. They are open-ended, yet carefully designed in a variety of colors, sizes, shapes, and textures that stimulate and develop perpetual, motor, and language skills. Learning Materials Workshops are designed for early childhood/primary grade teachers, paraprofessionals, curriculum coordinators, special education teachers, ESL teachers, and teachers of the gifted and talented to help develop the learning process.
Karen Hewitt, President

3845 Light Machines
444 E Industrial Park Avenue
Manchester, NH 03109-5317
800-221-2763
Fax: 603-625-2137
E-mail: industrialsales@intelitek_usa.com
http://www.lightmachines.com
Subjects include demonstrations and comprehensive training on CNC routers, turning machines and milling machines, and CAD/CAM software.

3846 MPulse Maintenance Software
PO Box 22906
Eugene, OR 97402
541-302-6677
800-944-1796
Fax: 541-302-6680

E-mail: info@mpulsesoftware.com
http://www.mpulsesoftware.com
Deliver simply better EAM / CMMS software that is easier to use and faster to implement. Keep it affordable by controlling the cost of sales and marketing. Design it to keep up with their needs today, their challenges of tomorrow, while maintaining the history of what they did yesterday. And do it better than anyone else

Steve Brous, President & CEO

3847 Marcraft International Corporation
1350 Spaulding Ave
Suite 302
Kennwick, WA 99352
509-374-1951
800-441-6006
Fax: 509-374-9250
E-mail: sales@marcraft.com
http://www.marcraft.com
s to develop exceptional products for effectively teaching and training people the technical IT, computer, and electronics training skills in demand today and in the future.

Robert Krug, National Sales Manager

3848 Maryland Center for Career and Technology Education
1415 Key Highway
Baltimore, MD 21230
410-685-1648
Fax: 410-685-0032
Subjects include technology education and occupational education certification.

3849 Media and American Democracy
Harvard Graduate School of Education
Programs in Professional Education
Appian Way
Cambridge, MA 02138
617-495-3572
800-545-1849
Fax: 617-496-8051
E-mail: ppe@harvard.edu
http://www.gse.harvard.edu/~ppe
Participants learn about the interaction between the media and American democratic process, develop curriculum units, and examine ways to help students become thoughtful consumers of media messages about politics. Designed for secondary school teachers of history, social studies, English, journalism, and humanities.

August

Tracy Ryder, Program Assistant

3850 Millersville University
PO Box 1002
1 South George Street
Millersvile, PA 17551
717-872-3011
800-426-4553
Fax: 877-327-8132
http://www.millersville.edu
With a student population of 7,259 undergraduate and 1,047 graduate students, Millersville University offers all the advantages you would expect from a university: competitive programs, great facilities, a diverse student community and a variety of campus programming all offered in an accessible, intimate and close-knit atmosphere more frequently found at a smaller college

Michael G Warfel, Chairman
Paul G Wedel, Vice Chairman

3851 Morehead State University
150 University Boulevard
Morehead, KY 40351
606-783-2221
Fax: 606-783-5000
E-mail: admissions@moreheadstate.edu
http://www.morehead-st.edu
Morehead State University was founded upon and continues to embrace the ideal that all persons should have opportunity to participate in higher education. With immense pride in its past and great promise for its future, the University intends to emerge in the first decade of the 21st century as an even stronger institution recognized for superb teaching and learning with exemplary programs in teacher education, space-related science and technology, entrepreneurship, visual and performing arts, r

Beth Patrick, Vice President
Dayna Seelig, Special Assistant to the Pre

3852 Musikgarten
507 Arlington Street
Greensboro, NC 27406
336-272-5303
800-216-6864
Fax: 336-272-0581
E-mail: musgarten@aol.com
http://www.musikgarten.org
Early childhood music education workshops teaching music and understanding children.

Lorna Heyge, President

3853 NASA Educational Workshop
NSTA
1840 Wilson Boulevard
Arlington, VA 22201-3000
703-243-7100
888-400-6782
Fax: 703-243-7177
E-mail: businessoffice@nsta.org
http://www.nsta.org
Two week workshop at a NASA Center, professional development opportunity for K-12 teachers in mathematics, science, and technology, teachers and curriculum specialists at the K-12 levels; media specialists, resource teachers, elementary curriculum developers, counselors, and others with special interest in mathematics, science, technology, and geography.

Karen Ostlund, President
Bill Badders, President-Elect

3854 NCSS Summer Workshops
National Council for the Social Studies
8555 Sixteenth Street
Suite 500
Silver Spring, MD 20910
301-588-1800
800-683-0812
Fax: 301-588-2049
E-mail: sgriffin@ncss.org
http://www.socialstudies.org
Social studies educators teach students the content knowledge, intellectual skills, and civic values necessary for fulfilling the duties of citizenship in a participatory democracy.

July

Susan Griffin, Executive Director
Sojan Alex, Finance Assistant

3855 National Center for Construction Education & Research
13614 Progress Boulevard
Alachua, FL 32615
386-518-6500
888-622-3720
Fax: 386-518-6303
E-mail: info@nccer.org
http://www.nccer.org
Our mission is to build a safe, productive, and sustainable workforce of craft professionals.

Don Whyte, President
Cathy Tyler, Executive Assistant

3856 National Computer Systems
4401 L Street NW
Suite 550
Edina, MN 55435
612-995-8997
800-328-6172
Fax: 952-830-8564
http://www.ncsus.net
Programs offer skills to teach technology in the classroom.

3857 National Head Start Association
1651 Prince Street
Alexandria, VA 22314-2818
703-739-0875
Fax: 703-739-0878
http://www.nhsa.org
The National Head Start Association is a private not-for-profit membership organization dedicated exclusively to meeting the needs of Head Start children and their families.

Ron Herndon, Chairman
Linda Broyles, Vice- Chairperson

3858 Northern Arizona University
South San Francisco Street
Flagstaff, AZ 86011
928-523-9011
Fax: 520-523-6395
E-mail: tlc2@dana.ucc.nau.edu
http://www.nau.edu
Provide an outstanding undergraduate residential education strengthened by research, graduate and professional programs, and sophisticated methods of distance delivery.

John D Haeger, President
Tracy Cooper, Lab Assistant

3859 Orff-Schulwerk Teacher Certification Program
DePaul University, School of Music
804 West Belden Avenue
Chicago, IL 60614
773-325-7260
Fax: 773-325-7264
E-mail: ahutchen@wppost.depaul.edu.
Music education, pedagogy and workshops.

Judy Bundra, Associate Dean

3860 Owens Community College
PO Box 10000
Toledo, OH 43699-1947
567-661-7000
800-466-9367
Fax: 419-661-7664
http://www.owens.edu
We believe in serving our students and our communities. Your success is our misssion.

Diana H Talmage, Chairman
R J Molter, Vice Chair

3861 Paideia Group
608 Garden Leaf Court
St. Louis, MO 63011
636-220-9300
Fax: 919-932-3905
E-mail: bethsymes@psideiagroup.com
http://www.paideiagroup.com
To help people understand what it means to be customer-focused. Participants focus on the skills, attitudes, and automatic behaviors that must be

developed to reach a common goal of becoming a customer-focused organization.

Beth Symes, Principal and Founder

3862 Pamela Sims & Associates
54 Mozart Crescent
Brampton, Ontario
Canada L6Y-2W7
905-455-7331
888-610-7467
Fax: 905-455-0207
E-mail: loveofkids@aol.com
http://www.pamelasims.com
Seminars and workshops for educators and parents.

Pamela Sims, President
Kelly Smith, Marketing Director

3863 Pennsylvania State University-Workforce Education & Development Program
411D Keller Building
University Park, PA 16802
814-863-3858
Fax: 814-863-7532
E-mail: eifl@psu.edu
http://www.ed.psu.edu/wfed
To promote excellence, opportunity, and leadership among professionals in the workforce education and development field including, but not limited to, those employed in secondary or postsecondary education institutions, social services industries, and employee groups and private businesses.

Edgar I Farmer, Department Head
Judith A Kolb, Professor-in-Charge

3864 Performance Learning Systems
72 Lone Oak Drive
Cadiz, KY 42211
270-522-2000
866-757-2527
Fax: 270-522-2010
E-mail: info@plsweb.com
http://www.plsweb.com
The mission of Performance Learning Systems, Inc. is to enhance education through the development of educational services.

Jackie Futrell, Resource Manager
Stephen G Barkley, Master teacher-of-teachers

3865 Piano Workshop
Goshen College
1700 S Main Street
Goshen, IN 46526
574-535-7000
Fax: 574-535-7949
E-mail: beverlykl@goshen.edu
http://www.goshen.edu/music/Piano%20Workshop/Main
The Goshen College Piano Workshop and Academy comprises lectures, master classes and recital performances presented by distinguished clinicians, composers and performers. Teachers participating in the Workshop hear inspiring lectures relevant to piano pedagogy, performance and literature.

Beverly K Lapp, Associate Professor of Music

3866 Pittsburg State University
College of Technology
1701 S Broadway
Pittsburg, KS 66762
620-231-7000
800-854-7488
Fax: 620-235-4343
E-mail: psuinfo@pittstate.edu
http://www.pittstate.edu
A comprehensive regional university, provides undergraduate and graduate programs

and services to the people of southeast Kansas, but also to others who seek the benefits offered.

Bruce Dallman, Dean, College of Technology
Steve Scott, President

3867 Polaroid Education Program
565 Technology Square
#3B
Cambridge, MA 02139-3539
781-386-2000
Fax: 781-386-3925
This program offers workshops for professional educators, preK-12; the Visual Learning Workshop and an Instant Image Portfolio Workshop.

3868 Professional Development Institutes
Center for Professional Development & Services
2730 University Boulevard
Suite 301
Kensington, MD 20895
301-949-1771
800-766-1156
Fax: 301-949-5441
E-mail: info@pditraining.net
http://www.pditraining.net
Offers a wide variety of courses for Real Estate professionals around the US to meet their pre-licensing, post-licensing, and continuing education needs. Also offers non-credit courses on Technology, Business, Accounting, and Project Management, among others to further any career.

3869 Professional Development Workshops
Rebus
4111 Jackson Road
Ann Arbor, MI 48103
734-668-4870
800-435-3085
Fax: 734-668-4728
http://www.rebusinc.com
Workshops that promote success by assessing children in the context of active learning.

June/July

Sam Meisels, CEO
Linda Borgsdorf, President

3870 Project Zero Classroom
Harvard Graduate School of Education
Programs in Professional Education
Appian Way
Cambridge, MA 02138
617-495-3572
800-545-1849
Fax: 617-496-8051
E-mail: ppe@harvard.edu
http://www.gse.harvard.edu/~ppe
Renowned educators Howard Gardner and David Perkins and their Project Zero colleagues work with K-12 educators to help them reshape their classroom practices to promote student understanding. The week focuses on five concepts: teaching for understanding, multiple intelligences, the thinking classroom, authentic assessment, and learning with and through the arts.

July

Tracy Ryder, Program Assistant

3871 Robert McNeel & Associates
3670 Woodland Park Avenue N
Seattle, WA 98103
206-545-7000
Fax: 206-545-7321
E-mail: bob@mcneelcom
http://www.en.na.mcneel.com
3D modeling workshop for design, drafting, graphics, and technology educators.

3872 Rockford Systems
4620 Hydraulic Road
Rockford, IL 61109-2695
815-874-7891
800-922-7533
Fax: 815-874-6144
E-mail: sales@rockfordsystems.com
http://www.rockfordsystems.com
Machine safegaurding seminar for technology educators.

3873 SUNY College at Oswego
7060 Route 104
Oswego, NY 13126-3599
315-312-2500
Fax: 315-312-2863
E-mail: stanley@oswego.edu
http://www.oswego.edu
The chief goal of the Oswego College Foundation, Inc. is to raise and manage private support to advance SUNY Oswego's mission.

October
26 booths with 350-400 attendees

Deborah F Stanley, President
Howard Gordon, Executive Assistant to Presi

3874 School of Music
Georgia State University
PO Box 4097
Atlanta, GA 30302-4097
404-413-5900
Fax: 404-413-5910
E-mail: music@gsu.edu
http://www.music.gsu.edu
The mission of the School of Music is to provide a comprehensive, rigorous, and innovative academic program that is consistent with the urban context and mission of Georgia State University, and that serves the pursuit of artistic, professional, and scholarly excellence through experiences of lasting value to all stakeholders.

W Dwight Coleman, Director
Robert J Ambrose, Associate Director

3875 Southern Polytechnic State University
1100 S Marietta Parkway
Marietta, GA 30060-2896
678-915-7778
800-635-3204
Fax: 678-915-7490
E-mail: coned@spsu.edu
http://www.oce.spsu.edu
Specialize in the delivery of comprehensive real-world training on a grand scale. Whether it be High-Tech, Business Professional or Engineering

3876 Southwestern Oklahoma State University
Industrial and Engineering Technology Department
100 Campus Drive
Weatherford, OK 73096
580-774-3063
Fax: 580-774-3795
E-mail: admissions@swosu.edu
http://www.swosu.edu
The mission of Southwestern Oklahoma State University is to provide educational opportunities in higher education that meet the needs of the state and region; contribute to the educational, economic, and cultural environment; and support scholarly activity.

Gary Bell, Chair
Jeff Short, Program Coordinator

3877 Specialized Solutions
24703 US Highway 19-N
Suite 200
Clearwater, FL 33763

240-252-5070
888-840-2378
Fax: 877-200-5959
E-mail:
cameron@specializedsolutions.com
http://www.specializedsolutions.com
Technology based training and certification self study programs.

Sheri Nash, Contact

3878 Staff Development Workshops & Training Sessions
National School Conference Institute
PO Box 37527
Phoenix, AZ 85069-7527
602-371-8655
Fax: 602-371-8790
Offers twenty relevant and leading edge programs including curriculum instruction assessment, restructuring your school, improving student performance and gifted at-risk students. Ten monthly sessions of each program are available, with monthly feedback to follow-up. Accelerates restructuring efforts and also offers graduate credit.

3879 Standards and Accountability: Their Impact on Teaching and Assessment
Harvard Graduate School of Education
Programs in Professional Education
339 Gutman Library
Cambridge, MA 02138
617-495-3572
800-545-1849
Fax: 617-496-8051
E-mail: ppe@harvard.edu
http://www.gse.harvard.edu/~ppe
Examines educational and policy issues by new approaches to standards, assessment, and accountability. Focuses on issues of excellence and equity, aligning assessments with standards, strengthening professional development, impacts of challenges on school communities, and political and legal issues surrounding standards and forms of accountability. Designed for public school leaders whose responsibilities include evaluation and testing.

July

Tracy Ryder, Program Assistant

3880 Storytelling for Educational Enrichment The Magic of Storytelling
2709 Oak Haven Drive
San Marcos, TX 78666-5065
512-392-0669
800-322-3199
Fax: 512-392-9660
E-mail: krieger@corridor.net
Teacher in-service and training in storytelling and puppetry for teachers of Pre-K through third grades. The Magic of Storytelling is for all ages and levels, specializing in original stories of enlightenment and environmental education. Over ten years experiences with many national and regional conferences and training.

Cherie Krieger, President

3881 Summer Institute in Siena
University of Siena-S/American
Universities
595 Prospect Road
Waterbury, CT 06706
203-754-5741
Fax: 203-753-8105
E-mail: siena@sienamusic.org
http://www.sienamusic.org

Programs offered in cooperation with the University of Siena-S and American Universities and Colleges. The program in Siena Italy is open to qualified graduates, undergraduates, professionals, teachers, 19 years of age or above. Special diploma; credit or non-credit; in-service credit; auditions; trips to Rome, Florence, Assisi, Venice, Pisa, three days in Switzerland; a Puccini Opera.

Joseph Del Principe, Music Director

3882 Summer Programs for School Teams
National Association of Elementary
School Principa
1615 Duke Street
Alexandria, VA 22314-3345
703-684-3345
800-386-2377
Fax: 703-518-6281
http://www.naesp.org
Events focused on the key to exceptional instruction. Effective teaching and learning for school teams, must include the principal.

Ann R Walker, Assistant Executive
Director
Herrie Hahn, Director Programs

3883 Supplemental Instruction, Supervisor Workshops
University of Missouri-Kansas City
5100 Rockhill Road
SASS 210
Kansas City, MO 64110-2499
816-235-1174
Fax: 816-235-5156
E-mail: cad@umkc.edu
http://www.umkc.edu/cad/si
Supplemental Instruction (SI) is an academic assistance program that utilizes peer-assisted study sessions.

Kim Wilcox, Coordinator of Training
Glen Jacobs, Executive Director

3884 THE Institute & Knowvation
1105 Media 9201 Oakdale Avenue
Suite 101
Chatsworth, CA 91311
818-734-1520
800-840-0003
Fax: 818-734-1522
E-mail: kodell@1105media.com
http://www.thejournal.com/institute
T.H.E. Institute believes that in order for students to be successful in the 21st century, technology must be an integral part of every aspect of education.

Geoffrey H Fletcher, Executive Director

3885 TUV Product Service
Westendstra e 199
Munich, MA D-806
49 -9 5-91 0
800-TUV-0123
Fax: 978-762-7637
E-mail: info@tuev-sued.de
http://www.tuvglobal.com
As process partners with comprehensive industry knowledge our teams of specialists provide early consultation and continuous guidance, thus achieving the optimisation of technology, systems and expertise

Axel Stepken, Chief Executive Officer
Manfred Bayerlein, Chief Operations
Officer

3886 Teacher Education Institute
1079 W Morse Boulevard
Suite A
Winter Park, FL 32789-3751
800-331-2208
Fax: 800-370-2600
E-mail: tei@teachereducation.com
http://www.teachereducation.com
TEI was founded in 1981 to meet the needs of classroom teachers for quality education and training in practical, proven skills and methods that make a tangible and positive difference in their relationships and interactions with students and colleagues.

Vince Welsh, President

3887 Teachers College: Columbia University
Center for Technology & School Change
525 W 120th Street
New York, NY 10027
212-678-3000
Fax: 212-678-4048
E-mail: webcomments@tc.columbia.edu
http://www.tc.columbia.edu
bring educational opportunities to all members of society, and whose faculty and students, time and again during more than a century of leadership, have demonstrated the power of ideas to change the world.

Howard Budin, Director Center for Technolo
Susan H Fuhrman, President

3888 Technology Training for Educators
Astronauts Memorial Foundation
Kennedy Space Center
, FL 32899
321-452-2887
800-792-3494
Fax: 321-452-6244
E-mail: amfreg@amfcse.org
http://www.amfcse.org
Microsoft NT Administration; Technology Specialist; Management of Technology; Advanced Technology Specialist.

3889 Tooling University
3615 Superior Avenue
Building 44,6th Floor
Cleveland, OH 44114-3898
216-706-6600
866-706-8665
Fax: 216-706-6601
E-mail: info@toolingu.com
http://www.toolingu.com
Toolingu.com is the leading online training provider focused on the unique needs of manufacturers. Our roots are in manufacturing, and our business started by recognizing the industry's specific needs

Gene Jones, Director Marketing

3890 Total Quality Schools Workshop
Pennsylvania State University
302F Rackley Building
University Park, PA 16802
814-843-3765
E-mail: hli@psu.edu
http://www.ed.psu.edu/ctqs/index.html
Designed for public school educators at the state, national, and international level, this training program provides information in the philosophy, tools, and techniques of total quality management in education. The three day-six week program focuses on leadership, reform models, and education decision making.

William Hartman, Director

3891 University of Arkansas at Little Rock
2801 S University Avenue
Little Rock, AR 72204-1099
501-683-7302
Fax: 501-683-7304

E-mail: admissions@ualr.edu
http://www.ualr.edu
With more than 100 programs of study, UALR has an academic program to suit your interests. We offer everything from computer science to fine arts, and we're sure you will find your niche on our campus

Sandra Bates, President
Tammy Starks, Vice President

3892 University of Central Florida

3100 Technology Parkway
Suite 264
Orlando, FL 32826-3281
407-823-4910
Fax: 407-207-4911
E-mail: distrib@ucf.edu
http://www.distrib.ucf.edu
The University of Central Florida is one of the most dynamic universities in the country. Offering 223 degree programs, it has become an academic and research leader in numerous fields, such as optics, modeling and simulation, engineering and computer science, business administration, education, science, hospitality management and digital media.

John C Hitt, President/Corporate Secretar
John Schell, Vice President

3893 University of Michigan-Dearborn Center for Corporate & Professional Development

4901 Evergreen Road
CCPD-2000
Dearborn, MI 48128-2406
313-593-5000
Fax: 313-593-5111
E-mail: info@umich.edu
http://www.umd.umich.edu
We offer undergraduate, graduate, and professional education to a diverse, highly motivated, and talented student body. Our programs are responsive to the changing needs of society; relevant to the goals of our students and community partners; rich in opportunities for independent and collaborative study, research, and practical application; and reflective of the traditions of excellence, innovation, and leadership that distinguish the University of Michigan

Daniel Little, Chancellor
Ray Metz, Chief of Staff

3894 Wavelength

4753 N Broadway
Suite 808
Chicago, IL 60640
773-784-1012
877-528-47 2
Fax: 773-784-1079
E-mail: info@wavelengthinc.com
http://www.wavelengthinc.com
Wavelength offers a fresh perspective on the key challenges in education today. Our programs are founded on the tenet that humor heals and enlightens.

3895 Wids Learning Design System

1 Foundation Circle
Waunakee, WI 53597
800-677-9437
800-821-6313
Fax: 608-849-2468
E-mail: info@wids.org
http://www.wids.org
WIDS strives to enhance the quality of learning through the development, implementation, support, and continuous improvement of the WIDS Learning Design System, a comprehensive methodology, supported by application and professional development tools, for designing and planning perfor-

mance-based assessment learning and teaching.

Lisa Laabs, Office Manager
Judy Neill, Director

3896 Workforce Education and Development

Southern Illinois University Carbondale
475 Clocktower Drive
Mailcode 4605
Carbondale, IL 62901-4605
618-453-3321
Fax: 618-453-1909
E-mail: wed@siu.edu
http://www.wed.siu.edu/Public/
The Department of Workforce Education and Development is one of the largest education, training, and development departments in the United States. A recent external evaluation team recognized the Department as among the top ten in the nation.

Keith Waugh, Associate
Professor/Chairman

Directories & Handbooks / *General*

3897 106 Ways Parents Can Help Students Achieve
American Association of School Administrators
1615 Duke Street
Suite 700
Alexandria, VA 22314-1730
703-528-0700
Fax: 703-841-1543
E-mail: info@aasa.org
http://www.aasa.org
Provides parents with useful information about the importance of parental involvement, concrete ways to work with children and schools to promote success, and a list of resources for further reading.
Set of 10
ISBN: 0-8108-4220-3

3898 A Personal Planner & Training Guide for the Substitute Teacher
Master Teacher
One Leadership Lane
PO Box 1207
Manhattan, KS 66502-1207
800-669-9633
Fax: 800-669-1132
http://www.masterteacher.com
Helps substitute teachers set the tone for a positive experience.
90 pages
ISBN: 0-914607-89-8
John Eller, Author

3899 Academic Year & Summer Programs Abroad
American Institute for Foreign Study
1 High Ridge Park
Stamford, CT 06905-5504
203-399-5000
866-906-2437
Fax: 203-399-5590
E-mail: info@aifs.com
http://www.aifs.com
Offers school names, addresses, courses offered, tuition and fee information.
224 pages Annual
Cyril Taylor, Founder/ Chairman
William L. Gertz, President/ CEO

3900 Accredited Institutions of Postsecondary Education
MacMillan Publishing Company
1633 Broadway
New York, NY 10019
212-654-8500
888-247-8269
Fax: 800-835-3202
http://ope.ed.gov/accreditation/
Lists over 5,000 accredited institutions and programs for postsecondary education in the United States.
600 pages Annual

3901 Activities and Strategies for Connecting Kids with Kids: Elementary Edition
Master Teacher
One Leadership Lane
PO Box 1207
Manhattan, KS 66502-1207
800-669-9633
Fax: 800-669-1132
http://www.masterteacher.com
Activities, lesson plans, and strategies that celebrate each student's individual differences while developing cooperation, tolerance, understanding, sharing and caring.
159 pages
ISBN: 0-914607-74-X

3902 Activities and Strategies for Connecting Kids with Kids: Secondary Edition
Master Teacher
One Leadership Lane
PO Box 1207
Manhattan, KS 66502-1207
800-669-9633
Fax: 800-669-1132
http://www.masterteacher.com
Activities, lesson plans, and strategies that celebrate each student's individual differences while developing cooperation, tolerance, understanding, sharing and caring.
136 pages
ISBN: 0-914607-75-8

3903 American School Directory
PO Box 20002
Murfreesboro, TN 37129
866-273-2797
Fax: 800-929-3408
E-mail: support@asddataservices.com
http://www.asd.com
More than 104,000 school sites are loaded with pictures, art, calendars, menus, local links and notes from students, parents and alumni. Choose the school by name, state list, or by ASD number.

3904 Amusing and Unorthodox Definitions
Careers/Consultants Consultants in Education
3050 Palm Aire Drive N
#310
Pompano Beach, FL 33069
954-974-5477
Fax: 954-974-5477
E-mail: carconed@aol.com
Collection of amusing and unorthodox definitions. The meanings, purposes and implications assigned to the words appearing here will delight audiences, enliven conversations and keep you chuckling.

ISBN: 0-7392-0089-5
ISSN: 99-94623

Dr. Robert M Bookbinder, President/Author

3905 Associated Schools Project in Education for International Co-operation
UNESCO Associated Schools Project Network
7 Place de Fontenoy
75352 Paris 07 SP
France
33 -0 1-45 6
1-45681000
http://www.unesco.org
Lists 1,970 secondary and primary schools, teacher training institutions and nursery schools in 95 countries that participate in the UNESCO Associated School Project.
200 pages Annual

3906 Association for Community-Based Education Directory of Members
Association for Community Based Education
1805 Florida Avenue NW
Washington, DC 20009-1708
202-462-6333

Offers information on 100 private community organizations concerned with alternative education including colleges that award degrees without residency requirements and more.
115 pages Annual

3907 Awakening Brilliance: How to Inspire Children to Become Successful Learners
Pamela Sims & Associates
54 Mozart Crescent
Canada L6Y 2W7
905-455-7331
888-610-7467
Fax: 905-455-0207
E-mail: loveofkids@aol.com
http://www.pamelasims.com
Seminars and workshops for educators and parents. Upcoming workshops include themes of awakening students' potential and team leadership skills.
248 pages Paperback
ISBN: 0-9651126-0-8

Pamela Sims, Author/Editor
Kelly Smith, Marketing Director

3908 Beyond the Bake Sale
Master Teacher
One Leadership Lane
PO Box 1207
Manhattan, KS 66502-1207
800-669-9633
Fax: 800-669-1132
http://www.masterteacher.com
A notebook containing 101 detailed plans that not only provide you with fundraising ideas, but get you started, keep you on track, and lead your team through the finishing touches.
101 pages
ISBN: 1-58992-119-4

3909 Biographical Membership Directory
American Educational Research Association
1430 K Street, NW
Suite 1200
Washington, DC 20005-3078
202-238-3200
Fax: 202-238-3250
http://www.aera.net
Membership directory of more than 23,000 persons involved in education research and development, including the names, addresses, phone numbers, highest degree held and year received, occupational specialization areas, e-mail addresses and more.
420 pages Bi-Annual

Felice J. Levine, Executive Director
Gerald E. Sroufe, Senior Advisor

3910 CASE Directory of Advancement Professionals in Education
Council for Advancement & Support of Education
1307 New York Avenue NW
Suite 1000
Washington, DC 20005-4701
202-328-2273
Fax: 202-387-4973
E-mail: info@case.org
http://www.case.org
Membership directory of 16,000 professionals in alumni relations, communications and fund raising at educational institutions worldwide.
Publication Date: 1995 200 pages Annual
ISBN: 0-899643-10-8

John Lippincott, President
Donald Falkenstein, Vice President

11 Cabells Directory of Publishing Opportunities in Educational Curriculum & Methods
Cabell Publishing Company
Box 5428
Tobe Hahn Station
Beaumont, TX 77726
409-898-0575
Fax: 409-866-9554
E-mail: info@cabells.com
http://www.cabells.com
Provides information on editor's contact information, manuscript guidelines, acceptance rate, review information and circulation data for over 350 academic journals.
799 pages Annual
ISBN: 0-911753-27-3
David WE Cabell, Editor
Deborah L English, Editor

12 Cadet Gray: Your Guide to Military Schools-Military Colleges & Cadet Programs
Reference Desk Books
PO Box 22925
Santa Barbara, CA 93121
805-772-8806
This is a comprehensive reference book which describes 55 American military schools, grade schools, high schools, junior colleges, senior colleges, and the federal service academies. Descriptions include school histories, academic requirements, military environment, extracurricular activities and costs.
Publication Date: 1990 212 pages
ISBN: 0-962574-90-2

13 Carnegie Communications, LLC
Porter Sargent Publishers
2 LAN Drive
Suite 100
Westford, MA 01886-3028
978-692-5092
800-342-7470
Fax: 978-692-4174
E-mail: info@carnegiecomm.com
http://www.carnegiecomm.com
Lists and authoritatively describes 800 elementary and secondary schools in 130 countries. Written for the educator, personnel advisor, student and parent as well as diplomatic and corporate officials, this unique guide is an indispensable reference for American students seeking preparatory schooling overseas. Hardcover.
Publication Date: 1991 544 pages BiAnnual
Joe Moore, President/ CEO
Meghan Dalesandro, EVP, Operation

14 Character Education Evaluation Tool Kit
Character Education Partnership
1634 I Street NW
Suite 550
Washington, DC 20036
202-296-7743
800-988-8081
Fax: 202-296-7779
E-mail: information@character.org
http://www.character.org
Julea Posey, Matthew Davison, Meg Korpi, Author
Becky Sipos, President and CEO
Sheril Morgan, Director

3915 Character Education Kit: 36 Weeks of Success: Elementary Edition
Master Teacher
One Leadership Lane
PO Box 1207
Manhattan, KS 66502-1207
800-669-9633
Fax: 800-669-1132
http://www.masterteacher.com
Takes the guesswork out of delivering your character education message by providing you with all the pieces of a well-rounded program including important components for 36 character traits.
428 pages
ISBN: 1-58992-096-1

3916 Choosing Your Independent School in the United Kingdom & Ireland
Independent Schools Information Service
56 Buckingham Gate
London SW1E 6AG
England
71-63087934
1,400 independent schools in the United Kingdom and Ireland with contact information, entry requirements, fees, scholarships available, subjects and exam boards.
293 pages Annual/September

3917 Classroom Teacher's Guide for Working with Paraeducators
Master Teacher
One Leadership Lane
PO Box 1207
Manhattan, KS 66502-1207
800-669-9633
Fax: 800-669-1132
http://www.masterteacher.com
This workbook includes numerous forms that allow teachers to communicate more effectively to paras the vital information they will need in working with special students.
60 pages
ISBN: 1-58992-127-5
Wendy Dover, Author

3918 Commonwealth Universities Yearbook
Association of Commonwealth Universities
20-24 Tavistock Square
London WC1H 0PF
England
207-380-6700
44-20-7380-6700
Fax: 207-387-2655
Fax: 44-20-738-2655
E-mail: info@acu.ac.uk
http://www.acu.ac.uk
Offers information on over 700 university institutions of recognized academic standing in 36 Commonwealth countries or regions, including Africa, Asia, Australia, Britain, Canada and the Pacific.
2,600 pages Annual
ISBN: 0-85143-188-7
ISSN: 0069-7745
Olive Mugenda, Chairman
Jan Thomas, Vice Chairman

3919 Complete Learning Disabilities Directory
Grey House Publishing
5979 North Elm Avenue
Suite 113
Millerton, NY 12546
518-789-8700
800-562-2139
Fax: 518-789-0556
E-mail: books@greyhouse.com
http://www.greyhouse.com

A one-stop sourcebook for people of all ages with learning disabilities and those who work with them. This comprehensive database in print includes information about associations and organizations, schools, government agencies, testing materials, camps, books, newsletters and more.
800 pages Annual/Softcover
ISBN: 1-59237-049-7
Leslie Mackenzie, Publisher
Richard Gottlieb, Editor

3920 Computer and Web Resources for People with Disabilities
Alliance for Technology Access/Hunter House
1119 Old Humboldt Road
Suite 240
Jackson, TN 38305
731-554-5282
800-914-3017
Fax: 731-554-5283
E-mail: atainfo@ataccess.org
http://www.ataccess.org
This directory shows how America's forty-five million people with disabilities can potentially benefit from using computer technology to achieve goals and change their lives. Written by experts in the field, this important work provides a comprehensive, step-by-step guide to approaching computer innovations. It explains how to identify the appropriate technology, how to seek funding, how to set it up and what to consider.
Publication Date: 1996 400 pages Paperback/CD ROM
ISBN: 0-89793-433-4
James Allison, President
Bob Van der Linde, Vice President

3921 Conservation Education and Outreach Techniques
North American Assoc for Environmental Education
2000 P Street NW
Suite 540
Washington, DC 20036
202-419-0412
Fax: 212-419-0415
E-mail: info@naaee.org
http://www.naaee.org
Presents the theory and practice for creating effective education and outreach programmes for conservation. An exciting array of techniques for enhancing school resources, marketing environmental messages, using mass media, developing partnerships for conservation, and designing on-site programmes for natural areas and community centres.

ISBN: 0-19-856772-3
Jose Marcos-Iga, President
Judy Braus, Executive Director

3922 Contemporary World Issues: Public Schooling in America
ABC-CLIO
130 Cremona Drive
#1911
Santa Barbara, CA 93117-5599
805-963-4221
800-368-6868
Fax: 805-685-9685
http://www.abc-clio.com
Offers information on organizations and agencies involved with public education systems.

3923 Cornocopia of Concise Quotations
Careers/Consultants Consultants in
Education
3050 Palm Aire Drive N
#310
Pompano Beach, FL 33069
954-974-5477
Fax: 954-974-5477
E-mail: carconed@aol.com
Wealth of practical reminders of the endur-
ing ideas. The book furthers humane un-
derstandings by gathering and preserving
the wisdom of the wise and experienced.

ISBN: 0-7392-0275-8
ISSN: 99-95201

Dr. Robert M Bookbinder, President

**3924 Council for Educational
Development and Research
Directory**
National Education Association (NEA)
1201 16th Street NW
Washington, DC 20036-3290
202-833-4000
Fax: 202-822-7974
E-mail: ncuea@nea.org
http://www.nea.org
Offers 15 member educational research
and development institutions.

50 pages Annual

Lily Eskelsen Garc¡a, President
Becky Pringle, Vice President

3925 Digest of Supreme Court Decisions
Phi Delta Kappa Educational Foundation
320 W. Eighth Street
Suite 216
Bloomington, IN 47404-0789
812-339-1156
800-786-1156
Fax: 812-339-0018
E-mail: memberservices@pdkintl.org
http://www.pdkintl.org
Designed as a ready reference, this edition
of a popular digest provides a concise set of
individual summaries of cases decided by
the Supreme Court. Fully indexed.

256 pages Paperback
ISBN: 0-87367-835-4

Perry A Zirkel, Author
Dan Brown, Executive Director
Bill Bushaw, Chief Executive Officer

3926 Directory for Exceptional Children
Porter Sargent Publishers, Inc.
2 LAN Drive
Suite 100
Westford, MA 01886-3028
978-692-5092
800-342-7470
Fax: 617-523-1021
E-mail: info@portersargent.com
http://www.portersargent.com
A comprehensive survey of 2,500 schools,
facilities and organizations across the
country serving children and young adults
with developmental, physical and medical
disabilities. With 15 distinct chapters covering a range of disabilities, this work is an
invaluable aid to parents and professionals
seeking the optimal environment for
special-needs children. Hardcover.

*Publication Date: 1994 1152 pages BiAn-
nual*
ISSN: 0070-5012

Dan McKeever, Senior Editor

**3927 Directory of Catholic Special
Educational Programs & Facilities**
National Catholic Educational
Association
1005 North Glebe Road
Suite 525
Arlington, VA 22201-3829
202-337-6232
800-711-6232
Fax: 703-243-0025
http://www.ncea.org
Lists approximately 950 Catholic schools
and day and residential school programs
for children and adolescents with special
education needs.

Publication Date: 1989 100 pages

Blas, Cupich, Chairman
Robert Bimonte, President

**3928 Directory of Central Agencies for
Jewish Education**
Jewish Education Service of North
America
247 West 37th Street
5th Floor
New York, NY 10018
212-284-6882
Fax: 212-284-6951
E-mail: info@jesna.org
http://www.jesna.org
Offers educational resources for professionals in Jewish education, including general education information, materials and
services.

Cass Gottlieb, Chair
Sandra Gold, Vice Chair

**3929 Directory of College Cooperative
Education Programs**
National Commission for Cooperative
Education
600 Suffolk Street
Suite 25
Lowell, MA 01854-5096
617-373-3770
Fax: 617-373-3463
E-mail: ncce@neu.edu
http://www.waceinc.org
A publication providing detailed informa-
tion on cooperative education programs at
460 colleges throughout the United States.

Publication Date: 1962 219 pages
ISBN: 0-89774-998-4

Mauritis van Rooijen, Chair
Sampan Silapanad, Chair

**3930 Directory of ERIC Information
Service Providers**
Educational Resources Information
Ctr./Access ERIC
1600 Research Boulevard
Rockville, MD 20850-3172
301-656-9723
http://eric.ed.gov
Offers information on more than 1,000
government agencies, nonprofit and profit
organizations, individuals and foreign organizations that provide access to ERIC
microfiche collections, search services and
abstract journal collections.

100 pages Biennial

3931 Directory of Graduate Programs
Graduate Record Examinations Program/
ETS
PO Box 6000
Princeton, NJ 08541-6000
609-771-7670
866-473-4373
Fax: 610-290-8975
http://www.ets.org/gre

Accredited institutions that offer graduate degrees.

1,400 pages 4 Volumes

3932 Directory of Indigenous Education
Floyd Beller - Wested
730 Harrison Street
San Francisco, CA 94107
415-565-3000
877-493-7833
Fax: 415-565-3012
E-mail: fbeller@WestEd.org
http://www.wested.org
This revised and expanded edition incorporates a
wider scope of information, including a list of
Head Start, Child Care and Title IX programs and
JOM contractors, which enhances our principal
goal of improving educational services to native
students and communities.

Publication Date: 1998 94 pages

Tacy C. Ashby, Vice President
Jorge Ayala, Superintendent

**3933 Directory of International Internships: A
World of Opportunities**
International Studies & Programs
Michigan State University
427 N. Shaw Lane, Room 207
East Lansing, MI 48824-1035
517-353-2350
Fax: 517-353-7254
E-mail: gliozzo@msu.edu
http://www.isp.msu.edu
A directory containing information about a wide
range of overseas internship oppotunities. Over
500 entries of international internships sponsored
by educational institutions, government agencies,
and private organizations. There are indexes of
topics in geographical areas listed by countries
and geographical areas listed by topic.

Adedayo Adekson, Assistant Dean
Deandra Beck, Associate Dean

**3934 Directory of Member Institutions and
Institutional Representatives**
Council of Graduate Schools
1 Dupont Circle NW
Suite 230
Washington, DC 20036-1136
202-223-3791
Fax: 202-331-7157
E-mail: general_inquiries@cgs.nche.edu
http://www.cgsnet.org
Offers listings of over 400 member graduate
schools in the US and Canada.

85 pages Annually

Barbara A. Knuth, Chair
Suzanne T. Ortega, President

**3935 Directory of Overseas Educational
Advising Centers**
College Board Publications
45 Columbus Avenue
New York, NY 10023-6917
212-713-8000
800-323-7155
Fax: 800-525-5562
http://www.collegeboard.org
This directory has been developed as a means
through which institutions of higher education
can communicate directly with overseas education advisers and through which advisers can
communicate more directly with each other.

Publication Date: 1995 165 pages

David Coleman, President/ CEO
Jeremy Singer, Chief Operating Officer

3936 Directory of Postsecondary Institutions
National Center for Education Statistics
K Street NW
Washington, DC 20006

202-502-7300
877-4ED-PUBS
Fax: 301-470-1244
E-mail: edpubs@inet.ed.gov
http://www.edpubs.gov
Postsecondary institutions in the US, Puerto Rico, Virgin Islands and territories in the Pacific United States. Two volumes: Volume I Degree-Granting Institutions, Volume II Non-Degree-Granting Institutions.
Publication Date: 1990 500 pages Biennial

937 Directory of Youth Exchange Programs
UN Educational, Scientific & Cultural Association
Youth Division, 1 Rue Miollis
Paris F-75015
France
1-4563842
Offers about 370 nonprofit organizations and governmental agencies in 95 countries that organize youth and student exchanges, study tours and correspondence exchanges.
Publication Date: 1992 225 pages

938 Diversity, Accessibility and Quality
College Board Publications
45 Columbus Avenue
New York, NY 10023-6917
212-713-8000
800-323-7155
Fax: 800-525-5562
http://www.collegeboard.org
Primarily for non-Americans, this overview is designed to examine aspects of US education that have particular importance in programs of student exchange.
Publication Date: 1995 47 pages
ISBN: 0-874474-24-8

Clifford F Sjogren, Author
David Coleman, President/ CEO
Jeremy Singer, Chief Operating Officer

939 Education Sourcebook: Basic Information about National Education Expectations and Goals
Omnigraphics
155 West Congress
Suite 200
Detroit, MI 48226
313-961-1340
800-234-1340
Fax: 313-961-1383
E-mail: contact@omnigraphics.com
http://www.omnigraphics.com
A collection of education-related documents and articles for parents and students.
1123 pages
ISBN: 0-7808-0179-2

Jeanne Gough, Author
Paul Rogers, Publicity Associate

940 Educational Placement Sources-Abroad
Education Information Services/Instant Alert
PO Box 620662
Newton, MA 02462-0662
617-433-0125
Lists 150 organizations, arranged by type, in the United States and abroad that place English-speaking teachers and education administrators in positions abroad.
19 pages Annual

FB Viaux, President

941 Educational Rankings Annual
Gale Group
27500 Drake Road
Farmington Hills, MI 48331-3535

248-699-GALE
800-877-4253
Fax: 301-363-4253
E-mail: galeord@galegroup.com
http://www.cengage.com
Top 10 lists from popular and scholarly periodicals, government publications, and others. The lists cover all facets of education.
890 pages Annual Hardcover
ISBN: 0-7876-7419-2

Lynn C Hattendorf Westney, Author
Josef Blumenfeld, Senior Vice President
Lindsay Stanley, Senior Director

3942 Educational Resources Catalog
CDE Press
1430 N Street
PO Box 271
Sacramento, CA 95814-0271
916-445-1260
800-995-4099
Fax: 916-323-0823
http://www.cde.ca.gov/cdepress
Resource catalog from the California Department of Education.

3943 Educator's Desk Reference: A Sourcebook of Educational Information & Research
MacMillan Publishing Company
1633 Broadway
New York, NY 10019
212-654-8500
Fax: 800-835-3202
Directory includes national and regional education organizations.
Publication Date: 1989

3944 Educator's Scrapbook
Careers/Consultants Consultants in Education
3050 Palm Aire Drive N
#310
Pompano Beach, FL 33069
954-974-5477
Fax: 954-974-5477
E-mail: carconed@aol.com
Collection of education morsels offered to those who would seek to redefine and clarify the aims and purposes of today's education. The book attepts to help its readers refocus upon the real purposes of education and their relationships to current education practices.

ISBN: 0-9703623-0-7
ISSN: 00-93185

Dr. Robert M Bookbinder, President

3945 Educators Guide to FREE Computer Materials and Internet Resources
Educators Progress Service
214 Center Street
Beaver Dam, WI 53956-1408
920-210-3684
888-951-4469
Fax: 920-326-3127
E-mail: info@monumentalhosting.com
http://www.monumentalhosting.com
Lists and describes almost 2000 web sites of educational value. Available in two grade specific editions.
317 pages Annual
ISBN: 87708-362-2

Kathy Nehmer, President

3946 Educators Guide to FREE Films, Filmstrips and Slides
Educators Progress Service
214 Center Street
Beaver Dam, WI 53956-1408

920-210-3684
888-951-4469
Fax: 920-326-3127
E-mail: info@monumentalhosting.com
http://www.monumentalhosting.com
Lists and describes free and free-loan films, filmstrips, slides, and audiotapes for all age levels.
135 pages Annual
ISBN: 87708-400-9

Kathy Nehmer, President

3947 Educators Guide to FREE Multicultural Material
Educators Progress Service
214 Center Street
Beaver Dam, WI 53956-1408
920-210-3684
888-951-4469
Fax: 920-326-3127
E-mail: info@monumentalhosting.com
http://www.monumentalhosting.com
Lists and describes FREE films, videotapes, filmstrips, slides, web sites, and hundreds of free printed materials in the field of multicultural and diversity education for all age levels.
198 pages Annual
ISBN: 87708-412-2

Kathy Nehmer, President

3948 El-Hi Textbooks and Serials in Print
RR Bowker Reed Reference
2104 21st Avenue South
Birmingham, NJ 35223-1541
205-870-4693
Fax: 908-665-6688
http://frankflemingart.com
Listing of about 995 publishers of elementary and secondary level textbooks and related teaching materials.
Annual

3949 Environmental Education Materials: Guidelines for Excellence
North American Assoc for Environmental Education
2000 P Street NW
Suite 540
Washington, DC 20036
202-419-0412
Fax: 212-419-0415
E-mail: info@naaee.org
http://www.naaee.org
A set of recommendations for developing and selecting environmental education materials. These guidelines aim to help developers of activity guides, lesson plans, and other instructional materials produce high wuality products, and to provide educators with a tool to evaluate the wide array of available environmental education materials.
23 pages
ISBN: 1-884008-41-0

Jose Marcos-Iga, President
Judy Braus, Executive Director

3950 Evaluating Your Environmental Education Programs: A Workbook for Practitioners
North American Assoc for Environmental Education
2000 P Street NW
Suite 540
Washington, DC 20036
202-419-0412
Fax: 212-419-0415
E-mail: info@naaee.org
http://www.naaee.org
Walks you through how to design and conduct an evaluation. Throughout the work-

book, 23 exercises as you to check your understanding (the answers are included). In addition, 47 application exercises point you to tasks that will help you develop your own evaluation.

Jose Marcos-Iga, President
Judy Braus, Executive Director

3951 Excellence in Environmental Education: Guidelines for Learning (PreK-12)
North American Assoc for Environmental Education
2000 P Street NW
Suite 540
Washington, DC 20036
202-419-0412
Fax: 212-419-0415
E-mail: info@naaee.org
http://www.naaee.org
The guidelines support state and local environmental education efforts by: setting expectations for performance and achievement in fourth, eighth, and twelfth grades; suggesting a framework for effective and comprehensive environmental education programs and curricula; demonstrating how environmental edcuation can be used to meet standards set by the traditional disciplines and to give students opportunities to synthesize knowledge and experience across disciplines.
121 pages
ISBN: 1-884008-75-5

Jose Marcos-Iga, President
Judy Braus, Executive Director

3952 Exceptional Children Education Resources
The Council for Exceptional Children
2900 Crystal Drive
Suite 1000
Arlington, VA 22202-3557
703-620-3660
888-232-7733
Fax: 703-264-9494
E-mail: cec@cec.sped.org
http://www.cec.sped.org/bk/catalog/journals.htm
A proprietary database that includes bibliographic data and abstract information on journal articles, and audiovisual materials in special education, and gifted education.

ISSN: 0160-4309

Robin D. Brewer, President
Sharon Raimondi, Treasurer

3953 Family Services Report
CD Publications
8204 Fenton Street
Sliver Spring, MD 20910
301-588-6380
855-237-1396
Fax: 301-588-0519
E-mail: info@cdpublications.com
http://cdpublications.com
Private grants for family service programs
18 pages
ISSN: 1524-9484

Ray Sweeney, Editor
Mary Crompton, Publisher

3954 Fifty State Educational Directories
Career Guidance Foundation
1327 E. Kemper Rd
Suite 3000
Cincinnati, OH 45246-1906
513-834-8780
Fax: 513-834-8779
http://collegesource.com

A collection on microfiche consisting of reproductions of the state educational directories published by each individual state department of education.

3955 Funny School Excuses
Careers/Consultants Consultants in Education
3050 Palm Aire Drive N
#310
Pompano Beach, FL 33069
954-974-5477
Fax: 954-974-5477
E-mail: carconed@aol.com
Collection of illustrations, cartoons and excuses gathered from authentic notes written by parents and sometimes their children. The book is wonderfully entertaining and recommended for its unusual humor, variety, and revelations of human nature.

ISBN: 0-7392-0309-6
ISSN: 99-95349

Dr. Robert M Bookbinder, President

3956 Ganley's Catholic Schools in America
Fisher Publishing Company
PO Box 15070
Sun City West, AZ 85376-5070
623-328-8326
800-759-7615
Fax: 480-657-9422
E-mail:
publisher@ganleyscatholicschools.com
http://www.ganleyscatholicschool.com
Comprehensive listings on all Catholic Schools in America. Listings include phone numbers, addresses, names of administrators, number of students, complete diocesan, state, regional and national statistics. Includes an extensive analysis of demographic trends within Catholic elementary and secondary education, prepared by the National Catholic Education Association.

450+ pages Annual/June
ISBN: 1-558331-59-0

Millard T Fischer, Publisher

3957 Graduate & Undergraduate Programs & Courses in Middle East Studies in the US, Canada
Middle East Studies Association of North America
University of Arizona
633 Third Ave
New York, NY 10017-6795
520-697-1505
Fax: 520-626-9095
E-mail: mesana@u.arizona.edu
http://www.acls.org

Pauline Yu, President
Steven C. Wheatley, Vice President

3958 Guide to International Exchange, Community Service & Travel for Persons with Disabilities
Mobility International USA
132 E. Broadway
Suite 343
Eugene, OR 97401
541-343-1284
Fax: 541-343-6812
E-mail: info@miusa.org
http://www.miusa.org
This directory lists an impressive array of information regarding international study,

living, travel, funding and contact organizations for people with disabilities.
Publication Date: 1981
ISBN: 1-880034-24-7

Susan Sygall, Chief Executive Officer
Cerise Roth-Vinson, Chief Operating Officer

3959 Guide to Schools and Departments of Religion and Seminaries
MacMillan Publishing Company
175 Fifth Avenue
New York, NY 10010
646-307-5151
800-858-7674
Fax: 201-767-5029
E-mail: press.inquiries@macmillanusa.com
http://us.macmillan.com
Over 700 accredited programs and institutions granting degrees in theology, divinity and religion.
Publication Date: 1952

3960 Guide to Summer Camps & Schools
Porter Sargent Publishers
2 LAN Drive
Suite 100
Westford, MA 01886-3028
978-692-5092
800-342-7470
Fax: 617-523-1021
E-mail: info@portersargent.com
http://www.portersargent.com
Covers the broad spectrum of recreational and educational summer opportunities. Current facts from 1,500 camps and schools, as well as programs for those with special needs or learning disabilities, makes the guide a comprehensive and convenient resource.

816 pages Biannual
ISBN: 0-875581-33-1

HJ Lane Coordinating Editor, Author
J Yonce, General Manager
Daniel McKeever, Sr Editor

3961 Guidelines for Effective Character Education Through Sports
Character Education Partnership
1634 I Street NW
Suite 550
Washington, DC 20036
202-296-7743
800-988-8081
Fax: 202-296-7779
E-mail: information@character.org
http://www.character.org
Guidelines for turning sports and physical education programs into the powerful, positive forces they should be.

Becky Sipos, President/ CEO
Sheril Morgan, Director

3962 Guidelines for the Preparation and Professional Development of Environmental Educato
North American Assoc for Environmental Education
2000 P Street NW
Suite 540
Washington, DC 20036
202-419-0412
Fax: 212-419-0415
E-mail: info@naaee.org
http://www.naaee.org
Recommendations about the basic knowledge and abilities educators need to provide high quality environmental education. The guidelines are designed to apply: within the context of pre-service teacher education programs and environmental education courses offered to students with varied

backgrounds such as environmental studies, geography, liberal studies, or natural resources.

43 pages
ISBN: 1-884008-78-X

Jose Marcos-Iga, President
Judy Braus, Executive Director

3963 Handbook of Private Schools
Porter Sargent Publishers
2 LAN Drive
Suite 100
Westford, MA 01886-3028
978-692-5092
800-342-7470
Fax: 617-523-1021
E-mail: info@portersargent.com
http://www.portersargent.com
Continuing a tradition that began in 1915, this handbook provides optimal guidance in the choice of educational environments and opportunities for students. Totally revised and updated, this 83rd edition presents current facts on 1,700 elementary and secondary boarding and day schools across the United States. Complete statistical data on enrollments, tuition, graduates, administrators and faculty have been compiled and objectively reported. Hardcover.

1472 pages Annual
ISBN: 0-875581-44-7

J Yonce, General Manager
Daniel McKeever, Sr Editor

3964 Handbook of United Methodist-Related Schools, Colleges, Universities & Theological Schools
General Board of Higher Education & Ministry/UMC
1001 19th Avenue
PO Box 340007
Nashville, TN 37203-0007
615-340-7400
Fax: 615-340-7379
E-mail: scu@gbhem.org
http://www.gbhem.org/highed.html
Includes two pages of information about each of United Methodist's 123 institutions, a chart indicating major areas of study, information about United Methodist loan and scholarship programs, as well as information about how to select a college. Published every four years.

344 pages Paperback

James E. Dorff, President
Lanther Marie Mills, Vice President

3965 Hidden America
Place in the Woods
3900 Glenwood Avenue
Golden Valley, MN 55422-5302
763-374-2120
Fax: 952-593-5593
E-mail: placewoods@aol.com
Set of five reference-essay books on American minorities (African America; Hispanic America, the People (Native Americans); American women; My Own Book! classroom reference for elementary through secondary).

36+ pages Paperback Book

Roger Hammer, Publisher

3966 Higher Education Directory
Higher Education Publications
1801 Robert Fulton Drive
Suite 555
Reston, VA 20191-5499
571-313-0478
888-349-7715
Fax: 571-313-0526

E-mail: info@hepinc.com
http://www.hepinc.com
Lists over 4,364 degree granting colleges and universities accredited by approved agencies, recognized by the US Secretary of Education successor to the Department of Education's: Education Directory, Colleges and Universities and Council for Higher Education Accreditation (CHEA).

Publication Date: 1994 1,040 pages Annual/Paperback
ISBN: 0-914927-44-2
ISSN: 0736-0197

Jeanne Burke, Editor
Fred Hafner JR, Vice President Operations

3967 Higher Education Opportunities for Women & Minorities: Annotated Selections
U.S. Office of Postsecondary Education
400 Maryland Avenue SW
Room 3915
Washington, DC 20202-0001
202-708-9180
Programs of public and private organizations and state and federal government agencies that offer loans, scholarships and fellowship opportunities for women and minorities.

143 pages Biennial

3968 Home from Home (Educational Exchange Programs)
Central Bureau for Educational Visits & Exchanges
10 Spring Gardens
London, SW1A 2BN, England
171-389-4004
Fax: 171-389-4426
150 organizations and agencies worldwide that arrange stays with families for paying guests or on an exchange basis. Organizations are geographically listed including a description of program, costs, insurance information, overseas representation and language instruction.

216 pages

3969 Homeschooler's Guide to FREE Teaching Aids
Educators Progress Service
214 Center Street
Beaver Dam, WI 53956-1408
920-210-3684
888-951-4469
Fax: 920-326-3127
E-mail: info@monumentalhosting.com
http://www.monumentalhosting.com
Lists and describes free print materials specifically available to homeschoolers with students of all age levels.

277 pages
ISBN: 87708-375-4

Kathy Nehmer, President

3970 Homeschooler's Guide to FREE Videotapes
Educators Progress Service
214 Center Street
Beaver Dam, WI 53956-1408
920-210-3684
888-951-4469
Fax: 920-326-3127
E-mail: info@monumentalhosting.com
http://www.monumentalhosting.com
Lists and describes free and free-loan videotapes specifically available to homeschoolers with students of all age levels.

248 pages Annual
ISBN: 87708-411-4

Kathy Nehmer, President

3971 IIEPassport: Academic Year Abroad 2007
Institute of International Education
809 United Nations Plaza
New York, NY 10017-3580
412-741-0930
Fax: 212-984-5496
E-mail: iiebooks@abdintl.com
http://www.iiebooks.org
Over 3,100 undergraduate and graduate study-abroad programs conducted worldwide during the academic year by United States and foreign colleges, universities, and private organizations.

Publication Date: 2007 Annual
ISBN: 87206-279-1

Marie O'Sullivan, Author
Daniel Obst, Sr Editor

3972 ISS Directory of Overseas Schools
International Schools Services
15 Roszel Road
PO Box 5910
Princeton, NJ 08540-6729
609-452-0990
Fax: 609-452-2690
E-mail: jlarsson@iss.edu
http://www.iss.edu
The only comprehensive guide to American and international schools around the world. The Directory is carefully researched and compiled to include current and complete information on over 600 international schools.

590 pages Paperback
ISBN: 0-913663-13-1

Jane Larsson, Director Of Education

3973 Inclusion Guide for Handling Chronically Disruptive Behavior
Master Teacher
One Leadership Lane
PO Box 1207
Manhattan, KS 66502-1207
800-669-9633
Fax: 800-669-1132
http://www.masterteacher.com
A comprehensive process for ensuring that no disruptive behavior is tolerated, no student is turned away, and all students are served.

150 pages
ISBN: 0-914607-40-5

Teresa VanDover, Author

3974 Incorporating Multiple Intelligences into the Curriculum and into the Classroom: Elementary
Master Teacher
One Leadership Lane
PO Box 1207
Manhattan, KS 66502-1207
800-669-9633
Fax: 800-669-1132
http://www.masterteacher.com
Contains lesson plans and teaching methods that address the needs of students and help them identify their strengths according to the domains of multiple intelligences.

181 pages
ISBN: 0-914607-63-4

3975 Incorporating Multiple Intelligences into the Curriculum and into the Classroom: Secondary
Master Teacher
One Leadership Lane
PO Box 1207
Manhattan, KS 66502-1207
800-669-9633
Fax: 800-669-1132
http://www.masterteacher.com

Contains lesson plans and teaching methods that address the needs of students and help them identify their strengths according to the domains of multiple intelligences.

147 pages
ISBN: 0-914607-64-2

3976 Independent Schools Association of the Southwest-Membership List

Independent Schools Association of the Southwest
Energy Square
505 North Big Spring Street, Suite 406
Midland, TX 79701
432-684-9550
800-688-5007
Fax: 432-684-9401
http://www.isasw.org
A geographical index of 65 independent elementary and secondary schools accredited by the association.

5 pages Annual/August

Rhonda Durham, Executive Director
Allison Rose, Director of IS

3977 Independent Study Catalog

Peterson's Guides
PO Box 2123
Princeton, NJ 08543-2123
800-338-3282
Fax: 609-896-4531
A comprehensive listing of over 10,000 correspondence course offerings at 100 accredited colleges and universities nationwide, for those seeking the flexibility and convenience of at-home study.

293 pages
ISBN: 1-560794-60-7

3978 International Federation of Organizations for School Correspondence/Exchange

FIOCES
29, rue d'ulm, F-75230 Paris
F-75230 Paris
France
Governmental agencies and other organizations concerned with scholastic correspondence and student exchange programs.

Publication Date: 1991 3 pages

3979 International Schools Directory

European Council of International Schools
Fourth Floor, 146 Buckingham Palace
London, SW1W 9TR
United Kingdom
44 -0 2- 782
1730-268244
Fax: 1730-267914
E-mail: ecis@ecis.org
http://www.ecis.org
Over 420 ECIS schools in more than 90 countries; 300 affiliated colleges and universities worldwide; educational publishers and equipment suppliers.

Publication Date: 1965 550 pages Annual

Kevin J. Ruth, Ph.D., Executive Director
Darlene Fisher, People & Programmes Lead

3980 International Study Telecom Directory

WorldWide Classroom
PO Box 1166
Milwaukee, WI 53201-1166
414-224-3476
Fax: 414-224-3466

E-mail: info@worldwide.edu
http://www.worldwide.edu
Comprehensive directory for locating educational resources both internationally and throughout the US Provides contact information on educational institutions including address, phone, fax, e-mail and URL. New icon system offers additional information on the type of programs offered. Resource guide at beginning includes useful web sites, airline and car rental contact numbers, currency converters, international organizations and international publications.

Mike Witley, President
Stacy Hargarten, Classroom Publications

3981 International Voluntary Service Directory

Volunteers for Peace
1034 Tiffany Road
Belmont, VT 05730
802-259-2759
Fax: 802-259-2922
E-mail: vfp@vfp.org
http://www.vfp.org
Comprehensive listing of over 3,400 workcamps in 100 countries around the world. Organized by country.

289 pages Annual
ISBN: 0-945617-20-B

Peter Coldwell, Director

3982 International Who's Who in Education

International Biographical Centre/Melrose Press
3 Regal Lane, Soham, Ely
Cambridgeshire CB7 5BA
United Kingdom
353-721091
Lists about 5,000 persons at all levels of teaching and educational administration.

1,000 pages

3983 International Yearbook of Education: Education in the World

UN Educational, Scientific & Cultural Assn.
7, place de Fontenoy
F-75700 Paris
France
1-45681000
Describes and offers information on educational systems worldwide.

Publication Date: 1989 200 pages

3984 Job Search Handbook for Educators

American Association for Employment in Education
947 E. Johnstown Road
#170
Gahanna, OH 43230
614-485-1111
Fax: 360-244-7802
E-mail: execdir@aaee.org
http://www.aaee.org
Resume writing, interviewing tips, as well as articles on how to select the kind of school system you want, job fair networking and other related articles.

212 pages Bi-Annually

Doug Peden, Executive Director
Todd Fukai, Board President

3985 Legal Basics: A Handbook for Educators

Phi Delta Kappa International
320 W. Eighth Street
Suite 216
Bloomington, IL 47404-0789
812-339-1156
800-766-1156
Fax: 812-339-0018
E-mail: memberservices@pdkintl.org
http://www.pdkintl.org
Superintendents, principals, counselors, teachers, and paraprofessionals need to pay close attention to their actions in schools and classrooms because, from a legal standpoint, those settings may contain hazardous conditions. Legal Basics points out the pitfalls and how to avoid them.

Publication Date: 1906 120 pages Paperback
ISBN: 0-8736-806-0

Evelyn B Kelly, Author
Patricia Williams, Chair
Douglas Christensen, Vice Chair

3986 Lesson Plans and Modifications for Inclusion and Collaborative Classrooms

Master Teacher
One Leadership Lane
PO Box 1207
Manhattan, KS 66502-1207
800-669-9633
Fax: 800-669-1132
http://www.masterteacher.com
Each modification is a complete lesson plan that gives the teacher a description of the activity and objetive the materials need and a step-by-step guide of how to carry out the learning process.

Publication Date: 1969 242 pages
ISBN: 0-914607-37-5

3987 Lesson Plans for Character Education: Elementary Edition

Master Teacher
One Leadership Lane
PO Box 1207
Manhattan, KS 66502-1207
800-669-9633
Fax: 800-669-1132
http://www.masterteacher.com
Gives you more than 140 practical lessons developed and tested by teachers across the curriculum and in all grade levels.

Publication Date: 1969 207 pages
ISBN: 0-914607-53-7

3988 List of Over 70 Higher Education Association

Educational Information Services
PO Box 662
Newton Lower Falls, MA 02162
617-964-4555
Provides descriptions and contact information on associations for individuals in higher education.

3989 List of State Boards of Higher Education

Educational Information Services
PO Box 662
Newton Lower Falls, MA 02162
617-964-4555
A compilation of the boards of education for all the states in the union.

3990 List of State Community & Junior College Board Offices

Educational Information Services
PO Box 662
Newton Lower Falls, MA 02162
617-964-4555
A list of the board officers and state officers within community, junior and university institutions.

991 MDR School Directory
Market Data Retrieval
6 Armstrong Road
Suite 301
Shelton, CT 06484-6216
203-926-4800
800-333-8802
Fax: 203-929-5253
E-mail: mdrinfo@dnb.com
http://schooldata.com
MDR's school directories provide comprehensive data on every public school district and school, Catholic and other independent schools, regional and county centers in all fifty states and the District of Columbia. Updated each year, each state directory contains current names and job titles of key decision makers, school and district addresses, phone numbers, current enrollments and much more. Also available on CD-ROM and diskette.

Publication Date: 1969 51 Volume Set

Mike Subrizi, Director Marketing

992 Minority Student Guide to American Colleges
Paoli Publishing
P.O. Box 190
Suite 287
Paoli, IN 47454-1553
812-723-2572
Fax: 812-723-2592
http://paolinewsrepublican.com
Covers colleges, military schools, and financial aid information for minority students.

89 pages

993 Monograph 1-Using a Logic Model to Review and Analyze an Environmental Education Program
North American Association for Environmental Educa
2000 P Street NW
Suite 540
Washington, DC 20036
202-419-0412
Fax: 212-419-0415
E-mail: info@naaee.org
http://www.naaee.org
Reviews and analyzes a long-standing and well-documented program in environmental education, Hungerford et al.'s issue-and-action instruction program (1973-). Logic models provide conceptual guidance and visual support for this review and analysis. These models were adapted from work in Aquatic Resource Education by Peyton, and the literature on logic modeling in program evaluation.

72 pages
ISBN: 1-884008-86-0

Jose Marcos-Iga, President
Susan McGuire, Secretary

994 Monograph 2-Preparing Effective Environmental Educators
North American Association for Environmental Educa
2000 P Street NW
Suite 540
Washington, DC 20036
202-419-0412
Fax: 212-419-0415
E-mail: info@naaee.org
http://www.naaee.org
Focuses on the methods used to prepare those who teach environmental education. Research and evaluation related to three main audiences for environmental education preparedness training - pre-service teachers, in-service teachers, and nonformal education - are examined. The five papers presented

represent an interesting and instructive array of research and evaluation that can be used to spur our thinking about the preparation of environmental educators.

89 pages
ISBN: 1-884008-88-7

Jose Marcos-Iga, President
Susan McGuire, Secretary

3995 NAFSA's Guide to Education Abroad for Advisers & Administrators
NAFSA: Association of International Educators
1307 New York Avenue NW
8th Floor
Washington, DC 20005-4701
202-737-3699
800-836-4994
Fax: 202-737-3657
E-mail: inbox@nafsa.org
http://www.nafsa.org

Publication Date: 1948

Marlene M Johnson, Executive Director & CEO
Vic Johnson, Senior Advisor

3996 NEA Almanac of Higher Education
National Education Association (NEA)
1201 16th Street NW
Washington, DC 20036-3290
202-833-4000
Fax: 202-822-7974
E-mail: nche@nea.org
http://www.nea.org

Publication Date: 1857 Annually
ISSN: 0743-670X

Con Lehane, Author
Lily Eskelsen Garcia, President
Becky Pringle, VP

3997 National Directory of Children, Youth & Families Services
Contexo Media
9737 Washingtonian Blvd
Suite 200
Gaithersburg, MD 20878
800-334-5724
Fax: 301-287-2535
E-mail:
customersupport@contexomedia.com
http://www.contexomedia.com
Organized by state and county, this directory lists over 30,000 organizations and 46,000 contacts that focus on helping anyone who is committed to providing the best possible service to our nation's at-risk children, youth and families.

Publication Date: 0 1456 pages Annually

Treavor Peterson, President
Kim Luna, Product Manager

3998 National Guide to Educational Credit for Training Programs
American Council on Education
1 Dupont Circle NW
Suite 535
Washington, DC 20036-1110
202-939-9430
Fax: 202-833-4762
http://www.acenet.edu
More than 4,500 courses offered by over 280 government agencies, business firms and nonprofit groups.

1,018 pages Annual

James H. Mullen Jr., Chair
Renu Khator, Vice Chair/ Chair-elect

3999 National Reference Directory of Year-Round Education Programs
National Association for Year-Round Education
PO Box 711386
San Diego, CA 92171-1386
619-276-5296
Fax: 858-571-5754
E-mail: info@nayre.org
http://www.nayre.org
Six hundred fifty school districts in the US with year-round programs are covered in this directory, listed by geographical location, including all contact information and descriptions.

178 pages Annual Paperback

Charles Ballinger, Executive Director Emeritus
Samuel Pepper, Executive Director

4000 National Schools of Character: Best Practices and New Perspectives
Character Education Partnership
1634 I Street NW
Suite 550
Washington, DC 20006
202-296-7743
800-988-8081
Fax: 202-296-7779
http://www.character.org

Becky Sipos, President and CEO
Sheril Morgan, Director

4001 National Schools of Character: Practices to Adopt & Adapt
Character Education Partnership
1634 I Street NW
Suite 550
Washington, DC 20006
202-296-7743
800-988-8081
Fax: 202-296-7779
http://www.character.org

Becky Sipos, President and CEO
Sheril Morgan, Director

4002 National Society for Experiential Education
19 Mantua Road
Suite 420
Mt. Royal, NJ 08061
856-423-3427
Fax: 856-423-3420
E-mail: nsee@talley.com
http://www.nsee.org

Publication Date: 1971 28 pages Quarterly

Linda Goff, Author
Jim Colbert, President
Gregg Lorenz, Vice President

4003 New England Association of Schools and Colleges
New England Association of Schools and Colleges
3 Burlington Woods Drive
Suite 100
Burlington, MA 01803-1433
781-425-7700
855-886-3272
Fax: 781-425-1001
http://www.neasc.org
Listing of over 1,575 institutions of higher education, public and independent schools and vocational-technical schools in New England.

Publication Date: 1885 65 pages Annual

Mary Lyons, Chair
William L. Burke III, Secretary-Treasurer̈

4004 Nonformal Environmental Education Programs: Guidelines for Excellence
North American Assoc for Environmental Education
2000 P Street NW
Suite 540
Washington, DC 20036
202-419-0412
Fax: 212-419-0415
E-mail: info@naaee.org
http://www.naaee.org
A set of recommendations for developing and administering high quality nonformal environmental education programs. These recommendations provide a tool that can be used to ensure a firm foundation for new programs or to trigger improvements in existing ones. The overall goal of these guidelines is to facilitate a superior educational process leading to the environmental quality that people desire.

ISBN: 1-884008-89-5

Jose Marcos-Iga, President
Susan McGuire, Secretary

4005 Overseas American-Sponsored Elementary and Secondary Schools
US Department of State, Office Overseas Schools
2201 C Street NW
Washington, DC 20520
202-647-4000
Fax: 202-261-8224
http://www.state.gov/m/a/os
Lists nearly 180 independent schools overseas and 10 regional associations of schools.

30 pages Annual

Antony Blinken, Deputy Secretary

4006 Paradigm Lost: Leading America Beyond It's Fear of Educational Change
American Association of School Administrators
1615 Duke Street
Suite 700
Alexandria, VA 22314-1730
703-528-0700
Fax: 703-841-1543
E-mail: info@aasa.org
http://www.aasa.org
Explores the beliefs and assumptions upon which schools operate, provides powerful and practical insights and improvement strategies.
Publication Date: 1998 158 pages Softcover
ISBN: 0-87652-232-0

Daniel A. Domenech, Executive Director
Sharon Adams-Taylor, Associate Executive Director

4007 Patterson's American Education
Educational Directories Inc
Po Box 68097
Schaumburg, IL 60168-97
847-891-1250
800-357-6183
Fax: 847-891-0945
E-mail: info@ediusa.com
http://www.ediusa.com
Lists more than 11,000 public school districts; 300 parochial superintendents; 400 territorial schools; 400 state department of education personnel; and 400 educational associations in one easy to use consistent format. Arranged alphabetically by state then by city. City listings include the city name, telephone area code, city population, county name, public school district

name, enrollment, grade range, superintendent's name, address and phone number. Index of secondary schools included.
Publication Date: 1904 974 pages Annual
ISBN: 0-9771602-3-8
ISSN: 0079-0230

Linda Moody, Office Manager

4008 Patterson's Schools Classified
Educational Directories Inc.
1025 W Wise Road
PO Box 68097
Schaumburg, IL 60168-97
847-891-1250
800-357-6183
Fax: 847-891-0945
E-mail: info@ediusa.org
http://www.ediusa.org
Contains 7,000 accredited postsecondary schools, the broadest assortment available in a single directory. Universities, colleges, community colleges, junior colleges, career schools and teaching hospitals are co-mingled under 50 academic disciplines but retain their school type identification. School professional accreditation is shown in 32 classifications. The basic entry includes school name, mailing address and contact person, with additional descriptive material supplied by the school.
Publication Date: 1904 302 pages Annual
ISBN: 0-9771602-2-X

Wayne Moody, Coordinating Education

4009 Persons as Resources
World Council for Curriculum & Instruction
10455 Pomerado Road
Alliant International University
San Diego, CA 92131
858-635-4718
Fax: 858-635-4714
E-mail: wcci@alliant.edu
http://www.wcci-international.org
Listing of about 600 member individuals and institutions concerned with curriculum and instruction in schools, colleges, universities and non-school agencies.

75 pages Triennial

Teresita Paed-Pedrajas, President
Benedicta Agusiobo, ViceÿPresident

4010 Peterson's Competitive Colleges
Peterson's, A Nelnet Company
Princeton Pike Corporate Center
461 From Road
Paramus, NJ 07652
609-896-1800
800-338-3282
Fax: 402-458-3042
E-mail: support@petersons.com
http://www.petersons.com
The most trusted source of advice for excellent students searching for high-quality schools. Provides objective criteria to compare more than 440 leading colleges and universities.
Publication Date: 1975 524 pages
ISBN: 1-560795-98-0

4011 Peterson's Guide to Four-Year Colleges
Peterson's, A Nelnet Company
Princeton Pike Corporate Center
461 From Road
Paramus, NJ 07652
609-896-1800
800-338-3282
Fax: 402-458-3042
E-mail: support@petersons.com
http://www.petersons.com

Includes descriptions of over 2,000 colleges, providing guidance on selecting the right school, getting in and financial aid.
Publication Date: 1975 2,922 pages

4012 Peterson's Guide to Two-Year Colleges
Peterson's, A Nelnet Company
Princeton Pike Corporate Center
461 From Road
Paramus, NJ 07652
609-896-1800
800-338-3282
Fax: 402-458-3042
E-mail: support@petersons.com
http://www.petersons.com
The only two-year college guide available, this new and expanded directory is the most complete source of information on institutions that grant an associate as their highest degree.
Publication Date: 1975 712 pages
ISBN: 1-560796-05-7

4013 Peterson's Regional College Guide Set
Peterson's, A Nelnet Company
Princeton Pike Corporate Center
461 From Road
Paramus, NJ 07652
609-896-1800
800-338-3282
Fax: 402-458-3042
E-mail: support@petersons.com
http://www.petersons.com
Six individual regional guides that help students compare colleges in a specific geographic area.

Publication Date: 1975

4014 Power of Public Engagement Book Set
Master Teacher
One Leadership Lane
PO Box 1207
Manhattan, KS 66502-1207
800-669-9633
Fax: 800-669-1132
http://www.masterteacher.com
Learn how to engage your community to make the changes needed to ensure the best education for its children.
Publication Date: 1969
ISBN: 1-58992-128-3

William G O'Callaghan Jr, Author

4015 PreK-12 Excellence In Environmental Educatio Education
North American Assoc for Environmental Education
2000 P Street NW
Suite 540
Washington, DC 20036
202-419-0412
Fax: 212-419-0415
E-mail: info@naaee.org
http://www.naaee.org
Offers a vision of environmental education and promotes progress toward sustaining a healthy environment and quality of life. The Guidelines support state and local environmental efforts by: setting expectations for performance and achievement in fourth, eighth, and twelfth grades; suggesting a framework for effective and comprehensive environmental education programs.

ISBN: 1-884008-77-1

Jose Marcos-Iga, President
Susan McGuire, Secretary

4016 Private Independent Schools
Bunting & Lyon
238 N Main Street
Wallingford, CT 06492-3728
203-269-3333
Fax: 203-269-5697

E-mail: BuntingandLyon@aol.com
http://www.macraesbluebook.com
Provides information on more than 1,100 elementary and secondary private schools and summer programs in the United States and abroad. This annual guide, now in its 56th edition, is the most concise, current resource available on private school programs.

Publication Date: 1996 644 pages Annual
Hardcover
ISBN: 0-913094-56-0
ISSN: 0079-5399

Peter G Bunting, Publisher

4017 Private School Law in America
Progressive Business Publications
370 Technology Drive
Malvern, PA 19355
610-695-8600
800-220-5000
Fax: 610-647-8089
E-mail: customer_service@pbp.com
http://www.pbp.com
An up-to-date compilation of summarized federal and state appellate court decisions which affect private education. The full legal citation is supplied for each case. A brief introductory note on the American judicial system is provided along with updated appendices of recent US Supreme Court cases and recently published law review articles. Also included are portions of the US Constitution which are most frequently cited in private education cases.

Publication Date: 1959 500 pages Annually
ISBN: 0-939675-80-3

Ed Satell, Founder

4018 Public Schools USA: A Comparative Guide to School Districts
Peterson's, A Nelnet Company
Princeton Pike Corporate Center
461 From Road
Paramus, NJ 07652
609-896-1800
800-338-3282
Fax: 402-458-3042
E-mail: support@petersons.com
http://www.petersons.com
Lists over 400 school districts in 52 metropolitan areas throughout the United States.

Publication Date: 1975 490 pages Annual

Charles Hampton Harrison, Author

4019 School Foodservice Who's Who
Information Central
PO Box 3900
Prescott, AZ 86302-3900
520-778-1513
Listing of over 2,500 food service programs in public and Catholic school systems.

110 pages Triennial

4020 School Guide
School Guide Publications
210 N Avenue
New Rochelle, NY 10801-6402
914-632-7771
800-433-7771
Fax: 914-632-3412
E-mail: mridder@schoolguides.com
http://schoolguides.com
Listing of over 3,000 colleges, vocational schools and nursing schools in the US.

Publication Date: 1886 280 pages Annual/Paperback
ISBN: 1-893275-30-2

Janette Aiello, Editor

4021 Schools-Business & Vocational Directory
American Business Directories
5711 S 86th Circle
Omaha, NE 68127-4146
402-593-4600
888-999-1307
Fax: 402-331-5481
http://www.americanbusinessandservicedirectory.com
A complete listing of business and vocational schools nationwide. Includes phone numbers, contact names, employee sizes and more.

Annual

Jerry Venner, Coordinating Education

4022 Treasury of Noteworthy Proverbs
Morris Publishing
P.O. Box 2110
Kearney, NE 68848
954-974-5477
800-650-7888
Fax: 308-237-0263
E-mail: carconed@aol.com
http://www.morrispublishing.com
Tapestry of maxims, aphorisims, and pithy sayings. A revealing picture of the wisdom, philosophy, and humor of the people of this and many other nations throughout the world.

Publication Date: 1933
ISBN: 0-7392-0208-1
ISSN: 99-943-75

Dr. Robert M Bookbinder, President

4023 US Supreme Court Education Cases
Progressive Business Publications
370 Technology Drive
Malvern, PA 19355
610-695-8600
800-220-5000
Fax: 610-647-8089
E-mail: customer_service@pbp.com
http://www.pbp.com
A compilation of summarized US Supreme Court decisions since 1954 which affect education. The full legal citation is supplied for each case. Also included are portions of the US Constitution which are most frequently cited in education cases.

Publication Date: 1959 Annually

Liz Webb, Senior Corporate Recruiter
Ed Satell, Founder

4024 VincentCurtis Educational Register
Vincent-Curtis
PO Box 724
Falmouth, MA 02541-0724
508-457-6473
Fax: 508-457-6499
E-mail: articles@vincentcurtis.com
http://www.vincentcurtis.com
An online guide to a variety of private boarding and day schools and resident summer programs in the United States, Canada and Europe, together with articles by school heads and camp directors of interest to educators and parents of students 10-18.

Publication Date: 1994 236 pages Annual/June

Stan Vincent, Editor

4025 Western Association of Schools and Colleges
Western Association of Schools and Colleges
533 Airport Boulevard
Suite 200
Burlingame, CA 94010-2009
650-696-1060
Fax: 650-696-1867

E-mail: mail@acswasc.org
http://www.acswasc.org
Listing of schools and colleges in California, Hawaii, Guam, American Samoa and East Asia.

130 pages Annual

Fred Van Leuven, Executive Director
Marilyn S. George, Associate Executive Director

4026 What's Fair Got to Do With It
North American Assoc for Environmental Education
2000 P Street NW
Suite 540
Washington, DC 20036
202-419-0412
Fax: 212-419-0415
E-mail: info@naaee.org
http://www.naaee.org
Educators will find these cases a powerful tool for professional development. Each case is a candid, dramatic, and highly readable first-person account that makes concrete the challenges of fairness, expectations, respect, and communication when people who share goals, perhaps, but not cultures, interact.

119 pages
ISBN: 0-914409-20-4

Jose Marcos-Iga, President
Susan McGuire, Secretary

4027 Whole Nonprofit Catalog
Grantmanship Center
PO Box 17720
Los Angeles, CA 90017
213-482-9860
800-421-9512
Fax: 213-482-9863
E-mail: Info@tgci.com
http://www.tgci.com
Offers information on training programs offered by the Center, publications and other services available to the nonprofit sector.

Publication Date: 1972

Cathleen Kiritz, President
Barbara Floersch, Executive Director

4028 Working Together: A Guide to Community-Based Educational Resources
Research, Advocacy & Legislation/Council of LaRaza
1126 16th Street, NW
Suite 600
Washington, DC 20036-4845
202-289-1380
E-mail: comments@nclr.org
http://www.nclr.org
Listing of about 30 community-based organizations nationwide providing educational services to Hispanic Americans.

35 pages

Jorge A. Plasencia, Chair
Renata Soto, Vice Chair

4029 World of Learning
Gale Group
27500 Drake Road
Farmington Hills, MI 48331
248-699-4253
800-877-4253
Fax: 877-363-4253
E-mail: galeord@galegroup.com
http://www.cengage.com
Contains information for over 26,000 universities, colleges, schools of art and music, libraries, archives, learned societies, research

institutes, museums and art galleries in more than 180 countries.

ISBN: 0-7876-5004-8

Michael E. Hansen, CEO
Fernando Bleichmar, Chief Strategy Officer

Directories & Handbooks / *Administration*

4030 American Association of Collegiate Registrars & Admissions Officers
American Association of Collegiate Registrars
1 Dupont Circle NW
Suite 520
Washington, DC 20036-1137
202-293-9161
Fax: 202-872-8857
http://www.aacrao.org
Offers more than 2,300 member institutions and 8,400 college and university registrars, financial aid information and admissions officers.

Publication Date: 1995 224 pages Annual

Brad Myers, President
Dan Garcia, President-Elect

4031 American School & University - Who's Who Directory & Buyer's Guide
Prism Business Media
9800 Metcalf Avenue
Overland Park, KS 66212-2286
913-967-1960
Fax: 913-967-1905
E-mail: jagron@asumag.com
http://www.asumag.com
Comprehensive directory of suppliers and products for facility needs; listings of architects by region; listing of associations affiliated with the education industry; article index for quick and easy reference; in-depth calendar of events.

Publication Date: 1928 Annual

Joe Agron, Editor-In-Chief
Gregg Herring, VP, Market Leader

4032 Bricker's International Directory
Peterson's, A Nelnet Company
Princeton Pike Corporate Center
461 From Road
Paramus, NJ 07652
609-896-1800
800-338-3282
Fax: 402-458-3042
E-mail: support@petersons.com
http://www.petersons.com
Offers over 400 residential management development programs at academic institutions in the United States and abroad.

Publication Date: 1975 Annual

4033 Cabells Directory of Publishing Opportunities in Educational Psychology and Administration
Cabell Publishing Company
Box 5428
Tobe Hahn Station
Beaumont, TX 77726
409-898-0575
Fax: 409-866-9554
E-mail: info@cabells.com
http://www.cabells.com
Provides information on editor contact information, manuscript guidelines, acceptance rate, review information and

circulation data for over 225 academic journals.

Publication Date: 1978 799 pages Annual
ISBN: 0-911753-28-1

David WE Cabell, Editor
Deborah L English, Associate Editor

4034 Character Education Questions & Answers
Character Education Partnership
1634 I Street NW
Suite 550
Washington, DC 20006
202-296-7743
800-988-8081
Fax: 202-296-7779
E-mail: information@character.org
http://www.character.org

Becky Sipos, President/ CEO
Sheril Morgan, Director

4035 Character Education Resource Guide
Character Education Partnership
1634 I Street NW
Suite 550
Washington, DC 20006
202-296-7743
800-988-8081
Fax: 202-296-7779
E-mail: information@character.org
http://www.character.org

Becky Sipos, President/ CEO
Sheril Morgan, Director

4036 Character Education: The Foundation for Teacher Education
Character Education Partnership
1634 I Street NW
Suite 550
Washington, DC 20006
202-296-7743
800-988-8081
Fax: 202-296-7779
E-mail: information@character.org
http://www.character.org

Becky Sipos, President/ CEO
Sheril Morgan, Director

4037 Continuing Education Guide
International Association for Continuing Education
7918 Jones Branch Drive
Suite 300
McLean, VA 22102-0001
703-506-3275
Fax: 703-506-3266
http://www.iacet.org
Explores how to interpret and use the Continuing Education Unit or other criteria used for continuing education programs. This guide, written by continuing education and training consultant, Louis Phillips, is a reference source complete with sample forms, charts, checklists and everything you need to plan, develop and evaluate your school's continuing education program.

Sandra Williams, President
Lori Schaeffer, President-Elect

4038 Creating Quality Reform: Programs, Communities and Governance
Pearson Education Communications
1 Lake Street
Upper Saddle River, NJ 07458
201-236-7000
Fax: 877-260-2530

E-mail: communications@pearsoned.com
http://www.pearsoned.com

Publication Date: 2002

J Thomas Owens, Editor
Jan C Simmons, Editor

4039 Designing & Implementing a Leadership Academy in Character Education
Character Education Partnership
1634 I Street NW
Suite 550
Washington, DC 20006
202-296-7743
800-988-8081
Fax: 202-296-7779
E-mail: information@character.org
http://www.character.org

Becky Sipos, President/ CEO
Sheril Morgan, Director

4040 Deskbook Encyclopedia of American School Law
Progressive Business Publications
370 Technology Drive
Malvern, PA 19355
610-695-8600
800-220-5000
Fax: 610-647-8089
E-mail: customer_service@pbp.com
http://www.pbp.com
An up-to-date compilation of summarized federal and state appellate court decisions which affect education. The full legal citation is supplied for each case with a brief introductory note on the American judicial system is provided along with updated appendices of recent US Supreme Court cases and recently published law review articles.

Publication Date: 1959 Annually

Liz Webb, Senior Corporate Recruiter
Ed Satell, Founder

4041 Developing a Character Education Program
Character Education Partnership
1634 I Street NW
Suite 550
Washington, DC 20006
202-296-7743
800-988-8081
Fax: 202-296-7779
E-mail: information@character.org
http://www.character.org

Henry Huffman, Author
Becky Sipos, President/ CEO
Sheril Morgan, Director

4042 Development Education: A Directory of Non-Governmental Practitioners
U.N. Non-Governmental Liaison Service
Palais des Nations, CH 1211
Geneva 10
Switzerland
E-mail: ngls@unctad.org
http://www.un-ngls.org
Lists about 800 national non-governmental organizations in industrialized countries and international non-governmental networks concerned with developmental education.

Publication Date: 1975 400 pages

Beth Peoch, Officer in Charge
David Vergari, Administration

4043 Directory of Chief Executive Officers of United Methodist Schools, Colleges & Universities
General Board of Higher Education & Ministry/UMC
1001 19th Avenue South
PO Box 340007
Nashville, TN 37203-0007

615-340-7406
Fax: 615-340-7379
E-mail: scu@gbhem.org
http://www.gbhem.org/highed.html
123 United Methodist educational institutions including theology schools, professional schools, two year colleges and colleges and universities with all contact information arranged by institution type. Paperback.

32 pages Annual

James E. Dorff, Presiden
Ianther Marie Mills, Vice President

4044 Directory of Organizations in Educational Management
ERIC Clearinghouse on Educational Management
1501 Kincaid Street
Eugene, OR 97403-1299
541-346-3053
800-438-8841
Fax: 541-346-3485
E-mail: sales@oregon.uoregon.edu
http://scholarsbank.uoregon.edu
Offers listings of 163 organizations in the field of educational management at the elementary and secondary school levels.

Dr. Philip Piele, Director
Stuart C Smith, Associate Director

4045 Directory of State Education Agencies
Council of Chief State School Officers
1 Massachusette Avenue NW
Suite 700
Washington, DC 20001-1431
202-336-7000
Fax: 202-408-8072
E-mail: communications@ccsso.org
http://www.ccsso.org
A reference to state and national education agency contracts. Arranged state-by-state, it includes state education agency personnel titles, addresses, phone numbers, and fax numbers when applicable. National information includes key contacts and information for 33 national education associations and 5 pages of names, titles, addresses, and numbers for the US Department of Education.

103 pages
ISBN: 1-884037-66-6

June Atkinson, President
Lillian Lowery, President-elect

4046 Educating for Character
Master Teacher
One Leadership Lane
PO Box 1207
Manhattan, KS 66502-1207
800-669-9633
Fax: 800-669-1132
http://www.masterteacher.com
Dr. Licona has developed a 12 point program that offers practical strategies designed to create a working coalition of parents, teachers and communities.

428 pages
ISBN: 0-553-37052-9

Thomas Lickona PhD, Author

4047 Educating for Character: How Our Schools Can Teach Respect and Responsibility
Character Education Partnership
1634 I Street NW
Suite 550
Washington, DC 20006
202-296-7743
800-988-8081
Fax: 202-296-7779

E-mail: information@character.org
http://www.character.org
Tom Likona, Author
Becky Sipos, President/ CEO
Sheril Morgan, Director

4048 Education Budget Alert
Committee for Education Funding
1640 Rhode Island Ave., NW
Suite 600
Washington, DC 20036-2109
202-383-0083
Fax: 202-463-4803
E-mail: jchang@cef.org
http://www.cef.org
Federal programs currently help over 63 million Americans to engage in formal learning. This guidebook explains what these programs do, what types of activities are supported, the reasons the federal government initiated these programs, and their level at funding.

Publication Date: 2012 150 pages Annually

Noelle Ellerson, President
Makese Motley, Vice-President

4049 Educational Consultants Directory
American Business and Service Directory
5711 S 86th Circle
PO Box 27347
Omaha, NE 68127
402-593-4600
800-555-6124
Fax: 402-331-5481
E-mail: info@usabsd.com
http://www.americanbusinessandservicedirectory.com
A list of more than 5,000 entries, including name, address, phone, size of advertisement, name of owner or manager and number of employees.

4050 Educational Dealer-Buyers' Guide Issue
Fahy-Williams Publishing
171 Reed St.
PO Box 1080
Geneva, NY 14456-2137
315-789-0458
800-344-0559
Fax: 315-789-4263
http://www.fwpi.com
List of approximately 2,000 suppliers of educational materials and equipment.

Annual

J. Kevin Fahy, Publisher
Tina Manzer, Editorial Director

4051 Executive Summary Set
Master Teacher
One Leadership Lane
PO Box 1207
Manhattan, KS 66502
800-669-9633
Fax: 800-669-1132
http://www.masterteacher.com
An easy, effective and practical way to orient new board members before they attend their first meeting. Executive Summary Sets cover the vital information board members must have in eight areas: tenets of education; powers and responsibilities; decision making; communication for maximum results; resource management; assessment of programs; assessment of personnel and conflict resolution.

Robert DeBruyn, Editor

4052 Grants and Contracts Handbook
Association of School Business Officials Int'l
11401 N Shore Drive
Reston, VA 20190-4232
703-478-0405
866-682-2729
Fax: 703-478-0205
http://asbointl.org
This is a basic reference for grant applicants, executors, project managers, administrators and staff. The ideas are school-tested and based on information gathered from institutions and agencies over the past two decades.

Publication Date: 1910 32 pages
ISBN: 0-910170-52-5

Mark C. Pepera, President
Brenda R. Burkett, Vice President

4053 Hispanic Yearbook-Anuario Hispano
TIYM Publishing
8370 Greensboro Dr.
#1009
McLean, VA 22102
703-734-1632
Fax: 703-356-0787
E-mail: TIYM@aol.com
http://www.tiym.com
This guide lists Hispanic organizations, publications, radio and TV stations, through not specifically for grant-giving purposes.

Publication Date: 1985 Annually

John O Zavala, COO
Ramon Palencia, Director PR

4054 Leading to Change: The Challenge of the New Superintendency
Jossey-Bass/Pfeiffer
One Montgomery Street
Suite 1200
San Francisco, CA 94104-1741
415-433-1740
Fax: 415-433-0499
http://www.josseybass.com
The challenge of the new superintendency.

Publication Date: 1814 352 pages
ISBN: 0-7879-0214-4

Susan Moore Johnson, Author
Stephen M. Smith, President and CEO
John Kritzmacher, EVP, CFO

4055 Legal Basics: A Handbook for Educators
Phi Delta Kappa International
320 W. Eighth Street
Suite 216
Bloomington, IL 47404-0789
812-339-1156
800-766-1156
Fax: 812-339-0018
E-mail: memberservices@pdkintl.org
http://www.pdkintl.org
Superintendents, principals, counselors, teachers, and paraprofessionals need to pay close attention to their actions in schools and classrooms because, from a legal standpoint, those settings may contain hazardous conditions. Legal Basics points out the pitfalls and how to avoid them.

Publication Date: 1906 120 pages Paperback
ISBN: 8-87367-806-0

Evelyn B Kelly, Author
Dan Brown, Executive Director
Douglas Christensen, Vice Chair

4056 Legal Issues and Education Technology
National School Board Association
1680 Duke Street
Alexandria, VA 22314

703-838-6722
800-706-6722
Fax: 703-683-7590
E-mail: info@nsba.org
http://www.nsba.org
Helps administrators craft an acceptable-use policy.

Publication Date: 1999
ISSN: 0314510

Thomas Gentzel, Executive Director
Heather Francis, Executive Assistant

4057 Lifeworld of Leadership: Creating Culture, Community, and Personal Meaning in Our Schools
Jossey-Bass Publishers
One Montgomery Street
Suite 1200
San Francisco, CA 94104-1741
415-433-1740
Fax: 415-433-0499
http://www.josseybass.com
Explores the crucial link between school improvement and school character.

Publication Date: 1814 240 pages Paperback
ISBN: 0-7879-7277-6

Stephen M. Smith, President and CEO
John Kritzmacher, EVP, CFO

4058 Looking at Schools: Instruments & Processes for School Analysis
Research for Better Schools
123 South Broad Street
Suite 1860
Philadelphia, PA 19109
215-568-6150
Fax: 215-568-7260
http://www.rbs.org
Thirty-five institutions that offer instruments and processes to assess the performance of students, teachers and administrators, school climate effectiveness and school-community relations.

Publication Date: 1966 140 pages

Carol Crociante, Executive Assistant
Keith M Kershner, Executive Director

4059 Market Data Retrieval-National School Market Index
Market Data Retrieval
6 Armstrong Road
Suite 301
Shelton, CT 06484-0947
203-926-4800
800-333-8802
Fax: 203-929-5253
E-mail: msubrizi@dnb.com
http://schooldata.com
An annual report on school spending patterns for instructional materials in the United States. The Index now in its twenty-fifth year of publication, lists the expenditures for instructional materials for all 15,000 US senior districts.

Publication Date: 1996
ISBN: 0-897708-25-3

Mike Subrizi, Marketing Director

4060 National Association of Principals of Schools for Girls Directory
National Association of Principals/Girls Schools
23490 Caraway Lakes Dr.
Bonita Springs, FL 34135-8317
239-947-4323
Fax: 828-693-1490
E-mail: bruce@headsnetwork.org
http://www.headsnetwork.org
List of 575 principals and deans of private and secondary schools for girls and coeducational schools, colleges and admissions officers.

Publication Date: 1920 Annual

Bruce W. Galbraith, Executive Director

4061 National School Public Relations Association Directory
National School Public Relations Association
15948 Derwood Road
Rockville, MD 20855-1109
301-519-0496
Fax: 301-519-0494
http://www.nspra.org
Lists over 2,800 school system public relations directors and school administration officers.

100 pages Annual

Rich Bagin, Executive Director
Karen H. Kleinz, Associate Director

4062 National School Supply & Equipment Association Membership/Buyers' Guide Directory
Education Market Association
8380 Colesville Rd
Suite 250
Silver Spring, MD 20910
301-495-0240
800-395-5550
Fax: 301-495-3330
E-mail: awatts@nssea.org
http://www.edmarket.org
Lists 1,500 member dealers, manufacturers and manufacturers' representatives for school supplies, equipment and instructional materials.

200 pages Annual

Adrienne Watts, Author
Jim McGarry, President/ CEO
Adrienne Dayton, VP, Marketing & Comm.

4063 National Schools of Character
Character Education Partnership
1634 I Street NW
Suite 550
Washington, DC 20006
202-296-7743
800-988-8081
Fax: 202-296-7779
E-mail: information@character.org
http://www.character.org

Becky Sipos, President/ CEO
Sheril Morgan, Director

4064 Proactive Leadership in the 21st Century
Master Teacher
One Leadership Lane
PO Box 1207
Manhattan, KS 66502-1207
800-669-9633
Fax: 800-669-1132
http://www.masterteacher.com
Contain the laws and principals of leadership and people management as they had never been defined and described before giving school administrators a set of guidelines that if followed would guarantee success.

ISBN: 0-914607-44-8

Robert L DeBruyn, Author

4065 QED's State School Guides
Quality Education Data
601 E. Marshall St
Suite 250
Sweet Springs, MO 65351
303-860-1832
800-776-6373
Fax: 660-335-4157
E-mail: info@qeddata.com
http://www.qeddata.com
Complete directories of every US school district and public, Catholic and private school. Directories are available for individual states, geographic regions and the entire United States. Each directory includes names of district administrators, school principals and school librarians, as well as addresses, phone numbers and enrollment information. QED's State school guide also includes key demographic and instructional technology data for each district and school.

Publication Date: 1993 Yearly
ISBN: 0-887476-49-0

John F. Hood, President
Peter Long, CEO

4066 School Promotion, Publicity & Public Relations: Nothing but Benefits
Master Teacher
One Leadership Lane
PO Box 1207
Manhattan, KS 66502-1207
785-539-0555
800-669-9633
Fax: 785-539-7739
http://www.masterteacher.com
Contains the vital foundations an administrator must have to understand and implement a program of publicity, promotion and public relations, in a school or school district.

327 pages
ISBN: 0-914607-25-1

Tracey H DeBruyn, Author

4067 Schoolwide Discipline Strategies that Make a Difference in Teaching & Learning
Master Teacher
One Leadership Lane
PO Box 1207
Manhattan, KS 66502-1207
800-669-9633
Fax: 800-669-1132
http://www.masterteacher.com
This approach to discipline will help your school or district eliminate the dependecy on one individual, provide guidance for present and new teachers, allow disipline to become a K-12 program, an bring about consistancy in the handling of all student misbehaviors.

150 pages
ISBN: 1-58992-000-7

Larry Dixon, Author

4068 The Teaching Professor
Magna Publications
2718 Dryden Drive
Madison, WI 53704
608-246-3590
Fax: 608-246-3597
E-mail: support@magnapubs.com
http://www.magnapubs.com
This newsletter has been a leading source of information and inspiration for educators committed to creating a better learning environment.

Publication Date: 1972 530 pages Paperback November
1000 attendees and 10+ exhibits

William Haight, President
Jody Glynn Patrick, Vice President

Directories & Handbooks / *Early Childhood Education*

969 Early Childhood Environmental Education Programs: Guidelines for Excellence
North American Association for Environmental Educa
2000 P Street NW
Suite 540
Washington, DC 20036
202-419-0412
Fax: 212-419-0415
E-mail: info@naaee.org
http://www.naaee.org
A set of recommendations for developing and administering high-quality environmental education programs for young children from birth to age eight, with a focus on ages three to six. These guidelines provide a tool that can be used to ensure a firm foundation for new programs or to trigger improvements in existing ones.

Jose Marcos-Iga, President
Susan McGuire, Secretary

Directories & Handbooks / *Elementary Education*

970 Educational Impressions
P.O. Box 377
Franklin, NJ 07414-0377
973-423-4666
800-451-7450
Fax: 201-644-0907
E-mail: awpeller@worldnet.att.net
http://www.edimpressions.com
Educational workbooks, activity books, literature guides, and audiovisuals. Grades K-8, with emphasis on intermediate and middle grades.

Paperback/Video/Audi

Neil Peller, Marketing Director
Lori Brown, Sales/Marketing

971 Educators Guide to FREE Videotapes-Elementary/ Middle School Edition
Educators Progress Service
214 Center Street
Randolph, WI 53956-1408
920-326-3126
888-951-4469
Fax: 920-326-3127
E-mail: epsinc@centurytel.net
http://www.freeteachingaids.com
Lists and describes free and free-loan videotapes for the elementary and middle school level.

Annual
ISBN: 0-877082-67-7

Kathy Nehmer, President

72 Educators Guide to FREE Videotapes-Secondary Edition
Educators Progress Service
214 Center Street
Randolph, WI 53956-1408
920-326-3126
888-951-4469
Fax: 920-326-3127
E-mail: epsinc@centurytel.net
http://www.freeteachingaids.com

Lists and describes free and free-loan videotapes for the elementary and middle school level.
Annual
ISBN: 0-877082-67-7

Kathy Nehmer, President

4073 Elementary Teachers Guide to FREE Curriculum Materials
Educators Progress Service
214 Center Street
Randolph, WI 53956-1408
920-326-3126
888-951-4469
Fax: 920-326-3127
E-mail: epsinc@centurytel.net
http://www.freeteachingaids.com
Lists and describes free supplementary teaching aids for the elementary level.

Annual
ISBN: 0-877082-64-2

Kathy Nehmer, President

4074 KIDSNET Media Guide and News
KIDSNET
6856 Eastern Avenue NW
Suite 208
Washington, DC 20012
202-291-1400
Fax: 202-882-7315
E-mail: kidsnet@kidsnet.org
http://www.kidsnet.org
Contains children's television, radio and video listings. Also lists related teaching materials and copyright guidelines.

150 pages Monthly

4075 Lesson Plans, Integrating Technology into the Classroom: Elementary Edition
Master Teacher
One Leadership Lane
PO Box 1207
Manhattan, KS 66502-1207
800-669-9633
Fax: 800-669-1132
http://www.masterteacher.com
Gives teachers practical lessons developed and tested by teachers across the curriculum, with students of all levels of ability in using technology.

Publication Date: 1969 130 pages
ISBN: 0-914607-59-6

4076 Nursery Schools & Kindergartens Directory
American Business Directories
5711 S 86th Circle
Omaha, NE 68127-4146
402-593-4600
888-999-1307
Fax: 402-331-5481
http://www.americanbusinessandservicedirectory.com
A geographical listing of 34,900 nursery schools and kindergartens including all contact information, first year in Yellow Pages and descriptions. Also available are regional editions and electronic formats.

Annual

Jerry Venner, Coordinating Education

4077 Parent Involvement Facilitator: Elementary Edition
Master Teacher
One Leadership Lane
PO Box 1207
Manhattan, KS 66502-1207
800-669-9633
Fax: 800-669-1132
http://www.masterteacher.com

Packed with ideas for you and your teachers to implement along with the exact steps for you to follow.

169 pages
ISBN: 0-914607-45-6

4078 Patterson's Elementary Education
Educational Directories Inc.
1025 W Wise Road
PO Box 68097
Schaumberg, IL 60168-97
847-891-1250
800-357-6183
Fax: 847-891-0945
E-mail: info@ediusa.org
http://www.ediusa.com
A directory to more than 13,000 public school districts; 71,000 public, private and Catholic elementary and middle schools; 1,600 territorial schools; and 400 state department of education personnel in one easy to use consistent format. Arranged alphabetically by state then city. City listings include city name, telephone area code, city population, county name, public school district name, enrollment, grade range, superintendent's name, address and phone number.

Publication Date: 1994 870 pages Annual
ISBN: 0-910536-59-7

Douglas Moody, Coordinating Education

4079 Teaching Our Youngest-A Guide for Preschool Teachers and Child Care and Family Providers
ED Pubs
P.O. Box 22207
Alexandria, VA 22304-1398
877-4ED-PUBS
Fax: 703-605-6794
E-mail: edpubs@inet.ed.gov
http://www.edpubs.org
This booklet draws from scientifically based research about what can be done to help children develop their language abilities, increase their knowledge, become familiar with books and other printed materials, learn letters and sounds, recognize numbers and learn to count.

Directories & Handbooks / *Employment*

4080 AAEE Job Search Handbook for Educators
American Association for Employment in Education
947 E. Johnstown Road
#170
Gahanna, OH 43230
614-485-1111
Fax: 614-485-9609
E-mail: aaee@osu.edu
http://www.aaee.org
Information for those pursuing work as educators.

72 pages Annually

Doug Peden, Executive Director
Deborah Snyder, President

4081 Cabell's Directory of Publishing Opportunities in Education
Cabell Publishing
Box 5428
Tobe Hahn Station
Beaumont, TX 77726-5428
409-898-0575
Fax: 409-866-9554
E-mail: info@cabells.com
http://www.cabells.com

Includes list of more than 430 education journals that consider manuscripts for publication. Includes contact names and addresses for submitting manuscripts, topics considered, publication guidelines, fees, and circulation information.

Publication Date: 1978 1,200 pages

David WE Cabell, Editor
Deborah L English, Associate Editor

4082 Cabell's Directory of Publishing Opportunities in Accounting

Cabell Publishing Company
Box 5428
Tobe Hahn Station
Beaumont, TX 77726
409-898-0575
Fax: 409-866-9554
E-mail: info@cabells.com
http://www.cabells.com
Contains information on 130 journal. Entries include manuscript guidelines for authors: editor's address, phone, fax and e-mail. Review process and the time required, acceptance rates, readership circulation and subscription prices. The Index classifies journals by 15 topics areas and provides information on type of review, acceptance rate and review time.

Publication Date: 1978 425 pages Annual
ISBN: 0-911753-13-3

David WE Cabell, Editor
Deborah L English, Editor

4083 Cabell's Directory of Publishing Opportunities in Economics & Finance

Cabell Publishing Company
Box 5428
Tobe Hahn Station
Beaumont, TX 77726-5428
409-898-0575
Fax: 409-866-9554
E-mail: info@cabells.com
http://www.cabells.com
Contains information on 350 journals. Each journal entry includes manuscript guidelines for authors: editor's address, phone, fax and e-mail, review process and time required, acceptance rates, readership, circulation and subscription prices. The Index classifies journals by 15 topic areas and provides information on type of review, acceptance rate and review time.

Publication Date: 1978 1100 pages Annual
ISBN: 0-911753-14-1

David WE Cabell, Editor
Deborah L English, Associate Editor

4084 Cabells Directory of Publishing Opportunities in Management

Cabell Publishing Company
Box 5428
Tobe Hahn Station
Beaumont, TX 77726
409-898-0575
Fax: 409-866-9554
E-mail: info@cabells.com
http://www.cabells.com
Provides editor contact information, acceptance rates, review information, manuscript guidelines and circulation data for over 540 academic journals.

Publication Date: 1978 648 pages
ISBN: 0-911753-15-X

David WE Cabell, Editor
Deborah L English, Associate Editor

4085 Career Book

VGM Career Books
4255 W Touhy Avenue
Lincolnwood, IL 60712
732-329-6991
Fax: 732-329-6994
Offers information on educational employment opportunities in America and abroad.

BiAnnual Hard/Paper

Joyce Lain Kennedy & Darryl Laramore, Author

4086 Career Development Activities for Every Classroom

University of Wisconsin-Madison
1025 W Johnson Street
Rm. 964
Madison, WI 53706-1796
608-265-6700
800-862-1071
Fax: 608-262-9197
E-mail: cewmail@soemadison.wisc.edu
http://www.cew.wisc.edu
Four volumes containing hundreds of career development activities, and separate activity masters to duplicate. All lessons are keyed to National Career Development Guidelines Competencies and subject matter areas. Each volume is available individually.

Publication Date: 1964

Rebecca M. Blank, Chancellor
Sarah Mangelsdorf, Provost and VC

4087 Career Information Center; 13 Volumes

MacMillan Publishers
175 Fifth Avenue
New York, NY 10010
646-307-5151
888-330-8477
Fax: 800-835-3202
E-mail: customerservice@mpsvirginia.com
http://us.macmillan.com
13 volumes covering 3,000 careers, 633 job summaries with 800 photos. Up-to-date information on salaries and occupational outlooks for nearly 3,000 careers.

2.6M pages Triennial
ISBN: 0-028974-52-2

4088 Careers Information Officers in Local Authorities

Careers Research & Advisory
Centre/Hobsons Pub.
Sheraton House, Castle Park
Cambridge CB3 0AX
England
44 -0 1-23 4
223-354551
E-mail: enquiries@crac.org.uk
http://www.crac.org.uk
1,100 United Kingdom institutions offering collections of career information and audio-visual materials covering career opportunities and current job markets. Arranged alphabetically listing address, phone, contact name and titles, type of materials held and a description of the facilities.

Publication Date: 1964 165 pages 12.95 pounds

Ellen Pearce, Chief Executive
Alison Mitchell, Director of Development

4089 Certification and Accreditation Programs Directory

Gale Research
27500 Drake Road
Farmington Hills, MI 48331-3535
248-699-4253
800-877-4253
Fax: 877-363-4253
E-mail: galeord@gale.com
http://www.cengage.com
Directory of private organizations that offer more than 1,700 voluntary certification programs and approximately 300 accreditation programs. Also on CD-ROM.

Publication Date: 1995 620 pages
ISSN: 1084-2128

Michael E. Hansen, CEO
Fernando Bleichmar, Chief Strategy Officer

4090 Council of British Independent Schools in the European Communities-Members Directory

Council of British International Schools
St Mary's University, Strawberry Hi
Twickenham, TW1 4SX
United Kingdom
44-1303-260857
Fax: 44-1303-260857
E-mail: ceo@cobis.org.uk
http://www.cobis.org.uk

Annual

Colin Bell, CEO
Sarah Wooldridge, Finance Officer

4091 Directory of English Language Schools in Japan Hiring English Teachers

Information Career Opportunities Research Center
Box 1100, Station F
Toronto M4Y 2T7
Canada
416-925-8878
English-language schools in Japan.

15 pages Annual

4092 Directory of International Internships Michigan State University

MSU: Dean's Office of Int'l Studies and Programs
427 N. Shaw Lane
Room 207
East Lansing, MI 48824-1035
517-355-2350
Fax: 517-353-7254
E-mail: infonew@isp.msu.edu
http://www.isp.msu.edu
International internships sponsored by academic institutions, private corporations and the federal government.

Publication Date: 1994 168 pages Paperback

Rachel Warner, Director of Communications
Julie Norton, Secretary

4093 Directory of Schools, Colleges, and Universities Overseas

Overseas Employment Services
EBSCO Industries
PO Box 1943
Birmingham, AL 35201
205-991-1330
Fax: 205-995-1582
Directory of 300 educational institutions worldwide that hire teachers to teach different subjects in English.

21 pages Annual

Leonard Simcoe, Editor

4094 Directory of Work and Study in Developing Countries
Vacation-Work Publishers
9 Park End Street
Oxford OX1 1HJ
England
865-241978
Offers information on about 420 organizations worldwide offering employment and study opportunities in over 100 developing countries.

215 pages

4095 Earn & Learn: Cooperative Education Opportunities
Octameron Associates
1900 Mount Vernon Avenue
PO Box 2748
Alexandria, VA 22301-0748
703-836-5480
Fax: 703-836-5650
E-mail: info@octameron.com
http://www.octameron.com
Explains how students may participate in cooperative work-study education programs with federal government agencies.

Publication Date: 1997 48 pages BiAnnual
ISBN: 1-57509-023-6

4096 English in Asia: Teaching Tactics for New English Teachers
Global Press
350 Rhode Island Street
Suite 240
San Francisco, CA 94103-1135
415-570-9114
E-mail: info@globalpressinstitute.org
http://globalpressinstitute.org
Directory covering 1,000 private English-language schools in Asia, to which applications can be sent to teach.

Publication Date: 1992 180 pages
Danforth Austin, Chairman
Cristi Hegranes, Secretary

4097 European Council of International Schools Directory
European Council of International Schools
Fourth Floor, 146 Buckingham Palace
London, SW1W 9TR, London
United Kingdom
004- 0-20 7
44-1730-26-8244
Fax: 44-1730-267914
E-mail: ecis@ecis.org
http://www.ecis.org
More than 420 member elementary and secondary international schools in Europe and worldwide.

Publication Date: 1965 480 pages Annual
Kevin J Ruth, PhD, President
Darlene Fisher, People & Programmes Lead

4098 Faculty Exchange Center Directory and House Exchange Supplement
Faculty Exchange Center
University of Dayton
300 College Park
Dayton, OH 45469-3116
937-229-1000
E-mail: info@udayton.edu
http://https://www.udayton.edu
Offers information for college and faculty members wishing to exchange positions and/or homes temporarily with faculty members at other institutions.

35 pages Annual
Steven D. Cobb, Chair
Rev. Martin A. Solma, Vice Chair

4099 Foreign Faculty and Administrative Openings
Education Information Services
PO Box 620662
Newton, MA 02462-0662
617-433-0125
150 specific openings in administration, counseling, library and other professional positions for American teachers in American schools overseas and in international schools in which teaching language is English.

15 pages Every 6 Weeks
FB Viaux, Coordinating Education

4100 Guide to Educational Opportunities in Japan
Embassy of Japan
2520 Massachusetts Avenue NW
Washington, DC 20008
202-238-6700
Fax: 202-328-2187
http://www.embjapan.org
This guide describes opportunities for study in Japan and outlines different forms of financial assistance.

4101 How to Create a Picture of Your Ideal Job or Next Career
Ten Speed Press
6001 Shellmound Street
Emeryville, CA 94608-0123
510-285-3000
800-841-BOOK
Fax: 510-285-2979
http://www.randomhouse.com
Offers handy tips on how to choose the right career, and then go out and get it.

Publication Date: 1989
Richard Nelson Bolles, Author

4102 How to Plan and Develop a Career Center
Center on Education and Work
964 Educational Sciences Building
1025 W Johnson Street Rm. 964
Madison, WI 53706-1796
608-265-6700
800-446-0399
Fax: 608-262-3063
E-mail: cewmail@soemadison.wisc.edu
http://www.cew.wisc.edu
High school, postsecondary, adult, and virtual career centers-a comprehensive blueprint that covers all the bases.

Publication Date: 1964
Rebecca M. Blank, Chancellor
Sarah Mangelsdorf, Provost and VC

4103 Leading Educational Placement Sources in the US
Educational Information Services
PO Box 662
Newton Lower Falls, MA 02162
617-964-4555
An index of the host placement agencies in America for education professionals.

4104 List of Over 200 Executive Search Consulting Firms in the US
Educational Information Services
PO Box 662
Newton Lower Falls, MA 02162
617-964-4555
http://http://www.nypl.org
Covers companies with active search committees in America.

4105 List of Over 600 Personnel & Employment Agencies
Educational Information Services
PO Box 662
Newton Lower Falls, MA 02162

617-964-4555
http://http://www.nypl.org
Contains information on personnel and employment agencies.

4106 Living in China: A Guide to Studying, Teaching & Working in the PRC & Taiwan
China Books & Periodicals
360 Swift Avenue
Suite 48
South San Francisco, CA 94080
650-872-7076
800-818-2017
Fax: 650-872-7808
E-mail: info@chinabooks.com
http://www.chinabooks.com
America's #1 source of publications about China since 1960.

284 pages Paperback
ISBN: 0835125823
November

Chellis Ying, Marketing Director
Chris Robyn, Senior Managing Editor

4107 National Directory of Internships
National Society for Experiential Education
19 Mantua Road
Suite 207
Mt. Royal, NJ 08061-7235
856-423-3427
Fax: 856-423-3420
E-mail: nsee@talley.com
http://www.nsee.org
Directory contains internship descriptions for hundreds of organizations in 85 fields in nonprofit organizations, government and corporations. Lists work and service experiences for high school, college and graduate students, people entering the job market, mid-career professionals and retired persons. Includes indexes by field of interest, location and host organization.

Publication Date: 1995 703 pages
ISBN: 0-536-01123-0

Jim Colbert, President
Stephanie Thomason, President Elect

4108 Opening List in US Colleges, Public & Private Schools
Education Information Services/Instant Alert
PO Box 620662
Newton, MA 02462-0662
617-433-0125
Offers about 150 current professional openings in US colleges and public and private schools.

10 pages Every 6 weeks
FB Viaux, Coordinating Education

4109 Opening List of Professional Openings in American Overseas Schools
Education Information Services/Instant Alert
PO Box 620662
Newton, MA 02462-0662
617-433-0125
About 150 current professional openings for teachers, administrators, counselors, librarians and educational specialists in American overseas schools and international schools at which the teaching language is primarily English.

FB Viaux, Coordinating Education

4110 Overseas Employment Opportunities for Educators
Department of Defense, Office of Dependent Schools
4800 Mark Center Drive
Alexandria, VA 22350-1400
571-372-0590
http://www.dodea.edu
This publication tells about teaching jobs in 250 schools operated for children of US military and civilian personnel stationed overseas. Applicants usually must qualify in two subject areas.

4111 Private School, Community & Junior College Four Year Colleges & Universities
Educational Information Services
PO Box 662
Newton Lower Falls, MA 02162
617-964-4555
Names, addresses and phones for any state or region in the United States offering employment opportunities.

4112 Research, Study, Travel, & Work Abroad
US Government Publishing Office
710 North Capitol Street N.W.
Washington, DC 20401-1
202-512-1800
866-512-1800
Fax: 202-512-2104
E-mail: ContactCenter@gpo.gov
http://www.gpo.gov
Publication Date: 1861

Davita Vance-Cooks, Director
Jim Bradley, Deputy Director

4113 Teaching Overseas
KSJ Publishing Company
PO Box 2311
Sebastopol, CA 95473-2311
A directory of information on how to find jobs teaching overseas.
Publication Date: 1992 89 pages 2nd Edition
ISBN: 0-962044-55-5

4114 Thirty-Four Activities to Promote Careers in Special Education
The Council for Exceptional Children
2900 Crystal Drive
Suite 1000
Arlington, VA 22202-3557
703-620-3660
888-232-7733
Fax: 703-264-1637
http://www.cec.sped.org
This guide introduces individuals to the opportunities, rewards and delights of working with children with exceptionalities. It provides directions on how to plan, develop, and implement activities in the school and community that will increase people's awareness of careers in special education and related services.
Publication Date: 1996 120 pages
ISBN: 0-865862-77-0

Robin D. Brewer, President
James P. Heiden, President Elect

4115 VGM's Careers Encyclopedia
VGM Career Books/National Textbook Company
4255 W Touhy Avenue
Lincolnwood, IL 60646-1933
708-679-5500
A list of over 200 professional associations that provide career guidance information.

4116 Work Abroad: The Complete Guide to Finding a Job Overseas
Transitions Abroad
P.O. Box 1369
Amherst, MA 01004
413-992-6486
Fax: 802-442-4827
E-mail: editor@transitionsabroad.com
http://www.transitionsabroad.com
Resource for finding both short- and long-term jobs abroad. Organized by region and country, includes websites and phone numbers.
Publication Date: 1977

Dr. Joanna Hubbs, President
Gregory Hubbs, Editor-in-Chief

4117 Workforce Preparation: An International Perspective
The Johns Hopkins University Press
2715 North Charles Street
Baltimore, MD 21218-4319
410-516-6989
800-530-9673
Fax: 410-516-8805
E-mail: muse@press.jhu.edu
http://muse.jhu.edu
Excellent collection of material by 20 prominent educators describes efforts in developed and developing countries worldwide to prepare youth and adults for work.

Dean Smith, Director
Wendy Queen, Deputy Director

4118 World of Learning
Europa Publications
18 Bedford Square
London WC1B 3JN
England
00 -00 - 7 8
171-580-8236
Fax: 171-636-1664
http://europa.eu
Details over 26,000 educational, cultural and scientific institutions throughout the world, together with an exhaustive directory of over 150,000 people active within them.
2,072 pages Annual
ISBN: 0-946653-92-5

Directories & Handbooks / *Financial Aid*

4119 Catalog of Federal Domestic Assistance
Office of Management & Budget
Washington, DC 20402

http://https://www.cfda.gov/
Offers information from all federal agencies that have assistance programs (loans, scholarships and technical assistance as well as grants) and compiles these into the CFDA. The individual entries are grouped by Department of Agency and includes an excellent set of instructions and several indices. Indices allow the user to search for grants by subject matter, agency, deadline date or eligibility criteria.

4120 Chronicle Financial Aid Guide
Chronicle Guidance Publications
66 Aurora Street
Moravia, NY 13118-3569
315-497-0330
800-622-7284
Fax: 315-497-3359
E-mail:

customerservice@chronicleguidance.com
http://www.chronicleguidance.com
Financial aid programs offered primarily by noncollegiate organizations, independent and AFL-CIO affiliated labor unions and federal and state governments for high school seniors and undergraduate and graduate students.
Publication Date: 1938 460 pages Annual
ISBN: 1-5563-310-1

Janet Seemann, Author
Cheryl Fickeisen, President and CEO
Gary Fickeisen, Vice President

4121 College Costs and Financial Aid Handbook
College Board Publications
45 Columbus Avenue
New York, NY 10023-6917
212-713-8000
800-323-7155
Fax: 888-321-7183
http://www.collegeboard.org
A step-by-step guide providing the most up-to-date facts on costs plus financial aid and scholarship availability at 3,200 two- and four-year institutions.
Publication Date: 1900
ISBN: 0-874476-83-6

David Coleman, President and CEO
Jeremy Singer, Chief Operating Officer

4122 College Financial Aid Annual
Arco/Macmillan
1633 Broadway
Floor 7
New York, NY 10019-6708
212-654-8933
Lists of private businesses, academic institutions and other organizations that provide awards and scholarships for financial aid; guide to federal and state financial aid.

4123 Directory of Educational Contests for Students K-12
ABC-CLIO
130 Cremona Drive
#1911
Santa Barbara, CA 93117-5599
805-895-5623
800-368-6868
Fax: 805-685-9685
E-mail: internationalsales@abc-clio.com
http://www.abc-clio.com
Offers about 200 competitive scholarship programs and other educational contests for elementary and secondary school students.
Publication Date: 1991 253 pages

4124 Directory of Financial Aid for Women
Reference Service Press
2310 Homestead Rd
Suite C1 #219
Los Altos, CA 94024
650-861-3170
Fax: 650-861-3171
E-mail: rspinfo@aol.com
http://www.rspfunding.com
Offers information on more than 1,500 scholarships, fellowships, loan sources, grants, awards and internships.
490 pages

Gail Schlachter, President
R. David Weber, Editor-in-Chief

4125 Directory of Institutional Projects Funded by Office of Educational Research
U.S. Office of Educational Research & Improvement
555 New Jersey Avenue NW
Washington, DC 20208-5573

202-219-2079
Fax: 202-219-2135
http://https://www2.ed.gov/pubs/TeachersGuide/oeri.html
Publication Date: 1990 60 pages

126 Directory of International Grants & Fellowships in the Health Sciences
National Institutes of Health
9000 Rockville Pike
Building 31, Room B2C29
Bethesda, MD 20892-2220
301-496-4000
Fax: 301-594-1211
E-mail: NIHinfo@od.nih.gov
http://www.nih.gov/fic
Fellowships and grants listed separately in this guide. Each listing includes a complete program description with contact information.
Publication Date: 1887

Francis S. Collins, M.D., Ph.D., Director

127 Don't Miss Out: The Ambitous Students Guide to Financial Aid
Octameron Associates
1900 Mt Vernon Avenue
P.O. Box 2748
Alexandria, VA 22301-0748
703-836-5480
Fax: 703-836-5650
E-mail: info2octameon.com
http://www.octameron.com
Publication Date: 0 192 pages Anually

128 Fellowships in International Affairs-A Guide to Opportunities in the US & Abroad
Lynne Rienner Publishing
1800 30th Street
Suite 314
Boulder, CO 80301
303-444-6684
Fax: 303-444-0824
E-mail: questions@rienner.com
http://www.rienner.com
This guide lists fellowships meant to encourage women to pursue careers in international security.
Publication Date: 1984

129 Fellowships, Scholarships and Related Opportunities
Center for International Ed./University of TN
1620 Melrose Avenue
University of Tennessee
Knoxville, TN 37996-3531
865-974-3177
Fax: 865-974-2985
E-mail: international@utk.edu
http://international.utk.edu
140 grants, scholarships and fellowships available to citizens of the United States for study or research abroad.
50 pages Biennial

130 Financial Aid for Research & Creative Activities Abroad
Reference Service Press
2310 Homestead Rd
Suite C1 #219
Los Altos, CA 94024
650-861-3170
Fax: 650-861-3171
E-mail: webagent@rspfunding.com
http://www.rspfunding.com
This book lists opportunities fir high school students and undergraduates, graduates,

postdoctoral students, professionals and others.
432 pages
ISBN: 1588410625

Gail Schlachter, President
R.David Weber, Editor-in-Chief

4131 Financial Aid for Study Abroad: a Manual for Advisers & Administrators
NAFSA: Association of International Educators
1307 New York Avenue NW
8th Floor
Washington, DC 20005-4701
202-737-3699
800-836-4994
Fax: 202-737-3657
E-mail: inbox@nafsa.org
http://www.nafsa.org
Publication Date: 1948 105 pages

Marlene M Johnson, Director/CEO
Vic Johnson, Senior Adviser

4132 Financial Resources for International Study
Institute of International Education
P.O. Box 1020
Sewickley, PA 15143-1020
412-741-0930
Fax: 212-984-5452
E-mail: iiebooks@abdintl.com
http://www.iiebooks.org
Directory of more than 600 awards that can be used for international study.
Publication Date: 1996 320 pages
ISBN: 087206-220-1

4133 Foundation Grants to Individuals
Foundation Center
79 Fifth Avenue/16th Street
New York, NY 10003-3076
212-260-4230
Fax: 212-807-3677
http://foundationcenter.org
Features current information for grant seekers.
Publication Date: 1956

Melissa Berman, President and CEO
Patrick Collins, CFO

4134 Free Money for College: Fifth Edition
Facts On File
132 West 31st Street
17th Floor
New York, NY 10001
800-322-8755
E-mail: custserv@factsonfile.com
http://www.factsonfile.com
1,000 grants and scholarships.
Publication Date: 1999 240 pages Annual Hardcover
ISBN: 081603947X

Laurie Blum, Author
Laurie Likoff, Editorial Director

4135 Free Money for Foreign Study: A Guide to 1,000 Grants for Study Abroad
Facts On File
132 West 31st Street
17th Floor
New York, NY 10001
800-322-8755
E-mail: custserv@factsonfile.com
http://www.factsonfile.com

Lists organizations and institutions worldwide offering scholarships and grants for study outside the United States.
262 pages

Laurie Likoff, Editorial Director

4136 Fulbright and Other Grants for USIA Graduate Study Abroad
U.S. Student Programs Division
809 United Nations Plaza
New York, NY 10017-3580
212-984-5330
Fax: 212-984-5325
http://www.iie.org
Mutual educational exchange grants for pre-doctoral students offered by foreign governments.
Publication Date: 1919 90 pages Annual

Allan E. Goodman, President and CEO
Reter Thompson, Executive Vice President

4137 Fund Your Way Through College: Uncovering 1,100 Opportunities in Aid
Visible Ink Press/Gale Research
43311 Joy Road
#414
Canton, MI 48187-2075
734-667-3211
Fax: 734-667-4311
http://www.visibleinkpress.com
1,100 scholarships, grants, loans, awards and prizes for undergraduate students.
470 pages

4138 German-American Scholarship Guide-Exchange Opportunities for Historians and Social Scientist
German Historical Institute
1607 New Hampshire Avenue NW
Washington, DC 20009-2562
202-387-3355
Fax: 202-387-6437
http://www.ghi-dc.org
This guide is divided into two sections: scholarships for study and research in the US and scholarships for study and research in Germany.

Hartmut Berghoff, Director
Uwe Spiekmann, Deputy Director

4139 Getting Funded: The Complete Guide to Writing Grant Proposals
Continuing Education Press
400 W First St
Chico, CA 95929-0250
530-898-6105
866-647-7377
Fax: 530-898-6105
E-mail: rce@csuchico.edu
http://rce.csuchico.edu
A step-by-step guide to writing successful grants and proposals. An indispensible reference for experienced and first-time grant writers alike.
180 pages Paperback
ISBN: 0-87678-071-0

Mary Hall, Author
Debra Barger, Administration
Joe Picard, Director

4140 Graduate Scholarship Book
Pearson Education
1 Lake Street
Upper Saddle River, NJ 07458
201-909-6200
Fax: 201-767-5029
http://www.pearsoned.com

A complete guide to scholarships, grants and loans for graduate and professional study.

441 pages Biennial

4141 Grant Opportunities for US Scholars & Host Opportunities for US Universities

International Research & Exchange Board
1275 K Street NW
Suite 600
Washington, DC 20005
202-628-8188
Fax: 202-628-8189
E-mail: irex@irex.org
http://www.irex.org
This pamphlet lists programs in advanced research, language and development, short-term travel, special projects and institutional opportunities.

Publication Date: 1968

Kristin M. Lord, President and CEO
Joyce Warner, SVP, Chied of Staff

4142 Grant Writing Beyond The Basics: Proven Strategies Professionals Use To Make Proposals

Continuing Education Press
400 W First St
Chico, CA 95929-0250
530-898-6105
866-647-7377
Fax: 530-898-6105
E-mail: rce@csuchico.edu
http://rce.csuchico.edu
Designed to inspire those with grant writing experience who want to take their development strategies to the next level.

128 pages Paperback
ISBN: 0-87678-117-2

Michael K Wells, Author
Debra Barger, Administration
Joe Picard, Director

4143 Grants & Awards Available to American Writers

PEN American Center
588 Broadway
Suite 303
New York, NY 10012
212-334-1660
Fax: 212-334-2181
E-mail: ftw@pen.org
http://www.pen.org
Includes a full program description and is then broken down by type of writing. Awards for work in a particular country are listed alphabetically by country.

340 pages Paperback
ISBN: 0-934638-20-9

Peter Godwinÿ, President
John Troubh, Executive Vice-President

4144 Grants Register

St. Martin's Press
175 5th Avenue
New York, NY 10010
212-674-5151
888-330-8477
Fax: 212-674-6132
E-mail:
firstname.lastname@stmartins.com
http://us.macmillan.com/smp
This directory offers a comprehensive list of programs organized alphabetically with special attention to eligibility requirements. Index by subject.

4145 Grants, Fellowships, & Prizes of Interest to Historians

American Historical Association
400 A Street SE
Washington, DC 20003-3889
202-544-2422
Fax: 202-544-8307
E-mail: aha@theaha.org
http://www.historians.org
This guide offers information on awards for historians from undergraduate to postgraduate grants, fellowships, prizes, internships and awards.

Publication Date: 1884

Jim Grossman, Executive Director
Shatha Almutawa, Associate Editor

4146 Guide to Department of Education Programs

US Department of Education
400 Maryland Avenue SW
Washington, DC 20202-0001
202-401-2000
800-872-5327
http://www.ed.gov
Programs of financial aid offered by the Department of Education.

Publication Date: 1980 35 pages Annual

Emma Vadehra, Chief of Staff
James Cole, Jr., General Counsel

4147 Harvard College Guide to Grants

Office of Career Services
Harvard University
54 Dunster Street
Cambridge, MA 02138
617-495-2595
Fax: 617-495-3584
http://www.ocs.fas.harvard.edu
This guide describes national and regional grants and fellowships for study in the US, study abroad and work and practical experience.

234 pages Paperback

4148 How to Find Out About Financial Aid & Funding

Reference Service Press
2310 Homestead Rd.
Suite C1 #219
Los Altos, CA 94024
650-861-3170
Fax: 650-861-3171
E-mail: rspinfo@aol.com
http://www.rspfunding.com
Over 700 financial aid directories and Internet sites described and evaluated.

432 pages Hardcover
ISBN: 1588410935

Gail A Schlachter, Author
Gail Schlachter, President
R. David Weber, Editor-in-Chief

4149 International Foundation Directory

Europa Publications
11 New Fetter Lane
London
England EC4P 4EE
00 -00 - 7 8
44-0-20-7842-2110
Fax: 44-0-20-7842-2249
http://europa.eu
A world directory of international foundations, trusts and similar non-profit institutions. Provides detailed information on over 1,200 institutions in some 70 countries throughout the world.

Publication Date: 1994 736 pages
ISBN: 1-857430-01-8

Paul Kelly, Editorial Director

4150 International Scholarship Book: The Complete Guide to Financial Aid

Pearson Education
1 Lake Street
Upper Saddle River, NJ 07458
201-909-6200
Fax: 201-767-5029
http://www.pearsoned.com
Offers information on private organizations providing financial aid for university students interested in studying in foreign countries.

335 pages Cloth

4151 Journal of Student Financial Aid

University of Notre Dame
Office of Financial Aid
Notre Dame, IN 46556
574-631-5000
http://www.nd.edu
Offers a listing of private and federal sources of financial aid for college bound students.

3x Year

Rev. John I. Jenkins, President
Thomas G. Burish, Provost

4152 Loans and Grants from Uncle Sam

Octameron Associates
1900 Mount Vernon Avenue
PO Box 2748
Alexandria, VA 22301-0748
703-836-5480
Fax: 703-836-5650
E-mail: info@octameron.com
http://www.octameron.com
Offers information on federal student loan and grant programs and state loan guarantee agencies.

72 pages Annual
ISBN: 1-57509-097-X

Anna Leider, Author

4153 Money for Film & Video Artists

American for the Art
1000 Vermont Avenue NW
6th Floor
Washington, DC 20005
202-371-2830
Fax: 202-371-0424
http://www.artsusa.org
The listings are organized by sponsoring organization and entries include basic application and program information.

Abel Lopez, Chair
Ramona Baker, Vice Chair

4154 Money for International Exchange in the Arts

American for the Art
1000 Vermont Avenue NW
6th Floor
Washington, DC 20005
202-371-2830
Fax: 202-371-0424
http://www.artsusa.org
A guide to the various resources available to support artists and arts organizations in international work.

Abel Lopez, Chair
Ramona Baker, Vice Chair

4155 Money for Visual Artists

America for the Art
1000 Vermont Avenue NW
6th Floor
Washington, DC 20005
202-371-2830
Fax: 202-371-0424
http://www.artsusa.org
Programs are listed alphabetically by sponsor with detailed program description.

Abel Lopez, Chair
Ramona Baker, Vice Chair

4156 National Association of State Scholarship and Grant Program Survey Report
National Association of State Scholarship Programs
8 W. 38TH ST
Suite 503
New York, NY 10018-1324
917-551-6770
E-mail: contact@nas.org
http://nas.org
Listing of over 50 member state agencies administering scholarship and grant programs for student financial aid.

Publication Date: 1987 150 pages

Peter Wyatt Wood, President
Ashley Thorne, ExecutiveyDirector

4157 National Association of Student Financial Aid Administrators Directory
1101 Connecticut Avenue NW
Suite 1100
Washington, DC 20036-4303
202-785-0453
Fax: 202-785-1487
http://www.nasfaa.org
Offers information on over 3,000 institutions of postsecondary education and their financial aid administrators.

230 pages Annual

Eileen O'Leary, National Chairÿ
Dan Mann, National Chair-Electÿ

4158 Need A Lift?
The American Legion
700 N Pennsylvania Street
P.O. Box 36460
Indianapolis, IN 46236-1050
317-630-1200
888-453-4466
Fax: 317-630-1381
E-mail: emblem@legion.org
http://www.EMBLEM.legion.org
Sources of career, scholarship and loan information or assistance.

144 pages Annual/Paperback

Robert Caudell, Author

4159 Peterson's Grants for Graduate and Postdoctoral Study
Peterson's, A Nelnet Company
Princeton Pike Corporate Center
461 From Road
Paramus, NJ 07652
609-698-1800
800-338-3282
Fax: 402-458-3042
E-mail: support@petersons.com
http://www.petersons.com
Only comprehensive source of current information on grants and fellowships exclusively for graduate and postdoctoral students.

Publication Date: 1998 5th Edition
ISBN: 1-560794-01-1

4160 Peterson's Sports Scholarships and College Athletic Programs
Peterson's, A Nelnet Company
Princeton Pike Corporate Center
461 From Road
Paramus, NJ 08648
609-896-1800
800-338-3282
Fax: 402-458-3042
E-mail: support@petersons.com
http://www.petersons.com

A college-by-college look at scholarships designated exclusively for student athletes in 32 men's and women's sports.
Publication Date: 2004 624 pages 5th Edition
ISBN: 0768915244

4161 Scholarship Handbook
The College Board
45 Columbus Avenue
New York, NY 10023
212-713-8000
800-323-7155
http://www.collegeboard.org
Useful text for college-bound students, their families and guidance counselors. Offers more than 2,000 descriptions of national and state level award programs, public and private education loan programs, intership opportunities and more.

David Coleman, President and CEO
Jeremy Singer, COO

4162 Scholarships for Emigres Training for Careers in Jewish Education
Jewish Foundation for Education of Women
135 E 64th Street
New York, NY 10065
212-288-3931
Fax: 212-288-5798
E-mail: fdnscholar@aol.com
http://www.jfew.org
Open to emigres from the former Soviet Union who are pursuing careers in Jewish education. Candidates in Jewish education, rabbinical and cantorial studies, and Jewish studies are invited to write the Foundation.

Elizabeth Leiman Kraiem, Executive Director
Jill Weber Smith, Chair

4163 Scholarships, Fellowships and Loans
Gale Research
27500 Drake Road
Farmington Hills, MI 48231-5477
800-877-4253
Fax: 877-363-4253
http://www.cengage.com
Written especially for professionals, students, counselors, parents and others interested in education. This resource provides more than 3,700 sources of education-related financial aid and awards at all levels of study.

Publication Date: 1995 1,290 pages Annual
ISBN: 0-810391-14-7

Michael E. Hansen, CEO
Fernando Bleichmar, Chief Strategy Officer

4164 Student Guide
Federal Student Aid Information Center
PO Box 84
Washington, DC 20044-0084
800-433-3243
800-433-3243
http://https://studentaid.ed.gov
Describes the federal student aid programs, and general information about the eligibility criteria, application procedures and award levels, and lists important deadlines and phone numbers.

54 pages

John J McCarthy, Director

4165 Study Abroad
U.N. Educational, Scientific & Cultural Assn.
7, place de Fontenoy
F-75700 Paris
France
1-45681123

Listing of over 200,000 scholarships, fellowships and educational exchange opportunities offered for study in 124 countries.
1,300 pages Biennial

4166 Write Now: A Complete Self-Teaching Programfor Better Handwriting
Continuing Education Press
400 W First St
Chico, CA 95929-0250
530-898-6105
866-647-7377
Fax: 530-898-4020
E-mail: rce@csuchico.edu
http://rce.csuchico.edu
A step-by-step guide to improving one's handwriting. Develop clean and legible italic handwriting with regular practice.

128 pages Paperback
ISBN: 0-87678-089-3

Barbara Getty & Inga Dubay, Author
Debra Barger, Administration
Joe Picard, Director

Directories & Handbooks / Guidance & Counseling

4167 Accredited Institutions of Postsecondary Education
MacMillan Publishers
175 Fifth Avenue
New York, NY 10010
646-307-5151
888-330-8477
Fax: 800-835-3202
E-mail: customerservice@mpsvirginia.com
http://us.macmillan.com
Lists over 5,000 accredited institutions and programs for postsecondary education in the United States.

600 pages Annual

4168 Adolescent Pregnancy Prevention Clearinghouse
Children's Defense Fund Education & Youth Develop.
25 E Street NW
#400
Washington, DC 20001-2109
202-628-8787
800-233-1200
Fax: 202-662-3560
E-mail: cdfinfo@childrensdefense.org
http://www.childrensdefense.org
Provides information and clarification on the connection between pregnancy and broader life questions for youth.

Marian Wright Edelman, President
Richard Gollub, Chief Financial Officer

4169 COLLEGESOURCE
Career Guidance Foundation
8090 Engineer Road
San Diego, CA 92111-1906
858-560-8051
800-854-2670
Fax: 858-278-8960
http://www.collegesource.org
CD-ROM and Web College Catalog Collection. Contains colleges and universitie's catalogs from throughout the US, over 2,600. Also a college search program that can be searched by major, tuition costs, and more. Foreign catalogs available.

Annette Crone, Account Coordinator
David Hunt, Account Coordinator

4170 Cabells Directory of Publishing Opportunities in Educational Psychology and Administration
Cabell Publishing Company
Box 5428
Tobe Hahn Station
Beaumont, TX 77726
409-898-0575
Fax: 409-866-9554
E-mail: info@cabells.com
http://www.cabells.com
Provides information on editor contact information, manuscript guidelines, acceptance rate, review information and circulation data for over 225 academic journals.
Publication Date: 1978 799 pages Annual
ISBN: 0-911753-19-2

David WE Cabell, Editor
Deborah L English, Associate Editor

4171 Career & Vocational Counseling Directory
American Business Directories
5711 S 86th Circle
Omaha, NE 68127-4146
402-593-4600
888-999-1307
Fax: 402-331-5481
http://http://www.americanbusinessandservicedirectory.com
Nationwide listing of 3,300 companies/consultants available in print, computer magnetic tape and diskette, mailing labels, and index cards listing the name, address, phone, size of advertisement, contact person and number of employees.
Annual

Jerry Venner, Coordinating Education

4172 College Handbook
College Board Publications
45 Columbus Avenue
New York, NY 10023-6992
212-713-8000
Fax: 800-525-5562
E-mail: puborderinfo@collegeboard.org
http://www.collegeboard.org
Descriptions of 3,200 colleges and universities.
Publication Date: 1994 1728 pages Annually

David Coleman, President and CEO
Jeremy Singer, COO

4173 College Handbook Foreign Student Supplement
College Board Publications
45 Columbus Avenue
New York, NY 10023-6917
212-713-8000
Fax: 800-525-5562
E-mail: aces@info.collegeboard.org
http://www.collegeboard.org
Lists about 2,800 colleges and universities that are open to foreign students.
Publication Date: 1994 288 pages Annual
ISBN: 0-877474-83-3

David Coleman, President and CEO
Jeremy Singer, COO

4174 College Transfer Guide
School Guide Publications
210 N Avenue
New Rochelle, NY 10801-6402
914-632-7771
800-433-7771
Fax: 914-632-3412
E-mail: mridder@schoolguides.com
http://www.schoolguides.com

Five hundred four-year colleges in the Northeast and Midwest that accept transfer students listing transfer requirements, deadlines, fees, enrollment, costs and contact information. Circulation, 60,000.
125 pages Annual/January

4175 Community College Exemplary Instructional Programs
Massachusetts Bay Community College Press
50 Oakland Street
Wellsley Hills, MA 02181
781-239-3000
Fax: 781-237-1061
http://www.massbay.edu
Community college programs identified as outstanding by the National Council of Instructional Administrators.
Publication Date: 1961

John O'Donnell, President

4176 Comparative Guide to American Colleges for Students, Parents & Counselors
HarperCollins
195 Broadway
New York, NY 10007-5244
212-207-7000
Fax: 212-207-7145
http://www.harpercollins.com
Accredited four-year colleges in the United States.
800 pages Cloth

4177 Directory of Play Therapy Training
University of North Texas
PO Box 310829
425 S. Welch St., Complex 2
Denton, TX 76203
940-565-3864
Fax: 940-565-4461
E-mail: cpt@unt.edu
http://www.centerforplaytherapy.com
Provides training, research publications and serves as a clearinghouse for literature in the field.
Paperback

Rinda Thomas, Office Manager
Sue C Bratton, Center Director

4178 Educators Guide to FREE Guidance Materials
Educators Progress Service
214 Center Street
Randolph, WI 53956-1408
920-326-3126
888-951-4469
Fax: 920-326-3127
E-mail: epsinc@centurytel.net
http://www.freeteachingaids.com
Lists and describes free films, videotapes, filmstrips, slides, web sites, and hundreds of free printed materials in the field of career education and guidance for all age levels.
190 pages Annual
ISBN: 87708-406-8

Kathy Nehmer, President

4179 Index of Majors and Graduate Degrees
College Board Publications
45 Columbus Avenue
New York, NY 10023-6992
212-713-8000
Fax: 800-525-5562
http://www.collegeboard.org

Includes descriptions of over 600 majors and identifies the 3,200 colleges, universities, and graduate schools that offer them.
Annual
ISBN: 0-87447-592-9

David Coleman, President and CEO
Jeremy Singer, COO

4180 Tests: a Comprehensive Reference for Psychology, Education & Business
PRO-ED
8700 Shoal Creek Boulevard
Austin, TX 78757-6897
512-451-3246
800-897-3202
Fax: 800-397-7633
E-mail: general@proedinc.com
http://www.proedinc.com
This fifth edition groups updated information on approximately 2,000 assessment instruments into three primary classifications-psychology, education, and business-and 89 subcategories, enabling users to readily identify the tests that meet their assessment needs. Each entry contains a statement of the instrument's purpose, a concise description of the instrument, scoring procedures, cost, and publisher information.
Publication Date: 1991 809 pages Paperback/Hardcover
ISBN: 0-89079-709-9

Taddy Maddox, General Editor

4181 Vocational Biographies
Vocational Biographies
PO Box 31
Sauk Centre, MN 56378-0031
320-352-6516
800-255-0752
Fax: 320-352-5546
E-mail: careers@vocbio.com
http://www.vocbio.com
Real life career success stories of persons in every walk of life that allow students to see a career through the eyes of a real person. New for 2005: Internet Access to 1001 Career Success Stories.

Toby Behnen, President
Roxann Behnen, Customer Service/Sales

4182 What Works and Doesn't With at Risk Students
BKS Publishing
3109 150th Place SE
Mill Creek, WA 98012-4864
425-745-3029
Fax: 425-337-4837
E-mail: DocBlokk@aol.com
http://www.literacyfirst.com
Publication Date: 1919 162 pages Paperback
ISBN: 0-9656713-0-5

Jan Glaes, Author
Bill Blokker, Owner

4183 World of Play Therapy Literature
Center for Play Therapy
PO Box 311337
5308 Valley Ridge Plaza
Middleton, WI 53562
608-203-8646
Fax: 608-203-5872
E-mail: cpt@coefs.coe.unt.edu
http://www.playtherapymadison.com
Author and topical listings of over 6,000 books, dissertations, documents, and journal articles on play therapy, updated every two years.
Publication Date: 1995 306 pages

Landreth, Homeyer, Bratton, Kale, Hipl, Schumann, Author

Directories & Handbooks / *Language Arts*

184 Classroom Strategies for the English Language Learner
Master Teacher
One Leadership Lane
PO Box 1207
Manhattan, KS 66502-1207
800-669-9633
Fax: 800-669-1132
http://www.masterteacher.com
A practical model for accelerating both oral language and literacy development, based on the latest research for effective instruction of both Native English speakers and English language learners.
266 pages
ISBN: 1-58992-068-6
Socrro Herrera EdD, Author

185 Italic Handwriting Series-Book A
Continuing Education Press
400 W First St
Chico, CA 95929-0250
530-898-6105
866-647-7377
Fax: 530-898-4020
E-mail: rce@csuchico.edu
http://rce.csuchico.edu
Book A is the first workbook of a seven-part series. Designed for the beginning reader and writer, it introduces the alphabet one letter at a time. Illustrated.
64 pages Paperback
ISBN: 0-87678-092-3
Barbara Getty & Inga Dubay, Author
Debra Barger, Administration
Joe Picard, Director

186 Italic Handwriting Series-Book B
Continuing Education Press
400 W First St
Chico, CA 95929-0250
530-898-6105
866-647-7377
Fax: 530-898-4020
E-mail: rce@csuchico.edu
http://rce.csuchico.edu
Book B is the second workbook of a seven-part series. Designed for the beginning reader and writer. Introduces words and sentences, lowercase and capitol print script, one letter per page. Illustrated.
59 pages Paperback
ISBN: 0-87678-093-1
Barbara Getty & Inga Dubay, Author
Debra Barger, Administration
Joe Picard, Director

187 Italic Handwriting Series-Book C
Continuing Education Press
400 W First St
Chico, CA 95929-0250
530-898-6105
866-647-7377
Fax: 530-898-4020
E-mail: rce@csuchico.edu
http://rce.csuchico.edu
Book C is the third workbook of a seven-part series. Covers basic italic and introduces the cursive. Words and sentences include days of week, months of year, modes of transportation, and tongue twisters. Illustrated.
60 pages Paperback
ISBN: 0-87678-094-X
Barbara Getty & Inga Dubay, Author
Debra Barger, Administration
Joe Picard, Director

4188 Italic Handwriting Series-Book D
Continuing Education Press
400 W First St
Chico, CA 95929-0250
530-898-6105
866-647-7377
Fax: 530-898-4020
E-mail: rce@csuchico.edu
http://rce.csuchico.edu
Book D is the fourth workbook of a seven-part series. Reviews basic italic and covers the total cursive program. Includes prefixes, suffixes, capitalization, and playful poems. Explores history of the alphabet. Illustrated.
80 pages Paperback
ISBN: 0-87678-095-8
Barbara Getty & Inga Dubay, Author
Debra Barger, Administration
Joe Picard, Director

4189 Italic Handwriting Series-Book E
Continuing Education Press
400 W First St
Chico, CA 95929-0250
530-898-6105
866-647-7377
Fax: 530-898-4020
E-mail: rce@csuchico.edu
http://rce.csuchico.edu
Book E is the fifth workbook of a seven-part series. Reviews basic italic and covers the total cursive program. Writing practice covers natural history— plants, volcanoes, cities. Explores history of the alphabet. Illustrated.
56 pages Paperback
ISBN: 0-87678-096-6
Barbara Getty & Inga Dubay, Author
Debra Barger, Administration
Joe Picard, Director

4190 Italic Handwriting Series-Book F
Continuing Education Press
400 W First St
Chico, CA 95929-0250
530-898-6105
866-647-7377
Fax: 530-898-4020
E-mail: rce@csuchico.edu
http://rce.csuchico.edu
Book F is the sixth workbook of a seven-part series. Reviews basic italic and covers the total cursive program. Writing practice emphasizes figures of speech (e.g. homophones, puns, metaphors, acronyms). Explores history of the alphabet. Illustrated.
56 pages Paperback
ISBN: 0-87678-097-4
Barbara Getty & Inga Dubay, Author
Debra Barger, Administration
Joe Picard, Director

4191 Italic Handwriting Series-Book G
Continuing Education Press
400 W First St
Chico, CA 95929-0250
530-898-6105
866-647-7377
Fax: 530-898-4020
E-mail: rce@csuchico.edu
http://rce.csuchico.edu
Book G is the seventh workbook of a seven-part series. A comprehensive self-instruction program in basic and cursive italic. Writing content follows a central theme- the history of our alphabet. Suitable for older students. Illustrated.
56 pages Paperback
ISBN: 0-87678-098-2
Barbara Getty & Inga Dubay, Author
Debra Barger, Administration
Joe Picard, Director

4192 Language Schools Directory
American Business Directories
5711 S 86th Circle
Omaha, NE 68127-4146
402-593-4600
888-999-1307
Fax: 402-331-5481
http://www.americanbusinessandservicedirectory.com
A listing of language schools, arranged by geographic location, offering contact information which is updated on a continual basis, and printed on request. Directory is also available in electronic formats.
Jerry Venner, Coordinating Education

4193 Picture Book Learning Volume-1
Picture Book Learning Inc.
PO Box 270075
Louisville, CO 80027
303-548-2809
E-mail: todd@picturebooklearning.com
http://www.picturebooklearning.com
Teachers can use this fun method of teaching elementary children basic language arts skills through the use of picture books.
60 pages
ISBN: 0-9760725-0-5
Todd Osborne, Co-President
Corinne Osborne, Editor

4194 Process of Elimination - a Method of Teaching Basic Grammar - Teacher Ed
Scott & McCleary Publishing Company
2482 11th Street SW
PO Box 3830
Akron, OH 44314-0830
702-566-8756
800-765-3564
Fax: 702-568-1378
E-mail: jscott7576@aol.com
http://www.scottmccleary.com
Series of 7 steps designed to teach basic grammar skills to students in middle grades through college. Available in a teacher edition and a student workbook.
50 pages
ISBN: 0-9636225-2-8
ISSN: 0-9636225-
Milton Metheny, Author
Janet Scott, Publisher
Sheila McCleary, Publisher

4195 Process of Elimination: A Method of Teaching Basic Grammar - Student Ed
Scott & McCleary Publishing Company
2482 11th Street SW
PO Box 3830
Akron, OH 44314-0830
702-566-8756
800-765-3564
Fax: 702-568-1378
E-mail: jscott7576@aol.com
http://www.scottmccleary.com
Series of 7 steps designed to teach basic grammar skills to students in middle grades through college. Available in a teacher edition and a student workbook.
Milton Metheny, Author
Janet Scott, Publisher
Sheila McCleary, Publisher

4196 Put Reading First: The Research Building Blocks For Teaching Children To Read
ED Pubs
P.O. Box 22207
Alexandria, VA 22304-1398
877-4ED-PUBS
Fax: 703-605-6794

E-mail: edpubs@inet.ed.gov
http://www.edpubs.org
Provides analysis and discussion in five areas of reading instruction: phonemic awareness, phonics, fluency, vocabulary and text comprehension.

4197 Write Now: A Complete Self Teaching Program for Better Handwriting
Continuing Education Press
400 W First St
Chico, CA 95929-0250
530-898-6105
866-647-7377
Fax: 530-898-4020
E-mail: rce@csuchico.edu
http://rce.csuchico.edu
Finally, a handwriting improvement book for adults. Teach yourself to write legibly and retain it over time using this step-by-step guide to modern italic handwriting with complete instructions as well as practice exercises and tips. The secret to legible handwriting is the absence of loops in letterform, making it easier to write and easier to read.

96 pages Paperback
ISBN: 0-87678-089-3

Barbara Getty & Inga Dubay, Author
Debra Barger, Administration
Joe Picard, Director

Directories & Handbooks / *Library Services*

4198 Directory of Manufacturers & Suppliers
Special Libraries Association
331 S Patrick Street
Alexandria, VA 22314-3501
703-647-4900
Fax: 703-647-4901
E-mail: sla@sla.org
http://www.sla.org
The SLA network consists of nearly 15,000 librarians and information professionals who specialize in the arts, communication, business, social science, biomedical sciences, geosciences and environmental studies, and industry, business, research, educational and technical institutions, government, special departments of public and university libraries, newspapers, museums, and public or private organizations that provide or require specialized information.

Doug Newcomb, Deputy CEO
Linda Broussard, Chief Financial Officer

4199 Directory of Members of the Association for Library and Information Science Education
Association for Library and Information Science Ed
2150 N 107th St
Suite 205
Seattle, WA 98133
206-209-5267
Fax: 206-367-8777
E-mail: office@alise.org
http://www.alise.org
The Directory is designed to serve as a handbook for the association, including a list of officers, committees, and interest groups and strategic planning information for the association. Also listed are graduate schools of library and information science and their faculty.

Annual Paperback

Clara Chu, President
Samantha K. Hastings, Vice President

4200 Libraries Unlimited Academic Catalog
Libraries Unlimited
88 Post Road W
Westport, CT 06881
203-226-3571
Fax: 203-222-1502
E-mail: lu-books@lu.com
http://www.abc-clio.com/LibrariesUnlimited.aspx
Catalog includes reference, collection development, library management, cataloging, and technology.

Kathryn Su rez, Publisher

4201 Managing Info Tech in School Library Media Center
Libraries Unlimited
88 Post Road West
Westport, CT 06881
203-226-3571
800-225-5800
Fax: 203-222-1502
E-mail: lu-books@lu.com
http://www.abc-clio.com/LibrariesUnlimited.aspx

Publication Date: 2000 290 pages Hardcover
ISBN: 1-56308-724-3

Kathryn Su rez, Publisher

4202 Managing Media Services Theory and Practice
Libraries Unlimited
88 Post Road West
Westport, CT 06881
203-226-3571
800-225-5800
Fax: 203-222-1502
E-mail: lu-books@lu.com
http://www.abc-clio.com/LibrariesUnlimited.aspx

Publication Date: 2002 418 pages Cloth
ISBN: 1-56308-530-5

Kathryn Su rez, Publisher

Directories & Handbooks / *Music & Art*

4203 College Guide for Visual Arts Majors
Peterson's, A Nelnet Company
Princeton Pike Corporate Center
461 From Road
Paramus, NJ 07652
609-896-1800
800-338-3282
Fax: 402-458-3042
E-mail: support@petersons.com
http://www.petersons.com
Offers descriptions of over 700 accredited US colleges and universities, music conservatories, and art/design schools that grant undergraduate degrees in the areas of studio art.

Publication Date: 2006 404 pages
ISBN: 1-560795-36-0

4204 Community Outreach and Education for the Arts Handbook
Music Teachers National Association
PO Box 261452
Littleton, CO 80163-1452
303-565-5351
888-512-5278
Fax: 555-555-1212
E-mail: mtnanet@mtaa.org
http://www.mtaa.org
Resource booklet for independent music teachers.

Paperback
March
150 booths with 2500 attendees

Chad Schwatbach, Pr/Marketing Associate

4205 Italic Letters
Continuing Education Press
400 W First St
Chico, CA 95929-0250
530-898-6105
866-647-7377
Fax: 530-898-4020
E-mail: rce@csuchico.edu
http://rce.csuchico.edu
Italic Letters is for professional and amateur calligraphers, art teachers, and enthusiasts of the book arts. Numerous tips on letter shapes, spacing, slant, pen edge angle, and other secrets to handsome writing.

128 pages Paperback
ISBN: 0-87678-091-5

Barbara Getty & Inga Dubay, Author
Debra Barger, Administration
Joe Picard, Director

4206 Money for Film & Video Artists
American for the Art
1000 Vermont Avenue NW
6th Floor
Washington, DC 20005
202-371-2830
Fax: 202-371-0424
http://www.artsusa.org
The listings are organized by sponsoring organization and entries include basic application and program information.

Abel Lopez, Chair
Ramona Baker, Vice Chair

4207 Money for Visual Artists
America for the Art
1000 Vermont Avenue NW
12th Floor
Washington, DC 20005
202-371-2830
Fax: 202-371-0424
http://www.artsusa.org
Programs are listed alphabetically by sponsor with detailed program description.

Abel Lopez, Chair
Ramona Baker, Vice Chair

4208 Music Teachers Guide to Music Instructional Software
Music Teachers National Association
1 W. 4th St.
Ste. 1550
Cincinnati, OH 45202-2811
513-421-1420
888-512-5278
Fax: 513-421-2503
E-mail: mtnanet@mtna.org
http://www.mtna.org
Evaluations of music software for the macintosh and PC, including CD-ROMs, music skills and keyboard technique drill software, sequencers and soundequipment controllers.

Publication Date: 1876

Kenneth J. Christensen, President
Rebecca Grooms Johnson, President-elect

209 Resource Booklet for Independent Music Teachers
Music Teachers National Association
1 W. 4th St.
Ste. 1550
Cincinnati, OH 45202-2811
513-421-1420
888-512-5278
Fax: 513-421-2503
E-mail: mtnanet@mtna.org
http://www.mtna.org
A booklet for organizing information about community resources.
Publication Date: 1876

Kenneth J. Christensen, President
Rebecca Grooms Johnson, President-elect

210 School Arts
Davis Publications, Inc.
50 Portland Street
Worcester, MA 01608
800-533-2847
Fax: 508-753-3834
http://www.schoolartsdigital.com
Companies offering products, materials, and art education resources or programs that focus on the history of art, multicultural resources such as Fine Art, reproductions, CD-Roms, museum education, programs, slides, books, videos, exhibits, architecture, timelines, and resource kits.

Directories & Handbooks / *Physical Education*

211 Educators Guide to FREE HPER Materials
Educators Progress Service
214 Center Street
Randolph, WI 53956-1408
920-326-3126
888-951-4469
Fax: 920-326-3127
E-mail: epsinc@centurytel.net
http://www.freeteachingaids.com
Lists and describes free films, videotapes, filmstrips, slides, web sites, and hundreds of free printed materials in the field of health, physical education, and recreation for all age levels.
184 pages Annual
ISBN: 87708-407-6

Kathy Nehmer, President

212 Schools & Colleges Directory
Association for Experiential Education
3775 Iris Avenue
Suite 4
Boulder, CO 80301-2043
303-440-8844
Fax: 303-440-9581
E-mail: publications@aee.org
http://www.aee.org
Provides information about many schools, colleges and universities that have programs or offer degrees related to the field of outdoor/experiential education. Listings include programs in high schools and independent organizations as well as institutions of higher learning. Paperback.
Publication Date: 1995 Paperback

Maurie Lung, President
Bobbi Beale, President-Elect

Directories & Handbooks / *Reading*

4213 Diagnostic Reading Inventory for Bilingual Students in Grades 1-8
Scott & McCleary Publishing Company
2482 11th Street SW
PO Box 3830
Akron, OH 44314-0830
702-566-8756
800-765-3564
Fax: 702-568-1378
E-mail: jscott7576@aol.com
http://www.scottmccleary.com
Series of 13 tests designed to access reading performance. IRI, spelling, phonics, visual and auditory discrimination and listening comprehension are just some of the tests included.
155 pages
ISBN: 0-9636225-1-X

Janet M Scott, Co-Author
Sheila C McCleary, Co-Author

4214 Diagnostic Reading Inventory for Primary and Intermediate Grades K-8
Scott & McCleary Publishing Company
2482 11th Street SW
PO Box 3830
Akron, OH 44314-0830
702-566-8756
800-765-3564
Fax: 702-568-1378
E-mail: jscott7576@aol.com
http://www.scottmccleary.com
Designed to assess reading performance in grades K-8. Tests include: word recognition, oral reading inventory, comprehension, listening comprehension, auditory and visual discrimination, auditory and visual memory, learning modalities inventory, phonics mastery tests, structural analysis, word association and a diagnostic spelling test.
260 pages
ISBN: 0-9636225-4-4

Janet M Scott, Co-Author
Sheila C McCleary, Co-Author

4215 Educational Leadership
Assn. for Supervision & Curriculum Dev. (ASCD)
1703 N Beauregard Street
Alexandria, VA 22311-1714
703-578-9600
800-933-2723
Fax: 703-575-5400
E-mail: el@ascd.org
http://www.ascd.org
For educators by educators. With a circulation of 175,000, Educational Leadership is acknowledged throughout the world as an authoritative source of information about teaching and learning, new ideas and practices relevant to practicing educators, and the latest trends and issues affecting prekindergarten through higher education.
Publication Date: 1943

Marge Scherer, Executive Editor

4216 Laubach Literacy Action Directory
Laubach Literacy Action
222 Waverly Avenue
Syracuse, NY 13244-2010
315-422-9121
888-528-2224
Fax: 315-422-6369
E-mail: info@laubach.org
http://library.syr.edu

Listing of over 1,100 local literacy councils and associates who teach the Laubach Method.
Publication Date: 1955 90 pages Annual

4217 Ready to Read, Ready to Learn
ED Pubs
P.O. Box 22207
Alexandria, VA 22304-1398
703-605-6794
Fax: 703-605-6794
E-mail: edpubs@inet.ed.gov
http://www.edpubs.org

4218 Tips for Reading Tutors
ED Pubs
P.O. Box 22207
Alexandria, VA 22304-1398
877-4ED-PUBS
Fax: 703-605-6794
E-mail: edpubs@inet.ed.gov
http://www.edpubs.org
Basic tips for reading tutors

Directories & Handbooks / *Secondary Education*

4219 College Board Guide to High Schools
College Board Publications
45 Columbus Avenue
New York, NY 10023-6917
212-713-8000
800-323-7155
Fax: 800-525-5562
http://www.collegeboard.org
Offers listings and information on over 25,000 public and private high schools nationwide.
Publication Date: 1994 2,024 pages
ISBN: 0-874474-66-3

David Coleman, President and CEO
Jeremy Singer, COO

4220 Compendium of Tertiary & Sixth Forum Colleges
SCOTVIC: S McDonald, Principal
Ridge College
Manchester
England
61-4277733
Offers listings of over 200 Sixth Form and Tertiary Colleges in the United Kingdom offering courses preparing secondary students for university study.
Publication Date: 1990 200 pages Biennial

4221 Directory of Public Elementary and Secondary Education Agencies
US National Center for Education Statistics
1990 K Street, NW
8th & 9th Floors
Washington, DC 20006-5651
202-502-7300
800-424-1616
Fax: 202-502-7466
http://nces.ed.gov
Directory of approximately 17,000 local education agencies that operate their own schools or pay tuition to other local education agencies.
400 pages Annual

Peggy G. Carr, Acting Commissioner
Lena McDowell, Contact

4222 Educators Guide to FREE Family and Consumer Education Materials
Educators Progress Service
214 Center Street
Randolph, WI 53956-1408

920-326-3126
888-951-4469
Fax: 920-326-3127
E-mail: epsinc@centurytel.net
http://www.freeteachingaids.com
Lists and describes free films, videotapes, filmstrips, slides, web sites, and hundreds of free printed materials in the field of home econominics and consumer education for all age levels.

161 pages Annual
ISBN: 87708-408-4

Kathy Nehmer, President

4223 Focus on School
ABC-CLIO
130 Cremona Drive
#1911
Santa Barbara, CA 93117-5599
805-968-1911
800-368-6868
Fax: 805-685-9685
http://www.abc-clio.com
Hotlines, print and nonprint resources on education for young adults.

Publication Date: 1990

4224 Great Source Catalog
Great Source Education Group
PO Box 7050
Wilmington, MA 01887
800-289-4490
Fax: 800-289-3994
http://www.hmco.com
Alternative, affordable, student-friendly K-12 materials to make teaching and learning fun for educators and students.

4225 Helping Your Child Succeed In School: Elementary and Secondary Editions
Master Teacher
One Leadership Lane
Manhattan, KS 66502-1207
785-539-0555
800-669-9633
Fax: 800-669-1132
http://www.masterteacher.com
Provides a way for school administrators to help parents help their children succeed in school. Published in English and Spanish.

Erica Paronson, Executive Editor

4226 Lesson Plans for Integrating Technology into the Classroom: Secondary Edition
Master Teacher
One Leadership Lane
PO Box 1207
Manhattan, KS 66502-1207
800-669-9633
Fax: 800-669-1132
http://www.masterteacher.com
Gives teachers practical lessons developed and tested by teachers across the curriculum, with students of all levels of ability in using technology.

104 pages
ISBN: 1-58992-152-6

4227 Lesson Plans for Problem-Based Learning: Secondary Edition
Master Teacher
One Leadership Lane
PO Box 1207
Manhattan, KS 66502-1207
800-669-9633
Fax: 800-669-1132
http://www.masterteacher.com
An instructional technique which organizes the curriculum around a major problem that students work to solve over the weeks or months.

117 pages
ISBN: 0-914607-87-1

4228 Lesson Plans for the Substitute Teacher: Secondary Edition
Master Teacher
One Leadership Lane
PO Box 1207
Manhattan, KS 66502-1207
800-669-9633
Fax: 800-669-1132
http://www.masterteacher.com
Gives you more than 100 lessons developed and tested by teachers across the curriculum and at all grade levels.

177 pages
ISBN: 1-58992-108-9

4229 Peterson's Private Secondary Schools
Peterson's, A Nelnet Company
Princeton Pike Corporate Center
461 From Road
Paramus, NJ 07652-2123
609-896-1800
800-338-3282
Fax: 402-458-3042
E-mail: support@petersons.com
http://www.petersons.com
Listing of over 1,400 accredited and state-approved private secondary schools in the US and abroad.

1,300 pages Annual

4230 Secondary Teachers Guide to FREE Curriculum Materials
Educators Progress Service
214 Center Street
Randolph, WI 53956-1408
920-326-3126
888-951-4469
Fax: 920-326-3127
E-mail: epsinc@centurytel.net
http://www.freeteachingaids.com
Lists and describes free supplementary teaching aids for the high school and college level.

296 pages Annual
ISBN: 87708-399-1

Kathy Nehmer, President

Directories & Handbooks / *Science*

4231 Earth Education: A New Beginning
Institute for Earth Education
Cedar Cove
PO Box 115
Greenville, WV 24945
304-832-6404
Fax: 304-832-6077
E-mail: info@ieetree.org
http://www.eartheducation.org
This book proposes another direction-an alternative that many environmental leaders and teachers around the world have already taken. It is called The Earth Education Path, and anyone can follow it in developing a genuine program made up of magical learning adventures.

334 pages Paperback
ISBN: 0917011023

Steve Van Matre, Chairman

4232 Earthkeepers
Institute for Earth Education
Cedar Cove
PO Box 115
Greenville, WV 24945
304-832-6404
Fax: 304-832-6077
E-mail: iee1@aol.com
http://www.eartheducation.org
This book will give you the best picture of what a complete earth education program involves. Even if you can't set up the complete Earthkeepers program, there are many activities you can use to build an earth education program in your own settting and situation.

108 pages Paperback
ISBN: 0917011015

Bruce Johnson, Chairman

4233 Educators Guide to FREE Science Materials
Educators Progress Service
214 Center Street
Randolph, WI 53956-1408
920-326-3126
888-951-4469
Fax: 920-326-3127
E-mail: epsinc@centurytel.net
http://www.freeteachingaids.com
Lists and describes free films, videotapes, filmstrips, slides, web sites, and hundreds of free printed materials in the field of science for all age levels.

Annual

Kathy Nehmer, President

4234 K-6 Science and Math Catalog
Carolina Biological Supply Co.
2700 York Road
PO Box 6010
Burlington, NC 27216-6010
336-584-0381
800-334-5551
Fax: 336-538-6330
E-mail: quotations@carolina.com
http://www.carolina.com
Service teaching materials for grades Pre K through 8, including charts, computers, software, books, living animals and plants, microscopes, microscope slides, models, teaching kits and more.

Publication Date: 1927

4235 Science for All Children; A Guide to Improving Science Education
National Academy Press
Smithsonian Information
P.O. Box 23293
Washington, DC 20026-3293
202-633-1000
Fax: 202-287-2070
E-mail: info@si.edu
http://www.si.edu/nsrc
Provides concise and practical guidelines for implementing science education reform at local level, including the elements of an effective, inquiry-based, hands-on science program. Produced by the National Science Resources Center. Published by National Academy Press.

240 pages
ISBN: 0-309-05297-1

National Science Resources Center, Author
John McCarter Jr., Chair
Shirley Ann Jackson, Vice Chair

4236 Sunship Earth
Institute for Earth Education
Cedar Cove
PO Box 115
Greenville, WV 24945
304-832-6404
Fax: 304-832-6077

E-mail: iee1@aol.com
http://www.eartheducation.org
Contains clear descriptions of key ecological concepts and concise reviews of important learning principals, plus over 200 additional pages of ideas, activities and guidelines for setting up a complete Sunship Earth Study Station.

265 pages Paperback
ISBN: 0876030460

Bruce Johnson, Chairman

237 Sunship III
Institute for Earth Education
Cedar Cove
PO Box 115
Greenville, WV 24945
304-832-6404
Fax: 304-832-6077
E-mail: iee1@aol.com
http://www.eartheducation.org
Examines perception and choice in our daily habits and routines. It is about exploration and discovery in the larger context of where and how we live, and examining alteratives and making sacrifices on behalf of a healthier home planet.

133 pages Paperback
ISBN: 0917011031

Bruce Johnson, Chairman

238 UNESCO Sourcebook for Out-of-School Science & Technology Education
U.N. Educational, Scientific & Cultural Assn.
7, place de Fontenoy
F-75700 Paris
France
Offers information on science clubs, societies and congresses, science fairs and museums.

145 pages

Directories & Handbooks / *Social Studies*

239 Directory of Central America Classroom Resources
Central American Resource Center
2845 West 7th Street
Los Angeles, CA 90005-2012
213-385-7800
Fax: 213-385-1094
E-mail: info@carecen-la.org
http://www.carecen-la.org
Offers information on suppliers of education resource materials about Central America, including curricula, materials, directories and organizations providing related services.

Publication Date: 1990 200 pages

Angela Sanbrano, President
Gloria Annicchiarico, Vice President

240 Educators Guide to FREE Social Studies Materials
Educators Progress Service
214 Center Street
Randolph, WI 53956-1408
920-326-3126
888-951-4469
Fax: 920-326-3127
E-mail: epsinc@centurytel.net
http://www.freeteachingaids.com
Lists and describes free films, videotapes, filmstrips, slides, web sites, and hundreds of free printed materials in the field of social studies for all age levels.

287 pages Annual
ISBN: 87708-405-X

Kathy Nehmer, President

4241 Geography: A Resource Guide for Secondary Schools
ABC-CLIO
130 Cremona Drive
#1911
Santa Barbara, CA 93117-5599
805-968-1911
800-368-6868
Fax: 805-685-9685
http://www.abc-clio.com
List of organizations and associations to use as resources for secondary education geography studies.

Directories & Handbooks / *Technology in Education*

4242 American Trade Schools Directory
Croner Publications
10951 Sorrento Valley Road
Suite 1D
San Diego, CA 92121
858-546-1954
800-441-4033
Fax: 858-546-1955
E-mail: paul@croner.com
http://www.croner.com
Loose leaf binder directory listing trade and technical schools throughout the United States, in alphabetical order, by state, then city, then school name.

411 pages
ISBN: 0-875140-02-5

Rosa Padilla, Office Manager

4243 Association for Educational Communications & Technology: Membership Directory
Association for Educational Communications & Tech.
320 W. 8th St.
Ste 101
Bloomington, IN 47404-3745
812-335-7675
877-677-AECT
E-mail: aect@aect.org
http://www.aect.org
Five thousand audiovisual and instructional materials specialists and school media specialists, with audio-visual and TV production personnel. Also listed are committees, task force divisions, auxiliary affiliates, state organizations and directory of corporate members.

200 pages Annual/Spring

Stephen Harmon, President
Ellen Hoffman, Executive Secretary

4244 Chronicle Vocational School Manual
Chronicle Guidance Publications
66 Aurora Street
Moravia, NY 13118-3569
315-497-0339
800-899-0454
Fax: 315-497-3359
E-mail: customerservice@chronicleguidance.com
http://www.chronicleguidance.com
A geographical index of more than 3,500 vocational schools including all contact information, programs, admissions requirements, costs, financial aid programs and student services.

Publication Date: 1938 300 pages Annual
ISBN: 1-556312-50-4

Cheryl Fickeisen, President/ CEO
Gary Fickeisen, Vice President

4245 Directory of Public Vocational-Technical Schools & Institutes in the US
Media Marketing Group
Voorhees Town Center
220 Laurel Road
Voorhees, NJ 08043-0611
856-782-6000
Fax: 856-385-7155
http://www.2mg.com
Offers information on over 1,400 post secondary vocational and technical education programs in public education; private trade and technical schools are not included.

Publication Date: 1994 400 pages Biennial
ISBN: 0-933474-51-2

Frank Palmieri, President

4246 Directory of Vocational-Technical Schools
Media Marketing Group
Voorhees Town Center
220 Laurel Road
Voorhees, NJ 08043-0611
856-782-6000
Fax: 856-385-7155
http://www.2mg.com
Offers information on public, postsecondary schools offering degree and non-degree occupational education.

Publication Date: 1996 450 pages Biennial
ISBN: 0-933474-52-0

Frank Palmieri, President

4247 Educational Film & Video Locator
RR Bowker Reed Reference
121 Chanlon Road
New Providence, NJ 07974-1541
908-665-2834
Fax: 908-464-3553
http://www.sabre.org
Producers and distributors of educational films.

Publication Date: 1990

4248 Guide to Vocational and Technical Schools East & West
Peterson's, A Nelnet Company
Princeton Pike Corporare Center
461 From Road
Paramus, NJ 07652
609-896-1800
800-338-3282
Fax: 402-458-3042
E-mail: support@petersons.com
http://www.petersons.com
These two directories cover the full range of training programs in over 240 career fields divided into the categories of Business, Technology, Trade, Personal Services, and Health Care. East edition covers East of Mississippi; West edition covers West of the Mississippi.

Publication Date: 2006 579 pages Per Volume

4249 Industrial Teacher Education Directory
National Assn. of Industrial Teacher Educators
University of Northern Iowa
Cedar Falls, IA 50614-0178
319-273-2561
Fax: 319-273-5818
http://www.uni.edu/indtech

Listing of about 2,800 industrial education faculty members at 250 universities and four-year colleges in the United States, Canada, Australia, Japan and Taiwan.

108 pages Annual

M Fahmy, Professor/Head of Department
Charles Johnson, Coordinator of Tech Ed. Prog

4250 Information Literacy: Essential Skills for the Information Age

Syracuse University
900 South Crouse Ave
Syracuse, NY 13244-0001
315-443-1870
800-464-9107
Fax: 315-443-5448
E-mail: eric@ericir.sye.edu
http://www.syr.edu
Traces history, development, and economic necessity of information literacy. Reports on related subject matter standards. Includes reports on the National Educational Goals (1991), the Secretary's Commission on Achieving Necessary Skills Report (1991), and the latest updates from ALA's Information Power (1998).

377 pages
ISBN: 0-937597-44-9

Richard L. Thompson, Chairman
Kenneth E. Goodman, Vice Chair

4251 Internet Resource Directory for Classroom Teachers

Regulus Communications
140 N 8th Street
Suite 201
Lincoln, NE 68508-1358
402-432-2680
http://regulus.com/
Directory offering information on all resources available on-line for classroom teachers, including e-mail addresses, Home Page URL's, phone and fax numbers, surface-mail addresses, classroom contacts and teaching resources. Available in paper and electronic formats.

Publication Date: 1996 272 pages Paper Format

Jane A Austin, Coordinating Education

4252 K-12 District Technology Coordinators

Quality Education Data
601 E. Marshall St
Suite 250
Sweet Springs, MO 65351-4715
303-860-1832
800-776-6373
Fax: 660-335-4157
E-mail: info@qeddata.com
http://www.qeddata.com
The first in QED's National Educator Directories, this comprehensive directory of technology coordinators combines QED's exclusive database of technology and demographic data with names of technology coordinators in the 7,000 largest US school districts. The directory includes district phone number, number of students in the district, number of computers, student/computer ratio and predominant computer brand.

Publication Date: 1994 400 pages

Peter Long, CEO
John F. Hood, President

4253 NetLingo Internet Dictionary

805-794-8687
E-mail: info@netlingo.com
http://www.netlingo.com

A smart looking easy-to-understand dictionary of 3000 internet terms, 1200 chat acronyms, and much more. Modem reference book for international students, educators, industry professionals and online businesses and organizations.

Publication Date: 0

Erin Jansen, Author

4254 Quick-Source

AM Educational Publishing
P.O. Box 247
Suite D
Harrisonburg, VA 22801-3048
866-293-5313
800-296-5750
Fax: 540-433-5640
E-mail: info@quicksourcelearning.com
http://https://www.quicksourcelearning.com/
Educational technology directory with over 1,100 names, addresses, phones/faxes, and brief descriptions of the products/services of companies/organizations; supports major works/word processors (MS-DOS/MAC); conferences and other educational technology listings.

Annual/September

4255 Schools Industrial, Technical & Trade Directory

American Business Directories
5711 S 86th Circle
Omaha, NE 68127-4146
402-593-4600
888-999-1307
Fax: 402-331-5481
http://www.americanbusinessandservicedirectory.com
A geographical listing of over 3,750 schools with all contact information, size of advertisement and first year in Yellow Pages. Also available in electronic formats.

Annual

Jerry Venner, Coordinating Education

4256 TESS: The Educational Software Selector

EPIE Institute
103 W Montauk Highway
PO Box 590
Hampton Bays, NY 11946-4003
631-728-9100
Fax: 631-728-9228
E-mail: kkomoski@epie.org
http://www.epie.org
A list of over 1,200 suppliers of educational software and over 18,000 educational software products (on CD-ROM) for pre-school through college information. Includes description of program, grade level data, price, platform and review citations.

Publication Date: 1967

Nancy Boland, Coordinating Education

4257 Tech Directions-Directory of Federal & Federal and State Officials Issue

Prakken Publications
416 Longshore Drive
PO Box 8623
Ann Arbor, MI 48107-8623
734-975-2800
Fax: 313-577-1672
http://https://www.techdirections.com
Listing of federal and state officials concerned with vocational, technical, indus-

trial trade and technology education in the United States and Canada.

Annual

Susanne Peckham, Managing Editor
Pam Moore, Assistant Editor

4258 Technology in Public Schools

Quality Education Data
601 E. Marshall St
Suite 250
Sweet Springs, MO 65351-4715
303-860-1832
800-776-6373
Fax: 660-335-4157
E-mail: info@qeddata.com
http://www.qeddata.com
Annual survey of instructional technology represents more than 67% of all US K-12 students. Includes computer brand and processor type market share, CD-ROM, networks, LAN, modem, cable and in-depth internet access installed base information.

Publication Date: 1994 160 pages Yearly
ISBN: 0-88947-925-1

Peter Long, CEO
John F. Hood, President

Periodicals / *General*

4259 AACS Newsletter

American Association of Christian Schools
602 Belvoir Avenue
East Ridge, TN 37412-2221
423-629-4280
Fax: 423-622-7461
http://www.aacs.org
Association news offering the most up-to-date information relating to Christian education.

Publication Date: 1972 4 pages Monthly

Dr. Carl Herbster, Contact

4260 AAHE Bulletin

American Association for Higher Education
4505 S. Maryland Parkway
Box 453068
Las Vegas, NV 89154-3068
702-895-2737
Fax: 702-895-4269
E-mail: ASHE@unlv.edu
http://www.ashe.ws
Electronic newsletter

16 pages Monthly

Kim Nehls, Ph.D, Executive Director
Holly Schneider, Conference Coordinator

4261 ACJS Today

Academy of Criminal Justice Services
7339 Hanover Parkway
Suite A
Greenbelta, MD 20770
301-446-6300
800-757-2257
Fax: 301-446-2819
http://www.acjs.org
Provides upcoming events, news releases, ACJS activities, ads, book reviews and miscellaneous information.

24-32 pages Quarterly

Brian Payne, President
Brandon Applegate, 1st Vice President

4262 ASCD Update

Assn. for Supervision & Curriculum Development
1703 N Beauregard Street
Alexandria, VA 22311-1714

703-578-9600
Fax: 703-575-5400
http://www.ascd.org
News on contemporary education issues and information on ASCD programs.

Publication Date: 1943

Ronald Brandt, Publisher
John O'Neil, Editor

263 ASSC Newsletter
Arkansas School Study Council
500 Woodlane Street
Suite 256
Little Rock, AR 72201
501-682-1010
Fax: 479-442-2038
http://www.sos.arkansas.gov
Monthly up-date on education, finance, new legislation, mandates for Arkansas public schools.

3-10 pages

Judith Crouch, Human Resources
Laura Labay, Public Affairs

264 AV Guide Newsletter
Educational Screen
380 E NW Highway
Des Plaines, IL 60016-2201
847-298-6622
Fax: 847-390-0408
Provides concise and practical information on audiovisually oriented products with an emphasis on new ideas and methods of using learning media, including educational computer software.

Monthly
ISSN: 0091-360X

HS Gillette, Publisher
Natalie Ferguson, Editor

265 Academe
American Association of University Professors
1133 Nineteenth Street, NW
Suite 200
Washington, DC 20036-3406
202-737-5900
Fax: 202-737-5526
E-mail: aaup@aaup.org
http://www.aaup.org
A thoughtful and provocative review of developments affecting higher education faculty. With timely features and informative departments, Academe delivers the latest on the state of the profession, legal and legislative trends, and issues in academia.

BiMonthly

Lawrence Hanley, Editor, Author
Julie Schmid, Executive Director
Elona M. Jouben, Executive Assistant

266 Aero Gramme
Alternative Education Resource Organizations
417 Roslyn Road
Roslyn Heights, NY 11577-2620
516-621-2195
800-769-4171
Fax: 516-625-3257
E-mail: info@educationrevolution.org
http://www.educationrevolution.org
Networks all forms of educational alternatives, from public and private alternative schools to homeschooling.

Quarterly

Jerry Mintz, Director
Chri Mercogliano, Course Instructor

4267 Agenda: Jewish Education
Jewish Education Service of North America
247 West 37th Street
5th Floor
New York, NY 10018
212-284-6950
Fax: 212-284-6951
E-mail: info@jesna.org
http://www.jesna.org
Seeks to create a community of discourse on issues of Jewish public policy dealing with Jewish education and the indications of policy options for the practice of Jewish education.

Quarterly
ISSN: 1072-1150

Cass Gottlieb, Chair
Sandra Gold, Vice Chair

4268 American Council on Education: GED Testing Service
American Council on Education
1 Dupont Circle NW
Suite 800
Washington, DC 20036-1193
202-939-9300
Fax: 202-833-4760
http://www.acenet.edu
Information relating to GED items and testing.

8 pages 5x Year

James H. Mullen Jr., Chair
Renu Khator, Vice Chair

4269 American Journal of Education
University of Chicago
5801 South Ellis Avenue
Chicago, IL 60637
773-702-1234
Fax: 773-702-6207
E-mail: aje@uchicago.edu
http://www.uchicago.edu

Quarterly

Robert Dreeben and Zalman Usiskin, Author
Robert J. Zimmer, President
Eric D. Isaacs, Provost

4270 American Scholar
1785 Massachusetts Avenue NW
4th Floor
Washington, DC 20036-2117
202-265-3808
A general interest magazine that includes articles on science, literature, and book reviews.

Quarterly

Anne Fadiman, Editor

4271 American Students & Teachers Abroad
US Government Printing Office
732 N Capitol Street NW
Washington, DC 20401
202-512-1800
Fax: 202-512-2104
E-mail: admin@access.gpo.gov
http://www.access.gpo.gov

4272 Annual Report
Jessie Ball duPont Fund
One Dependent Drive
Suite 1400
Jacksonville, FL 32202-5011
904-353-0890
800-252-3452
Fax: 904-353-3870
E-mail: contactus@dupontfund.org
http://www.dupontfund.org

Focused on a variety of good work aimed at growing the capacity of the nonprofit sector.
Publication Date: 0 Annually

4273 Association of Orthodox Jewish Teachers of the New York Public Schools
Association of Orthodox Jewish Teachers of the NY
1577 Coney Island Avenue
Brooklyn, NY 11230-4715
718-258-3585
Fax: 718-258-3586
E-mail: aojt@juno.com
http://www.aojt.org
Newsletter representing observant Jewish teachers in the New York City Public Schools.

Publication Date: 1963 8-12 pages Quarterly Newsletter

Nechemia Aaron Oberstein, President
Rachel B. Lieff, Vice President

4274 Between Classes-Elderhostel Catalog
Road Scholar
11 Avenue de Lafayette
Boston, MA 02111-1913
617-426-7788
Fax: 617-426-8351
http://www.roadscholar.org
Seasonal listings of elderhostel educational programs offered by educational cultural institutions in the US and 60 countries overseas.

120 pages Quarterly

Heather Baynes, Contact

4275 Blumenfeld Education Newsletter
PO Box 45161
Boise, ID 83711-5161

http://www.howtotutor.com/bel.htm
Providing knowledge to parents and educators who want to save children of America from destructive forces that endanger them. Children in public schools are at grave risk in 4 ways: academically, spiritually, morally, physically, and only a well-informed public will be able to reduce these risks.

8 pages

Peter F Watt, Publisher
Samuel L Blumenfeld, Editor

4276 Brighton Times
Brighton Academy/Foundation of Human Understanding
1121 NE 7th Street
PO Box 1000
Grants Pass, OR 97528-1421
541-474-6865
800-877-3227
Fax: 541-956-6705
http://https://www.fhu.com/aboutroy.html
Home schooling information.

Monthly

Cynthia Coumoyer, Contact

4277 Brochure of American-Sponsored Overseas Schools
Office of Overseas Schools, Department of State
Room H328
SA-1
Washington, DC 20522-132
202-261-8200
Fax: 202-261-8224
E-mail: OverseasSchools@state.gov
http://www.state.gov

Dr. Keith D. Miller, Director
Antony Blinken, Deputy Secretary

4278 Business-Education Insider
Heritage Foundation
214 Massachusetts Avenue NE
Washington, DC 20002-4999
202-546-4400
Fax: 202-546-8328
http://www.heritage.org
Deals with issues relating to the corporate/business world, and the effects it has on education.

Monthly

George Adams, Senior Production Specialist
David S. Addington, Group VP, Research

4279 CBE Report
Association for Community Based Education
1806 Vernon Street NW
PO BOX 70587
Washington, DC 20024-0587
202-462-6333
http://www.faqs.org
Educational institutions covering news, workshops and resources.

Monthly

4280 CEDS Communique
The Council for Exceptional Children
2900 Crystal Drive
Suite 1000
Arlington, VA 22202-1545
703-620-3660
888-232-7733
Fax: 703-264-9494
http://www.cec.sped.org
Reports on the activities of the Council for Educational Diagnostic Services and information about special programs, upcoming events, current trends and practices, and other topical matters.

Quarterly

Alison Heron, Director
Diane Shinn, Marketing & Communications

4281 Center Focus
Center of Concern
1225 Otis Street NE
Washington, DC 20017-2516
202-635-2757
Fax: 202-832-9494
E-mail: coc@coc.org
http://www.coc.org
Newsletters addressing the everchanging needs and concerns in the education field.

6 pages BiMonthly

Raymond W. Baker, President
Claire M. Cifaloglio, M.D., Pediatrician

4282 Center for Continuing Education of Women Newsletter
University of Michigan
Ann Arbor, MI 48109
734-763-1400
Fax: 734-936-1641
Association news focusing on the concerns of women in education.

4 pages

4283 Center for Parent Education Newsletter
81 Wyman Street
Wapham, MA 02160
617-964-2442
Offers information and tips to address parent involvement in the education of their children.

BiMonthly

4284 Change
Taylor & Francis
325 Chestnut Street
Suite 800
Philadelphia, PA 19106-1802
215-625-8900
800-365-9753
Fax: 202-296-5149
E-mail: customer.service@taylorandfrancis.com
http://www.heldref.org
Perspectives on the critical issues shaping the world of higher education. It is not only issue-oriented and reflective, but challenges the status quo in higher education.

BiMonthly

Margaret A Miller, President
Theodore J Marchese, VP/Editor

4285 Clearing House: A Journal of Educational Research
Taylor & Francis
325 Chestnut Street
Suite 800
Philadelphia, PA 19106-1826
215-625-8900
800-365-9753
Fax: 202-296-5149
E-mail: customer.service@taylorandfrancis.com
http://www.heldref.org
Each issue offers a variety of articles for teachers and administrators of middle schools and junior and senior high schools. It includes experiments, trends and accomplishments in courses, teaching methods, administrative procedures and school programs.

4 pages BiMonthly
ISSN: 0009-8655

Deborah N Cohen, Promotions Manager
Judy Cusick, Managing Editor

4286 Commuter Perspectives
National Clearinghouse for Commuter Programs
Western Illinois University
3300 River Drive
Moline, IL 61265-9634
309-762-8843
Fax: 301-314-9874
E-mail: nccp@accmail.umd.edu
http://www.wiu.edu
A quarterly newsletter published by the National Clearinghouse for Commuter Programs for professionals who work for, with, and on behalf of commuter students.

8 pages Quarterly

Dr. Kristi Mindrup, Co-Director
Dr. Melissa Mahan, Co-Director

4287 Congressional Digest
Congressional Digest Corp.
4416 East West Highway
Suite 400
Bethesda, MD 20814-4568
301-634-3113
800-637-9915
Fax: 301-634-3189
E-mail: griff.thomas@pro-and-con.org
http://www.pro-and-con.org
An independent publication featuring controversies in Congress, pro-and-con.

ISSN: 0010-5899

Delores Baisden, Assistant

4288 ConneXions
Association of International Schools in Africa
Peponi Road
PO Box 14103, Nairobi
Kenya 00800
254- 20- 269
254-20-2697442
Fax: 254- 20- 418
Fax: 254-20-4183272
E-mail: info@aisa.or.ke
http://www.aisa.or.ke
Published twice per year, ConneXions is AISA's print and online newsletter

Peter Bateman, Executive Director
Thomas Shearer, Chairperson

4289 Contemporary Education
Indiana State University, School of Education
200 North Seventh Street
Terre Haute, IN 47809-9989
877-856-8005
Fax: 812-856-8088
http://coe.indstate.edu
A readable and currently informative journal of topics in the mainstream of educational thought.

Quarterly
ISSN: 0010-7476

Todd Whitaker, Editor
Beth Whitaker, Editor

4290 Creative Child & Adult Quarterly
National Association for Gifted Children
1331 H Street, NW
Suite 1001
Washington, DC 20005-1352
202-785-4268
Fax: 202-785-4248
http://http://www.nagc.org

Quarterly

Tracy L. Cross, President
George Betts, President-Elect

4291 Creativity Research Journal
Lawrence Erlbaum Associates
10 Industrial Avenue
Mahwah, NJ 07430-2262
201-258-2200
800-926-6579
Fax: 201-236-0072
E-mail: journals@erlbaum.com
http://www.erlbaum.com
A peer-reviewed journal covering a full range of approaches including behavioral, cognitive, clinical developmental, educational, social and organizational. Online access is available by visiting LEAonline.com

Quarterly
ISSN: 1040-0419

Mark A Runco, PhD., Editor

4292 Currents
Council for Advancement & Support of Education
1307 New York Avenue NW
Suite 1000
Washington, DC 20005-4726
703-379-4611
Fax: 202-387-4973
E-mail: memberservicecenter@case.org
http://www.case.org
Published nine times a year and distributed to 19,000 professional members, Currents delivers essential information, insight and ideas that empower those who support education to master challenges and act decisively to create a better future for their institutions and the world.

John Lippincott, President
Donald Falkenstein, VP

293 DCDT Network
The Council for Exceptional Children
2900 Crystal Drive
Suite 1000
Arlington, VA 22202-1545
703-620-3660
888-232-7733
Fax: 703-264-9494
http://www.cec.sped.org
Newsletter of the Division on Career Development and Transition. Provides the latest information on legislation, projects, resource materials and implementation strategies in the field of career development and transition for persons with disabilities and/or who are gifted. Carries information about Division activities, upcoming events, announcements and reports of particular interest to DCDT members.

3x Year

Alison Heron, Director
Diane Shinn, Marketing & Communications

294 DECA Dimensions
1908 Association Drive
Reston, VA 20191-1503
703-860-5000
Fax: 703-860-4013
E-mail: info@deca.org
http://www.deca.org
An educational nonprofit association news management for marketing education students across the country, Canada, Guam and Puerto Rico. Offers information on DECA activities, leadership, business and career skills, which help develop future leaders in business, marketing and management.

36 pages Quarterly
ISSN: 1060-6106

Carol Lund, Author
Chuck Beatty, Project Manager
Cindy Allen, Director

295 DLD Times
The Council for Exceptional Children
2900 Crystal Drive
Suite 1000
Arlington, VA 22202-1589
703-620-3660
800-CEC-SPED
Fax: 703-264-1637
http://www.cec.sped.org
Information concerning education and welfare of children and youth with learning disabilities.

8 pages TriQuarterly

Alison Heron, Director
Diane Shinn, Marketing & Communications

296 Decision Line
Decision Sciences Institute
334 Melcher Hal
Suite 325
Houston, TX 77204-6021
713-743-4815
Fax: 713-743-8984
E-mail: info@decisionsciences.org
http://www.decisionsciences.org
Contains articles on education, business and decision sciences as well as available positions and textbook advertising.

32 pages 5x Year

E. Powell Robinson, Jr., Interim Executive Director
Dana L. Evans, Program Director

297 Desktop Presentations & Publishing
Doron & Associates
291 Farmington Avenue
Farmington, CT 6032-5421
860-677-8666
866-764-5378
Fax: 860-677-5839
E-mail: dental_associates@sbcglobal.net
http://www.dasmile.com/doc_doron.htm
Computer generated presentations and visual aids for education and business.

16 pages BiMonthly

Tom Doron, Contact

4298 Development and Alumni Relations Report
LRP Publications
360 Hiatt Drive
Suite 700
Palm Beach Gardens, FL 33418
561-622-6520
800-341-7874
Fax: 561-622-1375
E-mail: custserve@lrp.com
http://www.lrp.com
Provides colleges and universities with innovative ideas for improving: alumni relations; the involvement of alumni in clubs and chapters; annual giving; endowment and capital campaigns; and planned giving. Plus, you can recieve free e-mail updates on crucial news affecting your job with your paid subscription.

Monthly Newsletter

Kenneth F. Kahn, President

4299 Different Books
Place in the Woods
111 Third Avenue South
Suite 290
Minneapolis, MN 55401-5302
612-627-1970
Fax: 612-627-1980
E-mail: ump@umn.edu
http://www.upress.umn.edu
Special imprint of books by, for and about persons on a different path. Features main characters with disabilities as heroes and heroines in storyline. For hi-lo reading in early elementary grades (3-7).

Publication Date: 1925 Paperback

Roger Hammer, Publisher

4300 Directions
AFS Intercultural Programs USA
71 West 23rd Street
6th Floor
New York, NY 10010-4102
212-807-8686
Fax: 212-807-1001
http://www.afs.org
News of AFS US volunteers.

6 pages Monthly

Dr. Vincenzo Morlini, President/ CEO
Dr. Urs-Rainer von Arx, VP, CFO & Operation Officer

4301 Disability Compliance for Higher Education
LRP Publications
360 Hiatt Drive
Suite 700
Palm Beach Gardens, FL 33418
561-622-6520
800-341-7874
Fax: 561-622-1375
E-mail: custserve@lrp.com
http://www.lrp.com
Newsletter helps colleges determine if they're complying with the Americans with Disabilities Act (ADA) and Section 504 of the Rehabilitation Act- so they can avoid costly litigation. Gives tips on how to provide reasonable accommodations in test-taking, grading, admissions, and accessibility to programs and facilities.

Monthly
ISSN: 1086-1335

Edward Filo, Author
Kenneth F. Kahn, President

4302 Diversity 2000
Holocaust Resource Center
Kean College
1000 Morris Avenue
Union, NJ 07083
Offers ideas and issues on multicultural school education programs.

BiMonthly

Janice Kroposky, Director
Helen Walzer, Assistant Director

4303 ERIC/CRESS Bulletin
AEL, Inc.
102 E. Keefe Ave
Milwaukee, WI 53212-1348
414-265-7630
866-656-1486
Fax: 414-265-7628
E-mail: sales@aelseating.com
http://https://www.aelseating.com
Announces new developments in the ERIC system nationally, and publications and events relevant to American Indians, Alaska Natives, Mexican Americans, migrants, outdoor education and rural, small schools.

3x Year Newsletter

Patricia Hammer Cahape, Associate Director

4304 Eagle Forum
Eagle Education Fund
P.O. BOX 17113
Fountain Hills, AZ 85269-8110

http://www.fhgeef.org
News on the Eagle Education Fund.

Quarterly

Ralph Norman, President
Pam McNeil, 1st Vice President

4305 EdPress News
PreK-12 Learning Group
325 Chestnut St.
Ste. 1110
Philadelphia, PA 19106
267-351-4310
Fax: 267-351-4317
E-mail: prek12learning@publishers.org
http://www.aepweb.org
The Association supports the growth of educational publishing and it's positive effects on learning and teaching. EdPress provides information and analysis of markets and trends, education and legislative policy, learning and teaching research, and intellectual property. The Association also provides training and staff development programs, promotes supplemental learning resources as essential curriculum materials, and advocates on issues relevant to its constituents.

Jay Diskey, Executive Director
Stacey Pusey, Editorial Director

4306 Education
Project Innovation
1362 Santa Cruz Court
Chula Vista, CA 91910-7114
760-630-9938
E-mail: rcassel5@aol.com
http://www.rcassel.com
Original investigations and theoretical articles dealing with education. Preference given

to innovations, real or magical, which promise to improve learning.

160 pages Quarterly
ISSN: 0013-1172

Dr. Russell Cassel, Editor
Lan Mieu Cassel, Managing Editor

4307 Education Digest
Prakken Publications
PO Box 8623
3970 Varsity Drive
Ann Arbor, MI 48107-8623
734-975-2800
800-530-9673
Fax: 734-975-2787
E-mail: publisher@techdirectories.com
http://www.eddigest.com
Offers outstanding articles condensed for quick review from over 200 magazines, monthlies, books, newsletters and journals, timely and important for professional educators and others interested in the field.

80 pages Monthly
ISSN: 0013-127X

George F Kennedy, Publisher
Kenneth Schroeder, Managing Editor

4308 Education Hotline
Editorial Projects in Education
6935 Arlington Road
Suite 100
Bethesda, MD 20814
301-280-3100
800-445-8250
Fax: 301-280-3250
E-mail: ads@epe.org
http://www.edweek.org
Education newsletter.

4309 Education Newsletter Library Counterpoint
LRP Publications
360 Hiatt Drive
Suite 700
Palm Beach Gardens, FL 33418
561-622-6520
800-341-7874
Fax: 561-622-1375
E-mail: custserve@lrp.com
http://www.lrp.com
Offers its readers concise, informative and timely articles covering innovative practices in special education. Covers: special education news from the states; updates on curriculum; developments in special education technology; classified ads; descriptions of new products and publications; and more.

On-Line

Kenneth F. Kahn, President

4310 Education Newsline
National Association of Christian Educators
PO Box 3200
Costa Mesa, CA 92628-3200
949-251-9333
http://www.naceoffice.com
Articles pertinent to public education for teachers and parents, current trends and solutions and the work of Citizens for Excellence in Education.

Publication Date: 1972 8 pages BiMonthly

Robert Simonds, Publisher
Kathi Hudson, Editor

4311 Education Now and in the Future
Northwest Regional Educational Laboratory
101 SW Main Street
Suite 500
Portland, OR 97204-3213

503-275-9500
800-597-6339
Fax: 503-275-0458
E-mail: info@nwrel.org
http://www.nwrel.org
Contains articles about products, events, research and publications produced or sponsored by the NW Regional Educational Laboratory, a private nonprofit educational institution whose mission is to help schools improve outcomes for all students.

Steve Fleischman, CEO
Barbara Adams, Chairperson

4312 Education Quarterly
New Jersey State Department of Education
100 Riverview Plaza
PO Box 500
Trenton, NJ 08625-500
877-900-6960
http://www.state.nj.us/education
New Jersey education information and updates.

6 pages Quarterly

Richard Vespucci, Contact

4313 Education USA
LRP Publications
360 Hiatt Drive
Suite 1106
Palm Beach Gardens, FL 33418
561-622-6520
800-341-7874
Fax: 561-622-1375
E-mail: custserve@lrp.com
http://www.lrp.com
Offers information on court decisions, federal funding, the national debate over standards, education research, school finance, and more. Subscribers receive biweekly reports on Education Department policies on Title I, special education, bilingual education, drug-free schools and other issues affecting schools nationwide.

8-10 pages BiWeekly

Kenneth F. Kahn, President

4314 Education Update
Heritage Foundation
214 Massachusetts Avenue NE
Washington, DC 20002-4999
202-546-4400
Fax: 202-544-7330
http://www.heritage.org
Contains analyses of policy issues and trends in US education.

4315 Education Week
Editorial Projects in Education, Inc.
6935 Arlington Road
Suite 100
Bethesda, MD 20814-5233
301-280-3100
800-346-1834
Fax: 301-280-3250
E-mail: ads@epe.org
http://www.edweek.org
For principals, superintendents, director, managers and other administrators.

4316 Education in Focus
Books for All Times
PO Box 2
Alexandria, VA 22313-0002
703-548-0457
E-mail: jdavid@bfat.com

Examines failures and successes of public and private education by looking beneath the surface for answers and explanations.

6 pages BiAnnually
ISSN: 1049-7250

Joe David, Editor

4317 Educational Forum
University of Colorado-Denver, School of Education
PO Box 173364
Campus Box 106
Denver, CO 80217-3364
303-556-3402
Fax: 303-556-4479
E-mail: education@cudenver.edu
http://www.ucdenver.edu
The university is recognized as one of the leading public universities in the nation and offers a broad range of academic opportunities to students.

Quarterly

Hank Brown, President
Michel Dahlin, Interim Vice President

4318 Educational Freedom Spotlight On Homeschooling
Clonlara Home Based Education Programs
1289 Jewett Street
Ann Arbor, MI 48104-6201
734-769-4511
Fax: 734-769-9629
E-mail: clonlara@wash.k12.mi.us
http://www.clonlara.org
Clonlara School is committed to illuminating educational rights and freedoms through our actions and deep dedication to human rights and dignity.

12 pages Monthly

Susan Andrews, Editor
Carmen Amabile, Coordinator

4319 Educational Horizons
P. Lambda Theta, Int'l Honor & Professional Assn.
P.O. Box 7888
Bloomington, IN 47407-7888
812-339-1156
Fax: 812-339-0018
E-mail: root@pilambda.org
http://www.pilambda.org
Founded in the spirit of academic excellence in order to provide leadership in addressing educational, social and cultural issues of national and international significance and to enhance the status of educators by providing a recognized forum for sharing new perspectives, research findings and scholarly essays.

48 pages Quarterly
ISSN: 0013-175X

Dan Brown, Executive Director
Bill Bushaw, Chief Executive Officer

4320 Educational Research Forum
American Educational Research Association
1430 K Street, NW
Suite 1200
Washington, DC 20005-3078
202-238-3200
Fax: 202-238-3250
E-mail: aera@gmu.edu
http://www.aera.net
Contains news and information on educational research, teaching, counseling and school administration.

Felice J. Levine, Executive Director
Joyce E. King, President

4321 Educational Researcher
American Educational Research Association
1430 K Street, NW
Suite 1200
Washington, DC 20005-3078

202-238-3200
Fax: 202-238-3250
E-mail: aera@gmu.edu
http://www.aera.net
Publishes research news and commentary on events in the field of educational research and articles of a wide interest to anyone involved in education.

9x Year

Felice J. Levine, Executive Director
Joyce E. King, President

4322 Educational Theory

University of Illinois at Urbana
901 West Illinois Street
Urbana, IL 61801-6925
217-333-0302
Fax: 217-244-3711
E-mail: edtheory@uiuc.edu
http://illinois.edu
The purpose of this journal is to foster the continuing development of educational theory and encourage wide and effective discussion of theoretical problems with the educational profession. Publishes articles and studies in the foundations of education and in related disciplines outside the field of education which contribute to the advancement of education theory.

570 pages Quarterly
ISSN: 0013-2004

Nicholas C Burbules, Editor
Diane E Beckett, Business Manager

4323 Exceptional Children

The Council for Exceptional Children
2900 Crystal Drive
Suite 100
Arlington, VA 22202-3557
703-620-3660
888-232-7733
Fax: 703-264-3494
E-mail: service@cec.sped.org
http://www.cec.sped.org
Original research on the education and development of infants, toddlers, children and youth with exceptionalities and articles on professional issues of concern to special educators. Published quarterly, free to members or $86.00 per year to individuals.

Quarterly
ISSN: 0014-4029

Anitra Davis, Senior Customer Service Rep
Alison Heron, Director

4324 Focus on Autism

Pro-Ed., Inc.
8700 Shoal Creek Boulevard
Austin, TX 78757-6897
512-451-3246
800-897-3202
Fax: 512-451-8542
http://www.proedinc.com
Hands-on tips, techniques, methods and ideas from top authorities for improving the quality of assessment, instruction and management.

Brenda Smith Myles, PhD, Editor

4325 Focus on Research

The Council for Exceptional Children
2900 Crystal Drive
Suite 100
Arlington, VA 22202-1545
703-620-3660
888-232-7733
Fax: 703-264-9494
http://www.cec.sped.org
Contains member opinion articles, debates on research issues, descriptions and dates of specific projects, notices of funded program priorities in special education, the availabil-

ity of research dollars, and the discussion of emerging issues that may affect research in special education.

3x Year

Anitra Davis, Senior Customer Service Rep
Alison Heron, Director

4326 Foreign Student Service Council

2263 12th Place NW
Washington, DC 20009-4405
202-232-4979
Non-profit organization dedicated to promoting understanding between international students and Americans.

Quarterly

4327 Fortune Education Program

2890 Gateway Oaks Drive
Suite 100
Sacramento, CA 95833-1872
916-924-8633
800-448-3399
Fax: 916-924-8664
http://www.fortuneschool.us
Professional program that offers 75% off the cover price of Fortune magazine, a free educator's desk reference, a free 2-page teaching guide, fast delivery, choice of billing options. Plus quality customer service.

Paulette Brown Hinds, Managing Partner
Carolyn Lawson, Chief Information Officer

4328 Forum

Educators for Social Responsibility
23 Garden Street
Cambridge, MA 02138-3623
617-492-1764
Fax: 617-864-5164
E-mail: educators@esrnational.org
http://www.esrnational.org
Edited for educators concerned with teaching in the nuclear age.

12 pages Quarterly

Barry Berman, Chief Financial Officer
Deborah Childs-Bowen, Executive Director

4329 Foundation for Exceptional Children: Focus

The Council for Exceptional Children
2900 Crystal Drive
Suite 100
Arlington, VA 22202-1545
703-620-3660
888-232-7733
Fax: 703-264-9494
http://www.cec.sped.org
Membership and association news.

6 pages TriQuarterly

Anitra Davis, Senior Customer Service Rep
Alison Heron, Director

4330 Fulbright News

American Friends Service Committee
1501 Cherry St.
Room 450
Philadelphia, PA 19102-2269
215-241-7000
Fax: 212-941-6291
http://https://afsc.org
A four page newsletter distributed 5 times a year to visiting Fulbright scholars in the New York area. Contains a scholar profile, information about activities, tips for living in the United States, events in the New York area, and relevant announcements.

4 pages

Kristen Pendleton, Publisher

4331 GED Items

Adult Learning Center
1340 Braddock Place
7th Floor
Alexandria, VA 22314-1110
703-619-8027
http://www.acps.k12.va.us/adulted
Newsletter of the GED Testing Service with articles focusing on adult education programs, teaching tips, GED graduate success stories and administration of GED testing.

12 pages BiMonthly

4332 Gifted Child Society Newsletter

The Gifted Child Society
190 Rock Road
Glen Rock, NJ 07452-1736
201-444-6530
Fax: 201-444-9099
E-mail: admin@gifted.org
http://www.gifted.org
Provides educational enrichment and support for gifted children through national advocacy and various programs.

Publication Date: 1957 Bi-Annual

Janet L Chen, Executive Director

4333 Harvard Education Letter

Harvard Education Publishing Group
8 Story Street
1st Floor
Cambridge, MA 02138
617-495-3432
800-513-0763
Fax: 617-496-3584
E-mail: editor@edletter.org
http://www.edletter.org
Published by the Harvard Graduate School of Education and reports on current research and innovative practice in PreK-12.

Publication Date: 1985 8 pages Bi-Monthly
ISSN: 8755-3716

Douglas Clayton, Publisher
Nancy Walser, Editor

4334 Health in Action

American School Health Association
7918 Jones Branch Drive
Suite 300
McLean, VA 22102-0013
703-506-7675
800-445-2742
Fax: 703-506-3266
E-mail: info@ashaweb.org
http://www.ashaweb.org

24 pages Quarterly
ISSN: 1540-2479

Linda Morse, President
Ty Oehrtman, Vice President

4335 Help! I'm in Middle School... How Will I Survive?

Northern Research Station
11 Campus Blvd.
Suite 200
Newtown Square, PA 19073
610-557-4017
E-mail: info@englishthrough.com
http://www.nrs.fs.fed.us/pubs
The goal of NRS Publications is the success of every child. We provide a variety of books, educational games, posters, educational dice, overhead tiles, science kits, the SHAPES parts of speech learning system and creative play toys to help meet that goal.

Merry L Gumm, President
Tanya L Hein, Vice President

4336 Higher Education & National Affairs
American Council on Education
1 Dupont Circle NW
Suite 800
Washington, DC 20036-1132
202-939-9300
http://www.acenet.edu
National newsletter with Capitol Hill and Administration updates on issues that affect colleges and universities. Includes stories on the federal budget, student financial aid, tax laws, Education Department regulations and research, legal issues and minorities in higher education.

James H. Mullen Jr., Chair
Renu Khator, Vice Chair

4337 History of Education Quarterly
Indian University
School of Education
107 S. Indiana Ave.
Bloomington, IN 47405-7000
812-855-4848
Fax: 812-855-3631
http://www.iu.edu
Discusses current and historical movements in education.

Quarterly
Charles R. Bantz, Executive VP
MaryFrances McCourt, Senior VP, CFO

4338 Homeschooling Marketplace Newsletter
13106 Patrici Circle
Omaha, NE 68164
Offers information, strategies and tips for homeschooling.
Clarice Routh, Contact

4339 IDRA Newsletter
Intercultural Development Research Association
5835 Callaghan Road
Suite 101
San Antonio, TX 78228-1125
210-444-1710
Fax: 210-444-1714
E-mail: feedback@idra.org
http://www.idra.org
Mini-journal covering topics in the education of minority, poor and language-minority students in public institutions. It provides research-based solutions and editorial materials for education.

Monthly
Maria Robledo Montecel, President & CEO
Abelardo Villarreal, Chief of Operations

4340 IEA Reporter
Idaho Education Association
620 N 6th Street
P.O. Box 2638
Boise, ID 83701-5542
208-344-1341
800-727-9922
Fax: 208-336-6967
http://www.idahoea.org

Quarterly
Diana Mikesell, VP
Kathy Phelan, President

4341 Inclusive Education Programs
LRP Publications
360 Hiatt Drive
Suite 700
Palm Beach Gardens, FL 33418
561-622-6520
800-341-7874
Fax: 561-622-1375

E-mail: custserve@lrp.com
http://www.lrp.com
Newsletter covers the legal and practical issues of educating children with disabilities in regular education environments. It provides practical, how-to-advice, real life examples, and concise case summaries of the most recent judicial case laws.

Monthly
ISSN: 1076-8548
Kenneth F. Kahn, President

4342 Independent Scholar
National Coalition of Independent Scholars
PO Box 120182
San Antonio, TX 78212-0743
510-704-0990
http://www.ncis.org
A newsletter for independent scholars and their organizations.

Quarterly
Mona Berman, President
Janet Wasserman, Secretary

4343 Innovative Higher Education
Kluwer Academic/Human Sciences Press
233 Spring Street
New York, NY 10013
212-620-8000
800-221-9369
Fax: 212-463-0742
http://www.wkpa.nl
Provides educators and scholars with the latest creative strategies, programs and innovations designed to meet contemporary challenges in higher education. Professionals throughout the world contribute high-quality papers on the changing rules of vocational and liberal arts education, the needs of adults reentering the education process, and the reconciliation of faculty desires to economic realities, among other topics.

Quarterly
ISSN: 0742-5627
Carol Bischoff, Publisher
Ronald Simpson, Editor

4344 Insight
Independent Education Consultants Association
3251 Old Lee Highway
Suite 510
Fairfax, VA 22030-1504
703-591-4850
800-888-4322
Fax: 703-591-4860
E-mail: requests@IECAonline.com
http://www.IECAonline.com
Publication of national professional association of educational counselors working in private practice. Association provides counseling in college, secondary schools, learning disabilities and wilderness therapy programs.

Rebecca Peek, Author
Gail Meyer, President
Pamela Jobin, Vice President

4345 International Debates
Congressional Digest Corp.
4416 East West Highway
Suite 400
Bethesda, MD 20814-4568
301-634-3113
800-637-9915
Fax: 301-634-3189
E-mail: griff.thomas@pro-and-con.org
http://www.pro-and-con.org

An independent publication featuring global controversies in the United Nations and other international forums, pro and cons.

ISSN: 1542-0345
Delores Baisden, Assistant

4346 International Education
University of Tennessee
College of Education
Health & Human Services
Knoxville, TN 37996-3400
865-974-1000
Fax: 865-974-8718
E-mail: scarey@utk.edu
http://www.utk.edu
Publishes articles related to various international topics.

Publication Date: 1997 BiAnnual/Paperback
ISSN: 0160-5429
Sue Carey, Managing Editor

4347 International Journal of Qualitive Studies in Education
Taylor & Francis Group, LLC Books
6000 Broken Sound Parkway, NW
Suite 300
Boca Raton, FL 33487
561-994-0555
Fax: 561-241-7856
E-mail: orders@taylorandfrancis.com
http://www.tandF.co.uk/journals
Aims to enhance the theory of qualitative research in education.

6 Issues Per Year
Jim Scheurich, Editor
Angela Valenzuela, Editor

4348 International Volunteer
Volunteers for Peace
7 Kilburn Street
Suite 316
Burlington, VT 05401-9988
802-540-3060
Fax: 802-259-2922
E-mail: info@vfp.org
http://www.vfp.org
Newsletter of Volunteers for Peace, which provides intercultural education and community services.

8 pages Annual
Peter Coldwell, Author
Megan Brook, Executive Director
Maddie Craig, Coordinator

4349 Issues in Integrative Studies
Association for Integrative Studies
Miami University
Oxford, OH 45056
513-529-2659
Fax: 513-529-5849
E-mail: aisorg@muohio.edu
http://www.units.muohio.edu/aisorg
An annual, refereed professional journal for members.

ISBN: 1081-4760
Rick Szostak, Editor

4350 It Starts in the Classroom
National School Public Relations Association
15948 Derwood Road
Suite 201
Rockville, MD 20855-1109
301-519-0496
Fax: 301-519-0494
http://www.nspra.org

Devoted to classroom and teacher public relations techniques and ideas.

8 pages Monthly

Jim Cummings, President
Susan Hardy Brooks, President-elect

351 Journal of Behavioral Education

Kluwer Academic/Human Sciences Press
233 Spring Street
New York, NY 10013
212-620-8000
800-221-9369
Fax: 212-463-0742
http://www.wkpa.nl
Provides the first single-source forum for the publication of research on the application of behavioral principles and technology to education. Publishes original empirical research and brief reports covering behavioral education in regular, special and adult education settings. Subject populations include handicapped, at-risk, and non-handicapped students of all ages.

Quarterly
ISSN: 1053-0819

Carol Bischoff, Publisher
Christopher Skinner, Co-Editor

352 Journal of Creative Behavior

Creative Kids Education Foundation
11726 San Vicente Blvd.
Suite 370
Los Angeles, CA 90049
310-234-8604
800-447-2774
Fax: 413-559-6615
E-mail: creativekidsfoundation@gmail.com
http://creativekidseducationfoundation.org
Devoted to the serious general reader with vocational/avocational interests in the fields of creativity and problem solving. Its articles are authored not only by established writers in the field, but by up-and-coming contributors as well. The criteria for selecting articles include reference, clarity, interest and overall quality.

Quarterly

Jama Laurent, President
Byron Adams, Professor of Music

353 Journal of Curriculum Theorizing

Colgate University
Department of Education
13 Oak Drive
Hamilton, NY 13346
315-228-7000
Fax: 315-228-7998
http://www.colgate.edu
Analyzes and provides insights to curriculum movements and evolution.

Quarterly

JoAnne Pagano, Editor

354 Journal of Disability Policy Studies

Pro-Ed., Inc.
8700 Shoal Creek Boulevard
Austin, TX 78757-6897
512-451-3246
800-897-3202
Fax: 512-302-8542
E-mail: proed1@aol.com
http://www.proedinc.com
Devoted exclusively to disability policy topics and issues.

Quarterly Magazine
ISSN: 1044-2073

Craig R Fiedler, JD, PhD, Editor
Billie Jo Rylance, PhD, Editor

4355 Journal of Educational Research

Taylor & Francis
325 Chestnut Street
Suite 800
Philadelphia, PA 19106-1826
215-625-8900
800-354-1420
Fax: 202-296-5149
E-mail:
customer.service@taylorandfrancis.com
http://www.heldref.org
Since 1920, this journal has contributed to the advancement of educational practice in elementary and secondary schools. Authors experiment with new procedures, evaluate traditional practices, replicate previous research for validation and perform other work central to understanding and improving the education of today's students and teachers. This Journal is a valuable resource for teachers, counselors, supervisors, administrators, planners and educational researchers.

64 pages BiMonthly
ISSN: 0022-0671

Deborah Cohen, Promotions Editor

4356 Journal of Experimental Education

Taylor & Francis
325 Chestnut Street
Suite 800
Philadelphia, PA 19106-1826
215-625-8900
800-354-1420
Fax: 202-296-5149
E-mail:
customer.service@taylorandfrancis.com
http://www.heldref.org
Aims to improve educational practice by publishing basic and applied research studies using the range of quantitative and qualitative methodologies found in the behavioral, cognitive and social sciences. Published studies address all levels of schooling, from preschool through graduate and professional education, and various educational context, including public and private education in the United States and abroad.

96 pages Quarterly

Paige Jackson, Managing Editor

4357 Journal of Law and Education

University of South Carolina Law School
701 Main Street
Columbia, SC 29208
803-777-4155
Fax: 803-777-9405
E-mail: lawweb@law.sc.edu
http://www.law.sc.edu
A periodical offering information on the newest laws and legislation affecting education.

Quarterly

Ronbert M. Wilcox, Dean
Jaclyn A. Cherry, Associate Dean

4358 Journal of Learning Disabilities

Pro-Ed., Inc.
8700 Shoal Creek Boulevard
Austin, TX 78757-6897
512-451-3246
800-897-3202
Fax: 512-451-8542
E-mail: proed1@aol.com
http://www.proedinc.com
Special series, feature articles and research articles.

Bi-Monthly Magazine
ISSN: 0022-2194

Wayne P Hresko, PhD, Editor-in-Chief

4359 Journal of Negro Education

Howard University
2400 Sixth Street, NW
Washington, DC 20059-0001
202-806-6100
Fax: 202-806-8434
E-mail: jne@howard.edu
http://www.howard.edu
A Howard University quarterly review of issues incident to the education of Black people; tracing educational developments and presenting research on issues confronting Black students in the US and around the world.

120+ pages Quarterly
ISSN: 0022-2984

D. Kamili Anderson, Associate Editor
Dr. Sylvia T. Johnson, Editor-in-Chief

4360 Journal of Positive Behavior Interventions

Pro-Ed., Inc.
8700 Shoal Creek Boulevard
Austin, TX 78757-6897
512-451-3246
800-897-3202
Fax: 512-302-9129
http://www.proedinc.com
Sound, research-based principles of positive behavior support for use in home, school and community settings for people with challenges in behavioral adaptation.

Glen Dunlap, PhD, Editor
Robert L Koegel, PhD, Editor

4361 Journal of Research and Development in Education

University of Georgia, College of Education
G3 Aderhold Hall
110 Carlton Street,
Athens, GA 30602
404-542-1154
http://www.coe.uga.edu
A magazine offering insight and experimental and theoretical studies in education.

Quarterly

Craig H. Kennedy, Dean
Laura Lee Bierema, Associate Dean

4362 Journal of Research in Character Education

Character Education Partnership
1634 I Street NW
Suite 550
Washington, DC 20006
202-296-7743
800-988-8081
Fax: 202-296-7779
E-mail: information@character.org
http://www.character.org

Becky Sipos, President & CEO
Sheril Morgan, Director

4363 Journal of Research in Rural Education

University of Maine, College of Education
5766 Shibles Hall
Orono, ME 04469-5766
207-581-2493
Fax: 207-581-2423
http://www.umaine.edu
Publishes the results of educational research relevant to rural settings.

3x Year Journal

Theodore Coladarci, Editor
Sara Sheppard, Managing Editor

4364 Journal of School Health
American School Health Association
7918 Jones Branch Drive
Suite 300
McLean, VA 22102-0013
703-506-7675
800-445-2742
Fax: 703-506-3266
E-mail: info@ashaweb.org
http://www.ashaweb.org
Contains material related to health promotion in school settings. A non-profit organization founded in 1927, ASHA's mission is to protect and improve the health and well-being of children and youth by supporting comprehensive, preschool-12 school health programs. ASHA and its 4,000 members (school nurses, health educators, and physicians) work to improve school health services and school health environments.
40 pages Monthly
ISSN: 0022-4391

Linda Morse, President
Ty Oehrtman, Vice President

4365 Journal of Special Education
Pro-Ed., Inc.
8700 Shoal Creek Boulevard
Austin, TX 78757-6897
512-451-3246
800-897-3202
Fax: 512-302-9129
http://www.proedinc.com
Timely, sound special education research.

Lynn S Fuchs, PhD, Editor
Douglas Fuchs, PhD, Editor

4366 Journal of Urban & Cultural Studies
University of Massachusetts at Boston
Department of English
100 Morrissey Blvd.
Boston, MA 02125-3393
617-287-5000
Fax: 617-287-4000
http://www.umb.edu/
Explores various issues in education that deal with urban and cultural affairs.

Donaldo Macedo, Editor

4367 Kaleidoscope
Evansville-Vanderburgh School Corporation
951 Walnut St
Evansville, IN 47713-1821
812-435-8599
http://www.edlinesites.net/pages/EVSC
A staff publication for and about employees of the Evansville-Vanderburgh School Corporation.
8 pages Monthly

Patti S Coleman, Contact

4368 LD Forum
Council for Learning Disabilities
Box 405
11184 Antioch Road
Overland Park, KS 68210
913-491-1011
Fax: 913-491-1011
http://www.council-for-learning-disabiliti es.org/
Provides updated information and research on the activities of the Council for Learning Disabilities.
60 pages Quarterly
ISSN: 0731-9487

Steve Chamberlain, President
Mary Beth Calhoon, Vice President

4369 Learning Disability Quarterly
Council for Learning Disabilities
Box 405
11184 Antioch Road
Overland Park, KS 68210-4303
913-491-1011
Fax: 913-491-1011
http://www.council-for-learning-disabiliti es.org/
Aimed at learning disabled students, their parents and educators. Accepts advertising.
Quarterly

Steve Chamberlain, President
Mary Beth Calhoon, Vice President

4370 Learning Point Magazine Laboratory
North Central Regional Educational Laboratory
1000 Thomas Jefferson Street NW
Suite 300
Washington, DC 20007-1447
202-403-5000
Fax: 202-403-5001
E-mail: info@ncrel.org
http://www.ncrel.org
Applies research and technology to learning.
16 pages Quarterly

Jeri Nowakowski, Director

4371 Learning Unlimited Network of Oregon
31960 SE Chin Street
Boring, OR 97009-9708
503-663-5153
Cuts through all barriers to communication and learning; institutional, personal, physical, psychological, spiritual. It focuses on basic communication/language skills but sets no limits on means or tools, subjects or participants in seeking maximum balance and productivity for all.
10 pages 9x Year

Gene Lehman, Contact

4372 Let It Grow. Let It Grow. Let It Grow. Hands-on Activities to Explore the Planet Kingdom
NSR Publications
1482 51st Road
Douglass, KS 67039
620-986-5472
E-mail: info@englishthrough.com
http://www.nsrpublications.com
The goal of NSR Publication is the success of every child. We provide a variety of books, educational games, posters, educational dice, overhead tiles, science kits, the SHAPES parts of speech learning system and creative play toys to help meet that goal.
58 pages

Merry L Gumm, President
Tanya L Hein, Vice President

4373 Liaison Bulletin
National Assn. of State Directors of Special Ed.
225 Reinekers Lane
Suite 420
Alexandria, VA 22314-2840
703-519-3800
Fax: 703-519-3808
http://www.nasdse.org

Membership news for persons affiliated with the National Association of State Directors of Special Education.
BiWeekly

Dr. William Schipper, Editor
Frank Podobnik, Director

4374 Liberal Education
Association of American Colleges & Universities
1818 R Street NW
Washington, DC 20009-1604
202-387-3760
Fax: 202-265-9532
http://www.aacu-edu.org
Concentrates on issues currently affecting American higher education. Promotes and strengthens undergraduate curriculum, classroom teaching and learning, collaborative leadership, faculty leadership, diversity. Other publications on higher education include books, monographs, peer review, and on campus with women.
64 pages Quarterly
ISSN: 0024-1822

Kenneth P. Ruscio, Chair
Edward J. Ray, Vice Chair

4375 Link
AEL, Inc.
102 E. Keefe Ave
Milwaukee, WI 53212-1348
414-265-7630
866-656-1486
Fax: 414-265-7628
E-mail: sales@aelseating.com
http://www.aelseating.com
A newsletter for educators providing research summaries, education news, and news of AEL products, services and events.
12 pages Quarterly Newsletter

Patricia Hammer Cahape, Associate Director

4376 Lisle-Interaction
433 W Sterns Street
Temperance, MI 48182-9568
734-847-7126
800-477-1538
Fax: 512-259-0392
http://www.lisleinternational.org
Reports on domestic and international programs, annual meetings and board meetings of the Lisle Fellowship which seeks to broaden global awareness and appreciation of different cultures. Occasional special articles on topics such as racism, book reviews. News of members are also included.
16 pages Quarterly

Mark Kinney, Executive Director
Dianne Brause, VP

4377 MEA Today
Montana Education Association
1232 E 6th Avenue
Helena, MT 59601-3927
406-442-4250
800-398-0826
Fax: 406-443-5081
http://www.mea-mft.org
National and state association news, legislative policies, and classroom features.
8 pages Monthly

Eric Feaver, President
Melanie Charlsonÿ, VP

4378 Massachusetts Home Learning Association Newsletter
23 Mountain Street
Sharon, MA 02067-2234
781-784-8006
http://www.mhla.org

A source for information gleaned from all the major national magazines and many state newsletters. Calendar of events for Massachusetts homeschooling and several feature articles on legal, educational or familial issues.

24 pages Quarterly

Sharon Terry, Editor
Patrick Terry, Editor

379 Mel Gabler's Newsletter

Educational Research Analysts
PO Box 7518
Longview, TX 75607-7518
972-753-5993
http://www.textbookreviews.org/
Educational information pertaining to curricula used in schools.

8 pages SemiAnnually

Mel Gabler, Publisher
Chad Rosenberger, Editor

380 Minnesota Education Update

Office of Library Development & Services
200 West Baltimore Street
550 Cedar Street
Baltimore, MD 21201-2595
410-767-0444
Fax: 410-333-2507
http://www.marylandpublicschools.org
Policies and activities in elementary and secondary education in the state of Minnesota.

8 pages Monthly

Amber Massaquoi, Executive Assistant
Dennis Nangle, Branch Chief

381 Missouri Schools

Missouri Department of Education
PO Box 480
Jefferson City, MO 65102-0480
573-751-4212
Fax: 573-751-8613
http://dese.mo.gov
State education policy.

28 pages BiMonthly

Margie Vandeven, Commissioner
Jay Nixon, Governor

382 Momentum

National Catholic Educational Association
1005 North Glebe Road
Suite 525
Arlington, VA 22201
202-337-6232
800-711-6232
Fax: 703-243-0025
http://www.ncea.org
The association offers a quarterly publication, conducts research, works with voluntary groups and government agencies on educational problems, conducts seminars and workshops for all levels of educators.

Quarterly

Reverend Blase Cupich, Chairman
Brother Robert Bimonte, FSC, President

383 Montana Schools

Montana Office of Public Instruction
State Capitol
Helena, MT 59620
406-444-3095
Fax: 406-444-2893
http://opi.mt.gov
Information about people and programs in the Montana education system.

12 pages 5x Year

Ellen Meloy

4384 Montessori Observer

International Montessori Society
9525 Georgia Avenue
Suite 200
Silver Spring, MD 20910
301-589-1127
800-301-3131
Fax: 301-920-0764
E-mail: havis@imsmontessori.org
http://http://imsmontessori.org
Provides news and information about Montessori education and the work of the International Montessori Society.

Publication Date: 1979
ISSN: 0889-5643

Lee Havis, Editor

4385 NAEIR Advantage

Nat'l Assn. for Exchange of Industrial Resources
560 McClure Street
Galesburg, IL 61401-4286
309-343-0704
800-562-0955
Fax: 309-343-3519
E-mail: member.naeir@misslink.net
http://www.naeir.org
News of the National Association for the Exchange of Industrial Resources, which collects donations of new excess inventory from corporations and redistributes them to American schools and nonprofits.

Publication Date: 1977 8 pages BiMonthly

Gary C Smith, President/CEO
Robert B. Gilstrap, Vice President/CFO

4386 NAEN Bulletin

Nort American Association of Education Negotiators
PO Box 1068
Salem, OR 97308
519-503-0098
Fax: 503-588-2813
E-mail: execdir@naen.org
http://www.naen.org
Association news and notes.

Members Only

Tim Alexander, President
Michael R. Weinert, Executive Director

4387 NAFSA Newsletter

NAFSA: Association of International Educators
1307 New York Avenue NW
8th Floor
Washington, DC 20005-4701
202-737-3699
800-836-4994
Fax: 202-737-3657
E-mail: inbox@nafsa.org
http://www.nafsa.org
Publishes news and information related to international education and exchange.

Publication Date: 1948 40 pages Weekly & Quarterly

Fanta Aw, PhD, Chair/ President
Marlene Johnson, Executive Director/ CEO

4388 NAPSEC News

Assn. of Private Schools for Exceptional Children
1522 K Street NW
Suite 1032
Washington, DC 20005-1202
202-408-3338
Fax: 202-408-3340
http://www.napsec.org
Association news and events.

8-12 pages Quarterly

Sherry L Kolbe, Executive Director/CEO
Barb DeGroot, Manager

4389 NEA Higher Education Advocate

National Education Association (NEA)
1201 16th Street NW
Washington, DC 20036-3290
202-833-4000
Fax: 202-822-7974
E-mail: ncuea@nea.org
http://www.nea.org
Reports on NEA and general higher education news.

Publication Date: 1857 4 pages Monthly

Lily Eskelsen Garcia, President
Becky Pringle, Vice President

4390 NEA Today

National Education Association (NEA)
1201 16th Street NW
Washington, DC 20036-3290
202-833-4000
Fax: 202-822-7974
E-mail: ncuea@nea.org
http://www.nea.org
Contains news and features of interest to classroom teachers and other employees of schools.

Publication Date: 1857 8x Year

Lily Eskelsen Garcia, President
Becky Pringle, Vice President

4391 NEWSLINKS

International Schools Services
15 Roszel Road
P.O. Box 5910
Princeton, NJ 08543
609-452-0990
Fax: 609-452-2690
E-mail: newslinks@iss.edu
http://www.iss.edu
Regularly published newspaper of International Schools Services that is distributed free of charge to overseas teachers, school administrators and libraries, US universities, educational organizations, multinational corporations, school supply companies and educational publishers.

Publication Date: 1955 32-40 pages Quarterly

Roger Hove, President
Kristin Evins, Chief Financial Officer

4392 NJEA Review

New Jersey Education Association
180 W State Street
Trenton, NJ 08607-1211
609-599-4561
Fax: 609-392-6321
E-mail: webmaster@njea.org
http://www.njea.org
Monthly educational journal of the New Jersey Education Association which focuses on educational news and issues related to New Jersey public schools. Its readers are active and retired teaching staff members and support staff, administrators, board members, teacher education students, and others in New Jersey public schools and colleges.

Publication Date: 1853 80 pages Monthly
ISSN: 0027-6758

Wendell F. Steinhauer, Chair/ President
Marie Blistan, Vice President

4393 NREA News

National Rural Education Association
Colorado State University
Fort Collins, CO 80523
Fax: 970-491-1317
E-mail: jnewlin@lamar.colostate.edu
http://www.colostate.edu
Keeps all members up-to-date on Association activities, events, rural education confer-

ences and meetings, and research projects in progress.

Publication Date: 1870 8 pages Quarterly Newsletter
ISSN: 0273-4460

Joseph T Newlin, Editor

4394 National Accrediting Commission of Cosmetology, Arts and Sciences
National Accrediting Commission of Cosmetology
4401 Ford Avenue
Suite 1300
Arlington, VA 22302-1432
703-600-7600
Fax: 703-379-2200
E-mail: naccas@naccas.org
http://www.naccas.org
Information on accreditation, cosmetology schools and any federal regulations affecting accreditation and postsecondary education.

Publication Date: 1969 20 pages 6x Year

Tony Mirando, MS, DC, Executive Director
Eddie Broomfield, Asst. to Executive Director

4395 National Alliance of Black School Educators (NABSE)
National Alliance of Black School Educators
310 Pennsylvania Avenue SE
Washington, DC 20003
202-608-6310
800-221-2654
Fax: 202-608-6319
E-mail: info@nabse.org
http://www.nabse.org
For teachers, principals, specialists, superintendents, school board members and higher education personnel.

Publication Date: 1979 15-25 pages 3x Year

Nardos King, Chair
Bernard Hamilton, Ed.D, President

4396 National Homeschool Association Newsletter
National Homeschool Association
PO Box 290
Hartland, MI 48353-0290
425-432-1544
Information on what's happening in the homeschooling community.

28 pages Quarterly

4397 National Monitor of Education
CA Monitor of Education
1331 Fairmount Avenue
Suite 61
El Cerrito, CA 94530
510-527-4430
Fax: 510-528-9833
E-mail: jsod@aol.com
http://www.e-files.org
Supports traditional moral and academic values in education. Reports on litigation and reviews various education publications. Issues reported on include parents' rights and movement to restore basic academics.

8 pages Bi-Monthly/Paperback

Susan O'Donnell, Publisher
Susan Sweet, Newsletter Design

4398 New Hampshire Educator
National Education Association, New Hampshire
103 N State Street
Concord, NH 03301-2425

603-224-7751
Fax: 603-224-2648
http://neanh.org
Reports on the advancements in education in the state and nation and promotes the welfare of educators.

Publication Date: 1854 10 pages Monthly

Scott McGilvray, President
Megan Tuttle, Vice President

4399 New Images
METCO
55 Dimock Street
Boston, MA 02119-1029
617-427-1545
Mailed to METCO parents and educational institutions local and national.

4 pages Quarterly

JM Mitchell

4400 New York Teacher
New York State United Teachers
800 Troy-Schenectady Road
Latham, NY 12110-2455
518-213-6000
800-342-9810
Fax: 518-213-6415
E-mail: mediarel@nysutmail.org
http://www.nysut.org
Edited primarily for teaching personnel in elementary, intermediate and high schools and colleges. News and features cover organizations' development, progress of legislation affecting education at local state and national levels and news of the labor movement.

BiWeekly

Karen E. Magee, President
Andrew Pallotta, Executive Vice President

4401 News N' Notes
NTID at Rochester Institute of Technology
52 Lomb Memorial Drive
Rochester, NY 14623
585-475-6400
E-mail: gbuckley@ntid.rit.edu
http://www.ntid.rit.edu
Convention news, membership information, education legislation advocacy and personal contributions to the scholarly society.

Publication Date: 1829 12 pages Quarterly

Dr. Gerard J. Buckley, President
Bernard Hurwitz, J.D., Executive Assistant

4402 Non-Credit Learning News
Learning for All Seasons
6 Saddle Club Road
#579X
Lexington, MA 02420-2115
781-861-0379
Marketing information for directors and marketers of non-credit programs.

8 pages 10x Year

Susan Capon

4403 Notes from the Field
Jessie Ball duPont Fund
One Dependent Drive
Suite 1400
Jacksonville, FL 32202-5011
904-353-0890
800-252-3452
Fax: 904-353-3870
E-mail: contactus@dupontfund.org
http://www.dupontfund.org

Provides information on the various organizations and institutes the Jessie Ball duPont Fund reaches out to every year.

Publication Date: 1977 3x

Sherry P. Magill, President
Mark D. Constantine, Senior Vice President

4404 Occupational Programs in California Community Colleges
Leo A Myer Associates/LAMA Books
2381 Sleepy Hollow Avenue
Hayward, CA 94545-3429
510-785-1091
888-452-6244
Fax: 510-785-1099
E-mail: lama@lmabooks.com
http://www.lamabooks.com
Writers and publishers of HVAC books.

186 pages Bi-Annually
ISBN: 0-88069

Steve Meyer, President

4405 Our Children: The National PTA Magazine
1250 N. Pitt Street
Alexandria, VA 22314
703-518-1200
800-307-4782
Fax: 703-836-0942
E-mail: info@pta.org
http://www.pta.org
Written by, for and about the National PTA. A nonprofit organization of parents, educators, students, and other citizens active in their schools and communities.

5x Year

Otha Thornton, President
Shannon Sevier, Vice President Advocacy

4406 PTA National Bulletin
National Association of Hebrew Day School PTA'S
160 Broadway
New York, NY 10038-4201
212-227-1000
Fax: 212-406-6934
Educational events in day school relating to PTA movement. News of national and regional groups.

Quarterly

4407 PTA in Pennsylvania
Pennsylvania PTA
4804 Derry Street
Harrisburg, PA 17111-3440
717-564-8985
Fax: 717-564-9046
E-mail: info@papta.org
http://www.papta.org
Topical articles about issues affecting education and children, such as safety and health, AIDS, parents involvement and guidance, environmental concerns and special education.

24 pages Quarterly
ISSN: 1072-3242
250 attendees and 40-50 exhibits

Deborah Dunstone, President
Christine Harty, Secretary

4408 Parents as Teachers National Center
2228 Ball Drive
Saint Louis, MO 63146
314-432-4330
Fax: 314-432-8963
E-mail: patnc@patnc.org
http://www.parentsasteachers.org
Provides information, training and technical assistance for those interested in adopting the home-school-community partnership program. Offers parents the information and support

needed to give their children the best possible start in life.

Quarterly

Julie Robbens, Editor, Author
Scott Hippert, President/CEO
Cheryl Dyle-Palmer, M.A., EVP/ COO

409 Passing Marks
San Bernadino City Unified School District
777 N F Street
San Bernardino, CA 92410
909-381-1250
Fax: 909-388-1451
http://www.sbcusd.k12.ca.us
Educational resume of school activities, covering instruction, personnel, administration, board of education, etc.

12 pages Monthly

Michael J. Gallo, President
Bobbie Perong, Vice President

410 Pennsylvania Home Schoolers Newsletter
RR 2 Box 117
Kittanning, PA 16201-9311
724-783-6512
Fax: 724-783-6512
A support newsletter directed to homeschooling families in Pennsylvania. Articles, reviews of curriculum, advice, calendar, support group listing, children's writing section.

32 pages Quarterly

Howard Richman, Publisher
Susan Richman, Editor

411 Pennsylvania State Education Association
400 N 3rd Street
PO Box 1724
Harrisburg, PA 17105-1724
717-255-7000
800-944-7732
Fax: 717-255-7124
http://www.psea.org
Publication Date: 1852 16 pages 9x Year
ISSN: 0896-6605

Michael J. Crossey, President
W. Gerard Oleksiak, Vice President

412 Phi Delta Kappa Educational Foundation
P.O. Box 7888
Bloomington, IN 47407-7888
812-339-1156
800-766-1156
Fax: 812-339-0018
E-mail: memberservices@pdkintl.org
http://www.pdkintl.org
Articles concerned with educational research, service, and leadership; issues, trends and policy are emphazied.

Publication Date: 1906 350 pages 10x Year
ISBN: 0-87367-835-4
November
600 attendees and 30 exhibits

Perry A. Zirkel, Author
Patricia Williams, Chair
Douglas Christensen, Vice Chair

413 Phi Delta Kappan
Phi Delta Kappa International
320 W. Eighth Street
Suite 216
Bloomington, IN 47404
812-339-1156
800-766-1156
Fax: 812-339-0018
E-mail: memberservices@pdkintl.org
http://www.pdkintl.org

Published 8 times a year and is Phi Delta Kappa International's professional education magazine distributed to more than 35,000 individuals. Addresses policy/practice for teachers, administrators, education faculty. Advocates research-based school reform and covers professinal development, research, federal policy, and standards. Includes annual PDK/Gallup poll on public education and features full text of current issues available to online subscribers.

Publication Date: 1906
ISBN: 0031-7217

Patricia Williams, Chair
Douglas Christensen, Vice Chair

4414 Planning for Higher Education
Society for College and University Planning (SCUP)
1330 Eisenhower Place
Ann Arbor, MI 48108
734-669-3270
Fax: 734-661-0157
E-mail: info@scup.org
http://www.scup.org/phe
A quarterly, peer-reviewed journal devoted to the advancement and application of the best planning practices for colleges and universities.

70+ pages Quarterly Journal
ISSN: 0736-0983
July
150 booths with 1,200 attendees and 150 exhibits

Ellen Stanton Milstone, Chair
Philip G. Stack, Vice Chair

4415 Policy & Practice
American Public Human Services Association
1133 19th Street, NW
Suite 400
Washington, DC 20036
202-682-0100
Fax: 202-289-6555
http://www.aphsa.org
This quarterly magazine presents a comprehensive look at issues important to public human services administrators. It also features a wide spectrum of views by the best thinkers in social policy.

Publication Date: 1930 52 pages Quarterly
ISSN: 1520-801X

Reggie Bicha, President
Tracy Wareing, Executive Director

4416 Population Educator
Population Connection
1400 16th Street NW
Suite 320
Washington, DC 20036-2215
202-332-2200
800-767-1956
Fax: 202-332-2302
E-mail: poped@populationconnection.org
http://www.populationeducation.org
Offers population education news, classroom activities and workshop schedules for grades K-12.

4 pages Quarterly
Pamela Wasseman

4417 Public Education Alert
Public Education Association
39 W 32nd Street
New York, NY 10001-3803
212-868-1640
Fax: 212-302-0088
E-mail: info@peaonline
http://www.pea-online.org
Provides information and consumer-oriented analysis of law policy issues and current de-

velopments in New York City public education. PEA Alert back issues; e-guide to New York City's public high school offering comparative data.

Ray Domanico, Publisher
Jessica Wolfe, Editor

4418 QEG
Friends Council on Education
1507 Cherry Street
Philadelphia, PA 19102
215-241-7245
E-mail: info@friendscouncil.org
http://friendscouncil.org
Informal news sheet for Quaker schools.

4 pages BiMonthly
Irene McHenry

4419 QUIN: Quarterly University International News
University of Minnesota, Office in Education
231 Pillsbury Drive S.E
Minneapolis, MN 55455-213
612-625-1915
800-752-1000
Fax: 612-624-1693
http://admissions.tc.umn.edu
International campus update for students, faculty, staff and the community.

TriQuarterly
Rachelle Hernandez, Associate Vice Provost

4420 Reclaiming Children and Youth
Pro-Ed., Inc.
8700 Shoal Creek Boulevard
Austin, TX 78757-6897
512-451-3246
800-897-3202
Fax: 512-451-8542
E-mail: general@proedinc.com
http://www.proedinc.com
Provides positive, creative solutions to professionals serving youth in conflict.

Quarterly Magazine
Nicholas J Long, PhD, Editor
Larry K Brendtro, PhD, Editor

4421 Recognition Review
Awards and Recognition Association
8735 W. Higgins Road
Suite 300
Chicago, IL 60631
847-375-4800
800-344-2148
Fax: 847-375-6480
E-mail: info@ara.org
http://www.ara.org
Published monthly by the Awards and Recognition Association. Recognition Review is the leading voice of the awards, engraving and recognition industry.

Publication Date: 1964 Monthly
Jeanette Brewer Richardson, CRS, President
Louise Ristau, CAE, Executive Director

4422 Regional Spotlight
Southern Regional Education Board
592 10th Street NW
Atlanta, GA 30318-5776
404-875-9211
Fax: 404-872-1477
http://www.sreb.org
News of educational interest directed to 15 SREB-member states.

9 pages
Steve Beshear, Chair
Dave Spence, President

4423 Remedial and Special Education

Pro-Ed., Inc.
8700 Shoal Creek Boulevard
Austin, TX 78757-6897
512-451-3246
800-897-3202
Fax: 512-451-8542
E-mail: general@proedinc.com
http://www.proedinc.com
Highest-quality interdisciplinary scholarship that bridges the gap between theory and practice involving the education of individuals for whom typical instruction is not effective.

Bi-Monthly Magazine
ISSN: 0741-9325

Edward A Polloway, EdD,
Editor-in-Chief

4424 Renaissance Educator

Renaissance Educational Associates
4817 N County Road 29
Loveland, CO 80538-9515
970-679-4300
Quarterly publication highlighting educators around the world who are revealing the effectiveness of integrity in education.

8 pages Quarterly

Kristy Clark

4425 Research in Higher Education

Kluwer Academic/Human Sciences Press
233 Spring Street
New York, NY 10013
212-620-8000
800-221-9369
Fax: 212-463-0742
http://www.wkpa.nl
Essential source of new information for all concerned with the functioning of postsecondary educational institutions. Publishes original, quantitative research articles which contribute to an increased understanding of an institution, aid faculty in making more informed decisions about current or future operations, and improve the efficiency of an institution.

Bimonthly
ISSN: 0361-0365

Carol Bischoff, Publisher
John C Smart, Editor

4426 Research in the Schools

Mid-South Educational Research
Association
University of Alabama
Tuscaloosa, AL 35487-0001
Fax: 205-348-6873
E-mail: ktcampbell@selu.edu
http://msera.org
A nationally refereed journal sponsored by the Mid-South Educational Research Association and the University of Alabama. RITS publishes original contributions in the following areas: 1) Research in practice; 2) Topical Articles; 3) Methods and Techniques; 4) Assessment and 5) Other topics of interest dealing with school-based research. Contributions should follow the guidelines in the latest edition of the Publications Manual of the American Psychological Association.

Publication Date: 1972

Kathy Campbell, President
Cliff Hofwolt, Executive Director

4427 Roeper Review: A Journal on Gifted Education

Roeper Institute
PO Box 329
Bloomfield Hills, MI 48303-0329
248-203-7321
Fax: 248-203-7310
E-mail: tcross@bsu.edu
http://www.roeperreview.org
A journal that focuses on gifted and talented education, the Roeper Review applies the highest standards of peer review journalism to cover a broad range of issues. For professionals who work with teachers and for professionals who work directly with gifted and talented children and their families, the journal provides readable coverage of policy issues. Each issue covers one or more subjects. Regular departments include research reports and book reviews.

60-80 pages Quarterly
ISSN: 0278-3193

Tracy L Cross PhD, Editor
Vicki Rossbach, Subsciption

4428 Rural Educator: Journal for Rural and Small Schools

National Rural Education Association
Colorado State University
Fort Collins, CO 80523
970-491-7022
Fax: 970-491-1317
E-mail: jnewlin@lamar.colostate.edu
http://www.colostate.edu
Official journal of the NREA. A nationally recognized publication that features timely and informative articles written by leading rural educators from all levels of education. All NREA members are encouraged to submit research articles and items of general information for publication.

Publication Date: 1870 40 pages TriAnnual

Joseph T Newlin, Editor

4429 SEDL Letter

Southwestern Educational Development
Laboratory
4700 Mueller Boulevard
Austin, TX 78723
512-476-6861
800-476-6861
Fax: 512-476-2286
E-mail: information@sedl.org
http://www.sedl.org
A biannual letter that complements and draws on work and performed by SEDL under a variety of funding sources, including the US Department of Education and the US government.

Publication Date: 1960
ISBN: 520-7315

Linda Villarreal, Chair
Gwenneth Price-Picard, Vice Chair

4430 SKOLE: A Journal of Alternative Education

Down-To-Earth Books
72 Philip Street
Albany, NY 12202-1729
518-432-1578
Publishes articles, poems, and research by people engaged in alternative education.

200 pages SemiAnnually

Mary Leue

4431 SNEA Impact: The Student Voice of the Teaching Profession

National Education Association (NEA)
1201 16th Street NW
Washington, DC 20036-3290
202-833-4000
Fax: 202-822-7974
http://www.nea.org
Offers articles and views on current events and the educational system through students' eyes for education professionals.

Publication Date: 1857 7x Year

Lily Eskelsen, President
Becky Pringle, Vice President

4432 Safety Forum

Safety Society
1900 Association Drive
Reston, VA 20191-1502
703-476-3440
Offers articles and up-to-date information on school safety.

4 pages TriQuarterly

Linda Moore

4433 School Bus Fleet

Bobit Business Media
3520 Challenger Street
Torrance, CA 90503
310-533-2400
Fax: 310-533-2512
E-mail: info@schoolbusfleet.com
http://www.schoolbusfleet.com
Coverage of federal vehicle and education regulations that affect pupil transportation, policy and management issues and, of course, how to improve the safety of children riding yellow buses. Special sections include how to transport students with disabilities, a state report on regulations and legislation, and various other departments. School officials that manage finance operations at school districts, private contractors, school bus manufacturers are the audience.

Publication Date: 1956

James Blue, General Manager
Thomas McMahon, Executive Editor

4434 School Foodservice & Nutrition

School Nutrition Association
1600 Duke Street
Floor 7
Alexandria, VA 22314-3421
703-739-3900
800-877-8822
Fax: 703-739-3915
http://schoolnutrition.org
For foodservice professionals presenting current articles on industry issues, management events, legislative issues, public relations programs and professional development news.

11x Year

Adrienne Gall Tufts, Editor

4435 School Law Bulletin

Quinlan Publishing
23 Drydock Avenue
Boston, MA 02210-2336
617-542-0048
Covers cases and laws pertaining to schools.

8 pages Monthly

4436 School Safety

National School Safety Center
141 Duesenberg Drive
Suite 7B
Westlake Village, CA 91362
805-373-9977
800-453-7461
Fax: 805-373-9277
E-mail: info@schoolsafety.us
http://www.schoolsafety.us
For educators, law enforcers, judges and legislators on the prevention of drugs, gangs, weapons, bullying, discipline problems and vandalism; also

on-site security and character development as they relate to students and schools.

Monthly

Dr. Ronald D Stephens, Executive Director
June Lane Arnette, Editor

437 School Transportation News
STN Media Company Inc.
P.O. Box 789
Redondo Beach, CA 90277
310-792-2226
Fax: 310-792-2231
E-mail: bpaul@stnonline.com
http://www.stnonline.com
Covers school district and contractor fleets, special needs and prekindergarten transportation, Head Start, and more on a monthly basis. Reports developments affecting public school transportation supervisors and directors, state directors of school transportation, school bus contractors, special needs transportation, Head Start transportation, private school transportation, school business officials responsible for transportation and industry suppliers.

Publication Date: 1991 Magazine/Monthly 100 booths

Bill Paul, Author
Ryan Gray, Editor-in-Chief
Tony Corpin, Publisher

438 School Zone
West Aurora Public Schools, District 129
80 S River Street
#14
Aurora, IL 60506-5178
630-844-4400
http://www.sd129.org
Informs the community of what is happening in their schools, with their students, and with their tax dollars.

4 pages 5x Year

Laurel Chivari

439 Shaping the Future
Lutheran Education Association
7400 Augusta Street
River Forest, IL 60305
708-209-3343
Fax: 708-209-3458
E-mail: lea@lea.org
http://www.lea.org
Newsletter for LEA members to focus on the unique spiritual and professional needs of church workers and to celebrate life in the ministry. Resource information for the organization, upcoming events, encouragement for pre-planning.

Daniel Czaplewski, Chair
Candyce Seider, Vice Chair

440 Sharing Space
Creative Urethanes, Children's Creative Response
PO Box 271
Nyack, NY 10960-0271
845-358-4601
Trains all those working with children to communicate positivity and cooperation.

12 pages TriAnnually

441 Special Education Leadership
LifeWay Church Resources
One LifeWay Plaza
Nashville, TN 37234
615-251-2000
800-588-7222
Fax: 615-251-5933
http://www.lifeway.com

Covers special education issues relating to religious education.

Publication Date: 1891 52 pages Quarterly

Thom S. Rainer, President/ CEO
Brad Waggoner, Executive Vice President

4442 Special Educator
LRP Publications
360 Hiatt Drive
Palm Beach Gardens, FL 33418
703-516-7002
800-341-7874
Fax: 561-622-2423
E-mail: custserve@lrp.com
http://www.lrp.com
Covers important issues in the field of special education, including such topics as law and administrative policy.

Publication Date: 1977 22 pages 22 Issues Per Year
ISSN: 1047-1618

Kenneth F. Kahn, President

4443 Star News
Jefferson Center for Character Education
PO Box 1283
Monrovia, CA 91017-1283
949-770-7602
Fax: 949-450-1100
Mission is to produce and promote programs to teach children the concepts, skills and behavior of good character, common core values, personal and civic responsibility, workforce readiness and citizenship.

Quarterly

Robert Jamieson, CEO
Sharon McClenahan, Administrative Assistant

4444 Statewise: Statistical & Research Newsletter
State Board of Education, Planning & Research
PO Box 1402
Dover, DE 19903-1402
302-736-4601
Fax: 302-739-4654
Statistical data relating to Delaware public schools.

2 pages

4445 Street Scenes
(APO Street College of Education
610 W 112th Street
New York, NY 10025-1898
212-222-6700
Fax: 212-222-6700
New ideas in education.

8 pages SemiAnnually

Renee Creange

4446 Supreme Court Debates
Congressional Digest Corp.
4416 East West Highway
Suite 400
Bethesda, MD 20814-4568
301-528-7777
800-637-9915
Fax: 301-634-3189
E-mail: support@congressionaldigest.com
http://www.pro-and-con.org
An independent publication featuring controversies before the U.S. Supreme Court, pro-and-con.

Publication Date: 1921
ISSN: 1099-5390

Delores Baisden, Assistant

4447 Teacher$ Talk
Teachers Insurance and Annuity Association
730 3rd Avenue
New York, NY 10017-3206
212-490-9000
Fax: 800-914-8922
http://www.tiaa-cref.org
Offers timely information and helpful hints about savings, investments, finance and insurance for teachers and educators.

Publication Date: 1918 Quarterly

Roger Ferguson, President/ CEO
Ron Pressman, EVP/ COO

4448 Teaching Exceptional Children
Council for Exceptional Children
2900 Crystal Drive
Suite 1000
Arlington, VA 22202-3557
703-620-3660
888-232-7733
Fax: 703-264-9494
E-mail: robin.brewer@unco.edu
http://www.cec.sped.org
Features practical articles that present methods and materials for classroom use as well as current issues in special education teaching and learning. Published four times per year, free with membership or $86.00 for individual subscription.

Publication Date: 1922

Robin D. Brewer, President
Alexander T. Graham, Executive Director/Secretary

4449 Telluride Newsletter
217 West Ave.
Ithaca, NY 14850
607-273-5011
Fax: 607-272-2667
E-mail: telluride@tellurideassociation.org
http://www.tellurideassociation.org
News of interest to alumni of Telluride Association sponsored programs.

Publication Date: 1891 8 pages TriQuarterly

Eric Lemer

4450 Tennessee Education
University of Tennessee
College of Education
Knoxville, TN 37996-0001
865-974-5252
Fax: 865-974-8718
E-mail: admissions@utk.edu
http://www.utk.edu
Publishes articles on topics related to K through higher education.

BiAnnually
ISSN: 0739-0408

Mary Lucal, Assistant Vice Chancellor

4451 Tennessee School Board Bulletin
Tennessee School Boards Association
525 Brick Church Park Drive
Nashville, TN 37207
615-815-3900
800-448-6465
Fax: 615-815-3911
http://www.tsba.net
Articles of interest to boards of education.

Publication Date: 1939 6 pages

Susan Lodal, President
Wayne Blair, Vice President

4452 The Sounds and Spelling Patterns of English: P Honics for Teachers and Parents
Oxton House Publishers, LLC
Po Box 209
Farmington, ME 04938
207-779-1923
800-539-7323
Fax: 207-779-0623
E-mail: info@oxtonhouse.com
http://www.oxtonhouse.com
A clear, concise, practical, jargon-free overview of the sounds that make up the English language and the symbols that we use to represent them in writing. It includes a broad range of strategies for helping beginning readers develop fluent decoding skills.

62 pages

Jill Fulkerson, Representative, Colorado
Phillip Neill, Representative, Texas

4453 Theory Into Practice
Ohio State University, College of Education
122 Ramseyer Hall
29 W Woodruff Avenue
Columbus, OH 43210
614-292-3407
Fax: 614-292-7900
E-mail: tip@osu.edu
http://www.coe.ohio-state.edu
Nationally recognized for excellence in educational journalism; thematic format, providing comprehensive discussion of single topic with many diverse points of view.

Quarterly
ISSN: 0040-5841

Anita Woolfolk Hey, Author
Anita Woolfolk Hey, Editor

4454 This Active Life
National Education Association (NEA)
1201 16th Street NW
Washington, DC 20036-3290
202-833-4000
Fax: 202-822-7974
http://www.nea.org/retired
Serves as a resource in the maintenance of quality public education.

Publication Date: 1857 20 pages Bi-Monthly
ISSN: 1526-9342

Lily Eskelsen, President
Becky Pringle, Vice President

4455 Three R'S for Teachers: Research, Reports & Reviews
Master Teacher
Po Box 1207
Manhattan, KS 66502
785-539-0555
800-669-9633
Fax: 800-669-1132
http://www.masterteacher.com
The publication that synthesizes the most recent educational research, data and trends on specific topics for teachers.

Publication Date: 1969 Quarterly

Dr. Joanna Hubbs, President
Gregory Hubbs, Editor-in-Chief

4456 Tidbits
Assn. for Legal Support of Alternative Schools
PO Box 2823
Santa Fe, NM 87504-2823
505-471-6928

Information and legal advice to those involved in non-public educational facilities.

12 pages Quarterly
Ed Nagel

4457 Transitions Abroad: The Guide to Learning, Living, & Working Abroad
Transitions Abroad
P.O. Box 1369
Amherst, MA 1004
413-992-6486
Fax: 802-442-4827
E-mail: webeditor@TransitionsAbroad.com
http://www.transitionsabroad.com
This magazine contains articles and bibliographies on travel, study, teaching, internships and work abroad.

Publication Date: 1977 Bi-Monthly

4458 Unschoolers Network
Unschoolers Network
2 Smith Street
Farmingdale, NJ 07727
732-938-2473
E-mail: UnNet@unschooling.org
http://www.unschooling.org/UnNet
Information and support for families teaching their children at home.

Publication Date: 1977 14 pages Monthly

Nancy Plent

4459 VSBA Newsletter
Vermont School Boards Association
2 Prospect Street
Montpelier, VT 05602
802-223-3580
800-244-8722
E-mail: sdale@vtvsba.org
http://www.vtvsba.org
General information.

Publication Date: 1936 16 pages Monthly

Stephen Dale, Executive Director
Kerri Lamb, Operations Manager

4460 WCER Highlights
Wisconsin Center for Education Research
1025 W Johnson Street
Suite 785
Madison, WI 53706
608-263-4200
Fax: 608-263-6448
E-mail: uw-wcer@education.wisc.edu
http://www.wcer.wisc.edu
News about research conducted at the Wisconsin Center for Education Research.

Publication Date: 1964 8 pages Quarterly
ISSN: 1073-1882

Robert Mathieu, Director
Paul Baker, Specialist

4461 WestEd: Focus
WestEd
730 Harrison Street
San Francisco, CA 94107-1242
415-615-3144
877-493-7833
Fax: 415-512-2024
E-mail: info@WestEd .org
http://www.WestEd.org
Improving education through research, development and service.

Glen H. Harvey, CEO
Jacob Moore, Board Member

4462 Western Journal of Black Studies
Washington State University
Heritage House
Pullman, WA 99164-0001
509-335-3564
888-468-6978
Fax: 509-335-8338
E-mail: admissions@wsu.edu
http://www.wsu.edu
A journal which canvasses topical issues affecting Black studies and education.

Publication Date: 1890 Quarterly

Elson S. Floyd, Ph.D., President
Daniel J. Bernardo, Provost & EVP

4463 World Gifted
World Council for Gifted & Talented Children
Western Kentucky University
Gary A. Ransdell Hall, Room 2007, 1906 C
Bowling Green, KY 42101-1030
270-745-4123
Fax: 270-745-4124
E-mail: headquarters@world-gifted.org
http://www.world-gifted.org
Offers information and articles on gifted education for the professional.

4464 Young Audiences Newsletter
Young Audiences New York
One East 53rd Street
New York, NY 10128-1688
212-319-9269
Fax: 212-319-9272
E-mail: info@yany.org
http://www.yany.org
Organization news of performing arts education programs in schools and communities.

Publication Date: 1952 Annual

Kim Greenberg, Chair
Robert Riesenberg, President

Periodicals / *Administration*

4465 AACRAO Data Dispenser
American Association of Collegiate Registrars
1 Dupont Circle NW
Suite 520
Washington, DC 20036
202-293-9161
Fax: 202-872-8857
E-mail: myers.7@osu.edu
http://www.aacrao.org
Association newsletter for US and foreign postsecondary education institution professionals involved in admissions, records and registration.

12 pages 10x Year

Brad Myers, President
Nicole Rovig, VP, Information Technology

4466 AASA Bulletin
American Association of School Administrators
1615 Duke Street
Alexandria, VA 22314
703-528-0700
Fax: 703-841-1543
E-mail: info@aasa.org
http://www.aasa.org
The AASA Bulletin is a supplement to The School Administrator. It contains the Job Bulletin and information for school leaders about the many products, services and events available to them from AASA.

Publication Date: 1865

Ginger O'Neil, Editor
Kari Arfstrom, Project Director

467 ACCT Advisor
Association of Community College Trustees
1101 17th Street NW
Suite 300
Washington, DC 20036
202-775-4667
Fax: 202-223-1297
E-mail: acctinfo@acct.org
http://www.acct.org
Provides news of association events, federal regulations, activities, state activities, legal issues and other news of interest to community college governing board members.
Robin M. Smith, Chair
Bakari Lee, Vice Chair

468 AVA Update
Association for Volunteer Administration
PO Box 4584
Boulder, CO 80306-4584
303-447-0558
Information of value to administrators of volunteer services.
4 pages BiMonthly
Martha Martin

469 Accreditation Fact Sheet
NAPNSC Accrediting Commission for Higher Education
182 Thompson Road
Grand Junction, CO 81503-2246
970-243-5441
Fax: 970-242-4392
E-mail: director@napnsc.org
http://www.napnsc.org
Newsletter reporting on the origin, history, developments, procedures and changes of educational institution accreditation.
Annually
H. Earl Heusser, Author
H Earl Heusser, Executive Director

470 Administrative Information Report
Nat'l Association of Secondary School Principles
1904 Association Drive
Reston, VA 20191-1537
703-860-0200
800-253-7746
Fax: 703-620-6534
http://www.principals.org
Offers school statistics and administrative updates for secondary school principals and management officers.
Publication Date: 1916 4 pages Monthly
G.A. Buie, President
JoAnn D. Bartoletti, Executive Director

471 American School & University Magazine
Intertec Publishing
PO Box 12960
Overland Park, KS 66282-2960
913-967-1960
Fax: 913-967-1905
Directed at business and facilities administrators in the nation's public and private schools.
Monthly
Joe Agron, Editor

472 American School Board Journal
National School Boards Association
1680 Duke Street
Alexandria, VA 22314
703-838-6722
Fax: 703-683-7590
E-mail: info@nsba.org
http://www.nsba.org
Published primarily for school board members and school system superintendents serving public elementary and secondary schools in the United States and Canada.
Monthly
Anne M. Byrne, President
Heather Francis, Executive Asst.

4473 Board
Master Teacher
PO Box 1207
Manhattan, KS 66502
785-539-0555
800-669-9633
Fax: 800-669-1132
http://www.masterteacher.com
Designed to be a continuous form of communication to help board members know and understand the duties, responsibilities, and commitments of the office; view the superintendent of schools as the educational leader; improve administrator-board working relationships; better understand the purpose of education; and work at their responsibilities in a prudent, calm, and rational manner.
Publication Date: 1969 Monthly
Dr. Joanna Hubbs, President
Gregory Hubbs, Editor-in-Chief

4474 Building Leadership Bulletin
2990 Baker Drive
Springfield, IL 62703-2800
217-525-1383
Fax: 217-525-7264
http://www.ipa.vsta.net
Topical, timely issues.
8 pages 11x Year
Julie Weichert, Associate Director

4475 Business Education Forum
National Business Education Association
1914 Association Drive
Reston, VA 20191-1596
703-860-8300
Fax: 703-620-4483
http://www.nbea.org
A journal of distinctive articles dealing with current issues and trends, future directions and exemplary programs in business education at all instructional levels. Articles focus on international business, life-long learning, cultural diversity, critical thinking, economics, state-of-the-art technology and the latest research in the field.
Publication Date: 1939 200 pages Quarterly
Maurice S. Henderson, President
Janet M Treichel, Executive Director

4476 CASE Currents
1307 New York Avenue NW
Suite 1000
Washington, DC 20036-1226
202-328-2273
Fax: 202-387-4973
E-mail: MemberSupportCenter@case.org
http://www.case.org
Covers the world of fund raising, alumni administration, public relations, periodicals, publications and student recruitment in higher education.
Publication Date: 1974 10x Year
John Lippincott, President
Christina Antoniewicz, Educational Programs Manager

4477 CASE Newsletter
The Council for Exceptional Children
2900 Crystal Drive
Suite 1000
Arlington, VA 22202-3557
703-620-3660
888-232-7733
Fax: 703-264-9494
http://www.cec.sped.org
News about CASE activities, upcoming events, current trends and practices, state and national legislation, and other practical information relevant to the administration of special education programs.
Publication Date: 1922 5x Year
Robin D. Brewer, President
Alexander T. Graham, Executive Director/Secretary

4478 CASE in Point
The Council for Exceptional Children
2900 Crystal Drive
Suite 1000
Arlington, VA 22202-3557
703-620-3660
888-232-7733
Fax: 703-264-9494
http://www.cec.sped.org
A journal reporting on emerging promising practices, current research, contact points for expanded information, and field-based commentary relevant to the administration of special education programs.
Publication Date: 1922 BiAnnual
Robin D. Brewer, President
Alexander T. Graham, Executive Director/Secretary

4479 California Schools Magazine
California School Boards Association
3251 Beacon Boulevard
West Sacramento, CA 95691
916-371-4691
800-266-3382
Fax: 916-372-3369
http://www.csba.org
For school board members, superintendents and school business managers, responsible for the operation of California's public schools. Articles of interest to parents, teachers, community members and anyone else concerned with public education.
20 pages Quarterly
ISSN: 1081-8936
Jesus Holguin, President
Sherri Reusche, Vice President

4480 Clearing House: A Journal of Educational Research
Heldref Publications
325 Chestnut Street
Suite 800
Philadelphia, PA 19106
215-625-8900
800-365-9753
Fax: 202-296-5149
E-mail: customer.service@taylorandfrancis.com
http://www.heldref.org
Each issue offers a variety of articles for teachers and administrators of middle schools and junior and senior high schools. It includes experiments, trends and accomplishments in courses, teaching methods, administrative procedures and school programs.
4 pages BiMonthly
ISSN: 0009-8655
Deborah N Cohen, Promotions Manager
Judy Cusick, Managing Editor

4481 Connection
National Association of State Boards of Education
1680 Duke Street
Alexandria, VA 22314
703-838-6722
Fax: 703-683-7590

E-mail: info@nsba.org
http://www.nsba.org
Quarterly magazine for state board of education members.
10 pages
Anne M. Byrne, President
Heather Francis, Executive Asst.

4482 Developer
National Staff Development Council
504 South Locust St.
Oxford, OH 45056-0240
513-523-6029
Fax: 513-523-0638
http://learningforward.org
Devoted to staff development for educational personnel.
Publication Date: 1969 8 pages 10x Year
Deborah Jackson, President
Stephanie Hirsh, Executive Director

4483 ERS Spectrum
Educational Research Service
1001 N. Fairfax Street
Suite 500
Arlington, VA 22314-1587
703-243-2100
800-791-9308
Fax: 703-243-1985
E-mail: ers@ers.org
http://www.ers.org
A quarterly journal of school research and information. Publishes practical research and information for school decisions. Authors include practicing administrators and other educators in local school districts.
Publication Date: 1958 48 pages Quarterly
ISSN: 0740-7874
Lester Strong, Chair
Christopher Curran, Vice Chair

4484 Education Daily
LRP Publications
360 Hiatt Drive
Palm Beach Gardens, FL 33418
703-516-7002
800-341-7874
Fax: 561-622-2423
E-mail: custserve@lrp.com
http://www.lrp.com
News on national education policy. Offers daily reports of Education Department policies, initiatives and priorities— how they are developed and how they affect school programs.
Publication Date: 1977 6-8 pages Daily
Kenneth F. Kahn, President

4485 Educational Administration Quarterly
University of Wisconsin, Milwaukee
PO Box 413
Milwaukee, WI 53201-0413
414-229-1122
Fax: 414-229-5300
http://www4.uwm.edu
Deals with administrative issues and policy.
Quarterly
Mark Mone, Chancellor
Johannes Britz, Provost/ Vice Chancellor

4486 Electronic Learning
Scholastic
555 Broadway
New York, NY 10012-3919
212-343-6100
800-724-6527
Fax: 212-343-4801
Published for the administrative level, education professionals who are directly re-

sponsible for the implementing of electronic technology at the district, state and university levels.
8x Year
Lynn Diamond, Advertising Director
Therese Mageau, Editor

4487 Enrollment Management Report
LRP Publications
360 Hiatt Drive
Palm Beach Gardens, FL 33418
703-516-7002
800-341-7874
Fax: 561-622-2423
E-mail: custserve@lrp.com
http://www.lrp.com
Provides colleges and universities with solutions and strategies for recruitment, admissions, retention and financial aid. Reviews the latest trends, research studies and their findings and gives a profile on how other institutions are handling their enrollment management issues.
Publication Date: 1977 Monthly
ISSN: 1094-3757
Kenneth F. Kahn, President

4488 Galileo For Superintendents And District Level Administrators
Master Teacher
Po Box 1207
Manhattan, KS 66505
785-539-0555
800-669-9633
Fax: 800-669-1132
http://www.masterteacher.com
The monthly web and print service provides direction & strategies for superintendents and district level administrators.
Publication Date: 1969 Monthly Newsletter
Dr. Joanna Hubbs, President
Gregory Hubbs, Editor-in-Chief

4489 HR on Campus
LRP Publications
360 Hiatt Drive
Palm Beach Gardens, FL 33418
703-516-7002
800-341-7874
Fax: 561-622-2423
E-mail: custserve@lrp.com
http://www.lrp.com
This monthly newsletter provides coverage of the latest and most inovative programs higher education institutions use to handle their human resource challenges. Plus, you can recieve free e-mail updates on crucial news affecting your job with your paid subscription.
Publication Date: 1977 Monthly
ISSN: 1098-9293
Kenneth F. Kahn, President

4490 IPA Newsletter
2990 Baker Drive
Springfield, IL 62703-2800
217-525-1383
Fax: 217-525-7264
http://www.ipa.vsta.net
Provides current information on Illinois principals and the profession.
8 pages 11x Year
David Turner, Author
Julie Weichert, Associate Director

4491 Integrated Pathways
Association of Integrative Studies
Miami University
Oxford, OH 45056
513-529-2659
Fax: 513-529-5849

E-mail: rszostak@ualberta.ca
http://www.units.muohio.edu/aisorg
AIS news, including updates on AIS conferences, decisions of the AIS Board of Directors, and membership announcements. Published quarterly.
Publication Date: 1979
ISSN: 1081-647X
Rick Szostak, President
James Welch, Vice President, Development

4492 Journal of Curriculum & Supervision
Association for Supervision & Curriculum Develop.
1703 N Beauregard Street
Alexandria, VA 22311-1714
512-471-4611
800-933-ASCD
Fax: 512-471-8460
E-mail: oldavisjr@mail.uteyas.edu
http://www.ascd.org
Offers professional updates and news as well as membership/association information.
Publication Date: 1943 Quarterly Paperback
Nancy Gibson, President
Judy Seltz, Executive Director

4493 Journal of Education for Business
Heldref Publications
325 Chestnut Street
Suite 800
Philadelphia, PA 19106
215-625-8900
800-365-9753
Fax: 202-296-5149
E-mail: customer.service@taylorandfrancis.com
http://www.heldref.org
Offers information to instructors, supervisors, and administrators at the secondary, postsecondary and collegiate levels. The journal features basic and applied research-based articles in accounting, communications, economics, finance, information systems, management, marketing and other business disciplines.
BiMonthly

4494 Keystone Schoolmaster Newsletter
Pennsylvania Assn. of Secondary School Principals
PO Box 39
122 Valley Road
Summerdale, PA 17093
717-732-4999
Fax: 717-732-4890
http://www.paessp.org
Reports achievements, honors, problems and innovations by officers and established authorities.
Publication Date: 1960 4 pages Monthly
Jacqueline Clarke Havrilla, President
Paul M. Healey, PhD, Executive Director

4495 LSBA Quarter Notes
Louisiana School Boards Association
7912 Summa Avenue
Baton Rouge, LA 70809
225-769-3191
877-664-5722
Fax: 225-769-6108
http://www.lsba.com
News articles relative to the association, feature stories on research.
Publication Date: 1938 6 pages BiMonthly
John Smith, President
Russ Wise, Vice President

4496 Legal Notes for Education
Progressive Business Publications
370 Technology Drive
Malvern, PA 19355
610-695-8600
800-220-5000
Fax: 610-647-8089

E-mail: customer_service@pbp.com
http://www.pbp.com
Reports the latest school law cases and
late-breaking legislation along with the most
recent law review articles affecting education. Federal and state appellate court decisions are summarized and the full legal
citation is supplied for each case.

Publication Date: 1959 Monthly

Ed Satell, Founder
Liz Webb, Human Resources

4497 Maintaining Safe Schools
LRP Publications
360 Hiatt Drive
Palm Beach Gardens, FL 33418
703-516-7002
800-341-7874
Fax: 561-622-2423
E-mail: custserv@lrp.com
http://www.lrp.com
Focuses on the legal and practical issues involved in preventing and responding to vio-
lent acts by students in schools, and
highlights successful violence prevention
programs in school districts across the country. Offers strategies for mediation, discipline and crisis managment.

Publication Date: 1977 Monthly
ISSN: 1082-4774

Kenneth F. Kahn, President

4498 Managing School Business
LRP Publications
360 Hiatt Drive
Palm Beach Gardens, FL 33418
703-516-7002
800-341-7874
Fax: 561-622-2423
E-mail: custserve@lrp.com
http://www.lrp.com
Newsletter provides school business managers with tips on how to solve the problems
they face in managing finance, operations,
personnel, and their own career.

Publication Date: 1977 Biweekly
ISSN: 1092-2229

Angela Childers, Author
Kenneth F. Kahn, President

4499 Memo to the President
American Assn. of State Colleges &
Universities
1307 New York Avenue NW
5th Floor
Washington, DC 20005
202-293-7070
Fax: 202-296-5819
http://www.aascu.org
Monitors public policies at national, state
and campus level on higher education issues.
Reports on activities of the Association and
member institutions.

20 pages Monthly
November

J. Keith Motley, Chair
Muriel A. Howard, President

4500 NASPA Forum
National Assn. of Student Personnel
Administrators
111 K Street NE
10th Floor
Washington, DC 20002
202-265-7500
Fax: 202-797-1157
E-mail: office@naspa.org
http://www.naspa.org

Offers information for personnel administrators and strategies, updates and tips on the education system.

Publication Date: 1918 Monthly

Patricia Whitely, Chair
Kevin Kruger, President

4501 National Faculty Forum
National Faculty of Humanities, Arts &
Sciences
1676 Clifton Road NE
Atlanta, GA 30329-4050
404-727-5788
Offers administrative news and updates for
persons in higher education.

TriQuarterly

4502 Network
National School Public Relations
Association
15948 Derwood Road
Rockville, MD 20855
301-519-0496
Fax: 301-519-0494
E-mail: nspra@nspra.org
http://www.nspra.org
Monthly newsletter for and about our members. Some articles about school public relations, issues that affect school public
relations people.

Jim Cummings, APR, President
Stephen Nichols, VP for Diversity
Engagement

4503 OASCD Journal
Oklahoma Curriculum Development
3705 S. 98th East Avenue
Tulsa, OK 74146
918-627-4403
Fax: 918-627-4433
A refereed journal which prints contributions
on curriculum theory and practices, leadership in education, staff development and supervision. The Editorial Board welcomes
photographs, letters to the editor, program
descriptions, interviews, research reports,
theoretical pieces, reviews of books and
non-print media, poetry, humor, cartoons,
satire and children's art and writing, as well
as expository articles.

Annual

Blaine Smith, Executive Secretary

4504 On Board
New York State School Boards Association
24 Century Hill Drive
Suite 200
Latham, NY 12110-2125
518-783-0200
800-342-3360
Fax: 518-783-0211
E-mail: info@nyssba.org
http://www.nyssba.org
Contains general educational news, state and
federal legislative activity, legal and employee relations issues, commentary, issues
in education, and successful education programs around the state.

Publication Date: 1896 21x Year

Lynne L. Lenhardt, President
Susan Bergtraum, 1st VP & Area 11
Director

4505 Perspectives for Policymakers
New Jersey School Boards Association
413 W State Street
#909
Trenton, NJ 08618-5617
609-695-7600
888-88N-SBA

E-mail: info@njsba.org
http://www.njsba.org
Each issue focuses on a specific topic in education providing background, activities and
resources.

8 pages SemiAnnually

Donald Webster, Jr., President
Daniel T. Sinclair, VP, County Activities

4506 Planning & Changing
Illinois State University
College of Education
Campus Box 5300
Normal, IL 61790-5300
309-438-2399
Fax: 309-438-8683
http://http://coe.ilstu.edu/eafdept/pandc.htm

An educational leadership and policy journal. This journal attempts to disseminate
timely and useful reports of practice and theory with particular emphasis on change, and
planning in K-12 educational settings and
higher education settings. Paperback.

Publication Date: 1857 64 pages Quarterly
ISSN: 0032-0684

Perry Schoon, Chair, College Faculty
Alan Bates, College Faculty

4507 Principal
Nat'l Association of Elementary School
Principals
1615 Duke Street
Alexandria, VA 22314-3406
703-684-3345
Fax: 800-396-2377
A professional magazine edited for elemen-
tary and middle school principals and others
interested in education.

5x Year

Leon E Greene, Editor
Louanne M Wheeler, Production Manager

4508 Principal Communicator
National School Public Relations
Association
15948 Derwood Road
Rockville, MD 20855
301-519-0496
Fax: 301-519-0494
E-mail: nspra@nspra.org
http://www.napra.org
Tips for building public relations people.

6 pages Monthly

Andy Grunig, Manager of Communications

4509 Private Education Law Report
Progressive Business Publications
370 Technology Drive
Malvern, PA 19355
610-695-8600
800-220-5000
Fax: 610-647-8089
E-mail: customer_service@pbp.com
http://www.pbp.com
Reports the latest school law cases and
late-breaking legislation along with the most
recent law review articles affecting private
education. Federal and state appellate court
decisions are summarized and the full legal
citation is supplied for each case.

Publication Date: 1959 Monthly

Ed Satell, Founder
Liz Webb, Human Resources

4510 Public Personnel Management
International Personnel Management
Association
1617 Duke Street
Alexandria, VA 22314-3406

703-549-7100
Fax: 703-684-0948
Caters to those professionals in human resource management.
Quarterly
Sarah Al Shiffert, Editor

4511 Rural Educator-Journal for Rural and Small Schools
National Rural Education Association
Colorado State University
Fort Collins, CO 80523
970-491-7022
Fax: 970-491-1317
E-mail: jnewlin@lamar.colostate.edu
http://www.colostate.edu
Official journal of the NREA. A nationally recognized publication that features timely and informative articles written by leading rural educators from all levels of education. All NREA members are encouraged to submit research articles and items of general information for publication.
Publication Date: 1870 40 pages Quarterly Magazine
ISSN: 0273-446X
Joseph T Newlin, Editor

4512 School Administrator
American Association of School Administrators
801 N Quincy Street
Suite 700
Arlington, VA 22203-1730
703-528-0700
Fax: 703-841-1543
E-mail: info@aasa.org
http://www.aasa.org
Ensures the highest quality education systems for all learners through the support and development of leadership on the building, district and state levels.
52 pages Monthly
Paul D Houston, Executive Director

4513 School Business Affairs
Association of School Business Officials Int'l
11401 N Shore Drive
Reston, VA 20190-4232
703-478-0405
Fax: 703-478-0205
For school business administrators responsible for the administration and purchase of products and services for the schools.
Monthly
Peg D Kirkpatrick, Editor/Publisher
Robert Gluck, Managing Editor

4514 School Law Briefings
LRP Publications
360 Hiatt Drive
Palm Beach Gardens, FL 33418
703-516-7002
800-341-7874
Fax: 561-622-2423
E-mail: custserve@lrp.com
http://www.lrp.com
Gives you summaries of general education, special education, and early childhood court cases, as well as administrative hearings.
Publication Date: 1977 Monthly
ISSN: 1094-3749
Kenneth F. Kahn, President

4515 School Law News
LRP Publications
360 Hiatt Drive
Palm Beach Gardens, FL 33418

703-516-7002
800-341-7874
Fax: 561-622-2423
E-mail: custserve@lrp.com
http://www.lrp.com
Advises administrators to avoid legal pitfalls by monitoring education-related court action across the nation. With School Law News, administrators receive the latest information on issues like sexual harassment liability, special education, religion in the schools, affirmative action, youth violence, student-faculty rights, school finance, desegregation and much more.
Publication Date: 1977 8-10 pages Monthly
Kenneth F. Kahn, President

4516 School Planning & Management
Peter Li Education Group
2621 Dryden Road
Suite 300
Dayton, OH 45439
937-293-1415
800-523-4625
Fax: 800-370-4450
http://www.peterli.com
For the business needs of school administrators featuring issues, ideas and technology at work in public, private and independent schools.
Monthly
ISSN: 1086-4628
Peter J Li, Publisher
Deborah Moore, Editor

4517 Section 504 Compliance Advisor
LRP Publications
360 Hiatt Drive
Palm Beach Gardens, FL 33418
703-516-7002
800-341-7874
Fax: 561-622-2423
E-mail: custserve@lrp.com
http://www.lrp.com
Newsletter examines the requirements of Section 504 of the Rehabilitation Act and analyzes their impact on disciplining students. Provides educators and administrators with detailed tips and advice to help them solve the discipline problems they face everyday and keep their policies and programs in compliance.
Publication Date: 1977 Monthly
ISSN: 1094-3730
Kenneth F. Kahn, President

4518 Special Education Law Monthly
LRP Publications
360 Hiatt Drive
Palm Beach Gardens, FL 33418
703-516-7002
800-341-7874
Fax: 561-622-2423
E-mail: custserve@lrp.com
http://www.lrp.com
Covers court decisions and administrative rulings affecting the education of students with disabilities.
Publication Date: 1977 Monthly
ISSN: 1094-3773
Kenneth F. Kahn, President

4519 Special Education Law Report
Progressive Business Publications
370 Technology Drive
Malvern, PA 19355
610-695-8600
800-220-5000
Fax: 610-647-8089
E-mail: customer_service@pbp.com
http://www.pbp.com

Reports the latest school law cases and late-breaking legislation along with the most recent law review articles affecting special education. Federal and state appellate court decisions are summarized and the full legal citation is supplied for each case.
Publication Date: 1959 Monthly
Ed Satell, Founder
Liz Webb, Human Resources

4520 Special Education Report
LRP Publications
360 Hiatt Drive
Palm Beach Gardens, FL 33418
703-516-7002
800-341-7874
Fax: 561-622-2423
E-mail: custserve@lrp.com
http://www.lrp.com
The special education administrator's direct pipeline to federal legislation, regulation and funding of programs for children and youths with disabilities.
Publication Date: 1977 6-8 pages Monthly
Kenneth F. Kahn, President

4521 Student Affairs Today
LRP Publications
360 Hiatt Drive
Palm Beach Gardens, FL 33418
703-516-7002
800-341-7874
Fax: 561-622-2423
E-mail: custserve@lrp.com
http://www.lrp.com
Newsletter provides strategies and tips for handling higher education institutions' student affairs challenges and problems involving: sexual harassment, binge drinking, fraternity and sorority activities, student housing and more. Gives profiles of other colleges programs.
Publication Date: 1977 Monthly
ISSN: 1098-5166
Kenneth F. Kahn, President

4522 Superintendents Only Notebook
Master Teacher
Leadership Lane
PO Box 1207
Manhattan, KS 66502
800-669-9633
Fax: 800-669-1132
http://www.masterteacher.com
Offers superintendents hundreds of solid ideas to help their jobs run more smoothly. Written by practicing superintendents and business executives, this publication saves hundreds of hours of anguish over the course of the year.
Publication Date: 1969 Monthly
Dr. Joanna Hubbs, President
Gregory Hubbs, Editor-in-Chief

4523 THE Journal Technology Horizons in Education
T.H.E Journal
1105 Media
9201 Oakdale Ave., Suite 101

Chatsworth, CA 91311

818-734-1520
Fax: 818-734-1522
E-mail: editorial@thejournal.com
http://www.thejournal.com

A forum for administrators and managers in school districts to share their experiences in the use of technology-based educational aids.

Publication Date: 1972

Rajeev Kapur, Chief Executive Officer
Henry Allain, Chief Operating Officer

24 Thrust for Educational Leadership

Association of California School Administrators
1029 J Street
Suite 500
Sacramento, CA 95814
916-444-3216
800-608-2272
Fax: 916-444-3739
E-mail: rdelling@lausd.net
http://www.acsa.org
Designed for school administrators who must stay abreast of educational developments, management and personnel practices, social attitudes and issues that impact schools.

Publication Date: 1971 7x Year

Randall V. Delling, President
Ralph Gomez Porras, Vice President

25 Title I Handbook

Thompson Publishing Group, Inc.
P.O. Box 41868
Austin, TX 78704
800-677-3789
Fax: 800-999-5661
E-mail: service@thompson.com
http://www.titleionline.com
Two-volume looseleaf provides complete, up-to-date coverage of Title I, the largest federal program of aid for elementary and secondary education. The book contains all the laws, regulations and guidance needed to sucessfully operate the grant program, and insightful articles on key Title I topics, ongoing budget coverage, and special reports on issues like Title I testing, schoolwide programs, and audits. Also included is a compilation of official Title I policy letters, found nowhere else.

Publication Date: 1972 1,500 pages Quarterly

Cheryl L. Sattler, Author
Jeannette Burke, Director, Product Marketing
Mark Reishus, Energy Regulation

26 Title I Monitor

Thompson Publishing Group, Inc.
P.O. Box 41868
Austin, TX 78704
202-872-4000
800-677-3789
Fax: 800-999-5661
E-mail: service@thompson.com
http://www.titleionline.com
This newsletter provides continuing coverage of Title I, the largest federal program of aid for elementary and secondary education. Title I is at the heart of the debate over education reform, and the Monitor ensures that educators have the most up-to-date information about developments in this ever-changing program. Breaking news about the Title I budget, new legislation and regulations, court cases and other issues.

Publication Date: 1972 Monthly
ISSN: 1086-2455

Cheryl L Sattler, Author
Jeannette Burke, Director, Product Marketing
Mark Reishus, Energy Regulation

4527 Training Magazine

Lakewood Publications
P.O. Box 247
27020 Noble Road
Excelsior, MN 55331
847-559-7596
800-328-4329
Fax: 847-559-7596
E-mail: ntrn@omeda.com
http://www.trainingmag.com
Focuses on corporate training and employee development, as well as management and human performance issues.

Monthly

Mike Murrell, President/ Publisher
Bryan Powell, VP - Finance/Operations

4528 Updating School Board Policies

National School Boards Association
1680 Duke Street
Alexandria, VA 22314
703-838-6722
Fax: 703-683-7590
E-mail: info@nsba.org
http://www.nsba.org
Offers information and statistics for school boards and administrative offices across the country.

16 pages BiMonthly
ISSN: 1081-8286

Anne M. Byrne, President
Heather Francis, Executive Assistant

Periodicals / *Early Childhood Education*

4529 Child Development

Arizona State University
University Drive and Mill Avenue
Tempe, AZ 85287
480-965-9011
Fax: 480-965-8544
http://www.asu.edu
Offers professionals working with children news on childhood education, books, reviews, questions and answers and professional articles of interest.

BiMonthly

Michael M. Crow, President
Morgan R. Olsen, VP, Business & Finance

4530 Child Study Journal

Buffalo State College
1300 Elmwood Avenue
Buffalo, NY 14222
716-878-4000
http://suny.buffalostate.edu
Articles of interest related to childhood education.

Publication Date: 1871 Quarterly

Katherine S. Conway-Turner, President

4531 Children Today

ACF Office of Public Affairs
370 L'Enfant Promenade, S.W.
4th Floor
Washington, DC 20447
202-401-9215
888-747-1861
Fax: 202-205-9688
http://www.acf.hhs.gov/office-of-public-aff airs
An interdisciplinary magazine published by the Administration for Children and Families (ACF). The content is a mix of theory and practice, research and features, news and opinions for its audience.

Quarterly

Jeff Hild, Chief of Staff
Mark Greenberg, Assistant Secretary

4532 Children and Families

National Head Start Association
1651 Prince Street
Alexandria, VA 22314
703-739-0875
866-677-8724
Fax: 703-739-0878
http://www.nhsa.org
Designed to support the Head Start programs, directors, staff, parents and volunteers.

Publication Date: 1973 Quarterly
ISSN: 1091-7578

Vanessa Rich, Vice Chairman
Alvin Jones, Vice Chairman

4533 Division for Children with Communication Disorders Newsletter

The Council for Exceptional Children
2900 Crystal Drive
Suite 1000
Arlington, VA 22202-3557
703-620-3660
888-232-7733
Fax: 703-264-1637
http://www.cec.sped.org
Information concerning education and welfare of children with communication disorders.

Publication Date: 1922 12 pages SemiAnnually

Robin D. Brewer, President
Alexander T. Graham, Executive Dir./ Secretary

4534 Early Childhood Education Journal

Kluwer Academic/Human Sciences Press
233 Spring Street
New York, NY 10013
212-620-8000
Fax: 212-463-0742
http://www.wkpa.nl
Provides professional guidance on instructional methods and materials, child development trends, funding and administrative issues and the politics of day care.

Quarterly
ISSN: 1082-3301

Carol Bischoff, Publisher
Mary Renck Jalongo, Editor

4535 Early Childhood Report

LRP Publications
360 Hiatt Drive
Palm Beach Gardens, FL 33418
703-516-7002
800-341-7874
Fax: 561-622-2423
E-mail: custserve@lrp.com
http://www.lrp.com
Educational newsletter for parents and professionals involved at the local state and federal levels responsible for the design and implementation of early childhood programs.

Publication Date: 1977 Monthly
ISSN: 1058-6482

Kenneth F. Kahn, President

4536 Early Childhood Research Quarterly

Department of Individuals & Family Syudies
111 Alison Annex
University of Delaware
Newark, DE 19716

302-831-6500
Fax: 302-831-8776
E-mail: hdfs-dept@udel.edu
http://www.hdfs.udel.edu
Addresses various topics in the development and education of young children.

Quarterly
Dr. Marion Hyson, Editor

4537 Early Childhood Today
Scholastic
555 Broadway
New York, NY 10012
212-343-6100
800-724-6527
Fax: 212-343-4801
E-mail: ect@scholastic.com
http://www.scholastic.com
The magazine for all early childhood professionals working with infants to six-year-olds. Each issue provides child development information resources, staff development information and parent communication information.

Publication Date: 1920 8x Year
ISSN: 1070-1214

Richard Robinson, Chair/ President/ CEO
Maureen O'Connell, EVP/ CFO/ CAO

4538 Highlights for Children
Highlights for Children
PO Box 269
1800 Watermark Drive
Columbus, OH 43216-0269
888-372-6433
http://www.highlights.com/working-for-h
ighlights
Magazine featuring Fun with a Purpose, to all children preschool to preteen. Features stories, hidden pictures, reading and thinking exercises, crafts, puzzles, and more.

Publication Date: 1946

Kent S. Johnson, CEO
Christine French Cully, Editor in Chief

4539 Journal of Early Intervention
The Council for Exceptional Children
2900 Crystal Drive
Suite 1000
Arlington, VA 22202-3557
703-620-3660
888-232-7733
Fax: 703-264-1637
http://www.cec.sped.org

Publication Date: 1922 Quarterly
ISSN: 0885-3460

Robin D. Brewer, President
Alexander T. Graham, Executive Dir./
Secretary

4540 Journal of Research in Childhood Education
Association for Childhood Education International
1101 16th St. N.W.
Suite 300
Washington, DC 20036
202-372-9986
800-423-3563
Fax: 202-372-9989
http://acei.org
Current research in education and related fields. It is intended to advance knowledge and theory of the education of children, from infancy through early adolescence. The journal seeks to stimulate the exchange of research ideas through publication of: reports of empirical research; theroretical articles; ethnographic and case studies; cross-cultural studies and studies addressing international concerns; partici-

pant observation studies and, studies, deriving data collected.

142 pages BiAnnual
ISSN: 0256-8543

Carrie Whaley, President
Diane Whitehead, Executive Director

4541 NHSA Journal
National Head Start Association
1651 Prince Street
Alexandria, VA 22314
703-739-0875
866-677-8724
Fax: 703-739-0878
http://www.nhsa.org
Edited for Head Start communities serving children 3 to 5 years of age throughout the country. The journal is an invaluable resource containing current research, innovative programming ideas, details on the Head Start conferences and training events.

Publication Date: 1973 Quarterly

Vanessa Rich, Chairman
Alvin Jones, Vice Chairman

4542 National Guild of Community Schools of the Arts
National Guild of Community Schools of the Arts
520 8th Avenue
Suite 302
New York, NY 10018
212-268-3337
Fax: 212-268-3995
E-mail: info@natguild.org
http://www.nationalguild.org
National association of community based arts education institutions employment opportunities, guildnotes newsletter, and publications catalog. See www.nationalguild.org.

Monthly

Terry Hueneke, Chairman
Carol Ross, Vice Chairman

4543 Parents Make the Difference!: School Readiness Edition
The Parent Institute
PO Box 7474
Fairfax Station, VA 22039-7474
703-323-9170
800-756-5525
Fax: 703-323-9173
E-mail: support@parent-institute.com
http://www.parent-institute.com
Newsletter focusing on parent involvement in education. Focuses on parents of children ages infant to five.

Publication Date: 1989 Monthly
ISSN: 1089-3075

John H. Wherry, Ed.D., President

4544 Pre-K Today
Scholastic
555 Broadway
New York, NY 10012
212-343-6100
800-724-6527
Fax: 212-343-4801
http://www.scholastic.com
Edited to serve the needs of early childhood professionals, owners, directors, teachers and administrators in preschools and kindergarten.

Publication Date: 1920 8x Year

Richard Robinson, Chair/ President/ CEO
Maureen O'Connell, EVP/ CFO/ CAO

4545 Report on Preschool Programs
Business Publishers
2222 Sedwick Drive
Durham, NC 27713
301-587-6300
800-223-8720
Fax: 800-508-2592
E-mail: custserv@bpinews.com
http://www.bpinews.com
Reports on information about Head Start regulations, federal funding policies, state trends in Pre-K and research news. Also covers information on grant and contract opportunities.

Publication Date: 1963 8 pages BiWeekly

Eric Easton, Publisher
Chuck Devarics, Editor

4546 Topics in Early Childhood Special Education
Pro-Ed
8700 Shoal Creek Boulevard
Austin, TX 78757-6897
512-451-3246
800-897-3202
Fax: 512-451-8542
E-mail: general@proedinc.com
http://www.proedinc.com
Provides program developers, advocates, researchers, higher education faculty and other leaders with the most current, relevant research on all aspects of early childhood education for children with special needs.

Judith J Carta, PhD, Editor

4547 Totline Newsletter
Frank Schaffer Publications
23740 Hawthorne Boulevard
Torrance, CA 90505
310-378-1137
800-421-5533
Fax: 800-837-7260
E-mail: fspcustsrv@aol.com
http://www.frankschaffer.com
Creative activities for working with toddlers and preschool children.

32 pages BiMonthly

4548 Vision
SERVE
5900 Summit Avenue, #201
Browns Summit, NC 27214
336-315-7400
800-755-3277
Fax: 336-315-7457
E-mail: cahearn@serve.org
http://www.serve.org
Publication of the Regional Educational Laboratories, an educational research and development organization supported by contracts with the US Education Department, National Institute for Education Sciences. Specialty area: Extended Learning Opportunity including Before and After School programs and Early Childhood.

Quarterly

Charles Ahearn, Author
Wendy McColskey, Program Director
Elliot Wolf, Operations Director

Periodicals / *Elementary Education*

4549 Children's Literature in Education
Kluwer Academic/Human Sciences Press
233 Spring Street
New York, NY 10013
212-620-8000
Fax: 212-463-0742
http://www.wkpa.nl

Source for stimulating articles and interviews on noted children's authors, incisive critiques of classic and contemporary writing for young readers, and original articles describing successful classroom reading projects. Offers timely reviews on a variety of reading-related topics for teachers and teachers-in-training, librarians, writers and interested parents.

Quarterly
ISSN: 0045-6713

Margaret Mackey & Geoff Fox, Editors, Author
Carol Bischoff, Publisher

4550 Creative Classroom
Creative Classroom Publishing
149 5th Avenue
12th Floor
New York, NY 10010
212-353-3639
Fax: 212-353-8030
http://www.creativeclassroom.com
A magazine for teachers of K-8, containing innovative ideas, activities, classroom management tips and information on contemporary social problems facing teachers and students.

BiMonthly

Susan Eveno, Editorial Director
Laura Axler, Associate Editor

4551 Dragonfly
National Science Teachers Association
1840 Wilson Boulevard
Arlington, VA 22201
703-243-7100
800-782-6782
Fax: 703-243-7177
E-mail: boardofdirectors@nsta.org
http://www.nsta.org
A fun-filled interdisciplinary magazine for children grades 3-6. A teacher's companion is also available. The teacher's companion is designed to help you integrate Dragonfly into your curriculum.

Publication Date: 1944

Juliana Texley, President
Dr. David L. Evans, Executive Director

4552 Educate@Eight
US Department of Education, Region VIII
1244 Speer Boulevard
Suite 310
Denver, CO 80204-3582
303-844-3544
Fax: 303-844-2524
http://www.ed.gov

8 pages

Helen Littlejohn, Author

4553 Elementary School Journal
University of Missouri
1507 E Broadway
Hillcrest Hall
Columbia, MO 65211
573-882-2121
http://missouri.edu
Academic journal publishing primarily original studies but also reviews of research and conceptual analyses for researchers and practitioners interested in elementary schooling. Emphasizes papers dealing with educational theory and research and their implications.

Publication Date: 1839 5x Year

R. Bowen lLoftin, Chancellor
Kenneth D. Dean, Interim Provost

4554 Elementary Teacher's Ideas and Materials Workshop
Princeton Educational Publishers
117 Cuttermill Road
NY, NY 11021-3101
516-466-9300
Articles on teaching for elementary schools.

16 pages 10x Year

Barry Pavelec

4555 Helping Your Child Succeed in Elementary School
Rowman & Littlfield Education
4501 Forbes Boulevard
Suite 200
NY, MD 20706
301-459-3366
Fax: 301-429-5748
E-mail: customercare@rowman.com
http://www.rowmaneducation.com
Provides parents with useful information about the importance of parental involvement, concrete ways to work with children and schools to promote success, and a list of resources for further reading.

Tom Koerner, PhD, VP & Publisher
Dean Roxanis, Sr. Marketing Manager

4556 Highlights for Children
Highlights for Children
PO Box 269
1800 Watermark Drive
Columbus, OH 43216-0269
888-372-6433
Fax: 614-876-8564
http://www.highlights.com/working-for-highlights
Magazine featuring Fun with a Purpose, to all children preschool to preteen. Features stories, hidden pictures, reading and thinking exercises, crafts, puzzles, and more.

Publication Date: 1946

Kent S. Johnson, CEO
Christine French Cully, Editor in Chief

4557 Independent School
National Association of Independent Schools
1129 20th Street, NW
Suite 800
Washington, DC 20036-3425
202-973-9700
Fax: 888-316-3862
http://www.nais.org
Contains information and opinion about secondary and elementary education in general and independent education in particular.

TriAnnually

Thomas W Leonhardt, Editor
Kurt R Murphy, Advertising/Editor

4558 Instructor
Scholastic
555 Broadway
New York, NY 10012
212-343-6100
800-724-6527
Fax: 212-343-4801
http://www.scholastic.com
Edited for teachers, curriculum coordinators, principals and supervisors of primary grades through junior high school.

Publication Date: 1920 Monthly

Richard Robinson, Chair/ President/ CEO
Maureen O'Connell, EVP/ CFO/ CAO

4559 Journal of Research in Childhood Education
Association for Childhood Education International
1101 16th St., N.W.
Suite 300
Washington, DC 20036
202-372-9986
800-423-3563
Fax: 202-372-9989
E-mail: cwhaley@uu.edu
http://acei.org
Current research in education and related fields. It is intended to advance knowledge and theory of the education of children, from infancy through early adolescence. The journal seeks to stimulate the exchange of research ideas through publication of: reports of empirical research; theroretical articles; ethnographic and case studies; cross-cultural studies and studies addressing international concerns; participant observation studies and, studies, deriving data collected.

Publication Date: 1892 142 pages BiAnnual
ISSN: 0256-8543

Carrie Whaley, President
Diane Whitehead, Executive Director

4560 Montessori LIFE
American Montessori Society
281 Park Avenue S
6th Floor
New York, NY 10010
212-358-1250
Fax: 212-358-1256
E-mail: kate@amshq.org
http://www.amshq.org
Magazine for parents and educators.

Publication Date: 1960 Quarterly
ISSN: 1054-0040

Joy Turner, Author
Joyce S. Pickering, President
Dane L. Peters, Vice President

4561 Parents Make the Difference!
The Parent Institute
PO Box 7474
Fairfax Station, VA 22039-7474
703-323-9170
800-756-5525
Fax: 703-323-9173
E-mail: support@parent-institute.com
http://www.parent-institute.com
Newsletter focusing on parent involvement in children's education. Focuses on parents of preschool-aged children.

Publication Date: 1989 9x Year

John H. Wherry, Ed.D., President

4562 Teaching K-8 Magazine
Early Years
40 Richards Avenue
Norwalk, CT 06854-2319
203-855-2650
800-249-9363
Fax: 203-855-2656
E-mail: patricia@teachingk-8.com
http://www.teachingk-8.com
Written for teachers in the elementary grades, kindergarten through eighth, offering classroom tested ideas and methods.

Monthly Magazine
ISSN: 0891-4508
November-December

Allen A Raymond, Publisher
Patricia Broderick, Editorial Director

Periodicals / *Employment*

4563 AACE Careers Update
American Association for Career
Education
2900 Amby Place
Hermosa Beach, CA 90254
310-376-7378
Fax: 310-376-2926
Connects careers, education and work
through career education for all ages. Career awareness, exploration, decision making, and preparation. Employability,
transitions, continuing education, paid and
nonpaid work, occupations, career tips, resources, partnerships, conferences and
workshops. Awards and recognition,
trends and futures. A newsletter is
published.

8+ pages Quarterly/Newsletter
ISBN: 1074-9551

Dr.Pat Nellor Wickwire, Author
Dr. Pat Nellor Wickwire, Editor

**4564 Career Development for
Exceptional Individuals**
The Council for Exceptional Children
2900 Crystal Drive
Suite 1000
Arlington, VA 22202-3557
703-620-3660
888-232-7733
Fax: 703-264-9494
http://www.cec.sped.org
Contains articles dealing with the latest research activities, model programs, and issues in career development and transition
planning for individuals with disabilities
and/or who are gifted.

Publication Date: 1922 2x Year

Robin D. Brewer, President
Alexander T. Graham, Executive Dir./
Secretary

4565 Career Education News
Diversified Learning
72300 Vallat Road
Rancho Mirage, CA 92270-3906
619-346-3336
Reports on programs, materials and training for career educators.

4 pages BiWeekly

Webster Wilson Jr, Publisher
Webster Wilson, Editor

4566 Careers Bridge Newsletter
St. Louis Public Schools
801 N. 11th Street
Saint Louis, MO 63101
314-231-3720
http://www.slps.org
Available to educators and business/community persons on collaborative activities
and promotion of career and self-awareness education in preschool to grade 12.

BiMonthly

Dr. Kelvin Adams, Superintendent
Roger CayCe, Interim Chief of Staff

4567 Chronicle of Higher Education
Subscription Department
163 E. Center Street
Marion, OH 43302
740-387-0400
800-347-6969
http://www.marionstar.com

Newspaper published weekly advertising
many teaching opportunities overseas.
Weekly

Adam Trabitz, Sales Director
Kelly Gearhart, Sales Manager

**4568 Current Openings in Education in
the USA**
Education Information Services
100 Walnut Street
Newton, MA 02460
617-559-6000
http://www.newton.k12.ma.us
This publication is a booklet listing about
140 institutions or school systems, each
with one to a dozen or more openings for
teachers, librarians, counselors and other
personnel.

15 pages Every 6 Weeks

F Viaux, Coordinating Education

4569 Education Jobs
National Education Service Center
PO Box 1279
Riverton, WY 82501-1279
307-856-0170
Offers information on employment in the
education field.

Weekly

Lucretia Ficht, Contact

4570 Employment Opportunities
National Guild of Community Schools of
the Arts
520 8th Avenue
Suite 302
New York, NY 10018
212-268-3337
Fax: 212-268-3995
E-mail: info@natguild.org
http://www.nationalguild.org

Monthly

Terry Hueneke, Chairman
Carol Ross, Vice Chairman

**4571 Faculty, Staff & Administrative
Openings in US Schools & Colleges**
Educational Information Services
PO Box 662
Newton Lower Falls, MA 02162
617-964-4555
A listing of available positions in the educational system in the United States.

Monthly

4572 International Educator
The International Educator
PO Box 513
Cummaquid, MA 02637
508-790-1990
877-375-6668
Fax: 508-790-1922
E-mail: tie@tieonline.com
http://www.tieonline.com/contact_us.cfm
A newspaper listing over 100 teaching positions overseas.

Publication Date: 1986 Quarterly

Daniel Lincoln, Editor
Nikki Gundry, Ad Sales Rep.

4573 Jobs Clearinghouse
Association for Experiential Education
1435 Yarmouth Ave
#104
Boulder, CO 80304
303-440-8844
Fax: 303-440-9581
E-mail: jch@aee.org
http://www.aee.org

A newsletter that is one of the most comprehensive and widely-used monthly listings of
full-time, part-time, and seasonal employment
and internship opportunities in the experiential/adventure education field for both employers
and job seekers.

Monthly

Maurie Lung, President
Robert Smariga, CEO

4574 Journal of Cooperative Education
University of Waterloo
200 University Avenue West
Waterloo, ON N2L 3
519-888-4567
519-885-1211
http://uwaterloo.ca
Dedicated to the publication of thoughtful and
timely articles concerning work-integrated education. It invites manuscripts which are essays
that analyze issues, reports of research, descriptions of innovative practices.

Publication Date: 1957 3x Year

Feridun Hamdullahpur, President/
Vice-Chancellor
Ian Orchard, VP Academic & Provost

**4575 Journal of Vocational Education
Research**
Colorado State University
202 Education
Fort Collins, CO 80523
970-491-6835
Fax: 970-491-1317
E-mail: questions@online.colostate.edu
http://www.colostate.edu
Publishes refereed articles dealing with research
and research-related topics in vocational education. Manuscripts based on original investigations, comprehensive reviews of literature,
research methodology and theoretical constructs
in vocational education are encouraged.

Quarterly

Brian Cobb, Editor

4576 New Jersey Education Law Report
Whitaker Newsletters
313 S Avenue
#340
Fanwood, NJ 07023-1364
908-889-6336
800-359-6049
Fax: 908-889-6339
Court decisions and rulings on employment in
New Jersey schools.

8 pages
ISSN: 0279-8557

Joel Whitaker, Publisher
Fred Rossu, Editor

4577 SkillsUSA Champions
SkillsUSA Inc.
14001 SkillsUSA Way
Leesburg, VA 20176-5494
703-777-8810
Fax: 703-777-8999
E-mail: anyinfo@skillsusa.org
http://www.skillsusa.org
To individuals interested in cultivating leadership skills, SkillsUSA is a dynamic resource that
inspires and connencts all members creating a virtual community through its revalent and useful
content.

28 pages Quarterly
ISSN: 1040-4538

Ahmad Shawwal, President
Dalton Lee Crump, Vice President

4578 VEWAA Newsletter
Vocational Evaluation & Work Adjustment
Assn.
1234 Haley Circle
Auburn University
Auburn, AL 36849
334-844-3800
E-mail: Info@vewaa.com
http://www.vewaa.com
News and information about the practice of
vocational evaluation and work adjustment.

8 pages Quarterly

Ronald Fru, Publisher
Clarence D Brown, Editor

4579 Views & Visions
Wisconsin Vocational Association
44 E Mifflin Street
Suite 104
Madison, WI 53703-2800
608-283-2595
Fax: 608-283-2589
For teachers of vocational and adult educa-
tion.

8 pages BiMonthly

Linda Stemper

4580 Vocational Training News
Aston Publications
701 King Street
Suite 444
Alexandria, VA 22314-2944
703-683-4100
800-453-9397
Fax: 703-739-6517
Contains timely, useful reports on the federal
Job Training Partnership Act and the Carl D
Perkins Vocational Education Act. Other ar-
eas include literacy, private industry councils
and training initiatives.

10 pages Weekly

Cynthia Carter, Publisher
Matthew Dembicki, Editor

Periodicals / *Financial Aid*

**4581 American-Scandinavian Foundation
Magazine**
American-Scandinavian Foundation
58 Park Avenue
New York, NY 10016-5025
212-779-3587
E-mail: info@amscan.org
http://www.amscan.org
Covers politics, culture and lifestyles of Den-
mark, Finland, Iceland, Norway and Sweden.

100 pages Quarterly Magazine

Edward P Gallagher, President
Christian Sonne, Deputy Chairman

4582 Education Grants Alert
LPR Publications
360 Hiatt Drive
Palm Beach Gardens, FL 33418-2944
703-516-7002
800-341-7874
Fax: 561-622-2423
E-mail: custserve@lrp.com
http://www.lrp.com
Dedicated to helping schools increase funding for K-12 programs. This newsletter will
uncover new and recurring grant competitions from federal agencies that fund school
projects, plus scores of corporate and foundation sources.

Publication Date: 1977 Weekly

Kenneth F. Kahn, President

4583 Federal Research Report
Business Publishers
2222 Sedwick Drive
Durham, NC 27713
301-587-6300
800-223-8720
Fax: 800-508-2592
E-mail: custserv@bpinews.com
http://www.bpinews.com
Identifies critical funding sources supplying
administrator's with contact names, addresses, telephone numbers, RFP numbers
and other vital details.

Publication Date: 1963 8 pages Weekly

Eric Easton, Publisher
Leonard Eiserer, Editor

**4584 Foundation & Corporate Grants
Alert**
LRP Publishing
360 Hiatt Drive
Palm Beach Gardens, FL 33418
703-516-7002
800-341-7874
Fax: 561-622-2423
E-mail: custserve@lrp.com
http://www.lrp.com
Offers information on funding trends, new
foundations and hard-to-find regional
funders. You'll also get to foundation and
corporate funders from the inside, with foundation profiles and interviews with program
officers.

Publication Date: 1977 Monthly

Kenneth F. Kahn, President

4585 Grants for School Districts Monthly
Quinlan Publishing
23 Drydock Avenue
Boston, MA 02210-2336
617-542-0048
Listing of grants available for schools across
the country.

Monthly

4586 Informativo
LASPAU (Latin America Scholarship
Program)
25 Mount Auburn Street
Suite 300
Cambridge, MA 02138-6095
617-495-5255
E-mail: angelica_natera@harvard.edu
http://www.laspau.harvard.edu
Administers scholarships for staff members
nominated by Latin American and Caribbean
education and development organizations
and other public and private sector entities.

Publication Date: 1964 8 pages SemiAnnually

Jeff Coburn, Chair
Fernando Reimers, Vice Chair

4587 NASFAA Newsletter
National Assn. of Student Financial Aid
Admin.
1101 Connecticut Avenue NW
Suite 1100
Washington, DC 20036-4303
202-785-0453
Fax: 202-785-1487
http://www.nasfaa.org
News covering student financial aid legisla-
tion and regulations.

24 pages SemiMonthly

Eileen O'Leary, National Chair
Justin Draeger, President/ CEO

4588 United Student Aid Funds Newsletter
PO Box 6180
Indianapolis, IN 46206-6180
317-578-6094
USA Funds Education Loan products and ser-
vices information.

8 pages BiMonthly

Nelson Scharadin, Publisher
Dena Weisbard, Editor

Periodicals / *Guidance &
Counseling*

4589 ASCA Counselor
American Counseling Association
6101 Stevenson Ave.
Alexandria, VA 22304
703-823-9800
800-347-6647
Fax: 703-823-0252
E-mail: membership@counseling.org
http://www.counseling.org
Aimed at the guidance counselor.

16 pages BiMonthly

Robert L. Smith, Ph.D., NCC, FPPR,
President
Richard Yep, CEO

4590 Adolescence
Libra Publishers
3089C Clairemont Drive
San Diego, CA 92117-6802
858-571-1414
Fax: 858-571-1414
E-mail: librapublishers@juno.com
Articles contributed by professionals span-
ning issues relating to teenage education,
counseling and guidance. Paperback.

256 pages Quarterly
ISSN: 0001-8449

Jon Kroll, Editor
William Kroll, Author

**4591 Association for Play Therapy
Newsletter**
Association for Play Therapy Newsletter
3198 Willow Avenue
Suite 110
Clovis, CA 93612
559-294-2128
Fax: 559-294-2129
E-mail: info@a4pt.org
http://www.a4pt.org
Dedicated to the advancement of play therapy. APT is interdisciplinary and defines play
therapy as a distinct group of interventions
which use play as an integral component of
the therapeutic process.

Publication Date: 1982 Quarterly

Lawrence Rubin, PhD, LMHC, RPT-S,
Chair
Kathryn Lebby, CAE, CMP, President/ CEO

4592 Attention
CHADD
4601 Presidents Drive
Suite 300
Lanham, MD 20706
301-306-7070
800-233-4050
Fax: 301-306-7090
E-mail: help@chadd.org
http://www.chadd.org

Magazine for children and adults with Attention Deficit/Hyperactivity Disorder, and their families.

Publication Date: 1987 48 pages Bi-Monthly
ISSN: 1551-0980
70+ booths with 1,400 attendees and 70+ exhibits

Michael F. MacKay, JD, CPA, MSIA, President
Susan Buningh, MRE, Executive Editor

4593 Before You Can Discipline
Master Teacher
Leadership Lane
PO Box 1207
Manhattan, KS 66505-1207
800-669-9633
Fax: 800-669-1132
http://www.masterteacher.com
Understand exactly how student's primary and secondary needs can and do influence acceptable and unacceptable behavior. Develop professional attitudes toward discipline problems and learn the laws and principals of managing people.

Publication Date: 1969 170 pages
ISBN: 0-914607-03-0

Robert L DeBruyn, Author
Dr. Joanna Hubbs, President
Gregory Hubbs, Editor-in-Chief

4594 Child Psychiatry & Human Development
Kluwer Academic/Human Sciences Press
233 Spring Street
New York, NY 10013
212-620-8000
800-221-9369
Fax: 212-463-0742
http://www.wkpa.nl
Interdisciplinary international journal serving the groups represented by child psychiatry, clinical child/pediatric/family psychology, pediatrics, social science, and human development. Publishes research on diagnosis, assessment, treatment, epidemiology, development, advocacy, training, cultural factors, ethics, policy, and professional issues as related to clinical disorders in children, adolescents and families.

Quarterly
ISSN: 0009-398X

Carol Bischoff, Publisher
Kenneth J Tarnowski, Editor

4595 Child Welfare
Child Welfare League of America
440 1st Street NW
Suite 310
Washington, DC 20001-2085
202-688-4200
Fax: 202-833-1689
E-mail: cwla@cwla.org
http://www.cwla.org

Publication Date: 1920 BiMonthly

Joesph M. Costa, Chair
Julie Sweeney-Springwater, Vice Chair

4596 Child and Adolescent Social Work Journal
Kluwer Academic/Human Sciences Press
233 Spring Street
New York, NY 10013
212-620-8000
800-221-9369
Fax: 212-463-0742
http://www.wkpa.nl
Features original articles that focus on clinical social work practice with children, adolescents and their families. The journal

addresses current issues in the field of social work drawn from theory, direct practice, research, and social policy, as well as focuses on problems affecting specific populations in special settings.

Bimonthly
ISSN: 0738-0151

Carol Bischoff, Publisher
Thomas Kenemore, Editor

4597 College Board News
College Board Publications
45 Columbus Avenue
New York, NY 10023
212-713-8000
800-323-7155
Fax: 800-525-5562
http://www.collegeboard.org
Sent free to schools and colleges several times a year, the News reports on the activities of the College Board. Its articles inform readers about the Board's services in such areas as high school, guidance, college admission, curriculum and placement, testing, financial aid, adult education and research.

Publication Date: 1900

David Coleman, President/ CEO
Jeremy Singer, COO

4598 College Board Review
College Board Publications
45 Columbus Avenue
New York, NY 10023
212-713-8000
800-323-7155
Fax: 800-525-5562
http://www.collegeboard.org
Each issue of the Review probes key problems and trends facing education professionals concerned with student transition from high school to college.

Publication Date: 1900

David Coleman, President/ CEO
Jeremy Singer, COO

4599 College Times
College Board Publications
45 Columbus Avenue
New York, NY 10023
212-713-8000
800-323-7155
Fax: 800-525-5562
http://www.collegeboard.org
This annual magazine is a one-stop source to college admission. It provides valuable advice to help students through the complex college selection, application and admission process.

Publication Date: 1900 32 pages Package of 50

David Coleman, President/ CEO
Jeremy Singer, COO

4600 Communique
National Association of School Psychologists
4340 EW Highway
Suite 402
Bethesda, MD 20814
301-657-0270
866-331-NASP
Fax: 301-657-0275
E-mail: sgorin@naspweb.org
http://www.nasponline.org

50 pages 8x Year
ISSN: 0164-775X

Stephen E. Brock, President
Susan Gorin, Executive Director

4601 Counseling & Values
American Counseling Association
6101 Stevenson Ave.
Alexandria, VA 22304
703-823-9800
800-347-6647
Fax: 703-823-0252
E-mail: membership@counseling.org
http://www.counseling.org
Editorial content focuses on the roles of values and religion in counseling and psychology.

3x Year

Robert L. Smith, Ph.D., NCC, FPPR, President
Richard Yep, CEO

4602 Counseling Today
American Counseling Association
6101 Stevenson Ave.
Alexandria, VA 22304
703-823-9800
800-347-6647
Fax: 703-823-0252
E-mail: membership@counseling.org
http://www.counseling.org
Covers national and international counseling issues and reports legislative and governmental activities affecting counselors.

Monthly

Robert L. Smith, Ph.D., NCC, FPPR, President
Richard Yep, CEO

4603 Counselor Education & Supervision
American Counseling Association
6101 Stevenson Ave.
Alexandria, VA 22304
703-823-9800
800-347-6647
Fax: 703-823-0252
E-mail: membership@counseling.org
http://www.counseling.org
Covers counseling theories, techniques and skills, teaching and training.

Quarterly

Robert L. Smith, Ph.D., NCC, FPPR, President
Richard Yep, CEO

4604 ERIC Clearinghouse on Counseling & Student Services
ERIC Clearinghouse on Counseling and Student Servi
201 Ferguson Building UNCG
Greensboro, NC 27412
910-334-4114
800-414-9769
Fax: 910-334-4116
E-mail: ericcas2@hamlet.uncg.edu
http://cecp.air.org/teams/stratpart/ericccss.asp
Covers news about ERIC and the counseling clearinghouse and developments in the fields of education and counseling.

4 pages Quarterly

David Osher, Director
Mary Quinn, Deputy Director

4605 Educational & Psychological Measurement
Sage Publications
2455 Teller Road
Thousand Oaks, CA 91320
805-499-9774
800-818-7243
Fax: 800-583-2665
E-mail: journals@sagepub.com
http://www.sagepub.com

Quarterly

Sara Miller Mccune, Founder/ Chairman
Blaise R. Simqu, President & CEO

4606 Elementary School Guidance & Counseling
American Counseling Association
6101 Stevenson Ave.
Alexandria, VA 22304-3300
703-823-9800
800-347-6647
Fax: 703-823-0252
E-mail: membership@counseling.org
http://www.counseling.org
Journal concerned with enhancing the role of the elementary, middle school and junior high school counselor.

Quarterly
ISSN: 0013-5976

Robert L. Smith, Ph.D., NCC, FPPR, President
Richard Yep, CEO

4607 Family Relations
Miami University
501 E. High St.
Oxford, OH 45056
513-529-4909
Fax: 513-529-7270
http://miamioh.edu

Publication Date: 1809 Quarterly

Dr. David C. Hodge, President
Robin Parker, General Counsel

4608 Family Therapy: The Journal of the California Graduate School of Family Psychology
Libra Publishers
3089C Clairemont Drive
San Diego, CA 92117-6802
858-571-1414
Fax: 858-571-1414
Articles contributed by professionals spanning issues relating to teenage education, counseling and guidance. Paperback.

96 pages Quarterly
ISSN: 0091-6544

William Kroll, Editor

4609 Health & Social Work
National Association of Social Workers
750 First Street NE
Suite 800
Washington, DC 20002
202-408-8600
800-638-8799
Fax: 202-336-8311
E-mail: membership@naswdc.org
http://www.socialworkers.org
Covers practice, innovation, research, legislation, policy , planning, and all the professional issues relevant to social work services in all levels of education.

Publication Date: 1955

Darrell P. Wheeler, PhD, MPH, ACSW, President
Angelo McClain, PhD, LICSW, CEO

4610 ICA Quarterly
Western Illinois University
1 University Circle
Macomb, IL 61455
309-298-1414
Fax: 309-298-3253
E-mail: info@wiu.edu
http://www.wiu.edu
Official publication of the Illinois Counseling Association. Focus is on material of interest and value to professional counselors.

Publication Date: 1899 Quarterly

Dr. Jack Thomas, President
Dr. Kenneth Hawkinson, Provost & Academic VP

4611 International Journal of Play Therapy
Association for Play Therapy Newsletter
3198 Willow Avenue
Suite 110
Clovis, CA 93612-2831
559-294-2128
Fax: 559-294-2129
E-mail: info@a4pt.org
http://www.a4pt.org
Dedicated to the advancement of play therapy. APT is interdisciplinary and defines play therapy as a distinct group of interventions which use play as an integral component of the therapeutic process.

Publication Date: 1982 BiAnnual

Lawrence Rubin, PhD, LMHC, RPT-S, Chair
Kathryn Lebby, CAE, CMP, President/ CEO

4612 Journal for Specialists in Group Work
American Counseling Association
6101 Stevenson Ave.
Alexandria, VA 22304-3302
703-823-9800
800-347-6647
Fax: 703-823-0252
E-mail: membership@counseling.org
http://www.counseling.org
Contains theory, legal issues and current literature reviews.

Quarterly

Robert L. Smith, Ph.D., NCC, FPPR, President
Richard Yep, CEO

4613 Journal of At-Risk Issues
Clemson University
209 Martin Street
Clemson, SC 29631-1555
864-656-2599
800-443-6392
Fax: 864-656-0136
E-mail: ndpc@clemson.edu
http://www.dropoutprevention.org

Publication Date: 1986 36 pages
ISBN: 1098-1608

Dr. Judy Johnson, Author
Z. Annette Bassett, Administrative Asst.
Jennie Cole, Research Associate

4614 Journal of Child and Adolescent Group Therapy
Kluwer Academic/Human Sciences Press
233 Spring Street
New York, NY 10013
212-620-8000
800-221-9369
Fax: 212-463-0742
http://www.wkpa.nl
Addresses the whole spectrum of professional issues relating to juvenile and parent group treatment. Promotes the exchange of new ideas from a wide variety of disciplines concerned with enhancing treatments for this special population. The multidisciplinary contributions include clinical reports, illustrations of new technical methods, and studies that contribute to the advancement of therapeutic results, as well as articles on theoretical issues, applications, and the group process.

Quarterly
ISSN: 1053-0800

Carol Bischoff, Publisher
Edward S Soo, Editor

4615 Journal of College Admission
Nat'l Association for College Admission Counseling
1050 N Highland Street
Suite 400
Alexandria, VA 22201
703-836-2222
800-822-6285
Fax: 703-243-9375
E-mail: info@nacacnet.org
http://www.nacac.com
Membership association offering information to counselors and guidance professionals working in the college admissions office.

Publication Date: 1937 32 pages Quarterly
ISSN: 0734-6670

Elaina Loveland, Author
Jeff Fuller, President
Joyce E. Smith, CEO

4616 Journal of Counseling & Development
American Counseling Association
6101 Stevenson Ave.
Alexandria, VA 22304
703-823-9800
800-347-6647
Fax: 703-823-0252
E-mail: membership@counseling.org
http://www.counseling.org
A quarterly journal that publishe articles that have broad interest for a readership composed mostly of couselors and other mental health professionals who work in private practice, schools, colleges, community agencies, hospitals and government.

ISBN: 0748-9633

Robert L. Smith, Ph.D., NCC, FPPR, President
Richard Yep, CEO

4617 Journal of Counseling and Development
American Counseling Association
6101 Stevenson Ave.
Alexandria, VA 22304-3302
703-823-9800
800-347-6647
Fax: 703-823-0252
E-mail: membership@counseling.org
http://www.counseling.org
Edited for counseling and human development specialists in schools, colleges and universities.

Monthly

Robert L. Smith, Ph.D., NCC, FPPR, President
Richard Yep, CEO

4618 Journal of Drug Education
California State University
18111 Nordhoff Street
Northridge, CA 91330
818-677-1200
Fax: 818-677-2045
http://www.csun.edu
Offers information to counselors and guidance professionals dealing with areas of drug and substance abuse education in the school system.

Publication Date: 1958 Quarterly

Dianne F. Harrison, President
Colin Doanhue, VP & CFO

4619 Journal of Emotional and Behavioral Disorders
Pro-Ed
8700 Shoal Creek Boulevard
Austin, TX 78757-6897

512-451-3246
800-897-3202
Fax: 512-451-8542
E-mail: general@proedinc.com
http://www.proedinc.com
Presents high-quality interdisciplinary scholarship in the area of emotional and behavioral disabilities. Explores issues including youth violence, emotional problems among minority children, long-term foster care placement, mental health services, social development and educational strategies.

Michael H Epstein, EdD, Editor
Douglas Cullinan, EdD, Editor

4620 Journal of Employment Counseling
American Counseling Association
6101 Stevenson Ave.
Alexandria, VA 22304-3302
703-823-9800
800-347-6647
Fax: 703-823-0252
E-mail: membership@counseling.org
http://www.counseling.org
Editorial content includes developing trends in case studies and newest personnel practices.

Quarterly

Robert L. Smith, Ph.D., NCC, FPPR, President
Richard Yep, CEO

4621 Journal of Humanistic Education and Development
Ohio University
1 Ohio University
345 Baker University Center
Athens, OH 45701
740-593-1000
Fax: 740-593-0569
E-mail: deanofstudents@ohio.edu
http://www.ohio.edu
Focuses on the humanities and promotes their place in the educational system.

Publication Date: 1786 Quarterly

David Brightbill, Chair
David A. Wolfort, Vice Chair

4622 Journal of Multicultural Counseling & Development
American Counseling Association
6101 Stevenson Ave.
Alexandria, VA 22304-3302
703-823-9800
800-347-6647
Fax: 703-823-0252
E-mail: membership@counseling.org
http://www.counseling.org
Contains articles with focus on research, theory and program application related to multicultural counseling.

Quarterly

Robert L. Smith, Ph.D., NCC, FPPR, President
Richard Yep, CEO

4623 Journal of Sex Education & Therapy
American Association of Sexuality Educators Counse
1444 I Street, NW
Suite 700
Washington, DC 20005
202-449-1099
Fax: 202-216-9646
E-mail: info@aasect.org
http://www.aasect.org

Provides education and training in all areas of sexual health.

Publication Date: 1967 110 pages Quarterly
ISSN: 0161-4576

Michael Plant, Author
Pat Schiller, MA, JD, Founder

4624 Measurement & Evaluation in Counseling and Development
American Counseling Association
6101 Stevenson Ave.
Alexandria, VA 22304-3302
703-823-9800
800-347-6647
Fax: 703-823-0252
E-mail: membership@counseling.org
http://www.counseling.org
Editorial focuses on research and applications in counseling and guidance.

Quarterly

Robert L. Smith, Ph.D., NCC, FPPR, President
Richard Yep, CEO

4625 NACAC Bulletin
Nat'l Association for College Admission Counseling
1050 N Highland Street
Suite 400
Alexandria, VA 22201
703-836-2222
800-822-6285
Fax: 703-243-9375
E-mail: info@nacacnet.org
http://www.nacac.com
Membership association offering information to counselors and guidance professionals working in the college admissions office.

Publication Date: 1937 Monthly

Jeff Fuller, President
Joyce E. Smith, CEO

4626 NASW News
National Association of Social Workers
750 First Street NE
Suite 800
Washington, DC 20002
202-408-8600
800-638-8799
Fax: 301-206-7989
E-mail: membership@naswdc.org
http://www.naswdc.org
Features in-depth coverage of developments in social work practice, news of national social policy developments, political and legislative news in social services, noteworthy achievements of social workers and association news.

Publication Date: 1955 Monthly

Darrell P. Wheeler, PhD, MPH, ACSW, President
Angelo McClain, PhD, LICSW, CEO

4627 National Coalition for Sex Equity in Education
PO Box 534
Annandale, NJ 08801
908-735-5045
Fax: 908-735-9674
E-mail: info@ncsee.org
http://www.ncsee.org
The only national organization for gender equity specialists and educators. Individuals and organizations committed to reducing sex role stereotyping for females and males. Services include an annual national training conference, a quarterly newsletter and a membership directory. Members may join task forces dealing with equity related topics such as computer/technology issues,

early childhood, male issues, sexual harassment prevention, sexual orientation and vocational issues.

Quarterly Newsletter

Theodora Martin, Business Manager

4628 New Horizons
National Registration Center for Study Abroad
PO Box 1393
Milwaukee, WI 53201
414-278-0631
Fax: 414-271-8884
E-mail: study@nrcsa.com
http://www.nrcsa.com
Provides information about member institution's programs and establishes standards for treatment of visitors from abroad including the appointment of bilingual housing officers and counselors to deal with culture shock.

Publication Date: 1968 16 pages Quarterly
ISBN: 1-977864-43-3

Anne Wittig, Author
Mike Wittig, General Manager

4629 Rehabilitation Counseling Bulletin
Pro-Ed
8700 Shoal Creek Boulevard
Austin, TX 78757-6897
512-451-3246
800-897-3202
Fax: 512-451-8542
E-mail: general@proedinc.com
http://www.proedinc.com
International journal providing original empirical research, essays of a theoretical nature, methodological treatises and comprehensive reviews of the literature, intensive case studies and research critiques.

Quarterly Magazine
ISSN: 0034-3552

Douglas Strohmer, PhD, Editor

4630 School Counselor
American Counseling Association
6101 Stevenson Ave.
Alexandria, VA 22304-3302
703-823-9800
800-347-6647
Fax: 703-823-0252
E-mail: membership@counseling.org
http://www.counseling.org
Includes current issues and information affecting teens and how counselors can deal with them.

5x Year

Robert L. Smith, Ph.D., NCC, FPPR, President
Richard Yep, CEO

4631 School Psychology Review
National Association of School Psychologists
4340 EW Highway
Suite 402
Bethesda, MD 20814
301-657-0270
866-331-NASP
Fax: 301-657-0275
E-mail: sgorin@naspweb.org
http://www.nasponline.org

170 pages Quarterly
ISSN: 0279-6015

Susan Gorin, Executive Director
Laura Benson, COO

4632 Social Work Research Journal
National Association of Social Workers
750 First Street NE
Suite 800
Washington, DC 20002
202-408-8600
800-638-8799
Fax: 202-336-8311

E-mail: membership@naswdc.org
http://www.socialworkers.org
Contains orginal research papers that contribute to knowledge about social work issues and problems. Topics include new technology, strategies and methods, and resarch results.

Publication Date: 1955 Quarterly
ISSN: 1070-5309

Darrell P. Wheeler, PhD, MPH, ACSW, President
Angelo McClain, PhD, LICSW, CEO

4633 Social Work in Education
National Association of Social Workers
750 First Street NE
Suite 800
Washington, DC 20002
202-408-8600
Fax: 202-336-8310
E-mail: membership@naswdc.org
http://www.socialworkers.org
Covers practice, innovation, research, legislation, policy, planning, and all the professional issues relevant to social work services in all levels of education.

Publication Date: 1955

Darrell P. Wheeler, PhD, MPH, ACSW, President
Angelo McClain, PhD, LICSW, CEO

4634 SocialWork
National Association of Social Workers
750 First Street NE
Suite 800
Washington, DC 20002
202-408-8600
800-638-8799
Fax: 202-336-8311
E-mail: membership@naswdc.org
http://www.socialworkers.org
Covers important research findings, critical analyses, practice issues, and information on current social issues such as AIDS, homelessness, and federal regulation of social programs. Case management, third-party reimbursement, credentialing, and other professional issues are addressed.

Publication Date: 1955

Darrell P. Wheeler, PhD, MPH, ACSW, President
Angelo McClain, PhD, LICSW, CEO

4635 Today's School Psychologist
LRP Publications
360 Hiatt Drive
Palm Beach Gardens, FL 33418
703-516-7002
800-341-7874
Fax: 561-622-2423
E-mail: custserve@lrp.com
http://www.lrp.com/ed
An in-depth guide to a school psychologist's job, offering practical strategies and tips for handling day-to-day responsibilites, encouraging change, and improving professional standing and performance.

Publication Date: 1977 Monthly
ISSN: 1098-9277

Kenneth F. Kahn, President

4636 Washington Counseletter
Chronicle Guidance Publications
66 Aurora Street
Moravia, NY 13118-3569
315-497-0330
800-622-7284
Fax: 315-497-3359
E-mail:
customerservice@chronicleguidance.com
http://www.chronicleguidance.com

Monthly report highlighting federal, state, and local developments affecting the counseling and education professions. Items list events, programs, activities and publications of interest to counselors and educators.

Publication Date: 1938 8 pages 8x Year

Cheryl Fickeisen, President/ CEO
Gary Fickeisen, Vice President

Periodicals / *Language Arts*

4637 AATF National Bulletin
American Association of Teachers of French
P.O. Box 2617
Carbondale, IL 62902-2617
815-310-0490
Fax: 815-310-5754
E-mail: abrate@siu.edu
http://www.frenchteachers.org
Announcements and short articles relating to the association on French language and cultural activities.

Publication Date: 1995 30-50 pages 5x Year

Mary Helen Kashuba, SSJ, President
Jayne Abrate, Executive Director

4638 ACTFL Newsletters
American Council on the Teaching of Foreign Lang.
1001 N. Fairfax Street
Suite 200
Alexandria, VA 22314
703-894-2900
Fax: 914-963-1275
http://www.actfl.org/
A quarterly newsletter containing topical and timely information on matters of interest to foreign language educators. Regular columns include Languages in the News and Washington Watch.

20 pages Quarterly

Jacque Bott Van Houten, President
Marty Abbott, Executive Director

4639 ADE Bulletin
Association of Departments of English
26 Broadway
Third Floor
New York, NY 10004-1789
646-576-5133
Fax: 646-835-4056
E-mail: dlaurence@mla.org
http://www.ade.org
This bulletin concentrates on developments in scholarship, curriculum and teachers in English.

64 pages
ISSN: 0001-0888

David Laurence, Director
Doug Steward, Associate Director

4640 Beyond Words
1534 Wells Drive NE
Albuquerque, NM 87112-6383
505-275-2558
Offers information on literature, language arts and English for the teaching professional.

10x Year

4641 Bilingual Research Journal
National Association for Bilingual Education
8701 Georgia Ave.
Suite 700
Siver Spring, MD 20910
240-450-3700
Fax: 240-450-3799

E-mail: nabe@nabe.org
http://www.nabe.org
Journal published by National Association for Bilingual Education.

Publication Date: 1972 Quarterly
8,000 attendees

Julio Cruz, Ed.D., President
Jose A. Ruiz-Escalante, Ed.D., Vice President

4642 Bilingual Review Press
Arizona State University
PO Box 877705
Tempe, AZ 85287-7705
480-965-8972
Fax: 480-965-0865
http://www.asu.edu
Offers information and reviews on books, materials and the latest technology available to bilingual educators.

3x Year

Gary D Keller, President

4643 CEA Forum
College English Association
English Department
Youngstown State University
Youngstown, OH 44555-0001
330-941-3000
Fax: 330-941-2304
E-mail: Daniel.Robinson@widener.edu
http://web.ysu.edu/class/english
Publishes articles on professional issues and pedagogy related to the teaching of English. Subscription includes CEA Critic, a scholarly journal that appears 3x annually.

Publication Date: 1963 Newsletter
ISSN: 0007-8034

Carole S. Weimer, Chair
Leonard Schiavone, Vice Chair

4644 Classroom Notes Plus
National Council of Teachers of English
1111 W Kenyon Road
Urbana, IL 61801-1096
217-328-3870
877-369-6283
Fax: 217-328-9645
E-mail: executivecommittee@ncte.org
http://www.ncte.org
Secondary periodical for English/Language Arts featuring usable teaching ideas for teachers by teachers.

Publication Date: 1911 16 pages Quarterly

Kathy G. Short, President
Susan Houser, Vice President

4645 Communication Disorders Quarterly
Pro-Ed., Inc.
8700 Shoal Creek Boulevard
Austin, TX 78757-6897
512-451-3246
800-897-3202
Fax: 512-451-8542
E-mail: general@proedinc.com
http://www.proedinc.com
Research, intervention and practice in speech, language and hearing.

Quarterly Magazine
ISSN: 1525-7401

Alejandro Brice, Editor

4646 Communication: Journalism Education Today
Truman High School
3301 S Noland Road
Independence, MO 64055
816-521-2710
Fax: 816-521-2913
http://sites.isdschools.org/truman

Provides educational perspectives to JEA members— mostly high schools journalism editors— on a wide variety of topics such as teaching/advising issues, scholastic media strategy, pedagogical updates, current journalism research and other professional and technological concerns.

Publication Date: 1964 Quarterly
ISBN: 1536
ISSN: 9129

Pam Boatright, President
Bradley Wilson, Editor

4647 Composition Studies Freshman English News
De Paul University
1 E. Jackson Blvd.
Chicago, IL 60604
312-362-8000
800-4DE-PAUL
Fax: 773-325-7328
E-mail: dpcl@depaul.edu
http://www.depaul.edu/
Theoretical and practical articles on rhetorical theory.

Publication Date: 1898 44 pages SemiAnnually

Rev. Dennis H. Holtschneider, CM, EdD, President
Robert L. Kozoman, EVP

4648 Council-Grams
National Council of Teachers of English
1111 W Kenyon Road
Urbana, IL 61801-1096
217-328-3870
800-369-6283
Fax: 217-328-9645
E-mail: executivecommittee@ncte.org
http://www.ncte.org
Offers information and updates in the areas of English, language arts and reading.

Publication Date: 1911 16 pages 5x Year

Kathy G. Short, President
Susan Houser, Vice President

4649 Counterforce
Society for the Advancement of Good English
4501 Riverside Avenue
#30
Anderson, CA 96007-2759
530-365-8026
Offers updates and information for English teachers and professors.

Quarterly

4650 English Education
New York University
70 Washington Square South
New York, NY 10012
212-998-1212
Fax: 212-995-4661
E-mail: admissions.ops@nyu.edu
http://www.nyu.edu
Offers updates and information for reading and English teachers, and professors.

Publication Date: 1831 Quarterly

Martin Lipton, Chair
John Sexton, President

4651 English Journal
National Council of Teachers of English
1111 W Kenyon Road
Urbana, IL 61801-1096
217-328-3870
800-369-6283
Fax: 217-328-9645
E-mail: executivecommittee@ncte.org
http://www.ncte.org

An ideal magazine for middle school, junior and senior high school English teachers.

Publication Date: 1911 Biannual
ISSN: 0013-8274

Kathy G. Short, President
Susan Houser, Vice President

4652 English Leadership Quarterly
National Council of Teachers of English
1111 W Kenyon Road
Urbana, IL 61801-1096
217-328-3870
800-369-6283
Fax: 217-328-9645
E-mail: executivecommittee@ncte.org
http://www.ncte.org
Teaching of English for secondary school English Department chairpersons.

Publication Date: 1911 12 pages Quarterly

Kathy G. Short, President
Susan Houser, Vice President

4653 English for Specific Purposes
University of Michigan
500 South State Street
Ann Arbor, MI 48109
734-764-1817
Fax: 619-594-6530
E-mail: sgrafton@umich.edu
http://www.umich.edu
Concerned with English education and its importance to the developing student.

Publication Date: 1817 3x Year

Janey Lack, Chair
Steve Grafton, President/ CEO

4654 Foreign Language Annals
American Council on the Teaching of Foreign Lang.
1001 N. Fairfax Street
Suite 200
Alexandria, VA 22314
703-894-2900
Fax: 914-963-1275
http://www.actfl.org
Dedicated to advancing all areas of the profession of foreign language teaching. It seeks primarily to serve the interests of teachers, administrators and researchers, regardless of educational level of the language with which they are concerned. Preference is given in this scholarly journal to articles that describe innovative and successful teaching methods, that report educational research or experimentation, or that are relevant to the concerns and problems of the profession.

128 pages Quarterly

Jacque Bott Van Houten, President
Marty Abbott, Executive Director

4655 Journal of Basic Writing
City University of NY, Instructional Resource Ctr.
535 E 80th Street
New York, NY 10021-0767
212-794-5445
Fax: 212-794-5706
Publishes articles of theory, research and teaching practices related to basic writing. Articles are referred by members of the Editorial Board and the editors.

Spring & Fall

Karen Greenberg, Editor
Trudy Smoke, Editor

4656 Journal of Children's Communication Development
The Council for Exceptional Children
2900 Crystal Drive
Suite 1000
Arlington, VA 22202-3557
703-620-3660
888-232-7733
Fax: 703-264-9494
E-mail: robin.brewer@unco.edu
http://www.cec.sped.org
Provides in-depth research and practical application articles in communication assessment and intervention. The journal frequently contains a practitioner's section that addresses professional questions, reviews tests and therapy materials, and describes innovative programs and service delivery models.

Publication Date: 1922 2x Year
ISSN: 0735-3170

Robin D. Brewer, President
Alexander T. Graham, Executive Dir./ Secretary

4657 Journal of Teaching Writing
Indiana Teachers of Writing
425 University Boulevard CA 345
Indianapolis, IN 46202
317-274-4777
Fax: 317-278-1287
E-mail: jtw@iupui.edu
http://www.iupui.edu/~jtw
A refereed journal for classroom teachers and researchers at all academic levels whose interest or emphasis is the teaching of writing. Appearing semiannually, JTW publishes articles on the theory, practice, and teaching of writing throughout the curriculum. Each issue covers a range of topics, from composition theory and discourse analysis to curriculum development and innovative teaching techniques. Contributors are reminded to tailor their writing for a diverse readership.

12-20 pages Semiannually

Dr. Kim Brian Lovejoy, Editor
Kay Halasek, Reviews Editor

4658 Journalism Quarterly
George Washington University
2121 Eye Street, NW
Washington, DC 20052
202-994-1000
Fax: 202-994-5806
http://www.gwu.edu
Information on all facets of writing and journalism for the student and educator.

Publication Date: 1821 Quarterly

Nelson A. Carbonell, Jr., Chair
Steven Knapp, President

4659 Language & Speech
Kingston Press Services, Ltd.
43 Derwent Road, Whitton
Twickenham, Middlesex TW2 7HQ
United Kingdom
0-20-8893-3015
Fax: 208-893-3015
E-mail: sales@kingstonepress.com
http://www.kingstonepress.com
Includes psychological research articles, speech perception, speech production, psycholinguistics and reading.

Quarterly

4660 Language Arts
National Council of Teachers of English
1111 W Kenyon Road
Urbana, IL 61801-1096
217-328-3870
800-369-6283
Fax: 217-328-9645
E-mail: executivecommittee@ncte.org
http://www.ncte.org

Edited for instructors in language arts at the elementary level.

Publication Date: 1911 Monthly

Kathy G. Short, President
Susan Houser, Vice President

4661 Language, Speech & Hearing Services in School
Ohio State University
281 W. Lane Ave.
Columbus, OH 43210
614-292-OHIO
Fax: 614-292-7504
http://www.osu.edu
Interested in innovative technology and growth in language development in schools.

Jeffery Wadsworth, Chair
Ronald A. Ratner, Vice Chair

4662 Merlyn's Pen: Fiction, Essays and Poems by America's Teens
11 South Angell St.
Suite 301
Providence, RI 02906
401-751-3766
800-247-2027
Fax: 401-751-3766
E-mail: merlyn@merlynspen.org
http://www.merlynspen.com
Merlyns' Pen magazine is a selective publisher of model writing by America's students in grades 6-12. Products include Merlyn's Pen magazine (a reproducible annual magazine) and the American Teen Writer Series, collections of anthologized short fiction and nonfiction by brilliant teen writers. Used for models, inspiration, and instruction in literature and writing.

Publication Date: 1985 100 pages Annually
ISSN: 0882-2050

R. James Stahl, Editor

4663 Modern Language Journal
Case Western Reserve University
10900 Euclid Ave.
Cleveland, OH 44106
216-368-2000
Fax: 216-368-2216
http://www.case.edu

Publication Date: 1826 Quarterly

Barbara R. Snyder, President
William A. Baeslack III, Provost & EVP

4664 NABE News
National Association for Bilingual Education
8701 Georgia Ave.
Suite 700
Siver Spring, MD 20910-4018
240-450-3700
Fax: 240-450-3799
E-mail: nabe@nabe.org
http://www.nabe.org
Magazine published by the National Association for Bilingual Education.

Publication Date: 1972 Bi-Monthly

Julio Cruz, Ed.D., President
Jose A. Ruiz-Escalante, Ed.D., Vice President

4665 NASILP Journal
Temple University
1801 N. Broad Street
Philadelphia, PA 19122
215-204-7000
http://www.temple.edu
Articles, news and book reviews on language instructional methodology.

Publication Date: 1884 12 pages SemiAnnually

Neil D. Theobald, President

4666 National Clearinghouse for Bilingual Education Newsletter
George Washington University
2121 Eye Street, NW
Washington, DC 20052
202-994-1000
800-321-6223
E-mail: askncbe@ncbe.gwu.edu
http://www.gwu.edu
Provides information to practitioners on the education of language minority students.

Publication Date: 1821 Weekly

Nelson A. Carbonell, Jr., Chair
Steven Knapp, President

4667 PCTE Bulletin
Williamsport Area Community College
One College Avenue
Williamsport, PA 17701
570-326-3761
800-367-9222
http://www.pct.edu/about/history_wacc.htm
Focuses on Pennsylvania literacy issues.

Publication Date: 1970 SemiAnnually

Sen. Gene Yaw, Chair
Dave Jane Gilmour, Ph.D., President

4668 Quarterly Journal of Speech
National Communication Association
1765 N Street NW
Washington, DC 20036
202-464-4622
Fax: 202-464-4600
E-mail: inbox@natcom.org
http://www.natcom.org
Main academic journal in the speech/communication field of education.

Publication Date: 1914 Quarterly

Carole Blair, President
Christina S. Beck, 1st VP

4669 Quarterly Review of Doublespeak
National Council of Teachers of English
1111 W Kenyon Road
Urbana, IL 61801-1096
217-328-3870
800-369-6283
Fax: 217-328-9645
E-mail: executivecommittee@ncte.org
http://www.ncte.org
Provides information on the misuses and abuse of language.

Publication Date: 1911 8 pages Quarterly

Kathy G. Short, President
Susan Houser, Vice President

4670 Quarterly of the NWP
National Writing Project
2105 Bancroft Way
Suite 1042
Berkeley, CA 94720-1042
510-642-0963
Fax: 510-642-4545
E-mail: nwp@nwp.org
http://www.writingproject.org
Journal on the research in and practice of teaching writing at all grade levels.

40 pages Quarterly Magazine
ISSN: 0896-3592

Art Peterson, Amy Bauman; Editors, Author
Judith Warren Little, Chair
Elyse Eidman-Aadahl, Executive Director

4671 Quill and Scroll
University of Iowa School of Journalism
100 Adler Journalism Builing
Iowa City, IA 52242
319-335-3457
Fax: 319-335-3989

E-mail: quill-scroll@uiowa.edu
http://www.uiowa.edu/~quill-sc
Founded and distributed for the purpose of encouraging and rewarding individual achievements in journalism and allied fields. This magazine is published bimonthly during the school year and has a variety of pamphlets and lists of publications available as resources.

BiMonthly

Richard P Johns, Executive Director

4672 Research in the Teaching of English
Harvard Graduate School of Education
Larsen Hall
Appian Way
Cambridge, MA 02138
617-495-3521
Fax: 617-495-0540
http://www.gse.harvard.edu
A research journal devoted to original research on the relationships between teaching and learning for language development in reading, writing and speaking at all age levels.

Publication Date: 1920 Quarterly

Sandra Stotsky, Editor

4673 Rhetoric Review
University of Arizona
Department of English
Tucson, AZ 85721
520-621-2211
Fax: 520-621-7397
http://www.arizona.edu
A journal of rhetoric and composition publishing scholarly and historical studies, theoretical and practical articles, views of the profession, review essays of professional books, personal essays about writing and poems.

Publication Date: 1885 200+ pages Quarterly
ISSN: 0735-0198

Ann Weaver Hart, President
Andrew DuMont, Executive Communication Mngr

4674 Slate Newsletter
National Council of Teachers of English
1111 W Kenyon Road
Urbana, IL 61801-1096
217-328-3870
800-369-6283
Fax: 217-328-9645
E-mail: executivecommittee@ncte.org
http://www.ncte.org
Short articles on topics such as censorship, trends and issues and testing.

Publication Date: 1911

Kathy G. Short, President
Susan Houser, Vice President

4675 Studies in Second Language Acquisition
Cambridge University Press
1105 Atwater
Bloomington, IN 47401-5020
812-855-6874
Fax: 812-855-2386
E-mail: ssla@indiana.edu
http://www.indiana.edu/~ssla
Referred journal devoted to problems and issues in second and foreign language acquisition of any language.

140 pages Quarterly Paperback
ISSN: 0272-2631

Albert Valdman, Editor

4676 TESOL Journal: A Journal of Teaching and Classroom Research

Teachers of English to Speakers of Other Languages
1925 Ballenger Avenue
Suite 550
Alexandria, VA 22314-6820
703-836-0774
888-547-3369
Fax: 703-836-7864
E-mail: info@tesol.org
http://www.tesol.org
TESOL's mission is to develop the expertise of its members and others involved in teaching English to speakers of other languages to help them foster communication in diverse settings. The association advances standards for professional preparation and employment, continuing education, and student programs, produces programs, services, and products, and promotes advocacy to further the profession. TESOL has 91 affiliates worldwide.

Publication Date: 1963 50 pages Quarterly

Yilin Sun, President
Rosa Aronson, Executive Dir./ Secretary

4677 TESOL Quarterly

Teachers of English to Speakers of Other Languages
1925 Ballenger Avenue
Suite 550
Alexandria, VA 22314-6820
703-836-0774
888-547-3369
Fax: 703-836-7864
E-mail: info@tesol.org
http://www.tesol.org
TESOL Quarterly is our scholarly journal containing articles on academic research, theory, reports, reviews. Articles about linguistics, ethnographies, and more describe the theoretic basis for ESL/EFL teaching practices. Readership is approximately 23,400.

Publication Date: 1963 830 pages Quarterly

Yilin Sun, President
Rosa Aronson, Executive Dir./ Secretary

4678 Writing Lab Newsletter

Purdue University, Department of English
500 Oval Drive
W. Lafayette, IN 47907
765-494-3740
Fax: 765-494-3780
E-mail: wln@purdue.edudue.edu
http://www.cla.purdue.edu/english
Monthly newsletter for readers involved in writing centers and/or one-to-one instruction in writing skills.

Publication Date: 1955 16 pages Monthly/Newsletter
ISSN: 1040-3779

Nancy Peterson, Department Head
Ryan Schneider, Dir. Of Graduate Studies

Periodicals / *Library Services*

4679 ALA Editions Catalog

American Library Association
50 East Huron Street
Chicago, IL 60611-2795
312-944-6780
800-545-2433
Fax: 312-836-9958
E-mail: ala@ala.org
http://www.ala.org
Contains over 1,000 job listings, news and reports on the latest technologies in 11 issues annually. Also scholarships, grants and awards are possibilities.

Publication Date: 1853 Annually

Courtney Young, President
Keith Michael Fiels, Executive Director

4680 American Libraries

American Library Association
50 East Huron Street
Chicago, IL 60611-2795
312-944-6780
800-545-2433
Fax: 312-836-9958
E-mail: ala@ala.org
http://www.ala.org
The magazine of the American Library Association that is published six times a year and distributed to more than 65,000 individuals.

Publication Date: 1853
ISBN: 0002-9769

Courtney Young, President
Keith Michael Fiels, Executive Director

4681 Booklist

American Library Association
50 East Huron Street
Chicago, IL 60611-2795
312-944-6780
800-545-2433
Fax: 312-836-9958
E-mail: ala@ala.org
http://www.ala.org
A guide to current print and audiovisual materials worthy of consideration for purchase by small and medium-sized public libraries and school library media centers.

Publication Date: 1853 Semimonthly

Courtney Young, President
Keith Michael Fiels, Executive Director

4682 Catholic Library World

Catholic Library Association
8550 United Plaza Blvd.
Baton Rouge, LA 19041-1412
225-408-4417
E-mail: sbaron@regent.edu
http://www.cathla.org
A periodical geared toward the professional librarian in order to keep them abreast of new publications, library development, association news and technology.

Publication Date: 1921 Quarterly

Sara R. Baron, President
Mary Kelleher, VP/ Treasurer

4683 Choice

Current Reviews for Academic Libraries
100 Riverview Center
Middletown, CT 06457-3445
860-347-6933
Fax: 860-346-8586
E-mail: adsales@ala-choice.org
http://www.ala.org/acrl/choice
A magazine distributed to librarians and other organizations that analyzes various materials, offers book reviews and information on the latest technology available for the library acquisitions departments.

11x Year

Steven Conforti, Subscriptions Manager
Stuart Foster, Advertising Manager

4684 Emergency Librarian

Ken Haycock and Associates
101-1001 W Braodway
Vancouver
British Columbia
604-925-0266
604-925-056
E-mail: ken@kenhaycock.com
http://kenhaycock.com
Professional journal targeted to the specific needs and concerns of teachers and teacher-librarians.

Publication Date: 1991 5x Year

Dr. Ken Haycock, Senior Partner
Shelley Jackson, Dir. Of Client Studies

4685 ILA Reporter

The Illinois Library Association
33 W Grand Avenue
Suite 401
Chicago, IL 60654-6799
312-644-1896
Fax: 312-644-1899
E-mail: ila@ila.org
http://www.ila.org

30 pages
ISSN: 0018-9979

Jeannie Dilger, President
Betsy Adamowski, VP/ President Elect

4686 Information Technology & Libraries

University of the Pacific
3601 Pacific Avenue
Stockton, CA 95211
209-946-2285
Fax: 209-946-2805
E-mail: President@Pacific.edu
http://www.pacific.edu
Offers information on the latest technology, systems and electronics offered to the library market.

Quarterly

Pamela Eibeck, President
Ken Mullen, VP, Business & Finance

4687 Journal of Education for Library and Information Sciences

Kent State University
800 E. Summit St.
Kent, OH 44240
330-672-3000
Fax: 330-672-7965
E-mail: info@kent.edu
http://www.kent.edu
The latest information on books, publications, electronics and technology for the librarian.

Publication Date: 1910 Quarterly

Beverly Warren, President
Edward G. Mahon, Vice President

4688 Libraries & Culture

University of Texas at Austin/Univ. of Texas Press
PO Box 7819
Austin, TX 78713-7819
512-471-3434
Fax: 512-232-7178
E-mail: dgdavis@gslis.utexas.edu
http://www.utexas.edu
An interdisciplinary journal that explores the significance of collections of recorded knowledge. Scholarly articles and book reviews cover international topics dealing with libraries, books, reviews, archives, personnel, and their history; for scholars, librarians, historians, readers interested in the history of books and libraries.

Publication Date: 1883 100 pages Quarterly
ISSN: 0894-8631

William Powers, Jr., President
Gregory L. Fenves, EVP & Provost

4689 Library Collections, Acquisitions & Technical Services

Pergamon Press, Elsevier Science
The Boulevard, Lanngford Lane
Kidlington, Oxford
United Kingdom
614-292-4738
Fax: 614-292-7859

E-mail: deidrichs.1@osu.edu
http://www.elsvier.com
Offers information on policy, practice, and research on the collection management and technical service areas of libraries.

500 pages Quarterly
ISSN: 1464-9055

Carol Pitts Diedrichs, Editor

4690 Library Issues: Briefings for Faculty and Administrators
Mountainside Publishing Company
PO Box 8330
Ann Arbor, MI 48107
734-662-3925
Fax: 734-662-4450
E-mail: sales@libraryissues.com
http://www.libraryissues.com
Offers overviews of the trends and problems affecting campus libraries. Explained in layman's terms as they relate to faculty, administrators and the parent institution.

Publication Date: 1980 4-6 pages Bi-Monthly
ISSN: 0734-3035

Richard M. Dougherty, Editor
Ann P. Dougherty, Managing Editor

4691 Library Quarterly
Indiana University, School of Library Science
1320 E. 10th Street
LI 011
Bloomington, IN 47405-3907
812-855-2018
888-335-7547
Fax: 812-855-6166
E-mail: ilsmain@indiana.edu
http://www.ils.indiana.edu
Updates, information, statistics, book reviews and publications for librarians.

Quarterly

David Cole, Manager, IT Hardware
Jane M. Lewis, ILS Business Dir.

4692 Library Resources & Technical Services
Columbia University, School of Library Sciences
116th Street and Broadway
New York, NY 10027
212-854-1754
Fax: 212-854-8951
E-mail: askcuit@columbia.edu
http://www.columbia.edu

Publication Date: 1754 Quarterly

Lee C. Bollinger, President
John H. Coatsworth, Provost

4693 Library Trends
Grad. School Library & Info. Science
501 E Daniel Street
MC-493
Champaign, IL 61820-6211
217-333-3280
Fax: 217-244-3302
E-mail: dstroud@illinois.edu
http://www.lis.illinois.edu
A scholarly quarterly devoted to invited papers in library and information science. Each issue is devoted to a single theme.

208 pages Quarterly

Allen Renear, Chair
Carol Tilley, Chair, Admissions

4694 Media & Methods Magazine
American Society of Educators
1429 Walnut Street
Philadelphia, PA 19102-3218
215-563-6005
Fax: 215-587-9706

E-mail: info@media-methods.com
http://www.media-methods.com
Leading pragmatic magazine for K-12 educators and administrators. The focus is on how to integrate today's technologies and presentation tools into the curriculum. Very up-to-date and well respected national source publication. Loyal readers are media specialists, school librarians, technology coordinators, administrators and classroom teachers.

5x Year

Michele Sokoloff, Publisher
Christine Weiser, Editor

4695 NEWSletter
New Jersey Library Association
PO Box 1534
Trenton, NJ 08607
609-394-8032
Fax: 609-394-8164
E-mail: ptumulty@njla.org
http://njla.org
A quarterly newsletter and distributed to more than 1,800 members, serves as a vehicle for communication of library issues and activities among members of NJLA.

Terrie McColl, President
James Keehbler, Vice President

4696 Read, America!
Place in the Woods
3900 Glenwood Avenue
Golden Valley, MN 55422-5302
763-374-2120
Fax: 952-593-5593
E-mail: readamerica10732@aol.com
News, book reviews, ideas for librarians and reading program leaders; short stories and poetry pages for adults and children; and an annual Read America! collection with selections of new books solicited from 350 publishers.

12 pages Quarterly Newsletter
ISSN: 0891-4214

Roger Hammer, Editor/Publisher

4697 School Library Journal
School Library Journal
123 William St., Suite 802
New York, NY 10038
646-380-0700
Fax: 646-380-0756
E-mail: slj@mediasourceinc.com
http://www.schoollibraryjournal.com
For children, young adults and school librarians.

Kathy Ishizuka, Executive Editor
Rebecca T. Miller, Editor-in-Chief

4698 School Library Media Activities Monthly
LMS Associates
2205 West Division
Suite A-9
Arlington, TX 76012
301-685-8621
800-725-7377
E-mail: lms@lmsassociates.com
http://lmsassociates.com

Monthly

Steve Langston, President
Michael Fiedler, GM/ Sales Rep.

4699 School Library Media Quarterly
American Library Association
50 East Huron Street
Chicago, IL 60611-2795
312-944-6780
800-545-2433
Fax: 312-836-9958

E-mail: ala@ala.org
http://www.ala.org
For elementary and secondary building level library media specialists, district supervisors and others concerned with the selection and purchase of print and nonprint media.

Publication Date: 1853 Quarterly

Courtney Young, President
Keith Michael Fiels, Executive Director

4700 Southeastern Librarian (SELn)
Southeastern Library Association
PO Box 950
Rex, GA 30273
678-466-4334
Fax: 678-466-4349
E-mail: gordonbaker@clayton.edu
http://selaonline.org
This quarterly publication seeks to publish articles, announcements and news of professional interest to the library community in the southeast. The publication also represents a significant means for addressing the Association's research objective. Two newsletter-style issues serve as a vehicle for conducting Association business, and two issues include juried articles.

Publication Date: 1920

Camille McCutcheon, President
Sue Alexander, Secretary

4701 Special Libraries
Special Libraries Association
331 South Patrick Street
Alexandria, VA 22314-3501
703-647-4900
Fax: 703-647-4901
http://www.sla.org
Includes information and manuscripts on the administration, organization and operation of special libraries.

Publication Date: 1909 Quarterly

Jill Strand, President
Linda Broussard, CFO

4702 Specialist
Special Libraries Association
1700 18th Street NW
Washington, DC 20009-2514
703-647-4900
Fax: 703-647-4901
http://www.sla.org
Contains news and information about the special library/information field.

Publication Date: 1909 Monthly

Jill Strand, President
Linda Broussard, CFO

4703 TLACast
Texas Library Association
3355 Bee Cave Road
Suite 401
Austin, TX 78746-6763
512-328-1518
800-580-2852
Fax: 512-328-8852
E-mail: tla@txla.org
http://www.txla.org
The association's online newsletter that is published several times a year to keep members informed on TLA issues and events.

Publication Date: 1902

Sharon Amastae, President
Patricia H. Smith, Executive Director

4704 Texas Library Journal
Texas Library Association
3355 Bee Cave Road
Suite 401
Austin, TX 78746-6763

512-328-1518
800-580-2852
Fax: 512-328-8852
E-mail: tla@txla.org
http://www.txla.org
Publication Date: 1902
ISBN: 0040-4446

Sharon Amastae, President
Patricia H. Smith, Executive Director

Periodicals / *Mathematics*

4705 Focus on Learning Problems in Math
Center for Teaching/Learning Math
754 Old Connecticut Path
Framingham, MA 01701-7747
508-877-7895
Fax: 508-788-3600
E-mail: mahesh@mathematicsforall.org
http://www.mathematicsforall.org
An interdisciplinary journal. Edited jointly by the Research Council for Diagnostic and Prescription Mathematics and the Center for Teaching/Learning of Mathematics. The objective of focus is to make available the current research, methods of identification, diagnosis, and remediation of learning problems in mathematics. Contribution from the fields of education psychology and mathematics having the potential to import on classroom or clinical practice are valued.

64-96 pages Quarterly

Mahesh Sharma, Editor/ Founder

4706 Journal for Research in Mathematics Education
National Council of Teachers of Mathematics
1906 Association Drive
Reston, VA 20191-1502
703-620-9840
Fax: 703-476-2970
E-mail: nctm@nctm.org
http://www.nctm.org
A forum for disciplined inquiry into the teaching and learning of math at all levels— from preschool through adult. Available in print or online version.

5x Year
ISSN: 0021-8251

Diane J. Briars, President
Bob Doucette, Executive Director

4707 Journal of Computers in Math & Science
PO Box 2966
Charlottesville, VA 22902-2966
804-973-3087
Fax: 703-997-8760
Quarterly

4708 Journal of Recreational Mathematics
4761 Bigger Road
Kettering, OH 45440-1829
631-691-1470
Fax: 631-691-1770
Promotes the creative practice of mathematics for educational learning.

Quarterly

Joseph S Madachy, Editor

4709 Math Notebook
Center for Teacher/Learning Math
754 Old Connecticut Path
Framingham, MA 01701-7747

508-877-7895
Fax: 508-788-3600
E-mail: mahesh@mathematicsforall.org
http://www.mathematicsforall.org
A publication for teachers and parents to improve mathematics instruction.

4x/5x Year

Mahesh Sharma, Editor/ Founder

4710 Mathematics & Computer Education
MAYTC Journal
PO Box 158
Old Bethpage, NY 11804-0158
516-822-5475
Contains a variety of articles pertaining to the field of mathematics.

TriAnnually

George Miller, Editor

4711 Mathematics Teacher
National Council of Teachers of Mathematics
1906 Association Drive
Reston, VA 20191-1502
703-620-9840
Fax: 703-476-2970
E-mail: nctm@nctm.org
http://www.nctm.org
Devoted to the improvement of mathematics instruction in grades 9 and higher.

Monthly
ISSN: 0025-5769

Diane J. Briars, President
Bob Doucette, Executive Director

4712 Mathematics Teaching in the Middle School
National Council of Teachers of Mathematics
1906 Association Drive
Reston, VA 20191-1593
703-620-9840
Fax: 703-476-2970
E-mail: nctm@nctm.org
http://www.nctm.org
Addresses the learning needs of students in grades 5-9.

Monthly
ISSN: 1072-0839

Diane J. Briars, President
Bob Doucette, Executive Director

4713 NCTM News Bulletin
National Council of Teachers of Mathematics
1906 Association Drive
Reston, VA 20191-9988
703-620-9840
Fax: 703-476-2970
E-mail: nctm@nctm.org
http://www.nctm.org
Publication that reaches all of NCTM's individual and institutional members of more than 107,000 math teachers and school personnel.

Diane J. Briars, President
Bob Doucette, Executive Director

4714 Notices of the American Mathematical Society
American Mathematical Society
201 Charles Street
Providence, RI 2904-2294
401-455-4000
800-321-4267
Fax: 401-331-3842
http://www.ams.org

Announces programs, meetings, conferences and symposia of the AMS and other mathematical groups.

Publication Date: 1888 10x Year

David A. Vogan, Jr., President
Dr. Donald McClure, Executive Director

4715 SSMart Newsletter
School Science & Mathematics Association
University of Alabama Birmingham
School of Education EB 246B
Birmingham, AL 35924-1250
205-934-5067
Fax: 570-389-3894
E-mail: office@ssma.org
http://www.ssma.org
Membership news offering information, updates, reviews, articles and association news for professionals in the science and mathematics fields of education.

8 pages Quarterly

Gilbert Naizer, President
Carla Johnson, Editor

4716 Teaching Children Mathematics
National Council of Teachers of Mathematics
1906 Association Drive
Reston, VA 20191-1502
703-620-9840
Fax: 703-476-2970
E-mail: nctm@nctm.org
http://www.nctm.org
Concerned primarily with the teaching of mathematics from Pre-K through grade 6.

Monthly
ISSN: 1073-5836

Diane J. Briars, President
Bob Doucette, Executive Director

Periodicals / *Music & Art*

4717 American Academy of Arts & Sciences Bulletin
American Academy of Arts & Sciences
136 Irving Street
Cambridge, MA 02138
617-576-5000
Fax: 617-576-5050
http://www.amacad.org
Covers current news of the Academy as well as developments in the arts and sciences.

Publication Date: 1780

Don M. Randel, Chair
Jonathan F. Fanton, President

4718 Art Education
National Art Education Association
1806 Robert Fulton Drive
Suite 300
Reston, VA 20191
703-860-8000
Fax: 703-860-2960
E-mail: info@arteducators.org
http://www.arteducators.org
A professional journal in the field of art education devoted to articles on all education levels.

Publication Date: 1947 6x Year

Dennis Inhulsen, President
Dr. Deborah B. Reeve, Executive Director

4719 Arts & Activities
Arts & Activities Magazine
12345 World Trade Drive
San Diego, CA 92128
858-605-0242
E-mail: subs@artsandactivities.com
http://www.artsandactivities.com

For classroom teachers, art teachers and other school personnel teaching visual art from kindergarten through college levels.

Monthly
ISSN: 0004-3931

720 Arts Education Policy Review

Heldref Publications
325 Chestnut Street
Suite 800
Philadelphia, PA 19106
215-625-8900
800-365-9753
Fax: 202-296-5149
E-mail:
customer.service@taylorandfrancis.com
http://www.heldref.org
Discusses major policy issues concerning K-12 education in the various arts. The journal presents a variety of views rather than taking sides and emphasizes analytical exploration. Its goal is to produce the most insightful, comprehensive and rigorous exchange of ideas ever available on arts education. The candid discussions are a valuable resource for all those involved in the arts and concerned about their role in education.

40 pages BiWeekly
ISSN: 1063-2913

Leila Saad, Managing Editor

721 CCAS Newsletter

Council of Colleges of Arts & Sciences
c/o The College of William & Mary
PO Box 8795
Williamsburg, VA 23187-8795
757-221-1784
Fax: 757-221-1776
E-mail: ccas@wm.edu
http://www.ccas.net
Membership newsletter to inform deans about arts and sciences issues in education.

Publication Date: 1965 4-10 pages BiMonthly

Timothy D. Johnston, President
Kate Conley, Treasurer

722 Choral Journal

American Choral Directors Association
PO Box 6310
Lawton, OK 73506-0310
903-935-7963
Fax: 903-934-8114
E-mail: jmoore@etbu.edu
http://acda.org/page.asp%3Fpage%3Dwomenschoirhistory
Publishes scholarly, practical articles and regular columns of importance to professionals in the fields of choral music and music education. Articles explore conducting teachnique, rehearsal strategies, historical performance practice, choral music history and teaching materials.

Publication Date: 1980 Monthly

Amy Blosser, Chair
Karen Fulmer, President

723 Clavier

The Instrumentalist
200 Northfield Road
Northfield, IL 60093
847-446-5000
Fax: 847-446-6263
E-mail: members@schooltheatre.org
http://www.schooltheatre.org
Published 10 times each year for piano and organ teachers, with issues in all months except June and August.

Monthly

4724 Dramatics

Educational Theatre Association
2343 Auburn Avenue
Cincinnati, OH 45219-2815
513-421-3900
Fax: 513-421-7077
E-mail: members@schooltheatre.org
http://www.schooltheatre.org
Magazine published by Educational Theatre Association, a professional association for theatre educators/artists.

Monthly

Jay Seller, Ph.D., President
Frank Pruet, Vice President

4725 Flute Talk

The Instrumentalist
200 Northfield Road
Northfield, IL 60093
847-446-5000
888-446-6888
Fax: 847-446-6263
E-mail:
advertising@theinstrumentalist.com
http://theinstrumentalist.com
Published 10 times each year for flute teachers and intermediate or advanced students, with issues every month except June and August.

Monthly

4726 Instrumentalist

The Instrumentalist
200 Northfield Road
Northfield, IL 60093
847-446-5000
888-446-6888
Fax: 847-446-6263
E-mail:
advertising@theinstrumentalist.com
http://theinstrumentalist.com
Published 12 times each year for band and orchestra directors and teachers of instruments in these groups.

Monthly

4727 Journal of Experiential Education

Association of Experiential Education
1435 Yarmouth Ave
#104
Boulder, CO 80304
303-440-8844
Fax: 303-440-9581
E-mail: aewert@indiana.edu
http://www.aee.org
A professional journal that publishes articles in outdoor adventure programming, service learning, environmental education, therapeutic applications, research and theory, the creative arts, and much more. An invaluable reference tool for anyone in the field of experiential education.

3x Year
ISSN: 1053-8259

Maurie Lung, President
Robert Smariga, CEO

4728 Journal of the American Musicological Society

American Musicological Society
6010 College Station
Brunswick, ME 04011
207-798-4243
877-679-7648
Fax: 207-798-4254
E-mail: ams@ams-net.org
http://www.ams-net.org
One of the premier journals in the field, the Journal of the American Musicological Society(JAMS) publlishes scholarship from all fields of musicalinquiry:from historical musicology, critical theory, music analysis, iconographyand organology, to performance practice, aesthetics and hermeneutics, ethnomusicology, gender and sexuality, popular music and cultural studies.

ISBN: 0003
ISSN: 0139

Annegret Fauser, Editor-in-Chief
Louise Goldberg, Assistant Editor

4729 Music Educators Journal

National Association for Music Education
1806 Robert Fulton Drive
Reston, VA 20191
703-860-4000
Fax: 703-860-1531
E-mail: memberservices@nafme2.org
http://www.nafme.org
Offers informative, timely and accurate articles, editorials, and features to a national audience of music educators.

Publication Date: 1907 BiMonthly
ISSN: 0027-4321

Frances Ponick, Editor, Author
Glenn E. Nierman, President/ Chair
Michael A. Butera, Executive Director/ CEO

4730 Music Educators Journal and Teaching Music

National Association for Music Education
1806 Robert Fulton Drive
Reston, VA 20191
703-860-4000
Fax: 703-860-4826
E-mail: memberservices@nafme2.org
http://www.nafme.org
Informative, timely and accurate articles, editorials, and features to a national audience of music educators.

Publication Date: 1907 BiMonthly
ISSN: 1069-7446

Glenn E. Nierman, President/ Chair
Michael A. Butera, Executive Director/ CEO

4731 NAEA News

National Art Education Association
1806 Robert Fulton Drive
Suite 300
Reston, VA 20191
703-860-8000
Fax: 703-860-2960
E-mail: info@arteducators.org
http://www.naea-reston.org
National, state and local news affecting visual arts education.

24 pages BiMonthly

Dr. Thomas Hatfield, Executive Director

4732 National Guild of Community Schools of the Arts

National Guild of Community Schools of the Arts
520 8th Avenue
Suite 302
New York, NY 10018
212-268-3337
Fax: 212-268-3995
E-mail: info@natguild.org
http://www.nationalguild.org
National association of community based arts education institutions employment opportunities, guildnotes newsletter, and publications catalog.

Monthly

Terry Hueneke, Chairman
Carol Ross, Vice Chairman

4733 Oranatics Journal
Educational Theatre Association
2343 Auburn Avenue
Cincinnati, OH 45219-2815
513-451-3900
Fax: 513-421-7077
E-mail: members@schooltheatre.org
http://www.schooltheatre.org
Promotes and strengthens theatre in education - primarily middle school and high school. Sponsors an honor society, various events, numerous publications, and arts education advocacy activities.

9x Year

Jay Seller, Ph.D., President
Frank Pruet, Vice President

4734 SchoolArts
Davis Publications
50 Portland Street
Worcester, MA 01608
508-754-7201
800-533-2847
Fax: 508-791-3834
E-mail: VSullivan@DavisArt.com
http://www.davisart.com
Davis has promoted and advocated for art education at both the local and national levels, providing good ideas for teachers and celebrating cultural diversity and the contributions of world cultures through a wide range of art forms.

Publication Date: 1901

Wyatt Wade, President
Valerie Sullivan, Publications

4735 SchoolArts Magazine
Davis Publications
50 Portland Street
Worcester, MA 01608
508-754-7201
800-533-2847
Fax: 508-791-3834
E-mail: VSullivan@DavisArt.com
http://www.davisart.com
Aimed at art educators in public and private schools, elementary through high school. Articles offer ideas and information involving art media for the teaching profession and for use in classroom activities.

Publication Date: 1901 Monthly
ISSN: 0036-3463

Wyatt Wade, President
Valerie Sullivan, Publications

4736 Studies in Art Education
Louisiana State University, Dept. of Curriculum
Baton Rouge, LA 70803-0001
225-578-3202
Fax: 225-578-9135
E-mail: webmaster@lsu.edu
http://www.lsu.edu
Reports on developments in art education.

Quarterly

Karen A Hamblen, Editor

4737 Teaching Journal
Educational Theatre Association
2343 Auburn Avenue
Cincinnati, OH 45219-2815
513-421-3900
Fax: 513-421-7077
E-mail: members@schooltheatre.org
http://www.schooltheatre.org

Journal published by Educational Theatre Association, a professional association for theatre educators/artists.

Quarterly

Jay Seller, Ph.D., President
Frank Pruet, Vice President

4738 Teaching Music
National Association for Music Education
1806 Robert Fulton Drive
Reston, VA 20191-4348
703-860-4000
Fax: 703-860-4826
E-mail: memberservices@nafme2.org
http://www.nafme.org
Offers informative, timely and accurate articles, editorials, and features to a national audience of music educators.

Publication Date: 1907 BiMonthly
ISSN: 1069-7446

Glenn E. Nierman, President/ Chair
Michael A. Butera, Executive Director/ CEO

4739 Ultimate Early Childhood Music Resource
Miss Jackie Music Company
10001 El Monte Street
Shawnee Mission, KS 66207-3631
913-381-3672
E-mail: jsilberg@interserv.com
http://www.jackiesilberg.com
Designed to assist parents and teachers engaged in early childhood.

16 pages Quarterly

Jackie Weissman, Publisher
Emily Smith, Editor

Periodicals / *Physical Education*

4740 Athletic Director
National Association for Sport & Physical Ed.
1900 Association Drive
Reston, VA 20191
703-476-3410
800-213-7193
Fax: 703-476-9527
E-mail: board@shapeamerica.org
http://www.shapeamerica.org/standards/pe
Of interest to athletic directors and coaches.

Publication Date: 1885 4 pages SemiAnnually

Dolly D. Lambdin, Ed.D., President
E. Paul Roetert, CEO

4741 Athletic Management
College Athletic Administrator
2488 N Triphammer Road
Ithaca, NY 14850
607-274-3209
Fax: 607-273-0701
http://athletics.ithaca.edu/staff.aspx
Offers information on how athletic managers can improve their operations, focusing on high school and college athletic departments.

BiMonthly

Andrea McClatchie, Operations and Events
Kathy Farley, Administrative Assistant

4742 Athletic Training
National Athletic Trainers' Association
1620 Valwood Parkway
Suite 115
Carrollton, TX 75006
214-637-6282
860-437-5700
Fax: 214-637-2206
E-mail: jthornton@clarion.edu
http://www.nata.org
Edited for athletic trainers.

Publication Date: 1950 100 pages Quarterly Magazine

Jim Thornton, MS, ATC, CES, President
MaryBeth Horodyski, Vice President

4743 Athletics Administration
NACDA
PO Box 16428
Cleveland, OH 44116
440-892-4000
Fax: 440-892-4007
E-mail: burkeg@nsula.edu
http://www.nacda.com
The official publication of the National Association of Collegiate Directors of Athletics (NACDA), Athletics Administration focuses on athletics facilities, new ideas in marketing, promotions, development, legal ramifications and other current issues in collegiate athletics administrations.

Publication Date: 1965 44-48 pages BiMonthly
ISSN: 0044-9873

Jim Phillips, President
Bob Vecchione, Executive Dir.

4744 Journal of Environmental Education
Heldref Publications
325 Chestnut Street
Suite 800
Philadelphia, PA 19106
215-625-8900
800-365-9753
Fax: 202-296-5149
E-mail: customer.service@taylorandfrancis.com
http://www.heldref.org
An excellent resource for department chairpersons and directors of programs in environmental, resources, and outdoor education.

48 pages Quarterly
ISSN: 0095-8964

B Alison Panko, Managing Editor

4745 Journal of Experiential Education
Association for Experiential Education
1435 Yarmouth Ave
#104
Boulder, CO 80304
303-440-8844
800-787-7979
Fax: 303-440-9581
E-mail: simps_sv@mail.uwlax.edu
http://www.aee.org
A professional journal that publishes articles in outdoor adventure programming, service learning, environmental education, therapeutic applications, research and theory, the creative arts, and much more. An invaluable reference tool for anyone in the field of experiential education.

3x Year

Maurie Lung, President
Robert Smariga, CEO

4746 Journal of Physical Education, Recreation and Dance
American Alliance for Health, Phys. Ed. & Dance
1900 Association Drive
Reston, VA 20191-1502
703-476-3495
800-213-7193
Fax: 703-476-9527

E-mail: board@shapeamerica.org
http://www.shapeamerica.org/standards/pe
Presents new books, teaching aids, facilities, equipment, supplies, news of the profession and related groups.

Publication Date: 1885 9x Year

Dolly D. Lambdin, Ed.D., President
E. Paul Roetert, CEO

747 Journal of Teaching in Physical Education
Human Kinetics Incorporation
PO Box 5076
Champaign, IL 61825-5076
217-351-5076
800-747-4457
Fax: 217-351-1549
E-mail: info@hkusa.com
http://www.humankinetics.com/jtpe
Journal for in-service and pre-service teachers, teacher educators, and administrators, that presents research articles based on classroom and laboratory studies, descriptive and survey studies, summary and review articles, as well as discussions of current topics.

132 pages Quarterly
ISSN: 0273-5024

Brian Moore, Managing Editor
Skip Maier, Journals Division Dir.

748 Marketing Recreation Classes
Learning Resources Network
P.O. Box 9
River Falls, WI 54022
715-426-9777
800-678-5376
Fax: 888-234-8633
E-mail: info@lern.org
http://www.lern.org
Successful new class ideas and promotion techniques for recreation instructors.

8 pages Monthly

William A. Draves, President
Greg Marsello, VP, Development

49 National Association for Sport & Physical Education News
National Association for Sport & Physical Ed.
1900 Association Drive
Reston, VA 20191-1502
703-476-3410
800-213-7193
Fax: 703-476-9527
E-mail: board@shapeamerica.org
http://www.shapeamerica.org/standards/pe
News of conventions, new publications, workshops, and more, all tailored for people in the field of sports, physical education, coaching, etc. Legislative issues are covered as well as news about the over 20 structures in NASPE.

Publication Date: 1885 12 pages Monthly

Dolly D. Lambdin, Ed.D., President
E. Paul Roetert, CEO

50 National Standards for Dance Education News
National Dance Association
1900 Association Drive
Reston, VA 20191-1502
703-476-3400
800-213-7193
Fax: 703-476-9527
E-mail: board@shapeamerica.org
http://www.shapeamerica.org/standards/pe
News of the National Dance Association activities, national events in dance education

and topics of interest to recreation and athletic directors.

Publication Date: 1885 12 pages Quarterly

Dolly D. Lambdin, Ed.D., President
E. Paul Roetert, CEO

4751 Physical Education Digest
Physical Education Update
11 Cerilli Crescent
Sudbury
Ontario, Ca P3E5R
705-805-9245
800-455-8782
Fax: 705-805-9245
E-mail: coach@pedigest.com
http://www.physicaleducationupdate.com
Edited for physical educators and scholastic coaches. Condenses practical ideas from periodicals and books.

36 pages Quarterly
ISSN: 0843-2635

Dick Moss, Editor/ Publisher

4752 Physical Educator
Arizona State University
University Drive and Mill Avenue
Tempe, AZ 85287
480-965-9011
Fax: 480-965-2569
http://www.asu.edu
Offers articles for the physical educator.

Quarterly

Michael M. Crow, President
Morgan R. Olsen, VP, Business & Finance

4753 Quest
Louisiana State University/Dept. of Kinesiology
Huey Room 112
Baton Rouge, LA 70803-0001
225-388-2036
Fax: 225-388-3680
http://www.southeastern.edu
Publishes articles concerning issues critical to physical education in higher education. Its purpose is to stimulate professional development within the field.

Publication Date: 1925 Quarterly

Dr. John Crain, President
Dr. Tammy Bourg, Provost/ VP

4754 Teaching Elementary Physical Education
Human Kinetics Publishers
1607 N Market Street
P.O. Box 5076
Champaign, IL 61820
217-351-5076
800-747-4457
Fax: 217-351-1459
E-mail: info@hkusa.com
http://www.humankinetics.com
A resource for elementary physical educators, by physical educators. Each 32-page issue includes informative articles on current trends, teaching hints, activity ideas, current resources and events, and more.

32 pages BiMonthly Magazine
ISSN: 1045-4853

Brian Holding, CEO
Margery Robinson, Managing Editor

Periodicals / *Reading*

4755 Beyond Words
20827 NW Cornell Rd.
Suite 500
Hillsboro, OR 97124

503-531-8700
Fax: 503-531-8773
http://www.beyondword.com
Offers information on literature, language arts and English for the teaching professional.

Publication Date: 1983 10x Year

Richard Cohn, President/ Publisher
Tim Schroeder, Chief Operating Officer

4756 Christian Literacy Outreach
Christian Literacy Association
541 Perry Highway
Pittsburgh, PA 15229
412-364-3777
http://www.pghpresbytery.org/mission_agencies/miss_files/alghLitera
Association news offering membership information, convention news, books and articles for the Christian education professional.

Publication Date: 1975 4 pages Quarterly

Joseph Mosca

4757 Exercise Exchange
Appalachian State University
222 Duncan Hall
Boone, NC 28608
828-262-2000
Fax: 828-262-2128
E-mail: admissions@appstate.edu
http://www.appstate.edu
Bi-annual journal which features classroom-tested approaches to the teaching of English language arts from middle school through college; articles are written by classroom practitioners.

Publication Date: 1899 BiAnnual
ISSN: 0531-531X

Dr. Randy Edwards, Chief of Staff
Melody C. Miller, Executive Assistant

4758 Forum for Reading
Fitchburg State College, Education Department
160 Pearl Street
Fitchburg, MA 01420-2697
978-665-3000
800-705-9692
E-mail: admissions@fitchburgstate.edu
http://www.fitchburgstate.edu/academics/academic-departments/educat
Offers articles, reviews, question and answer columns and more for educators and students.

Publication Date: 1894 2x Year

Dr. Ronald P. Colbert, Chair
Beth Lawrence, Secretary

4759 Journal of Adolescent & Adult Literacy
International Reading Association
800 Barksdale Road
Newark, DE 19711-3204
302-731-1600
800-336-7323
Fax: 302-731-1057
E-mail: customerservice@reading.org
http://www.reading.org
Carries articles and departments for those who teach reading in adolescent and adult programs. Applied research, instructional techniques, program descriptions, training of teachers and professional issues.

Publication Date: 1956 80-96 pages 8x Year
ISSN: 1081-3004

Jill Lewis-Spector, President
Diane Barone, Vice President

4760 Journal of Reading Recovery
Reading Recovery Council of North
America
500 W. Wilson Bridge Road
Suite 250
Worthington, OH 43085
614-310-7323
877-883-7323
Fax: 614-310-7345
E-mail: jjohnson@readingrecovery.org
http://www.readingrecovery.org
The Journal of Reading Recovery is published twice per year, and is primarily a
practitioners journal offering current information on Reading Recovery teaching
theory, implementation and research for
K-6 classroom literacy.

Janet Behrend, President
Lindy Harmon, Vice President

4761 Laubach LitScape
Laubach Literacy Action
1320 Jamesville Avenue
Syracuse, NY 13210
315-422-9121
888-528-2224
Fax: 315-422-6369
E-mail: info@laubach.org
http://www.laubach.org
Includes articles about national literacy activities as well as support and information
on tutoring, resources, training, new readers, program management, and recruitment
and retention of students and volunteers.

12 pages Quarterly

Linda Church, Managing Editor

4762 Literacy Advocate
Laubach Literacy Action
1320 Jamesville Avenue
Syracuse, NY 13210
315-422-9121
888-528-2224
Fax: 315-422-6369
E-mail: info@laubach.org
http://www.laubach.org
Covers United States and international
programs and membership activities.

8 pages Quarterly

Beth Kogut, Editor

4763 News for You
Laubach Literacy Action
1320 Jamesville Avenue
Syracuse, NY 13210
315-422-9121
888-528-2224
Fax: 315-422-6369
E-mail: info@laubach.org
http://www.laubach.org
A newspaper for older teens and adults
with special reading needs. Includes US
and world news written at a 4th to 6th grade
reading level.

4 pages Weekly
ISSN: 0884-3910

Heidi Stephens, Editor

4764 Phonics Institute
The Phonics Instuite
PO Box 98682
Steilacoom, WA 98388
253-588-3436
E-mail: read@readingstore.com
http://www.readingstore.com
Restoration of intensive phonics to begin-
ning reading instruction.

8 pages 5x Year

4765 RIF Newsletter
Smithsonian Institution
PO Box 37012
SI Building, Room 153, MRC 010
Washington, DC 20013-7012
202-357-2888
Fax: 202-786-2564
E-mail: info@si.edu
http://www.si.edu
Describes RIF's nationwide reading moti-
vation program.

Publication Date: 1846 TriQuarterly

John W. McCarter, Jr., Chair
Shirley Ann Jackson, Vice Chair

4766 Read, America!
Place in the Woods
3900 Glenwood Avenue
Golden Valley, MN 55422-5302
763-374-2120
Fax: 952-593-5593
E-mail: readamerica10732@aol.com
News, book reviews, ideas for librarians
and reading program leaders; short stories
and poetry pages for adults and children;
and an annual Read America! collection
with selections of new books solicited
from 350 publishers.

12 pages Quarterly Newsletter
ISSN: 0891-4214

Roger Hammer, Editor/Publisher

4767 Reading Improvement
Project Innovation of Mobile
PO Box 8508
Mobile, AL 36608
334-633-7802
E-mail:
philfeldman@projectinnovation.com
http://www.projectinnovation.biz
A journal dedicated to improving reading
and literacy in America.

Quarterly

Dr. Phil Feldman, Editor

4768 Reading Psychology
Texas A&M University, College of
Education
Department of Education
College Station, TX 77843-0001
979-845-7093
Fax: 979-845-9663
http://www.tamu.edu/about/departments.
html

Publication Date: 1862 Quarterly

Dr. Mark A. Hussey, President
Dr. Karan L. Watson, Provost/ EVP

4769 Reading Research Quarterly
Ohio State University
281 W. Lane Ave.
Columbus, OH 43210
614-292-OHIO
Fax: 614-292-1816
http://www.osu.edu
Delves into reading ratings and special
concerns in the field of literacy.

Quarterly

Jeffery Wadsworth, Chair
Ronald A. Rtaner, Vice Chair

4770 Reading Research and Instruction
Appalachian State University, College of
Education
Dept. of Curriculum & Instruction
Boone, NC 28608

828-262-2000
E-mail: admissions@appstate.edu
http://www.appstate.edu

Publication Date: 1899 Quarterly

John C. Fennebresque, Chair
W. Louis Bissette, Jr., Vice Chair

4771 Reading Teacher
International Reading Association
800 Barksdale Road
Newark, DE 19711-3204
302-731-1600
800-336-7323
Fax: 301-731-1057
E-mail: customerservice@reading.org
http://www.reading.org
Carries articles and departments for those who
teach reading in preschool and elementary
schools. Applied research, instructional techniques, program descriptions, the training of
teachers, professional issues and special feature
reviews of children's books and ideas for
classroom practice.

Publication Date: 1956 8x Year

Jill Lewis-Spector, President
Marcie Craig Post, Executive Director

4772 Reading Today
International Reading Association
800 Barksdale Road
Newark, DE 19711-3204
302-731-1600
800-336-7323
Fax: 302-731-1057
E-mail: customerservice@reading.org
http://www.reading.org
Edited for IRA individual and institutional members offering information for teachers, news of the
education profession and information for and relating to parents, councils and international
issues.

Publication Date: 1956 36-44 pages BiMonthly

Jill Lewis-Spector, President
Marcie Craig Post, Executive Director

4773 Recording for the Blind & Dyslexic
Learning Ally
20 Roszel Road
Princeton, NJ 08540
609-750-1830
800-221-4792
Fax: 609-750-9653
E-mail: bvidialogue@LearningAlly.org
http://www.learningally.org
Textbooks on tape for students who cannot read
standard print.

Publication Date: 1948

Andrew Friedman, President/ CEO
Jim Halliday, Executive Vice President

4774 Report on Literacy Programs
Business Publishers
2222 Sedwick Drive
Durham, NC 27713
301-587-6300
800-223-8720
Fax: 800-508-2592
E-mail: custserv@bpinews.com
http://www.bpinews.com
Reports on the efforts of business and government
to provide literacy training to adults— focusing
on the effects of literacy on the workforce.

8-10 pages BiWeekly

Eric Easton, Publisher
Dave Speights, Editor

4775 Visual Literacy Review & Newsletter
International Visual Literacy Association
Virginia Tech
Old Security Building
Blacksburg, VA 24061

540-231-8992
E-mail: jhethorn@udel.edu
http://www.ivla.org
Forum for sharing research and practice within an educational context in the area of visual communication.

8 pages BiMonthly

Janet Hethorn, President
Cindy Kovalik, Vice President

776 WSRA Journal
University of Wisconsin - Oshkosh
1863 Doty Street
Oshkosh, WI 54901-6978
920-424-7231
Fax: 920-326-6280
E-mail: wsra@centurytel.net
A quarterly publication of the Wisconsin State Reading Association that publishes articles about literacy for academicians, teachers, libraries and literary workers.

Quarterly

Dr. Margaret Humadi Genisio, Editor

777 What's Working in Parent Involvement
The Parent Institute
PO Box 7474
Fairfax Station, VA 22039-7474
703-323-9170
800-756-5525
Fax: 703-323-9173
E-mail: custsvc@parent-institute.com
http://www.parent-institute.com
Focuses on parent involvement in children's reading education.

10x Year

John H.ÿ Wherry, Ed.D., President

Periodicals / *Secondary Education*

778 ACTIVITY
American College Testing
2201 Dodge
Iowa City, IA 52243-0001
319-337-1410
Fax: 319-337-1014
Distributed free of charge to more than 100,000 persons concerned with secondary and postsecondary education. ACT, an independent nonprofit organization provides a broad range of educational programs and services throughout this country and abroad.

Quarterly

Dan Lechay, Editor

779 Adolescence
Libra Publishers
3089C Clairemont Drive
PNB 383
San Diego, CA 92117-6802
858-571-1414
Fax: 858-571-1414
Articles contributed by professionals spanning issues relating to teenage education, counseling and guidance. Paperback.

256 pages Quarterly
ISSN: 0001-8449

William Kroll, Editor

780 American Secondary Education
Bowling Green State University
Education Room 531
Bowling Green, OH 43403-0001
419-372-2531
Fax: 419-372-8265

E-mail: joelo@bgsu.edu
http://www.bgsu.edu
Serves those involved in secondary education— administrators, teachers, university personnel and others. Examines and reports on current issues in secondary education and provides readers with information on a wide range of topics that impact secondary education professionals. Professionals are provided with the most up-to-date theories and practices in their field.

Quarterly

Joel O'Dorisio, Chair
Allen Rogel, Vice Chair

4781 Child and Youth Care Forum
Kluwer Academic/Human Sciences Press
233 Spring Street
New York, NY 10013
212-620-8000
800-221-9369
Fax: 212-463-0742
http://www.wkpa.nl
Independent, professional publication committed to the improvement of child and youth care practice in a variety of day and residential settings and to the advancement of this field. Designed to serve child and youth care practitioners, their supervisors, and other personnel in child and youth care settings, the journal provides a channel of communication and debate including material on practice, selection and training, theory and research, and professional issues.

Bimonthly
ISSN: 1053-1890

Carol Bischoff, Publisher
Doug Magnuson, Co-Editor

4782 Family Therapy: The Journal of the California Graduate School of Family Psychology
Libra Publishers
3089C Clairemont Drive
PNB 383
San Diego, CA 92117-6802
858-571-1414
Fax: 858-571-1414
Articles contributed by professionals spanning issues relating to teenage education, counseling and guidance. Paperback.

96 pages Quarterly
ISSN: 0091-6544

William Kroll, Editor

4783 High School Journal
University of North Carolina
CB 3500 Peabody Hall
Chapel Hill, NC 27599-3500
919-966-1346
Fax: 919-962-1533
http://soe.unc.edu/hsj
The Journal publishes articles dealing with adolescent growth, development, interests, beliefs, values, learning, etc., as they effect school practice. In addition, it reports on research dealing with teacher, administrator and student interaction within the school setting. The audience is primarily secondary school teachers and administrators, as well as college level educators.

Publication Date: 1918 60 pages Quarterly
ISSN: 0018-1498

Zan Crowder, Editor
Hillary Parkhouse, Associate Editor

4784 Independent School
National Association of Independent Schools
1129 20th Street, NW
Suite 800
Washington, DC 20036-3425
202-973-9700
Fax: 888-316-3862
http://www.nais.org
Contains information and opinion about secondary and elementary education in general and independent education in particular.

TriAnnually

John E. Chubb, President
Kurt R Murphy, Advertising/Editor

4785 Journal of At-Risk Issues
Clemson University
209 Martin Street
Clemson, SC 29631-1555
864-656-2599
800-443-6392
Fax: 864-656-0136
E-mail: NDPC@clemson.edu
http://www.dropoutprevention.org
Publication Date: 0 36 pages
ISBN: 1098-1608

Dr. Judy Johnson, Author
Raymond J. McNulty, Chair
Bob Collins, Vice Chair

4786 NASSP Bulletin
National Assn. of Secondary School Principals
1904 Association Drive
P.O. Box 417939
Reston, VA 20191-1537
703-860-0200
800-253-7746
Fax: 703-620-6534
E-mail: nassp@nassp.org
http://www.principals.org
For administrators at the secondary school level dealing with subjects that range from the philosophical to the practical.

TriAnnual

G.A. Buie, President
Michael Allison, President Elect

4787 Parents Still Make the Difference!
The Parent Institute
PO Box 7474
Fairfax Station, VA 22039-7474
703-323-9170
800-756-5525
Fax: 703-323-9173
E-mail: custsvc@parent-institute.com
http://www.parent-institute.com
Newsletter focusing on parent involvement in children's education. Focuses on parents of children in grades 7-12.

Monthly
ISSN: 1523-2395

Betsie Millar, Author
John H.ÿ Wherry, Ed.D., President

4788 Parents Still Make the Difference!: Middle School Edition
The Parent Institute
PO Box 7474
Fairfax Station, VA 22039-7474
703-323-9170
800-756-5525
Fax: 703-323-9173
E-mail: custsvc@parent-institute.com
http://www.parent-institute.com

Newsletter focusing on parent involvement in children's education. Focuses on parents of children in grades 7-12.

Monthly
ISSN: 1071-5118
John H.ÿ Wherry, Ed.D., President

Periodicals / *Science*

4789 American Biology Teacher
National Association of Biology Teachers
12100 Sunset Hills Road
Suite 130
Reston, VA 20190
703-264-9696
888-501-NABT
Fax: 703-435-4390
E-mail: office@nabt.org
http://www.nabt.org
Edited for elementary, secondary school, junior college, four-year college and university teachers of biology.

80 pages 9 times a year
Stacey Kiser, President
Jane Ellis, President Elect

4790 AnthroNotes
Smithsonian Information
PO Box 37012
SI Building, Room 153, MRC 010
Washington, DC 20013-7012
202-633-1000
Fax: 202-357-2208
E-mail: info@si.edu
http://www.mnh.si.edu
Offers archeological, anthropological research in an engaging style.

20 pages
Ann Krupp, Editor

4791 Appraisal: Science Books for Young People
Children's Science Book Review Committee
Boston University
School of Education
Boston, MA 02215
617-353-4150
This is a journal dedicated to the review of science books for children and young adults. Now in its 27th year of publication, Appraisal reviews nearly all of the science books published yearly for pre-school through high-school age young people. Each book is examined by a children's librarian and by a specialist in its particular discipline.

Quarterly
Diane Holzheimer, Editor

4792 Association of Science-Technology Centers Dimensions
818 Connecticut Avenue, NW
7th Floor
Washington, DC 20006-2734
202-783-7200
Fax: 202-783-7207
E-mail: info@astc.org
http://www.astc.org
Publication Date: 1973 20 pages
ISSN: 1528-820X
Carolyn Sutterfield, Author
Chevy Humphrey, Chair
Linda Conlon, Chair-Elect

4793 CCAS Newsletter
Council of Colleges of Arts & Sciences
PO Box 8795
Williamsburg, VA 23187-8795
757-221-1784
Fax: 757-221-1776
E-mail: ccas@wm.edu
http://www.ccas.net
Membership newsletter to inform deans about arts and sciences issues in education.

Publication Date: 1965 4-10 pages Bi-Monthly
Dr. Anne-Marieÿ McCartan, Executive Director
Nichelle Wright, Office Specialist

4794 Cream of the Crop
California Foundation for Agriculture
2300 River Plaza Drive
Sacramento, CA 95833-3293
916-561-5625
800-700-2482
Fax: 916-561-5697
E-mail: info@learnaboutag.org
http://www.LearnAboutAg.org
E-newsletter released monthly with articles about agriculture related resources, ideas, information and CFAITC event overviews.

Judy Culbertson, Executive Director
Mindy DeRohan, Communications Coordinator

4795 Journal of College Science Teaching
National Science Teachers Association
1840 Wilson Boulevard
Arlington, VA 22201-3000
703-243-7100
800-782-6782
Fax: 703-243-7177
http://www.nsta.org
Professional journal for college and university teachers of introductory and advanced science with special emphasis on interdisciplinary teaching of nonscience majors. Contains feature articles and departments including a science column, editorials, lab demonstrations, problem solving techniques and book reviews.

6x Year
Juliana Texley, President
Carolyn Hayes, President Elect

4796 Journal of Environmental Education
Taylor & Francis
325 Chestnut Street
Suite 800
Philadelphia, PA 19106
215-625-8900
800-354-1420
Fax: 202-296-5149
E-mail: customer.service@taylorandfrancis.com
http://www.heldref.org
A vital research journal for everyone teaching about the environment. Each issue features case studies of relevant projects, evaluation of new research, and discussion of public policy and philosophy in the area of environmental education. The Journal is an excellent resource for department chairpersons and directors of programs in outdoor education.

Quarterly
Kerri P Kilbane, Editor

4797 Journal of Research in Science Teaching
Wiley InterScience
Wiley Corporate Headquarters
111 River Street
Hoboken, NJ 07030-5774
866-465-3817
Fax: 201-748-5715
E-mail: onlinelibrarysales@wiley.com
http://www.interscience.wiley.com
10x Year

4798 NSTA Reports!
National Science Teachers Association
1840 Wilson Boulevard
Arlington, VA 22201-3000
703-243-7100
800-782-6782
Fax: 703-243-7177
http://www.nsta.org
The association's timely source of news on issues of interest to science teachers of all levels. Includes national news, information on teaching materials, announcements of programs for teachers and students, and advance notice about all NSTA programs, conventions and publications.

52 pages BiMonthly
Juliana Texley, President
Carolyn Hayes, President Elect

4799 Odyssey
Cobblestone Publishing
30 Grove Street
Suite C
Peterborough, NH 03458-1453
603-924-7209
800-821-0115
Fax: 603-924-7380
E-mail: custsvc@cobblestonepub.org
http://www.odysseymagazine.com
Secrets of science are probed with each theme issues's articles, interviews, activities and math puzzles. Astronomical concepts are experienced with Jack Horkheimer's Star Gazer cartoon and Night-Sky Navigation.

48 pages Monthly
ISSN: 0163-0946
Elizabeth E Lindstrom, Editor

4800 Physics Teacher
American Association of Physics Teachers
One Physics Ellipse
College Park, MD 20740-3845
301-209-3311
Fax: 301-209-0845
E-mail: webmaster@aapt.org
http://www.aapt.org
Published by the American Association of Physics Teachers and dedicated to the improvement of the teaching of introductory physics at all levels.

9x Year
Mary Elizabeth Mogge, President
Janelle M. Bailey, President Elect

4801 Quantum
National Science Teachers Association
1840 Wilson Boulevard
Arlington, VA 22201-3000
703-243-7100
800-782-6782
Fax: 703-243-7177
http://www.nsta.org
Illustrated magazine containing material translated from Russian magazine Kvant as well as original material specifically targeted to American students. In addition to feature articles and department pieces, Quantum offers olympiad-style problems and brainteasers. Each issue also contains an answer section.

BiMonthly
Juliana Texley, President
Carolyn Hayes, President Elect

4802 Reports of the National Center for Science Education
National Center for Science Education
420 40th Streetÿ
Suite 2
Oakland, CA 94609-2688
510-601-7203
800-290-6006
Fax: 510-601-7204
E-mail: info@ncse.com
http://www.ncseweb.org
An examination of issues and current events in science education with a focus on evolutionary science, and the evolution/creation controversy.

36-44 pages BiMonthly Newsletter
ISSN: 1064-2358

Brian Altersÿ, President
Lorne Trottier, Vice President/ Treasurer

4803 Science Activities
Heldref Publications
325 Chestnut Street
Suite 800
Philadelphia, PA 19106
215-625-8900
800-365-9753
Fax: 202-296-5149
E-mail: customer.service@taylorandfrancis.com
http://www.heldref.org
A storehouse of up-to-date creative science projects and curriculum ideas for the K-12 classroom teacher. A one-step source of experiments, projects and curriculum innovations in the biological, physical and behavioral sciences, the journal's ideas have been teacher tested, providing the best of actual classroom experiences. Regular departments feature news notes, computer news, book reviews and new products and resources for the classroom.

48 pages Quarterly
ISSN: 0036-8121

Betty Bernard, Managing Editor

4804 Science News Magazine
Society for Science & The Public
1719 N Street NW
Washington, DC 20036-2888
202-785-2255
800-552-4412
Fax: 202-659-0365
E-mail: member@societyforscience.org
http://www.societyforscience.org
Information and programs in all areas of science.

Publication Date: 1921 Weekly

Maya Ajmera, CEO/ President/ Publisher
Tom Bakry, Chief Technology Officer

4805 Science Scope
National Science Teachers Association
1840 Wilson Boulevard
Arlington, VA 22201-3000
703-243-7100
800-782-6782
Fax: 703-243-7177
http://www.nsta.org
Specifically for middle-school and junior-high science teachers. Science Scope addresses the needs of both new and veteran teachers. The publication includes classroom activities, posters and teaching tips, along with educational theory on the way adolescents learn.

8x Year

Juliana Texley, President
Carolyn Hayes, President Elect

4806 Science Teacher
National Science Teachers Association
1840 Wilson Boulevard
Arlington, VA 22201-3000
703-243-7100
800-782-6782
Fax: 703-243-7177
http://www.nsta.org
Professional journal for junior and senior high school science teachers. Offers articles on a wide range of scientific topics, innovative teaching ideas and experiments, and current research news. Also offers reviews, posters, information on free or inexpensive materials, and more.

9x Year

Juliana Texley, President
Carolyn Hayes, President Elect

4807 Science and Children
National Association of Science Teachers
1840 Wilson Boulevard
Arlington, VA 22201-3000
703-243-7100
800-782-6782
Fax: 703-243-7177
http://www.nsta.org
Dedicated to preschool through middle school science teaching provides lively how-to articles, helpful hints, software and book reviews, colorful posters and inserts, think pieces and on-the-scene reports from classroom teachers.

8x Year

Juliana Texley, President
Carolyn Hayes, President Elect

4808 Sea Frontiers
International Oceanographic Foundation
4600 Rickenbacker Causeway
Key Biscayne, FL 33149-1031
305-361-4888
A general interest magazine about science education including underwater studies.

BiMonthly

Bonnie Gordon, Editor

4809 Teacher Resource Guide
California Foundation for Agriculture
2300 River Plaza Drive
Sacramento, CA 95833
916-561-5625
800-722-2482
Fax: 916-561-5697
E-mail: infolearnaboutag.org
http://www.LearnAboutAg.org
This is a must have tool for professional and volunteers encouraging the agriculturalliteracy of California's youth. Resources that assist in teaching about agriculture are plentiful. This guide provides an all-encompassing look at the array of materials that readily support such an endeavor.

Judy Culbertson, Executive Director
Mindy DeRohan, Communications Coordinator

4810 Universe in the Classroom
Astronomical Society of the Pacific
390 Ashton Avenue
San Francisco, CA 94112-1722
415-337-1100
Fax: 415-337-5205
E-mail: astroed@astrosociety.org
http://www.astrosociety.org/uitc
On teaching astronomy in grades 3-12, including astronomical news, plain-English

explanations, teaching resources and classroom activities.

8 pages Quarterly

Gordon Myers, President
Connie Walker, Vice President

Periodicals / *Social Studies*

4811 Alumni Newsletter
Jewish Labor Committee
25 East 21st Street
Floor 2
New York, NY 10010-6207
212-477-0707
Fax: 212-477-1918
E-mail: JLCExec@aol.com
http://www.jewishfederations.org/IR/community-directory.aspx-id=496
Newsletter of American public secondary school teachers who teach about the Holocaust and Jewish Resistance to the Nazis during World War II.

8 pages SemiAnnually

Avram B.ÿ Lyon, Executive Director

4812 American Sociological Review
Pennsylvania State University
211 Oswald Tower, Department of Soc
University Park, PA 16802
814-865-2527
Fax: 814-863-7216
E-mail: sociology@la.psu.edu
http://www.psu.edu/
Addresses most aspects of sociology in a general range of categories for academic and professional sociologists.

Bimonthly

David Baker, Professor of Education
Duane Alwin, Director

4813 AnthroNotes
Smithsonian Information
PO Box 37012
SI Building, Room 153, MRC 010
Washington, DC 20013-7012
202-633-1000
Fax: 202-357-2208
E-mail: info@si.edu
http://www.mnh.si.edu
Offers archeological, anthropological research in an engaging style.

4814 AppleSeeds
Cobblestone Publishing
30 Grove Street
Suite C
Peterborough, NH 03458-1453
603-924-7209
800-821-0115
Fax: 603-924-7380
E-mail: custsvc@cobblestonepub.com
http://www.cobblestonepub.com
A delightful way to develop love of non-fiction reading in grades 2-4. Full color articles, photographs, maps, activities that grab student and teacher interest. Children's doings and thinking around the world in Mail Bag.

Publication Date: 1973 32 pages Monthly
ISSN: 1099-7725

Susan Buckey, Barb Burt, Editors, Author
Lou Waryncia, Managing Editor

4815 Boletin
Center for the Teaching of the Americas
Immaculata College
Immaculata, PA 19345
610-647-4400

School teaching of the Americas.

Quarterly

Sr. Mary Consuela

4816 California Weekly Explorer

California Weekly Reporter
285 E Main Street
Suite 3
Tustin, CA 92780-4429
714-730-5991
Fax: 714-730-3548
Resources, events, awards and reviews relating to California history.

16 pages Weekly

Don Oliver

4817 Calliope

Cobblestone Publishing
30 Grove Street
Suite C
Peterborough, NH 03458-1453
603-924-7209
800-821-0115
Fax: 603-924-7380
E-mail: custsvc@cobblestonepub.com
http://www.cobblestonepub.com
Invests in world history with reality not only through articles, stories and maps but also current events and resource lists. Calliope's themes are geared to topics studied in world history classrooms.

48 pages Monthly
ISSN: 1058-7086

Lou Waryncia, Managing Editor
Charles F Baker, Editors

4818 Capitalism for Kids

National Schools Commitee for Economic Education
250 East 73rd Street
Suite 12G
New York, NY 10021-8641
212-535-9534
Fax: 212-535-4167
E-mail: info@nscee.org
http://www.nscee.org
Teaches young people about capitalism and the free enterprise system in a clear and entertaining styl. Disscusses the practical aspects of starting a small business.

247 pages

Edward H. Crane, Jr., Chairman
John G. Murphy, Ph.D, President

4819 Cobblestone

Cobblestone Publishing
30 Grove Street
Suite C
Peterborough, NH 03458-1453
603-924-7209
800-821-0115
Fax: 603-924-7380
E-mail: custsvc@cobblestonepub.com
http://www.cobblestonepub.com
Blends sound information with excellent writing, a combination that parents and teachers appreciate. Cobblestone offers imaginative approaches to introduce young readers to the world of American history.

48 pages Monthly
ISSN: 0199-5197

Lou Waryncia, Managing Editor
Meg Chorlian, Editor

4820 Colloquoy on Teaching World Affairs

World Affairs Council of North California
312 Sutter Street
Suite 200
San Francisco, CA 94108-4311
415-293-4600
Fax: 415-982-5028
http://www.worldaffairs.org
Offers information, articles and updates for the history teacher.

3x Year

Peter J. Robertson, Chairman
Jane M. Wales, President/ CEO

4821 Faces

Cobblestone Publishing
30 Grove Street
Suite C
Peterborough, NH 03458-1453
603-924-7209
800-821-0115
Fax: 603-924-7380
E-mail: custsvc@cobblestonepub.com
http://www.cobblestonepub.com
The world is brought to the classroom through the faces of its people. World culture encourages young readers' perspectives through history, folk tales, news and activities.

48 pages Monthly
ISSN: 0749-1387

Lou Waryncia, Managing Editor
Elizabeth Crooker Carpentiere, Editor

4822 Focus

Freedoms Foundation at Valley Forge
PO Box 706
Valley Forge, PA 19482-0706
215-933-8825
800-896-5488
Fax: 610-935-0522
E-mail: tsueta@ffvf.org
http://www.ffvf.org
Strives to teach America and promote responsible citizenship through educational programs and awards designed to recognize outstanding Americans.

6 pages Quarterly

Thomas M Sueat, Editor

4823 Footsteps

Cobblestone Publishing
30 Grove Street
Suite C
Peterborough, NH 03458-1453
603-924-7209
800-821-0115
Fax: 603-924-7380
E-mail: custsvc@cobblestonepub.com
http://www.cobblestonepub.com
Celebrates heritage of African Americans and explores their contributions to culture from colonial times to present. Courage, perserverance mark struggle for freedom and equality in articles, maps, photos, etc.

48 pages 9x Year
ISSN: 1521-5865

Lou Waryncia, Managing Editor
Charles Baker, Editor

4824 History Matters Newsletter

National Council for History Education
13940 Cedar Rd. #393
University Heights, OH 44118
240-696-6600
Fax: 240-523-0245
E-mail: NCHE@nche.net
http://www.nche.net

Serves as a resource to help members improve the quality and quantity of history learning.

8 pages Monthly
ISSN: 1090-1450

Justin Jakovac, Executive Director
John Csepegi, Director of Membershipÿ

4825 Inquiry in Social Studies: Curriculum, Research & Instruction

University of North Carolina-Charlotte
Dept of Curriculum & Instruction
Charlotte, NC 28223
704-547-4500
Fax: 704-547-4705
An annual journal of North Carolina Council for the Social Studies with a readership of 1,400.

Annual

John A Gretes, Editor
Jeff Passe, Editor

4826 Journal of American History

Organization of American Historians
112 N. Bryan Avenue
Bloomington, IN 47408-4141
812-855-7311
800-446-8923
Fax: 812-855-0696
http://www.oah.org/meetings-events/2015/
Contains articles and essays concerning the study and investigation of American history.

Quarterly

Patricia Limerick, President
Jon Butler, President-Elect

4827 Journal of Economic Education

Heldref Publications
325 Chestnut Street
Suite 800
Philadelphia, PA 19106
215-625-8900
800-365-9753
Fax: 202-296-5149
E-mail: customer.service@taylorandfrancis.com
http://www.heldref.org
Offers original articles on innovations in and evaluations of teaching techniques, materials and programs in economics.

Quarterly
ISSN: 0022-4085

4828 Journal of Geography

National Council for Geographic Education
1101 14ÿStreet, NW
Suite 350
Washington, DC 20005-5647
202-216-0942
Fax: 202-618-6249
E-mail: ncge@jsu.edu
http://www.ncge.org
Stresses the essential value of geographic education and knowledge in schools.

Quarterly
ISSN: 0022-1341

Susan Hume, President
Eric J. Fournier, Board Chair

4829 Magazine of History

Organizations of American History
112 N. Bryan Avenue
Bloomington, IN 47408-4141
812-855-7311
800-446-8923
Fax: 812-855-0696
E-mail: oah@oah.org
http://www.oah.org
Includes informative articles, lesson plans, current historiography and reproducible classroom materials on a particular theme. In addition to topical articles, such columns as Dialogue, Studentspeak and History Headlines allow for the

exchange of ideas from all levels of the profession.

70-90 pages Quarterly Magazine
ISSN: 0882-228X

Patricia Limerick, President
Jon Butler, President-Elect

4830 New England Journal of History
Bentley College
Dept of History
175 Forest Street
Waltham, MA 02452
781-891-2000
Fax: 781-891-2896
http://www.bentley.edu
Covers all aspects of American history for the professional and student.

3x Year

Gloria Cordes Larson, Esq., President
Victor Schlitzer, Director, Marketing & Adv.

4831 News & Views
Pennsylvania Council for the Social Studies
11533 Clematis Boulevard
Pittsburgh, PA 15235-3105
717-238-8768
E-mail: lguru1@aol.com
http://www.pcss.org
Offers news, notes, and reviews of interest to social studies educators.

20 pages 5x Year
ISSN: 0894-8712

Jack Suskind, Executive Secretary
Leo R West, Editor

4832 Perspective
Association of Teachers of Latin American Studies
PO Box 620754
Flushing, NY 11362-0754
718-428-1237
Fax: 718-428-1237
Promotes the teaching of Latin America in US schools and colleges.

10 pages BiMonthly
Daniel Mugan

4833 Social Education
National Council for the Social Studies
8555 Sixteenth Street
Suite 500
Silver Spring, MD 20910
301-588-1800
800-683-0812
Fax: 301-588-2049
E-mail: sgriffin@ncss.org
http://www.socialstudies.org
Journal for the social studies profession serves middle school, high school and college and university teachers. Social Education features research on significant topics relating to social studies, lesson plans that can be applied to various disciplines, techniques for using teaching materials in the classroom and information on the latest instructional technology.

7x Year
ISSN: 0337-7724

Michelle Herczog, President
Kim O'Neil, President Elect

4834 Social Studies
Heldref Publications
325 Chestnut Street
Suite 800
Philadelphia, PA 19106
215-625-8900
800-365-9753
Fax: 202-296-5149
E-mail:

customer.service@taylorandfrancis.com
http://www.heldref.org
Offers K-12 classroom teachers, teacher educators and curriculum administrators an independent forum for publishing their ideas about the teaching of social studies at all levels. The journal presents teachers' methods and classroom-tested suggestions for teaching social studies, history, geography and the social sciences.

48 pages BiMonthly

Helen Kress, Managing Editor

4835 Social Studies Journal
Pennsylvania Council for the Social Studies
11533 Clematis Boulevard
Pittsburgh, PA 15235-3105
717-238-8768
E-mail: lguru1@aol.com
http://www.pcss.org
Delves into matters of social studies, history, research and statistics for the education professional and science community.

80 pages Annual

Leo R West, Editor
Dr. Saundra McKee, Editor

4836 Social Studies Professional
National Council for the Social Studies
8555 Sixteenth Street
Suite 500
Silver Spring, MD 20910
301-588-1800
800-683-0812
Fax: 301-588-2049
E-mail: sgriffin@ncss.org
http://www.socialstudies.org
Newsletter focusing on strategies, tips and techniques for the social studies educator. New product announcements, professional development opportunities, association news, state and regional meetings.

6 Times

Michelle Herczog, President
Kim O'Neil, President Elect

4837 Social Studies and the Young Learner
National Council for the Social Studies
8555 Sixteenth Street
Suite 500
Silver Spring, MD 20910
301-588-1800
800-683-0812
Fax: 301-588-2049
E-mail: sgriffin@ncss.org
http://www.socialstudies.org
This publication furthers creative teaching in grades K-6, meeting teachers' needs for new information and effective teaching activities.

Quarterly

Steven S. Lapham, Editor

4838 Society For History Education/History Teacher
California State University - Long Beach
CSULB, 1250 Bellflower Blvd.
Long Beach, CA 90840-1601
562-985-2573
Fax: 562-985-5431
E-mail: historyteacherjournal@gmail.com
http://www.thehistoryteacher.org
The most widely recognized journal in the United States suppoting all areas of history education, pre-collegiate through university level, with practical and insightful profes-

sional analyses of both traditional and innovative teaching techniques.

150 pages Quarterly
ISSN: 0018-2745

Jane Dabel, Editor
Elisa Herrera, Executive Director

4839 Teaching Georgia Government Newsletter
Carl Vinson Institute of Government
201 N Milledge Avenue
Athens, GA 30602-5482
706-542-2736
Fax: 706-542-9301
http://www.cviog.uga.edu
Substantive and supplementary material for social studies teachers in Georgia. Topics of government, history, archaeology, geography, citizenship, etc. are covered. Publications available and upcoming social studies meetings in the state are also announced.

8 pages TriAnnually

Stacy Jones, Associate Director
Laura Meadows, Director

4840 Theory and Research in Social Education
National Council for the Social Studies
8555 Sixteenth Street
Suite 500
Silver Spring, MD 20910
301-588-1800
800-683-0812
Fax: 301-588-2049
E-mail: sgriffin@ncss.org
http://www.socialstudies.org
Features articles covering a variety of topics: teacher training, learning theory, and child development research; instructional strategies; the relationship of the social sciences, philosophy, history and the arts to social education; models and theories used in developing social studies curriculum; and schemes for student participation and social action.

Quarterly

Michelle Herczog, President
Kim O'Neil, President Elect

4841 Wall Street Journal - Classroom Edition
PO Box 7019
Chicopee, MA 01021
800-544-0522
Fax: 413-598-2332
E-mail: classroom.edition@wsj.com
http://www.wsjclassroom.com
Monthly student newspaper, with stories drawn from the daily journal that show international, business, economic, and social issues affect students' lives and futures. The newspaper is supported by posters, monthly teacher guides, and videos. Regular features on careers, enterprise, marketing, personal finance and technology. Helps teachers prepare students for the world of work by combining timely articles with colorful graphics, etc.

Monthly

Krishnan Anantharamanz, Editor

4842 Women's History Project News
National Women's History Project
730 Second Street #469ÿ
PO Box 469
Santa Rosa, CA 95402
707-636-2888
Fax: 707-636-2909
E-mail: nwhp1980@gmail.com
http://www.nwhp.org
Monthly E-mail newsletter about US women's history, for educators, researchers,

program planners, and general women's history enthusiasts.

Monthly

Molly Murphy MacGregor, Chair/ Co-Founder
Shona Rocco, Financial Manager

Periodicals / *Technology in Education*

4843 Cable in the Classroom
CCI/Crosby Publishing
214 Lincoln Street
Suite 112
Boston, MA 02134
617-254-9481
Fax: 617-254-9776
http://www.ciconline.org
Most comprehensive guide to integrating educational video with the Internet and other curriculum resources for K-12 educators.

54 pages Monthly
ISSN: 1054-5409

Stephen P Crosby, Publisher
Al Race, Executive Editor

4844 Connections/EdTech News
Commonwealth of Learning
4710 Kingsway, Suite 2500
Burnaby, BC V5Hÿ-4M2
604-775-8200
Fax: 604-775-8210
E-mail: info@col.org
http://www.col.org/connections
Published three times per year to, these newsletters provide a continually updated mailing list of over 9,000 government officials, education leaders and international agencies with information on COL's work with its partners as well as other developments worldwide.

Asha S. Kanwar, President/ CEO
Vis Naidoo, Vice President

4845 E-School News
7920 Norfolk Avenue
Suite 900
Bethesda, MD 20814
301-913-0115
800-394-0115
Fax: 301-913-0119
E-mail: ndavid@eschoolnews.com
http://www.eschoolnews.com
Monthly newspaper dedicated to providing news and information to help educators use technology to improve education.

Monthly

Gregs Downey, Publisher
Nancy David, Customer Relations
Director

4846 EDUCAUSE Quarterly
EDUCAUSE
282 Century Place
Suite 5000
Louisville, CO 80027
303-449-4430
Fax: 303-440-0461
E-mail: info@educause.edu
http://www.educause.edu
Strategic policy advocacy; teaching and learning initiatives; applied research; special interest collaboration communities; awards for leadership and exemplary prac-

tices; and extensive online information services.

Quarterly Magazine
ISSN: 1528-5324

Nancy Hays, Author
Diana G. Oblinger, President/ CEO
Kay Rhodes, Asso. Vice Chancellor &
CIO

4847 EDUCAUSE Review
EDUCAUSE
282 Century Place
Suite 5000
Louisville, CO 80027-2408
303-449-4430
Fax: 303-440-0461
E-mail: info@educause.edu
http://www.educause.edu
Strategic policy advocacy; teaching and learning initiatives applied research; special interest collaboration communities; awards for leadership and exemplary practices; and extensive online information services.

Monthly
ISSN: 1527-6619

Nancy Hays, Author
Diana G. Oblinger, President/ CEO
Kay Rhodes, Asso. Vice Chancellor &
CIO

4848 Education Technology News
Business Publishers
2222 Sedwick Drive
Durham, NC 27713
301-587-6300
800-223-8720
Fax: 800-508-2592
E-mail: custserv@bpinews.com
http://www.bpinews.com
Offers information on computer hardware, multimedia products, software applications, public and private funding and integration of technology into K-12 classrooms.

8 pages BiWeekly

Eric Easton, Publisher
Brian Love, Editorial Coordinato

4849 Educational Technology
700 E Palisade Avenue
Englewood Cliffs, NJ 07632-3040
201-871-4007
800-952-BOOK
Fax: 201-871-4009
Published since 1961, periodical covering the entire field of educational technology. Issues feature essays by leading authorities plus a Research Section. With many special issues covering aspects of the field in depth. Readers are found in some 120 countries.

9x Year

Lawrence Lipsitz, Editor

4850 Electronic Learning
Scholastic
555 Broadway
New York, NY 10012-3919
212-343-6100
800-724-6527
Fax: 212-343-4801
Published for the administrative level, education professionals who are directly responsible for the implementing of electronic technology at the district, state and university levels.

8x Year

Lynn Diamond, Advertising Director
Therese Mageau, Editor

4851 Electronic School
1680 Duke Street
Alexandria, VA 22314
703-838-6722
Fax: 703-683-7590
E-mail: cwilliams@nsba.org
http://www.electronic-school.com
The school technology authority.

Cheryl S Williams, Director
Ann Lee Flynn, Director Education

4852 Information Searcher
Datasearch Group
14 Hadden Road
Scarsdale, NY 10583-3328
914-723-1995
Fax: 914-723-1995
http://www.infosearcher.com
Quarterly newsletter for the Internet and curriculum-technology integration in school.

32 pages

Pam Berger, President
Bill Berger, Treasurer

4853 Journal of Computing in Childhood Education
AACE
PO Box 2966
Charlottesville, VA 22902-2966
757-623-7588
Fax: 703-997-8760
http://www.aace.org
Discusses the realm of software and technology now merging with primary education.

Quarterly

4854 Journal of Educational Technology Systems
58 New Mill Road
Smithtown, NY 11787-3342
516-632-8767
A compendium of articles submitted by professionals regarding the newest technology in the educational field.

Quarterly

Dr. Thomas Liao, Editor

4855 Journal of Information Systems Education
Bryant University
1150 Douglas Pike
Smithfield, RI 02917-1284
401-232-6000
800-622-7001
Fax: 401-232-6319
E-mail: admission@bryant.edu
http://www.bryant.edu
Publishes original articles on current topics of special interest to Information Systems Educators and Trainers. Focus is applications-oriented articles describing curriculum, professional development or facilities issues. Topics include course projects/cases, lecture materials, curriculum design and/or implementation, workshops, faculty/student intern/extern programs, hardware/software selection and industry relations.

Quarterly

Richard Glass, Contact

4856 Journal of Research on Computing in Education
International Society for Technology in Education
1530 Wilson Boulevard
Suite 730
Arlington, VA 22209
703-348-4784
800-336-5191
Fax: 703-348-6459

E-mail: iste@iste.org
http://www.iste.org
A quarterly journal of original research and detailed system and project evaluations. It also defines the state of the art and future horizons of educational computing.

Quarterly

Diane McGrath, Editor
Brian Lewis, M.A., C.A.E., CEO

857 Journal of Special Education Technology
The Council for Exceptional Children
1920 Association Drive
Reston, VA 20191-1589
703-620-3660
888-232-7733
Fax: 703-264-9494
E-mail: cec@cec.sped.org
http://cecp.air.org/teams/stratpart/cec.asp
Provides professionals in the field with information on new technologies, current research, exemplary practices, relevant issues, legislative events and more concerning the availability and effective use of technology and media for individuals with disabilities and/or who are gifted.

Quarterly

Herbert Rieth, Editor

858 Matrix Newsletter
Department of CCTE, Teachers
College/Communication
PO Box 8
New York, NY 10027-0008
212-678-3344
Fax: 212-678-8227
Newsletter describing activities and interests of Department of Communication, Computing and Technology.

14 pages SemiAnnually
Marie Sayer

859 MultiMedia Schools
Information Today
143 Old Marlton Pike
Medford, NJ 08055-8750
609-654-6266
800-300-9868
Fax: 609-654-4309
E-mail: custserv@infotoday.com
http://www.infotoday.com
A practical journal of multimedia, CD-Rom, online and Internet in K-12.

Thomas H Hogan, Publisher
Ferdi Serim, Editor

860 National Forum of Instructional Technology Journal
McNeese State University
4205 Ryan Stree
Lake Charles, LA 70601-5915
337-475-5000
800-622-3352
Fax: 318-475-5467
http://www.mcneese.edu
Publication Date: 1939
Dr. J Mark Hunter, Editor

861 Society for Applied Learning Technology
50 Culpeper Street
Warrenton, VA 20186
540-347-0055
800-457-6812
Fax: 540-349-3169
E-mail: info@lti.org
http://www.salt.org
Publication Date: 1972 Quarterly

4862 TAM Connector
The Council for Exceptional Children
1920 Association Drive
Reston, VA 20191-1589
703-620-3660
888-232-7733
Fax: 703-264-9494
E-mail: cec@cec.sped.org
http://cecp.air.org/teams/stratpart/cec.asp
Contains information about upcoming events, current trends and practices, state and national legislation, recently published materials and practical information relative to the availability and effective use of technology and media for individuals who are gifted or are disabled.

Quarterly

Cynthia Warger, Editor

4863 TECHNOS Quarterly for Education & Technolgy
Agency for Instructional Technology
8111 N. Lee Paul Road
Bloomington, IN 47404-7916
812-339-2203
800-457-4509
Fax: 812-333-4218
E-mail: info@ait.net
http://www.ait.net
TECHNOS Quarterly is a forum for the discussion of ideas about the use of technology in education, with a focus on reform.

36 pages Quarterly
ISSN: 1060-5649

Michael F Sullivan, Executive Director
Carole Novak, Manager TECHNOS Press

4864 Tech Directions
Prakken Publications
275 Meity Drive
P.O. Box 8623
Ann Arbor, MI 48107-8623
734-975-2800
Fax: 734-975-2787
E-mail: publisher@techdirections.com
http://www.eddigest.com
Issues programs, projects for educators in career-technical and technology education and monthly features on technology, computers, tech careers.

Monthly
ISSN: 1062-9351

Tom Bowden, Managing Editor

4865 Technology & Learning
NewBay Media
28 East 28th Street
12th Floor
New York, NY 10016
212-378-0400
800-607-4410
Fax: 212-378-0470
http://www.techlearning.com
Product reviews; hard-hitting, straightforward editorial features; ideas on challenging classroom activities; and more. Tailor made to the special needs of a professional and an educator.

Publication Date: 2006 60-80 pages Monthly Magazine
ISSN: 1053-6728
March & October

Susan McLester, Author
Judy Salpeter, Editor-in-Chief
Jo-Ann McDevitt, Publisher

4866 Technology Integration for Teachers
Master Teacher
One Leadership Lane
PO Box 1207
Manhattan, KS 66502-1207

800-669-9633
Fax: 800-669-1132
http://www.masterteacher.com
4 pages Monthly

4867 Technology Teacher
International Technology Education Association
1914 Association Drive
Suite 201
Reston, VA 20191-1538
703-860-2100
Fax: 703-860-0353
E-mail: itea@iris.org
http://www.iteawww.org
Seeks to advance technological literacy through professional development activities and publications.

40 pages 8x Year

Kendall Starkweather, Executive Director
Kathleen de la Paz, Editor

4868 Technology in Education Newsletter
111 E 14th Street
#140
New York, NY 10003-4103
800-443-7432
This newsletter for K-12 educators and administrators, covers national trends of technology in education.

4869 Web Feet Guides
Thomson Gale
Thomson Gale World Headquarters
27500 Drake Road
Farmington Hills, MI 48331-3535
248-699-4253
800-877-4253
Fax: 877-363-4253
http://www.webfeetguides.com
The premier subject guides to the Internet, rigorously reviewed by librarians and educators, fully annotated, expanded and updated monthly. Appropriate for middle school through adult. Available in print, online, or MARC records. For more information, free trials and free samples.

Monthly

General

4870 ABC Feelings Adage Publications
Po Box 7280
Ketchum, ID 83340
208-788-5399
Fax: 208-788-4195
E-mail: info@abcfeelings.com
http://www.abcfeelings.com
Interactive line of children's products that relate feelings to each letter of the alphabet. Encourages dialogue, understanding, communication, enhances self-esteem. Books, audiotape, poster, placemats, charts, activity cards, t-shirts and multicultural activity guides, floor puzzles, feelings dictionary, carpets.

Ages 3-10

Dr. Alexandra Delis-Abrams, President

4871 ABDO Publishing Company
P.O Box 398166
Minneapolis, MN 55439-5300
452-831-2120
800-800-1312
Fax: 800-862-3480
E-mail: info@abdopublishing.com
http://www.abdopub.com
K-8 nonfiction books, including Abdo and Daughters imprint, high/low books for reluctant readers and Checkerboard Library with K-3 science, geography, and biographies for beginning readers. Sand Castle for pre-K to second grade, graduated reading program.

Jill Abdo Hansen, President
James Abdo, Publisher

4872 AGS
4201 Woodland Road
Circle Pines, MN 55014-1796
763-786-4343
800-328-2560
Fax: 800-471-8457
Major test publisher and distributor of tests for literature, reading, English, mathematics, sciences, aptitude, and various other areas of education. Includes information on timing, scoring, teacher's guides and student's worksheets.

4873 AIMS Education Foundation
1595 S Chestnut Avenue
Fresno, CA 93702-4706
559-255-4094
888-733-2467
Fax: 559-255-6396
E-mail: aimsed@fresno.edu
http://www.aimsedu.org
A nonprofit educational foundation that focuses on preparing materials for science and mathematics areas of education.

4874 Ablex Publishing Corporation
PO Box 811
Stamford, CT 06904-0811
201-767-8450
Fax: 201-767-8450
Publishes academic books and journals dealing with many different subject areas. Some of these include: education, linguistics, psychology, library science, computer and cognitive science, writing research and sociology.

Kristin K Butter, President

4875 Acorn Naturalists
155 El Camino Real
Tustin, CA 92780
714-838-4888
800-422-8886
Fax: 714-838-5309
http://www.acornnaturalists.com
Publishes and distributes science and environmental education materials for teachers, naturalists and outdoor educators. A complete catalog is available.
World Wildlife Fund, Author
Jennifer Rigby, Director
Mika Stonehawk, Operations Manager

4876 Active Child
PO Box 2346
Salem, OR 97308-2346
503-371-0865
Publishes creative curriculum for young children.

4877 Active Learning
10744 Hole Avenue
Riverside, CA 92505-2867
909-689-7022
Fax: 909-689-7142
Interactive learning center publishing materials for childhood education.

4878 Active Parenting Publishers
1220 Kennestone Circle
Suite 130
Marietta, GA 30066-6022
770-429-0565
800-825-0060
Fax: 770-429-0334
E-mail: cservice@activeparenting.com
http://www.activeparenting.com
Produces and sells books and innovative video-based programs for use in parent education, self-esteem education and loss education groups/classes.

4879 Addison-Wesley Publishing Company
2725 Sand Hill Road
Menlo Park, CA 94025-7019
650-854-0300
Publisher and distributor of a wide range of fiction, nonfiction and textbooks for grades K-12 in the areas of mathematics, reading, language arts, science, social studies and counseling.

4880 Advance Family Support & Education Program
301 S Frio Street
Suite 103
San Antonio, TX 78207-4422
210-270-4630
Fax: 210-270-4612
Offers books and publications on counseling and support for the family, student and educator.

4881 Alarion Press
PO Box 1882
Boulder, CO 80306-1882
303-443-9039
800-523-9177
Fax: 303-443-9098
E-mail: info@alarion.com
http://www.alarion.com
Video programs, posters, activities, manuals and workbooks dealing with History Through Art and Architecture for grades K-12.

4882 Albert Whitman & Company
250 South Northwest Highway
Suite 320
Park Ridge, IL 60068-2723
847-232-2800
800-255-7675
Fax: 847-581-0039
E-mail: mail@awhitmanco.com
http://www.albertwhitman.com
Children's books.

4883 Allyn & Bacon
160 Gould Street
Needham Heights, MA 02194
781-455-1250
Fax: 781-455-1220
Publisher of college textbooks and professional reference books.

4884 Alpha Publishing Company
1910 Hidden Point Road
Annapolis, MD 21401-6002
410-757-5404
Educational materials for K-12 curricula.

4885 American Association for State & Local History
1717 Church Street
Nashville, TN 37203-2921
615-320-3203
Fax: 615-327-9013
http://www.aaslh.org
How-to books for anyone teaching history or social studies.

4886 American Association of School Administrators
1615 Duke Street
Alexandria, VA 22314-1813
703-528-0700
Fax: 703-528-2146
E-mail: info@aasa.org
http://www.aasa.org
Paul Houston, Executive Director

4887 American Guidance Service
4201 Woodland Road
Circle Pines, MN 55014-1796
612-786-4343
800-328-2560
Fax: 763-783-4658
Largest distributor of educational materials focusing on guidance counselors and educators in the field of counseling. Materials include books, pamphlets, workshops and information on substance abuse, childhood education, alcoholism, inner-city subjects and more.

Matt Keller, Marketing Director

4888 American Institute of Physics
2 Huntington Quadrangle
Suite 1NO1
Melville, NY 11747
516-576-2200
Fax: 516-349-9704
http://www.aip.org
Physics books.

Marc Brodsky, Executive Director

4889 American Nuclear Society
Outreach Department
555 N Kensington Avenue
La Grange Park, IL 60526-5592
708-352-6611
800-323-3044
Fax: 708-352-0499
E-mail: outreach@ans.org
http://www.aboutnuclear.com
Nuclear science and technology, supplemental educational materials for grades K-12. ReActions newsletters.

4890 American Physiological Society
9650 Rockville Pike
Bethesda, MD 20814-3991
301-530-7132
Fax: 301-634-7098
http://www.the-aps.org
Videotapes, tracking materials and free teacher resource packets.

4891 American Technical Publishers
10100 Orland Parkway
Suite 200
Orland Parkway, IL 60467-5756
708-957-1100
800-323-3471
Fax: 708-957-1101
E-mail: service@americantech.net
http://www.go2atp.com
Offers instructional materials for a variety of vocational and technical training areas.

4892 American Water Works Association
6666 W Quincy Avenue
Denver, CO 80235-3098
303-794-7711
800-926-7337
Fax: 303-347-0804
http://www.awwa.org
Activity books, teacher guides and more on science education.

Gary McCoy, Director-at-large

4893 Ampersand Press
750 Lake Street
Port Townsend, WA 98368
360-379-5187
800-624-4263
Fax: 360-379-0324
E-mail: info@ampersandpress.com
http://www.ampersandpress.com
Nature and science educational games.

Lou Haller, Owner

4894 Amsco School Publications
315 Hudson Street
New York, NY 10013-1085
212-886-6500
800-969-8398
Fax: 212-675-7010
http://www.amscopub.com
Basal textbooks, workbooks and supplementary materials for grades 7-12.

4895 Anderson's Bookshops
123 West Jefferson
Naperville, IL 60540-3832
630-355-2665
Fax: 630-355-3470
http://www.andersonsbookshop.com
The very latest and best trade books to use in the classroom.

4896 Annenberg/CPB Project
1301 Pennsylvania Avenue NW
Suite 302
Washington, DC 20004-2037
202-783-0500
Fax: 202-783-0333
E-mail: order@learner.org
http://www.learner.org
Offers teaching resources in chemistry, geology, physics and environmental science.

Pete Neal, General Manager
Larisa M Kirgan, Operations Officer

4897 Art Image Publications
PO Box 160
Derby Line, VT 05830-0568
800-361-2598
Fax: 800-559-2598
http://www.artimagepublications.com
Offers various products including art appreciation kits, art image mini-kits and visual arts programs for grades K-12.

Rachel Ross, President
Rachel Ross, Art Educational Consultant

4898 Art Visuals
PO Box 925
Orem, UT 84059-0925
801-226-6115
Fax: 801-226-6115

E-mail: artvisuals@sisna.com
http://www.artvisuals.tripod.com
Social studies and art history products including an Art History Timeline, 20 feet long that represents over 50 different styles, ranging from prehistoric to contemporary art; Modern Art Styles, set of 30 posters depicting 20th century styles; Multicultural Posters, Africa, India, China, Japan and the World of Islam, with 18 posters in each culture. Sets on women artists and African American Artists. Each set is printed on hard cardstock, laminated and ultraviolet protected.

Diane Asay, Owner

4899 Asian American Curriculum Project
529 East Third Avenue
San Mateo, CA 94401
650-375-8286
800-874-2242
Fax: 650-375-8797
E-mail: aacpinc@best.com
http://www.asianamericanbooks.com
Develops, promotes and disseminates Asian-American books to schools, libraries and Asian-Americans. Over 1,500 titles.

Florence M Hongo, General Manager

4900 Association for Science Teacher Education
University of Florida
11000 University Parkway
Pensacola, FL 32514-5732
850-474-2000
Fax: 850-474-3205
http://www.theaste.org
Yearbooks, journals, newsletters and information on AETS.

John Tilloston, President

4901 Association for Supervision & Curriculum Development
ASCD
1703 N Beauregard Street
Alexandria, VA 22311-1717
703-578-9600
800-933-2723
Fax: 703-575-5400
E-mail: member@ascd.org
http://www.ascd.org
Publishers of educational leadership books, audios and videos focusing on teaching and learning in all subjects and grade levels.

4902 Association of American Publishers
71 5th Avenue
Floor 12
New York, NY 10003
212-255-0200
Fax: 212-255-7007
http://www.publishers.org
Association for the book publishing industry.

4903 Atheneum Books for Children
MacMillan Publishing Company
1633 Broadway
New York, NY 10019
212-512-2000
Fax: 800-835-3202
Hardcover trade books for children and young adults.

4904 Australian Press-Down Under Books
15235 Brand Boulevard
Suite A107
Mission Hills, CA 91345-1423
818-837-3755
Big Books, models for writing, small books and teacher's ideas books from Australia.

4905 Avon Books
1350 Avenue of the Americas
New York, NY 10019-4702

212-481-5600
Fax: 212-532-2172
Focuses on middle grade paperbacks for the classroom and features authors such as Cleary, Avi, Borks, Hous, Reeder, Hobbs, Hahn, Taylor and Prish.

4906 Ballantine/Del Rey/Fawcett/Ivy
201 E 50th Street
New York, NY 10022-7703
212-782-9000
800-638-6460
Fax: 212-782-8438
Offer paperback books for middle school and junior and senior high.

4907 Barron's Educational Series
250 Wireless Boulevard
Hauppauge, NY 11788-3924
631-434-3311
800-645-3476
Fax: 631-434-3217
E-mail: barrons@barronseduc.com
http://www.barronseduc.com
Educational books, including a full line of juvenile fiction and non-fiction, and titles for test prep and guidance, ESL, foreign language, art history and techniques, business, and reference.

Frederick Glasser, Director School/Library Sale

4908 Baylor College of Medicine
One Baylor Plaza
Houston, TX 77030
713-798-4951
Fax: 713-798-6521
http://www.bcm.edu
Offers materials and programs in the scientific area from Texas Scope, Sequence and Coordination projects.

Peter G Traber, President
Robert H Allen, Chairman

4909 Beech Tree Books
1350 Avenue of the Americas
New York, NY 10019-4702
212-261-6500
Fax: 212-261-6518
Curriculum offering reading materials, fiction and nonfiction titles.

4910 Black Butterfly Children's Books
625 Broadway
Floor 10
New York, NY 10012-2611
212-982-3158
A wide variety of books focusing on children, hardcover and paperback.

4911 Blake Books
2222 Beebee Street
San Luis Obispo, CA 93401-5505
805-543-7314
800-727-8550
Fax: 805-543-1150
Photo books on nature, endangered species, habitats, etc. for ages 10 and up.

Paige Torres, President

4912 Bluestocking Press Catalog
Bluestocking Press
PO Box 1014
Placerville, CA 95997-1014
530-622-8586
800-959-8586
Fax: 530-642-9222
E-mail: Jane@bluestockingpress.com
http://www.bluestockingpress.com
Approximately 800 items with a concentration in American History, economics and law. That includes fiction, nonfiction, primary source material, historical documents, fac-

simile newspapers, historical music, hands-on-kits, audio history, coloring books and more.

Jane A Williams, Coordinating Editor

4913 Boyds Mill Press
815 Church Street
Honesdale, PA 18431-1889
570-253-1164
Fax: 570-253-0179
Publishes books for children from pre-school to young adult.

4914 BridgeWater Books
100 Corporate Drive
Mahwah, NJ 07430-2041
Distinctive children's hardcover books featuring award-winning authors and illustrators, including Laurence Yep, Babette Cole, Joseph Bruchac and others. An imprint of Troll Associates.

4915 Bright Ideas Charter School
2507 Central Freeway East
Wichita Falls, TX 76302-5802
940-767-1561
Fax: 940-767-1904
E-mail: lydiaplmr@aol.com
K-12 curriculum framework for educators struggling to move toward a global tomorrow.

Lynda Plummer, President

4916 Brown & Benchmark Publishers
25 Kessel Court
Madison, WI 63711
608-273-0040
College textbooks in language arts and reading.

4917 Bureau for At-Risk Youth Guidance Channel
Guidance Channel
135 Dupont Street
PO Box 760
Plainview, NY 11803-0760
516-349-5520
800-999-6884
Fax: 800-262-1886
E-mail: info@at-risk.com
http://www.at-risk.com
Publisher and distributor of educational curriculums, videos, publications and products for at-risk youth and the counselors and others who work with them. Bureau products focus on areas such as violence and drug prevention, character education, parenting skills and more.

Sally Germain, Editor-in-Chief

4918 Business Publishers
PO Box 17592
Baltimore, MD 21297
301-587-6300
800-274-6737
Fax: 301-585-9075
E-mail: bpinews@bpinews.com
http://www.bpinews.com
Publishes education related materials.

4919 CLEARVUE/eav
6465 N Avondale Avenue
Chicago, IL 60631
773-775-9433
800-253-2788
Fax: 773-775-9855
E-mail: slucas@clearvue.com
http://www.clearvue.com
CLEARVUE/eav offers educators the largest line of curriculum-oriented media in the industry. CLEARVUE/eav programs have,

and will continue to enhance students' interest, learning, motivation and skills.

Sarah M Lucas, Communications Coordinator
Kelli Campbell, VP

4920 Calculators
7409 Fremont Avenue S
Minneapolis, MN 55423-3971
800-533-9921
Fax: 612-866-9030
Calculators and calculator books for K thru college level instruction. Calculator products by Texas Instruments, Casio, Sharp and Hewlett-Packard.

Richard Nelson, President

4921 Cambridge University Press
Edinburgh Building
Shaftesbury Road
Cambridge, England CB22RU

http://www.cup.cam.ac.uk
Curriculum materials and textbooks for science education for grades K-12.

4922 Candlewick Press
2067 Massachusetts Avenue
Cambridge, MA 02140-1340
617-661-3330
Fax: 617-661-0565
High quality trade hardcover and paperback books for children and young adults.

4923 Capstone Press
151 Good Counsel Drive
Mankato, MN 56001-3143
952-224-0529
888-262-6135
Fax: 888-262-0705
E-mail: timadsen@capstone-press.com
http://www.capstonepress.com
PreK-12 Nonfiction publisher

Tim Mandsen, Director Marketing

4924 Careers/Consultants in Education Press
3050 Palm Aire Drive N
#310
Pompano Beach, FL 33069
954-974-3511
Fax: 954-974-5477
E-mail: carconed@aol.com
Current education job lists for teacher and administrator positions in schools and colleges. Plus nine differently titled desk/reference paperback books.

Dr. Robert M Bookbinder, President

4925 Carolrhoda Books
A Division of Lerner Publishing Group
241 1st Avenue N
Minneapolis, MN 55401-1607
612-332-3344
800-328-4929
Fax: 612-332-7615
http://www.lernerbooks.com
Fiction and nonfiction for readers K through grade 6. List includes picture books, biographies, nature and science titles, multicultural and introductory geography books, and fiction for beginning readers.

Rebecca Poole, Submissions Editor

4926 Carson-Dellosa Publishing Company
PO Box 35665
Greensboro, NC 27425-5665
336-632-0084
800-321-0943
Fax: 336-632-087

Textbooks, manuals, workbooks and materials aimed at increasing students reading skills.

4927 Center for Play Therapy
University of North Texas
PO Box 311337
Denton, TX 76203
940-565-3864
Fax: 940-565-4461
E-mail: cpt@coefs.coe.unt.edu
http://www.centerforplaytherapy.com
Encourages the unique development and emotional growth of children through the process of play therapy, a dynamic interpersonal relationship between a child and a therapist trained in play therapy procedures. Provides training, research, publications, counseling services and acts as a clearinghouse for literature in the field.

Garry Landreth PhD, Director

4928 Central Regional Educational Laboratory
2550 S Parker Road
Suite 500
Aurora, CO 80014
303-337-0990
Fax: 303-337-3005
E-mail: twaters@mcrel.org
The Regional Educational Laboratories are educational research and development organizations supported by contracts with the US Education Department, Office of Educational Research and Improvement. Specialty area: curriculum, learning and instruction.

Dr. J Timothy Waters, Executive Director

4929 Charles Scribner & Sons
MacMillan Publishing Company
1633 Broadway
New York, NY 10019
212-632-4944
Fax: 800-835-3202
Hardcover trade books for children and young adults.

4930 Chicago Board of Trade
141 W Jackson Boulevard
Chicago, IL 60604-2992
312-435-3500
Educational materials including a new economics program entitled Commodity Challenge.

4931 Children's Book Council
12 West 37th Street
2nd Floor
New York, NY 10018-7480
212-966-1990
800-999-2160
Fax: 212-966-2073
E-mail: staff@cbcbooks.org
http://www.cbcbooks.org
The Children's Book Council, Inc is the nonprofit trade association of publishers and packagers of trade books and related materials for children and young adults.

JoAnn Sabatino-Falkenstein, VP Marketing

4932 Children's Press
Grolier Publishing
90 Sherman Turnpike
Danbury, CT 06816
800-621-1115
Fax: 800-374-4329
http://publishing.grolier.com
Leading supplier of reference and children's nonfiction and fiction books.

4933 Children's Press/Franklin Watts
PO Box 1330
Danbury, CT 06813-1330
203-797-3500
Fax: 203-797-3197
K-12 curriculum materials.

934 Children's Television Workshop
1 Lincoln Plaza
New York, NY 10023-7129
212-875-6809
Fax: 212-875-7388
Hands-on books for elementary school use in the area of science education.

Brenda Pilson, Review Coordinator
Elaine Israel, Editor-in-Chief

935 Chime Time
2440-C Pleasantdale Road
Atlanta, GA 30340-1562
770-662-5664
Early childhood products and publications.

936 Choices Education Project
Watson Institute for International Studies
Brown University
PO Box 1948
Providence, RI 02912-1948
401-863-3155
Fax: 401-863-1247
E-mail: choices@brown.edu
http://www.choices.edu
Develops interactive, supplementary curriculum resources on current and historical international issues. Makes complex current and historic international issues accessible for secondary school students. Materials are low-cost, reproducible, updated annually.

Annually

937 Close Up Publishing
44 Canal Center Plaza
Alexandria, VA 22314-1592
800-765-3131
Fax: 703-706-3564
Offers textbooks, workbooks and other publications focusing on self-esteem, learning and counseling.

38 Cognitive Concepts
PO Box 1363
Evanston, IL 60204-1363
888-328-8199
Fax: 847-328-5881
http://www.cogcon.com
Leading provider of language and literacy software, books, internet services and staff development. Specialize in integrating technology with scientific principles and proven instructional methods to offer effective and affordable learning solutions for educators, specialists and families.

39 College Board
45 Columbus Avenue
New York, NY 10023-6992
212-713-8000
Fax: 212-713-8282
http://www.collegeboard.org
Publishers of books of interest to educational researchers, policymakers, students, counselors, teachers; products to prepare students for college and test prep materials.

40 Coloring Concepts
1732 Jefferson Street
Suite 7
Napa, CA 94559-1737
707-257-1516
800-257-1516
Fax: 707-253-2019
E-mail: chris@coloringconcepts.com
http://www.coloringconcepts.com
Colorable active learning books for middle school through college that combine scientifically correct text with colorable illustrations to provide an enjoyable and educational experience that helps the user retain more information than during normal reading. Subjects include Anatomy, Marine Biology, Zoology,

Botany, Human Evolution, Human Brain, Microbiology and biology.

Christopher Elson, Operations

4941 Comprehensive Health Education Foundation
22419 Pacific Hwy S
Seattle, WA 98198-5106
206-824-2907
800-833-6388
E-mail: info@chef.org
http://www.chef.org
Primarily Health gives K-3 kids a dynamic, hands-on health program while teaching academic skills.

Larry Clark, President
Marvin Hamanishi, Vice President

4942 Computer Learning Foundation
PO Box 60007
Palo Alto, CA 94306-0007
408-720-8898
Fax: 408-730-1191
E-mail: clf@computerlearning.org
http://www.computerlearning.org
Publishes books and videos on using technology.

4943 Computer Literacy Press
Computer Literacy Press
PO Box 562
Earlysville, VA 22936
513-600-3455
513-530-0110
Fax: 800-833-5413
E-mail: info@complitpress.com
http://www.complitpress.com
Instructional materials using hands-on, step-by-step format, appropriate for courses in adult and continuing education, business education, computer literacy and applications, curriculum integration, Internet instruction, and training and staff development. Products are available for ranging from middle school through high school as well as post secondary, teacher training and adult/senior courses.

Robert First, President

4944 Concepts to Go
PO Box 10043
Berkeley, CA 94709-5043
510-848-3233
Fax: 510-486-1248
Develops and distributes manipulative activities for language arts and visual communications for ages 3-8.

4945 Congressional Quarterly
1414 22nd Street NW
Washington, DC 20037-1003
202-887-8500
Fax: 202-293-1487
Comprehensive publications and reference and paperback books pertaining to Congress, US Government and politics, the presidency, the Supreme Court, national affairs and current issues.

4946 Continental Press
520 E Bainbridge Street
Elizabethtown, PA 17022-2299
717-367-1836
800-233-0759
Fax: 717-367-5660
E-mail: cpeducation@continentalpress.com
http://www.continentalpress.com
Publisher of print for PreK-12 (plus adult education). Programs relate to skill areas in reading, math, comprehension, phonics, etc. Producers of Testlynx Software.

4947 Cottonwood Press
107 Cameron Drive
Suite 398
Fort Collins, CO 80525
970-204-0715
800-864-4297
Fax: 970-204-0761
E-mail: cottonwood@cottonwwodpress.com
http://www.cottonwoodpress.com
Publishes books focusing on teaching language arts and writing, grades 5-12.

Cheryl Thurston

4948 Council for Exceptional Children
The Council for Exceptional Children
1920 Association Drive
Reston, VA 20191-1589
703-620-3660
888-232-7733
Fax: 703-264-9494
E-mail: cec@cec.sped.org
http://cecp.air.org/teams/stratpart/cec.asp
The Council for Exceptional Children is a major publisher of special education literature and produces a catalog semiannually.

Marilyn Friend, President
Bruce Ramirez, Executive Director

4949 Creative Teaching Press
Po Box 2723
Huntington Beach, CA 92647-0723
800-287-8879
Fax: 800-229-9929
E-mail: customerservice@creativeteaching.com
http://www.creativeteaching.com
Offers language and literature-based books including Teaching Basic Skills through Literature, Literature-Based Homework Activities, I Can Read! I Can Write!, Multicultural Art Activities, Responding to Literature, and Linking Math and Literature.

Jim Connelly, President
Luella Connelly, Co-Founder

4950 Cricket Magazine Group
315 5th Street
Peru, IL 61354-2859
815-223-1500
Magazines of high quality children's literature.

4951 Curriculum Associates
PO Box 2001
North Billerica, MA 01862-0901
978-667-8000
800-225-0248
Fax: 800-366-1158
E-mail: cainfo@curriculumassociates.com
http://www.curriculumassociates.com
Supplementary educational materials; cross-curriculum, language arts, reading, study skills, test preparation, diagnostic assessments, emergent readers, videos, and software.

4952 DC Heath & Company
125 Spring Street
Lexington, MA 02421-7801
781-862-6650
Publishes resources for all academic levels ranging from textbooks, fiction and nonfiction titles to business and college guides.

4953 DLM Teaching Resources
PO Box 4000
Allen, TX 75013-1302
972-248-6300
800-527-4747
Offers a variety of teacher's resources and guides for testing in all areas of education.

4954 Dawn Publications
14618 Tyler Foote Road
Nevada City, CA 95959-9316
530-478-7540
800-545-7475
Fax: 530-478-0112
Specializes in nature, children and health and healing books, tapes and videos and dedicated to helping people experience unity and harmony.
Bob Rinzler, Publisher
Glenn Hoveman, Editor

4955 Delta Education
80 Northwest Blvd.
Nashua, NH 03061-3000
800-258-1302
Fax: 800-282-9560
Science programs, materials and curriculum kits.

4956 Dial Books for Young Readers
345 Hudson Street
New York, NY 10014-3658
212-366-2800
Fax: 212-366-2938
http://www.penguinputnam.com
General hardcover, children's books, from toddler through young adult, fiction and nonfiction.

4957 Didax Educational Resources
PO Box 507
Rowley, MA 01969-0907
978-948-2340
800-458-0024
Fax: 978-948-2813
E-mail: info@didaxinc.com
http://www.didaxinc.com
High quality educational materials featuring Unifix and hundreds of math and reading supplements.
Brian Scarlett, President
Martin Kennedy, VP

4958 Dinah-Might Activities
PO Box 39657
San Antonio, TX 78218-6657
210-698-0123
Fax: 210-698-0095
Learn how to integrate language arts, math, map and globe skills and more into a science curriculum. Books include The Big Book of Books and Activities, Organizing the Integrated Classroom, Write Your Own Thematic Units and Reading and Writing All Day Long.

4959 Dinocardz Company
146 5th Avenue
San Francisco, CA 94118-1310
415-751-5809
Dinosaur curriculums for grades 1-3 and 4-6.

4960 Disney Press
Disney Juvenile Publishing
114 5th Avenue
New York, NY 10011-5604
212-633-4400
Fax: 212-633-5929
Hardcover trade and library editions and paperback books for children, grades K-12.
Liisa-Ann Fink, President

4961 Dominic Press
1949 Kellogg Avenue
Carlsbad, CA 92008-6582
619-481-3838
Offers a range of materials for the Reading Recovery Program and Chapter 1 programs.

4962 Dorling Kindorley Company
95 Madison Avenue
New York, NY 10016
212-213-4800
Fax: 212-689-5254
Science books for all grade levels.

4963 Dover Publications
31 E 2nd Street
Mineola, NY 11501
516-294-7000
Fax: 516-742-6953
Fun and educational storybooks, coloring, activity, cut-and-assemble toy books, science for children.
Clarence Strowbridge, President

4964 Dutton Children's Books
375 Hudson Street
New York, NY 10014-3658
212-366-2000
Fax: 212-366-2948
General hardcover children's books from toddler through young adult, fiction and nonfiction.

4965 DynEd International
1350 Bayshore Highway
Suite 850
Burlingame, CA 94010
800-765-4375
Fax: 650-375-7017
http://www.dyned.com
Pre-K-adult listening and speaking skill development English language acquisition software.
Steven Kearney, Sales
Sue Young, Operations

4966 EBSCO Publishing
EBSCO Publishing
10 Estes Street
Ipswich, MA 01938
800-653-2726
Fax: 978-356-6565
E-mail: information@ebscohost.com
http://www.ebscohost.com
Database and eBook provider for libraries and other institutions — more than 375 full-text and secondary research databases and more than 300,000 eBooks available via the EBSCOhost platform. EBSCO's content services K-12 students to public library patrons, from academic, corporate and medical researchers to clinicians and governments around the world.
Tim Collins, President
Sam Brooks, EVP Sales/Marketing

4967 ETA - Math Catalog
620 Lakeview Parkway
Vernon Hills, IL 60061-1828
847-816-5050
800-445-5985
Fax: 847-816-5066
E-mail: info@etauniverse.com
http://www.etauniverse.com
Offers a full line of mathematics products, materials, books, textbooks and workbooks for grades K-12.
Mary Cooney, Product Development Manager
Monica Butler, Director Marketing

4968 ETR Associates
4 Carbonero Way
Scotts Valley, CA 95066
831-438-4060
800-321-4407
Fax: 800-435-8433
http://www.etr.org
ETR Associate's mission is to enhance the well-being of individuals, families and communities by providing leadership, educational resources, training and research in health promotion with an emphasis on sexuality and health education.
Robert Keet, President
Arnold W. Kriegel, Vice President

4969 EVAN-Motor Corporation
18 Lower Ragsdale Drive
Monterey, CA 93940-5728
831-649-5901
Fax: 800-777-4332
Resource materials for K-6 science educational programs.

4970 Early Start-Fun Learning
PO Box 350187
Jacksonville, FL 32235-0187
904-641-6138
Preschool materials for the educator.

4971 Earth Foundation
5151 Mitchelldale
B11
Houston, TX 77092-7200
713-686-9453
Fax: 713-686-6561
Join the largest active network of educators working to save endangered ecosystems and their species! Multi-disciplinary, hands-on curriculum and videos for the classroom.
Cynthia Everage, President

4972 Editorial Projects in Education
6935 Arlington Road
Suite 100
Bethesda, MD 20814-5233
301-280-3100
800-346-1834
Fax: 301-280-3250
E-mail: customercare@epe.org
http://www2.edweek.org
Publishes various newsletters and publications in the fields of history and education.
Christopher B Swanson, Director
Carole Vinograd Bausell, Assistant Director

4973 Edmark
Riverdeep Inc.
100 Pine Street
Suite 1900
San Francisco, CA 94111
415-659-2000
888-242-6747
Fax: 415-659-2020
E-mail: info@riverdeep.net
http://www.edmark.com
Develops innovative and effective educational materials for children.
Barry O'Callaghan, Chairman
Tony Mulderry, Executive Vice President

4974 Education Center
3515 W Market Street
Greensboro, NC 27403-1309
336-273-9409
Publishers of the Mailbox, teacher's helper magazines, learning centers clubs, classroom beautiful bulletin board clubs, the storybook club and more.

4975 Educational Marketer
SIMBA Information
11 Riverbend Drive
PO Box 4234
Stamford, CT 06907-0234
800-307-2529
Fax: 203-358-5824
Contains a range of print and electronic tools, including software and multimedia materials for educational institutions.

976 Educational Press Association of America
Glassboro State College
Glassboro, NJ 08028
609-445-7349
Offers various publications and bibliographic data focusing on all aspects of education.

977 Educational Productions
9000 SW Gemini Drive
Beaverton, OR 97008
503-644-7000
800-950-4949
Fax: 503-350-7000
E-mail: custserv@edpro.com
http://www.edpro.com
Video training programs that help increase parenting skills and help every teacher meet performance standards. Offers training on preventing discipline problems, increasing parenting skills, supporting literacy efforts and more.

978 Educational Teaching Aids
620 Lakeview Pkwy
Vernon Hills, IL 60061-1838
847-816-5050
800-445-5985
Fax: 847-816-5066
E-mail: info@etauniverse.com
http://www.etauniverse.com
Manipulatives to enhance understanding of basic concepts and to help bridge the gap between the concrete and the abstract.

979 Educators Progress Service
214 Center Street
Randolph, WI 53956
920-326-3127
888-951-4469
Fax: 920-326-3126
http://www.freeteachingaids.com
A complete spectrum of curriculum and mixed media resources for allgrade levels.

980 Educators Publishing Service
31 Smith Place
Cambridge, MA 02138-1089
617-547-6706
800-225-5750
Fax: 617-547-0412
http://www.epsbooks.com
Supplementary workbooks and teaching materials in reading, spelling, vocabulary, comprehension, and elementary math, as well as materials for assessment and learning differences.

981 Edumate-Educational Materials
2231 Morena Boulevard
San Diego, CA 92110-4134
619-275-7117
Multicultural and multilingual materials in the form of toys, puzzles, books, videos, music, visuals, games, dolls and teacher resources. Special emphasis on Spanish and other languages. Literature offered from North and South America.
Gustavo Blankenburg, President

982 Ellis
406 W 10600 S
Suite 610
Salt Lake City, UT 84003
801-374-3424
888-756-1570
Fax: 801-374-3495
http://www.ellis.com
Publish software that teaches English.

983 Encyclopaedia Britannica
333 N La Salle Street
Chicago, IL 60610
312-347-7159
800-323-1229
Fax: 312-294-2104
http://www.britannica.com
Books and related educational materials.

4984 Energy Learning Center
USCEA
1776 I Street NW
Suite 400
Washington, DC 20006-3700
703-741-5000
Fax: 703-741-6000
Energy learning materials.

4985 Essential Learning Products
PO Box 2590
Columbus, OH 43216-2590
800-357-3570
Fax: 614-487-2272
Publishers of phonics workbooks.

4986 Ethnic Arts & Facts
PO Box 20550
Oakland, CA 94620-0550
510-465-0451
888-278-5652
Fax: 510-465-7488
E-mail: eaf@ethnicartsnfacts.com
http://www.ethnicartsnfacts.com
Kit titles include: Traditional Africa, Urban Africa, China, Guatemala, Peru, Huichol Indians of Mexico, Chinese Shadow Puppet Kit. African-American Music History Mini-Kit. Artifact kits/resource booklets designed to enhance appreciation of cultural diversity, improve geographic literacy and sharpen critical thinking and writing skills.
Susan Drexler, Curriculum Specialist

4987 Evan-Moor Corporation
18 Lower Ragsdale Drive
Monterey, CA 93940-5728
How to Make Books with Children and other fine teacher resources and reproducible materials for all curriculum areas grades PreK-6.

4988 Everyday Learning Corporation
PO Box 812960
Chicago, IL 60681-2960
800-382-7670
Fax: 312-233-7860
University of Chicago school mathematics project. Everyday Mathematics enriched curriculum for grades K-6.

4989 Exploratorium
3601 Lyon Street
San Francisco, CA 94123-1099
415-563-7337
Fax: 415-561-0307
http://www.exploratorium.edu
Exploratorium is dedicated to the formal and informal teaching of science using innovative interactive methods of inquiry. It publishes materials for educators and provides professional development opportunities both in print and online.
Quarterly/Monthly

4990 Extra Editions K-6 Math Supplements
PO Box 38
Urbana, IL 61803-0038
Fax: 614-794-0107
Special needs math supplements offering 70 single-topic units from K-6 that reach students your basic math program misses. Extra Editions newspaper-like format uses animation with a hands-on approach to show real life necessity for computational skills, time, money, problem solving, critical thinking,
etc. Ideal for Chapter One, Peer-Tutoring, Parental Involvement, Home Use, and more.
Craig Rucker, General Manager
Earl Ockenga, Author/Owner

4991 F(G) Scholar
Future Graph
538 Street Road
Suite 200
Southhampton, PA 18966-3780
215-396-0721
Fax: 215-396-0724
A revolutionary program for teaching, learning and using math. This single program allows students and teachers easy answers to Algebra, Trigonometry, Pre-Calculus, Calculus, Statistics, Probability and more. It combines all of the power of a graphing calculator, spreadsheet, drawing tools, mathematics and programming/scripting language and much more, and makes it simple and fun to use.

4992 Facts on File
11 Penn Plaza
New York, NY 10001
212-967-8800
800-322-8755
Fax: 212-967-9196
E-mail: llikoff@factsonfile.com
http://www.factsonfile.com
Reference books for teacher education, software, hardware and educational computer systems.
9 Hardcover Books
Laurie Likoff, Editorial Director

4993 Farrar, Straus & Giroux
19 Union Square W
New York, NY 10003-3304
212-741-6900
Fax: 212-633-9385
Children's, young adult and adult trade books in hardcover and paperback, including Sunburst Books, Aerial Miraso/libros juveniles and Hill and Wang.

4994 First Years
1 Kiddie Drive
Avon, MA 02322-1171
508-588-1220
Early childhood books, hardcover and paperback.

4995 Forbes Custom Publishing
60 5th Avenue
New York, NY 10011-8802
513-229-1000
800-355-9983
Fax: 800-451-3661
E-mail: fcpinfo@forbes.com
http://www.forbescp.com
Offers educators and teachers the opportunity to select unique teaching material to create a book designed specifically for their courses.

4996 Formac Distributing
5502 Atlantic Street
Halifax, NS E3HIG-4
902-421-7022
800-565-1905
Fax: 902-425-0166
Contemporary and historical fiction for ages 6-15. Multicultural themes featuring Degrassi Y/A series; first novel chapter books.

4997 Frank Schaffer Publications
3195 Wilson Drive NW
Grand Rapids, MI 49534
800-417-3261
Fax: 888-203-9361
E-mail:

311

cpg_custserve@schoolspecialty.com
http://www.frankschaffer.com
Best-selling supplemental materials including charts, literature notes, resource materials and more.

4998 Franklin Watts
Grolier Publishing
Sherman Turnpike
Danbury, CT 06816
800-621-1115
800-843-3749
Fax: 800-374-4329
Publisher of library bound books, paperback and Big Books for literature based, multicultural classrooms and school libraries.

4999 Free Spirit Publishing
217 Fifth Avenue North
Suite 200
Minneapolis, MN 55401-1299
612-338-2068
800-736-7323
Fax: 612-337-5050
Free Spirit is the leading publisher of learning tools that support young people's social and emotional health.

5000 Frog Publications
PO Box 280996
Tampa, FL 33682
813-935-5845
Fax: 813-935-3764
http://www.frog.com
An organized system of cooperative games for K-5 reading, language arts, thinking skills, math, social studies, Spanish and multicultural studies. Parental Involvement Program, Learning Centers, Test Preperation, Afterschool Program Materials. Drops in the Bucket daily practice books.

5001 Gareth Stevens
330 W Olive Street
Suite 100
Milwaukee, WI 53212
414-332-3520
800-542-2595
Fax: 414-336-0156
E-mail: info@gsinc.com
http://www.garethstevens.com
Complete display of supplemental children's reading material for grades K-6, including our New World Almanac Library imprint grades 6-12.

Bi-Annually
ISSN: 0-8368

Mark Sachner, Author
Juanita Jones, Marketing Manager
Jonathan Strickland, National Sales Manager

5002 Glencoe/Div. of Macmillan/McGraw Hill
936 Eastwind Drive
Westerville, OH 43081-3329
708-615-3360
800-442-9685
Fax: 972-228-1982
Secondary science programs.

5003 Goethe House New York
1014 5th Avenue
New York, NY 10028-0104
Teaching materials on Germany for the social studies classroom in elementary, middle and high schools.

5004 Goodheart-Willcox Publisher
18604 W Creek Drive
Tinley Park, IL 60477-6243

800-323-0440
Fax: 888-409-3900
E-mail: custerv@goodheartwillcox.com
http://www.goodheartwillcox.com
Comprehensive text designed to help young students learn about themselves, others, and the environment. Readers will develop skills in clothing, food, decision making, and life management. Case studies throughout allow students to apply learning to real-life situations.

5005 Greenhaven Press
PO Box 9187
Farmington Hills, MI 48333-9187
800-231-5163
800-231-5163
Fax: 248-699-8035
E-mail: info@greenhaven.com
Publishers of the Opposing Viewpoints Series, presenting viewpoints in an objective, pro/con format on some of today's controversial subjects.

5006 Greenwillow Books
1350 Avenue of the Americas
New York, NY 10019-4702
212-261-6500
Fax: 212-261-6518
Offers publications for all reading levels.

5007 Grey House Publishing
4419 Route 22
Amenia, NY 12501
518-789-8700
800-562-2139
Fax: 518-789-0545
E-mail: books@greyhouse.com
http://www.greyhouse.com
Publisher of educational reference directories, and encyclopedias.

Richard Gottlieb, President
Leslie Mackenzie, Publisher

5008 Grolier Publishing
90 Sherman Turnpike
Danbury, CT 06816
203-797-3500
800-621-1115
Fax: 203-797-3197
http://www.publishing.grolier.com
Publisher of library bound and paperback books in the areas of social studies, science, reference, history, and biographies for schools and libraries for grades K-12.

5009 Gryphon House
Gryphon House
PO Box 275
Mount Rainier, MD 20712-0275
301-779-6200
Fax: 301-595-0051
E-mail: info@ghbooks.com
http://www.ghbooks.com
Resource and activity books for early childhood teachers and directors.

Cathy Calloitte, Marketing Director

5010 H. W. Wilson
Grey House Publishing
2 University Plaza
Suite 310
Hackensack, NJ 07601
201-968-0500
800-221-1592
Fax: 201-968-0511
E-mail: info@hwwilsoninprint.com
http://www.hwwilsoninprint.com
H. W. Wislon publishes database and reference resources to serve libraries, schools and corporations.

5011 Hands-On Prints
PO Box 5899-268
Berkeley, CA 94705
510-601-6279
Fax: 510-601-6278
Specializes in cultural and language materials for children with an emphasis on internationalism and multiculturalism.

Christina Cheung, President

5012 Hardcourt Religion Publishers
6277 Sea Harbor Drive
Orlando, FL 32887
563-557-3700
800-922-7696
Fax: 563-557-3719
E-mail: hardcourtreligion.com
Publishers of religion education materials for schools and parishes.

5013 Hazelden Educational Materials
PO Box 176
Center City, MN 55012-0176
651-257-4010
Fax: 651-213-4590
Educational publisher of materials supporting both students and faculty in areas of substance abuse and related topics.

5014 Heinemann
361 Hanover Street
Portsmouth, NH 03801-3959
603-431-7894
Fax: 203-750-9790
Holistic/student-centered publications, videotapes and workshops for parents, teachers and administrators.

5015 Henry Holt & Company
175 Fifth Avenue
New York, NY 10010
646-307-5095
800-628-9658
Fax: 212-633-0748
Books and materials for classroom teachers, grades 6-adult, including programs on science literacy.

5016 Henry Holt Books for Young Readers
115 W 18th Street
New York, NY 10011-4113
800-628-9658
Fax: 212-647-0490
Hardcover and paperback trade books for preschool through young adult, fiction and nonfiction. Also, big books and promotional materials are available.

5017 High Touch Learning
PO Box 754
Houston, MN 55943-0754
507-896-3500
800-255-0645
Fax: 507-896-3243
Classroom interactive learning maps promoting the hands-on approach to the teaching of social studies.

5018 High/Scope Educational Research Foundation
600 N River Street
Ypsilanti, MI 48198-2821
734-485-2000
800-40 -RESS
Fax: 734-485-4467
Early childhood, elementary, movement and music, and adolescent materials. Over 300 titles of books, videos, cassettes and CDs from which to choose. Research and training materials as well as curriculum and development materials are based on the acclaimed High/Scope active learning approach.

Emily Koepp, President

019 Holiday House
425 Madison Avenue
New York, NY 10017-1110
212-688-0085
Fax: 212-688-0395
Hardcover and paperback children's books. General fiction and nonfiction, preschool through high school.

020 Hoover's
5800 Airport
Dallas, TX 78752-3812
512-374-4500
Fax: 512-374-4501
Everything educational, for the early childhood and K-12 market. As a partner for over 100 years, the company is eager to extend their commitment to produce quality, timely shipping and customer service to the public. Offer over 10,000 products for infants, toddlers, pre-school and school age educational needs.

021 Horn Book Guide
Horn Book
56 Roland Street
Suite 200
Boston, MA 02129
617-628-0225
800-325-1170
Fax: 617-628-0882
E-mail: info@hbook.com
http://www.hbook.com
The most comprehensive review source of children's and young adult books available. Published each spring and fall, the Guide contains concise, critical reviews of almost every hardcover trade children's and young adult book published in the United States - nearly 2,000 books each issue.
BiAnnually
ISSN: 1044-405X

Anne Quirk, Marketing Manager
Roger Sutton, Editor

022 Houghton Mifflin Books for Children
222 Berkeley Street
Boston, MA 02116-3748
617-351-5000
800-225-3362
Fax: 617-351-1111
http://www.hmco.com
Wide variety of children's and young adult books, fiction and nonfiction.

023 Houghton Mifflin Company: School Division
222 Berkeley Street
Boston, MA 02116-3748
617-351-5000
Fax: 617-651-1106
Children's literature; K-12 reading and language arts print and software programs; and testing and evaluation for K-12.

024 Hyperion Books for Children
114 5th Avenue
New York, NY 10011-5604
212-633-4400
Fax: 212-633-5929
Children's books in paperback and hardcover editions.

025 ITP South-Western Publishing Company
5101 Madison Road
Cincinnati, OH 45227-1427
800-824-5179
Fax: 800-487-8488
Innovative instructional materials for teaching integrated science.

5026 Idea Factory
10710 Dixon Drive
Riverview, FL 33569-7406
813-677-6727
Teacher resource books, science project ideas, materials and more for elementary and middle school teachers.

5027 Institute for Chemical Education
University of Wisconsin
1101 University Avenue
Madison, WI 53706-1322
608-262-3033
800-991-5534
Fax: 608-265-8094
E-mail: ice@chem.wisc.edu
http://ice.chem.wisc.edu
Hands-on activities, publications, kits and videos.

5028 Institute for Educational Leadership
1001 Connecticut Avenue NW
Suite 310
Washington, DC 20036-5541
202-822-8405
Fax: 202-872-4050
The Institute's list of publications on educational trends and policies is available to the public.

Michael C Usdan, President

5029 IntelliTools
1720 Corporate Circle
Petaluma, CA 94954
707-773-2000
800-899-6687
Fax: 707-773-2001
http://www.intellitools.com
Provider of hardware and software giving students with special needs comprehensive access to learning.

5030 Intellimation
130 Cremona Drive
Santa Barbara, CA 93117-5599
805-968-2291
800-346-8355
Fax: 805-968-8899
Educational materials in all areas of curriculum for early learning through college level. Over 400 titles are available in video, and software and multimedia exclusively for the Macintosh. Free catalogs avaiable.

Karin Fisher, Marketing Associate
Marlene Carlyle, Marketing Supervisor

5031 Intercultural Press
100 City Hall Plaza
Suite 501
Boston, MA 02108
617-523-3801
888-273-2539
Fax: 617-523-3708
E-mail: books@interculturalpress.com
http://www.interculturalpress.com
Publishes over 100 titles.

Judy Carl-Hendrick, Managing Editor

5032 J Weston Walch, Publisher
PO Box 658
Portland, ME 04104-0658
207-772-2846
800-558-2846
Fax: 207-772-3105
http://www.walch.com
Walch Publishing is an independent, family-owned publisher of educational supplemental materials for grades 3 through 12 and adult makets.

5033 Jacaranda Designs
3000 Jefferson Street
Boulder, CO 80304-2638

707-374-2543
Fax: 707-374-2543
Authentic African children's books from Kenya, including modern concept stories for K-3 in bilingual editions, folktales, and traditional cultural stories for older readers. All books are written and illustrated by African Kenyans.

Carrie Jenkins Williams, President

5034 Jarrett Publishing Company
PO Box 1460
Ronkonkoma, NY 11779
631-981-4248
Fax: 631-588-4722
Offers a wide range of books for today's educational needs.

5035 JayJo Books
Guidance Channel
135 Dupont Street
PO Box 760
Plainview, NY 11803
516-349-5520
800-999-6884
Fax: 516-349-5521
E-mail: jayjobooks@guidancechannel.com
http://www.jayjo.com
Publisher of books to help teachers, parents and children cope with chronic illnesses, special needs and health education in classroom, family and social settings.

Sally Germain, Editor-in-Chief

5036 John Wiley & Sons
111 River Street
Hoboken, NJ 07030-5774
201-748-6000
Fax: 201-748-6088
Publish science and nature books for children and adults.

5037 Jossey-Bass: An Imprint of Wiley
Jossey-Bass/Pfeiffer
989 Market Street
San Francisco, CA 94103-1741
415-433-1740
Fax: 415-433-0499
http://www.josseybass.com
Creating educational incentives that work.

Adrianne Biggs, Publicity/Manager
Jennifer A O'Day, Editor

5038 Junior Achievement
1 Education Way
Colorado Springs, CO 80906-4477
719-540-8000
Fax: 719-540-6127
Provides business and economics-related materials and programs to students in grades K-12. All programs feature volunteers from the local business community. Materials are free, but available only from local Junior Achievement offices.

5039 Kaeden Corporation
PO Box 16190
19915 Lake Road
Rocky River, OH 44116
440-356-0030
800-890-7323
Fax: 440-356-5081
E-mail: lcowan@kaedeen.com
http://www.kaeden.com
Books for emergent readers at the K, 1 and 2 levels, ideal for Title 1 and Reading Recovery and other at-risk reading programs.

Laura Cowan, Sales Manager
Joan Hoyer, Office Manager

5040 Kane/Miller Book Publishers
PO Boxn 8515
La Jolla, CA 92038-0529

858-456-0540
Fax: 858-456-9641
E-mail: info@kanemiller.com
http://www.kanemiller.com
English translation of foreign children's picture books. Distributors of Spanish language children's books.

Byron Parnell, Sales Manager
Kira Lynn, President

5041 Keep America Beautiful
1010 Washington Boulevard
Stamford, CT 06901
203-323-8987
Fax: 203-325-9199
E-mail: info@kab.org
http://www.kab.org
K-12 curriculum specializing in litter prevention and environmental education. Education posters with lesson plans printed right on the back of each poster and school recycling guides.

5042 Kendall-Hunt Publishing Company
4050 Westmark Drive
Dubuque, IA 52002-2624
319-589-1000
800-228-0810
Fax: 800-772-9165
E-mail: webmaster@kendallhunt.com
http://www.kendallhunt.com
A leading custom publisher in the United States with over 6,000 titles in print. Kendall/Hunt publishes educational materials for kindergarten through college to continuing education creditation and distance learning courses.

Karen Berger, Customer Service Assistant

5043 Knowledge Adventure
2377 Crenshaw Blvd
Suite 302
Torrance, CA 90501
310-533-3400
Fax: 310-533-3700
E-mail: editorial@education.com
http://www.knowledgeadventure.com
Develops, publishes, and distributes best-selling multimedia educational software for use in both homes and schools.

5044 Knowledge Unlimited
PO Box 52
Madison, WI 53701-0052
800-356-2303
Fax: 608-831-1570
http://www.newscurrents.com
NewsCurrents, the most effective current events programs for grades 3-12. Now available on DVD or Online.

5045 Kraus International Publications
358 Saw Mill River Road
Millwood, NY 10546-1035
914-762-2200
800-223-8323
Fax: 914-762-1195
Offers teacher resource notebooks with complete resource information for teachers and administrators at all levels. Great for program planning, quick reference, inservice training. Also offers books on early childhood education, English/language arts, mathematics, science, health education and visual arts.

Barry Katzen, President

5046 Lake Education
AGS/Lake Publishing Company
500 Harbor Boulevard
Belmont, CA 94002-4075

650-592-1606
800-328-2560
Fax: 800-471-8457
Alternative learning materials for under-achieving students grades 6-12, RSL and adult basic education. High interest, low readability fiction, adapted classic literature, lifeskills and curriculum materials to supplement and support many basal programs.

Phil Schlenter
Carol Hegarty, VP Editorial

5047 Langenseheidt Publishing
515 Valley Street
Maplewood, NJ 07040-1337
800-526-4953
Fax: 908-206-1104
E-mail: edusales@hammond.com
http://www.hammondmap.com
World maps, atlases, general reference guides and CD-Roms.

5048 Lawrence Hall of Science
University of California
Berkeley, CA 94720
510-642-5132
Fax: 510-642-1055
E-mail: lhsinfo@uclink.berkeley.edu
http://www.lawrencehallofscience.org
Offers programs and materials in the field of science and math education for teachers, families and interested citizens. Exhibits include Equals, Family Math, CePUP and FOSS.

Linda Schneider, Marketing Manager
Mike Salter, Marketing/PR Associate

5049 Leap Frog Learning Materials
6401
Suite 100
Emeryville, CA 94608-1071
510-596-3333
800-701-5327
Learning materials, books, posters, games and toys for children.

5050 Learning Connection
19 Devane Street
Frostproof, FL 33843-2017
863-635-5610
800-338-2282
Fax: 863-635-4676
Thematic, literature-based units with award-winning books, media and hands-on for PK-12 including parent involvement, early childhood, bilingual, literacy, math, writing, science and multicultural.

5051 Learning Disabilities Association of America
Learning Disabilities Association of America
4156 Library Road
Pittsburgh, PA 15234-1349
412-341-1515
888-300-6710
Fax: 412-344-0224
E-mail: info@ldaamerica.org
http://www.ldaamerica.org
Has 50 state affiliates with more than 300 local chapters. The national office has a resource center of over 500 publications for sale.

5052 Learning Links
2300 Marcus Avenue
New Hyde Park, NY 11042-1083
516-437-9075
800-724-2616
Fax: 516-437-5392
E-mail: learningLx@aol.com
http://www.learinglinks.com

All you need for literature based instruction; Noveltie, study guides, thematic units books and more.

5053 Lee & Low Books
95 Madison Avenue
Suite 606
New York, NY 10016-3303
212-779-4400
Fax: 212-683-1894
E-mail: info@leeandlow.com
http://www.leeandlow.com
A multicultural children's book publisher. Our primary focus is on picture books, especially stories set in contemporary America. Spanish language titles are available.

Craig Low, VP Publisher
Louise May, Executive Editor

5054 Leo A Myer Associates/LAMA Books
20956 Corsair Boulevard
Hayward, CA 94545-1002
510-785-1091
Fax: 510-785-1099
E-mail: lama@lmabooks.com
Writers and publishers of HVAC books.

Barbara Ragura, Marketing Assistant

5055 Lerner Publishing Group
A Division Lerner Publications Group
241 1st Avenue N
Minneapolis, MN 55401-1607
612-332-3344
800-328-4929
Fax: 612-332-7615
http://www.lernerbooks.com
Primarily nonfiction for readers of all grade levels. List includes titles encompassing nature, geography, natural and physical science, current events, ancient and modern history, world art, special interests, sports, world cultures, and numerous biography series. Some young adult and middle grade fiction.

Jennifer Martin, Submissions Editor

5056 Linden Tree Children's Records & Books
170 State Street
Los Altos Hills, CA 94022-2863
650-949-3390
Fax: 650-949-0346
Offers a wide variety of books, audio cassettes and records for children.

5057 Listening Library
One Park Avenue
Old Greenwich, CT 06870-1727
203-637-3616
800-243-4504
Fax: 800-454-0606
E-mail: moreinfo@listeninglib.com
http://www.listeninglib.com
A producer of quality unabridged audiobooks for listeners of all ages. Specializing in children's literature and adult classics.

BiAnnually

Annette Imperati, Director Sales/Marketing

5058 Little, Brown & Company
3 Center Plaza
Boston, MA 02108-2084
617-227-0730
Fax: 617-263-2854
Trade books for children and young adults, hardcover and paper, including Sierra Club Books for Children.

5059 Lodestar Books
375 Hudson Street
New York, NY 10014-3658
212-366-2000

General hardcover children's books from toddler through young adult, fiction and non-fiction.

5060 Lothrop, Lee & Shepard Books
1350 Avenue of the Americas
New York, NY 10019-4702
212-261-6500
Fax: 212-261-6518
Children's books.

5061 Lynne Rienner Publishing
1800 30th Street
Suite 314
Boulder, CO 80301
303-333-3003
800-803-8488
Fax: 303-333-4037
E-mail: karen-hemmes@mindspring.com
http://www.fireflybooks.com
Publishes academic-level books with a focus on international and domestic social sciences.

Karen Hemmes, Publicist
Mary Kay Opicka, Publicist

5062 MHS
PO Box 950
North Tonawanda, NY 14120-0950
416-492-2627
800-456-3003
Fax: 416-492-3343
E-mail: customer_service@mhs.com
http://www.mhs.com
Publishers and distributors of professional assessment materials.

Steven J Stein, PhD, President

5063 MacMillan Children's Books
1633 Broadway
New York, NY 10019
212-512-2000
Fax: 800-835-3202
Hardcover trade books for children and young adults.

5064 MacMillan Reference
1633 Broadway
New York, NY 10019
212-512-2000
Fax: 800-835-3202
A wide variety of titles for students and teachers of all grade levels.

5065 Macmillan/McGraw-Hill School Division
1633 Broadwaty
New York, NY 10019
212-654-8500
800-442-9685
Fax: 800-835-3202
Quality literature for the student and excellent support for the teacher. Programs and educational materials for all grade levels.

5066 Macro Press
18242 Peters Court
Fountain Valley, CA 92708-5873
310-823-9556
Fax: 310-306-2296
Includes resources to conduct thematic hands-on science lessons and integrated curriculum; and, student materials offering a Scientist's Notebook and reading materials to integrate hands-on (grade specific) scientific thinking, problem solving and documenting skills to benefit all students. Nine award-winning K-6 teachers (200+ years combined experience) joined together to address the real needs of today's high student load.

Leigh Hoven Swenson, President

5067 Magna Publications
2718 Dryden Drive
Madison, WI 53704
608-227-8109
800-206-4805
Fax: 608-246-3597
E-mail: carriej@magnapubs.com
http://www.magnapubs.com
Produces eight subscriptions newsletters in the field of higher education.

Carrie Jenson, Conference Manager
David Burns, Associate Publisher

5068 Major Educational Resources Corporation
10153 York Road
Suite 107
Hunt Valley, MD 21030-3340
800-989-5353
Multimedia curriculum tools for educators.

5069 Margaret K McElderry Books
1633 Broadway
New York, NY 10019
212-512-2000
Fax: 800-835-3202
Hardcover trade books for children and young adults.

5070 Mari
3215 Pico Boulevard
Santa Monica, CA 90405-4603
310-829-2212
800-955-9494
Fax: 310-829-2317
http://www.mariinc.com
The best literature learning materials for K-12. Offers Mini-Units for writing and critical thinking skills, Literature Extenders that extend literature across the curriculum and Basic Skills Through Literature that combine literature and skill work.

5071 MasterTeacher
Leadership Lane
PO Box 1207
Manhattan, KS 66505-1207
800-669-9633
Fax: 800-669-1132
http://www.masterteacher.com
A publisher of videotapes for the professional. Offers programs on inclusion, tests and testing, student motivation, discipline and more.

5072 MathSoft
101 Main Street
Cambridge, MA 02142
617-577-1017
800-628-4223
Fax: 617-577-8829
http://www.mathsoft.com
Provider of math, science and engineering software for business, academia, research and government.

5073 McCracken Educational Services
PO Box 3588
Blaine, WA 98231
360-332-1881
800-447-1462
Fax: 360-332-7332
E-mail: mes@mccrackened.com
http://www.mccrackened.com
Materials for beginning reading, writing and spelling. Big Books, manipulative materials, teacher resource books, spelling through phonics, posters and both audio and video tapes.

Robert & Marlene McCracken, Author

5074 McGraw Hill Children's Publishing
PO Box 1650
Grand Rapids, MI 49501-1650

616-363-1290
Fax: 800-543-2690
New self-esteem literature based reading and multicultural literature based reading.

5075 Mel Bay Publications
4 Industrial Drive
PO Box 66
Pacific, MO 63069-0066
637-257-3970
800-863-5229
Fax: 636-257-5062
E-mail: email@melbay.com
http://www.melbay.com
Music supply distributors.

Sheri Stephens, Customer Service Supervisor

5076 Merriam-Webster
47 Federal Street
#281
Springfield, MA 01105-3805
413-734-3134
Fax: 413-734-0257
A wide variety of titles for students and teachers of all grade levels.

5077 Millbrook Press
1251 Washington Avenue N
Minneapolis, MN 55401
203-740-2220
800-328-4929
Fax: 800-332-1132
http://www.millbrookpress.com
Exceptional nonfiction juvenile and young adult books for schools and public libraries.

5078 Milton Roy Company
820 Linden Avenue
Rochester, NY 14625-2710
716-248-4000
Teacher support materials, scientific kits and manuals.

5079 Mimosa Publications
90 New Montgomery Street
San Francisco, CA 94105-4501
415-982-5350
A language based K-3 math program featuring big books, language and activity based math topics and multicultural math activities.

5080 Model Technologies
2420 Van Layden Way
Modesto, CA 95356-2454
209-575-3445
Curriculum guides and scientific instruction kits.

5081 Mondo Publishing
980 Avenue Of The Americas
New York, NY 10018
Fax: 888-532-4492
E-mail: mondopub@aol.com
http://www.mondopub.com
Offers multicultural big books and music cassettes: Folk Tales from Around the World series; Exploring Habitats series; and, Let's Write and Sing a Song, whole language activities through music.

5082 Morning Glory Press
6595 San Haroldo Way
Buena Park, CA 90620-3748
714-828-1998
888-612-8254
Fax: 714-828-2049
E-mail: info@morningglorypress.com
http://www.morningglorypress.com
Publishes books and materials for teenage parents.

Quarterly

Jeanne Lindsay, President
Carole Blum, Promotion Director

5083 Music for Little People
PO Box 1460
Redway, CA 95560-1460
707-923-3991
Fax: 707-923-3241
Science and environmental education materials set to music for younger students.

5084 N&N Publishing Company
18 Montgomery Street
Middletown, NY 10940-5116
Low-cost texts and workbooks.

5085 NASP Publications
National Association of School Psychologists
4340 EW Highway
Suite 402
Bethesda, MD 20814
301-657-0270
Fax: 301-657-0275
E-mail: center@naspweb.org
http://www.naspionline.org
Over 100 hard-to-find books and videos centering on counseling, psychology and guidance for students.

Betty Somerville, President

5086 NCTM Educational Materials
National Council of Teachers of Mathematics
1906 Association Drive
Reston, VA 20191-1502
703-620-9840
Fax: 703-476-2970
E-mail: nctm@nctm.org
http://www.nctm.org
Publications, videotapes, software, posters and information to improve the teaching and learning of mathematics.

Harry B Tunis, Publications Director
Cynthia C Rosso, Director Marketing Services

5087 NYSTROM
3333 N Elston Avenue
Chicago, IL 60618-5898
773-463-1144
800-621-8086
Fax: 773-463-0515
Maps, globes, hands-on geography and history materials.

5088 Narrative Press
PO Box 145
Crabtree, OR 97335
800-315-9005
Fax: 541-259-2154
E-mail: service@narrativepress.com
http://www.narrativepress.com
Publisher of first person narratives of adventure and exploration.

Vickie Zimmer, Editor

5089 National Aeronautics & Space Administration
NASA Headquarters
300 E Street SW
Washington, DC 20546
202-358-0000
Fax: 202-358-3251
Over 10 different divisions offering a wide variety of classroom and educational materials in the areas of science, physics, aeronautics and more.

5090 National Center for Science Teaching & Learning/Eisenhower Clearinghouse
1929 Kenny Road
Columbus, OH 43210-1015
Collects and creates the most up-to-date listing of science and mathematics curriculum materials in the nation.

5091 National Council for the Social Studies
8555 Sixteenth Street
Suite 500
Silver Spring, MD 20910
301-588-1800
800-683-0812
Fax: 301-588-2049
E-mail: sgriffin@ncss.org
http://www.ncss.org
Publishes books, videotapes and journals in the area of social education and social studies.

5092 National Council of Teachers of English
1111 W Kenyon Road
Urbana, IL 61801-1096
217-328-3870
800-369-6283
Fax: 217-328-9645
E-mail: public_info@ncte.org
http://www.ncte.org
Devoted to the advancement of English language and literature studies at all levels of education. Publishes 12 periodicals, a member newspaper, and 20-25 books a year, and holds conventions and workshops.

Lori Bianchini, Public Affairs

5093 National Council on Economic Education
1140 Avenue of the Americas
New York, NY 10036-5803
212-730-7007
Offers various programs including their latest, US History: Eyes on the Economy, a council program for secondary education teachers.

5094 National Geographic School Publishing
1145 17th Street NW
Washington, DC 20036
800-368-2728
Fax: 515-362-3366
Books, magazines, videos, and software in the areas of science, geography and social studies.

5095 National Geographic Society
PO Box 10041
Des Moines, IA 50340-0597
800-548-9797
Fax: 301-921-1575
http://www.nationalgeographic.com
Science materials, videos, CD-ROM's and telecommunications program.

5096 National Head Start Association
1651 Prince Street
Alexandria, VA 22314-2818
703-739-0875
Fax: 703-739-0878
http://www.nhsa.org
Dedicated to promoting and protecting the Head Start program. Advocates on the behalf of America's low-income children and families. Publishes many books, periodicals and resource guides. Offers a legislative hotline as well as training programs through the NHSA Academy.

Ron Herndon, President
Blanche Russ-Glover, VP

5097 National Textbook Company
4255 W Touhy Avenue
Lincolnwood, IL 60646-1975
847-679-5500
800-323-4900
Fax: 847-679-2494
Offers various textbooks for students grades K-college level.

5098 National Women's History Project
3343 Industrial Drive
Suite #4
Santa Rosa, CA 95403
707-636-2888
Fax: 707-636-2909
E-mail: nwhp@aol.com
http://www.nwhp.org
Non-profit organization, the clearinghouse for information about multicultural US women's history. Initiated March as National Women's History Month; issues a catalog of women's history materials. Provides teacher-training nationwide; coordinates the Women's History Network; produces videos, posters, curriculum units and other curriculum materials.

Molly Murphy MacGregor, Exec. Dir./Co-Founder

5099 National Writing Project
University of California, Berkeley
2105 Bancroft Way
#1042
Berkeley, CA 94720-1042
510-642-6096
Fax: 510-642-4545
http://www.writingproject.org
Technical reports and occasional paper series: a series of research reports and essays on the research in and practice of teaching writing at all grade levels.

5100 New Canaan Publishing Company
PO Box 752
New Canaan, CT 06840
203-966-3408
800-705-5698
Fax: 203-966-3408
http://www.newcanaanpublishing.com
Children's publications.

5101 New Press
38 Greene Street
4th Floor
New York, NY 10013
212-629-8802
Fax: 212-629-8617
Multicultural teaching materials, focusing on the social studies.

5102 NewsBank
5020 Tamiami Trail N
Suite 110
Naples, FL 34103-2837
941-263-6004
Electronic information services that support the science curriculum.

5103 North South Books
11 E 26th Street
17 Floor
New York, NY 10010-2007
212-706-4545
Fax: 212-706-4544
Publisher of quality children's books by authors and illustrators from around the world.

5104 Nystrom, Herff Jones
3333 N Elston Avenue
Chicago, IL 60618-5811
913-432-8100
Fax: 913-432-3958
Charts for earth, life and physical science for upper elementary and high school grades.

5105 Options Publishing
PO Box 1749
Merrimack, NH 03054

603-429-2698
800-782-7300
Fax: 603-424-4056
E-mail: serviceoptionspublishing.com m
http://www.optionspublishing.com
Publishers of supplemental materials in reading, math and language arts.

Marty Furlong, VP

106 Organization of American Historians
112 N Bryan Avenue
Bloomington, IN 47408-4136
812-855-7311
800-446-8923
Fax: 812-855-0696
E-mail: oah@oah.org
http://www.oah.org
Offers various products and literature dealing with American history, as well as job registries, Magazine of History, Journal of American History, OAH Newsletter, and more.

Damon Freeman, Marketing Manager
Michael Regoli, Publications Director

107 Oxton House Publishers, LLC
Po Box 209
Farmington, ME 04938
207-779-1923
800-539-7323
Fax: 207-779-0623
E-mail: info@oxtonhouse.com
http://www.oxtonhouse.com
Publishes high quality, innovative, affordable materials for teaching, reading and mathematics and for dealing with learning disabilities.

William Berlinghoff, Managing Editor
Bobby Brown, Marketing Director

108 PF Collier
1315 W 22nd Street
Suite 250
Oak Brook, IL 60523-2061
A leading educational publisher for more than 110 years, creating the home learning center. Products include: Collier's Encyclopedia, Quickstart and Early Learning Fun.

109 PRO-ED
8700 Shoal Creek Boulevard
Austin, TX 78757-6897
512-451-3246
800-897-3202
Fax: 800-397-7633
E-mail: info@proedinc.com
http://www.proedinc.com
A leading publisher of assessments, therapy materials and resource/reference books in the areas of speech, language, and hearing; psychology; special education; and occupational therapy.

110 Parenting Press
PO Box 75267
11065 5th Avenue NE
Seattle, WA 98125-0267
206-364-2900
800-992-6657
Fax: 206-364-0702
E-mail: office@ParentingPress.com
http://www.ParentingPress.com
Publishes books for parents, children, and professionals who work with them. Nonfiction books include topics on parenting, problem solving, dealing with feelings, safety, and special issues.

Carolyn J Threadgill, Publisher

111 Penguin USA
375 Hudson Street
New York, NY 10014-3658

212-366-2000
Fax: 212-366-2934
http://www.penguinputnam.com
Children's and adult hardcover and paperback general trade books, including classics and multiethnic literature.

5112 Perfection Learning Corporation
Perfection Learning
10520 New York Avenue
Des Moines, IA 50322
303-333-3003
800-803-8488
Fax: 303-333-4037
E-mail: karen-hemmes@mindspring.com
http://www.fireflybooks.com
Perfection Learning publishes high interest-low reading level fiction and non-fiction books for young adults.

Karen Hemmes, Publicist
Mary Kay Opicka, Publicist

5113 Perma Bound Books
E Vandalia Road
Jacksonville, IL 62650
217-243-5451
800-637-6581
Fax: 800-551-1169
Thematically arranged for K-12 classroom use with 480,000 titles available in durable Perma-Bound bindings; related library services also available.

Ben Mangum, President

5114 Personalizing the Past
1534 Addison Street
Berkeley, CA 94703-1454
415-388-9351
Museum quality artifact history kits complete with integrated lesson plan teachers guide. Copy-ready student worksheets, literature section, videos and audio tapes. United States and ancient world history.

5115 Perspectives on History Series
Discovery Enterprises, Ltd.
31 Laurelwood Drive
Carlisle, MA 01741
978-287-5401
800-729-1720
Fax: 978-287-5402
E-mail: ushistorydocs@aol.com
http://www.ushistorydocs.com
Primary and secondary source materials for middle school to college levels; bibliographies; plays for grades 5-9 on American history topics. Educators curriculum guides for using primary source documents. 75-volumes of primary source documents on American history may be purchased individually or in sets. New Researching American History Series presents documents with summaries and vocabulary on each page (20 volumes) sold individually or in sets.

JoAnne Deitch, President

5116 Peytral Publications Inc
PO Box 1162
Minnetonka, MN 55345
952-949-8707
877-739-8725
Fax: 952-906-9777
E-mail: inquiry@peytral.com
http://www.peytral.com
Books and videos for educators.

Peggy Hammeken, Owner

5117 Phelps Publishing
PO Box 22401
Cleveland, OH 44122
216-752-4938
Fax: 216-752-4941

E-mail: earl@phelpspublishing.com
http://www.phelpspublishing.com
Publisher of art instruction books for ages 8 to 108.

Earl Phelps, President

5118 Phoenix Learning Resources
12 W 31st Street
New York, NY 10001-4415
212-629-3887
800-221-1274
Fax: 212-629-5648
Phoenix Learning Resources provides all students with the skills to be successful, lifelong learners.

Alexander Burke, President
John Rothermich, Executive VP

5119 Pleasant Company Publications
8400 Fairway Pl
Middleton Branch, WI 53562-2554
608-836-4848
800-233-0264
Fax: 800-257-3865
The American Girls Collection historical fiction series.

5120 Pocket Books/Paramount Publishing
1230 Avenue of the Americas
New York, NY 10020-1513
212-698-7000
Books for children and young adults in hardcover and paperback originals and reprints of bestselling titles.

5121 Population Connection
1400 16th Street NW
Suite 320
Washington, DC 20036-2290
800-767-1956
Fax: 202-332-2302
E-mail: poped@populationconnection.org
http://www.populationconnection.org
Curriculum materials for grades K-12 to teach students about population dynamics and their social, political and environmental effects in the United States and the world.

Pamela Wasserman, Director Education

5122 Prentice Hall School Division
340 Rancheros Drive
Suite 160
San Marcos, CA 92069
760-510-0222
Fax: 760-510-0230
Superb language arts textbooks and ancillaries for students grades 6-12.

5123 Prentice Hall School Division - Science
1 Lake Street
Upper Saddle River, NJ 07458
201-236-7000
Fax: 201-236-3381
Science textbooks and ancillaries for grades 6-12 and advanced placement students.

5124 Prentice Hall/Center for Applied Researchin Education
1 Lake Street
Upper Saddle River, NJ 07458
201-236-7000
Fax: 201-236-3381
Publisher of practical, time and work saving teaching/learning resources for PreK-12 teachers and specialists in all content areas.

5125 Project Learning Tree
American Forest Foundation
1111 19th Street NW
Suite 780
Washington, DC 20036-3603

202-463-2462
Fax: 202-463-2461
Pre-K through grade 12 curriculum materials containing hundreds of hands-on science activities. PLT uses the forest as a window into the natural world to increase students' understanding of our complex environment. Stimulates critical and creative thinking; develops the ability to make informed decisions on environmental issues; and instills the confidence and commitment to take action on them.

Kathy McGlauflin, President

5126 Prufrock Press
PO Box 8813
Waco, TX 76714
800-998-2208
Fax: 800-240-0333
http://www.prufrock.com
Exciting classroom products for gifted and talented education.

5127 Puffin Books
375 Hudson Street
New York, NY 10014-3658
212-366-2819
Fax: 212-366-2040
Offers the Puffin Teacher Club set.

Lisa Crosby, President

5128 RR Bowker
ProQuest Affiliate
121 Chanlon Road
New Providence, NJ 07974-1541
908-464-6800
Fax: 908-665-6688
A leading information provider to schools and libraries for over one hundred years, RR Bowker provides quality resources to help teachers and librarians make informed reading selections for children and young adults.

5129 Raintree/Steck-Vaughn
Harcourt Achieve
6277 Sea Harbor Drive
Orlando, FL 32887
800-531-5015
Fax: 800-699-9459
http://www.steck-vaughn.com
Reference materials for K-8 students and texts for underachieving students K-12.

Tim McEwen, President
Martijn Tel, Chief Financial Officer

5130 Rand McNally
8255 Central Park Avenue
Skokie, IL 60076-2970
847-674-2151
Cross-curricular products featuring reading/language arts in the social studies.

5131 Random House
201 E 50th Street
New York, NY 10022-7703
212-751-2600
Fax: 212-572-8700
Offers a line of science trade books for grades K-8.

5132 Random House/Bullseye/Alfred A Knopf/Crown Books for Young Readers
201 E 50th Street
New York, NY 10022-7703
212-751-2600
Fax: 212-572-8700
Publisher of hardcover books, paperbacks, books and cassettes and videos for children.

5133 Recorded Books
270 Skipjack Road
Prince Frederick, MD 20678-3410
800-638-1304
Professionally narrated, unabridged books on standard-play audio cassettes, classroom ideas and combinations of print book, cassettes and teacher's guides.

Linda Hirshman, President

5134 Redleaf Press
10 Yorkton Court
Saint Paul, MN 55117-1065
800-428-8309
Fax: 800-641-0115
E-mail: jward@redleafpress.org
http://www.redleafpress.org
Publisher of curriculum, activity, and childrens books for early childhood professionals.

Sid Farrer, Editor In Chief
JoAnne Voltz, Marketing Manager

5135 Reference Desk Books
430 Quintana Road
Suite 146
Morro Bay, CA 93442-1948
805-772-8806
Offers a variety of books for the education professional.

5136 Rhythms Productions
PO Box 34485
Los Angeles, CA 90034-0485
310-836-4678
800-544-7244
Fax: 310-837-1534
Producer and publisher of songs and games for learning through music. Cassettes, CDs, books for birth through elementary featuring rhythms, puppet play, art activities, and more. Titles include Lullabies, Singing Games, Watch Me Grow series, Mr. Windbag concept stories, phonics, First Reader's Kit, Hear-See-Say-Do Musical Math series, Themes, and more. Also publishes a line of folk dances from elementary through adult.

Audio
Ruth White, President

5137 Richard C Owen Publishers
PO Box 585
Katonah, NY 10536
914-232-3903
800-336-5588
Fax: 914-232-3977
E-mail: mfrund@rcowen.com
http://www.rcowen.com
Focus child-centered learning, Books for Young Learners, professional books, the Learning Network and Meet the Author series.

Mary Frundt, Marketing

5138 Riverside Publishing Company
425 Spring Lake Drive
Ithaca, IL 60143
630-467-7000
800-323-9540
Fax: 630-467-7192
http://www.riverpub.com
Offers a full line of reading materials, including fiction and nonfiction titles for all grade levels.

5139 Roots & Wings Educational Catalog-Australiafor Kids
PO Box 19678
Boulder, CO 80308-2678
303-776-4796
800-833-1787

Fax: 303-776-6090
E-mail: roos@boulder.net
http://www.rootsandwingscatalog.com/
www.australiaforkids.com
Catalog company providing materials for the education of the young child, specializing in the following topics: Australia, multiculturalism, parenting and families, teaching, special needs, environment and peace.

Susan Ely, President/Sales
Anne Wilson, VP/Marketing

5140 Rosen Publishing Group
29 E 21st Street
New York, NY 10010-6209
212-777-3017
800-237-9932
Fax: 888-436-4643
Nonfiction books on self-help and guidance for young adults. Books also available for reluctant readers on self-esteem, values and drug abuse prevention.

5141 Routledge/Europa Library Reference
Taylor & Francis Books
29 W 35 Street
New York, NY 10001-2299
212-216-7800
800-634-7064
Fax: 212-564-7854
E-mail: reference@routledge-ny.com
http://www.reference.routlege-ny.com
Publisher of a wide range of print and online library reference titles, including the renowned Europa World Yearbook and the award-winning Routledge Encyclopedia of Philosophy (both available in online and print formats), Garland Encyclopedia of World Music, Routledge Religion and Society Encyclopedias, Chronological History of US Foreign Relations, and many other acclaimed resources.

Koren Thomas, Sr Marketing/Library Ref
Elizabeth Sheehan, Marketing/Library Reference

5142 Runestone Press
A Divisions of Lerner Publishing Group
241 1st Avenue N
Minneapolis, MN 55401-1607
612-332-3344
800-328-4929
Fax: 612-332-7615
http://www.lernerbooks.com
Nonfiction for readers in Grades 5 and up. Newly revised editions of previously out-of-print books. List includes Buried Worlds archaeology series and titles of Jewish and Native American interest. Complete catalog is available.

Harry J Lerner, President
Mary M Rodgers, Editorial Director

5143 Saddleback Educational
Three Watson
Irvine, CA 92618-2767
949-860-2500
800-637-8715
Fax: 888-734-4010
Supplementary curriculum materials for K-12 and adult students.

5144 SafeSpace Concepts
1424 N Post Oak Road
Houston, TX 77055-5401
713-956-0820
800-622-4289
Fax: 713-956-6416
E-mail: safespacec@aol.com
http://www.safespaceconcepts.com
Manufactures young children's play equipment and furnishings.

Barbara Carlson, PhD, President
Jerry Johnson, Marketing Director

145 Sage Publications
Sage Publications
2455 Teller Road
Thousand Oaks, CA 91320
303-333-3003
800-803-8488
Fax: 303-333-4037
E-mail: karen-hemmes@mindspring.com
http://www.fireflybooks.com
Sage Publications publishes handbooks and guides with a focus on research and science.

Karen Hemmes, Publicist
Mary Kay Opicka, Publicist

146 Salem Press
Grey House Publishing
2 University Plaza
Suite 310
Hackensack, NJ 07601
201-968-0500
Fax: 201-968-0511
E-mail: sales@salempress.com
http://www.salempress.com
Salem Press delivers award-winning literary, historical, medical and science reference content to the public library, academic and high school markets.

Richard Gottlieb, President
Pam Brunke, Sales Manager

147 Santillana Publishing
901 W Walnut Street
Compton, CA 90220-5109
310-763-0455
800-245-8584
Fax: 305-591-9145
Publishers of K-12 and adult titles in Spanish.Imprints include: Altea, Alfagunea, Taurus and Aguilar.

Marla Norman, Publisher/Trade Book
Antonio de Marco, President

148 Scholastic
555 Broadway
New York, NY 10012
212-343-6100
800-724-6527
Fax: 212-343-4801
http://www.scholastic.com
Publisher and distributor of children's books. Provides professional and classroom resources for K-12.

149 School Book Fairs
PO Box 835105
Richardson, TX 75083
972-231-9838
A children's book publisher that provides distribution of leisure reading materials to elementary and middle schools through book fair fund-raising events via a North American network with 97 locations.

150 Science Inquiry Enterprises
14358 Village View Lane
Chino Hills, CA 91709-1706
530-295-3338
Fax: 530-295-3334
Selected science teaching materials.

151 Scott & McCleary Publishing Company
2482 11th Street SW
Akron, OH 44314-1712
702-566-8756
800-765-3564
Fax: 702-568-1378
E-mail: jscott7576@aol.com
http://www.scottmccleary.com
Diagnostic reading and testing material.

Janet M Scott, Publisher
Sheila C McCleary, Publisher

5152 Scott Foresman Company
1900 E Lake Avenue
Glenview, IL 60025-2086
800-554-4411
Fax: 800-841-8939
Science tests and reading/language arts materials for teachers and students. Celebrate Reading! is the K-8 literature-based reading/integrated language arts program designed to meet the needs of all children. Book Festival is a literature learning center that offers teachers a collection of trade books for independent reading.

Bert Crossland, Reading Product Manager
Jim Fitzmaurice, VP Editor Group

5153 Sharpe Reference
M.E. Sharpe, Inc.
80 Business Park Drive
Armonk, NY 10504
914-273-1800
800-541-6563
Fax: 914-273-2106
E-mail: custserv@mesharpe.com
http://www.mesharpe.com
Historical, political, geographical and art reference books.

Diana McDermott, Director Marketing

5154 Signet Classics
375 Hudson Street
New York, NY 10014-3658
212-366-2000
Fax: 212-366-2888
Publishes books on literature, poetry and reading.

5155 Silver Moon Press
160 5th Avenue
Suite 622
New York, NY 10010-7003
212-242-6499
800-874-3320
Fax: 212-242-6799
Informational and entertaining books for young readers. Subjects include history, multiculturalism and science.

5156 Simon & Schuster Children's Publishing
1230 Avenue of the Americas
New York, NY 10020
212-698-7000
Fax: 212-698-7007
http://www.simonsayskids.com
Fiction and nonfiction, in hardcover and paperback editions, for preschool through young adult.

5157 Social Issues Resources Series
1100 Holland Drive
Boca Raton, FL 33487-2701
561-994-0079
Fax: 561-994-2014
Provides information systems in print format and CD-ROM format.

5158 Social Science Education Consortium
Box 21270
Boulder, CO 80308-4270
303-492-8154
Fax: 303-449-3925
E-mail: singletl@stripe.colorado.edu
http://www.ssecinc.org
Produces curriculum guides, instructional units and collections of lesson plans on US history, law-related education, global studies, public issues and geography. Develops projects for social studies teachers and evaluates social studies programs.

James Cooks, Executive Director
Laurel Singleton, Associate Director

5159 Social Studies School Service
10200 Jefferson Boulevard
Culver City, CA 90232-3598
310-839-2436
800-421-4246
Fax: 310-839-2249
E-mail: access@socialstudies.com
http://www.socialstudies.com
Supplemental materials in all areas of social studies, language arts.

5160 Special Education & Rehabilitation Services
330 C Street
Washington, DC 20202
202-205-5465
Fax: 202-260-7225
Judith E Heuman, Assistant Secretary

5161 Speech Bin
1965 25th Avenue
Vero Beach, FL 32960-3000
561-770-0007
800-477-3324
Fax: 561-770-0006
Publisher and distributor of books and materials for professionals in rehabilitation, speech-language pathology, occupational and physical therapy, special education, and related fields. Major product lines include professional and children's books, computer software, diagnostic tests.

Jan J Binney, VP

5162 Stack the Deck Writing Program
PO Box 5352
Chicago, IL 60680-0429
312-675-1000
Fax: 312-765-0453
E-mail: stockthedeck@sbcglobal.net
http://www.stackthedeck.com
Composition textbooks, grades 1-12, plus computer software.

5163 Stenhouse Publishers
477 Congress Street
Suite 4B
Portland, ME 04101-3417
888-363-0566
Fax: 800-833-9164
http://www.stenhouse.com
Professional materials for teachers by teachers.

5164 Story Teller
PO Box 921
Salem, UT 84653-0921
801-423-2560
Fax: 801-423-2568
E-mail: patti@thestoryteler.com
http://www.thestoryteller.com
Felt board stories books and educational sets.

Patti Gardner, VP Sales

5165 Summit Learning
7755 Rockwell Avenue
PO Box 755
Fort Atkinson, WI 53538-0755
800-777-8817
800-777-8817
Fax: 800-317-2194
E-mail: info@summitlearning.com
http://www.summitlearning.com
Summit learning is a distributor of manipulative-based math and science materials, provides you with a carefully selected group of the most popular high-quality products at low prices.

Gary Otto, Marketing Manager

5166 Sunburst Technology
1550 Executive Drive
Elgin, IL 60123

914-747-3310
800-338-3457
Fax: 914-747-4109
http://www.sunburst.com
K-12 educational software, guidance and health materials, and online teacher resources.

5167 Sundance Publishing
234 Taylor Street
PO Box 1326
Littleton, MA 01460
978-486-9201
800-343-8204
Fax: 978-486-8759
E-mail: kjasmine@sundancepub.com
http://www.sindancepub.com
A supplementary educational publisher of instructional materials for shared, guided, and independent reading, phonics, and comprehension skills for grades K-9. Some of its programs include AlphKids, SunLit Fluency, Popcorns and Little Readers. Its Second Chance Reading Program for below-level readers features high-interest titles, written for upper elementary/middle school students. It also distributes paperback editions of some of the most widely taught literature titles for grades K-1

Katherine Jasmine, VP Marketing

5168 Synergistic Systems
2297 Hunters Run Drive
Reston, VA 20191-2834
703-758-9213
Science education curriculum materials.

5169 TASA
PO Box 382
Brewster, NY 10509-0382
845-277-8100
800-800-2598
Fax: 845-277-3548
Degrees of Literacy Power Program; English Language Profiles, primary, standard and advanced DRP tests, Degrees of World Meaning Tests.

5170 TL Clark Incorporated
5111 SW Avenue
St. Louis, MO 63110
314-865-2525
800-859-3815
Fax: 314-865-2240
E-mail: general@tlclarkinc.com
http://www.tlclarkinc.com
Educational products for grades Pre-K-3. Rest time products including cots and mats, sand and water play tubs, active play items including tunnels, tricycles and foam play items.

Jim Fleminla, President

5171 TMC/Soundprints
353 Main Avenue
Norwalk, CT 06851-1508
203-846-2274
800-228-7839
Fax: 203-846-1776
E-mail: sndprnts@ixinctcom.com
http://www.soundprints.com
Children's story books for children ages 4 through 8 under the license of the Smithsonian Institute and the National Wildlife Federation. Each 32 page four color book highlights a unique aspect of the animal featured in the book so as to provide education while still being entertaining. Each book can be bought with an audiocassette read-a-long and plush toy. Over 80 books in print.

Ashley Anderson, Associate Publisher
Chelsea Shriver

5172 Tambourine Books
1350 Avenue of the Americas
New York, NY 10019-4702
212-261-6500
Fax: 212-261-6518
A wide variety of books to increase creativity and reading skills in students.

5173 Taylor & Francis Publishers
7625 Empire Drive
Florence, KY 41042
800-624-7064
Fax: 800-248-4724
Publisher of professional texts and references in several fields including the behavioral sciences; arts, humanities, social sciences, science technology and medicine.

Chris Smith, Customer Service Manager

5174 Teacher's Friend Publications
3240 Trade Center Drive
Riverside, CA 92507
909-682-4748
800-343-9680
Fax: 909-682-4680
Complete line of the original monthly and seasonal Creative Idea Books. Plus, two new cooperative-learning language series and much more.

Karen Sevaly, Author
Richard Sevaly, President/CEO
Kim Marsh, National Sales Manager

5175 Teaching Comprehension: Strategies for Stories
Oxton House Publishers, LLC
Po Box 209
Farmington, ME 04938
207-779-1923
800-539-7323
Fax: 207-779-0623
E-mail: info@oxtonhouse.com
http://www.oxtonhouse.com
A detailed roadmap for providing students with effective strategies for comprehending and remembering stories. It includes story-line masters for helping students to organize their thinking and to accurately depict character and sequence events.

62 pages

William Berlinghoff, Managing Editor
Bobby Brown, Marketing Director

5176 Theme Connections
Perfection Learning
PO Box 500
Logan, IA 51546-0500
800-831-4190
Fax: 712-644-2392
Features 135 best-selling literature titles and related theme libraries for students to develop lifelong learning strategies.

5177 Ther-A-Play Products
PO Box 2030
Lodi, CA 95241-2030
209-368-6787
800-308-6749
Fax: 209-365-2157
E-mail: madgic@attbi.com
Children's books, play therapy books, sandplay and sandtray manipulatives, puppets, games, doll houses and furniture. Playmobile and educational toys, specializing in counselors' tools. Books on abuses, illness, death, behavior and parenting.

Madge Geiszler, Owner

5178 Thomson Learning
115 5th Avenue
New York, NY 10003-1004
212-979-2210
800-880-4253
Fax: 248-699-8061
Book publisher of library and classroom-oriented educational resources for children and young adults. Over 200 books are available in 30 different subjects.

5179 Time-Life Books
2000 Duke Street
Alexandria, VA 22314-3414
703-838-7000
Fax: 703-838-7166
A wide-ranging selection of quality reference and supplemental books for students from elementary to high school.

5180 Tiny Thought Press
1427 S Jackson Street
Louisville, KY 40208-2720
502-637-6916
Fax: 502-634-1693
Children's books that build character and self-esteem.

5181 Tom Snyder Productions
80 Coolidge Hill Road
Watertown, MA 02472
800-342-0236
Fax: 800-304-1254
E-mail: ask@tomsynder.com
http://www.tomsynder.com
Developer and publisher of educational software.

John McAndrews, Contact

5182 Tor Books/Forge/SMP
175 5th Avenue
New York, NY 10010-7703
212-388-0100
Fax: 212-388-0191
Science-fiction and fantasy children's books, mysteries, Westerns, general fiction and classics publications.

5183 Tricycle Press
PO Box 7123
Berkeley, CA 94707-0123
510-559-1600
800-841-2665
Fax: 510-559-1637
Publisher of books and posters for children ages 2-12 and their grown-ups. Catalog available.

Christine Longmuir, Publicity/Marketing

5184 Troll Associates
100 Corporate Drive
Mahwah, NJ 07430-2322
201-529-4000
Fax: 201-529-8282
Publisher of children's books and products, including paperbacks and hardcovers, special theme units, read-alongs, videos, software and big books.

5185 Trumpet Club
1540 Broadway
New York, NY 10036-4039
212-492-9595
School book club featuring hardcover and paperback books, in class text sets and author video visits.

5186 Turn-the-Page Press
203 Baldwin Avenue
Roseville, CA 95678-5104
916-786-8756
800-959-5549
Fax: 916-786-9261
E-mail: mleeman@ibm.net
http://www.turnthepage.com

Books, cassettes and videos focusing on early childhood education.

Michael Leeman, President

187 USA Today
1000 Wilson Boulevard
Arlington, VA 22209-3901
703-276-3400
Fax: 703-854-2103
Educational programs focusing on social studies.

188 Upstart Books
PO Box 800
Fort Atkinson, WI 53538-0800
920-563-9571
800-558-2110
Fax: 920-563-7395
http://www.hpress.highsmith.com
Publishes teacher activity resources, reading activities, library and information seeking skills, Internet.

Matt Mulder, Director
Virginia Harrison, Editor

189 Useful Learning
711 Meadow Lane Court
Apartment 12
Mount Vernon, IA 52314-1549
319-895-6155
800-962-3855
The Useful Spelling Textbook series for Grades 2-8, represents a curriculum based upon the scientific knowledge of research studies conducted during the past 80 years at The University of Iowa, Iowa City, IA. Incorporates the New Iowa Spelling Scale and is composed of qualitative curriculum, qualitative learning practices and qualitative instructional procedures.

Larry D. Zenor, PhD, President
Bradley M Loomer, PhD, Board Chairman

190 VIDYA Books
PO Box 7788
Berkeley, CA 94707-0788
510-527-9932
Fax: 510-527-2936
Supplemental materials about India and the surrounding region for K-12 lesson plans.

191 Viking Children's Books
375 Hudson Street
New York, NY 10014-3658
212-941-8780
General hardcover children's books, from toddler through young adult, fiction and non-fiction.

192 Vision 23
Twenty-Third Publications
185 Willow Street
Mystic, CT 06355-2636
860-536-2611
Fax: 800-572-0788
A wide variety of children's products including books, games, clothing and toys.

193 WH Freeman & Company
41 Madison Avenue
New York, NY 10010-2202
212-576-9400
Fax: 212-481-1891
Books relating to the world of mathematics.

194 Wadsworth Publishing School Group
10 Davis Drive
Belmont, CA 94002-3002
650-595-2350
Fax: 800-522-4923
College and advanced placement/honors high school materials in biology, chemistry and environmental science.

5195 Walker & Company
104 Fifth Avenue
New York, NY 10011
212-727-8300
800-289-2553
Fax: 212-727-0984
http://www.walkerbooks.com
Hardcover and paperback trade titles for Pre-K-12th grade, including picture books, photo essays, fiction and nonfiction titles appropriate for every curriculum need.

5196 Warren Publishing House
11625-G Airport Road
Everett, WA 98204-3790
425-353-3100
New Totline Teaching Tales with related activities plus quality whole language teacher activity books including Alphabet Theme-A-Saurus and Piggyback Songs.

5197 Waterfront Books
85 Crescent Road
Burlington, VT 05401-4126
802-658-7477
800-639-6063
Fax: 802-860-1368
E-mail: helpkids@waterfrontbooks.com
http://www.waterfrontbooks.com
Publishes and distributes books on special issues for children: barriers to learning, coping skills, mental health, prevention strategies, family/parenting, etc. for grades K-12. Titles include: The Divorce Workbook; Josh, a Boy with Dyslexia; What's a Virus, Anyway? The Kids' Book About AIDS and more.

Sherrill N Musty, Publisher
Michelle Russell, Order Fulfillment

5198 Web Feet Guides
Rock Hill Communications
14 Rock Hill Road
Bala Cynwyd, PA 19004
610-667-2040
888-762-5445
Fax: 610-667-2291
E-mail: info@rockhillcommunications.com
http://www.webfeetguides.com
The premier subject guides to the Internet, rigorously reviewed by librarians and educators, fully annotated, expanded and updated monthly. Appropriate for middle school through adult. Available in print, online, or marc records. For more information, free trials and Web casts, and free interactive Web Quests for your K-8 students, visit our Web site.

Linda Smith, Marketing Coordinator

5199 West Educational Publishing
620 Opperman Drive
#645779
Saint Paul, MN 55123-1340
A leader in quality social studies textbooks and ancillaries for grades K-12.

5200 Western Psychological Services
12031 Wilshire Boulevard
Los Angeles, CA 90025-1251
310-478-2061
800-648-8857
Fax: 310-478-7838
http://www.wpspublish.com
Assessment tools for professionals in education, psychology and allied fields. Offer a variety of tests, books, software and therapeutic games.

5201 Wildlife Conservation Society
Bronx Zoo
Education Department
2300 Southern Boulevard
Bronx, NY 10460

718-220-5131
800-937-5131
Fax: 718-733-4460
E-mail: sscheio@wes.org
http://www.wcs.com
Environmental science and conservation biology curriculum materials and information regarding teacher training programming for Grades K-12, on site or off site, nationally and locally. Science programming for grades pre-K-12 available on site.

Sydell Schein, Manager/Program Services
Ann Robinson, Director National Programs

5202 William Morrow & Company
1350 Avenue of the Americas
New York, NY 10019-4702
212-261-6500
Fax: 212-261-6518
High quality hardcover and paperback books for children.

5203 Winston Derek Publishers
101 French Landing Drive
Nashville, TN 37228-1511
615-321-0535
A cross section of African American books and educational materials, including preschool and primary grade books.

5204 Wolfram Research, Inc.
100 Trade Center Drive
Champaign, IL 61820-7237
217-398-0700
800-965-3726
Fax: 217-398-0747
E-mail: info@wolfram.com
http://www.wolfram.com
Offers mathematics publications, statistics and information to educators of grades K-12.

Stephen Wolfram, Founder/CEO
Jean Buck, Dir., Corp Communications

5205 Workman Publishing
708 Broadway
New York, NY 10003-9508
212-254-5900
Fax: 212-254-8098
Children's curriculum, books, textbooks, workbooks, fiction and nonfiction titles.

5206 World & I
News World Communications
2800 New York Avenue NE
Washington, DC 20002-1945
202-636-3365
800-822-2822
Fax: 202-832-5780
E-mail: ckim@worldandimag.com
http://www.worldandi.com
With over 40 articles each month, The World & I presents an enlightening look at our changing world through the eyes of noted scholars and experts covering current issues, the arts, science, book reviews, lifestyles, cultural perspectives, philosophical trends, and the millennium. For educators, students and libraries. Free teacher's guides year round. Also, online archives available at www.worldandi.com.

Charles Kim, Business Director

5207 World Association of Publishers, Manufacturers& Distributors
Worlddidac
Bollwerk 21, PO Box 8866 CH-3001
Berne
Switzerland
41-31-3121744
Fax: 41-31-3121744
E-mail: info@worlddidac.org
A worldwide listing of over 330 publishers, manufacturers and distributors of educa-

tional materials. Listings include all contact information, products and school levels/grades.

160 pages Annual
Beat Jost, Coordinating Education

5208 World Bank
1818 H Street NW
Room T-8061
Washington, DC 20433-0002
202-477-1234
Fax: 202-477-6391
Maps, poster kits, case studies and videocassettes that teach about life in developing countries.

5209 World Book Educational Products
525 W Monroe Street
20th Floor
Chicago, IL 60661
312-729-5800
Fax: 312-729-5600
Reference books and the World Book Encyclopedia on CD-Rom.

5210 World Eagle
111 King Street
Littleton, MA 01460-1527
978-486-9180
800-854-8273
Fax: 978-486-9652
E-mail: info@ibaradio.org
http://www.worldeagle.com
Publishes an online, social studies educational resource magazine: comparative data, graphs, maps and charts on world issues. Publishes world regional atlases, and supplies maps and curriculum materials.

Valentina Bardawil Powers, Author
Martine Crandall-Hollick, President

5211 World Resources Institute
10 G Street, NE
Suite 800
Washington, DC 20002
202-729-7600
Fax: 202-729-7610
The world Resources Institute is an environmental think tank that goes beyond research to create practical ways to protect the Earth and improve people's lives. our mission is to move human society to live in ways that protect Earth's environment for surrent and future generations.

Jonathan Lash, President

5212 World Scientific Publishing Company
27 Warren Street
Suite 401-402
Hackensack, NJ 07601
201-487-9655
Fax: 201-487-9695
E-mail: wspc@wspc.com
http://www.wspc.com
This is one of the world's leading academic publishers. It now publishes more than 400 books and 100 journals a year in diverse fields of science technology, medicine, business and management.

Ruth Zhou, Marketing Executive

5213 World of Difference Institute
Anti-Defamation League
823 United Nations Plaza
New York, NY 10017-3518
212-490-2525
Fax: 212-867-0779
E-mail: webmaster@adl.org
http://www.adl.org

Materials and training, as well as Pre K-12 curriculum resources, Anti-bias and diversity.

Lindsay J Friedman, Director

5214 Worth Publishers
33 Irving Plaza
New York, NY 10003-2332
212-475-6000
Fax: 212-689-2383
A balanced and comprehensive account of the U.S. past is accompanied by an extensive set of supplements.

5215 Wright Group
19201 120th Avenue NE
Bothell, WA 98011-9507
800-523-2371
Fax: 425-486-7704
http://www.wrightgroup.com
Supplementary program materials for reading education.

5216 Write Source Educational Publishing House
PO Box 460
Burlington, WI 53105-0460
262-763-8258
Fax: 262-763-2651
Publishes Writers Express, a writing, thinking and learning handbook series for grades 4 and 5. Also offer the latest editions of Write Source 2000 and Writers INC for grades 6-8 and 9-12.

5217 Zaner-Bloser K-8 Catalog
2200 W 5th Avenue
Columbus, OH 43215
614-486-0221
800-421-3018
Fax: 614-487-2699
http://www.zaner-bloser.com
Publisher of handwriting materials and reading, writing, spelling and study skills programs.

Robert Page, President

5218 Zephyr Press
814 North Franklin Street
Chicago, IL 60610-3109
312-337-5985
800-232-2187
Fax: 312-337-5985
E-mail: neways2learn@zephyrpress.com
http://www.zephyrpress.com
Zephyr Press publishes effective, state-of-the-art-teaching materials for classroom use.

Joey Tanner MEd, President

5219 ZooBooks
ZooBooks/Wildlife Education. Ltd.
12233 Thatcher Court
Poway, CA 92064-6880
619-513-7600
800-477-5034
Fax: 858-513-7660
E-mail: animals@zoobooks.com
http://www.zoobooks.com
Reference books offering fascinating insights into the world of wildlife. Created in collaboration with leading scientists and educators, these multi-volume Zoobooks make important facts and concepts about nature, habitat and wildlife understandable to children. From alligators to zebras, aquatic to exotic, each Zoobook is colorful, scientifically accurate and easy to read.

General

5220 You Call This Living?
William Kingsley Publishing
3036 Big Oaks Drive
Garland, TX 75044
972-220-9959
E-mail: seabed999@yahoo.com
http://www.billkingsley.com
The book explored the human condition and the need for a drastic overhaul of the educational system.

274 pages
ISBN: 978-578-12522

Bill Kingsley, Author
Bill Kingsley

General

221 AVKO Educational Research Foundation
3084 Willard Road
Birch Run, MI 48415-9404
810-686-9283
866-285-6612
Fax: 810-686-1101
E-mail: avkoemail@aol.com
http://www.avko.org
Comprised of teachers and individuals interested in helping others learn to read and spell. Develops reading training materials for individuals with dyslexia or other learning disabilities using a method involving audio, visual, kinesthetic and oral diagnosis and remediation. Conducts research into the causes of reading, spelling, and writing disabilities.

Don McCabe, President/ Research Director
Linda Heck, Vice-President

222 Assistive Technology Clinics
Children's Hospital
1056 E 19th Avenue
#030
Denver, CO 80218-1007
303-861-6250
Fax: 303-764-8214
A diagnostic clinic providing evaluation, information and support to families with children with disabilities in the areas of seating and mobility. Offers augmentative communication and assistive technology access.

Tracey Kovach, Coordinator

223 Center for Equity and Excellence in Education
George Washington University
1555 Wilson Boulevard
Suite 515
Arlington, VA 22209-2004
703-528-3588
800-925-3223
Fax: 703-528-5973
E-mail: ceeeinfo@ceee.gwu.edu
http://www.ceee.gwu.edu
Mission is to advance education reform so that all students achieve high standards. Operates under the umbrella of the Institute for Education Policy Studies within the Graduate School of Education and Human Development. Designs and conducts program evaluation for states, districts and schools and conducts program evalutaion, policy and applied research effecting equitable educational opportunities for all students.

Charlene Rivera, Executive Director
Kristina Anstrom, Assistant Director

224 Center for Learning
The Center for Learning
PO Box 910
2105 Evergreen Road
Villa Maria, PA 16155
724-964-8083
800-767-9090
Fax: 724-964-8992
E-mail: customerservice@centerforlearning.org
http://www.centerforlearning.org
To improve education by writing and publishing values-based curriculum materials that enable teachers to foster student responsibility for learning

225 Center for Organization of Schools
Johns Hopkins University
2701 N Charles Street
Suite 300
Baltimore, MD 21218-2404

410-516-8800
Fax: 410-516-8890
E-mail: mmaushard@csos.jhu.edu
http://www.csos.jhu.edu
Conduct research, development, evaluation, and dissemination of replicable strategies designed to transform low-performing schools so that al lstudents graduate ready for college, career and life. Products include curricula that help all students achieve at a high level. Programs in early learning; school, family and community partnerships; a financial literacy program called Stocks ain the Future, and the Baltimore Education Research Consotrium, plus Talent development Secondary reform

James McPartland, Co-Director
Mary Maushard, Communication Director

5226 Center for Research on the Context of Teaching
Stanford University
CERAS Building
4th Floor 520 Galvez Mall
Stanford, CA 94305-3084
650-725-1845
Fax: 650-736-2296
http://www.stanford.edu/group/CRC/
Conducts research on ways in which secondary school teaching and learning are affected by their contexts.

Milbrey W McLaughlin, Co-Director
Joan E Talbert, Co-Director

5227 Center for Social Organization of Schools
Johns Hopkins University
3003 N Charles Street
Suite 200
Baltimore, MD 21218-3888
410-516-8800
Fax: 410-516-8890
E-mail: jmcpartland@csos.jhu.edu
http://www.csos.jhu.edu
Conduct programmatic research to improve the education system, as well as full-time support staff engaged in developing curricula and providing technical assistance to help schools use the Center's research.

Jim McPartland, Director
Mary Maushard, Communication Director

5228 Center for Technology in Education
Bank Street College of Education
6740 Alexander Bell Drive
Suite 302
Columbia, MD 21046-1898
410-516-9800
Fax: 410-516-9818
E-mail: cte@jhu.edu
http://cte.jhu.edu
Improve the quality of life of children and youth, particularly those with special needs, through teaching, research, and leadership in the use of technology.

Jacqueline A Nunn, Director
K Lynne Harper Mainzer, Deputy Director

5229 Center for the Study of Reading
University of Illinois
158 Children's Research Center
51 Gerty Drive
Champaign, IL 61820
217-333-2552
Fax: 217-244-4501
E-mail: csrrca@uiuc.edu
http://csr.ed.uiuc.edu
Conduct reading research and development must be to discover and put into practice the

means for reaching children who are failing to read.

Richard C Anderson, Director
Kim Nguyen-Jahiel, Associate Director

5230 Center for the Study of Small/Rural Schools
University of Oklahoma
555 E Constitution Street
Suite 138
Norman, OK 73072-7820
405-325-1450
Fax: 405-325-7075
E-mail: jcsimmons@ou.edu
http://cssrs.ou.edu
Assists small and rural schools in building and maintaining necessary knowledge bases, founded on state-of-the-art research in the areas of school improvement and reform, restructuring, staff development, administration, and teaching.

Jan C Simmons, Director

5231 Center on Families, Schools, Communities & Children's Learning
Northeastern University
50 Nightingale Hall
Boston, MA 02215
617-373-2595
Fax: 617-373-8924
Examines how families, communities and schools can work in partnership to promote children's motivation, learning and development, including disseminating information.

Nancy Ames, Vice President

5232 Center on Organization & Restructuring of Schools
1025 W Johnson Street
Madison, WI 53706-1706
608-263-7575
Fax: 608-263-6448
Focuses on restructuring K-12 schools in various areas of student development and progress.

Fred M Newman, Director

5233 Council for Educational Development and Research
National Education Association (NEA)
1201 16th Street NW
Washington, DC 20036-3290
202-833-4000
Fax: 202-822-7974
http://www.nea.org
The voice of education professionals. Advocate for education professionals

John I Wilson, Executive Director
Dennis Van Roekel, President

5234 Curriculum Research and Development Group
University of Hawaii
1776 University Avenue
Honolulu, HI 96822-2463
808-956-4969
800-799-8111
Fax: 808-956-6730
E-mail: crdg@hawaii.edu
http://www.hawaii.edu/crdg
Conducts research and creates, evaluates, disseminates, and supports educational programs that serve students, teachers, parents, and other educators in grades preK-12.

Helen Au, Assistant Director
Dr. Kathleen F. Berg, Director

5235 Division for Research
The Council for Exceptional Children
2000 Broadway
Oakland, CA 94612

510-891-3400
http://www.dor.kaiser.org
The Division of Research aims to conduct, publish, and disseminate high-quality epidemiologic and health services research to improve the health and medical care of Kaiser Permanente members and the society at large.

Joe Selby, Director
Morris Collen, Founder

5236 Educational Information & Resource Center
Research Department
606 Delsea Drive
Sewell, NJ 08080-9399
856-582-7000
Fax: 856-582-4206
E-mail: info@eirc.org
http://www.eirc.org
EIRC is committed to continuously improving the education, safety, physical and emotional health of children. EIRC meets this commitment by developing and delivering a comprehensive array of support services to those who teach, raise, care for and mentor children.

Charles Ivory, Executive Director
John Henry, Program Director

5237 Educational Research Service
1001 N Fairfax Street
Suite 500
Alexandria, VA 22314-1587
703-243-2100
800-791-9308
Fax: 703-243-1985
E-mail: ers@ers.org
http://www.ers.org
For over 30 years Educational Research Service has been the nonprofit organization serving the research and information needs of the nation's K-12 education leaders and the public.

John C Draper EdD, CEO
Katherine A Behrens, Chief Operating Officer

5238 Educational Testing Service
Rosedale Road
Princeton, NJ 08541
609-921-9000
Fax: 609-734-5410
http://www.ets.org
To advance quality and equity in education by providing fair and valid assessments, research and related services. Our products and services measure knowledge and skills, promote learning and educational performance, and support education and professional development for all people worldwide.

Susan Keipper, Program Director
Kurt Landgraf, President and CEO

5239 Florida Atlantic University-Multifunctional Resource Center
1515 W Commercial Boulevard
Suite 303
Boco Raton, FL 33309-3095
561-297-3000
800-328-6721
Fax: 561-297-2141
Provides training and technical assistance to Title VII-funded classroom instructional projects and other programs serving limited-English proficient students.

Dr Ann C Willig, Director
Elaine Sherr, Research Assistant

5240 Higher Education Center
National Education Association (NEA)
1201 16th Street NW
Washington, DC 20036-3290
202-833-4000
Fax: 202-822-7974
E-mail: ncuea@nea.org
http://www.nea.org
The center provides data and other research products to NEA higher education affiliates. The Research Advisory Group, composed of higher education leaders and staff, meets twice a year to review products from the NEA Research Center for Higher Education and make recommendations about additional research needs. The center currently provides salary reports, Higher Education Contract Analysis System, and budget analysis.

Dennis Van Roekel, President
John I Wilson, Executive Director

5241 Information Center on Education
Eba Room 385
Albany, NY 12234-1
518-474-8716
Fax: 518-473-7737
Coordinates data collection procedures within the New York State Education Department.

Leonard Powell, Director

5242 Information Exchange
Maine State Library
64 State House Station
Augusta, ME 04333-64
207-287-5620
800-322-8899
Fax: 207-287-5624
Provides access to the latest education research and information for teachers.

Edna M Comstock, Director

5243 Institute for Research in Learning Disabilities
The University of Kansas
3060 Robert
Lawrence, KS 66045-1
785-864-4780
Fax: 785-864-5728
Although the focus of the Institute's research is children, they have a sizeable publication list with some of their research having relevance for adults.

5244 Instructional Materials Laboratory
University of Missouri-Columbia
8 London Hall
Columbia, MO 65211-2230
800-669-2465
800-669-2465
Fax: 573-882-1992
E-mail: iml@missouri.edu
http://www.iml.missouri.edu/
Prepares and disseminates instructional materials for the vocational education community.

Dana Tannehill, Director
Richard Branton, Assistant Director

5245 Learning Research and Development Center
University of Pittsburgh
3939 O'Hara Street
Pittsburgh, PA 15260
412-624-7487
Fax: 412-624-3051
E-mail: lrangel@pitt.edu
http://www.lrdc.pitt.edu
LRDC fosters an environment in which research initiatives relating to the science, practice, organization and technology of

learning, teaching and training are born and thrive.

Charles Perfetti, Director
Alan Lesgold, Senior Scientist/Research Sc

5246 Life Lab Science Program
1156 High Street
Santa Cruz, CA 95064
831-459-2001
Fax: 831-459-3483
E-mail: lifelab@lifelab.org
http://www.lifelab.org
Life Lab Science Program is nationally acknowledged as an expert leader in the development and dissemination of garden-centered educational programs.

Gail Harlamoff, Executive Director
Whitney Cohen, Education Director

5247 Merrimack Education Center
101 Mill Road
Chelmsford, MA 01824-4899
978-256-3985
Fax: 978-256-6890
E-mail: cjeffers@meccorp.mec.edu
http://www.mec.edu/
Merrimack Education Center (MEC) is a diversified educational and technological resource for schools, cities and towns and other non-profit organizations. MEC offers a broad range of special education, professional development, facilities management and technology programs and solutions.

John Barranco, Director

5248 Mid-Atlantic Regional Educational Laboratory
1301 Cecil B Moore Avenue
Philadelphia, PA 19122-6091
215-204-3000
Fax: 215-204-5130
E-mail: robert.sullivan@temple.edu
http://www.temple.edu/lss
The Regional Educational Laboratories are educational research and development organizations supported by contracts with the US Education Department. Specialty area: Education Leadership.

William Evans, Director

5249 Mid-Continent Regional Educational Laboratory
2550 S Parker Road
Suite 500
Aurora, CO 80014-1678
303-337-0990
Fax: 303-337-3005
Focuses on improvement of education practices in Colorado, Kansas, Missouri, Nebraska, Wyoming, North Dakota and South Dakota.

C. Lawrence Hutchins, Director

5250 Midwestern Regional Educational Laboratory
1900 Spring Road
Suite 300
Oak Brook, IL 60521
630-649-6500
Fax: 630-649-6700
E-mail: nowakows@ncrel.org
The Regional Educational Laboratories are educational research and development organizations supported by contracts with the US Education Department, Office of Educational Research and Improvement. Specialty area: Technology.

Dr. Jeri Nowakowski, Executive Director

5251 Missouri LINC
401 E Stewart Road
Columbia, MO 65211

573-882-2733
800-392-0533
Fax: 573-882-5071
Serves students with special needs through a resource and technical assistance center.

Linda Bradley, Director

252 Music Teachers National Association
441 Vine Street
Suite 3100
Cincinnatti, OH 45202-3004
513-421-1420
888-512-5278
Fax: 513-421-2503
E-mail: mtnanet@mtna.org
http://www.mtna.org
Research reports dealing with any aspects of music, music teaching, music learning and related subjects.

Rachel Kramer, Member Liaison

253 NEA Foundatrion for the Improvement of Education
1201 16th Street NW
Washington, DC 20036
202-822-7840
Fax: 202-822-7779
E-mail: info@neafoundation@list.nea.org
http://www.neafoundation.org
The NEA Foundation, through the unique strength of its partnership with educators, advances student achievement by investing in public education that will prepare each of America's children to learn and thrive in a rapidly changing world.

Aaron J Pope, Communications Associate
John I Wilson, Executive Director

254 National Black Child Development Institute
1313 L Street, NW
Suite 110
Washington, DC 20005-4110
202-833-2220
800-556-2234
Fax: 202-833-8222
E-mail: moreinfo@nbcdi.org
http://www.nbcdi.org
NBCDI's mission is to improve and protect the quality of life of Black children and families.

Carol Brunson Day, President
Gillian Shurland, Contact

255 National Center for Improving Science Education
2000 L Street NW
Suite 616
Washington, DC 20036-4917
202-467-0652
Fax: 202-467-0659
Promotes change in state and local policies and practices in science curricula, teaching, and assessment.

Senta A Raizen, Director

256 National Center for Research in Mathematical Sciences Education
University of Wisconsin-Madison
1025 W Johnson Street
#557
Madison, WI 53706-1706
608-263-4285
Fax: 608-263-3406
Provides a research base for the reform of school mathematics.

Thomas A Romberg, Director

5257 National Center for Research in Vocational Education
University of California, Berkeley
2030 Addison Street
Suite 500
Berkeley, CA 94720-1674
510-642-4004
800-762-4093
Fax: 510-642-2124
E-mail: NCRVE@berkeley.edu
http://vocserve.berkeley.edu
The mission of the National Center for Research in Vocational Education (NCRVE) is to strengthen education to prepare all individuals for lasting and rewarding employment and lifelong learning.

David Stern, Director
Phyllis Hudecki, Associate Director

5258 National Center for Research on Teacher Learning
Michigan State University, College of Education
116 Erickson Hall
East Lansing, MI 48824-1034
517-355-9302
Fax: 517-432-2795
E-mail: floden_@_msu.edu
http://ncrtl.msu.edu
The NCRTL extended its findings about learning from students-as-learners to teachers-as-learners in order to understand how teachers learn to teach.

Robert E Floden, Director
G Williamson McDiarmid, Director

5259 National Center for Science Teaching & Learning
Ohio State University
1314 Kinnear Road
Columbus, OH 43212-1156
614-292-3339
Fax: 614-292-0263
Seeks to understand how non-curricular factors affect how science is taught in grades K-12.

Arthur L White, Director

5260 National Center for the Study of Privatizationin Education
525 W 120th Street
Box 181, 230 Thompson Hall
New York, NY 10027-6696
212-678-3259
Fax: 212-678-3474
E-mail: ncspe@columbia.edu
http://www.ncspe.org
The goal of the National Center for the Study of Privatization in Education is to provide an independent, non-partisan source of analysis and information on privatization in education.

Henry M Levin, Director
Clive Belfield, Associate Director

5261 National Center on Education & the Economy
555 13th Street, NW
Suite 500 W
Washington, DC 20004
202-783-3668
888-361-6233
Fax: 202-783-3672
E-mail: info@ncee.org
http://www.ncee.org
NCEE is committed not just to research, analysis and advocacy, but also to following through on its recommendations by creating the training, professional development, technical assistance and materials that profes-

sionals in the system need to implement the proposals we make.

Marc Tucker, President/Founder
Rich Moglia Cannon, Chief Financial Officer

5262 National Center on Education in the Inner Cities
Temple University
13th Street & Cecil B Moore Avenue
Philadelphia, PA 19122
215-893-8400
Fax: 215-735-9718
Conducts systematic studies of innovative initiatives for improving the quality and outcomes of schooling and broad-based efforts to strengthen and improve education.

Margaret C Wang, Director

5263 National Child Labor Committee
1501 Broadway
Suite 1908
New York, NY 10036-5592
212-840-1801
Fax: 212-768-0963
E-mail: info@nationalchildlabor.org
http://www.nationalchildlabor.org
The National Child Labor Committee (NCLC) is a private, non-profit organization founded in 1904 and incorporated by an Act of Congress in 1907 with the mission of promoting the rights, awareness, dignity, well-being and education of children and youth as they relate to work and working.

Jeffrey F Newman, President/Executive Director
Erik Butler, President

5264 National Clearinghouse for Alcohol & Drug Information
PO Box 2345
Rockville, MD 20847-2345
240-221-4019
800-729-6686
Fax: 240-221-4292
http://ncadi.samhsa.gov
SAMHSA's National Clearinghouse for Alcohol and Drug Information (NCADI) is the Nation's one-stop resource for information about substance abuse prevention and addiction treatment.

John Noble, Director

5265 National Clearinghouse for Bilingual Education
George Washington University
2011 Eye Street NW
Suite 300
Washington, DC 20006
202-467-0867
800-321-6223
Fax: 202-467-4283
E-mail: askncela@ncela.gwu.edu
http://www.ncela.gwu.edu
OELA's National Clearinghouse collects, coordinates and conveys a broad range of research and resources in support of an inclusive approach to high quality education for ELLs.

Nancy Zelasko, Director
Minerva Gorena, Director

5266 National Clearinghouse for Information on Business Involvement in Education
National Association for Industry-Education Co-op
235 Hendricks Boulevard
Buffalo, NY 14226-3304
716-834-7047
Fax: 718-834-7047

E-mail: www2.pecom/naiec
http://www2.pecom.net/naiec
Seeks to foster industry-education cooperation in the US and Canada in the areas of school improvement, career education and human resource/economic development.

Dr. Donald Clark, Director

5267 National Dropout Prevention Center
Clemson University
209 Martin Street
Clemson, SC 29631-1555
864-656-2599
Fax: 864-656-0136
E-mail: ndpc@clemson.edu
http://www.dropoutprevention.org
Provide knowledge and promote networking for researchers, practitioners, policymakers, and families to increase opportunities for youth in at-risk situations to receive the quality education and services to successfully graduate from high school.

Jay Smink, Executive Director
Marty Duckenfield, Public Information Director

5268 National Early Childhood Technical Assistance System
517 S Greensboro Street
Carrboro, NC 27510
919-962-2001
919-843-3269
Fax: 919-966-7463
E-mail: nectac@unc.edu
http://www.nectac.org
NECTAC is the national early childhood technical assistance center supported by the U.S. Department of Education's Office of Special Education Programs.

Lynne Kahn, Director
Joan Danaher, Associate Director

5269 National Information Center for Educational Media
PO Box 8640
Albuquerque, NM 87198-8640
505-998-0800
800-926-8328
Fax: 505-256-1080
E-mail: mhlava@accessinn.com
http://www.nicem.com
The world's most comprehensive audiovisual database for over 35 years and a crucial reference tool for librarians, media specialists, training directors, faculty, teachers and researchers.

Marjorie Hlava, President
Jay Van Eman, Chief Executive Officer

5270 National Research Center on the Gifted & Talented
University of Connecticut
2131 Hillside Road
Unit 3007
Storrs, CT 06269-3007
860-486-4826
Fax: 860-486-2900
http://www.gifted.uconn.edu
Studies focusing on meeting the needs of gifted and talented youth have received national and international attention for over 40 years.

Joseph S Renzulli, Director
Phillip E Austin, President

5271 National Resource Center on Self-Care & School-Age Child Care
American Home Economics Association
1555 King Street
Alexandria, VA 22314-2738

703-706-4620
800-252-SAFE
Fax: 703-706-4663
Provides materials to parents, educators, child care professionals and others concerned about the number of latchkey children and about quality school-age child care.

Dr. Margaret Plantz, Director

5272 National School Boards Association Library
1680 Duke Street
Alexandria, VA 22314-3455
703-838-6731
Fax: 703-683-7590
Maintains up-to-date collection of resources concerning education issues, with an emphasis on school board policy issues.

Adria Thomas, Director

5273 National School Safety Center
141 Duesenberg Drive
Suite 11
Westlake Village, CA 91362-3815
805-373-9977
Fax: 805-373-9277
E-mail: info@schoolsafety.us
http://www.schoolsafety.us
Serves as an advocate for safe, secure and peaceful schools worldwide and as a catalyst for the prevention of school crime and violence.

Ronald D Stephens, Executive Director
June Lane Arnette, Associate Director

5274 National Science Resources Center
901 D Street SW
Suite 704B
Washington, DC 20024
202-633-2966
Fax: 202-287-2070
E-mail: nsrcinfo@si.edu
http://www.nsrconline.org
Intermediary organization that bridges research on how children learn with best practices for the classroom.

Sally Shuler, Executive Director
Jennifer Childress, Director

5275 North Central Regional Educational Laboratory
1120 East Diehl Road
Suite 200
Naperville, IL 60563-1486
630-649-6500
Fax: 630-649-6700
E-mail: info@ncrel.org
http://www.ncrel.org
Being an educator is a great responsibility. At Learning Point Associates, we accept responsibility in order to deserve the trust that has been placed in us and our work

Gina Burkhard, Chief Executive Officer
Robert Davis, Chief Financial Officer

5276 Northeast Regional Center for Drug-Free Schools & Communities
12 Overton Avenue
Sayville, NY 11782-2437
718-340-7000
Fax: 516-589-7894
Works to support the prevention of alcohol and other drug use in the northeast region of the United States.

Dr. Gerald Edwards, Director

5277 Northeast and Islands Regional Educational Laboratory
222 Richmond Street
Suite 300
Providence, RI 02903
401-274-9548
800-521-9550
Fax: 401-421-7650
E-mail: info@lab.brown.edu
Promotes educational change to provide all students equitable opportunities to succeed. We advocate for populations whose access to excellent education has been limited or denied.

Oaxaca Schroder, Administrative Assistant
Sunitha Appikatla, Senior Programmer/Analyst

5278 Northwest Regional Educational Laboratory
101 SW Main Street
Suite 500
Portland, OR 97204-3213
503-275-9500
800-547-6339
Fax: 503-275-0660
E-mail: info@nwrel.org
http://www.nwrel.org
The mission of the Northwest Regional Educational Laboratory (NWREL) is to improve learning by building capacity in schools, families, and communities through applied research and development

Jerry Colonna, Chairperson
Rob Larson, Vice Chairperson

5279 Pacific Regional Educational Laboratory
1099 Alakea Street
Suite 2500
Honolulu, HI 96813
808-969-3482
Fax: 808-969-3483
E-mail: kofelj@prel.hawaii.edu
The Regional Educational Laboratories are educational research and development organizations supported by contracts with the U.S. Education Department, Office of Educational Research and Improvement. Specialty area: Language and Cultural Diversity.

Dr. John Kofel, Executive Director

5280 Parent Educational Advocacy Training Center
100 N Washington Street
Suite 234
Falls Church, VA 22046-4523
703-923-0010
800-869-6782
Fax: 800-693-3514
E-mail: partners@peatc.org
http://www.peatc.org
Mission is to build positive futures for children in Virginia by working collaboratively with families, schools and communities in order to improve opportunities for excellence in education and success in school and community life.

Michael Jefferson, President
Betsy McGuire, Vice President

5281 Parents as Teachers National Center
2228 Ball Drive
Saint Louis, MO 63146
314-432-4330
866-728-4968
Fax: 314-432-8963
E-mail: info@parentsasteachers.org
http://www.patnc.org
To provide the information, support and encouragement parents need to help their children develop optimally during the crucial early years of life.

Sue Stepleton, President/CEO
Cheryl Dyle-Palmer, COO

282 Public Education Fund Network
601 13th Street NW
Suite 710 S
Washington, DC 20005-3808
202-628-7460
Fax: 202-628-1893
E-mail: PEN@PublicEducation.org
http://www.publiceducation.org
To build public demand and mobilize resources for quality public education for all children through a national constituency of local education funds and individuals.

Wendy D Puriefoy, Director
Richard J. Vierk, Chairman

283 Quality Education Data
1050 Seventeenth Street
Suite 1100
Denver, CO 80265
303-209-9400
800-525-5811
Fax: 303-209-9444
E-mail: info@qeddata.com
http://www.qeddata.com
Gathers information about K-12 schools, colleges and other educational institutions, offers an on-line database on education, directories of public and nonpublic schools and research reports.

Jeanne Hayes, President
Katie Bukovsky, Sales Executive

284 Regional Laboratory for Educational Improvement of the Northeast
555 New Jersey Ave NW
Washington, DC 20208
800-347-4200
Fax: 781-481-1120
Seeks to improve education in Connecticut, Maine, Massachusetts, New Hampshire, New York, Rhode Island, Vermont, Puerto Rico and the Virgin Islands.

David P Crandall, Director

285 Research for Better Schools
112 N Broad Street
Philadelphia, PA 19102-2471
215-568-6150
Fax: 215-568-7260
E-mail: info@rbs.org
http://www.rbs.org
RBS is a private, nonprofit educational organization funded primarily through grants and contracts from the U.S. Department of Education, the National Science Foundation, Mid-Atlantic state departments of education, institutions of higher education, foundations, and school districts.

Dr. Keith M Kershner, Executive Director
Rev. John F Bloh, President

286 SERVE
PO Box 5367
Greensboro, NC 27435
336-315-7400
800-755-3277
Fax: 336-315-7457
E-mail: info@serve.org
http://www.serve.org
Its mission is to support and promote teaching and learning excellence in the Pre-kindergarten to Grade 12 education community.

Ludwig Van Broekhuizen, Executive Director
Francena Cummings, Director, Technical Assistan

287 SIGI PLUS
Educational Testing Service
105 Terry Drive
Suite 120
Newtown, PA 18940-1872

800-257-7444
Fax: 215-579-8589
A computerized career guidance program developed by Educational Testing Service. Covers all the major aspects of career decision making and planning through a carefully constructed system of nine separate but interrelated sections, including a Tech Prep module and Internet Hydrolink Connectivity.

Annie Schofer, Sales Manager

5288 Satellite Educational Resources Consortium
939 S Stadium Road
Columbia, SC 29201-4724
803-252-2782
Fax: 803-252-5320
http://www.adec.edu
Seeks to expand educational opportunities by employing the latest telecommunication technologies to make quality education in math, science, and foreign languages available equally and cost-effectively to students regardless of their geographic location.

Wilbur H Hinton, Executive Director

5289 Scientific Learning
300 Frank H Ogawa Plaza
Suite 600
Oakland, CA 94612-2040
888-665-9707
888-665-9707
Fax: 510-444-3580
E-mail: customerservice@scilearn.com
http://www.scientificlearning.com
Scientific Learning bases their products and services on neuroscience research and scientifically validated efficacy and deliver them using the most efficient technologies. We also provide beneficial products and services to our customers that are easy to use and access.

Robert C Bowen, Chairman/CEO
Andy Myers, President/COO

5290 Smithsonian Institution/Office of Elementary& Secondary Education
PO Box 37012
SI Building, Room 153, MRC 010
Washington, DC 20013-7012
202-633- 100
Fax: 202-357-2116
E-mail: info@si.edu
http://si.edu
Helps K-12 teachers incorporate museums and other community resources into their curricula.

Ann Bay, Director
G Wayne Clough, Secretary

5291 Society for Research in Child Development
University of Chicago Press
2950 S State Street
Suite 401
Ann Arbor, MI 48104
734-926-0600
Fax: 734-926-0601
E-mail: info@srcd.org
http://www.srcd.org
The Society is a multidisciplinary, not-for-profit, professional association with a membership

Barbara Kahn, Business Manager
Lonnie Sherrod, Executive Director

5292 Southeast Regional Center for Drug-Free Schools & Communities
Spencerian Office Plaza
Louisville, KY 40292-1

502-588-0052
800-621-7372
Fax: 502-588-1782
Works to support the prevention of alcohol and drug use among youth in the Southeast region.

Nancy J Cunningham, Director

5293 Southern Regional Education Board
592 10th Street NW
Atlanta, GA 30318-5776
404-875-9211
Fax: 404-872-1477
E-mail: evalutech@sreb.org
http://www.sreb.org
Nonprofit, nonpartisan organization that helps government and education leaders in its 16 member states work together to advance education and improve the social and economic life of the region.

Mark D Musick, Director
David S Spence, President

5294 Southwest Comprehensive Regional Assistance Center-Region IX
New Mexico Highlands University
121 Tijeras Avenue NE
Suite 2100
Albuquerque, NM 87102-3461
800-247-4269
Fax: 505-243-4456
National network of 15 technical assistance centers, funded through the US Department of Education, designed to support federally funded educational programs. Specifically, these centers will provide comprehensive training and technical assistance under the Improving America's Schools Act (IASA) to States, Tribes, community based organizations, local education agencies, schools and other recipients of funds under the Act.

Paul E Martinez EdD, Director

5295 Southwestern Educational Development Laboratory
4700 Mueller Boulevard
Austin, TX 78723
512-476-6861
800-476-6861
Fax: 512-476-2286
E-mail: information@sedl.org
http://www.sedl.org
SEDL is a private, nonprofit corporation dedicated to fulfilling its mission with clients and other education stakeholders on a national, regional, state, and local basis through diverse and interrelated funding, partnerships, and projects.

Dr. Wesley A Hoover, President/ CEO
Vicki Dimock, Chief Program Officer

5296 Special Interest Group for Computer Science Education
Computer Science Department
University of Texas at Austin
Austin, TX 78712
512-471-9539
Fax: 512-471-8885
http://www.sigcse.org
Provides a forum for solving problems common in developing, implementing and evaluating computer science education programs and courses.

Nell B Dale, Director

5297 TACS/WRRC
1268 University of Oregon
Eugene, OR 97403
541-346-5641
Fax: 541-346-0322
E-mail: wrrc@oregon.uoregon.edu
http://wrrc.uoregon.edu/tacs

Supports state education agencies in their task of ensuring quality programs and services for children with disabilities and their families.

Richard Zeller, Co-Director
Caroline Moore, Project Director

5298 TERC
2067 Massachusetts Avenue
Cambridge, MA 2140-1340
617-873-9600
Fax: 617-873-9601
E-mail: contactus@terc.edu
http://www.terc.edu
We imagine a future in which learners from diverse communities engage in creative, rigorous, and reflective inquiry as an integral part of their lives.

24 pages
ISSN: 0743-0221

Laurie Brennan, President
Nira Voss, Chief Financial Officer

5299 UCLA Statistical Consulting
University of California, Los Angeles
8130 MSB, UCLA
PO Box 951554
Los Angeles, CA 90095-1554
310-825-8299
Fax: 310-206-5658
http://www.ats.ucla.edu
Provides statistical consulting services to UCLA and off-campus students. The staff is faculty members, graduate students and the Department of Statistics. Specializes in the quantitative analysis of research problems in a wide variety of fields.

Debbie Barrera, Administrator
Richard Berk, Director

Audio Visual Materials

300 AGC/United Learning
Discovery Education
1560 Sherman Avenue
Suite 100
Evanston, IL 60201
847-328-6700
800-323-9084
Fax: 847-328-6706
http://www.discoveryed.com
A publisher/producer of educational videos and digital content K-College curriculum based.

Coni Rechner, Director Marketing
Ronald Reed, Sr. Vice President

301 Active Parenting Publishing
1220 Kennestone Circle
Suite 130
Marietta, GA 30066-6022
770-429-0565
800-825-0060
Fax: 770-429-0334
E-mail: cservice@activeparenting.com
http://www.activeparenting.com
Videos and books on parenting, character education, substance abuse prevention, divorce and step-parenting, ADHD and more.

Dr. Michael H. Popkin, Founder

302 Agency for Instructional Technology/AIT
8111 N. Lee Paul Road
Bloomington, IN 47404-7916
800-457-4509
E-mail: info@ait.net
http://www.ait.net
Videodiscs, videocassettes, films and electronics.

303 Allied Video Corporation
PO Box 702618
Tulsa, OK 74170-2618
918-587-6477
800-926-5892
Fax: 918-587-1550
E-mail: allied@farpointer.net
http://www.allied-video.com/default.aspx
Produces the educational video series, The Assistant Professor. Animations and three-dimensional graphics clearly illustrate concepts in mathematics, science and music. Companion supplementary materials are also available.

Video

Charles Brown, President

304 Altschul Group Corporation
1560 Sherman Avenue
Suite 100
Evanston, IL 60201-4817
800-323-9084
Video and film educational programs.

305 Ambrose Video Publishing Inc
145 West 45th Street
New York, NY 10036
212-768-7373
800-526-4663
Fax: 212-768-9282
E-mail:
customerservice@ambrosevideo.com
http://www.ambrosevideo.com
A leading distributor of broadcast quality documentation/educational videos to individuals (in the home) and schools, libraries and other institutions. The company also sells through catalog, sales staff and television advertising.

5306 Anchor Audio
5931 Darwin Court
Carlsbad, CA 92008
310-784-2300
800-262-4671
Fax: 760-827-7105
E-mail: sales@anchoraudio.com
http://www.anchoraudio.com
Various audio visual products for the school and library.

Alex Jacobs, VP, Sales
Nick Craig, Sales

5307 Association for Educational Communications & Technology
1025 Vermont Avenue NW
Suite 820
Washington, DC 20005-3516
202-347-7834
Offers a full line of videotapes and films for the various educational fields including language arts, science and social studies.

5308 BUILD Sucess Through the Values of Excellence
Center for the Study of Small/Rural Schools
555 E Constitution Street
Room 138
Norman, OK 73072-7820
405-325-1450
Fax: 405-325-7075
E-mail: jcsimmons@ou.edu
http://cssrs.ou.edu
Series IV

Video

Jan C Simmons, Ph.D., Program Director

5309 Bergwall Productions
540 Baltimore Pike
Chadds Ford, PA 19317-9304
800-645-3565
Educational videotapes and films.

5310 Cedrus
1420 Buena Vista Avenue
McLean, VA 22101-3510
703-883-0986
Videodiscs, videocassettes and filmstrips for educational purposes.

5311 Cengage Learning
2493 Du Bridge Avenue
Irvine, CA 92606-5022
949-660-0727
800-233-7078
Fax: 949-660-0206
E-mail: info@conceptmedia.com
http://http://www.cengage.co.in/
Videos for students and professionals focused on child development, early childhood education, and the challenges facing many young children. Effective educational media for development specialists, regular and special education staff in elementary school, preschool teachers, childcare providers, health care workers and parents.

Dennis Timmerman, Sr Account Executive

5312 Character Education
Center for the Study of Small/Rural Schools
555 E Constitution Street
Room 138
Norman, OK 73072-7820
405-325-1450
Fax: 405-325-7075
E-mail: jcsimmons@ou.edu
http://cssrs.ou.edu
Series IV

Video

Jan C Simmons, Ph.D., Program Director

5313 Chip Taylor Communications
2 East View Drive
Derry, NH 03038-5728
603-434-9262
800-876-2447
Fax: 603-432-2723
E-mail: chip.taylor@chiptaylor.com
http://www.chiptaylor.com
Quality educational videotapes and DVDs and multimedia in all areas of interest.

Video

Chip Taylor, President

5314 Churchill Media
6677 N NW Highway
Chicago, IL 60631-1304
310-207-6600
800-334-7830
Fax: 800-624-1678
Videos, videodiscs and curriculum packages for schools and libraries.

5315 College Board Publications
College Board Publications
45 Columbus Avenue
New York, NY 10023-6992
212-713-8000
800-323-7155
Fax: 800-525-5562
E-mail: aces@info.collegeboard.org
http://www.collegeboard.org
Offers a variety of educational videotapes and publications focusing on college issues.

David Coleman, President/ CEO
Jack Buckley, SVP, Research

5316 Computer Prompting & Captioning Company
1010 Rockville Pike
Suite 306
Rockville, MD 20852-3035
301-738-8487
800-977-6678
Fax: 301-738-8488
E-mail: info@cpcweb.com
http://www.cpcweb.com
Closed captioning systems and service.

Sid Hoffman, Project Manager

5317 Crystal Productions
5320 Carpinteria Ave
Suite K
Carpinteria, CA 93013-2107
847-657-8144
800-255-8629
Fax: 800-657-8149
E-mail: custserv@crystalproductions.com
http://www.crystalproductions.com
Producer and distributor of educational resource material in art and sciences. Resources include videotapes, posters, books, videodiscs, CD-Rom, reproductions, games.

132 pages

Amy Woodworth, President

5318 Dukane Corporation
Audio Visual Products Division
2900 Dukane Drive
St Charles, IL 60174-3395
630-584-2300
Fax: 630-584-5156
http://www.dukane.com
Full line of audio visual products, LCD display panels, computer data projectors, overhead projectors, microfilm readers and silent and sound filmstrip projectors.

Michael W. Ritschdorff, President/ CEO
Terry Goldman, VP, Administration

5319 Early Advantage
270 Monroe Turnpike
P.O. Box 743
Fairfield, CT 6824-9853
888-248-0480
Fax: 800-409-9928
E-mail:
customerservice@early-advantage.com
http://www.earlyadvantage.com
Features the Muzzy video collection for teaching children beginning second language skills.

5320 Educational Video Group
291 S Wind Way
Greenwood, IN 46142-9190
317-888-6581
Fax: 317-888-5857
E-mail: evg@insightbb.com
http://www.evgonline.com
Award-winning video programs and textbooks in education, presenting new offerings in speech, government and historic documentaries.

Roger Cook, President

5321 English as a Second Language Video Series
Master Teacher
One Leadership Lane
PO Box 1207
Manhattan, KS 66502-1207
800-669-9633
Fax: 800-669-1132
http://www.masterteacher.com
Assessing the needs of culturally diverse learners, you will learn what must be done to evaluate the learning needs and progress of ESL students.

ISBN: 1-58992-045-7

5322 Fase Productions
4801 Wilshire Boulevard
Suite 215
Los Angeles, CA 90010-3813
213-965-8794
Educational videotapes and films.

5323 Films for Humanities & Sciences
PO Box 2053
Princeton, NJ 08543-2053
609-419-8000
800-257-5126
Fax: 609-419-8071
http://www.wiley.com/legacy/college/geo
cases/cases/case6/videos.htm
A leading publisher/distributor of over four thousand educational programs, including NOVA and TV Ontario, for school and college markets. Also a leader in the production and distribution of videotapes and videodiscs to the educational, institutional and government markets.

5324 First Steps/Concepts in Motivation
18105 Town Center Drive
Olney, MD 20832-1479
301-774-9429
800-947-8377
Educational videotapes and accessories promoting physical fitness for preschoolers and young children. Using choreographed dance movement, familiar and fun children's music, colorful mats, bean bags and rhythm sticks, First Steps teaches balance, gross and fine motor skills, rhythm, coordination, and primary learning skills.

Dale Rimmey, Marketing Director
Larry Rose, President/Owner

5325 Future of Rural Education
Center for the Study of Small/Rural Schools
555 E Constitution Street
Room 138
Norman, OK 73072-7820
405-325-1450
Fax: 405-325-7075
E-mail: jcsimmons@ou.edu
http://cssrs.ou.edu
Series I

Video

Jan C Simmons, Ph.D., Program Director

5326 GPN Year 2005 Literacy Catalog
Destination Education
4910 S 75th St
Lincoln, NE 68516
402-472-2007
800-228-4630
Fax: 402-435-0110
E-mail: slenzen@shopdei.com
http://www.gpn.unl.edu
DVD, VHS, CD-ROM and slides for K-12 libraries and higher education. Free previews and satisfaction guaranteed. The sole source of Reading Rainbow and many other quality programs seen on PBS.

Annually/Video

Steve Lenzen, President and co-founder
John Vondracek, Director Marketing

5327 Gangs in Our Schools: Identification, Response, and Prevention Strategies
Center for the Study of Small/Rural Schools
555 E Constitution Street
Room 138
Norman, OK 73072-7820
405-325-1450
Fax: 405-325-7075
E-mail: jcsimmons@ou.edu
http://cssrs.ou.edu
Series III

Video

Jan C Simmons, Ph.D., Program Director

5328 Guidance Associates
31 Pine View Road
PO Box 1000
Mount Kisco, NY 10549-7000
800-431-1242
Fax: 914-666-5319
E-mail: willg1961@gmail.com
http://www.guidanceassociates.com
Curriculum based videos in health/guidance, social studies, math, science, English, the humanities and career education.

Will Goodman, President

5329 Health Connection
55 West Oak Ridge Drive
Hagerstown, MD 21740
800-548-8700
Fax: 888-294-8405
E-mail: sales@healthconnection.org
http://www.healthconnection.org
Tools for freedom from tobacco and other drugs.

5330 Human Relations Media
175 Tompkins Avenue
Pleasantville, NY 10570-3144
800-431-2050
Fax: 914-244-0485
Offers a wide variety of videotapes and videodiscs in the areas of guidance, social services, human relations, self-esteem and student services.

5331 IIEPassport: Short Term Study Abroad
Institute of International Education
809 United Nations Plaza
New York, NY 10017-3580
412-741-0930
Fax: 212-984-5496
E-mail: iiebooks@abdintl.com
http://www.iiebooks.org
Over 2,900 short-term study abroad programs offered by universities, schools, associations and other organizations.

Annual
ISBN: 087206-296-1

Daniel Obst, Sr Editor

5332 INSIGHTS Visual Productions
374-A N Highway 101
Encinitas, CA 92024-2527
760-942-0528
Fax: 760-944-7793
Science video for K-12 and teacher training.

5333 INTELECOM Intelligent Telecommunications
150 E Colorado Boulevard
Suite 300
Pasadena, CA 91105-1937
626-796-7300
800-576-2988
Fax: 626-577-4282
E-mail: wharden@intelecom.org
http://www.intelecomonline.net
Videos and educational films.

Bob Miller, VP Marketing/Sale

5334 In Search of Character
Performance Resource Press
1270 Rankin Drive
Suite F
Troy, MI 48083-2843
800-453-7733
Fax: 800-499-5718
http://www.pronline.net
Character education videos.

5335 Instructional Resources Corporation
1819 Bay Ridge Avenue
Annapolis, MD 21403-2835
800-922-1711
Fax: 410-268-8320
E-mail: bwhite@historypictures.com
http://www.historypictures.info
American History Videodisc.

5336 Intermedia
5600 Rainier Ave S
Suite 203
Seattle, WA 98118
206-284-2995
800-553-8336
Fax: 206-283-0778
E-mail: info@intermedia-inc.com
http://www.intermedia-inc.com
Distributes a wide range of high-quality, social interest videos on topics such as teen pregnancy prevention, substance abuse prevention, domestic violence, sexual harassment, dating violence, date rape, gang education, cultural diversity, AIDS prevention and teen patenting. Offer free 30 day previews of the programs which are developed to address the needs of educators who must deal with the pressing social problems of today.

Paperback/Video

Susan Hoffman, President
Ted Fitch, General Manager

5337 International Historic Films
3533 S Archer Avenue
Chicago, IL 60609-1135
773-927-2900
Fax: 773-927-9211
E-mail: intrvdeo@ix.netcom.com
http://www.ihffilm.com

Military, political and social history of the 20th century.

Video/Audio

338 January Productions
PO Box 66
Hawthorne, NJ 07507-0066
973-423-4666
800-451-7450
Fax: 973-423-5569
E-mail: anpeller@worldnet.att.net
Educational videotapes, read-a-long books, and CD-Rom.

Paperback/Video/Audi

Lori Brown, Sales/Marketing

339 Karol Media
375 Stewart Road
Hanover, PA 18706
570-822-8899
Fax: 570-822-8226
http://www.karolmedia.com
Science videos.

Carol Kincheloe, Founder
Mick Kincheloe, Founder

340 Kimbo Educational
PO Box 477
Long Branch, NJ 07740-0477
732-229-4949
800-631-2187
E-mail: service@kimboed.com
http://www.kimboeddownloads.com
Manufacturer of children's audio-musical learning fun. Also offers videos and music by other famous children's artists such as Raffi, Sharon, Lois and Bram.

Jim Kimble, President

341 Leadership: Rethinking the Future
Center for the Study of Small/Rural Schools
555 E Constitution Street
Room 138
Norman, OK 73072-7820
405-325-1450
Fax: 405-325-7075
E-mail: jcsimmons@ou.edu
http://cssrs.ou.edu
Series IV

Video

Jan C Simmons, Ph.D., Program Director

342 MPC Multimedia Products Corp
1010 Sherman Avenue
Hamden, CT 06514
203-407-4623
800-243-2108
Fax: 203-407-4636
E-mail: sales@800-pickmpc.com
http://www.800-pickmpc.com
Over 5,000 most frequently requested high quality audio, visual and video products and materials offered at deep discount prices. Manufacturer of high quality tape records, CD's record players, PA systems, headphones

148 pages BiAnnual

T. Guercia, Author
T Guercia, VP
A Melillo, Sales Manager

343 Main Street Foundations: Building Community Teams
Center for the Study of Small/Rural Schools
555 E Constitution Street
Room 138
Norman, OK 73072-7820
405-325-1450
Fax: 405-325-7075
E-mail: jcsimmons@ou.edu
http://cssrs.ou.edu

Prevention Series

Video

Jan C Simmons, Ph.D., Program Director

5344 Marshmedia
Marsh Media
P.O. Box 8082
Shawnee Mission, KS 66208-82
816-523-1059
800-821-3303
Fax: 816-333-7421
E-mail: info@marshmedia.com
http://www.marshmedia.com
Children's educational videotapes, books and teaching guides.

32 pages Bi-Annual
ISBN: 1-55942-xxx

Joan K Marsh, President

5345 Media Projects
5215 Homer Street
Dallas, TX 75206-6623
214-826-3863
Fax: 214-826-3919
E-mail: mail@mediaprojects.org
http://www.mediaprojects.org
Educational videotapes in all areas of interest, including drug education, violence prevention, women's studies, history, youth issues and special education.

Allen Mondell, Director, Writer, Producer

5346 Middle School: Why and How
Center for the Study of Small/Rural Schools
555 E Constitution Street
Room 138
Norman, OK 73072-7820
405-325-1450
Fax: 405-325-7075
E-mail: jcsimmons@ou.edu
http://cssrs.ou.edu
Series III

Video

Jan C Simmons, Ph.D., Program Director

5347 Multicultural Educations: Valuing Diversity
Center for the Study of Small/Rural Schools
555 E Constitution Street
Room 138
Norman, OK 73072-7820
405-325-1450
Fax: 405-325-7075
E-mail: jcsimmons@ou.edu
http://cssrs.ou.edu
Series I

Video

Jan C Simmons, Ph.D., Program Director

5348 NUVO, Ltd.
PO Box 1729
Chula Vista, CA 91912
619-426-8440
Fax: 619-691-1525
E-mail: nuvoltd@aol.com
Produces and distributes how-to videotapes for teens and adults on beginning reading and decorative napkin folding useful in classroom instruction and individual practice. Also distributes two bilingual (Spanish/English) books by psychologist Dr. Jorge Espinoza.

5349 National Film Board
1251 Avenue of the Americas
New York, NY 10020-1104
800-542-2164
Fax: 845-774-2945
Educational films and videos ranging from documentaries on nature and science to social issues such as teen pregnancy.

5350 National Geographic School Publishing
PO Box 10579
Washington, DC 20090-8019
800-368-2728
Fax: 515-362-3366
Offers a wide variety of videodiscs, videotapes and educational materials in the area of social studies, geography, science and social sciences.

5351 PBS Video
1320 Braddock Pl
Alexandria, VA 22314-1649
703-739-5380
800-424-7963
Fax: 703-739-5269
Award-winning programs from PBS, public television's largest video distributors. Video and multimedia programming including interactive videodiscs for schools, colleges and libraries. The PBS Video Resource Catalog is organized into detailed subject categories.

5352 PICS Authentic Foreign Video
University of Iowa
270 International Center
Iowa City, IA 52242-1802
319-335-3500
800-373-PICS
Fax: 319-335-0280
E-mail: webmaster@uiowa.edu
http://housing.uiowa.edu
Provides educators with authentic foreign language videos in French, German and Spanish on videotapes and videodisc. Also offers software to accompany the videodiscs as well as written materials in the form of transcripts and videoguides with pedagogical hints and tips.

Sally Mason, President
Anny Ewing, French Coll Editor

5353 Penton Overseas
2470 Impala Drive
Carlsbad, CA 92008-7226
800-748-5804
Fax: 760-431-8110
Educational videotapes and videodiscs in a wide variety of interests for classroom use.

5354 Phoenix Films/BFA Educ Media/Coronet/MII
Phoenix Learning Group
141 Millwell Dr.
Suite A
St. Louis, MO 63043
314-569-0211
800-221-1274
Fax: 314-569-2834
E-mail: phoenixdealer@aol.com
http://www.phoenixlearninggroup.com
Educational multi-media - VHS, CD-Rom, DVD, streaming & broadcast.

Video

Kathy Longsworth, Vice President, Market Dev

5355 Presidential Classroom
2201 Old Ivy Road
P.O. Box 400406
Charlottesville, VA 22904
434-924-7236
800-441-6533
Fax: 434-982-2739
E-mail: eriedel@presidentialclassroom.org
http://www.presidentialclassroom.org
Video of civic education programs in Washington, DC for high school juniors and seniors. Each one week program provides students with an inside view of the federal

government in action and their role as responsible citizens and future leaders.

Annual
400 attendees
Jack Buechner, President/CEO
William Antholis, Director and CEOÿ

5356 Rainbow Educational Media Charles Clark Company
4540 Preslyn Drive
Raleigh, NC 27616
919-954-7550
800-331-4047
Fax: 919-954-7554
E-mail: karencf@rainbowedumedia.com
http://www.rainbowedumedia.com
Educational videocassettes and CD-Roms.

Karen C Francis, Business Analyst

5357 Rainbow Educational Video
170 Keyland Court
Bohemia, NY 11716-2638
800-331-4047
Producer and distributor of educational videos.

Wesley Clark, Marketing Director

5358 Reading & O'Reilly: The Wilton Programs
PO Box 302
Wilton, CT 06897-0302
800-458-4274
Producers and distributors of award-winning audiovisual educational programs in art appreciation, history, multicultural education, social studies and music. Titles include: African-American Art and the Take-a-Bow, musical production series. Free catalog is available of full product line.

Lee Reading, President
Gretchen O'Reilly, VP

5359 SAP Today
Performance Resource Press
1270 Rankin Drive
Suite F
Troy, MI 48083-2843
800-453-7733
Fax: 800-499-5718
http://store.amplifiedlifenetwork.com
Overview offers the basics of student assistance.

5360 SVE: Society for Visual Education
55 E Monroe Street
Suite 3400
Chicago, IL 60603-5710
312-849-9100
800-829-1900
Fax: 800-624-1678
Producer and distributor of curriculum based instructional materials including videodisc, microcomputer software, video cassettes and filmstrips for grade levels PreK-12.

5361 Slow Learning Child Video Series
Master Teacher
One Leadership Lane
PO Box 1207
Manhattan, KS 66502-1207
800-669-9633
Fax: 800-669-1132
http://www.masterteacher.com
Provides a full understandging of the slow learning child and allows all educators to share in the excitment of teaching this

invidual in ways that develop his or her emerging potenial to the fullest.

ISBN: 1-58992-157-0
Mildred Odom Bradley, Author

5362 Spoken Arts
PO Box 100
New Rochelle, NY 10802-0100
727-578-7600
Literature-based audio and visual products for library and K-12 classrooms.

5363 Teacher's Video Company
8150 S Krene Road
Tempe, AZ 85284
800-262-8837
Fax: 800-434-5638
http://www.teachersvideo.com
Video for teachers.

5364 Teen Court: An Alternative Approach to Juvenile Justice
Center for the Study of Small/Rural Schools
555 E Constitution Street
Room 138
Norman, OK 73072-7820
405-325-1450
Fax: 405-325-7075
E-mail: jcsimmons@ou.edu
http://cssrs.ou.edu
Prevention Series

Video
Jan C Simmons, Ph.D., Program Director

5365 Tools to Help Youth
529 S 7 Street
Suite 570
Minneapolis, MN 55415
800-328-0417
Fax: 612-342-2388
http://www.communityintervention.com
Books and videos on counseling, character education, anger management, life skills, and achohol, tobacco and other drug uses.

5366 Training Video Series for the Professional School Bus Driver
Master Teacher
One Leadership Lane
PO Box 1207
Manhattan, KS 66502-1207
800-669-9633
Fax: 800-669-1132
http://www.masterteacher.com
Will help you provide bus drivers with consistent direction and training for the many situations thay will encounter beyond driving safety.

ISBN: 1-58992-082-1

5367 True Colors
Center for the Study of Small/Rural Schools
555 E Constitution Street
Room 138
Norman, OK 73072-7820
405-325-1450
Fax: 405-325-7075
E-mail: jcsimmons@ou.edu
http://cssrs.ou.edu
Series III

Video
Jan C Simmons, Ph.D., Program Director

5368 United Transparencies
435 Main Street
#104
Johnson City, NY 13790-1935

607-729-6512
800-477-6512
Fax: 607-729-4820
A full line of overhead transparencies for Junior-Senior high school and colleges and technical programs.

D Hetherington

5369 Video Project
P.O. Box 411376
San Francisco, CA 94141-1376
800-475-2638
Fax: 888-562-9012
E-mail: support@videoproject.com
http://www.videoproject.org
Distributor of environmental videos with a collection of over 500 programs for all grade levels, including Oscar and Emmy award winners. Many videotapes come with teacher's guides. Free catalogs available.

Steve Michelson, President
Craig Malina, Director of Business Affairs

5370 Weston Woods Studios
265 Post Road West
Westport, CT 06880
203-845-0197
800-243-5020
Fax: 203-845-0498
E-mail: wstnwoods@aol.com
Audiovisual adaptations of classic children's literature.

Video
Cindy Cardozo, Marketing Coordinator

Classroom Materials

5371 ABC School Supply
3312 N Berkeley Lake Road NW
Duluth, GA 30096-3024
Instructional materials and supplies.

5372 ADP Lemco
5970 W Dannon Way
West Jordan, UT 84081
801-280-4000
800-575-3626
Fax: 801-280-4040
E-mail: customerservice@adplemco.com
http://www.adplemco.com
Announcement boards, schedule boards, chalkboards, tackboard, marker boards, trophy cases, athletic equipment, gym divider curtains and basketball backstops.

David L Hall, Sr VP

5373 APCO
388 Grant Street SE
Atlanta, GA 30312-2227
404-688-9000
877-988-APCO
Fax: 404-577-3847
http://www.apcosigns.com
Classroom supplies including announcement and chalkboards.

Anne M Gallup

5374 AbleNet
2625 Patton Road
Roseville, MN 55113-1308
651-294-2200
800-322-0956
Fax: 651-294-2259
E-mail: customerservice@ablenetinc.com
http://www.ablenetinc.com

Adaptive devices for students with disabilities from Pre-K through adult, as well as activities and games for students of all abilities.

Bill Sproull, Board Chairman
Jennifer Thalhuber, President/CEO

5375 Accounter Systems USA
1107 S Mannheim Road
Suite 305
Westchester, IL 60154-2560
800-229-8765
Sports timers and clocks and classroom supplies.

5376 Accu-Cut Systems
1035 E Dodge Street
Fremont, NE 68025
402-721-4134
800-288-1670
Fax: 402-721-5778
E-mail: info@accucut.com
http://www.accucut.com
Manufacturer of die cutting machines dies.

5377 Airomat Corporation
2916 Engle Road
Fort Wayne, IN 46809-1198
260-747-7408
800-348-4905
Fax: 260-747-7409
E-mail: airomat@airomat.com
http://www.airomat.com
Mats and matting.

Jody Feasel, VP
Janie Feasel, President/CEO

5378 Airspace USA
89 Patton Avenue
Asheville, NC 28801
828-258-1319
800-872-1319
Fax: 828-258-1390
E-mail: sales@airspace-usa.com
http://www.airspacesolutions.com
Airspace Soft Center Play and Learn Systems provide a comprehensive range of play, learning and physical development opportunities using commercial grade and foam filled play equipment. Play manual provided.

Daniel Brenman, VP Sales/Marketing
Tracy Syxes, Administrator

5379 All Art Supplies
Art Supplies Wholesale
4 Enon Street
North Beverly, MA 01915
800-462-2420
Fax: 978-922-1495
E-mail: info@allartsupplies.com
http://www.allartsupplies.com
Art supplies at wholesale prices.

5380 American Foam
HC 37 Box 317 H
Lewisburg, WV 24901
304-497-3000
800-344-8997
Fax: 304-497-3001
http://www.bfoam.com
Carving blocks of foam.

5381 American Plastics Council
700 Second St., NE
Washington, DC 20002
202-249-7000
800-243-5790
Fax: 202-249-6100
http://www.plastics.org
Offers classroom materials on recycling and environmental education.

5382 Anatomical Chart Company
8221 Kimball Avenue
Skokie, IL 60076-2956
847-679-4700
http://www.anatomical.com
Maps and charts for educational purposes.

5383 Angels School Supply
600 E Colorado Boulevard
Pasadena, CA 91101-2006
626-584-0855
Fax: 626-584-0888
http://www.angelschoolsupply.com
School and classroom supplies.

Jennifer , Sales Representitive

5384 Aol@School
22070 Broderick Drive
Dulles, VA 20166
888-468-3768
E-mail: aol at school@aol.com
http://www.school.aol.com
Age-appropriate, high-quality educational content tailored for K-12 students and educators. Aol@School focuses and filters the Web for us, providing appropriate, developmental access to the vast educational resources on the internet.

5385 Armada Art Materials
Armada Art Inc.
142 Berkeley Street
Boston, MA 02116
617-859-3800
800-435-0601
Fax: 617-859-3808
E-mail: info@armadaart.com
http://www.armadaart.com

5386 Art Materials Catalog
United Art and Education
PO Box 9219
Fort Wayne, IN 46899-9219
260-478-1121
800-322-3247
Fax: 800-858-3247
http://www.unitednow.com
Art materials.

5387 Art Supplies Wholesale
4 Enon Street
North Beverly, MA 01915
800-462-2420
Fax: 978-922-1495
E-mail: info@allartsupplies.com
http://www.allartsupplies.com
Wholesale art supplies.

5388 Art to Remember
5535 Macy Drive
Indianapolis, IN 46235
317-826-0870
800-895-8777
Fax: 317-823-2822
E-mail: info@arttoremember.com
http://www.arttoremember.com
A unique program that encourages your students' artisic creativity while providing an opportunity to raise funds for schools.

Patty Arbuckle, Program Coordinator
Kathy Robinson, Program Coordinator

5389 Artix
PO Box 25008
Kelowna, BC V1W3Y
250-861-5345
800-665-5345
http://www.artix.bc.ca
Papermaking kits.

5390 Assessories by Velma
PO Box 2580
Shasta, CA 96087-2580
Multicultural education-related products.

5391 At-Risk Resources
135 Dupont Street
PO Box 760
Plainview, NY 11803-0706
800-999-6884
Fax: 800-262-1886
Dealing with drug violence prevention, character education, self-esteem, teen sexuality, dropout prevention, safe schoolks, career development, parenting crisis and trauma, and professional development.

5392 Atlas Track & Tennis
19495 SW Teton Avenue
Tualatin, OR 97062-8846
800-423-5875
Fax: 503-692-0491
Specialty sport surfaces; synthetic running tracks, tennis courts, and athletic flooring for schools.

5393 Audio Forum
69 Broad Street
Guildford, CT 06437
203-453-9794
Fax: 203-453-9774
E-mail: info@audioforum.com
http://www.audioforum.com
Cassettes, CD's and books for language study.

5394 Badge-A-Minit
345 N. Lewis Ave.
Oglesby, IL 61348
815-883-8822
800-223-4103
Fax: 815-883-9696
E-mail: questions@badgeaminit.com
http://www.badgeaminit.com
Awards, trophies, emblems and badges for educational purposes.

5395 Bag Lady School Supplies
9212 Marina Pacifica Drive N
Long Beach, CA 90803-3886
Classroom supplies.

5396 Bale Company
PO Box 6400
Providence, RI 02940-6400
800-822-5350
Fax: 401-831-5500
http://www.bale.com
Awards, medals, pins, plaques and trophies.

5397 Bangor Cork Company
William & D Streets
Pen Argyl, PA 18072
610-863-9041
Fax: 610-863-6275
http://www.bangorcork.com
Announcement boards.

Janice Cory, Customer Services Rep

5398 Baumgarten's
144 Ottley Drive NE
Atlanta, GA 30324-4016
404-874-7675
800-247-5547
Fax: 800-255-5547
E-mail: mlynch@baumgartens.com
http://www.baumgartens.com
Products available include pencil sharpeners, pencil grips, pocket binders, disposable aprons, American flags, practical colorful clips, fastening devices in a variety of shapes and sizes, identification security items, lamination, magnifiers and key chains.

David Baumgarten, Vice President
Michael Lynch, National Sales Manager

5399 Best Manufacturing Sign Systems
1202 N. Park Avenue
PO Box 577
Montrose, CO 81401-3171
970-249-2378
800-235-2378
Fax: 970-249-0223
E-mail: sales@bestsigns.com
http://www.bestsigns.com
Architectural and ADA signs, announcement boards.

Mary Phillips, Sales Manager

5400 Best-Rite
2885 Lorraine Avenue
Temple, TX 76501
254-778-4727
800-749-2258
Fax: 800-697-6258
E-mail: boards@bestrite.com
http://www.bestrite.com
Quality visual display products which include a complete line of chalk, marker, tack, bulletin, fabric and projection boards. Display and trophy cases, beginner boards, reversible boards, mobile easels, desk-top and floor carrels and early childhood products are also manufactured.

Bob Wilson, VP
Greg Moore, Executive VP

5401 Binney & Smith
1100 Church Lane
Easton, PA 18044-431
610-253-6271
800-CRA-YOLA
Fax: 610-250-5768
http://www.crayola.com
Crayons.

Mike Perry, President, CEO
Smith Holland, CFO, EVP

5402 Black History Month
Guidance Channel
135 Dupont Street
PO Box 760
Plainview, NY 44803-0706
800-999-6884
Fax: 800-262-1886
Products to celebrate Black history, multicultutral resources.

5403 Blackboard Resurfacing Company
50 N 7th Street
Bangor, PA 18013-1731
610-588-0965
Fax: 610-863-1997
Chalk and announcement boards.

Karin Karpinski, Administrative Assistant

5404 Bob's Big Pencils
1848 E 27th Street
Hays, KS 67601-2108
Large novelty pencils, plaques, bookends and many pencil related items.

5405 Book It!/Pizza Hut
9111 E Douglas Avenue
Wichita, KS 67207-1205
316-687-8401
National reading incentive program with materials, books and incentive display items to get students interested in reading.

5406 Borden
Home & Professional Products Group
180 E Broad Street
Columbus, OH 43215-3799
614-225-7479
Fax: 614-225-7167
Arts and crafts supplies, maintenance and repair supplies.

5407 Bulman Products
1650 Mc Reynolds Ave NW
Grand Rapids, MI 49504
616-363-4416
Fax: 616-363-0380
E-mail: bulman@macatawa.com
http://bulmanproducts.com
Art craft paper.

5408 Bydee Art
8603 Yellow Oak Street
Austin, TX 78729-3739
512-474-4343
Fax: 512-474-5749
Prints, books, T-shirts with the Bydee People focusing on education.

5409 C-Thru Ruler Company
6 Britton Drive
Bloomfield, CT 06002-3632
860-243-0303
Fax: 860-243-1856
http://www.CThruRuler.com
Arts, crafts and classroom supplies.

Ross Zachs, Manager

5410 CHEM/Lawrence Hall of Science
University of California
1 Centennial Drive #5200
Berkeley, CA 94720-5200
510-642-6000
Fax: 510-642-1055
E-mail: lhsinfo@uclink.berkley.edu
http://www.lawrencehallofscience.org
Activities for grades 5-6 and helps students understand the use of chemicals in our daily lives.

Elizabeth K. Stage, Director
Rena Dorph, Research

5411 CORD Communications
324 Kelly Street
Waco, TX 76710-5709
254-776-1822
Fax: 254-776-3906
Instructional materials for secondary and postsecondary applications in science education.

5412 Califone International
1145 Arroyo Avenue, # A
San Fernando, CA 91340
818-407-2400
800-722-0500
Fax: 877-402-2248
http://www.califone.com
Multisensory, supplemental curricula on magnetic cards for use with all Card Reader/Language master equipment.

Nelly Spievak, Sales Coordinator

5413 Cardinal Industries
PO Box 1430
Grundy, VA 24614-1430
276-935-4545
800-336-0551
Fax: 276-935-4970
Awards, emblems, trophies and badges.

5414 Carousel Productions
1100 Wilcrest Drive
Suite 100
Houston, TX 77042-1642
281-568-9300
Fax: 281-568-9498
Moments in History T-shirts, as well as other various educational gifts and products.

5415 Cascade School Supplies
1 Brown Street
PO Box 780
North Adams, MA 01247
800-628-5078
Fax: 866-298-6578
E-mail: president@cascadeschoolsupplies.com
http://cascadeschoolsupplies.com
Offers a variety of school supplies and more.

Peter L. Cote, President

5416 Celebrate Diversity
Guidance Channel
135 Dupont Street
PO Box 760
Plainview, NY 44803-0706
800-999-6884
Fax: 800-262-1886
Educational resources that celebrate diversity.

5417 Celebrate Earth Day
Guidance Channel
135 Dupont Street
PO Box 760
Plainview, NY 44803-0706
800-999-6884
Fax: 800-262-1886
Educational resources for celebrating earth day.

5418 Center Enterprises
PO Box 33161
West Hartford, CT 06110
860-953-4423
Fax: 800-373-2923
Clifford individual curriculum and storybook stamp sets, individual, grading, curriculum based and Sweet Arts rubber stamp line, stamp pads, embossing inks and powders.

5419 Center for Learning
10200 Jefferson Blvd.
Box 802
Culver City, CA 90232
440-331-1404
800-421-4246
Fax: 800-944-5432
E-mail: customerservice@centerforlearning.org
http://www.centerforlearning.org
Supplementary curriculum units for all grade levels in biography, language arts, novel/drama and social studies.

5420 Center for Teaching International Relations
University of Denver
2199 S. University Blvd.
Denver, CO 80208
303-871-3106
http://www.du.edu
Reproducible teaching activities and software promoting multicultural understanding and international relations in the classroom for grades K-adult.

Rebecca Chopp, Chancellor
Gregg Kvistad, Executive Vice Chancellor

5421 Childcraft Education Corporation
20 Kilmer Avenue
Edison, NJ 08817
732-572-6100
Distributes children's toys, products, materials and publications to schools.

5422 Childswork/Childsplay
The Guidence Channel
135 Dupont Street
PO Box 760
Plainview, NY 11803-0760
800-962-1141
Fax: 800-262-1886
http://www.childswork.com
Contains over 450 resources to address the social and emotional needs of children and adolescents.

Lawrence C Shapiro, PhD, President
Constance H Logan, Development Coordinator

423 Chroma
205 Bucky Drive
Lititz, PA 17543
717-626-8866
800-257-8278
Fax: 717-626-9292
E-mail: infousa@chromaonline.com
http://www.chromaonline.com
Tempera and acrylic paints.

424 Chroma-Vision Sign & Art System
PO Box 434
Greensboro, NC 27402-0434
336-275-0602
Refillable and renewable felt tip markers
used with non-toxic, water soluable, fast dry-
ing colors for making signs, posters, and general art work with no messy cleanup.

S Gray, President

**425 Citizenship Through Sports and Fine
Arts Curriculum**
National Federation of State High School
Assoc.
PO Box 690
Indianapolis, IN 46206
317-972-6900
800-776-3462
Fax: 317-822-5700
http://www.nfhs.org
High school activities curriculum package
that includes an introductory video, Rekin-
dling the Spirit, along with the Overview
booklet, plus two insightful books covering
eight targets of the curriculum.

Tom Mezzanotte, President
Tom Welter, Presideny- Elect

426 Claridge Products & Equipment
Claridge Products & Equipment
601 Highway 62-65 S
PO Box 910
Harrison, AR 72602-0910
870-743-2200
Fax: 870-743-1908
E-mail: claridge@claridgeproducts.com
http://www.claridgeproducts.com
Claridge manufactures chalkboards,
markerboards, bulletin boards, display and
trophy cases, bulletin and directory board
cabinets, easels, lecterns, speakers' stands,
wood lecture units with matching credenzas
and much more.

Terry McCutchen, Sales Manager

427 Collins & Aikman Floorcoverings
311 Smith Industrial Boulevard
Dalton, GA 30722
800-248-2878
Fax: 706-259-2666
E-mail: tellis@powerbond.com
http://www.powerbond.com
An alternative to conventional carpet to improve indoor air quality and reduce maintenance cost. Powerboard floor covering.

T Ellis, General Manager/Edu Markets

428 Columbia Cascade Company
1300 S.W. Sixth Avenue
Suite 310
Portland, OR 97201-3464
503-223-1157
800-547-1940
Fax: 503-223-4530
E-mail: hq@timberform.com
http://www.timberform.com
Playground equipment and site furniture.

Dale Gordon, Sales Manager

429 Creative Artworks Factory
19031 McGuire Road
Perris, CA 92570-8305
909-780-5950
Screenprinted T-shirts, posters and gifts for
educational purposes.

5430 Creative Educational Surplus
9801 James Avenue S
#C
Bloomington, MN 55431-2919
Art and classroom materials.

**5431 Crizmac Art & Cultural Education
Materials Inc**
1642 No. Alvernon Way
PO Box 65928
Tucson, AZ 85728-5928
520-323-8555
800-913-8555
Fax: 520-323-6194
E-mail: customerservice@crizmac.com
http://www.crizmac.com
Publisher of art and cultural education materials includes curriculum, books, music,and
folk art.

Stevie Mack, President

5432 Crown Mats & Matting
2100 Commerce Drive
Fremont, OH 43420-1048
419-332-5531
800-628-5463
Fax: 800-544-2806
E-mail: sales@crown-mats.com
http://www.crown-mats.com
Mats, matting and flooring for schools.

Vincent J. DePhillipsÿ, President

5433 Dahle USA
49 Vose Farm Road
Peterborough, NH 03458
603-924-0003
800-995-1379
Fax: 603-924-1616
E-mail: info@dahleusa.com
http://www.dahleusa.com
Arts and crafts supplies, school and office
products, office shreddars and more.

5434 Designer Artwear I
8475 C-1 Highway 6 N
Houston, TX 77095
281-446-6641
Specialty clothing, accessories, etc. all educationally designed.

5435 Dexter Educational Toys
Dexter Educational Toys, Inc.
PO Box 630861
Aventura, FL 33163-0861
305-931-7425
800-291-4515
Fax: 305-931-0552
E-mail: dexterplay@bellsouth.net
http://www.dexterplay.com
Manufacturer and distributor of education
material. Dress-ups for children 2-7 years.
Multicultural hand puppets, finger puppets,
head masks puppet theaters, rag dolls,
dress-ups for teddy bears and dolls, cloth
books, export manufacturing under special
designs and orders.

Genny Silverstein, VP Secretary

5436 Dick Blick Art Materials
PO Box 1267
Galesburg, IL 61402-1267
309-343-6181
800-723-2787
Fax: 800-621-8293
E-mail: info@dickblick.com
http://www.dickblick.com
Classroom art supplies.

5437 Dinorock Productions
407 Granville Drive
Silver Spring, MD 20901-3238
301-588-9300
http://www.dinorock.com
Musical, Broadway puppet shows for early
childhood fun and education.

5438 Discovery Toys
12443 Pine Creek Road
Cerritos, CA 90703-2044
562-809-0331
800-341-8697
Fax: 562-809-0331
E-mail: contact@discoverytoys.net
http://www.discoverytoyslink.com/elizabet
h
Emphasizes child physical, social and educational development through creative play.
Educational toys, games and books are available for all ages. Services include home demonstrations, fund raisers, phone and catalog
orders. New Book of Knowledge Encyclopedia and patenting video tapes are also
available.

Jerry Salerno, CEO
Jim Myers, COO

5439 Disney Educational Productions
500 S Buena Vista Street
Burbank, CA 91521-0001
800-777-8100
Creates and manufactures classroom aids for
the educational field.

5440 Dixie Art Supplies
5440 Mounes St.
Suite 108
New Orleans, LA 70123-3290
504-733-6509
800-783-2612
Fax: 504-733-0668
E-mail: artdixie@aol.com
http://www.dixieart.com
Fine art supplier.

5441 Dr. Playwell's Game Catalog
Guidance Channel
135 Dupont Street
PO Box 760
Plainview, NY 44803-0706
800-999-6884
Fax: 800-262-1886
Games that develop character and life skills.

5442 Draper
411 South Pearl Street
Spiceland, IN 47385
765-987-7999
800-238-7999
Fax: 765-987-7142
E-mail: draper@draper.com
http://www.draperinc.com
Projection screens, video projector mounts
and lifts, plasma display mounts, presentation easels, window shades and gymnasium
equipment.

Chris Broome, Contract Market Manager
Bob Mathes, AV/Video Market Manager

5443 Draw Books
Peel Productions
PO Box 546
Columbus, NC 28722-0546
828-859-3879
800-345-6665
Fax: 801-365-9898
http://www.drawbooks.com
How-to-draw books for elementary and mid-
dle school.

Paperback
ISBN: 0-939217

School Supplies / Classroom Materials

5444 Dupont Company
Corlan Products
CRP-702
Wilmington, DE 19880
302-774-1000
800-436-7426
Fax: 800-417-1266
http://http://www.dupont.com/
Arts and crafts supplies.

5445 Durable Corporation
75 N Pleasant Street
Norwalk, OH 44857-1218
419-668-8138
800-419-8622
Fax: 800-537-6287
http://www.durablecorp.com
Furniture, classroom supplies, arts and crafts and educational products.

5446 EZ Grader
PO Box 23698
Chagrin Falls, OH 44023
800-732-4018
Fax: 800-689-2772
E-mail: ezgrader@voyager.net
http://www.ezgrader.com
Electronic gradebook designed by teachers for teachers. It is an incredible time saver and computes percentage scores accurately, quickly and easily.

5447 Early Ed
3110 Sunrise Drive
Crown Point, IN 46307-8905
Teacher sweatshirts, cardigans, T-shirts, tote bags and jewelry.

5448 Education Department
Wildlife Conservation Society
2300 Southern Boulevard
Bronx, NY 10460
718-220-5100
800-937-5131
Fax: 718-733-4460
E-mail: membership@wcs.org
http://www.wcs.org
Year round programs for school and general audience. Teacher training, grades K-12.

Sydell Schein, Manager/Program Services
Ann Robinson, Director/National Programs

5449 Educational Equipment Corporation of Ohio
845 Overholt Road
Kent, OH 44240-7529
330-673-4881
Fax: 330-673-4915
E-mail: mkaufman@mkco.com
http://www.mkco.com
Chalkboards, tackboards, trophy cases, announcement boards.

Michael Kaufman, General Manager
Eric Baughman, Sales Manager

5450 Electronic Book Catalog
Franklin Learning Resources
1 Franklin Plaza
Burlington, NJ 08016-4908
800-BOO-MAN
Fax: 609-387-1787
Electronic translation machines, calculators and supplies.

5451 Ellison Educational Equipment
25862 Commercentre Drive
Lake Forest, CA 92630-8804
800-253-2238
Fax: 800-253-2240
E-mail:

europecustomerservices@ellison.com
http://www.ellison.com
Serves the educational and craft community with time-saving equipment, supplies and ideas.

5452 Endura Rubber Flooring
2 University Office Park
Waltham, MA 02453-3421
781-647-5375
Fax: 781-647-4543
Floorcoverings, mats and matting for schools.

5453 Fairgate Rule Company
3718 New York 9G
Sawkill Industrial Park
Rhinebeck, NY 12572
845-876-3063
Fax: 845-265-4128
E-mail: sales@fairgate.com
http://www.fairgate.com
Arts and crafts supplies.

5454 Family Reading Night Kit
Renaissance Learning
2911 Peach Street
PO Box 8036
Wisconsin Rapids, WI 54495-8036
715-424-3636
800-338-4204
Fax: 715-424-4242
E-mail: answers@renaissance.com
http://www.renlearn.com
Kit to start a family reading night where parents and children spent quality time together sharing enthusiasm over books.

Mary T. Minch, EVP, Finance, CFO
Samir Joglekar, EVP, Sales

5455 Fascinating Folds
PO Box 10070
Glendale, AZ 85318
602-375-9979
Fax: 602-375-9978
http://www.fascinating-folds.com
World's large supplier of origami and paper arts products.

5456 Fiskars Corporation
2537 Daniels St.
Madison, WI 53718
608-233-1649
866-348-5661
Fax: 608-294-4790
http://www.fiskars.com
School scissors.

5457 Fox Laminating Company
84 Custer Street
W Hartford, CT 06110-1955
860-953-4884
800-433-2468
Fax: 860-953-1277
E-mail: sales@foxlaminating.com
http://www.foxlam.com
Easy, simple, and inexpensive do-it-yourself laminators. A piece of paper can be laminated for just pennies. Badges, ID's and luggage tags can also be made. Also laminated plaques for awards, diplomas, and mission statements.

Joe Fox, President
John Mills, Marketing Manager

5458 George F Cram Company
PO Box 426
Indianapolis, IN 46206-0426
317-635-5564
Fax: 317-687-2845
Classroom geography maps, state maps, social studies skills and globes.

5459 Gift-in-Kind Clearinghouse
PO Box 850
Davidson, NC 28036-0850
704-892-7228
Fax: 704-892-3825
Educational and classroom supplies, computers and gifts for teachers.

5460 Gold's Artworks
2100 N Pine St.
Lumberton, NC 28358
910-739-9605
800-356-2306
Fax: 910-739-9605
http://www.goldsartworks.20m.com
Papermaking supplies.

5461 Golden Artist Colors
188 Bell Road
New Berlin, NY 13411-9527
607-847-6154
800-959-6543
Fax: 607-847-6767
E-mail: goldenart@goldenpaints.com
http://www.goldenpaints.com
Acrylic paints.

Barbara Schindler, President/ COO
Mark Golden, CEO

5462 Graphix
5800 Pennsylvania Ave.
Maple Heights, OH 44137
216-581-9050
800-447-2349
Fax: 216-581-9041
E-mail: info@grafixarts.com
http://www.grafixarts.com
Art and crafts supplies and a source for creative plastic films.

Tanya Lutz, National Sales Manager

5463 Grolier Multimedial Encyclopedia
Grolier Publishing
PO Box 1716
Danbury, CT 06816
203-797-3703
800-371-3908
Fax: 203-797-3899
Encyclopedia software.

5464 Hands-On Equations
Borenson & Associates
PO Box 3328
Allentown, PA 18106
610-398-6908
800-993-6284
Fax: 610-398-7863
E-mail: info@borenson.com
http://www.borenson.com
System to teach algebraic concepts to elementary and middle school students.

5465 Harrisville Designs
Center Village
PO Box 806
Harrisville, NH 03450
603-827-3333
800-338-9415
Fax: 603-827-3335
http://www.harrisville.com
Award-winning weaving products for children.

5466 Hayes School Publishing
7624 Reinhold Driveÿ
Cincinnati, OH 45237
513-527-4521
800-926-0704
Fax: 513-527-4526
E-mail: info@flipsideproducts.com
http://www.hayespub.com
Suppliers of certificates and awards.

336

467 Henry S Wolkins Company
605 Myles Standish Boulevard
Taunton, MA 02780
800-233-1844
Fax: 877-965-5467
http://www.wolkins.com
Art and craft materials, teaching aids, early
learning products, furniture, general school
equipment.

**468 Hooked on Phonics Classroom
Edition**
665 3rd Street
Suite 225
San Francisco, CA 94107
714-437-3450
800-222-3334
E-mail: customerservice@hop.com
http://www.hop.com
Program that teaches students to learn letters
and sounds to decoding words, and then reading books.

469 Hydrus Galleries
PO Box 4944
San Diego, CA 92164-4944
800-493-7299
Fax: 619-283-7466
E-mail: info@hydra9.com
http://www.hydra9.com
Curriculum-based classroom activities in-
cluding papyrus outlines for students to
paint.

470 Insect Lore
PO Box 1535
Shafter, CA 93263
800-548-3284
Fax: 661-746-0334
E-mail: livebug@insectlore.com
http://www.insectlore.com
Science materials for elementary and
preschool students.

471 J&A Handy-Crafts
165 S Pennsylvania Avenue
Lindenhurst, NY 11757-5058
631-226-2400
888-252-1130
Fax: 631-226-2564
E-mail: info@jacrafts.com
http://www.jacrafts.com
Arts, crafts and educational supplies.

Paul Siegelman, Marketing

472 Jiffy Printers Products
35070 Maria Road
Cathedral City, CA 92234
760-321-7335
Fax: 760-770-1955
E-mail: jiffyprod@aol.com
Adhesive wax sticks.

Ivan Zwelling, Owner

473 Key-Bak
Division of West Coast Chain
Manufacturing Co.
4245 Pacific Privado
Ontario, CA 91761
909-923-7800
800-685-2403
Fax: 909-923-0024
E-mail: sales@keybak.com
http://www.keybak.com
Badges, awards and emblems for educational
purposes.

474 Keyboard Instructor
Advanced Keyboard Technology, Inc.
PO Box 2418
Paso Robles, CA 93447-2418
805-237-2055
Fax: 805-239-8973
http://www.keyboardinstructor.com

Mobile keyboarding lab with individualized
instruction.

5475 Kids Percussion Buyer's Guide
Percussion Marketing Council
PO Box 33252
Cleveland, OH 44133
440-582-7006
Fax: 440-230-1346
E-mail: DLevine360@aol.com
http://www.playdrums.com
This guide is divided into two sections- recre-
ational instruments and those for beginning
traditional drummers.

**5476 Kids at Heart & School Art
Materials**
PO Box 94082
Seattle, WA 98124-9482
Classroom and art materials.

5477 Kidstamps
PO Box 18699
Cleveland Heights, OH 44118-0699
216-291-6884
Fax: 216-291-6887
E-mail: kidstamps@apk.net
http://www.kidstamps.com
Rubber stamps, T-shirts, bookplates and
mugs designed by leading children's illustra-
tors.

5478 Knex Education Catalog
Knex Education
2990 Bergey Road
PO Box 700
Hatfield, PA 19440-0700
800-KID-KNEX
E-mail: email@knex.com
http://www.knexeducation.com
Hands-on, award-winning curriculum supported K-12 math, science and technology
sets.

Joel Glickman, Chairman
Bob Glickman, Vice Chairman

5479 Lauri
PO Box 0263
Smethport, PA 16749
800-451-0520
Fax: 207-639-3555
Lacing puppets craft kits, crepe rubber picture puzzles, phonics kits and math
manipulatives for pre- K and up. Catalog offers 200 manipulatives for early childhood.

5480 Learning Materials Workshop
58 Henry Street
Burlington, VT 05401-3621
802-802-8399
800-693-7164
Fax: 802-862-0794
E-mail: info@learningmaterialswork.com
http://www.learningmaterialswork.com
Designs and produces open-ended blocks and
construction sets for early childhood classrooms. An education guide and video, as well
as training workshops are offered.

Karen Hewitt, President/ Founder

5481 Learning Needs Catalog
Riverdeep Interactive Learning
PO Box 97021
Redmond, WA 98073-9721
800-362-2890
http://www.learningneeds.com
Hardware, software and print products de-
signed for specialized student needs for
Pre-K to grade 12.

**5482 Learning Power and the Learning
Power Workbook**
Great Source Education Group
181 Ballardvale
Willmington, MA 01887
800-289-4490
Student materials for 8th and 9th grade critical thinking, study skills, life management,
and other student success course.

218 pages
ISBN: 0-963813-33-1

5483 Learning Well
111 Kane Street
Baltimore, MD 21224-1728
800-645-6564
Fax: 800-413-7442
E-mail: learningwell@wclm.com
Drawing compass/ruler.

5484 Linray Enterprises
167 Corporation Road
Hyannis, MA 02601-2204
800-537-9752
Mats and matting for gym classes.

5485 Loew-Coenell
300 Gap Way
Erlanger, KY 41018-3160
866-227-9206
Fax: 201-836-7070
E-mail: sales@loew-cornell.com
http://www.loew-cornell.com
Leader in art and craft brushes, painting accessories and artists' tools.

5486 Longstreth
28 Wells Road
Spring City, PA 19475-0475
610-495-7022
800-545-1329
Fax: 610-495-7023
http://www.longstreth.com
Awards, emblems, badges and trophies,
sports timers and clocks.

5487 Love to Teach
693 Glacier Pass
Westerville, OH 43081-1295
614-899-2115
800-326-8361
Fax: 614-899-2070
http://www.lovetoteach.com
Gifts for teachers.

Linda Vollmer, Contact

5488 Lyra
78 Browne Street
Suite 3
Brookline, MA 02146
888-PEN-LYRA
E-mail: mshoham@aol.com
Drawing supplies.

5489 MPI School & Instructional Supplies
PO Box 24155
Lansing, MI 48909-4155
517-393-0440
Fax: 517-393-8884
School and classroom supplies, arts and
crafts.

5490 Magnetic Aids
201 Ann Street
P.O. Box 2502
Newburgh, NY 12550
845-863-1400
800-426-9624
Fax: 845-863-1490
E-mail: info@magneticaids.com
http://www.magneticaids.com

Announcement and chalkboards, office supplies and equipment. Magnetic book supports.

Paul Pecka, VP Sales

5491 Mailer's Software
970 Calle Negocio
San Clemente, CA 92673-6201
949-492-7000
Fax: 949-589-5211
Charts, maps, globes and software for the classroom.

5492 Marsh Industries
Div. of Marsh Lumber Company
2301 E. High Avenue
PO Box 1000
New Philadelphia, OH 44663-5100
330-308-8667
800-426-4244
Fax: 330-308-5325
E-mail: vpsales@marsh-ind.com
http://www.marsh-ind.com
Marker boards chalkboards, and tacknoards for new rennovative construction projects. Glass enclosed bulletin and directory boards. Map rail and accessories.

William Singhaus, Sales Manager

5493 Master Woodcraft
1312 College Street
Oxford, NC 27565
919-693-8811
800-333-2675
Fax: 919-693-1707
Announcement and classroom chalkboards, arts and craft supplies. Cork bulletin boards, dry erase melamine boards, easels, floor and table top.

J Moss, VP

5494 Material Science Technology
Energy Concepts
595 Bond Street
Lincolnshire, IL 60069
800-621-1247
http://www.energy-concepts-inc.com
Provides practical knowledge of the use and development of materials in todays world. Each unit combines theory with hands-on experience.

5495 Math Through the Ages: A Gentle History for Teachers and Others
Oxton Publishers, LLC
124 Main St., Suite 203
PO Box 209
Farmington, ME 04938
207-779-1923
800-539-7323
Fax: 207-779-0623
E-mail: info@oxtonhouse.com
http://www.oxtonhouse.com
An easy-to-use tool for teachers who want some history for their math classes, this book contains 25 independent 4-to-6 page historical summaries of particular topics from elementary and secondary math, a 56-page overview and an extensive bibliography.

224 pages

William Berlinghoff, Managing Editor
Bobby Brown, Marketing Director

5496 Midwest Publishers Supply
4640 N Olcott Avenue
Harwood Heights, IL 60706
800-621-1507
Fax: 800-832-3189
E-mail: info@mps-co.com
http://www.mps-co.com

Arts and crafts supplies.
Bonnie Cready, Sales Manager

5497 Miller Multiplex
1555 Larkin Williams Road
Fenton, MO 63026-3008
636-343-5700
800-325-3350
Fax: 636-326-1716
E-mail: info@millermultiplex.com
Announcement boards, classroom displays, charts and photography, books towers, posters, frames, kiosk displays, presentation displays.

12 pages Annually

Kathy Webster, Director Marketing

5498 Monsanto Company
800 N Lindbergh Boulevard
Saint Louis, MO 63167-0001
314-694-1000
Fax: 314-694-7625
http://www.monsanto.com
Arts and crafts supplies.

Hugh Grant, Chairman/ CEO
Brett D. Begemann, President/ COO

5499 Morrison School Supplies
400 Industrial Road
San Carlos, CA 94070-6285
650-592-3000
800-950-4567
Fax: 650-592-1679
http://www.morrisonschoolsupplies.com
School supplies, classroom equipment, furniture and toys.

5500 Names Unlimited
2300 Spikes Lane
Lansing, MI 48906-3996
Chalkboard and markerboard slates and tablets.

5501 Nasco Arts & Crafts Catalog
Nasco
901 Janesville Avenue
PO Box 901
Fort Atkinson, WI 53538-0901
920-563-2446
800-558-9595
Fax: 920-563-8296
E-mail: custserv@enasco.com
http://www.eNASCO.com
Complete line of arts and craft materials for the art educator and individual artist.

Norman Eckley, Founder
Kris Bakke, Arts & Crafts Director

5502 Nasco Early Learning & Afterschool Essential Catalogs
Nasco
901 Janesville Avenue
PO Box 901
Fort Atkinson, WI 53538-0901
920-563-2446
800-558-9595
Fax: 920-563-8296
E-mail: custserv@enasco.com
http://www.eNasco.com
Features low prices on classroom supplies, materials, furniture and equipment for early childhood and afterschool programs.

Norman Eckley, Founder
Scott J Beyer, Director, Sales & Marketing

5503 Nasco Math Catalog
Nasco
901 Janesville Avenue
PO Box 901
Fort Atkinson, WI 53538-0901

920-563-2446
800-558-9595
Fax: 920-563-8296
E-mail: custserv@enasco.com
http://www.eNasco.com
Features hands-on manipulatives and real-life problem-solving projects.

Norman Eckley, Founder

5504 National Teaching Aids
401 Hickory Street
PO Box 2121
Fort Collins, CO 80522
970-484-7445
800-289-9299
Fax: 970-484-1198
E-mail: custserv@amep.com
http://www.hubbardscientific.com
Learning math, alphabet, and geography skills is easy with our Clever Catch Balls. These colorful 24-inch inflatable vinyl balls provide an excellent way for children to practice math, alphabet and geography skills. Excellent learning tool in organized classroom activities, on the playground, or at home.

Michael Warring, President
Candace Coffman, National Sales Manger

5505 New Hermes
2200 Northmont Parkway
Duluth, GA 30096
770-623-0331
800-843-7637
Fax: 770-814-7203
E-mail: sales@us.gravotech.com
http://www.newhermes.com
Announcement boards, trophies, badges, emblems.

Gerard Guyard, Chairman

5506 Newbridge Discovery Station
33 Boston Post Road Westÿ
Suite 440
Marlborough, MA 1752
800-867-0307
Fax: 800-456-2419
http://www.newbridgeonline.com
Monthly quick tips and activities for teachers.

5507 Newbridge Jumbo Seasonal Patterns
PO Box 5267
Clifton, NJ 07015
Art projects, games, bulletin boards, flannel boards, story starters, learning center displays, costumes, masks and more for grades Pre K-3.

5508 NewsCurrents
Knowledge Unlimited
2320 Pleasant View Roadÿ
PO Box 52
Madison, WI 53701
608-836-6660
800-356-2303
Fax: 800-618-1570
E-mail: csis@newscurrents.com
http://www.newscurrents.com
Current issues discussion programs for grades 3 and up.

5509 Partners in Learning Programs
1065 Bay Boulevard
Suite H
Chula Vista, CA 91911-1626
619-407-4744
Fax: 619-407-4755
Manufacturers and produces books, manuals, materials, supplies and gifts, such as banners for classroom purposes.

5510 Pearson Education Technologies
827 W Grove Avenue
Mesa, AZ 85210

520-615-7600
800-222-4543
Fax: 520-615-7601
http://www.pearsonedtech.com
SuccessMaker is a multimedia K-Adult learning system which includes math, reading, language arts and science courseware.

5511 Pentel of America
2715 Columbia Street
Torrance, CA 90503
310-320-3831
800-421-1419
Fax: 310-533-0697
http://www.pentel.com
Office supplies and equipment.

5512 Pin Man
Together Inc.
802 E 6th Street
PO Box 52528
Tulsa, OK 74105-3264
918-587-2405
800-282-0085
Fax: 918-382-0906
http://www.thepinmanok.com
Manufacturer of custom designed lapel pins, totes for Chapter 1, reading, scholastic achievement, honor roll, parent involvement, staff awards and incentives with over 25,000 items available for imprint.

Bern Gentry, CEO

5513 PlayConcepts
2275 Huntington Drive
#305
San Marino, CA 91108-2640
800-261-2584
Fax: 626-795-1177
Creative, 3-D scenery that stimulates dramatic play. The scenes complement integrated curriculum. They are age and developmentally appropriate, non-biased, and effective for groups or individuals.

5514 Polyform Products Company
1901 Estes Avenue
Elk Grove Village, IL 60007
847-427-0020
Fax: 847-427-0020
E-mail: polyform@sculpey.com
http://www.sculpey.com
Manufacturer of sculpey modeling clay.

5515 Presidential Classroom
2201 Old Ivy Road
P.O. Box 400406
Charlottesville, VA 22904
434-924-7236
800-441-6533
Fax: 434-982-2739
E-mail: eriedel@presidentialclassroom.org
http://www.presidentialclassroom.org
Civic education programs in Washington, DC for high school juniors and seniors. Each one week program provides students with an inside view of the federal government in action and their role as responsible citizens and future leaders.

Jan-March, June+July
400 attendees

Jack Buechner, President/CEO
William Antholis, Director/ CEOÿ

5516 Professor Weissman's Software
Professor Weissman's Software
246 Crafton Avenue
Staten Island, NY 10314-4227
347-528-7837
Fax: 718-698-5219
E-mail: mathprof@math911.com
http://www.math911.com
Algebra comic books, learn by example algebra flash cards, step-by-step software tutori-

als for algebra, trigonometry, precalculus, statistics, network versions for all software.
Martin Weissman, Owner
Keith Morse, VP

5517 Pumpkin Masters
PO Box 61456
Denver, CO 80206-8456
303-860-8006
Fax: 303-860-9826
Classroom pumpkin carving kits featuring whole language curriculum with safer and easier carving tools and patterns.

5518 Puppets on the Pier
Pier 39
Box H4
San Francisco, CA 94133
415-379-9544
800-443-4463
Fax: 415-379-9544
E-mail: puppetshop@gmail.com
http://www.puppetdream.com
Puppets, arts, crafts and other creative educational products for children.

Arthur Partner

5519 Qwik-File Storage Systems
1000 Allview Drive
Crozet, VA 22932-3144
804-823-4351
Schedule boards and classroom supplies.

5520 RC Musson Rubber Company
1320 East Archwood Avenue
P.O. Box 7038ÿ
Akron, OH 44306-2825
330-773-7651
800-321-3281
Fax: 330-773-3254
E-mail: info@mussonrubber.com
http://www.mussonrubber.com
Rubber floorcoverings, mats and athletic matting.

Mark Reese, Customer Service Manager
Robert Segers, VP

5521 RCA Rubber Company
1833 East Market St.ÿ
P.O. Box 9240
Akron, OH 44305-0240
330-784-1291
800-321-2340
Fax: 330-794-6446
E-mail: commercialsales@rcarubber.com
http://www.rcarubber.com
Floorcoverings, athletic mats and more for the physical education class.

5522 Reading is Fundamental
600 Maryland Avenue SW
Suite 600
Washington, DC 20024-2520
202-673-1641
Fax: 202-673-1633
Distributor of posters, bookmarks, and parent guide brochures.

5523 Reconnecting Youth
National Educational Service
304 W Kirkwood Avenue
Suite 2
Bloomington, IN 47404-5132
812-336-7700
800-733-6786
Fax: 812-336-7790
E-mail: nes@nesonline.com
http://www.nesonline.com
Curriculum to help discouraged learners achieve in school, manage their anger, and decrease drug use, depression, and suicide risk. The program was piloted for five years with over 600 urban Northwestern public

high school students with funding from the National Institute on Drug Abuse and the National Institute of Mental Health, and has since been successful in many educational settings.

3 Ring Binder Circul
ISBN: 1-879639-42-4

Jane St. John, Sales Marketing Director

5524 Red Ribbon Resources
135 Dupont Street
PO Box 760
Plainview, NY 11803
800-646-7999
Fax: 800-262-1886
http://www.redribbonresources.com
Over 250 low cost giveaways to promote your safe and drug-free school and community.

5525 Renaissance Graphic Arts
69 Steamwhistle Drive
Ivyland, PA 18974
215-357-5705
888-833-3398
Fax: 215-357-5258
E-mail: pat@printmaking-materials.com
http://www.printmaking-materials.com
Tools, papers, plates, inks and assorted products necessary for printmaking.

5526 Rock Paint Distributing Corporation
365 Sunnyside Drive
PO Box 482
Milton, WI 53563
608-868-6873
800-236-6873
Fax: 800-715-7625
E-mail: handyart@handyart.com
http://www.handyart.com
Tempera paint, India ink, acrylic paint, block inc, washable paint, fabric paint.

Chuck Jackson, President

5527 S&S Worldwide
S&S Arts & Crafts
75 Mill Street
PO Box 513ÿ
Colchester, CT 06415-1263
860-537-3451
800-243-9232
Fax: 800-566-6678
E-mail: cservice@ssww.com
http://www.ssww.com
Arts and crafts, classroom games and group paks.

5528 Safe & Drug Free Catalog
Performance Resource Press
1270 Rankin Drive
Suite F
Troy, MI 48083-2843
800-453-7733
Fax: 800-499-5718
http://www.pronline.net
Books, videos, CD-Roms, phamlets and posters toassist students with social skills, counseling, drug and violence prevention.

5529 Sakura of America
30780 San Clemente Street
Hayward, CA 94544-7131
510-475-8880
800-776-6257
Fax: 510-475-0973
E-mail: express@sakuraofamerica.com
http://www.gellyroll.com
Gelly Roll pens, Cray pas oil pastels, Fantasia watercolors, Pigma micron pens, Pentouch and Aqua Wipe markers and other art supplies for the classroom.

John Crook
Donna Wilson, Marketing Director

5530 Sanford Corporation
A Lifetime of Color
2711 Washington Boulevard
Bellwood, IL 60104-1970
708-547-6650
800-323-0749
Fax: 708-547-6719
E-mail:
consumer.service@sanfordcorp.com
http://www.sanfordcorp.com
Writing instruments, art supplies.

Angela Nigl, Author
Sharon Meyers, PR Manager

5531 Sax Visual Art Resources
Sax Arts and Crafts
2725 S Moorland Road
bept. SA
New Berlin, WI 53151
800-558-6696
Fax: 800-328-4729
E-mail: catalog@saxfcs.com
http://www.saxfcs.com
Variety of resources for slides, books, videos, fine art posters and CD-Roms.

5532 School Mate
PO Box 2225
Jackson, TN 38302
731-935-2000
Fax: 800-668-7610
E-mail: school@schoolmateinc.com
Pre-school and elementary art products.

5533 SchoolMatters
Current
The Current Building
Colorado Springs, CO 80941-0001
800-525-7170
Fax: 800-993-3232
Offers a variety of creative classroom ideas including stickers, mugs, posters, signs and more for everyday and holidays and everyday of the year.

5534 Scott Sign Systems
7525 Pennsylvania Avenue
Suite 101
Sarasota, FL 34243
941-355-5171
800-237-9447
Fax: 941-351-1787
E-mail: info@scottsigns.com
http://www.scottsigns.com
Educational supplies including announcement, letters, signs, graphics and chalkboards.

Kathy Hannon, Regional Sales Manager
Lisa Pyrcz, Account Mgr, Southeast/West

5535 Scratch-Art Company
PO Box 303
Avon, MA 02322
508-583-8085
800-377-9003
Fax: 508-583-8091
E-mail: info@scratchart.com
http://www.scratchart.com
Offers materials for drawing, sketching and rubbings.

5536 Sea Bay Game Company
77 Cliffwood Avenue, Suite 1-D
Cliffwood, NJ 07721
732-583-7902
800-568-0188
Fax: 732-583-7284
http://www.seabaygame.com
Manufacturer and distributor of products, games and creative play to nursery schools and preschools.

5537 Seton Identification Products
20 Thompson Road
PO Box 819
Branford, CT 06405-819
855-544-7992
800-243-6624
Fax: 800-345-7819
E-mail: help@seton.com
http://www.seton.com
Manufacturer of all types of identification products including signs, tags, labels, traffic control, OSHA, ADA and much more.

5538 Shapes, Etc.
532 North Plymouth Avenue
Rochester, NY 14608
585-335-6619
800-888-6580
Fax: 585-335-6070
E-mail: info@shapesetc.com
http://www.shapesetc.com
Notepads and craft materials for creative writing projects. Coordinates with literature themes. Perfect for storystarters, bulletin boards, awards and motivators.

5539 Sign Product Catalog
Scott Sign Systems, Inc.
7525 Pennsylvania Avenue
Suite 101
Sarasota, FL 34243
941-355-5171
800-237-9447
Fax: 941-351-1787
E-mail: info@scottsigns.com
http://www.scottsigns.com
Educational supplies including announcement, letters, signs, graphics and chalkboards.

Kathy Hannon, Regional Sales Manager
Lisa Pyrcz, Account Mgr, Southeast/West

5540 Small Fry Originals
2700 S Westmoreland Road
Dallas, TX 75233-1312
214-330-8671
800-248-9443
Children's original artwork preserved in plastic plates and mugs.

5541 Southwest Plastic Binding Corporation
109 Millwell Court
Maryland Heights, MO 63043-2509
314-739-4400
800-325-3628
Fax: 800-942-2010
http://www.swbindinglaminating.com
Overhead transparencies, maps, charts and classroom supplies.

5542 Spectrum Corporation
10048 Easthaven Boulevard
Houston, TX 77075-3298
713-944-6200
800-392-5050
Fax: 713-944-1290
E-mail: sherrig@specorp.com
http://www.spectrumstuff.com
Announcement boards, scoreboards and sports equipment, sports timers and clocks.

5543 Speedball Art Products Company
2301 Speedball Road
PO Box 5157
Statesville, NC 28677
704-838-1475
800-898-7224
Fax: 704-838-1472
E-mail: tonyahill@speedballart.com
http://www.speedballart.com

Art products for stamping, calligraphy, printmaking, drawing and painting.

Walt Glazer, CEO
Tonya Hill, Director of Sales

5544 Sponge Stamp Magic
525 S Anaheim Hills Road
Apartment C314
Anaheim, CA 92807-4726
Rubber stamps and games for classroom use.

5545 Staedtler
5725 McLaughlin Road
Mississauga, On L5R 3
905-501-9008
800-776-5544
Fax: 905-501-9117
E-mail: info@staedtler.ca
http://www.staedtler-usa.com
Arts and crafts supplies, office supplies and equipment.

Dick Hoye, National Sales Manager

5546 Sylvan Learning Systems
1000 Lancaster Street
Baltimore, MD 21202
410-843-6828
888-779-5826
Fax: 410-783-3832
http://www.sylvanlearning.com
Provides public school academic programs that are traditional sylvan programs modified to fit the needs of individual school districts and performance guarantees.

Jody Madron, Contact

5547 Tandy Leather Company
PO Box 791
Fort Worth, TX 76101-0791
817-451-1480
Fax: 817-451-5254
Arts and crafts supplies, computer peripherals and systems.

5548 Teacher Appreciation
Guidance Channel
135 Dupont Street
PO Box 760
Plainview, NY 44803-0706
800-999-6884
Fax: 800-262-1886
Products for celebrating teacher appreciation week.

5549 Teachers Store
PO Box 24155
Lansing, MI 48909-4155
517-393-0440
Fax: 517-393-8884
School and classroom supplies, arts and crafts.

5550 Texas Instruments
12500 TI Boulevard
P.O. Box 660199
Dallas, TX 75243-4136
972-995-2011
800-336-5236
Fax: 972-995-4360
http://www.ti.com
Manufacturer of calculators.

Rich Templeton, Chairman/ President
Brian Crutcher, EVP, Business Operations

5551 Triarco Arts & Crafts
9900 13th Ave. N.
Suite 1015
Plymouth, MN 55441-5035
763-559-5590
800-328-3360
Fax: 736-559-2215
E-mail: info@triarcoarts.com
http://www.etriarco.com
Art supplies.

552 Vanguard Crafts
1081 E 48th Street
Brooklyn, NY 11234
718-377-5188
800-662-7238
Fax: 888-692-0056
Arts and crafts supplier.

553 Wagner Zip-Change
3100 W Hirsch Avenue
Melrose Park, IL 60160-1741
708-681-4100
800-323-0744
Fax: 800-243-4924
E-mail: sales@wagnerzip.com
http://www.wagnerzip.com
Non-lighted changeable letter message activity signs, changeable letters in all sizes and colors.

CJ Krasula, Marketing VP
Jim Leone, Sales Manager

554 Walker Display
6520 Grand Avenue
P.O. Box 16955
Duluth, MN 55807-2242
218-624-8990
800-234-7614
Fax: 888-695-4647
http://www.walkerdisplay.com
Arts, crafts, classroom supplies and displays.

555 Wellness Reproductions
Guidance Channel
135 Dupont Street
PO Box 760
Plainview, NY 44803-0706
800-999-6884
Fax: 800-262-1886
Mental and life skills educational materials.

556 Wikki Stix One-of-a-Kind Creatables
Omnicor
11034 N. 23rd Drive
#103
Phoenix, AZ 85029-4735
602-870-9937
800-869-4554
Fax: 602-870-9877
E-mail: info@wikkistix.com
http://www.wikkistix.com
Unique, one-of-a-kind twistable, stickable, creatable, hands-on teaching tools. Ideal for Pre-K through 8 for science, language arts, math, arts and crafts, positive behavior rewards, rainy day recess, classroom display, diagrams and 3-D work. Self-stick; no glue needed.

Kem Clark, President
Gloria Porter, General Manager

557 Wilson Language Training
47 Old Webster Road
Oxford, MA 1540
508-368-2399
800-899-8454
Fax: 508-368-2300
http://www.wilsonlanguage.com
Multisensory language program.

558 Wilton Art Appreciation Programs
Reading & O'Reilley
PO Box 646
Botsford, CT 06404
203-270-6336
800-458-4274
Fax: 203-270-5569
E-mail: ror@wiltonart.com
http://www.wiltonart.com
Materials for art appreciation including CD-ROMS, videos, fine art prints, slides, workbooks, teacher' guides, lessons, puzzles and games.

Diana O'Neill, President

5559 Young Explorers
P.O. Box 3338
Chelmsford, MO 1824-938
800-239-7577
Fax: 888-876-8847
http://www.youngexplorers.com
Educational material for children.

Electronic Equipment

5560 AIMS Multimedia
9710 De Soto Avenue
Chatsworth, CA 91311-4409
818-773-4300
800-367-2467
Fax: 818-341-6700
E-mail: info@aimsmultimedia.com
http://www.aimsmultimedia.com
Film, video, laserdisc producer and distributor, offering a free catalog available materials. Also provides internet video streaming.

David Sherman, President
Biff Sherman, President

5561 Advance Products Company
1101 E Central Avenue
Wichita, KS 67214-3922
316-263-4231
Fax: 316-263-4245
Manufacturer of steel mobile projection and television tables, video cabinets, easels, computer furniture, wall and ceiling TV mounts, and study tables and carrels.

Paul Keck

5562 All American Scoreboards
Everbrite
401 South Main Street
Pardeeville, WI 53954
608-429-2121
800-356-8146
Fax: 877-505-9405
E-mail: scoreboardsales@everbrite.com
http://www.allamericanscoreboards.com
Scoreboards.

Doug Winkelmann, Product Manager

5563 American Time & Signal Company
140 3rd Avenue S
Dassel, MN 55325
800-328-8996
Fax: 800-789-1882
E-mail: theclockexperts@atsclock.com
http://www.atsclock.com
Sports timers and clocks.

Jeff Baumgartner, CEO/ Owner

5564 Arts & Entertainment Network
235 E 45th Street
Floor 9
New York, NY 10017-3354
212-210-1400
Fax: 212-210-9755
http://www.aenetworks.com
Cable network offering free educational programming to schools.

5565 Barr Media/Films
12801 Schabarum Avenue
Irwindale, CA 91706-6808
626-338-7878
K-12 film, video and interactive Level I and III laserdisc programs.

5566 C-SPAN Classroom
4000 N Capitol Street NW
Washington, DC 20001
202-737-3220
800-523-7586

Fax: 202-737-6226
http://www.c-span.org
C-SPAN School Bus travels through more than 80 communities during each school year. This bus is a mobile television production studio and learning center designed to give hands-on experience with C-SPAN's programming.

John Evans, CEO/ Chairman
Thomas O. Might, President/ CEO

5567 CASIO
570 Mount Pleasant Avenue
Dover, NJ 07801-1631
973-361-5400
Fax: 570-868-6898
http://www.casio.com
Cameras, overhead projectors and electronics.

5568 CASPR
100 Park Center Plaza
Suite 550
San Jose, CA 95113-2204
800-852-2777
http://www.caspr.com
Leader in the field of library automation for schools. Integrated library automation-cross platforms: Macintosh, Windows, Apple IIe/IIGS. Multimedia source.

Norman Kline, President

5569 Cable in the Classroom
1800 N Beauregard Street
Suite 100
Alexandria, VA 22311-1710
703-845-1400
Fax: 703-845-1409
http://www.ciconline.org
Represents the cable tele-communications industry's commitment to improving teaching and learning for children in schools, at home and in their communities.

5570 Canon USA
1 Canon Plaza
Melville, NY 11747
631-330-5000
Fax: 516-328-5069
E-mail: pr@cusa.canon.com
http://www.usa.canon.com/cusa/home
School equipment and supplies including a full line of electronics, cameras, calculators and other technology.

5571 Caulastics
5955 Mission Street
Daly City, CA 94014-1397
415-585-9600
Overhead projectors, transparencies and electronics.

5572 Cheshire Corporation
Cheshire Corporation
PO Box 61109
Denver, CO 80206-8109
303-333-3003
Fax: 303-333-4037
E-mail: karen-hemmes@mindspring.com
Cheshire corporation is a publicist for book, video, CD-ROM and internet publishers in the school and library market.

Karen Hemmes, Publicist
Mary Kay Opicka, Publicist

5573 Chief Manufacturing
6436 City West Parkway
Eden Prairie, MN 55344
952-894-6280
800-582-6480
Fax: 877-894-6918
E-mail: orders@chiefmfg.com
http://www.chiefmfg.com

Manufacturer of Communications Support Systems for audio visual and video equipment. Chief's product includes a full-line of mounts, electric lifts, carts, and accessories for LCD/DLP projectors, plasma displays and TV/monitors.

Liz Sorensen, Marketing Assistant
Sharon McCubbin, Marketing Manager

5574 Chisholm
7019 Realm Drive
San Jose, CA 95119-1321
408-329-4305
800-888-4210
E-mail: info@chisholm.com
http://www.chisholm.com
Computer peripherals, overhead projectors and overhead transparencies.

5575 Daktronics
201 Daktronics Dr.ÿ
Brookings, SD 57006-5128
605-697-4300
800-325-8766
Fax: 605-697-4300
E-mail: sales@daktronics.com
http://www.daktronics.com
Scoreboards, electronic message displays statistics software.

Gary Gramm, HSPR Market Manager

5576 Depco- Millennium 3000
3305 Airport Drive
PO Box 178
Pittsburg, KS 66762
316-231-0019
800-767-1062
Fax: 316-231-0024
E-mail: sales@depcoinc.com
http://www.depcoinc.com
Program tracks and schedules for you, the test taker delivers tests electronically, as well as, automatic final exams. There are workstation security features to help keep students focused on their activities.

5577 Discovery Networks
7700 Wisconsin Avenue
Bethesda, MD 20814-3578
301-986-0444
http://www.discovery.com
Manages and operates The Discovery Channel, offering the finest in nonfiction documentary programming, as well as The Learning Channel, representing a world of ideas to learners of all ages.

5578 Echolab
175 Bedford Street
Burlington, MA 01803-2794
781-273-1512
Fax: 978-250-3335
Cameras, equipment, projectors and electronics.

5579 Eiki International
Audio Visual/Video Products
26794 Vista Terrace Drive
Lake Forest, CA 92630
949-457-0200
Fax: 949-457-7878
Video projectors, overhead projectors and transparencies.

5580 Elmo Manufacturing Corporation
1478 Old Country Road
Plainview, NY 11803-5034
516-501-1400
800-947-3566
Fax: 516-501-0429
http://www.elmousa.com
Overhead projectors and transparencies.

5581 Fair-Play Scoreboards
1700 Delaware Avenue
Des Moines, IA 50317-2999
800-247-0265
Fax: 515-265-3364
E-mail: sales@fair-play.com
http://www.fair-play.com
Scoreboards and sports equipment.

5582 Festo Corporation
395 Moreland Road
PO Box 18023
Hauppauge, NY 11788
631-435-0800
800-993-3786
Fax: 631-435-3847
E-mail: product.support@us.festo.com
http://www.festo-usa.com

5583 General Audio-Visual
333 West Merrick Road
Valley Stream, NY 11580-5219
516-825-8500
Fax: 516-568-2057
http://www.gavi.com
Offers a full line of audio-visual equipment and supplies, cameras, projectors and various other electronics for the classroom.

5584 Hamilton Electronics
2003 W Fulton Street
Chicago, IL 60612-2365
312-421-5442
Fax: 312-421-0818
http://www.hamiltonbuhl.com
Electronics, equipment and supplies.

5585 JR Holcomb Company
3205 Harvard Avenue
Cleveland, OH 44101
216-341-3000
800-362-9907
Fax: 216-341-5151
A full line of electronics including calculators, overhead projectors and overhead transparencies.

5586 JVC Professional Products Company
41 Slater Drive
Elmwood Park, NJ 07407-1311
201-794-3900
Electronics line including cameras, projectors, transparencies and other technology for the classroom.

5587 Labelon Corporation
10 Chapin Street
Canandaigua, NY 14424-1589
585-394-6220
800-428-5566
Fax: 585-394-3154
http://www.labelon.com
Electronics, supplies and equipment for schools.

5588 Learning Channel
7700 Wisconsin Avenue
Bethesda, MD 20814
800-346-0032
Offers educational programming for schools.

5589 Learning Station/Hug-a-Chug Records
3950 Bristol Court
Melbourne, FL 32904-8712
321-728-8773
800-789-9990
Fax: 321-722-9121
E-mail: thelearningstation@cfl.rr.com
http://www.learningstationmusic.com
Early childhood products including OMH, cassettes, CD's and videos. Also, the Learning Station performs children and

family concerts and are internationally acclaimed for their concert/keynote presentations for early childhood conferences and other educational organizations.

Don Monopoli, President
Laurie Monopoli, VP

5590 Learning Well
2200 Marcus Avenue
#3759
New Hyde Park, NY 11042-1042
800-645-6564
Fax: 800-638-6499
Instructional material including computer and board games, videos, cassettes, audio tapes, theme units, manipulatives for grades PreK-8.

Mona Russo, President

5591 Leightronix
1125 N Cedar Rd
Mason, MI 48854
517-694-5589
800-243-5589
Fax: 517-694-1600
E-mail: sales@leightronix.com
http://www.leightronix.com
Educational cable programming for schools and institutions.

5592 MCM Electronics
650 Congress Park Drive
Centerville, OH 45459
888-235-4692
800-543-4330
Fax: 800-765-6960
http://www.mcmelectronics.com
Offers a full line of electronics products and components for use in the classroom or at home. Over 40,000 parts.

5593 Magna Plan Corporation
71 Meadowbank Drive
Ottawa, On K2G0P
613-563-8727
800-361-1192
Fax: 518-298-2368
E-mail: info@visualplanning.com
http://www.visualplanning.com
Overhead projectors.

Joseph P Josephson, Managing Director
Joel Boloten, Manager Consultation Service

5594 Mitsubishi Professional Electronics
200 Cottontail Lane
Somerset, NJ 08873-1231
732-560-4500
Fax: 732-560-4535
http://www.mitsubishielectric.com
Video projectors and electronics.

5595 Multi-Video
PO Box 35444
Charlotte, NC 28235-5444
704-563-4279
800-289-0111
Fax: 704-568-0219
Cameras, projectors and equipment.

5596 Naden Scoreboards
505 Fair Avenue
PO Box 636
Webster City, IA 50595-0636
515-832-4290
800-467-4290
Fax: 515-832-4293
E-mail: naden@ncn.net
http://www.naden.com
Electronic scoreboards for sports.

Russ Naden, President

5597 Navitar
200 Commerce Drive
Rochester, NY 14623

585-359-4000
800-828-6778
Fax: 585-359-4999
E-mail: info@navitar.com
http://www.navitar.com
Overhead projectors and transparencies.

Julian Goldstein, Co-President
Jeremy Goldstein, Co-President

598 Neumade Products Corporation
30 Pecks Lane
Newtown, CT 06470-2361
203-270-1100
Fax: 203-270-7778
E-mail: neumadeGJ@aol.com
http://www.neumade.com
Overhead projectors, overhead transparencies, video projectors and electronics.

Gregory Jones, VP Sales

599 Nevco Scoreboard Company
301 East Harris Avenue
Greenville, IL 62246-2151
618-664-0360
800-851-4040
Fax: 618-664-0398
E-mail: sales@nevco.com
http://www.nevco.com
Nevco is a premier manufacturer and distributor of scoreboards, message centers and video displays.

G.D. Moore, President
Phil Robertson, Sales Manager

600 Panasonic Communications & System Company
1 Panasonic Way
Secaucus, NJ 07094-2917
201-392-4818
800-524-1064
Fax: 201-392-4044
Cameras, projectors, equipment, players, CD-ROM equipment and school supplies.

601 Quickset International
3650 Woodhead Drive
Northbrook, IL 60062-1895
800-247-6563
Fax: 847-498-1258
http://www.moogs3.com
Telecommunication equipment, cameras, projectors and electronics.

602 RMF Products
1275 Paramount Pkwy.
PO Box 520
Batavia, IL 60510-0520
630-879-0020
Fax: 630-879-6749
E-mail: info@rmfproducts.com
http://www.rmfproducts.com
Complete line of slide-related products including two and three-projector dissolve controls, programmers, multi-track tape recorders, audio-visual cables, remote controls and slide mounts.

Richard Frieders, President

603 RTI-Research Technology International
4700 Chase
Lincolnwood, IL 60712-1689
847-677-3000
800-323-7520
Fax: 800-784-6733
E-mail: sales@rtico.com
http://www.rti-us.com
TapeChek Videotape Cleaner/Inspector/Rewinders make videotapes last longer and perform better. Find damage before tape

is circulated. Also available is videotape/laser disc storage, shipping and care products.
Ray Short, President/ CEO
Tom Boyle, Senior VP, RTI Sales

5604 Recreation Equipment Unlimited
PO Box 4700
Pittsburgh, PA 15206-0700
412-731-3000
Fax: 412-731-3052
Scoreboards and sports/recreation equipment.

5605 Reliance Plastics & Packaging
25 Prospect Street
Newark, NJ 07105-3300
973-473-7200
Fax: 973-589-6440
Vinyl albums for audio or video cassettes, video discs, slides, floppy disks, CDs Protect, store and circulate valuable media properly.

5606 Resolution Technology
26000 Avenida Aeropuerto Spc 22
San Juan Capistrano, CA 92675-4736
949-661-6162
Fax: 949-661-0114
Video systems and videomicroscopy equipment.

5607 RobotiKits Direct
17141 Kingsview Avenue
Suite B
Carson, CA 90746-1207
310-515-6800
877-515-6652
Fax: 310-515-0927
E-mail: info@owirobot.com
http://www.owirobot.com
New science and robotic kits for the millenium.

Craig Morioka, President
Armer Amante, General Manger

5608 S'Portable Scoreboards
3058 Alta Vista Drive
Fallbrook, CA 92028-8738
800-323-7745
Fax: 270-759-0066
Portable scoreboards, manual and electronic, sports timers and clocks.

5609 SONY Broadcast Systems Product Division
1 Sony Drive
Park Ridge, NJ 07656
800-472-SONY
Interactive videodisc players for multimedia applications, VTRs, monitors, projection systems, video cameras, editing systems, printers and scanners, video presentation stands, audio cassette duplicators and video library systems.

5610 Scott Resources/ Hubbard Scientific
National Training Aids
401 Hickory Street
PO Box 2121
Fort Collins, CO 80522-2121
970-484-7445
800-289-9299
Fax: 970-484-1198
E-mail: custserv@amep.com
http://www.hubbardscientific.com
Microslide system is a comprehensive, classroom-ready to help students learn. The microslide system combines superb photo-materials with detailed curriculum material and reproducible student activity sheets at an affrdable price.

Michael Warring, President
Candace Coffman, National Sales Manager

5611 Shure Brothers
222 Hartrey Avenue
Evanston, IL 60202-3696
847-866-2200
Fax: 847-866-2551
Electronics, hardware and classroom supplies.

5612 Swift Instruments
1190 N 4th Street
San Jose, CA 95112
408-293-2380
800-523-4544
Fax: 408-292-7967
http://www.swiftmicroscope.com
Capture live or still microscopic images through your compound or stereo microscope and background sound images through your VCR or computer.

5613 Tech World
Lab-Volt
PO Box 686
Farmingdale, NJ 07727
732-938-2000
800-522-8658
Fax: 732-774-8573
E-mail: us@labvolt.com
http://www.labvolt.com
Tech World provides superior hands-on instruction using state-of-the-art technology and equipment. Lab-Volt also offers a full line of attractive, durable, and flexible modular classroom furniture.

5614 Technical Education Systems
56 East End Drive
Gilberts, IL 60136
847-428-3085
800-451-2169
Fax: 847-428-3286
http://www.tii-tech.com
Hands-on application-oriented training systems integrating today's real world technologies in a flexible and easy-to-understand curriculum format.

5615 Telex Communications
12000 Portland Avenue S
Burnsville, MN 55337
952-884-4051
800-828-6107
Fax: 952-884-0043
http://www.telex.com
Telex manufactures a variety of products for the educational market, including multimedia headphones, headsets and microphones; LCD computer and multimedia projection panels, group listening centers, video projectors, slide projectors, portable sound systems, wired and wireless intercoms, and wired and wireless microphones.

Dawn Wiome, Marketing Coordinator

5616 The Transcription Studio
The Transcription Studio, LLC
2267 Honolulu Ave
Suite 2
Montrose, CA 91020
818-248-3400
Fax: 818-846-8933
E-mail:
Operations@TranscriptionStudio.com
http://www.transcriptionstudio.com
We transcribe and provide closed-captioning services to the education and academic fields.

Jeff Zedlar, CEO
Deborah Hargreaves, Director of Operations

5617 Three M Visual Systems
3M Austin Center
6801 River Place Boulevard
Austin, TX 78726-4530

512-984-1800
800-328-1371
Fax: 512-984-6529
http://www.solutions.3m.com
Overhead projectors, audiovisual carts and
tables, and overhead transparencies.

5618 Tom Snyder Productions
100 Talcott Avenue
Watertown, MA 02472-5703
617-926-6000
800-342-0236
Fax: 800-304-1254
E-mail: dealer@tomsnyder.com
http://www.tomsnyder.com
Educational videotapes, videodiscs and
computer programs.

Bridget Dalton, Ed.D., Author
Peggy Healy Stearns, Ph.D., Author

5619 Varitronics Systems
PO Box 234
Minneapolis, MN 55440
800-637-5461
Fax: 800-543-8966
Computer electronics, hardware, software
and systems.

5620 Wholesale Educational Supplies
PO Box 120123
East Haven, CT 06512-0123
800-243-2518
Fax: 800-452-5956
E-mail: wes4@snet.net
http://www.discountav.com
Over 5,000 audio visual and video equip-
ment and supplies offered at deep discount
prices. Free 148 page catalog.

J Fields, President

Furniture & Equipment

5621 ASRS of America
304 Park Avenue South
11th Floor
New York, NY 10010
212-760-1607
Fax: 212-760-1614
E-mail: info@elecompack.com
http://www.elecompack.com
Offers Elecompack, high density compact
shelving which offers double storage capacity, automatic passive safety systems
and custom front panels.

Walter M Kaufman

5622 Adden Furniture
710 Chelmsford Street
Lowell, MA 01851
978-454-7848
800-625-3876
Fax: 978-453-1449
E-mail: fsafran@addenfurniture.com
http://www.addenfurniture.com
Manufacturer of dormitory furniture,
bookcases and shelving products.

Linda Kane, President
Patrick Furnari, CEO

5623 Air Technologies Corporation
25641 White Sands Street
Dana Point, CA 92629
949-661-5060
800-759-5060
Fax: 949-661-2454
E-mail: ken@airtech.net
http://www.airtech.net
Develop and manufacture professional ergonomic computer products.

5624 Alma Industries
1300 Prospect Street
High Point, NC 27260-8329
336-578-5700
Fax: 336-578-0105
Bookcases and shelving for educational
purposes.

5625 Angeles Group
9 Capper Drive
Dailey Industrial Park
Pacific, MO 63069
636-257-0533
800-346-6313
Fax: 636-257-5473
http://www.angeles-group.com
Housekeeping furniture and children play
kitchen's made of durable and sturdy
molded polyethylene. Baseline Furniture:
tables, chairs, lockers, cubbies, bookcases,
bookracks, silver rider trikes, spaceline
cots, basic trikes, and bye bye buggies.

Tim Lynch, Director of Sales
David Curry, General Manager

**5626 Anthro Corporation Technology
Furniture**
10450 SW Manhasset Dr.
Tualatin, OR 97062
503-691-2556
800-325-3841
Fax: 800-325-0045
http://www.anthro.com
Durable computer workstations and accessories; educational discounts; and dozens
of shapes and sizes.

Shoaib Tureen, Co-Founder, President
Cathy Filgas, Co-Founder, VP-Sales

5627 Architectural Precast
10210 Winstead Lane
Cincinnati, OH 45246
513-772-4670
800-542-1738
Fax: 513-772-4672
E-mail: est@archprecast.com
http://www.archprecast.com
Furniture, tables, playground equipment,
desks.

5628 Blanton & Moore Company
PO Box 70
Barium Springs, NC 28010-0070
704-528-4506
Fax: 704-528-6519
http://www.blantonandmoore.com
Standard and custom library furniture
crafted from fine hardwoods.

Billy Galliher, Manager Sales
Administration

5629 Borroughs Corporation
3002 N Burdick Street
Kalamazoo, MI 49004-3483
616-342-0161
800-748-0227
Fax: 269-342-4161
http://www.borroughs.com
Bookcases and shelving products for educational purposes.

Zac Sweetland, VP, Sales
Tom Gambon, VP Finance &
Administration

5630 Brady Office Machine Security
11056 S Bell Avenue
Chicago, IL 60643-3935
773-779-8349
800-326-8349
Fax: 773-779-9712
E-mail: b.brady1060@aol.com
The Brady Office Machine Security physically protects all office machines, com-

puter components, faxes, printers, VCRs, have
wall and ceiling mounts for TVs.

Bernadette Brady, President
Don Brady, VP

5631 Bretford Manufacturing
9715 Soreng Avenue
Schiller Park, IL 60176-2186
540-678-2545
http://www.bretford.com
Manufacturer of a full line of AV and computer
projection screens, television mounts, wood office furniture and a full line of combination wood
shelving and steel library shelving.

5632 Brixey
13030 Inglewood Avenue
Suite 200
Hawthorne, CA 90250
310-263-7025
877-694-0752
Fax: 310-263-7250
E-mail: brixey@brixey.com
http://www.brixey.com
Furniture for the classroom.

5633 Brodart Company, Automation Division
500 Arch Street
Williamsport, PA 17701
570-326-2461
800-233-8467
Fax: 570-326-1479
E-mail: support@brodart.com
http://www.brodart.com
Brodart's Automation Division has been providing library systems, software, and services for
over 25 years. Products include: library management systems, media management systems,
Internet solutions, cataloged web sites, cataloging resource tools, union catalog solutions, public
access catalogs, and bibliographic services.

Kasey Dibble, Marketing Coordinator
Sally Wilmoth, Director Marketing/Sales

5634 Buckstaff Company
Buckstaff Company
PO Box 2851
Oshkosh, WI 54903
920-235-5890
800-755-5890
Fax: 920-235-2018
E-mail: sales@buckstaff.com
http://www.buckstaff.com
The premier manufacturer of library furniture in
the United States. Quality and durability has been
the Buckstaff trademark for 150 years.

Tom Mugerauer, Sales Manager, National

5635 Carpets for Kids Etc...
115 SE 9th Avenue
Portland, OR 97214-1301
503-232-1203
Fax: 503-232-1394
E-mail: customerservice@carpetsforkids.com
http://www.carpetsforkids.com
Carpets, flooring and floorcoverings for educational purposes.

5636 Children's Factory
505 N Kirkwood Road
Saint Louis, MO 63122-3913
314-821-1441
Fax: 877-726-1714
Manufactures children's indoor play furniture.

5637 Children's Furniture Company
Gressco Ltd.
328 Moravian Valley Road
Waunakee, WI 53597-339
608-849-6300
800-345-3480
Fax: 608-849-6304

E-mail: info@gresscoltd.com
http://www.gressco.com
Commercial quality furniture for children of
all ages.

Robert Childers, President
Caroline Ashmore, Marketing/Sales

5638 Community Playthings
PO Box 901
Rifton, NY 12471-0901
800-777-4244
Fax: 800-336-5948
E-mail: sales@bruderhof.com
Unstructured maple toys and furniture in-
cluding innovative products, especially for
infants and toddlers.

5639 Continental Film
1466 Riverside Drive, Suite E
PO Box 5126
Chattanooga, TN 37406
423-622-1193
888-909-3456
Fax: 423-629-0853
E-mail: info@continentalfilm.com
http://www.continentalfilm.com
LCD projectors, distance learning systems,
interactive white boards, document cameras.

Jim Webster, President
Courtney Sisk, VP

5640 Counterpoint
17237 Van Wagoner Road
Spring Lake, MI 49456-9702
800-628-1945
Fax: 616-847-3109
Audiovisual carts and tables.

5641 CyberStretch By Jazzercise
2460 Impala Drive
Carlsbad, CA 92010
760-476-1750
Fax: 760-602-7180
E-mail: customercare@jazzercise.com
http://www.jazzercise.com
To foster and promote wellness through the
production of free interactive software programs for business, government, educational
and personal use.

Kathy Missett, Contact

5642 Da-Lite Screen Company
3100 North Detroit Street
Warsaw, IN 46582
574-267-8101
800-622-3737
Fax: 877-325-4832
E-mail: info@da-lite.com
http://www.da-lite.com
Projection screens, monitor mounts, audiovisual carts and tables, overhead projectors and
transparencies.

5643 DeFoe Furniture 4 Kids
910 S Grove Avenue
Ontario, CA 91761-8011
909-947-4459
Fax: 909-947-3377
Furniture, floorcoverings, toys, constructive
playthings and more for children grades
PreK-5.

5644 Decar Corporation
7615 University Avenue
Middleton Branch, WI 53562-3142
606-836-1911
Library shelving, storage facilities and furniture.

5645 DecoGard Products
Construction Specialties
Route 405
PO Box 400
Muncy, PA 17756
570-546-5941
Fax: 570-546-5169
Physical fitness and athletic floor coverings
and mats.

5646 Engineering Steel Equipment Company
560 Central Drive
Suite 104
Virginia Beach, VA 23454
757-627-0762
Fax: 757-625-5754
E-mail: al@engineeringsteel.com
http://www.engineeringsteel.com
Audiovisual carts and tables, bookcases and
library shelving.

5647 Environments
PO Box 1348
Beaufort, SC 29901-1348
843-846-8155
800-348-4453
Fax: 843-846-2999
Publishes a catalog featuring equipment and
materials for child care and early education.
Offers durable and easy-to-maintain products with values that promote successful pre-
school, kindergarden, special needs and
multi-age programs.

5648 Flagship Carpets
PO Box 1189
Chatsworth, GA 30705-1189

http://www.flagshipcarpets.com
Carpets, flooring and floorcoverings.

5649 Fleetwood Group
PO Box 1259
Holland, MI 49422-1259
616-396-1142
800-257-6390
Fax: 616-820-8300
E-mail: www.fleetwoodfurniture.com
Offers library and school furniture including
shelving, check out desks and multimedia
units.

5650 Fordham Equipment Company
3308 Edson Avenue
New York, NY 10469
718-379-7300
800-249-5922
Fax: 718-379-7312
E-mail: alrobbi@attglobal.net
http://www.fordhamequip.com
Distributor and manufacturer of complete
line of library supplies. Specialize in professional library shelving and furniture (wood
and metal), mobile shelving and displayers.
Catalog on request.

Al Robbins, President

5651 Good Sports
6031 Broad Street Mall
Pittsburgh, PA 15206-3009
412-661-9500
Mats, matting, floorcoverings and athletic
training mats.

5652 Grafco
ERD
PO Box 71
Catasauqua, PA 18032-0071
800-367-6169
Fax: 610-782-0813
E-mail: info@grafco.com
http://www.grafco.com

GRAFCO manufacturers sturdy and durable
computer furniture and tables designed for
the educational environment.

Art Grafenberg, President

5653 Grammer
6989 N 55th Street
Suite A
Oakdale, MN 55128
651-770-6515
800-367-7328
http://www.grammerusa.com
Leading manufacturer and designer of
ergonomically sound seating. Offers a chair
designed especially for children.

5654 Greeting Tree
2709 Oak Haven Drive
San Marcos, TX 78666
512-392-0669
800-322-3199
Fax: 512-392-9660
E-mail: krieger@corridor.net
http://www.greetingtree.com
Solid wood furniture for Reading Recovery,
Reading Library, Primary and Early Childhood. Specializes in quality and customized
furniture for today's classroom. Kitchen
learning centers, storage units of all sizes and
sorts, easels with over fourteen different display front possibilities.
BiAnnually

Cherie Krieger, Owner

5655 Gressco Ltd.
Gressco
328 Moravian Valley Road
PO Box 339
Waunakee, WI 53597-339
608-849-6300
800-345-3480
Fax: 608-849-6304
E-mail: info@gresscoltd.com
http://www.gressco.com
Gressco is a supplier of a complete line of
commercial children's HABA furniture and
library displays for all types of medias.
Kwik-case for the security protection of CDs,
videos, and audiocassettes. Catalog
available.

Caroline Ashmore, Marketing/Sales

5656 H Wilson Company
2245 Delany Road
Waukegan, IL 60087
708-339-5111
800-245-7224
Fax: 800-245-8224
E-mail: info@hwilson.com
http://www.hwilson.com
Manufacturer of furniture for audio, video,
and computers. Complete line of TV wall and
ceiling mounts. Makers of the famous Tuffy
color carts.

Matthew Glowiak, Director
Sales/Marketing

5657 HON Company
200 Oak Street
Muscatine, IA 52761-4341
563-272-7100
800-466-8694
Fax: 563-264-7505
E-mail: HONGSATeam@honcompany.com
http://www.hon.com
Bookcases and shelving units.

5658 Haworth
One Haworth Center
Holland, MI 49423-9576
616-393-3000
800-344-2600

Fax: 616-393-1570
http://www.haworth.com
Steel and wood desks, systems furniture, seating, files, bookcases, shelving units, and tables.

5659 Joy Carpets
104 West Forrest Road
Fort Oglethorpe, GA 30742-3675
706-866-3335
800-645-2787
Fax: 706-866-7928
E-mail: joycarpets@joycarpets.com
http://www.joycarpets.com
Manufacturer of recreational and educational carpet for the classroom, home, or business. With a 10 year wear warranty, Class #1 Flammability rating, anti-stain and anti-bacterial treatment.

Joy Dobosh, Director Marketing

5660 KI
PO Box 8100
Green Bay, WI 54308-8100
920-468-8100
Fax: 920-468-2232
Library shelving, furniture, bookcases and more.

5661 Kensington Technology Group
2855 Campus Drive
San Mateo, CA 94403
650-572-2700
Fax: 650-572-9675
http://www.kensington.com
Offers several ergonomic mice.

5662 Kimball Office Furniture Company
1600 Royal Street
Jasper, IN 47549-1001
800-482-1818
800-482-1616
Fax: 812-482-8300
http://www.kimball.com
Bookcases, office equipment and shelving units for educational institutions.

5663 Lee Metal Products
PO Box 6
Littlestown, PA 17340-0006
717-359-4111
Fax: 717-359-4414
http://www.leemetal.com
Carts, tables, bookcases and storage cabinets.

Richard Kemper, President

5664 Library Bureau
172 Industrial Road
Fitchburg, MA 01420
978-345-7942
800-221-6638
Fax: 978-345-0188
E-mail: melvil@librarybureau.com
http://www.librarybureau.com
Library shelving, bookcases, cabinets, circulation desks, carrels, computer workstations, upholstered seating.

Dennis Ruddy, Sr Project Manager

5665 Library Store
Library Store
112 E S Street
PO Box 0964
Tremont, IL 61568-964
309-925-5571
800-548-7204
Fax: 800-320-7706
E-mail: customerservice@thelibrarystore.com
http://www.thelibrarystore.com

The Library Store offers through its full-line catalog, supplies and furniture items for librarians, schools, and churches. Free catalog available containing special product discounts.

Janice Smith, Marketing Director

5666 Little Tikes Company
2180 Barlow Road
Hudson, OH 44236-4199
330-656-3906
800-321-0183
Fax: 330-650-3221
http://www.littletikes.com
Offers a wide variety of furniture, educational games and toys and safety products for young children.

5667 Lucasey Manufacturing Company
2744 E 11th Street
Oakland, CA 94601-1429
510-534-1435
800-582-2739
Fax: 510-534-6828
E-mail: janrence@lucasey.com
http://www.lucasey.com
Audiovisual carts, tables, and TV mounts

Jan RenceTurnbull, National Accountant

5668 Lundia
600 Capitol Way
Jacksonville, IL 62650-1096
800-726-9663
Fax: 800-869-9663
http://www.lundiausa.com
Bookcases and shelving products, as well as furniture for educational institutions.

5669 Lyon Metal Products
PO Box 671
Aurora, IL 60507-0671
630-892-8941
800-433-8488
Fax: 630-892-8966
E-mail: lyon@lyonworkspace.com
http://www.lyonworkspace.com
Bookcases and library shelving.

5670 Mateflex-Mele Corporation
2007 Beechgrove Place
Utica, NY 13501
315-733-1412
844-244-8464
Fax: 315-735-4372
http://www.mateflex.com
Manufacturers of Mateflex gymnasium flooring for basketball/gym courts. Mateflex II tennis court surfaces and Mateflex/Versaflex gridded safety floor tiles.

Gabe Martini, Sales Manager

5671 Microsoft Corporation
One Microsoft Way
Redmond, WA 98502-6399
425-882-8080
Fax: 206-703-2641
http://www.microsoft.com
Strives to produce innovative products and services that meet our costomers' evolving needs.

5672 Miller Multiplex
1610 Design Way
Dupo, IL 62239-1820
636-343-5700
800-325-3350
Fax: 618-286-6202
E-mail: info@Miller-Group.com
http://www.multiplexdisplays.com
Announcement boards, classroom displays, charts and pghtography, books tow-

ers, posters, frames, kiosk displays, presentation displays.

12 pages

Kathy Webster, Director Marketing

5673 ModuForm
ModuForm, Inc.
172 Industry Road
Fitchburg,, MA 01420
978-345-7942
800-221-6638
Fax: 978-345-0188
E-mail: guestlog@moduform.com
http://www.moduform.com
Residence hall furniture, loung seating, tables, stacking chairs, fully upholstered seating.

Robert Kushnir, Nationals Sales Manager
Darlene Bailey, VP Sales/Marketing

5674 Morgan Buildings, Pools, Spas, RV's
12700 Hillcrest Rd Suite 278
PO Box 660280
Dallas, TX 75230
972-864-7300
800-935-0321
Fax: 972-864-7382
E-mail: rmoran@morganusa.com
http://www.morganusa.com
Classrooms, campus and other buildings custom designed to meet your projects needs. Permanent and relocatable modular classrooms or complete custom facilities. Rent, lease or purchase options available.

5675 Norco Products
Division of USA McDonald Corporation
4985 Blue Mountain Road
PO Box 4227
Missoula, MT 59806
406-251-3800
800-662-2300
Fax: 406-251-3824
E-mail: jim@norcoproducts.com
http://www.norcoproducts.com
Mobile cabinets, YRE funiture, tables, science labs, home economics displays, bookcases and shelving units, laboratory equipment, casework, cabinets, computer labs, podiums, award display cabinets, flags and flag poles.

Jim McDonald, President
Patti McDonald, Vice President

5676 Nova
421 W Industrial Avenue
PO Box 725
Effingham, IL 62401
800-730-6682
Fax: 800-940-6682
E-mail: novadesk@effingham.net
http://www.novadesk.com
Patented furniture solution for computer mounting incorporates the downward gaze, our visual system's natural way of viewing close objects. Scientific evidence indicates that viewing a computer monitor at a downward gaze angle is a better solution than with traditional monitor placement.

5677 Oscoda Plastics
5585 North Huron Avenue
PO Box 189
Oscoda, MI 48750
989-739-6900
800-544-9538
Fax: 800-548-7678
E-mail: sales@oscodaplastics.com
http://www.oscodaplastics.com
Oscoda Plastics manufactures Protect-All Specialty Flooring from 100% recycled post-industrial vinyls. Protect-All is perfect for use in locker rooms, kitchen/walk-in cooler floors, fitness ar-

eas, weight rooms, gym floors, or as a temporary gym floor cover.

Joe Brinn, National Sales Manager
Rick Maybury, Sales Coordinator

678 Palmer Snyder
201 High Street
Conneautville, PA 16406
814-587-6313
800-762-0415
Fax: 814-587-2375
Tables are built with the highest quality materials for long life and low maintenance. A complete range of rugged options.

679 Paragon Furniture
2224 East Randol Mill Road
Arlington, TX 76011
817-633-3242
800-451-8546
Fax: 817-633-2733
E-mail: customerservice@paragoninc.com
http://www.paragoninc.com
Offers a line of furniture for classroom, labs, science, and libraries.

Carl Brockway, VP Sales
Mark Hubbard, President

680 Pawling Corporation
Borden Lane
Wassaic, NY 12592
845-373-9300
800-431-3456
Fax: 800-451-2200
E-mail: sales@pawling.com
Pawling is an approved manufacturer by E&I cooperative buying for athletic flooring, traffic safety products, wall and corner protection and entrance mat systems.

Richard Meyer, Sales Manager

681 Peerless Sales Company
1980 N Hawthorne Avenue
Melrose Park, IL 60160-1167
708-865-8870
Fax: 708-865-2941
Auidovisual carts and tables.

682 RISO
300 Rosewood Drive
Suite 210
Danvers, MA 01923-4527
978-777-7377
800-876-7476
Fax: 978-777-2517
The Risograph digital printer offers high speed copy/duplicating at up to 130 pages per minute. A 50-sheet document feeder lets people print multi-page documents quickly and inexpensively. Specifically designed to handle medium run length jobs that are too strenuous for copiers. Offers various other products and office equipment available to the education community.

683 Research Technology International
4700 Chase Avenue
Lincolnwood, IL 60646-1689
847-677-3000
800-323-7520
Fax: 847-677-1311
E-mail: sales@rtico.com
http://www.ritco.com
Tape check, Video tape cleaner, disk chack optical, disc rejestor.

684 Russ Bassett Company
8189 Byron Road
Whittier, CA 90606-2615
562-945-2445
800-350-2445
Fax: 562-698-8972

E-mail: info@russbassett.com
http://www.russbassett.com
Shelving units, furniture and bookcases for educational institutions.

685 SNAP-DRAPE
2045 Westgate Drive
Suite 100
Carrollton, TX 75006-5116
972-466-1030
800-527-5147
Fax: 800-230-1330
E-mail: info@snapdrape.com
http://www.snapdrape.com
Table and stage skirting

Melissa Acton, Marketing/Sales Assistant

686 Screen Works
2201 W Fulton Street
Chicago, IL 60612
312-243-8265
800-294-8111
Fax: 312-243-8290
E-mail: screens@thescreenworks.com
http://www.thescreenworks.com
Manufacturers the E-Z Fold brand of portable projection screens and offers a full line of portable presentation accessories and services, including: an extensive screen rental inventory; audio-visula roll carts; lecterns and PaperStand flip charts. Custom screen sizes, screen surface cleaning and frame repair service also available.

David Hull, National Sales Manager

687 Spacemaster Systems
155 W Central Avenue
Zeeland, MI 49464-1601
616-772-2406
Fax: 616-772-2100
Standard and Custom Shelving Systems and USEFUL AISLE Storage Systems.

688 Spacesaver Corporation
1450 Janesville Avenue
Fort Atkinson, WI 53538-2798
920-563-6362
800-255-8170
Fax: 920-563-2702
E-mail: info@spacesaver.com
http://www.spacesaver.com
Flexible Spacesaver custom designs high-density mobile storage systems. Will double your storage and filing capacity while increasing usable floor space. Store files, supplies, manuals, books, drawings, multi-media, etc.

689 Synsor Corporation
1920 Merrill Creek Pkwy
Everett, WA 98203-5859
425-551-1300
800-426-0193
Fax: 425-551-1313
E-mail: info@synsor.com
http://www.synsor.com
Offers a full line of educational furniture.

690 Tab Products Company
1400 Page Mill Road
Palo Alto, CA 94304-1124
800-672-3109
Fax: 920-387-1802
Bookcases and shelving products for library/media centers.

691 Tepromark International
206 Mosher Avenue
Woodmere, NY 11598-1662
516-569-4533
800-645-2622
Fax: 516-295-5991
Trolley Rail wall guards, corner guards, wall guards with hand rails, door plates, chair

rolls, kick plates, vinyl floor mats and carpet mats. All mats promote safety from slipping in wet areas.

Robert Rymers

692 Tesco Industries
1038 E Hacienda Street
Bellville, TX 77418-2828
979-865-3176
800-699-5824
Fax: 979-865-9026
E-mail: tesco@tesco-ind.com
http://www.tesco-ind.com
Bookcases and shelving units.

693 Texwood Furniture
1353 N 2nd Street
Taylor, TX 76574
512-352-3000
888-878-0000
Fax: 512-352-3084
E-mail: ajohnson@texwood.com
http://www.texwood.com
Wood library furniture, shelving, computer tables and circulation desks and early childhood furniture.

Andrea Johnson, Director Marketing
Dave Gaskers, VP Sales/Marketing

694 Tot-Mate by Stevens Industries
704 West Main Street
Teutopolis, IL 62467-1212
217-857-7100
800-397-8687
Fax: 217-857-7101
E-mail: timw@stevens.com
http://www.stevensind.com
Early learning furniture manufactured by Stevens Industries. Features include 16 color choices, plastic laminate surfacing, rounded corners, beveled edges, safe and strong designs. Items offered include change tables, storage shelving, book displays, teacher cabinets, housekeeping sets and locker cubbies.

Randy Ruholl, Sales Representative
Paul Jones, Customer Service

695 University Products
University Products
517 Main Street
PO Box 101
Holyoke, MA 1040
413-532-3372
800-628-1912
Fax: 413-532-9281
E-mail: info@universityproducts.com
http://www.universityproducts.com
University Products specializes in top-quality archival materials for conservation and preservation as well as library and media centers supplies, equipment, and furnishings.

Scott E. Magoon, President/ COO

696 W. C. Heller & Company
Heller
201 W Wabash Avenue
Montpelier, OH 43543
419-485-3176
Fax: 419-485-8694
E-mail: wcheller@hotmail.com
Complete line of wood library furniture in oak and birch, custom cabinetry and special modifications. Over 110 years in business.

Robert L Heller II, VP Sales

697 Wheelit
PO Box 352800
Toledo, OH 43635-2800
419-531-4900
800-523-7508
Fax: 419-531-6415
Carts and storage containers.

5698 White Office Systems
50 Boright Avenue
Kenilworth, NJ 07033
908-272-6700
800-275-1442
Fax: 908-931-0840
http://whitesystems.com
Shelving, bookcases, furniture and products for libraries, media centers, schools and offices.

5699 Whitney Brothers Company
PO Box 644
Keene, NH 03431-0644
603-352-2610
Fax: 603-357-1559
http://www.whitneybros.com
Manufactures children's furniture products for preschools and day care centers.

5700 Winsted Corporation
10901 Hampshire Avenue S
Minneapolis, MN 55438
952-944-9050
800-447-2257
Fax: 800-421-3839
E-mail: info@winsted.com
http://www.winsted.com
Video furniture, accessories, tape storage systems and lan rack systems.

Rich McPherson, Western Regional Manager
Kim Richter, Western Regional Manager

5701 Wood Designs
PO Box 1308
Monroe, NC 28111-1308
704-283-7508
800-247-8465
Fax: 704-289-1899
E-mail: p.schneider@tip-me-not.com
http://www.wooddesigns.org
Manufactures wooden educational equipment and teaching toys for early learning environments. Sold through school supply dealers and stores.

Dennis Gosney, President
Paul Schneider, VP Sales/Marketing

5702 Worden Company
199 E 17th Street
Holland, MI 49423
800-748-0561
Fax: 616-392-2542
E-mail: info@wordencompany.com
http://www.wordencompany.com
Furniture for office, business, school or library.

Maintenance

5703 American Locker Security Systems
2701 Regent Blvd
Suite 200
DFW Airport, TX 75261
817-329-1600
800-828-9118
Fax: 817-421-8618
E-mail: info@americanlocker.com
http://www.americanlocker.com
Lockers featuring coin operated lockers.

David L Henderson, VP/General Manager

5704 Atlantic Fitness Products
PO Box 300
Linthicum Hts, MD 21090-0300
410-859-3907
800-445-1855
http://www.atlanticfitnessproducts.com
School lockers and fitness/physical education products and equipment.

5705 Barco Products
24 N. Washington Ave.
Batavia, IL 60510
800-338-2697
E-mail: sales@barcoproducts.com
http://www.barcoproducts.com
Maintenance and safety products made from recycled materials.

Cyril Matter, CEO
Judy Leonard, Marketing Manager

5706 Blaine Window Hardware
17319 Blaine Drive
Hagerstown, MD 21740
302-797-6500
800-678-1919
Fax: 888-250-3960
E-mail: info@Blainewindow.com
http://www.blainewindow.com
Window and door parts including window repair hardware, custom screens locker hardware, chair glides, panic exit hardware, balance systems, door closers and motorized operators.

William Pasquerette, VP
Robert Slick, Purchasing Agent

5707 Bleacherman, M.A.R.S.
105 Mill Street
Corinth, NY 12822
518-654-9084
800-628-1332
Fax: 518-654-2232
E-mail: info@bleacherman.com
http://www.mars-bleachers.com
School lockers.

5708 Burkel Equipment Company
14670 Hanks Drive
Red Bluff, CA 96080-9475
800-332-3993
School lockers, hardware and security equipment, maintenance and repair supplies.

5709 Chemtrol
Santa Barbara Control Systems
5375 Overpass Road
Santa Barbara, CA 93111-5879
800-621-2279
Fax: 805-683-1893
E-mail: chemtrol@slocontrol.com
http://www.ccdc.ucsb.edu
Maintenance supplies for educational institutions.

Karl Johan Astrom, Mechanical Engineering
Bassam Bamieh, Mechanical Engineering

5710 Contact East
Stanley Supply & Services, Inc.
335 Willow Street
North Andover, MA 01845-5995
978-682-9844
800-225-5370
Fax: 800-743-8141
E-mail: sales@contacteast.com
http://www.contacteast.com
Maintenance supplies and equipment.

5711 DeBourgh Manufacturing Company
27505 Otero Avenue
PO Box 981
La Junta, CO 81050
719-384-8161
800-328-8829
Fax: 719-384-7713
E-mail: sales@debourgh.com
http://www.debourgh.com
Security equipment, hardware, storage and school lockers.

Ralph Malers, Employee

5712 Dow Corning Corporation
2200 W. Salzburg Rd.
PO Box 0994
Midland, MI 48686-0994
989-496-4000
Fax: 989-496-4572
http://www.dowcorning.com/content/publishedli t/Global_Fast_Facts.pd
Maintenance supplies and equipment.

Robert D. Hansen, President/ CEO
Cathy Yang, Global Media Relations,China

5713 Dri-Dek Corporation
Kendall Products
P.O. Box 8656
Naples, FL 34101
239-643-0448
800-348-2398
Fax: 800-828-4248
E-mail: info@dri-dek.com
http://www.dri-dek.com
Oxy-BI vinyl compound in the Dri-Dek flooring systems helps halt the spread of infectious fungus and bacteria in areas with barefooted traffic. This compound makes Dri-Dek's anti-skid, self-draining surface ideal for use in the wettest conditions.

5714 Esmet
1406 5th Street SW
Canton, OH 44702
330-452-9132
800-321-0870
Fax: 330-452-2557
E-mail: info@esmet.com
http://www.esmet.com
Lockers for the educational institution.

5715 Ex-Cell Metal Products
11240 Melrose Avenue
Franklin, IL 60131
847-451-0451
Fax: 847-451-0458
Maintenance supplies and repair equipment.

5716 Facilities Network
PO Box 868
Mahopac, NY 10541-0868
845-621-1664
School lockers and security system units.

5717 Fibersin Industries
37031 E Wisconsin Avenue
PO Box 88
Oconomowoc, WI 53066-88
262-567-4427
Fax: 262-567-4814
E-mail: info@fiberesin.com
http://www.fiberesin.com
School lockers and maintenance supplies. Desks, cradenzas, bookcases for school adm. Tables for cafeteria and adm.

5718 Flagpole Components
4150A Kellway Circle
Addison, TX 75001
972-250-0893
800-634-4926
Fax: 972-380-5143
http://www.concordindustries.com
Maintenance and repair supplies and equipment.

5719 Flexi-Wall Systems
PO Box 89
208 Carolina Dr.
Liberty, SC 29657-0089
864-843-3104
800-843-5394
Fax: 864-843-9318
E-mail: flexiwall@bellsouth.net
http://www.flexiwall.com/pages/home_page.htm

Maintenance and repair supplies for educational institutions.

720 Flo-Pac Corporation
700 Washington Avenue N
Suite 400
Minneapolis, MN 55401-1130
612-332-6240
Fax: 612-344-1663
Maintenance and repair supplies.

721 Four Rivers Software Systems
400 Penn Center Blvd
Suite 450
Pittsburgh, PA 15235
412-256-9020
Fax: 412-273-6420
http://www.frsoft.com
Maintenance and repair supplies, business
and administrative software and supplies.

Pierre Harrison, Regional VP,Healthcare
M. Lynn O'Donnell, Dir. Of Marketing

722 Friendly Systems
3878 Oak Lawn Avenue
#1008-300
Dallas, TX 75219-4460
972-857-0399
Maintenance and repair supplies.

723 GE Capitol Modular Space
40 Liberty Boulevard
Malvern, PA 19355
610-225-2836
800-523-7918
Fax: 610-225-2762
http://www.modspace.com
School lockers, shelving and storage facilities.

724 Glen Products
13765 Alton Parkway
Suite A
Irvine, CA 92618-1627
800-486-4455
Storage facilities, lockers and security systems.

725 Global Occupational Safety
22 Harbor Park Drive
Port Washington, NY 11050-4650
516-625-4466
Safety storage facilities, shelving, lockers
and hardware.

726 Graffiti Gobbler Products
6428 Blarney Stone Court
Springfield, VA 22152-2106
800-486-2512
Educational maintenance and repair supplies
and equipment.

727 H&H Enterprises
PO Box 585
Grand Haven, MI 49417-9430
616-846-8972
800-878-7777
Fax: 616-846-1004
E-mail: hhenterprises@novagate.com
http://handhent.com
Maintenance and repair supplies.

728 HAZ-STOR
75 Camrose Cres.
Underwood., Ql 4119
073-341-6200
800-727-2067
Fax: 073-341-6211
E-mail: sales@haz-stor.net
http://haz-stor.net
Manufacturer of pre-fabricated steel structures including hazardous material storage
buildings and outdoor flammables lockers as
well as waste compactors and drum crushers,

secondary containment products and process
shelters.
Roger Quinlan, National Sales Manager
Antoinette Balthazor, Marketing
Coordinator

5729 HOST/Racine Industries
1405 16th Street
Racine, WI 53403-2249
800-558-9439
Fax: 262-637-1624
Maintenance and repair supplies.

5730 Hako Minuteman
14N845 U.S. Route 20
Pingree Grove, IL 60140
847-264-5400
Fax: 847-683-5207
http://www.minutemanintl.com
Maintenance and repair supplies for educational institutions.

5731 Haws Corporation
1455 Kleppe Ln
Sparks, NV 89431
775-359-4712
888-640-4297
Fax: 775-359-7424
E-mail: haws@hawsco.com
http://www.hawsco.com
Manufacturer of drinking fountains, electric
water coolers, emergency drench showers
and eyewashes.

Tom White, President
Aaron Cross, Jr., VP of Operations

5732 Honeywell
Home & Building Control
PO Box 524
Minneapolis, MN 55440-0524
973-455-2001
Fax: 973-455-4807
Maintenance and cleaning products for edu-
cational purposes.

5733 Insta-Foam Products
2050 N Broadway Street
Joliet, IL 60435-2571
800-800-FOAM
Fax: 800-326-1054
Maintenance supplies, cleaning products and
repair hardware.

5734 Interstate Coatings
1005 Highway 301 S
Wilson, NC 27895
800-533-7663
Hardware, repair, maintenance and cleaning
supplies.

5735 J.A. Sexauer
PO Box 1000
White Plains, NY 10602
800-431-1872
Fax: 888-499-0441
E-mail: customercare@sexauer.com
http://www.casinovendors.com/vendor/j-a-s
exauer
Cleaning and maintenance supplies for edu-
cational institutions.

5736 Karnak Corporation
330 Central Avenue
Clark, NJ 07066
732-388-0300
800-526-4236
Fax: 732-388-9422
http://www.karnakcorp.com/Contact.aspx
Maintenance and cleaning supplies.

Sarah J. Jelin, Chairwoman, President
John McDermott, Vice-Chairman

5737 Kool Seal
Unifex Professional Maintenance Products
1499 Enterprise Pkwy
Twinsburg, OH 44087-2241
800-321-0572
Fax: 330-425-9778
Maintenance, repair and cleaning supplies.

5738 LDSystems
407 Garden Oaks
Houston, TX 77018
713-695-9400
Fax: 713-695-8015
E-mail: info@ldsystems.com
http://www.ldsystems.com
Environmentally-safe bottom pump air pow-
ered spray containers to dispense cleaning
supplies such as window sprays, for cooling
during workouts and general storage
containers.

Dick Stark

5739 List Industries
401 Jim Moran Blvd.
PO Box 9601
Deerfield Beach, FL 33442
954-429-9155
800-776-1342
Fax: 954-428-3843
http://www.listindustries.com
School lockers and storage facilities.

JR List, President
Max H. List, Founder

5740 Maintenance
1051 W Liberty Street
Wooster, OH 44691-3307
330-264-6262
800-892-6701
Fax: 800-264-2578
Provides pavement maintenance products for
parking lots, driveways, tennis courts, etc.

Robert E Huebner

5741 Master Bond
154 Hobart Street
Hackensack, NJ 07601
201-343-8983
Fax: 201-343-2132
E-mail: main@masterbond.com
http://www.masterbond.com
Repair hardware, maintenance and cleaning
products for schools.

Dr. Walter Brenne, Technical Director

5742 Master Builders
Admixture Division
23700 Chagrin Boulevard
Cleveland, OH 44122-5554
216-831-5500
Fax: 216-839-8815
School hardware, maintenance and repair
supplies and equipment.

5743 Medart
Division of Carriage Industries
PO Box 435
Garrettsville, OH 44231-0435
662-453-2506
School lockers.

5744 Modular Hardware
8190 N Brookshire Court
Tucson, AZ 85741-4037
520-744-4424
800-533-0042
Fax: 800-533-7942
School hardware, for repair and maintenance
purposes.

5745 Penco Products
1820 Stonehenge Drive
Greenville, NC 27858

349

610-666-0500
800-562-1000
Fax: 610-666-7561
E-mail: general@pencoproducts.com
http://www.pencoproducts.com
School lockers.

L. Lewis Sagendorph, Founder
Sarah Crandell, Accounts Payable

5746 Permagile Industries

910 Manor Lane
Bay Shore, NY 11706-7512
516-349-1100
Maintenance and cleaning products and
supplies.

5747 Powr-Flite Commercial Floor Care Equipment

3301 Wichita Court
Fort Worth, TX 76140
817-551-0700
800-880-2913
Fax: 817-551-0719
E-mail: info@powr-flite.com
http://www.powrflite.com
School maintenance supplies focusing on
floor care equipment products, accessories
and parts.

Curtis Walton, Contact

5748 ProCoat Products

260 Centre Street
Suite D
Holbrook, MA 02343
781-767-2270
Fax: 781-767-2271
E-mail: info@procoat.com
http://www.procoat.com
Designed to restore aged and discolored
acoustical ceiling tiles. Acoustical and fire
retarding qualities are maintained. Ceiling
restoration is cost effective, time efficient
and avoids solid waste disposal. Products
available also for preventative
maintenance programs.

Kenneth Woolf, Borad Chairman,
Founder
Lisa Ploss, President

5749 Rack III High Security Bicycle Rack Company

675 Hartz Avenue
Suite 306
Danville, CA 94526-3859
800-733-1971
Lockers, bicycle racks, storage facilities
and hardware.

5750 Republic Storage Systems Company

1038 Belden Avenue NE
Canton, OH 44705-1454
330-438-5800
800-477-1255
Fax: 330-454-7772
http://republicstorage.com
Storage facilities, containers, maintenance
products, shelving and lockers.

John Berger, Co-Founder
Wilson Berger, Co-Founder

5751 Safety Storage

855 N. 5th Street
Charleston, IL 61920
800-344-6539
Fax: 831-637-7405
http://www.safetystorage.com
Equipment, supplies and storage containers for maintenance and educational purposes.

Lynn Dufek, CEO

5752 Salsbury Industries

1010 E 62nd Street
Los Angeles, CA 90001-1598
323-846-6700
800-624-5269
Fax: 323-846-6800
E-mail: salsbury@mailboxes.com
http://www.mailboxes.com
School lockers, maintenance products and
storage facilities.

5753 Servicemaster

Education Management Services
860 Ridge Lake Boulevard
Downers Grove, IL 60515
800-926-9700
http://ems.educationmgt.com
A provider of facility management support
services to education.

Mark A. Smith, Ed.D, President
Joshua T. Fischer, PhD, VP of Operations

5754 Sheffield Plastics

Bayer MaterialScience LLC
119 Salisbury Road
Sheffield, MA 01257
413-229-8711
800-628-5084
Fax: 413-229-8717
E-mail: sfdinfo@bayer.com
http://www.sheffieldplastics.com
Maintenance and cleaning products for
schools.

5755 Southern Sport Surfaces

PO Box 1817
Cumming, GA 30028-1817
770-887-3508
800-346-1632
Maintenance and cleaning products for
schools.

5756 System Works

3301 Windy Ridge Parkway
Marietta, GA 30067
770-952-8444
800-868-0497
Fax: 770-955-2977
Addresses the capacity, quality and safety
requirements of maintenance operations.
Comprehensive and interactive it maxi-
mizes maintenance resources, people,
tools and replacement parts, for increased
productivity and equipment reliability, reduced inventories and accurate cost
accounting.

Karen Kharlead

5757 TENTEL Corporation

330 Industrial Drive # 4
Placerville, CA 95667
530-344-0183
800-538-6894
Fax: 530-344-0186
E-mail: info@tentel.com
http://www.tentel.com
Cleaning, repair and maintenance products
for educational institutions.

5758 Tiffin Systems

450 Wall Street
Tiffin, OH 44883-1366
419-447-8414
800-537-0983
Fax: 419-447-8512
E-mail: mdysard@tiffinmetal.com
http://www.tiffinmetal.com
Lockers, storage containers and shelving.

Matt Dysard, President/ COO
Will Heddles, CEO

5759 Topog-E Gasket Company

1224 N Utica
Tulsa, OK 74110
918-587-6649
Fax: 918-587-6961
E-mail: info@topog-e.com
http://www.topog-e.com
Maintenance supplies and products.

5760 Tru-Flex Recreational Coatings

Touraine Paints
1760 Revere Beach Pkwy
Everett, MA 02149-5906
800-325-0017
Maintenance, floor care, coatings and repair supplies for upkeep of schools and institutions.

5761 Wagner Spray Tech Corporation

1770 Fernbrook Lane N
Minneapolis, MN 55447
763-553-0759
Fax: 763-553-7288
http://www.wagnerspraytech.com
Maintenance supplies, floor care, cleaning and repair products and equipment.

5762 Wilmar

303 Harper Drive
Moorestown, NJ 08057
800-345-3335
800-345-3000
Fax: 800-220-3291
E-mail: customercare@wilmar.com
http://www.wilmar.com
Maintenance and repair products, hardware and
supplies.

5763 Witt Company

4454 Steel Place
Cincinnati, OH 45209-1184
513-979-3127
800-543-7417
Fax: 513-979-3134
Lockers, maintenance supplies and storage containers for educational purposes.

5764 Zep Manufacturing

1310 Seaboard Industrial Dr.
Atlanta, GA 30318
404-352-1680
877-428-9937
http://www.zep.com
Maintenance and cleaning supplies.

Scientific Equipment

5765 Adventures Company

435 Main Street
Johnson City, NY 13790-1935
607-729-6512
800-477-6512
Fax: 607-729-4820
A full line of supplies and equipment for science
and technology education.

D Hetherington

5766 Alfa Aesar

26 Parkridge Rd
Ward Hill, MA 01835
978-521-6300
800-343-0660
Fax: 978-521-6350
http://www.alfa.com
Laboratory equipment and supplies.

5767 American Chemical Society

1155 16th Street NW
Washington, DC 20036
202-872-4600
800-333-9511
Fax: 202-833-7732

E-mail: service@acs.org
http://www.@acs.org
Exhibits hands-on activities and programs for K-12 and college science curriculum.

Pat N. Confalone, Chair
Diane Grob Schmidt, President

768 Arbor Scientific
PO Box 2750
Ann Arbor, MI 48106-2750
734-477-9370
800-367-6695
Fax: 734-477-9373
E-mail: mail@arborsci.com
http://www.arborsci.com
Innovative products for Science Education.

56 pages Bi-Annual Catalog

Dave Barnes, Marketing Director

769 Astronomy to Go
1115 Melrose Avenue
Melrose Park, PA 19027-3017
215-831-0485
Fax: 215-831-0486
E-mail: astro2go@aol.com
http://www.astronomytogo.com
Programs include Starlab Planetarium presentations, hands-on demonstrations, slides and lecture shows and energy observing sessions with our many telescopses. We are funded through our traveling museum shop which carries a large assortment of t-shirts, jewelry, gifts, books, and teaching supplies as well as an extensive selection of meteorites.

Bob Summerfield, Director/ Founder

770 CEM Corporation
3100 Smith Farm Road
Matthews, NC 28104
704-821-7015
Fax: 704-821-7894
http://www.cem.com
Laboratory and scientific supplies, furniture, casework and equipment.

771 Carolina Biological Supply Company
2700 York Road
Burlington, NC 27215-3398
336-584-0381
800-334-5551
Fax: 800-222-7112
E-mail: carolina@carolina.com
http://www.carolina.com
Educational products for teachers and students of biology, molecular biology, biotechnology, chemistry, earth science, space science, physics, and mathematics. Carolina serves elementary schools through universities with living and preserved animals and plants, prepared microscope slides, microscopes, audiovisuals, books, charts, models, computer software, games, apparatus, and much more.

772 Challenger Center for Space Science Education
422 1st St. SE
3rd Floor
Washington, DC 20003
202-827-1580
800-969-5747
Fax: 703-683-7546
E-mail: mail@challenger.org
http://www.challenger.org
Is a global not-for-profit education organization created in 1986 by familes of the astronauts tragically lost during the last flight of the Challenger Space Shuttle. Dedicated to the educaltional spirit of that mission, Challenger center develops Learning Centers and othe educational programs worldwide to con-

tinue the mission to engage students in science and math education

Dr. Lance Bush, President/ CEO
Steven Goldberg, CFO

5773 ChronTrol Corporation
7525-D Mission Gorge Rd.
San Diego, CA 92120
619-282-8686
800-854-1999
Fax: 619-563-6563
E-mail: info@chrontrol.com
http://www.chrontrol.com
Scientific equipment, laboratory supplies and furniture.

5774 Classic Modular Systems
1911 Columbus Street
Two Rivers, WI 54241
414-793-2269
800-558-7625
Fax: 414-793-2896
E-mail: info@classicmodular.com
http://www.classicmodular.com
Laboratory equipment, shelving, cabinets and markerboards.

Cathy Albers, Advertising Manager

5775 Columbia University's Biosphere 2 Center
Highway 77 & Biosphere Road
Oracle, AZ 85623
520-838-6155
Fax: 520-838-6136
E-mail: info@email.arizona.edu
http://b2science.org
Educational programs and products.

Pierre Meystre, Director
Joaquin Ruiz, Director

5776 Connecticut Valley Biological Supply Company
82 Valley Road
PO Box 326
Southampton, MA 01073
413-527-4030
800-628-7748
Fax: 800-355-6813
E-mail: connval@ctvalleybio.com
http://www.connecticutvalleybiological.com
Cultures and specimens, instruments, equipment, hands-on kits, books, software, audio-visuals, models and charts for teaching botany, zoology, life science, anatomy, physiology, genetics, astronomy, entomology, microscopy, AP Biology, microbiology, horticulture, biotechnology, earth science, natural history and environmental science.

Marschall P. Lohr, Founder

5777 Crow Canyon Archaeological Center
23390 Road K
Cortez, CO 81321
970-565-8975
800-422-8975
Fax: 970-565-4859
E-mail: webmanager@crowcanyon.org
http://www.crowcanyon.org
Experiential education programs in archaeology and Native American history. Programs offered for school groups, teachers and other adults.

ISBN: 0-7872-6748-1

M Elaine Davis and Marjorie R Connelly, Author
W. Bruce Milne, Chair
Barbara L. Schwietert, Vice-Chairman

5778 Cuisenaire Company of America
10 Bank Street
#5026
White Plains, NY 10606-1933
914-997-2600
Fax: 914-684-6137
Science materials and equipment.

5779 DISCOVER Science Program
105 Terry Drive
Suite 120
Newtown, PA 18940-1872
800-448-3399
Fax: 215-579-8589
Features the newest developments in a wide range of science topics and provides an easy way for teachers to stay current and up-to-date in the world of science. The DISCOVER Program offers the DISCOVER magazine at the lowest possible price.

5780 Delta Biologicals
PO Box 26666
Tucson, AZ 85726-6666
520-790-7737
800-821-2502
Fax: 520-745-7888
E-mail: customerservice@deltabio.com
http://www.deltabio.com
Products and supplies for science and biology educators for over 30 years. Preserves specimens, laboratory furniture, microscopes, anatomy models, balances and scales, dissection supplies, lab safety supplies, multimedia, plant presses.

Lynn Hugins, Marketing
Darlene Harris, Customer Service Manager

5781 Delta Biologicals Catalog
PO Box 26666
Tucson, AZ 85726-6666
520-790-7737
800-821-2502
Fax: 520-745-7888
E-mail: customerservice@deltabio.com
http://www.deltabio.com

96 pages

Lynn Hugins, Marketing
Darlene Harris, Customer Service Manager

5782 Detecto Scale Corporation
203 E Daugherty Street
Webb City, MO 64870
417-673-4631
800-641-2008
Fax: 417-673-5001
E-mail: detecto@cardet.com
http://www.detectoscale.com
Scientific equipment and supplies for educational laboratories.

Johnathan Sabo, VP Marketing

5783 Dickson Company
930 S Westwood Avenue
Addison, IL 60101-4997
630-543-3747
800-757-3747
Fax: 800-676-0498
E-mail: dicksoncsr@dicksondata.com
http://www.dicksondata.com
Laboratory instruments, electronics, furniture and equipment.

Mike Unger, President
Mark Kohlmeier, CFO

5784 Donald K. Olson & Associates
PO Box 858
Bonsall, CA 92003-0858
Fax: 19-4 -
Mineral and fossil samples for educational purposes.

5785 Dranetz Technologies
1000 New Durham Road
Edison, NJ 08818-4019
732-287-3680
800-372-6832
Fax: 732-287-9014
http://www.dranetz.com
Laboratory instruments, equipment and supplies.

5786 Edmund Scientific - Scientifics Catalog
E726 Edscorp Building
Department 16A1
Barrington, NJ 08007
856-547-3488
Fax: 856-573-6295
Over 5,000 products including a wide selection of microscopes, telescopes, astronomy aids, fiber optic kits, demonstration optics, magnets and science discover products used in science fair projects.

Nancy McGonigle, President

5787 Educational Products
1342 N I35 E
Carrollton, TX 75006
972-245-9512
Fax: 972-245-5468
Science display boards, workshop materials and science fair accessories.

5788 Edwin H. Benz Company
73 Maplehurst Avenue
Providence, RI 02908
401-331-5650
Fax: 401-331-5685
E-mail: engineering@benztesters.com
http://www.benztesters.com
Laboratory equipment.

Ted Benz, President

5789 Electro-Steam Generator Corporation
50 Indel Ave.
PO Box 438
Rancocas, NJ 08073-0438
609-288-9071
866-617-0764
Fax: 609-288-9078
E-mail: jharline@electrostream.com
http://www.electrosteam.com
Laboratory equipment and supplies. Manufacture steam generators for sterilizers, autoclaves, clean rooms, pure steam humidification, laboratories, steam rooms, and cleaning of all kinds.

Jack Harlin, Sales/Marketing Associate

5790 Estes-Cox Corporation
PO Box 227
Penrose, CO 81240-0227
719-372-6565
800-820-0202
Fax: 719-372-3217
E-mail: webcs@centurims.com
http://www.esteseducator.com
Supplier of model rockets, engines and supporting videos, curriculums and educational publications for K-12.

Ann Grimm, Director Education

5791 FOTODYNE
950 Walnut Ridge Drive
Hartland, WI 53029
262-369-7000
800-362-3642
Fax: 262-369-7017
E-mail: info@fotodyne.com
http://www.fotodyne.com

Biotechnology curriculum equipment.
Brian Walsh, President & Owner
Dennis Devitt, Board Member

5792 First Step Systems
PO Box 2304
Jackson, TN 38302-2304
800-831-0877
Fax: 216-361-0829
Developed an effective, safe and less expensive approach to blood exposure safety for schools and classrooms that both help comply with OSHA requirements and is easy to purchase and resupply.

Susan Staples, Account Manager
Renee Carr, Bid Support

5793 Fisher Scientific Company
1410 Wayne Avenue
Indiana, PA 15701-3940
724-357-1000
Fax: 724-357-1019
A full line of laboratory and scientific supplies and equipment for educational institutions.

5794 Fisher Scientific/EMD
3970 John Creek Court
Suite 500
Suwanee, GA 30024
770-871-4500
800-766-7000
Fax: 800-926-1166
Supplier of chemistry, biology and physics laboratory supplies and equipment.

5795 Fisons Instruments
8 Forge Parkway
Franklin, MA 02038-3157
978-524-1000
Laboratory equipment and instruments for the scientific classroom.

5796 Flinn Scientific
PO Box 219
Batavia, IL 60510
630-879-6900
800-452-1261
Fax: 866-452-1436
E-mail: flinn@flinnsci.com
http://www.flinnsci.com
Laboratory safety supplies.

5797 Forestry Supplies
PO Box 8397
205 West Rankin St.
Jackson, MS 39284-8397
601-354-3565
800-647-5368
Fax: 800-543-4203
E-mail: fsi@forestry-suppliers.com
http://www.forestry-suppliers.com
Field and lab equipment for earth, life and environmental sciences.

Ken Peacock, VP Marketing
Debbie Raddin, Education Specialist

5798 Frank Schaffer Publications
23740 Hawthorne Boulevard
Torrance, CA 90505-5927
310-378-1133
800-421-5565
Fax: 800-837-7260
Charts, animal posters, floor puzzles, resource books and more.

5799 Frey Scientific
PO Box 300
Nashua, NH 03061-3000
800-225-3739
Fax: 800-226-3739
E-mail:

customercare.frey@schoolspeciality
http://www.freyscientific.com
Name brand scientific products including Energy Physics, Earth Science, Chemistry and Applied Science. Over 12,000 products and kits for grades 5-14 are available.

5800 Great Adventure Tours
1717 Old Topanga Canyon Road
Topanga, CA 90290-3934
800-642-3933
Educational science field trips and adventures.

5801 Guided Discoveries
PO Box 1360
Claremont, CA 91711
800-45 -423
Fax: 909-625-7305
E-mail: info@guideddiscoveries.org
http://guideddiscoveries.org
Outdoor educational science programs.

Ross Turner, President/ CEO/ Co-Founder
Kristi Turner, CFO/ Co-Founder

5802 HACH Company
PO Box 389
Loveland, CO 80539
970-669-3050
800-227-4224
Fax: 970-669-2932
http://www.hach.com
Water and soil test kits for field and laboratory work.

5803 Heathkit Educational Systems
455 Riverview Drive
Benton Harbor, MI 49022-5015
616-925-6000
800-253-0570
Fax: 616-925-3895
Electronics educational products from basic electricity to high-tech lasers and microscopes and beyond. Comprehensive line of different media to fit varied applications. Including Computer-Aided Instruction and Computer-Aided Troubleshooting services and Heathkit's PC Servicing, Troubleshooting and Networking courses.

Carolyn Feltner, Sales Coordinator
Patrick Beckett, Marketing Manager

5804 Holometrix
25 Wiggins Avenue
Bedford, MA 01730-2314
781-275-3300
Fax: 781-275-3705
Laboratory instruments.

5805 Howell Playground Equipment
3728 Salem Rd.
Enterprise, AL 36330
217-442-0482
800-239-1370
Fax: 334-347-9563
E-mail: howellequipment@aol.com
http://www.primestripe.com
Playground equipment and bicycle racks.

Nina Payne, President

5806 Hubbard Scientific
PO Box 2121
401 Hickory St.
Fort Collins, CO 80522
970-484-7445
800-289-9299
Fax: 970-484-1198
E-mail: custserv@amep.ceom
http://www.amep.com
Earth science and life science models, kits, globes and curriculum materials.

5807 Innova Corporation
115 George Lamb Road
Bernardston, MA 01337-9742

Science kits and globes.

08 Insect Lore
PO Box 1535
Shafter, CA 93263
661-746-6047
800-548-3284
Fax: 661-746-0334
E-mail: orders@insectlore.com
http://www.insectlore.com
Science and nature materials for preschool through grade 6. Raises butterflies, frogs, ladybugs and more. Features books, curriculum units, videos, puppet, posters, and other nature oriented products.

09 Insights Visual Productions
PO Box 230644
Encinitas, CA 92023-0644
800-942-0528
Laboratory instruments, manuals, and supplies.

10 Instron Corporation
100 Royall Street
Canton, MA 02021-1089
781-828-2500
Fax: 781-575-5776
http://www.instron.com
Laboratory and scientific equipment, supplies and furniture.

11 Johnsonite
16910 Munn Road
Chagrin Falls, OH 44023
440-543-8916
800-899-8916
Fax: 440-543-8920
E-mail: info@johnsonite.com
http://www.johnsonite.com/ContactUs.aspx
Physical education mats, matting and floors.

12 Justrite Manufacturing Company
2454 E Dempster Street
Suite 300
Des Plaines, IL 60016
847-298-9250
800-798-9250
Fax: 847-298-9261
E-mail: justrite@justritemfg.com
http://www.justritemfg.com
Supplies and equipment aimed at the scientific classroom or laboratory.

13 KLM Bioscientific
8888 Clairemont Mesa Boulevard
Suite D
San Diego, CA 92123-1137
858-571-5562
Fax: 858-571-5587
http://labsuppliesUSA.com
A mail order company that provides high quality, reasonably priced, on time living and preserved biological specimens. The Biology Store also carries a wide range of instructional materials including books, charts, models and videos. Also available is a wide range of general labware.

Loli Victorio, President

14 Ken-a-Vision Manufacturing Company
5615 Raytown Road
Kansas City, MO 64133-3388
816-353-4787
Fax: 816-358-5072
E-mail: info@ken-a-vision.com
http://www.ken-a-vision.com
Video Flex, Vison Viewer, Pupil CAM, Microscopes and Microrojectors

Steve Dunn, Domestic/International Op.
Ben Hoke, Sales Manger

5815 Kepro Circuit Systems
3640 Scarlet Oak Boulevard
Kirkwood, MO 63122-6606
800-325-3878
Fax: 636-861-9109
Laboratory equipment.

5816 Kewaunee Scientific Corporation
2700 W Front Street
Statesville, NC 28677
704-873-7202
800-824-6626
Fax: 704-873-5160
E-mail: humanresources@kewaunee.com
http://www.kewaunee.com
Science and laboratory supplies.

David M. Rausch, President & CEO
Elizabeth D. Phillips, VP, Human Resources

5817 Knex Education Catalog
Knex Education
2990 Bergey Road
PO Box 700
Hatfield, PA 19440-0700
888-KID-KNEX
E-mail: email@knex.com
http://www.knexeducation.com
Hands-on, award-winning curriculum supported K-12 math, science and technology sets.

Michael Araten, President

5818 Koffler Sales Company
785 Oakwood Road
Suite C-100
Lake Zurich, IL 60047-1524
847-438-1152
800-355-MATS
Fax: 847-438-1514
E-mail: info@kofflersales.com
http://www.kofflersales.com
Floor mats, Matting and stair treads.

Ron Starr, President
Pat Starr, CEO

5819 Komodo Dragon
PO Box 822
The Dalles, OR 97058-0822
541-773-5808
Museum-quality fossils and minerals.

5820 Kreonite
715 E 10th Street N
Wichita, KS 67214-2918
316-263-1111
Fax: 316-263-6829
Laboratory equipment, furniture and hardware.

5821 Kruger & Eckels
1406 E Wilshire Avenue
Santa Ana, CA 92705
714-547-5165
Fax: 714-547-2009
http://www.krugerandeckels.com
Laboratory and scientific instruments for institutional or educational use.

5822 LEGO Data
PO Box 1600
Enfield, CT 06083-1600
860-749-2291
Fax: 860-763-7477
Curriculum programs and materials for science education.

5823 LINX System
Science Source
PO Box 727
Waldoboro, ME 04572-0727
207-832-6344
800-299-5469

Fax: 207-832-7281
E-mail: info@thesciencesource.com
http://www.thesciencesource.com
A building system that integrates science, mathematics and technology at the K-9 level.

5824 Lab Safety Supply
PO Box 1368
401 S Wright Rd.
Janesville, WI 53547-1368
608-754-2345
800-356-0783
Fax: 608-754-1806
E-mail: custserv@labsafety.com
http://www.labsafety.com
Extensive variety of school products, including lab and safety apparel and floorcoverings.

5825 Lab Volt Systems
PO Box 686
Farmingdale, NJ 07727-0686
Educational materials and equipment for the science educator.

5826 Lab-Aids
17 Colt Court
Ronkonkoma, NY 11779
631-737-1133
800-381-8003
Fax: 631-737-1286
E-mail: mkt@lab-aids.com
http://www.lab-aids.com
Science kits, published curriculum materials.

John Weatherby, Sales/Marketing Director
David M Frank, President

5827 Labconco Corporation
8811 Prospect Avenue
Kansas City, MO 64132-2696
816-333-8811
800-821-5525
Fax: 816-363-0130
E-mail: labconco@labconco.com
http://www.labconco.com
Laboratory equipment and supplies.

Mark Schmitz, VP, Research & Engineering

5828 Lakeside Manufacturing
1977 S Allis Street
Milwaukee, WI 53207-1295
414-481-3900
Fax: 414-481-9313
Laboratory and scientific instruments, equipment, furniture and supplies.

5829 Lane Science Equipment Company
225 W 34th Street
Suite 1412
New York, NY 10122-1496
212-563-0663
Fax: 212-465-9440
Scientific equipment, technology and supplies.

5830 Lasy USA
1309 Webster Avenue
Fort Collins, CO 80524-2756
800-444-2126
Fax: 970-221-4352
Building sets that encourage children to encounter technology through problem solving activities, planning, co-operation and perseverance. Allows students to build and learn programming skills in areas of communication, construction, manufacturing and transportation.

Dave Nayak

5831 Learning Technologies
40 Cameron Avenue
Somerville, MA 02144-2404

617-628-1459
800-537-8703
Fax: 617-628-8606
E-mail: starlab@starlab.com
http://www.starlab.com
STARLAB portable planetarium systems and the Project STAR hands-on science materials.

Jane Sadler, President

5832 Leica Microsystems EAD
PO Box 123
Buffalo, NY 14240-0123
716-686-3000
Fax: 716-686-3085
Educational microscopes for elementary through university applications.

5833 Life Technologies
7335 Executive Way
Frederick, MD 21704
240-379-4328
800-952-9166
Fax: 716-774-6727
http://learnlifetechnologies.com
Supplier of biology and cell culture products.

5834 Lyon Electric Company
1690 Brandywine Avenue
Chula Vista, CA 91911
619-216-3400
Fax: 619-216-3434
E-mail: lyonelec@acts.com
http://www.lyonelectric.com
Electrical tabletop incubators for science classrooms and tabletop animal intensive care units, hatchers and brooders.

Caroline Vazquez, Sales Manager
Jose Madrigal, Marketing Manager

5835 Magnet Source
747 S Gilbert Street
Castle Rock, CO 80104
303-688-3966
888-525-3536
Fax: 303-688-5303
E-mail: magnet@magnetsource.com
http://www.magnetsource.com
Educational magnetic products and magnetic toys designed to stimulate creativity and encourage exploration of science with fun magnets. Kits include experiments, fun games, activities and powerful magnets. Moo Magnets, rare earth magnets, horseshoes, and bulk magnets.

Jim Madsen, Sales Manager

5836 Meiji Techno America
Meiji Techno America
5895 Rue Ferrari
San Jose, CA 95138
408-226-3454
800-832-0060
Fax: 408-226-0900
E-mail: info@meijitechno.com
http://www.meijitechno.com
A full line of elementary, secondary, grade school and college-level microscopes and accessories.

James J Dutkiewicz, General Manager

5837 Metrologic Instruments
Coles Road at Route 42
Blackwood, NJ 08012
800-436-3876
Fax: 856-228-0653
Manufactures low-power lasers and laser accessories for the classroom, a range of helium-neon lasers, a modulated VLD laser, optics lab, sandbox holography kit, speed of light lab, optics bench system and digital laser power meter, as well as a selec-

tion of pin carriers, mounting pins, lenses and mirrors. Sponsors the Physics Bowl, a yearly national physics competition for high school students by the American Association of Physics Teachers.

Betty Williams

5838 Modern School Supplies
PO Box 958
Hartford, CT 06143
860-243-2329
Fax: 800-934-7206
E-mail: sales@modernss.com
http://www.modernss.com
Products for hands-on science education.

5839 Mohon International
1600 Porter Court
Paris, TN 38242
731-642-4251
Fax: 731-642-4262
Classroom equipment and supplies, directed at the scientific classroom and laboratory.

5840 Museum Products Company
84 Route 27
Mystic, CT 06355-1226
860-536-6433
800-395-5400
Fax: 860-572-9589
E-mail: museumprod@aol.com
http://www.museumproducts.net
Field guides, rock collections, environmental puzzles, posters, charts, books, magnets, magnifiers, microscopes and other lab equipment. Also weather simulators, physics demonstration, games, toys in space, animal track replicas and fossils. Free catalog.

John Bannister, President

5841 Nalge Company
PO Box 20365
Rochester, NY 14602-0365
585-586-8800
800-625-4327
Fax: 585-586-8987
Plastic labware and safety products for the scientific classroom.

5842 National Instruments
6504 Bridge Point Parkway
Austin, TX 78730-5039
512-794-0100
Fax: 512-683-5794
Laboratory/scientific instruments.

5843 National Optical & Scientific Instruments
6508 Tri-County Pkwy.
Schertz, TX 78154
210-590-7010
800-275-3716
Fax: 210-590-1104
E-mail: natlopt@sbcglobal.net
http://www.nationaloptical.com
Wholesale distributor of national comppound, stero and digital miocroscopes for K-12 and college.

Michael Hart, Sales Manager
Cynthia Syverson-Mercer, Director

5844 Ohaus Corporation
19-A Chapin Road
Pine Brook, NJ 07058
973-377-9000
800-672-7722
Fax: 973-593-0359
http://www.distribuidoramuller.com.ar/eq
uipos/ohaus/traveler.pdf
Scientific supplies and equipment for the classroom or laboratory.

5845 PASCO Scientific
10101 Foothills Boulevard
Roseville, CA 95747-7100
916-786-3800
800-772-8700
Fax: 916-786-7565
E-mail: jbrown@pasco.com
http://ww.pasco.com
US manufacturers of physics apparatus and probe warer that enable teachers to improve science literacy and meet the standards

Justine Brown, Copy Writer

5846 Quest Aerospace Education
350 E 18th Street
Yuma, AZ 85364
602-595-9506
Fax: 520-783-9534
A complete line of model rockets and related teaching materials.

5847 Resources for Teaching Elementary School Science
National Academy Press
Arts & Industries Bldg Room 1201
900 Jefferson Drive SW
Washington, DC 20560-0403
202-287-2063
Fax: 202-287-2070
E-mail: outreach@nas.edu
http://www.si.edu
Resource guides for elementary, middle school, and high school science teachers. Annotated guides to hands-on, inquiry-centered curriculum materials and sources of help in teaching science from kindergarten through sixth grades. Produced by the National Science Resources Center.

National Science Resources Center, Author
Douglas Lapp, Executive Director

5848 Rheometrics
1 Possumtown Road
Piscataway, NJ 08854-2100
732-560-8550
Laboratory/science supplies and equipment.

5849 SARUT
107 Horatio Street
New York, NY 10014-1569
212-691-9453
http://fair.mingluji.com/SARUT_INC
Science and nature-related educational tools.

5850 Safe-T-Rack Systems
4325 Dominguez Road
Suite A
Rocklin, CA 95677
916-632-1121
Fax: 916-632-1173
http://www.safe-t-racksystems.com
Laboratory furniture, safety storage containers and equipment.

5851 Sargent-Welch Scientific Company
PO Box 92912
Rochester, NY 14692-9012
847-459-6625
800-727-4368
Fax: 800-676-2540
http://www.sargentwelch.com
Models, books and instruments for the scientific classroom.

5852 Science Instruments Company
6122 Reisterstown Road
Baltimore, MD 21215-3423
410-358-7810
Develops, manufactures and markets unique hands-on programs in biotechnology, biomedical instrumentation, telecommunications, electronics and industrial controls.

5853 Science Source
86475 Gene Lasserre Blvd.
Yulee, FL 32097
904-225-5558
800-875-3214
Fax: 904-225-2228
E-mail: info@sciencefirst.com
http://www.thesciencesource.com
Design technology books, teacher resource
and student books on design and technology,
design technology materials, equipment and
supplies used in the construction of design
challenges.

Michelle Winter, Sales/Marketing Support
Rudolf Graf, President

5854 Science for Today & Tomorrow
1840 E 12th Street
Mishawaka, IN 46544
574-258-5397
Fax: 574-258-5594
Hands-on science activities packaged for K-3
students.

**5855 Scientific Laser Connection,
Incorporated**
5021 N 55th Avenue
Suite 10
Glendale, AZ 85301-7535
623-939-6711
877-668-7844
Fax: 623-939-3369
E-mail: sales@slclaser.com
http://www.slclasers.com
Laser education modules.

Don Morris, President
Travis Gatrin, Service

5856 Shain/Shop-Bilt
509 Hemlock Street
Philipsburg, PA 16866-2937
814-342-2820
Fax: 814-342-6180
Laboratory casework and cabinets.

5857 Sheldon Lab Systems
PO Box 836
Crystal Springs, MS 39059-0836
601-892-2731
Fax: 601-892-4364
Laboratory casework and technical equip-
ment for K-12, college and university level.

5858 Skilcraft
CRAFT House Corporation
328 N Westwood Avenue
Toledo, OH 43607-3317
419-537-9090
Fax: 419-537-9160
Microchemistry sets.

5859 Skullduggery Kits
624 S B Street
Tustin, CA 92780-4318
800-336-7745
Fax: 714-832-1215
Social studies kits offers hands-on learning,
art projects, complete lesson plans, authentic
replicas, and challenging products designed
for small groups of students with increasing
levels of difficulty.

5860 Skulls Unlimited International
10313 S Sunnylane
Oklahoma City, OK 73160
405-794-9300
800-659-SKUL
Fax: 405-794-6985
E-mail: sales@skullsunlimited.com
http://www.skullsunlimited.com
Leading supplier of specimen supplies to the
educational community.

Jay Villemarette, President

5861 Society of Automotive Engineers
400 Commonwealth Drive
Warrendale, PA 15086-7511
724-776-4841
877-606-7323
Fax: 724-776-5760
E-mail: info@sae.org
http://www.sae.org
Award-winning science unit for grades 4-6.

Jamie Ferguson, Development Officer
Lori Gatmaitan, Director

**5862 Southern Precision Instruments
Company**
3419 E Commerce Street
San Antonio, TX 78220-1322
210-212-5055
800-417-5055
Fax: 210-212-5062
E-mail: spico@flash.net
http://www.flash.net/spico
Microscopes and microprojectors for grades
K-1-K-12 and college levels. Stereo and compound microscopes, along with CCTV color
systems.

Victor Spiroff, VP/General Manager

5863 Southland Instruments
17741 Metzler Lane
Unit A
Huntington Beach, CA 92647-6246
714-847-5007
Fax: 714-893-3613
Microscopes.

5864 Spectronics Corporation
956 Brush Hollow Road
Westbury, NY 11590
516-333-4840
800-274-8888
Fax: 800-491-6868
E-mail: info@spectroline.com
http://www.spectroline.com
Laboratory and scientific classroom equipment, hardware and shelving.

Gloria Blusk, Manager Customer Service
Vincent McKenna, Publicist

5865 Spitz
700 Brandywine Drive
Chadds Ford, PA 19317
610-459-5200
Fax: 610-459-3830
E-mail: spitz@spitzinc.com
http://www.spitzinc.com
Offers scientific and laboratory instruments
and accessories.

Jon Shaw, President/ CEO
Paul Dailey, CFO

5866 Swift Instruments
1190 N 4th Street
San Jose, CA 95112-4946
408-293-2380
Educational microscopes and other laboratory instruments.

5867 TEDCO
498 S Washington Street
Hagerstown, IN 47346-1596
765-489-4527
800-654-6357
Fax: 765-489-5752
E-mail: sales@tedcotoys.com
http://www.tedcotoys.com
Bill Nye Extreme Gyro, Prisms, Educational
Toys Solar Science Kit.

Raplh Teetor, Founder
Marjorie Teetor, Owner

5868 Telaire Systems
6489 Calle Real
Goleta, CA 93117-1538
805-964-1699
Fax: 805-964-2129
Laboratory instruments and hardware.

5869 Tooltron Industries
103 Parkway
Boerne, TX 78006
830-249-8277
800-293-8134
Fax: 830-755-8134
E-mail: easykut@gvtc.com
http://www.tooltron.com
Scientific hardware and laboratory equipment, including instruments and accessories.
School scissors and craft supplies.

Thomas Love, Owner/VP Marketing

5870 Triops
PO Box 11369
Pensacola, FL 32524
850-479-4415
800-200-3466
Fax: 850-479-3315
E-mail: triopsinc@aol.com
http://www.triops.com
Classroom activities and kits in environmen-
tal, ecological and biological sciences.

Dr. Eugene Hull, President
Peter Bender, Office Manager

5871 Trippense Planetarium Company
Science First
86475 Gene Lasserre Blvd.
Yulee, FL 32097
904-225-5558
800-875-3214
Fax: 904-225-2228
E-mail: info@sciencefirst.com
http://www.sciencefirst.com
Astronomy and earth science models and ma-
terials, including the Trippense planetarium,
Elementary planetarium, Copernican and
Ptolemic solar systems, Milky Way model,
Explore Celestial Globes and the patented top
quality educational astronomy models since
1905.

Kris Spors, Customer Service Manager
Nancy Bell, President

5872 Unilab
967 Mabury Road
San Jose, CA 95133
800-288-9850
Fax: 408-975-1035
E-mail: unilab@richnet.net
http://www.unilabinc.com
Designs and manufactures products for
teaching science and technology.

Gerald A Beer, VP

5873 Vibrac Corporation
16 Columbia Drive
PO Box 840
Amherst, NH 03031
603-882-6777
Fax: 603-886-3857
E-mail: vibrac@concentric.net
http://www.vibrac.com
Scientific instruments and hardware.

5874 Wild Goose Company
5181 S 300 W
Murray, UT 84107-4709
801-466-1172
Hands-on science kits for elementary-aged
students 3 and up and resource books for all
levels of general science.

5875 Wildlife Supply Company
86475 Gene Lasserre Blvd.
Yulee, FL 32097
904-225-9889
800-799-8115
Fax: 904-225-2228
E-mail: goto@wildco.com
http://www.wildco.com
Aquatic sampling equipment including Fieldmaster Field Kits, Water Bottle Kits, Secchi Disks, line and messengers and a NEW Mini Ponar bottom grab. Also, a variety of professional Wildco bottom grabs, water bottles, plankton nets, hand corers and other materials.

Aaron Bell, Product Manager
Bruce Izard, Customer Service Manager

5876 WoodKrafter Kits
PO Box 808
Yarmouth, ME 04096-0808
207-846-3722
Fax: 207-846-1019
Science kits, hands-on curriculum-based science kits for ages 4 and up, classroom packs, supplies and science materials also available.

Sports & Playground Equipment

5877 American Playground Corporation
6406 Production Drive
Anderson, IN 46013-9408
765-642-0288
800-541-1602
Fax: 765-649-7162
E-mail: sales@american-playgroud.com
http://www.american-playground.com
Playground equipment and supplies.

Julie Morson, Inside Sales Manager
Marty Bloyd, General Manager

5878 American Swing Products
9120 Double Diamond Parkway #1062
Reno, NV 89521
800-433-2573
800-433-2573
Fax: 775-883-2384
E-mail: play@americanswing.com
http://www.americanswing.com
Replacement playground parts, including commercial and residential swing sets, swing hangers for pipes and wood beams, spring animals, S-hooks, spring connectors, and more.

Susan Watson, President

5879 BCI Burke Company
660 Van Dyne Road
PO Box 549
Fond Du Lac, WI 54936-0549
920-921-9220
800-266-1250
Fax: 920-921-9566
E-mail: pr@bciburke.com
http://www.bciburke.com
Playground equipment.

5880 Belson Manufacturing
111 N River Road
North Aurora, IL 60542-1396
800-323-5664
Playground equipment.

5881 Colorado Time Systems
1551 E 11th Street
Loveland, CO 80537
970-667-1000
800-279-0111
Fax: 970-667-5876
E-mail: sales@coloradotimes.com
http://www.coloradotime.com
Been the system of choice for sports timing and scoring. Has a timing system for almost every sport including swimming, basketball, football, baseball, track, soccer and most others. Has a wide variety of displays ranging from fixed digit scoreboards to animation LED boards to fullcolor video displays and ribbon boards.

Randy Flint, Sr Sales Representative
Rick Connell, CDS Sales Manager

5882 Constructive Playthings
Action For Children
1227 E 119th Street
Grandview, MO 64030-1178
312-823-1100
http://www.actforchildren.org/
Playground, recreational and indoor fun equipment for children grades PreK-3.

5883 Creative Outdoor Designs
142 Pond Drive
Lexington, SC 29073-8009
803-957-9259
Fax: 803-957-7152
Playground equipment.

5884 Curtis Marketing Corporation
2550 Rigel Road
Venice, FL 34293-3200
941-493-8085
Playground equipment.

5885 GameTime
150 PlayCore Dr. SE
Fort Payne, AL 35967
256-845-5610
800-235-2440
Fax: 256-845-9361
E-mail: info@gametime.com
http://www.gametime.com
Playground equipment.

Doris Dellinger, Marketing Service Manager

5886 Gared Sports
9200 East 146th St.
Bldg. A
Noblesville, IN 46060
317-774-9840
800-325-2682
Fax: 314-421-6014
E-mail: laura@garedsports.com
http://www.garedsports.com
Basketball, Volleyball, Soccer, Equipment and training aids for indoor and outdoor facilities.

Laura St George, Sales/Marketing Manager

5887 Gerstung/Gym-Thing
6308 Blair Hill Lane
Baltimore, MD 21209-2102
800-922-3575
Physical education mats, matting and floorcoverings.

5888 Grounds for Play
1050 Columbia Dr.
Carrollton, GA 30117
817-477-5482
800-552-7529
Fax: 817-477-1140
E-mail: jimdempsey@groundsforplay.com
http://www.groundsforplay.com
Playground equipment, flooring, floorcoverings, play eviroment design,
lanscape architecure, insatllation, and safety insepection.

Jim Dempsey, Senior VP
Emily Smith, Office Manager

5889 Iron Mountain Forge
One Iron Mountain Drive
Farmington, MO 63640
800-325-8828
Fax: 573-760-7441
Playground equipment.

5890 JCH International
978 E Hermitage Road NE
Rome, GA 30161-9641
800-328-9203
Coverings, mats and physical education matting.

5891 Jaypro
Jaypro Sports
976 Hartford Tpke
Waterford, CT 06385
860-447-3001
800-243-0533
Fax: 860-444-1779
E-mail: info@jaypro.com
http://www.jaypro.com
Sports equipment.

Linda Andels, Marketing Manager
Bill Wild, VP Sales/Marketing

5892 Kidstuff Playsystems
5400 Miller Avenue
Gary, IN 46403-2844
800-255-0153
Fax: 219-938-3340
E-mail: rhagelberg@kidstuffplaysystems.com
http://www.fun-zone.com
Preschool and grade school playground equipment, Health Trek Fitness Course, park site furnishings.

Dick Hagelberg, CEO

5893 Kompan
7717 New Market Street
Olympia, WA 98501
360-943-6374
800-426-9788
Fax: 360-943-5575
http://www.kompan.com
Unique playgrond equipment.

Tom Grover, Marketing Director

5894 LA Steelcraft Products
1975 Lincoln Avenue
Pasadena, CA 91103
626-798-7401
800-371-2438
Fax: 626-798-1482
E-mail: info@lasteelcraft.com
http://www.lasteelcraft.com
Manufacturer of quality athletic, park and playground equipment for schools, parks and industry. Features indoor/outdoor fiberglass furniture, court and field equipment, site furnishings, bike racks, flagpoles, baseball and basketball backstops.

James D Holt, President
John C Gaudesi, COO

5895 Landscape Structures
PO Box 198
601 7th St.
Delano, MN 55328-0198
763-972-3391
888-4FU-LSI
Fax: 763-972-3185
http://www.playlsi.com
Playground equipment.

Bill Jannott, Board Member
Rick Jannott, Board Member

96 MMI-Federal Marketing Service
PO Box 241367
Montgomery, AL 36124-1367
334-286-0700
Fax: 334-286-0711
Playground equipment, sports timers, clocks and school supplies.

97 Matworks
Division of Janitex Rug Service Corporation
11900 Old Baltimore Pike
Beltsville, MD 20705-1265
800-523-5179
Fax: 301-595-0740
E-mail: info@thematworks.com
http://www.thematworks.com
Mats, matting and floorcoverings for entrances, gymnasiums, and all other facilities where the potential for slip and fall exists.

Robert Burman, Chairman
Robert B. Collins, CEO and President

98 Miracle Recreation Equipment Company
878 E Highway 60
PO Box 420
Monett, MO 65708-0420
417-235-6917
888-458-2752
Fax: 417-235-6816
http://www.miracle-recreation.com
Playground and recreation equipment.

99 National Teaching Aids
401 Hickory Street
PO Box 2121
Fort Collins, CO 80522
970-484-7445
800-289-9299
Fax: 970-484-1198
E-mail: bevans@amep.com
http://www.amep.com
Learning math, alphabet, and geography skills is easy with our Clever Catch Balls. These colorful 24-inch inflatable vinyl balls provide an excellent way for children to practice math, alphabet and geography skills. Excellent learning tool in organized classroom activities, on the playground, or at home.

Michael Warring, President
Candace Coffman, National Sales Manger

00 New Braunfels General Store International
3150 Interstate H 35 S
New Braunfels, TX 78130-7927
830-620-4000
Fax: 830-620-0598
Playground equipment, supplies and classroom supplies.

01 Outback Play Centers
1280 W Main Street
Sun Prairie, WI 53590-0010
608-825-2140
800-338-0522
Fax: 608-825-2114
http://www.outbackplaycenters.com
Playground equipment.

Jack Garczynskl, President

02 Playground Environments
22 Old Country Road
PO Box 578
Quogue, NY 11959
516-653-5465
800-662-0922
Fax: 516-653-2933
E-mail: peplay@mindspring.com
http://www.ncsu.edu/project/design-project s/sites/cud/content/Lands
Designs and manufactures integrated play and recreational areas for children, providing

them with new experiences in a safe, accessible, educationally supportive and fun environment.

Suzanne Crocitto, Contact
Claire Dudley, Ass. Landscape Architect

5903 Playnix
5370 Broadway
Denver, CO 80216-3731
303-868-9916
Fax: 303-781-6749
E-mail: JDelmore10@gmail.com
http://www.playnix.com
Wood products and playground equipment.

5904 Playworld Systems
1000 Buffalo Road
Lewisburg, PA 17837-9795
570-522-9800
800-233-8404
Fax: 570-522-3030
E-mail: info@PlayworldSystems.com
http://www.playworldsystems.com
Playground and recreational equipment.

Mathew M. Miller, Chief Executive Officer

5905 Porter Athletic Equipment Company
Porter Athletic Equipment Company
601 Mercury Drive
Champaign, IL 61822-9648
217-367-8438
800-637-3090
Fax: 217-367-8440
E-mail: porter@porter-ath.com
http://www.porterathletic.com
Athletic equipment, floorcoverings, mats and supplies.

Dan Morgan, VP Sales/Marketing

5906 Quality Industries
130 Jones Boulevardÿ
PO Box 765
La Vergne, TN 37086-0765
800-745-8613
Fax: 615-793-2347
E-mail: sales@qualityind.com
http://www.qualityind.com
Recycled plastic park and playground equipment.

5907 Real ACT Prep Guide
Peterson's, A Nelnet Company
Princeton Pike Corporate Center
2000 Lenox Drive PO Box 67005
Lawrenceville, NJ 08648
609-896-1800
800-338-3282
Fax: 609-896-4531
Familiarizes students with the test's format, reviews skills, and provides the all-important practice that helps build confidence.

621 pages
ISBN: 0-768919-75-4

Elaine Bender, Mark Weinfeld, et al., Author

5908 Recreation Creations
PO Box 955
Hillsdale, MI 49242-0955
517-439-0300
800-888-0977
Fax: 517-439-0303
http://rec-creations.com
Heavy duty park and playground equipment for school and public use. Equipment is both colorful and safe.

DC Shaneour

5909 Roppe Corporation
1602 N Union Street
Fostoria, OH 44830-1158

419-435-8546
800-537-9527
Fax: 419-435-1056
E-mail: sales@roppe.com
http://www.roppe.com
Floorcoverings, mats and matting.

5910 Safety Play
10460 Roosevelt Boulevard
#295
St Petersburgh, FL 33716-3818
727-522-0061
888-878-0244
Fax: 727-522-0061
E-mail: safetyplay@mindspring.com
http://www.safetyplay.net
Playground and recreational accident consultants. Experienced in inspections, design, expert witness. Creators of Playground Safety Signs as required to be on the playground.

Scott Burmon, Contact

5911 Sport Court
5445 W Harold Gatty Dr.
Salt Lake City, UT 84116-1504
801-972-0260
800-421-8112
Fax: 801-401-3504
E-mail: info@sportcourt.com
http://www.sportcourt.com
Sport flooring, portable flooring, outdoor-indoor educational institutions.

Finnika Lundmark, Director Marketing

5912 Sport Floors
6651 Reese Road
PO Box 1478
Memphis, TN 38133-1478
901-452-9492
800-881-6440
Fax: 901-452-9250
http://www.sportsfloorsinc.com
Sport floors, flooring, floorcoverings, mats and matting.

5913 Sportmaster
6031 Broad Street Mall
Pittsburgh, PA 15206-3009
412-243-5100
Fax: 412-731-3052
Playground equipment, sports timers and clocks.

5914 Stackhouse Athletic Equipment Company
1450 McDonald St NE
Salem, OR 97301-6949
503-363-1840
800-285-3640
Fax: 503-363-0511
E-mail: bob@stackhouseathletic.com
http://www.stackhouseathletic.com
Volleyball, soccer, football and baseball hardgoods.

Greg Henshaw, VP Marketing

5915 Swedes Systems - HAGS Play USA
2180 Stratingham Drive
Dublin, OH 43016-8907
Fax: 614-889-9026
Playground safety consultants.

5916 Ultra Play Systems
Parek Stuff
1675 Locust Streetÿ
Red Bud, IL 62278-1000
800-458-5872
http://www.ultraplay.com
Playground and recreational equipment.

5917 Wausau Tile
PO Box 1520
Wausau, WI 54402-1520

715-359-3121
800-388-8728
Fax: 715-355-4627
E-mail: wtile@wausautile.com
http://www.wausautile.com
Playground and recreation equipment.

Rob Geurink, Furnishings Division
Manager

5918 Wear Proof Mat Company
2156 W Fulton Street
Chicago, IL 60612-2392
312-733-4570
Fax: 800-322-7105
http://www.notracks.com
Mats, matting and floorcoverings for the
physical education class.

5919 Wolverine Sports
745 State Circle
Ann Arbor, MI 48108-1647
734-761-5690
800-521-2832
Fax: 800-654-4321
http://www.wolverinesports.com
Playground, sports and physical fitness
furniture and equipment.

General

5920 A-V Online
National Information Center for
Educational Media
4725 Indian School Road NE
Suite 100
Albuquerque, NM 87198-8640
505-265-3591
800-926-8328
Fax: 505-256-1080
E-mail: info-request@nicem.com
http://www.nicem.com
A CD-ROM that contains over 400,000 ci-
tations with abstracts, to non-print educa-
tional materials for all educational levels.
It is available on an annual subscription ba-
sis and comes with semiannual updates.

Lisa Savard, Marketing and Sales

5921 AASA Daily News
American Association of School
Administrators
1615 Duke Street
Suite 700
Alexandria, VA 22314-1730
703-528-0700
Fax: 703-841-1543
E-mail: info@aasa.org
http://www.aasa.org

Daniel A. Domenech, Executive Director
Sharon Adams-Taylor, Associate
Executive Director

5922 ACT
2201 N Dodge Street
PO Box 168
Iowa City, IA 52243-0168
319-337-1000
Fax: 319-339-3021
http://www.act.org
Help individuals and organizations make
informed decisions about education and
work.

Jon L. Erickson, President
Jon Whitmore, Chief Executive Officer

5923 AMX Corporation
3000 Research Drive
Richardson, TX 75243-5481
469-624-7400
800-222-0193

Fax: 972-624-7153
http://www.amx.com
Multiple products, equipment and supplies.

Rashid Skaf, President

5924 ASC Electronics
2 Kees Pl
Merrick, NY 11566-3625
516-623-3206
Fax: 516-378-2672
High tech multimedia system. Completely
software driven, featuring interactive
video, audio and data student drills. Novell
network. System includes CD-ROM,
laserdisc and digital voice card technology.

5925 Accelerated Math
Renaissance Learning
2911 Peach Street
PO Box 8036
Wisconsin Rapids, WI 54495-8036
715-424-3636
800-338-4204
Fax: 715-424-4242
E-mail: answers@renaissance.com
http://www.renaissance.com
Math management software that helps
teachers increase student math achievement in grades 1 through calculus.

John J. Lynch, Chief Executive Officer
Mary T. Minch, EVP, Finance & CFO

5926 Accelerated Reader
Renaissance Learning
2911 Peach Street
PO Box 8036
Wisconsin Rapids, WI 54495-8036
715-424-3636
800-338-4204
Fax: 715-424-4242
E-mail: answers@renaissance.com
http://www.renaissance.com
Software program that helps teachers man-
age literature-based reading.

John J. Lynch, Chief Executive Officer
Mary T. Minch, EVP, Finance & CFO

5927 Actrix Systems
6315 San Ignacio Avenue
San Jose, CA 95119-1202
800-422-8749
Fax: 509-744-2851
Computer networks.

5928 Allen Communications
5 Triac Center
5th Floor
Salt Lake Cty, UT 84180
801-537-7800
Fax: 801-537-7805
Software.

5929 Alltech Electronics Company
602 Garrison Street
Oceanside, CA 92054-4865
760-721-0093
Fax: 760-732-1460
Computer hardware.

5930 Anchor Pad Products
Anchor Pad Products
11105 Dana Circle
Cypress, CA 90630-5133
714-799-4071
800-626-2467
Fax: 714-799-4094
E-mail: kris@anchor.com
http://www.anchorpad.com

Cost effective physical security systems for computers, computer peripherals and office
equipment.

Kris Jones, Marketing Associate
Melanie Rustle, Marketing Associate

5931 Apple Computer
1 Infinite Loop
Cupertino, CA 95014-2084
408-996-1010
800-692-7753
Fax: 408-974-2786
http://www.apple.com
Offers a wide selection of software systems and
programs for the student, educator, professional
and classroom use. Program areas include reading, science, social studies, history, language arts,
mathematics and more.

Tim Cook, CEO
Angela Ahrendts, Senior Vice Presidentÿ

5932 Ascom Timeplex
400 Chestnut Ridge Road
Woodcliff Lake, NJ 07675-7604
201-646-1571
Fax: 201-646-0485
Computer networks.

5933 BGS Systems
128 Technology Drive
Waltham, MA 02453-8909
617-891-0000
Facility planning and evaluation software.

5934 BLS Tutorsystems
5153 W Woodmill Drive
Wilmington, DE 19808-4067
800-545-7766
Computer software.

5935 Broderbund Software
500 Redwood Boulevard
Novato, CA 94947-6921
319-395-9626
800-223-8941
Fax: 319-395-7449
Educational software.

5936 Bulletin Boards for Busy Teachers

http://www.geocities.com/VisionTeacherwv/
Bulletin board tips and education links.

5937 CASL Software
6818 86th Street E
Puyallup, WA 98371-6450
206-845-7738
Educational software for schools and institutions
in all areas of interest.

5938 CCU Software
PO Box 6724
Charleston, WV 25362-0724
800-843-5576
Fax: 800-321-4297
Educational software.

5939 CCV Software
5602 36th Street S
Fargo, ND 58104-6768
800-541-6078
Fax: 800-457-6953
All varieties of software and hardware for the educational fields of interest including language arts,
math, social studies, science, history and more.

5940 Cambridge Development Laboratory
86 West Street
Waltham, MA 02451-1110
781-890-4640
800-637-0047
Fax: 781-890-2894
E-mail: customerservice@edumatch.com
http://www.edumatch.com

Meets all educational software needs in language arts, mathematics, science, social studies early learning and special education.

5941 Chariot Software Group
2645 Financial Court
Suite 1
San Diego, CA 92117-3002
858-270-0202
800-242-7468
Fax: 858-270-2027
E-mail: info@chariot.com
http://www.chariot.com
Academic software.

5942 Child's Play Software
5785 Emporium Square
Columbus, OH 43231-2802
614-833-1836
Fax: 614-833-1837
Markets learning games and creative software to schools.

5943 Claris Corporation
5201 Patrick Henry Drive
Santa Clara, CA 95054-1171
800-747-7483
Educational software.

5944 Classroom Direct
20200 E 9 Mile Road
Saint Clair Shores, MI 48080-1791
800-777-3642
Fax: 800-628-6250
Full line of hardware and software for Mac, IBM and Apple II at discount prices.

5945 College Board/SAT
45 Columbus Avenue
New York, NY 10023-6992
217-713-8000
877-999-7723
Fax: 646-607-2881
E-mail: SpringBoard@collegeboard.org
http://www.collegeboard.org
David Coleman, President and CEO
Jeremy Singer, Chief Operating Officer

5946 Computer City Direct
2000 Two Tandy Center
Fort Worth, TX 76102
800-538-0586
Hardware.

5947 Computer Friends
10200 SW Eastridge Street
Portland, OR 97225
800-547-3303
Fax: 503-643-5379
E-mail: cfi@cfriends.com
http://www.cfriends.com
Computer hardware, software and networks, printer support products.
Jimmy Moglia, Marketing Director

5948 Data Command
PO Box 548
Kankakee, IL 60901-0548
800-528-7390
Educational software.

5949 Davidson & Associates
19840 Pioneer Avenue
Torrance, CA 90503-1690
800-545-7677
Educational software and systems.

5950 Dell Computer Corporation
9595 Arboretum Boulevard
Austin, TX 78759-6337
512-338-4400
800-388-1450
Hardware.

5951 Digital Divide Network
19 Duncan Street
Suite 505
Toronto, ON
416-977-9363
Fax: 416-352-1898
http://www.digitaldivide.net
Knowledge to help everyone succeed in the digital age.
Adam Clare, Lead Editor
Kristen Jordan, Project Coordinator

5952 Digital Equipment Corporation
Educational Computer Systems Group
2 Iron Way
Marlboro, MA 01752
Computer hardware and networks.

5953 Don Johnston Developmental Equipment
26799 West Commerce Drive
Suite 115
Volo, IL 60073-1190
847-740-0749
800-999-4660
Fax: 847-740-7326
E-mail: info@donjohnston.com
http://donjohnston.com
Develops educational software for special needs. Products include the Ukandu Series for emergent literacy, LD, ESL, students Co-Writer and Write: OutLoud.

5954 Edmark Corporation
6727 185th Avenue NE
PO Box 97021
Redmond, WA 98052-5037
425-556-8400
800-691-2986
Fax: 425-556-8430
Markets educational software.

5955 EduQuest, An IBM Company
PO Box 2150
Atlanta, GA 30301-2150
Offers exciting educational software in various fields of interest including history, social studies, reading, math and language arts, as well as computers.

5956 Educational Activities
1937 Grand Avenue
P.O. Box 87
Baldwin, NY 11510-2889
516-223-4666
800-797-3223
Fax: 516-623-9282
http://www.edact.com
Supplemental materials.
Carol Stern, VP
Roni Hofbauer, Office Manager

5957 Educational Resources
1550 Executive Drive
Elgin, IL 60123-9330
630-213-8681
Fax: 630-213-8681
The largest distributor of educational software and technology in the education market. Features Mac, APL, ligs and IBM school versions, lab packs, site licenses, networking and academic versions. Hardware, accessories and multimedia is also available.

5958 Electronic Specialists Inc.
75 Middlesex Ave
PO Box 389
Natick, MA 01760-0004
508-655-1532
810-225-4876
Fax: 508-653-0268
E-mail: clipprx@ix.netcom.com
http://www.electspec.com

Computer and electronics, including networks and computer systems plus transformers and power converters.
Frank Stifter, President

5959 Environmental Systems Research Institute
380 New York Street
Redlands, CA 92373-8100
909-793-2853
888-377-4575
http://www.esri.com
Demonstrates a full range of geographic information system software products.
Jack Dangermond, Founder

5960 Eversan Inc.
34 Main Street
Whitesboro, NY 13492
315-736-3967
800-383-6060
Fax: 315-736-4058
E-mail: sales&eversan.com
http://www.eversan.com
Announcement boards, scoreboards and classroom supplies, sports timers and clocks.
Michelle Moran, Sales Representative
Elsa Kucherna, Sales Representative

5961 GAMCO Educational Materials
PO Box 1911
Big Spring, TX 79721-1911
800-351-1404
Publishes software in math, language arts, reading, social studies, early childhood education and teacher tools for Macintosh, Apple, IBM and MS-DOS compatible.

5962 Games2Learn
1936 East Deere Avenue
Suite 120
Santa Ana, CA 92705
714-751-4263
888-713-4263
Fax: 714-442-0869
E-mail: CustomerService@Games2Learn.com
http://www.games2learn.com
Develops, markets and provides children and adults with quality, fun, interactive educational products designed to increase their skills in language, math and general knowledge. Creator of The Phonics Game.

5963 Gateway Learning Corporation
665 3rd Street
Suite 225
San Francisco, CA 94107
800-544-7323
http://www.hop.com
Develop and sell innovative educational products for home learning.
Lionel Guerin, Chairman
Frederic Gagey, Chief Financial Officer

5964 Greene & Associates
1100 NW Loop 410
Suite 700
San Antonio, TX 78213-5857
210-366-8768
Fax: 210-366-0198
http://greeneandassociates.com
Educational software.
Barbara A. F. Greene, Chief Executive Officer

5965 Grolier
PO Box 1716
Danbury, CT 06816
800-371-3908
Fax: 800-456-4402
Multimedia software for education.

5966 Hubbell
Kellems Division
40 Waterview Drive
Shelton, CT 06378-2604
475-882-4800
800-288-6000
Fax: 203-882-4852
http://www.hubbell-wiring.com
Computer hardware, software, systems, and networks.

5967 Indiana Cash Drawer
1315 S Miller Street
Shelbyville, IN 46176-2424
317-398-6643
Fax: 317-392-0958
Computer peripherals.

5968 Ingenuity Works
325 Howe St
Suite 407
Vancouver, BC 98230-9702
604-484-8053
800-665-0667
Fax: 604-431-7996
E-mail:
information@ingenuityworks.com
http://www.ingenuityworks.com
Publishes K-12 educational software for classroom use. Key curriculum areas include geography, keyboarding, and math (K-9). Network and district licenses are available.

Brigetta , Director Marketing

5969 Instructional Design
WIDS-Worldwide Instructional Design System
1 Foundation Circle
Waunakee, WI 53597-8914
608-849-2411
800-677-9437
Fax: 608-849-2468
E-mail: info@wids.org
http://www.wids.org
Performance-based curriculum design software and professional devlopment tools. Use software to write curriculum, implement standards, create assessments, and build in learning styles. Excellent upfront online design tool.

Leah Osborn, Director
Terri Johnson, Associate Director

5970 Instructor
Scholastic
555 Broadway
New York, NY 10012-3919
212-343-6100
800-724-6527
Fax: 212-343-4801
http://www.scholastic.com/instructor
Edited for teachers, curriculum coordinators, principals and supervisors of primary grades through junior high school.

Monthly

Dick Robinson, President and CEO
Lynn Diamond, Advertising Director

5971 Jostens Learning Corporation
4920 Pacific Heights Boulevard
Suite 500
San Diego, CA 92121
858-587-0087
800-521-8538
Fax: 858-587-1629
Educational software and CD-ROM's.

5972 Journey Education
5212 Tennyson Pkwy.
Suite 130
Plano, TX 75024

800-876-3507
Fax: 972-245-3585
E-mail: sales@journeyed.com
http://www.journeyed.com
Software for students.

5973 Ken Cook Education Systems
9929 W Silver Spring Drive
PO Box 25267
Milwaukee, WI 53225-1024
414-466-6060
800-362-2665
Fax: 414-466-0840
E-mail: BoatingManuals@kencook.com
http://www.boatpubs.com
Classroom curricular software.

5974 Kensington Microwave
2855 Campus Drive
San Mateo, CA 94403-2510
650-572-2700
800-535-4242
Fax: 650-572-9675
http://www.kensington.com
Computer systems and peripherals.

5975 Lapis Technologies
1100 Marina Village Parkway
Alameda, CA 94501-1043
510-748-1600
Computer peripherals.

5976 Laser Learning Technologies
120 Lakeside Avenue
#3240
Seattle, WA 98122-6533
800-722-3505
Educational CD-ROM's and interactive videos.

5977 Lawrence Productions
6146 West Main St
Suite A
Kalamazoo, MI 49009-9687
269-903-2395
800-421-4157
Fax: 616-665-7060
E-mail: sales@lpi.com
http://www.lpi.com
More than 60 proven software titles for PreK to adult, covering problem solving, early learning and leadership skills.

5978 Learning Company
500 Redwood Boulevard
Novato, CA 94947
415-881-8000
800-825-4420
Fax: 877-864-2275
http://www.sphinxaur.com/learning-company/novato-ca/
School educational software.

5979 Library Corporation, Sales & Marketing
1501 Regency Way
Woodstock, GA 30189-5487
770-591-0089
Computer networks.

Gary Kirk, Branch Manager

5980 LinkNet
Introlink
1400 E Touhy Avenue
Suite 260
Des Plaines, IL 60018-3339
847-390-8700
Fax: 847-390-9435
Computer networks.

5981 MECC
6160 Summit Drive N
Minneapolis, MN 55430-2100

800-685-MECC
http://www.mecc.co
Educational software, hardware and overhead projectors.

5982 Mamopalire of Vermont
PO Box 24
Warren, VT 05674
802-496-4095
888-496-4094
Fax: 802-496-4096
E-mail: bethumpd@wcvt.com
http://www.bethumpd.com
Provides quality educational books and board games for the whole family.

Rebecca Cahilly, President
Glenn Cahilly, CEO

5983 McGraw-Hill Educational Resources
11 W 19th Street
New York, NY 10011-4209
800-442-9685
Fax: 972-228-1982
Educational software for all areas of interest including social studies, science, mathematics and reading.

5984 Microsoft Corporation
1 Microsoft Way
Redmond, WA 98052-8300
425-882-8080
Fax: 425-936-7329
http://www.microsoft.com
One of the largest publishers and distributors of educational software, hardware, equipment and supplies.

Bill Gates, Founder
Paul Allen, Founder

5985 Misty City Software
11866 Slater Avenue NE
Kirkland, WA 98034-4103
206-820-2219
800-795-0049
Fax: 425-820-4298
Publisher of Grade Machine, gradebook software for Macintosh, MS-DOS, and Apple II. Grade Machine used by thousands of teachers in hundreds of schools worldwide. Grade Machine has full-screen editing, flexible reports, large class capacity, excellent documentation and reasonable cost.

Roberta Spiro, Business Manager
Russell Cruickshanks, Sales Manager

5986 NCR Corporation
1700 S Patterson Boulevard
Dayton, OH 45479-0002
937-445-5000
Computer networks, systems (large, mini, micro, medium and personal).

5987 NetLingo The Internet Dictionary
PO Box 627
Ojai, CA 93024
805-794-8687
Fax: 805-640-3654
E-mail: info@netlingo.com
http://www.NetLingo.com
A smart-looking and easy to understand dictionary of 3000 internet terms, 1200 chat acronyms, and much more. NetLingo is a modern reference book fo international students, educators, industry professionals, and online businesses and organizations.

528 pages Paperback
ISBN: 0-9706396-7-8

Erin Jansen, Author
Erin Jansen, Author/Publisher

5988 NetZero
2555 Townsgate Road
Westlake Village, CA 91361-2650

805-418-2020
Fax: 805-418-2075
http://www.netzero.com
Free Internet access.

89 New Century Education Corporation
220 Old New Brunswick Road
P.O. Box 43052
Upper Montclair, NJ 07043
732-981-0820
800-833-6232
Fax: 732-981-0552
E-mail: jharrison@ncecorp.com
http://www.newcenturyeducation.org
ILS systems.

Janice Harrison, Marketing Representative

90 OnLine Educator

http://faldo.atmos.uiuc.edu/CLA
A comprehensive archive of educational sites
with useful search capabilities and descriptions of the sites.

91 Online Computer Systems
1 Progress Drive
Horsham, PA 19044-3502
CD-ROM networking, CD-ROM titles and
CD-ROM tower units.

92 PBS TeacherSource
2100 Crystal Drive
Arlington, VA 22202
http://www.pbslearningmedia.org
Includes an on-line inventory of more than
1,000 free lesson plans, teacher guides and
other activities designed to complement PBS
television programs.

93 Parent Link
Parlant Technology
290 N University Avenue
PO Box 50240
Provo, UT 84605
801-373-9669
800-735-2930
Fax: 801-373-9697
E-mail: info@parlant.com
http://www.parlant.com
School to home communication systems allow scholls to create messages — emails,
telephone calls, web content, printed letters,
about student information, grades, attendance, homework, and activities. Also provides inbound access via internet and
telephone.

George Joeckel, Marketing

94 Peopleware
1621 114th Avenue SE
Suite 120
Bellevue, WA 98004-6905
425-454-6444
Fax: 425-454-7634
http://peopleware.com
Classroom curricular software.

95 Phillips Broadband Networks
100 Fairgrounds Drive
Manlius, NY 13104-2437
315-682-9105
Fax: 315-682-1022
Computer networks.

96 Pioneer New Media Technologies
2265 E 220th Street
Long Beach, CA 90810-1639
800-LAS-R ON
http://www.pioneerelectronics.com
DRM-604X CD-ROM mini-changer, world's
fastest CD-ROM drive for multimedia. Also
offers special packages including The Mystery Reading Bundle, CLD-V2400RB which
includes the CLD-V2400 LaserDisc player,

educator's remote control, UC-V109BC
barcode reader and membership in the Pioneers in Learning Club and The Case of the
Missing Mystery Writer videodisc from
Houghton Mifflin.

5997 Polaroid Corporation
575 Tech Square
Cambridge, MA 02139
781-386-2000
Fax: 781-386-3925
Computer repair, hardware and peripherals,
equipment and various size systems.

5998 Power Industries
37 Walnut Street
Wellsley Hills, MA 02181
800-395-5009
Educational software.

5999 Quetzal Computers
1708 E 4th Street
Brooklyn, NY 11223-1925
718-375-1186
Computer systems and networks, peripherals
and hardware.

6000 RLS Groupware
Realtime Learning Systems
2700 Connecticut Avenue NW
Washington, DC 20008-5330
202-483-1510
Classroom curricular software.

6001 Radio Shack
100 Throckmorton Street
Suite 1800
Ft. Worth, TX 76102
817-415-3700
Fax: 817-415-2335
Computer networks and peripherals.

Laura Moore, Sr VP Public Relations

6002 Rose Electronics
10850 Wilcrest Drive
Suite 900
Houston, TX 77099-3599
281-933-7673
Fax: 281-933-0044
Computer peripherals and hardware.

6003 STAR Reading & STAR Math
Renaissance Learning
2911 Peach Street
PO Box 8036
Wisconsin Rapids, WI 54495-8036
715-424-3636
800-338-4204
Fax: 715-424-4242
E-mail: answers@renaissance.com
http://www.renaissance.com
Computer-adaptive tests provide instructional levels, grade equivalents and percentile ranks.

John J. Lynch, Chief Executive Officer
Mary T. Minch, EVP, Finance & CFO

6004 SVE & Churchill Media
6677 N NW Highway
Chicago, IL 60631
773-775-9550
800-829-1900
Fax: 773-775-5091
E-mail: slucas@svemedia.com
http://www.svemedia.com
Has brought innovative media technology
into america's pre-K through high school
classrooms. By producing programs to satisfy state curriculum standards, SVE
consistently provides educators with
high-quality and award-winning videos,

CD-ROMs, eLMods, and DVDs in science,
social studies, English and health/guidance.
Sarah M Lucas, Communications
Coordinator
Kelli Campbell, VP
Marketing/Development

6005 School Cruiser
Time Cruiser Computing Corporation
9 Law Drive
3rd Floor, Ottawa, Ontario
Canada K1N 7G1
613-562-9847
877-450-9482
Fax: 613-562-4768
http://www.epals.com
School Cruiser provides online tools and resources to promote academic and community
interaction. It lets you access and share
school calenders, lesson plans, homework assignments, announcements and other school
related information.

6006 SchoolHouse
http://www.encarta.msn.com/schoolhouse/
maincontent.asp
The Encarta Lesson Collection and other educational resources.

6007 Seaman Nuclear Corporation
7315 S 1st Street
Oak Creek, WI 53154-2095
414-762-5100
Fax: 414-762-5106
Facility planning and evaluation software.

Scott C. Seamen, President
Todd Seaman, Vice President

6008 Skills Bank Corporation
7104 Ambassador Road
Suite 1
Baltimore, MD 21244-2732
800-451-5726
Educational manufacturing company offering computer and electronic resources, software, programs and systems focusing on
home education and tutoring.

6009 Sleek Software Corporation
2404 Rutland Drive,Suite 600
P.O. Box 170100
Austin, TX 78717
512-833-0352
800-337-5335
Fax: 512-833-9718
E-mail: info@sleek.com
http://www.sleek.com
Specializes in Algorithm-Based tutorial and
test-generating software.

6010 Smartstuff Software
PO Box 82284
Portland, OR 97282-0284
415-763-4799
800-671-3999
Fax: 877-278-7456
E-mail: info@smartstuff.com
http://www.smartstuff.com
Foolproof Security is a dual platform desktop
security product that prevents unwanted
changes to the desktop and a product line for
the internet that protects browser settings, filters content, and allows guided activities.

6011 Society for Visual Education
1345 W Diversey Parkway
Chicago, IL 60614-1249
773-775-9550
Fax: 800-624-1678
Educational software dealing specifically
with special education.

6012 SofterWare
132 Welsh Road
Suite 140
Horsham, PA 19044-2217
215-628-0400
800-220-4111
Fax: 215-628-0585
E-mail: info@softerware.com
http://www.softerware.com
Offers software, support and administrative solutions to four markets: childcare centers, public and private schools, nonprofit organizations and institutions, and camps.

Nathan Relles, President and Co-Founder
Douglas Schoenberg, CEO/ Co-Founder

6013 SpecialNet
GTE Educational Network Services
5525 N Macarthur Boulevard
Suite 320
Irving, TX 75038-2600
214-518-8500
800-927-3000
Fax: 757-852-8277
Contains news and information on trends and developments in educational services and programs. Databases, bulletin boards, school packages, student/teacher packages, online magazines, distance learning, vocational education, school health, educational laws, and more.

6014 Student Software Guide
800-874-9001
E-mail: journey.com
Discounts on a variety of software materials.

6015 Sun Microsystems
2550 Garcia Avenue
#6-13
Mountain View, CA 94043-1100
714-643-2688
800-555-9786
Fax: 650-934-9776
Computer networks and peripherals.

6016 Sunburst/Wings for Learning
101 Castleton Street
Pleasantville, NY 10570-3405
914-747-3310
800-338-3457
Fax: 914-747-4109
Educational materials, including software, print materials, videotapes, videodisc and interdisciplinary packages.

6017 Support Systems International Corporation
136 S 2nd Street
Richmond, CA 94804-2110
510-234-9090
800-777-6269
Fax: 510-233-8888
E-mail: Sales@FiberMailbox.com
http://www.fiberopticcableshop.com
Fiber optic patch cables, converters, and switches.

Ben Parsons, General Manager

6018 Surfside Software
PO Box 1112
East Orleans, MA 02643-1112
800-942-9008
Educational software.

6019 Target Vision
1160 Pittsford Victor Road
Suite K
Pittsford, NY 14534-3825
800-724-4044
Fax: 585-248-2354

TVI DeskTop expands your show directly to desktop PC utilizing existing LANS. View information by topics or as a screen saver. Features: graphic importing, VCR interface, advanced scheduling and more.

6020 Teacher Universe
5900 Hollis Street
Suite A
Emeryville, CA 94608
877-248-3224
Fax: 415-763-4917
E-mail: info@teacheruniverse.com
http://www.teacheruniverse.com
Creates technology-rich solutions for improving the quality of life and work for teachers worldwide.

6021 Technolink Corporation
2609 Reach Rdÿ
Williamsport, PA 17701-4004
570-323-9057
Fax: 814-693-5901
E-mail: sales@technolinkcorp.com
http://www.technolinkcorp.com
Computer systems and electronics.

6022 Tom Snyder Productions
100 Talcott Avenue
Watertown, MA 02472-5703
800-342-0236
Fax: 800-304-1254
E-mail: dealer@tomsnyder.com
http://www.tomsnyder.com
Educational CD-ROM products and Internet services for schools.

Tom Synder, Founder

6023 Tripp Lite
1111 West 35th Street
Chicago, IL 60610-4117
773-869-1111
E-mail: international@tripplite.com
http://www.tripplite.com
Peripherals, hardware and computer systems.

Moti Shulak, Sales Representative

6024 True Basic
12 Commerce Avenue
West Lebanon, NH 03784-1669
800-436-2111
Fax: 603-298-7015
E-mail: john@truebasic.com
http://www.truebasic.com
Educational software.

6025 U.S. Public School Universe Database
U.S. National Center for Education Statistics
555 New Jersey Avenue NW
Washington, DC 20001-2029
202-219-1335
85,000 public schools of elementary and secondary levels, public special education, vocational/technical education and alternative education schools.

6026 USA CityLink Project
USA CityLink Project
Floppies for Kiddies
4060 Highway 59
Mandevelle, LA 70471
985-398-2158
Fax: 985-892-8535
http://www.usacitylink.com
Collects used and promotional disketts from the masses for redistribution to school groups and nonprofits throughout the county.

Carol Blake, Contact

6027 Unisys
PO Box 500
Blue Bell, PA 19424-0001
215-986-3501
Fax: 215-986-3279
http://www.unisys.com
A full line of computers (sizes ranging from mini/micro to medium/large and personal).

Peter Altabef, President and CEO
Quincy Allen, Chief Marketing Officer

6028 Ventura Educational Systems
910 Ramona Avenue
P.O. Box 1622ÿ
Arroyo Grande, CA 93421-1622
805-473-7383
800-336-1022
Fax: 805-556-4469
E-mail: sales@venturaes.com
http://www.venturaes.com
Publishers of curriculum based educational software for all grade levels, specializing in interactive math and science software. Programs include teacher's guide with student worksheets.

Fred Ventura, Software Developer
Marne Ventura, Teacher

6029 Viziflex Seels
406 N Midland Ave
Saddle Brook, NJ 07663-6895
201-487-8080
800-627-7752
Fax: 201-487-3266
E-mail: info@viziflex.com
http://www.viziflex.com
Peripherals, hardware and electronics, floorcoverings, mats and matting.

6030 Waterford Institute
1590 E 9400 S
Sandy, UT 84093-3009
801-349-2200
800-767-9976
Fax: 801-572-1667
http://www.waterford.org
Produces children's educational software for math and reading.

Dustin Heuston, Chairman
Benjamin Heuston, President and COO

6031 Web Connection
Education Week
6935 Arlington Road
Bethesda, MD 20814
301-280-3100
800-346-1834
E-mail: ads@epe.org
http://www.edweek.org
Information about education suppliers.

Larry Berger, Chairman
Gina Burkhardt, Secretary

6032 Wiremold Company
60 Woodlawn Street
W Hartford, CT 06110-2383
800-243-8421
Computer networks and peripherals.

6033 Wisconsin Technical College System Foundation
4622 University Avenue
PO Box 7874
Madison, WI 53707-7874
608-266-1207
800-821-6313
Fax: 608-266-1690
E-mail: foundation@wtcsf.tec.wi.us
http://www.wtcsystem.edu
Interactive videodiscs, self-paced instruction or with barcodes. Students learn faster, become more motivated and retain more information. Math, al-

gebra and electronics courseware are also available.

Drew Petersen, President
John Schwantes, Vice President

4 Word Associates
3226 Robincrest Drive
Northbrook, IL 60062-5125
847-291-1101
Fax: 847-291-0931
E-mail: microlrn@aol.com
http://www.wordassociates.com
Software tutorials featuring lessons in question format, with tutorial and test mode. 15 titles include Math SAT, 2 English SAT; US Constitution Tutor; Phraze Maze; Geometry: Planely Simple, Concepts and Proofs, Right Triangles; Life Skills Math; Algebra; Reading: Myths and More Myths, Magic and Monsters; Economics; American History. Windows, Macintosh, CD's or disks.

Software

Myrna Helfand, President
Sherry Azaria, Marketing

5 Ztek Company
PO Box 967
Lexington, KY 40588-1768
859-281-1611
800-247-1603
Fax: 859-281-1521
E-mail: cs@ztek.com
http://www.ztek.com
Offers physics multimedia lessons on CD-ROM, DVD, videodisc and videotape. Also, carries Pioneer New Media DVD and videodisc players as well as Bretford Manufacturing's line of audio-visual furniture.

6 ePALS.com
Classroom Exchange
World's largest online classroom community, connecting over 3 million students and teachers through 41,044 profiles.

7 http://ericir.syr.edu
AskERIC
Ask a question about education and receive a personalized e-mail response in two business days.

8 http://gsn.bilkent.edu.tr
Ballad of an EMail Terrorist
Global SchoolNet Foundation
One pitfall of the internet is danger of vulgarity and/or obscenity to a child via e-mail.

39 http://suzyred.home.texas.net
The Little Red School House
Offers sections on music, writing, quotes, web quests, jokes, poetry, games, activities and more.

40 www.FundRaising.Com
FundRaising.Com
800-443-5353
Internet fundraising company.

41 www.abcteach.com
P.O. Box 1217
Union Lake, MI 48387-1217
Fax: 248-493-6565
E-mail: support@abcteach.com
Offers ideas and activities for kids, parents, students and teachers. Features section on many topics in education, including writing, poetry, word searches, crosswords, games, maps, mazes and more.

42 www.abctooncenter.com
ABC Toon Center
This family orientated site offers games, cartoons, storybook, theater, information stations and more. This site is open to children of

differnt languages. Can be translated into Italian, French, Spanish, German and Russian.

6043 www.americatakingaction.com
America Taking Action
Provides every school with a free, 20 page website with resources for teachers, parents, students and the community. Created entirely by involved parents, teachers and community leaders as a public service.

6044 www.awesomelibrary.org
Awesome Library
Organizes the Web with 15,000 carefully reviewed resources, including the top 5 percent in education. Offers sections of mathematics, science, social studies, english, health, physical education, technology, languages, special education, the arts and more. Features a section involved with today's current issues facing our world, like pollution, gun control, tobacco, and other changing 'hot' topics. Site can be browsed in English, German, Spanish, French or Portuguese.

6045 www.bigchalk.com
Big Chalk-The Education Network
800-521-0600
Fax: 734-997-4268
Educational web site tailored to fit teachers' and students' needs.

6046 www.brunchbunch.org
Brunch Bunch
The foundation names all of the grants it makes after teachers who have demonstrated excellence. The foundation regularly makes significant grants to aid teachers' efforts.

6047 www.busycooks.com
BusyCooks.com
A hit with home economics teachers, enjoying free recipes and online cooking shows. Tapping into the experience of thousands to nuture your culinary creativity.

6048 www.chandra.harvard.edu
Chandra X-ray Observatory Center
60 Garden Street
Cambridge, MA 2138
617-496-7941
Fax: 617-495-7356
E-mail: cxcpub@cfa.harvard.edu
Find teacher-developed, classroom-ready materials based on results from the Chandra mission. Classroom-ready activities, interactive games, activities, quizzes, and printable activities which will keep students absorbed with interest.

6049 www.cherrydale.com
Cherrydale Farms
707 N. Valley Forge Rd.
Lansdale, PA 19446
800-333-4525
E-mail: CDFinfo@Cherrydale.com
Website offers company information, fund raising products and information, online mega mall, card shop, career opportunities and much more. Produces fine chocolates and confections. Many opportunities for schools to raise funds with various Cherrydale programs.

6050 www.cleverapple.com
Education Station
E-mail: info@cleverapple.com
Offers links to many sites involved with education.

6051 www.edhelper.com
edhelper.com
Keeps you up to date with the latest educational news.

6052 www.education-world.com
Education World
75 Mill St.
Colchester, CT 6415
800-227-0831
E-mail: webmaster@educationworld.com
Features and education-specific search engine with links to over 115,000 sites. Offers monthly reviews of other educational web sites, and other original content on a weekly basis.

6053 www.eduverse.com
Software developer building core technologies for powering international distance education. Features an online distance education engine, product information, news releases and more.

6054 www.efundraising.com
efundraising.com
C/O FedEx Trade Networks
156 Lawrence Paquette Ind'l Drive, PMW#
Champlain, NY 12919
866-825-2921
Fax: 877-275-8664
E-mail: online@fundraising.com
Provides non-profit groups with quality products, low prices and superior service. Helping thousands of schools, youth sports teams and community groups reach their fundraising goals each year.

6055 www.embracingthechild.com
Embracing the Child
E-mail: pk@embracingthechild.org
Educational resource for teachers and parents that provides a structural resource for home and classroom use, lesson planning, as well as a child-safe site, for children's research, classroom use and homework fulfillment.

6056 www.enc.org
ENC Learning Inc.
1585 Central Ave.
Ste C-5 #293
Summerville, SC 29483
614-378-4567
Fax: 843-832-2063
E-mail: info@goENC.com
For math and science teachers-anywhere in the K-12 spectrum. This organization contains a wealth of information, activities, resources, and demonstrations for the sciences and math.

6057 www.englishhlp.com
English Help
E-mail: englishhlpr@hotmail.com
This page is a walk through of Microsoft Power Point. The goal is to show in a few simple steps how to make your own website. Created by Rebecca Holland.

6058 www.expage.com/Just4teachers
Just 4 Teachers
The ultimate website for educators! Teaching tips, resources, themeunits, search engines, classroom management and sites for kids.

6059 www.fraboom.com
Fraboom
FR Productions, LLC
1427 NW Raleigh St
Portland, OR 97209
503-208-2315
E-mail: support@fraboom.com
This site's tools let you specify areas within your state's standards and search for a list of 'Flying Rhinoceros' lessons that meet your criteria. Offers other information sources for teachers and students.

6060 www.globalschoolnet.org
Global SchoolNet Foundation
270 N. El Camino Real
Ste. 395
Encinitas, CA 92024
760-635-0001
E-mail: helper2014@globalschoolnet.org
Connects teachers, administrators, and parents with options and possibilities the Internet has to offer the schools of the world.

Dr. Yvonne Marie Andres, President
John St. Clair, Vice President

6061 www.gradebook.org/
The Classroom
Dedicated to the students and teachers of the world.

6062 www.homeworkspot.com
HomeworkSpot
A free online homework resource center developed by educators, students, parents and journalists for K-12 students. It simplifies the search for homework help, features a top-notch reference cetner, current events, virtual field trips and expeditions, extracurricular activities and study breaks, parent and teacher resources and much more.

6063 www.iearn.org
iEARN USA
Utilizes projects for students ages 6 through 19. Projects are concerned with the environment as well as arts, politics, and the health and welfare of all the Earth's citizens.

6064 www.jasonproject.org
Jason Project
Founded in 1989 as a tool for live, interactive programs for students in the fourth through eighth grades. Annual projects are funded through a variety of public corporations and governmental organizations.

Dr. Eleanor Smalley, EVP/ COO
Sean Smith, SVP/ CTO

6065 www.junebox.com
School Specialty
800-513-2465
E-mail:
WebSupport@SchoolSpecialty.com
A classroom superstore that features the leading suppliers of educational products and services. A gateway to project ideas and educational links.

6066 www.k12planet.com
Chancery Software
Chancery Software is announcing a new school to home extension that will provide student information systems to give parents, students, and educators access to accurate information about students in one, easy-to-use website.

6067 www.kiddsmart.com
Institute for Child Development
E-mail: dcornell@kiddsmart.com
The ICD develops educational materials and resources designed to facilitate children's social and emotional development. Offers the previous materials as well as research summaries, lesson plans, training, workshops, games, multi-cultural materials and other resources to teachers, educational centers, parents, counselors, corporations, non-profits and others involved in the child-care professions.

6068 www.lessonplansearch.com
Lesson Plan Search
220 lesson plans from cooking to writing.

6069 www.lessonplanspage.com
HotChalk
1999 S. Bascom Avenue
Suite 1020
Campbell, CA 95008
888-468-2336
Fax: 408-608-1679
E-mail: support@hotchalk.com
A collection of over 1,000 free lesson plans for teachers to use in their classrooms. Lesson plans are organized by subject and grade level.

6070 www.library.thinkquest.org
Think Quest Library of Entries
The Arti FAQS 2100 Project is designed to predict how art will influence our lives in the next hundred years. Students can use available data to make reasonable predictions for the future.

6071 www.ncspearson.com
NCS Pearson
E-mail: info@ncs.com
NCS Pearson is at the forefront of the education space with curriculum, contant, tools, assessment, and interface to enterprise systems

6072 www.negaresa.org
Northeast Georgia RESA
E-mail: keith.everson@negaresa.org
For teachers, electronic web-based grade book aplication eGRader 2000. Many educational resource links as well has discussion groups, a news and events section, and even links to online shopping.

Dr. Keith Everson, Executive Director
Debra Wallace, Business/ Finance Director

6073 www.netrover.com/~kingskid/108.html
Room 108
An educational activity center for kids. Offers lots of fun for children with educational focus; like songs, art, math, kids games, children's stories and much more. Sections with pen pal information, puzzles, crosswords, teachers store, spelling, kids sites, email, music, games and more.

6074 www.pcg.cyberbee.com
IwayNet Communications
614-294-9292
E-mail: support@iwaynet.net
Offered to classes all over the world via the internet. Your class commits to exchanging picture postcards with all other participants. Appropriate for all ages, for public and private schools, for youth groups and for home- schools.

6075 www.pitt.edu
EdIndex
724-244-4939
E-mail: poole@pitt.edu
A web resource for teachers and students, offers course information, MS Office tutorials, personal and professional pages, and more.

6076 www.riverdeep.net
Riverdeep Interactive Learning
617-351-5316
800-426-657
E-mail: Sales_Support@hmhco.com
Riverdeep's interactive science, language and math arts programs deliver high quality educational experiences.

6077 www.safedayeducation.com
Safe Day Education
E-mail: info@safedayeducation.com
The leader in bully prevention and street proofing education for kids; safe dating preparation programs for teens; and re-empowerment and assault prevention training for women.

6078 www.safekids.com/child_safety.htm
SafeKids.Com
E-mail: larry@safekids.com
Cyberspace is a fabulous tool for learning, but some of it can be exploitative and even criminal.

Larry Magid, Founder/ Editor

6079 www.sdcoe.k12.ca.us
Researches a coral reef and creates a diorama for The Cay by Theodore Taylor.

6080 www.shop2gether.com
Collective Publishing Service
We are committed to helping all schools buy better by shopping together. Building upon a scalable, dynamic procurement platform and group buying technology, we also provide a unique ecommerce system, delivering next generation procurement services over the Internet.

6081 www.spaceday.com
Space Day
Program engineered to build problem-solving and teamwork skills.

6082 www.specialednews.com
Special Education News
E-mail: info@specialednews.com
Consists of breaking news stories from Washington and around the country. These stories are compiled together in the Special Education News letter is sent via e-mail once a week.

6083 www.straightscoop.org
Straight Scoop News Bureau
SSNB increases the frequency of anti-drug themes and messages in junior high and high school student media.

6084 www.tcta.org
Texas Classroom Teachers Association
PO Box 1489
Austin, TX 78767-1489
512-477-9415
888-879-8282
Fax: 512-469-9527
Compromised of Texas educators, provides interest for teachers everywhere. Education laws and codes are presented here.

Terrill Q. Littlejohn, President
Teresa Koehler, President-Elect

6085 www.teacherszone.com
TeachersZone.Com
Lesson plans, free stuff for teachers, contests, sites for kids, conferences and workshops, schools and organizations, job listings, products for school.

6086 www.teacherweb.com
TeacherWeb
PO BOX 06290
Chicago, IL 60606
TeacherWeb, your free personal website that's as easy to use as the bulletin board in your classroom. This site offers a secure, password-protected service.

6087 www.teachingheart.com
Teaching is A Work of Heart
Chock-full of ideas, projects, motivational thoughts, behavior ideas.

38 www.thelearningworkshop.com
Learning Workshop.com
Services for teachers, students, and parents. For teachers online gradebooks and grade tracking, students can check their grades online, parents enjoy articles written expressly for them and a tutor search by zip code.

39 www.tutorlist.com
TutorList.com
Offers information on tips on how to find and choose a tutor, what a tutor does, educational news and more.

90 www.worksafeusa.org
WorkSafeUSA
Addresses the alarming injury and death rates experienced by America's adolescent workers. This non-profit site publishes and distributes A Teen Guide to Workplace Safety, available in English and Spanish.

91 www1.hp.com
Hewlett-Packard Development Company
3000 Hanover Street
Palo Alto, CA 94304-1185
650-857-1501
Compaq is one of the leading corporations in educational technology, working on developing solutions that will connect students, teachers and the community.

Administration

92 ASQC
611 E Wisconsin Avenue
Milwaukee, WI 53202-4695
800-248-1946
Fax: 414-272-1734
Business and administrative software.

93 Anchor Pad
Anchor Pad Products
11105 Dana Cir
Cypress, CA 90630-5133
714-799-4071
800-626-2467
Fax: 714-799-4094
E-mail: anchor@anchor.com
Computer and office security

Caroline Jones, COO
Melanie Ruste, Sales/Marketing Associate

94 Applied Business Technologies
55 S.E. 2nd Avenue
Delray Beach, FL 33444
561-272-1232
800-683-6590
Fax: 610-359-9420
E-mail: info@appliedcorp.com
Computer networks and administrative software.

95 AskSam Systems
PO Box 1831
Perry, FL 32348
850-584-6590
800-800-1997
Fax: 850-584-7481
E-mail: info@asksam.com
Business and administrative free form database software.

Dottie Sheffield, Sales Manager

96 Autodesk Retail Products
1725 220th Street
Suite C101
Bothell, WA 98021-8809
425-487-2233
Fax: 425-486-1636
Administrative and business software.

6097 Avcom Systems
250 Cox Lane
PO Box 977
Cutchogue, NY 11935-1303
631-734-5080
800-645-1134
Fax: 631-734-7204
Supplies for making and mounting transparencies. Products includes economy and self-adhesive mounts; transparent rolls and sheets; markers, pens and cleaners; thermo, computer graphics and plain-paper copier transparency films and laminating supplies.

Joseph K Lukas

6098 Bobbing Software
67 Country Oaks Drive
Buda, TX 78610-9338
800-688-6812
Administrative software and systems.

6099 Bull HN Information Systems
285 Billerica Road
Chelmsford, MA 01824
978-294-6000
Fax: 978-244-0085
Computer networks, computers (large, medium, micro and mini), and supplies.

6100 Bureau of Electronic Publishing
745 Alexander Road
#728
Princeton, NJ 08540-6343
973-808-2700
Administrative software, hardware and systems.

6101 CRS
17440 Dallas Parkway
Suite 120
Dallas, TX 75287-7307
800-433-9239
Administrative software and systems.

6102 Campus America
900 E Hill Avenue
Suite 205
Knoxville, TN 37915-2580
865-523-4477
877-536-0222
Fax: 617-492-9081
Computer supplies, equipment, systems and networks.

6103 Century Consultants
150 Airport Road
Suite 1500
Lakewood, NJ 08701-3309
732-363-9300
Fax: 732-363-9374
E-mail: marketing@centuryltd.com
Develops, markets, and services Oracle based web-enabled Management software, STAR_BASE, for school districts K-12.

6104 Computer Resources
1037 Calef Highway
Barrington, NH 03825-0060
603-664-5811
888-641-9922
Fax: 603-664-5864
The Modular Management System for Schools is a school administrative software system designed to handle all student record keeping and course scheduling needs. A totally integrated modular system built around a central Student Master File. Additional modules handle student scheduling, grades, attendance and discipline reporting.

Raymond J Perreault, VP Marketing
Robert W Cook, National Sales Manager

6105 Computer Supply People (The)
N93 W14636 Whittaker Way
Menomonee Falls, WI 53051-1629
262-251-5511
800-242-2090
Fax: 262-251-4737
E-mail:
medmgt@computersupplypeople.com
http://www.computersupplypeople.com
Computer supplies, equipment and systems, Koss headphones.

John Schimberg, Education Sales

6106 Cyborg Systems
2 N Riverside Plaza
Chicago, IL 60606-2600
312-454-1865
Administrative and business software programs.

6107 Diskovery Educational Systems
1860 Old Okeechobee Road
Suite 105
West Palm Beach, FL 33409-5281
561-683-8410
800-331-5489
Fax: 561-683-8416
E-mail: info@diskovery.com
http://www.diskovery.com
Computer supplies, equipment, and various size systems.

6108 Doron Precision Systems
Doron Precision Systems
150 Corporate Drive
PO Box 400
Binghamton, NY 13902-0400
607-772-1610
Fax: 607-772-6760
E-mail: sales@doronprecision.com
http://www.doronprecision.com
Business and classroom curriculum software. Driving Simulation Systems and Entertainment Simulation Systems.

6109 Educational Data Center
180 De La Salle Drive
Romeoville, IL 60446-1895
800-451-7673
Fax: 815-838-9412
Administration software.

6110 EnrollForecast: K-12 Enrollment Forecasting Program
Association of School Business Officials Int'l
11401 N Shore Drive
Reston, VA 20190-4232
703-478-0405
Fax: 703-478-0205
A powerful planning tool that helps project student enrollment.

Peg D Kirkpatrick, Editor/Publisher
Robert Gluck, Managing Editor

6111 Epson America
3840 Kilroy Airport Way
Long Beach, CA 90806
800-289-7766
E-mail: Webmaster@ea.epson.com
http://www.epson.com
Computer repair and peripherals.

John Lang, President/ CEO
Keith Kratzberg, SVP, Sales & Marketing

6112 FMJ/PAD.LOCK Computer Security Systems
520 W. Central Ave.
Brea, CA 92821
714-990-3218
800-872-9562
Fax: 714-990-5409

E-mail: dealerinquiry@fmjpadlock.com
http://www.fmjpadlock.com
Computer peripherals, supplies and equipment.

Tom Separa

6113 Geist

Geist Manufacturing
1821 Yolande Avenue
Lincoln, NE 68521-1835
402-474-3400
800-432-3219
Fax: 402-474-4369
E-mail: products@geistmfg.com
http://www.geistmfg.com
Power distribution for racks, cabinets and data centers.

Terri Rockeman, Customer Service Supervisor

6114 Global Computer Supplies

11 Harbor Park Drive
Port Washington, NY 11050-4622
516-625-6200
800-446-9662
Fax: 516-484-8533
http://www.globalcomputer.com
Computer supplies, equipment, hardware, software and systems.

6115 Harrington Software

658 Ridgewood Road
Maplewood, NJ 07040-2536
201-761-5914
Administrative and business software.

6116 Information Design

7009 S Potomac Street
Suite 110
Englewood, CO 80112
303-792-2990
800-776-2469
Fax: 303-792-2378
E-mail: sales@idesgninc.com
http://www.idesigninc.com
Administrative and business software including systems focusing on payroll, personnel, financial accounting, purchasing, budgeting, fixed asset accounting and salary administration.

6117 International Rotex

7171 Telegraph Road
Los Angeles, CA 90040-3227
800-648-1871
Computer supplies.

6118 Jay Klein Productions Grade Busters

118 N. Tejon St.
Suite 304
Colorado Springs, CO 80903
719-599-8786
Fax: 719-380-9997
E-mail: support@gradebusters.com
http://www.gradebusters.com
A line of teacher productivity tools, the most highly recognized integrated gradebooks, attendance records, seating charts and scantron packages in K-12 education today (Mac, DOS, Windows, Apple II).

Jay A Klein, President
Angela C Wormley, Office Manager

6119 Jostens Learning Corporation

5521 Norman Center Drive
Minneapolis, MN 55437-1040
800-635-1429
The leading provider of comprehensive multimedia instruction, including hardware, software and service.

6120 MISCO Computer Supplies

1 Misco Plaza
Holmdel, NJ 07733-1033
800-876-4726
Computer supplies, networks, equipment and accessories.

6121 Mathematica

Wolfram Research, Inc.
100 Trade Centre Drive
Champaign, IL 61820-7237
217-398-0700
800-965-3726
Fax: 217-398-0747
E-mail: info@wolfram.com
http://www.wolfram.com
Classroom curricular software and business/administrative software.

Stephen Wolfram, Founder/CEO
Jean Buck, Dir., Corp Communications

6122 MicroAnalytics

Student Transportation Systems
2300 Clarendon Boulevard
Suite 404
Arlington, VA 22201-3331
703-841-0414
Fax: 703-527-1693
Automates bus routing and scheduling for school districts with fleets of 5 to 500 buses. BUSTOPS is flexible, affordable and easy to use. Offers color maps and graphics, efficient routing, report writing, planning and more to improve your pupil transportation system.

Mary Buchanan, Sales Manager

6123 MicroLearn Tutorial Series

Word Associates
3226 Robincrest Drive
Northbrook, IL 60062-5125
847-291-1101
Fax: 847-291-0931
E-mail: microlrn@aol.com
http://www.wordassociates.com
Software tutorials featuring lessons in question format, with tutorial and test mode. 15 titles include Math SAT, 2 English SAT; US Constitution Tutor; Phraze Maze; Geometry: Planely Simple, Concepts and Proofs, Right Triangles; Life Skills Math; Algebra; Reading: Myths and More Myths, Magic and Monsters; Economics; American History. Windows, Macintosh, CD's or disks.

Software

Myrna Helfand, President

6124 NCS Marketing

11000 Prairie Lakes Drive
Eden Prairie, MN 55344-3885
800-447-3269
Fax: 612-830-7788
http://www.ncspearson.com
OpScan optical mark reading scanners from NCS process data at speeds of up to 10,000 sheets per hour for improved accuracy and faster turnaround. Also provides software and scanning applications and services that manage student, financial, human resources, instructional and assessment information.

Sheryl Kyweriga

6125 National Computer Systems

11000 Prairie Lakes Drive
Minneapolis, MN 55440
800-447-3269
Fax: 952-830-8564
Administrative software and systems.

6126 Parlant Technologies

PO Box 50240
Provo, UT 84605
801-373-9669
800-735-2930
Fax: 801-373-9697
E-mail: info@parlant.com
http://www.parlant.com
Administrative software and systems.

6127 Quill Corporation

P.O. Box 37600
Philadelphia, PA 19101-0600
847-634-4800
800-982-3400
Fax: 800-789-8955
http://www.quill.com
Computer and office supplies and equipment.

6128 Rauland Borg

1802 West Central Road
Mount Prospect, IL 60056
847-679-0900
Fax: 800-217-0977
http://www.rauland.com
Administrative software and systems.

Kidder's Rauland-Borg, President/ CEO
Peipert , SVP, Finance

6129 Rediker Administration Software

2 Wileraham Road
Hampden, MA 01036-9685
413-566-3463
800-213-9860
Fax: 413-566-2274
E-mail: APSupport@rediker.com
http://www.rediker.com
School administrative software for the teaching professional.

Rich Rediker, CEO
Andrew Anderlonis, President

6130 Scantron Corporation

1313 Lone Oak Road
Eagan, MN 55121
949-639-7500
800-722-687
http://www.scantron.com
Computer peripherals, administrative software and services.

6131 SourceView Software International

PO Box 578
Concord, CA 94522-0578
925-825-1248
Classroom curricular, business and administrative software.

6132 Systems & Computer Technology Services

4 Country View Road
Malvern, PA 19355-1408
610-647-5930
Fax: 610-578-7778
Administrative and business software programs and services.

6133 Trapeze Software

8360 East Via de Ventura
Suite L-200
Scottsdale, AZ 85258
480-627-8400
Fax: 480-627-8411
E-mail: info@trapezegroup.com
http://www.trapezegroup.com
Computerized bus routing, boundary planning and redistricting software and services, and AVL (automatic vehicle locator software).

Clint Rooley, Director of Sales

34 University Research Company
7200 Wisconsin Avenue
Suite 600
Bethesda, MD 20814
301-654-8338
800-526-4972
Fax: 301-941-8427
http://www.urc-chs.com
Supplies Quiz-A-Matic electronics for quiz competitions.

Barbara N. Turner, President

35 Velan
4153 24th Street
Suite 1
San Francisco, CA 94114-3667
415-949-9150
Administrative software and systems.

36 WESTLAW
West Group
610 Opperman Drive
Eagan, MN 55123-1340
612-687-7000
800-937-8529
Fax: 651-687-5827
http://www.westlaw.com
Online service concerning the complete text of U.S. federal court decisions, state court decisions from all 50 states, regulations, specialized files, and texts dealing with education.

37 http://teacherfiles.homestead.com/index~ns4
Homestead
800-986-0958
http://www.homestead.com
Offers sections on clip art, quotes, slogans, lesson plans, organizations, web quests, political involvement, grants, publications, special education, professional development, humor and more.

38 www.abcteach.com
Abcteach
P.O. Box 1217
Union Lake, MI 48387-1217
Fax: 248-493-6565
E-mail: support@abcteach.com
http://www.abcteach.com
Free printable materials for kids, parents, student teachers and teachers. Theme units, spelling word searches, research help, writing skills and much more.

39 www.apple.com
PowerSchool
PowerSchool's web-based architecture makes it easy to learn and easy to use.

40 www.atozteacherstuff.com
A to Z Teacher Stuff
E-mail: webmaster@atozteacherstuff.com
http://atozteacherstuff.com
Features quick indexes to online lesson plans and teacher resources, educational sites for teachers, articles, teacher store and more.

41 www.awesomelibrary.org
Awesome Library

http://www.awesomelibrary.org
Organizes the Web with 15,000 carefully reviewed resources, including the top 5 percent in education. Offers sections of mathematics, science, social studies, english, health, physical education, technology, languages, special education, the arts and more. Features a section involved with today's current issues facing our world, like pollution, gun control, tobacco, and other changing 'hot' topics. Site can be browsed in English, German, Spanish, French or Portuguese.

6142 www.easylobby.com
HID Global
611 Center Ridge Drive
Austin, TX 78753

http://www.hidglobal.com
The complete electronic visitor management system.

Denis H,bert, President/ CEO
Michele DeWitt, SVP, Human Resources

6143 www.fraboom.com
FR Productions, LLC
1427 NW Raleigh St
Portland, OR 97209
503-208-2315
E-mail: support@fraboom.com
http://fraboom.com
This site's tools let's you specify areas within your state's standards and search for a list of 'Flying Rhinoceros' lessons that meet your criteria. Offers other information sources for teachers and students.

6144 www.fundraising.com
PO BOX 305142
Nashville, TN 37230-5142
800-443-5353
E-mail: filter.efr@gafundraising.com
http://www.fundraising.com
Internet fundraising company.

6145 www.hoagiesgifted.org
Hoagies Gifted Education Page
256 Eagleview Boulevard PMB 123
Exton, PA 19341
E-mail: webmaster@hoagiesgifted.org
http://www.hoagiesgifted.org
Features the latest research on parenting and educating gifted children. Offers ideas, solutions and other things to try for parents of gifted children. Sections with world issues facing children and other important social topics.

Carolyn K. Founder/ Director

6146 www.kiddsmart.com
Institute for Child Development
E-mail: dcornell@kiddsmart.com
The ICD develops educational materials and resources designed to facilitate children's social and emotional development. Offers the previous materials as well as research summaries, lesson plans, training, workshops, games, multi-cultural materials and other resources to teachers, educational centers, parents, counselors, corporations, non-profits and others involved in the child-care professions.

6147 www.nycteachers.com
NYCTeachers.com

http://www.nycteachers.com
Designed for NYC teachers that work within public school systems. Speaks out on controversial issues facing the broadening, funding, development, staffing and other concerns about public schools. Welcomes your suggestions and comments about the site and the issues involved.

6148 www.songs4teachers.com
O'Flynn Consulting
c/o Mary Flynn
494 St. Vincent Street
Barrie, ON L4M 7
705-728-6528
Fax: 705-728-6528
E-mail: mary@songs4teachers.com
http://www.songs4teachers.com
Offers many resources for teachers including songs made especially for your classroom. Sections with songs and activities for holi-

days, seasons and more. Features books and audios with 101 theme songs for use in the classroom or anywhere children gather to sing.

6149 www.thecanadianteacher.com
The Canadian Teacher Marketplace

http://www.thecanadianteacher.com
Site where educators can find the latest links to free resources, materials, lesson plans, software, samples and computers. Some links are for Canadians only.

6150 www.welligent.Com
Welligent
5205 Colley Avenue
Norfolk, VA 23508
888-317-5960
E-mail: info@welligent.com
http://www.welligent.com
A web-based software program that improves student health management and your school's finances at the same time.

Early Childhood Education

6151 Jump Start Math for Kindergartners
Knowledge Adventure
Torrance, CA
800-545-7677
http://www.knowledgeadventure.com
The program covers important and essential kindergarten math skills such as, writing numbers, sorting, and problem solving/following directions.

David Lord, President/ CEO
Jim Czulewicz, Chief Revenue Officer

6152 Mindplay
4400 E. Broadway Blvd.
Suite 400
Tucson, AZ 85711
520-888-1800
800-221-7911
Fax: 520-888-7904
E-mail: mail@mindplay.com
http://www.mindplay.com
Educational software focusing on early childhood education and adult literacy.

Stacie Johnson, Communication Coordinator
Judith Bliss, Founder/ Chairwoman

6153 Nordic Software
PO Box 5403
Lincoln, NE 68505
402-489-1557
800-306-6502
Fax: 402-489-1560
E-mail: info@nordicsoftware.com
http://www.nordicsoftware.com
Specializes in developing and publishing educational software titles. Well-known for its software titles that make it easy for children to learn while playing on the computer. Develops and publishes elementary software products for the Macintosh and Windows platforms. Products include Turbo Math Facts, Clock Shop, Coin Critters, Language Explorer and Preschool Parade, and more.

Tammy Hurlbut, Finance/Operations

6154 Personalized Software
PO Box 359
Phoenix, OR 97535
541-535-8085
800-553-2312
Fax: 541-535-8889
E-mail: info@childcaremanager.com
http://www.childcaremanager.com

Offers a full line of childcare management and development software programs.

6155 Science for Kids
9950 Concord Church Road
Lewisville, NC 27023-9720
336-945-9000
800-572-4362
Fax: 336-945-2500
E-mail: sci4kids@aol.com
http://www.scienceforkids.com
Developers and publishers of CD-ROM science and early learning programs for children ages 5-14; for Macintosh and Windows computers; school and home programs available.

Charles Moyer, Executive VP

**6156 http://daycare.about.com/parentin
g/daycare**
About Parenting/Family Daycare

6157 www.booksofwonder.com
Books of Wonder
18 West 18th St.
New York, NY 10011
212-989-3270
800-207-6968
E-mail: info@booksofwonder.com
http://www.booksofwonder.com
New and vintage childrens books.

6158 www.lil-fingers.com
Lil' Fingers

http://www.lil-fingers.com
A computer storybook site for toddlers. Parents and children are encouraged to enjoy the colorful drawings and animations. Offers games, storybooks, coloring pages, the Lil' Store and more.

Elementary Education

**6159 Educational Institutions
Partnership Program**
Defense Information Systems Agency
Automation Resources Information
701 S Courthouse Road
Arlington, VA 22204-2199
703-607-6900
Fax: 703-607-4371
Makes available used computer equipment for donation of transfer to eligible schools, including K-12 schools recognized by the US Department of Education, Universities, colleges, Minority Institutions and nonporfit groups.

6160 Houghton Mifflin Company
222 Berkeley Street
Boston, MA 02116-3748
617-351-5000
Fax: 617-351-1106
http://www.hmhco.com
Offers literature-based technology products for grades K-8 including CD's Story Time, a Macintosh based CD-ROM programs for grades 1 and 2 and Channel R.E.A.D., a videodisc series for grades 3-8.

Linda K. Zecher, President/ CEO/ Director
Eric Shuman, Chief Financial Officer

6161 Kid Keys 2.0
Knowledge Adventure
800-545-7677
E-mail: schoolsales@jumpstart.com
http://www.knowledgeadventure.com
Keyboarding for grades K-2.

6162 Kinder Magic
1680 Meadowglen Lane
Encinitas, CA 92024-5652
760-632-6693
Fax: 760-632-9995
http://www.kindermagic.com
Educational software for ages 4-11.

Dr. Ilse Ortabasi, President

6163 Micrograms Publishing
9934 N Alpine Road
Suite 108
Machesney Park, IL 61115-8240
800-338-4726
Fax: 815-877-1482
http://www.micrograms.com
Micrograms develops educational software for schools and homes.

6164 Tudor Publishing Company
17218 Preston Road
Suite 400
Dallas, TX 75252-4018
Grade level evaluation (GLE) is a computer-adaptive assessment program for elementary and secondary students.

6165 Wordware Publishing
2320 Los Rios Boulevard
#200
Plano, TX 75074-8157
214-423-0090
Fax: 972-881-9147
Publisher of computer reference tutorials, regional Texas and Christian books. Educational division produces a diagnostic and remediation software for grade levels 3-8. Content covers over 3,000 objectives in reading, writing and math. Contact publisher for dealer information.

Eileen Schnett, Product Manager

6166 World Classroom
Global Learning Corporation
PO Box 201361
Arlington, TX 76006-1361
214-641-3356
800-866-4452
An educational telecommunications network that prepares students, K-12 to use real-life data to make real-life decisions about themselves and their environment. Participating countries have included Argentina, Australia, Belgium, Canada, Denmark, France, Germany, Hungary, Iceland, Indonesia, Kenya, Russia, Lithuania, Mexico, Singapore, Taiwan, the Netherlands, the United States and Zimbabwe.

**6167 http://k-6educators....education/k-6
educators**
About Education Elementary Educators

**6168 http://www.etacuisenaire.com/inde
x.htm**
ETA hand2mind
500 Greenview Court
Vernon Hills, IL 60061
847-816-5050
800-288-9920
Fax: 800-875-9643
http://www.hand2mind.com
Over 5,000 manipulative-based education and supplemental materials for grades K-12.

Bill Chiasson, President
Dr. Barbara diSioudi, VP, Product Development

6169 http://www.wnet.org/wnetschool
wNet School
212-560-2713
http://www.wnet.org/education
Helps K-12 teachers by providing free standards based lesson plans, classroom activities, multimedia primers, online mentors, links to model technology schools, and more. Online workshops are also included in the WNET TV site.

Carole Wacey, Vice President
Christopher Brande, National Segment Producer

6170 www.cherrydale.com/
Cherrydale Farms
707 N. Valley Forge Rd.
Lansdale, PA 19446
800-333-4525
E-mail: CDFinfo@Cherrydale.com
http://www.cherrydale.com
Website offers company information, fund raising products and information, online mega mall, card shop, career opportunities and much more. Produces fine chocolates and confections. Many opportunities for schools to raise funds with various Cherrydale programs.

6171 www.efundraising.com
Fundraising
C/O FedEx Trade Networks
156 Lawrence Paquette Ind'l Drive, PMW#
Champlain, NY 12919
866-825-2921
Fax: 877-275-8664
E-mail: online@fundraising.com
http://www.efundraising.com
Provides non-profit groups with quality products, low prices and superior service. Helping thousands of schools, youth sports teams and community groups reach their fundraising goals each year.

6172 www.hoagiesgifted.org
Hoagies' Gifted Education Page
256 Eagleview Boulevard PMB 123
Exton, PA 19341
E-mail: webmaster@hoagiesgifted.org
http://www.hoagiesgifted.org
Features the latest research on parenting and educating gifted children. Offers ideas, solutions and other things to try for parents of gifted children. Sections with world issues facing children and other important social topics.

Carolyn K. Founder/ Director

6173 www.netrover.com/~kingskid/108.html
Room 108

http://www.netrover.com
An educational activity center for kids. Offers lots of fun for children with educational focus; like songs, art, math, kids games, children's stories and much more. Sections with pen pal information, puzzles, crosswords, teachers store, spelling, kids sites, email, music, games and more.

6174 www.netrox.net
Dr. Labush's Links to Learning

http://www.mylinkstolearning.com
General links for teachers with internet help, coloring pages, and enrichment programs.

6175 www.primarygames.com
PrimaryGames.com
E-mail: webmaster@primarygames.com
http://www.primarygames.com
Contains educational games for elementary students.

6176 www.usajobs.opm.gov/b1c.htm
Overseas Employment Info-Teachers

Employment

7 Educational Placement Service
90 S Cascade
Suite 1110
Colorado Springs, CO 80903

http://www.teacherjobs.com
Largest teacher placement service in the U.S.

8 Job Bulletin
American Association of School
Administrators
1615 Duke Street
Alexandria, VA 22314
703-528-0700
Fax: 703-841-1543
E-mail: info@aasa.org
http://www.aasa.org
The Job Bulletin was made to help employers
and job candidates save time finding one an-
other.

Jay Goldman, Editor
Kelly Beckwith, Project Director

9 Teachers@Work
PO Box 430
Vail, CO 81658
970-476-5008
Fax: 970-476-1496
E-mail: support@teachersatwork.com
http://www.teachersatwork.com
Electronic employment service designed to
match the professional staffing needs of
schools with teacher applicants.

0 www.SchoolJobs.com
SchoolJobs.com
Provides principals, superintendents and
other administrators the ability to market
their job openings to a national pool of candidates, also gives educational professionals
the chance to search for opportunities
matching their skills.

1 www.aasa.org
American Association of School
Administrators
1615 Duke Street
Suite 700
Alexandria, VA 22314-1730
703-528-0700
Fax: 703-841-1543
E-mail: info@aasa.org
http://www.aasa.org
Leadership news online.

Jay Goldman, Editor
Kelly Beckwith, Project Director

Guidance & Counseling

**2 Alcohol & Drug Prevention for
Teachers, Law Enforcement &
Parent Groups**
PO Box 4656
Reading, PA 19606
610-582-2090
Fax: 610-404-0406
E-mail: nodrugs@earthlink.net
http://www.nodrugs.com
Local organizations and international groups
against drugs.

3 Live Wire Media
P.O. Box 848
Mill Valley, CA 94942
415-564-9500
800-359-5437
Fax: 415-552-4087

E-mail: sales@livewiremedia.com
http://www.livewiremedia.com/
Videos for youth guidance and character development, and teacher training.

Christine Hollander, Director Marketing

6184 Phillip Roy Multimedia Materials
PO Box 130
Indian Rocks Beach, FL 34635
727-593-2700
800-255-9085
Fax: 727-595-2685
E-mail: ruth@philliproy.com
http://www.phillproy.com
Multimedia materials for use with alternative
education, Chapter 1, dropout prevention,
Even Start, Head Start, JTPA/PIC, special education students, at-risk students, transition
to work programs. Focuses on basic skills,
conflict resolution, remediation, vocational
education, critical thinking skills, communication skills, reasoning and decision making
skills. Materials can be duplicated networked
at no cost.

Phil Padol, Consultant
Regina Jacques, Customer Support

6185 www.goodcharacter.com
Character Education
P.O. BOX 848
Mill Valley, CA 94942
415-564-9500
800-359-KIDS
Fax: 415-552-4087
http://www.goodcharacter.com
Teaching guides for k-12 character education, packed with discussion questions, assignments, and activities that you can use as
your own lesson plans.

International

6186 www.aed.org
FHI 360
359 Blackwell Street
Suite 200
Durham, NC 27701
919-544-7040
Fax: 919-544-7261
http://www.fhi360.og
The site provides information on interna-
tional exchange, fellowshipand training.

Patrick C. Fine, Med, Chief Executive
Officer
Manisha Bharti, MPH, MBA, Chief Stategy
Officer

6187 www.asce.org
American Society of Civil Engineers
1801 Alexander Bell Drive
Reston, VA 20191
703-295-6300
800-548-2723
http://www.asce.org
This site lists scholarships and fellowships
available only to ASCE members.

Robert D. Stevens, President
Dennis D. Truax, Treasurer

6188 www.cie.uci.edu
International Opportunities Program
1100 Student Services II
Irvine, CA 92697-2475
949-824-6343
Fax: 949-824-9133
E-mail: studyabroad@uci.edu
http://www.cie.uci.edu

Valuable links for exploring opportunities
for study and research abroad.

Marcella Khelif, Associate Director
Sharon Parks, Assistant Director

6189 www.ciee.org
Council on International Educational
Exchange
300 Fore St.
Portland, ME 4101
207-553-4000
Fax: 207-553-4299
E-mail: contact@ciee.org
http://www.ciee.org
Study abroad programs by region, work
abroad opportunities, international volunteer
projects and Council-administered financial
aid and grant information .

Dr. James P. Pellow, President/ CEO
Jorge Barroso, Chief Information Officer

6190 www.cies.org
Council for International Exchange of
Scholars
1400 K Street, NW
Suite 700
Washington, DC 20005
202-686-4000
Fax: 202-686-4029
E-mail: Scholars@iie.org
http://www.cies.org
Information on the Fulbright Senior Scholar
Program which is made available to Fulbright
alumni,grantees, prospective applicants and
public at large.

Jeff Hopper, Director
Peter VanDerwater, Director of Outreach

6191 www.daad.org
German Academic Exchange Service
(DADD)
871 United Nations Plaza
New York, NY 10017
212-758-3223
Fax: 212-755-5780
E-mail: daadny@daad.org
http://www.daad.org
Promotes international academic relations
and contains links to research grants, summer
language grants,annual grants, grants in German studies andspecial programs.

Dr. Nina Lemmens, Director
Peter Kerrigan, Deputy & Marketing
Director

6192 www.ed.gov
US Department of Education
400 Maryland Avenue, SW
Washington, DC 20202
800-872-5327
E-mail: answers.ed.gov
http://www2.ed.gov
This site describes programs and fellowships
offered by the International Education and
Graduate Programs office of the US Department of Education.

Arne Duncan, Secretary of Education
Emma Vadehra, Chief of Staff

6193 www.finaid.org
FinAid
A free, comprehensive, independent and
ojective guide to student financial aid.

Mark Kantrowitz, Founder

6194 www.iie.org
Institute of International Education
P.O. Box 1020
Sewickley, PA 15143-1020
412-741-0930
Fax: 212-984-5452

E-mail: iiebooks@abdintl.com
http://www.iiebooks.org
The largest not-for-profit international educational organization in the United States. This site provides information regarding IIE's programs, services and resources, including the Filbright Fellowship.

6195 www.iiepasspport.org
Institute of International Education
IIE Passport: Study Abroad
1350 Edgmont Avenue Suite 1100
Chester, PA 19013
877-404-0338
Fax: 610-499-9205
E-mail: iiesupport@naylor.com
http://www.iiepassport.org
A student guide on the web to 5,000 learning oppurtunities worldwide.

6196 www.irex.org
International Research and Exchange Board
E-mail: questions@finaid.org
http://www.finaid.org
Academic exchanges between the United States and Russia. Lists a variety of programs as well as grant and fellowship oppurtunities.

6197 www.isp.msu.edu/ncsa
Michigan State University
National Consortium for Study in Af in Africa
E-mail: ncsa@msu.edu
http://www.istc.umn.edu
Provides a comprehensive lists of sponsors for African exchange.

6198 www.istc.umn.edu/
University of Minnesota
International Study and Travel Center
Comprehensive and searchable links to study, work and travel abroad opportunities.

6199 www.languagetravel.com
Language Travel Magazine
Resource for finding study abroad language immersion courses.

6200 www.nsf.gov/
National Science Foundation
4201 Wilson Blvd
Arlington, VA 22230
703-292-5111
E-mail: info@nsf.gov
http://www.nsf.gov
Encourages exchange in science and engineering. The site has inter-national component, providing links with valuable information on fellowships grants and awards, summer institutes, workshops,research and education projects and international programs.

Dr. France A. Cerdova, Director
Dr. Richard O. Buckius, Chief Operating Officer

6201 www.si.edu/
Smithsonian Institution
600 Maryland Ave.
Suite 1005
Washington, DC 20024
202-633-5330
Fax: 202-633-5489
E-mail: learning@si.edu
http://www.smithsonianeducation.org
Fellowships link to Smithsonian Oppurtunities for research and study.

Patricia Bartlett, Chief of Staff
Claudine Brown, Assistant Secretary

6202 www.studiesinaustralia.com/study
Studies in Australia
E-mail: enquiries@studiesinaustralia.com
http://www.studiesinaustralia.com
Listing of study abroad oppurtunities in Australia, providing details of academic and training institutions and the programs they offer to prospective international students and education professionals.

Denis Whelan, Vice President of Sales
Elysia Singam, Advertising Copy Controller

6203 www.studyabroad.com/
StudyAbroad.com
3803 West Chester Pk.
Suite 125
Newtown Sq, PA 19073
484-766-2920
Fax: 610-499-9205
E-mail: webmaster@studyabroad.com
http://www.studyabroad.com
Study abroad information resource listing study abroad programs worldwide.

6204 www.studyabroad.com/.
StudyAbroad.com
3803 West Chester Pk.
Suite 125
Newtown Sq, PA 19073
484-766-2920
Fax: 610-499-9205
E-mail: webmaster@studyabroad.com
http://www.studyabroad.com
A commercial site with thousands of study abroad programs in over 100 countries with links to study abroad program home pages.

6205 www.ucis.pitt.edu/crees
University of Pittsburgh
Center for Russian/European Studies
4400 Wesley W. Posvar Hall, 230 South Bo
Pittsburgh, PA 15260
412-648-7407
Fax: 412-648-7002
E-mail: crees@pitt.edu
http://www.ucis.pitt.edu/crees
Index of electronic resources for the student interested in Russian and European language and culture study.

Andrew Konitzer, Acting Director
Dawn Seckler, Acting Associate Director

6206 www.upenn.edu/oip/scholarships.html
University of Pennsylvania
Scholarships/Graduate Study Abroad
Provides links for graduate study abroad and scholarship opportunities.

6207 www.usc.edu
University of Southern California
Resources for Colleges and Universities in International Exchange
Links for browsing all aspects of international exchange, including study, research, work and teaching abroad, financial aid, grants and scholarships.

6208 www.usinfo.state/gov
US Department of State International Information Programs
Comprehensive desriptions of all IIP programs, sections on policy issues, global and regional issues and IIP publications.

6209 www.wes.org
World Education Services
Bowling Green Station
P.O. Box 5087
New York, NY 10274-5087

212-966-6311
Fax: 212-739-6100
http://www.wes.org
Features information on WES' foreign credentials evaluation services, world education workshops, and the journals World Education and News Reviews.

6210 www.world-arts-resources.com/
World Wide Arts Resources
P.O. Box 150
Granville, OH 43023
646-455-1425
http://wwar.com
Focuses solely on the arts, this site provides links for funding sources, university programs and arts organizations all over the world.

6211 www.yfu.org/
Youth for Understanding (YFU)
641 S Street, NW.
Suite 200
Washington, DC 20001
202-774-5200
http://yfuusa.org
Oppurtunities for young people around the world to spend a summer, semester or year with a host family in another country.

6212 wwww.sas.upenn.edu
African Studies Center, University of Pennsylvania
647 Williams Hall
255 S 36th Street
Philadelphia, PA 19104-6305
215-898-6971
Fax: 215-573-7379
http://www.africa.upenn.edu
Links to Africa-related internet sources, African Studies Association and UPenn African Studies Center.

Carol Muller, Ph.D, Director
Ali B. Ali-Dinar, Ph.D, Associate Director

Language Arts

6213 Advantage Learning Systems
Renaissance Learning
2911 Peach Street
Wisconsin Rapids, WI 54494
715-424-3636
800-338-4204
Fax: 715-424-4242
E-mail: answers@renlearn.com
http://www.renlearn.com
Accelerated Reader software and manuals that motivate K-12 students to read more and better books. The program boosts reading scores and library circulation. Lets educators quickly and accurately assess student reading while motivating students to read more and better books.

John J. Lynch Jr., Chief Executive Officer
Mary T. Minch, EVP, Finance & CFO

6214 Bytes of Learning Incorporated
266 Elmwood Avenue #256
Buffalo, NY 14222
905-947-4646
800-465-6428
Fax: 905-475-8650
http://www.bytesoflearning.com
Single and site licensed software for Macintosh, Apple II, DOS and Windows-network compatible too. Keyboarding, language arts, career exploration and more on diskette and CD-ROM.

6215 Humanities Software
408 Columbia Street
#950
Hood River, OR 97031-2044

503-386-6737
800-245-6737
Fax: 541-386-1410
Over 150 whole language, literature-based language arts software titles for grades K-12.

Karen Withrow, Marketing Assistant
Charlotte Arnold, Marketing Director

16 Teacher Support Software
3542 NW 97th Boulevard
Gainesville, FL 32606-7322
352-332-6404
800-228-2871
Fax: 352-332-6779
E-mail: tss@tssoftware.com
http://www.tssoftware.com
Language arts, Title 1, special ed, at-risk and ESL, curriculum-based networkable software for grades K-12. Vocabulary software that develops sight word recognition, provides basal correlated databases, tests reading comprehension, tracks student's progress and provides powerful teacher tools.

17 Weaver Instructional Systems
6161 28th Street SE
Grand Rapids, MI 49546-6931
616-942-2891
800-634-8916
Fax: 616-942-1796
E-mail: wisesoft@aol.com
http://www.wisesoft.com
Reading and language arts computer software programs for K-college.

18 www.caslt.org
Canadian Association of Second Language Teachers
2490 Don Reid Drive
Ottawa, ON K1H 1
613-727-0994
877-727-0994
E-mail: info@caslt.org
http://www.caslt.org
Promotes the advancement of second language education throughout Canada.

Guy Leclair, Executive Director
Diane Paquette, Finance Manager

19 www.riverdeep.net
Riverdeep Interactive Learning
617-351-5316
800-426-6577
E-mail: Sales_Support@hmhco.com
http://forms.hmhco.com
Riverdeep's interactive science, language and math arts programs deliver high quality educational experiences.

20 www.signit2.com
Aylmer Press
Box 2302
Madison, WI 53701
608-441-5277
E-mail: steve@signit2.com
http://www.signit2.com
Website hosted by Aylmer Press which produces video's to teach kids sign language as well as music.

21 www.usajobs.opm.gov/b1c.htm1
Overseas Employment Info- Teachers
US Office of Personnel Management

Library Services

22 American Econo-Clad Services
2101 N Topeka
Topeka, KS 66601
800-255-3502
Fax: 785-233-3129

A full service supplier of educational materials for the library, curriculum and software resource needs including MatchMaker, CD-ROM and ABLE (Analytically Budgeted Library Expenditures) computer systems.

6223 Anchor Audio Portable Sound Systems
5931 Darwin Court
Carlsbad, CA 92008
310-784-2300
800-262-4671
Fax: 760-827-7105
E-mail: sales@anchoraudio.com
http://www.anchoraudio.com
Various audio visual products for the school and library.

Alex Jacobs, VP, Sales

6224 Baker & Taylor
2550 West Tyvola Road
Suite 300
Charlotte, NC 28217
704-998-3100
800-775-1800
http://www.baker-taylor.com
Nation's leading wholesale supplier of audio, computer software, books, videocassettes and other accessories to schools and libraries.

George F. Coe, President/ CEO
Jeff Leonard, Chief Financial Officer

6225 Brodart Company, Automation Division
500 Arch Street
Williamsport, PA 17701
570-326-2461
800-233-8467
Fax: 570-326-1479
E-mail: support@brodart.com
http://www.brodart.com
Brodart's Automation Division has been providing library systems, software, and services for over 25 years. Products include: library management systems, media management systems, Internet solutions, cataloged web sites, cataloging resource tools, union catalog solutions, public access catalogs, and bibliographic services.

Kasey Dibble, Marketing Coordinator
Sally Wilmoth, Director Marketing/Sales

6226 Catalog Card Company
12219 Nicollet Avenue
Burnsville, MN 55337-1650
612-882-8558
800-442-7332
Fax: 785-290-1223
MARC records compatible with all software for retrospective conversions and new book orders. Catalog Card's conversion services include barcode labels to complement circulation software. MARC records generated from Dewey/Sears and Library of Congress databases are in standard USMARC or MicroLIF format.

6227 Data Trek
5838 Edison Place
Carlsbad, CA 92008-6519
800-876-5484
Turn-key library automation systems and computer networks.

6228 Demco
PO Box 7488
Madison, WI 53707-7488
800-356-1200
Fax: 800-245-1329
E-mail: custserv@demco.com
http://www.demco.com
A leader in educational and library supplies for more than 80 years, Demco offers library

audio and visual supplies and equipment plus display furniture.

6229 Dewey Decimal Classification
OCLC Forest Press
6565 Frantz Road
Dublin, OH 43017-3395
614-764-6000
800-848-5878
Fax: 614-764-6096
E-mail: oclc@oclc.org
http://www.oclc.org/fp
OCLC Forest Press publishes the Dewey Decimal Classification (DDC) system and many related print and CD-ROM products that teach librarians and library users about the DDC.

Skip Prichard, Chief Executive Officer
Rick Schwieterman, Chief Financial Officer

6230 Ebsco Subscription Services
International Headquarters
10 Estes Street
Ipswich, MA 01938
205-991-1480
800-653-2726
Fax: 978-356-6565
E-mail: information@ebsco.com
http://www.ebsco.com
Periodical subscription and ordering and customer service equipment, computer and CD-ROM supplies, products and hardware for libraries.

Tim Collins, President
Sam Brooks, EVP

6231 Electronic Bookshelf
5276 S Country Road, 700 W
Frankfort, IN 46041
765-324-2182
Fax: 765-324-2183
Reading motivation, testing management system and various computer systems and networks for educational purposes.

Rosalie Carter

6232 Filette Keez Corporation/Colorworks Diskette Organizing System
3204 Channing Lane
Bedford, TX 76021-6506
817-283-5428
Produces ten filing inventions for classroom library, lab and district technology resources management. SelecTsideS folders store multimedia in Press-an-Inch Technology Slings and keep instruction, printouts, pamphlets and blackliners altogether. The diskette/CD portfolio color coordinates with the student/magazine Spbinder, plastic LaceLox fastener and all systems paper supplies: CD envelopes, storage box dividers, sheeted cards, perforated tractor labels and keys, available in 7 tech colors.

Roxanne Kay Harbert, Founder/President
Ray L Harbert, VP

6233 Follett School Solutions
1391 Corporate Drive
McHenry, IL 60050-7041
815-344-8700
800-323-3397
Fax: 800-807-3623
E-mail: sales@winnebago.com
http://www.follettsoftware.com
Comprehensive, user-friendly circulation and catalog software for Windows, Mac OS, and MS-DOS systems-plus Internet technology, online periodical databases, outstanding customer support, and retrospective conversion services-all developed within the quality

guidelines of Winnebago's ISO 9001 certification with TickIT accreditation.

6234 Follett Software Company

1391 Corporate Drive
McHenry, IL 60050-7041
815-344-8700
800-323-3397
Fax: 815-344-8774
E-mail: marketing@fsc.follett.com
http://www.fsc.follett.com
Helping K-12 schools and districts create a vital library-to-classroom link to improve student achievement. FSC combines award-winning library automation with practical applications of the Internet. From OPAC data enhancement and easy-to-implement Internet technology to innovative information literacy solutions, FSC helps simplify resource management, increase access to resources inside and outside your collection and provide tools to integrate technology into the curriculum.

Patricia Yonushonis, Marketing Manager
Ann Reist, Conference Manager

6235 Foundation for Library Research

1200 Bigley Avenue
Charleston, WV 25302-3752
304-343-6480
Fax: 304-343-6489
The Automated Library Systems integrated library automation software.

Robert Evans

6236 Gaylord Brothers

PO Box 4901
Syracuse, NY 13221-4901
800-448-6160
Fax: 800-272-3412
http://www.gaylord.com
Library, AV supplies and equipment; security systems; and library furniture.

Tim Krein

6237 Highsmith Company

W5527 Highway 106
Fort Atkinson, WI 53538
414-563-9571
Catalog of microcomputer and multimedia curriculum products and software.

Barbara R Endl

6238 Information Access Company

362 Lakeside Drive
Foster City, CA 94404-1171
800-227-8431
Offers automation products and electronics for library/media centers.

6239 LePAC NET

Brodart Automation
500 Arch Street
Williamsport, PA 17701
570-326-2461
800-233-8467
Fax: 570-326-1479
E-mail: support@brodart.com
http://www.brodart.com
Software for searching thousands of library databases with a single search. Schools can use to take multiple individual library databases and consolidate them, while deleting duplicate listings, into a union database.

Shawn Knight, Assistant Marketing Manager
Denise Macafee, Marketing Manager

6240 Library Corporation

Library Corporation
Research Park
Inwood, WV 25428-9733
304-229-0100
800-325-7759
Fax: 304-229-0295
E-mail: info@TLCdelivers.com
http://www.tlcdelivers.com
Web-based library management systems allows patrons to have easy and immediate access to books and other library resources.

Annette Harwood Murphy, President/CEO/Chair
Calvin Whittington, Director, Finance & Admin

6241 Lingo Fun

International Software
PO Box 486
Westerville, OH 43086-0486
800-745-8258
Providers of microcomputer software including CD-ROM's for Macintosh and MPC, on-line dictionaries, translation assistants; teaching programs for elementary presentation, review and reinforcement, test preparation, and literary exploration.

6242 MARCIVE

PO Box 47508
San Antonio, TX 78265-7508
210-646-6161
800-531-7678
Fax: 210-646-0167
E-mail: info@marcive.com
http://www.marcive.com
Economical, fast 100% conversion. Full MARC records with SEARS or LC headings. Free authorities processing smart barcode labels, reclassification, MARC Record enrichment

Robert Fleming, President
Scott Fleming, Chief Operating Officer

6243 Medianet/Dymaxion Research Limited

5515 Cogswell Street
Halifax, No B3J 1
902-422-1973
Fax: 902-421-1267
E-mail: info@medianet.ns.ca
http://www.medianet.ns.ca
Medianet is the scheduling system for equipment and media that has consistently been rated as best in its class. Features include book library system integration, time-of-day booking, catalog production, WWW and touch tone phone booking by patrons.

Peter Mason, President

6244 Mitinet/Marc Software

PO Box 505
Bethany, MO 64424-0505
608-845-2300
800-824-6272
Fax: 660-425-3998
http://www.mitinet.com
Import/export USMARC, MICROLIF to USMARC conversions.

Bart Fitzgerald, Owner/ President
Cindy Beerkircher, Office Manager

6245 Orange Cherry Software

69 Westchester Avenue
PO Box 390
Pound Ridge, NY 10576-1702
914-764-4104
800-672-6002
Fax: 914-764-0104
http://www.orangecherry.com

Educational software products for libraries and media centers.

Biannual

Nicholas Vazzana, President

6246 Pearson Education

3001 Wayburne Drive
Burnbay
Canada V5G 4W3
604-294-1233
877-873-1550
Fax: 604-294-2225
E-mail: proded@pearson.com
http://www.pearsonschoolsystems.com
Online catalog searches and checking materials in and out.

6247 Right on Programs

27 Bowdon Road
Suite B
Greenlawn, NY 11740
631-424-7777
Fax: 631-424-7207
E-mail: riteonsoft@aol.com
http://www.rightonlibrarysoftware.com
Computer software for Windows and networks for library management including circulation, cataloging, periodicals, catalog cardmaking, inventory and thirty more. Used in more than 24,000 schools and libraries of all sizes.

D Farren, VP

6248 SOLINET, Southeastern Library Network

1438 W Peachtree Street NW
Suite 200
Atlanta, GA 30309-2955
404-892-0943
800-999-8558
Fax: 404-892-7879
E-mail: information@solinet.net
http://www.solinet.net
SOLINET provides access, training and support for OCLC products and services; offers discounted library products and services, including licensed databases; provides electronic information solutions; workflow consulting, training and customized workshops; and supports a regional preservation of materials program.

Cathie Gharing, Marketing Coordinator
Liz Hornsby, Editor

6249 SirsiDynix

3300 North Ashton Blvd
Suite 500
Lehi, UT 84043
801-223-5200
800-288-8020
Fax: 801-331-7770
E-mail: marketing@sirsidynix.com
http://www.sirsi.com
Unicorn Collection Management Systems are fully integrated UNIX-based library systems, automating all of a library's operation. Modules include: cataloging, authority control, public access, materials booking, circulation, academic reserves, acquisitions, serials control, reference database manager and electronic mail. Modules can be configured for all types and sizes of libraries.

Bill Davison, Chief Executive Officer
Scott Wheelhouse, SVP, Operations

6250 Social Issues Resources Series

PO Box 2348
Boca Raton, FL 33427
561-994-0079
800-521-0600
Fax: 561-994-4704
http://ars.sirs.com
Publisher of CD-ROM reference systems for PC and Macintosh computers. Databases of full-text

articles carefully selected from 1,000 domestic and international sources. Also provides PC-compatible and stand-alone and network packages.

Paula Jackson, Marketing Director
Suzanne Panek, Customer Service

51 TekData Systems Company
1111 W Park Avenue
Libertyville, IL 60048-2952
847-367-8800
Fax: 847-367-0235
E-mail: tekdata@tekdata.com
http://www.tekdata.com
Scheduling and booking systems for intranets and internets.

Randy Kick, Sales Manager

52 Three M Library Systems
Three M Center
Building 225-4N-14
St. Paul, MN 55144
800-328-0067
Fax: 800-223-5563
Materials Flow Management system is the first comprehensive system for optimizing the handling, processing and security of your library materials - from processing to checkout to check-in. The SelfCheck System and Staff Workstation automate the processing of virtually all of your library materials, while the Tattle-Tape Security Strips and Detection Systems help ensure the security of those materials.

53 UMI
300 N Zeeb Road
Ann Arbor, MI 48103-1553
800-521-0600
Fax: 800-864-0019
Information products in microform, CD-ROM, online and magnetic tape.

54 University Products
517 Main Street
#101
Holyoke, MA 01040-5514
413-532-3372
800-628-1912
Fax: 413-452-0618
E-mail: info@universityproducts.com
http://www.universityproducts.com
Complete selection of library and media center supplies and equipment.

Juhn Dunpay

55 WLN
PO Box 3888
Lacey, WA 98509-3888
360-923-4000
800-342-5956
Fax: 360-923-4009
School and media librarians experience 95% hit rates with WLN's LaserCat, CD-ROM database, a cataloging product and MARC record service.

56 www.awesomelibrary.org
Awesome Library

http://www.awesomelibrary.org
Organizes the Web with 15,000 carefully reviewed resources, including the top 5 percent in education. Offers sections of mathematics, science, social studies, english, health, physical education, technology, languages, special education, the arts and more. Features a section involved with today's current issues facing our world, like pollution, gun control, tobacco, and other changing 'hot' topics. Site can be browsed in English, German, Spanish, French or Portuguese.

6257 www.techlearning.com
Technology & Learning
28 East 28th Street
12th floor
New York, NY 10016
212-378-0400
Fax: 212-378-0470
http://www.techlearning.com
Open 24 hours, every day of the week, with an extensive and up-to-date catalog of over 53,000 software and hardware products. Powerful search engine will help you find the right education-specific products.

Mathematics

6258 Accelerated Math
Renaissance Learning
2911 Peach Street
Wisconsin Rapids, WI 54494
715-424-3636
800-338-4204
Fax: 715-424-4242
E-mail: answers@renlearn.com
http://www.renlearn.com
Accelerated Math provides 17 different reports, providing individualized, constructive feedback to students, parents, and teachers.

John J. Lynch Jr., Chief Executive Officer
Mary T. Minch, EVP, Finance & CFO

6259 Applied Mathematics Program
Prime Technology Corporation
PO Box 2407
Minneola, FL 34755-2407
352-394-7558
Fax: 352-394-3778
http://www.primetechnology.net
Provides students with comprehensive instruction in 11 math areas. In working with this program, students develop employment and life skills. The program will also lead the student to greater success on the mathematics sections of any standardized test.

Paul Scime, President

6260 CAE Software
3608 Shepherd Street
Chevy Chase, MD 20815-4132
301-907-9845
800-354-3462
Provides educational software for mathematics, grades 3-12. Simulations, tutorials, games, and problem solving. Titles include Mathematics Life Skills Services, Reading and Making Graphs Series, MathLab Series, Meaning of Fractions, Using Fractions and Using Decimals, ALG Football, GEO Pool and GEO Billiards, Paper Route, Mathematics Achievement Project, and others.

Alan R Chap, President

6261 EME Corporation
PO Box 1949
Stuart, FL 34995-1949
772-285-2131
800-848-2050
Fax: 561-219-2209
E-mail: emecorp@aol.com
http://www.emescience.com
Publishers of award-winning science and math software, elementary through high school levels.

6262 Logal Software
125 Cambridgepark Drive
Cambridge, MA 02140-2329
617-491-4440
Fax: 617-491-5855

Math and science products for high school through college.

Martha Cheng, President

6263 MathType
Design Science
140 Pine Avenue
4th Floor
Long Beach, CA 90803-1502
562-432-2920
800-827-0685
Fax: 562-432-2857
E-mail: info@dessci.com
http://www.dessci.com
Designed to make the creation of complex equations on a computer simple and fast. It works in conjunction with the software applications you already own, such as word processing programs, graphics programs, presentation programs, and web-authoring applications. Create research papers, tests, slides, books or web pages quickly and easily. MathType is the powerful, professional version of the Equation Editor in Microscoft Word, and Wordperfect.

Bruce Virga, EVP Sales/BD, COO
Paul R. Topping, President/ CEO

6264 Mathematica
Wolfram Research, Inc.
100 Trade Center Drive
Champaign, IL 61820-7237
217-398-0700
800-965-3726
Fax: 217-398-0747
E-mail: info@wolfram.com
http://www.wolfram.com
Mathematica is an indispensable tool for finding and communicating solutions quickly and easily.

Stephen Wolfram, Founder/CEO
Jean Buck, Dir., Corp Communications

6265 MindTwister Math
Edmark Corporation
PO Box 97021
Redmond, WA 98073-9721
425-556-8400
800-691-2986
Fax: 425-556-8430
E-mail: edmarkteam@edmark.com
http://www.edmark.com
Software to help students in grade 3 and 4 build math fact fluency, practice mental math and improve estimating skills as they compete in a series of math challenges.

6266 Multimedia - The Human Body
Sunburst Digital, Inc.
3150 W Higgins Rd
Ste 140
Hoffman Estates, IL 60169
914-747-3310
800-321-7511
Fax: 914-747-4109
E-mail: service@sunburst.com
http://www.sunburst.com
Multimedia production of the intricate workings of the human body.

6267 Texas Instruments
Consumer Relations
12500 TI Boulevard
Dallas, TX 75243
972-995-2011
800-842-2737
Fax: 972-917-0874
http://www.ti.com
Instructional calculators offer features matched to math concepts taught at each of conceptional development. Classroom accessories and teacher support programs that support the Texas Instruments products enhance

instruction and learning. TI also offers a complete range of powerful notebook computers and laser printers for every need.

Rich Templeton, Chairman/ President/ CEO
Steve Anderson Analog, SVP

6268 William K. Bradford Publishing Company
35 Forest Ridge Road
Concord, MA 01742-5414
800-421-2009
Fax: 978-318-9500
http://www.wkbradford.com
Educational software for grades K-12. Especially math and grade book.

Hal Wexler, VP

6269 www.mathgoodies.com
Mrs. Glosser's Math Goodies
75 Mill Street
Colchester, CT 6415
914-736-0286
Fax: 866-776-9170
http://www.mathgoodies.com
Free educational site featuring interactive math lessons. Use a problem-solving approach and actively engage students in the learning process.

6270 www.mathstories.com
MathStories.com
1426 Pine Grove Way
San Jose, CA 95129
E-mail: Customerservice@Mathstories.com
http://www.mathstories.com
The goal of this site is to help grade school children improve their math problem-solving and critical thinking skills. Offers over 4000 math word problems for children.

6271 www.riverdeep.net
Riverdeep Interactive Learning
617-351-5316
800-426-6577
E-mail: Sales_Support@hmhco.com
http://forms.hmhco.com
Riverdeep's interactive science, language and math arts programs deliver high quality educational experiences.

6272 www.themathemagician.8m.com
The Mathemagician
310-452-0655
E-mail: themathemagician_us@yahoo.com
http://www.themathemagician.8m.com
Offers the help of a real live person to help students correct and understand math and other home work problems.

Music & Art

6273 Harmonic Vision
1433 Rapids Trl
Nekoosa, WI 54457
715-325-3252
800-474-0903
Fax: 866-422-6686
http://www.harmonicvision.com
Leading musical education software to teach effectiveness of music in the home, school and studio.

6274 Midnight Play
Simon & Schuster Interactive
1230 Avenue of the Americas
New York, NY 10020
212-698-7000
800-793-9972
http://www.simonandschuster.com

Electronic picture book with an unusual look at creativity.

Carolyn Reidy, President/ CEO
Jon Anderson, EVP & Publisher

6275 Music Teacher Find
33 W 17th Street
10th Floor
New York, NY 10011
212-242-2464
http://www.MusicTeacherFind.com
Comprehensive Music Teacher Database designed to help music students find quality teachers in their neighborhood.

6276 Music and Guitar
http://www.nl-guitar.com
Original music programs for schools, courses and encounterswith music.

6277 Pure Gold Teaching Tools
PO Box 16622
Tuscon, AZ 85732
520-747-5600
866-692-6500
Fax: 520-571-9077
E-mail: info@puregoldteachingtools.com
http://www.puregoldteachingtools.com
Exciting teaching methods and fabulous gifts for teachers, parents, students, pre-schoolers, homeschoolers and music therapists.

Heidi Goldman, President

6278 http://library.thinkquest.org
Think Quest
http://gitso-outage.oracle.com/thinkquest
The Arti FAQS 2100 Project is designed to predict how art will influence our lives in the next hundred years. Students can use available data to make reasonable predictions for the future.

6279 http://members.truepath.com/head oftheclass
Head of The Class
Offers three galleries with clip art for teachers and children, several lesson plans, teaching tips, songs for teachers, lounge laughs, teacher tales and more.

6280 www.billharley.com
Round River Productions
301 Jacob Street
Seekonk, MA 2771
508-336-9703
800-682-9522
Fax: 508-336-2254
E-mail: debbie@billharley.com
http://www.billharley.com
Humerous, yet meaningful songs which chronicle the lives of children at school and at home. His recordings of songs and stories can be used most effectively in the classroom as inspirational tools for the motivation of learning.

6281 www.sanford-artedventures.com
Sanford- A Lifetime of Color
800-323-0749
Teaches students about art and color theory while they play a game. Lessons plans, newsletter and product information.

6282 www.songs4teachers.com
O'Flynn Consulting
E-mail: oflynn4@home.com
Offers many resources for teachers including songs made especially for your classroom. Sections with songs and activities for holidays, seasons and more. Features

books and audios with 101 theme songs for use in the classroom or anywhere children gather to sing.

6283 www.ushistory.com
History Happens
http://www.songsabouthistory.com
Teaches integrating art, music, literature, science, math, library skills, and American history. The Primary source is stories from American history presented in musci video style.

Physical Education

6284 InfoUse
2560 9th Street
Suite 216
Berkeley, CA 94710-2557
510-549-6520
Fax: 510-549-6512
An award-winning, multimedia development and products firm, features CD-ROM, websites on health, education and disability. For training, education or presentations, our services include: research, instructional design, interface design, graphics, animation, content acquisition, videoing, analog and digital editing and evaluation. Products include SafeNet, (HIV prevention for fifth and sixth grade children), Place Math and Math Pad (math tools and lessons for students with disabilities).

Lewis E Kraus, VP
Susan Stoddard, President

6285 www.sports-media.org
Sports Media
http://www.sports-media.org
A tool for p.e. teachers, coaches, students and everyone who is interested in p.e./fitness and sports. Interactive p.e. lesson plans, sports pen-apls for the kids, European p.e. mailing list, and developing teaching skills in physical education.

Dr. Zan Gao, Editor-in-Chief
Guy Van Damme, Co-Chief editor

Reading

6286 Accelerated Reader
Renaissance Learning
2911 Peach Street
Wisconsin Rapids, WI 54494
715-424-3636
800-338-4204
Fax: 715-424-4242
E-mail: answers@renlearn.com
http://www.renlearn.com
Helps teachers increase literature-based reading practice for all k-12 students

John J. Lynch Jr., Chief Executive Officer
Mary T. Minch, EVP, Finance & CFO

Secondary Education

6287 New York Times
New York, NY
646-698-8000
Fax: 646-698-8344
http://www.nytimes.com/learning
A resource for educators, parents and students in grades six through 12. Provides a daily lesson plan and comprehensive interactive resources based on newspaper content.

Katherine Schulte, Editor
Michael Gonchar, Deputy Editor

8 Wm. C. Brown Communications
2460 Kerper Boulevard
Dubuque, IA 52001-2224
College textbooks, software, CD-ROM and more for grades 10-12.

9 http://adulted.about.com/education/adulted
Adult/Continuing Education

0 http://englishhlp.www5.50megs.com
English Help
E-mail: englishhlpr@hotmail.com
This page is a walk through of Microsoft Power Point. The goal is to show in a few simple steps how to make your own website. Created by Rebecca Holland.

1 www.number2.com
Number2.com
Currently offer SAT and GRE prep along with a vocabulary builder. Practice questions and word drill are adapted to the ability level of the user.

Science

2 Academic Software Development Group
University of Maryland
University of Maryland
Computer Science Center
College Park, MD 20742-0001
301-405-5100
Fax: 301-405-0726
Offers BioQuest Library which is a set of peer-reviewed resources for science education.

3 Accu-Weather
385 Science Park Road
State College, PA 16803-2215
814-237-0309
Fax: 814-238-1339
http://www.accuweather.com
Offers a telecommunications weather and oceanography database.

Dr. Joel N. Myers, Founder/ Chairman/ President
Barry Lee Myers, CEO

4 AccuLab Products Group
614 Senic Drive
Suite 104
Modesto, CA 95350
209-522-8874
Fax: 209-522-8875
Science laboratory software.

5 Learning Team
10 Long Pond Road
Armonk, NY 10504-2625
914-273-2226
800-793-TEAM
Fax: 914-273-2227
Offers CD-ROM, including MathFinder, Science Helper and Small Blue Planet and Redshift, the Learning Team edition.

Thomas Laster

6 Problem Solving Concepts
611 N Capitol Avenue
Indianapolis, IN 46204-1205
317-267-9827
800-755-2150
Fax: 317-262-5044
Pro Solv provides students with a new approach to learning introductory physics problem solving techniques. Multi-experiential exercises with supporting text introduce students to relevant variables and their interrelations, principles, graphing and the development of problem solving skills through the quiz/tutorial mode.

Thomas D Feigenbaum, President
Gean R Shelor, Administrative Assistant

6297 Quantum Technology
PO Box 8252
Searcy, AR 72145-8252
A microcomputer database collection system that allows users to perform experiments in chemistry, biology and applied physics.

6298 SCI Technologies
SCI Technologies
2002 W. Huron St.
Chicago, IL 60612
312-243-1977
800-421-9881
Fax: 312-243-1972
E-mail: create@scitechnologies.com
http://www.scitechnologies.com
A computer-based interface with an integrated hardware and software package that allows the focus of a science lab to shift from data collection to data analysis and experiment design.

Colleen Greenblatt, Sales Manager
Michelle Trexler, Event Coordinator

6299 Videodiscovery
1700 Westlake Avenue N
Suite 600
Seattle, WA 98109-3040
206-285-5400
800-548-3472
Fax: 206-285-9245
Publishers of award winning science videodiscs and multimedia software for kindergarten through post-secondary classes.

6300 www.kidsastronomy.com
KidsAstronomy.com

http://www.kidsastronomy.com
Offers information on astronomy, deep space, the solar system, space exploration, a teachers corner and more.

6301 www.riverdeep.net
Riverdeep Interactive Learning
617-351-5316
800-426-6577
E-mail: Sales_Support@hmhco.com
Riverdeep's interactive science, language and math arts programs deliver high quality educational experiences.

Social Studies

6302 AccuNet/AP Multimedia Archive
AccuWeather, Inc.
385 Science Park Road
State College, PA 16803
814-235-8600
800-249-5389
Fax: 814-235-8669
E-mail: apsupport@accuweather.com
http://ap.accuweather.com
The Photo Archive is an on-line database containing almost a half-million of Associated Press's current and historic images for the last 150 years.

Michael Warfield, Southeastern Sales Manager
Richard Towne, Northeastern Sales Manager

6303 Cengage Learning
10650 Toebben Drive
Independence, KY 41051
800-354-9706
Fax: 800-487-8488
E-mail: order.samples@cengage.com
http://www.cengage.com
Offers CD-Rom information that offer students contextual understanding of the most commonly-studies persons, events and social movements in U.S. history; concepts, theories, discoveries and people involved in the study of science; current geopolitical data with cultural information on 200 nations of the world as well as all U.S. states and dependencies; poetry and literary information; and more in various databases for education.

Michael E. Hansen, Chief Executive Officer
Sandi Kirshner, Chief Marketing Officer

6304 World Geography Web Site
ABC-CLIO Schools
130 Cremona Drive
#1911
Santa Barbara, CA 93117-5599
805-968-1911
800-368-6868
Fax: 805-685-9685
http://www.abc-clio.com
Provides convenient internet access to curriculum-based reference and research materials for media specialist, educators and students.

CD-ROM

Judy Fay, Managing Editor
Valerie Mercado, Customer Service

6305 WorldView Software
76 N Broadway
Suite 2002
Hicksville, NY 11801-4241
516-681-1773
800-347-8839
Fax: 516-681-1775
E-mail: history@worldviewsoftware.com
http://www.worldviewsoftware.com
WorldView Software's interactive social studies programs for middle school and high school are comprehensive, curriculum-based tools that may be used along with or in place of textbooks. Each dynamic program contains Socratic learning sessions, writing activities and exams with instant feedback. Resource materials in every program include sketches and artwork. Used nationallly in classrooms, computer labs and learning centers.

Grades 7-12

Jerrold Kleinstein, President

6306 http://faculty.acu.edu
M.I. Smart Program
Abilene Christian University
Abilene, TX 79699
325-674-2000
800-460-6228
http://www.acu.edu
Site designed for teacher and students. Offers electronic resources for historical and cultural geography. Features games, quizzes, trivia and virtual tours for students and thier teachers.

Dr. Phil Schubert, President
Steven Holley, Chief Financial Officer

Technology in Education

6307 BLINKS.Net
PO Box 79321
Atlanta, GA 30357
404-243-5202
Fax: 404-241-4992

E-mail: info@blinks.net
http://www.blinks.net
Fastest growing free Internet service provider and community portal for information and resources for the African American, Caribbean, Latino, and African markets.

6308 Boyce Enterprises
360 Sharry Lane
Santa Maria, CA 93455
805-937-4353
Fax: 805-934-1765
Development of computer-based vocational curriculums.

6309 Center for Educational Outreach and Innovation
Teachers College-Columbia University
525 W 120th Street
Box 132
New York, NY 10027
212-678-3000
800-209-1245
Fax: 212-678-8417
E-mail: ceoi-mail@tc.columbia.edu
http://www.tc.columbia.edu
Lifelong learning programs, including distance learning courses, certificates and workshoops in education related topics.

Dr. Susan H. Fuhrman, President
Dr. Thomas James, Provost/ Dean

6310 Depco
3305 Airport Drive
PO Box 178
Pittsburg, KS 66762
316-231-0019
800-767-1062
Fax: 316-231-0024
E-mail: sales@depcoinc.com
http://www.depcoinc.com
Program tracks and schedules for you, the test taker delivers tests electronically, as well as, automatic final exams. There are workstation security features to help keep students focused on their activities.

6311 Dialog Information Services
Worldwide Headquaters
3460 Hillview Avenue
#10010
Palo Alto, CA 94304-1338
415-858-3785
800-334-2564
Fax: 650-858-7069
The world's most comprehensive online information source offering over 450 databases containing over 330 million articles, abstracts and citations - covering an unequaled variety of topics, with particular emphasis on news, business, science and technology. Dialog has offices throughout the United States and around the world.

6312 Distance Education Database
International Centre for Distance Learning
Open University, Walton Hall
Milton Keynes
England
441-085-3537
Fax: 441-086-4173
Contains information on distance education, including more than 22,000 distance-taught programs and courses in the Commonwealth of Learning, an organization created by the Commonwealth Heads of Government. On-line and CD-Rom versions of the database contain detailed information on over 30,000 distance-taught courses, 900 distance teaching instruc-

tions, and nearly 9,000 books, journals, reports and papers.

Keith Harry, Director

6313 EDUCAUSE
1150 18th Street, NW
Suite 900
Washington, DC 20036-4822
202-872-4200
Fax: 202-872-4318
E-mail: info@educause.edu
http://www.educause.edu
Aims to link practitioners in primary and secondary education through computer-mediated communications networks.

Malcolm Brown, Director
Dr. Diana G. Oblinger, President/ CEO

6314 Educational Structures
NCS Pearson
827 W Grove Avenue
Mesa, AZ 85210
800-736-4357
http://www.ncspearson.com
Features complete lesson plans and resources in social studies, mathematics, science, and language arts.

6315 Gibson Tech Ed
31500 Grape St. Bldg 3-364
Lake Elsinore, CA 92532
800-422-1100
Fax: 951-471-4981
E-mail: gary@gibsonteched.com
http://www.gibsonteched.com
Educational materials to teach electronics, from middle, junior, high school and college.

Gary Gibson, Founder
Tim Gibson, President

6316 Grolier Interactive
Grolier Publishing
90 Sherman Turnpike
Danbury, CT 06816
800-371-3908
Fax: 800-456-4402
http://http://publishing.grolier.com
Instructional software including reference, science, mathematics, music, social studies, early learning, art and art history, language arts/literature.

6317 Heifner Communications
4451 Interstate 70 Drive NW
Columbia, MO 65202-3271
573-445-6163
800-445-6164
Fax: 512-527-2395
Offers educational-merit, cable-programming available via satellite. HCI Distance Learning systems are designed for dependable services and ease of operation and competitive prices.

Vicky Roberts

6318 In Focus
27700 B SW Parkway Avenue
Wilsonville, OR 97070-9215
503-685-8887
800-294-6400
Fax: 503-685-8887
LCD panels, video projectors and systems.

6319 JonesKnowledge.com
Jones Knowledge Group
9697 E Mineral Avenue
Centennial, CO 80112
800-350-6914
http://www.jonesknowledge.com
For administrators, that means and integrated solution-with no minimum commitment, or upfront investment. For

instructors, it means getting your course online your way, without being a web expert, and for students it means, an accessible and convenient online experience.

6320 Mastercam
CNC Software
5717 Wollochet Drive NW
Suite 2A
Gig Harbor, WA 98335
800-275-6226
Fax: 253-858-6737
E-mail: mcinfo@mastercam.com
http://www.mastercamedu.com

6321 Merit Audio Visual
Merit Software
121 West 27th Street
Suite 1200
New York, NY 10001
212-675-8567
800-753-6488
Fax: 646-351-0423
E-mail: sales@meritsoftware.com
http://www.meritsoftware.com
Easy to use, interactive basic skills software for Windows 9x/ME/NT/2000/XP computers. Lessons for reading, writing, grammar and math with appropriate graphics for teens and adults.

Ben Weintraub, Marketing Manager

6322 National Information Center for Educational Media
4725 Indian School Road NE
Suite 100
Albuquerque, NM 87198-8640
505-265-3591
800-926-8328
Fax: 505-256-1080
E-mail: info-request@nicem.com
http://www.nicem.com
NICEM maintains a comprehensive database describing educational media materials for all ages and subjects. It is available on CD-ROM and online.

Lisa Savard, Sales/Marketing Director

6323 NoRad Corporation
4455 Torrance Boulevard
#2806513
Torrance, CA 90503-4398
310-605-0808
Fax: 323-934-2101
Mini, personal, medium and large computer systems for educational institutions.

6324 Proxima Corporation
9440 Carroll Park Drive
San Diego, CA 92121
858-457-5500
800-294-6400
Fax: 503-685-7239
http://www.proxima.com
Proxima Corporation is a global leader in the multimedia projection market, providing world class presentation solutions to corporate enterprises, workgroups, mobile professionals, trainers, and professional public speakers.

Kim Gallagher, Public Relations Manager
Kathy Bankerd, Director Marketing Programs

6325 RB5X: Education's Personal Computer Robot
General Robotics Corporation
760 S Youngfield Court
Suite 8
Lakewood, CO 80228-2813
303-988-5636
800-422-4265
Fax: 303-988-5303
E-mail: cbrown@generalrobotics.com
http://www.edurobot.com

RB5X: Education's Personal Computer Robot. All grade levels. Self learn, self teach, hands on modular system. Problem solving, basic learning skills, increases self-esteem. Expanable open-ended, motivation at its best.

Constant Brown, President

26 SEAL
550 Spring Street
Naugatuck, CT 06770-1906
203-729-5201
Complete line of systems and electronics for schools.

27 Sharp Electronics Corporation
LCD Products Group
Sharp Plaza
Mall Stop One
Mahwah, NJ 07430
201-529-8200
800-237-4277
Fax: 201-529-9636
E-mail: aquosadvantage@sharpusa.com
http://www.sharpusa.com
Offers a full line of LCD-based video and computer multimedia projectors and projection panels for use in a wide range of educational applications. Sharp's product line also includes industrial VHS format VCRs, color TV monitors.

J Ganguzza, Director/Marketing

28 Valiant
80 Little Falls Road
Fairfield, NJ 07004
800-825-4268
Fax: 800-453-6338
E-mail: sales@valiantnational.com
http://www.valiantnational.com
Distributors of LCD projection panels, P/A systems, overhead/slide and filmstrip projectors, cassette recorders, classroom record players, laser pointers, laminating equipment, lecturns, listening centers and headphones.

Sheldon Goldstein

29 Vernier Software
13979 SW Millikan Way
Beaverton, OR 97005
503-277-2299
888-VER-ER
Fax: 503-277-2440
E-mail: info@vernier.com
http://www.vernier.com
Laboratory interacting software for the Macintosh, IBM and Apple II.

30 Websense
10240 Sorrento Valley Road
San Diego, CA 92121
858-320-8000
800-723-1166
Fax: 858-458-2950
http://www.websense.com
Internet filtering.

John R. McCormack, Chief Executive Officer
John Borgerding, President/ COO

31 http://di...elearn/cs/eductechnology/index.htm
About Education Distance Learning

32 http://futurekids.com
FUTUREKIDS School Technology Solutions
330 East 85th Street
New York, NY 10028
212-717-0110
Fax: 212-717-0259

E-mail: info1@futurekidsnyc.com
http://www.futurekidsnyc.com
Helping schools use technology to transform education.

6333 http://online.uophx.edu
University of Phoenix Online

http://www.university-of-phoenix-online.net
Offers you the convenience and flexibility of attending classes from your personal computer. Students are discussing issues, sharing ideas, testing theories, essentially enjoying all of the advantages of an on-campus degree programs. Interaction is included like e-mail, so you practice at your convenience.

6334 http://www.crossteccorp.com
NetOp
500 NE Spanish River Blvd.
Suite 201
Boca Raton, FL 33431
561-391-6560
800-675-0729
Fax: 561-391-5820
E-mail: sales@crosstecsoftware.com
http://www.crossteccorp.com
A powerful combination of seven essential tools for networked classrooms. Based on the award winning technology of NetOp Remote Control and is easy-to-use software only solution.

6335 http://www.growsmartbrains.com
GrowSmartBrains.com
Website for parents and educators who want research based information and practical stradegies for raising children in a media age.

6336 http://www.zdnet.com
ZDNet

http://www.zdnet.com
Full-service destination for people looking to buy, use and learn more about technology.

Larry Dignan, Editor-in-Chief
David Grober, Senior Editor

6337 www.21ct.org
Twenty First Century Teachers Network
A nationwide, non-profit initiative of the McGuffey Project, dedicated to assisting k-12 teachers learn, use and effectively integrate technology in the curriculum for improved student learning.

6338 www.aboutonehandtyping.com/
One Hand Typing and Keyboarding Resources
740 Purdue Dr.
Claremont, CA 91711
909-398-1228
Fax: 408-228-8752
http://www.aboutonehandtyping.com
This site dishes up a blend of messages and stories, resources for one-hand typists, links to alternative keyboards, teaching links, and more.

6339 www.digitaldividenetwork.org
Digital Divide Network
c/o TakingITGlobal
19 Duncan Street, Suite 505
Toronto, ON M5H 3
416-977-9363
Fax: 416-352-1898
E-mail: ddn@takingitglobal . org
http://www.digitaldivide.net
The goal of bridging the divide is to use communications technology to help improve the quality of life of all communities and their citizens; provide them with the tools, skills and information they need to help them real-

ize their socioeconomic, educational and cultural potential.

Adam Clare, Volunteer Lead Editor
Kirsten Jordan, DDN Project Coordinator

6340 www.getquizzed.com
GetQuizzed
Designed as a free service that provides a database that allows users to create, store and edit Multiple Choice or Question and Answer quizzes, under password protected conditions.

6341 www.guidetogeekdom.com
Guide to Geekdom
E-mail: info@guidetogeekdom.com
http://www.guidetogeekdom.com
Designed especially for Homeschoolers, step-by-step lessons teach students how to use the computer and troubleshoot computer problems. Offers workbooks, sample lesson and more.

6342 www.happyteachers.com
HappyTeachers.com
Information about technical and vocational education programs, products and curriculum.

6343 www.integratingit.com
Integrating Information Technology for the Classroom, School, & District
Dedicated to providing the education community a place to find real world strategies, solutions, and resources for integrating technology. Organized by the perspective of the classroom teacher, the school administrator, and the district.

6344 www.livetext.com
LiveText Curriculum Manager
1 W. Harris Avenue
2nd Floor
La Grange, IL 60525
866-548-3839
Fax: 708-588-1793
E-mail: edu-solutions@livetext.com
http://www.livetext.com
Provides tools for engaged learning classroom projects and provides online professional development for teachers.

6345 www.ncrel.org
North Central Regional Educational Laboratory
1120 East Diehl Road
Suite 200
Naperville, IL 60563-1486
Fax: 630-649-6730
E-mail: info@ncrel.org
http://www.ncrel.org
Offers research results regarding the effective use of technology.

Gina Burkhardt, CEO
Sabrina Laine, Chief Officer, R&D

6346 www.ncrtec.org
N Central Regional Technology in Education Consortiums

http://www.ncrtec.org
Provides a variety of tools and information to improve technology-related professional development programs.

Elementary Education

6347 Curriculum Associates
153 Rangeway Road
No. Billerica, MA 01862
978-667-8000
800-225-0248
Fax: 800-366-1158
http://www.curriculumassociates.com
Test preparation material with a guarantee
of success; skill instruction and assessment.

Frank E. Ferguson, Chairman
Robert Waldron, Chief Executive Officer

**6348 Diagnostic Reading Inventory for
Primaryand Intermediate Grades
K-8**
Scott and McCleary Publishing Co.
PO Box 3830
Akron, OH 44314-0830
702-566-8756
800-765-3564
Fax: 702-568-1378
E-mail: jscott7576@aol.com
http://www.scottmccleary.com
A series of 13 tests at each grade level, 10
can be given in a group setting. 3 Forms of
the IRI teacher friendly. Easy to administer.

Spiral Paperback
ISBN: 0-9636225-4-4

Janet M. Scott and Sheila C. McCeary,
Author
Janet Scott, Co-Author
Sheila McCleary, Co-Author

6349 Lexia Learning Systems
200 Baker Ave Ext.
Concord, MA 01742
978-405-6200
800-435-3942
Fax: 978-287-0062
E-mail: info@lexialearning.com
http://www.lexialearning.com
Reading software and assessment programs for children and adults, professional
development programs for teachers, principals and administrators.

Elizabeth C. Crawford Brooke, VP,
Education & Research
Collin Earnst, VP, Marketing

**6350 National Study of School
Evaluation**
1699 E Woodfield Road
Suite 406
Schaumburg, IL 60173-4958
847-995-9080
800-843-6773
Fax: 847-995-9088
E-mail: schoolimprovement@nsse.org
http://www.nsse.org
Provides educational leaders with
state-of-the-art assessment and evaluation
materials to enhance and promote student
growth and school improvement.

Dr. Kathleen A. Fitzpatrick, Executive
Director

6351 Pro-Ed, Inc.
8700 Shoal Creek Blvd
Austin, TX 78757-6897
800-897-3202
Fax: 800-397-7633
E-mail: info@proedinc.com
http://www.linguisystems.com
Offers tests and print materials for speech
language pathologists, teachers of the
learning disabled, middle school language
arts and reading teachers.

6352 Testing Miss Malarky
Bloomsbury Publishing Inc.
1385 Broadway
5th Floor
New York, NY 10018
212-419-5300
888-330-8477
Fax: 212-727-0984
E-mail: ebookhelp@bloomsbury.com
http://www.bloomsbury.com
Author and artist exploit the mania that accompanies the classes first standardized
test.

32 pages
ISBN: 0-8027-8737-1

Judy Finchler, Contact

Language Arts

6353 CTB/McGraw-Hill
20 Ryan Ranch Road
Monterey, CA 93940-5703
831-393-0700
800-538-9547
Fax: 800-282-0266
E-mail: Customer_Service_Ind@ctb.com
http://www.ctb.com
K-12 achievement tests, early literacy assessment, language proficiency evaluation, adult basic skills tests, and test
management and instructional planning
software.

Ellen Haley, President
Sandor Nagy, Chief Operating Officer

6354 SLEP Program Office
PO Box 6155
Princeton, NJ 08541-6155
Offers information on the Secondary Level
English Proficiency Test.

Mathematics

**6355 Psychological Assessment
Resources**
16204 North Florida Avenue
Lutz, FL 33549
813-961-2196
800-331-TEST
Fax: 800-727-9329
http://www.parinc.com
Catalog of professional testing resources.

**6356 Summing It Up: College Board
Mathematics Assessment Programs**
College Board Publications
45 Columbus Avenue
New York, NY 10023-6992
212-713-8000
800-323-7155
Fax: 800-525-5562
http://www.collegeboard.org
An overview of SAT I: Reasoning Tests and
PSAT/NMSQT, SAT II: Subject Tests, Descriptive Tests of Mathematical Skills
(DTMS), CPTs in Mathematics, CLEP
Mathematics Examinations, AP Exams in
Mathematics, AP Exams in Computer Sciences, and Pacesetter Mathematics.

30 pages

David Coleman, President/ CEO
Jeremy Singer, Chief Operating Officer

Music & Art

6357 A&F Video's Art Catalog
PO Box 264
Geneseo, NY 14454

http://www.aandfvideo.com
New listing of titles for Art Teachers and Art Lovers.

6358 All Art Supplies
Art Supplies Wholesale
4 Enon Street
North Beverly, MA 01915
800-462-2420
Fax: 978-922-1495
E-mail: info@allartsupplies.com
http://www.allartsupplies.com
Art supplies at wholesale prices.

6359 American Art Clay Company
6060 Guion Road
Indianapolis, IN 46254
317-244-6871
800-374-1600
Fax: 317-248-9300
E-mail: salessupport@amaco.com
http://www.amaco.com
Provides ceramic materials and equipment.

6360 Arnold Grummer
PO Box 13245
Milwaukee, WI 53213
800-453-1485
Fax: 414-453-1495
E-mail: webmaster@arnoldgrummer.com
http://www.arnoldgrummer.com
Products and information to meet most any
papermaking need.

6361 Arrowmont School of Arts & Crafts
556 Parkway
Gainsburg, TN 37738
865-438-5860
Fax: 865-438-4101
E-mail: info@arrowmont.org
http://www.arrowmont.org
The art school of tomorrow.

Marty Begalla, President
Susie Glenn, Vice President

6362 Art & Creative Materials Institute
99 Derby St.
Suite 200
Hingham, MA 02043
781-556-1044
Fax: 781-207-5550
E-mail: debbiem@acminet.org
http://www.acminet.org
A non-profit trade association whose memebers
are manufacturers of art and creative materials.
Sponsors a certification program to ensure that art
materials are non-toxic or affixed with health
warning labels where appropriate. Publishes a
booklet on the safe use of art materials and a listing of products that are approved under its certification program. Both of these publications are
free of charge.

Debbie Gustafson, Deputy Director
David H Baker, Executive Director

6363 Art Instruction Schools
3309 Broadway Street NW
Minneapolis, MN 55413

http://www.artists-ais.com

6364 Art to Remember
5535 Macy Drive
Indianapolis, IN 46235
317-826-0870
800-895-8777
Fax: 317-823-2822

E-mail: info@arttoremember.com
http://www.arttoremember.com
A unique program that encourages your students' artisic creativity while providing an oppurtunity to raise funds for schools.

65 ArtSketchbook.com
487 Hulsetown Road
Campbell Hall, NY 10916
845-496-4709
http://www.artsketchbook.com
Provides instructions and work examples by an elementary student, secondary student and a professional artist.

66 Arts Institutes International
Education Management Corporation
210 Sixth Avenue
33rd Floor
Pittsburgh, PA 15222
888-624-0300
E-mail: csprogramadmin@edmc.edu
http://www.artinstitutes.edu
Post-secondary career education. Offers associate's, bachelor's and non-degree programs in design, media arts, technology, culinary arts and fashion.

67 Museum Stamps
PO Box 356
New Canaan, CT 06840
800-659-2787
Fax: 203-966-2729
http://www.museumstamps.com
Rubber stamps of famous works of art, stamp accessories, classroom projects.

68 Music Ace 2
Harmonic Vision
1433 Rapids Trl
Nekoosa, WI 54457
715-325-3252
800-474-0903
Fax: 866-422-6686
http://www.harmonicvision.com
Introduces concepts such as standard notation, rhythm, melody, time signatures, harmony, intervals and more.

69 http://www.ilford.com
Ilford

http://www.ilford.com
Partners in imaging.

70 www.schoolrenaissance.com
Renaissance Learning
2911 Peach Street
Wisconsin Rapids, WI 54494
715-424-3636
800-338-4204
Fax: 715-424-4242
E-mail: answers@renaissance.com
http://www.renaissance.com
The School Renaissance Model combines the #1 software in education with professional development and consulting services to help you dramatically improve student performance.

John J. Lynch Jr., Chief Executive Officer
Mary T. Minch, EVP, Finance & CFO

71 www.speedballart.com
2301 Speedball Road
Statesville, NC 28677
800-898-7224
http://www.speedballart.com
Speedball lesson plans and teaching aids for calligraphy, stamping, printmaking, drawing, painting and more.

Walt Glazer, Chief Executive

Reading

6372 Advantage Learning Systems
2911 Peach Street
PO Box 8036
Wisconsin Rapids, WI 54495-8036
800-338-4204
Fax: 715-424-4242
E-mail: mail@advlearn.com
http://www.advlearn.com
New computer-adaptive tests that assess student reading and math levels in just 15 minutes or less.

6373 Educational Testing Service/Library
Test Collection
Rosedale Road
Princeton, NJ 08541
609-734-5686
Fax: 609-734-5410
Provides information on tests and related materials to those in research and advisory services and educational activities.

Janet Williams, President

6374 National Foundation for Dyslexia
4801 Hermitage Road
Richmond, VA 23227-3332
804-262-0586
800-SOS-READ
Provides screenings for schools or individuals and assists individuals with IEP's. Provides information about support groups and organizations and teacher training workshops.

Jo Powell, Executive Director

6375 Psychological Assessment Resources
16204 North Florida Avenue
Lutz, FL 33549
813-961-2196
800-331-TEST
Fax: 800-727-9329
http://www.parinc.com
Catalog of professional testing resources.

6376 www.schoolrenaissance.com
Renaissance Learning
2911 Peach Street
Wisconsin Rapids, WI 54494
715-424-3636
800-338-4204
Fax: 715-424-4242
E-mail: answers@renaissance.com
http://www.renaissance.com
The School Renaissance Model combines the #1 software in education with professional development and consulting services to help you dramatically improve student performance.

John J. Lynch Jr., Chief Executive Officer
Mary T. Minch, EVP, Finance & CFO

6377 www.voyagerlearning.com
Cambium Learning Group
17855 Dallas Parkway
Suite 400
Dallas, TX 75287

http://www.voyagersopris.com
Improves students performance in reading for those at different grade levels.

Secondary Education

6378 ACT
PO Box 4060
Iowa City, IA 52243-0001
319-337-1000
800-498-6065

Offers a full-service catalog of tests for intermediate and secondary schools organized by assessment, career and educational planning, study skills, surveys and research services.
Catalog

6379 Admission Officer's Handbook for the New SAT Program
College Board Publications
45 Columbus Avenue
New York, NY 10023-6992
212-713-8000
800-323-7155
Fax: 800-525-5562
http://www.collegeboard.org
Designed to help college admission staff quickly find information on the new SAT program, the Handbook has detailed descriptions of score reports and special services for colleges.
56 pages
David Coleman, President/ CEO
Jeremy Singer, Chief Operating Officer

6380 American College Testing
ACT
2201 Dodge
#168
Iowa City, IA 52243-0001
319-337-1028
Fax: 319-337-1014
E-mail: gullettk@act.org
http://www.act.org
Provides educational assessment services to students and their parents, high schools, colleges and professional associations. Also workforce development services, including a network of ACT Centers and the Workkeys program.
Jon Whitmore, Chief Executive Officer
Janet E. Godwin, Chief Operating Officer

6381 College-Bound Seniors
College Board Publications
45 Columbus Avenue
New York, NY 10023-6992
212-713-8000
800-323-7155
Fax: 800-525-5562
http://www.collegeboard.org
Profile of SAT and achievement test takers, national report.
13 pages
David Coleman, President/ CEO
Jeremy Singer, Chief Operating Officer

6382 CollegeChoice, StudentChoice
College Board Publications
45 Columbus Avenue
New York, NY 10023-6992
212-713-8000
800-323-7155
Fax: 800-525-5562
http://www.collegeboard.org
This video provides a reassuring perspective on the SAT's importance and how the college admission process really works. It shows how SAT scores are only one of many elements in the admission picture and emphasizes academic preparation for college and discusses the SAT within the context of the entire admission process.
15 Minutes
David Coleman, President/ CEO
Jeremy Singer, Chief Operating Officer

6383 Counselor's Handbook for the SAT Program
College Board Publications
45 Columbus Avenue
New York, NY 10023-6992

212-713-8000
800-323-7155
Fax: 800-525-5562
http://www.collegeboard.org
Easy-to-use reference provides details on
the new SAT program tests and services.

64 pages

David Coleman, President/ CEO
Jeremy Singer, Chief Operating Officer

6384 Destination College: Planning with the PSAT/NMSQT

College Board Publications
45 Columbus Avenue
New York, NY 10023-6992
212-713-8000
800-323-7155
Fax: 800-525-5562
http://www.collegeboard.org
This new video offers schools an ideal format for explaining the features and benefits of the PSAT/NMSQT Score Report to groups of students.

18 Minutes

David Coleman, President/ CEO
Jeremy Singer, Chief Operating Officer

6385 Educational Testing Service

660 Rosedale Road
Princeton, NJ 08541
609-921-9000
Fax: 609-734-5410
http://www.ets.org
Private educational measurement institution and a leader in educational research.

Susan Keipper, Program Director

6386 Focus on the SAT: What's on it, How to Prepare & What Colleges Look For

College Board Publications
45 Columbus Avenue
New York, NY 10023-6992
212-713-8000
800-323-7155
Fax: 800-525-5562
http://www.collegeboard.org
The authoritative video for students on how to prepare for the SAT and PSAT/NMSQT. It provides test-taking tips, sample test questions, and an explanation of how SAT is developed.

20 Minutes

David Coleman, President/ CEO
Jeremy Singer, Chief Operating Officer

6387 GED Testing Service

American Council on Education
1 Dupont Cir NW
Washington, DC 20036-1110
202-939-9490
877-392-6433
Fax: 202-775-8578
E-mail: help@GEDtestingservice.com
http://www.gedtestingservice.com
The largest testing service in the United States. Maintains a full line of tests and testing resources for all areas of education and all grade levels K-college level testing.

Randy Trask, President/ CEO

6388 Guide to the College Board Validity Study Service

College Board Publications
45 Columbus Avenue
New York, NY 10023-6992
212-713-8000
800-323-7155
Fax: 800-525-5562
http://www.collegeboard.org

The purpose of this manual is to assist Validity Study Service users in designing and interpreting validity studies. It provides design suggestions, sample admission and placement studies, advice on interpreting studies, and a discussion of basic statistical concepts.

60 pages

David Coleman, President/ CEO
Jeremy Singer, Chief Operating Officer

6389 Look Inside the SAT I: Test Prep from the Test Makers Video

College Board Publications
45 Columbus Avenue
New York, NY 10023-6992
212-713-8000
800-323-7155
Fax: 800-525-5562
http://www.collegeboard.org
Brings the College Board's test-taking tips to life through interviews with people from different backgrounds who recount their SAT experiences.

30 Minutes
ISBN: 0-874475-29-5

David Coleman, President/ CEO
Jeremy Singer, Chief Operating Officer

6390 Master The GMAT

Peterson's, A Nelnet Company
461 From Road
Paramus, NJ 07652
609-896-1800
800-338-3282
Fax: 402-458-3042
E-mail: custsvc@petersons.com
http://www.petersons.com
Helps test takers get ready, develop test-preparation strategies and manage test anxiety constructively, whether they have seven weeks to prepare or just one day.

672 pages Book & Disk

Martinson, Author

6391 Master The SAT

Peterson's, A Nelnet Company
461 From Road
Paramus, NJ 07652
609-896-1800
800-338-3282
Fax: 402-458-3042
E-mail: custsvc@petersons.com
http://www.petersons.com
Features easily accessible Red Alert sections offering essential tips for test-taking success. Provides students with the critical skills they need to tackle the SAT.

821 pages Book & Disk
ISBN: 1-560796-06-5

John Davenport Carris with Michael R. Crystal, Author

6392 National Center for Fair & Open Testing

P.O. Box 300204
Jamaica Plain, MA 02130
617-477-9792
Fax: 617-497-2224
http://www.fairtest.org
Dedicated to ensuring that America's students and workers are assessed using fair, accurate, relevant and open tests.

Cinthia Schuman, President

6393 National Study of School Evaluation

1699 E Woodfield Road
Suite 406
Schaumburg, IL 60173-4958

847-995-9080
800-843-6773
Fax: 847-995-9088
E-mail: schoolimprovement@nsse.org
http://www.nsse.org
Provides educational leaders with state-of-the-art assessment and evaluation materials to enhance and promote student growth and school improvement.

Dr. Kathleen A. Fitzpatrick, Executive Director

6394 Official Guide to the SAT II: Subject Tests

College Board Publications
45 Columbus Avenue
New York, NY 10023-6992
212-713-8000
800-323-7155
Fax: 800-525-5562
http://www.collegeboard.org
The authoritative preparation guide for students taking the SAT II: Subject Tests. The guide includes full-length practice Subject Tests, along with answer sheets, answer keys, and scoring instructions for Writing, Literature, American History, World History, Math I, Math IIC, Biology, Chemistry and Physics. It also includes minitests in French (reading only), German (reading only), Italian, Latin, Modern Hebrew, and Spanish.

380 pages
ISBN: 0-874474-88-4

David Coleman, President/ CEO
Jeremy Singer, Chief Operating Officer

6395 One-On-One with the SAT

College Board Publications
45 Columbus Avenue
New York, NY 10023-6992
212-713-8000
800-323-7155
Fax: 800-525-5562
http://www.collegeboard.org
Gives students easy access to proven advice and test-taking strategies directly from the test makers, as well as a unique chance to take a real SAT on computer. This program also includes password protection for each student record and toll-free technical support.

Home License

David Coleman, President/ CEO
Jeremy Singer, Chief Operating Officer

6396 Panic Plan for the SAT

Peterson's, A Nelnet Company
461 From Road
Paramus, NJ 07652
609-896-1800
800-338-3282
Fax: 402-458-3042
E-mail: custsvc@petersons.com
http://www.petersons.com
An excellent, two-week review, featuring actual questions from the SAT. Helps students make the most out of the limited time they have left to study.

368 pages
ISBN: 1-560794-32-1

Michael R Crystal, Author

6397 Preventing School Failure

Taylor & Francis
325 Chestnut Street
Suite 800
Philadelphia, PA 19106
215-625-8900
800-354-1420
Fax: 202-296-5149
E-mail: customer.service@taylorandfrancis.com
http://www.heldref.org
The articles cover a broad array of specific topics, from important technical aspects and adaptions of functional behavioral assessment to descriptions of projects in which functional behavioral assess-

ment is being used to provide technical assistance to preschools, schools, and families who must deal eith children and adolescents who present serious challenging behaviors.

Quarterly
ISSN: 1045-988X

Sheldon Braaten, Executive Editor

6398 Psychological Corporation
555 Academic Court
San Antonio, TX 78204-2498
210-921-8701
Assessment materials for teachers in all areas of curricula.

6399 Psychometric Affiliates
PO Box 807
Murfreeboro, TN 37133
615-890-6296
Testing instruments for use by educational institutions.

Jeannette Heritage

6400 Real SAT's
College Board Publications
45 Columbus Avenue
New York, NY 10023-6992
212-713-8000
800-323-7155
Fax: 800-525-5562
http://www.collegeboard.org
The only preparation guide that contains actual scorable tests. It has been developed to help the millions of students taking the tests each year to do their best on the PSAT/NMSQT and SAT and to improve their scores.

396 pages
ISBN: 0-874475-11-2

David Coleman, President/ CEO
Jeremy Singer, Chief Operating Officer

6401 Registration Bulletin
College Board Publications
45 Columbus Avenue
New York, NY 10023-6992
212-713-8000
800-323-7155
Fax: 800-525-5562
http://www.collegeboard.org
Available in five regional and a New York State edition, the Bulletin provides information on how to register for the SAT I and SAT II, and on how to use the related services.

24 pages

David Coleman, President/ CEO
Jeremy Singer, Chief Operating Officer

6402 SAT Services for Students with Disabilities
College Board Publications
45 Columbus Avenue
New York, NY 10023-6992

212-713-8000
800-323-7155
Fax: 800-525-5562
http://www.collegeboard.org
Describes arrangements for students with physical, hearing, visual and learning disabilities who wish to take the SAT I and/or SAT II.

6 pages

David Coleman, President/ CEO
Jeremy Singer, Chief Operating Officer

6403 Scholastic Testing Service
480 Meyer Road
Bensenville, IL 60106-1617
630-766-7150
800-642-6787
Fax: 630-766-8054
E-mail: sts@ststesting.com
http://www.ststesting.com
Publisher of assessment materials from birth into adulthood, ability and achievement tests for kindergarten through grade twelve. Tests are also constructed on contract for educational agencies and school districts. Publish the Torrance Tests of Creative Thinking, Thinking Creatively in Action and Movement, the STS High School Placement Test and Educational Development Series.

OF Anderhalter, President
John D Kauffman, VP Marketing

6404 TOEFL Test and Score Manual
College Board Publications
45 Columbus Avenue
New York, NY 10023-6992
212-713-8000
800-323-7155
Fax: 800-525-5562
http://www.collegeboard.org
Focuses on information that college admissions officers, foreign student advisers and other users of TOEFL score reports need to know about the operation of the TOEFL program, the test itself, and the interpretation of scores.

48 pages

David Coleman, President/ CEO
Jeremy Singer, Chief Operating Officer

6405 Taking the SAT I: Reasoning Test
College Board Publications
45 Columbus Avenue
New York, NY 10023-6992
212-713-8000
800-323-7155
Fax: 800-525-5562
http://www.collegeboard.org
A complete guide for students who plan to take the SAT I: Reasoning Test.

80 pages

David Coleman, President/ CEO
Jeremy Singer, Chief Operating Officer

6406 Taking the SAT II: The Official Guide to the SAT II: Subject Tests
College Board Publications
45 Columbus Avenue
New York, NY 10023-6992
212-713-8000
800-323-7155
Fax: 800-525-5562
http://www.collegeboard.org
Provides information about the content and format of each of the SAT II: Subject Tests, as well as test-taking advice and sample questions.

95 pages

David Coleman, President/ CEO
Jeremy Singer, Chief Operating Officer

6407 TestSkills
College Board Publications
45 Columbus Avenue
New York, NY 10023-6992
212-713-8000
800-323-7155
Fax: 800-525-5562
http://www.collegeboard.org
A preparation program for the PSAT/NMSQT that helps students, particularly those from minority and disadvantaged groups, sharpen skills and increase confidence needed to succeed on the tests.

Spiral-Bound

David Coleman, President/ CEO
Jeremy Singer, Chief Operating Officer

6408 Think Before You Punch: Using Calculators on the New SAT I and PSAT/NMSQT
College Board Publications
45 Columbus Avenue
New York, NY 10023-6992
212-713-8000
800-323-7155
Fax: 800-525-5562
http://www.collegeboard.org
This video looks at the pros and cons of calculators usage on a test. In it, students talk about using them, and College Board and ETS staff explain the new calculator policy. It works through math questions that may or may not best be answered with the help of a calculator.

12 Minutes

David Coleman, President/ CEO
Jeremy Singer, Chief Operating Officer

EDUCATION STATISTICS

Rates of high school completion and bachelor's degree attainment among persons age 25 and over, by race/ethnicity and sex: Selected years, 1910 through 2013

[Standard errors appear in parentheses]

Sex, high school or bachelor's degree attainment, and year	Total, percent of all persons age 25 and over		White[1]		Black[1]		Hispanic		Asian/Pacific Islander Total		Asian		Pacific Islander		American Indian/ Alaska Native		Two or more races	
1	2		3		4		5		6		7		8		9		10	
Total																		
High school completion or higher[2]																		
1910[3]	13.5	(—)	—	(†)	—	(†)	—	(†)	—	(†)	—	(†)	—	(†)	—	(†)	—	(†)
1920[3]	16.4	(—)	—	(†)	—	(†)	—	(†)	—	(†)	—	(†)	—	(†)	—	(†)	—	(†)
1930[3]	19.1	(—)	—	(†)	—	(†)	—	(†)	—	(†)	—	(†)	—	(†)	—	(†)	—	(†)
1940	24.5	(—)	26.1	(—)	7.7	(—)	—	(†)	—	(†)	—	(†)	—	(†)	—	(†)	—	(†)
1950	34.3	(—)	36.4	(—)	13.7	(—)	—	(†)	—	(†)	—	(†)	—	(†)	—	(†)	—	(†)
1960	41.1	(—)	43.2	(—)	21.7	(—)	—	(†)	—	(†)	—	(†)	—	(†)	—	(†)	—	(†)
1970	55.2	(—)	57.4	(—)	36.1	(—)	—	(†)	—	(†)	—	(†)	—	(†)	—	(†)	—	(†)
1975	62.5	(—)	65.8	(—)	42.6	(—)	38.5	(—)	—	(†)	—	(†)	—	(†)	—	(†)	—	(†)
1980	68.6	(0.20)	71.9	(0.21)	51.4	(0.81)	44.5	(1.18)	—	(†)	—	(†)	—	(†)	—	(†)	—	(†)
1985	73.9	(0.18)	77.5	(0.19)	59.9	(0.74)	47.9	(0.99)	—	(†)	—	(†)	—	(†)	—	(†)	—	(†)
1986	74.7	(0.18)	78.2	(0.19)	62.5	(0.72)	48.5	(0.96)	—	(†)	—	(†)	—	(†)	—	(†)	—	(†)
1987	75.6	(0.17)	79.0	(0.18)	63.6	(0.71)	50.9	(0.94)	—	(†)	—	(†)	—	(†)	—	(†)	—	(†)
1988	76.2	(0.17)	79.8	(0.18)	63.5	(0.70)	51.0	(0.92)	—	(†)	—	(†)	—	(†)	—	(†)	—	(†)
1989	76.9	(0.17)	80.7	(0.18)	64.7	(0.69)	50.9	(0.89)	82.3	(1.17)	—	(†)	—	(†)	—	(†)	—	(†)
1990	77.6	(0.17)	81.4	(0.17)	66.2	(0.67)	50.8	(0.88)	84.2	(1.09)	—	(†)	—	(†)	—	(†)	—	(†)
1991	78.4	(0.16)	82.4	(0.17)	66.8	(0.66)	51.3	(0.86)	84.2	(1.05)	—	(†)	—	(†)	—	(†)	—	(†)
1992	79.4	(0.16)	83.4	(0.16)	67.7	(0.65)	52.6	(0.85)	83.7	(1.02)	—	(†)	—	(†)	—	(†)	—	(†)
1993	80.2	(0.16)	84.1	(0.16)	70.5	(0.63)	53.1	(0.83)	84.2	(1.00)	—	(†)	—	(†)	—	(†)	—	(†)
1994	80.9	(0.15)	84.9	(0.16)	73.0	(0.61)	53.3	(0.78)	84.8	(0.98)	—	(†)	—	(†)	—	(†)	—	(†)
1995	81.7	(0.15)	85.9	(0.16)	73.8	(0.61)	53.4	(0.78)	83.8	(1.06)	—	(†)	—	(†)	—	(†)	—	(†)
1996	81.7	(0.16)	86.0	(0.16)	74.6	(0.53)	53.1	(0.68)	83.5	(0.82)	—	(†)	—	(†)	—	(†)	—	(†)
1997	82.1	(0.14)	86.3	(0.15)	75.3	(0.52)	54.7	(0.54)	85.2	(0.75)	—	(†)	—	(†)	—	(†)	—	(†)
1998	82.8	(0.14)	87.1	(0.14)	76.4	(0.50)	55.5	(0.53)	84.9	(0.74)	—	(†)	—	(†)	—	(†)	—	(†)
1999	83.4	(0.14)	87.7	(0.14)	77.4	(0.49)	56.1	(0.52)	84.7	(0.73)	—	(†)	—	(†)	—	(†)	—	(†)
2000	84.1	(0.13)	88.4	(0.14)	78.9	(0.48)	57.0	(0.51)	85.7	(0.71)	—	(†)	—	(†)	—	(†)	—	(†)
2001	84.3	(0.13)	88.7	(0.13)	79.5	(0.47)	56.5	(0.50)	87.8	(0.60)	—	(†)	—	(†)	—	(†)	—	(†)
2002	84.1	(0.09)	88.7	(0.10)	79.2	(0.34)	57.0	(0.34)	87.7	(0.44)	—	(†)	—	(†)	—	(†)	—	(†)
2003	84.6	(0.09)	89.4	(0.09)	80.3	(0.33)	57.0	(0.33)	87.8	(0.43)	87.8	(0.44)	88.2	(1.87)	77.2	(1.64)	86.1	(0.97)
2004	85.2	(0.09)	90.0	(0.09)	81.1	(0.32)	58.4	(0.32)	86.9	(0.43)	86.9	(0.44)	88.5	(1.91)	77.8	(1.61)	87.2	(0.91)
2005	85.2	(0.14)	90.1	(0.16)	81.4	(0.44)	58.5	(0.53)	87.8	(0.62)	87.7	(0.62)	90.1	(2.69)	75.6	(2.02)	88.6	(0.83)
2006	85.5	(0.15)	90.5	(0.15)	81.2	(0.43)	59.3	(0.58)	87.5	(0.71)	87.5	(0.71)	85.7	(2.51)	78.5	(2.11)	88.1	(0.90)
2007	85.7	(0.15)	90.6	(0.15)	82.8	(0.39)	60.3	(0.56)	88.0	(0.79)	87.9	(0.81)	88.6	(2.30)	80.3	(2.27)	89.3	(0.87)
2008	86.6	(0.15)	91.5	(0.15)	83.3	(0.40)	62.3	(0.58)	89.0	(0.62)	88.8	(0.64)	94.4	(1.00)	78.4	(2.74)	89.5	(1.12)
2009	86.7	(0.15)	91.6	(0.15)	84.2	(0.44)	61.9	(0.56)	88.4	(0.61)	88.3	(0.63)	90.8	(1.76)	81.5	(1.83)	87.4	(0.96)
2010	87.1	(0.13)	92.1	(0.14)	84.6	(0.41)	62.9	(0.53)	89.1	(0.67)	89.1	(0.68)	90.2	(1.95)	80.8	(1.76)	88.9	(0.90)
2011	87.6	(0.13)	92.4	(0.14)	84.8	(0.41)	64.3	(0.54)	88.8	(0.55)	88.7	(0.57)	90.4	(1.61)	82.3	(1.77)	89.4	(1.00)
2012	87.6	(0.15)	92.5	(0.14)	85.7	(0.40)	65.0	(0.59)	89.2	(0.59)	89.0	(0.61)	91.6	(1.33)	81.8	(1.69)	91.0	(0.89)
2013	88.2	(0.14)	92.9	(0.13)	85.9	(0.42)	66.2	(0.52)	90.2	(0.51)	90.2	(0.53)	89.5	(1.72)	82.2	(1.68)	92.6	(0.75)
Bachelor's or higher degree[4]																		
1910[3]	2.7	(—)	—	(†)	—	(†)	—	(†)	—	(†)	—	(†)	—	(†)	—	(†)	—	(†)
1920[3]	3.3	(—)	—	(†)	—	(†)	—	(†)	—	(†)	—	(†)	—	(†)	—	(†)	—	(†)
1930[3]	3.9	(—)	—	(†)	—	(†)	—	(†)	—	(†)	—	(†)	—	(†)	—	(†)	—	(†)
1940	4.6	(—)	4.9	(—)	1.3	(—)	—	(†)	—	(†)	—	(†)	—	(†)	—	(†)	—	(†)
1950	6.2	(—)	6.6	(—)	2.2	(—)	—	(†)	—	(†)	—	(†)	—	(†)	—	(†)	—	(†)
1960	7.7	(—)	8.1	(—)	3.5	(—)	—	(†)	—	(†)	—	(†)	—	(†)	—	(†)	—	(†)
1970	11.0	(—)	11.6	(—)	6.1	(—)	—	(†)	—	(†)	—	(†)	—	(†)	—	(†)	—	(†)
1975	13.9	(—)	14.9	(—)	6.4	(—)	6.6	(—)	—	(†)	—	(†)	—	(†)	—	(†)	—	(†)
1980	17.0	(0.16)	18.4	(0.18)	7.9	(0.44)	7.6	(0.63)	—	(†)	—	(†)	—	(†)	—	(†)	—	(†)
1985	19.4	(0.16)	20.8	(0.19)	11.1	(0.47)	8.5	(0.55)	—	(†)	—	(†)	—	(†)	—	(†)	—	(†)
1986	19.4	(0.16)	20.9	(0.19)	10.9	(0.47)	8.4	(0.53)	—	(†)	—	(†)	—	(†)	—	(†)	—	(†)
1987	19.9	(0.16)	21.4	(0.19)	10.8	(0.46)	8.6	(0.53)	—	(†)	—	(†)	—	(†)	—	(†)	—	(†)
1988	20.3	(0.16)	21.8	(0.19)	11.2	(0.46)	10.0	(0.55)	—	(†)	—	(†)	—	(†)	—	(†)	—	(†)
1989	21.1	(0.16)	22.8	(0.19)	11.7	(0.46)	9.9	(0.53)	41.5	(1.51)	—	(†)	—	(†)	—	(†)	—	(†)
1990	21.3	(0.16)	23.1	(0.19)	11.3	(0.45)	9.2	(0.51)	41.7	(1.47)	—	(†)	—	(†)	—	(†)	—	(†)
1991	21.4	(0.16)	23.3	(0.19)	11.5	(0.45)	9.7	(0.51)	40.3	(1.42)	—	(†)	—	(†)	—	(†)	—	(†)
1992	21.4	(0.16)	23.2	(0.19)	11.9	(0.45)	9.3	(0.49)	39.3	(1.35)	—	(†)	—	(†)	—	(†)	—	(†)
1993	21.9	(0.16)	23.8	(0.19)	12.2	(0.45)	9.0	(0.48)	42.1	(1.35)	—	(†)	—	(†)	—	(†)	—	(†)
1994	22.2	(0.16)	24.3	(0.19)	12.9	(0.46)	9.1	(0.45)	41.3	(1.34)	—	(†)	—	(†)	—	(†)	—	(†)
1995	23.0	(0.16)	25.4	(0.19)	13.3	(0.47)	9.3	(0.45)	38.5	(1.40)	—	(†)	—	(†)	—	(†)	—	(†)
1996	23.6	(0.17)	25.9	(0.20)	13.8	(0.42)	9.3	(0.40)	42.3	(1.09)	—	(†)	—	(†)	—	(†)	—	(†)
1997	23.9	(0.16)	26.2	(0.19)	13.3	(0.41)	10.3	(0.33)	42.6	(1.04)	—	(†)	—	(†)	—	(†)	—	(†)
1998	24.4	(0.16)	26.6	(0.19)	14.8	(0.42)	11.0	(0.33)	42.3	(1.02)	—	(†)	—	(†)	—	(†)	—	(†)
1999	25.2	(0.16)	27.7	(0.19)	15.5	(0.43)	10.9	(0.33)	42.4	(1.01)	—	(†)	—	(†)	—	(†)	—	(†)
2000	25.6	(0.16)	28.1	(0.19)	16.6	(0.44)	10.6	(0.32)	44.4	(1.00)	—	(†)	—	(†)	—	(†)	—	(†)
2001	26.1	(0.16)	28.6	(0.19)	16.1	(0.43)	11.2	(0.32)	48.0	(0.92)	—	(†)	—	(†)	—	(†)	—	(†)
2002	26.7	(0.11)	29.4	(0.14)	17.2	(0.31)	11.1	(0.21)	47.7	(0.66)	—	(†)	—	(†)	—	(†)	—	(†)
2003	27.2	(0.11)	30.0	(0.14)	17.4	(0.31)	11.4	(0.21)	48.8	(0.65)	50.0	(0.67)	27.0	(2.56)	12.6	(1.30)	22.0	(1.17)
2004	27.7	(0.11)	30.6	(0.14)	17.7	(0.31)	12.1	(0.21)	48.9	(0.64)	49.7	(0.66)	32.4	(2.81)	14.3	(1.36)	21.8	(1.13)
2005	27.7	(0.23)	30.6	(0.29)	17.6	(0.45)	12.0	(0.31)	49.3	(0.91)	50.4	(0.93)	24.6	(3.67)	14.5	(1.51)	23.2	(1.19)

See notes at end of table.

Rates of high school completion and bachelor's degree attainment among persons age 25 and over, by race/ethnicity and sex: Selected years, 1910 through 2013—Continued

[Standard errors appear in parentheses]

Sex, high school or bachelor's degree attainment, and year	Total, percent of all persons age 25 and over		White[1]		Black[1]		Hispanic		Asian/Pacific Islander Total		Asian		Pacific Islander		American Indian/ Alaska Native		Two or more races	
1	2		3		4		5		6		7		8		9		10	
2006	28.0	(0.20)	31.0	(0.25)	18.6	(0.47)	12.4	(0.32)	49.1	(1.04)	50.0	(1.06)	26.9	(3.42)	12.9	(1.60)	23.1	(1.28)
2007	28.7	(0.21)	31.8	(0.27)	18.7	(0.51)	12.7	(0.31)	51.2	(1.02)	52.5	(1.03)	23.8	(3.30)	13.1	(1.24)	23.7	(1.30)
2008	29.4	(0.21)	32.6	(0.26)	19.7	(0.51)	13.3	(0.29)	51.9	(0.95)	52.9	(0.97)	28.4	(2.86)	14.9	(1.52)	24.4	(1.36)
2009	29.5	(0.21)	32.9	(0.26)	19.4	(0.45)	13.2	(0.34)	51.6	(0.91)	52.8	(0.95)	28.3	(2.68)	17.5	(2.08)	25.5	(1.34)
2010	29.9	(0.19)	33.2	(0.24)	20.0	(0.51)	13.9	(0.31)	51.6	(1.04)	52.8	(1.09)	25.6	(2.89)	16.0	(1.77)	25.3	(1.30)
2011	30.4	(0.19)	34.0	(0.24)	20.2	(0.50)	14.1	(0.34)	49.5	(0.92)	50.8	(0.96)	22.1	(2.73)	16.1	(1.73)	27.4	(1.27)
2012	30.9	(0.21)	34.5	(0.27)	21.4	(0.53)	14.5	(0.35)	50.7	(0.92)	51.9	(0.94)	24.5	(2.75)	16.7	(1.82)	27.1	(1.34)
2013	31.7	(0.21)	35.2	(0.26)	22.0	(0.49)	15.1	(0.34)	52.5	(0.92)	53.9	(0.93)	25.6	(2.66)	15.4	(1.72)	30.6	(1.35)
Males																		
High school completion or higher[2]																		
1940	22.7	(—)	24.2	(—)	6.9	(—)	—	(†)	—	(†)	—	(†)	—	(†)	—	(†)	—	(†)
1950	32.6	(—)	34.6	(—)	12.6	(—)	—	(†)	—	(†)	—	(†)	—	(†)	—	(†)	—	(†)
1960	39.5	(—)	41.6	(—)	20.0	(—)	—	(†)	—	(†)	—	(†)	—	(†)	—	(†)	—	(†)
1970	55.0	(—)	57.2	(—)	35.4	(—)	—	(†)	—	(†)	—	(†)	—	(†)	—	(†)	—	(†)
1980	69.2	(0.29)	72.4	(0.31)	51.2	(1.21)	44.9	(1.71)	—	(†)	—	(†)	—	(†)	—	(†)	—	(†)
1990	77.7	(0.24)	81.6	(0.25)	65.8	(1.01)	50.3	(1.25)	86.0	(1.49)	—	(†)	—	(†)	—	(†)	—	(†)
1995	81.7	(0.22)	86.0	(0.22)	73.5	(0.91)	52.9	(1.11)	85.8	(1.46)	—	(†)	—	(†)	—	(†)	—	(†)
1996	81.9	(0.23)	86.1	(0.23)	74.6	(0.80)	53.0	(0.97)	86.2	(1.10)	—	(†)	—	(†)	—	(†)	—	(†)
1997	82.0	(0.21)	86.3	(0.21)	73.8	(0.79)	54.9	(0.76)	87.5	(1.00)	—	(†)	—	(†)	—	(†)	—	(†)
1998	82.8	(0.20)	87.1	(0.21)	75.4	(0.77)	55.7	(0.74)	87.9	(0.98)	—	(†)	—	(†)	—	(†)	—	(†)
1999	83.4	(0.20)	87.7	(0.20)	77.2	(0.74)	56.0	(0.75)	86.9	(1.00)	—	(†)	—	(†)	—	(†)	—	(†)
2000	84.2	(0.19)	88.5	(0.20)	79.1	(0.72)	56.6	(0.73)	88.4	(0.94)	—	(†)	—	(†)	—	(†)	—	(†)
2001	84.4	(0.19)	88.6	(0.19)	80.6	(0.69)	55.6	(0.72)	90.6	(0.78)	—	(†)	—	(†)	—	(†)	—	(†)
2002	83.8	(0.14)	88.5	(0.14)	79.0	(0.51)	56.1	(0.48)	89.8	(0.58)	—	(†)	—	(†)	—	(†)	—	(†)
2003	84.1	(0.13)	89.0	(0.14)	79.9	(0.50)	56.3	(0.46)	89.8	(0.58)	89.8	(0.59)	89.8	(2.61)	76.5	(2.33)	87.2	(1.36)
2004	84.8	(0.13)	89.9	(0.13)	80.8	(0.49)	57.3	(0.45)	88.8	(0.59)	88.8	(0.60)	88.9	(2.65)	77.1	(2.31)	87.8	(1.29)
2005	84.9	(0.19)	89.9	(0.20)	81.4	(0.60)	57.9	(0.69)	90.4	(0.65)	90.5	(0.66)	88.5	(3.62)	75.6	(2.57)	89.0	(1.19)
2006	85.0	(0.20)	90.2	(0.21)	80.7	(0.63)	58.5	(0.77)	89.5	(0.84)	89.7	(0.86)	85.8	(3.10)	78.1	(2.77)	88.0	(1.36)
2007	85.0	(0.21)	90.2	(0.22)	82.5	(0.55)	58.2	(0.80)	90.0	(0.81)	90.1	(0.82)	88.1	(2.75)	78.3	(3.58)	89.4	(1.28)
2008	85.9	(0.19)	91.1	(0.20)	82.1	(0.61)	60.9	(0.72)	91.0	(0.66)	90.8	(0.67)	95.8	(1.40)	77.3	(3.37)	89.6	(1.21)
2009	86.2	(0.19)	91.4	(0.20)	84.2	(0.60)	60.6	(0.72)	90.8	(0.66)	90.7	(0.68)	92.1	(2.18)	80.0	(2.33)	87.3	(1.26)
2010	86.6	(0.17)	91.8	(0.19)	84.2	(0.57)	61.4	(0.68)	91.4	(0.78)	91.5	(0.79)	89.3	(2.84)	78.9	(2.46)	88.1	(1.36)
2011	87.1	(0.18)	92.0	(0.17)	84.2	(0.55)	63.6	(0.71)	90.6	(0.68)	90.6	(0.69)	91.5	(2.22)	80.6	(2.35)	88.1	(1.40)
2012	87.3	(0.19)	92.2	(0.18)	85.1	(0.56)	64.0	(0.73)	90.6	(0.68)	90.5	(0.70)	93.3	(1.84)	81.8	(2.39)	90.2	(1.45)
2013	87.6	(0.17)	92.7	(0.17)	84.9	(0.62)	64.6	(0.66)	91.6	(0.57)	91.7	(0.57)	89.3	(2.48)	81.0	(2.11)	93.3	(1.03)
Bachelor's or higher degree[4]																		
1940	5.5	(—)	5.9	(—)	1.4	(—)	—	(†)	—	(†)	—	(†)	—	(†)	—	(†)	—	(†)
1950	7.3	(—)	7.9	(—)	2.1	(—)	—	(†)	—	(†)	—	(†)	—	(†)	—	(†)	—	(†)
1960	9.7	(—)	10.3	(—)	3.5	(—)	—	(†)	—	(†)	—	(†)	—	(†)	—	(†)	—	(†)
1970	14.1	(—)	15.0	(—)	6.8	(—)	—	(†)	—	(†)	—	(†)	—	(†)	—	(†)	—	(†)
1980	20.9	(0.26)	22.7	(0.29)	7.7	(0.65)	9.2	(0.99)	—	(†)	—	(†)	—	(†)	—	(†)	—	(†)
1990	24.4	(0.25)	26.7	(0.28)	11.9	(0.69)	9.8	(0.74)	45.9	(2.14)	—	(†)	—	(†)	—	(†)	—	(†)
1995	26.0	(0.25)	28.9	(0.29)	13.7	(0.71)	10.1	(0.67)	42.3	(2.06)	—	(†)	—	(†)	—	(†)	—	(†)
1996	26.0	(0.26)	28.8	(0.30)	12.5	(0.61)	10.3	(0.59)	46.9	(1.59)	—	(†)	—	(†)	—	(†)	—	(†)
1997	26.2	(0.24)	29.0	(0.28)	12.5	(0.60)	10.6	(0.57)	48.0	(1.51)	—	(†)	—	(†)	—	(†)	—	(†)
1998	26.5	(0.24)	29.3	(0.28)	14.0	(0.62)	11.1	(0.47)	46.0	(1.50)	—	(†)	—	(†)	—	(†)	—	(†)
1999	27.5	(0.24)	30.6	(0.28)	14.3	(0.62)	10.7	(0.46)	46.3	(1.48)	—	(†)	—	(†)	—	(†)	—	(†)
2000	27.8	(0.24)	30.8	(0.28)	16.4	(0.65)	10.7	(0.45)	48.1	(1.47)	—	(†)	—	(†)	—	(†)	—	(†)
2001	28.0	(0.24)	30.9	(0.28)	15.9	(0.64)	11.1	(0.45)	52.9	(1.33)	—	(†)	—	(†)	—	(†)	—	(†)
2002	28.5	(0.17)	31.7	(0.20)	16.5	(0.47)	11.0	(0.30)	51.5	(0.96)	—	(†)	—	(†)	—	(†)	—	(†)
2003	28.9	(0.17)	32.3	(0.20)	16.8	(0.47)	11.2	(0.29)	52.8	(0.96)	54.2	(0.98)	25.7	(3.76)	13.1	(1.85)	21.9	(1.69)
2004	29.4	(0.17)	32.9	(0.20)	16.6	(0.46)	11.8	(0.30)	52.9	(0.93)	54.0	(0.95)	31.9	(3.94)	15.6	(1.99)	20.7	(1.60)
2005	28.9	(0.29)	32.4	(0.37)	16.0	(0.64)	11.8	(0.43)	53.0	(1.10)	54.3	(1.13)	25.1	(4.70)	17.0	(2.30)	23.1	(1.67)
2006	29.2	(0.24)	32.8	(0.31)	17.5	(0.63)	11.9	(0.40)	51.9	(1.33)	53.1	(1.35)	26.6	(4.67)	13.7	(2.07)	22.6	(1.75)
2007	29.5	(0.25)	33.2	(0.33)	18.1	(0.62)	11.8	(0.37)	54.2	(1.31)	55.8	(1.32)	19.2	(4.14)	12.7	(1.89)	21.5	(1.81)
2008	30.1	(0.25)	33.8	(0.33)	18.7	(0.67)	12.6	(0.39)	54.9	(1.24)	56.1	(1.24)	27.5	(3.64)	14.6	(2.15)	22.7	(1.62)
2009	30.1	(0.28)	33.9	(0.36)	17.9	(0.57)	12.5	(0.41)	54.8	(1.14)	56.5	(1.17)	23.0	(3.35)	16.1	(2.96)	24.4	(1.92)
2010	30.3	(0.23)	34.2	(0.30)	17.9	(0.59)	12.9	(0.37)	54.6	(1.26)	56.2	(1.30)	18.0	(3.74)	13.5	(2.61)	24.8	(1.86)
2011	30.8	(0.23)	35.0	(0.29)	18.4	(0.64)	13.1	(0.44)	52.4	(1.15)	54.0	(1.21)	19.1	(3.55)	14.1	(1.98)	25.7	(1.91)
2012	31.4	(0.27)	35.5	(0.33)	19.5	(0.62)	13.3	(0.45)	53.1	(1.26)	54.4	(1.29)	24.1	(3.34)	16.1	(2.27)	25.2	(1.85)
2013	32.0	(0.25)	36.0	(0.31)	20.2	(0.64)	13.9	(0.43)	55.1	(1.17)	56.9	(1.20)	23.1	(3.32)	14.0	(2.13)	29.0	(1.78)
Females																		
High school completion or higher[2]																		
1940	26.3	(—)	28.1	(—)	8.4	(—)	—	(†)	—	(†)	—	(†)	—	(†)	—	(†)	—	(†)
1950	36.0	(—)	38.2	(—)	14.7	(—)	—	(†)	—	(†)	—	(†)	—	(†)	—	(†)	—	(†)
1960	42.5	(—)	44.7	(—)	23.1	(—)	—	(†)	—	(†)	—	(†)	—	(†)	—	(†)	—	(†)
1970	55.4	(—)	57.7	(—)	36.6	(—)	—	(†)	—	(†)	—	(†)	—	(†)	—	(†)	—	(†)
1980	68.1	(0.28)	71.5	(0.30)	51.5	(1.08)	44.2	(1.63)	—	(†)	—	(†)	—	(†)	—	(†)	—	(†)
1990	77.5	(0.23)	81.3	(0.24)	66.5	(0.90)	51.3	(1.23)	82.5	(1.57)	—	(†)	—	(†)	—	(†)	—	(†)
1995	81.6	(0.21)	85.8	(0.22)	74.1	(0.81)	53.8	(1.09)	81.9	(1.54)	—	(†)	—	(†)	—	(†)	—	(†)

See notes at end of table.

Rates of high school completion and bachelor's degree attainment among persons age 25 and over, by race/ethnicity and sex: Selected years, 1910 through 2013—Continued

[Standard errors appear in parentheses]

Sex, high school or bachelor's degree attainment, and year	Total, percent of all persons age 25 and over	White[1]	Black[1]	Hispanic	Asian/Pacific Islander — Total	Asian	Pacific Islander	American Indian/ Alaska Native	Two or more races
1	2	3	4	5	6	7	8	9	10
1996	81.6 (0.22)	85.9 (0.22)	74.6 (0.71)	53.3 (0.97)	81.0 (1.21)	— (†)	— (†)	— (†)	— (†)
1997	82.2 (0.20)	86.3 (0.20)	76.5 (0.68)	54.6 (0.76)	82.9 (1.11)	— (†)	— (†)	— (†)	— (†)
1998	82.9 (0.19)	87.1 (0.20)	77.1 (0.67)	55.3 (0.75)	82.3 (1.09)	— (†)	— (†)	— (†)	— (†)
1999	83.3 (0.19)	87.6 (0.19)	77.5 (0.66)	56.3 (0.73)	82.8 (1.06)	— (†)	— (†)	— (†)	— (†)
2000	84.0 (0.19)	88.4 (0.19)	78.7 (0.64)	57.5 (0.71)	83.4 (1.03)	— (†)	— (†)	— (†)	— (†)
2001	84.2 (0.18)	88.8 (0.19)	78.6 (0.64)	57.4 (0.70)	85.2 (0.91)	— (†)	— (†)	— (†)	— (†)
2002	84.4 (0.13)	88.9 (0.13)	79.4 (0.45)	57.9 (0.48)	85.7 (0.64)	— (†)	— (†)	— (†)	— (†)
2003	85.0 (0.13)	89.7 (0.13)	80.7 (0.44)	57.8 (0.46)	86.1 (0.62)	86.1 (0.64)	86.9 (2.63)	77.9 (2.30)	85.1 (1.38)
2004	85.4 (0.12)	90.1 (0.12)	81.2 (0.43)	59.5 (0.46)	85.3 (0.63)	85.1 (0.64)	88.1 (2.76)	78.6 (2.24)	86.5 (1.29)
2005	85.5 (0.15)	90.3 (0.18)	81.5 (0.53)	59.1 (0.63)	85.4 (0.76)	85.2 (0.78)	91.7 (2.46)	75.6 (2.29)	88.1 (1.12)
2006	85.9 (0.16)	90.8 (0.17)	81.5 (0.51)	60.1 (0.59)	85.6 (0.82)	85.6 (0.81)	85.7 (3.08)	78.9 (2.18)	88.2 (1.11)
2007	86.4 (0.15)	91.0 (0.16)	83.0 (0.49)	62.5 (0.56)	86.1 (0.93)	86.0 (0.97)	89.1 (2.40)	81.9 (1.91)	89.2 (1.22)
2008	87.2 (0.17)	91.8 (0.18)	84.2 (0.49)	63.7 (0.61)	87.2 (0.75)	87.0 (0.78)	93.0 (1.57)	79.2 (2.95)	89.5 (1.53)
2009	87.1 (0.16)	91.9 (0.17)	84.2 (0.48)	63.3 (0.59)	86.4 (0.73)	86.3 (0.75)	89.7 (2.33)	82.7 (1.96)	87.6 (1.16)
2010	87.6 (0.15)	92.3 (0.17)	85.0 (0.46)	64.4 (0.59)	87.2 (0.72)	87.1 (0.75)	90.9 (2.41)	82.5 (1.95)	89.7 (1.13)
2011	88.0 (0.15)	92.8 (0.16)	85.3 (0.50)	65.1 (0.57)	87.1 (0.64)	87.0 (0.66)	89.5 (2.25)	83.8 (2.00)	90.7 (1.22)
2012	88.0 (0.17)	92.7 (0.18)	86.1 (0.46)	66.0 (0.65)	87.9 (0.64)	87.8 (0.66)	90.1 (2.11)	81.8 (1.84)	91.6 (1.13)
2013	88.6 (0.16)	93.2 (0.16)	86.6 (0.46)	67.9 (0.55)	89.0 (0.61)	88.9 (0.63)	89.6 (2.01)	83.1 (2.16)	92.0 (0.95)
Bachelor's or higher degree[4]									
1940	3.8 (—)	4.0 (—)	1.2 (—)	— (†)	— (†)	— (†)	— (†)	— (†)	— (†)
1950	5.2 (—)	5.4 (—)	2.4 (—)	— (†)	— (†)	— (†)	— (†)	— (†)	— (†)
1960	5.8 (—)	6.0 (—)	3.6 (—)	— (†)	— (†)	— (†)	— (†)	— (†)	— (†)
1970	8.2 (—)	8.6 (—)	5.6 (—)	— (†)	— (†)	— (†)	— (†)	— (†)	— (†)
1980	13.6 (0.20)	14.4 (0.23)	8.1 (0.59)	6.2 (0.79)	— (†)	— (†)	— (†)	— (†)	— (†)
1990	18.4 (0.21)	19.8 (0.25)	10.8 (0.59)	8.7 (0.69)	37.8 (2.01)	— (†)	— (†)	— (†)	— (†)
1995	20.2 (0.22)	22.1 (0.26)	13.0 (0.62)	8.4 (0.61)	35.0 (1.90)	— (†)	— (†)	— (†)	— (†)
1996	21.4 (0.23)	23.2 (0.27)	14.8 (0.58)	8.3 (0.53)	38.0 (1.50)	— (†)	— (†)	— (†)	— (†)
1997	21.7 (0.21)	23.7 (0.25)	14.0 (0.56)	10.1 (0.46)	37.4 (1.43)	— (†)	— (†)	— (†)	— (†)
1998	22.4 (0.21)	24.1 (0.25)	15.4 (0.58)	10.9 (0.47)	38.9 (1.39)	— (†)	— (†)	— (†)	— (†)
1999	23.1 (0.22)	25.0 (0.26)	16.5 (0.59)	11.0 (0.46)	39.0 (1.37)	— (†)	— (†)	— (†)	— (†)
2000	23.6 (0.22)	25.5 (0.26)	16.8 (0.59)	10.6 (0.44)	41.0 (1.37)	— (†)	— (†)	— (†)	— (†)
2001	24.3 (0.22)	26.5 (0.26)	16.3 (0.58)	11.3 (0.45)	43.4 (1.26)	— (†)	— (†)	— (†)	— (†)
2002	25.1 (0.15)	27.3 (0.19)	17.7 (0.42)	11.2 (0.31)	44.2 (0.91)	— (†)	— (†)	— (†)	— (†)
2003	25.7 (0.15)	27.9 (0.19)	18.0 (0.43)	11.6 (0.30)	45.3 (0.89)	46.3 (0.92)	28.0 (3.50)	12.2 (1.81)	22.2 (1.61)
2004	26.1 (0.15)	28.4 (0.19)	18.5 (0.43)	12.3 (0.35)	45.2 (0.88)	45.7 (0.90)	32.9 (4.01)	13.1 (1.84)	22.7 (1.59)
2005	26.5 (0.23)	28.9 (0.30)	18.9 (0.51)	12.1 (0.42)	46.0 (1.08)	46.8 (1.10)	24.1 (4.08)	12.2 (2.00)	23.3 (1.43)
2006	26.9 (0.22)	29.3 (0.28)	19.5 (0.55)	12.9 (0.39)	46.6 (1.11)	47.3 (1.15)	27.2 (4.03)	12.3 (1.81)	23.6 (1.70)
2007	28.0 (0.23)	30.6 (0.29)	19.2 (0.59)	13.7 (0.44)	48.6 (1.07)	49.5 (1.10)	27.9 (4.16)	13.4 (1.53)	25.8 (1.58)
2008	28.8 (0.24)	31.5 (0.29)	20.5 (0.58)	14.1 (0.37)	49.3 (0.99)	50.1 (1.02)	29.3 (3.82)	15.1 (1.75)	26.1 (1.92)
2009	29.1 (0.21)	31.9 (0.26)	20.6 (0.56)	14.0 (0.41)	48.8 (0.98)	49.7 (1.02)	32.9 (3.74)	18.8 (1.91)	26.6 (1.67)
2010	29.6 (0.21)	32.4 (0.26)	21.6 (0.63)	14.9 (0.42)	49.1 (1.12)	49.9 (1.19)	32.2 (4.11)	18.2 (1.83)	25.7 (1.59)
2011	30.1 (0.22)	33.1 (0.28)	21.7 (0.60)	15.2 (0.43)	47.0 (1.04)	48.0 (1.07)	24.7 (3.52)	17.9 (2.17)	28.9 (1.70)
2012	30.6 (0.23)	33.5 (0.30)	22.9 (0.61)	15.8 (0.45)	48.6 (0.93)	49.7 (0.94)	24.9 (3.70)	17.2 (2.13)	28.8 (1.88)
2013	31.4 (0.24)	34.4 (0.31)	23.4 (0.61)	16.2 (0.42)	50.2 (0.94)	51.3 (0.96)	28.0 (3.44)	16.6 (2.05)	32.0 (1.89)

—Not available.

†Not applicable.

[1]Includes persons of Hispanic ethnicity for years prior to 1980.

[2]Data for years prior to 1993 are for persons with 4 or more years of high school. Data for later years are for high school completers—i.e., those persons who graduated from high school with a diploma as well as those who completed high school through equivalency programs, such as a GED program.

[3]Estimates based on Census Bureau reverse projection of 1940 census data on education by age.

[4]Data for years prior to 1993 are for persons with 4 or more years of college.

NOTE: Beginning in 2005, standard errors were computed using replicate weights, which produced more precise values than the methodology used in prior years. For 1960 and prior years, data were collected in April. For all other years, data were collected in March. Race categories exclude persons of Hispanic ethnicity except where otherwise noted. SOURCE: U.S. Department of Commerce, Census Bureau, *U.S. Census of Population: 1960*, Vol. I, Part 1; J.K. Folger and C.B. Nam, *Education of the American Population* (1960 Census Monograph); Current Population Reports, Series P-20, various years; and Current Population Survey (CPS), March 1970 through March 2013. (This table was prepared February 2014.)

Educational Attainment

Percentage of persons 25 to 29 years old with selected levels of educational attainment, by race/ethnicity and sex: Selected years, 1920 through 2013

[Standard errors appear in parentheses]

Sex, selected level of educational attainment, and year	Total	White[1]	Black[1]	Hispanic	Asian/Pacific Islander — Total	Asian	Pacific Islander	American Indian/ Alaska Native	Two or more races
1	2	3	4	5	6	7	8	9	10
Total									
High school completion or higher[2]									
1920[3]	— (†)	22.0 (—)	6.3 (—)	— (†)	— (†)	— (†)	— (†)	— (†)	— (†)
1940	38.1 (—)	41.2 (—)	12.3 (—)	— (†)	— (†)	— (†)	— (†)	— (†)	— (†)
1950	52.8 (—)	56.3 (—)	23.6 (—)	— (†)	— (†)	— (†)	— (†)	— (†)	— (†)
1960	60.7 (—)	63.7 (—)	38.6 (—)	— (†)	— (†)	— (†)	— (†)	— (†)	— (†)
1970	75.4 (—)	77.8 (—)	58.4 (—)	— (—)	— (†)	— (†)	— (†)	— (†)	— (†)
1975	83.1 (—)	86.6 (—)	71.1 (—)	53.1 (—)	— (†)	— (†)	— (†)	— (†)	— (†)
1980	85.4 (0.40)	89.2 (0.40)	76.7 (1.64)	58.0 (2.59)	— (†)	— (†)	— (†)	— (†)	— (†)
1985	86.1 (0.37)	89.5 (0.38)	80.5 (1.42)	60.9 (2.17)	— (†)	— (†)	— (†)	— (†)	— (†)
1990	85.7 (0.38)	90.1 (0.37)	81.7 (1.37)	58.2 (1.94)	91.5 (2.09)	— (†)	— (†)	— (†)	— (†)
1995	86.8 (0.39)	92.5 (0.36)	86.7 (1.23)	57.1 (1.80)	90.8 (2.26)	— (†)	— (†)	— (†)	— (†)
2000	88.1 (0.37)	94.0 (0.33)	86.8 (1.13)	62.8 (1.22)	93.7 (1.27)	— (†)	— (†)	— (†)	— (†)
2003	86.5 (0.27)	93.7 (0.25)	88.5 (0.78)	61.7 (0.75)	96.3 (0.67)	97.3 (0.60)	‡ (†)	80.5 (4.33)	91.7 (2.18)
2005	86.2 (0.42)	92.8 (0.39)	87.0 (1.03)	63.3 (1.32)	95.6 (0.88)	95.5 (0.92)	‡ (†)	80.2 (4.77)	91.4 (3.91)
2006	86.4 (0.36)	93.4 (0.35)	86.3 (1.09)	63.2 (1.17)	96.4 (0.88)	96.6 (0.86)	‡ (†)	79.8 (5.19)	89.3 (3.96)
2007	87.0 (0.36)	93.5 (0.33)	87.7 (1.16)	65.0 (1.06)	96.8 (0.91)	97.5 (0.73)	‡ (†)	84.5 (4.41)	90.5 (4.30)
2008	87.8 (0.36)	94.2 (0.38)	87.5 (1.29)	68.3 (1.16)	95.9 (0.86)	95.8 (0.91)	— (†)	86.7 (3.36)	94.2 (3.82)
2009	88.6 (0.36)	94.6 (0.33)	88.9 (0.98)	68.9 (1.16)	95.4 (0.91)	95.8 (0.95)	91.6 (3.46)	81.1 (4.26)	88.5 (3.61)
2010	88.8 (0.32)	94.5 (0.31)	89.6 (0.93)	69.4 (1.22)	93.7 (1.18)	94.0 (1.24)	89.7 (5.05)	89.9 (2.98)	88.5 (3.86)
2011	89.0 (0.34)	94.4 (0.34)	88.1 (0.98)	71.5 (1.12)	95.4 (0.87)	95.3 (0.91)	— (†)	84.9 (3.95)	90.7 (3.79)
2012	89.7 (0.38)	94.6 (0.37)	88.5 (0.96)	75.0 (1.16)	96.2 (0.73)	96.1 (0.77)	98.6 (0.83)	84.5 (3.94)	92.8 (2.22)
2013	89.9 (0.35)	94.1 (0.35)	90.3 (0.92)	75.8 (1.10)	95.4 (0.77)	95.4 (0.81)	95.5 (2.72)	84.7 (3.47)	97.4 (1.11)
Bachelor's or higher degree[4]									
1920[3]	— (†)	4.5 (—)	1.2 (—)	— (†)	— (†)	— (†)	— (†)	— (†)	— (†)
1940	5.9 (—)	6.4 (—)	1.6 (—)	— (†)	— (†)	— (†)	— (†)	— (†)	— (†)
1950	7.7 (—)	8.2 (—)	2.8 (—)	— (†)	— (†)	— (†)	— (†)	— (†)	— (†)
1960	11.0 (—)	11.8 (—)	5.4 (—)	— (†)	— (†)	— (†)	— (†)	— (†)	— (†)
1970	16.4 (—)	17.3 (—)	10.0 (—)	— (†)	— (†)	— (†)	— (†)	— (†)	— (†)
1975	21.9 (—)	23.8 (—)	10.5 (—)	8.8 (—)	— (†)	— (†)	— (†)	— (†)	— (†)
1980	22.5 (0.47)	25.0 (0.55)	11.6 (1.24)	7.7 (1.39)	— (†)	— (†)	— (†)	— (†)	— (†)
1985	22.2 (0.45)	24.4 (0.53)	11.6 (1.15)	11.1 (1.39)	— (†)	— (†)	— (†)	— (†)	— (†)
1990	23.2 (0.46)	26.4 (0.55)	13.4 (1.20)	8.1 (1.07)	43.0 (3.71)	— (†)	— (†)	— (†)	— (†)
1995	24.7 (0.49)	28.8 (0.62)	15.4 (1.31)	8.9 (1.04)	43.1 (3.87)	— (†)	— (†)	— (†)	— (†)
2000	29.1 (0.52)	34.0 (0.67)	17.8 (1.28)	9.7 (0.75)	54.3 (2.60)	— (†)	— (†)	— (†)	— (†)
2003	28.4 (0.36)	34.2 (0.49)	17.5 (0.93)	10.0 (0.47)	60.0 (1.74)	62.1 (1.77)	‡ (†)	10.0 (3.28)	22.3 (3.28)
2005	28.8 (0.55)	34.5 (0.78)	17.6 (1.21)	11.2 (0.81)	60.0 (2.20)	62.1 (2.25)	‡ (†)	16.4 (3.56)	28.0 (3.79)
2006	28.4 (0.52)	34.3 (0.78)	18.7 (1.33)	9.5 (0.66)	59.6 (2.39)	61.9 (2.44)	‡ (†)	9.5! (4.26)	23.3 (3.14)
2007	29.6 (0.54)	35.5 (0.75)	19.5 (1.21)	11.6 (0.61)	59.4 (2.24)	61.5 (2.26)	‡ (†)	6.4! (2.99)	26.3 (3.44)
2008	30.8 (0.51)	37.1 (0.70)	20.4 (1.35)	12.4 (0.69)	57.9 (2.26)	60.2 (2.32)	‡ (†)	14.3 (3.17)	26.6 (3.75)
2009	30.6 (0.57)	37.2 (0.85)	18.9 (1.36)	12.2 (0.80)	56.4 (2.25)	60.3 (2.28)	12.5! (4.44)	15.9 (3.73)	29.7 (3.84)
2010	31.7 (0.51)	38.6 (0.72)	19.4 (1.20)	13.5 (0.80)	52.5 (2.32)	55.8 (2.47)	10.0! (4.40)	18.6 (4.80)	29.8 (3.22)
2011	32.2 (0.62)	39.2 (0.88)	20.1 (1.25)	12.8 (0.73)	56.0 (2.50)	57.2 (2.52)	‡ (†)	17.3 (4.45)	32.4 (3.85)
2012	33.5 (0.58)	39.8 (0.78)	23.2 (1.38)	14.8 (0.90)	59.6 (2.17)	61.7 (2.24)	25.5! (6.12)	10.4 (2.87)	32.9 (3.72)
2013	33.6 (0.55)	40.4 (0.77)	20.5 (1.38)	15.7 (0.82)	58.0 (2.16)	60.1 (2.18)	24.7! (7.54)	16.6 (4.89)	29.6 (3.45)
Master's or higher degree									
1995	4.5 (0.24)	5.3 (0.31)	1.8 (0.48)	1.6 (0.46)	10.9 (1.85)	— (†)	— (†)	— (†)	— (†)
2000	5.4 (0.26)	5.8 (0.33)	3.7 (0.63)	2.1 (0.36)	15.5 (1.70)	— (†)	‡ (†)	‡ (†)	— (†)
2003	5.7 (0.19)	6.6 (0.26)	2.6 (0.39)	1.4 (0.18)	18.4 (1.37)	19.1 (1.44)	‡ (†)	‡ (†)	4.4! (1.61)
2005	6.3 (0.31)	7.5 (0.45)	2.6 (0.44)	2.1 (0.38)	16.9 (1.93)	17.5 (2.01)	‡ (†)	‡ (†)	7.0! (2.49)
2006	6.4 (0.29)	7.5 (0.42)	3.2 (0.58)	1.5 (0.25)	20.1 (2.00)	21.1 (2.10)	‡ (†)	‡ (†)	7.1 (1.83)
2007	6.3 (0.30)	7.6 (0.42)	3.5 (0.59)	1.5 (0.25)	17.5 (1.84)	18.5 (1.93)	‡ (†)	‡ (†)	6.2! (2.38)
2008	7.0 (0.28)	8.2 (0.40)	4.4 (0.64)	2.0 (0.28)	19.9 (1.84)	21.0 (1.96)	‡ (†)	‡ (†)	6.9! (2.57)
2009	7.4 (0.30)	8.9 (0.45)	4.2 (0.54)	1.9 (0.26)	21.1 (1.98)	22.9 (2.16)	‡ (†)	‡ (†)	6.5! (2.02)
2010	6.8 (0.26)	7.7 (0.38)	4.7 (0.60)	2.5 (0.37)	17.9 (1.87)	19.2 (1.99)	‡ (†)	‡ (†)	5.3! (1.63)
2011	6.9 (0.32)	8.1 (0.45)	4.0 (0.52)	2.7 (0.37)	16.7 (1.78)	17.5 (1.85)	‡ (†)	‡ (†)	6.1 (1.59)
2012	7.2 (0.35)	8.2 (0.51)	5.1 (0.66)	2.7 (0.36)	17.8 (1.85)	18.9 (1.92)	# (†)	2.6! (1.28)	4.1! (1.49)
2013	7.4 (0.31)	8.6 (0.50)	3.3 (0.50)	3.0 (0.37)	20.6 (1.73)	21.8 (1.79)	‡ (†)	‡ (†)	4.8! (1.54)
Males									
High school completion or higher[2]									
1980	85.4 (0.49)	89.1 (0.48)	74.7 (1.97)	57.0 (3.45)	— (†)	— (†)	— (†)	— (†)	— (†)
1985	85.9 (0.49)	89.2 (0.49)	80.6 (1.75)	58.6 (2.62)	— (†)	— (†)	— (†)	— (†)	— (†)
1990	84.4 (0.56)	88.6 (0.57)	81.4 (2.03)	56.6 (2.69)	95.3 (1.78)	— (†)	— (†)	— (†)	— (†)
1995	86.3 (0.56)	92.0 (0.53)	88.4 (1.72)	55.7 (2.51)	90.5 (2.37)	— (†)	— (†)	— (†)	— (†)
2000	86.7 (0.55)	92.9 (0.51)	87.6 (1.67)	59.2 (1.76)	92.1 (1.83)	— (†)	— (†)	— (†)	— (†)
2003	84.9 (0.41)	92.8 (0.38)	87.4 (1.21)	59.6 (1.02)	96.1 (0.99)	97.7 (0.80)	‡ (†)	‡ (†)	94.8 (2.49)
2005	85.0 (0.58)	91.8 (0.53)	86.6 (1.76)	63.2 (1.72)	96.8 (1.09)	96.7 (1.15)	‡ (†)	‡ (†)	89.1 (3.07)
2006	84.4 (0.54)	92.3 (0.52)	84.2 (2.02)	60.5 (1.64)	97.2 (1.01)	97.2 (1.06)	‡ (†)	‡ (†)	89.2 (3.81)
2007	84.9 (0.50)	92.7 (0.48)	87.4 (1.65)	60.5 (1.59)	95.9 (1.13)	96.3 (1.10)	‡ (†)	‡ (†)	92.9 (2.64)
2008	85.8 (0.54)	92.6 (0.58)	85.7 (1.99)	65.6 (1.55)	95.6 (1.23)	95.4 (1.31)	‡ (†)	‡ (†)	92.7 (2.68)
2009	87.5 (0.51)	94.4 (0.46)	88.8 (1.56)	66.2 (1.54)	96.4 (1.17)	96.2 (1.25)	‡ (†)	‡ (†)	92.0 (3.01)
2010	87.4 (0.44)	94.6 (0.42)	87.9 (1.52)	65.7 (1.52)	93.8 (1.83)	93.5 (1.95)	‡ (†)	93.2 (3.47)	87.9 (4.32)
2011	87.5 (0.49)	93.4 (0.48)	88.0 (1.43)	69.2 (1.62)	94.2 (1.30)	93.9 (1.36)	‡ (†)	84.5 (5.28)	86.2 (4.41)
2012	88.4 (0.51)	93.8 (0.50)	86.2 (1.58)	73.3 (1.57)	96.1 (1.04)	96.0 (1.09)	‡ (†)	‡ (†)	91.0 (3.58)
2013	88.3 (0.52)	93.3 (0.53)	87.8 (1.60)	73.1 (1.64)	94.4 (1.13)	94.3 (1.21)	‡ (†)	‡ (†)	96.8 (1.77)
Bachelor's or higher degree[4]									
1980	24.0 (0.59)	26.8 (0.69)	10.5 (1.39)	8.4 (1.94)	— (†)	— (†)	— (†)	— (†)	— (†)
1985	23.1 (0.59)	25.5 (0.69)	10.3 (1.35)	10.9 (1.66)	— (†)	— (†)	— (†)	— (†)	— (†)
1990	23.7 (0.65)	26.6 (0.79)	15.1 (1.87)	7.3 (1.41)	47.6 (4.19)	— (†)	— (†)	— (†)	— (†)
1995	24.5 (0.70)	28.4 (0.88)	17.4 (2.04)	7.8 (1.35)	42.0 (3.98)	— (†)	— (†)	— (†)	— (†)

See notes at end of table.

Percentage of persons 25 to 29 years old with selected levels of educational attainment, by race/ethnicity and sex: Selected years, 1920 through 2013—Continued

[Standard errors appear in parentheses]

Sex, selected level of educational attainment, and year	Total		White[1]		Black[1]		Hispanic		Asian/Pacific Islander Total		Asian		Pacific Islander		American Indian/ Alaska Native		Two or more races	
1	2		3		4		5		6		7		8		9		10	
2000	27.9	(0.73)	32.3	(0.93)	18.4	(1.96)	8.3	(0.98)	55.5	(3.37)	—	(†)	—	(†)	—	(†)	—	(†)
2003	26.0	(0.50)	31.4	(0.68)	17.7	(1.39)	8.4	(0.58)	59.2	(2.52)	61.7	(2.58)	‡	(†)	‡	(†)	17.5	(4.27)
2005	25.5	(0.68)	30.7	(0.98)	14.2	(1.57)	10.2	(0.99)	58.5	(3.11)	61.0	(3.17)	‡	(†)	‡	(†)	24.5	(4.13)
2006	25.3	(0.67)	31.4	(0.98)	15.2	(1.66)	6.9	(0.70)	58.7	(3.46)	60.9	(3.52)	‡	(†)	‡	(†)	20.8	(4.65)
2007	26.3	(0.72)	31.9	(0.98)	18.9	(1.86)	8.6	(0.71)	58.5	(3.45)	60.4	(3.54)	‡	(†)	‡	(†)	23.3	(4.88)
2008	26.8	(0.64)	32.6	(0.89)	19.0	(1.94)	10.0	(0.86)	54.1	(3.41)	55.8	(3.53)	‡	(†)	‡	(†)	25.7	(4.45)
2009	26.6	(0.66)	32.6	(1.04)	14.8	(1.82)	11.0	(1.04)	55.2	(3.07)	59.2	(3.24)	‡	(†)	‡	(†)	24.6	(5.77)
2010	27.8	(0.68)	34.8	(0.96)	15.0	(1.72)	10.8	(1.06)	49.0	(3.12)	52.3	(3.31)	‡	(†)	18.9 !	(7.12)	24.9	(4.91)
2011	28.4	(0.82)	35.5	(1.16)	17.0	(1.83)	9.6	(0.90)	50.8	(3.42)	52.1	(3.55)	‡	(†)	15.4 !	(4.80)	34.1	(6.62)
2012	29.8	(0.82)	36.0	(1.06)	19.1	(1.74)	12.5	(1.20)	55.0	(3.15)	56.9	(3.16)	‡	(†)	‡	(†)	30.4	(5.44)
2013	30.2	(0.68)	37.1	(1.00)	17.4	(1.63)	13.1	(1.06)	53.0	(3.03)	55.1	(3.13)	‡	(†)	‡	(†)	29.3	(4.61)
Master's or higher degree																		
1995	4.9	(0.35)	5.6	(0.45)	2.2 !	(0.80)	2.0 !	(0.70)	12.6	(2.68)	—	(†)	—	(†)	—	(†)	—	(†)
2000	4.7	(0.34)	4.9	(0.43)	2.1 !	(0.72)	1.5	(0.43)	17.2	(2.56)	—	(†)	—	(†)	—	(†)	—	(†)
2003	5.0	(0.25)	5.8	(0.34)	1.6	(0.46)	1.2	(0.22)	19.3	(2.03)	20.6	(2.15)	‡	(†)	‡	(†)	‡	(†)
2005	5.2	(0.38)	6.2	(0.55)	1.1 !	(0.43)	1.7	(0.46)	19.7	(3.13)	20.5	(3.30)	‡	(†)	‡	(†)	‡	(†)
2006	5.1	(0.37)	5.8	(0.51)	1.7 !	(0.52)	1.1	(0.32)	20.5	(2.68)	21.8	(2.83)	‡	(†)	‡	(†)	5.9 !	(2.66)
2007	5.0	(0.39)	5.7	(0.50)	3.3	(0.99)	0.6 !	(0.19)	18.4	(2.89)	19.3	(3.00)	‡	(†)	‡	(†)	9.8 !	(4.28)
2008	5.3	(0.34)	5.9	(0.49)	3.4	(0.90)	1.2	(0.32)	20.9	(2.94)	22.1	(3.07)	‡	(†)	‡	(†)	7.8 !	(2.85)
2009	6.1	(0.37)	7.4	(0.60)	3.2	(0.73)	1.2	(0.28)	20.4	(2.48)	22.0	(2.69)	‡	(†)	‡	(†)	5.0 !	(2.38)
2010	5.2	(0.32)	6.3	(0.50)	2.9	(0.69)	1.5	(0.39)	15.0	(2.19)	16.2	(2.36)	‡	(†)	‡	(†)	#	(†)
2011	5.1	(0.38)	5.9	(0.49)	1.9	(0.54)	1.8	(0.41)	18.0	(2.58)	19.1	(2.71)	‡	(†)	‡	(†)	‡	(†)
2012	5.6	(0.42)	6.3	(0.59)	2.7	(0.72)	2.4	(0.50)	16.2	(2.46)	17.2	(2.60)	‡	(†)	‡	(†)	‡	(†)
2013	5.7	(0.38)	6.3	(0.53)	1.5 !	(0.56)	2.1	(0.43)	20.8	(2.49)	22.1	(2.60)	‡	(†)	‡	(†)	5.9 !	(2.47)
Females																		
High school completion or higher[2]																		
1980	85.5	(0.48)	89.2	(0.48)	78.3	(1.71)	58.9	(3.38)	—	(†)	—	(†)	—	(†)	—	(†)	—	(†)
1985	86.4	(0.47)	89.9	(0.48)	80.5	(1.61)	63.1	(2.48)	—	(†)	—	(†)	—	(†)	—	(†)	—	(†)
1990	87.0	(0.51)	91.7	(0.49)	82.0	(1.85)	59.9	(2.79)	85.1	(2.82)	—	(†)	—	(†)	—	(†)	—	(†)
1995	87.4	(0.54)	93.0	(0.50)	85.3	(1.75)	58.7	(2.60)	91.2	(2.50)	—	(†)	—	(†)	—	(†)	—	(†)
2000	89.4	(0.49)	95.2	(0.43)	86.2	(1.53)	66.4	(1.69)	95.2	(1.39)	—	(†)	—	(†)	—	(†)	—	(†)
2003	88.2	(0.37)	94.5	(0.33)	89.4	(1.01)	64.2	(1.11)	96.5	(0.90)	96.9	(0.88)	‡	(†)	‡	(†)	88.6	(3.50)
2005	87.4	(0.44)	93.8	(0.47)	87.3	(1.22)	63.4	(1.54)	94.6	(1.36)	94.4	(1.41)	‡	(†)	‡	(†)	94.2	(2.26)
2006	88.5	(0.44)	94.6	(0.41)	88.0	(1.14)	66.6	(1.41)	95.6	(1.44)	96.0	(1.31)	‡	(†)	‡	(†)	89.4	(3.81)
2007	89.1	(0.45)	94.2	(0.44)	87.9	(1.46)	70.7	(1.30)	97.7	(1.05)	98.5	(0.68)	‡	(†)	90.2	(4.49)	87.9	(3.82)
2008	89.9	(0.39)	94.7	(0.44)	89.2	(1.43)	71.9	(1.34)	96.1	(1.12)	96.2	(1.18)	‡	(†)	84.2	(4.68)	95.9	(2.44)
2009	89.8	(0.41)	94.8	(0.44)	89.0	(1.12)	72.5	(1.34)	94.5	(1.20)	95.3	(1.18)	‡	(†)	83.4	(4.81)	84.8	(3.57)
2010	90.2	(0.39)	94.4	(0.42)	91.2	(0.96)	74.1	(1.53)	93.6	(1.25)	94.5	(1.27)	‡	(†)	86.8	(4.80)	89.1	(3.55)
2011	90.7	(0.36)	95.5	(0.42)	88.2	(1.24)	74.3	(1.26)	96.6	(0.89)	96.6	(0.92)	‡	(†)	85.3	(6.02)	94.0	(2.52)
2012	91.1	(0.44)	95.3	(0.46)	90.6	(1.11)	76.9	(1.39)	96.3	(0.98)	96.1	(1.04)	‡	(†)	85.8	(4.53)	94.7	(2.35)
2013	91.5	(0.38)	94.9	(0.43)	92.5	(0.95)	78.8	(1.17)	96.2	(0.96)	96.3	(1.01)	‡	(†)	82.0	(5.40)	98.2	(1.15)
Bachelor's or higher degree[4]																		
1980	21.0	(0.56)	23.2	(0.65)	12.4	(1.36)	6.9	(1.74)	—	(†)	—	(†)	—	(†)	—	(†)	—	(†)
1985	21.3	(0.57)	23.3	(0.67)	12.6	(1.35)	11.2	(1.62)	—	(†)	—	(†)	—	(†)	—	(†)	—	(†)
1990	22.8	(0.64)	26.2	(0.78)	11.9	(1.56)	9.1	(1.64)	37.4	(3.83)	—	(†)	—	(†)	—	(†)	—	(†)
1995	24.9	(0.70)	29.2	(0.89)	13.7	(1.70)	10.1	(1.59)	44.5	(4.38)	—	(†)	—	(†)	—	(†)	—	(†)
2000	30.1	(0.73)	35.8	(0.96)	17.4	(1.69)	11.0	(1.12)	53.1	(3.26)	—	(†)	—	(†)	—	(†)	—	(†)
2003	30.9	(0.53)	37.1	(0.71)	17.4	(1.25)	12.0	(0.75)	60.7	(2.39)	62.4	(2.44)	‡	(†)	‡	(†)	26.9	(4.89)
2005	32.2	(0.75)	38.2	(1.00)	20.5	(1.68)	12.4	(1.07)	61.4	(3.06)	63.1	(3.11)	‡	(†)	‡	(†)	32.1	(5.70)
2006	31.6	(0.69)	37.2	(0.99)	21.7	(1.77)	12.8	(1.05)	60.4	(2.76)	62.8	(2.82)	‡	(†)	‡	(†)	25.7	(4.72)
2007	33.0	(0.72)	39.2	(1.03)	20.0	(1.38)	15.4	(1.10)	60.3	(2.83)	62.5	(2.88)	‡	(†)	‡	(†)	29.6	(5.17)
2008	34.9	(0.71)	41.7	(0.98)	21.6	(1.57)	15.5	(1.11)	61.6	(2.67)	64.4	(2.71)	‡	(†)	12.2 !	(3.69)	27.7	(5.57)
2009	34.8	(0.78)	42.0	(1.12)	22.6	(1.75)	13.8	(1.09)	57.6	(3.00)	61.3	(3.03)	‡	(†)	16.3	(4.42)	35.0	(5.07)
2010	35.7	(0.68)	42.4	(0.96)	23.3	(1.72)	16.8	(1.20)	55.8	(2.93)	58.9	(3.00)	‡	(†)	18.4 !	(6.68)	24.6	(4.96)
2011	36.1	(0.71)	43.0	(1.03)	22.9	(1.62)	16.8	(1.10)	61.0	(2.74)	62.0	(2.75)	‡	(†)	19.7 !	(6.64)	31.2	(4.36)
2012	37.2	(0.69)	43.6	(0.97)	26.7	(1.78)	17.4	(1.01)	64.0	(2.38)	66.2	(2.46)	‡	(†)	14.0 !	(4.55)	35.5	(5.50)
2013	37.0	(0.71)	43.8	(0.95)	23.2	(2.03)	18.6	(1.10)	62.4	(2.51)	64.3	(2.54)	‡	(†)	16.4 !	(6.57)	30.0	(5.26)
Master's or higher degree																		
1995	4.1	(0.32)	5.0	(0.42)	1.4 !	(0.59)	1.2 !	(0.58)	8.9	(2.50)	—	(†)	—	(†)	—	(†)	—	(†)
2000	6.2	(0.38)	6.7	(0.50)	4.9	(0.96)	2.7	(0.58)	13.9	(2.26)	—	(†)	—	(†)	—	(†)	—	(†)
2003	6.4	(0.28)	7.4	(0.38)	3.3	(0.59)	1.7	(0.30)	17.5	(1.86)	17.7	(1.93)	‡	(†)	‡	(†)	7.3 !	(2.86)
2005	7.3	(0.44)	8.8	(0.64)	4.0	(0.70)	2.6	(0.51)	14.4	(2.08)	15.0	(2.15)	‡	(†)	‡	(†)	10.0 !	(4.26)
2006	7.8	(0.42)	9.2	(0.63)	4.5	(0.93)	2.0	(0.41)	19.7	(2.33)	20.4	(2.44)	‡	(†)	‡	(†)	8.3 !	(2.89)
2007	7.6	(0.43)	9.4	(0.63)	3.7	(0.66)	2.6	(0.53)	16.5	(2.39)	17.7	(2.54)	‡	(†)	‡	(†)	‡	(†)
2008	8.7	(0.44)	10.4	(0.64)	5.2	(0.87)	2.9	(0.46)	18.9	(2.30)	19.9	(2.44)	‡	(†)	‡	(†)	‡	(†)
2009	8.8	(0.45)	10.4	(0.66)	5.1	(0.80)	2.7	(0.43)	21.7	(2.45)	23.7	(2.70)	‡	(†)	‡	(†)	7.9 !	(2.84)
2010	8.5	(0.39)	9.2	(0.56)	6.2	(0.94)	3.8	(0.56)	20.6	(2.60)	21.8	(2.75)	‡	(†)	‡	(†)	10.0 !	(3.06)
2011	8.8	(0.48)	10.4	(0.72)	5.8	(0.85)	3.8	(0.63)	15.4	(1.98)	15.9	(2.03)	‡	(†)	‡	(†)	9.9	(2.61)
2012	8.8	(0.45)	10.0	(0.67)	7.1	(1.00)	3.0	(0.45)	19.3	(2.23)	20.4	(2.31)	‡	(†)	‡	(†)	6.3 !	(2.49)
2013	9.2	(0.44)	10.8	(0.71)	4.8	(0.74)	4.0	(0.59)	20.4	(1.91)	21.6	(2.00)	‡	(†)	‡	(†)	3.3 !	(1.56)

—Not available.
†Not applicable.
#Rounds to zero.
!Interpret data with caution. The coefficient of variation (CV) for this estimate is between 30 and 50 percent.
‡Reporting standards not met. Either there are too few cases for a reliable estimate or the coefficient of variation (CV) is 50 percent or greater.
[1]Includes persons of Hispanic ethnicity for years prior to 1980.
[2]Data for years prior to 1993 are for persons with 4 or more years of high school. Data for later years are for high school completers—i.e., those persons who graduated from high school with a diploma as well as those who completed high school through equivalency programs, such as a GED program.

[3]Estimates based on Census Bureau reverse projection of 1940 census data on education by age.
[4]Data for years prior to 1993 are for persons with 4 or more years of college.
NOTE: Beginning in 2005, standard errors were computed using replicate weights, which produced more precise values than the methodology used in prior years. For 1960 and prior years, data were collected in April. For all other years, data were collected in March. Race categories exclude persons of Hispanic ethnicity except where otherwise noted.
SOURCE: U.S. Department of Commerce, Census Bureau, *U.S. Census of Population: 1960*, Vol. I, Part 1; J.K. Folger and C.B. Nam, *Education of the American Population* (1960 Census Monograph); Current Population Reports, Series P-20, various years; and Current Population Survey (CPS), March 1970 through March 2013. (This table was prepared October 2013.)

Number of persons age 18 and over, by highest level of educational attainment, sex, race/ethnicity, and age: 2013

[Numbers in thousands. Standard errors appear in parentheses]

Sex, race/ethnicity, and age	Total	Elementary school (kindergarten—8th grade)	High school: 1 to 3 years	High school: 4 years, no completion	High school: Completion	High school: Some college, no degree	Postsecondary: Associate's degree	Postsecondary: Bachelor's degree	Postsecondary: Master's degree	Postsecondary: First-professional or doctor's degree
1	2	3	4	5	6	7	8	9	10	11
Total, 18 and over	236,929 (99.1)	10,367 (191.3)	15,811 (222.5)	3,581 (101.3)	69,985 (427.8)	46,467 (312.0)	22,196 (237.1)	44,378 (351.6)	17,586 (221.5)	6,558 (145.5)
18 and 19 years old	7,876 (79.3)	97 (20.3)	2,485 (61.7)	572 (33.5)	2,129 (55.9)	2,480 (64.6)	81 (12.7)	2,774 (77.6)	‡	‡
20 to 24 years old	22,153 (21.6)	349 (35.5)	1,316 (57.9)	425 (30.9)	6,152 (104.6)	9,182 (145.3)	1,747 (67.7)	‡	191 (21.7)	‡
25 years old and over	206,899 (52.7)	9,922 (179.4)	12,011 (198.2)	2,585 (86.6)	61,704 (404.2)	34,805 (282.7)	20,367 (226.3)	41,575 (337.0)	17,395 (218.7)	6,536 (144.7)
25 to 29 years old	21,138 (40.0)	545 (39.5)	1,264 (55.8)	330 (28.6)	5,667 (97.6)	4,198 (100.0)	2,033 (67.7)	5,533 (110.8)	1,197 (55.5)	372 (33.6)
30 to 34 years old	20,659 (41.1)	750 (43.7)	1,201 (54.4)	321 (25.7)	5,284 (102.1)	3,521 (85.7)	2,203 (68.2)	4,820 (92.4)	1,960 (64.2)	599 (37.2)
35 to 39 years old	19,221 (31.3)	846 (47.5)	1,096 (48.7)	225 (21.8)	4,877 (97.1)	3,228 (73.2)	2,022 (58.5)	4,327 (83.3)	1,931 (62.7)	668 (39.3)
40 to 49 years old	41,717 (41.9)	1,601 (57.1)	2,135 (73.2)	509 (32.0)	11,766 (152.3)	6,876 (117.4)	4,631 (96.4)	9,164 (138.3)	3,745 (92.2)	1,289 (56.6)
50 to 59 years old	43,266 (71.3)	1,753 (61.4)	2,232 (71.7)	493 (37.3)	13,758 (178.9)	7,199 (120.2)	4,581 (93.7)	8,179 (139.5)	3,586 (85.2)	1,485 (64.1)
60 to 64 years old	17,611 (110.0)	791 (39.4)	737 (43.7)	140 (15.1)	5,232 (114.2)	3,194 (77.8)	1,813 (64.5)	3,338 (81.2)	1,721 (65.4)	646 (46.8)
65 years old and over	43,287 (95.8)	3,635 (87.2)	3,347 (82.9)	566 (42.9)	15,120 (181.5)	6,590 (126.7)	3,085 (90.5)	6,214 (129.5)	3,254 (90.4)	1,478 (64.8)
Males, 18 and over	114,447 (83.4)	5,219 (117.9)	8,069 (144.5)	1,909 (66.0)	34,637 (249.5)	21,983 (197.3)	9,558 (154.4)	21,112 (206.6)	7,879 (132.9)	4,080 (106.5)
18 and 19 years old	4,008 (58.4)	‡	1,361 (43.4)	327 (24.3)	1,135 (40.9)	1,088 (41.9)	‡	1,238 (57.0)	‡	‡
20 to 24 years old	11,134 (20.9)	207 (23.1)	721 (38.7)	256 (23.8)	3,487 (81.6)	4,387 (94.5)	753 (44.2)	‡	75 (15.9)	‡
25 years old and over	99,305 (51.6)	4,963 (109.3)	5,988 (133.5)	1,326 (54.4)	30,014 (227.4)	16,508 (185.8)	8,775 (142.7)	19,860 (202.5)	7,804 (132.7)	4,068 (106.3)
25 to 29 years old	10,628 (41.1)	304 (27.2)	746 (44.1)	195 (22.1)	3,183 (68.0)	2,104 (70.5)	889 (43.1)	2,604 (68.6)	421 (35.8)	183 (21.7)
30 to 34 years old	10,189 (40.3)	439 (30.2)	623 (39.7)	183 (18.3)	2,875 (68.1)	1,780 (58.7)	975 (46.0)	2,255 (64.0)	734 (38.8)	322 (26.3)
35 to 39 years old	9,461 (30.4)	496 (35.0)	542 (34.1)	135 (15.8)	2,696 (62.8)	1,613 (53.0)	836 (38.5)	1,959 (50.6)	837 (38.0)	347 (26.6)
40 to 49 years old	20,481 (40.5)	874 (42.8)	1,219 (57.5)	275 (22.8)	6,123 (101.4)	3,439 (86.0)	2,028 (63.3)	4,260 (83.6)	1,676 (55.7)	766 (39.8)
50 to 59 years old	21,025 (50.9)	887 (42.2)	1,149 (51.7)	266 (22.5)	6,965 (118.8)	3,260 (73.3)	1,923 (60.1)	3,825 (91.7)	1,660 (57.5)	909 (50.6)
60 to 64 years old	8,224 (102.1)	355 (26.4)	355 (29.0)	59 (10.4)	2,344 (75.8)	1,438 (57.9)	818 (42.9)	1,657 (60.0)	792 (34.8)	406 (34.8)
65 years old and over	19,298 (95.8)	1,609 (49.9)	1,353 (54.6)	212 (23.2)	5,828 (100.9)	2,873 (80.4)	1,305 (56.4)	3,299 (89.4)	1,684 (63.3)	1,134 (52.4)
Females, 18 and over	122,482 (58.6)	5,149 (108.7)	7,742 (132.4)	1,672 (63.3)	35,348 (284.9)	24,484 (205.8)	12,637 (162.2)	23,266 (236.0)	9,707 (150.6)	2,478 (74.0)
18 and 19 years old	3,869 (58.1)	49 (12.3)	1,124 (43.4)	245 (21.6)	994 (37.0)	1,391 (45.8)	51 (10.3)	1,536 (60.7)	‡	‡
20 to 24 years old	11,019 (12.5)	142 (19.3)	595 (39.0)	169 (19.3)	2,664 (68.0)	4,794 (95.1)	994 (49.4)	‡	116 (17.5)	‡
25 years old and over	107,594 (12.5)	4,958 (105.2)	6,023 (119.2)	1,259 (55.5)	31,690 (271.0)	18,298 (173.5)	11,592 (150.9)	21,715 (223.0)	9,591 (148.6)	2,469 (74.1)
25 to 29 years old	10,510 (6.3)	242 (24.3)	518 (30.0)	136 (15.6)	2,484 (64.5)	2,094 (57.0)	1,143 (48.3)	2,929 (75.0)	776 (41.8)	189 (22.1)
30 to 34 years old	10,470 (5.6)	311 (24.6)	578 (33.6)	137 (17.7)	2,408 (59.2)	1,740 (54.5)	1,228 (44.9)	2,565 (59.7)	1,226 (47.7)	277 (24.6)
35 to 39 years old	9,759 (5.6)	351 (23.2)	554 (30.8)	90 (13.3)	2,181 (59.0)	1,615 (46.9)	1,186 (43.4)	2,368 (58.9)	1,094 (45.5)	321 (25.3)
40 to 49 years old	21,236 (5.4)	727 (31.7)	917 (41.5)	234 (18.9)	5,642 (93.0)	3,616 (72.5)	2,603 (66.9)	4,904 (94.2)	2,069 (65.4)	523 (34.0)
50 to 59 years old	22,241 (44.7)	866 (38.8)	1,082 (46.8)	227 (25.3)	6,793 (107.2)	3,760 (80.8)	2,657 (64.2)	4,354 (84.8)	1,926 (64.4)	575 (35.4)
60 to 64 years old	9,387 (44.2)	436 (28.2)	382 (28.6)	81 (11.8)	2,889 (73.4)	1,756 (52.6)	994 (46.5)	1,681 (54.8)	929 (46.0)	240 (25.4)
65 years old and over	23,990 (0.5)	2,026 (62.6)	1,993 (65.6)	354 (32.8)	9,292 (132.3)	3,717 (86.7)	1,780 (64.7)	2,914 (80.6)	1,570 (61.5)	344 (31.7)
White, 18 and over	156,352 (123.3)	2,948 (104.0)	7,812 (149.0)	1,506 (73.3)	45,896 (356.7)	30,958 (271.4)	15,923 (211.9)	33,119 (297.0)	13,241 (185.6)	4,949 (122.6)
18 and 19 years old	4,292 (63.1)	50 (15.4)	1,370 (46.1)	241 (22.7)	1,116 (42.0)	1,457 (49.2)	‡	2,000 (64.9)	‡	‡
20 to 24 years old	12,375 (35.6)	92 (21.8)	478 (35.6)	140 (17.6)	3,113 (79.9)	5,347 (106.6)	1,066 (55.7)	‡	129 (18.3)	‡
25 years old and over	139,685 (102.5)	2,805 (96.6)	5,964 (139.6)	1,125 (63.7)	41,667 (347.7)	24,154 (257.0)	14,818 (202.0)	31,105 (290.2)	13,111 (183.9)	4,936 (121.9)
25 to 29 years old	12,126 (43.5)	100 (17.5)	508 (34.2)	109 (14.7)	2,850 (78.7)	2,370 (79.2)	1,286 (56.8)	3,865 (91.7)	802 (51.9)	236 (28.9)
30 to 34 years old	12,044 (44.1)	90 (18.5)	402 (33.0)	99 (11.5)	2,844 (76.4)	2,127 (70.8)	1,479 (55.7)	3,305 (78.5)	1,319 (52.5)	379 (28.5)
35 to 39 years old	11,102 (44.1)	99 (15.8)	333 (30.4)	59 (11.5)	2,677 (70.9)	1,928 (59.7)	1,356 (51.5)	2,952 (69.2)	1,256 (50.4)	442 (31.5)
40 to 49 years old	26,571 (55.2)	244 (26.2)	892 (51.0)	182 (20.5)	7,328 (124.7)	4,500 (96.9)	3,246 (83.9)	6,678 (114.8)	2,619 (74.5)	883 (45.9)
50 to 59 years old	30,549 (51.6)	371 (28.6)	1,161 (57.0)	228 (26.9)	9,794 (158.4)	5,197 (111.1)	3,506 (77.9)	6,267 (121.9)	2,858 (80.8)	1,166 (55.0)
60 to 64 years old	13,161 (94.5)	190 (22.4)	374 (29.8)	60 (13.2)	3,885 (103.2)	2,470 (74.5)	1,434 (63.3)	2,742 (76.0)	1,443 (62.2)	564 (43.8)
65 years old and over	34,131 (97.8)	1,712 (72.2)	2,293 (77.0)	387 (36.2)	12,289 (171.1)	5,562 (119.3)	2,510 (83.9)	5,296 (123.3)	2,814 (87.6)	1,267 (59.8)
Black, 18 and over	27,416 (85.7)	846 (51.9)	2,614 (86.9)	681 (44.3)	9,208 (144.0)	6,361 (119.0)	2,428 (64.9)	3,471 (90.7)	1,445 (62.3)	362 (29.8)
18 and 19 years old	1,155 (35.7)	‡	401 (25.3)	104 (14.7)	349 (23.1)	255 (20.1)	‡	195 (24.4)	‡	‡
20 to 24 years old	3,221 (27.2)	‡	255 (28.6)	91 (16.8)	1,066 (49.0)	1,406 (55.3)	183 (23.0)	‡	‡	‡
25 years old and over	23,041 (63.3)	811 (50.4)	1,959 (68.5)	486 (33.8)	7,794 (124.3)	4,699 (95.1)	2,233 (62.7)	3,267 (88.5)	1,433 (61.9)	359 (29.7)
25 to 29 years old	2,649 (23.3)	‡	163 (17.5)	‡	913 (41.4)	697 (37.4)	240 (20.8)	456 (30.3)	71 (11.9)	‡
30 to 34 years old	2,514 (29.5)	‡	180 (19.8)	‡	775 (39.0)	556 (31.1)	266 (22.3)	438 (30.3)	178 (19.3)	‡
35 to 39 years old	2,326 (22.8)	‡	160 (18.3)	‡	727 (34.7)	529 (31.6)	228 (20.6)	390 (30.3)	201 (19.0)	‡
40 to 49 years old	5,042 (28.5)	88 (18.3)	308 (26.1)	90 (13.7)	1,659 (53.8)	1,085 (45.7)	588 (33.0)	807 (40.4)	347 (25.8)	69 (12.2)
50 to 59 years old	4,942 (54.4)	164 (20.4)	454 (30.0)	118 (16.3)	1,723 (50.8)	951 (42.0)	472 (28.6)	654 (37.2)	304 (24.3)	102 (15.4)
60 to 64 years old	1,817 (49.7)	61 (10.0)	161 (17.7)	‡	628 (33.4)	374 (23.0)	162 (17.3)	226 (22.3)	129 (15.7)	36 (8.0)
65 years old and over	3,750 (38.3)	412 (26.6)	534 (29.3)	94 (12.7)	1,368 (42.9)	508 (28.5)	276 (21.1)	294 (22.0)	202 (19.4)	62 (9.4)

See notes at end of table.

Number of persons age 18 and over, by highest level of educational attainment, sex, race/ethnicity, and age: 2013—Continued

[Numbers in thousands. Standard errors appear in parentheses]

Sex, race/ethnicity, and age	Total	Elementary school (kindergarten–8th grade)	High school			Some college, no degree	Postsecondary education			
			1 to 3 years	4 years, no completion	Completion		Associate's degree	Bachelor's degree	Master's degree	First-professional or doctor's degree
1	2	3	4	5	6	7	8	9	10	11
Hispanic, 18 and over	35,441 (35.6)	5,836 (135.7)	4,510 (97.5)	1,127 (43.9)	10,911 (160.7)	5,973 (98.1)	2,440 (66.0)	3,361 (90.8)	992 (41.7)	290 (24.0)
18 and 19 years old	1,760 (35.0)	‡ (†)	547 (29.1)	179 (17.8)	477 (30.2)	515 (28.9)	‡ (†)	‡ (†)	‡ (†)	‡ (†)
20 to 24 years old	4,551 (6.3)	228 (26.9)	513 (32.8)	152 (16.0)	1,565 (50.2)	1,498 (47.0)	340 (25.8)	236 (23.1)	‡ (†)	‡ (†)
25 years old and over	29,130 (11.8)	5,591 (127.0)	3,450 (81.0)	797 (40.0)	8,869 (144.6)	3,960 (84.0)	2,079 (61.1)	3,121 (87.0)	978 (41.2)	285 (23.4)
25 to 29 years old	4,402 (34.5)	390 (30.6)	538 (34.1)	139 (17.3)	1,551 (51.3)	766 (39.2)	328 (25.5)	558 (32.4)	103 (13.5)	‡ (†)
30 to 34 years old	4,195 (34.0)	609 (39.7)	558 (36.8)	163 (19.1)	1,321 (43.9)	612 (39.5)	303 (26.9)	470 (29.8)	122 (14.1)	39 (8.6)
35 to 39 years old	3,978 (28.2)	684 (41.0)	549 (31.6)	114 (14.2)	1,178 (45.7)	530 (29.0)	292 (23.3)	448 (30.3)	146 (14.8)	‡ (†)
40 to 49 years old	6,853 (38.3)	1,195 (50.3)	814 (36.5)	189 (17.5)	2,116 (66.1)	884 (40.7)	521 (32.4)	775 (38.3)	265 (18.4)	94 (12.9)
50 to 59 years old	4,911 (50.4)	1,098 (48.8)	473 (30.9)	108 (13.8)	1,445 (51.4)	658 (31.2)	362 (24.4)	531 (33.2)	183 (17.2)	53 (8.5)
60 to 64 years old	1,579 (41.8)	452 (29.2)	162 (19.1)	‡ (†)	415 (27.4)	217 (19.0)	105 (13.6)	121 (12.7)	73 (11.7)	‡ (†)
65 years old and over	3,213 (8.5)	1,163 (37.5)	356 (23.7)	58 (10.4)	843 (34.4)	294 (18.1)	168 (15.7)	219 (16.7)	87 (12.5)	‡ (†)
Asian, 18 and over	12,475 (93.4)	602 (43.3)	487 (33.8)	158 (20.1)	2,338 (76.8)	1,822 (59.3)	873 (41.6)	3,652 (91.0)	1,660 (65.9)	882 (46.8)
18 and 19 years old	371 (19.9)	‡ (†)	95 (11.6)	‡ (†)	87 (11.3)	159 (16.4)	‡ (†)	‡ (†)	‡ (†)	‡ (†)
20 to 24 years old	1,211 (28.7)	‡ (†)	‡ (†)	‡ (†)	151 (19.5)	588 (31.5)	87 (12.7)	287 (23.9)	‡ (†)	‡ (†)
25 years old and over	10,894 (84.4)	585 (42.7)	358 (30.0)	125 (19.0)	2,101 (70.1)	1,075 (46.2)	782 (39.4)	3,364 (85.4)	1,624 (65.0)	881 (46.7)
25 to 29 years old	1,344 (32.2)	‡ (†)	‡ (†)	‡ (†)	172 (16.3)	206 (19.2)	96 (13.8)	513 (31.8)	211 (21.2)	83 (12.2)
30 to 34 years old	1,352 (33.0)	‡ (†)	‡ (†)	‡ (†)	181 (16.9)	118 (15.7)	88 (13.9)	494 (27.4)	307 (26.1)	120 (18.9)
35 to 39 years old	1,358 (37.9)	‡ (†)	‡ (†)	‡ (†)	168 (18.3)	113 (13.1)	105 (13.5)	455 (29.5)	292 (24.9)	151 (17.1)
40 to 49 years old	2,385 (46.4)	60 (10.5)	71 (15.3)	‡ (†)	406 (28.1)	226 (21.9)	178 (19.0)	742 (33.0)	450 (32.0)	224 (23.5)
50 to 59 years old	2,030 (45.3)	99 (15.1)	90 (14.8)	‡ (†)	516 (29.2)	214 (21.2)	137 (16.7)	606 (31.4)	189 (18.3)	151 (17.5)
60 to 64 years old	781 (30.1)	78 (13.6)	‡ (†)	‡ (†)	228 (21.8)	66 (10.3)	84 (12.8)	206 (18.6)	53 (8.8)	‡ (†)
65 years old and over	1,645 (34.9)	278 (24.6)	97 (13.0)	‡ (†)	430 (26.3)	132 (15.8)	94 (13.1)	347 (24.9)	122 (15.1)	120 (17.1)

†Not applicable.

‖Interpret data with caution. The coefficient of variation (CV) for this estimate is between 30 and 50 percent.

‡Reporting standards not met. Either there are too few cases for a reliable estimate or the coefficient of variation (CV) is 50 percent or greater.

NOTE: Total includes other racial/ethnic groups not shown separately. Race categories exclude persons of Hispanic ethnicity. Detail may not sum to totals because of rounding. Standard errors were computed using replicate weights.

SOURCE: U.S. Department of Commerce, Census Bureau, Current Population Survey (CPS), March 2013. (This table was prepared February 2014.)

Percentage of persons 18 to 24 years old and age 25 and over, by educational attainment and race/ethnicity (including selected subgroups): 2007 and 2012

[Standard errors appear in parentheses]

Year and race/ethnicity	18 to 24 years old							Age 25 and over					
	Less than high school completion	High school completion[1] or higher						Less than high school completion	High school completion[1] or higher				
		Total, high school or higher	High school only	At least some college					Total, high school or higher	High school only	Some college, no degree	Associate's degree	Bachelor's or higher degree
				Total, at least some college	Some college, no degree	Associate's degree	Bachelor's or higher degree						
1	2	3	4	5	6	7	8	9	10	11	12	13	14
2007													
Total[2]	**17.1 (0.09)**	**82.9 (0.09)**	**33.5 (0.12)**	**49.5 (0.13)**	**36.0 (0.11)**	**4.7 (0.06)**	**8.8 (0.08)**	**15.5 (0.04)**	**84.5 (0.04)**	**30.2 (0.05)**	**19.5 (0.04)**	**7.5 (0.03)**	**27.5 (0.05)**
White	12.3 (0.09)	87.7 (0.09)	32.1 (0.15)	55.6 (0.17)	39.6 (0.14)	5.3 (0.07)	10.7 (0.11)	10.6 (0.03)	89.4 (0.03)	30.7 (0.05)	20.4 (0.04)	7.9 (0.03)	30.5 (0.05)
Black	22.8 (0.29)	77.2 (0.29)	37.7 (0.35)	39.5 (0.34)	31.6 (0.34)	3.2 (0.13)	4.6 (0.15)	19.7 (0.09)	80.3 (0.09)	34.4 (0.14)	21.3 (0.13)	7.3 (0.07)	17.3 (0.08)
Hispanic	30.7 (0.26)	69.3 (0.26)	36.6 (0.29)	32.6 (0.29)	25.4 (0.28)	3.4 (0.10)	3.8 (0.11)	39.4 (0.15)	60.6 (0.15)	28.2 (0.14)	14.5 (0.10)	5.4 (0.06)	12.6 (0.10)
Mexican	33.2 (0.34)	66.8 (0.34)	37.8 (0.37)	29.0 (0.36)	23.3 (0.33)	3.0 (0.12)	2.8 (0.13)	45.7 (0.20)	54.3 (0.20)	27.9 (0.17)	13.3 (0.13)	4.4 (0.07)	8.6 (0.10)
Puerto Rican	25.7 (0.93)	74.3 (0.93)	37.4 (1.07)	36.9 (0.99)	28.9 (0.96)	3.4 (0.33)	4.7 (0.39)	27.5 (0.37)	72.5 (0.37)	30.9 (0.39)	18.2 (0.29)	7.8 (0.20)	15.6 (0.34)
Cuban	12.1 (0.88)	87.9 (0.88)	35.2 (1.57)	52.7 (1.71)	36.8 (1.59)	6.9 (0.90)	9.1 (1.10)	24.5 (0.61)	75.5 (0.61)	28.5 (0.63)	14.0 (0.36)	8.0 (0.32)	25.1 (0.60)
Dominican	26.0 (1.48)	74.0 (1.48)	30.5 (1.81)	43.5 (1.93)	31.5 (1.77)	6.1 (0.94)	5.8 (0.91)	37.4 (0.85)	62.6 (0.85)	26.7 (0.87)	14.0 (0.57)	6.8 (0.40)	15.1 (0.58)
Salvadoran	37.7 (1.78)	62.3 (1.78)	33.6 (1.64)	28.7 (1.29)	22.4 (1.20)	3.2 (0.61)	3.1 (0.56)	53.4 (0.74)	46.6 (0.74)	25.1 (0.62)	10.3 (0.41)	3.5 (0.28)	7.7 (0.37)
Other Central American	40.1 (1.36)	59.9 (1.36)	31.5 (1.13)	28.4 (1.06)	20.9 (1.06)	3.3 (0.43)	4.2 (0.49)	42.1 (0.69)	57.9 (0.69)	26.5 (0.62)	12.8 (0.45)	4.9 (0.29)	13.7 (0.43)
South American	16.7 (1.12)	83.3 (1.12)	31.5 (1.21)	51.8 (1.41)	35.4 (1.26)	6.4 (0.64)	10.0 (0.82)	16.4 (0.43)	83.6 (0.43)	28.6 (0.57)	16.7 (0.41)	7.7 (0.27)	30.7 (0.48)
Other Hispanic or Latino	22.3 (0.97)	77.7 (0.97)	36.5 (1.04)	41.2 (1.13)	32.8 (1.03)	3.6 (0.35)	4.8 (0.39)	23.8 (0.42)	76.2 (0.42)	29.8 (0.42)	21.6 (0.34)	6.8 (0.22)	17.9 (0.35)
Asian	8.1 (0.32)	91.9 (0.32)	23.2 (0.48)	68.7 (0.54)	44.5 (0.60)	4.9 (0.24)	19.3 (0.48)	14.1 (0.16)	85.9 (0.16)	17.7 (0.19)	11.6 (0.13)	6.9 (0.10)	49.8 (0.24)
Asian Indian	5.5 (0.61)	94.5 (0.61)	17.4 (1.20)	77.1 (1.29)	40.6 (1.51)	4.3 (0.60)	32.2 (1.44)	9.3 (0.32)	90.7 (0.32)	11.5 (0.39)	6.3 (0.24)	4.1 (0.19)	68.8 (0.58)
Chinese[3]	7.8 (0.62)	92.2 (0.62)	21.2 (1.01)	70.9 (1.10)	43.3 (1.23)	4.2 (0.45)	23.4 (1.07)	18.5 (0.39)	81.5 (0.39)	16.1 (0.39)	7.7 (0.22)	5.7 (0.20)	52.0 (0.51)
Filipino	6.8 (0.58)	93.2 (0.58)	27.2 (1.26)	66.0 (1.26)	45.4 (1.30)	6.9 (0.58)	13.8 (1.05)	7.9 (0.22)	92.1 (0.22)	16.2 (0.40)	17.8 (0.36)	9.9 (0.30)	48.2 (0.55)
Japanese	4.0 (1.12)	96.0 (1.12)	23.1 (2.10)	72.8 (2.43)	51.7 (2.82)	4.7 (0.93)	16.5 (1.97)	6.1 (0.32)	93.9 (0.32)	21.9 (0.62)	15.2 (0.55)	10.6 (0.44)	46.2 (0.71)
Korean	7.1 (0.63)	92.9 (0.63)	21.7 (1.56)	71.2 (1.63)	52.3 (1.80)	3.5 (0.61)	15.4 (1.25)	9.0 (0.40)	91.0 (0.40)	19.9 (0.64)	12.5 (0.42)	5.6 (0.30)	53.1 (0.73)
Vietnamese	9.1 (1.06)	90.9 (1.06)	24.9 (1.48)	66.0 (1.59)	45.5 (1.73)	6.9 (0.81)	13.6 (1.22)	26.6 (0.61)	73.4 (0.61)	24.9 (0.67)	13.8 (0.45)	7.7 (0.36)	27.0 (0.59)
Other Asian	14.8 (1.18)	85.2 (1.18)	28.9 (1.29)	56.3 (1.44)	40.9 (1.58)	4.6 (0.61)	10.8 (0.77)	22.1 (0.61)	77.9 (0.61)	23.2 (0.71)	12.7 (0.51)	7.3 (0.39)	34.6 (0.79)
Pacific Islander	13.5 (1.58)	86.5 (1.58)	43.5 (2.29)	43.0 (2.84)	34.1 (2.87)	4.9 (1.23)	4.0 (1.10)	15.4 (0.88)	84.6 (0.88)	39.0 (1.26)	21.6 (1.16)	8.2 (0.65)	15.8 (1.14)
American Indian/Alaska Native	27.8 (1.22)	72.2 (1.22)	41.1 (1.18)	31.0 (1.11)	24.3 (1.03)	3.7 (0.45)	3.0 (0.39)	21.5 (0.46)	78.5 (0.46)	34.0 (0.48)	23.1 (0.43)	8.2 (0.30)	13.1 (0.35)
Two or more races	16.2 (0.70)	83.8 (0.70)	34.2 (1.00)	49.7 (1.00)	37.9 (0.83)	4.7 (0.41)	7.1 (0.38)	12.8 (0.28)	87.2 (0.28)	27.9 (0.46)	25.6 (0.37)	9.0 (0.24)	24.7 (0.41)
White and Black	19.9 (1.34)	80.1 (1.34)	37.1 (1.95)	43.0 (1.97)	33.1 (1.78)	4.1 (0.85)	5.8 (0.73)	10.6 (0.86)	89.4 (0.86)	28.2 (1.47)	26.8 (1.09)	9.7 (0.81)	24.7 (1.12)
White and Asian	9.1 (0.93)	90.9 (0.93)	27.4 (1.55)	63.5 (1.62)	45.6 (1.61)	5.8 (0.87)	12.0 (1.03)	7.2 (0.58)	92.8 (0.58)	19.4 (0.94)	22.7 (0.87)	9.0 (0.58)	41.7 (1.11)
White and American Indian/Alaska Native	19.6 (1.26)	80.4 (1.26)	36.5 (1.77)	43.8 (1.66)	35.1 (1.61)	4.0 (0.63)	4.8 (0.64)	16.0 (0.50)	84.0 (0.50)	32.2 (0.67)	26.4 (0.62)	8.2 (0.34)	17.2 (0.50)
Other two or more races	16.1 (1.34)	83.9 (1.34)	35.8 (1.70)	48.2 (1.82)	37.8 (1.68)	4.8 (0.67)	5.6 (0.64)	12.3 (0.57)	87.7 (0.57)	26.7 (0.71)	25.5 (0.65)	9.9 (0.50)	25.6 (0.82)
2012													
Total[2]	**14.7 (0.09)**	**85.3 (0.09)**	**29.5 (0.11)**	**55.8 (0.12)**	**41.4 (0.13)**	**4.8 (0.05)**	**9.6 (0.07)**	**13.6 (0.04)**	**86.4 (0.04)**	**28.0 (0.04)**	**21.3 (0.03)**	**8.0 (0.02)**	**29.2 (0.05)**
White	10.9 (0.10)	89.1 (0.10)	28.6 (0.15)	60.6 (0.15)	43.1 (0.17)	5.6 (0.08)	11.8 (0.11)	8.5 (0.04)	91.5 (0.04)	28.7 (0.05)	21.7 (0.04)	8.5 (0.03)	32.6 (0.06)
Black	18.9 (0.24)	81.1 (0.24)	32.4 (0.32)	48.7 (0.34)	40.6 (0.35)	3.1 (0.12)	5.0 (0.14)	16.5 (0.12)	83.5 (0.12)	31.4 (0.14)	25.5 (0.14)	7.8 (0.08)	18.8 (0.13)
Hispanic	23.4 (0.26)	76.6 (0.26)	32.0 (0.26)	44.5 (0.30)	36.1 (0.29)	4.1 (0.12)	4.4 (0.13)	35.9 (0.16)	64.1 (0.16)	26.6 (0.13)	17.7 (0.11)	5.8 (0.06)	13.9 (0.12)
Mexican	24.7 (0.34)	75.3 (0.34)	33.6 (0.36)	41.6 (0.39)	34.7 (0.37)	3.6 (0.14)	3.4 (0.15)	41.5 (0.19)	58.5 (0.19)	26.6 (0.17)	16.9 (0.13)	5.0 (0.08)	10.0 (0.11)
Puerto Rican	21.8 (0.75)	78.2 (0.75)	32.4 (0.87)	45.9 (0.83)	36.7 (0.94)	4.6 (0.39)	4.6 (0.40)	23.2 (0.33)	76.8 (0.33)	29.3 (0.38)	22.0 (0.34)	8.6 (0.22)	17.0 (0.35)
Cuban	11.9 (0.93)	88.1 (0.93)	25.6 (1.46)	62.5 (1.61)	42.5 (1.73)	9.4 (0.90)	10.6 (1.16)	21.5 (0.49)	78.5 (0.49)	29.9 (0.66)	16.3 (0.42)	8.0 (0.32)	24.3 (0.50)
Dominican	20.7 (1.22)	79.3 (1.22)	24.4 (1.29)	54.8 (1.68)	43.1 (1.70)	5.2 (0.72)	6.5 (0.68)	33.3 (0.75)	66.7 (0.75)	25.7 (0.71)	18.2 (0.69)	6.2 (0.35)	16.6 (0.58)
Salvadoran	28.7 (1.43)	71.3 (1.43)	30.6 (1.25)	40.7 (1.46)	34.0 (1.60)	2.8 (0.45)	3.9 (0.52)	48.4 (0.71)	51.6 (0.71)	25.0 (0.60)	13.9 (0.47)	3.9 (0.23)	8.9 (0.36)
Other Central American	33.3 (1.17)	66.7 (1.17)	27.9 (0.97)	38.9 (1.21)	30.8 (1.17)	3.2 (0.34)	4.8 (0.52)	41.7 (0.64)	58.3 (0.64)	24.4 (0.50)	14.7 (0.40)	5.3 (0.25)	13.8 (0.37)
South American	11.4 (0.74)	88.6 (0.74)	26.2 (1.06)	62.3 (1.17)	46.0 (1.23)	7.4 (0.57)	9.0 (0.69)	15.8 (0.40)	84.2 (0.40)	24.7 (0.42)	19.7 (0.40)	8.0 (0.26)	31.8 (0.46)
Other Hispanic or Latino	16.6 (0.81)	83.4 (0.81)	31.1 (1.28)	52.3 (1.31)	41.0 (1.35)	4.4 (0.50)	6.9 (0.61)	18.5 (0.45)	81.5 (0.45)	26.1 (0.51)	24.8 (0.48)	8.0 (0.26)	22.7 (0.48)
Asian	7.7 (0.27)	92.3 (0.27)	19.9 (0.43)	72.5 (0.48)	46.6 (0.60)	5.0 (0.22)	20.9 (0.45)	14.2 (0.13)	85.8 (0.13)	15.3 (0.16)	12.9 (0.14)	6.8 (0.10)	50.9 (0.25)
Asian Indian	5.2 (0.61)	94.8 (0.61)	16.3 (0.88)	78.5 (0.98)	42.4 (1.48)	4.2 (0.59)	31.9 (1.38)	8.1 (0.27)	91.9 (0.27)	9.1 (0.31)	6.9 (0.26)	4.0 (0.17)	71.8 (0.58)
Chinese[3]	5.0 (0.44)	95.0 (0.44)	16.8 (0.70)	78.2 (0.82)	45.6 (1.17)	3.8 (0.40)	28.9 (0.99)	19.3 (0.37)	80.7 (0.37)	14.4 (0.35)	9.1 (0.25)	5.8 (0.18)	51.3 (0.50)
Filipino	7.9 (0.75)	92.1 (0.75)	22.7 (0.95)	69.4 (1.13)	49.5 (1.27)	6.8 (0.55)	13.1 (0.78)	7.5 (0.29)	92.5 (0.29)	15.2 (0.38)	19.5 (0.42)	9.2 (0.27)	48.7 (0.54)
Japanese	5.8 (1.47)	94.2 (1.47)	21.9 (2.76)	72.3 (3.12)	49.4 (3.73)	4.7 (1.00)	18.1 (2.39)	4.9 (0.32)	95.1 (0.32)	18.3 (0.54)	16.5 (0.57)	10.7 (0.48)	49.6 (0.60)
Korean	7.3 (0.91)	92.7 (0.91)	18.6 (1.39)	74.1 (1.49)	53.6 (1.77)	4.2 (0.70)	16.3 (1.12)	7.2 (0.31)	92.8 (0.31)	18.0 (0.56)	13.9 (0.38)	6.5 (0.31)	54.3 (0.71)
Vietnamese	8.6 (0.83)	91.4 (0.83)	19.5 (1.13)	71.9 (1.36)	52.0 (1.32)	6.7 (0.93)	13.2 (1.02)	29.4 (0.52)	70.6 (0.52)	21.5 (0.51)	15.8 (0.40)	7.2 (0.32)	26.1 (0.58)
Other Asian	13.2 (0.70)	86.8 (0.70)	25.4 (1.03)	61.5 (1.08)	41.8 (1.04)	5.3 (0.50)	14.3 (0.81)	20.8 (0.48)	79.2 (0.48)	17.5 (0.47)	14.7 (0.44)	7.2 (0.37)	39.9 (0.64)
Pacific Islander	19.6 (2.39)	80.4 (2.39)	41.6 (2.66)	38.8 (2.58)	32.9 (2.54)	4.2 (0.99)	1.7 ! (0.57)	13.4 (0.78)	86.6 (0.78)	34.0 (1.35)	27.0 (1.27)	9.6 (0.73)	16.1 (1.19)
American Indian/Alaska Native	25.2 (1.19)	74.8 (1.19)	35.5 (1.20)	39.3 (1.34)	34.1 (1.27)	2.8 (0.32)	2.4 (0.43)	18.6 (0.39)	81.4 (0.39)	31.9 (0.46)	26.8 (0.46)	8.7 (0.29)	14.1 (0.35)
Two or more races	14.4 (0.46)	85.6 (0.46)	28.7 (0.61)	56.9 (0.65)	43.7 (0.70)	4.6 (0.31)	8.6 (0.40)	10.6 (0.25)	89.4 (0.25)	22.9 (0.33)	27.1 (0.36)	9.3 (0.21)	30.0 (0.36)
White and Black	19.4 (1.09)	80.6 (1.09)	30.3 (1.15)	50.3 (1.27)	41.4 (1.17)	3.5 (0.52)	5.4 (0.71)	8.9 (0.58)	91.1 (0.58)	22.7 (0.97)	29.9 (1.01)	11.0 (0.74)	27.5 (0.94)
White and Asian	9.0 (0.80)	91.0 (0.80)	23.5 (1.31)	67.5 (1.62)	48.1 (1.58)	4.9 (0.49)	14.4 (0.94)	8.1 (0.54)	91.9 (0.54)	16.2 (0.65)	21.8 (0.69)	8.4 (0.42)	45.5 (0.84)
White and American Indian/Alaska Native	17.3 (1.02)	82.7 (1.02)	32.3 (1.52)	50.4 (1.59)	40.6 (1.61)	4.4 (0.71)	5.3 (0.83)	12.7 (0.44)	87.3 (0.44)	27.0 (0.61)	29.5 (0.59)	9.3 (0.37)	21.5 (0.47)
Other two or more races	11.5 (0.81)	88.5 (0.81)	29.1 (1.19)	59.4 (1.47)	44.5 (1.47)	5.7 (0.64)	9.2 (0.87)	10.8 (0.40)	89.2 (0.40)	23.1 (0.57)	27.0 (0.67)	9.3 (0.43)	29.8 (0.67)

!Interpret data with caution. The coefficient of variation (CV) for this estimate is between 30 and 50 percent.
[1]High school completers include diploma recipients and those completing high school through alternative credentials, such as a GED.
[2]Total includes other racial/ethnic groups not shown separately.
[3]Excludes Taiwanese. Taiwanese is included in "Other Asian."

NOTE: Race categories exclude persons of Hispanic ethnicity. Detail may not sum to totals because of rounding.
SOURCE: U.S. Department of Commerce, Census Bureau, American Community Survey, 2007 and 2012. (This table was prepared February 2014.)

Persons age 25 and over who hold a bachelor's or higher degree, by sex, race/ethnicity, age group, and field of bachelor's degree: 2012

[Standard errors appear in parentheses]

Field of bachelor's degree	Total[1]	Sex		Race/ethnicity[1]					Age		
		Males	Females	White	Black	Hispanic	Asian/Pacific Islander	American Indian/Alaska Native	25 to 29 years old	30 to 49 years old	50 years old and over
1	2	3	4	5	6	7	8	9	10	11	12
Total population, 25 and over (in thousands)	208,841 (47.5)	100,655 (28.5)	108,186 (29.5)	140,914 (29.5)	23,783 (22.8)	28,924 (20.0)	10,893 (18.1)	1,284 (10.9)	21,186 (22.7)	83,438 (30.0)	104,217 (38.9)
Percent of population with bachelor's degree	29.2 (0.02)	29.2 (0.06)	29.2 (0.06)	32.6 (0.06)	18.8 (0.13)	13.9 (0.11)	49.9 (0.24)	14.1 (0.35)	31.8 (0.17)	31.8 (0.08)	26.5 (0.05)
Bachelor's degree holders							Number (in thousands)				
Total	60,946 (117.0)	29,400 (64.4)	31,545 (68.1)	45,909 (83.4)	4,462 (29.9)	4,028 (33.8)	5,438 (30.1)	181 (4.8)	6,738 (36.8)	26,547 (69.7)	27,660 (60.0)
Agriculture/forestry	644 (9.5)	443 (8.0)	201 (5.2)	549 (8.7)	23 (2.1)	25 (2.2)	38 (2.4)	3 (0.6)	62 (2.6)	238 (6.1)	343 (6.4)
Art/architecture	2,941 (18.8)	1,271 (10.6)	1,670 (15.4)	2,300 (16.8)	136 (4.9)	205 (6.9)	241 (7.0)	7 (1.0)	433 (9.7)	1,329 (14.7)	1,179 (12.8)
Business/management	12,488 (43.0)	7,065 (34.9)	5,423 (26.5)	9,196 (38.0)	1,086 (12.7)	944 (12.7)	1,063 (14.0)	32 (2.1)	1,320 (14.0)	5,997 (30.8)	5,170 (27.1)
Communications	2,189 (18.3)	914 (10.5)	1,274 (14.1)	1,732 (15.3)	179 (6.9)	143 (4.9)	97 (4.1)	5 (1.0)	359 (7.6)	1,211 (14.6)	618 (9.4)
Computer and information sciences	1,701 (18.1)	1,205 (14.2)	497 (9.1)	994 (13.0)	158 (5.7)	119 (4.2)	394 (8.9)	3 (0.7)	227 (7.8)	1,074 (13.6)	401 (6.7)
Education	8,517 (36.6)	2,108 (19.7)	6,409 (28.5)	7,014 (32.5)	618 (9.3)	487 (9.7)	280 (5.9)	34 (2.1)	581 (10.7)	2,604 (21.0)	5,331 (28.1)
Engineering	4,759 (27.1)	4,101 (25.8)	658 (10.2)	3,188 (21.2)	193 (7.0)	347 (8.0)	938 (12.3)	9 (1.1)	467 (9.0)	2,073 (17.7)	2,218 (17.4)
English/literature	1,994 (17.7)	677 (9.5)	1,316 (14.5)	1,639 (14.7)	98 (4.9)	86 (3.9)	134 (5.3)	4 (0.8)	203 (5.8)	794 (10.1)	996 (12.4)
Foreign languages	675 (9.4)	188 (5.2)	487 (7.6)	505 (7.6)	28 (2.3)	66 (3.2)	65 (3.4)	† (†)	74 (3.6)	255 (5.9)	345 (5.6)
Health sciences	4,316 (24.9)	766 (11.1)	3,550 (21.7)	3,138 (20.3)	358 (8.8)	256 (7.8)	490 (8.2)	13 (1.2)	445 (8.3)	1,840 (19.4)	2,030 (15.7)
Liberal arts/humanities	890 (10.7)	354 (7.3)	536 (8.9)	663 (9.5)	63 (3.1)	77 (3.5)	70 (3.9)	3 (0.7)	84 (4.4)	396 (7.2)	411 (6.9)
Mathematics/statistics	930 (11.5)	551 (8.7)	379 (7.0)	706 (9.6)	55 (2.9)	39 (2.6)	117 (5.0)	† (†)	87 (3.6)	330 (6.3)	513 (8.2)
Natural sciences (biological and physical)	4,748 (25.3)	2,741 (18.4)	2,007 (16.5)	3,476 (20.1)	265 (7.2)	256 (6.5)	651 (10.5)	13 (1.3)	575 (9.8)	2,049 (16.0)	2,124 (16.7)
Philosophy/religion/theology	823 (10.9)	578 (9.0)	245 (5.9)	651 (10.2)	65 (3.2)	43 (2.7)	47 (2.7)	† (†)	86 (4.0)	305 (7.0)	432 (7.5)
Pre-professional	967 (11.7)	583 (9.2)	384 (8.5)	678 (9.4)	146 (5.8)	99 (4.5)	23 (1.9)	5 (1.0)	161 (5.5)	540 (9.7)	266 (5.9)
Psychology	2,832 (19.7)	901 (11.1)	1,931 (16.9)	2,158 (17.2)	240 (5.9)	219 (5.4)	148 (4.4)	12 (1.4)	394 (8.5)	1,353 (13.6)	1,085 (11.9)
Social sciences/history	5,871 (29.7)	3,352 (19.5)	2,519 (18.9)	4,591 (24.4)	401 (8.6)	359 (8.2)	401 (7.9)	16 (1.3)	673 (9.0)	2,448 (18.0)	2,750 (19.0)
Other fields	3,661 (22.4)	1,601 (15.7)	2,060 (17.3)	2,732 (19.3)	350 (8.2)	257 (7.0)	244 (5.8)	17 (1.4)	506 (8.5)	1,709 (15.3)	1,446 (13.2)
						Percentage distribution, by field					
Total	100.0	100.0	100.0	100.0	100.0	100.0	100.0	100.0	100.0	100.0	100.0
Agriculture/forestry	1.1 (0.02)	1.5 (0.03)	0.6 (0.02)	1.2 (0.02)	0.5 (0.05)	0.6 (0.05)	0.7 (0.04)	1.5 (0.35)	0.9 (0.04)	0.9 (0.02)	1.2 (0.02)
Art/architecture	4.8 (0.03)	4.3 (0.03)	5.3 (0.05)	5.0 (0.04)	3.1 (0.11)	5.1 (0.17)	4.4 (0.13)	3.7 (0.51)	6.4 (0.14)	5.0 (0.06)	4.3 (0.05)
Business/management	20.5 (0.06)	24.0 (0.11)	17.2 (0.08)	20.0 (0.07)	24.3 (0.27)	23.4 (0.27)	19.6 (0.22)	17.7 (1.10)	19.6 (0.18)	22.6 (0.10)	18.7 (0.09)
Communications	3.6 (0.03)	3.1 (0.03)	4.0 (0.04)	3.8 (0.03)	4.0 (0.15)	3.5 (0.12)	1.8 (0.08)	2.9 (0.55)	5.3 (0.12)	4.6 (0.05)	2.2 (0.03)
Computer and information sciences	2.8 (0.03)	4.1 (0.05)	1.6 (0.03)	2.2 (0.03)	3.5 (0.13)	3.0 (0.10)	7.2 (0.16)	1.9 (0.38)	3.4 (0.11)	4.0 (0.05)	1.4 (0.02)
Education	14.0 (0.05)	7.2 (0.07)	20.3 (0.08)	15.3 (0.06)	13.8 (0.18)	12.1 (0.22)	5.1 (0.11)	19.1 (1.11)	8.6 (0.15)	9.8 (0.07)	19.3 (0.10)
Engineering	7.8 (0.04)	13.9 (0.08)	2.1 (0.03)	6.9 (0.04)	4.3 (0.15)	8.6 (0.18)	17.3 (0.20)	4.8 (0.58)	6.9 (0.13)	7.8 (0.06)	8.0 (0.06)
English/literature	3.3 (0.03)	2.3 (0.03)	4.2 (0.04)	3.6 (0.03)	2.2 (0.11)	2.1 (0.10)	2.5 (0.10)	2.4 (0.43)	3.0 (0.08)	3.0 (0.04)	3.6 (0.04)
Foreign languages	1.1 (0.01)	0.6 (0.02)	1.5 (0.02)	1.1 (0.02)	0.6 (0.05)	1.6 (0.08)	1.2 (0.06)	0.5 ! (0.17)	1.1 (0.05)	1.0 (0.02)	1.2 (0.02)
Health sciences	7.1 (0.04)	2.6 (0.04)	11.3 (0.07)	6.8 (0.05)	8.0 (0.18)	6.4 (0.18)	9.0 (0.14)	6.9 (0.67)	6.6 (0.12)	6.9 (0.07)	7.3 (0.05)
Liberal arts/humanities	1.5 (0.02)	1.2 (0.02)	1.7 (0.03)	1.4 (0.02)	1.4 (0.07)	1.9 (0.08)	1.3 (0.07)	1.7 (0.36)	1.2 (0.07)	1.5 (0.03)	1.5 (0.03)
Mathematics/statistics	1.5 (0.02)	1.9 (0.03)	1.2 (0.02)	1.5 (0.02)	1.2 (0.06)	1.0 (0.06)	2.1 (0.09)	0.9 (0.21)	1.3 (0.05)	1.2 (0.02)	1.9 (0.03)
Natural sciences (biological and physical)	7.8 (0.04)	9.3 (0.06)	6.4 (0.05)	7.6 (0.04)	5.9 (0.16)	6.4 (0.16)	12.0 (0.18)	7.0 (0.67)	8.5 (0.14)	7.7 (0.06)	7.7 (0.06)
Philosophy/religion/theology	1.4 (0.02)	2.0 (0.03)	0.8 (0.02)	1.4 (0.02)	1.5 (0.07)	1.1 (0.07)	0.9 (0.05)	1.7 (0.36)	1.3 (0.06)	1.1 (0.03)	1.6 (0.03)
Pre-professional	1.6 (0.02)	2.0 (0.03)	1.2 (0.03)	1.5 (0.02)	3.3 (0.13)	2.5 (0.11)	0.4 (0.04)	2.8 (0.55)	2.4 (0.08)	2.0 (0.04)	1.0 (0.02)
Psychology	4.6 (0.03)	3.1 (0.04)	6.1 (0.05)	4.7 (0.04)	5.4 (0.13)	5.4 (0.13)	2.7 (0.08)	6.4 (0.76)	5.8 (0.12)	5.1 (0.05)	3.9 (0.04)
Social sciences/history	9.6 (0.04)	11.4 (0.06)	8.0 (0.05)	10.0 (0.05)	9.0 (0.18)	8.9 (0.17)	7.4 (0.14)	8.8 (0.69)	10.0 (0.12)	9.2 (0.06)	9.9 (0.06)
Other fields	6.0 (0.04)	5.4 (0.05)	6.5 (0.05)	5.9 (0.04)	7.8 (0.18)	6.4 (0.17)	4.5 (0.11)	9.2 (0.74)	7.5 (0.12)	6.4 (0.06)	5.2 (0.05)

†Not applicable.
!Interpret data with caution. The coefficient of variation (CV) for this estimate is between 30 and 50 percent.
[1]Totals include other racial/ethnic groups not separately shown.

NOTE: Race categories exclude persons of Hispanic ethnicity. Detail may not sum to totals because of rounding.
SOURCE: U.S. Department of Commerce, Census Bureau, American Community Survey, 2012. (This table was prepared January 2014.)

Number of persons 25 to 34 years old, percentage with a bachelor's or higher degree, and percentage distribution, by undergraduate field of study and selected student characteristics: 2012

[Standard errors appear in parentheses]

Sex, race/ethnicity, nativity, and citizenship status	Total population ages 25 to 34 (in thousands)	Percent of population with bachelor's or higher degree	Percentage distribution of bachelor's degree holders													
				Bachelor's degree in a science, technology, engineering, or mathematics (STEM) field									Bachelor's degree in a non-STEM field			
			Total, all fields	STEM total	Agriculture/natural resources	Architecture	Computer and information sciences	Engineering/engineering technologies	Biology/biomedical sciences	Mathematics/statistics	Physical/social sciences	Health studies	Non-STEM total	Business	Education	All other fields of study
1	2	3	4	5	6	7	8	9	10	11	12	13	14	15	16	17
Total[1]	42,012 (32.5)	32.4 (0.12)	100.0 (†)	38.6 (0.15)	1.2 (0.04)	0.7 (0.03)	4.1 (0.09)	7.7 (0.09)	5.7 (0.07)	1.2 (0.04)	11.3 (0.11)	6.7 (0.09)	61.4 (0.15)	20.7 (0.14)	8.9 (0.11)	31.8 (0.17)
Sex																
Male	21,158 (21.5)	28.3 (0.14)	100.0 (†)	41.8 (0.28)	1.3 (0.06)	0.9 (0.05)	7.0 (0.16)	13.6 (0.16)	5.4 (0.11)	1.5 (0.07)	9.6 (0.14)	2.6 (0.08)	58.2 (0.28)	23.8 (0.24)	4.2 (0.12)	30.2 (0.27)
Female	20,854 (20.1)	36.5 (0.15)	100.0 (†)	36.1 (0.20)	1.1 (0.04)	0.6 (0.04)	1.9 (0.07)	3.0 (0.07)	5.9 (0.09)	0.9 (0.04)	12.7 (0.16)	9.9 (0.14)	63.9 (0.20)	18.2 (0.17)	12.6 (0.16)	33.1 (0.19)
Race/ethnicity																
White	24,200 (12.6)	38.6 (0.15)	100.0 (†)	35.1 (0.19)	1.4 (0.05)	0.7 (0.04)	2.9 (0.07)	5.8 (0.11)	5.4 (0.30)	1.1 (0.04)	11.2 (0.21)	6.5 (0.09)	64.9 (0.19)	20.6 (0.17)	10.5 (0.13)	33.9 (0.19)
Black	5,371 (12.8)	19.4 (0.28)	100.0 (†)	37.8 (0.64)	0.8 (0.08)	0.4 (0.11)	4.6 (0.33)	5.1 (0.30)	4.7 (0.21)	0.9 (0.12)	13.1 (0.42)	8.2 (0.33)	62.2 (0.64)	23.2 (0.64)	7.1 (0.35)	31.9 (0.60)
Hispanic	8,575 (20.6)	14.2 (0.19)	100.0 (†)	35.5 (0.54)	0.5 (0.08)	0.8 (0.11)	3.4 (0.25)	7.8 (0.33)	4.7 (0.21)	0.8 (0.11)	11.3 (0.38)	6.3 (0.33)	64.5 (0.54)	22.6 (0.51)	8.0 (0.35)	33.9 (0.59)
Asian	2,596 (15.5)	63.1 (0.44)	100.0 (†)	60.5 (0.52)	0.6 (0.07)	0.8 (0.09)	11.5 (0.35)	19.5 (0.38)	8.2 (0.26)	1.9 (0.17)	10.7 (0.29)	7.7 (0.28)	39.5 (0.52)	18.8 (0.37)	2.5 (0.14)	18.2 (0.40)
Pacific Islander	87 (3.8)	16.6 (2.09)	100.0 (†)	52.2 (5.25)	‡	# (†)	6.1 (2.79)	4.3 (1.84) !	10.7 (3.27) !	‡	23.7 (5.00) !	5.5 (2.13) !	47.8 (5.25)	16.2 (4.66)	7.7 (2.93) !	23.9 (4.70)
American Indian/Alaska Native[2]	279 (6.4)	11.2 (0.77)	100.0 (†)	36.5 (3.40)	3.5 (1.20) !	‡	3.7 (1.35) !	5.2 (1.68) !	7.5 (1.56) !	‡	7.7 (1.75) !	6.6 (1.72) !	63.5 (3.40)	19.5 (2.57) !	9.8 (2.06) !	34.2 (3.24) !
American Indian	233 (5.3)	11.1 (0.80)	100.0 (†)	35.9 (3.66)	4.2 (1.45) !	‡	2.6 (1.15) !	5.7 (1.89) !	5.4 (1.36) !	‡	7.5 (2.00) !	8.0 (2.09) !	64.1 (3.66)	19.6 (2.78) !	8.7 (1.94) !	35.8 (3.49) !
Alaska Native	16 (1.5)	4.5 (2.01) !	‡	‡	‡	‡	‡	‡	‡	‡	‡	‡	‡	‡	‡	‡
Two or more races	804 (13.3)	32.7 (0.72)	100.0 (†)	42.5 (1.34)	0.7 (0.18)	0.8 (0.17)	4.3 (0.47)	9.2 (0.80)	6.6 (0.58)	1.2 (0.27)	13.6 (1.14)	6.1 (0.55)	57.5 (1.34)	17.6 (0.91)	5.1 (0.51)	34.8 (1.17)
Race/ethnicity by sex																
Male																
White	12,223 (9.7)	34.2 (0.19)	100.0 (†)	37.1 (0.33)	1.5 (0.08)	0.9 (0.05)	5.5 (0.14)	10.8 (0.20)	5.2 (0.12)	1.5 (0.07)	9.5 (0.20)	2.2 (0.09)	62.9 (0.33)	25.1 (0.30)	5.0 (0.14)	32.9 (0.33)
Black	2,567 (13.2)	15.5 (0.33)	100.0 (†)	38.6 (1.28)	0.6 (0.20)	0.7 (0.22)	7.7 (0.66)	9.7 (0.59)	4.0 (0.51)	1.4 (0.21)	10.7 (0.77)	3.6 (0.32)	61.4 (1.28)	25.7 (1.21)	4.7 (0.55)	31.0 (1.07)
Hispanic	4,507 (14.7)	11.6 (0.25)	100.0 (†)	40.3 (1.01)	0.6 (0.14)	1.2 (0.22)	6.2 (0.50)	14.4 (0.64)	4.7 (0.44)	1.0 (0.17)	9.1 (0.56)	3.2 (0.34)	59.7 (1.01)	23.9 (0.81)	3.5 (0.34)	32.3 (0.95)
Asian	1,219 (9.3)	61.1 (0.73)	100.0 (†)	69.5 (0.63)	0.5 (0.10)	0.8 (0.12)	15.2 (0.59)	29.7 (0.62)	7.4 (0.43)	2.4 (0.32)	9.5 (0.41)	4.1 (0.33)	30.5 (0.63)	16.3 (0.50)	0.9 (0.14)	13.3 (0.50)
Pacific Islander	46 (2.5)	14.4 (2.20)	100.0 (†)	63.6 (7.53)	# (†)	# (†)	13.3 (6.13)	8.5 (3.62)	‡	# (†)	34.3 (8.43)	‡	36.4 (7.53)	12.1 (4.79)	‡	23.4 (6.92)
American Indian/Alaska Native[2]	142 (4.6)	8.4 (0.93)	100.0 (†)	48.4 (5.95)	8.0 (2.97) !	‡	9.2 (3.42) !	12.1 (3.89) !	7.8 (2.84) !	‡	‡	‡	51.6 (5.95)	23.4 (4.93) !	‡	24.9 (4.74) !
American Indian	117 (3.2)	8.8 (1.07) !	100.0 (†)	44.6 (6.17)	9.3 (3.45) !	#	5.9 (2.77) !	12.8 (4.29) !	6.2 (2.84) !	‡	‡	‡	55.4 (6.17)	25.6 (5.34) !	‡	26.9 (4.93) !
Alaska Native	9 (1.3)	‡	‡	‡	‡	‡	‡	‡	‡	‡	‡	‡	‡	‡	‡	‡
Two or more races	404 (9.4)	28.1 (0.90)	100.0 (†)	45.9 (2.03)	0.6 (0.21)	0.7 (0.23)	7.5 (0.94)	16.5 (1.63)	6.4 (0.90)	1.7 (0.55)	10.2 (1.45)	2.3 (0.56)	54.1 (2.03)	19.2 (1.48)	3.1 (0.55)	31.9 (2.05)
Female																
White	11,976 (7.2)	43.2 (0.19)	100.0 (†)	33.5 (0.25)	1.3 (0.05)	0.6 (0.05)	0.9 (0.05)	1.8 (0.07)	5.6 (0.11)	0.9 (0.05)	12.5 (0.17)	9.9 (0.15)	66.5 (0.25)	16.9 (0.22)	14.9 (0.20)	34.7 (0.24)
Black	2,804 (13.6)	23.0 (0.39)	100.0 (†)	37.4 (0.82)	0.9 (0.18)	0.2 (0.09)	2.6 (0.32)	2.3 (0.27)	5.1 (0.35)	0.6 (0.15)	14.6 (0.52)	11.0 (0.52)	62.6 (0.82)	21.6 (0.74)	8.6 (0.55)	32.4 (0.70)
Hispanic	4,069 (12.1)	17.2 (0.24)	100.0 (†)	32.0 (0.66)	0.4 (0.10)	0.5 (0.09)	1.3 (0.17)	2.9 (0.26)	4.7 (0.26)	0.6 (0.13)	13.0 (0.52)	8.6 (0.51)	68.0 (0.66)	21.7 (0.62)	11.3 (0.55)	35.0 (0.69)
Asian	1,376 (10.5)	64.9 (0.46)	100.0 (†)	53.0 (0.77)	0.7 (0.11)	0.8 (0.14)	7.8 (0.36)	11.0 (0.43)	7.8 (0.33)	1.5 (0.13)	11.7 (0.41)	10.6 (0.41)	47.0 (0.77)	20.9 (0.64)	3.9 (0.23)	22.2 (0.49)
Pacific Islander	41 (2.3)	19.0 (2.98)	100.0 (†)	42.4 (6.01)	‡	‡	#	‡	15.9 (5.65)	‡	14.6 (4.10)	7.7 (3.16)	57.6 (6.01)	19.7 (7.69)	13.5 (5.02)	24.4 (6.09)
American Indian/Alaska Native[2]	137 (3.5)	14.1 (1.15)	100.0 (†)	29.2 (3.68)	‡	‡	‡	‡	7.3 (2.01) !	‡	9.5 (2.54)	7.6 (2.18) !	70.8 (3.68)	17.1 (2.87) !	13.8 (3.01) !	39.9 (3.53) !
American Indian	117 (3.4)	13.4 (1.13)	100.0 (†)	30.2 (4.14)	‡	‡	‡	‡	4.9 (1.70) !	‡	10.0 (2.81)	9.4 (2.69) !	69.8 (4.14)	15.6 (3.05) !	12.6 (2.74) !	41.6 (3.94) !
Alaska Native	7 (0.7)	8.4 (3.87) !	‡	‡	‡	‡	‡	‡	‡	‡	‡	‡	‡	‡	‡	‡
Two or more races	400 (8.3)	37.4 (0.98)	100.0 (†)	39.9 (1.68)	0.8 (0.23)	0.9 (0.24)	1.9 (0.45)	3.6 (0.56)	6.8 (0.76)	0.8 (0.24)	16.2 (1.43)	8.9 (0.93)	60.1 (1.68)	16.3 (1.20)	6.7 (0.85)	37.1 (1.40)
Nativity																
Hispanic																
U.S.-born[3]	4,453 (27.3)	19.0 (0.30)	100.0 (†)	34.1 (0.64)	0.4 (0.09)	0.6 (0.10)	3.2 (0.28)	5.9 (0.29)	4.7 (0.24)	0.7 (0.11)	12.0 (0.47)	6.5 (0.38)	65.9 (0.64)	20.5 (0.61)	7.8 (0.40)	37.6 (0.65)
Foreign-born	4,122 (26.4)	9.1 (0.23)	100.0 (†)	38.8 (1.16)	0.7 (0.17)	1.2 (0.24)	3.9 (0.47)	12.0 (0.73)	4.5 (0.47)	1.0 (0.22)	9.7 (0.63)	5.8 (0.55)	61.2 (1.16)	27.4 (1.02)	8.4 (0.61)	25.4 (1.05)
Asian																
U.S.-born[3]	734 (9.4)	60.4 (0.74)	100.0 (†)	50.0 (1.06)	0.3 (0.09)	1.0 (0.21)	4.7 (0.42)	12.2 (0.58)	11.4 (0.60)	1.1 (0.20)	14.2 (0.67)	7.1 (0.54)	50.0 (1.06)	21.8 (0.79)	2.5 (0.30)	25.7 (0.96)
Foreign-born	1,862 (15.1)	64.2 (0.47)	100.0 (†)	64.4 (0.57)	0.9 (0.09)	0.7 (0.11)	13.5 (0.42)	22.9 (0.44)	7.1 (0.32)	2.2 (0.21)	9.4 (0.32)	7.9 (0.32)	35.6 (0.57)	17.7 (0.43)	2.6 (0.18)	15.4 (0.48)
Citizenship status																
U.S.-born citizen	34,275 (45.6)	32.9 (0.13)	100.0 (†)	35.2 (0.17)	1.2 (0.04)	0.7 (0.03)	3.0 (0.07)	5.6 (0.09)	5.5 (0.08)	1.1 (0.04)	11.5 (0.11)	6.6 (0.09)	64.8 (0.17)	20.6 (0.15)	9.9 (0.09)	34.3 (0.20)
Naturalized citizen	2,183 (18.4)	38.7 (0.46)	100.0 (†)	47.5 (0.73)	0.6 (0.11)	0.9 (0.13)	6.5 (0.38)	10.3 (0.45)	7.8 (0.45)	1.3 (0.16)	11.9 (0.47)	8.2 (0.37)	52.5 (0.73)	25.7 (0.54)	4.7 (0.34)	22.2 (0.59)
Noncitizen	5,554 (37.0)	26.5 (0.24)	100.0 (†)	60.0 (0.68)	0.9 (0.10)	0.9 (0.11)	11.7 (0.42)	22.1 (0.40)	6.1 (0.23)	2.1 (0.20)	9.5 (0.28)	6.6 (0.29)	40.0 (0.68)	18.2 (0.47)	3.7 (0.21)	18.1 (0.49)

†Not applicable.

#Rounds to zero.

‡Reporting standards not met. Either there are too few cases for a reliable estimate or the coefficient of variation (CV) is 50 percent or greater.

!Interpret data with caution. The coefficient of variation (CV) for this estimate is between 30 and 50 percent.

[1]Total includes other racial/ethnic groups not shown separately.

[2]Includes persons reporting American Indian alone, persons reporting Alaska Native alone, and persons from American Indian and/or Alaska Native tribes specified or not specified.

[3]Includes those born in the 50 states, the District of Columbia, Puerto Rico, American Samoa, Guam, the U.S. Virgin Islands, and the Northern Marianas, as well as those born abroad to U.S.-citizen parents.

NOTE: Estimates are for the entire population in the indicated age range, including persons living in households and persons living in group quarters (such as college residence halls, residential treatment centers, military barracks, and correctional facilities). The first bachelor's degree major reported by respondents was used to classify their field of study, even though they were able to report a second bachelor's degree major and may possess advanced degrees in other fields. STEM fields, as defined here, consist of the fields specified in columns 6 through 13. Data were assembled based on major field aggregations, except that management of STEM activities was counted as a STEM field instead of a business field. Detail may not sum to totals because of rounding. Race categories exclude persons of Hispanic ethnicity. SOURCE: U.S. Department of Commerce, Census Bureau, American Community Survey (ACS), 2012. (This table was prepared January 2014.)

Percentage of persons 18 to 24 years old and age 25 and over, by educational attainment and state: 2000, 2011, and 2012

[Standard errors appear in parentheses]

State	Percent of 18- to 24-year-olds who were high school completers[1] — 2000	2011	2012	2000 Less than high school completion	2000 High school completion or higher	2000 Bachelor's or higher degree Total	2000 Bachelor's degree	2000 Graduate degree	2011 Less than high school completion	2011 High school completion or higher	2011 Bachelor's or higher degree Total	2011 Bachelor's degree	2011 Graduate degree	2012 Less than high school completion	2012 High school completion or higher	2012 Bachelor's or higher degree Total	2012 Bachelor's degree	2012 Graduate degree
1	2	3	4	5	6	7	8	9	10	11	12	13	14	15	16	17	18	19
United States	74.7 (0.02)	84.1 (0.10)	85.3 (0.09)	19.6 (0.01)	80.4 (0.01)	24.4 (0.01)	15.5 (0.01)	8.9 (#)	14.1 (0.04)	85.9 (0.04)	28.6 (0.06)	17.9 (0.04)	10.7 (0.03)	13.6 (0.04)	86.4 (0.04)	29.2 (0.05)	18.3 (0.04)	10.9 (0.03)
Alabama	72.2 (0.15)	81.8 (0.74)	84.5 (0.75)	24.7 (0.06)	75.3 (0.06)	19.0 (0.05)	12.1 (0.04)	6.9 (0.03)	17.3 (0.37)	82.7 (0.37)	22.5 (0.32)	13.9 (0.26)	8.6 (0.21)	16.2 (0.24)	83.8 (0.24)	23.4 (0.29)	14.6 (0.19)	8.7 (0.20)
Alaska	76.9 (0.40)	79.9 (2.15)	86.3 (2.28)	11.7 (0.12)	88.3 (0.12)	24.7 (0.16)	16.1 (0.13)	8.6 (0.10)	7.2 (0.50)	92.8 (0.50)	25.8 (0.90)	15.4 (0.90)	10.4 (0.87)	8.2 (0.56)	91.8 (0.56)	28.9 (1.22)	17.4 (0.93)	11.4 (0.82)
Arizona	69.2 (0.19)	81.1 (0.67)	81.9 (0.63)	19.0 (0.06)	81.0 (0.06)	23.5 (0.07)	15.1 (0.06)	8.4 (0.04)	14.3 (0.23)	85.7 (0.23)	26.4 (0.26)	17.0 (0.23)	9.4 (0.18)	14.2 (0.21)	85.8 (0.21)	27.5 (0.29)	17.2 (0.23)	10.2 (0.18)
Arkansas	75.4 (0.19)	84.5 (0.98)	84.5 (0.99)	24.7 (0.07)	75.3 (0.07)	16.7 (0.06)	11.0 (0.05)	5.7 (0.04)	16.3 (0.43)	83.7 (0.43)	20.4 (0.38)	13.2 (0.31)	7.2 (0.25)	14.9 (0.34)	85.1 (0.34)	21.2 (0.35)	13.9 (0.33)	7.3 (0.21)
California	70.7 (0.07)	84.4 (0.26)	85.1 (0.21)	23.2 (0.03)	76.8 (0.03)	26.6 (0.03)	17.1 (0.02)	9.5 (0.02)	18.9 (0.10)	81.1 (0.10)	30.3 (0.13)	19.2 (0.11)	11.1 (0.09)	18.6 (0.09)	81.4 (0.09)	31.0 (0.11)	19.7 (0.10)	11.3 (0.08)
Colorado	75.1 (0.15)	84.2 (0.74)	85.9 (0.75)	13.1 (0.05)	86.9 (0.05)	32.7 (0.06)	21.6 (0.06)	11.1 (0.04)	9.8 (0.21)	90.2 (0.21)	36.8 (0.37)	23.3 (0.31)	13.5 (0.21)	9.6 (0.20)	90.4 (0.20)	37.6 (0.34)	23.7 (0.29)	13.9 (0.22)
Connecticut	78.2 (0.21)	85.6 (0.78)	86.3 (0.81)	16.0 (0.06)	84.0 (0.06)	31.4 (0.08)	18.1 (0.07)	13.3 (0.06)	11.0 (0.27)	89.0 (0.27)	36.2 (0.42)	20.6 (0.35)	15.6 (0.32)	10.1 (0.26)	89.9 (0.26)	37.2 (0.35)	20.6 (0.28)	16.6 (0.27)
Delaware	77.6 (0.41)	84.1 (1.54)	82.3 (1.91)	17.4 (0.14)	82.6 (0.14)	25.0 (0.16)	15.6 (0.14)	9.4 (0.11)	12.7 (0.52)	87.3 (0.52)	28.2 (0.60)	16.9 (0.56)	11.3 (0.53)	11.7 (0.60)	88.3 (0.60)	30.2 (0.82)	19.0 (0.60)	11.2 (0.56)
District of Columbia	79.4 (0.40)	89.8 (1.27)	86.5 (1.42)	22.2 (0.18)	77.8 (0.18)	39.1 (0.21)	18.1 (0.17)	21.0 (0.18)	12.9 (0.73)	87.1 (0.73)	52.5 (0.80)	23.6 (0.69)	28.9 (0.72)	10.8 (0.46)	89.2 (0.46)	53.7 (0.76)	23.7 (0.77)	30.0 (0.74)
Florida	71.7 (0.11)	82.4 (0.39)	84.2 (0.30)	20.1 (0.04)	79.9 (0.04)	22.3 (0.04)	14.2 (0.03)	8.1 (0.02)	14.1 (0.12)	85.9 (0.12)	25.9 (0.16)	16.5 (0.12)	9.3 (0.10)	13.6 (0.13)	86.4 (0.13)	26.8 (0.15)	17.3 (0.13)	9.5 (0.09)
Georgia	70.0 (0.15)	79.5 (0.55)	81.5 (0.56)	21.4 (0.05)	78.6 (0.05)	24.3 (0.05)	16.0 (0.05)	8.3 (0.04)	15.7 (0.19)	84.3 (0.19)	27.6 (0.24)	17.8 (0.21)	9.8 (0.16)	14.8 (0.21)	85.2 (0.21)	28.3 (0.23)	17.9 (0.19)	10.4 (0.16)
Hawaii	85.8 (0.25)	89.6 (1.23)	92.1 (0.99)	15.4 (0.10)	84.6 (0.10)	26.2 (0.12)	17.8 (0.10)	8.4 (0.08)	9.5 (0.40)	90.5 (0.40)	29.7 (0.55)	19.8 (0.51)	9.9 (0.35)	10.0 (0.43)	90.0 (0.43)	30.1 (0.58)	19.8 (0.49)	10.3 (0.41)
Idaho	77.3 (0.25)	85.0 (1.11)	86.1 (1.31)	15.3 (0.09)	84.7 (0.09)	21.7 (0.10)	14.9 (0.09)	6.9 (0.06)	11.3 (0.35)	88.7 (0.35)	25.6 (0.68)	17.6 (0.54)	7.9 (0.39)	11.2 (0.40)	88.8 (0.40)	25.8 (0.70)	17.1 (0.54)	8.7 (0.42)
Illinois	76.0 (0.09)	84.9 (0.44)	85.7 (0.42)	18.6 (0.05)	81.4 (0.05)	26.1 (0.05)	16.6 (0.03)	9.5 (0.02)	12.7 (0.14)	87.3 (0.14)	31.0 (0.22)	19.2 (0.19)	11.7 (0.17)	12.3 (0.17)	87.7 (0.17)	31.5 (0.20)	19.6 (0.15)	11.8 (0.13)
Indiana	76.5 (0.15)	80.5 (0.74)	82.6 (0.68)	17.9 (0.05)	82.1 (0.05)	19.4 (0.05)	12.2 (0.04)	7.2 (0.04)	12.8 (0.20)	87.2 (0.20)	22.8 (0.27)	14.6 (0.22)	8.1 (0.19)	12.7 (0.22)	87.3 (0.22)	23.3 (0.29)	15.0 (0.21)	8.3 (0.18)
Iowa	81.4 (0.16)	87.5 (0.82)	88.0 (0.56)	13.9 (0.06)	86.1 (0.06)	21.2 (0.07)	14.7 (0.06)	6.5 (0.04)	9.0 (0.28)	91.0 (0.28)	25.8 (0.47)	17.6 (0.41)	8.2 (0.27)	7.9 (0.27)	92.1 (0.27)	26.8 (0.37)	18.4 (0.34)	8.4 (0.28)
Kansas	78.3 (0.18)	85.3 (0.85)	86.0 (0.85)	14.0 (0.06)	86.0 (0.06)	25.8 (0.08)	17.1 (0.06)	8.7 (0.05)	10.4 (0.32)	89.6 (0.32)	30.5 (0.51)	20.0 (0.39)	10.5 (0.33)	9.9 (0.30)	90.1 (0.30)	30.2 (0.44)	19.3 (0.36)	10.9 (0.36)
Kentucky	74.9 (0.15)	83.4 (0.88)	86.7 (0.72)	25.9 (0.06)	74.1 (0.06)	17.1 (0.05)	10.2 (0.04)	6.9 (0.03)	16.9 (0.31)	83.1 (0.31)	20.7 (0.33)	12.2 (0.24)	8.5 (0.24)	16.5 (0.29)	83.5 (0.29)	21.5 (0.31)	12.9 (0.25)	8.6 (0.20)
Louisiana	72.3 (0.15)	80.1 (0.77)	80.2 (0.88)	25.2 (0.06)	74.8 (0.06)	18.7 (0.05)	12.2 (0.04)	6.5 (0.03)	17.4 (0.29)	82.6 (0.29)	21.1 (0.36)	14.0 (0.27)	7.1 (0.21)	16.8 (0.31)	83.2 (0.31)	22.2 (0.31)	14.6 (0.26)	7.6 (0.16)
Maine	78.9 (0.28)	88.3 (1.19)	89.9 (1.09)	14.6 (0.08)	85.4 (0.08)	22.9 (0.10)	15.0 (0.09)	7.9 (0.06)	9.2 (0.40)	90.8 (0.40)	28.6 (0.70)	18.3 (0.53)	10.3 (0.44)	7.9 (0.38)	92.1 (0.38)	28.0 (0.71)	18.6 (0.52)	9.5 (0.42)
Maryland	79.6 (0.16)	86.3 (0.57)	88.0 (0.56)	16.2 (0.05)	83.8 (0.05)	31.4 (0.07)	18.0 (0.05)	13.4 (0.05)	11.0 (0.21)	89.0 (0.21)	37.0 (0.28)	20.5 (0.23)	16.6 (0.23)	10.8 (0.22)	89.2 (0.22)	37.0 (0.31)	20.2 (0.28)	16.8 (0.23)
Massachusetts	82.2 (0.13)	88.5 (0.53)	85.3 (0.85)	15.2 (0.05)	84.8 (0.05)	33.2 (0.08)	19.5 (0.05)	13.7 (0.04)	11.0 (0.20)	89.1 (0.20)	39.2 (0.44)	22.2 (0.34)	16.9 (0.34)	10.4 (0.17)	89.6 (0.17)	39.5 (0.30)	22.4 (0.24)	17.1 (0.21)
Michigan	76.5 (0.10)	85.9 (0.52)	86.8 (0.49)	16.6 (0.03)	83.4 (0.03)	21.8 (0.04)	13.7 (0.03)	8.1 (0.02)	11.3 (0.17)	88.7 (0.17)	25.8 (0.22)	15.7 (0.18)	10.0 (0.15)	10.4 (0.17)	89.6 (0.17)	26.3 (0.23)	16.2 (0.18)	10.1 (0.13)
Minnesota	79.3 (0.13)	87.5 (0.56)	86.9 (0.63)	12.1 (0.04)	87.9 (0.04)	27.4 (0.06)	19.1 (0.06)	8.3 (0.03)	7.9 (0.16)	92.1 (0.16)	32.6 (0.40)	21.8 (0.30)	10.8 (0.25)	7.6 (0.19)	92.4 (0.19)	32.7 (0.42)	22.1 (0.38)	10.6 (0.24)
Mississippi	71.3 (0.18)	81.6 (0.91)	82.2 (0.84)	27.1 (0.08)	72.9 (0.08)	16.9 (0.06)	11.1 (0.05)	5.8 (0.04)	19.2 (0.37)	80.8 (0.37)	20.1 (0.47)	12.9 (0.36)	7.2 (0.27)	17.5 (0.35)	82.5 (0.35)	20.6 (0.41)	12.8 (0.33)	7.8 (0.24)
Missouri	76.5 (0.13)	84.6 (0.62)	87.3 (0.53)	18.7 (0.05)	81.3 (0.05)	21.6 (0.05)	14.0 (0.04)	7.6 (0.03)	12.3 (0.21)	87.7 (0.21)	26.4 (0.34)	16.3 (0.28)	10.1 (0.19)	12.2 (0.21)	87.8 (0.21)	26.0 (0.30)	16.4 (0.24)	9.6 (0.19)
Montana	78.6 (0.31)	87.5 (1.57)	84.2 (1.86)	12.8 (0.10)	87.2 (0.10)	24.4 (0.13)	17.2 (0.11)	7.2 (0.08)	7.5 (0.47)	92.5 (0.47)	29.4 (0.82)	20.5 (0.68)	8.9 (0.46)	7.2 (0.46)	92.8 (0.46)	28.5 (0.71)	19.2 (0.58)	9.3 (0.49)
Nebraska	80.0 (0.21)	85.4 (1.13)	89.2 (0.97)	13.4 (0.07)	86.6 (0.07)	23.7 (0.09)	16.4 (0.08)	7.3 (0.06)	8.9 (0.32)	91.1 (0.32)	28.1 (0.54)	19.5 (0.40)	8.6 (0.31)	9.1 (0.29)	90.8 (0.29)	29.7 (0.50)	20.3 (0.42)	9.5 (0.32)
Nevada	66.7 (0.32)	78.9 (1.27)	78.3 (1.20)	19.3 (0.10)	80.7 (0.10)	18.2 (0.10)	12.1 (0.08)	6.1 (0.06)	15.0 (0.37)	85.0 (0.37)	22.4 (0.43)	14.8 (0.30)	7.5 (0.26)	14.4 (0.30)	85.6 (0.30)	22.6 (0.34)	15.0 (0.33)	7.7 (0.21)
New Hampshire	77.8 (0.29)	89.2 (0.96)	88.4 (1.26)	12.6 (0.08)	87.4 (0.08)	28.7 (0.11)	18.7 (0.11)	10.0 (0.07)	8.2 (0.42)	91.8 (0.42)	33.5 (0.65)	20.6 (0.50)	12.9 (0.45)	8.0 (0.46)	92.0 (0.46)	35.3 (0.74)	22.0 (0.54)	13.4 (0.49)
New Jersey	76.3 (0.14)	86.5 (0.45)	87.6 (0.46)	17.9 (0.04)	82.1 (0.04)	29.8 (0.05)	18.8 (0.04)	11.0 (0.04)	12.0 (0.15)	88.0 (0.15)	35.2 (0.24)	21.9 (0.18)	13.4 (0.16)	11.6 (0.18)	88.4 (0.18)	36.3 (0.26)	22.5 (0.20)	13.8 (0.18)
New Mexico	70.5 (0.24)	79.4 (1.33)	78.6 (1.27)	21.1 (0.09)	78.9 (0.09)	23.5 (0.09)	13.7 (0.07)	9.8 (0.06)	17.0 (0.42)	83.0 (0.42)	25.6 (0.49)	14.4 (0.47)	11.2 (0.34)	15.5 (0.38)	84.5 (0.38)	26.2 (0.43)	14.7 (0.40)	11.5 (0.33)
New York	76.1 (0.09)	85.4 (0.35)	86.6 (0.29)	20.9 (0.04)	79.1 (0.04)	27.4 (0.04)	15.6 (0.04)	11.8 (0.03)	14.9 (0.12)	85.1 (0.12)	33.1 (0.15)	18.8 (0.14)	14.3 (0.12)	14.6 (0.11)	85.4 (0.11)	33.5 (0.17)	19.2 (0.13)	14.3 (0.14)
North Carolina	74.2 (0.11)	83.1 (0.55)	83.2 (0.57)	21.9 (0.04)	78.1 (0.04)	22.5 (0.04)	15.3 (0.04)	7.2 (0.03)	15.2 (0.20)	84.8 (0.20)	26.7 (0.26)	17.7 (0.22)	9.0 (0.15)	14.9 (0.21)	85.1 (0.21)	27.3 (0.23)	18.0 (0.19)	9.3 (0.13)
North Dakota	84.4 (0.34)	92.3 (1.05)	90.9 (1.53)	16.1 (0.10)	83.9 (0.10)	22.0 (0.04)	16.5 (0.10)	5.5 (0.06)	9.2 (0.49)	90.8 (0.49)	26.2 (0.97)	19.9 (0.83)	6.3 (0.53)	8.2 (0.49)	91.8 (0.49)	28.8 (0.91)	20.2 (0.78)	8.6 (0.63)
Ohio	76.8 (0.09)	84.4 (0.51)	85.4 (0.37)	17.0 (0.03)	83.0 (0.03)	21.1 (0.03)	13.7 (0.03)	7.4 (0.02)	11.6 (0.14)	88.4 (0.14)	24.8 (0.21)	15.6 (0.16)	9.2 (0.13)	11.1 (0.15)	88.9 (0.15)	25.2 (0.19)	16.0 (0.17)	9.1 (0.14)
Oklahoma	74.8 (0.16)	81.5 (0.89)	83.7 (0.76)	19.4 (0.06)	80.6 (0.06)	20.3 (0.06)	13.5 (0.05)	6.8 (0.04)	13.9 (0.30)	86.1 (0.30)	23.8 (0.42)	16.0 (0.34)	7.8 (0.20)	13.4 (0.30)	86.6 (0.30)	23.7 (0.23)	15.4 (0.23)	8.3 (0.23)
Oregon	74.2 (0.17)	84.3 (0.82)	87.1 (0.86)	14.9 (0.05)	85.1 (0.05)	25.1 (0.06)	16.4 (0.06)	8.7 (0.04)	10.7 (0.27)	89.3 (0.27)	29.2 (0.33)	18.3 (0.27)	10.9 (0.27)	9.9 (0.23)	90.1 (0.23)	30.2 (0.35)	18.6 (0.31)	11.5 (0.23)
Pennsylvania	79.8 (0.09)	86.9 (0.38)	87.6 (0.48)	18.1 (0.03)	81.9 (0.03)	22.4 (0.03)	14.0 (0.03)	8.4 (0.02)	11.3 (0.17)	88.7 (0.17)	27.1 (0.20)	16.4 (0.16)	10.6 (0.14)	11.1 (0.15)	88.9 (0.15)	28.1 (0.23)	17.1 (0.17)	10.9 (0.15)
Rhode Island	81.3 (0.32)	88.2 (1.25)	88.3 (1.00)	22.0 (0.13)	78.0 (0.13)	25.6 (0.14)	15.9 (0.12)	9.7 (0.10)	15.5 (0.52)	84.5 (0.52)	31.0 (0.61)	18.8 (0.52)	12.2 (0.47)	14.2 (0.53)	85.8 (0.53)	31.2 (0.65)	18.2 (0.54)	13.1 (0.49)

See notes at end of table.

Percentage of persons 18 to 24 years old and age 25 and over, by educational attainment and state: 2000, 2011, and 2012—Continued

[Standard errors appear in parentheses]

State	Percent of 18- to 24-year-olds who were high school completers[1]			Percent of population 25 years old and over, by educational attainment														
				2000					2011					2012				
				Less than high school completion	High school completion or higher	Bachelor's or higher degree			Less than high school completion	High school completion or higher	Bachelor's or higher degree			Less than high school completion	High school completion or higher	Bachelor's or higher degree		
	2000	2011	2012			Total	Bachelor's degree	Graduate degree			Total	Bachelor's degree	Graduate degree			Total	Bachelor's degree	Graduate degree
1	2	3	4	5	6	7	8	9	10	11	12	13	14	15	16	17	18	19
South Carolina	74.3 (0.18)	81.9 (0.77)	83.7 (0.75)	23.7 (0.07)	76.3 (0.07)	20.4 (0.07)	13.5 (0.06)	6.9 (0.04)	15.8 (0.25)	84.2 (0.25)	23.8 (0.35)	15.7 (0.27)	8.1 (0.21)	15.1 (0.20)	84.9 (0.20)	25.3 (0.34)	16.3 (0.25)	9.0 (0.20)
South Dakota	78.2 (0.33)	82.8 (1.69)	85.0 (1.85)	15.4 (0.12)	84.6 (0.12)	21.5 (0.13)	15.5 (0.12)	6.0 (0.08)	9.6 (0.52)	90.4 (0.52)	25.7 (0.92)	17.8 (0.72)	7.9 (0.52)	9.4 (0.49)	90.6 (0.49)	26.7 (1.02)	18.4 (0.84)	8.3 (0.54)
Tennessee	75.1 (0.16)	86.1 (0.61)	87.9 (0.54)	24.1 (0.06)	75.9 (0.06)	19.6 (0.06)	12.8 (0.05)	6.8 (0.03)	15.8 (0.21)	84.2 (0.21)	23.7 (0.26)	15.3 (0.22)	8.4 (0.16)	14.9 (0.23)	85.1 (0.23)	24.6 (0.21)	15.8 (0.20)	8.8 (0.15)
Texas	68.6 (0.08)	80.8 (0.36)	82.2 (0.30)	24.3 (0.03)	75.7 (0.03)	23.2 (0.03)	15.6 (0.03)	7.6 (0.02)	18.9 (0.13)	81.1 (0.13)	26.5 (0.15)	17.8 (0.13)	8.7 (0.10)	18.5 (0.11)	81.5 (0.11)	26.9 (0.14)	17.9 (0.12)	9.1 (0.09)
Utah	80.3 (0.16)	88.0 (0.85)	86.5 (0.87)	12.3 (0.07)	87.7 (0.07)	26.1 (0.09)	17.8 (0.08)	8.3 (0.06)	9.3 (0.28)	90.7 (0.28)	29.7 (0.47)	20.1 (0.37)	9.6 (0.27)	8.7 (0.32)	91.3 (0.32)	30.7 (0.45)	20.4 (0.39)	10.3 (0.26)
Vermont	83.0 (0.28)	91.7 (1.20)	91.3 (1.56)	13.6 (0.10)	86.4 (0.10)	29.4 (0.13)	18.3 (0.11)	11.1 (0.09)	8.0 (0.50)	92.0 (0.50)	37.0 (1.20)	22.4 (0.98)	14.7 (0.84)	7.7 (0.51)	92.3 (0.51)	35.1 (1.07)	22.0 (0.81)	13.2 (0.68)
Virginia	79.4 (0.13)	87.5 (0.45)	88.9 (0.52)	18.5 (0.05)	81.5 (0.05)	29.5 (0.06)	17.9 (0.05)	11.6 (0.04)	12.2 (0.16)	87.8 (0.16)	35.4 (0.27)	20.6 (0.20)	14.7 (0.19)	11.9 (0.15)	88.1 (0.15)	35.7 (0.25)	20.7 (0.22)	15.1 (0.18)
Washington	75.3 (0.16)	83.4 (0.67)	84.5 (0.62)	12.9 (0.05)	87.1 (0.05)	27.7 (0.06)	18.4 (0.05)	9.3 (0.04)	10.0 (0.18)	90.0 (0.18)	31.8 (0.31)	20.1 (0.26)	11.7 (0.21)	9.4 (0.18)	90.6 (0.18)	31.8 (0.32)	20.6 (0.25)	11.2 (0.21)
West Virginia	78.2 (0.22)	84.0 (1.20)	87.7 (1.20)	24.8 (0.09)	75.2 (0.09)	14.8 (0.07)	8.9 (0.06)	5.9 (0.05)	16.1 (0.42)	83.9 (0.42)	18.6 (0.52)	11.7 (0.37)	6.9 (0.30)	16.1 (0.44)	83.9 (0.44)	18.2 (0.40)	11.1 (0.32)	7.2 (0.26)
Wisconsin	78.9 (0.13)	86.8 (0.55)	88.3 (0.57)	14.9 (0.04)	85.1 (0.04)	22.4 (0.05)	15.2 (0.04)	7.2 (0.04)	9.5 (0.22)	90.5 (0.22)	26.4 (0.34)	17.2 (0.30)	9.2 (0.22)	9.1 (0.21)	90.9 (0.21)	27.5 (0.36)	17.9 (0.27)	9.5 (0.23)
Wyoming	79.0 (0.41)	86.4 (1.95)	86.7 (1.77)	12.1 (0.13)	87.9 (0.13)	21.9 (0.16)	14.9 (0.14)	7.0 (0.10)	7.6 (0.52)	92.4 (0.52)	24.8 (1.04)	16.1 (0.79)	8.7 (0.54)	8.5 (0.58)	91.5 (0.58)	25.4 (1.02)	17.1 (0.76)	8.3 (0.57)

#Rounds to zero.

[1]High school completers include diploma recipients and those completing high school through alternative credentials, such as a GED.

NOTE: Detail may not sum to totals because of rounding.

SOURCE: U.S. Department of Commerce, Census Bureau, Census 2000 Summary File 3, retrieved October 11, 2006, from http://factfinder2.census.gov/faces/tableservices/jsf/pages/productview.xhtml?pid=DEC_00_SF3_QTP20&prodType=table; Census Briefs, *Educational Attainment: 2000*; and 2011 and 2012 American Community Survey (ACS) 1-Year Public Use Microdata Sample (PUMS) data. (This table was prepared January 2014.)

Rates of high school completion and bachelor's degree attainment among persons age 25 and over, by race/ethnicity and state: 2011 and 2012

[Standard errors appear in parentheses]

Year and state	Percent with high school completion or higher						Percent with bachelor's degree or higher					
	Total[1]	White	Black	Hispanic	Asian	Two or more races	Total[1]	White	Black	Hispanic	Asian	Two or more races
1	2	3	4	5	6	7	8	9	10	11	12	13
2011												
United States	85.9 (0.04)	91.1 (0.03)	82.7 (0.11)	63.1 (0.16)	85.2 (0.16)	88.7 (0.25)	28.6 (0.06)	31.8 (0.07)	18.7 (0.11)	13.4 (0.12)	50.3 (0.26)	28.3 (0.37)
Alabama	82.7 (0.37)	85.0 (0.39)	78.6 (0.69)	57.8 (2.68)	87.6 (2.30)	87.5 (2.56)	22.5 (0.32)	25.2 (0.38)	14.6 (0.55)	12.6 (1.79)	51.2 (3.82)	19.9 (2.93)
Alaska	92.8 (0.50)	96.4 (0.51)	87.5 (6.06)	62.6 (2.68)	72.5 (4.85)	92.0 (3.72)	25.8 (1.24)	29.6 (1.44)	26.9 (8.07)	27.7 (5.79)	24.5 (4.68)	15.5 (4.32)
Arizona	85.7 (0.23)	93.4 (0.21)	90.0 (0.82)	65.3 (0.70)	83.2 (1.50)	94.0 (1.25)	26.4 (0.26)	32.5 (0.35)	21.4 (1.23)	10.0 (0.39)	48.1 (2.42)	27.6 (2.47)
Arkansas	83.7 (0.43)	86.3 (0.38)	79.2 (1.00)	54.6 (3.20)	84.2 (4.54)	81.6 (3.42)	20.4 (0.38)	21.8 (0.44)	15.8 (1.03)	8.5 (1.45)	36.9 (4.24)	18.3 (3.61)
California	81.1 (0.10)	93.9 (0.10)	88.6 (0.32)	58.5 (0.29)	85.8 (0.26)	90.8 (0.62)	30.3 (0.13)	39.3 (0.22)	23.0 (0.42)	10.7 (0.18)	48.7 (0.39)	32.4 (0.86)
Colorado	90.2 (0.21)	95.3 (0.16)	88.6 (1.19)	68.3 (0.98)	86.6 (1.47)	92.1 (1.41)	36.8 (0.37)	42.4 (0.42)	25.0 (2.15)	13.2 (0.64)	46.6 (2.52)	36.1 (2.66)
Connecticut	89.0 (0.27)	93.0 (0.27)	83.0 (0.90)	67.8 (1.41)	87.7 (1.65)	90.9 (1.90)	36.2 (0.42)	40.4 (0.52)	17.4 (1.18)	14.9 (1.15)	61.6 (2.68)	29.3 (3.27)
Delaware	87.3 (0.52)	89.7 (0.52)	84.6 (1.42)	67.5 (4.48)	88.0 (2.62)	92.1 (4.98)	28.2 (0.68)	30.6 (0.86)	17.9 (1.54)	14.9 (2.31)	69.5 (3.93)	25.3 (7.89)
District of Columbia	87.1 (0.73)	99.8 (0.12)	80.7 (1.25)	65.2 (4.30)	84.8 (4.85)	98.6 (1.13)	52.5 (0.80)	90.2 (0.90)	22.8 (1.26)	36.2 (3.69)	77.2 (4.27)	74.5 (4.46)
Florida	85.9 (0.12)	91.0 (0.13)	79.4 (0.39)	75.0 (0.35)	85.0 (0.96)	86.9 (1.10)	25.9 (0.16)	29.0 (0.21)	16.0 (0.44)	20.4 (0.38)	45.9 (1.12)	25.1 (1.38)
Georgia	84.3 (0.19)	87.9 (0.25)	83.8 (0.41)	54.4 (1.45)	84.8 (1.14)	89.4 (1.71)	27.6 (0.24)	31.0 (0.32)	21.5 (0.44)	13.0 (0.80)	49.9 (1.70)	32.8 (3.12)
Hawaii	90.5 (0.40)	96.0 (0.51)	98.9 (0.79)	53.6 (1.81)	87.5 (0.74)	91.6 (1.10)	29.7 (0.55)	40.8 (1.61)	31.9 (6.05)	19.9 (2.21)	31.4 (4.88)	17.4 (1.44)
Idaho	88.7 (0.35)	92.1 (0.37)	86.6 (6.15)	53.6 (2.14)	86.6 (3.75)	93.7 (4.88)	25.6 (0.68)	27.1 (0.78)	32.8 (9.80)	9.1 (1.17)	58.9 (4.88)	14.8 (4.27)
Illinois	87.3 (0.14)	92.8 (0.13)	83.4 (0.48)	61.7 (0.70)	89.0 (0.83)	90.9 (1.48)	31.0 (0.22)	34.6 (0.42)	19.3 (0.47)	12.9 (0.47)	60.7 (1.50)	34.6 (2.19)
Indiana	87.2 (0.25)	89.0 (0.21)	82.9 (0.78)	61.7 (1.69)	84.4 (2.16)	87.1 (2.24)	22.8 (0.27)	23.4 (0.30)	15.0 (1.00)	12.9 (1.01)	58.9 (2.33)	27.5 (2.84)
Iowa	91.0 (0.28)	92.7 (0.24)	82.0 (2.94)	56.6 (3.16)	86.5 (2.66)	87.7 (3.28)	25.8 (0.47)	26.0 (0.52)	19.4 (2.85)	12.3 (1.84)	54.0 (4.88)	15.8 ! (5.19)
Kansas	89.6 (0.32)	93.0 (0.28)	87.9 (1.58)	57.5 (2.15)	77.6 (3.02)	87.4 (2.87)	30.5 (0.51)	32.7 (0.52)	19.1 (2.17)	12.3 (1.45)	43.4 (3.15)	24.1 (2.94)
Kentucky	83.1 (0.31)	83.5 (0.35)	82.9 (1.06)	64.4 (2.83)	83.9 (4.34)	86.2 (3.12)	20.7 (0.33)	20.9 (0.32)	15.1 (1.12)	13.9 (1.94)	57.7 (4.78)	24.9 (4.63)
Louisiana	82.6 (0.29)	86.9 (0.33)	74.9 (0.50)	73.2 (2.35)	74.9 (2.64)	90.9 (3.33)	21.1 (0.36)	24.9 (0.42)	12.7 (0.51)	15.4 (1.68)	36.9 (3.41)	20.3 (3.83)
Maine	90.8 (0.40)	91.2 (0.43)	78.1 (7.34)	77.9 (7.44)	73.9 (5.47)	88.2 (4.12)	28.6 (0.70)	28.8 (0.71)	17.5 ! (7.33)	24.1 (6.39)	31.1 (6.53)	21.5 ! (6.93)
Maryland	89.0 (0.21)	92.6 (0.21)	88.1 (0.38)	62.4 (1.76)	89.5 (0.98)	91.3 (1.45)	36.4 (0.28)	41.1 (0.42)	27.2 (0.60)	21.2 (1.23)	61.0 (1.61)	44.4 (3.27)
Massachusetts	89.1 (0.20)	92.4 (0.18)	81.9 (0.99)	66.6 (1.11)	81.9 (1.08)	85.7 (2.34)	39.2 (0.32)	41.6 (0.37)	23.7 (1.31)	17.1 (0.88)	55.0 (1.22)	37.7 (2.99)
Michigan	88.7 (0.17)	90.6 (0.17)	82.2 (0.66)	70.7 (1.46)	89.2 (1.19)	88.5 (1.20)	25.8 (0.22)	26.8 (0.25)	15.9 (0.50)	17.1 (1.25)	61.7 (2.09)	22.5 (1.76)
Minnesota	92.1 (0.18)	94.5 (0.15)	79.2 (1.79)	63.1 (2.70)	78.7 (1.91)	88.5 (3.03)	32.6 (0.40)	33.6 (0.42)	19.9 (1.99)	14.6 (1.77)	46.9 (2.21)	34.5 (3.72)
Mississippi	80.8 (0.37)	85.5 (0.41)	74.9 (0.71)	49.4 (3.94)	68.3 (4.30)	88.7 (4.12)	20.1 (0.47)	28.8 (0.62)	14.5 (0.63)	8.6 (1.68)	29.3 (4.10)	24.9 (5.37)
Missouri	87.7 (0.21)	88.9 (0.23)	83.5 (0.71)	66.2 (1.76)	87.9 (1.68)	88.0 (1.47)	26.4 (0.34)	27.2 (0.32)	17.8 (0.98)	17.9 (1.71)	59.4 (2.89)	17.3 (2.19)
Montana	92.5 (0.47)	93.0 (0.47)	‡ (†)	88.3 (3.59)	‡ (†)	82.6 (3.14)	29.4 (0.82)	30.4 (0.88)	‡ (†)	19.0 (4.79)	‡ (†)	16.8 ! (5.50)
Nebraska	91.1 (0.32)	95.0 (0.23)	84.9 (2.75)	48.7 (2.79)	76.2 (5.01)	91.1 (4.82)	28.1 (0.54)	29.8 (0.61)	22.6 (3.22)	9.4 (1.48)	38.7 (5.50)	24.7 (5.37)
Nevada	84.0 (0.37)	92.3 (0.39)	86.2 (1.57)	57.7 (1.20)	87.6 (1.44)	90.1 (1.87)	22.4 (0.43)	26.7 (0.64)	16.7 (1.75)	8.1 (0.60)	33.9 (2.01)	24.3 (3.10)
New Hampshire	91.8 (0.42)	92.2 (0.38)	72.4 (9.02)	73.4 (4.36)	89.3 (5.30)	86.1 (5.01)	33.5 (0.65)	33.1 (0.67)	14.5 (7.39)	24.5 (4.05)	63.3 (5.44)	29.6 (4.61)
New Jersey	88.0 (0.15)	92.4 (0.18)	85.4 (0.45)	70.9 (0.62)	91.1 (0.49)	89.0 (1.49)	35.2 (0.24)	38.3 (0.34)	22.1 (0.66)	15.7 (0.58)	67.9 (0.97)	32.2 (2.35)
New Mexico	83.0 (0.42)	94.2 (0.40)	90.8 (2.41)	70.3 (0.91)	93.1 (2.59)	87.9 (3.67)	25.6 (0.49)	39.0 (0.88)	16.8 (3.25)	12.8 (0.66)	54.3 (5.10)	26.6 (4.44)
New York	85.1 (0.12)	91.8 (0.12)	81.7 (0.38)	65.6 (0.53)	77.9 (0.59)	83.9 (1.25)	33.1 (0.15)	38.7 (0.21)	19.5 (0.40)	15.9 (0.38)	46.5 (0.80)	36.3 (1.51)
North Carolina	84.8 (0.20)	88.9 (0.21)	81.5 (0.45)	53.6 (1.24)	82.0 (1.68)	85.3 (1.95)	26.7 (0.26)	30.5 (0.33)	16.7 (0.56)	10.7 (0.64)	49.5 (2.26)	27.0 (2.44)
North Dakota	90.8 (0.49)	91.4 (0.51)	‡ (†)	69.4 (5.63)	90.5 (4.69)	92.4 (3.76)	26.2 (0.97)	26.9 (1.00)	16.7 (†)	10.7 (†)	70.8 (12.06)	‡ (†)
Ohio	88.4 (0.14)	89.5 (0.15)	83.0 (0.50)	73.7 (1.25)	88.9 (1.23)	86.8 (1.47)	24.8 (0.21)	25.4 (0.23)	15.0 (0.58)	18.5 (1.26)	65.0 (1.81)	24.9 (2.34)
Oklahoma	86.1 (0.33)	88.9 (0.37)	85.4 (1.25)	57.2 (1.84)	83.9 (3.26)	85.6 (1.07)	23.8 (0.42)	25.4 (0.44)	19.7 (1.70)	11.9 (1.26)	42.8 (4.01)	20.9 (1.82)
Oregon	89.3 (0.27)	92.6 (0.25)	87.8 (2.14)	59.2 (1.88)	86.6 (1.47)	87.6 (1.62)	29.2 (0.33)	30.8 (0.37)	22.4 (2.87)	11.0 (0.84)	44.3 (2.49)	27.4 (2.78)
Pennsylvania	88.7 (0.17)	90.7 (0.16)	83.0 (0.63)	65.6 (1.30)	82.5 (0.93)	90.4 (1.31)	27.1 (0.20)	28.3 (0.23)	14.8 (0.65)	11.0 (0.96)	53.0 (1.35)	27.9 (2.32)
Rhode Island	84.5 (0.52)	88.3 (0.48)	80.0 (2.84)	61.7 (2.72)	69.1 (4.61)	76.0 (6.68)	31.0 (0.61)	33.8 (0.71)	19.6 (2.69)	13.2 (1.64)	38.7 (5.55)	20.5 (5.26)
South Carolina	84.2 (0.25)	88.0 (0.28)	78.0 (0.55)	63.5 (2.75)	80.6 (3.07)	75.3 (4.05)	23.8 (0.35)	28.3 (0.44)	12.8 (0.52)	13.9 (1.65)	37.9 (3.06)	20.6 (3.26)
South Dakota	90.4 (0.52)	92.2 (0.52)	42.9 (11.29)	57.2 (7.07)	84.2 (6.33)	85.9 (5.91)	25.7 (0.92)	26.5 (1.01)	‡ (†)	21.4 (6.37)	56.6 (7.71)	16.4 ! (6.37)
Tennessee	84.2 (0.21)	85.6 (0.24)	82.2 (0.58)	61.0 (2.02)	84.6 (2.16)	84.4 (2.24)	24.8 (0.26)	24.8 (0.29)	18.3 (0.72)	12.4 (1.41)	49.1 (3.35)	21.4 (6.37)
Texas	81.1 (0.13)	92.6 (0.14)	86.3 (0.58)	60.3 (0.32)	86.1 (0.56)	89.9 (1.14)	26.5 (0.15)	35.0 (0.23)	20.2 (0.53)	12.0 (0.22)	51.9 (1.04)	33.1 (1.59)
Utah	90.7 (0.28)	94.6 (0.24)	80.9 (4.72)	64.7 (1.95)	87.7 (2.38)	91.8 (2.41)	29.7 (0.47)	32.2 (0.53)	15.4 (3.58)	12.3 (1.17)	41.8 (3.20)	32.9 (5.00)
Vermont	92.0 (0.50)	92.2 (0.52)	‡ (†)	70.7 (1.21)	90.8 (†)	97.2 (1.60)	37.1 (1.20)	38.5 (1.17)	‡ (†)	24.1 ! (1.08)	‡ (†)	18.1 ! (6.05)
Virginia	87.8 (0.16)	90.5 (0.17)	87.3 (1.37)	60.6 (1.20)	84.0 (0.89)	89.8 (1.44)	35.4 (0.27)	33.6 (0.32)	20.0 (1.77)	12.4 (0.79)	43.8 (1.26)	35.3 (3.04)
Washington	90.0 (0.18)	93.8 (0.18)	85.0 (1.26)	60.6 (4.76)	82.5 (4.82)	93.1 (1.13)	31.8 (0.31)	33.6 (0.36)	21.4 (2.95)	12.4 (0.96)	59.8 (1.39)	28.1 (1.94)
West Virginia	83.9 (0.40)	83.9 (0.45)	78.4 (1.26)	‡ (†)	‡ (†)	‡ (†)	18.6 (0.52)	18.5 (0.50)	16.6 (†)	32.6 (5.99)	63.0 (7.87)	12.6 (2.93)
Wisconsin	90.5 (0.22)	92.6 (0.19)	82.6 (†)	64.2 (1.74)	82.1 (2.42)	88.8 (2.35)	26.4 (0.34)	27.5 (0.36)	12.2 (1.27)	12.3 (1.38)	50.5 (3.16)	20.5 (3.38)
Wyoming	92.4 (0.52)	93.4 (0.45)	‡ (†)	81.9 (3.43)	98.8 (0.94)	71.2 (12.71)	24.8 (1.04)	25.9 (1.11)	‡ (†)	13.8 (2.84)	63.8 (10.32)	‡ (†)

See notes at end of table.

Rates of high school completion and bachelor's degree attainment among persons age 25 and over, by race/ethnicity and state: 2011 and 2012—Continued

[Standard errors appear in parentheses]

Year and state	Percent with high school completion or higher						Percent with bachelor's degree or higher					
	Total¹	White	Black	Hispanic	Asian	Two or more races	Total¹	White	Black	Hispanic	Asian	Two or more races
1	2	3	4	5	6	7	8	9	10	11	12	13
United States	86.4 (0.04)	91.5 (0.04)	83.5 (0.12)	64.1 (0.16)	85.8 (0.13)	89.4 (0.25)	29.2 (0.05)	32.6 (0.06)	18.8 (0.13)	13.9 (0.12)	50.9 (0.25)	30.0 (0.36)
2012												
Alabama	83.8 (0.24)	86.1 (0.28)	79.9 (0.67)	60.7 (2.38)	90.6 (1.91)	83.7 (2.71)	23.4 (0.29)	26.1 (0.36)	14.9 (0.54)	14.7 (1.65)	54.4 (4.42)	23.3 (3.04)
Alaska	91.8 (0.56)	95.8 (0.58)	90.3 (5.49)	90.0 (3.88)	79.5 (3.50)	84.4 (4.11)	28.9 (1.22)	35.1 (1.45)	26.7 (6.87)	19.8 (4.72)	19.7 (4.55)	17.5 (4.28)
Arizona	85.8 (0.21)	93.4 (0.18)	89.8 (0.89)	64.9 (0.65)	90.4 (1.05)	91.9 (1.29)	27.5 (0.29)	33.1 (0.38)	22.5 (1.48)	11.7 (0.42)	57.1 (1.73)	30.5 (2.74)
Arkansas	85.1 (0.34)	87.8 (0.32)	80.2 (0.96)	63.5 (3.11)	88.3 (2.35)	88.0 (2.34)	21.2 (0.35)	22.7 (0.41)	14.8 (1.09)	8.1 (1.29)	46.4 (4.72)	28.4 (4.10)
California	81.4 (0.09)	94.1 (0.09)	88.4 (0.40)	59.4 (0.25)	86.1 (0.23)	91.8 (0.46)	31.0 (0.11)	40.3 (0.19)	22.2 (0.47)	11.2 (0.15)	48.9 (0.40)	36.1 (0.89)
Colorado	90.4 (0.20)	95.7 (0.15)	88.8 (1.24)	67.9 (0.97)	83.7 (1.84)	94.6 (1.24)	37.6 (0.34)	43.4 (0.41)	25.8 (2.10)	12.6 (0.57)	48.8 (2.13)	38.9 (2.76)
Connecticut	89.9 (0.26)	93.2 (0.22)	87.5 (0.82)	70.4 (1.22)	89.4 (1.28)	91.3 (2.09)	37.2 (0.35)	41.1 (0.41)	19.2 (1.16)	16.7 (0.99)	62.8 (2.29)	33.4 (4.25)
Delaware	88.3 (0.60)	90.9 (0.71)	85.7 (1.25)	65.7 (3.90)	91.2 (2.74)	90.1 (5.82)	30.2 (0.82)	32.2 (0.99)	20.8 (1.69)	20.0 (2.93)	65.8 (4.64)	22.0 (6.34)
District of Columbia	89.2 (0.46)	99.4 (0.18)	83.6 (0.93)	72.2 (2.58)	93.8 (1.58)	93.7 (3.43)	53.7 (0.76)	89.5 (0.85)	25.4 (1.35)	35.5 (3.13)	81.2 (2.65)	64.1 (8.30)
Florida	86.4 (0.13)	91.3 (0.13)	80.3 (0.30)	76.1 (0.38)	85.5 (0.81)	88.4 (1.16)	26.8 (0.15)	30.0 (0.18)	16.7 (0.39)	21.3 (0.37)	47.3 (1.23)	29.4 (1.85)
Georgia	85.2 (0.21)	88.5 (0.22)	84.1 (0.28)	59.7 (1.39)	88.7 (0.99)	88.8 (1.54)	28.3 (0.23)	32.3 (0.27)	20.5 (0.49)	13.9 (0.80)	53.2 (1.49)	31.4 (2.21)
Hawaii	90.0 (0.43)	97.1 (0.39)	99.1 (0.78)	86.9 (2.00)	86.9 (0.81)	89.8 (1.18)	30.1 (0.58)	41.4 (1.33)	34.3 (4.90)	22.9 (2.38)	30.6 (0.94)	21.7 (1.10)
Idaho	89.8 (0.40)	92.8 (0.35)	‡	58.7 (2.54)	88.3 (3.24)	87.2 (3.22)	25.8 (0.70)	27.5 (0.78)	‡	8.0 (1.10)	42.5 (6.05)	17.1 (4.07)
Illinois	87.7 (0.17)	93.2 (0.14)	84.1 (0.36)	61.4 (0.77)	90.2 (0.67)	92.2 (1.25)	31.5 (0.20)	35.1 (0.14)	19.1 (0.56)	12.6 (0.44)	64.0 (1.10)	38.2 (2.70)
Indiana	87.3 (0.22)	89.1 (0.22)	84.3 (0.74)	61.3 (1.59)	85.8 (1.97)	86.1 (1.98)	23.3 (0.29)	24.1 (0.31)	16.3 (0.89)	12.8 (1.08)	51.6 (2.82)	25.1 (3.20)
Iowa	92.1 (0.27)	93.7 (0.24)	84.1 (2.90)	60.6 (3.12)	85.0 (3.02)	87.2 (4.37)	26.8 (0.37)	27.1 (0.40)	18.1 (2.80)	13.7 (1.66)	56.7 (4.33)	21.8 (4.42)
Kansas	90.1 (0.30)	93.2 (0.23)	88.3 (1.50)	59.5 (2.15)	88.0 (2.22)	91.4 (1.94)	30.2 (0.44)	32.5 (0.50)	17.7 (1.70)	11.7 (1.11)	46.4 (3.81)	22.2 (3.33)
Kentucky	83.5 (0.29)	83.9 (0.32)	84.3 (1.06)	71.0 (2.59)	83.1 (3.15)	78.1 (3.21)	21.5 (0.31)	21.9 (0.33)	13.7 (1.00)	16.9 (2.05)	52.0 (3.63)	20.1 (3.19)
Louisiana	83.2 (0.31)	89.1 (0.31)	76.2 (1.06)	70.3 (2.09)	81.2 (2.08)	83.2 (2.06)	21.5 (0.31)	26.1 (0.41)	13.1 (0.47)	16.7 (1.67)	44.9 (2.82)	24.0 (2.86)
Maine	92.1 (0.38)	92.6 (0.37)	81.2 (6.01)	85.6 (5.21)	60.1 (12.00)	88.7 (4.21)	28.0 (0.71)	28.1 (0.72)	36.0 (8.69)	24.6 (6.77)	26.6 (7.60)	25.8 (5.13)
Maryland	89.2 (0.22)	92.8 (0.21)	88.5 (0.36)	62.8 (1.66)	89.6 (0.74)	93.2 (1.15)	37.0 (0.31)	41.8 (0.40)	25.9 (0.58)	21.5 (1.07)	60.5 (1.29)	38.3 (2.59)
Massachusetts	89.7 (0.17)	92.9 (0.18)	81.6 (1.05)	68.5 (0.98)	84.7 (0.98)	88.6 (1.38)	39.5 (0.30)	42.0 (0.33)	20.3 (1.17)	16.7 (0.88)	57.4 (1.22)	36.3 (2.68)
Michigan	89.6 (0.15)	91.3 (0.15)	84.3 (0.58)	70.3 (1.55)	87.9 (1.26)	86.5 (1.32)	26.3 (0.23)	27.4 (0.25)	16.7 (0.54)	15.3 (1.01)	62.4 (2.22)	24.1 (2.19)
Minnesota	92.4 (0.17)	94.9 (0.16)	80.8 (1.69)	64.5 (2.85)	80.1 (1.89)	90.3 (2.04)	32.7 (0.24)	33.8 (0.43)	19.8 (2.05)	16.7 (1.65)	47.5 (2.55)	23.9 (3.65)
Mississippi	82.5 (0.35)	86.4 (0.44)	76.3 (0.63)	70.1 (2.74)	78.7 (4.71)	85.6 (4.27)	20.6 (0.41)	23.9 (0.59)	14.9 (0.59)	9.4 (1.76)	33.2 (5.31)	26.2 (4.82)
Missouri	87.8 (0.21)	89.3 (0.22)	81.8 (0.85)	69.0 (1.98)	83.1 (1.94)	86.1 (2.00)	26.0 (0.30)	27.1 (0.31)	16.4 (0.83)	18.4 (1.82)	52.4 (3.20)	22.1 (2.26)
Montana	92.8 (0.46)	93.8 (0.41)	81.0 (2.59)	79.8 (4.09)	80.7 (3.28)	91.2 (3.41)	28.5 (0.71)	29.9 (0.73)	20.2 (2.81)	13.8 (3.79)	51.1 (4.47)	23.6 (5.90)
Nebraska	90.8 (0.46)	92.8 (0.25)	84.5 (1.09)	54.2 (3.05)	88.6 (1.15)	88.3 (4.80)	29.7 (0.50)	31.5 (0.60)	16.2 (1.49)	10.3 (1.74)	35.9 (1.67)	25.4 (5.38)
Nevada	85.6 (0.30)	92.8 (0.25)	87.2 (5.43)	63.1 (1.24)	77.0 (6.02)	89.9 (1.81)	22.6 (0.34)	27.1 (0.50)	22.8 ! (7.88)	8.2 (0.55)	44.8 (5.63)	22.9 (3.32)
New Hampshire	92.0 (0.46)	92.6 (0.43)	88.6 (5.43)	85.7 (3.18)	‡	87.3 (5.15)	35.3 (0.74)	35.6 (0.72)	22.8 ! (7.88)	25.1 (4.42)	‡	28.7 (5.22)
New Jersey	88.4 (0.18)	92.9 (0.16)	85.9 (0.54)	71.1 (0.74)	92.5 (0.44)	89.8 (1.86)	36.3 (0.26)	39.9 (0.32)	21.1 (0.61)	16.4 (0.58)	68.2 (1.00)	38.2 (2.77)
New Mexico	84.5 (0.38)	94.3 (0.35)	83.9 (4.25)	74.4 (0.80)	82.0 (3.07)	95.2 (2.44)	26.3 (0.43)	38.9 (0.70)	21.6 (4.42)	13.6 (0.65)	50.3 (4.88)	41.2 (4.74)
New York	85.4 (0.11)	92.3 (0.11)	82.5 (0.34)	65.5 (0.48)	77.6 (0.56)	84.7 (1.15)	33.5 (0.17)	39.2 (0.21)	21.6 (0.46)	16.6 (0.36)	44.8 (0.72)	33.9 (1.57)
North Carolina	85.1 (0.21)	89.0 (0.20)	82.2 (0.40)	54.0 (1.45)	84.6 (1.34)	89.3 (1.64)	27.3 (0.23)	29.3 (0.27)	17.1 (0.52)	11.0 (0.67)	52.8 (1.93)	29.7 (2.47)
North Dakota	91.8 (0.49)	92.5 (0.44)	‡	83.6 (4.67)	‡	100.0 (#)	28.8 (0.91)	29.3 (0.96)	‡	25.6 (7.37)	‡	16.3 ! (7.17)
Ohio	88.9 (0.15)	90.2 (0.15)	82.8 (0.51)	72.2 (1.39)	88.2 (1.35)	86.2 (1.46)	25.2 (0.19)	26.1 (0.20)	15.3 (0.57)	16.0 (1.14)	60.4 (1.86)	22.9 (1.99)
Oklahoma	86.6 (0.30)	89.6 (0.28)	88.4 (1.06)	55.8 (2.07)	83.2 (2.52)	89.1 (1.08)	23.7 (0.38)	26.0 (0.47)	17.7 (1.46)	9.2 (1.09)	45.9 (3.74)	19.7 (1.39)
Oregon	89.9 (0.23)	90.9 (0.22)	90.2 (1.65)	68.3 (1.53)	87.4 (1.30)	90.0 (1.64)	30.1 (0.35)	31.7 (0.37)	21.8 (3.05)	13.8 (1.00)	46.1 (2.34)	26.4 (2.25)
Pennsylvania	88.9 (0.15)	90.9 (0.13)	84.5 (0.55)	61.3 (1.40)	85.0 (3.44)	86.5 (1.91)	28.1 (0.23)	29.3 (0.24)	16.3 (0.65)	14.9 (1.00)	54.6 (1.60)	26.9 (2.17)
Rhode Island	85.8 (0.53)	89.0 (0.48)	82.9 (2.53)	65.6 (2.21)	75.0 (3.44)	80.5 (4.10)	31.2 (0.65)	34.2 (0.79)	18.8 (3.00)	11.2 (1.81)	47.9 (3.72)	21.4 (4.41)
South Carolina	84.9 (0.20)	88.5 (0.23)	78.6 (0.59)	64.9 (2.22)	80.5 (2.23)	88.9 (2.41)	25.3 (0.34)	29.6 (0.23)	14.2 (0.56)	18.7 (1.76)	39.4 (2.84)	27.3 (3.45)
South Dakota	90.6 (0.49)	92.6 (0.53)	‡	69.5 (5.55)	67.5 (9.91)	90.9 (4.99)	26.7 (1.02)	28.2 (1.10)	‡	13.7 (1.33)	54.1 (10.46)	21.3 (9.09)
Tennessee	85.1 (0.23)	86.6 (0.25)	82.8 (0.63)	62.2 (1.81)	84.0 (1.68)	85.5 (1.91)	24.6 (0.21)	26.0 (0.25)	17.3 (0.66)	12.1 (1.22)	48.7 (2.32)	21.8 (2.31)
Texas	81.5 (0.11)	87.4 (0.13)	87.4 (0.31)	61.3 (0.29)	86.5 (0.56)	92.7 (0.90)	26.7 (0.14)	35.6 (0.51)	20.9 (0.47)	14.3 (1.13)	53.9 (0.99)	32.1 (1.60)
Utah	91.3 (0.32)	94.9 (0.22)	89.0 (2.95)	66.4 (1.90)	83.4 (2.28)	92.7 (2.36)	30.7 (0.45)	32.7 (0.51)	35.8 (5.02)	14.3 (1.13)	46.3 (2.66)	34.3 (4.50)
Vermont	92.3 (0.51)	92.7 (0.51)	‡	80.4 (7.20)	75.4 (10.19)	94.7 (3.74)	35.1 (1.07)	35.0 (1.09)	‡	25.4 (7.41)	49.6 (14.61)	38.7 (8.40)
Virginia	88.1 (0.15)	91.1 (0.15)	82.6 (0.42)	70.8 (1.31)	91.2 (0.74)	89.4 (1.38)	35.7 (0.25)	39.0 (0.29)	20.2 (0.48)	24.4 (1.04)	58.5 (1.15)	40.4 (2.02)
Washington	90.6 (0.18)	94.3 (0.14)	90.5 (0.97)	62.5 (1.16)	85.9 (0.73)	91.4 (0.93)	31.8 (0.32)	33.4 (0.37)	19.6 (1.46)	13.6 (0.67)	46.5 (1.03)	29.8 (1.43)
West Virginia	83.9 (0.44)	83.8 (0.45)	86.3 (2.20)	73.9 (5.42)	91.1 (3.73)	87.1 (3.18)	18.2 (0.40)	18.2 (0.41)	11.3 (2.20)	22.8 (4.49)	58.6 (7.85)	12.4 (3.04)
Wisconsin	90.9 (0.21)	93.0 (0.19)	78.0 (1.43)	66.7 (1.95)	85.1 (2.05)	90.4 (2.23)	27.5 (0.36)	28.6 (0.41)	14.1 (1.34)	13.1 (1.39)	45.6 (3.42)	30.3 (4.15)
Wyoming	91.5 (0.58)	93.4 (0.61)	‡	73.4 (3.27)	‡	87.2 (5.16)	25.4 (1.02)	26.5 (1.11)	‡	15.0 (2.57)	‡	20.9 ! (7.07)

†Not applicable.
#Rounds to zero.
!Interpret data with caution. The coefficient of variation (CV) for this estimate is between 30 and 50 percent.
‡Reporting standards not met. Either there are too few cases for a reliable estimate or the coefficient of variation (CV) is 50 percent or greater.

¹Total includes racial/ethnic groups not shown separately.
NOTE: Race categories exclude persons of Hispanic ethnicity.
SOURCE: U.S. Department of Commerce, Census Bureau, 2011 and 2012 American Community Survey (ACS) 1-Year Public Use Microdata Sample (PUMS) data. (This table was prepared January 2014.)

Rates of high school completion and bachelor's degree attainment among persons age 25 and over, by sex and state: 2011 and 2012

[Standard errors appear in parentheses]

State	2011 Percent with high school completion or higher — Total	Male	Female	2011 Percent with bachelor's or higher degree — Total	Male	Female	2012 Percent with high school completion or higher — Total	Male	Female	2012 Percent with bachelor's or higher degree — Total	Male	Female
	2	3	4	5	6	7	8	9	10	11	12	13
United States	85.9 (0.04)	85.2 (0.04)	86.5 (0.04)	28.6 (0.06)	28.8 (0.07)	28.4 (0.07)	86.4 (0.04)	85.7 (0.05)	87.0 (0.04)	29.2 (0.05)	29.2 (0.06)	29.2 (0.06)
Alabama	82.7 (0.37)	81.2 (0.48)	84.1 (0.40)	22.5 (0.32)	22.5 (0.40)	22.5 (0.40)	83.8 (0.24)	82.9 (0.37)	84.6 (0.32)	23.4 (0.29)	23.3 (0.36)	23.4 (0.39)
Alaska	92.8 (0.50)	93.7 (0.63)	91.9 (0.68)	25.8 (1.24)	22.2 (1.37)	29.6 (1.61)	91.8 (0.56)	92.2 (0.57)	91.4 (0.92)	28.9 (1.22)	25.6 (1.48)	32.4 (1.57)
Arizona	85.7 (0.23)	85.1 (0.31)	86.3 (0.31)	26.4 (0.26)	27.4 (0.37)	25.4 (0.30)	85.8 (0.21)	85.3 (0.29)	86.2 (0.25)	27.5 (0.29)	28.5 (0.37)	26.5 (0.36)
Arkansas	83.7 (0.43)	82.9 (0.56)	84.4 (0.48)	20.5 (0.38)	20.5 (0.49)	20.2 (0.48)	85.1 (0.34)	84.2 (0.48)	86.0 (0.42)	21.2 (0.35)	20.6 (0.51)	21.8 (0.44)
California	81.1 (0.10)	80.9 (0.12)	81.3 (0.11)	30.3 (0.13)	30.7 (0.18)	30.0 (0.15)	81.4 (0.09)	81.1 (0.13)	81.7 (0.12)	31.0 (0.11)	31.4 (0.16)	30.6 (0.13)
Colorado	90.2 (0.21)	89.5 (0.29)	91.0 (0.28)	36.8 (0.37)	37.2 (0.45)	36.5 (0.47)	90.4 (0.20)	89.7 (0.30)	91.1 (0.23)	37.7 (0.34)	37.7 (0.43)	37.5 (0.43)
Connecticut	89.0 (0.27)	88.4 (0.39)	89.5 (0.30)	36.2 (0.42)	36.6 (0.50)	35.8 (0.54)	89.9 (0.26)	89.3 (0.36)	90.4 (0.31)	37.2 (0.35)	37.8 (0.51)	36.7 (0.39)
Delaware	87.3 (0.52)	86.1 (0.75)	88.5 (0.57)	28.2 (0.68)	28.2 (0.92)	28.2 (0.97)	88.3 (0.60)	87.1 (0.81)	89.3 (0.67)	30.2 (0.82)	29.0 (1.00)	31.3 (1.06)
District of Columbia	87.1 (0.73)	85.9 (0.99)	88.1 (0.90)	52.5 (0.68)	52.5 (1.12)	52.5 (0.95)	88.9 (0.46)	88.9 (0.68)	89.5 (0.65)	53.7 (0.76)	55.5 (1.07)	52.1 (0.84)
Florida	85.9 (0.12)	84.9 (0.17)	86.9 (0.12)	25.9 (0.16)	26.7 (0.21)	25.1 (0.21)	86.4 (0.13)	85.5 (0.20)	87.3 (0.14)	26.8 (0.15)	27.8 (0.21)	25.9 (0.19)
Georgia	84.3 (0.19)	83.2 (0.25)	85.2 (0.26)	27.6 (0.24)	27.7 (0.28)	27.6 (0.37)	85.2 (0.21)	84.0 (0.30)	86.2 (0.23)	28.3 (0.23)	27.9 (0.27)	28.7 (0.30)
Hawaii	90.5 (0.40)	90.6 (0.52)	90.4 (0.55)	29.7 (0.55)	29.1 (0.79)	30.3 (0.74)	90.0 (0.43)	90.8 (0.54)	89.2 (0.59)	30.1 (0.58)	27.9 (0.70)	32.2 (0.82)
Idaho	88.7 (0.35)	87.9 (0.49)	89.4 (0.50)	25.6 (0.68)	26.5 (0.85)	24.6 (0.93)	89.8 (0.40)	89.1 (0.54)	90.4 (0.55)	25.8 (0.70)	26.5 (0.80)	25.1 (0.95)
Illinois	87.3 (0.14)	86.9 (0.20)	87.7 (0.18)	31.0 (0.22)	31.1 (0.27)	30.8 (0.27)	87.7 (0.17)	86.9 (0.23)	88.4 (0.21)	31.5 (0.20)	31.2 (0.26)	31.8 (0.25)
Indiana	87.2 (0.20)	86.5 (0.30)	87.8 (0.27)	22.8 (0.27)	23.3 (0.34)	22.3 (0.35)	87.3 (0.22)	86.7 (0.31)	87.9 (0.26)	23.3 (0.29)	23.3 (0.37)	23.4 (0.32)
Iowa	91.0 (0.28)	90.2 (0.33)	91.7 (0.35)	25.8 (0.47)	25.1 (0.63)	26.4 (0.56)	92.1 (0.27)	91.6 (0.37)	92.5 (0.32)	26.8 (0.37)	26.5 (0.50)	27.1 (0.48)
Kansas	89.6 (0.32)	88.6 (0.44)	90.4 (0.41)	30.5 (0.51)	30.3 (0.60)	30.6 (0.63)	90.1 (0.30)	89.3 (0.44)	90.9 (0.34)	30.2 (0.44)	29.6 (0.63)	30.7 (0.47)
Kentucky	83.1 (0.31)	82.1 (0.41)	84.1 (0.38)	20.7 (0.33)	20.6 (0.41)	20.9 (0.42)	83.5 (0.29)	82.3 (0.40)	84.6 (0.36)	21.5 (0.31)	21.0 (0.36)	22.1 (0.47)
Louisiana	82.6 (0.29)	80.6 (0.37)	84.4 (0.35)	21.1 (0.36)	20.3 (0.43)	21.8 (0.42)	83.2 (0.31)	81.3 (0.41)	85.0 (0.36)	21.3 (0.31)	21.3 (0.51)	23.0 (0.36)
Maine	90.8 (0.40)	89.6 (0.62)	91.9 (0.49)	28.6 (0.70)	27.5 (0.84)	29.5 (0.85)	92.1 (0.38)	90.9 (0.56)	93.3 (0.44)	28.0 (0.71)	27.0 (0.91)	29.0 (0.77)
Maryland	89.0 (0.21)	88.3 (0.28)	89.7 (0.23)	37.0 (0.28)	36.8 (0.39)	37.2 (0.35)	89.2 (0.22)	88.2 (0.28)	90.1 (0.25)	37.0 (0.31)	36.9 (0.41)	37.0 (0.38)
Massachusetts	89.1 (0.20)	88.8 (0.23)	89.3 (0.26)	39.2 (0.32)	39.8 (0.42)	38.7 (0.34)	89.7 (0.17)	89.2 (0.24)	90.2 (0.20)	39.5 (0.30)	39.8 (0.37)	39.2 (0.36)
Michigan	88.7 (0.17)	87.9 (0.22)	89.4 (0.23)	25.8 (0.22)	25.9 (0.29)	25.6 (0.29)	89.6 (0.17)	89.2 (0.21)	89.9 (0.20)	26.3 (0.23)	26.4 (0.28)	26.2 (0.26)
Minnesota	92.1 (0.16)	91.6 (0.25)	92.6 (0.21)	32.6 (0.40)	32.0 (0.56)	33.3 (0.44)	92.4 (0.19)	91.8 (0.26)	92.9 (0.23)	32.7 (0.42)	31.9 (0.54)	33.5 (0.51)
Mississippi	80.8 (0.37)	78.3 (0.55)	83.1 (0.42)	20.1 (0.47)	19.0 (0.56)	21.1 (0.54)	82.5 (0.35)	80.6 (0.54)	84.2 (0.37)	20.6 (0.41)	18.9 (0.49)	22.1 (0.52)
Missouri	87.7 (0.21)	87.4 (0.31)	88.0 (0.26)	26.4 (0.34)	26.9 (0.42)	25.9 (0.42)	87.8 (0.21)	87.3 (0.28)	88.2 (0.27)	26.0 (0.30)	25.4 (0.37)	26.6 (0.39)
Montana	92.5 (0.47)	91.9 (0.64)	93.2 (0.62)	29.4 (0.82)	29.5 (0.99)	29.3 (0.98)	92.8 (0.46)	92.3 (0.59)	93.3 (0.57)	29.4 (0.71)	27.6 (1.01)	29.4 (0.99)
Nebraska	91.1 (0.32)	90.5 (0.45)	91.6 (0.37)	28.1 (0.54)	28.1 (0.74)	28.2 (0.77)	90.8 (0.29)	90.4 (0.47)	91.1 (0.38)	29.7 (0.50)	29.2 (0.68)	30.2 (0.75)
Nevada	84.0 (0.37)	83.6 (0.49)	84.4 (0.45)	22.4 (0.43)	22.2 (0.62)	22.6 (0.52)	85.6 (0.30)	85.6 (0.44)	85.6 (0.38)	22.6 (0.34)	23.0 (0.44)	22.3 (0.48)
New Hampshire	91.8 (0.42)	90.9 (0.58)	92.6 (0.45)	33.5 (0.70)	33.0 (0.84)	33.9 (0.82)	92.0 (0.46)	91.0 (0.54)	92.9 (0.57)	35.3 (0.74)	34.5 (0.83)	36.1 (0.95)
New Jersey	88.0 (0.15)	87.7 (0.22)	88.2 (0.19)	35.2 (0.24)	36.4 (0.32)	34.2 (0.26)	88.4 (0.18)	88.1 (0.23)	88.6 (0.20)	36.3 (0.26)	36.8 (0.34)	35.8 (0.28)
New Mexico	83.0 (0.42)	81.7 (0.53)	84.2 (0.55)	25.6 (0.49)	25.8 (0.60)	25.3 (0.60)	84.5 (0.38)	83.5 (0.55)	85.5 (0.48)	26.2 (0.43)	26.0 (0.63)	26.4 (0.55)
New York	85.1 (0.12)	84.8 (0.18)	85.3 (0.14)	33.1 (0.15)	32.9 (0.22)	33.3 (0.16)	84.9 (0.11)	84.9 (0.17)	85.8 (0.13)	33.5 (0.17)	32.9 (0.28)	34.0 (0.23)
North Carolina	84.8 (0.20)	83.3 (0.25)	86.3 (0.25)	26.7 (0.26)	26.3 (0.33)	27.1 (0.32)	85.1 (0.21)	83.2 (0.31)	86.7 (0.20)	27.3 (0.23)	26.7 (0.28)	27.9 (0.29)
North Dakota	90.8 (0.49)	90.5 (0.72)	91.1 (0.71)	26.2 (0.97)	23.7 (1.18)	28.7 (1.29)	91.8 (0.49)	91.2 (0.57)	92.3 (0.69)	28.8 (0.91)	27.9 (1.29)	29.7 (1.14)
Ohio	88.4 (0.14)	87.8 (0.21)	88.9 (0.19)	24.8 (0.21)	25.5 (0.29)	24.2 (0.29)	88.9 (0.15)	88.3 (0.18)	89.4 (0.19)	25.5 (0.19)	25.7 (0.23)	24.9 (0.26)
Oklahoma	86.1 (0.33)	85.3 (0.44)	86.8 (0.40)	23.8 (0.42)	23.9 (0.52)	23.9 (0.54)	86.6 (0.30)	86.1 (0.43)	87.1 (0.36)	23.7 (0.38)	23.3 (0.48)	24.0 (0.48)
Oregon	89.3 (0.27)	88.5 (0.39)	90.1 (0.33)	29.2 (0.33)	29.6 (0.49)	28.8 (0.42)	90.1 (0.23)	89.1 (0.36)	91.1 (0.26)	30.2 (0.35)	30.3 (0.43)	30.0 (0.40)
Pennsylvania	88.7 (0.17)	88.5 (0.22)	88.9 (0.19)	27.1 (0.21)	27.3 (0.27)	26.8 (0.25)	88.9 (0.15)	88.6 (0.20)	89.2 (0.18)	28.1 (0.23)	28.5 (0.30)	27.7 (0.26)
Rhode Island	84.5 (0.52)	83.3 (0.69)	85.6 (0.67)	31.0 (0.61)	31.8 (0.81)	30.3 (0.78)	85.4 (0.53)	85.4 (0.76)	86.2 (0.57)	31.2 (0.65)	31.7 (0.90)	30.8 (0.71)
South Carolina	84.2 (0.25)	82.9 (0.40)	85.4 (0.31)	23.8 (0.35)	23.7 (0.43)	23.8 (0.40)	84.9 (0.20)	83.8 (0.31)	85.8 (0.29)	25.3 (0.34)	25.4 (0.47)	25.3 (0.38)
South Dakota	90.4 (0.52)	89.5 (0.69)	91.3 (0.67)	25.7 (0.92)	25.1 (1.09)	26.3 (1.25)	90.6 (0.49)	90.0 (0.74)	91.2 (0.70)	26.7 (1.02)	26.1 (1.33)	27.2 (1.16)
Tennessee	84.2 (0.21)	83.0 (0.30)	85.3 (0.26)	23.7 (0.26)	23.5 (0.36)	23.5 (0.30)	85.1 (0.23)	84.2 (0.30)	85.9 (0.28)	24.6 (0.21)	24.3 (0.31)	24.8 (0.29)
Texas	81.1 (0.13)	80.5 (0.17)	81.6 (0.17)	26.5 (0.15)	26.9 (0.20)	26.1 (0.18)	81.5 (0.11)	81.5 (0.18)	82.2 (0.14)	26.9 (0.14)	27.0 (0.18)	26.9 (0.19)
Utah	90.7 (0.28)	90.0 (0.39)	91.4 (0.31)	29.7 (0.47)	32.7 (0.64)	26.8 (0.60)	91.3 (0.32)	91.0 (0.41)	91.6 (0.42)	30.7 (0.45)	33.0 (0.53)	28.5 (0.64)
Vermont	92.0 (0.50)	90.6 (0.77)	93.3 (0.59)	37.0 (1.20)	33.0 (1.46)	40.9 (1.52)	93.3 (0.51)	90.9 (0.68)	93.6 (0.63)	35.1 (1.07)	32.9 (1.14)	37.3 (1.46)
Virginia	87.8 (0.16)	87.0 (0.23)	88.5 (0.21)	35.4 (0.27)	36.0 (0.32)	34.7 (0.35)	87.4 (0.15)	87.4 (0.23)	88.7 (0.21)	35.7 (0.25)	36.2 (0.38)	35.4 (0.31)
Washington	90.0 (0.18)	89.7 (0.26)	90.3 (0.23)	31.8 (0.31)	32.9 (0.40)	30.6 (0.37)	90.6 (0.18)	90.0 (0.25)	91.1 (0.21)	31.8 (0.32)	32.4 (0.38)	31.3 (0.39)
West Virginia	83.9 (0.42)	82.7 (0.59)	85.0 (0.52)	18.6 (0.52)	18.7 (0.69)	18.6 (0.57)	83.9 (0.44)	83.0 (0.67)	84.8 (0.52)	18.2 (0.40)	17.7 (0.52)	18.7 (0.52)
Wisconsin	90.5 (0.22)	89.5 (0.27)	91.4 (0.29)	26.4 (0.34)	27.3 (0.43)	25.5 (0.45)	90.0 (0.21)	90.0 (0.29)	91.7 (0.23)	27.5 (0.36)	26.8 (0.42)	28.1 (0.46)
Wyoming	92.4 (0.52)	91.3 (0.78)	93.5 (0.64)	24.8 (1.04)	23.1 (1.35)	26.5 (1.23)	91.5 (0.58)	91.5 (0.75)	91.6 (0.84)	25.4 (1.02)	25.0 (1.23)	25.8 (1.30)

NOTE: Detail may not sum to totals because of rounding.

SOURCE: U.S. Department of Commerce, Census Bureau, 2011 and 2012 American Community Survey (ACS) 1-Year Public Use Microdata Sample (PUMS) data. (This table was prepared January 2014.)

Educational Attainment

Number of persons age 25 and over in metropolitan areas with populations greater than 1 million and rates of high school completion and bachelor's degree attainment among persons in this age group, by sex: 2013

[Standard errors appear in parentheses]

Metropolitan area	Number of persons 25 years old and over (in thousands) — Total	Males	Females	Percent with high school completion or higher — Total	Male	Female	Percent with bachelor's or higher degree — Total	Male	Female
1	2	3	4	5	6	7	8	9	10
Atlanta-Sandy Springs-Marietta, GA CBSA	3,516 (205.4)	1,648 (101.9)	1,867 (111.2)	90.2 (1.43)	89.0 (1.92)	91.3 (1.40)	39.4 (2.47)	39.0 (3.11)	39.8 (2.31)
Austin-Round Rock, TX CBSA	1,282 (88.0)	666 (44.4)	616 (51.7)	90.6 (2.12)	89.2 (2.99)	92.1 (1.81)	49.0 (3.52)	49.5 (3.97)	48.5 (4.16)
Birmingham-Hoover, AL CBSA	818 (57.2)	396 (30.1)	422 (31.0)	87.9 (2.21)	85.7 (2.69)	90.0 (2.66)	27.7 (4.13)	27.6 (4.57)	27.7 (4.61)
Boston-Worcester-Manchester, MA-NH-CT-ME CSA	3,885 (101.4)	1,836 (58.1)	2,049 (52.5)	91.9 (1.07)	92.8 (1.08)	91.0 (1.34)	45.7 (2.01)	47.3 (2.28)	44.2 (2.17)
Buffalo-Niagara Falls, NY CBSA	800 (49.8)	396 (30.6)	404 (26.0)	89.8 (2.29)	90.9 (3.03)	88.7 (3.00)	26.5 (3.91)	28.1 (4.79)	24.9 (4.64)
Charlotte-Gastonia-Concord, NC-SC CBSA	1,143 (70.7)	544 (42.5)	600 (37.0)	86.9 (2.69)	84.6 (3.44)	89.0 (2.23)	33.8 (3.98)	36.7 (4.93)	31.2 (3.72)
Chicago-Naperville-Michigan City, IL-IN-WI CSA	6,339 (253.9)	3,045 (122.1)	3,295 (141.9)	90.7 (0.76)	90.2 (0.97)	91.2 (0.78)	39.0 (1.56)	40.3 (1.80)	37.9 (1.64)
Cincinnati-Middletown, OH-KY-IN CBSA[1]	1,313 (71.3)	634 (39.4)	679 (38.9)	88.9 (1.72)	88.6 (2.10)	89.2 (2.09)	27.1 (2.56)	29.5 (2.98)	24.9 (2.84)
Cleveland-Akron-Elyria, OH CSA	1,832 (78.1)	873 (47.7)	958 (43.0)	90.9 (1.47)	88.7 (2.38)	93.0 (1.29)	29.7 (2.67)	31.1 (3.34)	28.4 (2.80)
Columbus, OH CSA	1,133 (64.4)	551 (34.8)	583 (39.3)	93.2 (1.42)	92.8 (2.01)	93.6 (1.48)	33.0 (3.56)	34.8 (4.30)	31.3 (4.01)
Dallas-Fort Worth-Arlington, TX CBSA	4,482 (164.3)	2,268 (96.5)	2,214 (82.9)	83.4 (1.43)	82.2 (1.75)	84.7 (1.46)	33.4 (1.78)	33.4 (2.14)	33.4 (2.02)
Denver-Aurora-Boulder, CO CSA	1,968 (47.7)	971 (33.6)	997 (23.6)	91.3 (0.98)	91.1 (1.10)	91.5 (1.23)	48.5 (1.84)	49.9 (2.16)	47.2 (2.12)
Detroit-Warren-Flint, MI CSA	3,592 (188.3)	1,718 (96.3)	1,874 (99.0)	91.9 (0.97)	92.2 (1.49)	91.5 (1.08)	32.2 (1.89)	31.0 (2.21)	33.4 (2.19)
Fresno-Madera, CA CSA	734 (183.2)	361 (84.6)	372 (100.0)	77.6 (2.49)	75.7 (3.10)	79.4 (2.95)	24.9 (3.92)	22.2 (3.97)	27.5 (5.29)
Grand Rapids-Muskegon-Holland, MI CSA	911 (164.5)	428 (79.8)	483 (86.5)	95.3 (1.09)	94.4 (1.84)	96.2 (1.12)	29.7 (3.92)	28.9 (3.99)	30.4 (4.77)
Greensboro-Winston-Salem-High Point, NC CSA	1,015 (73.6)	478 (40.4)	537 (42.3)	87.8 (2.76)	87.6 (3.78)	88.0 (2.74)	28.9 (3.65)	24.9 (3.66)	32.5 (4.54)
Hartford-West Hartford, CT CBSA	753 (35.2)	351 (17.9)	402 (20.8)	90.5 (1.29)	88.7 (1.73)	92.0 (1.48)	40.6 (3.01)	38.8 (3.32)	42.2 (3.38)
Houston-Baytown-Sugarland, TX CBSA	4,014 (157.4)	1,995 (87.0)	2,019 (84.5)	83.5 (1.42)	82.8 (1.75)	84.2 (1.50)	29.6 (1.73)	31.4 (2.00)	27.8 (1.85)
Indianapolis-Anderson-Columbus, IN CSA	1,254 (116.1)	600 (53.5)	654 (67.2)	92.8 (1.37)	91.6 (1.88)	94.0 (1.45)	34.5 (3.73)	36.6 (4.53)	32.7 (3.74)
Jacksonville, FL CBSA	881 (61.5)	396 (33.7)	485 (36.5)	93.2 (1.47)	94.1 (2.11)	92.6 (1.78)	31.3 (3.27)	30.0 (4.78)	32.4 (3.54)
Kansas City, MO-KS CSBA	1,330 (62.6)	639 (34.3)	691 (35.3)	92.4 (1.53)	92.2 (1.88)	92.6 (1.54)	39.0 (2.67)	39.1 (3.11)	39.1 (2.90)
Las Vegas-Paradise, NV CBSA	1,282 (33.2)	628 (22.1)	654 (16.1)	88.9 (1.12)	88.3 (1.41)	89.4 (1.26)	22.5 (1.51)	23.0 (1.82)	22.0 (1.82)
Los Angeles-Long Beach-Riverside, CA CSA	11,805 (173.3)	5,719 (106.7)	6,086 (90.2)	80.6 (0.88)	80.3 (1.09)	80.9 (0.87)	30.8 (1.03)	31.7 (1.23)	30.0 (1.13)
Louisville, KY-IN CBSA	851 (84.5)	413 (52.0)	438 (37.3)	92.5 (0.69)	90.7 (0.83)	93.4 (0.86)	28.4 (3.41)	29.9 (4.70)	26.9 (3.89)
Memphis, TN-MS-AR CBSA[1]	847 (67.6)	394 (35.1)	453 (36.2)	87.2 (2.71)	86.3 (3.60)	88.0 (3.06)	28.3 (3.30)	24.2 (4.05)	31.9 (4.13)
Miami-Fort Lauderdale-Miami Beach, FL CBSA	4,055 (140.0)	1,875 (77.6)	2,180 (74.5)	87.8 (1.25)	86.9 (1.58)	88.6 (1.31)	31.2 (1.70)	32.0 (2.02)	30.5 (1.84)
Milwaukee-Racine-Waukesha, WI CSA	1,177 (148.8)	565 (78.9)	612 (72.5)	91.4 (1.53)	90.2 (2.28)	92.6 (1.52)	32.7 (2.90)	27.3 (3.18)	37.6 (3.12)
Minneapolis-St. Paul-St. Cloud, MN-WI CSA[1]	2,337 (49.0)	1,158 (35.9)	1,179 (21.6)	93.1 (0.72)	93.4 (0.89)	92.9 (0.88)	40.1 (1.69)	38.5 (1.89)	41.6 (2.05)
Nashville-Davidson-Murfreesboro, TN CBSA	1,188 (211.4)	595 (116.0)	593 (97.4)	88.5 (2.12)	90.1 (2.69)	87.0 (2.22)	39.5 (3.18)	42.4 (4.01)	36.7 (4.38)
New Orleans-Metairie-Kenner, LA CBSA	736 (47.0)	338 (27.7)	397 (29.4)	89.1 (1.97)	90.8 (2.65)	87.7 (2.21)	31.0 (3.38)	33.6 (5.13)	28.8 (3.50)
New York-Newark, NY-NJ-PA CSA	14,708 (208.1)	6,871 (124.1)	7,837 (106.5)	87.5 (0.56)	87.5 (0.68)	87.6 (0.68)	40.1 (0.91)	40.9 (1.19)	39.4 (0.95)
Oklahoma City, OK CBSA	904 (41.4)	407 (26.5)	497 (21.5)	91.2 (1.74)	90.2 (2.08)	92.1 (2.39)	26.5 (2.59)	27.6 (3.41)	25.5 (2.54)
Orlando, FL CBSA	1,437 (88.6)	702 (47.1)	735 (48.0)	90.7 (1.27)	88.8 (1.98)	92.5 (1.31)	34.9 (2.69)	34.1 (3.10)	35.8 (3.21)
Philadelphia-Camden-Vineland, PA-NJ-DE-MD CSA	4,132 (110.2)	1,859 (62.5)	2,273 (65.1)	92.5 (0.69)	91.5 (0.83)	93.4 (0.86)	35.8 (1.71)	37.8 (2.00)	34.1 (1.87)
Phoenix-Mesa-Scottsdale, AZ CBSA	2,840 (244.2)	1,435 (126.1)	1,405 (121.9)	85.3 (1.58)	85.1 (2.07)	85.5 (1.74)	32.1 (2.78)	34.2 (3.02)	30.0 (3.15)
Pittsburgh-New Castle, PA CSA	1,644 (80.8)	786 (44.1)	857 (47.6)	92.5 (1.14)	92.0 (1.54)	92.8 (1.47)	35.0 (2.62)	38.0 (3.15)	32.2 (2.94)
Portland-Vancouver-Beaverton, OR-WA CSA	1,455 (64.4)	693 (39.7)	762 (32.1)	93.4 (1.15)	92.8 (1.43)	93.9 (1.16)	34.6 (2.30)	34.6 (3.13)	34.6 (2.58)
Providence-Fall River-Warwick, RI-MA CBSA	876 (47.1)	418 (24.9)	459 (23.8)	87.9 (1.29)	88.4 (1.29)	87.5 (1.82)	37.3 (2.50)	40.8 (3.73)	34.2 (1.91)
Raleigh-Durham-Cary, NC CSA	1,259 (64.6)	613 (39.2)	646 (37.5)	88.5 (2.03)	88.3 (2.72)	89.1 (2.09)	42.7 (2.99)	43.7 (3.65)	41.7 (3.09)
Richmond, VA CBSA	985 (71.9)	466 (35.1)	519 (41.3)	88.5 (2.50)	88.0 (2.28)	89.0 (3.42)	33.3 (3.31)	31.3 (4.21)	35.1 (3.88)
Rochester, NY CBSA	698 (47.9)	336 (23.4)	361 (29.7)	92.3 (2.25)	92.4 (2.98)	92.2 (2.72)	39.7 (3.94)	40.7 (5.04)	38.8 (4.53)
Sacramento-Arden-Arcade-Roseville, CA CBSA	1,478 (79.7)	713 (45.5)	765 (42.8)	87.8 (2.13)	87.8 (2.78)	87.9 (2.17)	33.7 (3.32)	35.5 (4.26)	32.0 (3.03)
Salt Lake City-Ogden-Clearfield, UT CSA	1,029 (39.8)	504 (24.1)	525 (20.7)	92.7 (1.15)	92.1 (1.58)	93.2 (1.17)	33.7 (2.29)	35.3 (2.44)	32.2 (2.78)
San Antonio, TX CBSA	1,432 (82.6)	678 (47.3)	754 (44.5)	80.7 (2.57)	79.7 (3.13)	81.7 (2.57)	25.5 (2.79)	26.3 (3.33)	24.7 (3.01)
San Diego-Carlsbad-San Marcos, CA CBSA	2,004 (79.6)	961 (44.8)	1,043 (45.5)	89.4 (1.46)	91.1 (1.63)	87.8 (1.69)	41.1 (2.37)	43.4 (2.95)	38.9 (2.71)
San Jose-San Francisco-Oakland, CA CSA	5,716 (197.2)	2,880 (108.3)	2,836 (103.2)	88.5 (1.06)	87.3 (1.38)	89.7 (0.98)	46.2 (1.57)	47.3 (1.94)	45.0 (1.61)
Seattle-Tacoma-Olympia, WA CSA	2,939 (76.1)	1,417 (47.9)	1,521 (41.7)	94.0 (0.69)	94.1 (0.91)	93.9 (0.85)	41.7 (2.00)	41.2 (2.35)	42.2 (2.37)
St. Louis, MO-IL CBSA	1,890 (79.7)	898 (44.4)	992 (40.0)	91.6 (1.31)	92.2 (1.70)	91.0 (1.59)	34.9 (2.43)	35.9 (3.01)	33.9 (2.53)
Tampa-St. Petersburg-Clearwater, FL CBSA	2,242 (223.0)	1,066 (118.5)	1,176 (109.3)	91.7 (1.02)	91.6 (1.45)	91.8 (1.46)	28.1 (2.05)	26.3 (2.67)	30.1 (2.22)
Virginia Beach-Norfolk-Newport News, VA-NC CBSA[1]	1,052 (65.9)	476 (38.5)	576 (51.7)	95.1 (1.05)	95.1 (1.34)	95.9 (1.11)	30.5 (2.84)	32.3 (4.09)	29.0 (2.83)
Washington-Baltimore-Northern Virginia, DC-MD-VA-WV CSA[1]	5,854 (99.7)	2,774 (60.2)	3,080 (51.7)	91.6 (0.64)	90.5 (0.82)	92.6 (0.66)	49.2 (1.39)	50.3 (1.59)	48.2 (1.52)

[1]Information on metropolitan status was suppressed for a small portion of sample observations. As a result, population estimates for these areas may be slightly underestimated.

NOTE: CSA = Combined Statistical Area; CBSA = Core Based Statistical Area. Detail may not sum to totals because of rounding. Standard errors were computed using replicate weights.

SOURCE: U.S. Department of Commerce, Census Bureau, Current Population Survey (CPS), March 2013. (This table was prepared February 2014.)

Average National Assessment of Educational Progress (NAEP) reading scale score, by grade and selected student and school characteristics: Selected years, 1992 through 2013

[Standard errors appear in parentheses]

Grade and selected student or school characteristic	1992[1]	1994[1]	1998	2000	2002	2003	2005	2007	2009	2011	2013
1	2	3	4	5	6	7	8	9	10	11	12
4th grade, all students	217 (0.9)	214 (1.0)	215 (1.1)	213 (1.3)	219 (0.4)	218 (0.3)	219 (0.2)	221 (0.3)	221 (0.3)	221 (0.3)	222 (0.3)
Sex											
Male	213 (1.2)	209 (1.3)	212 (1.3)	208 (1.3)	215 (0.4)	215 (0.3)	216 (0.2)	218 (0.3)	218 (0.3)	218 (0.3)	219 (0.3)
Female	221 (1.0)	220 (1.1)	217 (1.3)	219 (1.4)	222 (0.5)	222 (0.3)	222 (0.3)	224 (0.3)	224 (0.3)	225 (0.3)	225 (0.3)
Gap between female and male score	8 (1.6)	10 (1.7)	5 (1.8)	11 (1.9)	6 (0.6)	7 (0.4)	6 (0.4)	7 (0.4)	7 (0.4)	7 (0.5)	7 (0.5)
Race/ethnicity											
White	224 (1.2)	224 (1.3)	225 (1.0)	224 (1.1)	229 (0.3)	229 (0.2)	229 (0.2)	231 (0.2)	230 (0.3)	231 (0.2)	232 (0.3)
Black	192 (1.7)	185 (1.8)	193 (1.9)	190 (1.8)	199 (0.5)	198 (0.4)	200 (0.3)	203 (0.4)	205 (0.5)	205 (0.5)	206 (0.5)
Hispanic	197 (2.6)	188 (3.4)	193 (3.2)	190 (2.9)	201 (1.3)	200 (0.6)	203 (0.5)	205 (0.5)	205 (0.5)	206 (0.5)	207 (0.5)
Asian/Pacific Islander	216 (2.9)	220 (3.8)	215 (5.6)	225 (5.2)	224 (1.6)	226 (1.2)	229 (0.7)	232 (1.0)	235 (1.0)	235 (1.2)	235 (1.1)
American Indian/Alaska Native	‡ (†)	211 (6.6)	‡ (†)	214 (6.0)	207 (2.0)	202 (1.4)	204 (1.3)	203 (1.2)	204 (1.3)	202 (1.3)	205 (1.3)
Gap between White and Black score	32 (2.1)	38 (2.2)	32 (2.2)	34 (2.1)	30 (0.6)	31 (0.5)	29 (0.4)	27 (0.5)	26 (0.6)	25 (0.5)	26 (0.6)
Gap between White and Hispanic score	27 (2.9)	35 (3.6)	32 (3.3)	35 (3.1)	28 (1.4)	28 (0.6)	26 (0.5)	26 (0.5)	25 (0.6)	24 (0.6)	25 (0.6)
Percentage of students in school eligible for free or reduced-price lunch											
0–25 percent (low poverty)	— (†)	— (†)	231 (1.4)	231 (1.5)	233 (0.4)	233 (0.4)	234 (0.3)	235 (0.4)	237 (0.4)	238 (0.5)	240 (0.4)
26–50 percent	— (†)	— (†)	218 (1.6)	218 (1.3)	221 (0.5)	221 (0.5)	221 (0.3)	223 (0.4)	223 (0.5)	226 (0.5)	227 (0.5)
51–75 percent	— (†)	— (†)	205 (1.8)	205 (2.1)	210 (0.7)	211 (0.5)	211 (0.4)	212 (0.4)	215 (0.5)	217 (0.4)	218 (0.4)
76–100 percent (high poverty)	— (†)	— (†)	187 (3.1)	184 (2.8)	196 (0.7)	194 (0.5)	197 (0.4)	200 (0.5)	202 (0.5)	203 (0.5)	203 (0.4)
Gap between low-poverty and high-poverty score	— (†)	— (†)	44 (3.4)	48 (3.2)	37 (0.9)	39 (0.7)	37 (0.5)	35 (0.7)	35 (0.6)	35 (0.7)	37 (0.6)
English language learner (ELL) status											
ELL	‡ (†)	‡ (†)	174 (5.2)	167 (5.2)	183 (2.1)	186 (0.8)	187 (0.5)	188 (0.6)	188 (0.8)	188 (0.8)	187 (0.7)
Non-ELL	‡ (†)	‡ (†)	217 (1.0)	216 (1.1)	221 (0.3)	221 (0.3)	222 (0.2)	224 (0.3)	224 (0.3)	225 (0.3)	226 (0.3)
Gap between non-ELL and ELL score	‡ (†)	‡ (†)	43 (5.3)	49 (5.3)	38 (2.1)	35 (0.8)	35 (0.6)	36 (0.6)	36 (0.8)	36 (0.9)	38 (0.7)
8th grade, all students	260 (0.9)	260 (0.8)	263 (0.8)	— (†)	264 (0.4)	263 (0.3)	262 (0.2)	263 (0.2)	264 (0.3)	265 (0.2)	268 (0.3)
Sex											
Male	254 (1.1)	252 (1.0)	256 (1.0)	— (†)	260 (0.5)	258 (0.3)	257 (0.2)	258 (0.3)	259 (0.3)	261 (0.3)	263 (0.3)
Female	267 (1.0)	267 (1.0)	270 (0.8)	— (†)	269 (0.5)	269 (0.3)	267 (0.2)	268 (0.3)	269 (0.3)	270 (0.2)	273 (0.3)
Gap between female and male score	13 (1.5)	15 (1.4)	14 (1.3)	— (†)	9 (0.7)	11 (0.4)	10 (0.3)	10 (0.4)	9 (0.5)	9 (0.4)	10 (0.4)
Race/ethnicity											
White	267 (1.1)	267 (1.0)	270 (0.9)	— (†)	272 (0.4)	272 (0.2)	271 (0.2)	272 (0.2)	273 (0.2)	274 (0.2)	276 (0.3)
Black	237 (1.7)	236 (1.8)	244 (1.2)	— (†)	245 (0.7)	244 (0.5)	243 (0.4)	245 (0.4)	246 (0.4)	249 (0.5)	250 (0.5)
Hispanic	241 (1.6)	243 (1.2)	243 (1.7)	— (†)	247 (0.4)	245 (0.7)	246 (0.4)	247 (0.4)	249 (0.6)	252 (0.5)	256 (0.5)
Asian/Pacific Islander	268 (3.9)	265 (3.0)	264 (7.1)	— (†)	267 (1.7)	270 (1.1)	271 (0.8)	271 (1.1)	274 (1.1)	275 (1.0)	280 (0.9)
American Indian/Alaska Native	‡ (†)	248 (4.7)	‡ (†)	— (†)	250 (3.5)	246 (3.0)	249 (1.4)	247 (1.2)	251 (1.2)	252 (1.2)	251 (1.0)
Gap between White and Black score	30 (2.0)	30 (2.1)	26 (1.5)	— (†)	27 (0.7)	28 (0.5)	28 (0.5)	27 (0.5)	26 (0.5)	25 (0.5)	26 (0.5)
Gap between White and Hispanic score	26 (2.0)	24 (1.5)	27 (1.9)	— (†)	26 (0.9)	27 (0.7)	25 (0.5)	25 (0.5)	24 (0.7)	22 (0.5)	21 (0.5)
Percentage of students in school eligible for free or reduced-price lunch											
0–25 percent (low poverty)	— (†)	— (†)	273 (1.1)	— (†)	276 (0.6)	275 (0.4)	274 (0.3)	275 (0.4)	277 (0.5)	279 (0.4)	282 (0.5)
26–50 percent	— (†)	— (†)	262 (1.3)	— (†)	264 (0.8)	263 (0.4)	262 (0.3)	263 (0.4)	265 (0.4)	268 (0.4)	270 (0.5)
51–75 percent	— (†)	— (†)	252 (2.1)	— (†)	254 (0.8)	253 (0.6)	252 (0.4)	253 (0.5)	256 (0.6)	258 (0.5)	261 (0.4)
76–100 percent (high poverty)	— (†)	— (†)	240 (1.8)	— (†)	240 (1.1)	239 (1.0)	240 (0.6)	241 (0.7)	243 (0.7)	247 (0.5)	249 (0.5)
Gap between low-poverty and high-poverty score	— (†)	— (†)	33 (2.1)	— (†)	36 (1.3)	36 (1.1)	34 (0.7)	34 (0.8)	34 (0.8)	32 (0.7)	33 (0.7)
English language learner (ELL) status											
ELL	‡ (†)	‡ (†)	218 (2.5)	— (†)	224 (1.4)	222 (1.5)	224 (0.9)	223 (1.1)	219 (1.0)	224 (1.0)	225 (0.9)
Non-ELL	‡ (†)	‡ (†)	264 (0.7)	— (†)	266 (0.4)	265 (0.3)	264 (0.2)	265 (0.2)	266 (0.2)	267 (0.2)	270 (0.2)
Gap between non-ELL and ELL score	‡ (†)	‡ (†)	46 (2.6)	— (†)	42 (1.4)	43 (1.5)	40 (0.9)	42 (1.1)	47 (1.0)	44 (1.0)	45 (1.0)
12th grade, all students	292 (0.6)	287 (0.7)	290 (0.6)	— (†)	287 (0.7)	— (†)	286 (0.6)	— (†)	288 (0.7)	— (†)	— (†)
Sex											
Male	287 (0.7)	280 (0.8)	282 (0.8)	— (†)	279 (0.9)	— (†)	279 (0.8)	— (†)	282 (0.7)	— (†)	— (†)
Female	297 (0.7)	294 (0.8)	298 (0.8)	— (†)	295 (0.7)	— (†)	292 (0.7)	— (†)	294 (0.8)	— (†)	— (†)
Gap between female and male score	10 (1.0)	14 (1.2)	16 (1.1)	— (†)	16 (1.1)	— (†)	13 (1.1)	— (†)	12 (1.1)	— (†)	— (†)
Race/ethnicity											
White	297 (0.6)	293 (0.7)	297 (0.7)	— (†)	292 (0.7)	— (†)	293 (0.7)	— (†)	296 (0.6)	— (†)	— (†)
Black	273 (1.4)	265 (1.6)	269 (1.4)	— (†)	267 (1.3)	— (†)	267 (1.2)	— (†)	269 (1.1)	— (†)	— (†)
Hispanic	279 (2.7)	270 (1.7)	275 (1.5)	— (†)	273 (1.5)	— (†)	272 (1.2)	— (†)	274 (1.0)	— (†)	— (†)
Asian/Pacific Islander	290 (3.2)	278 (2.4)	287 (2.7)	— (†)	286 (2.0)	— (†)	287 (1.9)	— (†)	298 (2.4)	— (†)	— (†)
American Indian/Alaska Native	‡ (†)	274 (5.8)	‡ (†)	— (†)	‡ (†)	— (†)	279 (6.3)	— (†)	283 (3.7)	— (†)	— (†)
Gap between White and Black score	24 (1.5)	29 (1.7)	27 (1.6)	— (†)	25 (1.5)	— (†)	26 (1.4)	— (†)	27 (1.3)	— (†)	— (†)
Gap between White and Hispanic score	19 (2.8)	23 (1.8)	22 (1.7)	— (†)	20 (1.7)	— (†)	21 (1.4)	— (†)	22 (1.2)	— (†)	— (†)
Percentage of students in school eligible for free or reduced-price lunch											
0–25 percent (low poverty)	— (†)	— (†)	296 (0.9)	— (†)	293 (0.9)	— (†)	292 (1.1)	— (†)	299 (1.1)	— (†)	— (†)
26–50 percent	— (†)	— (†)	284 (1.7)	— (†)	282 (1.6)	— (†)	282 (1.1)	— (†)	286 (0.8)	— (†)	— (†)
51–75 percent	— (†)	— (†)	275 (2.0)	— (†)	275 (2.6)	— (†)	273 (1.8)	— (†)	276 (1.1)	— (†)	— (†)
76–100 percent (high poverty)	— (†)	— (†)	272 (3.3)	— (†)	268 (2.4)	— (†)	266 (2.0)	— (†)	266 (1.0)	— (†)	— (†)
Gap between low-poverty and high-poverty score	— (†)	— (†)	23 (3.4)	— (†)	25 (2.6)	— (†)	26 (2.3)	— (†)	33 (1.5)	— (†)	— (†)
English language learner (ELL) status											
ELL	— (†)	— (†)	244 (2.6)	— (†)	245 (2.4)	— (†)	247 (2.4)	— (†)	240 (2.1)	— (†)	— (†)
Non-ELL	— (†)	— (†)	291 (0.6)	— (†)	288 (0.7)	— (†)	288 (0.6)	— (†)	290 (0.7)	— (†)	— (†)
Gap between non-ELL and ELL score	— (†)	— (†)	46 (2.7)	— (†)	43 (2.5)	— (†)	40 (2.4)	— (†)	50 (2.2)	— (†)	— (†)

—Not available.
†Not applicable.
‡Reporting standards not met (too few cases for a reliable estimate).
[1]Accommodations were not permitted for this assessment.
NOTE: Scale ranges from 0 to 500. Includes public and private schools. For 1998 and later years, includes students tested with accommodations (1 to 10 percent of all students, depending on grade level and year); excludes only those students with disabilities and English language learners who were unable to be tested even with accommodations (2 to 6 percent of all students). Race categories exclude persons of Hispanic ethnicity. Totals include other racial/ethnic groups not shown separately. Grade 12 results for the 2013 NAEP Reading Assessment were not yet available at the time this table was created.
SOURCE: U.S. Department of Education, National Center for Education Statistics, National Assessment of Educational Progress (NAEP), 1992, 1994, 1998, 2000, 2002, 2003, 2005, 2007, 2009, 2011, and 2013 Reading Assessments, retrieved November 14, 2013, from the Main NAEP Data Explorer (http://nces.ed.gov/nationsreportcard/naepdata/). (This table was prepared November 2013.)

Percentage of students at or above selected National Assessment of Educational Progress (NAEP) reading achievement levels, by grade and selected student characteristics: Selected years, 1998 through 2013

[Standard errors appear in parentheses]

Grade and selected student characteristic	1998		2000		2003		2005		2007		2009		2011		2013	
	At or above Basic[1]	At or above Proficient[2]	At or above Basic[1]	At or above Proficient[2]	At or above Basic[1]	At or above Proficient[2]	At or above Basic[1]	At or above Proficient[2]	At or above Basic[1]	At or above Proficient[2]	At or above Basic[1]	At or above Proficient[2]	At or above Basic[1]	At or above Proficient[2]	At or above Basic[1]	At or above Proficient[2]
1	2	3	4	5	6	7	8	9	10	11	12	13	14	15	16	17
4th grade, all students	60 (1.2)	29 (0.9)	59 (1.4)	29 (1.1)	63 (0.3)	31 (0.3)	64 (0.3)	31 (0.2)	67 (0.3)	33 (0.2)	67 (0.3)	33 (0.4)	67 (0.3)	34 (0.4)	68 (0.3)	35 (0.3)
Sex																
Male	57 (1.3)	27 (1.1)	55 (1.4)	25 (1.2)	60 (0.4)	28 (0.4)	61 (0.4)	29 (0.3)	64 (0.4)	30 (0.3)	64 (0.3)	30 (0.4)	64 (0.4)	31 (0.4)	65 (0.4)	32 (0.4)
Female	62 (1.5)	32 (1.2)	64 (1.6)	34 (1.4)	67 (0.4)	35 (0.4)	67 (0.3)	34 (0.4)	70 (0.3)	36 (0.4)	70 (0.4)	36 (0.4)	71 (0.4)	37 (0.5)	72 (0.4)	38 (0.4)
Race/ethnicity																
White	70 (1.3)	37 (1.2)	70 (1.2)	38 (1.2)	75 (0.3)	41 (0.3)	76 (0.3)	41 (0.3)	78 (0.3)	43 (0.4)	78 (0.3)	42 (0.4)	78 (0.6)	44 (0.5)	79 (0.3)	46 (0.4)
Black	36 (1.8)	10 (1.1)	35 (1.6)	13 (1.0)	40 (0.4)	13 (0.3)	42 (0.5)	13 (0.3)	46 (0.6)	14 (0.4)	49 (0.8)	16 (0.5)	49 (0.6)	17 (0.5)	50 (0.6)	18 (0.5)
Hispanic	37 (3.2)	13 (1.7)	37 (3.0)	13 (1.8)	44 (0.7)	15 (0.5)	46 (0.7)	16 (0.5)	50 (0.6)	17 (0.6)	49 (0.7)	17 (0.5)	51 (0.8)	18 (0.5)	53 (0.6)	20 (0.6)
Asian/Pacific Islander	58 (6.1)	30 (4.5)	70 (5.0)	41 (5.7)	70 (1.5)	38 (1.4)	73 (0.9)	42 (0.9)	77 (1.0)	46 (1.4)	80 (1.0)	49 (1.4)	80 (1.2)	49 (1.7)	80 (1.0)	51 (1.2)
American Indian/Alaska Native	‡ (†)	‡ (†)	63 (10.9)	28 (8.9)	47 (2.0)	16 (1.5)	48 (1.5)	18 (1.0)	49 (1.4)	18 (1.4)	50 (1.7)	20 (1.4)	47 (1.7)	18 (1.4)	51 (1.6)	21 (1.4)
Eligibility for free or reduced-price lunch																
Eligible	39 (1.8)	13 (1.0)	38 (1.8)	13 (1.1)	45 (0.4)	15 (0.3)	46 (0.4)	16 (0.3)	50 (0.4)	17 (0.3)	51 (0.4)	17 (0.3)	52 (0.4)	18 (0.3)	53 (0.4)	20 (0.3)
Not eligible	73 (0.9)	40 (1.2)	73 (1.4)	39 (1.5)	76 (0.3)	42 (0.3)	77 (0.2)	42 (0.3)	79 (0.3)	44 (0.3)	80 (0.3)	45 (0.4)	82 (0.3)	48 (0.5)	83 (0.3)	51 (0.3)
Unknown	69 (3.0)	37 (3.8)	71 (2.4)	40 (2.4)	81 (0.9)	43 (1.1)	77 (1.1)	45 (1.4)	80 (1.3)	46 (1.8)	81 (1.7)	50 (1.7)	82 (1.0)	48 (1.3)	83 (1.6)	51 (2.1)
8th grade, all students	73 (0.8)	32 (1.1)	— (†)	— (†)	74 (0.3)	32 (0.3)	73 (0.2)	31 (0.3)	74 (0.2)	31 (0.2)	75 (0.3)	32 (0.4)	76 (0.3)	34 (0.3)	78 (0.3)	36 (0.3)
Sex																
Male	67 (1.2)	26 (1.3)	—	—	69 (0.3)	27 (0.3)	68 (0.3)	26 (0.3)	69 (0.3)	26 (0.3)	71 (0.4)	28 (0.3)	72 (0.4)	29 (0.3)	74 (0.4)	31 (0.4)
Female	80 (0.9)	39 (1.3)	—	—	79 (0.3)	38 (0.3)	78 (0.2)	36 (0.3)	79 (0.3)	36 (0.3)	79 (0.4)	37 (0.5)	80 (0.3)	38 (0.4)	82 (0.3)	42 (0.3)
Race/ethnicity																
White	81 (0.9)	39 (1.3)	—	—	83 (0.2)	41 (0.3)	82 (0.2)	39 (0.3)	84 (0.3)	40 (0.3)	84 (0.3)	41 (0.4)	85 (0.3)	43 (0.4)	86 (0.2)	46 (0.4)
Black	53 (1.8)	13 (1.5)	—	—	54 (0.6)	13 (0.4)	52 (0.6)	12 (0.4)	55 (0.6)	14 (0.5)	57 (0.6)	14 (0.6)	61 (0.7)	15 (0.5)	61 (0.6)	17 (0.6)
Hispanic	53 (2.4)	14 (1.0)	—	—	56 (0.9)	15 (0.6)	56 (0.6)	15 (0.4)	58 (0.5)	15 (0.4)	61 (0.8)	17 (0.7)	64 (0.8)	19 (0.6)	68 (0.7)	22 (0.6)
Asian/Pacific Islander	75 (8.8)	33 (8.8)	—	—	79 (1.2)	40 (1.2)	80 (0.8)	40 (1.2)	80 (1.0)	41 (1.1)	83 (1.1)	45 (1.7)	83 (1.0)	47 (1.4)	86 (0.7)	52 (1.3)
American Indian/Alaska Native	‡ (†)	‡ (†)	—	—	57 (3.3)	17 (1.7)	59 (2.1)	17 (1.7)	56 (1.9)	18 (1.3)	62 (2.0)	21 (2.0)	63 (1.4)	22 (1.6)	62 (1.8)	19 (1.6)
Eligibility for free or reduced-price lunch																
Eligible	56 (1.3)	14 (1.0)	—	—	57 (0.5)	16 (0.3)	57 (0.4)	15 (0.3)	58 (0.4)	15 (0.3)	60 (0.5)	16 (0.3)	63 (0.5)	18 (0.3)	66 (0.4)	20 (0.2)
Not eligible	80 (1.0)	38 (1.5)	—	—	82 (0.3)	40 (0.4)	81 (0.3)	39 (0.4)	83 (0.4)	40 (0.3)	85 (0.3)	42 (0.5)	86 (0.3)	45 (0.4)	87 (0.3)	48 (0.4)
Unknown	80 (1.9)	43 (2.5)	—	—	81 (0.9)	42 (1.2)	84 (1.0)	45 (1.3)	86 (1.0)	48 (1.3)	89 (1.3)	51 (1.8)	90 (0.8)	54 (1.4)	92 (0.9)	59 (2.4)
12th grade, all students	76 (0.7)	40 (0.7)	(†)	(†)	—	—	73 (0.8)	35 (0.7)	—	—	74 (0.6)	38 (0.8)	—	—	—	—
Sex																
Male	70 (0.9)	32 (0.9)	(†)	(†)	—	—	67 (0.9)	29 (0.9)	—	—	69 (0.8)	32 (0.9)	—	—	—	—
Female	83 (0.8)	48 (1.1)	(†)	(†)	—	—	78 (0.9)	41 (0.9)	—	—	80 (0.6)	43 (1.0)	—	—	—	—
Race/ethnicity																
White	82 (0.7)	47 (0.9)	(†)	(†)	—	—	79 (0.8)	43 (0.9)	—	—	81 (0.5)	46 (0.8)	—	—	—	—
Black	57 (1.9)	17 (1.4)	(†)	(†)	—	—	54 (1.5)	16 (1.2)	—	—	57 (1.3)	17 (1.2)	—	—	—	—
Hispanic	62 (2.5)	24 (1.5)	(†)	(†)	—	—	60 (1.9)	20 (1.3)	—	—	61 (1.1)	22 (1.3)	—	—	—	—
Asian/Pacific Islander	74 (3.1)	38 (2.9)	(†)	(†)	—	—	74 (2.3)	36 (2.9)	—	—	81 (1.5)	49 (2.9)	—	—	—	—
American Indian/Alaska Native	‡ (†)	‡ (†)	(†)	(†)	—	—	67 (10.1)	26 (8.6)	—	—	70 (6.4)	29 (5.5)	—	—	—	—
Eligibility for free or reduced-price lunch																
Eligible	56 (1.6)	19 (1.4)	(†)	(†)	—	—	59 (1.4)	20 (0.8)	—	—	61 (1.1)	21 (1.1)	—	—	—	—
Not eligible	79 (0.6)	43 (0.8)	(†)	(†)	—	—	76 (0.8)	39 (0.8)	—	—	79 (0.6)	44 (0.9)	—	—	—	—
Unknown	81 (1.6)	45 (2.0)	(†)	(†)	—	—	80 (2.0)	46 (2.1)	—	—	81 (2.3)	48 (3.0)	—	—	—	—

—Not available.
†Not applicable.
‡Reporting standards not met (too few cases for a reliable estimate).
[1] Basic denotes partial mastery of the knowledge and skills that are fundamental for proficient work at a given grade.
[2] Proficient represents solid academic performance. Students reaching this level have demonstrated competency over challenging subject matter.
NOTE: Includes public and private schools. Includes students tested with accommodations (1 to 11 percent of all students, depending on grade level and year); excludes only those students with disabilities and English language learners who were unable to be tested even with accommodations (2 to 6 percent of all students). Race categories exclude persons of Hispanic ethnicity. Totals include other racial/ethnic groups not shown separately. Grade 12 results for the 2013 NAEP Reading Assessment were not yet available at the time this table was created.
SOURCE: U.S. Department of Education, National Center for Education Statistics, National Assessment of Educational Progress (NAEP), 1998, 2000, 2003, 2005, 2007, 2009, 2011, and 2013 Reading Assessments, retrieved November 13, 2013, from the Main NAEP Data Explorer (http://nces.ed.gov/nationsreportcard/naepdata/). (This table was prepared November 2013.)

Average National Assessment of Educational Progress (NAEP) reading scale score and percentage distribution of students, by age, amount of reading for school and for fun, and time spent on homework and watching TV/video: Selected years, 1984 through 2012

[Standard errors appear in parentheses]

Amount of reading for school and for fun, time spent on homework and watching TV/video	9-year-olds 1984	9-year-olds 1994	9-year-olds 1999	9-year-olds 2008	9-year-olds 2012	13-year-olds 1984	13-year-olds 1994	13-year-olds 1999	13-year-olds 2008	13-year-olds 2012	17-year-olds 1984	17-year-olds 1994	17-year-olds 1999	17-year-olds 2008	17-year-olds 2012
1	2	3	4	5	6	7	8	9	10	11	12	13	14	15	16
Average scale score[1]															
Pages read daily in school and for homework															
5 or fewer	208 (0.9)	203 (2.3)	202 (1.8)	210 (1.1)	207 (1.1)	250 (0.8)	249 (1.7)	249 (2.0)	250 (1.1)	251 (1.8)	273 (0.8)	271 (1.9)	273 (2.7)	271 (1.3)	274 (1.1)
6–10	215 (1.0)	214 (1.7)	212 (1.7)	219 (1.3)	219 (1.5)	261 (0.6)	261 (1.4)	262 (1.7)	258 (1.2)	261 (1.5)	287 (0.9)	284 (2.1)	285 (1.7)	284 (1.4)	283 (1.2)
11–15	220 (1.4)	209 (2.3)	221 (2.4)	224 (1.5)	225 (1.3)	264 (1.0)	266 (1.8)	264 (2.1)	263 (1.1)	266 (1.8)	294 (0.9)	288 (1.9)	292 (2.1)	290 (1.6)	289 (1.5)
16–20	215 (1.4)	209 (2.9)	214 (2.0)	225 (1.6)	226 (1.2)	263 (1.5)	263 (2.3)	264 (2.0)	267 (1.6)	268 (1.8)	296 (1.1)	298 (2.0)	292 (2.9)	296 (1.5)	297 (1.5)
More than 20	215 (1.6)	217 (2.4)	217 (2.1)	226 (1.2)	227 (1.0)	261 (1.5)	261 (2.0)	265 (2.0)	267 (1.4)	271 (1.3)	300 (1.2)	304 (2.2)	302 (1.9)	303 (1.3)	301 (1.5)
Frequency of reading for fun															
Almost every day	214 (1.1)	215 (2.3)	215 (2.4)	225 (1.2)	226 (0.9)	264 (1.4)	272 (3.2)	272 (3.2)	274 (1.4)	276 (1.4)	297 (1.5)	302 (4.2)	301 (4.9)	302 (1.3)	302 (1.3)
Once or twice a week	212 (1.7)	214 (3.1)	215 (2.6)	225 (1.3)	226 (0.9)	255 (1.4)	255 (3.1)	263 (3.2)	264 (1.1)	267 (1.4)	290 (1.7)	286 (4.1)	289 (2.9)	291 (1.7)	294 (1.4)
Once or twice a month	204 (3.3)	213 (5.8)	211 (4.2)	221 (1.7)	219 (2.0)	255 (2.1)	255 (5.7)	260 (3.7)	261 (1.3)	258 (1.7)	290 (1.8)	288 (4.5)	286 (4.8)	288 (1.5)	288 (1.5)
A few times a year	197 (4.2)	‡ (†)	195 (‡)	212 (1.9)	211 (1.9)	252 (3.6)	252 (5.4)	255 (4.4)	254 (1.3)	258 (1.9)	279 (2.7)	281 (8.2)	283 (4.4)	287 (1.6)	288 (1.4)
Never or hardly ever	198 (2.7)	193 (3.9)	195 (3.3)	211 (1.2)	208 (1.9)	239 (2.5)	237 (5.1)	242 (5.3)	247 (0.9)	249 (1.3)	269 (2.4)	258 (5.2)	262 (5.0)	269 (1.1)	272 (1.4)
TV/video watched on school day															
None	212 (3.4)	212 (4.8)	221 (4.6)	223 (3.0)	222 (3.1)	264 (2.7)	270 (5.1)	265 (6.0)	267 (3.0)	276 (3.5)	300 (1.6)	308 (3.4)	300 (2.8)	292 (2.4)	292 (2.5)
1 hour or less	217 (1.5)	216 (1.8)	218 (2.1)	225 (1.2)	229 (1.2)	269 (1.1)	270 (1.5)	270 (1.6)	266 (1.2)	269 (1.2)	300 (1.2)	299 (2.0)	298 (2.0)	293 (1.2)	290 (1.2)
2 hours	222 (1.1)	219 (2.1)	221 (1.7)	229 (1.1)	227 (1.1)	268 (0.7)	268 (1.4)	268 (1.6)	266 (1.3)	266 (1.5)	295 (0.9)	292 (1.8)	292 (2.1)	284 (1.1)	290 (1.3)
3 hours	220 (1.2)	218 (2.2)	218 (2.3)	227 (1.3)	226 (1.4)	264 (0.8)	262 (1.4)	263 (1.6)	262 (1.3)	261 (1.5)	288 (1.0)	284 (2.4)	282 (2.3)	276 (2.3)	284 (1.3)
4 hours	219 (1.0)	212 (1.8)	214 (2.4)	223 (1.4)	224 (1.4)	262 (0.9)	254 (2.0)	254 (2.4)	255 (1.5)	259 (1.5)	284 (1.0)	276 (4.1)	273 (2.2)	273 (2.4)	277 (2.1)
5 hours	214 (1.4)	209 (2.7)	208 (3.0)	219 (2.2)	213 (2.1)	257 (1.0)	250 (3.0)	253 (3.2)	255 (2.6)	255 (2.1)	277 (1.5)	269 (4.0)	275 (3.8)	273 (2.4)	275 (3.9)
6 hours or more	199 (0.8)	192 (2.7)	191 (1.7)	205 (1.2)	205 (1.9)	245 (1.0)	234 (3.1)	238 (1.8)	238 (1.4)	241 (1.4)	269 (1.5)	256 (3.7)	256 (5.2)	256 (2.3)	261 (2.6)
Percentage distribution															
Pages read daily in school and for homework															
5 or fewer	36 (0.8)	28 (1.4)	28 (1.4)	25 (0.9)	22 (0.7)	27 (0.7)	26 (0.9)	23 (1.0)	26 (0.8)	23 (0.8)	26 (0.8)	21 (1.2)	23 (1.4)	30 (0.9)	29 (0.7)
6–10	25 (0.4)	24 (0.6)	24 (0.9)	20 (0.5)	17 (0.6)	34 (0.5)	31 (0.9)	31 (1.1)	24 (0.6)	22 (0.5)	26 (0.3)	25 (0.6)	31 (0.8)	23 (0.5)	25 (0.6)
11–15	20 (0.4)	16 (0.5)	15 (0.7)	14 (0.5)	12 (0.6)	18 (0.4)	17 (0.6)	18 (0.7)	17 (0.5)	17 (0.5)	18 (0.3)	18 (0.6)	17 (0.8)	16 (0.4)	15 (0.5)
16–20	13 (0.4)	14 (0.9)	14 (0.7)	14 (0.6)	15 (0.6)	11 (0.2)	13 (0.6)	13 (0.7)	13 (0.6)	14 (0.6)	14 (0.3)	13 (0.5)	14 (1.2)	12 (0.5)	12 (0.5)
More than 20	13 (0.5)	17 (1.0)	19 (1.0)	28 (0.8)	34 (1.1)	11 (0.5)	14 (0.8)	16 (1.0)	22 (0.9)	24 (1.1)	21 (0.9)	23 (1.5)	22 (1.2)	19 (0.7)	22 (0.7)
Frequency of reading for fun															
Almost every day	53 (1.0)	58 (1.6)	54 (1.7)	48 (0.7)	53 (0.8)	35 (1.0)	32 (1.8)	28 (1.7)	26 (0.7)	27 (0.7)	31 (1.0)	30 (2.6)	25 (1.7)	20 (0.6)	19 (0.6)
Once or twice a week	28 (0.6)	25 (1.5)	25 (1.5)	23 (0.6)	23 (0.6)	35 (1.2)	32 (2.1)	36 (1.6)	25 (0.6)	26 (0.6)	33 (1.2)	31 (1.9)	28 (2.7)	26 (0.5)	21 (0.6)
Once or twice a month	7 (0.3)	5 (0.6)	6 (0.6)	8 (0.4)	7 (0.4)	14 (0.7)	14 (1.7)	13 (1.1)	14 (0.4)	14 (0.4)	14 (0.8)	15 (1.5)	19 (1.7)	17 (0.5)	16 (0.6)
A few times a year	3 (0.3)	3 (0.6)	4 (0.7)	8 (0.4)	7 (0.3)	7 (0.5)	10 (1.2)	10 (1.1)	12 (0.4)	11 (0.4)	10 (0.5)	12 (1.5)	12 (1.4)	16 (0.5)	18 (0.6)
Never or hardly ever	9 (0.5)	9 (0.8)	10 (0.8)	14 (0.6)	11 (0.4)	8 (0.6)	12 (1.7)	9 (1.4)	24 (0.7)	22 (0.7)	9 (0.6)	12 (1.4)	16 (2.4)	24 (0.6)	27 (0.6)
Time spent on homework yesterday															
No homework assigned	35 (1.3)	32 (2.1)	26 (1.6)	18 (1.3)	22 (1.6)	22 (0.7)	23 (1.4)	24 (1.2)	23 (1.2)	21 (1.2)	22 (0.9)	23 (1.4)	26 (1.0)	28 (0.8)	27 (0.9)
Didn't do assignment	4 (0.3)	4 (0.4)	4 (0.4)	4 (0.3)	4 (0.4)	4 (0.2)	6 (0.6)	6 (0.4)	7 (0.4)	4 (0.3)	11 (0.3)	11 (0.6)	13 (0.7)	12 (0.4)	11 (0.4)
Less than 1 hour	41 (1.0)	48 (1.7)	53 (1.4)	60 (1.2)	57 (1.3)	36 (0.5)	34 (1.0)	37 (1.4)	43 (1.2)	44 (0.8)	27 (0.4)	27 (0.9)	27 (1.0)	27 (0.5)	26 (0.6)
1 to 2 hours	13 (0.4)	11 (0.7)	12 (0.7)	12 (0.5)	12 (0.6)	29 (0.3)	28 (1.0)	26 (1.0)	21 (0.7)	23 (0.9)	27 (0.5)	26 (1.2)	23 (0.8)	22 (0.5)	23 (0.5)
More than 2 hours	6 (0.2)	4 (0.4)	5 (0.5)	5 (0.3)	5 (0.3)	9 (0.3)	9 (0.7)	8 (0.8)	6 (0.4)	7 (0.5)	13 (0.3)	13 (0.9)	12 (0.9)	10 (0.5)	13 (0.7)
TV/video watched on school day															
None	3 (0.2)	4 (0.2)	4 (0.8)	4 (0.3)	6 (0.3)	2 (0.2)	4 (0.6)	4 (0.6)	5 (0.3)	6 (0.3)	5 (0.2)	6 (0.8)	6 (0.3)	6 (0.3)	10 (0.3)
1 hour or less	14 (0.3)	23 (1.0)	24 (0.9)	24 (0.6)	27 (0.7)	12 (0.4)	23 (1.0)	29 (0.8)	25 (0.5)	29 (0.6)	25 (0.4)	31 (0.9)	34 (0.9)	33 (0.6)	34 (0.6)
2 hours	16 (0.3)	21 (0.7)	21 (0.9)	18 (0.6)	18 (0.5)	18 (0.5)	21 (0.7)	20 (0.8)	25 (0.5)	27 (0.5)	26 (0.3)	26 (0.9)	26 (0.9)	27 (0.6)	25 (0.6)
3 hours	15 (0.3)	16 (0.5)	14 (0.6)	13 (0.4)	12 (0.5)	23 (0.4)	16 (0.5)	20 (0.9)	18 (0.4)	15 (0.5)	20 (0.4)	18 (0.8)	17 (0.8)	16 (0.5)	16 (0.6)
4 hours	12 (0.2)	9 (0.5)	9 (0.4)	8 (0.3)	8 (0.4)	17 (0.3)	9 (0.4)	10 (0.6)	10 (0.3)	10 (0.4)	12 (0.2)	9 (0.5)	8 (0.5)	8 (0.4)	8 (0.3)
5 hours	9 (0.3)	6 (0.4)	6 (0.4)	6 (0.3)	6 (0.3)	10 (0.3)	6 (0.4)	5 (0.3)	5 (0.3)	4 (0.2)	6 (0.2)	5 (0.4)	4 (0.4)	4 (0.4)	3 (0.2)
6 hours or more	30 (0.7)	20 (0.8)	22 (1.2)	26 (0.8)	23 (0.8)	13 (0.4)	20 (0.8)	9 (0.6)	13 (0.4)	10 (0.5)	6 (0.4)	5 (0.6)	5 (0.6)	6 (0.5)	5 (0.3)

†Not applicable.

‡Reporting standards not met (too few cases for a reliable estimate).

[1]Scale ranges from 0 to 500. Students scoring 150 (or higher) are able to follow brief written directions and carry out simple, discrete reading tasks. Students scoring 200 are able to understand, combine ideas, and make inferences based on short uncomplicated passages about specific or sequentially related information. Students scoring 250 are able to search for specific information, interrelate ideas, and make generalizations about literature, science, and social studies materials. Students scoring 300 are able to find, understand, summarize, and explain relatively complicated literary and informational material.

NOTE: Includes public and private schools. For 1984, 1994, and 1999, accommodations were not permitted. For 2008 and later years, includes students tested with accommodations; excludes only those students with disabilities and English language learners who were unable to be tested even with accommodations (2 to 4 percent of all students, depending on age and assessment year). Detail may not sum to totals because of rounding.

SOURCE: U.S. Department of Education, National Center for Education Statistics, National Assessment of Educational Progress (NAEP), *NAEP Trends in Academic Progress*, 1996 and 1999; and 2008 and 2012 NAEP Long-Term Trend Reading Assessments, retrieved June 24, 2009, and July 02, 2013, from the Long-Term Trend NAEP Data Explorer (http://nces.ed.gov/nationsreportcard/naepdata/). (This table was prepared July 2013.)

Average National Assessment of Educational Progress (NAEP) reading scale score of 4th-grade public school students and percentage attaining reading achievement levels, by state: Selected years, 1992 through 2013

[Standard errors appear in parentheses]

State	Average scale score[1]									Percent attaining reading achievement levels, 2013		
	1992	1998	2002	2003	2005	2007	2009	2011	2013	At or above Basic[2]	At or above Proficient[3]	At Advanced[4]
1	2	3	4	5	6	7	8	9	10	11	12	13
United States	215 (1.0)	213 (1.2)	217 (0.5)	216 (0.3)	217 (0.2)	220 (0.3)	220 (0.3)	220 (0.3)	221 (0.3)	67 (0.3)	34 (0.3)	8 (0.2)
Alabama	207 (1.7)	211 (1.9)	207 (1.4)	207 (1.7)	208 (1.2)	216 (1.3)	216 (1.2)	220 (1.3)	219 (1.2)	65 (1.5)	31 (1.4)	6 (0.7)
Alaska	— (†)	— (†)	— (†)	212 (1.6)	211 (1.4)	214 (1.0)	211 (1.2)	208 (1.1)	209 (1.0)	58 (1.2)	27 (1.2)	6 (0.5)
Arizona	209 (1.2)	206 (1.4)	205 (1.5)	209 (1.2)	207 (1.6)	210 (1.6)	210 (1.2)	212 (1.2)	213 (1.4)	60 (1.6)	28 (1.4)	5 (0.6)
Arkansas	211 (1.2)	209 (1.6)	213 (1.4)	214 (1.4)	217 (1.1)	217 (1.2)	216 (1.1)	217 (1.0)	219 (0.9)	66 (1.1)	32 (1.3)	7 (0.7)
California[5,6]	202 (2.0)	202 (2.5)	206 (2.5)	206 (1.2)	207 (0.7)	209 (1.0)	210 (1.5)	211 (1.8)	213 (1.2)	58 (1.4)	27 (1.3)	6 (0.7)
Colorado	217 (1.1)	220 (1.4)	— (†)	224 (1.2)	224 (1.1)	224 (1.1)	226 (1.2)	223 (1.3)	227 (1.0)	74 (1.2)	41 (1.5)	10 (0.9)
Connecticut	222 (1.3)	230 (1.6)	229 (1.1)	228 (1.1)	226 (1.0)	227 (1.3)	229 (1.1)	227 (1.3)	230 (0.9)	76 (1.2)	43 (1.2)	12 (0.9)
Delaware[7]	213 (0.6)	207 (1.7)	224 (0.6)	224 (0.7)	226 (0.8)	225 (0.7)	226 (0.5)	225 (0.7)	226 (0.8)	73 (1.1)	38 (1.2)	9 (0.6)
District of Columbia	188 (0.8)	179 (1.2)	191 (0.9)	188 (0.9)	191 (1.0)	197 (0.9)	202 (1.0)	201 (0.8)	206 (0.9)	50 (1.2)	23 (0.9)	7 (0.6)
Florida	208 (1.2)	206 (1.4)	214 (1.4)	218 (1.1)	220 (0.9)	224 (0.8)	226 (1.0)	225 (1.1)	227 (1.1)	75 (1.2)	39 (1.5)	9 (0.8)
Georgia	212 (1.5)	209 (1.4)	215 (1.0)	214 (1.3)	214 (1.4)	219 (0.9)	218 (1.1)	221 (1.1)	222 (1.1)	67 (1.3)	34 (1.5)	9 (0.8)
Hawaii	203 (1.7)	200 (1.5)	208 (0.9)	208 (1.4)	210 (1.0)	213 (1.1)	211 (1.0)	214 (1.0)	215 (1.0)	62 (1.3)	30 (1.2)	7 (0.7)
Idaho	219 (0.9)	— (†)	220 (1.1)	218 (1.0)	222 (0.9)	223 (0.8)	221 (0.9)	221 (0.8)	219 (0.9)	68 (1.2)	33 (1.2)	7 (0.6)
Illinois	— (†)	‡ (‡)	‡ (†)	216 (1.6)	217 (1.2)	219 (1.2)	219 (1.4)	219 (1.1)	219 (1.4)	64 (1.5)	34 (1.4)	8 (0.8)
Indiana	221 (1.3)	— (†)	222 (1.4)	220 (1.0)	218 (1.1)	222 (0.9)	223 (1.1)	221 (0.9)	225 (1.0)	73 (1.2)	38 (1.5)	8 (0.8)
Iowa[5,6]	225 (1.1)	220 (1.6)	223 (1.1)	223 (1.1)	221 (0.9)	225 (1.1)	221 (1.2)	221 (0.8)	224 (1.1)	72 (1.3)	38 (1.4)	9 (0.9)
Kansas[5,6]	— (†)	221 (1.4)	222 (1.4)	220 (1.2)	221 (1.2)	225 (1.1)	224 (1.3)	224 (1.0)	223 (1.3)	71 (1.6)	38 (1.7)	8 (0.9)
Kentucky	213 (1.3)	218 (1.5)	219 (1.1)	219 (1.3)	220 (1.1)	222 (1.1)	226 (1.1)	225 (1.0)	224 (1.2)	71 (1.3)	36 (1.7)	9 (0.8)
Louisiana	204 (1.2)	200 (1.6)	207 (1.7)	205 (1.4)	209 (1.3)	207 (1.6)	207 (1.1)	210 (1.4)	210 (1.3)	56 (1.7)	23 (1.3)	4 (0.6)
Maine	227 (1.1)	225 (1.4)	225 (1.1)	224 (0.9)	225 (0.9)	226 (0.9)	224 (0.9)	222 (0.7)	225 (0.9)	71 (1.0)	37 (1.2)	9 (0.8)
Maryland	211 (1.6)	212 (1.6)	217 (1.5)	219 (1.4)	220 (1.3)	225 (1.1)	226 (1.4)	231 (0.9)	232 (1.3)	77 (1.2)	45 (1.8)	14 (1.3)
Massachusetts[5]	226 (0.9)	223 (1.4)	234 (1.1)	228 (1.2)	231 (0.9)	236 (1.1)	234 (1.1)	237 (1.0)	232 (1.1)	79 (1.1)	47 (1.5)	14 (1.0)
Michigan	216 (1.5)	216 (1.5)	219 (1.1)	219 (1.2)	218 (1.5)	220 (1.4)	218 (1.0)	219 (1.2)	217 (1.4)	64 (1.6)	31 (1.6)	6 (0.8)
Minnesota[5,6]	221 (1.2)	219 (1.7)	225 (1.0)	223 (1.1)	225 (1.3)	225 (1.1)	223 (1.3)	222 (1.2)	227 (1.2)	74 (1.5)	41 (1.4)	10 (0.8)
Mississippi	199 (1.3)	203 (1.3)	203 (1.3)	205 (1.3)	204 (1.4)	208 (1.0)	211 (1.1)	209 (1.2)	209 (0.9)	53 (1.3)	21 (1.0)	3 (0.5)
Missouri	220 (1.2)	216 (1.3)	220 (1.3)	222 (1.2)	221 (0.9)	221 (1.1)	224 (1.1)	220 (0.9)	222 (1.0)	70 (1.3)	35 (1.4)	7 (0.7)
Montana[5,6]	— (†)	225 (1.5)	224 (1.8)	223 (1.2)	225 (1.1)	227 (1.0)	225 (0.8)	225 (0.6)	223 (0.8)	70 (1.1)	35 (1.1)	7 (0.7)
Nebraska[7]	221 (1.1)	— (†)	222 (1.5)	221 (1.0)	221 (1.2)	223 (1.3)	223 (1.0)	223 (1.0)	223 (1.0)	71 (1.1)	37 (1.4)	8 (0.7)
Nevada	— (†)	206 (1.8)	209 (1.2)	207 (1.2)	207 (1.2)	211 (1.2)	211 (1.1)	213 (1.0)	214 (1.1)	61 (1.4)	27 (1.4)	5 (0.6)
New Hampshire[5,7]	228 (1.2)	226 (1.7)	— (†)	228 (1.0)	227 (0.9)	229 (0.9)	229 (1.0)	230 (0.8)	232 (0.9)	80 (1.0)	45 (1.5)	11 (0.9)
New Jersey[7]	223 (1.4)	— (†)	— (†)	225 (1.2)	223 (1.3)	231 (1.2)	229 (0.9)	231 (1.2)	229 (1.3)	75 (1.3)	42 (1.7)	12 (1.0)
New Mexico	211 (1.5)	205 (1.4)	208 (1.6)	203 (1.5)	207 (1.3)	212 (1.3)	208 (1.4)	208 (1.0)	206 (1.1)	52 (1.2)	21 (0.9)	4 (0.6)
New York[5,6,7]	215 (1.4)	215 (1.6)	222 (1.5)	222 (1.1)	223 (1.1)	224 (1.0)	224 (1.0)	222 (1.1)	224 (1.2)	70 (1.4)	37 (1.5)	9 (0.8)
North Carolina	212 (1.1)	213 (1.6)	222 (1.0)	221 (1.0)	217 (1.0)	218 (0.9)	219 (1.1)	221 (1.2)	222 (1.1)	69 (1.2)	35 (1.2)	8 (0.7)
North Dakota[6]	226 (1.1)	— (†)	224 (1.0)	222 (0.9)	225 (0.7)	226 (0.9)	226 (0.8)	226 (0.5)	224 (0.5)	73 (0.9)	34 (0.9)	6 (0.5)
Ohio	217 (1.3)	— (†)	222 (1.3)	222 (1.2)	223 (1.4)	226 (1.1)	225 (1.1)	224 (1.0)	224 (1.2)	71 (1.3)	37 (1.6)	9 (0.9)
Oklahoma	220 (0.9)	219 (1.2)	213 (1.2)	214 (1.2)	214 (1.1)	217 (1.1)	217 (1.1)	215 (1.1)	217 (1.1)	65 (1.3)	30 (1.3)	5 (0.6)
Oregon	— (†)	212 (1.8)	220 (1.4)	218 (1.3)	217 (1.4)	215 (1.4)	218 (1.2)	216 (1.1)	219 (1.3)	66 (1.4)	33 (1.6)	9 (1.0)
Pennsylvania	221 (1.3)	— (†)	221 (1.2)	219 (1.3)	223 (1.3)	226 (1.0)	224 (1.4)	227 (1.2)	226 (1.3)	73 (1.4)	40 (1.6)	10 (1.0)
Rhode Island	217 (1.8)	218 (1.4)	220 (1.2)	216 (1.3)	216 (1.2)	219 (1.0)	223 (1.1)	223 (1.2)	223 (0.9)	70 (1.2)	38 (1.2)	9 (0.7)
South Carolina	210 (1.3)	209 (1.4)	214 (1.3)	215 (1.3)	213 (1.3)	214 (1.2)	216 (1.1)	215 (1.2)	214 (1.2)	60 (1.4)	28 (1.5)	6 (0.8)
South Dakota	— (†)	— (†)	— (†)	222 (1.2)	222 (0.5)	223 (1.0)	222 (0.6)	220 (0.9)	218 (1.0)	66 (1.2)	32 (1.1)	6 (0.6)
Tennessee[6]	212 (1.4)	212 (1.4)	214 (1.2)	212 (1.6)	214 (1.4)	216 (1.2)	217 (1.2)	215 (1.1)	220 (1.4)	67 (1.5)	34 (1.6)	8 (0.9)
Texas	213 (1.6)	214 (1.9)	217 (1.7)	215 (1.0)	219 (0.8)	220 (0.9)	219 (1.2)	218 (1.5)	217 (1.1)	63 (1.3)	28 (1.2)	6 (0.7)
Utah	220 (1.1)	216 (1.2)	222 (1.0)	219 (1.0)	221 (1.1)	221 (1.2)	219 (1.0)	220 (1.0)	223 (1.1)	71 (1.2)	37 (1.4)	8 (0.7)
Vermont	— (†)	— (†)	227 (1.1)	226 (0.9)	227 (0.9)	228 (0.8)	229 (0.8)	227 (0.6)	228 (0.6)	75 (1.0)	42 (1.1)	12 (1.0)
Virginia	221 (1.4)	217 (1.2)	225 (1.3)	223 (1.5)	226 (0.8)	227 (1.1)	227 (1.2)	226 (1.1)	229 (1.3)	74 (1.3)	43 (1.6)	12 (1.2)
Washington[6]	— (†)	218 (1.4)	224 (1.2)	221 (1.1)	224 (1.1)	224 (1.4)	221 (1.2)	221 (1.1)	225 (1.4)	72 (1.3)	40 (1.7)	10 (1.1)
West Virginia	216 (1.3)	216 (1.7)	219 (1.2)	219 (1.0)	215 (0.8)	215 (1.1)	215 (1.0)	214 (0.8)	215 (0.8)	62 (1.3)	27 (1.1)	5 (0.6)
Wisconsin[5,6]	224 (1.0)	222 (1.1)	‡ (†)	221 (0.8)	221 (1.0)	223 (1.2)	220 (1.1)	221 (0.8)	221 (1.6)	68 (1.8)	35 (1.6)	8 (0.8)
Wyoming	223 (1.1)	218 (1.5)	221 (1.0)	222 (0.8)	223 (0.7)	225 (0.5)	223 (0.7)	224 (0.8)	226 (0.6)	75 (1.0)	37 (0.9)	7 (0.5)
Department of Defense dependents schools[8]	— (†)	220 (0.7)	224 (0.4)	224 (0.5)	226 (0.6)	229 (0.5)	228 (0.5)	229 (0.5)	232 (0.6)	82 (0.9)	43 (1.1)	8 (0.6)

—Not available.

†Not applicable.

‡Reporting standards not met. Participation rates fell below the required standards for reporting.

[1]Scale ranges from 0 to 500.

[2]*Basic* denotes partial mastery of the knowledge and skills that are fundamental for proficient work at the 4th-grade level.

[3]*Proficient* represents solid academic performance for 4th-graders. Students reaching this level have demonstrated competency over challenging subject matter.

[4]*Advanced* signifies superior performance.

[5]Did not satisfy one or more of the guidelines for school participation in 1998. Data are subject to appreciable nonresponse bias.

[6]Did not satisfy one or more of the guidelines for school participation in 2002. Data are subject to appreciable nonresponse bias.

[7]Did not satisfy one or more of the guidelines for school participation in 1992. Data are subject to appreciable nonresponse bias.

[8]Prior to 2005, NAEP divided the Department of Defense (DoD) schools into two jurisdictions, domestic and overseas. In 2005, NAEP began combining the DoD domestic and overseas schools into a single jurisdiction. Data shown in this table for years prior to 2005 were recalculated for comparability.

NOTE: With the exception of 1992, includes public school students who were tested with accommodations; excludes only those students with disabilities (SD) and English language learners (ELL) who were unable to be tested even with accommodations. SD and ELL populations, accommodation rates, and exclusion rates vary from state to state. Race categories exclude persons of Hispanic ethnicity.

SOURCE: U.S. Department of Education, National Center for Education Statistics, National Assessment of Educational Progress (NAEP), 1992, 1998, 2002, 2003, 2005, 2007, 2009, 2011, and 2013 Reading Assessments, retrieved November 8, 2013, from the Main NAEP Data Explorer (http://nces.ed.gov/nationsreportcard/naepdata/). (This table was prepared November 2013.)

Average National Assessment of Educational Progress (NAEP) reading scale score and percentage of 4th-grade public school students, by race/ethnicity and state: 2013

[Standard errors appear in parentheses]

State	Average scale score[1] White		Black		Hispanic		Asian		Pacific Islander		American Indian/ Alaska Native		Percent of students White		Black		Hispanic		Asian		Pacific Islander		American Indian/ Alaska Native	
1	2		3		4		5		6		7		8		9		10		11		12		13	
United States	231	(0.3)	205	(0.5)	207	(0.5)	237	(1.1)	210	(2.5)	206	(1.5)	51	(0.4)	15	(0.3)	25	(0.4)	5	(0.2)	#	(†)	1	(#)
Alabama	227	(1.3)	202	(1.8)	206	(4.1)	‡	(†)	‡	(†)	‡	(†)	60	(1.6)	30	(1.8)	7	(0.9)	2	(0.2)	#	(†)	1	(0.3)
Alaska	228	(1.1)	203	(4.3)	213	(2.9)	207	(2.9)	197	(5.1)	173	(2.1)	47	(1.0)	4	(0.3)	7	(0.4)	8	(0.5)	3	(0.3)	24	(1.0)
Arizona	228	(1.4)	206	(4.0)	202	(1.7)	219	(8.8)	‡	(†)	186	(3.9)	41	(1.5)	5	(0.4)	45	(1.5)	3	(0.5)	#	(†)	5	(0.6)
Arkansas	226	(1.0)	200	(2.4)	211	(2.8)	‡	(†)	‡	(†)	‡	(†)	64	(1.3)	21	(1.4)	11	(0.9)	2	(0.3)	#	(†)	1	(0.2)
California	232	(1.6)	202	(2.6)	201	(1.5)	229	(2.8)	‡	(†)	‡	(†)	26	(1.7)	6	(0.7)	54	(1.8)	11	(1.3)	1	(0.1)	1	(0.2)
Colorado	237	(1.2)	203	(4.5)	210	(1.6)	230	(5.0)	‡	(†)	‡	(†)	57	(1.1)	5	(0.5)	31	(1.2)	4	(0.4)	#	(†)	1	(0.2)
Connecticut	238	(1.0)	208	(2.6)	209	(2.2)	246	(3.2)	‡	(†)	‡	(†)	61	(1.3)	11	(0.7)	20	(1.1)	5	(0.4)	#	(†)	#	(†)
Delaware	235	(0.9)	213	(1.3)	216	(1.8)	249	(3.6)	‡	(†)	‡	(†)	47	(1.0)	31	(0.8)	15	(0.7)	4	(0.3)	#	(†)	1	(0.2)
District of Columbia	259	(2.3)	197	(1.0)	208	(2.1)	‡	(†)	‡	(†)	‡	(†)	10	(0.3)	73	(0.5)	14	(0.4)	2	(0.2)	#	(†)	#	(†)
Florida	236	(1.4)	212	(1.6)	225	(1.5)	248	(2.9)	‡	(†)	‡	(†)	40	(1.7)	22	(1.3)	31	(1.6)	3	(0.3)	#	(†)	#	(†)
Georgia	233	(1.5)	209	(1.7)	213	(2.0)	245	(3.5)	‡	(†)	‡	(†)	44	(1.4)	34	(1.9)	15	(1.2)	4	(0.4)	#	(†)	#	(†)
Hawaii	231	(1.9)	223	(6.4)	211	(3.2)	218	(1.7)	203	(1.5)	‡	(†)	15	(0.8)	2	(0.3)	6	(0.5)	36	(1.1)	33	(1.1)	1	(0.1)
Idaho	224	(1.0)	‡	(†)	198	(1.9)	‡	(†)	‡	(†)	‡	(†)	78	(0.8)	1	(0.2)	16	(0.7)	1	(0.2)	#	(†)	1	(0.3)
Illinois	231	(1.8)	199	(2.7)	204	(1.6)	242	(3.4)	‡	(†)	‡	(†)	48	(1.6)	17	(1.2)	27	(1.5)	5	(0.6)	#	(†)	#	(†)
Indiana	229	(1.1)	207	(3.0)	215	(2.3)	236	(7.3)	‡	(†)	‡	(†)	74	(1.6)	10	(1.6)	9	(0.9)	2	(0.4)	#	(†)	#	(†)
Iowa	227	(1.3)	200	(3.8)	210	(2.7)	224	(7.3)	‡	(†)	‡	(†)	80	(1.0)	5	(0.5)	8	(0.7)	3	(0.4)	#	(†)	#	(†)
Kansas	230	(1.2)	200	(3.9)	208	(2.1)	228	(5.6)	‡	(†)	‡	(†)	67	(1.4)	7	(0.8)	17	(1.4)	3	(0.4)	#	(†)	1	(0.2)
Kentucky	227	(1.3)	204	(2.3)	220	(3.1)	243	(4.9)	‡	(†)	‡	(†)	80	(1.0)	11	(0.8)	5	(0.7)	2	(0.3)	#	(†)	1	(†)
Louisiana	223	(1.3)	198	(1.5)	212	(3.4)	‡	(†)	‡	(†)	‡	(†)	44	(2.0)	48	(1.8)	4	(0.6)	1	(0.2)	#	(†)	1	(0.3)
Maine	226	(0.9)	192	(5.0)	‡	(†)	‡	(†)	‡	(†)	‡	(†)	92	(0.4)	3	(0.3)	2	(0.2)	2	(0.2)	#	(†)	1	(0.2)
Maryland	244	(1.6)	214	(1.3)	224	(2.7)	255	(3.8)	‡	(†)	‡	(†)	43	(1.9)	34	(1.7)	12	(0.9)	6	(1.0)	#	(†)	#	(†)
Massachusetts	241	(1.2)	209	(3.3)	208	(2.5)	239	(3.3)	‡	(†)	‡	(†)	64	(1.5)	7	(1.0)	18	(1.2)	7	(0.8)	#	(†)	#	(†)
Michigan	224	(1.8)	196	(2.3)	209	(3.1)	228	(7.4)	‡	(†)	‡	(†)	66	(1.9)	18	(2.1)	9	(1.8)	3	(0.7)	#	(†)	1	(0.3)
Minnesota	233	(1.0)	208	(3.2)	207	(3.1)	223	(5.6)	‡	(†)	‡	(†)	72	(1.7)	9	(1.2)	7	(0.7)	7	(1.0)	#	(†)	1	(0.2)
Mississippi	222	(1.0)	197	(1.5)	206	(3.0)	‡	(†)	‡	(†)	‡	(†)	44	(1.3)	52	(1.3)	3	(0.4)	1	(0.2)	#	(†)	#	(†)
Missouri	228	(1.0)	200	(2.0)	219	(4.6)	‡	(†)	‡	(†)	‡	(†)	72	(1.3)	19	(1.1)	5	(0.7)	2	(0.3)	#	(†)	1	(0.1)
Montana	228	(0.8)	‡	(†)	214	(4.2)	‡	(†)	‡	(†)	198	(2.4)	79	(1.0)	1	(0.2)	4	(0.3)	1	(0.2)	#	(†)	13	(0.9)
Nebraska	229	(1.1)	202	(3.1)	207	(2.1)	232	(6.1)	‡	(†)	‡	(†)	70	(1.3)	6	(0.6)	17	(1.0)	2	(0.3)	#	(†)	1	(0.3)
Nevada	226	(1.2)	201	(2.6)	202	(1.5)	227	(3.2)	‡	(†)	‡	(†)	36	(1.5)	10	(0.8)	41	(1.5)	5	(0.5)	1	(0.2)	1	(0.1)
New Hampshire	233	(0.9)	215	(5.0)	209	(4.1)	237	(4.4)	‡	(†)	‡	(†)	89	(0.8)	2	(0.2)	4	(0.5)	4	(0.4)	#	(†)	#	(†)
New Jersey	238	(1.3)	211	(2.2)	212	(2.3)	250	(2.4)	‡	(†)	‡	(†)	53	(1.6)	17	(1.3)	21	(1.7)	8	(1.3)	#	(†)	#	(†)
New Mexico	225	(1.8)	210	(5.8)	201	(1.2)	‡	(†)	‡	(†)	187	(3.4)	24	(1.1)	2	(0.2)	63	(1.0)	1	(0.2)	#	(†)	9	(1.1)
New York	233	(1.3)	211	(2.2)	210	(1.8)	237	(2.4)	‡	(†)	‡	(†)	48	(1.9)	18	(1.5)	23	(1.5)	9	(0.8)	#	(†)	#	(†)
North Carolina	232	(1.2)	210	(1.5)	210	(2.2)	238	(4.1)	‡	(†)	206	(7.3)	49	(1.5)	26	(1.2)	16	(1.1)	3	(0.3)	#	(†)	2	(0.8)
North Dakota	227	(0.5)	211	(4.4)	217	(4.2)	‡	(†)	‡	(†)	201	(2.1)	84	(0.4)	3	(0.2)	2	(0.2)	1	(0.1)	#	(†)	9	(0.3)
Ohio	231	(1.1)	195	(2.8)	214	(2.9)	244	(5.6)	‡	(†)	‡	(†)	71	(1.8)	17	(1.6)	4	(0.6)	2	(0.3)	#	(†)	#	(†)
Oklahoma	223	(1.3)	201	(2.5)	204	(2.0)	228	(5.1)	‡	(†)	217	(2.4)	52	(1.2)	11	(0.8)	14	(0.9)	2	(0.3)	#	(†)	15	(0.8)
Oregon	225	(1.3)	200	(4.0)	199	(2.0)	234	(6.6)	‡	(†)	‡	(†)	64	(1.1)	3	(0.4)	21	(1.1)	4	(0.7)	1	(0.1)	2	(0.4)
Pennsylvania	233	(1.2)	208	(3.0)	208	(3.6)	236	(3.4)	‡	(†)	‡	(†)	69	(1.9)	16	(1.4)	8	(1.1)	4	(0.5)	#	(†)	#	(†)
Rhode Island	233	(0.9)	205	(2.8)	201	(1.8)	224	(4.9)	‡	(†)	‡	(†)	63	(1.2)	9	(0.4)	22	(1.1)	3	(0.3)	#	(†)	1	(0.1)
South Carolina	224	(1.7)	197	(1.8)	211	(3.8)	‡	(†)	‡	(†)	‡	(†)	53	(1.3)	35	(1.4)	7	(0.7)	1	(0.2)	#	(†)	#	(†)
South Dakota	225	(0.8)	202	(6.1)	207	(4.2)	‡	(†)	‡	(†)	191	(2.5)	76	(1.1)	3	(0.3)	4	(0.4)	2	(0.3)	#	(†)	14	(1.2)
Tennessee	227	(1.3)	201	(2.7)	203	(3.6)	240	(5.4)	‡	(†)	‡	(†)	67	(1.7)	21	(1.4)	8	(0.7)	2	(0.3)	#	(†)	#	(†)
Texas	233	(1.6)	209	(2.1)	206	(1.2)	252	(4.5)	‡	(†)	‡	(†)	30	(1.4)	14	(1.0)	50	(1.4)	4	(0.8)	#	(†)	#	(†)
Utah	229	(0.9)	‡	(†)	196	(2.0)	‡	(†)	‡	(†)	‡	(†)	77	(1.3)	1	(0.2)	16	(1.1)	1	(0.2)	1	(0.2)	1	(0.3)
Vermont	229	(0.7)	‡	(†)	‡	(†)	‡	(†)	‡	(†)	‡	(†)	91	(0.4)	2	(0.2)	1	(0.2)	2	(0.2)	#	(†)	#	(†)
Virginia	236	(1.3)	211	(2.2)	211	(3.4)	248	(4.0)	‡	(†)	‡	(†)	54	(1.7)	20	(1.1)	12	(1.0)	9	(1.2)	#	(†)	#	(†)
Washington	232	(1.4)	211	(3.9)	205	(2.6)	243	(3.9)	‡	(†)	‡	(†)	58	(1.1)	4	(0.5)	21	(1.3)	8	(1.0)	1	(0.2)	1	(0.4)
West Virginia	215	(0.8)	203	(3.5)	‡	(†)	‡	(†)	‡	(†)	‡	(†)	92	(0.7)	5	(0.5)	1	(0.2)	1	(0.2)	#	(†)	#	(†)
Wisconsin	228	(1.1)	193	(3.0)	201	(3.5)	223	(3.9)	‡	(†)	211	(6.6)	71	(1.7)	10	(0.9)	12	(1.1)	4	(0.4)	#	(†)	2	(0.7)
Wyoming	229	(0.6)	‡	(†)	215	(1.6)	‡	(†)	‡	(†)	199	(2.7)	79	(0.4)	1	(0.1)	13	(0.3)	1	(0.2)	#	(†)	4	(0.2)
Department of Defense dependents schools	236	(0.9)	222	(1.6)	228	(1.5)	235	(2.5)	‡	(†)	‡	(†)	47	(0.5)	15	(0.4)	19	(0.5)	6	(0.3)	1	(0.2)	#	(†)

†Not applicable.
#Rounds to zero.
‡Reporting standards not met (too few cases for a reliable estimate).
[1]Scale ranges from 0 to 500.
NOTE: Includes public school students who were tested with accommodations; excludes only those students with disabilities (SD) and English language learners (ELL) who were unable to be tested even with accommodations. SD and ELL populations, accommodation rates, and exclusion rates vary from state to state. Race/ethnicity based on school records. Race categories exclude persons of Hispanic ethnicity. Detail may not sum to totals because of rounding and because table does not include students classified as "Two or more races."
SOURCE: U.S. Department of Education, National Center for Education Statistics, National Assessment of Educational Progress (NAEP), 2013 Reading Assessment, retrieved November 15, 2013, from the Main NAEP Data Explorer (http://nces.ed.gov/nationsreportcard/naepdata/). (This table was prepared November 2013.)

Average National Assessment of Educational Progress (NAEP) reading scale score of 8th-grade public school students and percentage attaining reading achievement levels, by locale and state: Selected years, 2003 through 2013

[Standard errors appear in parentheses]

State	Average scale score[1]												Percent attaining reading achievement levels, 2013				Average scale score[1] by school locale, 2013							
	2003		2005		2007		2009		2011		2013		At or above Basic[2]		At or above Proficient[3]		City		Suburb		Town		Rural	
1	2		3		4		5		6		7		8		9		10		11		12		13	
United States	261	(0.2)	260	(0.2)	261	(0.2)	262	(0.3)	264	(0.2)	266	(0.2)	77	(0.3)	34	(0.3)	260	(0.6)	270	(0.4)	263	(0.6)	268	(0.5)
Alabama	253	(1.5)	252	(1.4)	252	(1.0)	255	(1.1)	258	(1.5)	257	(1.2)	68	(1.3)	25	(1.5)	250	(3.5)	261	(3.4)	259	(1.8)	259	(1.4)
Alaska	256	(1.1)	259	(0.9)	259	(1.0)	259	(0.9)	261	(0.9)	261	(0.8)	71	(1.1)	31	(1.1)	‡	(†)	‡	(†)	‡	(†)	‡	(†)
Arizona	255	(1.4)	255	(1.0)	255	(1.2)	258	(1.2)	260	(1.2)	260	(1.1)	72	(1.3)	28	(1.5)	259	(1.5)	266	(2.3)	251	(3.4)	261	(2.2)
Arkansas	258	(1.3)	258	(1.1)	258	(1.0)	258	(1.2)	259	(0.9)	262	(1.1)	73	(1.2)	30	(1.5)	265	(1.5)	261	(2.5)	260	(2.0)	261	(2.0)
California[4]	251	(1.3)	250	(0.6)	251	(0.8)	253	(1.2)	255	(1.0)	262	(1.2)	72	(1.0)	29	(1.4)	261	(2.0)	263	(1.9)	254	(3.4)	266	(5.1)
Colorado	268	(1.2)	265	(1.1)	266	(1.0)	266	(0.8)	271	(1.4)	271	(1.1)	81	(1.1)	40	(1.5)	264	(2.5)	274	(2.1)	268	(3.0)	278	(1.9)
Connecticut	267	(1.1)	264	(1.3)	267	(1.6)	272	(0.9)	275	(0.9)	274	(1.0)	83	(1.0)	45	(1.3)	261	(2.7)	278	(1.1)	282	(2.8)	283	(1.9)
Delaware	265	(0.7)	266	(0.6)	265	(0.6)	265	(0.7)	266	(0.6)	266	(0.7)	77	(1.0)	33	(1.0)	263	(2.2)	264	(1.0)	268	(1.7)	269	(1.1)
District of Columbia	239	(0.8)	238	(0.9)	241	(0.7)	242	(0.9)	242	(0.9)	248	(0.9)	57	(1.3)	17	(0.9)	248	(0.9)	‡	(†)	‡	(†)	‡	(†)
Florida	257	(1.3)	256	(1.2)	260	(1.2)	264	(1.2)	262	(1.0)	266	(1.1)	77	(1.2)	33	(1.5)	265	(3.0)	266	(1.3)	263	(2.3)	267	(2.6)
Georgia	258	(1.1)	257	(1.3)	259	(1.0)	260	(1.0)	262	(1.1)	265	(1.2)	75	(1.4)	32	(1.5)	255	(2.6)	270	(1.9)	264	(3.0)	262	(2.1)
Hawaii	251	(0.9)	249	(0.9)	251	(0.8)	255	(0.6)	257	(0.7)	260	(0.8)	71	(1.0)	28	(1.1)	264	(1.5)	261	(1.5)	257	(1.5)	256	(2.0)
Idaho	264	(0.9)	264	(1.1)	265	(0.9)	265	(0.9)	268	(0.9)	270	(0.8)	82	(0.9)	38	(1.2)	273	(0.9)	271	(1.5)	268	(1.5)	269	(1.5)
Illinois	266	(1.0)	264	(1.0)	263	(1.0)	265	(1.2)	266	(0.8)	267	(1.0)	77	(0.9)	36	(1.4)	259	(2.5)	269	(1.5)	268	(1.5)	276	(2.8)
Indiana	265	(1.0)	261	(1.1)	264	(1.1)	266	(1.0)	265	(1.0)	267	(1.2)	79	(1.2)	35	(1.7)	261	(2.5)	269	(2.6)	267	(2.2)	271	(1.6)
Iowa	268	(0.8)	267	(0.9)	267	(0.9)	265	(0.9)	265	(1.0)	269	(0.8)	81	(0.9)	37	(1.3)	264	(2.0)	281	(2.2)	267	(1.7)	270	(1.0)
Kansas[4]	266	(1.5)	267	(1.0)	267	(0.8)	267	(1.1)	267	(1.0)	267	(1.0)	78	(1.2)	36	(1.2)	259	(2.8)	275	(2.2)	262	(1.6)	272	(1.3)
Kentucky	266	(1.3)	264	(1.1)	262	(1.0)	267	(0.9)	269	(0.8)	270	(0.8)	80	(0.9)	38	(1.4)	266	(1.4)	274	(1.9)	269	(1.7)	270	(1.5)
Louisiana	253	(1.6)	253	(1.6)	253	(1.1)	253	(1.6)	255	(1.5)	257	(1.0)	68	(1.4)	24	(1.3)	253	(2.1)	263	(2.6)	254	(2.0)	259	(1.8)
Maine	268	(1.0)	270	(1.0)	270	(0.8)	268	(0.7)	270	(0.8)	269	(0.8)	79	(1.0)	38	(1.3)	267	(2.6)	276	(2.3)	269	(1.7)	268	(1.0)
Maryland	262	(1.4)	261	(1.2)	265	(1.2)	267	(1.1)	271	(1.2)	274	(1.1)	82	(1.2)	42	(1.4)	269	(2.1)	274	(1.4)	‡	(†)	278	(2.4)
Massachusetts	273	(1.0)	274	(1.0)	273	(1.0)	274	(1.2)	275	(1.0)	277	(1.0)	84	(0.9)	48	(1.4)	263	(2.6)	281	(1.1)	‡	(†)	282	(3.7)
Michigan	264	(1.8)	261	(1.2)	260	(1.2)	262	(1.4)	265	(0.9)	266	(1.0)	77	(1.1)	33	(1.5)	257	(2.5)	271	(1.2)	268	(2.5)	266	(2.3)
Minnesota	268	(1.1)	268	(1.2)	268	(0.9)	270	(1.0)	270	(1.0)	271	(1.0)	82	(1.1)	41	(1.5)	267	(2.1)	274	(1.8)	270	(2.2)	272	(1.9)
Mississippi	255	(1.4)	251	(1.3)	250	(1.1)	251	(1.0)	254	(1.2)	253	(1.0)	64	(1.3)	20	(1.3)	249	(4.8)	258	(2.2)	245	(2.1)	257	(1.3)
Missouri	267	(1.0)	265	(1.0)	263	(1.0)	267	(1.0)	267	(1.1)	267	(1.1)	78	(1.3)	36	(1.4)	257	(4.2)	272	(1.8)	263	(2.6)	271	(1.4)
Montana	270	(0.9)	269	(0.7)	271	(0.9)	270	(0.6)	273	(0.6)	272	(0.8)	84	(0.8)	40	(1.2)	273	(1.6)	277	(3.4)	270	(1.3)	272	(1.2)
Nebraska	266	(0.9)	267	(0.9)	267	(0.9)	267	(0.9)	268	(0.7)	269	(0.8)	81	(0.9)	37	(1.3)	271	(1.5)	270	(1.7)	266	(1.8)	270	(1.6)
Nevada	252	(0.8)	253	(0.9)	252	(0.8)	254	(0.9)	258	(0.9)	262	(0.7)	72	(1.0)	30	(1.1)	262	(1.5)	258	(1.2)	263	(2.0)	266	(1.6)
New Hampshire	271	(0.9)	270	(1.2)	270	(0.9)	271	(1.0)	272	(0.7)	274	(0.8)	84	(0.8)	44	(1.3)	260	(2.0)	277	(1.8)	273	(1.5)	278	(1.2)
New Jersey	268	(1.2)	269	(1.2)	270	(1.1)	273	(1.3)	275	(1.2)	276	(1.1)	85	(1.0)	46	(1.4)	266	(4.5)	277	(1.2)	‡	(†)	280	(2.4)
New Mexico	252	(0.9)	251	(1.0)	251	(0.8)	254	(1.2)	256	(0.9)	256	(0.8)	67	(1.0)	22	(1.0)	257	(1.2)	258	(1.9)	257	(1.6)	253	(1.3)
New York	265	(1.3)	265	(1.0)	264	(1.0)	264	(1.0)	266	(1.1)	266	(1.1)	76	(1.0)	35	(1.6)	256	(1.3)	274	(2.0)	274	(5.3)	272	(2.5)
North Carolina	262	(1.0)	258	(0.9)	259	(1.1)	260	(1.2)	263	(0.9)	265	(1.1)	76	(1.1)	33	(1.6)	266	(2.2)	270	(5.4)	258	(2.0)	264	(1.5)
North Dakota	270	(0.8)	270	(0.6)	268	(0.7)	269	(0.6)	269	(0.7)	268	(0.6)	81	(1.0)	34	(0.9)	268	(1.2)	270	(2.0)	268	(1.2)	267	(0.8)
Ohio	267	(1.3)	267	(1.3)	268	(1.2)	269	(1.3)	268	(1.1)	269	(1.0)	79	(1.0)	39	(1.5)	251	(3.7)	274	(1.2)	265	(2.0)	274	(1.6)
Oklahoma	262	(0.9)	260	(1.1)	260	(0.8)	259	(0.9)	260	(1.1)	262	(0.9)	75	(1.1)	29	(1.2)	257	(2.5)	265	(1.8)	261	(1.3)	263	(1.7)
Oregon	264	(1.2)	263	(1.1)	266	(0.9)	265	(1.0)	264	(0.9)	268	(0.9)	79	(1.1)	37	(1.3)	271	(1.5)	269	(2.0)	264	(2.0)	269	(2.0)
Pennsylvania	264	(1.2)	267	(1.3)	268	(1.2)	271	(0.8)	268	(1.3)	272	(1.0)	81	(1.2)	42	(1.4)	246	(2.8)	280	(1.2)	273	(1.9)	275	(2.5)
Rhode Island	261	(0.7)	261	(0.7)	258	(0.9)	260	(0.6)	265	(0.7)	267	(0.6)	77	(0.9)	36	(1.2)	257	(1.3)	268	(1.0)	279	(4.5)	278	(1.3)
South Carolina	258	(1.3)	257	(1.1)	257	(0.9)	257	(1.2)	260	(0.9)	261	(1.0)	73	(1.4)	29	(1.2)	264	(3.6)	262	(1.9)	258	(2.2)	261	(1.2)
South Dakota	270	(0.8)	269	(0.6)	270	(0.7)	270	(0.5)	269	(0.8)	268	(0.8)	81	(0.9)	36	(1.1)	269	(1.3)	‡	(†)	268	(1.3)	268	(1.2)
Tennessee	258	(1.2)	259	(0.9)	259	(1.0)	261	(1.1)	259	(1.0)	265	(1.1)	77	(1.2)	33	(1.5)	256	(3.1)	275	(2.4)	265	(2.6)	267	(1.3)
Texas	259	(1.1)	258	(0.6)	261	(0.9)	260	(1.1)	261	(1.0)	264	(1.1)	76	(1.4)	31	(1.6)	258	(1.9)	266	(2.0)	260	(3.3)	272	(2.2)
Utah	264	(0.8)	262	(0.8)	262	(0.8)	266	(1.0)	266	(0.8)	270	(0.8)	81	(1.0)	39	(1.2)	272	(3.1)	271	(1.0)	265	(2.0)	270	(2.2)
Vermont	271	(0.8)	269	(0.7)	273	(0.8)	272	(0.6)	274	(0.9)	274	(0.7)	84	(0.9)	45	(1.0)	‡	(†)	‡	(†)	‡	(†)	‡	(†)
Virginia	268	(1.1)	268	(1.0)	267	(1.1)	266	(1.1)	267	(1.2)	268	(1.3)	78	(1.3)	36	(1.6)	262	(2.8)	272	(1.9)	260	(3.3)	267	(2.2)
Washington	264	(0.9)	265	(1.3)	265	(0.9)	267	(1.1)	268	(1.0)	272	(1.0)	81	(1.2)	42	(1.5)	270	(2.3)	275	(1.3)	270	(2.7)	270	(2.0)
West Virginia	260	(1.0)	255	(1.2)	255	(1.0)	255	(0.9)	256	(0.9)	257	(0.9)	70	(1.1)	25	(1.1)	260	(3.6)	260	(2.1)	256	(1.7)	257	(1.2)
Wisconsin	266	(1.3)	266	(1.1)	264	(1.0)	266	(1.0)	267	(0.9)	268	(0.9)	78	(0.9)	36	(1.4)	257	(2.0)	273	(2.3)	272	(1.6)	269	(1.6)
Wyoming	267	(0.5)	268	(0.7)	266	(0.7)	268	(1.0)	270	(1.0)	271	(0.6)	84	(0.7)	38	(1.0)	272	(1.1)	‡	(†)	272	(1.0)	268	(1.2)
Department of Defense dependents schools[5]	272	(0.6)	271	(0.7)	273	(1.0)	272	(0.7)	272	(0.7)	277	(0.7)	89	(0.8)	45	(1.2)	266	(2.6)	275	(1.6)	‡	(†)	275	(3.3)

†Not applicable.

‡Reporting standards not met. Either there are too few cases for a reliable estimate or item response rates fell below the required standards for reporting.

[1]Scale ranges from 0 to 500.

[2]Basic denotes partial mastery of the knowledge and skills that are fundamental for proficient work at the 8th-grade level.

[3]Proficient represents solid academic performance for 8th-graders. Students reaching this level have demonstrated competency over challenging subject matter.

[4]Did not satisfy one or more of the guidelines for school participation in 2003. Data are subject to appreciable nonresponse bias.

[5]Prior to 2005, NAEP divided the Department of Defense (DoD) schools into two jurisdictions, domestic and overseas. In 2005, NAEP began combining the DoD domestic and overseas schools into a single jurisdiction. Data shown in this table for 2003 were recalculated for comparability.

NOTE: Includes public school students who were tested with accommodations; excludes only those students with disabilities (SD) and English language learners (ELL) who were unable to be tested even with accommodations. SD and ELL populations, accommodation rates, and exclusion rates vary from state to state.

SOURCE: U.S. Department of Education, National Center for Education Statistics, National Assessment of Educational Progress (NAEP), 2003, 2005, 2007, 2009, 2011, and 2013 Reading Assessments, retrieved November 8, 2013, from the Main NAEP Data Explorer (http://nces.ed.gov/nationsreportcard/naepdata/). (This table was prepared November 2013.)

Average National Assessment of Educational Progress (NAEP) reading scale scores of 4th- and 8th-graders in public schools and percentage scoring at or above selected reading achievement levels, by English language learner (ELL) status and state: 2013
[Standard errors appear in parentheses]

State	4th-graders							8th-graders						
	English language learners				Not English language learners			English language learners				Not English language learners		
	Percent of all students assessed	Average scale score[1]	Percent At or above Basic[2]	Percent At or above Proficient[3]	Average scale score[1]	Percent At or above Basic[2]	Percent At or above Proficient[3]	Percent of all students assessed	Average scale score[1]	Percent At or above Basic[2]	Percent At or above Proficient[3]	Average scale score[1]	Percent At or above Basic[2]	Percent At or above Proficient[3]
1	2	3	4	5	6	7	8	9	10	11	12	13	14	15
United States	10 (0.3)	187 (0.7)	31 (0.8)	7 (0.4)	225 (0.3)	71 (0.3)	37 (0.4)	5 (0.1)	225 (0.9)	30 (1.4)	3 (0.4)	268 (0.2)	79 (0.3)	36 (0.3)
Alabama	2 (0.5)	‡ (†)	‡ (†)	‡ (†)	219 (1.2)	66 (1.5)	31 (1.5)	1 (0.2)	‡ (†)	‡ (†)	‡ (†)	258 (1.2)	69 (1.3)	25 (1.5)
Alaska	14 (0.9)	154 (3.0)	10 (2.3)	1 (0.6)	218 (1.0)	65 (1.3)	32 (1.3)	11 (0.7)	214 (2.5)	16 (2.9)	1 (†)	267 (0.7)	78 (1.0)	35 (1.2)
Arizona	7 (0.9)	159 (4.4)	8 (2.4)	1 (†)	217 (1.2)	63 (1.5)	30 (1.4)	1 (0.2)	‡ (†)	‡ (†)	‡ (†)	261 (1.1)	73 (1.3)	28 (1.5)
Arkansas	8 (0.8)	202 (2.8)	47 (3.8)	17 (2.6)	220 (1.0)	68 (1.2)	33 (1.4)	6 (0.5)	245 (3.2)	55 (4.7)	12 (3.8)	263 (1.2)	74 (1.2)	31 (1.6)
California	25 (1.4)	182 (1.8)	26 (1.8)	5 (0.8)	223 (1.1)	69 (1.4)	34 (1.5)	12 (0.9)	220 (2.2)	23 (3.5)	2 (1.0)	267 (1.2)	79 (1.1)	33 (1.4)
Colorado	14 (1.1)	192 (2.3)	37 (2.9)	8 (1.6)	232 (1.0)	80 (1.2)	46 (1.7)	8 (0.8)	232 (2.5)	37 (4.4)	3 (1.5)	274 (1.1)	85 (1.0)	43 (1.6)
Connecticut	5 (0.4)	181 (4.0)	25 (5.1)	4 (1.9)	232 (0.9)	79 (1.2)	45 (1.2)	3 (0.6)	222 (5.7)	27 (7.0)	1 (†)	276 (0.9)	85 (0.9)	47 (1.3)
Delaware	2 (0.2)	184 (5.5)	24 (6.7)	4 (1.9)	227 (0.7)	74 (1.1)	39 (1.2)	1 (0.2)	‡ (†)	‡ (†)	‡ (†)	267 (0.7)	77 (1.0)	34 (1.0)
District of Columbia	6 (0.3)	182 (3.7)	23 (4.8)	5 (2.6)	207 (1.0)	51 (1.2)	24 (0.9)	5 (0.3)	218 (3.9)	25 (5.4)	2 (†)	249 (0.9)	59 (1.3)	18 (0.9)
Florida	10 (0.8)	199 (2.4)	41 (3.7)	10 (1.9)	230 (1.0)	79 (1.1)	42 (1.5)	4 (0.3)	226 (3.3)	30 (4.8)	3 (1.4)	268 (1.1)	79 (1.0)	35 (1.5)
Georgia	3 (0.6)	189 (4.5)	29 (5.9)	8 (3.5)	223 (1.1)	68 (1.4)	35 (1.5)	2 (0.4)	220 (5.1)	21 (6.7)	4 (†)	265 (1.2)	76 (1.4)	32 (1.5)
Hawaii	7 (0.6)	166 (3.5)	14 (2.9)	3 (1.4)	219 (1.0)	65 (1.3)	32 (1.3)	10 (0.4)	224 (2.4)	29 (3.1)	3 (1.2)	264 (0.8)	76 (1.1)	31 (1.2)
Idaho	4 (0.5)	170 (4.2)	17 (4.3)	3 (1.4)	222 (0.9)	70 (1.1)	34 (1.2)	3 (0.4)	222 (3.8)	21 (5.7)	2 (†)	272 (0.8)	84 (0.8)	39 (1.2)
Illinois	8 (0.7)	174 (2.8)	18 (3.1)	3 (1.7)	222 (1.4)	68 (1.6)	36 (1.5)	5 (0.5)	219 (3.8)	23 (4.9)	1 (†)	269 (1.0)	80 (1.0)	38 (1.4)
Indiana	6 (0.8)	203 (3.5)	48 (5.6)	13 (3.1)	227 (1.1)	75 (1.2)	39 (1.6)	3 (0.4)	236 (4.6)	40 (6.0)	6 (2.3)	268 (1.1)	81 (1.3)	36 (1.8)
Iowa	5 (0.8)	195 (5.2)	41 (6.4)	11 (2.8)	225 (1.2)	73 (1.4)	39 (1.5)	2 (0.3)	226 (3.9)	27 (6.9)	2 (†)	270 (0.8)	83 (0.9)	38 (1.3)
Kansas	13 (1.3)	203 (2.5)	49 (3.4)	17 (2.4)	226 (1.2)	75 (1.5)	41 (1.8)	8 (1.3)	245 (2.4)	55 (3.6)	13 (2.3)	269 (1.1)	80 (1.4)	38 (1.4)
Kentucky	2 (0.3)	197 (6.0)	41 (7.9)	11 (5.9)	225 (1.2)	72 (1.4)	37 (1.7)	1 (0.2)	237 (4.5)	43 (8.1)	5 (†)	270 (0.9)	80 (0.9)	38 (1.4)
Louisiana	2 (0.3)	202 (4.7)	47 (7.8)	10 (5.2)	211 (1.3)	57 (1.7)	23 (1.3)	1 (0.3)	‡ (†)	‡ (†)	‡ (†)	258 (1.0)	68 (1.4)	24 (1.3)
Maine	2 (0.3)	190 (6.5)	35 (8.0)	9 (4.9)	226 (0.9)	72 (1.1)	38 (1.3)	2 (0.3)	‡ (†)	‡ (†)	‡ (†)	270 (0.8)	79 (1.0)	39 (1.3)
Maryland	4 (0.6)	207 (5.0)	51 (7.1)	18 (4.9)	233 (1.3)	78 (1.1)	46 (1.9)	1 (0.4)	‡ (†)	‡ (†)	‡ (†)	274 (1.0)	83 (1.1)	43 (1.4)
Massachusetts	10 (0.8)	192 (4.3)	40 (4.3)	12 (2.4)	237 (1.0)	83 (1.1)	51 (1.5)	5 (0.6)	224 (3.0)	28 (4.0)	4 (1.5)	280 (1.0)	87 (0.9)	50 (1.4)
Michigan	8 (1.6)	194 (4.3)	39 (5.8)	9 (2.3)	219 (1.4)	66 (1.4)	32 (1.7)	3 (0.7)	232 (5.3)	41 (6.7)	8 (3.9)	267 (1.1)	78 (1.2)	34 (1.6)
Minnesota	8 (0.9)	188 (2.9)	33 (4.7)	8 (1.9)	230 (1.1)	78 (1.4)	44 (1.4)	5 (0.8)	231 (5.1)	40 (7.7)	6 (2.6)	273 (1.0)	84 (1.0)	42 (1.6)
Mississippi	1 (0.3)	‡ (†)	‡ (†)	‡ (†)	209 (1.0)	54 (1.3)	21 (1.0)	1 (0.2)	‡ (†)	‡ (†)	‡ (†)	253 (1.0)	64 (1.3)	20 (1.3)
Missouri	2 (0.3)	197 (4.0)	37 (9.0)	6 (3.5)	223 (1.0)	70 (1.2)	36 (1.4)	1 (0.3)	‡ (†)	‡ (†)	‡ (†)	267 (1.1)	79 (1.3)	36 (1.4)
Montana	3 (0.5)	174 (4.3)	16 (4.6)	2 (1.6)	225 (0.8)	72 (1.1)	36 (1.1)	2 (0.3)	‡ (†)	‡ (†)	‡ (†)	273 (0.8)	85 (0.8)	41 (1.2)
Nebraska	7 (0.6)	190 (3.9)	34 (4.3)	7 (1.9)	226 (1.0)	74 (1.0)	39 (1.4)	2 (0.3)	‡ (†)	‡ (†)	‡ (†)	270 (0.8)	82 (0.9)	37 (1.3)
Nevada	22 (1.2)	185 (1.6)	30 (2.5)	6 (1.1)	222 (1.1)	71 (1.4)	33 (1.5)	7 (0.4)	217 (2.5)	21 (3.5)	2 (1.4)	265 (0.7)	76 (1.0)	33 (1.1)
New Hampshire	2 (0.4)	196 (5.7)	34 (7.3)	10 (4.6)	233 (0.9)	81 (1.0)	45 (1.5)	2 (0.2)	‡ (†)	‡ (†)	‡ (†)	275 (0.8)	85 (0.8)	44 (1.4)
New Jersey	3 (0.5)	188 (5.8)	33 (6.8)	9 (3.5)	230 (1.2)	76 (1.2)	43 (1.7)	1 (0.2)	‡ (†)	‡ (†)	‡ (†)	277 (1.0)	86 (1.0)	47 (1.4)
New Mexico	18 (1.3)	168 (1.8)	16 (1.8)	3 (1.0)	214 (1.0)	60 (1.3)	25 (1.0)	13 (0.6)	224 (1.7)	29 (2.8)	2 (1.2)	261 (0.8)	73 (1.1)	25 (1.1)
New York	7 (0.5)	182 (2.7)	25 (3.2)	4 (1.4)	227 (1.2)	74 (1.5)	40 (1.6)	6 (0.5)	215 (2.7)	20 (3.4)	1 (0.7)	270 (1.1)	80 (1.0)	37 (1.7)
North Carolina	6 (0.7)	183 (3.4)	23 (3.8)	4 (1.8)	225 (1.0)	72 (1.2)	37 (1.2)	4 (0.3)	232 (3.6)	41 (5.9)	7 (3.0)	266 (1.1)	77 (1.1)	34 (1.7)
North Dakota	2 (0.2)	‡ (†)	‡ (†)	‡ (†)	225 (0.5)	74 (0.9)	34 (0.9)	2 (0.2)	‡ (†)	‡ (†)	‡ (†)	269 (0.6)	82 (1.0)	35 (0.9)
Ohio	3 (0.5)	205 (5.1)	51 (7.1)	19 (5.2)	224 (1.2)	71 (1.3)	38 (1.6)	1 (0.3)	251 (6.4)	60 (9.0)	20 (8.3)	269 (1.0)	79 (1.0)	39 (1.5)
Oklahoma	6 (0.5)	186 (3.4)	30 (4.0)	6 (1.7)	219 (1.1)	68 (1.3)	31 (1.4)	4 (0.5)	229 (3.8)	39 (5.1)	6 (3.6)	263 (0.9)	76 (1.2)	30 (1.2)
Oregon	13 (0.9)	183 (2.7)	29 (2.8)	6 (1.7)	225 (1.3)	71 (1.4)	38 (1.7)	3 (0.4)	218 (4.5)	23 (5.4)	1 (†)	270 (0.9)	81 (1.1)	38 (1.3)
Pennsylvania	2 (0.3)	181 (7.4)	27 (6.9)	5 (2.5)	227 (1.3)	74 (1.4)	41 (1.6)	2 (0.4)	222 (5.2)	26 (5.3)	3 (1.5)	273 (1.0)	83 (1.1)	43 (1.4)
Rhode Island	6 (0.5)	168 (3.5)	17 (3.4)	4 (2.2)	226 (0.9)	73 (1.1)	40 (1.2)	4 (0.3)	216 (3.5)	20 (4.4)	3 (2.0)	269 (0.6)	79 (0.9)	37 (1.2)
South Carolina	6 (0.7)	206 (3.9)	54 (5.2)	18 (4.1)	214 (1.2)	61 (1.4)	29 (1.5)	3 (0.3)	242 (4.3)	54 (6.1)	10 (3.2)	262 (1.0)	73 (1.4)	30 (1.2)
South Dakota	3 (0.5)	160 (6.6)	20 (4.1)	5 (2.5)	220 (0.8)	67 (1.2)	33 (1.1)	2 (0.3)	‡ (†)	‡ (†)	‡ (†)	269 (0.7)	82 (0.9)	36 (1.1)
Tennessee	3 (0.4)	174 (5.4)	19 (4.6)	2 (†)	221 (1.3)	69 (1.5)	35 (1.6)	1 (0.2)	‡ (†)	‡ (†)	‡ (†)	266 (1.1)	77 (1.2)	33 (1.5)
Texas	22 (1.6)	194 (1.4)	36 (2.4)	9 (1.3)	223 (1.2)	70 (1.4)	34 (1.5)	7 (0.7)	227 (2.6)	32 (3.9)	2 (1.3)	267 (1.1)	79 (1.3)	33 (1.7)
Utah	5 (0.6)	159 (3.6)	9 (2.9)	1 (0.3)	226 (1.0)	74 (1.1)	39 (1.4)	4 (0.4)	220 (3.3)	21 (5.1)	3 (1.9)	272 (0.9)	83 (1.0)	40 (1.2)
Vermont	2 (0.2)	‡ (†)	‡ (†)	‡ (†)	229 (0.6)	76 (1.0)	43 (1.1)	1 (0.1)	‡ (†)	‡ (†)	‡ (†)	275 (0.7)	84 (0.9)	45 (1.0)
Virginia	7 (0.8)	186 (3.6)	28 (4.2)	5 (2.0)	232 (1.2)	77 (1.3)	46 (1.6)	5 (0.6)	242 (3.6)	51 (6.8)	7 (2.9)	269 (1.4)	79 (1.3)	38 (1.6)
Washington	9 (0.8)	179 (3.0)	20 (3.1)	3 (1.4)	229 (1.4)	77 (1.3)	43 (1.8)	5 (0.6)	222 (4.7)	26 (6.1)	3 (2.2)	275 (0.9)	84 (1.1)	44 (1.5)
West Virginia	1 (0.3)	‡ (†)	‡ (†)	‡ (†)	215 (0.8)	62 (1.2)	27 (1.0)	# (†)	‡ (†)	‡ (†)	‡ (†)	257 (0.9)	70 (1.1)	25 (1.1)
Wisconsin	8 (0.8)	190 (2.8)	34 (4.4)	9 (2.2)	223 (1.6)	70 (1.7)	37 (1.7)	5 (0.4)	242 (2.9)	51 (4.3)	9 (2.7)	269 (1.0)	79 (0.9)	38 (1.5)
Wyoming	3 (0.2)	196 (3.9)	37 (6.8)	9 (4.4)	227 (0.5)	76 (1.0)	38 (1.0)	2 (0.2)	‡ (†)	‡ (†)	‡ (†)	272 (0.6)	85 (0.8)	38 (1.0)
Department of Defense dependents schools	5 (0.3)	216 (2.5)	63 (4.7)	20 (4.0)	233 (0.6)	83 (0.9)	44 (1.1)	3 (0.3)	244 (3.7)	52 (7.4)	6 (3.8)	278 (0.7)	91 (0.8)	46 (1.2)

†Not applicable.
#Rounds to zero.
‡Reporting standards not met (too few cases for a reliable estimate).
[1]Scale ranges from 0 to 500.
[2]*Basic* denotes partial mastery of the knowledge and skills that are fundamental for proficient work at a given grade.
[3]*Proficient* represents solid academic performance. Students reaching this level have demonstrated competency over challenging subject matter.

NOTE: The results for English language learners are based on students who were assessed and cannot be generalized to the total population of such students. Although testing accommodations were permitted, some English language learners did not have a sufficient level of English proficiency to participate in the 2013 Reading Assessment.
SOURCE: U.S. Department of Education, National Center for Education Statistics, National Assessment of Educational Progress (NAEP), 2013 Reading Assessment, retrieved November 8, 2013, from the Main NAEP Data Explorer (http://nces.ed.gov/nationsreport card/naepdata/). (This table was prepared November 2013.)

Average National Assessment of Educational Progress (NAEP) reading scale score and standard deviation, by selected student characteristics, percentile, and grade: Selected years, 1992 through 2013
[Standard errors appear in parentheses]

Selected student characteristic, percentile, and grade	1992[1]	1998	2000	2002	2003	2005	2007	2009	2011	2013 Total	2013 Male	2013 Female
1	2	3	4	5	6	7	8	9	10	11	12	13

Average reading scale score[2]

All students												
4th grade	217 (0.9)	215 (1.1)	213 (1.3)	219 (0.4)	218 (0.3)	219 (0.2)	221 (0.3)	221 (0.3)	221 (0.3)	222 (0.3)	219 (0.3)	225 (0.3)
8th grade	260 (0.9)	263 (0.8)	— (†)	264 (0.4)	263 (0.3)	262 (0.2)	263 (0.2)	264 (0.3)	265 (0.2)	268 (0.3)	263 (0.3)	273 (0.3)
12th grade	292 (0.6)	290 (0.6)	— (†)	287 (0.7)	— (†)	286 (0.6)	— (†)	288 (0.7)	— (†)	— (†)	— (†)	— (†)
Eligibility for free or reduced-price lunch												
4th grade												
Eligible	— (†)	196 (1.7)	193 (1.7)	203 (0.7)	201 (0.3)	203 (0.3)	205 (0.3)	206 (0.2)	207 (0.3)	207 (0.3)	204 (0.4)	211 (0.3)
Not eligible	— (†)	227 (0.9)	226 (1.2)	230 (0.4)	229 (0.3)	230 (0.2)	232 (0.3)	232 (0.3)	235 (0.3)	236 (0.3)	233 (0.4)	239 (0.4)
Unknown	— (†)	223 (2.7)	225 (2.3)	226 (1.6)	230 (0.9)	232 (0.9)	233 (1.3)	236 (1.3)	235 (0.8)	237 (1.4)	233 (1.7)	240 (2.0)
8th grade												
Eligible	— (†)	245 (1.0)	— (†)	249 (0.5)	247 (0.4)	247 (0.3)	247 (0.3)	249 (0.3)	252 (0.3)	254 (0.2)	249 (0.3)	259 (0.3)
Not eligible	— (†)	269 (1.0)	— (†)	272 (0.4)	271 (0.3)	270 (0.2)	271 (0.3)	273 (0.3)	275 (0.3)	278 (0.3)	273 (0.3)	284 (0.3)
Unknown	— (†)	272 (2.0)	— (†)	271 (1.4)	272 (1.0)	275 (1.1)	277 (1.3)	280 (1.3)	283 (0.9)	286 (1.8)	281 (2.3)	291 (1.7)
12th grade												
Eligible	— (†)	270 (1.1)	— (†)	273 (1.4)	— (†)	271 (1.0)	— (†)	273 (0.7)	— (†)	— (†)	— (†)	— (†)
Not eligible	— (†)	293 (0.6)	— (†)	289 (0.9)	— (†)	290 (0.7)	— (†)	294 (0.8)	— (†)	— (†)	— (†)	— (†)
Unknown	— (†)	295 (1.6)	— (†)	294 (1.5)	— (†)	295 (1.9)	— (†)	296 (2.4)	— (†)	— (†)	— (†)	— (†)
Read for fun on own time												
4th grade												
Almost every day	223 (1.2)	219 (1.5)	218 (1.7)	225 (0.5)	225 (0.3)	225 (0.3)	227 (0.3)	228 (0.4)	228 (0.4)	229 (0.4)	226 (0.5)	231 (0.4)
1–2 times a week	218 (1.2)	217 (1.2)	216 (1.2)	220 (0.5)	219 (0.3)	220 (0.3)	223 (0.3)	221 (0.4)	221 (0.4)	223 (0.4)	220 (0.4)	225 (0.4)
1–2 times a month	210 (1.6)	211 (1.9)	212 (1.6)	210 (0.8)	211 (0.3)	213 (0.4)	216 (0.4)	214 (0.4)	214 (0.4)	216 (0.4)	214 (0.5)	219 (0.6)
Never or hardly ever	199 (1.8)	202 (1.9)	201 (1.8)	208 (0.5)	207 (0.4)	208 (0.3)	211 (0.4)	210 (0.3)	210 (0.3)	211 (0.4)	209 (0.5)	213 (0.7)
8th grade												
Almost every day	277 (1.1)	277 (1.0)	— (†)	279 (0.6)	279 (0.4)	279 (0.3)	281 (0.4)	282 (0.4)	284 (0.4)	286 (0.4)	281 (0.6)	289 (0.5)
1–2 times a week	263 (1.0)	267 (1.1)	— (†)	266 (0.5)	265 (0.4)	265 (0.3)	265 (0.3)	267 (0.4)	268 (0.3)	271 (0.4)	267 (0.6)	274 (0.5)
1–2 times a month	258 (1.2)	263 (0.9)	— (†)	264 (0.6)	262 (0.3)	261 (0.3)	261 (0.4)	261 (0.4)	263 (0.3)	266 (0.3)	262 (0.4)	269 (0.4)
Never or hardly ever	246 (1.4)	251 (1.1)	— (†)	255 (0.4)	253 (0.3)	252 (0.3)	253 (0.3)	253 (0.4)	255 (0.3)	257 (0.3)	255 (0.3)	260 (0.4)
12th grade												
Almost every day	304 (0.9)	304 (1.0)	— (†)	304 (1.1)	— (†)	302 (1.2)	— (†)	305 (0.9)	— (†)	— (†)	— (†)	— (†)
1–2 times a week	296 (0.7)	298 (0.9)	— (†)	292 (1.1)	— (†)	292 (1.0)	— (†)	295 (1.0)	— (†)	— (†)	— (†)	— (†)
1–2 times a month	290 (0.9)	289 (0.7)	— (†)	288 (0.9)	— (†)	285 (0.8)	— (†)	288 (0.8)	— (†)	— (†)	— (†)	— (†)
Never or hardly ever	279 (1.0)	275 (1.0)	— (†)	275 (1.0)	— (†)	274 (0.8)	— (†)	275 (0.6)	— (†)	— (†)	— (†)	— (†)
Percentile[3]												
4th grade												
10th	170 (1.9)	163 (2.1)	159 (2.3)	170 (0.9)	169 (0.5)	171 (0.4)	174 (0.4)	175 (0.5)	174 (0.4)	174 (0.6)	169 (0.8)	179 (0.6)
25th	194 (1.1)	191 (1.7)	189 (1.4)	196 (0.5)	195 (0.4)	196 (0.3)	199 (0.3)	199 (0.4)	200 (0.4)	200 (0.3)	197 (0.5)	204 (0.5)
50th	219 (1.3)	217 (1.3)	218 (1.7)	221 (0.5)	221 (0.3)	221 (0.2)	224 (0.3)	223 (0.3)	224 (0.3)	225 (0.3)	222 (0.4)	228 (0.4)
75th	242 (1.1)	242 (0.9)	243 (0.8)	244 (0.5)	244 (0.3)	244 (0.3)	246 (0.3)	245 (0.3)	246 (0.3)	247 (0.3)	245 (0.4)	250 (0.4)
90th	261 (1.4)	262 (0.9)	262 (1.4)	263 (0.4)	264 (0.3)	263 (0.3)	264 (0.4)	264 (0.3)	264 (0.4)	265 (0.4)	263 (0.5)	268 (0.4)
8th grade												
10th	213 (1.2)	216 (1.7)	— (†)	220 (0.5)	217 (0.6)	216 (0.3)	217 (0.4)	219 (0.4)	221 (0.3)	223 (0.4)	218 (0.6)	229 (0.5)
25th	237 (1.1)	241 (0.7)	— (†)	244 (0.5)	242 (0.4)	240 (0.4)	242 (0.3)	243 (0.4)	244 (0.3)	246 (0.2)	242 (0.4)	251 (0.3)
50th	262 (1.1)	266 (0.7)	— (†)	267 (0.5)	266 (0.3)	265 (0.2)	265 (0.2)	267 (0.3)	267 (0.3)	269 (0.3)	265 (0.3)	274 (0.4)
75th	285 (0.8)	288 (1.0)	— (†)	288 (0.4)	288 (0.3)	286 (0.2)	287 (0.2)	288 (0.4)	289 (0.3)	291 (0.3)	286 (0.4)	296 (0.4)
90th	305 (1.3)	306 (0.8)	— (†)	305 (0.5)	306 (0.2)	305 (0.2)	305 (0.2)	305 (0.4)	307 (0.2)	310 (0.4)	304 (0.4)	314 (0.4)
12th grade												
10th	249 (0.8)	240 (0.6)	— (†)	237 (1.5)	— (†)	235 (1.1)	— (†)	238 (0.8)	— (†)	— (†)	— (†)	— (†)
25th	271 (0.8)	267 (0.8)	— (†)	263 (1.3)	— (†)	262 (0.8)	— (†)	264 (0.8)	— (†)	— (†)	— (†)	— (†)
50th	294 (0.8)	293 (0.6)	— (†)	289 (0.7)	— (†)	288 (0.8)	— (†)	291 (0.7)	— (†)	— (†)	— (†)	— (†)
75th	315 (0.5)	317 (0.7)	— (†)	312 (0.6)	— (†)	313 (1.1)	— (†)	315 (0.9)	— (†)	— (†)	— (†)	— (†)
90th	333 (0.7)	336 (0.8)	— (†)	332 (0.9)	— (†)	333 (1.1)	— (†)	335 (0.9)	— (†)	— (†)	— (†)	— (†)

Standard deviation[4] of the reading scale score

All students												
4th grade	36 (0.6)	39 (0.7)	42 (0.9)	36 (0.3)	37 (0.2)	36 (0.1)	36 (0.2)	35 (0.2)	36 (0.1)	37 (0.2)	38 (0.3)	36 (0.2)
8th grade	36 (0.3)	35 (0.5)	— (†)	34 (0.3)	35 (0.2)	35 (0.1)	35 (0.2)	34 (0.2)	34 (0.1)	34 (0.1)	34 (0.2)	34 (0.2)
12th grade	33 (0.4)	38 (0.4)	— (†)	37 (0.4)	— (†)	38 (0.4)	— (†)	38 (0.3)	— (†)	— (†)	— (†)	— (†)

—Not available.
†Not applicable.
[1]Accommodations were not permitted for this assessment.
[2]Scale ranges from 0 to 500.
[3]The percentile represents a specific point on the percentage distribution of all students ranked by their reading score from low to high. For example, 10 percent of students scored at or below the 10th percentile score, while 90 percent of students scored above it.
[4]The standard deviation provides an indication of how much the test scores varied. The lower the standard deviation, the closer the scores were clustered around the average score. About two-thirds of the student scores can be expected to fall within the range of one standard deviation above and one standard deviation below the average score. For example, the average score for all 4th-graders in 2013 was 222, and the standard deviation was 37. This means that we would expect about two-thirds of the students to have scores between 259 (one standard deviation above the average) and 185 (one standard deviation below). Standard errors also must be taken into account when making comparisons of these ranges.
NOTE: Includes public and private schools. For 1998 and later years, includes students tested with accommodations (1 to 11 percent of all students, depending on grade level and year); excludes only those students with disabilities and English language learners who were unable to be tested even with accommodations (2 to 6 percent of all students). On the student questionnaire, the format of the question about reading for fun on your own time changed slightly beginning with the 2002 assessment year. In 1992 through 2000, reading for fun was one of several activities included in the same question ("How often do you do each of the following?"), and the response options were listed in order from most frequent to least frequent (that is, "Almost every day" was listed first, and "Never or hardly ever" was listed last); in 2002 through 2011, reading for fun was the only activity in the question, and the order of the response options was reversed. Grade 12 results for the 2013 NAEP Reading Assessment were not yet available at the time this table was created.
SOURCE: U.S. Department of Education, National Center for Education Statistics, National Assessment of Educational Progress (NAEP), 1992, 1998, 2000, 2002, 2003, 2005, 2007, 2009, 2011, and 2013 Reading Assessments, retrieved November 19, 2013, from the Main NAEP Data Explorer (http://nces.ed.gov/nationsreportcard/naepdata/). (This table was prepared November 2013.)

Average National Assessment of Educational Progress (NAEP) reading scale scores of 4th- and 8th-grade public school students and percentage attaining reading achievement levels, by race/ethnicity and jurisdiction or specific urban district: 2009, 2011, and 2013

[Standard errors appear in parentheses]

Grade level and jurisdiction or specific urban district	2009 All students	2011 All students[2]	White	Black	Hispanic	Asian	2013 All students[2]	White	Black	Hispanic	Asian	Percent of students 2013 At or above Basic[3]	At or above Proficient[4]
1	2	3	4	5	6	7	8	9	10	11	12	13	14
4th grade													
United States	220 (0.3)	220 (0.3)	230 (0.3)	205 (0.4)	205 (0.5)	236 (1.3)	221 (0.3)	231 (0.3)	205 (0.5)	207 (0.5)	237 (1.1)	67 (0.3)	34 (0.3)
All large cities	210 (0.7)	211 (0.7)	232 (0.9)	202 (0.7)	203 (0.8)	225 (2.5)	212 (0.7)	235 (1.0)	202 (0.8)	204 (0.8)	229 (2.5)	57 (0.8)	26 (0.7)
Selected urban districts													
Albuquerque	— (†)	209 (1.6)	231 (2.5)	‡ (†)	201 (1.7)	‡ (†)	207 (1.5)	232 (2.4)	‡ (†)	199 (1.7)	‡ (†)	54 (1.7)	24 (1.5)
Atlanta	209 (1.5)	212 (1.4)	251 (1.9)	203 (1.6)	215 (3.4)	‡ (†)	214 (1.3)	252 (1.9)	204 (1.4)	208 (3.5)	‡ (†)	57 (1.6)	27 (1.2)
Austin	220 (1.8)	224 (2.3)	249 (3.3)	215 (4.5)	210 (2.6)	‡ (†)	221 (1.6)	250 (2.2)	206 (5.4)	208 (2.1)	‡ (†)	65 (1.7)	36 (1.7)
Baltimore City	202 (1.7)	200 (1.7)	221 (3.3)	198 (1.7)	‡ (†)	‡ (†)	204 (1.6)	233 (5.2)	201 (1.7)	‡ (†)	‡ (†)	45 (2.2)	14 (1.4)
Boston	215 (1.4)	217 (0.8)	241 (2.5)	211 (1.7)	214 (1.1)	226 (3.8)	214 (1.1)	237 (2.2)	205 (1.9)	210 (1.7)	234 (3.3)	61 (1.4)	26 (1.3)
Charlotte	225 (1.6)	224 (1.2)	244 (1.5)	211 (1.9)	212 (2.6)	233 (5.3)	226 (1.6)	245 (1.8)	215 (2.0)	212 (2.9)	238 (4.9)	72 (1.8)	40 (1.9)
Chicago	202 (1.5)	203 (1.3)	229 (2.4)	197 (1.9)	201 (1.5)	228 (4.2)	206 (1.6)	239 (4.1)	198 (2.5)	203 (2.6)	235 (4.7)	51 (1.6)	20 (1.6)
Cleveland	194 (2.0)	193 (0.9)	209 (2.6)	187 (1.1)	196 (3.3)	‡ (†)	190 (1.9)	206 (3.7)	185 (2.2)	191 (4.1)	‡ (†)	33 (2.2)	9 (1.2)
Dallas	— (†)	204 (1.6)	237 (6.9)	204 (2.0)	200 (1.4)	‡ (†)	205 (1.4)	231 (4.9)	201 (2.1)	204 (1.8)	‡ (†)	49 (2.1)	16 (1.5)
Detroit	187 (1.9)	191 (2.0)	‡ (†)	190 (2.5)	199 (5.5)	‡ (†)	190 (2.2)	‡ (†)	188 (2.6)	199 (3.4)	‡ (†)	30 (2.7)	7 (1.3)
District of Columbia	203 (1.2)	201 (1.0)	255 (3.0)	191 (1.3)	204 (3.3)	‡ (†)	206 (1.2)	260 (2.6)	192 (1.4)	211 (2.6)	‡ (†)	49 (1.4)	25 (1.0)
Fresno	197 (1.7)	194 (2.4)	216 (3.9)	191 (4.3)	190 (2.5)	195 (3.0)	196 (1.7)	218 (2.9)	187 (3.0)	192 (1.9)	199 (3.0)	39 (1.9)	13 (1.0)
Hillsborough County (FL)	— (†)	231 (1.7)	242 (1.8)	218 (2.5)	223 (2.1)	‡ (†)	228 (1.3)	237 (1.8)	214 (3.1)	223 (1.6)	247 (4.0)	75 (1.4)	40 (2.0)
Houston	211 (1.4)	213 (1.6)	243 (3.0)	207 (1.7)	209 (1.6)	245 (6.3)	208 (1.3)	238 (3.3)	202 (2.7)	204 (1.3)	245 (4.7)	52 (1.6)	19 (1.3)
Jefferson County (KY)	219 (1.8)	223 (1.3)	230 (1.4)	208 (2.1)	221 (3.9)	256 (5.7)	221 (1.2)	233 (1.7)	203 (1.9)	221 (3.5)	‡ (†)	66 (1.6)	33 (1.6)
Los Angeles	197 (1.1)	201 (1.2)	225 (3.7)	196 (4.2)	196 (1.1)	226 (4.2)	205 (1.2)	237 (3.4)	204 (2.9)	199 (1.3)	222 (4.3)	50 (1.9)	19 (1.7)
Miami-Dade	221 (1.2)	221 (1.5)	240 (3.4)	210 (2.1)	222 (1.8)	‡ (†)	223 (1.5)	239 (2.8)	209 (2.2)	225 (1.7)	‡ (†)	70 (1.7)	35 (2.1)
Milwaukee	196 (2.0)	195 (1.7)	216 (3.9)	187 (2.0)	198 (2.7)	206 (3.3)	199 (1.9)	223 (3.8)	190 (2.3)	200 (2.6)	201 (8.2)	42 (2.1)	15 (1.8)
New York City	217 (1.4)	216 (1.2)	235 (3.3)	209 (1.7)	207 (1.5)	230 (3.6)	216 (1.4)	231 (3.1)	210 (1.8)	208 (1.6)	233 (3.2)	62 (1.6)	28 (1.7)
Philadelphia	195 (1.8)	199 (1.8)	217 (3.3)	195 (1.9)	191 (3.5)	212 (5.2)	200 (1.7)	214 (3.2)	196 (2.0)	193 (3.0)	215 (4.9)	44 (2.2)	14 (1.7)
San Diego	213 (2.1)	215 (1.7)	240 (2.3)	205 (3.0)	201 (2.2)	225 (3.3)	218 (1.6)	240 (2.2)	205 (4.0)	204 (2.4)	229 (3.9)	64 (2.0)	33 (1.8)
8th grade													
United States	262 (0.3)	264 (0.2)	272 (0.3)	248 (0.5)	251 (0.5)	277 (1.1)	266 (0.2)	275 (0.2)	250 (0.4)	255 (0.4)	280 (1.0)	77 (0.3)	34 (0.3)
All large cities	252 (0.5)	255 (0.5)	273 (1.0)	245 (0.8)	249 (0.8)	271 (1.5)	258 (0.8)	276 (1.0)	246 (0.9)	253 (0.7)	273 (2.8)	68 (0.7)	26 (0.9)
Selected urban districts													
Albuquerque	— (†)	254 (1.2)	271 (2.2)	‡ (†)	248 (1.6)	‡ (†)	256 (1.0)	275 (2.6)	‡ (†)	250 (1.1)	‡ (†)	66 (1.5)	23 (1.4)
Atlanta	250 (1.5)	253 (1.0)	287 (3.2)	249 (1.2)	‡ (†)	‡ (†)	255 (1.0)	294 (2.8)	249 (1.2)	254 (4.5)	‡ (†)	63 (1.5)	22 (1.3)
Austin	261 (2.0)	261 (1.5)	285 (1.8)	246 (3.6)	251 (2.2)	‡ (†)	261 (1.4)	286 (2.9)	245 (3.5)	251 (1.6)	‡ (†)	70 (1.5)	31 (2.1)
Baltimore City	245 (1.7)	246 (1.6)	267 (3.7)	242 (1.7)	‡ (†)	‡ (†)	252 (1.5)	275 (5.6)	249 (1.5)	‡ (†)	‡ (†)	61 (2.7)	16 (1.8)
Boston	257 (1.4)	255 (1.2)	281 (4.3)	246 (2.0)	245 (2.3)	280 (3.4)	257 (1.0)	281 (2.8)	247 (1.8)	250 (1.5)	278 (3.5)	66 (1.5)	28 (1.3)
Charlotte	259 (1.0)	265 (0.9)	283 (1.8)	253 (1.6)	256 (2.5)	264 (5.3)	266 (1.2)	286 (2.0)	253 (1.8)	259 (3.1)	‡ (†)	76 (1.4)	36 (1.7)
Chicago	249 (1.6)	253 (1.1)	271 (3.5)	245 (1.9)	255 (1.3)	262 (13.1)	253 (1.0)	279 (2.6)	244 (1.6)	255 (1.6)	278 (4.3)	64 (1.5)	21 (1.3)
Cleveland	242 (1.6)	240 (1.7)	260 (3.1)	234 (2.2)	241 (3.8)	‡ (†)	239 (1.6)	250 (3.2)	235 (1.8)	241 (3.6)	‡ (†)	49 (2.0)	11 (1.5)
Dallas	— (†)	248 (1.0)	276 (4.1)	244 (2.8)	246 (1.1)	‡ (†)	251 (1.3)	‡ (†)	244 (2.4)	253 (1.6)	‡ (†)	63 (2.0)	15 (1.4)
Detroit	232 (2.4)	237 (1.0)	‡ (†)	235 (1.1)	244 (4.2)	‡ (†)	239 (1.6)	‡ (†)	239 (1.6)	242 (4.7)	‡ (†)	46 (2.1)	9 (1.6)
District of Columbia	240 (1.5)	237 (1.0)	290 (3.4)	231 (1.2)	232 (3.8)	‡ (†)	245 (1.3)	301 (4.0)	237 (1.4)	247 (3.6)	‡ (†)	53 (1.8)	18 (1.1)
Fresno	240 (2.4)	238 (1.8)	257 (3.2)	230 (3.5)	234 (2.2)	241 (3.4)	245 (1.4)	265 (3.4)	236 (3.3)	241 (1.6)	247 (3.1)	54 (2.3)	13 (1.5)
Hillsborough County (FL)	— (†)	264 (1.5)	276 (1.5)	247 (2.4)	258 (2.3)	‡ (†)	267 (1.2)	277 (1.6)	252 (2.3)	263 (1.8)	‡ (†)	77 (1.6)	35 (1.6)
Houston	252 (1.2)	252 (0.9)	283 (2.2)	247 (2.4)	249 (1.3)	‡ (†)	252 (1.2)	284 (3.2)	245 (2.2)	250 (1.4)	284 (5.6)	63 (1.7)	19 (1.3)
Jefferson County (KY)	259 (1.0)	260 (1.1)	269 (1.7)	245 (1.7)	‡ (†)	‡ (†)	261 (1.0)	271 (1.6)	243 (1.6)	258 (4.5)	‡ (†)	69 (1.3)	29 (1.5)
Los Angeles	244 (1.1)	246 (1.1)	273 (3.6)	242 (3.3)	241 (1.2)	269 (4.5)	250 (1.2)	276 (3.2)	240 (3.8)	245 (1.1)	272 (3.1)	60 (1.6)	19 (1.5)
Miami-Dade	261 (1.4)	260 (1.4)	275 (2.4)	246 (1.8)	262 (1.5)	‡ (†)	259 (1.0)	278 (2.8)	245 (2.0)	261 (1.1)	‡ (†)	71 (1.3)	27 (1.5)
Milwaukee	241 (2.0)	238 (1.6)	255 (3.0)	232 (2.0)	243 (2.9)	248 (5.5)	242 (1.4)	262 (3.3)	232 (1.7)	253 (2.5)	‡ (†)	51 (2.0)	13 (1.4)
New York City	252 (1.4)	254 (1.8)	271 (3.6)	248 (2.3)	246 (2.4)	273 (3.3)	256 (1.2)	274 (4.0)	253 (2.0)	249 (2.0)	271 (3.1)	67 (1.2)	25 (1.6)
Philadelphia	247 (2.5)	247 (1.5)	264 (3.8)	244 (1.9)	239 (3.0)	258 (4.7)	249 (1.8)	261 (3.1)	244 (2.4)	243 (3.3)	265 (5.4)	58 (2.2)	16 (2.0)
San Diego	254 (2.8)	256 (2.1)	275 (2.6)	238 (4.8)	245 (3.2)	268 (4.2)	260 (1.5)	281 (2.4)	244 (3.7)	247 (2.1)	266 (3.6)	70 (1.8)	29 (2.3)

—Not available.

†Not applicable.

‡Reporting standards not met (too few cases for a reliable estimate).

[1]Scale ranges from 0 to 500.

[2]Includes data for students of two or more races, which are not separately shown.

[3]*Basic* denotes partial mastery of prerequisite knowledge and skills that are fundamental for proficient work at a given grade.

[4]*Proficient* represents solid academic performance. Students reaching this level have demonstrated competency over challenging subject matter.

NOTE: Race categories exclude persons of Hispanic ethnicity. Totals include racial/ethnic groups not shown separately.

SOURCE: U.S. Department of Education, National Center for Education Statistics, National Assessment of Educational Progress (NAEP), 2009, 2011, and 2013 Reading Assessments, retrieved December 30, 2013, from the Main NAEP Data Explorer (http://nces.ed.gov/nationsreportcard/naepdata/). (This table was prepared December 2013.)

Average National Assessment of Educational Progress (NAEP) reading scale score, by age and selected student characteristics: Selected years, 1971 through 2012

[Standard errors appear in parentheses]

Selected student characteristic	1971	1975	1980	1984	1988	1990	1992	1994	1996	1999	2004[1] Previous format	2004[1] Revised format	2008	2012
1	2	3	4	5	6	7	8	9	10	11	12	13	14	15
9-year-olds **All students**	208 (1.0)	210 (0.7)	215 (1.0)	211 (0.8)	212 (1.1)	209 (1.2)	211 (0.9)	211 (1.2)	212 (1.0)	212 (1.3)	219 (1.1)	216 (1.0)	220 (0.9)	221 (0.8)
Sex														
Male	201 (1.1)	204 (0.8)	210 (1.1)	207 (1.0)	207 (1.4)	204 (1.7)	206 (1.3)	207 (1.3)	207 (1.4)	209 (1.6)	216 (1.4)	212 (1.1)	216 (1.1)	218 (0.9)
Female	214 (1.0)	216 (0.8)	220 (1.1)	214 (0.9)	216 (1.3)	215 (1.2)	215 (0.9)	215 (1.4)	218 (1.1)	215 (1.5)	221 (1.0)	219 (1.1)	224 (0.9)	223 (0.9)
Gap between female and male score	13 (1.5)	12 (1.1)	10 (1.6)	7 (1.3)	9 (1.9)	11 (2.0)	10 (1.6)	7 (1.9)	11 (1.8)	6 (2.2)	5 (1.8)	8 (1.5)	7 (1.4)	5 (1.3)
Race/ethnicity														
White	214 [2] (0.9)	217 (0.7)	221 (0.8)	218 (0.9)	218 (1.4)	217 (1.3)	218 (1.0)	218 (1.3)	220 (1.2)	221 (1.6)	226 (1.1)	224 (0.9)	228 (1.0)	229 (0.8)
Black	170 [2] (1.7)	181 (1.2)	189 (1.8)	186 (1.3)	189 (2.4)	182 (2.9)	185 (2.2)	185 (2.3)	191 (2.6)	186 (2.3)	200 (2.2)	197 (1.8)	204 (1.7)	206 (1.9)
Hispanic	[3] (†)	183 (2.2)	190 (2.3)	187 (3.0)	194 (3.5)	189 (2.3)	192 (3.1)	186 (3.9)	195 (3.4)	193 (2.7)	205 (1.7)	199 (1.5)	207 (1.5)	208 (1.5)
Gap between White and Black score	44 (1.9)	35 (1.4)	32 (1.9)	32 (1.6)	29 (2.8)	35 (3.2)	33 (2.4)	33 (2.6)	29 (2.8)	35 (2.8)	26 (2.5)	27 (2.1)	24 (2.0)	23 (2.1)
Gap between White and Hispanic score	† (†)	34 (2.4)	31 (2.4)	31 (3.1)	24 (3.8)	28 (2.6)	26 (3.2)	32 (4.1)	25 (3.6)	28 (3.2)	21 (2.1)	25 (1.8)	21 (1.8)	21 (1.7)
13-year-olds **All students**	255 (0.9)	256 (0.8)	258 (0.9)	257 (0.6)	257 (1.0)	257 (0.8)	260 (1.2)	258 (0.9)	258 (1.0)	259 (1.0)	259 (1.0)	257 (1.0)	260 (0.8)	263 (1.0)
Sex														
Male	250 (1.0)	250 (0.8)	254 (1.1)	253 (0.7)	252 (1.3)	251 (1.1)	254 (1.7)	251 (1.2)	251 (1.2)	254 (1.3)	254 (1.2)	252 (1.1)	256 (1.0)	259 (1.3)
Female	261 (0.9)	262 (0.9)	263 (0.9)	262 (0.7)	263 (1.0)	263 (1.1)	265 (1.2)	266 (1.2)	264 (1.2)	265 (1.2)	264 (1.3)	262 (1.2)	264 (0.9)	267 (0.9)
Gap between female and male score	11 (1.3)	13 (1.2)	8 (1.4)	9 (1.0)	11 (1.7)	13 (1.6)	11 (2.1)	15 (1.7)	13 (1.7)	12 (1.8)	10 (1.8)	10 (1.6)	8 (1.3)	8 (1.6)
Race/ethnicity														
White	261 [2] (0.7)	262 (0.7)	264 (0.7)	263 (0.6)	261 (1.1)	262 (0.9)	266 (1.2)	265 (1.1)	266 (1.0)	267 (1.2)	266 (1.0)	265 (1.0)	268 (1.0)	270 (1.3)
Black	222 [2] (1.2)	226 (1.2)	233 (1.5)	236 (1.2)	243 (2.4)	241 (2.2)	238 (2.3)	234 (2.4)	234 (2.6)	238 (2.4)	244 (2.0)	239 (1.9)	247 (1.6)	247 (1.6)
Hispanic	[3] (†)	232 (3.0)	237 (2.0)	240 (2.0)	240 (3.5)	238 (2.3)	239 (3.5)	235 (1.9)	238 (2.9)	244 (2.9)	242 (1.6)	241 (2.1)	242 (1.5)	249 (1.3)
Gap between White and Black score	39 (1.4)	36 (1.4)	32 (1.6)	26 (1.3)	18 (2.6)	21 (2.4)	29 (2.7)	31 (2.7)	32 (2.8)	29 (2.7)	22 (2.3)	25 (2.1)	21 (1.9)	23 (2.1)
Gap between White and Hispanic score	† (†)	30 (3.1)	27 (2.1)	23 (2.1)	21 (3.6)	24 (2.5)	27 (3.7)	30 (2.2)	28 (3.1)	23 (3.1)	24 (1.9)	24 (2.4)	26 (1.8)	21 (1.8)
Parents' highest level of education														
Did not finish high school	— (†)	— (†)	239 (1.1)	240 (1.2)	246 (2.1)	241 (1.8)	239 (2.6)	237 (2.4)	239 (2.8)	238 (3.4)	240 (2.7)	238 (2.3)	239 (1.9)	248 (2.0)
Graduated high school	— (†)	— (†)	253 (0.9)	253 (0.8)	253 (1.2)	251 (0.9)	252 (1.7)	251 (1.4)	251 (1.5)	251 (1.8)	251 (1.6)	249 (1.1)	251 (1.1)	248 (1.7)
Some education after high school	— (†)	— (†)	268 (1.0)	266 (1.1)	265 (1.7)	267 (1.7)	265 (2.7)	266 (1.9)	268 (2.3)	269 (2.4)	264 (2.0)	261 (1.4)	265 (1.1)	264 (1.5)
Graduated college	— (†)	— (†)	273 (0.9)	268 (0.9)	265 (1.6)	267 (1.1)	271 (1.5)	269 (1.2)	269 (1.4)	270 (1.2)	270 (1.0)	266 (1.2)	270 (1.2)	273 (1.3)
17-year-olds **All students**	285 (1.2)	286 (0.8)	285 (1.2)	289 (0.8)	290 (1.0)	290 (1.1)	290 (1.1)	288 (1.3)	288 (1.1)	288 (1.3)	285 (1.2)	283 (1.1)	286 (0.9)	287 (0.9)
Sex														
Male	279 (1.2)	280 (1.0)	282 (1.3)	284 (0.8)	286 (1.5)	284 (1.6)	284 (1.5)	282 (2.2)	281 (1.5)	281 (1.6)	278 (1.5)	276 (1.4)	280 (1.1)	283 (1.1)
Female	291 (1.3)	291 (1.0)	289 (1.2)	294 (0.9)	294 (1.5)	296 (1.5)	296 (1.5)	295 (1.5)	295 (1.2)	295 (1.4)	292 (1.3)	289 (1.2)	291 (1.0)	291 (1.0)
Gap between female and male score	12 (1.8)	12 (1.4)	7 (1.8)	10 (1.2)	8 (2.1)	12 (2.0)	11 (1.9)	13 (2.7)	15 (1.8)	13 (2.1)	14 (2.0)	14 (1.8)	11 (1.5)	8 (1.5)
Race/ethnicity														
White	291 [2] (1.0)	293 (0.6)	293 (0.9)	295 (0.9)	295 (1.2)	297 (1.2)	297 (1.4)	296 (1.5)	295 (1.2)	295 (1.4)	293 (1.1)	289 (1.2)	295 (1.0)	295 (1.0)
Black	239 [2] (1.7)	241 (2.0)	243 (1.8)	264 (1.2)	274 (2.4)	267 (2.3)	261 (2.1)	266 (3.9)	266 (2.7)	264 (1.7)	264 (2.7)	262 (1.9)	266 (2.4)	269 (1.6)
Hispanic	[3] (†)	252 (3.6)	261 (2.7)	268 (2.9)	271 (4.3)	275 (3.6)	271 (3.7)	263 (4.9)	265 (4.1)	271 (3.9)	264 (2.9)	267 (2.5)	269 (1.3)	274 (1.5)
Gap between White and Black score	53 (2.0)	52 (2.1)	50 (2.0)	32 (1.5)	20 (2.7)	29 (2.6)	37 (2.5)	30 (4.2)	29 (3.0)	31 (2.3)	29 (2.9)	27 (2.3)	29 (2.6)	26 (1.9)
Gap between White and Hispanic score	† (†)	41 (3.6)	31 (2.9)	27 (3.0)	24 (4.4)	22 (3.8)	26 (3.9)	33 (5.2)	30 (4.2)	24 (4.2)	29 (3.1)	22 (2.8)	26 (1.6)	21 (1.9)
Parents' highest level of education														
Did not finish high school	— (†)	— (†)	262 (1.5)	269 (1.4)	267 (1.4)	270 (2.8)	271 (3.9)	268 (2.7)	267 (3.2)	265 (3.6)	259 (3.4)	259 (2.7)	266 (2.1)	266 (2.1)
Graduated high school	— (†)	— (†)	277 (1.0)	281 (0.8)	282 (1.3)	283 (1.4)	280 (1.6)	276 (1.9)	273 (1.7)	274 (2.1)	274 (1.6)	271 (1.4)	274 (1.4)	270 (1.6)
Some education after high school	— (†)	— (†)	295 (1.2)	298 (0.9)	299 (2.2)	295 (1.9)	293 (1.9)	294 (1.6)	295 (2.2)	295 (1.8)	286 (1.9)	285 (1.5)	288 (1.1)	287 (1.1)
Graduated college	— (†)	— (†)	301 (1.0)	302 (0.9)	300 (1.4)	302 (1.5)	301 (1.7)	300 (1.7)	299 (1.5)	298 (1.3)	298 (1.3)	295 (1.2)	298 (1.1)	300 (1.0)

—Not available.
†Not applicable.
[1]In 2004, two assessments were conducted—one using the same format that was used in previous assessments, and one using a revised assessment format that provides accommodations for students with disabilities and for English language learners. The 2004 data in column 12 are for the format that was used in previous assessment years, while the 2004 data in column 13 are for the revised format. In subsequent years, only the revised format was used.
[2]Data for 1971 include persons of Hispanic ethnicity.
[3]Test scores of Hispanics were not tabulated separately.
NOTE: Scale ranges from 0 to 500. Students scoring 150 (or higher) are able to follow brief written directions and carry out simple, discrete reading tasks. Students scoring 200 are able to understand, combine ideas, and make inferences based on short uncomplicated passages about specific or sequentially related information. Students scoring 250 are able to search for specific information, interrelate ideas, and make generalizations about literature, science, and social studies materials. Students scoring 300 are able to find, understand, summarize, and explain relatively complicated literary and informational material. Includes public and private schools. For assessment years prior to 2004, accommodations were not permitted. For 2004 (revised format) and later years, includes students tested with accommodations; excludes those students with disabilities and English language learners who were unable to be tested even with accommodations (2 to 5 percent of all students, depending on age and assessment year). Race categories exclude persons of Hispanic ethnicity, except where noted. Totals include other racial/ethnic groups not shown separately.
SOURCE: U.S. Department of Education, National Center for Education Statistics, National Assessment of Educational Progress (NAEP), *NAEP 2012 Trends in Academic Progress*; and 2012 NAEP Long-Term Trend Reading Assessment, retrieved June 27, 2013, from Long-Term Trend NAEP Data Explorer (http://nces.ed.gov/nationsreportcard/naepdata/). (This table was prepared June 2013.)

Percentage of students at or above selected National Assessment of Educational Progress (NAEP) reading score levels, by age, sex, and race/ethnicity: Selected years, 1971 through 2012

[Standard errors appear in parentheses]

Age, sex, race/ethnicity, and score level	1971	1975	1980	1984	1988	1990	1992	1994	1996	1999	2004	2008	2012
1	2	3	4	5	6	7	8	9	10	11	12	13	14
9-year-olds													
Total													
Level 150[1]	91 (0.5)	93 (0.4)	95 (0.4)	92 (0.4)	93 (0.7)	90 (0.9)	92 (0.4)	92 (0.7)	93 (0.6)	93 (0.7)	94 (0.5)	96 (0.4)	96 (0.4)
Level 200[2]	59 (1.0)	62 (0.8)	68 (1.0)	62 (0.8)	63 (1.3)	59 (1.3)	62 (1.1)	63 (1.4)	64 (1.3)	64 (1.4)	69 (1.0)	73 (0.9)	74 (0.9)
Level 250[3]	16 (0.6)	15 (0.6)	18 (0.8)	17 (0.7)	17 (1.1)	18 (1.0)	16 (0.8)	17 (1.2)	17 (0.8)	16 (1.0)	19 (0.7)	21 (0.8)	22 (0.7)
Male													
Level 150[1]	88 (0.7)	91 (0.5)	93 (0.5)	90 (0.5)	90 (0.9)	88 (1.4)	90 (0.8)	90 (1.0)	92 (0.8)	91 (1.1)	92 (0.6)	94 (0.6)	94 (0.6)
Level 200[2]	53 (1.2)	56 (1.0)	63 (1.1)	58 (1.0)	58 (1.8)	54 (1.9)	57 (1.6)	59 (1.5)	58 (2.0)	61 (1.8)	64 (1.3)	70 (1.2)	71 (1.0)
Level 250[3]	12 (0.6)	12 (0.6)	15 (0.9)	16 (0.8)	16 (1.4)	16 (1.2)	14 (1.0)	15 (1.2)	14 (1.3)	15 (1.3)	17 (0.8)	19 (1.0)	21 (0.8)
Female													
Level 150[1]	93 (0.5)	95 (0.3)	96 (0.4)	94 (0.5)	95 (1.0)	92 (1.1)	94 (0.6)	94 (0.8)	95 (0.6)	95 (0.8)	96 (0.5)	97 (0.4)	97 (0.4)
Level 200[2]	65 (1.1)	68 (0.8)	73 (1.0)	65 (1.0)	67 (1.4)	64 (1.2)	67 (1.2)	67 (1.9)	70 (1.6)	67 (1.6)	73 (1.2)	77 (1.1)	77 (1.1)
Level 250[3]	19 (0.8)	18 (0.8)	21 (1.0)	18 (0.8)	19 (1.2)	21 (1.2)	18 (1.1)	18 (1.5)	19 (1.3)	17 (1.3)	20 (1.0)	23 (1.0)	23 (0.9)
White													
Level 150[1]	94[5] (0.4)	96 (0.3)	97 (0.2)	95 (0.3)	95 (0.7)	94 (0.9)	96 (0.5)	96 (0.5)	96 (0.6)	97 (0.4)	97 (0.4)	98 (0.4)	98 (0.4)
Level 200[2]	65[5] (1.0)	69 (0.8)	74 (0.7)	69 (0.9)	68 (1.6)	66 (1.4)	69 (1.2)	70 (1.5)	71 (1.5)	73 (1.6)	77 (1.0)	81 (1.0)	82 (0.8)
Level 250[3]	18[5] (0.7)	17 (0.7)	21 (0.9)	21 (0.8)	20 (1.5)	23 (1.2)	20 (1.0)	20 (1.5)	20 (1.1)	20 (1.4)	24 (0.8)	27 (1.1)	28 (0.8)
Black													
Level 150[1]	70[5] (1.7)	81 (1.1)	85 (1.4)	81 (1.2)	83 (2.4)	77 (2.7)	80 (2.2)	79 (2.4)	84 (1.9)	82 (2.5)	88 (1.7)	91 (1.1)	94 (1.0)
Level 200[2]	22[5] (1.5)	32 (1.5)	41 (1.9)	37 (1.5)	39 (2.9)	34 (3.4)	37 (2.2)	38 (2.8)	42 (3.2)	36 (3.0)	50 (2.3)	58 (2.3)	61 (2.1)
Level 250[3]	2[5] (0.5)	2 (0.3)	4 (0.6)	5 (0.6)	6 (1.2)	5 (1.5)	5 (0.8)	4 (1.5)	6 (1.1)	4 (1.1)	7 (0.8)	9 (0.9)	10 (1.1)
Hispanic													
Level 150[1]	[6] (†)	81 (2.5)	84 (1.8)	82 (3.0)	86 (3.5)	84 (1.8)	83 (2.6)	80 (4.6)	86 (2.4)	87 (3.3)	89 (1.3)	93 (0.8)	92 (1.1)
Level 200[2]	[6] (†)	35 (3.0)	42 (2.6)	40 (2.7)	46 (3.3)	41 (2.7)	43 (3.5)	37 (4.6)	48 (3.8)	44 (3.4)	53 (1.7)	62 (1.7)	63 (1.8)
Level 250[3]	[6] (†)	3 (0.5)	5 (1.4)	4 (0.7)	9 (2.3)	6 (2.0)	7 (2.3)	6 (1.6)	7 (3.2)	6 (1.7)	7 (0.8)	10 (1.2)	11 (1.0)
13-year-olds													
Total													
Level 200[2]	93 (0.5)	93 (0.4)	95 (0.4)	94 (0.3)	95 (0.6)	94 (0.6)	93 (0.7)	92 (0.6)	92 (0.7)	93 (0.7)	92 (0.6)	94 (0.4)	94 (0.4)
Level 250[3]	58 (1.1)	59 (1.0)	61 (1.1)	59 (0.8)	59 (1.3)	59 (1.0)	62 (1.4)	60 (1.2)	60 (1.3)	61 (1.5)	59 (1.1)	63 (0.8)	66 (1.3)
Level 300[4]	10 (0.5)	10 (0.5)	11 (0.5)	11 (0.4)	11 (0.8)	11 (0.6)	15 (0.9)	14 (0.8)	14 (1.0)	15 (1.1)	12 (0.8)	13 (0.5)	15 (1.0)
Male													
Level 200[2]	91 (0.7)	91 (0.5)	93 (0.6)	92 (0.4)	93 (1.0)	91 (0.9)	90 (1.1)	89 (1.1)	89 (1.2)	91 (0.9)	89 (0.8)	92 (0.6)	93 (0.7)
Level 250[3]	52 (1.2)	52 (1.1)	56 (1.2)	54 (0.9)	52 (1.9)	52 (1.5)	55 (2.0)	53 (1.9)	53 (1.6)	55 (1.9)	55 (1.3)	59 (1.2)	62 (1.6)
Level 300[4]	7 (0.5)	7 (0.4)	9 (0.7)	9 (0.5)	9 (0.9)	9 (0.9)	8 (0.8)	13 (1.1)	10 (0.7)	10 (1.0)	11 (1.1)	11 (0.7)	13 (1.1)
Female													
Level 200[2]	95 (0.4)	95 (0.4)	96 (0.4)	96 (0.3)	97 (0.6)	96 (0.6)	95 (0.7)	95 (0.6)	95 (0.6)	96 (0.7)	95 (0.6)	96 (0.5)	96 (0.4)
Level 250[3]	64 (1.1)	65 (1.2)	65 (1.1)	64 (0.8)	65 (1.4)	65 (1.5)	68 (1.4)	68 (1.7)	66 (1.6)	66 (1.9)	65 (1.3)	66 (1.0)	69 (1.4)
Level 300[4]	12 (0.6)	13 (0.7)	13 (0.6)	13 (0.6)	13 (0.9)	13 (0.9)	14 (1.1)	18 (1.1)	18 (1.1)	17 (1.3)	14 (1.0)	16 (0.9)	17 (1.1)
White													
Level 200[2]	96[5] (0.3)	96 (0.4)	97 (0.2)	96 (0.2)	96 (0.6)	96 (0.6)	96 (0.6)	95 (0.7)	95 (0.5)	95 (0.6)	95 (0.5)	96 (0.4)	96 (0.6)
Level 250[3]	64[5] (0.9)	65 (0.9)	68 (0.8)	65 (0.8)	64 (1.5)	65 (1.2)	68 (1.4)	68 (1.3)	69 (1.4)	69 (1.7)	68 (1.1)	72 (1.2)	74 (1.8)
Level 300[4]	11[5] (0.5)	12 (0.5)	14 (0.6)	13 (0.6)	12 (0.9)	13 (0.9)	18 (1.1)	17 (1.0)	17 (1.3)	18 (1.4)	16 (0.9)	18 (0.8)	19 (1.0)
Black													
Level 200[2]	74[5] (1.7)	77 (1.3)	84 (1.7)	85 (1.2)	91 (2.2)	88 (2.3)	82 (2.7)	81 (2.3)	82 (3.2)	85 (2.3)	86 (1.5)	91 (1.1)	90 (1.3)
Level 250[3]	21[5] (1.2)	25 (1.6)	30 (2.0)	35 (1.3)	40 (2.3)	42 (3.5)	38 (2.7)	36 (3.5)	34 (3.9)	38 (2.7)	40 (2.3)	48 (2.3)	48 (2.5)
Level 300[4]	1[5] (0.2)	2 (0.3)	2 (0.5)	3 (0.6)	5 (1.2)	5 (1.2)	6 (1.4)	4 (1.2)	3 (0.9)	5 (1.4)	4 (0.7)	6 (0.8)	6 (0.9)
Hispanic													
Level 200[2]	[6] (†)	81 (2.3)	87 (2.4)	86 (1.7)	87 (2.6)	86 (2.4)	83 (3.5)	82 (2.7)	85 (3.2)	89 (2.8)	85 (1.9)	87 (1.3)	91 (1.2)
Level 250[3]	[6] (†)	32 (3.6)	35 (2.6)	39 (2.3)	38 (4.4)	37 (2.9)	41 (5.1)	34 (3.9)	38 (3.7)	43 (3.8)	44 (2.3)	44 (1.8)	51 (1.7)
Level 300[4]	[6] (†)	2 (1.0)	2 (0.6)	4 (1.0)	4 (1.9)	4 (1.2)	6 (1.9)	4 (1.8)	4 (1.7)	5 (1.2)	5 (1.2)	5 (0.6)	6 (0.5)
17-year-olds													
Total													
Level 250[3]	79 (0.9)	80 (0.7)	81 (0.9)	83 (0.6)	86 (0.8)	84 (1.0)	83 (0.8)	81 (1.0)	82 (0.8)	82 (1.0)	79 (0.9)	80 (0.6)	82 (0.6)
Level 300[4]	39 (1.0)	39 (0.8)	38 (1.1)	40 (1.0)	41 (1.5)	41 (1.0)	43 (1.1)	41 (1.2)	39 (1.4)	40 (1.4)	36 (1.2)	39 (0.8)	39 (0.9)
Male													
Level 250[3]	74 (1.0)	76 (0.8)	78 (1.0)	80 (0.7)	83 (1.4)	80 (1.4)	78 (1.2)	76 (1.5)	77 (1.2)	77 (1.5)	73 (1.2)	76 (0.8)	79 (0.8)
Level 300[4]	34 (1.1)	34 (1.0)	35 (1.3)	36 (1.0)	37 (2.3)	36 (1.5)	38 (1.6)	36 (1.9)	34 (1.9)	34 (1.7)	32 (1.2)	35 (0.9)	36 (1.2)
Female													
Level 250[3]	83 (1.0)	84 (0.9)	84 (1.2)	87 (0.6)	88 (1.1)	89 (1.0)	87 (1.1)	86 (1.2)	87 (1.0)	87 (1.0)	84 (0.9)	84 (0.8)	85 (0.7)
Level 300[4]	44 (1.2)	44 (0.9)	41 (1.2)	45 (1.1)	44 (2.0)	47 (1.3)	48 (1.5)	46 (1.5)	45 (1.7)	45 (1.8)	41 (1.6)	43 (1.0)	42 (1.1)
White													
Level 250[3]	84[5] (0.7)	86 (0.6)	87 (0.6)	88 (0.5)	89 (0.9)	88 (1.1)	88 (0.9)	86 (1.1)	87 (0.8)	87 (1.3)	83 (0.9)	87 (0.6)	87 (0.6)
Level 300[4]	43[5] (0.9)	44 (0.8)	43 (1.1)	47 (1.1)	45 (1.6)	48 (1.2)	50 (1.4)	48 (1.4)	46 (1.5)	46 (1.5)	42 (1.3)	47 (1.0)	47 (1.3)
Black													
Level 250[3]	40[5] (1.6)	43 (1.6)	44 (2.0)	65 (1.5)	76 (2.4)	69 (2.8)	61 (2.3)	66 (4.1)	68 (4.0)	66 (2.5)	64 (2.2)	67 (2.4)	70 (1.4)
Level 300[4]	8[5] (0.9)	8 (0.7)	7 (0.8)	16 (1.0)	25 (3.1)	20 (1.8)	17 (2.5)	17 (3.7)	18 (2.2)	17 (1.7)	16 (1.8)	21 (1.5)	22 (1.5)
Hispanic													
Level 250[3]	[6] (†)	53 (4.1)	62 (3.1)	68 (2.4)	71 (4.8)	75 (4.7)	69 (4.0)	63 (4.4)	65 (4.2)	68 (4.3)	67 (2.4)	70 (1.5)	74 (1.3)
Level 300[4]	[6] (†)	13 (2.7)	17 (2.1)	21 (3.0)	23 (3.7)	27 (3.3)	27 (3.2)	20 (3.0)	20 (4.8)	24 (3.8)	23 (2.1)	22 (1.0)	26 (1.3)

†Not applicable.
[1]Students scoring 150 (or higher) are able to follow brief written directions and carry out simple, discrete reading tasks.
[2]Students scoring 200 (or higher) are able to understand, combine ideas, and make inferences based on short uncomplicated passages about specific or sequentially related information.
[3]Students scoring 250 (or higher) are able to search for specific information, interrelate ideas, and make generalizations about literature, science, and social studies materials.
[4]Students scoring 300 (or higher) are able to find, understand, summarize, and explain relatively complicated literary and informational material.
[5]Data for 1971 include persons of Hispanic ethnicity.
[6]Test scores of Hispanics were not tabulated separately.

NOTE: The NAEP reading scores have been evaluated at certain performance levels, as outlined in footnotes 1 through 4. Scale ranges from 0 to 500. Includes public and private schools. For assessment years prior to 2004, accommodations were not permitted. For 2004 and later years, includes students tested with accommodations; excludes only those students with disabilities and English language learners who were unable to be tested even with accommodations (2 to 5 percent of all students, depending on age and assessment year). Race categories exclude persons of Hispanic ethnicity, except where noted. Totals include other racial/ethnic groups not shown separately.

SOURCE: U.S. Department of Education, National Center for Education Statistics, National Assessment of Educational Progress (NAEP), *NAEP 1999 Trends in Academic Progress*; and 2004, 2008, and 2012 Long-Term Trend Reading Assessments, retrieved May 12, 2009, and July 15, 2013, from the Long-Term Trend NAEP Data Explorer (http://nces.ed.gov/nationsreportcard/naepdata/). (This table was prepared July 2013.)

Average National Assessment of Educational Progress (NAEP) mathematics scale score, by grade and selected student and school characteristics: Selected years, 1990 through 2013

[Standard errors appear in parentheses]

Grade and selected student or school characteristic	1990[1]	1992[1]	1996	2000	2003	2005	2007	2009	2011	2013
1	2	3	4	5	6	7	8	9	10	11
4th grade, all students	213 (0.9)	220 (0.7)	224 (1.0)	226 (0.9)	235 (0.2)	238 (0.1)	240 (0.2)	240 (0.2)	241 (0.2)	242 (0.2)
Sex										
Male	214 (1.2)	221 (0.8)	224 (1.1)	227 (1.0)	236 (0.3)	239 (0.2)	241 (0.2)	241 (0.3)	241 (0.2)	242 (0.2)
Female	213 (1.1)	219 (1.0)	223 (1.1)	224 (0.9)	233 (0.2)	237 (0.2)	239 (0.2)	239 (0.3)	240 (0.2)	241 (0.2)
Gap between female and male score	-1 (1.7)	-2 (1.2)	# (†)	-3 (1.4)	-3 (0.3)	-3 (0.2)	-2 (0.3)	-2 (0.4)	-1 (0.3)	-1 (0.4)
Race/ethnicity										
White	220 (1.0)	227 (0.8)	232 (1.0)	234 (0.8)	243 (0.2)	246 (0.1)	248 (0.3)	248 (0.2)	249 (0.2)	250 (0.2)
Black	188 (1.8)	193 (1.4)	198 (1.6)	203 (1.2)	216 (0.4)	220 (0.3)	222 (0.3)	222 (0.3)	224 (0.4)	224 (0.3)
Hispanic	200 (2.2)	202 (1.5)	207 (1.9)	208 (1.5)	222 (0.4)	226 (0.3)	227 (0.3)	227 (0.4)	229 (0.3)	231 (0.4)
Asian[2]	225 (4.1)	231 (2.1)	229 (4.2)	‡ (†)	246 (1.1)	251 (0.7)	253 (0.8)	255 (1.0)	257 (1.0)	259 (0.8)
Pacific Islander	[2] (†)	[2] (†)	[2] (†)	[2] (†)	[2] (†)	[2] (†)	[2] (†)	[2] (†)	236 (2.1)	236 (2.0)
American Indian/Alaska Native	‡ (†)	‡ (†)	‡ (†)	217 (5.6)	208 (3.5)	223 (1.0)	226 (0.9)	228 (0.7)	225 (0.9)	227 (1.1)
Gap between White and Black score	32 (2.0)	35 (1.6)	34 (1.8)	31 (1.5)	27 (0.4)	26 (0.3)	26 (0.4)	26 (0.4)	25 (0.4)	26 (0.4)
Gap between White and Hispanic score	20 (2.4)	25 (1.7)	25 (2.1)	27 (1.7)	22 (0.5)	20 (0.3)	21 (0.4)	21 (0.5)	20 (0.4)	19 (0.5)
Percentage of students in school eligible for free or reduced-price lunch										
0–25 percent (low poverty)	— (†)	— (†)	— (†)	239 (1.2)	247 (0.3)	250 (0.3)	252 (0.3)	254 (0.4)	255 (0.4)	257 (0.4)
26–50 percent	— (†)	— (†)	— (†)	227 (1.2)	237 (0.3)	240 (0.3)	242 (0.3)	242 (0.4)	245 (0.4)	246 (0.4)
51–75 percent	— (†)	— (†)	— (†)	216 (1.3)	229 (0.4)	232 (0.3)	234 (0.3)	234 (0.4)	237 (0.3)	238 (0.5)
76–100 percent (high poverty)	— (†)	— (†)	— (†)	205 (1.2)	216 (0.5)	220 (0.4)	222 (0.4)	223 (0.4)	226 (0.3)	226 (0.5)
Gap between low-poverty and high-poverty score	— (†)	— (†)	— (†)	34 (1.7)	31 (0.6)	30 (0.4)	30 (0.5)	31 (0.6)	29 (0.6)	31 (0.6)
English language learner (ELL) status										
ELL	— (†)	— (†)	201 (3.6)	199 (2.0)	214 (0.6)	216 (0.5)	217 (0.5)	218 (0.6)	219 (0.5)	219 (0.6)
Non-ELL	— (†)	— (†)	225 (0.9)	227 (0.8)	237 (0.2)	240 (0.1)	242 (0.2)	242 (0.2)	243 (0.2)	244 (0.2)
Gap between non-ELL and ELL score	— (†)	— (†)	24 (3.7)	28 (2.1)	23 (0.6)	24 (0.5)	25 (0.5)	24 (0.7)	24 (0.5)	25 (0.6)
8th grade, all students	263 (1.3)	268 (0.9)	270 (0.9)	273 (0.8)	278 (0.3)	279 (0.2)	281 (0.3)	283 (0.3)	284 (0.2)	285 (0.3)
Sex										
Male	263 (1.6)	268 (1.1)	271 (1.1)	274 (0.9)	278 (0.3)	280 (0.2)	282 (0.3)	284 (0.3)	284 (0.3)	285 (0.3)
Female	262 (1.3)	269 (1.0)	269 (1.1)	272 (0.9)	277 (0.3)	278 (0.2)	280 (0.4)	282 (0.4)	283 (0.2)	284 (0.3)
Gap between female and male score	-1 (2.1)	1 (1.5)	-2 (1.5)	-2 (1.3)	-2 (0.4)	-2 (0.3)	-2 (0.4)	-2 (0.5)	-1 (0.4)	-1 (0.4)
Race/ethnicity										
White	270 (1.3)	277 (1.0)	281 (1.1)	284 (0.8)	288 (0.3)	289 (0.2)	291 (0.3)	293 (0.3)	293 (0.2)	294 (0.3)
Black	237 (2.7)	237 (1.3)	240 (1.9)	244 (1.2)	252 (0.5)	255 (0.4)	260 (0.4)	261 (0.5)	262 (0.5)	263 (0.4)
Hispanic	246 (4.3)	249 (1.2)	251 (1.7)	253 (1.3)	259 (0.6)	262 (0.4)	265 (0.4)	266 (0.6)	270 (0.5)	272 (0.5)
Asian[2]	275 (5.0)	290 (5.9)	‡ (†)	288 (3.5)	291 (1.3)	295 (0.9)	297 (0.9)	301 (1.2)	305 (1.1)	309 (1.1)
Pacific Islander	[2] (†)	[2] (†)	[2] (†)	[2] (†)	[2] (†)	[2] (†)	[2] (†)	[2] (†)	269 (2.4)	275 (2.3)
American Indian/Alaska Native	‡ (†)	‡ (†)	‡ (†)	259 (7.5)	263 (1.8)	264 (0.9)	264 (1.2)	266 (1.1)	265 (0.9)	269 (1.2)
Gap between White and Black score	33 (3.0)	40 (1.7)	41 (2.2)	40 (1.5)	35 (0.6)	34 (0.4)	32 (0.5)	32 (0.5)	31 (0.5)	31 (0.5)
Gap between White and Hispanic score	24 (4.5)	28 (1.5)	30 (2.0)	31 (1.6)	29 (0.7)	27 (0.5)	26 (0.5)	26 (0.6)	23 (0.5)	22 (0.5)
Percentage of students in school eligible for free or reduced-price lunch										
0–25 percent (low poverty)	— (†)	— (†)	— (†)	287 (1.1)	291 (0.4)	293 (0.4)	296 (0.4)	298 (0.5)	300 (0.5)	301 (0.5)
26–50 percent	— (†)	— (†)	— (†)	270 (1.4)	278 (0.4)	280 (0.3)	282 (0.4)	284 (0.5)	287 (0.5)	289 (0.5)
51–75 percent	— (†)	— (†)	— (†)	260 (1.8)	266 (0.7)	268 (0.4)	271 (0.4)	274 (0.7)	276 (0.7)	277 (0.4)
76–100 percent (high poverty)	— (†)	— (†)	— (†)	246 (2.2)	251 (0.7)	254 (0.6)	259 (0.7)	260 (0.7)	264 (0.7)	265 (0.6)
Gap between low-poverty and high-poverty score	— (†)	— (†)	— (†)	41 (2.4)	40 (0.8)	38 (0.7)	37 (0.8)	38 (0.8)	36 (0.9)	36 (0.8)
English language learner (ELL) status										
ELL	— (†)	— (†)	226 (3.2)	234 (2.7)	242 (1.0)	244 (0.8)	246 (0.8)	243 (0.9)	244 (1.0)	246 (0.8)
Non-ELL	— (†)	— (†)	272 (1.0)	274 (0.8)	279 (0.3)	281 (0.2)	283 (0.3)	285 (0.3)	286 (0.2)	287 (0.3)
Gap between non-ELL and ELL score	— (†)	— (†)	46 (3.4)	40 (2.8)	38 (1.0)	37 (0.8)	38 (0.8)	42 (0.9)	42 (1.0)	41 (0.8)
12th grade, all students	[3] (†)	[3] (†)	[3] (†)	[3] (†)	— (†)	150 (0.6)	— (†)	153 (0.7)	— (†)	— (†)
Sex										
Male	[3] (†)	[3] (†)	[3] (†)	[3] (†)	— (†)	151 (0.7)	— (†)	155 (0.9)	— (†)	— (†)
Female	[3] (†)	[3] (†)	[3] (†)	[3] (†)	— (†)	149 (0.7)	— (†)	152 (0.7)	— (†)	— (†)
Gap between female and male score	[3] (†)	[3] (†)	[3] (†)	[3] (†)	— (†)	-3 (1.0)	— (†)	-3 (1.1)	— (†)	— (†)
Race/ethnicity										
White	[3] (†)	[3] (†)	[3] (†)	[3] (†)	— (†)	157 (0.6)	— (†)	161 (0.6)	— (†)	— (†)
Black	[3] (†)	[3] (†)	[3] (†)	[3] (†)	— (†)	127 (1.1)	— (†)	131 (0.8)	— (†)	— (†)
Hispanic	[3] (†)	[3] (†)	[3] (†)	[3] (†)	— (†)	133 (1.3)	— (†)	138 (0.8)	— (†)	— (†)
Asian[2]	[3] (†)	[3] (†)	[3] (†)	[3] (†)	— (†)	163 (2.0)	— (†)	175 (2.7)	— (†)	— (†)
American Indian/Alaska Native	[3] (†)	[3] (†)	[3] (†)	[3] (†)	— (†)	134 (4.1)	— (†)	144 (2.8)	— (†)	— (†)
Gap between White and Black score	[3] (†)	[3] (†)	[3] (†)	[3] (†)	— (†)	31 (1.2)	— (†)	30 (1.0)	— (†)	— (†)
Gap between White and Hispanic score	[3] (†)	[3] (†)	[3] (†)	[3] (†)	— (†)	24 (1.4)	— (†)	23 (1.0)	— (†)	— (†)
Percentage of students in school eligible for free or reduced-price lunch										
0–25 percent (low poverty)	[3] (†)	[3] (†)	[3] (†)	[3] (†)	— (†)	158 (1.0)	— (†)	166 (1.3)	— (†)	— (†)
26–50 percent	[3] (†)	[3] (†)	[3] (†)	[3] (†)	— (†)	147 (1.0)	— (†)	150 (0.7)	— (†)	— (†)
51–75 percent	[3] (†)	[3] (†)	[3] (†)	[3] (†)	— (†)	136 (1.3)	— (†)	140 (1.2)	— (†)	— (†)
76–100 percent (high poverty)	[3] (†)	[3] (†)	[3] (†)	[3] (†)	— (†)	122 (2.7)	— (†)	130 (1.7)	— (†)	— (†)
Gap between low-poverty and high-poverty score	[3] (†)	[3] (†)	[3] (†)	[3] (†)	— (†)	36 (2.8)	— (†)	36 (2.1)	— (†)	— (†)

—Not available.
†Not applicable.
#Rounds to zero.
‡Reporting standards not met (too few cases for a reliable estimate).
[1]Accommodations were not permitted for this assessment.
[2]For assessment years prior to 2011, Pacific Islander students are included with Asian students.
[3]Because of major changes to the framework and content of the grade 12 assessment, scores from 2005 and later assessment years cannot be compared with scores from earlier assessment years. Therefore, this table does not include scores from the earlier grade 12 assessment years (1990, 1992, 1996, and 2000). For data pertaining to comparisons between earlier years, see the *Digest of Education Statistics 2009*, table 138 (http://nces.ed.gov/programs/digest/d09/tables/dt09_138.asp).
NOTE: For the grade 4 and grade 8 assessments, scale ranges from 0 to 500. For the grade 12 assessment, scale ranges from 0 to 300. Includes public and private schools. For 1996 and later years, includes students tested with accommodations (1 to 12 percent of all students, depending on grade level and year); excludes only those students with disabilities and English language learners who were unable to be tested even with accommodations (1 to 4 percent of all students). Race categories exclude persons of Hispanic ethnicity. Totals include other racial/ethnic groups not shown separately. Gaps are computed based on unrounded scores. Grade 12 results for the 2013 NAEP Mathematics Assessment were not yet available at the time this table was created.
SOURCE: U.S. Department of Education, National Center for Education Statistics, National Assessment of Educational Progress (NAEP), 1990, 1992, 1996, 2000, 2003, 2005, 2007, 2009, 2011, and 2013 Mathematics Assessments, retrieved November 9, 2013, from the Main NAEP Data Explorer (http://nces.ed.gov/nationsreportcard/naepdata/). (This table was prepared November 2013.)

Percentage of students at or above selected National Assessment of Educational Progress (NAEP) mathematics achievement levels, by grade and selected student characteristics: Selected years, 1996 through 2013

[Standard errors appear in parentheses]

Grade and selected student characteristic	1996 At or above Basic[1]	1996 At or above Proficient[2]	2000 At or above Basic[1]	2000 At or above Proficient[2]	2003 At or above Basic[1]	2003 At or above Proficient[2]	2005 At or above Basic[1]	2005 At or above Proficient[2]	2007 At or above Basic[1]	2007 At or above Proficient[2]	2009 At or above Basic[1]	2009 At or above Proficient[2]	2011 At or above Basic[1]	2011 At or above Proficient[2]	2013 At or above Basic[1]	2013 At or above Proficient[2]
1	2	3	4	5	6	7	8	9	10	11	12	13	14	15	16	17
4th grade, all students	63 (1.3)	21 (1.1)	65 (1.3)	24 (1.0)	77 (0.3)	32 (0.3)	80 (0.2)	36 (0.2)	82 (0.2)	39 (0.3)	82 (0.3)	39 (0.3)	82 (0.2)	40 (0.3)	83 (0.2)	42 (0.3)
Sex																
Male	63 (1.5)	22 (1.2)	67 (1.4)	26 (1.2)	78 (0.4)	35 (0.4)	81 (0.2)	38 (0.2)	82 (0.2)	41 (0.2)	82 (0.3)	41 (0.3)	83 (0.3)	42 (0.4)	82 (0.3)	43 (0.4)
Female	63 (1.4)	20 (1.4)	64 (1.5)	22 (1.1)	76 (0.3)	30 (0.3)	80 (0.2)	34 (0.3)	82 (0.2)	37 (0.2)	82 (0.3)	37 (0.3)	82 (0.3)	39 (0.4)	83 (0.2)	41 (0.4)
Race/ethnicity																
White	76 (1.2)	27 (1.3)	78 (1.4)	31 (1.2)	87 (0.2)	43 (0.4)	90 (0.2)	47 (0.3)	91 (0.2)	51 (0.2)	91 (0.6)	51 (0.5)	91 (0.2)	52 (0.4)	91 (0.6)	54 (0.5)
Black	27 (2.0)	3 (0.6)	36 (1.9)	5 (0.8)	54 (0.6)	10 (0.3)	60 (0.5)	13 (0.3)	64 (0.6)	15 (0.6)	64 (0.6)	16 (0.6)	66 (0.5)	17 (0.5)	66 (0.6)	18 (0.6)
Hispanic	40 (2.7)	7 (1.4)	42 (2.6)	7 (1.0)	62 (0.7)	16 (0.5)	68 (0.5)	19 (0.3)	70 (0.5)	22 (0.4)	71 (0.7)	22 (0.4)	72 (0.5)	24 (0.5)	73 (0.7)	26 (0.6)
Asian/Pacific Islander	67 (5.7)	27 (5.0)	‡ (†)	‡ (†)	87 (0.8)	48 (1.9)	90 (0.5)	55 (1.1)	91 (0.7)	58 (1.3)	92 (0.6)	60 (1.6)	91 (0.6)	62 (1.6)	91 (0.6)	64 (1.2)
American Indian/Alaska Native	57 (7.5)	‡ (†)	40 (6.1)	8 (4.5)	64 (1.7)	17 (1.2)	68 (1.5)	21 (1.2)	70 (1.2)	25 (1.2)	66 (1.6)	21 (1.1)	66 (1.2)	22 (1.2)	68 (1.7)	23 (1.4)
Eligibility for free or reduced-price lunch																
Eligible	40 (1.8)	8 (0.9)	43 (1.5)	8 (0.8)	62 (0.5)	15 (0.3)	67 (0.3)	19 (0.2)	70 (0.4)	22 (0.3)	70 (0.4)	22 (0.3)	72 (0.3)	24 (0.3)	73 (0.4)	25 (0.4)
Not eligible	76 (1.2)	27 (1.2)	78 (1.6)	32 (1.6)	88 (0.3)	45 (0.4)	90 (0.2)	49 (0.3)	91 (0.2)	53 (0.2)	91 (0.3)	54 (0.4)	92 (0.2)	57 (0.4)	93 (0.2)	59 (0.4)
Unknown	72 (3.0)	28 (4.1)	80 (2.2)	36 (2.2)	84 (0.9)	41 (1.2)	87 (0.7)	45 (1.2)	90 (0.9)	48 (1.2)	88 (1.3)	47 (1.7)	90 (0.8)	52 (1.4)	90 (1.0)	52 (2.2)
8th grade, all students	61 (1.0)	23 (1.0)	63 (0.9)	26 (0.8)	68 (0.3)	29 (0.3)	69 (0.2)	30 (0.2)	71 (0.3)	32 (0.3)	73 (0.3)	34 (0.3)	73 (0.2)	35 (0.2)	74 (0.3)	35 (0.3)
Sex																
Male	62 (1.2)	25 (1.2)	64 (1.1)	27 (1.0)	69 (0.4)	30 (0.4)	70 (0.3)	31 (0.3)	72 (0.3)	34 (0.3)	73 (0.3)	36 (0.3)	73 (0.4)	36 (0.3)	74 (0.3)	36 (0.4)
Female	60 (1.2)	22 (1.2)	63 (1.1)	24 (0.9)	67 (0.3)	27 (0.3)	69 (0.3)	28 (0.3)	71 (0.3)	30 (0.3)	72 (0.4)	32 (0.4)	73 (0.2)	34 (0.3)	74 (0.4)	35 (0.4)
Race/ethnicity																
White	73 (1.3)	30 (1.3)	76 (0.9)	34 (1.0)	80 (0.3)	37 (0.4)	80 (0.2)	39 (0.3)	82 (0.3)	42 (0.3)	83 (0.3)	44 (0.4)	84 (0.3)	44 (0.3)	84 (0.3)	45 (0.4)
Black	25 (2.0)	4 (0.8)	31 (1.5)	5 (0.6)	39 (0.8)	7 (0.3)	42 (0.6)	9 (0.3)	47 (0.7)	11 (0.3)	50 (0.6)	12 (0.5)	51 (0.6)	13 (0.6)	52 (0.7)	14 (0.5)
Hispanic	39 (2.0)	8 (1.1)	41 (1.9)	8 (1.0)	48 (0.8)	12 (0.5)	52 (0.6)	13 (0.4)	55 (0.7)	15 (0.4)	57 (0.8)	17 (0.6)	61 (0.7)	20 (0.6)	62 (0.6)	21 (0.5)
Asian/Pacific Islander	‡ (†)	‡ (†)	75 (2.8)	41 (4.4)	78 (1.1)	43 (1.3)	81 (0.8)	47 (1.2)	83 (0.8)	50 (1.0)	85 (1.0)	54 (1.8)	86 (1.0)	55 (1.2)	87 (0.8)	60 (1.3)
American Indian/Alaska Native	‡ (†)	‡ (†)	47 (10.4)	‡ (†)	52 (2.7)	15 (1.7)	53 (1.3)	14 (1.2)	53 (1.8)	16 (1.2)	56 (1.5)	18 (1.3)	55 (1.5)	17 (1.2)	59 (1.7)	21 (1.5)
Eligibility for free or reduced-price lunch																
Eligible	38 (2.1)	8 (1.0)	41 (1.3)	9 (0.8)	48 (0.5)	12 (0.4)	51 (0.4)	13 (0.2)	55 (0.5)	15 (0.3)	57 (0.5)	17 (0.3)	59 (0.4)	19 (0.3)	60 (0.4)	20 (0.4)
Not eligible	69 (1.5)	28 (1.3)	74 (1.1)	34 (1.3)	79 (0.3)	37 (0.4)	79 (0.2)	39 (0.3)	81 (0.3)	42 (0.3)	83 (0.3)	45 (0.4)	84 (0.2)	47 (0.4)	86 (0.3)	49 (0.4)
Unknown	70 (2.6)	30 (2.6)	67 (2.0)	29 (1.5)	75 (1.1)	36 (1.2)	79 (1.1)	40 (1.4)	81 (1.7)	43 (1.2)	83 (1.3)	48 (1.9)	85 (0.9)	48 (1.5)	84 (1.3)	50 (2.6)
12th grade, all students[3]	†	†	†	†	—	—	61 (0.8)	23 (0.7)	—	—	64 (0.8)	26 (0.8)	—	—	—	—
Sex																
Male	†	†	†	†	—	—	62 (1.0)	25 (1.0)	—	—	65 (0.9)	28 (1.0)	—	—	—	—
Female	†	†	†	†	—	—	60 (1.0)	21 (0.8)	—	—	63 (0.8)	24 (0.8)	—	—	—	—
Race/ethnicity																
White	†	†	†	†	—	—	70 (0.8)	29 (0.8)	—	—	75 (0.7)	33 (0.8)	—	—	—	—
Black	†	†	†	†	—	—	30 (1.7)	6 (0.8)	—	—	37 (1.2)	6 (0.6)	—	—	—	—
Hispanic	†	†	†	†	—	—	40 (2.1)	11 (1.0)	—	—	45 (1.1)	11 (0.8)	—	—	—	—
Asian/Pacific Islander	†	†	†	†	—	—	73 (2.6)	36 (3.0)	—	—	84 (1.9)	52 (3.4)	—	—	—	—
American Indian/Alaska Native	†	†	†	†	—	—	42 (8.6)	6 (2.9)	—	—	56 (5.4)	12 (3.3)	—	—	—	—
Eligibility for free or reduced-price lunch																
Eligible	†	†	†	†	—	—	39 (1.6)	8 (1.0)	—	—	45 (1.1)	10 (0.6)	—	—	—	—
Not eligible	†	†	†	†	—	—	66 (0.9)	27 (0.9)	—	—	72 (0.7)	32 (1.1)	—	—	—	—
Unknown	†	†	†	†	—	—	75 (2.7)	35 (2.3)	—	—	71 (3.3)	32 (3.0)	—	—	—	—

—Not available.
†Not applicable.
‡Reporting standards not met.

[1] *Basic* denotes partial mastery of the knowledge and skills that are fundamental for proficient work.

[2] *Proficient* represents solid academic performance. Students reaching this level have demonstrated competency over challenging subject matter.

[3] Because of major changes to the framework and content of the grade 12 assessment, results from 2005 and later assessment years cannot be compared with results from earlier assessment years. Therefore, this table excludes grade 12 results from 1996 and 2000.

NOTE: Includes public and private schools. Includes students tested with accommodations (1 to 12 percent of all students, depending on grade level and year); excludes only those students with disabilities and English language learners who were unable to be tested even with accommodations (1 to 4 percent of all students). Race categories exclude persons of Hispanic ethnicity. Totals include other racial/ethnic groups not shown separately. Grade 12 results for the 2013 NAEP Mathematics Assessment were not yet available at the time this table was created.

SOURCE: U.S. Department of Education, National Center for Education Statistics, National Assessment of Educational Progress (NAEP), 1996, 2000, 2003, 2005, 2007, 2009, 2011, and 2013 Mathematics Assessments, retrieved November 11, 2013, from the Main NAEP Data Explorer (http://nces.ed.gov/nationsreportcard/naepdata/). (This table was prepared November 2013.)

Average National Assessment of Educational Progress (NAEP) mathematics scale score of 8th-graders with various attitudes toward mathematics and percentage reporting these attitudes, by selected student and school characteristics: 2013

[Standard errors appear in parentheses]

Average scale score[1]

Student or school characteristic	Math work is engaging and interesting				Math work is challenging				Math work is too easy			
	Never or hardly ever	Sometimes	Often	Always/almost always	Never or hardly ever	Sometimes	Often	Always/almost always	Never or hardly ever	Sometimes	Often	Always/almost always
1	2	3	4	5	6	7	8	9	10	11	12	13
All students	280 (0.4)	284 (0.4)	289 (0.3)	287 (0.6)	295 (0.6)	286 (0.3)	284 (0.3)	275 (0.5)	285 (0.5)	283 (0.3)	287 (0.3)	290 (0.7)
Sex												
Male	281 (0.5)	285 (0.4)	290 (0.4)	287 (0.8)	297 (0.9)	287 (0.4)	284 (0.4)	274 (0.7)	284 (0.7)	284 (0.4)	289 (0.5)	292 (0.9)
Female	279 (0.5)	284 (0.4)	289 (0.4)	288 (0.7)	293 (0.7)	285 (0.3)	284 (0.5)	277 (0.7)	286 (0.6)	283 (0.4)	286 (0.5)	288 (1.0)
Race/ethnicity												
White	286 (0.4)	294 (0.3)	300 (0.4)	300 (0.7)	303 (0.5)	295 (0.3)	294 (0.4)	286 (0.7)	292 (0.5)	293 (0.3)	297 (0.4)	299 (0.8)
Black	260 (0.8)	263 (0.6)	267 (0.8)	266 (1.0)	273 (1.4)	265 (0.5)	263 (0.7)	255 (0.9)	264 (1.0)	262 (0.5)	266 (0.7)	269 (1.4)
Hispanic	268 (0.9)	271 (0.7)	275 (0.6)	275 (1.2)	279 (1.6)	273 (0.5)	271 (0.8)	264 (0.9)	272 (1.4)	270 (0.6)	275 (0.7)	277 (1.7)
Asian	303 (2.0)	306 (1.8)	314 (1.4)	311 (2.1)	324 (1.8)	310 (1.2)	303 (1.9)	296 (3.6)	311 (2.7)	307 (1.6)	310 (1.6)	316 (2.2)
Pacific Islander	269 (4.7)	278 (4.1)	273 (5.4)	277 (4.6)	289 (7.0)	278 (3.0)	271 (4.4)	265 (3.6)	277 (7.5)	274 (2.7)	275 (5.3)	283 (5.7)
American Indian/Alaska Native	270 (2.8)	269 (2.2)	272 (2.2)	271 (3.9)	281 (4.0)	270 (2.2)	271 (2.4)	262 (3.7)	268 (2.9)	268 (1.8)	277 (2.6)	276 (5.3)
Two or more races	281 (1.9)	285 (1.3)	290 (2.2)	302 (5.4)	299 (3.1)	290 (1.7)	285 (1.5)	277 (3.6)	286 (2.5)	285 (1.3)	293 (3.0)	299 (2.8)
Eligibility for free or reduced-price lunch												
Eligible	267 (0.5)	270 (0.4)	274 (0.4)	272 (0.6)	280 (0.9)	272 (0.3)	269 (0.4)	260 (0.6)	268 (0.7)	269 (0.3)	274 (0.4)	277 (0.9)
Not eligible	289 (0.5)	297 (0.4)	303 (0.4)	303 (0.6)	306 (0.6)	298 (0.4)	296 (0.4)	289 (0.8)	296 (0.5)	296 (0.4)	300 (0.5)	304 (1.0)
Unknown	284 (1.8)	297 (2.4)	306 (2.6)	305 (4.1)	308 (3.7)	299 (2.5)	295 (2.4)	292 (3.8)	296 (3.3)	297 (2.2)	304 (2.6)	302 (5.2)
Control of school												
Public	279 (0.4)	283 (0.3)	288 (0.3)	286 (0.5)	294 (0.6)	285 (0.3)	283 (0.3)	274 (0.4)	284 (0.5)	282 (0.3)	286 (0.4)	290 (0.7)
Private	284 (1.5)	295 (2.1)	303 (2.1)	303 (3.4)	307 (4.0)	298 (1.8)	292 (1.8)	292 (2.7)	295 (2.4)	294 (1.9)	303 (2.2)	301 (4.7)

Percent of students

Student or school characteristic	Math work is engaging and interesting				Math work is challenging				Math work is too easy			
	Never or hardly ever	Sometimes	Often	Always/almost always	Never or hardly ever	Sometimes	Often	Always/almost always	Never or hardly ever	Sometimes	Often	Always/almost always
1	2	3	4	5	6	7	8	9	10	11	12	13
All students	22 (0.2)	35 (0.2)	28 (0.2)	15 (0.2)	12 (0.2)	45 (0.3)	32 (0.2)	11 (0.1)	17 (0.2)	55 (0.2)	21 (0.2)	7 (0.1)
Sex												
Male	21 (0.3)	33 (0.3)	29 (0.3)	16 (0.2)	12 (0.2)	45 (0.3)	33 (0.3)	10 (0.2)	15 (0.2)	54 (0.3)	23 (0.2)	8 (0.1)
Female	22 (0.3)	37 (0.2)	27 (0.3)	14 (0.2)	11 (0.2)	45 (0.4)	32 (0.3)	12 (0.2)	20 (0.3)	55 (0.3)	19 (0.2)	6 (0.1)
Race/ethnicity												
White	25 (0.3)	36 (0.3)	27 (0.2)	12 (0.2)	12 (0.2)	45 (0.3)	32 (0.3)	11 (0.2)	20 (0.3)	54 (0.3)	19 (0.2)	6 (0.1)
Black	18 (0.5)	33 (0.4)	27 (0.4)	21 (0.4)	11 (0.3)	44 (0.5)	33 (0.5)	14 (0.4)	15 (0.4)	54 (0.5)	22 (0.5)	8 (0.3)
Hispanic	19 (0.5)	36 (0.5)	30 (0.5)	16 (0.4)	10 (0.4)	46 (0.6)	32 (0.6)	11 (0.3)	9 (0.4)	56 (0.5)	23 (0.3)	8 (0.2)
Asian	14 (0.8)	37 (1.0)	31 (0.9)	18 (0.8)	14 (0.8)	50 (1.2)	28 (1.2)	8 (0.6)	9 (0.8)	52 (1.2)	27 (0.9)	12 (0.7)
Pacific Islander	15 (1.9)	36 (2.7)	28 (3.1)	21 (2.4)	11 (2.5)	46 (3.0)	33 (2.9)	11 (1.7)	9 (1.5)	57 (3.2)	28 (3.1)	7 (1.9)
American Indian/Alaska Native	20 (1.4)	36 (1.5)	28 (1.4)	16 (1.3)	11 (1.3)	44 (1.7)	32 (1.6)	13 (1.0)	16 (1.2)	57 (1.8)	21 (1.2)	7 (1.0)
Two or more races	22 (1.0)	37 (1.3)	28 (1.3)	14 (1.1)	13 (0.9)	44 (1.5)	32 (1.2)	12 (0.8)	18 (0.9)	52 (1.1)	22 (0.9)	8 (0.7)
Eligibility for free or reduced-price lunch												
Eligible	20 (0.3)	35 (0.3)	28 (0.3)	16 (0.3)	11 (0.3)	45 (0.3)	32 (0.3)	12 (0.2)	14 (0.2)	55 (0.3)	23 (0.3)	8 (0.2)
Not eligible	23 (0.3)	36 (0.2)	28 (0.3)	13 (0.3)	12 (0.2)	45 (0.3)	32 (0.3)	10 (0.2)	19 (0.3)	54 (0.3)	20 (0.3)	7 (0.1)
Unknown	22 (1.3)	33 (1.1)	28 (1.3)	16 (1.1)	11 (0.8)	45 (1.5)	33 (1.2)	11 (0.8)	23 (1.2)	56 (1.3)	16 (0.7)	5 (0.5)
Control of school												
Public	22 (0.2)	36 (0.2)	28 (0.2)	15 (0.2)	12 (0.2)	45 (0.2)	32 (0.2)	11 (0.1)	17 (0.2)	54 (0.2)	21 (0.2)	8 (0.1)
Private	23 (0.9)	34 (1.0)	28 (1.0)	15 (0.9)	10 (0.6)	43 (1.3)	35 (1.1)	12 (0.7)	24 (1.0)	57 (1.1)	15 (0.7)	5 (0.4)

[1]Scale ranges from 0 to 500.

NOTE: Includes public and private schools. Includes students tested with accommodations (12 percent of all 8th-grade students); excludes only those students with disabilities and English language learners who were unable to be tested even with accommodations (1 percent of all 8th-grade students). Race categories exclude persons of Hispanic ethnicity. Detail may not sum to totals because of rounding.

SOURCE: U.S. Department of Education, National Center for Education Statistics, National Assessment of Educational Progress (NAEP), 2011 Mathematics Assessment, retrieved November 15, 2013, from the Main NAEP Data Explorer (http://nces.ed.gov/nationsreportcard/naepdata/). (This table was prepared November 2013.)

Average National Assessment of Educational Progress (NAEP) mathematics scale score of high school graduates at grade 12, by highest mathematics course taken in high school and selected student and school characteristics: 2009

[Standard errors appear in parentheses]

Selected student or school characteristic	Algebra I or below[1]	Geometry	Algebra II/ trigonometry	Analysis/ precalculus	Statistics/ probability	Advanced mathematics, other[2]	Calculus
1	2	3	4	5	6	7	8
Total[3]	**114** (1.1)	**127** (1.0)	**143** (0.6)	**166** (0.9)	**164** (1.8)	**154** (1.3)	**193** (1.2)
Sex							
Male	117 (1.7)	128 (1.2)	145 (0.8)	169 (1.0)	165 (2.2)	156 (1.5)	197 (1.4)
Female	111 (1.6)	126 (1.1)	142 (0.8)	163 (1.0)	162 (2.0)	153 (1.4)	190 (1.2)
Race/ethnicity							
White	117 (1.6)	133 (1.3)	150 (0.8)	172 (0.9)	169 (1.5)	160 (1.3)	194 (1.1)
Black	104 (2.8)	114 (1.8)	129 (0.9)	147 (1.6)	139 (4.0)	138 (2.1)	170 (2.7)
Hispanic	109 (2.2)	122 (1.0)	136 (0.8)	155 (1.6)	154 (3.2)	142 (2.3)	179 (2.5)
Asian/Pacific Islander	‡ (†)	129 (3.9)	149 (4.1)	170 (2.3)	176 (4.1)	164 (2.9)	203 (1.8)
American Indian/Alaska Native	‡ (†)	‡ (†)	143 (3.8)	‡ (†)	‡ (†)	‡ (†)	‡ (†)
Student with disabilities (SD) status							
SD[4]	103 (1.7)	114 (2.5)	126 (2.1)	166 (5.0)	136 (6.3)	134 (3.5)	197 (3.7)
Non-SD	122 (1.2)	129 (0.9)	144 (0.6)	166 (0.9)	164 (1.7)	156 (1.3)	193 (1.2)
English language learner (ELL) status							
ELL	104 (4.5)	113 (2.8)	121 (2.1)	144 (6.1)	‡ (†)	129 (4.8)	‡ (†)
Non-ELL	114 (1.2)	128 (1.0)	144 (0.6)	166 (0.9)	164 (1.8)	155 (1.3)	193 (1.2)
School type							
Traditional public	114 (1.2)	127 (1.0)	143 (0.7)	166 (0.9)	164 (1.8)	155 (1.4)	193 (1.3)
Public charter	‡ (†)	‡ (†)	137 (10.3)	141 (6.8)	132 (1.6)	‡ (†)	‡ (†)
Private	‡ (†)	123 (3.3)	146 (3.3)	169 (2.7)	168 (3.9)	146 (4.0)	193 (3.3)
Percentage of students eligible for free or reduced-price lunch							
0–25 percent	116 (3.0)	134 (2.0)	151 (1.3)	173 (1.5)	173 (1.5)	162 (1.9)	199 (1.6)
26–50 percent	115 (1.5)	127 (1.4)	144 (1.0)	165 (1.1)	162 (2.9)	154 (1.7)	189 (1.0)
51–75 percent	111 (3.0)	123 (1.8)	136 (1.1)	156 (1.3)	149 (3.6)	146 (3.7)	179 (2.8)
76–100 percent	107 (5.4)	115 (3.1)	126 (2.0)	144 (3.7)	137 (4.1)	131 (2.6)	163 (3.9)
School locale							
City	110 (2.6)	125 (1.7)	140 (1.8)	163 (2.1)	163 (3.3)	151 (3.0)	195 (2.3)
Suburban	112 (2.3)	127 (1.9)	144 (1.0)	169 (1.4)	167 (2.4)	157 (2.0)	195 (2.0)
Town	114 (2.5)	129 (1.9)	144 (1.6)	166 (1.6)	164 (3.1)	152 (3.8)	191 (2.1)
Rural	117 (2.0)	129 (1.4)	145 (1.3)	165 (1.9)	157 (4.9)	155 (2.1)	187 (2.0)

†Not applicable.

‡Reporting standards not met (too few cases for a reliable estimate).

[1]Includes basic math, general math, applied math, prealgebra, and algebra I.

[2]Includes courses such as actuarial sciences, pure mathematics, discrete math, and advanced functions and modeling.

[3]Includes other racial/ethnic groups not shown separately, as well as students for whom information on race/ethnicity or sex was missing.

[4]SD estimates include both students with an Individualized Education Plan (IEP) and students with a plan under Section 504 of the Rehabilitation Act (a "504 plan"). IEPs are only for students who require specialized instruction, whereas 504 plans apply to students who require accommodations but may not require specialized instruction.

NOTE: Scale ranges from 0 to 300. Includes students tested with accommodations (6 percent of all 12th-graders); excludes only those students with disabilities and English language learners who were unable to be tested even with accommodations (3 percent of all 12th-graders). For a transcript to be included in the analyses, it had to meet three requirements: (1) the graduate received either a standard or honors diploma, (2) the graduate's transcript contained 16 or more Carnegie credits, and (3) the graduate's transcript contained more than 0 Carnegie credits in English courses. Race categories exclude persons of Hispanic ethnicity.

SOURCE: U.S. Department of Education, National Center for Education Statistics, National Assessment of Educational Progress (NAEP), 2009 Mathematics Assessment; and 2009 High School Transcript Study (HSTS). (This table was prepared September 2012.)

Average National Assessment of Educational Progress (NAEP) mathematics scale score of 4th-grade public school students and percentage attaining mathematics achievement levels, by state: Selected years, 1992 through 2013
[Standard errors appear in parentheses]

State	1992		2000		2003		2005		2007		2009		2011		2013		At or above Basic[2]		At or above Proficient[3]		At Advanced[4]	
1	2		3		4		5		6		7		8		9		10		11		12	
United States	219	(0.8)	224	(1.0)	234	(0.2)	237	(0.2)	239	(0.2)	239	(0.2)	240	(0.2)	241	(0.2)	82	(0.2)	41	(0.3)	8	(0.2)
Alabama	208	(1.6)	217	(1.2)	223	(1.2)	225	(0.9)	229	(1.3)	228	(1.1)	231	(1.0)	233	(1.0)	75	(1.4)	30	(1.6)	3	(0.5)
Alaska	—	(†)	—	(†)	233	(0.8)	236	(1.0)	237	(1.0)	237	(0.9)	236	(0.9)	236	(0.8)	77	(1.1)	37	(1.1)	6	(0.6)
Arizona	215	(1.1)	219	(1.3)	229	(1.1)	230	(1.1)	232	(1.0)	230	(1.1)	235	(1.1)	240	(1.2)	82	(1.1)	40	(1.8)	7	(1.0)
Arkansas	210	(0.9)	216	(1.1)	229	(0.9)	236	(0.9)	238	(1.1)	238	(0.9)	238	(0.8)	240	(0.9)	83	(1.0)	39	(1.4)	5	(0.6)
California[5]	208	(1.6)	213	(1.6)	227	(0.9)	230	(0.6)	230	(0.7)	232	(1.2)	234	(1.4)	234	(1.2)	74	(1.5)	33	(1.7)	5	(0.7)
Colorado	221	(1.0)	—	(†)	235	(1.0)	239	(1.1)	240	(1.0)	243	(1.0)	244	(0.9)	247	(0.8)	87	(1.0)	50	(1.3)	11	(0.9)
Connecticut	227	(1.1)	234	(1.1)	241	(0.8)	242	(0.8)	243	(1.1)	245	(1.0)	242	(1.3)	243	(0.9)	83	(1.1)	45	(1.3)	9	(0.9)
Delaware	218	(0.8)	—	(†)	236	(0.5)	240	(0.5)	242	(0.4)	239	(0.5)	240	(0.6)	243	(0.7)	86	(0.9)	42	(1.1)	7	(0.6)
District of Columbia	193	(0.7)	192	(1.1)	205	(0.7)	211	(0.8)	214	(0.8)	219	(0.7)	222	(0.7)	229	(0.7)	66	(1.3)	28	(1.0)	6	(0.7)
Florida	214	(1.5)	—	(†)	234	(1.1)	239	(0.7)	242	(0.8)	242	(1.0)	240	(0.8)	242	(0.8)	84	(0.9)	41	(1.3)	6	(0.7)
Georgia	216	(1.2)	219	(1.1)	230	(1.0)	234	(1.0)	235	(0.8)	236	(0.9)	238	(0.7)	240	(1.0)	81	(1.2)	39	(1.5)	7	(0.7)
Hawaii	214	(1.3)	216	(1.0)	227	(1.0)	230	(0.8)	234	(0.8)	236	(1.1)	239	(0.9)	243	(0.8)	83	(0.8)	46	(1.3)	9	(0.7)
Idaho[5]	222	(1.0)	224	(1.4)	235	(0.7)	242	(0.7)	241	(0.7)	241	(0.8)	240	(0.6)	241	(0.9)	83	(1.0)	40	(1.5)	6	(0.8)
Illinois[5]	—	(†)	223	(1.9)	233	(1.1)	233	(1.0)	237	(1.1)	238	(1.0)	239	(1.1)	239	(1.2)	79	(1.1)	39	(1.7)	8	(1.0)
Indiana[5]	221	(1.0)	233	(1.1)	238	(0.9)	240	(0.9)	245	(0.8)	243	(0.9)	244	(1.0)	249	(0.9)	90	(0.8)	52	(1.5)	10	(1.0)
Iowa[5]	230	(1.0)	231	(1.2)	238	(0.7)	240	(0.7)	243	(0.8)	243	(0.8)	243	(0.8)	246	(0.9)	87	(0.9)	48	(1.6)	9	(0.9)
Kansas[5]	—	(†)	232	(1.6)	242	(1.0)	246	(1.0)	248	(0.9)	245	(1.0)	246	(0.9)	246	(0.8)	89	(0.9)	48	(1.4)	8	(0.7)
Kentucky	215	(1.0)	219	(1.4)	229	(1.1)	232	(0.9)	235	(0.9)	239	(1.1)	241	(0.8)	241	(0.9)	84	(0.9)	41	(1.4)	6	(0.7)
Louisiana	204	(1.5)	218	(1.4)	226	(1.0)	230	(0.9)	230	(1.0)	229	(1.0)	231	(1.0)	231	(1.2)	75	(1.4)	26	(1.8)	3	(0.6)
Maine[5]	232	(1.0)	230	(1.0)	238	(0.8)	241	(0.8)	242	(0.8)	242	(0.8)	244	(0.8)	242	(0.7)	88	(0.8)	47	(1.4)	9	(0.7)
Maryland	217	(1.3)	222	(1.2)	233	(1.3)	238	(1.0)	240	(0.9)	244	(0.9)	247	(0.9)	245	(1.3)	82	(1.1)	47	(1.7)	13	(1.5)
Massachusetts	227	(1.2)	233	(1.2)	242	(0.8)	247	(0.8)	252	(0.8)	252	(0.8)	253	(0.8)	253	(1.0)	90	(0.8)	58	(1.5)	16	(1.1)
Michigan[5]	220	(1.7)	229	(1.6)	236	(0.9)	238	(1.2)	238	(1.3)	236	(1.0)	236	(1.1)	237	(1.1)	77	(1.2)	37	(1.7)	7	(0.8)
Minnesota[5]	228	(0.9)	234	(1.3)	242	(0.9)	246	(1.0)	247	(1.0)	249	(1.1)	249	(0.9)	253	(1.1)	90	(1.0)	59	(1.7)	16	(1.1)
Mississippi	202	(1.1)	211	(1.1)	223	(1.0)	227	(0.9)	228	(0.8)	227	(1.0)	230	(0.9)	231	(0.7)	74	(1.2)	26	(1.2)	2	(0.4)
Missouri	222	(1.2)	228	(1.2)	235	(0.9)	235	(0.9)	239	(0.9)	241	(1.2)	240	(0.9)	240	(0.8)	83	(1.1)	39	(1.3)	5	(0.7)
Montana[5]	—	(†)	228	(1.7)	236	(0.8)	241	(0.8)	244	(0.8)	244	(0.7)	244	(0.6)	244	(0.6)	86	(0.9)	45	(1.2)	7	(0.6)
Nebraska	225	(1.2)	225	(1.8)	236	(0.8)	238	(0.9)	238	(1.1)	239	(1.0)	240	(1.0)	243	(1.0)	84	(1.1)	45	(1.5)	8	(0.7)
Nevada	—	(†)	220	(1.0)	228	(0.8)	230	(0.8)	232	(0.9)	235	(0.9)	237	(0.8)	236	(0.8)	80	(1.1)	34	(1.2)	4	(0.5)
New Hampshire	230	(1.2)	—	(†)	243	(0.9)	246	(0.9)	249	(0.8)	251	(0.8)	252	(0.6)	253	(0.8)	93	(0.8)	59	(1.2)	12	(0.8)
New Jersey	227	(1.5)	—	(†)	239	(1.1)	244	(1.1)	249	(1.1)	247	(1.0)	248	(0.9)	247	(1.1)	87	(0.9)	49	(1.7)	10	(1.1)
New Mexico	213	(1.4)	213	(1.5)	223	(1.1)	224	(0.8)	228	(0.9)	230	(1.0)	233	(0.8)	233	(0.7)	74	(1.0)	31	(1.0)	4	(0.4)
New York[5]	218	(1.2)	225	(1.4)	236	(0.9)	238	(0.9)	243	(0.8)	241	(0.7)	238	(0.8)	240	(1.0)	82	(1.2)	40	(1.5)	7	(0.6)
North Carolina	213	(1.1)	230	(1.1)	242	(0.8)	241	(0.9)	242	(0.8)	244	(0.8)	245	(0.7)	245	(0.9)	87	(0.9)	45	(1.4)	8	(0.8)
North Dakota	229	(0.8)	230	(1.2)	238	(0.7)	243	(0.5)	245	(0.5)	245	(0.6)	245	(0.4)	246	(0.5)	89	(0.6)	48	(1.0)	7	(0.6)
Ohio[5]	219	(1.2)	230	(1.5)	238	(1.0)	242	(1.0)	245	(1.0)	244	(1.1)	244	(0.8)	246	(1.1)	86	(0.9)	48	(1.7)	10	(1.0)
Oklahoma	220	(1.0)	224	(1.0)	229	(1.0)	234	(1.0)	237	(0.8)	237	(0.9)	237	(0.8)	239	(0.7)	83	(1.0)	36	(1.3)	5	(0.6)
Oregon[5]	—	(†)	224	(1.8)	236	(0.9)	238	(0.8)	236	(1.0)	238	(0.9)	237	(0.9)	240	(1.3)	81	(1.2)	40	(2.0)	8	(0.9)
Pennsylvania	224	(1.3)	—	(†)	236	(1.1)	241	(1.2)	244	(0.8)	244	(1.1)	246	(1.1)	244	(1.0)	85	(1.0)	44	(1.7)	8	(0.9)
Rhode Island	215	(1.5)	224	(1.1)	230	(1.0)	233	(0.9)	236	(0.9)	239	(0.8)	242	(0.7)	241	(0.8)	83	(1.0)	42	(1.2)	7	(0.6)
South Carolina	212	(1.1)	220	(1.4)	236	(0.9)	238	(0.9)	237	(0.8)	236	(0.9)	237	(1.1)	237	(1.0)	79	(1.3)	35	(1.5)	5	(0.7)
South Dakota	—	(†)	—	(†)	237	(0.7)	242	(0.5)	241	(0.7)	242	(0.5)	241	(0.6)	241	(0.5)	84	(1.0)	40	(1.1)	5	(0.6)
Tennessee	211	(1.4)	220	(1.4)	228	(1.0)	232	(1.2)	233	(0.9)	232	(1.1)	233	(0.9)	240	(0.9)	80	(1.2)	40	(1.4)	7	(0.9)
Texas	218	(1.2)	231	(1.1)	237	(0.9)	242	(0.6)	242	(0.7)	240	(0.7)	241	(1.1)	242	(0.9)	84	(1.0)	41	(1.5)	7	(0.9)
Utah	224	(1.0)	227	(1.3)	235	(0.8)	239	(0.8)	239	(0.9)	240	(1.0)	243	(0.8)	243	(0.9)	83	(1.0)	44	(1.4)	8	(0.9)
Vermont[5]	—	(†)	232	(1.6)	242	(0.8)	244	(0.5)	246	(0.5)	248	(0.4)	247	(0.5)	248	(0.6)	87	(0.7)	52	(1.1)	11	(0.7)
Virginia	221	(1.3)	230	(1.0)	239	(1.1)	241	(0.9)	244	(0.9)	243	(1.0)	245	(0.8)	246	(1.1)	88	(0.9)	47	(1.7)	9	(1.2)
Washington	—	(†)	—	(†)	238	(1.0)	242	(0.9)	243	(1.0)	242	(0.8)	243	(0.9)	246	(1.1)	86	(0.8)	48	(1.6)	10	(1.2)
West Virginia	215	(1.1)	223	(1.3)	231	(0.8)	231	(0.7)	236	(0.9)	233	(0.8)	235	(0.7)	237	(0.8)	81	(1.0)	35	(1.2)	4	(0.5)
Wisconsin[5]	229	(1.1)	—	(†)	237	(0.9)	241	(0.9)	244	(0.9)	244	(0.9)	245	(0.8)	245	(1.0)	85	(1.1)	47	(1.6)	9	(0.8)
Wyoming	225	(0.9)	229	(1.1)	241	(0.6)	243	(0.6)	244	(0.5)	242	(0.6)	244	(0.4)	247	(0.4)	90	(0.7)	48	(0.9)	7	(0.5)
Department of Defense dependents schools[6]	—	(†)	227	(0.6)	237	(0.4)	239	(0.5)	240	(0.4)	240	(0.5)	241	(0.4)	245	(0.4)	89	(0.6)	45	(0.8)	6	(0.6)

—Not available.
†Not applicable.
[1]Scale ranges from 0 to 500.
[2]*Basic* denotes partial mastery of the knowledge and skills that are fundamental for proficient work at the 4th-grade level.
[3]*Proficient* represents solid academic performance for 4th-graders. Students reaching this level have demonstrated competency over challenging subject matter.
[4]*Advanced* signifies superior performance.
[5]Did not meet one or more of the guidelines for school participation in 2000. Data are subject to appreciable nonresponse bias.
[6]Prior to 2005, NAEP divided the Department of Defense (DoD) schools into two jurisdictions, domestic and overseas. In 2005, NAEP began combining the DoD domestic and overseas schools into a single jurisdiction. Data shown in this table for years prior to 2005 were recalculated for comparability.
NOTE: With the exception of 1992, includes public school students who were tested with accommodations; excludes only those students with disabilities (SD) and English language learners (ELL) who were unable to be tested even with accommodations. SD and ELL populations, accommodation rates, and exclusion rates vary from state to state. Detail may not sum to totals because of rounding.
SOURCE: U.S. Department of Education, National Center for Education Statistics, National Assessment of Educational Progress (NAEP), 1992, 2000, 2003, 2005, 2007, 2009, 2011, and 2013 Mathematics Assessments, retrieved November 21, 2013, from the Main NAEP Data Explorer (http://nces.ed.gov/nationsreportcard/naepdata/). (This table was prepared November 2013.)

Average National Assessment of Educational Progress (NAEP) mathematics scale score of 8th-grade public school students and percentage attaining mathematics achievement levels, by state: Selected years, 1990 through 2013

[Standard errors appear in parentheses]

State	1990[2]	1996[3]	2000	2003	2005	2007	2009	2011	2013	At or above Basic[4]	At or above Proficient[5]	At Advanced[6]
1	2	3	4	5	6	7	8	9	10	11	12	13
United States	**262 (1.4)**	**271 (1.2)**	**272 (0.9)**	**276 (0.3)**	**278 (0.2)**	**280 (0.3)**	**282 (0.3)**	**283 (0.2)**	**284 (0.2)**	**73 (0.3)**	**34 (0.3)**	**8 (0.2)**
Alabama	253 (1.1)	257 (2.1)	264 (1.8)	262 (1.5)	262 (1.5)	266 (1.5)	269 (1.2)	269 (1.4)	269 (1.3)	60 (1.5)	20 (1.6)	3 (0.6)
Alaska	— (†)	278 (1.8)	— (†)	279 (0.9)	279 (0.8)	283 (1.1)	283 (1.0)	283 (0.8)	282 (0.9)	72 (1.1)	33 (1.1)	7 (0.7)
Arizona[7]	260 (1.3)	268 (1.6)	269 (1.8)	271 (1.2)	274 (1.1)	276 (1.2)	277 (1.4)	279 (1.2)	280 (1.2)	69 (1.3)	31 (1.3)	7 (0.9)
Arkansas	256 (0.9)	262 (1.5)	257 (1.5)	266 (1.2)	272 (1.2)	274 (1.1)	276 (1.1)	279 (1.0)	278 (1.1)	69 (1.4)	28 (1.3)	5 (0.6)
California[7]	256 (1.3)	263 (1.9)	260 (2.1)	267 (1.2)	269 (0.7)	270 (0.8)	270 (1.3)	273 (1.2)	276 (1.2)	65 (1.3)	28 (1.3)	6 (0.7)
Colorado	267 (0.9)	276 (1.1)	— (†)	283 (1.1)	281 (1.2)	286 (0.9)	287 (1.4)	292 (1.1)	290 (1.2)	77 (1.3)	42 (1.5)	12 (0.9)
Connecticut	270 (1.0)	280 (1.1)	281 (1.3)	284 (1.2)	281 (1.4)	282 (1.5)	289 (1.0)	287 (1.1)	285 (1.1)	74 (1.3)	37 (1.2)	10 (0.8)
Delaware	261 (0.9)	267 (0.9)	— (†)	277 (0.7)	281 (0.6)	283 (0.9)	284 (0.5)	283 (0.7)	282 (0.7)	71 (1.0)	33 (1.1)	8 (0.6)
District of Columbia	231 (0.9)	233 (1.3)	235 (1.1)	243 (0.8)	245 (0.9)	248 (0.9)	254 (0.9)	260 (0.7)	265 (0.9)	54 (1.3)	19 (1.0)	4 (0.5)
Florida	255 (1.2)	264 (1.8)	— (†)	271 (1.5)	274 (1.1)	277 (1.3)	279 (1.1)	278 (0.8)	281 (0.8)	70 (1.1)	31 (1.1)	7 (0.6)
Georgia	259 (1.3)	262 (1.6)	265 (1.2)	270 (1.2)	272 (1.1)	275 (1.0)	278 (0.9)	278 (1.0)	279 (1.2)	68 (1.4)	29 (1.3)	7 (0.8)
Hawaii	251 (0.8)	262 (1.0)	262 (1.4)	266 (0.8)	266 (0.7)	269 (0.8)	274 (0.7)	278 (0.7)	281 (0.8)	72 (1.0)	32 (1.1)	7 (0.6)
Idaho[7]	271 (0.8)	— (†)	277 (1.0)	280 (0.9)	281 (0.9)	284 (0.9)	287 (0.8)	287 (0.8)	286 (0.7)	78 (0.9)	36 (1.1)	7 (0.8)
Illinois[7]	261 (1.7)	— (†)	275 (1.7)	277 (1.2)	278 (1.1)	280 (1.1)	282 (1.2)	283 (1.1)	285 (1.0)	74 (1.1)	36 (1.3)	9 (0.9)
Indiana[7]	267 (1.2)	276 (1.4)	281 (1.4)	281 (1.1)	282 (1.0)	285 (1.1)	287 (0.9)	285 (1.0)	288 (1.1)	77 (1.1)	38 (1.4)	10 (0.9)
Iowa	278 (1.1)	284 (1.3)	— (†)	284 (0.8)	284 (0.9)	285 (0.9)	284 (1.0)	285 (0.9)	285 (0.9)	76 (0.9)	36 (1.3)	7 (0.6)
Kansas[7]	— (†)	— (†)	283 (1.7)	284 (1.3)	284 (1.0)	290 (1.1)	289 (1.0)	290 (0.9)	290 (1.0)	79 (1.2)	40 (1.1)	10 (0.8)
Kentucky	257 (1.2)	267 (1.1)	270 (1.3)	274 (1.2)	274 (1.2)	279 (1.1)	279 (1.1)	282 (0.9)	281 (0.9)	71 (1.2)	30 (1.2)	6 (0.6)
Louisiana	246 (1.2)	252 (1.6)	259 (1.5)	266 (1.5)	268 (1.4)	272 (1.1)	272 (1.6)	273 (1.2)	273 (0.9)	64 (1.2)	21 (1.0)	3 (0.4)
Maine[7]	— (†)	284 (1.3)	281 (1.1)	282 (0.9)	281 (1.1)	286 (0.8)	286 (0.7)	289 (0.8)	289 (0.7)	78 (1.0)	40 (1.2)	10 (0.7)
Maryland	261 (1.4)	270 (2.1)	272 (1.7)	278 (1.0)	278 (1.1)	286 (1.2)	288 (1.1)	288 (1.2)	287 (1.1)	74 (1.1)	37 (1.1)	12 (0.9)
Massachusetts	— (†)	278 (1.7)	279 (1.5)	287 (0.9)	292 (0.9)	298 (1.3)	299 (1.3)	299 (0.8)	301 (0.9)	86 (0.7)	55 (1.2)	18 (1.2)
Michigan[7]	264 (1.2)	277 (1.8)	277 (1.9)	276 (2.0)	277 (1.5)	277 (1.4)	278 (1.6)	280 (1.4)	280 (1.3)	70 (1.6)	30 (1.5)	7 (0.7)
Minnesota	275 (0.9)	284 (1.3)	287 (1.4)	291 (1.1)	290 (1.2)	292 (1.2)	294 (1.0)	295 (1.0)	295 (1.0)	83 (1.0)	47 (1.2)	14 (1.0)
Mississippi	— (†)	250 (1.2)	254 (1.1)	261 (1.1)	263 (1.2)	265 (0.8)	265 (1.2)	269 (1.4)	271 (0.9)	61 (1.3)	21 (1.2)	3 (0.4)
Missouri	— (†)	273 (1.4)	271 (1.5)	279 (1.1)	276 (1.3)	281 (1.0)	286 (1.0)	282 (1.1)	283 (1.0)	74 (1.3)	33 (1.3)	7 (0.7)
Montana[7]	280 (0.9)	283 (1.3)	285 (1.4)	286 (0.8)	286 (0.7)	287 (0.7)	292 (0.9)	293 (0.6)	289 (0.9)	80 (1.1)	40 (1.3)	9 (0.7)
Nebraska	276 (1.0)	283 (1.0)	280 (1.2)	282 (0.9)	284 (1.0)	284 (1.0)	284 (1.1)	283 (0.8)	285 (0.9)	76 (1.1)	36 (1.2)	7 (0.7)
Nevada	— (†)	— (†)	265 (0.8)	268 (0.8)	270 (0.8)	271 (0.8)	274 (0.7)	278 (0.8)	278 (0.7)	68 (1.1)	28 (1.0)	6 (0.5)
New Hampshire	273 (0.9)	— (†)	— (†)	286 (0.8)	285 (0.8)	288 (0.7)	292 (0.9)	292 (0.7)	296 (0.8)	84 (0.8)	47 (1.1)	13 (1.0)
New Jersey	270 (1.1)	— (†)	— (†)	281 (1.1)	284 (1.4)	289 (1.2)	293 (1.4)	294 (1.2)	296 (1.1)	82 (1.0)	49 (1.4)	16 (0.9)
New Mexico	256 (0.7)	262 (1.2)	259 (1.3)	263 (1.0)	263 (0.9)	268 (0.9)	270 (1.1)	274 (0.8)	273 (0.7)	63 (1.1)	23 (1.0)	4 (0.4)
New York[7]	261 (1.4)	270 (1.7)	271 (2.2)	280 (1.1)	280 (0.9)	280 (1.2)	283 (1.2)	280 (0.9)	282 (0.9)	72 (1.2)	32 (1.2)	8 (0.7)
North Carolina	250 (1.1)	268 (1.4)	276 (1.3)	281 (1.0)	282 (0.9)	284 (1.1)	284 (1.3)	286 (1.0)	286 (1.1)	75 (1.2)	36 (1.5)	9 (0.8)
North Dakota	281 (1.2)	284 (0.9)	282 (1.1)	287 (0.8)	287 (0.6)	292 (0.7)	293 (0.7)	292 (0.6)	291 (0.5)	82 (0.7)	41 (1.0)	8 (0.6)
Ohio	264 (1.0)	— (†)	281 (1.6)	282 (1.3)	283 (1.1)	285 (1.2)	286 (1.0)	289 (0.9)	290 (1.1)	79 (1.1)	40 (1.5)	11 (0.9)
Oklahoma	263 (1.3)	— (†)	270 (1.3)	272 (1.1)	271 (1.0)	275 (0.9)	276 (1.0)	279 (1.0)	276 (1.0)	68 (1.4)	25 (1.1)	4 (0.5)
Oregon[7]	271 (1.0)	276 (1.5)	280 (1.5)	281 (1.3)	282 (1.0)	284 (1.1)	285 (1.0)	283 (1.0)	284 (1.1)	73 (1.0)	34 (1.6)	8 (0.8)
Pennsylvania	266 (1.6)	— (†)	— (†)	279 (1.1)	281 (1.5)	286 (1.1)	288 (1.3)	286 (1.2)	290 (1.0)	78 (1.1)	42 (1.5)	10 (0.8)
Rhode Island	260 (0.6)	269 (0.9)	269 (1.3)	272 (0.7)	272 (0.8)	275 (0.7)	278 (0.8)	283 (0.5)	284 (0.6)	74 (0.9)	36 (0.8)	8 (0.7)
South Carolina	— (†)	261 (1.5)	265 (1.5)	277 (1.3)	281 (0.9)	282 (1.0)	280 (1.3)	281 (1.1)	280 (1.1)	69 (1.4)	31 (1.2)	8 (0.7)
South Dakota	— (†)	— (†)	— (†)	285 (0.8)	287 (0.6)	288 (0.8)	291 (0.5)	291 (0.5)	287 (0.7)	79 (0.9)	38 (1.0)	7 (0.6)
Tennessee	— (†)	263 (1.4)	262 (1.5)	268 (1.8)	271 (1.1)	274 (1.1)	275 (1.4)	274 (1.2)	278 (1.3)	69 (1.3)	28 (1.4)	5 (0.6)
Texas	258 (1.4)	270 (1.4)	273 (1.6)	277 (1.1)	281 (0.6)	286 (1.0)	287 (1.3)	290 (0.9)	288 (1.0)	80 (1.1)	38 (1.4)	8 (0.8)
Utah	— (†)	277 (1.0)	274 (1.2)	281 (1.0)	279 (0.7)	281 (0.9)	284 (0.9)	283 (0.8)	284 (0.9)	75 (1.1)	36 (1.1)	8 (0.7)
Vermont[7]	— (†)	279 (1.0)	281 (1.5)	286 (0.8)	287 (0.8)	291 (0.7)	293 (0.6)	294 (0.7)	295 (0.7)	84 (0.9)	47 (1.0)	14 (0.8)
Virginia	264 (1.5)	270 (1.6)	275 (1.3)	282 (1.3)	284 (1.1)	288 (1.1)	286 (1.1)	289 (1.1)	288 (1.2)	77 (1.2)	38 (1.5)	10 (1.2)
Washington	— (†)	276 (1.3)	— (†)	281 (0.9)	285 (1.0)	285 (1.0)	289 (1.0)	288 (1.0)	290 (1.0)	79 (1.0)	42 (1.4)	12 (0.9)
West Virginia	256 (1.0)	265 (1.0)	266 (1.2)	271 (1.2)	269 (1.0)	270 (1.0)	270 (1.0)	273 (0.7)	274 (0.9)	65 (1.2)	24 (1.1)	3 (0.5)
Wisconsin	274 (1.3)	283 (1.5)	— (†)	284 (1.3)	285 (1.2)	286 (1.1)	288 (0.9)	289 (1.0)	289 (0.9)	78 (0.9)	40 (1.2)	11 (0.7)
Wyoming	272 (0.7)	275 (0.9)	276 (1.0)	284 (0.7)	282 (0.8)	287 (0.7)	286 (0.6)	288 (0.6)	288 (0.5)	81 (0.8)	38 (1.1)	7 (0.5)
Department of Defense dependents schools[8]	— (†)	274 (0.9)	277 (1.1)	285 (0.7)	284 (0.7)	285 (0.8)	287 (0.9)	288 (0.8)	290 (0.8)	83 (0.9)	40 (1.2)	8 (0.7)

—Not available.
†Not applicable.
[1] Scale ranges from 0 to 500.
[2] Accommodations were not permitted for this assessment.
[3] The 1996 data in this table do not include students who were tested with accommodations. Data for students tested with accommodations are not available at the state level for 1996.
[4] Basic denotes partial mastery of the knowledge and skills that are fundamental for proficient work at the 8th-grade level.
[5] Proficient represents solid academic performance for 8th-graders. Students reaching this level have demonstrated competency over challenging subject matter.
[6] Advanced signifies superior performance.
[7] Did not meet one or more of the guidelines for school participation in 2000. Data are subject to appreciable nonresponse bias.

[8] Prior to 2005, NAEP divided the Department of Defense (DoD) schools into two jurisdictions, domestic and overseas. In 2005, NAEP began combining the DoD domestic and overseas schools into a single jurisdiction. Data shown in this table for years prior to 2005 were recalculated for comparability.
NOTE: For 2000 and later years, includes public school students who were tested with accommodations; excludes only those students with disabilities (SD) and English language learners (ELL) who were unable to be tested even with accommodations. SD and ELL populations, accommodation rates, and exclusion rates vary from state to state. Detail may not sum to totals because of rounding.
SOURCE: U.S. Department of Education, National Center for Education Statistics, National Assessment of Educational Progress (NAEP), 1990, 1996, 2000, 2003, 2005, 2007, 2009, 2011, and 2013 Mathematics Assessments, retrieved November 7, 2013, from the Main NAEP Data Explorer (http://nces.ed.gov/nationsreportcard/naepdata/). (This table was prepared November 2013.)

Average National Assessment of Educational Progress (NAEP) mathematics scale score of 8th-grade public school students, by race/ethnicity, highest level of parental education, and state: 2013
[Standard errors appear in parentheses]

State	Race/ethnicity[1] White		Black		Hispanic		Asian		Pacific Islander		American Indian/ Alaska Native		Highest level of education attained by parents[2] Did not finish high school		Graduated high school		Some education after high school		Graduated college	
1	2		3		4		5		6		7		8		9		10		11	
United States	**293**	**(0.3)**	**263**	**(0.4)**	**271**	**(0.4)**	**308**	**(1.1)**	**274**	**(2.3)**	**270**	**(1.3)**	**267**	**(0.5)**	**270**	**(0.4)**	**285**	**(0.4)**	**295**	**(0.3)**
Alabama	280	(1.6)	250	(1.4)	257	(3.5)	‡	(†)	‡	(†)	‡	(†)	252	(2.7)	253	(2.0)	274	(1.6)	279	(2.0)
Alaska	294	(1.0)	270	(3.9)	277	(2.4)	278	(2.5)	257	(4.7)	262	(2.3)	‡	(†)	‡	(†)	‡	(†)	‡	(†)
Arizona	294	(1.6)	266	(4.0)	269	(1.3)	306	(4.3)	‡	(†)	259	(3.4)	267	(2.3)	268	(2.1)	283	(2.0)	294	(1.8)
Arkansas	286	(1.2)	255	(1.7)	274	(2.4)	‡	(†)	‡	(†)	‡	(†)	267	(2.4)	266	(1.9)	281	(1.5)	288	(1.4)
California	291	(1.6)	258	(3.0)	263	(1.1)	307	(2.8)	‡	(†)	‡	(†)	260	(1.7)	266	(1.8)	279	(2.1)	292	(1.7)
Colorado	300	(1.3)	260	(3.8)	273	(1.8)	308	(5.4)	‡	(†)	‡	(†)	265	(3.4)	271	(2.3)	293	(1.8)	302	(1.3)
Connecticut	297	(1.0)	260	(2.6)	258	(2.3)	308	(3.6)	‡	(†)	‡	(†)	260	(4.3)	267	(2.0)	280	(2.2)	296	(1.2)
Delaware	293	(0.9)	264	(1.1)	276	(2.0)	312	(4.8)	‡	(†)	‡	(†)	268	(3.7)	271	(1.7)	282	(1.8)	292	(1.1)
District of Columbia	317	(3.5)	261	(1.0)	265	(2.7)	‡	(†)	‡	(†)	‡	(†)	257	(3.6)	253	(2.1)	271	(2.1)	277	(1.7)
Florida	291	(1.2)	264	(1.7)	274	(1.0)	310	(4.7)	‡	(†)	‡	(†)	266	(2.3)	269	(1.5)	286	(1.3)	290	(1.0)
Georgia	292	(1.4)	262	(1.4)	276	(2.8)	310	(6.6)	‡	(†)	‡	(†)	267	(2.4)	267	(1.6)	281	(1.8)	289	(1.5)
Hawaii	290	(2.3)	‡	(†)	280	(3.1)	291	(1.3)	267	(1.3)	‡	(†)	273	(4.0)	270	(1.4)	287	(1.7)	291	(1.2)
Idaho	291	(0.8)	‡	(†)	268	(1.6)	‡	(†)	‡	(†)	‡	(†)	268	(2.2)	270	(2.0)	288	(1.8)	296	(1.1)
Illinois	296	(1.3)	260	(1.3)	272	(1.4)	313	(6.2)	‡	(†)	‡	(†)	267	(2.3)	272	(2.0)	285	(1.8)	297	(1.2)
Indiana	293	(1.1)	265	(2.4)	278	(2.4)	‡	(†)	‡	(†)	‡	(†)	272	(2.9)	276	(1.9)	290	(1.7)	298	(1.5)
Iowa	289	(1.0)	255	(3.1)	265	(2.6)	301	(4.7)	‡	(†)	‡	(†)	261	(4.2)	272	(1.9)	287	(1.8)	294	(1.0)
Kansas	295	(1.1)	268	(3.2)	276	(3.0)	302	(7.1)	‡	(†)	‡	(†)	268	(3.3)	277	(2.0)	287	(1.9)	300	(1.2)
Kentucky	283	(1.0)	260	(1.6)	269	(3.0)	313	(7.1)	‡	(†)	‡	(†)	262	(2.5)	270	(1.4)	281	(1.7)	291	(1.2)
Louisiana	285	(0.8)	259	(1.1)	277	(3.7)	‡	(†)	‡	(†)	‡	(†)	266	(2.7)	265	(1.5)	279	(1.4)	279	(1.3)
Maine	290	(0.8)	262	(4.9)	‡	(†)	‡	(†)	‡	(†)	‡	(†)	270	(3.5)	275	(1.9)	285	(1.8)	298	(0.9)
Maryland	299	(1.6)	268	(1.4)	280	(2.3)	319	(4.1)	‡	(†)	‡	(†)	269	(2.7)	272	(1.7)	288	(1.8)	297	(1.4)
Massachusetts	307	(1.0)	277	(1.8)	277	(2.1)	324	(3.5)	‡	(†)	‡	(†)	274	(2.4)	283	(2.2)	298	(1.6)	311	(1.2)
Michigan	287	(1.2)	251	(2.2)	261	(2.6)	310	(7.7)	‡	(†)	‡	(†)	260	(3.9)	264	(2.2)	279	(1.9)	291	(1.6)
Minnesota	301	(1.1)	260	(3.5)	273	(3.1)	291	(3.1)	‡	(†)	‡	(†)	269	(4.5)	274	(2.3)	293	(2.3)	305	(1.2)
Mississippi	285	(1.1)	255	(1.1)	279	(3.7)	‡	(†)	‡	(†)	‡	(†)	265	(2.3)	259	(1.5)	278	(2.2)	279	(1.3)
Missouri	288	(0.9)	260	(3.1)	276	(2.9)	‡	(†)	‡	(†)	‡	(†)	265	(2.7)	269	(1.7)	289	(1.8)	292	(1.3)
Montana	293	(0.9)	‡	(†)	282	(4.0)	‡	(†)	‡	(†)	263	(2.2)	268	(2.5)	279	(1.6)	290	(1.8)	297	(1.1)
Nebraska	292	(0.9)	250	(4.2)	267	(1.7)	302	(4.9)	‡	(†)	‡	(†)	267	(2.7)	272	(1.9)	287	(1.8)	295	(1.0)
Nevada	289	(1.4)	263	(2.2)	268	(1.1)	300	(2.8)	‡	(†)	‡	(†)	265	(2.1)	271	(1.5)	288	(1.4)	289	(1.2)
New Hampshire	297	(0.8)	‡	(†)	270	(3.7)	313	(6.4)	‡	(†)	‡	(†)	274	(3.2)	282	(1.6)	293	(1.6)	304	(1.0)
New Jersey	303	(1.3)	274	(2.6)	283	(2.3)	323	(3.1)	‡	(†)	‡	(†)	279	(3.5)	277	(2.1)	292	(1.9)	306	(1.2)
New Mexico	289	(1.2)	258	(5.0)	268	(0.8)	‡	(†)	‡	(†)	260	(2.3)	264	(1.8)	262	(1.4)	277	(1.3)	285	(1.3)
New York	294	(1.1)	262	(1.9)	265	(1.8)	305	(2.4)	‡	(†)	‡	(†)	265	(2.7)	268	(1.9)	282	(1.8)	292	(1.1)
North Carolina	296	(1.5)	268	(1.6)	279	(2.0)	301	(6.4)	‡	(†)	‡	(†)	272	(2.7)	273	(1.8)	289	(1.8)	296	(1.3)
North Dakota	294	(0.6)	272	(4.1)	‡	(†)	‡	(†)	‡	(†)	265	(2.4)	270	(3.2)	274	(1.8)	290	(1.4)	297	(0.6)
Ohio	294	(1.1)	267	(1.8)	277	(3.9)	312	(5.8)	‡	(†)	‡	(†)	267	(3.3)	276	(1.8)	290	(1.6)	300	(1.2)
Oklahoma	281	(1.2)	256	(3.1)	265	(3.0)	299	(4.3)	‡	(†)	275	(1.9)	261	(2.7)	265	(1.9)	281	(1.6)	284	(1.2)
Oregon	290	(1.1)	‡	(†)	266	(1.8)	306	(5.6)	‡	(†)	‡	(†)	266	(2.3)	270	(1.7)	286	(1.8)	297	(1.6)
Pennsylvania	297	(1.0)	262	(2.1)	264	(2.4)	307	(4.4)	‡	(†)	‡	(†)	269	(3.3)	276	(1.5)	290	(1.6)	299	(1.4)
Rhode Island	294	(0.7)	263	(2.8)	263	(1.6)	285	(4.9)	‡	(†)	‡	(†)	264	(2.5)	269	(1.9)	284	(1.9)	297	(0.9)
South Carolina	292	(1.2)	261	(1.7)	272	(3.8)	‡	(†)	‡	(†)	‡	(†)	267	(2.9)	266	(1.8)	282	(1.8)	290	(1.4)
South Dakota	294	(0.7)	254	(5.5)	274	(3.8)	‡	(†)	‡	(†)	260	(1.7)	265	(3.0)	272	(1.9)	288	(1.9)	297	(0.8)
Tennessee	284	(1.2)	257	(2.8)	270	(3.3)	‡	(†)	‡	(†)	‡	(†)	261	(2.4)	268	(1.9)	282	(1.7)	287	(1.5)
Texas	300	(1.5)	273	(2.0)	281	(1.1)	321	(3.7)	‡	(†)	‡	(†)	277	(1.5)	278	(1.5)	289	(1.7)	299	(1.3)
Utah	291	(0.9)	‡	(†)	258	(1.9)	‡	(†)	‡	(†)	‡	(†)	258	(3.1)	264	(2.1)	284	(1.7)	297	(0.8)
Vermont	296	(0.6)	258	(5.4)	‡	(†)	‡	(†)	‡	(†)	‡	(†)	270	(3.3)	281	(1.4)	295	(1.7)	306	(0.9)
Virginia	296	(1.2)	267	(1.8)	279	(2.1)	311	(3.5)	‡	(†)	‡	(†)	269	(2.7)	271	(1.6)	284	(2.0)	300	(1.6)
Washington	296	(1.2)	269	(4.7)	273	(1.6)	310	(3.5)	‡	(†)	‡	(†)	270	(2.2)	275	(2.1)	290	(1.7)	303	(1.3)
West Virginia	275	(0.9)	264	(2.9)	‡	(†)	‡	(†)	‡	(†)	‡	(†)	259	(2.5)	265	(1.4)	279	(1.5)	284	(1.3)
Wisconsin	296	(0.8)	252	(2.3)	273	(2.2)	290	(3.4)	‡	(†)	‡	(†)	265	(3.1)	274	(1.7)	288	(1.5)	298	(1.0)
Wyoming	290	(0.6)	‡	(†)	278	(1.7)	‡	(†)	‡	(†)	269	(3.4)	272	(2.6)	275	(1.3)	291	(1.3)	296	(0.8)
Department of Defense dependents schools	296	(1.1)	276	(1.8)	283	(1.7)	301	(2.4)	‡	(†)	‡	(†)	‡	(†)	278	(2.0)	288	(1.7)	295	(0.8)

†Not applicable.
‡Reporting standards not met. Either there are too few cases for a reliable estimate or item response rates fell below the required standards for reporting.
[1]Data for students of two or more races are not separately shown.
[2]Excludes students who responded "I don't know" to the question about educational level of parents.
NOTE: Scale ranges from 0 to 500. Includes public school students who were tested with accommodations; excludes only those students with disabilities (SD) and English language learners (ELL) who were unable to be tested even with accommodations. SD and ELL populations, accommodation rates, and exclusion rates vary from state to state. Detail may not sum to totals because of rounding.
SOURCE: U.S. Department of Education, National Center for Education Statistics, National Assessment of Educational Progress (NAEP), 2013 Mathematics Assessment, retrieved November 11, 2013, from the Main NAEP Data Explorer (http://nces.ed.gov/nationsreportcard/naepdata/). (This table was prepared November 2013.)

Average National Assessment of Educational Progress (NAEP) mathematics scale scores of 4th- and 8th-grade public school students and percentage attaining achievement levels, by race/ethnicity and jurisdiction or specific urban district: 2009, 2011, and 2013
[Standard errors appear in parentheses]

Grade level and jurisdiction or specific urban district	2009 All students	2011 All students[2]	2011 White	2011 Black	2011 Hispanic	2011 Asian	2013 All students[2]	2013 White	2013 Black	2013 Hispanic	2013 Asian	2013 At or above Basic[3]	2013 At or above Proficient[4]
1	2	3	4	5	6	7	8	9	10	11	12	13	14
4th grade													
United States	239 (0.2)	240 (0.2)	249 (0.2)	224 (0.4)	229 (0.3)	257 (1.1)	241 (0.2)	250 (0.2)	224 (0.3)	230 (0.4)	260 (0.8)	82 (0.2)	41 (0.3)
All large cities	231 (0.5)	233 (0.6)	251 (0.8)	222 (0.5)	228 (0.6)	249 (2.1)	235 (0.7)	254 (0.9)	223 (0.6)	229 (0.8)	258 (2.1)	75 (0.7)	33 (0.8)
Selected urban districts													
Albuquerque	— (†)	235 (1.3)	254 (1.9)	‡ (†)	229 (1.3)	‡ (†)	235 (1.0)	253 (2.0)	‡ (†)	229 (1.2)	‡ (†)	75 (1.5)	34 (1.8)
Atlanta	225 (0.8)	228 (0.7)	269 (1.4)	219 (0.8)	230 (2.8)	‡ (†)	233 (0.7)	269 (1.4)	222 (0.9)	233 (2.7)	‡ (†)	72 (1.2)	31 (1.0)
Austin	240 (1.0)	245 (1.1)	266 (1.5)	232 (2.7)	237 (1.5)	‡ (†)	245 (0.9)	264 (1.7)	228 (3.4)	237 (1.2)	‡ (†)	85 (1.2)	46 (1.6)
Baltimore City	222 (1.0)	226 (1.1)	244 (2.6)	223 (1.2)	‡ (†)	‡ (†)	223 (1.2)	250 (4.0)	220 (1.2)	227 (3.9)	‡ (†)	62 (1.9)	19 (1.5)
Boston	236 (0.7)	237 (0.6)	255 (1.8)	230 (1.1)	234 (1.2)	259 (2.5)	237 (0.8)	255 (1.6)	228 (1.4)	233 (1.1)	259 (2.2)	80 (1.3)	34 (1.4)
Charlotte	245 (1.3)	247 (1.1)	264 (1.4)	232 (1.4)	240 (1.6)	259 (3.7)	247 (1.6)	264 (2.0)	235 (2.2)	242 (2.0)	255 (4.1)	87 (1.4)	50 (2.4)
Chicago	222 (1.2)	224 (0.9)	246 (2.5)	217 (1.9)	223 (1.3)	246 (3.2)	231 (1.3)	261 (2.8)	221 (2.1)	230 (1.2)	256 (5.8)	70 (1.6)	28 (1.5)
Cleveland	213 (1.0)	216 (0.7)	232 (2.0)	211 (0.9)	218 (1.8)	‡ (†)	216 (0.9)	233 (2.2)	210 (1.1)	221 (2.6)	‡ (†)	54 (1.7)	13 (1.1)
Dallas	— (†)	233 (1.3)	258 (3.5)	225 (2.0)	234 (1.2)	‡ (†)	234 (1.0)	‡ (†)	226 (1.7)	235 (1.1)	‡ (†)	78 (1.7)	30 (1.8)
Detroit	200 (1.7)	203 (1.4)	‡ (†)	201 (1.5)	215 (2.4)	‡ (†)	204 (1.6)	‡ (†)	201 (1.6)	214 (2.9)	‡ (†)	35 (2.5)	4 (1.1)
District of Columbia	220 (0.8)	222 (1.0)	272 (1.8)	212 (1.2)	223 (2.6)	‡ (†)	229 (0.8)	277 (2.2)	218 (1.0)	226 (2.3)	‡ (†)	64 (1.4)	30 (1.1)
Fresno	219 (1.4)	218 (0.9)	238 (2.2)	214 (2.3)	214 (1.0)	222 (2.0)	220 (1.2)	241 (2.2)	211 (2.5)	217 (1.5)	221 (2.7)	59 (2.2)	15 (1.2)
Hillsborough County (FL)	— (†)	243 (1.1)	253 (1.7)	228 (1.9)	239 (1.2)	‡ (†)	243 (0.9)	254 (1.4)	227 (1.9)	238 (1.3)	263 (3.2)	85 (1.3)	43 (1.6)
Houston	236 (1.2)	237 (0.8)	259 (2.1)	229 (1.4)	236 (0.9)	265 (3.4)	236 (1.1)	261 (1.9)	227 (2.3)	235 (1.0)	‡ (†)	80 (1.5)	32 (1.7)
Jefferson County (KY)	233 (1.6)	235 (0.9)	243 (1.2)	221 (1.3)	238 (3.1)	256 (4.3)	234 (1.0)	245 (1.2)	220 (1.4)	224 (3.0)	‡ (†)	75 (1.4)	33 (1.4)
Los Angeles	222 (1.2)	223 (0.8)	243 (1.6)	215 (3.0)	220 (0.8)	251 (2.6)	228 (1.3)	254 (3.4)	223 (2.3)	224 (0.9)	252 (2.4)	69 (1.5)	25 (2.0)
Miami-Dade	236 (1.3)	236 (1.0)	255 (2.0)	225 (1.5)	237 (1.0)	‡ (†)	237 (1.1)	251 (2.2)	227 (1.9)	238 (1.2)	‡ (†)	81 (1.3)	34 (1.8)
Milwaukee	220 (1.5)	220 (1.0)	239 (1.9)	211 (1.4)	221 (1.8)	230 (3.2)	221 (1.6)	246 (2.8)	209 (1.8)	227 (2.2)	234 (7.5)	61 (2.3)	18 (1.6)
New York City	237 (1.0)	234 (1.2)	248 (3.2)	226 (1.1)	227 (1.7)	252 (2.0)	236 (1.1)	251 (2.7)	225 (1.5)	228 (1.5)	257 (2.6)	77 (1.4)	34 (1.5)
Philadelphia	222 (1.4)	225 (1.2)	243 (3.0)	220 (0.9)	223 (2.4)	251 (2.8)	223 (1.5)	237 (3.3)	218 (1.3)	217 (2.2)	246 (3.9)	62 (2.2)	19 (1.9)
San Diego	236 (1.6)	239 (1.3)	258 (2.1)	222 (2.7)	229 (1.4)	248 (2.5)	241 (1.2)	260 (1.9)	228 (3.1)	228 (1.6)	253 (2.8)	81 (1.5)	42 (1.6)
8th grade													
United States	282 (0.3)	283 (0.2)	293 (0.2)	262 (0.5)	269 (0.5)	305 (1.1)	284 (0.2)	293 (0.3)	263 (0.4)	271 (0.4)	308 (1.1)	73 (0.3)	34 (0.3)
All large cities	271 (0.7)	274 (0.7)	295 (1.1)	261 (0.9)	267 (1.0)	298 (2.3)	276 (0.8)	295 (1.2)	261 (0.8)	269 (0.8)	301 (2.2)	65 (0.9)	27 (0.9)
Selected urban districts													
Albuquerque	— (†)	275 (1.0)	291 (2.3)	‡ (†)	269 (1.2)	‡ (†)	274 (1.2)	295 (2.6)	‡ (†)	267 (1.5)	‡ (†)	62 (1.6)	26 (1.6)
Atlanta	259 (1.6)	266 (1.3)	309 (2.8)	262 (1.4)	264 (3.5)	‡ (†)	267 (1.2)	311 (3.0)	261 (1.3)	262 (3.7)	‡ (†)	54 (1.6)	17 (1.1)
Austin	287 (0.9)	287 (1.2)	313 (1.8)	265 (5.3)	276 (1.7)	‡ (†)	285 (1.0)	312 (1.9)	267 (2.5)	273 (1.3)	‡ (†)	73 (1.3)	35 (1.5)
Baltimore City	257 (1.9)	261 (1.3)	280 (4.0)	259 (1.5)	‡ (†)	‡ (†)	260 (2.0)	286 (6.0)	257 (2.0)	‡ (†)	‡ (†)	46 (2.3)	13 (1.6)
Boston	279 (1.3)	282 (0.9)	305 (3.1)	272 (1.6)	271 (1.6)	319 (3.6)	283 (1.2)	309 (2.4)	271 (1.8)	275 (1.8)	318 (3.7)	70 (1.6)	36 (1.2)
Charlotte	283 (0.9)	285 (0.8)	311 (1.3)	268 (1.2)	272 (2.6)	304 (6.4)	289 (1.2)	313 (1.9)	271 (1.8)	279 (3.4)	314 (6.1)	75 (1.4)	40 (1.6)
Chicago	264 (1.4)	270 (1.0)	296 (4.3)	260 (1.4)	271 (1.4)	296 (3.3)	269 (1.0)	294 (2.4)	259 (1.5)	270 (1.4)	306 (5.4)	57 (1.6)	20 (1.1)
Cleveland	256 (1.0)	256 (1.2)	277 (3.4)	249 (2.1)	258 (4.4)	‡ (†)	253 (1.3)	265 (2.9)	249 (1.5)	252 (3.4)	‡ (†)	39 (1.7)	9 (0.9)
Dallas	— (†)	274 (0.9)	306 (4.5)	264 (2.2)	276 (1.1)	‡ (†)	275 (1.0)	304 (4.7)	263 (2.0)	277 (1.1)	‡ (†)	67 (1.4)	23 (1.4)
Detroit	238 (2.7)	246 (1.2)	‡ (†)	244 (1.4)	258 (2.8)	‡ (†)	240 (1.7)	‡ (†)	239 (1.7)	243 (4.0)	‡ (†)	24 (2.1)	3 (0.7)
District of Columbia	251 (1.3)	255 (0.9)	322 (3.0)	249 (1.2)	253 (2.8)	‡ (†)	260 (1.3)	315 (4.1)	253 (1.4)	262 (3.6)	‡ (†)	47 (1.8)	17 (1.2)
Fresno	258 (1.2)	256 (0.9)	281 (2.6)	243 (2.6)	251 (1.2)	265 (2.9)	260 (1.4)	279 (3.0)	247 (4.0)	256 (1.6)	270 (2.8)	48 (2.2)	12 (1.1)
Hillsborough County (FL)	— (†)	282 (1.5)	293 (2.1)	263 (1.9)	274 (2.4)	‡ (†)	284 (1.1)	296 (1.8)	264 (2.5)	278 (1.9)	‡ (†)	73 (1.3)	34 (1.7)
Houston	277 (1.2)	279 (1.0)	309 (3.0)	271 (1.9)	278 (1.1)	310 (5.2)	280 (1.1)	312 (3.1)	271 (1.7)	279 (1.2)	314 (7.2)	72 (1.4)	28 (1.4)
Jefferson County (KY)	271 (0.9)	274 (1.0)	285 (1.5)	257 (1.4)	270 (4.5)	‡ (†)	273 (1.0)	285 (1.5)	257 (1.7)	265 (3.7)	‡ (†)	61 (1.3)	25 (1.3)
Los Angeles	258 (1.0)	261 (1.3)	291 (4.6)	246 (3.9)	255 (1.3)	297 (3.9)	264 (1.5)	293 (3.2)	256 (3.4)	258 (1.3)	298 (3.3)	54 (1.8)	18 (1.5)
Miami-Dade	273 (1.1)	272 (1.1)	288 (3.1)	256 (2.2)	274 (1.0)	‡ (†)	274 (1.5)	295 (3.4)	259 (2.9)	275 (1.3)	‡ (†)	63 (1.8)	24 (1.5)
Milwaukee	251 (1.5)	254 (1.7)	274 (4.2)	246 (1.8)	259 (3.3)	271 (5.6)	257 (1.4)	282 (3.5)	247 (1.8)	266 (2.2)	‡ (†)	44 (2.1)	11 (1.3)
New York City	273 (1.5)	272 (1.6)	292 (3.2)	262 (2.1)	261 (1.6)	304 (3.2)	274 (1.1)	301 (3.8)	263 (1.9)	263 (1.7)	304 (3.1)	61 (1.3)	25 (1.4)
Philadelphia	265 (2.0)	265 (2.0)	281 (3.9)	260 (2.3)	256 (3.1)	295 (5.4)	266 (1.7)	287 (2.8)	258 (2.2)	261 (4.1)	297 (4.9)	54 (2.0)	19 (1.5)
San Diego	280 (2.0)	278 (1.7)	302 (2.3)	256 (4.0)	263 (2.6)	293 (3.3)	277 (1.4)	300 (2.3)	260 (4.5)	260 (2.2)	294 (2.9)	65 (1.7)	31 (1.6)

—Not available.
†Not applicable.
‡Reporting standards not met (too few cases for a reliable estimate).
[1]Scale ranges from 0 to 500.
[2]Includes data for students of two or more races, which are not separately shown.
[3]Basic denotes partial mastery of the knowledge and skills that are fundamental for proficient work at a given grade.

[4]Proficient represents solid academic performance. Students reaching this level have demonstrated competency over challenging subject matter.
NOTE: Race categories exclude persons of Hispanic ethnicity. Totals include racial/ethnic groups not shown separately.
SOURCE: U.S. Department of Education, National Center for Education Statistics, National Assessment of Educational Progress (NAEP), 2009, 2011, and 2013 Mathematics Assessments, retrieved December 30, 2013, from the Main NAEP Data Explorer (http://nces.ed.gov/nationsreportcard/naepdata/). (This table was prepared December 2013.)

Average National Assessment of Educational Progress (NAEP) mathematics scale score, by age and selected student characteristics: Selected years, 1973 through 2012

[Standard errors appear in parentheses]

Selected student characteristic	1973	1978	1982	1986	1990	1992	1994	1996	1999	2004[1] Previous format	2004[1] Revised format	2008	2012
1	2	3	4	5	6	7	8	9	10	11	12	13	14
9-year-olds													
All students	219 (0.8)	219 (0.8)	219 (1.1)	222 (1.0)	230 (0.8)	230 (0.8)	231 (0.8)	231 (0.8)	232 (0.8)	241 (0.9)	239 (0.9)	243 (0.8)	244 (1.0)
Sex													
Male	218 (0.7)	217 (0.7)	217 (1.2)	222 (1.1)	229 (0.9)	231 (1.0)	232 (1.0)	233 (1.2)	233 (1.0)	243 (1.1)	239 (1.0)	242 (0.9)	244 (1.2)
Female	220 (1.1)	220 (1.0)	221 (1.2)	222 (1.2)	230 (1.1)	228 (1.0)	230 (0.9)	229 (0.7)	231 (0.9)	240 (1.1)	240 (1.0)	243 (1.0)	244 (1.0)
Gap between female and male score	2 (1.3)	3 (1.3)	4 (1.7)	# (†)	1 (1.4)	-2 (1.4)	-2 (1.4)	-4 (1.4)	-2 (1.3)	-3 (1.5)	1 (1.4)	1 (1.3)	# (†)
Race/ethnicity													
White	225 (1.0)	224 (0.9)	224 (1.1)	227 (1.1)	235 (0.8)	235 (0.8)	237 (1.0)	237 (1.0)	239 (0.9)	247 (0.9)	245 (0.8)	250 (0.8)	252 (1.1)
Black	190 (1.8)	192 (1.1)	195 (1.6)	202 (1.6)	208 (2.2)	208 (2.0)	212 (1.6)	212 (1.4)	211 (1.6)	224 (2.1)	221 (2.1)	224 (1.9)	226 (1.8)
Hispanic	202 (2.4)	203 (2.2)	204 (1.3)	205 (2.1)	214 (2.1)	212 (2.3)	210 (2.3)	215 (1.7)	213 (1.9)	230 (2.0)	229 (2.0)	234 (1.2)	234 (0.9)
Gap between White and Black score	35 (2.1)	32 (1.5)	29 (2.0)	25 (2.0)	27 (2.4)	27 (2.2)	25 (1.8)	25 (1.8)	28 (1.8)	23 (2.2)	24 (2.2)	26 (2.1)	25 (2.1)
Gap between White and Hispanic score	23 (2.6)	21 (2.4)	20 (1.7)	21 (2.3)	21 (2.3)	23 (2.5)	27 (2.5)	22 (2.0)	26 (2.1)	18 (2.2)	16 (2.1)	16 (1.4)	17 (1.5)
13-year-olds													
All students	266 (1.1)	264 (1.1)	269 (1.1)	269 (1.2)	270 (0.9)	273 (0.9)	274 (1.0)	274 (0.8)	276 (0.8)	281 (1.0)	279 (1.0)	281 (0.9)	285 (1.1)
Sex													
Male	265 (1.3)	264 (1.3)	269 (1.4)	270 (1.1)	271 (1.2)	274 (1.1)	276 (1.3)	276 (0.9)	277 (0.9)	283 (1.2)	279 (1.0)	284 (1.1)	286 (1.3)
Female	267 (1.1)	265 (1.1)	268 (1.1)	268 (1.5)	270 (0.9)	272 (1.0)	273 (1.0)	272 (1.0)	274 (1.1)	279 (1.0)	278 (1.2)	279 (1.0)	284 (1.1)
Gap between female and male score	2 (1.7)	1 (1.7)	-1 (1.7)	-2 (1.9)	-2 (1.5)	-2 (1.5)	-3 (1.6)	-4 (1.4)	-3 (1.4)	-3 (1.6)	-1 (1.6)	-4 (1.4)	-2 (1.7)
Race/ethnicity													
White	274 (0.9)	272 (0.8)	274 (1.0)	274 (1.3)	276 (1.1)	279 (0.9)	281 (0.9)	281 (0.9)	283 (0.8)	288 (0.9)	287 (0.9)	290 (1.2)	293 (1.1)
Black	228 (1.9)	230 (1.9)	240 (1.6)	249 (2.3)	249 (2.3)	250 (1.9)	252 (3.5)	252 (1.3)	251 (2.6)	262 (1.6)	257 (1.8)	262 (1.2)	264 (1.9)
Hispanic	239 (2.2)	238 (2.0)	252 (1.7)	254 (2.9)	255 (1.4)	259 (1.9)	256 (1.9)	256 (1.6)	259 (1.7)	265 (2.0)	264 (1.5)	268 (1.2)	271 (1.4)
Gap between White and Black score	46 (2.1)	42 (2.1)	34 (1.9)	24 (2.6)	27 (2.6)	29 (2.1)	29 (3.7)	29 (1.6)	32 (2.7)	27 (1.8)	30 (2.1)	28 (1.7)	28 (2.2)
Gap between White and Hispanic score	35 (2.4)	34 (2.1)	22 (1.9)	19 (3.2)	22 (2.1)	20 (2.1)	25 (2.1)	25 (1.9)	24 (1.9)	23 (2.2)	23 (1.8)	23 (1.7)	21 (1.8)
Parents' highest level of education													
Did not finish high school	— (†)	245 (1.2)	251 (1.4)	252 (2.3)	253 (1.8)	256 (1.0)	255 (2.1)	254 (2.4)	256 (2.8)	262 (2.2)	263 (1.9)	268 (1.3)	266 (2.5)
Graduated high school	— (†)	263 (1.0)	263 (0.8)	263 (1.2)	263 (1.2)	263 (1.2)	266 (1.1)	267 (1.1)	264 (1.1)	271 (1.7)	270 (1.3)	272 (1.1)	270 (1.1)
Some education after high school	— (†)	273 (1.2)	275 (0.9)	274 (0.8)	277 (1.0)	278 (1.0)	277 (1.6)	277 (1.4)	279 (0.9)	283 (1.0)	282 (1.4)	285 (1.1)	286 (1.4)
Graduated college	— (†)	284 (1.2)	282 (1.5)	280 (1.4)	280 (1.0)	283 (1.0)	285 (1.2)	283 (1.2)	286 (1.0)	292 (0.9)	289 (1.1)	291 (1.0)	296 (1.3)
17-year-olds													
All students	304 (1.1)	300 (1.0)	298 (0.9)	302 (0.9)	305 (0.9)	307 (0.9)	306 (1.0)	307 (1.2)	308 (1.0)	307 (0.8)	305 (0.7)	306 (0.6)	306 (0.8)
Sex													
Male	309 (1.2)	304 (1.0)	301 (1.0)	305 (1.2)	306 (1.1)	309 (1.1)	309 (1.4)	310 (1.3)	310 (1.4)	308 (1.0)	307 (0.9)	309 (0.7)	308 (1.0)
Female	301 (1.1)	297 (1.0)	296 (1.0)	299 (1.0)	303 (1.1)	305 (1.1)	304 (1.1)	305 (1.4)	307 (1.4)	305 (0.9)	304 (0.8)	303 (0.8)	304 (0.8)
Gap between female and male score	-8 (1.6)	-7 (1.4)	-6 (1.4)	-5 (1.5)	-3 (1.5)	-4 (1.5)	-4 (1.8)	-5 (1.9)	-3 (1.7)	-3 (1.4)	-3 (1.2)	-5 (1.1)	-4 (1.3)
Race/ethnicity													
White	310 (1.1)	306 (0.9)	304 (0.9)	308 (1.0)	309 (1.0)	312 (0.8)	312 (1.1)	313 (1.4)	315 (1.1)	313 (0.7)	311 (0.7)	314 (0.7)	314 (1.0)
Black	270 (1.3)	268 (1.3)	272 (1.2)	279 (2.1)	289 (2.8)	286 (2.2)	286 (1.8)	286 (1.7)	283 (1.5)	285 (1.6)	284 (1.4)	287 (1.2)	288 (1.3)
Hispanic	277 (2.2)	276 (2.3)	277 (1.8)	283 (2.9)	284 (2.9)	292 (2.6)	291 (3.7)	292 (2.1)	293 (2.5)	289 (2.4)	292 (1.4)	293 (1.1)	294 (1.1)
Gap between White and Black score	40 (1.7)	38 (1.6)	32 (1.5)	29 (2.3)	21 (3.0)	26 (2.4)	27 (2.1)	27 (2.2)	31 (1.9)	28 (1.8)	27 (1.6)	26 (1.4)	26 (1.6)
Gap between White and Hispanic score	33 (2.5)	30 (2.4)	27 (2.0)	24 (3.0)	26 (3.1)	20 (2.8)	22 (3.9)	21 (2.5)	22 (2.7)	24 (1.9)	19 (1.4)	21 (1.3)	19 (1.5)
Parents' highest level of education													
Did not finish high school	— (†)	280 (1.2)	279 (1.0)	279 (2.3)	285 (2.2)	285 (2.3)	284 (2.4)	281 (2.4)	289 (1.8)	287 (2.4)	287 (1.2)	292 (1.3)	290 (1.4)
Graduated high school	— (†)	294 (0.8)	293 (0.8)	293 (1.0)	294 (0.9)	298 (1.7)	295 (1.1)	297 (2.4)	299 (1.6)	295 (1.1)	294 (0.9)	296 (1.2)	291 (1.1)
Some education after high school	— (†)	305 (0.9)	304 (0.9)	305 (1.2)	308 (1.0)	308 (1.1)	305 (1.3)	307 (1.5)	308 (1.6)	306 (1.1)	305 (0.9)	306 (0.8)	306 (0.9)
Graduated college	— (†)	317 (1.0)	312 (1.0)	314 (1.4)	316 (1.3)	316 (1.0)	318 (1.4)	317 (1.3)	317 (1.2)	317 (0.9)	315 (0.9)	316 (0.7)	317 (0.8)

—Not available.
†Not applicable.
#Rounds to zero.

[1]In 2004, two assessments were conducted—one using the same format that was used in previous assessments, and one using a revised assessment format that provides accommodations for students with disabilities and for English language learners. The 2004 data in column 11 are for the format that was used in previous assessment years, while the 2004 data in column 12 are for the revised format. In subsequent years, only the revised format was used.

NOTE: Scale ranges from 0 to 500. Students scoring 150 (or higher) know some basic addition and subtraction facts. Students scoring 200 have a considerable understanding of two-digit numbers and know some basic multiplication and division facts. Students scoring 250 have an initial understanding of the four basic operations and are developing an ability to analyze simple logical relations. Students scoring 300 can perform reasoning and problem solving involving fractions, decimals, percents, elementary geometry, and simple algebra. Students scoring 350 can perform reasoning and problem solving involving geometry, algebra, and beginning statistics and probability. Includes public and private schools. For assessment years prior to 2004, accommodations were not permitted. For 2004 (revised format) and later years, includes students tested with accommodations; excludes only those students with disabilities and English language learners who were unable to be tested even with accommodations (1 to 4 percent of all students, depending on age and assessment year). Race categories exclude persons of Hispanic ethnicity. Totals include other racial/ethnic groups not shown separately.

SOURCE: U.S. Department of Education, National Center for Education Statistics, National Assessment of Educational Progress (NAEP), *NAEP 2012 Trends in Academic Progress*; and 2012 NAEP Long-Term Trend Mathematics Assessment, retrieved August 29, 2013, from Long-Term Trend NAEP Data Explorer (http://nces.ed.gov/nationsreportcard/naepdata/). (This table was prepared August 2013.)

Percentage of students at or above selected National Assessment of Educational Progress (NAEP) mathematics score levels, by age, sex, and race/ethnicity: Selected years, 1978 through 2012

[Standard errors appear in parentheses]

Sex, race/ethnicity, and year	9-year-olds Level 150[1]	9-year-olds Level 200[2]	9-year-olds Level 250[3]	13-year-olds Level 200[2]	13-year-olds Level 250[3]	13-year-olds Level 300[4]	17-year-olds Level 250[3]	17-year-olds Level 300[4]	17-year-olds Level 350[5]
1	2	3	4	5	6	7	8	9	10
Total									
1978	96.7 (0.25)	70.4 (0.92)	19.6 (0.73)	94.6 (0.46)	64.9 (1.18)	18.0 (0.73)	92.0 (0.50)	51.5 (1.14)	7.3 (0.44)
1982	97.1 (0.35)	71.4 (1.18)	18.8 (0.96)	97.7 (0.37)	71.4 (1.18)	17.4 (0.95)	93.0 (0.50)	48.5 (1.28)	5.5 (0.43)
1986	97.9 (0.29)	74.1 (1.24)	20.7 (0.88)	98.6 (0.25)	73.3 (1.59)	15.8 (1.01)	95.6 (0.48)	51.7 (1.43)	6.5 (0.52)
1990	99.1 (0.21)	81.5 (0.96)	27.7 (0.86)	98.5 (0.21)	74.7 (1.03)	17.3 (0.99)	96.0 (0.52)	56.1 (1.43)	7.2 (0.63)
1996	99.1 (0.18)	81.5 (0.76)	29.7 (1.02)	98.8 (0.20)	78.6 (0.87)	20.6 (1.24)	96.8 (0.42)	60.1 (1.72)	7.4 (0.77)
1999	98.9 (0.17)	82.5 (0.84)	30.9 (1.07)	98.7 (0.25)	78.8 (1.02)	23.2 (0.95)	96.8 (0.45)	60.7 (1.63)	8.4 (0.83)
2004	98.7 (0.19)	87.0 (0.77)	40.9 (0.89)	98.1 (0.19)	81.1 (0.98)	27.8 (1.09)	95.8 (0.40)	58.3 (1.12)	6.1 (0.47)
2008	99.0 (0.18)	89.1 (0.69)	44.5 (1.01)	98.2 (0.19)	83.4 (0.63)	30.0 (1.08)	96.0 (0.37)	59.4 (0.87)	6.2 (0.40)
2012	98.7 (0.21)	88.7 (0.69)	46.7 (1.28)	98.5 (0.21)	84.7 (0.71)	34.0 (1.38)	95.7 (0.31)	59.7 (1.22)	7.0 (0.51)
Male									
1978	96.2 (0.48)	68.9 (0.98)	19.2 (0.64)	93.9 (0.49)	63.9 (1.32)	18.4 (0.85)	93.0 (0.52)	55.1 (1.21)	9.5 (0.57)
1982	96.5 (0.55)	68.8 (1.29)	18.1 (1.06)	97.5 (0.55)	71.3 (1.44)	18.9 (1.18)	93.9 (0.58)	51.9 (1.51)	6.9 (0.70)
1986	98.0 (0.51)	74.0 (1.45)	20.9 (1.10)	98.5 (0.32)	73.8 (1.76)	17.6 (1.12)	96.1 (0.63)	54.6 (1.78)	8.4 (0.91)
1990	99.0 (0.26)	80.6 (1.05)	27.5 (0.96)	98.2 (0.34)	75.1 (1.75)	19.0 (1.24)	95.8 (0.77)	57.6 (1.42)	8.8 (0.76)
1996	99.1 (0.20)	82.5 (1.10)	32.7 (1.74)	98.7 (0.25)	79.8 (1.43)	23.0 (1.64)	97.0 (0.66)	62.7 (1.77)	9.5 (1.32)
1999	98.8 (0.28)	82.6 (0.92)	32.4 (1.25)	98.5 (0.27)	79.3 (1.12)	25.4 (1.19)	96.5 (0.81)	63.1 (2.12)	9.8 (1.09)
2004	98.3 (0.27)	86.1 (0.89)	40.7 (1.03)	97.7 (0.29)	80.5 (1.08)	29.9 (1.27)	95.6 (0.45)	60.8 (1.31)	7.3 (0.68)
2008	99.0 (0.27)	88.4 (0.87)	44.4 (1.18)	98.2 (0.28)	84.3 (0.75)	33.4 (1.29)	96.2 (0.47)	62.9 (0.96)	7.6 (0.61)
2012	98.6 (0.24)	88.0 (0.79)	47.0 (1.47)	98.2 (0.27)	84.7 (0.84)	35.7 (1.55)	95.5 (0.43)	61.5 (1.33)	9.0 (0.75)
Female									
1978	97.2 (0.27)	72.0 (1.05)	19.9 (1.00)	95.2 (0.49)	65.9 (1.17)	17.5 (0.75)	91.0 (0.57)	48.2 (1.29)	5.2 (0.66)
1982	97.6 (0.33)	74.0 (1.30)	19.6 (1.11)	98.0 (0.27)	71.4 (1.29)	15.9 (1.00)	92.1 (0.56)	45.3 (1.37)	4.1 (0.42)
1986	97.8 (0.38)	74.3 (1.32)	20.6 (1.28)	98.6 (0.31)	72.7 (1.95)	14.1 (1.31)	95.1 (0.65)	48.9 (1.73)	4.7 (0.59)
1990	99.1 (0.26)	82.3 (1.26)	27.9 (1.31)	98.9 (0.18)	74.4 (1.32)	15.7 (1.00)	96.2 (0.84)	54.7 (1.84)	5.6 (0.79)
1996	99.1 (0.36)	80.7 (0.93)	26.7 (1.07)	98.8 (0.27)	77.4 (1.09)	18.4 (1.48)	96.7 (0.57)	57.6 (2.21)	5.3 (0.80)
1999	99.0 (0.19)	82.5 (1.15)	29.4 (1.36)	99.0 (0.40)	78.4 (1.22)	21.0 (1.38)	97.2 (0.40)	58.5 (1.89)	7.1 (1.06)
2004	99.0 (0.22)	87.8 (0.96)	41.1 (1.13)	98.4 (0.25)	81.7 (1.10)	25.7 (1.24)	95.9 (0.58)	55.9 (1.18)	4.9 (0.48)
2008	99.0 (0.21)	89.9 (0.78)	44.6 (1.18)	98.2 (0.25)	82.5 (0.86)	26.7 (1.13)	95.7 (0.43)	55.8 (1.25)	4.6 (0.34)
2012	98.8 (0.29)	89.4 (0.80)	46.5 (1.34)	98.8 (0.23)	84.7 (0.91)	32.2 (1.42)	96.0 (0.37)	57.9 (1.45)	5.1 (0.60)
White									
1978	98.3 (0.19)	76.3 (1.00)	22.9 (0.87)	97.6 (0.27)	72.9 (0.85)	21.4 (0.73)	95.6 (0.30)	57.6 (1.14)	8.5 (0.48)
1982	98.5 (0.25)	76.8 (1.22)	21.8 (1.13)	99.1 (0.14)	78.3 (0.94)	20.5 (1.00)	96.2 (0.33)	54.7 (1.41)	6.4 (0.54)
1986	98.8 (0.24)	79.6 (1.33)	24.6 (1.03)	99.3 (0.27)	78.9 (1.69)	18.6 (1.17)	98.0 (0.36)	59.1 (1.69)	7.9 (0.68)
1990	99.6 (0.16)	86.9 (0.86)	32.7 (1.04)	99.4 (0.14)	82.0 (1.01)	21.0 (1.23)	97.6 (0.28)	63.2 (1.59)	8.3 (0.73)
1996	99.6 (0.15)	86.6 (0.80)	35.7 (1.38)	99.6 (0.16)	86.4 (1.02)	25.4 (1.50)	98.7 (0.37)	68.7 (2.18)	9.2 (1.02)
1999	99.6 (0.12)	88.6 (0.78)	37.1 (1.35)	99.4 (0.29)	86.7 (0.92)	29.0 (1.26)	98.7 (0.40)	69.9 (1.96)	10.4 (1.07)
2004	99.2 (0.18)	91.9 (0.61)	47.2 (0.97)	99.1 (0.16)	89.3 (0.82)	35.1 (1.21)	97.5 (0.28)	66.8 (1.08)	7.6 (0.63)
2008	99.6 (0.12)	94.0 (0.52)	52.9 (1.29)	98.9 (0.17)	90.4 (0.83)	39.2 (1.60)	98.2 (0.26)	70.5 (1.09)	8.1 (0.55)
2012	99.4 (0.18)	93.2 (0.58)	55.9 (1.54)	99.2 (0.15)	91.6 (0.57)	41.4 (1.65)	97.9 (0.33)	70.3 (1.56)	9.1 (0.71)
Black									
1978	88.4 (1.01)	42.0 (1.44)	4.1 (0.64)	79.7 (1.48)	28.7 (2.06)	2.3 (0.48)	70.7 (1.73)	16.8 (1.57)	0.5 (—)
1982	90.2 (0.97)	46.1 (2.35)	4.4 (0.81)	90.2 (1.60)	37.9 (2.51)	2.9 (0.96)	76.4 (1.47)	17.1 (1.51)	0.5 (—)
1986	93.9 (1.37)	53.4 (2.47)	5.6 (0.92)	95.4 (0.95)	49.0 (3.70)	4.0 (1.42)	85.6 (2.53)	20.8 (2.83)	0.2 (—)
1990	96.9 (0.88)	60.0 (2.76)	9.4 (1.72)	95.4 (1.10)	48.7 (3.56)	3.9 (1.61)	92.4 (2.20)	32.8 (4.49)	2.0 (1.04)
1996	97.3 (0.84)	65.3 (2.38)	10.0 (1.24)	96.2 (1.27)	53.7 (2.26)	4.8 (1.08)	90.6 (1.33)	31.2 (2.51)	0.9 (—)
1999	96.4 (0.64)	63.3 (2.11)	12.3 (1.48)	96.5 (1.06)	50.8 (4.01)	4.4 (1.37)	88.6 (1.95)	26.6 (2.70)	1.0 (—)
2004	97.1 (0.65)	74.3 (2.61)	22.0 (1.72)	95.3 (0.78)	61.5 (2.47)	9.7 (1.35)	89.1 (1.63)	29.4 (2.07)	0.4 (—)
2008	96.9 (0.86)	75.6 (2.31)	24.6 (1.67)	96.6 (0.68)	67.6 (1.69)	10.2 (1.17)	90.6 (1.42)	31.8 (1.60)	0.8 (0.23)
2012	97.5 (0.66)	77.2 (1.56)	26.3 (2.01)	96.7 (0.66)	67.3 (2.10)	14.2 (1.61)	89.8 (1.03)	33.8 (2.04)	1.1 (0.32)
Hispanic									
1978	93.0 (1.20)	54.2 (2.80)	9.2 (2.49)	86.4 (0.94)	36.0 (2.92)	4.0 (0.95)	78.3 (2.29)	23.4 (2.67)	1.4 (0.58)
1982	94.3 (1.19)	55.7 (2.26)	7.8 (1.74)	95.9 (0.95)	52.2 (2.48)	6.3 (0.97)	81.4 (1.86)	21.6 (2.16)	0.7 (0.36)
1986	96.4 (1.29)	57.6 (2.95)	7.3 (2.81)	96.9 (1.43)	56.0 (5.01)	5.5 (1.15)	89.3 (2.52)	26.5 (4.48)	1.1 (—)
1990	98.0 (0.76)	68.4 (3.03)	11.3 (3.49)	96.8 (1.06)	56.7 (3.32)	6.4 (1.70)	85.8 (4.18)	30.1 (3.09)	1.9 (0.78)
1996	98.1 (0.73)	67.1 (2.14)	13.8 (2.26)	96.2 (0.78)	58.3 (2.28)	6.7 (1.17)	92.2 (2.24)	40.1 (3.47)	1.8 (—)
1999	98.1 (0.71)	67.5 (2.47)	10.5 (1.63)	97.2 (0.60)	62.9 (2.50)	8.2 (1.37)	93.6 (2.21)	37.7 (4.15)	3.1 (1.12)
2004	98.0 (0.46)	80.5 (2.03)	30.2 (2.17)	96.4 (0.66)	68.5 (1.86)	13.7 (1.44)	92.3 (1.05)	38.1 (2.12)	1.9 (0.60)
2008	98.9 (0.28)	85.1 (1.25)	33.5 (1.46)	97.0 (0.44)	73.3 (1.71)	14.4 (1.09)	92.2 (1.10)	41.1 (1.69)	1.5 (0.41)
2012	98.3 (0.40)	84.7 (1.00)	34.6 (1.22)	97.3 (0.54)	76.4 (1.94)	18.5 (1.45)	92.9 (0.59)	43.3 (1.91)	2.4 (0.44)

—Not available.

[1]Students scoring 150 (or higher) know some basic addition and subtraction facts.

[2]Students scoring 200 (or higher) have a considerable understanding of two-digit numbers and know some basic multiplication and division facts.

[3]Students scoring 250 (or higher) have an initial understanding of the four basic operations and are developing an ability to analyze simple logical relations.

[4]Students scoring 300 (or higher) can perform reasoning and problem solving involving fractions, decimals, percents, elementary geometry, and simple algebra.

[5]Students scoring 350 (or above) can perform reasoning and problem solving involving geometry, algebra, and beginning statistics and probability.

NOTE: The NAEP mathematics scores have been evaluated at certain performance levels, as outlined in footnotes 1 through 5. Scale ranges from 0 to 500. Includes public and private schools. For assessment years prior to 2004, accommodations were not permitted. For 2004 and later years, includes students tested with accommodations; excludes only those students with disabilities and English language learners who were unable to be tested even with accommodations (1 to 4 percent of all students, depending on age and assessment year). Race categories exclude persons of Hispanic ethnicity. Totals include other racial/ethnic groups not shown separately.

SOURCE: U.S. Department of Education, National Center for Education Statistics, National Assessment of Educational Progress (NAEP), *NAEP Trends in Academic Progress*, 1996 and 1999; and 2004, 2008, and 2012 Long-Term Trend Mathematics Assessments, retrieved May 4, 2009, and July 20, 2013, from the Long-Term Trend NAEP Data Explorer (http://nces.ed.gov/nationsreportcard/naepdata/). (This table was prepared July 2013.)

National Assessment of Educational Progress (NAEP) mathematics performance of 17-year-olds, by highest mathematics course taken, sex, and race/ethnicity: Selected years, 1978 through 2012

[Standard errors appear in parentheses]

Year, sex, and race/ethnicity	Percent of students	Average scale score by highest mathematics course taken						Percent of students at or above score levels			
		All students	Prealgebra or general mathematics	Algebra I	Geometry	Algebra II	Precalculus or calculus	200	250	300	350
1	2	3	4	5	6	7	8	9	10	11	12
1978											
All students	100 (†)	300 (1.0)	267 (0.8)	286 (0.7)	307 (0.7)	321 (0.7)	334 (1.4)	100 (†)	92 (0.5)	52 (1.1)	7 (0.4)
Sex											
Male	49 (0.5)	304 (1.0)	269 (1.0)	289 (0.9)	310 (1.0)	325 (0.8)	337 (2.0)	100 (†)	93 (0.5)	55 (1.2)	10 (0.6)
Female	51 (0.5)	297 (1.0)	264 (0.9)	284 (1.0)	304 (0.8)	318 (0.9)	329 (1.8)	100 (†)	91 (0.6)	48 (1.3)	5 (0.7)
Race/ethnicity											
White	83 (1.3)	306 (0.9)	272 (0.6)	291 (0.6)	310 (0.6)	325 (0.6)	338 (1.1)	100 (†)	96 (0.3)	58 (1.1)	8 (0.5)
Black	12 (1.1)	268 (1.3)	247 (1.6)	264 (1.5)	281 (1.9)	292 (1.4)	297 (6.5)	99 (0.3)	71 (1.7)	17 (1.6)	# (†)
Hispanic	4 (0.5)	276 (2.3)	256 (2.3)	273 (2.8)	294 (4.4)	303 (2.9)	‡ (†)	99 (0.4)	78 (2.3)	23 (2.7)	1 (0.6)
Other[1]	1 (0.1)	313 (3.3)	‡ (†)	‡ (†)	‡ (†)	323 (2.9)	‡ (†)	100 (†)	94 (2.6)	65 (4.9)	15 (3.2)
1990											
All students	100 (†)	305 (0.9)	273 (1.1)	288 (1.2)	299 (1.5)	319 (1.0)	344 (2.7)	100 (†)	96 (0.5)	56 (1.4)	7 (0.6)
Sex											
Male	49 (0.9)	306 (1.1)	274 (1.7)	291 (1.6)	302 (1.6)	323 (1.2)	347 (2.4)	100 (†)	96 (0.8)	58 (1.4)	9 (0.8)
Female	51 (0.9)	303 (1.1)	271 (1.8)	285 (1.8)	296 (1.8)	316 (1.1)	340 (4.0)	100 (†)	96 (0.8)	55 (1.8)	6 (0.8)
Race/ethnicity											
White	73 (0.5)	309 (1.0)	277 (1.1)	292 (1.6)	304 (1.3)	323 (0.9)	347 (2.8)	100 (†)	98 (0.3)	63 (1.6)	8 (0.7)
Black	16 (0.3)	289 (2.8)	264 (2.2)	278 (4.0)	285 (3.5)	302 (3.2)	‡ (†)	100 (†)	92 (2.2)	33 (4.5)	2 (1.0)
Hispanic	7 (0.4)	284 (2.9)	‡ (†)	‡ (†)	‡ (†)	306 (3.3)	‡ (†)	100 (†)	86 (4.2)	30 (3.1)	2 (0.8)
Other[1]	4 (0.5)	312 (5.2)	‡ (†)	‡ (†)	‡ (†)	321 (3.8)	‡ (†)	100 (†)	98 (‡)	62 (7.0)	16 (4.3)
1996											
All students	100 (†)	307 (1.2)	269 (1.9)	283 (1.3)	298 (1.3)	316 (1.3)	339 (1.7)	100 (†)	97 (0.4)	60 (1.7)	7 (0.8)
Sex											
Male	50 (1.2)	310 (1.3)	272 (2.5)	286 (1.5)	302 (1.7)	320 (1.7)	342 (2.3)	100 (†)	97 (0.7)	63 (1.8)	9 (1.3)
Female	50 (1.2)	305 (1.4)	265 (2.2)	278 (2.2)	294 (1.5)	313 (1.4)	335 (2.2)	100 (†)	97 (0.6)	58 (2.2)	5 (0.8)
Race/ethnicity											
White	71 (0.6)	313 (1.4)	273 (2.3)	287 (2.0)	304 (1.6)	320 (1.4)	342 (1.9)	100 (†)	99 (0.4)	69 (2.2)	9 (1.0)
Black	15 (0.3)	286 (1.7)	‡ (†)	272 (2.4)	280 (3.0)	299 (2.2)	‡ (†)	100 (†)	91 (1.3)	31 (2.5)	1 (—)
Hispanic	9 (0.7)	292 (2.1)	‡ (†)	‡ (†)	‡ (†)	306 (2.8)	‡ (†)	100 (†)	92 (2.2)	40 (3.5)	2 (—)
Other[1]	4 (0.7)	312 (5.7)	‡ (†)	‡ (†)	‡ (†)	‡ (†)	‡ (†)	100 (†)	97 (1.2)	64 (7.2)	14 (5.0)
1999											
All students	100 (†)	308 (1.0)	278 (2.8)	285 (1.7)	298 (1.2)	315 (0.8)	341 (1.4)	100 (†)	97 (0.5)	61 (1.6)	8 (0.8)
Sex											
Male	48 (1.0)	310 (1.4)	281 (3.2)	288 (2.6)	301 (1.8)	317 (1.3)	343 (1.9)	100 (†)	96 (0.8)	63 (2.1)	10 (1.1)
Female	52 (1.0)	307 (1.0)	274 (3.2)	282 (2.5)	295 (1.3)	314 (1.1)	340 (2.0)	100 (†)	97 (0.4)	58 (1.9)	7 (1.1)
Race/ethnicity											
White	72 (0.5)	315 (1.1)	282 (3.4)	290 (2.2)	303 (1.5)	320 (0.9)	343 (1.5)	100 (†)	99 (0.4)	70 (2.0)	10 (1.1)
Black	15 (0.4)	283 (1.5)	‡ (†)	267 (2.9)	281 (2.5)	293 (1.4)	‡ (†)	100 (†)	89 (2.0)	27 (2.7)	1 (—)
Hispanic	10 (0.5)	293 (2.5)	‡ (†)	‡ (†)	‡ (†)	308 (3.0)	‡ (†)	100 (†)	94 (2.2)	38 (4.1)	3 (1.1)
Other[1]	4 (0.2)	320 (4.0)	‡ (†)	‡ (†)	‡ (†)	320 (4.4)	‡ (†)	100 (†)	100 (†)	76 (6.3)	14 (4.1)
2008											
All students	100 (†)	306 (0.6)	270 (1.9)	280 (1.1)	295 (0.8)	307 (0.7)	333 (0.8)	— (†)	96 (0.4)	59 (0.9)	6 (0.4)
Sex											
Male	50 (0.5)	309 (0.7)	273 (2.9)	283 (1.5)	300 (0.8)	310 (0.8)	336 (1.1)	— (†)	96 (0.5)	63 (1.0)	8 (0.6)
Female	50 (0.5)	303 (0.8)	267 (2.8)	276 (1.6)	289 (1.0)	303 (0.8)	331 (0.9)	— (†)	96 (0.4)	56 (1.3)	5 (0.3)
Race/ethnicity											
White	59 (1.5)	314 (0.7)	275 (2.3)	287 (1.3)	301 (0.9)	314 (0.8)	337 (0.8)	— (†)	98 (0.3)	71 (1.1)	8 (0.5)
Black	14 (1.4)	287 (1.2)	‡ (†)	266 (2.6)	282 (1.5)	291 (1.5)	312 (2.6)	— (†)	91 (1.4)	32 (1.6)	1 (0.2)
Hispanic	19 (0.9)	293 (1.1)	261 (3.2)	274 (2.3)	289 (1.3)	296 (1.2)	320 (1.9)	— (†)	92 (1.1)	41 (1.7)	1 (0.4)
Other[1]	7 (0.5)	316 (1.8)	‡ (†)	‡ (†)	297 (2.8)	311 (1.9)	340 (2.2)	— (†)	98 (0.7)	71 (2.2)	13 (1.8)
2012											
All students	100 (†)	306 (0.8)	263 (3.6)	272 (1.5)	290 (1.3)	305 (1.0)	334 (0.8)	— (†)	96 (0.3)	60 (1.2)	7 (0.5)
Sex											
Male	49 (0.5)	308 (1.0)	266 (4.4)	276 (1.7)	293 (1.6)	308 (1.1)	337 (1.2)	— (†)	95 (0.4)	62 (1.3)	9 (0.8)
Female	51 (0.5)	304 (0.8)	‡ (†)	267 (2.0)	287 (1.3)	302 (1.1)	331 (1.0)	— (†)	96 (0.4)	58 (1.4)	5 (0.6)
Race/ethnicity											
White	56 (1.6)	314 (1.0)	268 (5.2)	278 (2.1)	298 (1.8)	311 (1.2)	337 (0.8)	— (†)	98 (0.3)	70 (1.6)	9 (0.7)
Black	13 (1.2)	288 (1.3)	‡ (†)	260 (2.7)	280 (1.6)	290 (1.0)	317 (2.5)	— (†)	90 (1.0)	34 (2.0)	1 (0.3)
Hispanic	22 (1.5)	294 (1.1)	‡ (†)	269 (2.5)	284 (1.4)	296 (1.0)	324 (2.0)	— (†)	93 (0.6)	43 (1.9)	2 (0.4)
Other[1]	8 (0.8)	318 (2.4)	‡ (†)	‡ (†)	293 (3.7)	308 (2.4)	338 (2.1)	— (†)	98 (0.8)	73 (3.0)	14 (2.3)

—Not available.
†Not applicable.
#Rounds to zero.
‡Reporting standards not met (too few cases for a reliable estimate).
[1]Includes Asians/Pacific Islanders and American Indians/Alaska Natives.
NOTE: Scale ranges from 0 to 500. Students scoring 200 (or higher) have a considerable understanding of two-digit numbers and know some basic multiplication and division facts. Students scoring 250 have an initial understanding of the four basic operations and are developing an ability to analyze simple logical relations. Students scoring 300 can perform reasoning and problem solving involving fractions, decimals, percents, elementary geometry, and simple algebra. Students scoring 350 can perform reasoning and problem solving involving geometry, alge-

bra, and beginning statistics and probability. Includes public and private schools. For assessment years prior to 2004, accommodations were not permitted. For 2004 and later years, includes students tested with accommodations; excludes only those students with disabilities and English language learners who were unable to be tested even with accommodations (1 to 4 percent of all students, depending on age and assessment year). Race categories exclude persons of Hispanic ethnicity. Detail may not sum to totals because of rounding.
SOURCE: U.S. Department of Education, National Center for Education Statistics, National Assessment of Educational Progress (NAEP), *NAEP Trends in Academic Progress*, 1996 and 1999; and 2004, 2008, and 2012 Long-Term Trend Mathematics Assessments, retrieved June 4, 2009, and August 12, 2013, from the Long-Term Trend NAEP Data Explorer (http://nces.ed.gov/nationsreportcard/naepdata/). (This table was prepared August 2013.)

Average National Assessment of Educational Progress (NAEP) science scale score, standard deviation, and percentage of students attaining science achievement levels, by grade level, selected student and school characteristics, and percentile: 2009 and 2011

[Standard errors appear in parentheses]

Selected characteristic, percentile, and achievement level	Grade 4 — 2009 Total, all students	Grade 4 — 2009 Male	Grade 4 — 2009 Female	Grade 8 — 2009 Total, all students	Grade 8 — 2009 Male	Grade 8 — 2009 Female	Grade 8 — 2011 Total, all students	Grade 8 — 2011 Male	Grade 8 — 2011 Female	Grade 12 — 2009 Total, all students	Grade 12 — 2009 Male	Grade 12 — 2009 Female
(column number) 1	2	3	4	5	6	7	8	9	10	11	12	13
All students	150 (0.3)	151 (0.3)	149 (0.3)	150 (0.3)	152 (0.4)	148 (0.3)	152 (0.3)	154 (0.3)	149 (0.3)	150 (0.8)	153 (0.9)	147 (0.9)
Average science scale score[1]												
Race/ethnicity												
White	163 (0.3)	164 (0.3)	162 (0.3)	162 (0.2)	164 (0.3)	160 (0.3)	163 (0.2)	166 (0.3)	161 (0.3)	159 (0.7)	162 (0.9)	156 (0.8)
Black	127 (0.4)	126 (0.6)	128 (0.3)	126 (0.4)	125 (0.6)	126 (0.5)	129 (0.5)	130 (0.8)	128 (0.6)	125 (1.2)	127 (1.6)	123 (1.5)
Hispanic	131 (0.5)	132 (0.7)	130 (0.6)	132 (0.6)	134 (0.8)	130 (0.7)	137 (0.5)	140 (0.8)	134 (0.8)	134 (1.3)	138 (2.3)	130 (1.5)
Asian/Pacific Islander	160 (1.2)	159 (1.4)	160 (1.4)	160 (1.4)	162 (1.3)	158 (1.3)	159 (1.3)	161 (1.6)	157 (1.7)	164 (3.0)	161 (2.9)	166 (3.8)
American Indian/Alaska Native	135 (1.3)	135 (1.5)	135 (1.8)	137 (1.4)	141 (1.8)	133 (2.0)	141 (1.4)	143 (2.1)	139 (1.5)	144 (3.7)	‡ (†)	‡ (†)
Highest education level of either parent												
Did not finish high school	†	†	†	132 (0.6)	135 (1.0)	128 (0.7)	136 (0.7)	136 (0.7)	130 (1.0)	136 (1.4)	136 (1.9)	128 (1.8)
Graduated high school	†	†	†	140 (0.4)	141 (0.6)	137 (0.5)	143 (0.4)	143 (0.7)	138 (0.6)	140 (0.9)	140 (1.5)	136 (1.4)
Some education after high school	†	†	†	153 (0.4)	154 (0.5)	150 (0.4)	156 (0.4)	156 (0.7)	151 (0.6)	150 (0.7)	150 (1.3)	144 (1.1)
Graduated college	†	†	†	162 (0.4)	162 (0.5)	159 (0.3)	164 (0.3)	164 (0.4)	160 (0.4)	163 (0.7)	163 (0.9)	159 (1.0)
Eligibility for free or reduced-price lunch												
Eligible	134 (0.4)	134 (0.4)	133 (0.3)	135 (0.4)	135 (0.5)	131 (0.4)	139 (0.3)	139 (0.4)	135 (0.4)	132 (1.0)	135 (1.1)	130 (1.1)
Not eligible	163 (0.3)	164 (0.3)	163 (0.3)	163 (0.3)	163 (0.4)	159 (0.4)	166 (0.3)	166 (0.4)	161 (0.4)	157 (0.9)	159 (1.1)	154 (1.0)
Unknown	162 (1.3)	163 (1.7)	161 (1.3)	167 (1.2)	167 (1.4)	161 (1.2)	168 (1.6)	168 (2.2)	159 (2.2)	156 (2.7)	156 (3.6)	156 (3.0)
School type												
Public	149 (0.3)	149 (0.3)	148 (0.3)	151 (0.3)	151 (0.4)	147 (0.3)	153 (0.2)	153 (0.3)	148 (0.3)	—	—	—
Private	163 (1.3)	165 (1.2)	162 (1.0)	167 (0.9)	167 (1.2)	161 (1.0)	168 (3.0)†	168 (3.6)†	158 (3.0)	—	—	—
School locale												
City	142 (0.6)	142 (0.6)	142 (0.7)	144 (0.6)	144 (0.7)	141 (0.7)	146 (0.6)	146 (0.8)	142 (0.7)	146 (1.8)	148 (1.6)	144 (2.2)
Suburban	154 (0.6)	154 (0.6)	153 (0.4)	155 (0.5)	155 (0.6)	152 (0.9)	158 (0.5)	158 (0.5)	153 (0.8)	154 (1.4)	157 (1.3)	150 (1.5)
Town	150 (0.6)	151 (0.8)	149 (0.6)	152 (1.0)	152 (1.1)	147 (1.0)	155 (0.7)	155 (0.5)	150 (0.8)	153 (1.2)	153 (1.3)	146 (1.6)
Rural	155 (0.5)	156 (0.7)	154 (0.5)	156 (0.4)	156 (0.5)	152 (0.5)	159 (0.6)	159 (0.6)	153 (0.6)	150 (1.2)	153 (1.5)	146 (1.4)
Percentile[2]												
10th	104 (0.6)	103 (0.6)	104 (0.5)	103 (0.6)	103 (0.7)	103 (0.6)	106 (0.5)	107 (0.9)	105 (0.7)	104 (1.2)	106 (1.8)	103 (1.1)
25th	128 (0.4)	128 (0.5)	128 (0.4)	130 (0.4)	130 (0.5)	127 (0.5)	131 (0.4)	133 (0.5)	129 (0.6)	126 (0.8)	128 (1.0)	125 (1.5)
50th	153 (0.4)	154 (0.4)	152 (0.4)	156 (0.4)	156 (0.4)	151 (0.4)	155 (0.4)	155 (0.5)	152 (0.6)	151 (1.1)	154 (1.4)	148 (1.1)
75th	175 (0.3)	176 (0.3)	174 (0.4)	178 (0.3)	178 (0.4)	172 (0.4)	176 (0.4)	179 (0.5)	173 (0.4)	174 (1.0)	178 (1.2)	171 (1.1)
90th	192 (0.3)	194 (0.3)	191 (0.5)	195 (0.2)	195 (0.3)	188 (0.5)	193 (0.4)	196 (0.4)	189 (0.5)	194 (1.0)	198 (0.9)	190 (1.4)
Standard deviation of the science scale score[3]												
All students	35 (0.2)	34 (0.2)	34 (0.2)	36 (0.2)	36 (0.2)	34 (0.2)	34 (0.2)	33 (0.2)	33 (0.3)	35 (0.4)	36 (0.5)	34 (0.5)
Percent of students attaining science achievement levels												
Achievement level												
Below Basic	28 (0.3)	27 (0.4)	28 (0.3)	37 (0.4)	35 (0.5)	38 (0.4)	35 (0.3)	32 (0.4)	37 (0.5)	40 (1.0)	37 (1.1)	42 (1.3)
At or above Basic[4]	72 (0.3)	73 (0.4)	72 (0.3)	63 (0.4)	65 (0.5)	62 (0.4)	65 (0.3)	68 (0.4)	63 (0.5)	60 (1.0)	63 (1.1)	58 (1.3)
At or above Proficient[5]	34 (0.3)	35 (0.4)	32 (0.3)	30 (0.3)	34 (0.4)	27 (0.3)	32 (0.4)	35 (0.5)	28 (0.4)	21 (0.8)	24 (1.0)	18 (0.8)
At Advanced[6]	1 (0.1)	1 (0.1)	1 (0.1)	2 (0.1)	2 (0.1)	2 (0.1)	2 (0.1)	2 (0.1)	1 (0.1)	1 (0.2)	2 (0.3)	1 (0.2)

—Not available.
†Not applicable.
‡Reporting standards not met (too few cases for a reliable estimate).
[1]Scale ranges from 0 to 300 for all three grades, but scores cannot be compared across grades. For example, the average score of 163 for White 4th-graders does not denote higher performance than the score of 159 for White 12th-graders.
[2]The percentile represents a specific point on the percentage distribution of all students ranked by their science score from low to high. For example, 10 percent of students scored at or below the 10th percentile score, while 90 percent of students scored above it.
[3]The standard deviation provides an indication of how much the test scores varied. The lower the standard deviation, the closer the scores were clustered around the average score. About two-thirds of the student scores can be expected to fall within the range of one standard deviation above and one standard deviation below the average score. For example, the average score for all 4th-graders was 150, and the standard deviation was 35. This means that we would expect about two-thirds of the students to have scores between 185 (one standard deviation above the average) and 115 (one standard deviation below the average). Standard errors also must be taken into account when making comparisons of these ranges. For a discussion of standard errors, see Appendix A: Guide to Sources.
[4]Basic denotes partial mastery of the knowledge and skills that are fundamental for proficient work.
[5]Proficient represents solid academic performance. Students reaching this level have demonstrated competency over challenging subject matter.
[6]Advanced signifies superior performance.

NOTE: In 2011, only 8th-grade students were assessed in science. Includes students tested with accommodations (7 to 11 percent of all students, depending on grade level and year); excludes only those students with disabilities and English language learners who were unable to be tested even with accommodations (2 to 3 percent of all students). Race categories exclude persons of Hispanic ethnicity.

SOURCE: U.S. Department of Education, National Center for Education Statistics, National Assessment of Educational Progress (NAEP), 2011 Science Assessment, retrieved August 1, 2012, from the Main NAEP Data Explorer (http://nces.ed.gov/nationsreportcard/naepdata/). (This table was prepared August 2012.)

Average National Assessment of Educational Progress (NAEP) science scale scores of 8th-grade public school students, by race/ethnicity and state: 2009 and 2011

[Standard errors appear in parentheses]

State	2009 Total, all students		2009 White		2009 Black		2009 Hispanic		2009 Asian/Pacific Islander		2011 Total, all students		2011 White		2011 Black		2011 Hispanic		2011 Asian/Pacific Islander	
1	2		3		4		5		6		7		8		9		10		11	
United States	149	(0.3)	161	(0.2)	125	(0.4)	131	(0.6)	159	(1.0)	151	(0.2)	163	(0.2)	128	(0.5)	136	(0.5)	159	(1.2)
Alabama	139	(1.1)	152	(1.1)	115	(1.8)	129	(3.5)	‡	(†)	140	(1.4)	152	(1.3)	118	(1.4)	136	(3.6)	‡	(†)
Alaska	—	(†)	—	(†)	—	(†)	—	(†)	—	(†)	153	(0.7)	166	(0.9)	133	(3.2)	147	(2.7)	145	(2.2)
Arizona	141	(1.3)	157	(1.3)	126	(3.2)	127	(1.5)	159	(5.5)	144	(1.3)	158	(1.3)	128	(2.9)	132	(1.6)	‡	(†)
Arkansas	144	(1.3)	154	(0.9)	111	(2.1)	134	(3.0)	‡	(†)	148	(1.1)	158	(1.0)	119	(2.1)	138	(2.1)	‡	(†)
California	137	(1.4)	157	(2.0)	122	(2.8)	122	(1.3)	154	(2.2)	140	(1.3)	159	(1.6)	124	(3.4)	128	(1.4)	157	(2.8)
Colorado	156	(1.0)	166	(1.0)	135	(3.7)	137	(1.6)	161	(3.7)	161	(1.3)	171	(1.4)	149	(3.7)	141	(1.8)	162	(4.5)
Connecticut	155	(0.9)	164	(0.8)	126	(2.3)	128	(1.8)	169	(3.5)	155	(1.1)	165	(1.0)	128	(2.3)	129	(2.5)	170	(4.2)
Delaware	148	(0.6)	159	(0.9)	133	(1.0)	141	(2.2)	160	(4.3)	150	(0.6)	161	(0.8)	134	(1.3)	139	(2.0)	168	(3.3)
District of Columbia	—	(†)	—	(†)	—	(†)	—	(†)	—	(†)	112	(1.0)	174	(3.3)	107	(1.1)	116	(2.6)	‡	(†)
Florida	146	(1.0)	158	(1.4)	126	(1.4)	139	(1.2)	163	(4.1)	148	(1.1)	161	(1.1)	127	(2.0)	144	(1.5)	161	(4.5)
Georgia	147	(1.0)	161	(1.2)	129	(1.3)	137	(2.2)	172	(2.7)	151	(1.4)	166	(1.6)	133	(1.8)	143	(3.1)	168	(3.9)
Hawaii	139	(0.7)	153	(1.5)	133	(5.0)	148	(4.3)	136	(1.0)	142	(0.7)	157	(1.8)	‡	(†)	144	(3.3)	139	(0.9)
Idaho	158	(0.9)	162	(0.9)	‡	(†)	137	(1.4)	‡	(†)	159	(0.7)	163	(0.7)	‡	(†)	139	(1.8)	‡	(†)
Illinois	148	(1.4)	162	(1.2)	118	(1.5)	131	(1.5)	167	(3.2)	147	(1.0)	161	(1.1)	120	(1.9)	135	(1.2)	163	(4.4)
Indiana	152	(1.2)	159	(1.0)	126	(3.9)	135	(3.5)	‡	(†)	153	(0.9)	160	(1.0)	125	(2.7)	136	(3.7)	‡	(†)
Iowa	156	(0.9)	160	(0.8)	127	(3.5)	133	(3.2)	‡	(†)	157	(0.8)	161	(0.8)	128	(3.7)	143	(3.1)	‡	(†)
Kansas	—	(†)	—	(†)	—	(†)	—	(†)	—	(†)	156	(0.8)	163	(0.8)	129	(3.2)	134	(2.1)	156	(5.2)
Kentucky	156	(0.8)	159	(0.9)	137	(1.8)	145	(3.5)	‡	(†)	157	(0.8)	160	(0.9)	135	(1.7)	149	(3.0)	‡	(†)
Louisiana	139	(1.7)	155	(1.5)	120	(1.9)	‡	(†)	‡	(†)	143	(1.7)	156	(1.6)	125	(2.1)	142	(5.2)	‡	(†)
Maine	158	(0.8)	159	(0.8)	126	(4.5)	‡	(†)	‡	(†)	160	(0.5)	160	(0.6)	‡	(†)	‡	(†)	‡	(†)
Maryland	148	(1.1)	164	(1.2)	127	(1.5)	136	(2.8)	169	(2.5)	152	(1.2)	167	(1.2)	131	(1.8)	142	(2.2)	164	(4.3)
Massachusetts	160	(1.1)	167	(1.1)	132	(2.6)	131	(2.7)	168	(4.1)	161	(1.1)	169	(1.1)	133	(4.3)	130	(2.6)	170	(4.1)
Michigan	153	(1.4)	162	(1.0)	121	(2.1)	139	(3.4)	‡	(†)	157	(1.0)	165	(0.8)	124	(2.8)	146	(3.3)	166	(6.9)
Minnesota	159	(1.0)	166	(0.9)	128	(2.8)	132	(3.7)	141	(3.0)	161	(1.0)	168	(1.0)	129	(2.5)	137	(4.0)	149	(3.9)
Mississippi	132	(1.2)	150	(1.2)	114	(1.1)	‡	(†)	‡	(†)	137	(1.3)	156	(1.1)	119	(1.4)	‡	(†)	‡	(†)
Missouri	156	(1.1)	161	(0.9)	129	(2.5)	150	(3.8)	167	(4.7)	156	(1.1)	162	(0.8)	130	(3.5)	‡	(†)	‡	(†)
Montana	162	(0.7)	166	(0.7)	‡	(†)	155	(3.3)	‡	(†)	163	(0.7)	167	(0.7)	‡	(†)	‡	(†)	‡	(†)
Nebraska	—	(†)	—	(†)	—	(†)	—	(†)	—	(†)	157	(0.7)	164	(0.7)	126	(3.5)	135	(1.9)	‡	(†)
Nevada	141	(0.7)	153	(0.9)	127	(2.4)	129	(1.0)	148	(2.4)	144	(0.8)	157	(1.3)	123	(3.3)	133	(1.1)	154	(2.6)
New Hampshire	160	(0.8)	161	(0.8)	‡	(†)	131	(4.2)	‡	(†)	162	(0.7)	164	(0.6)	‡	(†)	137	(4.3)	‡	(†)
New Jersey	155	(1.5)	165	(1.0)	127	(3.3)	138	(2.7)	174	(2.6)	155	(1.2)	166	(1.2)	131	(2.5)	134	(1.9)	173	(2.8)
New Mexico	143	(1.4)	163	(1.4)	‡	(†)	135	(1.4)	‡	(†)	145	(0.8)	161	(1.4)	‡	(†)	139	(0.8)	‡	(†)
New York	149	(1.2)	164	(1.0)	123	(1.8)	125	(1.7)	161	(2.3)	149	(1.0)	163	(1.3)	130	(2.2)	129	(1.7)	154	(2.6)
North Carolina	144	(1.3)	158	(1.3)	121	(1.6)	132	(2.3)	165	(7.1)	148	(1.1)	160	(1.1)	125	(1.8)	138	(2.4)	160	(6.5)
North Dakota	162	(0.5)	166	(0.6)	‡	(†)	‡	(†)	‡	(†)	164	(0.7)	168	(0.8)	‡	(†)	‡	(†)	‡	(†)
Ohio	158	(1.0)	164	(0.8)	126	(2.1)	140	(4.6)	‡	(†)	158	(1.0)	165	(1.0)	132	(2.6)	151	(5.3)	‡	(†)
Oklahoma	146	(0.9)	155	(1.0)	124	(2.6)	127	(2.6)	‡	(†)	148	(1.1)	156	(1.0)	126	(3.6)	135	(2.8)	‡	(†)
Oregon	154	(1.0)	160	(1.1)	135	(4.1)	130	(1.8)	160	(3.5)	155	(0.9)	162	(1.0)	‡	(†)	135	(1.4)	159	(4.3)
Pennsylvania	154	(1.1)	162	(0.9)	123	(2.0)	121	(4.4)	159	(4.1)	151	(1.3)	163	(0.9)	120	(2.3)	118	(4.8)	163	(4.9)
Rhode Island	146	(0.6)	155	(0.8)	125	(2.6)	119	(1.9)	146	(5.3)	149	(0.7)	161	(0.7)	122	(3.4)	120	(1.9)	151	(4.6)
South Carolina	143	(1.6)	158	(1.1)	124	(1.7)	129	(4.2)	‡	(†)	149	(1.0)	163	(1.0)	128	(1.6)	139	(3.0)	‡	(†)
South Dakota	161	(0.6)	165	(0.6)	141	(5.5)	135	(4.1)	‡	(†)	162	(0.5)	166	(0.6)	‡	(†)	151	(4.1)	‡	(†)
Tennessee	148	(1.2)	157	(0.9)	122	(2.0)	139	(3.8)	‡	(†)	150	(1.0)	160	(0.9)	121	(1.6)	137	(3.1)	‡	(†)
Texas	150	(1.2)	167	(1.4)	133	(2.5)	141	(1.5)	170	(3.6)	153	(1.0)	167	(1.2)	137	(2.3)	146	(1.3)	172	(4.3)
Utah	158	(1.0)	164	(1.1)	‡	(†)	129	(1.7)	147	(3.9)	161	(0.8)	167	(0.8)	‡	(†)	137	(2.0)	153	(4.7)
Vermont	—	(†)	—	(†)	—	(†)	—	(†)	—	(†)	163	(0.8)	164	(0.9)	‡	(†)	‡	(†)	‡	(†)
Virginia	156	(1.1)	166	(1.0)	135	(2.0)	144	(2.2)	168	(3.1)	160	(1.0)	169	(1.3)	138	(1.7)	145	(2.8)	172	(2.4)
Washington	155	(1.0)	161	(1.1)	135	(3.7)	132	(2.3)	157	(3.0)	156	(0.9)	163	(1.0)	133	(3.1)	141	(2.5)	156	(2.8)
West Virginia	145	(0.8)	146	(0.8)	127	(2.8)	‡	(†)	‡	(†)	149	(1.0)	150	(1.0)	136	(2.7)	‡	(†)	‡	(†)
Wisconsin	157	(0.9)	165	(0.8)	120	(1.5)	134	(3.9)	152	(3.5)	159	(1.0)	166	(0.9)	121	(3.1)	140	(4.8)	149	(4.7)
Wyoming	158	(0.7)	162	(0.7)	‡	(†)	137	(1.8)	‡	(†)	160	(0.5)	164	(0.6)	‡	(†)	143	(2.0)	‡	(†)
Department of Defense dependents schools	162	(0.7)	170	(1.0)	144	(1.4)	155	(2.0)	160	(2.3)	161	(0.8)	169	(1.1)	143	(2.2)	158	(2.5)	155	(3.2)

—Not available.

†Not applicable.

‡Reporting standards not met (too few cases for a reliable estimate).

NOTE: Scale ranges from 0 to 300. Includes students tested with accommodations (10 percent of all students in 2009 and 9 percent of all students in 2011); excludes only those students with disabilities and English language learners who were unable to be tested even with accommodations (2 percent of all students in both years). Race categories exclude persons of Hispanic ethnicity. Totals include other racial/ethnic groups not shown separately.

SOURCE: U.S. Department of Education, National Center for Education Statistics, National Assessment of Educational Progress (NAEP), 2009 and 2011 Science Assessment, retrieved August 12, 2012, from the Main NAEP Data Explorer (http://nces.ed.gov/nationsreportcard/naepdata/). (This table was prepared August 2012.)

Average National Assessment of Educational Progress (NAEP) science scale scores of 8th-graders with various attitudes toward science and percentage reporting these attitudes, by selected student characteristics: 2011

[Standard errors appear in parentheses]

Student characteristic	Take science only because it will help in future				Like science				Take science only because required			
	Strongly disagree	Disagree	Agree	Strongly agree	Strongly disagree	Disagree	Agree	Strongly agree	Strongly disagree	Disagree	Agree	Strongly agree
1	2	3	4	5	6	7	8	9	10	11	12	13
Average scale score[1]												
All students	154 (0.5)	161 (0.4)	150 (0.3)	143 (0.5)	136 (0.6)	144 (0.5)	155 (0.3)	166 (0.5)	164 (0.5)	160 (0.4)	146 (0.3)	138 (0.5)
Sex												
Male	156 (0.7)	163 (0.4)	153 (0.4)	145 (0.7)	136 (0.9)	146 (0.7)	157 (0.4)	168 (0.7)	166 (0.6)	162 (0.5)	148 (0.5)	140 (0.7)
Female	152 (0.9)	158 (0.5)	148 (0.5)	141 (0.6)	136 (0.8)	144 (0.6)	153 (0.5)	162 (0.7)	161 (0.7)	158 (0.6)	144 (0.5)	137 (0.6)
Race/ethnicity												
White	164 (0.6)	169 (0.4)	161 (0.3)	158 (0.6)	148 (0.6)	156 (0.5)	165 (0.3)	175 (0.5)	174 (0.5)	170 (0.4)	157 (0.4)	150 (0.6)
Black	132 (1.3)	137 (1.3)	130 (0.8)	123 (0.9)	120 (1.1)	124 (0.8)	131 (0.6)	141 (1.2)	139 (1.6)	137 (0.7)	126 (0.7)	121 (0.8)
Hispanic	140 (1.6)	145 (1.0)	135 (0.7)	132 (1.0)	124 (1.3)	129 (1.1)	140 (0.6)	151 (1.3)	149 (1.3)	144 (0.9)	132 (0.9)	129 (0.9)
Asian	165 (2.8)	170 (1.9)	159 (2.1)	156 (2.0)	140 (3.3)	151 (2.2)	162 (1.7)	177 (2.1)	176 (2.4)	167 (0.9)	155 (2.0)	144 (2.3)
Pacific Islander	143 (6.5)	146 (3.9)	139 (2.2)	137 (5.1)	117 (5.3)	130 (3.4)	147 (3.1)	153 (3.6)	150 (4.8)	150 (3.4)	134 (3.8)	126 (3.4)
American Indian/Alaska Native	140 (4.4)	151 (2.2)	141 (1.9)	134 (2.2)	126 (3.2)	138 (2.3)	146 (2.2)	150 (3.1)	149 (3.3)	150 (2.0)	140 (2.7)	132 (3.2)
Two or more races	158 (5.0)	161 (1.8)	153 (1.6)	155 (4.2)	139 (4.6)	147 (2.3)	159 (1.2)	170 (3.6)	167 (3.9)	163 (1.7)	152 (2.2)	139 (2.6)
Eligibility for free or reduced-price lunch												
Eligible	140 (0.7)	146 (0.5)	136 (0.4)	130 (0.6)	125 (0.7)	131 (0.7)	140 (0.4)	149 (0.6)	147 (0.5)	145 (0.5)	133 (0.5)	128 (0.6)
Not eligible	165 (0.7)	170 (0.4)	162 (0.4)	158 (0.9)	147 (0.9)	156 (0.6)	166 (0.4)	176 (0.5)	175 (0.6)	170 (0.5)	158 (0.5)	150 (0.5)
Unknown	168 (3.9)	170 (2.3)	161 (2.4)	154 (3.7)	147 (5.4)	156 (2.6)	166 (1.9)	177 (3.4)	174 (3.1)	170 (2.5)	157 (2.4)	147 (5.1)
Parents' highest level of education												
Did not finish high school	134 (1.9)	142 (1.3)	130 (1.4)	128 (1.5)	125 (1.8)	126 (1.6)	136 (0.9)	144 (1.8)	140 (1.6)	140 (1.3)	128 (1.2)	129 (1.5)
Graduated high school	143 (1.4)	148 (0.9)	139 (0.6)	132 (1.1)	129 (1.0)	135 (0.8)	143 (0.6)	153 (1.0)	151 (1.2)	148 (0.7)	136 (0.7)	132 (0.7)
Some education after high school	156 (1.3)	160 (0.8)	152 (0.6)	145 (0.9)	140 (1.3)	146 (0.9)	156 (0.5)	165 (1.0)	164 (0.9)	160 (0.8)	149 (0.7)	141 (0.9)
Graduated college	165 (0.8)	170 (0.4)	161 (0.4)	153 (0.7)	145 (0.9)	155 (0.6)	164 (0.4)	174 (0.5)	173 (0.6)	169 (0.4)	156 (0.5)	146 (0.8)
Percent of students												
All students	12 (0.2)	32 (0.3)	39 (0.3)	18 (0.2)	12 (0.2)	19 (0.3)	50 (0.3)	19 (0.3)	18 (0.2)	34 (0.3)	30 (0.2)	17 (0.2)
Sex												
Male	14 (0.3)	33 (0.4)	36 (0.4)	16 (0.3)	11 (0.2)	16 (0.3)	51 (0.4)	22 (0.4)	21 (0.3)	35 (0.4)	27 (0.3)	17 (0.2)
Female	10 (0.2)	30 (0.4)	41 (0.4)	19 (0.3)	12 (0.3)	23 (0.4)	49 (0.4)	16 (0.3)	15 (0.2)	34 (0.4)	33 (0.4)	18 (0.3)
Race/ethnicity												
White	13 (0.2)	36 (0.4)	37 (0.4)	13 (0.2)	10 (0.2)	16 (0.3)	50 (0.4)	20 (0.3)	20 (0.2)	37 (0.4)	28 (0.3)	16 (0.2)
Black	12 (0.5)	22 (0.7)	37 (0.7)	29 (0.6)	16 (0.5)	20 (0.6)	46 (0.6)	19 (0.6)	17 (0.7)	28 (0.6)	30 (0.7)	25 (0.5)
Hispanic	11 (0.4)	27 (0.6)	42 (0.6)	20 (0.6)	13 (0.6)	21 (0.7)	50 (0.6)	16 (0.5)	15 (0.5)	33 (0.6)	35 (0.6)	18 (0.5)
Asian	9 (0.8)	26 (1.4)	42 (1.7)	22 (1.1)	8 (0.8)	16 (0.8)	57 (1.4)	19 (0.9)	19 (0.9)	37 (1.4)	30 (1.4)	14 (0.8)
Pacific Islander	11 (2.5)	26 (3.3)	39 (3.7)	23 (3.3)	15 (2.9)	21 (3.1)	50 (4.3)	15 (2.6)	14 (2.9)	37 (3.9)	30 (2.8)	18 (2.9)
American Indian/Alaska Native	10 (1.2)	27 (1.8)	44 (2.0)	18 (1.1)	14 (1.3)	19 (1.2)	52 (1.6)	15 (1.3)	14 (1.3)	29 (1.5)	37 (1.7)	19 (1.5)
Two or more races	13 (1.4)	33 (2.0)	36 (1.9)	18 (1.7)	14 (1.8)	18 (1.0)	47 (2.0)	21 (1.8)	20 (2.4)	34 (1.9)	28 (1.7)	19 (1.5)
Eligibility for free or reduced-price lunch												
Eligible	12 (0.2)	27 (0.3)	40 (0.3)	21 (0.3)	14 (0.3)	20 (0.3)	49 (0.3)	17 (0.3)	16 (0.3)	31 (0.4)	32 (0.3)	21 (0.3)
Not eligible	12 (0.2)	35 (0.3)	38 (0.3)	15 (0.3)	10 (0.2)	18 (0.3)	51 (0.4)	20 (0.3)	20 (0.3)	37 (0.4)	28 (0.3)	15 (0.2)
Unknown	12 (1.9)	38 (2.9)	35 (2.7)	15 (1.6)	10 (1.2)	20 (2.1)	48 (2.5)	22 (2.1)	22 (2.1)	36 (2.5)	30 (2.4)	12 (1.4)
Parents' highest level of education												
Did not finish high school	12 (0.6)	27 (1.1)	40 (1.0)	20 (0.9)	16 (0.7)	23 (0.9)	45 (1.1)	15 (0.7)	14 (0.6)	29 (0.9)	34 (1.0)	23 (0.9)
Graduated high school	12 (0.4)	31 (0.6)	39 (0.6)	18 (0.5)	13 (0.4)	21 (0.4)	50 (0.6)	16 (0.6)	15 (0.5)	32 (0.6)	32 (0.6)	20 (0.4)
Some education after high school	12 (0.3)	31 (0.5)	39 (0.5)	17 (0.4)	12 (0.3)	20 (0.5)	50 (0.5)	18 (0.6)	18 (0.4)	35 (0.6)	29 (0.5)	18 (0.5)
Graduated college	12 (0.3)	33 (0.4)	38 (0.4)	17 (0.3)	10 (0.3)	18 (0.4)	51 (0.5)	21 (0.3)	21 (0.3)	37 (0.5)	28 (0.4)	15 (0.3)

[1]Scale ranges from 0 to 300.

NOTE: Includes public and private schools. Includes students tested with accommodations (11 percent of all 8th-graders); excludes only those students with disabilities and English language learners who were unable to be tested even with accommodations (2 percent of all 8th-graders). Detail may not sum to totals because of rounding. Race categories exclude persons of Hispanic ethnicity.

SOURCE: U.S. Department of Education, National Center for Education Statistics, National Assessment of Educational Progress (NAEP), 2011 Science Assessment, retrieved November 22, 2013, from the Main NAEP Data Explorer (http://nces.ed.gov/nationsreportcard/naepdata/). (This table was prepared November 2013.)

Average National Assessment of Educational Progress (NAEP) science scale scores of 12th-graders with various educational goals and attitudes toward science, and percentage reporting these goals and attitudes, by selected student characteristics: 2009

[Standard errors appear in parentheses]

Student characteristic	Educational goals[1]				Like science				Take science only because required			
	Graduate high school	Some education after high school	Graduate college	Go to graduate school	Strongly disagree	Disagree	Agree	Strongly agree	Strongly disagree	Disagree	Agree	Strongly agree
1	2	3	4	5	6	7	8	9	10	11	12	13
Average scale score[2]												
All students	114 (1.9)	131 (1.3)	148 (0.6)	171 (1.0)	132 (1.3)	141 (0.9)	153 (0.9)	172 (1.1)	169 (1.1)	159 (0.9)	142 (0.9)	134 (1.0)
Sex												
Male	121 (2.6)	134 (1.8)	152 (0.8)	177 (1.3)	130 (1.7)	141 (1.4)	155 (1.2)	175 (1.3)	172 (1.4)	162 (1.2)	143 (1.2)	134 (1.3)
Female	103 (2.6)	127 (1.9)	143 (0.8)	166 (1.2)	133 (1.8)	141 (1.1)	150 (0.9)	169 (1.8)	165 (1.8)	156 (0.9)	140 (1.2)	134 (1.4)
Race/ethnicity												
White	127 (2.1)	140 (1.6)	156 (0.7)	178 (1.0)	140 (1.6)	150 (1.1)	161 (0.9)	180 (1.0)	176 (1.1)	167 (0.8)	151 (1.0)	143 (1.4)
Black	89 (3.6)	107 (3.2)	124 (1.1)	144 (1.8)	113 (2.0)	120 (1.5)	128 (1.5)	142 (2.4)	140 (2.6)	135 (2.3)	121 (1.6)	115 (1.7)
Hispanic	106 (3.7)	122 (2.7)	136 (1.2)	154 (2.3)	123 (2.6)	127 (1.8)	135 (1.8)	157 (2.4)	152 (2.9)	143 (1.7)	128 (1.6)	125 (2.3)
Asian/Pacific Islander	‡ (†)	‡ (†)	154 (2.9)	181 (3.4)	141 (5.2)	149 (3.8)	166 (2.9)	188 (4.5)	181 (4.2)	171 (3.3)	154 (3.2)	141 (4.5)
American Indian/Alaska Native	‡ (†)	‡ (†)	‡ (†)	‡ (†)	‡ (†)	‡ (†)	‡ (†)	‡ (†)	‡ (†)	‡ (†)	‡ (†)	‡ (†)
Eligibility for free or reduced-price lunch												
Eligible	105 (2.9)	120 (2.0)	134 (0.8)	151 (2.0)	120 (1.8)	125 (1.4)	135 (1.1)	152 (2.0)	147 (2.7)	142 (1.4)	127 (1.1)	121 (1.6)
Not eligible	122 (2.0)	138 (1.8)	153 (0.8)	176 (1.0)	137 (1.5)	148 (1.1)	159 (1.1)	179 (1.3)	175 (1.2)	165 (1.0)	148 (1.1)	140 (1.4)
Unknown	‡ (†)	‡ (†)	151 (2.4)	169 (3.5)	139 (3.1)	146 (3.6)	158 (2.9)	177 (3.8)	175 (3.6)	164 (3.3)	149 (2.6)	138 (3.3)
Parents' highest level of education												
Did not finish high school	112 (3.7)	124 (2.8)	134 (1.5)	145 (3.1)	119 (2.7)	125 (2.5)	134 (2.0)	153 (3.5)	147 (3.1)	138 (2.5)	127 (2.3)	121 (2.2)
Graduated high school	109 (2.8)	129 (2.7)	141 (1.3)	158 (2.1)	124 (2.2)	132 (1.5)	141 (1.3)	158 (2.7)	149 (2.7)	149 (1.6)	133 (1.8)	126 (1.9)
Some education after high school	126 (4.0)	135 (2.2)	146 (0.9)	162 (2.1)	133 (1.5)	138 (1.2)	149 (1.2)	168 (1.7)	164 (2.3)	156 (1.3)	140 (1.1)	133 (1.7)
Graduated college	120 (3.9)	140 (2.4)	155 (0.8)	177 (0.9)	141 (1.7)	151 (1.3)	163 (1.0)	181 (1.3)	180 (1.3)	168 (1.0)	152 (1.0)	143 (1.2)
Percent of students												
All students	5 (0.3)	7 (0.3)	59 (0.7)	26 (0.8)	14 (0.4)	21 (0.4)	48 (0.5)	16 (0.3)	15 (0.4)	34 (0.5)	31 (0.4)	19 (0.4)
Sex												
Male	6 (0.4)	9 (0.4)	59 (0.8)	22 (0.8)	12 (0.5)	18 (0.5)	52 (0.7)	18 (0.5)	17 (0.5)	37 (0.6)	29 (0.7)	17 (0.5)
Female	4 (0.3)	6 (0.4)	58 (0.9)	31 (1.0)	16 (0.5)	25 (0.6)	45 (0.7)	14 (0.5)	14 (0.6)	31 (0.7)	33 (0.6)	21 (0.6)
Race/ethnicity												
White	4 (0.3)	7 (0.3)	60 (0.7)	26 (0.8)	13 (0.5)	21 (0.5)	49 (0.7)	17 (0.5)	17 (0.5)	36 (0.6)	29 (0.6)	18 (0.5)
Black	6 (0.8)	6 (0.6)	60 (1.3)	25 (1.4)	20 (1.0)	23 (0.9)	43 (1.3)	14 (0.9)	11 (0.8)	28 (1.2)	33 (1.0)	28 (1.1)
Hispanic	7 (0.7)	12 (0.8)	59 (1.1)	18 (1.1)	13 (0.7)	24 (0.9)	49 (1.1)	14 (1.1)	12 (0.8)	31 (1.1)	38 (1.0)	19 (0.9)
Asian/Pacific Islander	3 (0.8)	2 (0.5)	42 (2.6)	50 (2.8)	9 (1.0)	18 (1.7)	55 (1.5)	18 (1.5)	19 (1.6)	40 (1.3)	28 (1.9)	13 (1.1)
American Indian/Alaska Native	‡ (†)	‡ (†)	‡ (†)	‡ (†)	‡ (†)	‡ (†)	‡ (†)	‡ (†)	‡ (†)	‡ (†)	‡ (†)	‡ (†)
Eligibility for free or reduced-price lunch												
Eligible	8 (0.5)	10 (0.6)	60 (1.2)	18 (0.9)	16 (0.7)	23 (0.9)	47 (1.0)	14 (0.6)	13 (0.7)	30 (0.8)	34 (0.7)	22 (0.8)
Not eligible	4 (0.3)	7 (0.4)	59 (0.8)	29 (0.9)	13 (0.4)	21 (0.5)	49 (0.6)	17 (0.4)	16 (0.5)	35 (0.6)	30 (0.6)	18 (0.5)
Unknown	2 (0.7)	4 (1.0)	56 (2.4)	35 (2.7)	13 (1.2)	21 (1.3)	48 (1.9)	18 (1.6)	16 (1.6)	36 (2.3)	29 (1.8)	19 (1.6)
Parents' highest level of education												
Did not finish high school	11 (1.1)	13 (1.0)	53 (2.2)	16 (1.8)	19 (1.4)	22 (1.4)	47 (1.7)	13 (1.2)	13 (1.6)	30 (1.6)	35 (1.7)	23 (1.3)
Graduated high school	10 (0.6)	12 (0.8)	62 (1.4)	13 (1.0)	16 (0.8)	25 (1.0)	46 (1.0)	12 (0.7)	12 (1.3)	31 (1.3)	35 (1.1)	22 (1.1)
Some education after high school	4 (0.4)	9 (0.5)	65 (1.0)	20 (1.1)	15 (0.8)	22 (1.0)	48 (1.2)	15 (0.8)	14 (1.0)	33 (1.0)	32 (0.9)	21 (0.8)
Graduated college	2 (0.2)	4 (0.3)	56 (0.8)	37 (0.9)	12 (0.6)	19 (0.6)	50 (0.7)	19 (0.5)	18 (0.4)	37 (0.7)	28 (0.6)	17 (0.6)

†Not applicable.

‡Reporting standards not met (too few cases for a reliable estimate).

[1]The educational goals columns exclude the 1 percent of students who reported that they would not finish high school and the 2 percent who reported that they did not know how much education they would complete.

[2]Scale ranges from 0 to 300.

NOTE: Includes students tested with accommodations (7 percent of all 12th-graders); excludes only those students with disabilities and English language learners who were unable to be tested even with accommodations (3 percent of all 12th-graders). Race categories exclude persons of Hispanic ethnicity.

SOURCE: U.S. Department of Education, National Center for Education Statistics, National Assessment of Educational Progress (NAEP), 2009 Science Assessment, retrieved May 26, 2011, from the Main NAEP Data Explorer (http://nces.ed.gov/nationsreportcard/naepdata/). (This table was prepared May 2011.)

Average National Assessment of Educational Progress (NAEP) arts scale score of 8th-graders, percentage distribution by frequency of instruction, and percentage participating in selected activities, by subject and selected characteristics: 2008

[Standard errors appear in parentheses]

| Selected characteristic | Average score | | | Percentage distribution of students by school-reported frequency of instruction | | | | | | | | Percent of students reporting participation in musical activities in school | | |
	Music[1] responding scale score (0 to 300)	Visual arts[2] Responding scale score (0 to 300)	Visual arts[2] Creating task score (0 to 100)	Music Subject not offered	Music Less than once a week	Music Once or twice a week	Music At least 3 or 4 times a week	Visual arts Subject not offered	Visual arts Less than once a week	Visual arts Once or twice a week	Visual arts At least 3 or 4 times a week	Play in band	Play in orchestra	Sing in chorus or choir
1	2	3	4	5	6	7	8	9	10	11	12	13	14	15
All students	150 (1.2)	150 (1.2)	52 (0.6)	8 (2.0)	8 (2.0)	27 (3.1)	57 (3.2)	14 (2.4)	10 (2.5)	30 (3.5)	47 (3.9)	16 (0.9)	5 (0.5)	17 (1.2)
Sex														
Male	145 (1.3)	145 (1.4)	49 (0.7)	9 (2.1)	8 (2.1)	27 (3.1)	56 (3.2)	14 (2.6)	10 (2.5)	30 (3.6)	46 (4.1)	18 (1.0)	3 (0.5)	9 (1.2)
Female	155 (1.4)	155 (1.2)	54 (0.7)	8 (2.0)	7 (1.9)	28 (3.2)	57 (3.2)	13 (2.3)	10 (2.5)	29 (3.3)	48 (3.8)	14 (1.0)	6 (0.6)	26 (1.8)
Race/ethnicity														
White	161 (1.3)	160 (1.2)	55 (0.5)	6 (2.5)	8 (2.5)	29 (4.0)	57 (3.6)	11 (2.6)	11 (3.4)	34 (4.4)	44 (4.6)	19 (1.2)	5 (0.6)	16 (1.9)
Black	130 (2.0)	129 (2.4)	43 (1.5)	10 (2.9)	6 (4.5)	26 (5.5)	56 (7.0)	18 (4.9)	10 (4.9)	24 (4.5)	49 (5.7)	13 (1.2)	4 (1.0)	21 (1.9)
Hispanic	129 (1.9)	134 (1.9)	46 (1.1)	14 (4.3)	6 (2.3)	21 (4.1)	59 (4.5)	17 (4.5)	5 (2.0)	23 (4.7)	56 (6.0)	8 (1.2)	3 (0.6)	10 (1.6)
Asian/Pacific Islander	159 (4.7)	156 (4.2)	54 (2.0)	7 (4.1)	8 (3.4)	25 (6.6)	60 (8.7)	5 (2.5)	11 (4.6)	29 (6.0)	54 (8.4)	21 (3.5)	6 (2.1)	16 (2.9)
Free or reduced-price lunch eligibility														
Eligible	132 (1.3)	132 (1.4)	46 (1.0)	10 (2.1)	6 (2.1)	26 (3.4)	58 (3.9)	18 (3.4)	9 (3.2)	26 (3.7)	47 (4.7)	12 (1.2)	3 (0.6)	15 (1.4)
Not eligible	161 (1.4)	161 (1.2)	55 (0.6)	8 (2.6)	8 (2.6)	26 (4.0)	59 (4.0)	10 (2.4)	10 (3.2)	30 (4.1)	50 (4.6)	19 (1.0)	5 (0.6)	18 (1.6)
Unknown	156 (5.6)	156 (5.9)	57 (2.6)	4 (†)	19 (8.7)	54 (11.5)	23 (10.5)	16 (10.3)	13 (8.4)	47 (13.6)	24 (10.6)	14 (6.3)	5 (2.3)	13 (2.0)
Control of school														
Public	149 (1.3)	149 (1.2)	51 (0.7)	8 (2.1)	7 (2.1)	24 (3.2)	61 (3.5)	13 (2.4)	10 (2.7)	26 (3.5)	51 (4.2)	17 (0.9)	5 (0.5)	18 (1.3)
Private	163 (2.8)	159 (5.2)	60 (1.3)	10 (6.0)	15 (6.9)	71 (8.8)	3 (†)	17 (8.2)	10 (6.1)	70 (10.2)	3 (0.9)	9 (1.9)	1 (0.4)	13 (2.1)
School location														
City	142 (2.0)	144 (2.1)	49 (1.2)	13 (4.0)	10 (3.8)	24 (5.7)	52 (5.6)	12 (2.6)	9 (3.5)	24 (4.9)	55 (5.4)	14 (1.0)	4 (0.6)	16 (1.3)
Suburban	155 (1.9)	155 (1.8)	54 (0.7)	3 (2.2)	7 (3.5)	32 (5.6)	57 (6.3)	10 (3.1)	10 (4.6)	33 (6.4)	46 (6.1)	14 (1.5)	6 (1.0)	16 (1.6)
Town	156 (3.5)	149 (2.8)	50 (1.2)	4 (1.0)	# (†)	18 (9.0)	78 (9.0)	16 (8.4)	# (†)	23 (9.2)	60 (10.5)	23 (3.0)	4 (1.3)	23 (3.4)
Rural	150 (2.6)	151 (3.0)	52 (1.5)	13 (5.0)	8 (4.8)	29 (5.7)	50 (7.7)	20 (7.3)	17 (6.8)	35 (7.8)	28 (6.7)	18 (2.5)	3 (1.0)	21 (3.4)
Region														
Northeast	154 (3.1)	160 (2.3)	52 (0.9)	10 (5.3)	13 (5.8)	40 (9.0)	37 (8.6)	5 (3.3)	5 (†)	50 (6.2)	39 (9.3)	16 (2.7)	6 (0.9)	17 (2.6)
Midwest	158 (2.9)	155 (2.3)	53 (1.3)	12 (6.6)	# (†)	25 (7.2)	63 (5.8)	9 (2.0)	15 (7.7)	26 (6.7)	50 (7.3)	22 (2.1)	6 (1.3)	24 (3.1)
South	147 (1.9)	147 (2.2)	51 (1.0)	6 (1.8)	10 (4.0)	25 (3.9)	59 (5.7)	19 (5.3)	9 (3.8)	26 (5.0)	46 (6.4)	16 (1.2)	4 (0.6)	16 (2.0)
West	144 (2.0)	143 (2.1)	51 (1.1)	8 (3.7)	8 (3.5)	24 (6.9)	60 (5.4)	15 (4.9)	9 (4.0)	25 (9.0)	51 (8.2)	9 (1.2)	3 (0.6)	12 (1.7)
Frequency of instruction														
Subject not offered	139 (6.3)	138 (4.2)	—	†	†	†	†	†	†	†	†	17 (4.0)	4 (1.5)	11 (2.1)
Less than once a week	149 (6.4)	154 (5.3)	—	†	†	†	†	†	†	†	†	11 (2.4)	4 (1.5)	10 (2.0)
Once or twice a week	152 (2.8)	154 (2.6)	—	†	†	†	†	†	†	†	†	12 (1.7)	3 (0.8)	17 (2.2)
At least 3 or 4 times a week	149 (1.8)	149 (1.8)	—	†	†	†	†	†	†	†	†	17 (1.4)	5 (0.7)	20 (1.6)

—Not available.
†Not applicable.
#Rounds to zero.

[1] Students were asked to analyze and describe aspects of music they heard, critique instrumental and vocal performances, and demonstrate their knowledge of standard musical notation and music's role in society.

[2] The visual arts assessment measured students' ability to respond to and create visual arts. Responding questions asked students to analyze and describe works of art and design, while creating questions required students to create works of art and design of their own.

NOTE: Excludes students unable to be tested due to limited proficiency in English or due to a disability (if the accommodations provided were not sufficient to enable the test to properly reflect the students' music or visual arts proficiency). Detail may not sum to totals because of rounding. Race categories exclude persons of Hispanic ethnicity. Totals include other racial/ethnic groups not shown separately.

SOURCE: U.S. Department of Education, National Center for Education Statistics, National Assessment of Educational Progress (NAEP), 2008 Arts Assessment, retrieved June 30, 2009, from the Main NAEP Data Explorer (http://nces.ed.gov/nationsreportcard/naepdata/). (This table was prepared June 2009.)

Average National Assessment of Educational Progress (NAEP) civics scale score and percentage of students attaining civics achievement levels, by grade level and selected student characteristics: 1998, 2006, and 2010

[Standard errors appear in parentheses]

Selected student characteristic	Average scale score[1]						Percent of students attaining achievement levels							
							At or above *Basic*[2]				At or above *Proficient*[3]		At *Advanced*[4]	
	1998		2006		2010		1998		2010		1998	2010	1998	2010
1	2		3		4		5		6		7	8	9	10
4th-graders	**150**	**(0.7)**	**154**	**(1.0)**	**157**	**(0.8)**	**69**	**(1.0)**	**77**	**(1.0)**	**23 (0.9)**	**27 (0.9)**	**2 (0.3)**	**2 (0.2)**
Sex														
Male	149	(1.0)	153	(1.1)	153	(1.0)	68	(1.2)	73	(1.3)	22 (1.2)	24 (1.0)	2 (0.4)	1 (0.3)
Female	151	(0.9)	155	(1.1)	160	(0.8)	70	(1.0)	81	(1.0)	23 (1.2)	30 (1.2)	1 (0.4)	2 (0.3)
Race/ethnicity														
White	158	(0.9)	164	(0.9)	167	(0.8)	78	(1.3)	87	(0.9)	29 (1.2)	37 (1.3)	2 (0.4)	2 (0.3)
Black	130	(1.1)	140	(1.5)	143	(1.2)	45	(1.7)	62	(2.2)	7 (1.1)	12 (1.1)	1 (0.3)	# (†)
Hispanic	123	(2.2)	138	(1.3)	140	(1.6)	40	(2.8)	58	(2.3)	6 (1.1)	10 (1.2)	# (†)	# (†)
Asian/Pacific Islander	147	(4.0)	154	(3.8)	164	(2.0)	66	(5.5)	82	(2.3)	20 (3.5)	37 (4.4)	2 (0.9)	3 (1.4)
American Indian/Alaska Native	‡	(†)	124	(7.6)	143	(7.0)	‡	(†)	63	(10.9)	‡ (†)	12 (7.4)	‡ (†)	# (†)
Free or reduced-price lunch eligibility														
Eligible	132	(0.9)	139	(1.1)	143	(0.9)	49	(1.3)	62	(1.3)	9 (0.9)	11 (0.9)	# (†)	# (†)
Not eligible	160	(1.1)	166	(0.8)	169	(0.8)	80	(1.4)	90	(0.9)	30 (1.3)	40 (1.4)	2 (0.5)	3 (0.4)
Unknown	154	(2.2)	167	(2.1)	171	(2.7)	72	(3.1)	89	(2.9)	27 (2.5)	44 (3.4)	2 (0.9)	5 (1.4)
8th-graders	**150**	**(0.7)**	**150**	**(0.8)**	**151**	**(0.8)**	**70**	**(0.9)**	**72**	**(1.0)**	**22 (0.8)**	**22 (0.8)**	**2 (0.2)**	**1 (0.1)**
Sex														
Male	148	(0.9)	149	(1.0)	150	(0.9)	67	(1.1)	70	(1.1)	22 (1.0)	22 (0.9)	2 (0.3)	1 (0.2)
Female	152	(0.8)	151	(0.8)	152	(0.8)	73	(1.2)	74	(1.1)	22 (1.1)	22 (0.9)	1 (0.3)	1 (0.2)
Race/ethnicity														
White	158	(0.9)	161	(0.8)	160	(0.8)	78	(1.1)	82	(1.0)	28 (1.0)	29 (1.0)	2 (0.3)	2 (0.2)
Black	131	(1.2)	133	(1.5)	135	(1.6)	49	(1.7)	53	(2.3)	7 (1.0)	9 (1.1)	# (†)	# (†)
Hispanic	127	(1.3)	131	(1.1)	137	(1.1)	44	(2.3)	56	(1.4)	7 (1.0)	11 (0.9)	# (†)	# (†)
Asian/Pacific Islander	151	(8.9)	154	(3.2)	158	(2.5)	69	(9.5)	78	(2.5)	25 (5.8)	30 (3.1)	3 (1.3)	2 (0.8)
American Indian/Alaska Native	‡	(†)	127	(7.3)	136	(12.6)	‡	(†)	56	(18.0)	‡ (†)	11 (6.0)	‡ (†)	1 (†)
Parents' highest level of education[5]														
Did not finish high school	123	(3.2)	129	(1.6)	134	(1.3)	40	(3.8)	52	(2.1)	4 (1.2)	6 (1.2)	# (†)	# (†)
Graduated high school	144	(1.2)	140	(1.3)	139	(1.1)	65	(2.0)	60	(1.8)	14 (1.4)	10 (0.7)	# (†)	# (†)
Some education after high school	143	(1.0)	153	(1.0)	155	(1.1)	64	(1.5)	78	(1.5)	15 (1.2)	22 (1.3)	1 (0.2)	1 (0.4)
Graduated college	160	(0.8)	162	(0.9)	162	(0.8)	80	(1.0)	83	(1.0)	32 (1.2)	32 (1.2)	3 (0.4)	2 (0.3)
Free or reduced-price lunch eligibility														
Eligible	131	(1.1)	132	(1.0)	136	(0.9)	48	(1.6)	54	(1.4)	8 (0.8)	9 (0.6)	# (0.2)	# (†)
Not eligible	157	(1.0)	160	(0.8)	163	(0.7)	78	(1.2)	85	(0.8)	27 (1.2)	31 (1.0)	2 (0.3)	2 (0.3)
Unknown	156	(2.2)	171	(2.4)	166	(2.3)	76	(2.7)	88	(2.5)	29 (2.1)	35 (3.5)	3 (0.6)	3 (0.9)
12th-graders	**150**	**(0.8)**	**151**	**(0.9)**	**148**	**(0.8)**	**65**	**(0.9)**	**64**	**(1.0)**	**26 (0.9)**	**24 (0.9)**	**4 (0.4)**	**4 (0.3)**
Sex														
Male	148	(1.1)	150	(1.1)	148	(0.9)	62	(1.2)	63	(1.0)	27 (1.2)	25 (0.9)	5 (0.6)	5 (0.5)
Female	152	(0.8)	152	(1.0)	148	(0.9)	68	(1.2)	64	(1.3)	26 (1.1)	22 (1.1)	3 (0.4)	3 (0.4)
Race/ethnicity														
White	157	(1.0)	158	(1.0)	156	(0.9)	73	(1.1)	73	(1.0)	32 (1.3)	30 (1.1)	5 (0.6)	5 (0.4)
Black	130	(1.6)	131	(1.4)	127	(1.6)	41	(2.0)	38	(1.9)	9 (1.3)	8 (0.9)	1 (0.3)	1 (0.2)
Hispanic	132	(1.1)	134	(1.1)	137	(1.4)	45	(1.9)	50	(1.8)	10 (1.2)	13 (1.4)	1 (0.3)	2 (0.4)
Asian/Pacific Islander	149	(5.2)	155	(3.1)	153	(2.6)	63	(4.8)	70	(3.1)	27 (6.6)	29 (2.8)	5 (2.3)	5 (1.4)
American Indian/Alaska Native	‡	(†)	131	(3.5)	134	(14.6)	‡	(†)	47	(17.3)	‡ (†)	16 (9.0)	‡ (†)	1 (†)
Parents' highest level of education[5]														
Did not finish high school	124	(2.1)	126	(1.8)	128	(1.4)	38	(2.6)	40	(2.3)	6 (1.6)	8 (1.2)	# (†)	# (†)
Graduated high school	140	(1.2)	138	(1.0)	137	(1.2)	54	(1.8)	51	(1.7)	14 (1.4)	13 (1.1)	# (†)	1 (0.4)
Some education after high school	145	(1.1)	150	(0.9)	147	(1.1)	60	(1.3)	63	(1.5)	20 (1.4)	20 (1.4)	2 (0.4)	3 (0.6)
Graduated college	160	(0.9)	162	(1.1)	158	(0.9)	75	(1.0)	75	(1.0)	36 (1.3)	33 (1.2)	7 (0.8)	6 (0.5)
Free or reduced-price lunch eligibility														
Eligible	130	(1.4)	133	(1.0)	132	(1.0)	42	(2.1)	44	(1.4)	10 (1.7)	11 (0.8)	1 (0.4)	1 (0.2)
Not eligible	153	(1.0)	156	(1.0)	155	(0.9)	69	(1.1)	72	(1.0)	29 (1.3)	29 (1.2)	5 (0.5)	5 (0.4)
Unknown	153	(1.3)	160	(2.4)	159	(3.3)	68	(1.6)	75	(3.3)	29 (1.5)	35 (3.7)	5 (0.7)	7 (1.6)

†Not applicable.
#Rounds to zero.
‡Reporting standards not met (too few cases for a reliable estimate).
[1]Scale ranges from 0 to 300 for all three grades, but scores cannot be compared across grades. For example, the average score of 167 for White 4th-graders in 2010 does not denote higher performance than the score of 160 for White 8th-graders.
[2]*Basic* denotes partial mastery of the knowledge and skills that are fundamental for proficient work at a given grade.
[3]*Proficient* represents solid academic performance. Students reaching this level have demonstrated competency over challenging subject matter.
[4]*Advanced* signifies superior performance for a given grade.

[5]These data are based on students' responses to questions about their parents' education level. Because the wording of the questions was different in 1998 than in the later assessment years, data from 1998 are not directly comparable to data from 2006 and 2010.
NOTE: Includes students tested with accommodations (1 to 13 percent of all students, depending on grade level and year); excludes only those students with disabilities and English language learners who were unable to be tested even with accommodations (1 to 5 percent of all students). Race categories exclude persons of Hispanic ethnicity.
SOURCE: U.S. Department of Education, National Center for Education Statistics, National Assessment of Educational Progress (NAEP), 1998, 2006, and 2010 Civics Assessments, retrieved May 25, 2011, from the Main NAEP Data Explorer (http://nces.ed.gov/nations reportcard/naepdata/). (This table was prepared May 2011.)

Average National Assessment of Educational Progress (NAEP) economics scale score of 12th-graders, percentage attaining economics achievement levels, and percentage with different levels of economics coursework, by selected characteristics: 2006 and 2012

[Standard errors appear in parentheses]

Selected characteristic	Average scale score[1]		At or above Basic[2]		At or above Proficient[3]		At Advanced[4]		No economics courses		Combined course		Consumer economics/ business		General economics		Advanced economics[5]	
1	2		3		4		5		6		7		8		9		10	
2006																		
All students	**150**	**(0.9)**	**79**	**(0.8)**	**42**	**(1.1)**	**3**	**(0.3)**	**13**	**(0.9)**	**12**	**(0.7)**	**11**	**(0.7)**	**49**	**(1.4)**	**16**	**(0.7)**
Sex																		
Male	152	(1.0)	79	(0.8)	45	(1.3)	4	(0.5)	13	(1.0)	10	(0.6)	10	(0.7)	50	(1.4)	16	(0.8)
Female	148	(0.9)	79	(0.9)	38	(1.3)	2	(0.3)	12	(0.9)	13	(0.9)	11	(0.8)	48	(1.6)	15	(0.8)
Race/ethnicity																		
White	158	(0.8)	87	(0.7)	51	(1.2)	4	(0.4)	15	(1.1)	12	(0.8)	11	(0.8)	49	(1.6)	13	(0.9)
Black	127	(1.2)	57	(1.9)	16	(1.3)	#	(†)	8	(0.8)	11	(0.9)	11	(1.2)	49	(1.7)	21	(1.1)
Hispanic	133	(1.2)	64	(1.6)	21	(1.2)	#	(†)	8	(1.7)	13	(1.1)	7	(0.9)	55	(2.6)	18	(1.2)
Asian/Pacific Islander	153	(3.5)	80	(4.0)	44	(4.5)	4	(1.4)	13	(1.8)	10	(1.8)	10	(1.4)	45	(4.1)	22	(1.9)
American Indian/Alaska Native	137	(4.1)	72	(5.6)	26	(4.8)	2	(†)	11	(3.9)	18	(2.7)	17	(3.2)	41	(4.9)	13	(3.1)
Parents' highest level of education																		
Not high school graduate	129	(1.4)	59	(2.1)	17	(1.7)	#	(†)	10	(1.7)	13	(1.4)	10	(1.4)	53	(3.2)	14	(1.3)
Graduated high school	138	(1.2)	69	(1.5)	27	(1.4)	1	(0.3)	11	(1.2)	12	(1.0)	12	(1.0)	52	(1.7)	13	(0.9)
Some college	150	(0.8)	82	(1.1)	39	(1.4)	1	(0.4)	11	(1.0)	13	(0.9)	12	(1.0)	51	(1.9)	14	(1.0)
Graduated college	160	(0.9)	87	(0.8)	54	(1.3)	5	(0.6)	14	(1.0)	11	(0.8)	10	(0.7)	47	(1.5)	17	(1.0)
Free or reduced-price lunch eligibility																		
Eligible	132	(0.9)	62	(1.1)	20	(1.1)	1	(0.2)	9	(0.7)	13	(1.1)	10	(0.9)	50	(1.6)	18	(0.8)
Not eligible	155	(0.9)	84	(0.8)	48	(1.2)	4	(0.4)	13	(1.1)	12	(0.8)	12	(0.9)	48	(1.6)	16	(0.9)
Unknown	157	(1.9)	86	(1.7)	50	(2.8)	4	(1.1)	16	(3.0)	12	(1.6)	7	(1.1)	54	(3.1)	11	(1.4)
Region																		
Northeast	153	(2.0)	81	(1.7)	46	(2.6)	4	(0.9)	26	(2.6)	7	(1.1)	11	(1.3)	43	(3.2)	13	(1.4)
Midwest	153	(1.5)	83	(1.4)	45	(2.0)	3	(0.6)	12	(2.2)	12	(1.6)	15	(1.5)	51	(2.6)	10	(1.0)
South	147	(1.4)	77	(1.4)	37	(1.7)	2	(0.5)	6	(1.1)	14	(1.2)	9	(1.3)	49	(2.0)	22	(1.5)
West	‡	(†)	‡	(†)	‡	(†)	‡	(†)	‡	(†)	‡	(†)	‡	(†)	‡	(†)	‡	(†)
2012																		
All students	**152**	**(0.8)**	**82**	**(0.8)**	**42**	**(1.1)**	**3**	**(0.3)**	**9**	**(1.0)**	**9**	**(0.8)**	**10**	**(1.2)**	**54**	**(2.0)**	**18**	**(0.9)**
Sex																		
Male	155	(0.9)	83	(1.0)	47	(1.3)	4	(0.4)	8	(0.9)	9	(0.8)	10	(1.2)	54	(2.0)	18	(1.0)
Female	149	(0.9)	80	(1.0)	37	(1.3)	2	(0.2)	10	(1.2)	9	(0.9)	10	(1.3)	53	(2.2)	18	(1.1)
Race/ethnicity																		
White	160	(1.0)	89	(0.9)	53	(1.6)	4	(0.4)	10	(1.4)	9	(1.0)	11	(1.6)	54	(2.4)	15	(1.1)
Black	131	(1.4)	61	(2.1)	16	(1.3)	1	(0.2)	6	(1.2)	8	(1.1)	9	(1.2)	54	(2.9)	23	(1.4)
Hispanic	138	(1.4)	71	(2.0)	25	(1.4)	1	(0.3)	5	(1.1)	9	(1.0)	7	(1.2)	57	(2.9)	21	(2.0)
Asian	160	(1.9)	86	(1.9)	53	(2.4)	6	(1.3)	10	(1.5)	9	(1.2)	7	(1.2)	45	(2.7)	29	(2.6)
Pacific Islander	‡	(†)	‡	(†)	‡	(†)	‡	(†)	‡	(†)	‡	(†)	‡	(†)	‡	(†)	‡	(†)
American Indian/Alaska Native	136	(4.7)	72	(7.8)	20	(5.6)	2	(†)	4	(2.7)	7	(2.9)	19	(9.9)	54	(8.0)	16	(4.6)
Two or more races	154	(3.4)	87	(3.0)	42	(5.2)	3	(1.8)	10	(2.9)	6	(1.4)	7	(1.8)	57	(4.5)	20	(2.8)
Parents' highest level of education																		
Not high school graduate	134	(1.5)	66	(2.1)	21	(1.9)	#	(†)	4	(0.7)	10	(1.3)	10	(1.4)	59	(2.4)	17	(1.5)
Graduated high school	139	(1.1)	71	(1.7)	27	(1.6)	1	(0.2)	7	(1.2)	9	(1.1)	11	(1.2)	56	(2.3)	16	(1.0)
Some college	150	(0.8)	84	(1.0)	38	(1.2)	1	(0.3)	8	(1.2)	9	(0.9)	10	(1.5)	56	(2.3)	16	(1.6)
Graduated college	161	(0.9)	89	(1.0)	55	(1.4)	5	(0.5)	10	(1.4)	9	(1.0)	10	(1.3)	51	(2.3)	20	(1.2)
Free or reduced-price lunch eligibility																		
Eligible	138	(0.9)	70	(1.3)	25	(1.1)	#	(†)	7	(0.9)	9	(0.7)	10	(1.2)	57	(2.1)	18	(1.3)
Not eligible	159	(0.9)	88	(0.8)	52	(1.4)	4	(0.4)	10	(1.3)	9	(1.1)	11	(1.4)	51	(2.3)	19	(1.1)
Unknown	164	(3.3)	90	(2.3)	59	(4.2)	5	(1.4)	13	(4.7)	8	(1.8)	6	(1.6)	58	(5.0)	15	(1.9)
School location																		
City	147	(1.8)	77	(1.9)	37	(2.3)	3	(0.5)	8	(1.5)	9	(1.3)	8	(1.4)	54	(3.3)	22	(1.8)
Suburb	156	(0.9)	85	(1.0)	48	(1.1)	4	(0.4)	12	(1.8)	10	(1.1)	11	(1.6)	50	(2.1)	17	(1.5)
Town	149	(2.7)	81	(2.4)	39	(3.8)	2	(0.6)	9	(2.8)	8	(1.2)	10	(2.4)	57	(3.5)	16	(3.8)
Rural	152	(1.5)	83	(1.5)	42	(2.5)	2	(0.6)	5	(1.2)	9	(1.4)	12	(2.8)	57	(4.0)	17	(2.1)
Region																		
Northeast	154	(1.7)	84	(1.8)	46	(2.0)	3	(0.7)	27	(4.0)	9	(1.9)	11	(1.4)	39	(5.5)	14	(2.2)
Midwest	157	(1.6)	86	(1.1)	50	(2.2)	4	(0.7)	5	(1.2)	9	(2.3)	18	(3.4)	57	(4.3)	11	(1.0)
South	149	(1.8)	79	(1.7)	38	(2.7)	2	(0.5)	3	(1.5)	8	(1.2)	5	(0.9)	55	(3.6)	29	(2.0)
West	148	(1.1)	79	(1.4)	40	(1.5)	2	(0.3)	7	(1.2)	11	(1.1)	9	(3.1)	60	(3.0)	13	(1.0)

†Not applicable.

#Rounds to zero.

‡Reporting standards not met. Either there are too few cases for a reliable estimate or item response rates fell below the required standards for reporting.

[1]Scale ranges from 0 to 300.

[2]Basic denotes partial mastery of the knowledge and skills that are fundamental for proficient work at a given grade.

[3]Proficient represents solid academic performance. Students reaching this level have demonstrated competency over challenging subject matter.

[4]Advanced signifies superior performance for a given grade.

[5]Advanced economics includes Advanced Placement, International Baccalaureate, and honors courses.

NOTE: Includes public and private schools. Includes students tested with accommodations; excludes only those students with disabilities and English language learners who were unable to be tested even with accommodations (3 percent of all students in both assessment years). Detail may not sum to totals because of rounding. Race categories exclude persons of Hispanic ethnicity. Totals include other racial/ethnic groups not shown separately.

SOURCE: U.S. Department of Education, National Center for Education Statistics, National Assessment of Educational Progress (NAEP), 2006 and 2012 Economics Assessment, retrieved May 08, 2013, from the NAEP Data Explorer (http://nces.ed.gov/nationsreportcard/naepdata/). (This table was prepared May 2013.)

Average National Assessment of Educational Progress (NAEP) geography scale score, standard deviation, and percentage of students attaining geography achievement levels, by grade level, selected student characteristics, and percentile: 1994, 2001, and 2010

[Standard errors appear in parentheses]

Selected student characteristic	4th-graders						8th-graders						12th-graders					
	1994[1]		2001		2010		1994[1]		2001		2010		1994[1]		2001		2010	
1	2		3		4		5		6		7		8		9		10	
	Average geography scale score[2]																	
All students	206	(1.2)	208	(0.9)	213	(0.8)	260	(0.7)	260	(1.0)	261	(0.7)	285	(0.7)	284	(0.8)	282	(0.6)
Sex																		
Male................	208	(1.4)	210	(1.0)	215	(0.9)	262	(0.9)	262	(1.2)	263	(0.8)	288	(0.8)	287	(1.0)	285	(0.6)
Female................	203	(1.4)	206	(1.3)	211	(0.9)	258	(0.8)	258	(1.0)	259	(0.8)	281	(0.9)	281	(0.8)	280	(0.8)
Race/ethnicity																		
White................	218	(1.5)	219	(1.1)	224	(0.9)	269	(0.8)	269	(1.4)	272	(0.6)	290	(0.8)	291	(0.8)	290	(0.5)
Black................	166	(2.4)	180	(1.8)	192	(1.3)	229	(1.7)	233	(1.6)	241	(1.1)	258	(1.4)	258	(1.5)	261	(1.2)
Hispanic................	177	(3.3)	185	(2.5)	197	(1.2)	238	(2.0)	237	(2.0)	244	(1.0)	269	(1.7)	268	(1.6)	270	(1.2)
Asian/Pacific Islander................	211	(4.0)	214	(3.5)	224	(3.3)	262	(5.3)	264	(2.7)	268	(2.7)	283	(3.1)	284	(5.0)	285	(1.7)
American Indian/Alaska Native	‡	(†)	‡	(†)	201	(3.5)	251	(5.5)	261	(5.3)	250	(3.9)	‡	(†)	‡	(†)	277	(2.5)
Parents' highest level of education																		
Did not finish high school................	—	(†)	—	(†)	—	(†)	238	(1.7)	236	(1.8)	243	(1.3)	263	(1.2)	266	(1.7)	263	(1.2)
Graduated high school................	—	(†)	—	(†)	—	(†)	250	(1.2)	251	(1.2)	251	(1.1)	274	(1.1)	275	(0.9)	274	(0.8)
Some education after high school	—	(†)	—	(†)	—	(†)	265	(1.0)	264	(1.1)	262	(1.0)	286	(1.0)	284	(0.9)	280	(0.7)
Graduated college	—	(†)	—	(†)	—	(†)	272	(1.0)	273	(1.0)	272	(0.7)	294	(0.9)	293	(1.0)	291	(0.7)
Eligibility for free or reduced-price lunch																		
Eligible	—	(†)	185	(1.4)	197	(0.7)	—	(†)	239	(1.3)	246	(0.9)	—	(†)	268	(1.7)	269	(0.8)
Not eligible................	—	(†)	221	(1.1)	227	(0.8)	—	(†)	269	(1.2)	272	(0.7)	—	(†)	287	(1.0)	288	(0.5)
Unknown................	—	(†)	219	(2.8)	227	(3.7)	—	(†)	265	(2.3)	276	(2.6)	—	(†)	288	(1.6)	289	(2.2)
Percentile[3]																		
10th................	146	(1.9)	159	(2.6)	169	(1.8)	213	(1.3)	213	(1.2)	220	(1.2)	244	(0.9)	246	(1.1)	247	(0.8)
25th................	179	(1.5)	184	(1.4)	192	(1.2)	237	(1.0)	238	(1.3)	241	(0.7)	265	(1.1)	266	(1.2)	265	(0.8)
50th................	211	(1.1)	211	(1.0)	216	(1.1)	263	(1.1)	264	(1.2)	263	(0.9)	287	(0.9)	286	(0.9)	284	(0.7)
75th................	237	(1.3)	235	(1.4)	236	(0.7)	285	(0.9)	285	(1.1)	284	(0.9)	306	(1.0)	304	(0.9)	301	(0.7)
90th................	257	(2.0)	254	(1.3)	253	(0.9)	302	(1.9)	302	(1.1)	300	(0.7)	321	(1.0)	319	(1.3)	315	(0.7)
	Standard deviation of the geography scale score[4]																	
All students	44	(0.8)	37	(0.8)	33	(0.4)	35	(0.4)	35	(0.5)	31	(0.3)	30	(0.4)	28	(0.4)	26	(0.3)
	Percent of students achieving geography achievement levels																	
Achievement level																		
Below *Basic*	30	(1.1)	27	(1.0)	21	(0.9)	29	(1.0)	28	(1.2)	26	(0.9)	30	(0.9)	29	(1.0)	30	(0.9)
At or above *Basic*[5]	70	(1.1)	73	(1.0)	79	(0.9)	71	(1.0)	72	(1.2)	74	(0.9)	70	(0.9)	71	(1.0)	70	(0.9)
At or above *Basic* by sex																		
Male	71	(1.3)	74	(0.9)	80	(1.0)	72	(1.3)	73	(1.5)	75	(1.0)	73	(1.1)	74	(1.3)	73	(1.0)
Female	68	(1.4)	71	(1.5)	78	(1.1)	69	(1.1)	71	(1.1)	73	(1.1)	67	(1.2)	68	(1.2)	66	(1.2)
At or above *Basic* by race/ethnicity																		
White	81	(1.3)	84	(1.1)	89	(1.0)	81	(0.9)	82	(1.5)	86	(0.7)	78	(0.9)	81	(0.9)	81	(0.8)
Black................	33	(2.4)	43	(2.5)	57	(2.1)	34	(3.0)	39	(2.4)	49	(1.7)	33	(2.3)	33	(2.0)	36	(1.8)
Hispanic................	44	(3.1)	50	(3.1)	64	(1.7)	49	(3.8)	45	(2.5)	55	(1.5)	48	(3.0)	48	(2.9)	52	(2.0)
Asian/Pacific Islander	72	(4.4)	77	(4.2)	87	(3.2)	72	(6.7)	77	(3.6)	80	(3.3)	67	(3.8)	70	(6.2)	73	(2.7)
American Indian/Alaska Native	‡	(†)	‡	(†)	68	(6.4)	62	(7.7)	74	(4.8)	62	(7.2)	‡	(†)	‡	(†)	62	(5.1)
At or above *Proficient*[6]................	22	(1.2)	20	(0.9)	21	(0.8)	28	(1.0)	29	(1.3)	27	(0.8)	27	(1.2)	24	(1.2)	20	(0.8)
At *Advanced*[7]................	3	(0.4)	2	(0.3)	2	(0.2)	4	(0.4)	4	(0.5)	3	(0.2)	2	(0.5)	1	(0.3)	1	(0.1)

—Not available.
†Not applicable.
‡Reporting standards not met (too few cases for a reliable estimate).
[1]Accommodations were not permitted for this assessment.
[2]Scale ranges from 0 to 500.
[3]The percentile represents a specific point on the percentage distribution of all students ranked by their geography score from low to high. For example, 10 percent of students scored at or below the 10th percentile score, while 90 percent of students scored above it.
[4]The standard deviation provides an indication of how much the test scores varied. The lower the standard deviation, the closer the scores were clustered around the average score. About two-thirds of the student scores can be expected to fall within the range of one standard deviation above and one standard deviation below the average score. For example, the average score for all 4th-graders in 2010 was 213, and the standard deviation was 33. This means that we would expect about two-thirds of the students to have scores between 246 (one standard deviation above the average) and 180 (one standard deviation below). Standard errors also must be taken into account when making comparisons of these ranges. For a discussion of standard errors, see Appendix A: Guide to Sources.
[5]*Basic* denotes partial mastery of the knowledge and skills that are fundamental for proficient work.
[6]*Proficient* represents solid academic performance. Students reaching this level have demonstrated competency over challenging subject matter.
[7]*Advanced* signifies superior performance.
NOTE: For 2001 and later years, includes students tested with accommodations (3 to 13 percent of all students, depending on grade level and year); excludes only those students with disabilities and English language learners who were unable to be tested even with accommodations (1 to 4 percent of all students). Race categories exclude persons of Hispanic ethnicity. Detail may not sum to totals because of rounding.
SOURCE: U.S. Department of Education, National Center for Education Statistics, National Assessment of Educational Progress (NAEP), 1994, 2001, and 2010 Geography Assessments, retrieved July 22, 2011, from the Main NAEP Data Explorer (http://nces.ed.gov/nationreportcard/naepdata/). (This table was prepared July 2011.)

Average National Assessment of Educational Progress (NAEP) U.S. history scale score, standard deviation, and percentage of students attaining achievement levels, by grade level, selected characteristics, and percentile: Selected years, 1994 through 2010

[Standard errors appear in parentheses]

Selected characteristic	4th-graders 1994[1]	4th 2001	4th 2006	4th 2010	8th-graders 1994[1]	8th 2001	8th 2006	8th 2010	12th-graders 1994[1]	12th 2001	12th 2006	12th 2010
1	2	3	4	5	6	7	8	9	10	11	12	13
Average U.S. history scale score[2]												
All students	205 (1.0)	208 (0.9)	211 (1.1)	214 (0.8)	259 (0.6)	260 (0.8)	263 (0.8)	266 (0.8)	286 (0.8)	287 (0.9)	290 (0.7)	288 (0.8)
Sex												
Male	203 (1.5)	207 (1.1)	211 (1.2)	215 (1.0)	259 (0.8)	261 (0.9)	264 (0.9)	268 (0.8)	288 (0.8)	288 (1.1)	292 (0.9)	290 (0.8)
Female	206 (1.1)	209 (1.2)	211 (1.1)	213 (0.9)	259 (0.7)	260 (0.9)	261 (0.8)	263 (0.8)	285 (0.9)	286 (0.9)	288 (0.8)	286 (1.0)
Race/ethnicity												
White	214 (1.3)	217 (1.3)	223 (1.1)	224 (1.1)	266 (0.8)	268 (0.9)	273 (0.6)	274 (0.7)	292 (0.8)	292 (1.0)	297 (0.8)	296 (0.7)
Black	176 (1.6)	186 (2.0)	191 (1.9)	198 (1.9)	238 (1.6)	244 (1.9)	244 (1.2)	250 (1.1)	265 (1.5)	267 (1.4)	270 (1.1)	268 (1.5)
Hispanic	175 (2.6)	184 (2.6)	194 (1.9)	198 (1.2)	243 (1.4)	240 (2.0)	248 (1.2)	252 (1.0)	267 (1.7)	271 (1.9)	275 (1.0)	275 (1.5)
Asian/Pacific Islander	204 (3.6)	216 (3.7)	214 (5.1)	221 (2.4)	261 (5.0)	264 (2.8)	270 (3.0)	275 (1.8)	283 (3.5)	294 (6.0)	296 (2.6)	293 (2.5)
American Indian/Alaska Native	‡ (†)	‡ (†)	190 (5.9)	193 (6.2)	245 (3.4)	255 (4.4)	244 (6.3)	259 (5.0)	272 (3.0)	283 (4.2)	278 (4.1)	278 (4.2)
Parents' highest level of education[3]												
Did not finish high school	—	—	—	—	241 (1.3)	241 (2.8)	244 (0.9)	249 (0.9)	263 (1.4)	266 (1.6)	268 (1.3)	268 (1.7)
Graduated high school	—	—	—	—	251 (0.8)	251 (1.0)	252 (1.3)	255 (0.9)	276 (0.8)	274 (1.1)	278 (1.0)	277 (1.0)
Some education after high school	—	—	—	—	264 (0.8)	264 (1.0)	265 (0.9)	267 (0.9)	287 (1.2)	286 (0.8)	290 (1.0)	286 (1.0)
Graduated college	—	—	—	—	270 (0.8)	273 (0.9)	274 (0.8)	276 (0.8)	296 (0.9)	298 (1.2)	300 (0.8)	298 (0.8)
Eligibility for free or reduced-price lunch												
Eligible	— (†)	188 (1.4)	195 (1.1)	199 (0.9)	— (†)	242 (1.3)	247 (1.1)	253 (0.7)	— (†)	269 (1.4)	273 (1.0)	273 (1.0)
Not eligible	— (†)	219 (1.4)	224 (1.0)	227 (0.8)	— (†)	267 (1.1)	273 (0.7)	275 (0.8)	— (†)	289 (1.2)	295 (0.8)	294 (0.7)
Unknown	— (†)	217 (2.8)	227 (3.9)	225 (6.1)	— (†)	266 (2.0)	281 (2.7)	278 (2.0)	— (†)	294 (2.1)	300 (2.4)	300 (2.5)
Percentile[3]												
10th	147 (2.1)	157 (1.4)	165 (2.3)	169 (1.4)	217 (1.1)	216 (1.3)	221 (1.4)	227 (1.2)	244 (1.2)	244 (1.2)	249 (1.3)	246 (1.3)
25th	180 (1.5)	184 (1.4)	189 (1.3)	192 (1.6)	239 (0.9)	239 (1.1)	243 (0.9)	246 (0.9)	265 (1.5)	266 (1.1)	270 (1.0)	267 (1.3)
50th	210 (0.9)	211 (1.1)	213 (1.0)	216 (0.6)	261 (1.1)	261 (1.0)	265 (0.7)	267 (0.7)	288 (0.9)	288 (1.1)	291 (0.7)	286 (0.7)
75th	234 (1.2)	234 (1.0)	235 (1.0)	238 (0.9)	282 (0.7)	284 (1.0)	285 (0.7)	286 (0.7)	309 (0.9)	309 (1.0)	312 (0.7)	311 (0.6)
90th	253 (1.4)	254 (1.4)	254 (1.1)	256 (1.4)	299 (0.6)	302 (1.0)	302 (1.0)	302 (1.1)	326 (1.0)	326 (1.5)	329 (0.9)	328 (1.0)
Standard deviation of the U.S. history scale score[4]												
All students	41 (0.7)	38 (0.7)	34 (0.5)	34 (0.7)	32 (0.3)	33 (0.4)	32 (0.4)	29 (0.3)	32 (0.6)	32 (0.4)	31 (0.3)	32 (0.4)
Percent of students achieving U.S. history achievement levels												
Achievement level												
Below Basic	36 (1.1)	34 (1.2)	30 (1.3)	27 (0.8)	39 (0.9)	38 (1.0)	35 (1.0)	31 (1.0)	57 (1.2)	57 (1.2)	53 (1.1)	55 (1.0)
At or above Basic[5]	64 (1.1)	66 (1.2)	70 (1.3)	73 (0.8)	61 (0.9)	62 (1.0)	65 (1.0)	69 (1.0)	43 (1.2)	43 (1.2)	47 (1.1)	45 (1.0)
At or above Basic by race/ethnicity												
White	73 (1.3)	76 (1.5)	84 (1.1)	83 (1.0)	70 (1.1)	71 (1.1)	79 (0.8)	80 (0.9)	49 (1.3)	49 (1.5)	56 (1.3)	55 (1.2)
Black	35 (1.5)	41 (2.3)	46 (2.5)	54 (2.6)	32 (2.4)	35 (2.1)	40 (1.7)	48 (2.1)	19 (1.5)	19 (1.5)	20 (1.6)	20 (2.1)
Hispanic	36 (3.2)	40 (2.8)	49 (2.7)	56 (1.6)	41 (2.2)	36 (2.6)	46 (2.2)	52 (1.7)	24 (2.3)	24 (2.3)	27 (1.4)	28 (1.4)
Asian/Pacific Islander	62 (4.3)	74 (4.5)	71 (7.7)	82 (3.1)	60 (6.9)	65 (3.0)	75 (4.4)	78 (2.1)	51 (6.7)	51 (6.7)	54 (3.5)	50 (3.2)
American Indian/Alaska Native	‡ (†)	‡ (†)	41 (7.7)	49 (5.4)	42 (6.2)	43 (6.5)	43 (6.1)	61 (6.3)	37 (7.8)	37 (7.8)	32 (7.3)	29 (5.9)
At or above Proficient[6]	17 (1.0)	18 (0.9)	18 (1.0)	20 (0.7)	14 (0.6)	16 (0.7)	17 (0.8)	17 (0.8)	11 (0.9)	11 (0.9)	13 (0.7)	12 (0.5)
At Advanced[7]	2 (0.3)	2 (0.3)	2 (0.3)	2 (0.3)	1 (0.1)	1 (0.1)	1 (0.1)	1 (0.1)	1 (0.3)	1 (0.3)	1 (0.2)	1 (0.1)

—Not available.
†Not applicable.
‡Reporting standards not met (too few cases for a reliable estimate).
[1]Accommodations were not permitted for this assessment.
[2]Scale ranges from 0 to 500.
[3]The percentile represents a specific point on the percentage distribution of all students ranked by their U.S. history score from low to high. For example, 10 percent of students scored at or below the 10th percentile score, while 90 percent of students scored above it.
[4]The standard deviation provides an indication of how much the test scores varied. The lower the standard deviation, the closer the scores were clustered around the average score. About two-thirds of the student scores can be expected to fall within the range of one standard deviation above and one standard deviation below the average score. For example, the average score for all 4th-graders in 2010 was 214, and the standard deviation was 34. This means that we would expect about two-thirds of the students to have scores between 248 (one standard deviation above the average) and 180 (one standard deviation below). Stan-

dard errors also must be taken into account when making comparisons of these ranges. For a discussion of standard errors, see Appendix A: Guide to Sources.
[5]Basic denotes partial mastery of the knowledge and skills that are fundamental for proficient work.
[6]Proficient represents solid academic performance. Students reaching this level have demonstrated competency over challenging subject matter.
[7]Advanced signifies superior performance.

NOTE: For 2001 and later years, includes students tested with accommodations (3 to 13 percent of all students, depending on grade level and year); excludes only those students with disabilities and English language learners who were unable to be tested even with accommodations (2 to 3 percent of all students). Race categories exclude persons of Hispanic ethnicity.
SOURCE: U.S. Department of Education, National Center for Education Statistics, National Assessment of Educational Progress (NAEP), 1994, 2001, 2006, and 2010 U.S. History Assessments, retrieved June 27, 2010, from the Main NAEP Data Explorer (http://nces.ed.gov/nationsreportcard/naepdata/). (This table was prepared June 2011.)

Average National Assessment of Educational Progress (NAEP) writing scale score of 8th- and 12th-graders, standard deviation, and percentage of students attaining writing achievement levels, by selected student and school characteristics and percentile: 2011

[Standard errors appear in parentheses]

Selected student or school characteristic	8th-graders								12th-graders							
	Total, all students		Eligibility for free or reduced-price lunch						Total, all students		Eligibility for free or reduced-price lunch					
			Eligible		Not eligible		Unknown				Eligible		Not eligible		Unknown	
1	2		3		4		5		6		7		8		9	
Average writing scale score[1]																
All students	150	(0.7)	134	(0.6)	161	(0.8)	163	(2.2)	150	(0.5)	133	(0.7)	157	(0.6)	167	(1.7)
Sex																
Male	140	(0.7)	125	(0.7)	151	(0.9)	154	(2.6)	143	(0.6)	126	(0.8)	150	(0.6)	162	(1.9)
Female	160	(0.7)	144	(0.6)	171	(0.8)	171	(2.5)	157	(0.6)	140	(0.7)	165	(0.6)	173	(1.9)
Race/ethnicity																
White	158	(0.8)	142	(0.8)	163	(0.9)	166	(2.3)	159	(0.7)	144	(1.0)	161	(0.7)	172	(1.6)
Black	132	(1.1)	127	(1.1)	145	(1.4)	140	(4.6)	130	(1.0)	124	(1.1)	140	(1.2)	148	(3.6)
Hispanic	136	(0.7)	130	(0.8)	150	(1.0)	150	(5.4)	134	(0.7)	128	(0.8)	142	(1.0)	149	(3.6)
Asian/Pacific Islander	163	(2.4)	146	(2.8)	171	(2.4)	175	(4.0)	158	(1.6)	146	(2.3)	163	(2.0)	162	(4.9)
Asian	165	(2.0)	148	(2.7)	172	(2.2)	175	(4.0)	158	(1.5)	146	(2.5)	164	(1.7)	162	(5.0)
Native Hawaiian/Pacific Islander	141	(6.3)	‡	(†)	‡	(†)	‡	(†)	144	(6.0)	‡	(†)	‡	(†)	‡	(†)
American Indian/Alaska Native	145	(4.0)	139	(4.3)	‡	(†)	‡	(†)	145	(3.5)	135	(4.4)	153	(4.4)	‡	(†)
Two or more races	155	(1.9)	141	(2.3)	165	(2.5)	‡	(†)	158	(2.3)	137	(4.2)	163	(2.8)	‡	(†)
Parents' highest level of education																
Did not finish high school	133	(1.0)	131	(1.0)	142	(2.0)	‡	(†)	129	(0.9)	127	(1.0)	135	(1.6)	‡	(†)
Graduated high school	138	(0.8)	131	(0.8)	149	(1.3)	146	(4.4)	138	(0.7)	131	(1.0)	145	(0.9)	153	(3.5)
Some education after high school	150	(0.9)	143	(0.9)	158	(1.2)	155	(3.8)	149	(0.5)	140	(0.9)	155	(0.6)	158	(2.2)
Graduated college	160	(0.8)	141	(0.8)	166	(0.9)	167	(2.3)	160	(0.7)	139	(1.1)	164	(0.7)	173	(1.5)
Student's attitude and experience																
Agreed or strongly agreed that "Writing is one of my favorite activities"	157	(0.8)	141	(0.8)	170	(0.9)	172	(2.5)	157	(0.6)	139	(0.8)	165	(0.6)	175	(2.0)
Uses a computer for writing school assignments once or twice a week	157	(0.9)	140	(0.7)	168	(1.2)	169	(2.9)	154	(0.6)	136	(0.8)	161	(0.7)	167	(1.4)
School locale																
City	144	(1.2)	130	(1.0)	160	(1.4)	164	(4.3)	146	(1.0)	131	(0.8)	156	(1.2)	168	(2.5)
Suburban	155	(1.3)	137	(1.0)	165	(1.3)	164	(4.4)	154	(0.9)	135	(1.1)	160	(0.9)	167	(2.1)
Town	148	(1.1)	137	(1.3)	156	(1.3)	157	(3.8)	149	(2.0)	134	(3.1)	156	(1.8)	‡	(†)
Rural	150	(1.4)	137	(1.5)	158	(1.3)	158	(5.3)	149	(1.1)	135	(1.5)	154	(1.0)	164	(5.4)
Percentile[2]																
10th	104	(1.0)	92	(1.1)	119	(1.1)	121	(3.8)	104	(0.9)	90	(0.9)	114	(1.1)	126	(4.6)
25th	127	(0.8)	113	(0.6)	140	(1.0)	142	(2.6)	127	(0.8)	111	(0.9)	136	(0.8)	149	(2.3)
50th	151	(0.8)	135	(0.6)	163	(0.9)	163	(2.6)	152	(0.7)	135	(1.1)	159	(0.8)	170	(2.2)
75th	175	(0.7)	157	(0.8)	184	(1.1)	185	(2.6)	175	(0.6)	156	(0.6)	180	(0.5)	189	(1.7)
90th	194	(0.9)	176	(0.9)	201	(1.4)	203	(3.5)	194	(0.7)	176	(0.8)	198	(0.8)	205	(3.2)
Standard deviation of the writing scale score[3]																
All students	35	(0.3)	33	(0.3)	32	(0.3)	32	(1.1)	35	(0.3)	33	(0.3)	33	(0.3)	31	(0.9)
Percent of students attaining writing achievement levels																
Achievement level																
Below *Basic*[4]	20	(0.6)	32	(0.8)	10	(0.6)	10	(1.6)	21	(0.6)	36	(0.9)	14	(0.5)	9	(1.3)
At or above *Basic*	80	(0.6)	68	(0.8)	90	(0.6)	90	(1.6)	79	(0.6)	64	(0.9)	86	(0.5)	91	(1.3)
At or above *Basic* by race/ethnicity																
White	87	(0.6)	76	(1.1)	91	(0.6)	94	(1.6)	87	(0.6)	76	(1.2)	88	(0.6)	95	(1.1)
Black	65	(1.7)	59	(1.7)	79	(2.1)	74	(6.4)	61	(1.5)	54	(1.7)	71	(1.9)	82	(3.9)
Hispanic	69	(0.9)	63	(1.1)	82	(1.2)	80	(5.4)	65	(0.9)	59	(1.1)	74	(1.4)	79	(4.7)
Asian/Pacific Islander	88	(2.3)	76	(3.4)	93	(1.8)	96	(2.1)	85	(1.4)	78	(2.7)	89	(1.4)	83	(4.4)
Asian	89	(1.9)	79	(3.0)	94	(1.7)	95	(2.2)	85	(1.4)	78	(2.9)	89	(1.3)	83	(4.4)
Native Hawaiian/Pacific Islander	70	(7.3)	‡	(†)	‡	(†)	‡	(†)	78	(5.0)	‡	(†)	‡	(†)	‡	(†)
American Indian/Alaska Native	78	(4.7)	74	(6.6)	‡	(†)	‡	(†)	76	(4.3)	66	(7.2)	84	(5.0)	‡	(†)
Two or more races	87	(1.7)	79	(3.9)	92	(1.9)	‡	(†)	86	(2.7)	70	(7.1)	90	(3.1)	‡	(†)
At or above *Proficient*[5]	27	(0.7)	12	(0.4)	37	(1.0)	39	(2.9)	27	(0.6)	12	(0.5)	33	(0.7)	46	(2.3)
At *Advanced*[6]	3	(0.2)	1	(0.1)	5	(0.4)	5	(1.2)	3	(0.2)	1	(0.1)	4	(0.3)	7	(1.2)

†Not applicable.

‡Reporting standards not met (too few cases for a reliable estimate).

[1]Scale ranges from 0 to 300.

[2]The percentile represents a specific point on the percentage distribution of all students ranked by their writing score from low to high. For example, 10 percent of students scored at or below the 10th percentile score, while 90 percent of students scored above it.

[3]The standard deviation provides an indication of how much the test scores varied. The lower the standard deviation, the closer the scores were clustered around the average score. About two-thirds of the student scores can be expected to fall within the range of one standard deviation above and one standard deviation below the average score. For example, the average score for all 12th-graders was 150 and the standard deviation was 35. This means that we would expect about two-thirds of the students to have scores between 185 (one standard deviation above the average) and 115 (one standard deviation below). Standard errors also must be taken into account when making comparisons of these ranges.

[4]*Basic* denotes partial mastery of the knowledge and skills that are fundamental for proficient work.

[5]*Proficient* represents solid academic performance. Students reaching this level have demonstrated competency over challenging subject matter.

[6]*Advanced* signifies superior performance.

NOTE: Writing scores from 2011 cannot be compared with writing scores from earlier assessment years. The 2011 writing assessment was developed under a new framework and is NAEP's first computer-based writing assessment. Includes public and private schools. Includes students tested with accommodations (8 percent of all 8th-graders and 7 percent of all 12th-graders); excludes only those students with disabilities and English language learners who were unable to be tested even with accommodations (2 percent of all students at both grades). Race categories exclude persons of Hispanic ethnicity. Detail may not sum to totals because of rounding.

SOURCE: U.S. Department of Education, National Center for Education Statistics, National Assessment of Educational Progress (NAEP), 2011 Writing Assessment, retrieved October 1, 2012, from the Main NAEP Data Explorer (http://nces.ed.gov/nationsreportcard/naepdata/). (This table was prepared October 2012.)

Enrollment in public elementary and secondary schools, by level and grade: Selected years, fall 1980 through fall 2023

[In thousands]

Year	All grades	Elementary													Secondary					
		Total	Pre-kinder-garten	Kinder-garten	1st grade	2nd grade	3rd grade	4th grade	5th grade	6th grade	7th grade	8th grade	Un-graded	Total	9th grade	10th grade	11th grade	12th grade	Un-graded
1	2	3	4	5	6	7	8	9	10	11	12	13	14	15	16	17	18	19	20
1980	40,877	27,647	96	2,593	2,894	2,800	2,893	3,107	3,130	3,038	3,085	3,086	924	13,231	3,377	3,368	3,195	2,925	366
1985	39,422	27,034	151	3,041	3,239	2,941	2,895	2,771	2,776	2,789	2,938	2,982	511	12,388	3,439	3,230	2,866	2,550	303
1990	41,217	29,876	303	3,306	3,499	3,327	3,297	3,248	3,197	3,110	3,067	2,979	541	11,341	3,169	2,896	2,612	2,381	284
1991	42,047	30,503	375	3,311	3,556	3,360	3,334	3,315	3,268	3,239	3,181	3,020	542	11,544	3,313	2,915	2,645	2,392	278
1992	42,823	31,086	505	3,313	3,542	3,431	3,361	3,342	3,325	3,303	3,299	3,129	536	11,737	3,352	3,027	2,656	2,431	272
1993	43,465	31,502	545	3,377	3,529	3,429	3,437	3,361	3,350	3,356	3,355	3,249	513	11,963	3,487	3,050	2,751	2,424	250
1994	44,111	31,896	603	3,444	3,593	3,440	3,439	3,426	3,372	3,381	3,404	3,302	492	12,215	3,604	3,131	2,748	2,488	244
1995	44,840	32,338	637	3,536	3,671	3,507	3,445	3,431	3,438	3,395	3,422	3,356	500	12,502	3,704	3,237	2,826	2,487	247
1996	45,611	32,762	670	3,532	3,770	3,600	3,524	3,454	3,453	3,494	3,464	3,403	399	12,849	3,801	3,323	2,930	2,586	208
1997	46,127	33,071	695	3,503	3,755	3,689	3,597	3,507	3,458	3,492	3,520	3,415	440	13,056	3,819	3,376	2,972	2,673	216
1998	46,539	33,344	729	3,443	3,727	3,681	3,696	3,592	3,520	3,497	3,530	3,480	449	13,195	3,856	3,382	3,021	2,722	214
1999	46,857	33,486	751	3,397	3,684	3,656	3,691	3,686	3,604	3,564	3,541	3,497	415	13,371	3,935	3,415	3,034	2,782	205
2000	47,204	33,686	776	3,382	3,636	3,634	3,676	3,711	3,707	3,663	3,629	3,538	334	13,517	3,963	3,491	3,083	2,803	177
2001	47,672	33,936	865	3,379	3,614	3,593	3,653	3,695	3,727	3,769	3,720	3,616	304	13,736	4,012	3,528	3,174	2,863	159
2002	48,183	34,114	915	3,434	3,594	3,565	3,623	3,669	3,711	3,788	3,821	3,709	285	14,069	4,105	3,584	3,229	2,990	161
2003	48,540	34,201	950	3,503	3,613	3,544	3,611	3,619	3,685	3,772	3,841	3,809	255	14,339	4,190	3,675	3,277	3,046	150
2004	48,795	34,178	990	3,544	3,663	3,560	3,580	3,612	3,635	3,735	3,818	3,825	215	14,618	4,281	3,750	3,369	3,094	122
2005	49,113	34,204	1,036	3,619	3,691	3,606	3,586	3,578	3,633	3,670	3,777	3,802	205	14,909	4,287	3,866	3,454	3,180	121
2006	49,316	34,235	1,084	3,631	3,751	3,641	3,627	3,586	3,602	3,660	3,716	3,766	170	15,081	4,260	3,882	3,551	3,277	110
2007	49,293	34,205	1,081	3,609	3,750	3,704	3,659	3,624	3,600	3,628	3,701	3,709	139	15,087	4,200	3,863	3,558	3,375	92
2008	49,266	34,286	1,180	3,640	3,708	3,699	3,708	3,647	3,629	3,614	3,653	3,692	117	14,980	4,123	3,822	3,548	3,400	87
2009	49,361	34,409	1,223	3,678	3,729	3,665	3,707	3,701	3,652	3,644	3,641	3,651	119	14,952	4,080	3,809	3,541	3,432	90
2010	49,484	34,625	1,279	3,682	3,754	3,701	3,686	3,711	3,718	3,682	3,676	3,659	77	14,860	4,008	3,800	3,538	3,472	42
2011	49,522	34,773	1,291	3,746	3,773	3,713	3,703	3,672	3,699	3,724	3,696	3,679	77	14,749	3,957	3,751	3,546	3,452	43
Projected																			
2012	49,652	34,968	1,305	3,787	3,794	3,732	3,721	3,707	3,681	3,718	3,744	3,701	77	14,684	3,978	3,704	3,501	3,459	42
2013	49,750	35,111	1,302	3,777	3,834	3,754	3,741	3,725	3,716	3,699	3,738	3,749	77	14,639	4,003	3,724	3,456	3,415	42
2014	49,751	35,062	1,264	3,668	3,824	3,793	3,762	3,744	3,734	3,735	3,719	3,743	76	14,689	4,054	3,746	3,475	3,372	42
2015	49,839	35,069	1,267	3,677	3,713	3,783	3,801	3,766	3,754	3,753	3,755	3,725	76	14,770	4,048	3,795	3,496	3,390	42
2016	49,951	35,142	1,279	3,713	3,723	3,674	3,791	3,805	3,775	3,772	3,773	3,760	76	14,810	4,028	3,789	3,541	3,410	42
2017	50,280	35,412	1,342	3,895	3,759	3,683	3,682	3,795	3,814	3,794	3,793	3,779	77	14,868	4,066	3,770	3,535	3,454	42
2018	50,543	35,642	1,352	3,924	3,943	3,719	3,691	3,686	3,804	3,833	3,814	3,798	77	14,901	4,086	3,806	3,518	3,449	42
2019	50,834	35,878	1,361	3,951	3,973	3,901	3,727	3,695	3,695	3,823	3,854	3,820	78	14,957	4,107	3,825	3,552	3,432	42
2020	51,165	36,115	1,370	3,975	4,000	3,931	3,910	3,731	3,704	3,713	3,844	3,860	78	15,050	4,131	3,844	3,569	3,465	42
2021	51,485	36,335	1,377	3,997	4,025	3,958	3,939	3,914	3,740	3,722	3,733	3,850	79	15,151	4,174	3,866	3,587	3,482	42
2022	51,804	36,585	1,385	4,018	4,048	3,982	3,966	3,943	3,923	3,759	3,742	3,739	79	15,219	4,163	3,906	3,608	3,500	42
2023	52,113	36,967	1,391	4,037	4,069	4,005	3,991	3,970	3,953	3,943	3,779	3,748	80	15,146	4,043	3,896	3,645	3,520	42

NOTE: Due to changes in reporting and imputation practices, prekindergarten enrollment for years prior to 1992 represent an undercount compared to later years. The total ungraded counts of students were prorated to the elementary and secondary levels based on prior reports. Detail may not sum to totals because of rounding.

SOURCE: U.S. Department of Education, National Center for Education Statistics, *Statistics of Public Elementary and Secondary School Systems, 1980–81*; Common Core of Data (CCD), "State Nonfiscal Survey of Public Elementary/Secondary Education," 1985–86 through 2011–12; and National Elementary and Secondary Enrollment Projection Model, 1972 through 2023. (This table was prepared January 2014.)

Enrollment in public elementary and secondary schools, by region, state, and jurisdiction: Selected years, fall 1990 through fall 2023

Region, state, and jurisdiction	Actual total enrollment													Percent change in total enrollment, 2006 to 2011	Projected total enrollment						Percent change in total enrollment, 2011 to 2023
	Fall 1990	Fall 2000	Fall 2001	Fall 2002	Fall 2003	Fall 2004	Fall 2005	Fall 2006	Fall 2007	Fall 2008	Fall 2009	Fall 2010	Fall 2011		Fall 2012	Fall 2013	Fall 2014	Fall 2015	Fall 2020	Fall 2023	
1	2	3	4	5	6	7	8	9	10	11	12	13	14	15	16	17	18	19	20	21	22
United States	**41,216,683**	**47,203,539**	**47,671,870**	**48,183,086**	**48,540,215**	**48,795,465**	**49,113,298**	**49,315,842**	**49,292,507**	**49,265,572**	**49,360,982**	**49,484,181**	**49,521,669**	**0.4**	**49,651,900**	**49,750,400**	**49,751,300**	**49,839,400**	**51,165,200**	**52,112,800**	**5.2**
Region																					
Northeast	7,281,763	8,222,127	8,250,440	8,296,621	8,292,315	8,271,259	8,240,160	8,257,889	8,122,022	8,052,985	8,092,029	8,071,335	7,953,981	-3.7	7,901,300	7,852,600	7,800,800	7,766,800	7,768,400	7,791,000	-2.0
Midwest	9,943,761	10,729,987	10,744,536	10,818,970	10,808,977	10,775,409	10,818,815	10,819,248	10,770,212	10,742,973	10,672,171	10,609,604	10,573,792	-2.3	10,556,400	10,536,700	10,496,200	10,479,600	10,504,000	10,515,400	-0.6
South	14,807,016	17,007,261	17,236,914	17,471,440	17,672,745	17,891,987	18,103,166	18,293,633	18,424,719	18,490,770	18,651,889	18,805,000	18,955,932	3.6	19,115,700	19,236,100	19,300,200	19,385,600	20,060,900	20,542,600	8.4
West	9,184,143	11,244,164	11,439,980	11,596,055	11,766,178	11,856,810	11,951,157	11,945,072	11,975,554	11,978,844	11,944,893	11,998,242	12,037,964	0.8	12,078,600	12,125,000	12,154,200	12,207,300	12,832,000	13,263,700	10.2
State																					
Alabama	721,806	739,992	737,190	739,366	731,220	730,140	741,761	743,632	744,865	745,668	748,889	755,552	744,621	0.1	742,400	739,300	734,300	730,000	715,000	712,800	-4.3
Alaska	113,903	133,356	134,349	134,364	133,933	132,970	133,288	132,608	131,029	130,662	131,661	132,104	131,167	-1.1	131,000	132,300	133,400	135,000	147,200	155,200	18.3
Arizona	639,853	877,696	922,180	937,755	1,012,068	1,043,298	1,094,454	1,068,249	1,087,447	1,087,817	1,077,831	1,071,751	1,080,319	1.1	1,088,500	1,098,800	1,108,300	1,122,600	1,226,000	1,295,500	19.9
Arkansas	436,286	449,959	449,805	450,985	454,523	463,115	474,206	476,409	479,016	478,965	480,559	482,114	483,114	1.4	486,300	487,300	486,200	484,900	485,700	488,600	1.1
California	4,950,474	6,140,814	6,247,726	6,353,667	6,413,867	6,441,557	6,437,202	6,406,750	6,343,471	6,322,528	6,263,438	6,289,578	6,287,834	-1.9	6,282,200	6,278,800	6,268,600	6,271,000	6,543,800	6,742,400	7.2
Colorado	574,213	724,508	742,145	751,862	757,693	765,976	779,826	794,026	801,867	818,443	832,368	843,316	854,265	7.6	864,700	874,000	880,700	888,600	931,600	954,000	11.7
Connecticut	469,123	562,179	570,228	570,023	577,203	577,390	575,059	575,100	570,626	567,198	563,968	560,546	554,437	-3.6	548,000	542,700	536,500	532,100	528,500	533,500	-3.8
Delaware	99,658	114,676	115,555	116,342	117,668	119,091	120,937	122,254	122,574	125,430	126,801	129,403	128,946	5.5	129,500	130,400	131,100	132,100	138,200	140,100	8.7
District of Columbia	80,694	68,925	75,392	76,166	78,057	76,714	76,876	72,850	78,422	68,681	69,433	71,284	73,911	1.5	74,700	74,200	73,400	73,000	71,900	69,600	-5.8
Florida	1,861,592	2,434,821	2,500,478	2,539,929	2,587,628	2,639,336	2,675,024	2,671,513	2,666,811	2,631,020	2,634,522	2,643,347	2,668,156	-0.1	2,696,300	2,715,800	2,730,200	2,745,000	2,903,500	3,032,800	13.7
Georgia	1,151,687	1,444,937	1,470,634	1,496,012	1,522,611	1,553,437	1,598,461	1,629,157	1,649,589	1,655,792	1,667,685	1,677,067	1,685,016	3.4	1,695,700	1,704,600	1,707,500	1,712,200	1,760,500	1,809,700	7.4
Hawaii	171,708	184,360	184,546	183,829	183,609	183,185	182,818	180,728	179,897	179,478	180,196	179,601	182,706	1.1	182,600	182,600	182,000	181,500	180,600	178,000	-2.6
Idaho	220,840	245,117	246,521	248,604	252,120	256,084	261,982	267,380	272,119	275,051	276,299	275,859	279,873	4.7	283,000	286,600	289,200	292,500	307,800	314,000	12.2
Illinois	1,821,407	2,048,792	2,071,391	2,084,187	2,100,961	2,097,503	2,111,706	2,118,276	2,112,805	2,119,707	2,104,175	2,091,654	2,083,097	-1.7	2,084,100	2,077,500	2,069,700	2,067,400	2,061,600	2,053,000	-1.4
Indiana	954,525	989,267	996,133	1,003,875	1,011,130	1,021,348	1,035,074	1,045,940	1,046,766	1,046,147	1,046,661	1,047,232	1,040,765	-0.5	1,038,100	1,033,500	1,025,200	1,019,100	1,005,100	1,009,500	-3.0
Iowa	483,652	495,080	485,932	482,210	481,226	478,319	483,482	483,122	485,115	487,559	491,842	495,775	495,870	2.6	498,000	499,500	499,000	499,400	504,100	501,500	1.1
Kansas	437,034	470,610	470,205	470,957	470,490	469,136	467,525	469,506	468,295	471,060	474,489	483,701	486,108	3.5	488,000	489,700	490,200	491,700	498,900	499,300	2.7
Kentucky	636,401	665,850	654,363	660,782	663,369	674,796	679,878	683,152	666,225	670,030	680,089	673,128	681,987	-0.2	683,300	682,300	680,100	679,000	672,600	668,500	-2.0
Louisiana	784,757	743,089	731,328	730,464	727,709	724,281	654,526	675,851	681,038	684,873	690,915	696,558	703,390	4.1	710,400	712,000	709,700	709,200	697,900	686,300	-2.4
Maine	215,149	207,037	205,586	204,337	202,084	198,820	195,498	193,986	196,245	192,935	189,225	189,077	188,969	-2.6	187,500	186,900	186,200	185,900	187,300	187,200	-0.9
Maryland	715,176	852,920	860,640	866,743	869,113	865,561	860,020	851,640	845,700	843,861	848,412	852,211	854,086	0.3	857,600	862,300	866,600	873,000	934,200	969,000	13.5
Massachusetts	834,314	975,150	973,139	982,989	980,459	975,574	971,909	968,661	962,958	958,910	957,053	955,563	953,369	-1.6	950,300	945,200	938,200	932,600	923,300	926,100	-2.9
Michigan	1,584,431	1,720,626	1,730,669	1,785,160	1,757,604	1,751,290	1,742,282	1,722,656	1,692,739	1,659,921	1,649,082	1,587,067	1,573,537	-8.7	1,555,400	1,541,400	1,524,100	1,512,600	1,479,200	1,473,300	-6.4
Minnesota	756,374	854,340	851,384	846,891	842,854	838,503	839,243	840,565	837,578	836,048	837,053	838,037	839,738	-0.1	845,400	850,800	856,500	863,200	913,600	937,700	11.7
Mississippi	502,417	497,871	493,507	492,645	493,540	495,376	494,954	495,026	494,122	491,962	492,481	490,526	490,619	-0.9	491,700	489,400	486,100	482,900	468,200	458,600	-6.5
Missouri	816,558	912,744	909,792	906,499	905,941	905,449	917,705	920,353	917,188	917,871	917,982	918,710	916,584	-0.4	916,300	916,700	914,400	913,800	923,500	930,000	1.5
Montana	152,974	154,875	151,947	149,995	148,356	146,705	145,416	144,418	142,823	141,899	141,807	141,693	142,349	-1.4	143,100	143,800	143,900	144,300	147,100	146,800	3.1
Nebraska	274,081	286,199	285,095	285,402	285,542	285,761	286,646	287,580	291,244	292,590	295,368	298,500	301,296	4.8	304,100	306,200	307,000	308,700	316,700	316,400	5.0
Nevada	201,316	340,706	356,814	369,498	385,401	400,083	412,395	424,766	429,362	433,371	428,947	437,149	439,634	3.5	442,300	446,000	449,900	454,900	496,600	534,700	21.6
New Hampshire	172,785	208,461	206,847	207,671	207,417	206,852	205,767	203,572	200,772	197,934	197,140	194,711	191,900	-5.7	189,000	186,800	184,600	182,700	182,400	186,400	-2.9
New Jersey	1,089,646	1,313,405	1,341,656	1,367,438	1,380,753	1,393,347	1,395,602	1,388,850	1,382,348	1,381,420	1,396,029	1,402,548	1,356,431	-2.3	1,346,300	1,334,400	1,321,200	1,310,200	1,295,900	1,297,200	-4.4
New Mexico	301,881	320,306	320,260	320,234	323,066	326,102	326,758	328,220	329,040	330,245	334,419	338,122	337,225	2.7	337,800	339,400	340,200	340,800	342,900	339,600	0.7
New York	2,598,337	2,882,188	2,872,132	2,888,233	2,864,775	2,836,337	2,815,581	2,809,649	2,765,435	2,740,592	2,766,052	2,734,955	2,704,718	-3.7	2,691,100	2,676,500	2,662,400	2,654,700	2,657,700	2,652,600	-1.9
North Carolina	1,086,871	1,293,638	1,315,363	1,335,954	1,360,209	1,385,754	1,416,436	1,444,481	1,489,492	1,488,645	1,483,397	1,490,605	1,507,864	4.4	1,515,700	1,524,900	1,530,300	1,537,900	1,602,100	1,672,300	10.9
North Dakota	117,825	109,201	106,047	104,225	102,233	100,513	98,283	96,670	95,059	94,728	95,073	96,323	97,646	1.0	99,100	100,200	101,000	102,000	107,500	107,800	10.4
Ohio	1,771,089	1,835,049	1,830,985	1,838,285	1,845,428	1,840,032	1,839,683	1,836,722	1,827,184	1,817,163	1,764,297	1,754,191	1,740,030	-5.3	1,730,300	1,722,700	1,712,100	1,704,200	1,677,000	1,664,100	-4.4
Oklahoma	579,087	623,110	622,139	624,548	626,160	629,476	634,739	639,391	642,065	645,108	654,802	659,911	666,120	4.2	673,000	677,000	677,900	679,600	689,000	690,300	3.6
Oregon	472,394	546,231	551,480	554,071	551,273	552,505	552,194	562,574	565,586	575,393	582,839	570,720	568,208	1.0	569,900	572,500	573,800	576,600	603,600	626,600	10.3
Pennsylvania	1,667,834	1,814,311	1,821,627	1,816,747	1,821,146	1,828,089	1,830,684	1,871,060	1,801,971	1,775,029	1,785,993	1,793,284	1,771,395	-5.3	1,758,500	1,751,600	1,744,500	1,742,000	1,761,000	1,772,200	#
Rhode Island	138,813	157,347	158,046	159,205	159,375	156,498	153,422	151,612	147,629	145,342	145,118	143,793	142,854	-5.8	140,700	139,700	138,900	138,900	142,400	144,700	1.3
South Carolina	622,112	677,411	676,198	694,389	699,198	703,736	701,544	708,021	712,317	718,113	723,143	725,838	727,186	2.7	734,700	738,800	740,900	744,300	761,100	770,600	6.0
South Dakota	129,164	128,603	127,542	130,048	125,537	122,798	122,012	121,158	121,606	126,429	123,713	126,128	128,016	5.7	128,300	129,300	129,900	130,600	135,500	135,900	6.2
Tennessee	824,595	909,161	924,899	927,608	936,682	941,091	953,928	978,368	964,259	971,950	972,549	987,422	999,693	2.2	1,006,500	1,012,600	1,016,700	1,021,400	1,054,200	1,081,100	8.1
Texas	3,382,887	4,059,619	4,163,447	4,259,823	4,331,751	4,405,215	4,525,394	4,599,509	4,674,832	4,752,148	4,850,210	4,935,715	5,000,470	8.7	5,072,200	5,135,400	5,178,400	5,226,300	5,511,100	5,669,000	13.4
Utah	446,652	481,485	484,684	489,262	495,981	503,607	508,430	523,386	576,244	559,778	571,586	585,552	598,832	14.4	612,500	624,700	634,500	643,500	683,700	704,600	17.7

See notes at end of table.

Enrollment in public elementary and secondary schools, by region, state, and jurisdiction: Selected years, fall 1990 through fall 2023—Continued

	Actual total enrollment													Percent change in total enrollment, 2006 to 2011	Projected total enrollment						Percent change in total enrollment, 2011 to 2023
Region, state, and jurisdiction	Fall 1990	Fall 2000	Fall 2001	Fall 2002	Fall 2003	Fall 2004	Fall 2005	Fall 2006	Fall 2007	Fall 2008	Fall 2009	Fall 2010	Fall 2011		Fall 2012	Fall 2013	Fall 2014	Fall 2015	Fall 2020	Fall 2023	
1	2	3	4	5	6	7	8	9	10	11	12	13	14	15	16	17	18	19	20	21	22
Vermont	95,762	102,049	101,179	99,978	99,103	98,352	96,638	95,399	94,038	93,625	91,451	96,858	89,908	-5.8	89,900	89,000	88,200	87,800	89,800	91,200	1.4
Virginia	998,601	1,144,915	1,163,091	1,177,229	1,192,092	1,204,739	1,213,616	1,220,440	1,230,857	1,235,795	1,245,340	1,251,440	1,257,883	3.1	1,263,200	1,269,100	1,272,700	1,279,200	1,333,000	1,370,300	8.9
Washington	839,709	1,004,770	1,009,200	1,014,798	1,021,349	1,020,005	1,031,985	1,026,774	1,030,247	1,037,018	1,035,347	1,043,788	1,045,453	1.8	1,049,200	1,052,400	1,055,500	1,061,300	1,124,200	1,177,400	12.6
West Virginia	322,389	286,367	282,885	282,455	281,215	280,129	280,866	281,939	282,535	282,729	282,662	282,879	282,870	0.3	282,600	280,800	278,000	275,400	262,700	253,100	-10.5
Wisconsin	797,621	879,476	879,361	881,231	880,031	864,757	875,174	876,700	874,633	873,750	872,436	872,286	871,105	-0.6	869,400	869,300	867,000	867,200	881,300	886,900	1.8
Wyoming	98,226	89,940	88,128	88,116	87,462	84,733	84,409	85,193	86,422	87,161	88,155	89,009	90,099	5.8	91,900	93,100	94,100	94,800	96,900	94,900	5.3
Jurisdiction																					
Bureau of Indian Education	—	46,938	46,476	46,126	45,828	45,828	50,938	—	—	40,927	41,351	41,962	—	—	—	—	—	—	—	—	—
DoD, overseas	—	73,581	73,212	72,889	71,053	68,327	62,543	60,891	57,247	56,768	—	—	—	—	—	—	—	—	—	—	—
DoD, domestic	—	34,174	32,847	32,115	30,603	29,151	28,329	26,631	27,548	28,013	—	—	—	—	—	—	—	—	—	—	—
Other jurisdictions																					
American Samoa	12,463	15,702	15,897	15,984	15,893	16,126	16,438	16,400	—	—	—	—	—	—	—	—	—	—	—	—	—
Guam	26,391	32,473	31,992	—	31,572	30,605	30,996	—	—	—	—	31,618	31,243	—	—	—	—	—	—	—	—
Northern Marianas	6,449	10,004	10,479	11,251	11,244	11,601	11,718	11,695	11,299	10,913	10,961	11,105	11,011	-5.8	—	—	—	—	—	—	—
Puerto Rico	644,734	612,725	604,177	596,502	584,916	575,648	563,490	544,138	526,565	503,635	493,393	473,735	452,740	-16.8	—	—	—	—	—	—	—
U.S. Virgin Islands	21,750	19,459	18,780	18,333	17,716	16,429	16,750	16,284	15,903	15,768	15,493	15,495	15,711	-3.5	—	—	—	—	—	—	—

—Not available.
#Rounds to zero.
NOTE: DoD = Department of Defense. Detail may not sum to totals because of rounding. Some data have been revised from previously published figures.

SOURCE: U.S. Department of Education, National Center for Education Statistics, Common Core of Data (CCD), "State Non-fiscal Survey of Public Elementary/Secondary Education," 1990–91 through 2011–12; and State Public Elementary and Secondary Enrollment Projection Model, 1980 through 2023. (This table was prepared December 2013.)

Public school enrollment in prekindergarten through grade 8, by region, state, and jurisdiction: Selected years, fall 1990 through fall 2023

Region, state, and jurisdiction	Actual enrollment													Percent change in enrollment, 2006 to 2011	Projected enrollment						Percent change in enrollment, 2011 to 2023
	Fall 1990	Fall 2000	Fall 2001	Fall 2002	Fall 2003	Fall 2004	Fall 2005	Fall 2006	Fall 2007	Fall 2008	Fall 2009	Fall 2010	Fall 2011		Fall 2012	Fall 2013	Fall 2014	Fall 2015	Fall 2020	Fall 2023	
1	2	3	4	5	6	7	8	9	10	11	12	13	14	15	16	17	18	19	20	21	22
United States	**29,875,914**	**33,686,421**	**33,935,922**	**34,114,245**	**34,200,741**	**34,177,565**	**34,203,962**	**34,234,751**	**34,205,362**	**34,285,564**	**34,409,260**	**34,624,530**	**34,772,751**	**1.6**	**34,967,700**	**35,111,000**	**35,062,300**	**35,069,200**	**36,114,900**	**36,966,700**	**6.3**
Region																					
Northeast	5,188,795	5,839,970	5,823,249	5,809,545	5,751,561	5,689,094	5,622,955	5,573,729	5,504,400	5,476,224	5,494,080	5,540,276	5,479,174	-1.7	5,470,500	5,459,800	5,424,200	5,396,400	5,411,600	5,477,400	#
Midwest	7,129,501	7,523,246	7,516,458	7,534,620	7,501,579	7,438,674	7,425,308	7,404,578	7,359,028	7,373,391	7,361,959	7,349,334	7,358,792	-0.6	7,363,300	7,363,700	7,323,300	7,288,400	7,316,500	7,356,600	#
South	10,858,800	12,314,176	12,453,658	12,573,054	12,675,179	12,780,160	12,881,836	12,989,696	13,086,326	13,166,980	13,300,643	13,434,553	13,578,211	4.5	13,707,500	13,795,700	13,791,500	13,804,700	14,313,400	14,716,800	8.4
West	6,698,818	8,009,029	8,142,557	8,197,026	8,272,422	8,269,637	8,273,863	8,266,748	8,255,608	8,268,969	8,252,578	8,300,367	8,356,574	1.1	8,426,300	8,491,700	8,523,300	8,579,700	9,073,400	9,415,900	12.7
State																					
Alabama	527,097	538,634	535,580	533,207	525,313	521,757	529,347	528,664	527,259	528,078	529,394	533,612	527,006	-0.3	526,600	523,900	518,300	512,700	506,800	506,600	-3.9
Alaska	85,297	94,442	94,888	94,380	93,695	91,981	91,225	90,167	88,980	89,263	90,824	91,990	92,057	2.1	93,000	94,300	95,400	96,700	107,000	112,600	22.3
Arizona	479,046	640,564	671,652	660,359	704,322	722,203	739,535	759,656	771,056	771,749	760,420	751,992	759,494	#	773,000	786,400	796,200	806,100	879,000	936,700	23.3
Arkansas	313,505	318,023	317,923	318,826	321,508	328,187	335,746	336,552	339,920	341,603	344,209	345,808	346,022	2.8	348,500	348,400	346,400	344,400	344,000	348,500	0.7
California	3,613,734	4,407,035	4,478,326	4,525,385	4,539,777	4,507,355	4,465,615	4,410,105	4,328,968	4,306,258	4,264,022	4,293,968	4,308,447	-2.3	4,327,800	4,349,200	4,356,000	4,384,400	4,627,600	4,779,300	10.9
Colorado	419,910	516,566	529,156	534,465	536,325	540,695	549,875	559,041	565,726	580,304	591,378	601,077	610,854	9.3	619,100	625,900	628,200	630,600	653,100	673,800	10.3
Connecticut	347,396	406,445	410,017	405,998	407,794	404,169	399,705	398,063	394,034	392,218	389,964	387,475	383,377	-3.7	379,300	376,400	372,400	369,500	373,400	382,200	-0.3
Delaware	72,606	80,801	81,274	82,221	82,898	83,599	84,639	84,996	85,019	86,811	87,710	90,279	90,624	6.6	92,000	93,300	93,900	94,400	97,400	98,700	8.9
District of Columbia	61,282	53,692	57,967	58,802	59,489	57,118	55,646	52,391	55,836	50,779	51,656	53,548	56,195	7.3	57,300	57,300	56,700	56,400	55,400	52,900	-5.9
Florida	1,369,934	1,759,902	1,797,414	1,809,279	1,832,376	1,857,798	1,873,395	1,866,562	1,855,859	1,849,295	1,850,901	1,858,498	1,876,102	0.5	1,895,200	1,910,400	1,918,000	1,927,500	2,068,500	2,167,500	15.5
Georgia	849,082	1,059,983	1,075,195	1,088,561	1,103,181	1,118,379	1,145,446	1,166,508	1,178,577	1,185,684	1,194,751	1,202,479	1,211,250	3.8	1,217,300	1,221,500	1,218,200	1,217,200	1,266,700	1,308,600	8.0
Hawaii	122,840	132,293	131,881	130,862	130,054	128,788	127,472	126,008	125,556	125,910	127,477	127,525	131,005	4.0	131,500	131,400	130,600	130,300	127,700	126,600	-3.4
Idaho	160,091	170,421	171,423	173,249	175,424	178,221	182,829	187,005	191,171	193,554	194,728	194,144	198,064	5.9	201,100	203,600	205,400	206,900	215,500	219,500	10.8
Illinois	1,309,516	1,473,933	1,484,201	1,487,650	1,492,725	1,483,644	1,480,320	1,477,679	1,472,909	1,479,195	1,463,713	1,454,793	1,453,156	-1.7	1,453,700	1,452,600	1,443,300	1,434,200	1,422,800	1,430,700	-1.5
Indiana	675,804	703,261	711,455	714,003	716,819	720,006	724,467	730,108	729,550	730,021	730,599	729,414	724,605	-0.8	722,700	719,500	712,800	704,200	702,600	712,200	-1.7
Iowa	344,804	333,750	329,649	325,843	326,831	324,169	326,160	326,218	329,504	335,566	341,333	348,112	350,152	7.3	353,200	354,800	353,700	353,500	353,500	349,100	-0.3
Kansas	319,648	323,157	322,345	321,795	322,491	321,176	320,513	326,201	326,771	331,079	332,997	342,927	347,129	6.4	349,000	350,700	350,000	349,500	351,700	352,300	1.5
Kentucky	459,200	471,429	473,491	476,751	478,254	485,794	487,429	487,165	469,373	472,204	484,466	480,334	488,456	0.3	490,800	490,500	486,300	481,900	474,700	474,200	-2.9
Louisiana	586,202	546,579	536,953	536,882	536,390	533,751	482,082	492,116	499,549	504,213	509,883	512,266	518,802	5.4	524,400	525,400	519,500	515,100	502,000	493,700	-4.8
Maine	155,203	145,701	143,855	141,776	139,420	136,275	133,491	132,338	130,742	129,324	128,646	128,929	130,046	-1.7	129,600	129,600	129,300	129,100	130,800	130,600	0.4
Maryland	526,744	609,043	610,858	610,337	605,862	597,417	588,571	579,065	576,479	576,473	581,785	588,156	594,216	2.6	600,600	608,600	613,200	620,100	663,300	690,400	16.2
Massachusetts	604,234	702,575	699,495	701,050	692,130	682,175	675,398	670,628	666,926	666,538	666,551	666,402	666,314	-0.6	663,900	660,700	654,300	648,700	644,400	655,600	-1.6
Michigan	1,144,878	1,222,482	1,222,763	1,253,811	1,229,121	1,211,698	1,191,397	1,170,558	1,136,823	1,118,569	1,114,611	1,075,584	1,070,873	-8.5	1,060,000	1,052,000	1,039,300	1,028,500	1,024,100	1,028,000	-4.0
Minnesota	545,556	577,766	573,028	567,701	564,049	558,447	557,757	558,445	558,180	560,184	564,661	569,963	575,544	3.1	583,000	589,400	593,400	597,300	628,700	649,700	12.9
Mississippi	371,641	363,873	361,615	360,254	360,881	361,057	358,030	356,382	353,512	351,807	351,652	350,885	352,999	-0.9	355,800	354,500	350,200	346,600	334,400	327,000	-7.4
Missouri	588,070	644,766	642,492	634,667	632,227	628,667	635,142	634,275	631,746	635,411	638,082	642,991	645,376	1.8	645,900	647,100	644,800	643,700	653,100	657,300	1.8
Montana	111,169	105,226	102,721	101,177	100,160	98,673	97,770	97,021	96,354	96,869	97,868	98,491	99,725	2.8	100,900	101,600	102,000	102,200	103,100	102,300	2.6
Nebraska	198,080	195,486	194,653	195,113	195,417	194,816	195,055	195,769	200,095	202,912	206,860	210,292	213,504	9.1	216,500	218,700	219,000	219,300	219,600	219,200	2.7
Nevada	149,881	250,720	262,472	270,940	280,734	288,753	295,989	302,953	307,573	308,328	305,512	307,297	309,360	2.1	312,500	315,800	318,700	321,500	358,900	390,900	26.4
New Hampshire	126,301	147,121	144,487	143,616	142,031	140,241	138,584	136,188	134,359	132,995	132,768	131,576	129,632	-4.8	127,600	126,500	125,200	124,400	128,000	132,900	2.5
New Jersey	783,422	967,533	971,774	978,609	978,440	975,856	970,592	963,418	954,418	956,765	968,332	981,255	947,576	-1.6	943,900	938,100	929,400	921,200	915,800	929,300	-1.9
New Mexico	208,087	224,879	225,036	224,497	226,032	227,900	229,552	230,091	229,718	231,415	235,343	239,345	239,481	4.1	240,800	241,700	241,300	240,800	240,100	237,300	-0.9
New York	1,827,418	2,028,906	2,016,847	2,016,282	1,978,181	1,942,575	1,909,028	1,887,284	1,856,315	1,843,080	1,847,003	1,869,150	1,857,574	-1.6	1,861,300	1,862,100	1,850,600	1,842,700	1,835,100	1,847,300	-0.6
North Carolina	783,132	945,470	955,965	963,967	974,019	985,740	1,003,118	1,027,067	1,072,324	1,058,926	1,053,801	1,058,409	1,074,063	4.6	1,080,300	1,086,100	1,085,700	1,085,400	1,148,900	1,208,500	12.5
North Dakota	84,943	72,421	70,454	69,089	67,870	67,122	65,638	64,395	63,492	63,955	64,576	66,035	67,888	5.4	69,400	70,600	71,700	72,500	74,200	73,100	7.7
Ohio	1,257,580	1,293,646	1,286,632	1,283,795	1,278,202	1,267,088	1,261,331	1,253,193	1,241,322	1,239,494	1,225,346	1,222,808	1,217,226	-2.9	1,214,500	1,210,500	1,199,800	1,190,000	1,175,500	1,169,800	-3.9
Oklahoma	424,899	445,402	445,989	449,030	450,310	452,942	456,954	459,944	462,629	467,960	476,962	483,464	490,196	6.6	495,600	497,700	495,900	494,900	495,500	497,800	1.6
Oregon	340,243	379,264	381,678	381,988	378,052	376,933	379,680	380,576	383,598	395,421	404,451	392,601	391,310	2.8	393,200	395,500	396,500	398,300	423,500	442,000	13.0
Pennsylvania	1,172,164	1,257,824	1,254,692	1,241,636	1,235,624	1,234,828	1,227,625	1,220,074	1,205,351	1,194,327	1,200,446	1,209,766	1,204,850	-1.2	1,205,800	1,206,600	1,202,900	1,201,000	1,219,100	1,230,500	#
Rhode Island	101,797	113,545	112,783	112,544	111,209	107,040	103,870	101,996	99,159	97,983	98,184	97,734	97,659	-4.3	96,100	97,100	97,500	97,300	99,900	102,200	4.6
South Carolina	452,033	493,226	486,723	500,427	500,743	504,264	498,030	501,273	504,566	507,602	512,124	515,581	519,389	3.6	527,100	530,300	529,400	528,800	540,100	546,900	5.3
South Dakota	95,165	87,838	86,982	89,450	86,015	83,891	83,530	83,137	83,424	87,477	85,745	87,936	90,529	8.9	91,000	92,100	92,700	93,400	95,000	94,400	4.3
Tennessee	598,111	668,123	674,507	673,337	675,277	670,880	676,576	691,971	681,751	684,549	686,668	701,707	712,749	3.0	718,900	722,500	721,900	722,200	748,000	770,600	8.1
Texas	2,510,955	2,943,047	3,016,214	3,079,665	3,132,584	3,184,235	3,268,339	3,319,782	3,374,684	3,446,511	3,520,348	3,586,609	3,636,852	9.6	3,686,800	3,729,600	3,744,100	3,763,300	3,946,000	4,077,700	12.1
Utah	324,982	333,104	337,974	342,607	348,840	355,445	357,644	371,272	410,258	404,469	413,343	424,979	434,536	17.0	444,100	451,200	455,000	458,900	478,500	493,900	13.7

See notes at end of table.

Public school enrollment in prekindergarten through grade 8, by region, state, and jurisdiction: Selected years, fall 1990 through fall 2023—Continued

					Actual enrollment									Percent change in enrollment, 2006 to 2011	Projected enrollment						Percent change in enrollment, 2011 to 2023
Region, state, and jurisdiction	Fall 1990	Fall 2000	Fall 2001	Fall 2002	Fall 2003	Fall 2004	Fall 2005	Fall 2006	Fall 2007	Fall 2008	Fall 2009	Fall 2010	Fall 2011		Fall 2012	Fall 2013	Fall 2014	Fall 2015	Fall 2020	Fall 2023	
1	2	3	4	5	6	7	8	9	10	11	12	13	14	15	16	17	18	19	20	21	22
Vermont	70,860	70,320	69,299	68,034	66,732	65,935	64,662	63,740	63,096	62,994	62,186	67,989	62,146	-2.5	62,900	62,800	62,500	62,500	65,200	66,800	7.5
Virginia	728,280	815,748	826,184	831,504	837,258	839,687	841,299	841,685	850,444	855,008	864,020	871,446	881,225	4.7	888,100	894,600	895,700	898,100	938,400	970,700	10.2
Washington	612,597	694,367	696,257	697,191	699,248	695,405	699,482	694,858	697,407	704,794	705,387	714,172	718,184	3.4	723,700	728,400	731,000	735,400	792,900	837,200	16.6
West Virginia	224,097	201,201	199,806	200,004	198,836	197,555	197,189	197,573	198,545	199,477	200,313	201,472	202,065	2.3	202,300	201,200	198,100	195,400	183,300	176,600	-12.6
Wisconsin	565,457	594,740	591,804	591,703	589,812	577,950	583,998	584,600	585,212	589,528	593,436	598,479	602,810	3.1	604,500	605,700	602,900	602,300	615,700	620,900	3.0
Wyoming	70,941	60,148	59,093	59,926	59,759	57,285	57,195	57,995	59,243	60,635	61,825	62,786	64,057	10.5	65,700	66,700	67,100	67,600	66,500	63,900	-0.2
Jurisdiction																					
Bureau of Indian Education	—	35,746	35,021	34,392	33,671	33,671	36,133	—	—	30,612	31,381	31,985	—	—	—	—	—	—	—	—	—
DoD, overseas	—	59,299	58,750	58,214	56,226	53,720	48,691	47,589	44,418	43,931	—	—	—	—	—	—	—	—	—	—	—
DoD, domestic	—	30,697	29,389	28,759	27,500	26,195	25,558	24,052	24,807	25,255	—	—	—	—	—	—	—	—	—	—	—
Other jurisdictions																					
American Samoa	9,390	11,895	11,911	11,838	11,772	11,873	11,766	11,763	—	—	—	—	—	—	—	—	—	—	—	—	—
Guam	19,276	23,698	23,133	22,551	22,551	21,686	21,946	—	—	—	—	21,561	21,223	—	—	—	—	—	—	—	—
Northern Marianas	4,918	7,809	8,015	8,379	8,192	8,416	8,427	8,504	8,140	7,816	7,743	7,688	7,703	-9.4	—	—	—	—	—	—	—
Puerto Rico	480,356	445,524	438,115	429,413	418,649	408,671	399,447	382,647	372,514	355,115	347,638	334,613	318,924	-16.7	—	—	—	—	—	—	—
U.S. Virgin Islands	16,249	13,910	13,421	12,933	12,738	11,650	11,728	11,237	10,770	10,567	10,409	10,518	10,576	-5.9	—	—	—	—	—	—	—

—Not available.
#Rounds to zero.
NOTE: DoD = Department of Defense. Detail may not sum to totals because of rounding. Some data have been revised from previously published figures.

SOURCE: U.S. Department of Education, National Center for Education Statistics, Common Core of Data (CCD), State Nonfiscal Survey of Public Elementary/Secondary Education, 1990–91 through 2011–12; and State Public Elementary and Secondary Enrollment Projection Model, 1980 through 2023. (This table was prepared January 2014.)

Public school enrollment in grades 9 through 12, by region, state, and jurisdiction: Selected years, fall 1990 through fall 2023

Region, state, and jurisdiction	Fall 1990	Fall 2000	Fall 2001	Fall 2002	Fall 2003	Fall 2004	Fall 2005	Fall 2006	Fall 2007	Fall 2008	Fall 2009	Fall 2010	Fall 2011	Percent change in enrollment, 2006 to 2011	Fall 2012	Fall 2013	Fall 2014	Fall 2015	Fall 2020	Fall 2023	Percent change in enrollment, 2011 to 2023
1	2	3	4	5	6	7	8	9	10	11	12	13	14	15	16	17	18	19	20	21	22
United States	11,340,769	13,517,118	13,735,948	14,068,841	14,339,474	14,617,900	14,909,336	15,081,091	15,087,145	14,980,008	14,951,722	14,859,651	14,748,918	-2.2	14,684,200	14,639,400	14,689,000	14,770,300	15,050,300	15,146,100	2.7
Region																					
Northeast	2,092,968	2,382,157	2,427,191	2,487,076	2,540,754	2,582,165	2,617,205	2,684,160	2,617,622	2,576,761	2,597,949	2,531,059	2,474,807	-7.8	2,430,600	2,392,800	2,376,600	2,370,400	2,356,800	2,313,600	-6.5
Midwest	2,814,260	3,206,741	3,228,078	3,284,350	3,307,398	3,336,735	3,393,507	3,414,670	3,411,184	3,369,582	3,310,212	3,260,270	3,215,000	-5.8	3,193,000	3,173,000	3,172,900	3,191,200	3,187,500	3,158,800	-1.7
South	3,948,216	4,693,085	4,783,256	4,898,386	4,997,566	5,111,827	5,221,330	5,303,937	5,338,393	5,323,790	5,351,246	5,370,447	5,377,721	1.4	5,408,100	5,440,400	5,508,600	5,580,600	5,747,400	5,825,900	8.3
West	2,485,325	3,235,135	3,297,423	3,399,029	3,493,756	3,587,173	3,677,294	3,678,324	3,719,946	3,709,875	3,692,315	3,697,875	3,681,390	0.1	3,652,300	3,633,300	3,630,900	3,627,600	3,758,600	3,847,800	4.5
State																					
Alabama	194,709	201,358	201,610	206,159	205,907	208,383	212,414	214,968	217,606	217,590	219,495	221,940	217,615	1.2	215,800	215,400	216,000	217,300	218,100	206,100	-5.3
Alaska	28,606	38,914	39,461	39,984	40,238	40,989	42,063	42,441	42,049	41,399	40,837	40,114	39,110	-7.8	38,000	38,000	38,100	38,300	40,200	42,600	8.9
Arizona	160,807	237,132	250,528	277,396	307,746	321,035	354,919	308,593	316,391	316,068	317,411	319,759	320,825	4.0	315,500	312,400	312,100	316,600	347,000	359,800	11.8
Arkansas	122,781	131,936	131,882	132,159	133,015	134,928	138,460	139,857	139,096	137,362	136,350	136,306	137,092	-2.0	137,800	139,000	139,700	140,500	141,700	140,100	2.2
California	1,336,740	1,733,779	1,769,400	1,828,282	1,874,090	1,934,202	1,971,587	1,996,645	2,014,503	2,016,270	1,999,416	1,995,610	1,979,387	-0.9	1,954,400	1,929,600	1,912,600	1,886,600	1,916,200	1,963,100	-0.8
Colorado	154,303	207,942	212,989	217,397	221,368	225,281	229,951	234,985	236,141	238,139	240,990	242,239	241,411	3.6	245,600	248,100	252,500	258,000	278,600	280,200	15.1
Connecticut	121,727	155,734	160,211	164,025	169,409	173,221	175,354	177,003	176,592	174,980	174,004	173,071	171,060	-3.4	168,700	166,200	164,100	162,600	155,100	151,300	-11.6
Delaware	27,052	33,875	34,281	34,121	34,770	35,492	36,298	37,258	37,555	38,619	39,091	39,124	38,322	2.9	37,500	37,100	37,200	37,700	40,700	41,400	8.0
District of Columbia	19,412	15,233	17,425	17,364	18,568	19,596	21,230	20,459	22,586	17,902	17,777	17,736	17,716	-13.4	17,400	16,800	16,700	16,600	16,500	16,800	-5.2
Florida	491,658	674,919	703,064	730,650	755,252	781,538	801,629	804,951	810,952	781,725	783,621	784,849	792,054	-1.6	801,000	805,400	812,000	817,500	835,000	865,300	9.2
Georgia	302,605	384,954	395,439	407,451	419,430	435,058	453,015	462,649	471,012	470,108	472,934	474,588	473,766	2.4	478,400	483,100	489,300	495,000	493,800	501,100	5.8
Hawaii	48,868	52,067	52,666	52,967	53,555	54,397	55,346	54,720	54,341	53,568	52,719	52,076	51,701	-5.5	51,100	51,100	51,400	51,100	52,900	51,400	-0.6
Idaho	60,749	74,696	75,098	75,355	76,696	77,863	79,153	80,375	80,948	81,497	81,571	81,715	81,809	1.8	82,000	83,000	83,900	85,600	92,400	94,500	15.5
Illinois	511,891	574,859	587,190	596,537	608,236	613,859	631,396	640,597	639,896	640,512	640,462	636,861	629,941	-1.7	630,000	624,900	626,300	633,200	638,600	622,300	-1.2
Indiana	278,721	286,006	284,678	289,872	294,311	301,342	310,607	315,832	317,216	316,126	316,062	317,818	316,160	0.1	315,300	314,000	312,500	314,800	302,500	297,300	-6.0
Iowa	138,848	161,330	156,283	156,367	154,395	154,150	157,322	156,904	155,611	151,993	150,509	147,663	145,718	-7.1	144,800	144,700	145,400	145,900	150,600	152,400	4.6
Kansas	117,386	147,453	147,860	149,162	147,999	147,960	147,012	143,305	141,524	139,981	141,492	140,774	138,979	-3.0	139,000	139,100	140,200	142,100	152,900	147,000	5.8
Kentucky	177,201	194,421	180,872	184,031	185,115	189,002	189,591	195,987	196,652	197,826	195,623	192,794	193,531	-1.3	192,500	193,800	193,700	197,200	197,900	194,400	0.4
Louisiana	198,555	196,510	194,375	193,582	191,319	190,530	172,444	183,735	181,489	180,660	181,032	184,292	184,588	0.5	186,100	186,600	190,200	194,100	195,900	192,600	4.3
Maine	59,946	61,336	61,731	62,561	62,664	62,545	62,007	61,648	65,503	63,611	60,579	60,148	58,923	-4.4	58,000	57,300	56,900	56,800	56,500	56,600	-3.9
Maryland	188,432	243,877	249,782	256,406	263,251	268,144	271,449	272,575	269,221	267,388	266,627	264,055	259,870	-4.7	257,000	253,700	253,400	252,900	270,800	278,600	7.2
Massachusetts	230,080	272,575	273,644	286,406	288,329	293,399	296,511	296,400	296,032	290,502	290,372	289,161	287,055	-3.7	286,400	284,500	283,800	283,900	278,900	270,500	-5.8
Michigan	439,553	498,144	507,906	531,349	528,483	539,592	550,885	552,098	555,916	541,352	534,471	511,483	502,664	-9.0	495,500	489,400	484,800	484,100	455,100	445,200	-11.4
Minnesota	210,818	276,574	278,356	279,190	278,805	280,056	281,486	282,120	279,398	275,864	272,392	268,074	264,194	-6.4	262,400	261,400	263,200	265,900	284,900	288,000	9.0
Mississippi	130,776	133,998	131,892	132,391	132,659	134,319	136,924	138,644	140,610	140,155	140,829	139,641	137,620	-0.7	135,900	134,900	136,000	136,300	133,800	131,600	-4.4
Missouri	228,488	267,978	267,300	271,832	273,714	276,782	282,563	296,078	285,442	282,460	279,900	275,719	271,208	-5.2	270,500	269,500	269,600	270,000	270,400	272,700	0.6
Montana	41,805	49,649	49,226	48,818	48,196	48,032	47,646	47,397	46,469	45,030	43,939	43,202	42,624	-10.1	42,200	42,200	41,900	42,100	44,000	44,500	4.4
Nebraska	76,001	90,713	90,442	90,289	90,125	90,945	91,591	91,811	91,149	89,678	88,508	88,208	87,792	-4.4	87,600	87,500	88,000	89,400	97,100	97,200	10.7
Nevada	51,435	89,986	94,342	98,558	104,667	111,130	116,406	121,813	121,789	125,043	123,435	129,852	130,274	6.9	129,800	130,200	131,300	133,400	137,700	143,800	10.4
New Hampshire	46,484	61,340	62,360	64,055	65,386	66,611	67,183	67,384	66,413	64,939	64,372	63,135	62,268	-7.6	61,000	60,300	59,400	58,200	54,400	53,500	-14.1
New Jersey	306,224	345,872	369,882	388,829	402,313	417,491	425,010	425,432	427,930	424,655	427,697	421,293	408,855	-3.9	402,400	396,400	391,800	389,000	380,100	368,000	-10.0
New Mexico	93,794	95,427	95,224	95,737	97,034	98,202	97,206	98,129	99,322	98,830	99,076	98,777	99,744	-0.4	97,000	97,700	99,900	99,900	102,900	102,300	4.7
New York	770,919	853,282	855,285	881,961	886,594	893,762	906,553	922,365	909,120	897,512	919,049	865,805	847,144	-8.2	829,800	814,400	811,800	812,000	822,700	805,300	-4.9
North Carolina	303,739	348,168	359,398	371,987	386,190	400,014	413,318	417,414	417,168	429,596	429,556	432,196	433,801	3.9	435,400	438,800	444,600	452,500	453,000	463,900	6.9
North Dakota	32,882	36,780	35,593	35,136	34,363	33,391	32,645	32,275	31,567	30,773	30,497	30,288	29,758	-7.8	29,700	29,600	29,300	29,500	33,300	34,700	16.6
Ohio	513,509	541,403	544,353	554,490	567,226	572,944	578,352	583,529	585,862	577,669	538,951	531,383	522,804	-10.4	515,800	512,200	512,300	514,200	501,600	494,300	-5.5
Oklahoma	154,188	177,708	176,150	175,518	175,850	176,534	177,785	179,447	179,436	177,148	177,840	176,447	175,924	-2.0	177,300	179,300	184,700	184,700	183,500	192,400	9.4
Oregon	132,151	166,967	169,802	172,083	173,221	175,572	172,514	181,988	181,988	179,972	178,388	178,119	176,898	-2.8	176,700	177,000	177,300	178,200	180,100	184,100	4.4
Pennsylvania	495,670	556,487	566,935	575,111	585,522	593,261	603,059	650,986	596,620	580,702	585,547	583,518	566,545	-13.0	552,700	545,000	541,700	541,000	542,000	541,600	-4.4
Rhode Island	37,016	43,802	45,263	46,661	48,166	49,458	49,552	49,616	48,470	47,359	46,934	46,059	45,195	-8.9	44,500	42,500	41,400	41,500	42,500	42,300	-6.0
South Carolina	170,079	184,185	189,475	193,962	198,455	199,472	203,514	206,748	207,751	210,511	211,019	210,257	210,797	0.5	207,600	208,500	211,500	215,600	221,000	223,700	7.7
South Dakota	33,999	40,765	40,560	40,598	39,522	38,907	38,482	38,021	38,182	38,952	37,968	38,192	37,487	-1.4	37,200	37,200	37,300	37,200	40,500	41,500	10.7
Tennessee	226,484	241,038	250,392	254,271	261,405	270,211	277,352	286,397	282,508	287,401	285,881	285,715	286,944	0.2	287,600	290,100	294,800	299,200	306,200	310,500	8.2
Texas	871,932	1,116,572	1,147,233	1,180,158	1,199,167	1,220,980	1,257,055	1,279,727	1,300,148	1,305,637	1,329,862	1,349,106	1,363,618	6.6	1,385,400	1,405,900	1,434,300	1,463,000	1,565,100	1,591,300	16.7
Utah	121,670	148,381	146,710	146,655	147,141	148,162	150,786	152,114	165,986	155,309	158,243	160,573	164,296	8.0	168,400	173,500	179,500	184,600	205,200	210,700	28.2

See notes at end of table.

Public school enrollment in grades 9 through 12, by region, state, and jurisdiction: Selected years, fall 1990 through fall 2023—Continued

Region, state, and jurisdiction	Fall 1990	Fall 2000	Fall 2001	Fall 2002	Fall 2003	Fall 2004	Fall 2005	Fall 2006	Fall 2007	Fall 2008	Fall 2009	Fall 2010	Fall 2011	Percent change in enrollment, 2006 to 2011	Fall 2012	Fall 2013	Fall 2014	Fall 2015	Fall 2020	Fall 2023	Percent change in enrollment, 2011 to 2023
1	2	3	4	5	6	7	8	9	10	11	12	13	14	15	16	17	18	19	20	21	22
Vermont	24,902	31,729	31,880	31,944	32,371	32,417	31,976	31,659	30,942	30,631	29,265	28,869	27,762	-12.3	26,900	26,200	25,700	25,300	24,600	24,400	-12.1
Virginia	270,321	329,167	336,907	345,725	354,834	365,052	372,317	378,755	380,413	380,787	381,320	379,994	376,658	-0.6	375,100	374,500	377,000	380,800	394,600	399,600	6.1
Washington	227,112	310,403	312,943	317,607	322,101	324,600	332,503	332,840	332,224	331,916	329,960	329,616	327,269	-1.4	325,500	324,000	324,500	325,900	331,300	340,200	4.0
West Virginia	98,292	85,166	83,079	82,451	82,379	82,574	83,677	84,366	83,990	83,252	82,349	81,407	80,805	-4.2	80,300	79,600	80,000	80,000	79,400	76,500	-5.3
Wisconsin	232,164	284,736	287,557	289,528	290,219	286,807	291,176	292,100	289,421	284,222	279,000	273,807	268,295	-8.1	264,800	263,600	264,100	264,800	265,700	266,100	-0.8
Wyoming	27,285	29,792	29,035	28,190	27,703	27,448	27,214	27,198	27,179	26,526	26,330	26,223	26,042	-4.3	26,200	26,500	26,900	27,200	30,400	31,000	19.0
Jurisdiction																					
Bureau of Indian Education	—	11,192	11,455	11,734	12,157	12,157	14,805	—	—	10,315	9,970	9,977	—	—	—	—	—	—	—	—	—
DoD, overseas	—	14,282	14,462	14,675	14,827	14,607	13,852	13,302	12,829	12,837	—	—	—	—	—	—	—	—	—	—	—
DoD, domestic	—	3,477	3,458	3,356	3,103	2,956	2,771	2,579	2,741	2,758	—	—	—	—	—	—	—	—	—	—	—
Other jurisdictions																					
American Samoa	3,073	3,807	3,996	4,146	4,121	4,253	4,672	4,637	—	—	—	—	—	—	—	—	—	—	—	—	—
Guam	7,115	8,775	8,859	—	9,021	8,919	9,040	—	—	—	—	10,057	10,020	—	—	—	—	—	—	—	—
Northern Marianas	1,531	2,195	2,464	2,872	3,052	3,185	3,291	3,191	3,159	3,097	3,218	3,417	3,308	3.7	—	—	—	—	—	—	—
Puerto Rico	164,378	167,201	166,062	167,089	166,977	166,977	164,043	161,491	154,051	148,520	145,755	139,122	133,816	-17.1	—	—	—	—	—	—	—
U.S. Virgin Islands	5,501	5,549	5,359	5,400	4,978	4,779	5,022	5,047	5,133	5,201	5,084	4,977	5,135	1.7	—	—	—	—	—	—	—

—Not available.

NOTE: DoD = Department of Defense. Detail may not sum to totals because of rounding. Some data have been revised from previously published figures.

SOURCE: U.S. Department of Education, National Center for Education Statistics, Common Core of Data (CCD), "State Non-fiscal Survey of Public Elementary/Secondary Education," 1990–91 through 2011–12; and State Public Elementary and Secondary Enrollment Projection Model, 1980 through 2023. (This table was prepared January 2014.)

Enrollment in public elementary and secondary schools, by level, grade, and state or jurisdiction: Fall 2011

State or jurisdiction	Total, all grades	Elementary Total	Prekindergarten	Kindergarten	Grade 1	Grade 2	Grade 3	Grade 4	Grade 5	Grade 6	Grade 7	Grade 8	Elementary ungraded	Secondary Total	Grade 9	Grade 10	Grade 11	Grade 12	Secondary ungraded
1	2	3	4	5	6	7	8	9	10	11	12	13	14	15	16	17	18	19	20
United States	49,521,669	34,772,751	1,290,977	3,746,415	3,772,639	3,713,225	3,703,314	3,671,865	3,699,119	3,723,575	3,695,995	3,679,111	76,516	14,748,918	3,956,990	3,751,378	3,545,841	3,451,876	42,833
Alabama	744,621	527,006	8,282	57,602	57,859	56,315	55,991	56,491	58,415	59,082	59,050	57,919	0	217,615	61,412	55,908	50,785	49,510	0
Alaska	131,167	92,057	2,755	10,453	10,143	9,961	9,835	9,667	9,891	9,901	9,924	9,527	0	39,110	9,833	9,546	9,813	9,918	0
Arizona	1,080,319	759,494	8,860	84,433	85,535	83,843	83,546	82,566	83,185	83,150	82,879	81,294	203	320,825	82,089	80,788	76,751	81,179	18
Arkansas	483,114	346,022	14,466	37,305	37,491	36,702	36,452	36,662	36,856	36,592	36,832	36,339	325	137,092	38,078	35,729	32,711	30,441	133
California	6,287,834	4,308,447	73,630	488,070	489,961	471,993	467,539	462,082	452,305	466,942	464,260	467,626	4,039	1,979,387	501,073	494,739	487,113	494,144	2,318
Colorado	854,265	610,854	31,091	66,361	66,398	65,598	65,956	64,560	64,089	63,492	62,153	61,156	0	243,411	62,358	60,662	58,993	61,398	0
Connecticut	554,437	383,377	16,022	38,840	40,396	40,051	40,946	40,138	41,078	41,431	41,964	42,511	0	171,060	45,140	43,145	42,098	40,677	0
Delaware	128,946	90,624	1,402	10,116	10,220	9,943	10,138	9,691	9,900	9,887	9,758	9,569	0	38,322	11,168	9,809	8,775	8,570	0
District of Columbia	73,911	56,195	10,831	6,358	5,757	5,102	4,805	4,643	4,816	4,560	4,248	4,328	747	17,716	6,050	4,313	3,708	3,190	455
Florida	2,668,156	1,876,102	54,938	203,302	203,496	200,381	206,732	195,625	202,733	204,229	204,288	200,378	0	792,054	218,469	203,907	195,307	174,371	0
Georgia	1,685,016	1,211,250	45,353	133,372	131,044	128,319	128,647	128,827	131,075	130,164	127,664	126,785	0	473,766	144,204	124,998	105,939	98,625	0
Hawaii	182,706	131,005	1,492	16,827	15,156	14,810	14,672	14,353	13,598	13,919	13,274	12,783	121	51,701	14,830	13,443	12,241	11,084	103
Idaho	279,873	198,064	1,338	21,901	22,557	22,068	21,845	21,835	21,818	21,765	21,765	21,172	0	81,809	21,479	20,996	19,911	19,423	0
Illinois	2,083,097	1,453,156	80,723	145,489	151,937	153,299	153,362	151,870	153,769	155,517	153,362	153,828	0	629,941	165,849	163,897	155,148	145,047	0
Indiana	1,040,765	724,605	9,540	78,166	79,365	79,264	77,866	78,627	81,987	80,259	79,945	79,586	0	316,160	81,801	82,495	77,793	74,071	0
Iowa	495,870	350,152	26,930	40,187	35,807	35,364	35,320	34,951	35,116	35,509	35,470	35,498	4,107	145,718	36,726	36,333	35,590	37,069	1,524
Kansas	486,108	347,129	18,110	37,557	36,798	36,180	36,215	35,608	35,992	35,816	35,455	35,291		138,979	36,197	35,081	33,699	32,478	139
Kentucky	681,987	488,456	28,107	52,325	52,552	51,269	51,309	49,894	51,330	51,087	50,194	50,043	346	193,531	52,499	49,938	47,027	43,928	0
Louisiana	703,390	518,802	29,422	56,037	56,214	54,202	53,607	58,304	51,709	55,279	51,739	52,289		184,588	54,775	48,355	42,370	39,088	0
Maine	188,969	130,046	5,048	13,644	13,826	13,714	13,457	14,190	13,885	14,038	14,317	14,584	0	58,923	14,695	14,686	14,655	14,887	0
Maryland	854,086	594,216	28,850	64,727	64,300	63,976	63,421	63,118	61,111	61,901	60,895	61,917	0	259,870	71,862	65,895	61,824	60,289	0
Massachusetts	953,369	666,314	28,116	67,956	69,906	70,561	70,826	70,404	71,355	71,483	71,950	72,758	999	287,055	76,690	72,220	70,685	67,460	0
Michigan	1,573,537	1,070,873	37,020	107,852	112,451	113,884	111,984	112,465	115,681	117,691	117,802	118,628	5,415	502,664	129,661	130,276	119,607	120,498	2,622
Minnesota	839,738	575,544	14,568	64,133	63,117	63,340	62,311	60,917	61,972	61,580	62,032	61,574	0	264,194	64,074	63,908	64,629	71,583	0
Mississippi	490,619	352,999	3,842	41,048	39,291	38,456	37,067	37,715	37,983	38,800	37,689	36,071	5,037	137,620	37,856	35,235	31,952	29,115	3,462
Missouri	916,584	645,376	29,931	69,864	69,325	68,320	67,473	67,274	68,154	68,500	68,122	68,413	0	271,208	71,813	69,041	65,879	64,475	0
Montana	142,349	99,725	1,475	11,697	11,013	11,015	10,825	10,739	10,780	10,566	10,842	10,773	0	42,624	11,326	10,841	10,249	10,208	0
Nebraska	301,296	213,504	12,907	23,795	22,951	23,099	22,428	22,279	21,949	21,738	21,243	21,115	0	87,792	21,965	21,986	21,509	22,332	0
Nevada	439,634	309,360	4,408	33,502	34,405	33,644	33,316	33,608	34,001	33,911	34,177	33,745	643	130,274	33,511	33,402	33,017	30,322	22
New Hampshire	191,900	129,632	3,228	11,915	13,680	13,859	13,902	14,190	14,237	14,607	14,850	15,164	0	62,268	16,641	15,537	15,179	14,911	0
New Jersey	1,356,431	947,576	36,581	90,955	96,939	98,784	97,569	96,459	98,000	97,384	99,004	98,968	36,933	408,855	104,553	98,853	96,668	94,059	14,722
New Mexico	337,225	239,481	7,652	26,954	26,643	26,175	25,639	25,703	25,786	25,270	25,223	24,436	0	97,744	29,325	25,734	22,014	20,671	0
New York	2,704,718	1,857,574	49,569	197,458	199,702	199,594	199,611	196,082	198,007	201,429	200,192	201,190	14,740	847,144	226,304	218,032	196,644	190,732	15,432
North Carolina	1,507,864	1,074,063	33,603	117,944	117,693	107,431	117,034	116,325	118,534	117,223	115,038	113,238	0	433,801	125,149	111,972	102,663	94,017	0
North Dakota	97,646	67,888	1,706	8,236	7,521	7,490	7,229	7,028	7,029	6,887	7,326	7,436	0	29,758	7,483	7,551	7,376	7,348	0
Ohio	1,740,030	1,217,226	29,015	131,323	130,527	129,983	129,674	130,406	133,152	134,459	134,468	134,219	0	522,804	148,538	135,373	121,027	117,866	0
Oklahoma	666,120	490,196	42,145	53,053	53,145	50,090	49,523	48,690	48,456	48,469	47,869	47,321	1,435	175,924	48,154	45,332	42,450	39,447	541
Oregon	568,208	391,310	7,262	41,478	42,402	42,474	42,463	42,072	42,885	43,193	43,428	43,653	0	176,898	43,968	44,249	42,783	45,898	0
Pennsylvania	1,771,395	1,204,850	12,887	128,804	129,881	131,128	130,624	129,845	133,069	135,198	136,390	135,598	1,426	566,545	144,339	144,453	138,146	138,265	1,342
Rhode Island	142,854	97,659	1,979	10,164	10,762	10,989	10,799	10,827	10,841	10,222	9,930	11,146	0	45,195	12,277	11,492	10,868	10,558	0

See notes at end of table.

Enrollment in public elementary and secondary schools, by level, grade, and state or jurisdiction: Fall 2011—Continued

		Elementary												Secondary					
State or jurisdiction	Total, all grades	Total	Prekinder-garten	Kinder-garten	Grade 1	Grade 2	Grade 3	Grade 4	Grade 5	Grade 6	Grade 7	Grade 8	Elementary ungraded	Total	Grade 9	Grade 10	Grade 11	Grade 12	Secondary ungraded
1	2	3	4	5	6	7	8	9	10	11	12	13	14	15	16	17	18	19	20
South Carolina	727,186	519,389	23,551	56,065	55,995	54,373	53,730	54,157	55,713	56,312	55,250	54,243	0	207,797	60,710	54,075	48,328	44,684	0
South Dakota	128,016	90,529	2,996	11,375	10,326	9,787	9,531	9,364	9,207	9,437	9,367	9,139	0	37,487	10,209	9,740	8,876	8,662	0
Tennessee	999,693	712,749	27,982	79,803	77,853	75,660	75,220	75,146	76,079	75,908	75,373	73,725	0	286,944	76,970	73,216	69,121	67,637	0
Texas	5,000,470	3,636,852	249,524	379,446	392,291	383,411	379,421	375,756	377,729	372,846	366,149	360,279	0	1,363,618	394,326	347,268	323,387	298,637	0
Utah	598,832	434,536	11,972	48,953	48,829	48,768	48,039	46,758	46,198	45,951	45,097	43,971	0	164,296	42,540	41,498	40,565	39,693	0
Vermont	89,908	62,146	5,559	6,062	6,232	6,185	6,165	6,158	6,304	6,283	6,552	6,646	0	27,762	7,017	6,869	6,946	6,930	0
Virginia	1,257,883	881,225	31,805	95,574	95,019	95,322	93,829	93,770	94,316	94,863	93,366	93,361	0	376,658	100,701	95,596	91,037	89,324	0
Washington	1,045,453	718,184	12,268	78,014	78,889	78,338	77,865	77,051	78,848	79,109	78,911	78,891	0	327,269	83,237	80,316	79,627	84,089	0
West Virginia	282,870	202,065	15,280	21,172	21,026	20,623	20,225	20,748	20,491	21,085	20,637	20,778	0	80,805	22,569	20,479	19,259	18,498	0
Wisconsin	871,105	602,810	54,438	60,875	60,572	60,984	60,216	60,094	60,958	61,818	61,442	61,413	0	268,295	67,542	65,510	66,851	68,392	0
Wyoming	90,099	64,057	518	7,873	7,441	7,104	7,115	6,790	6,747	6,833	6,840	6,796	0	26,042	6,955	6,661	6,248	6,178	0
Bureau of Indian Education	—	—	—	—	—	—	—	—	—	—	—	—	—	—	—	—	—	—	—
DoD, overseas	—	—	—	—	—	—	—	—	—	—	—	—	—	—	—	—	—	—	—
DoD, domestic	—	—	—	—	—	—	—	—	—	—	—	—	—	—	—	—	—	—	—
Other jurisdictions																			
American Samoa	—	—	—	—	—	—	—	—	—	—	—	—	—	—	—	—	—	—	—
Guam	31,243	21,223	13	2,216	2,337	2,328	2,418	2,334	2,358	2,364	2,383	2,472	0	10,020	3,101	3,269	2,089	1,561	0
Northern Marianas	11,011	7,703	462	608	736	762	792	814	851	849	944	841	44	3,308	962	950	742	654	0
Puerto Rico	452,740	318,924	1,060	29,287	35,333	32,808	31,990	33,638	34,920	35,415	37,989	36,488	9,996	133,816	35,472	34,152	30,914	28,278	5,000
U.S. Virgin Islands	15,711	10,576	—	1,114	1,101	1,145	1,148	1,251	1,217	1,200	1,274	1,126	—	5,135	1,746	1,215	1,056	1,118	—

—Not available.

NOTE: DoD = Department of Defense. The total ungraded counts of students were prorated to the elementary and secondary levels based on prior reports.

SOURCE: U.S. Department of Education, National Center for Education Statistics, Common Core of Data (CCD), "State Nonfiscal Survey of Public Elementary/Secondary Education", 2011–12. (This table was prepared August 2013.)

Enrollment and percentage distribution of enrollment in public elementary and secondary schools, by race/ethnicity and region: Selected years, fall 1995 through fall 2023

Region and year	Enrollment (in thousands)							Percentage distribution						
	Total	White	Black	Hispanic	Asian/ Pacific Islander	American Indian/ Alaska Native	Two or more races	Total	White	Black	Hispanic	Asian/ Pacific Islander	American Indian/ Alaska Native	Two or more races
1	2	3	4	5	6	7	8	9	10	11	12	13	14	15
United States														
1995	44,840	29,044	7,551	6,072	1,668	505	—	100.0	64.8	16.8	13.5	3.7	1.1	†
2000	47,204	28,878	8,100	7,726	1,950	550	—	100.0	61.2	17.2	16.4	4.1	1.2	†
2001	47,672	28,735	8,177	8,169	2,028	564	—	100.0	60.3	17.2	17.1	4.3	1.2	†
2002	48,183	28,618	8,299	8,594	2,088	583	—	100.0	59.4	17.2	17.8	4.3	1.2	†
2003	48,540	28,442	8,349	9,011	2,145	593	—	100.0	58.6	17.2	18.6	4.4	1.2	†
2004	48,795	28,318	8,386	9,317	2,183	591	—	100.0	58.0	17.2	19.1	4.5	1.2	†
2005	49,113	28,005	8,445	9,787	2,279	598	—	100.0	57.0	17.2	19.9	4.6	1.2	†
2006	49,316	27,801	8,422	10,166	2,332	595	—	100.0	56.4	17.1	20.6	4.7	1.2	†
2007	49,293	27,456	8,392	10,454	2,396	594	—	100.0	55.7	17.0	21.2	4.9	1.2	†
2008	49,266	27,057	8,358	10,563	2,451	589	247 [1]	100.0	54.9	17.0	21.4	5.0	1.2	0.5 [1]
2009	49,361	26,702	8,245	10,991	2,484	601	338 [1]	100.0	54.1	16.7	22.3	5.0	1.2	0.7 [1]
2010	49,484	25,933	7,917	11,439	2,466	566	1,164	100.0	52.4	16.0	23.1	5.0	1.1	2.4
2011	49,522	25,602	7,827	11,759	2,513	547	1,272	100.0	51.7	15.8	23.7	5.1	1.1	2.6
2012[2]	49,652	25,334	7,775	12,157	2,532	539	1,315	100.0	51.0	15.7	24.5	5.1	1.1	2.6
2013[2]	49,750	25,066	7,728	12,510	2,553	533	1,360	100.0	50.4	15.5	25.1	5.1	1.1	2.7
2014[2]	49,751	24,766	7,675	12,814	2,565	526	1,405	100.0	49.8	15.4	25.8	5.2	1.1	2.8
2015[2]	49,839	24,497	7,638	13,148	2,587	522	1,448	100.0	49.2	15.3	26.4	5.2	1.0	2.9
2016[2]	49,951	24,250	7,597	13,481	2,613	516	1,494	100.0	48.5	15.2	27.0	5.2	1.0	3.0
2017[2]	50,280	24,108	7,611	13,854	2,651	513	1,543	100.0	47.9	15.1	27.6	5.3	1.0	3.1
2018[2]	50,543	23,952	7,618	14,188	2,681	511	1,592	100.0	47.4	15.1	28.1	5.3	1.0	3.2
2019[2]	50,834	23,818	7,642	14,506	2,717	510	1,643	100.0	46.9	15.0	28.5	5.3	1.0	3.2
2020[2]	51,165	23,719	7,682	14,806	2,754	510	1,694	100.0	46.4	15.0	28.9	5.4	1.0	3.3
2021[2]	51,485	23,622	7,734	15,086	2,788	511	1,744	100.0	45.9	15.0	29.3	5.4	1.0	3.4
2022[2]	51,804	23,539	7,791	15,346	2,824	513	1,791	100.0	45.4	15.0	29.6	5.5	1.0	3.5
2023[2]	52,113	23,477	7,845	15,572	2,865	515	1,838	100.0	45.1	15.1	29.9	5.5	1.0	3.5
Northeast														
1995	7,894	5,497	1,202	878	295	21	—	100.0	69.6	15.2	11.1	3.7	0.3	†
2000	8,222	5,545	1,270	1,023	361	24	—	100.0	67.4	15.4	12.4	4.4	0.3	†
2001	8,254	5,527	1,273	1,050	378	25	—	100.0	67.0	15.4	12.7	4.6	0.3	†
2004	8,271	5,384	1,292	1,155	414	27	—	100.0	65.1	15.6	14.0	5.0	0.3	†
2005	8,240	5,317	1,282	1,189	425	27	—	100.0	64.5	15.6	14.4	5.2	0.3	†
2006	8,258	5,281	1,279	1,230	440	28	—	100.0	64.0	15.5	14.9	5.3	0.3	†
2007	8,122	5,148	1,250	1,246	451	27	—	100.0	63.4	15.4	15.3	5.6	0.3	†
2008	8,053	5,041	1,226	1,267	467	27	25 [1]	100.0	62.6	15.2	15.7	5.8	0.3	0.3 [1]
2009	8,092	5,010	1,230	1,308	487	27	30 [1]	100.0	61.9	15.2	16.2	6.0	0.3	0.4 [1]
2010	8,071	4,876	1,208	1,364	500	27	96	100.0	60.4	15.0	16.9	6.2	0.3	1.2
2011	7,954	4,745	1,166	1,394	510	27	113	100.0	59.7	14.7	17.5	6.4	0.3	1.4
Midwest														
1995	10,512	8,335	1,450	438	197	92	—	100.0	79.3	13.8	4.2	1.9	0.9	†
2000	10,730	8,208	1,581	610	239	92	—	100.0	76.5	14.7	5.7	2.2	0.9	†
2001	10,746	8,144	1,602	657	248	94	—	100.0	75.8	14.9	6.1	2.3	0.9	†
2004	10,775	7,983	1,634	793	269	96	—	100.0	74.1	15.2	7.4	2.5	0.9	†
2005	10,819	7,950	1,654	836	283	96	—	100.0	73.5	15.3	7.7	2.6	0.9	†
2006	10,819	7,894	1,655	883	290	97	—	100.0	73.0	15.3	8.2	2.7	0.9	†
2007	10,770	7,808	1,642	922	300	99	—	100.0	72.5	15.2	8.6	2.8	0.9	†
2008	10,743	7,734	1,632	963	314	99	29 [1]	100.0	72.0	15.2	9.0	2.9	0.9	0.3 [1]
2009	10,672	7,622	1,606	1,000	318	98	294	100.0	71.4	15.0	9.4	3.0	0.9	2.8
2010	10,610	7,327	1,505	1,077	312	94	294	100.0	69.1	14.2	10.2	2.9	0.9	2.8
2011	10,574	7,240	1,485	1,127	321	90	311	100.0	68.5	14.0	10.7	3.0	0.9	2.9
South														
1995	16,118	9,565	4,236	1,890	280	148	—	100.0	59.3	26.3	11.7	1.7	0.9	†
2000	17,007	9,501	4,516	2,468	352	170	—	100.0	55.9	26.6	14.5	2.1	1.0	†
2001	17,231	9,477	4,556	2,649	373	175	—	100.0	55.0	26.4	15.4	2.2	1.0	†
2004	17,892	9,410	4,704	3,155	432	191	—	100.0	52.6	26.3	17.6	2.4	1.1	†
2005	18,103	9,381	4,738	3,334	456	194	—	100.0	51.8	26.2	18.4	2.5	1.1	†
2006	18,294	9,358	4,729	3,522	485	200	—	100.0	51.2	25.9	19.3	2.6	1.1	†
2007	18,425	9,287	4,751	3,674	511	201	—	100.0	50.4	25.8	19.9	2.8	1.1	†
2008	18,441	9,190	4,771	3,790	537	203	—	100.0	49.7	25.8	20.5	2.9	1.1	†
2009	18,652	9,074	4,710	4,039	555	219	55 [1]	100.0	48.6	25.3	21.7	3.0	1.2	0.3 [1]
2010	18,805	8,869	4,545	4,206	555	207	424	100.0	47.2	24.2	22.4	3.0	1.1	2.3
2011	18,956	8,830	4,535	4,353	577	198	463	100.0	46.6	23.9	23.0	3.0	1.0	2.4
West														
1995	10,316	5,648	662	2,866	896	244	—	100.0	54.7	6.4	27.8	8.7	2.4	†
2000	11,244	5,624	733	3,625	998	264	—	100.0	50.0	6.5	32.2	8.9	2.4	†
2001	11,441	5,586	746	3,813	1,028	269	—	100.0	48.8	6.5	33.4	9.0	2.3	†
2004	11,857	5,541	757	4,213	1,069	277	—	100.0	46.7	6.4	35.5	9.0	2.3	†
2005	11,951	5,356	771	4,428	1,115	281	—	100.0	44.8	6.5	37.1	9.3	2.4	†
2006	11,945	5,268	759	4,531	1,117	270	—	100.0	44.1	6.4	37.9	9.4	2.3	†
2007	11,976	5,213	750	4,611	1,134	267	—	100.0	43.5	6.3	38.5	9.5	2.2	†
2008	11,979	5,092	728	4,543	1,133	261	222 [1]	100.0	42.5	6.1	37.9	9.5	2.2	1.9 [1]
2009	11,945	4,997	699	4,645	1,124	256	223 [1]	100.0	41.8	5.9	38.9	9.4	2.1	1.9 [1]
2010	11,998	4,861	659	4,792	1,100	237	349	100.0	40.5	5.5	39.9	9.2	2.0	2.9
2011	12,038	4,787	642	4,886	1,105	233	385	100.0	39.8	5.3	40.6	9.2	1.9	3.2

—Not available.

†Not applicable.

[1]For this year, data on students of two or more races were reported by only a small number of states. Therefore, the data are not comparable to figures for 2010 and later years.

[2]Projected.

NOTE: Race categories exclude persons of Hispanic ethnicity. Enrollment data for students not reported by race/ethnicity were prorated by state and grade to match state totals. Prior to 2008, data on students of two or more races were not collected. Some data have been revised from previously published figures. Detail may not sum to totals because of rounding.

SOURCE: U.S. Department of Education, National Center for Education Statistics, Common Core of Data (CCD), "State Nonfiscal Survey of Public Elementary and Secondary Education," 1995–96 through 2011–12; and National Elementary and Secondary Enrollment by Race/Ethnicity Projection Model, 1972 through 2023. (This table was prepared December 2013.)

Enrollment and percentage distribution of enrollment in public elementary and secondary schools, by race/ethnicity and level of education: Fall 1998 through fall 2023

Level of education and year	Enrollment (in thousands)									Percentage distribution								
	Total	White	Black	His-panic	Asian/Pacific Islander Total	Asian	Pacific Islander	American Indian/ Alaska Native	Two or more races	Total	White	Black	His-panic	Asian/Pacific Islander Total	Asian	Pacific Islander	American Indian/ Alaska Native	Two or more races
1	2	3	4	5	6	7	8	9	10	11	12	13	14	15	16	17	18	19
Total																		
1998	46,539	29,239	7,945	6,981	1,839	—	—	534	—	100.0	62.8	17.1	15.0	4.0	†	†	1.1	†
1999	46,857	29,035	8,066	7,327	1,887	—	—	542	—	100.0	62.0	17.2	15.6	4.0	†	†	1.2	†
2000	47,204	28,878	8,100	7,726	1,950	—	—	550	—	100.0	61.2	17.2	16.4	4.1	†	†	1.2	†
2001	47,672	28,735	8,177	8,169	2,028	—	—	564	—	100.0	60.3	17.2	17.1	4.3	†	†	1.2	†
2002	48,183	28,618	8,299	8,594	2,088	—	—	583	—	100.0	59.4	17.2	17.8	4.3	†	†	1.2	†
2003	48,540	28,442	8,349	9,011	2,145	—	—	593	—	100.0	58.6	17.2	18.6	4.4	†	†	1.2	†
2004	48,795	28,318	8,386	9,317	2,183	—	—	591	—	100.0	58.0	17.2	19.1	4.5	†	†	1.2	†
2005	49,113	28,005	8,445	9,787	2,279	—	—	598	—	100.0	57.0	17.2	19.9	4.6	†	†	1.2	†
2006	49,316	27,801	8,422	10,166	2,332	—	—	595	—	100.0	56.4	17.1	20.6	4.7	†	†	1.2	†
2007	49,293	27,456	8,392	10,454	2,396	—	—	594	—	100.0	55.7	17.0	21.2	4.9	†	†	1.2	†
2008	49,266	27,057	8,358	10,563	2,451	2,405	46	589	247 [1]	100.0	54.9	17.0	21.4	5.0	4.9	0.1	1.2	0.5 [1]
2009	49,361	26,702	8,245	10,991	2,484	2,435	49	601	338 [1]	100.0	54.1	16.7	22.3	5.0	4.9	0.1	1.2	0.7 [1]
2010	49,484	25,933	7,917	11,439	2,466	2,296	171	566	1,164	100.0	52.4	16.0	23.1	5.0	4.6	0.3	1.1	2.4
2011	49,522	25,602	7,827	11,759	2,513	2,334	179	547	1,272	100.0	51.7	15.8	23.7	5.1	4.7	0.4	1.1	2.6
2012 [2]	49,652	25,334	7,775	12,157	2,532	2,344	188	539	1,315	100.0	51.0	15.7	24.5	5.1	4.7	0.4	1.1	2.6
2013 [2]	49,750	25,066	7,728	12,510	2,553	2,355	198	533	1,360	100.0	50.4	15.5	25.1	5.1	4.7	0.4	1.1	2.7
2014 [2]	49,751	24,766	7,675	12,814	2,565	2,359	207	526	1,405	100.0	49.8	15.4	25.8	5.2	4.7	0.4	1.1	2.8
2015 [2]	49,839	24,497	7,638	13,148	2,587	2,373	215	522	1,448	100.0	49.2	15.3	26.4	5.2	4.8	0.4	1.0	2.9
2016 [2]	49,951	24,250	7,597	13,481	2,613	2,390	223	516	1,494	100.0	48.5	15.2	27.0	5.2	4.8	0.4	1.0	3.0
2017 [2]	50,280	24,108	7,611	13,854	2,651	2,419	232	513	1,543	100.0	47.9	15.1	27.6	5.3	4.8	0.5	1.0	3.1
2018 [2]	50,543	23,952	7,618	14,188	2,681	2,441	240	511	1,592	100.0	47.4	15.1	28.1	5.3	4.8	0.5	1.0	3.2
2019 [2]	50,834	23,818	7,642	14,506	2,717	2,468	249	510	1,643	100.0	46.9	15.0	28.5	5.3	4.9	0.5	1.0	3.2
2020 [2]	51,165	23,719	7,682	14,806	2,754	2,498	256	510	1,694	100.0	46.4	15.0	28.9	5.4	4.9	0.5	1.0	3.3
2021 [2]	51,485	23,622	7,734	15,086	2,788	2,526	263	511	1,744	100.0	45.9	15.0	29.3	5.4	4.9	0.5	1.0	3.4
2022 [2]	51,804	23,539	7,791	15,346	2,824	2,556	268	513	1,791	100.0	45.4	15.0	29.6	5.5	4.9	0.5	1.0	3.5
2023 [2]	52,113	23,477	7,845	15,572	2,865	2,593	272	515	1,838	100.0	45.1	15.1	29.9	5.5	5.0	0.5	1.0	3.5
Prekindergarten through grade 8																		
1998	33,344	20,585	5,864	5,237	1,271	—	—	387	—	100.0	61.7	17.6	15.7	3.8	†	†	1.2	†
1999	33,486	20,327	5,952	5,512	1,303	—	—	391	—	100.0	60.7	17.8	16.5	3.9	†	†	1.2	†
2000	33,686	20,130	5,981	5,830	1,349	—	—	397	—	100.0	59.8	17.8	17.3	4.0	†	†	1.2	†
2001	33,936	19,960	6,004	6,159	1,409	—	—	405	—	100.0	58.8	17.7	18.1	4.2	†	†	1.2	†
2002	34,114	19,764	6,042	6,446	1,447	—	—	415	—	100.0	57.9	17.7	18.9	4.2	†	†	1.2	†
2003	34,201	19,558	6,015	6,729	1,483	—	—	415	—	100.0	57.2	17.6	19.7	4.3	†	†	1.2	†
2004	34,178	19,368	5,983	6,909	1,504	—	—	413	—	100.0	56.7	17.5	20.2	4.4	†	†	1.2	†
2005	34,204	19,051	5,954	7,216	1,569	—	—	412	—	100.0	55.7	17.4	21.1	4.6	†	†	1.2	†
2006	34,235	18,863	5,882	7,465	1,611	—	—	414	—	100.0	55.1	17.2	21.8	4.7	†	†	1.2	†
2007	34,205	18,680	5,821	7,633	1,660	—	—	412	—	100.0	54.6	17.0	22.3	4.9	†	†	1.2	†
2008	34,286	18,501	5,793	7,689	1,705	1,674	31	410	187 [1]	100.0	54.0	16.9	22.4	5.0	4.9	0.1	1.2	0.5 [1]
2009	34,409	18,316	5,713	7,977	1,730	1,697	33	419	254 [1]	100.0	53.2	16.6	23.2	5.0	4.9	0.1	1.2	0.7 [1]
2010	34,625	17,823	5,495	8,314	1,711	1,589	122	394	887	100.0	51.5	15.9	24.0	4.9	4.6	0.4	1.1	2.6
2011	34,773	17,654	5,470	8,558	1,744	1,616	128	384	963	100.0	50.8	15.7	24.6	5.0	4.6	0.4	1.1	2.8
2012 [2]	34,968	17,506	5,454	8,866	1,764	1,629	135	380	997	100.0	50.1	15.6	25.4	5.0	4.7	0.4	1.1	2.9
2013 [2]	35,111	17,342	5,439	9,137	1,786	1,645	141	375	1,031	100.0	49.4	15.5	26.0	5.1	4.7	0.4	1.1	2.9
2014 [2]	35,062	17,115	5,392	9,331	1,790	1,644	147	369	1,065	100.0	48.8	15.4	26.6	5.1	4.7	0.4	1.1	3.0
2015 [2]	35,069	16,899	5,366	9,539	1,805	1,653	152	365	1,095	100.0	48.2	15.3	27.2	5.1	4.7	0.4	1.0	3.1
2016 [2]	35,142	16,737	5,356	9,738	1,818	1,662	156	362	1,130	100.0	47.6	15.2	27.7	5.2	4.7	0.4	1.0	3.2
2017 [2]	35,412	16,668	5,403	9,969	1,839	1,678	161	363	1,170	100.0	47.1	15.3	28.2	5.2	4.7	0.5	1.0	3.3
2018 [2]	35,642	16,592	5,451	10,166	1,860	1,695	165	364	1,210	100.0	46.6	15.3	28.5	5.2	4.8	0.5	1.0	3.4
2019 [2]	35,878	16,546	5,503	10,330	1,886	1,720	167	366	1,247	100.0	46.1	15.3	28.8	5.3	4.8	0.5	1.0	3.5
2020 [2]	36,115	16,515	5,550	10,480	1,919	1,749	170	368	1,283	100.0	45.7	15.4	29.0	5.3	4.8	0.5	1.0	3.6
2021 [2]	36,335	16,487	5,586	10,623	1,953	1,780	172	370	1,317	100.0	45.4	15.4	29.2	5.4	4.9	0.5	1.0	3.6
2022 [2]	36,585	16,476	5,623	10,779	1,985	1,809	176	372	1,350	100.0	45.0	15.4	29.5	5.4	4.9	0.5	1.0	3.7
2023 [2]	36,967	16,517	5,680	10,985	2,028	1,848	180	375	1,381	100.0	44.7	15.4	29.7	5.5	5.0	0.5	1.0	3.7
Grades 9 through 12																		
1998	13,195	8,655	2,081	1,744	567	—	—	147	—	100.0	65.6	15.8	13.2	4.3	†	†	1.1	†
1999	13,371	8,708	2,114	1,815	584	—	—	151	—	100.0	65.1	15.8	13.6	4.4	†	†	1.1	†
2000	13,517	8,747	2,119	1,896	601	—	—	153	—	100.0	64.7	15.7	14.0	4.4	†	†	1.1	†
2001	13,736	8,774	2,173	2,011	619	—	—	159	—	100.0	63.9	15.8	14.6	4.5	†	†	1.2	†
2002	14,069	8,854	2,257	2,148	642	—	—	168	—	100.0	62.9	16.0	15.3	4.6	†	†	1.2	†
2003	14,339	8,884	2,334	2,282	663	—	—	177	—	100.0	62.0	16.3	15.9	4.6	†	†	1.2	†
2004	14,618	8,950	2,403	2,408	679	—	—	178	—	100.0	61.2	16.4	16.5	4.6	†	†	1.2	†
2005	14,909	8,954	2,490	2,570	709	—	—	186	—	100.0	60.1	16.7	17.2	4.8	†	†	1.2	†
2006	15,081	8,938	2,540	2,701	720	—	—	181	—	100.0	59.3	16.8	17.9	4.8	†	†	1.2	†
2007	15,087	8,776	2,571	2,821	736	—	—	183	—	100.0	58.2	17.0	18.7	4.9	†	†	1.2	†
2008	14,980	8,556	2,565	2,874	746	731	15	179	59 [1]	100.0	57.1	17.1	19.2	5.0	4.9	0.1	1.2	0.4 [1]
2009	14,952	8,385	2,532	3,014	754	738	16	182	84 [1]	100.0	56.1	16.9	20.2	5.0	4.9	0.1	1.2	0.6 [1]
2010	14,860	8,109	2,422	3,125	755	707	49	171	277	100.0	54.6	16.3	21.0	5.1	4.8	0.3	1.2	1.9
2011	14,749	7,948	2,357	3,202	769	719	50	163	309	100.0	53.9	16.0	21.7	5.2	4.9	0.3	1.1	2.1
2012 [2]	14,684	7,828	2,320	3,290	768	715	53	159	318	100.0	53.3	15.8	22.4	5.2	4.9	0.4	1.1	2.2

See notes at end of table.

Enrollment and percentage distribution of enrollment in public elementary and secondary schools, by race/ethnicity and level of education: Fall 1998 through fall 2023—Continued

Level of education and year	Enrollment (in thousands)				Asian/Pacific Islander			American Indian/ Alaska Native	Two or more races	Percentage distribution				Asian/Pacific Islander			American Indian/ Alaska Native	Two or more races
	Total	White	Black	His-panic	Total	Asian	Pacific Islander			Total	White	Black	His-panic	Total	Asian	Pacific Islander		
1	2	3	4	5	6	7	8	9	10	11	12	13	14	15	16	17	18	19
2013²	14,639	7,724	2,289	3,373	767	710	56	158	329	100.0	52.8	15.6	23.0	5.2	4.9	0.4	1.1	2.2
2014²	14,689	7,651	2,283	3,483	775	715	60	157	340	100.0	52.1	15.5	23.7	5.3	4.9	0.4	1.1	2.3
2015²	14,770	7,598	2,271	3,610	782	719	63	157	353	100.0	51.4	15.4	24.4	5.3	4.9	0.4	1.1	2.4
2016²	14,810	7,513	2,241	3,743	794	728	67	154	364	100.0	50.7	15.1	25.3	5.4	4.9	0.4	1.0	2.5
2017²	14,868	7,440	2,208	3,886	812	741	71	150	373	100.0	50.0	14.8	26.1	5.5	5.0	0.5	1.0	2.5
2018²	14,901	7,360	2,167	4,023	821	746	76	147	382	100.0	49.4	14.5	27.0	5.5	5.0	0.5	1.0	2.6
2019²	14,957	7,271	2,139	4,176	831	749	82	144	396	100.0	48.6	14.3	27.9	5.6	5.0	0.5	1.0	2.6
2020²	15,050	7,204	2,132	4,325	835	748	86	143	412	100.0	47.9	14.2	28.7	5.5	5.0	0.6	0.9	2.7
2021²	15,151	7,135	2,148	4,463	836	745	90	142	427	100.0	47.1	14.2	29.5	5.5	4.9	0.6	0.9	2.8
2022²	15,219	7,062	2,168	4,566	839	746	92	141	442	100.0	46.4	14.2	30.0	5.5	4.9	0.6	0.9	2.9
2023²	15,146	6,960	2,166	4,586	837	745	92	140	457	100.0	46.0	14.3	30.3	5.5	4.9	0.6	0.9	3.0

—Not available.
†Not applicable.
[1]For this year, data on students of two or more races were reported by only a small number of states. Therefore, the data are not comparable to figures for 2010 and later years.
[2]Projected.
NOTE: Race categories exclude persons of Hispanic ethnicity. Enrollment data for students not reported by race/ethnicity were prorated by state and grade to match state totals. Prior to 2008, data on students of two or more races were not collected separately. Total counts of ungraded students were prorated to prekindergarten through grade 8 and grades 9 through 12 based on prior reports. Some data have been revised from previously published figures. Detail may not sum to totals because of rounding.
SOURCE: U.S. Department of Education, National Center for Education Statistics, Common Core of Data (CCD), "State Nonfiscal Survey of Public Elementary and Secondary Education," 1998–99 through 2011–12; and National Elementary and Secondary Enrollment by Race/Ethnicity Projection Model, 1972 through 2023. (This table was prepared April 2014.)

Percentage distribution of enrollment in public elementary and secondary schools, by race/ethnicity and state or jurisdiction: Fall 2001 and fall 2011

	Percentage distribution, fall 2001						Percentage distribution, fall 2011							
State or jurisdiction	Total	White	Black	Hispanic	Asian/ Pacific Islander	American Indian/ Alaska Native	Total	White	Black	Hispanic	Asian	Pacific Islander	American Indian/ Alaska Native	Two or more races
1	2	3	4	5	6	7	8	9	10	11	12	13	14	15
United States	100.0	60.3	17.2	17.1	4.2	1.2	100.0	51.7	15.8	23.7	4.7	0.4	1.1	2.6
Alabama	100.0	60.5	36.5	1.5	0.8	0.7	100.0	58.1	34.2	4.7	1.3	#	0.8	0.8
Alaska	100.0	60.4	4.7	3.6	5.9	25.5	100.0	50.9	3.6	6.2	6.1	2.2	23.5	7.5
Arizona	100.0	51.3	4.7	35.3	2.1	6.6	100.0	42.1	5.4	42.8	2.8	0.3	5.1	1.6
Arkansas.....................	100.0	71.1	23.3	4.2	0.9	0.5	100.0	64.4	21.2	10.2	1.4	0.5	0.7	1.6
California	100.0	35.0	8.4	44.5	11.2	0.9	100.0	26.0	6.5	52.1	11.2	0.6	0.7	2.9
Colorado.....................	100.0	66.8	5.7	23.3	3.0	1.2	100.0	56.1	4.8	31.9	3.1	0.2	0.8	3.1
Connecticut.................	100.0	69.2	13.8	13.7	3.0	0.3	100.0	60.9	13.0	19.5	4.4	0.1	0.3	1.8
Delaware.....................	100.0	59.6	31.1	6.6	2.4	0.3	100.0	49.5	31.6	13.1	3.4	0.1	0.5	1.8
District of Columbia	100.0	4.6	84.4	9.4	1.6	#	100.0	7.7	76.4	13.1	1.4	0.1	0.1	1.1
Florida........................	100.0	52.5	24.9	20.4	1.9	0.3	100.0	42.4	23.0	28.6	2.5	0.1	0.4	3.0
Georgia.......................	100.0	53.8	38.2	5.5	2.4	0.2	100.0	44.1	37.0	12.2	3.4	0.1	0.2	3.0
Hawaii........................	100.0	20.3	2.4	4.5	72.3	0.4	100.0	14.3	2.4	6.4	34.2	33.9	0.5	8.2
Idaho.........................	100.0	85.4	0.8	11.2	1.3	1.3	100.0	78.0	1.0	16.3	1.3	0.3	1.3	1.7
Illinois........................	100.0	59.0	21.2	16.2	3.5	0.2	100.0	50.8	18.0	23.7	4.2	0.1	0.3	2.8
Indiana.......................	100.0	83.0	11.8	3.9	1.0	0.2	100.0	72.5	12.2	9.0	1.7	0.1	0.3	4.3
Iowa..........................	100.0	89.6	4.1	4.0	1.7	0.5	100.0	80.7	5.1	8.9	2.1	0.2	0.5	2.6
Kansas.......................	100.0	77.8	8.9	9.8	2.2	1.3	100.0	67.4	7.3	17.2	2.5	0.2	1.1	4.3
Kentucky.....................	100.0	87.7	10.3	1.1	0.7	0.2	100.0	81.1	10.8	4.3	1.4	0.1	0.1	2.2
Louisiana....................	100.0	48.7	47.8	1.6	1.3	0.7	100.0	47.4	45.1	4.0	1.5	0.1	0.8	1.2
Maine.........................	100.0	96.2	1.4	0.6	1.1	0.7	100.0	91.8	3.0	1.6	1.6	0.1	0.8	1.1
Maryland.....................	100.0	52.4	37.2	5.4	4.6	0.4	100.0	42.5	35.4	12.1	5.9	0.1	0.3	3.7
Massachusetts..............	100.0	75.7	8.6	10.8	4.5	0.3	100.0	67.0	8.3	16.1	5.7	0.1	0.2	2.5
Michigan.....................	100.0	73.4	20.0	3.6	2.0	1.0	100.0	69.2	18.8	6.2	2.7	0.1	0.8	2.2
Minnesota...................	100.0	82.0	7.0	3.8	5.2	2.0	100.0	73.0	9.2	7.4	6.2	0.1	1.8	2.3
Mississippi..................	100.0	47.3	51.0	0.9	0.7	0.2	100.0	46.0	49.6	2.6	1.0	#	0.2	0.6
Missouri......................	100.0	79.0	17.5	2.0	1.2	0.3	100.0	74.2	16.8	4.9	1.9	0.2	0.5	1.7
Montana......................	100.0	85.9	0.6	1.9	1.0	10.6	100.0	80.9	1.0	3.7	0.9	0.3	11.6	1.7
Nebraska.....................	100.0	81.8	6.9	8.2	1.6	1.6	100.0	70.2	6.7	16.4	2.1	0.1	1.5	3.1
Nevada.......................	100.0	54.5	10.3	27.4	6.1	1.7	100.0	37.4	9.6	39.6	5.6	1.3	1.1	5.3
New Hampshire..............	100.0	95.0	1.2	2.1	1.5	0.2	100.0	89.1	1.9	3.9	2.8	0.1	0.3	1.9
New Jersey..................	100.0	59.4	17.9	16.0	6.6	0.2	100.0	51.1	16.2	22.5	9.0	0.2	0.1	0.8
New Mexico..................	100.0	34.3	2.4	51.0	1.1	11.3	100.0	25.9	2.0	59.5	1.2	0.1	10.2	1.1
New York.....................	100.0	54.8	19.9	18.6	6.2	0.4	100.0	48.2	18.5	23.3	8.4	0.2	0.5	0.8
North Carolina..............	100.0	60.0	31.3	5.2	1.9	1.5	100.0	52.4	26.4	13.5	2.5	0.1	1.5	3.7
North Dakota	100.0	88.7	1.1	1.3	0.8	8.1	100.0	83.2	2.6	2.9	1.2	0.2	9.1	0.9
Ohio..........................	100.0	80.1	16.7	1.9	1.2	0.1	100.0	73.7	16.2	3.8	1.8	#	0.1	4.3
Oklahoma....................	100.0	63.7	10.8	6.5	1.5	17.5	100.0	53.7	9.8	13.1	1.9	0.3	16.6	4.7
Oregon.......................	100.0	79.1	3.0	11.5	4.2	2.2	100.0	65.3	2.5	21.1	3.9	0.6	1.8	4.7
Pennsylvania................	100.0	77.7	15.3	4.8	2.1	0.1	100.0	70.6	15.3	8.7	3.3	0.1	0.2	1.9
Rhode Island	100.0	73.4	8.1	14.8	3.2	0.6	100.0	64.0	8.1	21.6	2.9	0.2	0.6	2.7
South Carolina..............	100.0	54.9	41.6	2.3	1.0	0.3	100.0	53.2	35.6	6.7	1.4	0.1	0.3	2.7
South Dakota...............	100.0	86.2	1.3	1.4	1.0	10.2	100.0	78.4	2.6	3.9	1.5	0.1	11.7	1.7
Tennessee	100.0	71.8	24.8	2.1	1.2	0.2	100.0	67.1	23.3	6.6	1.7	0.1	0.2	1.0
Texas	100.0	40.9	14.4	41.7	2.8	0.3	100.0	30.6	12.8	50.8	3.5	0.1	0.4	1.7
Utah..........................	100.0	84.7	1.0	9.9	2.8	1.5	100.0	77.5	1.3	15.3	1.8	1.5	1.2	1.4
Vermont......................	100.0	95.8	1.2	1.0	1.5	0.5	100.0	92.5	1.9	1.4	1.7	0.1	0.4	2.1
Virginia.......................	100.0	62.8	27.1	5.5	4.3	0.3	100.0	53.5	23.8	11.9	6.0	0.1	0.3	4.3
Washington..................	100.0	73.5	5.4	10.9	7.5	2.6	100.0	60.3	4.6	19.6	7.1	0.9	1.5	6.0
West Virginia................	100.0	94.5	4.4	0.4	0.6	0.1	100.0	91.7	5.0	1.2	0.7	#	0.1	1.2
Wisconsin....................	100.0	80.1	10.2	5.0	3.4	1.4	100.0	73.7	9.8	9.7	3.5	0.1	1.3	1.9
Wyoming.....................	100.0	87.3	1.4	7.2	0.9	3.2	100.0	80.5	1.1	12.6	0.8	0.1	3.2	1.7
Bureau of Indian Education	100.0	0.0	0.0	0.0	0.0	100.0	—	—	—	—	—	—	—	—
DoD, overseas	100.0	61.6	19.1	9.3	9.1	1.0	—	—	—	—	—	—	—	—
DoD, domestic	100.0	51.6	25.8	18.5	3.5	0.6	—	—	—	—	—	—	—	—
Other jurisdictions														
American Samoa	100.0	0.0	0.0	0.0	100.0	0.0	—	—	—	—	—	—	—	—
Guam	100.0	1.5	0.3	0.2	97.9	0.1	100.0	0.7	0.2	0.1	23.7	73.2	#	2.1
Northern Marianas.......	100.0	0.4	0.1	0.0	99.6	0.0	100.0	0.7	0.0	#	39.1	59.8	0.0	0.4
Puerto Rico	100.0	0.0	0.0	100.0	0.0	0.0	100.0	0.1	#	99.8	#	#	0.1	#
U.S. Virgin Islands........	—	—	—	—	—	—	100.0	1.5	78.1	18.8	0.3	0.1	0.1	1.0

—Not available.
#Rounds to zero.
NOTE: Percentage distribution based on students for whom race/ethnicity was reported, which may be less than the total number of students in the state. Race categories exclude persons of Hispanic ethnicity. DoD = Department of Defense. Detail may not sum to totals because of rounding.

SOURCE: U.S. Department of Education, National Center for Education Statistics, Common Core of Data (CCD), "State Nonfiscal Survey of Public Elementary/Secondary Education," 2001–02 and 2011–12. (This table was prepared March 2014.)

Average daily attendance (ADA) as a percentage of total enrollment, school day length, and school year length in public schools, by school level and state: 2007–08 and 2011–12

[Standard errors appear in parentheses]

State	2007–08		2011–12								
	ADA as percent of enrollment	Average hours in school day	Total elementary, secondary, and combined elementary/secondary schools				Elementary schools		Secondary schools	
			ADA as percent of enrollment	Average hours in school day	Average days in school year	Average hours in school year	ADA as percent of enrollment	Average hours in school day	ADA as percent of enrollment	Average hours in school day
1	2	3	4	5	6	7	8	9	10	11
United States	**93.1** (0.22)	**6.6** (0.02)	**93.9** (0.12)	**6.7** (0.01)	**179** (0.1)	**1,203** (2.0)	**94.9** (0.12)	**6.7** (0.01)	**91.7** (0.34)	**6.7** (0.02)
Alabama	93.8 (1.24)	7.0 (0.07)	94.4 (0.94)	7.0 (0.04)	181 (0.8)	1,271 (8.5)	95.3 (0.92)	7.1 (0.04)	94.6 (0.65)	6.9 (0.13)
Alaska	89.9 (1.22)	6.5 (0.05)	91.4 (1.19)	6.7 (0.17)	177 (1.3)	1,183 (37.3)	‡ (†)	‡ (†)	‡ (†)	‡ (†)
Arizona	89.0 (2.95)	6.4 (0.09)	91.7 (0.99)	6.7 (0.08)	179 (1.3)	1,201 (12.5)	93.5 (0.53)	6.9 (0.06)	87.9 (2.40)	6.5 (0.26)
Arkansas	91.8 (1.35)	6.9 (0.06)	94.2 (0.58)	7.0 (0.07)	180 (0.5)	1,261 (14.1)	94.7 (0.36)	7.0 (0.08)	92.9 (1.93)	6.9 (0.14)
California	93.2 (0.71)	6.2 (0.07)	93.1 (0.46)	6.2 (0.05)	180 (0.3)	1,121 (9.0)	94.7 (0.51)	6.3 (0.06)	89.7 (1.08)	6.3 (0.08)
Colorado	93.9 (0.44)	7.0 (0.05)	93.1 (0.71)	7.1 (0.06)	172 (1.4)	1,215 (7.7)	94.6 (0.59)	7.0 (0.07)	88.0 (2.57)	7.1 (0.10)
Connecticut	87.9 (2.98)	6.5 (0.09)	94.9 (0.47)	6.6 (0.04)	181 (0.1)	1,201 (7.5)	95.4 (0.61)	6.6 (0.05)	94.3 (0.33)	6.7 (0.09)
Delaware	89.8 (1.75)	6.7 (0.09)	93.5 (0.50)	7.0 (0.10)	182 (1.2)	1,269 (23.7)	94.1 (0.50)	7.0 (0.12)	93.8 (0.71)	7.0 (0.09)
District of Columbia	91.2 (1.27)	6.9 (0.21)	‡ (†)	‡ (†)	‡ (†)	‡ (†)	‡ (†)	‡ (†)	‡ (†)	‡ (†)
Florida	92.7 (0.74)	6.4 (0.08)	93.2 (0.52)	6.6 (0.06)	181 (1.2)	1,193 (14.2)	94.3 (0.49)	6.6 (0.08)	90.7 (0.84)	6.7 (0.09)
Georgia	93.3 (1.28)	6.8 (0.06)	94.3 (0.53)	7.0 (0.04)	178 (0.4)	1,242 (8.5)	95.0 (0.59)	6.9 (0.05)	‡ (†)	‡ (†)
Hawaii	90.7 (4.58)	6.3 (0.10)	‡ (†)	‡ (†)	‡ (†)	‡ (†)	‡ (†)	‡ (†)	‡ (†)	‡ (†)
Idaho	92.4 (2.27)	6.6 (0.09)	94.1 (1.01)	6.7 (0.13)	166 (5.1)	1,110 (21.7)	94.4 (0.75)	6.7 (0.08)	93.1 (0.83)	6.7 (0.20)
Illinois	94.0 (0.71)	6.5 (0.09)	94.1 (0.40)	6.5 (0.04)	176 (0.4)	1,151 (7.7)	95.1 (0.29)	6.5 (0.05)	92.4 (1.29)	6.8 (0.08)
Indiana	95.7 (0.51)	6.8 (0.06)	95.9 (0.20)	6.8 (0.05)	180 (0.1)	1,226 (9.1)	96.1 (0.25)	6.7 (0.05)	95.5 (0.31)	7.0 (0.07)
Iowa	94.8 (0.65)	6.9 (0.09)	95.7 (0.36)	6.7 (0.12)	180 (0.2)	1,213 (21.8)	96.4 (0.21)	6.9 (0.05)	93.6 (1.39)	6.3 (0.47)
Kansas	95.4 (0.52)	7.0 (0.07)	94.9 (0.42)	7.0 (0.03)	177 (2.6)	1,245 (17.9)	95.5 (0.53)	7.0 (0.04)	94.0 (0.42)	7.1 (0.04)
Kentucky	93.1 (1.89)	6.7 (0.06)	93.2 (1.33)	6.8 (0.06)	179 (1.0)	1,211 (11.6)	95.9 (0.22)	6.8 (0.07)	87.0 (4.87)	6.8 (0.14)
Louisiana	90.3 (2.31)	7.1 (0.08)	92.8 (0.70)	7.2 (0.07)	178 (1.1)	1,283 (10.7)	93.0 (0.88)	7.3 (0.07)	93.5 (0.42)	7.1 (0.14)
Maine	90.3 (2.41)	6.5 (0.06)	94.2 (0.73)	6.6 (0.06)	176 (0.2)	1,156 (10.7)	94.4 (1.00)	6.6 (0.07)	93.8 (0.45)	6.3 (0.08)
Maryland	94.1 (0.44)	6.6 (0.07)	‡ (†)	‡ (†)	‡ (†)	‡ (†)	‡ (†)	‡ (†)	‡ (†)	‡ (†)
Massachusetts	94.6 (0.58)	6.5 (0.05)	93.5 (0.62)	6.4 (0.07)	180 (0.2)	1,157 (13.3)	94.4 (0.63)	6.4 (0.07)	90.3 (2.55)	6.6 (0.05)
Michigan	93.0 (1.01)	6.6 (0.08)	91.6 (0.71)	6.8 (0.03)	177 (0.5)	1,196 (5.9)	92.3 (0.99)	6.8 (0.03)	89.4 (1.28)	6.7 (0.07)
Minnesota	93.1 (0.91)	6.3 (0.12)	93.1 (0.49)	6.4 (0.08)	173 (1.3)	1,111 (14.0)	96.1 (0.19)	6.6 (0.07)	89.5 (1.21)	6.0 (0.20)
Mississippi	92.1 (2.00)	7.0 (0.12)	94.4 (0.47)	7.2 (0.09)	181 (0.4)	1,312 (16.4)	94.9 (0.57)	7.3 (0.06)	93.7 (0.86)	7.2 (0.24)
Missouri	94.8 (0.26)	6.7 (0.05)	95.1 (0.36)	6.9 (0.03)	175 (0.3)	1,197 (5.3)	95.6 (0.24)	6.9 (0.04)	94.3 (0.24)	6.8 (0.11)
Montana	91.3 (1.39)	6.8 (0.05)	93.9 (0.81)	6.6 (0.04)	179 (0.4)	1,189 (11.2)	94.3 (0.79)	6.6 (0.09)	93.0 (0.48)	6.7 (0.14)
Nebraska	94.9 (1.21)	6.9 (0.08)	94.8 (0.60)	7.1 (0.05)	177 (1.0)	1,257 (9.6)	96.0 (0.53)	7.1 (0.04)	94.5 (0.66)	6.8 (0.19)
Nevada	93.5 (1.27)	6.3 (0.06)	93.9 (0.39)	6.5 (0.07)	180 (1.1)	1,164 (10.9)	94.5 (0.30)	6.4 (0.10)	93.9 (0.70)	6.5 (0.07)
New Hampshire	92.2 (1.75)	6.5 (0.05)	91.1 (2.86)	6.6 (0.05)	180 (0.3)	1,181 (10.3)	95.9 (0.45)	6.5 (0.07)	75.1 (12.63)	6.7 (0.05)
New Jersey	94.6 (0.59)	6.4 (0.05)	93.5 (1.13)	6.6 (0.06)	181 (0.2)	1,201 (11.8)	93.7 (1.40)	6.6 (0.07)	92.6 (1.29)	6.7 (0.07)
New Mexico	91.9 (1.76)	6.8 (0.08)	92.8 (0.80)	6.9 (0.09)	177 (0.6)	1,216 (15.7)	93.8 (0.80)	6.7 (0.08)	88.5 (2.41)	7.1 (0.14)
New York	92.7 (1.30)	6.6 (0.06)	92.7 (0.94)	6.6 (0.06)	182 (0.2)	1,206 (10.6)	93.6 (1.28)	6.6 (0.07)	90.0 (1.32)	6.8 (0.07)
North Carolina	92.6 (1.73)	6.7 (0.06)	94.7 (0.37)	6.9 (0.04)	181 (0.2)	1,240 (7.4)	95.2 (0.23)	6.8 (0.04)	‡ (†)	‡ (†)
North Dakota	95.9 (0.59)	6.6 (0.04)	95.2 (0.46)	6.5 (0.06)	177 (0.3)	1,159 (10.0)	96.4 (0.35)	6.4 (0.08)	95.5 (0.45)	6.6 (0.14)
Ohio	91.8 (2.01)	6.6 (0.10)	93.8 (0.48)	6.6 (0.03)	180 (0.5)	1,191 (6.2)	95.0 (0.30)	6.6 (0.04)	91.0 (1.45)	6.7 (0.07)
Oklahoma	92.1 (2.24)	6.6 (0.06)	94.4 (0.32)	6.7 (0.04)	174 (0.7)	1,176 (8.6)	94.9 (0.38)	6.7 (0.04)	93.3 (0.74)	6.8 (0.10)
Oregon	94.4 (0.59)	6.6 (0.06)	94.2 (0.40)	6.6 (0.05)	170 (0.9)	1,118 (7.9)	95.1 (0.29)	6.5 (0.06)	91.1 (1.41)	6.7 (0.06)
Pennsylvania	94.9 (0.39)	6.4 (0.12)	94.4 (0.29)	6.7 (0.06)	181 (0.2)	1,212 (9.5)	94.9 (0.38)	6.7 (0.06)	92.9 (0.56)	6.9 (0.14)
Rhode Island	93.7 (1.27)	6.3 (0.03)	94.6 (0.36)	6.4 (0.05)	180 (0.1)	1,150 (8.2)	95.1 (0.38)	6.3 (0.05)	‡ (†)	‡ (†)
South Carolina	94.9 (0.71)	6.9 (0.07)	95.6 (0.26)	7.0 (0.04)	181 (0.4)	1,263 (7.3)	96.2 (0.27)	6.9 (0.05)	93.9 (0.84)	7.1 (0.05)
South Dakota	93.6 (2.53)	6.8 (0.08)	96.1 (0.24)	7.0 (0.07)	170 (1.1)	1,180 (6.7)	96.7 (0.30)	6.9 (0.08)	93.6 (0.53)	6.9 (0.17)
Tennessee	94.9 (0.23)	7.0 (0.05)	94.6 (0.30)	7.1 (0.03)	179 (0.4)	1,272 (7.8)	95.0 (0.28)	7.1 (0.04)	94.2 (0.45)	7.0 (0.02)
Texas	94.1 (1.34)	7.2 (0.11)	95.2 (0.43)	7.3 (0.04)	179 (0.7)	1,297 (8.8)	95.9 (0.41)	7.3 (0.03)	94.8 (0.29)	7.3 (0.06)
Utah	91.4 (1.56)	6.3 (0.29)	93.3 (0.80)	6.5 (0.08)	179 (0.3)	1,165 (13.5)	94.4 (0.80)	6.5 (0.08)	93.6 (0.74)	6.6 (0.09)
Vermont	92.7 (3.39)	6.7 (0.07)	94.0 (0.95)	6.7 (0.04)	178 (0.3)	1,183 (7.2)	93.7 (1.30)	6.8 (0.04)	94.7 (0.35)	6.2 (0.12)
Virginia	94.7 (0.46)	6.6 (0.05)	95.0 (0.32)	6.6 (0.03)	185 (3.4)	1,222 (18.8)	95.8 (0.32)	6.7 (0.03)	93.3 (0.65)	6.6 (0.10)
Washington	82.9 (3.06)	6.2 (0.08)	92.2 (0.67)	6.3 (0.06)	179 (0.3)	1,129 (11.3)	94.3 (0.55)	6.4 (0.04)	88.0 (2.00)	6.1 (0.19)
West Virginia	94.0 (0.99)	6.9 (0.07)	94.9 (0.46)	7.0 (0.05)	181 (0.4)	1,272 (9.8)	96.2 (0.27)	7.0 (0.07)	89.8 (1.98)	7.3 (0.09)
Wisconsin	95.0 (0.57)	6.9 (0.04)	94.9 (0.31)	6.9 (0.11)	179 (0.2)	1,234 (19.2)	95.7 (0.21)	7.0 (0.03)	91.9 (1.08)	7.0 (0.12)
Wyoming	92.4 (1.15)	6.9 (0.05)	93.6 (0.81)	7.0 (0.04)	174 (0.5)	1,209 (6.5)	94.8 (0.78)	6.9 (0.05)	89.9 (2.19)	7.0 (0.08)

†Not applicable.
‡Reporting standards not met. Either the response rate is under 50 percent or there are too few cases for a reliable estimate.
NOTE: Averages reflect data reported by schools rather than state requirements. School-reported length of day may exceed state requirements, and there is a range of statistical error in reported estimates.

SOURCE: U.S. Department of Education, National Center for Education Statistics, Schools and Staffing Survey (SASS), "Public School Data File," 2007–08 and 2011–12. (This table was prepared May 2013.)

High school graduates, by sex and control of school: Selected years, 1869–70 through 2023–24

School year	High school graduates							Averaged freshman graduation rate for public schools[3]	Population 17 years old[4]	Graduates as a ratio of 17-year-old population
	Total[1]	Sex		Control						
				Public[2]			Private			
		Males	Females	Total	Males	Females	Total			
1	2	3	4	5	6	7	8	9	10	11
1869–70	16,000	7,064	8,936	—	—	—	—	—	815,000	2.0
1879–80	23,634	10,605	13,029	—	—	—	—	—	946,026	2.5
1889–90	43,731	18,549	25,182	21,882	—	—	21,849 [5]	—	1,259,177	3.5
1899–1900	94,883	38,075	56,808	61,737	—	—	33,146 [5]	—	1,489,146	6.4
1909–10	156,429	63,676	92,753	111,363	—	—	45,066 [5]	—	1,786,240	8.8
1919–20	311,266	123,684	187,582	230,902	—	—	80,364 [5]	—	1,855,173	16.8
1929–30	666,904	300,376	366,528	591,719	—	—	75,185 [5]	—	2,295,822	29.0
1939–40	1,221,475	578,718	642,757	1,143,246	538,273	604,973	78,229 [5]	—	2,403,074	50.8
1949–50	1,199,700	570,700	629,000	1,063,444	505,394	558,050	136,256 [5]	—	2,034,450	59.0
1959–60	1,858,023	895,000	963,000	1,627,050	791,426	835,624	230,973	—	2,672,000	69.5
1969–70	2,888,639	1,430,000	1,459,000	2,588,639	1,285,895	1,302,744	300,000	78.7	3,757,000	76.9
1974–75	3,132,502	1,542,000	1,591,000	2,822,502	1,391,519	1,430,983	310,000 [5]	74.9	4,256,000	73.6
1975–76	3,142,120	1,552,000	1,590,000	2,837,129	1,401,064	1,436,065	304,991	74.9	4,272,000	73.6
1976–77	3,139,536	1,551,000	1,589,000	2,837,340	—	—	302,196	74.4	4,272,000	73.5
1977–78	3,128,824	1,546,000	1,583,000	2,824,636	—	—	304,188	73.2	4,286,000	73.0
1978–79	3,101,152	1,532,000	1,569,000	2,801,152	—	—	300,000 [5]	71.9	4,327,000	71.7
1979–80	3,042,214	1,503,000	1,539,000	2,747,678	—	—	294,536	71.5	4,262,000	71.4
1980–81	3,020,285	1,492,000	1,528,000	2,725,285	—	—	295,000 [5]	72.2	4,212,000	71.7
1981–82	2,994,758	1,479,000	1,515,000	2,704,758	—	—	290,000 [5]	72.9	4,134,000	72.4
1982–83	2,887,604	1,426,000	1,461,000	2,597,604	—	—	290,000 [5]	73.8	3,962,000	72.9
1983–84	2,766,797	—	—	2,494,797	—	—	272,000 [5]	74.5	3,784,000	73.1
1984–85	2,676,917	—	—	2,413,917	—	—	263,000 [5]	74.2	3,699,000	72.4
1985–86	2,642,616	—	—	2,382,616	—	—	260,000 [5]	74.3	3,670,000	72.0
1986–87	2,693,803	—	—	2,428,803	—	—	265,000 [5]	74.3	3,754,000	71.8
1987–88	2,773,020	—	—	2,500,020	—	—	273,000 [5]	74.2	3,849,000	72.0
1988–89	2,743,743	—	—	2,458,800	—	—	284,943	73.4	3,842,000	71.4
1989–90[6]	2,574,162	—	—	2,320,337	—	—	253,825 [7]	73.6	3,505,000	73.4
1990–91	2,492,988	—	—	2,234,893	—	—	258,095	73.7	3,417,913	72.9
1991–92	2,480,399	—	—	2,226,016	—	—	254,383 [7]	74.2	3,398,884	73.0
1992–93	2,480,519	—	—	2,233,241	—	—	247,278	73.8	3,449,143	71.9
1993–94	2,463,849	—	—	2,220,849	—	—	243,000 [5]	73.1	3,442,521	71.6
1994–95	2,519,084	—	—	2,273,541	—	—	245,543	71.8	3,635,803	69.3
1995–96	2,518,109	—	—	2,273,109	—	—	245,000 [5]	71.0	3,640,132	69.2
1996–97	2,611,988	—	—	2,358,403	—	—	253,585	71.3	3,792,207	68.9
1997–98	2,704,050	—	—	2,439,050	1,187,647	1,251,403	265,000 [5]	71.3	4,008,416	67.5
1998–99	2,758,655	—	—	2,485,630	1,212,924	1,272,706	273,025	71.1	3,917,885	70.4
1999–2000	2,832,844	—	—	2,553,844	1,241,631	1,312,213	279,000 [5]	71.7	4,056,639	69.8
2000–01	2,847,973	—	—	2,569,200	1,251,931	1,317,269	278,773	71.7	4,023,686	70.8
2001–02	2,906,534	—	—	2,621,534	1,275,813	1,345,721	285,000 [5]	72.6	4,023,968	72.2
2002–03	3,015,735	—	—	2,719,947	1,330,973	1,388,974	295,788	73.9	4,125,087	73.1
2003–04[6,8]	3,054,438	—	—	2,753,438	1,347,800	1,405,638	301,000 [5]	74.3	4,113,074	74.3
2004–05	3,106,499	—	—	2,799,250	1,369,749	1,429,501	307,249	74.7	4,120,073	75.4
2005–06[6]	3,122,544	—	—	2,815,544	1,376,458	1,439,086	307,000 [5]	73.4	4,200,554	74.3
2006–07	3,199,650	—	—	2,893,045	1,414,069	1,478,976	306,605	73.9	4,297,239	74.5
2007–08	3,312,337	—	—	3,001,337	1,467,180	1,534,157	311,000 [5]	74.7	4,436,955	74.7
2008–09[6]	3,347,828	—	—	3,039,015	1,490,317	1,548,698	308,813	75.5	4,336,950	77.2
2009–10	3,440,185	—	—	3,128,022	1,542,684 [9]	1,585,338 [9]	312,163 [5]	78.2	4,311,831	79.8
2010–11	3,449,719	—	—	3,143,879	—	—	305,840	79.6	4,366,292	79.0
2011–12	3,452,470	—	—	3,147,790	—	—	304,680 [5]	80.8	4,291,741	80.4
2012–13[10]	3,408,600	—	—	3,110,150	—	—	298,450	—	—	—
2013–14[10]	3,365,560	—	—	3,070,440	—	—	295,120	—	—	—
2014–15[10]	3,322,780	—	—	3,031,450	—	—	291,320	—	—	—
2015–16[10]	3,322,620	—	—	3,047,830	—	—	274,800	—	—	—
2016–17[10]	3,328,710	—	—	3,066,350	—	—	262,370	—	—	—
2017–18[10]	3,366,070	—	—	3,105,970	—	—	260,100	—	—	—
2018–19[10]	3,348,610	—	—	3,100,900	—	—	247,710	—	—	—
2019–20[10]	3,326,590	—	—	3,085,600	—	—	240,980	—	—	—
2020–21[10]	3,352,680	—	—	3,115,140	—	—	237,540	—	—	—
2021–22[10]	3,360,180	—	—	3,130,360	—	—	229,820	—	—	—
2022–23[10]	3,369,380	—	—	3,146,530	—	—	222,850	—	—	—
2023–24[10]	3,388,680	—	—	3,164,540	—	—	224,140	—	—	—

—Not available.
[1]Includes graduates of public and private schools.
[2]Data for 1929–30 and preceding years are from *Statistics of Public High Schools* and exclude graduates from high schools that failed to report to the Office of Education. Includes estimates for jurisdictions not reporting counts of graduates by sex.
[3]The averaged freshman graduation rate provides an estimate of the percentage of students who receive a regular diploma within 4 years of entering ninth grade. The rate uses aggregate student enrollment data to estimate the size of an incoming freshman class and aggregate counts of the number of diplomas awarded 4 years later. Averaged freshman graduation rates in this table are based on reported totals of enrollment by grade and high school graduates, rather than on details reported by race/ethnicity.
[4]Derived from Current Population Reports, Series P-25. For years 1869–70 through 1989–90, 17-year-old population is an estimate of the October 17-year-old population based on July data. Data for 1990–91 and later years are October resident population estimates prepared by the Census Bureau.
[5]Estimated.
[6]Includes imputations for nonreporting states.
[7]Projected by private schools responding to the Private School Universe Survey.
[8]Includes estimates for public schools in New York and Wisconsin. Without estimates for these two states, the averaged freshman graduation rate for the remaining 48 states and the District of Columbia is 75.0 percent.

[9]Includes estimate for Connecticut, which did not report graduates by sex.
[10]Projected by NCES.
NOTE: Includes graduates of regular day school programs. Excludes graduates of other programs, when separately reported, and recipients of high school equivalency certificates. Some data have been revised from previously published figures. Detail may not sum to totals because of rounding.
SOURCE: U.S. Department of Education, National Center for Education Statistics, *Annual Report of the Commissioner of Education*, 1870 through 1910; *Biennial Survey of Education in the United States*, 1919–20 through 1949–50; *Statistics of State School Systems*, 1951–52 through 1957–58; *Statistics of Public Elementary and Secondary School Systems*, 1958–59 through 1980–81; *Statistics of Nonpublic Elementary and Secondary Schools*, 1959 through 1980; Common Core of Data (CCD), "State Nonfiscal Survey of Public Elementary/Secondary Education," 1981–82 through 2009–10; "State Dropout and Completion Data File," 2005–06 through 2011–12; *Public School Graduates and Dropouts From the Common Core of Data*, 2007–08 and 2008–09; Private School Universe Survey (PSS), 1989 through 2011; and National High School Graduates Projection Model, 1972–73 through 2023–24. U.S. Department of Commerce, Census Bureau, Population Estimates, retrieved August 11, 2011, from http://www.census.gov/popest/national/asrh/2009-nat-res.html and Population Estimates, retrieved April 8, 2014, from http://www.census.gov/popest/data/national/asrh/2012/2012-nat-res.html. (This table was prepared April 2014.)

Public high school graduates, by region, state, and jurisdiction: Selected years, 1980–81 through 2023–24

Region, state, and jurisdiction	1980-81	1989-90	1999-2000	2004-05	2005-06	2006-07	2007-08	2008-09	2009-10	2010-11	2011-12	2012-13	2013-14	2014-15	2015-16	2016-17	2017-18	2018-19	2019-20	2020-21	2021-22	2022-23	2023-24	Percent change, 2009-10 to 2023-24
				Actual data							Projected data													
1	2	3	4	5	6	7	8	9	10	11	12	13	14	15	16	17	18	19	20	21	22	23	24	25
United States	2,725,285	2,320,337[1]	2,553,844	2,799,250	2,815,544[1]	2,893,045	3,001,337	3,039,015[1]	3,128,022	3,121,630	3,103,680	3,110,150	3,070,440	3,031,450	3,047,830	3,066,350	3,105,970	3,100,900	3,085,600	3,115,140	3,130,350	3,146,530	3,164,540	1.2
Region																								
Northeast	593,727	446,045	453,814	503,528	521,015	536,697	552,289	552,973	556,400	556,050	547,550	541,790	524,560	511,640	510,350	507,520	509,230	506,210	501,740	509,290	508,820	502,760	500,840	-10.0
Midwest	784,071	616,700	648,020	676,786	684,049	702,987	721,120	717,536	726,844	702,910	691,940	689,860	678,520	664,430	672,330	671,900	678,090	680,610	672,410	675,120	681,680	671,620	674,410	-7.2
South	868,068	796,385	861,498	953,206	962,327	986,801	1,031,773	1,068,270	1,104,770	1,107,200	1,104,730	1,121,500	1,121,040	1,116,370	1,130,480	1,146,370	1,172,040	1,177,910	1,171,170	1,177,790	1,181,520	1,198,710	1,211,510	9.7
West	479,419	461,207	590,512	665,730	648,153	666,560	696,055	700,236	740,008	755,490	759,460	757,010	749,140	739,010	734,670	740,720	746,600	736,170	740,290	752,940	758,340	773,430	777,780	5.1
State																								
Alabama	44,894	40,485	37,819	37,453	37,918	38,912	41,346	42,082	43,166	44,210	44,030	43,050	42,560	41,760	42,430	42,550	42,990	42,860	41,190	40,770	40,790	40,690	41,280	-4.4
Alaska	5,343	5,386	6,615	6,909	7,361	7,666	7,855	8,008	8,245	7,750	7,970	7,230	7,210	7,100	7,050	7,280	7,260	7,240	7,180	7,350	7,480	7,650	7,770	-5.8
Arizona	28,416	32,103	38,304	59,498	54,091	55,954	61,667	62,374	61,145	65,010	64,910	64,000	63,380	60,610	60,600	61,450	63,030	64,120	65,010	66,930	68,110	68,860	69,960	13.4
Arkansas	29,577	26,475	27,335	26,621	28,790	27,166	28,725	28,057	28,276	28,110	28,210	28,210	28,540	28,810	28,810	29,210	29,200	29,480	29,470	29,380	29,380	29,310	29,610	4.7
California	242,172	236,291	309,866	355,217	343,515	356,641	374,561	372,310[2]	404,987	414,180	415,600	415,570	409,660	403,390	394,330	394,770	395,410	382,150	384,890	390,070	391,920	403,260	404,410	-0.1
Colorado	35,897	32,967	38,924	44,532	44,424	45,628	46,082	47,459	49,321	51,000	51,430	52,150	52,110	52,180	53,280	54,290	55,930	56,830	57,640	59,260	58,980	59,700	59,890	21.4
Connecticut	38,369	27,878	31,562	35,515	36,222	37,541	38,419	34,968	34,495	36,910	36,290	35,820	35,200	34,280	34,300	33,790	33,420	33,000	32,330	32,960	32,090	31,510	31,510	-8.7
Delaware	7,349	5,550	6,108	6,934	7,275	7,398	7,398	7,839	8,133	8,220	8,320	8,140	7,950	7,820	7,610	7,770	7,970	8,160	8,100	8,560	8,380	8,510	8,680	6.7
District of Columbia[3]	4,848	3,626	2,695	2,781	3,150[4]	2,944	3,352	3,517	3,602	3,290	3,080	3,100	3,020	3,090	2,970	2,780	2,900	2,920	2,760	2,700	2,710	2,930	3,010	-16.4
Florida	88,755	88,934	106,708	133,318	134,696	142,284	149,046	153,461	156,130	160,570	157,050	164,800	163,860	166,690	165,210	168,260	169,620	171,050	166,750	167,980	170,560	172,930	176,580	13.1
Georgia	62,963	56,605	62,563	70,834	73,498	77,829	83,505	88,003	91,561	93,410	91,780	92,690	93,770	93,390	95,300	96,430	98,350	98,220	96,670	95,860	96,180	96,940	96,380	7.4
Hawaii	11,472	10,325	10,437	10,813	10,922	11,063	11,613	11,508	10,998	11,090	11,360	11,000	10,900	10,630	10,790	10,960	11,070	10,530	11,050	11,190	11,170	11,310	11,070	0.7
Idaho	12,679	11,971	16,170	15,768	16,096	16,242	16,567	16,807	17,793	17,440	17,500	17,330	17,620	17,150	17,600	18,180	18,340	18,620	18,830	19,000	19,460	20,050	19,930	12.0
Illinois	136,795	108,119	111,835	123,615	126,817	130,220	135,143	131,670	139,035	136,400	134,660	141,290	135,860	132,500	135,230	135,830	136,980	138,510	139,070	139,020	140,870	136,320	135,710	-2.4
Indiana	73,381	60,012	57,012	55,444	57,920	59,887	61,901	63,663	64,551	65,750	65,090	65,670	66,570	64,860	64,520	64,640	65,190	66,750	63,660	63,170	63,550	62,040	62,210	-3.6
Iowa	42,635	31,796	33,926	33,547	33,693	34,127	34,573	33,926	34,462	33,370	32,820	32,150	31,960	31,770	32,010	32,100	32,530	32,270	32,220	32,690	32,840	33,290	34,110	-1.0
Kansas	29,397	25,367	29,102	30,355	29,818	30,139	30,737	30,368	31,642	31,210	30,470	30,790	30,120	29,650	30,530	30,740	31,200	31,370	31,230	31,900	31,840	32,150	32,340	2.2
Kentucky	41,714	38,005	36,830	38,399	38,449	39,099	39,339	41,851	42,664	41,540	41,750	41,700	40,130	39,350	39,350	40,790	41,230	42,250	41,120	41,190	41,470	41,690	41,790	-2.0
Louisiana	46,199	36,053	38,430	36,000	33,275	34,274	34,401	35,622	36,573	34,330	34,900	35,510	36,510	34,150	35,870	35,880	38,490	37,580	37,260	37,350	37,140	37,190	37,710	3.1
Maine	15,554	13,839	12,211	13,077	12,950	13,151	14,350[5]	14,093[5]	14,069	14,040	13,650	13,250	12,850	12,660	12,810	12,610	12,560	12,490	12,330	12,350	12,580	12,740	12,570	-10.7
Maryland	54,050	41,566	47,849	54,170	55,536	57,564	59,171	58,304	59,078	58,010	57,770	57,220	55,910	55,390	55,190	54,310	55,520	54,930	56,960	57,740	58,440	59,170	59,890	1.4
Massachusetts	74,831	55,941[6]	52,950	59,665	61,272	63,903	65,197	65,258	64,462	63,200	63,090	63,370	62,250	61,490	62,440	61,730	61,660	61,650	60,910	61,520	61,250	60,370	59,930	-7.0
Michigan	124,372	93,807	97,679	101,582	102,582	111,838	115,183	112,742	110,682	107,080	105,580	102,770	101,970	98,030	99,420	97,710	98,110	97,490	94,460	93,630	94,170	90,480	90,460	-18.3
Minnesota	64,166	49,087	57,372	58,391	58,898	59,497	60,409	59,729	59,667	58,890	57,240	56,690	55,000	55,330	55,250	55,950	56,610	57,700	57,420	59,520	61,060	60,570	60,440	1.3
Mississippi	28,083	25,182	24,232	23,523	23,848	24,186	24,795	24,505	25,478	26,160	25,670	26,020	25,200	24,720	24,610	25,020	25,780	25,020	24,710	24,180	24,790	24,540	24,990	-1.9
Missouri	60,359	48,957	52,848	57,841	58,417	60,275	61,717	62,969	63,994	62,170	60,760	60,190	59,720	58,810	59,990	59,360	59,310	59,310	58,480	58,830	59,220	59,680	60,690	-5.2
Montana	11,634	9,370	10,903	10,235	10,283	10,122	10,396	10,077	10,075	9,700	9,600	9,260	9,350	9,180	9,190	9,280	9,340	9,340	9,350	9,480	9,650	9,610	9,780	-2.9
Nebraska	21,411	17,664	20,149	19,940	19,764	19,873	20,035	19,501	19,370	19,320	19,320	19,450	19,470	18,980	19,150	19,360	19,940	20,180	20,600	20,870	21,510	21,350	21,690	12.0
Nevada	9,069	9,087	14,551	15,740	16,455	17,149	18,815	19,904[2]	20,956	23,460	24,360	24,350	23,820	23,630	24,000	24,580	24,560	25,240	25,130	25,000	25,100	25,570	25,830	23.3
New Hampshire	11,552	10,766	11,829	13,775	13,988	14,452	14,982	14,757	15,034	14,330	14,230	14,160	13,770	13,710	13,450	13,170	12,980	12,690	12,660	12,460	12,410	12,030	11,920	-20.7
New Jersey	93,168	69,824	74,420	86,502	90,049	93,013	94,994	95,085	96,225	94,280	91,100	90,870	88,030	86,950	86,110	85,340	83,940	84,400	83,260	84,200	84,430	81,870	81,270	-15.5
New Mexico	17,915	14,884	18,031	17,353	17,822	16,131	18,264	17,931	18,595	18,900	18,980	18,470	18,130	18,310	18,280	18,850	18,960	19,140	19,170	19,190	19,450	19,580	19,340	4.0
New York	198,465	143,318	141,731	153,203	161,817	168,333	176,310	180,917	183,826	185,630	184,900	184,490	176,890	171,440	170,400	170,290	173,720	171,580	171,540	175,340	174,530	173,620	172,490	-6.2
North Carolina	69,395	64,782	62,140	75,010	76,710	76,031	83,307	86,712	88,704	86,580	88,940	89,120	89,170	88,620	90,120	91,600	93,600	95,100	94,050	94,630	87,510	94,680	94,710	6.8
North Dakota	9,924	7,690	8,606	7,555	7,192	7,159	6,999	7,232	7,155	7,060	6,840	6,830	6,720	6,660	6,790	6,730	6,480	6,790	6,870	7,180	7,520	7,560	7,990	11.7
Ohio	143,503	114,513	111,668	116,702	117,356	117,658	120,758	122,203	123,437	110,360	109,370	106,100	103,810	101,340	102,980	102,710	103,610	103,130	101,650	101,170	101,000	99,610	100,570	-18.5
Oklahoma	38,875	35,606	37,646	36,227	36,497	37,100	37,630	37,219	38,503	37,830	37,660	37,520	37,310	37,330	38,740	39,100	39,580	39,800	40,130	40,790	40,820	41,430	41,660	8.2
Oregon	28,729	25,473	30,151	32,602	32,394	33,446	34,949	35,138	34,671	34,690	34,460	34,010	34,160	33,650	34,300	34,260	34,430	34,370	33,820	34,430	34,580	34,580	35,080	1.2
Pennsylvania	144,645	110,527	113,959	124,758	127,830[4]	128,603	130,298	130,658	131,182	130,950	127,790	123,540	119,990	116,150	115,720	116,660	116,980	115,670	114,170	115,940	116,870	115,860	116,770	-11.0
Rhode Island	10,719	7,825	8,477	9,881	10,108	10,384	10,347	10,028	9,908	9,730	9,820	9,810	9,430	9,000	9,220	8,190	8,460	9,000	8,980	8,950	9,040	8,800	8,910	-10.1

See notes at end of table.

Public high school graduates, by region, state, and jurisdiction: Selected years, 1980–81 through 2023–24—Continued

Region, state, and jurisdiction	1980–81	1989–90	1999–2000	2004–05	2005–06	2006–07	2007–08	2008–09	2009–10	2010–11	2011–12	2012–13	2013–14	2014–15	2015–16	2016–17	2017–18	2018–19	2019–20	2020–21	2021–22	2022–23	2023–24	Percent change, 2009–10 to 2023–24
1	2	3	4	5	6	7	8	9	10	11	12	13	14	15	16	17	18	19	20	21	22	23	24	25
					Actual data									Projected data										
South Carolina	38,347	32,483	31,617	33,439	34,970 [4]	35,108	35,303	39,114	40,438	40,050	40,050	39,830	39,420	38,580	39,680	40,250	41,410	41,760	40,980	40,050	41,490	42,100	42,780	5.8
South Dakota	10,385	7,650	9,278	8,585	8,599	8,346	8,582	8,123	8,162	8,460	8,090	8,030	8,040	8,000	7,880	7,990	8,080	7,920	8,070	8,300	8,470	8,880	8,970	9.9
Tennessee	50,648	46,094	41,568	47,967	50,880	54,502	57,486	60,368	62,062	62,880	63,080	62,670	61,990	61,780	63,080	64,650	65,570	65,750	65,870	65,410	65,730	66,530	67,690	8.5
Texas	171,665	172,480	212,925	239,717	240,485	241,193	252,121	264,275	280,894	282,670	282,960	292,560	295,600	298,370	302,280	309,670	319,300	323,230	325,870	330,120	334,350	338,510	340,060	21.1
Utah	19,886	21,196	32,501	30,253	29,050	28,276	28,167	30,463	31,481	30,850	31,620	31,990	32,350	33,390	34,850	36,000	37,100	37,410	38,020	39,330	40,120	40,350	41,720	32.5
Vermont	6,424	6,127	6,675	7,152	6,779	7,317	7,392	7,209	7,199	6,850	6,670	6,480	6,140	5,960	5,900	5,840	5,630	5,660	5,560	5,590	5,620	5,640	5,480	−23.9
Virginia	67,126	60,605	65,596	73,667	69,597	73,997	77,369	79,651	81,511	82,080	82,150	82,080	81,080	79,740	80,740	81,370	83,090	83,120	83,160	83,850	85,270	84,970	86,030	5.5
Washington	50,046	45,941	57,597	61,094	60,213	62,801	61,625	62,764	66,046	65,830	66,140	66,350	65,080	64,260	64,660	65,080	65,600	65,410	64,330	65,480	66,110	66,430	66,940	1.4
West Virginia	23,580	21,854	19,437	17,137	16,763	17,407	17,489	17,690	17,651	17,260	17,320	17,100	16,710	16,590	16,800	16,570	16,950	16,650	16,880	16,450	16,680	16,600	16,680	−5.5
Wisconsin	67,743	52,038	58,545	63,229	63,003	63,968	65,183	65,410	64,687	63,020	61,710	59,890	59,140	58,500	58,610	58,780	59,590	59,180	58,480	58,850	59,640	59,120	59,210	−8.5
Wyoming	6,161	5,823	6,462	5,616	5,527	5,441	5,494	5,493	5,695	5,600	5,550	5,440	5,390	5,530	5,630	5,700	5,770	5,780	5,870	6,160	6,190	6,470	6,660	16.9
Jurisdiction																								
Bureau of Indian Education	—	—	—	—	—	—	—	—	—	—	—	—	—	—	—	—	—	—	—	—	—	—	—	—
DoD, overseas	—	—	2,642	—	—	—	—	—	—	—	—	—	—	—	—	—	—	—	—	—	—	—	—	—
DoD, domestic	—	—	560	—	—	—	—	—	—	—	—	—	—	—	—	—	—	—	—	—	—	—	—	—
Other jurisdictions																								
American Samoa	—	703	698	905	879	954	—	—	—	—	—	—	—	—	—	—	—	—	—	—	—	—	—	—
Guam	—	1,033	1,406	1,179	—	—	—	—	—	—	—	—	—	—	—	—	—	—	—	—	—	—	—	—
Northern Marianas	—	227	360	614	670	643	—	—	—	—	—	—	—	—	—	—	—	—	—	—	—	—	—	—
Puerto Rico	—	29,049	30,856	29,071	31,896	31,718	30,016	29,286	25,514	—	—	—	—	—	—	—	—	—	—	—	—	—	—	—
U.S. Virgin Islands	—	1,260	1,060	940	—	820	820	940	958	—	—	—	—	—	—	—	—	—	—	—	—	—	—	—

—Not available.

[1] U.S. total includes estimates for nonreporting states.
[2] Estimated high school graduates from NCES 2011-312, *Public School Graduates and Dropouts from the Common Core of Data: School Year 2008–09.*
[3] Beginning in 1989–90, graduates from adult programs are excluded.
[4] Projected data from NCES 2009-062, *Projections of Education Statistics to 2018.*
[5] Includes 1,161 graduates in 2007–08 and 1,169 graduates in 2008–09 from private high schools that received a majority of their funding from public sources.
[6] Projected data from NCES 91-490, *Projections of Education Statistics to 2002.*

NOTE: Data include regular diploma recipients, but exclude students receiving a certificate of attendance and persons receiving high school equivalency certificates. DoD = Department of Defense. Some data have been revised from previously published figures. Detail may not sum to totals because of rounding.

SOURCE: U.S. Department of Education, National Center for Education Statistics, Common Core of Data (CCD), "State Nonfiscal Survey of Public Elementary/Secondary Education," 1981–82 through 2005–06; "State Dropout and Completion Data File," 2005–06 through 2009–10; *Public School Graduates and Dropouts from the Common Core of Data,* 2007–08 and 2008–09; and State High School Graduates Projection Model, 1980–81 through 2023–24. (This table was prepared May 2014.)

Public high school graduates, by race/ethnicity: 1998–99 through 2023–24

Year	Number of high school graduates							Percentage distribution of graduates						
	Total	White	Black	Hispanic	Asian/ Pacific Islander	American Indian/ Alaska Native	Two or more races	Total	White	Black	Hispanic	Asian/ Pacific Islander	American Indian/ Alaska Native	Two or more races
1	2	3	4	5	6	7	8	9	10	11	12	13	14	15
1998–99	2,485,630	1,749,561	325,708	270,836	115,216	24,309	—	100.0	70.4	13.1	10.9	4.6	1.0	—
1999–2000	2,553,844	1,778,370	338,116	289,139	122,344	25,875	—	100.0	69.6	13.2	11.3	4.8	1.0	—
2000–01	2,569,200	1,775,036	339,578	301,740	126,465	26,381	—	100.0	69.1	13.2	11.7	4.9	1.0	—
2001–02	2,621,534	1,796,110	348,969	317,197	132,182	27,076	—	100.0	68.5	13.3	12.1	5.0	1.0	—
2002–03	2,719,947	1,856,454	359,920	340,182	135,588	27,803	—	100.0	68.3	13.2	12.5	5.0	1.0	—
2003–04	2,753,438	1,829,177	383,443	374,492	137,496	28,830	—	100.0	66.4	13.9	13.6	5.0	1.0	—
2004–05	2,799,250	1,855,198	385,987	383,714	143,729	30,622	—	100.0	66.3	13.8	13.7	5.1	1.1	—
2005–06	2,815,544	1,838,765	399,406	396,820	150,925	29,628	—	100.0	65.3	14.2	14.1	5.4	1.1	—
2006–07	2,893,045	1,868,056	418,113	421,036	154,837	31,003	—	100.0	64.6	14.5	14.6	5.4	1.1	—
2007–08	3,001,337	1,898,367	429,840	448,887	159,410	32,036	32,797[1]	100.0	63.3	14.3	15.0	5.3	1.1	1.1[1]
2008–09	3,039,015	1,883,382	451,384	481,698	163,575	32,213	26,763[1]	100.0	62.0	14.9	15.9	5.4	1.1	0.9[1]
2009–10	3,128,022	1,871,980	472,261	545,518	167,840	34,131	36,292[1]	100.0	59.8	15.1	17.4	5.4	1.1	1.2[1]
2010–11	3,143,879	1,835,156	471,410	583,907	168,880	32,778	51,748	100.0	58.4	15.0	18.6	5.4	1.0	1.6
2011–12	3,147,790	1,807,104	467,419	605,674	173,762	32,423	61,408	100.0	57.4	14.8	19.2	5.5	1.0	2.0
2012–13[2]	3,110,150	1,766,390	450,760	626,280	173,640	30,240	62,850	100.0	56.8	14.5	20.1	5.6	1.0	2.0
2013–14[2]	3,070,440	1,730,560	433,110	638,840	173,900	28,860	65,170	100.0	56.4	14.1	20.8	5.7	0.9	2.1
2014–15[2]	3,031,450	1,688,980	424,210	651,690	172,060	27,180	67,340	100.0	55.7	14.0	21.5	5.7	0.9	2.2
2015–16[2]	3,047,830	1,682,000	428,920	670,420	168,750	28,380	69,350	100.0	55.2	14.1	22.0	5.5	0.9	2.3
2016–17[2]	3,066,350	1,677,460	425,700	692,290	169,530	29,020	72,340	100.0	54.7	13.9	22.6	5.5	0.9	2.4
2017–18[2]	3,105,970	1,669,320	428,510	726,090	178,840	28,190	75,020	100.0	53.7	13.8	23.4	5.8	0.9	2.4
2018–19[2]	3,100,900	1,647,840	419,000	752,560	176,080	27,600	77,830	100.0	53.1	13.5	24.3	5.7	0.9	2.5
2019–20[2]	3,085,600	1,613,600	408,910	777,990	177,630	26,880	80,590	100.0	52.3	13.3	25.2	5.8	0.9	2.6
2020–21[2]	3,115,140	1,614,270	402,510	806,220	182,550	26,170	83,420	100.0	51.8	12.9	25.9	5.9	0.8	2.7
2021–22[2]	3,130,360	1,601,380	397,650	835,880	183,600	25,860	85,980	100.0	51.2	12.7	26.7	5.9	0.8	2.7
2022–23[2]	3,146,530	1,577,570	398,150	876,760	179,890	25,580	88,570	100.0	50.1	12.7	27.9	5.7	0.8	2.8
2023–24[2]	3,164,540	1,564,210	403,960	901,510	178,380	25,600	90,880	100.0	49.4	12.8	28.5	5.6	0.8	2.9

—Not available.

[1]Data on students of two or more races were not reported by all states; therefore, the data are not comparable to figures for 2010–11 and later years.

[2]Projected.

NOTE: Race categories exclude persons of Hispanic ethnicity. Prior to 2007–08, data on students of two or more races were not collected separately. Some data have been revised from previously published figures. Detail may not sum to totals because of rounding.

SOURCE: U.S. Department of Education, National Center for Education Statistics, Common Core of Data (CCD), "State Nonfiscal Survey of Public Elementary/Secondary Education," 1999–2000 through 2005–06; "State Dropout and Completion Data File," 2005–06 through 2011–12; and National Public High School Graduates by Race/Ethnicity Projection Model, 1995–96 through 2023–24. (This table was prepared May 2014.)

Number of people taking the general educational development (GED) test and percentage distribution of those who passed, by age group: 1971 through 2012

	Number of test takers (in thousands)			Percentage distribution of test passers, by age group[1]				
Year	Total[2]	Completing test battery[3]	Passing tests[4]	16 to 18 years old	19 to 24 years old	25 to 29 years old	30 to 34 years old	35 years old or over
1	2	3	4	5	6	7	8	9
1971[5]	377	—	227	—	—	—	—	—
1972[5]	419	—	245	—	—	—	—	—
1973[5]	423	—	249	—	—	—	—	—
1974	—	—	294	35 [6]	27 [6]	13	9	17
1975	—	—	340	33 [6]	26 [6]	14	9	18
1976	—	—	333	31 [6]	28 [6]	14	10	17
1977	—	—	330	40 [6]	24 [6]	13	8	14
1978	—	—	381	31 [6]	27 [6]	13	10	18
1979	—	—	426	37 [6]	28 [6]	12	13	11
1980	—	—	479	37 [6]	27 [6]	13	8	15
1981	—	—	489	37 [6]	27 [6]	13	8	14
1982	—	—	486	37 [6]	28 [6]	13	8	15
1983	—	—	465	34 [6]	29 [6]	14	8	15
1984	—	—	427	32 [6]	28 [6]	15	9	16
1985	—	—	413	32 [6]	26 [6]	15	10	16
1986	—	—	428	32 [6]	26 [6]	15	10	17
1987	—	—	444	33 [6]	24 [6]	15	10	18
1988	—	—	410	35 [6]	22 [6]	14	10	18
1989	632	541	357	22	37	13	—	—
1990	714	615	410	22	39	13	10	15
1991	755	657	462	20	40	13	10	16
1992	739	639	457	22	39	13	9	17
1993	746	651	469	22	38	13	10	16
1994	774	668	491	25	37	13	10	15
1995	787	682	504	27	36	13	9	15
1996	824	716	488	27	37	13	9	14
1997	785	681	460	31	36	12	8	13
1998	776	673	481	32	36	11	7	13
1999	808	702	498	32	37	11	7	13
2000	811	699	487	33	37	11	7	13
2001[7]	1,016	928	648	29	38	11	8	14
2002[7]	557	467	330	38	36	10	6	11
2003	657	552	387	35	37	10	7	11
2004	666	570	406	35	38	11	6	10
2005	681	588	424	34	37	12	7	11
2006	676	580	398	35	36	12	6	11
2007	692	600	429	35	35	12	7	11
2008	737	642	469	34	35	13	7	11
2009	748	645	448	31	36	13	8	12
2010	720	623	452	27	37	14	9	14
2011	691	602	434	27	37	13	9	14
2012	674	581	401	26	37	14	9	13

—Not available.

[1] Age data for 1988 and prior years are for all test takers and may not be comparable to data for later years. For 1989 and later years, age data are only for test passers. The less than 1 percent of people who failed to report their date of birth—245 of the 401,388 test passers in 2012—were excluded from the calculation.

[2] All people taking the GED tests (one or more subtests).

[3] People completing the entire GED battery of five tests.

[4] Data for 2002 and later years are for people passing the GED tests (i.e., earning both a passing total score on the test battery and a passing score on each individual test). Data for 2001 and prior years are for high school equivalency credentials issued by the states to GED test passers. In order to receive high school equivalency credentials in some states, GED test passers must meet additional state requirements (e.g., complete an approved course in civics or government).

[5] Includes other jurisdictions, such as Puerto Rico, Guam, and American Samoa.

[6] For 1988 and prior years, 19-year-olds are included with the 16- to 18-year-olds instead of the 19- to 24-year-olds.

[7] A revised GED test was introduced in 2002. In 2001, test takers were required to successfully complete all five components of the GED or else begin the five-part series again with the new test that was introduced in 2002.

NOTE: Data are for the United States only and exclude other jurisdictions, except where noted. Detail may not sum to totals because of rounding.

SOURCE: American Council on Education, General Educational Development Testing Service, the GED annual *Statistical Report*, 1971 through 1992; *Who Took the GED?* 1993 through 2001; *Who Passed the GED Tests?* 2002 through 2005; and *GED Testing Program Statistical Report*, 2006 through 2012, retrieved July 15, 2013, from http://www.gedtesting service.com/educators/historical-testing-data. (This table was prepared July 2013.)

Percentage of high school dropouts among persons 16 through 24 years old (status dropout rate), by sex and race/ethnicity: Selected years, 1960 through 2012

[Standard errors appear in parentheses]

Year	Total status dropout rate				Male status dropout rate				Female status dropout rate			
	All races[1]	White	Black	Hispanic	All races[1]	White	Black	Hispanic	All races[1]	White	Black	Hispanic
1	2	3	4	5	6	7	8	9	10	11	12	13
1960[2]	27.2 (—)	— (†)	— (†)	— (†)	27.8 (—)	— (†)	— (†)	— (†)	26.7 (—)	— (†)	— (†)	— (†)
1967[3]	17.0 (—)	15.4 (—)	28.6 (—)	— (†)	16.5 (—)	14.7 (—)	30.6 (—)	— (†)	17.3 (—)	16.1 (—)	26.9 (—)	— (†)
1968[3]	16.2 (—)	14.7 (—)	27.4 (—)	— (†)	15.8 (—)	14.4 (—)	27.1 (—)	— (†)	16.5 (—)	15.0 (—)	27.6 (—)	— (†)
1969[3]	15.2 (—)	13.6 (—)	26.7 (—)	— (†)	14.3 (—)	12.6 (—)	26.9 (—)	— (†)	16.0 (—)	14.6 (—)	26.7 (—)	— (†)
1970[3]	15.0 (0.29)	13.2 (0.30)	27.9 (1.22)	— (†)	14.2 (0.42)	12.2 (0.42)	29.4 (1.82)	— (†)	15.7 (0.41)	14.1 (0.42)	26.6 (1.65)	— (†)
1971[3]	14.7 (0.28)	13.4 (0.29)	24.0 (1.14)	— (†)	14.2 (0.41)	12.6 (0.41)	25.5 (1.70)	— (†)	15.2 (0.40)	14.2 (0.42)	22.6 (1.54)	— (†)
1972	14.6 (0.28)	12.3 (0.29)	21.3 (1.07)	34.3 (2.22)	14.1 (0.40)	11.6 (0.40)	22.3 (1.59)	33.7 (3.23)	15.1 (0.39)	12.8 (0.41)	20.5 (1.44)	34.8 (3.05)
1973	14.1 (0.27)	11.6 (0.28)	22.2 (1.06)	33.5 (2.24)	13.7 (0.38)	11.5 (0.39)	21.5 (1.53)	30.4 (3.16)	14.5 (0.38)	11.8 (0.39)	22.8 (1.47)	36.4 (3.16)
1974	14.3 (0.27)	11.9 (0.28)	21.2 (1.05)	33.0 (2.08)	14.2 (0.39)	12.0 (0.40)	20.1 (1.51)	33.8 (2.99)	14.3 (0.38)	11.8 (0.39)	22.1 (1.45)	32.2 (2.90)
1975	13.9 (0.27)	11.4 (0.27)	22.9 (1.06)	29.2 (2.02)	13.3 (0.37)	11.0 (0.38)	23.0 (1.56)	26.7 (2.84)	14.5 (0.38)	11.8 (0.39)	22.9 (1.44)	31.6 (2.86)
1976	14.1 (0.27)	12.0 (0.28)	20.5 (1.00)	31.4 (2.01)	14.1 (0.38)	12.1 (0.39)	21.2 (1.49)	30.3 (2.94)	14.2 (0.37)	11.8 (0.39)	19.9 (1.35)	32.3 (2.76)
1977	14.1 (0.27)	11.9 (0.28)	19.8 (0.99)	33.0 (2.02)	14.5 (0.38)	12.6 (0.40)	19.5 (1.45)	31.6 (2.89)	13.8 (0.37)	11.2 (0.38)	20.0 (1.36)	34.3 (2.83)
1978	14.2 (0.27)	11.9 (0.28)	20.2 (1.00)	33.3 (2.00)	14.6 (0.38)	12.2 (0.40)	22.5 (1.52)	33.6 (2.88)	13.9 (0.37)	11.6 (0.39)	18.3 (1.31)	33.1 (2.78)
1979	14.6 (0.27)	12.0 (0.28)	21.1 (1.01)	33.8 (1.98)	15.0 (0.39)	12.6 (0.40)	22.4 (1.52)	33.0 (2.83)	14.2 (0.37)	11.5 (0.38)	20.0 (1.35)	34.5 (2.77)
1980	14.1 (0.26)	11.4 (0.27)	19.1 (0.97)	35.2 (1.89)	15.1 (0.39)	12.3 (0.40)	20.8 (1.47)	37.2 (2.72)	13.1 (0.36)	10.5 (0.37)	17.7 (1.28)	33.2 (2.61)
1981	13.9 (0.26)	11.3 (0.27)	18.4 (0.93)	33.2 (1.80)	15.1 (0.38)	12.5 (0.40)	19.9 (1.40)	36.0 (2.61)	12.8 (0.35)	10.2 (0.36)	17.1 (1.24)	30.4 (2.48)
1982	13.9 (0.27)	11.4 (0.29)	18.4 (0.97)	31.7 (1.93)	14.5 (0.40)	12.0 (0.42)	21.2 (1.50)	30.5 (2.73)	13.3 (0.38)	10.8 (0.40)	15.9 (1.26)	32.8 (2.71)
1983	13.7 (0.27)	11.1 (0.29)	18.0 (0.97)	31.6 (1.93)	14.9 (0.41)	12.2 (0.43)	19.9 (1.46)	34.3 (2.84)	12.5 (0.37)	10.1 (0.39)	16.2 (1.28)	29.1 (2.61)
1984	13.1 (0.27)	11.0 (0.29)	15.5 (0.91)	29.8 (1.91)	14.0 (0.40)	11.9 (0.43)	16.8 (1.37)	30.6 (2.78)	12.3 (0.37)	10.1 (0.39)	14.3 (1.22)	29.0 (2.63)
1985	12.6 (0.27)	10.4 (0.29)	15.2 (0.92)	27.6 (1.93)	13.4 (0.40)	11.1 (0.42)	16.1 (1.37)	29.9 (2.76)	11.8 (0.37)	9.8 (0.39)	14.3 (1.23)	25.2 (2.68)
1986	12.2 (0.27)	9.7 (0.28)	14.2 (0.90)	30.1 (1.88)	13.1 (0.40)	10.3 (0.42)	15.0 (1.33)	32.8 (2.66)	11.4 (0.37)	9.1 (0.39)	13.5 (1.21)	27.2 (2.63)
1987	12.6 (0.28)	10.4 (0.30)	14.1 (0.90)	28.6 (1.84)	13.2 (0.40)	10.8 (0.43)	15.0 (1.35)	29.1 (2.57)	12.1 (0.38)	10.0 (0.41)	13.3 (1.21)	28.1 (2.64)
1988	12.9 (0.30)	9.6 (0.31)	14.5 (1.00)	35.8 (2.30)	13.5 (0.44)	10.3 (0.46)	15.0 (1.48)	36.0 (3.19)	12.2 (0.42)	8.9 (0.43)	14.0 (1.36)	35.4 (3.31)
1989	12.6 (0.31)	9.4 (0.32)	13.9 (0.98)	33.0 (2.19)	13.6 (0.45)	10.3 (0.47)	14.9 (1.46)	34.4 (3.08)	11.7 (0.42)	8.5 (0.43)	13.0 (1.32)	31.6 (3.11)
1990	12.1 (0.29)	9.0 (0.30)	13.2 (0.94)	32.4 (1.91)	12.3 (0.42)	9.3 (0.44)	11.9 (1.30)	34.3 (2.71)	11.8 (0.41)	8.7 (0.42)	14.4 (1.34)	30.3 (2.70)
1991	12.5 (0.30)	8.9 (0.31)	13.6 (0.95)	35.3 (1.93)	13.0 (0.43)	8.9 (0.44)	13.5 (1.37)	39.2 (2.74)	11.9 (0.41)	8.9 (0.43)	13.7 (1.31)	31.1 (2.70)
1992[4]	11.0 (0.28)	7.7 (0.29)	13.7 (0.95)	29.4 (1.86)	11.3 (0.41)	8.0 (0.42)	12.5 (1.32)	32.1 (2.67)	10.7 (0.39)	7.4 (0.40)	14.8 (1.36)	26.6 (2.56)
1993[4]	11.0 (0.28)	7.9 (0.29)	13.6 (0.94)	27.5 (1.79)	11.2 (0.40)	8.2 (0.42)	12.6 (1.32)	28.1 (2.54)	10.9 (0.40)	7.6 (0.41)	14.4 (1.34)	26.9 (2.52)
1994[4]	11.4 (0.26)	7.7 (0.27)	12.6 (0.75)	30.0 (1.16)	12.3 (0.38)	8.0 (0.38)	14.1 (1.14)	31.6 (1.60)	10.6 (0.36)	7.5 (0.37)	11.3 (0.99)	28.1 (1.66)
1995[4]	12.0 (0.27)	8.6 (0.28)	12.1 (0.74)	30.0 (1.15)	12.2 (0.38)	9.0 (0.40)	11.1 (1.05)	30.0 (1.59)	11.7 (0.37)	8.2 (0.39)	12.9 (1.05)	30.0 (1.66)
1996[4]	11.1 (0.27)	7.3 (0.27)	13.0 (0.80)	29.4 (1.19)	11.4 (0.38)	7.3 (0.38)	13.5 (1.18)	30.3 (1.67)	10.9 (0.38)	7.3 (0.39)	12.5 (1.08)	28.3 (1.69)
1997[4]	11.0 (0.27)	7.6 (0.28)	13.4 (0.80)	25.3 (1.11)	11.9 (0.39)	8.5 (0.41)	13.3 (1.16)	27.0 (1.55)	10.1 (0.36)	6.7 (0.37)	13.5 (1.11)	23.4 (1.59)
1998[4]	11.8 (0.27)	7.7 (0.28)	13.8 (0.81)	29.5 (1.12)	13.3 (0.40)	8.6 (0.41)	15.5 (1.24)	33.5 (1.59)	10.3 (0.36)	6.9 (0.37)	12.2 (1.05)	25.0 (1.56)
1999[4]	11.2 (0.26)	7.3 (0.27)	12.6 (0.77)	28.6 (1.11)	11.9 (0.38)	7.7 (0.39)	12.1 (1.10)	31.0 (1.58)	10.5 (0.36)	6.9 (0.37)	13.0 (1.08)	26.0 (1.54)
2000[4]	10.9 (0.26)	6.9 (0.26)	13.1 (0.78)	27.8 (1.08)	12.0 (0.38)	7.0 (0.37)	15.3 (1.20)	31.8 (1.56)	9.9 (0.35)	6.9 (0.37)	11.1 (1.00)	23.5 (1.48)
2001[4]	10.7 (0.25)	7.3 (0.26)	10.9 (0.71)	27.0 (1.06)	12.2 (0.38)	7.9 (0.39)	13.0 (1.12)	31.6 (1.55)	9.3 (0.34)	6.7 (0.36)	9.0 (0.90)	22.1 (1.42)
2002[4]	10.5 (0.24)	6.5 (0.24)	11.3 (0.70)	25.7 (0.93)	11.8 (0.35)	6.7 (0.35)	12.8 (1.07)	29.6 (1.32)	9.2 (0.32)	6.3 (0.34)	9.9 (0.91)	21.2 (1.27)
2003[4,5]	9.9 (0.23)	6.3 (0.24)	10.9 (0.69)	23.5 (0.90)	11.3 (0.34)	7.1 (0.35)	12.5 (1.05)	26.7 (1.29)	8.4 (0.30)	5.6 (0.32)	9.5 (0.89)	20.1 (1.23)
2004[4,5]	10.3 (0.23)	6.8 (0.24)	11.8 (0.70)	23.8 (0.89)	11.6 (0.34)	7.1 (0.35)	13.5 (1.08)	28.5 (1.30)	9.0 (0.31)	6.4 (0.34)	10.2 (0.92)	18.5 (1.18)
2005[4,5]	9.4 (0.22)	6.0 (0.23)	10.4 (0.66)	22.4 (0.87)	10.8 (0.33)	6.6 (0.34)	12.0 (1.02)	26.4 (1.26)	8.0 (0.29)	5.3 (0.31)	9.0 (0.86)	18.1 (1.16)
2006[4,5]	9.3 (0.22)	5.8 (0.23)	10.7 (0.66)	22.1 (0.86)	10.3 (0.33)	6.4 (0.33)	9.7 (0.91)	25.7 (1.25)	8.3 (0.30)	5.3 (0.31)	11.7 (0.96)	18.1 (1.15)
2007[4,5]	8.7 (0.21)	5.3 (0.22)	8.4 (0.59)	21.4 (0.83)	9.8 (0.32)	6.0 (0.32)	8.0 (0.82)	24.7 (1.22)	7.7 (0.29)	4.5 (0.28)	8.8 (0.84)	18.0 (1.13)
2008[4,5]	8.0 (0.20)	4.8 (0.21)	9.9 (0.63)	18.3 (0.78)	8.5 (0.30)	5.4 (0.30)	8.7 (0.85)	19.9 (1.12)	7.5 (0.28)	4.2 (0.28)	11.1 (0.93)	16.7 (1.08)
2009[4,5]	8.1 (0.20)	5.2 (0.21)	9.3 (0.61)	17.6 (0.76)	9.1 (0.31)	6.3 (0.33)	10.6 (0.93)	19.0 (1.10)	7.0 (0.27)	4.1 (0.27)	8.1 (0.80)	16.1 (1.06)
2010[4,5,6]	7.4 (0.27)	5.1 (0.30)	8.0 (0.76)	15.1 (0.87)	8.5 (0.40)	5.9 (0.42)	9.5 (1.11)	17.3 (1.24)	6.3 (0.28)	4.2 (0.35)	6.7 (0.85)	12.8 (0.97)
2011[4,5,6]	7.1 (0.26)	5.0 (0.31)	7.3 (0.67)	13.6 (0.78)	7.7 (0.36)	5.4 (0.41)	8.3 (0.98)	14.6 (1.09)	6.5 (0.34)	4.6 (0.38)	6.4 (0.94)	12.4 (0.97)
2012[4,5,6]	6.6 (0.25)	4.3 (0.31)	7.5 (0.76)	12.7 (0.72)	7.3 (0.36)	4.8 (0.40)	8.1 (1.15)	13.9 (1.04)	5.9 (0.33)	3.8 (0.37)	7.0 (1.01)	11.3 (1.00)

—Not available.
†Not applicable.
[1]Includes other racial/ethnic categories not separately shown.
[2]Based on the April 1960 decennial census.
[3]For 1967 through 1971, White and Black include persons of Hispanic ethnicity.
[4]Because of changes in data collection procedures, data may not be comparable with figures for years prior to 1992.
[5]White and Black exclude persons identifying themselves as two or more races.
[6]Beginning in 2010, standard errors were computed using replicate weights, which produced more precise values than the methodology used in prior years.

NOTE: "Status" dropouts are 16- to 24-year-olds who are not enrolled in school and who have not completed a high school program, regardless of when they left school. People who have received GED credentials are counted as high school completers. All data except for 1960 are based on October counts. Data are based on sample surveys of the civilian noninstitutionalized population, which excludes persons in prisons, persons in the military, and other persons not living in households. Race categories exclude persons of Hispanic ethnicity except where otherwise noted.
SOURCE: U.S. Department of Commerce, Census Bureau, Current Population Survey (CPS), October, 1967 through 2012. (This table was prepared May 2013.)

Percentage of high school dropouts among persons 16 through 24 years old (status dropout rate), by income level, and percentage distribution of status dropouts, by labor force status and years of school completed: 1970 through 2012

[Standard errors appear in parentheses]

Year	Status dropout rate	Status dropout rate, by family income quartile				Percentage distribution of status dropouts, by labor force status				Percentage distribution of status dropouts, by years of school completed				
		Lowest quartile	Middle low quartile	Middle high quartile	Highest quartile	Total	Employed[1]	Unemployed	Not in labor force	Total	Less than 9 years	9 years	10 years	11 or 12 years
1	2	3	4	5	6	7	8	9	10	11	12	13	14	15
1970	15.0 (0.29)	28.0 (0.92)	21.2 (0.65)	11.7 (0.50)	5.2 (0.34)	100.0 (†)	49.8 (1.06)	10.3 (0.65)	39.9 (1.04)	100.0 (†)	28.5 (0.96)	20.6 (0.86)	26.8 (0.94)	24.0 (0.91)
1971	14.7 (0.28)	28.8 (0.90)	20.7 (0.63)	10.9 (0.49)	5.1 (0.32)	100.0 (†)	49.5 (1.05)	10.9 (0.65)	39.6 (1.02)	100.0 (†)	27.9 (0.94)	21.7 (0.86)	27.8 (0.94)	22.7 (0.88)
1972	14.6 (0.28)	27.6 (0.85)	20.8 (0.62)	10.2 (0.46)	5.4 (0.33)	100.0 (†)	51.2 (1.03)	10.2 (0.63)	38.6 (1.01)	100.0 (†)	27.5 (0.92)	20.8 (0.84)	29.0 (0.94)	22.7 (0.87)
1973	14.1 (0.27)	28.0 (0.85)	19.6 (0.60)	9.9 (0.45)	4.9 (0.31)	100.0 (†)	53.2 (1.04)	9.2 (0.60)	37.5 (1.01)	100.0 (†)	26.5 (0.92)	20.9 (0.84)	27.4 (0.93)	25.3 (0.90)
1974	14.3 (0.27)	— (†)	— (†)	— (†)	— (†)	100.0 (†)	51.8 (1.02)	12.3 (0.67)	35.9 (0.98)	100.0 (†)	25.4 (0.89)	20.1 (0.82)	28.7 (0.93)	25.8 (0.90)
1975	13.9 (0.27)	28.8 (0.82)	18.0 (0.58)	10.2 (0.45)	5.0 (0.30)	100.0 (†)	46.0 (1.02)	15.6 (0.74)	38.4 (1.00)	100.0 (†)	23.5 (0.87)	21.1 (0.84)	27.5 (0.92)	27.9 (0.92)
1976	14.1 (0.27)	28.1 (0.79)	19.2 (0.60)	10.1 (0.46)	4.9 (0.29)	100.0 (†)	48.8 (1.01)	16.0 (0.74)	35.2 (0.97)	100.0 (†)	24.3 (0.87)	20.1 (0.81)	27.8 (0.91)	27.8 (0.91)
1977	14.1 (0.27)	28.5 (0.80)	19.0 (0.60)	10.4 (0.46)	4.5 (0.29)	100.0 (†)	52.9 (1.02)	13.6 (0.70)	33.6 (0.96)	100.0 (†)	24.3 (0.87)	21.2 (0.84)	27.3 (0.91)	26.6 (0.90)
1978	14.2 (0.27)	28.2 (0.79)	18.9 (0.60)	10.5 (0.46)	5.5 (0.31)	100.0 (†)	54.3 (1.01)	12.4 (0.67)	33.3 (0.95)	100.0 (†)	22.9 (0.85)	20.2 (0.81)	28.2 (0.91)	28.8 (0.91)
1979	14.6 (0.27)	28.1 (0.79)	18.5 (0.60)	11.5 (0.47)	5.6 (0.32)	100.0 (†)	54.0 (0.99)	12.7 (0.66)	33.3 (0.94)	100.0 (†)	22.6 (0.83)	21.0 (0.81)	28.6 (0.90)	27.8 (0.89)
1980	14.1 (0.26)	27.0 (0.77)	18.1 (0.60)	10.7 (0.46)	5.7 (0.32)	100.0 (†)	50.4 (1.01)	17.0 (0.76)	32.6 (0.95)	100.0 (†)	23.6 (0.86)	19.7 (0.80)	29.8 (0.93)	27.0 (0.90)
1981	13.9 (0.26)	26.4 (0.75)	17.8 (0.57)	11.1 (0.47)	5.2 (0.30)	100.0 (†)	49.8 (1.01)	18.3 (0.78)	31.9 (0.94)	100.0 (†)	24.3 (0.86)	18.6 (0.78)	30.2 (0.92)	26.9 (0.89)
1982	13.9 (0.27)	27.2 (0.78)	18.3 (0.63)	10.2 (0.48)	4.4 (0.29)	100.0 (†)	45.2 (1.06)	21.1 (0.87)	33.7 (1.01)	100.0 (†)	22.9 (0.90)	20.8 (0.87)	28.8 (0.96)	27.6 (0.95)
1983	13.7 (0.27)	26.5 (0.77)	17.8 (0.62)	10.5 (0.50)	4.1 (0.29)	100.0 (†)	48.4 (1.08)	18.2 (0.83)	33.4 (1.02)	100.0 (†)	23.0 (0.91)	19.3 (0.85)	28.8 (0.98)	28.8 (0.98)
1984	13.1 (0.27)	25.9 (0.76)	16.5 (0.61)	9.9 (0.48)	3.8 (0.29)	100.0 (†)	49.7 (1.11)	17.3 (0.84)	32.9 (1.05)	100.0 (†)	23.6 (0.95)	21.4 (0.91)	27.5 (1.00)	27.5 (0.99)
1985	12.6 (0.27)	27.1 (0.78)	14.7 (0.60)	8.3 (0.46)	4.0 (0.29)	100.0 (†)	50.1 (1.15)	17.5 (0.88)	32.4 (1.08)	100.0 (†)	23.9 (0.98)	21.0 (0.94)	27.9 (1.03)	27.2 (1.03)
1986	12.2 (0.27)	25.4 (0.75)	14.8 (0.60)	8.0 (0.45)	3.4 (0.28)	100.0 (†)	51.1 (1.18)	16.4 (0.87)	32.5 (1.10)	100.0 (†)	25.4 (1.03)	21.5 (0.97)	25.7 (1.03)	27.4 (1.05)
1987	12.6 (0.28)	25.5 (0.76)	16.6 (0.63)	8.0 (0.46)	2.4 (0.26)	100.0 (†)	52.4 (1.16)	13.6 (0.80)	34.0 (1.10)	100.0 (†)	25.9 (1.02)	20.7 (0.94)	26.0 (1.02)	27.5 (1.04)
1988	12.9 (0.30)	27.2 (0.85)	15.4 (0.68)	8.2 (0.51)	3.4 (0.30)	100.0 (†)	52.9 (1.27)	— (†)	33.0 (†)	100.0 (†)	28.9 (1.15)	19.3 (1.00)	25.1 (1.10)	26.8 (1.12)
1989	12.6 (0.31)	25.0 (0.84)	16.2 (0.71)	8.7 (0.52)	3.3 (0.31)	100.0 (†)	53.2 (1.30)	13.8 (0.90)	33.0 (1.22)	100.0 (†)	29.4 (1.18)	20.8 (1.05)	24.9 (1.12)	25.0 (1.13)
1990	12.1 (0.29)	24.3 (0.82)	15.1 (0.65)	8.7 (0.51)	2.9 (0.28)	100.0 (†)	52.5 (1.29)	13.3 (0.88)	34.2 (1.23)	100.0 (†)	28.6 (1.17)	20.9 (1.05)	24.4 (1.11)	26.1 (1.14)
1991	12.5 (0.30)	25.9 (0.83)	15.5 (0.66)	7.7 (0.49)	3.0 (0.29)	100.0 (†)	47.5 (1.28)	15.8 (0.93)	36.7 (1.23)	100.0 (†)	28.6 (1.15)	20.5 (1.03)	26.1 (1.12)	24.9 (1.10)
1992[2]	11.0 (0.28)	23.4 (0.79)	12.9 (0.62)	7.3 (0.48)	2.4 (0.26)	100.0 (†)	47.6 (1.36)	15.0 (0.97)	37.4 (1.32)	100.0 (†)	21.6 (1.12)	17.5 (1.04)	24.4 (1.17)	36.5 (1.31)
1993[2]	11.0 (0.28)	22.9 (0.77)	12.7 (0.58)	6.6 (0.46)	2.9 (0.26)	100.0 (†)	48.7 (1.37)	12.8 (0.91)	38.5 (1.33)	100.0 (†)	21.0 (1.10)	16.6 (1.00)	24.1 (1.17)	38.8 (1.33)
1994[2]	11.4 (0.26)	20.7 (0.71)	13.7 (0.58)	8.7 (0.45)	4.9 (0.33)	100.0 (†)	49.5 (1.21)	13.0 (0.81)	37.5 (1.17)	100.0 (†)	23.9 (1.03)	16.2 (0.89)	20.3 (0.97)	39.6 (1.18)
1995[2]	12.0 (0.27)	23.2 (0.69)	13.8 (0.59)	8.3 (0.46)	3.6 (0.29)	100.0 (†)	48.9 (1.19)	14.2 (0.83)	37.0 (1.14)	100.0 (†)	22.2 (0.99)	17.0 (0.89)	22.5 (0.99)	38.3 (1.15)
1996[2]	11.1 (0.27)	22.0 (0.72)	13.6 (0.60)	7.0 (0.45)	3.2 (0.28)	100.0 (†)	47.3 (1.28)	15.0 (0.91)	37.7 (1.24)	100.0 (†)	20.3 (1.03)	17.7 (0.98)	22.6 (1.07)	39.4 (1.25)
1997[2]	11.0 (0.27)	21.8 (0.71)	13.5 (0.59)	6.2 (0.42)	3.8 (0.27)	100.0 (†)	53.3 (1.28)	13.3 (0.86)	33.5 (1.21)	100.0 (†)	19.9 (1.02)	15.7 (0.93)	22.3 (1.06)	42.1 (1.26)
1998[2]	11.8 (0.27)	22.3 (0.71)	14.9 (0.62)	7.7 (0.45)	3.5 (0.26)	100.0 (†)	55.1 (1.22)	13.7 (0.84)	34.6 (1.17)	100.0 (†)	21.0 (1.00)	14.9 (0.87)	21.4 (1.01)	42.6 (1.21)
1999[2]	11.2 (0.26)	21.0 (0.70)	14.3 (0.60)	7.4 (0.44)	3.9 (0.30)	100.0 (†)	55.6 (1.24)	14.3 (0.83)	34.4 (1.18)	100.0 (†)	22.2 (1.03)	16.3 (0.92)	22.5 (1.04)	39.0 (1.21)
2000[2]	10.9 (0.26)	20.7 (0.70)	12.8 (0.56)	8.3 (0.46)	3.5 (0.29)	100.0 (†)	56.9 (1.24)	12.3 (0.82)	30.8 (1.16)	100.0 (†)	21.5 (1.03)	15.3 (0.90)	23.1 (1.06)	40.0 (1.23)
2001[2]	10.7 (0.25)	19.3 (0.68)	13.4 (0.57)	9.0 (0.47)	3.2 (0.27)	100.0 (†)	58.3 (1.24)	14.8 (0.89)	26.9 (1.11)	100.0 (†)	18.4 (0.97)	16.8 (0.94)	23.8 (1.07)	40.9 (1.23)
2002[2]	10.5 (0.24)	18.8 (0.62)	12.3 (0.53)	8.4 (0.43)	3.8 (0.25)	100.0 (†)	57.4 (1.18)	13.3 (0.81)	29.2 (1.09)	100.0 (†)	22.8 (1.00)	17.1 (0.90)	21.3 (0.98)	38.9 (1.17)
2003[2]	9.9 (0.23)	19.5 (0.64)	10.8 (0.49)	7.3 (0.40)	2.2 (0.21)	100.0 (†)	53.5 (1.22)	13.7 (0.84)	32.9 (1.15)	100.0 (†)	21.2 (1.00)	18.2 (0.94)	20.7 (0.99)	42.6 (1.20)
2004[2]	10.3 (0.23)	18.0 (0.60)	12.7 (0.52)	8.2 (0.42)	3.7 (0.27)	100.0 (†)	53.0 (1.19)	14.3 (0.83)	32.7 (1.12)	100.0 (†)	21.4 (0.97)	15.9 (0.87)	22.5 (0.99)	40.3 (1.17)
2005[2]	9.4 (0.22)	17.9 (0.60)	11.5 (0.51)	7.1 (0.39)	2.7 (0.23)	100.0 (†)	56.9 (1.23)	11.9 (0.80)	31.2 (1.15)	100.0 (†)	18.9 (0.97)	16.8 (0.93)	21.4 (1.02)	42.9 (1.23)
2006[2]	9.3 (0.21)	16.5 (0.59)	12.1 (0.51)	6.3 (0.37)	3.8 (0.27)	100.0 (†)	56.4 (1.23)	11.7 (0.80)	32.0 (1.16)	100.0 (†)	22.1 (1.03)	13.4 (0.85)	20.7 (1.01)	43.9 (1.23)
2007[2]	8.7 (0.21)	16.7 (0.58)	10.5 (0.48)	6.4 (0.36)	3.2 (0.25)	100.0 (†)	55.5 (1.27)	11.2 (0.81)	33.3 (1.20)	100.0 (†)	21.2 (1.04)	16.9 (0.96)	22.9 (1.07)	39.0 (1.24)
2008[2]	8.0 (0.20)	16.4 (0.58)	9.4 (0.45)	5.4 (0.34)	2.2 (0.21)	100.0 (†)	46.8 (1.33)	13.2 (0.98)	36.9 (1.28)	100.0 (†)	18.4 (1.03)	15.2 (0.96)	23.8 (1.13)	42.6 (1.32)
2009[2]	8.1 (0.20)	15.8 (0.57)	9.7 (0.45)	5.4 (0.34)	2.5 (0.22)	100.0 (†)	43.2 (1.31)	19.9 (1.06)	36.9 (1.28)	100.0 (†)	17.7 (1.01)	13.6 (0.91)	24.4 (1.14)	44.3 (1.32)
2010[2,3]	7.4 (0.27)	13.8 (0.83)	8.9 (0.54)	5.1 (0.48)	2.5 (0.31)	100.0 (†)	45.8 (1.64)	18.7 (1.38)	35.5 (1.70)	100.0 (†)	19.2 (1.48)	13.1 (1.07)	22.5 (1.59)	45.2 (1.89)
2011[2,3]	7.1 (0.26)	13.0 (0.73)	9.0 (0.53)	4.8 (0.45)	2.3 (0.32)	100.0 (†)	49.8 (1.77)	16.0 (1.33)	34.2 (1.69)	100.0 (†)	18.1 (1.72)	12.9 (1.15)	21.2 (1.39)	47.7 (1.87)
2012[2,3]	6.6 (0.25)	11.8 (0.70)	8.7 (0.65)	4.1 (0.44)	1.9 (0.31)	100.0 (†)	44.8 (2.07)	18.1 (1.49)	37.1 (1.83)	100.0 (†)	18.3 (1.76)	10.2 (1.21)	21.9 (1.57)	49.6 (2.20)

—Not available.
†Not applicable.
[1]Includes persons who were employed but not at work during the survey week.
[2]Because of changes in data collection procedures, data may not be comparable with figures for years prior to 1992.
[3]Beginning in 2010, standard errors were computed using replicate weights, which produced more precise values than the methodology used in prior years.

NOTE: "Status" dropouts are 16- to 24-year-olds who are not enrolled in school and who have not completed a high school program, regardless of when they left school. People who have received GED credentials are counted as high school completers. Data are based on sample surveys of the civilian noninstitutionalized population, which excludes persons in prisons, persons in the military, and other persons not living in households. Detail may not sum to totals because of rounding.
SOURCE: U.S. Department of Commerce, Census Bureau, Current Population Survey (CPS), October, 1970 through 2012. (This table was prepared May 2013.)

Percentage of high school dropouts among persons 16 through 24 years old (status dropout rate) and number of status dropouts, by noninstitutionalized or institutionalized status, birth in or outside of the United States, and selected characteristics: 2010 and 2011

[Standard errors appear in parentheses]

Selected characteristic	Total status dropout rate		Noninstitutionalized population[1]					Institutionalized population[2]	
			Number of status dropouts	Percentage distribution of status dropouts	Status dropout rate			Number of status dropouts	Status dropout rate
	2010	2011			Total for noninstitutionalized population	For those born in the United States[3]	For those born outside of the United States[3]		
	2	3	4	5	6	7	8	9	10
Total	8.3 (0.08)	7.7 (0.06)	2,866,410 (25,305)	100.0 (†)	7.3 (0.06)	6.2 (0.06)	16.1 (0.26)	177,100 (3,724)	35.4 (0.56)
Sex									
Male	10.0 (0.10)	9.0 (0.09)	1,671,090 (16,867)	58.3 (0.32)	8.4 (0.08)	7.0 (0.08)	18.8 (0.43)	165,050 (3,550)	37.1 (0.59)
Female	6.6 (0.08)	6.2 (0.07)	1,195,320 (14,261)	41.7 (0.32)	6.2 (0.07)	5.4 (0.08)	12.9 (0.34)	12,050 (1,165)	21.9 (1.95)
Race/ethnicity									
White	5.3 (0.07)	5.1 (0.07)	1,085,210 (15,090)	37.9 (0.40)	4.9 (0.07)	4.9 (0.07)	4.3 (0.32)	43,300 (1,628)	26.9 (0.83)
Black	10.3 (0.17)	9.6 (0.18)	477,010 (9,745)	16.6 (0.32)	8.5 (0.17)	8.8 (0.18)	5.2 (0.58)	81,270 (2,590)	40.1 (1.04)
Hispanic	16.7 (0.26)	14.5 (0.19)	1,143,830 (16,263)	39.9 (0.39)	14.1 (0.19)	9.2 (0.18)	27.9 (0.47)	45,160 (1,779)	40.6 (1.22)
Asian	2.8 (0.16)	2.7 (0.14)	49,700 (2,690)	1.7 (0.10)	2.7 (0.14)	1.7 (0.17)	3.6 (0.25)	‡ (†)	23.2 (6.25)
Pacific Islander	4.8 (0.95)	8.8 (1.62)	6,810 (1,254)	0.2 (0.04)	8.8 (1.64)	5.0 (1.11)	24.0 (5.28)	‡ (†)	‡ (†)
American Indian/Alaska Native	15.4 (0.80)	13.1 (0.75)	38,810 (2,239)	1.4 (0.08)	12.6 (0.68)	12.5 (0.67)	18.4 ! (8.79)	2,780 (782)	33.3 (6.83)
Two or more races	6.1 (0.30)	6.0 (0.33)	58,300 (3,251)	2.0 (0.11)	5.7 (0.33)	5.6 (0.38)	6.5 (1.53)	3,550 (595)	30.5 (5.11)
Race/ethnicity by sex									
Male									
White	6.1 (0.09)	5.8 (0.10)	619,080 (11,427)	37.0 (0.51)	5.5 (0.10)	5.5 (0.10)	3.9 (0.43)	38,840 (1,426)	28.5 (0.86)
Black	12.7 (0.26)	11.8 (0.25)	271,010 (6,709)	16.2 (0.41)	9.8 (0.24)	10.2 (0.25)	5.0 (0.72)	77,540 (2,577)	41.4 (1.11)
Hispanic	20.2 (0.34)	17.0 (0.27)	688,710 (12,064)	41.2 (0.54)	16.4 (0.28)	10.1 (0.24)	32.2 (0.71)	42,590 (1,652)	42.2 (1.34)
Asian	3.4 (0.25)	3.1 (0.19)	28,350 (1,899)	1.7 (0.12)	3.0 (0.19)	1.9 (0.23)	4.0 (0.38)	‡ (†)	26.0 (7.06)
Pacific Islander	4.9 (1.05)	9.2 (2.10)	3,610 (870)	0.2 (0.05)	9.1 (2.11)	4.5 (1.25)	29.3 ! (8.83)	1,820 ! (644)	31.5 (8.26)
American Indian/Alaska Native	17.6 (1.34)	14.8 (1.11)	22,100 (1,649)	1.3 (0.10)	14.2 (1.00)	14.3 (1.00)	‡ (†)	‡ (†)	‡ (†)
Two or more races	7.3 (0.49)	7.4 (0.57)	34,630 (2,801)	2.1 (0.17)	6.9 (0.56)	6.7 (0.61)	8.9 (2.61)	3,230 (581)	32.4 (5.21)
Female									
White	4.5 (0.09)	4.3 (0.08)	466,140 (8,663)	39.0 (0.61)	4.3 (0.08)	4.3 (0.09)	4.8 (0.52)	4,460 (683)	17.9 (2.48)
Black	7.8 (0.23)	7.3 (0.22)	206,000 (6,510)	17.2 (0.49)	7.2 (0.22)	7.4 (0.23)	5.4 (0.72)	3,730 (586)	24.5 (3.25)
Hispanic	12.8 (0.27)	11.7 (0.23)	455,110 (9,545)	38.1 (0.60)	11.7 (0.24)	8.2 (0.23)	22.6 (0.60)	2,580 (536)	25.2 (4.26)
Asian	2.3 (0.20)	2.4 (0.18)	21,350 (1,697)	1.8 (0.14)	2.4 (0.18)	1.6 (0.22)	3.1 (0.29)	‡ (†)	‡ (†)
Pacific Islander	4.8 ! (1.60)	8.4 (2.11)	‡ (†)	0.3 (0.07)	8.5 (2.11)	5.5 ! (1.91)	19.3 (5.60)	‡ (†)	‡ (†)
American Indian/Alaska Native	13.2 (1.15)	11.4 (0.86)	16,710 (1,365)	1.4 (0.11)	10.9 (0.86)	10.7 (0.81)	‡ (†)	‡ (†)	37.2 ! (12.96)
Two or more races	4.9 (0.41)	4.6 (0.41)	23,670 (2,112)	2.0 (0.18)	4.6 (0.41)	4.6 (0.45)	4.2 ! (1.46)	‡ (†)	19.0 ! (9.26)
Age									
16	2.5 (0.09)	2.2 (0.09)	88,030 (3,885)	3.1 (0.13)	2.1 (0.09)	2.0 (0.10)	3.5 (0.44)	2,760 (589)	8.9 (1.83)
17	4.0 (0.12)	3.8 (0.11)	153,870 (4,516)	5.4 (0.15)	3.6 (0.11)	3.4 (0.11)	6.5 (0.52)	7,660 (665)	19.4 (1.58)
18	6.7 (0.14)	6.2 (0.15)	276,460 (7,584)	9.6 (0.25)	5.9 (0.15)	5.5 (0.14)	10.0 (0.76)	14,660 (1,246)	36.3 (2.23)
19	8.9 (0.19)	7.7 (0.15)	315,110 (6,262)	11.0 (0.21)	7.3 (0.15)	6.8 (0.16)	11.8 (0.66)	20,320 (1,450)	42.6 (2.54)
20–24	10.6 (0.10)	9.8 (0.10)	2,032,940 (21,006)	70.9 (0.36)	9.3 (0.09)	7.7 (0.10)	20.1 (0.35)	131,680 (3,026)	38.6 (0.65)
Region									
Northeast	6.3 (0.13)	6.1 (0.13)	399,510 (8,950)	13.9 (0.29)	5.8 (0.13)	5.1 (0.12)	11.1 (0.51)	21,600 (1,532)	29.5 (1.78)
Midwest	7.2 (0.12)	6.8 (0.12)	544,490 (10,471)	19.0 (0.34)	6.5 (0.12)	5.9 (0.13)	14.4 (0.83)	32,790 (1,568)	32.3 (1.36)
South	9.6 (0.13)	8.7 (0.11)	1,191,580 (15,844)	41.6 (0.40)	8.2 (0.11)	7.0 (0.10)	18.6 (0.45)	87,200 (3,053)	39.6 (0.98)
West	8.9 (0.14)	8.0 (0.12)	730,840 (11,601)	25.5 (0.33)	7.8 (0.12)	6.2 (0.12)	17.1 (0.45)	35,510 (1,677)	33.8 (1.22)

†Not applicable.
!Interpret data with caution. The coefficient of variation (CV) for this estimate is between 30 and 50 percent.
‡Reporting standards not met. Either there are too few cases for a reliable estimate or the coefficient of variation (CV) is 50 percent or greater.
[1]Persons living in households as well as persons living in noninstitutionalized group quarters. Noninstitutionalized group quarters include college and university housing, military quarters, facilities for workers and religious groups, and temporary shelters for the homeless.
[2]Persons living in institutionalized group quarters, including adult and juvenile correctional facilities, nursing facilities, and other health care facilities.
[3]United States refers to the 50 states and the District of Columbia.
NOTE: "Status" dropouts are 16- to 24-year-olds who are not enrolled in school and who have not completed a high school program, regardless of when they left school and whether they ever attended school in the United States. People who have received GED credentials are counted as high school completers. Detail may not sum to totals because of rounding. Race categories exclude persons of Hispanic ethnicity. Status dropout rates in this table may differ from those in tables based on the Current Population Survey (CPS) because of differences in survey design and target populations.
SOURCE: U.S. Department of Commerce, Census Bureau, American Community Survey (ACS), 2010 and 2011. (This table was prepared June 2013.)

Number and percentage distribution of 14- through 21-year-old students served under Individuals with Disabilities Education Act, Part B, who exited school, by exit reason, age, and type of disability: 2009–10 and 2010–11

Year, age, and type of disability	Total	Graduated with diploma	Received a certificate of attendance	Reached maximum age[1]	Dropped out[2]	Died	Transferred to regular education[3]	Moved, known to be continuing[4]
1	2	3	4	5	6	7	8	9
2009–10								
Total number	408,642	255,800	59,973	5,071	86,244	1,554	66,782	199,833
Percentage distribution of total	100.0	62.6	14.7	1.2	21.1	0.4	†	†
Number by age								
14	3,226	5	5	†	3,024	192	16,898	38,790
15	6,741	44	26	†	6,445	226	15,247	43,303
16	19,878	3,243	823	†	15,504	308	14,785	44,988
17	149,616	108,083	16,664	†	24,542	327	12,141	39,687
18	153,432	107,004	23,524	8	22,670	226	5,715	22,826
19	46,315	26,623	9,703	65	9,796	128	1,369	7,119
20	17,908	7,766	5,299	1,354	3,392	97	430	2,401
21	11,526	3,032	3,929	3,644	871	50	197	719
Number by type of disability								
Autism	12,295	8,145	2,730	567	816	37	1,820	3,852
Deaf-blindness	90	54	17	5	12	2	8	35
Emotional disturbance	45,659	22,806	4,706	365	17,654	128	7,084	40,578
Hearing impairments	4,768	3,421	793	52	488	14	660	1,649
Intellectual disability	41,709	16,966	14,389	2,101	7,987	266	1,854	16,521
Multiple disabilities	8,919	4,245	2,511	626	1,238	299	286	3,826
Orthopedic impairments	3,762	2,361	691	151	467	92	432	1,282
Other health impairments[5]	49,743	34,400	5,383	200	9,515	245	9,890	24,428
Specific learning disabilities	227,048	153,017	26,899	871	45,846	415	33,983	100,786
Speech or language impairments	10,357	7,287	1,256	37	1,760	17	10,321	5,564
Traumatic brain injury	2,480	1,687	397	66	309	21	229	798
Visual impairments	1,812	1,411	201	30	152	18	215	514
2010–11								
Total number	402,038	255,512	58,938	5,245	80,839	1,504	61,102	181,554
Percentage distribution of total	100.0	63.6	14.7	1.3	20.1	0.4	†	†
Number by age								
14	3,023	1	4	†	2,808	210	15,836	35,708
15	6,051	35	29	†	5,735	252	13,769	38,361
16	18,118	3,429	658	†	13,743	288	13,386	40,515
17	145,037	105,110	16,384	†	23,225	318	10,996	35,865
18	152,198	107,659	23,017	0	21,323	199	5,160	21,103
19	47,013	28,176	9,102	29	9,589	117	1,346	6,899
20	18,595	7,845	5,659	1,548	3,458	85	441	2,251
21	12,003	3,257	4,085	3,668	958	35	168	832
Number by type of disability								
Autism	14,162	9,179	3,366	685	892	40	1,366	4,297
Deaf-blindness	93	48	21	8	14	2	6	35
Emotional disturbance	42,889	22,423	4,160	308	15,866	132	6,207	34,844
Hearing impairments	4,707	3,439	737	42	479	10	620	1,469
Intellectual disability	40,439	16,137	14,446	2,122	7,480	254	1,556	15,383
Multiple disabilities	8,523	4,019	2,456	665	1,116	267	267	3,133
Orthopedic impairments	3,605	2,243	673	172	416	101	458	1,141
Other health impairments[5]	52,682	36,883	5,598	238	9,683	280	9,806	23,862
Specific learning disabilities	220,902	150,974	25,806	861	42,894	367	31,676	91,302
Speech or language impairments	9,795	7,111	1,060	45	1,564	15	8,776	4,899
Traumatic brain injury	2,536	1,717	431	73	289	26	178	706
Visual impairments	1,705	1,339	184	26	146	10	186	483

†Not applicable.
[1]Students may exit special education services due to maximum age beginning at age 18 depending on state law or practice or order of any court.
[2]"Dropped out" is defined as the total who were enrolled at some point in the reporting year, were not enrolled at the end of the reporting year, and did not exit for any of the other reasons described. Includes students previously categorized as "moved, not known to continue."
[3]"Transferred to regular education" was previously labeled "no longer receives special education."
[4]"Moved, known to be continuing" is the total number of students who moved out of the administrative area or transferred to another district and are known to be continuing in an educational program.

[5]Other health impairments include having limited strength, vitality, or alertness due to chronic or acute health problems such as a heart condition, tuberculosis, rheumatic fever, nephritis, asthma, sickle cell anemia, hemophilia, epilepsy, lead poisoning, leukemia, or diabetes.
NOTE: Data are for the 50 states, the District of Columbia, and the Bureau of Indian Education schools. Detail may not sum to totals because of rounding.
SOURCE: U.S. Department of Education, Office of Special Education Programs, Individuals with Disabilities Education Act (IDEA) database. Retrieved June 6, 2013, from http://tadnet.public.tadnet.org/pages/712. (This table was prepared June 2013.)

Private elementary and secondary school enrollment and private enrollment as a percentage of total enrollment in public and private schools, by region and grade level: Selected years, fall 1995 through fall 2011

[Standard errors appear in parentheses]

Grade level and year	Total private enrollment		Private enrollment, by region							
	In thousands	Percent of total enrollment	Northeast In thousands	Percent of total enrollment in Northeast	Midwest In thousands	Percent of total enrollment in Midwest	South In thousands	Percent of total enrollment in South	West In thousands	Percent of total enrollment in West
1	2	3	4	5	6	7	8	9	10	11
Total, all grades										
1995	5,918 (31.8)	11.7 (0.06)	1,509 (18.8)	16.0 (0.20)	1,525 (14.2)	12.7 (0.12)	1,744 (12.8)	9.8 (0.07)	1,141 (11.5)	10.0 (0.10)
1997	5,944 (18.5)	11.4 (0.04)	1,496 (8.3)	15.6 (0.09)	1,528 (11.6)	12.5 (0.10)	1,804 (11.3)	9.8 (0.06)	1,116 (5.2)	9.4 (0.04)
1999	6,018 (30.2)	11.4 (0.06)	1,507 (7.9)	15.5 (0.08)	1,520 (10.3)	12.4 (0.09)	1,863 (26.7)	10.0 (0.14)	1,127 (5.4)	9.2 (0.04)
2001	6,320 (40.3)	11.7 (0.08)	1,581 (9.5)	16.1 (0.10)	1,556 (22.9)	12.6 (0.19)	1,975 (21.4)	10.3 (0.11)	1,208 (23.4)	9.6 (0.19)
2003	6,099 (41.2)	11.2 (0.08)	1,513 (25.8)	15.4 (0.27)	1,460 (15.1)	11.9 (0.12)	1,944 (21.0)	9.9 (0.11)	1,182 (19.1)	9.1 (0.15)
2005	6,073 (42.4)	11.0 (0.08)	1,430 (7.7)	14.8 (0.08)	1,434 (21.0)	11.7 (0.17)	1,976 (24.7)	9.8 (0.12)	1,234 (26.3)	9.4 (0.20)
2007	5,910 (28.4)	10.7 (0.05)	1,426 (11.0)	14.9 (0.12)	1,352 (8.3)	11.2 (0.07)	1,965 (21.5)	9.6 (0.11)	1,167 (12.3)	8.9 (0.09)
2009	5,488 (35.9)	10.0 (0.07)	1,310 (15.7)	14.0 (0.17)	1,296 (25.9)	10.8 (0.22)	1,842 (17.6)	9.1 (0.09)	1,041 (8.0)	8.0 (0.06)
2011	5,268 (24.9)	9.7 (0.04)	1,252 (18.0)	13.7 (0.17)	1,263 (17.1)	10.7 (0.13)	1,747 (2.6)	8.5 (0.01)	1,006 (0.4)	7.8 (#)
Prekindergarten through grade 8										
1995	4,756 (28.4)	12.8 (0.08)	1,174 (16.8)	17.2 (0.25)	1,238 (13.5)	14.3 (0.16)	1,413 (11.9)	10.7 (0.09)	931 (9.2)	11.1 (0.11)
1997	4,759 (17.3)	12.6 (0.05)	1,165 (8.3)	16.8 (0.12)	1,235 (11.0)	14.1 (0.13)	1,449 (10.0)	10.8 (0.07)	909 (4.4)	10.5 (0.05)
1999	4,789 (23.1)	12.5 (0.06)	1,168 (7.5)	16.7 (0.11)	1,222 (8.4)	13.9 (0.10)	1,487 (19.6)	10.9 (0.14)	913 (4.4)	10.4 (0.05)
2001	5,023 (36.1)	12.9 (0.09)	1,216 (9.4)	17.3 (0.14)	1,253 (21.2)	14.3 (0.24)	1,584 (17.8)	11.3 (0.13)	969 (21.2)	10.6 (0.23)
2003	4,788 (30.3)	12.3 (0.08)	1,131 (7.8)	16.4 (0.11)	1,167 (13.6)	13.5 (0.16)	1,547 (18.6)	10.9 (0.13)	944 (18.1)	10.2 (0.20)
2005	4,724 (33.0)	12.1 (0.09)	1,063 (6.6)	15.9 (0.10)	1,142 (19.3)	13.3 (0.23)	1,551 (21.2)	10.7 (0.15)	969 (15.0)	10.5 (0.16)
2007	4,546 (21.9)	11.7 (0.06)	1,047 (6.3)	16.0 (0.10)	1,065 (7.7)	12.6 (0.09)	1,525 (17.7)	10.4 (0.12)	909 (8.1)	9.9 (0.09)
2009	4,179 (33.2)	10.8 (0.09)	938 (12.6)	14.6 (0.20)	1,016 (25.1)	12.1 (0.30)	1,424 (16.2)	9.8 (0.11)	802 (7.2)	8.8 (0.08)
2011	3,977 (18.2)	10.3 (0.04)	898 (12.8)	14.1 (0.17)	967 (12.8)	11.7 (0.14)	1,337 (1.8)	9.0 (0.01)	774 (0.3)	8.6 (#)
Grades 9 through 12										
1995	1,163 (4.6)	8.5 (0.03)	335 (2.9)	13.0 (0.11)	287 (0.9)	8.6 (0.03)	331 (2.1)	7.1 (0.04)	209 (2.3)	6.8 (0.08)
1997	1,185 (2.4)	8.3 (0.02)	331 (0.5)	12.5 (0.02)	293 (0.7)	8.5 (0.02)	354 (1.7)	7.2 (0.03)	207 (1.2)	6.4 (0.04)
1999	1,229 (8.3)	8.4 (0.06)	340 (1.1)	12.6 (0.04)	299 (2.5)	8.6 (0.07)	376 (7.6)	7.5 (0.15)	215 (1.8)	6.3 (0.05)
2001	1,296 (6.7)	8.6 (0.04)	365 (0.8)	13.1 (0.03)	302 (2.0)	8.6 (0.06)	390 (4.4)	7.5 (0.08)	239 (4.5)	6.8 (0.13)
2003	1,311 (24.7)	8.4 (0.16)	382 (24.0)	13.1 (0.83)	294 (4.1)	8.2 (0.11)	397 (3.0)	7.4 (0.06)	238 (3.5)	6.4 (0.09)
2005	1,349 (18.1)	8.3 (0.11)	367 (1.7)	12.3 (0.06)	292 (5.0)	7.9 (0.14)	425 (7.2)	7.5 (0.13)	265 (15.7)	6.7 (0.40)
2007	1,364 (12.0)	8.3 (0.07)	379 (8.8)	12.7 (0.30)	287 (1.3)	7.8 (0.04)	440 (5.5)	7.6 (0.10)	257 (5.7)	6.5 (0.14)
2009	1,309 (6.5)	8.0 (0.04)	372 (5.7)	12.6 (0.20)	280 (2.2)	7.7 (0.06)	418 (1.7)	7.3 (0.03)	239 (1.1)	6.1 (0.03)
2011	1,291 (15.4)	8.1 (0.09)	353 (5.2)	12.6 (0.16)	295 (14.4)	8.4 (0.38)	411 (1.8)	7.1 (0.03)	232 (0.1)	5.9 (#)

#Rounds to zero.
NOTE: Includes enrollment in prekindergarten through grade 12 in schools that offer kindergarten or higher grade. Ungraded students are prorated into prekindergarten through grade 8 and grades 9 through 12. Detail may not sum to totals because of rounding.

SOURCE: U.S. Department of Education, National Center for Education Statistics, Private School Universe Survey (PSS), 1995–96 through 2011–12; and Common Core of Data (CCD), "State Nonfiscal Survey of Public Elementary/Secondary Education," 1995–96 through 2011–12. (This table was prepared May 2014.)

Enrollment and percentage distribution of students enrolled in private elementary and secondary schools, by school orientation and grade level: Selected years, fall 1995 through fall 2011

[Standard errors appear in parentheses]

Grade level and year	Total private enrollment	Catholic				Other religious				Nonsectarian
		Total	Parochial	Diocesan	Private (independent)	Total	Conservative Christian	Affiliated[1]	Unaffiliated[1]	
1	2	3	4	5	6	7	8	9	10	11
					Enrollment					
Total, all grades										
1995	5,918,040 (31,815)	2,660,450 (6,878)	1,458,990 (2,079)	850,560 (5,674)	350,900 (1,176)	2,094,690 (16,956)	786,660 (8,815)	697,280 (4,886)	610,750 (11,831)	1,162,900 (18,443)
1997	5,944,320 (18,543)	2,665,630 (5,472)	1,438,860 (5,331)	873,780 (761)	352,990 (1,405)	2,097,190 (13,733)	823,610 (7,342)	646,500 (3,104)	627,080 (11,133)	1,181,510 (12,013)
1999	6,018,280 (30,179)	2,660,420 (4,831)	1,397,570 (5,626)	880,650 (†)	382,190 (1,945)	2,193,370 (27,176)	871,060 (4,827)	646,280 (4,894)	676,030 (24,593)	1,164,500 (8,156)
2001	6,319,650 (40,272)	2,672,650 (12,460)	1,309,890 (5,626)	979,050 (6,976)	383,710 (3,152)	2,328,160 (17,281)	937,420 (6,070)	663,190 (8,636)	727,550 (13,303)	1,318,840 (27,300)
2003	6,099,220 (41,219)	2,520,120 (10,580)	1,183,250 (9,937)	963,140 (4,754)	373,740 (3,996)	2,228,230 (19,674)	889,710 (8,852)	650,530 (5,860)	688,000 (14,805)	1,350,870 (29,197)
2005	6,073,240 (42,446)	2,402,800 (9,293)	1,062,950 (6,355)	956,610 (6,325)	383,230 (3,996)	2,303,330 (22,368)	957,360 (9,561)	696,910 (6,677)	649,050 (14,200)	1,367,120 (27,558)
2007	5,910,210 (28,363)	2,308,150 (6,083)	945,860 (5,361)	969,940 (1,788)	392,340 (3,432)	2,283,210 (20,628)	883,180 (6,616)	527,040 (3,512)	872,990 (18,217)	1,318,850 (18,235)
2009	5,488,490 (35,857)	2,160,220 (3,494)	856,440 (3,088)	909,010 (4,393)	394,770 (1,087)	2,076,220 (32,751)	737,020 (1,891)	516,310 (4,366)	822,890 (31,180)	1,252,050 (8,849)
2011	5,268,090 (24,908)	2,087,870 (14,426)	804,410 (3,686)	899,810 (14,320)	383,650 (459)	1,991,950 (21,814)	730,570 (4,721)	565,340 (2,990)	696,040 (20,419)	1,188,270 (5,376)
Prekindergarten through grade 8										
1995	4,755,540 (28,435)	2,041,990 (5,249)	1,368,340 (2,079)	575,190 (3,528)	98,460 (1,176)	1,752,510 (14,834)	651,050 (7,219)	574,820 (4,581)	526,630 (11,121)	961,040 (17,471)
1997	4,759,060 (17,323)	2,046,620 (5,469)	1,352,620 (5,331)	598,380 (761)	95,620 (1,393)	1,744,500 (12,194)	678,660 (5,957)	529,050 (2,504)	536,790 (10,120)	967,940 (11,050)
1999	4,788,990 (23,055)	2,033,900 (4,830)	1,317,300 (4,421)	607,860 (†)	108,740 (1,943)	1,818,260 (19,897)	713,020 (3,748)	529,280 (3,866)	575,970 (17,632)	936,820 (7,302)
2001	5,023,160 (36,096)	2,032,080 (10,751)	1,226,960 (4,494)	687,540 (6,976)	117,580 (2,978)	1,926,870 (15,459)	765,080 (5,110)	535,860 (7,370)	625,940 (12,240)	1,064,210 (24,703)
2003	4,788,070 (30,338)	1,886,530 (11,055)	1,108,320 (9,937)	670,910 (4,754)	107,300 (337)	1,835,930 (16,931)	722,460 (6,517)	519,310 (4,134)	594,160 (13,504)	1,065,620 (15,379)
2005	4,724,310 (33,034)	1,779,830 (9,318)	993,390 (6,355)	673,110 (6,286)	113,330 (2,896)	1,865,430 (19,380)	764,920 (8,028)	561,320 (5,730)	539,190 (12,633)	1,079,050 (15,497)
2007	4,545,910 (21,853)	1,685,220 (5,288)	878,830 (4,562)	688,260 (1,640)	118,130 (3,104)	1,833,540 (18,364)	698,930 (5,885)	417,610 (3,218)	717,000 (16,573)	1,027,150 (11,379)
2009	4,179,060 (33,168)	1,541,830 (3,250)	782,050 (3,085)	642,720 (846)	117,050 (578)	1,665,680 (30,216)	579,190 (1,685)	401,430 (3,952)	685,050 (28,928)	971,550 (8,113)
2011	3,976,960 (18,241)	1,481,620 (3,867)	737,090 (3,675)	630,970 (321)	113,560 (459)	1,583,610 (16,558)	568,150 (3,607)	443,780 (2,604)	571,690 (15,197)	911,730 (3,469)
Grades 9 through 12										
1995	1,162,500 (4,625)	618,460 (2,786)	90,650 (†)	275,370 (2,786)	252,440 (†)	342,180 (3,174)	135,610 (2,338)	122,460 (645)	84,120 (1,720)	201,860 (1,495)
1997	1,185,260 (2,374)	619,010 (96)	86,240 (†)	275,400 (†)	257,370 (96)	352,690 (2,261)	144,950 (1,660)	117,450 (848)	90,290 (1,221)	213,560 (1,860)
1999	1,229,290 (8,260)	626,520 (70)	80,270 (†)	272,790 (†)	275,100 (70)	375,100 (7,920)	158,040 (1,640)	117,000 (1,237)	100,060 (7,461)	227,670 (2,208)
2001	1,296,480 (6,669)	640,570 (2,317)	82,930 (2,293)	291,520 (†)	266,130 (338)	401,290 (3,527)	172,340 (2,633)	127,340 (1,625)	101,600 (1,852)	254,620 (4,465)
2003	1,311,150 (24,733)	633,590 (3,888)	74,930 (†)	292,230 (†)	266,430 (3,888)	392,310 (4,195)	167,250 (3,144)	131,220 (1,924)	93,840 (2,031)	285,250 (23,952)
2005	1,348,930 (18,073)	622,970 (1,538)	69,560 (1,201)	283,510 (700)	269,900 (1,341)	437,900 (6,541)	192,440 (3,404)	135,590 (1,493)	109,860 (5,190)	288,070 (16,551)
2007	1,364,300 (11,958)	622,930 (1,377)	67,030 (42)	281,680 (566)	274,210 (364)	449,680 (3,796)	184,260 (1,768)	109,430 (374)	156,000 (3,052)	291,700 (11,156)
2009	1,309,430 (6,480)	618,390 (4,409)	74,380 (10)	266,290 (4,311)	277,720 (920)	410,540 (4,285)	157,830 (362)	114,880 (1,074)	137,840 (4,111)	280,500 (1,880)
2011	1,291,130 (15,396)	606,250 (14,313)	67,320 (10)	268,840 (14,313)	270,090 (†)	408,330 (5,747)	162,420 (1,349)	121,560 (513)	124,350 (5,792)	276,550 (3,485)
					Percentage distribution					
Total, all grades										
1995	100.0 (†)	45.0 (0.19)	24.7 (0.13)	14.4 (0.08)	5.9 (0.03)	35.4 (0.19)	13.3 (0.12)	11.8 (0.08)	10.3 (0.18)	19.7 (0.23)
1997	100.0 (†)	44.8 (0.13)	24.2 (0.09)	14.7 (0.05)	5.9 (0.03)	35.3 (0.18)	13.9 (0.12)	10.9 (0.06)	10.5 (0.17)	19.9 (0.17)
1999	100.0 (†)	44.2 (0.24)	23.2 (0.14)	14.6 (0.07)	6.4 (0.04)	36.4 (0.28)	14.5 (0.09)	10.7 (0.08)	11.2 (0.36)	19.3 (0.11)
2001	100.0 (†)	42.3 (0.25)	20.7 (0.14)	15.5 (0.12)	6.1 (0.04)	36.8 (0.22)	14.8 (0.13)	10.5 (0.13)	11.5 (0.18)	20.9 (0.33)
2003	100.0 (†)	41.3 (0.27)	19.4 (0.17)	15.8 (0.14)	6.1 (0.07)	36.5 (0.25)	14.6 (0.13)	10.7 (0.10)	11.3 (0.22)	22.1 (0.36)
2005	100.0 (†)	39.6 (0.26)	17.5 (0.13)	15.8 (0.14)	6.3 (0.07)	37.9 (0.25)	15.8 (0.14)	11.5 (0.09)	10.7 (0.26)	22.5 (0.34)
2007	100.0 (†)	39.1 (0.20)	16.0 (0.11)	16.4 (0.09)	6.6 (0.06)	38.6 (0.25)	14.9 (0.12)	8.9 (0.06)	14.8 (0.26)	22.3 (0.25)
2009	100.0 (†)	39.4 (0.25)	15.6 (0.11)	16.6 (0.13)	7.2 (0.05)	37.8 (0.37)	13.4 (0.09)	9.4 (0.07)	15.0 (0.48)	22.8 (0.16)
2011	100.0 (†)	39.6 (0.25)	15.3 (0.09)	17.1 (0.25)	7.3 (0.04)	37.8 (0.28)	13.9 (0.09)	10.7 (0.08)	13.2 (0.34)	22.6 (0.15)
Prekindergarten through grade 8										
1995	100.0 (†)	42.9 (0.20)	28.8 (0.17)	12.1 (0.06)	2.1 (0.02)	36.9 (0.22)	13.7 (0.13)	12.1 (0.09)	11.1 (0.21)	20.2 (0.28)
1997	100.0 (†)	43.0 (0.15)	28.4 (0.12)	12.6 (0.05)	2.0 (0.03)	36.7 (0.20)	14.3 (0.13)	11.1 (0.06)	11.3 (0.19)	20.3 (0.19)
1999	100.0 (†)	42.5 (0.23)	27.5 (0.16)	12.7 (0.06)	2.3 (0.04)	38.0 (0.26)	14.9 (0.09)	11.1 (0.07)	12.0 (0.32)	19.6 (0.12)
2001	100.0 (†)	40.5 (0.27)	24.4 (0.17)	13.7 (0.14)	2.3 (0.05)	38.4 (0.25)	15.2 (0.15)	10.7 (0.14)	12.5 (0.20)	21.2 (0.37)
2003	100.0 (†)	39.4 (0.25)	23.1 (0.18)	14.0 (0.13)	2.2 (0.01)	38.3 (0.23)	15.1 (0.12)	10.8 (0.09)	12.4 (0.24)	22.3 (0.22)

See notes at end of table.

Enrollment and percentage distribution of students enrolled in private elementary and secondary schools, by school orientation and grade level: Selected years, fall 1995 through fall 2011—Continued

[Standard errors appear in parentheses]

Grade level and year	Total private enrollment	Catholic				Other religious				Nonsectarian
		Total	Parochial	Diocesan	Private (independent)	Total	Conservative Christian	Affiliated[1]	Unaffiliated[1]	
1	2	3	4	5	6	7	8	9	10	11
2005	100.0 (†)	37.7 (0.25)	21.0 (0.14)	14.2 (0.15)	2.4 (0.06)	39.5 (0.21)	16.2 (0.16)	11.9 (0.09)	11.4 (0.22)	22.8 (0.23)
2007	100.0 (†)	37.1 (0.20)	19.3 (0.13)	15.1 (0.09)	2.6 (0.07)	40.3 (0.27)	15.4 (0.14)	9.2 (0.07)	15.8 (0.30)	22.6 (0.21)
2009	100.0 (†)	36.9 (0.29)	18.7 (0.15)	15.4 (0.12)	2.8 (0.03)	39.9 (0.43)	13.9 (0.11)	9.6 (0.10)	16.4 (0.57)	23.2 (0.20)
2011	100.0 (†)	37.3 (0.18)	18.5 (0.11)	15.9 (0.08)	2.9 (0.02)	39.8 (0.24)	14.3 (0.08)	11.2 (0.08)	14.4 (0.32)	22.9 (0.11)
Grades 9 through 12										
1995	100.0 (†)	53.2 (0.20)	7.8 (0.03)	23.7 (0.20)	21.7 (0.09)	29.4 (0.20)	11.7 (0.18)	10.5 (0.06)	7.2 (0.14)	17.4 (0.12)
1997	100.0 (†)	52.2 (0.10)	7.3 (0.01)	23.2 (0.05)	21.7 (0.04)	29.8 (0.16)	12.2 (0.13)	9.9 (0.08)	7.6 (0.10)	18.0 (0.14)
1999	100.0 (†)	51.0 (0.34)	6.5 (0.04)	22.2 (0.15)	22.2 (0.15)	30.5 (0.45)	12.9 (0.14)	9.5 (0.11)	8.1 (0.56)	18.5 (0.19)
2001	100.0 (†)	49.4 (0.26)	6.4 (0.17)	22.5 (0.12)	20.5 (0.10)	31.0 (0.19)	13.3 (0.17)	9.8 (0.12)	7.8 (0.13)	19.6 (0.28)
2003	100.0 (†)	48.3 (0.91)	5.7 (0.11)	22.3 (0.42)	20.3 (0.44)	29.9 (0.59)	12.8 (0.32)	10.0 (0.23)	7.2 (0.20)	21.8 (1.43)
2005	100.0 (†)	46.2 (0.60)	5.2 (0.07)	21.0 (0.28)	20.0 (0.27)	32.5 (0.52)	14.3 (0.28)	10.1 (0.16)	8.1 (0.37)	21.4 (0.97)
2007	100.0 (†)	45.7 (0.40)	4.9 (0.09)	20.6 (0.18)	20.1 (0.17)	33.0 (0.33)	13.5 (0.16)	8.0 (0.07)	11.4 (0.22)	21.4 (0.65)
2009	100.0 (†)	47.2 (0.25)	5.7 (0.03)	20.3 (0.27)	21.2 (0.12)	31.4 (0.25)	12.1 (0.06)	8.8 (0.08)	10.5 (0.28)	21.4 (0.15)
2011	100.0 (†)	47.0 (0.63)	5.2 (0.06)	20.8 (0.88)	20.9 (0.25)	31.6 (0.49)	12.6 (0.18)	9.4 (0.13)	9.6 (0.43)	21.4 (0.35)

†Not applicable.

[1] Affiliated schools belong to associations of schools with a specific religious orientation other than Catholic or conservative Christian. Unaffiliated schools have a religious orientation or purpose but are not classified as Catholic, conservative Christian, or affiliated.

NOTE: Includes enrollment in prekindergarten through grade 12 in schools that offer kindergarten or higher grade. Ungraded students are prorated into prekindergarten through grade 8 and grades 9 through 12. Detail may not sum to totals because of rounding.

SOURCE: U.S. Department of Education, National Center for Education Statistics, Private School Universe Survey (PSS), 1995–96 through 2011–12. (This table was prepared April 2013.)

Percentage distribution of students enrolled in private elementary and secondary schools, by school orientation and selected characteristics: Fall 2009 and fall 2011

[Standard errors appear in parentheses]

Selected characteristic	Total	Catholic — Total	Catholic — Parochial	Catholic — Diocesan	Catholic — Private (independent)	Other religious — Total	Other religious — Conservative Christian	Other religious — Affiliated[1]	Other religious — Unaffiliated[1]	Nonsectarian
	2	3	4	5	6	7	8	9	10	11
	(†)	(0.25)	(0.11)	(0.13)	(0.05)	(0.37)	(0.09)	(0.07)	(0.48)	(0.16)
Fall 2009										
Total	100.0	39.4	15.6	16.6	7.2	37.8	13.4	9.4	15.0	22.8
School level[2]										
Elementary	100.0	49.5 (0.44)	25.9 (0.24)	20.9 (0.19)	2.7 (0.03)	30.1 (0.58)	7.1 (0.08)	8.4 (0.12)	14.6 (0.68)	20.4 (0.22)
Secondary	100.0	74.7 (0.25)	8.5 (0.05)	33.2 (0.38)	33.0 (0.22)	13.6 (0.22)	2.3 (0.01)	5.5 (0.03)	5.8 (0.23)	11.7 (0.13)
Combined	100.0	6.7 (0.06)	1.6 (0.02)	2.0 (0.02)	3.1 (0.03)	61.5 (0.35)	28.9 (0.26)	12.8 (0.15)	19.7 (0.68)	31.8 (0.31)
Student race/ethnicity[3]										
White	100.0	41.7 (0.38)	16.2 (0.16)	17.9 (0.20)	7.6 (0.07)	39.2 (0.54)	13.7 (0.13)	10.1 (0.11)	15.5 (0.72)	19.0 (0.18)
Black	100.0	35.1 (0.21)	13.1 (0.08)	13.8 (0.08)	8.2 (0.05)	41.8 (0.20)	18.0 (0.14)	8.9 (0.09)	14.8 (0.27)	23.1 (0.24)
Hispanic	100.0	60.3 (0.55)	25.1 (0.24)	23.5 (0.22)	11.7 (0.11)	24.3 (0.14)	10.4 (0.11)	6.2 (0.10)	7.7 (0.21)	15.4 (0.53)
Asian	100.0	38.1 (0.29)	15.1 (0.12)	15.5 (0.12)	7.5 (0.06)	30.3 (0.25)	11.5 (0.09)	9.7 (0.08)	9.1 (0.14)	31.6 (0.52)
Pacific Islander	100.0	40.3 (1.28)	17.7 (0.56)	16.7 (0.53)	5.9 (0.19)	44.6 (1.75)	12.5 (0.40)	5.4 (0.17)	26.7 (2.32)	15.1 (0.48)
American Indian/Alaska Native	100.0	41.0 (0.32)	10.3 (0.08)	18.2 (0.14)	12.5 (0.10)	34.1 (0.40)	17.1 (0.32)	5.6 (0.25)	11.4 (0.29)	24.9 (0.43)
Two or more races	100.0	44.8 (0.26)	16.5 (0.10)	19.7 (0.11)	8.7 (0.09)	27.0 (0.39)	9.8 (0.07)	8.0 (0.05)	9.2 (0.48)	28.2 (0.21)
School enrollment										
Less than 50	100.0	2.3 (0.26)	0.7 (0.10)	0.7 (0.06)	0.9 (0.19)	57.7 (3.20)	12.1 (0.97)	6.9 (0.86)	38.8 (4.56)	40.0 (3.04)
50 to 149	100.0	15.6 (0.21)	6.9 (0.09)	6.6 (0.12)	2.1 (0.06)	47.2 (0.42)	16.3 (0.21)	9.2 (0.12)	21.7 (0.65)	37.2 (0.36)
150 to 299	100.0	44.8 (0.32)	21.8 (0.15)	19.6 (0.14)	3.5 (0.06)	36.5 (0.40)	12.8 (0.12)	9.2 (0.14)	14.4 (0.51)	18.7 (0.25)
300 to 499	100.0	50.0 (0.46)	23.3 (0.33)	20.1 (0.38)	6.7 (0.06)	32.6 (0.58)	12.7 (0.12)	9.4 (0.26)	10.6 (0.71)	17.3 (0.27)
500 to 749	100.0	53.7 (#)	19.7 (#)	23.3 (#)	10.7 (#)	30.4 (#)	13.4 (#)	9.3 (#)	7.8 (#)	15.9 (#)
750 or more	100.0	42.0 (0.31)	6.6 (0.05)	17.3 (0.13)	18.2 (0.13)	36.5 (0.46)	12.7 (0.09)	11.0 (0.08)	12.8 (0.64)	21.5 (0.16)
Region										
Northeast	100.0	45.6 (0.57)	19.4 (0.28)	16.8 (0.38)	9.4 (0.13)	28.0 (0.80)	4.9 (0.09)	9.5 (0.11)	13.6 (0.77)	26.4 (0.28)
Midwest	100.0	56.1 (1.08)	23.3 (0.44)	24.3 (0.49)	8.5 (0.18)	32.3 (1.26)	9.2 (0.19)	8.0 (0.22)	15.1 (1.58)	11.6 (0.35)
South	100.0	26.8 (0.25)	9.9 (0.09)	12.0 (0.11)	5.0 (0.05)	48.7 (0.42)	19.4 (0.19)	11.3 (0.11)	18.0 (0.65)	24.5 (0.25)
West	100.0	32.9 (0.25)	11.4 (0.09)	14.7 (0.11)	6.8 (0.05)	37.8 (0.35)	18.9 (0.15)	7.7 (0.13)	11.3 (0.39)	29.2 (0.34)
School locale										
City	100.0	44.2 (0.23)	16.0 (0.10)	18.2 (0.10)	10.0 (0.06)	33.8 (0.09)	10.8 (0.07)	10.2 (0.07)	12.8 (0.11)	21.9 (0.26)
Suburban	100.0	40.6 (0.38)	17.0 (0.16)	17.0 (0.24)	6.6 (0.06)	35.4 (0.48)	13.2 (0.13)	9.2 (0.12)	13.0 (0.54)	23.9 (0.28)
Town	100.0	47.1 (1.16)	22.5 (0.56)	22.4 (0.55)	2.2 (0.05)	39.6 (1.45)	15.1 (0.40)	7.7 (0.40)	16.7 (1.94)	13.3 (0.72)
Rural	100.0	15.8 (0.59)	6.2 (0.23)	6.8 (0.25)	2.9 (0.11)	56.7 (1.50)	21.6 (0.81)	8.2 (0.36)	26.9 (2.56)	27.5 (0.97)
Fall 2011										
Total	100.0	39.6 (0.25)	15.3 (0.09)	17.1 (0.25)	7.3 (0.04)	37.8 (0.28)	13.9 (0.09)	10.7 (0.08)	13.2 (0.34)	22.6 (0.15)
School level[2]										
Elementary	100.0	49.8 (0.16)	25.7 (0.12)	21.5 (0.07)	2.7 (0.02)	29.5 (0.19)	7.1 (0.05)	9.5 (0.05)	12.9 (0.23)	20.6 (0.12)
Secondary	100.0	74.0 (0.52)	8.1 (0.15)	34.3 (1.24)	31.6 (0.60)	14.1 (0.28)	2.6 (0.05)	5.9 (0.11)	5.7 (0.12)	11.9 (0.31)
Combined	100.0	8.3 (0.11)	1.7 (0.02)	2.6 (0.05)	4.1 (0.04)	61.4 (0.48)	29.6 (0.34)	14.8 (0.24)	17.1 (0.89)	30.3 (0.39)
Student race/ethnicity[3]										
White	100.0	41.9 (0.35)	15.9 (0.14)	18.3 (0.33)	7.7 (0.06)	39.5 (0.45)	14.3 (0.13)	11.5 (0.12)	13.7 (0.55)	18.7 (0.19)
Black	100.0	35.4 (0.15)	11.9 (0.05)	14.9 (0.32)	8.6 (0.03)	41.8 (0.18)	17.7 (0.08)	10.5 (0.10)	13.6 (0.06)	22.8 (0.30)
Hispanic	100.0	60.2 (0.22)	24.3 (0.12)	24.5 (0.08)	11.4 (0.05)	24.4 (0.19)	11.1 (0.19)	6.9 (0.04)	6.4 (0.06)	15.4 (0.10)
Asian	100.0	36.6 (0.10)	13.8 (0.02)	15.2 (0.11)	7.5 (0.01)	31.2 (0.05)	12.3 (0.04)	10.1 (0.01)	8.9 (0.06)	32.2 (0.07)
Pacific Islander	100.0	46.3 (0.33)	16.2 (0.08)	20.9 (0.36)	9.2 (0.04)	38.1 (0.28)	12.2 (0.18)	13.0 (0.06)	12.9 (0.06)	15.6 (0.30)
American Indian/Alaska Native	100.0	43.9 (0.18)	11.0 (0.05)	18.0 (0.08)	15.0 (0.06)	30.4 (0.29)	16.1 (0.35)	7.2 (0.03)	7.2 (0.06)	25.7 (0.11)
Two or more races	100.0	44.1 (0.14)	15.5 (0.04)	19.9 (0.14)	8.7 (0.06)	27.6 (0.10)	11.0 (0.04)	9.4 (0.02)	7.3 (0.09)	28.3 (0.12)
School enrollment										
Less than 50	100.0	2.9 (0.21)	0.8 (0.03)	0.8 (0.02)	1.4 (0.19)	54.4 (1.45)	14.5 (0.57)	8.2 (0.30)	31.7 (1.65)	42.7 (1.38)
50 to 149	100.0	15.4 (0.15)	6.7 (0.06)	6.5 (0.06)	2.2 (0.02)	46.9 (0.78)	16.1 (0.37)	11.1 (0.11)	19.7 (0.52)	37.7 (0.69)
150 to 299	100.0	44.0 (0.10)	21.2 (0.08)	19.5 (0.05)	3.3 (0.01)	37.3 (0.10)	14.4 (0.03)	10.8 (0.11)	12.2 (0.03)	18.7 (0.12)
300 to 499	100.0	51.2 (0.80)	23.1 (0.15)	21.6 (0.08)	6.5 (0.02)	31.9 (0.12)	12.9 (0.05)	9.6 (0.17)	9.4 (0.03)	16.8 (0.06)
500 to 749	100.0	55.6 (0.80)	18.6 (0.34)	24.9 (1.36)	12.2 (0.22)	29.7 (0.54)	12.5 (0.23)	9.5 (0.17)	7.7 (0.14)	14.7 (0.27)
750 or more	100.0	38.4 (0.80)	5.7 (0.12)	15.7 (0.33)	16.9 (0.35)	39.6 (1.25)	13.0 (0.27)	13.5 (0.28)	13.0 (1.80)	22.1 (0.46)

See notes at end of table.

Percentage distribution of students enrolled in private elementary and secondary schools, by school orientation and selected characteristics: Fall 2009 and fall 2011—Continued

[Standard errors appear in parentheses]

Selected characteristic	Total	Catholic				Other religious				Nonsectarian
		Total	Parochial	Diocesan	Private (independent)	Total	Conservative Christian	Affiliated[1]	Unaffiliated[1]	
1	2	3	4	5	6	7	8	9	10	11
Region										
Northeast	100.0 (†)	43.3 (0.66)	17.0 (0.25)	16.5 (0.27)	9.8 (0.14)	30.9 (0.89)	4.7 (0.07)	11.9 (0.30)	14.2 (1.24)	25.8 (0.28)
Midwest	100.0 (†)	56.8 (0.79)	24.3 (0.38)	24.5 (0.94)	8.0 (0.13)	31.5 (0.90)	10.2 (0.32)	8.9 (0.18)	12.4 (0.66)	11.6 (0.43)
South	100.0 (†)	27.8 (0.04)	9.8 (0.01)	12.9 (0.02)	5.1 (0.01)	47.9 (0.07)	20.2 (0.06)	12.2 (0.02)	15.5 (0.02)	24.3 (0.09)
West	100.0 (†)	34.0 (0.01)	11.2 (0.01)	15.8 (0.01)	7.0 (0.00)	36.8 (0.02)	18.8 (0.01)	9.0 (0.01)	9.0 (0.02)	29.2 (0.01)
School locale										
City	100.0 (†)	44.2 (0.37)	15.4 (0.10)	19.3 (0.53)	9.5 (0.06)	33.9 (0.23)	10.4 (0.07)	11.1 (0.10)	12.4 (0.08)	21.9 (0.17)
Suburban	100.0 (†)	40.9 (0.14)	16.8 (0.15)	17.0 (0.06)	7.2 (0.02)	35.0 (0.08)	13.8 (0.05)	11.1 (0.10)	10.2 (0.04)	24.0 (0.15)
Town	100.0 (†)	49.4 (0.43)	23.9 (0.21)	23.4 (0.20)	2.1 (0.02)	39.3 (0.53)	16.8 (0.36)	8.6 (0.08)	14.0 (0.67)	11.3 (0.10)
Rural	100.0 (†)	16.7 (0.47)	6.3 (0.18)	7.2 (0.20)	3.2 (0.09)	57.2 (1.41)	23.4 (0.76)	9.7 (0.28)	24.1 (2.10)	26.2 (0.98)

†Not applicable.
#Rounds to zero.
[1]Affiliated schools belong to associations of schools with a specific religious orientation other than Catholic or conservative Christian. Unaffiliated schools have a religious orientation or purpose but are not classified as Catholic, conservative Christian, or affiliated.
[2]Elementary schools have grade 6 or lower and no grade higher than 8. Secondary schools have no grade lower than 7. Combined schools include those that have grades lower than 7 and higher than 8, as well as those that do not classify students by grade level.

[3]Race/ethnicity was not collected for prekindergarten students (788,370 out of 5,488,490 students in 2009 and 773,240 out of 5,268,090 students in 2011). Percentage distribution is based on the students for whom race/ethnicity was reported.
NOTE: Includes enrollment in prekindergarten through grade 12 in schools that offer kindergarten or higher grade. Detail may not sum to totals because of rounding.
SOURCE: U.S. Department of Education, National Center for Education Statistics, Private School Universe Survey (PSS), 2009–10 and 2011–12. (This table was prepared April 2013.)

Number and percentage distribution of private elementary and secondary students, teachers, and schools, by orientation of school and selected characteristics: Fall 1999, fall 2009, and fall 2011

[Standard errors appear in parentheses]

Selected characteristic	Fall 1999, total number	Fall 2009, total number	Fall 2011 Total Number	Percent	Catholic Number	Percent	Other religious Number	Percent	Nonsectarian Number	Percent
1	2	3	4	5	6	7	8	9	10	11
Students[1]										
Total.................	6,018,280 (30,179)	5,488,490 (35,857)	5,268,090 (24,908)	100.0 (†)	2,087,870 (14,426)	100.0 (†)	1,991,950 (21,814)	100.0 (†)	1,188,270 (5,376)	100.0 (†)
School level[2]										
Elementary.............	3,595,020 (11,516)	2,937,090 (26,807)	2,775,270 (9,594)	52.7 (0.23)	1,383,420 (3,829)	66.3 (0.47)	819,070 (7,697)	41.1 (0.37)	572,790 (3,263)	48.2 (0.22)
Secondary.............	806,640 (2,395)	785,810 (4,810)	757,620 (14,401)	14.4 (0.25)	560,280 (14,312)	26.8 (0.51)	106,970 (444)	5.4 (0.06)	90,370 (1,827)	7.6 (0.14)
Combined.............	1,616,620 (23,949)	1,765,590 (15,909)	1,735,200 (16,892)	32.9 (0.21)	144,170 (475)	6.9 (0.05)	1,065,910 (18,183)	53.5 (0.41)	525,120 (3,824)	44.2 (0.23)
School enrollment										
Less than 50	238,980 (5,691)	296,000 (22,889)	242,910 (7,660)	4.6 (0.14)	7,030 (473)	0.3 (0.02)	132,200 (7,447)	6.6 (0.35)	103,690 (1,771)	8.7 (0.14)
50 to 149.............	939,110 (10,717)	950,050 (12,053)	886,240 (7,898)	16.8 (0.15)	136,680 (498)	6.5 (0.05)	415,450 (10,139)	20.9 (0.43)	334,110 (4,582)	28.1 (0.29)
150 to 299.............	1,615,970 (7,315)	1,423,220 (9,951)	1,379,070 (3,193)	26.2 (0.15)	606,670 (1,318)	29.1 (0.19)	514,970 (1,773)	25.9 (0.34)	257,430 (2,046)	21.7 (0.16)
300 to 499.............	1,419,360 (13,203)	1,154,950 (10,730)	1,104,910 (4,050)	21.0 (0.11)	566,000 (2,400)	27.1 (0.19)	352,970 (2,234)	17.7 (0.21)	185,950 (†)	15.6 (0.07)
500 to 749.............	917,670 (2,330)	768,540 (†)	790,830 (14,312)	15.0 (0.25)	439,990 (14,312)	21.1 (0.55)	234,500 (†)	11.8 (0.13)	116,340 (†)	9.8 (0.04)
750 or more.............	887,190 (18,232)	895,720 (6,538)	864,120 (17,908)	16.4 (0.29)	331,500 (†)	15.9 (0.11)	341,860 (17,908)	17.2 (0.77)	190,760 (†)	16.1 (0.07)
Student race/ethnicity[3]										
White.................	4,061,870 (24,242)	3,410,360 (31,067)	3,208,730 (23,933)	71.4 (0.14)	1,342,980 (11,961)	69.6 (0.09)	1,266,580 (21,804)	75.5 (0.32)	599,160 (3,387)	67.3 (0.15)
Black.................	494,530 (5,079)	430,970 (2,579)	400,260 (1,601)	8.9 (0.06)	141,670 (239)	7.3 (0.04)	167,280 (472)	10.0 (0.13)	91,310 (1,532)	10.3 (0.15)
Hispanic.................	435,890 (1,592)	443,290 (4,113)	441,680 (2,016)	9.8 (0.05)	265,880 (1,805)	13.8 (0.02)	107,860 (925)	6.4 (0.10)	67,930 (379)	7.6 (0.04)
Asian.................	239,510 (877)	239,320 (1,894)	245,640 (281)	5.5 (0.03)	89,810 (297)	4.7 (0.02)	76,710 (89)	4.6 (0.06)	79,130 (203)	8.9 (0.04)
Pacific Islander	[4] (†)	28,020 (884)	26,810 (117)	0.6 (#)	12,410 (108)	0.6 (#)	10,210 (39)	0.6 (0.01)	4,190 (94)	0.5 (0.01)
American Indian/ Alaska Native....	22,690 (164)	21,080 (162)	21,430 (91)	0.5 (#)	9,420 (5)	0.5 (#)	6,510 (90)	0.4 (0.01)	5,500 (5)	0.6 (#)
Two or more races....	— (†)	127,090 (781)	150,300 (370)	3.3 (0.01)	66,220 (300)	3.4 (0.01)	41,490 (141)	2.5 (0.03)	42,590 (216)	4.8 (0.03)
School locale										
City.................	— (†)	2,252,780 (12,708)	2,186,170 (14,689)	41.5 (0.27)	966,990 (14,322)	46.3 (0.39)	740,520 (1,602)	37.2 (0.46)	478,660 (2,558)	40.3 (0.21)
Suburban.................	— (†)	2,137,800 (20,891)	2,018,570 (6,493)	38.3 (0.20)	826,400 (3,857)	39.6 (0.30)	707,340 (2,728)	35.5 (0.39)	484,840 (3,400)	40.8 (0.22)
Town.................	— (†)	387,920 (9,565)	358,600 (3,130)	6.8 (0.05)	177,140 (113)	8.5 (0.06)	141,060 (3,128)	7.1 (0.13)	40,400 (31)	3.4 (0.02)
Rural.................	— (†)	709,990 (26,462)	704,750 (19,874)	13.4 (0.33)	117,350 (†)	5.6 (0.04)	403,030 (21,029)	20.2 (0.84)	184,370 (3,228)	15.5 (0.24)
Teachers[5]										
Total.................	408,400 (2,977)	437,410 (3,222)	420,880 (1,836)	100.0 (†)	138,070 (1,069)	100.0 (†)	163,140 (1,568)	100.0 (†)	119,670 (567)	100.0 (†)
School level[2]										
Elementary.............	200,910 (735)	194,480 (1,878)	184,130 (855)	43.7 (0.16)	84,340 (224)	61.1 (0.47)	57,310 (731)	35.1 (0.26)	42,480 (373)	35.5 (0.23)
Secondary.............	62,740 (229)	67,530 (553)	65,180 (1,055)	15.5 (0.22)	41,290 (1,051)	29.9 (0.54)	10,850 (72)	6.7 (0.07)	13,030 (95)	10.9 (0.09)
Combined.............	144,750 (2,682)	175,410 (1,853)	171,570 (918)	40.8 (0.14)	12,440 (49)	9.0 (0.08)	94,980 (1,049)	58.2 (0.26)	64,160 (388)	53.6 (0.22)
School enrollment										
Less than 50	25,970 (488)	34,120 (1,642)	30,960 (1,104)	7.4 (0.24)	1,000 (72)	0.7 (0.05)	16,700 (1,080)	10.2 (0.59)	13,260 (241)	11.1 (0.18)
50 to 149.............	70,800 (983)	82,460 (1,102)	76,830 (766)	18.3 (0.16)	11,960 (48)	8.7 (0.07)	35,720 (918)	21.9 (0.45)	29,150 (415)	24.4 (0.27)
150 to 299.............	102,240 (486)	107,490 (1,873)	103,940 (376)	24.7 (0.14)	39,210 (69)	28.4 (0.22)	39,730 (285)	24.4 (0.32)	25,000 (221)	20.9 (0.15)
300 to 499.............	90,010 (1,316)	86,850 (751)	83,150 (295)	19.8 (0.10)	36,100 (124)	26.1 (0.20)	27,590 (244)	16.9 (0.20)	19,460 (†)	16.3 (0.08)
500 to 749.............	57,930 (79)	56,920 (†)	58,070 (1,051)	13.8 (0.22)	27,770 (1,051)	20.1 (0.61)	17,840 (†)	10.9 (0.11)	12,460 (†)	10.4 (0.05)
750 or more.............	61,440 (2,143)	69,570 (566)	67,930 (696)	16.1 (0.16)	22,030 (†)	16.0 (0.12)	25,570 (696)	15.7 (0.41)	20,330 (†)	17.0 (0.08)
School locale										
City.................	— (†)	176,740 (799)	173,390 (1,121)	41.2 (0.24)	62,980 (1,051)	45.6 (0.42)	60,890 (283)	37.3 (0.44)	49,530 (248)	41.4 (0.20)
Suburban.................	— (†)	166,170 (2,463)	155,630 (591)	37.0 (0.18)	53,660 (240)	38.9 (0.32)	55,960 (324)	34.3 (0.34)	46,010 (423)	38.4 (0.23)
Town.................	— (†)	30,390 (663)	28,270 (598)	6.7 (0.13)	12,620 (8)	9.1 (0.07)	11,730 (598)	7.2 (0.31)	3,920 (1)	3.3 (0.02)
Rural.................	— (†)	64,120 (1,960)	63,590 (1,123)	15.1 (0.23)	8,810 (†)	6.4 (0.05)	34,560 (1,203)	21.2 (0.56)	20,210 (241)	16.9 (0.18)
Schools										
Total.................	33,000 (301)	33,370 (834)	30,860 (542)	100.0 (†)	6,870 (31)	100.0 (.00)	14,210 (551)	100.0 (†)	9,770 (87)	100.0 (†)
School level[2]										
Elementary.............	22,300 (242)	21,420 (745)	19,700 (414)	63.8 (0.43)	5,420 (23)	78.9 (0.35)	7,930 (407)	55.8 (1.04)	6,350 (66)	64.9 (0.42)
Secondary.............	2,540 (62)	2,780 (39)	2,680 (30)	8.7 (0.18)	1,050 (27)	15.2 (0.36)	760 (13)	5.3 (0.22)	870 (10)	8.9 (0.12)
Combined.............	8,150 (160)	9,160 (153)	8,490 (188)	27.5 (0.38)	410 (9)	5.9 (0.11)	5,530 (204)	38.9 (0.95)	2,560 (53)	26.1 (0.43)
School enrollment										
Less than 50	9,160 (210)	11,070 (801)	9,660 (520)	31.3 (1.15)	250 (20)	3.7 (0.28)	5,600 (517)	39.4 (2.21)	3,810 (54)	39.0 (0.41)
50 to 149.............	10,260 (134)	10,470 (154)	9,720 (120)	31.5 (0.65)	1,310 (7)	19.0 (0.12)	4,540 (151)	32.0 (1.32)	3,860 (64)	39.5 (0.46)
150 to 299.............	7,440 (34)	6,690 (46)	6,460 (16)	20.9 (0.37)	2,770 (6)	40.3 (0.14)	2,440 (9)	17.2 (0.67)	1,240 (10)	12.7 (0.13)
300 to 499.............	3,730 (41)	3,010 (30)	2,900 (10)	9.4 (0.17)	1,470 (5)	21.4 (0.07)	940 (5)	6.6 (0.26)	490 (†)	5.0 (0.04)
500 to 749.............	1,530 (3)	1,280 (†)	1,320 (27)	4.3 (0.12)	740 (27)	10.8 (0.37)	390 (†)	2.7 (0.11)	190 (†)	2.0 (0.02)
750 or more.............	870 (20)	850 (7)	800 (10)	2.6 (0.06)	330 (†)	4.7 (0.02)	300 (10)	2.1 (0.11)	180 (†)	1.8 (0.02)
School locale										
City......................	— (†)	10,810 (171)	10,000 (52)	32.4 (0.59)	2,830 (27)	41.2 (0.33)	3,830 (9)	26.9 (1.05)	3,350 (41)	34.2 (0.37)
Suburban	— (†)	11,610 (176)	10,910 (70)	35.4 (0.63)	2,490 (27)	36.3 (0.33)	3,960 (24)	27.8 (1.08)	4,460 (56)	45.6 (0.41)
Town......................	— (†)	3,340 (154)	2,900 (104)	9.4 (0.22)	930 (1)	13.6 (0.06)	1,530 (104)	10.8 (0.43)	430 (1)	4.4 (0.04)
Rural......................	— (†)	7,610 (799)	7,050 (453)	22.8 (1.07)	610 (†)	8.9 (0.04)	4,900 (463)	34.4 (1.94)	1,540 (46)	15.7 (0.41)

—Not available.
†Not applicable.
#Rounds to zero.
[1]Includes students in prekindergarten through grade 12 in schools that offer kindergarten or higher grade.
[2]Elementary schools have grade 6 or lower and no grade higher than 8. Secondary schools have no grade lower than 7. Combined schools include those that have grades lower than 7 and higher than 8, as well as those that do not classify students by grade level.
[3]Race/ethnicity was not collected for prekindergarten students (773,000 in fall 2011). Percentage distribution is based on the students for whom race/ethnicity was reported.

[4]For 1999, Pacific Islander students are included under Asian. Prior to 2009, data were not collected on Pacific Islander students as a separate category.
[5]Reported in full-time equivalents (FTE). Excludes teachers who teach only prekindergarten students.
NOTE: Tabulation includes schools that offer kindergarten or higher grade. Detail may not sum to totals because of rounding.
SOURCE: U.S. Department of Education, National Center for Education Statistics, Private School Universe Survey (PSS), 1999–2000, 2009–10, and 2011–12. (This table was prepared April 2013.)

Private elementary and secondary enrollment, number of schools, and average tuition, by school level, orientation, and tuition: Selected years, 1999–2000 through 2011–12

[Standard errors appear in parentheses]

School orientation and tuition	Kindergarten through 12th-grade enrollment[1]				Total schools	Average tuition charged[2] (in current dollars)				Average tuition charged[2] (in constant 2012–13 dollars), total
	Total	Elementary	Secondary	Combined		Total	Elementary	Secondary	Combined	
1	2	3	4	5	6	7	8	9	10	11
1999–2000										
Total	5,262,850 (131,001)	2,920,680 (55,057)	818,920 (34,102)	1,523,240 (88,816)	27,220 (239)	$4,980 (157)	$3,740 (249)	$6,080 (175)	$6,760 (261)	$6,820 (215)
Catholic	2,548,710 (23,352)	1,810,330 (18,134)	616,200 (25,935)	122,190 (15,613)	8,100 (24)	3,340 (57)	2,600 (47)	4,830 (92)	6,890 (690)	4,570 (78)
Other religious	1,871,850 (86,782)	831,060 (41,035)	115,010 (10,981)	925,780 (66,926)	13,270 (237)	4,440 (153)	4,070 (130)	6,400 (456)	4,520 (280)	6,080 (210)
Nonsectarian	842,290 (61,373)	279,290 (28,987)	87,720 (11,774)	475,270 (43,377)	5,850 (76)	11,120 (775)	10,130 (1,921)	14,450 (1,461)	11,090 (801)	15,220 (1,061)
2003–04										
Total	5,059,450 (104,287)	2,675,960 (55,714)	832,320 (54,051)	1,551,170 (82,059)	28,380 (262)	$6,600 (145)	$5,050 (120)	$8,410 (433)	$8,300 (290)	$8,220 (180)
Catholic	2,320,040 (49,156)	1,645,680 (41,231)	584,250 (32,236)	90,110 (14,746)	7,920 (35)	4,250 (96)	3,530 (106)	6,050 (131)	5,800 (883)	5,290 (119)
Other religious	1,746,460 (63,090)	714,860 (28,935)	107,980 ! (33,776)	923,630 (48,379)	13,660 (203)	5,840 (144)	5,400 (161)	9,540 (963)	5,750 (230)	7,270 (179)
Nonsectarian	992,940 (71,519)	315,430 (30,820)	140,080 (27,556)	537,440 (59,332)	6,810 (136)	13,420 (379)	12,170 (468)	17,410 (1,988)	13,110 (480)	16,720 (472)
2007–08										
Total	5,165,280 (104,435)	2,462,980 (58,830)	850,750 (38,553)	1,851,550 (91,348)	28,220 (328)	$8,550 (176)	$6,730 (181)	$10,550 (356)	$10,050 (372)	$9,360 (193)
Catholic	2,224,470 (49,385)	1,457,960 (32,114)	620,840 (32,581)	145,680 (25,445)	7,400 (34)	6,020 (180)	4,940 (212)	7,830 (232)	9,070 (964)	6,590 (197)
Less than $3,500	619,410 (37,867)	571,560 (34,303)	‡ (†)	‡ (†)	2,810 (132)	2,980 (55)	3,010 (57)	† (†)	† (†)	3,260 (60)
$3,500 to $5,999	826,120 (37,974)	683,980 (32,576)	111,770 (16,043)	‡ (†)	3,040 (131)	4,900 (49)	4,860 (57)	5,150 (80)	† (†)	5,360 (53)
$6,000 to $9,999	607,980 (49,329)	165,120 (28,123)	395,900 (30,158)	‡ (†)	1,170 (102)	7,680 (116)	7,790 (240)	7,650 (117)	† (†)	8,410 (127)
$10,000 to $14,999	‡ (†)	‡ (†)	‡ (†)	‡ (†)	‡ (†)	‡ (†)	‡ (†)	‡ (†)	‡ (†)	‡ (†)
$15,000 or more	‡ (†)	‡ (†)	‡ (†)	‡ (†)	‡ (†)	‡ (†)	‡ (†)	‡ (†)	‡ (†)	‡ (†)
Other religious	1,975,980 (81,216)	709,730 (36,666)	128,550 (15,136)	1,137,700 (75,038)	13,950 (282)	7,120 (237)	6,580 (241)	10,490 (1,336)	7,070 (359)	7,800 (260)
Less than $3,500	430,010 (31,875)	172,660 (14,154)	† (†)	252,490 (29,920)	6,180 (291)	2,520 (106)	2,550 (167)	† (†)	2,510 (133)	2,760 (116)
$3,500 to $5,999	860,370 (59,588)	340,150 (27,800)	† (†)	489,390 (49,116)	5,030 (257)	5,370 (75)	5,570 (111)	† (†)	5,270 (101)	5,880 (82)
$6,000 to $9,999	384,850 (39,687)	103,280 (15,561)	57,150 (10,809)	224,420 (33,273)	1,640 (137)	8,050 (155)	8,810 (430)	7,680 (188)	7,790 (164)	8,810 (170)
$10,000 to $14,999	167,770 (25,960)	† (†)	† (†)	† (†)	620 (83)	13,230 (401)	† (†)	† (†)	† (†)	14,490 (439)
$15,000 or more	132,980 (24,657)	† (†)	† (†)	† (†)	480 (91)	22,880 (1,053)	† (†)	† (†)	† (†)	25,050 (1,153)
Nonsectarian	964,830 (55,074)	295,280 (25,191)	101,370 (12,739)	568,180 (48,321)	6,860 (119)	17,320 (555)	15,940 (702)	27,300 (1,506)	16,250 (795)	18,960 (608)
Less than $3,500	72,890 (10,998)	‡ (†)	‡ (†)	59,910 (10,584)	1,030 (125)	1,610 (387)	‡ (†)	‡ (†)	1,640 (467)	1,760 (423)
$3,500 to $5,999	103,930 (18,494)	42,610 (7,809)	‡ (†)	‡ (†)	1,040 (143)	6,290 (352)	8,090 (687)	‡ (†)	‡ (†)	6,890 (386)
$6,000 to $9,999	162,450 (24,872)	98,070 (16,434)	‡ (†)	‡ (†)	1,650 (168)	10,960 (530)	12,110 (792)	‡ (†)	‡ (†)	12,000 (581)
$10,000 to $14,999	208,670 (29,194)	77,450 (15,769)	‡ (†)	126,610 (25,784)	1,150 (124)	14,890 (567)	17,750 (1,501)	‡ (†)	13,230 (336)	16,300 (621)
$15,000 or more	416,900 (39,779)	71,360 (14,776)	‡ (†)	259,670 (38,826)	2,000 (157)	26,500 (943)	25,010 (1,422)	‡ (†)	25,350 (1,334)	29,010 (1,033)
2011–12										
Total	4,479,530 (105,651)	2,133,810 (59,964)	731,620 (53,646)	1,614,100 (98,602)	26,230 (541)	$10,740 (316)	$7,770 (211)	$13,030 (727)	$13,640 (753)	$10,940 (321)
Less than $3,500	618,710 (45,753)	404,700 (36,956)	42,580 ! (13,642)	171,430 (23,140)	7,950 (581)	2,190 (112)	2,410 (139)	1,370 (392)	1,870 (182)	2,230 (114)
$3,500 to $5,999	1,351,550 (64,739)	946,810 (56,403)	‡ (†)	364,520 (30,056)	7,800 (326)	5,300 (58)	5,350 (67)	‡ (†)	5,250 (118)	5,400 (59)
$6,000 to $9,999	1,167,820 (80,517)	467,040 (41,842)	275,980 (29,528)	424,800 (62,852)	5,070 (279)	8,560 (124)	9,090 (230)	7,980 (172)	8,360 (251)	8,720 (126)
$10,000 to $14,999	534,560 (45,926)	143,500 (18,976)	208,750 (38,977)	182,310 (36,985)	1,840 (150)	13,400 (207)	15,050 (454)	11,960 (225)	13,750 (348)	13,650 (211)
$15,000 or more	806,880 (69,846)	171,760 (25,237)	164,090 (32,298)	471,040 (65,345)	3,570 (194)	27,820 (951)	24,020 (960)	28,000 (2,487)	29,140 (1,274)	28,340 (969)
Catholic	1,892,480 (59,899)	1,244,480 (36,762)	511,870 (43,761)	136,130 (19,283)	6,760 (185)	6,890 (123)	5,330 (128)	9,790 (405)	10,230 (1,230)	7,020 (188)
Less than $3,500	307,610 (35,036)	259,330 (33,704)	‡ (†)	‡ (†)	1,730 (123)	2,580 (170)	2,660 (122)	† (†)	† (†)	2,630 (125)
$3,500 to $5,999	781,420 (53,974)	716,630 (50,260)	‡ (†)	‡ (†)	3,070 (187)	5,110 (68)	5,120 (72)	† (†)	† (†)	5,200 (69)
$6,000 to $9,999	516,660 (48,765)	243,570 (35,924)	234,460 (29,418)	‡ (†)	1,320 (126)	7,850 (139)	7,820 (210)	7,970 (199)	† (†)	8,000 (141)
$10,000 to $14,999	221,150 (36,032)	‡ (†)	177,560 (34,919)	‡ (†)	440 (68)	12,290 (240)	† (†)	12,020 (252)	† (†)	12,520 (245)
$15,000 or more	‡ (†)	‡ (†)	‡ (†)	‡ (†)	‡ (†)	‡ (†)	† (†)	† (†)	† (†)	‡ (†)

See notes at end of table.

Private elementary and secondary enrollment, number of schools, and average tuition, by school level, orientation, and tuition: Selected years, 1999–2000 through 2011–12—Continued

[Standard errors appear in parentheses]

| School orientation and tuition | Kindergarten through 12th-grade enrollment[1] | | | | Total schools | Average tuition charged[2] (in current dollars) | | | | Average tuition charged[2] (in constant 2012–13 dollars), total |
| | Total | Elementary | Secondary | Combined | | Total | Elementary | Secondary | Combined | |
1	2	3	4	5	6	7	8	9	10	11
Other religious............	1,604,900 (84,424)	609,930 (38,479)	116,660 (31,187)	878,320 (77,923)	13,040 (550)	8,690 (397)	7,960 (447)	16,520 (2,288)	8,160 (518)	8,850 (405)
Less than $3,500........	243,840 (25,511)	136,240 (19,015)	‡ (†)	103,980 (13,231)	5,190 (518)	2,090 (156)	1,860 (245)	‡ (†)	2,440 (169)	2,130 (159)
$3,500 to $5,999........	507,660 (38,017)	214,270 (23,446)	‡ (†)	286,370 (28,337)	4,280 (259)	5,540 (101)	5,980 (183)	‡ (†)	5,220 (123)	5,640 (103)
$6,000 to $9,999........	532,720 (61,948)	144,110 (26,978)	40,740 (7,928)	347,870 (59,370)	2,220 (228)	8,460 (186)	9,010 (269)	8,030 (196)	8,280 (260)	8,620 (190)
$10,000 to $14,999......	165,130 (32,486)	‡ (†)	‡ (†)	‡ (†)	630 (89)	13,490 (359)	‡ (†)	‡ (†)	‡ (†)	13,740 (366)
$15,000 or more........	155,550 (33,317)	‡ (†)	‡ (†)	‡ (†)	720 (126)	25,000 (2,243)	‡ (†)	‡ (†)	‡ (†)	25,460 (2,285)
Nonsectarian..........	982,140 (67,032)	279,400 (21,508)	103,090 (19,049)	599,650 (61,512)	6,430 (68)	21,510 (1,018)	18,170 (906)	25,180 (2,907)	22,440 (1,503)	21,910 (1,037)
Less than $3,500........	67,260 (15,092)	‡ (†)	‡ (†)	47,370 (14,470)	1,040 (140)	740 ! (285)	‡ (†)	‡ (†)	490 ! (244)	750 ! (290)
$3,500 to $5,999........	‡ (†)	‡ (†)	‡ (†)	‡ (†)	‡ (†)	‡ (†)	‡ (†)	‡ (†)	‡ (†)	‡ (†)
$6,000 to $9,999........	118,440 (21,597)	79,370 (7,976)	‡ (†)	‡ (†)	1,530 (119)	12,130 (628)	13,140 (683)	‡ (†)	‡ (†)	12,350 (640)
$10,000 to $14,999......	148,280 (33,642)	59,130 (11,788)	‡ (†)	‡ (†)	770 (106)	14,950 (418)	15,960 (908)	‡ (†)	‡ (†)	15,230 (426)
$15,000 or more........	585,680 (66,696)	115,850 (20,781)	74,630 (16,406)	395,200 (61,972)	2,640 (165)	29,160 (1,092)	25,490 (1,219)	32,120 (3,206)	29,670 (1,368)	29,700 (1,112)

†Not applicable.
!Interpret data with caution. The coefficient of variation (CV) for this estimate is between 30 and 50 percent.
‡Reporting standards not met. Either there are too few cases for a reliable estimate or the coefficient of variation (CV) is 50 percent or greater.
[1]Only includes kindergarten students who attend schools that offer first or higher grade.
[2]Each school reports the highest annual tuition charged for a full-time student; this amount does not take into account discounts that individual students may receive. This amount is weighted by the number of students enrolled in each school and averaged.

NOTE: Excludes schools not offering first or higher grade. Elementary schools have grade 6 or lower and no grade higher than 8. Secondary schools have no grade lower than 7. Combined schools include those that have grades lower than 7 and higher than 8, as well as those that do not classify students by grade level. Excludes prekindergarten students. Includes a small percentage of schools reporting tuition of 0; these private schools are often under contract to public school districts to provide special education services. Detail may not sum to totals because of rounding and cell suppression. Some data have been revised from previously published figures.
SOURCE: U.S. Department of Education, National Center for Education Statistics, Schools and Staffing Survey (SASS), "Private School Data File," 1999–2000, 2003–04, 2007–08, and 2011–12. (This table was prepared in June 2013.)

Private elementary and secondary school full-time-equivalent (FTE) staff and student to FTE staff ratios, by orientation of school, school level, and type of staff: 2007–08 and 2011–12

[Standard errors appear in parentheses]

Type of staff	Total, 2007–08	2011–12							
		Total				Catholic			
		Total	Elementary[1]	Secondary[2]	Combined[3]	Total	Elementary[1]	Secondary[2]	Combined[3]
1	2	3	4	5	6	7	8	9	10
Number of schools	28,220 (328)	26,230 (541)	15,000 (434)	2,820 (153)	8,400 (220)	6,760 (39)	5,300 (24)	1,040 (37)	410 (26)
Enrollment (in thousands)	5,165 (104)	4,480 (106)	2,134 (60)	732 (54)	1,614 (99)	1,892 (60)	1,244 (37)	512 (44M)	136 (19)
Number of FTE staff									
Total FTE staff	786,250 (16,261)	733,560 (17,373)	296,720 (8,627)	118,740 (8,321)	318,100 (17,125)	224,790 (7,201)	138,980 (3,830)	62,650 (5,069)	23,160 (2,739)
Principals	30,550 (463)	26,290 (497)	12,670 (319)	3,040 (159)	10,580 (410)	7,070 (115)	5,240 (83)	1,250 (50)	580 (66)
Assistant principals	13,120 (487)	11,280 (418)	4,160 (274)	2,510 (253)	4,610 (326)	3,270 (208)	1,470 (147)	1,460 (138)	350 (68)
Other managers	26,110 (952)	25,950 (872)	9,710 (511)	5,160 (479)	11,070 (707)	6,690 (410)	3,010 (252)	2,710 (312)	970 (142)
Instruction coordinators	7,850 (538)	7,630 (733)	2,310 (296)	1,440 ! (443)	3,880 (572)	1,280 (176)	550 (124)	500 (107)	230 (54)
Teachers	436,910 (8,665)	413,140 (9,516)	174,930 (4,690)	64,390 (4,936)	173,810 (10,001)	130,210 (3,981)	82,300 (2,281)	36,000 (2,853)	11,900 (1,567)
Teacher aides	53,740 (2,591)	52,440 (3,563)	25,210 (1,664)	2,370 (384)	24,860 (2,940)	14,260 (1,102)	11,350 (720)	450 ! (136)	2,460 ! (763)
Other aides	11,350 (1,251)	11,060 (2,290)	3,480 (374)	1,250 ! (400)	6,330 ! (2,122)	2,040 (281)	1,800 (260)	70 ! (28)	‡ (†)
Guidance counselors	11,780 (506)	11,040 (501)	2,140 (188)	3,590 (288)	5,310 (390)	4,220 (259)	1,390 (146)	2,320 (209)	500 (86)
Librarians/media specialists	12,190 (351)	11,190 (393)	5,230 (228)	1,610 (134)	4,350 (319)	4,300 (164)	3,080 (147)	900 (78)	320 (51)
Library/media center aides	4,150 (261)	2,650 (443)	1,320 (246)	‡ (†)	900 (152)	1,210 (215)	910 (220)	200 (46)	100 ! (30)
Nurses	8,340 (399)	7,600 (372)	3,010 (203)	1,680 (246)	2,900 (279)	2,890 (180)	2,070 (158)	600 (122)	230 (51)
Student support staff	24,920 (1,236)	23,010 (1,629)	5,510 (482)	4,190 (617)	13,300 (1,516)	4,420 (468)	2,210 (230)	1,350 (254)	860 ! (298)
Secretaries/clerical staff	50,360 (1,441)	42,730 (1,382)	15,420 (586)	8,210 (753)	19,090 (1,203)	13,460 (584)	7,080 (208)	5,160 (471)	1,220 (186)
Food service personnel	28,080 (1,019)	25,040 (1,196)	9,620 (549)	5,220 (583)	10,210 (998)	10,470 (625)	6,530 (435)	3,000 (383)	940 (142)
Custodial and maintenance	45,660 (1,469)	38,300 (1,482)	14,450 (614)	7,230 (527)	16,630 (1,369)	12,820 (576)	7,410 ! (325)	4,210 (393)	1,210 ! (185)
Other employees[5]	21,140 (2,717)	24,230 (3,023)	7,550 (1,820)	6,420 (1,602)	10,260 (1,975)	6,180 (1,381)	2,570 ! (921)	2,480 (735)	1,120 ! (508)
Students per FTE staff member									
Total FTE staff	7 (0.1)	6 (0.1)	7 (0.1)	6 (0.3)	5 (0.2)	8 (0.1)	9 (0.1)	8 (0.2)	6 (0.6)
Principals	169 (2.9)	170 (3.4)	168 (4.1)	241 (16.1)	153 (6.4)	268 (7.7)	237 (7.2)	409 (28.9)	235 (23.1)
Assistant principals	394 (12.3)	397 (14.5)	512 (30.9)	292 (20.2)	350 (23.5)	579 (28.4)	847 (77.4)	352 (19.1)	394 (69.0)
Other managers	198 (6.0)	173 (6.0)	220 (11.2)	142 (11.0)	146 (9.3)	283 (14.1)	413 (33.4)	189 (15.0)	140 (21.5)
Instruction coordinators	658 (43.1)	587 (54.5)	925 (125.5)	507 (128.0)	416 (64.9)	1,480 (198.3)	2,253 (653.7)	1,022 (226.7)	605 ! (223.6)
Teachers	12 (0.1)	11 (0.2)	12 (0.2)	11 (0.5)	9 (0.2)	15 (0.2)	15 (0.3)	14 (0.3)	11 (0.5)
Teacher aides	96 (4.8)	85 (5.9)	85 (5.0)	308 (57.9)	65 (8.9)	133 (10.6)	110 (6.3)	‡ (†)	‡ (†)
Other aides	455 (52.2)	405 (78.2)	614 (64.7)	‡ (†)	255 ! (80.4)	929 (144.9)	692 (107.9)	‡ (†)	‡ (†)
Guidance counselors	439 (16.1)	406 (15.0)	998 (84.7)	204 (9.3)	304 (16.0)	448 (21.0)	894 (96.6)	220 (7.9)	270 (34.6)
Librarians/media specialists	424 (9.5)	400 (13.0)	408 (15.7)	455 (35.2)	371 (20.6)	440 (17.9)	404 (22.0)	571 (30.4)	421 (46.3)
Library/media center aides	1,243 (75.1)	1,692 (229.0)	1,615 (281.5)	1,696 ! (636.7)	1,803 (329.9)	1,570 (259.6)	1,374 (328.5)	2,512 (665.0)	1,416 ! (510.9)
Nurses	619 (26.1)	590 (31.8)	709 (41.8)	434 (83.1)	556 (55.8)	654 (45.4)	602 (39.8)	860 ! (269.8)	594 (152.5)
Student support staff[4]	207 (9.9)	195 (14.1)	387 (32.3)	174 (26.7)	121 (12.7)	428 (49.0)	562 (61.8)	380 (98.6)	‡ (†)
Secretaries/clerical staff	103 (2.1)	105 (2.6)	138 (4.2)	89 (4.9)	85 (3.5)	141 (4.6)	176 (5.9)	99 (5.2)	112 (13.1)
Food service personnel	184 (6.2)	179 (7.8)	222 (12.1)	140 (15.9)	158 (13.9)	181 (9.1)	191 (12.0)	171 (17.8)	144 (26.5)
Custodial and maintenance	113 (2.8)	117 (3.8)	148 (5.0)	101 (5.4)	97 (6.2)	148 (4.5)	168 (5.8)	122 ! (6.2)	113 (15.5)
Other employees[5]	244 (29.0)	185 (24.0)	283 (62.5)	114 (32.0)	157 (37.1)	306 (71.6)	‡ (†)	206 ! (66.7)	‡ (†)

See notes at end of table.

Private elementary and secondary school full-time-equivalent (FTE) staff and student to FTE staff ratios, by orientation of school, school level, and type of staff: 2007–08 and 2011–12—Continued

[Standard errors appear in parentheses]

2011–12

Type of staff	Other religious orientation				Nonsectarian			
	Total	Elementary[1]	Secondary[2]	Combined[3]	Total	Elementary[1]	Secondary[2]	Combined[3]
1	11	12	13	14	15	16	17	18
Number of FTE staff								
Number of schools	13,040 (550)	6,860 (433)	890 (146)	5,290 (226)	6,430 (68)	2,840 (48)	890 (19)	2,700 (65)
Enrollment (in thousands)	1,605 (84)	610 (38)	117 (31)	878 (78)	982 (67)	279 (22)	103 (19)	600 (62)
Total FTE staff	254,000 (11,431)	92,610 (6,078)	25,040 (6,246)	136,350 (10,252)	254,770 (14,961)	65,140 (3,983)	31,050 (4,110)	158,590 (13,610)
Principals	11,990 (419)	4,760 (291)	840 (141)	6,390 (350)	7,230 (249)	2,670 (106)	950 (63)	3,610 (215)
Assistant principals	4,000 (300)	1,320 (177)	540 ! (228)	2,140 (221)	4,020 (338)	1,380 (165)	510 (108)	2,130 (278)
Other managers	8,790 (592)	3,230 (280)	1,120 ! (377)	4,440 (375)	10,470 (734)	3,470 (322)	1,330 (238)	5,670 (620)
Instruction coordinators	2,790 (470)	790 (135)	‡ (†)	1,470 (236)	3,560 (529)	960 (200)	410 ! (125)	2,190 (487)
Teachers	154,650 (6,944)	56,490 (3,508)	13,990 (3,896)	84,170 (6,547)	128,280 (8,136)	36,140 (2,384)	14,400 (2,231)	77,740 (7,508)
Teacher aides	12,200 (1,070)	7,250 (987)	310 (132)	4,630 (522)	25,980 (3,077)	6,610 (809)	1,610 (354)	17,760 (2,705)
Other aides	2,990 (585)	780 (158)	320 ! (140)	1,900 (512)	6,020 ! (2,194)	900 (203)	870 ! (384)	4,260 ! (2,068)
Guidance counselors	3,080 (276)	370 (67)	600 ! (183)	2,120 (208)	3,740 (370)	380 (104)	670 (112)	2,690 (328)
Librarians/media specialists	3,630 (240)	1,290 (134)	390 (112)	1,960 (199)	3,260 (283)	870 (98)	320 (63)	2,070 (252)
Library/media center aides	730 ! (330)	240 (63)	‡ (†)	320 (88)	710 (146)	170 ! (60)	‡ (†)	470 (132)
Nurses	1,740 (182)	530 (71)	400 ! (121)	810 (115)	2,960 (310)	410 (74)	690 (190)	1,860 (258)
Student support staff	4,050 (436)	1,550 (245)	810 ! (405)	1,680 (335)	14,540 (1,529)	1,750 (342)	2,030 (448)	10,760 (1,372)
Secretaries/clerical staff	16,000 (966)	5,510 (457)	1,610 ! (593)	8,890 (730)	13,270 (1,017)	2,830 (293)	1,450 (333)	8,980 (900)
Food service personnel	8,290 (813)	2,300 (238)	1,050 (264)	4,940 (718)	6,280 (886)	790 (155)	1,170 ! (392)	4,320 (756)
Custodial and maintenance	13,150 (904)	4,250 (358)	1,410 ! (323)	7,480 (804)	12,330 (1,101)	2,790 (347)	1,600 (348)	7,930 (998)
Other employees[5]	5,910 (1,690)	‡ (†)	970 ! (450)	2,990 (762)	12,130 (2,194)	3,020 (831)	2,970 ! (1,293)	6,150 (1,810)
Students per FTE staff member								
Total FTE staff	6 (0.2)	7 (0.2)	5 (0.5)	6 (0.2)	4 (0.1)	4 (0.2)	3 (0.4)	4 (0.2)
Principals	134 (5.5)	128 (6.4)	140 (26.9)	137 (8.9)	136 (7.6)	105 (7.9)	108 (21.6)	166 (13.0)
Assistant principals	402 (30.3)	464 (58.8)	217 (49.8)	410 (44.2)	245 (18.1)	203 (23.1)	202 (42.8)	282 (30.8)
Other managers	183 (11.8)	189 (16.7)	104 (17.1)	198 (16.3)	94 (6.1)	80 (5.5)	78 (16.8)	106 (11.1)
Instruction coordinators	575 (88.4)	769 (136.5)	‡ (†)	598 (107.7)	276 (40.2)	291 (64.2)	250 ! (116.8)	274 (66.3)
Teachers	10 (0.3)	11 (0.3)	8 (1.1)	10 (0.4)	8 (0.2)	8 (0.3)	7 (0.7)	8 (0.3)
Teacher aides	132 (12.6)	84 (9.7)	‡ (†)	190 (23.3)	38 (4.8)	42 (5.9)	64 (16.6)	34 (6.1)
Other aides	536 (110.3)	785 (171.8)	‡ (†)	462 ! (141.0)	163 ! (64.9)	310 (82.7)	‡ (†)	‡ (†)
Guidance counselors	520 (36.9)	1,653 (313.9)	195 (46.5)	415 (24.6)	263 (20.3)	743 (219.1)	154 (22.6)	223 (20.8)
Librarians/media specialists	442 (26.3)	475 (37.3)	301 ! (99.7)	448 (39.1)	301 (15.9)	322 (29.6)	319 (44.4)	290 (20.1)
Library/media center aides	2,196 (593.2)	2,512 (626.7)	‡ (†)	2,711 ! (866.0)	1,381 (257.5)	‡ (†)	‡ (†)	1,262 (352.2)
Nurses	922 (107.2)	1,154 (131.9)	143 ! (65.7)	1,080 (160.3)	331 (34.0)	679 (160.0)	149 ! (54.5)	322 (46.9)
Student support staff	396 (43.6)	394 (51.9)	73 (11.9)	521 (105.2)	68 (7.4)	160 (33.7)	51 (14.7)	56 (7.4)
Secretaries/clerical staff	100 (4.6)	111 (6.7)	‡ (†)	99 (6.0)	74 (3.5)	99 (7.3)	71 (11.0)	67 (4.6)
Food service personnel	194 (17.2)	265 (27.7)	‡ (†)	178 (21.3)	156 (19.4)	354 (82.1)	88 ! (32.9)	139 (24.1)
Custodial and maintenance	122 (6.7)	143 (10.7)	82 (16.4)	117 (9.1)	80 (4.6)	100 (9.0)	64 (11.3)	76 (6.7)
Other employees[5]	271 (64.9)	311 ! (131.9)	‡ (†)	294 ! (90.0)	81 (18.5)	93 ! (36.7)	‡ (†)	98 ! (45.5)

†Not applicable.

!Interpret data with caution. The coefficient of variation (CV) for this estimate is between 30 and 50 percent.

‡Reporting standards not met. The coefficient of variation (CV) for this estimate is 50 percent or greater.

[1]Includes schools beginning with grade 6 or below and with no grade higher than 8.

[2]Schools with no grade lower than 7.

[3]Schools with grades lower than 7 and higher than 8, as well as schools that do not classify students by grade level.

[4]Includes student support services professional staff, such as school psychologists, social workers, and speech therapists or pathologists.

[5]Includes other employees not identified by function.

NOTE: FTE staff consists of the total number of full-time staff, plus 48 percent of the part-time staff; this percentage was estimated based on the number of hours that part-time staff reported working. Data are based on a sample survey and may not be strictly comparable with data reported elsewhere. Excludes all prekindergarten students from calculations, but includes kindergarten students attending schools that offer first or higher grade. Includes only schools that offer first or higher grade. Detail may not sum to totals because of rounding. Some data have been revised from previously published figures.

SOURCE: U.S. Department of Education, National Center for Education Statistics, Schools and Staffing Survey (SASS), "Private School Data File," 2007–08 and 2011–12. (This table was prepared June 2013.)

Enrollment and instructional staff in Catholic elementary and secondary schools, by level: Selected years, 1919–20 through 2012–13

	Number of schools			Enrollment[1]				Instructional staff[2]		
School year	Total	Elementary[3]	Secondary	Total	Pre-kindergarten	Elementary	Secondary	Total	Elementary[3]	Secondary
1	2	3	4	5	6	7	8	9	10	11
1919–20	8,103	6,551	1,552	1,925,521	([4])	1,795,673	129,848	49,516	41,592	7,924
1929–30	10,046	7,923	2,123	2,464,467	([4])	2,222,598	241,869	72,552	58,245	14,307
1939–40	10,049	7,944	2,105	2,396,305	([4])	2,035,182	361,123	81,057	60,081	20,976
1949–50	10,778	8,589	2,189	3,066,387	([4])	2,560,815	505,572	94,295	66,525	27,770
Fall 1960	12,893	10,501	2,392	5,253,791	([4])	4,373,422	880,369	151,902	108,169	43,733
1969–70	11,352	9,366	1,986	4,367,000	([4])	3,359,000	1,008,000	195,400 [5]	133,200 [5]	62,200 [5]
1970–71	11,350	9,370	1,980	4,363,566	([4])	3,355,478	1,008,088	166,208	112,750	53,458
1974–75	10,127	8,437	1,690	3,504,000	([4])	2,602,000	902,000	150,179	100,011	50,168
1975–76	9,993	8,340	1,653	3,415,000	([4])	2,525,000	890,000	149,276	99,319	49,957
1979–80	9,640	8,100	1,540	3,139,000	([4])	2,293,000	846,000	147,294	97,724	49,570
1980–81	9,559	8,043	1,516	3,106,000	([4])	2,269,000	837,000	145,777	96,739	49,038
1981–82	9,494	7,996	1,498	3,094,000	([4])	2,266,000	828,000	146,172	96,847	49,325
1982–83	9,432	7,950	1,482	3,007,189	([4])	2,211,412	795,777	146,460	97,337	49,123
1983–84	9,401	7,937	1,464	2,969,000	([4])	2,179,000	790,000	146,913	98,591	48,322
1984–85	9,325	7,876	1,449	2,903,000	([4])	2,119,000	784,000	149,888	99,820	50,068
1985–86	9,220	7,790	1,430	2,821,000	([4])	2,061,000	760,000	146,594	96,741	49,853
1986–87	9,102	7,693	1,409	2,726,000	([4])	1,998,000	728,000	141,930	93,554	48,376
1987–88	8,992	7,601	1,391	2,690,668	67,637	1,942,148	680,883	139,887	93,199	46,688
1988–89	8,867	7,505	1,362	2,627,745	76,626	1,911,911	639,208	137,700	93,154	44,546
1989–90	8,719	7,395	1,324	2,588,893	90,023	1,892,913	605,957	136,900	94,197	42,703
1990–91	8,587	7,291	1,296	2,575,815	100,376	1,883,906	591,533	131,198	91,039	40,159
1991–92	8,508	7,239	1,269	2,550,863	107,939	1,856,302	586,622	153,334	109,084	44,250
1992–93	8,423	7,174	1,249	2,567,630	122,788	1,860,937	583,905	154,816	109,825	44,991
1993–94	8,345	7,114	1,231	2,576,845	132,236	1,859,947	584,662	157,201	112,199	45,002
1994–95	8,293	7,055	1,238	2,618,567	143,360	1,877,782	597,425	164,219	117,620	46,599
1995–96	8,250	7,022	1,228	2,635,210	144,099	1,884,461	606,650	166,759	118,753	48,006
1996–97	8,231	7,005	1,226	2,645,462	148,264	1,885,037	612,161	153,276	107,548	45,728
1997–98	8,223	7,004	1,219	2,648,859	150,965	1,879,737	618,157	152,259	105,717	46,542
1998–99	8,217	6,990	1,227	2,648,844	152,356	1,876,211	620,277	153,081	105,943	47,138
1999–2000	8,144	6,923	1,221	2,653,038	152,622	1,877,236	623,180	157,134	109,404	47,730
2000–01	8,146	6,920	1,226	2,647,301	155,742	1,863,682	627,877	160,731	111,937	48,794
2001–02	8,114	6,886	1,228	2,616,330	159,869	1,827,319	629,142	155,658	108,485	47,173
2002–03	8,000	6,785	1,215	2,553,277	157,250	1,765,893	630,134	163,004	112,884	50,120
2003–04	7,955	6,727	1,228	2,484,252	150,422	1,708,501	625,329	162,337	112,303	50,034
2004–05	7,799	6,574	1,225	2,420,590	150,905	1,642,868	626,817	160,153	107,764	52,389
2005–06	7,589	6,386	1,203	2,325,220	146,327	1,568,687	610,206	152,502 [6]	103,481 [6]	49,021 [6]
2006–07	7,498	6,288	1,210	2,320,651	152,429	1,544,695	623,527	159,135	107,682	51,453
2007–08	7,378	6,165	1,213	2,270,913	152,980	1,494,979	622,954	160,075	107,217	52,858
2008–09	7,248	6,028	1,220	2,192,531	153,325	1,434,949	604,257	157,615	105,518	52,097
2009–10	7,094	5,889	1,205	2,119,341	150,262	1,375,982	593,097	154,316	103,460	50,856
2010–11	6,980	5,774	1,206	2,065,872	152,846	1,336,560	576,466	151,473	102,365	49,108
2011–12	6,841	5,636	1,205	2,031,455	154,282	1,303,028	574,145	151,395	100,365	51,030
2012–13	6,685	5,472	1,213	2,001,740	156,233	1,278,010	567,497	151,405	100,633	50,772

[1]Elementary enrollment is for kindergarten through grade 8, and secondary enrollment is for grades 9 through 12.
[2]From 1919–20 through fall 1960, includes part-time teachers. From 1969–70 through 1993–94, excludes part-time teachers. Beginning in 1994–95, reported in full-time equivalents (FTE). Prekindergarten teachers not counted separately but may be included with elementary teachers.
[3]Includes middle schools.
[4]Prekindergarten enrollment was not reported separately, but may be included in elementary enrollment.
[5]Includes estimates for the nonreporting schools.

[6]Excludes the Archdiocese of New Orleans.
NOTE: Data collected by the National Catholic Educational Association and data collected by the National Center for Education Statistics are not directly comparable because survey procedures and definitions differ.
SOURCE: National Catholic Educational Association, *A Statistical Report on Catholic Elementary and Secondary Schools for the Years 1967–68 to 1969–70; A Report on Catholic Schools*, 1970–71 through 1973–74; *A Statistical Report on U.S. Catholic Schools*, 1974–75 through 1980–81; and *United States Catholic Elementary and Secondary Schools*, 1981–82 through 2012–13, retrieved May 9, 2013, from http://www.ncea.org/news/AnnualDataReport.asp. (This table was prepared May 2013.)

Private elementary and secondary schools, enrollment, teachers, and high school graduates, by state: Selected years, 2001 through 2011

[Standard errors appear in parentheses]

State	Schools, fall 2011		Enrollment in prekindergarten through grade 12												Teachers,[1] fall 2011		High school graduates, 2010–11	
			Fall 2001		Fall 2003		Fall 2005		Fall 2007		Fall 2009		Fall 2011					
1	2		3		4		5		6		7		8		9		10	
United States	30,860	(542)	6,319,650	(40,272)	6,099,220	(41,219)	6,073,240	(42,446)	5,910,210	(28,363)	5,488,490	(35,857)	5,268,090	(24,908)	420,880	(1,836)	305,840	(3,479)
Alabama....................	400	(1)	92,380	(3,926)	99,580	(12,130)	92,280	(5,892)	83,840	(103)	95,570	(11,745)	81,070	(49)	6,210	(1)	4,720	(†)
Alaska......................	50	(†)	7,420	(†)	7,370	(424)	7,500	(1,028)	4,990	(†)	7,510 !	(2,740)	5,170	(†)	420	(1)	220	(†)
Arizona....................	340	(5)	78,660	(18,218)	75,360	(16,426)	66,840	(†)	64,910	(†)	55,390	(†)	53,120	(229)	3,810	(16)	2,650	(†)
Arkansas.................	230 !	(73)	32,570	(†)	31,300	(†)	35,390	(5,858)	40,120	(11,961)	28,900	(1,371)	29,930	(1,245)	2,640	(337)	1,490	(†)
California.................	3,480	(2)	757,750	(8,415)	740,460	(8,703)	737,490	(15,529)	703,810	(6,129)	623,150	(4,185)	608,070	(69)	44,270	(12)	34,380	(1)
Colorado	410	(2)	64,700	(†)	62,080	(476)	70,770	(1,160)	64,740	(†)	63,720	(3,486)	61,140	(148)	4,880	(4)	2,890	(†)
Connecticut	410	(18)	82,320	(†)	102,960	(25,024)	76,220	(1,619)	85,150	(9,241)	72,540	(464)	66,320	(142)	7,080	(68)	5,960	(†)
Delaware.................	120	(†)	31,690	(1,023)	33,020	(2,649)	29,830	(†)	32,520	(2,701)	26,640	(†)	25,090	(†)	2,060	(†)	1,770	(†)
District of Columbia......	80	(†)	33,660 !	(14,373)	23,510	(6,121)	19,880	(†)	19,640	(†)	17,810	(†)	16,950	(†)	1,960	(†)	1,510	(†)
Florida.....................	1,880	(2)	365,890	(8,301)	398,720	(14,590)	396,790	(7,429)	391,660	(6,123)	343,990	(1,023)	340,960	(230)	26,430	(37)	20,060	(†)
Georgia	710	(†)	137,060	(4,550)	144,850	(6,527)	152,600	(10,394)	157,430	(9,185)	150,300	(6,251)	138,080	(†)	13,010	(†)	7,760	(†)
Hawaii	130	(†)	42,980	(220)	39,940	(†)	32,810	(†)	37,300	(290)	37,130	(†)	37,530	(†)	3,010	(†)	2,760	(†)
Idaho.......................	120	(4)	12,050	(†)	12,570	(†)	15,320	(2,518)	24,700 !	(11,608)	18,680	(4,814)	13,670	(193)	990	(17)	580	(4)
Illinois.....................	1,570	(53)	357,390	(19,293)	316,430	(1,698)	317,940	(4,263)	312,270	(6,638)	289,720	(9,237)	271,030	(1,289)	19,150	(221)	14,500	(49)
Indiana....................	970	(198)	129,240	(326)	124,500	(455)	139,370	(17,870)	119,910	(2,284)	120,770	(5,919)	129,120	(12,177)	8,900	(995)	5,620	(374)
Iowa........................	300	(51)	51,540	(†)	53,850	(4,634)	60,960	(8,311)	47,820	(†)	45,160	(†)	63,840	(14,665)	4,700	(1,078)	‡	(†)
Kansas....................	400 !	(193)	51,540	(8,341)	47,710	(2,151)	47,130	(1,654)	47,780	(2,414)	44,680	(1,668)	43,100	(1,640)	3,530	(446)	2,260	(†)
Kentucky	330	(1)	85,230	(3,227)	82,100	(1,525)	78,880	(1,228)	76,140	(2,074)	70,590	(2,132)	69,410	(12)	5,240	(1)	4,130	(†)
Louisiana.................	390	(2)	159,910	(11,381)	155,780	(3,515)	138,270	(525)	137,460	(†)	147,040	(9,890)	125,720	(108)	8,830	(5)	7,510	(†)
Maine......................	160	(†)	20,820	(174)	24,740	(3,629)	20,680	(337)	21,260	(143)	18,310	(†)	18,350	(†)	2,000	(†)	2,600	(†)
Maryland.................	740	(8)	175,740	(†)	172,360	(†)	170,350	(4,201)	165,760	(1,160)	145,690	(160)	137,450	(564)	12,430	(42)	8,830	(†)
Massachusetts	800	(44)	177,490	(9,836)	164,390	(6,636)	157,770	(3,273)	151,640	(2,516)	137,110	(1,169)	130,940	(1,596)	14,060	(323)	10,130	(†)
Michigan..................	790	(7)	198,380	(†)	180,080	(†)	166,950	(407)	159,100	(2,047)	153,230	(5,828)	135,580	(544)	9,290	(52)	7,290	(†)
Minnesota................	500	(†)	112,310	(2,993)	106,010	(3,011)	104,730	(3,467)	101,740	(3,903)	89,530	(†)	87,620	(†)	6,420	(†)	4,710	(†)
Mississippi..............	220	(†)	67,380	(10,106)	57,110	(2,981)	57,930	(4,104)	55,270	(†)	54,650	(2,458)	52,060	(†)	4,120	(†)	3,250	(†)
Missouri...................	1,270 !	(468)	138,140	(4,321)	141,530	(9,966)	137,810	(10,580)	125,610	(3,685)	117,970	(2,065)	130,130	(8,715)	10,510	(951)	7,530	(89)
Montana...................	110	(†)	12,930	(1,895)	12,510	(2,091)	‡	(†)	15,030 !	(5,465)	10,390	(1,221)	10,550	(†)	980	(†)	430	(†)
Nebraska.................	220	(†)	45,590	(618)	41,650	(†)	42,420	(†)	40,320	(†)	39,040	(†)	40,750	(†)	2,840	(†)	2,300	(†)
Nevada....................	160	(†)	20,370	(385)	23,930	(†)	29,120	(†)	29,820	(2,009)	25,060	(†)	26,130	(†)	1,590	(†)	900	(†)
New Hampshire	280	(†)	38,650	(†)	33,780	(†)	33,220	(†)	30,920	(†)	26,470	(†)	27,350	(†)	2,670	(†)	2,520	(†)
New Jersey	1,290	(18)	282,450	(4,182)	269,530	(7,577)	256,160	(8,439)	253,250	(5,016)	232,020	(16,536)	210,220	(1,211)	16,850	(208)	12,980	(71)
New Mexico..............	170	(1)	26,510	(†)	29,310	(3,928)	25,030	(141)	27,290	(1,388)	23,730	(507)	22,680	(10)	1,940	(2)	1,280	(†)
New York..................	1,930	(31)	559,670	(1,669)	515,620	(4,071)	510,750	(3,596)	518,850	(7,196)	486,310	(5,211)	487,810	(19,574)	41,450	(821)	30,440	(1,462)
North Carolina............	640	(†)	116,500	(4,112)	126,230	(11,439)	117,280	(11,681)	121,660	(2,226)	110,740	(1,851)	119,070	(†)	10,680	(†)	6,310	(†)
North Dakota.............	50	(†)	7,180	(†)	6,840	(†)	7,290	(†)	7,430	(†)	7,750	(†)	7,770	(†)	590	(†)	410	(†)
Ohio........................	970	(59)	290,370	(7,180)	270,660	(7,094)	254,530	(9,821)	239,520	(2,741)	246,250	(24,214)	213,990	(3,419)	15,270	(396)	12,860	(124)
Oklahoma.................	180	(10)	46,570	(8,723)	34,300	(2,013)	35,350	(1,194)	40,320	(5,032)	34,000	(716)	35,750	(847)	3,000	(72)	1,760	(17)
Oregon....................	430	(†)	71,500	(15,519)	54,320	(†)	69,620	(14,139)	66,260	(5,188)	56,820	(3,502)	53,200	(†)	3,820	(†)	2,970	(†)
Pennsylvania............	2,320	(60)	374,490	(†)	357,580	(3,364)	332,740	(3,918)	324,020	(6,253)	301,640	(5,036)	276,300	(3,668)	21,960	(468)	16,370	(90)
Rhode Island............	140	(†)	30,970	(†)	31,960	(†)	30,600	(†)	28,260	(1,096)	24,940	(†)	25,420	(†)	2,360	(†)	2,020	(†)
South Carolina	380	(†)	70,950	(†)	73,800	(†)	70,240	(1,797)	71,430	(1,043)	62,320	(311)	60,890	(†)	5,000	(†)	2,960	(†)
South Dakota	70	(†)	11,740	(†)	11,980	(†)	12,700	(†)	12,280	(†)	11,470	(†)	12,490	(†)	970	(†)	650	(†)
Tennessee...............	510	(1)	98,790	(†)	93,390	(†)	105,240	(2,531)	117,540	(12,851)	98,310	(4,176)	92,430	(34)	8,150	(2)	5,860	(†)
Texas......................	1,500	(18)	314,210	(12,244)	271,380	(2,758)	304,170	(20,453)	296,540	(4,132)	313,360	(11,968)	285,320	(2,046)	23,360	(101)	12,840	(489)
Utah	160	(2)	20,040	(†)	19,990	(†)	21,220	(†)	20,860	(†)	21,990	(1,558)	18,660	(55)	1,620	(6)	1,210	(1)
Vermont...................	110	(†)	14,090	(†)	12,730	(†)	11,530	(†)	12,600	(232)	10,350	(†)	9,030	(†)	1,200	(†)	1,000	(†)
Virginia....................	750	(2)	129,470	(†)	131,160	(6,936)	155,220	(14,290)	143,140	(7,988)	128,140	(2,581)	123,780	(82)	10,980	(11)	6,400	(1)
Washington	630	(5)	91,150	(2,028)	101,130	(7,935)	119,640	(13,187)	104,070	(3,054)	94,340	(625)	93,630	(234)	7,130	(21)	4,210	(30)
West Virginia............	120	(1)	16,560	(†)	15,300	(†)	16,120	(†)	14,980	(†)	13,860	(†)	13,430	(1)	1,130	(1)	660	(1)
Wisconsin................	840	(†)	162,220	(9,080)	159,240	(11,743)	142,280	(137)	138,290	(1,597)	130,510	(†)	127,250	(†)	9,150	(†)	5,420	(†)
Wyoming..................	40	(†)	2,430	(†)	2,600	(†)	2,310	(†)	2,930	(†)	2,910	(†)	2,740	(†)	260	(†)	30	(†)

†Not applicable.
!Interpret data with caution. The coefficient of variation (CVV) for this estimate is between 30 and 50 percent.
‡Reporting standards not met. The coefficient of variation (CV) for this estimate is 50 percent or greater.
[1]Reported in full-time equivalents (FTE). Excludes teachers who teach only prekindergarten students.

NOTE: Includes special education, vocational/technical education, and alternative schools. Tabulation includes schools that offer kindergarten or higher grade. Includes enrollment of students in prekindergarten through grade 12 in schools that offer kindergarten or higher grade. Detail may not sum to totals because of rounding.
SOURCE: U.S. Department of Education, National Center for Education Statistics, Private School Universe Survey (PSS), 2001–02 through 2011–12. (This table was prepared May 2013.)

Revenues for public elementary and secondary schools, by source of funds: Selected years, 1919–20 through 2010–11

	Revenues (in thousands)							Revenues per pupil						
				Local (including intermediate sources below the state level)							Local (including intermediate sources below the state level)			
School year	Total	Federal	State	Total	Property taxes	Other public revenue	Private[1]	Total	Federal	State	Total	Property taxes	Other public revenue	Private[1]
1	2	3	4	5	6	7	8	9	10	11	12	13	14	15
					Current dollars									
1919–20	$970,121	$2,475	$160,085	$807,561	—	—	—	$45	#	$7	$37	—	—	—
1929–30	2,088,557	7,334	353,670	1,727,553	—	—	—	81	#	14	67	—	—	—
1939–40	2,260,527	39,810	684,354	1,536,363	—	—	—	89	$2	27	60	—	—	—
1949–50	5,437,044	155,848	2,165,689	3,115,507	—	—	—	217	6	86	124	—	—	—
1959–60	14,746,618	651,639	5,768,047	8,326,932	—	—	—	419	19	164	237	—	—	—
1969–70	40,266,922	3,219,557	16,062,776	20,984,589	—	—	—	884	71	353	461	—	—	—
1979–80	96,881,164	9,503,537	45,348,814	42,028,813	—	—	—	2,326	228	1,089	1,009	—	—	—
1989–90	208,547,573	12,700,784	98,238,633	97,608,157	$74,867,627	$17,084,494	$5,656,036	5,144	313	2,423	2,408	$1,847	$421	$140
1990–91	223,340,537	13,776,066	105,324,533	104,239,939	80,373,547	17,951,451	5,914,941	5,419	334	2,555	2,529	1,950	436	144
1991–92	234,581,384	15,493,330	108,783,449	110,304,605	85,874,700	18,213,748	6,216,157	5,579	368	2,587	2,623	2,042	433	148
1992–93	247,626,168	17,261,252	113,403,436	116,961,481	87,143,955	23,116,567	6,700,958	5,783	403	2,648	2,731	2,035	540	156
1993–94	260,159,468	18,341,483	117,474,209	124,343,776	97,762,990	19,661,128	6,919,657	5,986	422	2,703	2,861	2,249	452	159
1994–95	273,149,449	18,582,157	127,729,576	126,837,717	97,978,129	21,560,162	7,299,425	6,192	421	2,896	2,875	2,221	489	165
1995–96	287,702,844	19,104,019	136,670,754	131,928,071	101,785,858	22,522,345	7,619,869	6,416	426	3,048	2,942	2,270	502	170
1996–97	305,065,192	20,081,287	146,435,584	138,548,321	106,545,881	24,288,693	7,713,747	6,688	440	3,211	3,038	2,336	533	169
1997–98	325,925,708	22,201,965	157,645,372	146,078,370	111,184,150	26,676,244	8,217,977	7,066	481	3,418	3,167	2,410	578	178
1998–99	347,377,993	24,521,817	169,298,232	153,557,944	119,483,487	25,348,879	8,725,578	7,464	527	3,638	3,300	2,567	545	187
1999–2000	372,943,802	27,097,866	184,613,352	161,232,584	124,735,516	27,628,923	8,868,145	7,959	578	3,940	3,441	2,662	590	189
2000–01	401,356,120	29,100,183	199,583,097	172,672,840	132,575,925	30,889,273	9,207,643	8,503	616	4,228	3,658	2,809	654	195
2001–02	419,501,976	33,144,633	206,541,793	179,815,551	141,095,685	28,924,825	9,795,041	8,800	695	4,333	3,772	2,960	607	205
2002–03	440,111,653	37,515,909	214,277,407	188,318,337	148,511,786	29,579,240	10,227,310	9,134	779	4,447	3,908	3,082	614	212
2003–04	462,026,099	41,923,435	217,384,191	202,718,474	160,602,055	31,651,489	10,464,930	9,518	864	4,478	4,176	3,309	652	216
2004–05	487,753,525	44,809,532	228,553,579	214,390,414	167,909,883	35,433,486	11,047,044	9,996	918	4,684	4,394	3,441	726	226
2005–06	520,621,788	47,553,778	242,151,076	230,916,934	178,279,408	41,111,066	11,526,460	10,600	968	4,930	4,702	3,630	837	235
2006–07	555,710,762	47,150,608	263,608,741	244,951,413	188,287,298	44,806,422	11,857,694	11,281	957	5,351	4,972	3,822	910	241
2007–08	584,683,686	47,788,467	282,622,523	254,272,697	196,521,569	45,314,965	12,436,163	11,879	971	5,742	5,166	3,993	921	253
2008–09	592,422,033	56,670,261	276,525,603	259,226,169	205,821,844	41,195,313	12,209,012	12,032	1,151	5,616	5,265	4,180	837	248
2009–10[2]	596,390,664	75,997,858	258,863,973	261,528,833	210,837,095	38,771,186	11,920,551	12,089	1,540	5,247	5,301	4,274	786	242
2010–11	604,293,209	75,541,475	266,786,402	261,965,331	211,651,391	38,478,546	11,835,394	12,217	1,527	5,394	5,296	4,279	778	239
					Constant 2012–13 dollars[3]									
1919–20	$11,776,652	$30,045	$1,943,330	$9,803,277	—	—	—	$546	$1	$90	$454	—	—	—
1929–30	28,228,769	99,126	4,780,175	23,349,468	—	—	—	1,099	4	186	909	—	—	—
1939–40	37,422,357	659,043	11,329,278	25,434,036	—	—	—	1,471	26	445	1,000	—	—	—
1949–50	53,112,824	1,522,432	21,155,955	30,434,437	—	—	—	2,115	61	842	1,212	—	—	—
1959–60	116,109,981	5,130,789	45,415,690	65,563,502	—	—	—	3,300	146	1,291	1,864	—	—	—
1969–70	246,613,711	19,718,093	98,376,052	128,519,567	—	—	—	5,414	433	2,160	2,821	—	—	—
1979–80	288,712,932	28,321,233	135,142,772	125,248,927	—	—	—	6,932	680	3,245	3,007	—	—	—
1989–90	379,979,509	23,141,183	178,993,535	177,844,791	$136,410,910	$31,128,426	$10,305,455	9,372	571	4,415	4,387	$3,365	$768	$254
1990–91	385,838,094	23,799,222	181,956,296	180,082,576	138,851,533	31,012,524	10,218,519	9,361	577	4,415	4,369	3,369	752	248
1991–92	392,675,333	25,934,916	182,097,046	184,643,371	143,749,158	30,488,734	10,405,478	9,339	617	4,331	4,391	3,419	725	247
1992–93	401,956,213	28,019,120	184,080,770	189,856,323	141,455,382	37,523,691	10,877,250	9,386	654	4,299	4,433	3,303	876	254
1993–94	411,637,588	29,020,831	185,873,689	196,743,068	154,685,592	31,108,841	10,948,635	9,471	668	4,276	4,526	3,559	716	252
1994–95	420,148,339	28,582,384	196,468,890	195,097,065	150,706,319	33,163,041	11,227,705	9,525	648	4,454	4,423	3,416	752	255
1995–96	430,813,128	28,606,816	204,654,059	197,552,253	152,416,581	33,725,498	11,410,174	9,608	638	4,564	4,406	3,399	752	254
1996–97	444,140,271	29,236,073	213,193,579	201,710,620	155,118,702	35,361,578	11,230,340	9,738	641	4,674	4,422	3,401	775	246
1997–98	466,196,562	31,757,176	225,492,279	208,947,107	159,035,225	38,157,079	11,754,803	10,107	688	4,889	4,530	3,448	827	255
1998–99	488,426,016	34,478,562	238,039,434	215,908,021	167,998,102	35,641,441	12,268,478	10,495	741	5,115	4,639	3,610	766	264

See notes at end of table.

Revenues for public elementary and secondary schools, by source of funds: Selected years, 1919–20 through 2010–11—Continued

| | Revenues (in thousands) | | | | | | | Revenues per pupil | | | | | | |
| | | | | Local (including intermediate sources below the state level) | | | | | | | Local (including intermediate sources below the state level) | | | |
School year	Total	Federal	State	Total	Property taxes	Other public revenue	Private[1]	Total	Federal	State	Total	Property taxes	Other public revenue	Private[1]
1	2	3	4	5	6	7	8	9	10	11	12	13	14	15
1999–2000	509,659,608	37,031,552	252,289,938	220,338,118	170,461,753	37,757,286	12,119,079	10,877	790	5,384	4,702	3,638	806	259
2000–01	530,318,581	38,450,560	263,712,498	228,155,523	175,174,796	40,814,515	12,166,213	11,235	815	5,587	4,833	3,711	865	258
2001–02	544,651,955	43,032,668	268,159,383	233,459,904	183,188,746	37,553,965	12,717,194	11,425	903	5,625	4,897	3,843	788	267
2002–03	559,122,670	47,660,622	272,220,367	239,241,680	188,671,002	37,577,791	12,992,887	11,604	989	5,650	4,965	3,916	780	270
2003–04	574,396,869	52,119,761	270,254,859	252,022,249	199,662,568	39,349,544	13,010,137	11,833	1,074	5,568	5,192	4,113	811	268
2004–05	588,666,994	54,080,373	275,840,033	258,746,589	202,649,497	42,764,476	13,332,616	12,064	1,108	5,653	5,303	4,153	876	273
2005–06	605,285,096	55,286,954	281,529,588	268,468,554	207,271,134	47,796,531	13,400,889	12,324	1,126	5,732	5,466	4,220	973	273
2006–07	629,793,552	53,436,340	298,750,891	277,606,322	213,388,212	50,779,645	13,438,464	12,784	1,085	6,064	5,635	4,332	1,031	273
2007–08	638,953,529	52,224,151	308,855,305	277,874,073	214,762,534	49,521,061	13,590,477	12,981	1,061	6,275	5,645	4,363	1,006	276
2008–09	638,494,825	61,077,520	298,031,060	279,386,245	221,828,655	44,399,081	13,158,509	12,968	1,241	6,053	5,674	4,505	902	267
2009–10[2]	636,612,328	81,123,291	276,322,227	279,166,810	225,056,330	41,385,985	12,724,494	12,904	1,644	5,601	5,659	4,562	839	258
2010–11	632,350,353	79,048,842	279,173,211	274,128,299	221,478,298	40,265,093	12,384,908	12,784	1,598	5,644	5,542	4,478	814	250
				Percentage distribution										
1919–20	100.0	0.3	16.5	83.2	—	—	—	100.0	0.3	16.5	83.2	—	—	—
1929–30	100.0	0.4	16.9	82.7	—	—	—	100.0	0.4	16.9	82.7	—	—	—
1939–40	100.0	1.8	30.3	68.0	—	—	—	100.0	1.8	30.3	68.0	—	—	—
1949–50	100.0	2.9	39.8	57.3	—	—	—	100.0	2.9	39.8	57.3	—	—	—
1959–60	100.0	4.4	39.1	56.5	—	—	—	100.0	4.4	39.1	56.5	—	—	—
1969–70	100.0	8.0	39.9	52.1	—	—	—	100.0	8.0	39.9	52.1	—	—	—
1979–80	100.0	9.8	46.8	43.4	—	—	—	100.0	9.8	46.8	43.4	—	—	—
1989–90	100.0	6.1	47.1	46.8	35.9	8.2	2.7	100.0	6.1	47.1	46.8	35.9	8.2	2.7
1990–91	100.0	6.2	47.2	46.7	36.0	8.0	2.6	100.0	6.2	47.2	46.7	36.0	8.0	2.6
1991–92	100.0	6.6	46.4	47.0	36.6	7.8	2.6	100.0	6.6	46.4	47.0	36.6	7.8	2.6
1992–93	100.0	7.0	45.8	47.2	35.2	9.3	2.7	100.0	7.0	45.8	47.2	35.2	9.3	2.7
1993–94	100.0	7.1	45.2	47.8	37.6	7.6	2.7	100.0	7.1	45.2	47.8	37.6	7.6	2.7
1994–95	100.0	6.8	46.8	46.4	35.9	7.9	2.7	100.0	6.8	46.8	46.4	35.9	7.9	2.7
1995–96	100.0	6.6	47.5	45.9	35.4	7.8	2.6	100.0	6.6	47.5	45.9	35.4	7.8	2.6
1996–97	100.0	6.6	48.0	45.4	34.9	8.0	2.5	100.0	6.6	48.0	45.4	34.9	8.0	2.5
1997–98	100.0	6.8	48.4	44.8	34.1	8.2	2.5	100.0	6.8	48.4	44.8	34.1	8.2	2.5
1998–99	100.0	7.1	48.7	44.2	34.4	7.3	2.5	100.0	7.1	48.7	44.2	34.4	7.3	2.5
1999–2000	100.0	7.3	49.5	43.2	33.4	7.4	2.4	100.0	7.3	49.5	43.2	33.4	7.4	2.4
2000–01	100.0	7.3	49.7	43.0	33.0	7.7	2.3	100.0	7.3	49.7	43.0	33.0	7.7	2.3
2001–02	100.0	7.9	49.2	42.9	33.6	6.9	2.3	100.0	7.9	49.2	42.9	33.6	6.9	2.3
2002–03	100.0	8.5	48.7	42.8	33.7	6.7	2.3	100.0	8.5	48.7	42.8	33.7	6.7	2.3
2003–04	100.0	9.1	47.1	43.9	34.8	6.9	2.3	100.0	9.1	47.1	43.9	34.8	6.9	2.3
2004–05	100.0	9.2	46.9	44.0	34.4	7.3	2.3	100.0	9.2	46.9	44.0	34.4	7.3	2.3
2005–06	100.0	9.1	46.5	44.4	34.2	7.9	2.2	100.0	9.1	46.5	44.4	34.2	7.9	2.2
2006–07	100.0	8.5	47.4	44.1	33.9	8.1	2.1	100.0	8.5	47.4	44.1	33.9	8.1	2.1
2007–08	100.0	8.2	48.3	43.5	33.6	7.8	2.1	100.0	8.2	48.3	43.5	33.6	7.8	2.1
2008–09	100.0	9.6	46.7	43.8	34.7	7.0	2.1	100.0	9.6	46.7	43.8	34.7	7.0	2.1
2009–10[2]	100.0	12.7	43.4	43.9	35.4	6.5	2.0	100.0	12.7	43.4	43.9	35.4	6.5	2.0
2010–11	100.0	12.5	44.1	43.4	35.0	6.4	2.0	100.0	12.5	44.1	43.4	35.0	6.4	2.0

—Not available.
#Rounds to zero.
[1]Includes revenues from gifts, and tuition and fees from patrons.
[2]Data have been revised from previously published figures.
[3]Constant dollars based on the Consumer Price Index, prepared by the Bureau of Labor Statistics, U.S. Department of Labor, adjusted to a school-year basis.

NOTE: Beginning in 1989–90, revenues for state education agencies were excluded and new survey collection procedures were initiated; data may not be entirely comparable with figures for earlier years. Detail may not sum to totals because of rounding.
SOURCE: U.S. Department of Education, National Center for Education Statistics, Biennial Survey of Education in the United States, 1919–20 through 1949–50; Statistics of State School Systems, 1959–60 and 1969–70; Revenues and Expenditures for Public Elementary and Secondary Education, 1979–80; and Common Core of Data (CCD), "National Public Education Financial Survey," 1989–90 through 2010–11. (This table was prepared July 2013.)

Revenues for public elementary and secondary schools, by source of funds and state or jurisdiction: 2010–11

State or jurisdiction	Total (in thousands)	Federal — Amount (in thousands)	Federal — Per pupil	Federal — Percent of total	State — Amount (in thousands)	State — Percent of total	Local — Amount (in thousands)[1]	Local — Percent of total	Property taxes — Amount (in thousands)	Property taxes — Percent of total	Private[2] — Amount (in thousands)	Private[2] — Percent of total
1	2	3	4	5	6	7	8	9	10	11	12	13
United States	**$604,293,209**	**$75,541,475**	**$1,527**	**12.5**	**$266,786,402**	**44.1**	**$261,965,331**	**43.4**	**$211,651,391**	**35.0**	**$11,835,394**	**2.0**
Alabama	7,386,471	1,250,581	1,655	16.9	3,827,907	51.8	2,307,983	31.2	1,070,276	14.5	305,976	4.1
Alaska	2,470,274	422,422	3,213	17.2	1,524,083	61.7	361,768	21.2	297,708	12.1	251,508	0.9
Arizona	9,764,472	1,693,809	1,530	16.8	3,954,069	40.2	4,250,211	43.0	3,094,295	31.7	233,940	2.4
Arkansas	5,292,728	529,728	1,730	10.0	3,703,033	51.3	1,711,386	32.5	1,449,958	27.5	144,113	2.7
California	67,864,062	9,248,710	1,470	13.6	38,411,425	56.6	20,203,927	29.8	16,065,777	23.7	445,791	0.7
Colorado	8,820,783	991,623	1,176	11.2	3,540,865	40.1	4,288,294	48.6	3,470,848	39.3	328,898	3.7
Connecticut	9,999,988	827,618	1,476	8.3	3,434,642	34.3	5,739,726	57.5	5,568,317	55.7	112,250	1.1
Delaware	1,748,688	207,823	1,606	11.9	1,024,557	58.6	516,279	29.5	455,581	24.9	16,655	1.0
District of Columbia	1,895,826	297,198	1,814	18.2	†	†	1,698,628	88.2	553,482	28.7	10,651	0.6
Florida	26,358,355	4,796,329	1,814	18.2	9,069,113	34.4	12,492,913	47.4	10,549,648	40.0	945,427	3.6
Georgia	18,047,879	2,312,872	1,379	12.8	7,526,257	41.7	8,208,751	45.5	5,806,444	32.2	478,313	2.7
Hawaii	2,470,432	347,042	1,934	14.0	2,059,751	83.4	495,280	2.6	412,701	0	33,597	1.3
Idaho	2,183,491	305,826	1,109	14.0	1,382,092	63.3	495,614	22.7	412,701	18.9	33,597	1.5
Illinois	26,805,633	2,990,110	1,709	11.1	9,380,092	35.0	16,691,051	57.8	14,482,300	50.1	494,189	1.7
Indiana	11,761,793	1,046,267	1,399	8.9	6,534,419	55.6	4,181,108	35.5	2,810,010	23.9	332,819	2.8
Iowa	5,906,171	613,528	1,238	10.4	2,550,546	43.2	2,742,097	46.4	1,913,657	32.4	139,587	2.4
Kansas	5,670,547	662,971	1,377	11.7	2,979,230	52.5	2,028,345	35.8	1,537,008	27.1	139,159	2.4
Kentucky	6,993,349	1,149,658	1,708	16.4	3,622,461	51.8	2,221,230	31.8	1,584,905	22.7	111,343	1.6
Louisiana	8,246,484	1,153,440	2,201	14.0	3,655,648	44.3	3,437,396	41.6	1,389,367	16.8	96,866	0.8
Maine	2,597,927	289,249	1,530	11.1	1,062,058	40.5	1,256,620	48.4	1,191,068	45.8	39,584	1.5
Maryland	13,437,322	1,256,210	1,474	9.3	5,508,344	41.0	6,672,768	49.7	3,173,859	23.6	280,449	2.1
Massachusetts	15,367,042	1,381,908	1,331	9.0	5,790,874	37.8	8,022,705	53.5	7,801,657	50.8	203,610	1.3
Michigan	19,466,487	2,705,858	1,705	13.9	10,717,834	55.1	6,042,795	30.6	5,130,243	26.6	220,290	1.5
Minnesota	10,938,581	1,099,581	1,080	10.0	6,307,541	57.7	3,655,648	33.4	2,480,043	22.8	321,762	2.9
Mississippi	4,483,191	1,006,453	1,530	22.4	2,071,471	46.2	1,256,620	31.3	1,132,742	25.3	113,009	2.5
Missouri	10,169,473	1,381,908	1,504	13.6	3,008,369	29.6	5,779,196	56.8	4,563,463	44.9	347,661	3.4
Montana	1,654,729	291,964	2,110	18.1	723,125	43.7	632,641	38.2	402,720	24.3	58,662	3.5
Nebraska	3,911,430	634,411	2,219	16.2	1,186,279	30.3	2,090,741	53.5	1,844,669	47.2	156,193	4.0
Nevada	4,212,703	463,653	1,056	11.0	1,388,275	33.0	2,360,775	56.0	1,209,583	28.7	42,241	1.0
New Hampshire	2,844,769	205,572	1,056	7.2	1,041,561	36.6	1,597,636	56.2	1,521,271	53.5	48,241	1.7
New Jersey	25,217,564	1,336,982	953	5.3	9,403,391	37.3	14,477,191	57.4	13,665,700	54.2	559,163	2.2
New Mexico	3,744,076	721,936	2,135	19.3	2,423,599	64.7	598,541	16.0	480,051	12.8	349,305	0.6
New York	57,538,128	5,368,090	2,163	9.3	23,097,869	40.1	29,095,179	50.5	26,342,464	45.8	348,961	0.6
North Carolina	13,228,969	2,518,090	1,435	16.2	7,699,843	58.1	3,441,351	26.0	331,542	45.8	245,351	1.9
North Dakota	1,258,921	186,727	1,939	14.8	629,843	50.0	442,351	35.1	331,542	26.3	50,814	4.0
Ohio	22,973,368	2,702,863	1,541	11.8	9,921,997	43.2	10,348,507	45.0	8,514,889	37.1	681,257	3.0
Oklahoma	5,874,001	994,189	1,507	16.9	2,754,252	46.9	2,125,560	36.2	1,529,148	26.0	247,868	4.2
Oregon	6,120,056	864,118	1,514	14.1	2,702,707	44.2	2,463,231	40.2	1,960,832	32.0	150,560	2.5
Pennsylvania	27,174,139	3,318,681	1,851	12.2	10,479,294	38.5	14,449,984	53.2	11,663,220	42.9	426,946	1.6
Rhode Island	2,278,564	250,194	1,740	11.0	830,217	36.4	1,198,154	52.6	1,166,220	51.2	19,890	0.9
South Carolina	7,873,340	1,085,533	1,496	13.8	3,414,705	43.4	3,373,102	42.8	2,577,353	32.7	240,757	3.1
South Dakota	1,307,520	265,427	2,108	20.3	380,410	29.1	661,188	50.6	552,306	42.2	37,121	2.8
Tennessee	8,915,680	1,312,277	1,329	14.7	3,608,119	40.5	3,995,291	44.8	1,754,306	19.7	437,477	4.9
Texas	50,874,695	7,988,095	1,614	15.7	20,430,187	40.2	22,470,413	44.2	20,383,702	40.1	193,309	0.4
Utah	4,597,983	577,903	987	12.6	2,340,850	50.9	1,679,229	36.5	1,283,423	27.5	193,309	4.2
Vermont	1,641,955	175,721	1,814	10.7	1,340,743	81.7	125,491	7.6	1,276	0.1	21,928	1.3
Virginia	14,444,511	1,427,295	1,141	9.9	5,349,193	37.0	7,668,024	53.1	4,655,902	25.9	271,692	1.9
Washington	11,801,402	1,365,968	1,309	11.6	6,757,950	57.3	3,677,484	29.5	3,099,889	26.4	317,048	2.7
West Virginia	3,499,055	513,799	1,816	14.7	1,951,616	55.8	1,033,700	29.5	999,889	28.5	28,531	2.0
Wisconsin	11,429,211	1,045,227	1,208	9.1	5,246,795	44.9	5,137,189	44.2	4,714,226	41.2	225,258	2.0
Wyoming	1,647,905	155,403	1,757	9.4	878,878	53.3	613,623	37.2	417,124	25.3	18,376	1.1
Other jurisdictions												
American Samoa	82,921	72,007	—	86.8	10,689	12.9	225	0.3	0	0.0	37	#
Guam	333,235	142,766	5,189	42.8	190,469	57.2	0	0.0	0	0.0	793	0.2
Northern Marianas	87,377	57,619	2,918	65.9	29,758	34.1	0	0.0	0	#	0	0.0
Puerto Rico	3,711,167	1,382,157	2,918	37.2	2,328,968	62.8	43	#	0	#	42	#
U.S. Virgin Islands	243,250	44,858	2,895	18.4	—	—	198,392	81.6	0	0.0	48	#

—Not available.
†Not applicable.
#Rounds to zero.
[1]Includes other categories of revenue not separately shown.
[2]Includes revenues from gifts, and tuition and fees from patrons.

NOTE: Excludes revenues for state education agencies. Detail may not sum to totals because of rounding.

SOURCE: U.S. Department of Education, National Center for Education Statistics, Common Core of Data (CCD), "National Public Education Financial Survey," 2010–11. (This table was prepared July 2013.)

Summary of expenditures for public elementary and secondary education and other related programs, by purpose: Selected years, 1919–20 through 2010–11

School year	Total expenditures	Current expenditures for public elementary and secondary education								Current expenditures for other programs[2]	Capital outlay[3]	Interest on school debt
		Total	Administration	Instruction	Plant operation	Plant maintenance	Fixed charges	Other school services[1]				
1	2	3	4	5	6	7	8	9		10	11	12
Amounts in thousands of current dollars												
1919–20	$1,036,151	$861,120	$36,752	$632,556	$115,707	$30,432	$9,286	$36,387		$3,277	$153,543	$18,212
1929–30	2,316,790	1,843,552	78,680	1,317,727	216,072	78,810	50,270	101,993		9,825	370,878	92,536
1939–40	2,344,049	1,941,799	91,571	1,403,285	194,365	73,321	50,116	129,141		13,367	257,974	130,909
1949–50	5,837,643	4,687,274	220,050	3,112,340	427,587	214,164	261,469	451,663		35,614	1,014,176	100,578
1959–60	15,613,254	12,329,388	528,408	8,350,738	1,085,036	422,586	909,323	1,033,297		132,566	2,661,786	489,514
1969–70	40,683,429	34,217,773	1,606,646	23,270,158	2,537,257	974,941	3,266,920	2,561,856		635,803	4,659,072	1,170,782
1979–80	95,961,561	86,984,142	4,263,757	53,257,937	9,744,785	(4)	11,793,934	7,923,729		597,585	6,506,167	1,873,666
1989–90	212,769,564	188,229,359	16,346,991[5]	113,550,405[5]	20,261,415[5]	(4)	—	38,070,548[5]		2,982,543	17,781,342	3,776,321
1999–2000	381,838,155	323,888,508	25,079,298[5]	199,968,138[5]	31,190,295[5]	(4)	—	67,650,776[5]		5,457,015	43,357,186	9,135,445
2000–01	410,811,185	348,360,841	26,689,181[5]	214,333,003[5]	34,034,158[5]	(4)	—	73,304,498[5]		6,063,700	46,220,704	10,165,940
2001–02	435,364,404	368,378,006	28,309,047[5]	226,668,386[5]	34,829,109[5]	(4)	—	78,571,464[5]		6,530,554	49,960,542	10,495,301
2002–03	454,906,912	387,593,617	29,751,958[5]	237,731,734[5]	36,830,517[5]	(4)	—	83,279,408[5]		6,873,742	48,940,374	11,499,160
2003–04	474,241,531	403,390,369	30,864,875[5]	247,444,620[5]	38,720,429[5]	(4)	—	86,360,444[5]		6,927,551	50,842,973	13,080,638
2004–05	499,568,736	425,047,565	32,666,223[5]	260,046,266[5]	40,926,881[5]	(4)	—	91,408,195[5]		7,691,468	53,528,382	13,301,322
2005–06	528,268,772	449,131,342	34,197,083[5]	273,760,798[5]	44,313,835[5]	(4)	—	96,859,626[5]		7,415,575	57,375,299	14,346,556
2006–07	562,194,807	476,814,206	36,213,814[5]	290,678,482[5]	46,828,916[5]	(4)	—	103,092,995[5]		7,804,253	62,863,465	14,712,882
2007–08	597,313,726	506,884,219	38,203,341[5]	308,238,664[5]	49,362,661[5]	(4)	—	111,079,554[5]		8,307,720	66,426,299	15,695,488
2008–09	610,326,007	518,922,842	38,811,325[5]	316,075,710[5]	50,559,027[5]	(4)	—	113,476,779[5]		8,463,793	65,890,367	17,049,004
2009–10[6]	607,018,292	524,715,242	38,972,700[5]	321,213,401[5]	50,023,919[5]	(4)	—	114,505,223[5]		8,355,761	56,714,992	17,232,297
2010–11	604,214,912	527,166,106	39,098,595[5]	322,492,844[5]	50,182,060[5]	(4)	—	115,392,607[5]		8,187,042	50,927,540	17,934,224
Amounts in thousands of constant 2012–13 dollars[7]												
1919–20	$12,578,214	$10,453,449	$446,146	$7,678,828	$1,404,609	$369,425	$112,726	$441,715		$39,781	$1,863,914	$221,082
1929–30	31,313,548	24,917,301	1,063,433	17,810,293	2,920,412	1,065,190	679,445	1,378,529		132,794	5,012,757	1,250,709
1939–40	38,805,039	32,145,909	1,515,931	23,230,969	3,217,655	1,213,808	829,656	2,137,891		221,287	4,270,683	2,167,160
1949–50	57,026,153	45,788,540	2,149,601	30,403,500	4,176,967	2,092,103	2,554,211	4,412,158		347,902	9,907,176	982,516
1959–60	122,933,585	97,077,513	4,160,509	65,750,942	8,543,214	3,327,302	7,159,708	8,135,838		1,043,781	20,958,020	3,854,271
1969–70	249,164,597	209,565,887	9,839,861	142,517,474	15,539,364	5,971,001	20,008,166	15,690,020		3,893,959	28,534,365	7,170,424
1979–80	285,972,448	259,219,085	12,706,307	158,712,535	29,040,170	(4)	35,146,783	23,613,290		1,780,847	19,388,852	5,583,661
1989–90	387,672,094	342,959,155	29,784,675[5]	206,892,013[5]	36,916,865[5]	(4)	—	69,365,603[5]		5,434,277	32,398,102	6,880,562
1999–2000	521,814,502	442,621,353	34,273,006[5]	273,273,567[5]	42,624,206[5]	(4)	—	92,450,573[5]		7,457,478	59,251,304	12,484,368
2000–01	542,811,718	460,295,029	35,264,863[5]	283,201,797[5]	44,969,905[5]	(4)	—	96,858,464[5]		8,012,069	61,072,193	13,432,427
2001–02	565,246,620	478,276,177	36,754,482[5]	294,290,341[5]	45,219,673[5]	(4)	—	102,011,680[5]		8,478,814	64,865,265	13,626,363
2002–03	577,918,729	492,403,181	37,797,214[5]	302,017,002[5]	46,789,892[5]	(4)	—	105,799,073[5]		8,732,502	62,174,388	14,608,658
2003–04	589,583,253	501,500,164	38,371,615[5]	307,626,377[5]	48,137,742[5]	(4)	—	107,364,430[5]		8,612,422	63,208,647	16,262,020
2004–05	602,926,707	512,987,523	39,424,681[5]	313,848,380[5]	49,394,423[5]	(4)	—	110,320,039[5]		9,282,789	64,603,104	16,053,290
2005–06	614,175,630	522,168,903	39,758,199[5]	318,279,671[5]	51,520,133[5]	(4)	—	112,610,900[5]		8,621,493	66,705,647	16,679,587
2006–07	637,141,997	540,379,156	41,041,542[5]	329,429,347[5]	53,071,762[5]	(4)	—	116,836,505[5]		8,844,652	71,243,905	16,674,283
2007–08	652,755,879	553,932,782	41,749,343[5]	336,849,115[5]	53,944,461[5]	(4)	—	121,389,864[5]		9,078,835	72,591,931	17,152,330
2008–09	657,791,195	559,279,585	41,829,691[5]	340,656,987[5]	54,491,014[5]	(4)	—	122,301,893[5]		9,122,024	71,014,676	18,374,909
2009–10[6]	647,956,702	560,102,986	41,601,089[5]	342,876,613[5]	53,397,622[5]	(4)	—	122,227,662[5]		8,919,289	60,539,953	18,394,474
2010–11	632,268,421	551,642,262	40,913,931[5]	337,466,085[5]	52,511,997[5]	(4)	—	120,750,249[5]		8,567,164	53,292,089	18,766,905
Percentage distribution												
1919–20	100.0	83.1	3.5	61.0	11.2	2.9	0.9	3.5		0.3	14.8	1.8
1929–30	100.0	79.6	3.4	56.9	9.3	3.4	2.2	4.4		0.4	16.0	4.0
1939–40	100.0	82.8	3.9	59.9	8.3	3.1	2.1	5.5		0.6	11.0	5.6
1949–50	100.0	80.3	3.8	53.3	7.3	3.7	4.5	7.7		0.6	17.4	1.7
1959–60	100.0	79.0	3.4	53.5	6.9	2.7	5.8	6.6		0.8	17.0	3.1
1969–70	100.0	84.1	3.9	57.2	6.2	2.4	8.0	6.3		1.6	11.5	2.9
1979–80	100.0	90.6	4.4	55.5	10.2	(4)	12.3	8.3		0.6	6.8	2.0
1989–90	100.0	88.5	7.7[5]	53.4[5]	9.5[5]	(4)	—	17.9[5]		1.4	8.4	1.8
1999–2000	100.0	84.8	6.6[5]	52.4[5]	8.2[5]	(4)	—	17.7[5]		1.4	11.4	2.4
2000–01	100.0	84.8	6.5[5]	52.2[5]	8.3[5]	(4)	—	17.8[5]		1.5	11.3	2.5
2001–02	100.0	84.6	6.5[5]	52.1[5]	8.0[5]	(4)	—	18.0[5]		1.5	11.5	2.4
2002–03	100.0	85.2	6.5[5]	52.3[5]	8.1[5]	(4)	—	18.3[5]		1.5	10.8	2.5
2003–04	100.0	85.1	6.5[5]	52.2[5]	8.2[5]	(4)	—	18.2[5]		1.5	10.7	2.8
2004–05	100.0	85.1	6.5[5]	52.1[5]	8.2[5]	(4)	—	18.3[5]		1.5	10.7	2.7
2005–06	100.0	85.0	6.5[5]	51.8[5]	8.4[5]	(4)	—	18.3[5]		1.4	10.9	2.7
2006–07	100.0	84.8	6.4[5]	51.7[5]	8.3[5]	(4)	—	18.3[5]		1.4	11.2	2.6
2007–08	100.0	84.9	6.4[5]	51.6[5]	8.3[5]	(4)	—	18.6[5]		1.4	11.1	2.6
2008–09	100.0	85.0	6.4[5]	51.8[5]	8.3[5]	(4)	—	18.6[5]		1.4	10.8	2.8
2009–10[6]	100.0	86.4	6.4[5]	52.9[5]	8.2[5]	(4)	—	18.9[5]		1.4	9.3	2.8
2010–11	100.0	87.2	6.5[5]	53.4[5]	8.3[5]	(4)	—	19.1[5]		1.4	8.4	3.0

—Not available.

[1]Prior to 1959–60, items included under "other school services" were listed under "auxiliary services," a more comprehensive classification that also included community services.

[2]Includes expenditures for summer schools, adult education, community colleges, and community services.

[3]Prior to 1969–70, excludes capital outlay by state and local school housing authorities.

[4]Plant operation also includes plant maintenance.

[5]Data not comparable to figures prior to 1989–90.

[6]Data have been revised from previously published figures.

[7]Constant dollars based on the Consumer Price Index, prepared by the Bureau of Labor Statistics, U.S. Department of Labor, adjusted to a school-year basis.

NOTE: Beginning in 1959–60, includes Alaska and Hawaii. Beginning in 1989–90, state administration expenditures were excluded from both "total" and "current" expenditures. Beginning in 1989–90, extensive changes were made in the data collection procedures. Detail may not sum to totals because of rounding.

SOURCE: U.S. Department of Education, National Center for Education Statistics, *Biennial Survey of Education in the United States*, 1919–20 through 1949–50; *Statistics of State School Systems*, 1959–60 and 1969–70; *Revenues and Expenditures for Public Elementary and Secondary Education, 1979–80*; and Common Core of Data (CCD), "National Public Education Financial Survey," 1989–90 through 2010–11. (This table was prepared July 2013.)

Current expenditures and current expenditures per pupil in public elementary and secondary schools: 1989–90 through 2023–24

School year	Current expenditures in unadjusted dollars[1]			Current expenditures in constant 2012–13 dollars[2]					
	Total, in billions	Per pupil in fall enrollment	Per pupil in average daily attendance (ADA)	Total current expenditures		Per pupil in fall enrollment		Per pupil in average daily attendance (ADA)	
				In billions	Annual percentage change	Per pupil enrolled	Annual percentage change	Per pupil in ADA	Annual percentage change
1	2	3	4	5	6	7	8	9	10
1989–90	$188.2	$4,643	$4,980	$343.0	3.8	$8,459	2.9	$9,073	2.3
1990–91	202.0	4,902	5,258	349.0	1.8	8,468	0.1	9,083	0.1
1991–92	211.2	5,023	5,421	353.6	1.3	8,409	-0.7	9,075	-0.1
1992–93	220.9	5,160	5,584	358.7	1.4	8,375	-0.4	9,064	-0.1
1993–94	231.5	5,327	5,767	366.4	2.1	8,429	0.6	9,126	0.7
1994–95	243.9	5,529	5,989	375.1	2.4	8,504	0.9	9,212	0.9
1995–96	255.1	5,689	6,147	382.0	1.8	8,519	0.2	9,205	-0.1
1996–97	270.2	5,923	6,393	393.3	3.0	8,624	1.2	9,307	1.1
1997–98	285.5	6,189	6,676	408.4	3.8	8,853	2.7	9,549	2.6
1998–99	302.9	6,508	7,013	425.9	4.3	9,151	3.4	9,861	3.3
1999–2000	323.9	6,912	7,394	442.6	3.9	9,446	3.2	10,104	2.5
2000–01	348.4	7,380	7,904	460.3	4.0	9,751	3.2	10,443	3.4
2001–02	368.4	7,727	8,259	478.3	3.9	10,033	2.9	10,723	2.7
2002–03	387.6	8,044	8,610	492.4	3.0	10,219	1.9	10,938	2.0
2003–04	403.4	8,310	8,900	501.5	1.8	10,332	1.1	11,064	1.2
2004–05	425.0	8,711	9,316	513.0	2.3	10,513	1.8	11,243	1.6
2005–06	449.1	9,145	9,778	522.2	1.8	10,632	1.1	11,368	1.1
2006–07	476.8	9,679	10,336	540.4	3.5	10,969	3.2	11,714	3.0
2007–08	506.9	10,298	10,982	553.9	2.5	11,254	2.6	12,001	2.5
2008–09	518.9	10,540	11,239	559.3	1.0	11,359	0.9	12,113	0.9
2009–10	524.7	10,636	11,427	560.1	0.1	11,353	-0.1	12,198	0.7
2010–11	527.2	10,658	11,418	551.6	-1.5	11,153	-1.8	11,948	-2.0
2011–12[3]	527.5	10,650	11,400	536.3	-2.8	10,830	-2.9	11,590	-3.0
2012–13[3]	542.2	10,920	11,680	542.2	1.1	10,920	0.8	11,680	0.8
2013–14[3]	556.6	11,190	11,970	548.4	1.1	11,020	0.9	11,790	0.9
2014–15[3]	576.8	11,590	12,400	558.8	1.9	11,230	1.9	12,020	1.9
2015–16[3]	—	—	—	570.0	2.0	11,440	1.8	12,240	1.8
2016–17[3]	—	—	—	582.8	2.2	11,670	2.0	12,480	2.0
2017–18[3]	—	—	—	598.3	2.7	11,900	2.0	12,730	2.0
2018–19[3]	—	—	—	610.7	2.1	12,080	1.5	12,930	1.5
2019–20[3]	—	—	—	622.4	1.9	12,240	1.3	13,100	1.3
2020–21[3]	—	—	—	633.0	1.7	12,370	1.0	13,240	1.0
2021–22[3]	—	—	—	643.2	1.6	12,490	1.0	13,370	1.0
2022–23[3]	—	—	—	654.2	1.7	12,630	1.1	13,510	1.1
2023–24[3]	—	—	—	662.9	1.3	12,720	0.7	13,610	0.7

—Not available.

[1]Unadjusted (or "current") dollars have not been adjusted to compensate for inflation.

[2]Constant dollars based on the Consumer Price Index, prepared by the Bureau of Labor Statistics, U.S. Department of Labor, adjusted to a school-year basis.

[3]Projected.

NOTE: Current expenditures include instruction, support services, food services, and enterprise operations. Some data have been revised from previously published figures.

SOURCE: U.S. Department of Education, National Center for Education Statistics, Common Core of Data (CCD), "National Public Education Financial Survey," 1989–90 through 2010–11; National Elementary and Secondary Enrollment Projection Model, 1972 through 2023; and Public Elementary and Secondary Education Current Expenditure Projection Model, 1973–74 through 2023–24. (This table was prepared May 2014.)

Total expenditures for public elementary and secondary education and other related programs, by function and state or jurisdiction: 2010–11
[In thousands of current dollars]

State or jurisdiction	Total	Elementary/ secondary current expenditures, total	Instruction	Support services — Total	Student support[4]	Instructional staff[5]	General administration	School administration	Operation and maintenance	Student transportation	Other support services	Food services	Enterprise operations[3]	Current expenditures for other programs[1]	Capital outlay[2]	Interest on school debt
1	2	3	4	5	6	7	8	9	10	11	12	13	14	15	16	17
United States	$604,214,912	$527,166,106	$322,492,844	$183,017,473	$29,345,585	$24,873,764	$10,489,229	$28,609,366	$50,182,060	$22,345,048	$17,172,420	$20,394,757	$1,261,032	$8,187,042	$50,927,540	$17,934,224
Alabama	7,410,192	6,592,925	3,846,419	2,301,718	382,417	297,721	158,287	407,947	594,180	330,019	131,147	444,788	0	116,732	565,985	134,550
Alaska	2,430,593	2,201,270	1,218,685	913,896	180,052	154,044	30,576	133,786	269,143	64,056	82,239	60,491	8,198	8,633	181,341	39,349
Arizona	9,889,232	8,340,211	4,506,883	3,394,014	1,087,247	195,308	126,897	392,530	937,481	323,522	331,029	393,701	45,613	47,020	864,847	637,155
Arkansas	5,392,058	4,578,136	2,615,474	1,702,516	233,099	392,196	112,986	231,473	435,105	172,141	125,517	254,728	5,418	30,556	657,234	126,132
California	67,570,728	57,526,835	34,679,610	20,417,014	3,004,958	3,499,992	555,828	3,811,666	5,695,223	1,386,604	2,462,742	2,287,136	143,075	938,345	6,763,699	2,341,849
Colorado	8,743,142	7,409,462	4,250,693	2,868,302	361,218	420,592	159,259	495,909	695,046	217,522	518,757	254,581	35,885	58,479	835,266	439,936
Connecticut	9,944,121	9,094,036	5,768,873	3,031,013	555,702	281,253	178,833	515,530	842,535	449,863	207,308	219,101	75,049	145,124	563,519	141,441
Delaware	1,855,007	1,613,304	1,018,491	536,283	75,881	21,042	22,133	88,755	160,882	94,237	73,355	58,529	0	28,277	189,766	23,660
District of Columbia	2,063,029	1,482,202	754,464	670,690	86,134	114,951	61,731	110,235	165,485	100,107	32,047	54,224	2,824	37,802	391,652	151,373
Florida	27,433,536	23,870,090	14,566,298	8,237,108	1,066,264	1,541,508	253,657	1,343,045	2,471,262	959,102	602,272	1,066,684		570,458	2,217,064	775,923
Georgia	17,178,095	15,527,907	9,668,819	5,009,451	733,717	777,196	234,176	932,355	1,156,798	658,161	517,049	806,569	43,067	26,993	1,367,894	255,301
Hawaii	2,342,924	2,141,561	1,242,693	782,875	201,020	71,439	10,796	137,151	251,208	66,436	44,825	115,980		17,627	85,475	98,261
Idaho	2,107,272	1,881,746	1,148,131	637,447	106,724	75,237	42,676	105,642	171,558	91,532	44,077	95,780	389	4,151	160,083	61,292
Illinois	27,621,033	24,554,467	14,690,696	9,118,001	1,658,199	1,059,076	999,732	1,249,947	2,211,843	1,152,373	786,830	745,770	0	151,196	2,093,497	821,873
Indiana	11,037,564	9,687,949	5,702,356	3,555,487	456,293	367,738	251,190	558,236	1,097,726	582,621	241,642	430,106	0	139,215	871,863	338,537
Iowa	5,859,335	4,855,871	2,994,346	1,640,916	273,995	231,275	125,472	274,596	412,748	177,495	145,336	215,791	4,817	30,310	871,157	101,997
Kansas	5,824,926	4,741,372	2,873,575	1,651,762	275,382	202,415	139,658	271,235	443,398	191,568	128,107	216,035	0	4,295	869,746	209,512
Kentucky	7,200,059	6,211,453	3,641,680	2,197,751	279,805	337,676	137,247	345,210	576,020	376,894	144,898	356,658	15,365	83,981	747,269	157,355
Louisiana	8,502,295	7,522,098	4,380,197	2,743,272	369,620	410,213	177,276	437,419	700,509	435,310	212,926	398,537	92	45,343	812,767	122,086
Maine	2,630,548	2,377,878	1,442,329	859,075	155,421	124,072	76,259	127,845	232,893	114,101	28,484	76,393	80	28,301	172,590	51,778
Maryland	13,251,725	12,035,719	7,424,153	4,149,496	528,145	668,989	92,610	833,866	1,070,409	612,124	343,352	311,684	150,386	28,220	1,022,082	165,704
Massachusetts	14,715,706	13,649,965	8,867,542	4,419,333	953,027	611,858	182,474	554,090	1,239,104	559,868	318,911	363,090	0	55,711	758,688	251,343
Michigan	19,444,952	16,786,444	9,672,947	6,535,509	1,269,121	889,719	343,162	914,817	1,572,870	706,467	839,353	577,989	0	332,187	1,434,833	891,488
Minnesota	10,816,918	8,944,867	5,888,594	2,649,197	236,405	377,320	269,575	357,613	646,876	498,338	263,070	381,430	25,646	417,151	1,052,205	402,695
Mississippi	4,268,801	3,887,981	2,247,757	1,399,692	187,586	197,923	115,358	224,147	400,360	186,606	87,713	240,263	269	28,526	281,036	71,258
Missouri	10,072,167	8,691,887	5,208,082	3,090,488	406,335	389,078	274,499	496,717	871,391	444,318	208,149	393,317	0	198,591	854,963	326,725
Montana	1,653,315	1,518,818	909,036	543,485	93,752	57,707	43,611	81,039	158,869	72,215	36,291	62,689	3,607	11,231	107,204	16,062
Nebraska	3,739,179	3,298,536	2,185,379	892,158	119,384	101,175	102,258	125,196	282,923	93,628	67,594	135,430	85,569	2,629	356,643	81,372
Nevada	4,244,029	3,676,997	2,190,166	1,364,559	187,908	194,601	45,813	261,636	386,890	152,658	135,054	122,068	204	25,308	297,155	244,570
New Hampshire	2,896,807	2,637,911	1,712,141	855,470	190,003	81,626	85,942	140,018	217,962	111,866	28,052	70,300	0	7,823	206,275	44,799
New Jersey	25,308,865	23,639,281	14,209,004	8,659,183	2,290,750	732,617	483,063	1,117,966	2,345,908	1,169,718	519,162	510,851	260,243	146,882	855,532	667,171
New Mexico	3,641,735	3,127,463	1,793,031	1,191,752	325,026	88,261	70,665	187,111	322,521	103,320	94,849	140,845	1,836	3,862	510,320	90
New York	57,350,534	51,509,285	35,992,426	14,485,533	1,708,221	1,330,084	984,671	1,965,608	4,561,407	2,686,652	1,248,890	1,031,327	0	2,165,740	2,513,775	1,161,734
North Carolina	13,277,669	12,322,555	7,702,399	3,955,217	581,125	451,273	198,490	767,107	1,057,753	526,541	372,928	664,939	31,199	67,080	878,592	9,442
North Dakota	1,198,926	1,049,772	607,522	356,906	47,023	35,583	48,894	51,693	102,037	44,942	26,734	54,145		8,143	123,406	17,605
Ohio	23,500,247	19,988,921	11,372,653	7,956,671	1,268,590	1,335,790	598,776	1,130,956	1,782,173	949,390	890,996	658,520	1,077	436,310	2,535,352	539,664
Oklahoma	5,618,816	5,036,031	2,862,054	1,829,693	341,623	205,512	165,478	266,368	531,204	165,215	154,202	295,573	48,711	13,899	508,086	60,800
Oregon	6,201,702	5,430,888	3,165,170	2,067,274	387,583	219,223	71,446	340,070	447,946	249,061	351,945	195,412	3,032	25,737	461,338	283,739
Pennsylvania	27,393,554	23,485,203	14,382,313	8,213,549	1,215,179	866,873	692,759	1,028,872	2,327,779	1,188,411	893,677	786,566	102,775	569,951	2,271,818	1,066,582
Rhode Island	2,316,164	2,149,366	1,324,326	771,429	225,594	78,607	29,670	102,131	176,137	82,675	76,616	52,553	1,057	69,475	47,874	49,449
South Carolina	7,919,837	6,461,884	3,688,634	2,419,435	474,538	396,370	71,970	389,412	629,655	256,128	201,362	335,226	18,589	65,127	985,481	407,345
South Dakota	1,347,213	1,126,503	666,180	396,459	62,504	46,946	37,112	55,538	115,533	40,275	38,550	57,729	6,135	2,947	190,229	27,535
Tennessee	9,294,028	8,377,599	5,325,040	2,647,827	342,363	512,100	169,585	465,391	718,289	293,094	147,006	404,732	0	84,493	641,341	190,595
Texas	52,711,794	42,864,245	25,719,093	14,811,471	2,081,440	2,224,154	626,347	2,377,519	4,675,412	1,211,190	1,615,409	2,333,728	0	337,583	6,556,136	2,953,783
Utah	4,642,830	3,704,133	2,382,888	1,104,285	143,615	147,035	42,186	225,694	335,661	115,410	94,685	200,910	16,050	103,832	701,431	133,434

See notes at end of table.

Total expenditures for public elementary and secondary education and other related programs, by function and state or jurisdiction: 2010–11—Continued

[In thousands of current dollars]

State or jurisdiction	Total expenditures	Current expenditures for elementary and secondary programs												Current expenditures for other programs[1]	Capital outlay[2]	Interest on school debt
	Total	Elementary/ secondary current expenditures, total	Instruction	Support services												
				Total	Student support[4]	Instructional staff[5]	General administration	School administration	Operation and maintenance	Student transportation	Other support services	Food services	Enterprise operations[3]			
1	2	3	4	5	6	7	8	9	10	11	12	13	14	15	16	17
Vermont	1,515,638	1,424,507	876,070	507,645	111,637	63,719	31,782	95,207	122,930	48,791	33,579	40,024	769	13,106	63,945	14,079
Virginia	14,291,767	12,968,457	7,861,182	4,602,565	627,158	862,346	199,556	750,559	1,263,117	695,293	204,535	502,837	1,873	74,580	1,075,075	173,655
Washington	12,025,483	10,040,312	6,067,366	3,516,776	671,779	402,544	192,069	572,454	896,173	408,823	372,934	335,166	121,004	57,362	1,514,773	413,036
West Virginia	3,515,624	3,388,294	2,029,616	1,178,712	153,000	133,942	66,053	180,907	337,813	248,745	58,252	179,966	0	46,185	65,730	15,415
Wisconsin	11,359,841	10,333,016	6,322,480	3,648,765	490,843	504,489	270,163	504,803	928,720	415,340	534,406	361,656	115	265,689	539,098	222,038
Wyoming	1,643,359	1,398,444	826,891	528,345	81,181	91,318	28,523	74,347	135,194	64,292	53,490	42,193	1,015	8,844	234,410	1,660
Other jurisdictions																
American Samoa	84,478	75,355	32,770	22,938	535	7,983	2,089	5,338	4,803	1,014	1,176	19,647	0	2,084	7,039	0
Guam	342,273	266,952	149,292	105,475	27,736	5,319	2,225	16,482	35,068	7,616	11,029	12,186	0	0	72,196	3,124
Northern Marianas	2,405,388	84,657	36,014	40,089	11,416	4,848	3,141	4,384	8,492	2,089	5,719	8,554	0	2,319,587	1,145	0
Puerto Rico	3,664,247	3,519,547	1,460,167	1,779,736	235,775	289,143	331,065	144,192	401,622	72,901	305,037	279,644	0	82,528	62,172	0
U.S. Virgin Islands	215,278	212,112	108,061	91,752	15,828	5,922	7,504	11,060	14,151	15,088	22,199	11,596	703	3,071	94	0

[1]Includes expenditures for adult education, community colleges, community colleges, private school programs funded by local and state education agencies, and community services.

[2]Includes expenditures for property and for buildings and alterations completed by school district staff or contractors.

[3]Includes expenditures for operations funded by sales of products or services (e.g., school bookstore or computer time). Also includes small amounts for direct program support made by state education agencies for local school districts.

[4]Includes expenditures for guidance, health, attendance, and speech pathology services.

[5]Includes expenditures for curriculum development, staff training, libraries, and media and computer centers.

NOTE: Excludes expenditures for state education agencies. Detail may not sum to totals because of rounding.

SOURCE: U.S. Department of Education, National Center for Education Statistics, Common Core of Data (CCD), "National Public Education Financial Survey," 2010–11. (This table was prepared July 2013.)

Total and current expenditures per pupil in public elementary and secondary schools: Selected years, 1919–20 through 2010–11

School year	Expenditure per pupil in average daily attendance				Expenditure per pupil in fall enrollment[1]				
	Unadjusted dollars[2]		Constant 2012–13 dollars[3]		Unadjusted dollars[2]		Constant 2012–13 dollars[3]		
	Total expenditure[4]	Current expenditure	Total expenditure[4]	Current expenditure	Total expenditure[4]	Current expenditure	Total expenditure[4]	Current expenditure	Annual percent change in current expenditure
1	2	3	4	5	6	7	8	9	10
1919–20	$64	$53	$776	$647	$48	$40	$581	$484	—
1929–30	108	87	1,466	1,172	90	72	1,214	970	—
1931–32	97	81	1,555	1,301	82	69	1,316	1,102	—
1933–34	76	67	1,332	1,179	65	57	1,131	1,002	—
1935–36	88	74	1,481	1,251	74	63	1,252	1,058	—
1937–38	100	84	1,610	1,354	86	72	1,382	1,163	—
1939–40	106	88	1,750	1,458	92	76	1,517	1,264	—
1941–42	110	98	1,633	1,459	94	84	1,398	1,249	—
1943–44	125	117	1,655	1,553	105	99	1,395	1,309	—
1945–46	146	136	1,850	1,730	124	116	1,576	1,474	—
1947–48	205	181	2,034	1,802	179	158	1,776	1,574	—
1949–50	260	210	2,543	2,055	231	187	2,257	1,823	—
1951–52	314	246	2,768	2,166	275	215	2,424	1,896	—
1953–54	351	265	3,019	2,278	312	236	2,685	2,026	—
1955–56	387	294	3,331	2,532	354	269	3,045	2,315	—
1957–58	447	341	3,625	2,764	408	311	3,306	2,520	—
1959–60	471	375	3,709	2,954	440	350	3,465	2,759	—
1961–62	517	419	3,980	3,225	485	393	3,735	3,026	—
1963–64	559	460	4,191	3,453	520	428	3,901	3,214	—
1965–66	654	538	4,741	3,899	607	499	4,401	3,620	—
1967–68	786	658	5,350	4,478	732	612	4,977	4,166	—
1969–70	955	816	5,849	4,997	879	751	5,385	4,601	—
1970–71	1,049	911	6,112	5,306	970	842	5,650	4,905	6.6
1971–72	1,128	990	6,341	5,564	1,034	908	5,815	5,103	4.0
1972–73	1,211	1,077	6,543	5,820	1,117	993	6,035	5,368	5.2
1973–74	1,364	1,207	6,768	5,990	1,244	1,101	6,171	5,462	1.7
1974–75	1,545	1,365	6,900	6,095	1,423	1,257	6,357	5,615	2.8
1975–76	1,697	1,504	7,081	6,273	1,563	1,385	6,520	5,776	2.9
1976–77	1,816	1,638	7,159	6,455	1,674	1,509	6,597	5,948	3.0
1977–78	2,002	1,823	7,396	6,733	1,842	1,677	6,803	6,193	4.1
1978–79	2,210	2,020	7,464	6,824	2,029	1,855	6,854	6,267	1.2
1979–80	2,491	2,272	7,422	6,770	2,290	2,088	6,823	6,224	-0.7
1980–81	2,742 [5]	2,502	7,324 [5]	6,681	2,529 [5]	2,307	6,755 [5]	6,162	-1.0
1981–82	2,973 [5]	2,726	7,310 [5]	6,701	2,754 [5]	2,525	6,771 [5]	6,207	0.7
1982–83	3,203 [5]	2,955	7,551 [5]	6,966	2,966 [5]	2,736	6,992 [5]	6,450	3.9
1983–84	3,471 [5]	3,173	7,890 [5]	7,213	3,216 [5]	2,940	7,309 [5]	6,682	3.6
1984–85	3,722 [5]	3,470	8,141 [5]	7,591	3,456 [5]	3,222	7,559 [5]	7,048	5.5
1985–86	4,020 [5]	3,756	8,546 [5]	7,985	3,724 [5]	3,479	7,918 [5]	7,397	5.0
1986–87	4,308 [5]	3,970	8,960 [5]	8,258	3,995 [5]	3,682	8,309 [5]	7,658	3.5
1987–88	4,654 [5]	4,240	9,295 [5]	8,468	4,310 [5]	3,927	8,608 [5]	7,842	2.4
1988–89	5,108	4,645	9,751	8,867	4,737	4,307	9,042	8,222	4.8
1989–90	5,547	4,980	10,107	9,073	5,172	4,643	9,423	8,459	2.9
1990–91	5,882	5,258	10,161	9,083	5,484	4,902	9,473	8,468	0.1
1991–92	6,072	5,421	10,164	9,075	5,626	5,023	9,418	8,409	-0.7
1992–93	6,279	5,584	10,193	9,064	5,802	5,160	9,419	8,375	-0.4
1993–94	6,489	5,767	10,267	9,126	5,994	5,327	9,483	8,429	0.6
1994–95	6,723	5,989	10,341	9,212	6,206	5,529	9,546	8,504	0.9
1995–96	6,959	6,147	10,421	9,205	6,441	5,689	9,645	8,519	0.2
1996–97	7,297	6,393	10,624	9,307	6,761	5,923	9,844	8,624	1.2
1997–98	7,701	6,676	11,015	9,549	7,139	6,189	10,212	8,853	2.7
1998–99	8,115	7,013	11,411	9,861	7,531	6,508	10,589	9,151	3.4
1999–2000	8,589	7,394	11,738	10,104	8,030	6,912	10,973	9,446	3.2
2000–01	9,180	7,904	12,129	10,443	8,572	7,380	11,326	9,751	3.2
2001–02	9,611	8,259	12,479	10,723	8,993	7,727	11,676	10,033	2.9
2002–03	9,950	8,610	12,641	10,938	9,296	8,044	11,810	10,219	1.9
2003–04	10,308	8,900	12,815	11,064	9,625	8,310	11,966	10,332	1.1
2004–05	10,779	9,316	13,009	11,243	10,078	8,711	12,164	10,513	1.8
2005–06	11,338	9,778	13,181	11,368	10,603	9,145	12,328	10,632	1.1
2006–07	12,015	10,336	13,617	11,714	11,252	9,679	12,752	10,969	3.2
2007–08	12,759	10,982	13,943	12,001	11,965	10,298	13,075	11,254	2.6
2008–09	13,033	11,239	14,046	12,113	12,222	10,540	13,173	11,359	0.9
2009–10[6]	13,035	11,427	13,914	12,198	12,133	10,636	12,951	11,353	-0.1
2010–11	12,908	11,418	13,507	11,948	12,048	10,658	12,608	11,153	-1.8

—Not available.

[1] Data for 1919–20 to 1953–54 are based on school-year enrollment.
[2] Unadjusted (or "current") dollars have not been adjusted to compensate for inflation.
[3] Constant dollars based on the Consumer Price Index, prepared by the Bureau of Labor Statistics, U.S. Department of Labor, adjusted to a school-year basis.
[4] Excludes "Other current expenditures," such as community services, private school programs, adult education, and other programs not allocable to expenditures per student at public schools.
[5] Estimated.
[6] Revised from previously published figures.

NOTE: Beginning in 1980–81, state administration expenditures are excluded from both "total" and "current" expenditures. Current expenditures include instruction, support services, food services, and enterprise operations. Total expenditures include current expenditures, capital outlay, and interest on debt. Beginning in 1988–89, extensive changes were made in the data collection procedures.

SOURCE: U.S. Department of Education, National Center for Education Statistics, *Biennial Survey of Education in the United States*, 1919–20 through 1955–56; *Statistics of State School Systems*, 1957–58 through 1969–70; *Revenues and Expenditures for Public Elementary and Secondary Education*, 1970–71 through 1986–87; and Common Core of Data (CCD), "National Public Education Financial Survey," 1987–88 through 2010–11. (This table was prepared July 2013.)

Current expenditure per pupil in fall enrollment in public elementary and secondary schools, by state or jurisdiction: Selected years, 1969–70 through 2010–11

State or jurisdiction	Unadjusted dollars[1]													
	1969–70	1979–80	1989–90	1999–2000	2001–02	2002–03	2003–04	2004–05	2005–06	2006–07	2007–08	2008–09	2009–10	2010–11
1	2	3	4	5	6	7	8	9	10	11	12	13	14	15
United States	$751	$2,088	$4,643	$6,912	$7,727	$8,044	$8,310	$8,711	$9,145	$9,679	$10,298	$10,540	$10,636	$10,658
Alabama	512	1,520	3,144	5,638	6,029	6,300	6,581	7,073	7,683	8,398	9,197	8,964	8,907	8,726
Alaska	1,059	4,267	7,577	8,806	9,564	9,870	10,116	10,847	11,476	12,324	14,641	15,363	15,829	16,663
Arizona	674	1,865	3,717	5,030	5,851	6,283	5,999	6,307	6,515	7,316	7,727	8,022	7,870	7,782
Arkansas	511	1,472	3,229	5,277	6,276	6,482	6,842	7,659	8,030	8,391	8,677	8,854	9,281	9,496
California	833	2,227	4,502	6,314	7,405	7,552	7,673	7,905	8,301	8,952	9,706	9,503	9,300	9,146
Colorado	686	2,258	4,357	6,215	6,941	7,384	7,478	7,826	8,166	8,286	9,152	8,782	8,926	8,786
Connecticut	911	2,167	7,463	9,753	10,577	11,057	11,436	12,263	13,072	13,659	14,610	15,353	15,698	16,224
Delaware	833	2,587	5,326	8,310	9,285	9,693	10,212	10,911	11,621	11,760	12,153	12,109	12,222	12,467
District of Columbia	947	2,811	7,872	10,107	12,102	11,847	12,959	13,915	13,752	15,511	16,353	19,698	20,910	20,793
Florida	683	1,834	4,597	5,831	6,213	6,439	6,793	7,215	7,812	8,567	9,084	8,867	8,863	9,030
Georgia	539	1,491	4,000	6,437	7,380	7,774	7,742	8,065	8,595	9,102	9,718	9,649	9,432	9,259
Hawaii	792	2,086	4,130	6,530	7,306	8,100	8,533	8,997	9,876	11,316	11,800	12,400	11,855	11,924
Idaho	573	1,548	2,921	5,315	6,011	6,081	6,168	6,319	6,469	6,648	6,951	7,118	7,100	6,821
Illinois	816	2,241	4,521	7,133	7,956	8,287	8,606	8,896	9,113	9,596	10,353	11,097	11,739	11,742
Indiana	661	1,708	4,270	7,192	7,734	8,057	8,431	8,919	8,929	9,080	8,867	9,254	9,479	9,251
Iowa	798	2,164	4,190	6,564	7,338	7,574	7,626	7,962	8,355	8,791	9,520	9,704	9,748	9,795
Kansas	699	1,963	4,290	6,294	7,339	7,454	7,776	7,926	8,640	9,243	9,894	10,204	9,972	9,802
Kentucky	502	1,557	3,384	5,921	6,523	6,661	6,864	7,132	7,668	7,941	8,740	8,786	8,957	9,228
Louisiana	589	1,629	3,625	5,804	6,567	6,922	7,271	7,669	8,486	8,937	10,006	10,625	10,701	10,799
Maine	649	1,692	4,903	7,667	8,818	9,344	9,746	10,342	10,841	11,644	11,761	12,183	12,525	12,576
Maryland	809	2,293	5,573	7,731	8,692	9,153	9,433	10,031	10,909	11,989	13,257	13,737	14,007	14,123
Massachusetts	791	2,548	5,766	8,816	10,232	10,460	11,015	11,642	12,087	12,784	13,690	14,534	13,956	14,285
Michigan	841	2,495	5,090	8,110	8,653	8,781	9,094	9,338	9,575	9,876	10,075	10,373	10,447	10,577
Minnesota	855	2,296	4,698	7,190	7,736	8,109	8,405	8,718	9,159	9,589	10,060	10,983	10,665	10,674
Mississippi	457	1,568	2,934	5,014	5,354	5,792	6,199	6,548	7,173	7,459	7,890	8,064	8,104	7,926
Missouri	596	1,724	4,071	6,187	7,136	7,495	7,542	7,858	8,273	8,848	9,532	9,617	9,721	9,461
Montana	728	2,264	4,240	6,314	7,062	7,496	7,825	8,133	8,626	9,191	9,786	10,120	10,565	10,719
Nebraska	700	2,025	4,553	6,683	7,741	8,074	8,452	8,794	9,324	10,068	10,565	10,846	11,339	11,540
Nevada	706	1,908	3,816	5,760	6,079	6,092	6,410	6,804	7,177	7,796	8,187	8,321	8,376	8,411
New Hampshire	666	1,732	4,786	6,860	7,935	8,579	9,161	9,771	10,396	11,036	11,951	12,583	13,072	13,548
New Jersey	924	2,825	7,546	10,337	11,793	12,568	13,338	14,117	14,954	16,163	17,620	16,973	17,379	16,855
New Mexico	665	1,870	3,446	5,825	6,882	7,125	7,572	7,834	8,354	8,849	9,291	9,648	9,621	9,250
New York	1,194	2,950	7,051	9,846	11,218	11,961	12,638	13,703	14,615	15,546	16,794	17,746	18,167	18,834
North Carolina	570	1,635	4,018	6,045	6,495	6,562	6,613	7,098	7,396	7,878	7,798	8,463	8,225	8,267
North Dakota	662	1,941	3,899	5,667	6,709	6,870	7,333	8,279	8,728	8,671	9,324	9,802	10,519	10,898
Ohio	677	1,894	4,531	7,065	8,069	8,632	9,029	9,330	9,692	9,937	10,340	10,669	11,224	11,395
Oklahoma	554	1,810	3,293	5,395	6,229	6,092	6,154	6,610	6,941	7,430	7,683	7,878	7,929	7,631
Oregon	843	2,412	4,864	7,149	7,642	7,491	7,618	8,069	8,645	8,958	9,565	9,611	9,268	9,516
Pennsylvania	815	2,328	5,737	7,772	8,537	8,997	9,708	10,235	10,723	10,905	11,741	12,299	12,729	13,096
Rhode Island	807	2,340	5,908	8,904	9,703	10,349	11,078	11,667	12,609	13,453	14,459	14,719	14,723	14,948
South Carolina	567	1,597	3,769	6,130	7,017	7,040	7,177	7,549	8,120	8,507	9,060	9,228	9,080	8,903
South Dakota	656	1,781	3,511	5,632	6,424	6,547	7,068	7,464	7,775	8,064	8,535	8,543	9,020	8,931
Tennessee	531	1,523	3,405	5,383	5,948	6,118	6,466	6,850	7,004	7,129	7,820	7,992	8,117	8,484
Texas	551	1,740	3,835	6,288	6,771	7,136	7,151	7,246	7,480	7,850	8,350	8,562	8,788	8,685
Utah	595	1,556	2,577	4,378	4,899	4,838	4,991	5,216	5,464	5,709	5,978	6,612	6,452	6,326
Vermont	790	1,930	5,770	8,323	9,806	10,454	11,211	11,972	12,805	13,629	14,421	15,096	15,666	14,707
Virginia	654	1,824	4,690	6,841	7,496	7,822	8,219	8,886	9,452	10,214	10,664	10,928	10,594	10,363
Washington	853	2,387	4,382	6,376	7,039	7,252	7,391	7,717	7,984	8,524	9,058	9,585	9,497	9,619
West Virginia	621	1,749	4,020	7,152	7,844	8,319	8,588	9,024	9,440	9,727	10,059	10,606	11,774	11,978
Wisconsin	793	2,225	5,020	7,806	8,634	9,004	9,240	9,755	9,993	10,372	10,791	11,183	11,507	11,946
Wyoming	805	2,369	5,239	7,425	8,645	8,985	9,308	10,190	11,437	13,266	13,856	14,628	15,232	15,815
Other jurisdictions														
American Samoa	—	—	1,781	2,739	2,906	2,976	3,493	3,607	3,561	3,481	—	—	—	—
Guam	766	—	3,817	—	—	—	5,781	—	6,781	—	—	—	—	8,443
Northern Marianas	—	—	3,356	5,120	4,438	4,519	4,241	5,034	4,924	4,707	4,535	5,753	5,676	7,623
Puerto Rico	—	—	1,605	3,404	3,563	4,260	4,147	4,979	5,470	6,006	6,520	6,955	7,021	7,429
U.S. Virgin Islands	—	—	6,043	6,478	5,716	6,840	7,239	8,387	8,768	9,669	12,358	12,768	14,215	13,689

See notes at end of table.

Current expenditure per pupil in fall enrollment in public elementary and secondary schools, by state or jurisdiction: Selected years, 1969–70 through 2010–11—Continued

State or jurisdiction	Constant 2012–13 dollars[2]													
	1969–70	1979–80	1989–90	1999–2000	2001–02	2002–03	2003–04	2004–05	2005–06	2006–07	2007–08	2008–09	2009–10	2010–11
1	16	17	18	19	20	21	22	23	24	25	26	27	28	29
United States	$4,601	$6,224	$8,459	$9,446	$10,033	$10,219	$10,332	$10,513	$10,632	$10,969	$11,254	$11,359	$11,353	$11,153
Alabama	3,133	4,531	5,728	7,705	7,827	8,003	8,182	8,537	8,933	9,518	10,050	9,661	9,508	9,131
Alaska	6,487	12,716	13,806	12,035	12,417	12,539	12,576	13,091	13,342	13,967	16,000	16,557	16,896	17,437
Arizona	4,130	5,558	6,773	6,874	7,597	7,982	7,459	7,612	7,574	8,292	8,445	8,646	8,401	8,143
Arkansas	3,129	4,386	5,884	7,212	8,148	8,235	8,506	9,244	9,336	9,510	9,482	9,543	9,907	9,937
California	5,104	6,635	8,204	8,629	9,614	9,594	9,540	9,540	9,651	10,145	10,607	10,242	9,927	9,571
Colorado	4,202	6,729	7,938	8,494	9,011	9,380	9,297	9,445	9,494	9,390	10,002	9,465	9,527	9,194
Connecticut	5,578	6,458	13,597	13,328	13,732	14,047	14,217	14,800	15,197	15,480	15,966	16,547	16,757	16,977
Delaware	5,105	7,709	9,705	11,356	12,054	12,315	12,696	13,168	13,511	13,328	13,281	13,050	13,047	13,046
District of Columbia	5,799	8,378	14,343	13,812	15,713	15,050	16,111	16,794	15,988	17,579	17,871	21,230	22,321	21,758
Florida	4,181	5,466	8,376	7,969	8,067	8,180	8,446	8,708	9,082	9,709	9,927	9,556	9,461	9,450
Georgia	3,300	4,443	7,288	8,797	9,582	9,877	9,625	9,734	9,993	10,315	10,620	10,400	10,069	9,689
Hawaii	4,850	6,218	7,525	8,924	9,486	10,291	10,609	10,858	11,482	12,825	12,895	13,364	12,654	12,478
Idaho	3,511	4,614	5,322	7,263	7,804	7,726	7,668	7,626	7,521	7,534	7,596	7,671	7,579	7,138
Illinois	4,996	6,679	8,237	9,748	10,330	10,528	10,700	10,736	10,595	10,875	11,314	11,960	12,530	12,287
Indiana	4,049	5,090	7,781	9,829	10,042	10,236	10,482	10,764	10,381	10,290	9,690	9,974	10,118	9,681
Iowa	4,888	6,449	7,634	8,970	9,527	9,621	9,481	9,609	9,713	9,963	10,403	10,459	10,405	10,249
Kansas	4,280	5,849	7,816	8,601	9,529	9,470	9,667	9,565	10,045	10,475	10,813	10,997	10,645	10,257
Kentucky	3,074	4,641	6,165	8,091	8,469	8,463	8,533	8,607	8,916	8,999	9,551	9,469	9,561	9,656
Louisiana	3,610	4,855	6,604	7,932	8,526	8,794	9,039	9,256	9,866	10,129	10,935	11,451	11,423	11,300
Maine	3,976	5,042	8,934	10,478	11,448	11,870	12,116	12,482	12,604	13,196	12,853	13,130	13,370	13,160
Maryland	4,956	6,832	10,155	10,565	11,285	11,628	11,727	12,107	12,683	13,587	14,487	14,805	14,952	14,779
Massachusetts	4,842	7,592	10,506	12,048	13,285	13,288	13,694	14,051	14,052	14,488	14,961	15,665	14,897	14,948
Michigan	5,154	7,437	9,274	11,083	11,234	11,155	11,305	11,270	11,132	11,193	11,010	11,179	11,151	11,068
Minnesota	5,235	6,844	8,560	9,826	10,044	10,302	10,449	10,522	10,648	10,868	10,994	11,837	11,384	11,169
Mississippi	2,797	4,674	5,345	6,851	6,951	7,359	7,707	7,903	8,339	8,453	8,622	8,691	8,650	8,294
Missouri	3,650	5,138	7,417	8,455	9,264	9,521	9,376	9,484	9,619	10,027	10,417	10,365	10,376	9,900
Montana	4,456	6,746	7,725	8,628	9,168	9,522	9,728	9,816	10,029	10,417	10,695	10,907	11,278	11,217
Nebraska	4,286	6,033	8,295	9,133	10,050	10,257	10,508	10,613	10,840	11,410	11,545	11,689	12,104	12,075
Nevada	4,322	5,686	6,952	7,871	7,892	7,740	7,970	8,212	8,344	8,835	8,946	8,968	8,941	8,802
New Hampshire	4,079	5,162	8,720	9,375	10,303	10,899	11,390	11,793	12,086	12,508	13,060	13,562	13,953	14,177
New Jersey	5,658	8,420	13,749	14,127	15,312	15,967	16,582	17,037	17,386	18,318	19,256	18,293	18,551	17,637
New Mexico	4,073	5,574	6,278	7,961	8,936	9,051	9,413	9,455	9,712	10,029	10,153	10,398	10,269	9,679
New York	7,315	8,793	12,847	13,455	14,564	15,196	15,712	16,538	16,992	17,619	18,353	19,126	19,392	19,708
North Carolina	3,493	4,874	7,322	8,261	8,433	8,337	8,221	8,566	8,599	8,928	8,522	9,121	8,779	8,651
North Dakota	4,057	5,786	7,104	7,744	8,710	8,727	9,117	9,992	10,147	9,827	10,189	10,564	11,229	11,404
Ohio	4,143	5,645	8,255	9,654	10,476	10,966	11,225	11,261	11,268	11,262	11,299	11,499	11,980	11,924
Oklahoma	3,391	5,393	6,000	7,372	8,088	7,739	7,651	7,978	8,070	8,420	8,396	8,491	8,464	7,986
Oregon	5,164	7,189	8,863	9,769	9,922	9,517	9,471	9,738	10,051	10,152	10,452	10,358	9,893	9,958
Pennsylvania	4,993	6,939	10,453	10,622	11,084	11,429	12,070	12,353	12,467	12,359	12,831	13,256	13,587	13,704
Rhode Island	4,941	6,974	10,765	12,169	12,597	13,147	13,773	14,081	14,659	15,246	15,801	15,864	15,716	15,642
South Carolina	3,474	4,760	6,868	8,377	9,110	8,943	8,922	9,111	9,441	9,641	9,901	9,946	9,692	9,316
South Dakota	4,019	5,307	6,397	7,697	8,340	8,317	8,787	9,008	9,040	9,139	9,327	9,207	9,628	9,346
Tennessee	3,251	4,539	6,204	7,356	7,722	7,772	8,039	8,268	8,143	8,080	8,546	8,614	8,665	8,878
Texas	3,375	5,184	6,987	8,593	8,791	9,066	8,890	8,745	8,697	8,896	9,125	9,228	9,380	9,088
Utah	3,645	4,637	4,695	5,983	6,361	6,146	6,205	6,296	6,353	6,470	6,533	7,127	6,888	6,620
Vermont	4,836	5,752	10,514	11,373	12,731	13,281	13,937	14,449	14,887	15,445	15,760	16,270	16,723	15,390
Virginia	4,008	5,436	8,545	9,349	9,732	9,937	10,218	10,724	10,989	11,576	11,654	11,778	11,309	10,844
Washington	5,225	7,113	7,985	8,714	9,139	9,213	9,189	9,313	9,283	9,660	9,898	10,331	10,138	10,066
West Virginia	3,806	5,211	7,324	9,773	10,184	10,569	10,677	10,891	10,976	11,023	10,992	11,431	12,568	12,534
Wisconsin	4,857	6,630	9,146	10,668	11,209	11,439	11,487	11,773	11,618	11,755	11,793	12,053	12,283	12,501
Wyoming	4,930	7,060	9,546	10,147	11,224	11,415	11,572	12,298	13,296	15,035	15,142	15,766	16,259	16,549
Other jurisdictions														
American Samoa	—	—	3,246	3,743	3,773	3,781	4,343	4,353	4,140	3,945	—	—	—	—
Guam	4,694	—	6,955	—	—	7,187	—	7,884	—	—	—	—	—	8,835
Northern Marianas	—	—	6,115	6,998	5,762	5,741	5,272	6,076	5,724	5,334	4,956	6,201	6,058	7,977
Puerto Rico	—	—	2,925	4,651	4,626	5,413	5,155	6,009	6,360	6,807	7,125	7,496	7,494	7,774
U.S. Virgin Islands	—	—	11,010	8,853	7,421	8,690	9,000	10,122	10,194	10,958	13,505	13,761	15,174	14,325

—Not available.

[1]Unadjusted (or "current") dollars have not been adjusted to compensate for inflation.
[2]Constant dollars based on the Consumer Price Index (CPI), prepared by the Bureau of Labor Statistics, U.S. Department of Labor, adjusted to a school-year basis. The CPI does not account for differences in inflation rates from state to state.
NOTE: Current expenditures include instruction, support services, food services, and enterprise operations. Expenditures for state administration are excluded in all years except

1969–70 and 1979–80. Beginning in 1989–90, extensive changes were made in the data collection procedures. Some data have been revised from previously published figures.
SOURCE: U.S. Department of Education, National Center for Education Statistics, *Statistics of State School Systems*, 1969–70; *Revenues and Expenditures for Public Elementary and Secondary Schools*, 1979–80; and Common Core of Data (CCD), "National Public Education Financial Survey," 1989–90 through 2010–11. (This table was prepared July 2013.)

Total and current expenditures per pupil in fall enrollment in public elementary and secondary education, by function and state or jurisdiction: 2010–11

State or jurisdiction	Total[1]	Current expenditures, capital expenditures, and interest on school debt per pupil													Capital outlay[2]	Interest on school debt
		Current expenditures														
		Total	Instruction	Support services									Food services	Enterprise operations[3]		
				Total	Student support[4]	Instructional staff[5]	General administration	School administration	Operation and maintenance	Student transportation	Other support services				
1	2	3	4	5	6	7	8	9	10	11	12	13	14	15	16
United States	**$12,048**	**$10,658**	**$6,520**	**$3,700**	**$593**	**$503**	**$212**	**$578**	**$1,015**	**$452**	**$347**	**$412**	**$25**	**$1,028**	**$363**
Alabama	9,653	8,726	5,091	3,046	506	394	209	540	786	437	174	589	0	749	178
Alaska	18,333	16,663	9,225	6,918	1,363	1,166	231	1,013	2,037	485	623	458	62	1,372	298
Arizona	9,183	7,782	4,205	3,167	1,014	182	118	366	875	302	309	367	43	807	594
Arkansas	11,120	9,496	5,425	3,531	483	813	234	480	902	357	260	528	11	1,363	262
California	10,594	9,146	5,514	3,246	478	556	88	606	906	220	392	364	23	1,075	372
Colorado	10,298	8,786	5,040	3,401	428	499	189	588	824	258	615	302	43	990	522
Connecticut	17,480	16,224	10,292	5,407	991	502	319	920	1,503	803	370	391	134	1,004	252
Delaware	14,117	12,467	7,871	4,144	586	163	171	686	1,243	728	567	452	0	1,466	183
District of Columbia	28,403	20,793	10,584	9,409	1,208	1,613	866	1,546	2,321	1,404	450	761	40	5,487	2,124
Florida	10,162	9,030	5,511	3,116	403	583	96	508	935	363	228	404	0	838	294
Georgia	10,227	9,259	5,765	2,987	438	463	140	556	690	392	308	481	26	816	152
Hawaii	12,946	11,924	6,919	4,359	1,119	398	60	764	1,399	370	250	646	0	475	547
Idaho	7,624	6,821	4,162	2,311	387	273	155	383	622	332	160	347	1	580	222
Illinois	13,135	11,742	7,025	4,360	793	506	478	598	1,058	551	376	357	0	1,000	393
Indiana	10,405	9,251	5,445	3,395	436	351	240	533	1,048	556	231	411	0	831	323
Iowa	11,757	9,795	6,040	3,310	553	466	253	554	833	358	293	435	10	1,756	206
Kansas	12,033	9,802	5,941	3,415	569	418	289	561	917	396	265	447	0	1,798	433
Kentucky	10,570	9,228	5,410	3,265	416	502	204	513	856	560	215	530	23	1,109	234
Louisiana	12,141	10,799	6,288	3,938	531	589	255	628	1,006	625	306	572	0	1,167	175
Maine	13,761	12,576	7,628	4,544	822	656	403	676	1,232	603	151	404	0	911	274
Maryland	15,516	14,123	8,712	4,869	620	785	109	978	1,256	718	403	366	176	1,199	194
Massachusetts	15,342	14,285	9,280	4,625	997	640	191	580	1,297	586	334	380	0	794	263
Michigan	12,041	10,577	6,095	4,118	800	561	216	576	991	445	529	364	31	902	562
Minnesota	12,406	10,674	7,027	3,161	282	450	322	427	772	595	314	455	31	1,252	481
Mississippi	8,643	7,926	4,582	2,853	382	403	235	457	816	380	179	490	1	572	145
Missouri	10,746	9,461	5,669	3,364	442	424	299	541	948	484	227	428	0	929	356
Montana	11,572	10,719	6,416	3,836	662	407	308	572	1,121	510	256	442	25	739	113
Nebraska	13,072	11,540	7,645	3,121	418	354	358	438	990	328	236	474	299	1,248	285
Nevada	9,650	8,411	5,010	3,121	430	445	105	599	885	349	309	279	0	679	559
New Hampshire	14,836	13,548	8,793	4,394	976	419	441	719	1,119	575	144	361	0	1,058	230
New Jersey	17,940	16,855	10,131	6,174	1,633	522	344	797	1,673	834	370	364	186	609	476
New Mexico	10,759	9,250	5,303	3,525	961	261	209	553	954	306	281	417	5	1,509	0
New York	20,174	18,834	13,160	5,296	625	486	360	719	1,668	982	457	377	0	915	425
North Carolina	8,862	8,267	5,167	2,653	390	303	133	515	710	353	250	446	0	589	6
North Dakota	12,362	10,898	6,307	3,705	488	369	508	537	1,059	467	278	562	324	1,281	183
Ohio	13,130	11,395	6,483	4,536	723	761	341	645	1,016	541	508	375	1	1,427	308
Oklahoma	8,493	7,631	4,337	2,773	518	311	251	404	805	250	234	448	74	770	92
Oregon	10,821	9,516	5,546	3,622	679	384	125	596	785	436	617	342	5	808	497
Pennsylvania	14,956	13,096	8,020	4,580	678	483	386	574	1,298	663	498	439	57	1,265	595
Rhode Island	15,624	14,948	9,210	5,365	1,569	547	206	710	1,225	575	533	365	7	332	344
South Carolina	10,821	8,903	5,082	3,333	654	546	99	537	867	353	277	462	26	1,357	561
South Dakota	10,658	8,931	5,282	3,143	496	372	294	440	916	319	306	458	49	1,508	218
Tennessee	9,325	8,484	5,393	2,682	347	519	172	471	727	297	149	410	0	648	193
Texas	10,611	8,685	5,211	3,001	422	451	127	482	947	245	327	473	0	1,328	598
Utah	7,749	6,326	4,069	1,886	245	251	72	385	573	197	162	343	27	1,195	228
Vermont	15,511	14,707	9,045	5,241	1,153	658	328	983	1,269	504	347	413	8	659	145
Virginia	11,360	10,363	6,282	3,678	501	689	159	600	1,009	556	163	402	1	859	139
Washington	11,465	9,619	5,813	3,369	644	386	184	548	859	392	357	321	116	1,451	396
West Virginia	12,263	11,978	7,175	4,167	541	473	234	640	1,194	879	206	636	0	231	54
Wisconsin	12,823	11,946	7,309	4,218	567	583	312	584	1,074	480	618	418	0	620	257
Wyoming	18,474	15,815	9,351	5,975	918	1,033	323	841	1,529	727	605	477	11	2,640	19
Other jurisdictions															
American Samoa	—	—	—	—	—	—	—	—	—	—	—	—	—	—	—
Guam	10,825	8,443	4,722	3,336	877	168	70	521	1,109	241	349	385	0	2,283	99
Northern Marianas	7,726	7,623	3,243	3,610	1,028	437	283	395	765	188	515	770	0	103	0
Puerto Rico	7,561	7,429	3,082	3,757	498	610	699	304	848	154	644	590	0	131	0
U.S. Virgin Islands	13,695	13,689	6,974	5,921	1,021	382	484	714	913	974	1,433	748	45	6	0

—Not available.

[1] Excludes "Other current expenditures," such as community services, private school programs, adult education, and other programs not allocable to expenditures per pupil in public schools.

[2] Includes expenditures for property and for buildings and alterations completed by school district staff or contractors.

[3] Includes expenditures for operations funded by sales of products or services (e.g., school bookstore or computer time). Includes very small amounts for direct program support made by state education agencies for local school districts.

[4] Includes expenditures for guidance, health, attendance, and speech pathology services.

[5] Includes expenditures for curriculum development, staff training, libraries, and media and computer centers.

NOTE: Excludes expenditures for state education agencies. "0" indicates none or less than $0.50. Detail may not sum to totals because of rounding.

SOURCE: U.S. Department of Education, National Center for Education Statistics, Common Core of Data (CCD), "National Public Education Financial Survey," 2010–11. (This table was prepared July 2013.)

Students transported at public expense and current expenditures for transportation: Selected years, 1929–30 through 2010–11

School year	Average daily attendance, all students	Students transported at public expense		Expenditures for transportation (in unadjusted dollars)[1]		Expenditures for transportation (in constant 2012–13 dollars)[2]	
		Number	Percent of total	Total[3] (in thousands)	Average per student transported	Total[3] (in thousands)	Average per student transported
1	2	3	4	5	6	7	8
1929–30	21,265,000	1,902,826	8.9	$54,823	$29	$740,983	$389
1931–32	22,245,000	2,419,173	10.9	58,078	24	931,987	385
1933–34	22,458,000	2,794,724	12.4	53,908	19	941,831	337
1935–36	22,299,000	3,250,658	14.6	62,653	19	1,054,788	324
1937–38	22,298,000	3,769,242	16.9	75,637	20	1,221,555	324
1939–40	22,042,000	4,144,161	18.8	83,283	20	1,378,725	333
1941–42	21,031,000	4,503,081	21.4	92,922	21	1,378,764	306
1943–44	19,603,000	4,512,412	23.0	107,754	24	1,430,652	317
1945–46	19,849,000	5,056,966	25.5	129,756	26	1,645,615	325
1947–48	20,910,000	5,854,041	28.0	176,265	30	1,750,183	299
1949–50	22,284,000	6,947,384	31.2	214,504	31	2,095,424	302
1951–52	23,257,000	7,697,130	33.1	268,827	35	2,366,308	307
1953–54	25,643,871	8,411,719	32.8	307,437	37	2,644,882	314
1955–56	27,740,149	9,695,819	35.0	353,972	37	3,046,242	314
1957–58	29,722,275	10,861,689	36.5	416,491	38	3,374,047	311
1959–60	32,477,440	12,225,142	37.6	486,338	40	3,829,264	313
1961–62	34,682,340	13,222,667	38.1	576,361	44	4,436,166	335
1963–64	37,405,058	14,475,778	38.7	673,845	47	5,054,646	349
1965–66	39,154,497	15,536,567	39.7	787,358	51	5,708,814	367
1967–68	40,827,965	17,130,873	42.0	981,006	57	6,673,656	390
1969–70	41,934,376	18,198,577	43.4	1,218,557	67	7,463,020	410
1971–72	42,254,272	19,474,355	46.1	1,507,830	77	8,477,266	435
1973–74	41,438,054	21,347,039	51.5	1,858,141	87	9,220,046	432
1975–76	41,269,720	21,772,483	52.8	2,377,313	109	9,917,345	455
1977–78	40,079,590	21,800,000 [4]	54.4	2,731,041	125 [4]	10,087,842	463 [4]
1979–80	38,288,911	21,713,515	56.7	3,833,145	177	11,423,052	526
1980–81	37,703,744	22,272,000 [4]	59.1	4,408,000 [4]	198 [4]	11,772,579 [4]	529 [4]
1981–82	37,094,652	22,246,000 [4]	60.0	4,793,000 [4]	215 [4]	11,782,953 [4]	530 [4]
1982–83	36,635,868	22,199,000 [4]	60.6	5,000,000 [4]	225 [4]	11,785,634 [4]	531 [4]
1983–84	36,362,978	22,031,000 [4]	60.6	5,284,000 [4]	240 [4]	12,010,493 [4]	545 [4]
1984–85	36,404,261	22,320,000 [4]	61.3	5,722,000 [4]	256 [4]	12,516,155 [4]	561 [4]
1985–86	36,523,103	22,041,000 [4]	60.3	6,123,000 [4]	278 [4]	13,017,895 [4]	591 [4]
1986–87	36,863,867	22,397,000 [4]	60.8	6,551,000 [4]	292 [4]	13,625,336 [4]	608 [4]
1987–88	37,050,707	22,158,000 [4]	59.8	6,888,000 [4]	311 [4]	13,756,259 [4]	621 [4]
1988–89	37,268,072	22,635,000 [4]	60.7	7,550,000 [4]	334 [4]	14,412,730 [4]	637 [4]
1989–90	37,799,296	22,459,000 [4]	59.4	8,030,990	358 [4]	14,632,689	652 [4]
1990–91	38,426,543	22,000,000 [4]	57.3	8,678,954	394 [4]	14,993,567	682 [4]
1991–92	38,960,783	23,165,000 [4]	59.5	8,769,754	379 [4]	14,680,048	634 [4]
1992–93	39,570,462	23,439,000 [4]	59.2	9,252,300	395 [4]	15,018,686	641 [4]
1993–94	40,146,393	23,858,000 [4]	59.4	9,627,155	404 [4]	15,232,576	638 [4]
1994–95	40,720,763	23,693,000 [4]	58.2	9,889,034	417 [4]	15,210,944	642 [4]
1995–96	41,501,596	24,155,000 [4]	58.2	10,396,426	430 [4]	15,567,857	644 [4]
1996–97	42,262,004	24,090,000 [4]	57.0	10,989,809	456 [4]	15,999,914	664 [4]
1997–98	42,765,774	24,342,000 [4]	56.9	11,465,658	471 [4]	16,400,211	674 [4]
1998–99	43,186,715	24,898,000 [4]	57.7	12,224,454	491 [4]	17,188,025	690 [4]
1999–2000	43,806,726	24,951,000 [4]	57.0	13,007,625	521 [4]	17,776,033	712 [4]
2000–01	44,075,930	24,471,000 [4]	55.5	14,052,654	574 [4]	18,568,008	759 [4]
2001–02	44,604,592	24,529,000 [5]	55.0	14,799,365	603 [5]	19,214,459	783 [5]
2002–03	45,017,360	24,621,000 [5]	54.7	15,648,821	636 [5]	19,880,433	807 [5]
2003–04	45,325,731	25,159,000 [5]	55.5	16,348,784	650 [5]	20,325,021	808 [5]
2004–05	45,625,458	25,318,000 [5]	55.5	17,459,659	690 [5]	21,071,964	832 [5]
2005–06	45,931,617	25,252,000 [5]	55.0	18,850,234	746 [5]	21,915,651	868 [5]
2006–07	46,132,663	25,285,000 [5]	54.8	19,979,068	790 [5]	22,642,513	895 [5]
2007–08	46,155,880	25,221,000 [5]	54.6	21,536,978	854 [4]	23,536,022	933 [4]
2008–09	46,173,477	—	—	21,679,876	860 [4]	23,365,924	927 [4]
2009–10	45,919,206	—	—	21,819,304	870 [4]	23,290,837	929 [4]
2010–11	46,168,400	—	—	22,345,048	886 [4]	23,382,522	928 [4]

—Not available.

[1] Unadjusted (or "current") dollars have not been adjusted to compensate for inflation.
[2] Constant dollars based on the Consumer Price Index, prepared by the Bureau of Labor Statistics, U.S. Department of Labor, adjusted to a school-year basis.
[3] Excludes capital outlay for years through 1979–80, and 1989–90 to the latest year. From 1980–81 to 1988–89 total transportation figures include capital outlay.
[4] Estimate based on data appearing in January issues of *School Bus Fleet.*
[5] Estimate based on data reported by *School Transportation News.*
NOTE: Some data have been revised from previously published figures.

SOURCE: U.S. Department of Education, National Center for Education Statistics, *Statistics of State School Systems,* 1929–30 through 1975–76; *Revenues and Expenditures for Public Elementary and Secondary Education,* 1977–78 and 1979–80; Common Core of Data (CCD), "National Public Education Financial Survey," 1987–88 through 2010–11; Bobit Publishing Co., *School Bus Fleet,* "School Transportation: 2000–2001 School Year" and *"2010 Fact Book"*; *School Transportation News,* "K–12 Enrollment/Transportation Data," 2001–02 through 2007–08; and unpublished data. (This table was prepared July 2013.)

Number of public school districts and public and private elementary and secondary schools: Selected years, 1869–70 through 2011–12

School year	Regular public school districts[1]	Total, all public and private schools	Total, all public schools[4]	Total, schools with reported grade spans[5]	Schools with elementary grades — Total	Schools with elementary grades — One-teacher	Schools with secondary grades	Total, all private schools	Private — Schools with elementary grades	Private — Schools with secondary grades
1	2	3	4	5	6	7	8	9	10	11
1869–70	—	—	116,312	—	—	—	—	—	—	—
1879–80	—	—	178,122	—	—	—	—	—	—	—
1889–90	—	—	224,526	—	—	—	—	—	—	—
1899–1900	—	—	248,279	—	—	—	—	—	—	—
1909–10	—	—	265,474	—	—	212,448	—	—	—	—
1919–20	—	—	271,319	—	—	187,948	—	—	—	—
1929–30	—	—	248,117	—	238,306	148,712	23,930	—	9,275 [6]	3,258 [6]
1939–40	117,108 [7]	—	226,762	—	—	113,600	—	—	11,306 [6]	3,568 [6]
1949–50	83,718 [7]	—	—	—	128,225	59,652	24,542	—	10,375 [6]	3,331 [6]
1951–52	71,094 [7]	—	—	—	123,763	50,742	23,746	—	10,666 [6]	3,322 [6]
1959–60	40,520 [7]	—	—	—	91,853	20,213	25,784	—	13,574 [6]	4,061 [6]
1961–62	35,676 [7]	125,634	107,260	—	81,910	13,333	25,350	18,374	14,762 [6]	4,129 [6]
1963–64	31,705 [7]	—	104,015	—	77,584	9,895	26,431	—	—	4,451 [6]
1965–66	26,983 [7]	117,662	99,813	—	73,216	6,491	26,597	17,849 [6]	15,340 [6]	4,606 [6]
1967–68	22,010 [7]	—	—	94,197	70,879	4,146	27,011	—	—	—
1970–71	17,995 [7]	—	—	89,372	65,800	1,815	25,352	—	14,372 [6]	3,770 [6]
1973–74	16,730 [7]	—	—	88,655	65,070	1,365	25,906	—	—	—
1975–76	16,376 [7]	—	88,597	87,034	63,242	1,166	25,330	—	—	—
1976–77	16,271 [7]	—	—	86,501	62,644	1,111	25,378	19,910 [6]	16,385 [6]	5,904 [6]
1978–79	16,014 [7]	—	—	84,816	61,982	1,056	24,504	19,489 [6]	16,097 [6]	5,766 [6]
1979–80	15,944 [7]	—	87,004	—	—	—	—	—	—	—
1980–81	15,912 [7]	106,746	85,982	83,688	61,069	921	24,362	20,764 [6]	16,792 [6]	5,678 [6]
1982–83	15,824 [7]	—	84,740	82,039	59,656	798	23,988	—	—	—
1983–84	15,747 [7]	111,872	84,178	81,418	59,082	838	23,947	27,694	20,872	7,862
1984–85	—	—	84,007	81,147	58,827	825	23,916	—	—	—
1985–86	—	—	—	—	—	—	—	25,616	20,252	7,387
1986–87	15,713	—	83,421	82,316	60,811	763	23,481	—	—	—
1987–88	15,577	110,055	83,248	81,416	59,754	729	23,841	26,807	22,959	8,418
1988–89	15,376	—	83,165	81,579	60,176	583	23,638	—	—	—
1989–90	15,367	110,137	83,425	81,880	60,699	630	23,461	26,712	24,221	10,197
1990–91	15,358	109,228	84,538	82,475	61,340	617	23,460	24,690	22,223	8,989
1991–92	15,173	110,576	84,578	82,506	61,739	569	23,248	25,998	23,523	9,282
1992–93	15,025	—	84,497	82,896	62,225	430	23,220	—	—	—
1993–94	14,881	111,486	85,393	83,431	62,726	442	23,379	26,093	23,543	10,555
1994–95	14,772	—	86,221	84,476	63,572	458	23,668	—	—	—
1995–96	14,766	121,519	87,125	84,958	63,961	474	23,793	34,394	32,401	10,942
1996–97	14,841	—	88,223	86,092	64,785	487	24,287	—	—	—
1997–98	14,805	123,403	89,508	87,541	65,859	476	24,802	33,895	31,408	10,779
1998–99	14,891	—	90,874	89,259	67,183	463	25,797	—	—	—
1999–2000	14,928	125,007	92,012	90,538	68,173	423	26,407	32,995	30,457	10,693
2000–01	14,859	—	93,273	91,691	69,697	411	27,090	—	—	—
2001–02	14,559	130,007	94,112	92,696	70,516	408	27,468	35,895	33,191	11,846
2002–03	14,465	—	95,615	93,869	71,270	366	28,151	—	—	—
2003–04	14,383	130,407	95,726	93,977	71,195	376	28,219	34,681	31,988	11,188
2004–05	14,205	—	96,513	95,001	71,556	338	29,017	—	—	—
2005–06	14,166	132,436	97,382	95,731	71,733	326	29,705	35,054	32,127	12,184
2006–07	13,856	—	98,793	96,362	72,442	313	29,904	—	—	—
2007–08	13,838	132,656	98,916	97,654	73,011	288	30,542	33,740	30,808	11,870
2008–09	13,809	—	98,706	97,119	72,771	237	29,971	—	—	—
2009–10	13,625	132,183	98,817	97,521	72,870	217	30,381	33,366	30,590	11,491
2010–11	13,588	—	98,817	97,767	73,323	224	30,681	—	—	—
2011–12	13,567	129,189	98,328	97,357	73,000	205	30,668	30,861	28,184	11,165

—Not available.

[1]Regular districts exclude regional education service agencies and supervisory union administrative centers, state-operated agencies, federally operated agencies, and other types of local education agencies, such as independent charter schools.

[2]Schools with both elementary and secondary programs are included under elementary schools and also under secondary schools.

[3]Data for most years prior to 1976–77 are partly estimated. Prior to 1995–96, excludes schools with highest grade of kindergarten.

[4]Includes regular schools and special schools not classified by grade span.

[5]Includes elementary, secondary, and combined elementary/secondary schools.

[6]These data cannot be compared directly with the data for years after 1980–81.

[7]Because of expanded survey coverage, data are not directly comparable with figures after 1983–84.

SOURCE: U.S. Department of Education, National Center for Education Statistics, *Annual Report of the Commissioner of Education*, 1870 through 1910; *Biennial Survey of Education in the United States*, 1919–20 through 1949–50; *Statistics of State School Systems*, 1951–52 through 1967–68; *Statistics of Public Elementary and Secondary School Systems*, 1970–71 through 1980–81; *Statistics of Public and Nonpublic Elementary and Secondary Day Schools*, 1968–69; *Statistics of Nonpublic Elementary and Secondary Schools*, 1970–71; *Private Schools in American Education*; Schools and Staffing Survey (SASS), "Private School Questionnaire," 1987–88 and 1990–91; Private School Universe Survey (PSS), 1989–90 through 2009–10; and Common Core of Data (CCD), "Local Education Agency Universe Survey" and "Public Elementary/Secondary School Universe Survey," 1982–83 through 2011–12. (This table was prepared September 2013.)

Selected statistics on enrollment, teachers, dropouts, and graduates in public school districts enrolling more than 15,000 students: Selected years, 1990 through 2011

Column groups: columns "White" through "Two or more races" fall under **Percentage distribution of enrollment, by race/ethnicity, fall 2011**; "Number of classroom teachers" through "Teachers as a percentage of total staff" fall under **Teachers and staff, fall 2011**; "Percent dropping out of grades 9–12" through "Number of high school graduates, 2008–09" fall under **Dropouts and graduates**.

Name of district	State	Enrollment, fall 1990	Enrollment, fall 2000	Enrollment, fall 2010	Enrollment, fall 2011	Number of English language learners, 2011	Percent eligible for free or reduced-price lunch, 2011[1]	White	Black	Hispanic	Asian	Pacific Islander	American Indian/Alaska Native	Two or more races	Number of classroom teachers	Pupil/teacher ratio	Total number of staff	Student/staff ratio	Teachers as a percentage of total staff	Percent dropping out of grades 9–12	Averaged freshman graduation rate (AFGR)[2]	Number of high school graduates, 2008–09[3]	Number of schools, fall 2011
1	2	3	4	5	6	7	8	9	10	11	12	13	14	15	16	17	18	19	20	21	22	23	24
Districts with more than 15,000 students[4]	†	16,867,272	20,275,399	21,791,371	21,844,210	2,825,519	51.5	35.6	21.3	32.6	6.4	0.6	0.7	2.8	1,286,083	16.9	2,474,035	8.8	52.0	—	—	—	32,652
Baldwin County	AL	17,479	22,656	28,199	28,700	648	40.8	78.5	13.8	4.7	0.9	0.1	0.6	1.4	1,680	17.1	3,267	8.8	51.4	0.7	72.5	1,549	47
Birmingham City	AL	41,710	37,843	25,914	25,091	523	88.7	1.0	95.2	3.2	0.2	#	#	0.3	1,516	16.6	2,916	8.6	52.0	4.3	47.4	1,210	81
Huntsville City	AL	24,024	22,832	23,364	22,974	724	48.5	46.5	42.7	6.2	2.3	0.2	0.5	1.6	1,525	15.1	2,661	8.6	57.3	1.5	68.1	1,351	50
Jefferson County	AL	40,752	40,726	35,860	35,978	848	56.3	49.9	43.0	5.6	0.5	0.2	0.2	0.8	2,313	15.6	4,511	8.0	51.3	1.5	68.9	2,194	62
Madison County	AL	13,861	15,675	19,897	20,012	124	34.2	69.8	19.0	2.7	1.6	#	5.4	1.5	1,252	16.0	2,417	8.3	51.8	1.9	71.7	1,142	29
Mobile County	AL	67,286	64,976	62,016	61,462	914	71.3	43.4	50.7	2.0	2.3	#	1.1	0.5	3,838	16.0	7,961	7.7	48.2	1.4	65.2	3,369	109
Montgomery County	AL	35,973	33,267	31,464	31,359	1,183	72.8	14.1	78.0	4.0	3.0	#	0.1	0.8	1,854	16.9	3,747	8.4	49.5	0.6	52.4	1,279	63
Shelby County	AL	16,096	20,129	28,063	28,304	1,400	34.2	73.4	14.6	8.9	1.9	#	0.1	1.1	1,852	15.3	3,667	7.7	50.5	0.6	83.3	1,597	41
Tuscaloosa County	AL	14,514	15,666	17,785	17,631	293	52.7	67.3	28.0	3.2	0.6	#	0.2	0.7	1,108	15.9	2,062	8.6	53.7	2.9	69.4	878	34
Anchorage	AK	41,992	49,526	49,206	48,765	5,291	40.4	46.2	6.3	10.5	10.6	4.4	8.7	13.2	2,967	16.4	6,145	7.9	48.3	4.7	74.9	2,967	97
Matanuska-Susitna Borough	AK	9,810	13,008	17,079	17,480	435	32.8	74.7	2.3	3.0	2.8	1.1	16.0	0.1	914	19.1	1,853	9.4	49.3	7.0	76.4	1,012	44
Cartwright Elementary	AZ	14,368	17,746	17,672	18,359	4,806	89.5	4.5	4.5	88.7	0.4	0.1	1.2	0.7	1,167	15.7	2,124	8.6	55.0	—	—	—	21
Chandler Unified	AZ	11,041	21,703	38,876	39,555	1,768	27.7	57.1	6.5	25.9	8.1	0.2	1.7	0.6	1,961	20.2	3,621	10.9	54.2	4.1	85.6	2,083	42
Deer Valley Unified	AZ	15,899	27,158	35,190	34,662	867	20.7	71.9	2.9	17.8	3.4	0.4	0.9	2.7	1,776	19.5	3,275	10.6	54.2	2.7	76.3	2,182	38
Dysart Unified	AZ	3,804	5,459	24,175	24,756	878	51.3	50.3	8.1	35.6	2.6	0.2	1.0	2.4	1,237	20.0	2,143	11.6	57.7	3.7	88.4	1,084	25
Gilbert Unified	AZ	10,862	29,188	38,086	38,311	684	16.8	70.3	4.1	18.4	4.8	0.3	1.0	1.2	1,991	19.2	3,836	10.0	51.9	4.1	84.8	2,503	44
Kyrene Elementary	AZ	10,483	19,446	17,815	17,831	357	27.9	54.1	10.1	21.7	7.4	0.2	3.4	2.9	1,145	15.6	1,990	9.0	57.5	—	—	†	26
Mesa Unified	AZ	62,748	73,587	65,123	64,728	4,560	56.9	49.8	4.5	38.5	2.3	#	4.2	0.7	3,224	20.1	6,700	9.7	48.1	5.3	68.8	4,068	84
Paradise Valley Unified	AZ	26,696	34,882	33,017	33,017	1,846	32.7	62.1	3.0	26.8	3.4	0.2	1.1	3.5	1,787	18.5	2,955	11.2	60.5	2.0	78.7	2,263	48
Peoria Unified School	AZ	20,850	32,608	36,873	36,620	950	38.6	59.4	4.7	29.1	2.6	0.4	0.9	2.8	2,308	15.9	4,234	8.6	54.5	2.1	80.9	2,679	41
Phoenix Union High	AZ	18,297	22,192	24,949	25,881	1,139	78.1	5.9	9.5	78.8	2.4	0.1	2.8	0.5	1,412	18.3	2,188	11.8	64.5	4.1	—	4,260	15
Scottsdale Unified	AZ	19,752	26,958	26,235	25,762	936	24.3	69.4	3.4	19.0	5.1	0.1	2.1	0.9	1,654	15.6	3,087	8.3	53.6	2.2	89.1	1,924	31
Sunnyside Unified	AZ	13,067	14,518	17,323	17,615	2,749	7.3	4.6	2.3	88.2	0.5	0.4	3.9	0.3	931	18.9	1,925	9.2	48.4	8.0	57.0	746	22
Tucson Unified	AZ	56,174	61,869	53,275	51,720	4,159	59.8	24.4	5.5	61.2	2.0	0.4	3.9	2.7	2,875	18.0	5,432	9.5	52.9	4.5	69.0	3,317	104
Washington Elementary	AZ	22,446	24,723	22,349	22,456	3,552	77.5	34.1	7.7	49.7	2.9	0.2	4.1	1.3	1,225	18.3	2,437	9.2	50.3	—	—	†	32
Little Rock	AR	25,813	25,502	25,685	25,537	2,085	71.0	20.2	66.7	9.8	2.2	#	0.3	0.8	1,737	14.7	3,867	6.6	44.9	3.0	65.6	1,355	49
Pulaski County Special	AR	21,495	18,735	17,501	17,637	372	55.0	47.8	42.6	5.8	2.1	0.1	0.3	1.3	1,189	14.8	2,098	8.4	56.7	5.5	59.6	875	36
Springdale	AR	7,877	11,422	19,411	19,976	8,298	66.6	41.2	2.2	44.2	1.8	8.6	0.5	1.5	1,184	16.9	2,378	8.4	49.8	4.0	74.2	868	26
ABC Unified	CA	20,972	22,303	20,682	20,688	4,404	18.9	7.4	9.5	43.0	36.6	0.8	0.3	2.4	823	25.1	1,695	12.2	48.5	—	—	—	31
Alhambra Unified	CA	20,313	19,776	18,413	18,290	5,670	63.1	2.9	0.7	42.4	52.2	0.1	0.2	1.6	709	25.8	1,433	12.8	49.5	—	—	—	18
Alvord Unified	CA	14,853	17,664	19,803	19,741	8,585	37.8	11.9	4.1	77.2	4.9	0.4	0.3	1.2	733	26.9	1,417	13.9	51.7	—	—	—	21
Anaheim City	CA	14,972	22,275	19,095	19,312	12,315	83.1	4.6	1.5	86.2	6.3	0.6	0.3	0.6	747	25.9	1,474	13.1	50.7	—	—	—	24
Anaheim Union High	CA	23,086	29,363	33,156	32,704	7,690	14.6	12.9	2.9	65.2	16.0	0.8	0.2	2.0	1,264	25.9	2,566	12.7	49.3	—	—	—	21
Antelope Valley Union High	CA	10,937	19,056	26,084	25,543	3,377	18.0	19.8	18.7	54.9	2.9	0.3	0.8	2.4	1,052	24.3	2,197	11.6	47.9	—	—	—	14
Antioch Unified	CA	13,045	19,081	19,081	18,877	2,789	25.7	21.5	24.1	37.8	9.6	1.0	0.8	5.2	806	23.4	1,538	12.3	52.4	—	—	—	28
Bakersfield City	CA	24,911	27,674	27,590	28,321	9,026	61.1	10.4	8.8	77.7	1.3	0.1	0.7	1.1	1,298	21.8	2,335	12.1	55.6	—	—	†	41
Baldwin Park Unified	CA	15,878	17,473	19,923	19,238	5,521	32.3	3.7	3.6	86.4	5.5	0.1	0.2	0.5	883	21.8	1,527	12.6	57.8	—	—	—	22
Burbank Unified	CA	12,057	16,170	16,630	16,670	1,792	28.7	44.7	2.4	39.2	9.7	0.1	0.2	3.6	673	24.8	1,259	13.2	53.4	—	—	—	22
Cajon Valley Union	CA	17,328	19,059	16,065	16,057	5,341	72.8	46.5	7.1	36.6	2.9	0.5	0.5	6.0	668	24.1	1,335	12.0	50.0	—	—	—	30
Capistrano Unified	CA	13,505	45,074	53,192	53,170	5,496	22.3	61.1	1.3	24.8	7.0	0.1	0.3	5.4	2,003	26.5	3,810	14.0	52.6	—	—	—	63
Chaffey Joint Union High	CA	23,257	19,851	25,427	25,065	3,052	5.3	19.3	9.1	62.0	7.0	0.6	0.3	1.7	924	27.1	1,677	14.9	55.1	—	—	—	10
Chino Valley Unified	CA	23,224	31,763	31,608	31,313	4,499	19.3	22.2	3.8	55.9	7.0	0.2	0.2	2.2	1,161	27.0	2,283	13.7	50.9	—	—	—	36
Chula Vista Elementary	CA	23,224	33,132	27,723	28,101	10,298	48.7	13.2	4.1	68.3	15.5	0.6	0.2	3.0	1,352	20.8	2,688	10.5	50.3	—	—	—	45
Clovis Unified	CA	16,415	38,717	38,495	39,040	2,556	14.8	46.5	3.3	31.6	13.0	0.2	0.8	1.1	1,483	26.3	3,263	12.0	45.4	—	—	—	47
Coachella Valley Unified	CA	9,091	12,636	18,464	18,406	10,571	83.3	1.4	0.2	96.6	0.3	#	0.4	0.6	834	22.1	1,600	11.5	52.1	—	—	—	23
Colton Joint Unified	CA	27,585	22,118	23,382	23,192	6,574	25.0	8.0	5.9	81.8	2.9	0.4	0.5	3.3	987	23.5	1,882	12.3	52.4	—	—	—	26
Compton Unified	CA	17,209	31,037	24,224	24,781	11,286	44.1	0.3	16.9	78.8	0.1	0.5	0.1	0.2	1,066	23.3	2,432	10.2	43.8	—	—	—	38
Conejo Valley Unified	CA	23,036	20,999	21,091	20,722	2,247	34.7	62.6	1.6	22.2	10.3	0.2	0.5	2.6	888	23.3	1,526	13.6	58.2	—	—	—	27
Corona-Norco Unified	CA	23,036	37,487	53,149	53,467	7,556	22.5	30.5	6.2	50.9	10.0	0.4	0.3	1.7	2,140	25.0	4,006	13.3	53.4	—	—	—	52

See notes at end of table.

Selected statistics on enrollment, teachers, dropouts, and graduates in public school districts enrolling more than 15,000 students: Selected years, 1990 through 2011—Continued

Columns 9–15 are the "Percentage distribution of enrollment, by race/ethnicity, fall 2011." Columns 16–20 are "Teachers and staff, fall 2011." Columns 21–23 are "Dropouts and graduates, 2008–09."

Name of district	State	Enrollment, fall 1990	Enrollment, fall 2000	Enrollment, fall 2010	Enrollment, fall 2011	Number of English language learners, 2011	Percent eligible for free or reduced-price lunch, 2011	White	Black	Hispanic	Asian	Pacific Islander	American Indian/Alaska Native	Two or more races	Number of classroom teachers	Pupil/teacher ratio	Total number of staff	Student/staff ratio	Teachers as a percentage of total staff	Percent dropping out of grades 9-12	Averaged freshman graduation rate (AFGR)	Number of high school graduates	Number of schools, fall 2011
1	2	3	4	5	6	7	8	9	10	11	12	13	14	15	16	17	18	19	20	21	22	23	24
Cupertino Union	CA	12,227	15,670	18,370	18,650	1,654	4.4	19.2	1.0	5.3	72.8	0.2	0.2	1.2	768	24.3	1,361	13.7	56.5	—	—	—	25
Desert Sands Unified	CA	16,058	23,500	29,199	29,123	7,221	51.6	23.3	2.0	70.0	2.6	0.1	0.3	1.6	1,116	26.2	2,070	14.1	53.9	—	—	—	34
Downey Unified	CA	15,418	21,474	22,844	22,782	4,245	13.1	7.0	3.1	85.9	3.2	0.3	0.3	0.2	862	26.4	1,497	15.2	57.6	—	—	—	20
East Side Union High	CA	21,973	24,282	25,676	25,638	4,809	23.6	7.9	3.3	48.1	38.1	0.8	0.4	1.5	1,089	23.5	1,788	14.3	60.9	—	—	—	21
Elk Grove Unified	CA	27,246	47,736	62,455	62,126	10,860	28.8	23.7	15.6	25.5	26.4	1.8	0.6	6.4	2,610	23.8	4,928	12.6	53.0	—	—	—	66
Escondido Union	CA	14,663	19,312	19,242	19,093	8,770	63.4	21.1	2.0	64.8	4.1	0.2	0.2	7.5	808	23.6	1,650	11.6	49.0	—	—	—	25
Fairfield-Suisun Unified	CA	20,227	22,263	21,534	21,577	3,421	28.8	20.0	18.0	36.2	13.6	1.1	1.1	10.0	834	25.9	1,524	14.2	54.7	—	—	—	29
Folsom-Cordova Unified	CA	12,656	16,277	18,893	19,154	2,091	32.6	58.1	7.3	16.9	13.4	0.8	0.7	2.8	767	25.0	1,457	13.1	52.7	—	—	—	33
Fontana Unified	CA	27,043	37,244	40,841	40,592	15,369	17.3	5.2	6.3	85.1	2.3	0.3	0.2	0.4	1,640	24.8	3,268	12.4	50.2	—	—	—	43
Fremont Unified	CA	27,172	31,078	32,607	32,829	5,766	17.2	18.5	4.5	15.4	59.7	0.9	0.5	0.4	1,397	23.5	2,245	14.6	62.2	—	—	—	41
Fresno Unified	CA	71,500	79,007	74,633	74,235	17,536	63.6	12.6	9.9	63.4	12.5	0.4	0.6	0.7	3,053	24.3	6,642	11.2	46.0	—	—	—	106
Garden Grove Unified	CA	37,969	48,742	48,659	47,999	20,743	49.0	10.6	0.8	53.4	33.8	0.8	0.2	0.3	1,823	26.3	3,553	13.5	51.3	—	—	—	68
Glendale Unified	CA	25,459	30,329	26,371	26,228	7,126	45.1	55.0	1.3	23.1	18.8	0.1	0.2	1.5	1,099	23.9	2,084	12.6	52.7	—	—	—	33
Grossmont Union High	CA	18,647	23,639	24,224	23,677	2,972	24.8	48.4	7.1	32.9	3.3	0.8	0.8	6.7	974	24.3	1,933	12.3	50.4	—	—	—	20
Hacienda La Puente Unified	CA	23,267	24,646	20,942	20,849	4,395	46.2	4.3	1.1	79.9	13.4	0.4	0.2	0.8	904	23.1	1,960	10.6	46.1	—	—	—	36
Hayward Unified	CA	19,122	24,205	21,744	21,637	7,176	31.9	7.5	13.8	58.8	14.7	3.7	0.5	0.9	894	24.2	1,655	13.1	54.0	—	—	—	33
Hemet Unified	CA	12,811	17,451	22,294	21,977	3,224	60.8	35.4	7.3	50.4	2.4	0.5	1.2	2.8	888	24.8	1,853	11.9	47.9	—	—	—	27
Hesperia Unified	CA	13,113	15,360	23,137	23,444	4,522	27.4	28.9	8.0	58.3	1.6	0.4	0.5	2.1	873	26.0	1,859	12.6	47.0	—	—	—	31
Huntington Beach Union High	CA	14,039	14,359	16,320	16,442	1,562	5.8	41.4	1.3	23.7	24.0	0.8	0.5	3.1	631	26.0	1,253	13.1	50.4	—	—	—	9
Irvine Unified	CA	20,183	23,961	27,262	28,179	4,279	12.8	35.5	2.3	10.1	46.1	0.4	0.2	5.2	981	28.7	2,006	14.0	48.9	—	—	—	35
Jurupa Unified	CA	15,419	19,839	20,088	19,884	7,410	74.6	12.7	2.5	82.1	1.3	0.4	0.8	0.9	821	24.2	1,684	11.8	48.7	—	—	—	25
Kern Union High	CA	20,183	29,333	37,452	37,505	3,138	10.1	26.2	6.8	60.7	3.5	0.2	0.8	1.8	1,489	25.2	3,261	11.5	45.7	—	—	—	25
Lake Elsinore Unified	CA	11,000	17,178	22,065	22,171	8,355	34.8	35.2	4.9	52.7	2.6	0.4	0.6	3.3	897	24.7	1,771	12.5	50.6	—	—	—	25
Lodi Unified	CA	23,954	27,339	30,528	30,319	3,202	36.2	26.0	7.6	40.8	21.9	0.6	0.7	2.5	1,322	22.9	2,560	11.8	51.7	—	—	—	53
Long Beach Unified	CA	71,342	93,694	84,812	83,691	20,746	32.3	15.1	15.7	53.7	11.1	1.8	0.2	2.4	3,135	26.7	7,147	11.8	43.9	—	—	—	92
Los Angeles Unified	CA	625,073	721,346	667,273	669,639	152,592	42.0	9.0	9.5	73.4	6.2	0.4	0.5	1.1	28,769	22.9	62,855	10.5	45.8	—	—	—	939
Lynwood Unified	CA	15,469	18,237	16,360	15,515	6,641	38.3	0.5	5.6	93.4	0.2	0.3	#	0.7	592	26.2	1,157	13.4	51.1	—	—	—	19
Madera Unified	CA	13,728	15,957	19,576	19,936	7,135	49.9	9.3	2.3	85.7	1.5	0.1	0.5	0.7	794	25.1	1,543	12.9	51.5	—	—	—	27
Manteca Unified	CA	13,356	19,746	23,406	23,309	4,803	16.6	25.1	3.5	49.6	13.6	1.0	0.9	1.6	920	25.3	1,659	14.0	55.4	—	—	—	29
Modesto City Elementary	CA	17,405	18,740	15,088	15,254	6,082	76.0	19.5	0.3	66.2	4.6	0.6	0.3	4.9	710	21.5	1,346	11.3	52.7	†	—	†	26
Montebello Unified	CA	32,938	34,794	32,046	31,319	10,180	28.9	1.8	0.3	94.9	2.3	0.2	0.1	0.2	1,188	26.4	2,428	12.9	49.0	—	—	—	30
Moreno Valley Unified	CA	29,064	32,730	36,901	35,692	8,990	24.5	10.1	17.5	65.6	3.9	0.9	0.5	2.0	1,456	24.5	2,694	13.2	54.0	—	—	—	39
Mount Diablo Unified	CA	32,840	32,648	34,116	33,977	6,682	17.4	40.5	4.6	37.3	11.5	0.9	0.4	4.8	1,500	22.7	2,539	13.4	59.1	—	—	—	54
Murrieta Valley Unified	CA	3,990	12,065	22,318	22,693	933	21.6	47.1	5.3	33.2	8.3	0.5	0.4	5.2	883	25.7	1,768	12.8	49.9	—	—	—	20
Napa Valley Unified	CA	13,705	16,332	18,003	18,078	3,423	31.8	32.3	2.2	51.8	8.3	0.4	0.6	4.7	769	23.5	1,430	12.6	53.8	—	—	—	33
Newport-Mesa Unified	CA	16,434	21,658	21,811	21,857	5,740	56.9	48.9	1.3	42.8	5.4	0.7	0.3	0.6	921	23.7	1,962	11.1	46.9	—	—	—	31
Norwalk-La Mirada Unified	CA	19,179	23,610	20,421	20,208	4,500	29.5	10.3	2.7	78.3	6.0	0.6	0.2	1.8	817	24.7	1,611	12.5	50.7	—	—	—	28
Oakland Unified	CA	52,085	54,863	46,586	46,377	14,274	61.0	8.8	30.5	41.0	14.3	0.7	0.3	3.9	2,097	22.1	4,200	11.0	49.9	—	—	—	134
Oceanside Unified	CA	17,034	21,082	21,082	20,987	4,172	32.1	28.8	6.6	54.2	6.2	0.9	0.5	2.3	845	24.8	1,670	12.6	50.6	—	—	—	25
Ontario-Montclair Elementary	CA	21,033	26,407	22,591	22,569	11,010	83.1	4.4	2.7	88.1	2.0	0.5	0.4	1.3	1,020	22.1	1,893	11.9	53.9	†	†	†	32
Orange Unified	CA	25,224	31,097	30,373	30,136	7,705	37.8	33.1	1.4	51.0	11.5	0.4	0.4	2.2	1,155	26.1	2,247	13.4	51.4	—	—	—	41
Oxnard	CA	12,212	16,249	15,870	16,118	8,587	37.5	4.5	1.8	89.9	2.7	0.4	0.2	0.6	638	25.3	1,290	12.5	49.4	—	—	—	21
Oxnard Union High	CA	11,512	14,552	16,676	16,790	3,236	10.9	16.8	2.4	72.5	6.8	0.4	0.3	0.9	668	25.1	1,233	13.6	54.2	—	—	—	10
Pajaro Valley Unified	CA	16,355	19,864	19,542	19,914	10,012	42.0	17.0	0.5	79.8	2.0	0.1	0.5	0.3	805	24.7	1,734	11.5	46.4	—	—	—	33
Palm Springs Unified	CA	14,427	19,542	23,626	23,676	7,372	76.7	16.1	5.4	73.3	3.4	0.2	0.7	1.1	904	26.1	1,717	13.8	52.6	—	—	—	29
Palmdale Elementary	CA	13,199	20,847	21,049	20,585	6,237	31.9	6.1	16.6	69.5	2.3	0.5	0.6	2.4	789	26.1	1,507	13.7	52.4	—	—	—	26
Panama-Buena Vista Union	CA	10,066	20,853	16,562	16,810	2,592	57.7	27.4	11.1	51.3	8.8	0.3	0.6	0.7	587	28.6	1,495	11.2	39.3	—	—	—	23
Paramount Unified	CA	12,855	16,862	15,792	15,929	5,919	5.5	1.6	8.9	87.0	1.3	0.7	#	0.5	616	25.9	1,204	13.2	51.1	—	—	—	19
Pasadena Unified	CA	21,802	19,803	19,802	19,802	4,240	26.6	14.8	16.3	59.4	5.2	0.2	0.2	3.7	889	22.3	1,967	10.1	45.2	—	—	—	31
Placentia-Yorba Linda Unified	CA	21,438	23,559	25,821	25,747	3,690	22.5	44.0	1.8	38.3	13.4	0.2	0.2	2.1	977	26.3	1,976	13.0	49.5	—	—	—	34
Pomona Unified	CA	26,918	26,046	28,298	27,737	10,970	54.0	4.1	5.6	83.1	5.7	0.2	0.3	1.1	1,180	23.5	2,361	11.7	50.0	—	—	—	44
Poway Unified	CA	24,662	32,532	34,135	34,569	4,112	10.5	54.1	2.9	12.9	25.3	0.5	0.3	4.0	1,216	28.4	2,530	13.7	48.1	—	—	—	37
Redlands Unified	CA	16,002	19,411	21,398	21,408	2,161	39.0	33.2	6.9	44.5	10.8	0.5	0.5	3.6	882	24.3	1,480	14.5	59.6	—	—	—	25
Rialto Unified	CA	19,794	28,060	27,026	26,764	7,353	36.1	4.5	13.7	78.8	1.5	0.5	0.3	0.7	1,113	24.0	2,108	12.7	52.8	—	—	—	30

See notes at end of table.

Selected statistics on enrollment, teachers, dropouts, and graduates in public school districts enrolling more than 15,000 students: Selected years, 1990 through 2011—Continued

Name of district	State	Enrollment, fall 1990	Enrollment, fall 2000	Enrollment, fall 2010	Enrollment, fall 2011	Number of English language learners, 2011	Percent eligible for free or reduced-price lunch, 2011[1]	White	Black	Hispanic	Asian	Pacific Islander	American Indian/Alaska Native	Two or more races	Number of classroom teachers	Pupil/teacher ratio	Total number of staff	Student/staff ratio	Teachers as a percentage of total staff	Percent dropping out of grades 9-12	Averaged freshman graduation rate (AFGR)[2]	Number of high school graduates, 2008-09[3]	Number of schools, fall 2011
1	2	3	4	5	6	7	8	9	10	11	12	13	14	15	16	17	18	19	20	21	22	23	24
Riverside Unified	CA	31,326	38,124	42,532	42,406	7,720	15.1	26.5	7.9	57.6	4.4	0.5	0.4	2.7	1,620	26.2	3,122	13.6	51.9	—	—	—	49
Rowland Unified	CA	19,143	18,972	15,711	15,738	5,107	65.7	4.0	2.2	63.6	28.2	0.3	0.2	1.6	659	23.9	1,453	10.8	45.3	—	—	—	22
Sacramento City Unified	CA	49,557	52,734	47,897	47,940	12,149	35.7	18.5	17.9	36.6	19.1	1.7	0.8	5.4	1,673	28.7	3,350	14.3	49.9	—	—	—	87
Saddleback Valley Unified	CA	25,130	35,199	31,724	30,885	4,524	21.4	53.5	1.6	29.6	9.9	0.3	0.3	4.8	1,125	27.5	2,056	15.0	54.7	—	—	—	34
San Bernardino City Unified	CA	40,589	52,031	54,518	54,379	17,488	42.9	8.6	14.7	71.8	2.1	0.5	0.7	1.8	2,341	23.2	5,110	10.6	45.8	—	—	—	78
San Diego Unified	CA	121,107	141,804	131,785	131,044	36,453	38.8	23.2	10.7	46.2	14.1	0.7	0.3	4.8	6,706	19.5	13,637	9.6	49.2	—	—	—	223
San Francisco Unified	CA	61,688	59,979	55,571	56,310	17,083	57.3	12.0	10.6	25.0	44.1	1.2	0.5	6.7	2,921	19.3	5,128	11.0	57.0	—	—	—	116
San Jose Unified	CA	29,630	33,015	33,018	33,308	8,846	29.1	25.8	3.1	52.4	14.3	0.5	0.5	3.3	1,474	22.6	2,742	12.1	53.8	—	—	—	53
San Juan Unified	CA	47,690	50,266	47,116	47,245	4,575	39.2	62.8	7.7	19.2	6.1	0.6	1.3	2.0	1,961	24.1	4,237	11.2	46.3	—	—	—	73
San Marcos Unified	CA	9,108	12,804	18,642	19,117	4,297	8.9	40.7	2.8	46.4	7.6	0.6	0.5	1.4	668	28.6	1,520	12.6	44.0	—	—	—	19
San Ramon Valley Unified	CA	16,119	20,742	28,987	29,884	1,519	5.6	52.3	2.0	8.1	30.3	0.2	0.1	6.9	1,261	23.7	2,198	13.6	57.4	—	—	—	35
Santa Ana Unified	CA	45,964	60,643	57,319	57,250	32,170	35.9	2.8	0.5	93.1	2.9	0.1	0.1	0.5	2,276	25.2	4,077	14.0	55.8	—	—	—	60
Santa Barbara Unified	CA	13,370	16,957	16,003	15,326	5,113	30.9	34.0	1.3	57.9	3.3	0.1	0.6	2.8	654	23.4	1,274	12.0	51.3	—	—	—	27
Santa Clara Unified	CA	14,043	14,107	15,383	15,289	4,739	28.9	22.8	4.0	36.2	31.4	1.1	0.6	4.0	643	23.8	1,235	12.4	52.0	—	—	—	26
Simi Valley Unified	CA	18,262	21,181	19,933	19,432	1,979	31.3	57.9	1.1	29.1	9.0	0.1	0.5	2.2	789	24.6	1,557	12.5	50.7	—	—	—	29
Stockton Unified	CA	32,687	37,573	38,252	38,803	10,489	44.5	8.6	11.8	60.1	13.8	0.6	0.5	1.9	1,624	23.9	3,320	11.7	48.9	—	—	—	63
Sweetwater Union High	CA	27,894	35,330	41,426	40,619	9,764	19.8	8.3	3.3	74.3	10.1	0.5	0.4	3.0	1,618	25.1	3,451	11.8	46.9	—	—	—	30
Temecula Valley Unified	CA	7,596	18,980	30,272	30,267	1,685	17.7	47.6	3.9	30.6	9.4	0.4	1.2	6.8	1,235	24.5	2,376	12.7	52.0	—	—	—	33
Torrance Unified	CA	19,645	24,118	24,370	24,229	3,627	27.9	29.4	4.0	22.9	35.0	0.7	0.5	7.5	902	26.9	1,829	13.2	49.3	—	—	—	31
Tracy Joint Unified	CA	7,626	13,816	17,530	17,422	4,135	21.1	26.4	7.2	46.0	15.3	1.1	0.5	3.5	710	24.5	1,329	13.1	53.4	—	—	—	24
Tustin Unified	CA	10,831	16,963	23,093	23,507	5,899	17.2	31.0	2.3	45.7	18.1	0.5	0.2	2.2	811	29.0	1,536	15.3	52.8	—	—	—	29
Twin Rivers Unified	CA	—	—	31,632	31,637	8,472	43.1	30.7	15.1	37.3	9.6	1.5	0.9	4.9	1,321	23.9	2,824	11.2	46.8	—	—	—	54
Val Verde Unified	CA	—	11,242	19,687	19,615	5,039	14.8	6.0	14.0	72.7	3.4	0.3	0.2	3.4	756	26.0	1,412	13.9	53.5	—	—	—	21
Vallejo City Unified	CA	19,049	20,270	15,604	15,313	2,767	33.1	9.0	29.5	33.4	20.0	1.7	0.5	5.9	669	22.9	1,338	11.4	50.0	—	—	—	26
Ventura Unified	CA	16,383	17,527	17,509	17,429	2,754	41.3	44.1	1.5	47.1	3.3	0.2	0.6	3.2	700	24.9	1,483	11.8	47.2	—	—	—	30
Victor Valley Union High	CA	4,662	9,091	13,962	15,186	1,316	30.1	14.6	19.4	55.5	2.5	0.6	0.5	6.9	603	25.2	1,124	13.5	53.6	—	—	—	10
Visalia Unified	CA	21,309	23,989	27,118	27,268	4,694	25.7	26.7	2.3	62.3	5.3	0.2	1.1	1.8	1,051	25.9	2,142	12.7	49.1	—	—	—	38
Vista Unified	CA	18,489	27,651	25,843	25,738	6,983	17.4	27.6	4.5	59.6	3.8	1.2	0.5	2.8	1,071	24.0	2,141	12.0	50.0	—	—	—	34
West Contra Costa Unified	CA	31,292	34,499	29,842	29,883	10,208	32.1	11.1	20.5	50.5	16.3	0.7	0.2	0.8	1,352	22.1	2,646	11.3	51.1	—	—	—	59
West Covina Unified	CA	7,723	10,118	14,665	15,302	1,133	23.0	19.2	7.9	57.0	11.4	0.4	0.6	3.6	609	25.1	1,120	13.7	54.4	—	—	—	17
William S. Hart Union High	CA	10,278	17,001	26,161	26,449	2,308	14.3	47.0	5.2	33.5	10.7	0.3	0.4	2.9	1,029	25.7	1,910	13.8	53.9	—	—	—	20
Academy, No. 20	CO	10,996	17,628	23,119	23,657	335	12.0	75.6	3.0	11.9	3.7	0.4	0.4	5.0	1,419	16.7	2,888	8.2	49.1	1.1	93.1	1,554	32
Adams 12 Five Star Schools	CO	20,838	30,079	41,957	42,990	5,070	33.9	57.6	2.5	32.5	5.2	0.4	0.7	1.4	2,108	20.4	4,185	10.3	50.4	1.1	69.1	1,950	54
Aurora, Joint District No. 28	CO	25,897	30,453	38,605	39,696	13,778	65.1	21.2	17.3	52.3	4.4	0.4	0.7	3.5	1,977	20.1	4,341	9.1	45.5	13.2	52.6	1,360	59
Boulder Valley School, No. RE2	CO	21,502	27,508	29,526	29,780	2,429	18.7	70.6	0.8	17.4	5.9	0.1	0.5	4.7	1,707	17.4	3,703	8.0	46.1	2.4	92.5	2,114	55
Brighton, No. 27J	CO	3,953	5,796	15,089	15,671	1,897	34.8	48.8	1.7	43.8	1.7	0.1	0.6	2.5	767	20.4	1,573	10.0	48.8	8.6	72.5	554	24
Cherry Creek, No. 5	CO	29,210	42,320	52,232	52,655	3,971	25.8	56.7	12.2	17.6	8.1	0.3	0.3	4.6	2,894	18.2	6,254	8.4	46.3	5.4	86.9	3,337	58
Colorado Springs, No. 11	CO	32,440	32,699	29,498	29,543	2,663	52.9	53.2	7.2	29.2	1.9	0.3	0.9	7.3	1,792	16.5	3,914	7.5	45.8	6.3	78.3	1,872	60
Denver	CO	59,013	70,847	78,339	80,890	25,417	72.0	20.4	14.2	58.2	3.4	0.2	0.8	2.9	4,588	17.6	9,487	8.5	48.4	14.0	55.1	2,893	164
Douglas County, No. RE1	CO	13,125	34,918	61,465	63,114	2,345	10.9	76.5	2.0	13.2	3.9	0.1	0.5	3.7	2,977	21.2	6,337	10.0	47.0	2.8	97.5	3,347	82
Falcon, No. 49	CO	2,488	6,026	14,708	15,063	402	21.1	66.0	7.1	17.7	2.0	0.4	0.7	5.8	784	19.2	1,467	10.3	53.5	3.7	80.7	669	21
Greeley, No. 6	CO	11,657	15,998	19,623	19,840	4,029	59.7	36.7	1.9	58.0	1.6	0.1	0.4	1.2	1,101	18.0	2,123	9.3	51.8	5.7	69.8	980	31
Jefferson County, No. R1	CO	76,275	87,703	85,979	85,793	5,051	31.7	68.0	1.1	23.6	3.1	0.2	0.8	3.3	4,729	18.1	10,315	8.3	45.8	3.6	81.2	5,767	163
Littleton, No. 6	CO	17,024	16,516	15,733	15,571	686	21.0	75.1	1.3	16.1	3.1	0.1	0.6	3.7	821	19.0	1,755	8.9	46.8	1.7	91.7	1,222	23
Mesa County Valley, No. 51	CO	18,589	19,688	22,109	21,925	1,046	44.5	72.5	0.7	21.8	0.8	0.1	1.1	2.9	1,251	17.5	2,553	8.6	49.0	6.2	81.8	1,336	46
Poudre, No. R1	CO	18,364	24,052	26,923	27,510	1,793	30.1	74.1	1.4	17.6	3.2	0.1	0.6	3.0	1,551	17.7	3,301	8.3	47.0	2.7	89.3	1,813	50
Pueblo, No. 60	CO	18,049	17,636	18,443	17,902	994	66.9	28.1	2.3	67.3	0.8	0.2	0.6	0.9	1,042	17.2	2,068	8.7	50.4	8.7	69.7	978	37
Saint Vrain Valley, No. RE1J	CO	15,070	22,379	27,379	28,109	3,800	31.8	65.1	1.0	28.4	1.1	0.2	0.6	3.6	1,562	18.0	3,021	9.3	51.7	4.8	81.0	1,394	52
Thompson, No. R2J	CO	12,019	14,766	15,310	15,655	400	36.0	76.6	0.9	18.3	1.5	0.1	0.6	1.8	839	18.7	1,919	8.2	43.7	4.1	87.6	1,106	34
Bridgeport	CT	19,687	22,432	20,205	20,126	2,546	98.8	8.4	38.8	48.6	3.0	0.1	0.8	0.2	1,339	15.0	2,912	6.9	46.0	9.8	53.4	937	36
Hartford	CT	25,418	22,543	21,021	20,931	3,616	89.1	9.8	33.4	49.4	2.5	0.1	0.3	4.5	1,559	13.4	3,147	6.7	49.5	10.8	50.6	909	48
New Haven	CT	17,881	19,549	20,003	20,554	2,567	69.1	15.1	44.5	38.0	2.2	0.0	0.2	0.2	1,615	12.7	3,303	6.2	48.9	8.7	59.7	911	47

See notes at end of table.

Selected statistics on enrollment, teachers, dropouts, and graduates in public school districts enrolling more than 15,000 students: Selected years, 1990 through 2011—Continued

Name of district	State	Enrollment, fall 1990	Enrollment, fall 2000	Enrollment, fall 2010	Enrollment, fall 2011	Number of English language learners, 2011	Percent eligible for free or reduced-price lunch, 2011	White	Black	Hispanic	Asian	Pacific Islander	American Indian/Alaska Native	Two or more races	Number of classroom teachers	Pupil/teacher ratio	Total number of staff	Student/staff ratio	Teachers as a percentage of total staff	Percent dropping out of grades 9-12	Averaged freshman graduation rate (AFGR)[2]	Number of high school graduates[3]	Number of schools, fall 2011
1	2	3	4	5	6	7	8	9	10	11	12	13	14	15	16	17	18	19	20	21	22	23	24
Stamford	CT	11,574	14,791	15,309	15,493	2,045	48.2	35.8	20.3	34.9	8.3	#	0.1	0.7	1,222	12.7	2,219	7.0	55.1	2.5	88.6	1,018	21
Waterbury	CT	13,323	16,282	18,152	18,061	1,951	79.2	22.9	28.0	46.9	1.8	0.1	0.5	1.7	1,339	13.5	2,796	6.5	47.9	6.3	68.9	857	30
Christina	DE	17,872	19,882	17,190	16,303	1,224	59.1	35.1	40.5	17.6	4.4	0.1	0.3	2.0	1,195	13.6	2,354	6.9	50.8	10.8	51.7	877	31
Red Clay Consolidated	DE	14,551	15,827	15,954	15,970	1,644	50.8	46.4	23.4	24.4	4.7	#	0.2	0.9	1,002	15.9	1,721	9.3	58.2	5.3	60.9	814	27
District of Columbia	DC	80,694	68,925	44,199	44,618	3,745	54.4	10.5	71.0	14.9	1.9	0.1	0.1	1.5	3,472	12.8	6,073	7.3	57.2	8.6	65.0	2,679	127
Alachua	FL	26,387	29,712	27,513	27,480	452	48.2	46.8	36.0	7.7	4.1	0.1	0.2	5.0	1,752	15.7	3,861	7.1	45.4	3.0	76.2	1,864	69
Bay	FL	21,875	25,755	25,935	26,346	424	51.9	73.4	15.2	4.7	2.2	#	0.5	4.2	1,733	15.2	3,370	8.1	51.4	0.9	69.5	1,532	48
Brevard	FL	56,639	70,597	71,866	71,792	1,953	43.6	64.1	14.2	12.6	2.0	0.2	0.2	6.8	4,846	14.8	8,836	8.1	54.8	0.7	79.8	4,931	123
Broward	FL	161,100	251,129	256,472	258,478	24,143	57.1	25.7	39.1	28.6	3.5	0.1	0.3	2.6	14,533	17.8	27,041	9.6	53.7	2.4	70.9	15,663	329
Charlotte	FL	13,030	17,170	16,640	16,424	223	61.3	73.6	8.8	11.8	1.4	0.1	0.3	3.9	1,503	10.9	2,898	5.7	51.9	3.3	90.0	1,402	25
Citrus	FL	11,697	15,199	15,675	15,539	130	58.8	82.2	4.8	7.2	1.7	0.1	0.4	3.6	1,097	14.7	2,219	7.9	49.4	1.6	73.8	1,056	23
Clay	FL	21,933	28,115	35,812	35,669	519	39.8	70.1	13.3	9.7	2.5	0.3	0.2	3.9	2,431	14.7	4,488	8.0	54.2	1.3	84.8	2,469	47
Collier	FL	20,878	34,203	42,919	43,238	5,510	59.5	39.2	12.0	44.4	1.1	#	0.1	2.1	2,953	14.6	5,430	8.0	54.4	2.4	69.3	2,477	68
Dade	FL	292,000	368,625	347,366	350,239	66,497	71.9	8.3	23.9	65.9	1.2	#	0.1	0.5	21,117	16.6	37,735	8.0	56.0	4.7	61.6	19,207	524
Duval	FL	111,100	125,846	123,997	125,429	3,844	61.6	39.2	44.3	8.4	4.3	0.2	0.2	3.4	7,589	16.5	12,064	9.3	62.9	5.9	59.9	5,958	195
Escambia	FL	43,091	45,012	40,227	40,496	453	61.7	49.7	35.3	4.9	2.6	0.1	1.0	6.3	3,410	11.9	6,285	6.4	54.3	2.7	56.6	2,116	72
Hernando	FL	12,861	17,215	22,684	22,616	593	57.9	72.3	7.2	15.3	1.6	0.1	0.4	3.2	1,513	14.9	2,765	8.2	54.7	3.1	54.7	1,338	34
Hillsborough	FL	123,900	164,311	194,525	197,041	22,474	56.8	38.5	21.5	32.5	3.3	0.1	0.2	3.7	13,862	14.2	25,472	7.7	54.4	1.1	69.1	10,415	308
Indian River	FL	11,838	14,979	17,740	17,964	1,123	55.5	59.3	16.1	19.8	1.4	0.1	0.4	2.9	1,035	17.4	1,951	9.2	53.1	1.6	76.6	1,108	30
Lake	FL	21,065	29,293	41,110	41,319	1,502	56.2	58.1	15.7	20.0	1.5	0.1	0.5	3.1	2,631	15.7	5,513	7.5	47.7	3.2	76.6	2,354	59
Lee	FL	43,240	58,401	81,967	83,895	5,319	64.2	47.6	15.4	33.0	1.5	0.1	0.2	2.2	5,207	16.1	10,283	8.2	50.6	1.7	71.2	4,258	126
Leon	FL	27,241	32,050	33,326	33,218	466	45.3	46.6	42.0	4.7	3.4	0.1	0.2	3.1	2,036	16.3	4,363	7.6	46.7	3.6	73.6	1,857	60
Manatee	FL	26,326	36,569	44,249	44,986	4,022	54.6	52.1	14.6	28.9	1.7	0.1	0.2	2.5	3,075	14.6	6,318	7.1	48.7	4.3	71.6	2,438	80
Marion	FL	29,577	38,562	41,955	42,281	1,857	65.7	55.6	19.5	18.1	1.2	0.1	0.7	4.9	2,864	14.8	6,016	7.0	47.6	3.1	64.5	2,421	64
Martin	FL	11,808	16,308	18,170	18,368	2,178	40.7	63.7	7.7	24.2	1.6	0.1	0.3	2.4	1,174	15.7	2,339	7.9	50.2	0.7	76.8	1,242	38
Okaloosa	FL	26,140	30,344	28,695	29,385	601	38.2	70.1	12.6	7.6	2.4	0.2	0.4	6.7	1,871	15.7	3,010	9.8	62.1	0.8	80.7	2,089	52
Orange	FL	103,000	150,681	176,008	180,000	28,311	54.2	31.3	27.4	33.8	4.5	0.2	0.2	2.5	11,308	15.9	21,976	8.2	51.5	1.2	70.0	9,946	243
Osceola	FL	19,570	34,566	53,357	54,783	9,332	63.2	27.8	11.6	54.9	2.5	0.2	0.3	2.3	3,288	16.7	6,634	8.3	49.6	1.2	75.7	3,202	64
Palm Beach	FL	106,000	153,871	174,663	176,901	18,698	53.5	35.9	28.7	29.0	2.4	0.1	0.2	2.8	11,682	15.1	20,451	8.6	57.1	2.9	73.3	10,654	252
Pasco	FL	33,891	49,704	66,994	66,659	2,448	54.9	67.6	5.8	19.5	1.6	0.1	0.4	4.1	4,779	13.9	9,503	7.0	50.3	1.4	65.9	3,611	111
Pinellas	FL	94,364	113,027	104,001	103,776	4,598	53.6	59.2	19.1	13.4	4.0	0.1	0.4	3.7	7,289	14.2	14,075	7.4	51.8	2.6	65.8	6,711	169
Polk	FL	65,218	79,477	95,178	96,070	9,512	68.3	46.1	21.1	27.3	1.6	0.1	0.6	3.1	6,771	14.2	13,342	7.2	50.7	5.0	68.4	4,884	163
Saint Johns	FL	12,080	20,090	30,710	31,580	240	23.3	80.7	7.7	6.5	2.9	0.1	0.2	1.8	2,280	13.8	4,110	7.7	55.5	1.2	84.9	1,840	45
Saint Lucie	FL	22,224	29,540	39,259	39,444	2,659	62.9	39.5	29.7	25.2	1.7	0.1	0.2	3.4	2,588	15.2	4,957	8.0	52.2	1.8	67.6	2,052	50
Santa Rosa	FL	15,741	22,633	25,533	25,885	165	41.0	80.1	5.3	5.2	1.6	0.1	0.6	7.1	1,557	16.6	2,468	10.5	63.1	2.1	80.9	1,664	38
Sarasota	FL	27,888	35,533	40,899	41,083	2,351	50.9	66.8	9.0	17.2	2.1	0.1	0.3	4.3	3,390	12.1	6,153	6.7	55.1	2.1	74.5	2,607	59
Seminole	FL	49,027	60,869	64,229	64,344	2,361	45.3	56.1	13.8	22.2	4.1	0.1	0.3	3.3	4,280	15.0	7,459	8.6	57.4	0.4	76.1	4,373	74
Volusia	FL	48,403	61,517	61,559	61,524	3,060	57.5	61.4	15.1	17.8	1.6	0.1	0.5	3.6	4,100	15.0	7,676	8.0	53.4	1.4	63.9	3,633	93
Atlanta	GA	60,795	58,230	49,796	50,009	1,654	74.7	13.1	78.2	6.3	0.8	0.1	0.1	1.4	3,619	13.8	6,581	7.6	55.0	9.5	53.3	2,033	108
Bibb County	GA	24,413	24,739	24,961	24,730	344	78.0	20.6	72.8	3.0	1.6	0.1	0.1	1.8	1,585	15.6	3,525	7.0	45.0	7.1	49.0	979	43
Chatham County	GA	34,100	35,344	35,246	35,842	622	63.8	28.0	58.3	5.6	2.0	0.1	0.1	5.9	2,603	13.8	4,710	7.6	55.3	4.7	55.3	1,528	55
Cherokee County	GA	16,086	26,043	38,774	38,760	1,531	31.0	74.4	6.8	14.0	2.0	0.1	0.3	2.8	2,377	16.3	4,515	8.6	52.7	4.2	70.2	1,880	40
Clayton County	GA	34,754	46,930	50,366	51,018	3,612	85.2	3.5	71.2	17.5	4.7	0.1	0.3	2.8	3,242	15.7	6,531	7.8	49.6	5.8	45.8	1,944	63
Cobb County	GA	69,441	95,781	107,315	107,291	7,732	44.0	43.8	31.2	16.9	4.9	0.1	0.2	2.9	7,342	14.6	13,621	7.9	53.9	3.5	77.9	6,833	116
Columbia County	GA	14,096	18,756	23,722	23,792	271	33.0	66.0	17.8	7.5	4.0	#	0.3	4.3	1,419	16.8	3,013	7.9	47.1	3.6	74.1	1,380	31
Coweta County	GA	10,430	16,766	22,490	22,508	486	43.9	65.9	21.2	7.2	1.8	0.2	0.2	3.6	1,434	15.7	3,056	7.4	46.9	3.3	74.1	1,217	28
DeKalb County	GA	74,404	95,958	98,115	98,088	9,707	71.1	11.0	69.0	12.7	5.5	0.1	0.1	1.5	6,660	14.7	13,269	7.4	50.1	6.0	63.1	5,129	135
Dougherty County	GA	18,877	16,779	15,906	15,945	193	82.2	8.7	87.8	1.9	0.5	0.3	0.1	0.8	1,045	15.3	2,380	6.7	43.9	3.3	59.1	752	27
Douglas County	GA	14,002	17,489	24,601	24,742	1,134	59.0	34.1	48.4	11.7	1.3	0.1	0.1	4.1	1,636	15.1	3,320	7.5	49.3	2.7	77.6	1,459	36
Fayette County	GA	13,105	19,590	21,274	20,539	476	23.6	56.1	23.9	9.1	4.6	0.1	0.4	5.8	1,462	14.0	2,891	7.1	50.6	1.0	90.1	1,829	28
Forsyth County	GA	7,742	17,131	35,920	37,262	1,572	19.2	74.9	2.5	12.0	7.5	0.1	0.4	2.6	2,240	16.6	4,179	8.9	53.6	2.1	83.7	1,555	35
Fulton County	GA	41,935	68,583	91,864	92,604	4,997	44.7	33.0	42.0	12.7	9.3	#	0.1	2.9	6,195	14.9	11,765	7.9	52.7	4.6	81.5	5,090	104

See notes at end of table.

Selected statistics on enrollment, teachers, dropouts, and graduates in public school districts enrolling more than 15,000 students: Selected years, 1990 through 2011—Continued

Name of district	State	Enrollment, fall 1990	Enrollment, fall 2000	Enrollment, fall 2010	Enrollment, fall 2011	Number of English language learners, 2011	Percent eligible for free or reduced-price lunch, 2011[1]	White	Black	Hispanic	Asian	Pacific Islander	American Indian/Alaska Native	Two or more races	Number of classroom teachers	Pupil/teacher ratio	Total number of staff	Student/staff ratio	Teachers as a percentage of total staff	Percent dropping out of grades 9-12	Averaged freshman graduation rate (AFGR)[2]	Number of high school graduates[3], 2008-09	Number of schools, fall 2011
1	2	3	4	5	6	7	8	9	10	11	12	13	14	15	16	17	18	19	20	21	22	23	24
Gwinnett County	GA	64,980	110,075	160,744	162,370	18,968	53.7	30.7	29.8	25.1	10.2	0.1	0.3	3.7	10,324	15.7	19,733	8.2	52.3	3.4	71.5	8,327	133
Hall County	GA	13,833	20,330	25,946	26,261	3,879	59.0	54.7	4.6	37.1	1.4	0.1	0.2	1.9	1,662	15.8	3,110	8.4	53.4	3.3	62.2	1,273	33
Henry County	GA	10,929	23,601	40,909	39,909	686	49.6	39.3	46.2	7.6	2.8	0.1	0.2	3.8	2,629	15.2	5,013	8.0	52.4	5.1	77.8	2,395	50
Houston County	GA	16,249	21,529	27,061	27,435	734	52.4	50.2	35.7	7.0	2.7	0.1	0.2	4.1	1,822	15.1	3,761	7.3	48.4	3.6	76.8	1,523	39
Muscogee County	GA	30,125	32,916	32,288	32,231	484	64.9	29.2	57.9	5.9	2.2	0.1	0.2	4.5	2,308	14.0	5,022	6.4	46.0	3.3	64.7	1,791	59
Newton County	GA	8,054	11,734	19,478	19,168	476	65.7	38.1	51.5	5.6	0.9	0.1	0.1	3.6	1,230	15.6	2,407	8.0	51.1	2.9	62.4	858	23
Paulding County	GA	7,604	16,587	28,407	28,237	340	41.5	67.2	20.1	7.4	0.8	0.1	0.4	3.9	1,704	16.6	3,293	8.6	51.7	3.5	71.8	1,349	33
Richmond County	GA	33,660	35,424	32,322	31,829	110	76.2	20.2	72.9	3.0	0.9	0.8	0.1	2.0	2,111	15.1	4,325	7.4	48.8	3.7	52.9	1,529	60
Rockdale County	GA	10,942	13,519	15,864	15,608	601	63.8	22.0	60.4	12.3	1.9	0.2	0.2	3.1	1,082	14.4	2,261	6.9	47.9	2.9	69.5	1,033	18
Hawaii Department of Education	HI	159,285	184,360	179,601	182,706	24,750	49.3	14.3	2.4	6.4	34.2	33.9	0.5	8.2	11,458	15.9	22,065	8.3	51.9	4.9	75.3	11,508	287
Boise Independent	ID	23,394	26,598	25,039	25,476	1,998	42.4	79.1	2.8	11.0	4.3	0.6	0.5	1.8	1,530	16.6	2,719	9.4	56.3	1.2	86.9	1,809	53
Meridian Joint	ID	14,802	23,854	35,537	36,303	1,375	32.4	84.1	1.3	8.4	2.2	0.4	0.6	3.0	1,803	20.1	2,998	12.1	60.1	1.4	80.7	1,887	55
Nampa	ID	7,878	11,403	15,181	15,556	1,062	64.0	63.5	1.5	32.0	1.0	0.9	1.0	0.2	783	19.9	1,364	11.4	57.4	0.8	70.4	761	32
Carpentersville (CUSD 300)	IL	11,196	16,711	20,678	20,810	2,492	39.5	53.4	5.1	32.8	5.5	0.2	0.2	2.9	1,098	18.9	1,310	15.9	83.8	8.7	91.4	1,326	27
City of Chicago (SD 299)	IL	408,830	435,261	405,644	403,004	53,786	86.7	8.9	41.6	44.4	3.3	0.1	0.4	1.4	22,460	17.9	26,529	15.2	84.7	15.0	60.8	20,082	641
Elgin (SD U-46)	IL	27,726	36,767	40,683	40,687	7,617	54.9	32.2	6.6	49.9	8.4	0.1	0.5	2.4	2,049	19.9	2,353	17.3	87.1	9.1	80.2	2,455	57
Indian Prairie (CUSD 204)	IL	7,670	23,173	29,522	29,286	1,458	14.6	56.3	9.2	10.0	20.2	#	0.2	4.0	1,767	16.6	2,086	14.0	84.7	5.5	1.2	25[5]	33
Naperville (CUSD 203)	IL	16,212	18,762	17,834	17,768	638	10.9	68.5	5.2	8.3	14.6	0.1	0.2	3.1	1,048	17.0	1,294	13.7	81.0	5.4	100.0[5]	1,579	22
Oswego (CUSD 308)	IL	4,108	6,846	16,729	17,150	599	22.9	62.3	7.7	18.3	6.4	#	0.4	5.1	889	19.3	1,018	16.8	87.3	6.0	93.3	795	22
Plainfield (SD 202)	IL	3,324	11,986	28,921	28,904	1,820	20.2	59.0	8.9	22.9	5.3	0.1	0.2	3.3	1,623	17.8	1,912	15.1	84.9	8.1	96.9	1,643	30
Rockford (SD 205)	IL	27,255	27,399	28,961	28,118	2,939	78.5	34.2	29.7	25.9	4.0	#	0.2	6.0	1,675	16.8	1,997	14.1	83.8	22.7	55.0	1,367	50
Valley View (CUSD 365U)	IL	11,781	13,558	17,874	17,838	2,208	55.7	28.8	20.7	39.8	6.4	0.4	0.3	3.7	1,054	16.9	1,292	13.8	81.6	13.7	84.6	1,140	20
Waukegan (CUSD 60)	IL	12,116	15,510	16,462	16,597	4,598	61.9	4.3	15.8	76.2	1.3	0.3	0.4	1.7	1,070	15.5	1,276	13.0	83.9	17.8	65.2	811	24
Carmel Clay	IN	8,449	12,073	15,550	15,750	476	9.7	78.2	3.3	2.2	10.8	0.4	0.3	4.9	949	16.6	2,312	6.8	41.0	0.5	90.9	916	17
Evansville Vanderburgh	IN	22,918	22,875	23,440	22,799	369	56.8	73.0	13.7	2.9	1.2	0.1	0.4	8.9	1,551	14.7	3,421	6.7	45.3	1.8	75.7	1,416	40
Fort Wayne	IN	31,611	31,843	31,401	30,821	2,474	69.2	49.1	24.7	13.8	4.0	0.1	0.6	7.6	1,818	17.0	4,242	7.3	42.9	0.8	70.8	1,898	51
Hamilton Southeastern	IN	3,113	8,777	18,687	19,053	510	13.7	77.7	7.0	5.1	5.5	0.1	0.2	4.3	1,012	18.8	2,219	8.6	45.6	0.5	94.6	863	20
Indianapolis	IN	48,140	41,008	33,079	31,999	4,026	75.6	22.5	53.7	18.4	0.4	#	0.2	4.8	2,160	14.8	5,672	5.6	38.1	5.1	35.0	1,159	68
MSD Wayne Township	IN	12,229	13,263	16,002	16,276	2,148	70.7	43.3	31.1	18.6	1.0	#	0.2	5.8	941	17.3	2,017	8.1	46.7	2.4	67.6	786	18
South Bend	IN	21,425	21,536	19,998	20,077	2,420	70.0	37.1	34.5	17.7	1.6	#	0.4	9.0	1,170	17.2	2,882	7.0	40.6	3.2	66.3	1,109	39
Vigo County	IN	16,982	16,545	15,891	15,601	189	53.9	83.0	5.6	2.7	1.6	#	0.2	6.8	937	16.6	1,868	8.4	50.2	0.1	71.6	952	29
Cedar Rapids	IA	17,003	17,780	17,272	17,170	426	42.0	74.1	14.4	4.9	2.3	0.2	0.4	3.7	1,150	14.9	2,515	6.8	45.7	5.6	76.3	1,071	33
Davenport	IA	17,846	16,874	17,096	16,955	454	60.6	58.7	18.9	13.1	1.9	0.1	0.4	7.0	1,076	15.8	2,074	8.2	51.9	9.4	72.7	930	33
Des Moines Independent	IA	30,888	32,435	33,091	33,453	5,144	70.7	47.2	17.2	22.3	6.4	0.2	0.4	6.3	2,280	14.7	4,540	7.4	50.2	7.6	64.9	1,607	62
Blue Valley	KS	9,433	17,111	21,641	21,925	360	8.0	79.3	3.2	4.4	9.5	#	0.3	3.4	1,651	13.3	2,968	7.4	55.6	0.5	94.4	1,412	34
Kansas City	KS	22,118	21,173	20,229	20,499	6,301	89.0	14.1	35.6	43.4	4.6	0.2	0.4	1.7	1,397	14.7	2,716	7.5	51.4	3.3	53.9	911	43
Olathe	KS	14,870	20,703	27,882	28,182	1,499	26.4	71.9	6.9	13.0	4.5	0.2	0.4	3.2	1,974	14.3	3,720	7.6	53.1	0.8	95.0	1,788	47
Shawnee Mission	KS	30,619	30,765	27,822	27,760	2,165	35.5	66.6	8.6	16.0	3.1	0.2	0.3	5.2	1,794	15.5	3,217	8.6	55.8	2.2	87.1	2,061	44
Wichita	KS	47,222	48,228	49,329	49,389	7,647	76.1	35.6	18.5	31.2	4.8	0.1	1.4	8.3	3,063	16.1	5,872	8.4	52.2	2.9	72.0	2,635	90
Boone County	KY	9,911	13,445	19,306	19,577	811	29.3	86.1	3.4	5.3	2.4	0.2	0.2	2.4	1,159	16.9	2,633	7.4	44.0	1.5	80.9	1,079	24
Fayette County	KY	32,083	33,130	37,819	38,641	3,205	43.3	57.2	23.0	12.1	4.0	0.1	0.2	3.4	2,742	14.1	5,711	6.8	48.0	3.5	78.0	2,101	73
Jefferson County	KY	91,450	96,860	97,331	99,191	5,302	58.6	50.9	37.0	6.6	3.1	0.1	0.1	2.2	5,904	16.8	7,320	13.6	80.7	5.7	69.5	5,506	173
Ascension Parish	LA	13,001	15,038	19,953	20,465	308	49.2	61.8	30.3	5.4	1.4	0.1	0.3	1.0	1,356	15.1	2,745	7.5	49.4	4.8	78.9	1,083	27
Bossier Parish	LA	17,804	18,797	20,656	21,037	557	45.3	60.6	27.1	6.8	1.4	0.2	0.4	3.5	1,357	15.5	2,850	7.4	47.6	5.3	71.2	1,041	34
Caddo Parish	LA	51,375	45,119	41,894	41,667	396	64.9	32.2	63.3	2.2	1.1	0.1	0.2	0.9	2,890	14.4	6,609	6.3	43.7	10.0	60.5	2,126	66
Calcasieu Parish	LA	32,917	32,261	33,063	32,563	285	58.9	60.7	34.3	2.5	1.1	#	0.2	1.1	2,381	13.7	4,856	6.7	49.0	3.5	69.9	1,695	58
East Baton Rouge Parish	LA	61,669	54,246	42,723	42,854	1,383	82.2	10.9	81.2	4.1	3.0	0.1	0.1	0.7	3,234	13.3	6,374	6.7	50.7	9.9	61.7	1,839	81
Jefferson Parish	LA	58,177	50,891	45,230	45,688	3,786	77.4	29.7	45.6	17.0	4.8	0.1	0.7	1.9	3,039	15.0	6,466	7.1	50.7	8.1	59.7	2,093	90
Lafayette Parish	LA	29,403	28,931	30,218	30,451	880	61.4	49.4	43.4	4.3	2.0	#	0.3	0.5	2,040	14.9	4,264	7.1	47.8	6.6	70.9	1,652	44

See notes at end of table.

Selected statistics on enrollment, teachers, dropouts, and graduates in public school districts enrolling more than 15,000 students: Selected years, 1990 through 2011—Continued

Name of district	State	Enrollment, fall 1990	Enrollment, fall 2000	Enrollment, fall 2010	Enrollment, fall 2011	Number of English language learners, 2011	Percent eligible for free or reduced-price lunch, 2011[1]	White	Black	Hispanic	Asian	Pacific Islander	American Indian/ Alaska Native	Two or more races	Number of classroom teachers	Pupil/ teacher ratio	Total number of staff	Student/ staff ratio	Teachers as a percentage of total staff	Percent dropping out of grades 9–12	Averaged freshman graduation rate (AFGR)[2]	Number of high school graduates, 2008–09[3]	Number of schools, fall 2011
1	2	3	4	5	6	7	8	9	10	11	12	13	14	15	16	17	18	19	20	21	22	23	24
Livingston Parish	LA	16,310	19,723	24,468	24,773	238	50.2	89.0	7.0	2.9	0.6	#	0.2	0.2	1,647	15.0	3,319	7.5	49.6	4.0	73.1	1,203	44
Ouachita Parish	LA	17,667	17,479	19,680	19,718	149	57.7	64.0	33.1	1.7	0.8	#	0.1	0.2	1,322	14.9	3,014	6.5	43.9	6.8	68.9	1,057	36
Rapides Parish	LA	24,765	23,467	23,989	24,028	390	68.8	52.6	42.5	2.6	1.4	#	0.7	0.2	1,672	14.4	3,328	7.2	50.2	7.7	64.2	1,134	48
Saint Tammany Parish	LA	27,522	32,392	36,651	37,058	541	46.7	74.5	19.0	3.9	1.6	#	0.4	0.5	2,394	15.5	5,066	7.3	47.3	4.6	77.2	2,132	55
Tangipahoa Parish	LA	16,724	18,197	19,400	19,511	273	75.5	47.3	47.4	3.2	0.6	#	0.2	1.3	1,173	16.6	2,566	7.6	45.7	5.4	65.5	995	35
Terrebonne Parish	LA	21,116	18,774	18,722	18,589	265	66.9	56.4	28.2	3.8	1.2	#	9.3	1.1	1,289	14.4	2,476	7.5	52.0	6.7	69.6	1,003	38
Anne Arundel County	MD	65,011	74,491	75,481	76,303	3,023	29.0	61.1	20.6	9.3	3.5	0.3	0.3	4.9	5,117	14.9	9,439	8.1	54.2	—	81.2	4,908	121
Baltimore City	MD	108,663	99,859	83,800	84,212	2,496	83.9	8.0	85.5	4.6	1.1	0.2	0.4	0.4	5,533	15.2	10,573	8.0	52.3	—	56.4	4,285	195
Baltimore County	MD	86,737	106,898	104,160	105,153	3,627	44.9	45.2	38.6	6.3	6.2	0.1	0.4	3.3	7,219	14.6	14,157	7.4	51.0	—	81.1	7,299	173
Calvert County	MD	10,398	16,170	16,795	16,553	138	22.7	74.9	14.3	4.0	1.6	0.1	0.3	5.0	1,062	15.6	2,150	7.7	49.4	—	89.4	1,356	26
Carroll County	MD	21,835	27,528	27,082	27,082	172	16.9	88.4	3.6	3.7	2.0	0.1	0.2	2.0	1,883	14.4	3,473	7.8	54.2	—	93.5	2,359	49
Cecil County	MD	12,868	15,905	15,937	15,827	154	41.0	80.9	8.5	4.8	0.9	0.1	0.3	4.5	1,149	13.8	2,083	7.6	55.1	—	78.1	1,080	29
Charles County	MD	18,708	23,468	26,850	26,778	192	29.3	33.7	52.0	5.3	3.1	0.1	0.6	5.3	1,719	15.6	3,288	7.3	52.3	—	93.4	2,172	37
Frederick County	MD	26,848	36,885	40,188	40,413	1,593	23.2	67.2	10.8	11.4	4.9	0.1	0.4	5.2	2,747	14.7	5,560	7.3	49.4	—	92.3	3,022	65
Harford County	MD	31,500	39,520	38,394	38,224	393	27.5	68.1	17.7	5.4	3.2	0.2	0.4	5.1	2,752	13.9	5,248	7.3	52.4	—	90.7	2,666	54
Howard County	MD	29,949	44,946	50,994	51,555	2,223	17.6	47.4	20.9	8.5	16.7	0.1	0.2	6.2	3,757	13.7	7,532	6.8	49.9	—	90.4	3,711	74
Montgomery County	MD	103,757	134,180	144,023	146,459	20,580	32.2	33.8	21.2	26.0	14.3	0.1	0.2	4.4	9,622	15.2	19,870	7.4	48.4	—	89.0	10,129	205
Prince George's County	MD	108,868	133,723	126,671	123,833	15,099	57.8	4.6	67.5	22.4	2.9	0.2	0.6	1.7	7,796	15.9	15,828	7.8	49.3	—	69.5	8,266	208
Saint Marys County	MD	12,549	15,151	17,271	17,449	136	29.8	69.9	18.5	5.0	2.5	0.2	0.4	3.4	1,038	16.8	2,019	8.6	51.4	—	79.7	1,093	27
Washington County	MD	17,778	19,782	22,206	22,240	357	46.1	74.4	11.9	5.8	1.7	#	0.2	6.0	1,531	14.5	2,967	7.5	51.6	—	88.4	1,546	46
Boston	MA	60,543	63,024	56,037	55,027	15,653	69.8	12.6	33.7	43.0	8.3	0.1	0.3	1.9	4,261	12.9	7,030	7.8	60.6	7.2	71.3	3,549	117
Brockton	MA	14,529	16,791	15,828	16,162	3,067	70.8	26.0	52.8	14.4	2.5	0.2	0.5	3.6	1,089	14.8	2,003	8.1	54.4	5.4	69.8	909	22
Springfield	MA	24,194	26,526	25,213	25,185	3,535	85.6	13.7	20.7	59.8	2.4	#	0.1	3.2	2,078	12.1	3,684	6.8	56.4	9.6	52.7	1,099	53
Worcester	MA	21,066	25,828	24,192	24,411	6,005	72.1	35.6	13.5	39.0	8.3	#	0.3	3.4	1,584	15.4	3,094	7.9	51.2	5.1	78.7	1,535	45
Ann Arbor	MI	14,190	16,539	16,764	16,635	667	23.2	55.6	14.6	6.4	14.7	0.1	0.4	8.3	967	17.2	2,939	5.7	32.9	1.7	92.8	1,289	32
Chippewa Valley	MI	9,340	12,329	16,088	16,178	802	26.0	82.4	8.7	2.8	2.6	#	0.2	3.1	784	20.6	1,465	11.0	53.5	1.7	90.5	1,124	20
Dearborn City	MI	13,380	17,129	18,653	18,736	7,324	69.7	91.7	4.9	2.1	0.9	#	0.3	0.2	1,128	16.6	2,087	9.0	54.0	1.9	75.4	1,220	33
Detroit City	MI	138,986	162,194	77,757	67,064	6,522	81.6	2.5	86.4	9.7	1.0	#	0.3	#	4,204	16.0	8,705	7.7	48.3	6.0	45.1	5,634	129
Grand Rapids	MI	26,871	25,625	18,125	17,606	3,645	85.2	20.3	37.1	34.0	1.2	#	0.6	6.7	1,161	15.2	2,763	6.4	42.0	6.5	45.7	808	64
Livonia	MI	16,543	18,347	15,617	15,426	0	25.1	80.5	8.2	3.7	3.3	#	0.4	3.9	823	18.7	1,711	9.0	48.1	1.0	89.9	1,393	26
Plymouth-Canton	MI	14,955	16,518	18,905	18,426	680	14.8	73.0	9.2	3.0	11.0	0.1	0.4	3.3	932	19.8	1,849	10.0	50.4	2.0	93.7	1,379	25
Utica	MI	23,960	27,786	28,985	28,606	1,017	28.7	89.3	4.7	1.9	2.9	0.3	0.1	0.8	1,331	21.5	2,711	10.6	49.1	0.9	93.1	2,236	38
Walled Lake Consolidated	MI	9,555	14,438	15,455	15,467	1,431	26.6	80.1	9.5	3.1	5.7	#	0.1	1.3	781	19.8	1,505	10.3	51.9	2.4	90.1	1,193	22
Warren Consolidated	MI	14,336	14,602	15,820	15,414	2,147	53.9	75.5	12.1	1.3	8.3	0.2	0.3	2.2	780	19.8	1,486	10.4	52.5	2.2	88.8	1,136	25
Anoka-Hennepin	MN	34,524	41,314	39,158	38,748	2,363	30.9	77.6	9.2	4.1	6.1	0.1	1.1	1.8	2,167	17.9	4,421	8.8	49.0	1.6	85.0	2,870	50
Minneapolis	MN	41,050	48,834	34,934	35,046	7,198	65.4	34.7	35.1	16.7	7.7	0.2	4.6	0.9	2,389	14.7	5,505	6.4	43.4	5.8	55.1	1,724	90
Osseo	MN	19,579	22,017	21,053	20,917	1,819	38.1	51.1	21.5	7.4	15.1	#	0.5	4.4	1,243	16.8	2,683	7.8	46.3	0.7	78.2	1,353	34
Rochester	MN	14,045	15,929	16,353	16,317	1,697	34.2	66.7	11.1	8.4	10.2	0.1	0.4	3.0	997	16.4	1,942	8.4	51.3	1.4	84.2	1,194	38
Rosemount-Apple Valley-Eagan	MN	20,547	28,330	27,590	27,515	1,365	20.0	73.2	9.1	6.6	7.8	0.1	0.5	2.7	1,554	17.7	3,168	8.7	49.1	0.8	82.7	2,109	35
Saint Paul	MN	35,932	45,115	38,316	38,310	13,257	72.7	24.0	28.1	13.8	30.8	#	1.4	1.9	2,388	16.0	5,342	8.8	44.7	3.9	73.0	2,409	98
South Washington County	MN	11,417	14,953	17,456	17,858	722	19.2	73.7	7.2	6.0	9.0	#	0.3	3.7	1,055	16.9	2,024	8.8	52.1	0.6	97.7	1,248	26
Desoto County	MS	13,470	19,812	31,916	32,311	1,060	50.8	60.9	31.3	6.0	1.5	0.1	0.1	#	1,799	18.0	3,710	8.7	48.5	1.4	70.7	1,551	40
Jackson	MS	33,546	31,351	30,366	29,898	144	89.3	1.4	97.3	0.9	0.1	#	#	0.2	1,867	16.0	4,687	6.4	39.8	5.9	51.6	1,274	64
Rankin County	MS	12,824	15,013	18,937	19,376	355	40.1	74.0	22.0	1.9	1.5	#	0.1	0.4	1,312	14.8	2,210	8.8	59.3	3.0	66.9	890	27
Columbia, 93	MO	12,786	16,178	17,550	17,709	759	37.3	62.6	20.5	5.6	5.3	0.0	0.4	5.6	1,240	14.3	2,309	7.7	53.7	4.1	91.5	1,213	32
Fort Zumwalt, R-II	MO	10,110	16,521	18,951	18,977	331	20.5	84.8	5.5	3.5	3.0	0.2	0.2	2.8	1,226	15.5	2,566	7.4	47.8	3.2	87.0	1,297	24
Francis Howell, R-III	MO	13,391	19,497	19,981	19,626	270	17.4	86.3	6.7	2.5	3.6	0.1	0.2	0.6	1,147	17.1	1,939	10.1	59.1	1.8	96.5	1,488	23
Hazelwood	MO	16,985	18,855	18,655	17,772	317	—	25.1	71.3	1.9	1.1	#	0.4	#	1,200	14.8	1,954	9.1	61.4	2.6	75.1	1,386	30
Kansas City, 33	MO	34,486	37,298	17,326	16,610	3,582	79.7	9.2	61.2	26.3	3.2	#	0.2	0.0	1,094	15.2	2,228	7.5	49.1	5.4	43.3	1,032	34
Lee's Summit, R-VII	MO	7,132	14,340	17,803	17,825	175	21.0	77.8	13.7	5.3	2.6	0.2	0.5	0.0	1,091	16.3	2,381	7.5	45.8	3.1	90.1	1,189	27

See notes at end of table.

Selected statistics on enrollment, teachers, dropouts, and graduates in public school districts enrolling more than 15,000 students: Selected years, 1990 through 2011—Continued

Name of district	State	Enroll. fall 1990	Enroll. fall 2000	Enroll. fall 2010	Enroll. fall 2011	Number of English language learners, 2011	Percent eligible for free or reduced-price lunch, 2011[1]	White	Black	Hispanic	Asian	Pacific Islander	American Indian/Alaska Native	Two or more races	Number of classroom teachers	Pupil/teacher ratio	Total number of staff	Student/staff ratio	Teachers as a percentage of total staff	Percent dropping out of grades 9-12	Averaged freshman graduation rate (AFGR)[2]	Number of high school graduates[3]	Number of schools, fall 2011
1	2	3	4	5	6	7	8	9	10	11	12	13	14	15	16	17	18	19	20	21	22	23	24
North Kansas City, 74	MO	15,732	17,258	18,764	19,133	1,196	46.4	64.8	12.0	12.7	3.9	0.5	0.8	5.3	1,292	14.8	3,110	6.2	41.6	3.1	93.4	1,268	32
Parkway, C-2	MO	21,542	20,433	17,458	17,363	622	14.4	66.0	14.6	4.3	11.3	0.1	0.2	3.5	1,260	13.8	2,810	6.2	44.8	1.4	92.0	1,418	28
Rockwood, R-VI	MO	15,608	21,203	22,823	22,503	412	7.4	80.6	10.2	2.3	5.9	#	0.2	0.8	1,465	15.4	3,276	6.9	44.7	1.3	94.5	1,721	31
Saint Louis City	MO	43,284	44,412	25,084	24,665	1,764	79.9	13.5	80.3	3.2	2.8	0.0	0.3	0.0	1,904	13.0	2,658	9.3	71.6	25.9	51.9	1,643	75
Springfield, R-XII	MO	23,631	24,630	24,730	25,175	589	51.5	83.2	7.9	4.2	2.4	0.4	0.5	1.4	1,623	15.5	9,953	2.5	16.3	4.9	82.7	1,673	55
Lincoln	NE	27,996	31,354	35,896	36,528	2,208	43.7	69.8	6.6	11.7	4.5	0.1	0.9	6.4	2,549	14.3	5,267	6.9	48.4	3.9	79.4	1,954	69
Millard	NE	16,764	19,160	22,783	23,074	268	18.2	82.6	2.9	6.4	4.6	0.3	0.4	2.8	1,513	15.3	2,679	8.6	56.5	0.9	96.8	1,583	37
Omaha	NE	41,699	45,197	49,405	50,340	6,760	71.3	33.1	26.2	30.5	3.0	0.1	1.2	5.9	3,327	15.1	6,956	7.2	47.8	5.6	57.7	2,293	100
Clark County	NV	121,984	231,655	314,059	313,398	68,577	59.6	30.2	12.3	43.1	6.5	1.5	0.5	5.9	14,822	21.1	17,334	18.1	85.5	—	—	—	364
Washoe County	NV	38,466	56,268	64,380	64,740	11,102	44.3	48.3	2.6	37.3	4.7	0.8	1.8	4.5	3,145	20.6	3,555	18.2	88.4	—	—	—	105
Elizabeth	NJ	15,266	19,674	24,258	23,386	2,730	85.5	8.4	21.7	67.8	1.9	0.1	#	0.0	1,846	12.7	3,616	6.5	51.1	6.7	62.2	928	33
Jersey City	NJ	28,585	31,347	34,505	27,397	2,512	77.5	10.5	33.6	38.0	16.6	0.8	0.6	0.0	2,601	10.5	4,898	5.6	53.1	6.4	71.1	1,471	38
Newark	NJ	48,433	42,150	41,235	35,543	3,143	85.5	7.9	53.4	37.7	0.8	0.1	0.2	#	2,546	14.0	6,144	5.8	41.4	4.2	75.4	2,421	74
Paterson	NJ	22,109	24,629	31,350	24,365	4,749	85.7	5.5	28.4	62.2	3.6	0.2	0.1	#	1,845	13.2	3,350	7.3	55.1	4.3	52.7	991	46
Toms River Regional	NJ	16,002	17,621	17,285	16,981	123	23.3	79.3	4.8	10.5	3.9	0.1	0.1	1.3	1,167	14.6	2,154	7.9	54.2	2.2	89.2	1,315	18
Albuquerque	NM	88,295	85,276	95,415	94,318	16,253	63.8	22.3	2.4	66.0	2.1	0.1	4.4	2.8	6,157	15.3	12,275	7.7	50.2	2.7	61.9	4,784	162
Las Cruces	NM	19,216	22,185	25,488	25,353	3,561	68.9	20.9	2.5	74.2	1.1	0.3	0.9	0.1	1,569	16.2	3,223	7.9	48.7	6.6	63.3	1,268	41
Rio Rancho	NM	—	10,219	16,751	16,870	609	50.9	41.9	3.4	46.7	2.1	0.0	3.8	2.0	1,032	16.3	2,037	8.3	50.7	3.9	75.8	915	19
Brentwood Union Free	NY	11,749	15,565	16,833	17,143	4,706	61.1	7.4	13.9	76.2	2.1	#	0.2	0.1	1,107	15.5	2,224	7.7	49.8	2.0	73.1	1,029	17
Buffalo City	NY	47,224	45,721	33,543	32,723	3,643	79.0	22.3	52.8	16.1	5.6	#	1.3	2.0	2,751	11.9	5,005	6.5	55.0	9.3	61.4	1,538	56
New York City	NY	943,969	1,066,516	995,336	990,145	142,572	73.5	14.9	28.1	40.3	15.6	0.4	0.6	0.1	67,046	14.8	125,119	7.9	53.6	7.4	—	56,655	1,565
Rochester City	NY	32,730	36,294	32,223	31,432	2,899	87.4	10.4	62.0	24.2	3.1	#	0.3	0.4	2,603	12.1	4,742	6.6	54.9	11.3	43.9	1,406	67
Syracuse City	NY	22,561	23,015	21,247	20,491	2,524	79.4	25.9	50.0	12.8	6.3	0.1	1.4	3.4	1,557	13.2	3,491	5.9	44.6	11.0	52.3	847	32
Yonkers City	NY	18,621	26,237	25,568	25,326	3,094	72.6	18.2	21.5	53.3	5.6	#	0.3	0.9	1,496	16.9	3,059	8.3	48.9	4.7	64.3	1,361	39
Alamance-Burlington	NC	10,322	20,729	22,811	22,851	2,499	53.7	51.9	21.4	21.8	1.3	0.1	0.4	3.2	1,487	15.4	2,764	8.3	53.8	8.0	72.3	1,349	35
Buncombe County	NC	22,026	24,708	25,572	25,656	1,714	53.9	75.5	6.0	12.0	1.4	0.2	0.3	4.7	1,607	16.0	3,470	7.4	46.3	4.7	75.2	1,628	43
Cabarrus County	NC	12,853	19,115	28,960	29,747	1,961	39.8	62.3	18.0	13.0	2.5	0.1	0.3	3.6	1,852	16.1	3,723	8.0	49.8	5.0	80.4	1,591	38
Catawba County	NC	12,770	16,250	17,370	17,364	1,233	49.3	71.4	5.1	12.3	6.9	0.1	0.2	4.1	1,063	16.3	2,013	8.6	52.8	4.2	81.8	1,166	28
Charlotte-Mecklenburg	NC	77,069	103,336	135,954	141,728	13,866	54.7	32.3	42.1	17.6	5.1	0.0	0.5	2.5	8,791	16.1	17,176	8.3	51.2	6.3	69.2	7,052	173
Cleveland County	NC	8,131	9,663	16,417	16,229	284	59.9	63.4	26.0	4.9	0.8	#	1.1	4.7	1,116	14.5	2,200	7.4	50.7	8.1	68.6	1,027	29
Craven County	NC	14,239	14,829	15,048	15,229	691	52.8	53.9	29.2	8.2	3.3	0.2	0.4	4.9	942	16.2	1,775	8.6	53.1	5.0	74.2	867	25
Cumberland County	NC	44,612	50,850	53,307	53,053	1,062	56.1	33.7	44.9	11.0	1.7	0.3	1.9	6.5	3,588	14.8	7,115	7.5	50.4	3.8	76.4	3,327	86
Davidson County	NC	16,426	19,136	20,648	20,338	383	43.1	87.9	3.1	5.9	1.0	0.1	0.3	1.7	1,199	17.0	2,361	8.6	50.8	6.4	77.7	1,289	33
Durham	NC	18,517	29,728	32,479	33,256	4,477	58.7	20.6	50.9	22.7	2.4	0.1	0.3	2.9	2,138	15.6	4,317	7.7	49.5	5.1	70.1	1,813	55
Forsyth County	NC	37,625	44,769	53,367	53,340	6,300	54.0	43.3	29.3	20.9	2.2	0.1	0.2	4.0	3,626	14.7	6,793	7.9	53.4	6.0	78.3	3,150	81
Gaston County	NC	29,631	30,603	32,326	31,696	1,479	57.8	65.6	19.8	9.4	1.4	#	0.6	3.5	1,857	17.1	3,686	8.6	50.4	6.1	72.6	2,035	55
Guilford County	NC	24,575	63,417	73,205	74,086	5,848	54.7	37.9	40.7	11.2	5.6	0.2	0.6	3.9	4,938	15.0	9,842	7.5	50.2	3.1	80.4	4,616	121
Harnett County	NC	11,890	16,338	19,704	19,681	1,327	56.1	52.1	25.3	16.3	0.6	0.2	1.1	4.6	1,215	16.2	2,206	8.9	55.1	6.3	73.1	1,108	27
Iredell-Statesville	NC	10,610	17,235	21,393	21,494	1,078	42.2	70.3	14.1	10.6	2.7	0.1	0.2	2.0	1,318	16.3	2,528	8.5	52.1	3.6	85.9	1,407	36
Johnston County	NC	14,647	21,334	32,454	33,097	2,889	43.8	61.2	16.2	18.2	0.6	0.1	0.5	3.3	2,157	15.3	3,837	8.6	56.2	5.3	74.0	1,625	44
Nash-Rocky Mount	NC	11,653	18,342	17,448	16,952	778	64.5	34.9	49.6	9.8	0.7	#	0.6	4.4	1,075	15.8	2,228	7.6	48.2	7.0	72.1	1,049	27
New Hanover County	NC	19,090	21,605	24,806	25,131	883	43.8	63.9	22.4	8.1	1.6	0.1	0.4	3.5	1,614	15.6	3,256	7.7	49.6	5.8	81.9	1,462	40
Onslow County	NC	18,605	20,884	23,890	24,989	324	40.9	61.4	19.5	10.7	1.1	0.3	0.8	6.3	1,422	17.6	2,845	8.8	50.0	4.7	69.2	1,472	35
Pitt County	NC	17,693	20,040	23,630	23,919	968	55.4	38.1	48.3	9.4	1.3	#	0.7	2.7	1,599	15.0	3,010	7.9	53.1	6.6	69.2	1,298	37
Randolph County	NC	13,572	17,271	18,935	18,711	1,252	53.8	77.9	4.0	13.7	0.9	#	0.7	2.5	1,167	16.0	2,267	8.3	51.4	6.3	70.3	1,035	31
Robeson County	NC	23,251	23,911	23,933	24,996	1,563	78.8	15.6	25.4	11.4	1.2	0.1	43.0	3.6	1,512	16.5	2,943	8.5	51.4	6.7		1,389	42
Rowan-Salisbury	NC	16,403	20,472	20,460	20,340	1,444	60.2	64.6	19.0	12.5	1.1	0.1	0.3	2.5	1,354	15.0	2,680	7.6	50.5	6.1	75.9	1,352	35
Union County	NC	12,864	22,862	40,153	40,141	2,155	34.1	67.9	13.2	14.2	1.7	0.1	0.3	2.7	2,383	16.8	4,705	8.5	50.6	3.3	87.6	2,136	52
Wake County	NC	64,266	98,950	144,173	148,154	11,111	34.5	49.2	24.7	15.1	6.2	#	0.4	4.3	9,440	15.7	16,592	8.9	56.9	4.3	84.7	8,186	165
Wayne County	NC	13,653	19,279	19,471	19,912	1,529	60.5	41.3	34.6	17.0	1.1	0.1	0.2	5.7	1,261	15.8	2,497	8.0	50.5	5.6	75.5	1,170	31

See notes at end of table.

Selected statistics on enrollment, teachers, dropouts, and graduates in public school districts enrolling more than 15,000 students: Selected years, 1990 through 2011—Continued

Name of district	State	Enrollment, fall 1990	Enrollment, fall 2000	Enrollment, fall 2010	Enrollment, fall 2011	Number of English language learners, 2011	Percent eligible for free or reduced-price lunch, 2011[1]	White	Black	Hispanic	Asian	Pacific Islander	American Indian/Alaska Native	Two or more races	Number of classroom teachers	Pupil/teacher ratio	Total number of staff	Student/staff ratio	Teachers as a percentage of total staff	Percent dropping out of grades 9-12	Averaged freshman graduation rate (AFGR)[2]	Number of high school graduates, 2008–09[3]	Number of schools, fall 2011
											Percentage distribution of enrollment, by race/ethnicity, fall 2011												
1	2	3	4	5	6	7	8	9	10	11	12	13	14	15	16	17	18	19	20	21	22	23	24
Akron City	OH	33,213	31,464	23,113	22,678	865	71.6	40.2	46.3	2.8	3.7	0.1	0.1	6.9	1,569	14.5	4,744	4.8	33.1	6.3	65.0	1,484	53
Cincinnati City	OH	51,148	46,562	33,783	32,154	1,269	66.3	24.8	65.7	2.9	1.0	#	0.1	5.5	1,681	19.1	4,322	7.4	38.9	5.3	52.7	1,723	57
Cleveland Municipal	OH	70,019	75,684	44,974	42,805	2,598	82.8	14.6	67.6	13.8	0.8	#	0.2	3.0	3,516	12.2	8,736	4.9	40.2	12.9	42.3	2,187	98
Columbus City	OH	64,280	64,511	51,134	50,488	4,951	73.2	27.4	57.9	6.8	2.1	#	0.2	5.5	3,187	15.8	7,102	7.1	44.9	11.0	55.0	2,709	119
Hilliard City	OH	6,533	12,423	15,455	15,464	1,051	22.4	77.9	5.5	6.3	6.3	0.1	0.1	4.9	845	18.3	1,727	9.0	48.9	2.1	86.4	968	23
Lakota Local	OH	9,356	14,659	18,135	17,364	870	15.6	75.0	10.2	4.5	5.8	#	0.1	4.3	844	20.6	1,722	10.1	49.0	1.6	95.1	1,232	20
Olentangy Local	OH	2,140	5,417	15,815	16,690	305	8.0	82.3	3.9	2.3	7.7	0.1	0.1	3.7	879	19.0	1,748	9.5	50.3	0.4	100.0 [5]	733	33
South-Western City	OH	16,605	19,216	20,725	20,895	2,465	52.2	69.6	12.0	11.5	2.1	0.1	0.2	4.5	1,108	18.9	2,469	8.5	44.9	3.7	70.4	1,220	33
Toledo City	OH	40,452	37,738	24,283	23,115	321	70.0	40.1	42.8	9.3	0.6	#	0.1	7.1	1,438	16.1	2,952	7.8	48.7	4.2	48.9	1,276	51
Broken Arrow	OK	13,872	14,990	16,732	16,985	763	39.9	68.1	4.2	9.7	2.5	0.2	6.4	8.8	956	17.8	2,035	8.3	47.0	3.6	78.7	921	23
Edmond	OK	13,041	17,084	21,344	21,985	676	28.5	67.3	10.6	8.0	4.7	0.2	2.5	6.8	1,198	18.4	2,459	8.9	48.7	0.6	89.2	1,331	23
Lawton	OK	17,727	17,338	16,199	15,875	679	58.3	42.9	28.8	14.1	2.2	0.6	6.7	4.6	1,043	15.2	2,328	6.8	44.8	3.4	77.5	1,013	33
Moore	OK	16,630	18,101	22,226	22,672	676	47.0	59.9	7.4	12.0	5.0	0.4	7.8	7.5	1,320	17.2	2,553	8.9	51.7	3.4	80.0	1,233	31
Norman	OK	11,572	12,596	14,644	15,022	755	46.9	66.2	6.4	10.3	3.0	0.2	6.9	7.0	900	16.7	1,714	8.8	52.5	1.2	82.4	811	24
Oklahoma City	OK	36,066	39,750	42,989	43,212	12,775	87.8	18.5	27.2	45.9	2.4	0.2	4.3	1.6	2,567	16.8	5,130	8.4	50.0	4.9	58.3	1,657	93
Putnam City	OK	18,071	19,506	19,068	19,213	2,133	72.5	40.2	26.0	20.5	4.5	0.2	3.9	4.8	1,230	15.6	2,156	8.9	57.0	2.1	73.6	1,182	27
Tulsa	OK	40,732	42,812	41,501	41,199	6,534	81.5	29.0	29.3	25.9	1.4	0.2	7.5	6.7	2,457	16.8	5,605	7.4	43.8	0.4	58.0	1,652	81
Beaverton, 48J	OR	24,874	33,600	38,902	39,736	5,645	40.2	52.4	2.9	23.3	13.2	0.7	0.5	6.9	1,967	20.2	3,876	10.3	50.7	2.6	83.0	2,459	56
Bend-Lapine, SD1	OR	9,481	13,128	16,173	16,437	741	46.9	85.2	0.8	10.1	0.7	0.2	1.0	1.5	719	22.9	1,513	10.9	47.5	2.6	86.1	1,131	28
Eugene, SD4J	OR	17,904	18,432	17,379	17,368	380	41.6	70.4	2.0	12.6	3.7	0.4	1.7	9.2	734	23.6	1,697	10.2	43.3	1.5	91.3	1,353	36
Hillsboro, SD1J	OR	10,396	18,315	20,923	21,286	3,481	47.4	52.0	2.1	34.0	6.8	0.6	0.8	3.7	925	23.0	2,078	10.7	44.5	3.7	85.3	1,293	34
North Clackamas, SD12	OR	12,403	14,876	17,420	17,442	2,533	46.1	68.9	1.7	15.9	6.6	0.7	0.9	5.3	690	25.3	1,625	10.7	42.5	3.7	81.8	1,113	31
Portland, SD1J	OR	53,042	53,141	45,818	46,930	5,155	46.1	56.4	11.7	15.5	8.1	1.0	1.1	6.1	2,395	19.6	5,417	8.7	44.2	8.6	68.4	2,320	88
Salem-Keizer, SD24J	OR	27,756	35,108	40,403	40,756	8,572	60.5	51.2	1.0	38.0	2.2	1.9	1.2	4.5	1,813	22.5	4,107	9.9	44.1	4.5	81.7	2,474	66
Allentown City	PA	13,519	16,424	17,637	17,560	2,035	77.6	14.9	16.7	65.0	1.6	0.1	0.1	1.6	1,061	16.6	2,274	7.7	46.7	9.1	67.3	1,068	22
Central Bucks	PA	10,286	17,305	20,432	20,081	90	6.1	89.3	1.7	2.7	5.3	0.0	0.1	0.8	1,163	17.3	2,253	8.9	51.6	0.4	96.2	1,529	23
Philadelphia City	PA	190,979	201,190	166,233	154,262	11,885	79.4	14.1	56.2	18.3	7.5	0.0	0.2	3.7	9,299	16.6	20,072	7.7	46.3	7.0	53.5	8,377	251
Pittsburgh	PA	39,896	38,560	27,982	26,653	547	70.6	33.8	55.4	1.7	2.8	#	0.1	6.1	1,979	13.5	4,157	6.4	47.6	5.6	64.8	1,716	65
Reading	PA	11,965	15,487	18,194	18,060	3,372	90.2	8.8	10.5	77.2	0.7	#	0.1	2.8	1,113	16.2	2,197	8.2	50.7	10.0	55.5	760	24
Providence	RI	20,908	26,937	23,573	23,518	4,095	82.2	8.9	18.4	63.6	5.3	0.1	0.9	2.9	1,647	14.3	3,025	7.8	54.4	7.5	66.9	1,462	41
Aiken, 01	SC	23,970	25,147	24,632	24,729	1,344	58.3	56.0	33.4	6.8	0.7	0.1	0.2	2.8	1,508	16.4	2,360	10.5	63.9	4.7	62.5	1,276	40
Beaufort, 01	SC	12,518	16,721	19,648	19,992	3,172	52.7	44.5	31.4	20.2	1.0	0.2	0.3	2.4	1,393	14.4	2,094	9.5	66.5	0.9	63.7	995	31
Berkeley, 01	SC	27,384	26,635	29,400	30,085	1,729	57.4	53.2	31.5	7.6	1.6	0.1	0.4	5.4	1,788	16.8	2,671	11.3	66.9	5.5	64.6	1,422	39
Charleston, 01	SC	43,637	44,767	43,654	44,058	2,357	51.7	45.0	44.6	6.7	1.4	0.1	0.1	2.0	3,222	13.7	4,461	9.9	72.2	2.8	60.2	2,158	78
Dorchester, 02	SC	13,735	16,678	22,762	23,346	646	40.5	58.0	29.6	5.7	1.7	0.4	0.1	4.1	1,355	17.2	1,885	12.4	71.9	4.2	67.4	1,136	21
Florence, 01	SC	14,731	13,930	15,919	16,027	321	61.6	42.6	51.0	2.2	1.9	0.2	0.1	2.0	1,032	15.5	1,729	9.3	59.7	2.2	67.3	900	22
Greenville, 01	SC	51,434	59,875	71,930	72,153	7,399	48.1	59.0	23.4	11.9	2.2	0.1	0.2	3.3	4,376	16.5	6,747	10.7	64.9	3.5	69.0	3,805	95
Horry, 01	SC	24,080	29,894	38,534	38,957	2,585	63.3	65.2	20.6	8.3	1.1	0.2	0.3	4.3	2,564	15.2	3,986	9.8	64.3	4.8	72.1	2,091	51
Lexington, 01	SC	11,202	17,285	22,694	22,990	897	37.1	79.8	9.7	5.6	1.6	0.1	0.2	3.0	1,512	15.2	2,248	10.2	67.2	1.4	73.7	1,206	27
Lexington, 05	SC	11,683	15,064	16,699	16,560	468	32.8	62.4	27.7	3.3	2.6	0.3	0.4	3.3	1,147	14.4	1,532	10.8	74.8	1.7	80.8	1,186	19
Pickens, 01	SC	14,289	15,938	16,319	16,546	560	46.5	83.1	7.2	4.8	1.0	#	0.1	3.7	989	16.7	1,386	11.9	71.4	4.0	62.9	855	26
Richland, 01	SC	27,051	27,061	24,220	23,942	668	67.7	18.0	73.6	3.7	0.9	0.2	0.2	3.5	1,760	13.6	2,398	10.0	73.4	4.0	58.8	1,251	50
Richland, 02	SC	12,788	27,409	25,667	25,954	1,366	45.7	28.5	59.0	6.6	3.0	0.2	0.2	2.5	1,684	15.4	2,167	12.0	77.7	2.9	74.4	1,347	30
Sumter, 01	SC	18,531	19,063	17,060	16,915	208	70.5	33.1	60.8	3.0	0.8	0.2	0.2	2.1	1,006	16.8	1,672	10.1	60.2	—	—	—	27
York, 03	SC	12,665	14,925	17,343	17,217	861	53.7	52.5	36.1	6.4	1.6	0.1	1.5	1.8	1,124	15.3	1,463	11.8	76.9	2.8	67.5	997	28
Sioux Falls	SD	16,092	19,097	21,390	22,827	1,978	43.6	70.9	10.0	8.1	3.2	0.1	5.7	2.0	1,403	16.3	2,726	8.4	51.5	0.6	75.6	1,289	50
Davidson County	TN	68,452	67,669	78,782	80,393	8,697	71.0	32.3	45.8	17.3	3.9	0.1	0.1	0.5	5,377	15.0	10,209	7.9	52.7	5.7	70.4	3,978	144
Hamilton County	TN	22,785	39,915	42,589	43,296	1,457	59.6	58.8	31.4	6.9	2.1	0.1	0.2	0.5	3,020	14.3	5,083	8.5	59.4	5.7	71.8	2,367	78
Knox County	TN	50,750	51,944	57,977	58,639	1,567	45.9	76.4	14.4	5.2	2.0	0.1	0.2	1.7	3,806	15.4	6,983	8.4	54.5	4.0	79.2	3,500	88
Memphis	TN	107,103	113,730	111,834	110,952	6,409	83.8	7.3	82.4	8.5	1.3	0.1	0.1	0.4	7,027	15.8	12,316	9.0	57.1	10.5	67.3	6,559	216

See notes at end of table.

Selected statistics on enrollment, teachers, dropouts, and graduates in public school districts enrolling more than 15,000 students: Selected years, 1990 through 2011—Continued

Name of district	State	Enrollment, fall 1990	Enrollment, fall 2000	Enrollment, fall 2010	Enrollment, fall 2011	Number of English language learners, 2011	Percent eligible for free or reduced-price lunch, 2011	White	Black	Hispanic	Asian	Pacific Islander	American Indian/Alaska Native	Two or more races	Number of classroom teachers	Pupil/teacher ratio	Total number of staff	Student/staff ratio	Teachers as a percentage of total staff	Percent dropping out of grades 9-12	Averaged freshman graduation rate (AFGR)[2]	Number of high school graduates[3]	Number of schools, fall 2011
1	2	3	4	5	6	7	8	9	10	11	12	13	14	15	16	17	18	19	20	21	22	23	24
Montgomery County	TN	16,591	23,339	29,780	30,614	610	46.4	57.8	23.8	10.2	1.5	0.6	0.4	5.5	1,969	15.6	3,779	8.1	52.1	1.1	86.3	1,826	36
Rutherford County	TN	17,996	25,356	38,846	39,608	1,559	42.0	68.7	16.2	9.5	4.2	0.1	0.2	1.2	2,626	15.1	4,219	9.4	62.2	1.4	88.7	2,649	46
Shelby County	TN	37,675	46,972	47,706	46,423	937	35.0	51.6	36.9	4.9	4.8	0.1	0.2	1.4	3,036	15.3	5,501	8.4	55.2	0.3	76.1	2,727	52
Sumner County	TN	19,630	22,347	27,907	28,361	436	37.9	83.1	9.5	5.0	1.4	0.1	0.2	0.6	1,915	14.8	3,660	7.7	52.3	1.4	82.6	1,689	46
Williamson County	TN	11,472	19,545	31,616	32,983	419	11.6	88.3	4.3	3.3	3.5	0.3	0.1	0.3	2,033	16.2	3,777	8.7	53.8	0.8	100.0[5]	2,300	41
Wilson County	TN	10,175	11,430	15,705	20,075	184	26.9	86.5	7.1	3.3	1.9	0.2	0.3	0.8	1,026	19.6	1,999	10.0	51.3	1.6	91.4	1,175	21
Abilene ISD	TX	18,217	18,118	17,161	17,177	476	64.4	41.2	12.1	40.7	1.9	0.1	0.4	3.6	1,117	15.4	2,278	7.5	49.0	2.7	69.7	879	38
Aldine ISD	TX	41,372	52,520	63,154	64,300	16,110	84.5	2.1	25.9	69.7	1.4	0.1	0.1	0.8	3,782	17.0	7,896	8.1	47.9	5.6	59.0	2,652	75
Alief ISD	TX	29,774	42,151	45,768	45,410	14,082	80.4	3.6	32.0	50.5	12.7	0.2	0.6	0.5	2,968	15.3	5,886	7.7	50.4	5.0	64.6	2,270	46
Allen ISD	TX	5,240	10,604	18,888	19,505	1,111	16.5	58.0	10.0	13.3	13.5	0.3	0.6	4.3	1,189	16.4	2,092	9.3	56.8	0.3	98.5	1,230	23
Alvin ISD	TX	9,323	11,324	17,367	18,209	2,469	52.8	32.1	13.1	44.6	7.9	0.3	0.5	1.6	1,076	16.9	2,262	8.1	47.6	3.2	79.6	808	23
Amarillo ISD	TX	27,374	28,908	32,682	32,995	4,181	66.6	37.6	9.9	44.4	4.8	0.3	0.6	2.4	2,260	14.6	4,086	8.1	55.3	3.1	73.8	1,706	54
Arlington ISD	TX	44,958	58,866	64,484	64,703	10,972	65.3	25.1	23.3	42.7	6.8	0.1	0.4	1.7	3,931	16.5	7,705	8.4	51.0	2.9	68.1	3,441	77
Austin ISD	TX	65,885	77,816	85,697	86,528	21,751	63.9	24.5	9.1	60.5	3.3	0.1	0.3	2.3	5,758	15.0	11,169	7.7	51.6	4.9	68.6	3,914	122
Beaumont ISD	TX	20,627	20,696	19,893	19,870	1,149	66.6	14.0	61.8	19.1	4.8	0.1	0.2	1.9	1,404	14.1	2,861	6.9	49.1	3.1	70.2	1,091	30
Birdville ISD	TX	18,477	21,246	23,545	23,711	2,472	55.9	47.6	7.0	37.4	4.9	0.1	0.7	2.3	1,491	15.9	2,882	8.2	51.7	3.6	70.7	1,297	32
Brownsville ISD	TX	37,489	40,898	49,879	49,655	14,867	—	0.8	0.1	98.8	0.3	#	#	#	3,303	15.0	7,424	6.7	44.5	2.3	68.7	2,524	59
Bryan ISD	TX	11,413	13,501	15,751	16,611	2,776	71.9	26.4	20.8	51.0	1.1	0.1	0.2	1.1	1,145	14.5	2,189	7.1	49.3	4.4	72.1	747	27
Carrollton-Farmers Branch ISD	TX	17,561	24,134	26,159	26,423	5,455	62.1	18.5	16.0	53.1	10.7	0.1	0.4	1.2	1,634	16.2	3,063	8.6	53.3	1.6	73.7	1,553	43
Clear Creek ISD	TX	22,372	29,875	38,406	39,209	2,500	28.0	52.3	8.3	26.0	9.7	0.1	0.3	3.2	2,451	16.0	4,830	8.1	50.8	0.9	83.5	2,412	46
Comal ISD	TX	5,883	10,695	17,239	17,817	707	32.6	57.8	1.1	35.8	1.1	0.1	0.3	2.6	1,106	16.1	2,241	8.0	49.4	1.3	100.0[5]	1,072	30
Conroe ISD	TX	23,288	34,928	51,170	52,664	4,986	36.6	54.6	6.0	32.9	3.1	0.1	0.4	2.7	3,153	16.7	5,955	8.8	53.0	0.9	84.2	2,931	53
Corpus Christi ISD	TX	41,881	39,138	38,409	38,678	1,615	69.7	14.1	4.2	78.9	1.6	0.1	0.2	0.9	2,302	16.8	4,774	8.1	46.7	3.1	69.4	2,079	58
Crowley ISD	TX	5,832	9,137	15,240	15,101	1,145	53.4	24.8	40.4	22.9	4.3	0.1	0.3	1.6	900	16.8	1,519	9.9	59.3	1.2	74.1	808	23
Cypress-Fairbanks ISD	TX	41,196	63,497	106,097	107,960	13,200	48.3	30.0	16.1	42.8	8.1	#	0.3	2.6	6,243	17.3	12,363	8.7	50.5	6.0	85.9	5,614	83
Dallas ISD	TX	161,000	161,548	157,162	157,575	56,650	85.9	4.7	24.4	68.8	1.1	0.1	0.4	0.5	10,277	15.3	18,311	8.6	56.1	6.0	57.1	6,671	237
Denton ISD	TX	10,690	13,645	23,994	24,845	3,356	42.7	51.9	11.7	31.3	3.7	0.1	0.9	1.4	1,763	14.1	3,067	8.1	57.5	1.7	78.8	1,081	36
Eagle Mt.-Saginaw ISD	TX	4,691	6,567	16,709	17,155	1,021	39.4	48.5	9.1	34.9	0.2	0.2	0.6	3.0	1,030	16.7	2,008	8.5	51.3	3.5	93.9	821	25
Eagle Pass ISD	TX	10,584	12,515	14,850	15,012	4,849	55.1	1.2	0.1	97.1	0.2	#	1.3	0.1	875	16.8	2,013	7.5	43.5	4.4	61.6	797	24
Ector County ISD	TX	26,993	26,831	28,126	28,533	3,372	63.6	23.8	4.1	69.7	0.6	0.2	0.4	1.0	1,697	16.1	3,253	8.8	52.2	3.7	74.9	1,270	39
Edinburg CISD	TX	15,645	22,005	33,223	33,412	9,569	72.4	1.1	0.2	97.9	0.6	#	#	0.1	2,079	15.2	4,304	7.8	48.3	4.8	66.0	1,494	45
El Paso ISD	TX	64,092	62,325	64,330	64,214	13,277	77.2	10.9	4.1	82.6	1.1	0.1	0.2	1.0	4,223	15.2	8,194	7.8	51.5	4.8	66.0	3,396	96
Fort Bend ISD	TX	36,286	53,999	68,948	69,449	8,372	37.4	19.5	29.5	26.3	21.7	0.1	0.5	2.3	3,982	17.4	7,915	8.8	50.3	1.5	83.5	4,636	73
Fort Worth ISD	TX	69,163	79,661	81,651	83,109	21,913	77.0	13.7	23.2	59.8	1.8	#	0.5	1.2	5,126	16.2	9,898	8.4	51.8	6.5	62.4	3,568	144
Frisco ISD	TX	1,419	7,234	37,279	40,123	1,494	12.2	57.7	10.5	15.0	13.4	0.1	0.6	2.7	2,655	15.1	4,821	8.3	55.1	4.0	100.0[5]	1,270	51
Galena Park ISD	TX	15,593	18,885	21,680	21,861	5,807	78.7	5.7	16.7	75.5	0.8	0.1	0.5	0.8	1,492	14.6	2,974	7.4	50.2	4.6	59.2	1,298	24
Garland ISD	TX	37,978	50,312	57,833	58,151	10,818	59.9	23.4	17.0	48.8	8.0	0.1	0.5	2.0	3,651	15.9	7,240	8.0	50.4	2.7	92.0	3,562	74
Goose Creek CISD	TX	17,654	18,003	21,283	21,675	2,406	63.6	24.9	16.3	55.5	1.3	0.1	0.4	1.5	1,306	16.6	2,789	7.8	48.6	2.8	80.0	1,103	28
Grand Prairie ISD	TX	16,482	20,257	26,541	26,607	5,884	72.4	14.0	17.1	63.1	3.1	0.1	1.2	1.3	1,598	16.6	3,128	8.5	51.1	4.4	67.2	1,266	39
Harlingen CISD	TX	14,863	15,857	18,422	18,605	2,417	77.2	7.9	0.5	90.6	0.7	0.1	0.2	0.2	1,176	15.8	2,556	7.3	46.0	4.2	68.9	960	31
Hays CISD	TX	4,166	7,402	15,325	15,932	2,201	49.1	33.1	3.4	60.9	0.7	#	0.2	1.7	1,006	15.8	2,138	7.5	47.1	4.3	80.5	662	23
Houston ISD	TX	194,000	208,462	204,245	203,066	54,333	80.5	8.1	25.1	62.4	3.3	0.1	0.2	0.7	10,920	18.6	22,302	9.1	49.0	4.6	59.2	8,595	279
Humble ISD	TX	19,560	24,684	35,913	36,076	2,704	44.9	46.3	15.7	30.0	3.0	0.5	0.6	1.9	2,310	15.6	4,527	8.0	51.0	1.7	92.0	2,140	43
Hurst-Euless-Bedford ISD	TX	18,740	19,203	21,046	21,570	1,630	34.9	44.2	12.5	27.7	7.3	0.7	0.5	2.0	1,297	15.2	3,864	9.0	53.0	3.0	90.3	1,323	32
Irving ISD	TX	23,509	29,097	34,243	34,243	12,200	73.1	10.9	12.5	71.3	3.4	1.2	0.5	1.2	2,281	16.2	2,447	8.1	59.0	4.5	68.9	1,648	40
Judson ISD	TX	23,097	16,603	22,040	22,503	1,545	51.9	18.3	24.8	51.5	1.8	0.3	0.4	2.9	1,271	17.7	2,776	8.1	48.6	1.0	75.0	1,154	30
Katy ISD	TX	19,507	34,503	60,803	62,414	7,168	34.3	42.3	9.6	34.3	11.1	0.2	0.4	2.4	3,860	16.2	7,315	8.5	52.8	1.0	93.3	3,539	56
Keller ISD	TX	8,212	17,083	32,746	33,130	1,558	18.7	62.4	7.7	18.7	5.9	0.2	0.5	2.3	1,871	17.7	3,321	10.0	56.3	1.4	87.8	1,736	40
Killeen ISD	TX	22,131	29,687	40,231	40,998	2,889	54.6	29.3	33.6	26.3	2.8	1.4	0.8	2.7	2,755	14.9	5,918	6.9	46.6	2.6	69.1	1,660	55
Klein ISD	TX	26,220	29,687	45,310	46,002	4,776	41.9	37.7	14.0	36.6	8.4	0.0	0.4	2.7	2,917	15.8	5,580	8.2	52.3	2.8	79.7	2,760	45
La Joya ISD	TX	9,844	17,641	28,846	28,965	12,733	11.7	0.2	#	99.7	0.0	0.0	0.1	#	1,967	14.7	4,059	7.1	48.5	4.0	69.7	1,190	37
Lamar CISD	TX	12,335	15,159	24,637	25,278	2,693	47.2	28.6	18.6	46.1	5.4	#	0.3	1.1	1,499	16.9	3,072	8.2	48.8	2.7	82.7	1,228	36
Laredo ISD	TX	23,304	22,547	24,706	24,788	14,693	—	0.3	#	99.5	0.1	0.0	0.0	#	1,494	16.6	3,566	7.0	41.9	2.9	62.3	1,068	30

See notes at end of table.

Selected statistics on enrollment, teachers, dropouts, and graduates in public school districts enrolling more than 15,000 students: Selected years, 1990 through 2011—Continued

Columns 9–15 show the Percentage distribution of enrollment, by race/ethnicity, fall 2011. Columns 16–20 show Teachers and staff, fall 2011. Columns 21–23 show Dropouts and graduates, 2008-09.

Name of district	State	Enroll. fall 1990	Enroll. fall 2000	Enroll. fall 2010	Enroll. fall 2011	No. of English language learners, 2011	Percent eligible for free or reduced-price lunch, 2011	White	Black	Hispanic	Asian	Pacific Islander	American Indian/Alaska Native	Two or more races	No. of classroom teachers	Pupil/teacher ratio	Total no. of staff	Student/staff ratio	Teachers as % of total staff	Percent dropping out of grades 9-12	Averaged freshman graduation rate (AFGR)[2]	No. of high school graduates[3]	No. of schools, fall 2011
1	2	3	4	5	6	7	8	9	10	11	12	13	14	15	16	17	18	19	20	21	22	23	24
Leander ISD	TX	5,419	14,499	32,152	33,309	1,403	21.9	63.8	3.9	23.5	5.0	0.2	0.3	3.3	2,159	15.4	4,041	8.2	53.4	2.5	92.7	1,477	38
Lewisville ISD	TX	20,776	39,096	51,484	51,920	6,414	27.8	51.4	8.7	26.0	10.6	0.1	0.4	2.8	3,706	14.0	6,312	8.2	58.7	1.2	82.8	3,158	69
Lubbock ISD	TX	30,991	29,026	28,905	28,790	695	65.0	27.9	13.3	55.0	1.7	0.1	0.4	1.7	1,931	14.9	3,296	8.7	58.6	6.2	75.2	1,603	54
Mansfield ISD	TX	7,570	14,888	32,251	32,564	2,975	37.2	39.6	25.7	24.1	6.2	0.1	0.5	3.8	1,946	16.7	3,785	8.6	51.4	2.1	81.1	1,666	41
McAllen ISD	TX	21,120	21,747	25,622	25,252	6,550	—	5.0	0.4	92.5	1.7	#	0.2	0.3	1,575	16.0	3,143	8.0	50.1	4.2	68.9	1,306	34
McKinney ISD	TX	5,052	12,000	24,422	24,733	2,070	29.0	55.1	12.0	25.9	3.4	0.3	0.2	2.7	1,611	15.3	2,545	9.7	63.3	1.5	88.3	1,234	32
Mesquite ISD	TX	25,920	32,334	37,747	38,287	5,843	68.1	20.9	24.7	49.6	2.0	0.1	0.6	2.1	2,441	15.7	4,659	8.2	52.4	1.4	78.4	2,265	47
Midland ISD	TX	21,082	20,522	21,736	22,628	1,805	49.1	31.1	8.4	57.8	1.3	#	0.3	1.0	1,388	16.3	2,667	8.5	52.1	4.8	73.1	1,212	35
Mission CISD	TX	11,032	12,464	15,841	15,680	4,581	—	0.9	0.2	98.8	#	0.0	#	0.1	972	16.1	2,128	7.4	45.7	1.4	70.1	756	23
North East ISD	TX	39,909	50,875	66,604	67,439	4,726	45.1	31.0	7.0	55.2	3.6	0.2	0.2	2.7	4,299	15.7	8,418	8.0	51.1	1.3	81.0	3,961	75
Northside ISD	TX	30,229	63,739	95,581	98,110	6,106	53.2	19.6	6.1	68.3	2.9	0.2	0.2	2.7	5,881	15.7	11,937	8.2	49.3	1.1	80.4	5,000	111
Northwest ISD	TX	3,197	5,356	15,370	16,626	666	23.5	68.3	6.5	19.4	2.8	0.2	0.7	2.2	1,035	16.1	1,638	10.1	63.2	2.0	85.0	597	24
Pasadena ISD	TX	37,643	42,577	52,218	52,942	12,572	79.7	7.9	6.5	81.8	2.8	0.1	0.2	0.7	3,376	15.7	7,037	7.5	48.0	5.0	63.8	2,428	64
Pearland ISD	TX	6,739	10,618	18,769	19,205	1,108	26.8	43.9	16.4	26.7	9.7	0.1	0.1	2.5	1,083	17.7	2,133	9.0	50.8	1.6	90.6	991	24
Pflugerville ISD	TX	6,482	14,545	22,763	23,070	3,244	52.7	25.0	19.0	44.1	7.9	0.1	0.2	3.4	1,500	15.4	2,563	9.0	58.5	4.0	84.3	1,271	27
Pharr-San Juan-Alamo ISD	TX	18,773	22,537	31,508	31,634	12,348	—	0.7	0.1	99.0	0.2	0.0	#	#	2,047	15.5	4,325	7.3	47.3	1.6	78.6	1,594	45
Plano ISD	TX	30,585	47,161	55,568	55,659	5,403	25.8	42.9	11.0	22.0	20.4	0.1	0.3	3.4	3,822	14.6	6,537	8.5	58.5	0.8	86.6	3,449	78
Richardson ISD	TX	32,555	35,138	36,070	36,513	5,883	56.9	28.5	23.1	38.7	6.5	0.1	0.3	2.4	2,417	15.3	4,672	7.9	51.7	1.9	75.6	1,922	58
Round Rock ISD	TX	19,636	31,536	44,776	45,034	3,095	29.2	44.7	9.1	30.1	11.5	0.2	0.5	4.0	3,001	15.0	5,525	8.2	54.3	1.9	88.2	2,545	59
San Antonio ISD	TX	60,161	57,273	55,116	54,394	8,522	30.7	2.1	6.4	90.8	0.6	#	0.1	0.3	3,385	16.1	7,390	7.4	45.8	9.0	55.7	2,270	99
Socorro ISD	TX	14,350	26,711	42,569	43,672	7,927	72.1	5.6	5.1	90.9	0.9	0.1	0.4	0.3	2,414	18.1	4,688	9.3	51.5	2.3	77.7	2,336	44
Spring Branch ISD	TX	26,495	31,659	32,948	33,687	10,075	58.6	28.2	5.1	58.3	6.1	0.1	0.8	1.4	2,166	15.5	4,241	7.9	51.1	3.5	78.0	1,818	49
Spring ISD	TX	18,537	23,034	36,323	36,513	5,910	72.6	12.9	40.3	41.4	4.1	0.1	0.3	1.0	2,084	17.5	4,516	8.1	46.2	3.7	76.1	1,718	40
Tyler ISD	TX	16,182	16,626	18,549	18,393	3,385	69.6	24.8	29.5	42.5	0.9	0.1	0.3	1.4	1,285	14.3	2,594	7.1	49.5	0.4	66.5	901	28
United ISD	TX	12,553	27,556	41,876	42,179	16,869	74.4	1.2	0.1	98.3	0.3	#	0.5	0.1	2,504	16.8	6,001	7.0	41.7	7.5	80.4	2,140	41
Waco ISD	TX	14,304	15,433	15,305	15,329	1,610	87.7	11.0	30.6	56.1	0.3	#	0.1	1.4	962	15.9	1,987	7.7	48.4	2.3	66.9	722	32
Weslaco ISD	TX	11,903	13,407	17,839	17,788	4,362	—	1.2	1.2	98.2	0.3	0.1	0.1	0.1	1,054	16.9	2,301	7.7	45.8	2.3	67.6	801	21
Ysleta ISD	TX	49,974	46,394	44,746	44,376	9,645	74.6	2.2	0.8	96.6	0.1	#	0.1	0.2	3,074	14.4	6,296	7.0	48.8	4.0	77.9	2,915	63
Alpine	UT	38,854	47,117	67,076	69,639	2,164	29.5	86.9	0.7	8.8	1.0	1.3	0.5	0.7	2,821	24.7	5,535	12.4	50.4	2.2	76.4	3,032	80
Cache	UT	12,280	13,026	15,648	15,865	527	41.8	88.5	0.6	8.2	0.6	0.5	0.4	1.1	625	25.4	1,510	10.5	41.4	1.3	90.0	904	27
Canyons	UT	—	—	33,714	33,946	1,546	37.8	79.4	1.3	12.0	2.6	1.2	1.0	2.5	1,447	23.5	2,583	13.1	56.0	—	—	—	49
Davis	UT	54,558	59,578	67,452	69,285	1,467	33.4	85.2	1.4	8.7	1.6	1.1	0.5	1.4	2,792	24.8	5,895	11.8	47.4	2.9	83.9	3,837	98
Granite	UT	78,554	71,328	70,083	69,252	11,665	58.4	56.1	2.9	30.9	4.3	3.7	1.5	0.5	2,982	23.2	5,972	11.6	49.9	4.9	67.2	3,601	106
Jordan	UT	64,991	73,158	50,048	50,961	1,909	37.3	80.8	0.9	11.9	1.7	1.3	0.4	2.8	2,122	24.0	4,045	12.6	52.4	2.1	85.0	4,982	54
Nebo	UT	16,393	21,094	29,848	30,487	937	70.1	86.4	0.6	10.1	0.5	0.8	0.5	1.0	1,264	24.1	2,631	11.6	48.0	2.2	86.2	1,540	42
Salt Lake	UT	24,766	25,367	24,647	25,016	618	72.4	42.4	4.3	41.1	4.7	1.8	1.3	2.1	1,155	21.7	2,604	9.6	44.3	7.6	66.7	1,117	44
Washington	UT	13,264	18,374	26,091	26,883	1,552	58.9	82.2	0.9	12.1	0.7	1.8	1.8	0.5	1,171	23.0	2,306	11.6	50.7	2.8	76.7	1,280	48
Weber	UT	25,661	27,783	30,431	30,568	1,308	46.7	82.9	0.9	11.5	1.2	0.6	0.5	2.3	1,334	22.9	2,567	11.9	52.0	2.3	82.5	1,816	49
Arlington County	VA	14,825	18,870	21,485	21,892	5,159	31.9	45.5	11.2	28.6	9.6	0.1	0.3	4.7	1,810	12.1	3,625	6.0	49.9	2.7	82.3	1,124	35
Chesapeake City	VA	29,533	37,645	39,748	39,468	635	29.7	51.2	32.9	6.2	2.5	0.2	0.2	6.6	2,680	14.7	5,510	7.2	48.6	1.8	78.5	2,871	47
Chesterfield County	VA	44,480	51,212	59,243	59,200	2,826	30.1	55.4	26.7	10.2	3.6	0.1	0.3	3.7	3,861	15.3	6,996	8.5	55.2	1.7	85.7	4,103	62
Fairfax County	VA	128,840	156,412	174,479	177,606	36,551	25.9	43.4	10.4	21.9	19.4	0.1	0.2	4.6	13,878	12.8	28,861	6.2	48.1	2.0	89.6	12,003	209
Hampton City	VA	21,383	23,290	21,568	21,588	372	53.1	27.6	60.4	5.2	2.3	0.1	0.3	4.0	1,605	13.4	3,207	6.7	50.1	4.2	65.6	1,357	32
Hanover County[6]	VA	11,328	16,611	18,628	18,531	118	18.8	83.3	9.6	2.8	1.8	0.1	0.2	2.0	1,301	14.2	2,652	7.0	49.0	1.1	88.1	1,446	26
Henrico County	VA	32,638	41,655	49,405	49,654	2,506	38.0	44.8	37.0	6.7	7.9	0.1	0.3	3.2	3,116	15.9	4,528	11.0	68.8	3.3	80.0	3,090	79
Loudoun County	VA	14,485	31,804	63,142	65,585	4,639	16.6	57.0	7.0	15.1	15.4	0.1	0.2	4.7	4,702	13.9	10,320	6.4	45.6	1.0	95.1	3,389	80
Newport News City	VA	28,925	33,008	30,488	29,948	883	57.3	28.7	54.9	10.3	2.8	0.1	0.6	2.7	1,716	17.5	4,171	7.2	41.1	4.7	68.0	1,852	44
Norfolk City	VA	36,541	37,349	33,787	33,461	621	63.6	22.3	62.3	6.2	2.1	0.1	0.4	6.3	2,332	14.4	4,348	7.7	53.6	5.6	52.9	1,560	50
Portsmouth City	VA	18,405	16,473	15,126	15,261	59	70.5	22.4	69.2	3.2	0.7	0.2	0.2	4.0	960	15.9	2,051	7.4	46.8	7.4	57.9	826	25
Prince William County	VA	41,888	54,646	79,358	81,937	13,868	36.5	35.4	20.6	28.9	7.5	0.2	0.3	7.0	5,160	15.9	9,311	8.8	55.4	2.2	78.5	4,590	88
Richmond City[6]	VA	27,021	27,237	23,454	23,336	967	71.4	9.4	81.6	7.4	0.7	0.1	0.1	0.6	1,332	17.5	3,117	7.5	42.7	5.1	52.2	991	53
Spotsylvania County	VA	12,227	18,876	23,585	23,817	819	33.2	63.6	18.7	10.5	2.8	0.1	0.3	3.9	1,464	16.3	2,635	9.0	55.5	2.2	83.1	1,669	34

See notes at end of table.

Selected statistics on enrollment, teachers, dropouts, and graduates in public school districts enrolling more than 15,000 students: Selected years, 1990 through 2011—Continued

Name of district	State	Enrollment, fall 1990	Enrollment, fall 2000	Enrollment, fall 2010	Enrollment, fall 2011	Number of English language learners, 2011	Percent eligible for free or reduced-price lunch, 2011[1]	White	Black	Hispanic	Asian	Pacific Islander	American Indian/Alaska Native	Two or more races	Number of classroom teachers	Pupil/teacher ratio	Total number of staff	Student/staff ratio	Teachers as a percentage of total staff	Percent dropping out of grades 9-12	Averaged freshman graduation rate (AFGR)[2]	Number of high school graduates[3]	Number of schools, fall 2011
								(Percentage distribution of enrollment, by race/ethnicity, fall 2011)							_(Teachers and staff, fall 2011)_					_(Dropouts and graduates, 2008–09)_			
1	2	3	4	5	6	7	8	9	10	11	12	13	14	15	16	17	18	19	20	21	22	23	24
Stafford County	VA	12,555	21,124	27,257	27,333	1,160	22.7	58.1	18.3	13.6	2.8	0.2	0.4	6.6	1,819	15.0	3,551	7.7	51.2	1.5	88.4	1,960	30
Virginia Beach City	VA	70,266	76,596	71,185	70,978	1,004	38.1	52.5	24.3	9.4	5.5	0.5	0.3	7.5	4,398	16.1	9,377	7.6	46.9	1.9	75.7	4,789	85
Bellevue	WA	14,971	15,431	18,330	18,475	1,595	21.0	48.3	3.0	10.4	29.9	0.2	0.3	7.9	933	19.8	1,826	10.1	51.1	1.1	87.1	1,219	29
Bethel	WA	11,319	16,029	17,779	17,962	57	47.4	62.4	9.9	15.8	6.6	2.1	2.1	4.1	842	21.3	1,678	10.7	50.2	6.6	66.6	981	40
Edmonds	WA	18,452	22,067	20,757	20,587	1,975	38.6	54.8	5.7	15.8	13.6	0.7	0.7	8.8	948	21.7	1,854	11.1	51.1	5.5	75.5	1,355	40
Everett	WA	14,846	18,683	18,992	18,776	1,464	20.5	62.1	4.1	14.4	12.0	1.2	0.9	5.2	876	21.4	1,647	11.4	53.2	2.2	75.8	1,102	33
Evergreen (Clark)	WA	14,242	21,660	25,750	26,333	563	48.2	66.9	3.2	14.3	6.8	1.5	0.8	6.5	1,414	18.6	2,433	10.8	58.1	7.4	70.7	1,317	37
Federal Way	WA	17,263	22,623	22,258	22,279	2,737	56.3	36.8	12.7	23.0	12.7	4.1	0.9	11.5	1,174	19.0	2,145	10.4	54.7	3.4	64.0	1,291	48
Highline	WA	15,900	18,024	17,992	18,152	3,907	69.0	25.2	11.1	35.5	14.7	4.2	1.1	8.2	977	18.6	1,929	9.4	50.7	4.0	56.8	847	49
Issaquah	WA	8,533	14,259	17,358	17,825	649	10.4	64.1	2.0	6.9	22.3	0.3	0.4	4.0	836	21.3	1,556	11.5	53.8	1.5	88.7	1,146	27
Kennewick	WA	11,147	13,629	16,467	16,599	1,823	51.0	63.4	2.4	29.5	2.5	0.3	0.7	1.2	806	20.6	1,526	10.9	52.8	4.0	74.8	886	28
Kent	WA	20,212	26,535	27,079	27,160	3,751	48.6	41.4	12.1	18.6	16.9	2.2	0.7	8.0	1,346	20.2	2,497	10.9	53.9	5.8	64.3	1,533	42
Lake Washington	WA	22,431	23,662	24,677	24,924	1,386	14.8	65.2	1.8	9.4	17.9	0.4	0.3	5.2	1,277	19.5	2,226	11.2	57.4	1.6	86.0	1,597	54
Northshore	WA	17,213	20,255	19,750	19,811	962	18.3	67.0	1.8	11.3	12.7	0.4	0.6	6.3	957	20.7	1,765	11.2	54.2	1.9	86.1	1,491	34
Pasco	WA	6,677	8,850	15,164	15,708	5,131	71.8	26.4	2.0	68.2	1.2	0.2	0.6	1.8	816	19.2	1,510	10.4	54.1	8.7	62.1	615	19
Puyallup	WA	14,325	19,757	20,986	20,810	611	34.2	65.5	3.9	12.9	4.7	1.0	1.0	10.7	1,030	20.2	1,933	10.8	53.3	7.1	81.9	1,419	37
Seattle	WA	40,917	47,575	47,735	49,269	4,857	41.3	43.3	18.5	12.3	18.4	0.6	1.2	5.7	2,645	18.6	4,964	9.9	53.3	6.7	77.0	2,661	105
Spokane	WA	27,965	31,725	29,446	29,038	58	56.6	73.9	2.8	7.4	2.7	1.4	2.3	9.4	1,631	17.8	3,035	9.6	53.7	8.3	62.7	1,622	60
Tacoma	WA	29,465	34,093	28,540	28,540	1,960	44.0	44.4	17.1	15.8	9.9	1.9	1.3	9.7	1,613	17.7	3,049	9.4	52.9	6.3	54.3	1,460	67
Vancouver	WA	15,943	21,892	22,669	22,713	2,213	53.2	65.6	3.5	19.3	3.6	1.8	0.8	5.3	1,057	21.5	2,151	10.6	49.1	4.7	72.8	1,285	41
Yakima	WA	12,076	13,985	14,927	15,120	4,163	81.6	20.6	1.0	74.0	0.5	#	1.0	2.8	801	18.9	1,521	9.9	52.7	4.5	54.2	677	26
Berkeley County	WV	10,415	13,076	17,720	18,002	378	47.8	79.6	10.2	5.5	1.0	0.1	0.2	3.4	1,259	14.3	2,488	7.2	50.6	4.2	79.2	1,018	30
Kanawha County	WV	34,284	29,250	28,458	28,429	215	49.7	84.0	12.9	0.7	1.5	#	0.1	0.7	1,979	14.4	3,861	7.4	51.3	5.3	75.4	1,656	70
Appleton Area	WI	12,876	14,793	15,194	15,119	1,347	38.9	76.0	4.5	7.5	11.2	0.0	0.8	2.5	901	16.8	1,499	10.1	60.1	2.1	94.6	1,159	38
Green Bay Area	WI	18,048	20,104	20,376	20,636	4,023	52.1	55.0	8.3	23.3	6.8	#	4.1	2.5	1,364	15.1	2,360	8.7	57.8	5.8	83.8	1,381	39
Kenosha	WI	16,219	20,099	22,986	22,905	1,940	49.0	56.5	15.5	23.2	1.7	0.1	0.3	2.7	1,307	17.5	2,367	9.7	55.2	3.7	82.1	1,482	44
Madison Metropolitan	WI	23,214	25,087	24,806	26,817	4,475	49.3	45.3	20.1	17.9	9.4	0.1	0.5	6.7	1,842	14.6	3,738	7.2	49.3	3.6	82.5	1,674	55
Milwaukee	WI	92,789	97,985	80,934	79,130	7,772	83.6	14.2	55.6	23.8	5.3	#	0.8	0.3	3,961	20.0	9,091	8.7	43.6	8.9	66.0	4,745	177
Racine Unified	WI	22,159	21,102	21,100	20,809	2,002	62.0	44.4	26.3	25.1	1.4	#	0.3	2.5	1,399	14.9	2,447	8.5	57.2	5.6	73.9	1,250	35

—Not available.
†Not applicable.
#Rounds to zero.
[1]Percentages are for those schools that reported on free and reduced-price lunch eligibility.
[2]The averaged freshman graduation rate provides an estimate of the percentage of students who receive a regular diploma within 4 years of entering ninth grade. The rate uses aggregate student enrollment data to estimate the size of an incoming freshman class and aggregate counts of the number of diplomas awarded 4 years later.
[3]Includes regular diplomas only.
[4]Total for districts reporting data.

[5]Reported data indicated an averaged freshman graduation rate of greater than 100.0 percent.
[6]Number of teachers based on data reported through the "Public Elementary/Secondary School Universe Survey."
NOTE: Total enrollment, staff, and teacher data in this table reflect totals reported by school districts and may differ from data derived from summing school-level data to school district aggregates. ISD = independent school district. CISD = consolidated independent school district. Race categories exclude persons of Hispanic ethnicity. Detail may not sum to totals because of rounding.
SOURCE: U.S. Department of Education, National Center for Education Statistics, Common Core of Data (CCD), "Public Elementary/Secondary School Universe Survey," 2011–12; "Local Education Agency Universe Survey," 1990–91, 2000–01, 2010–11, and 2011–12; and "Local Education Agency-Level Public-Use Data File on Public School Dropouts: School Year 2008–09." (This table was prepared April 2014.)

Enrollment, poverty, and federal funds for the 100 largest school districts, by enrollment size in 2011: Selected years, 2010–11 through 2013

Name of district	State	Rank order	Enrollment, fall 2011	5- to 17-year-old population, 2012	5- to 17-year-olds in poverty, 2012	Poverty rate of 5- to 17-year-olds, 2012	Revenues by source of funds, 2010–11					Revenue for selected federal programs (in thousands), 2010–11					Title I allocations (in thousands), federal fiscal year 2013[a]				
							Total (in thousands)	Federal (in thousands)	Federal as a percent of total	Federal revenue per student[b]	Title I basic and concentration grants	School lunch	Individuals with Disabilities Education Act (IDEA)	Eisenhower math and science	Vocational education	Drug-free schools	Total	Basic grants	Concentration grants	Targeted grants	Education finance incentive grants
1	2	3	4	5	6	7	8	9	10	11	12	13	14	15	16	17	18	19	20	21	22
New York City	NY	1	990,145	1,240,981	370,085	29.8	$22,651,559	$3,120,314	13.8	$3,135	$1,140,596	$334,291	$464,415	—	$15,655	$8,714	$720,281	$271,556	$67,586	$208,814	$172,325
Los Angeles Unified	CA	2	659,639	761,829	223,372	29.3	9,445,475	1,535,645	16.3	2,301	675,588	253,310	189,695	$54,204	9,781	1,631	315,289	107,192	26,745	86,170	95,182
City of Chicago (SD 299)	IL	3	403,004	430,713	143,000	33.2	5,661,444	1,118,967	19.8	2,758	459,176	175,878	159,283	45,955	8,003	7,062	272,319	93,395	23,231	72,582	83,111
Dade	FL	4	350,239	394,758	110,156	27.9	3,458,517	663,341	19.2	1,910	177,056	110,504	102,526	17,329	5,758	218	122,152	46,271	10,042	33,836	32,004
Clark County	NV	5	313,398	350,540	76,030	21.7	2,927,746	311,131	10.6	991	99,418	71,989	66,986	9,097	2,576	306	81,535	32,294	7,009	22,851	19,382
Broward	FL	6	258,478	287,262	53,929	18.8	2,477,771	439,868	17.8	1,715	90,884	66,084	72,542	9,260	3,750	266	58,780	22,876	5,283	16,050	14,570
Houston ISD	TX	7	203,066	220,326	79,293	36.0	2,221,585	408,408	18.4	2,000	132,832	96,349	28,356	11,296	3,323	410	103,713	37,483	9,142	29,726	29,362
Hillsborough	FL	8	197,041	214,014	45,346	21.2	1,947,934	424,200	21.8	2,181	76,327	62,106	63,723	8,467	3,227	25	49,561	19,558	4,770	13,283	11,950
Hawaii Department of Education	HI	9	182,706	216,099	33,653	15.6	2,499,513	347,363	13.9	1,934	54,333	45,171	50,244	1,142	3,155	1,203	47,598	19,946	4,329	10,800	12,523
Orange	FL	10	180,000	198,168	47,746	24.1	1,889,105	311,541	16.5	1,770	58,871	52,466	60,353	7,595	2,443	153	50,006	20,001	4,341	13,189	12,475
Fairfax County	VA	11	177,606	191,047	15,042	7.9	2,371,770	136,207	5.7	781	25,149	26,524	45,065	3,343	1,614	154	19,164	7,771	1,687	4,364	5,342
Palm Beach	FL	12	176,901	199,586	43,819	22.0	1,922,511	296,851	15.4	1,700	58,400	44,029	56,733	0	1,643	—	45,864	18,478	4,052	11,992	11,343
Gwinnett County	GA	13	162,370	172,247	34,383	20.0	1,663,059	165,617	10.0	1,030	25,319	52,030	26,452	3,066	1,059	82	36,474	15,007	3,257	9,215	8,995
Dallas ISD	TX	14	157,575	186,720	68,895	36.9	1,736,994	353,634	20.4	2,250	114,415	67,637	20,106	11,165	2,855	30	88,848	32,442	7,634	23,619	25,154
Philadelphia City	PA	15	154,262	240,899	91,341	37.9	2,896,799	636,770	22.0	3,831	242,012	70,487	0	30,165	6,095	422	276,989	59,340	14,755	46,055	56,839
Wake County	NC	16	148,154	173,789	26,778	15.4	1,183,308	145,597	12.3	1,010	9,274	23,472	16,296	3,843			27,919	11,263	2,444	6,787	7,425
Montgomery County	MD	17	146,459	170,144	13,226	7.8	2,687,215	165,503	6.2	1,149	23,458	24,045	46,184	4,205	1,342	74	22,589	9,339	2,157	5,486	5,606
Charlotte-Mecklenburg	NC	18	141,728	168,478	36,759	21.8	1,378,746	179,719	13.0	1,322	18,328	40,431	20,053	5,601			38,994	15,471	3,358	9,629	10,535
San Diego Unified	CA	19	131,044	140,229	31,075	22.2	1,474,174	216,241	14.7	1,641	66,432	43,103	32,309	6,618	1,097	287	36,842	14,564	3,646	9,440	9,193
Duval	FL	20	125,429	143,040	33,685	23.5	1,210,443	224,407	18.5	1,810	56,626	33,604	38,198	5,777	1,435	127	34,398	14,203	3,243	8,712	8,240
Prince George's County	MD	21	123,833	145,787	16,020	11.0	1,910,110	246,936	12.9	1,949	49,487	39,250	40,188	5,306	1,239	223	25,149	10,305	2,380	6,145	6,320
Memphis	TN	22	110,952	117,393	41,168	35.1	1,170,410	232,924	19.9	2,083	91,486	44,898	28,862	—	2,863	274	54,806	20,141	4,912	13,533	16,220
Cypress-Fairbanks ISD	TX	23	107,960	109,903	18,069	16.4	953,005	130,329	13.7	1,228	12,868	26,596	10,233	1,898	719	132	18,496	7,844	1,721	4,530	4,401
Cobb County	GA	24	107,291	119,447	18,907	15.8	1,124,647	107,963	9.6	1,006	15,514	23,641	14,020	2,318	719	525	21,985	9,267	2,140	5,651	4,928
Baltimore County	MD	25	105,153	127,642	14,500	11.4	1,555,549	138,275	8.9	1,328	27,187	21,375	40,779	5,670	1,365	65	22,755	9,522	2,067	5,351	5,814
Pinellas	FL	26	103,776	118,415	25,823	21.8	1,036,307	175,861	17.0	1,691	32,777	24,713	40,901	5,803	2,317	82	26,050	10,917	2,369	6,560	6,205
Jefferson County	KY	27	99,191	122,120	28,919	23.7	1,204,917	201,021	16.7	2,065	55,294	32,593	14,272	—	948		35,648	13,974	3,033	8,486	10,156
Northside ISD	TX	28	98,110	101,894	17,255	16.9	927,836	110,664	11.9	1,158	19,823	26,371	12,896	2,509	1,133	94	17,862	7,593	1,674	4,365	4,230
DeKalb County	GA	29	98,088	109,167	30,367	27.8	1,126,337	136,572	12.1	1,392	32,524	35,701	29,266	4,003	1,452	326	34,551	13,342	3,359	8,604	9,247
Polk	FL	30	96,070	102,837	28,409	27.6	936,340	182,192	19.5	1,914	42,036	32,194		4,848		98	28,840	12,036	2,612	7,293	6,898
Albuquerque	NM	31	94,318	114,855	28,276	24.6	1,006,464	138,297	13.7	1,449	29,955	20,445	40,921	5,888	1,153	64	30,500	12,375	2,686	7,500	7,940
Fulton County	GA	32	92,604	108,098	19,462	18.0	1,118,648	93,481	8.4	1,018	20,183		15,305	1,828	749	106	20,073	8,532	1,852	4,974	4,715
Austin ISD	TX	33	86,528	94,329	26,696	28.3	1,096,563	155,833	14.2	1,818	45,259	27,874	13,438	4,011	1,285	0	28,649	11,621	2,722	7,254	7,053
Jefferson County, No. R1	CO	34	85,793	88,605	9,658	10.9	857,134	76,726	9.0	892	15,385	11,451	20,924	2,636	428	49	10,052	4,276	928	2,190	2,658
Baltimore City	MD	35	84,212	91,468	31,331	34.3	1,441,019	279,303	19.4	3,333	106,721	29,203	36,064	10,456	1,887	617	52,113	20,566	4,912	12,962	13,673
Lee	FL	36	83,895	89,605	20,919	23.3	827,211	142,228	17.2	1,735	24,968	26,174	26,172	0	1,215	44	22,823	9,490	2,192	5,849	5,292
Long Beach Unified	CA	37	83,691	89,507	23,333	26.1	851,802	149,698	17.6	1,765	51,959	27,156	22,371	3,792	929	205	30,167	11,943	3,033	7,729	7,462
Fort Worth ISD	TX	38	83,109	89,093	31,457	35.3	835,866	181,849	21.8	2,227	48,520	29,951	15,498	6,384	1,260	25	37,690	15,086	3,679	9,616	9,308
Prince William County	VA	39	81,937	84,571	7,744	9.2	902,165	72,626	8.1	915	15,401		11,913	1,771	667	62	8,879	4,024	873	1,910	2,071
Denver	CO	40	80,890	88,209	21,750	24.5	976,213	161,894	16.6	2,067	54,552	24,399	20,527	6,267	1,601	155	30,124	11,520	2,927	7,426	8,252
Davidson County	TN	41	80,393	93,535	25,839	27.6	822,265	130,054	15.8	1,651	44,616	27,650	26,117	—	2,374	76	28,958	11,128	2,629	6,966	8,234
Milwaukee	WI	42	79,130	112,298	42,455	37.8	1,310,838	265,333	20.2	3,278	127,141	35,555	37,601	—	1,825	—	78,992	28,094	6,947	19,227	24,724
Anne Arundel County	MD	43	76,303	90,463	7,343	8.1	1,102,787	78,339	7.1	1,038	10,334	9,812	26,055	3,119	747	56	10,227	4,645	1,008	2,192	2,382
Fresno Unified	CA	44	74,235	79,559	32,432	40.8	768,552	139,750	18.2	1,867	65,078	32,103	20,125	4,421	1,739	114	43,423	17,035	4,317	11,180	10,891
Guilford County	NC	45	74,086	83,981	18,299	21.8	795,228	96,060	12.1	1,312	10,807	21,609	6,040	4,626	—	—	21,166	8,462	1,954	5,148	5,601

See notes at end of table.

Enrollment, poverty, and federal funds for the 100 largest school districts, by enrollment size in 2011: Selected years, 2010–11 through 2013—Continued

Name of district	State	Rank order	Enrollment, fall 2011	5- to 17-year-old population, 2012	5- to 17-year-olds in poverty, 2012	Poverty rate of 5- to 17-year-olds, 2012	Revenues by source of funds, 2010–11				Revenue for selected federal programs (in thousands), 2010–11						Title I allocations (in thousands), federal fiscal year 2013[3]				
							Total (in thousands)	Federal (in thousands)	Federal as a percent of total	Federal revenue per student	Title I basic and concentration grants	School lunch	Individuals with Disabilities Education Act (IDEA)	Eisenhower math and science	Vocational education	Drug-free schools	Total	Basic grants	Concentration grants	Targeted grants	Education finance incentive grants
1	2	3	4	5	6	7	8	9	10	11	12	13	14	15	16	17	18	19	20	21	22
Greenville, 01	SC	46	72,153	81,629	18,739	23.0	701,103	82,614	11.8	1,149	24,592	18,170	15,406	2,316	1,179	101	21,079	8,336	1,809	4,841	6,093
Brevard	FL	47	71,792	79,162	16,431	20.8	665,068	108,726	16.3	1,513	20,759	15,345	24,352	2,895	662	55	16,136	6,938	1,506	3,954	3,740
Virginia Beach City	VA	48	70,978	75,131	8,713	11.6	769,740	88,488	11.5	1,243	13,556	11,669	22,018	2,435	833	50	10,232	4,517	980	2,233	2,501
Alpine	UT	49	69,639	76,703	8,221	10.7	436,619	48,206	11.0	719	5,846	10,584	16,799	1,340	684	0	8,614	3,641	841	1,894	2,237
Fort Bend ISD	TX	50	69,449	77,845	8,820	11.3	623,356	55,659	8.9	807	8,040	10,551	7,111	1,108	578	43	8,681	3,932	904	2,058	1,787
Davis	UT	51	69,285	75,387	7,036	9.3	454,945	51,425	11.3	762	4,450	11,386	17,164	1,515	615	42	6,658	2,983	666	1,412	1,598
Granite	UT	52	69,252	78,955	17,134	21.7	474,236	68,178	14.4	973	16,771	17,606	18,299	2,721	1,448	174	18,305	7,237	1,571	4,150	5,347
North East ISD	TX	53	67,439	74,866	12,094	16.2	685,916	74,207	10.8	1,114	15,550	14,755	10,189	2,175	664	62	12,194	5,320	1,223	2,963	2,689
Detroit City	MI	54	67,064	135,355	69,045	51.0	1,250,847	451,471	36.1	5,806	199,619	31,071	12,190	0	4,401	720	154,750	50,842	12,959	40,302	50,647
Pasco	FL	55	66,659	72,275	13,431	18.6	666,094	115,324	17.3	1,721	20,772	19,162	22,437	0	761	2,929	13,520	5,801	1,369	3,333	3,016
Loudoun County	VA	56	65,585	70,829	2,855	4.0	917,398	37,168	4.1	589	1,473	5,085	16,949	488	442	21	1,475	1,475	0	0	0
Washoe County	NV	57	64,740	71,426	11,461	16.0	618,416	71,782	11.6	1,115	17,914	13,545	12,255	2,554	758	46	11,972	5,300	1,224	2,991	2,457
Mesa Unified	AZ	58	64,728	80,101	20,171	25.2	610,696	105,472	17.3	1,620	36,441	20,629	19,768	4,499	1,636	190	23,412	9,206	2,245	5,675	6,287
Arlington ISD	TX	59	64,703	76,796	16,588	24.8	591,620	117,878	19.9	1,828	18,642	19,549	10,420	1,985	844	6	16,840	7,185	1,603	4,099	3,953
Seminole	FL	60	64,344	72,382	10,715	14.8	577,531	89,063	15.4	1,387	12,841	13,805	18,685	2,477	529	28	10,102	4,516	980	2,367	2,239
Aldine ISD	TX	61	64,300	61,405	23,524	38.3	603,132	116,869	19.4	1,851	25,863	32,681	8,878	2,755	881	91	24,820	10,213	2,347	6,246	6,015
El Paso ISD	TX	62	64,214	65,790	22,286	33.9	595,870	95,837	16.1	1,490	27,368	20,898	6,169	2,897	1,403	36	29,482	11,606	2,958	7,718	7,200
Douglas County, No. RE1	CO	63	63,114	66,570	2,678	4.0	597,377	34,224	5.7	557	1,032	3,575	11,356	585	169	84	1,184	1,184	0	0	0
Katy ISD	TX	64	62,414	61,366	6,829	11.1	599,020	56,482	9.4	929	5,300	9,668	7,371	912	335	40	6,194	2,978	646	1,394	1,175
Elk Grove Unified	CA	65	62,126	69,006	12,813	18.6	580,280	64,944	11.2	1,040	14,441	14,687	13,349	2,495	497	57	13,300	5,750	1,325	3,248	2,978
Volusia	FL	66	61,524	67,795	17,052	25.2	608,890	104,082	17.1	1,691	24,974	16,662	20,282	2,925	768	0	16,941	7,250	1,599	4,158	3,933
Mobile County	AL	67	61,462	72,082	19,529	27.1	587,680	110,840	18.9	1,787	40,040	22,476	24,751	5,016	1,518	92	21,199	8,316	2,112	5,230	5,541
Chesterfield County	VA	68	59,200	62,081	5,711	9.2	563,296	44,087	7.8	744	7,495	6,779	15,182	1,255	585	19	5,735	2,946	844	1,345	1,444
Knox County	TN	69	58,639	68,116	12,181	17.9	480,087	58,015	12.1	1,001	19,954	12,943	14,962	—	1,373	423	12,224	5,229	1,164	2,835	2,996
Garland ISD	TX	70	58,151	60,067	13,120	21.8	545,423	93,503	17.1	1,617	20,717	16,054	9,094	1,987	707	51	13,688	5,877	1,357	3,360	3,094
Santa Ana Unified	CA	71	57,250	55,247	15,281	27.7	648,953	105,933	16.3	1,848	39,310	27,283	14,059	2,870	457	156	15,875	6,771	1,548	3,907	3,649
San Francisco Unified	CA	72	56,310	73,120	12,378	16.9	684,462	82,824	12.1	1,490	25,508	13,261	0	4,036	357	73	12,237	5,530	1,210	3,004	2,493
Plano ISD	TX	73	55,659	62,713	5,809	9.3	633,556	56,088	8.9	1,009	6,098	6,976	8,181	1,018	532	3	4,669	2,533	0	1,163	973
Boston	MA	74	55,027	71,810	23,305	32.5	1,250,911	151,199	12.1	2,698	45,802	14,288	19,130	0	1,678	—	40,755	14,827	3,580	9,306	13,043
Osceola	FL	75	54,783	53,327	11,992	22.5	509,748	91,019	17.9	1,706	15,732	18,019	15,157	0	555	55	11,591	5,077	1,191	2,735	2,587
San Antonio ISD	TX	76	54,394	57,732	22,504	39.0	578,043	155,469	26.9	2,821	42,648	31,600	9,340	4,078	1,039	0	30,691	12,389	3,086	7,767	7,450
San Bernardino City Unified	CA	77	54,379	57,418	21,186	36.9	600,660	95,741	15.9	1,756	40,089	22,912	15,935	4,041	601	195	26,814	11,012	2,693	6,796	6,313
Corona-Norco Unified	CA	78	53,467	56,300	8,154	14.5	492,882	53,014	10.8	997	8,970	10,885	13,511	1,609	218	62	7,951	3,655	844	1,865	1,587
Forsyth County	NC	79	53,340	61,770	15,089	24.4	590,947	70,338	11.9	1,318	8,594	14,656	4,487	2,200	208	—	15,129	6,322	1,372	3,550	3,884
Capistrano Unified	CA	80	53,170	64,183	5,346	8.3	416,481	29,877	7.2	562	4,408	4,420	13,750	1,109	208	62	4,295	2,369	0	1,072	854
Cumberland County	NC	81	53,053	55,198	14,220	25.8	501,648	89,294	17.8	1,675	8,417	16,341	8,709	2,335	715	—	14,443	6,054	1,322	3,375	3,692
Pasadena ISD	TX	82	52,942	53,946	15,918	29.5	506,146	96,482	19.1	1,848	20,809	22,572	6,341	2,214	417	0	16,094	6,910	1,500	3,919	3,765
Conroe ISD	TX	83	52,664	54,004	8,617	16.0	472,852	52,409	11.1	1,024	7,006	8,161	4,725	1,255	208	0	8,043	3,757	815	1,853	1,617
Cherry Creek, No. 5	CO	84	52,655	54,786	5,047	9.2	537,255	42,944	8.0	822	5,494	7,156	12,619	995	342	28	4,317	2,210	0	991	1,116
Lewisville ISD	TX	85	51,920	58,110	5,036	8.7	547,507	51,783	9.5	1,006	1,479	7,998	7,172	863	—	18	3,992	2,192	0	982	818
Tucson Unified	AZ	86	51,720	73,903	22,918	31.0	522,657	86,179	16.5	1,618	32,214	16,031	15,796	4,091	1,239	1,650	24,783	10,107	2,286	6,030	6,360
Howard County	MD	87	51,555	56,854	3,739	6.6	890,726	39,988	4.5	784	1,708	3,991	13,855	955	343	63	4,442	2,363	0	996	1,083
Clayton County	GA	88	51,018	54,137	17,621	32.5	500,420	64,312	12.9	1,277	11,340	22,819	6,183	1,156	412	68	18,479	7,851	1,813	4,648	4,167
Jordan	UT	89	50,961	58,400	5,709	9.8	339,004	36,432	10.7	728	1,811	7,268	14,895	1,036	466	21	4,832	2,453	0	1,124	1,255
Columbus City	OH	90	50,488	69,180	27,482	39.7	980,035	175,203	17.9	3,426	87,441	19,194	24,830	—	2,260	278	49,549	18,213	4,442	11,558	15,337

See notes at end of table.

Enrollment, poverty, and federal funds for the 100 largest school districts, by enrollment size in 2011: Selected years, 2010–11 through 2013—Continued

Name of district	State	Rank order	Enrollment, fall 2011	5- to 17-year-old population, 2012	5- to 17-year-olds in poverty, 2012[1]	Poverty rate of 5- to 17-year-olds, 2012[1]	Revenues by source of funds, 2010–11				Revenue for selected federal programs (in thousands), 2010–11						Title I allocations (in thousands), federal fiscal year 2013[2]				
							Total (in thousands)	Federal (in thousands)	Federal as a percent of total	Federal revenue per student[3]	Title I basic and concentration grants	School lunch	Individuals with Disabilities Education Act (IDEA)	Eisenhower math and science	Vocational education	Drug-free schools	Total	Basic grants	Concentration grants	Targeted grants	Education finance incentive grants
1	2	3	4	5	6	7	8	9	10	11	12	13	14	15	16	17	18	19	20	21	22
Omaha	NE	91	50,340	62,094	13,582	21.9	620,026	130,856	21.1	2,649	19,457	18,597	13,306	2,555	1,072	209	22,826	8,619	1,991	5,079	7,138
Atlanta	GA	92	50,009	55,895	21,876	39.1	757,348	103,765	13.7	2,084	32,474	20,344	12,094	5,673	962	702	34,936	13,550	3,305	8,490	9,590
Brownsville ISD	TX	93	49,655	48,027	22,524	46.9	504,356	117,817	23.4	2,362	30,156	28,518	7,375	5,264	1,059	115	26,698	10,475	2,662	7,045	6,516
Henrico County	VA	94	49,654	53,845	7,073	13.1	562,102	45,035	8.0	912	10,537	8,037	10,989	1,380	914	69	8,045	3,665	795	1,722	1,862
Wichita	KS	95	49,389	56,915	13,995	24.6	586,367	98,180	16.7	1,990	27,736	16,620	—	—	0	32	19,324	7,196	1,742	4,079	6,307
Seattle	WA	96	49,269	61,872	8,251	13.3	679,225	68,850	10.1	1,442	18,627	9,030	10,720	265	384	0	9,530	4,043	931	2,090	2,465
Anchorage	AK	97	48,765	53,683	6,136	11.4	732,488	114,561	15.6	2,328	12,476	13,206	12,186	3,913	974	588	13,711	5,601	901	3,572	3,636
Garden Grove Unified	CA	98	47,999	51,249	11,967	23.4	451,091	62,943	14.0	1,294	16,730	16,636	11,264	460	358	82	12,181	5,302	1,471	2,855	2,553
Sacramento City Unified	CA	99	47,940	52,274	16,142	30.9	512,325	101,180	19.7	2,112	34,818	15,237	13,047	5,537	537	3	20,829	8,870	2,163	5,328	4,467
San Juan Unified	CA	100	47,245	49,853	10,200	20.5	439,234	56,546	12.9	1,200	16,229	9,202	13,160	2,210	416	30	10,622	4,729	1,153	2,567	2,173

—Not available.

[1]Poverty is defined based on the number of persons and related children in the family and their income. For information on poverty thresholds, see http://www.census.gov/hhes/www/poverty/data/threshld/.

[2]Fiscal year 2013 Department of Education funds available for spending by school districts in the 2013–14 school year.

[3]Federal revenue per student is based on fall enrollment collected through the "Local Education Agency (School District) Finance Survey (F33)."

NOTE: Detail may not sum to totals because of rounding. ISD = independent school district.

SOURCE: U.S. Department of Education, National Center for Education Statistics, Common Core of Data (CCD), "Local Education Agency Universe Survey," 2011–12; "Local Education Agency (School District) Finance Survey (F33)," 2010–11; and unpublished Department of Education budget data. U.S. Department of Commerce, Census Bureau, Small Area Income and Poverty Estimates (SAIPE) Program, 2012 Poverty Estimates for School Districts. (This table was prepared May 2014.)

Public elementary and secondary schools, by level of school: Selected years, 1967–68 through 2011–12

Year	Total, all public schools	Schools with reported grade spans											Other schools[1]
		Total	Elementary schools				Secondary schools					Combined elementary/ secondary schools[2]	
			Total[3]	Middle schools[4]	One-teacher schools	Other elementary schools	Total[5]	Junior high[6]	3-year or 4-year high schools	5-year or 6-year high schools	Other secondary schools		
1	2	3	4	5	6	7	8	9	10	11	12	13	14
1967–68	—	94,197	67,186	—	4,146	63,040	23,318	7,437	10,751	4,650	480	3,693	—
1970–71	—	89,372	64,020	2,080	1,815	60,125	23,572	7,750	11,265	3,887	670	1,780	—
1972–73	—	88,864	62,942	2,308	1,475	59,159	23,919	7,878	11,550	3,962	529	2,003	—
1974–75	—	87,456	61,759	3,224	1,247	57,288	23,837	7,690	11,480	4,122	545	1,860	—
1975–76	88,597	87,034	61,704	3,916	1,166	56,622	23,792	7,521	11,572	4,113	586	1,538	1,563
1976–77	—	86,501	61,123	4,180	1,111	55,832	23,857	7,434	11,658	4,130	635	1,521	—
1978–79	—	84,816	60,312	5,879	1,056	53,377	22,834	6,282	11,410	4,429	713	1,670	—
1980–81	85,982	83,688	59,326	6,003	921	52,402	22,619	5,890	10,758	4,193	1,778	1,743	2,294
1982–83	84,740	82,039	58,051	6,875	798	50,378	22,383	5,948	11,678	4,067	690	1,605	2,701
1983–84	84,178	81,418	57,471	6,885	838	49,748	22,336	5,936	11,670	4,046	684	1,611	2,760
1984–85	84,007	81,147	57,231	6,893	825	49,513	22,320	5,916	11,671	4,021	712	1,596	2,860
1986–87	83,421	82,316	58,835	7,483	763	50,589	21,505	5,109	11,430	4,196	770	1,976	1,105 [7]
1987–88	83,248	81,416	57,575	7,641	729	49,205	21,662	4,900	11,279	4,048	1,435	2,179	1,832 [7]
1988–89	83,165	81,579	57,941	7,957	583	49,401	21,403	4,687	11,350	3,994	1,372	2,235	1,586 [7]
1989–90	83,425	81,880	58,419	8,272	630	49,517	21,181	4,512	11,492	3,812	1,365	2,280	1,545 [7]
1990–91	84,538	82,475	59,015	8,545	617	49,853	21,135	4,561	11,537	3,723	1,314	2,325	2,063
1991–92	84,578	82,506	59,258	8,829	569	49,860	20,767	4,298	11,528	3,699	1,242	2,481	2,072
1992–93	84,497	82,896	59,676	9,152	430	50,094	20,671	4,115	11,651	3,613	1,292	2,549	1,601
1993–94	85,393	83,431	60,052	9,573	442	50,037	20,705	3,970	11,858	3,595	1,282	2,674	1,962
1994–95	86,221	84,476	60,808	9,954	458	50,396	20,904	3,859	12,058	3,628	1,359	2,764	1,745
1995–96	87,125	84,958	61,165	10,205	474	50,486	20,997	3,743	12,168	3,621	1,465	2,796	2,167
1996–97	88,223	86,092	61,805	10,499	487	50,819	21,307	3,707	12,424	3,614	1,562	2,980	2,131
1997–98	89,508	87,541	62,739	10,944	476	51,319	21,682	3,599	12,734	3,611	1,738	3,120	1,967
1998–99	90,874	89,259	63,462	11,202	463	51,797	22,076	3,607	13,457	3,707	1,305	3,721	1,615
1999–2000	92,012	90,538	64,131	11,521	423	52,187	22,365	3,566	13,914	3,686	1,199	4,042	1,474
2000–01	93,273	91,691	64,601	11,696	411	52,494	21,994	3,318	13,793	3,974	909	5,096	1,582
2001–02	94,112	92,696	65,228	11,983	408	52,837	22,180	3,285	14,070	3,917	908	5,288	1,416
2002–03	95,615	93,869	65,718	12,174	366	53,178	22,599	3,263	14,330	4,017	989	5,552	1,746
2003–04	95,726	93,977	65,758	12,341	376	53,041	22,782	3,251	14,595	3,840	1,096	5,437	1,749
2004–05	96,513	95,001	65,984	12,530	338	53,116	23,445	3,250	14,854	3,945	1,396	5,572	1,512
2005–06	97,382	95,731	66,026	12,545	326	53,155	23,998	3,249	15,103	3,910	1,736	5,707	1,651
2006–07	98,793	96,362	66,458	12,773	313	53,372	23,920	3,112	15,043	4,048	1,717	5,984	2,431
2007–08	98,916	97,654	67,112	13,014	288	53,810	24,643	3,117	16,146	3,981	1,399	5,899	1,262
2008–09	98,706	97,119	67,148	13,060	237	53,851	24,348	3,037	16,246	3,761	1,304	5,623	1,587
2009–10	98,817	97,521	67,140	13,163	217	53,760	24,651	2,953	16,706	3,778	1,214	5,730	1,296
2010–11	98,817	97,767	67,086	13,045	224	53,817	24,544	2,855	16,321	4,047	1,321	6,137	1,050
2011–12	98,328	97,357	66,689	12,963	205	53,521	24,357	2,865	16,586	3,899	1,007	6,311	971

—Not available.
[1]Includes special education, alternative, and other schools not reported by grade span.
[2]Includes schools beginning with grade 6 or below and ending with grade 9 or above.
[3]Includes schools beginning with grade 6 or below and with no grade higher than 8.
[4]Includes schools with grade spans beginning with 4, 5, or 6 and ending with 6, 7, or 8.
[5]Includes schools with no grade lower than 7.
[6]Includes schools with grades 7 and 8 or grades 7 through 9.

[7]Because of revision in data collection procedures, figures not comparable to data for other years.
SOURCE: U.S. Department of Education, National Center for Education Statistics, *Statistics of State School Systems*, 1967–68 and 1975–76; *Statistics of Public Elementary and Secondary Day Schools*, 1970–71, 1972–73, 1974–75, and 1976–77 through 1980–81; and Common Core of Data (CCD), "Public Elementary/Secondary School Universe Survey," 1982–83 through 2011–12. (This table was prepared August 2013.)

Public elementary and secondary schools, by level, type, and state or jurisdiction: 1990–91, 2000–01, 2010–11, and 2011–12

State or jurisdiction	Total, all schools, 1990–91	Total, all schools, 2000–01	Total, all schools, 2010–11	Schools by level, 2011–12			Combined elementary/secondary[3]					Selected types of schools, 2011–12		
				Total, all schools	Elementary[1]	Secondary[2]	Total	Prekindergarten, kindergarten, or 1st grade to grade 12	Other schools ending with grade 12	Other combined schools	Other[4]	Alternative[5]	Special education[5]	One-teacher schools[5]
1	2	3	4	5	6	7	8	9	10	11	12	13	14	15
United States	84,538	93,273	98,817	98,328	66,689	24,357	6,311	3,111	2,369	831	971	6,144	2,087	205
Alabama	1,297	1,517	1,600	1,618	712	415	459	122	64	273	32	118	42	0
Alaska	498	515	509	511	201	82	228	212	14	2	0	65	3	8
Arizona	1,049	1,724	2,265	2,252	1,323	744	160	89	49	22	25	67	20	6
Arkansas	1,098	1,138	1,110	1,108	716	384	8	4	2	2	0	11	4	0
California	7,913	8,773	10,124	10,170	6,925	2,624	570	433	118	19	51	1,305	146	39
Colorado	1,344	1,632	1,796	1,813	1,295	393	125	49	61	15	0	87	7	1
Connecticut	985	1,248	1,157	1,150	817	279	37	11	18	8	17	47	48	0
Delaware	173	191	214	221	158	39	17	12	5	0	7	6	21	0
District of Columbia	181	198	228	228	170	37	13	3	5	5	8	11	7	0
Florida	2,516	3,316	4,131	4,212	2,756	683	632	244	368	20	141	413	183	3
Georgia	1,734	1,946	2,449	2,388	1,797	470	55	12	27	16	66	62	58	0
Hawaii	235	261	289	287	206	52	28	22	3	3	1	1	2	0
Idaho	582	673	748	762	448	230	84	52	23	9	0	91	15	12
Illinois	4,239	4,342	4,361	4,336	3,170	989	173	55	103	15	4	150	141	2
Indiana	1,915	1,976	1,936	1,933	1,372	454	107	58	38	11	0	11	34	0
Iowa	1,588	1,534	1,436	1,411	980	387	44	3	41	0	0	33	6	5
Kansas	1,477	1,430	1,378	1,359	949	365	41	13	28	0	4	2	10	0
Kentucky	1,400	1,526	1,554	1,565	995	441	116	33	76	7	13	172	10	0
Louisiana	1,533	1,530	1,471	1,437	978	288	167	100	63	4	4	266	35	0
Maine	747	714	631	621	448	148	12	10	2	0	13	0	3	1
Maryland	1,220	1,383	1,449	1,451	1,129	258	46	21	19	6	18	56	40	1
Massachusetts	1,842	1,905	1,829	1,835	1,414	370	44	14	25	5	7	19	22	0
Michigan	3,313	3,998	3,877	3,550	2,269	958	288	157	111	20	35	277	197	5
Minnesota	1,590	2,362	2,392	2,392	1,263	849	278	134	132	12	2	484	276	0
Mississippi	972	1,030	1,083	1,069	625	324	109	65	43	1	11	63	4	0
Missouri	2,199	2,368	2,410	2,408	1,581	646	161	74	85	2	20	105	64	0
Montana	900	879	827	826	479	347	0	0	0	0	0	4	2	60
Nebraska	1,506	1,326	1,096	1,090	718	317	27	17	9	1	28	29	25	7
Nevada	354	511	645	649	479	129	39	13	26	0	2	35	12	11
New Hampshire	439	526	480	477	373	104	0	0	0	0	0	0	0	1
New Jersey	2,272	2,410	2,607	2,596	1,946	544	57	28	19	10	49	107	69	0
New Mexico	681	765	862	866	604	239	23	8	12	3	0	39	8	0
New York	4,010	4,336	4,757	4,752	3,279	1,105	278	111	124	43	90	26	122	0
North Carolina	1,955	2,207	2,567	2,577	1,887	536	146	77	62	7	8	88	30	0
North Dakota	663	579	516	513	297	184	0	0	0	0	32	0	33	6
Ohio	3,731	3,916	3,758	3,714	2,544	1,004	158	50	69	39	8	6	57	0
Oklahoma	1,880	1,821	1,785	1,774	1,213	554	6	1	3	2	1	4	4	0
Oregon	1,199	1,273	1,296	1,261	890	294	77	54	20	3	0	41	2	11
Pennsylvania	3,260	3,252	3,233	3,181	2,252	824	100	47	39	14	5	12	8	0
Rhode Island	309	328	317	308	227	76	5	3	1	1	0	5	2	0
South Carolina	1,097	1,127	1,214	1,223	907	277	31	9	17	5	8	21	10	1
South Dakota	802	769	710	704	434	246	24	10	14	0	0	37	10	13
Tennessee	1,543	1,624	1,784	1,802	1,295	349	139	62	47	30	19	22	15	0
Texas	5,991	7,519	8,732	8,697	5,918	2,113	662	295	218	149	4	1,032	22	0
Utah	714	793	1,016	1,020	630	301	89	55	5	29	0	44	85	0
Vermont	397	393	320	320	235	69	16	11	5	0	0	1	0	1
Virginia	1,811	1,969	2,175	2,170	1,503	399	36	24	11	1	232	192	54	0
Washington	1,936	2,305	2,338	2,365	1,517	631	216	150	60	6	1	338	104	3
West Virginia	1,015	840	757	759	571	127	61	45	15	1	0	33	3	0
Wisconsin	2,018	2,182	2,238	2,243	1,553	583	103	32	67	4	4	87	11	7
Wyoming	415	393	360	354	241	96	16	7	3	6	1	19	1	1
Bureau of Indian Education..................	—	189	173	173	109	19	45	39	3	3	0	0	0	—
DoD, domestic and overseas	—	227	191	191	142	35	14	10	4	0	0	0	0	0
Other jurisdictions														
American Samoa	30	31	28	28	22	6	0	0	0	0	0	0	0	0
Guam	35	38	40	40	35	5	0	0	0	0	0	0	0	0
Northern Marianas......	26	29	30	29	21	7	0	0	0	0	1	0	0	0
Puerto Rico	1,619	1,543	1,473	1,464	865	397	172	2	3	167	30	9	23	0
U.S. Virgin Islands.......	33	36	32	31	22	9	0	0	0	0	0	0	0	0

—Not available.
[1]Includes schools beginning with grade 6 or below and with no grade higher than 8.
[2]Includes schools with no grade lower than 7.
[3]Includes schools beginning with grade 6 or below and ending with grade 9 or above.
[4]Includes schools not reported by grade span.

[5]Schools are also included under elementary, secondary, combined, or other as appropriate.
NOTE: DoD = Department of Defense.
SOURCE: U.S. Department of Education, National Center for Education Statistics, Common Core of Data (CCD), "Public Elementary/Secondary School Universe Survey," 1990–91, 2000–01, 2010–11, and 2011–12. (This table was prepared August 2013.)

Public elementary schools, by grade span, average school enrollment, and state or jurisdiction: 2011–12

State or jurisdiction	Total, all elementary schools	Total, all regular elementary schools[1]	Prekinder-garten, kindergarten, or 1st grade to grades 3 or 4	Prekinder-garten, kindergarten, or 1st grade to grade 5	Prekinder-garten, kindergarten, or 1st grade to grade 6	Prekinder-garten, kindergarten, or 1st grade to grade 8	Grade 4, 5, or 6 to grade 6, 7, or 8	Other grade spans	All elementary schools	Regular elementary schools[1]
1	2	3	4	5	6	7	8	9	10	11
United States	**66,689**	**65,461**	**4,979**	**25,115**	**10,801**	**6,428**	**12,963**	**6,403**	**479**	**484**
Alabama	712	703	83	311	172	3	33	110	483	487
Alaska	201	192	4	46	89	28	23	11	325	320
Arizona	1,323	1,304	48	250	344	458	164	59	513	515
Arkansas	716	713	128	142	181	7	154	104	425	427
California	6,925	6,705	131	2,435	2,170	957	1,036	196	559	570
Colorado	1,295	1,289	32	617	203	115	242	86	431	431
Connecticut	817	806	98	256	72	97	155	139	438	442
Delaware	158	153	15	80	5	9	38	11	558	565
District of Columbia	170	164	11	63	11	39	24	22	313	313
Florida	2,756	2,687	25	1,671	135	216	577	132	657	671
Georgia	1,797	1,791	42	1,070	37	27	466	155	658	660
Hawaii	206	206	0	82	86	8	27	3	557	557
Idaho	448	444	32	145	140	27	75	29	386	387
Illinois	3,170	3,133	295	800	330	709	580	456	433	437
Indiana	1,372	1,366	177	456	329	40	259	111	472	472
Iowa	980	977	130	346	141	13	230	120	325	325
Kansas	949	945	99	336	177	66	199	72	333	335
Kentucky	995	980	25	481	115	78	202	94	471	478
Louisiana	978	843	81	341	118	110	210	118	474	483
Maine	448	448	62	91	57	86	84	68	263	263
Maryland	1,129	1,115	9	655	96	89	222	58	515	519
Massachusetts	1,414	1,402	185	472	121	107	286	243	441	442
Michigan	2,269	2,220	229	832	213	222	483	290	418	421
Minnesota	1,263	1,104	104	355	325	74	230	175	424	467
Mississippi	625	622	65	131	103	38	155	133	510	510
Missouri	1,581	1,569	143	502	296	114	317	209	379	381
Montana	479	476	17	55	212	112	54	29	181	182
Nebraska	718	712	50	169	283	30	99	87	273	274
Nevada	479	470	10	260	83	20	92	14	619	630
New Hampshire	373	373	57	113	36	50	81	36	337	337
New Jersey	1,946	1,927	270	561	153	300	352	310	461	465
New Mexico	604	593	16	234	142	21	127	64	366	371
New York	3,279	3,259	292	1,260	372	230	730	395	526	527
North Carolina	1,887	1,875	77	1,089	67	110	457	87	552	554
North Dakota	297	296	11	56	126	62	27	15	204	205
Ohio	2,544	2,516	361	671	337	261	555	359	429	433
Oklahoma	1,213	1,209	62	338	138	292	238	145	383	384
Oregon	890	883	31	400	142	116	174	27	398	399
Pennsylvania	2,252	2,251	288	705	427	197	424	211	472	472
Rhode Island	227	226	36	77	42	4	39	29	399	400
South Carolina	907	904	39	460	45	35	228	100	550	552
South Dakota	434	430	17	134	69	96	98	20	202	204
Tennessee	1,295	1,288	96	421	196	245	281	56	515	517
Texas	5,918	5,770	618	2,657	535	130	1,332	646	562	573
Utah	630	592	10	85	433	26	34	42	543	568
Vermont	235	235	12	25	106	64	17	11	220	220
Virginia	1,503	1,503	51	845	151	13	311	132	560	560
Washington	1,517	1,435	58	604	377	75	262	141	436	450
West Virginia	571	570	72	271	36	35	119	38	346	346
Wisconsin	1,553	1,547	150	603	144	154	317	185	367	368
Wyoming	241	240	25	56	83	13	44	20	228	229
Bureau of Indian Education	109	109	6	5	25	67	4	2	—	—
DoD, domestic and overseas	142	142	20	43	26	9	28	16	—	—
Other jurisdictions										
American Samoa	22	22	0	0	0	22	0	0	—	—
Guam	35	35	0	25	0	0	8	2	606	606
Northern Marianas	21	21	0	0	12	0	0	9	280	280
Puerto Rico	865	865	42	1	793	0	17	12	242	242
U.S. Virgin Islands	22	22	1	1	17	1	2	0	397	397

—Not available.
[1]Excludes special education and alternative schools.
[2]Average for schools reporting enrollment data. Enrollment data were available for 66,286 out of 66,689 public elementary schools in 2011–12.

NOTE: Includes schools beginning with grade 6 or below and with no grade higher than 8. Excludes schools not reported by grade level, such as some special education schools for the disabled. DoD = Department of Defense.
SOURCE: U.S. Department of Education, National Center for Education Statistics, Common Core of Data (CCD), "Public Elementary/Secondary School Universe Survey," 2011–12. (This table was prepared August 2013.)

Public secondary schools, by grade span, average school enrollment, and state or jurisdiction: 2011–12

State or jurisdiction	Total, all secondary schools	Total, all regular secondary schools[1]	Schools, by grade span							Vocational schools[2]	Average school enrollment[2]	
			Grades 7 to 8 and 7 to 9	Grades 7 to 12	Grades 8 to 12	Grades 9 to 12	Grades 10 to 12	Other spans ending with grade 12	Other grade spans		All secondary schools	Regular secondary schools[1]
1	2	3	4	5	6	7	8	9	10	11	12	13
United States	24,357	19,441	2,865	3,126	773	15,891	695	327	680	1,434	690	788
Alabama	415	314	29	90	245	8	30	3	10	72	712	720
Alaska	82	62	14	19	1	47	1	0	0	3	460	559
Arizona	744	508	80	42	5	592	7	5	13	221	600	694
Arkansas	384	349	56	129	9	137	34	1	18	26	495	504
California	2,624	1,623	379	309	14	1,848	46	12	16	88	873	1,267
Colorado	393	338	42	49	3	287	4	1	7	5	627	706
Connecticut	279	204	33	13	7	185	20	15	6	16	672	852
Delaware	39	31	2	1	14	21	0	0	1	6	974	989
District of Columbia	37	28	0	3	2	29	1	0	2	4	425	481
Florida	683	507	17	44	34	561	7	12	8	52	1,199	1,479
Georgia	470	440	18	11	7	390	4	2	38	1	1,020	1,080
Hawaii	52	51	12	7	0	33	0	0	0	0	1,144	1,165
Idaho	230	148	40	54	2	114	17	2	1	9	437	598
Illinois	989	820	147	71	15	686	11	32	27	51	732	818
Indiana	454	439	81	93	4	264	3	1	8	28	836	844
Iowa	387	356	45	71	0	256	8	3	4	0	416	447
Kansas	365	359	42	84	3	231	1	2	2	1	430	435
Kentucky	441	250	28	37	9	354	4	6	3	126	649	801
Louisiana	288	204	31	48	93	95	16	0	5	8	654	745
Maine	148	119	13	11	0	112	6	0	6	27	492	500
Maryland	258	200	11	6	2	223	2	8	6	24	1,064	1,239
Massachusetts	370	317	30	40	9	284	2	3	2	39	829	849
Michigan	958	708	73	104	37	680	29	15	20	9	554	692
Minnesota	849	460	46	285	29	388	47	46	8	11	395	610
Mississippi	324	230	24	64	3	207	22	2	2	90	644	644
Missouri	646	563	63	181	1	357	20	9	15	66	533	537
Montana	347	344	176	0	0	171	0	0	0	0	161	162
Nebraska	317	311	28	173	0	111	1	4	0	0	359	359
Nevada	129	115	19	8	1	96	1	4	0	1	1,024	1,128
New Hampshire	104	104	16	0	0	86	0	1	1	0	636	636
New Jersey	544	406	49	43	18	396	9	7	22	56	932	1,036
New Mexico	239	209	39	31	0	152	8	9	9	1	479	523
New York	1,105	1,032	71	137	15	795	27	1	59	29	772	782
North Carolina	536	512	27	10	3	472	4	6	14	1	823	855
North Dakota	184	174	10	94	0	74	3	1	2	10	205	205
Ohio	1,004	917	132	117	42	666	18	11	18	72	592	605
Oklahoma	554	550	80	0	0	427	30	3	14	0	355	356
Oregon	294	268	32	50	3	203	4	2	0	0	620	667
Pennsylvania	824	728	108	151	11	469	62	8	15	87	802	813
Rhode Island	76	62	13	2	1	58	0	0	2	11	740	784
South Carolina	277	226	19	9	2	222	13	4	8	39	898	944
South Dakota	246	224	63	0	0	180	1	1	1	3	165	175
Tennessee	349	328	11	41	7	280	7	2	1	17	844	867
Texas	2,113	1,535	291	161	55	1,277	54	44	231	0	726	964
Utah	301	245	103	54	7	72	51	2	12	5	781	909
Vermont	69	53	8	18	0	28	0	0	15	15	511	520
Virginia	399	341	31	8	29	320	4	1	6	50	1,156	1,183
Washington	631	428	101	57	25	384	36	16	12	17	627	824
West Virginia	127	103	3	22	2	93	2	1	4	30	607	736
Wisconsin	583	518	60	62	3	408	16	28	6	7	484	528
Wyoming	96	80	19	12	1	62	2	0	0	0	332	388
Bureau of Indian Education	19	19	1	5	0	13	0	0	0	0	—	—
DoD, domestic and overseas	35	35	3	11	0	21	0	0	0	0	—	—
Other jurisdictions												
American Samoa	6	5	0	0	0	6	0	0	0	1	—	—
Guam	5	5	0	0	0	5	0	0	0	0	2,004	2,004
Northern Marianas	7	7	2	2	0	3	0	0	0	0	728	728
Puerto Rico	397	366	195	26	2	6	157	1	10	30	454	439
U.S. Virgin Islands	9	8	4	0	0	5	0	0	1	1	873	873

—Not available.

[1]Excludes vocational, special education, and alternative schools.

[2]Vocational schools are also included under appropriate grade span. Includes vocational schools not classified as secondary schools.

[3]Average for schools reporting enrollment data. Enrollment data were available for 22,753 out of 24,357 public secondary schools in 2011–12.

NOTE: Includes schools with no grade lower than 7. Excludes schools not reported by grade level, such as some special education schools for the disabled. DoD = Department of Defense.

SOURCE: U.S. Department of Education, National Center for Education Statistics, Common Core of Data (CCD), "Public Elementary/Secondary School Universe Survey," 2011–12. (This table was prepared August 2013.)

Public elementary and secondary charter schools and enrollment, by state: Selected years, 1999–2000 through 2011–12

State	Number of charter schools					Charter school enrollment					Charter schools as a percent of total public schools				Charter school enrollment as a percent of total public school enrollment			
	1999–2000	2005–06	2009–10	2010–11	2011–12	1999–2000	2005–06	2009–10	2010–11	2011–12	1999–2000	2005–06	2010–11	2011–12	1999–2000	2005–06	2010–11	2011–12
1	2	3	4	5	6	7	8	9	10	11	12	13	14	15	16	17	18	19
United States	1,524	3,780	4,952	5,274	5,696	339,678	1,012,906	1,610,285	1,787,091	2,057,599	1.7	3.9	5.3	5.8	0.7	2.1	3.6	4.2
Alabama	0	0	0	0	0	0	0	0	0	0	0.0	0.0	0.0	0.0	0.0	0.0	0.0	0.0
Alaska	18	23	25	27	27	2,300	4,660	5,196	5,751	5,922	3.6	4.6	5.3	5.3	1.7	3.5	4.4	4.5
Arizona	245	501	504	519	531	31,176	90,597	113,974	124,467	136,323	14.9	24.1	22.9	23.6	3.7	8.3	11.6	12.6
Arkansas	0	19	38	40	41	0	4,006	8,662	10,209	11,395	0.0	1.7	3.6	3.7	0.0	0.8	2.1	2.4
California	238	543	813	908	985	104,730	195,876	316,658	363,916	413,124	2.8	5.6	9.0	9.7	1.8	3.1	5.9	6.7
Colorado	69	121	158	168	178	17,822	44,254	66,826	74,685	83,478	4.3	7.1	9.4	9.8	2.5	5.7	8.9	9.8
Connecticut	16	14	18	18	17	2,148	2,927	5,215	5,139	6,098	1.5	1.3	1.6	1.5	0.4	0.5	0.9	1.1
Delaware	0	13	18	19	22	115	6,566	9,173	9,525	10,322	0.5	5.9	8.9	10.0	0.1	5.4	7.4	8.0
District of Columbia	27	52	99	97	100	6,432	17,260	25,813	26,910	29,002	14.3	22.7	42.5	43.9	8.3	22.5	37.8	39.3
Florida	113	342	412	458	519	17,251	92,335	137,887	154,703	180,880	3.5	9.2	11.1	12.3	0.7	3.5	5.9	6.8
Georgia	18	58	63	67	128	11,005	26,440	37,545	41,981	79,989	1.0	2.4	2.7	5.4	0.8	1.7	2.5	4.7
Hawaii	2	27	31	31	31	790	6,498	7,869	8,289	9,165	0.8	9.5	10.7	10.8	0.4	3.5	4.6	5.0
Idaho	8	26	36	40	45	915	8,003	14,529	15,330	17,257	1.2	3.7	5.3	5.9	0.4	3.1	5.6	6.2
Illinois	17	29	39	50	52	6,152	16,968	35,836	43,049	49,070	0.4	0.7	1.1	1.2	0.3	0.8	2.1	2.4
Indiana	0	29	53	60	65	0	7,409	18,488	22,472	28,270	0.0	1.5	3.1	3.4	0.0	0.7	2.2	2.7
Iowa	0	6	9	7	7	0	520	593	298	403	0.0	0.4	0.5	0.5	0.0	0.1	0.1	0.1
Kansas	0	26	35	25	17	0	1,914	4,684	4,618	3,122	0.0	1.8	1.8	1.3	0.0	0.4	1.0	0.6
Kentucky	0	0	0	0	0	0	0	0	0	0	0.0	0.0	0.0	0.0	0.0	0.0	0.0	0.0
Louisiana	16	26	77	78	99	2,449	8,315	31,467	29,199	44,330	1.0	1.9	5.3	6.9	0.3	1.3	4.2	6.3
Maine	0	0	0	0	0	0	0	0	0	0	0.0	0.0	0.0	0.0	0.0	0.0	0.0	0.0
Maryland	0	15	42	44	50	0	3,363	11,995	14,492	17,273	0.0	1.0	3.0	3.4	0.0	0.4	1.7	2.0
Massachusetts	40	59	62	63	72	12,518	21,958	27,393	28,422	30,595	2.1	3.1	3.4	3.9	1.3	2.3	3.0	3.2
Michigan	193	264	294	300	306	46,078	91,384	110,504	111,344	118,177	4.9	6.5	7.7	8.6	2.8	5.3	7.2	7.7
Minnesota	62	161	181	176	174	7,794	20,603	35,375	37,253	39,143	2.6	6.1	7.4	7.3	0.9	2.5	4.4	4.7
Mississippi	1	1	1	0	0	347	374	375	—	0	0.1	0.1	0.0	0.0	0.1	0.1	0.0	0.0
Missouri	15	23	48	53	61	4,303	10,972	18,415	20,076	21,472	0.6	1.0	2.2	2.5	0.5	1.2	2.2	2.3
Montana	0	0	0	0	0	0	0	0	0	0	0.0	0.0	0.0	0.0	0.0	0.0	0.0	0.0
Nebraska	0	0	0	0	0	0	0	0	0	0	0.0	0.0	0.0	0.0	0.0	0.0	0.0	0.0
Nevada	5	19	35	34	39	898	4,818	11,613	14,127	18,255	1.0	3.4	5.3	6.0	0.3	1.2	3.2	4.2
New Hampshire	0	6	15	14	15	0	200	816	983	1,169	0.0	1.3	2.9	3.1	0.0	0.1	0.5	0.6
New Jersey	0	54	70	76	86	0	14,937	22,981	24,591	29,007	0.0	2.2	2.9	3.3	0.0	1.1	1.8	2.1
New Mexico	1	53	72	81	84	22	8,595	13,090	15,290	16,864	0.1	6.2	9.4	9.7	#	2.6	4.6	5.0
New York	5	79	140	170	183	—	21,539	43,963	54,443	60,137	0.1	1.7	3.6	3.9	—	0.8	2.0	2.2
North Carolina	82	99	96	99	100	12,691	27,441	38,973	42,141	45,496	3.8	4.2	3.9	3.9	1.0	1.9	2.8	3.0
North Dakota	0	0	0	0	0	0	0	0	0	0	0.0	0.0	0.0	0.0	0.0	0.0	0.0	0.0
Ohio	48	316	323	339	355	9,809	68,679	90,989	96,669	107,089	1.2	7.9	9.0	9.6	0.5	3.7	5.5	6.2
Oklahoma	0	14	18	18	21	0	4,081	6,315	6,585	9,229	0.0	0.8	1.0	1.2	0.0	0.6	1.0	1.4
Oregon	1	54	102	108	115	109	5,192	18,334	20,372	24,205	0.1	4.3	8.3	9.1	#	1.0	3.7	4.4
Pennsylvania	47	116	134	145	162	11,413	55,630	79,167	90,063	104,967	1.5	3.6	4.5	5.1	0.6	3.0	5.1	6.0
Rhode Island	2	11	12	16	18	446	2,571	3,233	3,971	4,662	0.6	3.3	5.0	5.8	0.3	1.7	2.8	3.3
South Carolina	7	27	39	44	47	327	4,104	13,035	16,390	17,034	0.6	2.3	3.6	3.8	#	0.6	2.3	2.3
South Dakota	0	0	0	0	0	0	0	0	0	0	0.0	0.0	0.0	0.0	0.0	0.0	0.0	0.0
Tennessee	0	12	20	29	40	0	1,685	4,343	6,517	9,104	0.0	0.7	1.6	2.2	0.0	0.2	0.7	0.9
Texas	176	319	536	561	581	25,687	70,895	148,392	164,940	189,654	2.4	3.7	6.4	6.7	0.6	1.6	3.3	3.8
Utah	6	36	72	78	81	390	11,439	33,968	39,862	44,687	0.8	3.8	7.7	7.9	0.1	2.2	6.8	7.5
Vermont	0	0	0	0	0	0	0	0	0	0	0.0	0.0	0.0	0.0	0.0	0.0	0.0	0.0
Virginia	0	3	3	4	4	0	210	179	348	393	0.0	0.1	0.2	0.2	0.0	#	#	#
Washington	0	0	0	0	0	0	0	0	0	0	0.0	0.0	0.0	0.0	0.0	0.0	0.0	0.0
West Virginia	0	0	0	0	0	0	0	0	0	0	0.0	0.0	0.0	0.0	0.0	0.0	0.0	0.0
Wisconsin	45	181	206	207	234	3,561	27,450	36,153	36,863	40,531	2.1	8.1	9.2	10.4	0.4	3.1	4.2	4.7
Wyoming	0	3	3	3	4	0	238	269	258	306	0.0	0.8	0.8	1.1	0.0	0.3	0.3	0.3

—Not available.
#Rounds to zero.

SOURCE: U.S. Department of Education, National Center for Education Statistics, Common Core of Data (CCD), "Public Elementary/Secondary School Universe Survey," 1999–2000 through 2011–12. (This table was prepared September 2013.)

Functional age of public schools' main instructional buildings and percentage of schools with permanent and portable (temporary) buildings, by selected school characteristics and condition of permanent and portable buildings: 2012

[Standard errors appear in parentheses]

Functional age of main instructional building; presence and condition of permanent and portable buildings	All public schools[1]	Instructional level: Elementary	Secondary	Combined	Community type: City	Suburban	Town	Rural	Percent of students eligible for free or reduced-price lunch: Less than 35 percent	35 to 49 percent	50 to 74 percent	75 percent or more
1	2	3	4	5	6	7	8	9	10	11	12	13
Estimated number of schools	84,000 (†)	62,600 (†)	18,900 (†)	2,400 (†)	21,200 (†)	23,500 (†)	10,900 (†)	28,400 (†)	31 (†)	18 (†)	27 (†)	23 (†)
Main instructional building												
Percent of schools, by functional age[2]												
Less than 5 years old	21 (1.1)	19 (1.2)	25 (2.2)	27 (6.8)	24 (2.6)	23 (2.2)	19 (2.9)	17 (1.9)	20 (2.0)	23 (2.9)	18 (2.0)	24 (2.5)
5 to 14 years old	38 (1.2)	37 (1.4)	39 (2.3)	34 (7.2)	33 (2.5)	39 (2.7)	37 (4.1)	40 (2.3)	40 (2.2)	34 (3.3)	39 (2.6)	35 (3.0)
15 to 34 years old	23 (1.2)	25 (1.6)	17 (1.8)	28 (7.5)	20 (2.3)	20 (1.8)	27 (3.6)	28 (2.3)	25 (2.1)	22 (2.9)	25 (2.3)	20 (2.7)
35 or more years old	18 (1.2)	19 (1.4)	18 (1.7)	11 ! (4.3)	22 (2.4)	19 (2.2)	17 (3.0)	15 (1.9)	15 (2.0)	21 (2.9)	17 (2.1)	21 (2.8)
Average years												
Since construction	44 (0.7)	45 (0.9)	43 (1.2)	50 (4.2)	50 (1.7)	43 (1.2)	48 (1.8)	40 (1.2)	42 (1.3)	46 (1.8)	43 (1.4)	48 (1.9)
Since major renovation[3]	12 (0.4)	12 (0.5)	11 (0.7)	12 (2.0)	11 (0.7)	11 (0.7)	14 (1.2)	12 (0.8)	11 (0.6)	12 (1.1)	12 (0.8)	11 (0.8)
Permanent buildings (percent of schools)												
School has permanent buildings[4]	99 (0.2)	99 (0.3)	100 (0.3)	100 (#)	99 (0.7)	100 (0.4)	99 (0.6)	100 (0.3)	100 (0.4)	99 (0.6)	100 (#)	98 (0.8)
Overall condition of buildings[4]												
Excellent	20 (1.1)	20 (1.4)	20 (1.5)	15 ! (5.5)	17 (2.0)	23 (2.2)	18 (3.3)	20 (1.8)	24 (2.0)	18 (2.3)	20 (2.1)	16 (2.0)
Good	56 (1.4)	57 (1.7)	57 (2.2)	44 (7.0)	55 (2.6)	56 (2.6)	57 (3.8)	57 (2.5)	56 (2.3)	63 (3.5)	56 (2.7)	52 (3.2)
Fair	21 (1.0)	21 (1.3)	20 (2.0)	38 (7.4)	23 (2.3)	20 (2.1)	23 (3.2)	20 (2.0)	18 (1.9)	17 (2.5)	22 (2.0)	28 (2.7)
Poor	3 (0.5)	3 (0.6)	2 ! (0.7)	‡ (†)	5 (1.3)	‡ (†)	‡ (†)	2 ! (0.8)	2 ! (0.8)	2 ! (0.9)	2 ! (1.0)	4 (1.3)
Environmental factors are unsatisfactory[5]												
Lighting, artificial	8 (0.9)	8 (1.1)	7 (1.4)	‡ (†)	9 (1.6)	7 (1.4)	8 (2.1)	9 (1.4)	6 (1.4)	7 (1.8)	8 (1.8)	11 (1.9)
Lighting, natural	16 (1.1)	17 (1.4)	16 (1.7)	15 ! (5.3)	16 (2.2)	15 (2.0)	20 (3.2)	16 (1.9)	14 (1.7)	17 (2.7)	17 (2.0)	19 (2.6)
Heating	14 (0.9)	13 (1.2)	16 (2.1)	20 ! (6.2)	16 (2.1)	10 (1.6)	14 (2.4)	14 (1.7)	12 (1.6)	14 (2.4)	14 (2.2)	15 (2.3)
Air conditioning	17 (1.1)	16 (1.4)	20 (2.3)	21 (6.7)	21 (2.5)	13 (1.9)	18 (3.2)	17 (2.0)	17 (1.9)	16 (2.7)	15 (2.5)	19 (2.7)
Ventilation	17 (1.2)	16 (1.4)	16 (1.8)	28 (7.3)	18 (2.0)	12 (1.9)	16 (3.2)	20 (2.1)	15 (1.9)	9 (2.1)	16 (2.0)	20 (2.7)
Indoor air quality	9 (0.8)	9 (1.0)	9 (1.4)	13 ! (5.0)	6 (1.5)	4 (1.0)	7 (2.2)	7 (1.7)	7 (1.8)	9 (2.1)	11 (1.8)	10 (1.9)
Water quality	5 (0.6)	5 (0.8)	6 (1.1)	16 ! (6.4)	6 (1.5)	3 (0.9)	5 (1.6)	7 (1.3)	4 (1.0)	5 (1.5)	6 (1.4)	7 (1.4)
Acoustics or noise control	14 (1.0)	14 (1.3)	12 (1.5)	25 (6.2)	14 (2.1)	10 (1.5)	15 (3.0)	16 (2.0)	12 (1.7)	13 (2.4)	13 (1.8)	17 (2.3)
Portable (temporary) buildings (percent of schools)												
School has portable buildings[6]	31 (1.4)	33 (1.8)	24 (2.0)	29 (6.8)	40 (2.8)	32 (2.2)	27 (3.6)	25 (2.1)	25 (2.0)	30 (2.9)	31 (2.2)	39 (3.4)
Overall condition of buildings[6]												
Excellent	6 (1.1)	6 (1.4)	5 ! (1.5)	‡ (†)	4 ! (1.8)	5 ! (1.8)	10 ! (4.7)	7 ! (2.3)	8 ! (2.7)	7 ! (3.0)	4 ! (1.9)	5 ! (2.0)
Good	49 (2.8)	49 (3.2)	46 (4.4)	56 (14.2)	53 (4.2)	51 (4.9)	43 (7.7)	44 (5.0)	51 (4.8)	53 (6.1)	45 (4.4)	48 (5.0)
Fair	36 (2.4)	36 (2.9)	43 (4.8)	‡ (†)	34 (4.1)	38 (4.8)	38 (7.5)	36 (4.8)	29 (4.1)	36 (5.9)	41 (4.2)	38 (4.6)
Poor	9 (1.4)	9 (1.7)	7 ! (2.3)	‡ (†)	8 ! (2.6)	6 ! (2.0)	9 ! (4.1)	13 (3.5)	12 (3.2)	‡ (†)	10 ! (3.2)	8 ! (3.0)
Environmental factors are unsatisfactory[7]												
Lighting, artificial	11 (1.8)	11 (2.1)	12 (3.3)	# (†)	10 (2.9)	6 ! (2.6)	14 (5.7)	15 (4.0)	10 ! (3.0)	8 ! (3.5)	12 (3.3)	12 (3.3)
Lighting, natural	28 (2.5)	29 (3.0)	28 (4.3)	‡ (†)	26 (4.2)	26 (4.4)	41 (8.0)	28 (4.4)	26 (4.1)	28 (4.9)	29 (4.8)	30 (4.5)
Heating	12 (1.8)	11 (2.0)	16 (3.5)	‡ (†)	11 (2.9)	7 ! (2.4)	17 ! (5.7)	16 (4.0)	13 (3.5)	8 ! (3.5)	15 (3.9)	10 (3.1)
Air conditioning	15 (2.2)	16 (2.6)	14 (3.3)	‡ (†)	15 (3.6)	12 (3.1)	14 (5.3)	18 (4.3)	17 (4.1)	13 ! (4.1)	16 (3.9)	14 (3.7)
Ventilation	19 (2.2)	19 (2.6)	22 (3.9)	‡ (†)	18 (3.7)	14 (3.1)	26 (6.7)	24 (4.4)	18 (3.9)	18 ! (5.7)	23 (4.6)	18 (4.0)
Indoor air quality	16 (2.0)	17 (2.3)	14 (3.0)	‡ (†)	17 (3.6)	11 (2.8)	18 ! (6.5)	19 (4.2)	14 (3.4)	15 ! (4.4)	19 (4.1)	16 (3.6)
Water quality	10 (1.7)	10 (2.0)	8 ! (3.1)	‡ (†)	7 ! (3.6)	7 ! (2.9)	16 ! (6.7)	14 ! (4.6)	9 (3.8)	11 ! (†)	11 (3.8)	14 (3.8)
Acoustics or noise control	21 (2.5)	21 (2.9)	21 (4.1)	‡ (†)	19 (3.6)	17 (3.9)	24 (7.1)	26 (4.6)	19 (4.2)	11 ! (4.2)	26 (4.6)	23 (4.7)

†Not applicable.
#Rounds to zero.
!Interpret data with caution. The coefficient of variation (CV) for this estimate is between 30 and 50 percent.
‡Reporting standards not met. Either there are too few cases for a reliable estimate or the coefficient of variation (CV) for this estimate is 50 percent or greater.
[1]Excludes special education, vocational, and alternative schools; schools without enrollment data; and schools offering only preprimary education.
[2]The functional age of the main instructional building is the number of years since its most recent major renovation or since its construction if no major renovation has ever occurred.
[3]Based on schools whose main instructional building has undergone a major renovation.
[4]Based on the 99 percent of public schools with permanent buildings.
[5]Based on schools with the specified environmental factor in their permanent buildings. Includes ratings of "unsatisfactory" and "very unsatisfactory."
[6]Based on the 31 percent of public schools with portable (temporary) buildings.
[7]Based on schools with the specified environmental factor in their portable (temporary) buildings. Includes ratings of "unsatisfactory" and "very unsatisfactory."
NOTE: Detail may not sum to totals because of rounding.
SOURCE: U.S. Department of Education, National Center for Education Statistics, Fast Response Survey System (FRSS), Condition of Public School Facilities: 2012–13, FRSS 105, 2013. (This table was prepared June 2014.)

Age range for compulsory school attendance and special education services, and policies on year-round schools and kindergarten programs, by state: Selected years, 2000 through 2014

State	Compulsory attendance							Compulsory special education services, 2004[1]	Year-round schools, 2008		Kindergarten programs, 2014		
									Has policy on year-round schools	Has districts with year-round schools	School districts required to offer		
	2000	2002	2004	2006	2008	2010	2013				Program	Full-day program	Attendance required
1	2	3	4	5	6	7	8	9	10	11	12	13	14
Alabama	7 to 16	7 to 16	7 to 16[2]	7 to 16	7 to 16	7 to 17	6 to 17	6 to 21		Yes	X	X	
Alaska	7 to 16	7 to 16	7 to 16	7 to 16	7 to 16	7 to 16	7 to 16	3 to 22		Yes			
Arizona	6 to 16[2]	6 to 16[2]	6 to 16[2]	6 to 16[2]	6 to 16[2]	6 to 16[2]	6 to 16[2]	3 to 21	—	—	X		
Arkansas	5 to 17[2,3]	5 to 17[2,3]	5 to 17[2,3]	5 to 17[2,3]	5 to 17[2,3]	5 to 17[2,3]	5 to 17	5 to 21	X	Yes	X	X	X
California	6 to 18[2]	6 to 18	6 to 18	6 to 18	6 to 18	6 to 18	6 to 18	Birth to 21[4]	X	Yes	X	X	
Colorado	—	—	7 to 16	7 to 16	6 to 17	6 to 17	6 to 17	3 to 21		Yes	X		
Connecticut	7 to 16	7 to 18[2]	7 to 18[2]	5 to 18[3]	5 to 18[3]	5 to 18[3]	5 to 18	3 to 21		—	X		X
Delaware	5 to 16	5 to 16	5 to 16[2]	5 to 16	5 to 16	5 to 16	5 to 16	Birth to 20		Yes	X	X	X
District of Columbia	—	5 to 18[5]	5 to 18[5]	5 to 18	5 to 18	5 to 18	5 to 18	—	—	—	X	X	X
Florida	6 to 16[5]	6 to 16[5]	6 to 16[5]	6 to 16[5]	6 to 16[5]	6 to 16[5]	6 to 16	3 to 21	X	Yes	X	X	
Georgia	6 to 16	6 to 16	6 to 16	6 to 16	6 to 16	6 to 16	6 to 16	Birth to 21[6]		Yes	X		
Hawaii	6 to 18	6 to 18	6 to 18	6 to 18	6 to 18	6 to 18	6 to 18	Birth to 19		(7)	X		
Idaho	7 to 16	7 to 16	7 to 16	7 to 16	7 to 16	7 to 16	7 to 16	3 to 21		Yes	X		
Illinois	7 to 16	7 to 16	7 to 17	7 to 17	7 to 17	7 to 17	7 to 17	3 to 21	X	Yes	X		
Indiana	7 to 16	7 to 16	7 to 16	7 to 18[2]	7 to 18[2]	7 to 18[2]	7 to 18	3 to 22		Yes	X		
Iowa	6 to 16[2]	6 to 16[2]	6 to 16	6 to 16	6 to 16	6 to 16	6 to 16	Birth to 21	X	Yes	X		
Kansas	7 to 18[2]	7 to 18[2]	7 to 18[2]	7 to 18[2]	7 to 18[2]	7 to 18[2]	7 to 18	3 to 21[8]		—	X		
Kentucky	6 to 16	6 to 16	6 to 16[2]	6 to 16	6 to 16	6 to 16	6 to 16	Birth to 21		Yes	X		
Louisiana	7 to 17	7 to 17	7 to 17[2]	7 to 18[2]	7 to 18[2]	7 to 18[2]	7 to 18	3 to 21[9]		Yes	X	X	X
Maine	7 to 17	7 to 17	7 to 17[2]	7 to 17[2]	7 to 17[2]	7 to 17[2]	7 to 17	5 to 19[9,10]		—	X		
Maryland	5 to 16	5 to 16	5 to 16	5 to 16	5 to 16	5 to 16	5 to 16[3]	Birth to 21		—	X	X	X
Massachusetts	6 to 16	6 to 16	6 to 16	6 to 16[2]	6 to 16[2]	6 to 16	6 to 16	3 to 21[6]	(11)	—	X		
Michigan	6 to 16	6 to 16	6 to 16	6 to 16	6 to 16	6 to 18	6 to 16	Birth to 25	X	Yes	X		
Minnesota	7 to 18[2]	7 to 16	7 to 16	7 to 16[2]	7 to 16[2]	7 to 16	7 to 16	Birth to 21	X	Yes	X		
Mississippi	6 to 17	6 to 17	6 to 16	6 to 16	6 to 17	6 to 17	6 to 17	Birth to 20		—	X	X	
Missouri	7 to 16	7 to 16	7 to 16	7 to 16	7 to 16	7 to 17	7 to 17	Birth to 20		Yes[12]	X		
Montana	7 to 16[2]	7 to 16[2]	7 to 16[2]	7 to 16[2]	7 to 16[2]	7 to 16[2]	7 to 16	3 to 18[9]		—	X		
Nebraska	7 to 16	7 to 16	7 to 16	6 to 18	6 to 18	6 to 18	6 to 18	Birth to 20		Yes	X		
Nevada	7 to 17	7 to 17	7 to 17	7 to 17	7 to 18[2]	7 to 18[2]	7 to 18	Birth to 21[4]		Yes	X	13	X
New Hampshire	6 to 16	6 to 16	6 to 16	6 to 16	6 to 16	6 to 18	6 to 18	3 to 21		—	X		
New Jersey	6 to 16	6 to 16	6 to 16	6 to 16	6 to 16	6 to 16	6 to 16	5 to 21		—	X	14	
New Mexico	5 to 18	5 to 18	5 to 18[2]	5 to 18[2]	5 to 18[2]	5 to 18	5 to 18	3 to 21	X	Yes	X		X
New York	6 to 16[2]	6 to 16	6 to 16[15]	6 to 16[15]	6 to 16[15]	6 to 16	6 to 16	Birth to 20		—	X		
North Carolina	7 to 16	7 to 16	7 to 16	7 to 16	7 to 16	7 to 16	7 to 16	5 to 20	X	Yes	X	X	
North Dakota	7 to 16	7 to 16	7 to 16	7 to 16	7 to 16	7 to 16	7 to 16	3 to 21		No	X		
Ohio	6 to 18	6 to 18	6 to 18	6 to 18	6 to 18	6 to 18	6 to 18	3 to 21	X	—	X		X
Oklahoma	5 to 18	5 to 18	5 to 18	5 to 18	5 to 18	5 to 18	5 to 18	Birth to 21[9]		Yes	X	X	X
Oregon	7 to 18	7 to 18	7 to 18[2]	7 to 18	7 to 18	7 to 18[2]	7 to 18	3 to 20		Yes	X		
Pennsylvania	8 to 17	8 to 17	8 to 17[2]	8 to 17[2]	8 to 17[2]	8 to 17[2]	8 to 17	6 to 21	X[12]	—[12]	X		
Rhode Island	6 to 16	6 to 16	6 to 16	6 to 16	6 to 16	6 to 16	6 to 16[2]	3 to 21		—	X		X
South Carolina	5 to 16	5 to 16	5 to 16	5 to 17[3]	5 to 17[3]	5 to 17[3]	5 to 17	3 to 21[16]		—	X	X	X
South Dakota	6 to 16	6 to 16	6 to 16	6 to 16	6 to 16	6 to 18[2]	6 to 18[2]	Birth to 21	X	—	X		X[17]
Tennessee	6 to 17	6 to 17	6 to 17	6 to 17[3]	6 to 17[3]	6 to 17[3]	6 to 17	3 to 21[4]	X	Yes	X	X	X
Texas	6 to 18	6 to 18	6 to 18	6 to 18	6 to 18	6 to 18	6 to 18	3 to 21	X	Yes	X		
Utah	6 to 18	6 to 18	6 to 18	6 to 18	6 to 18	6 to 18	6 to 18	3 to 22		Yes	X		
Vermont	7 to 16	6 to 16	6 to 16	6 to 16[2]	6 to 16[2]	6 to 16[2]	6 to 16[2]	3 to 21		—[12]	X		
Virginia	5 to 18	5 to 18	5 to 18	5 to 18[2]	5 to 18[2]	5 to 18[2,3]	5 to 18	2 to 21	X	Yes	X		X
Washington	8 to 17[2]	8 to 17[2]	8 to 16[2]	8 to 18	8 to 18	8 to 18	8 to 18	3 to 21[16]		Yes	X	18	
West Virginia	6 to 16	6 to 16	6 to 16	6 to 16	6 to 16	6 to 17	6 to 17	5 to 21[19]	X	Yes	X	X	X
Wisconsin	6 to 18	6 to 18	6 to 18	6 to 18	6 to 18	6 to 18	6 to 18	3 to 21		Yes	X		
Wyoming	6 to 16[2]	6 to 16[2]	7 to 16[2]	7 to 16[2]	7 to 16[2]	7 to 16[2]	7 to 16	3 to 21			X	20	

—Not available.

X Denotes that the state has a policy. A blank denotes that the state does not have a policy.

[1]Most states have a provision whereby education is provided up to a certain age or completion of secondary school, whichever comes first.

[2]Child may be exempted from compulsory attendance if he/she meets state requirements for early withdrawal with or without meeting conditions for a diploma or equivalency.

[3]Parent/guardian may delay child's entry until a later age per state law/regulation.

[4]Student may continue in the program if 22nd birthday falls before the end of the school year.

[5]Attendance is compulsory until age 18 for Manatee County students, unless they earn a high school diploma prior to reaching their 18th birthday.

[6]Through age 21 or until child graduates with a high school or special education diploma or equivalent.

[7]Some districts operate on a multitrack system; the schools are open year-round, but different cohorts start and end at different times.

[8]To be determined by rules and regulations adopted by the state board.

[9]Children from birth through age 2 are eligible for additional services.

[10]Must be age 5 before October 15, and not age 20 before start of school year.

[11]Policies about year-round schools are decided locally.

[12]State did not participate in 2008 online survey. Data are from 2006.

[13]In certain school districts in Nevada, the lowest performing schools with the highest numbers of limited English proficient students will start offering full-day kindergarten programs.

[14]The Abbott District is required to offer full-day kindergarten.

[15]New York City and Buffalo require school attendance until age 17 unless employed; Syracuse requires kindergarten attendance at age 5.

[16]Student may complete school year if 21st birthday occurs while attending school.

[17]All children must attend kindergarten before age 7.

[18]Full-day kindergarten is being phased in beginning in the 2012–13 school year, beginning with the highest poverty schools. Statewide implementation will be achieved by 2017–18.

[19]Severely handicapped children may begin receiving services at age 3.

[20]Statute requires one full-day program per district.

NOTE: The Education of the Handicapped Act (EHA) Amendments of 1986 make it mandatory for all states receiving EHA funds to serve all 3- to 18-year-old disabled children.

SOURCE: Council of Chief State School Officers, *Key State Education Policies on PK–12 Education*, 2000, 2002, 2004, and 2008; Education Commission of the States (ECS), ECS StateNotes, *Compulsory School Age Requirements*, retrieved August 9, 2010, from http://www.ecs.org/clearinghouse/86/62/8662.pdf; ECS StateNotes, *Special Education: State Special Education Definitions, Ages Served*, retrieved August 9, 2010, from http://www.ecs.org/clearinghouse/52/29/5229.pdf; ECS StateNotes, *Compulsory School Age Requirements*, retrieved April 18, 2014, from http://www.ecs.org/clearinghouse/01/07/03/10703.pdf; ECS StateNotes, *District Must Offer Kindergarten*, retrieved April 18, 2014, from http://ecs.force.com/mbdata/mbquestRT?rep=Kq1416; ECS StateNotes, *Child Must Attend Kindergarten*, retrieved April 18, 2014, from http://ecs.force.com/mbdata/mbquestRT?rep=Kq1403; and supplemental information retrieved from various state websites. (This table was prepared April 2014.)

Minimum amount of instructional time per year and policy on textbook selection, by state: Selected years, 2000 through 2013

State	Minimum amount of instructional time per year					State policy on textbook selection				
	In days				In hours	State recommends or selects textbooks			Local decision, 2008	State standards used
	2000	2006	2011	2013	2013	Recommends	Selects	Either recommends or selects		
1	2	3	4	5	6	7	8	9	10	11
Alabama	175	175	180	180	†					X
Alaska	180	180	170[1]	170[1]	740 (K-3); 900 (4-12)			X	X	
Arizona	—	180	180[2]	180[2]	356 (K); 712 (1-3); 890 (4-6); 1,000 (7-8); 720[9] (9-12)	X			X	
Arkansas	178	178	178[1]	178[1]	†	X			X	
California	175	180	180/175[4]	180/175[4]	600 (K); 840 (1-3); 900 (4-8); 1,080 (9-12)	X				
Colorado	[2]	160	160	160	435/870 (K); 968 (1-5); 1,056 (6-12)				X	X
Connecticut	180	180	180	180	450/900 (K); 900 (1-12)				X	X
Delaware	[2]	†	†	†	1,060[6] (K); 1,060 (1-11); 1,032 (12)				X	X
District of Columbia	—	180	178	180	†				X	
Florida	180	180	180	180	720[7] (K-3); 900[7] (4-12)	X			X	X
Georgia	—	180	180	180	810 (K-3); 900 (4-5); 990 (6-12)	X				X
Hawaii	184	179	180[8]	180[8]	915 (K-6)[8,9]; 990 (7-12)[8,9]	X				X
Idaho	180[12]	†	†	†	450[10] (K); 810[10] (1-3); 900[10] (4-8); 990[10,11] (9-12)	X				X
Illinois	180	176	176	176	†				X	
Indiana	180	180	180	180	†	X			X	X
Iowa	180	180	180	180	†				X	
Kansas	186	186 (K-11);181 (12)	186 (K-11);181 (12)	186 (K-11);181 (12)	465 (K); 1,116 (1-11); 1,086 (12)				X	
Kentucky	175	175	175[1]	175[1]	1,062				X	
Louisiana	175	177	177[1]	177[1]	1,062	X				
Maine	175	175	175[1]	175[1]	†				X	
Maryland	180	180	180	180	1,080				X	
Massachusetts	180	180	180	180	425 (K); 900 (1-5); 990 (6-12)				X	
Michigan	[2]	180	165	170	1,098				X	
Minnesota	[2]	[2]	†	†	425 (K); 935 (1-6); 1,020 (7-12)				X	
Mississippi	180	180	180	180	†		X		X	
Missouri	174	174	174/142[13]	174/142[13]	1,044		—	—	—	
Montana	[2]	90 (K);180 (K-12)	†	†	360/720[1] (K); 720[1] (1-3); 1,080[1,11] (4-12)				X	
Nebraska	[2]	180	180	180	400 (K); 1,032 (1-8); 1,080 (9-12)				X	
Nevada	180	180	180	180	450 (K); 945 (1-5); 990 (6-12)		X		X	
New Hampshire	180	180	180	180	†				X	
New Jersey	180	180	180	180	†				X	
New Mexico	—	180	180	180	450/990[14] (K); 990[14] (1-6); 1,080 (7-12)		X		X	
New York	180	180	180	190	†				X	
North Carolina	180	180	180	185	1,025		X		X	
North Dakota	173	173	175[1]	175[1]	951.5 (K-8); 1,038 (9-12)				X	
Ohio	182	182	182[10]	182[10]	910				X	
Oklahoma	180	180	180[10]	180[10]	900[10] (1-6); 1,080[10] (7-12)		X		X	
Oregon	[2]	†	†	†	405 (K); 810 (1-3); 900 (4-8); 990[11] (9-12)				X	
Pennsylvania	180	180	180	180	450 (K); 900 (1-8); 990 (9-12)				X	
Rhode Island	180	180	180	180	†			X	X	
South Carolina	180	180	180[1]	180[1]	437.5 (K); 875 (1-3); 962.5[11] (4-12)			X		
South Dakota	—	180	180[1]	180[1]	†			—	X	
Tennessee	180	180	180	180	†			X		X
Texas	187	180	180	180	†		X	X		
Utah	180	180	180	180	450 (K); 810 (1); 990 (2-12)			X	X	

See notes at end of table.

Minimum amount of instructional time per year and policy on textbook selection, by state: Selected years, 2000 through 2013—Continued

State	Minimum amount of instructional time per year					State policy on textbook selection, 2008				
	In days				In hours	State recommends or selects textbooks			Local decision	State standards used
	2000	2006	2011	2013	2013	Recommends	Selects	Either recommends or selects		
1	2	3	4	5	6	7	8	9	10	11
Vermont	175	175	175	175	†	—	—	—	—	
Virginia	180	180	180	180	540 (K); 990 (1-12)	X			X	X
Washington	180[12]	180	180	180	450 (K); 1,000 (1-6); 1,080 (7-12)				X	X
West Virginia	180	180	180	180	†			X		
Wisconsin	180	180	180	180	437 (K); 1,050 (1-6); 1,137 (7-12)				X	X
Wyoming	175	175	175	175	450 (K); 900 (Elementary); 1,050 (Middle/Jr. High); 1,100 (Secondary)				X	X

— Not available.
† Not applicable.
X Denotes that the state has a policy. A blank denotes that the state does not have a policy.
[1] Does not include time for in-service or staff development or parent-teacher conferences.
[2] Or an equivalent number of minutes of instruction per year.
[3] Students must enroll in at least 4 subjects that meet at least 720 hours.
[4] Through 2014–15, charter schools and districts are allowed to shorten the 180-day instructional year to 175 days without fiscal penalty.
[5] No statewide policy; varies by district.
[6] 1,060-hour requirement for kindergarten waived if district shows inability to implement full-day program.
[7] For schools on double-session or approved experimental calendar: 630 (K–3); 810 (4–12).
[8] Does not apply to charter and multitrack schools.
[9] For the 2014–15 and 2015–16 school years.
[10] Includes time for in-service or staff development or parent-teacher conferences.
[11] Instructional time for graduating seniors may be reduced.
[12] 1998 data.
[13] 174 days required for a 5-day week; 142 days required for a 4-day week.
[14] Teachers may use 33 hours of the full-day kindergarten program and 22 hours of the grades 1 through 5 programs for home visits or parent-teacher conferences.

NOTE: Minimum number of instructional days refers to the actual number of days that pupils have contact with a teacher. Some states allow for different types of school calendars by setting instructional time in both days and hours, while others use only days or only hours. For states in which the number of days or hours varies by grade, the relevant grade(s) appear in parentheses.

SOURCE: Council of Chief State School Officers, Key State Education Policies on PK–12 Education, 2000, 2006, and 2008; Education Commission of the States, StateNotes, Number of Instructional Days/Hours in the School Year (March 2013 revision), retrieved May 1, 2014, from http://www.ecs.org/clearinghouse/01/06/68/10668.pdf; and supplemental information retrieved from various state websites. (This table was prepared May 2014.)

Course credit requirements and exit exam requirements for a standard high school diploma and the use of other high school completion credentials, by state: 2013

State	Total required credits for standard diploma, all courses	English/language arts	Social studies	Science	Mathematics	Other credits	Exit exam required for standard diploma	Subjects tested[1]	Exam based on standards for 10th grade or higher	Appeals or alternative route to standard diploma if exam failed	Advanced recognition for exceeding standard requirements	Alternative credential for not meeting all standard requirements[2]
1	2	3	4	5	6	7	8	9	10	11	12	13
Alabama	24.0	4.0	4.0	4.0	4.0	8.0	Yes	EMSH	Yes	Yes	Yes	Yes
Alaska	21.0	4.0	3.0	2.0	2.0	10.0	Yes	EM	Yes	Yes	No	Yes
Arizona	22.0	4.0	3.0	3.0	4.0	8.0	Yes	EM	Yes	Yes	Yes	No
Arkansas	22.0	4.0	3.0	3.0	4.0	8.0	Yes	M	No	Yes	Yes	No
California	13.0	3.0	3.0	2.0	2.0	3.0	Yes	EM	Yes	Yes	Yes	Yes
Colorado	—	—	0.5	—	—	—	No	†	†	†	No	No
Connecticut	20.0	4.0	3.0	2.0	3.0	8.0	No [3]	†	†	†	No	No
Delaware	22.0	4.0	3.0	3.0	4.0	8.0	No	†	†	†	No	Yes
District of Columbia	24.0	4.0	4.0	4.0	4.0	8.0	No	†	†	†	No	Yes
Florida	24.0	4.0	3.0	3.0	4.0	10.0	Yes	EM	Yes	Yes	No	Yes
Georgia	23.0	4.0	3.0	4.0	4.0	8.0	Yes	EMSH	Yes	Yes	No	Yes
Hawaii	24.0	4.0	4.0	3.0	3.0	10.0	No	†	†	†	Yes	Yes
Idaho	23.0	4.5	2.5	3.0	3.0	10.0	Yes	EM	Yes	Yes	No	No
Illinois	16.0	4.0	2.0	2.0	3.0	5.0	No	†	†	†	No	No
Indiana	20.0	4.0	3.0	3.0	3.0	7.0	Yes	EM	Yes	Yes	Yes	Yes
Iowa	14.0	4.0	3.0	3.0	3.0	1.0	No	†	†	†	Yes	No
Kansas	21.0	4.0	3.0	3.0	3.0	8.0	No	†	†	†	No	No
Kentucky	22.0	4.0	3.0	3.0	3.0	9.0	No	†	†	†	Yes	Yes
Louisiana	24.0	4.0	4.0	4.0	4.0	8.0	Yes	EMSH [4]	Yes	Yes	Yes	Yes
Maine	16.0	4.0	2.0	2.0	2.0	6.0	No	†	†	†	No	Yes
Maryland	21.0	4.0	3.0	3.0	3.0	8.0	Yes	EMS	Yes	Yes	No	Yes
Massachusetts	—	—	—	—	—	—	Yes	EMS	Yes	Yes	No	No
Michigan	16.0	4.0	3.0	3.0	4.0	2.0	No	†	†	†	No	No
Minnesota	21.5	4.0	3.5	3.0	3.0	8.0	Yes	EM [5]	Yes	Yes	No	No
Mississippi	24.0	4.0	4.0	4.0	4.0	8.0	Yes	EMSH	†	†	No	No
Missouri	24.0	4.0	3.0	3.0	3.0	11.0	No	†	†	†	No	No
Montana	20.0	4.0	2.0	2.0	2.0	10.0	No	†	†	†	No	No
Nebraska	200.0 [6]	—	—	—	—	—	No	†	†	†	No	No
Nevada	22.5	4.0	2.0	2.0	2.0	11.5	Yes	EMS	Yes	Yes	Yes	Yes
New Hampshire	20.0	4.0	2.5	2.0	3.0	8.5	No	†	†	†	Yes	Yes
New Jersey	24.0	4.0	3.0	3.0	3.0	11.0	Yes	EM	Yes	Yes	No	No
New Mexico	24.0	4.0	3.5	3.0	4.0	9.5	Yes	EMSH	Yes	Yes	No	Yes
New York	22.0	4.0	4.0	3.0	3.0	8.0	Yes	EMSH	Yes	Yes	Yes	Yes
North Carolina	21.0	4.0	3.0	3.0	4.0	7.0	No	†	†	†	Yes	Yes
North Dakota	22.0	4.0	3.0	3.0	3.0	9.0	No	†	†	†	No	No
Ohio	20.0	4.0	3.0	3.0	3.0	7.0	Yes	EMSH	Yes	Yes	Yes	No
Oklahoma	23.0	4.0	3.0	3.0	3.0	10.0	Yes	EMSH [7]	Yes	Yes	Yes	No
Oregon	24.0	4.0	3.0	3.0	3.0	11.0	No	†	†	†	No	No
Pennsylvania	—	—	—	—	—	—	No	†	†	†	No	No
Rhode Island	20.0	4.0	3.0	3.0	4.0	6.0	No [8]	†	†	†	No	No
South Carolina	24.0	4.0	3.0	3.0	4.0	10.0	Yes	EM	Yes	No	Yes	Yes
South Dakota	22.0	4.0	3.0	3.0	3.0	9.0	No	†	†	†	Yes	No
Tennessee	22.0	4.0	3.0	3.0	4.0	8.0	No	†	†	No	Yes	Yes
Texas	26.0	4.0	4.0	4.0	4.0	10.0	Yes	EMSH	Yes	Yes	Yes	Yes
Utah	24.0	4.0	3.0	3.0	3.0	11.0	No	†	†	†	No	Yes
Vermont	20.0	4.0	3.0	3.0	3.0	7.0	No	†	†	†	No	No
Virginia	22.0	4.0	3.0	3.0	3.0	9.0	Yes	EMSH [9]	Yes	Yes	Yes	Yes
Washington	20.0	3.0	2.5	2.0	3.0	9.5	Yes	EM	Yes	Yes	No	No
West Virginia	24.0	4.0	4.0	3.0	4.0	9.0	No	†	†	†	Yes	Yes
Wisconsin	13.0	4.0	3.0	2.0	2.0	2.0	No	†	†	†	No	Yes
Wyoming	13.0	4.0	3.0	3.0	3.0	0.0	No	†	†	†	Yes	No

—Not available.

†Not applicable.

[1] Exit exam subjects tested: E = English (including writing), M = Mathematics, S = Science, and H = History/social studies.

[2] A certificate of attendance is an example of an alternative credential for students who do not meet all requirements for a standard diploma. Depending on an individual state's policies, alternative credentials may be offered to students with disabilities, students who fail exit exams, or other students who do not meet all requirements.

[3] Requirement takes effect for class of 2020.

[4] Students must pass either the science or social studies components of the Graduation Exit Examination (GEE) to receive a standard diploma.

[5] Students can graduate by passing statewide reading and writing assessments and either passing mathematics assessments or meeting other requirements.

[6] Expressed in semester credits instead of Carnegie units.

[7] To receive the standard diploma, students must pass tests in algebra 1, English 2, and two of the following five subjects: algebra 2, biology 1, English 3, geometry, and U.S. history.

[8] Requirement takes effect for class of 2014.

[9] To receive the standard diploma, students must earn at least six verified credits by passing end-of-course assessments. One of those credits may be earned by passing a student-selected test in computer science, technology, career and technical education, or other areas.

NOTE: Local school districts frequently have other graduation requirements in addition to state requirements. The Carnegie unit is a standard of measurement that represents one credit for the completion of a 1-year course.

SOURCE: Editorial Projects in Education Research Center, custom table, retrieved August 27, 2013, from Education Counts database (http://www.edcounts.org/createtable/step1.php). (This table was prepared August 2013.)

States that use criterion-referenced tests (CRTs) aligned to state standards, by subject area and level: 2006–07

State	Aligned to state standards		Off-the-shelf/ norm-referenced test (NRT)[1]	CRTs,[2] by subject area and level			
	CRT[2]	Augmented or hybrid test[3]		English/ language arts	Mathematics	Science	Social studies/ history
1	2	3	4	5	6	7	8
Alabama	X		X	ES, MS, HS	ES, MS, HS	HS	HS
Alaska	X		X	ES, MS, HS	ES, MS, HS		
Arizona	X	X	X	ES, MS, HS	ES, MS, HS		
Arkansas	X		X	ES, MS, HS	ES, MS, HS	ES, MS	
California	X		X	ES, MS, HS	ES, MS, HS	ES, MS, HS	MS, HS
Colorado	X		X	ES, MS, HS	ES, MS, HS	ES, MS, HS	
Connecticut	X			ES, MS, HS	ES, MS, HS	HS	
Delaware		X		ES, MS, HS	ES, MS, HS	ES, MS, HS	ES, MS, HS
District of Columbia	X			ES, MS, HS	ES, MS, HS		
Florida	X		X	ES, MS, HS	ES, MS, HS	ES, MS, HS	
Georgia	X		X	ES, MS, HS	ES, MS, HS	ES, MS, HS	ES, MS, HS
Hawaii		X		ES, MS, HS	ES, MS, HS		
Idaho	X			ES, MS, HS	ES, MS, HS		
Illinois	X	X		ES, MS, HS	ES, MS, HS	HS	
Indiana	X			ES, MS, HS	ES, MS, HS	ES, MS	
Iowa			X	ES, MS, HS	ES, MS, HS	ES, MS, HS	
Kansas	X			ES, MS, HS	ES, MS, HS		
Kentucky	X		X	ES, MS, HS	ES, MS, HS	ES, MS, HS	ES, MS, HS
Louisiana	X	X		ES, MS, HS	ES, MS, HS	ES, MS, HS	ES, MS, HS
Maine	X		X	ES, MS, HS	ES, MS, HS	ES, MS	
Maryland	X	X		ES, HS	ES, MS, HS	HS	HS
Massachusetts	X			ES, HS	ES, MS, HS	ES, MS, HS	
Michigan	X		X	ES, MS, HS	ES, MS, HS	ES, MS, HS	MS, HS
Minnesota	X			ES, MS, HS	ES, MS, HS		
Mississippi	X		X	ES, MS, HS	ES, MS, HS	ES, MS, HS	HS
Missouri		X		ES, MS, HS	ES, MS, HS		
Montana	X		X	ES, MS, HS	ES, MS, HS		
Nebraska	X			ES, MS, HS			
Nevada	X		X	ES, MS, HS	ES, MS, HS		
New Hampshire	X			ES, MS	ES, MS		
New Jersey	X			ES, MS, HS	ES, MS, HS	ES, MS	
New Mexico	X		X	ES, MS, HS	ES, MS, HS	ES, MS, HS	
New York	X			ES, MS, HS	ES, MS, HS	ES, MS, HS	ES, MS, HS
North Carolina	X			ES, MS, HS	ES, MS, HS	HS	HS
North Dakota	X			ES, MS, HS	ES, MS, HS	ES, MS, HS	
Ohio	X			ES, MS, HS	ES, MS, HS	ES, MS, HS	ES, MS, HS
Oklahoma	X			ES, MS, HS	ES, MS, HS	ES, MS, HS	ES, MS, HS
Oregon	X			ES, MS, HS	ES, MS, HS	MS, HS	
Pennsylvania	X			ES, MS, HS	ES, MS, HS		
Rhode Island	X	X		ES, MS, HS	ES, MS, HS		
South Carolina	X			ES, MS, HS	ES, MS, HS	ES, MS, HS	ES, MS, HS
South Dakota		X	X	ES, MS, HS	ES, MS, HS	ES, MS, HS	
Tennessee	X			ES, MS, HS	ES, MS, HS	ES, MS, HS	ES, MS, HS
Texas	X			ES, MS, HS	ES, MS, HS	ES, MS, HS	MS, HS
Utah	X		X	ES, MS, HS	ES, MS, HS	ES, MS, HS	
Vermont	X			ES, MS	ES, MS		
Virginia	X			ES, MS, HS	ES, MS, HS	ES, MS, HS	ES, MS, HS
Washington	X			ES, MS, HS	ES, MS, HS	ES, MS, HS	
West Virginia	X		X	ES, MS, HS	ES, MS, HS	ES, MS, HS	ES, MS
Wisconsin		X		ES, MS, HS	ES, MS, HS	ES, MS, HS	ES, MS, HS
Wyoming	X			ES, MS, HS	ES, MS, HS		

X State has a test. A blank denotes that the state does not have this type of test.
[1]Off-the-shelf/norm-referenced tests (NRTs) are commercially developed tests that have not been modified to reflect state content standards.
[2]Criterion-referenced tests (CRTs) are custom-developed and explicitly designed to measure state content standards.

[3]Augmented or hybrid tests incorporate elements of both NRTs and CRTs. These tests include NRTs that have been augmented or modified to reflect state standards.
NOTE: ES = elementary school, MS = middle school, and HS = high school.
SOURCE: Quality Counts 2007, Cradle to Career, *Education Week*, 2007. (This table was prepared September 2008.)

Required testing for initial certification of elementary and secondary school teachers, by type of assessment and state: 2012 and 2013

State	Assessment for certification, 2012				Assessment for certification, 2013			
	Basic skills exam	Subject-matter exam	Knowledge of teaching exam	Assessment of teaching performance	Basic skills exam	Subject-matter exam	Knowledge of teaching exam	Assessment of teaching performance
1	2	3	4	5	6	7	8	9
Alabama	X	X	X	X	X	X	X	X
Alaska	X				X			
Arizona		X	X			X	X	
Arkansas	X	X	X	X	X	X	X	X
California	X	—		X	X	—		X
Colorado		X				X		
Connecticut	X	X	X	X	X	X	—	
Delaware	X	X			X	X		
District of Columbia	X	X	X		X	X	X	
Florida	X				X			X
Georgia	X	X			X	X		
Hawaii	X	X		—	X	X		X
Idaho						X		X
Illinois	X	X	X		X	X	X	X
Indiana	X	X		X	X	X		X
Iowa								
Kansas		X	X			X	X	
Kentucky	X	X	X	X	X	X	X	X
Louisiana	X	X	X	X	X	X	X	X
Maine	—		—		—		—	
Maryland	X	X	X	X	X	X	X	X
Massachusetts	X	X		X	X	X		X
Michigan	X	X		X	X	X		X
Minnesota	X	X	X		X	X	X	
Mississippi	—	—	—	—	—	—	—	—
Missouri	X	X		X	X	X		X
Montana								
Nebraska	X				X			
Nevada	—	X	—	—	—	X	—	—
New Hampshire	X	X			X	X		
New Jersey	—	—		—	—	—	—	—
New Mexico	X	X	X	X	X	X	X	X
New York		X	X			X	X	
North Carolina	—	—	—	—	—	—	—	—
North Dakota	—	X	—	—	—	X	—	—
Ohio		X	X	X		X	X	X
Oklahoma	—	—	—		—	—	—	—
Oregon	X	X		X	X	X		X
Pennsylvania	X	X	X	X		X	X	X
Rhode Island			X	X			X	X
South Carolina		X	X			X	X	
South Dakota	X	X	X	X	X	X	X	X
Tennessee	X	X	X		X	X	X	
Texas	X	X	X	X	X	X	X	X
Utah		X				X		X
Vermont	X	X			X	X		
Virginia	X	X	X		X	X	X	
Washington	X	X		X	X	X		X
West Virginia	X	X	X	X	X	X	X	X
Wisconsin	X	X			X	X		
Wyoming	—		—	—	—		—	—

—Not available.
X Denotes that the state requires testing. A blank denotes that the state does not require testing.

SOURCE: National Association of State Directors of Teacher Education and Certification (NASDTEC), NASDTEC Knowledgebase, retrieved August 8, 2013, from https://www.nasdtec.info/. (This table was prepared August 2013.)

Percentage of 4th-, 8th-, and 12th-graders absent from school in the last month, by selected student and school characteristics and number of days absent: 2002, 2009, and 2013

[Standard errors appear in parentheses]

Year, grade level, and days absent from school in the last month	All students	Sex — Male	Sex — Female	Race/ethnicity — White	Black	Hispanic	Asian/Pacific Islander	American Indian/Alaska Native	Two or more races	Eligibility — Eligible	Not eligible	Unknown	Control — Public	Catholic	Other private
	2	3	4	5	6	7	8	9	10	11	12	13	14	15	16
2002															
4th-graders															
None	52 (0.3)	55 (0.4)	50 (0.5)	52 (0.4)	52 (0.7)	50 (0.9)	66 (1.5)	42 (1.5)	55 (1.9)	49 (0.5)	55 (0.4)	53 (1.1)	52 (0.3)	55 (1.2)	55 (1.4)
1–2 days	30 (0.3)	28 (0.3)	32 (0.4)	31 (0.3)	27 (0.5)	31 (0.9)	22 (0.9)	34 (1.8)	29 (1.8)	30 (0.4)	29 (0.4)	30 (0.8)	30 (0.3)	31 (1.0)	28 (1.1)
3–4 days	11 (0.1)	11 (0.2)	12 (0.2)	11 (0.2)	12 (0.4)	11 (0.4)	7 (0.6)	14 (1.1)	10 (1.3)	13 (0.3)	10 (0.2)	11 (0.5)	11 (0.1)	10 (0.6)	12 (0.9)
5–10 days	4 (0.1)	4 (0.2)	4 (0.2)	4 (0.1)	4 (0.2)	4 (0.4)	3 (0.5)	6 (0.7)	5 (1.5)	5 (0.2)	4 (0.1)	4 (0.3)	4 (0.1)	3 (0.3)	4 (0.5)
More than 10 days	2 (0.1)	3 (0.1)	2 (0.1)	2 (0.1)	4 (0.2)	3 (0.3)	2 (0.5)	4 (0.6)	1 (0.6)	3 (0.2)	2 (0.1)	2 (0.2)	2 (0.1)	1 (0.2)	1 (0.3)
8th-graders															
None	45 (0.3)	47 (0.4)	43 (0.4)	44 (0.4)	46 (0.7)	44 (1.1)	62 (1.8)	31 (2.8)	50 (5.2)	41 (0.5)	46 (0.4)	46 (0.9)	44 (0.4)	49 (1.2)	47 (1.1)
1–2 days	35 (0.3)	34 (0.4)	37 (0.4)	37 (0.4)	31 (0.6)	34 (0.8)	26 (1.6)	37 (1.9)	33 (3.7)	34 (0.5)	36 (0.4)	36 (0.8)	35 (0.3)	37 (1.1)	37 (1.1)
3–4 days	13 (0.2)	12 (0.3)	14 (0.2)	13 (0.2)	15 (0.5)	14 (0.6)	7 (0.8)	20 (3.4)	9 (1.7)	15 (0.3)	12 (0.2)	12 (0.5)	13 (0.2)	10 (0.7)	11 (0.9)
5–10 days	5 (0.1)	5 (0.2)	5 (0.2)	5 (0.1)	5 (0.3)	5 (0.3)	3 (0.4)	8 (1.2)	6 (3.5)	6 (0.2)	4 (0.1)	4 (0.3)	5 (0.1)	3 (0.4)	4 (0.4)
More than 10 days	2 (0.1)	2 (0.1)	2 (0.1)	2 (0.1)	2 (0.2)	3 (0.2)	2 (0.2)	4 (1.0)	1 (1.1)	3 (0.2)	2 (0.1)	2 (0.2)	2 (0.1)	1 (0.1)	1 (0.3)
12th-graders															
None	36 (0.7)	39 (0.9)	32 (0.8)	35 (0.8)	37 (1.4)	34 (1.6)	41 (2.4)	‡	23 (5.5)	35 (1.3)	36 (0.8)	34 (1.4)	—	—	—
1–2 days	40 (0.6)	38 (0.8)	42 (0.8)	40 (0.8)	36 (1.1)	42 (1.7)	36 (1.8)	‡	51 (10.4)	37 (1.0)	40 (0.8)	42 (1.2)	—	—	—
3–4 days	17 (0.5)	14 (0.6)	19 (0.6)	17 (0.6)	17 (0.9)	16 (1.3)	15 (2.4)	‡	22 (4.4)	19 (1.0)	16 (0.5)	16 (1.2)	—	—	—
5–10 days	6 (0.3)	6 (0.3)	6 (0.3)	6 (0.3)	7 (0.8)	5 (0.9)	5 (0.9)	‡	4 (‡)	7 (0.6)	6 (0.3)	6 (0.7)	—	—	—
More than 10 days	2 (0.2)	3 (0.3)	2 (0.1)	2 (0.2)	2 (0.3)	3 (0.6)	3 (0.8)	‡	1 (0.3)	2 (0.4)	2 (0.3)	2 (0.4)	—	—	—
2009															
4th-graders															
None	52 (0.2)	54 (0.3)	51 (0.3)	52 (0.3)	51 (0.4)	52 (0.6)	65 (0.9)	42 (1.4)	53 (1.4)	49 (0.3)	56 (0.3)	53 (1.0)	52 (0.2)	54 (1.5)	†
1–2 days	29 (0.2)	28 (0.3)	31 (0.2)	31 (0.2)	28 (0.3)	29 (0.4)	24 (0.7)	32 (1.2)	29 (1.3)	30 (0.2)	29 (0.3)	30 (1.0)	30 (0.2)	31 (1.4)	†
3–4 days	11 (0.1)	11 (0.2)	12 (0.1)	11 (0.1)	12 (0.2)	12 (0.3)	6 (0.4)	15 (1.0)	12 (1.0)	13 (0.2)	10 (0.1)	10 (0.7)	11 (0.1)	10 (0.8)	†
5–10 days	5 (0.1)	4 (0.1)	5 (0.1)	5 (0.1)	5 (0.2)	5 (0.3)	3 (0.3)	7 (0.8)	4 (0.6)	5 (0.1)	4 (0.1)	5 (0.5)	4 (0.1)	4 (0.5)	†
More than 10 days	2 (0.1)	3 (0.1)	2 (0.1)	2 (0.1)	4 (0.2)	3 (0.2)	2 (0.3)	4 (0.5)	1 (0.3)	3 (0.1)	1 (0.1)	1 (0.3)	2 (0.1)	1 (0.3)	†
8th-graders															
None	46 (0.3)	48 (0.3)	44 (0.3)	45 (0.3)	45 (0.4)	45 (0.6)	65 (1.2)	33 (1.4)	45 (2.0)	43 (0.4)	48 (0.3)	49 (1.1)	45 (0.3)	54 (1.7)	†
1–2 days	35 (0.2)	33 (0.3)	36 (0.3)	37 (0.2)	32 (0.3)	33 (0.4)	25 (0.9)	39 (1.5)	32 (1.8)	34 (0.3)	36 (0.3)	35 (1.0)	35 (0.2)	34 (1.3)	†
3–4 days	13 (0.2)	13 (0.2)	14 (0.2)	12 (0.2)	15 (0.3)	13 (0.4)	7 (0.5)	18 (0.9)	13 (1.4)	15 (0.3)	11 (0.2)	11 (0.7)	13 (0.2)	9 (0.8)	†
5–10 days	5 (0.1)	5 (0.1)	5 (0.1)	5 (0.1)	6 (0.3)	6 (0.2)	2 (0.3)	7 (0.6)	7 (0.9)	6 (0.2)	4 (0.1)	5 (0.7)	5 (0.1)	3 (0.5)	†
More than 10 days	2 (0.1)	2 (0.1)	2 (0.1)	2 (0.1)	2 (0.1)	2 (0.2)	1 (0.2)	3 (0.6)	3 (0.7)	3 (0.1)	1 (0.1)	1 (0.3)	2 (0.1)	1 (0.2)	†
12th-graders															
None	38 (0.5)	41 (0.5)	35 (0.6)	36 (0.5)	39 (1.0)	38 (0.8)	50 (1.7)	30 (3.9)	39 (3.2)	36 (0.7)	38 (0.6)	43 (1.2)	—	—	—
1–2 days	39 (0.3)	37 (0.4)	41 (0.5)	40 (0.4)	38 (0.8)	39 (0.7)	33 (1.6)	36 (4.0)	37 (3.2)	39 (0.6)	40 (0.4)	39 (0.9)	—	—	—
3–4 days	15 (0.3)	13 (0.3)	17 (0.4)	15 (0.4)	16 (0.5)	15 (0.7)	11 (1.0)	23 (3.2)	16 (2.4)	16 (0.5)	15 (0.4)	12 (0.7)	—	—	—
5–10 days	6 (0.2)	5 (0.2)	6 (0.2)	6 (0.2)	6 (0.4)	6 (0.3)	4 (0.5)	8 (2.3)	6 (1.5)	7 (0.3)	5 (0.2)	5 (0.4)	—	—	—
More than 10 days	2 (0.1)	3 (0.1)	2 (0.1)	2 (0.1)	2 (0.2)	3 (0.2)	1 (0.3)	3 (1.6)	1 (0.5)	2 (0.2)	2 (0.1)	2 (0.4)	—	—	—
2013															
4th-graders															
None	51 (0.2)	53 (0.3)	48 (0.3)	50 (0.3)	50 (0.5)	50 (0.5)	65 (0.8)	40 (1.5)	49 (1.1)	47 (0.3)	54 (0.3)	55 (1.5)	50 (0.2)	54 (1.5)	†
1–2 days	30 (0.2)	29 (0.3)	31 (0.3)	32 (0.2)	29 (0.4)	29 (0.4)	21 (0.8)	32 (1.6)	30 (1.0)	30 (0.2)	30 (0.3)	28 (1.1)	30 (0.2)	30 (1.3)	†
3–4 days	12 (0.1)	11 (0.2)	13 (0.2)	12 (0.1)	13 (0.3)	13 (0.3)	8 (0.3)	16 (0.8)	13 (0.7)	14 (0.2)	11 (0.1)	10 (0.6)	12 (0.1)	10 (0.7)	†
5–10 days	5 (0.1)	5 (0.1)	5 (0.1)	5 (0.1)	5 (0.2)	5 (0.2)	4 (0.3)	7 (0.7)	5 (0.5)	6 (0.1)	5 (0.1)	5 (0.1)	5 (0.1)	5 (0.3)	†
More than 10 days	1 (#)	2 (0.1)	2 (0.1)	1 (#)	2 (0.1)	3 (0.2)	2 (0.2)	4 (0.6)	3 (0.3)	3 (0.1)	1 (0.1)	1 (0.1)	1 (#)	1 (0.2)	†
8th-graders															
None	44 (0.2)	47 (0.3)	42 (0.3)	43 (0.3)	46 (0.5)	44 (0.6)	63 (1.0)	36 (1.5)	42 (1.2)	41 (0.3)	46 (0.3)	51 (1.2)	44 (0.2)	50 (1.5)	†
1–2 days	36 (0.2)	35 (0.3)	38 (0.3)	39 (0.2)	33 (0.5)	36 (0.5)	27 (0.9)	37 (1.7)	36 (1.0)	36 (0.2)	37 (0.3)	34 (1.0)	37 (0.2)	37 (1.2)	†
3–4 days	13 (0.1)	12 (0.1)	14 (0.2)	13 (0.1)	13 (0.3)	13 (0.4)	7 (0.5)	18 (1.2)	15 (0.8)	15 (0.2)	11 (0.2)	10 (0.8)	13 (0.1)	9 (0.8)	†
5–10 days	5 (0.1)	5 (0.1)	5 (0.1)	5 (0.1)	5 (0.2)	5 (0.2)	2 (0.3)	6 (0.5)	6 (0.6)	6 (0.2)	4 (0.1)	4 (0.3)	5 (0.1)	3 (0.4)	†
More than 10 days	1 (#)	2 (0.1)	1 (0.1)	1 (#)	2 (0.1)	2 (0.1)	1 (0.2)	3 (0.4)	2 (0.3)	2 (0.1)	1 (#)	1 (0.3)	1 (#)	1 (0.2)	†

—Not available.
†Not applicable.
#Rounds to zero.
‡Reporting standards not met (too few cases for a reliable estimate).
NOTE: Includes public and private schools unless otherwise noted. Race categories exclude persons of Hispanic ethnicity. Prior to 2011, students in the "two or more races" category were categorized as "unclassified." Detail may not sum to totals because of rounding. Grade 12 results for the 2013 National Assessment of Educational Progress (NAEP) Reading Assessment were not yet available at the time this table was created.
SOURCE: U.S. Department of Education, National Center for Education Statistics, National Assessment of Educational Progress (NAEP), 2002, 2009, 2011, and 2013 Reading Assessments, retrieved December 19, 2013, from the Main NAEP Data Explorer (http://nces.ed.gov/nationsreportcard/naepdata/). (This table was prepared December 2013.)

Percentage of students in grades 9–12 who reported having been in a physical fight at least one time during the previous 12 months, by location and selected student characteristics: Selected years, 1993 through 2011

[Standard errors appear in parentheses]

Location and student characteristic	1993	1995	1997	1999	2001	2003	2005	2007	2009	2011
	2	3	4	5	6	7	8	9	10	11
Anywhere (including on school property)[1]										
Total	41.8 (0.99)	38.7 (1.14)	36.6 (1.01)	35.7 (1.17)	33.2 (0.71)	33.0 (0.99)	35.9 (0.77)	35.5 (0.77)	31.5 (0.70)	32.8 (0.65)
Sex										
Male	51.2 (1.05)	46.1 (1.09)	45.5 (1.07)	44.0 (1.27)	43.1 (0.84)	40.5 (1.32)	43.4 (1.01)	44.4 (0.89)	39.3 (1.20)	40.7 (0.74)
Female	31.7 (1.19)	30.6 (1.49)	26.0 (1.26)	27.3 (1.70)	23.9 (0.95)	25.1 (0.85)	28.1 (0.94)	26.5 (0.99)	22.9 (0.74)	24.4 (0.92)
Race/ethnicity[2]										
White	40.3 (1.13)	36.0 (1.06)	33.7 (1.29)	33.1 (1.45)	32.2 (0.95)	30.5 (1.11)	33.1 (0.88)	31.7 (0.96)	27.8 (0.88)	29.4 (0.74)
Black	49.5 (1.82)	41.6 (1.99)	43.0 (1.92)	41.4 (3.12)	36.5 (1.60)	39.7 (1.23)	43.1 (1.74)	44.7 (1.33)	41.1 (1.71)	39.1 (1.52)
Hispanic	43.2 (1.58)	47.9 (2.69)	40.7 (1.68)	39.9 (1.65)	35.8 (0.91)	36.1 (0.98)	41.0 (1.64)	40.4 (1.25)	36.2 (0.95)	36.8 (1.44)
Asian[3]	— (†)	— (†)	— (†)	22.7 (2.71)	22.3 (2.73)	25.9 (2.99)	21.6 (2.43)	24.3 (3.50)	18.9 (1.72)	18.4 (1.87)
American Indian/Alaska Native	49.8 (4.79)	47.2 (6.44)	54.7 (5.75)	48.7 (6.78)	49.2 (6.58)	46.6 (6.53)	44.2 (3.40)	36.0 (1.49)	42.4 (5.23)	42.4 (2.12)
Pacific Islander[3]	— (†)	— (†)	— (†)	50.7 (3.42)	51.7 (6.25)	30.0 (5.21)	34.4 (5.58)	42.6 (7.74)	32.6 (3.50)	43.0 (5.14)
Two or more races[3]	— (†)	— (†)	— (†)	40.2 (2.76)	39.6 (2.85)	38.2 (3.64)	46.9 (4.16)	47.8 (3.30)	34.2 (3.51)	45.0 (2.60)
Grade										
9th	50.4 (1.54)	47.3 (2.22)	44.8 (1.98)	41.1 (1.96)	39.5 (1.27)	38.6 (1.38)	43.5 (1.15)	40.9 (1.16)	37.0 (1.21)	37.7 (1.11)
10th	42.2 (1.45)	40.4 (1.49)	40.2 (1.91)	37.7 (2.11)	34.7 (1.37)	33.5 (1.20)	36.6 (1.09)	36.2 (1.34)	33.5 (1.19)	35.3 (1.35)
11th	40.5 (1.52)	36.9 (1.48)	34.2 (1.72)	31.3 (1.55)	29.1 (1.10)	30.9 (1.38)	31.6 (1.44)	34.8 (1.36)	28.6 (0.93)	29.7 (1.14)
12th	34.8 (1.56)	31.0 (1.71)	28.8 (1.36)	30.4 (1.91)	26.5 (1.01)	26.5 (1.08)	29.1 (1.26)	28.0 (1.42)	24.9 (0.99)	26.9 (0.95)
Urbanicity[4]										
Urban	— (†)	— (†)	38.2 (2.00)	37.0 (2.66)	36.8 (1.53)	35.5 (2.17)	— (†)	— (†)	— (†)	— (†)
Suburban	— (†)	— (†)	36.7 (1.59)	35.0 (1.56)	31.3 (0.80)	33.1 (1.23)	— (†)	— (†)	— (†)	— (†)
Rural	— (†)	— (†)	32.9 (2.91)	36.6 (2.14)	33.8 (2.58)	29.7 (1.61)	— (†)	— (†)	— (†)	— (†)
On school property[5]										
Total	16.2 (0.59)	15.5 (0.79)	14.8 (0.64)	14.2 (0.62)	12.5 (0.49)	12.8 (0.76)	13.6 (0.56)	12.4 (0.48)	11.1 (0.54)	12.0 (0.39)
Sex										
Male	23.5 (0.71)	21.0 (0.90)	20.0 (1.04)	18.5 (0.66)	18.0 (0.74)	17.1 (0.92)	18.2 (0.93)	16.3 (0.60)	15.1 (1.05)	16.0 (0.58)
Female	8.6 (0.73)	9.5 (1.03)	8.6 (0.78)	9.8 (0.95)	7.2 (0.47)	8.0 (0.70)	8.8 (0.52)	8.5 (0.62)	6.7 (0.42)	7.8 (0.43)
Race/ethnicity[2]										
White	15.0 (0.68)	12.9 (0.62)	13.3 (0.84)	12.3 (0.86)	11.2 (0.60)	10.0 (0.73)	11.6 (0.66)	10.2 (0.56)	8.6 (0.58)	9.9 (0.51)
Black	22.0 (1.39)	20.3 (1.25)	20.7 (1.20)	18.7 (1.51)	16.8 (1.26)	17.1 (1.30)	16.9 (1.39)	17.6 (1.10)	17.4 (0.99)	16.4 (0.89)
Hispanic	17.9 (1.75)	21.1 (1.68)	19.0 (1.50)	15.7 (0.91)	14.1 (0.89)	16.7 (1.14)	18.3 (1.62)	15.5 (0.81)	13.5 (0.82)	14.4 (0.79)
Asian[3]	— (†)	— (†)	— (†)	10.4 (0.95)	10.8 (1.92)	13.1 (2.26)	5.9 (1.53)	8.5 (1.99)	7.7 (1.09)	6.2 (1.06)
American Indian/Alaska Native	18.6 (2.74)	31.4 (5.58)	18.9 (5.55)	16.2 ! (5.23)	18.2 (4.41)	24.2 (5.03)	24.5 (3.16)	15.0 (1.12)	20.7 (3.73)	12.0 (1.77)
Pacific Islander[3]	— (†)	— (†)	— (†)	25.3 (4.60)	29.1 (7.63)	22.2 (4.82)	15.8 (5.60)	9.6 ! (3.47)	14.8 (2.37)	20.9 (4.41)
Two or more races[3]	— (†)	— (†)	— (†)	16.9 (2.40)	14.7 (1.97)	20.2 (3.83)	15.8 (2.61)	19.6 (2.39)	12.4 (2.19)	16.6 (1.41)
Grade										
9th	23.1 (1.55)	21.6 (1.79)	21.3 (1.29)	18.6 (1.02)	17.3 (0.77)	18.0 (1.24)	18.9 (0.93)	17.0 (0.67)	14.9 (0.98)	16.2 (0.77)
10th	17.2 (1.07)	16.5 (1.57)	17.0 (1.67)	17.2 (1.23)	13.5 (0.88)	12.8 (0.89)	14.4 (1.08)	11.7 (0.86)	12.1 (0.83)	12.8 (0.86)
11th	13.8 (1.27)	13.6 (1.00)	12.5 (0.87)	10.8 (1.01)	9.4 (0.71)	10.4 (0.89)	10.4 (0.75)	11.0 (0.73)	9.5 (0.63)	9.2 (0.55)
12th	11.4 (0.66)	10.6 (0.73)	9.5 (0.73)	8.1 (1.00)	7.5 (0.56)	7.3 (0.70)	8.5 (0.70)	8.6 (0.62)	6.6 (0.59)	8.8 (0.69)
Urbanicity[4]										
Urban	— (†)	— (†)	15.8 (1.50)	14.4 (1.08)	14.8 (0.90)	14.8 (1.31)	— (†)	— (†)	— (†)	— (†)
Suburban	— (†)	— (†)	14.2 (0.95)	13.7 (0.86)	11.0 (0.75)	12.8 (1.23)	— (†)	— (†)	— (†)	— (†)
Rural	— (†)	— (†)	14.7 (2.09)	16.3 (2.33)	13.8 (1.10)	10.0 (1.36)	— (†)	— (†)	— (†)	— (†)

—Not available.
†Not applicable.
! Interpret data with caution. The coefficient of variation (CV) for this estimate is between 30 and 50 percent.
[1]The term "anywhere" is not used in the Youth Risk Behavior Survey (YRBS) questionnaire; students were simply asked how many times in the past 12 months they had been in a physical fight.
[2]Race categories exclude persons of Hispanic ethnicity.
[3]Before 1999, Asian students and Pacific Islander students were not categorized separately, and students were not given the option of choosing two or more races. Because the response categories changed in 1999, caution should be used in comparing data on race from 1993, 1995, and 1997 with data from later years.
[4]Refers to the Standard Metropolitan Statistical Area (MSA) status of the respondent's household as defined in 2000 by the U.S. Census Bureau. Categories include "central city of an MSA (Urban)," "in MSA but not in central city (Suburban)," and "not MSA (Rural)."
[5]In the question asking students about physical fights at school, "on school property" was not defined for survey respondents.
SOURCE: Centers for Disease Control and Prevention, Division of Adolescent and School Health, Youth Risk Behavior Surveillance System (YRBSS), 1993 through 2011. (This table was prepared September 2013.)

Percentage of public school students in grades 9–12 who reported having been in a physical fight at least one time during the previous 12 months, by location and state: Selected years, 2003 through 2011

[Standard errors appear in parentheses]

State	Anywhere (including on school property)[1]					On school property[2]				
	2003	2005	2007	2009	2011	2003	2005	2007	2009	2011
1	2	3	4	5	6	7	8	9	10	11
United States[3]	33.0 (0.99)	35.9 (0.77)	35.5 (0.77)	31.5 (0.70)	32.8 (0.65)	12.8 (0.76)	13.6 (0.56)	12.4 (0.48)	11.1 (0.54)	12.0 (0.39)
Alabama	30.0 (1.78)	31.7 (1.84)	— (†)	31.7 (2.44)	28.4 (1.79)	12.9 (1.21)	14.6 (1.29)	— (†)	13.1 (1.41)	11.8 (1.30)
Alaska	27.1 (1.55)	— (†)	29.2 (1.77)	27.8 (1.52)	23.7 (1.17)	8.6 (0.92)	— (†)	10.4 (1.17)	9.8 (1.04)	7.7 (0.90)
Arizona	32.4 (1.79)	32.4 (1.43)	31.3 (1.54)	35.9 (1.83)	27.7 (1.41)	11.4 (0.86)	11.7 (0.87)	11.3 (0.72)	12.0 (0.82)	10.8 (0.78)
Arkansas	— (†)	32.1 (1.67)	32.8 (1.79)	34.7 (2.08)	29.1 (1.76)	— (†)	13.9 (1.33)	13.0 (1.03)	14.8 (1.30)	11.0 (1.36)
California	— (†)	— (†)	— (†)	— (†)	— (†)	— (†)	— (†)	— (†)	— (†)	— (†)
Colorado	— (†)	32.2 (1.54)	— (†)	32.0 (1.51)	24.9 (1.69)	— (†)	12.1 (0.89)	— (†)	10.7 (0.83)	— (†)
Connecticut	— (†)	32.7 (1.45)	31.4 (1.39)	28.3 (1.26)	25.1 (1.53)	— (†)	10.5 (0.72)	10.5 (0.83)	9.6 (0.79)	8.7 (0.84)
Delaware	34.9 (1.15)	30.3 (1.38)	33.0 (1.31)	30.4 (1.22)	28.0 (1.59)	11.4 (0.70)	9.8 (0.82)	10.5 (0.72)	8.6 (0.72)	8.8 (1.02)
District of Columbia	38.0 (1.61)	36.3 (1.26)	43.0 (1.45)	— (†)	37.9 (1.71)	15.2 (1.07)	16.4 (0.88)	19.8 (1.21)	— (†)	15.8 (1.55)
Florida	32.1 (0.74)	30.0 (0.94)	32.3 (1.24)	29.8 (0.83)	28.0 (0.72)	13.3 (0.65)	11.5 (0.77)	12.5 (0.84)	10.5 (0.47)	10.2 (0.44)
Georgia	31.4 (1.20)	33.8 (1.40)	34.0 (1.26)	32.3 (1.76)	33.1 (1.65)	11.1 (0.74)	12.1 (1.01)	13.1 (1.07)	11.7 (1.21)	11.9 (1.07)
Hawaii	— (†)	27.0 (1.37)	28.6 (2.20)	29.5 (1.92)	22.3 (1.11)	— (†)	10.0 (1.01)	7.0 (0.78)	10.2 (0.99)	8.2 (0.75)
Idaho	28.3 (2.00)	32.3 (1.38)	30.0 (1.39)	29.0 (1.08)	26.4 (1.45)	11.7 (1.20)	12.1 (1.14)	12.3 (0.98)	10.2 (0.79)	9.4 (0.81)
Illinois	— (†)	— (†)	33.9 (1.91)	33.0 (1.38)	29.5 (1.41)	— (†)	— (†)	11.3 (1.11)	11.5 (0.82)	9.8 (0.69)
Indiana	30.6 (2.01)	29.3 (1.51)	29.5 (1.35)	29.1 (1.51)	29.0 (1.34)	10.9 (1.14)	11.2 (0.98)	11.5 (0.92)	9.5 (1.18)	8.9 (0.80)
Iowa	— (†)	28.3 (1.61)	24.0 (1.39)	— (†)	24.4 (1.87)	— (†)	11.3 (1.12)	9.1 (0.96)	— (†)	9.6 (0.89)
Kansas	— (†)	27.9 (1.51)	30.3 (1.62)	27.8 (1.37)	22.4 (1.40)	— (†)	10.1 (0.92)	10.6 (1.04)	9.0 (0.81)	7.8 (0.84)
Kentucky	26.4 (1.66)	29.6 (1.17)	27.0 (0.98)	28.7 (1.66)	28.7 (1.65)	10.1 (1.05)	12.7 (0.81)	10.6 (0.65)	9.5 (0.93)	11.4 (0.93)
Louisiana	— (†)	— (†)	— (†)	36.1 (1.60)	36.0 (2.72)	— (†)	— (†)	— (†)	13.7 (1.28)	15.8 (2.17)
Maine	26.5 (1.39)	28.2 (1.11)	26.5 (1.93)	22.8 (0.55)	19.5 (0.46)	9.1 (1.01)	10.0 (1.03)	10.1 (1.09)	9.1 (0.33)	7.9 (0.27)
Maryland	— (†)	36.6 (1.83)	35.7 (2.62)	32.5 (2.23)	29.1 (1.80)	— (†)	14.9 (1.33)	12.4 (1.69)	11.2 (1.30)	11.1 (1.24)
Massachusetts	30.7 (1.05)	28.6 (1.33)	27.5 (1.34)	29.2 (1.24)	25.4 (0.92)	10.2 (0.67)	10.2 (0.67)	9.1 (0.81)	8.7 (0.68)	7.1 (0.65)
Michigan	30.8 (1.51)	30.1 (2.02)	30.7 (1.89)	31.6 (1.72)	27.4 (1.32)	12.2 (1.02)	11.4 (1.11)	11.4 (0.89)	11.3 (1.02)	9.1 (0.68)
Minnesota	— (†)	— (†)	— (†)	— (†)	— (†)	— (†)	— (†)	— (†)	— (†)	— (†)
Mississippi	30.6 (1.66)	— (†)	30.6 (1.43)	34.1 (1.73)	29.3 (1.72)	10.2 (1.26)	— (†)	11.9 (0.96)	12.6 (1.02)	12.3 (1.06)
Missouri	28.2 (2.07)	29.8 (2.12)	30.9 (2.18)	28.7 (1.34)	— (†)	9.8 (0.95)	10.2 (1.31)	10.7 (1.21)	9.0 (0.97)	— (†)
Montana	28.6 (1.16)	30.5 (1.19)	32.8 (1.08)	31.7 (2.25)	25.4 (0.73)	10.3 (0.68)	10.9 (0.67)	12.0 (0.75)	10.8 (1.33)	9.1 (0.51)
Nebraska	29.6 (1.14)	28.5 (1.02)	— (†)	— (†)	26.7 (1.09)	10.6 (0.81)	9.3 (0.60)	— (†)	— (†)	7.4 (0.68)
Nevada	35.0 (1.56)	34.5 (1.78)	31.6 (1.53)	35.0 (1.45)	— (†)	12.6 (1.01)	14.2 (1.32)	11.3 (1.10)	10.0 (0.82)	— (†)
New Hampshire	30.5 (1.84)	26.4 (1.84)	27.0 (1.40)	25.9 (1.59)	23.8 (1.27)	11.6 (1.20)	10.7 (1.06)	11.3 (0.70)	9.1 (0.87)	9.9 (0.89)
New Jersey	— (†)	30.7 (2.18)	— (†)	27.5 (1.46)	23.9 (1.56)	— (†)	10.1 (1.31)	— (†)	— (†)	— (†)
New Mexico	— (†)	36.7 (1.47)	37.1 (1.06)	37.3 (1.07)	31.5 (1.02)	— (†)	15.6 (1.19)	16.9 (0.70)	15.0 (0.85)	11.3 (0.78)
New York	32.1 (0.82)	32.1 (1.01)	31.7 (1.08)	29.6 (1.23)	27.0 (1.25)	14.6 (0.73)	12.5 (0.74)	12.2 (0.91)	11.4 (0.91)	— (†)
North Carolina	30.9 (1.41)	29.9 (1.41)	30.1 (1.54)	28.6 (0.96)	27.6 (1.37)	10.7 (1.00)	11.6 (0.85)	10.4 (0.84)	9.4 (0.43)	10.6 (1.01)
North Dakota	27.2 (1.60)	— (†)	— (†)	— (†)	— (†)	8.6 (0.96)	10.7 (1.13)	9.6 (0.79)	7.4 (0.78)	8.2 (0.73)
Ohio[3]	31.5 (2.83)	30.2 (1.95)	30.4 (1.57)	— (†)	31.2 (1.58)	11.3 (1.67)	10.2 (1.17)	9.4 (0.82)	— (†)	8.8 (0.68)
Oklahoma	28.4 (2.61)	31.1 (1.63)	29.2 (1.37)	30.8 (2.10)	28.5 (1.96)	11.4 (1.15)	12.1 (1.13)	10.6 (0.81)	12.8 (1.43)	9.4 (1.25)
Oregon	— (†)	— (†)	— (†)	— (†)	— (†)	— (†)	— (†)	— (†)	— (†)	— (†)
Pennsylvania	— (†)	— (†)	— (†)	29.6 (1.76)	— (†)	— (†)	— (†)	— (†)	9.9 (1.01)	— (†)
Rhode Island	27.6 (1.59)	28.4 (1.34)	26.3 (1.61)	25.1 (0.83)	23.5 (0.81)	11.4 (1.18)	11.2 (0.80)	9.6 (0.93)	9.1 (0.73)	7.8 (0.52)
South Carolina	— (†)	31.3 (1.68)	29.1 (1.37)	36.4 (2.06)	32.6 (2.04)	— (†)	12.7 (1.18)	10.8 (0.86)	12.1 (1.43)	12.2 (1.48)
South Dakota[3]	27.0 (2.72)	26.5 (2.86)	29.8 (2.00)	27.1 (1.36)	24.5 (2.22)	9.0 (1.12)	8.4 (1.56)	9.3 (1.32)	8.3 (0.52)	8.2 (0.92)
Tennessee	28.3 (1.94)	30.9 (1.66)	31.8 (1.55)	32.3 (1.31)	30.8 (1.24)	12.2 (1.33)	10.9 (1.00)	12.4 (1.13)	11.3 (0.96)	10.5 (0.83)
Texas	— (†)	34.2 (1.57)	34.9 (1.17)	33.3 (1.05)	34.1 (0.92)	— (†)	14.5 (0.94)	13.9 (0.90)	13.2 (0.67)	12.5 (0.65)
Utah	28.7 (2.74)	25.9 (1.84)	30.1 (2.01)	28.2 (1.61)	23.9 (1.88)	11.9 (1.80)	10.4 (1.57)	11.6 (1.36)	10.6 (0.84)	8.1 (1.18)
Vermont	26.9 (0.92)	24.3 (1.36)	26.0 (1.44)	25.6 (0.71)	23.1 (1.42)	12.2 (0.71)	12.2 (0.98)	11.5 (0.88)	11.0 (0.36)	8.8 (0.72)
Virginia	— (†)	— (†)	— (†)	— (†)	24.9 (1.71)	— (†)	— (†)	— (†)	— (†)	7.9 (0.93)
Washington	— (†)	— (†)	— (†)	— (†)	— (†)	— (†)	— (†)	— (†)	— (†)	— (†)
West Virginia	26.5 (1.62)	29.1 (1.88)	29.9 (2.39)	31.7 (1.96)	25.7 (1.66)	10.3 (1.39)	12.1 (1.41)	12.9 (1.70)	11.3 (1.07)	10.3 (1.02)
Wisconsin	31.4 (1.68)	32.6 (1.51)	31.2 (1.46)	25.8 (1.52)	25.3 (1.72)	11.6 (0.92)	12.2 (1.03)	11.4 (0.97)	9.6 (0.87)	9.1 (0.95)
Wyoming	31.2 (1.23)	30.4 (1.08)	27.9 (1.12)	30.9 (1.17)	26.5 (1.08)	12.7 (0.93)	12.2 (0.72)	11.6 (0.83)	12.6 (0.73)	11.3 (0.65)

—Not available.

†Not applicable.

[1]The term "anywhere" is not used in the Youth Risk Behavior Survey (YRBS) questionnaire; students were simply asked how many times in the past 12 months they had been in a physical fight.

[2]In the question asking students about physical fights at school, "on school property" was not defined for survey respondents.

[3]Data include both public and private schools.

NOTE: State-level data include public schools only, with the exception of data for Ohio and South Dakota. Data for the United States total, Ohio, and South Dakota include both public and private schools.

SOURCE: Centers for Disease Control and Prevention, Division of Adolescent and School Health, Youth Risk Behavior Surveillance System (YRBSS), 2003 through 2011. (This table was prepared September 2013.)

Percentage distribution of students in grades 9–12, by number of days they reported carrying a weapon anywhere or on school property during the previous 30 days and selected student characteristics: 2011

[Standard errors appear in parentheses]

Student characteristic	Anywhere (including on school property)[1]				On school property[2]			
	0 days	1 day	2 to 5 days	6 or more days	0 days	1 day	2 to 5 days	6 or more days
1	2	3	4	5	6	7	8	9
Total	83.4 (0.65)	3.5 (0.18)	5.6 (0.27)	7.5 (0.45)	94.6 (0.35)	1.6 (0.16)	1.4 (0.12)	2.4 (0.23)
Sex								
Male	74.1 (1.07)	4.8 (0.23)	8.5 (0.46)	12.6 (0.82)	91.8 (0.59)	2.5 (0.26)	2.1 (0.21)	3.7 (0.39)
Female	93.2 (0.41)	2.1 (0.27)	2.6 (0.21)	2.2 (0.19)	97.7 (0.19)	0.7 (0.12)	0.6 (0.09)	1.0 (0.13)
Race/ethnicity[3]								
White	83.0 (1.05)	3.2 (0.21)	5.9 (0.48)	8.0 (0.68)	94.9 (0.40)	1.6 (0.21)	1.3 (0.16)	2.3 (0.33)
Black	85.8 (0.85)	3.1 (0.41)	5.2 (0.46)	6.0 (0.56)	95.4 (0.67)	1.7 (0.46)	1.2 (0.26)	1.6 (0.34)
Hispanic	83.8 (0.82)	4.4 (0.44)	5.2 (0.50)	6.7 (0.70)	94.2 (0.70)	1.4 (0.20)	2.0 (0.32)	2.4 (0.46)
Asian	90.9 (1.57)	1.9 (0.54)	1.8! (0.78)	5.4 (1.57)	95.7 (1.66)	‡ (†)	‡ (†)	‡ (†)
Pacific Islander	79.3 (5.00)	3.0! (1.37)	7.6! (2.75)	10.1! (3.53)	89.1 (3.73)	6.5! (2.63)	‡ (†)	4.4! (1.89)
American Indian/Alaska Native	72.4 (2.41)	5.3 (0.91)	12.1 (1.52)	10.2 (1.23)	92.5 (1.62)	2.7 (0.68)	3.2! (1.23)	1.6 (0.48)
Two or more races	76.3 (2.58)	5.6 (1.18)	7.1 (1.32)	10.9 (1.92)	92.5 (1.87)	1.6! (0.52)	1.2! (0.42)	4.7! (1.81)
Grade								
9th	82.7 (1.07)	4.3 (0.47)	6.5 (0.46)	6.5 (0.58)	95.2 (0.50)	1.8 (0.28)	1.3 (0.19)	1.8 (0.31)
10th	83.4 (0.89)	3.2 (0.36)	5.7 (0.50)	7.7 (0.62)	93.9 (0.72)	1.9 (0.41)	1.7 (0.25)	2.4 (0.39)
11th	83.8 (0.84)	3.3 (0.32)	5.5 (0.46)	7.5 (0.46)	95.3 (0.44)	1.3 (0.26)	1.2 (0.23)	2.2 (0.33)
12th	84.2 (0.90)	3.0 (0.36)	4.6 (0.40)	8.1 (0.84)	94.4 (0.51)	1.4 (0.31)	1.3 (0.24)	2.9 (0.40)

†Not applicable.

!Interpret data with caution. The coefficient of variation (CV) for this estimate is between 30 and 50 percent.

‡Reporting standards not met. Either there are too few cases for a reliable estimate or the coefficient of variation (CV) is 50 percent or greater.

[1]The term "anywhere" is not used in the Youth Risk Behavior Survey (YRBS) questionnaire; students were simply asked how many days they carried a weapon during the past 30 days.

[2]In the question asking students about carrying a weapon at school, "on school property" was not defined for survey respondents.

[3]Race categories exclude persons of Hispanic ethnicity.

NOTE: Respondents were asked about carrying "a weapon such as a gun, knife, or club." Detail may not sum to totals because of rounding.

SOURCE: Centers for Disease Control and Prevention, Division of Adolescent and School Health, Youth Risk Behavior Surveillance System (YRBSS), 2011. (This table was prepared September 2013.)

Percentage of public school students in grades 9–12 who reported carrying a weapon at least 1 day during the previous 30 days, by location and state: Selected years, 2003 through 2011

[Standard errors appear in parentheses]

State	Anywhere (including on school property)[1]					On school property[2]				
	2003	2005	2007	2009	2011	2003	2005	2007	2009	2011
1	2	3	4	5	6	7	8	9	10	11
United States[3]	17.1 (0.90)	18.5 (0.80)	18.0 (0.87)	17.5 (0.73)	16.6 (0.65)	6.1 (0.57)	6.5 (0.46)	5.9 (0.37)	5.6 (0.32)	5.4 (0.35)
Alabama	19.9 (1.44)	21.0 (1.72)	— (†)	22.9 (2.27)	21.5 (1.54)	7.3 (1.35)	8.4 (1.44)	— (†)	8.7 (1.42)	8.2 (1.02)
Alaska	18.4 (1.14)	— (†)	24.4 (1.61)	20.0 (1.30)	19.0 (1.19)	7.1 (0.81)	— (†)	8.4 (1.07)	7.8 (0.83)	5.7 (0.72)
Arizona	18.4 (0.82)	20.6 (0.84)	20.5 (0.91)	19.9 (1.25)	17.5 (1.17)	5.8 (0.68)	7.4 (0.53)	7.0 (0.75)	6.5 (0.64)	5.7 (0.59)
Arkansas	— (†)	25.9 (1.15)	20.7 (1.36)	22.9 (1.82)	21.1 (1.76)	— (†)	10.5 (1.10)	6.8 (0.85)	8.4 (1.02)	6.5 (0.95)
California	— (†)	— (†)	— (†)	— (†)	— (†)	— (†)	— (†)	— (†)	— (†)	— (†)
Colorado	— (†)	17.0 (1.57)	— (†)	16.7 (1.27)	15.5 (1.31)	— (†)	5.4 (0.81)	— (†)	5.5 (0.90)	5.5 (0.69)
Connecticut	— (†)	16.3 (1.30)	17.2 (1.72)	12.4 (0.89)	— (†)	— (†)	6.4 (0.83)	5.5 (1.03)	3.9 (0.45)	6.6 (0.67)
Delaware	16.0 (0.88)	16.6 (1.04)	17.1 (1.00)	18.5 (0.92)	13.5 (0.88)	5.0 (0.47)	5.7 (0.54)	5.4 (0.55)	5.1 (0.59)	5.2 (0.57)
District of Columbia	25.0 (1.40)	17.2 (1.11)	21.3 (1.45)	— (†)	18.9 (1.34)	10.6 (0.96)	6.7 (0.60)	7.4 (0.76)	— (†)	5.5 (0.88)
Florida	17.2 (0.76)	15.2 (0.68)	18.0 (0.93)	17.3 (0.60)	15.6 (0.76)	5.3 (0.38)	4.7 (0.41)	5.6 (0.41)	4.7 (0.35)	— (†)
Georgia	18.7 (1.17)	22.1 (1.99)	19.5 (0.96)	18.8 (1.11)	22.8 (2.25)	5.0 (0.52)	7.5 (1.50)	5.3 (0.48)	6.0 (0.90)	8.6 (1.80)
Hawaii	— (†)	13.3 (1.03)	14.8 (1.56)	15.9 (2.06)	13.9 (0.81)	— (†)	4.9 (0.72)	3.7 (0.92)	4.7 (0.63)	4.2 (0.45)
Idaho	— (†)	23.9 (1.45)	23.6 (1.35)	21.8 (1.15)	22.8 (1.30)	7.7 (0.90)	— (†)	8.9 (0.96)	6.7 (0.59)	6.3 (0.78)
Illinois	— (†)	— (†)	14.3 (1.01)	16.0 (1.04)	12.6 (0.91)	— (†)	— (†)	3.7 (0.67)	4.8 (0.59)	3.9 (0.53)
Indiana	17.8 (1.93)	19.2 (1.25)	20.9 (0.80)	18.1 (1.58)	17.0 (1.46)	6.2 (0.91)	5.8 (0.71)	6.9 (0.64)	5.7 (0.80)	3.7 (0.46)
Iowa	— (†)	15.7 (1.49)	12.8 (1.13)	— (†)	15.8 (1.26)	— (†)	4.3 (0.70)	4.4 (0.61)	— (†)	4.5 (0.76)
Kansas	— (†)	16.2 (1.37)	18.4 (1.19)	16.0 (1.26)	— (†)	— (†)	4.9 (0.85)	5.7 (0.75)	5.1 (0.65)	5.2 (0.72)
Kentucky	18.5 (1.20)	23.1 (1.49)	24.4 (1.08)	21.7 (1.72)	22.8 (1.72)	7.4 (0.86)	6.8 (0.72)	8.0 (0.59)	6.5 (0.77)	7.4 (1.25)
Louisiana	— (†)	— (†)	— (†)	19.6 (1.73)	22.2 (0.98)	— (†)	— (†)	— (†)	5.8 (1.12)	4.2 (1.01)
Maine	16.5 (1.20)	18.3 (2.00)	15.0 (1.47)	— (†)	— (†)	6.6 (0.91)	5.9 (1.03)	4.9 (0.70)	— (†)	8.0 (0.45)
Maryland	— (†)	19.1 (1.59)	19.3 (1.51)	16.6 (1.19)	15.9 (1.10)	— (†)	6.9 (0.88)	5.9 (0.81)	4.6 (0.58)	5.3 (0.55)
Massachusetts	13.5 (0.89)	15.2 (0.88)	14.9 (0.88)	12.8 (1.00)	12.3 (0.95)	5.0 (0.50)	5.8 (0.59)	5.0 (0.48)	4.4 (0.58)	3.7 (0.46)
Michigan	15.2 (0.89)	15.8 (1.49)	17.9 (1.30)	16.6 (0.69)	15.7 (0.94)	5.1 (0.66)	4.7 (0.54)	5.0 (0.66)	5.4 (0.33)	3.5 (0.37)
Minnesota	— (†)	— (†)	— (†)	— (†)	— (†)	— (†)	— (†)	— (†)	— (†)	— (†)
Mississippi	20.0 (1.78)	— (†)	17.3 (1.33)	17.2 (1.02)	18.0 (1.39)	5.2 (0.78)	— (†)	4.8 (0.60)	4.5 (0.48)	4.2 (0.76)
Missouri	16.8 (1.87)	19.4 (1.79)	18.6 (1.48)	16.0 (1.44)	— (†)	5.5 (1.04)	7.3 (0.99)	4.6 (0.83)	5.3 (1.02)	— (†)
Montana	19.4 (0.88)	21.4 (1.20)	22.1 (0.76)	23.0 (1.07)	23.5 (0.96)	7.2 (0.56)	10.2 (0.89)	9.7 (0.57)	7.9 (0.67)	9.3 (0.69)
Nebraska	16.0 (1.06)	17.9 (0.89)	— (†)	— (†)	18.6 (0.90)	5.0 (0.53)	4.8 (0.48)	— (†)	— (†)	3.8 (0.45)
Nevada	14.9 (1.09)	18.4 (1.32)	14.5 (1.08)	19.1 (1.08)	— (†)	6.3 (0.67)	6.8 (0.91)	4.7 (0.61)	6.2 (0.62)	— (†)
New Hampshire	15.1 (1.59)	16.2 (1.26)	18.1 (1.46)	— (†)	14.5 (1.04)	5.8 (1.00)	6.5 (0.93)	5.8 (0.61)	8.8 (1.00)	— (†)
New Jersey	— (†)	10.5 (0.95)	— (†)	9.6 (0.81)	9.6 (1.17)	— (†)	3.1 (0.53)	— (†)	3.1 (0.45)	— (†)
New Mexico	— (†)	24.5 (1.44)	27.5 (1.20)	27.4 (0.90)	22.8 (0.93)	— (†)	8.0 (0.29)	9.3 (0.66)	8.1 (0.59)	6.5 (0.51)
New York	13.5 (1.01)	14.3 (0.74)	14.2 (0.76)	13.9 (0.98)	12.6 (0.76)	5.2 (0.51)	5.2 (0.42)	4.7 (0.41)	4.8 (0.64)	4.2 (0.32)
North Carolina	19.2 (1.49)	21.5 (1.35)	21.2 (1.19)	19.6 (0.95)	20.8 (1.24)	6.3 (0.79)	6.4 (0.77)	6.8 (0.94)	4.7 (0.57)	6.1 (0.64)
North Dakota	— (†)	— (†)	— (†)	— (†)	— (†)	5.7 (0.98)	6.0 (0.74)	5.0 (0.57)	5.4 (0.64)	5.7 (0.73)
Ohio[3]	12.5 (1.40)	15.2 (1.27)	16.6 (1.42)	— (†)	16.4 (1.37)	3.6 (0.75)	4.4 (0.63)	4.1 (0.51)	— (†)	— (†)
Oklahoma	21.8 (1.72)	18.9 (1.38)	22.3 (1.65)	19.0 (1.44)	19.4 (1.86)	8.0 (1.01)	7.0 (0.77)	9.0 (1.43)	5.6 (0.79)	6.1 (1.14)
Oregon	— (†)	— (†)	— (†)	— (†)	— (†)	— (†)	— (†)	— (†)	— (†)	— (†)
Pennsylvania	— (†)	— (†)	— (†)	14.8 (1.28)	— (†)	— (†)	— (†)	— (†)	3.3 (0.47)	— (†)
Rhode Island	12.3 (1.01)	12.4 (0.90)	12.0 (0.74)	10.4 (0.50)	11.2 (0.82)	5.9 (0.85)	4.9 (0.41)	4.9 (0.63)	4.0 (0.33)	4.0 (0.39)
South Carolina	— (†)	20.5 (1.42)	19.8 (1.69)	20.4 (2.22)	23.4 (1.86)	— (†)	6.7 (0.82)	4.8 (0.79)	4.6 (0.67)	6.3 (0.89)
South Dakota[3]	— (†)	— (†)	— (†)	— (†)	— (†)	7.1 (0.73)	8.3 (0.72)	6.3 (0.80)	9.2 (0.76)	5.7 (0.52)
Tennessee	21.3 (2.06)	24.1 (1.58)	22.6 (1.41)	20.5 (1.64)	21.1 (1.34)	5.4 (0.80)	8.1 (0.92)	5.6 (0.70)	5.1 (0.70)	5.2 (0.80)
Texas	— (†)	19.3 (0.93)	18.8 (0.71)	18.2 (0.89)	17.6 (0.73)	— (†)	7.9 (0.63)	6.8 (0.55)	6.4 (0.76)	4.9 (0.45)
Utah	15.3 (1.80)	17.7 (1.70)	17.1 (1.38)	16.0 (1.40)	16.8 (1.48)	5.6 (1.24)	7.0 (1.03)	7.5 (1.00)	4.6 (0.63)	5.9 (1.01)
Vermont	— (†)	— (†)	— (†)	— (†)	— (†)	8.3 (0.31)	9.1 (0.90)	9.6 (1.05)	9.0 (0.61)	9.1 (0.73)
Virginia	— (†)	— (†)	— (†)	— (†)	20.4 (1.26)	— (†)	— (†)	— (†)	— (†)	5.7 (0.64)
Washington	— (†)	— (†)	— (†)	— (†)	— (†)	— (†)	— (†)	— (†)	— (†)	— (†)
West Virginia	20.7 (1.37)	22.3 (1.32)	21.3 (1.52)	24.4 (1.05)	20.7 (1.64)	6.6 (1.25)	8.5 (1.00)	6.9 (0.89)	6.5 (0.72)	5.5 (0.75)
Wisconsin	13.2 (0.81)	15.8 (1.19)	12.7 (0.76)	10.9 (0.81)	10.4 (0.66)	3.2 (0.43)	3.9 (0.54)	3.6 (0.49)	3.4 (0.50)	3.1 (0.41)
Wyoming	24.6 (1.49)	28.0 (1.17)	26.8 (1.28)	26.0 (1.04)	27.1 (1.19)	10.1 (0.91)	10.0 (0.71)	11.4 (0.76)	11.5 (0.81)	10.5 (0.71)

—Not available.

†Not applicable.

[1]The term "anywhere" is not used in the Youth Risk Behavior Survey (YRBS) questionnaire; students were simply asked how many days they carried a weapon during the past 30 days.

[2]In the question asking students about carrying a weapon at school, "on school property" was not defined for survey respondents.

[3]Data include both public and private schools.

NOTE: Respondents were asked about carrying "a weapon such as a gun, knife, or club." State-level data include public schools only, with the exception of data for Ohio and South Dakota. Data for the United States total, Ohio, and South Dakota include both public and private schools.

SOURCE: Centers for Disease Control and Prevention, Division of Adolescent and School Health, Youth Risk Behavior Surveillance System (YRBSS), 2003 through 2011. (This table was prepared September 2013.)

Percentage of students in grades 9–12 who reported using alcohol at least 1 day during the previous 30 days, by location and selected student characteristics: Selected years, 1993 through 2011

[Standard errors appear in parentheses]

Location and student characteristic	1993	1995	1997	1999	2001	2003	2005	2007	2009	2011
	2	3	4	5	6	7	8	9	10	11
Anywhere (including on school property)[1]										
Total	48.0 (1.06)	51.6 (1.19)	50.8 (1.43)	50.0 (1.30)	47.1 (1.11)	44.9 (1.21)	43.3 (1.38)	44.7 (1.15)	41.8 (0.80)	38.7 (0.75)
Sex										
Male	50.1 (1.23)	53.2 (1.33)	53.3 (1.22)	52.3 (1.47)	49.2 (1.42)	43.8 (1.31)	43.8 (1.40)	44.7 (1.39)	40.8 (1.11)	39.5 (0.93)
Female	45.9 (1.32)	49.9 (1.79)	47.8 (1.99)	47.7 (1.45)	45.0 (1.11)	45.8 (1.29)	42.8 (1.56)	44.6 (1.42)	42.9 (0.85)	37.9 (0.91)
Race/ethnicity[2]										
White	49.9 (1.26)	54.1 (1.77)	54.0 (1.51)	52.5 (1.62)	50.4 (1.12)	47.1 (1.51)	46.4 (1.84)	47.3 (1.67)	44.7 (1.16)	40.3 (0.97)
Black	42.5 (1.82)	42.0 (2.24)	36.9 (1.46)	39.9 (4.07)	32.7 (2.33)	37.4 (1.67)	31.2 (1.05)	34.5 (1.65)	33.4 (1.45)	30.5 (1.40)
Hispanic	50.8 (2.82)	54.7 (2.56)	53.9 (1.96)	52.8 (2.41)	49.2 (1.52)	45.6 (1.39)	46.8 (1.39)	47.6 (1.80)	42.9 (1.43)	42.3 (1.38)
Asian[3]	— (†)	— (†)	— (†)	25.7 (2.24)	28.4 (3.22)	27.5 (3.47)	21.5 (1.98)	25.4 (2.17)	18.3 (1.60)	25.6 (2.90)
American Indian/Alaska Native	45.3 (7.18)	51.4 (7.18)	57.6 (3.79)	49.4 (6.43)	51.4 (3.97)	51.9 (5.29)	57.4 (4.13)	34.5 (1.77)	42.8 (1.60)	44.9 (2.26)
Pacific Islander[3]	— (†)	— (†)	— (†)	60.8 (5.11)	52.3 (8.54)	40.0 (7.04)	38.7 (8.43)	48.8 (6.58)	34.8 (5.43)	38.4 (6.40)
Two or more races[3]	— (†)	— (†)	— (†)	51.1 (3.98)	45.4 (4.11)	47.1 (3.59)	39.0 (3.59)	46.2 (2.89)	44.3 (2.42)	36.9 (3.08)
Grade										
9th	40.5 (1.79)	45.6 (1.87)	44.2 (3.12)	40.6 (2.17)	41.1 (1.82)	36.2 (1.43)	36.2 (1.23)	35.7 (1.15)	31.5 (1.28)	29.8 (1.35)
10th	44.0 (2.00)	49.5 (2.38)	47.2 (2.19)	49.7 (1.89)	45.2 (1.29)	43.5 (1.66)	42.0 (1.95)	41.8 (1.68)	40.6 (1.42)	35.7 (1.37)
11th	49.7 (1.73)	53.7 (1.51)	53.2 (1.49)	50.9 (1.98)	49.3 (1.70)	47.0 (2.08)	46.0 (1.98)	49.0 (1.83)	45.7 (2.05)	42.7 (1.28)
12th	56.4 (1.35)	56.5 (1.64)	57.3 (2.50)	61.7 (2.25)	55.2 (1.53)	55.9 (1.65)	50.8 (2.12)	54.9 (2.09)	51.7 (1.37)	48.4 (1.29)
Urbanicity[4]										
Urban	— (†)	— (†)	48.9 (2.07)	46.5 (2.75)	45.2 (1.97)	41.5 (1.48)	— (†)	— (†)	— (†)	— (†)
Suburban	— (†)	— (†)	50.5 (2.11)	51.4 (1.32)	47.6 (1.26)	46.5 (2.10)	— (†)	— (†)	— (†)	— (†)
Rural	— (†)	— (†)	55.4 (5.36)	52.2 (4.51)	50.2 (1.91)	45.3 (2.35)	— (†)	— (†)	— (†)	— (†)
On school property[5]										
Total	5.2 (0.39)	6.3 (0.45)	5.6 (0.34)	4.9 (0.39)	4.9 (0.28)	5.2 (0.46)	4.3 (0.30)	4.1 (0.32)	4.5 (0.29)	5.1 (0.33)
Sex										
Male	6.2 (0.39)	7.2 (0.50)	7.2 (0.66)	6.1 (0.54)	6.1 (0.43)	6.0 (0.61)	5.3 (0.39)	4.6 (0.35)	5.3 (0.41)	5.4 (0.43)
Female	4.2 (0.54)	5.3 (0.70)	3.6 (0.37)	3.6 (0.39)	3.8 (0.39)	4.2 (0.41)	3.3 (0.32)	3.6 (0.37)	3.6 (0.34)	4.7 (0.35)
Race/ethnicity[2]										
White	4.6 (0.44)	5.6 (0.62)	4.8 (0.42)	4.8 (0.55)	4.2 (0.26)	3.9 (0.45)	3.8 (0.38)	3.2 (0.35)	3.3 (0.27)	4.0 (0.38)
Black	6.9 (0.98)	7.6 (0.87)	5.6 (0.72)	4.3 (0.52)	5.3 (0.65)	5.8 (0.80)	3.2 (0.45)	3.4 (0.63)	5.4 (0.59)	5.1 (0.50)
Hispanic	6.8 (0.84)	9.6 (1.73)	8.2 (0.96)	7.0 (0.88)	7.0 (0.71)	7.6 (1.08)	7.7 (1.04)	7.5 (0.86)	6.9 (0.70)	7.3 (0.68)
Asian[3]	— (†)	— (†)	— (†)	2.0 (0.42)	6.8 (1.42)	5.6 (1.55)	1.3! (0.62)	4.4 (1.17)	2.9 (0.65)	3.5! (1.21)
American Indian/Alaska Native	6.7! (3.06)	8.1! (3.30)	8.6! (4.15)	‡ (†)	8.2 (1.69)	7.1! (2.61)	6.2! (2.05)	5.0 (0.89)	4.3! (1.58)	20.9 (4.15)
Pacific Islander[3]	— (†)	— (†)	— (†)	6.7 (1.59)	12.4 (3.50)	8.5! (3.29)	‡ (†)	‡ (†)	10.0 (2.34)	8.3! (3.61)
Two or more races[3]	— (†)	— (†)	— (†)	5.2 (1.09)	7.0! (2.36)	13.3 (2.93)	3.5 (1.02)	5.4 (1.25)	6.7 (1.37)	5.8 (1.32)
Grade										
9th	5.2 (0.38)	7.5 (0.90)	5.9 (0.83)	4.4 (0.60)	5.3 (0.47)	5.1 (0.69)	3.7 (0.48)	3.4 (0.43)	4.4 (0.37)	5.4 (0.56)
10th	4.7 (0.43)	5.9 (0.88)	4.6 (0.71)	5.0 (0.67)	5.1 (0.45)	5.6 (0.60)	4.5 (0.45)	4.1 (0.50)	4.8 (0.46)	4.4 (0.51)
11th	5.2 (0.80)	5.7 (0.86)	6.0 (0.86)	4.7 (0.57)	4.7 (0.45)	5.0 (0.57)	4.0 (0.47)	4.2 (0.54)	4.6 (0.44)	5.2 (0.56)
12th	5.5 (0.64)	6.2 (0.58)	5.9 (0.66)	5.0 (0.89)	4.3 (0.44)	4.5 (0.68)	4.8 (0.57)	4.8 (0.55)	4.1 (0.44)	5.1 (0.48)
Urbanicity[4]										
Urban	— (†)	— (†)	— (†)	— (†)	— (†)	— (†)	— (†)	— (†)	— (†)	— (†)
Suburban	— (†)	— (†)	— (†)	— (†)	— (†)	— (†)	— (†)	— (†)	— (†)	— (†)
Rural	— (†)	— (†)	— (†)	— (†)	— (†)	— (†)	— (†)	— (†)	— (†)	— (†)

—Not available.
†Not applicable.
‡Reporting standards not met. The coefficient of variation (CV) for this estimate is 50 percent or greater.
!Interpret data with caution. The coefficient of variation (CV) for this estimate is between 30 and 50 percent.

[1]The term "anywhere" is not used in the Youth Risk Behavior Survey (YRBS) questionnaire; students were simply asked how many days during the previous 30 days they had at least one drink of alcohol.

[2]Race categories exclude persons of Hispanic ethnicity.

[3]Before 1999, Asian students and Pacific Islander students were not categorized separately, and students were not given the option of choosing two or more races. Because the response categories changed in 1999, caution should be used in comparing data on race from 1993, 1995, and 1997 with data from later years.

[4]Refers to the Standard Metropolitan Statistical Area (MSA) status of the respondent's household as defined in 2000 by the U.S. Census Bureau. Categories include "central city of an MSA (Urban)," "in MSA but not in central city (Suburban)," and "not MSA (Rural)."

[5]In the question about drinking alcohol at school, "on school property" was not defined for survey respondents.

SOURCE: Centers for Disease Control and Prevention, Division of Adolescent and School Health, Youth Risk Behavior Surveillance System (YRBSS), 1993 through 2011. (This table was prepared September 2013.)

Percentage of public school students in grades 9–12 who reported using alcohol at least 1 day during the previous 30 days, by location and state: Selected years, 2003 through 2011

[Standard errors appear in parentheses]

State	Anywhere (including on school property)[1]					On school property[2]				
	2003	2005	2007	2009	2011	2003	2005	2007	2009	2011
1	2	3	4	5	6	7	8	9	10	11
United States[3]	44.9 (1.21)	43.3 (1.38)	44.7 (1.15)	41.8 (0.80)	38.7 (0.75)	5.2 (0.46)	4.3 (0.30)	4.1 (0.32)	4.5 (0.29)	5.1 (0.33)
Alabama	40.2 (2.04)	39.4 (2.55)	— (†)	39.5 (2.22)	35.6 (1.99)	4.1 (0.82)	4.5 (0.59)	— (†)	5.4 (0.76)	5.7 (1.08)
Alaska	38.7 (2.05)	— (†)	39.7 (2.11)	33.2 (1.66)	28.6 (1.95)	4.9 (0.81)	— (†)	4.1 (0.58)	3.0 (0.48)	3.4 (0.52)
Arizona	51.8 (1.93)	47.1 (1.73)	45.6 (1.73)	44.5 (1.67)	43.8 (1.47)	7.1 (0.67)	7.5 (0.88)	6.0 (0.54)	5.9 (0.61)	6.2 (0.55)
Arkansas	— (†)	43.1 (1.99)	42.2 (1.75)	39.7 (1.91)	33.9 (1.81)	— (†)	5.2 (0.62)	5.1 (0.65)	6.1 (0.89)	4.2 (0.68)
California	— (†)	— (†)	— (†)	— (†)	— (†)	— (†)	— (†)	— (†)	— (†)	— (†)
Colorado	— (†)	47.4 (4.42)	— (†)	40.8 (2.44)	36.4 (2.29)	— (†)	5.9 (1.08)	— (†)	4.1 (0.61)	5.3 (0.87)
Connecticut	— (†)	45.3 (2.16)	46.0 (2.13)	43.5 (2.22)	41.5 (1.90)	— (†)	6.6 (0.71)	5.6 (0.99)	5.0 (0.47)	4.6 (0.61)
Delaware	45.4 (1.30)	43.1 (1.16)	45.2 (1.40)	43.7 (1.65)	40.4 (1.55)	4.8 (0.44)	5.5 (0.66)	4.5 (0.48)	5.0 (0.73)	5.0 (0.50)
District of Columbia	33.8 (1.72)	23.1 (1.40)	32.6 (1.47)	— (†)	32.8 (1.89)	4.9 (0.64)	4.6 (0.55)	6.1 (0.92)	— (†)	6.8 (0.91)
Florida	42.7 (1.10)	39.7 (1.43)	42.3 (1.30)	40.5 (1.03)	37.0 (0.98)	5.1 (0.36)	4.5 (0.30)	5.3 (0.31)	4.9 (0.26)	5.1 (0.29)
Georgia	37.7 (1.41)	39.9 (2.12)	37.7 (1.52)	34.3 (1.65)	34.6 (1.93)	3.7 (0.55)	4.3 (0.67)	4.4 (0.58)	4.2 (0.48)	5.4 (0.80)
Hawaii	— (†)	34.8 (2.05)	29.1 (2.93)	37.8 (3.02)	29.1 (1.64)	— (†)	8.8 (0.93)	6.0 (0.93)	7.9 (1.31)	5.0 (0.42)
Idaho	34.8 (2.44)	39.8 (2.62)	42.5 (2.73)	34.2 (1.97)	36.2 (2.28)	3.8 (0.56)	4.3 (0.69)	6.2 (0.81)	3.5 (0.53)	4.1 (0.50)
Illinois	— (†)	— (†)	43.7 (2.72)	39.8 (1.91)	37.8 (1.87)	— (†)	— (†)	5.5 (0.75)	4.4 (0.64)	3.3 (0.40)
Indiana	44.9 (1.57)	41.4 (2.12)	43.9 (2.24)	38.5 (2.13)	33.5 (1.65)	3.9 (0.57)	3.4 (0.64)	4.1 (0.47)	3.5 (0.52)	2.0 (0.36)
Iowa	— (†)	43.8 (2.56)	41.0 (2.36)	— (†)	37.1 (2.58)	— (†)	4.6 (0.89)	3.4 (0.78)	— (†)	2.3 (0.41)
Kansas	— (†)	43.9 (1.74)	42.4 (1.69)	38.7 (1.93)	32.6 (1.53)	— (†)	5.1 (0.74)	4.8 (0.66)	3.2 (0.55)	2.9 (0.45)
Kentucky	45.1 (1.87)	37.4 (1.77)	40.6 (1.25)	37.8 (1.30)	34.6 (1.56)	4.8 (0.69)	3.5 (0.37)	4.7 (0.47)	5.2 (0.87)	4.1 (0.53)
Louisiana	— (†)	— (†)	— (†)	47.5 (2.80)	44.4 (2.00)	— (†)	— (†)	— (†)	5.6 (1.33)	6.0 (1.36)
Maine	42.2 (1.78)	43.0 (2.15)	39.3 (2.29)	32.2 (0.66)	28.7 (0.69)	3.7 (0.48)	3.9 (0.44)	5.6 (0.89)	4.0 (0.23)	3.1 (0.21)
Maryland	— (†)	39.8 (2.17)	42.9 (3.13)	37.0 (1.44)	34.8 (1.98)	— (†)	3.2 (0.42)	6.2 (1.10)	4.8 (0.67)	5.4 (0.63)
Massachusetts	45.7 (1.19)	47.8 (1.36)	46.2 (1.57)	43.6 (1.28)	40.1 (1.54)	5.3 (0.50)	4.2 (0.32)	4.7 (0.45)	3.8 (0.48)	3.6 (0.44)
Michigan	44.0 (1.40)	38.1 (1.73)	42.8 (1.70)	37.0 (1.28)	30.6 (1.64)	4.6 (0.33)	3.6 (0.46)	3.6 (0.51)	3.7 (0.40)	2.7 (0.37)
Minnesota	— (†)	— (†)	— (†)	— (†)	— (†)	— (†)	— (†)	— (†)	— (†)	— (†)
Mississippi	41.8 (1.74)	— (†)	40.6 (1.57)	39.2 (1.43)	36.2 (2.07)	4.9 (0.70)	— (†)	5.1 (0.71)	4.3 (0.45)	4.6 (0.67)
Missouri	49.2 (2.16)	40.8 (2.04)	44.4 (2.35)	39.3 (2.71)	— (†)	2.6 (0.58)	3.3 (0.57)	3.4 (0.74)	3.0 (0.55)	— (†)
Montana	49.5 (1.68)	48.6 (1.50)	46.5 (1.39)	42.8 (1.81)	38.3 (1.08)	6.7 (0.70)	6.4 (0.73)	5.7 (0.47)	5.1 (0.69)	3.5 (0.35)
Nebraska	46.5 (1.29)	42.9 (1.27)	— (†)	— (†)	26.6 (1.24)	4.6 (0.61)	3.6 (0.42)	— (†)	— (†)	3.0 (0.41)
Nevada	43.4 (1.51)	41.4 (1.73)	37.0 (1.52)	38.6 (1.66)	— (†)	7.4 (0.74)	6.8 (0.92)	4.4 (0.58)	4.4 (0.52)	— (†)
New Hampshire	47.1 (2.70)	44.0 (2.31)	44.8 (1.83)	39.3 (2.18)	38.4 (1.83)	4.0 (0.79)	— (†)	5.1 (0.73)	4.3 (0.68)	5.6 (0.70)
New Jersey	— (†)	46.5 (2.65)	— (†)	45.2 (2.21)	42.9 (2.46)	— (†)	3.7 (0.42)	— (†)	— (†)	— (†)
New Mexico	— (†)	42.3 (1.93)	43.2 (1.07)	40.5 (1.41)	36.9 (1.40)	— (†)	7.6 (0.87)	8.7 (1.35)	8.0 (0.90)	6.4 (0.54)
New York	44.2 (1.53)	43.4 (1.47)	43.7 (1.41)	41.4 (1.38)	38.4 (1.96)	5.2 (0.39)	4.1 (0.45)	5.1 (0.58)	— (†)	— (†)
North Carolina	39.4 (2.68)	42.3 (2.16)	37.7 (1.36)	35.0 (2.43)	34.3 (1.41)	3.6 (0.47)	5.4 (0.74)	4.7 (0.65)	4.1 (0.57)	5.5 (0.77)
North Dakota	54.2 (1.74)	49.0 (1.89)	46.1 (1.82)	43.3 (1.79)	38.8 (1.67)	5.1 (0.79)	3.6 (0.52)	4.4 (0.65)	4.2 (0.53)	3.1 (0.51)
Ohio[3]	42.2 (2.40)	42.4 (1.96)	45.7 (1.70)	— (†)	38.0 (2.94)	3.9 (0.69)	3.2 (0.59)	3.2 (0.50)	— (†)	— (†)
Oklahoma	47.8 (1.41)	40.5 (1.62)	43.1 (1.88)	39.0 (1.97)	38.3 (1.75)	3.2 (0.64)	3.8 (0.49)	5.0 (0.59)	3.9 (0.55)	2.6 (0.65)
Oregon	— (†)	— (†)	— (†)	— (†)	— (†)	— (†)	— (†)	— (†)	— (†)	— (†)
Pennsylvania	— (†)	— (†)	— (†)	38.4 (2.10)	— (†)	— (†)	— (†)	— (†)	2.8 (0.50)	— (†)
Rhode Island	44.5 (1.92)	42.7 (1.15)	42.9 (1.76)	34.0 (2.01)	34.0 (1.25)	4.6 (0.73)	5.3 (0.66)	4.8 (0.54)	3.2 (0.50)	— (†)
South Carolina	— (†)	43.2 (1.64)	36.8 (2.31)	35.2 (2.80)	39.7 (1.72)	— (†)	6.0 (0.96)	4.7 (0.73)	3.6 (0.79)	5.9 (0.90)
South Dakota[3]	50.2 (2.58)	46.6 (2.12)	44.5 (1.80)	40.1 (1.54)	39.3 (2.14)	5.4 (1.13)	4.0 (0.70)	3.6 (0.92)	— (†)	— (†)
Tennessee	41.1 (2.04)	41.8 (1.90)	36.7 (1.90)	33.5 (1.71)	33.3 (1.39)	4.2 (0.48)	3.7 (0.66)	4.1 (0.54)	3.0 (0.38)	3.2 (0.34)
Texas	— (†)	47.3 (1.93)	48.3 (1.64)	44.8 (1.25)	39.7 (1.15)	— (†)	5.7 (0.56)	4.9 (0.57)	4.7 (0.36)	3.9 (0.35)
Utah	21.3 (2.19)	15.8 (1.92)	17.0 (1.88)	18.2 (2.72)	15.1 (1.54)	3.8 (0.74)	2.1 (0.39)	4.7 ! (1.69)	2.7 (0.45)	2.7 (0.54)
Vermont	43.5 (1.48)	41.8 (1.53)	42.6 (1.04)	39.0 (1.57)	35.3 (1.10)	5.3 (0.60)	4.8 (0.54)	4.6 (0.40)	3.3 (0.28)	3.3 (0.50)
Virginia	— (†)	— (†)	— (†)	— (†)	30.5 (2.49)	— (†)	— (†)	— (†)	— (†)	3.3 (0.59)
Washington	— (†)	— (†)	— (†)	— (†)	— (†)	— (†)	— (†)	— (†)	— (†)	— (†)
West Virginia	44.4 (1.81)	41.5 (1.41)	43.5 (1.45)	40.4 (1.10)	34.3 (2.40)	4.1 (0.84)	6.4 (1.08)	5.5 (0.89)	5.7 (0.61)	4.2 (0.67)
Wisconsin	47.3 (1.63)	49.2 (1.51)	48.9 (1.56)	41.3 (1.83)	39.2 (1.35)	— (†)	— (†)	— (†)	— (†)	— (†)
Wyoming	49.0 (2.16)	45.4 (1.47)	42.4 (1.22)	41.7 (1.36)	36.1 (1.34)	6.2 (0.75)	6.2 (0.56)	6.9 (0.63)	6.4 (0.50)	5.1 (0.48)

—Not available.
†Not applicable.
!Interpret data with caution. The coefficient of variation (CV) for this estimate is between 30 and 50 percent.
[1]The term "anywhere" is not used in the Youth Risk Behavior Survey (YRBS) questionnaire; students were simply asked how many days during the previous 30 days they had at least one drink of alcohol.
[2]In the question about drinking alcohol at school, "on school property" was not defined for survey respondents.
[3]Data include both public and private schools.
NOTE: State-level data include public schools only, with the exception of data for Ohio and South Dakota. Data for the United States total, Ohio, and South Dakota include both public and private schools.
SOURCE: Centers for Disease Control and Prevention, Division of Adolescent and School Health, Youth Risk Behavior Surveillance System (YRBSS), 2003 through 2011. (This table was prepared September 2013.)

Percentage distribution of students in grades 9–12, by number of times they reported using marijuana anywhere or on school property during the previous 30 days and selected student characteristics: 2011

[Standard errors appear in parentheses]

Student characteristic	Anywhere (including on school property)[1]				On school property[2]			
	0 times	1 or 2 times	3 to 39 times	40 or more times	0 times	1 or 2 times	3 to 39 times	40 or more times
1	2	3	4	5	6	7	8	9
Total	76.9 (0.80)	7.4 (0.30)	10.9 (0.42)	4.8 (0.30)	94.1 (0.39)	2.8 (0.22)	2.3 (0.21)	0.7 (0.09)
Sex								
Male	74.1 (1.01)	7.1 (0.40)	11.8 (0.57)	7.0 (0.47)	92.5 (0.56)	3.1 (0.28)	3.2 (0.31)	1.2 (0.17)
Female	79.9 (0.95)	7.7 (0.48)	9.9 (0.56)	2.4 (0.26)	95.9 (0.32)	2.5 (0.21)	1.4 (0.19)	0.2 (0.04)
Race/ethnicity[3]								
White	78.3 (1.09)	6.9 (0.42)	10.2 (0.59)	4.6 (0.44)	95.5 (0.42)	2.2 (0.26)	1.9 (0.23)	0.4 (0.09)
Black	74.9 (1.35)	7.9 (0.69)	12.5 (0.81)	4.7 (0.63)	93.3 (0.77)	3.2 (0.43)	2.8 (0.52)	0.7 (0.18)
Hispanic	75.6 (1.27)	8.3 (0.59)	11.5 (0.67)	4.7 (0.46)	92.3 (0.54)	3.6 (0.26)	3.1 (0.40)	1.0 (0.21)
Asian	86.4 (3.75)	‡ (†)	5.5 (0.96)	3.2 ! (1.34)	95.5 (1.34)	2.4 ! (1.15)	‡ (†)	1.5 ! (0.70)
Pacific Islander	68.9 (7.08)	11.3 (3.34)	13.2 ! (5.20)	6.6 ! (2.27)	87.5 (4.94)	5.6 ! (2.24)	‡ (†)	‡ (†)
American Indian/Alaska Native	52.6 (3.20)	10.5 (2.82)	23.6 (2.57)	13.2 (1.81)	79.1 (4.05)	8.6 (2.18)	9.8 (1.79)	2.5 (0.67)
Two or more races	73.2 (2.10)	7.2 (1.20)	12.9 (1.44)	6.7 (1.33)	91.9 (1.79)	3.7 (0.98)	2.4 ! (0.86)	2.0 ! (0.69)
Grade								
9th	82.0 (1.11)	6.2 (0.47)	8.2 (0.63)	3.6 (0.42)	94.6 (0.65)	2.7 (0.41)	2.2 (0.33)	0.5 (0.11)
10th	78.4 (1.15)	7.4 (0.60)	10.0 (0.65)	4.3 (0.50)	93.8 (0.63)	3.2 (0.38)	2.3 (0.40)	0.7 (0.16)
11th	74.5 (1.44)	8.0 (0.59)	12.9 (0.82)	4.5 (0.50)	93.8 (0.70)	3.2 (0.47)	2.3 (0.35)	0.7 (0.16)
12th	72.0 (1.08)	8.3 (0.59)	13.0 (0.69)	6.7 (0.53)	94.6 (0.39)	2.2 (0.30)	2.4 (0.30)	0.8 (0.18)

†Not applicable.

!Interpret data with caution. The coefficient of variation (CV) for this estimate is between 30 and 50 percent.

‡Reporting standards not met. Either there are too few cases for a reliable estimate or the coefficient of variation (CV) is 50 percent or greater.

[1]The term "anywhere" is not used in the Youth Risk Behavior Survey (YRBS) questionnaire; students were simply asked how many times during the previous 30 days they had used marijuana.

[2]In the question about using marijuana at school, "on school property" was not defined for survey respondents.

[3]Race categories exclude persons of Hispanic ethnicity.

NOTE: Detail may not sum to totals because of rounding.

SOURCE: Centers for Disease Control and Prevention, Division of Adolescent and School Health, Youth Risk Behavior Surveillance System (YRBSS), 2011. (This table was prepared September 2013.)

Percentage of public school students in grades 9–12 who reported using marijuana at least one time during the previous 30 days, by location and state: Selected years, 2003 through 2011

[Standard errors appear in parentheses]

State	Anywhere (including on school property)[1]					On school property[2]				
	2003	2005	2007	2009	2011	2003	2005	2007	2009	2011
1	2	3	4	5	6	7	8	9	10	11
United States[3]	22.4 (1.09)	20.2 (0.84)	19.7 (0.97)	20.8 (0.70)	23.1 (0.80)	5.8 (0.68)	4.5 (0.32)	4.5 (0.46)	4.6 (0.35)	5.9 (0.39)
Alabama	17.7 (1.38)	18.5 (1.49)	— (†)	16.2 (1.28)	20.8 (1.62)	2.6 (0.54)	3.5 (0.80)	— (†)	4.6 (0.81)	4.0 (0.68)
Alaska	23.9 (1.29)	— (†)	20.5 (1.47)	22.7 (1.65)	21.2 (1.68)	6.5 (0.80)	— (†)	5.9 (0.70)	5.9 (0.69)	4.3 (0.59)
Arizona	25.6 (1.08)	20.0 (1.08)	22.0 (1.38)	23.7 (1.90)	22.9 (1.59)	6.5 (0.52)	5.1 (0.63)	6.1 (0.68)	6.4 (0.74)	5.6 (0.75)
Arkansas	— (†)	18.9 (1.70)	16.4 (1.08)	17.8 (1.24)	16.8 (1.72)	— (†)	4.1 (0.61)	2.8 (0.50)	4.5 (1.02)	3.9 (0.78)
California	— (†)	— (†)	— (†)	— (†)	— (†)	— (†)	— (†)	— (†)	— (†)	— (†)
Colorado	— (†)	22.7 (2.99)	— (†)	24.8 (2.22)	22.0 (1.16)	— (†)	6.0 (0.88)	— (†)	6.1 (0.89)	6.0 (0.77)
Connecticut	— (†)	23.1 (1.37)	23.2 (1.35)	21.8 (1.52)	24.2 (1.44)	— (†)	5.1 (0.49)	5.9 (0.77)	6.2 (0.76)	5.2 (0.68)
Delaware	27.3 (1.13)	22.8 (1.12)	25.1 (1.03)	25.8 (1.30)	27.6 (1.37)	6.0 (0.54)	5.6 (0.57)	5.4 (0.53)	5.6 (0.71)	6.1 (0.65)
District of Columbia	23.5 (1.23)	14.5 (1.08)	20.8 (1.33)	— (†)	26.1 (1.29)	7.5 (0.88)	4.8 (0.62)	5.8 (0.66)	— (†)	7.9 (0.91)
Florida	21.4 (0.89)	16.8 (0.86)	18.9 (0.88)	21.4 (0.72)	22.5 (0.86)	4.9 (0.41)	4.0 (0.31)	4.7 (0.40)	5.2 (0.39)	6.3 (0.39)
Georgia	19.5 (0.94)	18.9 (1.59)	19.6 (0.96)	18.3 (1.02)	21.2 (1.23)	3.2 (0.45)	3.3 (0.58)	3.6 (0.58)	3.4 (0.62)	5.6 (0.70)
Hawaii	— (†)	17.2 (1.73)	15.7 (1.78)	22.1 (2.03)	22.0 (1.32)	— (†)	7.2 (1.14)	5.7 (0.85)	8.3 (1.86)	7.6 (0.67)
Idaho	14.7 (1.56)	17.1 (1.32)	17.9 (1.73)	13.7 (1.07)	18.8 (1.76)	2.7 (0.55)	3.9 (0.61)	4.7 (0.80)	3.0 (0.44)	4.9 (0.73)
Illinois	— (†)	— (†)	20.3 (1.38)	21.0 (1.53)	23.1 (1.59)	— (†)	— (†)	4.2 (0.76)	5.0 (0.77)	4.7 (0.50)
Indiana	22.1 (1.19)	18.9 (1.38)	18.9 (1.19)	20.9 (1.83)	20.0 (1.13)	3.8 (0.67)	3.4 (0.57)	4.1 (0.45)	4.4 (0.62)	3.3 (0.66)
Iowa	— (†)	15.6 (1.74)	11.5 (1.53)	— (†)	14.6 (1.99)	— (†)	2.7 (0.64)	2.5 (0.66)	— (†)	3.4 (0.88)
Kansas	— (†)	15.6 (1.46)	15.3 (0.93)	14.7 (1.19)	16.8 (0.87)	— (†)	3.2 (0.51)	3.8 (0.53)	2.7 (0.35)	2.9 (0.53)
Kentucky	21.1 (1.09)	15.8 (1.19)	16.4 (1.07)	16.1 (1.15)	19.2 (1.47)	4.3 (0.55)	3.2 (0.45)	3.9 (0.44)	3.1 (0.54)	4.2 (0.65)
Louisiana	— (†)	— (†)	— (†)	16.3 (1.29)	16.8 (1.02)	— (†)	— (†)	— (†)	3.6 (0.89)	4.1 (0.59)
Maine	26.4 (1.69)	22.2 (2.13)	22.0 (1.55)	20.5 (0.57)	21.2 (0.72)	6.3 (0.76)	4.6 (0.72)	5.2 (0.65)	— (†)	— (†)
Maryland	— (†)	18.5 (2.25)	19.4 (1.91)	21.9 (1.57)	23.2 (1.51)	— (†)	3.7 (0.82)	4.7 (1.13)	5.0 (0.65)	5.7 (0.70)
Massachusetts	27.7 (1.39)	26.2 (1.22)	24.6 (1.43)	27.1 (1.24)	27.9 (1.31)	6.3 (0.44)	5.3 (0.54)	4.8 (0.44)	5.9 (0.79)	6.3 (0.51)
Michigan	24.0 (1.96)	18.8 (1.29)	18.0 (1.10)	20.7 (0.91)	18.6 (1.15)	7.0 (1.20)	3.7 (0.50)	4.0 (0.57)	4.8 (0.59)	3.3 (0.44)
Minnesota	— (†)	— (†)	— (†)	— (†)	— (†)	— (†)	— (†)	— (†)	— (†)	— (†)
Mississippi	20.6 (1.57)	— (†)	16.7 (1.02)	17.7 (1.21)	17.5 (1.18)	4.4 (0.90)	— (†)	2.7 (0.35)	2.5 (0.46)	3.2 (0.58)
Missouri	21.8 (1.37)	18.1 (2.23)	19.0 (1.23)	20.6 (2.02)	— (†)	3.0 (0.58)	4.0 (0.82)	3.6 (0.63)	3.4 (0.48)	— (†)
Montana	23.1 (1.45)	22.3 (1.43)	21.0 (1.44)	23.1 (1.58)	21.2 (1.50)	6.4 (0.70)	6.1 (0.70)	5.0 (0.49)	5.8 (0.67)	5.5 (0.59)
Nebraska	18.3 (1.23)	17.5 (1.05)	— (†)	— (†)	12.7 (1.06)	3.9 (0.51)	3.1 (0.41)	— (†)	— (†)	2.7 (0.43)
Nevada	22.3 (1.31)	17.3 (1.34)	15.5 (1.07)	20.0 (1.36)	— (†)	5.3 (0.69)	5.7 (0.81)	3.6 (0.55)	4.9 (0.53)	— (†)
New Hampshire	30.6 (2.51)	25.9 (1.69)	22.9 (1.39)	25.6 (1.86)	28.4 (1.82)	6.6 (0.86)	— (†)	4.7 (0.64)	6.8 (0.78)	7.3 (0.87)
New Jersey	— (†)	19.9 (2.18)	— (†)	20.3 (1.53)	21.1 (1.33)	— (†)	3.4 (0.67)	— (†)	— (†)	— (†)
New Mexico	— (†)	26.2 (2.00)	25.0 (2.07)	28.0 (1.52)	27.6 (1.58)	— (†)	8.4 (0.98)	7.9 (0.86)	9.7 (1.06)	9.7 (0.84)
New York	20.7 (1.05)	18.3 (1.13)	18.6 (0.78)	20.9 (1.32)	20.6 (1.07)	4.5 (0.41)	3.6 (0.41)	4.1 (0.44)	— (†)	— (†)
North Carolina	24.3 (1.99)	21.4 (1.61)	19.1 (1.27)	19.8 (1.67)	24.2 (1.25)	3.5 (0.71)	4.1 (0.65)	4.3 (0.54)	4.0 (0.63)	5.2 (0.91)
North Dakota	20.6 (1.58)	15.5 (1.62)	14.8 (1.18)	16.9 (1.55)	15.3 (1.52)	6.3 (0.98)	4.0 (0.71)	2.7 (0.43)	3.8 (0.59)	3.4 (0.45)
Ohio[3]	21.4 (2.33)	20.9 (1.79)	17.7 (1.50)	— (†)	23.6 (1.95)	4.2 (0.96)	4.3 (0.62)	3.7 (0.67)	— (†)	— (†)
Oklahoma	22.0 (2.20)	18.7 (1.12)	15.9 (1.37)	17.2 (2.04)	19.1 (1.90)	4.3 (0.70)	3.0 (0.38)	2.6 (0.40)	2.9 (0.70)	2.4 (0.58)
Oregon	— (†)	— (†)	— (†)	— (†)	— (†)	— (†)	— (†)	— (†)	— (†)	— (†)
Pennsylvania	— (†)	— (†)	— (†)	19.3 (1.43)	— (†)	— (†)	— (†)	— (†)	3.5 (0.58)	— (†)
Rhode Island	27.6 (1.11)	25.0 (1.16)	23.2 (1.85)	26.3 (1.33)	26.3 (1.35)	7.4 (0.70)	7.2 (0.65)	6.5 (0.93)	5.1 (0.60)	— (†)
South Carolina	— (†)	19.0 (1.24)	18.6 (1.44)	20.4 (1.56)	24.1 (1.99)	— (†)	4.6 (0.64)	3.3 (0.52)	3.7 (0.63)	5.2 (0.75)
South Dakota[3]	21.5 (3.35)	16.8 (1.87)	17.7 (3.72)	15.2 (1.36)	17.8 (3.57)	4.5 ! (1.50)	2.9 (0.73)	5.0 ! (2.41)	2.9 (0.49)	— (†)
Tennessee	23.6 (2.10)	19.5 (1.38)	19.4 (1.29)	20.1 (1.31)	20.6 (0.96)	4.1 (0.86)	3.5 (0.67)	4.1 (0.60)	3.8 (0.65)	3.6 (0.40)
Texas	— (†)	21.7 (0.99)	19.3 (1.01)	19.5 (0.71)	20.8 (1.30)	— (†)	3.8 (0.52)	3.6 (0.30)	4.6 (0.51)	4.8 (0.47)
Utah	11.4 (1.28)	7.6 (1.18)	8.7 (2.00)	10.0 (1.53)	9.6 (1.26)	3.7 (0.59)	1.7 (0.42)	3.8 ! (1.24)	2.5 (0.48)	4.0 (0.72)
Vermont	28.2 (1.58)	25.3 (1.59)	24.1 (0.88)	24.6 (1.14)	24.4 (1.43)	8.0 (0.44)	7.0 (0.80)	6.3 (0.63)	6.3 (0.57)	6.0 (0.84)
Virginia	— (†)	— (†)	— (†)	— (†)	18.0 (1.79)	— (†)	— (†)	— (†)	— (†)	3.5 (0.70)
Washington	— (†)	— (†)	— (†)	— (†)	— (†)	— (†)	— (†)	— (†)	— (†)	— (†)
West Virginia	23.1 (2.13)	19.6 (1.70)	23.5 (1.05)	20.3 (1.73)	19.7 (1.61)	4.5 (0.72)	4.9 (0.85)	5.8 (0.97)	3.9 (0.37)	3.0 (0.45)
Wisconsin	21.8 (1.18)	15.9 (1.07)	20.3 (1.30)	18.9 (1.64)	21.6 (1.78)	— (†)	— (†)	— (†)	— (†)	— (†)
Wyoming	20.4 (1.56)	17.8 (1.05)	14.4 (0.79)	16.9 (0.91)	18.5 (1.23)	5.1 (0.66)	4.0 (0.43)	4.7 (0.52)	5.3 (0.45)	4.7 (0.44)

—Not available.

†Not applicable.

!Interpret data with caution. The coefficient of variation (CV) for this estimate is between 30 and 50 percent.

[1]The term "anywhere" is not used in the Youth Risk Behavior Survey (YRBS) questionnaire; students were simply asked how many times during the previous 30 days they had used marijuana.

[2]In the question about using marijuana at school, "on school property" was not defined for survey respondents.

[3]Data include both public and private schools.

NOTE: State-level data include public schools only, with the exception of data for Ohio and South Dakota. Data for the United States total, Ohio, and South Dakota include both public and private schools.

SOURCE: Centers for Disease Control and Prevention, Division of Adolescent and School Health, Youth Risk Behavior Surveillance System (YRBSS), 2003 through 2011. (This table was prepared September 2013.)

Percentage of public school students in grades 9–12 who reported that illegal drugs were made available to them on school property during the previous 12 months, by state: Selected years, 2003 through 2011

[Standard errors appear in parentheses]

State	2003		2005		2007		2009		2011	
1	2		3		4		5		6	
United States[1]	28.7	(1.95)	25.4	(1.05)	22.3	(1.04)	22.7	(1.04)	25.6	(0.99)
Alabama	26.0	(1.78)	26.2	(1.90)	—	(†)	27.6	(1.30)	20.3	(1.32)
Alaska	28.4	(1.24)	—	(†)	25.1	(1.36)	24.8	(1.25)	23.2	(0.98)
Arizona	28.6	(1.23)	38.7	(1.18)	37.1	(1.45)	34.6	(1.43)	34.6	(1.55)
Arkansas	—	(†)	29.2	(1.35)	28.1	(1.28)	31.4	(1.56)	26.1	(1.30)
California	—	(†)	—	(†)	—	(†)	—	(†)	—	(†)
Colorado	—	(†)	21.2	(1.81)	—	(†)	22.7	(1.52)	17.2	(1.28)
Connecticut	—	(†)	31.5	(0.90)	30.5	(1.52)	28.9	(1.25)	27.8	(1.43)
Delaware	27.9	(0.90)	26.1	(1.05)	22.9	(0.99)	20.9	(0.87)	23.1	(1.20)
District of Columbia	30.2	(1.46)	20.3	(1.18)	25.7	(1.20)	—	(†)	22.6	(1.53)
Florida	25.7	(0.81)	23.2	(0.85)	19.0	(0.80)	21.8	(0.72)	22.9	(0.84)
Georgia	33.3	(1.00)	30.7	(1.25)	32.0	(1.23)	32.9	(1.22)	32.1	(1.34)
Hawaii	—	(†)	32.7	(1.74)	36.2	(2.46)	36.1	(1.51)	31.7	(1.48)
Idaho	19.6	(1.26)	24.8	(1.52)	25.1	(1.63)	22.7	(1.39)	24.4	(1.56)
Illinois	—	(†)	—	(†)	21.2	(1.18)	27.5	(1.97)	27.3	(1.46)
Indiana	28.3	(1.55)	28.9	(1.33)	20.5	(1.02)	25.5	(1.24)	28.3	(1.33)
Iowa	—	(†)	15.5	(1.37)	10.1	(1.08)	—	(†)	11.9	(1.16)
Kansas	—	(†)	16.7	(1.27)	15.0	(1.24)	15.1	(0.78)	24.9	(1.19)
Kentucky	30.4	(1.51)	19.8	(1.23)	27.0	(1.11)	25.6	(1.49)	24.4	(1.40)
Louisiana	—	(†)	—	(†)	—	(†)	22.8	(1.66)	25.1	(1.82)
Maine	32.6	(1.73)	33.5	(1.89)	29.1	(1.67)	21.2	(0.51)	21.7	(0.80)
Maryland	—	(†)	28.9	(2.04)	27.4	(1.46)	29.3	(1.35)	30.4	(1.99)
Massachusetts	31.9	(1.08)	29.9	(1.09)	27.3	(1.06)	26.1	(1.34)	27.1	(1.04)
Michigan	31.3	(1.50)	28.8	(1.37)	29.1	(1.07)	29.5	(0.90)	25.4	(0.90)
Minnesota	—	(†)	—	(†)	—	(†)	—	(†)	—	(†)
Mississippi	22.3	(1.31)	—	(†)	15.6	(1.53)	18.0	(1.07)	15.9	(0.89)
Missouri	21.6	(2.09)	18.2	(1.92)	17.8	(1.49)	17.3	(1.32)	—	(†)
Montana	26.9	(1.23)	25.3	(1.09)	24.9	(0.83)	20.7	(1.10)	25.2	(0.93)
Nebraska	23.3	(1.04)	22.0	(0.82)	—	(†)	—	(†)	20.3	(1.01)
Nevada	34.5	(1.30)	32.6	(1.53)	28.8	(1.39)	35.6	(1.30)	—	(†)
New Hampshire	28.2	(1.87)	26.9	(1.40)	22.5	(1.25)	22.1	(1.44)	23.2	(1.44)
New Jersey	—	(†)	32.6	(1.32)	—	(†)	32.2	(1.38)	27.3	(1.41)
New Mexico	—	(†)	33.5	(1.37)	31.3	(1.39)	30.9	(1.54)	34.5	(1.24)
New York	23.0	(0.97)	23.7	(0.76)	26.6	(1.09)	24.0	(1.05)	—	(†)
North Carolina	31.9	(1.74)	27.4	(1.66)	28.5	(1.37)	30.2	(1.51)	29.8	(1.87)
North Dakota	21.3	(1.07)	19.6	(1.10)	18.7	(1.05)	19.5	(1.16)	20.8	(1.03)
Ohio[1]	31.1	(1.68)	30.9	(1.88)	26.7	(1.26)	—	(†)	24.3	(1.70)
Oklahoma	22.2	(1.23)	18.4	(1.49)	19.1	(1.12)	16.8	(1.50)	17.2	(1.36)
Oregon	—	(†)	—	(†)	—	(†)	—	(†)	—	(†)
Pennsylvania	—	(†)	—	(†)	—	(†)	16.1	(1.07)	—	(†)
Rhode Island	26.0	(1.26)	24.1	(1.11)	25.3	(1.33)	25.2	(1.52)	22.4	(0.95)
South Carolina	—	(†)	29.1	(1.45)	26.6	(1.58)	27.6	(1.74)	29.3	(1.83)
South Dakota[1]	22.1	(1.25)	20.9	(2.30)	21.1	(1.98)	17.7	(0.64)	16.0	(1.81)
Tennessee	24.3	(2.25)	26.6	(1.21)	21.6	(1.35)	18.8	(1.06)	16.6	(0.88)
Texas	—	(†)	30.7	(1.73)	26.5	(0.83)	25.9	(1.25)	29.4	(1.34)
Utah	24.7	(2.04)	20.6	(1.36)	23.2	(1.83)	19.7	(1.52)	21.4	(1.55)
Vermont	29.4	(1.67)	23.1	(1.59)	22.0	(0.99)	21.1	(1.21)	17.6	(1.51)
Virginia	—	(†)	—	(†)	—	(†)	—	(†)	24.0	(1.67)
Washington	—	(†)	—	(†)	—	(†)	—	(†)	—	(†)
West Virginia	26.5	(2.06)	24.8	(1.36)	28.6	(2.76)	28.0	(1.27)	17.3	(1.04)
Wisconsin	26.3	(1.18)	21.7	(1.18)	22.7	(1.34)	20.5	(1.03)	20.9	(1.29)
Wyoming	18.1	(0.99)	22.7	(0.97)	24.7	(1.08)	23.7	(0.93)	25.2	(0.97)

— Not available.
†Not applicable.
[1]Data include both public and private schools.
NOTE: "On school property" was not defined for survey respondents. State-level data include public schools only, with the exception of data for Ohio and South Dakota. Data for the United States total, Ohio, and South Dakota include both public and private schools.
SOURCE: Centers for Disease Control and Prevention, Division of Adolescent and School Health, Youth Risk Behavior Surveillance System (YRBSS), 2003 through 2011. (This table was prepared September 2013.)

Percentage of high school seniors reporting use of alcohol and illicit drugs, by frequency of use and substance used: Selected years, 1975 through 2012

[Standard errors appear in parentheses]

Frequency of use and substance used	Class of 1975	Class of 1980	Class of 1985	Class of 1990	Class of 1995	Class of 2000	Class of 2005	Class of 2006	Class of 2007	Class of 2008	Class of 2009	Class of 2010	Class of 2011	Class of 2012
1	2	3	4	5	6	7	8	9	10	11	12	13	14	15
Ever used														
Alcohol[1]	90.4 (0.69)	93.2 (0.46)	92.2 (0.48)	89.5 (0.57)	80.7 (0.73)	80.3 (0.80)	75.1 (0.81)	72.7 (0.85)	72.2 (0.83)	71.9 (0.85)	72.3 (0.85)	71.0 (0.84)	70.0 (0.88)	69.4 (0.90)
Any illicit drug	55.2 (1.68)	65.4 (1.23)	60.6 (1.26)	47.9 (1.33)	48.4 (1.32)	54.0 (1.44)	50.4 (1.35)	48.2 (1.37)	46.8 (1.33)	47.4 (1.35)	46.7 (1.36)	48.2 (1.33)	49.9 (1.38)	49.1 (1.40)
Marijuana only	19.0 (1.32)	26.7 (1.15)	20.9 (1.05)	18.5 (1.03)	20.3 (1.06)	25.0 (1.25)	23.0 (1.14)	21.3 (1.12)	21.3 (1.09)	22.5 (1.13)	22.7 (1.15)	23.5 (1.13)	25.0 (1.19)	25.0 (1.21)
Any illicit drug other than marijuana[2]	36.2 (1.33)	38.7 (1.04)	39.7 (1.04)	29.4 (0.99)	28.1 (0.97)	29.0 (1.08)	27.4 (0.99)	26.9 (1.00)	25.5 (0.95)	24.9 (0.96)	24.0 (0.96)	24.7 (0.94)	24.9 (0.98)	24.1 (0.98)
Selected drugs														
Cocaine	9.0 (0.73)	15.7 (0.72)	17.3 (0.74)	9.4 (0.59)	6.0 (0.48)	8.6 (0.62)	8.0 (0.56)	8.5 (0.58)	7.8 (0.54)	7.2 (0.53)	6.0 (0.49)	5.5 (0.46)	5.2 (0.47)	4.9 (0.46)
Heroin	2.2 (0.21)	1.1 (0.12)	1.2 (0.12)	1.3 (0.13)	1.6 (0.14)	2.4 (0.19)	1.5 (0.14)	1.4 (0.14)	1.5 (0.14)	1.3 (0.13)	1.2 (0.13)	1.6 (0.14)	1.4 (0.14)	1.1 (0.13)
LSD	11.3 (0.81)	9.3 (0.57)	7.5 (0.52)	8.7 (0.57)	11.7 (0.64)	11.1 (0.69)	3.5 (0.38)	3.3 (0.37)	3.4 (0.37)	4.0 (0.40)	3.1 (0.36)	4.0 (0.40)	4.0 (0.41)	3.8 (0.41)
Marijuana/hashish	47.3 (1.68)	60.3 (1.27)	54.2 (1.83)	40.7 (1.30)	41.7 (1.30)	48.8 (1.45)	44.8 (1.34)	42.3 (1.36)	41.8 (1.31)	42.6 (1.34)	42.0 (1.35)	43.8 (1.32)	45.5 (1.37)	45.2 (1.39)
PCP	— (†)	9.6 (0.33)	4.9 (0.24)	2.8 (0.19)	2.7 (0.18)	3.4 (0.23)	2.4 (0.18)	2.2 (0.17)	2.1 (0.17)	1.8 (0.16)	1.7 (0.15)	1.8 (0.15)	2.3 (0.18)	1.6 (0.15)
Used during past 12 months														
Alcohol[1]	84.8 (0.84)	87.9 (0.59)	85.6 (0.63)	80.6 (0.73)	73.7 (0.81)	73.2 (0.89)	68.6 (0.87)	66.5 (0.90)	66.4 (0.88)	65.5 (0.90)	66.2 (0.90)	65.2 (0.88)	63.5 (0.92)	63.5 (0.94)
Any illicit drug	45.0 (1.64)	53.1 (1.26)	46.3 (1.26)	32.5 (1.21)	39.0 (1.26)	40.9 (1.39)	38.4 (1.28)	36.5 (1.29)	35.9 (1.25)	36.6 (1.27)	36.5 (1.29)	38.3 (1.26)	40.0 (1.32)	39.7 (1.34)
Marijuana only	18.8 (1.29)	22.7 (1.06)	18.9 (0.99)	14.6 (0.91)	19.6 (1.02)	20.5 (1.14)	18.8 (1.03)	17.3 (1.01)	17.4 (0.99)	18.3 (1.02)	19.5 (1.06)	21.0 (1.06)	22.4 (1.12)	22.7 (1.14)
Any illicit drug other than marijuana[2]	26.2 (1.15)	30.4 (0.92)	27.4 (0.89)	17.9 (0.79)	19.4 (0.81)	20.4 (0.90)	19.7 (0.83)	19.2 (0.84)	18.5 (0.80)	18.3 (0.81)	17.0 (0.79)	17.3 (0.78)	17.6 (0.81)	17.0 (0.81)
Selected drugs														
Cocaine	5.6 (0.52)	12.3 (0.58)	13.1 (0.59)	5.3 (0.40)	4.0 (0.35)	5.0 (0.43)	5.1 (0.40)	5.7 (0.43)	5.2 (0.40)	4.4 (0.38)	3.4 (0.34)	2.9 (0.30)	2.9 (0.31)	2.7 (0.31)
Heroin	1.0 (0.13)	0.5 (0.07)	0.6 (0.07)	0.5 (0.07)	1.1 (0.10)	1.5 (0.13)	0.8 (0.09)	0.8 (0.09)	0.9 (0.09)	0.7 (0.08)	0.7 (0.09)	0.9 (0.09)	0.8 (0.09)	0.6 (0.08)
LSD	7.2 (0.59)	6.5 (0.43)	4.4 (0.36)	5.4 (0.41)	8.4 (0.49)	6.6 (0.49)	1.8 (0.24)	1.7 (0.24)	2.1 (0.26)	2.7 (0.30)	1.9 (0.25)	2.6 (0.29)	2.7 (0.30)	2.4 (0.29)
Marijuana/hashish	40.0 (1.61)	48.8 (1.27)	40.6 (1.24)	27.0 (1.15)	34.7 (1.23)	36.5 (1.36)	33.6 (1.24)	31.5 (1.24)	31.7 (1.21)	32.4 (1.24)	32.8 (1.25)	34.8 (1.24)	36.4 (1.29)	36.4 (1.31)
PCP	— (†)	4.4 (0.20)	2.9 (0.16)	1.2 (0.11)	1.8 (0.13)	2.3 (0.16)	1.3 (0.11)	0.7 (0.09)	0.9 (0.09)	1.1 (0.11)	1.0 (0.10)	1.0 (0.10)	1.3 (0.12)	0.9 (0.10)
Used during past 30 days														
Alcohol[1]	68.2 (1.10)	72.0 (0.81)	65.9 (0.85)	57.1 (0.92)	51.3 (0.92)	50.0 (1.01)	47.0 (0.94)	45.3 (0.95)	44.4 (0.92)	43.1 (0.93)	43.5 (0.95)	41.2 (0.91)	40.0 (0.94)	41.5 (0.96)
Any illicit drug	30.7 (1.35)	37.2 (1.09)	29.7 (1.03)	17.2 (0.87)	23.8 (0.98)	24.9 (1.09)	23.1 (0.99)	21.5 (0.98)	21.9 (0.96)	22.3 (0.98)	23.3 (1.01)	23.8 (0.99)	25.2 (1.04)	25.2 (1.06)
Marijuana only	15.3 (1.06)	18.8 (0.88)	14.8 (0.80)	9.2 (0.67)	13.8 (0.79)	14.5 (0.89)	12.8 (0.78)	11.7 (0.77)	12.4 (0.76)	13.0 (0.79)	14.7 (0.84)	15.2 (0.83)	16.3 (0.89)	16.8 (0.91)
Any illicit drug other than marijuana[2]	15.4 (0.80)	18.4 (0.66)	14.9 (0.60)	8.0 (0.47)	10.0 (0.52)	10.4 (0.58)	10.3 (0.54)	9.8 (0.54)	9.5 (0.51)	9.3 (0.52)	8.6 (0.50)	8.6 (0.49)	8.9 (0.51)	8.4 (0.51)
Selected drugs														
Cocaine	1.9 (0.25)	5.2 (0.31)	6.7 (0.35)	1.9 (0.20)	1.8 (0.19)	2.1 (0.23)	2.3 (0.22)	2.5 (0.23)	2.0 (0.20)	1.9 (0.20)	1.3 (0.17)	1.3 (0.16)	1.1 (0.16)	1.1 (0.16)
Heroin	0.4 (0.08)	0.2 (0.04)	0.3 (0.05)	0.2 (0.04)	0.6 (0.08)	0.7 (0.09)	0.5 (0.07)	0.6 (0.06)	0.4 (0.06)	0.4 (0.06)	0.4 (0.06)	0.4 (0.06)	0.4 (0.07)	0.3 (0.06)
LSD	2.3 (0.28)	2.3 (0.21)	1.6 (0.18)	1.9 (0.20)	4.0 (0.28)	1.6 (0.20)	0.7 (0.12)	0.6 (0.12)	0.6 (0.11)	1.1 (0.15)	0.5 (0.11)	0.4 (0.13)	0.6 (0.13)	0.8 (0.14)
Marijuana/hashish	27.1 (1.30)	33.7 (1.07)	25.7 (0.98)	14.0 (0.80)	21.2 (0.94)	21.6 (1.04)	19.8 (0.94)	18.3 (0.92)	18.8 (0.90)	19.4 (0.93)	20.6 (0.96)	21.4 (0.95)	22.6 (1.00)	22.9 (1.02)
PCP	— (†)	1.4 (0.11)	1.6 (0.12)	0.4 (0.06)	0.6 (0.08)	0.9 (0.10)	0.7 (0.08)	0.4 (0.06)	0.5 (0.07)	0.6 (0.08)	0.5 (0.07)	0.8 (0.09)	0.8 (0.09)	0.5 (0.07)

—Not available.
†Not applicable.
[1]Survey question changed in 1993; later data are not comparable to figures for earlier years.
[2]Other illicit drugs include any use of LSD or other hallucinogens, crack or other cocaine, or heroin, or any use of other narcotics, amphetamines, barbiturates, or tranquilizers not under a doctor's orders.

NOTE: Detail may not sum to totals because of rounding. Standard errors were calculated from formulas to perform trend analysis over an interval greater than 1 year (for example, a comparison between 1975 and 1990). A revised questionnaire was used in 1982 and later years to reduce the inappropriate reporting of nonprescription stimulants. This slightly reduced the positive responses for some types of drug abuse.
SOURCE: University of Michigan, Institute for Social Research, Monitoring the Future, selected years, 1975 through 2012, retrieved April 15, 2013, from http://monitoringthefuture.org/data/12data.html. (This table was prepared April 2013.)

Percentage of 12- to 17-year-olds reporting use of illicit drugs, alcohol, and cigarettes during the past 30 days and the past year, by substance used, sex, and race/ethnicity: Selected years, 1985 through 2011

[Standard errors appear in parentheses]

Year, sex, and race/ethnicity	Percent reporting use during past 30 days					Percent reporting use during past year				
	Illicit drugs			Alcohol	Cigarettes	Illicit drugs			Alcohol	Cigarettes
	Any[1]	Marijuana	Cocaine			Any[1]	Marijuana	Cocaine		
1	2	3	4	5	6	7	8	9	10	11
1985	13.2 (—)	10.2 (—)	1.5	41.2 (—)	29.4 (—)	20.7 (—)	16.7 (—)	3.4	52.7 (—)	29.9 (—)
1990	7.1 (—)	4.4 (—)	0.6	32.5 (—)	22.4 (—)	14.1 (—)	9.6 (—)	1.9	41.8 (—)	26.2 (—)
1994	8.2 (—)	6.0 (—)	0.3	21.6 (—)	18.9 (—)	15.5 (—)	11.4 (—)	1.1	36.2 (—)	24.5 (—)
1995	10.9 (—)	8.2 (—)	0.8	21.1 (—)	20.2 (—)	18.0 (—)	14.2 (—)	1.7	35.1 (—)	26.6 (—)
1996	9.0 (—)	7.1 (—)	0.6	18.8 (—)	18.3 (—)	16.7 (—)	13.0 (—)	1.4	32.7 (—)	24.2 (—)
1997	11.4 (—)	9.4 (—)	1.0	20.5 (—)	19.9 (—)	18.8 (—)	15.8 (—)	2.2	34.0 (—)	26.4 (—)
1998	9.9 (—)	8.3 (—)	0.8	19.1 (—)	18.2 (—)	16.4 (—)	14.1 (—)	1.7	31.8 (—)	23.8 (—)
1999	9.8 (0.23)	7.2 (0.20)	0.5 (0.06)	16.5 (0.30)	14.9 (0.31)	19.8 (0.32)	14.2 (0.29)	1.6 (0.10)	34.1 (0.41)	23.4 (0.37)
2000	9.7 (0.24)	7.2 (0.21)	0.6 (0.07)	16.4 (0.29)	13.4 (0.28)	18.6 (0.31)	13.4 (0.27)	1.7 (0.12)	33.0 (0.39)	20.8 (0.34)
2001	10.8 (0.26)	8.0 (0.24)	0.4 (0.06)	17.3 (0.33)	13.0 (0.28)	20.8 (0.36)	15.2 (0.32)	1.5 (0.10)	33.9 (0.39)	20.0 (0.35)
2002	11.6 (0.29)	8.2 (0.24)	0.6 (0.07)	17.6 (0.32)	13.0 (0.30)	22.2 (0.38)	15.8 (0.32)	2.1 (0.13)	34.6 (0.42)	20.3 (0.35)
2003	11.2 (0.27)	7.9 (0.24)	0.6 (0.06)	17.7 (0.33)	12.2 (0.29)	21.8 (0.36)	15.0 (0.31)	1.8 (0.11)	34.3 (0.42)	19.0 (0.36)
2004	10.6 (0.27)	7.6 (0.23)	0.5 (0.06)	17.6 (0.32)	11.9 (0.30)	21.0 (0.34)	14.5 (0.31)	1.6 (0.11)	33.9 (0.41)	18.4 (0.35)
2005	9.9 (0.25)	6.8 (0.22)	0.6 (0.06)	16.5 (0.32)	10.8 (0.28)	19.9 (0.35)	13.3 (0.30)	1.7 (0.11)	33.3 (0.41)	17.3 (0.36)
2006	9.8 (0.27)	6.7 (0.21)	0.4 (0.05)	16.6 (0.32)	10.4 (0.26)	19.6 (0.37)	13.2 (0.31)	1.6 (0.11)	32.9 (0.42)	17.0 (0.35)
2007	9.5 (0.27)	6.7 (0.22)	0.4 (0.05)	15.9 (0.34)	9.8 (0.26)	18.7 (0.35)	12.5 (0.30)	1.5 (0.11)	31.8 (0.42)	15.7 (0.34)
2008	9.3 (0.24)	6.7 (0.22)	0.4 (0.05)	14.6 (0.31)	9.1 (0.24)	19.0 (0.35)	13.0 (0.29)	1.2 (0.10)	30.8 (0.40)	15.0 (0.31)
2009	10.0 (0.27)	7.3 (0.24)	0.3 (0.05)	14.7 (0.32)	8.9 (0.26)	19.5 (0.36)	13.6 (0.31)	1.0 (0.09)	30.3 (0.42)	15.0 (0.33)
2010[2]	10.1 (0.29)	7.4 (0.25)	0.2 (0.05)	13.6 (0.33)	8.4 (0.26)	19.5 (0.38)	14.0 (0.34)	1.0 (0.09)	28.7 (0.43)	14.2 (0.34)
Sex										
Male	10.4 (0.42)	8.4 (0.37)	0.3 (0.07)	13.7 (0.46)	8.6 (0.36)	19.4 (0.53)	14.9 (0.49)	0.9 (0.13)	27.8 (0.58)	14.4 (0.46)
Female	9.8 (0.41)	6.4 (0.34)	0.2 (0.05)	13.5 (0.45)	8.2 (0.34)	19.5 (0.54)	13.1 (0.45)	1.0 (0.14)	29.6 (0.61)	14.0 (0.46)
Race/ethnicity										
White	9.7 (0.35)	7.5 (0.31)	0.2 ! (0.06)	15.0 (0.44)	9.8 (0.35)	19.1 (0.47)	14.1 (0.41)	1.1 (0.12)	30.2 (0.54)	16.2 (0.44)
Black	10.8 (0.66)	7.5 (0.57)	‡ (†)	10.8 (0.75)	4.4 (0.48)	19.4 (0.90)	13.6 (0.77)	0.1 ! (0.04)	23.7 (0.95)	8.3 (0.66)
Hispanic	11.8 (0.76)	8.0 (0.62)	0.5 ! (0.16)	13.9 (0.76)	7.9 (0.58)	22.3 (0.98)	15.7 (0.88)	1.4 (0.26)	30.2 (1.07)	14.0 (0.78)
Asian	4.0 (1.00)	2.6 ! (0.81)	# (†)	4.9 (1.08)	3.6 (1.04)	9.4 (1.51)	5.9 (1.27)	‡ (†)	17.5 (1.90)	6.8 (1.40)
Pacific Islander	4.6 ! (1.55)	1.8 ! (0.65)	‡ (†)	‡ (†)	3.1 ! (1.26)	8.2 ! (2.81)	5.1 ! (2.24)	‡ (†)	‡ (†)	6.1 ! (1.88)
American Indian/Alaska Native	12.7 (2.54)	9.1 (2.13)	‡ (†)	11.1 (2.18)	14.9 (2.88)	28.3 (3.58)	19.7 (3.20)	0.8 ! (0.30)	27.1 (3.36)	22.7 (3.44)
Two or more races	13.4 (1.91)	8.2 (1.35)	‡ (†)	13.0 (1.52)	9.1 (1.47)	23.0 (2.31)	15.4 (1.82)	0.9 (0.08)	32.1 (2.50)	16.1 (1.93)
2011	10.1 (0.27)	7.9 (0.24)	0.3 (0.05)	13.3 (0.31)	7.8 (0.24)	19.0 (0.37)	14.2 (0.33)	0.9 (0.08)	27.8 (0.43)	13.2 (0.31)
Sex										
Male	10.8 (0.39)	9.0 (0.36)	0.2 (0.04)	13.3 (0.42)	8.2 (0.36)	19.1 (0.53)	15.1 (0.46)	0.9 (0.11)	27.0 (0.58)	13.7 (0.43)
Female	9.3 (0.36)	6.7 (0.31)	0.4 (0.08)	13.3 (0.43)	7.3 (0.33)	18.8 (0.50)	13.3 (0.45)	0.9 (0.12)	28.6 (0.59)	12.6 (0.42)
Race/ethnicity										
White	9.8 (0.33)	7.9 (0.30)	0.3 (0.06)	14.6 (0.42)	9.3 (0.33)	18.6 (0.45)	14.3 (0.41)	0.9 (0.10)	29.8 (0.53)	15.2 (0.41)
Black	11.1 (0.81)	8.2 (0.72)	# (†)	10.5 (0.78)	4.9 (0.51)	19.8 (0.97)	14.2 (0.87)	0.1 ! (0.04)	23.7 (1.06)	9.0 (0.65)
Hispanic	10.3 (0.66)	7.7 (0.60)	0.4 ! (0.13)	12.6 (0.68)	6.1 (0.54)	19.7 (0.84)	14.2 (0.77)	1.5 (0.23)	26.9 (0.94)	11.1 (0.69)
Asian	5.0 (1.13)	3.7 (1.01)	‡ (†)	7.4 (1.24)	3.3 (0.94)	9.4 (1.46)	6.6 (1.28)	‡ (†)	17.1 (1.82)	6.5 (1.22)
Pacific Islander	‡ (†)	‡ (†)	‡ (†)	‡ (†)	‡ (†)	‡ (†)	‡ (†)	‡ (†)	‡ (†)	‡ (†)
American Indian/Alaska Native	16.3 (3.16)	10.4 (2.22)	‡ (†)	15.2 (2.60)	12.3 (2.55)	28.5 (3.75)	18.9 (2.85)	‡ (†)	29.0 (3.43)	20.2 (3.04)
Two or more races	16.6 (2.05)	13.8 (1.99)	‡ (†)	17.5 (2.11)	10.7 (1.77)	29.5 (2.53)	24.8 (2.52)	1.7 ! (0.69)	33.2 (2.61)	19.9 (2.24)

—Not available.
†Not applicable.
#Rounds to zero.
!Interpret data with caution. The coefficient of variation (CV) for this estimate is between 30 and 50 percent.
‡Reporting standards not met (too few cases for a reliable estimate).
[1]Includes other illegal drug use not shown separately—specifically, the use of heroin, hallucinogens, and inhalants, as well as the nonmedical use of prescription-type pain relievers, tranquilizers, stimulants, and sedatives.
[2]Some data have been revised from previously published figures.

NOTE: Marijuana includes hashish usage. Data for 1999 and later years were gathered using Computer Assisted Interviewing (CAI) and may not be directly comparable to previous years. Because of survey improvements in 2002, the 2002 data constitute a new baseline for tracking trends. Valid trend comparisons can be made for 1985 through 1998, 1999 through 2001, and 2002 through 2011. Race categories exclude persons of Hispanic ethnicity.
SOURCE: U.S. Department of Health and Human Services, Substance Abuse and Mental Health Services Administration, *National Household Survey on Drug Abuse: Main Findings*, selected years, 1985 through 2001, and National Survey on Drug Use and Health, 2002 through 2011. Retrieved May 20, 2013, from http://www.samhsa.gov/data/NSDUH.aspx. (This table was prepared May 2013.)

Number and percentage of public schools that took a serious disciplinary action in response to specific offenses, number of serious actions taken, and percentage distribution of actions, by type of offense, school level, and type of action: Selected years, 1999–2000 through 2009–10

[Standard errors appear in parentheses]

Year, school level, and type of serious disciplinary action	Total	Physical attacks or fights	Insubordination	Distribution, possession, or use of alcohol	Distribution, possession, or use of illegal drugs	Use or possession of a firearm or explosive device	Use or possession of a weapon other than a firearm or explosive device[1]
1	2	3	4	5	6	7	8
Number of schools taking at least one action							
2009–10	32,300 (940)	24,000 (770)	— (†)	7,600 (320)	16,100 (400)	2,500 (340)	11,200 (650)
Percent of schools taking at least one action							
1999–2000[2]	— (†)	35.4 (1.02)	18.3 (0.79)	— (†)	— (†)	— (†)	— (†)
2003–04	45.7 (1.15)	32.0 (0.94)	21.6 (0.85)	9.2 (0.50)	21.2 (0.58)	3.9 (0.40)	16.8 (0.84)
2005–06	48.0 (1.18)	31.5 (1.02)	21.2 (0.85)	10.2 (0.47)	20.8 (0.61)	4.5 (0.35)	19.3 (0.91)
2007–08	46.4 (1.16)	31.5 (0.89)	21.4 (0.95)	9.8 (0.48)	19.3 (0.53)	2.8 (0.26)	15.3 (0.77)
2009–10[3]	39.1 (1.14)	29.0 (0.94)	— (†)	9.2 (0.39)	19.5 (0.48)	3.0 (0.41)	13.5 (0.78)
Primary school[4]	18.1 (1.51)	13.2 (1.26)	— (†)	1.0! (0.33)	2.0 (0.47)	1.7! (0.57)	6.4 (0.93)
Middle school[4]	67.0 (1.68)	49.7 (1.87)	— (†)	13.6 (1.17)	36.9 (1.19)	4.1 (0.65)	25.1 (1.70)
High school[4]	82.7 (1.57)	62.6 (1.63)	— (†)	36.1 (1.47)	66.1 (1.39)	7.3 (1.05)	28.9 (1.39)
Combined school[4]	49.2 (5.31)	35.6 (4.26)	— (†)	9.9 (2.54)	22.7 (3.57)	‡ (†)	10.9 (2.72)
Number of actions taken							
1999–2000[2]	— (†)	332,500 (27,420)	253,500 (27,720)	— (†)	— (†)	— (†)	— (†)
2003–04	655,700 (29,160)	273,500 (14,450)	220,400 (16,990)	25,500 (1,600)	91,100 (3,410)	9,900! (4,300)	35,400 (1,470)
2005–06	830,700 (45,710)	323,900 (16,690)	309,000 (33,840)	30,100 (1,880)	106,800 (4,950)	14,300 (2,690)	46,600 (2,040)
2007–08	767,900 (44,010)	271,800 (15,180)	327,100 (38,470)	28,400 (1,470)	98,700 (5,780)	5,200 (910)	36,800 (2,630)
2009–10[3]	433,800 (22,880)	265,100 (22,170)	— (†)	28,700 (1,920)	105,400 (4,070)	5,800 (1,360)	28,800 (1,580)
Percentage distribution of actions, 2009–10							
Out-of-school suspensions lasting 5 days or more	73.9 (1.79)	81.2 (2.18)	— (†)	74.3 (2.23)	59.6 (1.70)	55.5 (9.64)	62.2 (2.44)
Removal with no services for remainder of school year	6.1 (0.86)	5.0 (1.22)	— (†)	4.0 (0.92)	8.0 (0.94)	22.2 (4.96)	8.8 (1.31)
Transfer to specialized schools	20.0 (1.36)	13.9 (1.57)	— (†)	21.7 (2.27)	32.4 (1.57)	22.3! (7.91)	29.0 (2.32)

—Not available.
†Not applicable.
!Interpret data with caution. The coefficient of variation (CV) for this estimate is between 30 and 50 percent.
‡Reporting standards not met. Either there are too few cases for a reliable estimate or the coefficient of variation (CV) is 50 percent or greater.
[1]Prior to 2005–06, the questionnaire wording was simply "a weapon other than a firearm" (instead of "a weapon other than a firearm or explosive device").
[2]In the 1999–2000 questionnaire, only two items are the same as in questionnaires for later years—the item on physical attacks or fights and the item on insubordination. There are no comparable 1999–2000 data for serious disciplinary actions taken in response to the other specific offenses listed in this table, nor for total actions taken in response to all the listed offenses.
[3]Totals for 2009–10 are not comparable to totals for other years, because the 2009–10 questionnaire did not include an item on insubordination.
[4]Primary schools are defined as schools in which the lowest grade is not higher than grade 3 and the highest grade is not higher than grade 8. Middle schools are defined as schools in which the lowest grade is not lower than grade 4 and the highest grade is not higher than grade 9. High schools are defined as schools in which the lowest grade is not lower than grade 9 and the highest grade is not higher than grade 12. Combined schools include all other combinations of grades, including K–12 schools.

NOTE: Serious disciplinary actions include out-of-school suspensions lasting 5 or more days, but less than the remainder of the school year; removals with no continuing services for the remainder of the school year; and transfers to specialized schools for disciplinary reasons. Responses were provided by the principal or the person most knowledgeable about crime and safety issues at the school. Respondents were instructed to respond only for those times that were during normal school hours or when school activities or events were in session, unless the survey specified otherwise. Detail may not sum to totals because of rounding and because schools that reported serious disciplinary actions in response to more than one type of offense were counted only once in the total number or percentage of schools.
SOURCE: U.S. Department of Education, National Center for Education Statistics, 1999–2000, 2003–04, 2005–06, 2007–08, and 2009–10 School Survey on Crime and Safety (SSOCS), 2000, 2004, 2006, 2008, and 2010. (This table was prepared September 2013.)

Percentage of public and private schools with various safety and security measures, by school level: 2003–04, 2007–08, and 2011–12

[Standard errors appear in parentheses]

School control and school safety and security measure	Total[1] 2003–04	Total[1] 2007–08	Total[1] 2011–12	Elementary schools[2] 2003–04	Elementary schools[2] 2007–08	Elementary schools[2] 2011–12	Secondary schools[3] 2003–04	Secondary schools[3] 2007–08	Secondary schools[3] 2011–12
1	2	3	4	5	6	7	8	9	10
Public schools									
Controlled access during school hours									
Buildings (e.g., locked or monitored doors)	81.5 (0.60)	88.8 (0.63)	88.2 (0.56)	84.7 (0.65)	92.1 (0.71)	90.4 (0.67)	75.0 (1.33)	82.1 (1.42)	83.9 (1.04)
Grounds (e.g., locked or monitored gates)	39.4 (0.83)	44.9 (1.12)	44.1 (0.72)	39.0 (1.03)	45.7 (1.61)	45.4 (0.94)	41.4 (1.38)	43.3 (1.53)	39.6 (1.13)
Student dress, IDs, and school supplies									
Required students to wear uniforms	13.5 (0.53)	16.5 (0.83)	19.3 (0.54)	14.7 (0.67)	17.5 (1.05)	20.3 (0.76)	8.8 (1.11)	12.1 (1.19)	12.2 (0.69)
Enforced a strict dress code	49.3 (0.70)	54.0 (0.99)	49.1 (0.68)	45.2 (0.94)	50.0 (1.38)	44.6 (0.94)	59.7 (1.33)	64.4 (1.87)	58.3 (1.02)
Required students to wear badges or picture IDs	6.1 (0.31)	7.5 (0.53)	7.4 (0.33)	3.5 (0.35)	4.1 (0.57)	4.6 (0.32)	14.1 (0.74)	16.8 (1.15)	14.3 (1.02)
Required clear book bags or banned book bags on school grounds	6.0 (0.31)	6.8 (0.43)	5.7 (0.28)	3.3 (0.32)	4.7 (0.54)	3.2 (0.28)	11.3 (0.74)	10.5 (1.07)	9.3 (0.72)
Metal detectors, dogs, sweeps, and cameras									
Random metal detector checks on students	5.7 (0.32)	5.9 (0.45)	5.0 (0.32)	3.4 (0.33)	3.3 (0.48)	2.6 (0.28)	10.2 (0.64)	11.9 (1.05)	7.9 (0.63)
Students required to pass through metal detectors daily	2.0 (0.21)	2.3 (0.31)	2.7 (0.33)	0.8 (0.23)	0.3 ! (0.14)	0.8 (0.16)	3.7 (0.38)	5.2 (1.03)	4.6 (0.65)
Random dog sniffs to check for drugs	23.6 (0.59)	25.0 (0.68)	24.0 (0.40)	10.8 (0.62)	13.2 (0.83)	10.6 (0.39)	56.5 (1.59)	54.6 (1.59)	57.3 (1.28)
Random sweeps[4] for contraband (e.g., drugs or weapons)	12.8 (0.48)	14.8 (0.76)	12.1 (0.44)	5.6 (0.44)	7.6 (0.84)	5.0 (0.39)	28.2 (1.33)	30.5 (1.59)	26.1 (1.16)
Security cameras used to monitor the school	32.5 (0.68)	51.8 (0.94)	64.3 (0.75)	26.3 (0.77)	46.1 (1.29)	57.7 (0.97)	51.1 (1.55)	68.7 (1.77)	81.2 (1.07)
Daily presence of police or security personnel	24.8 (0.59)	27.2 (0.99)	28.1 (0.51)	15.5 (0.62)	16.2 (1.14)	17.1 (0.57)	53.9 (1.61)	58.3 (1.93)	57.6 (1.44)
Private schools									
Controlled access during school hours									
Buildings (e.g., locked or monitored doors)	73.5 (1.02)	81.5 (1.15)	80.1 (1.50)	79.5 (1.19)	84.1 (1.35)	82.0 (2.22)	62.9 (3.65)	76.9 (2.83)	71.5 (3.50)
Grounds (e.g., locked or monitored gates)	40.2 (1.08)	42.4 (1.22)	42.1 (1.43)	44.9 (1.32)	45.6 (1.50)	44.0 (1.99)	32.2 (3.80)	34.7 (3.37)	34.0 (4.67)
Student dress, IDs, and school supplies									
Required students to wear uniforms	55.5 (1.06)	55.4 (1.19)	56.9 (1.77)	60.6 (1.27)	62.2 (1.68)	60.0 (2.21)	44.9 (3.53)	42.8 (3.22)	49.2 (4.55)
Enforced a strict dress code	73.7 (1.00)	76.3 (1.08)	71.3 (1.49)	74.1 (1.32)	75.9 (1.48)	71.2 (2.12)	70.0 (3.78)	75.3 (3.36)	70.8 (3.13)
Required students to wear badges or picture IDs	2.2 (0.30)	2.9 (0.42)	2.7 (0.48)	1.0 (0.27)	1.6 (0.38)	1.4 (0.40)	9.8 (2.10)	6.2 (1.27)	8.2 (1.91)
Required clear book bags or banned book bags on school grounds	2.3 (0.35)	3.2 (0.43)	1.7 (0.33)	1.0 (0.30)	1.7 (0.46)	0.9 ! (0.30)	9.4 (2.59)	7.5 (2.11)	5.2 (1.47)
Metal detectors, dogs, sweeps, and cameras									
Random metal detector checks on students	0.7 (0.20)	1.1 (0.24)	1.2 ! (0.42)	‡ (†)	‡ (†)	‡ (†)	‡ (†)	‡ (†)	‡ (†)
Students required to pass through metal detectors daily	0.8 (0.21)	0.6 ! (0.19)	0.4 ! (0.16)	‡ (†)	‡ (†)	‡ (†)	‡ (†)	‡ (†)	‡ (†)
Random dog sniffs to check for drugs	3.4 (0.35)	3.9 (0.43)	4.1 (0.45)	‡ (†)	0.4 ! (0.20)	‡ (†)	15.0 (2.04)	17.0 (2.32)	16.3 (2.36)
Random sweeps[4] for contraband (e.g., drugs or weapons)	7.7 (0.61)	8.8 (0.69)	7.5 (0.93)	2.4 (0.52)	2.1 (0.42)	1.5 ! (0.68)	23.3 (3.75)	26.0 (3.64)	20.4 (2.95)
Security cameras used to monitor the school	19.4 (0.79)	32.9 (1.21)	40.6 (1.51)	19.9 (0.97)	31.4 (1.65)	39.8 (2.18)	24.3 (3.11)	43.1 (3.64)	52.0 (5.46)
Daily presence of police or security personnel	5.9 (0.50)	6.4 (0.54)	7.2 (0.77)	3.1 (0.50)	4.3 (0.61)	3.9 (0.80)	16.2 (2.99)	11.8 (2.46)	19.2 (4.77)

†Not applicable.

!Interpret data with caution. The coefficient of variation (CV) for this estimate is between 30 and 50 percent.

‡Reporting standards not met. Either there are too few cases for a reliable estimate or the coefficient of variation (CV) is 50 percent or greater.

[1]Includes combined elementary/secondary schools not separately shown.

[2]Elementary schools are those with any of grades kindergarten through grade 6 and none of grades 9 through 12.

[3]Secondary schools have any of grades 7 through 12 and none of grades kindergarten through grade 6.

[4]Does not include random dog sniffs.

NOTE: Responses were provided by the principal.

SOURCE: U.S. Department of Education, National Center for Education Statistics, Schools and Staffing Survey (SASS), "Public School Principal Data File" and "Private School Principal Data File," 2003–04, 2007–08, and 2011–12. (This table was prepared August 2013.)

Percentage of public and private schools with various safety and security measures, by school control and selected characteristics: 2011–12

[Standard errors appear in parentheses]

School control and selected characteristic	Total schools — Number	Total schools — Percentage distribution	Controlled access — School buildings[1]	Controlled access — School grounds[2]	Student dress, IDs, school supplies — School uniforms required	Strict dress code enforced	Badges or picture IDs required	Bookbags must be clear or are banned	Metal detectors, dogs, sweeps, cameras — Random metal detector checks	Daily metal detector checks[3]	Random dog sniffs for drugs	Random sweeps for contraband[4]	Security cameras	Daily presence of police or security
1	2	3	4	5	6	7	8	9	10	11	12	13	14	15
Public total	89,800 (410)	100.0 (†)	88.2 (0.56)	44.1 (0.72)	19.3 (0.54)	49.1 (0.68)	7.4 (0.33)	5.7 (0.28)	5.0 (0.32)	2.7 (0.33)	24.0 (0.40)	12.1 (0.44)	64.3 (0.75)	28.1 (0.51)
School enrollment														
Under 100	6,600 (400)	7.3 (0.44)	80.8 (1.98)	43.2 (3.20)	21.8 (2.54)	44.3 (3.15)	4.8 (1.38)	15.2 (2.11)	14.5 (2.22)	14.1 (2.22)	22.6 (2.46)	28.6 (2.45)	52.5 (3.13)	29.0 (2.92)
100 to 299	16,600 (560)	18.5 (0.60)	85.5 (1.57)	32.7 (1.92)	18.5 (1.66)	43.6 (2.21)	6.0 (1.00)	4.7 (0.68)	4.3 (0.77)	2.8 (0.57)	25.0 (1.36)	12.8 (1.06)	55.6 (2.56)	17.8 (1.54)
300 to 499	27,000 (630)	30.1 (0.68)	89.1 (0.98)	42.5 (1.49)	19.8 (1.08)	43.8 (1.45)	5.4 (0.64)	4.2 (0.43)	3.8 (0.58)	1.6! (0.56)	16.7 (0.73)	8.4 (0.66)	64.6 (1.59)	15.1 (0.99)
500 to 999	30,500 (600)	34.0 (0.69)	91.1 (0.81)	48.9 (1.41)	20.0 (1.04)	54.3 (1.15)	7.0 (0.59)	5.0 (0.54)	3.7 (0.45)	1.4! (0.43)	22.2 (0.80)	9.5 (0.56)	65.5 (1.19)	30.0 (1.05)
1,000 to 1,499	5,300 (240)	5.9 (0.27)	87.1 (1.63)	52.5 (2.35)	19.0 (2.47)	62.1 (2.24)	15.8 (1.72)	7.6 (1.18)	5.4 (0.94)	1.4! (0.49)	48.4 (2.64)	16.2 (1.60)	81.8 (2.40)	70.5 (2.37)
1,500 or more	3,700 (220)	4.2 (0.25)	85.4 (1.87)	57.9 (2.40)	9.9 (1.64)	60.0 (2.67)	24.9 (2.18)	7.8 (1.53)	11.4 (1.50)	2.6! (0.81)	55.1 (2.62)	22.4 (2.58)	87.2 (1.90)	90.4 (1.61)
Percent of students approved for free or reduced-price school lunch														
School does not participate	3,100 (260)	3.4 (0.29)	76.1 (4.70)	40.6 (5.40)	27.6 (4.48)	47.9 (5.64)	11.0 (2.19)	12.5 (3.41)	12.2 (3.48)	10.6! (3.56)	21.8 (2.92)	29.3 (5.28)	56.2 (5.44)	30.3 (4.42)
0 to 25 percent	18,600 (560)	20.7 (0.62)	89.0 (1.18)	38.3 (1.61)	6.5 (0.98)	37.8 (1.54)	4.0 (0.55)	3.6 (0.46)	1.9 (0.45)	1.1! (0.36)	25.2 (1.19)	9.6 (0.92)	65.2 (1.66)	26.3 (1.39)
26 to 50 percent	23,600 (710)	26.3 (0.77)	86.8 (1.04)	38.2 (1.71)	6.5 (0.68)	42.9 (1.50)	4.9 (0.66)	4.7 (0.57)	2.2 (0.40)	0.6! (0.24)	29.3 (1.02)	9.7 (0.66)	64.6 (1.63)	24.1 (0.99)
51 to 75 percent	22,700 (540)	25.2 (0.62)	90.4 (0.93)	43.4 (1.67)	15.8 (1.33)	50.4 (1.37)	8.5 (0.74)	5.4 (0.52)	5.3 (0.65)	2.4 (0.42)	24.8 (1.05)	11.5 (0.81)	66.4 (1.52)	25.8 (1.21)
76 to 100 percent	21,800 (640)	24.3 (0.70)	88.7 (1.10)	56.8 (1.75)	46.6 (1.63)	64.3 (1.61)	11.4 (0.96)	7.9 (0.62)	9.5 (0.88)	5.4 (1.16)	16.9 (1.00)	15.1 (1.10)	62.3 (1.86)	36.2 (1.52)
School locale														
City	23,400 (270)	26.1 (0.28)	88.5 (1.22)	54.9 (1.79)	39.9 (1.67)	56.5 (1.81)	11.8 (0.87)	6.0 (0.55)	8.3 (0.90)	5.2 (1.12)	13.4 (0.65)	11.0 (0.93)	59.2 (1.74)	38.8 (1.53)
Suburban	24,500 (360)	27.3 (0.36)	90.5 (0.90)	46.4 (1.33)	16.1 (0.95)	48.0 (1.57)	7.7 (0.75)	4.3 (0.55)	3.8 (0.55)	1.8 (0.31)	17.8 (0.79)	8.6 (0.62)	66.7 (1.34)	29.3 (1.17)
Town	12,300 (340)	13.7 (0.40)	87.4 (1.32)	36.9 (1.88)	12.1 (1.41)	45.9 (1.83)	4.6 (0.59)	6.5 (0.70)	5.1 (1.01)	1.6 (0.38)	32.4 (1.32)	14.3 (1.13)	67.0 (1.86)	22.5 (1.33)
Rural	29,500 (430)	32.9 (0.43)	86.6 (0.80)	46.1 (1.32)	8.6 (0.66)	45.6 (1.26)	4.9 (0.55)	6.3 (0.54)	3.4 (0.45)	1.8 (0.43)	34.1 (0.83)	15.0 (0.71)	65.3 (1.14)	21.0 (0.79)
School level[5]														
Elementary	61,200 (440)	68.2 (0.38)	90.4 (0.67)	45.4 (0.94)	20.3 (0.76)	44.6 (0.94)	4.6 (0.32)	3.2 (0.28)	2.6 (0.28)	0.8 (0.16)	10.6 (0.39)	5.0 (0.39)	57.7 (0.97)	17.1 (0.57)
Secondary	20,500 (540)	22.8 (0.56)	83.9 (1.04)	39.6 (1.13)	12.2 (0.69)	58.3 (1.02)	14.3 (1.02)	9.3 (0.72)	7.9 (0.63)	4.6 (0.65)	57.3 (1.28)	26.1 (1.16)	81.2 (1.07)	57.6 (1.44)
Combined	8,100 (660)	9.0 (0.74)	83.1 (2.43)	46.1 (2.62)	30.0 (2.51)	60.5 (2.35)	11.2 (1.55)	15.3 (1.96)	16.4 (1.68)	12.3 (2.32)	41.5 (2.58)	30.8 (2.90)	71.9 (2.53)	37.1 (2.25)
Private total	25,700 (610)	100.0 (†)	80.1 (1.50)	42.1 (1.43)	56.9 (1.77)	71.3 (1.49)	2.7 (0.48)	1.7 (0.33)	1.2! (0.42)	0.4! (0.16)	4.1 (0.45)	7.5 (0.93)	40.6 (1.51)	7.2 (0.77)
School enrollment														
Under 100	12,700 (580)	49.5 (1.32)	72.7 (2.57)	38.2 (2.45)	43.8 (2.66)	59.3 (2.67)	2.2 (0.64)	2.4 (0.61)	1.8! (0.83)	‡ (†)	1.6! (0.58)	10.2 (1.50)	24.7 (2.23)	3.7 (0.85)
100 to 299	8,400 (300)	32.8 (1.13)	89.2 (1.43)	46.1 (2.15)	69.0 (2.21)	81.2 (1.74)	1.7! (0.68)	1.0! (0.46)	‡ (†)	‡ (†)	2.7 (0.58)	3.1 (0.75)	50.4 (2.34)	4.7! (1.63)
300 to 499	2,800 (190)	10.8 (0.83)	84.2 (2.56)	48.1 (3.84)	71.6 (3.77)	88.7 (2.35)	3.8! (1.20)	‡ (†)	‡ (†)	‡ (†)	11.1 (2.49)	10.4 (2.33)	56.7 (3.98)	15.1 (2.74)
500 to 999	1,500 (120)	5.7 (0.51)	83.6 (2.87)	39.4 (3.84)	72.6 (4.36)	86.3 (3.17)	9.0 (2.41)	‡ (†)	‡ (†)	‡ (†)	18.9 (3.26)	5.0! (1.92)	80.8 (3.86)	24.2 (3.56)
1,000 or more	300 (60)	1.2 (0.24)	81.6 (7.85)	52.8 (11.06)	55.0 (10.35)	70.6 (9.34)	12.1! (4.88)	‡ (†)	‡ (†)	‡ (†)	13.5! (6.51)	‡ (†)	92.2 (4.54)	66.4 (9.60)
Percent of students approved for free or reduced-price school lunch														
School does not participate	18,900 (590)	73.6 (1.15)	76.6 (1.81)	41.3 (1.76)	52.3 (2.23)	69.5 (1.94)	2.3 (0.53)	1.1 (0.25)	‡ (†)	‡ (†)	4.4 (0.58)	7.5 (1.01)	36.4 (1.73)	7.7 (0.94)
0 to 25 percent	3,400 (240)	13.2 (0.89)	91.2 (2.67)	36.5 (4.08)	75.1 (3.38)	80.2 (2.71)	2.6! (0.83)	‡ (†)	‡ (†)	‡ (†)	3.9 (0.87)	1.5! (0.63)	56.1 (3.33)	2.7! (0.99)
26 to 100 percent	3,400 (230)	13.2 (0.94)	88.5 (3.55)	51.7 (3.79)	64.4 (3.67)	72.9 (3.69)	5.2! (1.91)	4.9! (1.52)	6.1! (2.85)	2.5! (1.13)	2.5! (0.80)	13.4 (3.59)	48.8 (3.71)	9.1 (2.32)
School level[5]														
Elementary	14,500 (500)	56.4 (0.90)	82.0 (2.22)	44.0 (1.99)	60.0 (2.21)	71.2 (2.12)	1.4 (0.40)	0.9! (0.30)	‡ (†)	‡ (†)	‡ (†)	1.5! (0.68)	39.8 (2.18)	3.9 (0.80)
Secondary	2,700 (140)	10.3 (0.57)	71.5 (3.50)	34.0 (4.67)	49.2 (4.55)	70.8 (3.13)	8.2 (1.91)	5.2 (1.47)	‡ (†)	‡ (†)	16.3! (2.36)	20.4 (2.95)	52.0 (5.46)	19.2 (4.77)
Combined	8,600 (210)	33.3 (0.71)	79.6 (2.19)	41.3 (2.49)	53.9 (2.73)	71.7 (2.22)	3.3 (0.97)	2.1! (0.70)	3.0! (1.20)	‡ (†)	7.1 (1.16)	13.7 (2.14)	38.4 (2.61)	9.1 (1.41)

†Not applicable.

‡Reporting standards not met. Either there are too few cases for a reliable estimate or the coefficient of variation (CV) is 50 percent or greater.

!Interpret data with caution. The coefficient of variation (CV) for this estimate is between 30 and 50 percent.

[1]Access to buildings is controlled during school hours (e.g., by locked or monitored doors).

[2]Access to grounds is controlled during school hours (e.g., by locked or monitored gates).

[3]All students must pass through a metal detector each day.

[4]Examples of contraband include drugs and weapons. The "sweeps" category does not include dog sniffs.

[5]Elementary schools have grade 6 or below, with no grade higher than 8; secondary schools have no grade lower than 7; and combined schools have grades lower than 7 and higher than 8.

NOTE: Responses were provided by the principal. Detail may not sum to totals because of rounding.

SOURCE: U.S. Department of Education, National Center for Education Statistics, Schools and Staffing Survey (SASS), "Public School Principal Data File" and "Private School Principal Data File," 2011–12. (This table was prepared October 2013.)

Public and private elementary and secondary teachers, enrollment, pupil/teacher ratios, and new teacher hires: Selected years, fall 1955 through fall 2023

Year	Teachers (in thousands)			Enrollment (in thousands)			Pupil/teacher ratio			Number of new teacher hires (in thousands)[1]		
	Total	Public	Private	Total	Public	Private	Total	Public	Private	Total	Public	Private
1	2	3	4	5	6	7	8	9	10	11	12	13
1955	1,286	1,141	145 [2]	35,280	30,680	4,600 [2]	27.4	26.9	31.7 [2]	—	—	—
1960	1,600	1,408	192 [2]	42,181	36,281	5,900 [2]	26.4	25.8	30.7 [2]	—	—	—
1965	1,933	1,710	223	48,473	42,173	6,300	25.1	24.7	28.3	—	—	—
1970	2,292	2,059	233	51,257	45,894	5,363	22.4	22.3	23.0	—	—	—
1971	2,293	2,063	230 [2]	51,271	46,071	5,200 [2]	22.4	22.3	22.6 [2]	—	—	—
1972	2,337	2,106	231 [2]	50,726	45,726	5,000 [2]	21.7	21.7	21.6 [2]	—	—	—
1973	2,372	2,136	236 [2]	50,445	45,445	5,000 [2]	21.3	21.3	21.2 [2]	—	—	—
1974	2,410	2,165	245 [2]	50,073	45,073	5,000 [2]	20.8	20.8	20.4 [2]	—	—	—
1975	2,453	2,198	255 [2]	49,819	44,819	5,000 [2]	20.3	20.4	19.6 [2]	—	—	—
1976	2,457	2,189	268	49,478	44,311	5,167	20.1	20.2	19.3	—	—	—
1977	2,488	2,209	279	48,717	43,577	5,140	19.6	19.7	18.4	—	—	—
1978	2,479	2,207	272	47,637	42,551	5,086	19.2	19.3	18.7	—	—	—
1979	2,461	2,185	276 [2]	46,651	41,651	5,000 [2]	19.0	19.1	18.1 [2]	—	—	—
1980	2,485	2,184	301	46,208	40,877	5,331	18.6	18.7	17.7	—	—	—
1981	2,440	2,127	313 [2]	45,544	40,044	5,500 [2]	18.7	18.8	17.6 [2]	—	—	—
1982	2,458	2,133	325 [2]	45,166	39,566	5,600 [2]	18.4	18.6	17.2 [2]	—	—	—
1983	2,476	2,139	337	44,967	39,252	5,715	18.2	18.4	17.0	—	—	—
1984	2,508	2,168	340 [2]	44,908	39,208	5,700 [2]	17.9	18.1	16.8 [2]	—	—	—
1985	2,549	2,206	343	44,979	39,422	5,557	17.6	17.9	16.2	—	—	—
1986	2,592	2,244	348 [2]	45,205	39,753	5,452 [2]	17.4	17.7	15.7 [2]	—	—	—
1987	2,631	2,279	352	45,488	40,008	5,479	17.3	17.6	15.6	—	—	—
1988	2,668	2,323	345 [2]	45,430	40,189	5,242 [2]	17.0	17.3	15.2 [2]	—	—	—
1989	2,713	2,357	356	46,141	40,543	5,599	17.0	17.2	15.7	—	—	—
1990	2,759	2,398	361 [2]	46,864	41,217	5,648 [2]	17.0	17.2	15.6 [2]	—	—	—
1991	2,797	2,432	365	47,728	42,047	5,681	17.1	17.3	15.6	—	—	—
1992	2,823	2,459	364 [2]	48,694	42,823	5,870 [2]	17.2	17.4	16.1 [2]	—	—	—
1993	2,868	2,504	364	49,532	43,465	6,067	17.3	17.4	16.7	—	—	—
1994	2,922	2,552	370 [2]	50,106	44,111	5,994 [2]	17.1	17.3	16.2 [2]	—	—	—
1995	2,974	2,598	376	50,759	44,840	5,918	17.1	17.3	15.7	—	—	—
1996	3,051	2,667	384 [2]	51,544	45,611	5,933 [2]	16.9	17.1	15.5 [2]	—	—	—
1997	3,138	2,746	391	52,071	46,127	5,944	16.6	16.8	15.2	—	—	—
1998	3,230	2,830	400 [2]	52,526	46,539	5,988 [2]	16.3	16.4	15.0 [2]	—	—	—
1999	3,319	2,911	408	52,875	46,857	6,018	15.9	16.1	14.7	305	222	83
2000	3,366	2,941	424 [2]	53,373	47,204	6,169 [2]	15.9	16.0	14.5 [2]	—	—	—
2001	3,440	3,000	441	53,992	47,672	6,320	15.7	15.9	14.3	—	—	—
2002	3,476	3,034	442 [2]	54,403	48,183	6,220 [2]	15.7	15.9	14.1 [2]	—	—	—
2003	3,490	3,049	441	54,639	48,540	6,099	15.7	15.9	13.8	311	236	74
2004	3,536	3,091	445 [2]	54,882	48,795	6,087 [2]	15.5	15.8	13.7 [2]	—	—	—
2005	3,593	3,143	450	55,187	49,113	6,073	15.4	15.6	13.5	—	—	—
2006	3,622	3,166	456 [2]	55,307	49,316	5,991 [2]	15.3	15.6	13.2 [2]	—	—	—
2007	3,634	3,178	456	55,203	49,293	5,910	15.2	15.5	13.0	327	246	80
2008	3,670	3,222	448 [2]	54,973	49,266	5,707 [2]	15.0	15.3	12.8 [2]	—	—	—
2009	3,647	3,210	437	54,849	49,361	5,488	15.0	15.4	12.5	—	—	—
2010	3,529	3,099	429 [2]	54,867	49,484	5,382 [2]	15.5	16.0	12.5 [2]	—	—	—
2011	3,524	3,103	421	54,790	49,522	5,268	15.5	16.0	12.5	241	173	68
2012[3]	3,525	3,111	414	54,833	49,652	5,181	15.6	16.0	12.5	245	171	74
2013[3]	3,524	3,118	407	54,842	49,750	5,091	15.6	16.0	12.5	239	170	69
2014[3]	3,515	3,118	397	54,725	49,751	4,974	15.6	16.0	12.5	232	166	66
2015[3]	3,514	3,123	391	54,731	49,839	4,892	15.6	16.0	12.5	241	175	67
2016[3]	3,544	3,155	390	54,790	49,951	4,839	15.5	15.8	12.4	272	202	70
2017[3]	3,593	3,199	394	55,132	50,280	4,852	15.3	15.7	12.3	293	217	76
2018[3]	3,630	3,235	395	55,380	50,543	4,837	15.3	15.6	12.3	289	214	74
2019[3]	3,666	3,269	397	55,671	50,834	4,836	15.2	15.5	12.2	292	217	75
2020[3]	3,699	3,300	398	56,010	51,165	4,844	15.1	15.5	12.2	291	216	76
2021[3]	3,736	3,335	401	56,343	51,485	4,857	15.1	15.4	12.1	296	219	77
2022[3]	3,776	3,371	405	56,684	51,804	4,880	15.0	15.4	12.1	303	225	79
2023[3]	3,817	3,408	409	57,023	52,113	4,910	14.9	15.3	12.0	308	227	80

—Not available.

[1] A teacher is considered to be a new hire for a public or private school if the teacher had not taught in that control of school in the previous year. A teacher who moves from a public to private or a private to public school is considered a new teacher hire, but a teacher who moves from one public school to another public school or one private school to another private school is not considered a new teacher hire.

[2] Estimated.

[3] Projected.

NOTE: Data for teachers are expressed in full-time equivalents (FTE). Counts of private school teachers and enrollment include prekindergarten through grade 12 in schools offering kindergarten or higher grades. Counts of public school teachers and enrollment include prekindergarten through grade 12. The pupil/teacher ratio includes teachers for students with disabilities and other special teachers, while these teachers are generally excluded from class size calculations. Ratios for public schools reflect totals reported by states and differ from totals reported for schools or school districts. Some data have been revised from previously published figures. Detail may not sum to totals because of rounding.

SOURCE: U.S. Department of Education, National Center for Education Statistics, *Statistics of Public Elementary and Secondary Day Schools*, 1955–56 through 1980–81; Common Core of Data (CCD), "State Nonfiscal Survey of Public Elementary/Secondary Education," 1981–82 through 2011–12; Private School Universe Survey (PSS), 1989–90 through 2011–12; Schools and Staffing Survey (SASS), "Public School Teacher Data File" and "Private School Teacher Data File," 1999–2000 through 2011–12; Elementary and Secondary Teacher Projection Model, 1973 through 2023; and New Teacher Hires Projection Model, 1988 through 2023. (This table was prepared February 2014.)

Public elementary and secondary teachers, by level and state or jurisdiction: Selected years, fall 2000 through fall 2011

State or jurisdiction	Fall 2000	Fall 2005	Fall 2007	Fall 2008	Fall 2009	Fall 2010				Fall 2011			
						Total	Elementary	Secondary	Ungraded	Total	Elementary	Secondary	Ungraded
1	2	3	4	5	6	7	8	9	10	11	12	13	14
United States	2,941,461 [1]	3,143,003 [1]	3,178,142 [1]	3,222,154 [1]	3,209,672 [1]	3,099,095 [1]	1,708,057 [1]	1,199,589	191,449	3,103,263 [1]	1,734,606 [1]	1,194,504	174,153
Alabama	48,194 [2]	57,757	50,420	47,818	47,492	49,363	28,057	21,306	0	47,723	26,963	20,759	0
Alaska	7,880	7,912	7,613	7,927	8,083	8,171	5,340	2,830	0	8,088	4,309	3,779	0
Arizona	44,438	51,376	54,032	54,696	51,947	50,031	35,188	14,843	0	50,800	36,058	14,742	0
Arkansas	31,947	32,997	33,882	37,162	37,240	34,273	17,701	14,077	2,496	33,983	17,407	13,974	2,601
California	298,021 [2]	309,222 [2]	305,230 [2]	303,647 [2]	316,299 [2]	260,806 [2]	176,602 [2]	84,199	5	268,689 [2]	174,194 [2]	85,727	8,768
Colorado	41,983	45,841	47,761	48,692	49,060	48,543	27,971	20,572	0	48,078	27,656	20,421	0
Connecticut	41,044	39,687	39,304	48,463	43,593	42,951	27,890	14,030	1,032	43,805	29,185	13,310	1,310
Delaware	7,469	7,998	8,198	8,322	8,640	8,933	4,457	4,476	0	8,587	4,255	4,332	0
District of Columbia	4,949	5,481 [3]	6,347	5,321	5,854	5,925	3,395	2,049	481	6,278	3,781	1,930	568
Florida	132,030	158,962	168,737	186,361	183,827	175,609	76,415	66,619	32,575	175,006	76,703	65,633	32,670
Georgia	91,043	108,535	116,857	118,839	115,918	112,460	68,631	43,775	54	111,133	52,141	43,441	15,551
Hawaii	10,927	11,226	11,397	11,295	11,472	11,396	6,191	5,127	78	11,458	6,278	5,113	68
Idaho	13,714	14,521	15,013	15,148	15,201	15,673	7,486	8,186	0	15,990	7,640	8,351	0
Illinois	127,620	133,857	136,571	135,704	138,483	132,983	90,610	42,373	0	131,777	89,868	41,910	0
Indiana	59,226	60,592	62,334	62,668	62,258	58,121 [2]	32,216 [2]	25,843	62	62,339	42,599	19,740	0
Iowa	34,636	35,181	36,089	35,961	35,842	34,642	24,039	10,604	0	34,658	24,093	10,565	0
Kansas	32,742	33,608	35,359	35,883	34,700	34,644	16,985	16,792	867	37,407	19,700	17,024	684
Kentucky	39,589	42,413	43,536	43,451	41,981	42,042	21,394	9,883	10,765	41,860	21,169	9,907	10,783
Louisiana	49,915	44,660	48,610	49,377	49,646	48,655	33,195	15,460	0	48,657	33,214	15,443	0
Maine	16,559	16,684	16,558	15,912	16,331	15,384	10,596	4,788	0	14,888	10,286	4,602	0
Maryland	52,433	56,685	59,320	58,940	58,463	58,428	34,424	24,004	0	57,589	34,188	23,401	0
Massachusetts	67,432	73,596	70,719	70,398	69,909	68,754	45,441	23,313	0	69,342	45,772	23,571	0
Michigan	97,031	98,069	96,204	94,754	92,691	88,615	35,735	34,850	18,030	86,997	35,137	34,385	17,475
Minnesota	53,457	51,107	52,975	53,083	52,839	52,672	27,629	23,577	1,466	52,832	27,991	23,338	1,503
Mississippi	31,006	31,433	33,560	33,358	33,103	32,255	15,215	12,891	4,149	32,007	15,391	12,557	4,058
Missouri	64,735	67,076	68,430	68,015	67,796	66,735	34,305	32,430	0	66,252	34,141	32,111	0
Montana	10,411	10,369	10,519	10,467	10,521	10,361	7,054	3,307	0	10,153	6,981	3,172	0
Nebraska	20,983	21,359	21,930	22,057	22,256	22,345	13,839	8,506	0	22,182	13,842	8,340	0
Nevada	18,293	21,744	23,423	21,993	22,104	21,839	10,842	8,041	2,956	21,132	10,317	7,769	3,046
New Hampshire	14,341	15,536	15,484	15,661	15,491	15,365	10,402	4,963	0	15,049	10,180	4,869	0
New Jersey	99,061	112,673	111,500	114,713	115,248	110,202	59,333	38,278	12,591	109,719	58,767	37,691	13,262
New Mexico	21,042	22,021	22,300	22,825	22,724	22,437	9,832	8,563	4,043	21,957	9,739	8,182	4,035
New York	206,961	218,989	211,854	217,944	214,804	211,606	101,708	69,357	40,541	209,527	121,569	87,687	271
North Carolina	83,680	95,664	106,562	109,634	105,036 [4]	98,357	49,681	47,549	1,128	97,308	64,599	31,706	1,003
North Dakota	8,141	8,003	8,068	8,181	8,366	8,417	5,431	2,986	0	8,525	5,499	3,026	0
Ohio	118,361	117,982	109,766	112,845	111,378	109,282	53,650	51,887	3,745	107,972	52,065	49,614	6,292
Oklahoma	41,318	41,833	46,735	46,571	42,615	41,278	22,292	18,986	0	41,349	22,545	18,804	0
Oregon	28,094	28,346	30,013	30,152	28,768	28,109	19,717	8,392	0	26,791	18,801	7,990	0
Pennsylvania	116,963	122,397	135,234	129,708	130,984	129,911	61,575	58,513	9,824	124,646	59,431	55,684	9,530
Rhode Island	10,645	14,180 [2]	11,271	11,316	11,366	11,212	5,294	5,918	0	11,414	5,472	5,942	0
South Carolina	45,380	48,212	47,382	49,941	46,980	45,210	31,715	13,495	0	46,782	32,577	14,205	0
South Dakota	9,397	9,129	9,416	9,244	9,326	9,512	6,056	2,573	883	9,247	5,890	2,514	843
Tennessee	57,164	59,596	64,659	64,926	65,361	66,558	45,093	19,315	2,151	66,382	45,212	19,066	2,104
Texas	274,826	302,425	321,929	327,905	333,164	334,997	167,161	133,218	34,618	324,282	162,768	130,424	31,090
Utah	22,008	22,993	24,336	23,657	25,615	25,677	12,859	10,132	2,686	25,970	13,032	10,333	2,605
Vermont	8,414	8,851	8,749	8,766	8,734	8,382	3,315	3,306	1,761	8,364	3,360	3,206	1,798
Virginia	86,977 [2]	103,944	71,861	71,415	70,827	70,947	34,169	36,779	0	90,832	41,909	48,923	0
Washington	51,098	53,508	53,960	54,428	53,448	53,934	28,128	23,490	2,317	53,119	28,113	22,934	2,072
West Virginia	20,930	19,940	20,306	20,209	20,299	20,338	9,509	10,830	0	20,247	9,483	10,765	0
Wisconsin	60,165	60,127	58,914	59,401	58,426	57,625	28,529	28,949	148	56,245	27,873	28,209	163
Wyoming	6,783	6,706	6,915	7,000	7,166	7,127	3,767	3,360	0	7,847	4,461	3,385	0
Bureau of Indian Education	—	—	—	—	—	—	—	—	—	—	—	—	—
DoD, overseas	5,105	5,726	4,147	4,551	—	—	—	—	—	—	—	—	—
DoD, domestic	2,399	2,033	2,243	2,145	—	—	—	—	—	—	—	—	—
Other jurisdictions													
American Samoa	820	989	—	—	—	—	—	—	—	—	—	—	—
Guam	1,975	1,804	—	—	—	1,843	911	932	0	2,291	925	991	375
Northern Marianas	526	614	550	514	552	607	338	266	3	496	292	200	4
Puerto Rico	37,620	42,036	40,826	39,356	39,102	36,506	16,865	14,151	5,490	33,079	15,140	12,618	5,321
U.S. Virgin Islands	1,511	1,434	1,518	1,331	1,425	1,457	617	471	369	1,217	522	399	296

—Not available.
[1] Includes imputed values for states.
[2] Includes imputations for underreporting of prekindergarten teachers.
[3] Imputed.
[4] Includes imputations for underreporting of kindergarten teachers.

NOTE: Distribution of elementary and secondary teachers determined by reporting units. Teachers reported in full-time equivalents (FTE). DoD = Department of Defense. Some data have been revised from previously published figures.
SOURCE: U.S. Department of Education, National Center for Education Statistics, Common Core of Data (CCD), "State Nonfiscal Survey of Public Elementary/Secondary Education," 2000–01 through 2011–12. (This table was prepared August 2013.)

Public elementary and secondary teachers, enrollment, and pupil/teacher ratios, by state or jurisdiction: Selected years, fall 2000 through fall 2011

State or jurisdiction	Pupil/teacher ratio				Fall 2009			Fall 2010			Fall 2011		
	Fall 2000	Fall 2006	Fall 2007	Fall 2008	Teachers	Enrollment	Pupil/teacher ratio	Teachers	Enrollment	Pupil/teacher ratio	Teachers	Enrollment	Pupil/teacher ratio
1	2	3	4	5	6	7	8	9	10	11	12	13	14
United States	16.0 [1]	15.6 [1]	15.5 [1]	15.3 [1]	3,209,672 [1]	49,360,982	15.4 [1]	3,099,095 [1]	49,484,181	16.0 [1]	3,103,263 [1]	49,521,669	16.0 [1]
Alabama	15.4 [2]	13.2	14.8	15.6	47,492	748,889	15.8	49,363	755,552	15.3	47,723	744,621	15.6
Alaska	16.9	16.8	17.2	16.5	8,083	131,661	16.3	8,171	132,104	16.2	8,088	131,167	16.2
Arizona	19.8	20.3	20.1	19.9	51,947	1,077,831	20.7	50,031	1,071,751	21.4	50,800	1,080,319	21.3
Arkansas	14.1	13.6	14.1	12.9	37,240	480,559	12.9	34,273	482,114	14.1	33,983	483,114	14.2
California	20.6 [2]	20.8 [2]	20.8 [2]	20.8 [2]	316,299 [2]	6,263,438	19.8 [2]	260,806 [2]	6,289,578	24.1 [2]	268,689 [2]	6,287,834	23.4 [2]
Colorado	17.3	16.9	16.8	16.8	49,060	832,368	17.0	48,543	843,316	17.4	48,078	854,265	17.8
Connecticut	13.7	14.7	14.5	11.7	43,593	563,968	12.9	42,951	560,546	13.1	43,805	554,437	12.7
Delaware	15.4	15.2	15.0	15.1	8,640	126,801	14.7	8,933	129,403	14.5	8,587	128,946	15.0
District of Columbia	13.9	13.5 [3]	12.4	12.9	5,854	69,433	11.9	5,925	71,284	12.0	6,278	73,911	11.8
Florida	18.4	16.4	15.8	14.1	183,827	2,634,522	14.3	175,609	2,643,347	15.1	175,006	2,668,156	15.2
Georgia	15.9	14.3	14.1	13.9	115,918	1,667,685	14.4	112,460	1,677,067	14.9	111,133	1,685,016	15.2
Hawaii	16.9	16.0	15.8	15.9	11,472	180,196	15.7	11,396	179,601	15.8	11,458	182,706	15.9
Idaho	17.9	18.1	18.1	18.2	15,201	276,299	18.2	15,673	275,859	17.6	15,990	279,873	17.5
Illinois	16.1	15.0	15.5	15.6	138,483	2,104,175	15.2	132,983	2,091,654	15.7	131,777	2,083,097	15.8
Indiana	16.7	17.0	16.8	16.7	62,258	1,046,661	16.8	58,121 [2]	1,047,232	18.0 [2]	62,339	1,040,765	16.7
Iowa	14.3	13.6	13.4	13.6	35,842	491,842	13.7	34,642	495,775	14.3	34,658	495,870	14.3
Kansas	14.4	13.3	13.2	13.1	34,700	474,489	13.7	34,644	483,701	14.0	37,407	486,108	13.0
Kentucky	16.8	15.8	15.3	15.4	41,981	680,089	16.2	42,042	673,128	16.0	41,860	681,987	16.3
Louisiana	14.9	14.7	14.0	13.9	49,646	690,915	13.9	48,655	696,558	14.3	48,657	703,390	14.5
Maine	12.5	11.5	11.9	12.1	16,331	189,225	11.6	15,384	189,077	12.3	14,888	188,969	12.7
Maryland	16.3	14.6	14.3	14.3	58,463	848,412	14.5	58,428	852,211	14.6	57,589	854,086	14.8
Massachusetts	14.5	13.2	13.6	13.6	69,909	957,053	13.7	68,754	955,563	13.9	69,342	953,369	13.7
Michigan	17.7 [2]	17.6	17.6	17.5	92,691	1,649,082	17.8	88,615	1,587,067	17.9	86,997	1,573,537	18.1
Minnesota	16.0	16.2	15.8	15.7	52,839	837,053	15.8	52,672	838,037	15.9	52,832	839,738	15.9
Mississippi	16.1	15.3	14.7	14.7	33,103	492,481	14.9	32,255	490,526	15.2	32,007	490,619	15.3
Missouri	14.1	13.6	13.4	13.5	67,796	917,982	13.5	66,735	918,710	13.8	66,252	916,584	13.8
Montana	14.9	13.9	13.6	13.6	10,521	141,807	13.5	10,361	141,693	13.7	10,153	142,349	14.0
Nebraska	13.6	13.4	13.3	13.3	22,256	295,368	13.3	22,345	298,500	13.4	22,182	301,296	13.6
Nevada	18.6	18.5	18.3	19.7	22,104	428,947	19.4	21,839	437,149	20.0	21,132	439,634	20.8
New Hampshire	14.5	13.1	13.0	12.6	15,491	197,140	12.7	15,365	194,711	12.7	15,049	191,900	12.8
New Jersey	13.3	12.4	12.4	12.0	115,248	1,396,029	12.1	110,202	1,402,548	12.7	109,719	1,356,431	12.4
New Mexico	15.2	14.9	14.8	14.5	22,724	334,419	14.7	22,437	338,122	15.1	21,957	337,225	15.4
New York	13.9	13.1	13.1	12.6	214,804	2,766,052	12.9	211,606	2,734,955	12.9	209,527	2,704,718	12.9
North Carolina	15.5	12.9	14.0	13.6	105,036 [4]	1,483,397	14.1	98,357	1,490,605	15.2	97,308	1,507,864	15.5
North Dakota	13.4	12.1	11.8	11.6	8,366	95,073	11.4	8,417	96,323	11.4	8,525	97,646	11.5
Ohio	15.5	16.6	16.6	16.1	111,378	1,764,297	15.8	109,282	1,754,191	16.1	107,972	1,740,030	16.1
Oklahoma	15.1	15.1	13.7	13.9	42,615	654,802	15.4	41,278	659,911	16.0	41,349	666,120	16.1
Oregon	19.4	18.8	18.8	19.1	28,768	582,839	20.3	28,109	570,720	20.3	26,791	568,208	21.2
Pennsylvania	15.5	15.2	13.3	13.7	130,984	1,785,993	13.6	129,911	1,793,284	13.8	124,646	1,771,395	14.2
Rhode Island	14.8	13.3	13.1	12.8	11,366	145,118	12.8	11,212	143,793	12.8	11,414	142,854	12.5
South Carolina	14.9	14.4	15.0	14.4	46,980	723,143	15.4	45,210	725,838	16.1	46,782	727,186	15.5
South Dakota	13.7	13.4	12.9	13.7	9,326	123,713	13.3	9,512	126,128	13.3	9,247	128,016	13.8
Tennessee	15.9 [2]	15.7	14.9	15.0	65,361	972,549	14.9	66,558	987,422	14.8	66,382	999,693	15.1
Texas	14.8	14.8	14.5	14.5	333,164	4,850,210	14.6	334,997	4,935,715	14.7	324,282	5,000,470	15.4
Utah	21.9	22.1	23.7	23.7	25,615	571,586	22.3	25,677	585,552	22.8	25,970	598,832	23.1
Vermont	12.1	10.8	10.7	10.7	8,734	91,451	10.5	8,382	96,858	11.6	8,364	89,908	10.7
Virginia	13.2 [2]	15.3	17.1	17.3	70,827	1,245,340	17.6	70,947	1,251,440	17.6	90,832	1,257,883	13.8
Washington	19.7	19.1	19.1	19.1	53,448	1,035,347	19.4	53,934	1,043,788	19.4	53,119	1,045,453	19.7
West Virginia	13.7	14.4	13.9	14.0	20,299	282,662	13.9	20,338	282,879	13.9	20,247	282,870	14.0
Wisconsin	14.6	14.8	14.8	14.7	58,426	872,436	14.9	57,625	872,286	15.1	56,245	871,105	15.5
Wyoming	13.3	12.6	12.5	12.5	7,166	88,155	12.3	7,127	89,009	12.5	7,847	90,099	11.5
Bureau of Indian Education	—	—	—	—	—	41,351	—	—	41,962	—	—	—	—
DoD, overseas	14.4	11.7	13.8	12.5	—	—	—	—	—	—	—	—	—
DoD, domestic	14.2	13.1	12.3	13.1	—	—	—	—	—	—	—	—	—
Other jurisdictions													
American Samoa	19.1	16.9	—	—	—	—	—	—	—	—	—	—	—
Guam	16.4	—	—	—	—	—	—	1,843	31,618	17.2	2,291	31,243	13.6
Northern Marianas	19.0	20.2	20.5	21.2	552	10,961	19.9	607	11,105	18.3	496	11,011	22.2
Puerto Rico	16.3	13.5	12.9	12.8	39,102	493,393	12.6	36,506	473,735	13.0	33,079	452,740	13.7
U.S. Virgin Islands	12.9	10.6	10.5	11.8	1,425	15,493	10.9	1,457	15,495	10.6	1,217	15,711	12.9

—Not available.
[1]Includes imputed values for states.
[2]Includes imputations to correct for underreporting of prekindergarten teachers/enrollment.
[3]Imputed.
[4]Includes imputations to correct for underreporting of kindergarten teachers.
NOTE: Teachers reported in full-time equivalents (FTE). DoD = Department of Defense. The pupil/teacher ratio includes teachers for students with disabilities and other special teachers, while these teachers are generally excluded from class size calculations. Ratios reflect totals reported by states and differ from totals reported for schools or school districts.
SOURCE: U.S. Department of Education, National Center for Education Statistics, Common Core of Data (CCD), "State Nonfiscal Survey of Public Elementary/Secondary Education," 2000–01 through 2011–12. (This table was prepared August 2013.)

Highest degree earned, years of full-time teaching experience, and average class size for teachers in public elementary and secondary schools, by state: 2011–12

[Standard errors appear in parentheses]

State	Total number of teachers (in thousands)	Percent of teachers, by highest degree earned — Less than bachelor's	Bachelor's	Master's	Education specialist[2] or doctor's	Percent of teachers, by years of full-time teaching experience — Less than 3	3 to 9	10 to 20	Over 20	Average class size, by level of instruction[1] — Elementary	Secondary
1	2	3	4	5	6	7	8	9	10	11	12
United States	3,385.2 (41.42)	3.8 (0.24)	39.9 (0.52)	47.7 (0.57)	8.7 (0.28)	9.0 (0.29)	33.3 (0.52)	36.4 (0.51)	21.3 (0.54)	21.2 (0.18)	26.8 (0.22)
Alabama	45.0 (2.61)	3.8 ! (1.51)	34.5 (2.69)	52.8 (2.81)	8.9 (1.64)	8.0 (1.28)	30.9 (2.75)	39.2 (2.85)	21.9 (2.34)	19.2 (0.42)	27.4 (0.94)
Alaska	7.5 (0.70)	4.4 ! (1.78)	45.6 (4.44)	41.9 (4.01)	8.2 (2.37)	12.9 (3.30)	30.8 (4.15)	39.6 (4.16)	16.7 (3.76)	18.3 (1.35)	18.7 (1.22)
Arizona	61.7 (2.61)	4.6 ! (1.16)	44.4 (3.67)	44.1 (3.49)	6.9 (1.71)	16.4 (2.29)	38.0 (2.75)	37.8 (2.60)	17.2 (2.02)	24.1 (0.67)	27.7 (0.96)
Arkansas	37.7 (2.01)	3.7 ! (1.45)	54.7 (3.36)	35.0 (3.13)	6.6 (1.72)	11.5 (2.03)	28.9 (3.38)	32.3 (3.93)	27.3 (3.37)	20.4 (0.73)	25.4 (1.69)
California	285.5 (7.27)	4.8 (0.91)	43.4 (2.33)	39.2 (2.18)	12.7 (1.56)	9.4 (1.29)	29.1 (2.13)	42.3 (2.25)	19.1 (1.89)	25.0 (0.52)	32.0 (0.53)
Colorado	55.9 (3.14)	2.8 ! (1.00)	36.1 (3.51)	49.9 (4.26)	11.2 (2.79)	10.8 (2.25)	33.4 (3.50)	42.9 (3.96)	12.9 (2.51)	20.3 (1.29)	29.1 (1.25)
Connecticut	44.9 (2.51)	‡ (†)	15.3 (1.86)	64.4 (3.01)	17.7 (2.37)	10.0 (1.43)	29.1 (2.66)	37.1 (2.43)	23.8 (3.34)	19.6 (0.68)	22.0 (0.71)
Delaware	9.3 (0.70)	4.0 ! (1.50)	34.5 (4.36)	49.7 (4.55)	11.8 (2.85)	12.6 (3.31)	35.0 (3.59)	33.8 (4.04)	18.6 (2.75)	20.3 (0.82)	25.8 (2.09)
District of Columbia	‡ (†)	‡ (†)	‡ (†)	‡ (†)	‡ (†)	‡ (†)	‡ (†)	‡ (†)	‡ (†)	‡ (†)	‡ (†)
Florida	‡ (†)	‡ (†)	‡ (†)	‡ (†)	‡ (†)	‡ (†)	‡ (†)	‡ (†)	‡ (†)	‡ (†)	‡ (†)
Georgia	123.3 (3.97)	3.4 ! (1.15)	29.5 (3.48)	43.5 (3.79)	23.6 (3.00)	6.3 (1.70)	34.2 (3.42)	39.8 (3.34)	19.7 (2.58)	21.0 (0.91)	27.5 (1.42)
Hawaii	‡ (†)	‡ (†)	‡ (†)	‡ (†)	‡ (†)	‡ (†)	‡ (†)	‡ (†)	‡ (†)	‡ (†)	‡ (†)
Idaho	16.3 (1.83)	4.6 (1.37)	55.6 (3.30)	35.3 (3.18)	4.4 (1.20)	10.4 (1.93)	30.4 (3.18)	35.2 (3.02)	24.0 (2.89)	24.5 (0.63)	25.4 (2.13)
Illinois	140.9 (9.09)	2.7 ! (0.81)	32.6 (2.53)	57.8 (2.44)	7.0 (1.34)	9.3 (1.56)	36.4 (2.59)	34.4 (2.85)	20.0 (2.51)	22.9 (1.26)	25.7 (1.00)
Indiana	64.0 (2.98)	2.2 (0.52)	43.6 (3.04)	47.4 (3.29)	6.9 (1.45)	10.0 (1.92)	26.1 (2.42)	35.6 (3.01)	28.3 (3.02)	21.4 (0.45)	27.3 (1.07)
Iowa	36.5 (2.28)	3.5 ! (0.83)	52.8 (3.89)	39.7 (3.66)	4.1 ! (1.26)	8.8 (1.85)	29.0 (2.98)	33.0 (2.77)	29.2 (2.55)	20.3 (0.93)	27.4 (1.35)
Kansas	36.5 (2.27)	3.8 (0.83)	43.8 (3.52)	47.0 (2.58)	5.4 (1.38)	12.5 (2.98)	27.4 (3.00)	32.7 (3.15)	27.4 (2.83)	20.4 (0.86)	24.6 (1.21)
Kentucky	46.8 (2.51)	5.1 (1.72)	17.5 (2.24)	57.5 (2.68)	20.0 (2.11)	10.1 (1.83)	32.2 (2.82)	38.5 (2.81)	19.2 (2.10)	23.3 (1.92)	26.6 (1.09)
Louisiana	44.5 (2.39)	3.5 ! (1.22)	61.9 (3.12)	27.0 (2.68)	6.0 (1.55)	8.6 (1.51)	31.2 (3.13)	38.1 (2.31)	22.0 (3.10)	19.6 (0.80)	23.4 (0.78)
Maine	18.4 (0.90)	4.9 ! (1.60)	46.3 (3.41)	42.8 (3.30)	6.0 (1.36)	5.8 (1.47)	24.1 (2.57)	39.4 (3.32)	30.6 (2.81)	17.6 (0.64)	19.9 (1.76)
Maryland	‡ (†)	‡ (†)	‡ (†)	‡ (†)	‡ (†)	‡ (†)	‡ (†)	‡ (†)	‡ (†)	‡ (†)	‡ (†)
Massachusetts	79.2 (4.42)	3.9 (1.08)	21.8 (2.33)	67.5 (2.54)	6.8 (1.48)	12.4 (1.96)	33.4 (3.04)	36.8 (3.02)	17.4 (3.09)	19.9 (1.72)	24.5 (1.18)
Michigan	96.7 (3.73)	2.3 (0.55)	29.8 (2.50)	62.9 (2.52)	5.0 (1.40)	7.3 (1.00)	31.4 (2.68)	42.7 (2.44)	18.7 (2.12)	23.8 (0.93)	28.9 (0.81)
Minnesota	62.3 (2.99)	4.4 (0.77)	35.3 (3.16)	50.1 (2.80)	10.2 (1.40)	9.5 (1.20)	27.4 (2.05)	40.3 (2.14)	22.9 (2.00)	21.6 (0.70)	22.9 (0.86)
Mississippi	37.6 (2.11)	5.3 (1.45)	54.4 (3.87)	35.2 (3.57)	5.1 (1.51)	10.3 (1.97)	41.0 (3.45)	35.6 (3.35)	18.2 (3.18)	21.6 (1.01)	22.8 (1.15)
Missouri	68.7 (2.34)	4.4 (0.91)	33.3 (2.90)	57.5 (2.96)	4.8 (0.94)	10.4 (1.90)	35.3 (2.21)	35.2 (2.31)	19.2 (2.31)	20.2 (0.83)	26.8 (1.18)
Montana	12.4 (0.90)	6.4 (1.32)	55.2 (3.34)	34.6 (3.39)	3.7 ! (1.66)	9.6 (2.33)	37.2 (3.17)	34.6 (3.04)	28.6 (3.65)	18.9 (0.80)	21.7 (1.81)
Nebraska	23.9 (1.73)	5.5 (1.31)	44.9 (3.29)	45.9 (3.15)	3.8 ! (0.98)	10.6 (1.74)	27.4 (2.52)	36.2 (2.63)	27.6 (2.54)	23.0 (0.72)	23.5 (0.99)
Nevada	25.2 (2.63)	4.5 ! (1.85)	25.1 (3.92)	49.8 (4.26)	20.6 (3.23)	6.5 ! (2.17)	39.0 (4.02)	36.2 (4.29)	18.2 (3.55)	25.3 (1.41)	34.5 (1.54)
New Hampshire	15.7 (1.05)	3.0 ! (1.12)	40.2 (3.49)	48.7 (3.55)	8.1 (1.82)	8.1 (1.54)	32.8 (3.41)	31.5 (3.57)	27.5 (3.54)	20.4 (3.09)	21.7 (1.16)
New Jersey	125.2 (4.16)	3.0 ! (0.74)	48.5 (2.47)	40.8 (2.30)	7.6 (1.60)	7.3 (1.24)	35.4 (2.45)	37.4 (2.66)	20.0 (2.03)	18.5 (0.81)	23.7 (0.68)
New Mexico	21.7 (2.83)	4.3 ! (2.01)	43.3 (3.80)	42.1 (3.72)	10.3 (2.82)	8.0 (2.46)	30.9 (3.73)	40.3 (5.11)	20.8 (5.19)	19.8 (0.76)	23.7 (1.58)
New York	241.4 (14.58)	2.8 ! (1.00)	4.4 ! (1.09)	84.2 (1.56)	8.6 (1.32)	5.3 (1.38)	30.0 (2.81)	34.8 (2.35)	30.0 (2.41)	20.7 (1.36)	25.1 (0.96)
North Carolina	104.3 (5.71)	4.1 ! (1.57)	54.2 (3.16)	33.8 (2.80)	7.8 (1.84)	8.4 (1.52)	35.8 (3.13)	34.5 (3.05)	21.1 (2.74)	18.8 (0.65)	25.8 (0.96)
North Dakota	10.3 (0.74)	6.9 (1.63)	59.2 (3.08)	30.1 (2.60)	3.9 (1.13)	12.2 (2.09)	24.6 (3.06)	30.6 (3.28)	32.6 (3.45)	17.8 (0.60)	19.2 (1.41)
Ohio	122.1 (4.29)	5.3 (1.17)	24.0 (1.79)	64.5 (2.16)	6.2 (1.28)	7.1 (1.11)	28.8 (2.48)	40.8 (2.67)	23.3 (2.00)	20.7 (0.99)	26.7 (0.85)
Oklahoma	46.2 (2.49)	4.3 (1.04)	65.6 (2.66)	26.9 (2.56)	3.2 ! (1.12)	9.8 (1.84)	30.1 (2.58)	36.9 (2.93)	23.3 (2.27)	20.4 (0.56)	23.3 (1.31)
Oregon	31.8 (1.28)	4.2 (1.53)	26.3 (3.18)	59.8 (3.62)	9.7 (1.94)	7.2 (1.54)	37.0 (2.55)	35.6 (3.58)	20.2 (2.45)	26.4 (0.88)	30.0 (1.60)
Pennsylvania	148.8 (7.48)	4.5 ! (1.94)	32.9 (2.52)	53.9 (3.34)	8.7 (1.77)	6.2 (1.78)	37.0 (2.55)	35.8 (2.17)	21.0 (2.30)	22.4 (0.99)	25.2 (1.05)
Rhode Island	‡ (†)	‡ (†)	‡ (†)	‡ (†)	‡ (†)	‡ (†)	‡ (†)	‡ (†)	‡ (†)	‡ (†)	‡ (†)
South Carolina	51.8 (1.76)	3.0 ! (1.34)	28.8 (3.14)	57.9 (3.95)	10.3 (2.15)	8.4 (1.58)	30.5 (3.22)	32.3 (3.54)	28.9 (3.38)	19.1 (0.75)	26.0 (1.98)
South Dakota	10.8 (0.92)	2.3 ! (0.73)	68.8 (3.52)	26.6 (3.13)	2.3 ! (1.14)	8.8 (1.65)	24.6 (2.76)	33.7 (3.63)	33.7 (3.28)	20.4 (0.66)	22.3 (1.31)
Tennessee	76.5 (2.91)	4.4 ! (1.52)	35.1 (3.54)	46.3 (3.44)	14.2 (2.83)	8.6 (1.80)	34.0 (3.66)	34.1 (3.48)	21.3 (1.74)	17.7 (0.52)	26.9 (1.60)
Texas	350.8 (22.99)	3.3 (0.65)	66.4 (2.09)	25.8 (2.12)	4.6 (0.77)	9.0 (0.95)	40.4 (2.05)	34.1 (1.88)	19.7 (2.73)	18.2 (0.82)	26.5 (1.07)
Utah	27.9 (1.67)	4.2 (1.10)	56.8 (3.96)	27.3 (3.88)	11.7 (3.94)	15.0 (2.43)	39.9 (4.49)	25.6 (4.52)	19.5 (3.12)	27.4 (2.09)	31.5 (1.29)
Vermont	9.4 (0.34)	6.6 (1.46)	35.4 (2.78)	52.0 (2.87)	6.0 (1.59)	12.9 (1.60)	22.1 (2.38)	37.0 (2.56)	28.0 (2.73)	16.6 (0.40)	19.8 (1.25)
Virginia	88.5 (3.35)	3.3 ! (1.07)	47.5 (3.08)	41.6 (3.17)	7.6 (1.26)	7.6 (1.68)	31.5 (3.20)	34.2 (2.73)	25.2 (2.43)	20.4 (1.27)	23.8 (0.90)
Washington	55.5 (3.15)	2.9 (0.59)	23.1 (2.61)	62.9 (2.92)	11.1 (1.96)	6.2 (1.45)	32.2 (3.00)	34.8 (2.82)	26.8 (3.03)	23.7 (0.60)	29.7 (0.99)
West Virginia	24.2 (0.79)	3.1 (0.90)	46.6 (4.82)	43.2 (4.71)	7.1 (1.73)	12.0 (2.26)	31.2 (4.12)	30.5 (3.82)	26.3 (3.24)	18.7 (1.00)	24.0 (1.65)
Wisconsin	66.8 (3.42)	2.7 (0.79)	36.7 (2.96)	55.1 (2.98)	5.5 (1.41)	10.5 (1.67)	26.2 (3.21)	42.1 (3.24)	21.3 (2.73)	20.8 (0.55)	20.9 (0.95)
Wyoming	8.5 (0.57)	7.0 ! (3.08)	44.3 (4.47)	41.2 (4.18)	7.5 ! (2.74)	7.6 ! (2.62)	25.2 (4.09)	35.1 (3.73)	32.1 (4.30)	17.0 (1.05)	19.6 (1.22)

†Not applicable.

!Interpret data with caution. The coefficient of variation (CV) for this estimate is between 30 and 50 percent.

‡Reporting standards not met. Data may be suppressed because the response rate is under 50 percent, there are too few cases for a reliable estimate, or the coefficient of variation (CV) is 50 percent or greater.

[1] Elementary teachers are those who teach self-contained classes at the elementary level, and secondary teachers are those who taught departmentalized classes (e.g., science, art, social science, or other course subjects) at the secondary level. Teachers were classified as elementary or secondary on the basis of the grades they taught, rather than on the level of the school in which they taught. In general, elementary teachers include those teaching prekindergarten through grade 5 and those teaching multiple grades, with a preponderance of grades taught being kindergarten through grade 6. In general, secondary teachers include those teaching any of grades 7 through 12 and those teaching multiple grades, with a preponderance of grades taught being grades 7 through 12 and usually with no grade taught being lower than grade 5.

[2] Education specialist degrees or certificates are generally awarded for 1 year's work beyond the master's level. Includes certificate of advanced graduate studies.

NOTE: Data are based on a head count of all teachers rather than on the number of full-time-equivalent teachers appearing in other tables. Excludes prekindergarten teachers. Detail may not sum to totals because of rounding and cell suppression.

SOURCE: U.S. Department of Education, National Center for Education Statistics, Schools and Staffing Survey (SASS), "Public School Teacher Data File, 2011–12. (This table was prepared May 2013.)

Percentage of teachers indicating that certain issues are serious problems in their schools, by level and control of school: Selected years, 1987–88 through 2011–12

[Standard errors appear in parentheses]

Control of school and issue	1987–88 total	1993–94 total	1999–2000 total	2003–04 Total[1]	2003–04 Elementary schools	2003–04 Secondary schools	2007–08 Total	2007–08 Elementary schools	2007–08 Secondary schools	2007–08 Combined schools	2011–12 Total	2011–12 Elementary schools	2011–12 Secondary schools	2011–12 Combined schools
1	2	3	4	5	6	7	8	9	10	11	12	13	14	15
Public schools														
Student tardiness	10.5 (0.18)	10.5 (0.28)	10.2 (0.22)	13.8 (0.29)	9.8 (0.38)	23.1 (0.58)	9.8 (0.33)	5.8 (0.37)	17.9 (0.65)	9.0 (1.36)	11.9 (0.33)	8.5 (0.49)	17.6 (0.55)	16.4 (1.11)
Student absenteeism	16.4 (0.23)	14.4 (0.29)	13.9 (0.26)	13.1 (0.31)	8.3 (0.36)	23.7 (0.59)	11.7 (0.36)	6.5 (0.42)	21.4 (0.63)	14.2 (0.95)	13.9 (0.35)	8.6 (0.49)	22.6 (0.63)	21.9 (1.48)
Teacher absenteeism	2.3 (0.09)	1.5 (0.09)	2.2 (0.10)	1.1 (0.08)	0.9 (0.12)	1.7 (0.15)	1.5 (0.15)	1.2 (0.20)	2.0 (0.20)	2.3 (0.48)	1.6 (0.14)	1.3 (0.16)	1.8 (0.20)	3.3 (0.58)
Students cutting class	5.9 (0.16)	5.1 (0.12)	4.7 (0.13)	5.5 (0.23)	1.5 (0.12)	14.5 (0.59)	4.0 (0.20)	0.5 (0.12)	10.9 (0.52)	4.0 (0.64)	4.9 (0.22)	1.2 (0.16)	10.8 (0.47)	10.4 (1.05)
Physical conflicts among students	5.8 (0.18)	8.2 (0.25)	4.8 (0.19)	12.1 (0.29)	13.7 (0.43)	9.3 (0.38)	— (†)	— (†)	— (†)	— (†)	— (†)	— (†)	— (†)	— (†)
Robbery or theft	3.7 (0.15)	4.1 (0.17)	2.4 (0.11)	3.7 (0.17)	2.9 (0.23)	5.9 (0.24)	— (†)	— (†)	— (†)	— (†)	— (†)	— (†)	— (†)	— (†)
Vandalism of school property	6.1 (0.15)	6.7 (0.23)	3.4 (0.15)	3.7 (0.16)	2.5 (0.21)	6.3 (0.33)	— (†)	— (†)	— (†)	— (†)	— (†)	— (†)	— (†)	— (†)
Student pregnancy	6.9 (0.17)	7.3 (0.24)	3.7 (0.12)	2.4 (0.12)	‡ (†)	7.0 (0.34)	— (†)	— (†)	— (†)	— (†)	— (†)	— (†)	— (†)	— (†)
Student use of alcohol	11.4 (0.21)	9.3 (0.17)	7.4 (0.14)	3.0 (0.10)	0.3 (0.07)	9.0 (0.28)	— (†)	— (†)	— (†)	— (†)	— (†)	— (†)	— (†)	— (†)
Student drug abuse	8.0 (0.14)	5.7 (0.14)	6.0 (0.11)	4.5 (0.14)	0.5 (0.10)	13.0 (0.35)	— (†)	— (†)	— (†)	— (†)	— (†)	— (†)	— (†)	— (†)
Student possession of weapons	1.7 (0.06)	2.8 (0.12)	0.8 (0.06)	0.5 (0.05)	‡ (†)	1.2 (0.12)	— (†)	— (†)	— (†)	— (†)	— (†)	— (†)	— (†)	— (†)
Verbal abuse of teachers	8.1 (0.21)	11.1 (0.26)	— (†)	11.8 (0.31)	9.3 (0.39)	17.1 (0.50)	— (†)	— (†)	— (†)	— (†)	— (†)	— (†)	— (†)	— (†)
Student disrespect for teachers	— (†)	18.5 (0.35)	17.2 (0.34)	21.6 (0.45)	18.6 (0.62)	28.3 (0.58)	— (†)	— (†)	— (†)	— (†)	— (†)	— (†)	— (†)	— (†)
Students dropping out	— (†)	5.8 (0.16)	4.6 (0.11)	3.3 (0.13)	0.4 (0.08)	9.6 (0.41)	3.5 (0.19)	0.8 (0.19)	8.7 (0.41)	5.3 (0.77)	3.1 (0.17)	0.9 (0.16)	6.3 (0.39)	7.7 (0.85)
Student apathy	— (†)	23.6 (0.35)	20.6 (0.30)	16.6 (0.34)	9.9 (0.40)	30.4 (0.56)	16.5 (0.45)	10.0 (0.55)	28.5 (0.67)	21.4 (1.16)	20.0 (0.44)	13.4 (0.61)	31.4 (0.74)	27.3 (1.41)
Lack of parental involvement	— (†)	27.6 (0.45)	23.7 (0.36)	21.6 (0.42)	19.3 (0.58)	26.3 (0.59)	19.5 (0.49)	16.8 (0.68)	24.0 (0.69)	23.5 (1.42)	24.6 (0.54)	22.1 (0.77)	28.3 (0.65)	29.4 (1.55)
Poverty	— (†)	19.5 (0.52)	19.2 (0.43)	21.4 (0.45)	22.4 (0.64)	19.0 (0.57)	22.1 (0.59)	22.8 (0.83)	20.2 (0.68)	26.7 (1.36)	29.0 (0.59)	29.5 (0.86)	26.8 (0.79)	32.4 (2.00)
Students come unprepared to learn	— (†)	28.8 (0.39)	29.5 (0.36)	26.8 (0.46)	23.7 (0.68)	33.5 (0.69)	24.2 (0.56)	20.7 (0.84)	30.5 (0.77)	28.5 (1.45)	30.2 (0.59)	27.1 (0.86)	35.4 (0.85)	34.9 (1.54)
Poor student health	— (†)	— (†)	— (†)	— (†)	— (†)	— (†)	3.3 (0.20)	3.4 (0.30)	2.8 (0.21)	4.2 (0.50)	5.0 (0.25)	5.1 (0.38)	4.4 (0.37)	6.3 (0.63)
Private schools														
Student tardiness	3.6 (0.38)	2.6 (0.23)	2.9 (0.21)	2.8 (0.40)	2.1 (0.45)	5.0 (0.83)	2.5 (0.28)	2.3 (0.37)	3.0 (0.83)	2.6 (0.47)	3.8 (0.59)	3.7 (0.61)	4.9 (1.11)	‡ (†)
Student absenteeism	3.7 (0.39)	2.2 (0.19)	2.5 (0.22)	1.9 (0.23)	0.9 (0.17)	4.0 (0.75)	2.0 (0.23)	0.9 (0.23)	3.9 (0.99)	2.3 (0.40)	3.0 (0.34)	2.1 (0.44)	4.6 (0.99)	‡ (†)
Teacher absenteeism	0.8 (0.13)	0.8 (0.10)	0.8 (0.11)	‡ (†)	‡ (†)	‡ (†)	0.5 (0.13)	0.3 ! (0.08)	‡ (†)	1.0 ! (0.32)	0.5 (0.12)	‡ (†)	0.7 ! (0.28)	‡ (†)
Students cutting class	0.9 (0.16)	0.7 (0.11)	0.8 (0.12)	0.5 (0.11)	‡ (†)	‡ (†)	0.5 ! (0.18)	‡ (†)	1.1 ! (0.41)	‡ (†)	0.7 (0.20)	‡ (†)	‡ (†)	‡ (†)
Physical conflicts among students	1.3 (0.19)	1.5 (0.15)	1.0 (0.18)	2.4 (0.31)	2.7 (0.55)	‡ (†)	— (†)	— (†)	— (†)	— (†)	— (†)	— (†)	— (†)	— (†)
Robbery or theft	1.3 (0.19)	0.8 (0.10)	0.9 (0.11)	0.4 (0.10)	‡ (†)	1.3 ! (0.40)	— (†)	— (†)	— (†)	— (†)	— (†)	— (†)	— (†)	— (†)
Vandalism of school property	1.3 (0.19)	1.2 (0.11)	0.7 (0.11)	0.5 (0.11)	‡ (†)	‡ (†)	— (†)	— (†)	— (†)	— (†)	— (†)	— (†)	— (†)	— (†)
Student pregnancy	0.6 (0.12)	0.4 (0.06)	0.4 (0.09)	0.7 (†)	‡ (†)	3.3 (0.86)	— (†)	— (†)	— (†)	— (†)	— (†)	— (†)	— (†)	— (†)
Student use of alcohol	3.6 (0.30)	3.1 (0.19)	3.1 (0.16)	1.1 (0.17)	‡ (†)	5.2 (1.31)	— (†)	— (†)	— (†)	— (†)	— (†)	— (†)	— (†)	— (†)
Student drug abuse	1.8 (0.18)	1.3 (0.15)	1.8 (0.14)	1.1 (0.25)	‡ (†)	— (†)	— (†)	— (†)	— (†)	— (†)	— (†)	— (†)	— (†)	— (†)
Student possession of weapons	0.4 (0.11)	0.3 (0.06)	0.3 (0.06)	# (†)	# (†)	# (†)	— (†)	— (†)	— (†)	— (†)	— (†)	— (†)	— (†)	— (†)
Verbal abuse of teachers	2.0 (0.24)	2.3 (0.25)	2.5 (0.22)	2.4 (0.40)	1.1 (0.29)	4.0 (0.84)	— (†)	— (†)	— (†)	— (†)	— (†)	— (†)	— (†)	— (†)
Student disrespect for teachers	— (†)	3.4 (0.27)	3.8 (0.31)	5.1 (0.37)	3.6 (0.54)	6.3 (1.05)	— (†)	— (†)	— (†)	— (†)	— (†)	— (†)	— (†)	— (†)
Students dropping out	— (†)	0.6 (0.09)	0.5 (0.10)	0.3 ! (0.09)	‡ (†)	‡ (†)	0.4 ! (0.13)	0.4 (0.13)	0.5 ! (0.22)	‡ (†)	0.3 ! (0.13)	‡ (†)	‡ (†)	‡ (†)
Student apathy	1.3 (0.19)	4.5 (0.28)	4.3 (0.29)	3.0 (0.39)	1.4 (0.23)	6.6 (0.95)	3.9 (0.34)	1.7 (0.30)	6.9 (1.06)	5.1 (0.74)	3.6 (0.38)	1.7 (0.42)	7.1 (1.32)	‡ (†)
Lack of parental involvement	— (†)	4.0 (0.26)	3.4 (0.30)	2.5 (0.37)	1.6 (0.28)	3.6 (0.77)	2.5 (0.24)	1.9 (0.36)	2.8 (0.67)	3.0 (0.46)	2.7 (0.32)	1.8 (0.34)	3.2 (0.80)	3.0 (0.46)
Poverty	— (†)	2.7 (0.23)	2.1 (0.21)	2.2 (0.26)	1.7 (0.31)	3.4 (0.78)	2.0 (0.21)	1.4 (0.28)	2.0 (0.56)	2.6 (0.44)	2.6 (0.33)	2.7 (0.52)	2.8 (0.79)	2.6 (0.44)
Students come unprepared to learn	— (†)	4.1 (0.28)	4.9 (0.36)	3.5 (0.30)	2.1 (0.53)	6.8 (0.99)	3.6 (0.34)	1.9 (0.33)	6.2 (1.51)	4.4 (0.85)	3.9 (0.41)	2.0 (0.41)	6.7 (1.07)	4.4 (0.85)
Poor student health	— (†)	— (†)	— (†)	— (†)	— (†)	— (†)	0.7 (0.13)	0.3 ! (0.12)	‡ (†)	1.0 (0.25)	0.8 (0.21)	0.4 ! (0.17)	0.5 ! (0.25)	1.0 (0.25)

—Not available.
†Not applicable.
#Rounds to zero.
!Interpret data with caution. The coefficient of variation (CV) for this estimate is between 30 and 50 percent.
‡Reporting standards not met. Data may be suppressed because the response rate is under 50 percent, there are too few cases for a reliable estimate, or the coefficient of variation (CV) is 50 percent or greater.
[1]For 2003–04, combined schools are included in the total but not shown separately.

NOTE: Elementary schools are those with any of grades kindergarten through grade 6 and none of grades 9 through 12. Secondary schools have any of grades 7 through 12, and none of grades kindergarten through grade 6. Combined schools have both elementary and secondary grades, or have all students in ungraded classrooms.

SOURCE: U.S. Department of Education, National Center for Education Statistics, Schools and Staffing Survey (SASS), "Public School Teacher Data File," selected years, 1987–88 through 2011–12; "Private School Teacher Data File," selected years, 1987–88 through 2011–12; and "Charter School Teacher Data File," 1999–2000. (This table was prepared May 2013.)

Estimated average annual salary of teachers in public elementary and secondary schools: Selected years, 1959–60 through 2012–13

School year	Current dollars					Average public school teachers' salary in constant 2012–13 dollars[2]		
	Average public school teachers' salary			Wage and salary accruals per full-time-equivalent (FTE) employee[1]	Ratio of average teachers' salary to accruals per FTE employee			
	All teachers	Elementary teachers	Secondary teachers			All teachers	Elementary teachers	Secondary teachers
1	2	3	4	5	6	7	8	9
1959–60	$4,995	$4,815	$5,276	$4,749	1.05	$39,329	$37,912	$41,542
1961–62	5,515	5,340	5,775	5,063	1.09	42,448	41,101	44,449
1963–64	5,995	5,805	6,266	5,478	1.09	44,970	43,545	47,003
1965–66	6,485	6,279	6,761	5,934	1.09	47,020	45,527	49,021
1967–68	7,423	7,208	7,692	6,533	1.14	50,498	49,035	52,328
1969–70	8,626	8,412	8,891	7,486	1.15	52,830	51,519	54,453
1970–71	9,268	9,021	9,568	7,998	1.16	53,975	52,537	55,723
1971–72	9,705	9,424	10,031	8,521	1.14	54,563	52,983	56,396
1972–73	10,174	9,893	10,507	9,056	1.12	54,985	53,466	56,784
1973–74	10,770	10,507	11,077	9,667	1.11	53,441	52,136	54,964
1974–75	11,641	11,334	12,000	10,411	1.12	52,000	50,628	53,603
1975–76	12,600	12,280	12,937	11,194	1.13	52,563	51,228	53,969
1976–77	13,354	12,989	13,776	11,971	1.12	52,639	51,200	54,302
1977–78	14,198	13,845	14,602	12,811	1.11	52,444	51,140	53,937
1978–79	15,032	14,681	15,450	13,807	1.09	50,769	49,584	52,181
1979–80	15,970	15,569	16,459	15,050	1.06	47,592	46,397	49,049
1980–81	17,644	17,230	18,142	16,461	1.07	47,122	46,017	48,452
1981–82	19,274	18,853	19,805	17,795	1.08	47,383	46,348	48,688
1982–83	20,695	20,227	21,291	18,873	1.10	48,781	47,678	50,186
1983–84	21,935	21,487	22,554	19,781	1.11	49,858	48,840	51,265
1984–85	23,600	23,200	24,187	20,694	1.14	51,622	50,747	52,906
1985–86	25,199	24,718	25,846	21,685	1.16	53,575	52,552	54,950
1986–87	26,569	26,057	27,244	22,700	1.17	55,261	54,196	56,665
1987–88	28,034	27,519	28,798	23,777	1.18	55,988	54,959	57,514
1988–89	29,564	29,022	30,218	24,752	1.19	56,437	55,402	57,685
1989–90	31,367	30,832	32,049	25,762	1.22	57,152	56,177	58,394
1990–91	33,084	32,490	33,896	26,935	1.23	57,155	56,129	58,558
1991–92	34,063	33,479	34,827	28,169	1.21	57,020	56,042	58,298
1992–93	35,029	34,350	35,880	29,245	1.20	56,860	55,758	58,242
1993–94	35,737	35,233	36,566	30,030	1.19	56,545	55,748	57,857
1994–95	36,675	36,088	37,523	30,857	1.19	56,412	55,509	57,717
1995–96	37,642	37,138	38,397	31,822	1.18	56,366	55,611	57,497
1996–97	38,443	38,039	39,184	33,058	1.16	55,969	55,381	57,048
1997–98	39,350	39,002	39,944	34,635	1.14	56,285	55,788	57,135
1998–99	40,544	40,165	41,203	36,306	1.12	57,006	56,474	57,933
1999–2000	41,807	41,306	42,546	38,176	1.10	57,133	56,448	58,143
2000–01	43,378	42,910	44,053	39,722	1.09	57,316	56,698	58,208
2001–02	44,655	44,177	45,310	40,579	1.10	57,977	57,356	58,827
2002–03	45,686	45,408	46,106	41,704	1.10	58,040	57,687	58,574
2003–04	46,542	46,187	46,976	43,301	1.07	57,862	57,420	58,401
2004–05	47,516	47,122	47,688	44,941	1.06	57,347	56,871	57,554
2005–06	49,086	48,573	49,496	46,755	1.05	57,068	56,472	57,545
2006–07	51,052	50,740	51,529	48,867	1.04	57,858	57,504	58,399
2007–08	52,800	52,385	53,262	50,670	1.04	57,701	57,247	58,206
2008–09	54,319	53,998	54,552	51,608	1.05	58,544	58,198	58,795
2009–10	55,202	54,918	55,595	52,533	1.05	58,925	58,622	59,344
2010–11	55,623	55,217	56,225	53,974	1.03	58,206	57,781	58,836
2011–12	55,418	54,704	56,226	—	—	56,340	55,614	57,162
2012–13	56,383	55,747	57,243	—	—	56,383	55,747	57,243

—Not available.
[1]The average monetary remuneration earned by FTE employees across all industries in a given year, including wages, salaries, commissions, tips, bonuses, voluntary employee contributions to certain deferred compensation plans, and receipts in kind that represent income. Calendar-year data from the U.S. Department of Commerce, Bureau of Economic Analysis, have been converted to a school-year basis by averaging the two appropriate calendar years in each case.
[2]Constant dollars based on the Consumer Price Index, prepared by the Bureau of Labor Statistics,

U.S. Department of Labor, adjusted to a school-year basis.
NOTE: Some data have been revised from previously published figures. Standard errors are not available for these estimates, which are based on state reports.
SOURCE: National Education Association, *Estimates of School Statistics*, 1959–60 through 2012–13; and unpublished tabulations. U.S. Department of Commerce, Bureau of Economic Analysis, National Income and Product Accounts, tables 6.6B-D, retrieved November 2, 2011, from http://www.bea.gov/national/nipaweb/SelectTable.asp. (This table was prepared April 2013.)

Estimated average annual salary of teachers in public elementary and secondary schools, by state: Selected years, 1969–70 through 2012–13

State	Current dollars							Constant 2012–13 dollars[1]							Percent change, 1999–2000 to 2012–13
	1969–70	1979–80	1989–90	1999–2000	2009–10	2011–12	2012–13	1969–70	1979–80	1989–90	1999–2000	2009–10	2011–12	2012–13	
1	2	3	4	5	6	7	8	9	10	11	12	13	14	15	16
United States...	$8,626	$15,970	$31,367	$41,807	$55,202	$55,418	$56,383	$52,830	$47,592	$57,152	$57,133	$58,925	$56,340	$56,383	-1.3
Alabama	6,818	13,060	24,828	36,689	47,571	48,003	47,949	41,757	38,920	45,237	50,139	50,779	48,802	47,949	-4.4
Alaska	10,560	27,210	43,153	46,462	59,672	62,425	65,468	64,675	81,088	78,626	63,495	63,696	63,464	65,468	3.1
Arizona	8,711	15,054	29,402	36,902	46,952	48,691	49,885	53,350	44,862	53,571	50,430	50,119	49,501	49,885	-1.1
Arkansas	6,307	12,299	22,352	33,386	46,700	46,314	46,632	38,627	36,652	40,726	45,625	49,850	47,085	46,632	2.2
California	10,315	18,020	37,998	47,680	68,203	68,531	69,324	63,174	53,701	69,234	65,159	72,803	69,672	69,324	6.4
Colorado	7,761	16,205	30,758	38,163	49,202	49,049	49,844	47,532	48,292	56,042	52,153	52,520	49,865	49,844	-4.4
Connecticut	9,262	16,229	40,461	51,780	64,350	69,465	69,766	56,725	48,363	73,721	70,762	68,690	70,621	69,766	-1.4
Delaware	9,015	16,148	33,377	44,435	57,080	58,800	59,679	55,212	48,122	60,814	60,724	60,930	59,779	59,679	-1.7
District of Columbia ..	10,285	22,190	38,402	47,076	64,548	68,720	70,906	62,990	66,128	69,970	64,334	68,901	69,864	70,906	10.2
Florida	8,412	14,149	28,803	36,722	46,708	46,479	46,944	51,519	42,165	52,480	50,184	49,858	47,253	46,944	-6.5
Georgia	7,276	13,853	28,006	41,023	53,112	52,938	52,880	44,562	41,283	51,028	56,062	56,694	53,819	52,880	-5.7
Hawaii	9,453	19,920	32,047	40,578	55,063	54,070	54,300	57,895	59,363	58,391	55,453	58,777	54,970	54,300	-2.1
Idaho	6,890	13,611	23,861	35,547	46,283	48,551	49,734	42,198	40,562	43,475	48,578	49,404	49,359	49,734	2.4
Illinois	9,569	17,601	32,794	46,486	62,077	57,636	59,113	58,605	52,452	59,752	63,527	66,264	58,595	59,113	-6.9
Indiana	8,833	15,599	30,902	41,850	49,986	50,516	51,456	54,098	46,486	56,304	57,192	53,357	51,357	51,456	-10.0
Iowa	8,355	15,203	26,747	35,678	49,626	50,240	51,528	51,170	45,306	48,734	48,757	52,973	51,076	51,528	5.7
Kansas	7,612	13,690	28,744	34,981	46,657	46,718	47,464	46,620	40,797	52,372	47,805	49,804	47,496	47,464	-0.7
Kentucky	6,953	14,520	26,292	36,380	49,543	49,730	50,326	42,584	43,271	47,905	49,717	52,884	50,558	50,326	1.2
Louisiana	7,028	13,760	24,300	33,109	48,903	50,179	51,381	43,043	41,006	44,275	45,246	52,201	51,014	51,381	13.6
Maine	7,572	13,071	26,881	35,561	46,106	47,338	48,119	46,375	38,952	48,978	48,597	49,216	48,126	48,119	-1.0
Maryland	9,383	17,558	36,319	44,048	63,971	63,634	65,265	57,466	52,324	66,174	60,196	68,285	64,693	65,265	8.4
Massachusetts	8,764	17,253	34,712	46,580	69,273	71,721	73,129	53,675	51,415	63,246	63,656	73,945	72,915	73,129	14.9
Michigan	9,826	19,663	37,072	49,044	57,958	61,560	61,560	60,179	58,597	67,546	67,023	61,867	62,585	61,560	-8.2
Minnesota	8,658	15,912	32,190	39,802	52,431	54,959	56,268	53,026	47,419	58,651	54,393	55,967	55,874	56,268	3.4
Mississippi	5,798	11,850	24,292	31,857	45,644	41,646	41,994	35,510	35,314	44,261	43,535	48,722	42,339	41,994	-3.5
Missouri	7,799	13,682	27,094	35,656	45,317	46,406	47,517	47,765	40,773	49,366	48,727	48,373	47,178	47,517	-2.5
Montana	7,606	14,537	25,081	32,121	45,759	48,546	49,999	46,583	43,321	45,698	43,896	48,845	49,354	49,999	13.9
Nebraska	7,375	13,516	25,522	33,237	46,227	48,154	48,931	45,168	40,279	46,502	45,421	49,345	48,955	48,931	7.7
Nevada	9,215	16,295	30,590	39,390	51,524	54,559	55,957	56,437	48,560	55,736	53,830	54,999	55,467	55,957	4.0
New Hampshire	7,771	13,017	28,986	37,734	51,443	54,177	55,599	47,593	38,791	52,813	51,567	54,912	55,079	55,599	7.8
New Jersey	9,130	17,161	35,676	52,015	65,130	67,078	68,797	55,917	51,141	65,003	71,083	69,523	68,194	68,797	-3.2
New Mexico	7,796	14,887	24,756	32,554	46,258	45,622	46,573	47,746	44,364	45,106	44,488	49,378	46,381	46,573	4.7
New York	10,336	19,812	38,925	51,020	71,633	73,398	75,279	63,303	59,041	70,923	69,723	76,464	74,620	75,279	8.0
North Carolina	7,494	14,117	27,883	39,404	46,850	45,947	45,947	45,897	42,070	50,804	53,849	50,010	46,712	45,947	-14.7
North Dakota	6,696	13,263	23,016	29,863	42,964	46,058	47,344	41,010	39,525	41,936	40,810	45,862	46,825	47,344	16.0
Ohio	8,300	15,269	31,218	41,436	55,958	56,715	58,092	50,833	45,503	56,880	56,626	59,732	57,659	58,092	2.6
Oklahoma	6,882	13,107	23,070	31,298	47,691	44,391	44,128	42,149	39,060	42,034	42,772	50,907	45,130	44,128	3.2
Oregon	8,818	16,266	30,840	42,336	55,224	57,348	58,758	54,006	48,474	56,191	57,856	58,948	58,302	58,758	1.6
Pennsylvania	8,858	16,515	33,338	48,321	59,156	61,934	63,521	54,251	49,216	60,743	66,035	63,146	62,965	63,521	-3.8
Rhode Island	8,776	18,002	36,057	47,041	59,686	62,186	63,474	53,748	53,647	65,697	64,286	63,711	63,221	63,474	-1.3
South Carolina	6,927	13,063	27,217	36,081	47,508	47,428	47,924	42,424	38,929	49,590	49,308	50,712	48,217	47,924	-2.8
South Dakota	6,403	12,348	21,300	29,071	38,837	38,804	39,580	39,215	36,798	38,809	39,728	41,456	39,450	39,580	-0.4
Tennessee	7,050	13,972	27,052	36,328	46,290	47,082	48,289	43,178	41,637	49,290	49,645	49,412	47,866	48,289	-2.7
Texas	7,255	14,132	27,496	37,567	48,261	48,373	48,110	44,433	42,114	50,099	51,339	51,516	49,178	48,110	-6.3
Utah	7,644	14,909	23,686	34,946	45,885	48,159	49,393	46,816	44,430	43,157	47,757	48,980	48,961	49,393	3.4
Vermont	7,968	12,484	29,012	37,758	49,084	51,306	52,526	48,800	37,203	52,861	51,600	52,394	52,160	52,526	1.8
Virginia	8,070	14,060	30,938	38,744	50,015	48,703	49,869	49,425	41,900	56,370	52,947	53,388	49,514	49,869	-5.8
Washington	9,225	18,820	30,457	41,043	53,003	52,232	53,571	56,498	56,085	55,494	56,089	56,578	53,101	53,571	-4.5
West Virginia	7,650	13,710	22,842	35,009	45,959	45,320	46,405	46,852	40,857	41,619	47,843	49,059	46,074	46,405	-3.0
Wisconsin	8,963	16,006	31,921	41,153	51,264	53,792	55,171	54,894	47,699	58,161	56,239	54,721	54,687	55,171	-1.9
Wyoming	8,232	16,012	28,141	34,127	55,861	57,222	57,920	50,417	47,717	51,274	46,638	59,628	58,174	57,920	24.2

[1]Constant dollars based on the Consumer Price Index (CPI), prepared by the Bureau of Labor Statistics, U.S. Department of Labor, adjusted to a school-year basis. The CPI does not account for differences in inflation rates from state to state.
NOTE: Some data have been revised from previously published figures. Standard errors are not available for these estimates, which are based on state reports.
SOURCE: National Education Association, *Estimates of School Statistics*, 1969–70 through 2012–13. (This table was prepared April 2013.)

Number and internet access of instructional computers and rooms in public schools, by selected school characteristics: Selected years, 1995 through 2008

[Standard errors appear in parentheses]

Instructional computers and rooms, and access	All public schools	Instructional level[1]		Size of school enrollment			Community type[2]				Percent of students eligible for free or reduced-price lunch[3]			
		Elementary	Secondary	Less than 300	300 to 999	1,000 or more	City	Suburban	Town	Rural	Less than 35 percent	35 to 49 percent	50 to 74 percent	75 percent or more
1	2	3	4	5	6	7	8	9	10	11	12	13	14	15
Computers for instructional purposes														
Number (in thousands)														
1995[4]	5,621 (—)	3,453 (—)	2,021 (—)	850 (—)	3,600 (—)	1,171 (—)	1,497 (—)	1,526 (—)	1,404 (—)	1,195 (—)	2,905 (—)	806 (—)	950 (—)	882 (—)
2000	8,776 (174)	5,296 (149)	3,271 (113)	1,135 (73)	5,524 (121)	2,117 (103)	2,537 (179)	3,396 (213)	1,155 (132)	1,689 (131)	4,394 (147)	1,373 (93)	1,606 (112)	1,384 (107)
2005	12,672 (281)	7,701 (251)	4,783 (148)	1,566 (98)	7,966 (243)	3,139 (163)	3,132 (177)	4,058 (242)	1,819 (193)	3,663 (255)	5,352 (261)	2,193 (185)	2,687 (244)	2,440 (152)
2008	15,434 (193)	9,711 (159)	5,415 (125)	1,746 (68)	9,486 (144)	4,202 (130)	3,611 (155)	5,787 (255)	2,062 (159)	3,974 (180)	6,195 (174)	2,364 (155)	3,805 (190)	3,070 (175)
Average number per school														
1995[4]	72 (—)	60 (—)	112 (—)	41 (—)	72 (—)	164 (—)	84 (—)	83 (—)	72 (—)	54 (—)	78 (—)	59 (—)	74 (—)	67 (—)
2000	110 (2.0)	89 (2.4)	178 (5.3)	57 (3.1)	106 (2.3)	259 (9.0)	120 (4.9)	128 (4.3)	97 (5.6)	82 (3.6)	120 (3.4)	111 (5.9)	94 (5.7)	99 (5.5)
2005	154 (3.4)	124 (3.8)	253 (6.8)	75 (4.2)	149 (4.2)	388 (13.5)	165 (7.2)	170 (6.3)	154 (13.4)	132 (5.9)	166 (5.5)	153 (9.3)	147 (6.9)	139 (7.4)
2008	189 (2.9)	157 (2.8)	301 (6.5)	87 (3.4)	179 (2.9)	486 (10.4)	205 (7.5)	221 (6.1)	189 (8.0)	147 (4.2)	209 (5.6)	182 (7.7)	181 (6.8)	170 (8.2)
Number with internet access (in thousands)														
1995[4]	447 (—)	232 (—)	187 (—)	59 (—)	315 (—)	73 (—)	96 (—)	131 (—)	126 (—)	94 (—)	286 (—)	46 (—)	57 (—)	36 (—)
2000	6,759 (174)	3,813 (136)	2,779 (113)	882 (69)	4,191 (114)	1,686 (97)	1,782 (148)	2,688 (178)	955 (111)	1,335 (91)	3,608 (139)	1,064 (80)	1,215 (93)	858 (87)
2005	12,245 (274)	7,361 (246)	4,706 (151)	1,515 (98)	7,642 (239)	3,089 (162)	3,009 (173)	3,912 (238)	1,784 (193)	3,541 (239)	5,239 (259)	2,090 (176)	2,583 (228)	2,332 (146)
2008	15,162 (204)	9,508 (169)	5,356 (128)	1,710 (69)	9,308 (153)	4,144 (130)	3,517 (154)	5,716 (253)	2,028 (154)	3,901 (178)	6,131 (174)	2,321 (153)	3,739 (188)	2,971 (175)
Percent with internet access														
1995[4]	8 (—)	7 (—)	9 (—)	7 (—)	9 (—)	6 (—)	6 (—)	9 (—)	9 (—)	8 (—)	10 (—)	6 (—)	6 (—)	4 (—)
2000	77 (1.1)	72 (1.5)	85 (1.2)	78 (2.6)	76 (1.3)	80 (1.8)	70 (2.1)	79 (1.7)	83 (2.5)	79 (2.1)	82 (1.2)	77 (2.9)	76 (2.6)	62 (3.1)
2005	97 (0.4)	96 (0.5)	98 (0.4)	97 (0.7)	96 (0.5)	98 (0.5)	96 (0.7)	96 (1.1)	98 (0.6)	97 (0.7)	98 (0.6)	95 (1.0)	96 (1.0)	96 (0.8)
2008	98 (0.2)	98 (0.3)	99 (0.2)	98 (0.7)	98 (0.3)	99 (0.4)	97 (0.5)	99 (0.3)	98 (0.7)	98 (0.4)	99 (0.3)	98 (0.5)	98 (0.4)	97 (0.7)
Ratio of students to instructional computers with internet access[5]														
2000	6.6 (0.10)	7.8 (0.20)	5.2 (0.20)	3.9 (0.30)	7.0 (0.20)	7.2 (0.30)	8.2 (0.40)	6.6 (0.20)	6.2 (0.30)	5.0 (0.30)	6.0 (0.20)	6.3 (0.40)	7.2 (0.40)	9.1 (0.70)
2005	3.8 (0.10)	4.1 (0.10)	3.3 (0.10)	2.4 (0.10)	3.9 (0.10)	4.0 (0.10)	4.2 (0.20)	4.1 (0.10)	3.4 (0.20)	3.0 (0.10)	3.8 (0.10)	3.4 (0.20)	3.6 (0.20)	4.0 (0.20)
2008	3.1 (0.04)	3.2 (0.05)	2.9 (0.05)	2.2 (0.07)	3.2 (0.05)	3.2 (0.06)	3.4 (0.12)	3.2 (0.08)	2.7 (0.09)	2.9 (0.07)	3.1 (0.06)	3.2 (0.08)	2.9 (0.08)	3.2 (0.14)
Instructional rooms[5]														
Number (in thousands)														
2000	2,905 (35)	1,864 (28)	972 (24)	377 (22)	1,871 (23)	657 (23)	866 (56)	1,086 (61)	413 (47)	541 (39)	1,380 (46)	465 (46)	570 (36)	482 (29)
2005	3,283 (71)	2,152 (70)	1,078 (27)	426 (23)	2,152 (70)	705 (30)	849 (62)	1,050 (61)	439 (41)	945 (67)	1,339 (50)	593 (51)	695 (56)	655 (39)
2008[6]	2,663 (21)	1,723 (20)	887 (15)	282 (9)	1,692 (20)	689 (18)	639 (26)	1,003 (35)	338 (24)	683 (28)	1,053 (27)	425 (26)	653 (27)	532 (22)
Percent with internet access[6]														
1995	8 (0.7)	8 (1.0)	8 (1.0)	9 (1.6)	8 (1.0)	4 (1.0)	6 (1.3)	8 (1.4)	8 (2.0)	8 (1.5)	10 (1.2)	6 (1.4)	6 (1.9)	3¹ (1.0)
2000	77 (1.1)	76 (1.5)	79 (1.6)	83 (2.8)	78 (1.5)	70 (2.2)	66 (2.2)	78 (1.8)	87 (2.6)	85 (1.7)	82 (1.5)	81 (2.9)	77 (2.8)	60 (3.3)
2005	94 (1.3)	93 (1.9)	95 (0.9)	92 (1.9)	94 (1.9)	94 (1.5)	88 (3.7)	96 (0.8)	98 (0.7)	95 (1.8)	96 (0.8)	88 (4.3)	96 (—)	91 (2.5)
2008	— (†)	— (†)	— (†)	— (†)	— (†)	— (†)	— (†)	— (†)	— (†)	— (†)	— (†)	— (†)	— (†)	— (†)

—Not available.
†Not applicable.
¹Interpret data with caution. The coefficient of variation (CV) for this estimate is between 30 and 50 percent.
[1]Data for combined schools are included in the totals and in analyses by other school characteristics, but are not shown separately.
[2]Due to definitional changes by community type, estimates for years prior to 2005 may not be directly comparable with estimates for later years.
[3]Free or reduced-price lunch information was obtained on the questionnaire and supplemented, if necessary, with data from the Common Core of Data (CCD).
[4]Includes computers used for instructional or administrative purposes.
[5]In 2008, instructional rooms included classrooms only and excluded computer labs and library/media centers. Prior to 2008, instructional rooms included classrooms, computer labs and other labs, library/media centers, and other rooms used for instructional purposes.
[6]Some data differ slightly (e.g., by 1 percent) from previously published figures.

NOTE: Detail may not sum to totals because of rounding.
SOURCE: U.S. Department of Education, National Center for Education Statistics, Fast Response Survey System (FRSS), Internet Access in U.S. Public Schools and Classrooms: 1994–2005 and Educational Technology in U.S. Public Schools: Fall 2008, and unpublished tabulations. (This table was prepared August 2010.)

Percentage of public school districts with students enrolled in technology-based distance education courses and number of enrollments in such courses, by instructional level and district characteristics: 2002–03, 2004–05, and 2009–10

[Standard errors appear in parentheses]

District characteristic	Percent of districts enrolling distance education students		Number of enrollments in technology-based distance education courses,[1] by instructional level								
			All instructional levels		Elementary schools		Middle or junior high schools		High schools		Combined or ungraded schools[2]	
1	2		3		4		5		6		7	
2002–03												
Total	36	(1.2)	317,070	(27,437)	2,780 !	(977)	6,390	(1,067)	214,140	(16,549)	93,760	(22,593)
District enrollment size												
Less than 2,500	37	(1.5)	116,300	(21,698)	‡	(†)	1,250 !	(450)	72,730	(6,924)	42,240 !	(20,502)
2,500 to 9,999	32	(1.8)	82,370	(6,384)	230 !	(109)	1,870 !	(642)	44,170	(5,832)	36,110	(1,210)
10,000 or more	50	(2.1)	118,390	(15,703)	2,480 !	(968)	3,270	(723)	97,240	(13,853)	‡	(†)
Region												
Northeast	21	(2.2)	41,950 !	(20,821)	100 !	(49)	‡	(†)	17,300	(3,656)	‡	(†)
Southeast	45	(2.6)	59,240	(6,251)	‡	(†)	2,530	(632)	50,640	(5,698)	4,680	(1,254)
Central	46	(2.3)	106,690	(7,726)	940 !	(441)	1,050 !	(412)	59,110	(6,455)	45,590	(2,529)
West	32	(2.2)	109,190	(16,010)	350 !	(165)	2,620	(782)	87,090	(14,825)	19,130 !	(8,619)
Poverty concentration												
Less than 10 percent	33	(2.1)	75,740	(11,177)	‡	(†)	2,020	(564)	55,670	(7,556)	17,470 !	(8,591)
10 to 19 percent	42	(2.1)	95,510	(7,962)	‡	(†)	1,830	(392)	78,680	(7,050)	13,560	(2,446)
20 percent or more	42	(2.5)	86,110	(13,518)	760 !	(249)	2,540 !	(837)	75,930	(13,532)	6,880	(1,557)
2004–05												
Total	37	(1.2)	506,950	(56,959)	12,540 !	(6,107)	15,150	(3,367)	309,630	(24,350)	169,630 !	(51,753)
District enrollment size												
Less than 2,500	37	(1.6)	210,200	(54,063)	610 !	(275)	‡	(†)	103,190	(17,659)	‡	(†)
2,500 to 9,999	35	(1.6)	102,730	(13,404)	‡	(†)	2,570	(731)	48,420	(5,136)	45,080	(9,429)
10,000 or more	50	(2.5)	193,440	(16,415)	5,280 !	(2,202)	6,520	(1,101)	157,440	(16,044)	24,210	(5,298)
Region												
Northeast	22	(2.0)	108,300 !	(49,777)	570 !	(206)	‡	(†)	16,860	(2,621)	‡	(†)
Southeast	46	(3.2)	112,830	(6,341)	‡	(†)	5,030	(732)	89,800	(5,276)	16,090	(1,913)
Central	45	(2.4)	128,650	(22,055)	‡	(†)	2,130 !	(953)	70,450	(13,024)	46,190 !	(15,067)
West	35	(2.1)	157,180	(22,608)	200 !	(161)	4,110 !	(1,732)	132,520	(21,287)	20,350 !	(7,587)
Poverty concentration												
Less than 10 percent	35	(1.9)	112,320	(16,778)	‡	(†)	4,070	(1,123)	80,150	(10,651)	‡	(†)
10 to 19 percent	42	(2.2)	151,050	(12,379)	‡	(†)	4,800	(602)	124,540	(10,283)	19,700	(5,835)
20 percent or more	43	(2.7)	106,610	(14,709)	‡	(†)	6,280 !	(3,111)	78,590	(13,367)	21,340	(2,905)
2009–10												
Total	55	(1.4)	1,816,390	(251,054)	78,040 !	(25,180)	154,970	(30,828)	1,348,920	(135,979)	‡	(†)
District enrollment size												
Less than 2,500	51	(1.8)	509,030 !	(167,570)	‡	(†)	‡	(†)	408,030 !	(123,883)	6,570 !	2,753
2,500 to 9,999	66	(1.5)	579,250 !	(185,243)	‡	(†)	23,960 !	(9,196)	312,130	(50,963)	‡	(†)
10,000 or more	74	(0.8)	728,110	(27,105)	11,540	(1,862)	77,750	(4,730)	628,760	(23,545)	10,060	2,756
Metropolitan status												
City	37	(4.0)	653,660 !	(201,665)	‡	(†)	40,400 !	(15,671)	405,740	(79,507)	‡	(†)
Suburban	47	(2.6)	527,250	(34,188)	22,900 !	(11,293)	62,210	(4,106)	434,260	(30,904)	7,880	2,347
Town	67	(2.7)	306,840 !	(145,000)	‡	(†)	‡	(†)	246,850 !	(107,079)	9,310 !	3,908
Rural	59	(2.5)	328,640	(36,233)	‡	(†)	15,360	(2,420)	262,070	(27,077)	‡	(†)
Region												
Northeast	39	(3.3)	77,670	(7,358)	‡	(†)	4,970	(989)	71,330	(6,651)	‡	(†)
Southeast	78	(3.7)	518,770	(63,187)	12,070 !	(4,154)	57,500	(9,828)	443,770	(50,079)	5,440 !	1,678
Central	62	(2.2)	697,140 !	(235,103)	37,920 !	(18,915)	‡	(†)	416,550	(122,633)	‡	(†)
West	51	(2.4)	522,810	(42,673)	‡	(†)	41,620	(3,384)	417,270	(33,400)	36,510 !	14,278
Poverty concentration												
Less than 10 percent	54	(2.5)	287,680	(34,577)	‡	(†)	12,620	(2,997)	231,890	(27,672)	‡	(†)
10 to 19 percent	56	(2.1)	1,009,290	(193,646)	23,540 !	(11,116)	97,220	(16,126)	682,380	(78,795)	‡	(†)
20 percent or more	56	(2.4)	519,420	(146,507)	‡	(†)	‡	(†)	434,640	(108,046)	5,750 !	2,484

†Not applicable.

!Interpret data with caution. The coefficient of variation (CV) for this estimate is between 30 and 50 percent.

‡Reporting standards not met. Either there are too few cases for a reliable estimate or the coefficient of variation (CV) is 50 percent or greater.

[1]Based on students regularly enrolled in the districts. Enrollments may include duplicated counts of students, since districts were instructed to count a student enrolled in multiple courses for each course in which he or she was enrolled.

[2]Combined or ungraded schools are those in which the grades offered in the school span both elementary and secondary grades or that are not divided into grade levels.

NOTE: Percentages are based on unrounded numbers. For the 2002–03 FRSS study sample, there were 3 cases for which district enrollment size was missing and 112 cases for which poverty concentration was missing. For the 2004–05 FRSS study sample, there were 7 cases for which district enrollment size was missing and 103 cases for which poverty concentration was missing. Detail may not sum to totals because of rounding or missing data.

SOURCE: U.S. Department of Education, National Center for Education Statistics, Fast Response Survey System (FRSS), *Technology-Based Distance Education Courses for Public Elementary and Secondary Schools: 2002–03 and 2004–05* and "Distance Education Courses for Public Elementary and Secondary School Students: 2009–10," FRSS 98. (This table was prepared November 2011.)

. **Federal support and estimated federal tax expenditures for education, by category: Selected fiscal years, 1965 through 2013**

[In millions of dollars]

Current dollars

Fiscal year	Total on-budget support, off-budget support, and nonfederal funds generated by federal legislation	On-budget support[1] Total	Elementary and secondary	Post-secondary	Other education[3]	Research at educational institutions	Off-budget support and nonfederal funds Total	Off-budget support Direct Loan Program[4]	Federal Family Education Loan Program[5]	Perkins Loans[6]	Income Contingent Loans[7]	Leveraging Educational Assistance Partnerships[8]	Supplemental Educational Opportunity Grants[9]	Work-Study Aid[10]	Estimated federal tax expenditures for education[2]
1	2	3	4	5	6	7	8	9	10	11	12	13	14	15	16
1965	$5,354.7	$5,331.0	$1,942.6	$1,197.5	$374.7	$1,816.3	$23.7	†	†	$16.1	†	†	†	$7.6	—
1970	13,359.1	12,526.5	5,830.4	3,447.7	964.7	2,283.6	832.6	†	$770.0	21.0	†	†	†	41.6	—
1975	24,691.5	23,288.1	10,617.2	7,644.0	1,608.5	3,418.4	1,403.4	†	1,233.0	35.7	†	$20.0	†	114.7	$8,605.0
1980	39,349.5	34,493.5	16,027.7	11,115.9	1,548.7	5,801.2	4,856.0	†	4,598.0	31.8	†	76.8	†	149.4	13,320.0
1985	47,753.4	39,027.9	16,901.3	11,174.4	2,107.6	8,844.6	8,725.5	†	8,467.0	21.4	†	76.0	†	161.1	19,105.0
1986	48,357.3	39,962.9	17,049.9	11,283.6	2,620.0	9,009.4	8,394.4	†	8,142.0	20.2	†	72.7	†	159.5	20,425.0
1987	50,724.6	41,194.7	17,535.7	11,300.0	2,820.4	10,538.6	9,529.8	†	9,272.0	20.9	$0.6	76.0	†	160.4	20,830.0
1988	54,078.7	43,454.4	18,564.9	10,657.5	2,981.6	11,250.5	10,624.3	†	10,380.0	20.6	0.5	72.8	†	150.4	17,025.0
1989	59,537.4	48,269.6	19,809.5	13,269.9	3,180.3	12,009.8	11,267.8	†	10,938.0	20.4	0.5	71.9	$22.0	215.0	17,755.0
1990	62,811.5	51,624.3	21,984.4	13,650.9	3,383.0	12,606.0	11,187.2	†	10,826.0	15.0	0.5	59.2	48.8	237.7	19,040.0
1991	70,375.6	57,599.5	25,418.0	14,707.4	3,698.6	13,775.4	12,776.1	†	12,372.0	17.3	0.5	63.5	87.7	235.0	18,995.0
1992	74,481.1	60,483.1	27,926.9	14,387.4	3,992.0	14,176.9	13,998.0	†	13,568.0	17.3	0.5	72.4	97.2	242.9	19,950.0
1993	84,741.5	67,740.6	30,834.3	17,844.0	4,107.2	14,955.1	17,000.8	†	16,524.0	29.3	†	72.4	184.6	190.5	21,010.0
1994	92,781.5	68,254.2	32,304.4	16,177.1	4,483.7	15,289.1	24,527.3	$813.0	23,214.0	52.7	†	72.4	184.6	190.5	22,630.0
1995	95,810.8	71,639.5	33,623.8	17,618.1	4,719.7	15,677.9	24,171.2	5,161.0	18,519.0	52.7	†	63.4	184.6	190.5	24,600.0
1996	96,833.0	71,327.4	34,391.5	15,775.5	4,828.0	16,332.3	25,505.6	8,357.0	16,711.0	31.1	†	31.4	184.6	190.5	26,340.0
1997	103,259.8	73,731.8	35,478.9	15,959.4	5,021.2	17,272.4	29,528.0	9,838.0	19,163.0	52.7	†	50.0	184.6	239.7	28,125.0
1998	107,810.5	76,909.2	37,486.2	15,799.6	5,148.5	18,475.0	30,901.3	10,400.1	20,002.5	45.0	†	25.0	194.3	234.4	29,540.0
1999	113,417.2	82,863.6	39,937.9	17,651.2	5,318.0	19,956.5	30,553.6	9,953.0	20,107.0	33.3	†	25.0	195.9	239.4	37,360.0
2000	119,541.6	85,944.2	43,790.8	15,008.7	5,484.6	21,660.1	33,597.4	10,347.0	22,711.0	33.3	†	50.0	199.7	256.4	39,475.0
2001	130,668.5	94,846.5	48,530.1	14,938.3	5,880.0	25,498.1	35,822.0	10,635.0	24,694.0	25.0	†	80.0	184.0	204.0	41,460.0
2002	150,034.5	109,211.5	52,754.1	22,964.2	6,297.7	27,195.5	40,823.0	11,689.0	28,606.0	25.0	†	104.0	192.0	207.0	—
2003	170,671.5	124,374.5	59,274.2	29,499.7	6,532.5	29,068.1	46,297.0	11,969.0	33,791.0	33.0	†	103.0	202.0	199.0	—
2004	185,176.7	132,420.7	62,653.2	32,433.0	6,576.8	30,757.7	52,756.0	12,840.0	39,266.0	33.0	†	102.0	244.0	271.0	—
2005	203,036.0	146,207.0	68,957.7	38,587.3	6,908.5	31,753.5	56,829.0	12,930.0	43,284.0	0.0	†	101.0	246.0	268.0	—
2006	226,978.7	166,495.7	70,948.2	57,757.7	7,074.5	30,715.2	60,483.0	12,677.0	47,307.0	0.0	†	100.0	205.0	194.0	—
2007	210,536.0	145,698.0	70,735.9	37,465.3	7,214.9	30,281.9	64,838.0	13,022.0	51,320.0	0.0	†	100.0	205.0	191.0	—
2008	220,336.9	144,338.9	71,272.6	36,386.3	7,882.2	28,797.8	75,998.0	18,213.0	57,296.0	0.0	†	98.0	201.0	190.0	—
2009[11]	368,349.6	271,297.6	172,660.8	53,085.4	8,853.7	36,697.7	97,052.0	29,738.0	66,778.0	0.0	†	98.0	201.0	237.0	—
2010	288,009.7	183,199.7	86,681.8	50,197.8	9,326.7	36,993.3	104,810.0	84,703.0	19,618.0	0.0	†	98.0	201.0	190.0	—
2011	292,962.0	183,655.7	76,118.9	64,400.2	11,133.7	32,002.9[12]	109,306.3	108,926.3	0.0	0.0	†	0.0	195.0	185.0	—
2012[12]	296,199.5	190,468.5	78,087.1	70,054.2	9,395.3	32,931.8[12]	105,731.0	105,351.0	0.0	0.0	†	0.0	195.0	185.0	—
2013[12]	—	—	80,444.4	62,448.9	9,659.5	—	106,932.7	106,434.0	0.0	0.0	†	0.0	188.2	310.5	—

Constant fiscal year 2013 dollars[13]

Fiscal year	Total on-budget support, off-budget support, and nonfederal funds generated by federal legislation	On-budget support[1] Total	Elementary and secondary	Post-secondary	Other education[3]	Research at educational institutions	Off-budget support and nonfederal funds Total	Off-budget support Direct Loan Program[4]	Federal Family Education Loan Program[5]	Perkins Loans[6]	Income Contingent Loans[7]	Leveraging Educational Assistance Partnerships[8]	Supplemental Educational Opportunity Grants[9]	Work-Study Aid[10]	Estimated federal tax expenditures for education[2]
1	2	3	4	5	6	7	8	9	10	11	12	13	14	15	16
1965	$36,902.7	$36,739.3	$13,387.5	$8,252.8	$2,582.0	$12,517.1	$163.4	†	†	$111.0	†	†	†	$52.4	—
1970	75,224.9	70,536.7	32,831.2	19,414.0	5,432.3	12,859.2	4,688.2	†	$4,335.9	118.1	†	†	†	234.2	—
1975	97,904.4	92,339.9	42,098.3	30,309.4	6,377.8	13,554.4	5,564.5	†	4,889.0	141.4	†	$79.3	†	454.8	$34,119.8
1980	106,439.9	93,304.5	43,354.7	30,068.3	4,189.3	15,692.2	13,135.4	†	12,437.5	86.0	†	207.7	†	404.1	36,030.4
1985	95,632.1	78,158.2	33,847.0	22,378.1	4,220.7	17,712.4	17,473.9	†	16,956.2	42.8	†	152.2	†	322.6	38,260.1
1986	94,313.1	77,941.2	33,253.1	22,006.8	5,109.9	17,571.3	16,371.9	†	15,879.7	39.4	†	141.8	†	311.1	39,835.6
1987	96,224.4	78,146.3	33,265.2	19,539.1	5,350.3	19,991.7	18,078.1	†	17,589.0	39.6	$1.05	144.2	†	304.3	39,514.5
1988	99,255.9	79,756.0	34,073.9	19,560.8	5,472.4	20,649.0	19,499.8	†	19,051.4	37.9	0.9	133.6	†	276.0	31,247.6
1989	105,242.2	85,324.4	35,016.6	23,456.7	5,621.8	21,229.3	19,917.8	†	19,334.7	36.0	1.0	127.1	$38.9	380.0	31,384.9

See notes at end of table.

Federal support and estimated federal tax expenditures for education, by category: Selected fiscal years, 1965 through 2013—Continued

[In millions of dollars]

Fiscal year	Total on-budget support, off-budget support, and nonfederal funds generated by federal legislation	On-budget support[1]					Off-budget support and nonfederal funds generated by federal legislation	Off-budget support	Nonfederal funds						Estimated federal tax expenditures for education[2]
		Total	Elementary and secondary	Post-secondary	Other education[3]	Research at educational institutions	Total	Direct Loan Program[4]	Federal Family Education Loan Program[5]	Perkins Loans[6]	Income Contingent Loans[7]	Leveraging Educational Assistance Partnerships[8]	Supplemental Educational Opportunity Grants[9]	Work-Study Aid[10]	
1	2	3	4	5	6	7	8	9	10	11	12	13	14	15	16
1990	107,766.3	88,572.3	37,718.8	23,421.0	5,804.3	21,628.3	19,194.0	†	18,574.3	25.8	0.9	101.5	83.7	407.8	32,667.1
1991	115,387.8	94,440.2	41,675.4	24,114.3	6,064.3	22,586.2	20,947.7	†	20,285.1	28.4	0.8	104.2	143.8	385.3	31,144.2
1992	117,728.2	95,602.3	44,142.5	22,741.4	6,309.9	22,408.6	22,125.9	†	21,446.2	27.4	0.9	113.8	153.7	384.0	31,533.9
1993	130,096.1	103,996.2	47,337.2	27,394.3	6,305.4	22,959.2	26,099.9	†	25,367.8	44.9	†	111.2	283.4	292.5	32,254.8
1994	139,846.4	102,877.3	48,691.3	24,383.1	6,758.1	23,044.7	36,969.1	$1,225.4	34,989.7	79.4	†	109.2	278.3	287.2	34,109.4
1995	140,314.0	104,915.5	49,241.8	25,801.6	6,911.9	22,960.2	35,398.6	7,558.2	27,120.9	77.1	†	92.8	270.4	279.0	36,026.5
1996	138,804.3	102,243.5	49,298.2	22,613.3	6,920.7	23,411.4	36,560.8	11,979.3	23,954.2	44.6	†	45.0	264.6	273.1	37,756.8
1997	145,096.2	103,604.8	49,853.4	22,425.5	7,055.5	24,270.4	41,491.5	13,823.9	26,927.0	74.1	†	70.3	259.4	336.8	39,520.0
1998	150,147.6	107,111.4	52,206.9	22,000.0	7,170.3	25,730.1	43,036.2	14,484.2	27,857.5	62.7	†	34.8	270.6	326.4	41,140.3
1999	155,963.2	113,948.1	54,919.8	24,272.7	7,313.0	27,442.7	42,015.1	13,686.7	27,649.7	45.8	†	34.4	269.4	329.2	51,374.8
2000	160,379.7	115,304.7	58,750.7	20,136.0	7,358.2	29,059.7	45,075.0	13,881.8	30,469.6	44.7	†	67.1	267.9	344.0	52,960.6
2001	170,740.1	123,932.7	63,412.6	19,519.3	7,683.2	33,317.6	46,807.4	13,896.4	32,266.8	32.7	†	104.5	240.4	266.6	54,174.4
2002	192,790.6	140,334.1	67,787.7	29,508.4	8,092.4	34,945.5	52,456.5	15,020.1	36,758.0	32.1	†	133.6	246.7	266.0	—
2003	213,379.3	155,497.2	74,106.6	36,881.5	8,167.2	36,341.9	57,882.1	14,964.1	42,246.7	41.3	†	128.8	252.5	248.8	—
2004	225,445.4	161,217.0	76,277.8	39,485.9	8,007.0	37,446.3	64,228.4	15,632.2	47,804.8	40.2	†	124.2	297.1	329.9	—
2005	238,858.0	172,002.6	81,124.0	45,395.3	8,127.4	37,355.8	66,855.4	15,211.3	50,920.7	0.0	†	118.8	289.4	315.3	—
2006	258,099.4	189,323.7	80,675.9	65,676.8	8,044.5	34,926.5	68,775.8	14,415.1	53,793.2	0.0	†	113.7	233.1	220.6	—
2007	233,220.5	161,396.4	78,357.4	41,502.0	7,992.3	33,544.7	71,824.1	14,425.1	56,849.6	0.0	†	110.8	227.1	211.6	—
2008	235,835.5	154,491.8	76,285.9	38,945.7	8,436.7	30,823.5	81,343.8	19,494.1	61,326.2	0.0	†	104.9	215.1	203.4	—
2009[11]	393,471.0	289,800.1	184,436.2	56,705.8	9,457.5	39,200.5	103,670.9	31,766.1	71,332.3	0.0	†	104.7	214.7	253.2	—
2010	304,064.0	193,411.6	91,513.6	52,996.0	9,846.6	39,055.4	110,652.3	89,424.5	20,711.6	0.0	†	103.5	212.2	200.6	—
2011	303,326.5	190,153.2	78,811.8	66,678.6	11,527.6	33,135.1 [12]	113,173.4	112,779.9	0.0	0.0	†	0.0	201.9	191.5	—
2012	301,018.2	193,567.1	79,357.5	71,193.9	9,548.1	33,467.6 [12]	107,451.1	107,064.9	0.0	0.0	†	0.0	198.2	188.0	—
2013[12]	—	—	80,444.4	62,448.9	9,659.5	—	106,932.7	106,434.0	0.0	0.0	†	0.0	188.2	310.5	—

—Not available.
†Not applicable.

[1]On-budget support includes federal funds for education programs tied to appropriations. Excludes appropriations. Excludes federal support for medical education benefits under Medicare in the U.S. Department of Health and Human Services. Benefits excluded because data before fiscal year (FY) 1990 are not available. This program existed since Medicare began, but was not available as a separate budget item until FY 1990. Excluded amounts range from $4,440,000,000 in FY 1990 to an estimated $10,000,000,000 in FY 2013.

[2]Losses of tax revenue attributable to provisions of the federal income tax laws that allow a special exclusion, exemption, or deduction from gross income or provide a special credit, preferential rate of tax, or a deferral of tax liability affecting individual or corporate income tax liabilities.

[3]Other education includes libraries, museums, cultural activities, and miscellaneous research.

[4]The William D. Ford Federal Direct Loan Program (commonly referred to as the Direct Loan Program) provides students with the same benefits they were eligible to receive under the Federal Family Education Loan (FFEL) Program, but provides loans to students through federal capital rather than through private lenders.

[5]The Federal Family Education Loan (FFEL) Program, formerly known as the Guaranteed Student Loan Program, provided student loans guaranteed by the federal government and disbursed to borrowers. After June 30, 2010, no new FFEL loans have been originated; all new loans are originated through the Direct Loan Program.

[6]Student loans created from institutional matching funds (since 1993 one-third of federal capital contributions). Excludes repayments of outstanding loans.

[7]Student loans created from institutional matching funds (one-ninth of the federal contribution). This was a demonstration project that involved only 10 institutions and had unsubsidized interest rates. Program repealed in fiscal year 1992.

[8]Formerly the State Student Incentive Grant Program. Starting in fiscal year 2000, amounts under $30.0 million have required dollar-for-dollar state matching contributions, while amounts over $30.0 million have required two-to-one state matching contributions.

[9]Institutions award grants to undergraduate students, and the federal share of such grants may not exceed 75 percent of the total grant.

[10]Employer contributions to student earnings are generally one-third of federal allocation.

[11]All education funds from the American Recovery and Reinvestment Act of 2009 (ARRA) are included in the FY 2009 row of this table. Most of these funds had a 2-year availability, meaning that they were available for the Department of Education to obligate during FY 2009 and FY 2010.

[12]Estimated.

[13]Data adjusted by the federal funds composite deflator reported in the U.S. Office of Management and Budget, *Budget of the U.S. Government, Historical Tables, Fiscal Year 2014.*

NOTE: To the extent possible, federal education funds data represent outlays rather than obligations. Some data have been revised from previously published figures. Detail may not sum to totals because of rounding. The increase in postsecondary expenditures in 2006 resulted primarily from an accounting adjustment. SOURCE: U.S. Department of Education, Budget Service, unpublished tabulations. U.S. Department of Education, National Center for Education Statistics, unpublished tabulations. U.S. Office of Management and Budget, *Budget of the U.S. Government, Appendix,* fiscal years 1967 through 2014. National Science Foundation, *Federal Funds for Research and Development,* fiscal years 1967 through 2012. (This table was prepared May 2014.)

Federal on-budget funds for education, by agency: Selected fiscal years, 1970 through 2012

[In thousands]

Agency	1970	1980	1990[1]	2000[1]	2005[1]	2008[1]	2009[1,2]	2010[1]	2011[1,3]	2012[1,3]
1	2	3	4	5	6	7	8	9	10	11
Total	**$12,526,499**	**$34,493,502**	**$51,624,342**	**$85,944,203**	**$146,206,999**	**$144,338,888**	**$271,297,567**	**$183,199,676**	**$183,655,692**	**$190,468,459**
Department of Education[2]	4,625,224	13,137,785	23,198,575	34,106,697	72,893,301	72,177,819	187,733,247	91,893,199	93,777,295	99,128,616
Department of Agriculture	960,910	4,562,467	6,260,843	11,080,031	13,817,553	16,588,529	16,603,791	19,260,881	20,396,195	22,212,582
Department of Commerce	13,990	135,561	53,835	114,575	243,948	193,612	263,000	303,000	296,489	307,919
Department of Defense	821,388	1,560,301	3,605,509	4,525,080	6,320,454	6,578,416	6,894,895	7,686,288	7,234,113	7,328,795
Department of Energy	551,527	1,605,558	2,561,950	3,577,004	4,339,879	2,469,637	3,747,800	3,402,600	2,807,045	3,219,690
Department of Health and Human Services	1,796,854	5,613,930	7,956,011	17,670,867	26,107,860	26,470,379	31,860,858	31,962,136	28,932,720	29,706,125
Department of Homeland Security	†	†	†	†	624,860	410,580	508,920	540,229	2,081,111	426,821
Department of Housing and Urban Development	114,709	5,314	118	1,400	1,100	400	200	400	1,300	1,400
Department of the Interior	190,975	440,547	630,537	959,802	1,254,533	1,066,457	1,010,559	1,039,367	1,000,447	981,255
Department of Justice	15,728	60,721	99,775	278,927	608,148	168,776	186,215	205,692	203,488	196,150
Department of Labor	424,494	1,862,738	2,511,380	4,696,100	5,764,500	5,070,500	6,073,300	6,826,000	6,121,000	5,662,000
Department of State	59,742	25,188	51,225	388,349	533,309	636,627	676,520	778,180	741,670	725,222
Department of Transportation	27,534	54,712	76,186	117,054	126,900	143,378	138,433	165,246	154,035	212,120
Department of the Treasury	18	1,247,463	41,715	83,000	†	100	†	†	†	100
Department of Veterans Affairs	1,032,918	2,351,233	757,476	1,577,374	4,293,624	4,527,232	4,763,479	8,802,944	10,293,752	10,603,821
Other agencies and programs										
ACTION	88,034	2,833	8,472	332,500	602,100	635,320	642,225	557,900	614,900	613,400
Agency for International Development	37,838	176,770	249,786	7,243	8,542	7,176	6,106	5,070	11,902	11,124
Appalachian Regional Commission	†	19,032	93	3,000	3,000	3,000	3,000	4,000	3,000	4,000
Barry Goldwater Scholarship and Excellence in Education Foundation	†	†	1,033	3,000	3,000	3,000	3,000	3,000	3,000	†
Corporation for National and Community Service	†	†	†	386,000	472,000	333,000	401,000	965,000	983,000	757,000
Environmental Protection Agency	19,446	41,083	87,481	98,900	83,400	44,500	52,900	54,700	53,600	53,800
Estimated education share of federal aid to the District of Columbia	33,019	81,847	104,940	127,127	154,962	149,722	157,465	159,670	155,643	151,381
Federal Emergency Management Agency	290	1,946	215	14,894	†	†	†	†	†	†
General Services Administration	14,775	34,800	†	†	†	†	†	†	†	†
Harry S Truman Scholarship fund	†	-1,895	2,883	3,000	3,000	3,000	2,000	2,000	1,000	1,200
Institute of American Indian and Alaska Native Culture and Arts Development	†	†	4,305	2,000	6,000	7,000	8,000	8,000	8,284	8,500
Institute of Museum and Library Services	†	†	†	166,000	250,000	253,000	265,000	265,000	274,000	243,000
James Madison Memorial Fellowship Foundation	†	†	191	7,000	2,000	2,000	2,000	2,000	2,000	2,000
Japanese-United States Friendship Commission	†	2,294	2,299	3,000	3,000	2,000	2,000	2,000	3,700	3,700
Library of Congress	29,478	151,871	189,827	299,000	430,000	434,000	468,000	516,000	521,000	521,000
National Aeronautics and Space Administration	258,366	255,511	1,093,303	2,077,830	2,763,120	1,154,900	1,754,100	1,585,500	1,430,761	1,277,997
National Archives and Records Administration	†	†	77,397	121,879	276,000	279,000	329,000	339,000	349,000	339,000
National Commission on Libraries and Information Science	†	2,090	3,281	2,000	1,000	1,000	†	†	†	†
National Endowment for the Arts	340	5,220	5,577	10,048	10,976	12,808	12,918	14,413	13,495	16,595
National Endowment for the Humanities	8,459	142,586	141,048	100,014	117,825	124,162	134,533	142,654	131,135	136,100
National Science Foundation	295,628	808,392	1,588,891	2,955,244	3,993,216	4,298,290	6,464,300	5,560,700	4,918,290	5,484,138
Nuclear Regulatory Commission	†	32,590	42,328	12,200	15,100	2,200	8,200	14,500	14,200	14,900
Office of Economic Opportunity	1,092,410	†	†	†	†	†	†	†	†	†
Smithsonian Institution	2,461	5,153	5,779	25,764	45,890	64,768	61,104	63,107	67,322	65,109
U.S. Arms Control and Disarmament Agency	100	661	25	†	†	†	†	†	†	†
United States Information Agency	8,423	66,210	201,547	†	†	†	†	†	†	†
United States Institute of Peace	†	†	7,621	13,000	28,000	17,000	49,000	58,000	47,000	44,000
Other agencies	1,421	990	885	300	7,900	8,600	13,500	14,300	11,700	7,900

See notes at end of table.

Federal Programs for Education & Related Activities

Federal on-budget funds for education, by agency: Selected fiscal years, 1970 through 2012—Continued

[In thousands]

Agency	Constant fiscal year 2013 dollars[4]									
	1970	1980	1990[1]	2000[1]	2005[1]	2008[1]	2009[1,2]	2010[1]	2011[1,3]	2012[1,3]
1	2	3	4	5	6	7	8	9	10	11
Total	$70,536,670	$93,304,530	$88,572,313	$115,304,694	$172,002,551	$154,491,784	$289,800,061	$193,411,636	$190,153,155	$193,567,128
Department of Education[2]	26,044,619	35,537,559	39,801,988	45,758,319	85,753,991	77,254,856	200,536,654	97,015,532	97,094,995	100,741,307
Department of Agriculture	5,410,881	12,341,421	10,741,780	14,865,221	16,255,408	17,755,377	17,736,169	20,334,526	21,117,782	22,573,951
Department of Commerce	78,778	366,691	92,365	153,716	286,998	207,231	280,937	319,890	306,978	312,928
Department of Defense	4,625,233	4,220,596	6,186,002	6,070,950	7,435,583	7,041,146	7,365,127	8,114,739	7,490,045	7,448,024
Department of Energy	3,105,647	4,343,016	4,395,559	4,798,990	5,105,571	2,643,353	4,003,400	3,592,269	2,906,354	3,272,070
Department of Health and Human Services	10,118,078	15,185,617	13,650,194	23,707,636	30,714,115	28,332,323	34,033,769	33,743,777	29,956,316	30,189,404
Department of Homeland Security	†	†	†	†	735,105	439,460	543,628	570,343	2,154,737	433,765
Department of Housing and Urban Development	645,926	14,374	202	1,878	1,294	428	214	422	1,346	1,423
Department of the Interior	1,075,380	1,191,675	1,081,818	1,287,692	1,475,872	1,141,472	1,079,479	1,097,304	1,035,841	997,219
Department of Justice	88,564	164,250	171,185	374,215	715,445	180,648	198,915	217,158	210,687	199,341
Department of Labor	2,390,324	5,038,685	4,308,796	6,300,394	6,781,541	5,427,162	6,487,499	7,206,497	6,337,552	5,754,113
Department of State	336,407	68,133	87,887	521,018	627,402	681,408	722,659	821,557	767,909	737,020
Department of Transportation	155,044	147,995	130,713	157,042	149,289	153,463	147,874	174,457	159,485	215,571
Department of the Treasury	101	3,374,373	71,571	111,355	†	107	†	†	104	102
Department of Veterans Affairs	5,816,357	6,360,058	1,299,608	2,116,241	5,051,155	4,845,681	5,088,348	9,293,640	10,657,930	10,776,331
Other agencies and programs										
ACTION	†	7,663	14,535	†	†	†	†	†	†	†
Agency for International Development	495,719	478,161	428,560	446,090	708,330	680,009	686,025	588,999	636,654	623,379
Appalachian Regional Commission	213,066	51,481	160	9,717	10,049	7,681	6,522	5,353	12,323	11,305
Barry Goldwater Scholarship and Excellence in Education Foundation	†	†	1,772	4,025	3,529	3,211	3,205	4,223	3,106	4,065
Corporation for National and Community Service	†	†	†	517,866	555,276	356,423	428,348	1,018,791	1,017,777	769,315
Environmental Protection Agency	109,500	111,129	150,092	132,686	98,114	47,630	56,508	57,749	55,496	54,675
Estimated education share of federal aid to the District of Columbia	185,930	221,395	180,046	170,556	182,302	160,254	168,204	168,570	161,149	153,844
Federal Emergency Management Agency	1,633	5,264	369	19,982	†	†	†	†	†	†
General Services Administration	83,198	94,134	4,946	4,025	3,529	3,211	2,136	2,111	1,035	1,220
Harry S Truman Scholarship fund	†	-5,126	7,386	2,683	7,059	7,492	8,546	8,446	8,577	8,638
Institute of American Indian and Alaska Native Culture and Arts Development	†	†	328	†	†	†	†	†	†	†
Institute of Museum and Library Services	†	†	†	222,709	294,108	270,796	283,073	279,772	283,694	246,953
James Madison Memorial Fellowship Foundation	†	†	3,944	9,391	2,353	2,141	2,136	2,111	2,071	2,033
Japanese-United States Friendship Commission	†	6,205	†	4,025	3,529	2,141	2,136	2,111	3,831	3,760
Library of Congress	165,991	410,809	325,688	401,145	505,866	464,528	499,918	544,763	539,432	529,476
National Aeronautics and Space Administration	1,454,858	691,154	1,875,789	2,787,664	3,250,622	1,236,136	1,873,730	1,673,879	1,481,379	1,298,788
National Archives and Records Administration	†	†	132,791	163,516	324,695	298,625	351,438	357,897	361,347	344,515
National Commission on Libraries and Information Science	†	5,653	5,629	2,683	1,176	1,070	†	†	†	†
National Endowment for the Arts	1,915	14,120	9,569	13,480	12,913	13,709	13,799	15,216	13,972	16,865
National Endowment for the Humanities	47,633	385,694	241,997	134,182	138,613	132,896	143,708	150,605	135,774	138,314
National Science Foundation	1,664,680	2,186,691	2,726,074	3,964,822	4,697,746	4,600,635	6,905,165	5,870,666	5,092,292	5,573,357
Nuclear Regulatory Commission	†	88,156	72,623	16,368	17,764	2,355	8,759	15,308	14,702	15,142
Office of Economic Opportunity	6,151,357	†	†	†	†	†	†	†	†	†
Smithsonian Institution	13,858	13,939	9,915	34,566	53,986	69,324	65,271	66,625	69,704	66,168
U.S. Arms Control and Disarmament Agency	563	1,788	43	†	†	†	†	†	†	†
United States Information Agency	47,430	179,097	345,796	†	†	†	†	†	†	†
United States Institute of Peace	†	†	13,075	17,441	32,940	18,196	52,342	61,233	48,663	44,716
Other agencies	8,002	2,678	1,518	402	9,294	9,205	14,421	15,097	12,114	8,029

†Not applicable.

[1]Excludes federal support for medical education benefits under Medicare in the U.S. Department of Health and Human Services. Benefits excluded from total because data before fiscal year (FY) 1990 are not available. This program existed since Medicare began, but was not available as a separate budget item until FY 1990. Excluded amounts are as follows: $4,440,000,000 in FY 1990, $8,020,000,000 in FY 2000, $8,290,000,000 in FY 2005, $9,600,000,000 in FY 2008, $8,800,000,000 in FY 2009, $9,080,000,000 in FY 2010, $9,200,000,000 in FY 2011, and $9,800,000,000 in FY 2012.

[2]All education funds from the American Recovery and Reinvestment Act of 2009 (ARRA) are included in the Department of Education amount for FY 2009. Most of these funds had a 2-year availability, meaning that they were available for the Department of Education to obligate during FY 2009 and FY 2010.

[3]Estimated.

[4]Data adjusted by the federal budget composite deflator reported in U.S. Office of Management and Budget, *Budget of the U.S. Government, Historical Tables, Fiscal Year 2014*.

NOTE: To the extent possible, amounts reported represent outlays rather than obligations. Negative amounts occur when program receipts exceed outlays. Starting in FY 2010, amounts for the U.S. Department of Education are appropriations, not outlays. Some data have been revised from previously published figures. Detail may not sum to totals because of rounding.

SOURCE: U.S. Department of Education, National Center for Education Statistics, unpublished tabulations. U.S. Office of Management and Budget, *Budget of the U.S. Government, Appendix*, fiscal years 1972 through 2014. National Science Foundation, *Federal Funds for Research and Development*, fiscal years 1970 to 2012. (This table was prepared April 2014.)

Federal on-budget funds for education, by level/educational purpose, agency, and program: Selected fiscal years, 1970 through 2013

[In thousands of current dollars]

Level/educational purpose, agency, and program	1970	1980	1990[1]	1995[1]	2000[1]	2005[1]	2010[1]	2011[1,2]	2012[1,2]	2013[3]
1	2	3	4	5	6	7	8	9	10	11
Total	$12,526,499	$34,493,502	$51,624,342	$71,639,520	$85,944,203	$146,206,999	$183,199,676	$183,655,692	$190,468,459	—
Elementary/secondary education	5,830,442	16,027,686	21,984,361	33,623,809	43,790,783	68,957,711	86,681,807	76,118,858	78,087,148	$80,444,438
Department of Education[3]	2,719,204	6,629,095	9,681,313	14,029,000	20,039,563	37,477,594	49,621,475	38,652,240	38,600,066	38,705,852
Education for the disadvantaged	1,339,014	3,204,664	4,494,111	6,808,000	8,529,111	14,635,566	15,864,666	15,515,444	15,741,703	15,590,733
Impact aid program[4]	656,372	690,170	816,366	808,000	877,101	1,262,174	1,276,183	1,273,631	1,291,186	1,299,088
School improvement programs[5]	288,304	788,918	1,189,158	1,397,000	2,549,971	7,918,091	16,999,862	6,738,485	6,327,886	6,543,628
Indian education	†	93,365	69,451	71,000	65,285	121,911	127,282	127,027	130,779	131,579
English Language Acquisition	21,250	169,540	188,919	225,000	362,662	667,485	750,000	733,530	732,144	736,624
Special education	79,090	821,777	1,616,623	3,177,000	4,948,977	10,940,312	12,587,035	12,526,672	12,640,709	12,661,256
Vocational and adult education	335,174	860,661	1,306,685	1,482,000	1,462,977	1,967,086	2,016,447	1,737,451	1,735,659	1,742,944
Education Reform—Goals 2000[6]	†	†	†	61,000	1,243,479	−35,031	†	†	†	†
Hurricane Education Recovery	†	†	†	†	†	†	†	†	†	†
Department of Agriculture	760,477	4,064,497	5,528,950	8,201,294	10,051,278	12,577,265	17,875,561	18,843,607	20,849,143	21,781,420
Child nutrition programs[7]	299,131	3,377,056	4,977,075	7,644,789	9,554,028	11,901,943	16,383,421	17,290,601	19,504,343	20,487,229
McGovern-Dole International Food for Education and Child Nutrition Program[8]	†	†	†	†	†	86,000	210,000	343,500	196,400	197,126
Agricultural Marketing Service—commodities[9]	341,597	388,000	350,441	400,000	400,000	399,322	1,100,000	1,006,000	952,000	903,000
Special Milk Program	83,800	159,293	18,707	(7)	(7)	(7)	(7)	(7)	(7)	(7)
Estimated education share of Forest Service permanent appropriations	35,949	140,148	182,727	156,505	97,250	190,000	182,140	203,506	196,400	194,065
Department of Commerce	†	54,816	†	†	†	†	†	†	†	†
Local public works program—school facilities[10]	†	54,816	†	†	†	†	†	†	†	†
Department of Defense	143,100	370,846	1,097,876	1,295,547	1,485,611	1,786,253	1,981,321	2,047,825	2,132,046	2,220,611
Junior Reserve Officers Training Corps (JROTC)	12,100	32,000	39,300	155,600	210,432	315,122	359,689	377,526	391,682	407,335
Overseas dependents schools	131,000	338,846	864,958	855,772	904,829	1,060,920	1,186,560	1,193,636	1,235,707	1,262,545
Domestic schools[11]	†	†	193,618	284,175	370,350	410,211	435,072	476,663	504,657	550,731
Department of Energy	200	77,633	15,563	12,646	†	†	†	†	†	†
Energy conservation for school buildings[11]	200	77,240	15,213	10,746	†	†	†	†	†	†
Pre-engineering program	†	393	350	1,900	†	†	†	†	†	†
Department of Health and Human Services	167,333	1,077,000	2,396,793	5,116,559	6,011,036	8,003,348	8,547,000	8,871,364	9,298,710	9,433,300
Head Start[12]	†	735,000	1,447,758	3,534,000	5,267,000	6,842,348	7,234,000	7,559,164	7,969,210	8,107,000
Payments to states for Aid to Families with Dependent Children (AFDC) work programs[13]	†	†	459,221	953,000	15,000	—	—	—	—	—
Social Security student benefits[14]	167,333	342,000	489,814	629,559	729,036	1,161,000	1,313,000	1,312,200	1,329,500	1,326,300
Department of Homeland Security	†	†	†	†	†	500	505	504	454	364
Tuition assistance to educational accreditation—Coast Guard personnel[15]	†	†	†	†	†	500	505	504	454	364
Department of the Interior	140,705	318,170	445,267	493,124	725,423	938,506	781,075	815,877	782,335	766,043
Mineral Leasing Act and other funds										
Payments to states—estimated education share	12,294	62,636	123,811	18,750	24,610	60,290	23,000	24,380	26,450	26,420
Payments to counties—estimated education share	16,359	48,953	102,522	37,490	53,500	79,686	50,000	53,000	58,000	57,570
Indian Education										
Bureau of Indian Education schools	95,850	178,112	192,841	411,524	466,905	517,647	580,492	583,572	631,477	597,412
Johnson-O'Malley assistance[16]	16,080	28,081	25,556	24,359	17,387	16,510	13,589	13,415	13,304	12,615
Education construction	†	†	†	†	161,021	263,373	112,994	140,509	52,104	71,026
Education expenses for children of employees, Yellowstone National Park	122	388	538	1,000	2,000	1,000	1,000	1,000	1,000	1,000
Department of Justice	8,237	23,890	65,997	128,850	224,800	554,500	137,529	140,525	149,587	160,684
Advanced occupational education	†	†	†	†	†	†	137,529	140,525	149,587	160,684
Vocational training expenses for prisoners in federal prisons	2,720	4,966	2,066	3,000	1,000	0	†	†	†	†
Inmate programs[17]	5,517	18,924	63,931	125,850	223,800	554,500	†	†	†	†

See notes at end of table.

Federal on-budget funds for education, by level/educational purpose, agency, and program: Selected fiscal years, 1970 through 2013—Continued

[In thousands of current dollars]

Level/educational purpose, agency, and program	1970	1980	1990[1]	1995[1]	2000[1]	2005[1]	2010[1]	2011[1,2]	2012[1,2]	2013[1]
1	2	3	4	5	6	7	8	9	10	11
Department of Labor	420,927	1,849,800	2,505,487	3,957,800	4,683,200	5,654,000	6,826,000	6,121,000	5,662,000	6,650,000
Job Corps	†	469,800	739,376	1,029,000	1,256,000	1,521,000	1,850,000	1,660,000	1,789,000	1,650,000
Training programs—estimated funds for education programs[18]	420,927	1,380,000	1,766,111	2,928,800	3,427,200	4,133,000	4,976,000	4,461,000	3,873,000	5,000,000
Department of Transportation	45	60	46	62	188	†	†	†	†	†
Tuition assistance for educational accreditation—Coast Guard personnel[15]	45	60	46	62	188	†	†	†	†	†
Department of the Treasury	†	935,903	†	†	†	†	†	†	†	†
Estimated education share of general revenue sharing[19]										
State[20]	†	525,019	†	†	†	†	†	†	†	†
Local	†	410,884	†	†	†	†	†	†	†	†
Department of Veterans Affairs	338,910	545,786	155,351	311,768	445,052	1,815,000	760,500	472,000	488,769	534,796
Noncollegiate and job training programs[21]	281,640	439,993	12,848	†	†	†	†	†	†	†
Vocational rehabilitation for disabled veterans[22]	41,700	87,980	136,780	298,132	438,635	1,815,000	760,500	472,000	488,769	534,796
Dependents' education[23]	15,570	17,813	5,723	5,961	6,417	†	—	—	—	—
Service members occupational conversion training act of 1992	†	†	†	7,675	†	†	†	†	†	†
Other agencies										
Appalachian Regional Commission	33,161	9,157	93	2,173	2,588	2,962	986	2,290	962	1,689
National Endowment for the Arts	†	4,989	4,641	7,117	6,002	8,470	11,530	12,125	10,450	10,427
Arts in education	†	4,989	4,641	7,117	6,002	8,470	11,530	12,125	10,450	10,427
National Endowment for the Humanities	20	330	404	997	812	603	125	75	100	333
Office of Economic Opportunity	1,072,375	†	†	†	†	†	†	†	†	†
Head Start[24]	325,700	†	†	†	†	†	†	†	†	†
Other elementary and secondary programs[25]	42,809	†	†	†	†	†	†	†	†	†
Job Corps[26]	144,000	†	†	†	†	†	†	†	†	†
Youth Corps and other training programs[26]	553,368	†	†	†	†	†	†	†	†	†
Volunteers in Service to America (VISTA)[27]	6,498	†	†	†	†	†	†	†	†	†
Other programs										
Estimated education share of federal aid to the District of Columbia	25,748	65,714	86,579	66,871	115,230	138,710	138,200	139,426	112,526	178,919
Postsecondary education	**$3,447,697**	**$11,115,882**	**$13,650,915**	**$17,618,137**	**$15,008,715**	**$38,587,287**	**$50,197,838**	**$64,400,219**	**$70,054,237**	**$62,448,915**
Department of Education[3]	1,187,962	5,682,242	11,175,978	14,234,000	10,727,315	31,420,023	36,539,655	49,260,330	54,470,178	45,942,515
Student financial assistance	†	3,682,789	5,920,328	7,047,000	9,060,317	15,209,515	25,959,478	43,753,247	43,324,872	37,130,405
Direct Loan Program[28]	†	†	†	840,000	-2,862,240	3,020,992	3,481,859	2,781,709	6,917,373	3,273,880
Federal Family Education Loan Program[29]	2,323	1,407,977	4,372,446	5,190,000	2,707,473	10,777,470	3,932,994	-91,796	1,498,353	2,787,755
Higher education	1,029,131	399,787	659,492	871,000	1,530,779	2,053,288	2,740,665	2,388,946	2,297,656	2,302,753
Facilities—loans and insurance	114,199	-19,031	19,219	-6,000	-2,174	-1,464	-8,360	-4,607	-8,513	-129
College housing loans[30]	774	14,082	-57,167	-46,000	-41,886	-33,521	-16,725	-13,265	-16,725	-1,176
Educational activities overseas	†	3,561	82	†	150	169	23,330	23,289	32,160	21,424
Historically Black Colleges and Universities Capital Financing, Program Account	†	†	†	†	†	†	†	†	†	†
Gallaudet College and Howard University	38,559	176,829	230,327	292,000	291,060	339,823	357,977	357,261	359,580	361,781
National Technical Institute for the Deaf	2,976	16,248	31,251	46,000	43,836	53,751	68,437	65,546	65,422	65,822
Hurricane Katrina, aid to institutions	†	†	†	†	†	†	†	†	†	†
Department of Agriculture	†	10,453	31,273	33,373	30,676	61,957	80,697	81,658	81,658	79,089
Agriculture Extension Service, Second Morrill Act payments to agricultural and mechanical colleges and Tuskegee Institute	†	10,453	31,273	33,373	30,676	61,957	80,697	81,658	81,658	79,089
Department of Commerce	8,277	29,971	3,312	3,487	3,800	—	—	—	—	—
Sea Grant Program[31]	—	3,123	3,312	3,487	3,800	†	—	—	—	†
Merchant Marine Academy[32]	6,160	14,809	†	†	†	†	†	†	†	†
State marine schools[32]	2,117	12,039	†	†	†	†	†	†	†	†

See notes at end of table.

T Federal on-budget funds for education, by level/educational purpose, agency, and program: Selected fiscal years, 1970 through 2013—Continued

[In thousands of current dollars]

Level/educational purpose, agency, and program	1970	1980	1990	1995[1]	2000[1]	2005[1]	2010[1]	2011[1,2]	2012[1,2]	2013[1]
1	2	3	4	5	6	7	8	9	10	11
Department of Defense	322,100	545,000	635,769	729,500	1,147,759	1,858,301	2,550,667	2,297,234	2,407,629	2,272,909
Tuition assistance for military personnel	57,500	—	95,300	127,000	263,303	608,109	669,892	567,412	590,626	564,604
Service academies	78,700	106,100	120,613	163,300	212,678	300,760	402,640	348,836	375,250	224,677
Senior Reserve Officers Training Corps (SROTC)[33]	108,100	—	193,056	219,400	363,461	537,525	885,500	851,910	844,498	843,018
Professional development education[33]	77,800	—	226,800	219,800	308,317	411,907	592,635	529,076	597,255	640,610
Department of Energy	3,000	57,701	25,502	28,027	†	†	†	†	†	†
University laboratory cooperative program	3,000	2,800	9,402	8,552	†	†	†	†	†	†
Teacher development projects	†	1,400	†	†	†	†	†	†	†	†
Energy conservation for buildings—higher education[11]	†	53,501	7,459	7,381	†	†	†	†	†	†
Minority honors vocational training	†	†	†	†	†	†	†	†	†	†
Honors research program	†	†	6,472	2,221	†	†	†	†	†	†
Students and teachers	†	†	2,169	9,873	†	†	†	†	†	†
Department of Health and Human Services	981,483	2,412,058	578,542	796,035	954,190	1,433,516	1,278,936	1,367,895	1,331,410	1,295,616
Health professions training programs[34]	353,029	460,736	230,600	298,302	340,361	581,661	406,000	498,000	459,000	438,039
Indian health manpower	†	7,187	9,508	27,000	16,000	27,000	46,000	41,000	41,000	41,000
National Health Service Corps scholarships	†	70,667	4,759	78,206	33,300	45,000	41,000	46,400	42,940	39,868
National Institutes of Health training grants[35]	†	176,388	241,356	380,502	550,220	756,014	775,186	771,766	777,761	766,000
National Institute of Occupational Safety and Health training grants[36]	8,088	12,899	10,461	11,660	14,198	23,841	10,750	10,729	10,709	10,709
Alcohol, drug abuse, and mental health training programs[37]	118,366	122,103	81,353	†	110	†	†	†	†	†
Health teaching facilities[38]	†	3,078	505	365	†	†	†	†	†	†
Social Security postsecondary students' benefits[39]	502,000	1,559,000	†	†	†	†	†	†	†	†
Department of Homeland Security[15]	†	†	†	†	†	36,400	45,824	49,604	48,592	43,468
Coast Guard Academy[15]	†	†	†	†	†	16,400	26,326	27,581	26,803	24,359
Postgraduate training for Coast Guard officers[40]	†	†	†	†	†	8,700	4,645	4,883	5,891	6,198
Tuition assistance to Coast Guard military personnel[15]	†	†	†	†	†	11,300	14,853	17,140	15,898	12,911
Department of Housing and Urban Development[30]	114,199	†	†	†	†	†	†	†	†	†
College housing loans[30]	114,199	†	†	†	†	†	†	†	†	†
Department of the Interior	31,749	80,202	135,480	159,054	187,179	249,227	174,092	112,970	120,720	108,837
Shared revenues, Mineral Leasing Act and other receipts—estimated education share	6,949	35,403	69,980	82,810	98,740	146,235	16,250	20,430	29,900	21,670
Indian programs										
Continuing education	9,380	16,909	34,911	43,907	57,576	76,271	126,791	61,603	61,435	58,832
Higher education scholarships	15,420	27,890	30,589	32,337	30,863	26,721	31,051	30,937	29,385	28,335
Department of State	30,850	†	2,167	3,000	319,000	424,000	657,660	620,050	601,770	605,641
Educational exchange[41]	30,850	†	†	†	319,000	424,000	657,660	620,050	601,770	605,641
Mutual educational and cultural exchange activities	30,454	†	†	†	303,000	402,000	635,000	599,550	583,200	586,957
International educational exchange activities	396	†	†	†	16,000	22,000	22,660	20,500	18,570	18,684
Russian, Eurasian, and East European Research and Training	†	†	2,167	3,000	†	†	†	†	†	†
Department of Transportation	11,197	12,530	46,025	59,257	60,300	73,000	95,000	77,000	118,000	130,000
Merchant Marine Academy[22]	11,197	12,530	20,926	30,850	34,000	61,000	79,000	61,000	101,000	109,000
State marine schools[32]	†	†	8,269	8,980	7,000	12,000	16,000	16,000	17,000	21,000
Coast Guard Academy[15]	9,342	10,000	12,074	13,500	15,500	†	†	†	†	†
Postgraduate training for Coast Guard officers[40]	1,655	2,230	4,173	5,513	2,500	†	†	†	†	†
Tuition assistance to Coast Guard military personnel[15]	200	300	582	414	1,300	†	†	†	†	†
Department of the Treasury	†	296,750	†	†	†	†	†	†	†	†
General revenue sharing—estimated state share to higher education[19,20]	†	296,750	†	†	†	†	†	†	†	†
Department of Veterans Affairs	693,490	1,803,847	599,825	1,010,114	1,132,322	2,478,624	8,042,444	9,821,752	10,115,052	11,162,755
Vietnam-era veterans	638,260	1,579,974	46,998	†	†	†	†	†	†	†
College student support	†	1,560,081	39,458	†	†	†	†	†	†	†
Work-study	†	19,893	7,540	†	†	†	†	†	†	†

See notes at end of table.

Federal on-budget funds for education, by level/educational purpose, agency, and program: Selected fiscal years, 1970 through 2013—Continued

[In thousands of current dollars]

Level/educational purpose, agency, and program	1970	1980	1990	1995[1]	2000[1]	2005[1]	2010[1]	2011[1,2]	2012[1,2]	2013[1]
1	2	3	4	5	6	7	8	9	10	11
Service persons college support	18,900	46,617	8,911	†	†	†	†	†	†	†
Post-Vietnam veterans	†	922	161,475	33,596	3,958	1,136	894	1,343	932	848
All-volunteer-force educational assistance	†	†	269,947	868,394	984,068	2,070,996	1,854,917	1,587,376	1,086,585	885,715
Veterans	†	†	183,765	760,390	876,434	1,887,239	1,659,694	1,385,943	931,756	726,697
Reservists	†	†	86,182	108,004	107,634	183,757	195,223	201,433	154,829	159,018
Post 9-11 GI Bill[42]	†	†	†	†	†	†	5,542,843	7,656,490	8,476,227	9,716,174
Veteran dependents' education	36,330	176,334	100,494	95,124	131,296	388,719	507,294	462,877	455,318	486,705
Payments to state education agencies	†	†	12,000	13,000	13,000	17,773	—	18,342	19,000	19,000
Reserve Education Assistance Program (REAP)[43]	†	†	†	†	†	†	136,496	95,324	76,990	54,313
Other agencies										
Appalachian Regional Commission	4,105	1,751	—	2,741	2,286	4,407	2,464	6,098	6,653	4,443
National Endowment for the Humanities	3,349	56,451	50,938	56,481	28,395	29,253	47,949	40,168	45,000	39,399
National Science Foundation	42,000	64,583	161,884	211,800	389,000	490,000	646,000	636,060	654,000	710,000
Science and engineering education programs	37,000	64,583	161,884	211,800	389,000	490,000	646,000	636,060	654,000	710,000
Sea Grant Program[51]	5,000	†	†	†	†	†	†	†	†	†
United States Information Agency[44]	8,423	51,095	181,172	260,800	†	†	†	†	†	†
Educational and cultural affairs[51]	†	49,546	35,862	13,600	†	†	†	†	†	†
Educational and cultural exchange programs[45]	†	†	145,307	247,200	†	†	†	†	†	†
Educational exchange activities, international	†	1,549	3	†	†	†	†	†	†	†
Information center and library activities	8,423	†	†	†	†	†	†	†	†	†
Other programs										
Barry Goldwater Scholarship and Excellence in Education Foundation	†	†	†	3,000	3,000	3,000	4,000	3,000	4,000	4,000
Estimated education share of federal aid to the District of Columbia[46]	5,513	13,143	14,637	9,468	11,493	14,578	20,450	15,115	37,875	37,193
Harry S Truman Scholarship fund	†	-1,895	2,883	3,000	3,000	3,000	2,000	1,000	1,200	1,500
Institute of American Indian and Alaska Native Culture and Arts Development	†	†	4,305	13,000	2,000	6,000	8,000	8,284	8,500	9,550
James Madison Memorial Fellowship Foundation	†	†	191	2,000	7,000	2,000	2,000	2,000	2,000	2,000
Other education	**$964,719**	**$1,548,730**	**$3,383,031**	**$4,719,655**	**$5,484,571**	**$6,908,504**	**$9,326,725**	**$11,133,686**	**$9,395,279**	**$9,659,535**
Department of Education[3]	630,235	747,706	2,251,801	2,861,000	3,223,801	3,538,862	5,073,063	5,255,939	5,464,708	5,641,061
Administration	47,456	187,317	328,293	404,000	458,054	548,842	1,531,232	1,755,384	1,928,821	2,048,098
Libraries[47]	108,284	129,127	137,264	117,000	†	†	†	†	†	†
Rehabilitative services and disability research	473,091	426,886	1,780,360	2,333,000	2,755,468	2,973,346	3,506,861	3,474,718	3,511,281	3,622,925
American Printing House for the Blind	1,404	4,349	5,736	7,000	9,368	16,538	24,600	24,551	24,505	24,655
Trust funds and contributions	0	27	148	0	465	136	10,370	1,286	101	-54,617
Department of Agriculture	135,637	271,112	352,511	422,878	444,477	468,631	567,423	552,030	547,081	534,371
Extension Service	131,734	263,584	337,907	405,371	424,174	445,631	543,423	530,030	526,081	513,371
National Agricultural Library	3,903	7,528	14,604	17,507	20,303	23,000	24,000	22,000	21,000	21,000
Department of Commerce	1,226	2,479	†	†	†	†	†	†	†	†
Maritime Administration										
Training for private sector employees[32]	1,226	2,479	†	†	†	†	†	†	†	†
Department of Health and Human Services	24,273	37,819	77,962	138,000	214,000	313,000	340,000	337,000	337,639	339,705
National Library of Medicine	24,273	37,819	77,962	138,000	214,000	313,000	340,000	337,000	337,639	339,705
Department of Homeland Security	†	†	†	†	†	278,243	341,100	1,892,000	215,471	258,000
Federal Law Enforcement Training Center[48]	†	†	†	†	†	159,000	323,000	311,000	271,000	258,000
Estimated disaster relief[49]	†	†	†	†	†	119,243	18,100	1,581,000	-55,529	—
Department of Justice	5,546	27,642	26,920	36,296	34,727	26,148	33,563	33,563	33,563	33,563
Federal Bureau of Investigation National Academy	2,066	7,234	6,028	12,831	22,479	15,619	19,443	19,443	19,443	19,443
Federal Bureau of Investigation Field Police Academy	2,500	7,715	10,548	11,140	11,962	10,456	14,120	14,120	14,120	14,120
Narcotics and dangerous drug training	980	2,416	850	325	286	73	†	†	†	†
National Institute of Corrections	†	10,277	9,494	12,000	†	†	†	†	†	†

See notes at end of table.

Federal on-budget funds for education, by level/educational purpose, agency, and program: Selected fiscal years, 1970 through 2013—Continued

[In thousands of current dollars]

Level/educational purpose, agency, and program	1970	1980	1990	1995	2000[1]	2005[1]	2010[1]	2011[1,2]	2012[1,2]	2013[1]
1	2	3	4	5	6	7	8	9	10	11
Department of State	20,672	25,000	47,539	51,648	69,349	109,309	120,520	121,620	123,452	219,238
Foreign Service Institute[41]	15,857	25,000	47,539	51,648	69,349	109,309	120,520	121,620	123,452	219,238
Center for Cultural and Technical Interchange[41]	4,815	†	†	†	†	†	†	†	†	†
Department of Transportation	3,964	10,212	1,507	650	700	1,100	146	135	120	—
Highways training and education grants	2,418	3,412	—	—	—	—	—	—	—	—
Maritime Administration										
Training for private sector employees[30]	†	†	1,507	650	700	1,100	146	135	120	—
Urban mass transportation—managerial training grants	1,546	500	—	—	—	—	—	—	—	—
Federal Aviation Administration										
Air traffic controllers second career program	—	6,300	—	—	—	—	—	—	—	—
Department of the Treasury	18	14,584	41,488	48,000	83,000	†	†	†	†	†
Federal Law Enforcement Training Center[48]	18	14,584	41,488	48,000	83,000	†	†	†	†	†
Other agencies										
ACTION[50]	†	2,833	8,472	†	†	†	†	†	†	†
Estimated education funds	†	2,833	8,472	†	†	†	†	†	†	†
Agency for International Development	88,034	99,707	170,371	260,408	299,000	574,000	542,700	599,500	598,800	602,369
Education and human resources	61,570	80,518	142,801	248,408	299,000	574,000	542,700	599,500	598,800	602,369
American schools and hospitals abroad	26,464	19,189	27,570	12,000	—	—	—	—	—	—
Appalachian Regional Commission	572	8,124	†	5,709	2,369	1,173	1,620	3,514	3,510	6,938
Corporation for National and Community Service[50]	†	†	†	214,600	386,000	472,000	965,000	983,000	757,000	760,498
Federal Emergency Management Agency[51]	290	281	215	170,400	14,894	†	†	†	†	†
Estimated architect/engineer student development program	40	31	200	—	—	—	—	—	—	—
Estimated other training programs[52]	250	250	15	—	—	—	—	—	—	—
Estimated disaster relief[49]	—	—	†	170,400	14,894	†	†	†	†	†
General Services Administration										
Libraries and other archival activities[53]	14,775	34,800	†	†	†	†	†	†	†	†
Institute of Museum and Library Services[57]	†	†	†	†	166,000	250,000	265,000	274,000	243,000	226,000
Japanese-United States Friendship Commission	†	2,294	2,299	2,000	3,000	3,000	2,000	3,700	3,700	3,700
Library of Congress	29,478	151,871	189,827	241,000	299,000	430,000	516,000	521,000	521,000	470,202
Salaries and expenses	20,700	102,364	148,985	198,000	247,000	383,000	439,000	446,000	442,000	422,625
Books for the blind and the physically handicapped	6,195	31,436	37,473	39,000	46,000	47,000	77,000	75,000	79,000	47,577
Special foreign currency program	2,273	3,492	10	—	—	—	—	—	—	—
Furniture and furnishings	310	14,579	3,359	4,000	6,000	—	—	—	—	—
National Aeronautics and Space Administration										
Aerospace education services project	350	882	3,300	5,923	6,800	—	—	—	—	—
National Archives and Records Administration										
Libraries and other archival activities[53]	†	†	77,397	105,172	121,879	276,000	339,000	349,000	339,000	373,000
National Commission on Libraries and Information Science[54]	†	231	936	1,000	2,000	1,000	†	†	†	†
National Endowment for the Arts	340	2,090	3,281	2,304	4,046	2,506	2,883	1,370	6,145	3,483
National Endowment for the Humanities	5,090	85,805	89,706	94,249	70,807	87,969	94,580	90,891	91,000	74,439
Smithsonian Institution	2,461	5,153	5,779	9,961	25,764	45,890	63,107	67,322	65,109	64,920
Museum programs and related research	2,261	3,254	690	3,190	18,000	32,000	52,000	56,000	54,000	54,313
National Gallery of Art extension service	200	426	474	771	764	890	107	119	122	115
Woodrow Wilson International Center for Scholars	†	1,473	4,615	6,000	7,000	13,000	11,000	11,203	10,987	10,492

See notes at end of table.

Federal on-budget funds for education, by level/educational purpose, agency, and program: Selected fiscal years, 1970 through 2013—Continued

[In thousands of current dollars]

Level/educational purpose, agency, and program	1970	1980	1990[1]	1995[1]	2000[1]	2005[1]	2010[1]	2011[1,2]	2012[1,2]	2013[1]
1	2	3	4	5	6	7	8	9	10	11
U.S. Information Agency—Center for Cultural and Technical Interchange[41]	†	15,115	20,375	34,000	†	†	†	†	†	†
United States Institute of Peace	†	†	7,621	12,000	13,000	28,000	58,000	47,000	44,000	47,000
Other programs										
Estimated education share of federal aid for the District of Columbia	1,758	2,990	3,724	2,457	404	1,674	1,020	1,102	980	1,048
Research programs at universities and related institutions[55]	$2,283,641	$5,801,204	$12,606,035	$15,677,919	$21,660,134	$31,753,498	$36,993,306	$32,002,929	$32,931,796	—
Department of Education[56]	87,823	78,742	89,483	279,000	116,464	456,822	659,006	608,786	593,664	$597,297
Department of Agriculture	64,796	216,405	348,109	434,544	553,600	709,700	737,200	918,900	734,700	—
Department of Commerce	4,487	48,295	50,523	85,442	110,775	243,948	303,000	296,489	307,919	—
Department of Defense	356,188	644,455	1,871,864	1,853,955	1,891,710	2,675,900	3,154,300	2,889,054	2,789,120	—
Department of Energy	548,327	1,470,224	2,520,885	2,651,641	3,577,004	4,339,879	3,402,600	2,807,045	3,219,690	—
Department of Health and Human Services	623,765	2,087,053	4,902,714	6,418,969	10,491,641	16,357,996	21,796,200	18,356,461	18,738,366	—
Department of Homeland Security	—	—	—	†	†	309,717	152,800	139,003	162,304	—
Department of Housing and Urban Development	510	5,314	118	1,613	1,400	1,100	400	1,300	1,400	—
Department of the Interior	18,521	42,175	49,790	50,618	47,200	66,800	84,200	71,600	78,200	—
Department of Justice	1,945	9,189	6,858	7,204	19,400	27,500	34,600	29,400	13,000	—
Department of Labor	3,567	12,938	5,893	10,114	12,900	110,500	†	†	†	†
Department of State	8,220	188	1,519	23	†	†	†	†	†	—
Department of Transportation	12,328	31,910	28,608	75,847	55,866	52,800	70,100	76,900	94,000	—
Department of the Treasury	†	226	227	1,496	†	†	†	100	100	—
Department of Veterans Affairs	518	1,600	2,300	2,500	†	†	†	†	†	—
Agency for International Development	†	77,063	79,415	30,172	33,500	28,100	15,200	15,400	14,600	—
Environmental Protection Agency	19,446	41,083	87,481	125,721	98,900	83,400	54,700	53,600	53,800	—
Federal Emergency Management Agency		1,665								
National Aeronautics and Space Administration	258,016	254,629	1,090,003	1,751,977	2,071,030	2,763,120	1,585,500	1,430,761	1,277,997	—
National Science Foundation	253,628	743,809	1,427,007	1,874,395	2,566,244	3,503,216	4,914,700	4,282,230	4,830,138	—
Nuclear Regulatory Commission	†	32,590	42,328	22,188	12,200	15,100	14,500	14,200	14,900	—
Office of Economic Opportunity	20,035			†	†	†	†	†	†	—
U.S. Arms Control and Disarmament Agency	100	661	25	†	†	†	†	†	†	—
Other agencies	1,421	990	885	500	300	7,900	14,300	11,700	7,900	—

See notes at end of table.

Federal on-budget funds for education, by level/educational purpose, agency, and program: Selected fiscal years, 1970 through 2012—Continued

—Not available.

†Not applicable.

[1]Excludes federal support for medical education benefits under Medicare in the U.S. Department of Health and Human Services. Benefits excluded from total because data before fiscal year (FY) 1990 are not available. This program existed since Medicare began, but was not available as a separate budget item until FY 1990. Excluded amounts are as follows: $4,440,000,000 in FY 1990, $7,510,000,000 in FY 1995, $8,020,000,000 in FY 2000, $8,290,000,000 in FY 2005, $9,080,000,000 in FY 2010, $9,200,000,000 in FY 2011, $9,800,000,000 in FY 2012, and an estimated $10,000,000,000 in FY 2013.

[2]Data for research programs at universities and related institutions are estimated.

[3]The U.S. Department of Education was created in May 1980. It formerly was the Office of Education in the U.S. Department of Health, Education, and Welfare.

[4]Arranges for the education of children who reside on federal property when no suitable local school district can or will provide for the education of these children.

[5]Includes many programs, such as No Child Left Behind, 21st Century Community Learning Centers, Class Size Reduction, Charter Schools, Safe and Drug-Free Schools, and Innovative programs.

[6]Included the School-To-Work Opportunities program, which initiated a national system to be administered jointly by the U.S. Departments of Education and Labor. Programs in the Education Reform program were transferred to the school improvement programs or discontinued in FY 2002. Amounts after FY 2002 reflect balances that are spending out from prior-year appropriations.

[7]Starting in FY 1994, the Special Milk Program has been included in the child nutrition programs.

[8]The Farm Security and Rural Investment Act of 2002 (Public Law 107-171) carries out preschool and school feeding programs in foreign countries to help reduce the incidence of hunger and malnutrition, and improve literacy and primary education.

[9]These commodities are purchased under Section 32 of the Act of August 24, 1935, for use in the child nutrition programs.

[10]Assisted in the construction of public facilities, such as vocational schools, through grants or loans. No funds have been appropriated for this program since FY 1977, and it was completely phased out in FY 1984.

[11]Established in 1979, with funds first appropriated in FY 1980.

[12]Formerly in the Office of Economic Opportunity. In FY 1972, funds were transferred to the U.S. Department of Health, Education, and Welfare, Office of Child Development.

[13]Created by the Family Support Act of 1988 to provide funds for the Job Opportunities and Basic Skills Training program. Later incorporated into the Temporary Assistance for Needy Families program.

[14]After age 18, benefits terminate at the end of the school term or in 3 months, whichever comes first.

[15]Transferred from the U.S. Department of Transportation to the U.S. Department of Homeland Security in March 2003.

[16]Provides funding for supplemental programs for eligible American Indian students in public schools.

[17]Finances the cost of academic, social, and occupational education courses for inmates in federal prisons.

[18]Some of the work and training programs were in the Office of Economic Opportunity and were transferred to the U.S. Department of Labor in FYs 1971 and 1972. From FY 1994 through FY 2001, included the School-to-Work Opportunities program, which was administered jointly by the U.S. Departments of Education and Labor.

[19]Established in FY 1972 and closed in FY 1986.

[20]The states' share of revenue-sharing funds could not be spent on education in FYs 1981 through 1986.

[21]Provided educational assistance allowances in order to restore lost educational opportunities to those individuals whose careers were interrupted or impeded by reason of active military service between January 31, 1955, and January 1, 1977.

[22]This program is in "Readjustment Benefits" program, Chapter 31, and covers the costs of subsistence, tuition, books, supplies, and equipment for disabled veterans requiring vocational rehabilitation.

[23]This program is in "Readjustment Benefits" program, Chapter 35, and provides benefits to children and spouses of veterans.

[24]Head Start program funds were transferred to the U.S. Department of Health, Education, and Welfare, Office of Child Development, in FY 1972.

[25]Most of these programs were transferred to the U.S. Department of Health, Education, and Welfare, Office of Education, in FY 1972.

[26]Transferred to the U.S. Department of Labor in FYs 1971 and 1972.

[27]Transferred to the ACTION Agency in FY 1972.

[28]Under the William D. Ford Federal Direct Loan Program (commonly referred to as the Direct Loan Program), the federal government uses Treasury funds to provide loan capital directly to schools, which then disburse loan funds to students.

[29]The Federal Family Education Loan (FFEL) Program eliminated the authorization to originate new FFEL loans after June 30, 2010; all new loans are originated through the Direct Loan Program. The FFEL Program made loan capital available to students and their families through private lenders. State and private nonprofit guaranty agencies administer the federal guarantee protecting FFEL lenders against losses related to borrower default. These agencies also collect on defaulted loans and provide other services to lenders.

[30]Transferred from the U.S. Department of Housing and Urban Development to the U.S. Department of Health, Education, and Welfare, Office of Education, in FY 1979.

[31]Transferred from the National Science Foundation to the U.S. Department of Commerce in October 1970.

[32]Transferred from the U.S. Department of Commerce to the U.S. Department of Transportation in FY 1981.

[33]Includes special education programs (military and civilian); legal education program; flight training; advanced degree program; college degree program (officers); and "Armed Forces Health Professions Scholarship" program.

[34]Does not include higher education assistance loans.

[35]Alcohol, drug abuse, and mental health training programs are included starting in FY 1992.

[36]From 2008 onward, funding came from "Harwood Training Grants."

[37]Beginning in FY 1992, data were included in the National Institutes of Health training grants program.

[38]This program closed in FY 2004.

[39]Postsecondary student benefits were ended by the Omnibus Budget Reconciliation Act of 1981 (Public Law 97-35) and were completely phased out by August 1985.

[40]Includes flight training. Transferred to the U.S. Department of Homeland Security in March 2003.

[41]Transferred from the U.S. Department of State to the United States Information Agency in 1977, then transferred back to the U.S. Department of State in FY 1998.

[42]Chapter 33 was enacted in the "Post 9-11 Veterans Educational Assistance Act of 2008" (Public Law 110-252).

[43]Part of the Ronald W. Reagan National Defense Authorization Act for FY 2005 (Public Law 108-375), enacted October 28, 2004. The Reserve Education Assistance Program (REAP) provides educational assistance to members of the National Guard and Reserves who serve on active duty in support of a contingency operation under federal authority on or after September 11, 2001.

[44]Abolished in FY 1998, with functions transferred to the U.S. Department of State and the newly created Broadcasting Board of Governors.

[45]Included in the "Educational and Cultural Affairs" program in FYs 1980 through 1983, and became an independent program in FY 1984.

[46]Includes funding for D.C. College Tuition Assistance Grant (DC TAG), D.C. Adoption Scholarship Program, Robert C. Byrd Honors Scholarship Program, United States Senate Youth Program (USSYP), Advanced Placement Test Fee Program, the Early College Grant, and the College Access Challenge Grant.

[47]Transferred from U.S. Department of Education to the Institute of Museum and Library Services in FY 1997.

[48]Transferred to the U.S. Department of Homeland Security in FY 2003.

[49]The disaster relief program repairs and replaces damaged and destroyed school buildings. This program was transferred from the Federal Emergency Management Agency to the U.S. Department of Homeland Security in FY 2003.

[50]The National Service Trust Act of 1993 established the Corporation for National and Community Service. In 1993, ACTION became part of this agency.

[51]The Federal Emergency Management Agency was created in 1979, representing a combination of five existing agencies. The funds for the Federal Emergency Management Agency in FY 1970 to FY 1975 were in other agencies. This agency was transferred to the U.S. Department of Homeland Security in March 2003.

[52]These programs include the Fall-Out Shelter Analysis, Blast Protection Design through FY 1992. Starting in FY 1993, earthquake training and safety for teachers and administrators for grades 1 through 12 are included.

[53]Transferred from the General Services Administration to the National Archives and Records Administration in April 1985.

[54]Public Law 110-161 transferred the National Commission on Libraries and Information Science to the Institute of Museum and Library Services starting in FY 2008.

[55]Includes federal obligations for research and development centers and R & D plant administered by colleges and universities. FY 2011 and FY 2012 data are estimated, except the U.S Department of Education data, which are actual numbers.

[56]FY 1970 includes outlays for the "National Institute of Education" program. FY 1990 through FY 2000 amounts are outlays for the Office of Educational Research and Improvement. Amounts for FY 2005 and later years are for the Institute of Education Sciences; these amounts are outlays for years prior to FY 2010 and appropriations for later years.

NOTE: To the extent possible, amounts reported represent outlays rather than obligations. Negative amounts occur when program receipts exceed outlays. Starting in FY 2010, amounts for the U.S. Department of Education are appropriations, not outlays. Some data have been revised from previously published figures. Detail may not sum to totals because of rounding.

SOURCE: U.S. Department of Education, Budget Service, unpublished tabulations. U.S. Office of Management and Budget, *Budget of the U.S. Government, Appendix*, fiscal years 1972 through 2014. National Science Foundation, *Federal Funds for Research and Development*, fiscal years 1970 through 2012. (This table was prepared May 2014.)

U.S. Department of Education appropriations for major programs, by state or jurisdiction: Fiscal year 2012

[In thousands of current dollars]

State or jurisdiction	Total	Grants for the disadvantaged[1]	Block grants to states for school improvement[2]	School assistance in federally affected areas[3]	Career/technical and adult education[4]	Special education[5]	Language assistance[6]	American Indian education	Student financial assistance[7]	Rehabilitation services[8]
1	2	3	4	5	6	7	8	9	10	11
Total, 50 states and D.C.[9]	$72,528,405	$14,805,310	$4,159,353	$1,200,579	$1,656,054	$12,103,118	$672,514	$105,921	$34,698,008	$3,127,548
Total, 50 states, D.C., other activities, and other jurisdictions	75,175,878	15,493,477	4,401,536	1,219,394	1,718,024	12,393,210	729,654	105,921	35,766,437	3,348,225
Alabama	1,229,656	242,268	70,561	2,859	28,995	193,241	3,882	1,673	628,187	57,990
Alaska	332,407	46,221	21,820	143,650	5,253	39,884	1,057	12,043	48,535	13,944
Arizona	2,749,652	335,274	78,443	179,851	36,218	203,368	18,303	11,267	1,820,058	66,870
Arkansas	733,907	167,121	47,358	493	17,289	121,266	3,112	309	329,489	47,469
California	8,489,412	1,852,037	458,794	67,010	214,447	1,316,596	161,603	6,070	4,097,299	315,556
Colorado	1,059,344	160,854	50,175	20,205	22,375	166,213	9,901	708	585,213	43,700
Connecticut	655,679	111,438	38,613	4,436	14,966	141,654	5,765	0	303,918	34,889
Delaware	196,104	45,705	21,814	48	6,349	37,854	1,231	0	69,875	13,228
District of Columbia	303,627	48,386	21,357	928	5,514	19,733	779	0	191,665	15,265
Florida	4,245,103	787,624	196,933	7,127	100,426	672,126	43,011	94	2,287,165	150,596
Georgia	2,442,012	530,703	129,001	22,617	56,151	352,372	15,211	0	1,231,515	104,442
Hawaii	286,756	48,562	21,960	51,620	7,647	43,004	3,499	0	95,097	15,367
Idaho	375,232	61,650	23,955	6,099	8,757	59,835	1,948	412	193,856	18,719
Illinois	3,102,934	674,596	176,196	14,187	62,599	540,519	28,373	170	1,487,216	119,078
Indiana	1,552,154	279,553	75,018	115	35,573	275,037	8,310	0	812,408	66,141
Iowa	1,082,778	89,474	35,952	192	15,644	129,841	3,216	271	779,966	28,221
Kansas	648,937	122,519	38,871	27,537	14,008	112,810	4,095	1,299	296,816	30,982
Kentucky	1,055,935	237,372	69,602	975	27,012	173,551	3,712	0	494,677	49,033
Louisiana	1,124,940	302,720	89,168	8,752	30,360	201,807	3,057	955	449,605	38,515
Maine	292,600	54,984	24,735	2,111	7,369	59,284	720	152	124,141	19,103
Maryland	1,046,363	198,900	58,628	6,593	25,135	213,960	10,001	75	482,234	50,837
Massachusetts	1,271,597	222,219	71,248	259	28,103	300,719	13,035	79	569,080	66,854
Michigan	2,502,887	565,606	159,423	4,355	52,673	424,224	10,570	2,681	1,172,816	110,539
Minnesota	1,220,169	165,421	58,344	20,774	22,783	203,985	8,590	4,035	684,639	51,598
Mississippi	859,440	196,857	63,415	2,284	19,744	128,559	1,642	456	399,470	47,013
Missouri	1,397,389	244,057	79,183	20,988	30,903	240,655	5,066	88	707,139	69,310
Montana	278,398	47,860	27,179	44,285	6,506	40,556	511	3,363	92,183	15,955
Nebraska	419,559	78,342	26,948	18,254	9,242	79,448	2,667	858	181,439	22,360
Nevada	412,299	111,017	26,814	3,565	14,938	76,890	8,799	755	154,605	14,915
New Hampshire	242,643	41,227	24,240	6	7,226	51,095	931	0	103,575	14,343
New Jersey	1,605,369	317,358	92,716	11,582	38,388	382,975	21,706	55	678,007	62,581
New Mexico	658,954	124,990	36,076	98,094	12,416	97,119	4,047	8,914	250,871	26,428
New York	4,795,922	1,182,857	315,524	34,490	94,947	815,307	55,533	1,934	2,136,538	158,792
North Carolina	2,002,790	422,198	107,323	16,990	53,163	350,250	15,381	3,688	921,956	111,842
North Dakota	203,814	37,099	22,457	27,120	5,235	30,935	507	1,888	64,043	14,531
Ohio	2,632,547	612,269	160,555	1,599	59,041	463,737	9,599	0	1,222,011	103,736
Oklahoma	906,988	168,971	58,392	37,914	21,293	156,615	4,499	25,541	386,874	46,890
Oregon	886,723	163,469	45,976	3,569	19,042	137,424	7,668	2,167	465,376	42,032
Pennsylvania	2,597,888	605,092	160,016	858	60,959	454,732	14,209	0	1,172,771	129,251
Rhode Island	284,594	51,328	21,934	1,581	7,841	47,485	2,437	0	136,565	15,422
South Carolina	1,041,816	224,458	60,285	1,855	27,367	189,959	4,469	20	474,316	59,088
South Dakota	299,540	46,116	22,834	52,678	5,423	36,933	738	4,132	117,640	13,045
Tennessee	1,404,514	291,669	79,982	4,016	35,770	251,628	5,670	0	665,991	69,788
Texas	6,022,685	1,499,509	363,983	103,314	148,174	1,043,536	101,415	399	2,510,206	252,148
Utah	759,759	99,508	30,310	8,636	15,216	118,396	4,813	1,347	442,173	39,360
Vermont	173,880	36,999	21,438	7	5,150	29,983	504	237	61,041	18,521
Virginia	1,549,671	240,392	75,757	40,353	37,744	300,918	11,625	15	766,559	76,301
Washington	1,219,371	237,616	70,101	45,422	30,203	237,842	17,374	4,415	518,037	58,360
West Virginia	536,981	99,026	35,747	15	12,320	81,436	610	0	262,073	45,753
Wisconsin	1,162,854	238,115	70,756	13,338	27,129	224,319	6,612	2,529	520,862	59,193
Wyoming	171,835	35,699	21,441	14,969	5,026	31,500	500	828	50,219	11,652
Other activities/jurisdictions										
Indian Tribe (Set-Aside)	280,521	101,541	23,687	0	14,038	98,252	5,000	0	0	38,003
Other nonstate allocations	319,299	47,040	72,601	17,441	13,313	25,000	45,100	0	0	98,805
American Samoa	33,482	11,518	4,835	0	583	6,951	959	0	7,119	1,517
Freely Associated States[10]	26,526	0	0	0	177	6,579	0	0	19,771	0
Guam	57,718	12,158	7,052	0	1,068	15,548	1,436	0	17,055	3,401
Northern Marianas	20,304	4,184	2,719	0	696	5,286	1,203	0	4,964	1,253
Puerto Rico	1,867,682	496,248	125,132	1,239	31,006	122,743	3,379	0	1,012,866	75,069
U.S. Virgin Islands	41,940	15,477	6,159	135	1,089	9,733	63	0	6,654	2,630

[1]Title I includes Grants to Local Education Agencies (Basic, Concentration, Targeted, and Education Finance Incentive Grants); School Turnaround Grants; Migrant Education Grants; and Neglected and Delinquent Children Grants.

[2]Title VI includes Improving Teacher Quality State Grants; Mathematics and Science Partnerships; Educational Technology State Grants; 21st Century Community Learning Centers; Assessing Achievement, including No Child Left Behind; Education for the Homeless Children and Youth; Rural and Low-Income Schools Program; and Small, Rural School Achievement Program.

[3]Includes Impact Aid—Basic Support Payments; Impact Aid—Payments for Children with Disabilities; and Impact Aid—Construction.

[4]Includes Career and Technical Education State Grants; English Literacy and Civics Education State Grants; and Adult Basic and Literacy Education State Grants.

[5]Includes Special Education—Grants to States; Preschool Grants; and Grants for Infants and Families.

[6]Includes English Learner Education.

[7]Includes Pell Grants; Federal Supplemental Educational Opportunity Grants; Federal Work-Study; College Access Challenge Grant; and Student Loan Program interest subsidies.

[8]Includes Vocational Rehabilitation State Grants; Supported Employment State Grants; Client Assistance State Grants; Independent Living State Grants; Services for Older Blind Individuals; Centers for Independent Living; Protection and Advocacy for Assistive Technology; Assistive Technology State Grant Program; and Protection and Advocacy of Individual Rights.

[9]Total excludes other activities and other jurisdictions.

[10]Includes the Marshall Islands, the Federated States of Micronesia, and Palau.

NOTE: Data reflect revisions to figures in the *Budget of the United States Government, Fiscal Year 2014*. Detail may not sum to totals because of rounding.

SOURCE: U.S. Department of Education, Budget Service, retrieved December 6, 2013, from http://www2.ed.gov/about/overview/budget/statetables/14stbyprogram.pdf; and unpublished tabulations. (This table was prepared January 2014.)

Appropriations for Title I and selected other programs under the No Child Left Behind Act of 2001, by program and state or jurisdiction: Fiscal years 2012 and 2013

[In thousands of current dollars]

State or jurisdiction	Title I total, 2012	Title I, 2013						Improving Teacher Quality State Grants, 2013
		Total	Grants to local education agencies[1]	State agency programs		Turn-around Grants	Assessing Achievement, 2013	
				Neglected and Delinquent	Migrant			
1	2	3	4	5	6	7	8	9
Total, 50 states and D.C.[2]	$14,805,310	$14,036,475	$13,164,974	$45,763	$362,751	$462,988	$351,136	$2,196,936
Total, 50 states, D.C., other activities, and other jurisdictions	15,493,477	14,686,340	13,760,219	47,614	372,751	505,756	368,900	2,337,830
Alabama	242,268	225,523	215,160	951	2,021	7,391	6,033	36,446
Alaska	46,221	46,332	37,767	210	6,836	1,520	3,493	10,869
Arizona	335,274	329,654	311,045	1,342	6,450	10,817	7,329	35,693
Arkansas	167,121	157,652	147,089	374	5,173	5,015	4,894	22,067
California	1,852,037	1,726,778	1,540,847	1,348	127,557	57,026	27,810	254,874
Colorado	160,854	152,033	139,574	529	6,905	5,024	6,272	25,502
Connecticut	111,438	113,713	107,665	1,192	976	3,881	5,234	21,661
Delaware	45,705	44,782	42,595	446	286	1,455	3,549	10,869
District of Columbia	48,386	45,653	44,013	216	0	1,424	3,255	10,869
Florida	787,624	750,985	701,541	1,172	22,302	25,970	13,758	103,193
Georgia	530,703	506,837	481,413	1,206	7,742	16,477	9,656	60,014
Hawaii	48,562	50,526	47,598	357	788	1,783	3,796	10,869
Idaho	61,650	59,635	53,679	438	3,502	2,016	4,138	10,886
Illinois	674,596	653,514	627,985	1,598	1,871	22,060	11,364	94,180
Indiana	279,553	262,746	248,168	544	5,390	8,644	7,303	39,054
Iowa	89,474	88,444	83,471	367	1,577	3,029	4,935	17,933
Kansas	122,519	111,823	96,510	327	11,315	3,671	4,917	18,274
Kentucky	237,372	226,111	210,475	926	7,247	7,463	5,726	36,017
Louisiana	302,720	293,028	279,286	1,746	2,422	9,573	5,953	52,216
Maine	54,984	51,867	48,799	217	1,146	1,704	3,743	10,869
Maryland	198,900	190,388	181,688	1,585	495	6,620	6,613	33,309
Massachusetts	222,219	215,355	204,213	2,336	1,577	7,229	6,830	41,975
Michigan	565,606	537,497	511,731	621	8,387	16,758	9,306	91,628
Minnesota	165,421	152,790	145,454	321	2,029	4,987	6,409	31,352
Mississippi	196,857	184,133	176,722	750	1,015	5,646	4,993	34,059
Missouri	244,057	235,146	224,772	1,356	1,486	7,532	6,787	39,562
Montana	47,860	45,559	42,989	97	986	1,486	3,592	10,869
Nebraska	78,342	73,006	65,230	335	4,989	2,454	4,211	11,146
Nevada	111,017	105,776	101,368	451	232	3,726	4,759	11,441
New Hampshire	41,227	41,800	39,809	476	143	1,372	3,782	10,869
New Jersey	317,358	290,960	278,123	1,429	1,922	9,486	8,553	52,275
New Mexico	124,990	117,059	112,088	314	902	3,754	4,377	18,128
New York	1,182,857	1,126,996	1,078,369	2,900	9,680	36,046	14,505	188,660
North Carolina	422,198	400,309	379,295	1,885	5,519	13,611	9,109	49,941
North Dakota	37,099	33,886	32,448	99	229	1,110	3,391	10,869
Ohio	612,269	578,176	555,292	1,128	2,599	19,158	10,306	86,229
Oklahoma	168,971	154,908	148,120	335	1,503	4,951	5,468	26,278
Oregon	163,469	162,632	145,927	1,139	10,035	5,531	5,311	22,277
Pennsylvania	605,092	560,176	532,380	570	8,870	18,355	10,507	93,850
Rhode Island	51,328	49,365	47,193	495	65	1,612	3,602	10,869
South Carolina	224,458	214,794	205,586	1,464	550	7,195	5,866	28,646
South Dakota	46,116	43,885	41,482	143	819	1,440	3,529	10,869
Tennessee	291,669	274,364	264,087	500	563	9,214	7,006	38,983
Texas	1,499,509	1,417,633	1,311,223	1,916	57,720	46,774	21,428	187,803
Utah	99,508	90,695	84,915	853	1,807	3,120	5,278	15,003
Vermont	36,999	34,284	31,925	613	621	1,125	3,349	10,869
Virginia	240,392	230,229	220,136	1,722	777	7,593	7,950	40,865
Washington	237,616	227,536	203,756	1,382	14,793	7,605	7,194	37,530
West Virginia	99,026	94,217	89,837	1,125	79	3,177	4,037	19,728
Wisconsin	238,115	220,871	211,698	1,301	622	7,250	6,580	37,830
Wyoming	35,699	34,415	32,439	618	228	1,129	3,351	10,869
Other activities/jurisdictions								
Indian Tribe Set-Aside	101,541	96,451	93,299	0	0	3,152	1,801	11,631
Other nonstate allocations	47,040	45,255	8,777	1,190	10,000	25,288	8,733	46,757
American Samoa	11,518	10,939	10,583	0	0	356	350	2,657
Guam	12,158	11,632	11,171	0	0	460	790	4,474
Northern Marianas	4,184	4,289	4,039	0	0	250	256	1,634
Puerto Rico	496,248	467,547	453,904	661	0	12,983	5,429	70,876
U.S. Virgin Islands	15,477	13,751	13,473	0	0	279	405	2,867

[1]Includes Basic, Concentration, Targeted, and Education Finance Incentive Grants.
[2]Total excludes other activities and other jurisdictions.
NOTE: Detail may not sum to totals because of rounding. Estimates for fiscal year 2013 are preliminary.

SOURCE: U.S. Department of Education, Budget Service, Elementary, Secondary, and Vocational Education Analysis Division, retrieved December 6, 2013, from http://www2.ed.gov/about/overview/budget/statetables/14stbyprogram.pdf. (This table was prepared December 2013.)

Selected population and enrollment statistics for countries with populations of at least 10 million in 2011, by continent and country: Selected years, 1990 through 2011

Continent and country[1]	Midyear population (in millions)			Persons per square kilometer, 2011	First level[2]					Second level[3]					Third level[4]				
					Enrollment (in thousands)		Gross enrollment ratio[5]			Enrollment (in thousands)		Gross enrollment ratio[5]			Enrollment (in thousands)		Gross enrollment ratio[5]		
	1991	2000	2011	2011	1999-2000	2010-11	1990-91	1999-2000	2010-11	1999-2000	2010-11	1990-91	1999-2000	2010-11	1999-2000	2010-11	1990-91	1999-2000	2010-11
1	2	3	4	5	6	7	8	9	10	11	12	13	14	15	16	17	18	19	20
World total[6]	5,371	6,090	6,943	53	654,723	699,301[7]	99	99	107[7]	450,397	543,989[7]	52	60	71[7]	99,511	182,963[7]	14	19	30[7]
Africa																			
Algeria[8]	26	31	37	15	4,843	3,363	100	103	115	2,994	4,573	61	62	98	—	1,189	11	—	30
Angola	10	13	18	14	—	5,027	92	—	140	355	885	12	15	32	—	143	1	—	7
Burkina Faso	9	12	17	61	852	2,205	33	45	82	190	604	7	10	24	11[7]	61	1	1[7]	4
Cameroon	12	16	21	45	2,237[9]	3,585	101	83[9]	106	700	1,574	28	27	47	66	244	3	5	12
Chad	6	8	11	9	914	1,929	54	64	91	137	457	8[10]	11	23	6	24	1[11,12]	1	2
Cote d'Ivoire	13	17	22	68	1,944	2,758	67	77	90	620[7]	—	22	25[7]	—	—	—	—	—	—
Democratic Rep. of the Congo	41	52	72	32	—	11,083	70	—	105	—	3,783	21[13]	—	43	—	488	2	—	8
Egypt[8]	56	65	82	83	7,947[7]	10,266	94	101[7]	109	8,028[7]	4,542	76	86[7]	—	—	2,246	16[14,15]	1	29
Ethiopia	49	64	89	89	5,847	14,298	33	55	95	1,195	2,148	14	14	36	68	632	1	1	8
Ghana[8]	16	19	24	106	2,561	3,860	75	86	107	1,057	640	36	41	57	—	286	1[11]	—	12
Guinea[8]	7	8	11	43	790	1,537	37	57	89	—	—	10	—	38	—	103	1	—	10
Kenya[8]	24	31	42	74	5,035	4,305	95	96	—	1,909	736	24[10]	39	—	89	—	2[11]	3	—
Madagascar	12	16	21	37	2,208	3,564	103	100	144	487	821	18[10]	32	34	32	86	3	2	4
Malawi	10	12	16	169	2,695	3,564	68	138	140	258[7]	2,479	8	19[7]	44	4	12	1	—	1
Mali	9	11	15	12	1,017	2,115	26	62	92	1,541	716	7	—	—	20	88	1	2	7
Morocco[8]	24	28	32	72	3,670	4,001	67	92	115	124	342	35	38	66	276	506	11	9	16
Mozambique[8]	13	18	23	29	2,544	5,254	67	74	107	486	716	8	6	26	12	113	#[12]	1	5
Niger	8	11	16	13	579	1,910	29	34	69	106[7]	342	7	7[7]	15	—	18	1	—	2
Nigeria[8]	99	124	164	181	19,151	—	91	98	128	4,104	—	25	24	32	—	—	4[11,16]	—	—
Rwanda	7	8	11	461	1,432	2,341	70	111	84	130	486	8	11	—	9	74	#[17]	1	7
Senegal	8	9	13	66	1,108	1,726	59	68	—	250	834[18]	16	16	41[18]	—	—	3	—	—
South Africa	39	45	49	40	7,445	—	122	107	—	4,142	—	74	84	—	—	—	13[19]	—	—
South Sudan[8]	5	6	10	16	—	1,028	—	—	—	—	—	—	—	—	—	—	—	—	—
Sudan[8]	22	27	34	18	2,567	—	53	—	—	980	1,152	24	—	—	204[7]	362	3[11]	—	35
Tunisia	8	10	11	68	1,414	1,028	113	116	108	1,104[7]	—	45	75[7]	91	180	290	9	19	9
Uganda	17	23	33	165	6,559	8,098	74[20,21]	129	110	547	—	13[10,21]	16	—	56	—	1	3	—
United Republic of Tanzania	26	33	46	52	4,382	—	70	68	—	—	—	5	—	—	—	—	#[13]	—	—
Zambia	8	10	13	18	1,590	3,030	99	84	113	844	—	24	—	—	25[7]	—	2	2[7]	—
Zimbabwe	10	12	12	31	2,461	—	116	101	—	—	—	50	43	—	—	93	5	—	6
Asia																			
Afghanistan[8]	14	22	30	46	749	5,292	27	21	97	—	2,209	9	—	52	—	98	2	—	4
Bangladesh[8]	114	132	159	1,218	—	18,432[18]	72	—	114[18]	10,329	11,543	19	48	51	727	2,008	4	5	13
Cambodia	10	12	15	83	2,248	2,224	121	106	126	351	—	32	17	—	22	223	1	2	16
China	1,164	1,264	1,337	140	113,613	99,708	125	96	128	81,488	97,452	49	58	87	7,364	31,308	3	8	24
India	854	1,006	1,189	400	—	137,747	97	110	113	71,031	113,728	44[10]	46	69	9,404	26,651	6	10	23
Indonesia	185	214	246	136	28,509	30,662	115	101	109	14,720	20,778	44	56	81	3,126	5,364	9[13]	15	27
Iran, Islamic Republic of	60	69	78	51	8,288	5,678	112	96	106	9,955	7,237	55[10]	79	84	1,405	4,117	10[14]	19	49
Iraq	17	23	30	70	3,639	—	111	111	103	1,224	—	47[10]	37	—	289	—	12[17]	12	—
Japan	124	127	127	350	7,529	7,029	100	101	102	8,782	7,285	97	102	102	3,982	3,881	30[13]	49	60
Kazakhstan	17	16	17	6	1,208	986	87	99	105	2,003	1,680	98	96	97	370	638	40	29	42
Korea, North (DPR)	21	23	24	203	—	—	—	—	—	—	—	—	—	—	—	—	—	—	—
Korea, South (Republic of)	43	47	49	503	4,030	3,140	105	102	104	3,959	3,868	90	99	97	3,003	3,356	39	79	101

See notes at end of table.

Selected population and enrollment statistics for countries with populations of at least 10 million in 2011, by continent and country: Selected years, 1990 through 2011—Continued

Continent and country[1]	Midyear population (in millions) 1991	2000	2011	Persons per square kilometer, 2011	First level[2] Enrollment (in thousands) 1999–2000	2010–11	First level Gross enrollment ratio[5] 1990–91	1999–2000	2010–11	Second level[3] Enrollment (in thousands) 1999–2000	2010–11	Second level Gross enrollment ratio[5] 1990–91	1999–2000	2010–11	Third level[4] Enrollment (in thousands) 1999–2000	2010–11	Third level Gross enrollment ratio[5] 1990–91	1999–2000	2010–11
1	2	3	4	5	6	7	8	9	10	11	12	13	14	15	16	17	18	19	20
Malaysia	18	23	29	87	3,026	—	94	98	—	2,205	—	56	66	—	549	—	7	26	—
Myanmar[8]	41	47	54	83	4,858	—	106	98	—	2,268	—	23	36	—	—	660	4[13]	—	14
Nepal[8]	19	25	29	205	3,780[9]	4,952	108	126[9]	143	1,348	2,830	33	37	63	94	385	5	4	14
Pakistan	122	152	187	243	13,987[18]	18,051	61[22]	70[18]	92	—	9,939	23	—	35	—	1,573	3	—	8
Philippines	67	81	102	342	12,708	—	111	110	—	—	—	73	—	—	—	—	28	—	—
Saudi Arabia	16	21	26	12	—	3,348	73	—	101	—	3,153[7]	44	—	114[7]	404	1,021	12	23	43
Sri Lanka[8]	17	19	21	329	—	1,735	106	—	99	—	2,574	74	—	99	—	232	5[13,23]	—	14
Syrian Arab Republic	13	16	23	123	2,775	2,507	108	108	121	1,069	2,821	52	44	74	—	571	18	—	26
Taiwan	20	22	23	718	—	—	—	—	—	—	—	—	—	—	—	—	—	—	—
Thailand	57	63	67	131	6,101	—	99	98	102	5,658	4,893	30	—	87	1,900	2,497	19[12]	35	53
Turkey	58	67	79	102	6,562	6,581	99	103	102	3,566	7,966	47	73	89	—	3,817	13	—	61
Uzbekistan	21	25	28	66	2,602	1,948	81	99	93	—	4,370	99	88	105	305	277	30	13	9
Vietnam	69	79	91	292	10,063	7,048	103	107	105	—	—	32	—	—	732	2,229	2	9	24
Yemen	13	17	24	45	—	3,641	79[16]	—	97	—	1,643	23[16]	—	46	—	267	4[13]	—	10
Europe																			
Belgium	10	10	10	345	774	736	101	105	104	1,058	803	103	145	106	356	462	40	58	69
Czech Republic	10	10	11	137	645	468	96	103	102	958	805	91	89	96	254	446	16[24]	28	65
France	59	61	65	102	3,885	4,172	108	104	108	5,929	5,888	99	106	110	2,015	2,259	40	57	57
Germany[25]	80	82	81	234	3,656	2,990	101	103	101	8,307	7,528	98	96	102	—	2,763	34	—	57
Greece	10	11	11	82	645	—	98	96	100	739	—	93	89	102	422	—	36	51	57
Italy[8]	57	58	61	207	2,836	2,828	103	103	100	4,404	4,630	83	93	101	1,770	1,968	32	49	64
Netherlands[8]	15	16	17	491	1,279	1,292	102	109	108	1,379	1,539	120	123	128	488	780	40	53	76
Poland[8]	38	39	38	126	3,319	2,192	98	99	99	3,988	2,726	81	100	97	1,580	2,080	22	50	74
Portugal	10	10	11	118	811	—	123	122	—	831	—	67	105	—	374	—	23	48	—
Romania[8]	23	22	22	95	1,189	826	91	106	104	2,226	1,778	92	81	96	453	872	10	24	52
Russian Federation	148	147	143	9	6,138	—	109	93	96	3,246	—	93	—	—	6,331	—	52	55	76
Spain[8]	39	41	47	94	2,540	2,773	109	103	—	5,204	3,248	104	111	129	1,829	1,950	37	59	83
Ukraine[8]	52	49	45	78	2,079	1,563	89	109	106	—	2,926	93	99	96	1,812	2,566	47	49	79
United Kingdom[8]	58	59	63	259	4,632	4,420	104	101	107	5,315	5,000	85	102	97	2,024	2,492	30	58	61
North America																			
Canada	28	31	34	4	2,456	—	103	100	—	2,519	—	101	102	—	1,212	—	95	59	—
Cuba	11	11	11	101	1,046	828	98	101	101	790	798	89	82	90	159	665	21	22	80
Guatemala	9	11	14	129	1,909	2,645	78	104	114	504	1,114	23[13]	38	65	—	—	8[12]	—	—
Mexico	86	100	116	60	14,766	14,935	114	106	104	9,094	11,836	53	70	84	1,963	2,981	15	19	28
United States	253	282	312	34	24,973	24,432	102	101	99	22,594	24,214	93	92	94	13,203	21,016	75	68	95
South America																			
Argentina	34	37	42	15	4,728	—	106	114	—	3,428	—	71	87	—	1,767[7]	—	38[13]	53[7]	—
Bolivia[8]	7	8	10	9	1,492	1,390	95	112	94	877[7]	1,060	37	78[7]	77	279	—	21	35	—
Brazil	152	174	198	23	—	—	106	—	—	—	—	38	82	90	2,781	6,929	11[26]	—	—
Chile	13	15	17	23	1,799	1,520	100	100	102	1,391	1,493	73	82	90	452	1,062	21[13]	37	71
Colombia	34	39	45	43	5,221	4,924	102	119	111	3,569	5,131	50[13]	72	97	934	1,849	13	24	43

See notes at end of table.

Selected population and enrollment statistics for countries with populations of at least 10 million in 2011, by continent and country: Selected years, 1990 through 2011—Continued

Continent and country[1]	Midyear population (in millions)			Persons per square kilometer, 2011	First level[2]					Second level[3]					Third level[4]				
	1991	2000	2011		Enrollment (in thousands)		Gross enrollment ratio[5]			Enrollment (in thousands)		Gross enrollment ratio[5]			Enrollment (in thousands)		Gross enrollment ratio[5]		
					1999–2000	2010–11	1990–91	1999–2000	2010–11	1999–2000	2010–11	1990–91	1999–2000	2010–11	1999–2000	2010–11	1990–91	1999–2000	2010–11
1	2	3	4	5	6	7	8	9	10	11	12	13	14	15	16	17	18	19	20
Ecuador	10	12	15	54	1,925	2,121	116	113	115	917	1,488	55	59	85	—	—	20	—	—
Peru	22	26	29	23	4,338	3,671	118	122	105	2,374	2,640	67	85	91	—	—	30	—	—
Venezuela	20	23	28	31	3,328	3,466	96	101	102	1,543	2,287	35	60	83	668	—	29	28	—
Oceania																			
Australia[8]	17	19	22	3	1,906	2,042	108	100	104	2,589	2,328	82	161	133	845	1,324	35 [27]	65	83

—Not available.
#Rounds to zero.
[1]Selection based on total population for midyear 2011.
[2]First-level enrollment consists of elementary school, typically corresponding to grades 1–6 in the United States.
[3]Second-level enrollment includes general education, teacher training (at the second level), and technical and vocational education. This level generally corresponds to secondary education in the United States, grades 7–12.
[4]Third-level enrollment includes college and university enrollment and technical and vocational education beyond the secondary school level.
[5]Data represent the total enrollment of all ages in the school level divided by the population of the specific age groups that correspond to the school level. Adjustments have been made for the varying lengths of first- and second-level programs. Ratios may exceed 100 because some countries have many students from outside the normal age range.
[6]Enrollment totals and ratios exclude Democratic People's Republic of Korea.
[7]Estimated by the UNESCO Institute for Statistics.
[8]Classification or data coverage of levels has been revised. Data by level may not be comparable over time.
[9]Policy change in 1999–2000: introduction of free universal primary education.
[10]General education enrollment only. Excludes teacher training and vocational education enrollments.
[11]Excludes nonuniversity institutions (such as teacher training colleges and technical colleges) and excludes distance-learning universities.
[12]Data for 1992–93.
[13]Data for 1991–92.

[14]Excludes private institutions.
[15]Data refer to universities and exclude Al Azhar.
[16]Data for 1993–94.
[17]Data for 1985–86.
[18]National estimation.
[19]Not including the former Independent States of Transkei, Bophuthatswana, Venda, and Ciskei.
[20]Estimated.
[21]Data refer to government aided and maintained schools only.
[22]Includes preprimary education.
[23]Excludes some nonuniversity institutions.
[24]Includes full-time students only.
[25]Data include both former East and West Germany.
[26]Excludes enrollments in programs formerly classified as doctoral.
[27]Data do not include Vocational Education and Training Institutes (VETS).
NOTE: Data do not include adult education or special education provided outside regular schools. Some data have been revised from previously published figures.
SOURCE: United Nations Educational, Scientific, and Cultural Organization (UNESCO), Statistical Yearbook, 1999, unpublished tabulations; and tabulations from the UNESCO Institute for Statistics Online Data Center, retrieved December 16, 2013, from http://data.uis.unesco.org/; U.S. Department of Commerce, Census Bureau, International Data Base, retrieved December 16, 2013, from http://www.census.gov/population/international/data/idb/informationGateway.php. (This table was prepared January 2014.)

Pupil/teacher ratios in public and private elementary and secondary schools, by level of education and country: Selected years, 2000 through 2011

Country	Elementary							Junior high school (lower secondary)							Senior high school (upper secondary)						
	2000	2005	2007	2008	2009	2010	2011	2000	2005	2007	2008	2009	2010	2011	2000	2005	2007	2008	2009	2010	2011
1	2	3	4	5	6	7	8	9	10	11	12	13	14	15	16	17	18	19	20	21	22
OECD average[1]	17.7	17.0	16.2	16.4	16.0	15.9	15.4	—	14.0	13.4	13.7	13.5	13.5	13.2	13.7	13.5	13.1	13.3	13.4	13.6	13.7
Australia	17.3	16.2	15.9	15.8	15.8	15.7	15.6	—	10.6	10.3	9.9	9.6	9.3	9.1[8]	—	12.1[2,3]	12.1[2,3]	12.0[2,3]	12.0[2,3]	12.0[2,3]	12.0
Austria	—	14.1	13.6	12.9	12.6	12.2	12.1	—	9.4	9.2[5]	8.1[5]	8.1[5]	8.1[5]	8.1[5]	—	11.3	11.0	10.5	10.2	10.1	9.8
Belgium	15.0[4]	12.8	12.6[5]	12.6[5]	12.5[5]	12.4[5]	12.4[5]	—	9.4[5]	9.2[5]	16.6[4,7]	17.7[4,7]	15.9[4,7]	—	9.7[3,6]	9.9[6]	10.2[3,6]	10.6[5,6]	10.2[5,6]	10.1[5,6]	10.1[5,6]
Canada	18.1	—	—	—	—	—	—	18.1	—	—	—	—	—	—	19.5	—	16.4[3,4,7,8]	14.7	15.8	14.2	—
Chile	—	25.9	24.7	24.1	22.4	24.6	23.1	—	25.9	24.7	24.1	22.4	25.1	23.6	—	26.6	25.7	25.2	24.7	26.1	25.4
Czech Republic	19.7	17.5	18.7	18.1	18.4	18.7	18.7	14.7	13.5	12.3	11.8	11.5	11.2	11.1	11.5	12.8	12.3	12.2	12.2	12.1	11.7
Denmark	10.4	—	—	—	—	—	—	11.4	11.9[7]	11.2[7]	10.7[7]	9.9[7]	11.5[7]	11.8[7]	14.4	—	—	—	—	—	—
Estonia	—	—	14.4	16.4	16.2	16.2	13.2	10.7	9.9	11.4	16.0	15.7	14.9	10.1	—	—	12.6	12.4[6]	16.8[6]	16.6[6]	13.7
Finland	16.9	15.9	15.0	14.4	13.6	14.0	13.7	10.7	10.4	9.9[5]	10.3[5]	10.1[5]	9.8[5]	9.3[5]	17.0[6,9]	18.0[6,9]	15.9[6]	15.9[6]	16.6[6]	17.1[6]	16.3[6]
France	19.8	19.4	19.7[5]	19.9[5]	19.7[5]	18.7[5]	18.4[5]	14.7	14.2	14.3[5]	14.6[5]	14.9[5]	15.0[5]	14.8[5]	10.4	10.3	9.6	9.5	9.6	9.7[5]	10.0[5]
Germany	19.8	18.8	18.3	18.0	17.4	16.7	16.3	15.7	15.5	15.2	15.0	15.1	14.9	14.2	13.9	14.0	14.3	14.0	13.9	13.2	13.8
Greece	13.4	11.1	10.1	10.0	10.7	10.8	10.7	10.8	7.9	7.7	—	—	—	—	10.5	8.8	7.3	—	—	—	—
Hungary	10.9	10.6	10.2	10.6	10.7	10.8	10.7	10.9	10.4	10.2	10.9	10.8	10.7	10.5	11.4[6]	12.2	12.1	12.3	12.8	12.5	12.4
Iceland	—	—	—	—	—	—	—	12.7	11.3[7]	10.4[7]	10.0[7]	9.9[7]	10.3[7]	10.6	9.7	10.8[6]	10.2[6]	10.6	10.9	11.3	11.5[6]
Ireland	21.5	17.9	17.9	17.8	15.9	15.9	15.7	—	—	14.3[5]	14.6[5]	14.9[5]	15.0[5]	14.8[5]	15.9[3,6]	15.5	13.2[3,6,8]	12.8[3,6,8]	12.6[3,6,8]	14.4[3,6]	14.4[3,6]
Israel	—	17.3	16.4	16.3	17.0	20.6[8]	15.9[8]	—	13.4	12.4	12.2	13.7	12.8[8]	13.6[8]	—	13.4	14.3	10.9	10.8	11.0[8]	11.3[8]
Italy	11.0	10.6	10.5	10.6[8]	10.7[8]	11.3[8]	11.7[8]	10.4	10.1	9.4	9.7[8]	10.0[8]	11.9[8]	11.5[8]	10.2	11.0	11.8	11.8	11.8	12.1	12.8
Japan	20.9	19.4	19.0	18.8	18.6	18.4	18.1	16.8	15.1	14.8	14.7	14.5	14.4	14.2	14.0	13.0	12.5	12.3	12.2	12.6	12.2
Korea, Republic of	32.1	28.0	25.6	24.1	22.5	21.1	19.6	21.5	20.8	20.5	20.2	19.9	19.7	18.8	20.9	16.0	16.2	16.5	16.7	16.5	15.8
Luxembourg	15.9[8]	—	11.2[8]	12.1[8]	11.6	10.1	9.9	—	—	9.0[3,8]	10.0[8]	9.2[3,8]	9.3[3,8]	—	9.2[3,8]	9.0[3,8]	9.1[3,8]	9.1[3,8]	9.1[3]	9.1[3]	9.6[3]
Mexico	27.2	28.3	28.0	28.0	28.1	28.1	28.1	34.8	33.7	33.3	33.9	33.0	32.7	31.9	26.5	25.8	25.7	25.8	25.6	26.9	26.8
Netherlands	16.8[4]	15.9[4]	15.6[4]	15.8[4,8]	15.8[4,8]	15.7[4,8]	15.8	19.9	16.8	16.2	16.2	16.3	16.3	15.3	17.1[3]	16.2[3]	15.7[3,6]	15.8[3,6]	16.1[3,6]	16.5[3,6,8]	18.2
New Zealand	20.6	18.1	17.5	17.1	16.3	16.2	16.3	19.9	—	16.2	16.1	16.3	9.9[8]	16.3	13.1	12.9	13.3	12.8	12.8	14.4	13.9
Norway	12.4	—	11.0[8]	10.8[8]	10.7[8]	10.5[8]	10.4[8]	9.9	—	10.2[8]	10.1[8]	9.9[8]	9.9[8]	10.0[8]	9.7	—	9.8[6,8]	9.9[6,8]	9.4[6,8]	9.4[6,8]	9.7[6,8]
Poland	12.7	11.7	11.0	10.5	10.2	10.0	11.0	11.5	12.7	12.4	12.9	12.9	12.7	10.0	16.9	12.9	12.2	12.2	12.0	12.1	11.1
Portugal	12.1	10.8	11.8	11.3	11.3	10.9	11.2	10.4	8.2	7.9	8.1	7.6	7.9	8.2	7.9	8.0	8.4[6]	7.3[6]	7.7[6]	7.2[6]	7.3[6]
Slovak Republic	18.3	18.9	17.9	18.6	17.7	17.1	16.9	13.5	14.1	13.9	14.5	14.0	13.6	13.1	12.8	14.3	14.1	15.1	15.1	14.6	14.3
Slovenia	14.9	15.0	15.2	15.8	16.7	16.2	16.0	—	11.1	9.5	8.9	7.9	8.0	7.9	11.9[3]	14.6	13.9[6]	13.7[6]	14.3[6]	14.3[6]	14.3[6]
Spain	14.9	14.3	13.6	13.1	13.3	13.2	13.2	12.8	12.5	11.7	10.3	10.1	10.1	10.3	15.2	8.1	7.7	8.7	9.3	9.6	9.8
Sweden	12.8	12.2	12.3	12.2	12.1	11.7	11.3	15.2	12.0	11.5	11.4	11.3	11.4	11.3	—	14.0	13.6	14.7	13.2	13.1	13.0
Switzerland[8]	—	14.6	14.8	15.4	15.4	14.9	15.4	—	11.7	12.3	12.1	12.0	11.8	15.2	14.0	10.5[2]	10.2[2]	10.4[2]	10.4[2]	10.3[2]	—
Turkey	30.5	25.8	26.2	24.4	22.9	21.7	21.0	17.6[2]	17.0	16.7	15.0	16.1	17.1	15.2	12.5[2]	11.8[2,6]	11.3[2,6]	17.0	16.9	17.6	17.8
United Kingdom	21.2	20.7	19.4	20.2	19.9	19.8	19.9	16.3	17.0	16.7	15.0	16.1	17.1	15.2	14.1	11.8[2,6]	11.3[2,6]	12.4[6]	12.3[6]	15.2[6]	17.3
United States	15.8	14.9	14.6	15.0	14.8	14.5	15.3	16.3	15.1	14.7	14.8	14.3	14.0	15.2	14.1	16.0	15.6	15.6	15.1	15.0	15.3
Other reporting countries																					
Brazil	—	22.9	25.8	24.5	24.0	23.4	22.5	—	18.1	22.3	21.2	21.0	20.4	19.8	—	17.6	20.2	18.4	18.1	17.3	16.9
Russian Federation	—	—	17.0[8]	17.3[8]	17.9[8]	19.2[8]	20.0[8]	—	—	—	—	—	—	—	—	11.2[6,10]	8.8[3,6,11]	8.7[3,6,11]	8.7[3,6,11]	11.3[3,6,11]	8.7[3,6,8]

—Not applicable.
†Not applicable. This level of education does not exist within the national education structure; students in the age group normally associated with this education level are reported in other levels.
[1]Refers to the mean of the data values for all reporting Organization for Economic Cooperation and Development (OECD) countries, to which each country reporting data contributes equally. The average includes all current OECD countries for which a given year's data are available, even if they were not members of OECD in that year. However, if data were reported for less than 75 percent of the countries, the average for that year is omitted.
[2]Includes only general programs.
[3]Includes junior high school data.
[4]Includes preprimary data.
[5]Excludes independent private institutions.
[6]Includes postsecondary non-higher-education.
[7]Includes elementary school data.
[8]Public schools only.
[9]Includes occupation-specific education corresponding to that offered at the vocational associate's degree level in the United States.
[10]Includes general programs.
[11]Excludes part-time personnel in public institutions.

NOTE: The pupil/teacher ratio is the number of full-time-equivalent students divided by the number of full-time-equivalent teachers, including teachers for students with disabilities and other special teachers. In this table, elementary school corresponds to International Standard Classification of Education (ISCED) level 1 (U.S. grades 1 through 6), junior high school corresponds to ISCED level 2 (U.S. grades 7 through 9), and senior high school corresponds to ISCED level 3 (U.S. grades 10 through 12).

SOURCE: Organization for Economic Cooperation and Development (OECD), Online Education Database; and Education at a Glance, 2002 through 2013. (This table was prepared December 2013.)

Average reading literacy scale scores of fourth-graders and percentage whose schools emphasize reading skills and strategies at or before second grade or at third grade, by sex and country or other education system: 2001, 2006, and 2011

[Standard errors appear in parentheses]

Country or other education system[1]	Average reading literacy scale score[2]		2011			Percent of fourth-graders in 2011, by grade at which reading skills and strategies emphasized[3]	
	2001	2006	Total	Male	Female	At or before second grade	At third grade
1	2	3	4	5	6	7	8
PIRLS average[4]	500 (†)	500 (†)	500 (†)	504 (0.5)	520 (0.5)	28 (0.5)	68 (0.5)
Australia	— (†)	— (†)	527 (2.2)	519 (2.7)	536 (2.2)	73 (4.0)	27 (4.0)
Austria	— (†)	538 (2.2)	529 (2.0)	525 (2.3)	533 (2.2)	29 (4.2)	71 (4.2)
Azerbaijan[5]	— (†)	— (†)	462[6] (3.3)	456[6] (3.5)	470[6] (3.6)	19 (3.6)	79 (3.8)
Belgium (French)-BEL	— (†)	500 (2.6)	506[6,7] (2.9)	504[6,7] (3.1)	509[6,7] (3.1)	29 (5.0)	70 (5.1)
Bulgaria	550 (3.8)	547 (4.4)	532 (4.1)	524 (4.3)	539 (4.5)	25 (3.5)	74 (3.6)
Canada	— (†)	— (†)	548[6] (1.6)	542[6] (2.1)	555[6] (1.7)	55 (2.7)	44 (2.7)
Chinese Taipei-CHN	— (†)	535 (2.0)	553 (1.9)	546 (2.1)	561 (2.1)	17 (3.0)	80 (3.0)
Colombia	422 (4.4)	— (†)	448 (4.1)	448 (4.6)	447 (4.6)	13 (3.3)	81 (3.6)
Croatia	— (†)	— (†)	553[6] (1.9)	546[6] (2.2)	560[6] (2.1)	31 (4.1)	68 (4.2)
Czech Republic	537 (2.3)	— (†)	545 (2.2)	542 (2.5)	549 (2.5)	24 (3.8)	74 (4.0)
Denmark	— (†)	546 (2.3)	554[6] (1.7)	548[6] (2.1)	560[6] (1.9)	21 (2.4)	79 (2.4)
England-GBR	553[4,5] (3.4)	539 (2.6)	552[7] (2.6)	540[7] (3.1)	563[7] (3.0)	84 (3.3)	15 (3.2)
Finland	— (†)	— (†)	568 (1.9)	558 (2.2)	578 (2.3)	10 (2.6)	87 (2.8)
France	525 (2.4)	522 (2.1)	520 (2.6)	518 (2.4)	522 (3.4)	18 (3.3)	81 (3.4)
Georgia[5]	— (†)	471[6,8] (3.1)	488[8] (3.1)	477[8] (4.0)	499[8] (2.7)	20 (2.8)	79 (2.9)
Germany	539 (1.9)	548 (2.2)	541 (2.2)	537 (2.7)	545 (2.3)	30 (3.4)	69 (3.3)
Hong Kong-CHN	528 (3.1)	564 (2.4)	571[9] (2.3)	563[9] (2.5)	579[9] (2.3)	16 (3.5)	81 (3.8)
Hungary	543 (2.2)	551 (3.0)	539 (2.9)	532 (3.2)	547 (3.2)	28 (4.1)	71 (4.0)
Indonesia	— (†)	405 (4.1)	428 (4.2)	419 (4.3)	437 (4.5)	‡ (†)	88 (3.2)
Iran, Islamic Republic of	414 (4.2)	421 (3.1)	457 (2.8)	448 (4.3)	467 (4.3)	7 (1.6)	85 (2.4)
Ireland	— (†)	— (†)	552 (2.3)	544 (3.0)	559 (2.9)	40 (4.0)	60 (4.0)
Israel	509[10] (2.8)	512[10] (3.3)	541[9] (2.7)	538[9] (3.4)	544[9] (3.1)	59 (4.7)	41 (4.7)
Italy	541 (2.4)	551 (2.9)	541 (2.2)	540 (2.7)	543 (2.4)	15 (2.5)	84 (2.5)
Lithuania	543[8] (2.6)	537[8] (1.6)	528[6,8] (2.0)	520[6,8] (2.4)	537[6,8] (2.4)	23 (3.3)	76 (3.4)
Malta	— (†)	— (†)	477 (1.4)	468 (2.0)	486 (1.9)	14 (0.1)	86 (0.1)
Morocco	350[11] (9.6)	323 (5.9)	310[12] (3.9)	296[12] (4.6)	326[12] (4.0)	‡ (†)	48[13] (4.0)
Netherlands	554[7] (2.5)	547[7] (1.5)	546[7] (1.9)	543[7] (2.2)	549[7] (2.1)	22[13] (4.4)	78[13] (4.4)
New Zealand	529 (3.6)	532 (2.0)	531 (1.9)	521 (2.7)	541 (2.2)	73[13] (3.6)	27[13] (3.6)
Northern Ireland-GBR	— (†)	— (†)	558[7] (2.4)	550[7] (3.2)	567[7] (2.5)	55[13] (4.6)	45[13] (4.6)
Norway	499 (2.9)	498[13] (2.6)	507[11] (1.9)	500[11] (2.7)	514[11] (2.2)	14 (3.4)	83 (3.9)
Oman	— (†)	— (†)	391[14] (2.8)	371[14] (3.4)	411[14] (3.0)	4 (0.9)	86 (2.0)
Poland	— (†)	519 (2.4)	526 (2.1)	519 (2.7)	533 (2.5)	6! (2.1)	94 (2.1)
Portugal	— (†)	— (†)	541 (2.6)	534 (2.8)	548 (3.0)	25 (4.1)	75 (4.1)
Qatar	— (†)	353 (1.1)	425[6] (3.5)	411[6] (4.2)	441[6] (4.7)	24 (3.0)	66 (3.4)
Romania	512 (4.6)	489 (5.0)	502 (4.3)	495 (4.3)	510 (4.8)	14 (3.4)	85 (3.5)
Russian Federation	528[6] (4.4)	565[6] (3.4)	568 (2.7)	559 (3.1)	578 (2.8)	50 (3.7)	50 (3.7)
Saudi Arabia	— (†)	— (†)	430 (4.4)	402 (8.2)	456 (3.1)	7 (1.7)	78 (3.5)
Singapore	528 (5.2)	558 (2.9)	567[6] (3.3)	559[6] (3.6)	576[6] (3.1)	46 (#)	54 (#)
Slovak Republic	518 (2.8)	531 (2.8)	535 (2.8)	530 (2.8)	540 (3.1)	24 (3.2)	76 (3.3)
Slovenia	502 (2.0)	522 (2.1)	530 (2.0)	523 (2.7)	539 (2.2)	8 (1.8)	87 (2.4)
Spain	— (†)	513 (2.5)	513 (2.3)	511 (2.8)	516 (2.5)	29 (3.2)	71 (3.2)
Sweden	561 (2.2)	549 (2.3)	542 (2.1)	535 (2.5)	549 (2.4)	37[13] (4.5)	63[13] (4.5)
Trinidad and Tobago	— (†)	436 (4.9)	471 (3.8)	456 (4.3)	487 (4.5)	32 (3.8)	66 (4.0)
United Arab Emirates	— (†)	— (†)	439 (2.2)	425 (3.5)	452 (3.0)	15 (1.3)	68 (2.2)
United States	542[6,7] (3.8)	540[7] (3.5)	556[6] (1.5)	551[6] (1.7)	562[6] (1.9)	75[13] (2.7)	24[13] (2.7)
Benchmarking education systems							
Abu Dhabi-UAE	— (†)	— (†)	424 (4.7)	406 (6.3)	442 (5.5)	11 (2.6)	61 (4.4)
Alberta-CAN	— (†)	560[6] (2.4)	548[6] (2.9)	543[6] (3.1)	553[6] (3.1)	52 (4.5)	48 (4.5)
Andalusia-ESP	— (†)	— (†)	515 (2.3)	511 (2.8)	519 (2.4)	26 (3.6)	74 (3.6)
Dubai-UAE	— (†)	— (†)	476 (2.0)	470 (3.5)	483 (3.9)	28 (0.3)	66 (0.3)
Florida-USA[15]	— (†)	— (†)	569[8,10] (2.9)	561[8,10] (3.0)	576[8,10] (3.4)	82[13] (4.7)	18[13] (4.7)
Maltese-MLT	— (†)	— (†)	457 (1.5)	445 (2.2)	470 (2.0)	14 (0.1)	86 (0.1)
Ontario-CAN	548[6] (3.3)	555[6] (2.7)	552[6] (2.6)	546[6] (2.8)	558[6] (3.3)	75 (4.0)	25 (4.0)
Quebec-CAN	537 (3.0)	533 (2.8)	538 (2.1)	531 (2.4)	544 (2.6)	23 (3.9)	75 (4.1)

—Not available.

†Not applicable.

#Rounds to zero.

!Interpret data with caution. The coefficient of variation (CV) for this estimate is between 30 and 50 percent.

‡Reporting standards not met. The coefficient of variation (CV) for this estimate is 50 percent or greater.

[1]Most of the education systems represent complete countries, but some represent subnational entities such as U.S. states, Canadian provinces, and England (which is part of the United Kingdom). The name of each subnational entity appears in italics and includes as a suffix the three-letter International Organization for Standardization (ISO) abbreviation for its complete country. Examples include Florida-USA, Ontario-CAN, and England-GBR.

[2]Progress in International Reading Literacy Study (PIRLS) scores are reported on a scale from 0 to 1,000, with the scale average set at 500 and the standard deviation set at 100.

[3]Based on principals' reports of the earliest grade at which each of 11 reading skills and strategies first receive a major emphasis in instruction. A school is counted as emphasizing reading skills and strategies at a certain grade (or before) only if its principal reported that all 11 skills and strategies are emphasized at that grade (or before). A small percentage of fourth-graders (1 percent in the United States) are not shown because their schools first emphasized reading skills and strategies at fourth grade or later.

[4]The PIRLS average includes only education systems that are members of the International Association for the Evaluation of Educational Achievement (IAE), which develops and implements PIRLS at the international level. "Benchmarking" education systems are not members of the IEA and are therefore not included in the average.

[5]Exclusion rates for Azerbaijan and Georgia are slightly underestimated as some conflict zones were not covered and no official statistics were available for 2011.

[6]National Defined Population covers 90 percent to 95 percent of National Target Population.

[7]Met guidelines for sample participation rates only after replacement schools were included.

[8]National Target Population does not include all of the International Target Population.

[9]National Defined Population covers less than 90 percent of National Target Population.

[10]National Defined Population covers less than 80 percent of National Target Population.

[11]Nearly satisfied guidelines for sample participation rates after replacement schools were included.

[12]The TIMSS & PIRLS International Study Center has reservations about the reliability of the average achievement score because the percentage of students with achievement too low for estimation exceeds 25 percent.

[13]Data are available for at least 70 percent but less than 85 percent of students.

[14]The TIMSS & PIRLS International Study Center has reservations about the reliability of the average achievement score because the percentage of students with achievement too low for estimation exceeds 15 percent, though it is less than 25 percent.

[15]All data for Florida are based on public schools only.

SOURCE: International Association for the Evaluation of Educational Achievement (IEA), Progress in International Reading Literacy Study (PIRLS), 2001, 2006, and 2011. (This table was prepared February 2013).

Average fourth-grade scores and annual instructional time in mathematics and science, by country or other education system: 2011
[Standard errors appear in parentheses]

Country or other education system[1]	Total instructional hours per year		Mathematics					Science				
			Average score[2]		Instructional time in mathematics			Average score[2]		Instructional time in science		
					Hours per year		As a percent of total instructional hours			Hours per year		As a percent of total instructional hours
1	2		3		4		5	6		7		8
TIMSS average[3]	897	(2.0)	500	(†)	162	(0.5)	18	(0.1)	500	(†)	85	(0.5)	10	(0.1)
Armenia	851 [4]	(17.1)	452	(3.5)	139 [4]	(1.7)	16	(0.2)	416	(3.8)	54 [5]	(0.6)	6	(0.1)
Australia	1,008	(6.9)	516	(2.9)	230 [5]	(5.8)	23	(0.6)	516	(2.8)	65 [5]	(2.3)	6	(0.2)
Austria	808	(6.9)	508	(2.6)	146	(2.1)	18	(0.3)	532	(2.8)	96	(2.3)	12	(0.3)
Azerbaijan[6,7]	804	(27.7)	463	(5.8)	130	(3.3)	18	(0.7)	438	(5.6)	61	(1.4)	8	(0.3)
Bahrain	964	(10.8)	436	(3.3)	131 [4]	(4.4)	14	(0.4)	449	(3.5)	85 [4]	(2.7)	9	(0.3)
Belgium (Flemish)-BEL	1,010 [4]	(16.8)	549	(1.9)	224 [4]	(4.1)	21	(0.3)	509	(2.0)	—	(†)	—	(†)
Chile	1,228 [4]	(22.6)	462	(2.3)	231 [5]	(6.7)	19	(0.6)	480	(2.4)	161 [5]	(6.4)	13	(0.5)
Chinese Taipei-CHN	989 [4]	(13.4)	591	(2.0)	133	(3.9)	12	(0.4)	552	(2.2)	90	(2.3)	9	(0.3)
Croatia[6]	776	(19.4)	490	(1.9)	134	(2.3)	18	(0.4)	516	(2.1)	95	(2.4)	13	(0.4)
Czech Republic	782	(8.2)	511	(2.4)	163	(3.0)	21	(0.4)	536	(2.5)	60	(2.2)	8	(0.3)
Denmark[6]	863 [4]	(9.4)	537	(2.6)	124 [5]	(2.0)	15	(0.3)	528	(2.8)	62 [5]	(1.9)	7	(0.2)
England-GBR	970 [4]	(8.3)	542	(3.5)	188 [5]	(3.3)	19	(0.4)	529	(2.9)	76 [5]	(3.2)	8	(0.3)
Finland	779	(9.8)	545	(2.3)	139	(2.5)	18	(0.4)	570	(2.6)	98	(1.9)	13	(0.4)
Georgia[7,8]	748 [4]	(18.7)	450	(3.7)	148 [4]	(3.9)	21	(0.6)	455	(3.8)	110 [4]	(2.7)	16	(0.4)
Germany	863 [4]	(11.2)	528	(2.2)	163 [4]	(3.1)	19	(0.3)	528	(2.9)	75 [5]	(3.5)	8	(0.4)
Hong Kong-CHN[6]	1,059 [4]	(11.2)	602	(3.4)	158 [4]	(3.0)	15	(0.3)	535	(3.8)	88 [4]	(4.2)	8	(0.4)
Hungary	760	(12.2)	515	(3.4)	148	(3.3)	20	(0.5)	534	(3.7)	72	(2.2)	10	(0.3)
Iran, Islamic Republic of	727	(11.2)	431	(3.5)	146	(3.9)	20	(0.4)	453	(3.7)	106	(3.2)	14	(0.4)
Ireland	854	(#)	527	(2.6)	150	(2.8)	18	(0.3)	516	(3.4)	63	(6.6)	7	(0.8)
Italy	1,085	(12.6)	508	(2.6)	214	(3.9)	20	(0.4)	524	(2.7)	78 [4]	(1.8)	7	(0.2)
Japan	891	(3.7)	585	(1.7)	150	(1.6)	17	(0.1)	559	(1.9)	91	(0.8)	10	(0.1)
Kazakhstan[6]	779	(10.6)	501	(4.5)	140	(2.7)	18	(0.4)	495	(5.1)	57	(1.3)	8	(0.2)
Korea, Republic of	789	(11.4)	605	(1.9)	121	(3.0)	15	(0.4)	587	(2.0)	92	(2.5)	11	(0.4)
Kuwait[8]	928 [4]	(23.1)	342 [9]	(3.4)	120 [4]	(4.9)	13	(0.4)	347 [10]	(4.7)	85 [5]	(5.8)	10	(0.6)
Lithuania[6,8]	649	(9.0)	534	(2.4)	133	(2.6)	21	(0.5)	515	(2.4)	60	(1.5)	9	(0.3)
Malta	891 [4]	(0.2)	496	(1.3)	183 [4]	(0.1)	21	(#)	446	(1.9)	39 [4]	(0.1)	4	(#)
Morocco	1,040 [4]	(23.6)	335 [9]	(4.0)	174 [5]	(3.5)	17	(0.4)	264 [9]	(4.5)	44 [5]	(5.5)	5	(0.6)
Netherlands[11]	1,074 [5]	(9.9)	540	(1.7)	195 [5]	(7.0)	18	(0.5)	531	(2.2)	42 [5]	(2.4)	4	(0.3)
New Zealand	925	(3.9)	486	(2.6)	168	(2.4)	18	(0.3)	497	(2.3)	52 [5]	(3.0)	6	(0.3)
Northern Ireland-GBR[11]	970 [4]	(11.0)	562	(2.9)	232 [5]	(6.1)	24	(0.6)	517	(2.6)	72 [5]	(3.9)	8	(0.4)
Norway[12]	817	(10.7)	495	(2.8)	157	(4.1)	19	(0.6)	494	(2.3)	55	(2.2)	7	(0.3)
Oman	999 [5]	(17.4)	385 [10]	(2.9)	170 [5]	(3.1)	17	(0.3)	377	(4.3)	120 [5]	(2.4)	12	(0.2)
Poland	764	(13.5)	481	(2.2)	157 [4]	(3.0)	21	(0.5)	505	(2.6)	64 [4]	(3.1)	8	(0.4)
Portugal	940 [4]	(13.1)	532	(3.4)	250 [4]	(4.3)	27	(0.4)	522	(3.9)	162 [4]	(4.1)	17	(0.8)
Qatar[6]	1,068	(9.1)	413	(3.5)	185	(6.3)	17	(0.6)	394	(4.3)	135	(6.8)	13	(0.6)
Romania	796	(17.9)	482	(5.8)	148	(3.9)	19	(0.5)	505	(5.9)	56	(6.2)	7	(0.8)
Russian Federation	660 [4]	(8.0)	542	(3.7)	104	(1.0)	16	(0.2)	552	(3.5)	49	(0.7)	8	(0.2)
Saudi Arabia	977 [4]	(19.4)	410	(5.3)	147 [4]	(6.6)	15	(0.5)	429	(5.4)	82 [4]	(4.2)	8	(0.5)
Serbia[6]	778	(18.5)	516	(3.0)	153	(2.1)	20	(0.5)	516	(3.1)	72	(5.0)	10	(0.9)
Singapore[6]	1,012	(#)	606	(3.2)	208	(3.2)	21	(0.3)	583	(3.4)	96	(2.1)	9	(0.2)
Slovak Republic	780	(8.8)	507	(3.8)	147	(1.4)	19	(0.1)	532	(3.8)	101	(4.3)	13	(0.6)
Slovenia	684	(#)	513	(2.2)	169	(2.6)	25	(0.4)	520	(2.7)	101	(1.2)	15	(0.2)
Spain	884 [4]	(9.7)	482	(2.9)	167 [4]	(2.3)	19	(0.2)	505	(3.0)	145 [4]	(2.6)	16	(0.3)
Sweden	849 [4]	(11.3)	504	(2.0)	138 [5]	(3.8)	17	(0.5)	533	(2.7)	75 [5]	(3.0)	9	(0.4)
Thailand	1,201 [4]	(20.9)	458	(4.8)	167	(5.2)	14	(0.4)	472	(5.6)	109	(4.9)	9	(0.4)
Tunisia	963 [4]	(22.9)	359 [10]	(3.9)	175 [4]	(2.9)	19	(0.3)	346 [10]	(5.3)	93 [4]	(5.4)	10	(0.6)
Turkey	900	(19.3)	469	(4.7)	126	(2.5)	15	(0.4)	463	(4.5)	94	(1.8)	11	(0.4)
United Arab Emirates	1,025 [4]	(8.5)	434	(2.0)	154 [5]	(2.4)	15	(0.2)	428	(2.5)	108 [5]	(3.0)	11	(0.3)
United States[6]	1,078	(7.3)	541	(1.8)	206 [4]	(4.6)	19	(0.5)	544	(2.1)	105 [4]	(3.1)	10	(0.3)
Yemen	831 [4]	(14.1)	248 [9]	(6.0)	135 [4]	(6.4)	16	(0.7)	209 [9]	(7.3)	91 [4]	(5.6)	11	(0.6)
Benchmarking education systems													
Abu Dhabi-UAE	1,033 [4]	(18.1)	417	(4.6)	150 [5]	(4.3)	15	(0.4)	411	(4.9)	110 [5]	(6.8)	11	(0.6)
Alberta-CAN[6]	1,006	(8.8)	507	(2.5)	169 [5]	(3.2)	17	(0.4)	541	(2.4)	130 [5]	(4.1)	13	(0.6)
Dubai-UAE	993 [4]	(0.7)	468	(1.6)	158 [5]	(2.3)	16	(0.2)	461	(2.3)	99 [5]	(1.6)	10	(0.2)
Florida-USA[6,13,14]	1,073 [4]	(19.7)	545	(2.9)	217 [5]	(8.8)	20	(0.9)	545	(3.7)	113 [5]	(9.6)	10	(0.8)
North Carolina-USA[6,8,14]	1,113 [4]	(22.9)	554	(4.2)	221 [4]	(13.5)	20	(1.2)	538	(4.6)	94 [4]	(6.0)	9	(0.4)
Ontario-CAN	969	(7.4)	518	(3.1)	201 [4]	(4.1)	21	(0.5)	528	(3.0)	92 [4]	(3.2)	10	(0.3)
Quebec-CAN	916	(5.1)	533	(2.4)	229	(5.0)	25	(0.6)	516	(2.7)	50	(1.7)	5	(0.2)

—Not available.
†Not applicable.
#Rounds to zero.
[1]Most of the education systems represent complete countries, but some represent subnational entities such as U.S. states, Canadian provinces, and England (which is part of the United Kingdom). The name of each subnational entity appears in italics and includes as a suffix three-letter International Organization for Standardization (ISO) abbreviation for its complete country. Examples include *Florida-USA*, *Ontario-CAN*, and *England-GBR*.
[2]Trends in International Mathematics and Science Study (TIMSS) scores are reported on a scale from 0 to 1,000, with the scale average set at 500 and the standard deviation set at 100.
[3]The TIMSS average includes only education systems that are members of the International Association for the Evaluation of Educational Achievement (IAE), which develops and implements TIMSS at the international level. "Benchmarking" education systems are not members of the IEA and are therefore not included in the average.
[4]Data are available for at least 70 percent but less than 85 percent of students.
[5]Data are available for at least 50 percent but less than 70 percent of students.
[6]National Defined Population covers 90 to 95 percent of National Target Population.
[7]Exclusion rates for Azerbaijan and Georgia are slightly underestimated as some conflict zones were not covered and no official statistics were available.
[8]National Target Population does not include all of the International Target Population defined by TIMSS.
[9]The TIMSS & PIRLS International Study Center has reservations about the reliability of the average achievement score because the percentage of students with achievement too low for estimation exceeds 25 percent.

[10]The TIMSS & PIRLS International Study Center has reservations about the reliability of the average achievement score because the percentage of students with achievement too low for estimation exceeds 15 percent, though it is less than 25 percent.
[11]Met guidelines for sample participation rates only after replacement schools were included.
[12]Nearly satisfied guidelines for sample participation rates after replacement schools were included.
[13]National Defined Population covers less than 90 percent of National Target Population (but at least 77 percent).
[14]All U.S. state data are based on public school students only.
NOTE: Countries were required to sample students in the grade that corresponded to the end of 4 years of formal schooling, providing that the mean age at the time of testing was at least 9.5 years. Instructional times shown in this table are actual or implemented times (as opposed to intended times prescribed by the curriculum). Principals reported total instructional hours per day and school days per year. Total instructional hours per year were calculated by multiplying the number of school days per year by the number of instructional hours per day. Teachers reported instructional hours per week in mathematics and science. Instructional hours per year in mathematics and science were calculated by dividing weekly instructional hours by the number of school days per week and then multiplying by the number of school days per year.
SOURCE: International Association for the Evaluation of Educational Achievement (IEA), Trends in International Mathematics and Science Study (TIMSS), 2011; *TIMSS 2011 International Results in Mathematics*, by Ina V.S. Mullis et al.; and *TIMSS 2011 International Results in Science*, by Michael O. Martin et al. (This table was prepared December 2012.)

Average eighth-grade scores and annual instructional time in mathematics and science, by country or other education system: 2011

[Standard errors appear in parentheses]

Country or other education system[1]	Total instructional hours per year		Mathematics					Science					
			Average score[2]		Instructional time in mathematics				Average score[2]		Instructional time in science[3]			
					Hours per year		As a percent of total instructional hours				Hours per year		As a percent of total instructional hours	
1	2		3		4		5		6		7		8	
TIMSS average[4]	1,031	(2.3)	500	(†)	138	(0.5)	14	(0.1)	500	(†)	158	(0.8)	11	(0.1)
Armenia	979 [5]	(12.8)	467	(2.7)	143 [5]	(3.0)	15	(0.2)	437	(3.1)	240 [6]	(4.9)	‡	(†)
Australia	1,039	(7.2)	505	(5.1)	143 [6]	(3.5)	14	(0.3)	519	(4.8)	131 [6]	(4.5)	12	(0.4)
Bahrain	1,019	(1.1)	409 [7]	(2.0)	142 [5]	(2.5)	14	(0.3)	452	(2.0)	130 [5]	(2.8)	13	(0.3)
Chile	1,245 [5]	(23.5)	416	(2.6)	193 [5]	(4.5)	15	(0.3)	461	(2.5)	134 [5]	(3.8)	11	(0.3)
Chinese Taipei-CHN	1,153	(11.7)	609	(3.2)	166	(2.4)	15	(0.2)	564	(2.3)	157	(2.7)	14	(0.3)
England-GBR[8]	992 [5]	(8.4)	507	(5.5)	116	(2.1)	11	(0.3)	533	(4.9)	102 [6]	(3.1)	10	(0.4)
Finland	934	(11.7)	514	(2.5)	105	(1.8)	11	(0.2)	552	(2.5)	190 [5]	(6.0)	‡	(†)
Georgia[9,10]	833 [5]	(10.8)	431	(3.8)	123 [5]	(3.3)	15	(0.5)	420	(3.0)	198 [5]	(6.8)	‡	(†)
Ghana	1,153 [5]	(18.9)	331 [11]	(4.3)	165 [5]	(6.8)	14	(0.6)	306 [7]	(5.2)	148 [5]	(6.1)	13	(0.4)
Hong Kong-CHN	1,026 [5]	(11.3)	586	(3.8)	138 [5]	(2.9)	13	(0.3)	535	(3.4)	103 [5]	(4.6)	10	(0.4)
Hungary	836	(12.2)	505	(3.5)	119	(1.9)	15	(0.3)	522	(3.1)	236	(4.8)	28 !	(13.1)
Indonesia	1,494 [5]	(40.9)	386 [7]	(4.3)	173 [5]	(7.9)	12	(0.6)	406	(4.5)	190 [5]	(12.2)	10	(0.5)
Iran, Islamic Republic of	994	(15.9)	415 [7]	(4.3)	124	(3.3)	13	(0.3)	474	(4.0)	120	(3.6)	12	(0.4)
Israel[12]	1,108 [5]	(14.1)	516	(4.1)	165 [5]	(3.0)	15	(0.2)	516	(4.0)	132	(3.9)	12	(0.4)
Italy	1,085	(9.4)	498	(2.4)	155	(2.5)	14	(0.2)	501	(2.5)	73	(1.0)	7	(0.1)
Japan	1,016	(6.7)	570	(2.6)	108	(1.4)	11	(0.1)	558	(2.4)	128	(1.7)	12	(0.3)
Jordan	1,041	(11.9)	406 [7]	(3.7)	130	(3.8)	13	(0.4)	449	(4.0)	134	(3.1)	13	(0.4)
Kazakhstan	920	(9.9)	487	(4.0)	117	(3.2)	13	(0.4)	490	(4.3)	244	(4.8)	27 !	(11.0)
Korea, Republic of	1,006	(12.1)	613	(2.9)	137	(1.8)	13	(0.2)	560	(2.0)	126	(2.5)	11	(0.2)
Lebanon	1,028 [5]	(12.7)	449	(3.7)	178 [5]	(3.9)	17	(0.4)	406	(4.9)	‡	(†)	‡	(†)
Lithuania[9]	898	(13.9)	502	(2.5)	132	(2.7)	15	(0.4)	514	(2.6)	251 [5]	(5.2)	‡	(†)
Macedonia, Republic of	1,023 [5]	(21.4)	426 [7]	(5.2)	122 [6]	(4.6)	13	(0.6)	407	(5.4)	334 [6]	(14.7)	‡	(†)
Malaysia	1,198 [5]	(13.7)	440	(5.4)	123 [5]	(3.4)	10	(0.3)	426	(6.3)	126	(3.6)	10	(0.3)
Morocco	1,303 [5]	(24.9)	371 [11]	(2.0)	148 [5]	(2.1)	12	(0.2)	376	(2.2)	144 [5]	(2.0)	‡	(†)
New Zealand	959	(4.4)	488	(5.5)	141	(1.8)	15	(0.2)	512	(4.6)	130 [5]	(2.6)	14	(0.3)
Norway	880	(6.3)	475	(2.4)	125	(3.4)	14	(0.4)	494	(2.6)	101	(3.3)	11	(0.4)
Oman	1,044 [5]	(17.7)	366 [7]	(2.8)	161 [5]	(5.1)	16	(0.4)	420	(3.2)	161 [6]	(3.8)	16	(0.3)
Palestinian National Authority	918	(7.3)	404 [7]	(3.5)	134	(4.0)	15	(0.4)	420	(3.2)	107	(3.3)	12	(0.4)
Qatar	1,054	(1.3)	410 [7]	(3.1)	162	(3.6)	15	(0.4)	419	(3.4)	131	(6.9)	12	(0.5)
Romania	984	(15.5)	458	(4.0)	145	(3.7)	15	(0.3)	465	(3.5)	281	(10.1)	‡	(†)
Russian Federation[13]	882	(8.7)	539	(3.6)	142	(2.0)	16	(0.3)	542	(3.2)	208	(1.6)	24 !	(8.8)
Saudi Arabia	1,050 [5]	(20.9)	394 [7]	(4.6)	134 [5]	(5.4)	13	(0.4)	436	(3.9)	124 [5]	(6.8)	12	(0.5)
Singapore[13]	1,106	(#)	611	(3.8)	138	(1.7)	13	(0.2)	590	(4.3)	115	(2.1)	11	(0.2)
Slovenia	798	(#)	505	(2.2)	121	(1.5)	15	(0.2)	543	(2.7)	251	(4.6)	31	(4.6)
Sweden	969 [5]	(13.4)	484	(1.9)	97 [6]	(2.2)	10	(0.3)	509	(2.5)	94 [6]	(3.1)	9	(0.4)
Syrian Arab Republic	811	(14.2)	380 [7]	(4.5)	118 [5]	(4.7)	15	(0.5)	426	(3.9)	150 [5]	(7.5)	‡	(†)
Thailand	1,270 [5]	(15.1)	427	(4.3)	129	(4.3)	10	(0.3)	451	(3.9)	119	(2.9)	9	(0.3)
Tunisia	1,299 [5]	(25.4)	425	(2.8)	131 [5]	(3.0)	10	(0.2)	439	(2.5)	64 [5]	(1.9)	5	(0.1)
Turkey	889	(16.7)	452	(3.9)	117	(1.8)	14	(0.3)	483	(3.4)	99	(1.1)	12	(0.2)
Ukraine	901	(10.7)	479	(3.9)	132	(3.5)	15	(0.4)	501	(3.4)	239	(4.0)	27 !	(11.4)
United Arab Emirates	1,046 [5]	(8.0)	456	(2.1)	157 [5]	(2.9)	15	(0.3)	465	(2.4)	115 [6]	(2.7)	11	(0.3)
United States[13]	1,114	(6.6)	509	(2.6)	157 [6]	(3.2)	14	(0.3)	525	(2.6)	139 [14]	(2.4)	13 [14]	(0.2)
Benchmarking education systems														
Abu Dhabi-UAE	1,045 [5]	(16.6)	449	(3.7)	158 [5]	(5.8)	15	(0.5)	461	(4.0)	111 [6]	(4.8)	11	(0.5)
Alabama-USA[9,15]	1,135 [5]	(16.0)	466	(5.9)	166 [6]	(8.9)	15	(0.9)	485	(6.2)	167 [6]	(6.0)	15	(0.5)
Alberta-CAN[13]	1,031	(10.0)	505	(2.6)	156	(4.2)	19	(0.4)	546	(2.4)	145 [5]	(4.0)	10	(0.4)
California-USA[9,13,15]	1,040 [5]	(15.2)	493	(4.9)	172 [6]	(8.0)	17	(0.7)	499	(4.6)	‡	(†)	14	(0.7)
Colorado-USA[9,15]	1,148	(17.0)	518	(4.9)	173 [5]	(8.6)	15	(0.8)	542	(4.4)	138 [6]	(6.0)	12	(0.5)

See notes at end of table.

Average eighth-grade scores and annual instructional time in mathematics and science, by country or other education system: 2011—Continued

[Standard errors appear in parentheses]

Country or other education system[1]	Total instructional hours per year	Mathematics Average score[2]	Instructional time in mathematics Hours per year	As a percent of total instructional hours	Science Average score[2]	Instructional time in science[3] Hours per year	As a percent of total instructional hours
1	2	3	4	5	6	7	8
Connecticut-USA[9,13,15]	1,071 (19.3)	518 (4.8)	144 [5] (4.4)	14 (0.5)	532 (4.6)	139 [6] (6.2)	13 (0.6)
Dubai-UAE	1,022 [5] (1.5)	478 (2.1)	155 [5] (3.6)	15 (0.3)	485 (2.5)	125 [6] (3.6)	11 (0.3)
Florida-USA[9,13,15]	1,119 [5] (17.0)	513 (6.4)	144 [6] (7.4)	13 (0.7)	530 (7.3)	‡ (†)	13 (0.8)
Indiana-USA[9,13,15]	1,133 [5] (14.9)	522 (5.1)	149 [6] (6.9)	13 (0.7)	533 (4.8)	132 [6] (6.5)	12 (0.6)
Massachusetts-USA[9,13,15]	1,087 (13.6)	561 (5.3)	154 [5] (5.4)	14 (0.6)	567 (5.1)	156 [6] (6.1)	15 (0.6)
Minnesota-USA[8,15]	1,043 (14.8)	545 (4.6)	142 [5] (7.5)	14 (0.7)	553 (4.6)	140 [6] (8.3)	14 (0.9)
North Carolina-USA[9,12,15]	1,159 (16.0)	537 (6.8)	185 [6] (9.7)	16 (0.8)	532 (6.3)	‡ (†)	16 (1.2)
Ontario-CAN[13]	971 [5] (7.5)	512 (2.5)	181 [5] (3.9)	16 (0.5)	521 (2.5)	96 [5] (3.5)	11 (0.3)
Quebec-CAN	913 (3.3)	532 (2.3)	147 (4.1)	15 (0.5)	520 (2.5)	102 [5] (3.0)	14 (0.4)

†Not applicable.

#Rounds to zero.

!Interpret data with caution. The coefficient of variation (CV) for this estimate is between 30 and 50 percent.

‡Reporting standards not met. Either data are available for less than 50 percent of the students or the coefficient of variation (CV) is 50 percent or greater.

[1]Most of the education systems represent complete countries, but some represent subnational entities such as U.S. states, Canadian provinces, and England (which is part of the United Kingdom). The name of each subnational entity appears in italics and includes as a suffix the three-letter International Organization for Standardization (ISO) abbreviation for its complete country. Examples include *Florida-USA*, *Ontario-CAN*, and *England-GBR*.

[2]Trends in International Mathematics and Science Study (TIMSS) scores are reported on a scale from 0 to 1,000, with the scale average set at 500 and the standard deviation set at 100.

[3]General/integrated science instructional time is shown for the 27 participating countries that teach science as a general or integrated subject at the eighth grade. For the 15 participating countries that teach the sciences as separate subjects (biology, chemistry, etc.) at the eighth grade, total instructional time across science subjects is shown.

[4]The TIMSS average includes only education systems that are members of the International Association for the Evaluation of Educational Achievement (IAE), which develops and implements TIMSS at the international level. "Benchmarking" education systems are not members of the IEA and are therefore not included in the average.

[5]Data are available for at least 70 percent but less than 85 percent of students.

[6]Data are available for at least 50 percent but less than 70 percent of students.

[7]The TIMSS & PIRLS International Study Center has reservations about the reliability of the average achievement score because the percentage of students with achievement too low for estimation exceeds 15 percent, though it is less than 25 percent.

[8]Nearly satisfied guidelines for sample participation rate after replacement schools were included.

[9]National Target Population does not include all of the International Target Population defined by TIMSS.

[10]Exclusion rates for Georgia are slightly underestimated as some conflict zones were not covered and no official statistics were available.

[11]The TIMSS & PIRLS International Study Center has reservations about the reliability of the average achievement score because the percentage of students with achievement too low for estimation exceeds 25 percent.

[12]National Defined Population covers less than 90 percent of National Target Population (but at least 77 percent).

[13]National Defined Population covers 90 to 95 percent of National Target Population.

[14]Data are for 2007 and are from *TIMSS 2007 International Results in Science*. Met guidelines for sample participation rates only after replacement schools were included. Data are available for at least 50 percent but less than 70 percent of students.

[15]All U.S. state data are based on public school students only.

NOTE: Countries were required to sample students in the grade that corresponded to the end of 8 years of formal schooling, providing that the mean age at the time of testing was at least 13.5 years. Instructional times shown in this table are actual or implemented times (as opposed to intended times prescribed by the curriculum). Principals reported total instructional hours per day and school days per year. Total instructional hours per year were calculated by multiplying the number of school days per year by the number of instructional hours per day. Teachers reported instructional hours per week in mathematics and science. Instructional hours per year in mathematics and science were calculated by dividing weekly instructional hours by the number of school days per week and then multiplying by the number of school days per year.

SOURCE: International Association for the Evaluation of Educational Achievement (IEA), Trends in International Mathematics and Science Study (TIMSS), 2011; *TIMSS 2011 International Results in Mathematics*, by Ina V.S. Mullis et al.; and *TIMSS 2011 International Results in Science*, by Michael O. Martin et al. (This table was prepared December 2012.)

Average reading literacy, mathematics literacy, and science literacy scores of 15-year-old students, by sex and country or other education system: 2009 and 2012

[Standard errors appear in parentheses]

Country or other education system	Reading literacy								Mathematics literacy								Science literacy							
	2009		2012						2009		2012						2009		2012					
			Total		Male		Female				Total		Male		Female				Total		Male		Female	
1	2		3		4		5		6		7		8		9		10		11		12		13	
OECD average[1]	**493**	**(0.5)**	**496**	**(0.5)**	**478**	**(0.6)**	**515**	**(0.5)**	**496**	**(0.5)**	**494**	**(0.5)**	**499**	**(0.6)**	**489**	**(0.5)**	**501**	**(0.5)**	**501**	**(0.5)**	**502**	**(0.6)**	**500**	**(0.5)**
Australia	515	(2.3)	512	(1.6)	495	(2.3)	530	(2.0)	514	(2.5)	504	(1.6)	510	(2.4)	498	(2.0)	527	(2.5)	521	(1.8)	524	(2.5)	519	(2.1)
Austria	470	(2.9)	490	(2.8)	471	(4.0)	508	(3.4)	496	(2.7)	506	(2.7)	517	(3.9)	494	(3.3)	494	(3.2)	506	(2.7)	510	(3.9)	501	(3.4)
Belgium	506	(2.3)	509	(2.3)	493	(3.0)	525	(2.7)	515	(2.3)	515	(2.1)	520	(2.9)	509	(2.6)	507	(2.5)	505	(2.2)	507	(3.0)	503	(2.6)
Canada	524	(1.5)	523	(1.9)	506	(2.3)	541	(2.1)	527	(1.6)	518	(1.8)	523	(2.1)	513	(2.1)	529	(1.6)	525	(1.9)	527	(2.4)	524	(2.0)
Chile	449	(3.1)	441	(2.9)	430	(3.8)	452	(2.9)	421	(3.1)	423	(3.1)	436	(3.8)	411	(3.1)	447	(2.9)	445	(2.9)	448	(3.7)	442	(2.9)
Czech Republic	478	(2.9)	493	(2.9)	474	(3.3)	513	(3.4)	493	(2.8)	499	(2.9)	505	(3.7)	493	(3.6)	500	(3.0)	508	(3.0)	509	(3.7)	508	(3.5)
Denmark	495	(2.1)	496	(2.6)	481	(3.3)	512	(2.6)	503	(2.6)	500	(2.3)	507	(2.9)	493	(2.3)	499	(2.5)	498	(2.7)	504	(3.5)	493	(2.5)
Estonia	501	(2.6)	516	(2.0)	494	(2.4)	538	(2.3)	512	(2.6)	521	(2.0)	523	(2.6)	518	(2.2)	528	(2.7)	541	(1.9)	540	(2.5)	543	(2.3)
Finland	536	(2.3)	524	(2.4)	494	(3.1)	556	(2.4)	541	(2.2)	519	(1.9)	517	(2.6)	520	(2.2)	554	(2.3)	545	(2.2)	537	(3.0)	554	(2.3)
France	496	(3.4)	505	(2.8)	483	(3.8)	527	(3.0)	497	(3.1)	495	(2.5)	499	(3.4)	491	(2.5)	498	(3.6)	499	(2.6)	498	(3.8)	500	(2.4)
Germany	497	(2.7)	508	(2.8)	486	(2.9)	530	(3.1)	513	(2.9)	514	(2.9)	520	(3.0)	507	(3.4)	520	(2.8)	524	(3.0)	524	(3.1)	524	(3.5)
Greece	483	(4.3)	477	(3.3)	452	(4.1)	502	(3.1)	466	(3.9)	453	(2.5)	457	(3.3)	449	(2.6)	470	(4.0)	467	(3.1)	460	(3.8)	473	(3.0)
Hungary	494	(3.2)	488	(3.2)	468	(3.9)	508	(3.3)	490	(3.5)	477	(3.2)	482	(3.7)	473	(3.6)	503	(3.1)	494	(2.9)	496	(3.4)	493	(3.3)
Iceland	500	(1.4)	483	(1.8)	457	(2.4)	508	(2.5)	507	(1.4)	493	(1.7)	490	(2.3)	496	(2.3)	496	(1.4)	478	(2.1)	477	(2.7)	480	(2.9)
Ireland	496	(3.0)	523	(2.6)	509	(3.5)	538	(3.0)	487	(2.5)	501	(2.2)	509	(3.3)	494	(2.6)	508	(3.3)	522	(2.5)	524	(3.4)	520	(3.1)
Israel	474	(3.6)	486	(5.0)	463	(8.2)	507	(3.9)	447	(3.3)	466	(4.7)	472	(7.8)	461	(3.5)	455	(3.1)	470	(5.0)	470	(7.9)	470	(4.0)
Italy	486	(1.6)	490	(2.0)	471	(2.5)	510	(2.3)	483	(1.9)	485	(2.0)	494	(2.4)	476	(2.2)	489	(1.8)	494	(1.9)	495	(2.2)	492	(2.4)
Japan	520	(3.5)	538	(3.7)	527	(4.7)	551	(3.6)	529	(3.3)	536	(3.6)	545	(4.6)	527	(3.6)	539	(3.4)	547	(3.6)	552	(4.7)	541	(3.5)
Korea, Republic of	539	(3.5)	536	(3.9)	525	(5.0)	548	(4.5)	546	(4.0)	554	(4.6)	562	(5.8)	544	(5.1)	538	(3.4)	538	(3.7)	539	(4.7)	536	(4.2)
Luxembourg	472	(1.3)	488	(1.5)	473	(1.9)	503	(1.8)	489	(1.2)	490	(1.1)	502	(1.5)	477	(1.4)	484	(1.2)	491	(1.3)	499	(1.7)	483	(1.7)
Mexico	425	(2.0)	424	(1.5)	411	(1.7)	435	(1.6)	419	(1.8)	413	(1.4)	420	(1.6)	406	(1.4)	416	(1.8)	415	(1.3)	418	(1.5)	412	(1.3)
Netherlands	508	(5.1)	511	(3.5)	498	(4.0)	525	(3.5)	526	(4.7)	523	(3.5)	528	(3.6)	518	(3.9)	522	(5.4)	522	(3.5)	524	(3.7)	520	(3.9)
New Zealand	521	(2.4)	512	(2.4)	495	(3.3)	530	(3.5)	519	(2.3)	500	(2.2)	507	(3.2)	492	(2.9)	532	(2.6)	516	(2.1)	518	(3.2)	513	(3.3)
Norway	503	(2.6)	504	(3.2)	481	(3.3)	528	(3.9)	498	(2.4)	489	(2.7)	490	(2.8)	488	(3.4)	500	(2.6)	495	(3.1)	493	(3.2)	496	(3.7)
Poland	500	(2.6)	518	(3.1)	497	(3.7)	539	(3.1)	495	(2.8)	518	(3.6)	520	(4.3)	516	(3.8)	508	(2.4)	526	(3.1)	524	(3.7)	527	(3.2)
Portugal	489	(3.1)	488	(3.8)	468	(4.2)	508	(3.7)	487	(2.9)	487	(3.8)	493	(4.1)	481	(3.9)	493	(2.9)	489	(3.7)	488	(4.1)	490	(3.8)
Slovak Republic	477	(2.5)	463	(4.2)	444	(4.6)	483	(5.1)	497	(3.1)	482	(3.4)	486	(4.1)	477	(4.1)	490	(3.0)	471	(3.6)	475	(4.3)	467	(4.2)
Slovenia	483	(1.0)	481	(1.2)	454	(1.7)	510	(1.8)	501	(1.2)	501	(1.2)	503	(2.0)	499	(2.0)	512	(1.1)	514	(1.3)	510	(1.9)	519	(1.9)
Spain	481	(2.0)	488	(1.9)	474	(2.3)	503	(1.9)	483	(2.1)	484	(1.9)	492	(2.4)	476	(2.0)	488	(2.1)	496	(1.8)	500	(2.3)	493	(1.9)
Sweden	497	(2.9)	483	(3.0)	458	(4.0)	509	(2.8)	494	(2.9)	478	(2.3)	477	(3.0)	480	(2.4)	495	(2.7)	485	(3.0)	481	(3.9)	489	(2.8)
Switzerland	501	(2.4)	509	(2.6)	491	(3.1)	527	(2.5)	534	(3.3)	531	(3.0)	537	(3.5)	524	(3.1)	517	(2.8)	515	(2.7)	518	(3.3)	512	(2.7)
Turkey	464	(3.5)	475	(4.2)	453	(4.6)	499	(4.3)	445	(4.4)	448	(4.8)	452	(5.1)	444	(5.7)	454	(3.6)	463	(3.9)	458	(4.5)	469	(4.3)
United Kingdom	494	(2.3)	499	(3.5)	487	(4.5)	512	(3.8)	492	(2.4)	494	(3.3)	500	(4.2)	488	(3.8)	514	(2.5)	514	(3.4)	521	(4.5)	508	(3.7)
United States	500	(3.7)	498	(3.7)	482	(4.1)	513	(3.8)	487	(3.6)	481	(3.6)	484	(3.8)	479	(3.9)	502	(3.6)	497	(3.8)	497	(4.1)	498	(4.0)
Non-OECD education systems																								
Albania	385	(4.0)	394	(3.2)	387	(3.8)	401	(3.7)	377	(4.0)	394	(2.0)	394	(2.6)	395	(2.6)	391	(3.9)	397	(2.4)	394	(3.0)	401	(2.9)
Argentina	398	(4.6)	396	(3.7)	377	(4.5)	414	(3.6)	388	(4.1)	388	(3.5)	396	(4.2)	382	(3.4)	401	(4.6)	406	(3.9)	402	(4.5)	409	(4.0)
Brazil	412	(2.7)	410	(2.1)	394	(2.4)	425	(2.2)	386	(2.4)	391	(2.1)	401	(2.2)	383	(2.3)	405	(2.4)	405	(2.1)	406	(2.3)	404	(2.3)
Bulgaria	429	(6.7)	436	(6.0)	403	(6.3)	472	(5.6)	428	(5.9)	439	(4.0)	438	(4.7)	440	(4.2)	439	(5.9)	446	(4.8)	437	(5.6)	457	(4.6)
Chinese Taipei	—	(†)	523	(3.0)	507	(4.3)	539	(4.3)	—	(†)	560	(3.3)	563	(5.4)	557	(5.7)	—	(†)	523	(2.3)	524	(3.9)	523	(4.0)
Colombia	413	(3.7)	403	(3.4)	394	(3.9)	412	(3.8)	381	(3.2)	376	(2.9)	390	(3.4)	364	(3.2)	402	(3.6)	399	(3.1)	408	(3.4)	390	(3.6)
Connecticut-USA[2]	—	(†)	521	(6.5)	510	(7.1)	532	(6.7)	—	(†)	506	(6.2)	513	(6.9)	499	(6.3)	—	(†)	521	(5.7)	528	(6.2)	514	(6.1)
Costa Rica	—	(†)	441	(3.5)	427	(3.9)	452	(3.5)	—	(†)	407	(3.0)	420	(3.6)	396	(3.1)	—	(†)	429	(2.9)	436	(3.5)	424	(3.2)
Croatia	476	(2.9)	485	(3.3)	461	(4.1)	509	(3.3)	460	(3.1)	471	(3.5)	477	(4.4)	465	(3.7)	486	(2.8)	491	(3.1)	490	(3.9)	493	(3.3)
Cyprus	—	(†)	449	(1.2)	418	(1.9)	481	(1.9)	—	(†)	440	(1.1)	440	(1.5)	440	(1.6)	—	(†)	438	(1.2)	431	(1.8)	444	(1.7)
Florida-USA[2]	—	(†)	492	(6.1)	481	(7.0)	503	(5.9)	—	(†)	467	(5.8)	474	(6.3)	460	(6.0)	—	(†)	485	(6.4)	491	(7.4)	478	(6.2)
Hong Kong-China	533	(2.1)	545	(2.8)	533	(3.8)	558	(3.3)	555	(2.7)	561	(3.2)	568	(4.6)	553	(3.9)	549	(2.8)	555	(2.6)	558	(3.6)	551	(3.1)
Indonesia	402	(3.7)	396	(4.2)	382	(4.8)	410	(4.3)	371	(3.7)	375	(4.0)	377	(4.4)	373	(4.3)	383	(3.8)	382	(3.8)	380	(4.1)	383	(4.1)
Jordan	405	(3.3)	399	(3.6)	361	(5.5)	436	(3.1)	387	(3.7)	386	(3.1)	375	(5.4)	396	(3.1)	415	(3.5)	409	(3.1)	388	(5.4)	430	(2.9)
Kazakhstan	390	(3.1)	393	(2.7)	374	(3.4)	411	(2.6)	405	(3.0)	432	(3.0)	432	(3.4)	432	(3.3)	400	(3.1)	425	(3.0)	420	(3.4)	429	(3.2)
Latvia	484	(3.0)	489	(2.4)	462	(3.3)	516	(2.7)	482	(3.1)	491	(2.8)	489	(3.4)	493	(3.2)	494	(3.1)	502	(2.8)	495	(3.6)	510	(2.8)
Liechtenstein	499	(2.8)	516	(4.1)	504	(6.2)	529	(5.8)	536	(4.1)	535	(4.0)	546	(6.0)	523	(5.8)	520	(3.4)	525	(3.5)	533	(5.8)	516	(5.7)
Lithuania	468	(2.4)	477	(2.5)	450	(2.8)	505	(2.6)	477	(2.6)	479	(2.6)	479	(2.8)	479	(3.0)	491	(2.9)	496	(2.6)	488	(3.0)	503	(2.6)
Macao-China	487	(0.9)	509	(0.9)	492	(1.4)	527	(1.1)	525	(0.9)	538	(1.0)	540	(1.4)	537	(1.3)	511	(1.0)	521	(0.8)	520	(1.3)	521	(1.2)
Malaysia	—	(†)	398	(3.3)	377	(3.9)	418	(3.3)	—	(†)	421	(3.2)	416	(3.7)	424	(3.7)	—	(†)	420	(3.0)	414	(3.8)	425	(3.1)
Montenegro, Republic of	408	(1.7)	422	(1.2)	391	(2.3)	453	(1.5)	403	(2.0)	410	(1.1)	410	(1.6)	410	(1.6)	401	(2.0)	410	(1.1)	402	(1.6)	419	(1.6)
Peru	370	(4.0)	384	(4.3)	373	(4.0)	395	(5.4)	365	(4.0)	368	(3.7)	378	(3.6)	359	(4.8)	369	(3.5)	373	(3.6)	376	(3.5)	370	(4.6)
Massachusetts-USA[2]	—	(†)	527	(6.1)	511	(6.2)	542	(6.6)	—	(†)	514	(6.2)	518	(6.3)	509	(7.1)	—	(†)	527	(6.0)	529	(6.1)	526	(6.8)
Qatar	372	(0.8)	388	(0.8)	354	(1.1)	424	(1.2)	368	(0.7)	376	(0.8)	369	(1.1)	385	(0.9)	379	(0.9)	384	(0.7)	367	(1.2)	402	(1.1)
Romania	424	(4.1)	438	(4.0)	417	(4.5)	457	(4.2)	427	(3.4)	445	(3.8)	447	(4.3)	443	(4.0)	428	(3.4)	439	(3.3)	436	(3.7)	441	(3.5)
Russian Federation	459	(3.3)	475	(3.0)	455	(3.5)	495	(3.2)	468	(3.3)	482	(3.0)	481	(3.7)	483	(3.1)	478	(3.3)	486	(2.9)	484	(3.5)	489	(2.9)
Serbia, Republic of	442	(2.4)	446	(3.4)	423	(3.9)	469	(3.8)	442	(2.9)	449	(3.4)	453	(4.1)	444	(3.7)	443	(2.4)	445	(3.4)	443	(4.0)	447	(3.8)
Shanghai-China	556	(2.4)	570	(2.9)	557	(3.3)	581	(2.8)	600	(2.8)	613	(3.3)	616	(4.0)	610	(3.4)	575	(2.3)	580	(3.0)	583	(3.5)	578	(3.1)
Singapore	526	(1.1)	542	(1.4)	527	(1.9)	559	(1.9)	562	(1.4)	573	(1.3)	572	(1.9)	575	(1.8)	542	(1.4)	551	(1.5)	551	(2.1)	552	(1.9)
Thailand	421	(2.6)	441	(3.1)	410	(3.6)	465	(3.3)	419	(3.2)	427	(3.4)	419	(3.6)	433	(4.1)	425	(3.0)	444	(2.9)	433	(3.3)	452	(3.4)
Tunisia	404	(2.9)	404	(4.5)	388	(5.0)	418	(4.4)	371	(3.0)	388	(3.9)	396	(4.3)	381	(4.0)	401	(2.7)	398	(3.5)	399	(3.9)	398	(3.6)
United Arab Emirates	—	(†)	442	(2.5)	413	(3.9)	469	(3.2)	—	(†)	434	(2.4)	432	(3.8)	436	(3.0)	—	(†)	448	(2.8)	434	(4.1)	462	(3.7)
Uruguay	426	(2.6)	411	(3.2)	392	(3.9)	428	(3.2)	427	(2.6)	409	(2.8)	415	(3.5)	404	(2.9)	427	(2.6)	416	(2.8)	415	(3.4)	416	(3.1)
Vietnam	—	(†)	508	(4.4)	492	(5.0)	523	(4.0)	—	(†)	511	(4.8)	517	(5.6)	507	(4.7)	—	(†)	528	(4.3)	529	(5.0)	528	(4.1)

—Not available.
†Not applicable.
[1]Refers to the mean of the data values for all Organization for Economic Cooperation and Development (OECD) countries, to which each country contributes equally regardless of the absolute size of the student population of each country.
[2]Results are for public school students only.
NOTE: Program for International Student Assessment (PISA) scores are reported on a scale from 0 to 1,000.
SOURCE: Organization for Economic Cooperation and Development (OECD), Program for International Student Assessment (PISA), 2009 and 2012. (This table was prepared July 2014.)

Average reading literacy scores of 15-year-old students and percentage attaining reading literacy proficiency levels, by country or other education system: 2012

[Standard errors appear in parentheses]

Country or other education system	Average reading literacy score	Below level 2				At level 2	At level 3	At level 4	At or above level 5		
		Total below level 2	Below level 1b	At level 1b	At level 1a				Total at or above level 5	At level 5	At level 6
1	2	3	4	5	6	7	8	9	10	11	12
OECD average[2]	**496** (0.5)	**18.0** (0.18)	**1.3** (0.05)	**4.4** (0.08)	**12.3** (0.13)	**23.5** (0.16)	**29.1** (0.17)	**21.0** (0.16)	**8.4** (0.12)	**7.3** (0.10)	**1.1** (0.04)
Australia	512 (1.6)	14.2 (0.46)	0.9 (0.11)	3.1 (0.21)	10.2 (0.42)	21.6 (0.47)	29.1 (0.53)	23.3 (0.51)	11.7 (0.54)	9.8 (0.46)	1.9 (0.19)
Austria	490 (2.8)	19.5 (1.07)	0.8 (0.24)	4.8 (0.64)	13.8 (0.84)	24.2 (0.89)	29.6 (0.92)	21.2 (0.94)	5.5 (0.61)	5.2 (0.59)	0.3 (0.10)
Belgium	509 (2.3)	16.2 (0.77)	1.6 (0.31)	4.1 (0.40)	10.4 (0.55)	20.4 (0.62)	27.3 (0.70)	24.4 (0.71)	12.3 (0.55)	10.4 (0.54)	1.4 (0.17)
Canada	523 (1.9)	10.9 (0.45)	0.5 (0.09)	2.4 (0.19)	8.0 (0.36)	19.4 (0.55)	31.0 (0.72)	25.8 (0.59)	12.9 (0.62)	10.8 (0.53)	2.1 (0.22)
Chile	441 (2.9)	33.0 (1.67)	1.0 (0.19)	8.1 (0.79)	23.9 (1.08)	35.1 (1.08)	24.3 (1.06)	6.9 (0.62)	0.6 (0.10)	0.6 (0.11)	‡ (†)
Czech Republic	493 (2.9)	16.9 (1.21)	0.6 ! (0.27)	3.5 (0.56)	12.7 (0.94)	26.4 (1.30)	31.3 (1.23)	19.4 (1.13)	6.1 (0.55)	5.3 (0.49)	0.8 (0.16)
Denmark	496 (2.6)	14.6 (1.07)	0.8 ! (0.30)	3.1 (0.39)	10.7 (0.77)	25.8 (0.92)	33.6 (0.85)	20.5 (0.86)	5.4 (0.62)	5.1 (0.58)	0.4 ! (0.12)
Estonia	516 (2.0)	9.1 (0.65)	‡ (†)	1.3 (0.28)	7.7 (0.61)	22.7 (0.94)	35.0 (1.06)	24.9 (1.08)	8.3 (0.72)	7.5 (0.71)	0.9 (0.18)
Finland	524 (2.4)	11.3 (0.71)	0.7 (0.16)	2.4 (0.38)	8.2 (0.57)	19.1 (0.81)	29.3 (0.70)	26.8 (0.84)	13.5 (0.64)	11.3 (0.60)	2.2 (0.26)
France	505 (2.8)	18.9 (0.98)	2.1 (0.40)	4.9 (0.43)	11.9 (0.70)	18.9 (0.85)	26.3 (0.84)	23.0 (0.67)	12.9 (0.85)	10.6 (0.62)	2.3 (0.41)
Germany	508 (2.8)	14.5 (0.91)	0.5 ! (0.18)	3.3 (0.40)	10.7 (0.67)	22.1 (0.93)	29.9 (0.86)	24.6 (0.88)	8.9 (0.70)	8.3 (0.64)	0.7 ! (0.23)
Greece	477 (3.3)	22.6 (1.24)	2.6 (0.40)	5.9 (0.60)	14.2 (0.83)	25.1 (1.06)	30.0 (1.02)	17.2 (1.19)	5.1 (0.61)	4.6 (0.59)	0.5 (0.13)
Hungary	488 (3.2)	19.7 (1.22)	0.7 ! (0.24)	5.2 (0.64)	13.8 (0.88)	24.3 (1.17)	29.9 (1.00)	20.4 (1.05)	5.6 (0.75)	5.3 (0.68)	0.4 ! (0.13)
Iceland	483 (1.8)	21.0 (0.72)	2.3 (0.33)	5.4 (0.47)	13.3 (0.63)	24.7 (0.92)	29.9 (1.09)	18.6 (1.12)	5.8 (0.51)	5.2 (0.41)	0.6 ! (0.21)
Ireland	523 (2.6)	9.6 (0.88)	0.3 ! (0.13)	1.9 (0.35)	7.5 (0.69)	19.6 (1.19)	33.4 (1.17)	26.0 (0.90)	11.4 (0.65)	10.1 (0.67)	1.3 (0.35)
Israel	486 (5.0)	23.6 (1.64)	3.8 (0.59)	6.9 (0.74)	12.9 (0.96)	20.8 (0.87)	25.3 (0.81)	20.6 (1.03)	9.6 (0.84)	8.1 (0.77)	1.5 (0.30)
Italy	490 (2.0)	19.5 (0.67)	1.6 (0.15)	5.2 (0.29)	12.7 (0.48)	23.7 (0.57)	29.7 (0.53)	20.5 (0.62)	6.7 (0.35)	6.1 (0.33)	0.6 (0.07)
Japan	538 (3.7)	9.8 (0.92)	0.6 (0.16)	2.4 (0.37)	6.7 (0.67)	16.6 (0.89)	26.7 (0.98)	28.4 (1.08)	18.5 (1.27)	14.6 (0.99)	3.9 (0.59)
Korea, Republic of	536 (3.9)	7.6 (0.89)	0.4 (0.13)	1.7 (0.39)	5.5 (0.60)	16.4 (0.94)	30.8 (1.00)	31.0 (1.06)	14.1 (1.24)	12.6 (1.05)	1.6 (0.32)
Luxembourg	488 (1.5)	22.2 (0.74)	2.0 (0.21)	6.3 (0.33)	13.8 (0.81)	23.4 (0.71)	25.8 (0.64)	19.7 (0.64)	8.9 (0.39)	7.5 (0.35)	1.4 (0.20)
Mexico	424 (1.5)	41.1 (0.90)	2.6 (0.22)	11.0 (0.53)	27.5 (0.70)	34.5 (0.62)	19.6 (0.54)	4.5 (0.25)	0.4 (0.09)	0.4 (0.08)	‡ (†)
Netherlands	511 (3.5)	14.0 (1.23)	‡ (†)	2.8 (0.49)	10.3 (0.93)	21.0 (1.27)	29.2 (1.32)	26.1 (1.36)	9.8 (0.82)	9.0 (0.72)	0.8 (0.19)
New Zealand	512 (2.4)	16.3 (0.83)	1.3 (0.28)	4.0 (0.46)	11.0 (0.67)	20.8 (0.76)	26.3 (1.06)	22.7 (1.06)	14.0 (0.77)	10.9 (0.62)	3.0 (0.37)
Norway	504 (3.2)	16.2 (1.03)	1.7 (0.31)	3.7 (0.36)	10.8 (0.69)	21.9 (1.03)	29.4 (1.35)	22.3 (1.21)	10.2 (0.74)	8.5 (0.61)	1.7 (0.31)
Poland	518 (3.1)	10.6 (0.80)	0.3 ! (0.11)	2.1 (0.35)	8.1 (0.74)	21.4 (0.90)	32.0 (0.89)	26.0 (0.96)	10.0 (0.93)	8.6 (0.76)	1.4 (0.37)
Portugal	488 (3.8)	18.8 (1.42)	1.3 (0.30)	5.1 (0.53)	12.3 (0.98)	25.5 (1.16)	30.2 (1.46)	19.7 (1.07)	5.8 (0.61)	5.3 (0.57)	0.5 ! (0.15)
Slovak Republic	463 (4.2)	28.2 (1.78)	4.1 (0.77)	7.9 (0.80)	16.2 (1.06)	25.0 (1.08)	26.8 (1.38)	15.7 (0.96)	4.4 (0.68)	4.1 (0.60)	‡ (†)
Slovenia	481 (1.2)	21.1 (0.68)	1.2 (0.14)	4.9 (0.37)	15.0 (0.71)	27.2 (0.77)	28.4 (0.94)	18.2 (0.63)	5.0 (0.43)	4.7 (0.45)	0.3 ! (0.12)
Spain	488 (1.9)	18.3 (0.76)	1.3 (0.17)	4.4 (0.38)	12.6 (0.47)	25.8 (0.81)	31.2 (0.68)	19.2 (0.62)	5.5 (0.30)	5.0 (0.30)	0.5 (0.10)
Sweden	483 (3.0)	22.7 (1.15)	2.9 (0.39)	6.0 (0.64)	13.9 (0.72)	23.5 (0.88)	27.3 (0.73)	18.6 (0.93)	7.9 (0.64)	6.7 (0.53)	1.2 (0.20)
Switzerland	509 (2.6)	13.7 (0.76)	0.5 (0.14)	2.9 (0.34)	10.3 (0.59)	21.9 (0.86)	31.5 (0.71)	23.8 (0.84)	9.1 (0.68)	8.2 (0.60)	1.0 (0.25)
Turkey	475 (4.2)	21.6 (1.43)	0.6 (0.15)	4.5 (0.57)	16.6 (1.07)	30.8 (1.39)	28.7 (1.34)	14.5 (1.39)	4.3 (0.85)	4.1 (0.79)	0.3 ! (0.13)
United Kingdom	499 (3.5)	16.6 (1.30)	1.5 (0.27)	4.0 (0.54)	11.2 (0.79)	23.5 (1.01)	29.9 (1.08)	21.3 (1.14)	8.8 (0.74)	7.5 (0.59)	1.3 (0.24)
United States	498 (3.7)	16.6 (1.26)	0.8 ! (0.49)	3.6 (0.49)	12.3 (0.89)	24.9 (0.99)	30.5 (0.88)	20.1 (1.08)	7.9 (0.67)	6.9 (0.59)	1.0 (0.22)

Percentage attaining reading literacy proficiency levels[1]

See notes at end of table.

International Comparisons of Education

Average reading literacy scores of 15-year-old students and percentage attaining reading literacy proficiency levels, by country or other education system: 2012—Continued

[Standard errors appear in parentheses]

Country or other education system	Average reading literacy score	Percentage attaining reading literacy proficiency levels[1]									
		Below level 2				At level 2	At level 3	At level 4	At or above level 5		
		Total below level 2	Below level 1b	At level 1b	At level 1a				Total at or above level 5	At level 5	At level 6
1	2	3	4	5	6	7	8	9	10	11	12
Non-OECD education systems											
Albania	394 (3.2)	52.3 (1.28)	12.0 (0.84)	15.9 (1.00)	24.4 (1.23)	24.7 (1.01)	15.9 (0.73)	5.9 (0.61)	1.2 (0.25)	1.1 (0.24)	‡ (†)
Argentina	396 (3.7)	53.6 (1.73)	8.1 (0.80)	17.7 (1.20)	27.7 (1.34)	27.3 (1.12)	14.6 (0.91)	4.0 (0.57)	0.5 (0.14)	0.5 (0.15)	‡ (†)
Brazil	410 (2.1)	49.2 (1.13)	4.0 (0.36)	14.8 (0.64)	30.4 (0.79)	30.1 (0.77)	15.8 (0.63)	4.4 (0.37)	0.5 (0.12)	0.5 (0.12)	‡ (†)
Bulgaria	436 (6.0)	39.4 (2.21)	8.0 (1.07)	12.8 (1.15)	18.6 (1.10)	22.2 (1.16)	21.4 (1.10)	12.7 (1.03)	4.3 (0.64)	3.8 (0.56)	0.5 ! (0.18)
Chinese Taipei	523 (3.0)	11.5 (0.87)	0.6 (0.15)	2.5 (0.32)	8.4 (0.65)	18.1 (0.83)	29.9 (0.92)	28.7 (1.01)	11.8 (0.84)	10.4 (0.73)	1.4 (0.32)
Colombia	403 (3.4)	51.4 (1.78)	5.0 (0.76)	15.4 (0.98)	31.0 (1.29)	30.5 (1.22)	14.5 (0.91)	3.2 (0.50)	0.3 ! (0.13)	0.3 ! (0.12)	‡ (†)
Connecticut-USA[3]	521 (6.5)	13.2 (1.76)	‡ (†)	3.2 (0.87)	9.7 (1.26)	19.6 (1.49)	28.2 (1.32)	24.4 (1.83)	14.5 (1.68)	11.7 (1.38)	2.9 (0.54)
Costa Rica	441 (3.5)	32.4 (1.81)	0.8 ! (0.24)	7.3 (1.02)	24.3 (1.25)	38.1 (1.40)	22.9 (1.42)	6.0 (0.78)	0.6 ! (0.19)	0.6 ! (0.19)	0.2 ! (0.11)
Croatia	485 (3.3)	18.7 (1.29)	0.7 ! (0.25)	4.0 (0.59)	13.9 (0.97)	27.8 (1.07)	31.2 (1.24)	17.8 (1.09)	4.4 (0.69)	4.2 (0.66)	0.2 ! (0.11)
Cyprus	449 (1.2)	32.8 (0.67)	6.1 (0.32)	9.7 (0.44)	17.0 (0.61)	25.1 (0.78)	24.9 (0.75)	13.2 (0.64)	4.0 (0.32)	3.5 (0.34)	0.5 (0.12)
Florida-USA[3]	492 (6.1)	17.5 (2.00)	0.7 ! (0.31)	3.6 (0.75)	13.2 (1.46)	25.8 (1.56)	30.9 (1.50)	20.4 (2.06)	5.5 (1.02)	4.9 (1.00)	‡ (†)
Hong Kong-China	545 (2.8)	6.8 (0.72)	0.2 ! (0.09)	1.3 (0.24)	5.3 (0.61)	14.3 (0.79)	29.2 (1.21)	32.9 (1.39)	16.8 (1.16)	14.9 (1.00)	1.9 (0.39)
Indonesia	396 (4.2)	55.2 (2.18)	4.1 (0.81)	16.3 (1.28)	34.8 (1.56)	31.6 (1.54)	11.5 (1.28)	1.5 ! (0.53)	‡ (†)	‡ (†)	‡ (†)
Jordan	399 (3.6)	50.7 (1.57)	7.5 (0.84)	14.9 (0.79)	28.3 (1.01)	30.8 (1.14)	15.5 (0.83)	2.9 (0.63)	‡ (†)	‡ (†)	‡ (†)
Kazakhstan	393 (2.7)	57.1 (1.56)	4.2 (0.47)	17.3 (1.24)	35.6 (1.15)	31.3 (1.12)	10.4 (0.87)	1.2 (0.24)	‡ (†)	‡ (†)	‡ (†)
Latvia	489 (2.4)	17.0 (1.14)	0.7 ! (0.24)	3.7 (0.54)	12.6 (0.96)	26.7 (1.31)	33.1 (1.05)	19.1 (0.88)	4.2 (0.55)	3.9 (0.56)	0.3 ! (0.11)
Liechtenstein	516 (4.1)	12.4 (1.88)	# (†)	‡ (†)	10.5 (1.85)	22.4 (3.44)	28.6 (4.53)	25.7 (2.44)	10.9 (2.89)	10.4 (2.44)	‡ (†)
Lithuania	477 (2.5)	21.2 (1.18)	1.0 (0.19)	4.6 (0.49)	15.6 (1.06)	28.1 (1.13)	31.1 (0.94)	16.3 (0.78)	3.3 (0.37)	3.1 (0.35)	0.2 ! (0.07)
Macao-China	509 (0.9)	11.5 (0.42)	0.3 ! (0.11)	2.1 (0.22)	9.0 (0.42)	23.3 (0.58)	34.3 (0.67)	24.0 (0.60)	7.0 (0.41)	6.4 (0.48)	0.6 ! (0.21)
Malaysia	398 (3.3)	52.7 (1.71)	5.8 (0.59)	16.4 (1.03)	30.5 (0.99)	31.0 (1.09)	13.6 (1.11)	2.5 (0.45)	‡ (†)	‡ (†)	‡ (†)
Massachusetts-USA[3]	527 (6.1)	11.5 (1.37)	‡ (†)	2.3 (0.55)	8.6 (1.19)	18.5 (1.76)	29.8 (1.52)	24.2 (1.82)	16.1 (1.98)	12.9 (1.59)	3.2 (0.86)
Montenegro, Republic of	422 (1.2)	43.3 (1.66)	4.4 (0.53)	13.2 (0.62)	25.7 (0.94)	29.2 (0.77)	19.9 (0.76)	6.6 (0.53)	1.0 (0.19)	0.9 (0.19)	‡ (†)
Peru	384 (4.3)	59.9 (1.95)	9.8 (0.87)	20.6 (1.11)	29.5 (0.98)	24.9 (1.02)	11.4 (0.96)	3.3 (0.61)	0.5 ! (0.21)	0.5 ! (0.21)	‡ (†)
Qatar	388 (0.8)	57.1 (0.42)	13.6 (0.32)	18.9 (0.48)	24.6 (0.44)	21.9 (0.50)	13.5 (0.43)	5.8 (0.21)	1.6 (0.14)	1.4 (0.13)	0.2 (0.05)
Romania	438 (4.0)	37.3 (1.87)	2.5 (0.38)	10.3 (0.82)	24.4 (1.28)	30.6 (1.12)	21.8 (1.17)	8.7 (0.88)	1.6 (0.38)	1.5 (0.35)	‡ (†)
Russian Federation	475 (3.0)	22.3 (1.29)	1.1 (0.18)	5.2 (0.49)	16.0 (1.03)	29.5 (1.08)	28.3 (1.05)	15.3 (0.93)	4.6 (0.58)	4.2 (0.51)	0.5 (0.12)
Serbia, Republic of	446 (3.4)	33.1 (1.66)	2.6 (0.40)	9.3 (0.73)	21.3 (1.09)	30.8 (1.20)	23.3 (1.15)	10.5 (0.81)	2.2 (0.41)	2.0 (0.39)	0.2 ! (0.08)
Shanghai-China	570 (2.9)	2.9 (0.39)	‡ (†)	0.3 ! (0.11)	2.5 (0.34)	11.0 (0.85)	25.3 (0.85)	35.7 (1.07)	25.1 (1.19)	21.3 (0.98)	3.8 (0.65)
Singapore	542 (1.4)	9.9 (0.42)	0.5 (0.12)	1.9 (0.27)	7.5 (0.41)	16.7 (0.66)	25.4 (0.79)	26.8 (0.79)	21.2 (0.60)	16.2 (0.73)	5.0 (0.43)
Thailand	441 (3.1)	33.0 (1.40)	1.2 (0.29)	7.7 (0.77)	24.1 (0.98)	36.0 (1.12)	23.5 (1.13)	6.7 (0.79)	0.8 (0.22)	0.8 (0.21)	‡ (†)
Tunisia	404 (4.5)	49.3 (2.24)	6.2 (0.91)	15.5 (1.20)	27.6 (1.31)	31.4 (1.43)	15.6 (1.15)	3.5 (0.69)	‡ (†)	‡ (†)	‡ (†)
United Arab Emirates	442 (2.5)	35.5 (1.08)	3.3 (0.34)	10.4 (0.65)	21.8 (0.72)	28.6 (0.72)	24.0 (0.77)	9.7 (0.58)	2.2 (0.29)	2.1 (0.28)	0.2 ! (0.06)
Uruguay	411 (3.2)	47.0 (1.42)	6.4 (0.70)	14.7 (0.84)	25.9 (0.88)	28.9 (1.00)	17.4 (0.71)	5.7 (0.62)	0.9 (0.27)	0.9 (0.26)	‡ (†)
Vietnam	508 (4.4)	9.4 (1.43)	‡ (†)	1.5 ! (0.48)	7.8 (1.10)	23.7 (1.40)	39.0 (1.47)	23.4 (1.47)	4.5 (0.81)	4.2 (0.71)	0.4 ! (0.16)

†Not applicable.
#Rounds to zero.
!Interpret data with caution. The coefficient of variation (CV) for this estimate is between 30 and 50 percent.
‡Reporting standards not met. Either there are too few cases for a reliable estimate or the coefficient of variation (CV) is 50 percent or greater.

[1]To reach a particular proficiency level, a student must correctly answer a majority of items at that level. Students were classified into reading literacy levels according to their scores. Exact cut scores are as follows: below level 1b (a score less than or equal to 262.04); level 1b (a score greater than 262.04 and less than or equal to 334.75); level 1a (a score greater than 334.75 and less than or equal to 407.47); level 2 (a score greater than 407.47 and less than or equal to 480.18); level 3 (a score greater than 480.18 and less than or equal to 552.89); level 4 (a score greater than 552.89 and less than or equal to 625.61); level 5 (a score greater than 625.61 and less than or equal to 698.32); and level 6 (a score greater than 698.32).

[2]Refers to the mean of the data values for all Organization for Economic Cooperation and Development (OECD) countries, to which each country contributes equally, regardless of the absolute size of the student population of each country.

[3]Results are for public school students only.

NOTE: Program for International Student Assessment (PISA) scores are reported on a scale from 0 to 1,000. Detail may not sum to totals because of rounding.

SOURCE: Organization for Economic Cooperation and Development (OECD), Program for International Student Assessment (PISA), 2012. (This table was prepared November 2013.)

Average mathematics literacy scores of 15-year-old students and percentage attaining mathematics literacy proficiency levels, by country or other education system: 2012

[Standard errors appear in parentheses]

Country or other education system	Average mathematics literacy score	Below level 2 — Total below level 2	Below level 2 — Below level 1	At level 1	At level 2	At level 3	At level 4	At or above level 5 — Total at or above level 5	At or above level 5 — At level 5	At or above level 5 — At level 6
1	2	3	4	5	6	7	8	9	10	11
OECD average[2]	494 (0.5)	23.0 (0.17)	8.0 (0.12)	15.0 (0.13)	22.5 (0.15)	23.7 (0.15)	18.1 (0.14)	12.7 (0.14)	9.3 (0.11)	3.3 (0.08)
Australia	504 (1.6)	19.7 (0.60)	6.1 (0.35)	13.5 (0.57)	21.9 (0.76)	24.6 (0.65)	19.0 (0.50)	14.8 (0.64)	10.5 (0.43)	4.3 (0.36)
Austria	506 (2.7)	18.7 (0.96)	5.7 (0.59)	13.0 (0.74)	21.9 (0.87)	24.2 (0.84)	21.0 (0.90)	14.3 (0.95)	11.0 (0.75)	3.3 (0.41)
Belgium	515 (2.1)	19.0 (0.82)	7.0 (0.58)	12.0 (0.52)	18.4 (0.58)	22.4 (0.70)	20.6 (0.63)	19.5 (0.76)	13.4 (0.73)	6.1 (0.43)
Canada	518 (1.8)	13.8 (0.55)	3.6 (0.29)	10.2 (0.45)	21.0 (0.64)	26.4 (0.63)	22.4 (0.49)	16.4 (0.64)	12.1 (0.47)	4.3 (0.29)
Chile	423 (3.1)	51.5 (1.67)	22.0 (1.35)	29.5 (1.01)	25.3 (1.00)	15.4 (0.78)	6.2 (0.60)	1.6 (0.22)	1.5 (0.21)	0.1 ! (0.04)
Czech Republic	499 (2.9)	21.0 (1.20)	6.8 (0.76)	14.2 (0.97)	21.7 (0.83)	24.8 (1.07)	19.7 (0.90)	12.9 (0.82)	9.6 (0.66)	3.2 (0.31)
Denmark	500 (2.3)	16.8 (0.98)	4.4 (0.49)	12.5 (0.70)	24.4 (0.97)	29.0 (1.03)	19.8 (0.69)	10.0 (0.66)	8.3 (0.57)	1.7 (0.32)
Estonia	521 (2.0)	10.5 (0.63)	2.0 (0.26)	8.6 (0.57)	22.0 (0.84)	29.4 (0.79)	23.4 (0.91)	14.6 (0.76)	11.0 (0.67)	3.6 (0.37)
Finland	519 (1.9)	12.3 (0.67)	3.3 (0.39)	8.9 (0.49)	20.5 (0.66)	28.8 (0.78)	23.2 (0.78)	15.3 (0.74)	11.7 (0.60)	3.5 (0.30)
France	495 (2.5)	22.4 (0.87)	8.7 (0.72)	13.6 (0.76)	22.1 (0.95)	23.8 (0.82)	18.9 (0.79)	12.9 (0.77)	9.8 (0.55)	3.1 (0.40)
Germany	514 (2.9)	17.7 (1.03)	5.5 (0.65)	12.2 (0.81)	19.4 (0.81)	23.7 (0.79)	21.7 (0.73)	17.5 (0.94)	12.8 (0.71)	4.7 (0.49)
Greece	453 (2.5)	35.7 (1.34)	14.5 (0.92)	21.2 (0.85)	27.2 (1.02)	22.1 (0.86)	11.2 (0.79)	3.9 (0.43)	3.3 (0.43)	0.6 (0.15)
Hungary	477 (3.2)	28.1 (1.31)	9.9 (0.77)	18.2 (1.04)	25.3 (1.21)	23.0 (1.02)	14.4 (0.86)	9.3 (1.12)	7.1 (0.73)	2.1 (0.51)
Iceland	493 (1.7)	21.5 (0.74)	7.5 (0.54)	14.0 (0.83)	23.6 (0.89)	25.7 (0.95)	18.1 (0.79)	11.2 (0.69)	8.9 (0.61)	2.3 (0.35)
Ireland	501 (2.2)	16.9 (0.99)	4.8 (0.55)	12.1 (0.70)	23.9 (0.72)	28.2 (0.87)	20.3 (0.76)	10.7 (0.54)	8.5 (0.51)	2.2 (0.23)
Israel	466 (4.7)	33.5 (1.68)	15.9 (1.23)	17.6 (0.93)	21.6 (0.93)	21.0 (0.87)	14.6 (0.88)	9.4 (0.99)	7.2 (0.74)	2.2 (0.39)
Italy	485 (2.0)	24.7 (0.76)	8.5 (0.39)	16.1 (0.51)	24.1 (0.55)	24.6 (0.62)	16.7 (0.48)	9.9 (0.57)	7.8 (0.44)	2.2 (0.25)
Japan	536 (3.6)	11.1 (0.98)	3.2 (0.49)	7.9 (0.69)	16.9 (0.85)	24.7 (1.00)	23.7 (0.89)	23.7 (1.46)	16.0 (0.89)	7.6 (0.84)
Korea, Republic of	554 (4.6)	9.1 (0.95)	2.7 (0.46)	6.4 (0.62)	14.7 (0.85)	21.4 (0.99)	23.9 (1.23)	30.9 (1.83)	18.8 (0.92)	12.1 (1.26)
Luxembourg	490 (1.1)	24.3 (0.54)	8.8 (0.54)	15.5 (0.54)	22.3 (0.72)	23.6 (0.72)	18.5 (0.58)	11.2 (0.42)	8.6 (0.38)	2.6 (0.25)
Mexico	413 (1.4)	54.7 (0.82)	22.8 (0.68)	31.9 (0.58)	27.8 (0.53)	13.1 (0.41)	3.7 (0.23)	0.6 (0.08)	0.6 (0.07)	‡ (†)
Netherlands	523 (3.5)	14.8 (1.28)	3.8 (0.57)	11.0 (0.93)	17.9 (1.08)	24.2 (1.19)	23.8 (1.11)	19.3 (1.21)	14.9 (0.99)	4.4 (0.56)
New Zealand	500 (2.2)	22.6 (0.80)	7.5 (0.58)	15.1 (0.66)	21.6 (0.83)	22.7 (0.76)	18.1 (0.84)	15.0 (0.88)	10.5 (0.75)	4.5 (0.40)
Norway	489 (2.7)	22.3 (1.06)	7.2 (0.78)	15.1 (0.88)	24.3 (0.84)	25.7 (1.01)	18.3 (0.96)	9.4 (0.67)	7.3 (0.56)	2.1 (0.30)
Poland	518 (3.6)	14.4 (0.89)	3.3 (0.38)	11.1 (0.77)	22.1 (0.93)	25.5 (0.94)	21.3 (1.12)	16.7 (1.33)	11.7 (0.78)	5.0 (0.80)
Portugal	487 (3.8)	24.9 (1.52)	8.9 (0.79)	16.0 (0.98)	22.8 (0.88)	24.0 (0.84)	17.7 (0.88)	10.6 (0.79)	8.5 (0.73)	2.1 (0.33)
Slovak Republic	482 (3.4)	27.5 (1.28)	11.1 (1.03)	16.4 (0.94)	23.1 (1.10)	22.1 (1.09)	16.4 (1.08)	11.0 (0.94)	7.8 (0.64)	3.1 (0.55)
Slovenia	501 (1.2)	20.1 (0.65)	5.1 (0.48)	15.0 (0.69)	23.6 (0.95)	23.9 (0.96)	18.7 (0.80)	13.7 (0.55)	10.3 (0.64)	3.4 (0.43)
Spain	484 (1.9)	23.6 (0.85)	7.8 (0.50)	15.8 (0.57)	24.9 (0.65)	26.0 (0.59)	17.6 (0.56)	8.0 (0.43)	6.7 (0.42)	1.3 (0.15)
Sweden	478 (2.3)	27.1 (1.12)	9.5 (0.68)	17.5 (0.76)	24.7 (0.92)	23.9 (0.78)	16.3 (0.69)	8.0 (0.52)	6.5 (0.49)	1.6 (0.25)
Switzerland	531 (3.0)	12.4 (0.70)	3.6 (0.35)	8.9 (0.59)	17.8 (1.06)	24.5 (1.02)	23.9 (0.80)	21.4 (1.19)	14.6 (0.78)	6.8 (0.69)
Turkey	448 (4.8)	42.0 (1.93)	15.5 (1.08)	26.5 (1.28)	25.5 (1.16)	16.5 (1.05)	10.1 (1.09)	5.9 (1.13)	4.7 (0.81)	1.2 ! (0.46)
United Kingdom	494 (3.3)	21.8 (1.30)	7.8 (0.77)	14.0 (0.76)	23.2 (0.81)	24.8 (0.85)	18.4 (0.78)	11.8 (0.81)	9.0 (0.63)	2.9 (0.42)
United States	481 (3.6)	25.8 (1.39)	8.0 (0.73)	17.9 (0.98)	26.3 (0.84)	23.3 (0.93)	15.8 (0.91)	8.8 (0.78)	6.6 (0.61)	2.2 (0.34)

See notes at end of table.

Average mathematics literacy scores of 15-year-old students and percentage attaining mathematics literacy proficiency levels, by country or other education system: 2012—Continued

[Standard errors appear in parentheses]

Country or other education system	Average mathematics literacy score	Below level 2 — Total below level 2	Below level 2 — Below level 1	Below level 2 — At level 1	At level 2	At level 3	At level 4	At or above level 5 — Total at or above level 5	At or above level 5 — At level 5	At level 6
1	2	3	4	5	6	7	8	9	10	11
Non-OECD education systems										
Albania	394 (2.0)	60.7 (0.95)	32.5 (1.03)	28.1 (0.97)	22.9 (0.91)	12.0 (0.92)	3.6 (0.35)	0.8 ! (0.19)	0.8 ! (0.20)	‡ (†)
Argentina	388 (3.5)	66.5 (2.03)	34.9 (1.95)	31.6 (1.22)	22.2 (1.36)	9.2 (0.88)	1.8 (0.35)	0.3 ! (0.10)	0.3 ! (0.10)	‡ (†)
Brazil	391 (2.1)	67.1 (1.03)	35.2 (0.93)	31.9 (0.70)	20.4 (0.67)	8.9 (0.47)	2.9 (0.35)	0.8 (0.20)	0.7 (0.19)	‡ (†)
Bulgaria	439 (4.0)	43.8 (1.78)	20.0 (1.45)	23.8 (0.95)	24.4 (1.12)	17.9 (0.91)	9.9 (0.83)	4.1 (0.62)	3.4 (0.50)	0.7 (0.19)
Chinese Taipei	560 (3.3)	12.8 (0.84)	4.5 (0.53)	8.3 (0.61)	13.1 (0.61)	17.1 (0.65)	19.7 (0.75)	37.2 (1.24)	19.2 (0.89)	18.0 (1.00)
Colombia	376 (2.9)	73.8 (1.43)	41.6 (1.71)	32.2 (1.05)	17.8 (0.90)	6.4 (0.61)	1.6 (0.28)	0.3 ! (0.11)	0.3 ! (0.10)	‡ (†)
Connecticut-USA[3]	506 (6.2)	20.6 (2.14)	6.8 (1.18)	13.8 (1.33)	20.0 (1.28)	24.3 (1.36)	18.6 (1.79)	16.4 (1.91)	11.5 (1.46)	4.9 (0.83)
Costa Rica	407 (3.0)	59.9 (1.87)	23.6 (1.68)	36.2 (1.22)	26.8 (1.29)	10.1 (0.99)	2.6 (0.46)	0.6 ! (0.19)	0.5 ! (0.16)	‡ (†)
Croatia	471 (3.5)	29.9 (1.36)	9.5 (0.74)	20.4 (1.02)	26.7 (0.95)	22.9 (1.12)	13.5 (0.80)	7.0 (1.15)	5.4 (0.76)	1.6 ! (0.51)
Cyprus	440 (1.1)	42.0 (0.63)	19.0 (0.58)	23.0 (0.65)	25.5 (0.62)	19.2 (0.58)	9.6 (0.44)	3.7 (0.27)	3.1 (0.25)	0.6 ! (0.20)
Florida-USA[3]	467 (5.8)	30.4 (2.65)	9.7 (1.44)	20.6 (1.87)	27.9 (1.42)	23.0 (1.64)	13.0 (1.34)	5.8 (1.18)	4.9 (1.04)	0.9 ! (0.39)
Hong Kong-China	561 (3.2)	8.5 (0.79)	2.6 (0.36)	5.9 (0.61)	12.0 (0.77)	19.7 (0.97)	26.1 (1.09)	33.7 (1.35)	21.4 (0.96)	12.3 (0.95)
Indonesia	375 (4.0)	75.7 (2.05)	42.3 (2.14)	33.4 (1.59)	16.8 (1.12)	5.7 (0.90)	1.5 ! (0.54)	‡ (†)	‡ (†)	‡ (†)
Jordan	386 (3.1)	68.6 (1.50)	36.5 (1.59)	32.1 (0.95)	21.0 (1.04)	8.1 (0.63)	1.8 (0.33)	‡ (†)	‡ (†)	‡ (†)
Kazakhstan	432 (3.0)	45.2 (1.70)	14.5 (0.90)	30.7 (1.40)	31.5 (0.95)	16.9 (1.11)	5.4 (0.79)	0.9 ! (0.29)	0.9 ! (0.27)	‡ (†)
Latvia	491 (2.8)	19.9 (1.13)	4.8 (0.53)	15.1 (0.96)	26.6 (1.29)	27.8 (0.92)	17.6 (0.90)	8.0 (0.78)	6.5 (0.65)	1.5 (0.28)
Liechtenstein	535 (4.0)	14.1 (2.02)	3.5 ! (1.31)	10.6 (1.81)	15.2 (2.52)	22.7 (2.81)	23.2 (3.01)	24.8 (2.55)	17.4 (3.17)	7.4 (1.86)
Lithuania	479 (2.6)	26.0 (1.18)	8.7 (0.68)	17.3 (0.89)	25.9 (0.80)	24.6 (1.01)	15.4 (0.70)	8.1 (0.60)	6.6 (0.49)	1.4 (0.24)
Macao-China	538 (1.0)	10.8 (0.49)	3.2 (0.29)	7.6 (0.53)	16.4 (0.71)	24.0 (0.69)	24.4 (0.87)	24.3 (0.56)	16.8 (0.63)	7.6 (0.35)
Malaysia	421 (3.2)	51.8 (1.68)	23.0 (1.19)	28.8 (1.12)	26.0 (0.95)	14.9 (0.93)	6.0 (0.69)	1.3 (0.30)	1.2 (0.28)	0.1 ! (0.05)
Massachusetts-USA[3]	514 (6.2)	17.8 (1.46)	5.3 (0.83)	12.5 (1.17)	20.4 (1.61)	24.3 (1.49)	18.9 (1.18)	18.5 (2.47)	12.7 (1.61)	5.8 (1.11)
Montenegro, Republic of	410 (1.1)	56.6 (1.02)	27.5 (0.64)	29.1 (1.14)	24.2 (1.06)	13.1 (0.73)	4.9 (0.48)	1.0 (0.20)	0.9 (0.20)	‡ (†)
Peru	368 (3.7)	74.6 (1.75)	47.0 (1.79)	27.6 (0.88)	16.1 (1.00)	6.7 (0.68)	2.1 (0.38)	0.6 ! (0.21)	0.5 ! (0.20)	‡ (†)
Qatar	376 (0.8)	69.6 (0.46)	47.0 (0.42)	22.6 (0.53)	15.2 (0.39)	8.8 (0.34)	4.5 (0.28)	2.0 (0.21)	1.7 (0.20)	0.3 (0.07)
Romania	445 (3.8)	40.8 (1.93)	14.0 (1.15)	26.8 (1.23)	28.3 (1.09)	19.2 (1.07)	8.4 (0.81)	3.2 (0.61)	2.6 (0.45)	0.6 ! (0.27)
Russian Federation	482 (3.0)	24.0 (1.13)	7.5 (0.70)	16.5 (0.80)	26.6 (0.99)	26.0 (0.97)	15.7 (0.78)	7.8 (0.85)	6.3 (0.64)	1.5 (0.31)
Serbia, Republic of	449 (3.4)	38.9 (1.54)	15.5 (1.16)	23.4 (0.93)	26.5 (1.12)	19.5 (1.03)	10.5 (0.69)	4.6 (0.71)	3.5 (0.52)	1.1 (0.31)
Shanghai-China	613 (3.3)	3.8 (0.55)	0.8 (0.21)	2.9 (0.46)	7.5 (0.64)	13.1 (0.77)	20.2 (0.83)	55.4 (1.37)	24.6 (1.04)	30.8 (1.24)
Singapore	573 (1.3)	8.3 (0.48)	2.2 (0.23)	6.1 (0.40)	12.2 (0.68)	17.5 (0.66)	22.0 (0.62)	40.0 (0.71)	21.0 (0.58)	19.0 (0.51)
Thailand	427 (3.4)	49.7 (1.74)	19.1 (1.07)	30.6 (1.20)	27.3 (1.00)	14.5 (1.15)	5.8 (0.74)	2.6 (0.51)	2.0 (0.38)	0.5 ! (0.19)
Tunisia	388 (3.9)	67.7 (1.83)	36.5 (1.88)	31.3 (1.09)	21.1 (1.17)	8.0 (0.79)	2.3 (0.68)	0.8 ! (0.37)	0.7 ! (0.32)	‡ (†)
United Arab Emirates	434 (2.4)	46.3 (1.22)	20.5 (0.92)	25.8 (0.81)	24.9 (0.69)	16.9 (0.64)	8.5 (0.54)	3.5 (0.29)	2.9 (0.25)	0.5 (0.11)
Uruguay	409 (2.8)	55.8 (1.31)	29.2 (1.20)	26.5 (0.76)	23.0 (0.93)	14.4 (0.87)	5.4 (0.60)	1.4 (0.32)	1.3 (0.28)	‡ (†)
Vietnam	511 (4.8)	14.2 (1.75)	3.6 (0.80)	10.6 (1.26)	22.8 (1.28)	28.4 (1.52)	21.3 (1.22)	13.3 (1.47)	9.8 (0.99)	3.5 (0.75)

†Not applicable.
#Rounds to zero.
!Interpret data with caution. The coefficient of variation (CV) for this estimate is between 30 and 50 percent.
‡Reporting standards not met. Either there are too few cases for a reliable estimate or the coefficient of variation (CV) is 50 percent or greater.
[1]To reach a particular proficiency level, a student must correctly answer a majority of items at that level. Students were classified into mathematics literacy levels according to their scores. Exact cut scores are as follows: below level 1 (a score less than or equal to 357.77); level 1 (a score greater than 357.77 and less than or equal to 420.07); level 2 (a score greater than 420.07 and less than or equal to 482.38); level 3 (a score greater than 482.38 and less than or equal to 544.68); level 4 (a score greater than 544.68 and less than or equal to 606.99); level 5 (a score greater than 606.99 and less than or equal to 669.30); and level 6 (a score greater than 669.30).

[2]Refers to the mean of the data values for all Organization for Economic Cooperation and Development (OECD) countries, to which each country contributes equally, regardless of the absolute size of the student population of each country.
[3]Results are for public school students only.
NOTE: Program for International Student Assessment (PISA) scores are reported on a scale from 0 to 1,000. Detail may not sum to totals because of rounding.
SOURCE: Organization for Economic Cooperation and Development (OECD), Program for International Student Assessment (PISA), 2012. (This table was prepared November 2013.)

Average science literacy scores of 15-year-old students and percentage attaining science literacy proficiency levels, by country or other education system: 2012

[Standard errors appear in parentheses]

Country or other education system	Average science literacy score	Percentage attaining science literacy proficiency levels[1]								
		Below level 2			At level 2	At level 3	At level 4	At or above level 5		
		Total below level 2	Below level 1	At level 1				Total at or above level 5	At level 5	At level 6
1	2	3	4	5	6	7	8	9	10	11
OECD average[2]	**501** (0.5)	**17.8** (0.17)	**4.8** (0.09)	**13.0** (0.14)	**24.5** (0.16)	**28.8** (0.17)	**20.5** (0.15)	**8.4** (0.11)	**7.2** (0.10)	**1.1** (0.04)
Australia	521 (1.8)	13.6 (0.48)	3.4 (0.25)	10.2 (0.41)	21.5 (0.47)	28.5 (0.68)	22.8 (0.63)	13.6 (0.55)	10.9 (0.47)	2.6 (0.25)
Austria	506 (2.7)	15.8 (1.00)	3.6 (0.54)	12.2 (0.92)	24.3 (1.05)	30.1 (0.85)	21.9 (0.81)	7.9 (0.70)	7.0 (0.62)	0.8 (0.20)
Belgium	505 (2.2)	17.7 (0.86)	5.9 (0.53)	11.8 (0.58)	21.5 (0.63)	28.7 (0.71)	23.0 (0.66)	9.1 (0.43)	8.1 (0.42)	0.9 (0.16)
Canada	525 (1.9)	10.4 (0.47)	2.4 (0.24)	8.0 (0.38)	21.0 (0.65)	32.0 (0.54)	25.3 (0.58)	11.3 (0.55)	9.5 (0.47)	1.8 (0.20)
Chile	445 (2.9)	34.5 (1.58)	8.1 (0.80)	26.3 (1.11)	34.6 (1.06)	22.4 (0.96)	7.5 (0.60)	1.0 (0.15)	1.0 (0.15)	# (†)
Czech Republic	508 (3.0)	13.8 (1.13)	3.3 (0.62)	10.5 (1.03)	24.7 (0.99)	31.7 (1.23)	22.2 (0.96)	7.6 (0.58)	6.7 (0.53)	0.9 (0.18)
Denmark	498 (2.7)	16.7 (0.97)	4.7 (0.55)	12.0 (0.69)	25.7 (0.80)	31.3 (0.90)	19.6 (0.79)	6.8 (0.70)	6.1 (0.67)	0.7 (0.17)
Estonia	541 (1.9)	5.0 (0.45)	0.5 (0.14)	4.5 (0.43)	19.0 (0.87)	34.5 (0.87)	28.7 (0.96)	12.8 (0.73)	11.1 (0.66)	1.7 (0.25)
Finland	545 (2.2)	7.7 (0.58)	1.8 (0.28)	5.9 (0.48)	16.8 (0.69)	29.6 (0.77)	28.8 (0.73)	17.1 (0.66)	13.9 (0.62)	3.2 (0.38)
France	499 (2.6)	18.7 (1.01)	6.1 (0.67)	12.6 (0.71)	22.9 (1.08)	29.2 (1.12)	21.3 (0.87)	7.9 (0.77)	6.9 (0.68)	1.0 (0.21)
Germany	524 (3.0)	12.2 (0.90)	2.9 (0.46)	9.3 (0.73)	20.5 (0.82)	28.9 (0.89)	26.2 (1.05)	12.2 (0.95)	10.6 (0.80)	1.6 (0.28)
Greece	467 (3.1)	25.5 (1.47)	7.4 (0.70)	18.1 (1.14)	31.0 (1.10)	28.8 (1.02)	12.2 (0.81)	2.5 (0.40)	2.3 (0.40)	‡ (†)
Hungary	494 (2.9)	18.0 (1.14)	4.1 (0.61)	14.0 (1.04)	26.4 (1.08)	30.9 (1.16)	18.7 (0.98)	5.9 (0.75)	5.5 (0.73)	0.5! (0.18)
Iceland	478 (2.1)	24.0 (0.78)	8.0 (0.56)	16.0 (0.72)	27.5 (0.87)	27.2 (0.86)	16.2 (0.74)	5.2 (0.61)	4.6 (0.60)	0.6 (0.17)
Ireland	522 (2.5)	11.1 (0.88)	2.6 (0.40)	8.5 (0.76)	22.0 (1.15)	31.1 (1.03)	25.0 (0.94)	10.7 (0.58)	9.3 (0.63)	1.5 (0.25)
Israel	470 (5.0)	28.9 (1.67)	11.2 (1.08)	17.7 (0.93)	24.8 (0.93)	24.4 (1.19)	16.1 (1.12)	5.8 (0.65)	5.2 (0.58)	0.6 (0.22)
Italy	494 (1.9)	18.7 (0.68)	4.9 (0.35)	13.8 (0.52)	26.0 (0.58)	30.1 (0.66)	19.1 (0.59)	6.1 (0.41)	5.5 (0.37)	0.6 (0.08)
Japan	547 (3.6)	8.5 (0.88)	2.0 (0.39)	6.4 (0.61)	16.3 (0.79)	27.5 (0.92)	29.5 (1.06)	18.2 (1.21)	14.8 (0.93)	3.4 (0.49)
Korea, Republic of	538 (3.7)	6.6 (0.77)	1.2 (0.25)	5.5 (0.60)	18.0 (1.02)	33.6 (1.11)	30.1 (1.24)	11.7 (1.13)	10.6 (0.93)	1.1! (0.39)
Luxembourg	491 (1.3)	22.2 (0.63)	7.2 (0.42)	15.1 (0.67)	24.2 (0.63)	26.2 (0.60)	19.2 (0.53)	8.2 (0.54)	7.0 (0.49)	1.2 (0.17)
Mexico	415 (1.3)	47.0 (0.81)	12.6 (0.52)	34.4 (0.58)	37.0 (0.59)	13.8 (0.52)	2.1 (0.16)	0.1 (0.04)	0.1! (0.04)	† (†)
Netherlands	522 (3.5)	13.1 (1.12)	3.1 (0.53)	10.1 (0.83)	20.1 (1.35)	29.1 (1.28)	25.8 (1.24)	11.8 (1.06)	10.5 (0.98)	1.3 (0.28)
New Zealand	516 (2.1)	16.3 (0.86)	4.7 (0.39)	11.6 (0.76)	21.7 (0.94)	26.4 (0.95)	22.3 (0.85)	13.4 (0.69)	10.7 (0.62)	2.7 (0.25)
Norway	495 (3.1)	19.6 (1.10)	6.0 (0.63)	13.6 (0.71)	24.8 (0.80)	28.9 (0.91)	19.0 (0.79)	7.5 (0.57)	6.4 (0.56)	1.1 (0.24)
Poland	526 (3.1)	9.0 (0.75)	1.3 (0.32)	7.7 (0.70)	22.5 (0.98)	33.1 (0.92)	24.5 (0.96)	10.8 (1.01)	9.1 (0.76)	1.7 (0.35)
Portugal	489 (3.7)	19.0 (1.44)	4.7 (0.66)	14.3 (1.09)	27.3 (0.96)	31.4 (1.25)	17.8 (1.06)	4.5 (0.55)	4.2 (0.55)	0.3! (0.11)
Slovak Republic	471 (3.6)	26.9 (1.58)	9.2 (0.95)	17.6 (1.14)	27.0 (1.30)	26.2 (1.62)	15.0 (1.02)	4.9 (0.72)	4.3 (0.58)	0.6! (0.25)
Slovenia	514 (1.3)	12.9 (0.56)	2.4 (0.19)	10.4 (0.55)	24.5 (1.00)	30.0 (1.02)	23.0 (0.92)	9.6 (0.72)	8.4 (0.71)	1.2 (0.24)
Spain	496 (1.8)	15.7 (0.71)	3.7 (0.33)	12.0 (0.51)	27.3 (0.64)	32.8 (0.60)	19.4 (0.53)	4.8 (0.29)	4.5 (0.26)	0.3 (0.08)
Sweden	485 (3.0)	22.2 (1.11)	7.3 (0.62)	15.0 (0.80)	26.2 (0.84)	28.0 (0.84)	17.2 (0.77)	6.3 (0.50)	5.6 (0.45)	0.7 (0.14)
Switzerland	515 (2.7)	12.8 (0.72)	3.0 (0.31)	9.8 (0.62)	22.8 (0.82)	31.3 (0.74)	23.7 (0.86)	9.3 (0.77)	8.3 (0.70)	1.0 (0.22)
Turkey	463 (3.9)	26.4 (1.50)	4.4 (0.50)	21.9 (1.27)	35.4 (1.43)	25.1 (1.28)	11.3 (1.28)	1.8 (0.36)	1.8 (0.34)	‡ (†)
United Kingdom	514 (3.4)	15.0 (1.07)	4.3 (0.48)	10.7 (0.86)	22.4 (1.00)	28.4 (0.98)	23.0 (0.91)	11.2 (0.79)	9.3 (0.70)	1.8 (0.34)
United States	497 (3.8)	18.1 (1.33)	4.2 (0.54)	14.0 (1.08)	26.7 (1.08)	28.9 (1.07)	18.8 (1.07)	7.5 (0.74)	6.3 (0.64)	1.1 (0.20)

See notes at end of table.

Average science literacy scores of 15-year-old students and percentage attaining science literacy proficiency levels, by country or other education system: 2012—Continued

[Standard errors appear in parentheses]

Country or other education system	Average science literacy score	Total below level 2	Below level 1	At level 1	At level 2	At level 3	At level 4	Total at or above level 5	At level 5	At level 6
			Below level 2			Percentage attaining science literacy proficiency levels[1]			At or above level 5	
1	2	3	4	5	6	7	8	9	10	11
Non-OECD education systems										
Albania	397 (2.4)	53.1 (1.20)	23.5 (1.04)	29.6 (0.94)	28.5 (1.19)	14.4 (0.78)	3.6 (0.41)	0.4! (0.13)	0.4! (0.14)	‡ (†)
Argentina	406 (3.9)	50.9 (2.21)	19.8 (1.39)	31.0 (1.46)	31.1 (1.33)	14.8 (1.20)	3.0 (0.43)	0.2! (0.10)	0.2! (0.10)	‡ (†)
Brazil	405 (2.1)	53.7 (1.14)	18.6 (0.78)	35.1 (0.79)	30.7 (0.78)	12.5 (0.68)	2.8 (0.37)	0.3! (0.10)	0.3! (0.10)	‡ (†)
Bulgaria	446 (4.8)	36.9 (2.02)	14.4 (1.34)	22.5 (1.15)	26.3 (1.07)	22.5 (1.09)	11.2 (0.84)	3.1 (0.58)	2.8 (0.50)	0.3! (0.12)
Chinese Taipei	523 (2.3)	9.8 (0.77)	1.6 (0.25)	8.2 (0.64)	20.8 (0.89)	33.7 (0.97)	27.3 (1.00)	8.3 (0.61)	7.8 (0.56)	0.6 (0.13)
Colombia	399 (3.1)	56.2 (1.61)	19.8 (1.36)	36.3 (1.10)	30.8 (1.08)	11.0 (0.83)	1.9 (0.25)	‡ (†)	‡ (†)	‡ (†)
Connecticut-USA[3]	521 (5.7)	13.5 (1.70)	3.3 (0.82)	10.2 (1.36)	21.4 (1.58)	29.4 (1.69)	22.8 (1.46)	12.9 (1.34)	10.7 (1.13)	2.2 (0.60)
Costa Rica	429 (2.9)	39.3 (1.75)	8.6 (0.79)	30.7 (1.30)	39.2 (1.25)	17.8 (1.12)	3.4 (0.57)	0.2! (0.10)	0.2! (0.11)	‡ (†)
Croatia	491 (3.1)	17.3 (0.93)	3.2 (0.38)	14.0 (0.74)	39.1 (0.99)	31.4 (1.19)	17.6 (1.16)	4.6 (0.79)	4.3 (0.75)	‡ (†)
Cyprus	438 (1.2)	38.0 (0.67)	14.4 (0.47)	23.7 (0.66)	30.3 (0.89)	21.3 (0.73)	8.4 (0.43)	2.0 (0.29)	1.8 (0.29)	0.2! (0.08)
Florida-USA[3]	485 (6.4)	21.3 (2.15)	5.1 (0.96)	16.1 (1.61)	28.4 (1.61)	28.2 (2.00)	16.6 (1.64)	5.5 (1.05)	4.9 (1.01)	‡ (†)
Hong Kong-China	555 (2.6)	5.6 (0.62)	1.2 (0.23)	4.4 (0.52)	13.0 (0.72)	29.8 (1.06)	34.9 (0.99)	16.7 (1.05)	14.9 (0.91)	1.8 (0.36)
Indonesia	382 (3.8)	66.6 (2.20)	24.7 (1.96)	41.9 (1.42)	26.3 (1.54)	6.5 (1.02)	‡ (†)	‡ (†)	‡ (†)	‡ (†)
Jordan	409 (3.1)	49.6 (1.55)	18.2 (1.21)	31.4 (0.96)	32.2 (1.04)	15.0 (0.86)	3.0 (0.57)	‡ (†)	‡ (†)	‡ (†)
Kazakhstan	425 (3.0)	41.9 (1.83)	11.3 (0.99)	30.7 (1.49)	36.8 (1.16)	17.8 (1.19)	3.3 (0.45)	0.2! (0.09)	0.2! (0.09)	‡ (†)
Latvia	502 (2.8)	12.4 (0.96)	1.8 (0.39)	10.5 (0.90)	28.2 (1.20)	35.1 (1.02)	20.0 (1.05)	4.4 (0.51)	4.0 (0.47)	0.4! (0.13)
Liechtenstein	525 (3.5)	10.4 (1.96)	‡ (†)	9.6 (1.94)	22.0 (3.94)	30.8 (3.79)	26.7 (2.58)	10.1 (1.80)	9.1 (1.47)	0.4! (0.47)
Lithuania	496 (2.6)	16.1 (1.08)	3.4 (0.48)	12.7 (0.84)	27.6 (1.00)	32.9 (1.08)	18.3 (0.88)	5.1 (0.49)	4.7 (0.47)	0.4 (0.09)
Macao-China	521 (0.8)	8.8 (0.46)	1.4 (0.20)	7.4 (0.49)	22.2 (0.60)	36.2 (0.81)	26.2 (0.73)	6.7 (0.36)	6.2 (0.35)	0.4 (0.10)
Malaysia	420 (3.0)	45.5 (1.55)	14.5 (1.13)	31.0 (1.21)	33.9 (1.10)	16.5 (1.07)	3.7 (0.54)	0.3! (0.12)	0.3! (0.13)	‡ (†)
Massachusetts-USA[3]	527 (6.0)	11.5 (1.18)	2.6 (0.65)	8.9 (1.03)	21.2 (1.96)	29.4 (1.50)	23.8 (1.84)	14.2 (1.94)	11.3 (1.48)	2.9 (0.73)
Montenegro, Republic of	410 (1.1)	50.7 (0.72)	18.7 (0.74)	32.0 (0.98)	29.7 (0.94)	15.4 (0.76)	3.8 (0.47)	0.4! (0.14)	0.4! (0.14)	‡ (†)
Peru	373 (3.6)	68.5 (1.95)	31.5 (1.61)	37.0 (1.26)	23.5 (1.29)	7.0 (0.85)	1.0 (0.28)	‡ (†)	‡ (†)	‡ (†)
Qatar	384 (0.7)	62.6 (0.53)	34.6 (0.38)	28.0 (0.58)	19.6 (0.71)	11.2 (0.39)	5.1 (0.40)	1.5 (0.12)	1.3 (0.11)	0.1! (0.04)
Romania	439 (3.3)	37.3 (1.64)	8.7 (0.77)	28.7 (1.32)	34.6 (1.23)	21.0 (1.12)	6.2 (0.77)	0.9! (0.29)	0.9 (0.26)	‡ (†)
Russian Federation	486 (2.9)	18.8 (1.15)	3.6 (0.39)	15.1 (0.96)	30.1 (1.08)	31.2 (0.89)	15.7 (0.98)	4.3 (0.59)	3.9 (0.51)	0.3! (0.16)
Serbia, Republic of	445 (3.4)	35.0 (1.81)	10.3 (0.99)	24.7 (1.15)	32.4 (1.21)	22.8 (1.06)	8.1 (0.63)	1.7 (0.36)	1.6 (0.35)	‡ (†)
Shanghai-China	580 (3.0)	2.7 (0.41)	0.3! (0.11)	2.4 (0.36)	10.0 (0.86)	24.6 (0.87)	35.5 (1.11)	27.2 (1.32)	23.0 (1.09)	4.2 (0.57)
Singapore	551 (1.5)	9.6 (0.51)	2.2 (0.27)	7.4 (0.48)	16.7 (0.73)	24.0 (0.73)	27.0 (0.87)	22.7 (0.81)	16.9 (0.94)	5.8 (0.41)
Thailand	444 (2.9)	33.6 (1.56)	7.0 (0.64)	26.6 (1.33)	37.5 (1.07)	21.6 (1.14)	6.4 (0.74)	0.9 (0.27)	0.9! (0.27)	‡ (†)
Tunisia	398 (3.5)	55.3 (1.87)	21.3 (1.45)	34.0 (1.07)	31.1 (1.36)	11.7 (1.00)	1.8 (0.49)	‡ (†)	‡ (†)	‡ (†)
United Arab Emirates	448 (2.8)	35.2 (1.30)	11.3 (0.76)	23.8 (0.99)	29.9 (0.83)	22.3 (0.88)	10.1 (0.60)	2.5 (0.27)	2.3 (0.25)	0.3! (0.07)
Uruguay	416 (2.8)	46.9 (1.25)	19.7 (1.06)	27.2 (0.92)	29.3 (1.00)	17.1 (0.95)	5.6 (0.53)	1.0 (0.25)	1.0 (0.24)	‡ (†)
Vietnam	528 (4.3)	6.7 (1.09)	0.9! (0.26)	5.8 (0.90)	20.7 (1.40)	37.5 (1.48)	27.0 (1.50)	8.1 (1.09)	7.1 (0.90)	1.0! (0.32)

†Not applicable.

#Rounds to zero.

!Interpret data with caution. The coefficient of variation (CV) for this estimate is between 30 and 50 percent.

‡Reporting standards not met. Either there are too few cases for a reliable estimate or the coefficient of variation (CV) is 50 percent or greater.

[1]To reach a particular proficiency level, a student must correctly answer a majority of items at that level. Students were classified into science literacy levels according to their scores. Exact cut scores are as follows: below level 1 (a score less than or equal to 334.94); level 1 (a score greater than 334.94 and less than or equal to 409.54); level 2 (a score greater than 409.54 and less than or equal to 484.14); level 3 (a score greater than 484.14 and less than or equal to 558.73 and less than or equal to 633.33); level 5 (a score greater than 633.33 and less than or equal to 707.93); and level 6 (a score greater than 707.93).

[2]Refers to the mean of the data values for all Organization for Economic Cooperation and Development (OECD) countries, to which each country contributes equally, regardless of the absolute size of the student population of each country.

[3]Results are for public school students only.

NOTE: Program for International Student Assessment (PISA) scores are reported on a scale from 0 to 1,000. Detail may not sum to totals because of rounding.

SOURCE: Organization for Economic Cooperation and Development (OECD), Program for International Student Assessment (PISA), 2012. (This table was prepared November 2013.)

Percentage of the population 25 to 64 years old who completed high school, by age group and country: Selected years, 2001 through 2011

[Standard errors appear in parentheses]

Country	2001 Total, 25 to 64 years old	2001 25 to 34 years old	2005 Total, 25 to 64 years old	2005 25 to 34 years old	2010 Total, 25 to 64 years old		2010 25 to 34 years old		2011 Total, 25 to 64 years old		2011 25 to 34 years old		2011 35 to 44 years old		2011 45 to 54 years old		2011 55 to 64 years old	
1	2	3	4	5	6		7		8		9		10		11		12	
OECD average[1]	64.2	74.0	72.8	82.6	74.0	(0.03)	81.9	(0.06)	74.8	(0.04)	82.2	(0.07)	78.5	(0.06)	72.6	(0.07)	63.8	(0.08)
Australia	58.9	70.7	65.0	78.6	73.2	(0.41)	84.8	(0.62)	74.1	(0.25)	84.4	(0.41)	78.4	(0.45)	69.2	(0.51)	60.8	(0.59)
Austria[2,3]	75.7	83.3	80.6	87.5	82.5	(0.12)	88.0	(0.23)	82.5	(0.26)	88.2	(0.44)	86.0	(0.43)	81.9	(0.50)	72.3	(0.65)
Belgium[2]	58.5	75.3	66.1	80.9	70.5	(0.19)	82.1	(0.34)	71.3	(0.19)	81.9	(0.35)	79.0	(0.35)	68.0	(0.38)	55.5	(0.43)
Canada	81.9	89.3	85.2	90.8	88.4	(0.12)	92.2	(0.20)	88.8	(0.13)	92.5	(0.19)	91.8	(0.19)	87.8	(0.21)	82.8	(0.28)
Chile[4]	—	—	50.0	64.3	71.4	(0.19)	86.6	(0.24)	72.3	(0.18)	87.8	(0.23)	76.9	(0.28)	67.0	(0.32)	55.5	(0.40)
Czech Republic	86.2	92.5	89.9	93.9	91.9	(0.08)	94.2	(0.14)	92.3	(0.07)	94.3	(0.14)	95.5	(0.11)	92.6	(0.15)	86.6	(0.18)
Denmark	80.2	86.3	81.0	87.4	75.7	(0.17)	79.8	(0.42)	76.9	(0.17)	80.3	(0.38)	81.7	(0.30)	76.0	(0.30)	69.8	(0.36)
Estonia	—	—	89.1	87.4	89.1	(0.30)	86.4	(0.73)	88.9	(0.29)	85.7	(0.71)	89.3	(0.55)	93.8	(0.42)	86.6	(0.64)
Finland	73.8	86.8	78.8	89.4	83.0	(0.12)	90.8	(0.20)	83.7	(0.18)	90.2	(0.31)	89.3	(0.31)	85.9	(0.32)	71.3	(0.41)
France[5]	63.9	78.4	66.3	81.1	70.8	(0.09)	83.8	(0.16)	71.6	(0.09)	83.3	(0.16)	78.3	(0.16)	67.7	(0.17)	57.6	(0.19)
Germany	82.6	85.5	83.1	84.1	85.8	(0.06)	86.5	(0.12)	86.3	(0.12)	86.8	(0.21)	86.9	(0.30)	87.0	(0.28)	84.1	(0.31)
Greece	51.4	72.6	57.1	73.6	65.2	(0.12)	78.9	(0.21)	67.1	(0.12)	80.1	(0.22)	73.6	(0.23)	64.4	(0.24)	47.2	(0.26)
Hungary	70.2	80.9	76.4	85.0	81.3	(0.10)	86.3	(0.19)	81.8	(0.27)	87.3	(0.32)	83.3	(0.41)	80.7	(0.46)	75.3	(0.50)
Iceland	56.9	61.2	62.9	69.0	66.5	(0.50)	72.4	(0.92)	70.7	(0.48)	74.7	(0.90)	74.8	(0.93)	68.8	(0.94)	63.3	(1.09)
Ireland	57.6	73.4	64.5	81.1	73.5	(0.12)	86.9	(0.18)	73.4	(0.13)	85.0	(0.20)	79.8	(0.22)	68.4	(0.27)	52.3	(0.33)
Israel	—	—	79.2	85.7	82.1	(0.15)	88.1	(0.24)	83.0	(0.15)	89.7	(0.23)	84.6	(0.28)	79.5	(0.35)	74.2	(0.41)
Italy	43.3	57.5	50.1	65.9	55.2	(0.08)	71.0	(0.18)	56.0	(0.14)	71.3	(0.36)	60.3	(0.29)	51.8	(0.28)	40.3	(0.28)
Japan	83.1	93.6	—	—	—	(†)	—	(†)	—	(†)	—	(†)	—	(†)	—	(†)	—	(†)
Korea, Republic of	68.0	94.6	75.5	97.3	80.4	(0.20)	97.8	(0.14)	81.4	(0.20)	98.0	(0.14)	95.6	(0.19)	75.4	(0.42)	45.1	(0.63)
Luxembourg	52.7	59.4	65.9	76.5	77.7	(0.40)	84.0	(0.80)	77.3	(0.40)	83.4	(0.76)	78.0	(0.71)	75.2	(0.77)	70.9	(0.94)
Mexico	21.6	25.4	21.3	24.0	36.2	(0.06)	43.6	(0.12)	36.3	(0.06)	44.0	(0.12)	36.9	(0.12)	33.7	(0.13)	23.3	(0.15)
Netherlands[2,5]	65.0	74.0	71.8	81.3	73.0	(0.09)	82.7	(0.18)	72.3	(0.09)	81.7	(0.18)	77.2	(0.17)	70.6	(0.17)	60.3	(0.20)
New Zealand	75.7	81.8	78.7	85.2	73.0	(0.37)	79.4	(0.73)	74.1	(0.36)	80.4	(0.71)	77.8	(0.66)	73.2	(0.70)	63.7	(0.83)
Norway[2]	85.2	93.4	77.2	83.5	80.6	(0.16)	83.0	(0.34)	81.9	(0.16)	83.8	(0.33)	84.6	(0.29)	77.6	(0.34)	81.4	(0.33)
Poland	45.9	51.7	51.4	62.5	88.7	(0.07)	93.7	(0.10)	89.1	(0.06)	94.1	(0.10)	91.9	(0.12)	89.5	(0.12)	80.0	(0.16)
Portugal	19.9	32.5	26.5	42.8	31.9	(0.16)	52.1	(0.39)	35.0	(0.16)	55.7	(0.39)	38.7	(0.34)	24.3	(0.27)	18.4	(0.26)
Slovak Republic	85.1	93.7	85.7	93.0	91.0	(0.12)	94.1	(0.20)	91.3	(0.23)	94.1	(0.46)	94.1	(0.41)	91.7	(0.44)	84.1	(0.57)
Slovenia	—	—	80.3	91.2	83.3	(0.19)	93.5	(0.27)	84.5	(0.19)	94.0	(0.27)	87.3	(0.38)	83.1	(0.36)	72.9	(0.45)
Spain	40.0	57.1	48.8	63.9	52.9	(0.08)	64.7	(0.16)	54.0	(0.29)	64.8	(0.59)	61.1	(0.53)	50.0	(0.55)	33.8	(0.57)
Sweden	80.6	90.7	83.6	90.6	86.5	(0.08)	91.1	(0.13)	87.0	(0.08)	90.9	(0.14)	91.4	(0.13)	87.4	(0.15)	78.2	(0.18)
Switzerland	87.4	91.8	83.0	87.9	86.1	(0.12)	90.2	(0.24)	85.6	(0.12)	89.1	(0.24)	87.4	(0.21)	84.6	(0.23)	80.7	(0.26)
Turkey	24.3	30.2	27.2	35.7	31.2	(0.09)	42.2	(0.18)	32.1	(0.09)	43.5	(0.18)	29.8	(0.17)	24.6	(0.17)	19.4	(0.18)
United Kingdom[3,5]	63.0	68.0	66.7	72.9	75.1	(0.18)	82.9	(0.35)	76.8	(0.09)	84.3	(0.17)	80.3	(0.17)	74.7	(0.18)	66.7	(0.20)
United States	87.7	88.1	87.8	86.7	89.0	(0.14)	88.4	(0.24)	89.3	(0.13)	89.0	(0.25)	89.0	(0.22)	89.3	(0.25)	89.6	(0.21)
Other reporting countries																		
Brazil[4]	—	—	29.5	38.0	—	(†)	—	(†)	43.3	(0.11)	56.7	(0.19)	44.0	(0.21)	36.4	(0.22)	26.2	(0.25)
Russian Federation[6]	88.0	91.0	—	—	—	(†)	—	(†)	94.1	(0.05)	94.0	(0.10)	95.2	(0.10)	95.5	(0.09)	91.0	(0.15)

—Not available.
†Not applicable.
[1]Refers to the mean of the data values for all reporting Organization for Economic Cooperation and Development (OECD) countries, to which each country reporting data contributes equally. The average includes all current OECD countries for which a given year's data are available, even if they were not members of OECD in that year.
[2]Data from 2000 reported for 2001.
[3]Data in 2005 columns include some International Standard Classification of Education (ISCED) 3C short programs.
[4]Data from 2004 reported for 2005.

[5]Data in 2001 columns include some ISCED 3C short programs.
[6]Data from 2002 reported for 2001.
NOTE: Data in this table refer to degrees classified as International Standard Classification of Education (ISCED) level 3. ISCED level 3 corresponds to high school completion in the United States. ISCED 3C short programs do not correspond to high school completion; these short programs are excluded from this table except where otherwise noted. Standard errors are not available for 2001 and 2005.
SOURCE: Organization for Economic Cooperation and Development (OECD), *Education at a Glance*, 2002, 2007, 2012, and 2013. (This table was prepared July 2013.)

Percentage of the population 25 to 64 years old who attained selected levels of postsecondary education, by age group and country: 2001 and 2011

[Standard errors appear in parentheses]

Country	Total, any postsecondary degree — 2001 Total, 25 to 64 years old	2001 25 to 34 years old	2011 Total, 25 to 64 years old	2011 25 to 34 years old	Vocational degree[1] Total, 25 to 64 years old	25 to 34 years old	35 to 44 years old	45 to 54 years old	55 to 64 years old	Bachelor's or higher degree[2] Total, 25 to 64 years old	25 to 34 years old	35 to 44 years old	45 to 54 years old	55 to 64 years old
1	2	3	4	5	6	7	8	9	10	11	12	13	14	15
OECD average[3]	22.6	27.3	31.5 (0.04)	38.6 (0.09)	9.9 (0.03)	10.3 (0.06)	10.9 (0.06)	10.0 (0.06)	8.3 (0.06)	22.8 (0.04)	29.5 (0.08)	24.7 (0.07)	19.4 (0.07)	16.6 (0.07)
Australia	29.0	33.5	38.3 (0.27)	44.6 (0.56)	10.4 (0.17)	9.6 (0.33)	11.1 (0.34)	11.7 (0.36)	9.1 (0.35)	27.9 (0.25)	35.0 (0.53)	29.9 (0.50)	23.6 (0.47)	21.1 (0.50)
Austria	14.1	14.3	19.3 (0.24)	21.2 (0.60)	7.3 (0.18)	5.5 (0.36)	7.5 (0.26)	8.3 (0.23)	7.7 (0.38)	12.0 (0.18)	15.7 (0.49)	13.8 (0.42)	10.4 (0.35)	7.9 (0.34)
Belgium	27.6	37.5	34.6 (0.20)	42.5 (0.45)	17.6 (0.16)	19.3 (0.36)	19.9 (0.34)	17.1 (0.31)	13.7 (0.30)	17.0 (0.16)	23.1 (0.39)	19.5 (0.34)	14.2 (0.28)	11.4 (0.27)
Canada[1]	41.6	50.5	51.3 (0.22)	56.7 (0.39)	24.6 (0.16)	25.6 (0.33)	26.4 (0.31)	25.1 (0.27)	20.8 (0.27)	26.8 (0.23)	31.1 (0.41)	31.6 (0.40)	22.9 (0.32)	21.8 (0.34)
Chile[1]	10.1	12.3	28.9 (0.18)	41.3 (0.34)	12.1 (0.13)	14.5 (0.23)	15.1 (0.22)	11.2 (0.20)	6.5 (0.18)	16.8 (0.15)	26.8 (0.30)	14.7 (0.23)	11.5 (0.22)	14.9 (0.28)
Czech Republic[5]	11.1	11.3	18.2 (0.11)	25.1 (0.26)	[5]	[5]	[5]	[5]	[5]	18.2 (0.11)	25.1 (0.26)	17.9 (0.21)	17.1 (0.22)	12.1 (0.17)
Denmark	26.8	27.5	33.7 (0.19)	38.6 (0.47)	5.6 (0.09)	5.4 (0.22)	6.4 (0.19)	5.6 (0.16)	5.0 (†)	28.1 (0.18)	33.2 (0.45)	31.1 (0.36)	25.9 (0.31)	22.9 (0.33)
Estonia	—	—	36.7 (0.45)	39.0 (0.99)	12.1 (0.30)	12.3 (0.67)	11.7 (0.57)	13.1 (0.58)	11.1 (0.59)	24.6 (0.40)	26.7 (0.90)	23.4 (0.75)	24.2 (0.74)	24.1 (0.81)
Finland	32.3	38.2	39.3 (0.24)	39.4 (0.50)	14.4 (0.17)	1.6 (0.13)	16.7 (0.39)	21.7 (0.40)	16.6 (0.35)	24.9 (0.21)	37.8 (0.50)	30.1 (0.48)	19.4 (0.39)	14.7 (0.33)
France	23.0	34.2	29.8 (0.09)	43.0 (0.21)	11.5 (0.06)	16.0 (0.16)	14.3 (0.13)	9.3 (0.11)	6.5 (0.09)	18.3 (0.07)	27.0 (0.19)	21.3 (0.16)	13.2 (0.13)	12.1 (0.12)
Germany	23.2	21.8	27.6 (0.08)	27.7 (0.19)	11.2 (0.06)	9.4 (0.18)	11.4 (0.12)	12.4 (0.11)	11.2 (0.12)	16.4 (0.07)	18.3 (0.16)	17.5 (0.14)	15.0 (0.19)	15.0 (0.14)
Greece	17.8	24.0	26.1 (0.12)	32.5 (0.26)	7.7 (0.07)	11.8 (0.11)	8.7 (0.14)	6.3 (0.12)	3.4 (0.09)	18.3 (0.10)	20.7 (0.23)	19.1 (0.20)	17.9 (0.19)	15.1 (0.19)
Hungary	14.1	14.7	21.1 (0.12)	28.1 (0.26)	0.6 (0.04)	1.6 (0.11)	0.5 (0.07)	0.3 (†)	‡ (†)	20.5 (0.26)	26.5 (0.43)	20.9 (0.44)	17.7 (0.47)	16.3 (0.48)
Iceland	24.8	26.6	33.9 (0.50)	39.4 (1.01)	3.9 (0.10)	2.5 (0.32)	4.9 (0.47)	4.1 (0.40)	3.9 (0.44)	30.0 (0.49)	36.9 (0.99)	34.2 (1.02)	27.0 (0.90)	20.1 (0.91)
Ireland	35.6	47.8	37.7 (0.14)	47.2 (0.28)	14.7 (0.10)	16.1 (0.20)	17.5 (0.20)	13.4 (0.20)	9.9 (0.19)	23.1 (0.12)	31.1 (0.26)	25.9 (0.24)	17.5 (0.22)	12.9 (0.22)
Israel	—	—	46.4 (0.20)	45.0 (0.38)	15.4 (0.14)	13.4 (0.25)	15.5 (0.29)	16.5 (0.30)	17.1 (0.32)	31.0 (0.18)	31.6 (0.35)	34.1 (0.37)	28.8 (0.37)	28.2 (0.38)
Italy	10.0	11.8	14.9 (0.08)	21.0 (0.20)	0.3 (0.01)	0.2 (0.02)	0.3 (0.02)	0.5 (0.02)	0.3 (0.02)	14.6 (0.08)	20.7 (0.20)	16.3 (0.16)	11.0 (0.14)	10.5 (0.15)
Japan	33.8	47.7	46.4 (0.19)	58.7 (0.40)	20.1 (0.15)	23.8 (0.35)	24.7 (0.33)	20.3 (0.34)	12.2 (0.30)	26.3 (0.17)	34.9 (0.39)	26.5 (0.33)	26.7 (0.37)	18.5 (0.36)
Korea, Republic of	24.2	39.5	39.5 (0.25)	63.8 (0.46)	12.6 (0.17)	24.9 (0.43)	14.9 (0.31)	6.1 (0.22)	2.1 (0.16)	27.8 (0.23)	38.9 (0.47)	34.6 (0.44)	21.8 (0.40)	10.7 (0.40)
Luxembourg	18.1	23.4	37.0 (0.46)	46.6 (1.02)	12.0 (0.31)	14.5 (0.72)	12.8 (0.57)	10.5 (0.55)	9.6 (0.61)	25.1 (0.41)	32.2 (0.96)	27.1 (0.76)	20.7 (0.73)	18.7 (0.80)
Mexico	15.0	17.9	17.3 (#)	22.5 (0.23)	1.1 (#)	1.2 (0.07)	1.1 (0.07)	1.2 (#)	0.7 (#)	16.2 (#)	21.3 (0.22)	14.3 (0.19)	15.1 (#)	11.3 (#)
Netherlands	23.2	26.5	32.0 (0.09)	39.8 (0.90)	2.5 (0.03)	2.2 (0.07)	2.9 (0.07)	2.8 (0.06)	2.2 (0.06)	29.5 (0.09)	37.6 (0.84)	31.3 (0.70)	26.5 (0.16)	23.6 (0.64)
New Zealand	29.2	28.5	39.3 (0.41)	46.0 (0.45)	15.5 (0.30)	14.6 (0.64)	14.8 (0.57)	16.4 (0.58)	16.2 (0.63)	23.8 (0.35)	31.4 (0.45)	26.2 (0.64)	20.4 (0.38)	16.5 (0.64)
Norway[6]	30.2	37.9	38.1 (0.20)	46.8 (0.45)	5.2 (0.10)	1.1 (0.09)	2.2 (0.12)	2.9 (0.14)	2.8 (0.14)	35.8 (0.20)	45.7 (0.45)	39.4 (0.39)	31.0 (0.15)	26.5 (0.37)
Poland[6]	11.9	15.2	23.7 (0.09)	39.2 (0.21)	2.2 (†)	[5]	[5]	[5]	[5]	23.7 (0.09)	39.2 (0.21)	24.4 (0.19)	15.6 (0.15)	12.8 (0.13)
Portugal[5]	9.0	13.7	17.3 (0.13)	26.9 (0.35)	[5]	[5]	[5]	[5]	[5]	17.3 (0.13)	26.9 (0.35)	18.6 (0.27)	11.5 (0.20)	10.9 (0.21)
Slovak Republic	10.9	11.9	18.8 (0.32)	25.7 (0.86)	1.3 (0.09)	1.3 (0.27)	1.2 (0.36)	1.4 (0.19)	1.2 (0.17)	17.5 (0.31)	24.4 (0.85)	16.1 (0.63)	14.9 (0.57)	12.7 (0.52)
Slovenia	—	—	13.9 (0.23)	33.8 (0.53)	11.2 (0.17)	12.6 (0.37)	11.6 (0.35)	11.7 (0.31)	8.7 (0.29)	13.9 (0.18)	21.2 (0.46)	16.5 (0.42)	10.1 (0.29)	7.7 (0.27)
Spain	23.6	35.5	31.6 (0.27)	39.2 (0.60)	9.3 (0.17)	12.4 (0.41)	11.6 (0.41)	7.3 (0.28)	4.1 (0.24)	22.3 (0.24)	26.7 (0.54)	25.5 (0.47)	19.8 (0.43)	14.5 (0.42)
Sweden	31.6	36.9	35.2 (0.11)	42.9 (0.23)	9.0 (0.07)	8.6 (0.13)	8.5 (0.13)	9.2 (0.13)	9.7 (0.13)	26.2 (0.10)	34.2 (0.22)	30.5 (0.21)	21.4 (0.19)	18.5 (0.17)
Switzerland	25.4	25.6	35.2 (0.16)	39.8 (0.38)	10.7 (0.10)	9.5 (0.23)	11.8 (0.20)	11.5 (0.20)	9.4 (0.19)	24.5 (0.14)	30.3 (0.35)	27.7 (0.28)	21.9 (0.26)	17.7 (0.25)
Turkey[6]	8.9	10.2	14.0 (0.07)	18.9 (0.14)	[5]	[5]	[5]	[5]	[5]	14.0 (0.07)	18.9 (0.14)	13.5 (0.13)	9.5 (0.12)	9.8 (0.14)
United Kingdom	26.0	30.0	39.4 (0.10)	46.9 (0.23)	9.8 (0.06)	7.6 (0.12)	10.6 (0.13)	11.7 (0.13)	9.3 (0.12)	29.6 (0.10)	39.3 (0.22)	32.0 (0.20)	24.1 (0.18)	22.0 (0.18)
United States	37.3	39.1	42.4 (0.22)	43.1 (0.46)	10.3 (0.11)	10.1 (0.24)	10.4 (0.22)	10.7 (0.21)	9.8 (0.25)	32.2 (0.22)	33.0 (0.45)	34.2 (0.40)	30.2 (0.39)	31.4 (0.39)
Other reporting countries														
Brazil[4,5]	7.7	6.7	11.6 (0.07)	12.7 (0.12)	[5]	[5]	[5]	[5]	[5]	11.6 (0.07)	12.7 (0.12)	11.8 (0.13)	11.4 (0.14)	9.5 (0.16)
China[4,6]	4.6	6.1	3.6 (†)	(†)	(†)	(†)	(†)	(†)	(†)	(†)	(†)	(†)	(†)	(†)
Russian Federation[1]	54.0	55.5	53.5 (†)	56.5 (†)	26.4 (†)	22.4 (†)	26.9 (†)	28.4 (†)	28.7 (†)	27.1 (†)	34.1 (†)	27.9 (†)	23.9 (†)	20.8 (†)

—Not available.
†Not applicable.
#Rounds to zero.
‡Reporting standards not met (too few cases for a reliable estimate).
[1]The vocational degree data in this table refer to degrees classified as International Standard Classification of Education (ISCED) level 5B. ISCED level 5B corresponds to the associate's degree in the United States.
[2]The data for bachelor's degree or higher in this table refer to degrees classified as ISCED level 5A (first and second award) and as level 6. ISCED 5A, first award, corresponds to the bachelor's degree in the United States; ISCED 5A, second award, corresponds to master's and first-professional degrees in the United States; and ISCED 6 corresponds to doctor's degrees.
[3]Refers to the mean of the data values for all reporting Organization for Economic Cooperation and Development (OECD) countries, to which each country reporting data contributes equally. The average includes all current OECD countries for which a given year's data are available, even if they were not members of OECD in that year.
[4]Data from 2000 reported for 2001.
[5]Columns for bachelor's or higher degree include vocational degree data.
[6]Data from 2010 reported for 2011.
[7]Data from 2002 reported for 2001.
NOTE: Standard errors are not available for 2001.
SOURCE: Organization for Economic Cooperation and Development (OECD), Education at a Glance, 2002 and 2013. (This table was prepared July 2013.)

Percentage of the population 25 to 64 years old who attained a bachelor's or higher level degree, by age group and country: Selected years, 1999 through 2011

[Standard errors appear in parentheses]

Country	1999 Total, 25 to 64	1999 25 to 34	2001 Total, 25 to 64	2001 25 to 34	2005 Total, 25 to 64	2005 25 to 34	2006 Total, 25 to 64	2006 25 to 34	2007 Total, 25 to 64	2007 25 to 34	2008 Total, 25 to 64	2008 25 to 34	2009 Total, 25 to 64	2009 25 to 34	2010 Total, 25 to 64	2010 25 to 34	2011 Total, 25 to 64	2011 25 to 34
1	2	3	4	5	6	7	8	9	10	11	12	13	14	15	16	17	18	19
OECD average[1]	14.0	16.5	15.1	18.2	18.8	23.9	19.5	24.6	20.0	25.4	20.8	26.6	21.4 (0.03)	27.7 (0.08)	22.0 (0.04)	28.5 (0.09)	22.8 (0.04)	29.5 (0.08)
Australia	17.7	20.1	19.2	23.9	22.7	29.2	23.8	29.2	24.1	30.6	25.5	31.9	26.8 (0.29)	34.6 (0.62)	26.9 (0.41)	34.2 (0.81)	27.9 (0.25)	35.0 (0.53)
Austria[2]	6.1	6.8	6.8	6.9	9.1	11.6	10.1	12.9	10.4	13.3	10.7	13.5	11.4 (0.10)	15.3 (0.25)	12.0 (0.25)	15.4 (0.49)	12.0 (0.18)	15.7 (0.49)
Belgium	12.0	16.0	12.7	17.8	13.8	19.1	14.1	19.4	14.0	18.2	16.4	22.8	17.5 (0.16)	24.2 (0.38)	17.2 (0.16)	23.3 (0.37)	17.0 (0.16)	23.1 (0.39)
Canada[2,3]	19.1	23.1	20.4	25.1	23.3	28.2	24.0	29.3	24.6	29.5	25.2	29.8	25.4 (0.16)	30.1 (0.34)	26.4 (0.22)	30.7 (0.42)	26.8 (0.23)	31.1 (0.41)
Chile[2,3]	8.2	9.6	9.0	10.7	—	—	—	—	—	—	15.7	22.3	16.4 (0.15)	24.0 (0.30)	16.5 (0.15)	25.4 (0.30)	16.8 (0.15)	26.8 (0.30)
Czech Republic[4]	10.8	10.9	11.1	—	13.1	14.2	13.5	15.2	13.7	15.5	14.5	17.7	15.5 (0.10)	20.2 (0.23)	16.8 (0.10)	22.6 (0.25)	18.2 (0.11)	25.1 (0.26)
Denmark[4]	—	—	21.5	21.7	26.0	30.7	27.1	31.7	25.5	32.0	27.3	34.9	27.1 (0.18)	36.2 (0.60)	26.8 (0.17)	31.4 (0.48)	28.1 (0.18)	33.2 (0.45)
Estonia[2]	—	—	—	—	22.2	24.1	22.2	24.1	22.2	25.2	22.3	23.5	22.7 (0.41)	21.7 (1.59)	21.9 (0.71)	23.8 (1.59)	24.6 (0.40)	26.7 (0.90)
Finland	13.9	15.6	14.8	18.0	18.1	26.6	19.2	29.4	20.9	31.8	21.5	32.9	22.6 (0.13)	36.0 (0.34)	23.5 (0.21)	36.7 (0.52)	24.9 (0.21)	37.8 (0.50)
France[2]	11.0	15.3	11.9	17.5	14.8	22.3	15.6	23.7	15.9	23.8	16.4	23.7	17.3 (0.08)	25.7 (0.20)	17.5 (0.08)	26.0 (0.19)	18.3 (0.07)	27.0 (0.19)
Germany	13.0	12.9	13.5	13.5	14.8	15.1	15.1	15.1	15.6	16.1	16.4	16.4	17.1 (0.06)	18.9 (0.14)	17.0 (0.07)	18.9 (0.16)	16.4 (0.07)	18.3 (0.16)
Greece[3]	13.2	16.6	12.4	14.7	14.5	17.0	15.1	17.4	15.4	17.7	16.8	18.6	16.9 (0.09)	19.3 (0.21)	17.5 (0.29)	20.0 (0.51)	18.3 (0.10)	20.7 (0.23)
Hungary[3]	13.5	13.7	14.1	14.7	16.9	19.1	17.4	20.1	17.7	21.1	18.7	22.9	19.4 (0.10)	24.1 (0.23)	19.6 (0.10)	24.7 (0.24)	20.5 (0.26)	26.5 (0.43)
Iceland[3]	17.8	22.3	18.8	21.1	25.9	32.5	25.6	28.5	26.1	27.9	27.9	27.9	28.8 (0.48)	33.4 (0.96)	28.7 (0.48)	34.0 (0.98)	30.0 (0.49)	36.9 (0.99)
Ireland[2]	10.6	16.1	14.0	19.8	18.4	26.2	19.9	28.2	21.1	29.9	22.2	30.6	20.9 (0.11)	28.8 (0.23)	21.8 (0.11)	29.7 (0.24)	23.1 (0.12)	31.1 (0.26)
Israel	9.3	—	—	11.8	29.8	34.8	29.8	34.8	28.3	28.1	28.8	28.9	29.4 (0.18)	29.5 (0.35)	30.5 (0.18)	31.8 (0.35)	31.0 (0.18)	31.6 (0.35)
Italy[3]	—	10.0	—	11.8	11.7	15.5	12.4	16.7	13.0	18.3	14.0	19.6	14.1 (0.06)	19.9 (0.15)	14.4 (0.07)	20.5 (0.19)	14.6 (0.08)	20.7 (0.20)
Japan	18.3	23.0	19.2	24.3	22.3	27.9	23.5	29.7	23.1	29.0	24.3	30.9	24.6 (0.11)	31.8 (0.27)	25.3 (0.18)	33.0 (0.38)	26.3 (0.17)	34.9 (0.39)
Korea, Republic of	16.9	23.2	17.5	25.0	22.7	31.7	23.5	32.9	24.4	33.9	25.6	34.5	27.1 (0.23)	37.6 (0.47)	27.5 (0.23)	39.0 (0.47)	27.8 (0.23)	38.9 (0.47)
Luxembourg	11.7	13.1	11.4	15.1	17.0	23.8	16.4	22.7	17.7	23.8	20.0	27.9	20.2 (0.39)	24.1 (0.93)	20.8 (0.39)	26.1 (0.96)	25.1 (0.41)	32.2 (0.96)
Mexico	11.9	14.1	13.3	15.3	13.8	17.0	14.4	17.5	14.9	18.4	14.9	18.5	15.9 (0.05)	20.2 (0.10)	16.2 (0.00)	20.6 (0.00)	16.2 (#)	21.3 (0.22)
Netherlands	20.1	22.7	20.9	24.1	28.3	33.8	28.4	34.3	29.1	35.1	29.8	37.5	30.0 (0.09)	37.6 (0.22)	29.8 (0.10)	38.4 (0.23)	29.5 (0.09)	37.6 (0.84)
New Zealand	13.1	15.6	13.9	16.9	19.7	26.2	23.0	28.0	25.3	33.0	25.1	33.6	23.2 (0.41)	30.8 (0.96)	24.3 (0.36)	31.5 (0.83)	23.8 (0.35)	31.4 (0.84)
Norway[2]	25.3	30.6	27.6	35.4	30.3	38.9	30.5	39.8	31.9	40.8	33.6	43.8	34.5 (0.20)	45.5 (0.45)	35.2 (0.20)	46.2 (0.45)	35.8 (0.20)	45.7 (0.45)
Poland[2,4]	11.3	12.3	11.9	15.2	16.9	25.5	17.9	28.0	18.7	30.0	19.6	32.1	21.2 (0.12)	35.4 (0.29)	22.9 (0.09)	37.4 (0.21)	23.7 (0.09)	39.2 (0.21)
Portugal[6]	7.1	9.3	6.6	10.3	12.8	19.1	13.5	20.0	13.7	21.4	14.3	23.2	14.7 (0.12)	23.3 (0.32)	15.4 (0.51)	24.8 (1.02)	17.5 (0.13)	26.9 (0.35)
Slovak Republic	—	—	10.3	11.2	12.8	15.4	13.3	15.7	13.3	16.8	14.0	17.8	15.0 (0.15)	19.7 (0.34)	16.6 (0.16)	23.5 (0.28)	17.5 (0.31)	24.4 (0.85)
Slovenia	—	—	—	—	10.6	15.2	10.6	15.2	11.7	17.6	11.8	18.4	12.6 (0.17)	18.7 (0.42)	13.1 (0.17)	19.2 (0.43)	13.9 (0.18)	21.2 (0.46)
Spain	14.8	22.1	16.9	23.9	19.9	27.0	19.8	26.0	20.0	26.0	20.0	23.4	20.1 (0.07)	25.0 (0.26)	21.5 (0.07)	26.9 (0.15)	22.3 (0.24)	26.7 (0.54)
Sweden	14.5	16.6	15.9	19.7	20.6	29.6	21.7	29.9	22.7	30.9	23.6	31.5	24.3 (0.11)	33.9 (0.26)	25.4 (0.10)	34.0 (0.22)	26.2 (0.10)	34.2 (0.22)
Switzerland	14.5	16.6	15.8	15.9	19.0	21.9	19.9	23.2	21.3	25.6	23.3	28.8	24.7 (0.24)	30.5 (0.56)	24.3 (0.15)	30.6 (0.37)	24.5 (0.14)	30.3 (0.35)
Turkey[4]	7.1	7.6	8.9	10.2	9.7	11.8	10.4	12.8	10.8	13.6	12.0	15.5	12.7 (0.07)	16.6 (0.13)	13.1 (0.07)	17.4 (0.13)	14.0 (0.07)	18.9 (0.14)
United Kingdom	16.6	18.8	18.0	21.0	20.8	26.9	21.7	28.6	22.7	29.4	23.6	30.7	26.9 (0.09)	36.3 (0.45)	28.0 (0.19)	37.9 (0.45)	29.6 (0.10)	39.3 (0.22)
United States	27.5	28.7	28.3	29.9	29.6	30.3	29.9	30.3	30.9	31.0	31.5	32.3	31.4 (0.16)	32.1 (0.32)	31.7 (0.22)	32.8 (0.36)	32.2 (0.22)	33.0 (0.45)
Other reporting countries																		
Brazil[2,4]	7.5	—	7.6	—	—	—	—	—	9.6	10.0	10.8	11.0	10.9 (0.07)	11.6 (0.12)	— (†)	— (†)	11.6 (0.07)	12.7 (0.12)
Russian Federation[7]	—	—	20.8	21.3	—	—	—	—	—	—	—	—	— (†)	— (†)	— (†)	— (†)	27.1 (†)	34.1 (†)

—Not available.
†Not applicable.
#Rounds to zero.

[1]Refers to the mean of the data values for all reporting Organization for Economic Cooperation and Development (OECD) countries, to which each country reporting data contributes equally. The average includes all current OECD countries for which a given year's data are available, even if they were not members of OECD in that year.
[2]Data from 1998 reported for 1999.
[3]Data from 2000 reported for 2001.
[4]Data include vocational degrees.
[5]Data for 1999 and 2001 include vocational degrees.
[6]Data for 2005 to 2011 include vocational degrees.
[7]Data from 2002 are reported for 2001.

NOTE: Data in this table refer to degrees classified as International Standard Classification of Education (ISCED) level 5A (first and second award) and as level 6. ISCED 5A, first award, corresponds to the bachelor's degree in the United States; ISCED 5A, second award, corresponds to master's and first-professional degrees in the United States; and ISCED 6 corresponds to doctor's degrees. Standard errors are not available for years prior to 2009.
SOURCE: Organization for Economic Cooperation and Development (OECD), *Education at a Glance*, 2001 through 2013. (This table was prepared July 2013.)

Percentage of the population 25 to 64 years old who attained a postsecondary vocational degree, by age group and country: Selected years, 1999 through 2011

[Standard errors appear in parentheses]

Country	1999 Total, 25 to 64 yrs	1999 25 to 34 yrs	2001 Total, 25 to 64 yrs	2001 25 to 34 yrs	2005 Total, 25 to 64 yrs	2005 25 to 34 yrs	2006 Total, 25 to 64 yrs	2006 25 to 34 yrs	2007 Total, 25 to 64 yrs	2007 25 to 34 yrs	2008 Total, 25 to 64 yrs	2008 25 to 34 yrs	2009 Total, 25 to 64 yrs	2009 25 to 34 yrs	2010 Total, 25 to 64 yrs	2010 25 to 34 yrs	2011 Total, 25 to 64 yrs	2011 25 to 34 yrs
1	2	3	4	5	6	7	8	9	10	11	12	13	14	15	16	17	18	19
OECD average[1]	8.4	10.5	8.9	10.8	8.6	9.6	9.0	10.0	9.4	10.1	9.7	10.4	10.4 (0.03)	11.0 (0.07)	10.2 (0.03)	10.9 (0.07)	9.9 (0.03)	10.3 (0.06)
Australia	9.0	8.8	9.7	9.7	9.0	8.9	9.2	9.6	9.6	10.2	10.1	9.8	10.1 (0.20)	10.2 (0.39)	10.7 (0.29)	10.2 (0.52)	10.4 (0.17)	9.6 (0.33)
Austria[2]	4.7	5.8	7.3	7.4	8.7	8.1	7.5	6.3	7.2	5.6	7.4	5.9	7.6 (0.08)	5.8 (0.16)	7.3 (0.19)	5.4 (0.29)	7.3 (0.18)	5.5 (0.36)
Belgium	13.9	17.9	14.9	19.7	17.3	21.5	17.7	22.5	18.1	23.1	15.9	19.5	15.9 (0.15)	18.3 (0.34)	17.8 (0.16)	20.5 (0.36)	17.6 (0.16)	19.3 (0.36)
Canada	20.2	23.7	21.2	25.4	22.8	25.6	22.9	25.5	23.7	26.3	23.6	26.1	24.1 (0.16)	26.0 (0.32)	24.2 (0.17)	25.8 (0.38)	24.6 (0.16)	25.6 (0.33)
Chile[2,3,4]	0.9	1.4	1.0	1.6	2.8	4.1	—	—	—	—	8.5	11.5	8.0 (0.11)	11.0 (0.22)	10.3 (0.13)	13.1 (0.23)	12.1 (0.13)	14.5 (0.23)
Denmark	—	—	5.3	5.8	7.6	9.1	7.6	9.1	6.7	8.1	7.0	8.2	7.2 (0.11)	8.5 (0.35)	6.3 (0.10)	6.2 (0.25)	5.6 (0.09)	5.4 (0.22)
Estonia	—	—	—	—	11.1	8.7	11.1	8.7	11.1	9.4	12.0	12.3	13.2 (0.33)	14.8 (0.75)	13.3 (0.55)	14.0 (1.24)	12.1 (0.30)	12.3 (0.67)
Finland	17.4	21.8	17.5	20.2	16.6	17.0	15.9	17.7	15.4	17.5	15.0	16.9	14.7 (0.11)	17.5 (0.13)	14.7 (0.18)	16.9 (0.16)	14.4 (0.17)	16.0 (0.13)
France	10.5	15.6	11.2	16.7	10.0	17.0	10.6	17.7	10.9	17.7	11.1	16.9	11.6 (0.07)	16.9 (0.18)	11.5 (0.06)	16.9 (0.16)	11.5 (0.06)	16.0 (0.13)
Germany	9.9	8.6	9.7	8.2	9.7	7.4	8.9	6.8	8.7	6.5	9.0	6.5	9.3 (0.05)	6.8 (0.09)	9.6 (0.05)	7.2 (0.10)	11.2 (0.06)	9.4 (0.11)
Greece	5.5	8.6	5.4	7.4	6.7	8.4	7.0	9.0	7.4	9.4	6.6	9.6	6.7 (0.06)	10.1 (0.16)	7.2 (0.16)	10.9 (0.34)	7.7 (0.07)	11.8 (0.18)
Hungary	—	—	—	—	0.2	0.5	0.3	0.6	0.5	0.9	#	1.0	# (†)	1.0 (#)	0.6 (0.02)	1.4 (0.06)	0.6 (0.04)	1.6 (0.11)
Iceland	4.6	5.3	6.0	5.5	4.7	3.3	3.9	3.0	3.7	3.2	3.4	2.2	3.9 (0.21)	2.5 (0.31)	3.8 (0.20)	2.2 (0.30)	3.9 (0.20)	2.5 (0.32)
Ireland[2]	10.5	13.4	21.6	28.1	10.6	14.4	10.9	14.0	11.1	14.0	11.7	14.5	14.9 (0.10)	18.7 (0.20)	15.6 (0.10)	18.4 (0.20)	14.7 (0.10)	16.1 (0.20)
Israel	—	—	—	—	16.0	15.1	16.0	15.1	15.2	13.4	15.1	13.4	15.5 (0.14)	13.4 (0.26)	15.0 (0.14)	12.4 (0.25)	15.4 (0.14)	13.4 (0.25)
Italy	—	—	—	—	0.5	0.6	0.5	0.6	0.5	0.6	#	#	# (†)	# (†)	# (†)	# (†)	0.3 (0.01)	0.2 (0.02)
Japan	13.4	22.1	23.4	—	17.7	25.3	17.5	24.4	17.9	24.6	18.5	24.1	19.1 (0.10)	23.9 (0.25)	19.5 (0.16)	23.7 (0.34)	20.1 (0.15)	23.8 (0.35)
Korea, Republic of	5.8	11.9	6.7	14.5	8.9	19.3	9.5	20.1	10.2	21.6	10.9	23.3	11.6 (0.16)	25.5 (0.42)	12.2 (0.17)	26.0 (0.43)	12.6 (0.17)	24.9 (0.43)
Luxembourg	6.6	8.1	6.7	8.3	9.6	13.2	7.6	10.8	8.8	11.9	7.7	10.8	14.6 (0.34)	20.4 (0.87)	14.7 (0.34)	18.1 (0.84)	12.0 (0.31)	14.5 (0.72)
Mexico	1.3	2.2	1.7	2.7	1.1	1.2	1.0	1.1	1.0	1.1	1.1	1.2	1.1 (0.01)	1.2 (0.03)	1.1 (#)	1.3 (#)	1.1 (#)	1.2 (#)
Netherlands	2.5	2.4	2.3	2.4	1.8	1.6	1.8	1.7	1.7	1.6	2.4	2.2	2.8 (0.03)	2.5 (0.07)	2.5 (0.03)	2.4 (0.07)	2.5 (0.03)	2.2 (0.07)
New Zealand	13.9	10.4	15.3	11.6	7.4	4.6	15.3	13.8	15.7	14.3	14.9	13.9	16.9 (0.36)	15.9 (0.76)	16.4 (0.31)	14.9 (0.64)	15.5 (0.30)	14.6 (0.64)
Norway[2]	2.0	2.2	2.6	2.6	2.4	1.9	2.4	1.7	2.4	1.9	2.4	1.8	2.2 (0.06)	1.4 (0.11)	2.1 (0.06)	1.0 (0.09)	2.2 (0.06)	1.1 (0.09)
Portugal	2.7	3.0	2.4	3.1	0.8	0.9	0.9	0.9	0.7	0.7	0.8	0.6	0.8 (0.04)	0.9 (0.08)	0.7 (0.04)	0.6 (0.05)	†	†
Slovak Republic	—	—	0.6	0.6	0.8	0.9	0.9	0.9	0.7	0.7	0.8	0.6	0.8 (0.04)	0.9 (0.08)	0.7 (0.04)	0.6 (0.05)	1.3 (0.09)	1.3 (0.22)
Slovenia	—	—	—	—	9.6	9.5	9.6	9.5	10.6	12.4	10.8	11.7	10.8 (0.16)	11.7 (0.35)	10.6 (0.16)	12.2 (0.36)	11.2 (0.17)	12.6 (0.37)
Spain	6.2	11.4	6.7	11.6	8.3	12.8	8.7	13.2	9.0	13.0	9.2	13.0	9.5 (0.05)	13.2 (0.11)	9.2 (0.05)	12.2 (0.11)	9.3 (0.17)	12.4 (0.41)
Sweden	15.6	20.7	14.7	17.1	9.1	8.9	8.8	8.5	8.7	8.5	8.6	8.4	8.7 (0.07)	8.5 (0.15)	8.8 (0.06)	8.2 (0.13)	9.0 (0.07)	8.6 (0.13)
Switzerland	9.1	9.3	9.6	9.7	9.7	9.1	9.9	9.0	10.0	9.5	10.4	9.7	10.3 (0.17)	9.4 (0.36)	10.8 (0.11)	8.2 (0.13)	10.7 (0.10)	8.6 (0.13)
United Kingdom	8.2	8.4	8.0	9.0	8.8	8.1	8.7	8.2	9.1	7.7	9.0	7.7	10.0 (0.06)	8.5 (0.12)	10.2 (0.13)	8.1 (0.25)	9.8 (0.06)	7.6 (0.12)
United States	8.3	8.7	9.0	9.2	9.4	9.0	9.6	9.3	9.4	9.3	9.6	9.3	9.8 (0.08)	8.9 (0.15)	10.0 (0.13)	9.5 (0.22)	10.3 (0.11)	10.1 (0.24)
Other reporting countries																		
Russian Federation[5]	—	—	33.5	34.2	—	—	—	—	—	—	—	—	— (†)	— (†)	26.4 (†)	— (†)	22.4 (†)	— (†)

—Not available.
†Not applicable.
#Rounds to zero.

[1]Refers to the mean of the data values for all reporting Organization for Economic Cooperation and Development (OECD) countries, to which each country reporting data contributes equally. The average includes all current OECD countries for which a given year's data are available, even if they were not members of OECD in that year.
[2]Data from 1998 reported for 1999.
[3]Data from 2000 reported for 2001.
[4]Data from 2004 reported for 2005.
[5]Data from 2002 reported for 2001.

NOTE: Data in this table refer to degrees classified as International Standard Classification of Education (ISCED) level 5B. ISCED level 5B corresponds to the associate's degree in the United States. Data for the Czech Republic, Poland, and Turkey are not shown because these countries are not able to separate tertiary degrees at this level. Standard errors are not available for years prior to 2009.
SOURCE: Organization for Economic Cooperation and Development (OECD), Education at a Glance, 2001 through 2013. (This table was prepared September 2013.)

Number of bachelor's degree recipients per 100 persons at the typical age of graduation, by sex and country: 2005 through 2011

Country	Typical age of graduation, 2011	Total							Male							Female						
		2005	2006	2007	2008	2009	2010	2011	2005	2006	2007	2008	2009	2010	2011	2005	2006	2007	2008	2009	2010	2011
1	2	3	4	5	6	7	8	9	10	11	12	13	14	15	16	17	18	19	20	21	22	23
OECD average[1]	—	34.7	36.2	37.5	39.1	38.9	39.8	39.7	27.5	28.7	30.0	31.0	31.0	31.5	31.8	42.3	44.0	45.3	47.5	47.1	48.5	48.0
Australia	21–22	59.9	59.6	60.7	58.9	58.5	58.6	59.0	47.9	47.4	48.6	47.0	46.9	46.5	47.0	72.5	72.5	73.4	71.4	70.8	71.4	71.8
Austria	22–25	20.4	21.7	22.4	25.8	30.3	30.7	33.7	19.0	20.4	20.8	22.7	25.9	26.3	28.5	21.8	22.9	24.0	29.1	34.7	35.2	39.0
Belgium (Flemish)[2]	21	18.4	19.0	35.4	27.0	—	—	—	17.0	17.9	32.6	24.4	—	—	—	19.8	20.2	38.2	29.6	—	—	—
Canada	22	33.6	39.3	35.2	39.5	38.9	38.6	37.6	29.3	29.1	26.5	29.1	29.3	29.1	28.5	44.3	49.7	44.3	50.6	49.0	48.6	47.2
Chile	23–26	11.5	15.0	14.5	14.7	17.6	18.1	18.5	9.7	13.0	11.9	11.7	13.2	14.9	15.5	13.4	17.0	17.3	17.8	22.1	21.5	21.6
Czech Republic	22–26	26.0	30.7	36.4	39.2	39.7	42.3	42.8	22.6	26.5	31.0	32.2	30.4	31.1	30.8	29.5	35.2	42.1	46.6	49.7	54.4	55.5
Denmark	24–26	52.9	50.3	50.9	50.3	48.3	50.7	50.6	37.2	37.0	38.3	38.3	35.3	37.5	38.3	69.2	63.7	63.9	62.6	61.7	64.3	63.3
Estonia	22–24	28.5	26.4	27.3	23.8	22.9	22.3	23.8	17.6	15.4	17.6	14.9	13.7	14.0	15.4	39.5	37.8	37.3	32.8	32.7	31.6	32.6
Finland[3]	24	53.8	57.3	58.8	79.8	42.3	46.4	50.3	38.8	40.6	41.3	55.3	28.7	33.1	36.4	69.7	74.5	77.4	105.6	56.6	60.3	65.0
France	19–24	—	34.2	33.8	33.9	33.0	—	—	—	30.6	30.2	30.3	29.8	—	—	—	37.9	37.5	37.6	36.3	—	—
Germany	24–27	20.5	21.0	23.2	25.5	28.9	30.4	31.0	20.0	20.0	22.0	24.0	27.4	28.7	29.6	21.1	22.0	24.4	27.0	30.5	32.2	32.5
Greece[2]	23–24	23.9	23.5	21.7	26.6	—	25.4	27.3	16.3	16.1	14.7	18.3	—	17.5	18.6	32.2	31.7	29.4	35.5	30.5	34.0	36.7
Hungary	21–24	41.5	38.2	38.8	37.6	39.0	38.4	32.8	29.0	26.1	26.2	25.2	27.1	25.4	25.0	54.5	51.0	51.8	50.4	51.2	49.1	41.0
Iceland	23–25	56.3	62.8	62.8	55.9	50.7	65.4	46.8	33.6	37.7	38.0	34.1	30.7	40.1	40.0	80.5	89.6	88.0	78.9	72.2	91.3	53.5
Ireland	21	40.7	42.8	44.8	46.0	47.1	52.2	—	33.3	33.4	36.4	36.9	38.5	45.3	—	48.0	52.5	53.4	55.2	55.4	58.9	—
Israel	26–29	32.9	33.4	36.1	36.3	36.4	36.8	38.5	25.7	26.8	29.1	29.6	30.8	30.6	31.8	40.2	40.3	43.1	43.1	42.0	43.1	45.3
Italy	23–25	44.8	42.7	38.7	35.8	34.6	33.6	34.3	37.3	35.1	31.6	28.5	28.5	26.9	27.3	52.7	50.6	46.1	42.3	40.9	40.6	41.6
Japan	21–23	36.9	38.7	38.8	40.6	41.5	41.3	44.8	41.3	42.9	42.9	44.8	46.1	45.4	49.1	32.2	34.3	34.4	36.0	36.7	37.1	40.2
Korea, Republic of	22–26	35.5	41.0	42.9	48.7	50.0	50.7	49.9	34.8	41.0	42.7	48.7	51.0	50.9	49.2	36.2	41.7	43.2	48.5	48.8	50.4	50.7
Mexico	23	15.2	18.1	18.2	17.8	19.0	19.5	20.9	14.5	16.7	16.8	16.2	17.4	17.7	19.3	15.9	19.5	19.7	19.3	20.7	21.2	22.4
Netherlands	23	47.2	49.2	47.8	46.0	45.6	44.7	45.3	40.2	42.9	41.7	39.8	39.4	38.6	38.5	54.3	55.7	54.1	52.3	51.9	51.0	52.2
New Zealand	21–23	49.0	53.5	53.8	50.0	50.7	47.3	51.0	36.6	40.6	41.6	37.6	38.9	36.7	37.6	62.0	67.0	66.0	63.0	63.1	58.6	65.1
Norway	22–25	42.1	45.1	45.0	46.1	44.3	46.1	46.1	28.8	31.9	31.8	33.9	32.0	33.7	33.4	55.8	58.8	58.7	58.8	57.3	58.8	59.3
Poland	22	45.0	44.8	46.6	48.2	49.4	56.9	60.6	32.8	32.9	34.4	35.0	35.9	40.5	42.9	57.6	57.1	59.2	61.9	63.3	73.8	79.1
Portugal	22	33.7	34.9	46.0	50.4	44.3	44.6	42.9	21.7	22.7	34.7	40.3	35.0	34.5	34.2	46.0	47.4	57.4	60.9	53.1	55.2	52.1
Slovak Republic	21–24	30.1	33.7	37.9	57.6	61.7	50.9	48.6	25.6	21.6	26.6	37.6	41.8	34.7	33.9	34.8	41.8	49.6	77.3	81.5	67.3	63.6
Slovenia	23–25	21.6	21.6	21.1	22.6	27.9	34.7	38.1	14.3	14.2	13.9	14.4	17.2	21.7	25.2	29.4	29.3	29.0	31.7	39.6	49.2	52.1
Spain	20–23	35.0	35.3	34.7	35.5	37.4	39.5	45.1	27.1	27.0	26.6	27.3	28.8	30.7	35.7	43.3	43.8	43.3	44.2	46.4	48.5	54.9
Sweden	25	44.0	43.3	42.2	40.9	38.1	35.7	38.5	30.8	29.8	29.1	27.9	25.8	23.6	25.0	57.6	57.2	55.8	54.7	51.0	48.6	52.7
Switzerland	24–26	25.0	27.0	28.9	30.6	29.2	28.8	28.0	26.1	26.8	28.7	29.2	27.0	26.7	25.4	23.9	27.1	29.2	32.0	31.5	31.0	30.7
Turkey	23–24	11.3	15.4	17.0	19.5	20.8	23.1	22.7	11.8	16.3	17.9	20.6	22.4	24.9	23.9	10.7	14.5	15.9	18.4	19.2	21.2	21.4
United Kingdom	20–24	39.8	39.0	39.0	40.2	39.9	41.9	43.4	34.1	33.0	32.9	33.5	33.8	35.6	36.6	45.7	45.2	45.4	47.2	46.3	48.6	50.6
United States	21	34.2	35.5	36.5	37.3	37.8	38.2	38.8	28.1	29.1	30.1	31.0	31.4	31.8	32.4	40.7	42.4	43.4	43.9	44.5	45.0	45.4
Other reporting countries																						
Brazil	22	17.5	21.3	22.7	25.6	24.9	23.1	25.9	13.3	16.2	18.4	19.9	17.9	16.9	19.0	21.6	26.4	27.0	31.3	32.0	29.4	32.8
Russian Federation	21–22	45.9	43.7	48.6	52.7	51.8	55.1	58.6	—	—	—	—	—	—	—	—	—	—	—	—	—	—

—Not available.

[1]Refers to the mean of the data values for all reporting Organization for Economic Cooperation and Development (OECD) countries, to which each country reporting data contributes equally. The average includes all current OECD countries for which a given year's data are available, even if they were not members of OECD in that year.

[2]Reference year for typical age of graduation is 2008.

[3]Structural changes in the Finnish higher education system accounted for much of the increase in Finnish degree recipients in 2008, as well as the decrease in 2009. Students had a strong incentive to complete their degrees in 2008. Students who did not complete their degrees in 2008 may have had to spend extra time or take additional courses in order to meet new requirements that went into effect in 2009.

NOTE: Data in this table refer to degrees classified by OECD as International Standard Classification of Education (ISCED) level 5A, first award. This level corresponds to the bachelor's degree in the United States. The recipients-per-100-persons ratio relates the number of people of all ages earning bachelor's degrees in a particular year to the number of people in the population at the typical minimum age of graduation. In countries where there are two types of first awards (corresponding with different typical ages of graduation), the recipients-per-100-persons ratio is the sum of the two different award types. The typical age is based on full-time attendance and normal progression through the education system (without repeating coursework, taking time off, etc.); this age varies across countries because of differences in their education systems and differences in program duration. This age is presented for the most recent year of data and may differ from previous years; please see previously published volumes of the Digest of Education Statistics for the typical age of graduation in previous years. Data for Luxembourg are not shown because students generally attend no more than 1 year of higher education in Luxembourg and must complete their degrees in other countries.

SOURCE: Organization for Economic Cooperation and Development (OECD), Education at a Glance, 2006 through 2013; and Online Education Database, retrieved August 24, 2013, from http://stats.oecd.org/Index.aspx. (This table was prepared September 2013.)

Percentage of bachelor's and higher level degrees awarded to women, by field of study and country: 2011

Country	All fields[1]	Education	Humanities and arts	Health and welfare	Social sciences, business, and law	Personal, transport, environmental protection, and security services	Engineering, manufacturing, and construction	Sciences, mathematics, and computer science					Agriculture
								Total	Life sciences	Physical sciences	Mathematics and statistics	Computer science	
1	2	3	4	5	6	7	8	9	10	11	12	13	14
OECD average[2]	58.0	77.1	66.0	74.8	57.6	52.9	27.1	41.3	63.7	43.2	45.0	19.4	54.2
Australia[3]	56.6	74.7	63.8	74.7	54.3	54.4	24.6	36.6	54.2	47.3	39.1	19.8	59.2
Austria	53.7	79.2	68.0	68.0	56.3	42.6	25.0	35.9	70.2	32.0	35.8	15.2	63.4
Belgium	55.0	75.3	65.4	66.5	58.4	41.1	25.7	35.9	52.3	33.9	44.1	9.9	57.5
Canada[3]	59.9	76.7	65.0	82.5	57.7	60.9	23.1	48.6	61.5	44.2	41.1	16.9	58.9
Chile	56.9	71.9	59.5	69.7	51.6	49.0	26.2	31.9	55.4	40.3	39.0	15.5	47.5
Czech Republic	61.2	82.0	71.2	79.8	68.0	46.5	26.6	39.4	71.5	49.8	52.1	12.2	61.0
Denmark	59.2	74.4	65.0	80.7	53.5	23.2	32.4	38.7	63.0	39.9	43.2	25.0	71.6
Estonia	66.5	91.8	76.6	86.2	70.1	64.0	35.1	49.3	72.9	48.3	74.6	27.4	54.5
Finland	61.3	81.2	73.7	85.3	65.3	68.2	22.4	44.7	76.0	46.9	43.8	27.5	60.1
France[3]	54.5	77.1	71.3	61.3	60.7	43.7	30.4	37.6	62.2	37.4	36.7	16.8	56.1
Germany	54.5	72.6	72.8	69.1	53.8	53.5	22.1	43.8	67.2	42.0	59.4	15.4	53.7
Greece	—	—	—	—	—	—	—	—	—	—	—	—	—
Hungary	62.3	80.7	70.2	75.5	67.7	60.6	23.2	36.3	63.0	40.8	40.2	16.3	49.2
Iceland[3]	67.0	83.8	68.8	87.6	59.0	69.8	40.3	47.9	73.5	43.4	23.1	18.8	63.2
Ireland	57.2	76.2	61.5	80.7	54.1	51.5	20.7	42.4	62.3	41.3	30.4	24.5	43.5
Israel	58.1	82.3	61.5	77.7	55.8	81.2	27.3	44.1	64.0	40.0	38.6	25.5	54.1
Italy	60.5	87.6	73.6	67.6	58.5	65.7	33.0	53.9	71.1	40.9	54.9	23.5	47.3
Japan	41.9	59.5	68.9	56.8	35.4	90.9	11.2	25.7	—	43.7	45.6	—	39.3
Korea, Republic of	47.3	70.6	66.8	65.3	44.2	36.2	23.8	40.0	49.3	45.6	54.7	21.9	40.2
Mexico	54.5	72.4	59.1	66.3	59.2	23.1	28.9	46.8	58.9	41.0	43.6	40.2	35.9
Netherlands	56.9	80.0	56.7	74.7	53.6	52.3	20.1	25.3	60.6	26.7	32.2	12.8	56.0
New Zealand	61.7	81.0	64.6	78.3	58.1	54.6	31.1	45.0	60.3	46.9	46.9	22.2	58.5
Norway	61.0	75.1	59.6	83.5	57.4	45.0	26.5	33.8	66.2	39.8	34.5	13.2	55.9
Poland	65.9	81.6	76.2	75.9	68.9	55.6	33.9	44.8	72.5	67.4	64.0	15.6	55.5
Portugal	60.4	81.5	60.3	78.9	62.4	49.5	31.2	55.1	71.2	49.1	59.4	22.4	57.4
Slovak Republic	63.9	77.4	69.8	83.1	69.1	45.9	30.5	42.6	71.4	54.1	56.8	12.1	46.7
Slovenia	64.0	84.0	77.8	76.7	69.1	60.2	33.9	43.0	71.5	43.7	58.3	9.7	60.9
Spain	58.9	74.1	63.5	75.6	60.3	53.5	32.1	43.2	61.6	49.3	47.2	21.5	50.1
Sweden	63.8	79.3	62.3	82.4	60.6	49.3	30.4	43.1	61.9	46.2	36.9	22.4	58.5
Switzerland	51.2	72.3	62.6	69.3	48.6	49.4	19.8	34.8	52.1	32.3	27.6	10.3	67.1
Turkey	46.7	57.2	56.6	59.6	43.2	33.7	29.8	50.5	67.0	47.4	54.6	26.9	33.9
United Kingdom	55.1	75.8	62.1	73.7	54.4	62.2	22.6	37.4	50.4	41.9	41.0	18.9	65.3
United States	57.7	77.8	58.8	79.3	54.3	54.9	21.8	43.3	58.3	38.7	41.6	20.9	50.8
Other reporting countries													
Argentina[3]	59.7	77.1	67.3	68.7	61.1	45.9	33.5	48.6	70.1	52.1	70.6	24.6	40.7
Brazil	62.9	77.2	51.9	76.4	57.5	68.4	30.2	39.5	72.4	46.5	44.1	17.5	41.2
China	48.3	—	—	—	—	—	—	—	—	—	—	—	—
Indonesia[3]	49.3	—	—	—	—	—	—	—	—	—	—	—	—
Saudi Arabia	66.3	66.4	73.7	58.3	63.6	80.2	7.5	73.4	84.9	76.2	80.5	52.8	#
South Africa	58.5	73.5	61.8	72.7	58.3	88.9	27.7	48.6	62.5	46.9	41.3	34.6	48.1

—Not available.
#Rounds to zero.
[1]May contain fields not shown in this table.
[2]Refers to the mean of the data values for all reporting Organization for Economic Cooperation and Development (OECD) countries, to which each country reporting data contributes equally.
[3]Data are for 2010 instead of 2011.
NOTE: Data in this table refer to degrees classified as International Standard Classification of Education (ISCED) level 5A (first and second award) or level 6. ISCED 5A, first award, corresponds to the bachelor's degree in the United States; ISCED 5A, second award, corresponds to master's and first-professional degrees in the United States; and ISCED 6 corresponds to doctor's degrees. Data for Luxembourg are not shown because students generally attend no more than 1 year of higher education in Luxembourg and must complete their degrees in other countries.
SOURCE: Organization for Economic Cooperation and Development (OECD), *Education at a Glance, 2013*. (This table was prepared September 2013.)

Percentage of bachelor's degrees awarded in mathematics, science, and engineering, by field of study and country: Selected years, 1990 through 2010

Country	All mathematics, science, and engineering degrees[1]							Natural sciences[2]							Mathematics and computer science[3]							Engineering						
	1990	1995	2000	2005	2008	2009	2010	1990	1995	2000	2005	2008	2009	2010	1990	1995	2000	2005	2008	2009	2010	1990	1995	2000	2005	2008	2009	2010
1	2	3	4	5	6	7	8	9	10	11	12	13	14	15	16	17	18	19	20	21	22	23	24	25	26	27	28	29
OECD average[4]	—	—	**22.7**	**22.7**	**21.9**	**21.0**	**21.0**	—	—	**5.7**	**4.8**	**4.7**	**4.6**	**4.6**	—	—	**4.1**	**5.3**	**4.8**	**4.2**	**4.1**	—	—	**13.6**	**12.8**	**12.4**	**12.3**	**12.6**
Australia	—	19.3	21.1	21.1	19.2	18.2	17.0	—	9.9	7.6	5.9	6.4	6.3	5.9	—	3.8	5.1	8.2	5.7	4.8	4.2	—	5.6	8.5	7.0	7.0	7.1	6.9
Austria	19.6	21.1	25.7	26.8	25.6	24.9	25.1	—	6.0	5.0	5.4	4.7	5.0	5.7	5.2	5.3	3.4	7.2	6.9	6.8	5.4	—	9.9	17.3	14.2	13.9	13.1	14.0
Belgium	—	—	23.6	24.7	21.3	19.3	20.0	—	—	6.4	5.7	3.8	4.3	3.7	—	—	2.3	5.2	2.5	1.7	1.7	—	—	14.9	13.8	15.0	13.3	14.0
Canada	16.4	16.7	20.0	20.7	20.0	20.3	19.9	—	6.5	8.1	6.5	9.4	9.3	9.1	4.2	3.8	4.3	5.9	3.6	3.4	3.4	6.2	6.4	7.6	8.2	7.5	7.6	7.4
Chile	—	—	22.9	22.9	20.0	18.9	18.2	6.0	—	—	3.2	2.0	1.5	1.5	—	—	4.3	2.6	2.3	2.6	2.2	—	—	—	17.2	15.6	14.8	14.5
Czech Republic	(5)	—	29.5	26.7	29.1	24.0	21.7	(5)	—	4.2	3.9	4.6	4.1	4.1	(5)	—	8.4	3.8	5.5	5.5	5.1	(5)	—	16.9	19.0	18.9	14.4	12.4
Denmark	—	—	10.5	16.3	18.7	17.5	16.4	4.4	2.5	6.8	2.4	2.7	3.0	3.1	—	—	3.1	3.1	2.7	2.8	3.1	21.7	17.0	—	10.8	13.3	11.7	10.2
Estonia	(5)	—	32.2	23.8	21.8	20.1	21.1	(5)	—	—	6.3	5.6	4.6	4.9	(5)	—	12.6	6.2	6.0	5.1	5.3	(5)	—	—	11.3	10.2	10.4	11.0
Finland	33.5	37.2	32.2	30.0	26.6	25.3	27.4	—	4.0	3.9	2.7	5.0	2.5	2.7	5.9	6.9	3.3	5.6	6.4	4.1	4.4	23.4	26.3	24.9	21.7	15.1	18.7	20.3
France	—	—	30.1	26.0	26.1	26.1	21.6	—	—	12.2	6.5	6.3	6.0	5.7	—	—	5.5	5.5	5.5	5.8	4.4	—	—	12.4	14.0	14.3	14.4	11.6
Germany	31.3	31.6	31.7	31.3	28.2	28.2	29.0	7.2	6.7	6.4	6.3	7.6	7.8	8.1	3.5	5.2	4.9	8.1	8.2	8.0	7.6	20.5	19.7	20.3	16.9	12.4	12.4	13.3
Greece	—	—	—	25.9	23.8	21.1	26.1	—	—	—	8.3	5.3	2.8	5.9	—	—	—	8.4	7.4	8.0	7.4	—	—	—	9.2	11.2	9.7	12.8
Hungary	—	—	12.6	11.0	15.1	17.1	18.9	—	—	1.1	1.2	1.4	2.8	3.7	—	—	1.2	2.4	5.3	4.5	4.2	—	—	10.4	7.4	8.4	9.7	10.9
Iceland	—	16.8	16.5	14.1	14.9	15.2	16.6	—	—	6.0	5.0	3.5	3.4	3.5	—	—	4.0	3.5	5.3	4.5	3.0	—	—	6.5	5.5	8.5	8.7	10.1
Ireland	34.1	32.3	29.3	17.7	22.8	19.4	21.6	14.1	16.9	11.5	3.5	—	5.9	5.7	6.3	—	7.2	4.4	—	3.5	4.4	14.1	10.7	10.6	9.9	9.5	9.9	11.6
Israel	—	—	19.0	26.7	21.0	21.3	21.0	—	—	3.1	5.1	5.2	5.0	4.6	—	—	6.8	7.5	4.1	4.2	4.5	—	—	9.1	14.1	11.7	12.1	11.9
Italy	19.7	19.5	27.5	23.9	22.0	22.6	22.9	7.6	6.8	5.9	4.8	4.8	5.0	5.2	3.2	3.8	3.2	2.2	2.1	2.2	2.3	8.3	8.9	18.4	16.9	15.1	15.4	15.5
Japan	—	—	22.3	23.0	21.8	19.5	16.1	2.4	3.4	—	5.2	4.8	5.0	5.1	3.9	3.8	—	2.2	2.1	2.2	2.3	7.6	19.3	18.9	17.4	16.6	16.3	16.1
Korea, Republic of	15.0	—	36.9	37.0	35.1	34.7	34.4	—	—	6.3	2.6	2.8	2.8	2.7	—	—	4.3	9.3	8.3	7.9	7.8	—	19.3	26.3	26.3	24.5	24.0	23.9
Mexico	—	—	23.0	27.3	26.8	25.9	25.6	—	—	2.2	2.6	2.8	2.8	2.7	—	—	6.7	9.3	8.3	7.4	3.7	—	—	14.1	15.3	15.7	15.6	19.2
Netherlands	21.1	—	16.2	14.9	13.7	13.5	13.4	7.1	—	3.2	2.5	1.2	1.2	1.3	1.6	1.6	1.9	4.6	4.8	4.6	4.4	12.4	—	11.1	7.7	7.7	7.7	7.7
New Zealand	19.5	—	17.8	19.9	20.7	21.1	22.1	8.2	—	11.2	6.7	7.7	8.0	8.3	5.5	—	1.9	7.6	5.7	6.0	6.0	5.8	3.2	4.7	5.6	7.3	7.0	7.7
Norway	12.9	16.8	11.6	13.7	13.4	14.2	15.0	2.1	3.1	0.7	0.8	1.7	1.9	2.1	0.6	0.5	3.4	4.7	3.2	3.0	3.1	10.2	13.2	7.5	8.2	8.5	9.3	9.8
Poland	—	—	16.7	17.7	19.9	19.0	19.2	—	3.1	2.7	2.3	3.8	3.7	3.9	—	—	2.0	5.3	5.0	4.7	4.5	—	—	12.0	10.1	11.1	10.7	10.8
Portugal	15.0	15.0	17.5	25.6	34.2	24.8	22.0	6.7	2.2	1.7	6.0	5.5	3.8	3.5	2.8	2.8	3.6	6.2	8.0	2.4	1.9	6.7	9.9	12.2	13.4	20.7	18.6	16.6
Slovak Republic	(5)	—	21.9	24.6	19.0	18.9	19.7	(5)	—	2.0	3.7	3.3	3.3	3.5	(5)	—	4.6	4.4	4.0	3.8	4.2	(5)	—	15.3	16.5	11.7	11.8	11.9
Slovenia	—	—	—	17.7	16.9	15.8	19.9	—	—	—	4.1	3.0	3.2	3.4	—	—	—	2.0	2.5	2.1	2.7	—	—	—	11.7	11.4	10.6	13.7
Spain	15.0	18.2	22.7	24.1	22.9	24.3	24.0	5.7	4.3	5.3	4.2	3.5	3.3	3.2	2.6	4.5	4.3	5.2	5.5	5.3	5.1	6.7	9.4	13.1	14.7	16.9	15.7	15.7
Sweden	24.0	26.4	27.7	26.9	22.9	22.9	22.1	4.1	3.9	3.7	3.6	3.5	3.7	3.2	4.7	5.5	3.7	4.0	2.6	2.6	2.3	15.2	17.0	20.3	19.2	16.9	16.6	16.5
Switzerland	23.0	22.3	25.1	24.2	20.8	20.4	18.5	—	10.4	6.0	6.9	6.2	6.4	5.7	4.0	3.7	1.8	4.7	3.9	3.0	2.7	8.1	8.3	17.3	12.7	10.7	10.7	10.8
Turkey	20.6	20.9	24.1	22.3	18.0	18.1	15.7	4.6	5.1	7.4	6.1	5.3	5.3	4.2	2.1	2.7	3.6	4.1	3.5	3.6	3.1	13.8	13.1	13.1	12.0	9.2	9.2	8.4
United Kingdom	—	—	28.5	26.0	24.0	24.3	24.3	—	—	12.5	9.2	9.2	9.5	9.3	—	—	5.8	8.3	6.2	6.0	5.9	—	—	10.2	8.4	8.6	8.8	9.1
United States	16.9	—	17.1	16.7	15.8	15.7	16.0	5.1	—	6.6	5.8	6.4	6.4	6.7	4.0	3.3	3.9	4.8	3.4	3.3	3.4	7.8	6.7	6.6	6.2	6.0	5.9	6.0
Other reporting countries																												
Brazil	(5)	—	—	11.4	11.1	11.0	10.1	(5)	—	—	3.2	3.3	2.9	1.8	(5)	—	—	3.5	2.9	2.9	2.5	(5)	—	—	4.8	4.9	5.2	5.7
Russian Federation	—	—	—	—	—	24.3	24.4	—	—	—	—	—	1.5	1.5	—	—	—	—	—	5.2	5.7	—	—	—	—	—	17.6	17.2

—Not available.

[1]Includes life sciences, physical sciences, mathematics/statistics, computer science, and engineering.
[2]Includes life sciences and physical sciences.
[3]Includes mathematics/statistics and computer science.
[4]Refers to the mean of the data values for all reporting Organization for Economic Cooperation and Development (OECD) countries for which each country reporting data contributes equally. The average includes all current OECD countries, to which each year's data are available, even if they were not members of OECD in that year. However, if data were reported for less than 75 percent of the countries that were members of OECD in a given year, the average for that year is omitted.
[5]Country did not exist in its current form in the given year.

NOTE: Data in this table refer to degrees classified as International Standard Classification of Education (ISCED) level 5A, first award. This level corresponds to the bachelor's degree in the United States. Data for Luxembourg are not shown because students generally attend no more than 1 year of higher education in Luxembourg and must complete their degrees in other countries. Detail may not sum to totals because of rounding.
SOURCE: Organization for Economic Cooperation and Development (OECD), Online Education Database, retrieved April 10, 2013, from http://stats.oecd.org/Index.aspx; and unpublished tabulations. (This table was prepared April 2013.)

Percentage of graduate degrees awarded in mathematics, science, and engineering degrees, by field of study and country: Selected years, 1990 through 2010

Country	All mathematics, science, and engineering degrees[1]							Natural sciences[2]							Mathematics and computer science[3]							Engineering						
	1990	1996	2000	2005	2008	2009	2010	1990	1996	2000	2005	2008	2009	2010	1990	1996	2000	2005	2008	2009	2010	1990	1996	2000	2005	2008	2009	2010
1	2	3	4	5	6	7	8	9	10	11	12	13	14	15	16	17	18	19	20	21	22	23	24	25	26	27	28	29
OECD average[4]	—	—	28.5	24.7	23.3	22.6	23.2	—	—	11.1	8.9	7.4	6.9	6.6	—	—	5.4	4.9	5.0	4.2	4.4	—	—	12.7	11.4	11.2	11.7	12.4
Australia	37.7	14.0	15.2	20.0	18.8	18.9	18.8	12.3	5.4	4.0	3.1	3.1	3.0	3.0	—	3.8	4.9	8.7	8.3	7.6	7.1	—	4.7	6.3	8.1	7.5	8.3	8.7
Austria	—	38.8	39.2	38.6	31.8	33.4	31.8	—	17.5	16.7	15.0	7.5	7.6	6.4	4.6	4.7	4.7	6.6	11.3	10.8	9.4	20.8	16.6	17.7	16.9	13.0	14.9	16.0
Belgium	—	—	19.7	18.7	18.0	21.2	22.1	—	—	—	9.3	5.4	5.7	5.3	—	—	—	3.3	3.7	3.2	2.5	—	—	7.0	6.2	8.9	12.3	14.3
Canada	20.0	22.3	22.4	18.8	26.3	26.0	26.0	7.8	7.7	7.4	5.0	9.9	10.1	10.1	3.4	3.5	4.1	4.0	4.3	4.1	4.1	8.8	11.2	10.9	9.8	12.1	11.9	11.9
Chile	—	—	—	8.5	11.4	7.9	10.5	—	—	—	2.2	2.8	2.1	2.8	—	—	—	1.6	2.3	2.2	2.2	—	—	—	4.6	6.3	3.6	5.5
Czech Republic	22.2[5]	—	21.0	26.1	22.2	26.9	29.4	5.8[5]	—	5.3	8.3	5.7	6.5	6.2	[5]	—	7.9	5.6	3.8	3.9	4.2	[5]	—	7.7	12.3	12.7	16.5	19.0
Denmark	—	12.3	27.8	23.4	21.3	23.3	24.5	—	3.1	9.8	7.5	5.9	5.7	5.5	4.8	1.5	2.5	9.2	7.6	7.9	9.0	11.6[5]	7.8	15.4	6.7	7.8	9.7	10.0
Estonia	—	—	28.7	23.9	28.6	27.3	28.0	—	—	11.3	10.0	8.2	8.3	9.3	[5]	4.0	2.4	5.0	7.7	5.7	6.5	10.5[5]	12.7	14.9	8.9	12.6	13.3	12.3
Finland	30.6	28.3	28.7	30.5	31.7	34.3	39.8	14.7	11.6	11.3	11.6	12.5	5.8	5.1	5.4	4.0	2.4	4.1	4.0	3.7	3.7	10.5	—	14.9	14.8	15.2	24.8	30.8
France	—	—	26.4	28.4	28.8	28.0	28.0	—	—	13.5	12.5	10.8	11.0	—	[5]	—	5.6	7.0	6.8	6.7	—	10.5	—	7.3	8.9	11.2	10.3	—
Germany	33.2	38.6	38.1	30.9	33.7	32.2	33.1	23.5	25.5	24.9	14.8	15.1	14.7	14.4	2.3	3.5	3.7	4.8	6.3	6.1	7.3	7.4	9.5	9.5	11.3	12.3	11.4	11.5
Greece	—	—	—	42.8	33.0	32.2	31.9	—	—	—	22.3	6.2	2.8	6.8	—	—	—	5.3	11.0	13.1	13.1	—	—	7.5	15.2	15.7	6.0	11.9
Hungary	—	—	9.9	6.4	8.3	10.0	9.5	—	—	1.7	1.8	2.6	2.8	2.6	—	—	0.7	1.7	1.4	1.2	1.3	—	—	7.5	2.9	4.4	6.0	5.6
Iceland	—	—	35.9	23.0	10.6	12.7	14.0	—	—	19.4	9.5	5.8	4.6	5.8	—	—	#	3.0	1.1	0.9	0.9	—	—	16.5	10.5	3.7	7.2	7.3
Ireland	34.5	23.1	28.1	16.8	19.0	16.3	17.3	19.5	10.9	6.9	4.1	—	5.1	3.4	5.8	3.0	15.2	6.3	—	6.2	7.1	9.3	9.2	6.0	6.4	6.1	5.1	6.8
Israel	—	—	18.1	17.9	18.6	18.4	16.7	—	—	9.2	8.9	9.2	8.8	8.2	—	—	2.8	3.2	3.3	3.2	3.0	—	—	6.1	5.9	6.0	6.3	5.5
Italy	—	—	11.7	15.9	18.6	18.4	16.7	—	—	0.3	3.5	—	—	—	—	—	5.8	3.5	—	—	—	—	—	5.7	8.9	—	—	—
Japan	—	—	54.4	50.9	47.1	46.8	46.4	—	—	9.2	8.9	4.4	4.7	4.7	—	—	5.7	2.0	1.2	1.4	1.6	45.1	44.4	41.9	38.0	34.7	34.7	34.5
Korea, Republic of	48.4	38.3	48.4	43.9	24.1	24.2	24.1	—	—	8.5	9.5	4.4	4.7	4.7	—	—	—	3.2	3.3	2.3	1.5	—	—	34.3	32.4	18.4	18.1	17.8
Mexico	—	—	31.4[6]	14.7	12.1	12.1	12.7	—	—	18.9[6]	3.3	2.9	2.3	3.4	—	—	4.1[6]	3.2	3.3	2.3	1.5	—	—	8.4[6]	8.2	5.9	6.9	7.0
Netherlands	28.9	18.6	—	21.3	14.6	15.1	15.5	17.7	4.4	11.6	7.2	—	—	—	1.5	3.7	1.4	5.2	4.1	4.6	4.1	9.7	10.6	—	11.9	7.6	7.9	8.3
New Zealand	22.6	16.7	20.5	16.6	18.5	20.1	20.2	13.8	12.7	14.9	7.8	—	—	—	4.7	1.1	4.6	5.2	4.1	4.6	4.1	4.0	3.0	7.5	4.2	5.3	5.9	6.9
Norway	33.4	38.3	22.0	25.8	22.2	19.1	19.8	8.0	8.7	14.9	—	—	—	—	2.1	1.9	4.6	11.9	10.8	—	—	23.3	27.7	2.5	6.1	5.3	4.3	6.4
Poland	—	—	—	9.1	11.1	11.5	11.4	—	—	—	3.3	4.4	4.7	4.2	—	—	—	—	—	2.3	2.0	—	—	—	3.5	5.0	6.5	6.5
Portugal	—	—	39.3[6]	33.8	49.2	32.7	31.3	—	—	11.7[6]	12.0	12.2	7.2	7.2	—	—	9.4[6]	10.0	11.2	2.3	2.0	—	—	18.2[6]	11.9	25.8	23.2	22.1
Slovak Republic	[5]	—	38.1	36.8	28.0	25.4	22.5	[5]	—	12.6	10.8	6.3	5.3	4.9	[5]	—	4.7	4.2	2.2	3.7	3.4	[5]	—	20.9	21.8	19.6	16.5	14.2
Slovenia	[5]	—	—	24.2	19.9	18.2	22.9	[5]	—	—	6.4	7.2	6.1	9.5	[5]	—	—	4.2	2.7	2.4	2.5	[5]	—	—	13.6	10.1	9.7	10.9
Spain	26.9	36.0	40.5	37.5[6]	26.6	24.5	23.2	19.7	24.8	23.9[6]	23.8[6]	14.0	12.3	9.7	1.4	4.1	5.4[6]	4.6[6]	3.9	3.5	3.4	5.7	7.1	6.8[6]	9.1[6]	8.7	8.7	10.1
Sweden	48.5	32.3	40.5	23.7	28.1	32.0	40.1	19.4	9.2	14.3	8.0	8.5	8.3	5.5	9.2	5.9	4.0	2.8	4.0	5.2	5.5	19.9	17.1	22.2	12.9	15.6	18.5	25.6
Switzerland	30.2	40.1	42.7	32.0	28.9	29.5	25.2	22.0	25.8	11.7	11.7	12.4	12.5	3.5	1.7	4.1	19.5	3.4	3.1	3.9	2.9	6.5	10.1	11.6	16.9	13.3	13.1	11.8
Turkey	24.0	—	25.7	21.4	18.8	18.3	16.5	7.6	—	7.6	6.7	5.4	5.3	5.0	3.3	—	3.0	3.4	3.1	3.0	2.9	13.2	—	15.2	11.2	10.4	9.9	8.6
United Kingdom	—	—	21.7	20.3	20.3	20.4	21.4	—	—	7.4	5.5	5.5	5.8	5.6	—	—	5.0	5.7	5.2	4.8	5.3	—	—	9.2	9.0	9.7	9.8	10.6
United States	14.5	13.8	13.0	13.5	13.0	13.1	13.0	4.2	4.0	3.4	3.3	3.5	3.4	3.5	3.4	3.2	3.4	3.5	3.2	3.2	3.1	6.9	6.7	6.2	6.7	6.3	6.5	6.4

—Not available.

#Rounds to zero.

[1]Includes life sciences, physical sciences, mathematics/statistics, computer science, and engineering.

[2]Includes life sciences and physical sciences.

[3]Includes mathematics/statistics and computer science.

[4]Refers to the mean of the data values for all reporting Organization for Economic Cooperation and Development (OECD) countries, to which each country reporting data contributes equally. The average includes all current OECD countries in that year. However, if data are reported which a given year's data are available, even if they were not members of OECD in that year. However, if data were reported for less than 75 percent of the countries that were members of OECD in a given year, the average for that year is omitted.

[5]Country did not exist in its current form in the given year.

[6]Only includes doctor's (Ph.D.) degrees.

NOTE: Data in this table refer to degrees classified as International Standard Classification of Education (ISCED) level 5A, second award, and as ISCED 6. ISCED 5A, second award, corresponds to master's and first-professional degrees in the United States, and ISCED 6 corresponds to doctor's degrees. Data for Luxembourg are not shown because students generally attend no more than 1 year of higher education in Luxembourg and must complete their degrees in other countries. Detail may not sum to totals because of rounding.

SOURCE: Organization for Economic Cooperation and Development (OECD), Online Education Database, retrieved April 11, 2013, from http://stats.oecd.org/index.aspx; and unpublished tabulations. (This table was prepared April 2013.)

Employment to population ratios of 25- to 64-year-olds, by sex, highest level of educational attainment, and country: 2011

Country	Total population, 25 to 64 years old				Male				Female			
	All levels of education	Less than high school completion	High school completion	Associate's or higher degree	All levels of education	Less than high school completion	High school completion	Associate's or higher degree	All levels of education	Less than high school completion	High school completion	Associate's or higher degree
1	2	3	4	5	6	7	8	9	10	11	12	13
OECD average[1]	**72.7**	**55.5**	**73.8**	**83.0**	**80.2**	**66.2**	**81.1**	**87.6**	**65.2**	**45.5**	**65.9**	**78.4**
Australia	78.2	65.8	80.7	84.1	86.4	76.6	88.9	90.3	70.2	56.3	70.1	79.1
Austria	75.8	56.2	77.9	86.5	81.6	65.7	81.9	89.9	70.0	50.9	73.6	82.4
Belgium	70.0	47.7	74.0	84.2	76.0	57.9	80.7	86.9	63.9	37.0	66.7	81.8
Canada	75.9	55.0	74.3	81.6	80.0	63.8	79.3	85.0	71.8	44.2	68.2	78.8
Chile	72.1	63.4	72.8	79.4	87.2	83.4	89.2	87.7	57.7	44.9	57.2	71.2
Czech Republic	74.2	42.2	75.3	83.1	83.4	50.8	83.6	91.5	64.8	38.0	66.2	74.4
Denmark	77.5	62.6	79.0	85.8	80.8	70.0	81.5	88.2	74.1	55.3	75.9	83.9
Estonia	73.3	48.4	74.0	80.0	76.5	53.6	78.2	84.6	70.5	40.7	69.2	77.4
Finland	75.4	55.5	74.7	84.3	77.4	60.3	77.3	87.2	73.4	48.9	71.6	82.2
France	71.6	55.7	73.7	83.8	76.4	62.7	78.1	87.2	67.0	49.4	69.0	81.0
Germany	77.5	56.5	77.6	87.9	83.0	66.7	82.1	91.0	72.0	49.2	73.1	84.0
Greece	62.5	52.6	62.6	74.8	74.1	67.5	75.9	79.7	50.8	37.6	49.4	69.9
Hungary	63.8	37.7	66.3	79.3	70.4	46.5	71.8	84.7	57.6	31.5	60.0	75.2
Iceland	82.6	74.4	83.4	88.8	86.0	81.5	86.1	90.3	79.2	68.3	79.2	87.8
Ireland	65.9	45.7	65.1	80.8	71.1	54.2	71.9	84.8	60.8	35.3	58.3	77.6
Israel	72.1	45.6	70.9	82.8	77.8	60.6	76.8	85.9	66.6	28.8	64.5	80.2
Italy	63.7	50.8	71.9	79.0	75.7	67.9	81.3	84.9	51.9	33.1	62.6	74.3
Japan	75.9	—	72.8	79.6	88.4	—	85.2	92.0	63.5	—	60.6	66.9
Korea, Republic of	72.2	65.2	70.8	76.9	85.5	77.7	83.7	89.7	58.6	57.2	57.7	60.5
Luxembourg	73.9	62.0	70.4	85.0	82.4	74.9	79.0	89.8	65.2	50.9	61.8	79.4
Mexico	67.0	62.5	71.2	79.3	87.7	87.2	90.1	87.2	48.7	41.7	55.0	70.5
Netherlands	77.4	62.1	80.0	87.4	83.6	74.4	84.9	89.6	71.1	50.9	75.2	85.0
New Zealand	79.3	68.0	82.1	84.4	86.4	76.5	89.1	90.3	72.7	60.5	72.9	80.0
Norway	82.5	68.0	81.7	90.5	85.3	72.4	85.4	91.9	79.7	63.3	76.9	89.3
Poland	67.5	39.8	65.9	84.7	75.0	49.3	75.0	89.1	60.3	30.8	56.0	81.7
Portugal	71.3	65.9	79.4	83.4	75.9	72.9	81.2	83.5	66.9	58.5	77.7	83.3
Slovak Republic	68.9	30.2	70.2	81.6	76.4	35.4	77.6	87.3	61.5	27.0	62.1	77.0
Slovenia	70.8	46.7	70.6	86.4	74.2	55.5	74.0	87.4	67.3	39.5	66.0	85.7
Spain	64.0	52.1	67.5	78.9	70.6	61.6	74.2	82.1	57.3	41.9	60.8	75.8
Sweden	83.0	65.2	83.5	88.7	85.9	74.5	86.7	89.8	80.0	53.0	79.7	87.8
Switzerland	82.7	68.4	82.5	88.8	89.7	78.7	89.1	93.5	75.6	61.7	76.7	81.9
Turkey	56.3	50.7	61.7	76.1	77.9	75.2	81.7	84.0	31.3	26.1	29.9	64.2
United Kingdom	75.0	55.9	78.2	83.2	81.3	66.1	82.8	87.7	68.9	47.9	72.9	78.9
United States	70.9	51.1	67.1	80.0	75.7	61.0	71.8	84.7	66.1	39.7	62.3	75.8
Other reporting countries												
Brazil	70.2	67.1	70.1	85.3	86.3	83.9	89.3	91.5	55.5	50.4	54.0	80.8
Russian Federation	76.7	49.0	72.8	82.8	81.9	56.6	79.3	88.2	72.2	40.3	64.9	79.1

—Not available.

[1]Refers to the mean of the data values for all reporting OECD countries, to which each country reporting data contributes equally.

NOTE: The "high school completion" columns include International Standard Classification of Education (ISCED) levels 3 and 4, with the exception of ISCED level 3C short programs. (ISCED 3C short programs do not correspond to high school completion in the United States and are included in the "less than high school completion" columns in this table.) ISCED level 5B corresponds to the associate's degree in the United States in this table. Also included in the "associate's or higher degree" columns are the following higher level degrees: ISCED 5A, first award, which corresponds to the bachelor's degree in the United States; ISCED 5A, second award, which corresponds to master's and first-professional degrees in the United States; and ISCED 6, which corresponds to doctor's degrees. For each country, the employment to population ratio of 25- to 64-year-olds is the number of persons in this age group who are employed as a percentage of the total civilian population in this age group.

SOURCE: Organization for Economic Cooperation and Development (OECD), *Education at a Glance, 2013.* (This table was prepared December 2013.)

Public and private direct expenditures on education institutions as a percentage of gross domestic product, by level of education and country: Selected years, 1995 through 2010

Column groups: columns 2–9 = **All institutions** (including preprimary education and subsidies to households, not separately shown); columns 10–17 = **Elementary and secondary institutions**; columns 18–25 = **Higher education institutions**. Within each group, columns = Public direct expenditures (1995, 2000[1], 2005[1], 2008[1], 2009[1]) and Direct expenditures, 2010 (Public[1], Private, Total).

Country (1)	All: 1995 (2)	2000[1] (3)	2005[1] (4)	2008[1] (5)	2009[1] (6)	2010 Pub[1] (7)	2010 Priv (8)	2010 Tot (9)	E/S: 1995 (10)	2000[1] (11)	2005[1] (12)	2008[1] (13)	2009[1] (14)	2010 Pub[1] (15)	2010 Priv (16)	2010 Tot (17)	Higher: 1995 (18)	2000[1] (19)	2005[1] (20)	2008[1] (21)	2009[1] (22)	2010 Pub[1] (23)	2010 Priv (24)	2010 Tot (25)
OECD average[2]	4.9	4.9	5.0	5.1	5.4	5.4	0.9	6.3	3.5	3.4	3.5	3.5	3.7	3.7	0.3	4.0	0.9	1.0	1.0	1.1	1.1	1.1	0.5	1.6
Australia	4.5	4.6	4.3	3.7	4.5	4.6	1.5	6.1	3.2	3.7	3.4	3.0	3.6	3.7	0.6	4.3	1.2	0.8	0.8	0.7	0.7	0.8	0.9	1.6
Austria	5.3	5.4[3]	5.2	5.2	5.7	5.6	0.2	5.8	3.8	3.7[3]	3.5	3.5	3.8	3.5	0.1	3.6	0.9	1.2[3]	1.2	1.2	1.4	1.5	0.1	1.5
Belgium	5.0	5.1	5.8	6.3	5.9	6.4	0.2	6.6	3.4	3.7[3]	4.3	4.3	4.1	4.3	0.1	4.4	0.9	1.2[4]	1.2	1.2	1.4	1.4	0.1	1.4
Canada	5.8	5.2	4.8	6.1	5.0	6.4	0.2	6.8	4.0	3.3	3.3[5,6]	3.6[6]	3.4[6]	—	—	—	1.5	1.6[5]	1.5[5]	2.5[5]	1.5[5]	—	—	—
Chile	—	4.2	3.3	3.7	4.1	4.3	2.6	6.8	—	3.2	2.7	3.0	3.3	2.9	0.8	3.6	—	0.6	0.3	0.3	0.3	0.8	1.6	2.5
Czech Republic	4.8	4.2	4.1	3.9	4.2	4.1	0.6	4.7	3.4	2.8[4]	2.7	2.5	2.6	2.6	0.3	2.8	0.7	0.8[4]	0.8	0.9	1.0	1.0	0.2	1.2
Denmark	6.5	6.4[3]	6.8	6.5	7.5	7.6	0.4	8.0	4.2	4.1[3,7]	4.4[7]	4.2[7]	4.7[7]	4.7[7]	0.1	4.8	1.3	1.5[3,7]	1.6[7]	1.6[7]	1.8[7]	1.8[7]	0.1	1.9[7]
Estonia	—	—	—	5.5	5.9	5.6	0.4	6.0	—	—	—	3.8	4.1	3.9	0.1	4.1	—	—	0.9	1.1	1.3	1.5	0.1	1.6
Finland	6.6	5.5	5.9	5.7	6.3	6.4	0.1	6.5	4.2	3.5	3.5	3.8	4.1	4.1	#	4.1	1.7	1.7	1.7	1.6	1.8	1.6	#	1.6
France	5.8	5.7	5.6	5.5	5.8	5.8	0.5	6.3	4.1	4.0	3.8	3.7	3.8	3.8	0.3	4.1	1.0	1.0	1.1	1.2	1.3	1.3	0.2	1.5
Germany	4.5	4.3[3]	4.2	4.1	4.5	—	—	—	2.9	2.9	2.8	2.6	2.9	—	—	—	1.0	1.0	0.9	1.0	1.1	—	—	—
Greece	3.7	3.7[3]	4.0	—	—	—	—	—	2.8	2.7[3,6]	2.5[6]	—	—	—	—	—	0.8	0.9[3]	1.4	0.9	—	—	—	—
Hungary	4.9	4.4	5.1	4.8	4.8	4.6	—	—	3.3	2.8	3.3	3.0	3.0	2.8	0.1	—	0.8	0.9	0.9	0.9	1.0	0.8	0.1	1.2
Iceland	4.5	5.7[3]	7.2	7.2	7.3	7.0	0.7	7.7	3.4	4.6[3]	5.2[7]	4.9	5.0	4.7	0.2	4.9	0.7	0.8[3]	1.1	1.2	1.2	1.2	#	1.2
Ireland	4.7	4.1	4.3	5.2	6.0	6.0	0.5	6.4	3.3	2.9	3.3	4.0	4.6	4.6	0.2	4.8	0.9	1.2[4]	1.0	1.2	1.4	1.3	0.3	1.6
Israel	—	6.6	6.2	5.9	5.8	5.9	1.5	7.4	—	4.5	4.2	4.0	3.8	4.0	0.3	4.3	—	—	1.0	0.9	0.8	1.0	0.7	1.7
Italy	4.5	4.5	4.3	4.5	4.5	4.3	0.4	4.7	3.2	3.2	3.2	3.2	3.3	3.1	0.1	3.2	0.7	0.7	0.6	0.8	0.8	0.8	0.2	1.0
Japan	3.6	3.5	3.4	3.3	3.6	3.6	1.5	5.1	2.8	2.7	2.6[7]	2.5[7]	2.7	2.8	0.2	3.0	0.4	0.5[7]	0.5[7]	0.5[7]	0.5[7]	0.5[7]	1.0[7]	1.5[7]
Korea, Republic of	3.6	4.3	4.3	4.7	4.9	4.8	2.8	7.6	3.0	3.3	3.4	3.4	3.6	3.4	0.9	4.2	0.3	0.6	0.6	0.6	0.7	0.7	1.9	2.6
Luxembourg	4.3	—	—	—	—	—	—	—	4.2	—	3.7[6]	2.8	3.2	3.4	0.1	3.5	0.1	—	—	—	—	—	—	—
Mexico	4.6	4.7	5.3	4.7	5.0	5.1	1.1	6.2	3.4	3.3	3.7	3.1	3.3	3.4	0.6	4.0	0.8	0.8	0.9	0.9	1.0	1.0	0.4	1.4
Netherlands	4.6	4.3	4.6	4.8	5.3	5.4	0.9	6.3	3.0	3.0	3.3	3.3	3.7	3.7	0.4	4.1	1.1	1.0	1.0	1.1	1.2	1.3	0.5	1.7
New Zealand	5.3	5.8	5.7	5.4	6.1	6.1	1.3	7.3	3.8	4.6	4.0	3.8	4.5	4.5	0.6	5.1	1.1	0.9	0.9	1.1	1.1	1.0	0.5	1.6
Norway	6.8	5.8	5.7	7.3	7.3	7.5	—	—	4.1	3.6	3.8	5.0	4.2	5.1	—	5.1	1.5	1.2	1.3	1.6	1.3	1.6	—	1.7
Poland	5.2	5.2[3]	5.4	5.0	5.0	5.0	0.8	5.8	3.3	3.7[3]	3.7	3.4	3.5	3.4	0.2	3.6	0.8	0.8[3]	1.2	1.0	1.1	1.0	0.4	1.5
Portugal	5.4	5.6[3]	5.3	4.7	5.5	5.4	0.4	5.8	4.1	4.1[3]	3.8	3.4	4.0	3.9	#	3.9	1.0	1.0[3]	0.9	0.9	0.7[7,8]	0.7[8]	0.3[8]	1.1
Slovak Republic	4.6	4.0[3]	3.7	3.5	4.1	4.0	0.7	4.6	—	2.7[3,4,8]	2.9	2.2[8]	2.7[7,8]	2.8	0.3	3.1	—	0.7[3,4,8]	0.7	0.7	1.1	0.7[8]	0.3[8]	0.9[8]
Slovenia	4.8	—	—	4.8	4.9	4.8	0.8	5.9	3.5	3.1	2.7	3.4	3.6	3.0	0.3	3.3	0.8	0.9	1.0	1.0	1.1	1.1	0.3	1.3
Spain	4.6	4.3	4.1	4.5	4.9	4.8	0.8	5.6	3.5	3.1	2.7	2.9	3.1	2.8	0.3	3.0	0.8	0.9	0.9	1.0	1.1	1.1	0.2	1.3
Sweden	6.6	6.3	6.2	6.1	6.6	6.3	0.2	6.5	4.4	4.4	4.2	4.0	4.2	4.0	#	4.0	1.6	1.5[4]	1.5	1.4	1.6	1.6	0.2	1.8
Switzerland	5.5	5.3[3]	5.6	5.3	5.5	5.2	—	—	4.1	3.8	3.9	3.8	3.8	3.6	—	—	1.1	1.2[3]	1.4	1.3	1.4	1.3	—	—
Turkey	2.2	3.4	2.2	—	—	—	—	—	1.4	2.4[3]	—	—	—	—	—	—	0.8	1.0[3]	—	—	—	0.7	#	—
United Kingdom	4.6	4.5	5.0	5.1	5.3	5.9	0.6	6.5	3.8	3.4	3.8	4.2	4.5	4.8	#	4.8	0.7	0.7[3]	0.9	0.6	0.6	0.7	0.6	1.4
United States	5.0	4.6	4.9	5.0	5.3	5.1	2.2	7.3	3.5	3.5[5]	3.6	3.7	3.8	3.7	0.3	4.0	1.1	0.8[5]	1.0	1.0	1.1	1.0	1.8	2.8
Other reporting countries																								
Brazil	3.4	—	4.4	5.3	5.5	5.6	—	—	1.9	—	3.3	4.1	4.3	4.3	0.1	—	0.7	—	0.8	0.8	0.8	0.9	—	—
Russian Federation	—	3.0[3]	3.8	4.1	4.7	4.1	0.8	4.9	—	1.7	1.9	2.0	2.3	2.0	0.1	2.1	—	0.5	0.8	0.9	1.2	1.0	0.6	1.6

—Not available.
#Rounds to zero.

[1]Unless otherwise noted, includes public subsidies to households for payments to education institutions and direct expenditures on education institutions from international sources.
[2]Refers to the mean of the data values for all reporting Organization for Economic Cooperation and Development (OECD) countries, to which each country reporting data contributes equally. The average includes all current OECD countries for which a given year's data are available, even if they were not members of OECD in that year.
[3]Public subsidies to households not included in public expenditures.
[4]Direct expenditures on education institutions from international sources exceed 1.5 percent of all public expenditures.
[5]Postsecondary non-higher-education included in higher education.
[6]Preprimary education (for children ages 3 and older) included in elementary and secondary education.
[7]Postsecondary non-higher-education included in both secondary and higher education.
[8]Occupation-specific education corresponding to that offered at the vocational associate's degree level in the United States is included in secondary education.

NOTE: Public direct expenditures on education include both amounts spent directly by governments to hire educational personnel and to procure other resources, and amounts provided by governments to public or private institutions. Private direct expenditures exclude public subsidies that are used for payments to education institutions. Postsecondary non-higher-education is included in elementary and secondary education unless otherwise noted. All institutions total includes expenditures that could not be reported by level of education. Some data have been revised from previously published figures. Detail may not sum to totals because of rounding.
SOURCE: Organization for Economic Cooperation and Development (OECD), Online Education Database; and Education at a Glance, 2008 through 2013. U.S. Department of Education, National Center for Education Statistics, International Education Indicators: A Time Series Perspective, 1985–1995 (NCES 2000-021). (This table was prepared May 2013.)

Selected statistics on public school libraries/media centers, by level of school: Selected years, 1999–2000 through 2011–12

[Standard errors appear in parentheses]

Selected statistic	1999–2000	2003–04	2007–08 Total	2007–08 Elementary	2007–08 Secondary	2007–08 Combined elem./sec.	2011–12 Total	2011–12 Elementary	2011–12 Secondary	2011–12 Combined elem./sec.
	2	3	4	5	6	7	8	9	10	11
Number of schools with libraries/media centers	77,300 (421)	78,300 (548)	81,900 (634)	59,700 (492)	17,800 (414)	4,400 (239)	81,200 (510)	58,000 (418)	17,100 (357)	6,100 (373)
Average number of staff per library/media center	1.89 (0.018)	1.76 (0.014)	1.72 (0.017)	1.65 (0.019)	2.04 (0.039)	1.42 (0.057)	1.77 (0.017)	1.72 (0.020)	1.93 (0.027)	1.42 (0.056)
Certified library/media specialists	0.81 (0.007)	0.79 (0.009)	0.78 (0.011)	0.73 (0.013)	0.98 (0.019)	0.66 (0.033)	0.90 (0.012)	0.88 (0.014)	0.99 (0.017)	0.88 (0.031)
Full-time	0.65 (0.007)	0.65 (0.009)	0.66 (0.010)	0.61 (0.012)	0.88 (0.018)	0.49 (0.032)	0.71 (0.010)	0.67 (0.012)	0.84 (0.017)	0.69 (0.029)
Part-time	0.16 (0.006)	0.14 (0.007)	0.13 (0.007)	0.13 (0.010)	0.10 (0.009)	0.18 (0.020)	0.20 (0.008)	0.21 (0.010)	0.15 (0.010)	0.19 (0.020)
Other professional staff	0.17 (0.007)	0.19 (0.008)	0.22 (0.010)	0.22 (0.010)	0.21 (0.021)	0.24 (0.027)	0.19 (0.007)	0.18 (0.009)	0.17 (0.014)	0.27 (0.026)
Full-time	0.12 (0.005)	0.13 (0.007)	0.13 (0.008)	0.13 (0.010)	0.14 (0.017)	0.15 (0.022)	0.12 (0.006)	0.11 (0.007)	0.13 (0.013)	0.16 (0.022)
Part-time	0.06 (0.004)	0.05 (0.005)	0.08 (0.007)	0.08 (0.009)	0.07 (0.013)	0.08 (0.017)	0.07 (0.005)	0.07 (0.007)	0.05 (0.005)	0.11 (0.014)
Other paid employees	0.91 (0.014)	0.78 (0.011)	0.72 (0.013)	0.70 (0.016)	0.86 (0.027)	0.51 (0.036)	0.68 (0.011)	0.66 (0.012)	0.76 (0.021)	0.61 (0.040)
Full-time	0.49 (0.008)	0.46 (0.009)	0.43 (0.013)	0.39 (0.016)	0.60 (0.022)	0.27 (0.028)	0.40 (0.008)	0.37 (0.012)	0.52 (0.017)	0.39 (0.031)
Part-time	0.41 (0.014)	0.33 (0.012)	0.29 (0.011)	0.31 (0.014)	0.26 (0.018)	0.24 (0.028)	0.28 (0.009)	0.29 (0.012)	0.24 (0.012)	0.22 (0.027)
Percent of libraries/media centers with certain media equipment										
Automated catalog	72.8 (0.69)	82.7 (0.66)	87.2 (0.71)	87.5 (0.94)	90.6 (1.08)	69.8 (2.88)	88.3 (0.49)	89.1 (0.60)	90.3 (0.78)	74.4 (2.16)
Automated circulation system	74.4 (0.65)	86.9 (0.61)	89.5 (0.68)	89.9 (0.87)	92.6 (0.98)	72.4 (3.15)	90.3 (0.47)	91.7 (0.59)	90.1 (0.75)	77.8 (2.17)
Media retrieval system[1]	— (†)	— (†)	34.9 (1.05)	35.9 (1.33)	35.1 (1.66)	20.6 (2.32)	32.5 (0.76)	33.6 (0.99)	32.3 (0.91)	22.4 (1.92)
Connection to Internet	90.1 (0.57)	95.1 (0.35)	96.7 (0.40)	96.5 (0.51)	98.6 (0.51)	91.6 (1.90)	95.9 (0.34)	96.2 (0.46)	97.3 (0.49)	89.6 (1.82)
Digital video disc (DVD) player/video cassette recorder (VCR)	— (†)	87.8 (0.60)	87.2 (0.77)	86.7 (1.02)	89.6 (1.00)	84.5 (2.20)	83.2 (0.76)	82.8 (0.98)	86.7 (0.76)	77.7 (2.00)
Disability assistance technologies, such as TDD	— (†)	11.9 (0.50)	23.9 (1.05)	23.0 (1.33)	26.4 (1.34)	25.9 (2.76)	31.0 (0.75)	29.9 (0.94)	34.3 (1.02)	31.9 (1.95)
Percent of libraries/media centers with certain services										
Students permitted to check out laptops	— (†)	— (†)	27.5 (1.02)	26.9 (1.27)	29.8 (1.34)	26.1 (2.57)	40.2 (0.69)	39.3 (0.85)	42.4 (1.08)	41.8 (2.67)
Staff permitted to check out laptops	— (†)	— (†)	45.9 (1.07)	45.2 (1.35)	50.1 (1.50)	38.5 (2.85)	54.3 (0.85)	53.9 (0.99)	55.5 (1.23)	54.2 (2.43)
Number of library computer workstations per 100 students	— (†)	2.3 (0.04)	2.6 (0.05)	2.5 (0.07)	2.9 (0.06)	3.0 (0.17)	3.1 (0.05)	2.8 (0.06)	3.6 (0.08)	3.3 (0.23)
Number of holdings per 100 students at the end of the school year[2]										
Books (number of volumes)	1,803 (19.7)	1,891 (45.1)	2,015 (30.5)	2,316 (40.2)	1,432 (36.6)	2,439 (132.3)	2,188 (42.4)	2,570 (58.5)	1,474 (24.7)	2,066 (87.3)
Audio and video materials	59 (0.9)	80 (3.7)	90 (3.8)	93 (5.6)	81 (5.2)	107 (13.3)	81 (2.4)	85 (3.3)	71 (2.9)	97 (8.3)
Number of additions per 100 students during the school year[2]										
Books (number of volumes)	— (†)	99.3 (2.08)	95.3 (2.21)	113.3 (3.26)	62.1 (2.67)	103.4 (7.41)	89.4 (3.47)	104.8 (5.45)	58.9 (2.08)	92.5 (6.54)
Audio and video materials	— (†)	5.1 (0.19)	5.4 (0.49)	5.9 (0.77)	4.5 (0.41)	5.7 (0.84)	4.3 (0.37)	3.8 (0.32)	4.2 (0.70)	8.2 ! (3.28)
Expenditures for library/media materials per pupil[3] in current dollars										
Total[3]	$23.37 (0.438)	$16.24 (0.322)	$16.11 (0.461)	$16.18 (0.591)	$15.90 (0.647)	$17.00 (1.216)	$16.00 (0.691)	$16.48 (1.099)	$14.80 (0.584)	$17.26 (1.215)
Books	9.97 (0.153)	10.99 (0.299)	11.40 (0.291)	11.99 (0.389)	10.26 (0.504)	12.10 (1.094)	10.28 (0.343)	10.73 (0.480)	9.41 (0.526)	10.27 (0.830)
Audio and video materials	1.66 (0.032)	1.14 (0.045)	1.08 (0.055)	1.06 (0.088)	1.11 (0.054)	1.16 (0.152)	0.84 (0.072)	0.80 (0.113)	0.89 (0.062)	0.89 (0.131)
Current serial subscriptions	1.26 (0.016)	1.38 (0.025)	(†)	(†)	(†)	(†)	(†)	(†)	(†)	(†)
Electronic subscriptions	0.81 (0.018)	0.88 (0.033)	(†)	(†)	(†)	(†)	(†)	(†)	(†)	(†)
Expenditures for library/media materials per pupil[3] in constant 2012–13 dollars[4]										
Total[3]	$31.94 (0.599)	$20.19 (0.400)	$17.60 (0.503)	$17.68 (0.645)	$17.38 (0.707)	$18.57 (1.329)	$16.27 (0.703)	$16.76 (1.117)	$15.04 (0.593)	$17.54 (1.235)
Books	13.62 (0.209)	13.66 (0.371)	12.46 (0.319)	13.10 (0.425)	11.22 (0.551)	13.23 (1.196)	10.45 (0.349)	10.91 (0.488)	9.57 (0.534)	10.44 (0.844)
Audio and video materials	2.27 (0.044)	1.42 (0.055)	1.18 (0.061)	1.16 (0.096)	1.21 (0.059)	1.27 (0.166)	0.85 (0.074)	0.81 (0.115)	0.91 (0.063)	0.91 (0.133)
Current serial subscriptions	1.72 (0.022)	1.72 (0.031)	(†)	(†)	(†)	(†)	(†)	(†)	(†)	(†)
Electronic subscriptions	1.11 (0.025)	1.10 (0.041)	(†)	(†)	(†)	(†)	(†)	(†)	(†)	(†)

—Not available.
†Not applicable.
! Interpret data with caution. The coefficient of variation (CV) for this estimate is between 30 percent and 50 percent.
[1]Centralized video distribution equipment with a scheduling and control server that telecasts video to classrooms.
[2]Holdings, additions, and expenditures are from the prior school year, while enrollment counts are from the current school year.
[3]Includes other expenditures not separately shown.
[4]Constant dollars based on the Consumer Price Index, prepared by the Bureau of Labor Statistics, U.S. Department of Labor, adjusted to a school-year basis.
NOTE: Detail may not sum to totals because of rounding.
SOURCE: U.S. Department of Education, National Center for Education Statistics, Schools and Staffing Survey (SASS), "Public School Library Media Center Questionnaire," 1999–2000, 2003–04, 2007–08, and 2011–12; and "Charter School Questionnaire," 1999–2000. (This table was prepared December 2013.)

Libraries & Educational Technology

Selected statistics on public school libraries/media centers, by state: 2011–12

[Standard errors appear in parentheses]

Columns 2–8 fall under the spanning header: **Percent of libraries/media centers offering selected services/equipment**

State	Automated catalog	Automated circulation system	Laptops for student use outside of library/media center	Laptops for staff use outside of library/media center	Media retrieval system[1]	Connection to the Internet	DVD player/VCR	Average number of staff per library/media center[2]	Books (number of volumes) held at end of year per 100 students[3]	Books (number of volumes) acquired during year per 100 students[3]	Total expenditure for materials per student[3]	Number of library computer workstations per 100 students
1	2	3	4	5	6	7	8	9	10	11	12	13
United States	88.3 (0.49)	90.3 (0.47)	40.2 (0.69)	54.3 (0.85)	32.5 (0.76)	95.9 (0.34)	83.2 (0.76)	1.8 (0.02)	2,188 (42.4)	89 (3.5)	$16.00 (0.691)	3.1 (0.05)
Alabama	96.0 (1.59)	98.5 (0.74)	46.7 (4.48)	59.9 (3.98)	29.6 (3.44)	97.2 (1.38)	95.4 (1.47)	1.6 (0.05)	2,114 (117.4)	48 (4.0)	7.31 (0.630)	2.4 (0.13)
Alaska	63.1 (5.91)	58.0 (6.01)	50.6 (5.32)	46.2 (3.49)	10.0! (3.22)	79.7 (6.31)	69.9 (6.51)	1.2 (0.11)	5,077 (351.4)	190 (29.7)	25.19 (3.742)	5.9 (0.66)
Arizona	77.5 (5.11)	78.5 (4.74)	33.0 (4.44)	51.4 (3.89)	35.2 (3.94)	88.7 (3.97)	78.8 (4.58)	1.5 (0.09)	1,988 (97.3)	57 (7.8)	9.60 (1.505)	2.7 (0.15)
Arkansas	97.4 (1.15)	97.4 (1.15)	29.5 (3.73)	48.1 (5.16)	30.6 (4.85)	100.0 (†)	84.2 (2.46)	1.8 (0.05)	1,880 (102.6)	96 (9.5)	16.00 (1.328)	2.7 (0.27)
California	78.5 (3.00)	82.5 (2.27)	20.8 (2.96)	40.7 (4.08)	13.1 (2.55)	93.6 (1.77)	58.9 (4.36)	1.5 (0.05)	2,065 (161.6)	75 (13.4)	10.25 (2.611)	2.2 (0.17)
Colorado	93.2 (3.07)	88.9 (3.73)	52.7 (4.25)	64.5 (4.58)	34.7 (4.91)	98.2 (0.90)	91.1 (2.64)	1.8 (0.10)	2,101 (137.0)	89 (8.4)	11.23 (1.648)	4.3 (0.30)
Connecticut	84.5 (4.76)	84.1 (4.79)	46.5 (7.41)	61.1 (6.05)	21.5 (4.98)	96.9 (2.11)	86.6 (3.83)	2.0 (0.08)	2,405 (105.1)	111 (29.0)	17.01 (1.330)	4.8 (0.46)
Delaware	95.1 (1.69)	97.1 (1.57)	41.6 (5.83)	48.6 (5.83)	24.4 (5.13)	98.2 (1.45)	81.4 (4.88)	2.0 (0.07)	2,835 (752.6)	61 (6.0)	9.41 (0.690)	3.0 (0.25)
District of Columbia	‡ (†)	—	—	—	—	—	—	—	—	—	—	—
Florida	93.9 (2.05)	91.4 (2.67)	40.5 (4.01)	70.2 (4.51)	73.9 (3.17)	97.4 (0.94)	89.6 (2.88)	1.6 (0.05)	1,904 (114.0)	68 (5.9)	10.98 (1.115)	2.6 (0.11)
Georgia	96.3 (1.26)	98.2 (0.78)	51.2 (4.92)	78.7 (3.79)	73.1 (4.13)	99.3 (0.37)	97.6 (1.38)	2.0 (0.06)	1,909 (81.2)	85 (7.8)	13.06 (0.806)	2.3 (0.16)
Hawaii	75.5 (5.06)	85.6 (3.70)	9.9 (2.35)	22.1 (4.21)	24.5 (4.39)	97.4 (1.81)	81.5 (6.08)	1.6 (0.12)	2,378 (179.4)	64 (6.9)	8.45 (0.954)	3.0 (0.22)
Idaho	80.3 (3.31)	81.6 (3.25)	39.4 (4.92)	48.1 (4.94)	15.2 (2.39)	94.9 (2.41)	79.9 (4.00)	2.1 (0.21)	2,453 (206.1)	110 (17.5)	20.31 (3.342)	3.6 (0.27)
Illinois	89.7 (3.52)	88.9 (4.46)	33.2 (4.58)	50.2 (5.73)	31.7 (5.41)	96.9 (1.75)	89.6 (3.38)	2.0 (0.09)	2,486 (142.5)	84 (7.5)	14.54 (1.057)	2.9 (0.27)
Indiana	—	—	—	—	—	—	—	—	—	—	—	—
Iowa	94.5 (2.53)	95.8 (1.94)	59.5 (4.38)	66.3 (4.73)	26.5 (5.18)	98.0 (1.26)	96.4 (3.45)	2.3 (0.09)	2,603 (132.0)	101 (9.8)	22.42 (1.432)	5.8 (0.59)
Kansas	92.2 (4.50)	99.2 (0.40)	58.0 (4.86)	58.2 (5.34)	58.3 (4.63)	93.9 (3.36)	97.7 (1.27)	2.0 (0.09)	3,564 (259.0)	101 (14.2)	42.42 (5.435)	4.2 (0.43)
Kentucky	91.0 (2.31)	93.0 (2.16)	48.4 (4.76)	51.3 (4.59)	56.3 (4.89)	95.0 (2.02)	86.6 (3.27)	1.5 (0.08)	2,026 (91.2)	96 (8.4)	17.68 (1.388)	3.5 (0.14)
Louisiana	83.9 (4.21)	86.9 (3.53)	48.4 (5.33)	66.8 (5.40)	56.1 (5.98)	98.1 (1.48)	85.9 (4.22)	1.4 (0.11)	1,951 (119.4)	66 (7.2)	17.58 (4.543)	2.6 (0.31)
Maine	85.6 (4.05)	88.6 (3.44)	48.1 (4.85)	53.1 (4.18)	11.3 (3.20)	84.7 (3.91)	75.8 (4.94)	1.7 (0.10)	3,393 (283.8)	109 (9.9)	22.60 (1.615)	2.6 (0.22)
Maryland	68.1 (4.03)	70.9 (4.42)	33.6 (4.95)	42.6 (5.18)	20.0 (4.09)	96.8 (1.82)	84.5 (3.77)	1.3 (0.10)	1,664 (121.0)	61 (7.5)	13.79 (2.749)	3.4 (0.26)
Massachusetts	83.6 (2.79)	87.1 (2.74)	39.9 (3.62)	51.3 (3.63)	45.9 (3.56)	98.3 (0.77)	80.8 (3.40)	1.7 (0.07)	2,065 (117.9)	58 (5.1)	10.13 (1.086)	4.5 (0.30)
Michigan	91.5 (2.23)	92.1 (2.41)	39.8 (3.67)	57.6 (4.04)	34.4 (3.13)	94.4 (1.86)	86.3 (3.43)	2.2 (0.06)	2,760 (139.9)	105 (24.4)	16.40 (2.140)	5.4 (0.35)
Minnesota	71.9 (5.72)	86.5 (3.53)	22.7 (3.97)	46.3 (5.13)	26.8 (3.50)	97.0 (1.86)	88.5 (3.43)	1.5 (0.08)	1,862 (110.5)	106 (22.0)	13.03 (1.871)	1.9 (0.15)
Mississippi	—	—	—	—	—	—	—	—	—	—	—	—
Missouri	93.8 (1.87)	97.3 (1.37)	34.8 (3.06)	44.1 (3.32)	19.8 (2.78)	98.2 (1.40)	89.2 (2.91)	1.9 (0.09)	2,624 (93.4)	106 (6.2)	21.23 (0.896)	4.4 (0.20)
Montana	77.6 (6.74)	87.9 (4.59)	34.8 (6.14)	50.6 (7.14)	17.0! (5.97)	96.2 (2.14)	92.5 (2.57)	1.8 (0.10)	3,570 (325.3)	118 (9.4)	21.64 (2.129)	6.1 (0.73)
Nebraska	90.0 (2.94)	93.6 (2.83)	71.8 (4.06)	71.8 (4.32)	33.6 (4.96)	95.0 (4.33)	65.2 (5.29)	2.1 (0.11)	3,629 (430.3)	137 (18.6)	21.64 (1.246)	5.8 (0.44)
Nevada	97.8 (1.08)	98.3 (0.96)	28.6 (4.31)	41.2 (4.77)	34.4 (3.34)	97.4 (1.78)	65.9 (5.29)	1.6 (0.07)	1,674 (55.0)	74 (5.3)	10.23 (0.490)	1.9 (0.13)
New Hampshire	91.3 (4.46)	94.4 (4.05)	58.4 (7.08)	66.7 (6.26)	7.9! (3.66)	100.0 (†)	56.1 (2.84)	1.8 (0.12)	2,134 (283.8)	81 (5.5)	21.78 (1.383)	3.7 (0.31)
New Jersey	85.7 (3.03)	86.5 (2.85)	46.5 (4.19)	45.4 (4.10)	20.7 (3.29)	96.0 (2.08)	79.9 (3.22)	1.4 (0.06)	2,172 (121.3)	68 (8.2)	15.47 (1.072)	3.1 (0.19)
New Mexico	87.3 (10.18)	86.3 (10.49)	38.3 (3.90)	65.2 (5.93)	37.6 (7.31)	95.8 (2.70)	83.7 (6.05)	1.8 (0.24)	3,057 (631.5)	95 (16.1)	‡ (†)	2.5! (1.21)
New York	94.2 (2.17)	93.8 (2.33)	57.3 (3.37)	45.8 (4.46)	21.2 (3.23)	98.7 (0.98)	81.3 (2.94)	2.0 (0.06)	1,898 (97.1)	101 (17.8)	19.25 (1.274)	3.5 (0.18)
North Carolina	95.9 (1.97)	95.5 (1.67)	57.3 (3.37)	86.1 (2.53)	55.4 (3.83)	98.5 (1.01)	93.6 (2.74)	1.6 (0.09)	1,940 (97.3)	88 (10.1)	15.85 (1.164)	3.5 (0.26)
North Dakota	77.6 (3.93)	80.5 (3.66)	45.1 (5.00)	52.7 (4.42)	20.1 (3.23)	96.6 (1.43)	75.6 (3.99)	2.0 (0.09)	3,728 (230.1)	172 (16.8)	24.28 (1.378)	4.8 (0.61)
Ohio	91.1 (2.26)	94.1 (2.23)	45.5 (3.69)	48.5 (3.52)	42.0 (4.60)	94.4 (1.88)	81.5 (3.43)	1.8 (0.07)	1,889 (75.4)	62 (4.0)	9.06 (0.502)	3.3 (0.20)
Oklahoma	84.1 (4.75)	86.4 (4.26)	42.3 (5.72)	46.2 (5.42)	26.7 (5.71)	94.1 (2.45)	87.7 (3.89)	1.9 (0.10)	2,676 (229.2)	133 (33.8)	11.28 (2.051)	4.0 (0.42)
Oregon	90.0 (3.18)	93.3 (1.71)	35.3 (5.01)	50.4 (4.96)	28.7 (5.09)	97.5 (1.54)	74.4 (5.11)	1.7 (0.08)	2,569 (116.8)	77 (10.6)	16.68 (1.792)	3.3 (0.22)
Pennsylvania	89.4 (3.12)	91.0 (2.86)	39.5 (3.37)	46.3 (3.89)	19.9 (3.71)	92.1 (3.19)	75.7 (4.33)	1.6 (0.06)	2,302 (181.0)	81 (10.1)	23.54 (2.067)	3.3 (0.22)
Rhode Island	72.9 (5.12)	76.7 (4.20)	26.0 (5.81)	22.9 (4.42)	5.1! (2.06)	94.3 (3.60)	72.4 (7.05)	1.7 (0.13)	1,993 (110.8)	62 (9.1)	9.22 (0.978)	4.8 (0.40)
South Carolina	97.2 (1.55)	97.2 (1.55)	49.1 (5.49)	79.0 (3.80)	85.0 (3.67)	100.0 (†)	96.1 (1.89)	1.8 (0.07)	2,246 (401.6)	79 (5.9)	15.47 (1.105)	3.0 (0.24)
South Dakota	75.1 (4.80)	69.3 (5.65)	44.6 (5.49)	51.9 (6.10)	21.6 (4.22)	84.2 (5.62)	77.5 (5.53)	1.8 (0.08)	3,370 (329.1)	81 (9.3)	22.94 (1.947)	3.5 (0.45)
Tennessee	92.3 (1.98)	98.1 (0.90)	46.3 (4.83)	57.9 (4.83)	28.0 (3.68)	98.1 (1.23)	90.5 (3.57)	1.7 (0.06)	1,756 (60.8)	81 (23.0)	11.96 (1.448)	2.3 (0.21)
Texas	96.8 (1.98)	96.8 (1.28)	42.1 (3.37)	59.2 (3.89)	32.9 (3.82)	96.9 (1.41)	84.8 (2.07)	1.7 (0.13)	2,261 (250.8)	113 (12.2)	23.54 (4.438)	2.3 (0.10)
Utah	86.1 (5.81)	85.8 (6.20)	28.0 (5.07)	34.2 (5.33)	44.5 (5.72)	84.8 (5.15)	84.8 (5.98)	1.7 (0.07)	1,652 (90.6)	85 (12.2)	10.03 (0.862)	2.1 (0.18)
Vermont	84.5 (4.69)	80.6 (4.24)	58.5 (5.72)	64.5 (4.95)	11.2 (2.48)	93.1 (2.97)	80.2 (4.12)	1.9 (0.09)	4,010 (145.6)	155 (9.1)	32.89 (1.796)	4.8 (0.48)
Virginia	95.7 (2.26)	97.3 (1.38)	60.8 (3.91)	74.7 (4.14)	11.2 (4.90)	96.8 (1.33)	90.1 (3.92)	1.9 (0.09)	2,018 (78.9)	122 (24.9)	22.06 (3.017)	3.1 (0.50)
Washington	92.2 (2.67)	93.6 (1.81)	29.0 (4.20)	47.5 (4.47)	28.1 (4.08)	96.3 (2.48)	84.1 (3.53)	1.0 (0.11)	2,325 (107.8)	82 (9.4)	9.46 (0.680)	3.9 (0.27)
West Virginia	69.0 (4.92)	74.9 (5.24)	50.4 (4.40)	47.5 (5.04)	27.2 (2.97)	92.8 (2.80)	86.6 (5.32)	1.0 (0.07)	1,923 (109.7)	110 (33.3)	15.04 (2.674)	4.5 (0.80)
Wisconsin	96.0 (2.31)	97.9 (1.07)	50.4 (4.28)	63.0 (4.28)	27.2 (3.97)	98.6 (1.35)	95.7 (2.36)	2.4 (0.09)	3,125 (149.7)	159 (8.7)	37.93 (2.217)	5.2 (0.41)
Wyoming	95.5 (4.10)	95.5 (4.07)	56.8 (5.80)	51.1 (4.62)	19.3 (5.06)	98.7 (0.80)	81.2 (5.71)	1.8 (0.10)	3,714 (330.4)	211 (33.4)	32.02 (5.222)	4.8 (0.67)

†Not applicable.

!Interpret data with caution. The coefficient of variation (CV) for this estimate is between 30 percent and 50 percent.

‡Reporting standards not met. Either the response rate is under 50 percent or there are too few cases for a reliable estimate.

[1]Centralized video distribution equipment with a scheduling and control server that telecasts video to classrooms.

[2]Includes professional and nonprofessional staff.

[3]Books held, books acquired, and expenditures are from the current school year, while enrollment counts are from the prior school year.

SOURCE: U.S. Department of Education, National Center for Education Statistics, Schools and Staffing Survey (SASS), "Public School Library Media Center Questionnaire," 2011–12. (This table was prepared December 2013.)

Collections, staff, and operating expenditures of degree-granting postsecondary institution libraries: Selected years, 1981–82 through 2011–12

Collections, staff, and operating expenditures	1981–82	1987–88	1991–92	1997–98	2001–02	2005–06	2007–08	2009–10	2011–12 Total	Public	Private nonprofit	Private for-profit
1	2	3	4	5	6	7	8	9	10	11	12	13
Number of libraries	3,104	3,438	3,274	3,658	3,568	3,617	3,827	3,689	3,793	1,560	1,461	772
Percentage of institutions with libraries	—	—	—	90.0	85.0	84.6	87.9	82.1	80.6	94.6	88.4	55.0
Number of circulation transactions (in thousands)	—	—	—	216,067	189,248	187,236	178,766	176,736	154,409	99,897	51,930	2,582
Number of circulation transactions per full-time equivalent (FTE) student	—	—	—	20	16	14	13	11	10	9	16	2
Enrollment (in thousands)												
Total enrollment[1]	12,372	12,767	14,359	14,502	15,928	17,487	18,248	20,428	20,994	15,110	3,927	1,957
Full-time-equivalent (FTE) enrollment[1]	9,015	9,230	10,361	10,615	11,766	13,201	13,783	15,496	15,886	10,949	3,321	1,616
Collections (in thousands)												
Number of volumes at end of year	567,826	718,504	749,429	878,906	954,030	1,015,658	1,052,531	1,076,027	1,099,951	669,521	424,671	5,760
Number of volumes added during year	19,507	21,907	20,982	24,551	24,574	22,241	23,990	27,164	27,605	17,134	9,984	488
Number of serial subscriptions at end of year[2]	4,890	6,416	6,966	10,908	9,855	16,361	25,342	25,041	—	—	—	—
Microform units at end of year	—	—	—	1,062,082	1,143,678	1,166,295	1,157,365	1,124,941	1,044,521	705,525	337,405	1,591
E-books at end of year	—	—	—	—	10,318	64,366	102,502	158,652	252,599	136,181	102,413	14,006
Number of volumes per FTE student	63	78	72	83	81	77	76	69	69	61	128	4
Full-time-equivalent (FTE) library staff												
Total staff in regular positions[3]	58,476	67,251	67,166	68,337	69,526	69,615	69,328	66,562	65,242	39,776	23,770	1,696
Librarians and professional staff	23,816	25,115	26,341	30,041	32,053	33,265	34,520	34,147	34,423	19,601	13,382	1,440
Other paid staff	34,660	40,733	40,421	38,026	37,473	36,350	34,808	32,415	30,819	20,175	10,388	256
Contributed services	—	1,403	404	270								
Student assistants	—	33,821	29,075	28,373	25,305	23,976	24,110	22,382	20,509	11,288	8,498	724
FTE student enrollment per FTE staff member	154	137	154	155	169	190	199	233	243	275	140	953
Library operating expenditures[4]												
Total operating expenditures (in thousands of current dollars)	$1,943,769	$2,770,075	$3,648,654	$4,592,657	$5,416,716	$6,234,192	$6,785,542	$6,829,108	$7,008,114	$4,077,793	$2,803,864	$126,457
Salaries and wages	914,379 [5]	1,451,551	1,889,368	2,314,380	2,753,404	3,102,561	3,342,082	3,401,649	3,443,831	2,060,066	1,308,607	75,158
Student hourly wages	100,847	(6)	(6)	(6)	(6)	(6)	(6)	(6)	(6)	(6)	(6)	(6)
Fringe benefits	167,515											
Furniture/equipment	—	—	—	57,013	—	—	—	—	—	—	—	—
Computer hardware/software	—	—	—	164,379	155,791	153,002	158,698	142,652	143,660	90,583	51,050	2,028
Bibliographic utilities/networks/consortia	—	—	—	89,618	92,242	106,268	113,427	117,838	123,650	71,925	50,694	1,031
Information resources	591,550	925,425	1,240,419	1,643,914	1,990,989	2,375,485	2,663,082	2,680,298	2,790,039	1,572,279	1,172,378	45,383
Books and serial backfiles—paper	—	—	—	514,048	563,007	572,228	611,192	515,942	503,851	248,460	244,454	10,938
Books and serial backfiles—electronic	—	—	—	28,061	44,792	93,778	133,586	152,359	180,570	100,553	74,724	5,292
Current serials—paper	—	—	—	849,399	926,105	830,137	699,906	536,357	487,265	272,219	207,707	7,339
Current serials—electronic	—	—	—	125,470	297,657	691,585	1,004,393	1,249,726	1,436,671	856,062	562,111	18,498
Audiovisual materials	—	—	23,879	30,623	37,041	39,029	43,849	55,659	37,022	19,486	15,609	1,926
Document delivery/interlibrary loan	—	—	—	19,309	22,913	26,513	30,496	33,679	32,490	20,069	11,768	652
Preservation	30,351	34,144	43,126	42,919	46,499	41,102	41,591	31,212	26,838	14,382	12,392	63
Other collection expenditures	561,199	891,281	1,173,414	34,086	52,976	81,113	98,069	105,364	85,334	41,047	43,612	675
Other library operating expenditures	169,478	393,099	518,867	323,354	424,290	496,877	508,253	486,672	506,934	282,941	221,136	2,857
Operating expenditures per full-time-equivalent (FTE) student												
In current dollars	216	300	352	433	460	472	492	441	441	372	844	78
In constant 2012–13 dollars[7]	530	599	590	619	598	549	538	470	448	379	858	80
Information resource expenditures per FTE student												
In current dollars	66	100	120	155	169	180	193	173	176	144	353	28
In constant 2012–13 dollars[7]	161	200	200	222	220	209	211	185	179	146	359	29
Operating expenditures (percentage distribution)	100.0	100.0	100.0	100.0	100.0	100.0	100.0	100.0	100.0	100.0	100.0	100.0
Salaries and wages	47.0	52.4	51.8	50.4	50.8	49.8	49.3	49.8	49.1	50.5	46.7	59.4
Student hourly wages	5.2	(6)	(6)	(6)	(6)	(6)	(6)	(6)	(6)	(6)	(6)	(6)
Fringe benefits	8.6	—	—	—	—	—	—	—	—	—	—	—
Preservation	1.6	1.2	1.2	0.9	0.9	0.7	0.6	0.5	0.4	0.4	0.4	0.1
Information resources	28.9	32.2	32.8	34.9	35.9	37.4	38.6	38.8	39.4	38.2	41.4	35.8
Other[8]	8.7	14.2	14.2	13.8	12.4	12.1	11.5	10.9	11.0	10.9	11.5	4.7
Library operating expenditures as a percent of total institutional expenditures for educational and general purposes	3.5	3.2	3.0	—	—	—	—	—	—	—	—	—

—Not available.

[1]Fall enrollment for the academic year specified.
[2]For 1997–98 and later years, includes microform and electronic serials.
[3]Excludes student assistants.
[4]Excludes capital outlay.
[5]Includes salary equivalents of contributed services staff.
[6]Included under salaries and wages.
[7]Constant dollars based on the Consumer Price Index, prepared by the Bureau of Labor Statistics, U.S. Department of Labor, adjusted to a school-year basis.
[8]Includes furniture/equipment, computer hardware/software, and bibliographic utilities/networks/consortia as well as expenditures classified as "other library operating expenditures."

NOTE: Data through 1995 are for institutions of higher education, while later data are for degree-granting institutions. Degree-granting institutions grant associate's or higher degrees and participate in Title IV federal financial aid programs. The degree-granting classification is very similar to the earlier higher education classification, but it includes more 2-year colleges and excludes a few higher education institutions that did not grant degrees. Detail may not sum to totals because of rounding.
SOURCE: U.S. Department of Education, National Center for Education Statistics, *Library Statistics of Colleges and Universities*, 1981–82; Integrated Postsecondary Education Data System (IPEDS), "Academic Libraries Survey" (IPEDS-L:88–98), "Fall Enrollment Survey" (IPEDS-EF:87–98), and IPEDS Spring 2002 through Spring 2012, Enrollment component; Academic Libraries Survey (ALS), 2000 through 2012. (This table was prepared May 2014.)

Collections, staff, operating expenditures, public service hours, and reference services of the 60 largest college and university libraries: Fiscal year 2012

Institution	Rank order, by number of volumes	Number of volumes at end of year (in thousands)	Number of e-books at end of year	Full-time-equivalent staff		Operating expenditures (in thousands of current dollars)		Public service hours per typical week	Gate count per typical week[1]	Annual reference information services to individuals[2]
				Total	Librarians	Total	Salaries and wages			
1	2	3	4	5	6	7	8	9	10	11
Harvard University (MA)	1	17,225	402,473	1,073	400	$134,533	$83,834	168	27,194 [3]	187,903
Yale University (CT)	2	13,504	1,090,187	600	163	81,221	35,235	111	27,194 [3]	31,783
University of Illinois at Urbana-Champaign	3	12,937	645,398	437	77	43,703	20,744	152	93,818	110,973
University of California, Berkeley	4	11,537	1,097,969	434	74	47,325	24,022	77	39,081 [3]	70,986
University of Michigan, Ann Arbor	5	11,458	1,926,938	690	186	63,828	32,553	168	114,557	211,469
University of Chicago (IL)	6	11,397	1,251,085	309	68	36,112	13,450	148	28,732	16,610
Columbia University in the City of New York	7	11,291	1,329,421	526	162	57,422	26,244	107	84,930	58,489
University of Texas at Austin	8	10,185	752,892	489	104	43,968	20,476	120	101,797	119,058
University of California, Los Angeles	9	9,981	1,288,821	527	133	50,171	27,406	96	81,905	113,725
Indiana University, Bloomington	10	9,276	1,363,894	395	90	33,371	15,259	101	64,700	138,542
Stanford University (CA)	11	9,025	841,538	653	153	69,922	31,704	105	20,491 [3]	105,636
University of Wisconsin, Madison	12	7,841	656,536	533	202	38,018	18,778	148	103,845	650
Tarrant County College District (TX)	13	7,828	83,036	73	24	3,878	2,723	84	26,583	—
Cornell University (NY)	14	7,684	903,397	468	110	45,471	21,917	145	73,193	62,429
Princeton University (NJ)	15	7,486	322,690	382	87	50,222	20,476	120	8,508	19,018
University of Washington, Seattle Campus	16	7,375	460,477	385	122	36,649	17,592	135	135,000	56,062
University of Minnesota, Twin Cities	17	6,918	484,151	355	87	39,526	17,992	107	45,000	46,021
Michigan State University	18	6,702	2,715,914	236	70	27,496	10,389	140	37,453	50,633
University of Pittsburgh, Main Campus (PA)	19	6,663	988,230	319	118	31,800	11,881	118	39,081 [3]	80,695
Duke University (NC)	20	6,540	875,488	321	114	41,043	17,127	149	95,437	80,518
University of Colorado at Boulder	21	6,510	675,723	232	62	24,263	10,114	128	66,545	57,345
University of North Carolina at Chapel Hill	22	6,437	996,453	409	130	38,135	18,921	146	90,160	84,345
University of Pennsylvania	23	6,108	1,100,111	416	137	41,535	19,601	116	31,779	6,500
Ohio State University, Main Campus	24	6,050	526,075	449	75	43,185	17,349	168	128,852	27,876
University of Arizona	25	6,030	1,184,441	194	51	23,350	8,410	142	38,585	17,247
University of Florida	26	5,611	815,537	301	90	28,657	13,434	138	53,235	44,945
Rutgers University, New Brunswick (NJ)	27	5,478	595,141	272	56	25,958	14,493	115	60,618	25,656
Pennsylvania State University, Main Campus	28	5,351	316,913	539	143	50,972	25,757	148	139,775	85,211
University of Iowa	29	5,310	772,023	221	66	24,728	9,883	116	34,623	52,416
University of Virginia, Main Campus	30	5,247	460,840	344	97	33,796	16,775	149	76,921	76,853
University of California, Davis	31	5,204	582,966	185	54	18,506	8,783	102	34,482	78,595
New York University	32	5,196	1,101,383	465	68	51,534	21,977	126	65,163	132,850
Northwestern University (IL)	33	5,140	139,418	362	111	32,029	14,629	122	21,560	23,444
University of Oklahoma, Norman Campus	34	5,139	1,168,077	142	34	17,000	4,727	117	26,456	21,693
University of Georgia	35	4,947	555,015	283	76	24,101	10,262	109	61,786	42,991
University of Southern California	36	4,845	877,824	329	84	66,405	17,589	159	53,335	110,159
Brown University (RI)	37	4,724	979,523	172	48	21,368	8,709	112	27,890	11,568
Texas A&M University, College Station	38	4,531	1,073,198	321	78	35,350	12,945	145	63,798	44,988
Arizona State University	39	4,531	403,504	288	73	25,459	9,795	149	39,081 [3]	42,726
University of South Carolina, Columbia	40	4,460	206,886	265	71	21,752	7,785	111	38,470	85,215
Johns Hopkins University (MD)	41	4,396	985,644	271	29	37,396	13,445	120	34,500	28,667
University of Cincinnati, Main Campus (OH)	42	4,336	1,243,527	188	44	21,019	8,588	106	33,229	119,451
Tulane University of Louisiana	43	4,320	927,113	172	55	17,813	6,275	118	20,000	21,633
Auburn University (AL)	44	4,318	821,083	106	29	12,762	4,502	146	28,066	98,072
University of Kansas	45	4,285	404,676	249	59	20,282	9,362	140	42,000	91,236
Miami University-Oxford (OH)	46	4,225	595,932	121	44	9,654	4,533	168	29,976	12,947
University at Buffalo (NY)	47	4,119	726,127	173	52	19,414	9,663	168	48,000	35,367
University of Maryland, College Park	48	4,094	599,198	250	80	29,353	11,724	138	58,461	386,001
University of Utah	49	4,068	334,463	322	79	25,130	12,508	142	55,008	165,837
University of Kentucky	50	4,023	588,428	238	74	21,285	8,741	140	51,632	29,825
University of Alabama	51	3,974	855,794	200	64	19,417	7,290	135	35,307	29,854
Brigham Young University (UT)	52	3,946	526,051	352	61	26,686	11,771	101	72,336	57,917
Washington University in St. Louis (MO)	53	3,890	590,299	245	97	32,570	10,042	120	28,000	52,905
Emory University (GA)	54	3,878	555,313	287	97	37,737	14,269	106	35,117	8,935
Syracuse University (NY)	55	3,815	942,224	207	59	19,271	8,613	136	34,993	21,395
Louisiana State University and Agricultural & Mechanical College	56	3,802	402,264	124	43	15,718	—	99	34,772	28,978
University of Notre Dame (IN)	57	3,796	466,168	249	77	26,934	10,880	147	26,544	20,612
Vanderbilt University (TN)	58	3,720	606,267	196	61	23,624	9,181	147	40,417	18,507
North Carolina State University at Raleigh	59	3,653	514,635	280	103	27,504	12,395	146	44,540	32,916
Temple University (PA)	60	3,573	635,008	196	55	23,382	8,263	145	80,009	73,889

—Not available.

[1]The number of entries into the library in an average week. A single person can be counted more than once.

[2]Includes both in-person and virtual services.

[3]Imputed.

SOURCE: U.S. Department of Education, National Center for Education Statistics, Academic Libraries Survey (ALS), fiscal year 2012. (This table was prepared March 2014.)

Public libraries, books and serial volumes, library visits, circulation, and reference transactions, by state: Fiscal years 2009 and 2010

State	Number of public libraries		Number of books and serial volumes				Library visits per capita[1]		Circulation per capita[2]		Reference transactions per capita[3]	
			In thousands		Per capita							
	2009	2010	2009	2010	2009	2010	2009	2010	2009	2010	2009	2010
1	2	3	4	5	6	7	8	9	10	11	12	13
United States	9,225 [4]	8,951 [4]	815,909	808,402	2.7	2.7	5.4	5.3	8.1	8.3	1.0	1.0
Alabama	210	212	9,546	9,649	2.1	2.1	3.7	3.7	4.6	4.6	0.9	0.9
Alaska	87	75	2,532	2,366	3.7	3.4	5.1	4.8	6.4	6.3	0.7	0.6
Arizona	89	89	8,807	8,946	1.3	1.4	4.4	4.6	7.4	8.2	0.7	0.7
Arkansas	52	55	6,578	6,569	2.5	2.5	4.0	4.0	5.3	5.5	0.7	0.8
California	181	181	75,299	74,754	2.0	1.9	4.8	4.6	6.2	6.3	0.9	0.9
Colorado	114	114	11,916	11,752	2.4	2.4	6.7	6.8	13.0	13.3	1.2	1.1
Connecticut	195	183	15,646	14,679	4.5	4.4	7.0	7.2	9.7	10.2	1.3	1.2
Delaware	21	21	1,701	1,858	2.2	2.4	5.6	5.8	10.5	11.5	0.6	0.7
District of Columbia	1	1	2,130	1,904	3.6	3.2	4.9	4.6	3.9	4.5	1.4	1.4
Florida	80	80	32,643	33,057	1.7	1.8	4.8	4.8	6.8	7.1	1.6	1.7
Georgia	61	61	16,341	16,765	1.7	1.7	4.3	3.9	5.1	4.7	0.9	1.1
Hawaii	1	1	3,383	3,466	2.6	2.7	4.7	4.1	5.6	5.4	0.7	0.6
Idaho	104	102	4,275	4,316	3.2	3.2	6.8	6.4	10.3	10.7	0.9	1.0
Illinois	634	622	45,250	45,223	3.8	3.8	7.0	7.0	9.7	10.3	1.2	1.2
Indiana	238	238	25,672	25,628	4.5	4.5	7.4	7.1	14.1	13.7	1.0	1.1
Iowa	541	531	12,143	12,117	4.1	4.1	6.5	6.6	9.7	9.9	0.6	0.6
Kansas	328	311	10,314	10,060	4.3	4.2	6.6	6.5	11.8	11.6	1.1	0.9
Kentucky	117	117	8,849	9,028	2.1	2.1	4.5	4.6	6.9	7.0	0.7	0.8
Louisiana	68	68	11,651	11,913	2.6	2.6	3.5	3.7	4.2	4.4	1.4	1.5
Maine	269	215	6,536	6,010	5.4	5.3	5.9	6.0	7.9	8.4	0.6	0.5
Maryland	24	24	13,892	13,954	2.5	2.5	6.1	6.0	10.7	10.7	1.3	1.4
Massachusetts	370	360	32,969	32,789	5.1	5.0	6.5	6.5	8.9	9.8	0.8	0.8
Michigan	384	384	35,539	35,322	3.6	3.6	6.0	6.0	8.6	9.0	1.0	1.0
Minnesota	138	138	15,535	15,592	2.9	2.9	5.6	5.3	11.2	11.1	0.7	0.7
Mississippi	50	50	5,556	5,569	1.9	1.9	3.2	3.4	3.0	3.0	0.6	0.6
Missouri	150	147	17,592	17,328	3.4	3.4	5.9	6.2	10.1	10.6	1.1	1.0
Montana	80	80	2,731	2,794	3.0	3.1	4.9	5.0	6.9	7.5	0.5	0.5
Nebraska	269	216	6,345	5,856	4.7	4.4	6.8	6.5	10.4	10.3	0.8	0.8
Nevada	22	22	4,782	4,545	1.8	1.7	4.3	4.3	7.2	7.6	0.6	0.6
New Hampshire	230	221	6,217	5,968	4.7	6.0	5.9	8.2	8.9	12.2	0.6	0.8
New Jersey	301	284	30,230	29,635	3.6	3.6	6.1	6.1	7.8	7.6	1.0	1.0
New Mexico	91	81	4,615	4,426	2.9	2.8	5.0	5.2	6.5	6.7	0.8	0.7
New York	756	756	75,760	73,078	4.0	3.9	6.3	6.2	8.4	8.7	1.5	1.4
North Carolina	77	77	16,907	16,755	1.8	1.8	4.8	4.7	6.0	6.0	1.4	1.4
North Dakota	85	73	2,575	2,374	4.5	4.1	4.4	4.2	7.8	7.2	0.8	0.7
Ohio	251	251	45,818	45,224	4.0	3.9	8.0	7.6	17.0	16.3	1.8	1.8
Oklahoma	115	116	7,278	7,352	2.4	2.4	7.0	5.2	7.1	7.4	0.7	0.7
Oregon	127	126	9,927	10,048	2.7	2.7	6.8	6.8	15.4	16.2	0.8	0.7
Pennsylvania	458	457	28,180	27,790	2.4	2.3	4.1	3.9	6.0	5.8	0.7	0.8
Rhode Island	48	48	4,334	4,636	4.1	4.4	6.4	6.0	7.3	7.4	0.8	0.7
South Carolina	42	42	9,430	9,575	2.2	2.2	4.2	4.2	6.1	6.2	1.2	1.2
South Dakota	112	102	3,096	2,926	4.2	4.0	5.4	5.5	8.4	8.2	0.9	0.6
Tennessee	186	186	11,754	11,837	1.9	1.9	3.5	3.4	4.0	4.2	0.6	0.6
Texas	559	549	41,749	41,832	1.8	1.8	3.5	3.4	5.1	5.2	0.7	0.7
Utah	71	72	6,744	6,873	2.5	2.5	7.0	7.0	13.4	13.7	1.9	1.2
Vermont	184	159	2,964	2,908	4.9	5.4	6.5	7.1	7.8	8.8	0.8	0.9
Virginia	91	91	19,151	18,921	2.5	2.5	5.5	5.5	9.8	10.0	1.0	1.0
Washington	63	61	15,377	14,878	2.3	2.3	6.7	6.8	12.9	13.1	0.9	0.9
West Virginia	97	97	5,213	5,264	2.9	2.9	3.4	3.4	4.3	4.4	0.5	0.5
Wisconsin	380	381	19,956	19,794	3.5	3.5	6.4	6.4	11.5	11.4	0.9	0.9
Wyoming	23	23	2,484	2,498	4.7	4.6	7.1	7.1	9.5	9.8	1.2	1.0

[1]The number of visits (entering the library for any purpose) per person during the year.
[2]The number of library materials lent per person during the year.
[3]A reference transaction is an information contact that involves the knowledge, use, recommendations, interpretation, or instructions in the use of one or more information sources by a member of the library staff.
[4]In 2009, of the 9,225 public libraries in the 50 states and the District of Columbia, 7,466 were single-outlet libraries and 1,759 were multiple-outlet libraries. In 2010, of the 8,951 public libraries in the 50 states and the District of Columbia, 7,204 were single-outlet libraries and 1,747 were multiple-outlet libraries. Single-outlet libraries consist of a central library, bookmobile, or books-by-mail-only outlet. Multiple-outlet libraries have two or more direct service outlets, including some combination of one central library, branch(es), bookmobile(s), and/or books-by-mail-only outlets.

NOTE: Data include imputations for nonresponse. Detail may not sum to totals because of rounding. Per capita figures are based on unduplicated populations of the areas served by public libraries.

SOURCE: Institute of Museum and Library Services, Public Libraries Survey, fiscal years 2009 and 2010, retrieved December 13, 2013, from http://www.imls.gov/research/public_libraries_in_the_united_states_survey.aspx. (This table was prepared December 2013.)

Labor force participation, employment, and unemployment of persons 25 to 64 years old, by sex, race/ethnicity, age group, and educational attainment: 2010, 2011, and 2012

[Standard errors appear in parentheses]

Sex, race/ethnicity, age group, and educational attainment	Labor force participation rate[1] 2010	2011	2012	Number of participants (in thousands) 2012	Employment to population ratio[2] 2010	2011	2012	Number employed (in thousands) 2012	Unemployment rate[3] 2010	2011	2012	Number unemployed (in thousands) 2012
1	2	3	4	5	6	7	8	9	10	11	12	13
All persons 25 to 64 years old, all education levels	77.9 (0.04)	77.5 (0.04)	77.5 (0.04)	127,929 (69.2)	70.7 (0.04)	70.8 (0.04)	71.5 (0.04)	117,957 (76.3)	9.2 (0.03)	8.6 (0.03)	7.8 (0.03)	9,971 (38.0)
Less than high school completion	61.3 (0.14)	61.0 (0.13)	60.7 (0.14)	12,029 (51.7)	51.1 (0.14)	51.4 (0.14)	52.1 (0.14)	10,337 (47.0)	16.6 (0.13)	15.7 (0.14)	14.1 (0.14)	1,692 (18.2)
High school completion[4]	74.1 (0.08)	73.6 (0.09)	73.2 (0.09)	32,141 (72.6)	65.4 (0.09)	65.5 (0.10)	65.9 (0.09)	28,912 (66.0)	11.7 (0.08)	10.9 (0.07)	10.0 (0.07)	3,229 (23.7)
Some college, no degree	78.9 (0.09)	78.3 (0.10)	78.0 (0.10)	28,252 (64.9)	70.7 (0.09)	70.3 (0.11)	71.2 (0.10)	25,800 (64.5)	10.0 (0.08)	9.7 (0.07)	8.7 (0.09)	2,452 (19.4)
Associate's degree	83.1 (0.13)	82.4 (0.12)	82.2 (0.13)	11,886 (41.5)	76.9 (0.14)	76.7 (0.15)	76.7 (0.15)	11,098 (41.9)	7.5 (0.08)	6.9 (0.09)	6.6 (0.09)	788 (10.1)
Bachelor's or higher degree	86.1 (0.06)	85.8 (0.06)	86.1 (0.06)	43,620 (100.3)	81.8 (0.07)	81.9 (0.07)	82.5 (0.07)	41,810 (98.9)	5.0 (0.04)	4.5 (0.04)	4.2 (0.04)	1,810 (16.4)
Sex												
Male, all education levels	83.2 (0.04)	82.9 (0.05)	82.9 (0.05)	67,409 (45.2)	75.1 (0.06)	75.5 (0.05)	76.4 (0.05)	62,098 (47.0)	9.8 (0.05)	8.8 (0.05)	7.9 (0.04)	5,311 (25.3)
Less than high school completion	70.5 (0.16)	70.1 (0.16)	69.7 (0.19)	7,561 (36.6)	59.2 (0.17)	59.7 (0.19)	60.7 (0.20)	6,581 (34.3)	16.1 (0.16)	14.8 (0.17)	13.0 (0.14)	980 (11.1)
High school completion[4]	80.0 (0.11)	79.3 (0.11)	79.2 (0.11)	18,377 (45.9)	69.8 (0.12)	70.3 (0.13)	71.0 (0.13)	16,473 (42.4)	12.7 (0.10)	11.3 (0.11)	10.4 (0.10)	1,905 (19.1)
Some college, no degree	83.7 (0.11)	83.0 (0.13)	83.0 (0.13)	14,456 (38.6)	75.1 (0.15)	75.1 (0.15)	76.1 (0.15)	13,254 (38.5)	10.2 (0.11)	9.5 (0.11)	8.3 (0.09)	1,202 (13.8)
Associate's degree	87.2 (0.16)	86.9 (0.17)	86.6 (0.16)	5,343 (27.0)	80.3 (0.20)	80.8 (0.22)	81.0 (0.18)	4,994 (26.6)	8.0 (0.13)	8.0 (0.14)	6.5 (0.13)	349 (6.0)
Bachelor's or higher degree	91.4 (0.07)	91.1 (0.07)	91.5 (0.06)	21,672 (56.5)	86.8 (0.08)	87.1 (0.09)	87.8 (0.08)	20,797 (55.8)	5.0 (0.05)	4.4 (0.05)	4.0 (0.05)	875 (10.8)
Female, all education levels	72.8 (0.06)	72.3 (0.06)	72.2 (0.06)	60,520 (56.1)	66.5 (0.06)	66.3 (0.06)	66.7 (0.07)	55,859 (60.0)	8.6 (0.05)	8.4 (0.05)	7.7 (0.04)	4,660 (27.2)
Less than high school completion	50.2 (0.18)	50.1 (0.21)	49.8 (0.23)	4,469 (29.5)	41.4 (0.19)	41.5 (0.22)	41.8 (0.23)	3,756 (27.1)	17.5 (0.21)	17.1 (0.29)	15.9 (0.26)	712 (12.6)
High school completion[4]	67.8 (0.11)	67.2 (0.14)	66.5 (0.14)	13,764 (45.2)	60.7 (0.12)	60.2 (0.15)	60.1 (0.15)	12,440 (43.4)	10.5 (0.10)	10.4 (0.11)	9.6 (0.10)	1,324 (14.5)
Some college, no degree	74.6 (0.11)	73.9 (0.12)	73.4 (0.16)	13,796 (53.7)	67.3 (0.11)	66.7 (0.13)	66.7 (0.15)	12,546 (51.1)	9.8 (0.10)	9.8 (0.09)	9.1 (0.10)	1,250 (14.9)
Associate's degree	80.1 (0.16)	79.1 (0.16)	78.9 (0.16)	6,543 (28.3)	74.4 (0.19)	73.6 (0.18)	73.6 (0.20)	6,105 (28.3)	7.2 (0.13)	6.9 (0.12)	6.7 (0.13)	439 (8.1)
Bachelor's or higher degree	81.4 (0.08)	81.0 (0.08)	81.3 (0.09)	21,948 (58.2)	77.4 (0.09)	77.3 (0.10)	77.8 (0.11)	21,013 (58.0)	4.9 (0.06)	4.7 (0.06)	4.3 (0.05)	935 (10.2)
Race/ethnicity												
White, all education levels	78.9 (0.05)	78.5 (0.05)	78.5 (0.05)	83,498 (57.9)	72.7 (0.05)	72.8 (0.05)	73.4 (0.06)	78,090 (66.9)	7.9 (0.04)	7.3 (0.04)	6.5 (0.04)	5,408 (30.2)
Less than high school completion	55.3 (0.24)	55.2 (0.24)	54.3 (0.23)	3,750 (37.0)	45.1 (0.23)	45.5 (0.25)	45.7 (0.21)	3,158 (23.9)	18.3 (0.22)	17.6 (0.24)	15.8 (0.20)	592 (9.1)
High school completion[4]	74.6 (0.10)	73.9 (0.11)	73.5 (0.11)	20,763 (59.3)	66.7 (0.11)	66.7 (0.12)	67.1 (0.12)	18,962 (53.8)	10.6 (0.08)	9.6 (0.09)	8.7 (0.08)	1,801 (17.8)
Some college, no degree	78.7 (0.09)	78.1 (0.12)	78.0 (0.12)	18,565 (37.6)	71.7 (0.11)	71.5 (0.13)	72.3 (0.13)	17,207 (52.9)	8.9 (0.08)	8.5 (0.10)	7.3 (0.08)	1,358 (16.3)
Associate's degree	83.5 (0.15)	82.7 (0.13)	82.5 (0.13)	8,427 (36.0)	78.0 (0.17)	77.8 (0.16)	77.8 (0.19)	7,941 (38.0)	6.6 (0.10)	6.0 (0.10)	5.8 (0.12)	486 (9.7)
Bachelor's or higher degree	86.2 (0.06)	85.8 (0.07)	86.1 (0.07)	31,993 (73.9)	82.3 (0.06)	82.4 (0.07)	83.0 (0.08)	30,822 (72.3)	4.5 (0.04)	4.0 (0.04)	3.7 (0.04)	1,171 (13.9)
Black, all education levels	73.5 (0.12)	73.1 (0.14)	72.9 (0.13)	14,604 (32.1)	62.6 (0.12)	62.5 (0.14)	62.9 (0.15)	12,617 (33.5)	14.8 (0.12)	14.4 (0.13)	13.6 (0.11)	1,986 (16.9)
Less than high school completion	48.7 (0.39)	48.1 (0.44)	47.3 (0.43)	1,286 (17.5)	35.2 (0.36)	35.2 (0.37)	34.9 (0.39)	949 (14.0)	27.7 (0.54)	26.7 (0.43)	26.2 (0.48)	336 (7.9)
High school completion[4]	69.6 (0.26)	69.0 (0.28)	68.3 (0.26)	4,305 (28.5)	57.2 (0.23)	57.1 (0.28)	57.1 (0.30)	3,598 (23.9)	17.8 (0.25)	17.2 (0.28)	16.4 (0.22)	707 (11.1)
Some college, no degree	78.2 (0.25)	77.1 (0.24)	76.8 (0.24)	4,148 (30.1)	66.9 (0.23)	65.8 (0.27)	66.2 (0.30)	3,578 (29.8)	14.5 (0.23)	14.6 (0.22)	13.7 (0.26)	569 (10.6)
Associate's degree	82.1 (0.36)	82.0 (0.46)	81.9 (0.42)	1,373 (14.6)	73.0 (0.42)	73.0 (0.51)	73.3 (0.46)	1,229 (14.2)	11.1 (0.36)	11.0 (0.39)	10.5 (0.32)	145 (4.6)
Bachelor's or higher degree	88.9 (0.18)	88.5 (0.18)	88.5 (0.18)	3,492 (26.2)	82.2 (0.20)	82.1 (0.32)	82.7 (0.27)	3,263 (26.1)	7.4 (0.15)	7.3 (0.22)	6.5 (0.19)	228 (6.5)
Hispanic, all education levels	77.3 (0.11)	77.1 (0.10)	77.3 (0.09)	19,879 (27.1)	68.9 (0.12)	69.2 (0.12)	70.3 (0.11)	18,064 (31.9)	10.9 (0.09)	10.1 (0.10)	9.1 (0.09)	1,815 (18.0)
Less than high school completion	70.6 (0.19)	70.0 (0.18)	70.1 (0.19)	6,099 (34.4)	61.2 (0.21)	61.4 (0.20)	62.6 (0.22)	5,445 (33.2)	13.3 (0.17)	12.3 (0.19)	10.7 (0.16)	654 (11.9)
High school completion[4]	77.1 (0.20)	77.1 (0.20)	77.3 (0.23)	5,407 (33.3)	68.4 (0.24)	68.7 (0.27)	69.6 (0.28)	4,868 (31.1)	11.3 (0.19)	10.9 (0.19)	10.0 (0.16)	539 (9.0)
Some college, no degree	81.4 (0.24)	80.8 (0.26)	80.8 (0.26)	3,836 (26.3)	73.3 (0.25)	73.5 (0.31)	73.4 (0.28)	3,486 (24.6)	10.3 (0.22)	10.3 (0.23)	9.7 (0.19)	350 (7.6)
Associate's degree	84.2 (0.36)	83.1 (0.41)	83.7 (0.38)	1,309 (16.4)	76.3 (0.47)	76.3 (0.46)	77.5 (0.38)	1,212 (15.2)	9.4 (0.36)	8.2 (0.27)	7.4 (0.27)	96 (3.8)
Bachelor's or higher degree	86.8 (0.36)	86.7 (0.21)	87.1 (0.23)	3,228 (28.8)	81.2 (0.31)	81.8 (0.26)	82.4 (0.26)	3,052 (27.5)	6.4 (0.15)	5.6 (0.16)	5.4 (0.16)	176 (5.3)
Asian, all education levels	79.0 (0.15)	78.7 (0.18)	78.4 (0.16)	7,046 (19.1)	73.1 (0.17)	73.3 (0.18)	73.5 (0.18)	6,608 (20.6)	7.5 (0.13)	6.9 (0.12)	6.2 (0.12)	438 (8.7)
Less than high school completion	65.7 (0.48)	64.4 (0.59)	64.5 (0.52)	665 (10.4)	58.0 (0.57)	57.7 (0.62)	58.5 (0.54)	603 (9.6)	11.8 (0.54)	10.4 (0.47)	9.3 (0.43)	62 (3.1)
High school completion[4]	74.6 (0.48)	75.1 (0.52)	74.3 (0.49)	958 (13.7)	67.3 (0.49)	67.3 (0.56)	67.9 (0.50)	876 (11.8)	9.8 (0.34)	9.4 (0.45)	8.6 (0.37)	82 (4.1)
Some college, no degree	79.0 (0.52)	78.7 (0.52)	78.0 (0.48)	928 (11.4)	71.7 (0.47)	71.5 (0.55)	71.3 (0.49)	848 (10.7)	9.1 (0.34)	9.2 (0.36)	8.6 (0.39)	80 (3.8)
Associate's degree	80.5 (0.64)	79.1 (0.66)	76.4 (0.68)	474 (8.9)	74.4 (0.70)	73.4 (0.73)	71.3 (0.70)	443 (8.3)	7.7 (0.44)	7.2 (0.41)	6.6 (0.41)	31 (2.1)
Bachelor's or higher degree	83.0 (0.21)	82.8 (0.23)	82.7 (0.21)	4,022 (23.7)	78.3 (0.23)	78.5 (0.24)	79.0 (0.26)	3,839 (23.1)	5.7 (0.16)	5.2 (0.13)	4.5 (0.13)	183 (5.2)
American Indian/Alaska Native, all education levels	67.0 (0.63)	66.6 (0.62)	66.2 (0.56)	725 (8.2)	56.8 (0.61)	57.0 (0.65)	57.2 (0.60)	626 (7.6)	15.2 (0.46)	14.5 (0.50)	13.7 (0.44)	99 (3.4)
Less than high school completion	46.9 (1.54)	44.9 (1.46)	44.0 (1.21)	77 (3.0)	35.1 (1.36)	32.7 (1.41)	33.0 (1.13)	58 (2.5)	25.3 (1.74)	27.2 (2.22)	24.9 (1.88)	19 (1.7)
High school completion[4]	64.4 (1.06)	63.1 (1.08)	64.7 (0.96)	230 (5.1)	52.4 (1.08)	52.4 (1.08)	54.4 (1.03)	194 (4.7)	18.7 (0.92)	17.0 (0.91)	16.0 (0.94)	37 (2.3)
Some college, no degree	71.0 (0.88)	71.9 (1.01)	68.5 (1.14)	209 (5.7)	61.0 (0.84)	61.8 (1.12)	59.0 (0.87)	180 (5.3)	14.1 (0.87)	13.8 (0.78)	13.8 (0.85)	29 (1.9)
Associate's degree	75.5 (1.78)	74.1 (1.70)	75.0 (1.75)	77 (3.2)	66.3 (1.87)	67.3 (1.95)	67.4 (1.69)	69 (2.9)	12.1 (1.46)	9.2 (1.23)	10.0 (1.04)	8 (0.9)
Bachelor's or higher degree	83.5 (1.19)	82.5 (0.93)	84.4 (1.13)	132 (4.0)	78.5 (1.36)	77.3 (1.11)	79.9 (1.16)	125 (3.9)	6.0 (0.73)	6.3 (0.77)	5.2 (0.65)	7 (0.9)

See notes at end of table.

Labor force participation, employment, and unemployment of persons 25 to 64 years old, by sex, race/ethnicity, age group, and educational attainment: 2010, 2011, and 2012—Continued

[Standard errors appear in parentheses]

Sex, race/ethnicity, age group, and educational attainment	Labor force participation				Employment				Unemployment			
	Labor force participation rate[1]			Number of participants (in thousands)	Employment to population ratio[2]			Number employed (in thousands)	Unemployment rate[3]			Number unemployed (in thousands)
	2010	2011	2012	2012	2010	2011	2012	2012	2010	2011	2012	2012
1	2	3	4	5	6	7	8	9	10	11	12	13
Age group												
25 to 34, all education levels	**82.1** (0.09)	**81.8** (0.08)	**82.0** (0.06)	**34,149** (37.7)	**73.1** (0.11)	**73.2** (0.08)	**74.1** (0.07)	**30,845** (36.7)	**11.0** (0.08)	**10.6** (0.08)	**9.7** (0.06)	**3,304** (21.3)
Less than high school completion	66.8 (0.29)	66.0 (0.31)	65.5 (0.17)	3,200 (27.1)	53.4 (0.28)	53.2 (0.32)	53.7 (0.32)	2,624 (24.0)	20.1 (0.28)	19.5 (0.28)	18.0 (0.31)	575 (11.0)
High school completion[4]	78.5 (0.16)	78.1 (0.19)	78.0 (0.17)	7,767 (35.2)	66.3 (0.20)	66.8 (0.20)	67.2 (0.17)	6,690 (32.6)	15.5 (0.17)	14.5 (0.20)	13.9 (0.15)	1,077 (12.3)
Some college, no degree	82.8 (0.16)	82.2 (0.17)	82.1 (0.17)	7,952 (41.0)	72.9 (0.18)	72.1 (0.20)	72.9 (0.20)	7,063 (40.5)	12.0 (0.17)	12.3 (0.17)	11.2 (0.15)	889 (11.9)
Associate's degree	87.4 (0.24)	86.3 (0.25)	86.7 (0.22)	3,127 (22.6)	80.3 (0.28)	79.4 (0.28)	80.1 (0.26)	2,887 (21.1)	8.1 (0.20)	8.0 (0.20)	7.7 (0.22)	240 (7.3)
Bachelor's or higher degree	89.5 (0.11)	89.3 (0.11)	89.7 (0.10)	12,103 (47.0)	84.9 (0.14)	84.9 (0.13)	85.8 (0.11)	11,580 (47.3)	5.1 (0.09)	4.9 (0.10)	4.3 (0.08)	522 (9.8)
35 to 44, all education levels	**82.7** (0.06)	**82.5** (0.08)	**82.5** (0.08)	**33,611** (37.1)	**75.3** (0.07)	**75.7** (0.09)	**76.3** (0.09)	**31,075** (38.5)	**9.0** (0.07)	**8.2** (0.07)	**7.5** (0.06)	**2,537** (21.4)
Less than high school completion	68.1 (0.23)	68.5 (0.29)	68.4 (0.24)	3,454 (24.4)	57.1 (0.30)	58.2 (0.29)	59.3 (0.26)	2,992 (21.8)	16.1 (0.29)	15.1 (0.27)	13.4 (0.22)	463 (8.4)
High school completion[4]	79.7 (0.16)	79.3 (0.15)	79.0 (0.18)	7,953 (36.1)	70.2 (0.17)	70.4 (0.20)	70.9 (0.18)	7,135 (32.0)	12.0 (0.15)	11.2 (0.15)	10.3 (0.16)	818 (13.8)
Some college, no degree	84.1 (0.15)	83.6 (0.15)	83.1 (0.18)	7,214 (31.6)	75.9 (0.17)	76.0 (0.19)	76.1 (0.23)	6,602 (32.3)	9.7 (0.13)	9.2 (0.13)	8.5 (0.15)	612 (10.4)
Associate's degree	87.0 (0.22)	86.9 (0.23)	86.5 (0.24)	3,172 (19.3)	80.7 (0.24)	81.1 (0.27)	80.8 (0.27)	2,963 (20.5)	7.3 (0.18)	6.7 (0.19)	6.6 (0.22)	209 (6.7)
Bachelor's or higher degree	88.9 (0.09)	88.7 (0.09)	89.1 (0.11)	11,818 (33.8)	85.0 (0.12)	85.3 (0.12)	85.8 (0.12)	11,383 (35.2)	4.4 (0.08)	3.8 (0.08)	3.7 (0.08)	435 (8.9)
45 to 54, all education levels	**80.9** (0.07)	**80.4** (0.07)	**80.3** (0.07)	**35,434** (41.2)	**74.0** (0.08)	**74.0** (0.08)	**74.6** (0.08)	**32,941** (45.6)	**8.5** (0.05)	**7.9** (0.06)	**7.0** (0.05)	**2,493** (17.4)
Less than high school completion	62.8 (0.25)	62.1 (0.26)	61.9 (0.26)	3,312 (19.5)	53.1 (0.27)	53.2 (0.29)	53.8 (0.27)	2,881 (18.7)	15.5 (0.25)	14.4 (0.25)	13.0 (0.22)	431 (7.8)
High school completion[4]	78.1 (0.14)	77.4 (0.14)	76.9 (0.16)	9,905 (34.7)	70.1 (0.14)	69.9 (0.15)	70.3 (0.17)	9,054 (34.1)	10.2 (0.12)	9.7 (0.13)	8.6 (0.10)	851 (9.9)
Some college, no degree	81.9 (0.15)	81.4 (0.17)	81.3 (0.13)	7,657 (27.6)	74.5 (0.17)	74.6 (0.18)	75.3 (0.18)	7,095 (29.5)	9.0 (0.13)	8.4 (0.11)	7.3 (0.11)	562 (8.2)
Associate's degree	85.7 (0.21)	85.4 (0.21)	84.6 (0.21)	3,346 (21.1)	79.6 (0.23)	79.9 (0.26)	79.5 (0.27)	3,146 (22.3)	7.1 (0.15)	6.4 (0.16)	6.0 (0.17)	201 (5.2)
Bachelor's or higher degree	89.6 (0.11)	89.3 (0.10)	89.4 (0.12)	11,212 (43.2)	85.2 (0.12)	85.4 (0.11)	85.9 (0.14)	10,765 (42.9)	4.8 (0.07)	4.4 (0.07)	4.0 (0.07)	448 (8.1)
55 to 64, all education levels	**64.3** (0.09)	**64.0** (0.09)	**64.1** (0.08)	**24,735** (31.4)	**59.1** (0.08)	**59.3** (0.09)	**59.9** (0.08)	**23,097** (33.7)	**8.2** (0.07)	**7.5** (0.06)	**6.6** (0.06)	**1,639** (13.8)
Less than high school completion	45.1 (0.25)	45.4 (0.28)	45.5 (0.26)	2,063 (16.1)	39.1 (0.26)	39.7 (0.29)	40.5 (0.26)	1,839 (15.2)	13.3 (0.25)	12.7 (0.30)	10.8 (0.24)	223 (5.1)
High school completion[4]	59.2 (0.16)	59.2 (0.16)	59.3 (0.15)	6,516 (25.7)	53.7 (0.16)	54.3 (0.16)	54.9 (0.15)	6,033 (24.4)	9.2 (0.13)	8.2 (0.14)	7.4 (0.11)	483 (7.8)
Some college, no degree	65.0 (0.18)	64.7 (0.23)	64.4 (0.19)	5,429 (26.6)	59.1 (0.18)	59.2 (0.22)	59.8 (0.20)	5,040 (25.7)	9.1 (0.13)	8.4 (0.14)	7.2 (0.12)	389 (7.0)
Associate's degree	70.2 (0.28)	69.1 (0.31)	69.2 (0.31)	2,241 (16.5)	64.7 (0.27)	64.4 (0.32)	65.0 (0.34)	2,102 (15.3)	7.8 (0.19)	6.7 (0.08)	6.2 (0.19)	138 (4.5)
Bachelor's or higher degree	74.9 (0.14)	74.4 (0.14)	74.5 (0.15)	8,487 (29.3)	70.7 (0.13)	70.5 (0.15)	71.0 (0.16)	8,082 (28.9)	5.2 (0.10)	5.2 (0.08)	4.8 (0.09)	405 (7.2)

[1] Percentage of the civilian population who are employed or seeking employment.
[2] Number of persons employed as a percentage of the civilian population.
[3] The percentage of persons in the civilian labor force who are not working and who made specific efforts to find employment sometime during the prior 4 weeks.
[4] Includes equivalency credentials, such as the General Educational Development (GED) credential.

NOTE: Race categories exclude persons of Hispanic ethnicity. Totals include racial/ethnic groups not separately shown. Standard errors were computed using replicate weights.
SOURCE: U.S. Department of Commerce, Census Bureau, American Community Survey, 2010, 2011, and 2012, unpublished tabulations. (This table was prepared January 2014.)

Labor force participation, employment, and unemployment of persons 16 to 24 years old who are not enrolled in school, by age group, sex, race/ethnicity, and educational attainment: 2010, 2011, and 2012

[Standard errors appear in parentheses]

Age group, sex, race/ethnicity, and educational attainment	Labor force participation rate[1] 2010	2011	2012	Number of participants (in thousands) 2012	Employment to population ratio[2] 2010	2011	2012	Number employed (in thousands) 2012	Unemployment rate[3] 2010	2011	2012	Number unemployed (in thousands) 2012
1	2	3	4	5	6	7	8	9	10	11	12	13
16 to 19 years old												
All persons, all education levels	62.7 (0.36)	62.7 (0.43)	64.1 (0.39)	1,571 (17.2)	41.7 (0.34)	41.7 (0.42)	43.5 (0.41)	1,066 (13.9)	33.4 (0.49)	33.5 (0.52)	32.1 (0.50)	505 (9.7)
Less than high school completion	48.6 (0.62)	47.2 (0.75)	47.9 (0.72)	366 (8.1)	29.1 (0.51)	26.6 (0.71)	27.6 (0.63)	211 (6.2)	40.2 (0.79)	43.6 (1.12)	42.5 (1.06)	156 (5.1)
High school completion[4]	70.2 (0.49)	70.0 (0.47)	70.3 (0.53)	986 (14.2)	47.9 (0.52)	47.9 (0.53)	48.6 (0.54)	682 (11.1)	32.4 (0.69)	31.6 (0.61)	30.8 (0.61)	304 (7.8)
At least some college	75.1 (0.99)	74.7 (1.13)	77.1 (1.03)	219 (5.4)	57.9 (1.22)	57.9 (1.22)	61.1 (1.22)	173 (4.9)	22.6 (1.08)	22.5 (1.35)	20.8 (1.12)	46 (2.7)
Male, all education levels	65.2 (0.49)	64.4 (0.58)	66.0 (0.52)	924 (12.3)	42.5 (0.48)	42.0 (0.55)	44.9 (0.49)	628 (9.4)	34.8 (0.62)	34.9 (0.60)	32.0 (0.59)	296 (7.0)
Less than high school completion	53.0 (0.86)	50.9 (1.04)	51.2 (1.09)	234 (6.7)	32.3 (0.82)	28.9 (0.97)	30.1 (0.90)	138 (5.0)	39.0 (1.12)	43.2 (1.36)	41.2 (1.30)	97 (4.2)
High school completion[4]	73.1 (0.65)	71.6 (0.59)	72.5 (0.63)	582 (9.7)	48.1 (0.61)	47.9 (0.71)	50.7 (0.65)	407 (7.9)	34.2 (0.80)	33.1 (0.78)	30.1 (0.75)	175 (5.4)
At least some college	74.3 (1.51)	75.9 (1.54)	77.2 (1.43)	108 (4.1)	55.9 (1.59)	59.0 (1.79)	60.2 (1.58)	84 (3.6)	24.8 (1.51)	22.3 (1.79)	22.1 (1.75)	24 (2.2)
Female, all education levels	59.5 (0.52)	60.4 (0.65)	61.5 (0.66)	647 (10.7)	40.8 (0.56)	41.3 (0.62)	41.6 (0.65)	438 (9.1)	31.4 (0.72)	31.6 (0.75)	32.3 (0.82)	209 (6.3)
Less than high school completion	41.8 (0.91)	41.4 (1.04)	43.0 (1.05)	132 (4.4)	24.0 (0.84)	23.1 (0.90)	23.8 (0.89)	73 (3.3)	42.4 (1.46)	44.3 (1.46)	44.7 (1.70)	59 (2.9)
High school completion[4]	66.7 (0.69)	68.0 (0.77)	67.2 (0.78)	404 (9.1)	46.7 (0.83)	48.0 (0.78)	45.9 (0.92)	275 (7.7)	29.9 (0.99)	29.4 (0.90)	31.8 (1.03)	128 (4.8)
At least some college	75.7 (1.25)	73.6 (1.59)	77.0 (1.34)	111 (4.0)	60.1 (1.52)	57.0 (1.91)	62.0 (1.56)	90 (3.6)	20.7 (1.56)	22.6 (1.78)	19.5 (1.57)	22 (2.0)
White, all education levels	67.5 (0.45)	67.4 (0.55)	68.8 (0.51)	819 (11.1)	46.2 (0.51)	47.4 (0.55)	50.4 (0.58)	600 (9.9)	31.5 (0.62)	29.7 (0.66)	26.7 (0.57)	219 (5.1)
Less than high school completion	49.4 (0.88)	47.5 (1.24)	49.6 (1.07)	162 (5.4)	29.1 (0.72)	28.3 (1.00)	29.1 (1.01)	95 (4.3)	41.0 (1.16)	40.5 (1.52)	41.3 (1.47)	67 (3.0)
High school completion[4]	74.8 (0.52)	74.9 (0.63)	74.8 (0.64)	533 (8.9)	53.4 (0.73)	53.4 (0.67)	56.3 (0.71)	401 (8.1)	30.3 (0.86)	28.7 (0.73)	24.8 (0.70)	132 (4.1)
At least some college	81.2 (1.06)	79.8 (1.30)	81.8 (1.20)	124 (4.3)	64.7 (1.56)	65.0 (1.50)	68.5 (1.36)	104 (3.9)	20.4 (1.51)	18.6 (1.66)	16.2 (1.27)	20 (1.7)
Black, all education levels	52.6 (0.97)	51.4 (1.03)	55.6 (1.12)	242 (6.8)	26.6 (0.88)	26.1 (0.90)	27.6 (1.02)	120 (4.8)	49.5 (1.32)	49.3 (1.31)	50.3 (1.39)	122 (4.8)
Less than high school completion	37.1 (1.48)	35.4 (1.56)	35.4 (1.75)	50 (2.9)	14.1 (1.04)	12.0 (1.16)	12.6 (1.25)	18 (1.8)	62.1 (2.27)	66.2 (2.75)	64.4 (2.97)	32 (2.3)
High school completion[4]	62.6 (1.39)	60.5 (1.34)	63.2 (1.36)	155 (5.9)	33.3 (1.23)	33.0 (1.26)	31.8 (1.47)	78 (4.5)	46.7 (1.68)	45.5 (1.63)	49.6 (1.85)	77 (3.7)
At least some college	66.9 (2.86)	63.3 (3.03)	75.8 (2.88)	37 (3.1)	44.0 (2.99)	42.9 (3.34)	50.1 (2.69)	24 (2.3)	33.2 (3.64)	32.2 (3.71)	33.9 (2.90)	13 (1.5)
Hispanic, all education levels	61.8 (0.76)	63.4 (0.71)	61.9 (0.72)	407 (7.4)	44.2 (0.80)	43.9 (0.87)	42.1 (0.67)	277 (6.0)	28.6 (0.97)	30.8 (1.10)	32.0 (0.96)	130 (4.8)
Less than high school completion	55.2 (1.19)	52.8 (1.09)	52.8 (1.48)	128 (4.9)	38.3 (1.12)	34.7 (1.23)	34.7 (1.27)	84 (3.8)	30.7 (1.48)	36.2 (1.86)	34.2 (1.79)	44 (2.9)
High school completion[4]	66.9 (1.21)	68.9 (1.11)	66.6 (1.05)	235 (5.7)	48.0 (1.13)	49.4 (1.43)	44.8 (1.11)	158 (4.9)	28.2 (1.27)	28.3 (1.58)	32.7 (1.33)	77 (3.7)
At least some college	70.2 (2.49)	73.6 (2.12)	71.2 (2.70)	44 (2.7)	55.6 (2.79)	54.7 (2.58)	56.1 (2.83)	34 (2.4)	20.7 (2.56)	25.6 (2.85)	21.2 (2.42)	9 (1.2)
Asian, all education levels	55.3 (2.92)	55.1 (3.11)	57.5 (3.08)	24 (1.9)	39.5 (2.70)	38.2 (2.84)	48.3 (3.36)	20 (1.9)	28.5 (3.03)	30.6 (3.20)	16.0 (2.76)	4 (0.6)
Less than high school completion	38.5 (5.13)	36.7 (5.19)	34.6 (5.69)	3 (0.7)	26.2 (4.81)	21.3 (4.16)	27.5 (5.25)	‡ (†)	31.8 (7.67)	41.9 (9.67)	20.5 (5.60)	‡ (†)
High school completion[4]	60.2 (3.81)	61.0 (3.85)	65.3 (4.12)	17 (1.5)	40.6 (3.52)	42.0 (3.76)	56.0 (4.27)	15 (1.4)	32.5 (4.35)	31.1 (4.27)	14.3 (3.29)	‡ (†)
At least some college	64.5 (5.61)	61.7 (8.02)	61.8 (7.32)	4 (0.8)	53.9 (6.16)	49.9 (6.86)	49.6 (8.50)	‡ (†)	16.5 ! (5.23)	19.1 ! (6.74)	19.8 ! (8.49)	‡ (†)
American Indian/Alaska Native, all education levels	44.0 (3.34)	47.8 (3.08)	56.1 (3.26)	20 (1.8)	28.5 (2.87)	28.3 (2.78)	28.3 (3.43)	10 (1.4)	35.3 (4.18)	51.1 (4.89)	49.6 (5.04)	10 (1.2)
Less than high school completion	30.4 (4.50)	37.8 (4.83)	45.7 (5.02)	7 (1.2)	15.7 (3.21)	17.3 (3.90)	17.3 (3.98)	‡ (†)	48.3 (7.43)	54.3 (8.63)	62.1 (8.22)	4 (1.0)
High school completion[4]	55.6 (4.89)	55.3 (4.38)	63.6 (4.40)	11 (1.2)	38.4 (4.64)	27.3 (4.55)	36.4 (4.67)	6 (1.1)	30.9 (5.48)	50.6 (6.87)	42.7 (5.70)	5 (0.7)
At least some college	‡ (†)	49.3 (9.42)	66.7 (7.65)	2 (0.5)	44.8 (10.11)	27.6 ! (8.42)	38.3 (8.74)	‡ (†)	‡ (†)	19.1 ! (†)	42.6 (11.01)	‡ (†)
20 to 24 years old												
All persons, all education levels	80.2 (0.14)	79.9 (0.13)	80.5 (0.13)	10,170 (33.4)	65.3 (0.18)	65.1 (0.17)	66.6 (0.18)	8,407 (32.1)	18.6 (0.17)	18.6 (0.18)	17.3 (0.18)	1,763 (19.1)
Less than high school completion	65.5 (0.38)	64.5 (0.42)	64.2 (0.47)	1,295 (17.6)	46.3 (0.41)	45.5 (0.46)	45.3 (0.44)	913 (14.0)	29.3 (0.53)	29.5 (0.57)	29.5 (0.58)	382 (9.5)
High school completion[4]	78.8 (0.20)	77.9 (0.23)	78.4 (0.24)	4,013 (23.1)	61.6 (0.28)	61.0 (0.28)	62.4 (0.30)	3,193 (20.3)	21.8 (0.30)	21.8 (0.30)	20.4 (0.30)	820 (13.8)
Some college, no degree	85.0 (0.30)	85.1 (0.30)	85.3 (0.27)	2,663 (20.3)	71.6 (0.39)	72.1 (0.44)	72.7 (0.36)	2,272 (19.2)	15.8 (0.31)	15.2 (0.31)	14.7 (0.33)	391 (9.2)
Associate's degree	90.6 (0.47)	90.1 (0.54)	89.4 (0.60)	544 (10.4)	82.3 (0.60)	81.6 (0.79)	81.2 (0.72)	494 (9.7)	9.2 (0.55)	9.4 (0.71)	9.2 (0.53)	50 (3.1)
Bachelor's or higher degree	93.3 (0.26)	93.4 (0.25)	93.8 (0.25)	1,654 (17.8)	86.0 (0.34)	86.2 (0.40)	87.0 (0.35)	1,535 (17.2)	7.9 (0.28)	7.8 (0.31)	7.2 (0.27)	120 (4.7)

See notes at end of table.

Labor force participation, employment, and unemployment of persons 16 to 24 years old who are not enrolled in school, by age group, sex, race/ethnicity, and educational attainment: 2010, 2011, and 2012—Continued

[Standard errors appear in parentheses]

Age group, sex, race/ethnicity, and educational attainment	Labor force participation rate[1] 2010	Labor force participation rate[1] 2011	Labor force participation rate[1] 2012	Number of participants (in thousands) 2012	Employment to population ratio[2] 2010	Employment to population ratio[2] 2011	Employment to population ratio[2] 2012	Number employed (in thousands) 2012	Unemployment rate[3] 2010	Unemployment rate[3] 2011	Unemployment rate[3] 2012	Number unemployed (in thousands) 2012
1	2	3	4	5	6	7	8	9	10	11	12	13
Male, all education levels	83.0 (0.19)	82.6 (0.19)	83.0 (0.17)	5,624 (25.8)	66.3 (0.23)	66.6 (0.25)	67.8 (0.24)	4,598 (25.0)	20.1 (0.22)	19.4 (0.23)	18.2 (0.23)	1,026 (13.7)
Less than high school completion	71.8 (0.47)	71.0 (0.47)	69.7 (0.57)	843 (13.0)	51.8 (0.55)	52.1 (0.53)	50.7 (0.65)	614 (10.6)	27.8 (0.63)	26.6 (0.62)	27.1 (0.74)	229 (7.6)
High school completion[4]	82.6 (0.30)	81.9 (0.27)	81.9 (0.27)	2,448 (16.7)	63.9 (0.36)	63.6 (0.36)	65.1 (0.39)	1,947 (15.5)	22.7 (0.35)	22.3 (0.39)	20.5 (0.38)	502 (10.3)
Some college, no degree	87.4 (0.41)	87.6 (0.42)	88.2 (0.31)	1,390 (16.2)	73.4 (0.54)	73.4 (0.60)	74.7 (0.45)	1,178 (15.2)	16.1 (0.43)	16.2 (0.52)	15.2 (0.41)	212 (6.0)
Associate's degree	92.9 (0.66)	92.3 (0.68)	92.2 (0.70)	263 (6.7)	83.4 (0.83)	83.9 (0.95)	82.8 (1.02)	236 (6.3)	10.3 (0.83)	9.1 (0.81)	10.2 (0.85)	27 (2.4)
Bachelor's or higher degree	95.3 (0.34)	93.8 (0.44)	94.9 (0.30)	680 (11.9)	86.5 (0.56)	85.7 (0.62)	87.0 (0.50)	623 (11.4)	9.3 (0.50)	8.6 (0.48)	8.4 (0.39)	57 (2.8)
Female, all education levels	76.9 (0.23)	76.7 (0.21)	77.7 (0.21)	4,545 (21.8)	64.0 (0.29)	63.3 (0.26)	65.1 (0.27)	3,809 (21.7)	16.7 (0.25)	17.5 (0.26)	16.2 (0.24)	737 (11.2)
Less than high school completion	55.5 (0.73)	54.8 (0.71)	56.0 (0.81)	452 (10.4)	37.6 (0.75)	35.5 (0.73)	37.0 (0.74)	299 (8.2)	32.2 (0.96)	35.2 (1.05)	33.9 (1.07)	153 (6.2)
High school completion[4]	73.6 (0.33)	72.5 (0.46)	73.6 (0.39)	1,565 (12.8)	58.5 (0.43)	57.3 (0.48)	58.6 (0.48)	1,246 (12.6)	20.6 (0.50)	21.0 (0.44)	20.4 (0.46)	319 (7.7)
Some college, no degree	82.7 (0.44)	82.6 (0.43)	82.3 (0.42)	1,273 (14.5)	70.9 (0.52)	69.8 (0.53)	70.7 (0.54)	1,094 (13.6)	14.2 (0.39)	15.4 (0.48)	14.0 (0.47)	179 (6.4)
Associate's degree	88.6 (0.73)	88.4 (0.78)	87.0 (0.89)	282 (7.9)	81.3 (0.91)	79.7 (1.11)	79.7 (1.01)	258 (7.3)	8.3 (0.72)	9.7 (1.02)	8.3 (0.65)	23 (2.0)
Bachelor's or higher degree	92.0 (0.35)	93.1 (0.34)	93.0 (0.32)	974 (11.8)	85.6 (0.44)	86.5 (0.47)	87.0 (0.41)	911 (11.7)	6.9 (0.32)	7.2 (0.38)	6.4 (0.33)	63 (3.3)
White, all education levels	84.0 (0.19)	83.4 (0.22)	84.1 (0.17)	5,777 (25.1)	70.9 (0.22)	70.5 (0.26)	72.4 (0.20)	4,970 (22.4)	15.6 (0.17)	15.4 (0.21)	14.0 (0.20)	806 (12.4)
Less than high school completion	65.2 (0.67)	63.6 (0.83)	64.6 (0.80)	462 (9.3)	44.9 (0.70)	42.4 (0.67)	45.0 (0.70)	322 (7.6)	31.1 (0.88)	33.4 (0.77)	30.2 (1.00)	140 (5.7)
High school completion[4]	81.5 (0.27)	80.4 (0.36)	81.1 (0.34)	2,175 (17.6)	65.3 (0.38)	65.1 (0.37)	66.6 (0.39)	1,788 (15.7)	19.8 (0.38)	19.0 (0.35)	17.8 (0.35)	387 (8.4)
Some college, no degree	86.8 (0.36)	86.9 (0.33)	87.1 (0.35)	1,537 (15.9)	75.5 (0.48)	75.7 (0.49)	75.7 (0.45)	1,359 (15.2)	13.0 (0.37)	12.9 (0.40)	11.6 (0.38)	177 (6.1)
Associate's degree	92.5 (0.49)	91.7 (0.59)	91.5 (0.61)	382 (9.6)	86.2 (0.59)	84.9 (0.79)	84.5 (0.78)	353 (8.8)	6.9 (0.52)	7.5 (0.70)	7.7 (0.59)	29 (2.5)
Bachelor's or higher degree	95.4 (0.23)	94.9 (0.30)	95.6 (0.24)	1,220 (15.4)	89.1 (0.33)	88.7 (0.48)	88.9 (0.31)	1,148 (15.1)	6.6 (0.26)	6.6 (0.36)	6.0 (0.27)	73 (3.4)
Black, all education levels	71.4 (0.44)	71.9 (0.43)	73.0 (0.45)	1,451 (15.1)	48.5 (0.48)	48.8 (0.51)	50.4 (0.61)	1,003 (15.1)	32.2 (0.57)	32.1 (0.56)	30.9 (0.61)	449 (9.1)
Less than high school completion	50.2 (1.14)	51.3 (1.08)	53.3 (1.09)	209 (7.0)	24.0 (0.75)	23.7 (0.94)	25.6 (0.95)	97 (4.5)	52.1 (1.24)	53.8 (1.54)	52.1 (1.60)	106 (5.1)
High school completion[4]	71.8 (0.63)	71.4 (0.64)	71.1 (0.61)	637 (11.4)	47.1 (0.75)	46.1 (0.86)	47.7 (0.76)	428 (8.9)	34.5 (0.86)	35.4 (0.90)	32.9 (0.81)	210 (6.6)
Some college, no degree	83.4 (0.71)	81.8 (0.81)	84.0 (0.72)	442 (8.4)	63.7 (0.90)	62.8 (0.96)	63.0 (1.08)	332 (8.5)	23.6 (0.94)	23.3 (1.02)	25.0 (1.01)	110 (4.5)
Associate's degree	85.5 (2.18)	88.9 (1.79)	86.3 (1.98)	50 (3.0)	68.9 (2.68)	74.1 (2.46)	73.0 (2.75)	42 (3.0)	19.3 (2.66)	16.6 (2.59)	15.4 (2.47)	8 (1.3)
Bachelor's or higher degree	91.1 (1.30)	94.7 (0.93)	92.9 (1.03)	119 (4.3)	77.1 (1.72)	82.1 (1.38)	81.1 (1.46)	104 (3.8)	15.4 (1.43)	13.3 (1.41)	12.7 (1.37)	15 (1.8)
Hispanic, all education levels	77.8 (0.28)	77.9 (0.26)	77.8 (0.32)	2,293 (17.6)	64.1 (0.34)	63.9 (0.37)	64.5 (0.38)	1,900 (17.8)	17.6 (0.38)	18.0 (0.35)	17.1 (0.38)	393 (9.0)
Less than high school completion	72.2 (0.53)	71.6 (0.65)	69.4 (0.72)	564 (11.8)	57.1 (0.60)	58.2 (0.74)	55.0 (0.83)	447 (10.7)	20.9 (0.71)	18.7 (0.69)	20.7 (0.81)	117 (5.0)
High school completion[4]	78.4 (0.46)	77.8 (0.48)	78.3 (0.51)	977 (12.6)	64.4 (0.53)	63.0 (0.59)	64.3 (0.60)	803 (12.3)	17.8 (0.53)	19.0 (0.55)	17.9 (0.57)	175 (5.7)
Some college, no degree	82.7 (0.77)	83.4 (0.68)	83.4 (0.54)	523 (9.5)	70.6 (0.82)	68.9 (0.93)	71.2 (0.73)	446 (8.6)	14.6 (0.59)	18.0 (0.79)	14.6 (0.67)	77 (3.8)
Associate's degree	87.7 (1.44)	84.9 (1.69)	84.0 (1.80)	84 (3.9)	73.7 (1.81)	73.7 (2.36)	74.5 (1.90)	75 (3.6)	13.4 (1.63)	13.2 (1.91)	11.4 (1.46)	10 (1.3)
Bachelor's or higher degree	87.7 (1.03)	90.3 (1.06)	91.2 (0.85)	144 (5.6)	79.8 (1.34)	81.4 (1.51)	81.7 (1.31)	129 (4.9)	9.0 (0.98)	10.4 (1.07)	10.4 (1.30)	15 (2.1)
Asian, all education levels	79.1 (1.00)	80.3 (0.87)	78.9 (0.73)	291 (6.9)	67.4 (1.06)	68.3 (1.12)	68.9 (0.97)	252 (6.8)	14.8 (0.80)	14.2 (1.03)	13.4 (0.83)	39 (2.4)
Less than high school completion	66.5 (3.14)	72.1 (2.63)	61.2 (3.18)	24 (1.9)	48.8 (3.41)	54.6 (2.95)	49.3 (3.69)	19 (1.8)	26.6 (3.69)	24.3 (3.30)	19.5 (3.45)	5 (0.9)
High school completion[4]	78.2 (1.93)	78.1 (2.03)	78.9 (1.75)	70 (3.5)	64.6 (2.19)	65.1 (2.36)	65.6 (2.13)	59 (3.1)	17.4 (2.01)	16.7 (1.99)	16.9 (1.93)	12 (1.4)
Some college, no degree	79.2 (1.87)	80.3 (1.68)	80.0 (2.00)	57 (3.5)	70.4 (2.03)	69.5 (2.23)	68.2 (2.29)	49 (3.1)	11.2 (1.20)	13.4 (2.02)	14.8 (2.29)	8 (1.1)
Associate's degree	84.7 (3.31)	86.3 (3.13)	81.2 (3.87)	15 (1.5)	70.4 (3.70)	74.9 (3.48)	75.7 (4.44)	13 (1.5)	16.8 (3.26)	13.2 (2.38)	6.8 ! (3.42)	‡ (†)
Bachelor's or higher degree	82.6 (1.28)	83.3 (1.50)	82.7 (1.23)	125 (4.2)	72.7 (1.49)	73.4 (1.85)	74.4 (1.42)	112 (4.0)	12.0 (0.99)	11.9 (1.30)	10.0 (1.07)	13 (1.4)
American Indian/Alaska Native, all education levels	67.7 (1.96)	65.9 (1.51)	71.8 (1.39)	83 (3.4)	45.1 (1.71)	48.2 (1.93)	50.6 (1.72)	58 (3.0)	33.4 (2.12)	26.9 (2.17)	29.5 (1.82)	24 (1.7)
Less than high school completion	54.0 (4.60)	51.6 (3.44)	55.9 (3.41)	13 (2.1)	23.9 (3.00)	30.6 (3.27)	32.1 (3.53)	8 (2.0)	55.7 (5.32)	40.7 (4.85)	42.5 (4.49)	6 (0.7)
High school completion[4]	69.6 (2.20)	68.3 (2.13)	73.0 (2.25)	41 (2.4)	47.4 (2.57)	50.3 (3.02)	52.8 (3.13)	29 (2.0)	31.9 (3.00)	24.7 (3.23)	31.0 (3.13)	13 (1.2)
Some college, no degree	71.9 (4.82)	74.4 (4.82)	79.0 (2.84)	23 (2.2)	56.0 (3.63)	54.6 (4.15)	61.2 (3.13)	18 (1.9)	22.1 (4.22)	26.6 (3.94)	22.5 (2.76)	5 (0.7)
Associate's degree	80.3 (8.90)	84.0 (6.15)	86.3 (5.12)	3 (0.5)	70.4 (9.36)	76.3 (7.99)	70.4 (5.12)	2 (0.5)	‡ (†)	‡ (†)	‡ (†)	‡ (†)
Bachelor's or higher degree	99.5 (0.53)	82.0 (8.14)	89.7 (4.84)	‡ (†)	96.2 (3.64)	77.9 (8.00)	77.9 (10.74)	‡ (†)	‡ (†)	‡ (†)	‡ (†)	‡ (†)

†Not applicable.

!Interpret data with caution. The coefficient of variation (CV) for this estimate is between 30 and 50 percent.

‡Reporting standards not met. Either there are too few cases for a reliable estimate or the coefficient of variation (CV) is 50 percent or greater.

[1]Percentage of the civilian population who are employed or seeking employment.

[2]Number of persons employed as a percentage of the civilian population.

[3]The percentage of persons in the civilian labor force who are not working and who made specific efforts to find employment sometime during the prior 4 weeks.

[4]Includes equivalency credentials, such as the General Educational Development (GED) credential.

NOTE: Table excludes persons enrolled in school. Race categories exclude persons of Hispanic ethnicity. Totals include racial/ethnic groups not separately shown. Standard errors were computed using replicate weights.

SOURCE: U.S. Department of Commerce, Census Bureau, American Community Survey, 2010, 2011, and 2012, unpublished tabulations. (This table was prepared January 2014.)

Number and percentage of persons 16 to 24 years old who were neither enrolled in school nor working, by educational attainment, age group, family poverty status, and race/ethnicity: 2013

[Standard errors appear in parentheses]

Age group, family poverty status, and race/ethnicity	All 16- to 24-year-olds (in thousands)	Neither enrolled in school nor working						
		Number (in thousands)	Percentage distribution	Percent, by educational attainment				
				Total	Less than high school completion	High school completion[1]	Some college, no bachelor's degree[2]	Bachelor's or higher degree
1	2	3	4	5	6	7	8	9
Total, 16 to 24 years old	39,013 (22.4)	5,584 (126.2)	100.0 (†)	14.3 (0.32)	11.9 (0.46)	29.7 (0.88)	8.4 (0.41)	9.1 (1.00)
White	21,704 (41.9)	2,618 (88.8)	46.9 (1.04)	12.1 (0.41)	9.8 (0.58)	26.8 (1.20)	7.2 (0.52)	8.0 (1.09)
Black	5,617 (32.4)	1,119 (51.0)	20.0 (0.78)	19.9 (0.90)	15.5 (1.36)	37.0 (1.92)	13.0 (1.26)	9.4 (2.79)
Hispanic	8,207 (6.0)	1,392 (48.3)	24.9 (0.79)	17.0 (0.59)	14.8 (0.89)	30.2 (1.45)	9.1 (0.78)	12.2 (3.12)
Asian	1,984 (23.3)	178 (17.8)	3.2 (0.32)	9.0 (0.90)	5.5 (1.48)	19.0 (3.46)	7.0 (1.24)	12.4 (2.33)
Pacific Islander	155 (19.6)	‡ (†)	0.4 (0.12)	14.9 (3.50)	‡ (†)	‡ (†)	‡ (†)	‡ (†)
American Indian/Alaska Native	352 (46.8)	128 (28.8)	2.3 (0.51)	36.5 (4.48)	33.0 (9.21)	52.1 (5.59)	18.1 (5.36)	‡ (†)
Two or more races	993 (43.8)	125 (17.5)	2.2 (0.32)	12.6 (1.67)	10.0 (2.06)	31.2 (4.85)	6.1 ! (2.01)	‡ (†)
Family poverty status								
Poor[3]	7,628 (163.2)	2,077 (78.0)	100.0 (†)	27.2 (0.89)	24.6 (1.15)	45.4 (1.99)	15.8 (1.45)	11.4 (3.15)
White	3,113 (108.2)	835 (53.4)	40.2 (1.95)	26.8 (1.47)	28.3 (2.08)	43.6 (3.13)	15.5 (2.05)	11.3 ! (3.78)
Black	1,685 (65.0)	505 (41.4)	24.3 (1.70)	30.0 (2.16)	24.1 (2.47)	46.7 (3.87)	21.3 (3.77)	‡ (†)
Hispanic	2,105 (77.1)	546 (36.6)	26.3 (1.67)	25.9 (1.47)	22.3 (1.94)	43.2 (3.10)	12.8 (2.33)	‡ (†)
Asian	393 (36.3)	57 (12.2)	2.8 (0.57)	14.6 (2.77)	15.8 ! (5.27)	‡ (†)	8.6 ! (3.21)	‡ (†)
Pacific Islander	‡ (†)	‡ (†)	‡ (†)	‡ (†)	‡ (†)	‡ (†)	‡ (†)	‡ (†)
American Indian/Alaska Native	147 (31.3)	81 (16.8)	3.9 (0.78)	55.3 (5.64)	‡ (†)	‡ (†)	‡ (†)	‡ (†)
Two or more races	167 (20.3)	48 (10.0)	2.3 (0.48)	29.1 (4.81)	‡ (†)	‡ (†)	‡ (†)	‡ (†)
Nonpoor[3]	31,385 (164.4)	3,507 (100.4)	100.0 (†)	11.2 (0.32)	8.3 (0.45)	24.6 (0.95)	7.0 (0.38)	8.8 (1.06)
White	18,591 (115.8)	1,783 (74.5)	50.8 (1.20)	9.6 (0.40)	6.9 (0.56)	22.7 (1.27)	6.0 (0.49)	7.6 (1.17)
Black	3,932 (73.4)	615 (36.7)	17.5 (0.92)	15.6 (0.87)	10.4 (1.38)	31.8 (2.22)	10.7 (1.18)	9.8 ! (2.96)
Hispanic	6,102 (78.7)	846 (37.0)	24.1 (0.99)	13.9 (0.57)	11.2 (0.84)	25.5 (1.61)	8.3 (0.78)	10.9 (2.99)
Asian	1,592 (41.2)	121 (14.9)	3.4 (0.42)	7.6 (0.92)	3.1 ! (1.18)	14.0 (3.41)	6.6 (1.38)	12.9 (2.54)
Pacific Islander	138 (19.1)	‡ (†)	0.6 ! (0.17)	14.2 (3.77)	‡ (†)	‡ (†)	‡ (†)	‡ (†)
American Indian/Alaska Native	205 (25.2)	47 ! (16.3)	1.3 ! (0.46)	23.0 (6.44)	26.9 ! (12.55)	‡ (†)	‡ (†)	‡ (†)
Two or more races	827 (42.9)	76 (13.6)	2.2 (0.39)	9.2 (1.59)	8.1 (2.03)	22.0 (5.06)	4.6 ! (1.76)	‡ (†)
Total, 16 to 19 years old	16,859 (5.0)	1,445 (55.7)	100.0 (†)	8.6 (0.33)	6.0 (0.33)	26.4 (1.40)	4.7 (0.59)	‡ (†)
White	9,329 (26.2)	729 (39.8)	50.4 (1.97)	7.8 (0.43)	5.7 (0.43)	24.9 (1.93)	3.7 (0.78)	‡ (†)
Black	2,396 (20.5)	252 (22.8)	17.4 (1.41)	10.5 (0.95)	6.6 (0.89)	29.4 (3.25)	9.0 (2.34)	‡ (†)
Hispanic	3,655 (3.5)	359 (26.2)	24.9 (1.60)	9.8 (0.72)	6.9 (0.68)	28.8 (2.61)	6.0 (1.20)	‡ (†)
Asian	774 (21.7)	‡ (†)	2.8 (0.59)	5.2 (1.10)	3.1 ! (1.04)	19.4 ! (5.95)	‡ (†)	‡ (†)
Pacific Islander	‡ (†)	‡ (†)	‡ (†)	‡ (†)	‡ (†)	‡ (†)	‡ (†)	‡ (†)
American Indian/Alaska Native	145 (26.1)	‡ (†)	‡ (†)	19.2 ! (8.82)	‡ (†)	‡ (†)	‡ (†)	‡ (†)
Two or more races	495 (28.6)	‡ (†)	2.3 (0.57)	6.6 (1.64)	5.6 (1.64)	‡ (†)	‡ (†)	‡ (†)
Poor[3]	3,051 (79.5)	482 (32.2)	33.4 (1.78)	15.8 (0.93)	11.4 (0.99)	39.6 (3.46)	10.2 (2.45)	‡ (†)
Nonpoor[3]	13,808 (79.8)	963 (44.6)	66.6 (1.78)	7.0 (0.32)	4.7 (0.31)	22.8 (1.61)	3.9 (0.59)	‡ (†)
Total, 20 to 24 years old	22,153 (21.6)	4,139 (106.0)	100.0 (†)	18.7 (0.48)	45.5 (1.76)	30.9 (1.00)	9.3 (0.48)	9.2 (1.02)
White	12,375 (35.6)	1,890 (72.4)	45.7 (1.12)	15.3 (0.58)	48.1 (2.83)	27.6 (1.40)	8.1 (0.59)	8.1 (1.11)
Black	3,221 (27.2)	868 (48.7)	21.0 (0.97)	26.9 (1.50)	58.4 (4.68)	39.6 (2.27)	13.7 (1.46)	9.4 ! (2.96)
Hispanic	4,551 (6.3)	1,032 (39.6)	24.9 (0.94)	22.7 (0.87)	37.6 (2.45)	30.7 (1.71)	10.0 (1.01)	12.5 (3.22)
Asian	1,211 (28.7)	138 (16.6)	3.3 (0.40)	11.4 (1.33)	‡ (†)	18.8 (4.32)	8.1 (1.47)	12.2 (2.40)
Pacific Islander	90 (15.8)	‡ (†)	0.5 ! (0.15)	20.9 (5.83)	‡ (†)	‡ (†)	‡ (†)	‡ (†)
American Indian/Alaska Native	207 (26.5)	101 (18.2)	2.4 (0.43)	48.7 (5.60)	‡ (†)	56.8 (8.52)	‡ (†)	‡ (†)
Two or more races	498 (29.7)	92 (14.7)	2.2 (0.35)	18.5 (2.76)	‡ (†)	36.2 (5.81)	7.1 ! (2.49)	‡ (†)
Poor[3]	4,577 (120.0)	1,594 (69.2)	38.5 (1.35)	34.8 (1.39)	58.8 (2.62)	47.2 (2.20)	16.9 (1.63)	11.4 (3.15)
Nonpoor[3]	17,577 (121.7)	2,545 (86.0)	61.5 (1.35)	14.5 (0.48)	36.2 (2.43)	25.2 (1.07)	7.8 (0.45)	8.9 (1.09)

†Not applicable.

!Interpret data with caution. The coefficient of variation (CV) for this estimate is between 30 and 50 percent.

‡Reporting standards not met. Either there are too few cases for a reliable estimate or the coefficient of variation (CV) is 50 percent or greater.

[1]Includes equivalency credentials, such as the General Educational Development (GED) credential.

[2]Includes persons with no college degree as well as those with an associate's degree.

[3]Poor is defined to include families with incomes below the poverty threshold. Nonpoor is defined to include families with incomes at or above the poverty threshold. For information about how the Census Bureau determines who is in poverty, see http://www.census.gov/hhes/www/poverty/about/overview/measure.html.

NOTE: Race categories exclude persons of Hispanic ethnicity. Standard errors were computed using replicate weights. Detail may not sum to totals because of rounding.

SOURCE: U.S. Department of Commerce, Census Bureau, Current Population Survey (CPS), March 2013, unpublished data. (This table was prepared October 2013.)

Unemployment rates of persons 16 to 64 years old, by age group and educational attainment: Selected years, 1975 through 2013

[Standard errors appear in parentheses]

Age group and educational attainment	1975	1980	1985	1990	1995	2000	2003	2005	2006	2007	2008	2009	2010	2011	2012	2013
1	2	3	4	5	6	7	8	9	10	11	12	13	14	15	16	17
16 to 19 years old, all education levels[1]	— (†)	— (†)	— (†)	17.0 (1.83)	21.0 (2.06)	17.2 (1.89)	27.0 (1.73)	22.8 (1.39)	20.6 (1.18)	19.5 (1.23)	20.9 (1.36)	30.3 (1.59)	31.9 (1.59)	28.8 (1.62)	30.6 (1.57)	29.4 (1.57)
Less than high school completion	— (†)	— (†)	— (†)	26.2 (3.54)	30.3 (3.67)	21.4 (3.23)	34.6 (2.96)	30.3 (2.34)	25.8 (2.24)	28.6 (2.42)	30.8 (2.40)	38.9 (3.05)	41.7 (3.14)	35.1 (3.42)	41.1 (3.01)	36.3 (2.70)
High school completion[2]	— (†)	— (†)	— (†)	11.7 (2.05)	15.1 (2.59)	15.3 (2.54)	22.4 (2.25)	19.1 (2.02)	17.6 (1.43)	15.1 (1.59)	17.2 (1.62)	29.1 (1.80)	29.6 (2.08)	28.9 (2.18)	28.7 (2.00)	29.2 (2.12)
At least some college	— (†)	— (†)	— (†)	‡! (†)	12.4! (5.19)	‡ (†)	20.9 (5.33)	15.8 (3.54)	17.7 (3.54)	8.9 (2.44)	11.3 (2.99)	18.1 (3.68)	18.1 (3.65)	16.2 (3.55)	19.6 (3.83)	16.2 (3.32)
20 to 24 years old, all education levels[1]	— (†)	— (†)	— (†)	8.2 (0.63)	10.7 (0.72)	9.2 (0.63)	11.4 (0.55)	10.9 (0.48)	9.3 (0.46)	9.9 (0.42)	10.7 (0.43)	17.0 (0.62)	18.8 (0.66)	18.1 (0.60)	15.5 (0.55)	15.2 (0.62)
Less than high school completion	— (†)	— (†)	— (†)	17.4 (2.15)	19.5 (2.37)	16.6 (2.18)	17.6 (1.55)	18.9 (1.34)	15.7 (1.34)	18.6 (1.47)	19.2 (1.66)	29.0 (1.69)	32.3 (1.80)	30.1 (1.95)	27.6 (2.12)	29.2 (2.27)
High school completion[2]	— (†)	— (†)	— (†)	7.8 (0.88)	12.0 (1.18)	10.0 (1.12)	11.7 (0.86)	12.0 (0.73)	10.4 (0.70)	9.4 (0.70)	13.0 (0.70)	20.3 (1.05)	22.3 (0.95)	21.6 (1.02)	18.3 (0.96)	17.5 (0.91)
Some college, no bachelor's degree[3]	— (†)	— (†)	— (†)	4.8 (1.09)	7.3 (1.13)	5.2 (1.02)	9.8 (0.97)	7.3 (0.76)	7.1 (0.68)	7.2 (0.72)	6.8 (0.67)	12.1 (0.94)	14.2 (1.07)	14.0 (0.98)	12.7 (0.89)	12.2 (1.02)
Bachelor's or higher degree	— (†)	— (†)	— (†)	3.1! (1.12)	4.1! (1.26)	5.0 (1.43)	5.8 (0.91)	5.4 (0.91)	3.9 (0.72)	3.4 (0.68)	5.4 (0.78)	7.9 (1.02)	7.9 (1.15)	8.7 (1.05)	6.0 (0.95)	7.0 (1.09)
25 to 64 years old, all education levels	6.8 (0.21)	5.0 (0.17)	6.1 (0.18)	3.6 (0.14)	4.8 (0.15)	3.3 (0.13)	5.3 (0.11)	4.4 (0.09)	4.1 (0.09)	3.9 (0.08)	4.4 (0.09)	8.1 (0.12)	9.1 (0.13)	8.3 (0.13)	6.6 (0.11)	6.6 (0.12)
Less than high school completion	10.5 (0.49)	8.4 (0.48)	11.4 (0.61)	7.7 (0.55)	10.0 (0.66)	7.9 (0.63)	9.9 (0.48)	9.0 (0.36)	8.3 (0.41)	8.5 (0.44)	10.1 (0.44)	15.8 (0.54)	16.8 (0.54)	16.2 (0.55)	14.3 (0.49)	12.7 (0.46)
High school completion[2]	6.8 (0.34)	5.1 (0.27)	6.9 (0.31)	3.8 (0.23)	5.2 (0.28)	3.8 (0.25)	6.4 (0.23)	5.5 (0.17)	4.7 (0.16)	4.7 (0.15)	5.8 (0.18)	10.4 (0.21)	12.1 (0.26)	10.9 (0.27)	9.2 (0.25)	8.7 (0.27)
Some college, no bachelor's degree[3]	5.5 (0.50)	4.3 (0.42)	4.7 (0.37)	3.1 (0.29)	4.5 (0.29)	3.0 (0.24)	5.2 (0.21)	4.2 (0.17)	3.9 (0.17)	3.7 (0.18)	4.2 (0.17)	8.0 (0.22)	8.8 (0.23)	8.1 (0.20)	7.9 (0.24)	6.5 (0.21)
Bachelor's or higher degree	2.4 (0.30)	1.9 (0.23)	2.4 (0.24)	1.7 (0.19)	2.5 (0.21)	1.5 (0.16)	3.0 (0.15)	2.3 (0.13)	2.3 (0.11)	2.0 (0.10)	2.1 (0.11)	4.3 (0.15)	4.7 (0.15)	4.4 (0.15)	4.1 (0.14)	3.8 (0.13)
25 to 34 years old, all education levels	8.6 (0.41)	6.8 (0.32)	7.3 (0.33)	4.8 (0.27)	5.8 (0.30)	4.0 (0.27)	6.3 (0.24)	5.8 (0.18)	5.5 (0.19)	4.9 (0.18)	5.9 (0.21)	10.1 (0.27)	10.8 (0.28)	10.0 (0.28)	9.2 (0.26)	8.0 (0.23)
Less than high school completion	17.2 (1.36)	13.7 (1.24)	15.5 (1.38)	12.0 (1.21)	12.9 (1.32)	10.3 (1.33)	12.4 (0.96)	11.6 (0.69)	11.0 (0.84)	10.3 (0.91)	14.2 (0.93)	19.9 (1.05)	20.3 (1.02)	19.7 (1.18)	16.8 (1.09)	15.1 (0.97)
High school completion[2]	9.4 (0.67)	7.9 (0.55)	9.1 (0.57)	5.1 (0.44)	6.8 (0.56)	4.8 (0.54)	8.0 (0.50)	7.7 (0.41)	6.5 (0.40)	6.2 (0.36)	8.5 (0.49)	14.1 (0.57)	15.9 (0.62)	14.3 (0.55)	12.8 (0.57)	12.1 (0.57)
Some college, no bachelor's degree[3]	6.7 (0.85)	6.0 (0.64)	5.4 (0.60)	3.8 (0.51)	5.0 (0.52)	3.6 (0.49)	5.8 (0.43)	5.4 (0.36)	5.3 (0.35)	4.6 (0.34)	6.0 (0.33)	9.8 (0.46)	10.6 (0.44)	10.1 (0.46)	10.1 (0.51)	8.0 (0.42)
Bachelor's or higher degree	2.9 (0.50)	2.5 (0.39)	2.8 (0.41)	1.9 (0.34)	2.7 (0.40)	1.6 (0.31)	3.1 (0.30)	2.6 (0.26)	2.8 (0.25)	2.2 (0.23)	2.2 (0.21)	4.5 (0.29)	4.5 (0.28)	4.3 (0.31)	4.1 (0.28)	3.6 (0.25)
35 to 44 years old, all education levels	6.4 (0.41)	4.3 (0.31)	5.6 (0.33)	3.3 (0.24)	4.6 (0.27)	3.5 (0.23)	5.5 (0.21)	4.2 (0.14)	4.1 (0.17)	3.7 (0.15)	4.3 (0.17)	7.9 (0.18)	9.2 (0.24)	8.2 (0.23)	7.1 (0.22)	6.4 (0.19)
Less than high school completion	11.2 (1.02)	9.0 (1.00)	12.4 (1.29)	8.3 (1.17)	10.5 (1.28)	8.4 (1.14)	10.2 (0.86)	8.7 (0.63)	8.6 (0.70)	9.3 (0.80)	9.1 (0.79)	15.3 (0.87)	17.8 (1.07)	15.9 (1.04)	14.1 (0.88)	11.5 (0.80)
High school completion[2]	5.7 (0.60)	4.2 (0.49)	6.1 (0.55)	3.7 (0.41)	5.1 (0.48)	3.9 (0.43)	6.7 (0.41)	5.2 (0.31)	5.1 (0.31)	4.8 (0.29)	6.0 (0.35)	10.6 (0.44)	11.9 (0.51)	11.3 (0.44)	9.1 (0.48)	8.5 (0.50)
Some college, no bachelor's degree[3]	4.6 (0.95)	3.1 (0.64)	4.8 (0.69)	2.8 (0.47)	4.7 (0.49)	3.9 (0.41)	5.0 (0.38)	3.9 (0.32)	3.7 (0.32)	3.0 (0.28)	3.8 (0.27)	7.2 (0.36)	9.2 (0.42)	7.5 (0.39)	7.4 (0.44)	6.7 (0.40)
Bachelor's or higher degree	2.3 (0.59)	1.6 (0.41)	2.2 (0.39)	1.6 (0.31)	2.2 (0.34)	1.8 (0.31)	3.0 (0.28)	2.0 (0.19)	2.0 (0.19)	1.5 (0.14)	1.9 (0.17)	4.2 (0.26)	4.6 (0.26)	4.6 (0.29)	3.6 (0.26)	3.6 (0.23)
45 to 54 years old, all education levels	5.9 (0.39)	3.9 (0.32)	5.4 (0.39)	2.5 (0.26)	3.9 (0.29)	2.4 (0.22)	4.8 (0.21)	3.9 (0.16)	3.4 (0.15)	3.5 (0.17)	3.9 (0.16)	7.4 (0.21)	8.4 (0.22)	7.5 (0.20)	6.8 (0.18)	6.0 (0.18)
Less than high school completion	8.5 (0.81)	6.6 (0.78)	10.2 (1.16)	4.7 (0.89)	7.9 (1.24)	6.1 (1.16)	8.4 (0.93)	7.0 (0.66)	5.9 (0.73)	7.3 (0.71)	8.9 (0.74)	13.6 (0.95)	15.6 (0.98)	16.3 (0.92)	13.5 (0.92)	12.3 (0.94)
High school completion[2]	5.6 (0.60)	3.4 (0.48)	5.4 (0.60)	2.3 (0.39)	4.0 (0.53)	2.7 (0.42)	5.6 (0.41)	4.6 (0.33)	3.9 (0.30)	4.0 (0.31)	4.7 (0.34)	8.8 (0.42)	11.0 (0.43)	9.3 (0.42)	7.8 (0.36)	7.8 (0.40)
Some college, no bachelor's degree[3]	4.7 (1.00)	3.0 (0.78)	3.2 (0.79)	2.6 (0.62)	3.9 (0.56)	2.4 (0.40)	5.1 (0.44)	3.7 (0.30)	3.4 (0.20)	3.7 (0.33)	4.0 (0.32)	7.5 (0.39)	7.6 (0.40)	7.1 (0.35)	6.9 (0.36)	5.2 (0.35)
Bachelor's or higher degree	2.0! (0.61)	1.3! (0.44)	2.1 (0.54)	1.4 (0.38)	2.4 (0.41)	1.3 (0.28)	2.9 (0.28)	2.5 (0.26)	2.3 (0.20)	1.8 (0.18)	1.9 (0.18)	4.3 (0.29)	4.8 (0.30)	4.0 (0.27)	3.9 (0.27)	3.8 (0.26)
55 to 64 years old, all education levels	5.5 (0.46)	3.2 (0.35)	4.6 (0.44)	2.8 (0.36)	3.9 (0.42)	2.8 (0.35)	4.2 (0.27)	3.7 (0.20)	2.9 (0.18)	3.1 (0.19)	3.3 (0.18)	6.7 (0.25)	7.3 (0.25)	6.9 (0.25)	6.6 (0.23)	5.7 (0.23)
Less than high school completion	7.1 (0.79)	5.2 (0.77)	7.1 (1.01)	3.9 (0.90)	6.7 (1.35)	5.2 (1.28)	6.5 (1.02)	7.5 (0.90)	6.0 (0.82)	5.3 (0.72)	5.6 (0.77)	12.7 (1.25)	10.1 (0.99)	11.5 (1.02)	11.5 (1.05)	11.2 (1.19)
High school completion[2]	5.1 (0.76)	2.7 (0.51)	4.5 (0.69)	3.0 (0.59)	3.4 (0.65)	3.2 (0.62)	4.5 (0.54)	4.3 (0.39)	2.9 (0.29)	3.7 (0.38)	3.4 (0.35)	7.8 (0.50)	9.3 (0.56)	8.4 (0.58)	7.1 (0.50)	6.4 (0.47)
Some college, no bachelor's degree[3]	4.1! (1.26)	2.0! (0.77)	3.0! (1.00)	2.2! (0.82)	3.2 (0.80)	2.8 (0.70)	4.4 (0.54)	3.5 (0.37)	3.1 (0.34)	3.5 (0.39)	3.7 (0.37)	7.0 (0.50)	7.7 (0.52)	7.3 (0.45)	7.1 (0.44)	5.8 (0.40)
Bachelor's or higher degree	1.5! (0.75)	‡! (†)	2.2! (0.70)	1.8! (0.62)	3.3 (0.79)	1.4! (0.46)	3.1 (0.41)	2.3 (0.30)	2.0 (0.22)	1.8 (0.22)	2.4 (0.26)	4.3 (0.33)	5.0 (0.34)	4.9 (0.35)	4.8 (0.38)	4.2 (0.29)

—Not available.
†Not applicable.
!Interpret data with caution. The coefficient of variation (CV) for this estimate is between 30 and 50 percent.
‡Reporting standards not met. The coefficient of variation (CV) for this estimate is 50 percent or greater.
[1]Data for 16- to 19-year-olds and 20- to 24-year-olds exclude persons enrolled in school.
[2]Includes equivalency credentials, such as the General Educational Development (GED) credential.
[3]Includes persons with no college degree as well as those with an associate's degree.

NOTE: The unemployment rate is the percentage of persons in the civilian labor force who are not working and who made specific efforts to find employment sometime during the prior 4 weeks. The civilian labor force consists of all civilians who are employed or seeking employment. Some data have been revised from previously published figures. SOURCE: U.S. Department of Labor, Bureau of Labor Statistics, Office of Employment and Unemployment Statistics, unpublished annual average data from the Current Population Survey (CPS), selected years, 1975 through 2013. (This table was prepared November 2013.)

Occupation of employed persons 25 years old and over, by highest level of educational attainment and sex: 2012

[Standard errors appear in parentheses]

Sex and occupation	Total employed (in thousands)	Percentage distribution, by highest level of educational attainment				College		
		Total	Less than high school completion	High school completion (includes equivalency)	Some college, no degree	Associate's degree	Bachelor's degree	Master's or higher degree
1	2	3	4	5	6	7	8	9
All persons	**124,635** (231.4)	**100.0**	**8.0** (0.09)	**27.1** (0.15)	**16.8** (0.12)	**11.0** (0.10)	**23.6** (0.14)	**13.6** (0.11)
Management, professional, and related	51,013 (221.9)	100.0	1.3 (0.06)	11.1 (0.16)	11.4 (0.16)	10.7 (0.16)	36.8 (0.25)	28.8 (0.23)
Management, business, and financial operations	21,794 (160.2)	100.0	2.2 (0.12)	16.6 (0.29)	14.6 (0.28)	9.2 (0.23)	38.2 (0.38)	19.3 (0.31)
Professional and related	29,219 (181.2)	100.0	0.7 (0.06)	7.0 (0.17)	9.0 (0.19)	11.8 (0.22)	35.7 (0.32)	35.8 (0.32)
Education, training, and library	7,828 (100.1)	100.0	0.6 (0.10)	6.5 (0.32)	7.0 (0.33)	5.4 (0.30)	34.9 (0.62)	45.6 (0.65)
Preschool and kindergarten teachers	593 (28.1)	100.0	1.2! (0.51)	14.2 (1.66)	17.4 (1.80)	13.2 (1.60)	38.1 (2.31)	15.9 (1.73)
Elementary and middle school teachers	2,713 (59.8)	100.0	0.2! (0.10)	2.3 (0.33)	2.7 (0.36)	2.2 (0.33)	44.7 (1.10)	47.8 (1.11)
Secondary school teachers	1,071 (37.7)	100.0	‡ (†)	1.2! (0.39)	1.7 (0.45)	1.6 (0.44)	42.7 (1.75)	52.8 (1.76)
Special education teachers	351 (21.6)	100.0	# (†)	3.1! (1.08)	3.4! (1.12)	3.7! (1.17)	34.5 (2.93)	55.3 (3.07)
Postsecondary teachers	1,249 (40.7)	100.0	‡ (†)	1.4 (0.38)	2.0 (0.46)	2.5 (0.51)	13.9 (1.13)	80.0 (1.31)
Other education, training, and library workers	675 (30.0)	100.0	2.2 (0.66)	10.7 (1.37)	14.2 (1.55)	8.7 (1.26)	39.0 (2.17)	25.3 (1.94)
Service occupations	19,730 (153.4)	100.0	16.3 (0.30)	37.4 (0.40)	19.8 (0.33)	11.9 (0.27)	12.1 (0.27)	2.5 (0.13)
Sales and office occupations	27,462 (176.7)	100.0	4.6 (0.15)	31.4 (0.32)	24.1 (0.30)	12.4 (0.23)	22.6 (0.29)	4.8 (0.15)
Natural resources, construction, and maintenance	11,458 (119.8)	100.0	19.5 (0.43)	42.9 (0.53)	17.4 (0.41)	11.7 (0.35)	7.2 (0.28)	1.4 (0.12)
Production, transportation, and material moving	14,972 (135.6)	100.0	16.9 (0.35)	47.8 (0.47)	17.5 (0.36)	8.1 (0.26)	7.9 (0.25)	1.8 (0.12)
Males	**66,455** (155.7)	**100.0**	**9.5** (0.13)	**28.9** (0.20)	**16.3** (0.16)	**9.6** (0.13)	**22.6** (0.18)	**13.1** (0.15)
Management, professional, and related	24,884 (153.4)	100.0	1.7 (0.09)	11.5 (0.23)	11.4 (0.23)	8.3 (0.20)	37.1 (0.35)	30.0 (0.33)
Management, business, and financial operations	12,334 (117.6)	100.0	2.7 (0.17)	17.1 (0.39)	14.0 (0.36)	8.0 (0.28)	38.2 (0.50)	20.0 (0.41)
Professional and related	12,551 (118.5)	100.0	0.7 (0.09)	6.0 (0.24)	8.9 (0.29)	8.7 (0.29)	35.9 (0.49)	39.8 (0.50)
Education, training, and library	2,054 (51.0)	100.0	0.5! (0.17)	3.2 (0.44)	4.2 (0.51)	3.0 (0.43)	33.5 (1.18)	55.6 (1.25)
Service occupations	8,541 (100.2)	100.0	16.5 (0.46)	35.8 (0.59)	20.1 (0.49)	10.9 (0.38)	13.8 (0.43)	2.9 (0.21)
Sales and office occupations	10,398 (109.3)	100.0	4.7 (0.24)	28.3 (0.50)	22.3 (0.46)	10.3 (0.34)	28.2 (0.50)	6.3 (0.27)
Natural resources, construction, and maintenance	10,984 (111.9)	100.0	19.4 (0.43)	43.4 (0.54)	17.3 (0.41)	11.7 (0.35)	6.9 (0.28)	1.3 (0.12)
Production, transportation, and material moving	11,648 (114.8)	100.0	16.1 (0.39)	47.9 (0.53)	17.8 (0.40)	8.5 (0.29)	7.9 (0.29)	1.7 (0.14)
Females	**58,180** (160.3)	**100.0**	**6.2** (0.11)	**25.0** (0.20)	**17.3** (0.17)	**12.7** (0.15)	**24.7** (0.20)	**14.1** (0.16)
Management, professional, and related	26,129 (150.4)	100.0	1.0 (0.07)	10.7 (0.21)	11.3 (0.22)	12.9 (0.23)	36.5 (0.33)	27.6 (0.30)
Management, business, and financial operations	9,461 (101.4)	100.0	1.6 (0.14)	15.9 (0.41)	15.3 (0.41)	10.7 (0.35)	38.2 (0.55)	18.4 (0.44)
Professional and related	16,668 (128.5)	100.0	0.7 (0.07)	7.7 (0.23)	9.1 (0.24)	14.2 (0.30)	35.5 (0.41)	32.8 (0.40)
Education, training, and library	5,774 (81.0)	100.0	0.6 (0.11)	7.7 (0.39)	8.0 (0.39)	6.3 (0.35)	35.4 (0.69)	42.0 (0.72)
Service occupations	11,189 (109.1)	100.0	16.1 (0.38)	38.6 (0.51)	19.6 (0.41)	12.6 (0.35)	10.8 (0.32)	2.2 (0.15!)
Sales and office occupations	17,063 (129.7)	100.0	4.6 (0.18)	33.4 (0.40)	25.2 (0.37)	13.7 (0.29)	19.3 (0.33)	3.9 (0.16)
Natural resources, construction, and maintenance	474 (23.9)	100.0	22.6 (2.11)	31.2 (2.34)	18.8 (1.97)	10.5 (1.55)	14.1 (1.76)	3.0 (0.86)
Production, transportation, and material moving	3,324 (62.3)	100.0	19.8 (0.76)	47.5 (0.95)	16.2 (0.70)	6.7 (0.48)	7.8 (0.51)	2.0 (0.27)

†Not applicable.
#Rounds to zero.
!Interpret data with caution. The coefficient of variation (CV) for this estimate is between 30 and 50 percent.
‡Reporting standards not met. The coefficient of variation (CV) for this estimate is 50 percent or greater.

NOTE: Detail may not sum to totals because of rounding.
SOURCE: U.S. Department of Labor, Bureau of Labor Statistics, Office of Employment and Unemployment Statistics, unpublished 2012 annual average data from the Current Population Survey (CPS). (This table was prepared April 2013.)

Median annual earnings of full-time year-round workers 25 years old and over, by highest level of educational attainment and sex: 1990 through 2012

[Standard errors appear in parentheses]

		Elementary/secondary			College			Bachelor's or higher degree[4]			
Sex and year	Total	Less than 9th grade	Some high school, no completion[1]	High school completion (includes equivalency)[2]	Some college, no degree[3]	Associate's degree	Total	Bachelor's degree[5]	Master's degree	Professional degree	Doctor's degree
1	2	3	4	5	6	7	8	9	10	11	12
					Current dollars						
Males											
1990	$30,730 (—)	$17,390 (—)	$20,900 (—)	$26,650 (—)	$31,730 (—)	$33,820[6] (†)	$42,670 (—)	$39,240 (—)	$49,730[6] (†)	$74,000 (†)	$57,190[6] (†)
1991	31,610 (—)	17,620 (—)	21,400 (—)	26,780 (—)	31,660 (—)	33,430 (—)	45,140 (—)	40,910 (—)	49,970 (—)	76,220 (—)	57,420 (—)
1992	32,060 (120)	17,290 (—)	21,270 (—)	27,280 (175)	32,100 (—)	33,690 (—)	45,800 (—)	41,360 (304)	51,870 (—)	76,550 (—)	63,150 (—)
1993	32,360 (124)	16,860 (—)	21,750 (—)	27,370 (204)	32,080 (—)	33,690 (—)	47,740 (—)	42,760 (536)	53,500 (—)	80,550 (—)	61,920 (—)
1994	33,440 (246)	17,530 (453)	22,050 (319)	28,040 (322)	32,280 (300)	35,790 (430)	49,230 (707)	43,660 (633)	(854)	75,010 (3,040)	(1,619)
1995	34,550 (275)	18,350 (545)	22,190 (342)	29,510 (358)	33,880 (517)	35,200 (535)	50,480 (312)	45,270 (510)	55,220 (973)	79,670 (2,582)	65,340 (2,188)
1996	35,620 (150)	17,960 (594)	22,720 (414)	30,710 (184)	34,850 (456)	37,130 (435)	51,440 (303)	45,850 (458)	60,510 (945)	85,960 (3,317)	71,230 (3,362)
1997	36,680 (149)	19,290 (629)	24,730 (466)	31,220 (171)	35,950 (293)	38,020 (774)	53,450 (755)	48,620 (851)	61,690 (771)	85,010 (4,253)	76,230 (3,611)
1998	37,910 (291)	19,380 (600)	23,960 (547)	31,480 (169)	36,930 (291)	40,270 (539)	56,520 (421)	51,410 (349)	62,240 (847)	94,740 (12,105)	75,080 (2,507)
1999	40,330 (144)	20,430 (444)	25,040 (535)	33,180 (388)	39,220 (581)	41,640 (459)	60,200 (439)	52,990 (722)	66,240 (690)	100,000 ! (37,836)	81,690 (3,953)
2000	41,060 (156)	20,790 (376)	25,100 (436)	34,300 (457)	40,340 (312)	41,950 (460)	61,870 (303)	56,330 (573)	68,320 (1,506)	99,410 (20,832)	80,250 (2,446)
2001	41,620 (104)	21,360 (235)	26,210 (251)	34,720 (299)	41,050 (214)	42,780 (561)	62,220 (279)	55,930 (335)	70,900 (687)	100,000	86,970 (3,013)
2002	41,150 (100)	20,920 (213)	25,960 (207)	33,210 (311)	40,850 (195)	42,860 (673)	61,700 (201)	56,080 (385)	67,280 (1,294)	100,000	83,310 (2,076)
2003	41,940 (90)	21,220 (227)	26,470 (280)	35,410 (168)	41,350 (182)	42,870 (719)	62,000 (187)	56,500 (365)	70,640 (562)	100,000	87,130 (2,528)
2004	42,090 (89)	21,660 (191)	26,280 (234)	35,730 (148)	41,900 (175)	44,400 (931)	62,800 (798)	57,220 (393)	71,530 (490)	100,000	82,400 (2,423)
2005	43,320 (367)	22,330 (220)	27,190 (237)	36,300 (141)	42,420 (323)	47,180 (367)	66,170 (356)	60,020 (653)	75,030 (1,229)	100,000	85,860 (3,061)
2006	45,760 (134)	22,710 (398)	27,650 (573)	37,030 (164)	43,830 (812)	47,070 (390)	66,930 (346)	60,910 (235)	75,430 (859)	100,000	100,000
2007	47,000 (130)	23,380 (544)	29,320 (590)	37,860 (406)	44,900 (585)	49,040 (801)	70,400 (241)	62,090 (236)	76,280 (416)	100,000	92,090 (1,894)
2008	49,000 (339)	24,260 (631)	29,680 (458)	39,010 (399)	45,820 (276)	50,150 (344)	72,220 (236)	65,800 (388)	80,960 (468)	100,000	100,000 (—)
2009	49,990 (201)	23,950 (394)	28,020 (542)	39,480 (379)	47,100 (347)	50,300 (238)	71,470 (239)	62,440 (707)	79,340 (1,568)	123,240 (2,539)	100,740 (519)
2010	50,360 (93)	24,450 (597)	29,440 (684)	40,060 (237)	46,370 (348)	50,280 (245)	71,780 (267)	63,740 (1,115)	80,960 (453)	115,300 (4,891)	101,220 (653)
2011	50,660 (25)	25,220 (23)	30,420 (300)	40,450 (87)	47,070 (78)	50,930 (212)	73,850 (490)	66,200 (25)	83,030 (755)	119,470 (1,917)	100,770 (192)
2012	50,950 (144)	25,130 (440)	30,330 (430)	40,350 (194)	47,190 (407)	50,960 (329)	75,320 (565)	66,150 (570)	85,120 (1,412)	116,350 (5,632)	106,470 (4,656)
Females											
1990	$21,370 (—)	$12,250 (—)	$14,430 (—)	$18,320 (—)	$22,230 (—)	$25,000[6] (†)	$30,380 (—)	$28,020 (—)	$34,950[6] (†)	$46,740 (†)	$43,300 (†)
1991	22,040 (—)	12,070 (—)	14,460 (—)	18,840 (—)	22,140 (—)	25,620 (—)	31,310 (—)	29,080 (294)	36,040 (—)	46,260 (—)	45,790 (—)
1992	23,140 (159)	12,960 (—)	14,560 (—)	19,430 (176)	23,160 (—)	25,880 (—)	32,300 (—)	30,330 (310)	38,610 (—)	50,210 (—)	47,250 (—)
1993	23,630 (166)	12,420 (—)	15,390 (—)	19,960 (173)	23,060 (—)	25,940 (—)	34,310 (—)	31,200 (314)	39,460 (—)	50,620 (2,154)	51,120 (2,888)
1994	24,400 (165)	12,430 (427)	15,130 (328)	20,370 (158)	23,510 (327)	(295)	35,380 (280)	31,740 (—)	(606)		
1995	24,880 (160)	13,580 (490)	15,830 (293)	20,460 (162)	24,000 (274)	27,310 (428)	35,260 (313)	32,050 (273)	40,260 (556)	50,000 (2,532)	48,140 (2,373)
1996	25,810 (131)	14,410 (559)	16,950 (333)	21,180 (143)	25,170 (267)	28,080 (526)	36,460 (296)	33,530 (437)	41,900 (564)	57,620 (3,635)	56,270 (3,300)
1997	26,970 (134)	14,160 (492)	16,700 (335)	22,070 (148)	26,340 (291)	28,810 (660)	38,040 (481)	35,380 (285)	44,950 (837)	61,050 (4,737)	53,040 (3,626)
1998	27,960 (199)	14,470 (429)	16,480 (322)	22,780 (254)	27,420 (271)	29,920 (513)	39,790 (408)	36,560 (305)	45,280 (760)	57,570 (1,705)	57,800 (1,881)
1999	28,840 (216)	15,100 (492)	17,020 (298)	23,060 (279)	27,760 (369)	30,920 (318)	41,750 (275)	37,990 (614)	48,100 (862)	59,900 (4,479)	60,080 (3,130)
2000	30,330 (138)	15,800 (327)	17,920 (434)	24,970 (236)	28,700 (364)	31,070 (307)	42,710 (439)	40,420 (284)	50,140 (735)	58,960 (3,552)	57,080 (2,999)
2001	31,360 (91)	16,690 (255)	19,160 (359)	25,300 (121)	30,420 (186)	32,150 (231)	44,780 (367)	40,990 (231)	50,670 (328)	61,750 (3,976)	62,120 (2,228)
2002	31,010 (83)	16,510 (297)	19,130 (360)	25,180 (121)	29,400 (299)	31,630 (211)	43,250 (568)	40,850 (173)	48,890 (595)	57,020 (2,421)	65,720 (2,268)
2003	31,570 (85)	16,910 (256)	18,940 (327)	26,070 (118)	30,140 (176)	32,250 (241)	45,120 (291)	41,330 (204)	50,160 (454)	66,490 (3,469)	67,210 (2,462)
2004	31,990 (80)	17,020 (241)	19,160 (319)	26,030 (116)	30,820 (135)	33,480 (489)	45,910 (229)	41,680 (172)	51,320 (263)	75,040 (2,436)	68,880 (2,450)
2005	33,080 (242)	16,140 (250)	20,130 (274)	26,290 (134)	31,400 (165)	33,940 (497)	46,950 (232)	42,170 (179)	51,410 (283)	80,460 (2,774)	66,850 (2,490)
2006	35,100 (113)	18,130 (408)	20,130 (270)	26,740 (136)	31,950 (165)	35,160 (376)	49,570 (441)	45,410 (259)	52,440 (561)	76,240 (2,488)	70,520 (1,779)
2007	36,090 (105)	18,260 (461)	20,400 (292)	27,240 (133)	32,840 (415)	36,330 (283)	50,400 (158)	45,770 (262)	55,430 (412)	71,100 (910)	68,990 (2,155)
2008	36,700 (109)	18,630 (494)	20,410 (295)	28,380 (283)	32,630 (355)	36,760 (243)	51,410 (145)	47,030 (237)	57,510 (745)	71,300 (2,859)	74,030 (2,144)
2009	37,260 (107)	18,480 (451)	21,230 (301)	29,150 (273)	34,090 (483)	37,270 (310)	51,880 (169)	46,830 (260)	61,070 (304)	83,910 (3,210)	76,580 (912)
2010	38,290 (272)	18,240 (592)	20,880 (334)	29,860 (260)	33,400 (410)	37,770 (588)	51,940 (159)	47,440 (336)	59,100 (1,021)	76,740 (2,723)	77,390 (2,174)
2011	38,910 (216)	20,100 (250)	21,110 (131)	30,010 (145)	34,590 (512)	39,290 (40)	52,140 (88)	49,110 (103)	60,300 (533)	80,720 (135)	77,460 (21)
2012	39,980 (294)	20,060 (514)	21,390 (285)	30,410 (165)	35,060 (452)	37,320 (455)	53,690 (888)	50,170 (290)	60,930 (464)	94,470 (6,655)	77,900 (3,616)

See notes at end of table.

Median annual earnings of full-time year-round workers 25 years old and over, by highest level of educational attainment and sex: 1990 through 2012—Continued

[Standard errors appear in parentheses]

[In constant 2012 dollars][7]

Sex and year	Total	Elementary/secondary				College					
		Less than 9th grade	Some high school, no completion[1]	High school completion (includes equivalency)[2]	Some college, no degree[3]	Associate's degree	Total (Bachelor's or higher degree[4])	Bachelor's degree[5]	Master's degree	Professional degree	Doctor's degree
1	2	3	4	5	6	7	8	9	10	11	12
Males											
1990	54,400 (—)	30,790 (—)	37,000 (—)	47,180 (—)	56,170 (—)	57,440 [6] (†)	75,530 (—)	69,460 (—)	84,480 [6] (—)	125,690 [6] (—)	97,140 [6] (—)
1991	53,700 (—)	29,930 (—)	36,350 (—)	45,490 (289)	53,780 (—)	55,130 (—)	76,670 (—)	69,480 (—)	82,400 (—)	125,860 (—)	94,680 (—)
1992	52,860 (198)	28,520 (—)	35,080 (—)	44,980 (327)	52,940 (—)	53,940 (—)	75,530 (—)	68,190 (501)	83,040 (—)	128,960 (—)	101,100 (—)
1993	51,810 (199)	27,000 (—)	34,830 (—)	43,820 (503)	51,360 (—)	53,580 (—)	76,430 (—)	68,460 (858)	83,520 (1,333)	117,100 (4,746)	96,660 (2,527)
1994	52,200 (384)	27,370 (707)	34,420 (498)	43,770 (—)	50,390 (468)	55,880 (671)	76,850 (1,104)	68,160 (988)	—	—	—
1995	52,450 (417)	27,860 (827)	33,680 (519)	44,800 (543)	51,440 (785)	53,440 (812)	76,630 (474)	68,720 (774)	83,820 (1,477)	120,940 (3,920)	99,180 (3,322)
1996	52,530 (221)	26,490 (876)	33,500 (610)	45,280 (271)	51,380 (672)	54,750 (641)	75,840 (447)	67,600 (675)	89,220 (1,393)	126,750 (4,891)	105,030 (4,957)
1997	52,870 (215)	27,810 (907)	35,640 (672)	44,990 (246)	51,810 (422)	54,810 (1,116)	77,050 (1,088)	70,080 (1,227)	88,920 (1,111)	122,540 (6,130)	109,890 (5,205)
1998	53,800 (413)	27,510 (852)	34,000 (776)	44,680 (240)	52,420 (413)	57,160 (765)	80,230 (598)	72,960 (495)	88,350 (1,202)	134,460 (17,181)	106,560 (3,558)
1999	56,010 (200)	28,370 (617)	34,770 (743)	46,080 (539)	54,460 (807)	57,820 (637)	83,600 (610)	73,580 (1,003)	91,990 (958)	138,870 [!] (52,542)	113,440 (5,489)
2000	55,160 (210)	27,930 (505)	33,720 (586)	46,090 (614)	54,190 (419)	56,360 (618)	83,120 (407)	75,690 (770)	91,790 (2,023)	133,560 (27,988)	107,820 (3,286)
2001	54,370 (136)	27,900 (307)	34,240 (328)	45,360 (391)	53,620 (280)	55,880 (733)	81,280 (364)	73,060 (438)	92,620 (897)	130,630 (—)	113,610 (3,936)
2002	52,920 (129)	26,680 (274)	33,310 (266)	42,700 (400)	52,530 (251)	55,110 (865)	79,350 (258)	72,120 (495)	86,520 (1,664)	128,600 (—)	107,130 (2,670)
2003	52,730 (113)	26,680 (285)	33,280 (352)	44,530 (211)	51,990 (229)	53,900 (904)	78,050 (235)	71,040 (459)	88,820 (707)	125,730 (—)	109,550 (3,179)
2004	51,540 (109)	26,530 (234)	32,180 (287)	43,750 (181)	51,310 (214)	54,380 (1,140)	76,910 (977)	70,080 (481)	87,610 (600)	122,470 (—)	100,920 (2,968)
2005	51,310 (435)	26,450 (261)	32,210 (281)	43,000 (167)	50,250 (383)	55,890 (435)	78,380 (422)	71,100 (774)	88,870 (1,456)	118,460 (—)	101,710 (3,626)
2006	52,510 (154)	26,060 (457)	31,730 (658)	42,500 (188)	50,300 (932)	54,020 (448)	76,560 (397)	69,890 (270)	86,560 (986)	114,760 (—)	114,760 (2,113)
2007	52,450 (145)	26,080 (607)	32,710 (607)	42,240 (453)	50,100 (653)	54,720 (894)	78,550 (269)	69,280 (263)	85,120 (464)	111,580 (—)	102,750 (560)
2008	52,650 (364)	26,060 (678)	31,890 (492)	41,920 (429)	49,240 (297)	53,890 (370)	77,600 (254)	70,700 (417)	87,000 (503)	107,450 (2,738)	107,450 (—)
2009	53,910 (217)	25,820 (425)	30,220 (584)	42,570 (409)	50,790 (374)	54,250 (257)	77,070 (258)	67,340 (762)	85,560 (1,691)	132,900 (—)	108,640 (—)
2010	53,430 (99)	25,940 (633)	31,230 (726)	42,500 (251)	49,270 (369)	53,350 (260)	76,150 (283)	67,620 (1,183)	85,890 (481)	122,330 (5,189)	107,390 (693)
2011	52,100 (26)	25,940 (24)	31,290 (309)	41,600 (89)	48,410 (80)	52,380 (218)	75,960 (504)	68,080 (26)	85,390 (777)	122,880 (1,972)	103,640 (197)
2012	50,950 (144)	25,130 (440)	30,330 (430)	40,350 (194)	47,190 (407)	50,960 (329)	75,320 (565)	66,150 (570)	85,120 (1,412)	116,350 (5,632)	106,470 (4,656)
Females											
1990	37,830 (—)	21,690 (—)	25,540 (—)	32,430 (—)	39,340 (—)	42,470 [6] (†)	53,770 (—)	49,590 (—)	59,370 [6] (—)	79,400 [6] (—)	73,560 [6] (—)
1991	37,440 (—)	20,500 (—)	24,550 (—)	32,000 (—)	37,610 (—)	42,250 (—)	53,180 (—)	49,390 (—)	59,420 (—)	76,280 (—)	75,510 (—)
1992	38,160 (262)	21,370 (—)	24,010 (—)	32,030 (290)	38,190 (—)	41,440 (—)	53,270 (—)	50,010 (485)	61,820 (—)	80,390 (—)	75,650 (—)
1993	37,830 (266)	19,880 (—)	24,630 (—)	31,960 (277)	36,910 (—)	40,490 (—)	54,930 (—)	49,950 (496)	61,600 (946)	79,010 (3,363)	79,800 (4,508)
1994	38,090 (258)	19,400 (667)	23,620 (512)	31,800 (247)	36,710 (510)	—	55,230 (437)	49,550 (490)	—	—	—
1995	37,760 (243)	20,610 (744)	24,020 (445)	31,060 (211)	36,430 (416)	41,460 (650)	53,530 (475)	48,660 (414)	61,120 (844)	75,900 (3,844)	73,080 (3,602)
1996	38,050 (193)	21,250 (824)	25,000 (491)	31,220 (213)	37,110 (394)	41,410 (776)	53,760 (436)	49,430 (644)	61,760 (832)	84,970 (5,360)	82,970 (4,866)
1997	38,880 (193)	20,410 (709)	24,070 (483)	31,810 (148)	37,960 (419)	41,530 (951)	54,830 (693)	51,000 (425)	64,790 (1,206)	88,000 (6,828)	82,030 (5,227)
1998	39,680 (282)	20,530 (609)	23,390 (457)	32,330 (361)	38,920 (385)	42,470 (728)	56,470 (579)	51,890 (433)	64,270 (1,079)	81,700 (2,420)	82,030 (—)
1999	40,050 (300)	20,970 (683)	23,630 (414)	32,020 (387)	38,550 (512)	42,940 (442)	57,970 (382)	52,760 (853)	66,790 (1,197)	83,190 (6,220)	83,430 (4,347)
2000	40,740 (185)	21,220 (439)	24,070 (583)	33,550 (317)	38,550 (489)	41,740 (412)	57,380 (590)	54,300 (382)	67,360 (987)	79,210 (4,772)	76,690 (4,029)
2001	40,960 (119)	21,800 (333)	25,020 (469)	33,050 (156)	39,740 (243)	42,000 (302)	58,490 (479)	53,550 (302)	66,190 (428)	80,660 (5,194)	81,150 (2,911)
2002	39,880 (107)	21,230 (382)	24,830 (463)	32,380 (157)	37,810 (385)	40,670 (271)	55,610 (730)	52,540 (222)	62,870 (765)	73,330 (3,113)	84,510 (2,917)
2003	39,690 (107)	21,260 (322)	23,810 (411)	32,780 (148)	37,900 (221)	40,550 (303)	56,730 (366)	51,960 (256)	63,070 (571)	83,600 (4,362)	84,510 (3,096)
2004	39,180 (98)	20,850 (295)	23,470 (391)	31,880 (142)	37,740 (165)	41,010 (599)	56,230 (280)	51,050 (211)	62,850 (322)	91,900 (2,983)	84,350 (3,001)
2005	39,180 (287)	19,120 (296)	23,840 (325)	31,140 (159)	37,200 (195)	40,200 (589)	55,610 (275)	49,960 (212)	60,900 (335)	95,310 (3,286)	79,190 (2,950)
2006	40,270 (130)	20,810 (468)	23,100 (310)	30,680 (156)	36,670 (189)	40,350 (431)	56,890 (506)	52,110 (297)	60,180 (644)	87,490 (2,855)	80,930 (2,042)
2007	40,260 (117)	20,380 (514)	22,760 (326)	30,390 (304)	36,640 (463)	40,540 (316)	56,230 (176)	51,070 (292)	61,840 (460)	79,330 (1,015)	79,540 (2,405)
2008	39,430 (117)	20,020 (531)	21,930 (317)	30,500 (148)	35,060 (381)	39,500 (261)	55,940 (156)	50,530 (255)	61,800 (801)	76,610 (3,072)	82,580 (2,304)
2009	40,180 (115)	19,930 (486)	22,890 (325)	31,430 (294)	36,760 (521)	40,190 (334)	55,940 (182)	50,500 (280)	65,850 (328)	90,480 (3,462)	—
2010	40,630 (289)	19,350 (628)	22,160 (354)	31,680 (276)	35,440 (435)	40,080 (624)	55,110 (169)	50,330 (356)	62,700 (1,083)	81,420 (2,889)	82,110 (2,307)
2011	40,020 (222)	20,680 (257)	21,710 (135)	30,870 (149)	35,580 (527)	40,410 (41)	53,620 (91)	50,510 (106)	62,020 (548)	83,020 (139)	79,670 (22)
2012	39,980 (294)	20,060 (514)	21,390 (285)	30,410 (165)	35,060 (452)	37,320 (455)	53,690 (888)	50,170 (290)	60,930 (464)	94,470 (6,655)	77,900 (3,616)

See notes at end of table.

Median annual earnings of full-time year-round workers 25 years old and over, by highest level of educational attainment and sex: 1990 through 2012—Continued

[Standard errors appear in parentheses]

Number of persons with earnings who worked full time, year round (in thousands)

Sex and year	Total	Elementary/secondary				College		Bachelor's or higher degree[4]				
		Less than 9th grade	Some high school, no completion[1]	High school completion (includes equivalency)[2]	Some college, no degree[3]	Associate's degree	Total	Bachelor's degree[5]	Master's degree	Professional degree[4]	Doctor's degree
1	2	3	4	5	6	7	8	9	10	11	12

Males

Year	Total	Less than 9th grade	Some HS, no completion	HS completion	Some college, no degree	Associate's degree	Total (Bach. or higher)	Bachelor's	Master's	Professional	Doctor's
1990	44,406 (268.6)	2,250 (73.9)	3,315 (89.3)	16,394 (188.0)	9,113 (144.6)	†[6]	13,334 (171.8)	7,569 (132.6)	†[6]	†[6]	†[6]
1991	44,199 (268.3)	1,807 (66.3)	3,083 (86.2)	15,025 (181.1)	8,034 (136.6)	2,899 (83.6)	13,350 (171.9)	8,456 (139.7)	3,073 (86.1)	1,147 (53.0)	674 (40.7)
1992	44,752 (269.1)	1,815 (66.5)	3,009 (85.2)	14,722 (179.5)	8,067 (136.6)	3,203 (87.8)	13,937 (175.2)	8,719 (141.7)	3,178 (87.5)	1,295 (56.5)	745 (42.8)
1993	45,873 (270.6)	1,790 (66.0)	3,083 (86.2)	14,604 (178.9)	8,493 (140.0)	3,557 (92.4)	14,346 (177.5)	9,178 (145.1)	3,131 (86.8)	1,231 (54.9)	808 (44.5)
1994	47,566 (303.0)	1,895 (69.2)	3,057 (87.6)	15,109 (188.5)	8,783 (146.2)	3,735 (96.6)	14,987 (187.8)	9,636 (152.8)	3,225 (89.9)	1,258 (56.4)	868 (46.9)
1995	48,500 (306.1)	1,946 (72.8)	3,335 (94.9)	15,331 (195.6)	8,908 (152.3)	3,926 (102.8)	15,054 (194.0)	9,597 (157.8)	3,395 (95.7)	1,208 (57.5)	853 (48.4)
1996	49,764 (301.1)	2,041 (69.2)	3,441 (89.6)	15,840 (186.5)	9,173 (144.2)	3,931 (95.6)	15,339 (183.7)	9,898 (149.6)	3,272 (87.4)	1,277 (54.8)	893 (45.9)
1997	50,807 (299.0)	1,914 (67.0)	3,548 (90.9)	16,225 (187.8)	9,170 (143.9)	4,086 (97.4)	15,864 (185.9)	10,349 (152.4)	3,228 (86.7)	1,321 (55.8)	966 (47.7)
1998	52,381 (306.4)	1,870 (66.3)	3,613 (91.7)	16,442 (189.7)	9,375 (145.7)	4,347 (100.1)	16,733 (191.2)	11,058 (157.6)	3,414 (89.2)	1,264 (54.6)	998 (48.5)
1999	53,062 (307.8)	1,993 (68.4)	3,295 (87.7)	16,589 (190.5)	9,684 (148.0)	4,359 (100.6)	17,142 (193.3)	11,142 (158.2)	3,725 (93.1)	1,267 (54.6)	1,008 (48.8)
2000	54,065 (309.7)	1,968 (68.0)	3,354 (88.4)	16,634 (191.7)	9,792 (148.8)	4,729 (104.7)	17,387 (194.6)	11,395 (159.9)	3,680 (92.6)	1,274 (54.8)	1,038 (49.5)
2001	54,013 (224.8)	2,207 (51.4)	3,503 (64.5)	16,314 (135.4)	9,494 (104.9)	4,714 (72.2)	17,780 (140.9)	11,479 (114.8)	3,961 (68.5)	1,298 (39.6)	1,041 (35.4)
2002	54,108 (225.0)	2,154 (50.7)	3,680 (66.1)	16,005 (134.2)	9,603 (105.5)	4,399 (74.5)	18,267 (142.7)	11,829 (116.5)	4,065 (69.4)	1,308 (39.6)	1,065 (35.8)
2003	54,253 (225.2)	2,209 (51.4)	3,369 (63.3)	16,513 (135.3)	9,340 (104.1)	4,696 (76.2)	18,354 (143.0)	11,846 (116.6)	4,124 (69.9)	1,348 (40.2)	1,037 (35.3)
2004	55,469 (227.0)	2,427 (53.8)	3,468 (64.2)	17,067 (138.3)	9,257 (103.4)	4,913 (77.0)	18,338 (142.9)	11,701 (115.9)	4,243 (70.9)	1,305 (39.6)	1,088 (36.1)
2005	56,717 (228.7)	2,425 (53.8)	3,652 (65.9)	17,266 (139.0)	9,532 (105.1)	5,022 (77.7)	18,820 (144.7)	12,032 (117.4)	4,275 (71.2)	1,369 (40.5)	1,144 (37.1)
2006	58,109 (230.6)	2,361 (53.1)	3,872 (67.8)	17,369 (139.4)	9,493 (104.9)	5,110 (78.7)	19,903 (148.4)	12,764 (120.7)	4,542 (73.3)	1,425 (41.3)	1,172 (37.5)
2007	58,147 (230.7)	2,142 (50.6)	3,451 (64.0)	17,224 (138.9)	9,867 (106.8)	5,244 (77.0)	20,218 (149.5)	12,962 (121.6)	4,800 (75.3)	1,332 (40.0)	1,125 (36.7)
2008	55,655 (227.2)	1,982 (48.7)	3,118 (60.9)	16,195 (135.0)	9,515 (105.0)	5,020 (75.5)	19,825 (148.1)	12,609 (120.0)	4,709 (74.6)	1,388 (40.8)	1,119 (36.7)
2009	52,445 (222.5)	1,561 (43.2)	2,795 (57.7)	15,258 (131.3)	8,609 (100.1)	4,828 (76.2)	19,395 (146.7)	12,290 (118.6)	4,575 (73.6)	1,319 (39.8)	1,212 (38.1)
2010	52,890 (223.2)	1,600 (43.8)	2,615 (55.9)	15,104 (130.7)	8,541 (99.7)	5,042 (77.2)	19,990 (148.7)	12,836 (121.1)	4,670 (74.3)	1,237 (38.5)	1,246 (38.7)
2011	54,279 (225.2)	1,848 (47.0)	2,715 (56.9)	15,335 (131.6)	8,752 (101.8)	5,206 (78.4)	20,423 (150.1)	13,013 (121.8)	4,889 (75.6)	1,300 (39.5)	1,271 (39.0)
2012	55,208 (226.6)	1,793 (46.3)	2,671 (56.4)	15,295 (131.4)	8,974 (102.1)	5,423 (80.0)	21,052 (152.2)	13,315 (123.2)	5,003 (76.9)	1,301 (39.5)	1,433 (41.4)

Females

Year	Total	Less than 9th grade	Some HS, no completion	HS completion	Some college, no degree	Associate's degree	Total (Bach. or higher)	Bachelor's	Master's	Professional	Doctor's
1990	28,636 (234.7)	847 (45.6)	1,861 (67.3)	11,810 (162.8)	6,462 (123.1)	†[6]	7,655 (133.3)	4,704 (105.8)	†[6]	†[6]	†[6]
1991	29,474 (237.1)	733 (42.4)	1,819 (66.5)	10,959 (157.4)	5,633 (115.3)	2,523 (78.1)	7,807 (134.6)	5,263 (111.6)	2,025 (70.1)	312 (27.7)	206 (22.5)
1992	30,346 (239.6)	734 (42.4)	1,659 (63.6)	11,039 (157.9)	5,904 (117.9)	2,655 (80.1)	8,355 (138.9)	5,604 (115.0)	2,192 (72.9)	334 (28.7)	225 (23.5)
1993	30,683 (240.5)	765 (43.3)	1,576 (62.0)	10,513 (154.4)	6,279 (121.4)	3,067 (86.0)	8,483 (139.9)	5,735 (116.3)	2,166 (72.5)	323 (28.2)	260 (25.3)
1994	31,379 (259.2)	696 (42.0)	1,675 (65.1)	10,785 (161.2)	6,256 (124.2)	3,210 (89.7)	8,756 (146.0)	5,901 (120.8)	2,174 (74.0)	398 (31.8)	283 (26.8)
1995	32,673 (268.2)	774 (46.1)	1,763 (69.3)	11,064 (168.6)	6,329 (129.5)	3,336 (94.9)	9,406 (156.3)	6,434 (130.5)	2,268 (78.5)	421 (34.0)	283 (27.9)
1996	33,549 (259.0)	750 (42.1)	1,751 (64.1)	11,363 (159.7)	6,582 (122.9)	3,468 (89.9)	9,636 (147.7)	6,689 (123.9)	2,213 (72.0)	413 (31.2)	322 (27.6)
1997	34,624 (260.1)	791 (43.2)	1,765 (64.4)	11,475 (160.0)	6,628 (123.2)	3,538 (90.7)	10,427 (153.0)	7,173 (128.0)	2,448 (75.7)	488 (34.0)	318 (27.4)
1998	35,628 (265.4)	814 (43.8)	1,878 (66.4)	11,613 (161.3)	7,070 (127.3)	3,527 (90.7)	10,725 (155.4)	7,288 (129.2)	2,639 (78.6)	468 (33.3)	329 (27.9)
1999	37,091 (269.7)	886 (45.7)	1,883 (66.5)	11,824 (162.7)	7,453 (130.6)	3,804 (94.1)	11,242 (158.9)	7,607 (131.9)	2,818 (81.2)	470 (33.3)	346 (28.6)
2000	37,762 (271.6)	930 (46.8)	1,950 (67.7)	11,789 (162.5)	7,391 (130.0)	4,118 (74.9)	11,584 (161.1)	7,899 (134.3)	2,823 (81.2)	509 (34.7)	353 (28.9)
2001	38,228 (197.0)	927 (33.4)	1,869 (47.3)	11,690 (115.8)	7,283 (92.0)	4,190 (75.0)	12,269 (118.5)	8,257 (98.1)	3,089 (60.6)	531 (25.3)	392 (21.7)
2002	38,510 (197.6)	858 (32.1)	1,841 (46.9)	11,687 (115.8)	7,354 (92.7)	4,285 (76.5)	12,484 (119.5)	8,229 (97.9)	3,281 (62.5)	572 (26.2)	402 (22.0)
2003	38,587 (197.9)	882 (32.6)	1,739 (45.6)	11,587 (115.3)	7,341 (92.6)	4,397 (76.3)	12,735 (120.8)	8,330 (98.5)	3,376 (63.4)	567 (26.1)	462 (23.6)
2004	39,072 (198.7)	917 (33.2)	1,797 (46.4)	11,392 (114.4)	7,330 (92.6)	4,505 (73.0)	13,131 (122.4)	8,664 (100.4)	3,451 (64.0)	564 (26.0)	452 (23.3)
2005	40,021 (200.6)	902 (32.9)	1,740 (45.6)	11,419 (114.5)	7,452 (93.3)	4,751 (74.9)	13,758 (125.1)	9,074 (102.6)	3,591 (65.3)	657 (28.1)	437 (22.9)
2006	41,311 (203.2)	934 (33.5)	1,802 (46.4)	11,652 (115.6)	7,613 (94.3)	4,760 (75.0)	14,549 (128.4)	9,645 (105.7)	3,746 (66.7)	662 (28.2)	497 (24.5)
2007	42,196 (204.9)	823 (31.5)	1,649 (44.4)	11,447 (114.7)	7,916 (96.1)	4,891 (76.5)	15,469 (132.1)	9,931 (107.2)	4,389 (72.1)	666 (28.3)	484 (24.1)
2008	40,979 (202.5)	814 (31.3)	1,568 (43.3)	10,851 (111.8)	7,456 (93.3)	4,955 (76.3)	15,335 (131.6)	9,856 (106.8)	4,176 (70.3)	753 (30.1)	550 (25.7)
2009	40,376 (201.4)	776 (30.5)	1,519 (42.7)	10,467 (109.9)	7,164 (91.6)	4,924 (73.0)	15,526 (132.4)	10,066 (107.9)	4,261 (71.0)	606 (27.0)	592 (26.7)
2010	40,196 (201.0)	732 (29.7)	1,371 (40.5)	10,117 (108.1)	7,150 (91.5)	4,999 (76.8)	15,826 (133.5)	9,903 (107.0)	4,576 (73.6)	622 (27.4)	725 (29.5)
2011	40,885 (202.4)	779 (30.6)	1,380 (40.7)	10,040 (107.7)	6,989 (90.5)	5,131 (77.8)	16,566 (136.4)	10,537 (110.2)	4,700 (74.6)	635 (27.6)	694 (29.8)
2012	41,319 (203.2)	690 (28.8)	1,351 (40.3)	9,870 (106.8)	6,899 (89.9)	5,246 (78.7)	17,263 (139.0)	10,961 (112.3)	4,887 (76.0)	670 (28.4)	745 (29.9)

See notes at end of table.

Median annual earnings of full-time year-round workers 25 years old and over, by highest level of educational attainment and sex: 1990 through 2012—Continued

[Standard errors appear in parentheses]

Percent of persons with earnings who worked full time, year round[8]

Sex and year	Total	Elementary/secondary			College		Bachelor's or higher degree[4]				
		Less than 9th grade	Some high school, no completion[1]	High school completion (includes equivalency)[2]	Some college, no degree[3]	Associate's degree	Total	Bachelor's degree[5]	Master's degree	Professional degree	Doctor's degree
1	2	3	4	5	6	7	8	9	10	11	12
Males											
1996	78.2 (0.25)	64.5 (1.31)	66.9 (1.01)	77.2 (0.45)	78.8 (0.58)	83.8 (0.83)	82.9 (0.43)	83.2 (0.53)	80.6 (0.95)	85.4 (1.40)	85.1 (1.69)
1997	81.6 (0.24)	63.9 (1.35)	69.5 (0.99)	78.7 (0.44)	79.5 (0.58)	81.7 (0.84)	83.3 (0.42)	83.9 (0.51)	80.8 (0.96)	85.4 (1.38)	83.4 (1.68)
1998	81.0 (0.24)	66.8 (1.37)	73.5 (0.97)	81.0 (0.43)	81.0 (0.56)	84.6 (0.76)	84.6 (0.39)	85.9 (0.47)	81.6 (0.92)	86.0 (1.39)	80.0 (1.74)
1999	81.1 (0.24)	70.3 (1.32)	71.5 (1.02)	80.3 (0.43)	81.3 (0.55)	84.2 (0.78)	84.7 (0.39)	85.3 (0.48)	83.5 (0.86)	85.6 (1.40)	81.8 (1.69)
2000	81.7 (0.23)	69.2 (1.33)	71.8 (1.01)	80.9 (0.42)	82.2 (0.54)	86.6 (0.71)	84.8 (0.39)	85.6 (0.47)	82.8 (0.87)	85.8 (1.39)	82.5 (1.65)
2001	80.1 (0.17)	69.7 (0.90)	70.9 (0.71)	79.4 (0.31)	80.2 (0.40)	84.1 (0.54)	83.3 (0.28)	83.6 (0.35)	82.4 (0.60)	84.6 (1.01)	82.2 (1.18)
2002	79.4 (0.17)	70.1 (0.91)	71.3 (0.69)	77.8 (0.32)	78.8 (0.41)	81.4 (0.58)	83.9 (0.27)	84.4 (0.34)	82.2 (0.60)	85.7 (0.99)	82.8 (1.16)
2003	79.5 (0.17)	71.5 (0.89)	70.1 (0.73)	78.7 (0.31)	78.8 (0.41)	82.1 (0.56)	83.1 (0.28)	84.0 (0.34)	81.1 (0.60)	84.4 (1.00)	80.3 (1.22)
2004	80.0 (0.17)	74.7 (0.84)	71.2 (0.71)	79.1 (0.30)	79.3 (0.41)	83.6 (0.53)	83.0 (0.28)	83.1 (0.35)	83.1 (0.58)	83.3 (1.03)	81.7 (1.16)
2005	80.3 (0.16)	74.0 (0.84)	73.8 (0.69)	79.5 (0.30)	80.0 (0.40)	82.5 (0.54)	82.9 (0.27)	83.0 (0.34)	82.7 (0.58)	83.7 (1.00)	82.4 (1.12)
2006	81.1 (0.16)	73.6 (0.85)	72.9 (0.67)	79.6 (0.30)	80.1 (0.40)	85.3 (0.50)	84.7 (0.26)	85.2 (0.32)	83.5 (0.55)	83.9 (0.94)	83.4 (1.09)
2007	80.5 (0.16)	71.1 (0.91)	70.8 (0.72)	79.4 (0.30)	79.5 (0.40)	83.3 (0.52)	84.5 (0.26)	85.1 (0.32)	83.5 (0.54)	83.1 (1.03)	83.5 (1.11)
2008	77.0 (0.17)	66.3 (0.95)	64.6 (0.76)	74.6 (0.32)	76.5 (0.42)	79.4 (0.56)	82.6 (0.27)	83.2 (0.33)	80.9 (0.57)	82.4 (1.02)	83.1 (1.12)
2009	73.9 (0.18)	56.2 (1.03)	61.8 (0.79)	70.1 (0.34)	73.4 (0.45)	77.9 (0.58)	80.8 (0.28)	79.9 (0.35)	82.0 (0.56)	85.1 (0.99)	81.2 (1.11)
2010	74.8 (0.18)	58.8 (1.04)	61.6 (0.82)	71.9 (0.34)	72.9 (0.45)	78.2 (0.56)	81.4 (0.27)	81.8 (0.34)	80.0 (0.58)	81.4 (1.10)	82.2 (1.08)
2011	76.6 (0.17)	67.2 (0.98)	64.2 (0.81)	74.2 (0.33)	75.2 (0.44)	78.0 (0.56)	82.0 (0.27)	82.1 (0.33)	82.3 (0.55)	81.6 (1.07)	81.0 (1.09)
2012	76.5 (0.17)	65.4 (1.00)	64.4 (0.82)	74.5 (0.33)	73.7 (0.44)	78.8 (0.54)	82.1 (0.26)	82.5 (0.33)	80.8 (0.55)	84.4 (1.01)	81.4 (1.02)
Females											
1996	60.7 (0.32)	47.9 (1.94)	49.4 (1.29)	60.0 (0.55)	62.0 (0.73)	63.7 (1.00)	63.5 (0.60)	63.4 (0.70)	62.4 (1.25)	68.4 (2.91)	70.0 (3.29)
1997	61.7 (0.32)	48.7 (1.91)	49.3 (1.29)	61.0 (0.55)	61.9 (0.72)	64.3 (0.99)	65.4 (0.58)	64.6 (0.70)	65.7 (1.20)	73.6 (2.63)	72.1 (3.29)
1998	62.5 (0.31)	51.8 (1.94)	53.1 (1.29)	61.9 (0.55)	63.3 (0.70)	64.9 (1.00)	65.0 (0.57)	64.0 (0.69)	66.2 (1.15)	71.9 (2.71)	68.5 (3.26)
1999	63.7 (0.31)	53.0 (1.88)	54.0 (1.30)	63.0 (0.54)	64.8 (0.69)	65.1 (0.96)	66.2 (0.56)	65.9 (0.68)	66.5 (1.12)	68.4 (2.73)	68.2 (3.18)
2000	64.6 (0.30)	53.5 (1.84)	56.5 (1.30)	64.1 (0.54)	65.3 (0.69)	66.6 (0.92)	66.6 (0.55)	66.7 (0.67)	64.9 (1.11)	70.6 (2.61)	71.5 (3.13)
2001	64.3 (0.22)	54.0 (1.32)	55.5 (0.94)	63.5 (0.39)	65.1 (0.49)	65.8 (0.65)	66.6 (0.38)	66.6 (0.47)	65.6 (0.76)	70.3 (2.12)	70.9 (2.12)
2002	64.1 (0.21)	52.6 (1.36)	55.5 (0.95)	63.2 (0.39)	65.0 (0.49)	65.6 (0.65)	66.5 (0.38)	65.9 (0.47)	66.1 (0.74)	74.3 (1.73)	73.8 (2.07)
2003	64.4 (0.21)	55.6 (1.38)	53.8 (0.96)	64.3 (0.39)	64.2 (0.49)	65.6 (0.64)	66.4 (0.37)	66.3 (0.46)	66.3 (0.73)	72.3 (1.75)	71.9 (1.95)
2004	64.5 (0.21)	56.3 (1.35)	56.1 (0.96)	64.5 (0.40)	64.2 (0.49)	64.6 (0.63)	66.7 (0.37)	66.3 (0.45)	66.3 (0.72)	71.5 (1.77)	71.2 (1.97)
2005	65.3 (0.21)	56.5 (1.36)	54.5 (0.97)	65.1 (0.40)	63.5 (0.49)	67.2 (0.61)	68.2 (0.36)	68.0 (0.44)	68.3 (0.70)	71.2 (1.64)	67.3 (2.02)
2006	66.2 (0.21)	58.5 (1.35)	56.0 (0.96)	65.6 (0.39)	65.9 (0.48)	67.3 (0.61)	68.6 (0.35)	68.4 (0.43)	67.5 (0.69)	73.6 (1.61)	74.0 (1.86)
2007	66.7 (0.21)	56.8 (1.43)	55.3 (1.00)	65.7 (0.39)	66.7 (0.48)	67.3 (0.60)	69.3 (0.34)	68.4 (0.42)	70.6 (0.63)	74.1 (1.60)	71.2 (1.91)
2008	64.4 (0.21)	51.6 (1.38)	52.8 (1.01)	62.4 (0.40)	64.7 (0.49)	65.5 (0.60)	67.9 (0.34)	67.8 (0.43)	66.9 (0.65)	74.0 (1.51)	70.0 (1.80)
2009	64.3 (0.21)	52.0 (1.42)	54.5 (1.04)	62.4 (0.41)	63.9 (0.50)	64.5 (0.60)	68.0 (0.34)	68.3 (0.42)	67.5 (0.65)	66.4 (1.72)	68.3 (1.74)
2010	64.4 (0.21)	51.7 (1.46)	52.4 (1.07)	62.6 (0.42)	63.3 (0.50)	64.3 (0.60)	68.5 (0.34)	67.7 (0.42)	68.5 (0.62)	73.9 (1.66)	76.3 (1.51)
2011	65.0 (0.21)	52.2 (1.42)	49.1 (1.04)	63.0 (0.42)	62.9 (0.50)	66.3 (0.59)	69.6 (0.33)	69.4 (0.41)	69.0 (0.60)	72.8 (1.65)	73.6 (1.58)
2012	64.8 (0.21)	50.0 (1.48)	51.1 (1.07)	62.3 (0.42)	61.7 (0.50)	64.7 (0.58)	70.0 (0.33)	70.6 (0.40)	68.0 (0.60)	73.2 (1.61)	73.9 (1.52)

—Not available.
†Not applicable.
!Interpret data with caution. The coefficient of variation (CV) for this estimate is between 30 and 50 percent.
[1]Includes 1 to 3 years of high school for 1990.
[2]Includes 4 years of high school for 1990.
[3]Includes 1 to 3 years of college and associate's degrees for 1990.
[4]Includes 4 or more years of college for 1990.
[5]Includes 4 years of college for 1990.
[6]Not reported separately for 1990.
[7]Constant dollars based on the Consumer Price Index, prepared by the Bureau of Labor Statistics, U.S. Department of Labor.
[8]Data not available for 1990 through 1995.
NOTE: Detail may not sum to totals because of rounding.
SOURCE: U.S. Department of Commerce, Census Bureau, Current Population Reports, Series P-60, *Money Income of Households, Families, and Persons in the United States* and *Income, Poverty, and Valuation of Noncash Benefits,* 1990 through 1994; Series P-60, *Money Income in the United States,* 1995 through 2002; Current Population Survey (CPS), 2004 through 2013 Annual Social and Economic Supplement, retrieved December 26, 2013, from http://www.census.gov/hhes/www/cpstables/032013/perinc/pinc03_000.htm. (This table was prepared December 2013.)

Median annual earnings of full-time year-round workers 25 to 34 years old and full-time year-round workers as a percentage of the labor force, by sex, race/ethnicity, and educational attainment: Selected years, 1995 through 2012

[Amounts in constant 2012 dollars. Standard errors appear in parentheses]

Sex, race/ethnicity, and educational attainment	1995	2000	2002	2005	2006	2007	2008	2009	2010	2011	2012
	2	3	4	5	6	7	8	9	10	11	12
Total, all full-time year-round workers 25 to 34 years old											
Median annual earnings, all education levels	$37,670 (209)	$40,000 (127)	$39,800 (132)	$38,770 (1,059)	$38,930 (1,042)	$38,760 (#)	$38,380 (819)	$40,630 (1,057)	$39,360 (815)	$38,740 (96)	$38,000 (874)
Less than high school completion	23,880 (379)	24,130 (524)	25,530 (274)	24,150 (754)	22,780 (778)	24,270 (685)	22,790 (745)	22,300 (773)	22,110 (828)	23,340 (842)	22,910 (814)
High school completion[1]	31,320 (299)	31,330 (234)	33,180 (207)	32,790 (1,102)	32,960 (1,121)	32,070 (694)	31,960 (5)	32,020 (16)	31,490 (32)	30,570 (24)	29,960 (15)
Some college, no degree	35,020 (652)	38,460 (501)	38,270 (264)	36,890 (754)	35,750 (924)	36,400 (854)	34,080 (462)	35,500 (1,225)	34,650 (909)	32,660 (510)	32,850 (718)
Associate's degree	37,390 (613)	39,990 (378)	40,670 (545)	39,930 (1,012)	38,500 (1,248)	38,530 (152)	38,320 (775)	38,420 (1,031)	38,940 (1,085)	37,800 (1,479)	35,720 (1,450)
Bachelor's or higher degree	49,680 (848)	53,320 (276)	54,020 (559)	51,570 (1,044)	51,090 (146)	52,990 (1,423)	53,260 (15)	53,340 (34)	51,310 (1,057)	51,030 (348)	49,950 (16)
Bachelor's degree	46,650 (379)	53,210 (394)	51,050 (291)	47,570 (1,296)	49,530 (1,183)	49,630 (877)	49,050 (923)	47,380 (290)	46,320 (654)	45,900 (641)	46,900 (893)
Master's or higher degree	59,730 (1,098)	63,880 (1,973)	63,820 (1,128)	58,710 (53)	56,950 (2,494)	61,640 (2,176)	58,590 (733)	63,370 (2,164)	57,540 (1,043)	60,450 (1,533)	59,620 (1,133)
Percent,[2] all education levels	63.6 (0.44)	68.4 (0.32)	66.3 (0.32)	66.6 (0.37)	68.0 (0.41)	67.8 (0.36)	64.6 (0.41)	61.0 (0.41)	61.9 (0.42)	63.3 (0.41)	64.2 (0.44)
Less than high school completion	49.6 (1.37)	59.4 (1.02)	60.0 (1.01)	60.0 (1.32)	61.7 (1.13)	56.5 (1.26)	50.2 (1.32)	47.0 (1.25)	44.9 (1.52)	48.1 (1.43)	48.6 (1.38)
High school completion[1]	62.8 (0.79)	67.2 (0.59)	64.2 (0.62)	66.9 (0.75)	66.2 (0.72)	67.0 (0.71)	61.7 (0.75)	55.3 (0.74)	57.0 (0.80)	59.1 (0.78)	60.3 (0.80)
Some college, no degree	61.5 (0.99)	67.8 (0.71)	64.9 (0.74)	63.5 (0.83)	64.8 (0.90)	64.8 (0.92)	62.9 (0.79)	58.7 (0.91)	58.1 (0.92)	59.0 (0.99)	59.2 (1.00)
Associate's degree	67.4 (1.41)	70.9 (1.01)	67.4 (1.07)	67.8 (1.16)	69.8 (1.16)	67.8 (1.23)	66.3 (1.30)	65.1 (1.18)	63.6 (1.29)	65.4 (1.17)	64.8 (1.18)
Bachelor's or higher degree	70.4 (0.79)	72.3 (0.55)	70.9 (0.56)	70.2 (0.67)	72.9 (0.65)	73.5 (0.59)	71.6 (0.56)	69.4 (0.63)	71.4 (0.59)	71.4 (0.62)	72.8 (0.62)
Bachelor's degree	70.5 (0.90)	73.1 (0.62)	71.2 (0.64)	70.9 (0.76)	73.0 (0.73)	73.2 (0.70)	71.6 (0.70)	69.1 (0.77)	71.2 (0.71)	71.1 (0.72)	72.9 (0.75)
Master's or higher degree	69.8 (1.65)	69.6 (1.18)	70.1 (1.18)	68.2 (1.27)	72.4 (1.11)	74.4 (1.21)	71.5 (1.05)	70.0 (1.10)	71.7 (1.23)	72.2 (1.25)	72.5 (1.20)
Male											
Median annual earnings, all education levels	40,580 (277)	42,660 (204)	43,360 (529)	41,150 (#)	39,860 (696)	42,010 (97)	42,650 (1)	42,810 (#)	41,990 (31)	40,750 (33)	40,000 (1)
Less than high school completion	26,750 (706)	26,560 (332)	26,610 (307)	25,760 (1,023)	24,980 (449)	25,460 (555)	25,570 (834)	24,250 (1,042)	25,270 (816)	25,480 (1,081)	24,600 (978)
High school completion[1]	36,070 (592)	38,420 (630)	36,940 (577)	35,130 (48)	34,150 (446)	34,140 (1,034)	34,080 (705)	35,200 (1,207)	34,530 (881)	33,120 (844)	32,830 (720)
Some college, no degree	39,090 (539)	42,400 (357)	43,000 (1,316)	41,040 (309)	39,560 (186)	40,620 (1,519)	38,620 (1,408)	41,390 (952)	39,880 (969)	37,450 (1,219)	37,670 (842)
Associate's degree	38,860 (998)	46,630 (522)	47,020 (1,370)	45,700 (1,823)	42,880 (1,832)	43,990 (368)	42,940 (1,696)	44,610 (1,646)	42,020 (453)	42,710 (1,767)	43,640 (2,742)
Bachelor's or higher degree	56,010 (868)	61,220 (552)	61,250 (1,154)	58,750 (1,875)	56,590 (188)	57,110 (1,085)	58,490 (408)	58,250 (588)	55,550 (1,873)	55,490 (1,056)	54,840 (513)
Bachelor's degree	52,690 (697)	59,690 (799)	57,400 (640)	52,860 (1,264)	56,420 (1,737)	55,240 (51)	56,420 (1,731)	54,020 (1,374)	52,420 (160)	50,790 (124)	49,970 (584)
Master's or higher degree	66,690 (2,138)	73,180 (1,981)	75,650 (1,490)	64,650 (3,922)	65,940 (3,256)	68,310 (3,330)	68,590 (1,875)	74,100 (3,106)	67,560 (1,475)	69,400 (2,399)	65,000 (2,361)
Percent,[2] all education levels	69.7 (0.57)	75.1 (0.40)	72.1 (0.42)	72.5 (0.48)	72.9 (0.54)	72.2 (0.51)	68.5 (0.57)	62.8 (0.58)	64.5 (0.56)	67.4 (0.57)	68.4 (0.53)
Less than high school completion	54.3 (1.71)	67.8 (1.22)	66.8 (1.19)	66.7 (1.54)	67.8 (1.34)	61.1 (1.51)	55.7 (1.54)	49.2 (1.71)	47.4 (1.81)	55.5 (1.74)	54.1 (1.88)
High school completion[1]	69.3 (1.00)	73.6 (0.73)	70.3 (0.77)	73.5 (0.91)	71.1 (0.88)	71.9 (0.94)	64.8 (0.95)	57.4 (1.01)	60.6 (1.01)	65.5 (1.00)	65.5 (1.00)
Some college, no degree	68.5 (1.31)	76.1 (0.91)	71.1 (0.97)	70.7 (1.13)	71.3 (1.21)	71.1 (1.31)	68.2 (1.12)	62.7 (1.31)	62.0 (1.17)	63.8 (1.33)	64.3 (1.41)
Associate's degree	78.6 (1.81)	80.9 (1.31)	74.7 (1.44)	75.1 (1.67)	78.4 (1.61)	73.4 (1.70)	73.2 (1.82)	70.1 (1.65)	68.6 (1.77)	71.6 (1.61)	71.8 (1.70)
Bachelor's or higher degree	75.9 (1.04)	78.0 (0.72)	76.3 (0.74)	74.6 (0.93)	76.7 (0.82)	77.7 (0.94)	76.6 (0.90)	71.8 (0.94)	75.0 (0.80)	75.3 (0.84)	77.1 (0.87)
Bachelor's degree	76.4 (1.19)	78.8 (0.81)	76.6 (0.85)	74.5 (1.01)	77.1 (1.07)	78.0 (1.07)	76.3 (1.10)	70.6 (1.15)	75.4 (0.91)	74.7 (0.98)	77.3 (0.94)
Master's or higher degree	74.6 (2.11)	75.3 (1.58)	75.4 (1.53)	75.1 (2.00)	75.5 (1.58)	76.8 (1.93)	77.2 (1.50)	75.6 (1.61)	74.0 (1.88)	77.3 (1.63)	76.4 (1.82)
Female											
Median annual earnings, all education levels	32,850 (270)	36,950 (318)	37,390 (327)	35,220 (34)	35,300 (440)	36,480 (429)	36,230 (508)	37,370 (223)	36,730 (36)	35,680 (20)	35,000 (786)
Less than high school completion	19,490 (760)	19,970 (558)	21,110 (600)	19,750 (751)	20,300 (489)	19,730 (894)	17,610 (746)	20,290 (620)	18,710 (694)	19,320 (480)	17,900 (773)
High school completion[1]	26,530 (448)	29,220 (319)	29,600 (515)	28,010 (192)	26,810 (695)	26,610 (1,070)	26,300 (128)	26,700 (27)	26,300 (66)	24,980 (748)	24,980 (9)
Some college, no degree	30,120 (435)	33,300 (326)	32,830 (349)	32,820 (467)	31,830 (596)	33,120 (795)	30,860 (931)	31,250 (1,048)	31,070 (1,069)	29,540 (1,117)	29,350 (627)
Associate's degree	36,080 (1,344)	35,520 (478)	35,600 (931)	34,470 (123)	34,120 (838)	34,320 (1,151)	34,650 (1,049)	33,060 (1,291)	36,500 (899)	32,740 (1,363)	31,610 (969)
Bachelor's or higher degree	44,850 (634)	48,000 (332)	46,750 (439)	46,750 (123)	46,590 (1,031)	47,510 (1,060)	47,920 (28)	48,110 (26)	46,320 (1,237)	45,830 (58)	46,840 (694)
Bachelor's degree	42,040 (911)	46,520 (371)	48,280 (708)	44,090 (1,076)	45,400 (482)	44,120 (103)	44,400 (580)	42,910 (1,245)	42,100 (1,190)	41,800 (1,361)	42,950 (1,236)
Master's or higher degree	52,040 (1,437)	55,440 (1,116)	55,260 (1,469)	55,190 (2,162)	54,490 (2,164)	55,570 (1,672)	54,170 (1,554)	57,790 (2,261)	52,470 (94)	52,530 (1,585)	53,520 (1,458)
Percent,[2] all education levels	56.6 (0.67)	60.7 (0.49)	59.5 (0.50)	59.6 (0.57)	62.1 (0.60)	62.7 (0.57)	60.0 (0.51)	58.9 (0.53)	58.7 (0.53)	58.6 (0.52)	59.3 (0.63)
Less than high school completion	41.3 (2.24)	45.3 (1.68)	46.4 (1.77)	45.9 (1.83)	48.5 (2.01)	45.9 (2.22)	38.6 (1.91)	42.7 (2.03)	39.4 (2.22)	34.1 (2.03)	37.8 (1.96)
High school completion[1]	54.4 (1.23)	58.5 (0.96)	55.7 (0.98)	57.0 (1.11)	58.8 (1.28)	59.4 (1.13)	56.6 (1.11)	51.8 (1.12)	51.1 (1.19)	51.6 (1.19)	51.9 (1.24)
Some college, no degree	53.9 (1.46)	59.2 (1.08)	58.1 (1.10)	55.7 (1.19)	57.6 (1.31)	57.9 (1.22)	56.6 (1.26)	54.1 (1.28)	53.6 (1.29)	53.3 (1.33)	53.3 (1.22)
Associate's degree	57.6 (2.05)	62.7 (1.45)	60.8 (1.54)	60.8 (1.57)	62.1 (1.64)	62.7 (1.75)	60.1 (1.68)	60.8 (1.65)	59.1 (1.67)	59.5 (1.75)	58.8 (1.69)
Bachelor's or higher degree	64.7 (1.17)	66.8 (0.82)	65.7 (0.82)	66.0 (0.99)	69.3 (0.90)	69.9 (0.76)	67.2 (0.71)	67.2 (0.82)	68.0 (0.77)	68.9 (0.84)	68.9 (0.90)
Bachelor's degree	64.9 (1.32)	67.6 (0.93)	65.9 (0.95)	67.4 (1.18)	69.2 (1.06)	68.7 (0.92)	67.3 (0.88)	67.9 (1.03)	67.2 (0.94)	67.8 (1.06)	68.5 (1.13)
Master's or higher degree	63.9 (2.57)	64.2 (1.71)	65.3 (1.60)	62.6 (1.76)	69.8 (1.62)	72.6 (1.52)	67.1 (1.44)	65.7 (1.58)	70.0 (1.63)	68.6 (1.76)	69.7 (1.71)

See notes at end of table.

Median annual earnings of full-time year-round workers 25 to 34 years old and full-time year-round workers as a percentage of the labor force, by sex, race/ethnicity, and educational attainment: Selected years, 1995 through 2012—Continued

[Amounts in constant 2012 dollars. Standard errors appear in parentheses]

Sex, race/ethnicity, and educational attainment	1995	2000	2002	2005	2006	2007	2008	2009	2010	2011	2012
1	2	3	4	5	6	7	8	9	10	11	12
White											
Median annual earnings, all education levels	39,160 (237)	43,630 (374)	44,410 (206)	41,150 (91)	42,130 (888)	44,260 (1,317)	42,650 (1)	42,810 (#)	42,070 (23)	40,820 (148)	40,960 (1,230)
Less than high school completion	26,470 (1,057)	27,720 (550)	29,360 (842)	26,980 (1,539)	28,460 (478)	26,520 (1,592)	27,290 (1,376)	26,390 (1,050)	26,310 (417)	26,310 (1,206)	24,630 (1,078)
High school completion[1]	33,110 (372)	36,820 (493)	35,660 (495)	35,170 (42)	34,120 (21)	33,200 (20)	33,220 (1,212)	34,180 (761)	33,640 (900)	32,610 (632)	32,330 (691)
Some college, no degree	36,160 (682)	39,870 (342)	39,140 (355)	37,480 (399)	37,770 (969)	38,660 (832)	35,220 (1,212)	37,480 (207)	36,670 (798)	35,430 (1,124)	34,930 (1,113)
Associate's degree	39,050 (760)	42,260 (412)	42,160 (1,415)	40,730 (439)	39,400 (604)	40,720 (1,463)	41,630 (1,071)	42,640 (1,572)	41,770 (791)	40,350 (1,361)	38,640 (1,868)
Bachelor's or higher degree	51,160 (899)	53,330 (305)	54,510 (826)	52,470 (886)	51,080 (500)	53,090 (1,051)	53,250 (22)	53,340 (39)	52,160 (836)	50,670 (91)	49,950 (19)
Bachelor's degree	48,200 (468)	53,240 (351)	52,190 (317)	48,110 (1,053)	50,410 (979)	49,720 (66)	50,010 (1,190)	48,160 (847)	48,340 (1,191)	47,910 (1,186)	47,430 (1,060)
Master's or higher degree	59,880 (1,043)	63,780 (2,192)	63,820 (1,462)	58,710 (59)	56,750 (643)	60,520 (924)	58,450 (349)	61,620 (1,817)	57,200 (903)	59,950 (1,641)	56,950 (2,474)
Percent,[2] all education levels	64.5 (0.52)	68.2 (0.39)	66.0 (0.41)	66.9 (0.49)	68.0 (0.51)	68.3 (0.47)	65.7 (0.54)	62.5 (0.52)	63.3 (0.52)	65.6 (0.54)	66.0 (0.54)
Less than high school completion	48.6 (2.03)	55.2 (1.76)	57.0 (1.85)	58.7 (2.29)	56.4 (2.41)	51.8 (2.28)	44.3 (2.56)	41.0 (2.43)	39.5 (2.78)	41.2 (2.70)	45.0 (2.44)
High school completion[1]	62.7 (0.94)	66.6 (0.75)	62.5 (0.80)	66.6 (0.92)	64.7 (1.06)	61.9 (0.89)	61.9 (1.04)	55.9 (1.04)	57.1 (1.08)	60.8 (1.15)	61.7 (1.10)
Some college, no degree	62.3 (1.18)	67.6 (0.88)	63.4 (0.94)	64.2 (1.02)	64.5 (1.12)	63.7 (1.18)	63.2 (1.02)	59.0 (1.14)	57.0 (1.20)	60.7 (1.25)	59.2 (1.39)
Associate's degree	66.7 (1.63)	68.2 (1.23)	66.9 (1.25)	66.9 (1.41)	69.9 (1.36)	69.6 (1.51)	66.3 (1.59)	65.4 (1.54)	63.9 (1.60)	65.7 (1.29)	66.2 (1.45)
Bachelor's or higher degree	70.5 (0.87)	72.2 (0.63)	71.2 (0.64)	69.8 (0.79)	72.8 (0.75)	72.8 (0.65)	71.5 (0.66)	69.5 (0.77)	71.7 (0.69)	72.4 (0.76)	72.8 (0.74)
Bachelor's degree	70.6 (0.99)	72.9 (0.72)	71.7 (0.74)	70.1 (0.92)	73.1 (0.86)	72.7 (0.77)	71.5 (0.82)	69.4 (0.90)	71.5 (0.79)	72.2 (0.84)	73.2 (0.87)
Master's or higher degree	70.3 (1.84)	69.9 (1.36)	69.6 (1.32)	68.8 (1.56)	71.9 (1.42)	73.3 (1.48)	71.5 (1.32)	69.5 (1.43)	72.3 (1.47)	72.8 (1.44)	71.9 (1.38)
Black											
Median annual earnings, all education levels	31,570 (543)	33,330 (351)	35,230 (740)	33,580 (1,190)	34,110 (1,379)	33,140 (43)	31,990 (1,388)	32,090 (129)	33,260 (754)	32,540 (742)	31,790 (467)
Less than high school completion	20,810 (1,638)	22,090 (1,034)	24,840 (1,504)	23,970 (1,392)	20,310 (1,352)	20,800 (2,024)	19,270 (1,437)	23,770 (3,751)	21,340 (1,945)	19,850 (748)	21,090 (1,695)
High school completion[1]	27,050 (869)	29,140 (482)	30,500 (796)	26,980 (1,186)	28,440 (813)	28,610 (1,452)	27,660 (1,295)	26,710 (928)	26,320 (770)	25,820 (1,070)	26,430 (1,330)
Some college, no degree	33,100 (1,281)	34,580 (692)	34,670 (1,032)	34,130 (1,646)	31,620 (1,171)	33,080 (166)	31,640 (470)	31,050 (1,652)	30,820 (409)	29,930 (591)	30,000 (1,291)
Associate's degree	33,020 (1,364)	33,190 (950)	37,200 (2,432)	32,720 (1,481)	32,860 (2,590)	32,620 (805)	32,750 (2,255)	29,680 (2,042)	30,820 (2,276)	34,350 (2,403)	31,600 (2,532)
Bachelor's or higher degree	41,250 (1,409)	46,090 (1,247)	48,050 (1,130)	45,540 (1,705)	45,080 (815)	44,060 (1,215)	47,240 (912)	47,700 (916)	43,200 (1,507)	42,380 (1,832)	44,080 (1,947)
Bachelor's degree	39,120 (1,282)	43,660 (1,908)	47,300 (1,390)	41,470 (2,528)	41,890 (2,725)	43,190 (1,265)	42,640 (957)	42,800 (1,663)	41,580 (518)	39,960 (1,004)	39,460 (821)
Master's or higher degree	49,890 (1,880)	53,840 (2,476)	48,460 (1,753)	50,630 (3,569)	53,870 (5,052)	49,770 (2,588)	55,940 (4,135)	56,820 (2,870)	51,700 (6,270)	51,030 (1,057)	54,660 (2,210)
Percent,[2] all education levels	62.4 (1.30)	69.7 (1.28)	65.5 (1.37)	64.5 (1.19)	66.6 (1.14)	65.0 (1.21)	60.5 (1.12)	57.4 (1.13)	57.7 (1.26)	55.7 (1.33)	58.5 (1.23)
Less than high school completion	42.4 (4.02)	48.8 (4.46)	46.5 (5.06)	40.3 (3.98)	53.4 (3.72)	43.9 (4.11)	38.3 (3.96)	38.1 (4.26)	30.3 (3.73)	30.3 (3.80)	27.5 (4.20)
High school completion[1]	60.7 (2.11)	68.3 (2.16)	64.2 (2.20)	64.0 (2.01)	64.9 (1.97)	60.4 (2.11)	57.8 (1.83)	48.9 (1.93)	53.6 (2.03)	50.8 (2.16)	51.4 (2.22)
Some college, no degree	62.2 (2.51)	69.8 (2.57)	65.9 (2.62)	59.3 (2.65)	63.6 (2.42)	65.5 (2.78)	60.0 (2.13)	57.7 (2.21)	56.2 (2.42)	50.8 (2.40)	58.0 (2.18)
Associate's degree	69.2 (4.29)	78.0 (3.79)	68.6 (4.70)	72.2 (3.57)	68.9 (3.34)	57.9 (3.78)	58.6 (3.75)	63.2 (3.58)	61.5 (3.25)	69.0 (3.32)	58.9 (3.34)
Bachelor's or higher degree	77.3 (2.85)	78.6 (2.58)	73.9 (2.85)	79.0 (1.94)	76.4 (2.39)	82.0 (1.95)	73.5 (2.15)	73.5 (2.05)	72.4 (2.11)	69.1 (2.13)	76.2 (2.12)
Bachelor's degree	76.1 (3.15)	79.4 (2.80)	72.7 (3.23)	79.9 (2.14)	77.0 (2.70)	82.5 (2.44)	72.2 (2.49)	73.1 (2.46)	71.1 (2.70)	68.5 (2.41)	75.1 (2.47)
Master's or higher degree	84.0 (6.41)	74.9 (6.52)	78.8 (5.96)	76.5 (3.95)	74.2 (4.56)	80.5 (3.78)	77.2 (3.80)	74.7 (3.60)	76.5 (3.65)	70.6 (4.32)	79.3 (3.96)
Hispanic											
Median annual earnings, all education levels	28,230 (658)	29,860 (607)	31,360 (438)	29,370 (9)	29,450 (232)	29,880 (745)	30,880 (1,134)	30,850 (1,357)	31,540 (622)	30,570 (21)	29,900 (43)
Less than high school completion	22,400 (607)	22,660 (468)	23,200 (533)	23,380 (73)	22,780 (#)	22,790 (794)	21,310 (560)	21,290 (80)	20,970 (273)	22,110 (958)	22,430 (1,168)
High school completion[1]	28,370 (1,178)	30,610 (795)	31,470 (724)	28,140 (1,024)	29,280 (926)	28,570 (918)	28,570 (1,561)	27,540 (851)	29,310 (951)	28,520 (1,313)	27,570 (764)
Some college, no degree	29,400 (1,342)	35,260 (939)	35,630 (958)	36,840 (1,675)	33,470 (632)	34,230 (1,063)	32,010 (1,810)	34,530 (982)	33,400 (1,448)	30,600 (796)	31,770 (1,356)
Associate's degree	35,790 (2,151)	39,480 (1,693)	37,840 (2,073)	39,870 (1,910)	35,930 (1,812)	33,990 (1,440)	33,990 (1,915)	32,880 (1,561)	35,680 (1,379)	35,410 (1,477)	33,340 (1,737)
Bachelor's or higher degree	44,890 (1,747)	48,450 (1,716)	48,000 (1,401)	47,670 (2,202)	47,670 (1,429)	47,950 (1,750)	47,600 (1,752)	48,780 (1,607)	46,430 (2,080)	42,050 (1,790)	44,650 (574)
Bachelor's degree	42,280 (2,013)	46,670 (1,279)	49,230 (2,004)	46,390 (816)	45,390 (1,883)	44,290 (2,309)	44,280 (2,256)	47,460 (1,041)	43,920 (3,175)	40,430 (303)	42,670 (2,041)
Master's or higher degree	‡ (†)	50,880 (3,119)	58,750 (5,469)	53,830 (4,139)	53,830 (3,200)	54,100 (2,975)	55,380 (3,513)	56,640 (4,245)	51,410 (3,765)	51,940 (2,549)	50,000 (4,043)
Percent,[2] all education levels	60.5 (1.32)	68.7 (1.14)	68.8 (1.08)	68.1 (0.82)	69.4 (0.89)	67.9 (0.86)	63.3 (0.93)	58.2 (0.96)	59.4 (0.85)	61.4 (0.89)	61.8 (0.87)
Less than high school completion	53.5 (2.27)	64.4 (2.00)	64.6 (1.87)	64.9 (1.67)	65.4 (1.43)	61.1 (1.72)	55.2 (1.80)	51.8 (1.67)	50.4 (1.77)	54.9 (1.69)	54.4 (1.81)
High school completion[1]	66.0 (2.31)	70.5 (2.00)	70.6 (1.93)	71.3 (1.40)	72.3 (1.30)	72.1 (1.31)	64.3 (1.40)	58.2 (1.57)	59.0 (1.64)	61.5 (1.49)	63.3 (1.53)
Some college, no degree	58.4 (3.18)	69.5 (2.89)	72.3 (2.60)	66.6 (1.93)	68.0 (2.13)	67.9 (2.06)	66.8 (2.02)	61.1 (2.28)	64.5 (1.85)	63.0 (2.09)	61.7 (2.13)
Associate's degree	67.0 (5.34)	79.0 (3.95)	69.8 (4.59)	70.0 (2.63)	71.2 (3.03)	67.9 (3.15)	71.0 (2.68)	66.2 (3.03)	65.1 (2.70)	65.3 (3.06)	65.2 (2.90)
Bachelor's or higher degree	66.9 (3.73)	70.1 (3.27)	71.4 (3.06)	69.5 (2.11)	73.8 (2.10)	73.5 (1.92)	71.0 (2.06)	64.4 (2.12)	68.1 (2.10)	68.3 (1.84)	68.4 (1.96)
Bachelor's degree	66.3 (4.12)	71.1 (3.57)	70.6 (3.45)	69.3 (2.40)	73.3 (2.38)	71.6 (2.15)	71.5 (2.28)	64.2 (2.23)	68.1 (2.29)	68.6 (2.13)	67.6 (2.21)
Master's or higher degree	69.8 (8.84)	65.5 (8.05)	74.6 (6.60)	70.4 (4.19)	75.5 (3.73)	80.2 (3.55)	68.7 (4.10)	65.3 (4.32)	68.2 (3.89)	67.1 (3.97)	71.3 (4.09)

See notes at end of table.

Median annual earnings of full-time year-round workers 25 to 34 years old and full-time year-round workers as a percentage of the labor force, by sex, race/ethnicity, and educational attainment: Selected years, 1995 through 2012—Continued

[Amounts in constant 2012 dollars. Standard errors appear in parentheses]

Sex, race/ethnicity, and educational attainment	1995	2000	2002	2005	2006	2007	2008	2009	2010	2011	2012
1	2	3	4	5	6	7	8	9	10	11	12
Asian[3]											
Median annual earnings, all education levels	38,100 (1,061)	47,810 (811)	50,330 (2,281)	46,850 (1,907)	50,980 (1,319)	49,540 (2,025)	52,860 (744)	52,650 (790)	48,150 (2,697)	50,240 (2,679)	53,830 (2,499)
Less than high school completion	‡ (†)	‡ (†)	‡ (†)	‡ (†)	‡ (†)	‡ (†)	‡ (†)	‡ (†)	‡ (†)	‡ (†)	‡ (†)
High school completion[1]	29,900 (2,188)	33,320 (1,206)	31,160 (1,462)	31,620 (1,660)	31,170 (2,892)	30,870 (2,827)	29,820 (2,633)	27,690 (2,165)	30,750 (1,813)	25,460 (1,313)	29,530 (816)
Some college, no degree	27,900 (2,624)	38,350 (1,985)	34,540 (1,735)	34,870 (2,448)	36,000 (2,771)	38,550 (2,665)	35,120 (4,560)	40,650 (3,513)	36,580 (1,503)	31,520 (1,835)	33,210 (2,634)
Associate's degree	30,130 (1,847)	39,330 (1,965)	‡ (†)	40,000 (4,961)	40,580 (5,146)	38,890 (5,042)	33,690 (2,682)	38,830 (4,093)	37,780 (2,826)	35,300 (6,650)	43,100 (3,162)
Bachelor's or higher degree	49,570 (2,135)	65,750 (1,360)	63,370 (1,167)	58,770 (1,070)	61,560 (3,077)	60,850 (5,043)	63,500 (898)	63,440 (1,500)	63,020 (1,137)	62,370 (2,413)	64,220 (1,674)
Bachelor's degree	45,430 (958)	59,790 (2,408)	57,070 (1,452)	58,760 (3,821)	56,360 (908)	54,580 (1,896)	58,260 (2,230)	53,300 (1,202)	56,870 (4,176)	52,350 (3,384)	59,280 (1,925)
Master's or higher degree	57,170 (5,473)	76,270 (5,852)	75,750 (2,112)	63,980 (4,692)	68,140 (2,035)	71,710 (2,408)	73,860 (2,998)	74,910 (3,219)	71,900 (5,165)	74,740 (4,556)	69,720 (1,963)
Percent[2] all education levels	63.4 (2.98)	68.5 (1.78)	65.8 (1.91)	64.8 (1.57)	69.3 (1.75)	71.2 (1.63)	68.8 (1.72)	66.7 (1.51)	65.1 (1.46)	65.1 (1.73)	67.9 (1.57)
Less than high school completion	46.6 (9.98)	61.6 (8.31)	‡ (†)	49.4 (7.62)	‡ (†)	‡ (†)	‡ (†)	‡ (†)	‡ (†)	‡ (†)	50.9 (7.17)
High school completion[1]	66.9 (7.05)	68.9 (4.59)	67.2 (4.64)	62.5 (4.82)	63.3 (4.18)	68.5 (4.09)	63.0 (4.17)	59.3 (4.15)	55.9 (3.97)	53.7 (4.47)	64.6 (3.35)
Some college, no degree	51.8 (8.46)	63.4 (4.59)	63.8 (5.54)	66.5 (4.65)	64.7 (4.97)	73.4 (4.48)	63.8 (4.70)	57.4 (5.03)	58.2 (4.93)	58.3 (4.37)	51.7 (4.31)
Associate's degree	77.1 (8.01)	72.2 (5.92)	67.3 (8.22)	66.3 (5.93)	74.1 (5.81)	70.6 (5.49)	78.4 (5.36)	70.3 (4.25)	56.5 (5.57)	55.1 (5.88)	60.6 (5.79)
Bachelor's or higher degree	65.6 (4.18)	69.9 (2.35)	67.4 (2.40)	66.0 (2.07)	71.0 (2.17)	72.4 (2.04)	71.9 (1.93)	70.5 (1.84)	71.1 (1.89)	70.4 (2.08)	72.9 (1.80)
Bachelor's degree	68.0 (5.27)	70.8 (2.87)	66.8 (3.05)	68.7 (2.69)	69.5 (2.78)	71.6 (2.40)	72.7 (2.48)	69.7 (2.46)	72.2 (2.22)	69.6 (2.59)	73.7 (2.31)
Master's or higher degree	62.0 (6.80)	67.9 (4.11)	68.4 (3.91)	61.3 (3.08)	73.3 (3.23)	73.6 (3.25)	70.9 (2.79)	71.6 (3.17)	69.4 (3.15)	71.8 (3.20)	71.7 (2.85)
Median annual earnings for other race groups, all education levels											
Pacific Islander[4]	[3] (†)	[3] (†)	‡ (†)	‡ (†)	33,140 (3,052)	38,060 (3,583)	‡ (†)	‡ (†)	‡ (†)	32,090 (2,623)	32,090 (4,904)
American Indian/Alaska Native[4]	29,880 (372)	33,310 (493)	31,620 (2,332)	34,680 (2,002)	29,550 (2,782)	33,980 (1,932)	30,710 (2,447)	32,110 (4,220)	33,160 (3,330)	32,890 (1,710)	32,880 (2,715)
Two or more races[4]	[3]	—	41,760 (2,265)	39,970 (1,676)	39,050 (1,364)	35,900 (3,411)	35,750 (3,003)	35,960 (2,881)	36,640 (1,466)	37,460 (1,680)	35,570 (1,515)
Percent[2] for other race groups, all education levels											
Pacific Islander[4]	[3] (†)	[3] (†)	66.2 (7.71)	53.7 (6.81)	68.1 (5.94)	70.2 (5.06)	58.6 (4.76)	46.9 (7.15)	62.2 (6.71)	56.9 (5.50)	69.4 (6.03)
American Indian/Alaska Native[4]	46.9 (8.10)	57.6 (4.94)	50.3 (6.16)	60.2 (4.01)	56.2 (4.86)	64.3 (4.58)	52.7 (4.28)	59.8 (4.30)	52.9 (4.14)	52.2 (4.58)	55.8 (5.05)
Two or more races[4]	[3]	—	56.1 (4.59)	61.9 (3.46)	60.9 (3.18)	59.5 (3.21)	59.5 (2.89)	50.2 (2.95)	60.2 (2.87)	58.1 (2.93)	59.0 (2.94)

—Not available.
†Not applicable.
#Rounds to zero.
‡Reporting standards not met (too few cases for a reliable estimate).
[1]Includes equivalency credentials, such as the General Educational Development (GED) credential.
[2]Full-time year-round workers as a percentage of the population ages 25 through 34 who reported working or looking for work in the given year.
[3]For 1995 and 2000, data for Asians and Pacific Islanders were not reported separately; therefore, Pacific Islanders are included with Asians for 1995 and 2000.
[4]For Pacific Islanders, American Indians/Alaska Natives, and persons of two or more races, data by educational attainment are omitted because these data did not meet reporting standards. All data shown for these three race categories are for persons of all education levels.

NOTE: Beginning in 2005, standard errors were computed using replicate weights, which produced more precise values than the methodology used in prior years. Race categories exclude persons of Hispanic ethnicity. Constant dollars based on the Consumer Price Index, prepared by the Bureau of Labor Statistics, U.S. Department of Labor.
SOURCE: U.S. Department of Commerce, Census Bureau, Current Population Survey (CPS), March 1996 through March 2013. (This table was prepared October 2013.)

Distribution of earnings and median earnings of persons 25 years old and over, by highest level of educational attainment and sex: 2012

[Standard errors appear in parentheses]

Sex and earnings	Total	Elementary/secondary			College			Bachelor's or higher degree			
		Less than 9th grade	Some high school, no completion	High school completion (includes equivalency)	Some college, no degree	Associate's degree	Total	Bachelor's degree	Master's degree	Professional degree	Doctor's degree
1	2	3	4	5	6	7	8	9	10	11	12
Number of persons (in thousands)	206,899 (210.7)	9,922 (109.1)	14,595 (131.0)	61,704 (240.9)	34,805 (193.4)	20,367 (152.9)	65,506 (245.7)	41,575 (208.0)	17,395 (142.2)	3,066 (61.5)	3,470 (65.4)
With earnings	135,931 (278.2)	4,123 (71.2)	6,795 (90.9)	36,375 (197.0)	23,359 (162.6)	14,990 (132.7)	50,289 (224.0)	31,682 (185.9)	13,384 (125.8)	2,456 (55.1)	2,768 (58.5)
Distribution of persons with earnings, by total annual earnings	100.0 (†)	100.0 (†)	100.0 (†)	100.0 (†)	100.0 (†)	100.0 (†)	100.0 (†)	100.0 (†)	100.0 (†)	100.0 (†)	100.0 (†)
$1 to $4,999 or loss[1]	5.2 (0.07)	7.6 (0.46)	10.2 (0.41)	5.9 (0.14)	6.4 (0.18)	5.1 (0.20)	3.4 (0.09)	3.6 (0.12)	3.2 (0.17)	2.3 (0.34)	2.4 (0.32)
$5,000 to $9,999	5.3 (0.07)	10.0 (0.52)	10.8 (0.42)	6.8 (0.15)	5.8 (0.17)	4.4 (0.19)	3.2 (0.09)	3.5 (0.12)	3.0 (0.17)	1.2 (0.25)	1.9 (0.29)
$10,000 to $14,999	6.8 (0.08)	16.3 (0.64)	14.2 (0.47)	8.5 (0.16)	7.3 (0.19)	6.5 (0.22)	3.6 (0.09)	3.9 (0.12)	3.2 (0.15)	2.3 (0.34)	2.3 (0.32)
$15,000 to $19,999	6.8 (0.08)	18.6 (0.68)	14.2 (0.46)	9.0 (0.17)	7.2 (0.19)	6.1 (0.22)	3.3 (0.09)	3.8 (0.12)	2.6 (0.16)	1.5 (0.27)	2.1 (0.31)
$20,000 to $24,999	7.8 (0.08)	15.7 (0.63)	13.6 (0.46)	10.5 (0.18)	8.9 (0.21)	7.9 (0.25)	4.0 (0.10)	4.9 (0.14)	2.8 (0.17)	1.9 (0.31)	2.0 (0.29)
$25,000 to $29,999	7.2 (0.08)	11.0 (0.55)	8.7 (0.38)	9.6 (0.17)	8.6 (0.20)	8.0 (0.25)	4.0 (0.10)	4.7 (0.13)	3.2 (0.17)	1.9 (0.31)	2.3 (0.32)
$30,000 to $34,999	7.8 (0.08)	6.7 (0.44)	7.3 (0.35)	10.0 (0.18)	8.9 (0.21)	9.3 (0.26)	5.3 (0.11)	6.3 (0.15)	4.1 (0.19)	2.8 (0.37)	2.4 (0.33)
$35,000 to $39,999	6.6 (0.08)	3.6 (0.33)	5.5 (0.31)	8.0 (0.16)	7.8 (0.20)	7.3 (0.24)	5.2 (0.11)	6.2 (0.15)	4.2 (0.19)	2.1 (0.32)	1.4 (0.25)
$40,000 to $49,999	11.1 (0.10)	4.8 (0.37)	6.5 (0.34)	11.2 (0.18)	11.7 (0.24)	13.4 (0.31)	11.3 (0.16)	12.5 (0.21)	10.7 (0.30)	4.7 (0.48)	7.2 (0.55)
$50,000 to $74,999	18.0 (0.12)	4.0 (0.34)	6.5 (0.33)	13.9 (0.20)	16.8 (0.27)	20.3 (0.37)	23.4 (0.21)	23.2 (0.27)	25.6 (0.42)	17.4 (0.85)	20.2 (0.85)
$75,000 to $99,999	7.7 (0.08)	0.9 (0.16)	1.5 (0.16)	3.9 (0.11)	5.9 (0.17)	7.3 (0.24)	12.7 (0.17)	12.0 (0.20)	14.4 (0.34)	12.7 (0.75)	13.6 (0.73)
$100,000 or more	9.7 (0.09)	0.8 (0.16)	1.1 (0.14)	2.7 (0.10)	4.7 (0.15)	4.4 (0.19)	20.6 (0.20)	15.4 (0.23)	22.9 (0.41)	49.2 (1.13)	42.3 (1.05)
Median earnings[2]	$36,630 (121)	$19,210 (372)	$20,150 (241)	$29,770 (314)	$32,030 (185)	$36,360 (342)	$55,140 (386)	$50,280 (192)	$61,040 (345)	$97,200 (3,645)	$82,880 (3,072)
Number of males (in thousands)	99,305 (124.7)	4,963 (77.0)	7,314 (92.4)	30,014 (166.1)	16,508 (132.7)	8,775 (100.6)	31,731 (169.0)	19,860 (143.1)	7,804 (95.3)	1,876 (48.0)	2,192 (51.8)
With earnings	72,128 (181.3)	2,742 (57.8)	4,150 (70.7)	20,533 (144.9)	12,181 (116.5)	6,879 (89.8)	25,642 (157.5)	16,146 (131.5)	6,196 (85.5)	1,540 (43.6)	1,760 (46.5)
Distribution of males with earnings, by total annual earnings	100.0 (†)	100.0 (†)	100.0 (†)	100.0 (†)	100.0 (†)	100.0 (†)	100.0 (†)	100.0 (†)	100.0 (†)	100.0 (†)	100.0 (†)
$1 to $4,999 or loss[1]	3.9 (0.08)	4.5 (0.44)	7.6 (0.46)	4.5 (0.16)	4.3 (0.21)	3.9 (0.22)	2.4 (0.11)	2.7 (0.14)	2.1 (0.20)	1.3 (0.33)	2.3 (0.40)
$5,000 to $9,999	3.9 (0.08)	7.6 (0.57)	8.2 (0.48)	4.8 (0.17)	4.5 (0.21)	2.8 (0.22)	2.0 (0.10)	2.1 (0.13)	2.0 (0.20)	0.5 (0.21)	2.0 (0.38)
$10,000 to $14,999	5.2 (0.09)	13.5 (0.73)	10.5 (0.53)	6.2 (0.19)	5.1 (0.22)	4.7 (0.28)	2.8 (0.12)	2.9 (0.15)	2.9 (0.24)	1.9 (0.39)	2.0 (0.37)
$15,000 to $19,999	5.7 (0.10)	18.5 (0.83)	13.3 (0.59)	7.2 (0.20)	5.2 (0.23)	3.8 (0.26)	2.6 (0.11)	3.0 (0.15)	2.2 (0.21)	1.1 (0.29)	1.6 (0.33)
$20,000 to $24,999	6.6 (0.10)	16.3 (0.79)	13.4 (0.59)	8.8 (0.22)	7.1 (0.26)	5.3 (0.30)	3.0 (0.12)	3.7 (0.17)	2.0 (0.20)	1.4 (0.33)	1.6 (0.33)
$25,000 to $29,999	6.6 (0.10)	12.7 (0.71)	8.9 (0.49)	8.6 (0.22)	8.0 (0.27)	6.5 (0.33)	3.3 (0.12)	3.6 (0.16)	3.2 (0.25)	1.7 (0.36)	2.1 (0.38)
$30,000 to $34,999	7.2 (0.11)	8.3 (0.59)	9.2 (0.50)	10.0 (0.23)	7.7 (0.27)	7.8 (0.36)	4.3 (0.14)	5.1 (0.19)	3.0 (0.24)	2.6 (0.46)	2.2 (0.39)
$35,000 to $39,999	6.2 (0.10)	4.6 (0.45)	7.1 (0.44)	8.4 (0.22)	7.1 (0.26)	6.7 (0.34)	3.8 (0.13)	4.8 (0.19)	2.3 (0.21)	2.1 (0.41)	0.9 (0.25)
$40,000 to $49,999	11.4 (0.13)	6.5 (0.52)	8.7 (0.49)	13.1 (0.26)	13.1 (0.34)	14.1 (0.47)	9.4 (0.20)	11.2 (0.28)	7.0 (0.36)	4.3 (0.58)	6.2 (0.64)
$50,000 to $74,999	20.1 (0.17)	5.3 (0.48)	9.5 (0.51)	18.6 (0.30)	21.8 (0.42)	26.3 (0.59)	22.2 (0.29)	23.4 (0.37)	21.9 (0.59)	15.0 (1.02)	17.6 (1.02)
$75,000 to $99,999	9.7 (0.12)	1.2 (0.23)	2.3 (0.26)	5.9 (0.18)	8.9 (0.29)	11.0 (0.42)	14.9 (0.25)	14.7 (0.31)	16.5 (0.53)	12.8 (0.95)	12.2 (0.87)
$100,000 or more	13.6 (0.14)	0.9 (0.20)	1.4 (0.20)	4.0 (0.15)	7.2 (0.26)	7.2 (0.35)	29.4 (0.32)	22.7 (0.37)	34.8 (0.68)	55.3 (1.42)	49.4 (1.33)
Median earnings[2]	$42,310 (142)	$21,320 (280)	$23,280 (664)	$34,960 (529)	$40,470 (311)	$45,590 (608)	$66,870 (508)	$60,300 (406)	$76,020 (843)	$101,890 (1,766)	$96,910 (5,001)

See notes at end of table.

Distribution of earnings and median earnings of persons 25 years old and over, by highest level of educational attainment and sex: 2012—Continued

[Standard errors appear in parentheses]

Sex and earnings	Total	Elementary/secondary			College		Bachelor's or higher degree				
		Less than 9th grade	Some high school, no completion	High school completion (includes equivalency)	Some college, no degree	Associate's degree	Total	Bachelor's degree	Master's degree	Professional degree	Doctor's degree
1	2	3	4	5	6	7	8	9	10	11	12
Number of females (in thousands)	107,594 (136.5)	4,958 (77.1)	7,282 (92.5)	31,690 (171.9)	18,298 (139.7)	11,592 (114.6)	33,775 (175.4)	21,715 (149.7)	9,591 (105.2)	1,191 (38.4)	1,278 (39.7)
With earnings	63,802 (197.4)	1,380 (41.3)	2,644 (56.9)	15,842 (131.4)	11,178 (112.7)	8,111 (97.3)	24,647 (152.2)	15,536 (130.3)	7,188 (92.0)	915 (33.7)	1,008 (35.3)
Distribution of females with earnings, by total annual earnings	100.0 (†)	100.0 (†)	100.0 (†)	100.0 (†)	100.0 (†)	100.0 (†)	100.0 (†)	100.0 (†)	100.0 (†)	100.0 (†)	100.0 (†)
$1 to $4,999 or loss[1]	6.8 (0.11)	13.8 (1.04)	14.4 (0.76)	7.8 (0.24)	8.7 (0.30)	6.2 (0.30)	4.4 (0.15)	4.6 (0.19)	4.2 (0.27)	3.8 (0.71)	2.5 (0.55)
$5,000 to $9,999	6.9 (0.11)	14.7 (1.07)	15.0 (0.78)	9.3 (0.26)	7.2 (0.27)	5.7 (0.29)	4.4 (0.15)	4.9 (0.19)	3.9 (0.25)	2.3 (0.56)	1.6 (0.45)
$10,000 to $14,999	8.6 (0.12)	21.7 (1.24)	20.0 (0.87)	11.5 (0.28)	9.7 (0.31)	8.0 (0.34)	4.3 (0.15)	4.9 (0.19)	3.4 (0.24)	3.1 (0.64)	2.8 (0.58)
$15,000 to $19,999	8.1 (0.12)	18.6 (1.17)	15.6 (0.79)	11.4 (0.28)	9.4 (0.31)	8.0 (0.34)	4.1 (0.14)	4.7 (0.19)	3.0 (0.22)	2.2 (0.54)	3.2 (0.62)
$20,000 to $24,999	9.2 (0.13)	14.5 (1.06)	13.8 (0.75)	12.7 (0.30)	10.9 (0.33)	10.1 (0.37)	5.1 (0.16)	6.1 (0.21)	3.5 (0.24)	2.9 (0.62)	2.7 (0.57)
$25,000 to $29,999	7.8 (0.12)	7.7 (0.80)	8.4 (0.60)	10.8 (0.28)	9.3 (0.31)	9.2 (0.36)	4.7 (0.15)	5.7 (0.21)	3.1 (0.23)	2.4 (0.56)	2.5 (0.55)
$30,000 to $34,999	8.4 (0.12)	3.5 (0.55)	4.4 (0.44)	10.0 (0.27)	10.2 (0.32)	10.6 (0.38)	6.4 (0.17)	7.5 (0.24)	5.0 (0.29)	3.1 (0.64)	2.7 (0.55)
$35,000 to $39,999	7.1 (0.11)	1.7 (0.39)	3.0 (0.37)	7.6 (0.23)	8.5 (0.29)	7.8 (0.33)	6.7 (0.18)	7.7 (0.24)	5.8 (0.31)	2.1 (0.52)	2.4 (0.54)
$40,000 to $49,999	10.9 (0.14)	1.5 (0.37)	3.1 (0.38)	8.8 (0.25)	10.2 (0.32)	12.8 (0.41)	13.3 (0.24)	13.8 (0.31)	13.9 (0.46)	5.3 (0.83)	9.1 (1.01)
$50,000 to $74,999	15.5 (0.16)	1.4 (0.35)	1.6 (0.28)	7.8 (0.24)	11.2 (0.33)	15.3 (0.45)	24.7 (0.31)	23.0 (0.38)	28.8 (0.60)	21.4 (1.51)	24.5 (1.52)
$75,000 to $99,999	5.4 (0.10)	‡ (†)	0.3 ! (0.11)	1.3 (0.10)	2.7 (0.17)	4.2 (0.25)	10.5 (0.22)	9.1 (0.26)	12.6 (0.44)	12.5 (1.22)	16.0 (1.29)
$100,000 or more[2]	5.3 (0.10)	0.7 ! (0.25)	0.5 ! (0.16)	1.0 (0.09)	1.9 (0.15)	2.1 (0.18)	11.3 (0.23)	7.9 (0.24)	12.7 (0.44)	39.0 (1.80)	29.9 (1.61)
Median earnings[2]	$30,990 (119)	$14,930 (566)	$15,150 (301)	$23,500 (324)	$26,620 (274)	$30,890 (272)	$46,710 (269)	$41,570 (237)	$51,570 (330)	$76,050 (2,191)	$70,810 (1,925)

†Not applicable.
!Interpret data with caution. The coefficient of variation (CV) for this estimate is between 30 and 50 percent.
‡Reporting standards not met. The coefficient of variation (CV) for this estimate is 50 percent or greater.
[1] A negative amount (a net loss) may be reported by self-employed persons.
[2] Excludes persons without earnings.

NOTE: Detail may not sum to totals because of rounding.
SOURCE: U.S. Department of Commerce, Census Bureau, Current Population Survey (CPS), 2013 Annual Social and Economic Supplement, retrieved December 26, 2013, from http://www.census.gov/hhes/www/cpstables/032013/perinc/pinc03_000.htm. (This table was prepared December 2013.)

Table. Labor force status of 2010, 2011, and 2012 high school completers, by college enrollment status, sex, and race/ethnicity: October 2010, 2011, and 2012

[Standard errors appear in parentheses]

Selected characteristic	Total number of high school completers (in thousands)	Percent of high school completers — Separately for those enrolled in college vs. those not enrolled	Percent of high school completers — For all high school completers	Percentage distribution of all high school completers — Employed	Percentage distribution — Unemployed (seeking employment)	Percentage distribution — Not in labor force	Labor force participation rate of all high school completers[1]	HS completers in civilian labor force[2] — Number — Total, all completers in labor force	Number — Employed	Number — Unemployed (seeking employment)	Unemployment rate	High school completers not in labor force (in thousands)
1	2	3	4	5	6	7	8	9	10	11	12	13
2010 high school completers[3]												
Total	**3,160** (91.8)	†	**100.0** (†)	**37.3** (1.73)	**14.4** (1.18)	**48.3** (1.77)	**51.7** (1.77)	**1,633** (70.7)	**1,179** (64.9)	**454** (38.1)	**27.8** (2.14)	**1,528** (74.0)
Male	1,679 (64.6)	† (†)	53.1 (1.30)	39.3 (2.31)	15.9 (1.71)	44.8 (2.26)	55.2 (2.26)	926 (51.5)	659 (49.2)	267 (28.2)	28.9 (2.91)	752 (48.0)
Female	1,482 (58.4)	† (†)	46.9 (1.30)	35.1 (2.32)	12.6 (1.50)	52.3 (2.52)	47.7 (2.52)	706 (45.2)	520 (38.0)	187 (23.9)	26.4 (2.85)	775 (49.5)
White	1,937 (68.7)	† (†)	61.3 (1.41)	40.9 (2.18)	12.9 (1.34)	46.2 (2.10)	53.8 (2.10)	1,041 (55.1)	792 (52.1)	249 (26.7)	23.9 (2.43)	896 (51.7)
Black	461 (36.9)	† (†)	14.6 (1.11)	24.5 (3.74)	23.3 (4.22)	52.2 (4.50)	47.8 (4.50)	220 (27.2)	113 (19.8)	107 (20.9)	48.7 (6.96)	241 (28.3)
Hispanic	507 (37.3)	† (†)	16.0 (1.05)	42.5 (4.60)	12.3 (2.68)	45.1 (4.60)	54.9 (4.60)	278 (30.6)	215 (27.9)	‡ (†)	22.5 (4.71)	229 (29.1)
Enrolled in college, 2010	2,152 (78.8)	100.0 (†)	68.1 (1.49)	30.9 (1.94)	9.1 (1.22)	60.0 (2.13)	40.0 (2.13)	860 (51.9)	664 (46.9)	196 (26.4)	22.8 (2.77)	1,292 (70.3)
Male	1,055 (50.5)	49.0 (1.64)	33.4 (1.24)	30.1 (2.67)	11.0 (1.81)	58.9 (3.05)	41.1 (3.05)	433 (37.4)	317 (31.7)	116 (19.6)	26.8 (3.87)	621 (44.8)
Female	1,097 (55.2)	51.0 (1.64)	34.7 (1.44)	31.6 (2.68)	7.3 (1.52)	61.1 (2.84)	38.9 (2.84)	427 (37.4)	347 (34.0)	‡ (†)	18.7 (3.66)	670 (46.3)
2-year	842 (55.9)	39.2 (2.02)	39.2 (2.02)	42.6 (3.21)	9.8 (1.93)	47.6 (3.43)	52.4 (3.43)	441 (39.3)	359 (36.1)	‡ (†)	18.7 (3.39)	401 (41.0)
4-year	1,309 (61.1)	60.9 (2.02)	60.9 (2.02)	23.3 (2.14)	8.7 (1.50)	68.0 (2.33)	32.0 (2.33)	419 (35.5)	305 (30.9)	114 (20.4)	27.1 (4.25)	890 (52.5)
Full-time students	1,946 (76.2)	90.4 (1.11)	90.4 (1.11)	27.6 (1.91)	9.1 (1.24)	63.3 (2.16)	36.7 (2.16)	714 (48.1)	537 (41.6)	176 (24.7)	24.7 (3.01)	1,233 (67.2)
Part-time students	206 (24.7)	9.6 (1.11)	9.6 (1.11)	61.7 (5.96)	9.5 ! (3.27)	28.7 (5.55)	71.3 (5.55)	147 (21.0)	127 (19.9)	‡ (†)	13.4 ! (4.54)	‡ (†)
White	1,365 (56.9)	63.5 (1.81)	43.2 (1.40)	34.3 (2.41)	9.1 (1.39)	56.7 (2.51)	43.3 (2.51)	592 (41.0)	468 (37.6)	124 (19.4)	21.0 (3.03)	774 (48.7)
Black	286 (33.4)	13.3 (1.42)	9.1 (1.01)	22.4 (4.79)	13.3 ! (4.58)	64.2 (5.48)	35.8 (5.48)	‡ (†)	‡ (†)	‡ (†)	‡ (†)	184 (26.3)
Hispanic	302 (31.5)	14.1 (1.30)	9.6 (0.96)	30.8 (5.59)	6.8 ! (2.60)	62.4 (5.72)	37.6 (5.72)	114 (20.6)	93 (19.1)	‡ (†)	18.1 ! (6.83)	189 (26.8)
Not enrolled in college, 2010	1,009 (54.9)	100.0 (†)	31.9 (1.49)	51.0 (2.98)	25.6 (2.38)	23.4 (2.29)	76.6 (2.29)	773 (49.7)	515 (42.9)	258 (27.4)	33.4 (3.07)	236 (25.4)
Male	624 (40.4)	61.9 (2.77)	19.7 (1.15)	54.8 (3.66)	24.2 (2.99)	21.0 (2.67)	79.0 (2.67)	493 (38.9)	342 (35.6)	151 (19.9)	30.7 (3.75)	131 (17.0)
Female	385 (37.4)	38.1 (2.77)	12.2 (1.13)	45.0 (4.64)	27.8 (3.95)	27.3 (4.11)	72.7 (4.11)	280 (30.8)	173 (24.6)	107 (17.8)	38.2 (5.13)	105 (19.2)
White	571 (39.3)	56.7 (2.72)	18.1 (1.13)	56.8 (3.94)	21.9 (3.02)	21.4 (3.15)	78.6 (3.15)	449 (36.0)	324 (33.6)	125 (18.1)	27.8 (3.79)	122 (19.7)
Black	175 (24.9)	17.3 (2.11)	5.5 (0.80)	27.8 (6.61)	39.6 (6.95)	32.6 (6.23)	67.4 (6.23)	118 (21.7)	‡ (†)	‡ (†)	58.7 (9.00)	‡ (†)
Hispanic	204 (25.4)	20.3 (2.34)	6.5 (0.76)	59.9 (5.86)	20.5 (5.10)	19.6 (5.11)	80.4 (5.11)	164 (23.9)	122 (19.9)	‡ (†)	25.5 (6.01)	‡ (†)
2011 high school completers[3]												
Total	**3,079** (88.3)	†	**100.0** (†)	**35.2** (1.40)	**12.9** (1.12)	**51.9** (1.60)	**48.1** (1.60)	**1,482** (58.7)	**1,084** (50.0)	**398** (34.8)	**26.8** (2.01)	**1,597** (73.3)
Male	1,611 (60.6)	† (†)	52.3 (1.30)	34.2 (2.00)	16.0 (1.62)	49.8 (2.40)	50.2 (2.40)	808 (46.2)	551 (36.3)	258 (27.3)	31.9 (2.67)	802 (51.6)
Female	1,468 (58.4)	† (†)	47.7 (1.30)	36.3 (2.22)	9.5 (1.32)	54.1 (2.28)	45.9 (2.28)	674 (40.4)	534 (37.3)	140 (19.7)	20.8 (2.69)	795 (48.6)
White	1,747 (60.6)	† (†)	56.7 (1.38)	42.7 (1.85)	10.2 (1.25)	47.1 (2.15)	52.9 (2.15)	925 (46.9)	746 (39.7)	179 (22.4)	19.3 (2.08)	822 (49.5)
Black	464 (36.1)	† (†)	15.1 (1.08)	23.1 (3.76)	17.5 (3.65)	59.4 (4.49)	40.6 (4.49)	189 (25.6)	107 (20.8)	‡ (†)	43.2 (7.23)	275 (29.2)
Hispanic	623 (42.0)	† (†)	20.2 (1.20)	28.4 (3.25)	15.9 (2.72)	55.7 (3.60)	44.3 (3.60)	276 (29.2)	177 (23.6)	99 (18.0)	35.9 (5.33)	347 (32.0)
Enrolled in college, 2011	2,101 (77.2)	100.0 (†)	68.2 (1.45)	30.4 (1.69)	8.2 (1.17)	61.4 (1.92)	38.6 (1.92)	810 (49.2)	638 (42.1)	172 (25.1)	21.2 (2.68)	1,291 (63.1)
Male	1,041 (55.6)	49.6 (1.70)	33.8 (1.44)	26.2 (2.33)	10.1 (1.96)	63.7 (2.86)	36.3 (2.86)	378 (35.7)	273 (27.2)	106 (21.6)	27.9 (4.47)	663 (46.2)
Female	1,060 (49.1)	50.4 (1.70)	34.4 (1.29)	34.5 (2.57)	6.3 (1.15)	59.2 (2.62)	40.8 (2.62)	432 (34.3)	365 (32.4)	‡ (†)	15.3 (2.73)	628 (40.0)
2-year	798 (49.2)	38.0 (1.89)	25.9 (1.49)	37.9 (3.07)	11.8 (2.32)	50.3 (3.30)	49.7 (3.30)	397 (36.0)	303 (30.0)	94 (19.8)	23.7 (4.21)	401 (35.9)
4-year	1,303 (62.2)	62.0 (1.89)	42.3 (1.44)	25.7 (2.08)	6.0 (1.23)	68.3 (2.14)	31.7 (2.14)	413 (33.8)	336 (32.2)	78 (15.9)	18.9 (3.67)	890 (51.2)
Full-time students	1,930 (74.2)	91.9 (1.11)	62.7 (1.42)	27.0 (1.71)	7.9 (1.20)	65.1 (1.95)	34.9 (1.95)	674 (44.0)	522 (36.8)	152 (24.0)	22.6 (3.02)	1,256 (63.0)
Part-time students	170 (24.1)	8.1 (1.11)	5.5 (0.78)	68.3 (6.42)	11.4 ! (4.38)	20.3 (4.97)	79.7 (4.97)	136 (20.8)	116 (18.8)	‡ (†)	14.3 ! (5.53)	‡ (†)

See notes at end of table.

Labor force status of 2010, 2011, and 2012 high school completers, by college enrollment status, sex, and race/ethnicity: October 2010, 2011, and 2012—Continued

[Standard errors appear in parentheses]

Selected characteristic	Total number of high school completers (in thousands)	Percent of high school completers — Separately for those enrolled in college vs. those not enrolled	Percent of high school completers — For all high school completers	Percentage distribution of all high school completers — Employed	Percentage distribution — Unemployed (seeking employment)	Percentage distribution — Not in labor force	Labor force participation rate of all high school completers[1]	High school completers in civilian labor force[2] Number (in thousands) — Total, all completers in labor force	Number — Employed	Number — Unemployed (seeking employment)	Unemployment rate	High school completers not in labor force (in thousands)
1	2	3	4	5	6	7	8	9	10	11	12	13
White	1,193 (52.9)	56.8 (1.73)	38.7 (1.43)	37.4 (2.27)	6.4 (1.33)	56.2 (2.69)	43.8 (2.69)	522 (40.1)	446 (33.1)	‡ (†)	14.6 (2.66)	670 (43.0)
Black	312 (31.6)	14.8 (1.44)	10.1 (0.96)	19.9 (4.50)	7.7! (3.02)	72.4 (4.76)	27.6 (4.76)	86 (17.2)	‡ (†)	‡ (†)	28.0! (10.19)	226 (26.9)
Hispanic	415 (33.9)	19.7 (1.39)	13.5 (1.02)	24.9 (3.96)	12.5 (3.31)	62.6 (4.45)	37.4 (4.45)	155 (22.3)	103 (18.5)	‡ (†)	33.5 (7.70)	260 (28.0)
Not enrolled in college, 2011	978 (51.1)	100.0 (†)	31.8 (1.45)	45.6 (2.88)	23.1 (2.58)	31.3 (2.74)	68.7 (2.74)	672 (42.5)	446 (34.7)	226 (27.9)	33.6 (3.40)	306 (32.3)
Male	569 (38.2)	58.2 (2.65)	18.5 (1.20)	48.8 (3.94)	26.7 (3.33)	24.5 (3.42)	75.5 (3.42)	430 (34.3)	278 (27.4)	152 (22.5)	35.4 (4.17)	139 (21.7)
Female	409 (34.4)	41.8 (2.65)	13.3 (1.03)	41.1 (4.39)	18.0 (3.43)	40.8 (4.77)	59.2 (4.77)	242 (24.5)	168 (21.8)	74 (13.9)	30.5 (5.11)	167 (26.5)
White	554 (37.4)	56.7 (2.58)	18.0 (1.14)	54.1 (3.72)	18.5 (2.97)	27.4 (3.32)	72.6 (3.32)	402 (31.6)	300 (26.6)	103 (18.4)	25.5 (3.89)	152 (21.7)
Black	152 (21.3)	15.6 (2.01)	5.0 (0.69)	29.7 (6.97)	37.6 (7.13)	32.6 (7.91)	67.4 (7.91)	103 (19.8)	‡ (†)	‡ (†)	55.9 (8.44)	‡ (†)
Hispanic	208 (26.8)	21.3 (2.38)	6.8 (0.84)	35.4 (6.04)	22.6 (5.12)	42.0 (6.75)	58.0 (6.75)	121 (19.4)	74 (15.0)	‡ (†)	39.0 (7.47)	‡ (†)
2012 high school completers[3]												
Total	3,203 (96.2)	† (†)	100.0 (†)	36.3 (1.53)	12.6 (1.15)	51.2 (1.61)	48.8 (1.61)	1,563 (67.9)	1,161 (57.7)	402 (38.9)	25.7 (2.13)	1,639 (73.1)
Male	1,622 (70.1)	† (†)	50.6 (1.25)	33.7 (2.21)	14.5 (1.75)	51.8 (2.29)	48.2 (2.29)	783 (49.3)	547 (42.8)	235 (29.5)	30.0 (3.29)	840 (52.7)
Female	1,581 (54.0)	† (†)	49.4 (1.25)	38.8 (1.92)	10.6 (1.29)	50.6 (2.16)	49.4 (2.16)	781 (42.2)	614 (36.0)	167 (21.1)	21.4 (2.31)	800 (44.7)
White	1,820 (62.8)	† (†)	56.8 (1.52)	42.5 (2.07)	10.9 (1.31)	46.6 (2.02)	53.4 (2.02)	971 (49.9)	774 (46.1)	198 (24.8)	20.3 (2.35)	849 (46.7)
Black	413 (33.9)	† (†)	12.9 (0.98)	26.4 (4.59)	23.2 (4.11)	50.4 (4.88)	49.6 (4.88)	205 (26.1)	109 (19.8)	96 (19.3)	46.8 (7.23)	208 (26.4)
Hispanic	697 (54.9)	† (†)	21.8 (1.41)	32.1 (3.10)	10.2 (2.13)	57.6 (3.29)	42.4 (3.29)	296 (28.7)	224 (25.2)	‡ (†)	24.2 (4.60)	402 (42.7)
Enrolled in college, 2012	2,121 (76.4)	100.0 (†)	66.2 (1.59)	31.5 (1.66)	6.8 (0.92)	61.8 (1.84)	38.2 (1.84)	811 (46.7)	667 (41.0)	143 (20.0)	17.7 (2.18)	1,310 (63.9)
Male	994 (53.3)	46.9 (1.66)	31.0 (1.31)	27.4 (2.39)	7.0 (1.37)	65.6 (2.58)	34.4 (2.58)	342 (29.7)	272 (27.0)	‡ (†)	20.4 (3.65)	652 (45.6)
Female	1,127 (49.9)	53.1 (1.66)	35.2 (1.41)	35.1 (2.19)	6.5 (1.20)	58.4 (2.43)	41.6 (2.43)	469 (32.6)	395 (29.0)	‡ (†)	15.7 (2.60)	658 (42.0)
2-year	921 (57.7)	43.4 (2.07)	28.8 (1.57)	39.9 (3.10)	8.0 (1.57)	52.1 (3.22)	47.9 (3.22)	441 (35.2)	367 (32.0)	‡ (†)	16.7 (3.09)	480 (47.1)
4-year	1,200 (58.3)	56.6 (2.07)	37.5 (1.60)	25.0 (1.92)	5.8 (1.14)	69.2 (2.17)	30.8 (2.17)	370 (31.8)	300 (27.6)	‡ (†)	18.8 (3.32)	830 (47.5)
Full-time students	1,863 (71.3)	87.8 (1.31)	58.2 (1.61)	28.1 (1.74)	5.8 (0.87)	66.1 (1.89)	33.9 (1.89)	632 (41.6)	523 (36.6)	109 (16.8)	17.2 (2.34)	1,231 (60.3)
Part-time students	258 (29.7)	12.2 (1.31)	8.1 (0.90)	55.9 (5.63)	13.4 (3.98)	30.8 (5.73)	69.2 (5.73)	179 (25.8)	144 (22.3)	‡ (†)	19.3 (5.36)	‡ (†)
White	1,196 (52.7)	56.4 (1.88)	37.3 (1.50)	35.0 (2.32)	6.6 (1.16)	58.3 (2.46)	41.7 (2.46)	498 (35.5)	419 (32.1)	79 (14.3)	15.9 (2.61)	698 (44.0)
Black	233 (30.4)	11.0 (1.38)	7.3 (0.93)	24.4 (5.79)	10.8! (4.25)	64.7 (6.27)	35.3 (6.27)	‡ (†)	‡ (†)	‡ (†)	‡ (†)	151 (24.1)
Hispanic	490 (43.3)	23.1 (1.71)	15.3 (1.16)	31.7 (3.98)	4.7! (1.83)	63.6 (4.00)	36.4 (4.00)	178 (22.7)	155 (22.0)	‡ (†)	12.9! (4.91)	312 (36.1)
Not enrolled in college, 2012	1,082 (63.3)	100.0 (†)	33.8 (1.59)	45.7 (2.52)	23.9 (2.62)	30.4 (2.69)	69.6 (2.69)	753 (53.4)	494 (40.9)	259 (31.4)	34.4 (3.24)	329 (34.5)
Male	628 (45.9)	58.1 (2.47)	19.6 (1.22)	43.8 (3.64)	26.3 (3.63)	29.8 (3.64)	70.2 (3.64)	441 (39.1)	275 (31.1)	166 (25.0)	37.5 (4.55)	187 (27.0)
Female	454 (37.3)	41.9 (2.47)	14.2 (1.09)	48.2 (3.92)	20.5 (3.35)	31.3 (3.78)	68.7 (3.78)	312 (29.8)	219 (25.1)	93 (16.5)	29.9 (4.50)	142 (21.3)
White	624 (42.3)	57.7 (2.63)	19.5 (1.21)	56.9 (3.29)	18.9 (2.69)	24.2 (3.11)	75.8 (3.11)	473 (39.3)	355 (34.3)	118 (17.9)	25.0 (3.32)	151 (20.9)
Black	180 (22.0)	16.6 (1.84)	5.6 (0.66)	28.8 (6.82)	39.2 (7.43)	31.9 (7.23)	68.1 (7.23)	122 (19.9)	‡ (†)	‡ (†)	57.6 (9.06)	‡ (†)
Hispanic	207 (28.4)	19.1 (2.25)	6.5 (0.85)	33.2 (6.32)	23.4 (5.69)	43.4 (5.64)	56.6 (5.64)	117 (18.0)	‡ (†)	‡ (†)	41.4 (9.35)	90 (18.2)

†Not applicable.
!Interpret data with caution. The coefficient of variation (CV) for this estimate is between 30 and 50 percent.
‡Reporting standards not met (too few cases for a reliable estimate).
[1]The labor force participation rate is the percentage of persons who are either employed or seeking employment.
[2]The labor force includes all employed persons plus those seeking employment. The unemployment rate is the percentage of persons in the labor force who are not working and who made specific efforts to find employment sometime during the prior 4 weeks.
[3]Includes 16- to 24-year-olds who completed high school between October of the previous year and October of the given year. Includes recipients of equivalency credentials as well as diploma recipients.

NOTE: Data are for October of given year. Data are based on sample surveys of the civilian noninstitutional population. Percentages are only shown when the base is 75,000 or greater. Standard errors were computed using replicate weights. Totals include race categories not separately shown. Race categories exclude persons of Hispanic ethnicity. Detail may not sum to totals because of rounding.
SOURCE: U.S. Department of Commerce, Census Bureau, Current Population Survey (CPS), October 2010, 2011, and 2012. (This table was prepared June 2013.)

Outcomes of Education

Labor force status of high school dropouts, by sex and race/ethnicity: October, selected years, 1980 through 2012

[Standard errors appear in parentheses]

Year, sex, and race/ethnicity	Number of dropouts (in thousands)	Percent of all dropouts	Percentage distribution of dropouts — Employed	Percentage distribution of dropouts — Unemployed (seeking employment)	Percentage distribution of dropouts — Not in labor force	Labor force participation rate of dropouts[1]	Dropouts in civilian labor force[2] — Number (in thousands) — Total	Dropouts in civilian labor force[2] — Number (in thousands) — Unemployed (seeking employment)	Unemployment rate	Dropouts not in labor force (in thousands)
1	2	3	4	5	6	7	8	9	10	11
All dropouts										
1980	738 (44.0)	100.0 (†)	43.8 (2.97)	20.0 (2.37)	36.2 (2.87)	63.8 (2.87)	471 (35.2)	148 (19.5)	31.4 (3.44)	267 (26.5)
1985	610 (42.3)	100.0 (†)	43.5 (3.45)	24.0 (2.94)	32.5 (3.25)	67.5 (3.25)	412 (34.8)	147 (20.6)	35.6 (4.01)	198 (24.1)
1990	412 (36.0)	100.0 (†)	46.3 (4.37)	21.6 (3.57)	32.2 (4.09)	67.8 (4.09)	279 (29.7)	89 (16.6)	31.8 (4.90)	132 (20.4)
1995	604 (43.6)	100.0 (†)	47.7 (3.61)	20.0 (2.86)	32.3 (3.38)	67.7 (3.38)	409 (35.9)	121 (19.3)	29.6 (3.97)	195 (24.8)
2000	515 (28.5)	100.0 (†)	48.7 (2.77)	19.2 (3.01)	32.0 (2.59)	68.0 (2.59)	350 (23.5)	99 (17.2)	28.1 (4.16)	165 (16.2)
2005	407 (35.3)	100.0 (†)	38.3 (4.22)	18.9 (3.42)	42.8 (3.32)	57.2 (4.30)	233 (26.7)	77 (15.4)	32.9 (5.42)	174 (17.9)
2010[3]	340 (29.0)	100.0 (†)	30.9 (4.24)	23.0 (4.29)	46.1 (4.78)	53.9 (4.78)	183 (21.5)	78 (16.0)	42.7 (6.67)	157 (21.9)
2011[3]	372 (33.4)	100.0 (†)	33.9 (4.09)	21.1 (4.18)	44.9 (4.78)	55.1 (4.78)	2045 (24.2)	79 (15.9)	38.4 (6.26)	167 (24.5)
2012[3]	370 (37.1)	100.0 (†)	23.8 (4.56)	23.4 (4.69)	52.8 (5.64)	47.2 (5.64)	174 (27.0)	‡ (†)	49.6 (7.82)	195 (28.8)
Male										
1980	422 (32.5)	57.2 (2.89)	50.3 (3.86)	22.0 (3.20)	27.7 (3.45)	72.3 (3.45)	305 (27.7)	93 (15.3)	30.5 (4.18)	117 (17.1)
1985	319 (29.9)	52.3 (3.39)	50.8 (4.69)	30.6 (4.32)	18.6 (3.65)	81.4 (3.65)	260 (27.0)	98 (16.6)	37.6 (5.04)	59 (12.9)
1990	217 (25.6)	52.8 (4.27)	51.3 (5.89)	28.0 (5.29)	20.7 (4.77)	79.3 (4.77)	172 (22.8)	61 (13.5)	35.3 (6.32)	45 (11.6)
1995	339 (31.5)	56.2 (3.45)	52.8 (4.64)	21.3 (3.80)	26.0 (4.07)	74.0 (4.07)	251 (27.1)	72 (14.5)	28.7 (4.88)	88 (16.1)
2000	295 (29.3)	57.3 (3.73)	74.6 (4.34)	18.2 (3.85)	25.6 (4.35)	74.4 (4.35)	220 (25.3)	‡ (†)	24.5 (4.96)	76 (14.9)
2005	227 (25.9)	55.8 (4.24)	59.9 (5.61)	21.6 (4.71)	40.3 (5.61)	59.7 (5.61)	136 (20.1)	‡ (†)	35.9 (7.09)	91 (16.4)
2010[3]	179 (21.3)	52.7 (4.17)	25.9 (4.96)	17.2 (4.40)	56.9 (5.70)	43.1 (5.70)	77 (14.4)	‡ (†)	39.8 (8.62)	102 (17.2)
2011[3]	204 (24.5)	54.7 (4.00)	42.1 (5.91)	16.0 ! (4.85)	41.8 (6.25)	58.2 (6.25)	118 (18.1)	‡ (†)	27.5 (7.53)	85 (17.4)
2012[3]	192 (27.1)	51.9 (5.42)	31.1 (6.58)	26.8 (6.34)	42.1 (6.64)	57.9 (6.64)	111 (20.9)	‡ (†)	46.3 (9.59)	‡ (†)
Female										
1980	316 (27.0)	42.8 (2.77)	35.0 (4.08)	17.4 (3.24)	47.6 (4.28)	52.4 (4.28)	165 (19.6)	55 (11.3)	33.2 (5.57)	150 (18.7)
1985	291 (27.4)	47.7 (3.25)	35.5 (4.51)	16.8 (3.52)	47.8 (4.71)	52.2 (4.71)	152 (19.8)	49 (11.2)	32.1 (6.09)	139 (18.9)
1990	194 (23.2)	47.2 (4.10)	55.0 (5.94)	14.4 (4.19)	45.0 (5.94)	55.0 (5.94)	107 (17.2)	‡ (†)	26.1 (7.08)	87 (15.6)
1995	265 (26.6)	43.8 (3.31)	59.5 (4.95)	18.4 (3.91)	40.5 (4.95)	59.5 (4.95)	157 (20.6)	‡ (†)	30.9 (6.05)	107 (17.0)
2000	220 (24.3)	42.7 (3.58)	59.5 (5.43)	20.3 (4.45)	40.6 (5.43)	59.4 (5.43)	131 (18.8)	‡ (†)	34.2 (6.80)	90 (15.6)
2005	180 (22.4)	44.2 (4.11)	53.9 (6.20)	15.6 (4.51)	46.0 (6.20)	54.0 (6.20)	97 (16.4)	‡ (†)	28.8 (7.67)	83 (15.2)
2010[3]	161 (19.3)	47.3 (4.17)	36.4 (6.46)	29.6 (7.15)	34.0 (6.82)	66.0 (6.82)	106 (17.0)	‡ (†)	44.8 (9.14)	‡ (†)
2011[3]	169 (20.4)	45.3 (4.00)	24.1 (5.60)	27.3 (6.92)	48.7 (7.45)	51.3 (7.45)	87 (14.9)	‡ (†)	53.1 (9.84)	82 (17.0)
2012[3]	178 (27.1)	48.1 (5.42)	15.9 ! (5.41)	19.7 ! (6.66)	64.5 (8.03)	35.5 (8.03)	‡ (†)	‡ (†)	‡ (†)	115 (24.8)
White										
1980	489 (35.9)	66.2 (2.83)	50.3 (3.67)	18.0 (2.79)	31.7 (3.42)	68.3 (3.42)	334 (29.7)	88 (15.1)	26.3 (3.87)	155 (20.2)
1985	354 (32.3)	58.1 (3.43)	49.2 (4.56)	23.3 (3.82)	27.5 (4.07)	72.5 (4.07)	257 (27.5)	83 (15.4)	32.2 (4.95)	98 (16.9)
1990	242 (27.6)	58.8 (4.31)	75.0 (4.95)	18.7 (4.41)	25.0 (4.95)	75.0 (4.95)	181 (23.9)	‡ (†)	25.0 (5.65)	60 (13.8)
1995	316 (31.6)	52.3 (3.61)	69.9 (4.59)	18.3 (3.83)	30.1 (4.59)	69.9 (4.59)	221 (26.4)	‡ (†)	26.2 (5.21)	95 (17.3)
2000	288 (21.4)	55.9 (2.76)	76.6 (3.14)	16.5 (3.79)	23.4 (3.14)	76.6 (3.14)	221 (18.7)	‡ (†)	21.5 (4.79)	‡ (†)
2005	194 (24.4)	47.6 (4.34)	60.3 (6.16)	20.0 (5.05)	39.7 (6.16)	60.3 (6.16)	117 (18.9)	‡ (†)	33.2 (7.67)	77 (15.4)
2010[3]	148 (18.9)	43.5 (4.57)	31.4 (6.58)	20.4 (5.46)	48.3 (6.82)	51.7 (6.82)	77 (13.6)	‡ (†)	39.4 (9.52)	71 (14.1)
2011[3]	181 (25.3)	48.5 (4.76)	32.8 (5.71)	18.2 (5.05)	49.0 (6.21)	51.0 (6.21)	92 (15.9)	‡ (†)	35.7 (8.57)	88 (17.6)
2012[3]	86 (15.3)	23.2 (4.16)	24.7 ! (7.85)	11.6 ! (5.44)	63.7 (8.29)	36.3 (8.29)	‡ (†)	‡ (†)	‡ (†)	‡ (†)
Black										
1980	141 (19.9)	19.1 (2.43)	49.3 (7.09)	28.4 (6.40)	50.7 (7.09)	49.3 (7.09)	69 (14.0)	‡ (†)	‡ (†)	71 (14.2)
1985	130 (20.2)	21.4 (2.95)	52.5 (7.78)	22.7 (6.52)	47.5 (7.78)	52.5 (7.78)	68 (14.7)	‡ (†)	‡ (†)	62 (14.0)
1990	82 (16.6)	19.9 (3.62)	66.1 (9.64)	35.2 (9.74)	33.9 (9.64)	66.1 (9.64)	‡ (†)	‡ (†)	‡ (†)	‡ (†)
1995	104 (18.5)	17.2 (2.79)	59.2 (8.75)	25.8 ! (7.78)	40.8 (8.75)	59.2 (8.75)	‡ (†)	‡ (†)	‡ (†)	‡ (†)
2000	106 (18.7)	20.6 (3.24)	52.2 (8.80)	25.5 ! (7.68)	47.8 (8.80)	52.2 (8.80)	‡ (†)	‡ (†)	‡ (†)	‡ (†)
2005	108 (19.3)	26.5 (4.07)	26.5 (7.89)	16.0 ! (6.56)	57.5 (8.84)	42.5 (8.84)	‡ (†)	‡ (†)	‡ (†)	‡ (†)
2010[3]	‡ (†)	18.7 (3.94)	‡ (†)	‡ (†)	‡ (†)	‡ (†)	‡ (†)	‡ (†)	‡ (†)	‡ (†)
2011[3]	‡ (†)	19.1 (3.77)	‡ (†)	‡ (†)	‡ (†)	‡ (†)	‡ (†)	‡ (†)	‡ (†)	‡ (†)
2012[3]	114 (22.9)	30.8 (5.01)	‡ (†)	35.6 (9.75)	57.3 (10.21)	42.7 (10.21)	‡ (†)	‡ (†)	‡ (†)	‡ (†)
Hispanic										
1980	91 (18.9)	12.3 (2.41)	65.2 (9.94)	17.9 ! (8.00)	34.8 (9.94)	65.2 (9.94)	59 (15.3)	‡ (†)	‡ (†)	‡ (†)
1985	105 (18.2)	17.3 (2.72)	69.9 (7.95)	32.0 (8.09)	30.1 (7.95)	69.9 (7.95)	74 (15.2)	‡ (†)	‡ (†)	‡ (†)
1990	72 (15.6)	17.4 (3.44)	‡ (†)	‡ (†)	‡ (†)	‡ (†)	‡ (†)	‡ (†)	‡ (†)	‡ (†)
1995	174 (23.8)	28.8 (3.34)	68.6 (6.40)	20.1 (5.52)	31.4 (6.40)	68.6 (6.40)	119 (19.7)	‡ (†)	29.3 (7.57)	‡ (†)
2000	101 (18.2)	19.6 (3.18)	61.1 (8.82)	22.1 ! (7.52)	38.9 (8.82)	61.1 (8.82)	‡ (†)	‡ (†)	‡ (†)	‡ (†)
2005	86 (17.2)	21.1 (3.76)	45.1 (9.96)	66.1 (9.64)	35.2 (9.74)	33.9 (9.64)	66 (9.6)	‡ (†)	‡ (†)	‡ (†)
2010[3]	93 (15.8)	27.3 (3.95)	33.9 (8.72)	52.2 (8.80)	25.5 ! (7.68)	47.8 (8.80)	52 (8.8)	‡ (†)	‡ (†)	‡ (†)
2011[3]	99 (17.4)	26.6 (4.14)	28.3 (7.34)	20.1 ! (6.43)	51.6 (8.76)	48.4 (8.76)	‡ (†)	‡ (†)	‡ (†)	‡ (†)
2012[3]	134 (24.2)	36.3 (5.08)	33.9 (8.08)	21.0 ! (7.47)	45.1 (10.42)	54.9 (10.42)	‡ (†)	‡ (†)	‡ (†)	‡ (†)

†Not applicable.

!Interpret data with caution. The coefficient of variation (CV) for this estimate is between 30 and 50 percent.

‡Reporting standards not met. Either there are too few cases for a reliable estimate or the coefficient of variation (CV) is 50 percent or greater.

[1]The labor force participation rate is the percentage of persons who are either employed or seeking employment.

[2]The labor force includes all employed persons plus those seeking employment. The unemployment rate is the percentage of persons in the labor force who are not working and who made specific efforts to find employment sometime during the prior 4 weeks.

[3]Beginning in 2010, standard errors were computed using replicate weights, which produced more precise values than the generalized variance function methodology used in prior years.

NOTE: Data are based on sample surveys of the civilian noninstitutional population. Data are for October of a given year. Dropouts are considered persons 16 to 24 years old who dropped out of school in the 12-month period ending in October of years shown. Includes dropouts from any grade, including a small number from elementary and middle schools. Percentages are only shown when the base is 75,000 or greater. Totals include race categories not separately shown. Race categories exclude persons of Hispanic ethnicity. Detail may not sum to totals because of rounding.

SOURCE: U.S. Department of Commerce, Census Bureau, Current Population Survey (CPS), October, selected years, 1980 through 2012. (This table was prepared April 2014.)

Graduation rates of first-time, full-time bachelor's degree-seeking students at 4-year postsecondary institutions, by race/ethnicity, time to completion, sex, and control of institution: Selected cohort entry years, 1996 through 2006

Time to completion, sex, control of institution, and cohort entry year	Total	White	Black	Hispanic	Asian/Pacific Islander			American Indian/ Alaska Native	Two or more races	Nonresident alien
					Total	Asian	Pacific Islander			
1	2	3	4	5	6	7	8	9	10	11
Graduating within 4 years after start, males and females										
All 4-year institutions										
1996 starting cohort	33.7	36.3	19.5	22.8	37.5	—	—	18.8	—	41.7
2000 starting cohort	36.1	38.9	21.3	25.9	41.0	—	—	21.0	—	41.9
2002 starting cohort	36.4	39.3	20.4	26.4	42.8	—	—	20.5	—	38.7
2003 starting cohort	36.7	40.0	19.9	26.5	43.8	—	—	20.4	—	37.3
2004 starting cohort	37.9	41.1	20.4	27.9	45.0	—	—	21.8	—	43.7
2005 starting cohort	38.6	41.9	20.8	28.6	45.1	45.5	22.7	22.5	44.0	44.0
2006 starting cohort	39.0	42.6	20.5	29.2	45.8	46.3	24.2	21.9	46.5	44.1
Public institutions										
1996 starting cohort	26.0	28.3	15.0	15.8	28.5	—	—	14.5	—	30.9
2000 starting cohort	29.0	31.4	17.9	18.9	33.7	—	—	16.4	—	32.7
2002 starting cohort	29.9	32.3	16.9	20.1	35.8	—	—	16.0	—	33.4
2003 starting cohort	30.7	33.4	16.5	20.6	37.5	—	—	17.0	—	33.7
2004 starting cohort	31.3	34.2	16.4	21.5	37.9	—	—	17.2	—	34.4
2005 starting cohort	32.0	35.2	16.6	22.5	38.8	39.1	16.9	17.9	28.8	33.5
2006 starting cohort	32.8	36.0	17.0	23.1	39.8	40.2	18.6	17.9	30.5	33.8
Nonprofit institutions										
1996 starting cohort	48.6	51.3	29.3	39.9	57.9	—	—	33.7	—	50.4
2000 starting cohort	50.3	53.5	28.2	42.9	58.8	—	—	36.0	—	50.3
2002 starting cohort	51.0	54.0	29.4	44.1	61.0	—	—	36.6	—	54.8
2003 starting cohort	51.5	54.6	29.7	43.9	61.4	—	—	34.3	—	55.1
2004 starting cohort	52.4	55.3	30.5	46.1	62.8	—	—	39.0	—	57.4
2005 starting cohort	51.9	55.0	29.2	44.9	62.0	62.5	35.1	35.1	59.7	57.3
2006 starting cohort	52.9	56.2	29.7	47.4	62.8	63.5	37.2	38.2	61.9	56.8
For-profit institutions										
1996 starting cohort	21.8	26.3	14.8	20.1	24.6	—	—	16.5	—	33.8
2000 starting cohort	25.7	30.3	22.5	27.4	42.7	—	—	28.0	—	36.5
2002 starting cohort	14.2	17.5	10.0	19.1	29.4	—	—	11.2	—	3.4
2003 starting cohort	12.7	16.0	8.9	17.9	24.1	—	—	6.8	—	3.6
2004 starting cohort	20.4	27.0	13.2	20.6	31.5	—	—	9.3	—	10.5
2005 starting cohort	35.4	38.9	27.7	27.6	40.8	43.0	20.0	33.6	24.1	15.3
2006 starting cohort	22.8	32.6	12.7	23.0	30.1	32.4	9.4	13.0	27.6	22.4
Graduating within 4 years after start, males										
All 4-year institutions										
1996 starting cohort	28.5	30.6	13.9	19.0	32.2	—	—	15.1	—	38.6
2000 starting cohort	31.1	33.4	15.5	21.8	35.7	—	—	17.1	—	39.3
2002 starting cohort	31.3	33.8	14.7	21.8	37.4	—	—	17.2	—	36.6
2003 starting cohort	31.9	34.6	14.6	22.3	38.9	—	—	17.5	—	36.1
2004 starting cohort	32.9	35.6	15.0	23.2	39.9	—	—	18.9	—	39.7
2005 starting cohort	34.1	36.6	16.3	24.8	40.0	40.3	20.8	20.1	40.1	40.2
2006 starting cohort	34.2	37.1	15.6	24.9	41.1	41.5	21.6	17.6	43.1	39.6
Public institutions										
1996 starting cohort	20.8	22.6	9.9	12.5	23.4	—	—	10.9	—	28.6
2000 starting cohort	23.6	25.5	11.7	14.5	27.8	—	—	11.9	—	30.2
2002 starting cohort	24.5	26.6	11.0	15.8	30.4	—	—	12.7	—	30.3
2003 starting cohort	25.6	27.8	10.9	16.4	32.5	—	—	14.1	—	30.6
2004 starting cohort	26.1	28.4	11.2	16.9	32.8	—	—	14.5	—	30.1
2005 starting cohort	27.1	29.7	11.5	18.4	33.5	33.8	14.0	15.0	26.5	29.9
2006 starting cohort	27.8	30.3	11.9	18.7	34.8	35.1	15.4	13.7	29.2	29.5
Nonprofit institutions										
1996 starting cohort	43.6	46.2	22.1	35.0	53.5	—	—	28.9	—	47.0
2000 starting cohort	46.0	48.9	22.3	38.2	56.1	—	—	33.2	—	48.0
2002 starting cohort	46.3	49.1	22.9	38.8	57.6	—	—	32.1	—	50.6
2003 starting cohort	46.9	49.7	23.1	39.8	58.4	—	—	30.6	—	51.1
2004 starting cohort	47.7	50.5	23.2	41.1	59.1	—	—	35.4	—	53.2
2005 starting cohort	47.2	50.2	22.6	40.5	58.4	58.9	29.9	30.7	55.5	52.6
2006 starting cohort	48.2	51.2	23.5	42.4	60.2	60.9	34.6	34.3	58.2	52.2
For-profit institutions										
1996 starting cohort	22.3	25.5	16.1	23.0	27.7	—	—	25.6	—	33.1
2000 starting cohort	30.1	34.3	23.7	30.9	44.5	—	—	28.7	—	36.7
2002 starting cohort	17.0	20.9	11.8	20.1	33.3	—	—	17.6	—	4.0
2003 starting cohort	15.3	18.9	10.6	19.4	27.0	—	—	9.4	—	4.8
2004 starting cohort	23.3	30.2	14.8	21.6	36.6	—	—	12.3	—	10.7
2005 starting cohort	42.1	44.6	36.0	32.5	42.6	43.6	31.0	47.6	24.2	16.5
2006 starting cohort	27.8	37.3	16.6	26.0	33.7	35.2	17.2	14.7	30.1	23.7
Graduating within 4 years after start, females										
All 4-year institutions										
1996 starting cohort	38.0	41.1	23.2	25.8	42.2	—	—	21.7	—	45.8
2000 starting cohort	40.2	43.5	25.2	29.0	45.7	—	—	24.0	—	45.3
2002 starting cohort	40.5	43.9	24.3	29.9	47.4	—	—	23.0	—	41.0
2003 starting cohort	40.6	44.4	23.6	29.5	48.0	—	—	22.5	—	38.4
2004 starting cohort	42.1	45.8	24.1	31.3	49.4	—	—	23.9	—	48.1
2005 starting cohort	42.3	46.3	23.9	31.4	49.6	50.1	24.2	24.4	47.3	48.4
2006 starting cohort	43.0	47.3	23.7	32.5	50.1	50.6	26.1	25.1	49.0	49.3

See notes at end of table.

Graduation rates of first-time, full-time bachelor's degree-seeking students at 4-year postsecondary institutions, by race/ethnicity, time to completion, sex, and control of institution: Selected cohort entry years, 1996 through 2006—Continued

Time to completion, sex, control of institution, and cohort entry year	Total	White	Black	Hispanic	Asian/Pacific Islander Total	Asian	Pacific Islander	American Indian/ Alaska Native	Two or more races	Nonresident alien
1	2	3	4	5	6	7	8	9	10	11
Public institutions										
1996 starting cohort	30.3	33.3	18.3	18.4	33.2	—	—	17.3	—	34.1
2000 starting cohort	33.5	36.3	22.0	22.2	39.1	—	—	19.9	—	36.2
2002 starting cohort	34.3	37.2	20.9	23.4	40.8	—	—	18.5	—	37.0
2003 starting cohort	34.9	38.2	20.2	23.8	42.0	—	—	19.2	—	37.1
2004 starting cohort	35.7	39.2	19.8	24.9	42.6	—	—	19.3	—	39.6
2005 starting cohort	36.2	40.0	20.0	25.5	43.5	43.9	19.0	20.2	30.8	37.7
2006 starting cohort	37.0	41.0	20.4	26.4	44.5	45.0	21.3	21.1	31.5	39.2
Nonprofit institutions										
1996 starting cohort	52.6	55.5	34.2	43.5	61.6	—	—	37.5	—	54.4
2000 starting cohort	53.7	57.3	32.3	46.2	60.9	—	—	38.1	—	53.2
2002 starting cohort	54.7	57.8	34.0	47.8	63.6	—	—	39.9	—	59.2
2003 starting cohort	55.1	58.4	34.3	46.6	63.6	—	—	36.9	—	59.5
2004 starting cohort	56.2	59.1	35.8	49.5	65.6	—	—	41.5	—	61.9
2005 starting cohort	55.6	58.9	34.0	47.9	64.6	65.2	38.6	38.4	62.9	62.6
2006 starting cohort	56.7	60.2	34.5	50.8	64.9	65.6	39.1	40.7	64.3	61.8
For-profit institutions										
1996 starting cohort	21.1	27.5	13.7	16.1	20.3	—	—	9.6	—	34.6
2000 starting cohort	20.7	24.5	21.4	23.1	39.3	—	—	27.2	—	36.3
2002 starting cohort	11.6	14.0	8.7	18.1	23.9	—	—	6.0	—	3.1
2003 starting cohort	10.6	13.6	7.9	16.6	21.2	—	—	5.2	—	2.9
2004 starting cohort	17.7	23.6	12.2	19.7	25.3	—	—	7.2	—	10.4
2005 starting cohort	27.9	31.5	21.0	22.7	37.9	41.8	5.9	21.4	24.0	14.4
2006 starting cohort	18.1	26.7	10.2	20.3	26.2	29.3	3.7	11.8	24.1	21.3
Graduating within 5 years after start, males and females										
All 4-year institutions										
1996 starting cohort	50.2	53.3	33.3	38.9	56.4	—	—	33.3	—	54.3
2000 starting cohort	52.6	55.7	36.0	42.4	60.1	—	—	35.1	—	55.2
2002 starting cohort	52.3	55.7	34.3	42.5	61.0	—	—	33.8	—	50.6
2003 starting cohort	52.8	56.6	33.8	42.7	62.0	—	—	33.4	—	49.5
2004 starting cohort	53.9	57.5	34.2	44.0	62.9	—	—	34.7	—	57.2
2005 starting cohort	54.3	58.0	34.6	44.7	63.1	63.5	40.8	35.3	58.6	58.0
2006 starting cohort	54.9	58.7	34.9	45.8	64.3	64.8	41.7	35.6	61.8	59.0
Public institutions										
1996 starting cohort	45.9	49.0	30.5	34.1	51.3	—	—	30.0	—	46.5
2000 starting cohort	49.1	51.9	34.6	38.0	56.8	—	—	31.9	—	49.8
2002 starting cohort	49.2	52.2	32.9	38.8	57.7	—	—	30.8	—	50.4
2003 starting cohort	50.2	53.5	32.3	39.4	59.0	—	—	31.6	—	51.2
2004 starting cohort	50.6	54.0	32.0	40.2	59.3	—	—	31.7	—	51.9
2005 starting cohort	51.1	54.7	32.4	41.3	59.9	60.2	38.9	32.5	47.8	51.3
2006 starting cohort	51.9	55.5	33.5	42.1	61.5	61.9	41.3	32.9	50.2	52.0
Nonprofit institutions										
1996 starting cohort	59.2	61.8	40.2	51.4	68.7	—	—	45.2	—	60.4
2000 starting cohort	60.8	63.8	39.9	55.1	70.0	—	—	46.9	—	60.4
2002 starting cohort	61.3	64.2	40.2	55.7	71.1	—	—	46.7	—	64.7
2003 starting cohort	62.1	65.1	41.1	56.0	71.9	—	—	44.3	—	65.4
2004 starting cohort	62.9	65.6	41.7	57.7	73.1	—	—	47.9	—	67.8
2005 starting cohort	62.3	65.3	40.4	56.4	72.8	73.2	49.4	43.9	71.3	67.8
2006 starting cohort	63.2	66.2	41.2	59.0	73.5	74.2	47.4	48.7	74.2	68.6
For-profit institutions										
1996 starting cohort	25.4	30.1	17.8	23.1	27.3	—	—	19.8	—	51.6
2000 starting cohort	30.0	34.8	28.0	31.3	45.1	—	—	29.4	—	44.0
2002 starting cohort	17.2	20.7	12.5	22.7	32.0	—	—	12.6	—	6.0
2003 starting cohort	17.7	21.4	13.8	22.7	28.7	—	—	9.8	—	7.9
2004 starting cohort	25.8	32.6	19.0	25.7	36.5	—	—	15.5	—	17.6
2005 starting cohort	39.4	43.3	31.5	33.0	46.1	48.1	27.1	36.9	26.8	24.0
2006 starting cohort	28.0	37.2	17.9	29.8	38.0	40.2	18.7	16.8	30.5	30.3
Graduating within 5 years after start, males										
All 4-year institutions										
1996 starting cohort	46.2	49.2	27.0	34.4	51.8	—	—	31.2	—	51.5
2000 starting cohort	49.0	52.0	29.9	37.8	56.5	—	—	31.6	—	53.0
2002 starting cohort	48.7	52.1	28.2	37.5	57.4	—	—	30.9	—	49.3
2003 starting cohort	49.6	53.3	28.3	38.4	58.5	—	—	30.8	—	48.8
2004 starting cohort	50.5	54.0	28.6	39.2	59.3	—	—	31.9	—	53.5
2005 starting cohort	51.3	54.7	29.8	41.0	59.4	59.7	39.5	34.2	55.5	54.2
2006 starting cohort	51.6	55.2	29.8	41.4	61.0	61.4	39.8	31.7	59.2	54.4
Public institutions										
1996 starting cohort	41.6	44.6	24.0	29.4	46.4	—	—	27.7	—	44.1
2000 starting cohort	44.8	47.6	27.4	32.6	52.1	—	—	27.7	—	47.2
2002 starting cohort	45.3	48.3	26.0	33.7	53.7	—	—	27.5	—	47.0
2003 starting cohort	46.6	49.9	26.3	34.6	55.1	—	—	28.6	—	48.0
2004 starting cohort	46.8	50.2	26.0	35.1	55.3	—	—	28.6	—	47.2
2005 starting cohort	47.8	51.3	26.7	37.1	56.0	56.3	36.9	31.2	44.9	46.9
2006 starting cohort	48.3	51.8	27.8	37.4	57.7	58.0	38.8	29.0	48.7	46.9

See notes at end of table.

Graduation rates of first-time, full-time bachelor's degree-seeking students at 4-year postsecondary institutions, by race/ethnicity, time to completion, sex, and control of institution: Selected cohort entry years, 1996 through 2006—Continued

Time to completion, sex, control of institution, and cohort entry year	Total	White	Black	Hispanic	Asian/Pacific Islander			American Indian/ Alaska Native	Two or more races	Nonresident alien
					Total	Asian	Pacific Islander			
1	2	3	4	5	6	7	8	9	10	11
Nonprofit institutions										
1996 starting cohort	55.8	58.5	34.0	47.4	65.9	—	—	42.9	—	57.7
2000 starting cohort	58.5	61.3	35.1	51.7	69.9	—	—	45.9	—	58.9
2002 starting cohort	58.5	61.5	34.7	51.4	70.0	—	—	44.0	—	61.9
2003 starting cohort	59.3	62.3	35.0	53.1	70.6	—	—	41.5	—	62.1
2004 starting cohort	60.0	62.8	35.5	53.9	71.1	—	—	45.9	—	64.4
2005 starting cohort	59.2	62.2	34.7	53.2	70.2	70.6	45.2	40.3	69.1	63.8
2006 starting cohort	60.1	63.2	35.6	55.4	72.2	72.9	44.7	45.7	72.5	64.4
For-profit institutions										
1996 starting cohort	25.6	29.2	18.1	25.4	29.9	—	—	30.8	—	51.0
2000 starting cohort	33.6	38.1	27.6	34.4	46.4	—	—	28.7	—	43.1
2002 starting cohort	19.9	24.1	14.3	23.6	35.4	—	—	18.5	—	6.3
2003 starting cohort	20.0	24.1	14.5	23.4	30.7	—	—	13.3	—	7.8
2004 starting cohort	27.6	34.8	18.9	26.0	41.5	—	—	15.1	—	16.8
2005 starting cohort	45.6	48.5	38.8	36.7	47.3	48.1	39.1	50.9	27.5	24.8
2006 starting cohort	32.5	41.5	20.9	32.0	40.8	42.1	25.9	18.2	34.0	32.4
Graduating within 5 years after start, females										
All 4-year institutions										
1996 starting cohort	53.6	56.8	37.5	42.4	60.5	—	—	34.9	—	57.9
2000 starting cohort	55.6	58.8	40.2	45.9	63.4	—	—	37.8	—	58.0
2002 starting cohort	55.2	58.6	38.4	46.2	64.1	—	—	36.0	—	52.0
2003 starting cohort	55.4	59.4	37.6	45.8	64.9	—	—	35.3		50.1
2004 starting cohort	56.8	60.5	38.1	47.5	66.0	—	—	36.8	—	61.3
2005 starting cohort	56.8	60.8	37.9	47.4	66.4	66.9	41.8	36.1	61.2	62.4
2006 starting cohort	57.6	61.7	38.4	49.0	67.3	67.9	43.2	38.5	63.6	64.2
Public institutions										
1996 starting cohort	49.5	52.7	34.8	37.8	56.0	—	—	31.8	—	50.0
2000 starting cohort	52.7	55.5	39.3	42.1	61.0	—	—	35.1	—	53.5
2002 starting cohort	52.5	55.4	37.6	42.6	61.5	—	—	33.2	—	54.4
2003 starting cohort	53.2	56.6	36.4	43.1	62.5	—	—	33.8	—	54.8
2004 starting cohort	53.7	57.3	35.9	44.0	62.9	—	—	34.0	—	57.5
2005 starting cohort	53.9	57.7	36.1	44.4	63.3	63.7	40.4	33.5	50.3	56.5
2006 starting cohort	54.9	58.7	37.2	45.7	65.1	65.5	43.3	36.0	51.4	58.2
Nonprofit institutions										
1996 starting cohort	61.8	64.5	44.5	54.3	71.0	—	—	47.0	—	63.7
2000 starting cohort	62.7	65.8	43.2	57.4	70.0	—	—	47.7	—	62.3
2002 starting cohort	63.5	66.4	44.0	58.7	71.9	—	—	48.6	—	67.7
2003 starting cohort	64.4	67.3	45.4	57.9	72.9	—	—	46.3	—	69.1
2004 starting cohort	65.2	67.8	46.2	60.3	74.6	—	—	49.2	—	71.5
2005 starting cohort	64.8	67.7	44.6	58.6	74.7	75.2	52.3	46.6	72.9	72.3
2006 starting cohort	65.7	68.5	45.5	61.5	74.5	75.2	49.3	50.6	75.3	73.2
For-profit institutions										
1996 starting cohort	25.1	31.4	17.6	20.0	23.7	—	—	11.5	—	52.2
2000 starting cohort	25.9	30.0	28.4	27.5	42.6	—	—	30.4	—	45.1
2002 starting cohort	14.7	17.3	11.2	21.7	27.1	—	—	8.0	—	5.8
2003 starting cohort	15.9	19.1	13.4	22.1	26.7	—	—	7.6	—	8.0
2004 starting cohort	24.1	30.3	19.1	25.4	30.5	—	—	15.8	—	18.2
2005 starting cohort	32.5	36.5	25.5	29.3	44.1	48.0	11.8	24.7	26.0	23.5
2006 starting cohort	23.8	31.8	15.8	27.8	35.1	38.1	13.6	15.8	25.9	28.5
Graduating within 6 years after start, males and females										
All 4-year institutions										
1996 starting cohort	55.4	58.1	38.9	45.7	63.4	—	—	38.0	—	58.0
2000 starting cohort	57.5	60.2	42.1	49.1	66.7	—	—	40.2	—	59.6
2002 starting cohort	57.2	60.2	40.1	48.9	67.1	—	—	38.3	—	55.3
2003 starting cohort	57.4	60.8	39.1	48.7	68.0	—	—	38.3	—	53.3
2004 starting cohort	58.3	61.5	39.5	50.1	68.7	—	—	39.4	—	61.5
2005 starting cohort[1]	58.7	62.1	39.9	51.0	69.2	69.6	48.5	39.8	64.3	62.6
2006 starting cohort[1]	59.2	62.5	40.2	51.9	70.1	70.6	48.5	40.2	66.6	63.6
Open admissions	32.8	41.3	19.3	30.3	37.8	40.1	21.3	17.6	36.8	38.1
90 percent or more accepted	47.6	50.2	32.7	40.1	49.5	49.8	38.2	29.2	46.5	48.0
75.0 to 89.9 percent accepted	55.9	58.8	38.3	47.4	61.2	61.3	54.5	40.9	59.8	59.6
50.0 to 74.9 percent accepted	60.5	63.9	43.2	51.9	67.8	68.2	49.6	42.2	60.4	62.3
25.0 to 49.9 percent accepted	72.4	76.6	51.6	65.1	80.2	80.5	57.5	55.0	79.1	73.5
Less than 25.0 percent accepted	85.6	88.9	58.7	85.0	91.8	92.3	68.1	79.4	91.6	88.5
Public institutions										
1996 starting cohort	51.7	54.3	36.8	42.1	59.5	—	—	35.3	—	51.3
2000 starting cohort	54.8	57.1	40.8	46.0	64.1	—	—	37.5	—	54.6
2002 starting cohort	54.9	57.4	39.4	46.3	64.7	—	—	35.7	—	55.5
2003 starting cohort	55.7	58.6	38.6	46.9	65.8	—	—	37.1	—	56.2
2004 starting cohort	56.0	58.9	38.3	47.8	66.2	—	—	37.0	—	57.2
2005 starting cohort[1]	56.5	59.6	38.6	48.7	67.0	67.2	49.5	37.8	55.9	57.3
2006 starting cohort[1]	57.2	60.2	39.7	49.5	68.2	68.5	49.1	38.2	57.0	57.7
Open admissions	32.2	38.5	18.2	29.0	34.8	36.0	10.0	13.7	31.4	44.4
90 percent or more accepted	47.9	50.3	32.4	40.1	50.3	50.5	25.0	29.6	57.1	45.8
75.0 to 89.9 percent accepted	54.0	56.9	37.4	46.0	60.9	61.0	52.1	40.3	50.8	58.2
50.0 to 74.9 percent accepted	60.0	63.3	44.3	50.8	67.5	67.9	49.0	41.0	54.6	59.7
25.0 to 49.9 percent accepted	70.0	73.5	50.2	61.6	78.6	78.8	55.8	50.7	76.5	64.5
Less than 25.0 percent accepted	70.4	80.4	34.6	70.1	69.6	70.0	63.2	70.2	79.7	74.8

See notes at end of table.

Graduation rates of first-time, full-time bachelor's degree-seeking students at 4-year postsecondary institutions, by race/ethnicity, time to completion, sex, and control of institution: Selected cohort entry years, 1996 through 2006—Continued

Time to completion, sex, control of institution, and cohort entry year	Total	White	Black	Hispanic	Asian/Pacific Islander Total	Asian	Pacific Islander	American Indian/ Alaska Native	Two or more races	Nonresident alien
1	2	3	4	5	6	7	8	9	10	11
Nonprofit institutions										
1996 starting cohort	63.1	65.7	44.6	55.7	73.5	—	—	48.1	—	63.4
2000 starting cohort	64.5	67.0	45.9	59.0	75.2	—	—	50.9	—	64.5
2002 starting cohort	64.6	67.2	44.9	59.5	75.3	—	—	49.8	—	68.3
2003 starting cohort	65.1	67.7	45.0	59.4	75.9	—	—	47.6	—	69.1
2004 starting cohort	65.4	67.9	44.9	60.5	76.2	—	—	50.7	—	71.2
2005 starting cohort[1]	65.1	67.8	43.8	60.4	76.4	76.9	52.6	46.4	75.2	71.0
2006 starting cohort[1]	65.5	68.1	44.5	62.0	76.8	77.5	52.6	51.3	77.5	71.9
Open admissions	38.1	44.8	22.4	34.4	43.4	44.7	36.5	28.6	45.1	47.2
90 percent or more accepted	48.5	51.2	38.5	42.9	43.5	44.3	40.3	28.9	37.9	56.0
75.0 to 89.9 percent accepted	61.1	63.8	42.5	53.0	63.0	63.2	56.4	45.7	73.6	61.8
50.0 to 74.9 percent accepted	62.3	65.8	41.3	56.5	69.4	70.0	51.3	48.1	69.3	65.6
25.0 to 49.9 percent accepted	77.5	81.0	55.0	76.2	84.9	85.1	62.1	66.3	84.7	79.6
Less than 25.0 percent accepted	90.6	92.2	73.7	90.0	95.3	95.6	71.4	82.1	94.4	89.3
For-profit institutions										
1996 starting cohort	28.0	33.2	19.2	24.6	28.9	—	—	23.1	—	54.0
2000 starting cohort	32.6	38.1	29.7	33.8	47.3	—	—	30.4	—	47.5
2002 starting cohort	22.0	25.5	16.3	27.5	35.5	—	—	17.1	—	12.5
2003 starting cohort	20.4	24.5	16.1	24.9	31.3	—	—	11.9	—	9.3
2004 starting cohort	28.4	35.3	21.3	28.9	38.9	—	—	19.2	—	21.7
2005 starting cohort	42.0	45.5	34.4	36.5	49.2	51.1	31.0	39.3	27.2	28.3
2006 starting cohort	31.5	40.3	21.1	33.7	42.5	44.4	25.2	18.8	32.4	35.5
Graduating within 6 years after start, males										
All 4-year institutions										
1996 starting cohort	52.0	54.8	32.8	41.3	59.5	—	—	36.2	—	55.4
2000 starting cohort	54.3	57.1	35.6	44.6	62.9	—	—	37.1	—	56.8
2002 starting cohort	54.1	57.3	34.0	44.1	64.0	—	—	35.1	—	53.9
2003 starting cohort	54.8	58.2	33.9	44.6	65.0	—	—	36.4	—	52.8
2004 starting cohort	55.5	58.8	34.2	45.6	65.7	—	—	37.5	—	58.5
2005 starting cohort[1]	56.3	59.5	35.1	47.4	66.3	66.6	49.0	38.9	61.3	59.2
2006 starting cohort[1]	56.5	59.8	35.2	47.7	67.4	67.8	46.5	37.2	64.5	60.1
Open admissions	33.1	41.3	17.8	28.6	36.7	39.1	18.9	19.4	34.9	38.4
90 percent or more accepted	44.8	47.4	29.1	36.3	47.0	47.4	25.8	26.9	46.1	42.9
75.0 to 89.9 percent accepted	53.1	56.0	33.6	43.6	58.2	58.2	56.2	36.6	57.8	57.1
50.0 to 74.9 percent accepted	57.3	60.7	38.1	47.2	65.0	65.4	47.2	39.5	56.9	57.4
25.0 to 49.9 percent accepted	70.1	74.5	44.7	61.0	78.0	78.2	51.4	48.5	74.3	71.4
Less than 25.0 percent accepted	84.2	87.7	53.9	81.6	89.8	90.1	70.5	77.0	90.3	86.8
Public institutions										
1996 starting cohort	48.1	50.8	30.3	37.5	55.2	—	—	33.1	—	48.8
2000 starting cohort	51.3	53.8	34.1	41.1	60.0	—	—	33.6	—	52.1
2002 starting cohort	51.7	54.4	32.9	41.4	61.3	—	—	32.2	—	52.5
2003 starting cohort	52.9	55.9	32.9	42.3	62.7	—	—	34.9	—	53.3
2004 starting cohort	53.0	56.0	32.7	43.0	62.9	—	—	34.9	—	53.0
2005 starting cohort[1]	53.9	57.1	33.2	44.8	64.0	64.2	50.7	36.8	52.7	53.3
2006 starting cohort[1]	54.4	57.4	34.2	45.0	65.1	65.4	47.2	35.2	56.1	53.7
Open admissions	29.5	35.6	15.3	24.9	28.9	30.2	9.5	15.2	27.8	38.7
90 percent or more accepted	0.0	47.9	29.4	36.2	47.9	48.0	25.0	27.9	57.6	41.1
75.0 to 89.9 percent accepted	51.7	54.5	32.5	42.7	57.8	57.9	52.3	36.1	53.8	55.7
50.0 to 74.9 percent accepted	56.9	60.2	38.9	45.7	64.5	64.9	47.2	38.9	48.9	54.8
25.0 to 49.9 percent accepted	66.9	70.4	43.3	58.0	76.0	76.3	50.6	43.7	74.0	62.7
Less than 25.0 percent accepted	71.3	80.3	32.2	68.1	65.6	65.8	62.5	57.1	79.7	77.8
Nonprofit institutions										
1996 starting cohort	60.4	63.0	38.9	52.1	71.5	—	—	46.7	—	60.9
2000 starting cohort	61.7	64.4	39.3	55.3	73.1	—	—	50.1	—	61.7
2002 starting cohort	61.9	64.8	38.6	55.4	73.8	—	—	46.6	—	65.4
2003 starting cohort	62.4	65.2	38.9	56.6	74.2	—	—	45.4	—	65.6
2004 starting cohort	63.0	65.7	39.2	57.0	74.4	—	—	49.3	—	68.2
2005 starting cohort[1]	62.4	65.2	38.1	57.2	74.6	75.0	49.2	42.7	73.5	67.4
2006 starting cohort[1]	62.9	65.6	39.2	58.7	75.7	76.3	49.2	48.6	76.2	68.8
Open admissions	36.6	44.1	19.2	32.4	41.4	43.1	34.5	27.1	38.5	51.2
90 percent or more accepted	43.4	46.1	31.8	38.7	39.7	42.2	26.1	14.3	27.6	50.2
75.0 to 89.9 percent accepted	57.5	60.4	38.1	48.5	61.2	61.3	60.5	42.8	64.3	59.4
50.0 to 74.9 percent accepted	58.9	62.5	37.2	52.9	67.3	67.9	47.8	44.0	70.0	60.9
25.0 to 49.9 percent accepted	76.4	80.2	48.7	72.1	83.8	84.1	52.9	61.9	82.0	77.3
Less than 25.0 percent accepted	89.7	91.5	68.8	88.1	95.2	95.4	80.0	84.7	94.8	87.4
For-profit institutions										
1996 starting cohort	28.0	32.3	19.4	26.7	31.7	—	—	30.8	—	53.0
2000 starting cohort	35.5	40.2	29.8	36.2	48.4	—	—	30.3	—	46.3
2002 starting cohort	23.6	27.8	16.6	26.7	38.4	—	—	23.5	—	11.7
2003 starting cohort	22.7	26.7	16.6	25.2	33.6	—	—	16.0	—	9.3
2004 starting cohort	30.2	37.0	21.2	29.1	43.5	—	—	18.5	—	23.6
2005 starting cohort	47.4	50.2	40.8	39.1	50.4	51.2	41.4	53.3	27.5	29.2
2006 starting cohort	35.4	43.9	23.5	35.3	44.0	45.5	27.6	19.6	34.6	37.4

See notes at end of table.

Graduation rates of first-time, full-time bachelor's degree-seeking students at 4-year postsecondary institutions, by race/ethnicity, time to completion, sex, and control of institution: Selected cohort entry years, 1996 through 2006—Continued

Time to completion, sex, control of institution, and cohort entry year	Total	White	Black	Hispanic	Asian/Pacific Islander Total	Asian	Pacific Islander	American Indian/ Alaska Native	Two or more races	Nonresident alien
1	2	3	4	5	6	7	8	9	10	11
Graduating within 6 years after start, females										
All 4-year institutions										
1996 starting cohort	58.2	60.9	43.0	49.1	66.8	—	—	39.5	—	61.5
2000 starting cohort	60.2	62.8	46.4	52.4	70.1	—	—	42.7	—	63.1
2002 starting cohort	59.7	62.5	44.2	52.5	69.8	—	—	40.7	—	56.7
2003 starting cohort	59.5	63.0	42.7	51.8	70.5	—	—	39.7	—	53.8
2004 starting cohort	60.6	63.8	43.1	53.4	71.3	—	—	40.9	—	64.9
2005 starting cohort[1]	60.8	64.2	43.1	53.7	71.7	72.2	48.1	40.5	66.8	66.5
2006 starting cohort[1]	61.4	64.9	43.6	54.9	72.6	73.1	50.1	42.4	68.1	67.6
Open admissions	32.5	41.4	20.5	31.7	38.8	41.1	23.4	16.3	38.5	37.8
90 percent or more accepted	50.2	52.8	35.5	43.2	51.9	52.2	44.8	31.1	46.8	55.6
75.0 to 89.9 percent accepted	58.2	61.2	41.5	50.1	64.0	64.2	52.8	44.4	61.4	63.1
50.0 to 74.9 percent accepted	63.0	66.6	46.5	55.3	70.3	70.8	51.4	44.1	62.6	67.8
25.0 to 49.9 percent accepted	74.3	78.3	56.0	67.9	82.1	82.3	62.5	59.5	82.3	75.4
Less than 25.0 percent accepted	87.2	90.5	62.6	88.9	93.9	94.5	66.0	81.7	92.8	90.6
Public institutions										
1996 starting cohort	54.7	57.4	41.0	45.7	63.5	—	—	37.0	—	54.9
2000 starting cohort	57.7	59.9	45.2	49.7	67.8	—	—	40.5	—	58.1
2002 starting cohort	57.5	59.9	43.7	50.0	67.7	—	—	38.3	—	59.0
2003 starting cohort	58.1	61.0	42.4	50.4	68.7	—	—	38.8	—	59.5
2004 starting cohort	58.5	61.4	42.1	51.4	69.2	—	—	38.5	—	62.2
2005 starting cohort[1]	58.8	61.9	42.2	51.7	69.7	70.0	48.6	38.6	58.7	61.9
2006 starting cohort[1]	59.6	62.7	43.3	52.9	71.1	71.5	50.7	40.5	57.8	62.6
Open admissions	34.6	41.3	20.6	32.7	41.9	42.9	11.1	12.4	34.4	50.9
90 percent or more accepted	50.1	52.5	34.6	43.2	52.8	53.0	25.0	30.9	56.8	53.0
75.0 to 89.9 percent accepted	55.9	58.9	40.6	48.4	64.0	64.1	51.8	43.9	48.4	61.9
50.0 to 74.9 percent accepted	62.6	66.0	47.7	54.6	70.3	70.8	50.5	42.5	58.3	65.6
25.0 to 49.9 percent accepted	72.3	76.0	54.7	64.0	80.7	80.9	59.6	55.2	78.4	66.2
Less than 25.0 percent accepted	68.7	80.6	36.8	74.5	78.3	79.4	64.3	89.5	79.5	68.4
Nonprofit institutions										
1996 starting cohort	65.4	67.9	48.4	58.3	75.0	—	—	49.2	—	66.4
2000 starting cohort	66.7	69.1	50.4	61.7	76.7	—	—	51.5	—	67.9
2002 starting cohort	66.7	69.1	49.4	62.2	76.3	—	—	52.1	—	71.5
2003 starting cohort	67.1	69.7	49.2	61.2	77.2	—	—	49.2	—	73.0
2004 starting cohort	67.3	69.6	49.1	62.8	77.6	—	—	51.6	—	74.4
2005 starting cohort[1]	67.2	69.7	48.0	62.6	77.8	78.3	54.9	49.2	76.5	75.0
2006 starting cohort[1]	67.6	70.1	48.5	64.2	77.7	78.4	55.0	52.9	78.3	75.4
Open admissions	39.6	45.4	25.7	36.4	45.1	46.0	39.1	29.5	52.0	40.0
90 percent or more accepted	53.1	55.9	43.9	46.1	46.2	46.0	46.9	37.5	41.1	64.0
75.0 to 89.9 percent accepted	63.7	66.3	45.8	55.9	64.3	64.7	53.7	47.4	80.8	65.0
50.0 to 74.9 percent accepted	64.8	68.3	44.5	58.8	71.0	71.6	53.8	50.6	68.9	70.3
25.0 to 49.9 percent accepted	78.4	81.7	58.8	79.0	85.8	85.9	71.9	69.3	86.2	81.8
Less than 25.0 percent accepted	91.4	92.9	77.3	91.7	95.3	95.8	66.7	80.0	94.1	91.5
For-profit institutions										
1996 starting cohort	27.9	34.5	19.0	21.9	24.9	—	—	17.3	—	55.1
2000 starting cohort	29.1	35.1	29.7	30.9	45.2	—	—	30.4	—	48.9
2002 starting cohort	20.5	23.1	16.1	28.3	31.3	—	—	12.0	—	13.0
2003 starting cohort	18.7	22.7	15.8	24.7	29.1	—	—	9.3	—	9.4
2004 starting cohort	26.8	33.4	21.3	28.7	33.3	—	—	19.6	—	20.3
2005 starting cohort[1]	35.9	39.4	29.1	34.0	47.3	50.9	17.6	27.2	26.9	27.7
2006 starting cohort	28.0	35.8	19.5	32.1	40.8	43.3	23.5	18.2	29.3	33.9

—Not available.

[1]Includes data for institutions not reporting admissions data, which are not separately shown.
NOTE: Data are for 4-year degree-granting postsecondary institutions participating in Title IV federal financial aid programs. Graduation rates refer to students receiving bachelor's degrees from their initial institutions of attendance only. Totals include data for persons whose race/ethnicity was not reported. Race categories exclude persons of Hispanic ethnicity. Some data have been revised from previously published figures.
SOURCE: U.S. Department of Education, National Center for Education Statistics, Integrated Postsecondary Education Data System (IPEDS), Fall 2001 and Spring 2007 through Spring 2013, Graduation Rates component. (This table was prepared January 2014.)

Graduation rates of first-time, full-time degree/certificate-seeking students at 2-year postsecondary institutions who completed a credential within 150 percent of normal time, by race/ethnicity, sex, and control of institution: Selected cohort entry years, 2000 through 2009

Sex, control of institution, and cohort entry year	Percent graduating with a certificate or associate's degree within 150 percent of normal time									
					Asian/Pacific Islander			American Indian/ Alaska Native	Two or more races	Nonresident alien
	Total	White	Black	Hispanic	Total	Asian	Pacific Islander			
1	2	3	4	5	6	7	8	9	10	11
Males and females										
All 2-year institutions										
2000 starting cohort	30.5	31.5	26.1	30.1	33.3	—	—	29.3	—	25.5
2002 starting cohort	29.3	30.4	24.2	30.7	31.4	—	—	26.3	—	26.7
2003 starting cohort	29.1	29.9	24.2	30.2	31.7	—	—	25.9	—	27.2
2004 starting cohort	27.8	29.0	22.9	26.3	30.2	—	—	26.7	—	32.9
2005 starting cohort	27.5	28.5	22.6	25.7	31.5	—	—	24.9	—	32.2
2006 starting cohort	29.2	29.3	24.5	30.8	34.0	—	—	24.2	—	30.0
2007 starting cohort	29.9	29.5	25.3	33.4	33.6	—	—	25.6	—	30.8
2008 starting cohort	31.3	30.2	27.7	35.2	34.3	35.2	24.0	25.7	33.1	33.7
2009 starting cohort	31.0	30.2	26.4	36.4	35.1	36.0	25.0	25.7	30.5	34.6
Public institutions										
2000 starting cohort	23.6	25.7	17.8	16.8	25.5	—	—	19.6	—	23.2
2002 starting cohort	21.9	24.5	13.2	16.7	23.8	—	—	18.8	—	25.5
2003 starting cohort	21.5	24.1	12.7	16.3	24.8	—	—	17.9	—	25.8
2004 starting cohort	20.3	22.9	11.5	15.0	24.2	—	—	17.8	—	30.5
2005 starting cohort	20.6	22.9	12.1	15.6	25.8	—	—	18.2	—	29.9
2006 starting cohort	20.4	23.1	12.0	15.6	25.4	—	—	17.0	—	24.9
2007 starting cohort	20.4	23.0	11.9	16.0	25.6	—	—	17.4	—	25.4
2008 starting cohort	20.2	22.8	11.8	15.8	26.2	27.2	15.3	15.5	17.1	30.6
2009 starting cohort	19.8	22.5	11.3	15.9	26.1	27.3	11.9	15.9	18.3	32.6
Nonprofit institutions										
2000 starting cohort	50.1	49.6	37.5	56.3	61.4	—	—	62.1	—	43.1
2002 starting cohort	49.1	55.1	36.5	46.1	49.5	—	—	20.3	—	45.3
2003 starting cohort	49.0	56.0	35.8	39.4	50.1	—	—	17.9	—	64.2
2004 starting cohort	44.4	48.9	37.3	35.6	36.6	—	—	19.5	—	54.7
2005 starting cohort	48.2	52.3	41.6	47.3	41.6	—	—	14.8	—	51.7
2006 starting cohort	52.8	55.0	46.5	47.5	51.2	—	—	22.6	—	69.3
2007 starting cohort	51.0	56.1	43.6	46.1	51.0	—	—	15.3	—	63.9
2008 starting cohort	56.5	59.4	53.4	62.4	52.8	53.7	30.8	25.0	55.8	59.5
2009 starting cohort	62.3	66.0	59.7	68.3	57.9	57.7	64.0	30.4	66.5	50.0
For-profit institutions										
2000 starting cohort	59.1	63.1	47.6	60.3	64.4	—	—	60.3	—	55.4
2002 starting cohort	57.1	61.0	49.3	59.7	61.7	—	—	58.1	—	58.9
2003 starting cohort	57.2	61.8	48.4	60.0	55.8	—	—	59.1	—	36.5
2004 starting cohort	58.2	64.3	48.4	59.6	65.4	—	—	59.0	—	71.1
2005 starting cohort	57.7	62.9	47.8	61.4	65.8	—	—	55.8	—	57.7
2006 starting cohort	58.6	63.0	47.5	63.0	71.8	—	—	57.6	—	63.5
2007 starting cohort	60.3	65.0	49.2	64.9	68.5	—	—	59.2	—	66.9
2008 starting cohort	61.8	64.3	52.7	68.0	69.8	70.1	66.1	60.2	57.3	62.0
2009 starting cohort	62.8	65.1	53.0	68.8	70.8	71.6	64.1	60.8	59.9	61.7
Males										
All 2-year institutions										
2000 starting cohort	28.7	30.0	23.1	27.9	30.1	—	—	28.3	—	22.9
2002 starting cohort	27.2	28.6	21.3	27.0	28.7	—	—	23.7	—	22.5
2003 starting cohort	27.2	28.5	20.6	26.8	29.4	—	—	22.4	—	22.6
2004 starting cohort	25.7	27.3	19.1	22.6	27.9	—	—	23.6	—	30.1
2005 starting cohort	25.3	27.0	18.6	21.8	28.4	—	—	23.4	—	29.4
2006 starting cohort	26.4	27.2	20.5	25.5	30.5	—	—	22.1	—	27.4
2007 starting cohort	26.4	27.2	20.4	26.7	29.7	—	—	23.9	—	26.9
2008 starting cohort	27.4	27.8	22.8	29.1	30.3	30.8	23.8	23.1	28.6	30.5
2009 starting cohort	27.3	27.9	22.1	30.2	30.9	31.7	21.6	23.7	24.5	31.5
Public institutions										
2000 starting cohort	22.2	24.2	16.5	15.4	22.6	—	—	19.3	—	20.4
2002 starting cohort	20.9	23.2	13.1	15.2	21.8	—	—	16.9	—	21.4
2003 starting cohort	20.8	23.0	12.5	15.2	22.7	—	—	16.4	—	21.3
2004 starting cohort	19.6	21.8	11.5	13.8	22.6	—	—	17.5	—	27.8
2005 starting cohort	19.9	22.1	12.0	14.6	23.5	—	—	18.7	—	27.4
2006 starting cohort	19.9	22.3	12.2	14.7	23.7	—	—	16.3	—	22.5
2007 starting cohort	19.9	22.3	12.0	15.2	24.0	—	—	18.6	—	22.0
2008 starting cohort	19.6	22.1	12.0	14.9	24.3	25.1	15.3	15.2	16.7	28.1
2009 starting cohort	19.4	22.0	11.4	14.8	24.4	25.4	12.4	16.0	16.8	29.9
Nonprofit institutions										
2000 starting cohort	49.5	49.3	31.7	54.3	62.5	—	—	64.5	—	42.6
2002 starting cohort	51.1	58.8	33.0	42.9	56.0	—	—	21.7	—	35.3
2003 starting cohort	49.6	57.0	31.4	42.4	48.1	—	—	16.8	—	51.6
2004 starting cohort	43.2	46.4	38.3	36.4	40.3	—	—	17.5	—	52.0
2005 starting cohort	44.5	49.1	38.7	42.9	43.7	—	—	10.4	—	47.7
2006 starting cohort	51.3	52.6	45.1	45.6	54.0	—	—	21.8	—	68.2
2007 starting cohort	50.0	56.4	45.5	41.1	49.3	—	—	10.3	—	58.1
2008 starting cohort	49.7	53.4	47.2	49.4	45.4	46.3	30.8	14.6	46.7	52.1
2009 starting cohort	53.6	57.5	51.0	58.2	47.4	47.7	37.5	22.4	56.1	45.1

See notes at end of table.

Graduation rates of first-time, full-time degree/certificate-seeking students at 2-year postsecondary institutions who completed a credential within 150 percent of normal time, by race/ethnicity, sex, and control of institution: Selected cohort entry years, 2000 through 2009—Continued

Sex, control of institution, and cohort entry year	Percent graduating with a certificate or associate's degree within 150 percent of normal time									
	Total	White	Black	Hispanic	Asian/Pacific Islander			American Indian/ Alaska Native	Two or more races	Nonresident alien
					Total	Asian	Pacific Islander			
1	2	3	4	5	6	7	8	9	10	11
For-profit institutions										
2000 starting cohort	59.3	63.7	45.6	58.2	63.1	—	—	55.9	—	55.0
2002 starting cohort	56.6	62.0	45.9	56.1	59.7	—	—	58.4	—	61.9
2003 starting cohort	58.0	63.7	45.7	56.9	62.0	—	—	59.5	—	36.7
2004 starting cohort	58.1	65.4	44.6	55.4	64.3	—	—	59.6	—	69.4
2005 starting cohort	57.7	64.8	43.1	57.5	65.7	—	—	56.3	—	56.3
2006 starting cohort	56.8	62.3	43.0	58.3	69.4	—	—	57.2	—	61.6
2007 starting cohort	58.3	65.3	44.6	59.3	66.3	—	—	56.9	—	66.7
2008 starting cohort	59.1	64.4	48.2	63.0	67.7	68.0	65.1	54.9	58.3	54.6
2009 starting cohort	59.8	63.7	49.3	64.6	67.7	68.7	59.2	59.4	55.2	59.9
Female										
All 2-year institutions										
2000 starting cohort	32.1	33.0	28.1	31.8	36.3	—	—	30.0	—	28.3
2002 starting cohort	30.9	32.0	26.1	33.4	33.9	—	—	28.2	—	30.4
2003 starting cohort	30.7	31.2	26.3	32.7	33.9	—	—	28.4	—	31.5
2004 starting cohort	29.6	30.5	25.2	29.0	32.6	—	—	28.8	—	35.3
2005 starting cohort	29.3	29.9	25.2	28.6	34.6	—	—	25.9	—	34.8
2006 starting cohort	31.6	31.2	27.1	34.5	37.5	—	—	25.8	—	32.4
2007 starting cohort	32.7	31.6	28.4	37.9	37.4	—	—	26.8	—	34.4
2008 starting cohort	34.4	32.3	31.0	39.5	38.3	39.5	24.1	27.8	36.1	36.8
2009 starting cohort	34.1	32.3	29.4	40.9	39.3	40.4	28.0	27.3	34.9	37.6
Public institutions										
2000 starting cohort	24.8	27.1	18.8	17.9	28.4	—	—	19.9	—	26.2
2002 starting cohort	22.8	25.8	13.2	17.8	25.9	—	—	20.2	—	29.2
2003 starting cohort	22.2	25.1	12.8	17.3	27.1	—	—	19.0	—	30.0
2004 starting cohort	21.0	24.0	11.5	16.0	26.1	—	—	17.9	—	32.8
2005 starting cohort	21.2	23.8	12.1	16.4	28.2	—	—	17.8	—	32.2
2006 starting cohort	21.0	23.9	11.8	16.3	27.3	—	—	17.5	—	27.3
2007 starting cohort	20.8	23.7	11.8	16.8	27.5	—	—	16.5	—	28.7
2008 starting cohort	20.7	23.5	11.7	16.5	28.3	29.6	15.3	15.7	17.4	33.0
2009 starting cohort	20.2	23.1	11.2	16.8	28.1	29.6	11.4	15.8	19.8	35.3
Nonprofit institutions										
2000 starting cohort	50.7	50.0	43.1	58.3	60.1	—	—	60.2	—	43.8
2002 starting cohort	47.3	51.4	39.2	48.9	44.3	—	—	19.3	—	55.0
2003 starting cohort	48.5	55.0	38.8	37.5	51.4	—	—	18.7	—	75.4
2004 starting cohort	45.4	51.1	36.3	35.1	34.3	—	—	21.0	—	57.4
2005 starting cohort	51.3	54.9	44.9	49.6	40.1	—	—	18.0	—	55.2
2006 starting cohort	54.0	56.7	47.7	48.5	48.8	—	—	23.2	—	70.4
2007 starting cohort	51.8	55.8	41.6	49.5	52.2	—	—	18.9	—	69.9
2008 starting cohort	59.7	63.0	55.7	67.6	56.6	57.4	30.8	31.5	58.3	66.8
2009 starting cohort	66.6	70.8	63.4	72.5	63.2	62.7	76.5	34.5	70.3	54.5
For-profit institutions										
2000 starting cohort	58.9	62.6	48.6	61.8	65.3	—	—	63.8	—	55.7
2002 starting cohort	57.4	60.3	50.8	61.7	63.3	—	—	58.0	—	56.7
2003 starting cohort	56.8	60.4	49.4	61.9	52.1	—	—	59.0	—	36.4
2004 starting cohort	58.3	63.4	49.9	61.9	66.2	—	—	58.7	—	72.3
2005 starting cohort	57.7	61.6	49.4	63.3	65.8	—	—	55.7	—	58.6
2006 starting cohort	59.6	63.4	49.3	65.2	73.4	—	—	57.9	—	65.1
2007 starting cohort	61.3	64.8	50.8	67.3	69.8	—	—	60.2	—	67.1
2008 starting cohort	63.2	64.3	54.7	70.5	71.0	71.2	67.1	63.6	56.9	67.7
2009 starting cohort	64.5	66.0	54.7	70.9	72.7	73.4	67.0	61.5	61.9	62.8

—Not available.
NOTE: Data are for 2-year degree-granting postsecondary institutions participating in Title IV federal financial aid programs. Graduation rates refer to students receiving associate's degrees or certificates from their initial institutions of attendance only. Totals include data for persons whose race/ethnicity was not reported. Race categories exclude persons of Hispanic ethnicity. Some data have been revised from previously published figures.

SOURCE: U.S. Department of Education, National Center for Education Statistics, Integrated Postsecondary Education Data System (IPEDS), Fall 2001 and Spring 2002 through Spring 2013, Graduation Rates component. (This table was prepared January 2014.)

Retention of first-time degree-seeking undergraduates at degree-granting postsecondary institutions, by attendance status, level and control of institution, and percentage of applications accepted: 2006 to 2012

Level, control, and percent of applications accepted	First-time degree-seekers (adjusted entry cohort),[1] by entry year						Students from adjusted cohort returning in the following year						Percent of first-time undergraduates retained					
	2006	2007	2008	2009	2010	2011	2007	2008	2009	2010	2011	2012	2006 to 2007	2007 to 2008	2008 to 2009	2009 to 2010	2010 to 2011	2011 to 2012
1	2	3	4	5	6	7	8	9	10	11	12	13	14	15	16	17	18	19
Full-time student retention																		
All institutions	2,171,714	2,269,712	2,296,305	2,386,597	2,341,321	2,270,919	1,542,175	1,619,269	1,647,198	1,714,013	1,679,620	1,630,899	71.0	71.3	71.7	71.8	71.7	71.8
Public institutions	1,524,044	1,603,819	1,654,779	1,743,668	1,696,663	1,665,771	1,072,644	1,132,790	1,167,180	1,229,276	1,192,769	1,170,408	70.4	70.6	70.5	70.5	70.2	70.3
Nonprofit institutions	466,139	477,369	476,153	478,708	487,864	484,498	369,084	375,721	378,111	381,423	389,217	396,716	79.2	78.7	79.4	79.7	79.8	79.8
For-profit institutions	181,531	188,524	165,373	164,221	154,794	120,650	100,447	110,758	101,907	103,314	97,634	73,775	55.3	58.8	61.6	62.9	63.1	61.1
4-year institutions	1,458,731	1,505,161	1,511,976	1,465,669	1,461,703	1,472,550	1,115,529	1,152,921	1,176,973	1,153,975	1,152,644	1,160,025	76.5	76.6	77.8	78.7	78.9	78.8
Public institutions	912,401	936,000	973,089	945,951	941,098	958,009	711,490	732,384	765,163	751,623	746,633	758,805	78.0	78.2	78.6	79.5	79.3	79.2
Open admissions	62,724	60,815	81,559	47,943	43,261	41,327	38,839	38,724	52,988	30,079	26,633	25,148	61.9	63.7	65.0	62.7	61.6	60.9
90 percent or more accepted	68,835	66,114	58,002	60,147	74,731	49,819	49,274	46,731	39,851	43,654	54,244	35,005	71.6	70.7	68.7	72.6	72.6	70.3
75.0 to 89.9 percent accepted	244,177	237,913	213,388	213,441	205,404	230,328	185,457	180,287	164,559	164,061	158,677	176,676	76.0	75.8	77.1	76.9	77.3	76.7
50.0 to 74.9 percent accepted	417,093	439,824	473,007	468,817	469,055	450,981	336,199	356,969	382,451	380,473	379,448	363,114	80.6	81.2	80.9	81.2	80.9	80.5
25.0 to 49.9 percent accepted	103,118	107,824	127,960	134,042	131,782	170,541	88,908	90,123	108,601	114,477	112,006	145,617	86.2	83.6	84.9	85.4	85.0	85.4
Less than 25.0 percent accepted	7,716	10,223	13,479	14,326	13,996	9,468	7,048	9,479	12,785	13,649	13,302	9,013	91.3	92.7	94.9	95.3	95.0	95.2
Information not available	8,738	13,287	5,694	7,235	2,889	5,545	5,765	10,071	3,928	5,230	2,323	4,232	66.0	75.8	69.0	72.3	80.4	76.3
Nonprofit institutions	457,566	468,995	468,220	470,748	476,912	473,800	363,760	370,740	373,352	376,726	382,520	380,279	79.5	79.1	79.7	80.0	80.2	80.3
Open admissions	26,679	26,571	24,220	22,613	22,861	21,962	16,116	15,227	16,499	14,349	14,330	13,835	60.4	57.3	68.1	63.5	62.7	63.0
90 percent or more accepted	13,684	16,008	16,738	15,066	13,922	13,393	9,549	11,249	11,899	10,898	9,720	9,174	69.8	70.3	71.1	72.3	69.8	68.5
75.0 to 89.9 percent accepted	102,218	93,360	81,056	80,332	80,816	79,225	78,495	71,066	62,246	61,725	62,865	61,606	76.8	76.1	76.8	76.8	77.8	77.8
50.0 to 74.9 percent accepted	190,079	196,121	210,894	218,136	224,992	219,751	148,781	152,948	164,566	170,310	176,699	171,851	78.3	78.0	78.0	78.1	78.5	78.2
25.0 to 49.9 percent accepted	93,560	100,121	98,546	98,239	92,996	93,743	81,880	86,755	84,760	84,926	79,847	80,260	87.5	86.7	86.0	86.4	85.9	85.6
Less than 25.0 percent accepted	26,696	28,631	32,190	32,980	38,926	44,290	25,639	27,621	30,570	31,790	37,396	42,698	96.0	96.5	95.0	96.4	96.0	96.4
Information not available	4,650	8,143	4,576	3,382	2,399	1,436	3,300	5,874	3,333	2,207	1,673	855	71.0	72.1	72.8	65.3	69.7	59.5
For-profit institutions	88,764	100,206	70,667	48,970	43,693	40,741	40,279	49,797	38,458	25,626	23,491	20,941	45.4	49.7	54.4	52.3	53.8	51.4
Open admissions	45,273	46,801	20,894	16,997	16,350	20,661	18,735	22,723	12,459	9,329	8,990	10,758	41.4	48.6	59.6	54.9	55.0	52.1
90 percent or more accepted	6,285	5,347	4,632	3,713	2,900	5,234	3,454	2,764	2,465	1,301	1,524	2,426	55.0	51.7	53.2	35.0	52.6	46.4
75.0 to 89.9 percent accepted	3,703	6,157	6,384	3,224	2,428	2,860	2,081	3,129	3,085	1,549	1,284	1,354	56.2	50.8	48.3	48.0	52.9	47.3
50.0 to 74.9 percent accepted	12,845	19,724	8,874	15,929	10,122	4,854	6,536	10,249	5,602	8,243	5,443	2,691	50.9	52.0	63.1	51.7	53.8	55.4
25.0 to 49.9 percent accepted	18,142	18,118	28,288	6,098	7,214	6,860	8,036	8,672	14,094	3,423	3,942	3,547	44.3	47.9	49.8	56.1	54.6	51.7
Less than 25.0 percent accepted	0	0	0	0	0	0	0	0	0	0	0	0	†	†	†	†	†	†
Information not available	2,516	4,059	1,595	3,009	4,679	272	1,437	2,260	753	1,781	2,308	165	57.1	55.7	47.2	59.2	49.3	60.7
2-year institutions	712,983	764,551	784,329	920,928	879,618	798,369	426,646	466,348	470,225	560,038	526,976	470,874	59.8	61.0	60.0	60.8	59.9	59.0
Public institutions	611,643	667,819	681,690	797,717	757,565	707,762	361,154	400,406	402,017	477,653	446,136	411,603	59.0	60.0	59.0	59.9	58.9	58.2
Nonprofit institutions	8,573	8,414	7,933	7,960	10,952	10,698	5,324	4,981	4,759	4,697	6,697	6,437	62.1	59.2	60.0	59.0	61.1	60.2
For-profit institutions	92,767	88,318	94,706	115,251	111,101	79,909	60,168	60,961	63,449	77,688	74,143	52,834	64.9	69.0	67.0	67.4	66.7	66.1
Part-time student retention																		
All institutions	463,234	532,827	519,619	551,181	545,227	532,000	191,586	219,857	210,836	231,593	228,460	224,512	41.4	41.3	40.6	42.0	41.9	42.2
Public institutions	419,006	475,209	477,242	502,825	497,707	494,287	171,746	194,321	192,225	211,093	210,585	209,121	41.0	40.9	40.3	42.0	42.3	42.3
Nonprofit institutions	14,585	14,414	11,213	10,369	9,861	9,757	7,018	6,523	5,477	4,899	4,360	4,384	48.1	45.3	48.8	47.2	44.2	44.9
For-profit institutions	29,643	43,204	31,164	37,987	37,659	27,956	12,822	19,013	13,134	15,601	13,515	11,007	43.3	44.0	42.1	41.1	35.9	39.4
4-year institutions	82,367	95,410	97,051	73,376	69,350	58,104	38,257	43,441	45,678	32,720	29,048	25,327	46.4	45.5	47.1	44.6	41.9	43.6
Public institutions	48,353	48,190	63,932	34,504	29,922	28,594	23,631	23,006	31,910	17,240	15,361	14,235	48.9	47.7	49.9	50.0	51.3	49.8
Open admissions	20,223	20,645	38,295	9,470	6,318	6,291	8,298	9,122	17,982	3,852	2,626	2,443	41.0	44.2	47.0	40.7	41.6	38.8
90 percent or more accepted	8,960	8,145	2,707	3,735	4,930	2,263	4,196	3,818	1,205	1,861	2,784	998	46.8	46.9	44.5	49.8	56.5	44.1
75.0 to 89.9 percent accepted	11,599	12,236	7,476	6,544	5,650	5,993	6,245	6,766	3,872	3,277	2,856	3,106	53.8	55.3	51.8	50.1	50.5	51.8
50.0 to 74.9 percent accepted	3,373	3,023	11,969	11,496	10,667	10,801	1,866	1,992	6,649	6,131	5,699	5,802	55.3	65.9	55.6	53.3	53.4	53.7
25.0 to 49.9 percent accepted	65	44	3,084	3,125	2,262	2,965	34	42	1,745	2,023	1,466	1,746	52.3	95.5	56.6	64.7	64.8	58.9
Less than 25.0 percent accepted	379	647	359	130	43	240	189	254	176	105	35	114	49.9	39.3	49.0	80.8	81.4	47.5

See notes at end of table.

Retention of first-time degree-seeking undergraduates at degree-granting postsecondary institutions, by attendance status, level and control of institution, and percentage of applications accepted: 2006 to 2012—Continued

Level, control, and percent of applications accepted	First-time degree-seekers (adjusted entry cohort),[1] by entry year						Students from adjusted cohort returning in the following year						Percent of first-time undergraduates retained					
	2006	2007	2008	2009	2010	2011	2007	2008	2009	2010	2011	2012	2006 to 2007	2007 to 2008	2008 to 2009	2009 to 2010	2010 to 2011	2011 to 2012
1	2	3	4	5	6	7	8	9	10	11	12	13	14	15	16	17	18	19
Nonprofit institutions	12,828	12,886	9,883	9,609	9,110	8,802	6,045	5,614	4,772	4,499	3,992	3,870	47.1	43.6	48.3	46.8	43.8	44.0
Open admissions	5,446	5,330	3,369	3,821	3,949	4,220	2,579	2,306	1,504	1,693	1,614	1,636	47.4	43.3	44.6	44.3	40.9	38.8
90 percent or more accepted	523	1,272	971	393	478	843	237	434	421	199	180	357	45.3	34.1	43.4	50.6	37.7	42.3
75.0 to 89.9 percent accepted	2,459	2,132	1,307	1,177	951	1,254	1,047	895	633	558	456	671	42.6	42.0	48.4	47.4	47.9	53.5
50.0 to 74.9 percent accepted	3,131	2,899	2,016	3,256	2,955	1,868	1,406	1,307	1,029	1,531	1,333	844	44.9	45.1	51.0	47.0	45.1	45.2
25.0 to 49.9 percent accepted	853	917	1,963	712	647	466	452	478	1,016	366	319	240	53.0	52.1	51.8	51.4	49.3	51.5
Less than 25.0 percent accepted	112	94	78	93	84	116	86	84	70	78	67	104	76.8	89.4	89.7	83.9	79.8	89.7
Information not available	304	242	179	157	46	35	238	110	99	74	23	18	78.3	45.5	55.3	47.1	50.0	51.4
For-profit institutions	21,186	34,334	23,236	29,263	30,318	20,708	8,581	14,821	8,996	10,981	9,695	7,222	40.5	43.2	38.7	37.5	32.0	34.9
Open admissions	10,515	20,602	10,933	10,996	13,052	10,632	4,105	9,896	4,296	4,333	4,767	4,251	39.0	48.0	39.3	39.4	36.5	40.0
90 percent or more accepted	2,212	1,616	3,518	1,375	2,549	2,246	639	735	1,037	379	569	643	28.9	45.5	29.5	27.6	22.3	28.6
75.0 to 89.9 percent accepted	2,838	2,702	2,057	3,151	2,407	4,145	1,342	959	697	1,093	527	1,106	47.3	35.5	33.9	34.7	21.9	26.7
50.0 to 74.9 percent accepted	2,774	4,360	3,686	4,661	6,237	525	1,134	1,399	1,707	2,283	1,996	221	40.9	32.1	46.3	49.0	32.0	42.1
25.0 to 49.9 percent accepted	2,033	3,185	2,584	1,099	1,826	2,933	627	951	1,116	342	583	936	30.8	29.9	43.2	31.1	31.9	31.9
Less than 25.0 percent accepted	0	170	48	0	0	0	0	67	22	0	0	0	†	39.4	45.8	†	†	†
Information not available	814	1,699	410	7,981	4,247	227	734	814	121	2,551	1,253	65	90.2	47.9	29.5	32.0	29.5	28.6
2-year institutions	380,867	437,417	422,568	477,805	475,877	473,896	153,329	176,416	165,158	198,873	199,412	199,185	40.3	40.3	39.1	41.6	41.9	42.0
Public institutions	370,653	427,019	413,310	468,321	467,785	465,693	148,115	171,315	160,315	193,853	195,224	194,886	40.0	40.1	38.8	41.4	41.7	41.8
Nonprofit institutions	1,757	1,528	1,330	760	751	955	973	909	705	400	368	514	55.4	59.5	53.0	52.6	49.0	53.8
For-profit institutions	8,457	8,870	7,928	8,724	7,341	7,248	4,241	4,192	4,138	4,620	3,820	3,785	50.1	47.3	52.2	53.0	52.0	52.2

†Not applicable.

[1]Adjusted student counts exclude students who died or were totally and permanently disabled, served in the armed forces (including those called to active duty), served with a foreign aid service of the federal government (e.g., Peace Corps), or served on official church missions.

SOURCE: U.S. Department of Education, National Center for Education Statistics, Integrated Postsecondary Education Data System (IPEDS), Spring 2008 through 2013, Enrollment component; and IPEDS Fall 2006 through Fall 2011, Institutional Characteristics component. (This table was prepared January 2014.)

Degrees conferred by degree-granting postsecondary institutions, by level of degree and sex of student: Selected years, 1869–70 through 2023–24

	Associate's degrees				Bachelor's degrees				Master's degrees				Doctor's degrees[1]			
Year	Total	Males	Females	Percent female	Total	Males	Females	Percent female	Total	Males	Females	Percent female	Total	Males	Females	Percent female
1	2	3	4	5	6	7	8	9	10	11	12	13	14	15	16	17
1869–70	—	—	—	—	9,371[2]	7,993[2]	1,378[2]	14.7	0	0	0	—	1	1	0	0.0
1879–80	—	—	—	—	12,896[2]	10,411[2]	2,485[2]	19.3	879	868	11	1.3	54	51	3	5.6
1889–90	—	—	—	—	15,539[2]	12,857[2]	2,682[2]	17.3	1,015	821	194	19.1	149	147	2	1.3
1899–1900	—	—	—	—	27,410[2]	22,173[2]	5,237[2]	19.1	1,583	1,280	303	19.1	382	359	23	6.0
1909–10	—	—	—	—	37,199[2]	28,762[2]	8,437[2]	22.7	2,113	1,555	558	26.4	443	399	44	9.9
1919–20	—	—	—	—	48,622[2]	31,980[2]	16,642[2]	34.2	4,279	2,985	1,294	30.2	615	522	93	15.1
1929–30	—	—	—	—	122,484[2]	73,615[2]	48,869[2]	39.9	14,969	8,925	6,044	40.4	2,299	1,946	353	15.4
1939–40	—	—	—	—	186,500[2]	109,546[2]	76,954[2]	41.3	26,731	16,508	10,223	38.2	3,290	2,861	429	13.0
1949–50	—	—	—	—	432,058[2]	328,841[2]	103,217[2]	23.9	58,183	41,220	16,963	29.2	6,420	5,804	616	9.6
1959–60	—	—	—	—	392,440[2]	254,063[2]	138,377[2]	35.3	74,435	50,898	23,537	31.6	9,829	8,801	1,028	10.5
1969–70	206,023	117,432	88,591	43.0	792,316	451,097	341,219	43.1	213,589	130,799	82,790	38.8	59,486	53,792	5,694	9.6
1970–71	252,311	144,144	108,167	42.9	839,730	475,594	364,136	43.4	235,564	143,083	92,481	39.3	64,998	58,137	6,861	10.6
1971–72	292,014	166,227	125,787	43.1	887,273	500,590	386,683	43.6	257,201	155,010	102,191	39.7	71,206	63,353	7,853	11.0
1972–73	316,174	175,413	140,761	44.5	922,362	518,191	404,171	43.8	268,654	159,569	109,085	40.6	79,512	69,959	9,553	12.0
1973–74	343,924	188,591	155,333	45.2	945,776	527,313	418,463	44.2	282,074	162,606	119,468	42.4	82,591	71,131	11,460	13.9
1974–75	360,171	191,017	169,154	47.0	922,933	504,841	418,092	45.3	297,545	166,318	131,227	44.1	84,904	71,025	13,879	16.3
1975–76	391,454	209,996	181,458	46.4	925,746	504,925	420,821	45.5	317,477	172,519	144,958	45.7	91,007	73,888	17,119	18.8
1976–77	406,377	210,842	195,535	48.1	919,549	495,545	424,004	46.1	323,025	173,090	149,935	46.4	91,730	72,209	19,521	21.3
1977–78	412,246	204,718	207,528	50.3	921,204	487,347	433,857	47.1	317,987	166,857	151,130	47.5	92,345	70,283	22,062	23.9
1978–79	402,702	192,091	210,611	52.3	921,390	477,344	444,046	48.2	307,686	159,111	148,575	48.3	94,971	70,452	24,519	25.8
1979–80	400,910	183,737	217,173	54.2	929,417	473,611	455,806	49.0	305,196	156,882	148,314	48.6	95,631	69,526	26,105	27.3
1980–81	416,377	188,638	227,739	54.7	935,140	469,883	465,257	49.8	302,637	152,979	149,658	49.5	98,016	69,567	28,449	29.0
1981–82	434,526	196,944	237,582	54.7	952,998	473,364	479,634	50.3	302,447	151,349	151,098	50.0	97,838	68,630	29,208	29.9
1982–83	449,620	203,991	245,629	54.6	969,510	479,140	490,370	50.6	296,415	150,092	146,323	49.4	99,335	67,757	31,578	31.8
1983–84	452,240	202,704	249,536	55.2	974,309	482,319	491,990	50.5	291,141	149,268	141,873	48.7	100,799	67,769	33,030	32.8
1984–85	454,712	202,932	251,780	55.4	979,477	482,528	496,949	50.7	293,472	149,276	144,196	49.1	100,785	66,269	34,516	34.2
1985–86	446,047	196,166	249,881	56.0	987,823	485,923	501,900	50.8	295,850	149,373	146,477	49.5	100,280	65,215	35,065	35.0
1986–87	436,304	190,839	245,465	56.3	991,264	480,782	510,482	51.5	296,530	147,063	149,467	50.4	98,477	62,790	35,687	36.2
1987–88	435,085	190,047	245,038	56.3	994,829	477,203	517,626	52.0	305,783	150,243	155,540	50.9	99,139	63,019	36,120	36.4
1988–89	436,764	186,316	250,448	57.3	1,018,755	483,346	535,409	52.6	316,626	153,993	162,633	51.4	100,571	63,055	37,516	37.3
1989–90	455,102	191,195	263,907	58.0	1,051,344	491,696	559,648	53.2	330,152	158,052	172,100	52.1	103,508	63,963	39,545	38.2
1990–91	481,720	198,634	283,086	58.8	1,094,538	504,045	590,493	53.9	342,863	160,842	182,021	53.1	105,547	64,242	41,305	39.1
1991–92	504,231	207,481	296,750	58.9	1,136,553	520,811	615,742	54.2	358,089	165,867	192,222	53.7	109,554	66,603	42,951	39.2
1992–93	514,756	211,964	302,792	58.8	1,165,178	532,881	632,297	54.3	375,032	173,354	201,678	53.8	112,072	67,130	44,942	40.1
1993–94	530,632	215,261	315,371	59.4	1,169,275	532,422	636,853	54.5	393,037	180,571	212,466	54.1	112,636	66,773	45,863	40.7
1994–95	539,691	218,352	321,339	59.5	1,160,134	526,131	634,003	54.6	403,609	183,043	220,566	54.6	114,266	67,324	46,942	41.1
1995–96	555,216	219,514	335,702	60.5	1,164,792	522,454	642,338	55.1	412,180	183,481	228,699	55.5	115,507	67,189	48,318	41.8
1996–97	571,226	223,948	347,278	60.8	1,172,879	520,515	652,364	55.6	425,260	185,270	239,990	56.4	118,747	68,387	50,360	42.4
1997–98	558,555	217,613	340,942	61.0	1,184,406	519,956	664,450	56.1	436,037	188,718	247,319	56.7	118,735	67,232	51,503	43.4
1998–99	564,984	220,508	344,476	61.0	1,202,239	519,961	682,278	56.8	446,038	190,230	255,808	57.4	116,700	65,340	51,360	44.0
1999–2000	564,933	224,721	340,212	60.2	1,237,875	530,367	707,508	57.2	463,185	196,129	267,056	57.7	118,736	64,930	53,806	45.3
2000–01	578,865	231,645	347,220	60.0	1,244,171	531,840	712,331	57.3	473,502	197,770	275,732	58.2	119,585	64,171	55,414	46.3
2001–02	595,133	238,109	357,024	60.0	1,291,900	549,816	742,084	57.4	487,313	202,604	284,709	58.4	119,663	62,731	56,932	47.6
2002–03	634,016	253,451	380,565	60.0	1,348,811	573,258	775,553	57.5	518,699	215,172	303,527	58.5	121,579	62,730	58,849	48.4
2003–04	665,301	260,033	405,268	60.9	1,399,542	595,425	804,117	57.5	564,272	233,056	331,216	58.7	126,087	63,981	62,106	49.3
2004–05	696,660	267,536	429,124	61.6	1,439,264	613,000	826,264	57.4	580,151	237,155	342,996	59.1	134,387	67,257	67,130	50.0
2005–06	713,066	270,095	442,971	62.1	1,485,242	630,600	854,642	57.5	599,731	241,656	358,075	59.7	138,056	68,912	69,144	50.1
2006–07	728,114	275,187	452,927	62.2	1,524,092	649,570	874,522	57.4	610,597	242,189	368,408	60.3	144,690	71,308	73,382	50.7
2007–08	750,164	282,521	467,643	62.3	1,563,069	667,928	895,141	57.3	630,666	250,169	380,497	60.3	149,378	73,453	75,925	50.8
2008–09	787,325	298,141	489,184	62.1	1,601,368	685,382	915,986	57.2	662,079	263,538	398,541	60.2	154,425	75,639	78,786	51.0
2009–10	849,452	322,916	526,536	62.0	1,650,014	706,633	943,381	57.2	693,025	275,197	417,828	60.3	158,558	76,605	81,953	51.7
2010–11	942,327	361,309	581,018	61.7	1,715,913	734,133	981,780	57.2	730,635	291,551	439,084	60.1	163,765	79,654	84,111	51.4
2011–12	1,017,538	391,990	625,548	61.5	1,791,046	765,317	1,025,729	57.3	754,229	302,191	452,038	59.9	170,062	82,611	87,451	51.4
2012–13[3]	1,042,000	406,000	636,000	61.0	1,818,000	777,000	1,041,000	57.3	762,000	306,000	456,000	59.8	173,900	85,900	88,000	50.6
2013–14[3]	1,031,000	409,000	623,000	60.4	1,844,000	788,000	1,056,000	57.3	791,000	316,000	475,000	60.1	177,000	87,300	89,700	50.7
2014–15[3]	1,046,000	418,000	628,000	60.0	1,835,000	778,000	1,057,000	57.6	821,000	327,000	495,000	60.3	177,500	88,000	89,600	50.5
2015–16[3]	1,074,000	431,000	643,000	59.9	1,850,000	786,000	1,064,000	57.5	844,000	333,000	511,000	60.5	182,400	90,100	92,300	50.6
2016–17[3]	1,116,000	445,000	671,000	60.1	1,882,000	789,000	1,093,000	58.1	867,000	340,000	527,000	60.8	187,600	92,300	95,300	50.8
2017–18[3]	1,156,000	460,000	696,000	60.2	1,902,000	793,000	1,109,000	58.3	892,000	348,000	544,000	61.0	190,900	93,500	97,300	51.0
2018–19[3]	1,197,000	476,000	721,000	60.2	1,926,000	800,000	1,127,000	58.5	915,000	356,000	559,000	61.1	194,100	94,900	99,200	51.1
2019–20[3]	1,239,000	492,000	746,000	60.2	1,953,000	808,000	1,145,000	58.6	935,000	361,000	575,000	61.5	197,600	96,500	101,100	51.2
2020–21[3]	1,279,000	508,000	771,000	60.3	1,978,000	816,000	1,162,000	58.7	957,000	366,000	592,000	61.9	200,300	97,700	102,600	51.2
2021–22[3]	1,321,000	524,000	797,000	60.3	2,004,000	824,000	1,180,000	58.9	981,000	371,000	610,000	62.2	202,800	98,500	104,300	51.4
2022–23[3]	1,365,000	540,000	825,000	60.4	2,031,000	832,000	1,199,000	59.0	1,007,000	378,000	629,000	62.5	205,500	99,300	106,200	51.7
2023–24[3]	1,410,000	556,000	854,000	60.6	2,061,000	842,000	1,219,000	59.1	1,032,000	385,000	647,000	62.7	208,500	100,300	108,100	51.8

—Not available.

[1] Includes Ph.D., Ed.D., and comparable degrees at the doctoral level. Includes most degrees formerly classified as first-professional, such as M.D., D.D.S., and law degrees.

[2] Includes some degrees classified as master's or doctor's degrees in later years.

[3] Projected.

NOTE: Data through 1994–95 are for institutions of higher education, while later data are for degree-granting institutions. Degree-granting institutions grant associate's or higher degrees and participate in Title IV federal financial aid programs. Some data have been revised from previously published figures. Detail may not sum to totals because of rounding.

SOURCE: U.S. Department of Education, National Center for Education Statistics, *Earned Degrees Conferred*, 1869–70 through 1964–65; Higher Education General Information Survey (HEGIS), "Degrees and Other Formal Awards Conferred" surveys, 1965–66 through 1985–86; Integrated Postsecondary Education Data System (IPEDS), "Completions Survey" (IPEDS-C:87–99); IPEDS Fall 2000 through Fall 2012, Completions component; and Degrees Conferred Projection Model, 1980–81 through 2023–24. (This table was prepared March 2014.)

Bachelor's, master's, and doctor's degrees conferred by degree-granting institutions, by field of study: Selected years, 1970–71 through 2011–12

Degree and year	Number of degrees conferred								Percentage distribution of degrees conferred							
	Total degrees	Humanities[1]	Social and behavioral sciences[2]	Natural sciences and mathematics[3]	Computer sciences and engineering[4]	Education	Business	Other fields[5]	Total degrees	Humanities[1]	Social and behavioral sciences[2]	Natural sciences and mathematics[3]	Computer sciences and engineering[4]	Education	Business	Other fields[5]
1	2	3	4	5	6	7	8	9	10	11	12	13	14	15	16	17
Bachelor's degrees																
1970–71	839,730	143,549	193,511	81,916	52,570	176,307	115,396	76,481	100.0	17.1	23.0	9.8	6.3	21.0	13.7	9.1
1975–76	925,746	150,736	176,674	91,596	52,328	154,437	143,171	156,804	100.0	16.3	19.1	9.9	5.7	16.7	15.5	16.9
1980–81	935,140	134,139	141,581	78,092	90,476	108,074	200,521	182,257	100.0	14.3	15.1	8.4	9.7	11.6	21.4	19.5
1985–86	987,823	132,891	134,468	76,228	139,459	87,147	236,700	180,930	100.0	13.5	13.6	7.7	14.1	8.8	24.0	18.3
1990–91	1,094,538	172,485	183,762	70,209	104,910	110,807	249,165	203,200	100.0	15.8	16.8	6.4	9.6	10.1	22.8	18.6
1995–96	1,164,792	193,404	199,895	93,443	102,503	105,384	226,623	243,540	100.0	16.6	17.2	8.0	8.8	9.0	19.5	20.9
2000–01	1,244,171	214,107	201,681	89,772	117,011	105,458	263,515	252,627	100.0	17.2	16.2	7.2	9.4	8.5	21.2	20.3
2005–06	1,485,242	261,696	249,619	105,899	128,886	107,238	318,042	313,862	100.0	17.6	16.8	7.1	8.7	7.2	21.4	21.1
2007–08	1,563,069	274,535	259,950	117,200	122,084	102,582	335,254	351,464	100.0	17.6	16.6	7.5	7.8	6.6	21.4	22.5
2008–09	1,601,368	278,387	262,771	121,009	122,408	101,708	347,985	367,100	100.0	17.4	16.4	7.6	7.6	6.4	21.7	22.9
2009–10	1,650,014	280,993	269,996	125,809	128,318	101,265	358,293	385,340	100.0	17.0	16.4	7.6	7.8	6.1	21.7	23.4
2010–11	1,715,913	288,371	278,037	131,897	136,189	103,992	365,093	412,334	100.0	16.8	16.2	7.7	7.9	6.1	21.3	24.0
2011–12	1,791,046	295,221	287,529	141,354	145,924	105,785	366,815	448,418	100.0	16.5	16.1	7.9	8.1	5.9	20.5	25.0
Master's degrees																
1970–71	235,564	34,510	22,256	17,152	18,535	87,666	26,490	28,955	100.0	14.6	9.4	7.3	7.9	37.2	11.2	12.3
1975–76	317,477	37,079	26,120	15,742	19,403	126,061	42,592	50,480	100.0	11.7	8.2	5.0	6.1	39.7	13.4	15.9
1980–81	302,637	35,130	22,168	13,579	21,434	96,713	57,888	55,725	100.0	11.6	7.3	4.5	7.1	32.0	19.1	18.4
1985–86	295,850	34,834	20,409	14,055	30,216	74,816	66,676	54,844	100.0	11.8	6.9	4.8	10.2	25.3	22.5	18.5
1990–91	342,863	35,984	23,582	13,664	34,774	87,352	78,255	69,252	100.0	10.5	6.9	4.0	10.1	25.5	22.8	20.2
1995–96	412,180	40,795	30,164	16,154	39,422	104,936	93,554	87,155	100.0	9.9	7.3	3.9	9.6	25.5	22.7	21.1
2000–01	473,502	40,625	30,321	15,360	44,098	127,829	115,602	99,658	100.0	8.6	6.4	3.2	9.3	27.0	24.4	21.0
2005–06	599,731	49,584	37,139	19,574	50,444	174,620	146,406	121,964	100.0	8.3	6.2	3.3	8.4	29.1	24.4	20.3
2007–08	630,666	52,087	39,926	20,730	51,517	175,880	155,637	134,889	100.0	8.3	6.3	3.3	8.2	27.9	24.7	21.4
2008–09	662,079	53,198	42,655	21,090	55,908	178,564	168,375	142,289	100.0	8.0	6.4	3.2	8.4	27.0	25.4	21.5
2009–10	693,025	54,927	43,974	22,422	57,299	182,139	177,684	154,580	100.0	7.9	6.3	3.2	8.3	26.3	25.6	22.3
2010–11	730,635	57,137	46,135	23,556	62,680	185,009	187,213	168,905	100.0	7.8	6.3	3.2	8.6	25.3	25.6	23.1
2011–12	754,229	59,979	48,723	25,570	66,014	178,062	191,571	184,310	100.0	8.0	6.5	3.4	8.8	23.6	25.4	24.4
Doctor's degrees[6]																
1970–71	64,998	4,402	5,804	9,126	3,816	6,041	774	35,035	100.0	6.8	8.9	14.0	5.9	9.3	1.2	53.9
1975–76	91,007	5,461	7,314	7,591	3,118	7,202	906	59,415	100.0	6.0	8.0	8.3	3.4	7.9	1.0	65.3
1980–81	98,016	4,827	6,698	7,473	2,860	7,279	808	68,071	100.0	4.9	6.8	7.6	2.9	7.4	0.8	69.4
1985–86	100,280	4,648	6,548	7,668	3,800	6,610	923	70,083	100.0	4.6	6.5	7.6	3.8	6.6	0.9	69.9
1990–91	105,547	4,858	6,944	9,378	6,006	6,189	1,185	70,987	100.0	4.6	6.6	8.9	5.7	5.9	1.1	67.3
1995–96	115,507	6,356	7,901	10,997	7,223	6,246	1,366	75,418	100.0	5.5	6.8	9.5	6.3	5.4	1.2	65.3
2000–01	119,585	6,466	9,021	10,190	6,315	6,284	1,180	80,129	100.0	5.4	7.5	8.5	5.3	5.3	1.0	67.0
2005–06	138,056	6,628	8,835	12,097	8,734	7,584	1,711	92,467	100.0	4.8	6.4	8.8	6.3	5.5	1.2	67.0
2007–08	149,378	7,049	9,355	13,754	9,675	8,491	2,084	98,970	100.0	4.7	6.3	9.2	6.5	5.7	1.4	66.3
2008–09	154,425	7,261	9,711	14,271	9,381	9,028	2,123	102,650	100.0	4.7	6.3	9.2	6.1	5.8	1.4	66.5
2009–10	158,558	7,739	9,778	14,321	9,370	9,233	2,245	105,872	100.0	4.9	6.2	9.0	5.9	5.8	1.4	66.8
2010–11	163,765	8,360	10,241	14,574	10,013	9,623	2,286	108,668	100.0	5.1	6.3	8.9	6.1	5.9	1.4	66.4
2011–12	170,062	8,733	10,525	14,974	10,554	9,990	2,531	112,755	100.0	5.1	6.2	8.8	6.2	5.9	1.5	66.3

[1] Includes degrees in Area, ethnic, cultural, gender, and group studies; English language and literature/letters; Foreign languages, literatures, and linguistics; Liberal arts and sciences, general studies, and humanities; Multi/interdisciplinary studies; Philosophy and religious studies; Theology and religious vocations; and Visual and performing arts.

[2] Includes Psychology; Social sciences; and History.

[3] Includes Biological and biomedical sciences; Mathematics and statistics; and Physical sciences and science technologies.

[4] Includes Computer and information sciences; Engineering; and Engineering technologies.

[5] Includes Agriculture and natural resources; Architecture and related services; Communication, journalism, and related programs; Communications technologies; Family and consumer sciences/human sciences; Health professions and related programs; Homeland security, law enforcement, and firefighting; Legal professions and studies; Library science; Military technologies and applied sciences; Parks, recreation, leisure, and fitness studies; Precision production; Public administration and social services; Transportation and materials moving; and Not classified by field of study.

[6] Includes Ph.D., Ed.D., and comparable degrees at the doctoral level. Includes most degrees formerly classified as first-professional, such as M.D., D.D.S., and law degrees.

NOTE: Data are for postsecondary institutions participating in Title IV federal financial aid programs. The new Classification of Instructional Programs was initiated in 2009–10. The figures for earlier years have been reclassified when necessary to make them conform to the new taxonomy. To facilitate trend comparisons, certain aggregations have been made of the degree fields as reported in the Integrated Postsecondary Education Data System (IPEDS): "Agriculture and natural resources" includes Agriculture, agriculture operations, and related sciences and Natural resources and conservation; "Business" includes Business, management, marketing, and related support services and Personal and culinary services; and "Engineering technologies" includes Engineering technologies and engineering-related fields, Construction trades, and Mechanic and repair technologies/technicians. Detail may not sum to totals because of rounding.

SOURCE: U.S. Department of Education, National Center for Education Statistics, Higher Education General Information Survey (HEGIS), "Degrees and Other Formal Awards Conferred" surveys, 1970–71 through 1985–86; Integrated Postsecondary Education Data System (IPEDS), "Completions Survey" (IPEDS-C:91–96); and IPEDS Fall 2001 through Fall 2012, Completions component. (This table was prepared July 2013.)

Degrees conferred by postsecondary institutions, by control, level of degree, and state or jurisdiction: 2011–12

State or jurisdiction	Public				Private nonprofit				Private for-profit			
	Associate's degrees	Bachelor's degrees	Master's degrees	Doctor's degrees[1]	Associate's degrees	Bachelor's degrees	Master's degrees	Doctor's degrees[1]	Associate's degrees	Bachelor's degrees	Master's degrees	Doctor's degrees[1]
1	2	3	4	5	6	7	8	9	10	11	12	13
United States	756,084	1,131,886	349,311	84,727	54,346	526,506	325,427	79,483	207,108	132,654	79,491	5,852
Alabama	10,284	21,529	9,288	1,733	144	3,619	674	520	2,724	2,291	1,440	3
Alaska	1,120	1,612	650	50	15	80	53	0	571	58	0	0
Arizona	16,823	23,775	7,121	1,787	8	937	1,298	595	46,159	39,995	27,759	1,151
Arkansas	8,122	11,458	4,775	855	121	2,558	487	58	402	173	58	0
California	89,284	125,326	29,548	6,900	1,189	34,681	33,074	10,141	24,139	12,403	5,880	407
Colorado	7,814	22,575	6,980	1,668	351	3,996	4,655	589	8,774	4,565	3,771	95
Connecticut	5,420	11,145	3,253	801	832	9,112	6,021	1,153	259	453	183	0
Delaware	1,735	4,040	897	277	199	1,821	1,764	308	13	24	19	0
District of Columbia	170	398	65	93	156	8,439	9,841	3,474	137	375	307	0
Florida	79,362	61,446	17,149	4,395	7,419	22,527	13,376	3,895	15,778	7,006	3,334	1,195
Georgia	14,496	33,656	10,928	2,341	1,212	9,886	4,923	1,542	3,020	2,679	1,939	385
Hawaii	3,054	4,055	1,287	494	554	1,858	685	0	591	103	143	39
Idaho	2,847	5,980	1,765	331	1,385	3,667	248	0	708	134	28	0
Illinois	32,516	34,658	12,630	2,970	1,687	30,227	26,245	5,007	7,415	7,570	4,763	152
Indiana	12,267	29,853	9,275	2,549	1,822	14,752	4,757	913	5,341	927	183	0
Iowa	12,735	11,672	2,976	1,480	645	10,558	2,264	1,353	7,135	18,446	6,860	124
Kansas	8,925	15,004	5,306	1,324	624	3,935	1,702	128	669	60	13	0
Kentucky	9,757	16,202	6,057	1,631	727	4,667	2,996	215	4,196	662	358	89
Louisiana	5,938	18,582	5,142	1,583	595	3,202	1,994	1,002	1,174	231	139	0
Maine	2,593	4,581	927	153	230	3,098	970	230	498	5	0	0
Maryland	14,250	23,931	9,892	2,142	18	6,401	7,626	680	888	531	327	0
Massachusetts	10,998	18,121	5,823	678	1,589	37,246	30,038	7,468	1,058	456	94	0
Michigan	27,059	43,645	16,582	4,008	4,838	13,591	4,709	1,876	1,425	579	101	0
Minnesota	16,575	21,319	5,349	1,703	700	10,850	5,043	1,163	3,205	2,811	10,217	1,417
Mississippi	12,305	11,214	3,452	1,050	61	2,302	1,355	167	630	0	2	0
Missouri	11,575	20,984	6,808	1,446	2,959	17,867	13,557	3,223	5,361	4,837	614	0
Montana	2,201	4,680	1,209	372	163	704	77	0	0	0	0	0
Nebraska	4,870	8,401	2,764	732	249	5,675	2,397	660	642	172	17	0
Nevada	3,853	6,625	1,880	573	0	309	361	377	1,497	705	363	0
New Hampshire	2,143	5,244	1,170	67	377	3,637	2,632	413	599	389	23	0
New Jersey	20,516	29,144	8,544	2,177	195	9,847	6,871	945	932	813	75	0
New Mexico	6,992	7,281	2,881	614	0	110	151	0	717	868	227	0
New York	50,397	58,090	19,653	2,919	8,907	67,696	50,855	11,888	10,350	3,640	898	2
North Carolina	24,874	35,589	11,445	2,300	1,252	14,361	4,922	1,891	1,546	772	581	229
North Dakota	1,972	5,060	1,244	443	244	616	481	37	35	3	0	0
Ohio	23,897	44,626	15,324	4,373	2,829	21,094	8,326	1,619	9,145	1,016	498	0
Oklahoma	9,824	15,965	5,164	1,319	198	3,653	1,260	409	1,491	228	57	0
Oregon	11,212	15,800	4,228	1,003	55	4,827	3,238	907	1,370	487	75	0
Pennsylvania	16,988	46,493	12,009	3,429	3,065	42,326	24,397	5,946	9,822	1,850	379	0
Rhode Island	1,545	3,921	811	234	1,992	7,093	1,755	511	0	0	0	0
South Carolina	8,953	16,566	4,367	1,313	429	5,275	1,140	53	1,408	1,132	465	238
South Dakota	2,119	4,040	1,084	353	213	1,002	225	0	367	350	158	0
Tennessee	9,497	19,981	5,885	1,763	744	11,363	5,648	1,376	3,307	965	396	13
Texas	59,683	89,186	35,319	7,499	1,300	19,775	9,035	2,571	6,369	2,363	953	34
Utah	10,662	14,426	3,429	817	469	11,185	3,613	239	2,170	943	627	128
Vermont	923	3,517	522	207	200	2,703	1,952	208	73	63	0	0
Virginia	18,074	35,099	11,967	3,250	811	13,888	7,694	1,948	7,314	4,011	1,855	130
Washington	27,833	24,384	5,531	1,689	66	7,232	3,841	851	1,078	760	223	21
West Virginia	3,056	9,102	2,701	880	93	1,083	252	106	1,782	3,099	2,939	0
Wisconsin	13,288	26,178	5,757	1,762	415	9,175	3,949	828	2,588	649	150	0
Wyoming	2,688	2,062	489	197	0	0	0	0	236	2	0	0
U.S. Service Academies	0	3,665	9	0	†	†	†	†	†	†	†	†
Other jurisdictions	3,288	8,170	942	514	3,418	11,240	3,864	891	2,429	948	503	0
American Samoa	269	2	0	0	0	0	0	0	0	0	0	0
Federated States of Micronesia	262	0	0	0	0	0	0	0	0	0	0	0
Guam	274	386	129	0	4	22	3	0	0	0	0	0
Marshall Islands	71	0	0	0	0	0	0	0	0	0	0	0
Northern Marianas	103	14	0	0	0	0	0	0	0	0	0	0
Palau	85	0	0	0	0	0	0	0	0	0	0	0
Puerto Rico	2,151	7,531	760	514	3,414	11,218	3,861	891	2,429	948	503	0
U.S. Virgin Islands	73	237	53	0	0	0	0	0	0	0	0	0

†Not applicable.
[1]Includes Ph.D., Ed.D., and comparable degrees at the doctoral level. Includes most degrees formerly classified as first-professional, such as M.D., D.D.S., and law degrees.
NOTE: Data are for postsecondary institutions participating in Title IV federal financial aid programs.

SOURCE: U.S. Department of Education, National Center for Education Statistics, Integrated Postsecondary Education Data System (IPEDS), Fall 2012, Completions component. (This table was prepared August 2013.)

Degrees conferred by postsecondary institutions, by level of degree and state or jurisdiction: 2008–09 through 2011–12

State or jurisdiction	2009–10				2010–11				2011–12			
	Associate's degrees	Bachelor's degrees	Master's degrees	Doctor's degrees[1]	Associate's degrees	Bachelor's degrees	Master's degrees	Doctor's degrees[1]	Associate's degrees	Bachelor's degrees	Master's degrees	Doctor's degrees[1]
1	2	3	4	5	6	7	8	9	10	11	12	13
United States	**849,452**	**1,650,014**	**693,025**	**158,558**	**942,327**	**1,715,913**	**730,635**	**163,765**	**1,017,538**	**1,791,046**	**754,229**	**170,062**
Alabama	10,198	25,686	11,291	2,079	11,795	27,248	11,888	2,144	13,152	27,439	11,402	2,256
Alaska	1,182	1,619	681	45	1,523	1,770	693	46	1,706	1,750	703	50
Arizona	50,252	44,339	34,860	2,684	58,991	50,928	36,231	2,937	62,990	64,707	36,178	3,533
Arkansas	7,172	12,523	4,126	804	10,181	13,259	4,793	813	8,645	14,189	5,320	913
California	102,018	164,234	65,050	16,382	107,675	169,623	67,439	17,140	114,612	172,410	68,502	17,448
Colorado	14,552	28,546	13,054	2,205	16,145	29,540	14,246	2,170	16,939	31,136	15,406	2,352
Connecticut	5,523	19,483	8,639	1,834	6,079	19,735	9,131	1,808	6,511	20,710	9,457	1,954
Delaware	1,712	5,505	2,452	528	1,820	5,877	2,705	546	1,947	5,885	2,680	585
District of Columbia	447	8,927	9,285	3,394	555	8,402	10,078	3,458	463	9,212	10,213	3,567
Florida	79,644	83,471	29,726	9,107	86,254	86,281	31,766	9,297	102,559	90,979	33,859	9,485
Georgia	15,583	42,452	16,304	3,958	17,949	45,075	17,533	4,005	18,728	46,221	17,790	4,268
Hawaii	3,238	5,401	2,028	381	3,766	5,751	2,062	529	4,199	6,016	2,115	533
Idaho	3,490	9,466	1,680	306	3,919	9,171	1,790	321	4,940	9,781	2,041	331
Illinois	38,263	70,847	41,548	7,625	40,009	71,580	43,011	7,846	41,618	72,455	43,638	8,129
Indiana	16,727	41,687	13,673	3,250	18,603	43,519	14,337	3,386	19,430	45,532	14,215	3,462
Iowa	15,834	30,323	7,452	2,744	19,290	36,266	9,982	3,112	20,515	40,676	12,100	2,957
Kansas	8,424	17,835	6,722	1,388	9,501	18,191	7,227	1,476	10,218	18,999	7,021	1,452
Kentucky	11,707	20,389	7,976	1,591	13,029	21,078	8,350	1,812	14,680	21,531	9,411	1,935
Louisiana	5,849	20,893	6,641	2,381	7,236	21,509	7,017	2,236	7,707	22,015	7,275	2,585
Maine	2,718	7,088	1,829	348	3,309	7,347	1,766	367	3,321	7,684	1,897	383
Maryland	12,446	28,012	16,019	2,665	13,921	29,247	16,975	2,652	15,156	30,863	17,845	2,822
Massachusetts	12,396	52,223	32,136	7,485	12,900	53,749	33,905	7,637	13,645	55,823	35,955	8,146
Michigan	29,318	56,061	21,176	5,589	30,859	56,217	21,252	5,807	33,322	57,815	21,392	5,884
Minnesota	18,453	31,952	21,015	4,173	20,480	33,386	21,823	4,352	20,480	34,980	20,609	4,283
Mississippi	9,824	12,953	4,203	1,154	11,440	13,230	4,676	1,170	12,996	13,516	4,809	1,217
Missouri	15,802	39,670	19,403	4,651	18,534	41,648	20,697	4,656	19,895	43,688	20,979	4,669
Montana	1,745	5,232	1,140	309	2,058	5,512	1,201	357	2,364	5,384	1,286	372
Nebraska	4,860	12,596	4,364	1,392	5,351	13,510	4,684	1,371	5,761	14,248	5,178	1,392
Nevada	4,068	7,345	2,652	830	4,997	7,556	2,720	839	5,350	7,639	2,604	950
New Hampshire	2,933	9,396	3,458	459	3,062	9,479	3,666	448	3,119	9,270	3,825	480
New Jersey	19,268	36,025	14,146	3,011	21,124	37,087	14,427	3,101	21,643	39,804	15,490	3,122
New Mexico	5,234	7,774	3,057	544	6,552	8,179	3,266	583	7,709	8,259	3,259	614
New York	61,618	123,703	68,258	14,155	66,644	127,205	70,225	14,230	69,654	129,426	71,406	14,809
North Carolina	22,879	46,826	15,395	3,955	25,154	48,670	16,226	4,116	27,672	50,722	16,948	4,420
North Dakota	2,411	5,727	1,392	447	2,552	5,674	1,572	456	2,251	5,679	1,725	480
Ohio	29,332	61,085	22,187	5,828	33,479	63,882	22,636	6,033	35,871	66,736	24,148	5,992
Oklahoma	9,723	19,535	5,947	1,586	10,710	19,511	6,356	1,611	11,513	19,846	6,481	1,728
Oregon	9,129	18,873	6,779	1,849	10,945	19,542	7,326	1,849	12,637	21,114	7,541	1,910
Pennsylvania	27,517	87,162	33,902	9,135	29,241	88,205	36,016	9,316	29,875	90,669	36,785	9,375
Rhode Island	3,590	10,647	2,396	746	3,461	10,863	2,545	709	3,537	11,014	2,566	745
South Carolina	8,727	21,905	5,676	1,496	9,771	23,034	5,849	1,606	10,790	22,973	5,972	1,604
South Dakota	1,952	4,976	1,309	307	2,601	5,211	1,427	300	2,699	5,392	1,467	353
Tennessee	10,645	29,857	10,627	2,655	12,478	31,026	11,099	2,989	13,548	32,309	11,929	3,152
Texas	55,048	104,657	39,739	9,318	58,609	107,438	42,039	9,705	67,352	111,324	45,307	10,104
Utah	11,054	21,931	5,804	936	12,398	24,461	6,995	1,087	13,301	26,554	7,669	1,184
Vermont	1,266	5,888	2,244	381	1,223	6,100	2,377	388	1,196	6,283	2,474	415
Virginia	21,010	45,324	18,889	4,633	24,193	49,077	20,697	4,923	26,199	52,998	21,516	5,328
Washington	23,068	30,551	9,766	2,366	27,045	31,398	9,850	2,412	28,977	32,376	9,595	2,561
West Virginia	3,989	12,032	5,064	943	4,688	12,978	5,884	1,007	4,931	13,284	5,892	986
Wisconsin	12,752	34,110	9,476	2,347	15,012	35,279	9,695	2,418	16,291	36,002	9,856	2,590
Wyoming	2,862	1,791	388	179	3,216	1,860	482	188	2,924	2,064	489	197
U.S. Service Academies	0	3,481	1	0	0	3,549	2	0	0	3,665	9	0
Other jurisdictions	**6,982**	**18,213**	**5,503**	**1,342**	**7,690**	**18,316**	**5,820**	**1,421**	**9,135**	**20,358**	**5,309**	**1,405**
American Samoa	242	0	0	0	216	0	0	0	269	2	0	0
Federated States of Micronesia	222	0	0	0	267	0	0	0	262	0	0	0
Guam	185	338	121	0	119	375	134	0	278	408	132	0
Marshall Islands	49	0	0	0	68	0	0	0	71	0	0	0
Northern Marianas	60	19	0	0	105	14	0	0	103	14	0	0
Palau	46	0	0	0	26	0	0	0	85	0	0	0
Puerto Rico	6,104	17,604	5,327	1,342	6,814	17,698	5,652	1,421	7,994	19,697	5,124	1,405
U.S. Virgin Islands	74	252	55	0	75	229	34	0	73	237	53	0

[1]Includes Ph.D., Ed.D., and comparable degrees at the doctoral level. Includes most degrees formerly classified as first-professional, such as M.D., D.D.S., and law degrees.
NOTE: Data are for postsecondary institutions participating in Title IV federal financial aid programs.

SOURCE: U.S. Department of Education, National Center for Education Statistics, Integrated Postsecondary Education Data System (IPEDS), Fall 2010 through Fall 2012, Completions component. (This table was prepared August 2013.)

Bachelor's degrees conferred by postsecondary institutions, by field of study and state or jurisdiction: 2011–12

State or jurisdiction	Total	Humanities[1]	Psychology	Social sciences and history	Natural sciences[2]	Computer sciences	Engineering[3]	Education	Business/ management	Health professions and related programs	Other fields[4]
1	2	3	4	5	6	7	8	9	10	11	12
United States	1,791,046	295,221	108,986	178,543	141,354	47,384	98,540	105,785	366,815	163,440	284,978
Alabama	27,439	2,581	1,475	1,780	1,986	584	2,080	2,576	6,648	2,795	4,934
Alaska	1,750	299	117	147	152	35	152	102	310	163	273
Arizona	64,707	8,671	2,101	2,733	2,482	3,711	1,528	3,400	21,202	9,274	9,605
Arkansas	14,189	2,202	725	950	1,124	287	561	1,416	2,783	1,769	2,372
California	172,410	35,416	12,570	24,661	16,776	3,905	9,982	2,626	30,771	10,373	25,330
Colorado	31,136	5,217	1,802	3,411	2,747	864	2,042	235	7,401	2,197	5,220
Connecticut	20,710	4,128	1,640	3,003	1,713	244	924	690	3,466	1,908	2,994
Delaware	5,885	707	305	562	307	127	314	460	1,456	600	1,047
District of Columbia	9,212	1,279	532	2,768	536	179	266	69	1,745	663	1,175
Florida	90,979	10,891	6,024	8,375	5,816	2,369	4,411	5,581	21,957	8,955	16,600
Georgia	46,221	6,904	2,672	4,234	3,778	1,425	2,451	4,289	10,072	3,742	6,654
Hawaii	6,016	898	409	726	387	132	139	403	1,358	610	954
Idaho	9,781	1,469	465	703	738	239	488	1,201	1,603	1,215	1,660
Illinois	72,455	12,475	4,103	6,217	5,247	2,501	3,628	5,897	15,340	5,692	11,355
Indiana	45,532	6,969	1,859	3,297	2,991	1,313	3,514	3,612	9,712	4,908	7,357
Iowa	40,676	3,716	3,417	4,034	1,851	955	1,332	3,335	10,493	3,772	7,771
Kansas	18,999	2,755	718	1,387	1,120	432	1,205	1,779	4,633	1,936	3,034
Kentucky	21,531	3,097	1,151	1,650	1,544	349	1,029	2,195	3,933	2,070	4,513
Louisiana	22,015	3,922	1,217	1,711	1,793	320	1,377	1,644	4,462	2,408	3,161
Maine	7,684	1,340	470	1,049	828	78	431	580	902	830	1,176
Maryland	30,863	4,321	2,118	4,103	2,764	1,977	1,352	1,446	5,584	2,432	4,766
Massachusetts	55,823	10,060	3,989	7,279	4,984	1,346	3,351	1,449	10,779	4,483	8,103
Michigan	57,815	7,455	3,214	4,466	4,659	1,566	4,608	3,743	12,104	5,923	10,077
Minnesota	34,980	5,582	2,200	3,105	3,618	959	1,423	2,722	7,158	2,866	5,347
Mississippi	13,516	1,822	812	852	1,168	167	705	1,855	2,729	1,383	2,023
Missouri	43,688	5,688	2,570	2,524	2,695	1,066	2,157	3,300	9,777	7,147	6,764
Montana	5,384	807	254	503	487	65	485	505	885	407	986
Nebraska	14,248	1,346	663	1,000	855	395	508	1,451	3,873	1,768	2,389
Nevada	7,639	995	460	655	515	194	345	459	2,024	789	1,203
New Hampshire	9,270	1,529	743	1,134	682	176	462	480	1,927	590	1,547
New Jersey	39,804	7,590	3,317	4,852	3,516	826	1,968	2,115	7,197	2,733	5,690
New Mexico	8,259	1,597	476	619	662	147	622	813	1,559	600	1,164
New York	129,426	26,738	9,837	15,279	10,433	3,041	6,228	7,011	23,911	9,896	17,052
North Carolina	50,722	6,375	3,473	5,302	4,701	1,106	2,863	4,083	9,014	4,092	9,713
North Dakota	5,679	493	224	225	377	126	454	572	1,122	787	1,299
Ohio	66,736	8,826	3,411	5,684	4,803	1,352	4,375	5,586	13,314	8,460	10,925
Oklahoma	19,846	3,554	905	1,041	1,382	424	1,341	1,748	4,183	1,712	3,556
Oregon	21,114	4,628	1,413	2,869	1,535	408	1,100	600	3,352	1,645	3,564
Pennsylvania	90,669	14,279	5,220	8,531	7,962	2,655	5,608	6,308	17,248	9,654	13,204
Rhode Island	11,014	1,548	569	1,001	843	258	443	488	2,866	625	2,373
South Carolina	22,973	3,151	1,332	2,328	2,463	361	1,031	1,915	5,519	1,620	3,253
South Dakota	5,392	560	235	402	421	186	428	475	779	875	1,031
Tennessee	32,309	6,026	1,864	2,735	2,289	593	1,618	2,529	5,971	3,149	5,535
Texas	111,324	23,326	5,905	8,871	8,993	2,030	6,835	2,130	22,700	10,217	20,317
Utah	26,554	3,316	1,287	2,371	1,801	1,311	1,299	3,008	4,744	3,313	4,104
Vermont	6,283	1,450	422	871	557	180	266	282	813	333	1,109
Virginia	52,998	11,000	4,018	6,605	4,308	2,274	2,859	1,336	10,081	3,633	6,884
Washington	32,376	7,272	1,843	4,517	3,055	849	1,745	1,393	5,237	2,072	4,393
West Virginia	13,284	2,980	554	1,122	771	399	719	848	2,189	919	2,783
Wisconsin	36,002	5,283	1,725	3,327	3,474	776	1,978	2,767	7,484	3,225	5,963
Wyoming	2,064	209	136	156	194	18	201	278	249	212	411
U.S. Service Academies	3,665	479	25	816	471	104	1,309	0	196	0	265
Other jurisdictions	20,358	1,020	927	750	1,711	650	1,378	2,269	5,586	3,116	2,951
American Samoa	2	0	0	0	0	0	0	2	0	0	0
Guam	408	59	15	18	21	11	0	78	80	33	93
Northern Marianas	14	0	0	0	0	0	0	14	0	0	0
Puerto Rico	19,697	951	889	723	1,659	629	1,378	2,145	5,406	3,070	2,847
U.S. Virgin Islands	237	10	23	9	31	10	0	30	100	13	11

[1]Includes degrees in area, ethnic, cultural, and gender studies; English language and literature/letters; foreign languages, literatures, and linguistics; liberal arts and sciences, general studies and humanities; multi/interdisciplinary studies; philosophy and religious studies; theology and religious vocations; and visual and performing arts.
[2]Includes biological and biomedical sciences; physical sciences; science technologies/technicians; and mathematics and statistics.
[3]Includes engineering; engineering technologies/technicians; mechanic and repair technologies/technicians; and construction trades.
[4]Includes agriculture, agricultural operations, and related sciences; natural resources and conservation; architecture and related services; communication, journalism, and related programs; communications technologies/technicians and support services; family and consumer sciences/human sciences; legal professions and studies; library science; military technologies and applied sciences; parks, recreation, leisure, and fitness studies; homeland security, law enforcement, and firefighting; public administration and social service professions; transportation and materials moving; and not classified by field of study.
NOTE: Data are for postsecondary institutions participating in Title IV federal financial aid programs. This table includes only those jurisdictions with 4-year institutions.
SOURCE: U.S. Department of Education, National Center for Education Statistics, Integrated Postsecondary Education Data System (IPEDS), Fall 2012, Completions component. (This table was prepared August 2013.)

Master's degrees conferred by postsecondary institutions, by field of study and state or jurisdiction: 2011–12

State or jurisdiction	Total	Humanities[1]	Psychology	Social sciences and history	Natural sciences[2]	Computer sciences	Engineering[3]	Education	Business/ management	Health professions and related programs	Other fields[4]
1	2	3	4	5	6	7	8	9	10	11	12
United States	754,229	59,979	26,834	21,889	25,570	20,917	45,097	178,062	191,571	83,893	100,417
Alabama	11,402	386	384	225	241	163	901	2,860	3,074	1,540	1,628
Alaska	703	52	37	14	35	7	69	296	82	15	96
Arizona	36,178	757	2,512	234	388	425	800	10,707	13,728	4,168	2,459
Arkansas	5,320	227	38	77	163	66	341	2,510	695	577	626
California	68,502	7,588	4,038	2,142	2,349	2,161	6,282	12,821	14,724	7,325	9,072
Colorado	15,406	935	893	530	457	783	1,031	2,708	5,178	982	1,909
Connecticut	9,457	911	289	275	556	233	645	2,315	2,053	1,007	1,173
Delaware	2,680	83	41	62	112	38	62	822	921	216	323
District of Columbia	10,213	1,196	124	1,309	550	254	520	781	2,010	785	2,684
Florida	33,859	1,637	1,117	694	1,040	493	2,311	5,284	11,431	4,385	5,467
Georgia	17,790	1,729	259	417	639	501	1,110	3,950	4,880	2,391	1,914
Hawaii	2,115	200	160	76	79	25	73	507	497	159	339
Idaho	2,041	130	18	48	115	12	184	607	290	237	400
Illinois	43,638	3,077	1,793	1,076	1,499	1,657	2,019	10,006	13,038	3,856	5,617
Indiana	14,215	1,379	289	292	562	288	1,039	2,741	4,229	1,530	1,866
Iowa	12,100	564	232	73	207	396	327	3,133	4,566	1,352	1,250
Kansas	7,021	657	151	196	181	114	462	1,970	1,409	672	1,209
Kentucky	9,411	719	449	197	303	155	316	3,392	1,395	1,159	1,326
Louisiana	7,275	563	168	142	423	125	342	1,466	1,689	1,195	1,162
Maine	1,897	151	27	7	29	3	34	792	243	342	269
Maryland	17,845	1,212	295	1,013	1,058	1,374	1,014	3,130	5,170	1,907	1,672
Massachusetts	35,955	3,107	980	1,442	1,110	929	2,149	7,969	9,782	3,377	5,110
Michigan	21,392	1,240	446	452	898	566	2,097	4,542	5,599	2,167	3,385
Minnesota	20,609	937	1,403	173	348	587	527	5,904	4,212	3,849	2,669
Mississippi	4,809	184	85	93	475	49	150	1,771	838	529	635
Missouri	20,979	1,189	792	589	445	390	843	4,204	7,717	2,380	2,430
Montana	1,286	116	35	55	76	9	75	368	116	127	309
Nebraska	5,178	277	109	282	189	138	171	1,668	1,162	579	603
Nevada	2,604	112	41	79	83	40	112	913	599	360	265
New Hampshire	3,825	135	32	69	75	86	172	1,063	1,451	418	324
New Jersey	15,490	1,409	473	357	708	678	1,474	3,569	3,327	1,584	1,911
New Mexico	3,259	309	66	135	159	43	279	865	680	438	285
New York	71,406	7,647	2,025	2,770	2,581	2,359	3,708	18,432	13,296	6,988	11,600
North Carolina	16,948	1,293	174	537	657	613	1,179	3,591	4,219	2,274	2,411
North Dakota	1,725	42	43	26	56	33	73	336	328	513	275
Ohio	24,148	2,031	657	663	950	313	1,619	5,928	5,858	3,169	2,960
Oklahoma	6,481	795	236	133	227	165	594	1,280	1,618	625	808
Oregon	7,541	759	242	143	268	77	372	2,759	1,329	801	791
Pennsylvania	36,785	2,781	1,286	860	1,197	1,275	2,407	9,758	7,550	5,001	4,670
Rhode Island	2,566	251	87	117	170	57	113	518	713	128	412
South Carolina	5,972	476	131	111	245	54	367	1,779	1,300	688	821
South Dakota	1,467	80	77	28	66	68	126	334	328	181	179
Tennessee	11,929	948	395	223	328	106	425	3,474	2,942	1,843	1,245
Texas	45,307	3,775	1,416	1,133	1,784	1,620	3,329	10,594	11,729	4,516	5,411
Utah	7,669	316	186	125	191	194	374	2,038	2,506	908	831
Vermont	2,474	585	63	471	37	67	57	405	356	121	312
Virginia	21,516	2,856	1,144	616	468	766	1,120	5,026	4,835	1,729	2,956
Washington	9,595	735	486	156	346	167	490	2,290	2,217	1,058	1,650
West Virginia	5,892	751	59	643	117	59	143	1,179	1,089	474	1,378
Wisconsin	9,856	621	344	287	288	131	606	2,615	2,530	1,218	1,216
Wyoming	489	69	7	22	42	5	55	92	43	50	104
U.S. Service Academies	9	0	0	0	0	0	9	0	0	0	0
Other jurisdictions	5,309	220	300	43	122	98	269	1,451	1,565	606	635
American Samoa	0	0	0	0	0	0	0	0	0	0	0
Guam	132	8	3	0	3	0	0	84	15	0	19
Northern Marianas	0	0	0	0	0	0	0	0	0	0	0
Puerto Rico	5,124	212	297	43	119	98	269	1,338	1,542	606	600
U.S. Virgin Islands	53	0	0	0	0	0	0	29	8	0	16

[1]Includes degrees in area, ethnic, cultural, and gender studies; English language and literature/letters; foreign languages, literatures, and linguistics; liberal arts and sciences, general studies and humanities; multi/interdisciplinary studies; philosophy and religious studies; theology and religious vocations; and visual and performing arts.
[2]Includes biological and biomedical sciences; physical sciences; science technologies/technicians; and mathematics and statistics.
[3]Includes engineering; engineering technologies/technicians; mechanic and repair technologies/technicians; and construction trades.
[4]Includes agriculture, agricultural operations, and related sciences; natural resources and conservation; architecture and related services; communication, journalism, and related programs; communications technologies/technicians and support services; family and consumer services/human sciences; legal professions and studies; library science; military technologies and applied sciences; parks, recreation, leisure, and fitness studies; homeland security, law enforcement, and firefighting; public administration and social service professions; transportation and materials moving; and not classified by field of study.

NOTE: Data are for postsecondary institutions participating in Title IV federal financial aid programs. This table includes only those jurisdictions with 4-year institutions.

SOURCE: U.S. Department of Education, National Center for Education Statistics, Integrated Postsecondary Education Data System (IPEDS), Fall 2012, Completions component. (This table was prepared August 2013.)

Certificates below the associate's degree level conferred by postsecondary institutions, by length of curriculum, sex of student, institution level and control, and discipline division: 2011–12

Discipline division	Less-than-1-year awards								1- to less-than-4-year awards							
	Total	Sex Males	Sex Females	Non-degree-granting (less-than-2-year)	Degree-granting (2-year and 4-year)	Public	Nonprofit	For-profit	Total	Sex Males	Sex Females	Non-degree-granting (less-than-2-year)	Degree-granting (2-year and 4-year)	Public	Nonprofit	For-profit
1	2	3	4	5	6	7	8	9	10	11	12	13	14	15	16	17
Total	463,849	194,832	269,017	125,908	337,941	306,815	13,772	143,262	523,866	178,652	345,214	223,633	300,233	217,571	19,100	287,195
Agriculture and natural resources	3,380	2,366	1,014	150	3,230	3,274	23	83	2,397	1,516	881	130	2,267	2,226	99	72
Agriculture, agriculture operations, and related sciences	2,442	1,564	878	150	2,292	2,345	16	81	2,247	1,405	842	130	2,117	2,091	84	72
Natural resources and conservation	938	802	136	0	938	929	7	2	150	111	39	0	150	135	15	0
Architecture and related services	196	121	75	0	196	148	47	1	127	64	63	10	117	110	17	0
Area, ethnic, cultural, gender, and group studies	461	124	337	0	461	432	29	0	87	32	55	0	87	83	4	0
Biological and biomedical sciences	115	55	60	13	102	100	5	10	102	34	68	47	55	88	1	13
Business, management, marketing, and support services	44,223	13,667	30,556	3,912	40,311	39,323	1,244	3,656	23,566	6,330	17,236	4,126	19,440	19,316	1,448	2,802
Accounting and related services	9,259	2,310	6,949	792	8,467	8,058	106	1,095	5,576	1,388	4,188	933	4,643	4,567	481	528
Business/commerce, general	1,925	978	947	4	1,921	1,718	182	25	1,548	809	739	11	1,537	1,502	1	45
Business administration, management, and operations	7,539	2,841	4,698	49	7,490	7,118	266	155	2,967	1,019	1,948	99	2,868	2,775	35	157
Management information systems and services	676	392	284	302	374	378	53	245	509	313	196	180	329	496	0	13
Business operations support and assistant services	12,316	2,375	9,941	1,965	10,351	10,743	103	1,470	8,785	1,284	7,501	2,170	6,615	6,613	532	1,640
Business and management, other	12,508	4,771	7,737	800	11,708	11,308	534	666	4,181	1,517	2,664	733	3,448	3,363	399	419
Communication, journalism, and related programs	1,735	905	830	798	937	895	73	767	1,257	746	511	769	488	309	158	790
Communications technologies	2,537	1,620	917	821	1,716	1,603	26	908	2,988	2,253	735	1,844	1,144	1,384	27	1,577
Computer and information sciences and support services	16,930	11,680	5,250	2,240	14,690	13,824	209	2,897	9,326	7,111	2,215	2,227	7,099	6,012	446	2,868
Construction trades	10,885	10,384	501	2,101	8,784	9,538	650	697	14,430	13,714	716	4,229	10,201	8,790	618	5,022
Education	5,197	807	4,390	102	5,095	4,121	309	767	3,160	374	2,786	407	2,753	2,123	572	465
Engineering	456	343	113	61	395	455	1	0	226	199	27	66	160	177	28	21
Engineering technologies and engineering-related fields	15,984	13,851	2,133	2,612	13,372	13,555	99	2,330	15,920	14,432	1,488	4,085	11,835	7,670	410	7,840
English language and literature/letters	1,595	567	1,028	610	985	559	635	401	330	105	225	65	265	101	18	211
Family and consumer sciences/human sciences	13,579	1,551	12,028	1,115	12,464	13,433	50	96	3,354	242	3,112	273	3,081	3,319	35	0
Foreign languages, literatures, and linguistics	1,043	218	825	0	1,043	927	83	33	623	98	525	5	618	599	24	0
Health professions and related programs	189,739	35,918	153,821	61,307	128,432	100,631	6,468	82,640	227,547	32,743	194,804	86,998	140,549	73,762	10,018	143,767
Dental assisting	8,136	790	7,346	2,888	5,248	1,438	278	6,420	15,623	1,557	14,066	5,107	10,516	4,228	42	11,353
Emergency medical technician (EMT paramedic)	16,166	10,778	5,388	1,362	14,804	15,818	57	291	4,830	1,169	3,661	442	4,388	4,240	239	351
Medical lab technician	13,257	2,406	10,851	3,051	10,206	9,071	275	3,911	4,955	1,313	3,642	1,465	3,490	2,903	515	1,537
Medical assisting	45,230	7,214	38,016	17,638	27,592	8,948	2,927	33,355	84,434	10,254	74,180	36,152	48,282	9,424	2,020	72,990
Nursing assisting	45,078	5,907	39,171	11,359	33,719	38,066	807	6,205	874	90	784	203	671	358	41	475
Practical nursing	5,878	701	5,177	466	5,412	5,454	31	393	56,797	7,048	49,749	19,097	37,700	36,882	2,256	17,659
Nursing, R.N. and other	1,851	207	1,644	31	1,820	1,695	2	154	3,948	525	3,423	2,298	1,650	1,301	2,404	243
Health sciences, other	54,143	7,915	46,228	24,512	29,631	20,141	2,091	31,911	56,086	8,295	47,791	22,234	33,852	14,426	2,501	39,159
Homeland security, law enforcement, and firefighting	23,308	17,844	5,464	3,093	20,215	21,922	373	1,013	6,280	4,104	2,176	299	5,981	5,336	157	787
Criminal justice and corrections	15,699	11,021	4,678	1,227	14,472	15,217	304	178	4,963	2,965	1,998	289	4,674	4,154	37	772
Fire control and safety	6,499	6,049	450	1,498	5,001	6,469	15	15	1,136	1,052	84	10	1,126	1,136	0	0
Homeland security and related protective services, other	1,110	774	336	368	742	236	54	820	181	87	94	0	181	46	120	15
Legal professions and studies	2,221	339	1,882	256	1,965	1,474	76	671	3,252	518	2,734	596	2,656	2,304	205	743
Liberal arts and sciences, general studies, and humanities	5,736	2,138	3,598	0	5,736	5,732	4	0	28,029	11,183	16,846	0	28,029	28,022	7	0
Library science	221	34	187	0	221	221	0	0	127	8	119	0	127	123	4	0
Mathematics and statistics	39	35	4	4	35	30	9	0	13	9	4	13	0	11	2	0
Mechanic and repair technologies/technicians	33,741	31,773	1,968	4,499	29,242	30,196	660	2,885	52,053	49,994	2,059	25,211	26,842	21,607	805	29,641
Military technologies and applied sciences	39	33	6	6	33	27	0	12	13	3	10	10	3	3	0	10
Multi/interdisciplinary studies	1,315	538	777	14	1,301	830	62	423	1,080	512	568	0	1,080	1,044	36	0
Parks, recreation, leisure, and fitness studies	836	448	388	203	633	499	30	307	816	482	334	231	585	349	0	467
Personal and culinary services	39,649	7,159	32,490	27,846	11,803	8,546	310	30,793	100,077	13,165	86,912	85,038	15,039	14,112	1,241	84,724
Philosophy and religious studies	67	32	35	35	32	50	17	0	38	19	19	0	38	0	38	0

See notes at end of table.

Certificates below the associate's degree level conferred by postsecondary institutions, by length of curriculum, sex of student, institution level and control, and discipline division: 2011–12—Continued

| Discipline division | Less-than-1-year awards | | | | | | | | 1- to less-than-4-year awards | | | | | | | |
| | Sex | | | Institution level | | Institution control | | | Sex | | | Institution level | | Institution control | | |
	Total	Males	Females	Non-degree-granting (less-than-2-year)	Degree-granting (2-year and 4-year)	Public	Nonprofit	For-profit	Total	Males	Females	Non-degree-granting (less-than-2-year)	Degree-granting (2-year and 4-year)	Public	Nonprofit	For-profit
1	2	3	4	5	6	7	8	9	10	11	12	13	14	15	16	17
Physical sciences and science technologies	558	421	137	108	450	468	0	90	497	362	135	3	494	488	0	17
Physical sciences	42	30	12	0	42	42	0	0	17	13	4	0	17	17	0	0
Science technologies/technicians	516	391	125	108	408	426	0	90	480	349	131	3	477	471	0	9
Precision production	15,380	14,620	760	2,011	13,369	14,135	531	714	13,059	12,430	629	4,090	8,969	9,515	635	2,909
Psychology	23	9	14	0	23	17	6	0	84	15	69	0	84	77	7	0
Public administration and social services	1,275	264	1,011	8	1,267	1,208	67	0	687	123	564	0	687	679	8	0
Social sciences and history	726	428	298	0	726	651	75	0	373	204	169	0	373	325	48	0
Social sciences	700	421	279	0	700	627	73	0	371	204	167	0	371	324	47	0
History	26	7	19	0	26	24	2	0	2	0	2	0	2	1	1	0
Theology and religious vocations	146	64	82	0	146	4	142	0	1,153	545	608	670	483	0	1,153	0
Transportation and materials moving	23,686	21,641	2,045	9,869	13,817	14,755	771	8,160	824	766	58	313	511	571	20	233
Visual and performing arts	6,828	2,835	3,993	2,159	4,669	3,232	688	2,908	9,981	4,217	5,764	1,901	8,080	6,936	811	2,234
Fine and studio arts	841	298	543	714	127	123	526	192	4,722	1,781	2,941	9	4,713	4,700	22	0
Music and dance	473	371	102	0	473	226	3	244	713	521	192	200	513	159	179	375
Visual and performing arts, other[2]	5,514	2,166	3,348	1,445	4,069	2,883	159	2,472	4,546	1,915	2,631	1,692	2,854	2,077	610	1,859

[1]Excludes "Construction trades" and "Mechanic and repair technologies/technicians," which are listed separately.
[2]Includes design and applied arts, drama and theatre arts, film and photographic arts, and all other arts not included under "Fine and studio arts" or "Music and dance."

NOTE: Data are for postsecondary institutions participating in Title IV federal financial aid programs. Degree-granting institutions grant degrees at the associate's or higher level, while non-degree-granting institutions grant only awards below that level.
SOURCE: U.S. Department of Education, National Center for Education Statistics, Integrated Postsecondary Education Data System (IPEDS), Fall 2012, Completions component. (This table was prepared October 2013.)

Certificates below the associate's degree level conferred by postsecondary institutions, by race/ethnicity and sex of student: 1998–99 through 2011–12

Year and sex	Number of certificates conferred to U.S. citizens and nonresident aliens								Percentage distribution of certificates conferred to U.S. citizens						
	Total	White	Black	Hispanic	Asian/ Pacific Islander	American Indian/ Alaska Native	Two or more races	Non-resident alien	Total	White	Black	Hispanic	Asian/ Pacific Islander	American Indian/ Alaska Native	Two or more races
1	2	3	4	5	6	7	8	9	10	11	12	13	14	15	16
Total															
1998–99	555,883	345,359	92,800	76,833	27,920	7,510	—	5,461	100.0	62.7	16.9	14.0	5.1	1.4	—
1999–2000	558,129	337,546	97,329	81,132	29,361	6,966	—	5,795	100.0	61.1	17.6	14.7	5.3	1.3	—
2000–01	552,503	333,478	99,397	78,528	28,123	6,598	—	6,379	100.0	61.1	18.2	14.4	5.1	1.2	—
2001–02	584,248	352,559	106,647	83,950	27,490	7,430	—	6,172	100.0	61.0	18.4	14.5	4.8	1.3	—
2002–03	646,425	382,289	120,582	95,499	32,981	8,117	—	6,957	100.0	59.8	18.9	14.9	5.2	1.3	—
2003–04	687,787	402,989	129,891	107,216	32,819	8,375	—	6,497	100.0	59.2	19.1	15.7	4.8	1.2	—
2004–05	710,873	415,670	133,601	114,089	32,783	8,150	—	6,580	100.0	59.0	19.0	16.2	4.7	1.2	—
2005–06	715,401	412,077	135,460	118,853	34,110	8,400	—	6,501	100.0	58.1	19.1	16.8	4.8	1.2	—
2006–07	729,037	420,585	139,995	119,501	32,962	8,793	—	7,201	100.0	58.3	19.4	16.6	4.6	1.2	—
2007–08	749,883	430,187	145,181	122,676	35,985	8,596	—	7,258	100.0	57.9	19.5	16.5	4.8	1.2	—
2008–09	805,755	451,107	161,954	138,550	37,804	9,510	—	6,830	100.0	56.5	20.3	17.3	4.7	1.2	—
2009–10	935,789	511,270	191,646	171,874	41,404	12,125	—	7,470	100.0	55.1	20.6	18.5	4.5	1.3	—
2010–11	1,029,557	557,163	207,389	186,943	44,431	11,194	15,142	7,295	100.0	54.5	20.3	18.3	4.3	1.1	1.5
2011–12	987,715	534,931	190,120	186,738	42,985	10,608	14,114	8,219	100.0	54.6	19.4	19.1	4.4	1.1	1.4
Males															
1998–99	219,872	144,735	29,875	27,719	11,742	3,061	—	2,740	100.0	66.7	13.8	12.8	5.4	1.4	—
1999–2000	226,110	143,634	33,792	30,337	13,082	2,862	—	2,403	100.0	64.2	15.1	13.6	5.8	1.3	—
2000–01	223,951	143,144	34,381	28,685	12,072	2,719	—	2,950	100.0	64.8	15.6	13.0	5.5	1.2	—
2001–02	235,275	152,226	36,482	29,749	10,938	3,226	—	2,654	100.0	65.4	15.7	12.8	4.7	1.4	—
2002–03	254,238	161,001	40,080	33,925	12,930	3,506	—	2,796	100.0	64.0	15.9	13.5	5.1	1.4	—
2003–04	257,138	161,684	40,809	36,157	12,713	3,135	—	2,640	100.0	63.5	16.0	14.2	5.0	1.2	—
2004–05	259,261	161,126	41,644	38,297	12,448	3,068	—	2,678	100.0	62.8	16.2	14.9	4.9	1.2	—
2005–06	259,737	158,747	41,863	40,752	12,790	3,219	—	2,366	100.0	61.7	16.3	15.8	5.0	1.3	—
2006–07	269,589	164,939	44,870	40,958	12,622	3,527	—	2,673	100.0	61.8	16.8	15.3	4.7	1.3	—
2007–08	283,266	172,398	48,024	43,085	13,527	3,452	—	2,780	100.0	61.5	17.1	15.4	4.8	1.2	—
2008–09	302,615	179,968	53,948	47,876	14,354	3,862	—	2,607	100.0	60.0	18.0	16.0	4.8	1.3	—
2009–10	355,380	205,335	65,492	60,820	15,933	5,079	—	2,721	100.0	58.2	18.6	17.2	4.5	1.4	—
2010–11	391,683	223,759	71,853	66,374	16,997	4,761	4,982	2,957	100.0	57.6	18.5	17.1	4.4	1.2	1.3
2011–12	373,484	213,520	65,143	65,744	16,154	4,497	4,940	3,486	100.0	57.7	17.6	17.8	4.4	1.2	1.3
Females															
1998–99	336,011	200,624	62,925	49,114	16,178	4,449	—	2,721	100.0	60.2	18.9	14.7	4.9	1.3	—
1999–2000	332,019	193,912	63,537	50,795	16,279	4,104	—	3,392	100.0	59.0	19.3	15.5	5.0	1.2	—
2000–01	328,552	190,334	65,016	49,843	16,051	3,879	—	3,429	100.0	58.5	20.0	15.3	4.9	1.2	—
2001–02	348,973	200,333	70,165	54,201	16,552	4,204	—	3,518	100.0	58.0	20.3	15.7	4.8	1.2	—
2002–03	392,187	221,288	80,502	61,574	20,051	4,611	—	4,161	100.0	57.0	20.7	15.9	5.2	1.2	—
2003–04	430,649	241,305	89,082	71,059	20,106	5,240	—	3,857	100.0	56.5	20.9	16.6	4.7	1.2	—
2004–05	451,612	254,544	91,957	75,792	20,335	5,082	—	3,902	100.0	56.9	20.5	16.9	4.5	1.1	—
2005–06	455,664	253,330	93,597	78,101	21,320	5,181	—	4,135	100.0	56.1	20.7	17.3	4.7	1.1	—
2006–07	459,448	255,646	95,125	78,543	20,340	5,266	—	4,528	100.0	56.2	20.9	17.3	4.5	1.2	—
2007–08	466,617	257,789	97,157	79,591	22,458	5,144	—	4,478	100.0	55.8	21.0	17.2	4.9	1.1	—
2008–09	503,140	271,139	108,006	90,674	23,450	5,648	—	4,223	100.0	54.3	21.6	18.2	4.7	1.1	—
2009–10	580,409	305,935	126,154	111,054	25,471	7,046	—	4,749	100.0	53.1	21.9	19.3	4.4	1.2	—
2010–11	637,874	333,404	135,536	120,569	27,434	6,433	10,160	4,338	100.0	52.6	21.4	19.0	4.3	1.0	1.6
2011–12	614,231	321,411	124,977	120,994	26,831	6,111	9,174	4,733	100.0	52.7	20.5	19.9	4.4	1.0	1.5

—Not available.
NOTE: Includes less-than-1-year awards and 1- to less-than-4-year awards (excluding associate's degrees) conferred by postsecondary institutions participating in Title IV federal financial aid programs. Race categories exclude persons of Hispanic ethnicity. Reported racial/ethnic distributions of students by level of degree, field of degree, and sex were used to estimate race/ethnicity for students whose race/ethnicity was not reported. Detail may not sum to totals because of rounding.
SOURCE: U.S. Department of Education, National Center for Education Statistics, Integrated Postsecondary Education Data System (IPEDS), "Completions Survey" (IPEDS-C:99); and IPEDS Fall 2000 through Fall 2012, Completions component. (This table was prepared July 2013.)

Associate's degrees conferred by postsecondary institutions, by sex of student and discipline division: 2001–02 through 2011–12

Discipline division	2001–02	2002–03	2003–04	2004–05	2005–06	2006–07	2007–08	2008–09	2009–10	2010–11	2011–12 Total	2011–12 Males	2011–12 Females
1	2	3	4	5	6	7	8	9	10	11	12	13	14
Total	595,133	634,016	665,301	696,660	713,066	728,114	750,164	787,325	849,452	942,327	1,017,538	391,990	625,548
Agriculture and natural resources	6,494	6,210	6,283	6,404	6,168	5,838	5,738	5,724	5,894	6,425	7,066	4,606	2,460
Agriculture, agriculture operations, and related sciences	5,125	4,892	4,959	5,137	4,958	4,638	4,554	4,525	4,615	4,920	5,398	3,356	2,042
Natural resources and conservation	1,369	1,318	1,324	1,267	1,210	1,200	1,184	1,199	1,279	1,505	1,668	1,250	418
Architecture and related services	443	440	492	583	656	517	568	596	552	569	593	332	261
Area, ethnic, cultural, gender, and group studies	94	120	105	115	124	164	169	173	199	209	194	62	132
Biological and biomedical sciences	1,534	1,496	1,456	1,709	1,827	2,060	2,200	2,364	2,664	3,245	3,834	1,280	2,554
Business, management, marketing, and support services	86,713	89,627	92,065	96,067	96,933	99,998	104,566	111,521	116,904	121,728	121,972	42,916	79,056
Accounting and related services	12,315	13,229	14,506	13,988	13,620	14,232	15,965	16,731	17,994	20,179	20,142	5,023	15,119
Business/commerce, general	12,936	13,054	13,387	12,050	13,297	12,725	12,473	13,067	14,547	15,083	17,303	7,157	10,146
Business administration, management, and operations	26,890	28,943	31,522	37,258	39,152	43,667	47,911	52,938	46,137	46,249	45,248	18,629	26,619
Management information systems and services	6,417	5,600	4,214	2,812	2,179	2,007	1,237	1,103	1,221	1,244	1,017	671	346
Business operations support and assistant services	11,508	11,524	11,400	11,196	10,044	8,864	7,841	7,549	7,388	8,257	8,950	877	8,073
Business and management, other	16,647	17,277	17,036	18,763	18,641	18,503	19,139	20,133	29,617	30,716	29,312	10,559	18,753
Communication, journalism, and related programs	2,819	2,589	2,444	2,545	2,629	2,609	2,620	2,722	2,839	3,051	3,495	1,625	1,870
Communications technologies	3,006	3,304	3,401	3,516	3,380	3,095	4,237	4,803	4,419	4,209	5,000	3,429	1,571
Computer and information sciences and support services	40,127	46,234	41,845	36,173	31,246	27,712	28,296	30,030	32,466	37,677	41,161	32,290	8,871
Construction trades	2,639	3,009	3,560	3,512	3,850	3,895	4,309	4,252	4,617	5,402	5,752	5,483	269
Education	9,611	11,205	12,465	13,329	14,475	13,021	13,108	14,123	17,048	20,459	20,531	2,633	17,898
Engineering	1,681	2,166	2,726	2,430	2,154	2,128	2,279	2,177	2,508	2,825	3,382	2,931	451
Engineering technologies and engineering-related fields[1]	40,217	39,998	36,915	33,548	30,461	29,199	29,334	30,434	31,850	35,521	36,510	32,224	4,286
English language and literature/letters	864	896	828	995	1,105	1,249	1,402	1,525	1,658	2,019	2,137	708	1,429
Family and consumer sciences/human sciences	9,208	9,496	9,478	9,707	9,488	9,124	8,613	9,020	9,573	8,532	9,503	369	9,134
Foreign languages, literatures, and linguistics	1,085	1,050	1,047	1,234	1,161	1,207	1,258	1,627	1,683	1,876	1,980	417	1,563
Health professions and related programs	82,361	90,716	106,208	122,520	134,931	145,436	155,816	165,163	177,686	201,831	218,041	34,018	184,023
Dental assisting	5,237	5,498	5,652	5,813	6,085	6,313	6,642	6,633	7,063	7,481	7,790	359	7,431
Emergency medical technician (EMT paramedic)	1,203	1,410	1,617	1,825	1,980	2,008	2,140	2,270	2,412	2,895	3,352	2,366	986
Medical lab technician	5,134	5,146	5,571	6,346	6,411	7,171	6,617	6,822	7,798	9,334	10,949	2,451	8,498
Medical assisting	11,102	11,920	15,543	19,005	22,267	23,491	24,276	25,981	29,985	39,232	46,598	6,252	40,346
Nursing assisting	0	8	38	38	101	158	329	385	1	38	36	4	32
Practical nursing	814	916	1,049	1,388	1,481	1,509	1,417	1,299	1,999	2,069	2,081	220	1,861
Nursing, R.N. and other	40,800	45,117	51,552	58,007	62,095	66,516	73,277	77,929	81,277	83,021	84,379	11,974	72,405
Health sciences, other	18,071	20,701	25,220	30,098	34,511	38,270	41,118	43,844	47,151	57,761	62,856	10,392	52,464
Homeland security, law enforcement, and firefighting	16,689	18,614	20,573	23,749	26,425	28,208	29,590	33,033	37,260	44,923	50,695	27,045	23,650
Criminal justice and corrections	13,603	15,155	17,040	19,942	22,351	23,917	25,588	28,996	32,754	40,023	45,525	22,352	23,173
Fire control and safety	2,619	2,941	3,012	3,366	3,554	3,811	3,937	3,970	4,307	4,603	4,602	4,300	302
Homeland security and related protective services, other	467	518	521	441	520	480	65	67	199	297	568	393	175
Legal professions and studies	7,815	8,412	9,466	9,885	10,509	10,391	9,465	9,062	10,003	11,620	12,182	1,679	10,503
Liberal arts and sciences, general studies, and humanities	207,163	217,361	227,650	240,131	244,689	250,030	254,012	263,853	284,775	306,670	336,554	129,179	207,375
Library science	96	87	114	108	136	84	117	116	131	112	160	19	140
Mathematics and statistics	685	732	801	807	753	827	855	930	1,051	1,644	1,529	1,050	479
Mechanic and repair technologies/technicians	12,063	12,028	12,553	13,619	14,454	15,432	15,297	16,066	16,305	19,969	20,714	19,709	1,005
Military technologies and applied sciences	62	85	293	355	610	781	851	721	668	856	986	770	216
Multi/interdisciplinary studies	13,205	14,067	14,794	13,888	14,473	15,838	16,255	15,459	17,671	23,729	27,267	10,171	17,096
Parks, recreation, leisure, and fitness studies	764	805	923	966	1,128	1,251	1,344	1,587	2,016	2,366	3,123	1,998	1,125
Personal and culinary services	9,325	12,607	14,239	16,311	17,162	16,103	16,592	16,327	16,467	18,258	20,366	9,103	11,263
Philosophy and religious studies	359	379	404	422	367	375	458	191	256	283	308	181	127
Physical sciences and science technologies	2,318	2,201	2,687	2,825	2,910	3,412	3,395	3,621	4,140	5,078	5,824	3,404	2,420
Physical sciences	1,356	1,152	1,599	1,637	1,741	2,023	1,980	2,194	2,378	3,148	3,652	2,072	1,580
Science technologies/technicians	962	1,049	1,088	1,188	1,169	1,389	1,415	1,427	1,762	1,930	2,172	1,332	840
Precision production	2,260	2,287	1,968	2,039	1,977	1,973	1,968	2,126	2,787	3,254	3,320	3,118	202
Psychology	1,705	1,785	1,887	1,942	1,944	2,213	2,412	3,949	6,582	3,866	4,717	1,093	3,624
Public administration and social services	3,323	3,534	3,728	4,027	4,415	4,338	4,192	4,178	4,526	7,472	9,143	1,382	7,761
Social sciences and history	5,593	5,720	6,245	6,533	6,730	7,080	7,812	9,142	10,649	12,767	14,132	5,139	8,993
Social sciences	5,304	5,404	5,875	6,233	6,308	6,673	7,358	8,657	10,108	12,067	13,321	4,650	8,671
History	289	316	370	300	422	407	454	485	541	700	811	489	322
Theology and religious vocations	414	425	492	581	570	608	582	675	613	758	839	423	416
Transportation and materials moving	1,122	1,211	1,217	1,435	1,472	1,674	1,550	1,430	1,444	1,697	2,098	1,782	316
Visual and performing arts	20,911	23,120	23,949	22,650	21,754	20,244	18,890	18,629	19,567	21,379	22,431	9,422	13,009
Fine and studio arts	1,518	1,760	1,450	1,614	1,638	1,753	1,705	2,015	2,277	2,405	2,341	746	1,595
Music and dance	1,637	2,093	2,584	2,333	2,389	2,290	1,317	1,151	1,335	1,356	1,683	1,084	599
Visual and performing arts, other[2]	17,756	19,267	19,915	18,703	17,727	16,201	15,868	15,463	15,955	17,618	18,407	7,592	10,815
Not classified by field of study	365	0	0	0	0	0	14	0	0	0	0	0	0

[1]Excludes "Construction trades" and "Mechanic and repair technologies/technicians," which are listed separately.

[2]Includes design and applied arts, drama and theatre arts, film and photographic arts, and all other arts not included under "Fine and studio arts" or "Music and dance."

NOTE: Data are for postsecondary institutions participating in Title IV federal financial aid programs.

SOURCE: U.S. Department of Education, National Center for Education Statistics, Integrated Postsecondary Education Data System (IPEDS), "Completions Survey" (IPEDS-C:98–99); and IPEDS Fall 2002 through Fall 2012, Completions component. (This table was prepared July 2013.)

Associate's degrees conferred by postsecondary institutions, by race/ethnicity and sex of student: Selected years, 1976–77 through 2011–12

Year and sex	Number of degrees conferred to U.S. citizens and nonresident aliens								Percentage distribution of degrees conferred to U.S. citizens						
	Total	White	Black	Hispanic	Asian/ Pacific Islander	American Indian/ Alaska Native	Two or more races	Non-resident alien	Total	White	Black	Hispanic	Asian/ Pacific Islander	American Indian/ Alaska Native	Two or more races
1	2	3	4	5	6	7	8	9	10	11	12	13	14	15	16
Total															
1976–77[1]	404,956	342,290	33,159	16,636	7,044	2,498	—	3,329	100.0	85.2	8.3	4.1	1.8	0.6	—
1980–81[2]	410,174	339,167	35,330	17,800	8,650	2,584	—	6,643	100.0	84.0	8.8	4.4	2.1	0.6	—
1990–91	481,720	391,264	38,835	25,540	15,257	3,871	—	6,953	100.0	82.4	8.2	5.4	3.2	0.8	—
1995–96	555,216	426,106	52,014	38,254	23,138	5,573	—	10,131	100.0	78.2	9.5	7.0	4.2	1.0	—
1996–97	571,226	429,464	56,306	43,549	25,159	5,984	—	10,764	100.0	76.6	10.0	7.8	4.5	1.1	—
1997–98	558,555	413,561	55,314	45,876	25,196	6,246	—	12,362	100.0	75.7	10.1	8.4	4.6	1.1	—
1998–99	564,984	412,985	58,417	48,845	27,628	6,395	—	10,714	100.0	74.5	10.5	8.8	5.0	1.2	—
1999–2000	564,933	408,822	60,208	51,563	27,778	6,474	—	10,088	100.0	73.7	10.9	9.3	5.0	1.2	—
2000–01	578,865	411,075	63,855	57,288	28,463	6,623	—	11,561	100.0	72.5	11.3	10.1	5.0	1.2	—
2001–02	595,133	417,733	67,343	60,003	30,945	6,832	—	12,277	100.0	71.7	11.6	10.3	5.3	1.2	—
2002–03	634,016	438,261	75,609	66,673	32,629	7,461	—	13,383	100.0	70.6	12.2	10.7	5.3	1.2	—
2003–04	665,301	456,047	81,183	72,270	33,149	8,119	—	14,533	100.0	70.1	12.5	11.1	5.1	1.2	—
2004–05	696,660	475,513	86,402	78,557	33,669	8,435	—	14,084	100.0	69.7	12.7	11.5	4.9	1.2	—
2005–06	713,066	485,297	89,784	80,854	35,201	8,552	—	13,378	100.0	69.4	12.8	11.6	5.0	1.2	—
2006–07	728,114	491,572	91,529	85,410	37,266	8,583	—	13,754	100.0	68.8	12.8	12.0	5.2	1.2	—
2007–08	750,164	501,079	95,702	91,274	38,843	8,849	—	14,417	100.0	68.1	13.0	12.4	5.3	1.2	—
2008–09	787,325	522,985	101,487	97,921	40,914	8,834	—	15,184	100.0	67.7	13.1	12.7	5.3	1.1	—
2009–10	849,452	552,863	113,905	112,211	44,021	10,337	—	16,115	100.0	66.3	13.7	13.5	5.3	1.2	—
2010–11	942,327	604,110	128,703	125,616	45,876	10,173	11,275	16,574	100.0	65.3	13.9	13.6	5.0	1.1	1.2
2011–12	1,017,538	632,802	141,886	151,621	48,707	10,711	14,759	17,052	100.0	63.2	14.2	15.2	4.9	1.1	1.5
Males															
1976–77[1]	209,672	178,236	15,330	9,105	3,630	1,216	—	2,155	100.0	85.9	7.4	4.4	1.7	0.6	—
1980–81[2]	183,819	151,242	14,290	8,327	4,557	1,108	—	4,295	100.0	84.2	8.0	4.6	2.5	0.6	—
1990–91	198,634	161,858	14,143	10,738	7,164	1,439	—	3,292	100.0	82.9	7.2	5.5	3.7	0.7	—
1995–96	219,514	169,230	17,941	15,740	10,229	1,993	—	4,381	100.0	78.7	8.3	7.3	4.8	0.9	—
1996–97	223,948	168,882	19,394	17,990	10,937	2,068	—	4,677	100.0	77.0	8.8	8.2	5.0	0.9	—
1997–98	217,613	161,212	18,686	19,108	10,953	2,252	—	5,402	100.0	76.0	8.8	9.0	5.2	1.1	—
1998–99	220,508	162,339	19,844	19,484	11,688	2,234	—	4,919	100.0	75.3	9.2	9.0	5.4	1.0	—
1999–2000	224,721	164,317	20,968	20,947	12,009	2,222	—	4,258	100.0	74.5	9.5	9.5	5.4	1.0	—
2000–01	231,645	166,322	22,147	23,350	12,339	2,294	—	5,193	100.0	73.4	9.8	10.3	5.4	1.0	—
2001–02	238,109	170,622	22,806	23,963	13,256	2,308	—	5,154	100.0	73.2	9.8	10.3	5.7	1.0	—
2002–03	253,451	179,163	25,591	26,461	14,057	2,618	—	5,561	100.0	72.3	10.3	10.7	5.7	1.1	—
2003–04	260,033	183,819	25,961	27,828	13,907	2,740	—	5,778	100.0	72.3	10.2	10.9	5.5	1.1	—
2004–05	267,536	188,569	27,151	29,658	13,802	2,774	—	5,582	100.0	72.0	10.4	11.3	5.3	1.1	—
2005–06	270,095	190,139	27,619	30,040	14,224	2,774	—	5,299	100.0	71.8	10.4	11.3	5.4	1.0	—
2006–07	275,187	191,565	28,273	31,646	15,510	2,873	—	5,320	100.0	71.0	10.5	11.7	5.7	1.1	—
2007–08	282,521	194,099	30,016	33,817	15,936	3,003	—	5,650	100.0	70.1	10.8	12.2	5.8	1.1	—
2008–09	298,141	203,086	31,994	36,739	17,156	3,074	—	6,092	100.0	69.5	11.0	12.6	5.9	1.1	—
2009–10	322,916	216,072	36,136	42,232	18,264	3,624	—	6,588	100.0	68.3	11.4	13.4	5.8	1.1	—
2010–11	361,309	238,078	41,596	47,682	19,181	3,724	4,257	6,791	100.0	67.2	11.7	13.4	5.4	1.0	1.2
2011–12	391,990	250,994	46,124	57,840	20,462	3,916	5,543	7,111	100.0	65.2	12.0	15.0	5.3	1.0	1.4
Females															
1976–77[1]	195,284	164,054	17,829	7,531	3,414	1,282	—	1,174	100.0	84.5	9.2	3.9	1.8	0.7	—
1980–81[2]	226,355	187,925	21,040	9,473	4,093	1,476	—	2,348	100.0	83.9	9.4	4.2	1.8	0.7	—
1990–91	283,086	229,406	24,692	14,802	8,093	2,432	—	3,661	100.0	82.1	8.8	5.3	2.9	0.9	—
1995–96	335,702	256,876	34,073	22,514	12,909	3,580	—	5,750	100.0	77.9	10.3	6.8	3.9	1.1	—
1996–97	347,278	260,582	36,912	25,559	14,222	3,916	—	6,087	100.0	76.4	10.8	7.5	4.2	1.1	—
1997–98	340,942	252,349	36,628	26,768	14,243	3,994	—	6,960	100.0	75.6	11.0	8.0	4.3	1.2	—
1998–99	344,476	250,646	38,573	29,361	15,940	4,161	—	5,795	100.0	74.0	11.4	8.7	4.7	1.2	—
1999–2000	340,212	244,505	39,240	30,616	15,769	4,252	—	5,830	100.0	73.1	11.7	9.2	4.7	1.3	—
2000–01	347,220	244,753	41,708	33,938	16,124	4,329	—	6,368	100.0	71.8	12.2	10.0	4.7	1.3	—
2001–02	357,024	247,111	44,537	36,040	17,689	4,524	—	7,123	100.0	70.6	12.7	10.3	5.1	1.3	—
2002–03	380,565	259,098	50,018	40,212	18,572	4,843	—	7,822	100.0	69.5	13.4	10.8	5.0	1.3	—
2003–04	405,268	272,228	55,222	44,442	19,242	5,379	—	8,755	100.0	68.7	13.9	11.2	4.9	1.4	—
2004–05	429,124	286,944	59,251	48,899	19,867	5,661	—	8,502	100.0	68.2	14.1	11.6	4.7	1.3	—
2005–06	442,971	295,158	62,165	50,814	20,977	5,778	—	8,079	100.0	67.9	14.3	11.7	4.8	1.3	—
2006–07	452,927	300,007	63,256	53,764	21,756	5,710	—	8,434	100.0	67.5	14.2	12.1	4.9	1.3	—
2007–08	467,643	306,980	65,686	57,457	22,907	5,846	—	8,767	100.0	66.9	14.3	12.5	5.0	1.3	—
2008–09	489,184	319,899	69,493	61,182	23,758	5,760	—	9,092	100.0	66.6	14.5	12.7	4.9	1.2	—
2009–10	526,536	336,791	77,769	69,979	25,757	6,713	—	9,527	100.0	65.1	15.0	13.5	5.0	1.3	—
2010–11	581,018	366,032	87,107	77,934	26,695	6,449	7,018	9,783	100.0	64.1	15.2	13.6	4.7	1.1	1.2
2011–12	625,548	381,808	95,762	93,781	28,245	6,795	9,216	9,941	100.0	62.0	15.6	15.2	4.6	1.1	1.5

—Not available.
[1]Excludes 1,170 males and 251 females whose racial/ethnic group was not available.
[2]Excludes 4,819 males and 1,384 females whose racial/ethnic group was not available.
NOTE: Data through 1990–91 are for institutions of higher education, while later data are for postsecondary institutions participating in Title IV federal financial aid programs. Race categories exclude persons of Hispanic ethnicity. For 1989–90 and later years, reported racial/ethnic distributions of students by level of degree, field of degree, and sex were used to estimate race/ethnicity for students whose race/ethnicity was not reported. Detail may not sum to totals because of rounding.
SOURCE: U.S. Department of Education, National Center for Education Statistics, Higher Education General Information Survey (HEGIS), "Degrees and Other Formal Awards Conferred" surveys, 1976–77 and 1980–81; Integrated Postsecondary Education Data System (IPEDS), "Completions Survey" (IPEDS-C:90–99); and IPEDS Fall 2000 through Fall 2012, Completions component. (This table was prepared July 2013.)

Associate's degrees conferred by postsecondary institutions, by race/ethnicity and field of study: 2010–11 and 2011–12

Field of study	2010–11				Asian/Pacific Islander			American Indian/ Alaska Native	Two or more races	Non-resident alien	2011–12				Asian/Pacific Islander			American Indian/ Alaska Native	Two or more races	Non-resident alien
	Total	White	Black	Hispanic	Total	Asian	Pacific Islander				Total	White	Black	Hispanic	Total	Asian	Pacific Islander			
1	2	3	4	5	6	7	8	9	10	11	12	13	14	15	16	17	18	19	20	21
All fields, total	942,327	604,110	128,703	125,616	45,876	41,474	4,402	10,173	11,275	16,574	1,017,538	632,802	141,886	151,621	48,707	44,829	3,878	10,711	14,759	17,052
Agriculture and natural resources	6,425	5,942	56	209	54	42	12	93	39	32	7,066	6,473	81	259	58	44	14	114	57	24
Architecture and related services	569	310	24	161	53	51	2	4	2	15	593	291	33	188	52	49	3	1	7	21
Area, ethnic, cultural, gender, and group studies	209	45	24	38	4	3	1	90	3	5	194	37	18	45	13	10	3	72	4	5
Biological and biomedical sciences	3,245	1,656	281	653	480	436	44	50	36	89	3,834	1,841	325	939	509	499	10	70	57	93
Business	139,986	84,192	23,901	16,601	7,701	6,979	722	1,660	1,789	4,142	142,338	83,468	24,090	18,924	7,923	7,342	581	1,614	2,149	4,170
Communication, journalism, and related programs	3,051	1,955	286	506	153	131	22	20	30	101	3,495	2,104	379	655	156	133	23	27	61	113
Communications technologies	4,209	2,956	535	414	134	126	8	39	67	64	5,000	3,376	585	600	206	194	12	41	124	68
Computer and information sciences	37,677	25,050	5,911	3,730	1,747	1,613	134	349	335	555	41,161	26,919	6,303	4,532	2,028	1,863	165	392	494	493
Construction trades	5,402	4,282	518	385	83	76	7	78	44	12	5,752	4,461	632	387	92	75	17	91	75	14
Education	20,459	13,278	2,948	2,952	416	329	87	477	195	193	20,531	12,957	3,056	3,230	373	332	41	482	213	220
Engineering	2,825	1,794	187	367	229	207	22	43	25	180	3,382	2,121	241	423	305	283	22	27	27	238
Engineering technologies and engineering-related fields[1]	35,521	25,100	4,296	3,958	1,187	1,087	100	393	310	277	36,510	25,631	4,449	4,276	1,179	1,091	88	381	347	247
English language and literature/letters	2,019	1,080	244	476	161	150	11	15	17	26	2,137	1,141	232	512	150	139	11	22	38	42
Family and consumer sciences/human sciences	8,532	4,430	1,893	1,602	336	305	31	76	65	130	9,503	4,839	2,093	1,843	422	391	31	99	90	117
Foreign languages, literatures, and linguistics	1,876	1,193	84	421	62	48	14	16	29	71	1,980	1,215	104	519	56	51	5	6	24	56
Health professions and related programs	201,831	139,071	28,024	19,513	9,524	8,655	869	1,804	2,208	1,687	218,041	146,666	31,225	23,793	9,966	9,256	710	1,995	2,769	1,627
Homeland security, law enforcement, and firefighting	44,923	27,248	7,667	7,691	1,039	827	212	466	670	142	50,695	28,818	8,814	10,538	1,189	970	219	499	650	187
Legal professions and studies	11,620	7,440	1,967	1,534	322	269	53	112	176	69	12,182	7,594	2,063	1,846	300	276	24	132	181	66
Liberal arts and sciences, general studies, and humanities	306,670	192,864	37,996	47,746	14,728	13,287	1,441	3,023	3,996	6,317	336,554	204,241	44,336	57,252	15,483	14,207	1,276	3,215	5,428	6,599
Library science	160	128	5	20	3	3	0	3	3	0	159	128	1	18	7	6	1	3	1	1
Mathematics and statistics	1,644	778	103	385	256	254	2	24	23	75	1,529	703	64	420	212	207	5	23	21	86
Mechanic and repair technologies/technicians	19,969	14,078	2,077	2,493	685	601	84	304	222	110	20,714	14,302	2,031	2,861	704	613	91	325	350	141
Military technologies and applied sciences	886	582	96	110	47	40	7	8	13	0	986	663	150	101	55	45	10	7	20	0
Multi/interdisciplinary studies	23,729	13,787	2,111	4,038	2,775	2,625	150	208	242	568	27,267	15,174	2,386	5,240	3,234	3,079	155	201	442	590
Parks, recreation, leisure, and fitness studies	2,366	1,457	350	372	88	64	24	38	21	40	3,123	1,889	404	533	106	92	14	53	58	80
Philosophy and religious studies	283	152	47	53	25	24	1	4	1	1	308	166	75	50	3	3	0	3	5	6
Physical sciences and science technologies	5,078	2,866	618	644	524	493	31	65	66	295	5,824	3,107	669	908	644	620	24	63	100	333
Precision production	3,254	2,741	153	216	79	68	11	39	20	6	3,320	2,784	151	220	74	69	5	50	32	9
Psychology	3,866	2,125	334	1,003	204	185	19	87	57	56	4,717	2,317	446	1,453	280	259	21	94	90	37
Public administration and social services	7,472	3,889	2,181	1,040	132	100	32	131	67	32	9,143	4,697	2,709	1,319	133	108	25	134	97	54
Social sciences and history	12,767	6,316	1,464	3,056	1,261	1,110	151	241	207	222	14,132	6,695	1,390	3,902	1,353	1,202	151	234	329	229
Social sciences	12,067	5,856	1,433	2,888	1,244	1,096	148	236	195	215	13,321	6,166	1,359	3,703	1,328	1,182	146	226	317	222
History	700	460	31	168	17	14	3	5	12	7	811	529	31	199	25	20	5	8	12	7
Theology and religious vocations	758	520	167	36	13	10	3	7	1	14	839	558	189	67	8	5	3	2	7	8
Transportation and materials moving	1,697	1,137	126	253	94	90	4	14	29	44	2,098	1,446	134	294	111	97	14	22	20	71
Visual and performing arts	21,379	13,668	2,029	2,940	1,277	1,186	91	194	267	1,004	22,431	13,990	2,028	3,474	1,323	1,219	104	217	392	1,007
Other and not classified	0	0	0	0	0	0	0	0	0	0	0	0	0	0	0	0	0	0	0	0

[1]Excludes "Construction trades" and "Mechanic and repair technologies/technicians," which are listed separately.
NOTE: Data are for postsecondary institutions participating in Title IV federal financial aid programs. Race categories exclude persons of Hispanic ethnicity. Reported racial/ethnic distributions of students by level of degree, field of degree, and sex were used to estimate race/ethnicity for students whose race/ethnicity was not reported in the Integrated Postsecondary Education Data System (IPEDS): "Agriculture and natural resources" includes Agriculture, agriculture operations, and related sciences and Natural resources and conservation; and "Business" includes Business management, marketing, and related support services and Personal and culinary services.
SOURCE: U.S. Department of Education, National Center for Education Statistics, Integrated Postsecondary Education Data System (IPEDS), Fall 2011 and Fall 2012, Completions component. (This table was prepared July 2013.)

Bachelor's degrees conferred by postsecondary institutions, by field of study: Selected years, 1970–71 through 2010–11

Field of study	1970-71	1975-76	1980-81	1985-86	1990-91	1995-96	2000-01	2001-02	2002-03	2003-04	2004-05	2005-06	2006-07	2007-08	2008-09	2009-10	2010-11	2011-12
1	2	3	4	5	6	7	8	9	10	11	12	13	14	15	16	17	18	19
Total	839,730	925,746	935,140	987,823	1,094,538	1,164,792	1,244,171	1,291,900	1,348,811	1,399,542	1,439,264	1,485,242	1,524,092	1,563,069	1,601,368	1,650,014	1,715,913	1,791,046
Agriculture and natural resources	12,672	19,402	21,886	16,823	13,124	21,425	23,370	23,331	23,348	22,835	23,002	23,053	23,133	24,113	24,988	26,336	28,623	30,929
Architecture and related services	5,570	9,146	9,455	9,119	9,781	8,352	8,480	8,808	9,056	8,838	9,237	9,515	9,717	9,805	10,119	10,051	9,832	9,728
Area, ethnic, cultural, gender, and group studies	2,579	3,577	2,887	3,021	4,776	5,633	6,160	6,390	6,634	7,181	7,569	7,879	8,194	8,454	8,772	8,621	9,100	9,232
Biological and biomedical sciences	35,705	54,154	43,078	38,395	39,482	61,014	60,576	60,309	61,294	62,624	65,915	70,607	76,832	79,829	82,825	86,400	90,003	95,849
Business	115,396	143,171	200,521	236,700	249,165	226,623	263,515	278,217	293,391	307,149	311,574	318,042	327,531	335,254	347,985	358,293	365,093	366,815
Communication, journalism, and related programs	10,324	20,045	29,428	41,666	51,650	47,320	58,013	62,791	67,895	70,968	72,715	73,955	74,783	76,382	78,009	81,266	83,274	83,770
Communications technologies	478	1,237	1,854	1,479	1,397	853	1,178	1,245	1,933	2,034	2,523	2,981	3,637	4,666	5,100	4,782	4,858	4,982
Computer and information sciences	2,388	5,652	15,121	42,337	25,159	24,506	44,142	50,365	57,433	59,488	54,111	47,480	42,170	38,476	37,994	39,589	43,072	47,384
Education	176,307	154,437	108,074	87,147	110,807	105,384	105,458	106,295	105,845	106,278	105,451	107,238	105,641	102,582	101,708	101,265	103,992	105,785
Engineering	45,034	38,733	63,642	77,391	62,448	62,168	58,209	59,536	62,567	63,410	64,707	66,841	66,874	68,431	68,911	72,654	76,376	81,382
Engineering technologies	5,148	7,943	11,713	19,731	17,303	15,829	14,660	15,052	14,664	14,669	14,837	14,565	14,980	15,177	15,503	16,075	16,741	17,158
English language and literature/letters	63,914	41,452	31,922	34,083	51,064	49,928	50,569	52,375	53,699	53,984	54,379	55,096	55,122	55,038	55,462	53,231	52,744	53,767
Family and consumer sciences/human sciences	11,167	17,409	18,370	13,847	13,920	14,353	16,421	16,938	17,929	19,172	20,074	20,775	21,400	21,870	21,905	21,818	22,444	23,428
Foreign languages, literatures, and linguistics	20,988	17,068	11,638	11,550	13,937	14,832	16,128	16,258	16,912	17,754	18,386	19,410	20,275	20,977	21,158	21,516	21,706	21,764
Health professions and related programs	25,223	53,885	63,665	65,309	59,875	86,087	75,933	72,887	71,261	73,934	80,685	91,973	101,810	111,478	120,488	129,634	143,430	163,440
Homeland security, law enforcement, and firefighting	2,045	12,507	13,707	12,704	16,806	24,810	25,211	25,536	26,200	28,175	30,723	35,319	39,206	40,235	41,800	43,667	47,602	53,767
Legal professions and studies	545	531	776	1,223	1,827	2,123	1,991	2,003	2,474	2,841	3,161	3,302	3,596	3,771	3,822	3,886	4,429	4,592
Liberal arts and sciences, general studies, and humanities	7,481	18,855	21,643	21,336	30,526	33,997	37,962	39,333	40,480	42,106	43,751	44,898	44,255	46,940	47,096	46,953	46,727	46,925
Library science	1,013	843	375	155	90	58	52	74	99	72	76	76	82	68	78	85	96	95
Mathematics and statistics	24,801	15,984	11,078	16,122	14,393	12,713	11,171	11,950	12,505	13,327	14,351	14,770	14,954	15,192	15,496	16,030	17,182	18,842
Military technologies and applied sciences	357	952	42	255	183	7	21	3	6	10	40	33	168	39	55	56	64	86
Multi/interdisciplinary studies	6,324	13,709	12,986	13,754	17,774	26,885	26,478	28,049	27,449	28,047	28,939	30,583	32,111	34,174	35,375	37,648	42,228	45,716
Parks, recreation, leisure and fitness studies	1,621	5,182	5,729	4,623	4,315	12,974	17,948	18,885	21,432	22,164	22,888	25,490	27,430	29,931	31,667	33,318	35,924	38,993
Philosophy and religious studies	8,149	8,447	6,776	6,396	7,423	7,541	8,717	9,473	10,344	11,152	11,584	11,985	11,969	12,257	12,444	12,504	12,836	12,651
Physical sciences and science technologies	21,410	21,458	23,936	21,711	16,334	19,716	18,025	17,890	18,038	18,131	19,104	20,522	21,291	22,179	22,688	23,379	24,712	26,663
Precision production	0	0	0	2	2	12	31	47	42	61	64	55	23	33	29	29	43	37
Psychology	38,187	50,278	41,068	40,628	58,655	73,416	73,645	76,775	78,650	82,098	85,614	88,134	90,039	92,587	94,271	97,216	100,893	108,986
Public administration and social services	5,466	15,440	16,707	11,887	14,350	19,849	19,447	19,392	19,900	20,552	21,769	21,986	23,147	23,493	23,851	25,414	26,774	29,695
Social sciences and history	155,324	126,396	100,513	93,840	125,107	126,479	128,036	132,874	143,256	150,357	156,892	161,485	164,183	167,363	168,500	172,780	177,144	178,543
Theology and religious vocations	3,720	5,490	5,808	5,510	4,799	5,292	6,945	7,762	7,962	8,126	9,284	8,548	8,696	8,992	8,940	8,718	9,074	9,369
Transportation and materials moving	0	225	263	1,838	2,622	3,561	3,748	4,020	4,631	4,824	4,904	5,349	5,657	5,203	5,189	4,998	4,941	4,876
Visual and performing arts	30,394	42,138	40,479	37,241	42,186	49,296	61,148	66,773	71,482	77,181	80,955	83,297	85,186	87,703	89,140	91,802	93,956	95,797
Not classified by field of study	0	0	0	0	13,258	1,756	783	264	0	0	0	0	0	377	0	0	0	0

NOTE: Data through 1990–91 are for institutions of higher education, while later data are for postsecondary institutions that participate in Title IV federal financial aid programs. The new Classification of Instructional Programs was initiated in 2009–10. The figures for earlier years have been reclassified when necessary to make them conform to the new taxonomy. To facilitate trend comparisons, certain aggregations have been made of the degree fields as reported in the Integrated Postsecondary Education Data System (IPEDS): "Agriculture and natural resources" includes Agriculture, agriculture operations, and related sciences and Natural resources and conservation; "Business" includes Business, management, marketing, and related support services and Personal and culinary services; and "Engineering technologies" includes Engineering technologies and engineering-related fields, Construction trades, and Mechanic and repair technologies/technicians.

SOURCE: U.S. Department of Education, National Center for Education Statistics, Higher Education General Information Survey (HEGIS), "Degrees and Other Formal Awards Conferred" surveys, 1970–71 through 1985–86; Integrated Postsecondary Education Data System (IPEDS), "Completions Survey" (IPEDS-C:91–99); and IPEDS Fall 2000 through Fall 2012, Completions component. (This table was prepared July 2013.)

Bachelor's degrees conferred by postsecondary institutions, by race/ethnicity and sex of student: Selected years, 1976–77 through 2011–12

Year and sex	Number of degrees conferred to U.S. citizens and nonresident aliens								Percentage distribution of degrees conferred to U.S. citizens						
	Total	White	Black	Hispanic	Asian/ Pacific Islander	American Indian/ Alaska Native	Two or more races	Non-resident alien	Total	White	Black	Hispanic	Asian/ Pacific Islander	American Indian/ Alaska Native	Two or more races
1	2	3	4	5	6	7	8	9	10	11	12	13	14	15	16
Total															
1976–77[1]	917,900	807,688	58,636	18,743	13,793	3,326	—	15,714	100.0	89.5	6.5	2.1	1.5	0.4	—
1980–81[2]	934,800	807,319	60,673	21,832	18,794	3,593	—	22,589	100.0	88.5	6.7	2.4	2.1	0.4	—
1990–91	1,094,538	914,093	66,375	37,342	42,529	4,583	—	29,616	100.0	85.8	6.2	3.5	4.0	0.4	—
1995–96	1,164,792	905,846	91,496	58,351	64,433	6,976	—	37,690	100.0	80.4	8.1	5.2	5.7	0.6	—
1996–97	1,172,879	900,809	94,349	62,509	68,859	7,425	—	38,928	100.0	79.4	8.3	5.5	6.1	0.7	—
1997–98	1,184,406	901,344	98,251	66,005	71,678	7,903	—	39,225	100.0	78.7	8.6	5.8	6.3	0.7	—
1998–99	1,202,239	909,562	101,910	69,735	74,126	8,658	—	38,248	100.0	78.1	8.8	6.0	6.4	0.7	—
1999–2000	1,237,875	929,102	108,018	75,063	77,909	8,717	—	39,066	100.0	77.5	9.0	6.3	6.5	0.7	—
2000–01	1,244,171	927,357	111,307	77,745	78,902	9,049	—	39,811	100.0	77.0	9.2	6.5	6.6	0.8	—
2001–02	1,291,900	958,597	116,623	82,966	83,093	9,165	—	41,456	100.0	76.7	9.3	6.6	6.6	0.7	—
2002–03	1,348,811	994,616	124,253	89,029	87,964	9,875	—	43,074	100.0	76.2	9.5	6.8	6.7	0.8	—
2003–04	1,399,542	1,026,114	131,241	94,644	92,073	10,638	—	44,832	100.0	75.7	9.7	7.0	6.8	0.8	—
2004–05	1,439,264	1,049,141	136,122	101,124	97,209	10,307	—	45,361	100.0	75.3	9.8	7.3	7.0	0.7	—
2005–06	1,485,242	1,075,561	142,420	107,588	102,376	10,940	—	46,357	100.0	74.7	9.9	7.5	7.1	0.8	—
2006–07	1,524,092	1,099,850	146,653	114,936	105,297	11,455	—	45,901	100.0	74.4	9.9	7.8	7.1	0.8	—
2007–08	1,563,069	1,122,675	152,457	123,048	109,058	11,509	—	44,322	100.0	73.9	10.0	8.1	7.2	0.8	—
2008–09	1,601,368	1,144,614	156,615	129,527	112,508	12,221	—	45,883	100.0	73.6	10.1	8.3	7.2	0.8	—
2009–10	1,650,014	1,167,499	164,844	140,316	117,422	12,399	—	47,534	100.0	72.9	10.3	8.8	7.3	0.8	—
2010–11	1,715,913	1,182,405	173,017	154,063	121,066	11,933	20,804	52,625	100.0	71.1	10.4	9.3	7.3	0.7	1.3
2011–12	1,791,046	1,211,565	185,518	169,646	126,147	11,483	27,181	59,506	100.0	70.0	10.7	9.8	7.3	0.7	1.6
Males															
1976–77[1]	494,424	438,161	25,147	10,318	7,638	1,804	—	11,356	100.0	90.7	5.2	2.1	1.6	0.4	—
1980–81[2]	469,625	406,173	24,511	10,810	10,107	1,700	—	16,324	100.0	89.6	5.4	2.4	2.2	0.4	—
1990–91	504,045	421,290	24,800	16,598	21,203	1,938	—	18,216	100.0	86.7	5.1	3.4	4.4	0.4	—
1995–96	522,454	409,565	32,974	25,029	30,669	2,885	—	21,332	100.0	81.7	6.6	5.0	6.1	0.6	—
1996–97	520,515	403,366	33,616	26,318	32,521	2,996	—	21,698	100.0	80.9	6.7	5.3	6.5	0.6	—
1997–98	519,956	399,553	34,510	27,677	33,445	3,151	—	21,620	100.0	80.2	6.9	5.6	6.7	0.6	—
1998–99	519,961	398,310	34,856	28,477	34,179	3,407	—	20,732	100.0	79.8	7.0	5.7	6.8	0.7	—
1999–2000	530,367	402,954	37,029	30,304	35,853	3,463	—	20,764	100.0	79.1	7.3	5.9	7.0	0.7	—
2000–01	531,840	401,780	38,103	31,368	35,865	3,700	—	21,024	100.0	78.7	7.5	6.1	7.0	0.7	—
2001–02	549,816	414,892	39,196	32,951	37,660	3,624	—	21,493	100.0	78.5	7.4	6.2	7.1	0.7	—
2002–03	573,258	430,248	41,494	35,101	40,230	3,870	—	22,315	100.0	78.1	7.5	6.4	7.3	0.7	—
2003–04	595,425	445,483	43,851	37,288	41,360	4,244	—	23,199	100.0	77.9	7.7	6.5	7.2	0.7	—
2004–05	613,000	456,592	45,810	39,490	43,143	4,143	—	23,254	100.0	77.4	7.8	6.7	7.4	0.7	—
2005–06	630,600	467,467	48,079	41,814	45,809	4,203	—	23,228	100.0	77.0	7.9	6.9	7.5	0.7	—
2006–07	649,570	480,558	49,685	44,750	47,582	4,505	—	22,490	100.0	76.6	7.9	7.1	7.6	0.7	—
2007–08	667,928	492,137	52,247	47,884	49,485	4,523	—	21,652	100.0	76.1	8.1	7.4	7.7	0.7	—
2008–09	685,382	503,357	53,473	50,629	50,741	4,849	—	22,333	100.0	75.9	8.1	7.6	7.7	0.7	—
2009–10	706,633	513,717	56,171	55,092	53,377	4,875	—	23,401	100.0	75.2	8.2	8.1	7.8	0.7	—
2010–11	734,133	519,883	59,119	60,742	55,290	4,798	8,123	26,178	100.0	73.4	8.4	8.6	7.8	0.7	1.1
2011–12	765,317	532,077	63,610	67,060	57,510	4,468	10,922	29,670	100.0	72.3	8.6	9.1	7.8	0.6	1.5
Females															
1976–77[1]	423,476	369,527	33,489	8,425	6,155	1,522	—	4,358	100.0	88.2	8.0	2.0	1.5	0.4	—
1980–81[2]	465,175	401,146	36,162	11,022	8,687	1,893	—	6,265	100.0	87.4	7.9	2.4	1.9	0.4	—
1990–91	590,493	492,803	41,575	20,744	21,326	2,645	—	11,400	100.0	85.1	7.2	3.6	3.7	0.5	—
1995–96	642,338	496,281	58,522	33,322	33,764	4,091	—	16,358	100.0	79.3	9.3	5.3	5.4	0.7	—
1996–97	652,364	497,443	60,733	36,191	36,338	4,429	—	17,230	100.0	78.3	9.6	5.7	5.7	0.7	—
1997–98	664,450	501,791	63,741	38,328	38,233	4,752	—	17,605	100.0	77.6	9.9	5.9	5.9	0.7	—
1998–99	682,278	511,252	67,054	41,258	39,947	5,251	—	17,516	100.0	76.9	10.1	6.2	6.0	0.8	—
1999–2000	707,508	526,148	70,989	44,759	42,056	5,254	—	18,302	100.0	76.3	10.3	6.5	6.1	0.8	—
2000–01	712,331	525,577	73,204	46,377	43,037	5,349	—	18,787	100.0	75.8	10.6	6.7	6.2	0.8	—
2001–02	742,084	543,705	77,427	50,015	45,433	5,541	—	19,963	100.0	75.3	10.7	6.9	6.3	0.8	—
2002–03	775,553	564,368	82,759	53,928	47,734	6,005	—	20,759	100.0	74.8	11.0	7.1	6.3	0.8	—
2003–04	804,117	580,631	87,390	57,356	50,713	6,394	—	21,633	100.0	74.2	11.2	7.3	6.5	0.8	—
2004–05	826,264	592,549	90,312	61,634	53,498	6,164	—	22,107	100.0	73.7	11.2	7.7	6.7	0.8	—
2005–06	854,642	608,094	94,341	65,774	56,567	6,737	—	23,129	100.0	73.1	11.3	7.9	6.8	0.8	—
2006–07	874,522	619,292	96,968	70,186	57,715	6,950	—	23,411	100.0	72.8	11.4	8.2	6.8	0.8	—
2007–08	895,141	630,538	100,210	75,164	59,573	6,986	—	22,670	100.0	72.3	11.5	8.6	6.8	0.8	—
2008–09	915,986	641,257	103,142	78,898	61,767	7,372	—	23,550	100.0	71.9	11.6	8.8	6.9	0.8	—
2009–10	943,381	653,782	108,673	85,224	64,045	7,524	—	24,133	100.0	71.1	11.8	9.3	7.0	0.8	—
2010–11	981,780	662,522	113,898	93,321	65,776	7,135	12,681	26,447	100.0	69.3	11.9	9.8	6.9	0.7	1.3
2011–12	1,025,729	679,488	121,908	102,586	68,637	7,015	16,259	29,836	100.0	68.2	12.2	10.3	6.9	0.7	1.6

—Not available.

[1] Excludes 1,121 males and 528 females whose racial/ethnic group was not available.

[2] Excludes 258 males and 82 females whose racial/ethnic group was not available.

NOTE: Data through 1990–91 are for institutions of higher education, while later data are for postsecondary institutions participating in Title IV federal financial aid programs. Race categories exclude persons of Hispanic ethnicity. For 1989–90 and later years, reported racial/ethnic distributions of students by level of degree, field of degree, and sex were used to estimate race/ethnicity for students whose race/ethnicity was not reported. Detail may not sum to totals because of rounding.

SOURCE: U.S. Department of Education, National Center for Education Statistics, Higher Education General Information Survey (HEGIS), "Degrees and Other Formal Awards Conferred" surveys, 1976–77 and 1980–81; Integrated Postsecondary Education Data System (IPEDS), "Completions Survey" (IPEDS-C:90–99); and IPEDS Fall 2000 through Fall 2012, Completions component. (This table was prepared July 2013.)

Bachelor's degrees conferred by postsecondary institutions, by race/ethnicity and field of study: 2010–11 and 2011–12

Field of study	2010–11 Total	White	Black	Hispanic	Asian/Pacific Islander Total	Asian	Pacific Islander	American Indian/ Alaska Native	Two or more races	Nonresident alien	2011–12 Total	White	Black	Hispanic	Asian/Pacific Islander Total	Asian	Pacific Islander	American Indian/ Alaska Native	Two or more races	Nonresident alien
(1)	2	3	4	5	6	7	8	9	10	11	12	13	14	15	16	17	18	19	20	21
All fields, total	**1,715,913**	**1,182,405**	**173,017**	**154,063**	**121,066**	**116,794**	**4,272**	**11,933**	**20,804**	**52,625**	**1,791,046**	**1,211,565**	**185,518**	**169,646**	**126,147**	**121,521**	**4,626**	**11,483**	**27,181**	**59,506**
Agriculture and natural resources	28,623	24,278	811	1,469	1,121	1,080	41	240	268	436	30,929	25,948	937	1,610	1,258	1,204	54	256	454	466
Architecture and related services	9,832	6,619	493	1,228	874	857	17	51	116	451	9,728	6,421	504	1,174	884	871	13	48	126	571
Area, ethnic, cultural, gender, and group studies	9,100	4,534	1,447	1,446	986	943	43	206	266	215	9,232	4,502	1,323	1,593	1,088	1,043	45	192	294	240
Biological and biomedical sciences	90,003	56,460	6,885	6,960	15,234	15,008	226	567	1,178	2,719	95,849	59,565	7,231	7,872	16,169	15,907	262	590	1,631	2,791
Business	365,093	238,786	42,572	32,394	27,510	26,583	927	2,269	3,541	18,021	366,815	232,695	44,246	34,349	28,054	26,970	1,084	2,142	4,348	20,981
Communication, journalism, and related programs	83,274	60,577	8,761	6,958	3,674	3,492	182	486	1,008	1,810	83,770	59,834	9,209	7,356	3,624	3,428	196	427	1,290	2,030
Communications technologies	4,858	3,360	519	494	264	257	7	27	69	125	4,982	3,248	545	563	268	258	10	26	119	213
Computer and information sciences	43,072	28,031	4,914	3,390	3,916	3,804	112	251	545	2,025	47,384	30,211	5,410	4,008	4,413	4,254	159	257	725	2,360
Construction trades	328	295	8	11	8	5	3	1	1	4	377	326	10	26	9	9	0	1	2	3
Education	103,992	85,234	7,115	6,585	2,290	1,843	447	856	787	1,125	105,785	86,084	7,641	6,966	2,150	1,954	196	768	1,051	1,125
Engineering	76,376	51,718	3,245	5,549	9,344	9,220	124	334	925	5,261	81,382	54,237	3,327	6,268	9,733	9,561	172	318	1,161	6,338
Engineering technologies and engineering-related fields	16,187	11,989	1,506	1,229	711	694	17	155	137	460	16,531	12,176	1,683	1,161	689	666	23	149	178	495
English language and literature/letters	52,744	40,147	3,942	4,507	2,473	2,367	106	332	786	557	53,767	40,160	4,138	4,982	2,511	2,410	101	319	1,111	546
Family and consumer sciences/human sciences	22,444	16,065	2,623	1,837	1,171	1,132	39	196	238	314	23,428	16,471	2,932	2,015	1,202	1,166	36	164	311	333
Foreign languages, literatures, and linguistics	21,706	14,821	922	3,684	1,321	1,297	24	128	384	446	21,764	14,612	944	3,975	1,261	1,235	26	99	442	431
Health professions and related programs	143,430	102,055	17,119	9,882	9,914	9,506	408	963	1,412	2,085	163,440	114,113	19,766	11,993	12,138	11,563	575	956	2,168	2,306
Homeland security, law enforcement, and firefighting	47,602	28,088	9,687	7,241	1,349	1,225	124	439	538	260	53,767	31,051	11,089	8,472	1,569	1,390	179	434	842	310
Legal professions and studies	4,429	2,769	787	547	219	211	8	26	53	28	4,592	2,785	821	586	232	223	9	29	71	68
Liberal arts and sciences, general studies, and humanities	46,727	31,056	6,853	4,911	1,680	1,552	128	532	632	1,063	46,925	31,138	6,764	5,029	1,737	1,605	132	521	821	915
Library science	96	85	3	3	3	3	0	0	2	0	95	89	2	3	1	1	0	0	0	0
Mathematics and statistics	17,182	11,836	840	1,158	1,858	1,822	36	85	216	1,189	18,842	12,737	976	1,308	1,876	1,837	39	59	247	1,639
Mechanic and repair technologies/technicians	226	158	13	18	14	13	1	4	1	18	250	171	12	17	12	12	0	5	1	32
Military technologies and applied sciences	64	43	16	2	0	0	0	1	1	0	86	51	25	6	0	0	0	1	1	2
Multi/interdisciplinary studies	42,228	28,286	4,375	5,254	2,656	2,557	99	352	516	789	45,716	30,096	5,054	5,951	2,639	2,532	107	357	707	912
Parks, recreation, leisure, and fitness studies	35,924	26,998	3,548	2,763	1,363	1,246	117	284	394	574	38,993	29,174	3,750	3,178	1,498	1,387	111	267	523	603
Philosophy and religious studies	12,836	9,752	963	970	689	660	29	79	191	192	12,651	9,474	964	1,052	622	598	24	85	254	200
Physical sciences and science technologies	24,712	17,842	1,329	1,466	2,538	2,491	47	149	340	1,048	26,663	18,983	1,541	1,681	2,741	2,702	39	154	447	1,116
Precision production	43	29	4	4	5	5	0	0	0	5	37	30	5	1	2	2	0	0	2	0
Psychology	100,893	66,122	12,397	11,629	6,797	6,583	214	691	1,580	1,677	108,986	70,011	13,524	13,326	7,330	7,085	245	753	2,037	2,005
Public administration and social services	26,774	15,336	6,093	3,305	968	876	92	293	497	282	29,695	16,967	6,914	3,732	1,013	907	106	287	462	320
Social sciences and history	177,144	118,979	16,682	18,108	13,670	13,261	409	1,238	2,556	5,911	178,543	117,854	17,145	19,548	13,020	12,550	470	1,115	3,463	6,398
Social sciences	142,145	90,734	15,051	15,192	12,442	12,077	365	1,001	2,073	5,652	143,422	89,730	15,425	16,581	11,791	11,382	409	887	2,860	6,148
History	34,999	28,245	1,631	2,916	1,228	1,184	44	237	483	259	35,121	28,124	1,720	2,967	1,229	1,168	61	228	603	250
Theology and religious vocations	9,074	7,555	585	380	240	215	25	39	58	217	9,369	7,750	637	385	232	216	16	42	88	235
Transportation and materials moving	4,941	3,812	285	379	215	206	9	42	58	150	4,876	3,737	343	380	185	163	22	44	53	134
Visual and performing arts	93,956	68,690	5,679	8,302	5,991	5,780	211	616	1,510	3,168	95,797	68,864	6,109	9,080	5,987	5,812	175	618	1,751	3,388
Other and not classified																				

¹Excludes "Construction trades" and "Mechanic and repair technologies/technicians," which are listed separately.

NOTE: Data are for postsecondary institutions participating in Title IV federal financial aid programs. Race categories exclude persons of Hispanic ethnicity. Reported racial/ethnic distributions of students by level of degree, field of degree, and sex were used to estimate race/ethnicity for students whose race/ethnicity was not reported. To facilitate trend comparisons, certain aggregations have been made of the degree fields as reported in the Integrated Postsecondary Education Data System (IPEDS): "Agriculture and natural resources" includes Agriculture, agriculture operations, and related sciences and Natural resources and conservation; and "Business" includes Business management, marketing, and related support services and Personal and culinary services.

SOURCE: U.S. Department of Education, National Center for Education Statistics, Integrated Postsecondary Education Data System (IPEDS), Fall 2011 and Fall 2012, Completions component. (This table was prepared July 2013.)

Master's degrees conferred by postsecondary institutions, by field of study: Selected years, 1970–71 through 2011–12

Field of study	1970–71	1975–76	1980–81	1985–86	1990–91	1995–96	2000–01	2001–02	2002–03	2003–04	2004–05	2005–06	2006–07	2007–08	2008–09	2009–10	2010–11	2011–12
1	2	3	4	5	6	7	8	9	10	11	12	13	14	15	16	17	18	19
Total	235,564	317,477	302,637	295,850	342,863	412,180	473,502	487,313	518,699	564,272	580,151	599,731	610,597	630,666	662,079	693,025	730,635	754,229
Agriculture and natural resources	2,457	3,340	4,003	3,801	3,295	4,551	4,272	4,503	4,492	4,783	4,746	4,640	4,623	4,684	4,877	5,211	5,773	6,390
Architecture and related services	1,705	3,215	3,153	3,260	3,490	3,993	4,302	4,566	4,925	5,424	5,674	5,743	5,951	6,065	6,587	7,280	7,788	8,448
Area, ethnic, cultural, gender, and group studies	1,032	993	802	915	1,233	1,652	1,555	1,541	1,509	1,683	1,755	2,080	1,699	1,778	1,779	1,775	1,914	1,947
Biological and biomedical sciences	5,625	6,457	5,766	5,064	4,834	6,593	7,017	7,011	7,050	7,732	8,284	8,781	8,898	9,689	10,017	10,725	11,327	12,415
Business	26,490	42,592	57,888	66,676	78,255	93,554	115,602	119,725	127,685	139,347	142,617	146,406	150,211	155,637	168,375	177,684	187,213	191,571
Communication, journalism, and related programs	1,770	2,961	2,896	3,500	4,123	5,080	5,218	5,510	6,053	6,535	6,762	7,244	6,773	6,915	7,092	7,636	8,303	9,005
Communications technologies	86	165	209	308	204	481	427	470	442	365	433	501	499	631	475	463	502	491
Computer and information sciences	1,588	2,603	4,218	8,070	9,324	10,579	16,911	17,173	19,509	20,143	18,416	17,055	16,232	17,087	17,907	17,953	19,446	20,917
Education	87,666	126,061	96,713	74,816	87,352	104,936	127,829	135,189	147,883	162,345	167,490	174,620	176,572	175,880	178,564	182,139	185,009	178,062
Engineering	16,813	16,472	16,893	21,529	24,454	26,789	25,174	24,838	28,251	32,554	32,488	30,848	29,299	31,557	34,546	35,088	38,719	40,323
Engineering technologies	134	328	323	617	996	2,054	2,013	2,149	2,332	2,499	2,500	2,541	2,690	2,873	3,455	4,258	4,515	4,774
English language and literature/letters	10,441	8,599	5,742	5,335	6,784	7,657	6,763	7,097	7,428	7,956	8,468	8,845	8,742	9,161	9,261	9,201	9,476	9,939
Family and consumer sciences/human sciences	1,452	2,179	2,570	2,011	1,541	1,712	1,838	1,683	1,607	1,794	1,827	1,983	2,080	2,199	2,453	2,580	2,918	3,157
Foreign languages, literatures, and linguistics	5,480	4,432	2,934	2,690	3,049	3,443	3,035	3,075	3,049	3,124	3,407	3,539	3,443	3,565	3,592	3,755	3,727	3,827
Health professions and related programs	5,330	12,164	16,176	18,603	21,354	33,920	43,623	43,560	42,748	44,939	46,703	51,380	54,531	58,120	62,620	69,084	75,579	83,893
Homeland security, law enforcement, and firefighting	194	1,197	1,538	1,074	1,108	1,812	2,514	2,935	2,956	3,717	3,991	4,277	4,906	5,760	6,128	6,714	7,433	8,402
Legal professions and studies	955	1,442	1,832	1,924	2,057	2,751	3,829	4,053	4,141	4,243	4,170	4,453	4,486	4,815	5,150	5,734	6,300	6,614
Liberal arts and sciences, general studies, and humanities	885	2,633	2,375	1,586	2,213	2,778	3,193	2,754	3,314	3,697	3,680	3,702	3,634	3,797	3,728	3,804	3,971	3,791
Library science	7,001	8,037	4,859	3,564	4,763	5,099	4,727	5,113	5,295	6,015	6,213	6,448	6,767	7,162	7,091	7,448	7,727	7,441
Mathematics and statistics	5,191	3,857	2,567	3,131	3,549	3,651	3,209	3,350	3,620	4,191	4,477	4,730	4,884	4,980	5,211	5,634	5,843	6,245
Military technologies and applied sciences	2	0	43	83	0	136	0	0	0	0	0	0	202	0	3	0	0	29
Multi/interdisciplinary studies	924	1,283	2,356	2,869	2,079	2,713	3,413	3,634	3,721	3,972	4,167	4,391	4,611	5,165	5,225	5,973	6,748	7,745
Parks, recreation, leisure, and fitness studies	218	571	643	570	483	1,684	2,354	2,580	2,978	3,199	3,740	3,992	4,110	4,440	4,822	5,617	6,553	7,047
Philosophy and religious studies	1,326	1,358	1,231	1,193	1,471	1,363	1,386	1,371	1,578	1,578	1,647	1,739	1,716	1,879	1,859	2,043	1,833	2,003
Physical sciences and science technologies	6,336	5,428	5,246	5,860	5,281	5,910	5,134	5,082	5,196	5,714	5,823	6,063	6,012	6,061	5,862	6,063	6,386	6,910
Precision production	0	0	0	0	0	8	2	2	3	13	6	9	5	3	10	10	5	11
Psychology	5,717	10,167	10,223	9,845	11,349	15,152	16,539	16,357	17,161	17,898	18,830	19,770	21,037	21,431	23,415	23,752	25,051	26,834
Public administration and social services	7,785	15,209	17,803	15,692	17,905	24,229	25,268	25,448	25,903	28,250	29,552	30,510	31,131	33,029	33,933	35,729	38,634	41,680
Social sciences and history	16,539	15,953	11,945	10,564	12,233	15,012	13,791	14,112	14,630	16,110	16,952	17,369	17,665	18,495	19,240	20,222	21,084	21,889
Theology and religious vocations	7,747	8,964	11,061	11,826	10,498	10,909	9,876	10,104	10,493	10,818	11,348	11,758	12,436	12,578	12,836	12,824	13,191	13,396
Transportation and materials moving	0	0	0	454	406	919	756	709	765	728	802	784	985	982	1,048	1,074	1,390	1,702
Visual and performing arts	6,675	8,817	8,629	8,420	8,657	10,280	11,404	11,595	11,982	12,906	13,183	13,550	13,767	14,164	14,918	15,552	16,277	17,331
Not classified by field of study	0	0	0	0	8,523	780	528	24	0	0	0	0	0	0	0	0	0	0

NOTE: Data through 1990–91 are for institutions of higher education, while later data are for postsecondary institutions that participate in Title IV federal financial aid programs. The new Classification of Instructional Programs was initiated in 2009–10. The figures for earlier years have been reclassified when necessary to make them conform to the new taxonomy. To facilitate trend comparisons, certain aggregations have been made of the degree fields as reported in the Integrated Postsecondary Education Data System (IPEDS): "Agriculture and natural resources" includes Agriculture, agriculture operations, and related sciences and Natural resources and conservation; "Business" includes Business, management, marketing, and related support services and Personal and culinary services; and "Engineering technologies" includes Engineering technologies and engineering-related fields, Construction trades, and Mechanic and repair technologies/technicians. SOURCE: U.S. Department of Education, National Center for Education Statistics, Higher Education General Information Survey (HEGIS), "Degrees and Other Formal Awards Conferred" surveys, 1970–71 through 1985–86; Integrated Postsecondary Education Data System (IPEDS), "Completions Survey" (IPEDS-C:91–99); and IPEDS Fall 2000 through Fall 2012, Completions component. (This table was prepared July 2013.)

Master's degrees conferred by postsecondary institutions, by race/ethnicity and sex of student: Selected years, 1976–77 through 2011–12

Year and sex	Number of degrees conferred to U.S. citizens and nonresident aliens								Percentage distribution of degrees conferred to U.S. citizens						
	Total	White	Black	Hispanic	Asian/ Pacific Islander	American Indian/ Alaska Native	Two or more races	Non-resident alien	Total	White	Black	Hispanic	Asian/ Pacific Islander	American Indian/ Alaska Native	Two or more races
1	2	3	4	5	6	7	8	9	10	11	12	13	14	15	16
Total															
1976–77[1]	322,463	271,402	21,252	6,136	5,127	1,018	—	17,528	100.0	89.0	7.0	2.0	1.7	0.3	—
1980–81[2]	301,081	247,475	17,436	6,534	6,348	1,044	—	22,244	100.0	88.8	6.3	2.3	2.3	0.4	—
1990–91	342,863	265,927	17,023	8,981	11,869	1,189	—	37,874	100.0	87.2	5.6	2.9	3.9	0.4	—
1995–96	412,180	302,790	26,323	14,553	18,505	1,793	—	48,216	100.0	83.2	7.2	4.0	5.1	0.5	—
1996–97	425,260	309,637	28,875	15,560	19,372	1,954	—	49,862	100.0	82.5	7.7	4.1	5.2	0.5	—
1997–98	436,037	312,752	30,703	16,370	21,415	2,068	—	52,729	100.0	81.6	8.0	4.3	5.6	0.5	—
1998–99	446,038	318,555	33,010	17,781	22,262	2,075	—	52,355	100.0	80.9	8.4	4.5	5.7	0.5	—
1999–2000	463,185	324,990	36,606	19,379	23,523	2,263	—	56,424	100.0	79.9	9.0	4.8	5.8	0.6	—
2000–01	473,502	324,211	38,853	21,661	24,544	2,496	—	61,737	100.0	78.7	9.4	5.3	6.0	0.6	—
2001–02	487,313	331,427	41,006	22,517	25,681	2,632	—	64,050	100.0	78.3	9.7	5.3	6.1	0.6	—
2002–03	518,699	346,003	45,150	25,200	27,492	2,886	—	71,968	100.0	77.5	10.1	5.6	6.2	0.6	—
2003–04	564,272	373,448	51,402	29,806	31,202	3,206	—	75,208	100.0	76.4	10.5	6.1	6.4	0.7	—
2004–05	580,151	383,246	55,330	31,639	33,042	3,310	—	73,584	100.0	75.7	10.9	6.2	6.5	0.7	—
2005–06	599,731	397,439	59,806	32,567	34,289	3,519	—	72,111	100.0	75.3	11.3	6.2	6.5	0.7	—
2006–07	610,597	403,562	63,412	34,967	36,491	3,589	—	68,576	100.0	74.5	11.7	6.5	6.7	0.7	—
2007–08	630,666	413,179	65,914	36,972	37,722	3,777	—	73,102	100.0	74.1	11.8	6.6	6.8	0.7	—
2008–09	662,079	427,891	70,839	39,582	40,257	3,777	—	79,733	100.0	73.5	12.2	6.8	6.9	0.6	—
2009–10	693,025	445,038	76,458	43,535	42,702	3,960	—	81,332	100.0	72.8	12.5	7.1	7.0	0.6	—
2010–11	730,635	462,903	80,706	46,787	43,728	3,948	6,700	85,863	100.0	71.8	12.5	7.3	6.8	0.6	1.0
2011–12	754,229	469,639	85,315	51,264	45,400	3,674	9,780	89,157	100.0	70.6	12.8	7.7	6.8	0.6	1.5
Males															
1976–77[1]	172,703	144,042	7,970	3,328	3,128	565	—	13,670	100.0	90.6	5.0	2.1	2.0	0.4	—
1980–81[2]	151,602	120,927	6,418	3,155	3,830	507	—	16,765	100.0	89.7	4.8	2.3	2.8	0.4	—
1990–91	160,842	117,993	6,201	4,017	6,765	495	—	25,371	100.0	87.1	4.6	3.0	5.0	0.4	—
1995–96	183,481	128,325	8,758	5,940	9,644	713	—	30,101	100.0	83.7	5.7	3.9	6.3	0.5	—
1996–97	185,270	128,946	9,252	6,335	9,488	743	—	30,506	100.0	83.3	6.0	4.1	6.1	0.5	—
1997–98	188,718	128,987	9,978	6,612	10,500	792	—	31,849	100.0	82.2	6.4	4.2	6.7	0.5	—
1998–99	190,230	129,912	10,346	7,044	10,638	794	—	31,496	100.0	81.8	6.5	4.4	6.7	0.5	—
1999–2000	196,129	131,221	11,642	7,738	11,299	845	—	33,384	100.0	80.6	7.2	4.8	6.9	0.5	—
2000–01	197,770	128,516	11,878	8,371	11,561	925	—	36,519	100.0	79.7	7.4	5.2	7.2	0.6	—
2001–02	202,604	131,316	12,119	8,539	11,956	995	—	37,679	100.0	79.6	7.3	5.2	7.2	0.6	—
2002–03	215,172	135,938	13,224	9,389	12,704	1,043	—	42,874	100.0	78.9	7.7	5.4	7.4	0.6	—
2003–04	233,056	146,369	15,027	10,929	14,551	1,137	—	45,043	100.0	77.9	8.0	5.8	7.7	0.6	—
2004–05	237,155	150,076	16,136	11,501	15,238	1,167	—	43,037	100.0	77.3	8.3	5.9	7.8	0.6	—
2005–06	241,656	153,666	17,384	11,739	16,001	1,252	—	41,584	100.0	76.8	8.7	5.9	8.0	0.6	—
2006–07	242,189	154,241	18,333	12,473	16,728	1,275	—	39,139	100.0	76.0	9.0	6.1	8.2	0.6	—
2007–08	250,169	157,596	18,761	13,189	17,476	1,293	—	41,854	100.0	75.7	9.0	6.3	8.4	0.6	—
2008–09	263,538	162,994	20,174	14,324	18,724	1,350	—	45,972	100.0	74.9	9.3	6.6	8.6	0.6	—
2009–10	275,197	170,203	22,120	15,525	19,535	1,415	—	46,399	100.0	74.4	9.7	6.8	8.5	0.6	—
2010–11	291,551	177,780	23,741	17,213	20,050	1,409	2,594	48,764	100.0	73.2	9.8	7.1	8.3	0.6	1.1
2011–12	302,191	182,960	25,143	18,849	20,774	1,297	3,512	49,656	100.0	72.4	10.0	7.5	8.2	0.5	1.4
Females															
1976–77[1]	149,760	127,360	13,282	2,808	1,999	453	—	3,858	100.0	87.3	9.1	1.9	1.4	0.3	—
1980–81[2]	149,479	126,548	11,018	3,379	2,518	537	—	5,479	100.0	87.9	7.7	2.3	1.7	0.4	—
1990–91	182,021	147,934	10,822	4,964	5,104	694	—	12,503	100.0	87.3	6.4	2.9	3.0	0.4	—
1995–96	228,699	174,465	17,565	8,613	8,861	1,080	—	18,115	100.0	82.8	8.3	4.1	4.2	0.5	—
1996–97	239,990	180,691	19,623	9,225	9,884	1,211	—	19,356	100.0	81.9	8.9	4.2	4.5	0.5	—
1997–98	247,319	183,765	20,725	9,758	10,915	1,276	—	20,880	100.0	81.2	9.2	4.3	4.8	0.6	—
1998–99	255,808	188,643	22,664	10,737	11,624	1,281	—	20,859	100.0	80.3	9.6	4.6	4.9	0.5	—
1999–2000	267,056	193,769	24,964	11,641	12,224	1,418	—	23,040	100.0	79.4	10.2	4.8	5.0	0.6	—
2000–01	275,732	195,695	26,975	13,290	12,983	1,571	—	25,218	100.0	78.1	10.8	5.3	5.2	0.6	—
2001–02	284,709	200,111	28,887	13,978	13,725	1,637	—	26,371	100.0	77.5	11.2	5.4	5.3	0.6	—
2002–03	303,527	210,065	31,926	15,811	14,788	1,843	—	29,094	100.0	76.5	11.6	5.8	5.4	0.7	—
2003–04	331,216	227,079	36,375	18,877	16,651	2,069	—	30,165	100.0	75.4	12.1	6.3	5.5	0.7	—
2004–05	342,996	233,170	39,194	20,138	17,804	2,143	—	30,547	100.0	74.6	12.5	6.4	5.7	0.7	—
2005–06	358,075	243,773	42,422	20,828	18,258	2,267	—	30,527	100.0	74.4	13.0	6.4	5.6	0.7	—
2006–07	368,408	249,321	45,079	22,494	19,763	2,314	—	29,437	100.0	73.6	13.3	6.6	5.8	0.7	—
2007–08	380,497	255,583	47,153	23,783	20,246	2,484	—	31,248	100.0	73.2	13.5	6.8	5.8	0.7	—
2008–09	398,541	264,897	50,665	25,258	21,533	2,427	—	33,761	100.0	72.6	13.9	6.9	5.9	0.7	—
2009–10	417,828	274,835	54,338	28,010	23,167	2,545	—	34,933	100.0	71.8	14.2	7.3	6.1	0.7	—
2010–11	439,084	285,123	56,965	29,574	23,678	2,539	4,106	37,099	100.0	70.9	14.2	7.4	5.9	0.6	1.0
2011–12	452,038	286,679	60,172	32,415	24,626	2,377	6,268	39,501	100.0	69.5	14.6	7.9	6.0	0.6	1.5

—Not available.
[1]Excludes 387 males and 175 females whose racial/ethnic group was not available.
[2]Excludes 1,377 males and 179 females whose racial/ethnic group was not available.
NOTE: Data through 1990–91 are for institutions of higher education, while later data are for postsecondary institutions participating in Title IV federal financial aid programs. Race categories exclude persons of Hispanic ethnicity. For 1989–90 and later years, reported racial/ethnic distributions of students by level of degree, field of degree, and sex were used to estimate race/ethnicity for students whose race/ethnicity was not reported. Detail may not sum to totals because of rounding.
SOURCE: U.S. Department of Education, National Center for Education Statistics, Higher Education General Information Survey (HEGIS), "Degrees and Other Formal Awards Conferred" surveys, 1976–77 and 1980–81; Integrated Postsecondary Education Data System (IPEDS), "Completions Survey" (IPEDS-C:90–99); and IPEDS Fall 2000 through Fall 2012, Completions component. (This table was prepared July 2013.)

Master's degrees conferred by postsecondary institutions, by race/ethnicity and field of study: 2010–11 and 2011–12

Field of study	2010–11										2011–12									
	Total	White	Black	Hispanic	Asian/Pacific Islander Total	Asian	Pacific Islander	American Indian/Alaska Native	Two or more races	Nonresident alien	Total	White	Black	Hispanic	Asian/Pacific Islander Total	Asian	Pacific Islander	American Indian/Alaska Native	Two or more races	Nonresident alien
1	2	3	4	5	6	7	8	9	10	11	12	13	14	15	16	17	18	19	20	21
All fields, total	730,635	462,903	80,706	46,787	43,728	42,381	1,347	3,948	6,700	85,863	754,229	469,639	85,315	51,264	45,400	43,773	1,627	3,674	9,780	89,157
Agriculture and natural resources	5,773	4,166	218	222	233	229	4	38	53	843	6,390	4,699	194	255	261	253	8	37	79	865
Architecture and related services	7,788	5,017	336	538	549	542	7	37	72	1,239	8,448	5,395	361	645	562	552	10	29	105	1,351
Area, ethnic, cultural, gender, and group studies	1,914	1,071	213	200	115	109	6	26	34	255	1,947	1,057	181	245	119	104	15	32	60	253
Biological and biomedical sciences	11,327	6,461	691	600	1,464	1,437	27	46	129	1,936	12,415	6,979	750	665	1,634	1,605	29	55	185	2,147
Business	187,213	105,520	26,712	11,680	15,378	14,906	472	921	1,618	25,384	191,571	105,268	28,086	12,865	16,196	15,667	529	882	2,222	26,052
Communication, journalism, and related programs	8,303	5,136	868	577	365	359	6	38	106	1,213	9,005	5,444	982	641	388	374	14	35	166	1,349
Communications technologies	502	214	46	23	27	27	0	2	0	190	491	211	35	36	19	19	0	5	2	183
Computer and information sciences	19,446	6,501	1,417	688	1,926	1,893	33	56	125	8,733	20,917	6,947	1,648	857	1,834	1,814	20	60	209	9,362
Construction trades	0	0	0	0	0	0	0	0	0	0	5	1	0	0	0	0	0	0	0	4
Education	185,009	139,909	19,816	12,925	5,002	4,679	323	1,088	1,507	4,762	178,062	132,477	19,486	13,442	5,094	4,722	372	929	2,124	4,510
Engineering	38,719	14,807	1,139	1,547	4,102	4,081	21	73	298	16,753	40,323	15,980	1,185	1,735	3,961	3,926	35	82	392	16,988
Engineering technologies and engineering-related fields¹	4,515	2,190	372	220	373	372	1	29	46	1,285	4,769	2,313	372	286	328	318	10	32	51	1,387
English language and literature/letters	9,476	7,529	462	566	347	334	13	69	148	355	9,939	7,824	598	591	343	329	14	61	185	337
Family and consumer sciences/human sciences	2,918	2,056	412	152	77	76	1	17	22	182	3,157	2,204	440	166	106	101	5	19	38	184
Foreign languages, literatures, and linguistics	3,727	2,114	79	592	166	163	3	21	36	719	3,827	2,133	101	637	148	137	11	9	59	740
Health professions and related programs	75,579	52,288	8,452	4,547	5,823	5,689	134	481	545	3,443	83,893	57,582	9,684	5,105	6,500	6,255	245	464	988	3,570
Homeland security, law enforcement, and firefighting	7,433	4,664	1,715	640	197	176	21	56	50	111	8,402	5,184	1,853	824	204	185	19	72	106	159
Legal professions and studies	6,300	2,185	386	287	365	361	4	21	42	3,014	6,614	2,081	489	291	217	211	6	35	45	3,456
Liberal arts and sciences, general studies, and humanities	3,971	2,859	378	206	187	181	6	24	56	261	3,791	2,667	412	237	151	150	1	28	81	215
Library science	7,727	6,474	381	372	284	280	4	45	48	123	7,441	6,068	326	501	285	271	14	32	110	119
Mathematics and statistics	5,843	2,636	171	220	521	517	4	16	37	2,242	6,245	2,757	190	232	501	495	6	11	62	2,492
Mechanic and repair technologies/technicians	0	0	0	0	0	0	0	0	0	0	0	0	0	0	0	0	0	0	0	0
Military technologies and applied sciences	5	4	0	0	0	0	0	0	0	1	29	23	1	3	0	0	0	0	1	1
Multi/interdisciplinary studies	6,748	4,576	543	495	374	356	18	39	84	637	7,745	5,305	603	561	407	395	12	42	133	694
Parks, recreation, leisure, and fitness studies	6,553	4,882	631	334	174	156	18	38	73	421	7,047	5,208	749	347	166	151	15	34	116	427
Philosophy and religious studies	1,833	1,400	121	79	54	52	2	10	30	139	2,003	1,448	191	103	91	89	2	9	31	130
Physical sciences and science technologies	6,386	3,707	185	268	404	394	10	28	46	1,748	6,910	4,005	230	245	330	325	5	30	90	1,980
Precision production	5	4	0	0	0	0	0	0	0	1	11	10	0	0	1	1	0	0	0	0
Psychology	25,051	17,066	3,425	2,255	979	928	51	151	292	883	26,834	18,063	3,726	2,378	1,146	1,084	62	139	495	887
Public administration and social services	38,634	22,912	7,344	3,696	1,654	1,561	93	340	618	2,070	41,680	24,700	7,986	4,183	1,743	1,657	86	298	797	1,973
Social sciences and history	21,084	13,469	1,404	1,362	1,020	997	23	108	301	3,420	21,889	13,750	1,488	1,541	1,053	1,025	28	105	402	3,550
Social sciences	17,081	10,096	1,278	1,129	935	915	20	84	252	3,307	17,734	10,311	1,341	1,287	973	950	23	77	340	3,405
History	4,003	3,373	126	233	85	82	3	24	49	113	4,155	3,439	147	254	80	75	5	28	62	145
Theology and religious vocations	13,191	9,088	1,817	507	648	618	30	60	83	988	13,396	9,119	2,007	480	635	612	23	41	139	975
Transportation and materials moving	1,390	1,105	92	85	41	39	2	8	18	41	1,702	1,340	124	114	66	61	5	9	41	41
Visual and performing arts	16,277	10,897	880	904	879	869	10	62	183	2,472	17,331	11,397	837	1,053	911	885	26	58	299	2,776
Other and not classified	0	0	0	0	0	0	0	0	0	0	0	0	0	0	0	0	0	0	0	0

¹Excludes "Construction trades" and "Mechanic and repair technologies/technicians," which are listed separately.

NOTE: Data are for postsecondary institutions participating in Title IV federal financial aid programs. Race categories exclude persons of Hispanic ethnicity. Reported racial/ethnic distributions of students by level of degree, field of degree, and sex were used to estimate race/ethnicity for students whose race/ethnicity was not reported. To facilitate trend comparisons, certain aggregations have been made of the degree fields as reported in the Integrated Postsecondary Education Data System (IPEDS): "Agriculture and natural resources" includes Agriculture, agriculture operations, and related sciences and Natural resources and conservation; and "Business" includes Business management, marketing, and related support services and Personal and culinary services.

SOURCE: U.S. Department of Education, National Center for Education Statistics, Integrated Postsecondary Education Data System (IPEDS), Fall 2011 and Fall 2012, Completions component. (This table was prepared July 2013.)

Doctor's degrees conferred by postsecondary institutions, by field of study: Selected years, 1970–71 through 2011–12

Field of study	1970–71	1975–76	1980–81	1985–86	1990–91	1995–96	2000–01	2001–02	2002–03	2003–04	2004–05	2005–06	2006–07	2007–08	2008–09	2009–10	2010–11	2011–12
1	2	3	4	5	6	7	8	9	10	11	12	13	14	15	16	17	18	19
Total	64,998	91,007	98,016	100,280	105,547	115,507	119,585	119,663	121,579	126,087	134,387	138,056	144,690	149,378	154,425	158,558	163,765	170,062
Agriculture and natural resources	1,086	928	1,067	1,158	1,185	1,259	1,127	1,148	1,229	1,185	1,173	1,194	1,272	1,257	1,328	1,147	1,246	1,333
Architecture and related services	36	82	93	73	135	141	153	183	152	173	179	201	178	199	212	210	205	255
Area, ethnic, cultural, gender, and group studies	143	186	161	156	159	183	216	212	186	209	189	226	233	270	239	253	278	302
Biological and biomedical sciences	3,603	3,347	3,640	3,405	4,152	5,250	5,225	5,104	5,268	5,538	5,935	6,162	6,764	7,400	7,499	7,666	7,693	7,935
Business	774	906	808	923	1,185	1,366	1,180	1,156	1,252	1,481	1,498	1,711	2,029	2,084	2,123	2,245	2,286	2,531
Communication, journalism, and related programs	145	196	171	212	259	338	368	374	394	418	465	461	479	489	533	570	577	563
Communications technologies	0	8	11	6	13	7	2	9	4	8	3	3	1	7	2	3	1	4
Computer and information sciences	128	244	252	344	676	869	768	752	816	909	1,119	1,416	1,595	1,698	1,580	1,599	1,588	1,698
Education	6,041	7,202	7,279	6,610	6,189	6,246	6,284	6,549	6,832	7,088	7,681	7,584	8,261	8,491	9,028	9,233	9,623	9,990
Engineering	3,687	2,872	2,598	3,444	5,316	6,304	5,485	5,123	5,195	5,801	6,413	7,243	7,867	7,922	7,742	7,704	8,369	8,722
Engineering technologies	1	2	10	12	14	50	62	58	57	58	54	75	61	55	59	67	56	134
English language and literature/letters	1,554	1,514	1,040	895	1,056	1,395	1,330	1,291	1,246	1,207	1,212	1,254	1,178	1,262	1,271	1,332	1,344	1,427
Family and consumer sciences/human sciences	123	178	247	307	229	375	354	311	376	329	331	340	337	323	333	296	320	325
Foreign languages, literatures, and linguistics	1,084	1,245	931	768	889	1,020	1,078	1,003	1,042	1,031	1,027	1,074	1,059	1,078	1,111	1,091	1,158	1,231
Health professions and related programs	15,988	25,267	29,595	31,922	29,842	32,678	39,019	39,435	39,799	41,861	44,201	45,677	48,943	51,675	54,709	57,746	60,153	62,090
Homeland security, law enforcement, and firefighting	1	9	21	21	28	38	44	49	72	54	94	80	85	88	97	106	131	117
Legal professions and studies	17,441	32,369	36,391	35,898	38,035	39,919	38,190	39,060	39,172	40,328	43,521	43,569	43,629	43,880	44,304	44,626	44,877	46,836
Liberal arts and sciences, general studies, and humanities	32	162	121	90	70	75	102	113	78	95	109	84	77	76	67	96	95	93
Library science	39	71	71	62	56	53	58	45	62	47	42	44	52	64	35	64	50	60
Mathematics and statistics	1,199	856	728	742	978	1,158	997	923	1,007	1,060	1,176	1,293	1,351	1,360	1,535	1,592	1,586	1,669
Multi/interdisciplinary studies	101	156	236	352	306	549	512	484	634	580	626	600	683	660	731	631	660	727
Parks, recreation, leisure, and fitness studies	2	15	42	39	28	104	177	151	199	222	207	194	218	228	285	266	257	288
Philosophy and religious studies	555	556	411	480	464	550	600	610	662	595	586	578	637	635	686	667	805	778
Physical sciences and science technologies	4,324	3,388	3,105	3,521	4,248	4,589	3,968	3,824	3,939	3,937	4,248	4,642	5,041	4,994	5,237	5,063	5,295	5,370
Psychology	2,144	3,157	3,576	3,593	3,932	4,141	5,091	4,759	4,835	4,827	5,106	4,921	5,153	5,296	5,477	5,540	5,851	5,928
Public administration and social services	174	292	362	382	430	499	574	571	599	649	673	704	726	760	812	838	851	884
Social sciences and history	3,660	4,157	3,122	2,955	3,012	3,760	3,930	3,902	3,850	3,811	3,819	3,914	3,844	4,059	4,234	4,238	4,390	4,597
Theology and religious vocations	312	1,022	1,273	1,185	1,076	1,517	1,461	1,350	1,329	1,304	1,422	1,429	1,573	1,615	1,587	2,070	2,374	2,447
Transportation and materials moving	0	0	0	3	0	0	0	0	0	0	0	0	0	0	0	0	0	0
Visual and performing arts	621	620	654	722	838	1,067	1,167	1,114	1,293	1,282	1,278	1,383	1,364	1,453	1,569	1,599	1,646	1,728
Not classified by field of study	0	0	0	0	747	7	63	0	0	0	0	0	0	0	0	0	0	0

NOTE: Data through 1990–91 are for institutions of higher education, while later data are for postsecondary institutions that participate in Title IV federal financial aid programs. The new Classification of Instructional Programs was initiated in 2009–10. Includes Ph.D., Ed.D., and comparable degrees at the doctoral level, as well as such degrees as M.D., D.D.S., and law degrees that were formerly classified as first-professional degrees. The figures for earlier years have been reclassified when necessary to make them conform to the new taxonomy. To facilitate trend comparisons, certain aggregations have been made of the degree fields as reported in the Integrated Postsecondary Education Data System (IPEDS): "Agriculture and natural resources" includes Agriculture, agriculture operations, and related sciences and Natural resources and conservation;

"Business" includes Business, management, marketing, and related support services and Personal and culinary services; and "Engineering technologies" includes Engineering technologies and engineering-related fields, Construction trades, and Mechanic and repair technologies/technicians.

SOURCE: U.S. Department of Education, National Center for Education Statistics, Higher Education General Information Survey (HEGIS), "Degrees and Other Formal Awards Conferred" surveys, 1970–71 through 1985–86; Integrated Postsecondary Education Data System (IPEDS), "Completions Survey" (IPEDS-C:91–99); and IPEDS Fall 2000 through Fall 2012, Completions component. (This table was prepared July 2013.)

Doctor's degrees conferred by postsecondary institutions, by race/ethnicity and sex of student: Selected years, 1976–77 through 2011–12

Year and sex	Number of degrees conferred[1] to U.S. citizens and nonresident aliens								Percentage distribution of degrees conferred[1] to U.S. citizens						
	Total	White	Black	Hispanic	Asian/ Pacific Islander	American Indian/ Alaska Native	Two or more races	Non-resident alien	Total	White	Black	Hispanic	Asian/ Pacific Islander	American Indian/ Alaska Native	Two or more races
1	2	3	4	5	6	7	8	9	10	11	12	13	14	15	16
Total															
1976–77[2]	91,218	79,932	3,575	1,533	1,674	240	—	4,264	100.0	91.9	4.1	1.8	1.9	0.3	—
1980–81[3]	97,281	84,200	3,893	1,924	2,267	312	—	4,685	100.0	90.9	4.2	2.1	2.4	0.3	—
1990–91	105,547	81,791	4,429	3,210	5,120	356	—	10,641	100.0	86.2	4.7	3.4	5.4	0.4	—
1995–96	115,507	82,641	6,153	4,361	8,979	607	—	12,766	100.0	80.4	6.0	4.2	8.7	0.6	—
1996–97	118,747	84,244	6,694	4,615	9,730	675	—	12,789	100.0	79.5	6.3	4.4	9.2	0.6	—
1997–98	118,735	83,690	7,018	4,705	9,814	732	—	12,776	100.0	79.0	6.6	4.4	9.3	0.7	—
1998–99	116,700	82,066	7,004	4,959	10,025	774	—	11,872	100.0	78.3	6.7	4.7	9.6	0.7	—
1999–2000	118,736	82,984	7,078	5,042	10,682	708	—	12,242	100.0	77.9	6.6	4.7	10.0	0.7	—
2000–01	119,585	82,321	7,035	5,204	11,587	705	—	12,733	100.0	77.0	6.6	4.9	10.8	0.7	—
2001–02	119,663	81,995	7,570	5,267	11,633	753	—	12,445	100.0	76.5	7.1	4.9	10.8	0.7	—
2002–03	121,579	82,549	7,537	5,503	12,008	759	—	13,223	100.0	76.2	7.0	5.1	11.1	0.7	—
2003–04	126,087	84,695	8,089	5,795	12,371	771	—	14,366	100.0	75.8	7.2	5.2	11.1	0.7	—
2004–05	134,387	89,763	8,527	6,115	13,176	788	—	16,018	100.0	75.8	7.2	5.2	11.1	0.7	—
2005–06	138,056	91,050	8,523	6,202	13,686	929	—	17,666	100.0	75.6	7.1	5.2	11.4	0.8	—
2006–07	144,690	94,248	9,377	6,593	14,924	918	—	18,630	100.0	74.8	7.4	5.2	11.8	0.7	—
2007–08	149,378	97,839	9,463	6,949	15,203	932	—	18,992	100.0	75.0	7.3	5.3	11.7	0.7	—
2008–09	154,425	101,303	10,183	7,490	15,809	978	—	18,662	100.0	74.6	7.5	5.5	11.6	0.7	—
2009–10	158,558	104,426	10,417	8,085	16,625	952	—	18,053	100.0	74.3	7.4	5.8	11.8	0.7	—
2010–11	163,765	105,932	10,925	8,650	17,078	947	1,271	18,962	100.0	73.2	7.5	6.0	11.8	0.7	0.9
2011–12	170,062	109,270	11,740	9,215	17,893	913	1,569	19,462	100.0	72.6	7.8	6.1	11.9	0.6	1.0
Males															
1976–77[2]	71,709	62,977	2,338	1,216	1,311	182	—	3,685	100.0	92.6	3.4	1.8	1.9	0.3	—
1980–81[3]	68,853	59,574	2,206	1,338	1,589	223	—	3,923	100.0	91.8	3.4	2.1	2.4	0.3	—
1990–91	64,242	48,812	1,991	1,835	3,038	196	—	8,370	100.0	87.4	3.6	3.3	5.4	0.4	—
1995–96	67,189	47,420	2,526	2,364	4,987	328	—	9,564	100.0	82.3	4.4	4.1	8.7	0.6	—
1996–97	68,387	48,113	2,704	2,481	5,334	368	—	9,387	100.0	81.5	4.6	4.2	9.0	0.6	—
1997–98	67,232	47,189	2,808	2,525	5,171	364	—	9,175	100.0	81.3	4.8	4.3	8.9	0.6	—
1998–99	65,340	45,802	2,793	2,533	5,382	402	—	8,428	100.0	80.5	4.9	4.5	9.5	0.7	—
1999–2000	64,930	45,308	2,762	2,602	5,467	333	—	8,458	100.0	80.2	4.9	4.6	9.7	0.6	—
2000–01	64,171	44,131	2,655	2,564	5,759	346	—	8,716	100.0	79.6	4.8	4.6	10.4	0.6	—
2001–02	62,731	43,014	2,821	2,586	5,645	357	—	8,308	100.0	79.0	5.2	4.8	10.4	0.7	—
2002–03	62,730	42,569	2,735	2,671	5,683	358	—	8,714	100.0	78.8	5.1	4.9	10.5	0.7	—
2003–04	63,981	43,014	2,888	2,731	5,620	357	—	9,371	100.0	78.8	5.3	5.0	10.3	0.7	—
2004–05	67,257	44,749	2,904	2,863	5,913	370	—	10,458	100.0	78.8	5.1	5.0	10.4	0.7	—
2005–06	68,912	45,476	2,949	2,850	5,977	429	—	11,231	100.0	78.8	5.1	4.9	10.4	0.7	—
2006–07	71,308	46,228	3,225	3,049	6,597	421	—	11,788	100.0	77.7	5.4	5.1	11.1	0.7	—
2007–08	73,453	48,203	3,296	3,146	6,535	447	—	11,826	100.0	78.2	5.3	5.1	10.6	0.7	—
2008–09	75,639	49,861	3,528	3,385	6,904	460	—	11,501	100.0	77.7	5.5	5.3	10.8	0.7	—
2009–10	76,605	50,705	3,622	3,641	7,230	430	—	10,977	100.0	77.3	5.5	5.5	11.0	0.7	—
2010–11	79,654	51,666	3,836	3,985	7,545	454	571	11,597	100.0	75.9	5.6	5.9	11.1	0.7	0.8
2011–12	82,611	53,444	4,108	4,215	7,792	418	701	11,933	100.0	75.6	5.8	6.0	11.0	0.6	1.0
Females															
1976–77[2]	19,509	16,955	1,237	317	363	58	—	579	100.0	89.6	6.5	1.7	1.9	0.3	—
1980–81[3]	28,428	24,626	1,687	586	678	89	—	762	100.0	89.0	6.1	2.1	2.5	0.3	—
1990–91	41,305	32,979	2,438	1,375	2,082	160	—	2,271	100.0	84.5	6.2	3.5	5.3	0.4	—
1995–96	48,318	35,221	3,627	1,997	3,992	279	—	3,202	100.0	78.1	8.0	4.4	8.8	0.6	—
1996–97	50,360	36,131	3,990	2,134	4,396	307	—	3,402	100.0	76.9	8.5	4.5	9.4	0.7	—
1997–98	51,503	36,501	4,210	2,180	4,643	368	—	3,601	100.0	76.2	8.8	4.6	9.7	0.8	—
1998–99	51,360	36,264	4,211	2,426	4,643	372	—	3,444	100.0	75.7	8.8	5.1	9.7	0.8	—
1999–2000	53,806	37,676	4,316	2,440	5,215	375	—	3,784	100.0	75.3	8.6	4.9	10.4	0.7	—
2000–01	55,414	38,190	4,380	2,640	5,828	359	—	4,017	100.0	74.3	8.5	5.1	11.3	0.7	—
2001–02	56,932	38,981	4,749	2,681	5,988	396	—	4,137	100.0	73.8	9.0	5.1	11.3	0.8	—
2002–03	58,849	39,980	4,802	2,832	6,325	401	—	4,509	100.0	73.6	8.8	5.2	11.6	0.7	—
2003–04	62,106	41,681	5,201	3,064	6,751	414	—	4,995	100.0	73.0	9.1	5.4	11.8	0.7	—
2004–05	67,130	45,014	5,623	3,252	7,263	418	—	5,560	100.0	73.1	9.1	5.3	11.8	0.7	—
2005–06	69,144	45,574	5,574	3,352	7,709	500	—	6,435	100.0	72.7	8.9	5.3	12.3	0.8	—
2006–07	73,382	48,020	6,152	3,544	8,327	497	—	6,842	100.0	72.2	9.2	5.3	12.5	0.7	—
2007–08	75,925	49,636	6,167	3,803	8,668	485	—	7,166	100.0	72.2	9.0	5.5	12.6	0.7	—
2008–09	78,786	51,442	6,655	4,105	8,905	518	—	7,161	100.0	71.8	9.3	5.7	12.4	0.7	—
2009–10	81,953	53,721	6,795	4,444	9,395	522	—	7,076	100.0	71.7	9.1	5.9	12.5	0.7	—
2010–11	84,111	54,266	7,089	4,665	9,533	493	700	7,365	100.0	70.7	9.2	6.1	12.4	0.6	0.9
2011–12	87,451	55,826	7,632	5,000	10,101	495	868	7,529	100.0	69.9	9.5	6.3	12.6	0.6	1.1

—Not available.
[1] Includes Ph.D., Ed.D., and comparable degrees at the doctoral level, as well as such degrees as M.D., D.D.S., and law degrees that were formerly classified as first-professional degrees.
[2] Excludes 500 males and 12 females whose racial/ethnic group was not available.
[3] Excludes 714 males and 21 females whose racial/ethnic group was not available.
NOTE: Data through 1990–91 are for institutions of higher education, while later data are for postsecondary institutions participating in Title IV federal financial aid programs. Race categories exclude persons of Hispanic ethnicity. For 1989–90 and later years, reported racial/ethnic distributions of students by level of degree, field of degree, and sex were used to estimate race/ethnicity for students whose race/ethnicity was not reported. Detail may not sum to totals because of rounding.
SOURCE: U.S. Department of Education, National Center for Education Statistics, Higher Education General Information Survey (HEGIS), "Degrees and Other Formal Awards Conferred" surveys, 1976–77 and 1980–81; Integrated Postsecondary Education Data System (IPEDS), "Completions Survey" (IPEDS-C:90–99); and IPEDS Fall 2000 through Fall 2012, Completions component. (This table was prepared July 2013.)

Doctor's degrees conferred by postsecondary institutions, by race/ethnicity and field of study: 2010–11 and 2011–12

Field of study	2010–11										2011–12									
	Total	White	Black	Hispanic	Asian/Pacific Islander Total	Asian	Pacific Islander	American Indian/ Alaska Native	Two or more races	Non-resident alien	Total	White	Black	Hispanic	Asian/Pacific Islander Total	Asian	Pacific Islander	American Indian/ Alaska Native	Two or more races	Non-resident alien
1	2	3	4	5	6	7	8	9	10	11	12	13	14	15	16	17	18	19	20	21
All fields, total	163,765	105,932	10,925	8,650	17,078	16,730	348	947	1,271	18,962	170,062	109,270	11,740	9,215	17,893	17,559	334	913	1,569	19,462
Agriculture and natural resources	1,246	610	25	48	40	39	1	7	6	510	1,333	637	42	47	41	41	0	9	4	553
Architecture and related services	205	68	8	9	41	41	0	0	4	75	255	95	12	9	28	27	0	1	5	105
Area, ethnic, cultural, gender, and group studies	278	141	38	16	27	26	1	7	2	47	302	134	42	29	28	28	0	8	4	57
Biological and biomedical sciences	7,693	4,214	285	342	688	673	15	28	49	2,087	7,935	4,304	300	352	746	738	8	35	63	2,135
Business	2,286	1,089	338	96	148	145	3	10	6	599	2,531	1,237	397	83	170	167	3	15	12	617
Communication, journalism, and related programs	577	358	36	14	17	17	0	4	2	146	563	352	33	23	29	27	2	2	8	116
Communications technologies	1	0	0	0	0	0	0	0	0	1	4	4	0	0	0	0	0	0	0	0
Computer and information sciences	1,588	581	41	21	146	144	2	3	3	793	1,698	597	46	31	146	146	0	2	5	871
Construction trades	0	0	0	0	0	0	0	0	0	0	0	0	0	0	0	0	0	0	0	0
Education	9,623	6,172	1,743	593	326	310	16	81	63	645	9,990	6,365	1,901	678	361	346	15	72	71	542
Engineering	8,369	2,599	155	200	644	640	4	15	36	4,720	8,722	2,775	185	198	623	621	2	11	43	4,887
Engineering technologies and engineering-related fields[1]	56	32	1	1	3	3	0	0	0	19	134	74	9	2	5	5	0	2	2	40
English language and literature/letters	1,344	1,044	59	54	50	50	0	5	17	115	1,427	1,085	64	71	49	47	2	11	10	137
Family and consumer sciences/human sciences	320	189	30	7	11	11	0	1	0	81	325	191	41	3	17	16	1	1	2	70
Foreign languages, literatures, and linguistics	1,158	625	23	84	48	47	1	2	3	374	1,231	657	17	117	60	59	1	2	12	366
Health professions and related programs	60,153	41,177	3,480	2,875	9,933	9,799	134	340	430	1,918	62,090	41,820	3,771	2,942	10,591	10,452	139	344	550	2,072
Homeland security, law enforcement, and firefighting	131	89	16	5	5	5	0	0	0	16	117	81	7	7	6	6	0	0	1	19
Legal professions and studies	44,877	32,762	3,207	3,290	3,686	3,532	154	361	480	1,091	46,836	34,329	3,398	3,561	3,679	3,545	134	330	560	979
Liberal arts and sciences, general studies, and humanities	95	73	4	1	5	5	0	0	0	11	93	68	7	2	3	3	0	3	1	9
Library science	50	26	1	1	1	1	0	0	0	21	60	32	0	1	6	6	0	0	1	20
Mathematics and statistics	1,586	685	25	31	98	97	1	5	2	740	1,669	696	23	43	79	77	2	0	10	818
Mechanics and repair technologies/technicians	0	0	0	0	0	0	0	0	0	0	0	0	0	0	0	0	0	0	0	0
Military technologies and applied sciences	0	0	0	0	0	0	0	0	0	0	0	0	0	0	0	0	0	0	0	0
Multi/interdisciplinary studies	660	372	71	34	38	38	0	3	9	133	727	432	67	38	34	32	2	5	6	145
Parks, recreation, leisure, and fitness studies	257	163	19	5	6	6	0	1	1	62	288	187	17	8	8	7	1	1	3	65
Philosophy and religious studies	805	550	54	25	23	23	0	1	9	143	778	541	36	27	33	33	0	1	9	130
Physical sciences and science technologies	5,295	2,579	100	144	272	265	7	13	30	2,157	5,370	2,622	104	155	288	283	5	1	40	2,152
Precision production	0	0	0	0	0	0	0	0	0	0	0	0	0	0	0	0	0	0	0	0
Psychology	5,851	4,303	430	376	300	299	1	34	56	352	5,928	4,306	441	396	357	354	3	0	70	331
Public administration and social services	851	458	145	50	45	45	0	3	6	144	884	493	140	50	44	43	1	0	9	148
Social sciences and history	4,390	2,509	194	194	202	197	5	16	37	1,238	4,597	2,611	214	214	210	207	3	12	39	1,297
Social sciences	3,482	1,846	148	152	175	170	5	11	25	1,125	3,628	1,918	149	172	179	178	1	10	30	1,170
History	908	663	46	42	27	27	0	5	12	113	969	693	65	42	31	29	2	9	9	127
Theology and religious vocations	2,374	1,417	362	74	167	165	2	1	8	345	2,447	1,468	386	65	155	149	6	7	19	347
Transportation and materials moving	0	0	0	0	0	0	0	0	0	0	0	0	0	0	0	0	0	0	0	0
Visual and performing arts	1,646	1,047	35	61	108	107	1	7	9	379	1,728	1,077	40	63	102	99	3	2	10	434
Other and not classified	0	0	0	0	0	0	0	0	0	0	0	0	0	0	0	0	0	0	0	0

[1] Excludes "Construction trades" and "Mechanic and repair technologies/technicians," which are listed separately.

NOTE: Data are for postsecondary institutions participating in Title IV federal financial aid programs. Race categories exclude persons of Hispanic ethnicity. Reported racial/ethnic distributions of students by level of degree, field of degree, and sex were used to estimate race/ethnicity for students whose race/ethnicity was not reported. To facilitate trend comparisons, certain aggregations have been made of the degree fields as reported in the Integrated Postsecondary Education Data System (IPEDS): "Agriculture and natural resources" includes Agriculture, agriculture operations, and related sciences and Natural resources and conservation; and "Business" includes Business management, marketing, and related support services and Personal and culinary services.

SOURCE: U.S. Department of Education, National Center for Education Statistics, Integrated Postsecondary Education Data System (IPEDS), Fall 2011 and Fall 2012, Completions component. (This table was prepared July 2013.)

Degrees conferred by postsecondary institutions in selected professional fields, by sex of student, control of institution, and field of study: Selected years, 1985–86 through 2011–12

Control of institution and field of study	1985–86	1990–91	1995–96	2000–01	2001–02	2002–03	2003–04	2004–05	2005–06	2006–07	2007–08	2008–09	2009–10 Total	2009–10 Males	2009–10 Females	2010–11 Total	2010–11 Males	2010–11 Females	2011–12 Total	2011–12 Males	2011–12 Females
1	2	3	4	5	6	7	8	9	10	11	12	13	14	15	16	17	18	19	20	21	22
Total, all institutions	73,910	71,948	76,734	79,707	80,698	80,897	83,041	87,289	87,655	90,064	91,309	92,004	94,103	47,538	46,565	95,749	48,801	46,948	98,710	50,334	48,376
Dentistry (D.D.S. or D.M.D.)	5,046	3,699	3,697	4,391	4,239	4,345	4,335	4,454	4,389	4,596	4,795	4,918	5,062	2,745	2,317	5,071	2,764	2,307	5,109	2,748	2,361
Medicine (M.D.)	15,938	15,043	15,341	15,403	15,237	15,034	15,442	15,461	15,455	15,730	15,646	15,987	16,356	8,468	7,888	16,863	8,701	8,162	16,927	8,809	8,118
Optometry (O.D.)	1,029	1,115	1,231	1,289	1,280	1,281	1,275	1,252	1,198	1,311	1,304	1,338	1,335	457	878	1,322	475	847	1,361	476	885
Osteopathic medicine (D.O.)	1,547	1,459	1,895	2,450	2,416	2,596	2,722	2,762	2,718	2,992	3,232	3,665	3,890	1,979	1,911	4,141	2,121	2,020	4,336	2,283	2,053
Pharmacy (Pharm.D.)	903	1,244	2,555	6,324	7,076	7,474	8,221	8,885	9,292	10,439	10,932	11,291	11,873	4,297	7,576	12,274	4,694	7,580	12,943	4,971	7,972
Podiatry (Pod.D. or D.P.) or podiatric medicine (D.P.M.)	612	589	650	528	474	439	382	343	347	331	555	431	491	276	215	543	318	225	535	342	193
Veterinary medicine (D.V.M.)	2,270	2,032	2,109	2,248	2,289	2,354	2,228	2,354	2,370	2,443	2,504	2,377	2,478	555	1,923	2,564	580	1,984	2,616	588	2,028
Chiropractic (D.C. or D.C.M.)	3,395	2,640	3,379	3,796	3,284	2,718	2,730	2,560	2,564	2,525	2,639	2,512	2,601	1,610	991	2,694	1,666	1,028	2,496	1,538	958
Law (LL.B. or J.D.)	35,844	37,945	39,828	37,904	38,981	39,067	40,209	43,423	43,440	43,486	43,769	44,045	44,345	23,394	20,951	44,445	23,493	20,952	46,445	24,576	21,869
Theology (M.Div, M.H.L., B.D., or Ord. and M.H.L./Rav., B.D., or Ord.)	7,283	5,695	5,879	5,026	5,195	5,360	5,332	5,533	5,666	5,990	5,751	5,362	5,672	3,757	1,915	5,832	3,989	1,843	5,942	4,003	1,939
Other[1]	43	487	170	348	227	229	165	262	216	221	182	78	0	0	0	0	0	0	0	0	0
Total, public institutions	29,568	29,554	29,882	32,633	33,439	33,549	34,499	35,768	36,269	36,855	37,278	37,357	38,132	18,432	19,700	39,071	19,027	20,044	39,776	19,589	20,187
Dentistry (D.D.S. or D.M.D.)	2,827	2,308	2,198	2,477	2,525	2,493	2,498	2,577	2,669	2,769	2,760	2,870	2,984	1,694	1,290	3,008	1,687	1,321	3,053	1,708	1,345
Medicine (M.D.)	9,991	9,364	9,370	9,408	9,390	9,276	9,418	9,536	9,650	9,733	9,646	9,795	10,043	5,208	4,835	10,577	5,522	5,055	10,626	5,591	5,035
Optometry (O.D.)	441	477	499	497	503	481	476	477	462	518	492	517	507	158	349	515	180	335	508	178	330
Osteopathic medicine (D.O.)	486	493	528	562	538	571	586	568	585	637	634	679	817	384	433	856	429	427	841	442	399
Pharmacy (Pharm.D.)	473	808	1,557	3,876	4,382	4,558	4,930	5,352	5,523	5,903	6,218	6,395	6,587	2,416	4,171	6,888	2,643	4,245	6,919	2,679	4,240
Podiatry (Pod.D. or D.P.) or podiatric medicine (D.P.M.)	0	0	0	0	75	81	64	64	65	66	73	68	85	45	40	87	41	46	204	128	76
Veterinary medicine (D.V.M.)	1,931	1,814	1,889	2,017	2,052	2,023	1,912	2,033	2,048	2,116	2,123	1,968	2,048	465	1,583	2,134	485	1,649	2,168	493	1,675
Chiropractic (D.C. or D.C.M.)	0	0	0	0	0	0	0	0	0	0	0	0	0	0	0	0	0	0	0	0	0
Law (LL.B. or J.D.)	13,419	14,290	13,841	13,712	13,974	14,066	14,615	15,161	15,267	15,113	15,332	15,065	15,061	8,062	6,999	15,006	8,040	6,966	15,457	8,370	7,087
Theology (M.Div, M.H.L., B.D., or Ord. and M.H.L./Rav., B.D., or Ord.)	0	0	0	0	0	0	0	0	0	0	0	0	0	0	0	0	0	0	0	0	0
Other[1]	0	0	0	0	0	0	0	0	0	0	0	0	0	0	0	0	0	0	0	0	0
Total, private institutions	44,342	42,394	46,852	47,074	47,259	47,348	48,542	51,521	51,386	53,209	54,031	54,647	55,971	29,106	26,865	56,678	29,774	26,904	58,934	30,745	28,189
Dentistry (D.D.S. or D.M.D.)	2,219	1,391	1,499	1,914	1,714	1,852	1,837	1,877	1,720	1,827	2,035	2,048	2,078	1,051	1,027	2,063	1,077	986	2,056	1,040	1,016
Medicine (M.D.)	5,947	5,679	5,971	5,995	5,847	5,758	6,024	5,925	5,805	5,997	6,000	6,192	6,313	3,260	3,053	6,286	3,179	3,107	6,301	3,218	3,083
Optometry (O.D.)	588	638	732	792	777	800	799	775	736	793	812	821	828	299	529	807	295	512	853	298	555
Osteopathic medicine (D.O.)	1,061	966	1,367	1,888	1,878	2,025	2,136	2,194	2,133	2,355	2,598	2,986	3,073	1,595	1,478	3,285	1,692	1,593	3,495	1,841	1,654
Pharmacy (Pharm.D.)	430	436	998	2,448	2,694	2,916	3,291	3,533	3,769	4,536	4,714	4,896	5,286	1,881	3,405	5,386	2,051	3,335	6,024	2,292	3,732
Podiatry (Pod.D. or D.P.) or podiatric medicine (D.P.M.)	612	589	650	528	399	358	318	279	282	265	482	363	406	231	175	456	277	179	331	214	117
Veterinary medicine (D.V.M.)	339	218	220	231	237	331	316	321	322	327	381	409	430	90	340	430	95	335	448	95	353
Chiropractic (D.C. or D.C.M.)	3,395	2,640	3,379	3,796	3,284	2,718	2,730	2,560	2,564	2,525	2,639	2,512	2,601	1,610	991	2,694	1,666	1,028	2,496	1,538	958
Law (LL.B. or J.D.)	22,425	23,655	25,987	24,192	25,007	25,001	25,594	28,262	28,173	28,373	28,437	28,980	29,284	15,332	13,952	29,439	15,453	13,986	30,988	16,206	14,782
Theology (M.Div, M.H.L., B.D., or Ord. and M.H.L./Rav., B.D., or Ord.)	7,283	5,695	5,879	5,026	5,195	5,360	5,332	5,533	5,666	5,990	5,751	5,362	5,672	3,757	1,915	5,832	3,989	1,843	5,942	4,003	1,939
Other[1]	43	487	170	348	227	229	165	262	216	221	182	78	0	0	0	0	0	0	0	0	0

[1]Includes naturopathic medicine and degrees that were not classified by field by the reporting institution.
NOTE: Data are for postsecondary institutions participating in Title IV federal financial aid programs. Includes degrees that require at least 6 years of college work for completion (including at least 2 years of preprofessional training).

SOURCE: U.S. Department of Education, National Center for Education Statistics, Higher Education General Information Survey (HEGIS), "Degrees and Other Formal Awards Conferred," 1985–86; Integrated Postsecondary Education Data System (IPEDS), "Completions Survey" (IPEDS-C:91–99); and IPEDS Fall 2000 through Fall 2012, Completions component. (This table was prepared July 2013.)

Degrees conferred by postsecondary institutions in selected professional fields, by race/ethnicity and field of study: 2010–11 and 2011–12

Field of study	2010–11										2011–12									
					Asian/Pacific Islander			American Indian/ Alaska Native	Two or more races	Non-resident alien					Asian/Pacific Islander			American Indian/ Alaska Native	Two or more races	Non-resident alien
	Total	White	Black	Hispanic	Total	Asian	Pacific Islander				Total	White	Black	Hispanic	Total	Asian	Pacific Islander			
1	2	3	4	5	6	7	8	9	10	11	12	13	14	15	16	17	18	19	20	21
All fields, total	**95,749**	**66,211**	**6,915**	**5,800**	**12,843**	**12,561**	**282**	**662**	**842**	**2,476**	**98,710**	**68,003**	**7,255**	**6,042**	**13,318**	**13,054**	**264**	**618**	**1,076**	**2,398**
Dentistry (D.D.S. or D.M.D.)	5,071	3,094	278	323	934	915	19	25	37	380	5,109	3,039	262	276	1,038	1,028	10	35	37	422
Medicine (M.D.)	16,863	10,713	1,129	967	3,570	3,547	23	100	161	223	16,927	10,683	1,190	935	3,557	3,528	29	114	229	219
Optometry (O.D.)	1,322	785	32	49	348	346	2	6	3	99	1,361	802	37	41	370	364	6	1	7	103
Osteopathic medicine (D.O.)	4,141	2,986	137	159	804	783	21	25	15	15	4,336	3,131	135	186	790	768	22	28	32	34
Pharmacy (Pharm.D.)	12,274	7,598	849	540	2,786	2,747	39	56	76	369	12,943	7,829	897	534	3,167	3,133	34	64	104	348
Podiatry (Pod.I.D or D.P) or podiatric medicine (D.P.M.)	543	372	55	21	71	71	0	12	0	12	535	366	41	32	68	68	0	3	4	21
Veterinary medicine (D.V.M.)	2,564	2,233	59	117	99	96	3	21	24	11	2,616	2,247	70	141	106	106	0	19	21	12
Chiropractic (D.C. or D.C.M.)	2,694	2,114	139	129	190	179	11	23	17	82	2,496	1,959	130	136	182	172	10	8	20	61
Law (LL.B or J.D.)	44,445	32,599	3,186	3,271	3,664	3,512	152	360	476	889	46,445	34,192	3,377	3,545	3,659	3,525	134	328	557	787
Theology (M.Div, M.H.L./Rav., B.D., or Ord.)	5,832	3,717	1,051	224	377	365	12	34	33	396	5,942	3,755	1,116	216	381	362	19	18	65	391

NOTE: Data are for postsecondary institutions participating in Title IV federal financial aid programs. Includes degrees that require at least 6 years of college work for completion (including at least 2 years of preprofessional training). Race categories exclude persons of Hispanic ethnicity. Reported racial/ethnic distributions of students by level of degree, field of degree, and sex were used to estimate race/ethnicity for students whose race/ethnicity was not reported.

SOURCE: U.S. Department of Education, National Center for Education Statistics, Integrated Postsecondary Education Data System (IPEDS), Fall 2011 and Fall 2012, Completions component. (This table was prepared July 2013.)

Historical summary of faculty, enrollment, degrees, and finances in degree-granting postsecondary institutions: Selected years, 1869–70 through 2011–12

Selected characteristic	1869–70	1879–80	1889–90	1899–1900	1909–10	1919–20	1929–30	1939–40	1949–50	1959–60	1969–70	1979–80	1989–90	1999–2000	2009–10	2011–12
1	2	3	4	5	6	7	8	9	10	11	12	13	14	15	16	17
Total institutions[1]	563	811	998	977	951	1,041	1,409	1,708	1,851	2,004	2,525	3,152	3,535	4,084	4,495	4,706
Total faculty[2]	5,553 [3]	11,522 [3]	15,809	23,868	36,480	48,615	82,386	146,929	246,722	380,554	450,000 [4]	675,000 [4]	824,220 [5]	1,027,830 [5]	1,439,144 [5]	1,523,615 [5]
Males	4,887 [3]	7,328 [3]	12,704 [3]	19,151	29,132	35,807	60,017	105,328	186,189	296,773	346,000 [4]	479,000 [4]	534,254 [5]	602,469 [5]	761,035 [5]	789,197 [5]
Females	666 [3]	4,194 [3]	3,105 [3]	4,717	7,348	12,808	22,369	40,601	60,533	83,781	104,000 [4]	196,000 [4]	289,966 [5]	425,361 [5]	678,109 [5]	734,418 [5]
Total fall enrollment[6]	52,286	115,817	156,756	237,592	355,213	597,880	1,100,737	1,494,203	2,444,900	3,639,847	8,004,660	11,569,899	13,538,560	14,849,691	20,427,711	20,994,113
Males	41,160 [3]	77,972 [3]	100,453 [3]	152,254	214,648 [3]	314,938	619,935	893,250	1,721,572	2,332,617	4,746,201	5,682,877	6,190,015	6,515,164	8,769,504	9,026,499
Females	11,126 [3]	37,845 [3]	56,303 [3]	85,338	140,565 [3]	282,942	480,802	600,953	723,328	1,307,230	3,258,459	5,887,022	7,348,545	8,334,527	11,658,207	11,967,614
Degrees conferred																
Associate's, total	—	—	—	—	—	—	—	—	—	—	206,023	400,910	455,102	564,933	849,452	1,017,538
Males	—	—	—	—	—	—	—	—	—	—	117,432	183,737	191,195	224,721	322,916	391,990
Females	—	—	—	—	—	—	—	—	—	—	88,591	217,173	263,907	340,212	526,536	625,548
Bachelor's, total[7]	9,371	12,896	15,539	27,410	37,199	48,622	122,484	186,500	432,058	392,440	792,316	929,417	1,051,344	1,237,875	1,650,014	1,791,046
Males	7,993	10,411	12,857	22,173	28,762	31,980	73,615	109,546	328,841	254,063	451,097	473,611	491,696	530,367	706,633	765,317
Females	1,378	2,485	2,682	5,237	8,437	16,642	48,869	76,954	103,217	138,377	341,219	455,806	559,648	707,508	943,381	1,025,729
Master's, total[8]	0	879	1,015	1,583	2,113	4,279	14,969	26,731	58,183	74,435	213,589	305,196	330,152	463,185	693,025	754,229
Males	0	868	821	1,280	1,555	2,985	8,925	16,508	41,220	50,898	130,799	156,882	158,052	196,129	275,197	302,191
Females	0	11	194	303	558	1,294	6,044	10,223	16,963	23,537	82,790	148,314	172,100	267,056	417,828	452,038
Doctor's, total[9]	1	54	149	382	443	615	2,299	3,290	6,420	9,829	59,486	95,631	103,508	118,736	158,558	170,062
Males	1	51	147	359	399	522	1,946	2,861	5,804	8,801	53,792	69,526	63,963	64,930	76,605	82,611
Females	0	3	2	23	44	93	353	429	616	1,028	5,694	26,105	39,545	53,806	81,953	87,451
Finances														*In thousands of current dollars*		
Current-fund revenue	—	—	$21,464	$35,084	$76,883	$199,922	$554,511	$715,211	$2,374,645	$5,786,537	$21,515,242	$58,519,982	$139,635,477	—	—	—
Educational and general income	—	—	—	—	67,917	172,929	483,065	571,288	1,833,845	4,688,352	16,486,177	—	—	—	—	—
Expenditures[10]	—	—	—	—	—	—	507,142	674,688	2,246,661	5,601,376	21,043,113	56,913,588	134,655,571	—	—	—
Value of physical property	—	—	95,426	253,599	457,594	747,333	2,065,049	2,753,780 [11]	4,799,964	13,548,548	42,093,580	83,733,387	164,635,000	236,784,000	446,484,000	488,444,000
Market value of endowment funds	—	—	78,788 [12]	194,998 [12]	323,661 [12]	569,071 [12]	1,372,068 [12]	1,686,283 [12]	2,601,223 [12]	5,322,080 [12]	11,206,632	20,743,045	67,978,726	—	355,790,614	424,587,666
Finances														*In thousands of constant 2012–13 dollars[13]*		
Current-fund revenue	—	—	—	—	—	—	$7,494,726	$11,840,107	$23,197,182	$45,553,400	$131,769,537	$174,393,813	$254,419,743	—	—	—
Educational and general income	—	—	—	—	—	—	6,529,068	9,457,504	17,914,272	36,914,529	100,969,160	—	—	—	—	—
Expenditures[10]	—	—	—	—	—	—	6,854,491	11,169,261	21,937,177	44,103,377	128,877,995	169,606,642	245,346,215	—	—	—
Value of physical property	—	—	—	—	—	—	27,911,037	45,588,015 [11]	46,889,384	106,676,775	257,801,030	249,531,598	299,969,573	323,586,000	476,596,000	496,572,000
Market value of endowment funds	—	—	—	—	—	—	18,544,761 [12]	27,915,917 [12]	25,410,554 [12]	41,904,293 [12]	68,634,725	61,815,786	123,859,139	—	379,788,776	431,653,399

—Not available.
[1] Prior to 1979–80, excludes branch campuses.
[2] Total number of different individuals (not reduced to full-time equivalent). Beginning in 1959–60, data are for the academic year.
[3] Estimated.
[4] Estimated number of senior instructional staff based on actual enrollment data for the designated year and enrollment/staff ratios for the prior staff survey. Excludes graduate assistants.
[5] Because of revised survey procedures, data may not be directly comparable with figures prior to 1989–90. Excludes graduate assistants.
[6] Data for 1869–70 to 1939–40 are for resident degree-credit students who enrolled at any time during the academic year.
[7] From 1869–70 to 1959–60, bachelor's degrees include degrees formerly classified as first-professional, such as M.D., D.D.S., and law degrees.
[8] Figures for years prior to 1969–70 are not precisely comparable with later data.
[9] Includes Ph.D., Ed.D., and comparable degrees at the doctoral level. Includes most degrees formerly classified as first-professional, such as M.D., D.D.S., and law degrees.
[10] Data for 1929–30 and 1939–40 include current-fund expenditures and additions to plant value. Data for 1949–50 through 1989–90 are current-fund expenditures only. Data for 1999–2000 include total expenditures for private institutions and current-fund expenditures for public institutions. Data for later years are for total expenditures.
[11] Includes unexpended plant funds.
[12] Book value. Includes other nonexpendable funds.
[13] Constant dollars based on the Consumer Price Index, prepared by the Bureau of Labor Statistics, U.S. Department of Labor, adjusted to a school-year basis.
NOTE: Data from 1989–90 are for institutions of higher education, while later data are for degree-granting institutions. Degree-granting institutions grant associate's or higher degrees and participate in Title IV federal financial aid programs. The degree-granting classification is very similar to the earlier higher education classification, but it includes more 2-year colleges and excludes a few higher education institutions that did not grant degrees. Detail may not sum to totals because of rounding.
SOURCE: U.S. Department of Education, National Center for Education Statistics, Biennial Survey of Education in the United States; Education Directory, Colleges and Universities; Faculty and Other Professional Staff in Institutions of Higher Education; Fall Enrollment in Colleges and Universities; Earned Degrees Conferred; Financial Statistics of Institutions of Higher Education; Higher Education General Information Survey (HEGIS), "Fall Enrollment in Institutions of Higher Education," "Degrees and Other Formal Awards Conferred," and "Financial Statistics of Institutions of Higher Education" surveys; Integrated Postsecondary Education Data System (IPEDS), "Fall Enrollment Survey" (IPEDS-EF-89–99), "Fall Staff Survey" (IPEDS-S-89–99), "Finance Survey" (IPEDS-F-FY90–00), "Completions Survey" (IPEDS-C-90–00), and "Institutional Characteristics Survey" (IPEDS-IC-89–99); IPEDS Winter 2009–10 and Winter 2011–12, Human Resources component, Fall Staff section; IPEDS Spring 2010 and Spring 2012, Enrollment component; IPEDS Fall 2010 and Fall 2012, Completions component; and IPEDS Spring 2010 and Spring 2012, Finance component. (This table was prepared March 2014.)

Recent high school completers and their enrollment in 2-year and 4-year colleges, by sex: 1960 through 2012
[Standard errors appear in parentheses]

Year	Number of high school completers[1] (in thousands)			Percent of high school completers enrolled in college[2]								
	Total	Males	Females	Total			Males			Females		
				Total	2-year	4-year	Total	2-year	4-year	Total	2-year	4-year
1	2	3	4	5	6	7	8	9	10	11	12	13
1960	1,679 (43.8)	756 (31.8)	923 (29.6)	45.1 (2.13)	— (†)	— (†)	54.0 (3.18)	— (†)	— (†)	37.9 (2.80)	— (†)	— (†)
1961	1,763 (46.0)	790 (33.2)	973 (31.3)	48.0 (2.09)	— (†)	— (†)	56.3 (3.10)	— (†)	— (†)	41.3 (2.77)	— (†)	— (†)
1962	1,838 (43.6)	872 (31.5)	966 (30.0)	49.0 (2.05)	— (†)	— (†)	55.0 (2.96)	— (†)	— (†)	43.5 (2.80)	— (†)	— (†)
1963	1,741 (44.2)	794 (32.1)	947 (30.0)	45.0 (2.09)	— (†)	— (†)	52.3 (3.11)	— (†)	— (†)	39.0 (2.78)	— (†)	— (†)
1964	2,145 (43.0)	997 (31.9)	1,148 (28.5)	48.3 (1.89)	— (†)	— (†)	57.2 (2.75)	— (†)	— (†)	40.7 (2.54)	— (†)	— (†)
1965	2,659 (47.7)	1,254 (35.1)	1,405 (32.0)	50.9 (1.70)	— (†)	— (†)	57.3 (2.45)	— (†)	— (†)	45.3 (2.33)	— (†)	— (†)
1966	2,612 (45.0)	1,207 (33.8)	1,405 (29.0)	50.1 (1.72)	— (†)	— (†)	58.7 (2.49)	— (†)	— (†)	42.7 (2.32)	— (†)	— (†)
1967	2,525 (37.9)	1,142 (28.4)	1,383 (24.3)	51.9 (1.42)	— (†)	— (†)	57.6 (2.09)	— (†)	— (†)	47.2 (1.92)	— (†)	— (†)
1968	2,606 (37.3)	1,184 (28.2)	1,422 (23.8)	55.4 (1.39)	— (†)	— (†)	63.2 (2.00)	— (†)	— (†)	48.9 (1.89)	— (†)	— (†)
1969	2,842 (36.0)	1,352 (26.8)	1,490 (23.7)	53.3 (1.34)	— (†)	— (†)	60.1 (1.90)	— (†)	— (†)	47.2 (1.85)	— (†)	— (†)
1970	2,758 (37.4)	1,343 (26.1)	1,415 (26.8)	51.7 (1.36)	— (†)	— (†)	55.2 (1.94)	— (†)	— (†)	48.5 (1.90)	— (†)	— (†)
1971	2,875 (38.0)	1,371 (26.6)	1,504 (27.1)	53.5 (1.33)	— (†)	— (†)	57.6 (1.90)	— (†)	— (†)	49.8 (1.84)	— (†)	— (†)
1972	2,964 (37.8)	1,423 (27.0)	1,542 (26.4)	49.2 (1.31)	— (†)	— (†)	52.7 (1.89)	— (†)	— (†)	46.0 (1.81)	— (†)	— (†)
1973	3,058 (37.1)	1,460 (27.6)	1,599 (24.6)	46.6 (1.29)	14.9 (0.92)	31.6 (1.20)	50.0 (1.87)	14.6 (1.32)	35.4 (1.79)	43.4 (1.77)	15.2 (1.28)	28.2 (1.61)
1974	3,101 (38.6)	1,491 (27.8)	1,611 (26.8)	47.6 (1.28)	15.2 (0.92)	32.4 (1.20)	49.4 (1.85)	16.6 (1.37)	32.8 (1.74)	45.9 (1.77)	13.9 (1.23)	32.0 (1.66)
1975	3,185 (38.6)	1,513 (27.3)	1,672 (27.2)	50.7 (1.26)	18.2 (0.98)	32.6 (1.19)	52.6 (1.83)	19.0 (1.44)	33.6 (1.73)	49.0 (1.75)	17.4 (1.32)	31.6 (1.62)
1976	2,986 (39.8)	1,451 (28.9)	1,535 (27.3)	48.8 (1.31)	15.6 (0.95)	33.3 (1.23)	47.2 (1.87)	14.5 (1.32)	32.7 (1.76)	50.3 (1.82)	16.6 (1.35)	33.8 (1.72)
1977	3,141 (40.7)	1,483 (29.7)	1,659 (26.7)	50.6 (1.29)	17.5 (0.98)	33.1 (1.21)	52.1 (1.87)	17.2 (1.41)	35.0 (1.79)	49.3 (1.77)	17.8 (1.36)	31.5 (1.65)
1978	3,163 (39.7)	1,485 (29.3)	1,677 (26.7)	50.1 (1.28)	17.0 (0.96)	33.1 (1.21)	51.1 (1.87)	15.6 (1.36)	35.5 (1.79)	49.3 (1.76)	18.3 (1.36)	31.0 (1.63)
1979	3,160 (40.0)	1,475 (29.2)	1,685 (26.2)	49.3 (1.28)	17.5 (0.98)	31.8 (1.20)	50.4 (1.88)	16.9 (1.41)	33.5 (1.78)	48.4 (1.76)	18.1 (1.35)	30.3 (1.62)
1980	3,088 (39.4)	1,498 (28.4)	1,589 (27.3)	49.3 (1.30)	19.4 (1.03)	29.9 (1.19)	46.7 (1.86)	17.1 (1.40)	29.7 (1.70)	51.8 (1.81)	21.6 (1.49)	30.2 (1.66)
1981	3,056 (42.2)	1,491 (30.4)	1,565 (29.1)	53.9 (1.30)	20.5 (1.05)	33.5 (1.23)	54.8 (1.86)	20.9 (1.52)	33.9 (1.77)	53.1 (1.82)	20.1 (1.46)	33.0 (1.72)
1982	3,100 (40.4)	1,509 (29.0)	1,592 (28.2)	50.6 (1.36)	19.1 (1.07)	31.5 (1.26)	49.1 (1.95)	17.5 (1.48)	31.6 (1.81)	52.0 (1.90)	20.6 (1.54)	31.4 (1.76)
1983	2,963 (41.6)	1,389 (30.4)	1,573 (28.2)	52.7 (1.39)	19.2 (1.10)	33.5 (1.31)	51.9 (2.03)	20.2 (1.63)	31.7 (1.89)	53.4 (1.91)	18.4 (1.48)	35.1 (1.82)
1984	3,012 (36.5)	1,429 (28.7)	1,584 (21.9)	55.2 (1.37)	19.4 (1.09)	35.8 (1.32)	56.0 (1.99)	17.7 (1.53)	38.4 (1.95)	54.5 (1.90)	21.0 (1.55)	33.5 (1.80)
1985	2,668 (40.1)	1,287 (28.7)	1,381 (27.9)	57.7 (1.45)	19.6 (1.16)	38.1 (1.43)	58.6 (2.08)	19.9 (1.69)	38.8 (2.06)	56.8 (2.02)	19.3 (1.61)	37.5 (1.97)
1986	2,786 (38.6)	1,332 (28.5)	1,454 (26.0)	53.8 (1.43)	19.2 (1.13)	34.5 (1.37)	55.8 (2.06)	21.3 (1.70)	34.5 (1.97)	51.9 (1.99)	17.3 (1.50)	34.6 (1.89)
1987	2,647 (40.9)	1,278 (29.8)	1,369 (28.0)	56.8 (1.46)	18.9 (1.15)	37.9 (1.43)	58.3 (2.09)	17.3 (1.60)	41.0 (2.09)	55.3 (2.04)	20.3 (1.65)	35.0 (1.95)
1988	2,673 (47.0)	1,334 (34.1)	1,339 (32.3)	58.9 (1.57)	21.9 (1.32)	37.1 (1.54)	57.1 (2.24)	21.3 (1.85)	35.8 (2.17)	60.7 (2.20)	22.4 (1.88)	38.3 (2.19)
1989	2,450 (46.5)	1,204 (32.9)	1,246 (32.8)	59.6 (1.64)	20.7 (1.35)	38.9 (1.63)	57.6 (2.35)	18.3 (1.84)	39.3 (2.32)	61.6 (2.27)	23.1 (1.97)	38.5 (2.28)
1990	2,362 (43.0)	1,173 (30.6)	1,189 (30.2)	60.1 (1.60)	20.1 (1.31)	40.0 (1.60)	58.0 (2.29)	19.6 (1.85)	38.4 (2.26)	62.2 (2.24)	20.6 (1.87)	41.6 (2.28)
1991	2,276 (41.0)	1,140 (29.0)	1,136 (29.0)	62.5 (1.62)	24.9 (1.44)	37.7 (1.62)	57.9 (2.33)	22.9 (1.98)	35.0 (2.25)	67.1 (2.22)	26.8 (2.09)	40.3 (2.32)
1992	2,397 (40.4)	1,216 (29.1)	1,180 (28.1)	61.9 (1.58)	23.0 (1.37)	38.9 (1.59)	60.0 (2.24)	22.1 (1.89)	37.8 (2.21)	63.8 (2.23)	23.9 (1.98)	40.0 (2.27)
1993	2,342 (41.4)	1,120 (30.6)	1,223 (27.7)	62.6 (1.59)	22.8 (1.38)	39.8 (1.61)	59.9 (2.33)	22.9 (2.00)	37.0 (2.30)	65.2 (2.17)	22.8 (1.91)	42.4 (2.25)
1994	2,517 (38.1)	1,244 (27.9)	1,273 (25.9)	61.9 (1.43)	21.0 (1.20)	40.9 (1.45)	60.6 (2.05)	23.0 (1.76)	37.5 (2.03)	63.2 (1.99)	19.1 (1.63)	44.1 (2.05)
1995	2,599 (40.9)	1,238 (29.9)	1,361 (27.7)	61.9 (1.41)	21.5 (1.19)	40.4 (1.42)	62.6 (2.03)	25.3 (1.82)	37.4 (2.03)	61.3 (1.95)	18.1 (1.54)	43.2 (1.98)
1996	2,660 (40.5)	1,297 (29.5)	1,363 (27.7)	65.0 (1.42)	23.1 (1.26)	41.9 (1.47)	60.1 (2.09)	21.5 (1.76)	38.5 (2.08)	69.7 (1.92)	24.6 (1.80)	45.1 (2.07)
1997	2,769 (41.8)	1,354 (31.0)	1,415 (27.9)	67.0 (1.38)	22.8 (1.23)	44.3 (1.45)	63.6 (2.01)	21.4 (1.71)	42.2 (2.07)	70.3 (1.87)	24.1 (1.75)	46.2 (2.04)
1998	2,810 (43.9)	1,452 (31.0)	1,358 (31.0)	65.6 (1.38)	24.4 (1.25)	41.3 (1.43)	62.4 (1.96)	24.4 (1.74)	38.0 (1.96)	69.1 (1.93)	24.3 (1.79)	44.8 (2.08)
1999	2,897 (41.5)	1,474 (29.9)	1,423 (28.8)	62.9 (1.38)	21.0 (1.17)	41.9 (1.41)	61.4 (1.95)	21.0 (1.63)	40.5 (1.97)	64.4 (1.95)	21.1 (1.67)	43.3 (2.02)
2000	2,756 (45.3)	1,251 (33.6)	1,505 (29.7)	63.3 (1.41)	21.4 (1.20)	41.9 (1.45)	59.9 (2.13)	23.1 (1.83)	36.8 (2.10)	66.2 (1.88)	20.0 (1.59)	46.2 (1.98)
2001	2,549 (46.5)	1,277 (33.7)	1,273 (32.0)	61.8 (1.48)	19.6 (1.21)	42.1 (1.51)	60.1 (2.11)	18.6 (1.68)	41.4 (2.12)	63.5 (2.08)	20.6 (1.75)	42.8 (2.13)
2002	2,796 (42.7)	1,412 (31.3)	1,384 (29.0)	65.2 (1.31)	21.6 (1.14)	43.6 (1.37)	62.1 (1.88)	20.4 (1.57)	41.7 (1.92)	68.4 (1.82)	22.8 (1.65)	45.6 (1.95)
2003	2,677 (42.2)	1,306 (29.9)	1,372 (29.7)	63.9 (1.35)	21.5 (1.16)	42.5 (1.39)	61.2 (1.97)	21.9 (1.67)	39.3 (1.97)	66.5 (1.86)	21.0 (1.61)	45.5 (1.96)
2004	2,752 (40.0)	1,327 (29.1)	1,425 (27.3)	66.7 (1.31)	22.4 (1.16)	44.2 (1.38)	61.4 (1.95)	21.8 (1.65)	39.6 (1.96)	71.5 (1.74)	23.1 (1.63)	48.5 (1.93)
2005	2,675 (40.8)	1,262 (31.5)	1,414 (24.9)	68.6 (1.31)	24.0 (1.21)	44.6 (1.40)	66.5 (1.94)	24.7 (1.77)	41.8 (2.03)	70.4 (1.77)	23.4 (1.64)	47.0 (1.94)
2006	2,692 (44.6)	1,328 (32.7)	1,363 (30.1)	66.0 (1.33)	24.7 (1.21)	41.3 (1.39)	65.8 (1.90)	24.9 (1.73)	40.9 (1.97)	66.1 (1.87)	24.5 (1.70)	41.7 (1.95)
2007	2,955 (42.6)	1,511 (30.0)	1,444 (30.3)	67.2 (1.26)	24.1 (1.15)	43.1 (1.33)	66.1 (1.78)	22.7 (1.57)	43.4 (1.86)	68.3 (1.79)	25.5 (1.67)	42.8 (1.90)
2008	3,151 (42.8)	1,640 (29.6)	1,511 (30.9)	68.6 (1.21)	27.7 (1.16)	40.9 (1.28)	65.9 (1.71)	24.9 (1.56)	41.0 (1.77)	71.6 (1.69)	30.6 (1.73)	40.9 (1.85)
2009	2,937 (45.0)	1,407 (32.8)	1,531 (30.6)	70.1 (1.23)	27.7 (1.21)	42.4 (1.33)	66.0 (1.84)	25.1 (1.69)	40.9 (1.91)	73.8 (1.64)	30.1 (1.71)	43.8 (1.85)
2010[3]	3,160 (91.8)	1,679 (64.6)	1,482 (58.4)	68.1 (1.49)	26.7 (1.52)	41.4 (1.61)	62.8 (1.88)	28.5 (2.03)	34.3 (1.97)	74.0 (2.31)	24.6 (2.32)	49.5 (2.59)
2011[3]	3,079 (88.3)	1,611 (60.6)	1,468 (58.4)	68.2 (1.45)	25.9 (1.49)	42.3 (1.44)	64.7 (2.16)	24.7 (1.79)	40.0 (2.10)	72.2 (1.98)	27.3 (2.17)	44.9 (2.37)
2012[3]	3,203 (96.2)	1,622 (70.1)	1,581 (54.0)	66.2 (1.59)	28.8 (1.57)	37.5 (1.60)	61.3 (2.17)	26.9 (2.20)	34.4 (2.15)	71.3 (2.11)	30.7 (2.09)	40.6 (2.21)

—Not available.
†Not applicable.
[1]Individuals ages 16 to 24 who graduated from high school or completed a GED during the preceding 12 months.
[2]Enrollment in college as of October of each year for individuals ages 16 to 24 who completed high school during the preceding 12 months.
[3]Beginning in 2010, standard errors were computed using replicate weights, which produced more precise values than the methodology used in prior years.

NOTE: Data are based on sample surveys of the civilian population. High school completion data in this table differ from figures appearing in other tables because of varying survey procedures and coverage. High school completers include GED recipients. Detail may not sum to totals because of rounding.
SOURCE: American College Testing Program, unpublished tabulations, derived from statistics collected by the Census Bureau, 1960 through 1969. U.S. Department of Commerce, Census Bureau, Current Population Survey (CPS), October, 1970 through 2012. (This table was prepared May 2013.)

Percentage of recent high school completers enrolled in 2- and 4-year colleges, by race/ethnicity: 1960 through 2012
[Standard errors appear in parentheses]

Year	Percent of recent high school completers[1] enrolled in college[2] (annual data)					3-year moving averages[3] — Percent of recent high school completers[1] enrolled in college[2]					Difference between percent enrolled		
	Total	White	Black	Hispanic	Asian	Total	White	Black	Hispanic	Asian	White-Black	White-Hispanic	White-Asian
1	2	3	4	5	6	7	8	9	10	11	12	13	14
1960[4]	45.1 (2.13)	45.8 (2.21)	— (†)	— (†)	— (†)	46.6 (1.49)	47.7 (1.56)	— (†)	— (†)	— (†)	— (†)	— (†)	— (†)
1961[4]	48.0 (2.09)	49.5 (2.19)	— (†)	— (†)	— (†)	47.4 (1.21)	48.7 (1.26)	— (†)	— (†)	— (†)	— (†)	— (†)	— (†)
1962[4]	49.0 (2.05)	50.6 (2.15)	— (†)	— (†)	— (†)	47.4 (1.20)	48.6 (1.25)	— (†)	— (†)	— (†)	— (†)	— (†)	— (†)
1963[4]	45.0 (2.09)	45.6 (2.17)	— (†)	— (†)	— (†)	47.5 (1.16)	48.5 (1.21)	— (†)	— (†)	— (†)	— (†)	— (†)	— (†)
1964[4]	48.3 (1.89)	49.2 (1.98)	— (†)	— (†)	— (†)	48.5 (1.08)	49.2 (1.13)	— (†)	— (†)	— (†)	— (†)	— (†)	— (†)
1965[4]	50.9 (1.70)	51.7 (1.78)	— (†)	— (†)	— (†)	49.9 (1.02)	51.0 (1.07)	— (†)	— (†)	— (†)	— (†)	— (†)	— (†)
1966[4]	50.1 (1.72)	51.7 (1.79)	— (†)	— (†)	— (†)	51.0 (0.99)	52.1 (1.04)	— (†)	— (†)	— (†)	— (†)	— (†)	— (†)
1967[4]	51.9 (1.42)	53.0 (1.50)	— (†)	— (†)	— (†)	52.5 (0.81)	53.8 (0.85)	— (†)	— (†)	— (†)	— (†)	— (†)	— (†)
1968[4]	55.4 (1.39)	56.6 (1.47)	— (†)	— (†)	— (†)	53.6 (0.80)	55.0 (0.84)	— (†)	— (†)	— (†)	— (†)	— (†)	— (†)
1969[4]	53.3 (1.34)	55.2 (1.41)	— (†)	— (†)	— (†)	53.5 (0.79)	54.6 (0.83)	— (†)	— (†)	— (†)	— (†)	— (†)	— (†)
1970[4]	51.7 (1.36)	52.0 (1.44)	— (†)	— (†)	— (†)	52.9 (0.77)	53.8 (0.82)	— (†)	— (†)	— (†)	— (†)	— (†)	— (†)
1971[4]	53.5 (1.33)	54.0 (1.40)	— (†)	— (†)	— (†)	51.5 (0.77)	51.9 (0.82)	— (†)	— (†)	— (†)	— (†)	— (†)	— (†)
1972	49.2 (1.31)	49.7 (1.42)	44.6 (4.62)	45.0 (9.74)	— (†)	49.7 (0.76)	50.5 (0.81)	38.4 (3.18)	49.9 (6.64)	— (†)	12.1 (3.28)	‡ (†)	— (†)
1973	46.6 (1.29)	47.8 (1.40)	32.5 (4.30)	54.1 (9.01)	— (†)	47.8 (0.75)	48.2 (0.81)	41.4 (2.62)	48.8 (5.33)	— (†)	6.8 ! (2.74)	‡ (†)	— (†)
1974	47.6 (1.28)	47.2 (1.39)	47.2 (4.58)	46.9 (8.94)	— (†)	48.3 (0.74)	48.7 (0.80)	45.0 (2.63)	53.1 (5.09)	— (†)	8.3 ! (2.75)	‡ (†)	— (†)
1975	50.7 (1.26)	51.1 (1.37)	41.7 (3.97)	58.0 (8.44)	— (†)	49.1 (0.74)	49.1 (0.81)	44.5 (2.29)	52.7 (4.88)	— (†)	‡ (†)	‡ (†)	— (†)
1976	48.8 (1.31)	48.8 (1.43)	44.4 (4.08)	52.7 (7.97)	— (†)	50.1 (0.74)	50.3 (0.81)	45.3 (2.30)	53.6 (4.68)	— (†)	5.0 ! (2.44)	‡ (†)	— (†)
1977	50.6 (1.29)	50.8 (1.41)	49.5 (4.65)	50.8 (7.96)	— (†)	49.9 (0.75)	50.1 (0.82)	46.8 (2.70)	48.8 (4.72)	— (†)	‡ (†)	‡ (†)	— (†)
1978	50.1 (1.28)	50.5 (1.41)	46.4 (4.51)	42.0 (8.44)	— (†)	50.0 (0.74)	50.4 (0.81)	47.5 (2.67)	46.1 (4.69)	— (†)	‡ (†)	‡ (†)	— (†)
1979	49.3 (1.28)	49.9 (1.41)	46.7 (4.69)	45.0 (7.92)	— (†)	49.6 (0.74)	50.1 (0.82)	45.2 (2.62)	46.3 (4.83)	— (†)	‡ (†)	‡ (†)	— (†)
1980	49.3 (1.30)	49.8 (1.43)	42.7 (4.44)	52.3 (8.70)	— (†)	50.8 (0.75)	51.5 (0.82)	44.0 (2.61)	49.6 (4.78)	— (†)	7.5 ! (2.74)	‡ (†)	— (†)
1981	53.9 (1.30)	54.9 (1.44)	42.7 (4.44)	52.1 (8.19)	— (†)	51.3 (0.75)	52.4 (0.83)	40.3 (2.50)	48.7 (4.68)	— (†)	12.2 (2.64)	‡ (†)	— (†)
1982	50.6 (1.36)	52.7 (1.52)	35.8 (4.33)	43.2 (7.96)	— (†)	52.4 (0.79)	54.2 (0.88)	38.8 (2.57)	49.4 (4.94)	— (†)	15.4 (2.70)	‡ (†)	— (†)
1983	52.7 (1.39)	55.0 (1.55)	38.2 (4.34)	54.2 (8.96)	— (†)	52.8 (0.79)	55.5 (0.89)	38.0 (2.47)	46.7 (4.72)	— (†)	17.5 (2.62)	‡ (†)	— (†)
1984	55.2 (1.37)	59.0 (1.54)	39.8 (4.15)	44.3 (7.67)	— (†)	55.1 (0.81)	57.9 (0.91)	39.9 (2.54)	49.3 (4.89)	— (†)	18.0 (2.70)	‡ (†)	— (†)
1985	57.7 (1.45)	60.1 (1.62)	42.2 (4.78)	51.0 (9.76)	— (†)	55.5 (0.82)	58.6 (0.92)	39.5 (2.55)	46.1 (5.18)	— (†)	19.1 (2.71)	12.5 ! (5.27)	— (†)
1986	53.8 (1.43)	56.8 (1.62)	36.9 (4.38)	44.0 (8.85)	— (†)	56.1 (0.84)	58.5 (0.94)	43.5 (2.71)	42.3 (5.20)	— (†)	15.0 (2.87)	16.2 ! (5.28)	— (†)
1987	56.8 (1.46)	58.6 (1.65)	52.2 (4.82)	33.5 (8.25)	— (†)	56.5 (0.83)	58.8 (0.95)	44.2 (2.65)	45.0 (5.04)	— (†)	14.6 (2.82)	13.8 ! (5.13)	— (†)
1988	58.9 (1.57)	61.1 (1.79)	44.4 (4.91)	57.1 (10.14)	— (†)	58.4 (0.92)	60.1 (0.96)	49.7 (2.98)	48.5 (5.99)	— (†)	10.4 ! (3.13)	‡ (†)	— (†)
1989	59.6 (1.64)	60.7 (1.85)	53.4 (5.27)	55.1 (10.51)	— (†)	59.5 (0.94)	61.6 (1.06)	48.0 (2.98)	52.7 (6.33)	— (†)	13.6 (3.16)	‡ (†)	— (†)
1990	60.1 (1.60)	63.0 (1.80)	46.8 (5.08)	42.7 (10.82)	— (†)	60.7 (0.92)	63.0 (1.08)	48.9 (2.97)	52.5 (5.70)	— (†)	14.0 (3.16)	‡ (†)	— (†)
1991	62.5 (1.62)	65.4 (1.82)	46.4 (5.25)	57.2 (9.58)	— (†)	61.5 (0.92)	64.2 (1.05)	47.2 (2.93)	52.6 (5.52)	— (†)	17.0 (3.11)	11.7 ! (5.62)	— (†)
1992	61.9 (1.58)	64.3 (1.84)	48.2 (4.92)	55.0 (8.50)	— (†)	62.3 (0.92)	64.2 (1.06)	50.0 (2.98)	58.2 (5.04)	— (†)	14.2 (3.16)	‡ (†)	— (†)
1993	62.6 (1.59)	62.9 (1.85)	55.6 (5.28)	62.2 (8.22)	— (†)	62.1 (0.91)	63.9 (1.04)	51.3 (2.97)	55.0 (4.97)	— (†)	12.6 (3.14)	‡ (†)	— (†)
1994	61.9 (1.43)	64.5 (1.61)	50.8 (4.42)	49.1 (6.28)	— (†)	62.1 (0.83)	64.0 (1.03)	52.4 (2.52)	55.0 (3.23)	— (†)	11.5 (2.72)	8.9 ! (3.39)	— (†)
1995	61.9 (1.41)	64.3 (1.64)	51.2 (4.20)	53.7 (4.92)	— (†)	63.0 (0.81)	65.4 (0.93)	52.9 (2.40)	51.6 (3.18)	— (†)	12.5 (2.57)	13.8 (3.31)	— (†)
1996	65.0 (1.42)	67.4 (1.67)	56.0 (4.03)	50.8 (5.79)	— (†)	64.7 (0.82)	66.6 (0.93)	55.4 (2.41)	57.6 (2.96)	— (†)	11.3 (2.58)	9.0 ! (3.10)	— (†)
1997	67.0 (1.38)	68.2 (1.64)	58.5 (4.12)	65.6 (4.53)	— (†)	65.9 (0.80)	68.1 (0.95)	58.8 (2.35)	55.3 (2.93)	— (†)	9.3 (2.53)	12.8 (3.08)	— (†)
1998	65.6 (1.38)	68.5 (1.61)	61.9 (4.05)	47.4 (4.92)	— (†)	65.2 (0.80)	67.7 (0.94)	59.8 (2.31)	51.9 (2.77)	— (†)	7.9 ! (2.50)	15.7 (2.94)	— (†)
1999	62.9 (1.38)	66.3 (1.64)	58.9 (3.86)	42.3 (4.76)	— (†)	64.0 (0.80)	66.8 (0.94)	58.6 (2.31)	47.4 (2.84)	— (†)	8.3 ! (2.50)	19.5 (2.99)	— (†)
2000	63.3 (1.41)	65.7 (1.66)	54.9 (4.11)	52.9 (5.03)	— (†)	62.7 (0.82)	65.4 (0.97)	56.4 (2.37)	48.6 (2.96)	— (†)	9.1 (2.53)	16.9 (3.11)	— (†)
2001	61.8 (1.48)	64.3 (1.72)	55.0 (4.17)	51.7 (5.63)	— (†)	63.5 (0.82)	66.3 (0.97)	56.4 (2.39)	52.8 (2.93)	— (†)	10.0 (2.58)	13.5 (3.09)	— (†)
2002	65.2 (1.31)	69.1 (1.55)	59.4 (3.90)	53.6 (4.46)	— (†)	63.7 (0.78)	66.5 (0.97)	57.3 (2.33)	54.8 (2.75)	— (†)	9.3 (2.52)	11.7 (2.92)	— (†)
2003[5]	63.9 (1.35)	66.2 (1.61)	57.5 (4.25)	58.6 (4.61)	84.1 (5.10)	65.3 (0.77)	68.0 (0.91)	59.9 (2.29)	57.7 (2.66)	80.0 (3.99)	8.1 ! (2.46)	10.3 (2.81)	-11.9 ! (4.10)
2004[5]	66.7 (1.31)	68.8 (1.57)	62.5 (3.77)	61.8 (4.76)	75.6 (6.13)	66.4 (0.77)	69.4 (0.91)	58.8 (2.34)	57.7 (2.60)	81.6 (3.37)	10.6 (2.51)	11.7 (2.75)	-12.2 (3.49)
2005[5]	68.6 (1.31)	73.2 (1.52)	55.7 (4.15)	54.0 (4.18)	86.7 (5.99)	67.1 (0.76)	70.2 (0.90)	58.2 (2.35)	57.5 (2.52)	80.9 (3.64)	12.0 (2.52)	12.6 (2.67)	-10.7 ! (3.75)
2006[5]	66.0 (1.33)	68.5 (1.60)	55.5 (4.33)	57.9 (4.18)	82.3 (5.32)	67.2 (0.75)	70.4 (0.89)	55.6 (2.35)	58.5 (2.43)	85.1 (3.64)	14.7 (2.51)	11.9 (2.59)	-14.7 (3.74)
2007[5]	67.2 (1.26)	69.5 (1.49)	55.7 (3.78)	64.0 (4.22)	88.8 (6.26)	67.3 (0.73)	70.0 (0.87)	55.7 (2.27)	62.0 (2.33)	85.8 (3.45)	14.3 (2.43)	8.0 ! (2.48)	-15.8 (3.56)
2008[5]	68.6 (1.21)	71.7 (1.44)	55.7 (3.78)	63.9 (3.72)	88.4 (5.08)	68.6 (0.71)	70.8 (0.86)	60.3 (2.25)	62.3 (2.25)	90.1 (3.01)	10.5 (2.31)	8.6 (2.41)	-19.2 (3.13)
2009[5]	70.1 (1.23)	71.3 (1.53)	69.5 (3.51)	59.3 (3.80)	92.1 (3.90)	68.9 (0.70)	72.1 (0.86)	62.4 (2.09)	60.9 (2.14)	88.1 (2.85)	8.8 (2.26)	10.3 (2.31)	-16.9 (2.98)
2010[5,6]	68.1 (1.49)	70.5 (1.68)	62.0 (4.81)	59.7 (4.18)	84.7 (5.27)	68.8 (0.71)	70.1 (0.90)	66.1 (2.01)	62.3 (2.01)	87.4 (2.78)	‡ (†)	7.8 (2.21)	-17.3 (2.92)
2011[5,6]	68.2 (1.45)	68.3 (1.86)	67.1 (4.01)	66.6 (3.50)	86.1 (4.25)	67.5 (0.89)	68.2 (1.03)	62.1 (2.86)	66.1 (2.17)	83.9 (2.79)	6.1 ! (3.04)	‡ (†)	-15.7 (2.97)
2012[5,6]	66.2 (1.59)	65.7 (1.94)	56.4 (4.84)	70.3 (3.22)	81.5 (5.15)	67.2 (1.17)	67.0 (1.37)	62.1 (3.16)	68.5 (2.44)	83.6 (3.48)	‡ (†)	‡ (†)	-16.6 (3.74)

—Not available.
†Not applicable.
!Interpret data with caution. The coefficient of variation (CV) for this estimate is between 30 and 50 percent.
‡Reporting standards not met. The coefficient of variation (CV) for this estimate is 50 percent or greater.
[1]Individuals ages 16 to 24 who graduated from high school or completed a GED during the preceding 12 months.
[2]Enrollment in college as of October of each year for individuals ages 16 to 24 who completed high school during the preceding 12 months.
[3]A 3-year moving average is an arithmetic average of the year indicated, the year immediately preceding, and the year immediately following. For the first and final years of available data, a 2-year moving average is used: The moving average for 1960 reflects an average of 1960 and 1961; for Black and Hispanic data, the moving average for 1972 reflects an average of 1972 and 1973; for Asian data, the moving average for 2003 reflects an average of 2003 and 2004; and the moving average for 2012 reflects an average of 2011 and 2012. Moving averages are used to produce more stable estimates.
[4]Prior to 1972, White data include persons of Hispanic ethnicity.
[5]White, Black, and Asian data exclude persons identifying themselves as two or more races.
[6]Beginning in 2010, standard errors were computed using replicate weights, which produced more precise values than the methodology used in prior years.
NOTE: Race categories exclude persons of Hispanic ethnicity except where otherwise noted. Total includes persons of other racial/ethnic groups not separately shown.
SOURCE: American College Testing Program, unpublished tabulations, derived from statistics collected by the Census Bureau, 1960 through 1969. U.S. Department of Commerce, Census Bureau, Current Population Survey (CPS), October, 1970 through 2012. (This table was prepared May 2013.)

Percentage of recent high school completers enrolled in 2-year and 4-year colleges, by income level: 1975 through 2012

[Standard errors appear in parentheses]

Year	Percent of recent high school completers[1] enrolled in college[2] (annual data)				3-year moving averages[3] Percent of recent high school completers[1] enrolled in college[2]				Difference between percent enrolled	
	Total	Low income	Middle income	High income	Total	Low income	Middle income	High income	High-low income	High-middle income
1	2	3	4	5	6	7	8	9	10	11
1975	50.7 (1.26)	31.2 (3.59)	46.2 (1.69)	64.5 (2.09)	49.1 (0.74)	34.7 (2.74)	43.5 (1.22)	63.7 (1.47)	29.0 (3.11)	20.2 (1.91)
1976	48.8 (1.31)	39.1 (4.20)	40.5 (1.76)	63.0 (2.06)	50.1 (0.74)	32.3 (2.17)	43.8 (1.00)	64.6 (1.18)	32.3 (2.47)	20.8 (1.55)
1977	50.6 (1.29)	27.7 (3.54)	44.2 (1.76)	66.3 (2.01)	49.9 (0.75)	32.4 (2.22)	43.1 (1.02)	64.4 (1.18)	32.1 (2.51)	21.4 (1.56)
1978	50.1 (1.28)	31.4 (3.74)	44.3 (1.74)	64.0 (2.05)	50.0 (0.74)	29.8 (2.13)	43.9 (1.01)	64.5 (1.17)	34.6 (2.43)	20.5 (1.55)
1979	49.3 (1.28)	30.5 (3.78)	43.2 (1.74)	63.2 (2.04)	49.6 (0.74)	31.6 (2.11)	43.4 (1.01)	64.1 (1.19)	32.6 (2.42)	20.8 (1.56)
1980	49.3 (1.30)	32.5 (3.47)	42.5 (1.78)	65.2 (2.08)	50.8 (0.75)	32.2 (2.14)	45.0 (1.02)	65.3 (1.20)	33.0 (2.45)	20.2 (1.57)
1981	53.9 (1.30)	33.6 (3.90)	49.2 (1.75)	67.6 (2.09)	51.3 (0.75)	32.9 (2.11)	44.5 (1.01)	67.9 (1.19)	34.9 (2.42)	23.4 (1.57)
1982	50.6 (1.36)	32.8 (3.81)	41.7 (1.81)	70.9 (2.13)	52.4 (0.79)	33.6 (2.29)	45.4 (1.06)	69.6 (1.25)	36.0 (2.61)	24.2 (1.64)
1983	52.7 (1.39)	34.6 (4.02)	45.2 (1.88)	70.3 (2.17)	52.8 (0.79)	34.0 (2.20)	45.1 (1.08)	71.7 (1.23)	37.8 (2.52)	26.7 (1.63)
1984	55.2 (1.37)	34.5 (3.62)	48.4 (1.89)	74.0 (2.09)	55.1 (0.81)	36.3 (2.26)	48.0 (1.11)	72.9 (1.24)	36.6 (2.58)	24.9 (1.66)
1985	57.7 (1.45)	40.2 (4.14)	50.6 (2.02)	74.6 (2.16)	55.5 (0.82)	35.9 (2.18)	49.1 (1.13)	73.2 (1.26)	37.3 (2.51)	24.1 (1.69)
1986	53.8 (1.43)	33.9 (3.59)	48.5 (1.97)	71.0 (2.28)	56.1 (0.84)	36.8 (2.23)	49.6 (1.17)	73.2 (1.27)	36.4 (2.57)	23.5 (1.72)
1987	56.8 (1.46)	36.9 (3.88)	50.0 (2.07)	73.8 (2.16)	56.5 (0.83)	37.6 (2.21)	51.1 (1.16)	72.6 (1.30)	35.0 (2.57)	21.5 (1.74)
1988	58.9 (1.57)	42.5 (4.39)	54.7 (2.14)	72.8 (2.62)	58.4 (0.92)	42.4 (2.54)	53.4 (1.28)	72.5 (1.44)	30.2 (2.92)	19.1 (1.93)
1989	59.6 (1.64)	48.1 (4.56)	55.4 (2.28)	70.7 (2.61)	59.5 (0.94)	45.6 (2.66)	54.9 (1.28)	73.2 (1.50)	27.6 (3.06)	18.4 (1.97)
1990	60.1 (1.60)	46.7 (4.76)	54.4 (2.14)	76.6 (2.54)	60.7 (0.92)	44.8 (2.63)	56.0 (1.27)	75.0 (1.44)	30.2 (3.00)	19.0 (1.92)
1991	62.5 (1.62)	39.5 (4.50)	58.4 (2.25)	78.2 (2.39)	61.5 (0.92)	42.2 (2.62)	56.5 (1.26)	78.0 (1.40)	35.8 (2.97)	21.4 (1.88)
1992	61.9 (1.58)	40.9 (4.37)	57.0 (2.18)	79.0 (2.35)	62.3 (0.92)	43.6 (2.60)	57.4 (1.26)	78.8 (1.38)	35.3 (2.94)	21.4 (1.86)
1993	62.6 (1.59)	50.4 (4.56)	56.9 (2.15)	79.3 (2.46)	62.1 (0.91)	44.7 (2.55)	57.3 (1.23)	78.7 (1.39)	34.0 (2.90)	21.5 (1.86)
1994	61.9 (1.43)	43.3 (3.96)	57.8 (1.94)	77.9 (2.22)	62.1 (0.83)	42.0 (2.27)	57.0 (1.14)	80.4 (1.22)	38.4 (2.57)	23.4 (1.67)
1995	61.9 (1.41)	34.2 (3.56)	56.0 (2.00)	83.5 (1.86)	63.0 (0.81)	42.1 (2.16)	58.9 (1.12)	79.9 (1.20)	37.8 (2.47)	21.0 (1.64)
1996	65.0 (1.42)	48.6 (3.78)	62.7 (1.95)	78.0 (2.27)	64.7 (0.82)	47.1 (2.18)	59.9 (1.16)	81.3 (1.19)	34.3 (2.49)	21.4 (1.66)
1997	67.0 (1.38)	57.0 (3.66)	60.7 (1.97)	82.2 (1.98)	65.9 (0.80)	50.6 (2.14)	62.7 (1.12)	79.3 (1.24)	28.7 (2.47)	16.6 (1.67)
1998	65.6 (1.38)	46.4 (3.62)	64.7 (1.89)	77.5 (2.21)	65.2 (0.80)	50.3 (2.14)	61.9 (1.10)	78.4 (1.24)	28.1 (2.47)	16.6 (1.66)
1999	62.9 (1.38)	47.6 (3.77)	60.2 (1.87)	75.4 (2.26)	64.0 (0.80)	47.9 (2.13)	61.5 (1.10)	76.6 (1.29)	28.7 (2.49)	15.1 (1.70)
2000	63.3 (1.41)	49.7 (3.67)	59.5 (1.97)	76.9 (2.22)	62.7 (0.82)	47.1 (2.17)	58.8 (1.14)	77.4 (1.29)	30.3 (2.52)	18.6 (1.72)
2001	61.8 (1.48)	43.8 (3.81)	56.4 (2.07)	80.0 (2.19)	63.5 (0.82)	49.9 (2.19)	59.1 (1.14)	78.3 (1.28)	28.4 (2.53)	19.3 (1.71)
2002	65.2 (1.31)	56.3 (3.64)	60.9 (1.78)	78.2 (2.12)	63.7 (0.78)	50.9 (2.14)	58.4 (1.08)	79.5 (1.20)	28.6 (2.45)	21.0 (1.61)
2003	63.9 (1.35)	52.8 (3.83)	57.6 (1.87)	80.1 (2.02)	65.3 (0.77)	52.5 (2.20)	60.6 (1.05)	79.5 (1.18)	27.0 (2.49)	18.9 (1.58)
2004	66.7 (1.31)	47.8 (3.95)	63.3 (1.79)	80.1 (1.98)	66.4 (0.77)	51.4 (2.24)	62.0 (1.05)	80.5 (1.15)	29.0 (2.52)	18.5 (1.56)
2005	68.6 (1.31)	53.5 (3.86)	65.1 (1.81)	81.2 (1.98)	67.1 (0.76)	50.8 (2.26)	63.3 (1.04)	80.7 (1.15)	29.9 (2.53)	17.4 (1.55)
2006	66.0 (1.33)	50.9 (3.92)	61.4 (1.82)	80.7 (2.01)	67.2 (0.75)	54.5 (2.18)	63.3 (1.03)	80.0 (1.15)	25.5 (2.47)	16.7 (1.55)
2007	67.2 (1.26)	58.4 (3.57)	63.3 (1.73)	78.2 (2.01)	67.3 (0.73)	55.3 (2.11)	63.5 (0.99)	80.2 (1.14)	24.9 (2.40)	16.8 (1.51)
2008	68.6 (1.21)	55.9 (3.50)	65.2 (1.62)	81.9 (1.90)	68.6 (0.71)	56.1 (2.08)	65.1 (0.96)	81.4 (1.11)	25.3 (2.36)	16.2 (1.47)
2009	70.1 (1.23)	53.9 (3.75)	66.7 (1.66)	84.2 (1.84)	68.9 (0.70)	53.3 (2.02)	66.2 (0.94)	82.8 (1.10)	29.5 (2.30)	16.6 (1.44)
2010[4]	68.1 (1.49)	50.7 (3.88)	66.7 (1.59)	82.2 (2.34)	68.8 (0.71)	52.6 (1.97)	66.5 (0.94)	83.0 (1.12)	30.4 (2.27)	16.4 (1.46)
2011[4]	68.2 (1.45)	53.5 (4.25)	66.2 (1.63)	82.4 (2.46)	67.5 (0.89)	51.6 (2.47)	65.9 (1.11)	81.7 (1.42)	30.1 (2.85)	15.9 (1.81)
2012[4]	66.2 (1.59)	50.9 (4.39)	64.7 (2.10)	80.7 (2.54)	67.2 (1.17)	52.1 (3.24)	65.5 (1.47)	81.5 (1.86)	29.4 (3.74)	16.0 (2.37)

[1]Individuals ages 16 to 24 who graduated from high school or completed a GED during the preceding 12 months.

[2]Enrollment in college as of October of each year for individuals ages 16 to 24 who completed high school during the preceding 12 months.

[3]A 3-year moving average is an arithmetic average of the year indicated, the year immediately preceding, and the year immediately following. For 1975 and 2012, a 2-year moving average is used: The moving average for 1975 reflects an average of 1975 and 1976, and the moving average for 2012 reflects an average of 2011 and 2012. Moving averages are used to produce more stable estimates.

[4]Beginning in 2010, standard errors were computed using replicate weights, which produced more precise values than the methodology used in prior years.

NOTE: Low income refers to the bottom 20 percent of all family incomes, high income refers to the top 20 percent of all family incomes, and middle income refers to the 60 percent in between.

SOURCE: U.S. Department of Commerce, Census Bureau, Current Population Survey (CPS), October, 1975 through 2012. (This table was prepared May 2013.)

Percentage of 18- to 24-year-olds enrolled in degree-granting institutions, by level of institution and sex and race/ethnicity of student: 1967 through 2012

[Standard errors appear in parentheses]

Year	Total, all students	Level of institution — 2-year	Level of institution — 4-year	Sex — Male	Sex — Female	Race/ethnicity — White	Black	Hispanic	Asian	Pacific Islander	American Indian/Alaska Native	Two or more races	Race/ethnicity by sex — White Male	White Female	Black Male	Black Female	Hispanic Male	Hispanic Female
1967	25.5 (0.44)	—	—	33.1 (0.71)	19.2 (0.54)	26.9 (0.48)	13.0 (1.16)	—	—	—	—	—	—	—	—	—	—	—
1968	26.1 (0.44)	—	—	34.1 (0.70)	19.5 (0.54)	27.5 (0.48)	14.5 (1.18)	—	—	—	—	—	—	—	—	—	—	—
1969	27.3 (0.44)	—	—	35.2 (0.69)	20.9 (0.54)	28.7 (0.47)	16.0 (1.20)	—	—	—	—	—	—	—	—	—	—	—
1970	25.7 (0.42)	—	—	32.1 (0.65)	20.3 (0.52)	27.1 (0.45)	15.5 (1.15)	—	—	—	—	—	—	—	—	—	—	—
1971	26.2 (0.41)	—	—	32.5 (0.63)	20.8 (0.52)	27.2 (0.44)	18.2 (1.19)	—	—	—	—	—	—	—	—	—	—	—
1972	25.5 (0.37)	—	—	30.2 (0.56)	21.2 (0.47)	27.2 (0.41)	18.3 (1.18)	13.4 (1.83)	—	—	—	—	32.3 (0.63)	22.5 (0.54)	21.1 (1.83)	15.9 (1.51)	15.1 (2.85)	12.0 (2.37)
1973	24.0 (0.35)	6.9 (0.21)	17.1 (0.31)	27.7 (0.54)	20.5 (0.46)	25.5 (0.40)	15.9 (1.09)	16.1 (2.02)	—	—	—	—	29.6 (0.60)	21.8 (0.53)	18.7 (1.77)	13.5 (1.39)	16.7 (2.94)	15.5 (2.77)
1974	24.6 (0.35)	7.6 (0.22)	17.0 (0.31)	27.7 (0.53)	21.7 (0.47)	25.8 (0.40)	17.6 (1.14)	18.0 (1.95)	—	—	—	—	28.9 (0.60)	22.9 (0.53)	19.8 (1.77)	15.9 (1.47)	19.7 (2.92)	16.5 (2.60)
1975	26.3 (0.36)	9.0 (0.23)	17.3 (0.31)	29.0 (0.53)	23.7 (0.48)	27.4 (0.40)	20.4 (1.18)	20.0 (2.09)	—	—	—	—	30.7 (0.59)	24.3 (0.54)	19.9 (1.74)	20.8 (1.61)	21.4 (3.10)	19.5 (2.81)
1976	26.7 (0.35)	6.4 (0.20)	20.2 (0.32)	28.0 (0.52)	25.2 (0.48)	27.6 (0.40)	22.5 (1.20)	20.0 (2.00)	—	—	—	—	29.3 (0.58)	21.3 (0.55)	22.0 (1.77)	22.9 (1.64)	21.3 (3.05)	18.8 (2.64)
1977	26.1 (0.38)	6.8 (0.22)	19.4 (0.35)	28.1 (0.56)	24.3 (0.52)	27.2 (0.43)	21.1 (1.18)	17.2 (1.87)	—	—	—	—	29.4 (0.64)	25.1 (0.59)	20.3 (1.70)	21.9 (1.61)	18.3 (2.80)	16.3 (2.50)
1978	25.3 (0.38)	6.6 (0.22)	18.7 (0.34)	27.1 (0.55)	23.6 (0.51)	26.5 (0.43)	20.1 (1.15)	15.2 (1.74)	—	—	—	—	28.4 (0.63)	24.6 (0.59)	19.7 (1.70)	20.4 (1.56)	16.1 (2.61)	14.3 (2.33)
1979	25.0 (0.37)	6.3 (0.21)	18.7 (0.34)	25.9 (0.54)	24.2 (0.52)	26.3 (0.43)	19.8 (1.13)	16.7 (1.77)	—	—	—	—	27.1 (0.61)	25.5 (0.59)	19.1 (1.67)	20.3 (1.54)	18.3 (2.65)	15.2 (2.35)
1980	25.7 (0.37)	7.1 (0.21)	18.6 (0.33)	25.6 (0.54)	25.0 (0.52)	27.3 (0.43)	19.4 (1.12)	16.7 (1.64)	—	—	—	—	28.4 (0.63)	26.3 (0.60)	17.5 (1.60)	20.9 (1.55)	15.9 (2.33)	15.9 (2.32)
1981	26.1 (0.37)	7.5 (0.22)	18.6 (0.33)	27.1 (0.54)	25.2 (0.51)	27.7 (0.43)	19.9 (1.09)	16.6 (1.63)	—	—	—	—	28.7 (0.62)	26.6 (0.60)	18.9 (1.58)	20.7 (1.51)	16.6 (2.35)	16.7 (2.27)
1982	26.6 (0.39)	7.7 (0.24)	18.9 (0.35)	27.2 (0.57)	26.0 (0.55)	28.1 (0.46)	19.9 (1.14)	16.8 (1.77)	—	—	—	—	28.9 (0.66)	27.4 (0.64)	18.7 (1.64)	21.0 (1.59)	14.9 (2.45)	18.6 (2.52)
1983	26.2 (0.40)	7.4 (0.24)	18.8 (0.35)	27.3 (0.57)	25.1 (0.54)	27.9 (0.46)	19.2 (1.12)	17.3 (1.77)	—	—	—	—	29.4 (0.66)	26.5 (0.64)	18.1 (1.60)	20.1 (1.56)	15.6 (2.46)	18.8 (2.54)
1984	27.1 (0.40)	7.3 (0.24)	19.8 (0.36)	28.6 (0.58)	25.6 (0.54)	28.9 (0.47)	20.3 (1.15)	18.0 (1.80)	—	—	—	—	30.8 (0.65)	27.1 (0.65)	20.3 (1.67)	20.3 (1.57)	16.1 (2.51)	19.6 (2.57)
1985	27.8 (0.41)	7.4 (0.24)	20.4 (0.37)	28.4 (0.60)	27.2 (0.57)	30.0 (0.49)	19.6 (1.16)	16.9 (1.84)	—	—	—	—	30.9 (0.70)	29.2 (0.67)	20.2 (1.72)	19.1 (1.56)	14.9 (2.46)	18.9 (2.75)
1986	27.9 (0.42)	7.6 (0.25)	20.3 (0.37)	28.2 (0.60)	27.6 (0.58)	29.7 (0.50)	21.9 (1.21)	17.6 (1.76)	—	—	—	—	30.6 (0.72)	28.8 (0.68)	20.0 (1.72)	23.4 (1.69)	16.7 (2.36)	18.7 (2.64)
1987	29.6 (0.43)	8.1 (0.26)	21.5 (0.39)	30.6 (0.62)	28.7 (0.59)	31.9 (0.51)	22.8 (1.25)	17.5 (1.73)	—	—	—	—	33.0 (0.74)	30.8 (0.71)	22.6 (1.83)	22.9 (1.70)	18.5 (2.46)	16.5 (2.43)
1988	30.3 (0.48)	8.8 (0.28)	21.5 (0.42)	30.2 (0.68)	30.4 (0.67)	33.2 (0.58)	21.2 (1.23)	17.0 (2.00)	—	—	—	—	33.4 (0.82)	33.0 (0.79)	18.5 (1.89)	23.5 (1.97)	19.7 (2.74)	17.6 (2.93)
1989	30.9 (0.47)	8.0 (0.28)	22.9 (0.44)	30.2 (0.68)	31.6 (0.67)	34.2 (0.57)	23.4 (1.38)	16.1 (1.90)	46.1 (3.92)	—	15.7 (5.33)‡	—	34.1 (0.83)	34.4 (0.80)	19.7 (1.89)	26.7 (1.89)	14.6 (2.55)	17.6 (2.81)
1990	32.0 (0.47)	8.7 (0.28)	23.3 (0.43)	32.3 (0.68)	31.8 (0.66)	35.1 (0.57)	25.4 (1.37)	15.8 (1.67)	56.9 (3.56)	—	15.8 (5.08)‡	—	35.5 (0.83)	34.7 (0.80)	26.0 (2.03)	24.8 (1.86)	15.3 (2.31)	16.4 (2.42)
1991	33.3 (0.42)	9.7 (0.30)	23.6 (0.43)	34.1 (0.66)	33.6 (0.67)	36.8 (0.58)	23.5 (1.34)	17.6 (1.72)	57.1 (3.19)	—	15.9 (5.45)‡	—	36.5 (0.83)	37.0 (0.82)	22.2 (1.95)	23.8 (1.84)	14.0 (2.15)	22.2 (2.70)
1992	34.4 (0.49)	9.9 (0.31)	24.4 (0.44)	32.7 (0.68)	36.0 (0.69)	37.3 (0.59)	25.2 (1.37)	21.9 (1.87)	58.4 (3.28)	—	18.5 (6.18)‡	—	36.2 (0.83)	38.3 (0.83)	21.3 (1.87)	28.8 (1.96)	17.8 (2.47)	24.7 (2.80)
1993	34.0 (0.49)	9.8 (0.30)	24.2 (0.44)	33.6 (0.69)	34.4 (0.69)	36.8 (0.59)	24.5 (1.35)	21.7 (1.88)	61.2 (3.66)	—	18.9 (5.66)	—	36.5 (0.84)	37.1 (0.83)	22.9 (1.84)	26.0 (1.90)	16.4 (2.59)	23.7 (2.71)
1994	34.6 (0.42)	9.1 (0.27)	25.5 (0.44)	33.1 (0.63)	36.0 (0.60)	38.1 (0.53)	27.7 (1.17)	18.8 (1.10)	62.7 (2.81)	—	29.4 (5.64)	—	37.0 (0.74)	39.2 (0.74)	25.6 (1.66)	29.5 (1.64)	16.5 (1.43)	21.5 (1.71)
1995	34.3 (0.44)	8.9 (0.27)	25.4 (0.41)	33.1 (0.62)	35.5 (0.65)	37.9 (0.55)	27.5 (1.18)	20.7 (1.13)	54.6 (3.10)	—	27.6 (6.14)	—	37.0 (0.81)	38.8 (0.78)	25.6 (1.71)	28.7 (1.72)	18.7 (1.49)	23.0 (1.71)
1996	35.5 (0.47)	9.5 (0.29)	26.1 (0.43)	34.1 (0.66)	37.0 (0.67)	39.5 (0.57)	27.4 (1.23)	21.7 (1.18)	53.9 (2.42)	—	30.3 (5.25)	—	38.3 (0.83)	37.0 (0.84)	25.7 (1.70)	28.8 (1.70)	16.5 (1.52)	26.1 (1.81)
1997	36.8 (0.47)	9.9 (0.29)	27.0 (0.43)	35.0 (0.66)	38.7 (0.67)	40.6 (0.59)	29.8 (1.25)	22.4 (1.21)	55.1 (2.60)	—	27.1 (4.63)	—	39.3 (0.82)	41.8 (0.84)	25.4 (1.75)	33.7 (1.75)	19.2 (1.56)	26.1 (1.88)
1998	36.5 (0.46)	10.2 (0.30)	26.3 (0.42)	34.5 (0.65)	38.6 (0.66)	40.6 (0.59)	29.8 (1.24)	20.4 (1.11)	60.4 (2.49)	—	20.3 (4.91)	—	39.4 (0.82)	41.9 (0.84)	26.1 (1.76)	32.9 (1.73)	16.4 (1.41)	24.9 (1.73)
1999	35.6 (0.45)	9.1 (0.27)	26.5 (0.42)	34.1 (0.64)	37.0 (0.65)	39.4 (0.53)	30.4 (1.21)	18.7 (1.12)	55.7 (2.42)	—	19.5 (4.71)	—	38.3 (0.81)	40.6 (0.82)	28.9 (1.81)	31.6 (1.70)	15.8 (1.41)	21.9 (1.65)
2000	35.5 (0.45)	9.4 (0.28)	26.0 (0.41)	34.0 (0.62)	37.0 (0.65)	38.7 (0.55)	30.5 (1.21)	20.6 (1.12)	55.9 (2.42)	—	15.9 (4.30)	—	38.3 (0.79)	41.3 (0.81)	25.1 (1.67)	35.2 (1.72)	18.5 (1.45)	25.4 (1.72)
2001	36.3 (0.45)	9.8 (0.28)	26.6 (0.41)	33.6 (0.63)	39.0 (0.64)	39.5 (0.57)	31.4 (1.22)	21.7 (1.10)	61.3 (2.35)	—	23.3 (4.29)	—	37.2 (0.79)	41.9 (0.82)	26.7 (1.70)	35.5 (1.71)	17.4 (1.42)	26.1 (1.67)
2002	36.7 (0.43)	9.7 (0.26)	27.0 (0.39)	33.7 (0.59)	39.7 (0.61)	40.9 (0.55)	31.9 (1.18)	19.9 (0.94)	60.9 (2.10)	—	23.6 (3.96)	—	38.9 (0.77)	42.8 (0.78)	26.3 (1.63)	36.9 (1.68)	16.2 (1.17)	24.4 (1.51)
2003	37.8 (0.43)	10.2 (0.27)	27.7 (0.39)	34.3 (0.59)	41.3 (0.61)	41.6 (0.55)	32.3 (1.20)	23.5 (1.02)	61.2 (2.27)	43.3 (9.97)	17.7 (4.45)	41.6 (3.58)	38.5 (0.76)	44.5 (0.78)	28.2 (1.68)	36.0 (1.69)	18.3 (1.27)	29.4 (1.60)
2004	38.0 (0.43)	9.4 (0.26)	28.6 (0.40)	34.7 (0.59)	41.2 (0.61)	41.7 (0.55)	31.8 (1.18)	24.7 (1.02)	60.2 (2.24)	55.8 (8.99)	24.4 (4.52)	36.8 (3.44)	38.4 (0.76)	45.0 (0.78)	26.5 (1.64)	36.6 (1.64)	21.7 (1.33)	28.2 (1.56)
2005[2]	38.9 (0.43)	9.6 (0.26)	29.2 (0.40)	35.3 (0.59)	42.5 (0.61)	42.8 (0.55)	33.1 (1.16)	24.8 (1.02)	60.6 (2.26)	50.6 (10.95)	27.8 (4.88)	41.8 (3.48)	39.4 (0.76)	46.1 (0.79)	28.2 (1.64)	37.6 (1.69)	20.0 (1.31)	27.6 (1.58)
2006	37.3 (0.42)	9.6 (0.25)	27.8 (0.39)	34.1 (0.58)	40.6 (0.60)	41.0 (0.54)	31.4 (1.16)	23.6 (0.99)	58.3 (2.28)	39.1 (8.36)	26.2 (5.18)	38.5 (3.51)	37.9 (0.75)	44.1 (0.78)	28.1 (1.60)	36.9 (1.65)	20.0 (1.29)	27.6 (1.52)
2007	38.8 (0.42)	10.9 (0.27)	27.9 (0.39)	35.5 (0.58)	42.1 (0.60)	42.6 (0.54)	33.1 (1.15)	26.6 (1.02)	57.2 (2.28)	37.1 (9.07)	24.7 (4.63)	39.2 (3.48)	39.6 (0.76)	45.7 (0.78)	32.2 (1.63)	34.0 (1.61)	20.7 (1.29)	33.0 (1.57)
2008[3]	39.6 (0.42)	11.8 (0.27)	27.8 (0.39)	37.0 (0.58)	42.3 (0.60)	42.2 (0.54)	32.1 (1.13)	25.8 (1.01)	59.3 (2.22)	27.3 (8.92)‡	23.7 (4.22)	45.7 (3.55)	41.7 (0.76)	41.7 (0.78)	29.7 (1.61)	34.2 (1.59)	23.0 (1.35)	30.0 (1.50)
2009[3]	41.3 (0.42)	11.7 (0.27)	29.6 (0.40)	38.4 (0.59)	44.2 (0.60)	45.0 (0.55)	37.7 (1.17)	27.5 (1.01)	65.2 (2.17)	33.4 (7.45)	29.8 (5.10)	39.3 (3.32)	47.7 (1.00)	47.7 (0.78)	33.2 (1.17)	41.9 (2.16)	24.2 (1.35)	31.0 (1.54)
2010[1,3]	41.2 (0.57)	12.9 (0.35)	28.2 (0.53)	38.3 (0.78)	44.1 (0.84)	43.3 (0.81)	38.4 (1.66)	31.9 (1.15)	63.6 (2.70)	36.0 (8.36)	41.4 (6.60)	38.3 (4.38)	40.6 (1.00)	46.1 (1.17)	35.2 (2.13)	41.4 (2.16)	27.9 (1.57)	36.1 (1.60)
2011[1,3]	42.0 (0.57)	12.0 (0.35)	30.0 (0.53)	39.1 (0.80)	44.1 (0.84)	44.7 (0.55)	37.1 (1.53)	34.8 (1.20)	60.1 (2.45)	37.8 (7.93)	23.5 (5.30)	38.8 (3.60)	47.1 (1.00)	47.1 (1.08)	34.0 (1.08)	39.9 (1.90)	31.0 (1.57)	39.4 (1.58)
2012[1,3]	41.0 (0.62)	12.7 (0.38)	28.3 (0.58)	37.6 (0.79)	44.5 (0.86)	42.1 (0.83)	36.4 (1.62)	37.5 (1.18)	59.8 (2.61)	50.3 (9.60)	27.8 (4.43)	39.4 (3.64)	38.3 (1.06)	46.0 (1.08)	33.9 (2.04)	38.7 (1.94)	41.7 (1.58)	41.7 (1.73)

—Not available.
†Not applicable.
‡Interpret data with caution. The coefficient of variation (CV) for this estimate is between 30 and 50 percent.
[1]Prior to 1972, White and Black data include persons of Hispanic ethnicity.
[2]After 2002, data for individual race categories exclude persons identifying themselves as two or more races.
[3]Beginning in 2010, standard errors were computed using replicate weights, which produced more precise values than the methodology used in prior years.
NOTE: Data are based on sample surveys of the civilian noninstitutional population. Totals include other racial/ethnic groups not separately shown. Race categories exclude persons of Hispanic ethnicity except where otherwise noted.
SOURCE: U.S. Department of Commerce, Census Bureau, Current Population Survey (CPS), October, 1967 through 2012. (This table was prepared May 2013.)

Total fall enrollment in degree-granting postsecondary institutions, by attendance status, sex of student, and control of institution: Selected years, 1947 through 2023

Year	Total enrollment	Attendance status			Sex of student			Control of institution			
		Full-time	Part-time	Percent part-time	Male	Female	Percent female	Public	Private		
									Total	Nonprofit	For-profit
1	2	3	4	5	6	7	8	9	10	11	12
1947[1]	2,338,226	—	—	—	1,659,249	678,977	29.0	1,152,377	1,185,849	—	—
1948[1]	2,403,396	—	—	—	1,709,367	694,029	28.9	1,185,588	1,217,808	—	—
1949[1]	2,444,900	—	—	—	1,721,572	723,328	29.6	1,207,151	1,237,749	—	—
1950[1]	2,281,298	—	—	—	1,560,392	720,906	31.6	1,139,699	1,141,599	—	—
1951[1]	2,101,962	—	—	—	1,390,740	711,222	33.8	1,037,938	1,064,024	—	—
1952[1]	2,134,242	—	—	—	1,380,357	753,885	35.3	1,101,240	1,033,002	—	—
1953[1]	2,231,054	—	—	—	1,422,598	808,456	36.2	1,185,876	1,045,178	—	—
1954[1]	2,446,693	—	—	—	1,563,382	883,311	36.1	1,353,531	1,093,162	—	—
1955[1]	2,653,034	—	—	—	1,733,184	919,850	34.7	1,476,282	1,176,752	—	—
1956[1]	2,918,212	—	—	—	1,911,458	1,006,754	34.5	1,656,402	1,261,810	—	—
1957	3,323,783	—	—	—	2,170,765	1,153,018	34.7	1,972,673	1,351,110	—	—
1959	3,639,847	2,421,016	1,218,831 [2]	33.5	2,332,617	1,307,230	35.9	2,180,982	1,458,865	—	—
1961	4,145,065	2,785,133	1,359,932 [2]	32.8	2,585,821	1,559,244	37.6	2,561,447	1,583,618	—	—
1963	4,779,609	3,183,833	1,595,776 [2]	33.4	2,961,540	1,818,069	38.0	3,081,279	1,698,330	—	—
1964	5,280,020	3,573,238	1,706,782 [2]	32.3	3,248,713	2,031,307	38.5	3,467,708	1,812,312	—	—
1965	5,920,864	4,095,728	1,825,136 [2]	30.8	3,630,020	2,290,844	38.7	3,969,596	1,951,268	—	—
1966	6,389,872	4,438,606	1,951,266 [2]	30.5	3,856,216	2,533,656	39.7	4,348,917	2,040,955	—	—
1967	6,911,748	4,793,128	2,118,620 [2]	30.7	4,132,800	2,778,948	40.2	4,816,028	2,095,720	2,074,041	21,679
1968	7,513,091	5,210,155	2,302,936	30.7	4,477,649	3,035,442	40.4	5,430,652	2,082,439	2,061,211	21,228
1969	8,004,660	5,498,883	2,505,777	31.3	4,746,201	3,258,459	40.7	5,896,868	2,107,792	2,087,653	20,139
1970	8,580,887	5,816,290	2,764,597	32.2	5,043,642	3,537,245	41.2	6,428,134	2,152,753	2,134,420	18,333
1971	8,948,644	6,077,232	2,871,412	32.1	5,207,004	3,741,640	41.8	6,804,309	2,144,335	2,121,913	22,422
1972	9,214,860	6,072,389	3,142,471	34.1	5,238,757	3,976,103	43.1	7,070,635	2,144,225	2,123,245	20,980
1973	9,602,123	6,189,493	3,412,630	35.5	5,371,052	4,231,071	44.1	7,419,516	2,182,607	2,148,784	33,823
1974	10,223,729	6,370,273	3,853,456	37.7	5,622,429	4,601,300	45.0	7,988,500	2,235,229	2,200,963	34,266
1975	11,184,859	6,841,334	4,343,525	38.8	6,148,997	5,035,862	45.0	8,834,508	2,350,351	2,311,448	38,903
1976	11,012,137	6,717,058	4,295,079	39.0	5,810,828	5,201,309	47.2	8,653,477	2,358,660	2,314,298	44,362
1977	11,285,787	6,792,925	4,492,862	39.8	5,789,016	5,496,771	48.7	8,846,993	2,438,794	2,386,652	52,142
1978	11,260,092	6,667,657	4,592,435	40.8	5,640,998	5,619,094	49.9	8,785,893	2,474,199	2,408,331	65,868
1979	11,569,899	6,794,039	4,775,860	41.3	5,682,877	5,887,022	50.9	9,036,822	2,533,077	2,461,773	71,304
1980	12,096,895	7,097,958	4,998,937	41.3	5,874,374	6,222,521	51.4	9,457,394	2,639,501	2,527,787	111,714 [3]
1981	12,371,672	7,181,250	5,190,422	42.0	5,975,056	6,396,616	51.7	9,647,032	2,724,640	2,572,405	152,235 [3]
1982	12,425,780	7,220,618	5,205,162	41.9	6,031,384	6,394,396	51.5	9,696,087	2,729,693	2,552,739	176,954 [3]
1983	12,464,661	7,261,050	5,203,611	41.7	6,023,725	6,440,936	51.7	9,682,734	2,781,927	2,589,187	192,740
1984	12,241,940	7,098,388	5,143,552	42.0	5,863,574	6,378,366	52.1	9,477,370	2,764,570	2,574,419	190,151
1985	12,247,055	7,075,221	5,171,834	42.2	5,818,450	6,428,605	52.5	9,479,273	2,767,782	2,571,791	195,991
1986	12,503,511	7,119,550	5,383,961	43.1	5,884,515	6,618,996	52.9	9,713,893	2,789,618	2,572,479	217,139 [4]
1987	12,766,642	7,231,085	5,535,557	43.4	5,932,056	6,834,586	53.5	9,973,254	2,793,388	2,602,350	191,038 [4]
1988	13,055,337	7,436,768	5,618,569	43.0	6,001,896	7,053,441	54.0	10,161,388	2,893,949	2,673,567	220,382
1989	13,538,560	7,660,950	5,877,610	43.4	6,190,015	7,348,545	54.3	10,577,963	2,960,597	2,731,174	229,423
1990	13,818,637	7,820,985	5,997,652	43.4	6,283,909	7,534,728	54.5	10,844,717	2,973,920	2,760,227	213,693
1991	14,358,953	8,115,329	6,243,624	43.5	6,501,844	7,857,109	54.7	11,309,563	3,049,390	2,819,041	230,349
1992	14,487,359	8,162,118	6,325,241	43.7	6,523,989	7,963,370	55.0	11,384,567	3,102,792	2,872,523	230,269
1993	14,304,803	8,127,618	6,177,185	43.2	6,427,450	7,877,353	55.1	11,189,088	3,115,715	2,888,897	226,818
1994	14,278,790	8,137,776	6,141,014	43.0	6,371,898	7,906,892	55.4	11,133,680	3,145,110	2,910,107	235,003
1995	14,261,781	8,128,802	6,132,979	43.0	6,342,539	7,919,242	55.5	11,092,374	3,169,407	2,929,044	240,363
1996	14,367,520	8,302,953	6,064,567	42.2	6,352,825	8,014,695	55.8	11,120,499	3,247,021	2,942,556	304,465
1997	14,502,334	8,438,062	6,064,272	41.8	6,396,028	8,106,306	55.9	11,196,119	3,306,215	2,977,614	328,601
1998	14,506,967	8,563,338	5,943,629	41.0	6,369,265	8,137,702	56.1	11,137,769	3,369,198	3,004,925	364,273
1999	14,849,691	8,803,139	6,046,552	40.7	6,515,164	8,334,527	56.1	11,375,739	3,473,952	3,055,029	418,923
2000	15,312,289	9,009,600	6,302,689	41.2	6,721,769	8,590,520	56.1	11,752,786	3,559,503	3,109,419	450,084
2001	15,927,987	9,447,502	6,480,485	40.7	6,960,815	8,967,172	56.3	12,233,156	3,694,831	3,167,330	527,501
2002	16,611,711	9,946,359	6,665,352	40.1	7,202,116	9,409,595	56.6	12,751,993	3,859,718	3,265,476	594,242
2003	16,911,481	10,326,133	6,585,348	38.9	7,260,264	9,651,217	57.1	12,858,698	4,052,783	3,341,048	711,735
2004	17,272,044	10,610,177	6,661,867	38.6	7,387,262	9,884,782	57.2	12,980,112	4,291,932	3,411,685	880,247
2005	17,487,475	10,797,011	6,690,464	38.3	7,455,925	10,031,550	57.4	13,021,834	4,465,641	3,454,692	1,010,949
2006	17,758,870	10,957,305	6,801,565	38.3	7,574,815	10,184,055	57.3	13,180,133	4,578,737	3,512,866	1,065,871
2007	18,248,128	11,269,892	6,978,236	38.2	7,815,914	10,432,214	57.2	13,490,780	4,757,348	3,571,150	1,186,198
2008	19,102,814	11,747,743	7,355,071	38.5	8,188,895	10,913,919	57.1	13,972,153	5,130,661	3,661,519	1,469,142
2009	20,427,711	12,722,782	7,704,929	37.7	8,769,504	11,658,207	57.1	14,810,642	5,617,069	3,765,083	1,851,986
2010	21,016,126	13,082,267	7,933,859	37.8	9,044,811	11,971,315	57.0	15,142,809	5,873,317	3,854,920	2,018,397
2011	20,994,113	13,001,457	7,992,656	38.1	9,026,499	11,967,614	57.0	15,110,196	5,883,917	3,927,186	1,956,731
2012	20,642,819	12,737,013	7,905,806	38.3	8,919,087	11,723,732	56.8	14,880,343	5,762,476	3,953,578	1,808,898
2013[5]	20,597,000	12,742,000	7,855,000	38.1	8,985,000	11,612,000	56.4	14,857,000	5,740,000	—	—
2014[5]	21,011,000	12,992,000	8,019,000	38.2	9,037,000	11,974,000	57.0	15,140,000	5,871,000	—	—

See notes at end of table.

Total fall enrollment in degree-granting postsecondary institutions, by attendance status, sex of student, and control of institution: Selected years, 1947 through 2023—Continued

Year	Total enrollment	Full-time	Part-time	Percent part-time	Male	Female	Percent female	Public	Total	Nonprofit	For-profit
1	2	3	4	5	6	7	8	9	10	11	12
2015[5]	21,266,000	13,112,000	8,154,000	38.3	9,073,000	12,193,000	57.3	15,319,000	5,947,000	—	—
2016[5]	21,586,000	13,278,000	8,308,000	38.5	9,146,000	12,441,000	57.6	15,545,000	6,041,000	—	—
2017[5]	21,946,000	13,468,000	8,478,000	38.6	9,243,000	12,703,000	57.9	15,802,000	6,144,000	—	—
2018[5]	22,227,000	13,618,000	8,609,000	38.7	9,323,000	12,904,000	58.1	16,004,000	6,223,000	—	—
2019[5]	22,512,000	13,774,000	8,737,000	38.8	9,408,000	13,104,000	58.2	16,208,000	6,304,000	—	—
2020[5]	22,797,000	13,929,000	8,868,000	38.9	9,491,000	13,306,000	58.4	16,410,000	6,388,000	—	—
2021[5]	23,141,000	14,122,000	9,020,000	39.0	9,599,000	13,543,000	58.5	16,652,000	6,489,000	—	—
2022[5]	23,499,000	14,329,000	9,170,000	39.0	9,712,000	13,786,000	58.7	16,905,000	6,594,000	—	—
2023[5]	23,834,000	14,520,000	9,314,000	39.1	9,817,000	14,017,000	58.8	17,143,000	6,691,000	—	—

—Not available.
[1]Degree-credit enrollment only.
[2]Includes part-time resident students and all extension students (students attending courses at sites separate from the primary reporting campus). In later years, part-time student enrollment was collected as a distinct category.
[3]Large increases are due to the addition of schools accredited by the Accrediting Commission of Career Schools and Colleges of Technology.
[4]Because of imputation techniques, data are not consistent with figures for other years.
[5]Projected.
NOTE: Data through 1995 are for institutions of higher education, while later data are for degree-granting institutions. Degree-granting institutions grant associate's or higher degrees and partici-

pate in Title IV federal financial aid programs. The degree-granting classification is very similar to the earlier higher education classification, but it includes more 2-year colleges and excludes a few higher education institutions that did not grant degrees.
SOURCE: U.S. Department of Education, National Center for Education Statistics, *Biennial Survey of Education in the United States; Opening Fall Enrollment in Higher Education*, 1963 through 1965; Higher Education General Information Survey (HEGIS), "Fall Enrollment in Colleges and Universities" surveys, 1966 through 1985; Integrated Postsecondary Education Data System (IPEDS), "Fall Enrollment Survey" (IPEDS-EF:86–99); IPEDS Spring 2001 through Spring 2013, Enrollment component; and Enrollment in Degree-Granting Institutions Projection Model, 1980 through 2023. (This table was prepared July 2014.)

Total fall enrollment in all postsecondary institutions participating in Title IV programs and annual percentage change in enrollment, by degree-granting status and control of institution: 1995 through 2012

Year	All Title IV institutions[1]				Degree-granting institutions[2]					Non-degree-granting institutions[3]			
	Total	Public	Private		Total	Public	Private			Total	Public	Private	
			Nonprofit	For-profit			Total	Nonprofit	For-profit			Nonprofit	For-profit
1	2	3	4	5	6	7	8	9	10	11	12	13	14
	Enrollment												
1995	14,836,338	11,312,491	2,977,794	546,053	14,261,781	11,092,374	3,169,407	2,929,044	240,363	574,557	220,117	48,750	305,690
1996	14,809,897	11,312,775	2,976,850	520,272	14,367,520	11,120,499	3,247,021	2,942,556	304,465	442,377	192,276	34,294	215,807
1997	14,900,416	11,370,755	3,012,106	517,555	14,502,334	11,196,119	3,306,215	2,977,614	328,601	398,082	174,636	34,492	188,954
1998	14,923,839	11,330,811	3,040,251	552,777	14,506,967	11,137,769	3,369,198	3,004,925	364,273	416,872	193,042	35,326	188,504
1999	15,262,888	11,556,731	3,088,233	617,924	14,849,691	11,375,739	3,473,952	3,055,029	418,923	413,197	180,992	33,204	199,001
2000	15,701,409	11,891,450	3,137,108	672,851	15,312,289	11,752,786	3,559,503	3,109,419	450,084	389,120	138,664	27,689	222,767
2001	16,334,134	12,370,079	3,198,354	765,701	15,927,987	12,233,156	3,694,831	3,167,330	527,501	406,147	136,923	31,024	238,200
2002	17,035,027	12,883,071	3,299,094	852,862	16,611,711	12,751,993	3,859,718	3,265,476	594,242	423,316	131,078	33,618	258,620
2003	17,330,775	12,965,502	3,372,647	992,626	16,911,481	12,858,698	4,052,783	3,341,048	711,735	419,294	106,804	31,599	280,891
2004	17,710,798	13,081,358	3,440,559	1,188,881	17,272,044	12,980,112	4,291,932	3,411,685	880,247	438,754	101,246	28,874	308,634
2005	17,921,804	13,115,177	3,484,013	1,322,614	17,487,475	13,021,834	4,465,641	3,454,692	1,010,949	434,329	93,343	29,321	311,665
2006	18,205,474	13,281,664	3,543,455	1,380,355	17,758,870	13,180,133	4,578,737	3,512,866	1,065,871	446,604	101,531	30,589	314,484
2007	18,671,084	13,595,849	3,595,207	1,480,028	18,248,128	13,490,780	4,757,348	3,571,150	1,186,198	422,956	105,069	24,057	293,830
2008	19,574,395	14,092,109	3,684,723	1,797,563	19,102,814	13,972,153	5,130,661	3,661,519	1,469,142	471,581	119,956	23,204	328,421
2009	20,966,826	14,936,382	3,791,418	2,239,026	20,427,711	14,810,642	5,617,069	3,765,083	1,851,986	539,115	125,740	26,335	387,040
2010	21,588,124	15,280,273	3,881,906	2,425,945	21,016,126	15,142,809	5,873,317	3,854,920	2,018,397	571,998	137,464	26,986	407,548
2011	21,557,259	15,244,288	3,954,529	2,358,442	20,994,113	15,110,196	5,883,917	3,927,186	1,956,731	563,146	134,092	27,343	401,711
2012	21,147,055	14,996,482	3,975,542	2,175,031	20,642,819	14,880,343	5,762,476	3,953,578	1,808,898	504,236	116,139	21,964	366,133
	Annual percentage change												
1995 to 1996	-0.2	#	#	-4.7	0.7	0.3	2.4	0.5	26.7	-23.0	-12.6	-29.7	-29.4
1996 to 1997	0.6	0.5	1.2	-0.5	0.9	0.7	1.8	1.2	7.9	-10.0	-9.2	0.6	-12.4
1997 to 1998	0.2	-0.4	0.9	6.8	#	-0.5	1.9	0.9	10.9	4.7	10.5	2.4	-0.2
1998 to 1999	2.3	2.0	1.6	11.8	2.4	2.1	3.1	1.7	15.0	-0.9	-6.2	-6.0	5.6
1999 to 2000	2.9	2.9	1.6	8.9	3.1	3.3	2.5	1.8	7.4	-5.8	-23.4	-16.6	11.9
2000 to 2001	4.0	4.0	2.0	13.8	4.0	4.1	3.8	1.9	17.2	4.4	-1.3	12.0	6.9
2001 to 2002	4.3	4.1	3.1	11.4	4.3	4.2	4.5	3.1	12.7	4.2	-4.3	8.4	8.6
2002 to 2003	1.7	0.6	2.2	16.4	1.8	0.8	5.0	2.3	19.8	-1.0	-18.5	-6.0	8.6
2003 to 2004	2.2	0.9	2.0	19.8	2.1	0.9	5.9	2.1	23.7	4.6	-5.2	-8.6	9.9
2004 to 2005	1.2	0.3	1.3	11.2	1.2	0.3	4.0	1.3	14.8	-1.0	-7.8	1.5	1.0
2005 to 2006	1.6	1.3	1.7	4.4	1.6	1.2	2.5	1.7	5.4	2.8	8.8	4.3	0.9
2006 to 2007	2.6	2.4	1.5	7.2	2.8	2.4	3.9	1.7	11.3	-5.3	3.5	-21.4	-6.6
2007 to 2008	4.8	3.7	2.5	21.5	4.7	3.6	7.8	2.5	23.9	11.5	14.2	-3.5	11.8
2008 to 2009	7.1	6.0	2.9	24.6	6.9	6.0	9.5	2.8	26.1	14.3	4.8	13.5	17.8
2009 to 2010	3.0	2.3	2.4	8.3	2.9	2.2	4.6	2.4	9.0	6.1	9.3	2.5	5.3
2010 to 2011	-0.1	-0.2	1.9	-2.8	-0.1	-0.2	0.2	1.9	-3.1	-1.5	-2.5	1.3	-1.4
2011 to 2012	-1.9	-1.6	0.5	-7.8	-1.7	-1.5	-2.1	0.7	-7.6	-10.5	-13.4	-19.7	-8.9

#Rounds to zero.
[1]Includes degree-granting and non-degree-granting institutions.
[2]Data for 1995 are for institutions of higher education, while later data are for degree-granting institutions. Degree-granting institutions grant associate's or higher degrees and participate in Title IV federal financial aid programs. The degree-granting classification is very similar to the earlier higher education classification, but it includes more 2-year colleges and excludes a few higher education institutions that did not grant degrees.

[3]Data are for institutions that did not offer accredited 4-year or 2-year programs, but were participating in Title IV federal financial aid programs. Includes some institutions transitioning to higher level offerings, though still classified at a lower level.
SOURCE: U.S. Department of Education, National Center for Education Statistics, Integrated Postsecondary Education Data System (IPEDS), "Fall Enrollment Survey" (IPEDS-EF:95–99); and IPEDS Spring 2001 through Spring 2013, Enrollment component. (This table was prepared October 2013.)

Total fall enrollment in degree-granting postsecondary institutions, by control and level of institution: 1970 through 2012

	All institutions			Public institutions			All private institutions			Private institutions					
										Nonprofit			For-profit		
Year	Total	4-year	2-year	Total	4-year	2-year	Total	4-year	2-year	Total	4-year	2-year	Total	4-year	2-year
1	2	3	4	5	6	7	8	9	10	11	12	13	14	15	16
1970	8,580,887	6,261,502	2,319,385	6,428,134	4,232,722	2,195,412	2,152,753	2,028,780	123,973	2,134,420	2,021,121	113,299	18,333	7,659	10,674
1971	8,948,644	6,369,355	2,579,289	6,804,309	4,346,990	2,457,319	2,144,335	2,022,365	121,970	2,121,913	2,011,682	110,231	22,422	10,683	11,739
1972	9,214,860	6,458,674	2,756,186	7,070,635	4,429,696	2,640,939	2,144,225	2,028,978	115,247	2,123,245	2,019,380	103,865	20,980	9,598	11,382
1973	9,602,123	6,590,023	3,012,100	7,419,516	4,529,895	2,889,621	2,182,607	2,060,128	122,479	2,148,784	2,045,804	102,980	33,823	14,324	19,499
1974	10,223,729	6,819,735	3,403,994	7,988,500	4,703,018	3,285,482	2,235,229	2,116,717	118,512	2,200,963	2,098,599	102,364	34,266	18,118	16,148
1975	11,184,859	7,214,740	3,970,119	8,834,508	4,998,142	3,836,366	2,350,351	2,216,598	133,753	2,311,448	2,198,451	112,997	38,903	18,147	20,756
1976	11,012,137	7,128,816	3,883,321	8,653,477	4,901,691	3,751,786	2,358,660	2,227,125	131,535	2,314,298	2,206,457	107,841	44,362	20,668	23,694
1977	11,285,787	7,242,845	4,042,942	8,846,993	4,945,224	3,901,769	2,438,794	2,297,621	141,173	2,386,652	2,277,072	109,580	52,142	20,549	31,593
1978	11,260,092	7,231,625	4,028,467	8,785,893	4,912,203	3,873,690	2,474,199	2,319,422	154,777	2,408,331	2,299,132	109,199	65,868	20,290	45,578
1979	11,569,899	7,353,233	4,216,666	9,036,822	4,980,012	4,056,810	2,533,077	2,373,221	159,856	2,461,773	2,351,364	110,409	71,304	21,857	49,447
1980	12,096,895	7,570,608	4,526,287	9,457,394	5,128,612	4,328,782	2,639,501	2,441,996	197,505 [1]	2,527,787	2,413,693	114,094	111,714	28,303	83,411 [1]
1981	12,371,672	7,655,461	4,716,211	9,647,032	5,166,324	4,480,708	2,724,640	2,489,137	235,503 [1]	2,572,405	2,453,239	119,166	152,235	35,898	116,337 [1]
1982	12,425,780	7,654,074	4,771,706	9,696,087	5,176,434	4,519,653	2,729,693	2,477,640	252,053 [1]	2,552,739	2,437,763	114,976	176,954	39,877	137,077 [1]
1983	12,464,661	7,741,195	4,723,466	9,682,734	5,223,404	4,459,330	2,781,927	2,517,791	264,136	2,589,187	2,472,894	116,293	192,740	44,897	147,843
1984	12,241,940	7,711,167	4,530,773	9,477,370	5,198,273	4,279,097	2,764,570	2,512,894	251,676	2,574,419	2,466,172	108,247	190,151	46,722	143,429
1985	12,247,055	7,715,978	4,531,077	9,479,273	5,209,540	4,269,733	2,767,782	2,506,438	261,344	2,571,791	2,463,000	108,791	195,991	43,438	152,553
1986	12,503,511	7,823,963	4,679,548	9,713,893	5,300,202	4,413,691	2,789,618	2,523,761	265,857 [2]	2,572,479	2,470,981	101,498	217,139	52,780	164,359 [2]
1987	12,766,642	7,990,420	4,776,222	9,973,254	5,432,200	4,541,054	2,793,388	2,558,220	235,168 [2]	2,602,350	2,512,248	90,102	191,038	45,972	145,066 [2]
1988	13,055,337	8,180,182	4,875,155	10,161,388	5,545,901	4,615,487	2,893,949	2,634,281	259,668	—	—	—	—	—	—
1989	13,538,560	8,387,671	5,150,889	10,577,963	5,694,303	4,883,660	2,960,597	2,693,368	267,229	—	—	—	—	—	—
1990	13,818,637	8,578,554	5,240,083	10,844,717	5,848,242	4,996,475	2,973,920	2,730,312	243,608	2,760,227	2,671,069	89,158	213,693	59,243	154,450
1991	14,358,953	8,707,053	5,651,900	11,309,563	5,904,748	5,404,815	3,049,390	2,802,305	247,085	2,819,041	2,729,752	89,289	230,349	72,553	157,796
1992	14,487,359	8,764,969	5,722,390	11,384,567	5,900,012	5,484,555	3,102,792	2,864,957	237,835	2,872,523	2,789,235	83,288	230,269	75,722	154,547
1993	14,304,803	8,738,936	5,565,867	11,189,088	5,851,760	5,337,328	3,115,715	2,887,176	228,539	2,888,897	2,802,540	86,357	226,818	84,636	142,182
1994	14,278,790	8,749,080	5,529,710	11,133,680	5,825,213	5,308,467	3,145,110	2,923,867	221,243	2,910,107	2,824,500	85,607	235,003	99,367	135,636
1995	14,261,781	8,769,252	5,492,529	11,092,374	5,814,545	5,277,829	3,169,407	2,954,707	214,700	2,929,044	2,853,890	75,154	240,363	100,817	139,546
1996	14,367,520	8,804,193	5,563,327	11,120,499	5,806,036	5,314,463	3,247,021	2,998,157	248,864	2,942,556	2,867,181	75,375	304,465	130,976	173,489
1997	14,502,334	8,896,765	5,605,569	11,196,119	5,835,433	5,360,686	3,306,215	3,061,332	244,883	2,977,614	2,905,820	71,794	328,601	155,512	173,089
1998	14,506,967	9,017,653	5,489,314	11,137,769	5,891,806	5,245,963	3,369,198	3,125,847	243,351	3,004,925	2,939,055	65,870	364,273	186,792	177,481
1999	14,849,160	9,196,160	5,653,531	11,375,739	5,977,678	5,398,061	3,473,952	3,218,482	255,470	3,055,029	2,991,728	63,301	418,923	226,754	192,169
2000	15,312,289	9,363,858	5,948,431	11,752,786	6,055,398	5,697,388	3,559,503	3,308,460	251,043	3,109,419	3,050,575	58,844	450,084	257,885	192,199
2001	15,927,987	9,677,408	6,250,579	12,233,156	6,236,455	5,996,701	3,694,831	3,440,953	253,878	3,167,330	3,119,781	47,549	527,501	321,172	206,329
2002	16,611,711	10,082,332	6,529,379	12,751,993	6,481,613	6,270,380	3,859,718	3,600,719	258,999	3,265,476	3,218,389	47,087	594,242	382,330	211,912
2003	16,911,481	10,417,247	6,494,234	12,858,698	6,649,441	6,209,257	4,052,783	3,767,806	284,977	3,341,048	3,297,180	43,868	711,735	470,626	241,109
2004	17,272,044	10,726,181	6,545,863	12,980,112	6,736,536	6,243,576	4,291,932	3,989,645	302,287	3,411,685	3,369,435	42,250	880,247	620,210	260,037
2005	17,487,475	10,999,420	6,488,055	13,021,834	6,837,605	6,184,229	4,465,641	4,161,815	303,826	3,454,692	3,411,170	43,522	1,010,949	750,645	260,304
2006	17,758,870	11,240,330	6,518,540	13,180,133	6,955,013	6,225,120	4,578,737	4,285,317	293,420	3,512,866	3,473,710	39,156	1,065,871	811,607	254,264
2007	18,248,128	11,630,198	6,617,930	13,490,780	7,166,661	6,324,119	4,757,348	4,463,537	293,811	3,571,150	3,537,664	33,486	1,186,198	925,873	260,325
2008	19,102,814	12,131,436	6,971,378	13,972,153	7,331,809	6,640,344	5,130,661	4,799,627	331,034	3,661,519	3,626,168	35,351	1,469,142	1,173,459	295,683
2009	20,427,711	12,906,305	7,521,406	14,810,642	7,709,197	7,101,445	5,617,069	5,197,108	419,961	3,765,083	3,730,316	34,767	1,851,986	1,466,792	385,194
2010	21,016,126	13,335,251	7,680,875	15,142,809	7,924,771	7,218,038	5,873,317	5,410,480	462,837	3,854,920	3,822,260	32,660	2,018,397	1,588,220	430,177
2011	20,994,113	13,494,131	7,499,982	15,110,196	8,047,729	7,062,467	5,883,917	5,446,402	437,515	3,927,186	3,887,322	39,864	1,956,731	1,559,080	397,651
2012	20,642,819	13,478,846	7,163,973	14,880,343	8,092,683	6,787,660	5,762,476	5,386,163	376,313	3,953,578	3,915,972	37,606	1,808,898	1,470,191	338,707

—Not available.

[1] Large increases are due to the addition of schools accredited by the Accrediting Commission of Career Schools and Colleges of Technology.

[2] Because of imputation techniques, data are not consistent with figures for other years.

NOTE: Data through 1995 are for institutions of higher education, while later data are for degree-granting institutions. Degree-granting institutions grant associate's or higher degrees and participate in Title IV federal financial aid programs. The degree-granting classification is very similar to the earlier higher education classification, but it includes more 2-year colleges and excludes a few higher education institutions that did not grant degrees.

SOURCE: U.S. Department of Education, National Center for Education Statistics, Higher Education General Information Survey (HEGIS), "Fall Enrollment in Institutions of Higher Education" surveys, 1970 through 1985; Integrated Postsecondary Education Data System (IPEDS), "Fall Enrollment Survey" (IPEDS-EF:86–99); and IPEDS Spring 2001 through Spring 2013, Enrollment component. (This table was prepared October 2013.)

Total fall enrollment in degree-granting postsecondary institutions, by level and control of institution, attendance status, and sex of student: Selected years, 1970 through 2023

Level and control of institution, attendance status, and sex of student	Actual													
	1970	1975	1980¹	1985	1990	1995	2000	2005	2007	2008	2009	2010	2011	2012
1	2	3	4	5	6	7	8	9	10	11	12	13	14	15
Total	8,580,887	11,184,859	12,096,895	12,247,055	13,818,637	14,261,781	15,312,289	17,487,475	18,248,128	19,102,814	20,427,711	21,016,126	20,994,113	20,642,819
Full-time	5,816,290	6,841,334	7,097,958	7,075,221	7,820,985	8,128,802	9,009,600	10,797,011	11,269,892	11,747,743	12,722,782	13,082,267	13,001,457	12,737,013
Males	3,504,095	3,926,753	3,689,244	3,607,720	4,013,233	4,321,410	4,898,507	5,993,623	6,240,448	6,513,386	7,052,138	7,245,210	7,208,046	7,027,221
Females	2,312,195	2,914,581	3,408,714	3,467,501	3,807,752	3,807,392	4,111,093	4,803,388	5,029,444	5,234,357	5,670,644	5,837,057	5,793,411	5,709,792
Part-time	2,764,597	4,343,525	4,998,937	5,171,834	5,997,652	6,132,979	6,302,689	6,690,464	6,978,236	7,355,071	7,704,929	7,933,859	7,992,656	7,905,806
Males	1,539,547	2,222,244	2,185,130	2,210,730	2,476,157	2,535,147	2,610,676	2,652,537	2,786,470	2,954,538	3,098,860	3,207,754	3,233,088	3,209,295
Females	1,225,050	2,121,281	2,813,807	2,961,104	3,521,495	3,597,832	3,692,013	4,037,927	4,191,766	4,400,533	4,606,069	4,726,105	4,759,568	4,696,511
4-year	6,261,502	7,214,740	7,570,608	7,715,978	8,578,554	8,769,252	9,363,858	10,999,420	11,630,198	12,131,436	12,906,305	13,335,251	13,494,131	13,478,846
Full-time	4,587,379	5,080,256	5,344,163	5,384,614	5,937,023	6,151,755	6,792,551	8,150,209	8,577,299	8,915,546	9,474,059	9,717,074	9,841,421	9,794,436
Males	2,732,796	2,891,192	2,809,528	2,781,412	2,926,360	2,929,177	3,115,252	3,649,622	3,839,336	3,984,494	4,222,234	4,353,627	4,405,066	4,403,960
Females	1,854,583	2,189,064	2,534,635	2,603,202	3,010,663	3,222,578	3,677,299	4,500,587	4,737,963	4,931,052	5,251,825	5,363,447	5,436,355	5,390,476
Part-time	1,674,123	2,134,484	2,226,445	2,331,364	2,641,531	2,617,497	2,571,307	2,849,211	3,052,899	3,215,890	3,432,246	3,618,177	3,652,710	3,684,410
Males	936,189	1,092,461	1,017,813	1,034,804	1,124,780	1,084,753	1,047,917	1,125,935	1,206,007	1,268,517	1,350,710	1,426,058	1,449,779	1,470,423
Females	737,934	1,042,023	1,208,632	1,296,560	1,516,751	1,532,744	1,523,390	1,723,276	1,846,892	1,947,373	2,081,536	2,192,119	2,202,931	2,213,987
Public 4-year	4,232,722	4,998,142	5,128,612	5,209,540	5,848,242	5,814,545	6,055,398	6,837,605	7,166,661	7,331,809	7,709,197	7,924,771	8,047,729	8,092,683
Full-time	3,086,491	3,469,821	3,592,193	3,623,341	4,033,654	4,084,711	4,371,218	5,021,745	5,244,841	5,378,123	5,649,713	5,811,370	5,889,009	5,910,198
Males	1,813,584	1,947,823	1,873,397	1,863,689	1,982,369	1,951,140	2,008,618	2,295,456	2,417,717	2,488,168	2,626,170	2,707,453	2,743,324	2,756,941
Females	1,272,907	1,521,998	1,718,796	1,759,652	2,051,285	2,133,571	2,362,600	2,726,289	2,827,124	2,889,955	3,023,543	3,103,917	3,145,685	3,153,257
Part-time	1,146,231	1,528,321	1,536,419	1,586,199	1,814,588	1,729,834	1,684,180	1,815,860	1,921,820	1,953,686	2,059,484	2,113,401	2,158,720	2,182,485
Males	609,422	760,469	685,051	693,115	764,248	720,402	683,100	724,375	772,563	788,594	833,156	861,091	885,565	901,197
Females	536,809	767,852	851,368	893,084	1,050,340	1,009,432	1,001,080	1,091,485	1,149,257	1,165,092	1,226,328	1,252,310	1,273,155	1,281,288
Private 4-year	2,028,780	2,216,598	2,441,996	2,506,438	2,730,312	2,954,707	3,308,460	4,161,815	4,463,537	4,799,627	5,197,108	5,410,480	5,446,402	5,386,163
Full-time	1,500,888	1,610,435	1,751,970	1,761,273	1,903,369	2,067,044	2,421,333	3,128,464	3,332,458	3,537,423	3,824,346	3,905,704	3,952,412	3,884,238
Males	919,212	943,369	936,131	917,723	943,991	978,037	1,106,634	1,354,166	1,421,619	1,496,326	1,596,064	1,646,174	1,661,742	1,647,019
Females	581,676	667,066	815,839	843,550	959,378	1,089,007	1,314,699	1,774,298	1,910,839	2,041,097	2,228,282	2,259,530	2,290,670	2,237,219
Part-time	527,892	606,163	690,026	745,165	826,943	887,663	887,127	1,033,351	1,131,079	1,262,204	1,372,762	1,504,776	1,493,990	1,501,925
Males	326,767	331,992	332,762	341,689	360,532	364,351	364,817	401,560	433,444	479,923	517,554	564,967	564,214	569,226
Females	201,125	274,171	357,264	403,476	466,411	523,312	522,310	631,791	697,635	782,281	855,208	939,809	929,776	932,699
Nonprofit 4-year	2,021,121	2,198,451	2,413,693	2,463,000	2,671,069	2,853,890	3,050,575	3,411,170	3,537,664	3,626,168	3,730,316	3,822,260	3,887,322	3,915,972
Full-time	1,494,625	1,596,074	1,733,014	1,727,707	1,859,124	1,989,457	2,226,028	2,534,793	2,643,207	2,698,819	2,783,162	2,865,417	2,907,240	2,928,938
Males	914,020	930,842	921,253	894,080	915,100	931,956	996,113	1,109,075	1,159,775	1,184,895	1,221,375	1,259,919	1,276,006	1,290,080
Females	580,605	665,232	811,761	833,627	944,024	1,057,501	1,229,915	1,425,718	1,483,432	1,513,924	1,561,787	1,605,498	1,631,234	1,638,858
Part-time	526,496	602,377	680,679	735,293	811,945	864,433	824,547	876,377	894,457	927,349	947,154	956,843	980,082	987,034
Males	325,693	329,662	327,986	336,168	352,106	351,874	332,814	339,572	344,325	357,974	364,432	366,645	375,304	377,740
Females	200,803	272,715	352,693	399,125	459,839	512,559	491,733	536,805	550,132	569,375	582,722	590,198	604,778	609,294
For-profit 4-year	7,659	18,147	28,303	43,438	59,243	100,817	257,885	750,645	925,873	1,173,459	1,466,792	1,588,220	1,559,080	1,470,191
2-year	2,319,385	3,970,119	4,526,287	4,531,077	5,240,083	5,492,529	5,948,431	6,488,055	6,617,930	6,971,378	7,521,406	7,680,875	7,499,982	7,163,973
Full-time	1,228,911	1,761,078	1,753,795	1,690,607	1,883,962	1,977,047	2,217,049	2,646,802	2,692,593	2,832,197	3,248,723	3,365,193	3,160,036	2,942,577
Males	771,299	1,035,561	879,716	826,308	881,392	878,215	995,841	1,153,766	1,190,108	1,249,863	1,448,410	1,483,430	1,388,345	1,305,832
Females	457,612	725,517	874,079	864,299	1,002,570	1,098,832	1,221,208	1,493,036	1,502,485	1,582,334	1,800,313	1,881,763	1,771,691	1,636,745
Part-time	1,090,474	2,209,041	2,772,492	2,840,470	3,356,121	3,515,482	3,731,382	3,841,253	3,925,337	4,139,181	4,272,683	4,315,682	4,339,946	4,221,396
Males	603,358	1,129,783	1,167,317	1,175,926	1,351,377	1,450,394	1,562,759	1,526,602	1,580,463	1,686,021	1,748,150	1,781,696	1,783,309	1,738,872
Females	487,116	1,079,258	1,605,175	1,664,544	2,004,744	2,065,088	2,168,623	2,314,651	2,344,874	2,453,160	2,524,533	2,533,986	2,556,637	2,482,524
Public 2-year	2,195,412	3,836,366	4,328,782	4,269,733	4,996,475	5,277,829	5,697,388	6,184,229	6,324,119	6,640,344	7,101,445	7,218,038	7,062,467	6,787,660
Full-time	1,129,165	1,662,621	1,595,493	1,496,905	1,716,843	1,840,590	2,000,008	2,387,016	2,442,140	2,548,488	2,880,631	2,952,480	2,776,731	2,615,620
Males	720,440	988,701	811,871	742,673	810,664	818,605	891,282	1,055,029	1,098,772	1,152,037	1,317,630	1,342,140	1,258,460	1,197,173
Females	408,725	673,920	783,622	754,232	906,179	1,021,985	1,108,726	1,331,987	1,343,368	1,396,451	1,563,001	1,610,340	1,518,271	1,418,447
Part-time	1,066,247	2,173,745	2,733,289	2,772,828	3,279,632	3,437,239	3,697,380	3,797,213	3,881,979	4,091,856	4,220,814	4,265,558	4,285,736	4,172,040
Males	589,439	1,107,680	1,152,268	1,138,011	1,317,730	1,417,488	1,549,407	1,514,363	1,568,247	1,671,716	1,732,613	1,768,853	1,768,887	1,725,988
Females	476,808	1,066,065	1,581,021	1,634,817	1,961,902	2,019,751	2,147,973	2,282,850	2,313,732	2,420,140	2,488,201	2,496,705	2,516,849	2,446,052
Private 2-year	123,973	133,753	197,505	261,344	243,608	214,700	251,043	303,826	293,811	331,034	419,961	462,837	437,515	376,313
Full-time	99,746	98,457	158,302	193,702	167,119	136,457	217,041	259,786	250,453	283,709	368,092	412,713	383,305	326,957
Males	50,859	46,860	67,845	83,635	70,728	59,610	104,559	98,737	91,336	97,826	130,780	141,290	129,885	108,659
Females	48,887	51,597	90,457	110,067	96,391	76,847	112,482	161,049	159,117	185,883	237,312	271,423	253,420	218,298
Part-time	24,227	35,296	39,203	67,642	76,489	78,243	34,002	44,040	43,358	47,325	51,869	50,124	54,210	49,356
Males	13,919	22,103	15,049	37,915	33,647	32,906	13,352	12,239	12,216	14,305	15,537	12,843	14,422	12,884
Females	10,308	13,193	24,154	29,727	42,842	45,337	20,650	31,801	31,142	33,020	36,332	37,281	39,788	36,472
Nonprofit 2-year	113,299	112,997	114,094	108,791	89,158	75,154	58,844	43,522	33,486	35,351	34,767	32,660	39,864	37,606
Full-time	91,514	82,158	83,000	76,547	62,003	54,033	46,670	28,939	21,295	23,270	23,483	23,101	30,579	29,320
Males	46,030	40,548	34,968	30,878	25,946	23,265	21,950	12,086	8,691	9,244	9,578	9,918	11,296	10,459
Females	45,484	41,610	48,041	45,669	36,057	30,768	24,720	16,853	12,604	14,026	13,905	13,183	19,283	18,861
Part-time	21,785	30,839	31,085	32,244	27,155	21,121	12,174	14,583	12,191	12,081	11,284	9,559	9,285	8,286
Males	12,097	18,929	11,445	10,786	7,970	6,080	4,499	3,566	3,003	2,867	2,721	2,586	2,544	2,465
Females	9,688	11,910	19,640	21,458	19,185	15,041	7,675	11,017	9,188	9,214	8,563	6,973	6,741	5,821
For-profit 2-year	10,674	20,756	83,411	152,553	154,450	139,546	192,199	260,304	260,325	295,683	385,194	430,177	397,651	338,707

See notes at end of table.

Total fall enrollment in degree-granting postsecondary institutions, by level and control of institution, attendance status, and sex of student: Selected years, 1970 through 2023—Continued

Level and control of institution, attendance status, and sex of student	Projected										
	2013	2014	2015	2016	2017	2018	2019	2020	2021	2022	2023
1	16	17	18	19	20	21	22	23	24	25	26
Total	**20,597,000**	**21,011,000**	**21,266,000**	**21,586,000**	**21,946,000**	**22,227,000**	**22,512,000**	**22,797,000**	**23,141,000**	**23,499,000**	**23,834,000**
Full-time	12,742,000	12,992,000	13,112,000	13,278,000	13,468,000	13,618,000	13,774,000	13,929,000	14,122,000	14,329,000	14,520,000
Males	5,766,000	5,783,000	5,807,000	5,860,000	5,932,000	5,990,000	6,048,000	6,101,000	6,169,000	6,244,000	6,312,000
Females	6,976,000	7,209,000	7,305,000	7,418,000	7,536,000	7,629,000	7,726,000	7,828,000	7,953,000	8,085,000	8,207,000
Part-time	7,855,000	8,019,000	8,154,000	8,308,000	8,478,000	8,609,000	8,737,000	8,869,000	9,020,000	9,170,000	9,314,000
Males	3,219,000	3,254,000	3,266,000	3,285,000	3,311,000	3,334,000	3,360,000	3,390,000	3,430,000	3,468,000	3,504,000
Females	4,636,000	4,765,000	4,888,000	5,022,000	5,167,000	5,275,000	5,377,000	5,478,000	5,590,000	5,702,000	5,810,000
4-year	**13,407,000**	**13,691,000**	**13,856,000**	**14,061,000**	**14,291,000**	**14,468,000**	**14,649,000**	**14,840,000**	**15,068,000**	**15,303,000**	**15,521,000**
Full-time	9,759,000	9,954,000	10,046,000	10,169,000	10,310,000	10,419,000	10,534,000	10,655,000	10,803,000	10,958,000	11,101,000
Males	4,420,000	4,437,000	4,457,000	4,498,000	4,552,000	4,594,000	4,637,000	4,680,000	4,733,000	4,790,000	4,842,000
Females	5,339,000	5,517,000	5,589,000	5,671,000	5,758,000	5,825,000	5,897,000	5,975,000	6,069,000	6,167,000	6,258,000
Part-time	3,648,000	3,737,000	3,810,000	3,892,000	3,981,000	4,048,000	4,115,000	4,185,000	4,266,000	4,345,000	4,420,000
Males	1,483,000	1,502,000	1,512,000	1,525,000	1,541,000	1,555,000	1,570,000	1,587,000	1,610,000	1,632,000	1,652,000
Females	2,165,000	2,235,000	2,298,000	2,367,000	2,440,000	2,494,000	2,545,000	2,598,000	2,656,000	2,713,000	2,768,000
Public 4-year	8,047,000	8,209,000	8,302,000	8,420,000	8,553,000	8,656,000	8,763,000	8,874,000	9,008,000	9,144,000	9,272,000
Full-time	5,877,000	5,987,000	6,038,000	6,109,000	6,190,000	6,254,000	6,322,000	6,393,000	6,480,000	6,570,000	6,654,000
Males	2,760,000	2,769,000	2,780,000	2,804,000	2,836,000	2,862,000	2,888,000	2,914,000	2,947,000	2,982,000	3,014,000
Females	3,117,000	3,219,000	3,259,000	3,305,000	3,354,000	3,392,000	3,434,000	3,478,000	3,532,000	3,588,000	3,640,000
Part-time	2,170,000	2,222,000	2,264,000	2,311,000	2,363,000	2,402,000	2,440,000	2,481,000	2,528,000	2,574,000	2,618,000
Males	909,000	921,000	926,000	934,000	944,000	952,000	961,000	971,000	985,000	998,000	1,010,000
Females	1,261,000	1,301,000	1,338,000	1,377,000	1,419,000	1,450,000	1,480,000	1,510,000	1,543,000	1,576,000	1,608,000
Private 4-year	5,360,000	5,482,000	5,554,000	5,641,000	5,738,000	5,811,000	5,887,000	5,966,000	6,061,000	6,159,000	6,249,000
Full-time	3,882,000	3,967,000	4,008,000	4,061,000	4,120,000	4,165,000	4,212,000	4,262,000	4,323,000	4,388,000	4,447,000
Males	1,660,000	1,668,000	1,677,000	1,694,000	1,716,000	1,732,000	1,749,000	1,765,000	1,786,000	1,808,000	1,828,000
Females	2,222,000	2,298,000	2,330,000	2,366,000	2,404,000	2,432,000	2,463,000	2,497,000	2,537,000	2,579,000	2,618,000
Part-time	1,478,000	1,515,000	1,546,000	1,581,000	1,618,000	1,647,000	1,675,000	1,704,000	1,738,000	1,771,000	1,803,000
Males	574,000	581,000	585,000	591,000	597,000	603,000	609,000	616,000	625,000	634,000	642,000
Females	904,000	934,000	961,000	990,000	1,021,000	1,044,000	1,065,000	1,088,000	1,112,000	1,137,000	1,160,000
Nonprofit 4-year	—	—	—	—	—	—	—	—	—	—	—
Full-time	—	—	—	—	—	—	—	—	—	—	—
Males	—	—	—	—	—	—	—	—	—	—	—
Females	—	—	—	—	—	—	—	—	—	—	—
Part-time	—	—	—	—	—	—	—	—	—	—	—
Males	—	—	—	—	—	—	—	—	—	—	—
Females	—	—	—	—	—	—	—	—	—	—	—
For-profit 4-year	—	—	—	—	—	—	—	—	—	—	—
2-year	**7,191,000**	**7,320,000**	**7,410,000**	**7,525,000**	**7,655,000**	**7,760,000**	**7,862,000**	**7,957,000**	**8,073,000**	**8,196,000**	**8,313,000**
Full-time	2,983,000	3,038,000	3,066,000	3,109,000	3,158,000	3,199,000	3,240,000	3,274,000	3,319,000	3,371,000	3,419,000
Males	1,346,000	1,346,000	1,350,000	1,362,000	1,379,000	1,395,000	1,411,000	1,421,000	1,436,000	1,453,000	1,470,000
Females	1,637,000	1,692,000	1,717,000	1,747,000	1,779,000	1,804,000	1,829,000	1,853,000	1,883,000	1,918,000	1,949,000
Part-time	4,208,000	4,282,000	4,344,000	4,416,000	4,497,000	4,560,000	4,622,000	4,683,000	4,754,000	4,825,000	4,893,000
Males	1,736,000	1,752,000	1,754,000	1,761,000	1,770,000	1,779,000	1,790,000	1,803,000	1,820,000	1,836,000	1,852,000
Females	2,471,000	2,530,000	2,589,000	2,655,000	2,727,000	2,781,000	2,832,000	2,881,000	2,934,000	2,988,000	3,041,000
Public 2-year	6,810,000	6,931,000	7,017,000	7,126,000	7,249,000	7,348,000	7,445,000	7,536,000	7,645,000	7,760,000	7,871,000
Full-time	2,653,000	2,700,000	2,725,000	2,762,000	2,806,000	2,842,000	2,879,000	2,909,000	2,948,000	2,994,000	3,037,000
Males	1,234,000	1,234,000	1,237,000	1,248,000	1,265,000	1,279,000	1,293,000	1,303,000	1,316,000	1,332,000	1,348,000
Females	1,419,000	1,466,000	1,488,000	1,514,000	1,541,000	1,563,000	1,585,000	1,606,000	1,632,000	1,662,000	1,689,000
Part-time	4,158,000	4,231,000	4,292,000	4,363,000	4,443,000	4,506,000	4,567,000	4,627,000	4,696,000	4,766,000	4,834,000
Males	1,723,000	1,738,000	1,741,000	1,747,000	1,757,000	1,765,000	1,777,000	1,789,000	1,806,000	1,822,000	1,838,000
Females	2,435,000	2,493,000	2,551,000	2,616,000	2,686,000	2,740,000	2,790,000	2,838,000	2,891,000	2,944,000	2,996,000
Private 2-year	380,000	389,000	393,000	399,000	406,000	412,000	417,000	422,000	428,000	435,000	442,000
Full-time	330,000	338,000	341,000	346,000	352,000	357,000	361,000	365,000	371,000	377,000	382,000
Males	112,000	112,000	112,000	113,000	115,000	116,000	117,000	118,000	119,000	121,000	122,000
Females	218,000	226,000	229,000	233,000	237,000	241,000	244,000	247,000	251,000	256,000	260,000
Part-time	50,000	51,000	52,000	53,000	54,000	55,000	56,000	57,000	57,000	58,000	59,000
Males	13,000	13,000	13,000	13,000	13,000	14,000	14,000	14,000	14,000	14,000	14,000
Females	37,000	38,000	38,000	39,000	41,000	41,000	42,000	43,000	44,000	44,000	45,000
Nonprofit 2-year	—	—	—	—	—	—	—	—	—	—	—
Full-time	—	—	—	—	—	—	—	—	—	—	—
Males	—	—	—	—	—	—	—	—	—	—	—
Females	—	—	—	—	—	—	—	—	—	—	—
Part-time	—	—	—	—	—	—	—	—	—	—	—
Males	—	—	—	—	—	—	—	—	—	—	—
Females	—	—	—	—	—	—	—	—	—	—	—
For-profit 2-year	—	—	—	—	—	—	—	—	—	—	—

—Not available.

[1]Large increase in private 2-year institutions in 1980 is due to the addition of schools accredited by the Accrediting Commission of Career Schools and Colleges of Technology. NOTE: Data through 1995 are for institutions of higher education, while later data are for degree-granting institutions. Degree-granting institutions grant associate's or higher degrees and participate in Title IV federal financial aid programs. The degree-granting classification is very similar to the earlier higher education classification, but it includes more 2-year colleges and excludes a few higher education institutions that did not grant degrees. SOURCE: U.S. Department of Education, National Center for Education Statistics, Higher Education General Information Survey (HEGIS), "Fall Enrollment in Colleges and Universities" surveys, 1970 through 1985; Integrated Postsecondary Education Data System (IPEDS), "Fall Enrollment Survey" (IPEDS-EF:90–99); IPEDS Spring 2001 through Spring 2013, Enrollment component; and Enrollment in Degree-Granting Institutions Projection Model, 1980 through 2023. (This table was prepared July 2014.)

Total fall enrollment in degree-granting postsecondary institutions, by attendance status, sex, and age: Selected years, 1970 through 2023

[In thousands]

Attendance status, sex, and age	1970	1980	1990	2000	2003	2004	2005	2006	2007	2008	2009	2010	2011	2012	Projected 2013	2014	2016	2023
1	2	3	4	5	6	7	8	9	10	11	12	13	14	15	16	17	18	19
All students	8,581	12,097	13,819	15,312	16,911	17,272	17,487	17,759	18,248	19,103	20,428	21,016	20,994	20,643	20,597	21,011	21,586	23,834
14 to 17 years old	263	257	153	131	169	166	187	184	200	195	217	202	221	216	224	227	237	262
18 and 19 years old	2,579	2,852	2,777	3,258	3,355	3,367	3,444	3,561	3,690	3,813	4,041	4,056	3,954	3,790	3,932	3,946	3,992	4,275
20 and 21 years old	1,885	2,395	2,593	3,005	3,391	3,516	3,563	3,573	3,570	3,649	3,945	4,101	4,267	4,240	4,462	4,459	4,429	4,614
22 to 24 years old	1,469	1,947	2,202	2,600	3,086	3,166	3,114	3,185	3,280	3,443	3,594	3,758	3,790	3,871	4,036	4,162	4,196	4,425
25 to 29 years old	1,091	1,843	2,083	2,044	2,311	2,418	2,469	2,506	2,651	2,840	3,096	3,253	3,268	3,218	3,105	3,233	3,501	3,846
30 to 34 years old	527	1,227	1,384	1,333	1,418	1,440	1,438	1,472	1,519	1,609	1,741	1,805	1,786	1,731	1,636	1,698	1,795	2,224
35 years old and over	767	1,577	2,627	2,942	3,181	3,199	3,272	3,277	3,339	3,554	3,794	3,840	3,707	3,577	3,203	3,286	3,437	4,188
Males	5,044	5,874	6,284	6,722	7,260	7,387	7,456	7,575	7,816	8,189	8,770	9,045	9,026	8,919	8,985	9,037	9,145	9,817
14 to 17 years old	125	106	66	58	67	62	68	69	88	93	103	94	104	109	112	114	118	127
18 and 19 years old	1,355	1,368	1,298	1,464	1,474	1,475	1,523	1,604	1,669	1,704	1,806	1,820	1,782	1,712	1,749	1,729	1,732	1,841
20 and 21 years old	1,064	1,219	1,259	1,411	1,541	1,608	1,658	1,628	1,634	1,695	1,876	1,948	1,984	1,962	2,072	2,048	2,015	2,074
22 to 24 years old	1,004	1,075	1,129	1,222	1,411	1,437	1,410	1,445	1,480	1,555	1,606	1,723	1,767	1,862	1,978	2,012	2,013	2,069
25 to 29 years old	796	983	1,024	908	1,007	1,039	1,057	1,040	1,148	1,222	1,382	1,410	1,402	1,347	1,328	1,366	1,454	1,555
30 to 34 years old	333	564	605	581	602	619	591	628	638	691	709	731	699	678	643	657	681	820
35 years old and over	366	559	902	1,077	1,158	1,147	1,149	1,160	1,159	1,228	1,287	1,320	1,288	1,249	1,102	1,111	1,134	1,330
Females	3,537	6,223	7,535	8,591	9,651	9,885	10,032	10,184	10,432	10,914	11,658	11,971	11,968	11,724	11,613	11,974	12,441	14,017
14 to 17 years old	137	151	87	73	102	104	119	115	112	102	114	108	116	107	112	113	119	135
18 and 19 years old	1,224	1,484	1,479	1,794	1,880	1,892	1,920	1,956	2,021	2,109	2,236	2,236	2,172	2,078	2,182	2,218	2,260	2,434
20 and 21 years old	821	1,177	1,334	1,593	1,851	1,908	1,905	1,945	1,936	1,954	2,069	2,154	2,283	2,278	2,390	2,411	2,414	2,540
22 to 24 years old	464	871	1,073	1,378	1,675	1,729	1,704	1,740	1,800	1,888	1,987	2,036	2,023	2,009	2,058	2,150	2,183	2,356
25 to 29 years old	296	859	1,059	1,136	1,304	1,379	1,413	1,466	1,502	1,618	1,713	1,844	1,866	1,870	1,777	1,867	2,047	2,292
30 to 34 years old	194	663	779	752	816	821	847	844	881	918	1,032	1,074	1,087	1,053	993	1,041	1,114	1,403
35 years old and over	401	1,018	1,725	1,865	2,023	2,052	2,123	2,117	2,180	2,326	2,507	2,520	2,419	2,328	2,101	2,175	2,303	2,858
Full-time	5,816	7,098	7,821	9,010	10,326	10,610	10,797	10,957	11,270	11,748	12,723	13,082	13,001	12,737	12,742	12,992	13,278	14,520
14 to 17 years old	246	231	134	121	146	138	152	148	169	168	181	170	185	187	182	185	193	213
18 and 19 years old	2,374	2,544	2,471	2,823	2,934	2,960	3,026	3,120	3,244	3,359	3,513	3,495	3,351	3,236	3,229	3,254	3,297	3,546
20 and 21 years old	1,649	2,007	2,137	2,452	2,841	2,926	2,976	2,972	2,985	3,043	3,271	3,363	3,427	3,392	3,453	3,459	3,442	3,606
22 to 24 years old	904	1,181	1,405	1,714	2,083	2,143	2,122	2,127	2,205	2,347	2,535	2,584	2,580	2,585	2,659	2,747	2,775	2,951
25 to 29 years old	426	641	791	886	1,086	1,132	1,174	1,225	1,299	1,369	1,520	1,605	1,600	1,558	1,505	1,571	1,703	1,887
30 to 34 years old	113	272	383	418	489	517	547	571	556	571	663	744	763	735	723	753	797	997
35 years old and over	104	221	500	596	747	795	800	794	812	890	1,041	1,121	1,096	1,044	991	1,022	1,071	1,321
Males	3,504	3,689	3,808	4,111	4,638	4,739	4,803	4,879	5,029	5,234	5,671	5,837	5,793	5,710	5,766	5,783	5,860	6,312
14 to 17 years old	121	95	55	51	58	49	53	52	74	73	78	71	85	94	90	92	95	103
18 and 19 years old	1,261	1,219	1,171	1,252	1,291	1,297	1,339	1,404	1,465	1,516	1,580	1,574	1,510	1,473	1,457	1,441	1,449	1,552
20 and 21 years old	955	1,046	1,035	1,156	1,305	1,360	1,398	1,372	1,366	1,407	1,547	1,586	1,587	1,556	1,584	1,564	1,545	1,609
22 to 24 years old	686	717	768	834	995	1,001	982	992	1,043	1,105	1,177	1,214	1,217	1,253	1,313	1,333	1,341	1,401
25 to 29 years old	346	391	433	410	503	498	506	533	578	597	665	714	727	706	703	725	777	849
30 to 34 years old	77	142	171	186	209	231	225	235	231	249	281	301	299	291	290	297	310	383
35 years old and over	58	80	174	222	277	302	300	291	273	287	343	376	369	337	329	332	342	415
Females	2,312	3,409	4,013	4,899	5,688	5,871	5,994	6,078	6,240	6,513	7,052	7,245	7,208	7,027	6,976	7,209	7,418	8,207
14 to 17 years old	125	136	78	70	88	89	98	95	95	95	103	99	100	93	92	93	98	110
18 and 19 years old	1,113	1,325	1,300	1,571	1,643	1,662	1,687	1,716	1,779	1,843	1,933	1,921	1,841	1,763	1,772	1,813	1,848	1,993
20 and 21 years old	693	961	1,101	1,296	1,536	1,566	1,578	1,601	1,619	1,636	1,724	1,777	1,840	1,836	1,869	1,895	1,897	1,997
22 to 24 years old	218	464	638	880	1,088	1,142	1,140	1,135	1,163	1,242	1,358	1,370	1,363	1,332	1,346	1,414	1,434	1,550
25 to 29 years old	80	250	358	476	583	634	668	692	721	772	855	890	872	852	802	847	926	1,038
30 to 34 years old	37	130	212	232	280	286	322	336	324	322	382	444	464	444	433	456	487	614
35 years old and over	46	141	326	374	471	493	500	503	539	603	697	745	726	707	662	690	729	906
Part-time	2,765	4,999	5,998	6,303	6,585	6,662	6,690	6,802	6,978	7,355	7,705	7,934	7,993	7,906	7,855	8,019	8,308	9,314
14 to 17 years old	16	26	19	10	23	28	36	36	31	27	36	32	36	29	42	42	44	49
18 and 19 years old	205	308	306	435	421	407	417	440	446	453	528	561	603	554	703	693	695	729
20 and 21 years old	236	388	456	553	551	590	586	601	585	606	674	739	840	848	1,009	1,000	987	1,008
22 to 24 years old	564	765	796	886	1,003	1,023	992	1,058	1,074	1,096	1,059	1,174	1,210	1,286	1,377	1,415	1,421	1,474
25 to 29 years old	665	1,202	1,291	1,158	1,224	1,286	1,296	1,282	1,352	1,471	1,576	1,649	1,669	1,659	1,599	1,661	1,797	1,959
30 to 34 years old	414	954	1,001	915	929	923	891	901	963	1,037	1,078	1,060	1,023	997	914	945	998	1,227
35 years old and over	663	1,356	2,127	2,345	2,434	2,404	2,472	2,483	2,527	2,664	2,753	2,719	2,612	2,532	2,212	2,264	2,365	2,867
Males	1,540	2,185	2,476	2,611	2,622	2,648	2,653	2,696	2,786	2,955	3,099	3,208	3,233	3,209	3,219	3,254	3,285	3,504
14 to 17 years old	4	12	11	7	9	13	15	17	14	20	25	23	20	14	22	22	23	24
18 and 19 years old	94	149	127	212	183	178	184	200	204	188	226	245	272	239	292	288	283	288
20 and 21 years old	108	172	224	255	236	248	260	257	269	289	329	362	397	406	488	484	470	466
22 to 24 years old	318	359	361	388	416	436	428	452	438	450	430	508	551	609	665	679	672	668
25 to 29 years old	450	592	591	498	504	540	551	507	570	625	717	695	675	641	624	641	677	706
30 to 34 years old	257	422	435	395	392	388	365	393	406	442	428	430	400	388	353	360	371	437
35 years old and over	309	479	728	855	882	845	850	869	886	941	944	944	919	912	774	779	791	915
Females	1,225	2,814	3,521	3,692	3,963	4,014	4,038	4,106	4,192	4,401	4,606	4,726	4,760	4,697	4,636	4,765	5,022	5,810
14 to 17 years old	12	14	9	3	14	15	21	20	17	7	11	9	16	15	19	20	21	25
18 and 19 years old	112	159	179	223	238	230	233	240	242	265	303	316	331	315	411	405	412	441
20 and 21 years old	128	216	233	298	315	342	327	344	317	318	345	377	443	442	521	516	518	543
22 to 24 years old	246	407	435	497	587	588	564	605	637	646	629	666	659	677	711	736	749	806
25 to 29 years old	216	609	700	660	721	746	745	774	781	846	858	953	994	1,018	975	1,020	1,121	1,254
30 to 34 years old	158	532	567	520	537	535	526	508	557	595	651	630	623	609	561	585	627	790
35 years old and over	354	876	1,399	1,491	1,552	1,560	1,623	1,614	1,640	1,723	1,810	1,775	1,693	1,621	1,438	1,484	1,574	1,952

NOTE: Distributions by age are estimates based on samples of the civilian noninstitutional population from the U.S. Census Bureau's Current Population Survey. Data through 1995 are for institutions of higher education, while later data are for degree-granting institutions. Degree-granting institutions grant associate's or higher degrees and participate in Title IV federal financial aid programs. The degree-granting classification is very similar to the earlier higher education classification, but it includes more 2-year colleges and excludes a few higher education institutions that did not grant degrees. Some data have been revised from previously published figures. Detail may not sum to totals because of rounding.

SOURCE: U.S. Department of Education, National Center for Education Statistics, Higher Education General Information Survey (HEGIS), "Fall Enrollment in Colleges and Universities" surveys, 1970 and 1980; Integrated Postsecondary Education Data System (IPEDS), "Fall Enrollment Survey" (IPEDS-EF:90–99); IPEDS Spring 2001 through Spring 2012, Enrollment component; and Enrollment in Degree-Granting Institutions Projection Model, 1980 through 2023. U.S. Department of Commerce, Census Bureau, Current Population Survey (CPS), October, selected years, 1970 through 2012. (This table was prepared June 2014.)

Total undergraduate fall enrollment in degree-granting postsecondary institutions, by attendance status, sex of student, and control and level of institution: Selected years, 1970 through 2023

Level and year	Total	Full-time	Part-time	Males	Females	Males: Full-time	Males: Part-time	Females: Full-time	Females: Part-time	Public	Private: Total	Private: Nonprofit	Private: For-profit
1	2	3	4	5	6	7	8	9	10	11	12	13	14
Total, all levels													
1970	7,368,644	5,280,064	2,088,580	4,249,702	3,118,942	3,096,371	1,153,331	2,183,693	935,249	5,620,255	1,748,389	1,730,133	18,256
1975	9,679,455	6,168,396	3,511,059	5,257,005	4,422,450	3,459,328	1,797,677	2,709,068	1,713,382	7,826,032	1,853,423	1,814,844	38,579
1980	10,475,055	6,361,744	4,113,311	5,000,177	5,474,878	3,226,857	1,773,320	3,134,887	2,339,991	8,441,955	2,033,100	1,926,703	106,397
1981	10,754,522	6,449,068	4,305,454	5,108,271	5,646,251	3,260,473	1,847,798	3,188,595	2,457,656	8,648,363	2,106,159	1,958,848	147,311
1982	10,825,062	6,483,805	4,341,257	5,170,494	5,654,568	3,299,436	1,871,058	3,184,369	2,470,199	8,713,073	2,111,989	1,939,389	172,600
1983	10,845,995	6,514,034	4,331,961	5,158,300	5,687,695	3,304,247	1,854,053	3,209,787	2,477,908	8,697,118	2,148,877	1,961,076	187,801
1984	10,618,071	6,347,653	4,270,418	5,006,813	5,611,258	3,194,930	1,811,883	3,152,723	2,458,535	8,493,491	2,124,580	1,940,310	184,270
1985	10,596,674	6,319,592	4,277,082	4,962,080	5,634,594	3,156,446	1,805,634	3,163,146	2,471,448	8,477,125	2,119,549	1,928,996	190,553
1986	10,797,975	6,352,073	4,445,902	5,017,505	5,780,470	3,146,330	1,871,175	3,205,743	2,574,727	8,660,716	2,137,259	1,928,294	208,965
1987	11,046,235	6,462,549	4,583,686	5,068,457	5,977,778	3,163,676	1,904,781	3,298,873	2,678,905	8,918,589	2,127,646	1,939,942	187,704
1988	11,316,548	6,642,428	4,674,120	5,137,644	6,178,904	3,206,442	1,931,202	3,435,986	2,742,918	9,103,146	2,213,402	—	—
1989	11,742,531	6,840,696	4,901,835	5,310,990	6,431,541	3,278,647	2,032,343	3,562,049	2,869,492	9,487,742	2,254,789	—	—
1990	11,959,106	6,976,030	4,983,076	5,379,759	6,579,347	3,336,535	2,043,224	3,639,495	2,939,852	9,709,596	2,249,510	2,043,407	206,103
1991	12,439,287	7,221,412	5,217,875	5,571,003	6,868,284	3,435,526	2,135,477	3,785,886	3,082,398	10,147,957	2,291,330	2,072,354	218,976
1992	12,537,700	7,244,442	5,293,258	5,582,936	6,954,764	3,424,739	2,158,197	3,819,703	3,135,061	10,216,297	2,321,403	2,101,721	219,682
1993	12,323,959	7,179,482	5,144,477	5,483,682	6,840,277	3,381,997	2,101,685	3,797,485	3,042,792	10,011,787	2,312,172	2,099,197	212,975
1994	12,262,608	7,168,706	5,093,902	5,422,113	6,840,495	3,341,591	2,080,522	3,827,115	3,013,380	9,945,128	2,317,480	2,100,465	217,015
1995	12,231,719	7,145,268	5,086,451	5,401,130	6,830,589	3,296,610	2,104,520	3,848,658	2,981,931	9,903,626	2,328,093	2,104,693	223,400
1996	12,326,948	7,298,839	5,028,109	5,420,672	6,906,276	3,339,108	2,081,564	3,959,731	2,946,545	9,935,283	2,391,665	2,112,318	279,347
1997	12,450,587	7,418,598	5,031,989	5,468,532	6,982,055	3,379,597	2,088,935	4,039,001	2,943,054	10,007,479	2,443,108	2,139,824	303,284
1998	12,436,937	7,538,711	4,898,226	5,446,133	6,990,804	3,428,161	2,017,972	4,110,550	2,880,254	9,950,212	2,486,725	2,152,655	334,070
1999	12,739,445	7,753,548	4,985,897	5,584,234	7,155,211	3,524,586	2,059,648	4,228,962	2,926,249	10,174,228	2,565,217	2,185,290	379,927
2000	13,155,393	7,922,926	5,232,467	5,778,268	7,377,125	3,588,246	2,190,022	4,334,680	3,042,445	10,539,322	2,616,071	2,213,180	402,891
2001	13,715,610	8,327,640	5,387,970	6,004,431	7,711,179	3,768,630	2,235,801	4,559,010	3,152,169	10,985,871	2,729,739	2,257,718	472,021
2002	14,257,077	8,734,252	5,522,825	6,192,390	8,064,687	3,934,168	2,258,222	4,800,084	3,264,603	11,432,855	2,824,222	2,306,091	518,131
2003	14,480,364	9,045,253	5,435,111	6,227,372	8,252,992	4,048,682	2,178,690	4,996,571	3,256,421	11,523,103	2,957,261	2,346,673	610,588
2004	14,780,630	9,284,336	5,496,294	6,340,048	8,440,582	4,140,628	2,199,420	5,143,708	3,296,874	11,650,580	3,130,050	2,389,366	740,684
2005	14,963,964	9,446,430	5,517,534	6,408,871	8,555,093	4,200,863	2,208,008	5,245,567	3,309,526	11,697,730	3,266,234	2,418,368	847,866
2006	15,184,302	9,571,079	5,613,223	6,513,756	8,670,546	4,264,606	2,249,150	5,306,473	3,364,073	11,847,426	3,336,876	2,448,240	888,636
2007	15,603,771	9,840,978	5,762,793	6,727,600	8,876,171	4,396,868	2,330,732	5,444,110	3,432,061	12,137,583	3,466,188	2,470,327	995,861
2008	16,365,738	10,254,930	6,110,808	7,066,623	9,299,115	4,577,431	2,489,192	5,677,499	3,621,616	12,591,217	3,774,521	2,536,532	1,237,989
2009	17,565,320	11,143,499	6,421,821	7,595,481	9,969,839	4,976,727	2,618,754	6,166,772	3,803,067	13,386,593	4,178,727	2,593,361	1,585,366
2010	18,078,672	11,451,568	6,627,104	7,835,163	10,243,509	5,117,497	2,717,666	6,334,071	3,909,438	13,704,290	4,374,382	2,653,404	1,720,978
2011	18,063,037	11,359,068	6,703,969	7,816,975	10,246,062	5,070,529	2,746,446	6,288,539	3,957,523	13,688,792	4,374,245	2,718,880	1,655,365
2012	17,732,431	11,097,779	6,634,652	7,713,901	10,018,530	4,984,696	2,729,205	6,113,083	3,905,447	13,473,743	4,258,688	2,745,075	1,513,613
2013[1]	17,650,000	11,052,000	6,598,000	7,729,000	9,921,000	4,999,000	2,730,000	6,053,000	3,867,000	13,428,000	4,222,000	—	—
2014[1]	17,968,000	11,242,000	6,726,000	7,759,000	10,209,000	5,001,000	2,758,000	6,241,000	3,968,000	13,666,000	4,302,000	—	—
2015[1]	18,155,000	11,325,000	6,830,000	7,777,000	10,378,000	5,012,000	2,765,000	6,313,000	4,065,000	13,812,000	4,343,000	—	—
2016[1]	18,397,000	11,448,000	6,949,000	7,827,000	10,571,000	5,049,000	2,778,000	6,400,000	4,171,000	14,000,000	4,397,000	—	—
2017[1]	18,677,000	11,596,000	7,082,000	7,899,000	10,778,000	5,103,000	2,796,000	6,493,000	4,286,000	14,218,000	4,459,000	—	—
2018[1]	18,904,000	11,720,000	7,184,000	7,962,000	10,942,000	5,151,000	2,812,000	6,570,000	4,372,000	14,394,000	4,510,000	—	—
2019[1]	19,134,000	11,850,000	7,284,000	8,030,000	11,104,000	5,199,000	2,831,000	6,651,000	4,453,000	14,571,000	4,563,000	—	—
2020[1]	19,360,000	11,974,000	7,386,000	8,095,000	11,265,000	5,242,000	2,853,000	6,733,000	4,533,000	14,744,000	4,616,000	—	—
2021[1]	19,634,000	12,130,000	7,504,000	8,180,000	11,454,000	5,296,000	2,883,000	6,834,000	4,621,000	14,953,000	4,681,000	—	—
2022[1]	19,917,000	12,296,000	7,621,000	8,269,000	11,648,000	5,356,000	2,912,000	6,939,000	4,708,000	15,169,000	4,747,000	—	—
2023[1]	20,186,000	12,452,000	7,734,000	8,353,000	11,833,000	5,413,000	2,940,000	7,039,000	4,794,000	15,375,000	4,810,000	—	—
2-year institutions[2]													
1970	2,318,956	1,228,909	1,090,047	1,374,426	944,530	771,298	603,128	457,611	486,919	2,194,983	123,973	113,299	10,674
1975	3,965,726	1,761,009	2,204,717	2,163,604	1,802,122	1,035,531	1,128,073	725,478	1,076,644	3,831,973	133,753	112,997	20,756
1980	4,525,097	1,753,637	2,771,460	2,046,642	2,478,455	879,619	1,167,023	874,018	1,604,437	4,327,592	197,505	114,094	83,411
1981	4,715,403	1,795,858	2,919,545	2,124,136	2,591,267	897,657	1,226,479	898,201	1,693,066	4,479,900	235,503	119,166	116,337
1982	4,770,712	1,839,704	2,931,008	2,169,802	2,600,910	930,606	1,239,196	909,098	1,691,812	4,518,659	252,053	114,976	137,077
1983	4,723,466	1,826,801	2,896,665	2,131,109	2,592,357	914,704	1,216,405	912,097	1,680,260	4,459,330	264,136	116,293	147,843
1984	4,530,337	1,703,786	2,826,551	2,016,463	2,513,874	841,347	1,175,116	862,439	1,651,435	4,278,661	251,676	108,247	143,429
1985	4,531,077	1,690,607	2,840,470	2,002,234	2,528,843	826,308	1,175,926	864,299	1,664,544	4,269,733	261,344	108,791	152,553
1986	4,679,548	1,696,261	2,983,287	2,060,932	2,618,616	824,551	1,236,381	871,710	1,746,906	4,413,691	265,857	101,498	164,359
1987	4,776,222	1,708,669	3,067,553	2,072,823	2,703,399	820,167	1,252,656	888,502	1,814,897	4,541,054	235,168	90,102	145,066
1988	4,875,155	1,743,592	3,131,563	2,089,689	2,785,466	818,593	1,271,096	924,999	1,860,467	4,615,487	259,668	—	—
1989	5,150,889	1,855,701	3,295,188	2,216,800	2,934,089	869,688	1,347,112	986,013	1,948,076	4,883,660	267,229	—	—
1990	5,240,083	1,883,962	3,356,121	2,232,769	3,007,314	881,392	1,351,377	1,002,570	2,004,744	4,996,475	243,608	89,158	154,450
1991	5,651,900	2,074,530	3,577,370	2,401,910	3,249,990	961,397	1,440,513	1,113,133	2,136,857	5,404,815	247,085	89,289	157,796
1992	5,722,349	2,080,005	3,642,344	2,413,266	3,309,083	951,816	1,461,450	1,128,189	2,180,894	5,484,514	237,835	83,288	154,547
1993	5,565,561	2,043,319	3,522,242	2,345,396	3,220,165	928,216	1,417,180	1,115,103	2,105,062	5,337,022	228,539	86,357	142,182
1994	5,529,609	2,031,713	3,497,896	2,323,161	3,206,448	911,589	1,411,572	1,120,124	2,086,324	5,308,366	221,243	85,607	135,636
1995	5,492,098	1,977,046	3,515,052	2,328,500	3,163,598	878,215	1,450,285	1,098,831	2,064,767	5,277,398	214,700	75,154	139,546
1996	5,562,780	2,072,215	3,490,565	2,358,792	3,203,988	916,452	1,442,340	1,155,763	2,048,225	5,314,038	248,742	75,253	173,489
1997	5,605,569	2,095,171	3,510,398	2,389,711	3,215,858	931,394	1,458,317	1,163,777	2,052,081	5,360,686	244,883	71,794	173,089
1998	5,489,314	2,085,906	3,403,408	2,333,334	3,155,980	936,421	1,396,913	1,149,485	2,006,495	5,245,963	243,351	65,870	177,481
1999	5,653,256	2,167,242	3,486,014	2,413,322	3,239,934	979,203	1,434,119	1,188,039	2,051,895	5,397,786	255,470	63,301	192,169
2000	5,948,104	2,217,044	3,731,060	2,558,520	3,389,584	995,839	1,562,681	1,221,205	2,168,379	5,697,061	251,043	58,844	192,199
2001	6,250,529	2,374,490	3,876,039	2,675,193	3,575,336	1,066,281	1,608,912	1,308,209	2,267,127	5,996,651	253,878	47,549	206,329
2002	6,529,198	2,556,032	3,973,166	2,753,405	3,775,793	1,135,669	1,617,736	1,420,363	2,355,430	6,270,199	258,999	47,087	211,912
2003	6,493,862	2,650,337	3,843,525	2,689,928	3,803,934	1,162,555	1,527,373	1,487,782	2,316,152	6,208,885	284,977	43,868	241,109
2004	6,545,570	2,683,489	3,862,081	2,697,507	3,848,063	1,166,554	1,530,953	1,516,935	2,331,128	6,243,344	302,226	42,250	259,976

See notes at end of table.

Total undergraduate fall enrollment in degree-granting postsecondary institutions, by attendance status, sex of student, and control and level of institution: Selected years, 1970 through 2023—Continued

Level and year	Total	Full-time	Part-time	Males	Females	Males Full-time	Males Part-time	Females Full-time	Females Part-time	Public	Private Total	Private Nonprofit	Private For-profit
1	2	3	4	5	6	7	8	9	10	11	12	13	14
2005	6,487,826	2,646,763	3,841,063	2,680,299	3,807,527	1,153,759	1,526,540	1,493,004	2,314,523	6,184,000	303,826	43,522	260,304
2006	6,518,291	2,643,222	3,875,069	2,704,654	3,813,637	1,159,800	1,544,854	1,483,422	2,330,215	6,224,871	293,420	39,156	254,264
2007	6,617,621	2,692,491	3,925,130	2,770,457	3,847,164	1,190,067	1,580,390	1,502,424	2,344,740	6,323,810	293,811	33,486	260,325
2008	6,971,105	2,832,110	4,138,995	2,935,793	4,035,312	1,249,832	1,685,961	1,582,278	2,453,034	6,640,071	331,034	35,351	295,683
2009	7,521,405	3,248,723	4,272,682	3,196,560	4,324,845	1,448,410	1,748,150	1,800,313	2,524,532	7,101,444	419,961	34,767	385,194
2010	7,680,875	3,365,193	4,315,682	3,265,126	4,415,749	1,483,430	1,781,696	1,881,763	2,533,986	7,218,038	462,837	32,660	430,177
2011	7,499,982	3,160,036	4,339,946	3,171,654	4,328,328	1,388,345	1,783,309	1,771,691	2,556,637	7,062,467	437,515	39,864	397,651
2012	7,163,973	2,942,577	4,221,396	3,044,704	4,119,269	1,305,832	1,738,872	1,636,745	2,482,524	6,787,660	376,313	37,606	338,707
2013[1]	7,191,000	2,983,000	4,208,000	3,082,000	4,108,000	1,346,000	1,736,000	1,637,000	2,471,000	6,810,000	380,000	—	—
2014[1]	7,320,000	3,038,000	4,282,000	3,098,000	4,222,000	1,346,000	1,752,000	1,692,000	2,530,000	6,931,000	389,000	—	—
2015[1]	7,410,000	3,066,000	4,344,000	3,104,000	4,306,000	1,350,000	1,754,000	1,717,000	2,589,000	7,017,000	393,000	—	—
2016[1]	7,525,000	3,109,000	4,416,000	3,122,000	4,402,000	1,362,000	1,761,000	1,747,000	2,655,000	7,126,000	399,000	—	—
2017[1]	7,655,000	3,158,000	4,497,000	3,150,000	4,505,000	1,379,000	1,770,000	1,779,000	2,727,000	7,249,000	406,000	—	—
2018[1]	7,760,000	3,199,000	4,560,000	3,174,000	4,585,000	1,395,000	1,779,000	1,804,000	2,781,000	7,348,000	412,000	—	—
2019[1]	7,862,000	3,240,000	4,622,000	3,201,000	4,662,000	1,411,000	1,790,000	1,829,000	2,832,000	7,445,000	417,000	—	—
2020[1]	7,957,000	3,274,000	4,683,000	3,224,000	4,734,000	1,421,000	1,803,000	1,853,000	2,881,000	7,536,000	422,000	—	—
2021[1]	8,073,000	3,319,000	4,754,000	3,255,000	4,818,000	1,436,000	1,820,000	1,883,000	2,934,000	7,645,000	428,000	—	—
2022[1]	8,196,000	3,371,000	4,825,000	3,290,000	4,906,000	1,453,000	1,836,000	1,918,000	2,988,000	7,760,000	435,000	—	—
2023[1]	8,313,000	3,419,000	4,893,000	3,322,000	4,990,000	1,470,000	1,852,000	1,949,000	3,041,000	7,871,000	442,000	—	—
4-year institutions													
1970	5,049,688	4,051,155	998,533	2,875,276	2,174,412	2,325,073	550,203	1,726,082	448,330	3,425,272	1,624,416	1,616,834	7,582
1975	5,713,729	4,407,387	1,306,342	3,093,401	2,620,328	2,423,797	669,604	1,983,590	636,738	3,994,059	1,719,670	1,701,847	17,823
1980	5,949,958	4,608,107	1,341,851	2,953,535	2,996,423	2,347,238	606,297	2,260,869	735,554	4,114,363	1,835,595	1,812,609	22,986
1981	6,039,119	4,653,210	1,385,909	2,984,135	3,054,984	2,362,816	621,319	2,290,394	764,590	4,168,463	1,870,656	1,839,682	30,974
1982	6,054,350	4,644,101	1,410,249	3,000,692	3,053,658	2,368,830	631,862	2,275,271	778,387	4,194,414	1,859,936	1,824,413	35,523
1983	6,122,529	4,687,233	1,435,296	3,027,191	3,095,338	2,389,543	637,648	2,297,690	797,648	4,237,788	1,884,741	1,844,783	39,958
1984	6,087,734	4,643,867	1,443,867	2,990,350	3,097,384	2,353,583	636,767	2,290,284	807,100	4,214,830	1,872,904	1,832,063	40,841
1985	6,065,597	4,628,985	1,436,612	2,959,846	3,105,751	2,330,138	629,708	2,298,847	806,904	4,207,392	1,858,205	1,820,205	38,000
1986	6,118,427	4,655,812	1,462,615	2,956,573	3,161,854	2,321,779	634,794	2,334,033	827,821	4,247,025	1,871,402	1,826,796	44,606
1987	6,270,013	4,753,880	1,516,133	2,995,634	3,274,379	2,343,509	652,125	2,410,371	864,008	4,377,535	1,892,478	1,849,840	42,638
1988	6,441,393	4,898,836	1,542,557	3,047,955	3,393,438	2,387,849	660,106	2,510,987	882,451	4,487,659	1,953,734	—	—
1989	6,591,642	4,984,995	1,606,647	3,094,190	3,497,452	2,408,959	685,231	2,576,036	921,416	4,604,082	1,987,560	—	—
1990	6,719,023	5,092,068	1,626,955	3,146,990	3,572,033	2,455,143	691,847	2,636,925	935,108	4,713,121	2,005,902	1,954,249	51,653
1991	6,787,387	5,146,882	1,640,505	3,169,093	3,618,294	2,474,129	694,964	2,672,753	945,541	4,743,142	2,044,245	1,983,065	61,180
1992	6,815,351	5,164,437	1,650,914	3,169,670	3,645,681	2,472,923	696,747	2,691,514	954,167	4,731,783	2,083,568	2,018,433	65,135
1993	6,758,398	5,136,163	1,622,235	3,138,286	3,620,112	2,453,781	684,505	2,682,382	937,730	4,674,765	2,083,633	2,012,840	70,793
1994	6,732,999	5,136,993	1,596,006	3,098,952	3,634,047	2,430,002	668,950	2,706,991	927,056	4,636,762	2,096,237	2,014,858	81,379
1995	6,739,621	5,168,222	1,571,399	3,072,630	3,666,991	2,418,395	654,235	2,749,827	917,164	4,626,228	2,113,393	2,029,539	83,854
1996	6,764,168	5,226,624	1,537,544	3,061,880	3,702,288	2,422,656	639,224	2,803,968	898,320	4,621,245	2,142,923	2,037,065	105,858
1997	6,845,018	5,323,427	1,521,591	3,078,821	3,766,197	2,448,203	630,618	2,875,224	890,973	4,646,793	2,198,225	2,068,030	130,195
1998	6,947,623	5,452,805	1,494,818	3,112,799	3,834,824	2,491,740	621,059	2,961,065	873,759	4,704,249	2,243,374	2,086,785	156,589
1999	7,086,189	5,586,306	1,499,883	3,170,912	3,915,277	2,545,383	625,529	3,040,923	874,354	4,776,442	2,309,747	2,121,989	187,758
2000	7,207,289	5,705,882	1,501,407	3,219,748	3,987,541	2,592,407	627,341	3,113,475	874,066	4,842,261	2,365,028	2,154,336	210,692
2001	7,465,081	5,953,150	1,511,931	3,329,238	4,135,843	2,702,349	626,889	3,250,801	885,042	4,989,220	2,475,861	2,210,169	265,692
2002	7,727,879	6,178,220	1,549,659	3,438,985	4,288,894	2,798,499	640,486	3,379,721	909,173	5,162,656	2,565,223	2,259,004	306,219
2003	7,986,502	6,394,916	1,591,586	3,537,444	4,449,058	2,886,127	651,317	3,508,789	940,269	5,314,218	2,672,284	2,302,805	369,479
2004	8,235,060	6,600,847	1,634,213	3,642,541	4,592,519	2,974,074	668,467	3,626,773	965,746	5,407,236	2,827,824	2,347,116	480,708
2005	8,476,138	6,799,667	1,676,471	3,728,572	4,747,566	3,047,104	681,468	3,752,563	995,000	5,513,730	2,962,408	2,374,846	587,562
2006	8,666,011	6,927,857	1,738,154	3,809,102	4,856,909	3,104,806	704,296	3,823,051	1,033,858	5,622,555	3,043,456	2,409,084	634,372
2007	8,986,150	7,148,487	1,837,663	3,957,143	5,029,007	3,206,801	750,342	3,941,686	1,087,321	5,813,773	3,172,377	2,436,841	735,536
2008	9,394,633	7,422,820	1,971,813	4,130,830	5,263,803	3,327,599	803,231	4,095,221	1,168,582	5,951,146	3,443,487	2,501,181	942,306
2009	10,043,915	7,894,776	2,149,139	4,398,921	5,644,994	3,528,317	870,604	4,366,459	1,278,535	6,285,149	3,758,766	2,558,594	1,200,172
2010	10,397,797	8,086,375	2,311,422	4,570,037	5,827,760	3,634,067	935,970	4,452,308	1,375,452	6,486,252	3,911,545	2,620,744	1,290,801
2011	10,563,055	8,199,032	2,364,023	4,645,321	5,917,734	3,682,184	963,137	4,516,848	1,400,886	6,626,325	3,936,730	2,679,016	1,257,714
2012	10,568,458	8,155,202	2,413,256	4,669,197	5,899,261	3,678,864	990,333	4,476,338	1,422,923	6,686,083	3,882,375	2,707,469	1,174,906
2013[1]	10,459,000	8,069,000	2,390,000	4,647,000	5,812,000	3,653,000	994,000	4,416,000	1,396,000	6,618,000	3,841,000	—	—
2014[1]	10,648,000	8,205,000	2,444,000	4,661,000	5,987,000	3,655,000	1,006,000	4,549,000	1,438,000	6,735,000	3,913,000	—	—
2015[1]	10,745,000	8,259,000	2,486,000	4,673,000	6,072,000	3,663,000	1,011,000	4,597,000	1,475,000	6,795,000	3,950,000	—	—
2016[1]	10,873,000	8,340,000	2,533,000	4,704,000	6,168,000	3,687,000	1,017,000	4,653,000	1,516,000	6,875,000	3,998,000	—	—
2017[1]	11,022,000	8,438,000	2,584,000	4,749,000	6,273,000	3,724,000	1,026,000	4,714,000	1,559,000	6,969,000	4,053,000	—	—
2018[1]	11,144,000	8,521,000	2,623,000	4,788,000	6,357,000	3,755,000	1,033,000	4,766,000	1,591,000	7,046,000	4,099,000	—	—
2019[1]	11,272,000	8,610,000	2,662,000	4,829,000	6,442,000	3,788,000	1,041,000	4,821,000	1,621,000	7,126,000	4,146,000	—	—
2020[1]	11,403,000	8,700,000	2,703,000	4,871,000	6,532,000	3,820,000	1,051,000	4,880,000	1,652,000	7,208,000	4,194,000	—	—
2021[1]	11,561,000	8,811,000	2,750,000	4,924,000	6,637,000	3,861,000	1,064,000	4,950,000	1,686,000	7,308,000	4,253,000	—	—
2022[1]	11,721,000	8,925,000	2,796,000	4,979,000	6,742,000	3,903,000	1,076,000	5,022,000	1,720,000	7,409,000	4,312,000	—	—
2023[1]	11,873,000	9,033,000	2,840,000	5,031,000	6,842,000	3,943,000	1,088,000	5,090,000	1,752,000	7,504,000	4,369,000	—	—

—Not available.

[1]Projected.

[2]Beginning in 1980, 2-year institutions include schools accredited by the Accrediting Commission of Career Schools and Colleges of Technology.

NOTE: Data include unclassified undergraduate students. Data through 1995 are for institutions of higher education, while later data are for degree-granting institutions. Degree-granting institutions grant associate's or higher degrees and participate in Title IV federal financial aid programs. The degree-granting classification is very similar to the earlier higher education classification, but it includes more 2-year colleges and excludes a few higher education institutions that did not grant degrees.

SOURCE: U.S. Department of Education, National Center for Education Statistics, Higher Education General Information Survey (HEGIS), "Fall Enrollment in Colleges and Universities" surveys, 1970 through 1985; Integrated Postsecondary Education Data System (IPEDS), "Fall Enrollment Survey" (IPEDS-EF:86–99); IPEDS Spring 2001 through Spring 2013, Enrollment component; and Enrollment in Degree-Granting Institutions Projection Model, 1980 through 2023. (This table was prepared July 2014.)

Total postbaccalaureate fall enrollment in degree-granting postsecondary institutions, by attendance status, sex of student, and control of institution: 1967 through 2023

Year	Total	Full-time	Part-time	Males	Females	Males Full-time	Males Part-time	Females Full-time	Females Part-time	Males Public	Males Private	Females Public	Females Private
1	2	3	4	5	6	7	8	9	10	11	12	13	14
1967	896,065	448,238	447,827	630,701	265,364	354,628	276,073	93,610	171,754	351,947	278,754	170,676	94,688
1968	1,037,377	469,747	567,630	696,649	340,728	358,686	337,963	111,061	229,667	410,609	286,040	238,048	102,680
1969	1,120,175	506,833	613,342	738,673	381,502	383,630	355,043	123,203	258,299	457,126	281,547	281,425	100,077
1970	1,212,243	536,226	676,017	793,940	418,303	407,724	386,216	128,502	289,801	496,757	297,183	311,122	107,181
1971	1,204,390	564,236	640,154	789,131	415,259	428,167	360,964	136,069	279,190	513,570	275,561	305,604	109,655
1972	1,272,421	583,299	689,122	810,164	462,257	436,533	373,631	146,766	315,491	506,950	303,214	341,081	121,176
1973	1,342,452	610,935	731,517	833,453	508,999	444,219	389,234	166,716	342,283	523,274	310,179	373,830	135,169
1974	1,425,001	643,927	781,074	856,847	568,154	454,706	402,141	189,221	378,933	538,573	318,274	418,197	149,957
1975	1,505,404	672,938	832,466	891,992	613,412	467,425	424,567	205,513	407,899	560,041	331,951	448,435	164,977
1976	1,577,546	683,825	893,721	904,551	672,995	459,286	445,265	224,539	448,456	555,912	348,639	477,203	195,792
1977	1,569,084	698,902	870,182	891,819	677,265	462,038	429,781	236,864	440,401	535,748	356,071	468,265	209,000
1978	1,575,693	704,831	870,862	879,931	695,762	458,865	421,066	245,966	449,796	519,150	360,781	479,458	216,304
1979	1,571,922	714,624	857,298	862,754	709,168	456,197	406,557	258,427	450,741	503,949	358,805	486,042	223,126
1980	1,621,840	736,214	885,626	874,197	747,643	462,387	411,810	273,827	473,816	507,587	366,610	507,852	239,791
1981	1,617,150	732,182	884,968	866,785	750,365	452,364	414,421	279,818	470,547	496,825	369,960	501,844	248,521
1982	1,600,718	736,813	863,905	860,890	739,828	453,519	407,371	283,294	456,534	493,122	367,768	489,892	249,936
1983	1,618,666	747,016	871,650	865,425	753,241	455,540	409,885	291,476	461,765	493,356	372,069	492,260	260,981
1984	1,623,869	750,735	873,134	856,761	767,108	452,579	404,182	298,156	468,952	484,963	371,798	498,916	268,192
1985	1,650,381	755,629	894,752	856,370	794,011	451,274	405,096	304,355	489,656	484,940	371,430	517,208	276,803
1986	1,705,536	767,477	938,059	867,010	838,526	452,717	414,293	314,760	523,766	503,107	363,903	550,070	288,456
1987	1,720,407	768,536	951,871	863,599	856,808	447,212	416,387	321,324	535,484	497,117	366,482	557,548	299,260
1988	1,738,789	794,340	944,449	864,252	874,537	455,337	408,915	339,003	535,534	495,461	368,791	562,781	311,756
1989	1,796,029	820,254	975,775	879,025	917,004	461,596	417,429	358,658	558,346	504,528	374,497	585,693	331,311
1990	1,859,531	844,955	1,014,576	904,150	955,381	471,217	432,933	373,738	581,643	522,136	382,014	612,985	342,396
1991	1,919,666	893,917	1,025,749	930,841	988,825	493,849	436,992	400,068	588,757	535,422	395,419	626,184	362,641
1992	1,949,659	917,676	1,031,983	941,053	1,008,606	502,166	438,887	415,510	593,096	537,471	403,582	630,799	377,807
1993	1,980,844	948,136	1,032,708	943,768	1,037,076	508,574	435,194	439,562	597,514	537,245	406,523	640,056	397,020
1994	2,016,182	969,070	1,047,112	949,785	1,066,397	513,592	436,193	455,478	610,919	535,759	414,026	652,793	413,604
1995	2,030,062	983,534	1,046,528	941,409	1,088,653	510,782	430,627	472,752	615,901	527,605	413,804	661,143	427,510
1996	2,040,572	1,004,114	1,036,458	932,153	1,108,419	512,100	420,053	492,014	616,405	519,702	412,451	665,514	442,905
1997	2,051,747	1,019,464	1,032,283	927,496	1,124,251	510,845	416,651	508,619	615,632	515,823	411,673	672,817	451,434
1998	2,070,030	1,024,627	1,045,403	923,132	1,146,898	505,492	417,640	519,135	627,763	507,763	415,369	679,794	467,104
1999	2,110,246	1,049,591	1,060,655	930,930	1,179,316	508,930	422,000	540,661	638,655	510,779	420,151	690,732	488,584
2000	2,156,896	1,086,674	1,070,222	943,501	1,213,395	522,847	420,654	563,827	649,568	510,309	433,192	703,155	510,240
2001	2,212,377	1,119,862	1,092,515	956,384	1,255,993	531,260	425,124	588,602	667,391	523,597	432,787	723,688	532,305
2002	2,354,634	1,212,107	1,142,527	1,009,726	1,344,908	566,930	442,796	645,177	699,731	551,729	457,997	767,409	577,499
2003	2,431,117	1,280,880	1,150,237	1,032,892	1,398,225	589,190	443,702	691,690	706,535	555,903	476,989	779,692	618,533
2004	2,491,414	1,325,841	1,165,573	1,047,214	1,444,200	598,727	448,487	727,114	717,086	550,236	496,978	779,296	664,904
2005	2,523,511	1,350,581	1,172,930	1,047,054	1,476,457	602,525	444,529	748,056	728,401	543,221	503,833	780,883	695,574
2006	2,574,568	1,386,226	1,188,342	1,061,059	1,513,509	614,709	446,350	771,517	741,992	545,554	515,505	787,153	726,356
2007	2,644,357	1,428,914	1,215,443	1,088,314	1,556,043	632,576	455,738	796,338	759,705	556,727	531,587	796,470	759,573
2008	2,737,076	1,492,813	1,244,263	1,122,272	1,614,804	656,926	465,346	835,887	778,917	568,550	553,722	812,386	802,418
2009	2,862,391	1,579,283	1,283,108	1,174,023	1,688,368	693,917	480,106	885,366	803,002	592,273	581,750	831,776	856,592
2010	2,937,454	1,630,699	1,306,755	1,209,648	1,727,806	719,560	490,088	911,139	816,667	603,406	606,242	835,113	892,693
2011	2,931,076	1,642,389	1,288,687	1,209,524	1,721,552	722,882	486,642	919,507	802,045	600,748	608,776	820,656	900,896
2012	2,910,388	1,639,234	1,271,154	1,205,186	1,705,202	725,096	480,090	914,138	791,064	597,849	607,337	808,751	896,451
2013[1]	2,947,000	1,690,000	1,258,000	1,255,000	1,692,000	767,000	489,000	923,000	769,000	623,000	632,000	806,000	886,000
2014[1]	3,043,000	1,750,000	1,294,000	1,278,000	1,765,000	782,000	496,000	968,000	798,000	634,000	643,000	840,000	925,000
2015[1]	3,111,000	1,787,000	1,324,000	1,296,000	1,815,000	795,000	501,000	992,000	823,000	643,000	653,000	864,000	951,000
2016[1]	3,189,000	1,830,000	1,359,000	1,319,000	1,870,000	811,000	508,000	1,019,000	851,000	654,000	664,000	890,000	980,000
2017[1]	3,269,000	1,873,000	1,396,000	1,344,000	1,925,000	829,000	515,000	1,044,000	881,000	667,000	677,000	917,000	1,008,000
2018[1]	3,323,000	1,898,000	1,425,000	1,361,000	1,962,000	839,000	522,000	1,059,000	903,000	675,000	686,000	935,000	1,027,000
2019[1]	3,378,000	1,925,000	1,453,000	1,378,000	2,000,000	849,000	529,000	1,076,000	924,000	684,000	694,000	953,000	1,047,000
2020[1]	3,437,000	1,955,000	1,482,000	1,396,000	2,041,000	860,000	537,000	1,095,000	945,000	693,000	703,000	973,000	1,068,000
2021[1]	3,507,000	1,992,000	1,516,000	1,419,000	2,088,000	873,000	546,000	1,119,000	969,000	704,000	715,000	995,000	1,093,000
2022[1]	3,582,000	2,033,000	1,549,000	1,443,000	2,138,000	888,000	556,000	1,145,000	993,000	716,000	727,000	1,019,000	1,119,000
2023[1]	3,648,000	2,068,000	1,580,000	1,464,000	2,184,000	899,000	565,000	1,169,000	1,016,000	727,000	737,000	1,041,000	1,143,000

[1]Projected.

NOTE: Data include unclassified graduate students. Data through 1995 are for institutions of higher education, while later data are for degree-granting institutions. Degree-granting institutions grant associate's or higher degrees and participate in Title IV federal financial aid programs. The degree-granting classification is very similar to the earlier higher education classification, but it includes more 2-year colleges and excludes a few higher education institutions that did not grant degrees.

SOURCE: U.S. Department of Education, National Center for Education Statistics, Higher Education General Information Survey (HEGIS), "Fall Enrollment in Colleges and Universities" surveys, 1967 through 1985; Integrated Postsecondary Education Data System (IPEDS), "Fall Enrollment Survey" (IPEDS-EF:86–99); IPEDS Spring 2001 through Spring 2013, Enrollment component; and Enrollment in Degree-Granting Institutions Projection Model, 1980 through 2023. (This table was prepared July 2014.)

Fall enrollment and number of degree-granting postsecondary institutions, by control and religious affiliation of institution: Selected years, 1980 through 2012

Control and religious affiliation of institution	Total enrollment						Enrollment, fall 2012					Number of institutions[1]				
							Total	Full-time Males	Full-time Females	Part-time Males	Part-time Females					
	Fall 1980	Fall 1990	Fall 2000	Fall 2009	Fall 2010	Fall 2011						Fall 1980	Fall 1990	Fall 2000	Fall 2010	Fall 2012
1	2	3	4	5	6	7	8	9	10	11	12	13	14	15	16	17
All institutions	**12,096,895**	**13,818,637**	**15,312,289**	**20,427,711**	**21,016,126**	**20,994,113**	**20,642,819**	**5,709,792**	**7,027,221**	**3,209,295**	**4,696,511**	**3,226**	**3,501**	**4,056**	**4,589**	**4,726**
Public institutions	9,457,394	10,844,717	11,752,786	14,810,642	15,142,809	15,110,196	14,880,343	3,954,114	4,571,704	2,627,185	3,727,340	1,493	1,548	1,676	1,652	1,623
Federal	50,989	50,669	16,917	21,722	21,622	21,304	20,691	13,745	5,228	554	1,164	12	17	12	14	14
State	(²)	7,181,380	9,548,090	12,104,170	12,366,422	12,346,172	12,195,526	3,441,305	3,995,532	1,959,329	2,799,360	(²)	978	1,355	1,331	1,315
Local	(²)	3,508,941	2,078,090	2,478,076	2,541,036	2,526,884	2,453,053	444,170	506,234	631,280	871,369	(²)	523	277	261	256
Other public	9,406,405	103,727	109,689	206,674	213,729	215,836	211,073	54,894	64,710	36,022	55,447	1,481	30	32	46	38
Private institutions	2,639,501	2,973,920	3,559,503	5,617,069	5,873,317	5,883,917	5,762,476	1,755,678	2,455,517	582,110	969,171	1,733	1,953	2,380	2,937	3,103
Independent nonprofit	1,521,614	1,474,818	1,577,242	1,953,136	1,995,440	2,054,854	2,064,076	703,075	849,765	202,650	308,586	795	709	729	736	765
For-profit	111,714	213,693	450,084	1,851,986	2,018,397	1,956,731	1,808,898	455,139	797,798	201,905	354,056	164	322	724	1,310	1,451
Religiously affiliated³	1,006,173	1,285,409	1,532,177	1,811,947	1,859,480	1,872,332	1,889,502	597,464	807,954	177,555	306,529	774	922	927	891	887
Advent Christian Church	143	—	—	—	—	—	—	—	—	—	—	1	—	—	—	—
African Methodist Episcopal Zion Church	1,091	88	34	1,485	1,536	1,537	1,459	784	609	36	30	3	1	1	3	3
African Methodist Episcopal	4,541	3,220	5,980	2,677	2,674	2,355	2,491	1,117	1,222	68	84	6	5	6	5	6
American Baptist	6,131	10,800	15,410	14,716	15,120	15,027	14,229	4,207	5,475	1,520	3,027	11	15	17	18	18
American Evangelical Lutheran Church	—	—	743	1,387	1,340	1,415	1,315	593	660	28	34	—	—	1	1	1
American Lutheran and Lutheran Church in America	3,092	—	1,460	—	—	—	—	—	—	—	—	3	—	1	—	—
American Lutheran	21,608	—	—	—	—	—	—	—	—	—	—	13	—	—	—	—
Assemblies of God Church	7,814	8,307	14,272	15,137	15,806	15,451	15,320	5,275	6,453	1,653	1,939	10	11	14	16	15
Baptist	38,231	99,510	107,610	165,848	174,481	172,946	112,351	36,221	47,394	11,685	17,051	33	69	68	69	70
Brethren Church	3,925	958	2,088	8,191	8,449	7,766	7,979	2,189	2,939	1,486	1,365	3	3	3	3	3
Brethren in Christ Church	1,301	2,239	2,797	6,331	6,465	6,536	6,688	2,156	2,952	616	964	1	1	4	4	4
Christian and Missionary Alliance Church	1,705	2,519	5,278	50,064	52,839	54,401	54,915	15,585	23,297	6,328	9,705	3	4	16	18	18
Christian Church (Disciples of Christ)	14,913	30,397	35,984	9,263	10,128	10,483	10,700	4,277	4,499	1,034	890	12	18	18	18	18
Christian Churches and Churches of Christ	1,342	2,263	7,277	4,901	4,817	4,514	4,048	2,014	1,901	53	80	7	8	8	4	4
Christian Methodist Episcopal	2,486	2,174	1,502	—	—	—	—	—	—	—	—	4	4	3	—	—
Christian Reformed Church	5,408	4,488	5,999	5,665	5,625	5,647	5,697	2,623	2,722	197	155	3	2	3	3	3
Church of Christ (Scientist)	2,773	2,557	—	—	—	—	—	—	—	—	—	6	8	—	—	—
Church of God of Prophecy	—	249	—	—	—	—	—	—	—	—	—	—	1	—	—	—
Church of God	6,082	5,627	12,540	15,117	16,731	17,093	17,821	5,114	7,863	2,021	2,823	9	9	7	7	8
Church of New Jerusalem	170	—	—	—	—	—	—	—	—	—	—	1	1	—	—	—
Church of the Brethren	8,482	4,463	4,187	5,861	6,154	6,028	6,261	2,431	3,148	283	399	6	5	4	5	6
Church of the Nazarene	11,716	10,779	16,661	21,389	21,144	20,866	21,401	6,159	9,976	1,944	3,322	10	9	12	10	10
Churches of Christ	9,343	14,611	30,140	34,996	35,538	36,450	35,871	11,567	14,866	3,511	5,927	9	19	19	17	17
Cumberland Presbyterian	594	746	1,112	3,247	4,652	5,744	6,500	2,332	2,915	503	750	2	1	1	2	2
Episcopal Church, Reformed	67	—	—	—	—	—	1,204	56	406	92	650	1	—	—	—	1
Evangelical Christian	—	—	—	—	—	—	74,372	14,974	19,470	15,801	24,127	—	—	1	1	1
Evangelical Congregational Church	80	88	148	159	153	125	123	21	15	57	30	—	—	1	1	1
Evangelical Covenant Church of America	1,401	1,035	2,387	3,186	3,233	3,220	3,141	742	1,182	399	818	1	1	3	2	2
Evangelical Free Church of America	833	2,355	4,022	3,106	2,926	3,215	2,651	782	538	802	529	1	2	3	3	3
Evangelical Lutheran Church	743	49,210	49,085	56,088	56,162	55,889	52,122	20,597	26,321	2,057	3,147	3	33	34	33	31
Free Methodist	5,543	5,902	7,323	12,090	12,270	12,412	12,254	3,323	6,044	839	2,048	5	4	4	5	5
Free Will Baptist Church	1,132	1,177	2,378	574	528	534	568	226	181	92	69	4	3	3	3	3
Friends United Meeting	5,157	5,844	10,898	13,786	13,876	13,570	12,921	4,523	5,699	1,101	1,598	5	6	8	7	7
Friends	1,109	1,243	1,059	—	—	—	—	—	—	—	—	2	1	1	—	—
General Conference Mennonite Church	820	—	—	—	—	—	—	—	—	—	—	—	—	—	1	1
Greek Orthodox	204	148	132	203	220	222	209	151	55	2	1	1	1	1	1	1
Interdenominational	1,254	11,103	14,182	23,060	30,162	34,475	39,376	13,088	15,898	4,887	5,503	4	17	14	30	32
Jewish	5,738	12,217	14,182	8,468	12,755	14,716	15,120	9,551	3,510	614	1,445	24	63	62	36	35
Latter-Day Saints	39,172	42,274	44,680	53,249	53,514	57,150	63,027	24,587	25,230	5,991	7,219	4	4	4	4	4
Lutheran Church—Missouri Synod	11,727	13,827	18,866	26,384	28,255	29,288	30,332	7,366	11,476	3,588	7,902	15	14	13	12	12

See notes at end of table.

Fall enrollment and number of degree-granting postsecondary institutions, by control and religious affiliation of institution: Selected years, 1980 through 2012—Continued

Control and religious affiliation of institution	Total enrollment						Enrollment, fall 2012					Number of institutions[1]				
	Fall 1980	Fall 1990	Fall 2000	Fall 2009	Fall 2010	Fall 2011	Total	Full-time Males	Full-time Females	Part-time Males	Part-time Females	Fall 1980	Fall 1990	Fall 2000	Fall 2010	Fall 2012
1	2	3	4	5	6	7	8	9	10	11	12	13	14	15	16	17
Lutheran Church in America	23,877	5,796	4,322	8,264	8,240	8,111	8,193	3,244	4,160	264	525	20	5	2	3	3
Mennonite Brethren Church	1,344	1,864	2,390	3,426	4,136	4,302	4,121	1,150	1,848	368	755	3	3	3	3	2
Mennonite Church	4,008	2,859	3,553	4,325	4,263	4,366	4,236	1,472	1,943	277	544	6	5	5	6	6
Missionary Church Inc.	487	699	1,647	2,165	2,152	2,074	1,963	509	929	163	362	1	1	1	1	1
Moravian Church	2,434	2,511	2,939	3,042	3,095	3,132	3,075	630	1,679	151	615	2	2	2	2	2
Multiple Protestant denominations	5,526	211	4,690	5,341	5,350	5,400	5,274	1,282	1,474	1,581	937	8	1	7	6	6
North American Baptist	155	—	124	125	120	141	148	30	29	55	34	1	1	1	1	1
Original Free Will Baptist	—	—	—	3,569	3,855	3,825	3,714	590	939	638	1,547	—	—	—	1	1
Pentecostal Holiness Church	767	566	976	1,124	1,272	1,504	1,524	598	600	130	196	3	3	2	3	3
Presbyterian U.S.A.	47,144	77,700	78,950	84,691	85,692	86,441	86,699	31,683	42,539	3,979	8,498	57	70	64	58	59
Presbyterian Church in America	—	1,877	4,499	2,174	2,071	1,792	1,803	722	668	271	142	—	1	5	2	2
Protestant Episcopal	5,396	4,559	5,479	5,036	5,006	4,604	4,202	1,879	2,029	143	151	12	9	12	11	9
Protestant, other	4,072	38,136	30,116	16,207	13,361	14,628	16,167	5,149	5,770	2,445	2,803	11	44	34	22	24
Reformed Church in America	2,713	5,525	6,002	6,514	6,555	6,501	6,502	2,610	3,448	196	248	4	4	4	5	5
Reformed Presbyterian Church	2,014	1,556	2,355	2,949	2,982	2,866	2,700	1,136	1,175	231	158	4	2	5	3	3
Reorganized Latter-Day Saints Church	4,274	4,793	3,390			—	—					2	1	2		
Roman Catholic	422,842	530,585	636,336	735,713	751,089	749,877	746,942	219,870	323,224	67,493	136,355	229	239	239	237	234
Russian Orthodox	47	38	106	79	60	53	55	42	4	8	1	1	1	1	1	1
Seventh-Day Adventists	19,168	15,771	19,223	24,818	25,430	25,751	26,343	8,360	11,358	2,258	4,367	11	11	13	14	13
Southern Baptist	85,281	49,493	54,275	46,689	49,882	51,832	52,610	14,586	20,099	7,025	10,900	54	29	32	22	22
Undenominational	—	6,758	23,573	27,071	27,745	29,650	29,966	8,556	11,631	4,476	5,303	—	14	16	16	18
Unitarian Universalist	87	82	132	171	166	190	227	31	57	55	84	1	2	2	2	2
United Brethren Church	545	601	938	1,270	1,260	1,260	1,204	441	628	55	80	2	2	1	1	1
United Church of Christ	14,169	20,175	23,709	27,507	20,528	17,724	17,473	5,434	7,012	1,711	3,316	16	18	18	17	15
United Methodist	127,099	148,851	171,109	202,913	206,744	206,268	204,506	74,113	95,123	12,899	22,371	91	96	100	96	94
Wesleyan Church	3,583	5,311	11,128	20,492	20,670	20,577	20,160	6,252	11,425	920	1,563	5	4	4	2	6
Wisconsin Evangelical Lutheran Synod	808	931	1,660	1,603	1,677	1,799	1,889	799	870	112	112	1	3	2	2	2
Other religiously affiliated	462	5,743	2,534	8,041	8,526	8,589	5,340	1,665	2,377	367	931	1	9	4	13	11

—Not available.

[1]Counts of institutions in this table may be lower than reported in other tables, because counts in this table include only institutions reporting separate enrollment data.

[2]Included under "Other public."

[3]Religious affiliation as reported by institution.

NOTE: Data for 1980 and 1990 are for institutions of higher education, while later data are for degree-granting institutions. Degree-granting institutions grant associate's or higher degrees and participate in Title IV federal financial aid programs. The degree-granting classification is very similar to the earlier higher education classification, but it includes more 2-year colleges and excludes a few higher education institutions that did not grant degrees. Some data have been revised from previously published figures.

SOURCE: U.S. Department of Education, National Center for Education Statistics, Higher Education General Information Survey (HEGIS), "Fall Enrollment in Institutions of Higher Education" and "Institutional Characteristics" surveys, 1980; Integrated Postsecondary Education Data System (IPEDS), "Fall Enrollment Survey" (IPEDS-EF:90) and "Institutional Characteristics Survey" (IPEDS-IC:90); and IPEDS Spring 2001 through Spring 2013, Enrollment component. (This table was prepared March 2014.)

Total fall enrollment in degree-granting postsecondary institutions, by state or jurisdiction: Selected years, 1970 through 2012

State or jurisdiction	Fall 1970	Fall 1980	Fall 1990	Fall 2000	Fall 2007	Fall 2008	Fall 2009	Fall 2010	Fall 2011	Fall 2012	Percent change, 2007 to 2012
1	2	3	4	5	6	7	8	9	10	11	12
United States	8,580,887	12,096,895	13,818,637	15,312,289	18,248,128	19,102,814	20,427,711	21,016,126	20,994,113	20,642,819	13.1
Alabama	103,936	164,306	218,589	233,962	268,183	310,941	311,740	327,327	318,686	310,311	15.7
Alaska	9,471	21,296	29,833	27,953	30,616	30,717	32,406	33,653	34,932	32,797	7.1
Arizona	109,619	202,716	264,148	342,490	624,147	704,245	828,631	795,388	796,986	736,379	18.0
Arkansas	52,039	77,607	90,425	115,172	152,168	158,374	168,352	175,895	179,281	176,458	16.0
California	1,257,245	1,790,993	1,808,740	2,256,708	2,529,522	2,652,241	2,735,579	2,714,172	2,685,893	2,621,460	3.6
Colorado	123,395	162,916	227,131	263,872	310,637	325,232	352,034	372,025	365,820	362,935	16.8
Connecticut	124,700	159,632	168,604	161,243	179,005	184,178	191,806	199,384	201,638	201,658	12.7
Delaware	25,260	32,939	42,004	43,897	52,343	53,088	55,174	55,731	56,516	58,128	11.1
District of Columbia	77,158	86,675	79,551	72,689	115,153	126,110	136,851	91,992	90,213	90,150	-21.7
Florida	235,525	411,891	588,086	707,684	913,793	972,699	1,053,221	1,125,469	1,143,698	1,154,929	26.4
Georgia	126,511	184,159	251,786	346,204	453,711	476,581	532,493	568,723	565,459	545,358	20.2
Hawaii	36,562	47,181	56,436	60,182	66,601	70,104	74,809	78,073	79,018	78,456	17.8
Idaho	34,567	43,018	51,881	65,594	78,846	80,456	84,450	85,201	90,142	108,008	37.0
Illinois	452,146	644,245	729,246	743,918	837,018	859,242	900,824	906,889	892,881	867,110	3.6
Indiana	192,668	247,253	284,832	314,334	380,477	401,956	441,294	459,423	457,824	447,262	17.6
Iowa	108,902	140,449	170,515	188,974	256,259	286,891	350,631	381,842	372,146	361,183	40.9
Kansas	102,485	136,605	163,733	179,968	194,102	198,991	210,843	214,859	216,662	213,786	10.1
Kentucky	98,591	143,066	177,852	188,341	258,213	257,583	277,907	291,102	293,766	282,125	9.3
Louisiana	120,728	160,058	186,840	223,800	224,754	236,375	251,853	263,638	265,856	258,825	15.2
Maine	34,134	43,264	57,186	58,473	67,173	67,796	70,170	72,985	72,297	72,810	8.4
Maryland	149,607	225,526	259,700	273,745	327,597	338,914	358,941	377,967	380,097	374,496	14.3
Massachusetts	303,809	418,415	417,833	421,142	463,366	477,056	497,290	508,302	508,554	516,331	11.4
Michigan	392,726	520,131	569,803	567,631	643,279	652,799	686,049	698,125	685,526	663,825	3.2
Minnesota	160,788	206,691	253,789	293,445	392,393	411,055	442,281	465,336	457,752	451,661	15.1
Mississippi	73,967	102,364	122,883	137,389	155,232	160,441	173,136	178,197	179,090	176,665	13.8
Missouri	183,930	234,421	289,899	321,348	384,366	396,409	424,944	444,695	456,997	441,371	14.8
Montana	30,062	35,177	35,876	42,240	47,371	47,840	51,588	53,312	54,042	53,254	12.4
Nebraska	66,915	89,488	112,831	112,117	127,378	130,458	138,645	144,682	142,875	139,578	9.6
Nevada	13,669	40,455	61,728	87,893	116,276	120,490	125,320	129,360	121,013	118,300	1.7
New Hampshire	29,400	46,794	59,510	61,718	70,724	71,739	74,234	75,594	77,444	82,678	16.9
New Jersey	216,121	321,610	324,286	335,945	398,136	410,160	432,127	444,091	443,750	439,965	10.5
New Mexico	44,461	58,283	85,500	110,739	134,375	142,413	152,752	162,652	157,555	156,424	16.4
New York	806,479	992,237	1,048,286	1,043,395	1,172,811	1,234,858	1,289,604	1,305,595	1,318,142	1,309,986	11.7
North Carolina	171,925	287,537	352,138	404,652	502,330	528,977	568,865	586,042	585,013	578,031	15.1
North Dakota	31,495	34,069	37,878	40,248	49,945	51,327	54,433	56,903	55,772	55,169	10.5
Ohio	376,267	489,145	557,690	549,553	630,497	653,585	711,095	744,947	735,026	709,818	12.6
Oklahoma	110,155	160,295	173,221	178,016	206,382	206,757	220,650	230,573	230,154	228,464	10.7
Oregon	122,177	157,458	165,741	183,065	202,928	220,474	243,412	250,331	259,061	254,695	25.5
Pennsylvania	411,044	507,716	604,060	609,521	725,397	740,288	778,123	803,593	787,789	777,242	7.1
Rhode Island	45,898	66,869	78,273	75,450	82,900	83,893	84,673	85,110	84,644	83,952	1.3
South Carolina	69,518	132,476	159,302	185,931	217,755	230,695	246,667	257,293	260,002	259,617	19.2
South Dakota	30,639	32,761	34,208	43,221	49,747	50,444	53,342	58,370	55,899	56,058	12.7
Tennessee	135,103	204,581	226,238	263,910	297,785	307,610	332,918	351,988	350,275	343,641	15.4
Texas	442,225	701,391	901,437	1,033,973	1,269,098	1,327,148	1,447,868	1,536,858	1,564,387	1,540,298	21.4
Utah	81,687	93,987	121,303	163,776	203,679	217,224	236,590	252,107	264,396	267,309	31.2
Vermont	22,209	30,628	36,398	35,489	42,191	42,946	44,975	45,572	45,143	44,703	6.0
Virginia	151,915	280,504	353,442	381,893	478,268	500,796	545,036	576,010	588,465	588,696	23.1
Washington	183,544	303,603	263,384	320,840	352,075	362,535	382,532	388,110	372,841	365,514	3.8
West Virginia	63,153	81,973	84,790	87,888	116,848	125,333	142,484	152,431	162,308	162,179	38.8
Wisconsin	202,058	269,086	299,774	307,179	343,747	352,875	373,228	383,986	376,603	369,732	7.6
Wyoming	15,220	21,147	31,326	30,004	35,246	35,936	37,093	38,298	38,092	37,812	7.3
U.S. Service Academies[1]	17,079	49,808	48,692	13,475	15,285	15,539	15,748	15,925	15,692	15,227	-0.4
Other jurisdictions	67,237	137,749	164,618	194,633	226,849	236,167	243,792	264,237	267,159	259,943	14.6
American Samoa	0	976	1,219	297	1,767	1,806	2,189	2,193	2,091	1,795	1.6
Federated States of Micronesia	0	224	975	1,576	2,379	2,457	3,401	2,699	2,915	2,744	15.3
Guam	2,719	3,217	4,741	5,215	5,244	5,351	5,755	6,188	6,360	5,924	13.0
Marshall Islands	0	0	0	328	557	689	847	869	989	1,123	101.6
Northern Marianas	0	0	661	1,078	901	791	989	1,137	1,046	1,178	30.7
Palau	0	0	491	581	668	502	651	694	742	680	1.8
Puerto Rico	63,073	131,184	154,065	183,290	212,949	222,178	227,358	247,724	250,402	244,076	14.6
U.S. Virgin Islands	1,445	2,148	2,466	2,268	2,384	2,393	2,602	2,733	2,614	2,423	1.6

[1]Data for 2000 and later years reflect a substantial reduction in the number of Department of Defense institutions included in the IPEDS survey.
NOTE: Data through 1990 are for institutions of higher education, while later data are for degree-granting institutions. Degree-granting institutions grant associate's or higher degrees and participate in Title IV federal financial aid programs. The degree-granting classification is very similar to the earlier higher education classification, but it includes more 2-year colleges and excludes a few higher education institutions that did not grant degrees.

SOURCE: U.S. Department of Education, National Center for Education Statistics, Higher Education General Information Survey (HEGIS), "Fall Enrollment in Colleges and Universities" surveys, 1970 and 1980; Integrated Postsecondary Education Data System (IPEDS), "Fall Enrollment Survey" (IPEDS-EF:90); and IPEDS Spring 2001 through Spring 2013, Enrollment component. (This table was prepared November 2013.)

Total fall enrollment in public degree-granting postsecondary institutions, by state or jurisdiction: Selected years, 1970 through 2012

State or jurisdiction	Fall 1970	Fall 1980	Fall 1990	Fall 2000	Fall 2007	Fall 2008	Fall 2009	Fall 2010	Fall 2011	Fall 2012	Percent change, 2007 to 2012
1	2	3	4	5	6	7	8	9	10	11	12
United States	6,428,134	9,457,394	10,844,717	11,752,786	13,490,780	13,972,153	14,810,642	15,142,809	15,110,196	14,880,343	10.3
Alabama	87,884	143,674	195,939	207,435	237,632	245,040	260,277	267,083	260,523	251,045	5.6
Alaska	8,563	20,561	27,792	26,559	29,381	29,167	30,493	32,303	32,158	30,595	4.1
Arizona	107,315	194,034	248,213	284,522	332,154	331,310	350,435	366,976	366,116	359,229	8.2
Arkansas	43,599	66,068	78,645	101,775	135,525	140,706	149,474	155,780	158,760	157,224	16.0
California	1,123,529	1,599,838	1,594,710	1,927,771	2,136,087	2,239,487	2,289,470	2,223,648	2,178,629	2,129,152	-0.3
Colorado	108,562	145,598	200,653	217,897	227,984	235,265	255,438	269,407	269,298	272,444	19.5
Connecticut	73,391	97,788	109,556	101,027	114,072	118,694	123,211	127,194	126,487	124,952	9.5
Delaware	21,151	28,325	34,252	34,194	39,092	38,952	40,428	40,408	40,698	41,113	5.2
District of Columbia	12,194	13,900	11,990	5,499	5,608	5,584	5,253	5,840	5,280	5,476	-2.4
Florida	189,450	334,349	489,081	556,912	683,328	709,593	759,479	790,027	803,200	804,693	17.8
Georgia	101,900	140,158	196,413	271,755	359,883	376,468	418,037	436,109	428,708	422,189	17.3
Hawaii	32,963	43,269	45,728	44,579	50,454	53,526	57,945	60,090	60,330	60,295	19.5
Idaho	27,072	34,491	41,315	53,751	60,526	61,190	63,261	64,204	65,753	78,781	30.2
Illinois	315,634	491,274	551,333	534,155	550,940	560,411	588,741	585,515	577,043	557,137	1.1
Indiana	136,739	189,224	223,953	240,023	278,951	296,950	325,072	337,705	340,264	333,769	19.7
Iowa	68,390	97,454	117,834	135,008	154,644	157,019	170,870	177,781	178,491	173,558	12.2
Kansas	88,215	121,987	149,117	159,976	170,054	172,640	182,736	185,623	186,475	183,976	8.2
Kentucky	77,240	114,884	147,095	151,973	211,234	208,970	221,508	229,725	233,427	224,092	6.1
Louisiana	101,127	136,703	158,290	189,213	193,316	203,098	215,511	224,811	225,210	220,971	14.3
Maine	25,405	31,878	41,500	40,662	48,357	48,191	49,668	51,482	50,253	50,270	4.0
Maryland	118,988	195,051	220,783	223,797	269,719	280,603	298,185	309,779	314,383	310,503	15.1
Massachusetts	116,127	183,765	186,035	183,248	198,700	205,820	218,999	224,493	227,005	228,178	14.8
Michigan	339,625	454,147	487,359	467,861	519,449	528,040	553,022	562,444	554,741	540,242	4.0
Minnesota	130,567	162,379	199,211	218,617	250,397	256,633	270,336	276,176	274,192	272,290	8.7
Mississippi	64,968	90,661	109,038	125,355	139,931	144,224	155,517	159,695	160,611	157,995	12.9
Missouri	132,540	165,179	200,093	201,509	223,155	228,737	245,568	256,119	260,585	257,430	15.4
Montana	27,287	31,178	31,865	37,387	42,857	43,565	46,653	48,261	48,912	48,333	12.8
Nebraska	51,454	73,509	94,614	88,531	96,680	99,593	104,149	107,980	106,794	104,166	7.7
Nevada	13,576	40,280	61,242	83,120	104,797	108,559	112,397	113,103	105,048	103,619	-1.1
New Hampshire	15,979	24,119	32,163	35,870	41,982	42,192	43,507	44,072	43,333	43,289	3.1
New Jersey	145,373	247,028	261,601	266,921	318,296	328,838	348,934	358,256	359,458	356,456	12.0
New Mexico	40,795	55,077	83,403	101,450	124,773	132,983	143,101	150,856	146,515	146,792	17.6
New York	449,437	563,251	616,884	583,417	652,428	675,892	712,466	723,500	731,914	722,274	10.7
North Carolina	123,761	228,154	285,405	329,422	410,746	434,976	470,239	475,598	470,989	465,684	13.4
North Dakota	30,192	31,709	34,690	36,014	43,016	44,268	46,727	48,904	48,868	48,929	13.7
Ohio	281,099	381,765	427,613	411,161	460,240	475,521	522,002	547,551	542,774	524,338	13.9
Oklahoma	91,438	137,188	151,073	153,699	177,643	178,253	189,953	197,642	197,373	195,111	9.8
Oregon	108,483	140,102	144,427	154,756	165,260	181,515	201,246	208,002	215,466	212,310	28.5
Pennsylvania	232,982	292,499	343,478	339,229	396,774	404,976	425,979	432,889	428,269	425,890	7.3
Rhode Island	25,527	35,052	42,350	38,458	41,503	42,601	43,409	43,224	43,254	43,204	4.1
South Carolina	47,101	107,683	131,134	155,519	180,479	187,253	200,204	205,080	208,302	209,023	15.8
South Dakota	23,936	24,328	26,596	34,857	38,917	39,743	41,674	44,569	43,729	44,185	13.5
Tennessee	98,897	156,835	175,049	202,530	208,524	214,140	231,741	242,486	241,917	235,010	12.7
Texas	365,522	613,552	802,314	896,534	1,109,666	1,163,132	1,258,841	1,334,885	1,367,005	1,347,860	21.5
Utah	49,588	59,598	86,108	123,046	147,982	158,037	170,921	178,599	179,208	171,001	15.6
Vermont	12,536	17,984	20,910	20,021	24,829	25,552	27,028	27,524	27,132	26,501	6.7
Virginia	123,279	246,500	291,286	313,780	370,486	383,121	401,093	409,004	413,761	409,753	10.6
Washington	162,718	276,028	227,632	273,928	301,793	312,071	328,391	330,874	317,066	311,497	3.2
West Virginia	51,363	71,228	74,108	76,136	87,838	88,695	94,533	96,104	95,634	93,017	5.9
Wisconsin	170,374	235,179	253,529	249,737	273,708	280,394	295,090	301,212	296,795	293,416	7.2
Wyoming	15,220	21,121	30,623	28,715	33,705	34,426	35,682	36,292	36,368	35,859	6.4
U.S. Service Academies[1]	17,079	49,808	48,692	13,475	15,285	15,539	15,748	15,925	15,692	15,227	-0.4
Other jurisdictions	46,680	60,692	66,244	84,464	80,958	82,424	87,030	83,719	78,928	78,369	-3.2
American Samoa	0	976	1,219	297	1,767	1,806	2,189	2,193	2,091	1,795	1.6
Federated States of Micronesia	0	224	975	1,576	2,379	2,457	3,401	2,699	2,915	2,744	15.3
Guam	2,719	3,217	4,741	5,215	5,077	5,202	5,661	6,103	6,274	5,847	15.2
Marshall Islands	0	0	0	328	557	689	847	869	989	1,123	101.6
Northern Marianas	0	0	661	1,078	901	791	989	1,137	1,046	1,178	30.7
Palau	0	0	491	581	668	502	651	694	742	680	1.8
Puerto Rico	42,516	54,127	55,691	73,121	67,225	68,584	70,690	67,291	62,257	62,579	-6.9
U.S. Virgin Islands	1,445	2,148	2,466	2,268	2,384	2,393	2,602	2,733	2,614	2,423	1.6

[1]Data for 2000 and later years reflect a substantial reduction in the number of Department of Defense institutions included in the IPEDS survey.
NOTE: Data through 1990 are for institutions of higher education, while later data are for degree-granting institutions. Degree-granting institutions grant associate's or higher degrees and participate in Title IV federal financial aid programs. The degree-granting classification is very similar to the earlier higher education classification, but it includes more 2-year colleges and excludes a few higher education institutions that did not grant degrees.

SOURCE: U.S. Department of Education, National Center for Education Statistics, Higher Education General Information Survey (HEGIS), "Fall Enrollment in Colleges and Universities" surveys, 1970 and 1980; Integrated Postsecondary Education Data System (IPEDS), "Fall Enrollment Survey" (IPEDS-EF:90); and IPEDS Spring 2001 through Spring 2013, Enrollment component. (This table was prepared November 2013.)

Total fall enrollment in private degree-granting postsecondary institutions, by state or jurisdiction: Selected years, 1970 through 2012

State or jurisdiction	Fall 1970	Fall 1980	Fall 1990	Fall 2000	Fall 2007	Fall 2008	Fall 2009	Fall 2010	Fall 2011	Fall 2012	Percent change, 2007 to 2012
1	2	3	4	5	6	7	8	9	10	11	12
United States	2,152,753	2,639,501	2,973,920	3,559,503	4,757,348	5,130,661	5,617,069	5,873,317	5,883,917	5,762,476	21.1
Alabama	16,052	20,632	22,650	26,527	30,551	65,901	51,463	60,244	58,163	59,266	94.0
Alaska	908	735	2,041	1,394	1,235	1,550	1,913	1,350	2,774	2,202	78.3
Arizona	2,304	8,682	15,935	57,968	291,993	372,935	478,196	428,412	430,870	377,150	29.2
Arkansas	8,440	11,539	11,780	13,397	16,643	17,668	18,878	20,115	20,521	19,234	15.6
California	133,716	191,155	214,030	328,937	393,435	412,754	446,109	490,524	507,264	492,308	25.1
Colorado	14,833	17,318	26,478	45,975	82,653	89,967	96,596	102,618	96,522	90,491	9.5
Connecticut	51,309	61,844	59,048	60,216	64,933	65,484	68,595	72,190	75,151	76,706	18.1
Delaware	4,109	4,614	7,752	9,703	13,251	14,136	14,746	15,323	15,818	17,015	28.4
District of Columbia	64,964	72,775	67,561	67,190	109,545	120,526	131,598	86,152	84,933	84,674	-22.7
Florida	46,075	77,542	99,005	150,772	230,465	263,106	293,742	335,442	340,498	350,236	52.0
Georgia	24,611	44,001	55,373	74,449	93,828	100,113	114,456	132,614	136,751	123,169	31.3
Hawaii	3,599	3,912	10,708	15,603	16,147	16,578	16,864	17,983	18,688	18,161	12.5
Idaho	7,495	8,527	10,566	11,843	18,320	19,266	21,189	20,997	24,389	29,227	59.5
Illinois	136,512	152,971	177,913	209,763	286,078	298,831	312,083	321,374	315,838	309,973	8.4
Indiana	55,929	58,029	60,879	74,311	101,526	105,006	116,222	121,718	117,560	113,493	11.8
Iowa	40,512	42,995	52,681	53,966	101,615	129,872	179,761	204,061	193,655	187,625	84.6
Kansas	14,270	14,618	14,616	19,992	24,048	26,351	28,107	29,236	30,187	29,810	24.0
Kentucky	21,351	28,182	30,757	36,368	46,979	48,613	56,399	61,377	60,339	58,033	23.5
Louisiana	19,601	23,355	28,550	34,587	31,438	33,277	36,342	38,827	40,646	37,854	20.4
Maine	8,729	11,386	15,686	17,811	18,816	19,605	20,502	21,503	22,044	22,540	19.8
Maryland	30,619	30,475	38,917	49,948	57,878	58,311	60,756	68,188	65,714	63,993	10.6
Massachusetts	187,682	234,650	231,798	237,894	264,666	271,236	278,291	283,809	281,549	288,153	8.9
Michigan	53,101	65,984	82,444	99,770	123,830	124,759	133,027	135,681	130,785	123,583	-0.2
Minnesota	30,221	44,312	54,578	74,828	141,996	154,422	171,945	189,160	183,560	179,371	26.3
Mississippi	8,999	11,703	13,845	12,034	15,301	16,217	17,619	18,502	18,479	18,670	22.0
Missouri	51,390	69,242	89,806	119,839	161,211	167,672	179,376	188,576	196,412	183,941	14.1
Montana	2,775	3,999	4,011	4,853	4,514	4,275	4,935	5,051	5,130	4,921	9.0
Nebraska	15,461	15,979	18,217	23,586	30,698	30,865	34,496	36,702	36,081	35,412	15.4
Nevada	93	175	486	4,773	11,479	11,931	12,923	16,257	15,965	14,681	27.9
New Hampshire	13,421	22,675	27,347	25,848	28,742	29,547	30,727	31,522	34,111	39,389	37.0
New Jersey	70,748	74,582	62,685	69,024	79,840	81,322	83,193	85,835	84,292	83,509	4.6
New Mexico	3,666	3,206	2,097	9,289	9,602	9,430	9,651	11,796	11,040	9,632	0.3
New York	357,042	428,986	431,402	459,978	520,383	558,966	577,138	582,095	586,228	587,712	12.9
North Carolina	48,164	59,383	66,733	75,230	91,584	94,001	98,626	110,444	114,024	112,347	22.7
North Dakota	1,303	2,360	3,188	4,234	6,929	7,059	7,706	7,999	6,904	6,240	-9.9
Ohio	95,168	107,380	130,077	138,392	170,257	178,064	189,093	197,396	192,252	185,480	8.9
Oklahoma	18,717	23,107	22,148	24,317	28,739	28,504	30,697	32,931	32,781	33,353	16.1
Oregon	13,694	17,356	21,314	28,309	37,668	38,959	42,166	42,329	43,595	42,385	12.5
Pennsylvania	178,062	215,217	260,582	270,292	328,623	335,312	352,144	370,704	359,520	351,352	6.9
Rhode Island	20,371	31,817	35,923	36,992	41,397	41,292	41,264	41,886	41,390	40,748	-1.6
South Carolina	22,417	24,793	28,168	30,412	37,276	43,442	46,463	52,213	51,700	50,594	35.7
South Dakota	6,703	8,433	7,612	8,364	10,830	10,701	11,668	13,801	12,170	11,873	9.6
Tennessee	36,206	47,746	51,189	61,380	89,261	93,470	101,177	109,502	108,358	108,631	21.7
Texas	76,703	87,839	99,123	137,439	159,432	164,016	189,027	201,973	197,382	192,438	20.7
Utah	32,099	34,389	35,195	40,730	55,697	59,187	65,669	73,508	85,188	96,308	72.9
Vermont	9,673	12,644	15,488	15,468	17,362	17,394	17,947	18,048	18,011	18,202	4.8
Virginia	28,636	34,004	62,156	68,113	107,782	117,675	143,943	167,006	174,704	178,943	66.0
Washington	20,826	27,575	35,752	46,912	50,282	50,464	54,141	57,236	55,775	54,017	7.4
West Virginia	11,790	10,745	10,682	11,752	29,010	36,638	47,951	56,327	66,674	69,162	138.4
Wisconsin	31,684	33,907	46,245	57,442	70,039	72,481	78,138	82,774	79,808	76,316	9.0
Wyoming	0	26	703	1,289	1,541	1,510	1,411	2,006	1,724	1,953	26.7
Other jurisdictions	20,557	77,057	98,374	110,169	145,891	153,743	156,762	180,518	188,231	181,574	24.5
American Samoa	0	0	0	0	0	0	0	0	0	0	†
Federated States of Micronesia	0	0	0	0	0	0	0	0	0	0	†
Guam	0	0	0	0	167	149	94	85	86	77	-53.9
Marshall Islands	0	0	0	0	0	0	0	0	0	0	†
Northern Marianas	0	0	0	0	0	0	0	0	0	0	†
Palau	0	0	0	0	0	0	0	0	0	0	†
Puerto Rico	20,557	77,057	98,374	110,169	145,724	153,594	156,668	180,433	188,145	181,497	24.5
U.S. Virgin Islands	0	0	0	0	0	0	0	0	0	0	†

†Not applicable.
NOTE: Data through 1990 are for institutions of higher education, while later data are for degree-granting institutions. Degree-granting institutions grant associate's or higher degrees and participate in Title IV federal financial aid programs. The degree-granting classification is very similar to the earlier higher education classification, but it includes more 2-year colleges and excludes a few higher education institutions that did not grant degrees.

SOURCE: U.S. Department of Education, National Center for Education Statistics, Higher Education General Information Survey (HEGIS), "Fall Enrollment in Colleges and Universities" surveys, 1970 and 1980; Integrated Postsecondary Education Data System (IPEDS), "Fall Enrollment Survey" (IPEDS-EF:90); and IPEDS Spring 2001 through Spring 2013, Enrollment component. (This table was prepared November 2013.)

Total fall enrollment in degree-granting postsecondary institutions, by control, level of enrollment, level of institution, and state or jurisdiction: 2012

	Public				Private							
	Undergraduate			Post-bacca-laureate	Undergraduate					Postbaccalaureate		
State or jurisdiction	Total	4-year	2-year		Total	Nonprofit 4-year	For-profit 4-year	Nonprofit 2-year	For-profit 2-year	Total	Nonprofit 4-year	For-profit 4-year
1	2	3	4	5	6	7	8	9	10	11	12	13
United States	13,473,743	6,686,083	6,787,660	1,406,600	4,258,688	2,707,469	1,174,906	37,606	338,707	1,503,788	1,208,503	295,285
Alabama	216,535	130,260	86,275	34,510	49,382	21,674	24,045	518	3,145	9,884	3,917	5,967
Alaska	28,034	27,276	758	2,561	1,984	497	1,259	0	228	218	218	0
Arizona	332,352	114,685	217,667	26,877	289,258	3,503	274,906	0	10,849	87,892	5,598	82,294
Arkansas	141,323	81,479	59,844	15,901	16,181	13,973	1,704	319	185	3,053	2,860	193
California	2,023,402	564,081	1,459,321	105,750	336,257	161,047	105,455	1,665	68,090	156,051	134,542	21,509
Colorado	238,951	141,157	97,794	33,493	66,283	19,606	36,360	245	10,072	24,208	13,668	10,540
Connecticut	111,481	53,253	58,228	13,471	55,331	47,176	7,883	0	272	21,375	20,589	786
Delaware	37,012	22,079	14,933	4,101	10,804	10,297	296	211	0	6,211	6,120	91
District of Columbia	4,857	4,857	0	619	42,842	39,085	3,757	0	0	41,832	39,915	1,917
Florida	738,862	666,812	72,050	65,831	284,521	124,905	114,259	1,630	44,157	65,285	53,397	11,888
Georgia	382,476	234,809	147,667	39,713	94,337	51,705	33,780	504	8,348	28,832	21,024	7,808
Hawaii	53,935	24,602	29,333	6,360	15,337	12,131	1,495	0	1,711	2,824	2,161	663
Idaho	71,476	45,836	25,640	7,305	28,425	25,977	1,940	0	508	802	772	30
Illinois	507,197	148,467	358,730	49,940	206,514	137,447	60,339	718	8,010	103,459	89,662	13,797
Indiana	295,297	195,025	100,272	38,472	97,328	72,773	18,411	439	5,705	16,165	15,703	462
Iowa	158,615	58,207	100,408	14,943	156,803	44,565	111,751	203	284	30,822	11,439	19,383
Kansas	162,950	79,719	83,231	21,026	24,918	18,706	2,383	2,280	1,549	4,892	4,885	7
Kentucky	200,102	102,520	97,582	23,990	45,840	29,709	12,818	0	3,313	12,193	10,514	1,679
Louisiana	197,648	119,606	78,042	23,323	29,621	19,897	3,238	1,054	5,432	8,233	7,930	303
Maine	46,007	27,739	18,268	4,263	17,077	15,383	952	285	457	5,463	5,453	10
Maryland	265,180	120,166	145,014	45,323	37,305	29,564	5,057	0	2,684	26,688	25,353	1,335
Massachusetts	201,040	95,746	105,294	27,138	180,792	173,059	4,910	959	1,864	107,361	107,101	260
Michigan	473,592	235,479	238,113	66,650	101,918	93,559	6,646	80	1,633	21,665	21,159	506
Minnesota	247,522	112,388	135,134	24,768	88,225	50,565	35,722	87	1,851	91,146	20,794	70,352
Mississippi	141,605	64,045	77,560	16,390	13,781	11,275	453	0	2,053	4,889	4,778	111
Missouri	230,947	121,899	109,048	26,483	132,361	103,671	20,518	1,207	6,965	51,580	49,347	2,233
Montana	43,667	34,425	9,242	4,666	4,757	4,350	0	407	0	164	164	0
Nebraska	90,630	45,250	45,380	13,536	25,091	22,378	1,943	161	609	10,321	10,242	79
Nevada	95,487	83,884	11,603	8,132	11,367	884	5,718	0	4,765	3,314	2,537	777
New Hampshire	39,172	24,525	14,647	4,117	27,598	23,723	3,591	284	0	11,791	11,674	117
New Jersey	318,677	145,889	172,788	37,779	58,224	49,637	5,684	0	2,903	25,285	24,754	531
New Mexico	133,345	52,226	81,119	13,447	8,428	684	6,068	0	1,676	1,204	650	554
New York	652,778	323,712	329,066	69,496	418,273	364,666	29,081	4,175	20,351	169,439	166,835	2,604
North Carolina	420,434	175,760	244,674	45,250	87,836	72,615	11,013	706	3,502	24,511	20,734	3,777
North Dakota	42,738	35,870	6,868	6,191	5,385	4,385	1,000	0	0	855	855	0
Ohio	464,084	274,612	189,472	60,254	154,803	114,940	21,604	2,020	16,239	30,677	29,311	1,366
Oklahoma	173,639	104,886	68,753	21,472	28,425	19,228	4,723	0	4,474	4,928	4,760	168
Oregon	194,691	85,844	108,847	17,619	30,503	21,722	5,218	0	3,563	11,882	11,648	234
Pennsylvania	378,805	234,456	144,349	47,085	261,543	199,686	22,031	8,511	31,315	89,809	88,494	1,315
Rhode Island	38,813	20,929	17,884	4,391	34,525	34,525	0	0	0	6,223	6,223	0
South Carolina	189,392	87,432	101,960	19,631	44,443	30,043	9,396	950	4,054	6,151	3,608	2,543
South Dakota	38,626	32,279	6,347	5,559	10,633	6,217	4,122	294	0	1,240	762	478
Tennessee	209,423	117,121	92,302	25,587	85,866	60,506	13,788	1,509	10,063	22,765	20,801	1,964
Texas	1,210,112	509,101	701,011	137,748	152,740	95,856	27,404	3,635	25,845	39,698	36,634	3,064
Utah	158,627	128,630	29,997	12,374	80,398	64,939	11,373	2,191	1,895	15,910	14,140	1,770
Vermont	24,179	17,868	6,311	2,322	13,619	13,102	517	0	0	4,583	4,583	0
Virginia	360,859	166,432	194,427	48,894	131,693	86,643	35,835	326	8,889	47,250	41,340	5,910
Washington	288,656	149,345	139,311	22,841	40,961	30,851	5,760	33	4,317	13,056	12,278	778
West Virginia	80,594	59,433	21,161	12,423	55,561	6,683	46,581	0	2,297	13,601	997	12,604
Wisconsin	269,565	158,586	110,979	23,851	60,208	47,457	11,974	0	777	16,108	15,580	528
Wyoming	33,150	10,194	22,956	2,709	1,953	0	145	0	1,808	0	0	0
U.S. Service Academies	15,202	15,202	0	25	†	†	†	†	†	†	†	†
Other jurisdictions	71,872	62,004	9,868	6,497	159,491	116,551	11,058	804	31,078	22,083	21,305	778
American Samoa	1,795	1,795	0	0	0	0	0	0	0	0	0	0
Federated States of Micronesia	2,744	0	2,744	0	0	0	0	0	0	0	0	0
Guam	5,556	3,411	2,145	291	75	75	0	0	0	2	2	0
Marshall Islands	1,123	0	1,123	0	0	0	0	0	0	0	0	0
Northern Marianas	1,178	1,178	0	0	0	0	0	0	0	0	0	0
Palau	680	0	680	0	0	0	0	0	0	0	0	0
Puerto Rico	56,556	53,380	3,176	6,023	159,416	116,476	11,058	804	31,078	22,081	21,303	778
U.S. Virgin Islands	2,240	2,240	0	183	0	0	0	0	0	0	0	0

†Not applicable.
NOTE: Degree-granting institutions grant associate's or higher degrees and participate in Title IV federal financial aid programs.

SOURCE: U.S. Department of Education, National Center for Education Statistics, Integrated Postsecondary Education Data System (IPEDS), Spring 2013, Enrollment component. (This table was prepared November 2013.)

Total fall enrollment of first-time degree/certificate-seeking students in degree-granting postsecondary institutions, by attendance status, sex of student, and level and control of institution: 1955 through 2023

Year	Total	Full-time	Part-time	Males Total	Males Full-time	Males Part-time	Females Total	Females Full-time	Females Part-time	4-year Public	4-year Private	2-year Public	2-year Private
1	2	3	4	5	6	7	8	9	10	11	12	13	14
1955[1]	670,013	—	—	415,604	—	—	254,409	—	—	283,084 [2]	246,960 [2]	117,288 [2]	22,681 [2]
1956[1]	717,504	—	—	442,903	—	—	274,601	—	—	292,743 [2]	261,951 [2]	137,406 [2]	25,404 [2]
1957[1]	723,879	—	—	441,969	—	—	281,910	—	—	293,544 [2]	262,695 [2]	140,522 [2]	27,118 [2]
1958[1]	775,308	—	—	465,422	—	—	309,886	—	—	328,242 [2]	272,117 [2]	146,379 [2]	28,570 [2]
1959[1]	821,520	—	—	487,890	—	—	333,630	—	—	348,150 [2]	291,691 [2]	153,393 [2]	28,286 [2]
1960[1]	923,069	—	—	539,512	—	—	383,557	—	—	395,884 [2]	313,209 [2]	181,860 [2]	32,116 [2]
1961[1]	1,018,361	—	—	591,913	—	—	426,448	—	—	438,135 [2]	336,449 [2]	210,101 [2]	33,676 [2]
1962[1]	1,030,554	—	—	598,099	—	—	432,455	—	—	445,191 [2]	324,923 [2]	224,537 [2]	35,903 [2]
1963[1]	1,046,424	—	—	604,282	—	—	442,142	—	—	—	—	—	—
1964[1]	1,224,840	—	—	701,524	—	—	523,316	—	—	539,251 [2]	363,348 [2]	275,413 [2]	46,828 [2]
1965[1]	1,441,822	—	—	829,215	—	—	612,607	—	—	642,233 [2]	398,792 [2]	347,788 [2]	53,009 [2]
1966	1,554,337	—	—	889,516	—	—	664,821	—	—	626,472 [2]	382,889 [2]	478,459 [2]	66,517 [2]
1967	1,640,936	1,335,512	305,424	931,127	761,299	169,828	709,809	574,213	135,596	644,525	368,300	561,488	66,623
1968	1,892,849	1,470,653	422,196	1,082,367	847,005	235,362	810,482	623,648	186,834	724,377	378,052	718,562	71,858
1969	1,967,104	1,525,290	441,814	1,118,269	876,280	241,989	848,835	649,010	199,825	699,167	391,508	814,132	62,297
1970	2,063,397	1,587,072	476,325	1,151,960	896,281	255,679	911,437	690,791	220,646	717,449	395,886	890,703	59,359
1971	2,119,018	1,606,036	512,982	1,170,518	895,715	274,803	948,500	710,321	238,179	704,052	384,695	971,295	58,976
1972	2,152,778	1,574,197	578,581	1,157,501	858,254	299,247	995,277	715,943	279,334	680,337	380,982	1,036,616	54,843
1973	2,226,041	1,607,269	618,772	1,182,173	867,314	314,859	1,043,868	739,955	303,913	698,777	378,994	1,089,182	59,088
1974	2,365,761	1,673,333	692,428	1,243,790	896,077	347,713	1,121,971	777,256	344,715	745,637	386,391	1,175,759	57,974
1975	2,515,155	1,763,296	751,859	1,327,935	942,198	385,737	1,187,220	821,098	366,122	771,725	395,440	1,283,523	64,467
1976	2,347,014	1,662,333	684,681	1,170,326	854,597	315,729	1,176,688	807,736	368,952	717,373	413,961	1,152,944	62,736
1977	2,394,426	1,680,916	713,510	1,155,856	839,848	316,008	1,238,570	841,068	397,502	737,497	404,631	1,185,648	66,650
1978	2,389,627	1,650,848	738,779	1,141,777	817,294	324,483	1,247,850	833,554	414,296	736,703	406,669	1,173,544	72,711
1979	2,502,896	1,706,732	796,164	1,179,846	840,315	339,531	1,323,050	866,417	456,633	760,119	415,126	1,253,854	73,797
1980	2,587,644	1,749,928	837,716	1,218,961	862,458	356,503	1,368,683	887,470	481,213	765,395	417,937	1,313,591	90,721 [3]
1981	2,595,421	1,737,714	857,707	1,217,680	851,833	365,847	1,377,741	885,881	491,860	754,007	419,257	1,318,436	103,721 [3]
1982	2,505,466	1,688,620	816,846	1,199,237	837,223	362,014	1,306,229	851,397	454,832	730,775	404,252	1,254,193	116,246 [3]
1983	2,443,703	1,678,071	765,632	1,159,049	824,609	334,440	1,284,654	853,462	431,192	728,244	403,882	1,189,869	121,708
1984	2,356,898	1,613,185	743,713	1,112,303	786,099	326,204	1,244,595	827,086	417,509	713,790	402,959	1,130,311	109,838
1985	2,292,222	1,602,038	690,184	1,075,736	774,858	300,878	1,216,486	827,180	389,306	717,199	398,556	1,060,275	116,192
1986	2,219,208	1,589,451	629,757	1,046,527	768,856	277,671	1,172,681	820,595	352,086	719,974	391,673	990,973	116,588
1987	2,246,359	1,626,719	619,640	1,046,615	779,226	267,389	1,199,744	847,493	352,251	757,833	405,113	979,820	103,593
1988	2,378,803	1,698,927	679,876	1,100,026	807,319	292,707	1,278,777	891,608	387,169	783,358	425,907	1,048,914	120,624
1989	2,341,035	1,656,594	684,441	1,094,750	791,295	303,455	1,246,285	865,299	380,986	762,217	413,836	1,048,529	116,453
1990	2,256,624	1,617,118	639,506	1,045,191	771,372	273,819	1,211,433	845,746	365,687	727,264	400,120	1,041,097	88,143
1991	2,277,920	1,652,983	624,937	1,068,433	798,043	270,390	1,209,487	854,940	354,547	717,697	392,904	1,070,048	97,271
1992	2,184,113	1,603,737	580,376	1,013,058	760,290	252,768	1,171,055	843,447	327,608	697,393	408,306	993,074	85,340
1993	2,160,710	1,608,274	552,436	1,007,647	762,240	245,407	1,153,063	846,034	307,029	702,273	410,688	973,545	74,204
1994	2,133,205	1,603,106	530,099	984,558	751,081	233,477	1,148,647	852,025	296,622	709,042	405,917	952,468	65,778
1995	2,168,831	1,646,812	522,019	1,001,052	767,185	233,867	1,167,779	879,627	288,152	731,836	419,025	954,595	63,375
1996	2,274,319	1,739,852	534,467	1,046,662	805,982	240,680	1,227,657	933,870	293,787	741,164	427,442	989,536	116,177
1997	2,219,255	1,733,512	485,743	1,026,058	806,054	220,004	1,193,197	927,458	265,739	755,362	442,397	923,954	97,542
1998	2,212,593	1,775,412	437,181	1,022,656	825,577	197,079	1,189,937	949,835	240,102	792,772	460,948	858,417	100,456
1999	2,357,590	1,849,741	507,849	1,094,539	865,545	228,994	1,263,051	984,196	278,855	819,503	474,223	955,499	108,365
2000	2,427,551	1,918,093	509,458	1,123,948	894,432	229,516	1,303,603	1,023,661	279,942	842,228	498,532	952,175	134,616
2001	2,497,078	1,989,179	507,899	1,152,837	926,393	226,444	1,344,241	1,062,786	281,455	866,619	508,030	988,726	133,703
2002	2,570,611	2,053,065	517,546	1,170,609	945,938	224,671	1,400,002	1,107,127	292,875	886,297	517,621	1,037,267	129,426
2003	2,591,754	2,102,394	489,360	1,175,856	965,075	210,781	1,415,898	1,137,319	278,579	918,602	537,726	1,004,428	130,998
2004	2,630,243	2,147,546	482,697	1,190,268	981,591	208,677	1,439,975	1,165,955	274,020	925,249	562,485	1,009,082	133,427
2005	2,657,338	2,189,884	467,454	1,200,055	995,610	204,445	1,457,283	1,194,274	263,009	953,903	606,712	977,224	119,499
2006	2,707,213	2,219,853	487,360	1,228,665	1,015,585	213,080	1,478,548	1,204,268	274,280	990,262	598,412	1,013,080	105,459
2007	2,776,168	2,293,855	482,313	1,267,030	1,052,600	214,430	1,509,138	1,241,255	267,883	1,023,543	633,296	1,016,262	103,067
2008	3,024,723	2,427,740	596,983	1,389,302	1,115,500	273,802	1,635,421	1,312,240	323,181	1,053,838	673,581	1,186,576	110,728
2009	3,210,237	2,586,840	623,397	1,479,801	1,192,553	287,248	1,730,436	1,394,287	336,149	1,090,769	713,284	1,275,630	130,554
2010	3,156,949	2,532,858	624,091	1,461,707	1,171,619	290,088	1,695,242	1,361,239	334,003	1,110,675	676,027	1,236,477	133,770
2011	3,093,077	2,479,137	613,940	1,424,596	1,140,566	284,030	1,668,481	1,338,571	329,910	1,131,807	656,938	1,195,286	109,046
2012	2,990,280	2,406,038	584,242	1,385,096	1,114,025	271,071	1,605,184	1,292,013	313,171	1,127,832	642,686	1,133,486	86,276
2013[4]	2,979,000	—	—	1,390,000	—	—	1,589,000	—	—	—	—	—	—
2014[4]	3,031,000	—	—	1,395,000	—	—	1,636,000	—	—	—	—	—	—
2015[4]	3,061,000	—	—	1,399,000	—	—	1,663,000	—	—	—	—	—	—
2016[4]	3,101,000	—	—	1,407,000	—	—	1,694,000	—	—	—	—	—	—
2017[4]	3,147,000	—	—	1,421,000	—	—	1,727,000	—	—	—	—	—	—
2018[4]	3,185,000	—	—	1,432,000	—	—	1,753,000	—	—	—	—	—	—
2019[4]	3,223,000	—	—	1,444,000	—	—	1,779,000	—	—	—	—	—	—
2020[4]	3,261,000	—	—	1,456,000	—	—	1,805,000	—	—	—	—	—	—
2021[4]	3,306,000	—	—	1,471,000	—	—	1,835,000	—	—	—	—	—	—
2022[4]	3,353,000	—	—	1,487,000	—	—	1,866,000	—	—	—	—	—	—
2023[4]	3,398,000	—	—	1,502,000	—	—	1,896,000	—	—	—	—	—	—

—Not available.
[1]Excludes first-time degree/certificate-seeking students in occupational programs not creditable towards a bachelor's degree.
[2]Data for 2-year branches of 4-year college systems are aggregated with the 4-year institutions.
[3]Large increases are due to the addition of schools accredited by the Accrediting Commission of Career Schools and Colleges of Technology.
[4]Projected.
NOTE: Data through 1995 are for institutions of higher education, while later data are for degree-granting institutions. Degree-granting institutions grant associate's or higher degrees and participate in Title IV federal financial aid programs. The degree-granting classification is very similar to the earlier higher education classification, but it includes more 2-year colleges and excludes a few higher education institutions that did not grant degrees. Alaska and Hawaii are included in all years.
SOURCE: U.S. Department of Education, National Center for Education Statistics, Biennial Survey of Education in the United States; Opening Fall Enrollment in Higher Education, 1963 through 1965; Higher Education General Information Survey (HEGIS), "Fall Enrollment in Colleges and Universities" surveys, 1966 through 1985; Integrated Postsecondary Education Data System (IPEDS), "Fall Enrollment Survey" (IPEDS-EF:86–99); IPEDS Spring 2001 through Spring 2013, Enrollment component; and First-Time Freshmen Projection Model, 1975 through 2023. (This table was prepared July 2014.)

Acceptance rates; number of applications, admissions, and enrollees; and enrollees' SAT and ACT scores for degree-granting postsecondary institutions with first-year undergraduates, by control and level of institution: 2012–13

Acceptance rates, applications, admissions, enrollees, and SAT and ACT scores	All institutions			Public institutions			Private institutions								
							Total			Nonprofit			For-profit		
	Total	4-year	2-year	Total	4-year	2-year	Total	4-year	2-year	Total	4-year	2-year	Total	4-year	2-year
	2	3	4	5	6	7	8	9	10	11	12	13	14	15	16
Number of institutions reporting application data[1]	4,264	2,585	1,679	1,579	646	933	2,685	1,939	746	1,335	1,242	93	1,350	697	653
Percentage distribution of institutions by their acceptance of applications	100.0	100.0	100.0	100.0	100.0	100.0	100.0	100.0	100.0	100.0	100.0	100.0	100.0	100.0	100.0
No application criteria	51.0	26.4	88.9	65.0	17.8	97.6	42.8	29.3	77.9	16.5	13.8	51.6	68.8	56.8	81.6
90 percent or more accepted	6.2	7.7	3.9	2.8	5.9	0.6	8.2	8.3	7.9	4.6	4.4	6.5	11.8	15.1	8.3
75.0 to 89.9 percent accepted	12.0	17.8	2.9	9.4	22.4	0.3	13.5	16.3	6.2	11.1	11.2	6.5	9.0	9.0	6.1
50.0 to 74.9 percent accepted	21.5	33.7	2.8	16.1	37.9	1.0	24.7	32.2	5.1	40.0	41.2	19.4	11.7	16.9	3.1
25.0 to 49.9 percent accepted	7.6	11.7	1.3	6.1	14.4	0.3	8.5	10.8	2.5	26.5	27.6	14.0	4.3	8.5	0.9
10.0 to 24.9 percent accepted	1.3	2.1	0.2	0.5	1.1	0.1	1.8	2.4	0.3	3.2	3.5	1.1	0.6	1.4	0.0
Less than 10 percent accepted	0.4	0.6	0.1	0.2	0.5	0.1	0.5	0.6	0.1	0.8	1.0	0.9	0.2	0.4	0.0
Number of applications (in thousands)	8,847	8,739	108	4,814	4,754	60	4,033	3,986	47	3,871	3,856	15	162	130	32
Percentage distribution of applications by institutions' acceptance of applications	100.0	100.0	100.0	100.0	100.0	100.0	100.0	100.0	100.0	100.0	100.0	100.0	100.0	100.0	100.0
No application criteria	†	†	†	†	†	†	†	†	†	†	†	†	†	†	†
90 percent or more accepted	3.2	2.8	38.0	3.9	3.4	45.2	2.4	2.1	28.7	1.7	1.7	4.1	20.0	15.0	40.1
75.0 to 89.9 percent accepted	15.5	15.5	16.8	18.4	18.6	8.0	12.0	11.8	28.2	11.1	11.2	2.6	32.5	30.6	40.0
50.0 to 74.9 percent accepted	44.2	44.4	29.3	46.9	47.1	32.2	40.9	41.1	25.5	41.3	41.2	46.9	32.8	37.0	15.6
25.0 to 49.9 percent accepted	27.3	27.5	12.9	27.5	27.7	10.0	27.1	27.2	16.6	27.6	27.6	43.3	14.7	17.3	4.2
10.0 to 24.9 percent accepted	6.8	6.8	2.7	2.3	2.2	4.7	12.2	12.3	0.1	12.7	12.7	0.3	0.1	0.1	0.0
Less than 10 percent accepted	3.0	3.0	0.4	1.0	1.0	0.0	5.3	5.4	0.9	5.6	5.6	2.9	#	#	0.0
Number of admissions (in thousands)	4,922	4,840	82	2,874	2,827	47	2,048	2,012	35	1,931	1,923	8	117	90	27
Percentage distribution of admissions by institutions' acceptance of applications	100.0	100.0	100.0	100.0	100.0	100.0	100.0	100.0	100.0	100.0	100.0	100.0	100.0	100.0	100.0
No application criteria	†	†	†	†	†	†	†	†	†	†	†	†	†	†	†
90 percent or more accepted	5.4	4.7	49.2	6.1	5.2	58.2	4.5	4.0	37.3	3.2	3.2	6.9	26.6	20.6	46.4
75.0 to 89.9 percent accepted	22.6	22.7	18.3	25.1	25.3	8.6	19.2	18.9	31.1	18.1	18.1	4.0	36.9	36.3	39.2
50.0 to 74.9 percent accepted	50.1	50.5	25.0	49.5	49.9	27.0	50.9	51.4	22.4	52.2	52.2	56.0	28.8	33.8	12.3
25.0 to 49.9 percent accepted	19.3	19.5	7.1	18.4	18.6	5.5	20.6	20.8	9.2	21.4	21.3	32.7	7.6	9.3	2.1
10.0 to 24.9 percent accepted	2.2	2.2	0.4	0.8	0.8	0.7	4.1	4.2	#	4.3	4.4	0.0	#	#	0.0
Less than 10 percent accepted	0.4	0.4	#	0.1	0.1	0.0	0.8	0.8	0.1	0.8	0.8	0.4	0.0	0.0	0.0
Number of enrollees (in thousands)	1,551	1,503	48	997	971	26	554	532	22	486	482	5	67	50	17
Percentage distribution of enrollees by institutions' acceptance of applications	100.0	100.0	100.0	100.0	100.0	98.7	100.0	100.0	100.0	100.0	100.0	100.0	100.0	100.0	100.0
No application criteria	†	†	†	†	†	†	†	†	†	†	†	†	†	†	†
90 percent or more accepted	7.1	5.9	44.3	7.3	6.2	48.4	6.9	5.6	39.5	4.5	4.5	9.8	23.9	15.9	47.5
75.0 to 89.9 percent accepted	22.7	22.8	20.9	24.8	25.1	12.9	19.0	18.5	30.5	16.6	16.7	5.1	36.2	35.8	37.4
50.0 to 74.9 percent accepted	48.8	49.4	27.8	49.9	50.4	32.1	46.7	47.6	22.7	48.8	48.7	60.4	30.9	37.2	12.5
25.0 to 49.9 percent accepted	17.7	18.0	6.1	16.8	17.1	5.3	19.2	19.7	7.1	20.6	20.6	23.9	8.9	11.1	2.6
10.0 to 24.9 percent accepted	2.8	2.9	0.7	0.8	0.8	#	6.3	6.6	#	7.2	7.3	0.1	#	#	0.0
Less than 10 percent accepted	0.9	0.9	0.1	0.3	0.3	0.0	1.9	2.0	0.1	2.2	2.2	0.7	0.0	0.0	0.0
SAT scores of enrollees															
Critical reading, 25th percentile[2]	469	470	409	457	458	408	476	476	411	476	477	404	437	434	‡
Critical reading, 75th percentile[2]	579	581	504	564	565	519	588	590	488	589	590	486	541	546	‡
Mathematics, 25th percentile[2]	478	479	404	471	472	414	482	483	391	483	484	388	433	434	‡
Mathematics, 75th percentile[2]	587	588	514	579	580	530	592	594	495	593	594	490	552	553	‡
ACT scores of enrollees															
Composite, 25th percentile[2]	20.4	20.4	17.0	19.7	19.8	16.5	20.7	20.8	18.0	20.8	20.8	18.0	18.8	18.8	‡
Composite, 75th percentile[2]	25.3	25.4	21.4	24.5	24.6	21.1	25.8	25.9	21.9	25.9	25.9	21.9	23.8	23.8	‡
English, 25th percentile[2]	19.3	19.4	15.6	18.6	18.7	15.2	19.8	19.8	16.4	19.8	19.1	16.4	19.1	19.1	‡
English, 75th percentile[2]	25.6	25.7	21.3	24.7	24.8	21.4	26.1	26.2	21.1	26.2	25.1	21.1	25.1	25.1	‡
Mathematics, 25th percentile[2]	19.4	19.5	16.6	19.0	19.0	16.1	19.7	19.7	17.5	19.7	18.8	17.5	18.8	18.8	‡
Mathematics, 75th percentile[2]	25.2	25.2	21.3	24.6	24.7	20.8	25.5	25.6	22.1	25.5	24.3	22.1	24.3	24.3	‡

†Not applicable.
#Rounds to zero.
‡Reporting standards not met (too few cases).
[1]The total on this table differs slightly from other counts of institutions with first-year undergraduates because approximately 0.7 percent of these institutions did not report application information.
[2]Data are only for institutions that require test scores for admission. Relatively few 2-year institutions require test scores for admission. The SAT Critical reading and Mathematics scales range from 200 to 800. The ACT Composite, English, and Mathematics scales range from 1 to 36.

NOTE: Degree-granting institutions grant associate's or higher degrees and participate in Title IV federal financial aid programs. Excludes institutions not enrolling any first-time degree/certificate-seeking undergraduates. Detail may not sum to totals because of rounding.
SOURCE: U.S. Department of Education, National Center for Education Statistics, Integrated Postsecondary Education Data System (IPEDS), Fall 2012, Institutional Characteristics component. (This table was prepared August 2013.)

Total fall enrollment in degree-granting postsecondary institutions, by level of enrollment, sex, attendance status, and race/ethnicity of student: Selected years, 1976 through 2012

Level of enrollment, sex, attendance status, and race/ethnicity of student	Fall enrollment (in thousands)											Percentage distribution of U.S. residents										
	1976	1980	1990	2000	2005	2007	2008	2009	2010	2011	2012	1976	1980	1990	2000	2005	2007	2008	2009	2010	2011	2012
1	2	3	4	5	6	7	8	9	10	11	12	13	14	15	16	17	18	19	20	21	22	23
All students, total	10,985.6	12,086.8	13,818.6	15,312.3	17,487.5	18,248.1	19,102.8	20,427.7	21,016.1	20,994.1	20,642.8	100.0	100.0	100.0	100.0	100.0	100.0	100.0	100.0	100.0	100.0	100.0
White	9,076.1	9,833.0	10,722.5	10,462.1	11,495.4	11,756.2	12,088.8	12,730.8	12,722.5	12,394.2	11,981.1	84.3	83.5	79.9	70.8	68.0	66.7	65.5	64.5	62.7	61.2	60.3
Total, selected races/ethnicities	1,690.8	1,948.8	2,704.7	4,321.5	5,407.2	5,867.4	6,353.5	7,012.1	7,584.0	7,859.5	7,878.4	15.7	16.5	20.1	29.2	32.0	33.3	34.5	35.5	37.3	38.8	39.7
Black	1,033.0	1,106.8	1,247.0	1,730.3	2,214.6	2,383.4	2,584.5	2,919.8	3,038.8	3,067.9	2,962.1	9.6	9.4	9.3	11.7	13.1	13.5	14.0	14.8	15.0	15.1	14.9
Hispanic	383.8	471.7	782.4	1,461.8	1,882.0	2,076.2	2,272.9	2,546.7	2,741.4	2,890.1	2,979.4	3.6	4.0	5.8	9.9	11.1	11.8	12.3	12.9	13.5	14.3	15.0
Asian/Pacific Islander	197.9	286.4	572.4	978.2	1,134.4	1,217.9	1,302.8	1,337.7	1,282.2	1,282.5	1,259.2	1.8	2.4	4.3	6.6	6.7	6.9	7.1	6.8	6.3	6.3	6.3
Asian	—	—	—	—	—	—	—	—	1,218.1	1,216.6	1,195.6	—	—	—	—	—	—	—	—	6.0	6.0	6.0
Pacific Islander	—	—	—	—	—	—	—	—	64.0	65.9	63.6	—	—	—	—	—	—	—	—	0.3	0.3	0.3
American Indian/Alaska Native	76.1	83.9	102.8	151.2	176.3	190.0	193.2	207.9	196.4	186.1	172.9	0.7	0.7	0.8	1.0	1.0	1.1	1.0	1.1	1.0	0.9	0.9
Two or more races	—	—	—	—	—	—	—	—	325.3	432.9	505.1	—	—	—	—	—	—	—	—	1.6	2.1	2.5
Nonresident alien	218.7	305.0	391.5	528.7	584.8	624.5	660.6	684.8	709.6	740.5	782.9	†	†	†	†	†	†	†	†	†	†	†
Male	5,794.4	5,868.1	6,283.9	6,721.8	7,455.9	7,815.9	8,188.9	8,769.5	9,044.8	9,026.5	8,919.1	100.0	100.0	100.0	100.0	100.0	100.0	100.0	100.0	100.0	100.0	100.0
White	4,813.7	4,772.9	4,861.0	4,634.6	5,007.2	5,146.1	5,302.9	5,594.4	5,606.8	5,453.8	5,285.0	85.3	84.4	80.5	72.1	70.1	68.8	67.7	66.6	64.7	63.2	62.2
Total, selected races/ethnicities	826.6	884.4	1,176.6	1,789.8	2,139.2	2,336.6	2,532.8	2,808.4	3,057.6	3,173.6	3,209.4	14.7	15.6	19.5	27.9	29.9	31.2	32.3	33.4	35.3	36.8	37.8
Black	469.9	463.7	484.7	635.3	774.1	838.1	911.8	1,037.1	1,089.1	1,103.5	1,079.4	8.3	8.2	8.0	9.9	10.8	11.2	11.6	12.3	12.6	12.8	12.7
Hispanic	209.7	231.6	353.9	627.1	774.6	861.6	946.7	1,066.3	1,154.6	1,214.2	1,254.3	3.7	4.1	5.9	9.8	10.8	11.5	12.1	12.7	13.3	14.1	14.8
Asian/Pacific Islander	108.4	151.3	294.9	465.9	522.0	562.5	597.4	621.5	600.8	602.4	593.7	1.9	2.7	4.9	7.3	7.3	7.5	7.6	7.4	6.9	7.0	7.0
Asian	—	—	—	—	—	—	—	—	572.3	573.4	565.3	—	—	—	—	—	—	—	—	6.6	6.6	6.7
Pacific Islander	—	—	—	—	—	—	—	—	28.6	29.0	28.5	—	—	—	—	—	—	—	—	0.3	0.3	0.3
American Indian/Alaska Native	38.5	37.8	43.1	61.4	68.4	74.4	76.9	83.4	78.8	73.7	68.6	0.7	0.7	0.7	1.0	1.0	1.0	1.0	1.0	0.9	0.9	0.8
Two or more races	—	—	—	—	—	—	—	—	134.3	179.8	213.3	—	—	—	—	—	—	—	—	1.5	2.1	2.5
Nonresident alien	154.1	210.8	246.3	297.3	309.5	333.2	353.3	366.7	380.3	399.1	424.7	†	†	†	†	†	†	†	†	†	†	†
Female	5,191.2	6,218.7	7,534.7	8,590.5	10,031.6	10,432.2	10,913.9	11,658.2	11,971.3	11,967.6	11,723.7	100.0	100.0	100.0	100.0	100.0	100.0	100.0	100.0	100.0	100.0	100.0
White	4,262.4	5,060.1	5,861.5	5,827.5	6,488.2	6,610.1	6,785.9	7,136.4	7,115.7	6,940.3	6,696.1	83.1	82.6	79.3	69.7	66.5	65.2	64.0	62.9	61.1	59.7	58.9
Total, selected races/ethnicities	864.2	1,064.4	1,528.1	2,531.7	3,268.0	3,530.9	3,820.7	4,203.7	4,526.4	4,685.9	4,669.4	16.9	17.4	20.7	30.3	33.5	34.8	36.0	37.1	38.9	40.3	41.1
Black	563.1	643.0	762.3	1,095.0	1,440.4	1,545.3	1,672.7	1,882.7	1,949.7	1,964.5	1,882.7	11.0	10.5	10.3	13.1	14.8	15.2	15.8	16.6	16.7	16.9	16.6
Hispanic	174.1	240.1	428.5	834.7	1,107.3	1,214.5	1,326.1	1,480.4	1,586.9	1,676.0	1,725.1	3.4	3.9	5.8	10.0	11.4	12.0	12.5	13.1	13.6	14.4	15.2
Asian/Pacific Islander	89.4	135.2	277.5	512.3	612.4	655.4	705.4	716.1	681.3	680.1	665.5	1.7	2.2	3.8	6.1	6.3	6.5	6.7	6.3	5.9	5.8	5.9
Asian	—	—	—	—	—	—	—	—	645.9	643.2	630.3	—	—	—	—	—	—	—	—	5.5	5.5	5.5
Pacific Islander	—	—	—	—	—	—	—	—	35.5	36.9	35.2	—	—	—	—	—	—	—	—	0.3	0.3	0.3
American Indian/Alaska Native	37.6	46.1	59.7	89.7	107.9	115.6	116.4	124.5	117.6	112.4	104.3	0.7	0.8	0.8	1.1	1.1	1.1	1.1	1.1	1.0	1.0	0.9
Two or more races	—	—	—	—	—	—	—	—	191.0	253.1	291.8	—	—	—	—	—	—	—	—	1.6	2.2	2.6
Nonresident alien	64.6	94.2	145.2	231.4	275.3	291.2	307.3	318.1	329.2	341.4	358.2	†	†	†	†	†	†	†	†	†	†	†
Full-time	6,703.6	7,088.9	7,821.0	9,009.6	10,797.0	11,269.9	11,747.7	12,722.8	13,082.3	13,001.5	12,737.0	100.0	100.0	100.0	100.0	100.0	100.0	100.0	100.0	100.0	100.0	100.0
White	5,512.6	5,717.0	6,016.5	6,231.1	7,220.5	7,394.2	7,593.5	8,078.8	8,051.1	7,781.2	7,485.6	84.2	83.4	79.9	72.5	69.8	68.6	67.6	66.3	64.3	62.7	61.9
Total, selected races/ethnicities	1,030.9	1,137.5	1,514.9	2,368.5	3,117.1	3,382.0	3,631.9	4,101.7	4,465.1	4,622.3	4,610.0	15.8	16.6	20.1	27.5	30.2	31.4	32.4	33.7	35.7	37.3	38.1
Black	659.2	685.6	718.3	982.6	1,321.7	1,416.1	1,530.7	1,763.7	1,809.3	1,807.9	1,720.1	10.1	10.0	9.5	11.4	12.8	13.1	13.6	14.5	14.5	14.6	14.2
Hispanic	211.1	247.0	394.7	710.3	979.7	1,082.9	1,177.2	1,364.2	1,499.7	1,593.2	1,632.4	3.2	3.6	5.2	8.3	9.5	10.0	10.5	11.2	12.0	12.8	13.5
Asian/Pacific Islander	117.7	162.0	347.4	591.2	710.1	770.0	808.9	848.6	821.0	821.7	815.4	1.8	2.4	4.6	6.9	6.9	7.1	7.2	7.0	6.6	6.6	6.7
Asian	—	—	—	—	—	—	—	—	783.3	782.6	778.5	—	—	—	—	—	—	—	—	6.3	6.3	6.4
Pacific Islander	—	—	—	—	—	—	—	—	37.7	39.1	36.9	—	—	—	—	—	—	—	—	0.3	0.3	0.3
American Indian/Alaska Native	43.0	43.0	54.4	84.4	105.6	113.0	115.1	127.0	118.2	110.7	102.1	0.7	0.6	0.7	1.0	1.0	1.0	1.0	1.0	0.9	0.9	0.8
Two or more races	—	—	—	—	—	—	—	—	216.9	289.7	340.0	—	—	—	—	—	—	—	—	1.7	2.3	2.8
Nonresident alien	160.0	234.4	289.6	410.0	459.4	493.7	522.3	542.3	566.1	598.0	641.4	†	†	†	†	†	†	†	†	†	†	†
Part-time	4,282.1	4,997.9	5,997.7	6,302.7	6,690.5	6,978.2	7,355.1	7,704.9	7,933.9	7,992.7	7,905.8	100.0	100.0	100.0	100.0	100.0	100.0	100.0	100.0	100.0	100.0	100.0
White	3,563.5	4,116.0	4,706.0	4,231.0	4,274.9	4,362.1	4,495.3	4,651.9	4,671.4	4,613.0	4,495.5	84.4	83.5	79.8	68.4	65.1	63.7	62.3	61.5	60.0	58.8	57.9
Total, selected races/ethnicities	659.9	811.3	1,189.8	1,953.0	2,290.1	2,485.4	2,721.5	2,910.4	3,118.9	3,237.2	3,268.8	15.6	16.5	20.2	31.6	34.9	36.3	37.7	38.5	40.0	41.2	42.1
Black	373.8	421.2	528.7	747.7	892.9	967.2	1,053.7	1,146.2	1,229.5	1,260.1	1,242.1	8.9	8.5	9.0	12.1	13.6	14.1	14.6	15.2	15.8	16.1	16.0
Hispanic	172.7	224.8	387.7	751.5	902.2	993.2	1,095.7	1,182.5	1,241.6	1,297.0	1,347.0	4.1	4.6	6.6	12.2	13.7	14.5	15.2	15.6	15.9	16.5	17.3
Asian/Pacific Islander	80.2	124.4	225.1	387.1	424.3	447.9	493.9	489.1	461.2	460.8	443.8	1.9	2.5	3.8	6.3	6.5	6.5	6.8	6.5	5.9	5.9	5.7
Asian	—	—	—	—	—	—	—	—	434.9	434.0	417.1	—	—	—	—	—	—	—	—	5.6	5.5	5.4
Pacific Islander	—	—	—	—	—	—	—	—	26.3	26.8	26.7	—	—	—	—	—	—	—	—	0.3	0.3	0.3
American Indian/Alaska Native	33.1	40.9	48.4	66.8	70.7	77.0	78.2	80.9	78.2	75.4	70.8	0.8	0.8	0.8	1.1	1.1	1.1	1.1	1.1	1.0	1.0	0.9
Two or more races	—	—	—	—	—	—	—	—	108.4	143.2	165.0	—	—	—	—	—	—	—	—	1.4	1.8	2.1
Nonresident alien	58.7	70.6	101.8	118.7	125.5	130.8	138.3	142.6	143.5	143.2	141.5	†	†	†	†	†	†	†	†	†	†	†

See notes at end of table.

Total fall enrollment in degree-granting postsecondary institutions, by level of enrollment, sex, attendance status, and race/ethnicity of student: Selected years, 1976 through 2012—Continued

Level of enrollment, sex, attendance status, and race/ethnicity of student	Fall enrollment (in thousands)											Percentage distribution of U.S. residents										
	1976	1980	1990	2000	2005	2007	2008	2009	2010	2011	2012	1976	1980	1990	2000	2005	2007	2008	2009	2010	2011	2012
1	2	3	4	5	6	7	8	9	10	11	12	13	14	15	16	17	18	19	20	21	22	23
Undergraduate, total	**9,419.0**	**10,469.1**	**11,959.1**	**13,155.4**	**14,964.0**	**15,603.8**	**16,365.7**	**17,565.3**	**18,078.7**	**18,063.0**	**17,732.4**	**100.0**	**100.0**	**100.0**	**100.0**	**100.0**	**100.0**	**100.0**	**100.0**	**100.0**	**100.0**	**100.0**
White	7,740.5	8,480.7	9,272.6	8,983.5	9,828.6	10,046.6	10,339.2	10,915.3	10,897.7	10,611.6	10,247.4	83.4	82.7	79.0	69.8	67.1	65.8	64.6	63.5	61.6	60.2	59.3
Total, selected races/ethnicities	1,535.3	1,778.5	2,467.7	3,884.0	4,820.7	5,221.9	5,666.2	6,271.6	6,780.7	7,029.1	7,034.6	16.6	17.3	21.0	30.2	32.9	34.2	35.4	36.5	38.4	39.8	40.7
Black	943.4	1,018.8	1,147.2	1,548.9	1,955.4	2,092.6	2,269.3	2,577.4	2,676.5	2,698.9	2,592.8	10.2	9.9	9.8	12.0	13.3	13.7	14.2	15.0	15.1	15.3	15.0
Hispanic	352.9	433.1	724.6	1,351.0	1,733.6	1,915.9	2,103.5	2,362.5	2,543.6	2,685.1	2,766.1	3.8	4.2	6.2	10.5	11.8	12.5	13.1	13.7	14.4	15.2	16.0
Asian/Pacific Islander	169.3	248.7	500.5	845.5	971.4	1,042.1	1,117.9	1,142.3	1,087.9	1,085.1	1,063.2	1.8	2.4	4.3	6.6	6.6	6.8	7.0	6.6	6.2	6.2	6.2
Asian	—	—	—	—	—	—	—	—	1,030.3	1,025.8	1,006.5	—	—	—	—	—	—	—	—	5.8	5.8	5.8
Pacific Islander	—	—	—	—	—	—	—	—	57.6	59.3	56.7	—	—	—	—	—	—	—	—	0.3	0.3	0.3
American Indian/Alaska Native	69.7	77.9	95.5	138.5	160.4	171.3	175.6	189.4	179.3	169.9	157.5	0.8	0.8	0.8	1.1	1.1	1.1	1.1	1.1	1.0	1.0	0.9
Two or more races	—	—	—	—	—	—	—	—	293.5	390.2	455.0	†	†	†	†	†	†	†	†	1.7	2.2	2.6
Nonresident alien	143.2	209.9	218.7	288.0	314.7	335.3	360.3	378.4	400.3	422.3	450.5											
Male	4,896.8	4,997.4	5,379.8	5,778.3	6,408.9	6,727.6	7,066.6	7,595.5	7,835.2	7,817.0	7,713.9	100.0	100.0	100.0	100.0	100.0	100.0	100.0	100.0	100.0	100.0	100.0
White	4,052.2	4,054.9	4,184.4	4,010.1	4,330.4	4,455.9	4,598.6	4,860.2	4,861.9	4,722.9	4,571.9	84.4	83.5	79.6	71.3	69.2	67.9	66.8	65.6	63.7	62.1	61.1
Total, selected races/ethnicities	748.2	802.7	1,069.3	1,618.0	1,926.6	2,107.5	2,290.3	2,546.2	2,771.0	2,876.5	2,904.9	15.6	16.5	20.4	28.7	30.8	32.1	33.2	34.4	36.3	37.9	38.9
Black	430.7	428.2	448.0	577.0	697.5	754.1	821.3	938.3	982.9	994.9	969.7	9.0	8.8	8.5	10.3	11.1	11.5	11.9	12.7	12.9	13.1	13.0
Hispanic	191.7	211.2	326.9	582.6	718.5	802.0	884.0	997.3	1,079.9	1,136.2	1,173.0	4.0	4.3	6.2	10.4	11.5	12.2	12.8	13.5	14.1	15.0	15.7
Asian/Pacific Islander	91.1	128.5	254.5	401.9	448.1	483.6	514.6	534.0	513.6	513.9	505.5	1.9	2.6	4.8	7.1	7.2	7.4	7.5	7.2	6.7	6.8	6.8
Asian	—	—	—	—	—	—	—	—	487.6	487.4	479.9	—	—	—	—	—	—	—	—	6.4	6.4	6.4
Pacific Islander	—	—	—	—	—	—	—	—	26.0	26.4	25.6	—	—	—	—	—	—	—	—	0.3	0.3	0.3
American Indian/Alaska Native	34.8	34.8	39.9	56.4	62.5	67.8	70.3	76.5	72.4	67.8	62.9	0.7	0.7	0.8	1.0	1.0	1.0	1.0	1.0	0.9	0.9	0.8
Two or more races	—	—	—	—	—	—	—	—	123.3	163.6	193.8	†	†	†	†	†	†	†	†	1.6	2.2	2.6
Nonresident alien	96.4	139.8	126.1	150.2	151.8	164.2	177.7	189.1	202.2	217.6	237.1											
Female	4,522.1	5,471.7	6,579.3	7,377.1	8,555.1	8,876.2	9,299.1	9,969.8	10,243.5	10,246.1	10,018.5	100.0	100.0	100.0	100.0	100.0	100.0	100.0	100.0	100.0	100.0	100.0
White	3,688.3	4,425.8	5,088.2	4,973.3	5,498.2	5,590.6	5,740.6	6,055.0	6,035.7	5,888.6	5,675.5	82.4	81.9	78.4	68.7	65.5	64.2	63.0	61.9	60.1	58.6	57.9
Total, selected races/ethnicities	787.0	975.8	1,398.5	2,266.0	2,894.0	3,114.4	3,375.9	3,725.4	4,009.7	4,152.7	4,129.7	17.6	18.1	21.6	31.3	34.5	35.8	37.0	38.1	39.9	41.4	42.1
Black	512.7	590.6	699.2	971.9	1,257.8	1,338.5	1,448.0	1,639.1	1,693.7	1,703.9	1,623.1	11.5	11.2	10.8	13.4	15.0	15.4	15.9	16.8	16.9	17.0	16.6
Hispanic	161.2	221.8	397.6	768.4	1,015.0	1,113.9	1,219.5	1,365.1	1,463.7	1,548.8	1,593.0	3.6	4.1	6.1	10.6	12.1	12.8	13.4	14.0	14.6	15.4	16.2
Asian/Pacific Islander	78.2	120.2	246.0	443.6	523.2	558.5	603.2	608.3	574.3	571.2	557.7	1.7	2.2	3.8	6.1	6.2	6.4	6.6	6.2	5.7	5.7	5.7
Asian	—	—	—	—	—	—	—	—	542.7	538.3	526.6	—	—	—	—	—	—	—	—	5.4	5.4	5.4
Pacific Islander	—	—	—	—	—	—	—	—	31.6	32.9	31.1	—	—	—	—	—	—	—	—	0.3	0.3	0.3
American Indian/Alaska Native	34.9	43.1	55.5	82.1	98.0	103.6	105.2	112.9	106.9	102.1	94.6	0.8	0.8	0.9	1.1	1.2	1.2	1.2	1.2	1.1	1.0	1.0
Two or more races	—	—	—	—	—	—	—	—	170.2	226.6	261.3	†	†	†	†	†	†	†	†	1.7	2.3	2.7
Nonresident alien	46.8	70.1	92.6	137.8	162.9	171.2	182.6	189.4	198.1	204.7	213.3											
Postbaccalaureate, total	**1,566.6**	**1,617.7**	**1,859.5**	**2,156.9**	**2,523.5**	**2,644.4**	**2,737.1**	**2,862.4**	**2,937.5**	**2,931.1**	**2,910.4**	**100.0**	**100.0**	**100.0**	**100.0**	**100.0**	**100.0**	**100.0**	**100.0**	**100.0**	**100.0**	**100.0**
White	1,335.6	1,352.4	1,449.8	1,478.6	1,666.8	1,709.7	1,749.6	1,815.5	1,824.9	1,782.6	1,733.8	89.6	88.8	86.0	77.2	74.0	72.6	71.8	71.0	69.4	68.2	67.3
Total, selected races/ethnicities	155.5	170.3	237.0	437.5	586.6	645.5	687.2	740.5	803.3	830.4	844.2	10.4	11.2	14.0	22.8	26.0	27.4	28.2	29.0	30.6	31.8	32.7
Black	78.4	87.9	99.8	171.9	212.5	229.1	242.5	262.2	286.6	297.1	309.7	6.0	5.8	5.9	9.5	11.5	12.3	12.9	13.4	13.8	14.1	14.3
Hispanic	30.9	38.6	57.9	110.8	148.4	160.3	169.4	184.2	197.9	205.0	213.4	2.1	2.5	3.4	5.8	6.6	6.8	7.0	7.2	7.5	7.8	8.3
Asian/Pacific Islander	28.6	37.7	72.0	132.7	163.0	175.8	184.9	195.4	194.3	197.4	196.0	1.9	2.5	4.3	6.9	7.2	7.5	7.6	7.6	7.4	7.6	7.6
Asian	—	—	—	—	—	—	—	—	187.8	190.8	189.1	—	—	—	—	—	—	—	—	7.1	7.3	7.3
Pacific Islander	—	—	—	—	—	—	—	—	6.5	6.6	6.9	—	—	—	—	—	—	—	—	0.2	0.3	0.3
American Indian/Alaska Native	6.4	6.0	7.3	12.6	15.9	18.7	17.7	18.5	17.1	16.1	15.4	0.4	0.4	0.4	0.7	0.7	0.8	0.7	0.7	0.7	0.6	0.6
Two or more races	—	—	—	—	—	—	—	—	31.8	42.7	50.1	†	†	†	†	†	†	†	†	1.2	1.6	1.9
Nonresident alien	75.5	95.1	172.7	240.7	270.1	289.1	300.3	306.4	309.3	318.1	332.4											
Male	897.6	870.7	904.2	943.5	1,047.1	1,088.3	1,122.3	1,174.0	1,209.6	1,209.5	1,205.2	100.0	100.0	100.0	100.0	100.0	100.0	100.0	100.0	100.0	100.0	100.0
White	761.6	718.1	676.6	624.5	676.8	690.2	704.3	734.2	744.9	730.9	713.1	90.7	89.8	86.3	78.4	76.1	75.1	74.4	73.7	72.2	71.1	70.1
Total, selected races/ethnicities	78.4	81.7	107.4	171.9	212.5	229.1	242.5	262.2	286.6	297.1	309.7	9.3	10.2	13.7	21.6	23.9	24.9	25.6	26.3	27.8	28.9	29.9
Black	39.2	35.5	36.7	58.3	76.6	84.0	90.5	98.8	106.2	108.5	109.7	4.7	4.4	4.7	7.3	8.6	9.1	9.6	9.9	10.3	10.6	10.8
Hispanic	18.1	20.4	27.0	44.5	56.1	59.6	62.7	69.0	74.7	77.9	81.3	2.2	2.5	3.4	5.6	6.3	6.5	6.6	6.9	7.2	7.6	8.0
Asian/Pacific Islander	17.4	22.8	40.4	64.0	73.9	78.9	82.7	87.5	87.2	88.6	88.3	2.1	2.8	5.2	8.0	8.3	8.6	8.7	8.8	8.5	8.6	8.7
Asian	—	—	—	—	—	—	—	—	84.7	86.0	85.4	—	—	—	—	—	—	—	—	8.2	8.4	8.4
Pacific Islander	—	—	—	—	—	—	—	—	2.5	2.6	2.8	—	—	—	—	—	—	—	—	0.2	0.3	0.3
American Indian/Alaska Native	3.7	3.0	3.2	5.0	5.9	6.6	6.5	6.9	6.4	5.9	5.7	0.4	0.4	0.4	0.6	0.7	0.7	0.7	0.7	0.6	0.6	0.6
Two or more races	—	—	—	—	—	—	—	—	12.0	16.2	19.6	†	†	†	†	†	†	†	†	1.2	1.6	1.9
Nonresident alien	57.7	71.0	120.2	147.1	157.7	169.1	175.5	177.7	178.1	181.5	187.5											

See notes at end of table.

Total fall enrollment in degree-granting postsecondary institutions, by level of enrollment, sex, attendance status, and race/ethnicity of student: Selected years, 1976 through 2012—Continued

Level of enrollment, sex, attendance status, and race/ethnicity of student	Fall enrollment (in thousands)											Percentage distribution of U.S. residents										
	1976	1980	1990	2000	2005	2007	2008	2009	2010	2011	2012	1976	1980	1990	2000	2005	2007	2008	2009	2010	2011	2012
1	2	3	4	5	6	7	8	9	10	11	12	13	14	15	16	17	18	19	20	21	22	23
Female	669.1	747.0	955.4	1,213.4	1,476.5	1,556.0	1,614.8	1,688.4	1,727.8	1,721.6	1,705.2	100.0	100.0	100.0	100.0	100.0	100.0	100.0	100.0	100.0	100.0	100.0
White	574.1	634.3	773.2	854.1	990.0	1,019.5	1,045.3	1,081.4	1,080.0	1,051.7	1,020.6	88.1	87.7	85.6	76.3	72.6	71.0	70.2	69.3	67.6	66.4	65.4
Total, selected races/ethnicities	77.2	88.6	129.6	265.7	374.0	416.5	444.8	478.3	516.7	533.3	539.7	11.9	12.3	14.4	23.7	27.4	29.0	29.8	30.7	32.4	33.6	34.6
Black	50.5	52.4	63.1	123.1	182.6	206.8	224.7	243.6	256.0	260.6	259.6	7.7	7.2	7.0	11.0	13.4	14.4	15.1	15.6	16.0	16.4	16.6
Hispanic	12.8	18.3	30.9	66.3	92.3	100.7	106.7	115.2	123.2	127.1	132.1	2.0	2.5	3.4	5.9	6.8	7.0	7.2	7.4	7.7	8.0	8.5
Asian/Pacific Islander	11.2	15.0	31.5	68.7	89.1	97.0	102.2	107.9	107.1	108.9	107.8	1.7	2.1	3.5	6.1	6.5	6.8	6.9	6.9	6.7	6.9	6.9
Asian	—	—	—	—	—	—	—	—	103.1	104.8	103.7	—	—	—	—	—	—	—	—	6.5	6.6	6.6
Pacific Islander	—	—	—	—	—	—	—	—	3.9	4.0	4.1	—	—	—	—	—	—	—	—	0.2	0.3	0.3
American Indian/Alaska Native	2.7	3.0	4.1	7.6	10.0	12.1	11.2	11.6	10.7	10.3	9.8	0.4	0.4	0.5	0.7	0.7	0.8	0.8	0.7	0.7	0.6	0.6
Two or more races	—	—	—	—	—	—	—	—	19.7	26.5	30.5	—	—	—	—	—	—	—	—	1.2	1.7	2.0
Nonresident alien	17.8	24.1	52.5	93.6	112.4	120.1	124.8	128.7	131.1	136.6	144.9	†	†	†	†	†	†	†	†	†	†	†

—Not available.
†Not applicable.
NOTE: Race categories exclude persons of Hispanic ethnicity. Because of underreporting and nonreporting of racial/ethnic data, some figures are slightly lower than corresponding data in other tables. Data through 1990 are for institutions of higher education, while later data are for degree-granting institutions. Degree-granting institutions grant associate's or higher degrees and participate in Title IV federal financial aid programs. The degree-granting classification is very similar to the ear-lier higher education classification, but it includes more 2-year colleges and excludes a few higher education institutions that did not grant degrees. Detail may not sum to totals because of rounding.
SOURCE: U.S. Department of Education, National Center for Education Statistics, Higher Education General Information Survey (HEGIS), "Fall Enrollment in Colleges and Universities" surveys, 1976 and 1980; Integrated Postsecondary Education Data System (IPEDS), "Fall Enrollment Survey" (IPEDS-EF:90); and IPEDS Spring 2001 through Spring 2013, Enrollment component. (This table was prepared November 2013.)

Total fall enrollment in degree-granting postsecondary institutions, by level and control of institution and race/ethnicity of student: Selected years, 1976 through 2012

Level and control of institution and race/ethnicity of student	Fall enrollment (in thousands)											Percentage distribution of U.S. residents										
	1976	1980	1990	2000	2005	2007	2008	2009	2010	2011	2012	1976	1980	1990	2000	2005	2007	2008	2009	2010	2011	2012
1	2	3	4	5	6	7	8	9	10	11	12	13	14	15	16	17	18	19	20	21	22	23
All students, total	10,985.6	12,086.8	13,818.6	15,312.3	17,487.5	18,248.1	19,102.8	20,427.7	21,016.1	20,994.1	20,642.8	100.0	100.0	100.0	100.0	100.0	100.0	100.0	100.0	100.0	100.0	100.0
White	9,076.1	9,833.0	10,722.5	10,462.1	11,495.4	11,756.2	12,088.8	12,730.8	12,722.5	12,394.2	11,981.1	84.3	83.5	79.9	70.8	68.0	66.7	65.5	64.5	62.7	61.2	60.3
Total, selected races/ethnicities	1,690.8	1,948.8	2,704.7	4,321.5	5,407.2	5,867.4	6,353.5	7,012.1	7,584.0	7,859.5	7,878.8	15.7	16.5	20.1	29.2	32.0	33.3	34.5	35.5	37.3	38.8	39.7
Black	1,033.0	1,106.8	1,247.0	1,730.3	2,214.6	2,383.4	2,584.5	2,919.8	3,038.8	3,067.9	2,962.1	9.6	9.4	9.3	11.7	13.1	13.5	14.0	14.8	15.0	15.1	14.9
Hispanic	383.8	471.7	782.4	1,461.8	1,882.0	2,076.2	2,272.9	2,546.7	2,741.4	2,890.1	2,979.4	3.6	4.0	5.8	9.9	11.1	11.8	12.3	12.9	13.5	14.3	15.0
Asian/Pacific Islander	197.9	286.4	572.4	978.2	1,134.4	1,217.9	1,302.8	1,337.7	—	—	—	1.8	2.4	4.3	6.6	6.7	6.9	7.1	6.8	—	—	—
Asian	—	—	—	—	—	—	—	—	1,218.1	1,216.6	1,195.6	—	—	—	—	—	—	—	—	6.0	6.0	6.0
Pacific Islander	—	—	—	—	—	—	—	—	64.0	65.9	63.6	—	—	—	—	—	—	—	—	0.3	0.3	0.3
American Indian/Alaska Native	76.1	83.9	102.8	151.2	176.3	190.0	193.3	207.9	196.4	186.1	172.9	0.7	0.7	0.8	1.0	1.0	1.1	1.0	1.1	1.0	0.9	0.9
Two or more races	—	—	—	—	—	—	—	—	325.3	432.9	505.1	—	—	—	—	—	—	—	—	1.6	2.1	2.5
Nonresident alien	218.7	305.0	391.5	528.7	584.8	624.5	660.6	684.8	709.6	740.5	782.9	†	†	†	†	†	†	†	†	†	†	†
Public	8,641.0	9,456.4	10,844.7	11,752.8	13,021.8	13,490.8	13,972.2	14,810.6	15,142.8	15,110.2	14,880.3	100.0	100.0	100.0	100.0	100.0	100.0	100.0	100.0	100.0	100.0	100.0
White	7,094.5	7,656.1	8,385.4	7,963.4	8,518.2	8,640.3	8,817.7	9,234.6	9,187.1	8,935.1	8,634.3	83.5	82.7	79.2	69.8	67.3	66.0	65.1	64.3	62.5	61.0	60.0
Total, selected races/ethnicities	1,401.2	1,596.2	2,199.2	3,446.3	4,130.8	4,448.8	4,727.5	5,135.2	5,501.4	5,703.4	5,747.5	16.5	17.3	20.8	30.2	32.7	34.0	34.9	35.7	37.5	39.0	40.0
Black	831.2	876.1	976.4	1,319.2	1,580.4	1,667.6	1,759.2	1,937.2	1,988.6	2,013.3	1,937.0	9.8	9.5	9.2	11.6	12.5	12.7	13.0	13.5	13.5	13.8	13.5
Hispanic	336.8	406.2	671.4	1,229.3	1,525.6	1,685.4	1,832.4	2,017.7	2,157.4	2,275.8	2,365.9	4.0	4.4	6.3	10.8	12.1	12.9	13.5	14.0	14.7	15.5	16.5
Asian/Pacific Islander	165.7	239.7	461.0	770.5	881.9	942.5	982.9	1,018.5	—	—	—	2.0	2.6	4.4	6.8	7.0	7.2	7.3	7.1	—	—	—
Asian	—	—	—	—	—	—	—	—	925.5	915.3	901.1	—	—	—	—	—	—	—	—	6.3	6.3	6.3
Pacific Islander	—	—	—	—	—	—	—	—	44.0	43.0	41.4	—	—	—	—	—	—	—	—	0.3	0.3	0.3
American Indian/Alaska Native	67.5	74.2	90.4	127.3	143.0	153.3	153.0	161.8	151.0	142.4	131.7	0.8	0.8	0.9	1.0	1.1	1.1	1.1	1.1	1.0	1.0	0.9
Two or more races	—	—	—	—	—	—	—	—	234.9	313.5	370.4	—	—	—	—	—	—	—	—	1.6	2.1	2.6
Nonresident alien	145.3	204.2	260.0	343.1	372.8	401.7	427.0	440.8	454.3	471.7	498.6	†	†	†	†	†	†	†	†	†	†	†
Private	2,344.6	2,630.4	2,973.9	3,559.5	4,465.6	4,757.3	5,130.7	5,617.1	5,873.3	5,883.9	5,762.5	100.0	100.0	100.0	100.0	100.0	100.0	100.0	100.0	100.0	100.0	100.0
White	1,981.6	2,176.9	2,337.0	2,498.7	2,977.3	3,116.0	3,271.1	3,496.2	3,535.4	3,459.1	3,346.9	87.3	86.1	82.2	74.1	70.0	68.7	66.8	65.1	62.9	61.6	61.1
Total, selected races/ethnicities	289.6	352.7	505.5	875.2	1,276.4	1,418.6	1,625.9	1,876.9	2,082.6	2,156.1	2,131.3	12.7	13.9	17.8	25.9	30.0	31.3	33.2	34.9	37.1	38.4	38.9
Black	201.8	230.7	270.6	411.1	634.2	715.7	825.3	982.7	1,050.1	1,054.6	1,025.1	8.9	9.1	9.5	12.2	14.9	15.8	16.9	18.3	18.7	18.8	18.7
Hispanic	47.0	65.6	111.0	232.5	356.4	390.7	440.5	529.0	584.1	614.3	613.6	2.1	2.6	3.9	6.9	8.4	8.6	9.0	9.8	10.4	10.9	11.2
Asian/Pacific Islander	32.2	46.7	111.5	207.7	252.4	275.4	319.9	319.1	—	—	—	1.4	1.8	3.9	6.2	5.9	6.1	6.5	5.9	—	—	—
Asian	—	—	—	—	—	—	—	—	292.6	301.2	294.5	—	—	—	—	—	—	—	—	5.6	5.8	5.8
Pacific Islander	—	—	—	—	—	—	—	—	20.0	22.9	22.2	—	—	—	—	—	—	—	—	0.4	0.4	0.4
American Indian/Alaska Native	8.6	9.7	12.4	23.9	33.3	36.7	40.3	46.1	45.4	43.6	41.2	0.4	0.4	0.4	0.7	0.8	0.8	0.8	0.9	0.8	0.8	0.8
Two or more races	—	—	—	—	—	—	—	—	90.4	119.3	134.7	—	—	—	—	—	—	—	—	1.6	2.1	2.5
Nonresident alien	73.4	100.8	131.4	185.6	212.0	222.8	233.6	244.0	255.3	268.7	284.3	†	†	†	†	†	†	†	†	†	†	†
4-year, total	7,106.5	7,565.4	8,578.6	9,363.9	10,999.4	11,630.2	12,131.4	12,906.3	13,335.3	13,494.1	13,478.8	100.0	100.0	100.0	100.0	100.0	100.0	100.0	100.0	100.0	100.0	100.0
White	5,999.0	6,274.5	6,768.1	6,658.0	7,496.9	7,781.0	7,987.1	8,357.4	8,398.2	8,307.0	8,144.2	86.6	85.7	82.0	74.6	71.4	70.1	69.0	67.8	66.0	64.6	63.7
Total, selected races/ethnicities	931.0	1,049.9	1,486.1	2,266.1	3,009.5	3,320.5	3,588.4	3,964.4	4,328.2	4,542.6	4,645.4	13.4	14.3	18.0	25.4	28.6	29.9	31.0	32.2	34.0	35.4	36.3
Black	603.7	634.3	722.8	995.4	1,313.4	1,441.7	1,565.0	1,767.0	1,841.0	1,870.9	1,845.4	8.7	8.7	8.8	11.2	12.5	13.0	13.5	14.3	14.5	14.6	14.4
Hispanic	173.6	216.6	358.2	617.9	900.5	1,008.7	1,092.2	1,237.7	1,355.1	1,453.5	1,533.3	2.5	3.0	4.3	6.9	8.6	9.1	9.4	10.0	10.6	11.3	12.0
Asian/Pacific Islander	118.7	162.1	357.2	576.3	700.0	761.5	823.4	842.0	—	—	—	1.7	2.2	4.3	6.5	6.7	6.9	7.1	6.8	—	—	—
Asian	—	—	—	—	—	—	—	—	818.4	837.8	835.4	—	—	—	—	—	—	—	—	6.1	6.2	6.2
Pacific Islander	—	—	—	—	—	—	—	—	35.9	38.6	38.8	—	—	—	—	—	—	—	—	0.3	0.3	0.3
American Indian/Alaska Native	35.0	36.9	47.9	76.5	95.6	108.6	107.8	117.7	109.0	105.1	93.0	0.5	0.5	0.6	0.9	0.9	1.0	0.9	1.0	0.9	0.8	0.8
Two or more races	—	—	—	—	—	—	—	—	204.8	275.3	333.0	—	—	—	—	—	—	—	—	1.6	2.1	2.6
Nonresident alien	176.5	240.9	324.3	439.7	493.1	528.7	555.9	584.6	608.9	644.6	689.2	†	†	†	†	†	†	†	†	†	†	†
Public	4,892.9	5,127.6	5,848.2	6,055.4	6,837.6	7,166.7	7,331.8	7,709.2	7,924.8	8,047.7	8,092.7	100.0	100.0	100.0	100.0	100.0	100.0	100.0	100.0	100.0	100.0	100.0
White	4,120.2	4,243.0	4,605.6	4,311.2	4,678.1	4,813.6	4,879.2	5,057.8	5,070.4	5,027.7	4,952.2	86.1	85.1	81.5	74.4	71.4	70.2	69.6	68.7	67.0	65.6	64.4
Total, selected races/ethnicities	666.7	740.8	1,046.2	1,486.4	1,876.9	2,045.3	2,128.2	2,307.6	2,496.6	2,640.8	2,733.1	13.9	14.9	18.5	25.6	28.6	29.8	30.4	31.3	33.0	34.4	35.6
Black	421.8	438.2	495.1	627.8	754.0	801.7	827.3	896.7	912.6	931.9	922.6	8.8	8.8	8.8	10.8	11.5	11.7	11.8	12.1	12.1	12.2	12.0
Hispanic	129.3	156.4	262.5	420.0	595.6	668.6	709.9	794.1	869.2	945.7	1,007.8	2.7	3.1	4.6	7.2	9.1	9.7	10.1	10.8	11.5	12.3	13.1
Asian/Pacific Islander	87.5	117.2	250.6	381.3	460.1	498.5	518.3	540.1	—	—	—	1.8	2.4	4.4	6.6	7.0	7.3	7.4	7.3	—	—	—
Asian	—	—	—	—	—	—	—	—	522.8	531.5	535.1	—	—	—	—	—	—	—	—	6.9	6.9	7.0
Pacific Islander	—	—	—	—	—	—	—	—	18.1	19.0	19.0	—	—	—	—	—	—	—	—	0.2	0.2	0.2
American Indian/Alaska Native	28.2	29.0	38.0	57.2	67.2	76.5	72.6	76.7	69.5	66.1	61.3	0.6	0.6	0.7	1.0	1.0	1.1	1.0	1.0	0.9	0.9	0.8
Two or more races	—	—	—	—	—	—	—	—	122.4	165.6	206.3	—	—	—	—	—	—	—	—	1.6	2.2	2.7
Nonresident alien	106.0	143.8	196.4	257.8	282.6	307.8	324.4	343.7	357.8	379.2	407.3	†	†	†	†	†	†	†	†	†	†	†

See notes at end of table.

Total fall enrollment in degree-granting postsecondary institutions, by level and control of institution and race/ethnicity of student: Selected years, 1976 through 2012—Continued

Level and control of institution and race/ethnicity of student	Fall enrollment (in thousands)											Percentage distribution of U.S. residents										
	1976	1980	1990	2000	2005	2007	2008	2009	2010	2011	2012	1976	1980	1990	2000	2005	2007	2008	2009	2010	2011	2012
1	2	3	4	5	6	7	8	9	10	11	12	13	14	15	16	17	18	19	20	21	22	23
Private	2,213.6	2,437.8	2,730.3	3,308.5	4,161.8	4,463.5	4,799.6	5,197.1	5,410.5	5,446.4	5,386.2	100.0	100.0	100.0	100.0	100.0	100.0	100.0	100.0	100.0	100.0	100.0
White	1,878.8	2,031.5	2,162.5	2,346.9	2,818.8	2,967.5	3,107.9	3,299.5	3,327.7	3,279.3	3,191.9	87.7	86.8	83.1	75.1	71.3	69.9	68.0	66.6	64.5	63.3	62.5
Total, selected races/ethnicities	264.3	309.2	439.8	779.7	1,132.5	1,275.3	1,460.2	1,656.7	1,831.6	1,901.8	1,912.3	12.3	13.2	16.9	24.9	28.7	30.1	32.0	33.4	35.5	36.7	37.5
Black	182.0	196.1	227.7	367.6	559.4	640.0	737.6	870.3	928.4	939.0	923.1	8.5	8.4	8.7	11.8	14.2	15.1	16.1	17.6	18.0	18.1	18.1
Hispanic	44.3	60.2	95.7	197.9	304.9	340.1	382.3	443.6	485.9	507.8	525.5	2.1	2.6	3.7	6.3	7.7	8.0	8.4	9.0	9.4	9.8	10.3
Asian/Pacific Islander	31.2	44.9	106.6	195.0	239.8	263.1	305.1	301.8	295.5	306.3	300.3	1.5	1.9	4.1	6.2	6.1	6.2	6.7	6.1	5.7	5.9	5.9
Asian	—	—	—	—	—	—	—	—	277.7	286.6	280.6	—	—	—	—	—	—	—	—	5.4	5.5	5.5
Pacific Islander	—	—	—	—	—	—	—	—	17.8	19.7	19.8	—	—	—	—	—	—	—	—	0.3	0.4	0.4
American Indian/Alaska Native	6.8	7.9	9.9	19.3	28.4	32.1	35.2	41.0	39.5	39.0	36.7	0.3	0.3	0.4	0.6	0.7	0.8	0.8	0.8	0.8	0.8	0.7
Two or more races	—	—	—	—	—	—	—	—	82.4	109.7	126.7	—	—	—	—	—	—	—	—	1.6	2.1	2.5
Nonresident alien	70.5	97.1	127.9	181.9	210.4	220.8	231.5	240.8	251.2	265.4	281.9	†	†	†	†	†	†	†	†	†	†	†
2-year, total	3,879.1	4,521.4	5,240.1	5,948.4	6,488.1	6,617.9	6,971.4	7,521.4	7,680.9	7,500.0	7,164.0	100.0	100.0	100.0	100.0	100.0	100.0	100.0	100.0	100.0	100.0	100.0
White	3,077.1	3,558.5	3,954.3	3,804.1	3,998.6	3,975.2	4,101.6	4,373.4	4,324.4	4,087.2	3,837.0	80.2	79.8	76.4	64.9	62.5	60.9	59.7	58.9	57.0	55.2	54.3
Total, selected races/ethnicities	759.8	898.9	1,218.6	2,055.4	2,397.7	2,546.9	2,765.0	3,047.8	3,255.9	3,316.9	3,233.3	19.8	20.2	23.6	35.1	37.5	39.1	40.3	41.1	43.0	44.8	45.7
Black	429.3	472.5	524.3	734.9	901.1	941.7	1,019.5	1,152.8	1,197.7	1,197.1	1,116.4	11.2	10.6	10.1	12.5	14.1	14.4	14.8	15.5	15.8	16.2	15.8
Hispanic	210.2	255.1	424.2	843.9	981.5	1,067.4	1,180.7	1,309.0	1,386.4	1,436.6	1,446.1	5.5	5.7	8.2	14.4	15.3	16.4	17.2	17.6	18.3	19.4	20.5
Asian/Pacific Islander	79.2	124.3	215.2	401.9	434.4	456.4	479.4	495.7	463.8	444.7	423.7	2.1	2.8	4.2	6.9	6.8	7.0	7.0	6.7	6.1	6.0	6.0
Asian	—	—	—	—	—	—	—	—	435.7	417.4	398.9	—	—	—	—	—	—	—	—	5.7	5.6	5.6
Pacific Islander	—	—	—	—	—	—	—	—	28.1	27.3	24.8	—	—	—	—	—	—	—	—	0.4	0.4	0.4
American Indian/Alaska Native	41.2	47.0	54.9	74.7	80.7	81.4	85.5	90.3	87.4	81.0	74.9	1.1	1.1	1.1	1.3	1.3	1.2	1.2	1.2	1.2	1.1	1.1
Two or more races	—	—	—	—	—	—	—	—	120.5	157.6	172.1	—	—	—	—	—	—	—	—	1.6	2.1	2.4
Nonresident alien	42.2	64.1	67.1	89.0	91.8	95.8	104.7	100.2	100.6	95.9	93.6	†	†	†	†	†	†	†	†	†	†	†
Public	3,748.1	4,328.8	4,996.5	5,697.4	6,184.2	6,324.1	6,640.3	7,101.4	7,218.0	7,062.5	6,787.7	100.0	100.0	100.0	100.0	100.0	100.0	100.0	100.0	100.0	100.0	100.0
White	2,974.3	3,413.1	3,779.8	3,652.2	3,840.1	3,826.7	3,938.5	4,176.8	4,116.7	3,907.4	3,682.0	80.2	80.0	76.6	65.1	63.0	61.4	60.2	59.6	57.8	56.1	55.0
Total, selected races/ethnicities	734.5	855.4	1,153.0	1,959.9	2,253.9	2,403.6	2,599.3	2,827.6	3,004.8	3,062.6	3,014.4	19.8	20.0	23.4	34.9	37.0	38.6	39.8	40.4	42.2	43.9	45.0
Black	409.5	437.9	481.4	691.4	826.3	865.9	931.9	1,040.4	1,076.0	1,081.4	1,014.4	11.0	10.3	9.8	12.3	13.6	13.9	14.3	14.9	15.1	15.5	15.1
Hispanic	207.5	249.8	408.9	809.2	930.0	1,016.8	1,122.5	1,223.6	1,288.2	1,330.1	1,358.1	5.6	5.9	8.3	14.4	15.3	16.3	17.2	17.5	18.1	19.1	20.3
Asian/Pacific Islander	78.2	122.5	210.3	389.2	421.8	444.1	464.5	478.4	446.7	426.8	407.4	2.1	2.9	4.3	6.9	6.9	7.1	7.1	6.8	6.3	6.1	6.1
Asian	—	—	—	—	—	—	—	—	420.8	402.8	385.0	—	—	—	—	—	—	—	—	5.9	5.8	5.7
Pacific Islander	—	—	—	—	—	—	—	—	25.9	24.0	22.4	—	—	—	—	—	—	—	—	0.4	0.3	0.3
American Indian/Alaska Native	39.3	45.2	52.4	70.1	75.7	76.8	80.4	85.1	81.5	76.3	70.4	1.1	1.1	1.1	1.2	1.2	1.2	1.2	1.2	1.1	1.1	1.1
Two or more races	—	—	—	—	—	—	—	—	112.5	147.9	164.1	—	—	—	—	—	—	—	—	1.6	2.1	2.4
Nonresident alien	39.2	60.3	63.6	85.2	90.2	93.9	102.6	97.1	96.5	92.5	91.2	†	†	†	†	†	†	†	†	†	†	†
Private	131.0	192.6	243.6	251.0	303.8	293.8	331.0	420.0	462.8	437.5	376.3	100.0	100.0	100.0	100.0	100.0	100.0	100.0	100.0	100.0	100.0	100.0
White	102.8	145.4	174.5	151.8	158.4	148.5	163.2	196.6	207.7	179.8	154.9	80.3	77.0	72.7	61.4	52.4	50.9	49.6	47.2	45.3	41.4	41.4
Total, selected races/ethnicities	25.3	43.5	65.6	95.5	143.8	143.3	165.7	220.2	251.0	254.3	219.0	19.7	23.0	27.3	38.6	47.6	49.1	50.4	52.8	54.7	58.6	58.6
Black	19.8	34.6	42.9	43.5	74.8	75.7	87.7	112.4	121.8	115.6	102.1	15.5	18.3	17.9	17.6	24.7	26.0	26.7	27.0	26.5	26.6	27.3
Hispanic	2.6	5.3	15.3	34.7	51.4	50.6	58.2	85.4	98.2	106.5	88.0	2.1	2.8	6.4	14.0	17.0	17.3	17.7	20.5	21.4	24.5	23.5
Asian/Pacific Islander	0.9	1.8	4.9	12.7	12.6	12.3	14.8	17.3	17.1	17.9	16.3	0.7	1.0	2.0	5.1	4.2	4.2	4.5	4.2	3.7	4.1	4.4
Asian	—	—	—	—	—	—	—	—	14.9	14.6	13.9	—	—	—	—	—	—	—	—	3.3	3.4	3.7
Pacific Islander	—	—	—	—	—	—	—	—	2.2	3.3	2.4	—	—	—	—	—	—	—	—	0.5	0.8	0.6
American Indian/Alaska Native	1.8	1.8	2.5	4.5	5.0	4.6	5.0	5.1	5.9	4.7	4.5	1.4	1.0	1.1	1.8	1.6	1.6	1.5	1.2	1.3	1.1	1.2
Two or more races	—	—	—	—	—	—	—	—	8.0	9.6	8.0	—	—	—	—	—	—	—	—	1.8	2.2	2.1
Nonresident alien	3.0	3.7	3.5	3.8	1.6	2.0	2.1	3.2	4.1	3.4	2.4	†	†	†	†	†	†	†	†	†	†	†

—Not available.
†Not applicable.
NOTE: Race categories exclude persons of Hispanic ethnicity. Because of underreporting and nonreporting of racial/ethnic data, some figures are slightly lower than corresponding data in other tables. Data through 1990 are for institutions of higher education, while later data are for degree-granting institutions. Degree-granting institutions grant associate's or higher degrees and participate in Title IV federal financial aid programs. The degree-granting classification is very similar to the earlier higher education classification, but it includes more 2-year colleges and excludes a few higher education institutions that did not grant degrees. Detail may not sum to totals because of rounding.
SOURCE: U.S. Department of Education, National Center for Education Statistics, Higher Education General Information Survey (HEGIS), "Fall Enrollment in Colleges and Universities" surveys, 1976 and 1980; Integrated Postsecondary Education Data System (IPEDS), "Fall Enrollment Survey" (IPEDS-EF:90); and IPEDS Spring 2001 through Spring 2013, Enrollment component. (This table was prepared November 2013.)

Total fall enrollment in degree-granting postsecondary institutions, by control and level of institution, level of enrollment, and race/ethnicity of student: 2012—Continued

Level of enrollment and race/ethnicity of student	Total, all institutions	Public institutions									Nonprofit institutions									For-profit institutions		
		Total	4-year							2-year	Total	4-year							2-year	Total	4-year	2-year
			Total	Research university, very high[1]	Research university, high[2]	Doctoral/research university[3]	Master's[4]	Bacca-laureate[5]	Special focus[6]			Total	Research university, very high[1]	Research university, high[1]	Doctoral/research university[3]	Master's[4]	Bacca-laureate[5]	Special focus[6]				
1	2	3	4	5	6	7	8	9	10	11	12	13	14	15	16	17	18	19	20	21	22	23
Postbaccalaureate	100.0	100.0	100.0	100.0	100.0	100.0	100.0	100.0	100.0	†	100.0	100.0	100.0	100.0	100.0	100.0	100.0	100.0	†	100.0	100.0	†
White	67.3	71.0	71.0	74.1	74.0	62.8	67.6	72.3	62.9	†	68.3	68.3	66.5	65.7	64.7	70.0	75.8	68.3	†	47.7	47.7	†
Black	14.3	10.6	10.6	6.8	9.2	22.8	14.5	13.3	9.2	†	12.6	12.6	7.3	14.3	13.9	15.4	13.4	10.2	†	36.3	36.3	†
Hispanic	8.3	8.6	8.6	7.4	8.8	8.9	10.3	5.9	8.1	†	7.9	7.9	8.0	9.9	10.9	7.5	5.1	6.1	†	8.3	8.3	†
Asian	7.3	7.0	7.0	8.8	5.2	3.4	5.1	5.0	17.2	†	8.5	8.5	14.9	7.5	7.9	4.8	3.4	12.2	†	4.3	4.3	†
Pacific Islander	0.3	0.2	0.2	0.2	0.2	0.1	0.2	0.6	0.1	†	0.3	0.3	0.2	0.3	0.3	0.3	0.2	0.4	†	0.6	0.6	†
American Indian/Alaska Native	0.6	0.6	0.6	0.6	0.7	0.5	0.7	0.7	0.6	†	0.5	0.5	0.3	0.5	0.5	0.5	0.7	0.5	†	0.9	0.9	†
Two or more races	1.9	1.9	1.9	2.2	1.9	1.6	1.7	2.3	1.8	†	2.0	2.0	2.7	2.0	1.9	1.5	1.3	2.4	†	1.9	1.9	†

†Not applicable.

[1]Research universities with a very high level of research activity.

[2]Research universities with a high level of research activity.

[3]Institutions that award at least 20 doctor's degrees per year, but did not have high levels of research activity.

[4]Institutions that award at least 50 master's degrees per year.

[5]Institutions that primarily emphasize undergraduate education. Also includes institutions classified as 4-year under the IPEDS system, which had been classified as 2-year in the Carnegie system because they primarily award associate's degrees.

[6]Four-year institutions that award degrees primarily in single fields of study, such as medicine, business, fine arts, theology, and engineering.

NOTE: Relative levels of research activity for research universities were determined by an analysis of research and development expenditures, science and engineering research staffing, and doctoral degrees conferred, by field. Further information on the research index ranking may be obtained from http://classifications.carnegiefoundation.org/resources/. Degree-granting institutions grant associate's or higher degrees and participate in Title IV federal financial aid programs. Race categories exclude persons of Hispanic ethnicity.

SOURCE: U.S. Department of Education, National Center for Education Statistics, Integrated Postsecondary Education Data System (IPEDS), Spring 2013, Enrollment component. (This table was prepared November 2013.)

Employees in degree-granting postsecondary institutions, by sex, employment status, control and level of institution, and primary occupation: Selected years, fall 1991 through fall 2011

Sex, employment status, control and level of institution, and primary occupation	1991	1993	1995	1997	1999	2001	2003	2005	2007	2009	2011	Percent change, 2001 to 2011
1	2	3	4	5	6	7	8	9	10	11	12	13
All institutions	2,545,235	2,602,612	2,662,075	2,752,504	2,883,175	3,083,353	3,187,907	3,379,087	3,561,428	3,723,419	3,840,980	24.6
Professional staff	1,595,460	1,687,287	1,744,867	1,835,916	1,950,861	2,132,150	2,268,268	2,459,885	2,629,401	2,782,149	2,923,961	37.1
Executive/administrative/managerial	144,755	143,675	147,445	151,363	159,888	152,038	184,913	196,324	217,518	230,579	238,718	57.0
Faculty (instruction/research/public service)	826,252	915,474	931,706	989,813	1,027,830	1,113,183	1,173,593	1,290,426	1,371,390	1,439,144	1,523,615	36.9
Graduate assistants	197,751	202,819	215,909	222,724	239,738	261,136	292,061	317,141	328,979	342,393	355,916	36.3
Other professional	426,702	425,319	449,807	472,016	523,405	605,793	617,701	655,994	711,514	770,033	805,712	33.0
Nonprofessional staff	949,775	915,325	917,208	916,588	932,314	951,203	919,639	919,202	932,027	941,270	917,019	-3.6
Males	1,227,591	1,256,037	1,274,676	1,315,311	1,365,812	1,451,773	1,496,867	1,581,498	1,650,350	1,709,636	1,754,713	20.9
Professional staff	895,591	930,933	946,134	982,870	1,026,882	1,105,053	1,160,417	1,240,030	1,302,131	1,353,915	1,402,698	26.9
Executive/administrative/managerial	85,423	82,748	82,127	81,931	83,883	79,348	91,604	95,223	102,258	106,892	109,374	37.8
Faculty (instruction/research/public service)	525,599	561,123	562,893	587,420	602,469	644,514	663,723	714,453	743,812	761,035	789,197	22.4
Graduate assistants	119,125	120,384	123,962	125,873	132,607	142,120	156,881	167,529	173,121	180,941	188,468	32.6
Other professional	165,444	166,678	177,152	187,646	207,923	239,071	248,209	262,825	282,940	305,047	315,659	32.0
Nonprofessional staff	332,000	325,104	328,542	332,441	338,930	346,720	336,450	341,468	348,219	355,721	352,015	1.5
Females	1,317,644	1,346,575	1,387,399	1,437,193	1,517,363	1,631,580	1,691,040	1,797,589	1,911,078	2,013,783	2,086,267	27.9
Professional staff	699,869	756,354	798,733	853,046	923,979	1,027,097	1,107,851	1,219,855	1,327,270	1,428,234	1,521,263	48.1
Executive/administrative/managerial	59,332	60,927	65,318	69,432	76,005	72,690	93,309	101,101	115,260	123,687	129,344	77.9
Faculty (instruction/research/public service)	300,653	354,351	368,813	402,393	425,361	468,669	509,870	575,973	627,578	678,109	734,418	56.7
Graduate assistants	78,626	82,435	91,947	96,851	107,131	119,016	135,180	149,612	155,858	161,452	167,448	40.7
Other professional	261,258	258,641	272,655	284,370	315,482	366,722	369,492	393,169	428,574	464,986	490,053	33.6
Nonprofessional staff	617,775	590,221	588,666	584,147	593,384	604,483	583,189	577,734	583,808	585,549	565,004	-6.5
Full-time	1,812,912	1,783,510	1,801,371	1,828,507	1,918,676	2,043,208	2,083,142	2,179,864	2,281,223	2,381,702	2,435,533	19.2
Professional staff	1,031,797	1,039,094	1,066,510	1,104,834	1,180,173	1,283,684	1,337,568	1,432,107	1,526,823	1,619,517	1,693,088	31.9
Executive/administrative/managerial	139,116	137,834	140,990	144,529	153,722	146,523	178,691	190,078	210,257	222,282	231,602	58.1
Faculty (instruction/research/public service)	535,623	545,706	550,822	568,719	590,937	617,868	630,092	675,624	703,463	728,977	761,619	23.3
Other professional	357,058	355,554	374,698	391,586	435,514	519,293	528,785	566,405	613,103	668,258	699,867	34.8
Nonprofessional staff	781,115	744,416	734,861	723,673	738,503	759,524	745,574	747,757	754,400	762,185	742,445	-2.2
Part-time	732,323	819,102	860,704	923,997	964,499	1,040,145	1,104,765	1,199,223	1,280,205	1,341,717	1,405,447	35.1
Professional staff	563,663	648,193	678,357	731,082	770,688	848,466	930,700	1,027,778	1,102,578	1,162,632	1,230,873	45.1
Executive/administrative/managerial	5,639	5,841	6,455	6,834	6,166	5,515	6,222	6,246	7,261	8,297	7,116	29.0
Faculty (instruction/research/public service)	290,629	369,768	380,884	421,094	436,893	495,315	543,501	614,802	667,927	710,167	761,996	53.8
Graduate assistants	197,751	202,819	215,909	222,724	239,738	261,136	292,061	317,141	328,979	342,393	355,916	36.3
Other professional	69,644	69,765	75,109	80,430	87,891	86,500	88,916	89,589	98,411	101,775	105,845	22.4
Nonprofessional staff	168,660	170,909	182,347	192,915	193,811	191,679	174,065	171,445	177,627	179,085	174,574	-8.9
Public 4-year	1,341,914	1,333,533	1,383,476	1,418,661	1,470,842	1,558,576	1,569,870	1,656,709	1,741,699	1,803,724	1,843,204	18.3
Professional staff	826,633	855,913	893,345	932,972	987,622	1,069,161	1,115,312	1,200,168	1,278,894	1,336,958	1,390,625	30.1
Executive/administrative/managerial	63,674	59,678	60,590	61,984	64,336	60,245	70,397	74,241	81,364	84,355	84,911	40.9
Faculty (instruction/research/public service)	358,376	374,021	384,399	404,109	417,086	438,459	450,123	486,691	518,221	539,901	575,534	31.3
Graduate assistants	144,344	170,916	178,342	182,481	196,393	218,260	239,600	257,578	266,429	275,872	285,905	31.0
Other professional	260,239	251,298	270,014	284,398	309,807	352,197	355,192	381,658	412,880	436,830	444,275	26.1
Nonprofessional staff	515,281	477,620	490,131	485,689	483,220	489,415	454,558	456,541	462,805	466,766	452,579	-7.5
Private 4-year	734,509	762,034	770,004	786,634	857,820	912,924	988,895	1,073,764	1,157,226	1,229,784	1,297,486	42.1
Professional staff	442,524	473,372	495,383	517,485	569,579	627,364	701,244	789,179	867,234	934,298	1,008,814	60.8
Executive/administrative/managerial	57,148	59,230	62,314	62,580	69,626	65,739	84,306	90,415	103,183	111,616	118,268	79.9
Faculty (instruction/research/public service)	232,893	251,948	262,660	278,541	296,737	325,713	364,166	430,305	472,628	498,582	540,093	65.8
Graduate assistants	23,989	28,880	33,853	36,064	38,597	41,611	52,101	59,147	62,550	66,521	70,011	68.3
Other professional	128,494	133,314	136,556	140,300	164,619	194,301	200,671	209,312	228,873	257,579	280,442	44.3
Nonprofessional staff	291,985	288,662	274,621	269,149	288,241	285,560	287,651	284,585	289,992	295,486	288,672	1.1
Public 2-year	441,414	478,980	482,454	512,086	517,967	578,394	593,466	610,978	620,784	638,352	641,616	10.9
Professional staff	306,631	337,371	336,661	358,367	364,703	408,792	422,756	440,536	449,372	467,760	474,644	16.1
Executive/administrative/managerial	20,772	21,531	21,806	22,822	21,459	22,566	25,872	26,770	27,363	27,827	27,562	22.1
Faculty (instruction/research/public service)	222,532	276,413	272,434	290,451	296,239	332,665	341,643	354,497	358,925	373,778	377,696	13.5
Graduate assistants	29,216	2,762	3,401	3,561	4,170	1,215	323	374	0	0	0	-100.0
Other professional	34,111	36,665	39,020	41,533	42,835	52,346	54,918	58,895	63,084	66,155	69,386	32.6
Nonprofessional staff	134,783	141,609	145,793	153,719	153,264	169,602	170,710	170,442	171,412	170,592	166,972	-1.6
Private 2-year	27,398	28,065	26,141	35,123	36,546	33,459	35,676	37,636	41,719	51,559	58,674	75.4
Professional staff	19,672	20,631	19,478	27,092	28,957	26,833	28,956	30,002	33,901	43,133	49,878	85.9
Executive/administrative/managerial	3,161	3,236	2,735	3,977	4,467	3,488	4,338	4,898	5,608	6,781	7,977	128.7
Faculty (instruction/research/public service)	12,451	13,092	12,213	16,712	17,768	16,346	17,661	18,933	21,616	26,883	30,292	85.3
Graduate assistants	202	261	313	618	578	50	37	42	0	0	0	-100.0
Other professional	3,858	4,042	4,217	5,785	6,144	6,949	6,920	6,129	6,677	9,469	11,609	67.1
Nonprofessional staff	7,726	7,434	6,663	8,031	7,589	6,626	6,720	7,634	7,818	8,426	8,796	32.7

NOTE: Data through 1995 are for institutions of higher education, while later data are for degree-granting institutions. Degree-granting institutions grant associate's or higher degrees and participate in Title IV federal financial aid programs. The degree-granting classification is very similar to the earlier higher education classification, but it includes more 2-year colleges and excludes a few higher education institutions that did not grant degrees. Beginning in 2007, includes institutions with fewer than 15 full-time employees; these institutions did not report staff data prior to 2007. By definition, all graduate assistants are part time. SOURCE: U.S. Department of Education, National Center for Education Statistics, Integrated Postsecondary Education Data System (IPEDS), "Fall Staff Survey" (IPEDS-S:91–99); and IPEDS Winter 2001–02 through Winter 2011–12, Human Resources component, Fall Staff section. (This table was prepared July 2012.)

Full-time instructional faculty in degree-granting postsecondary institutions, by race/ethnicity, sex, and academic rank: Fall 2007, fall 2009, and fall 2011

Sex and academic rank	Total	White	Black, Hispanic, Asian, Pacific Islander, American Indian/Alaska Native, and two or more races							American Indian/ Alaska Native	Two or more races	Race/ ethnicity unknown	Non-resident-alien[2]
			Total	Percent[1]	Black	Hispanic	Asian/Pacific Islander						
							Total	Asian	Pacific Islander				
1	2	3	4	5	6	7	8	9	10	11	12	13	14
2007													
Total	703,463	540,460	119,906	18.2	37,930	24,975	53,661	—	—	3,340	—	11,875	31,222
Professors	173,395	147,867	22,734	13.3	5,839	4,128	12,239	—	—	528	—	1,309	1,485
Associate professors	143,692	115,274	24,255	17.4	7,855	4,714	11,082	—	—	604	—	1,628	2,535
Assistant professors	168,508	117,618	34,940	22.9	10,642	6,329	17,290	—	—	679	—	3,593	12,357
Instructors	101,429	77,609	19,470	20.1	7,480	5,800	5,225	—	—	965	—	2,350	2,000
Lecturers	31,264	23,470	5,326	18.5	1,602	1,492	2,081	—	—	151	—	661	1,807
Other faculty	85,175	58,622	13,181	18.4	4,512	2,512	5,744	—	—	413	—	2,334	11,038
2009													
Total	728,977	551,271	130,903	19.2	39,715	28,040	59,691	—	—	3,457	—	16,058	30,745
Professors	177,581	149,568	24,633	14.1	6,086	4,683	13,284	—	—	580	—	1,923	1,457
Associate professors	148,981	117,270	26,779	18.6	8,163	5,383	12,632	—	—	601	—	2,387	2,545
Assistant professors	171,639	117,892	37,199	24.0	10,979	6,789	18,712	—	—	719	—	4,617	11,931
Instructors	104,521	78,329	20,951	21.1	7,806	6,577	5,566	—	—	1,002	—	3,396	1,845
Lecturers	33,332	24,895	5,851	19.0	1,812	1,583	2,318	—	—	138	—	882	1,704
Other faculty	92,923	63,317	15,490	19.7	4,869	3,025	7,179	—	—	417	—	2,853	11,263
Males	415,821	314,712	71,889	18.6	18,026	14,865	37,261	—	—	1,737	—	8,973	20,247
Professors	127,931	107,315	18,013	14.4	3,755	3,209	10,684	—	—	365	—	1,405	1,198
Associate professors	87,965	68,747	15,935	18.8	4,180	3,096	8,338	—	—	321	—	1,497	1,786
Assistant professors	88,665	59,607	18,954	24.1	4,568	3,422	10,658	—	—	306	—	2,477	7,627
Instructors	46,762	35,137	9,003	20.4	2,880	3,078	2,568	—	—	477	—	1,583	1,039
Lecturers	15,724	11,702	2,620	18.3	822	650	1,084	—	—	64	—	466	936
Other faculty	48,774	32,204	7,364	18.6	1,821	1,410	3,929	—	—	204	—	1,545	7,661
Females	313,156	236,559	59,014	20.0	21,689	13,175	22,430	—	—	1,720	—	7,085	10,498
Professors	49,650	42,253	6,620	13.5	2,331	1,474	2,600	—	—	215	—	518	259
Associate professors	61,016	48,523	10,844	18.3	3,983	2,287	4,294	—	—	280	—	890	759
Assistant professors	82,974	58,285	18,245	23.8	6,411	3,367	8,054	—	—	413	—	2,140	4,304
Instructors	57,759	43,192	11,948	21.7	4,926	3,499	2,998	—	—	525	—	1,813	806
Lecturers	17,608	13,193	3,231	19.7	990	933	1,234	—	—	74	—	416	768
Other faculty	44,149	31,113	8,126	20.7	3,048	1,615	3,250	—	—	213	—	1,308	3,602
2011													
Total	761,619	563,689	147,517	20.7	41,649	31,331	66,887	65,438	1,449	3,529	4,121	17,000	33,413
Professors	181,508	150,334	27,588	15.5	6,517	5,180	14,646	14,425	221	589	656	2,202	1,384
Associate professors	155,200	119,371	30,648	20.4	8,695	6,143	14,409	14,129	280	597	804	2,477	2,704
Assistant professors	174,045	118,014	39,988	25.3	10,994	7,428	19,822	19,443	379	701	1,043	4,926	11,117
Instructors	109,054	80,703	23,160	22.3	8,600	6,906	5,808	5,449	359	981	865	3,263	1,928
Lecturers	34,477	25,823	6,262	19.5	1,688	1,773	2,456	2,421	35	135	210	849	1,543
Other faculty	107,335	69,444	19,871	22.2	5,155	3,901	9,746	9,571	175	526	543	3,283	14,737
Males	426,982	315,801	79,805	20.2	18,660	16,345	41,057	40,357	700	1,749	1,994	9,602	21,774
Professors	128,648	106,039	19,841	15.8	3,984	3,499	11,579	11,420	159	362	417	1,643	1,125
Associate professors	89,741	68,447	17,865	20.7	4,373	3,437	9,305	9,142	163	313	437	1,574	1,855
Assistant professors	88,168	58,531	19,881	25.4	4,458	3,692	10,974	10,820	154	303	454	2,693	7,063
Instructors	48,130	35,870	9,749	21.4	3,136	3,133	2,669	2,526	143	463	348	1,487	1,024
Lecturers	15,689	11,720	2,740	18.9	751	753	1,110	1,090	20	47	79	410	819
Other faculty	56,606	35,194	9,729	21.7	1,958	1,831	5,420	5,359	61	261	259	1,795	9,888
Females	334,637	247,888	67,712	21.5	22,989	14,986	25,830	25,081	749	1,780	2,127	7,398	11,639
Professors	52,860	44,295	7,747	14.9	2,533	1,681	3,067	3,005	62	227	239	559	259
Associate professors	65,459	50,924	12,783	20.1	4,322	2,706	5,104	4,987	117	284	367	903	849
Assistant professors	85,877	59,483	20,107	25.3	6,536	3,736	8,848	8,623	225	398	589	2,233	4,054
Instructors	60,924	44,833	13,411	23.0	5,464	3,773	3,139	2,923	216	518	517	1,776	904
Lecturers	18,788	14,103	3,522	20.0	937	1,020	1,346	1,331	15	88	131	439	724
Other faculty	50,729	34,250	10,142	22.8	3,197	2,070	4,326	4,212	114	265	284	1,488	4,849

—Not available.
[1]Combined total of faculty who were Black, Hispanic, Asian, Pacific Islander, American Indian/Alaska Native, and of two or more races as a percentage of total faculty, excluding race/ethnicity unknown and nonresident alien.
[2]Race/ethnicity not collected.
NOTE: Degree-granting institutions grant associate's or higher degrees and participate in Title IV federal financial aid programs. Includes institutions with fewer than 15 full-time employees; these institutions did not report staff data prior to 2007. Race categories exclude persons of Hispanic ethnicity.
SOURCE: U.S. Department of Education, National Center for Education Statistics, Integrated Postsecondary Education Data System (IPEDS), Winter 2007–08, Winter 2009–10, and Winter 2011–12, Human Resources component, Fall Staff section. (This table was prepared July 2012.)

Average salary of full-time instructional faculty on 9-month contracts in degree-granting postsecondary institutions, by academic rank, control and level of institution, and sex: Selected years, 1970–71 through 2012–13

Sex and academic year	All faculty	Academic rank						Public institutions			Private institutions		
		Professor	Associate professor	Assistant professor	Instructor	Lecturer	No rank	Total	4-year	2-year	Total	4-year	2-year
1	2	3	4	5	6	7	8	9	10	11	12	13	14
						Current dollars							
Total													
1970–71	$12,710	$17,958	$13,563	$11,176	$9,360	$11,196	$12,333	$12,953	$13,121	$12,644	$11,619	$11,824	$8,664
1975–76	16,659	22,649	17,065	13,986	13,672	12,906	15,196	16,942	17,400	15,820	15,921	16,116	10,901
1980–81	23,302	30,753	23,214	18,901	15,178	17,301	22,334	23,745	24,373	22,177	22,093	22,325	15,065
1982–83	27,196	35,540	26,921	22,056	17,601	20,072	25,557	27,488	28,293	25,567	26,393	26,691	16,595
1984–85	30,447	39,743	29,945	24,668	20,230	22,334	27,683	30,646	31,764	27,864	29,910	30,247	18,510
1985–86	32,392	42,268	31,787	26,277	20,918	23,770	29,088	32,750	34,033	29,590	31,402	31,732	19,436
1987–88	35,897	47,040	35,231	29,110	22,728	25,977	31,532	36,231	37,840	32,209	35,049	35,346	21,867
1989–90	40,133	52,810	39,392	32,689	25,030	28,990	34,559	40,416	42,365	35,516	39,464	39,817	24,601
1990–91	42,165	55,540	41,414	34,434	26,332	30,097	36,395	42,317	44,510	37,055	41,788	42,224	24,088
1991–92	43,851	57,433	42,929	35,745	30,916	30,456	37,783	43,641	45,638	38,959	44,376	44,793	25,673
1992–93	44,714	58,788	43,945	36,625	28,499	30,543	37,771	44,197	46,515	38,935	45,985	46,427	26,105
1993–94	46,364	60,649	45,278	37,630	28,828	32,729	40,584	45,920	48,019	41,040	47,465	47,880	28,435
1994–95	47,811	62,709	46,713	38,756	29,665	33,198	41,227	47,432	49,738	42,101	48,741	49,379	25,613
1995–96	49,309	64,540	47,966	39,696	30,344	34,136	42,996	48,837	51,172	43,295	50,466	50,819	31,915
1996–97	50,829	66,659	49,307	40,687	31,193	34,962	44,200	50,303	52,718	44,584	52,112	52,443	32,628
1997–98	52,335	68,731	50,828	41,830	32,449	35,484	45,268	51,638	54,114	45,919	54,039	54,379	33,592
1998–99	54,097	71,322	52,576	43,348	33,819	36,819	46,250	53,319	55,948	47,285	55,981	56,284	34,821
1999–2000	55,888	74,410	54,524	44,978	34,918	38,194	47,389	55,011	57,950	48,240	58,013	58,323	35,925
2001–02	59,742	80,792	58,724	48,796	46,959	41,798	46,569	58,524	62,013	50,837	62,818	63,088	33,139
2002–03	61,330	83,466	60,471	50,552	48,304	42,622	46,338	60,014	63,486	52,330	64,533	64,814	34,826
2003–04	62,579	85,333	61,746	51,798	49,065	43,648	47,725	60,874	64,340	53,076	66,666	66,932	36,322
2004–05	64,234	88,158	63,558	53,308	49,730	44,514	48,942	62,346	66,053	53,932	68,755	68,995	37,329
2005–06	66,172	91,208	65,714	55,106	50,883	45,896	50,425	64,158	67,951	55,405	71,016	71,263	38,549
2006–07	68,585	94,870	68,153	57,143	53,278	47,478	52,161	66,566	70,460	57,466	73,419	73,636	41,138
2007–08	71,085	98,548	70,826	59,294	55,325	49,392	54,405	68,981	72,857	59,646	76,133	76,341	43,402
2008–09	73,570	102,346	73,439	61,550	56,918	51,188	56,370	71,237	75,245	61,433	79,147	79,410	43,542
2009–10	74,625	103,684	74,126	62,246	57,797	52,177	56,807	72,183	76,153	62,265	80,385	80,603	44,748
2010–11	75,472	104,957	75,103	63,140	57,943	52,549	56,549	72,704	76,861	62,301	81,892	82,094	45,146
2011–12	76,570	107,091	76,175	64,009	58,349	53,361	56,922	73,503	77,843	62,568	83,534	83,695	47,805
2012–13	77,301	108,310	77,089	64,632	57,495	53,394	58,254	73,909	78,111	62,781	85,000	85,167	44,978
Males													
1975–76	17,414	22,902	17,209	14,174	14,430	13,579	15,761	17,661	18,121	16,339	16,784	16,946	11,378
1980–81	24,499	31,082	23,451	19,227	15,545	18,281	23,170	24,873	25,509	22,965	23,493	23,669	16,075
1982–83	28,664	35,956	27,262	22,586	18,160	21,225	26,541	28,851	29,661	26,524	28,159	28,380	17,346
1984–85	32,182	40,269	30,392	25,330	21,159	23,557	28,670	32,240	33,344	28,891	32,028	32,278	19,460
1985–86	34,294	42,833	32,273	27,094	21,693	25,238	30,267	34,528	35,786	30,758	33,656	33,900	20,412
1987–88	38,112	47,735	35,823	30,086	23,645	27,652	32,747	38,314	39,898	33,477	37,603	37,817	22,641
1989–90	42,763	53,650	40,131	33,781	25,933	31,162	35,980	42,959	44,834	37,081	42,312	42,595	25,218
1990–91	45,065	56,549	42,239	35,636	27,388	32,398	38,036	45,084	47,168	38,787	45,019	45,319	25,937
1991–92	46,848	58,494	43,814	36,969	33,359	32,843	39,422	46,483	48,401	40,811	47,733	48,042	26,825
1992–93	47,866	59,972	44,855	37,842	29,583	32,512	39,365	47,175	49,392	40,725	49,518	49,837	27,402
1993–94	49,579	61,857	46,229	38,794	29,815	34,796	42,251	48,956	50,989	42,938	51,076	51,397	30,783
1994–95	51,228	64,046	47,705	39,923	30,528	35,082	43,103	50,629	52,874	44,020	52,653	53,036	29,639
1995–96	52,814	65,949	49,037	40,858	30,940	36,135	44,624	52,163	54,448	45,209	54,364	54,649	33,301
1996–97	54,465	68,214	50,457	41,864	31,738	36,932	45,688	53,737	56,162	46,393	56,185	56,453	34,736
1997–98	56,115	70,468	52,041	43,017	33,070	37,481	46,822	55,191	57,744	47,690	58,293	58,576	36,157
1998–99	58,048	73,260	53,830	44,650	34,741	38,976	47,610	57,038	59,805	48,961	60,392	60,641	38,040
1999–2000	60,084	76,478	55,939	46,414	35,854	40,202	48,788	58,984	62,030	50,033	62,631	62,905	38,636
2001–02	64,320	83,356	60,300	50,518	48,844	44,519	48,049	62,835	66,577	52,360	67,871	68,100	33,395
2002–03	66,126	86,191	62,226	52,441	50,272	45,469	47,412	64,564	68,322	53,962	69,726	69,976	34,291
2003–04	67,485	88,262	63,466	53,649	50,985	46,214	48,973	65,476	69,248	54,623	72,021	72,250	35,604
2004–05	69,337	91,290	65,394	55,215	51,380	46,929	50,102	67,130	71,145	55,398	74,318	74,540	34,970
2005–06	71,569	94,733	67,654	57,099	52,519	48,256	51,811	69,191	73,353	56,858	76,941	77,143	38,215
2006–07	74,167	98,563	70,168	59,150	55,061	49,641	53,665	71,797	76,072	58,971	79,491	79,663	41,196
2007–08	76,935	102,555	72,940	61,368	57,116	51,804	56,196	74,389	78,673	61,166	82,681	82,850	42,995
2008–09	79,706	106,759	75,634	63,726	58,819	53,777	58,341	76,897	81,394	62,870	86,008	86,205	43,871
2009–10	80,885	108,227	76,401	64,450	59,799	54,946	58,649	77,951	82,428	63,698	87,386	87,549	44,500
2010–11	81,868	109,656	77,423	65,392	59,792	55,435	58,392	78,603	83,288	63,683	88,996	89,155	44,542
2011–12	83,154	112,068	78,559	66,300	60,064	56,363	58,833	79,550	84,443	63,932	90,838	90,974	45,250
2012–13	84,026	113,595	79,508	66,937	59,161	56,190	60,386	80,072	84,822	64,152	92,485	92,632	42,906

See notes at end of table.

Average salary of full-time instructional faculty on 9-month contracts in degree-granting postsecondary institutions, by academic rank, control and level of institution, and sex: Selected years, 1970–71 through 2012–13—Continued

Sex and academic year	All faculty	Academic rank						Public institutions			Private institutions		
		Professor	Associate professor	Assistant professor	Instructor	Lecturer	No rank	Total	4-year	2-year	Total	4-year	2-year
1	2	3	4	5	6	7	8	9	10	11	12	13	14
Females													
1975–76	14,308	20,308	16,364	13,522	12,572	11,901	14,094	14,762	14,758	14,769	13,030	13,231	10,201
1980–81	19,996	27,959	22,295	18,302	14,854	16,168	20,843	20,673	20,608	20,778	18,073	18,326	13,892
1982–83	23,261	32,221	25,738	21,130	17,102	18,830	23,855	23,892	23,876	23,917	21,451	21,785	15,845
1984–85	25,941	35,824	28,517	23,575	19,362	21,004	26,050	26,566	26,813	26,172	24,186	24,560	17,575
1985–86	27,576	38,252	30,300	24,966	20,237	22,273	27,171	28,299	28,680	27,693	25,523	25,889	18,504
1987–88	30,499	42,371	33,528	27,600	21,962	24,370	29,605	31,215	31,820	30,228	28,621	28,946	21,215
1989–90	34,183	47,663	37,469	31,090	24,320	26,995	32,528	34,796	35,704	33,307	32,650	33,010	24,002
1990–91	35,881	49,728	39,329	32,724	25,534	28,111	34,179	36,459	37,573	34,720	34,359	34,898	22,585
1991–92	37,534	51,621	40,766	34,063	28,873	28,550	35,622	37,800	38,634	36,517	36,828	37,309	24,683
1992–93	38,385	52,755	41,861	35,032	27,700	28,922	35,792	38,356	39,470	36,710	38,460	38,987	25,068
1993–94	40,058	54,746	43,178	36,169	28,136	31,048	38,474	40,118	41,031	38,707	39,902	40,378	26,142
1994–95	41,369	56,555	44,626	37,352	29,072	31,677	38,967	41,548	42,663	39,812	40,908	41,815	22,851
1995–96	42,871	58,318	45,803	38,345	29,940	32,584	41,085	42,871	43,986	41,086	42,871	43,236	30,671
1996–97	44,325	60,160	47,101	39,350	30,819	33,415	42,474	44,306	45,402	42,531	44,374	44,726	30,661
1997–98	45,775	61,965	48,597	40,504	32,011	33,918	43,491	45,648	46,709	43,943	46,106	46,466	30,995
1998–99	47,421	64,236	50,347	41,894	33,152	35,115	44,723	47,247	48,355	45,457	47,874	48,204	31,524
1999–2000	48,997	67,079	52,091	43,367	34,228	36,607	45,865	48,714	50,168	46,340	49,737	50,052	32,951
2001–02	52,662	72,542	56,186	46,824	45,262	39,538	45,003	52,123	53,895	49,290	54,149	54,434	32,921
2002–03	54,105	75,028	57,716	48,380	46,573	40,265	45,251	53,435	55,121	50,717	55,881	56,158	35,296
2003–04	55,378	76,652	59,095	49,689	47,404	41,536	46,519	54,408	56,117	51,591	57,921	58,192	36,896
2004–05	56,926	79,160	60,809	51,154	48,351	42,455	47,860	55,780	57,714	52,566	59,919	60,143	39,291
2005–06	58,665	81,514	62,860	52,901	49,533	43,934	49,172	57,462	59,437	54,082	61,830	62,092	38,786
2006–07	61,016	85,090	65,237	54,974	51,832	45,693	50,812	59,781	61,875	56,127	64,246	64,481	41,099
2007–08	63,347	88,301	67,816	57,111	53,889	47,407	52,837	62,129	64,226	58,318	66,528	66,745	43,670
2008–09	65,638	91,522	70,375	59,286	55,424	49,078	54,649	64,231	66,393	60,195	69,300	69,593	43,344
2009–10	66,653	92,835	71,019	60,001	56,246	49,945	55,211	65,144	67,283	61,047	70,516	70,756	44,892
2010–11	67,461	94,032	72,001	60,893	56,506	50,227	54,985	65,615	67,937	61,138	72,088	72,302	45,518
2011–12	68,470	95,840	73,053	61,761	57,013	51,001	55,319	66,375	68,897	61,433	73,617	73,776	49,382
2012–13	69,114	96,680	73,991	62,382	56,188	51,200	56,461	66,706	69,150	61,652	75,002	75,166	46,407
					Constant 2012–13 dollars[1]								
Total													
1970–71	74,019	104,582	78,991	65,087	54,509	65,204	71,827	75,438	76,417	73,637	67,664	68,863	50,458
1975–76	69,494	94,485	71,190	58,345	57,037	53,839	63,392	70,676	72,587	65,994	66,416	67,232	45,474
1980–81	62,233	82,133	61,998	50,479	40,536	46,206	59,648	63,416	65,094	59,229	59,004	59,624	40,235
1982–83	64,104	83,772	63,456	51,989	41,488	47,312	60,241	64,793	66,690	60,265	62,212	62,914	39,117
1984–85	66,599	86,933	65,501	53,958	44,251	48,853	60,553	67,034	69,480	60,949	65,424	66,162	40,488
1985–86	68,867	89,865	67,581	55,867	44,473	50,537	61,843	69,629	72,356	62,910	66,763	67,464	41,322
1987–88	71,691	93,945	70,361	58,137	45,390	51,879	62,974	72,358	75,572	64,326	69,998	70,591	43,671
1989–90	73,123	96,221	71,774	59,560	45,605	52,821	62,967	73,639	77,190	64,712	71,904	72,548	44,824
1990–91	72,844	95,950	71,545	59,488	45,490	51,996	62,875	73,107	76,894	64,015	72,192	72,946	41,614
1991–92	73,405	96,139	71,860	59,836	51,751	50,981	63,247	73,053	76,395	65,216	74,282	74,980	42,975
1992–93	72,581	95,426	71,333	59,451	46,261	49,578	61,311	71,742	75,505	63,201	74,644	75,362	42,375
1993–94	73,360	95,962	71,640	59,540	45,613	51,785	64,214	72,657	75,978	64,935	75,102	75,758	44,991
1994–95	73,542	96,456	71,853	59,613	45,629	51,064	63,414	72,958	76,505	64,758	74,971	75,953	39,396
1995–96	73,837	96,644	71,825	59,442	45,439	51,116	64,383	73,130	76,627	64,831	75,569	76,098	47,790
1996–97	74,002	97,048	71,786	59,235	45,414	50,900	64,351	73,235	76,751	64,909	75,869	76,351	47,503
1997–98	74,859	98,312	72,703	59,832	46,414	50,756	64,750	73,861	77,404	65,682	77,297	77,783	48,049
1998–99	76,062	100,282	73,923	60,949	47,550	51,768	65,030	74,969	78,664	66,484	78,712	79,137	48,959
1999–2000	76,376	101,688	74,511	61,467	47,718	52,195	64,761	75,178	79,193	65,925	79,280	79,703	49,094
2001–02	77,564	104,895	76,243	63,353	60,968	54,268	60,462	75,983	80,513	66,003	81,558	81,910	43,025
2002–03	77,914	106,037	76,822	64,222	61,366	54,148	58,869	76,243	80,653	66,481	81,984	82,341	44,243
2003–04	77,799	106,088	76,763	64,396	60,998	54,264	59,333	75,679	79,989	65,985	82,880	83,210	45,155
2004–05	77,524	106,398	76,708	64,337	60,019	53,724	59,068	75,244	79,719	65,090	82,980	83,270	45,052
2005–06	76,933	106,040	76,400	64,067	59,157	53,360	58,625	74,592	79,001	64,415	82,565	82,852	44,817
2006–07	77,728	107,517	77,238	64,760	60,380	53,808	59,115	75,440	79,853	65,127	83,207	83,453	46,623
2007–08	77,683	107,695	77,400	64,798	60,461	53,976	59,454	75,384	79,619	65,182	83,199	83,427	47,431
2008–09	79,292	110,306	79,150	66,337	61,344	55,169	60,754	76,777	81,097	66,211	85,302	85,585	46,928
2009–10	79,658	110,677	79,125	66,444	61,695	55,696	60,638	77,051	81,289	66,464	85,806	86,039	47,766
2010–11	78,976	109,830	78,590	66,071	60,633	54,989	59,175	76,079	80,430	65,193	85,695	85,905	47,242
2011–12	77,845	108,873	77,443	65,074	59,320	54,249	57,870	74,726	79,138	63,610	84,925	85,088	48,601
2012–13	77,301	108,310	77,089	64,632	57,495	53,394	58,254	73,909	78,111	62,781	85,000	85,167	44,978

See notes at end of table.

Average salary of full-time instructional faculty on 9-month contracts in degree-granting postsecondary institutions, by academic rank, control and level of institution, and sex: Selected years, 1970–71 through 2012–13—Continued

Sex and academic year	All faculty	Academic rank						Public institutions			Private institutions		
		Professor	Associate professor	Assistant professor	Instructor	Lecturer	No rank	Total	4-year	2-year	Total	4-year	2-year
1	2	3	4	5	6	7	8	9	10	11	12	13	14
Males													
1975–76	72,644	95,539	71,788	59,130	60,196	56,647	65,749	73,677	75,593	68,163	70,018	70,692	47,464
1980–81	65,430	83,012	62,631	51,350	41,517	48,824	61,881	66,429	68,128	61,333	62,743	63,214	42,932
1982–83	67,565	84,753	64,260	53,238	42,805	50,030	62,561	68,005	69,915	62,520	66,374	66,895	40,887
1984–85	70,394	88,083	66,479	55,406	46,283	51,528	62,712	70,521	72,936	63,195	70,057	70,604	42,566
1985–86	72,911	91,066	68,614	57,604	46,121	53,658	64,350	73,409	76,083	65,394	71,555	72,074	43,397
1987–88	76,114	95,332	71,543	60,087	47,222	55,225	65,400	76,518	79,682	66,858	75,098	75,526	45,217
1989–90	77,916	97,752	73,119	61,550	47,250	56,777	65,556	78,272	81,689	67,563	77,095	77,608	45,949
1990–91	77,854	97,693	72,970	61,563	47,316	55,970	65,710	77,887	81,486	67,008	77,774	78,293	44,808
1991–92	78,421	97,915	73,342	61,883	55,841	54,978	65,990	77,810	81,020	68,316	79,902	80,419	44,903
1992–93	77,697	97,349	72,811	61,426	48,020	52,775	63,899	76,576	80,176	66,106	80,380	80,898	44,479
1993–94	78,446	97,873	73,146	61,381	47,175	55,055	66,851	77,460	80,677	67,938	80,815	81,323	48,707
1994–95	78,797	98,514	73,378	61,408	46,957	53,962	66,300	77,876	81,328	67,710	80,989	81,578	45,590
1995–96	79,085	98,754	73,430	61,181	46,331	54,110	66,822	78,110	81,532	67,697	81,406	81,833	49,866
1996–97	79,294	99,312	73,459	60,950	46,207	53,768	66,517	78,235	81,765	67,542	81,799	82,189	50,571
1997–98	80,266	100,796	74,438	61,530	47,303	53,612	66,973	78,944	82,596	68,215	83,381	83,787	51,718
1998–99	81,618	103,007	75,686	62,779	48,847	54,801	66,942	80,198	84,089	68,841	84,913	85,263	53,486
1999–2000	82,110	104,513	76,445	63,428	48,998	54,939	66,673	80,606	84,769	68,375	85,591	85,965	52,799
2001–02	83,509	108,223	78,289	65,589	63,415	57,801	62,384	81,580	86,439	67,981	88,119	88,416	43,357
2002–03	84,008	109,498	79,052	66,621	63,866	57,764	60,233	82,023	86,797	68,554	88,580	88,898	43,563
2003–04	83,898	109,728	78,902	66,697	63,385	57,453	60,884	81,400	86,090	67,908	89,538	89,822	44,264
2004–05	83,683	110,177	78,923	66,639	62,010	56,639	60,468	81,019	85,865	66,860	89,694	89,962	42,205
2005–06	83,208	110,139	78,655	66,384	61,060	56,104	60,236	80,443	85,282	66,104	89,453	89,688	44,430
2006–07	84,054	111,702	79,522	67,036	62,402	56,259	60,819	81,369	86,213	66,833	90,088	90,283	46,688
2007–08	84,076	112,074	79,710	67,065	62,418	56,612	61,412	81,294	85,976	66,843	90,356	90,540	46,986
2008–09	85,904	115,062	81,516	68,682	63,393	57,959	62,878	82,877	87,724	67,759	92,696	92,910	47,282
2009–10	86,340	115,526	81,554	68,797	63,832	58,652	62,604	83,208	87,987	67,994	93,279	93,454	47,501
2010–11	85,669	114,747	81,018	68,428	62,569	58,009	61,103	82,252	87,155	66,640	93,128	93,295	46,610
2011–12	84,537	113,933	79,866	67,404	61,063	57,301	59,812	80,874	85,849	64,996	92,350	92,488	46,003
2012–13	84,026	113,595	79,508	66,937	59,161	56,190	60,386	80,072	84,822	64,152	92,485	92,632	42,906
Females													
1975–76	59,686	84,718	68,264	56,409	52,445	49,645	58,795	61,584	61,567	61,610	54,359	55,194	42,553
1980–81	53,404	74,671	59,544	48,880	39,671	43,180	55,666	55,212	55,038	55,492	48,268	48,944	37,102
1982–83	54,829	75,949	60,668	49,806	40,312	44,385	56,229	56,316	56,279	56,375	50,563	51,350	37,349
1984–85	56,743	78,360	62,377	51,567	42,352	45,944	56,981	58,110	58,650	57,248	52,904	53,722	38,443
1985–86	58,628	81,326	64,420	53,079	43,025	47,354	57,767	60,166	60,976	58,877	54,264	55,042	39,341
1987–88	60,911	84,621	66,960	55,121	43,861	48,670	59,125	62,341	63,549	60,369	57,160	57,809	42,369
1989–90	62,282	86,843	68,269	56,646	44,311	49,186	59,267	63,400	65,054	60,686	59,488	60,145	43,732
1990–91	61,986	85,910	67,945	56,534	44,112	48,565	59,046	62,986	64,911	59,982	59,357	60,289	39,018
1991–92	62,829	86,410	68,240	57,019	48,332	47,790	59,630	63,275	64,671	61,128	61,648	62,453	41,318
1992–93	62,307	85,635	67,950	56,866	44,964	46,948	58,099	62,260	64,069	59,590	62,430	63,285	40,691
1993–94	63,383	86,622	68,318	57,228	44,518	49,126	60,875	63,476	64,921	61,244	63,136	63,888	41,363
1994–95	63,633	86,990	68,642	57,453	44,718	48,724	59,937	63,907	65,622	61,237	62,923	64,318	35,149
1995–96	64,196	87,326	68,587	57,419	44,833	48,792	61,522	64,196	65,865	61,524	64,196	64,743	45,928
1996–97	64,532	87,586	68,574	57,289	44,869	48,649	61,838	64,504	66,100	61,920	64,603	65,116	44,639
1997–98	65,475	88,633	69,513	57,936	45,788	48,516	62,208	65,294	66,811	62,855	65,949	66,464	44,335
1998–99	66,675	90,318	70,790	58,904	46,613	49,373	62,882	66,431	67,988	63,914	67,313	67,777	44,324
1999–2000	66,958	91,669	71,186	59,265	46,775	50,027	62,678	66,572	68,559	63,328	67,970	68,401	45,030
2001–02	68,372	94,183	72,948	60,793	58,765	51,333	58,428	67,673	69,974	63,994	70,303	70,674	42,742
2002–03	68,735	95,316	73,324	61,462	59,167	51,153	57,487	67,885	70,026	64,432	70,992	71,344	44,841
2003–04	68,846	95,295	73,468	61,775	58,933	51,638	57,833	67,641	69,766	64,139	72,009	72,345	45,870
2004–05	68,704	95,538	73,390	61,738	58,354	51,239	57,762	67,321	69,655	63,442	72,316	72,586	47,420
2005–06	68,205	94,769	73,082	61,504	57,589	51,079	57,169	66,807	69,102	62,877	71,885	72,190	45,094
2006–07	69,150	96,434	73,934	62,303	58,742	51,785	57,586	67,751	70,124	63,609	72,811	73,077	46,579
2007–08	69,227	96,497	74,111	62,412	58,891	51,807	57,742	67,896	70,187	63,731	72,703	72,941	47,724
2008–09	70,743	98,639	75,848	63,897	59,734	52,895	58,899	69,226	71,556	64,877	74,690	75,005	46,714
2009–10	71,148	99,096	75,808	64,047	60,040	53,313	58,935	69,537	71,821	65,164	75,272	75,527	47,919
2010–11	70,593	98,398	75,344	63,721	59,130	52,559	57,538	68,662	71,092	63,976	75,435	75,659	47,632
2011–12	69,609	97,435	74,269	62,789	57,962	51,850	56,240	67,480	70,043	62,456	74,842	75,004	50,204
2012–13	69,114	96,680	73,991	62,382	56,188	51,200	56,461	66,706	69,150	61,652	75,002	75,166	46,407

[1]Constant dollars based on the Consumer Price Index, prepared by the Bureau of Labor Statistics, U.S. Department of Labor, adjusted to an academic-year basis.
NOTE: Data through 1995–96 are for institutions of higher education, while later data are for degree-granting institutions. Degree-granting institutions grant associate's or higher degrees and participate in Title IV federal financial aid programs. Data for 1987–88 and later years include imputations for nonrespondent institutions.

SOURCE: U.S. Department of Education, National Center for Education Statistics, Higher Education General Information Survey (HEGIS), "Faculty Salaries, Tenure, and Fringe Benefits" surveys, 1970–71 through 1985–86; Integrated Postsecondary Education Data System (IPEDS), "Salaries, Tenure, and Fringe Benefits of Full-Time Instructional Faculty Survey" (IPEDS-SA:87–99); and IPEDS Winter 2001–02 through Winter 2011–12 and Spring 2013, Human Resources component, Salaries section. (This table was prepared March 2014.)

Average salary of full-time instructional faculty on 9-month contracts in degree-granting postsecondary institutions, by academic rank, sex, and control and level of institution: Selected years, 1999–2000 through 2012–13

Academic year, control and level of institution	Constant 2012–13 dollars[1]	Current dollars												
	All faculty, total	All faculty			Academic rank									No academic rank
		Total	Males	Females	Professor			Associate professor			Assistant professor	Instructor	Lecturer	
					Total	Males	Females	Total	Males	Females				
1	2	3	4	5	6	7	8	9	10	11	12	13	14	15
1999–2000														
All institutions	$76,376	$55,888	$60,084	$48,997	$74,410	$76,478	$67,079	$54,524	$55,939	$52,091	$44,978	$34,918	$38,194	$47,389
Public	75,178	55,011	58,984	48,714	72,475	74,501	65,568	54,641	55,992	52,305	45,285	35,007	37,403	47,990
4-year	79,193	57,950	62,030	50,168	75,204	76,530	69,619	55,681	56,776	53,599	45,822	33,528	37,261	40,579
Doctoral[2]	85,073	62,253	66,882	52,287	81,182	82,445	74,653	57,744	58,999	55,156	48,190	33,345	38,883	39,350
Master's[3]	72,119	52,773	55,565	48,235	66,588	67,128	64,863	53,048	53,686	51,977	43,396	33,214	34,448	43,052
Other 4-year	65,415	47,867	49,829	44,577	60,360	60,748	59,052	49,567	50,133	48,548	42,306	35,754	36,088	38,330
2-year	65,925	48,240	50,033	46,340	57,806	59,441	55,501	48,056	49,425	46,711	41,984	37,634	40,061	48,233
Nonprofit	79,496	58,172	62,788	49,881	78,512	80,557	70,609	54,300	55,836	51,687	44,423	34,670	40,761	41,415
4-year	79,843	58,425	63,028	50,117	78,604	80,622	70,774	54,388	55,898	51,809	44,502	34,813	40,783	41,761
Doctoral[2]	98,220	71,873	77,214	59,586	95,182	96,768	87,342	62,503	63,951	59,536	52,134	39,721	42,693	45,887
Master's[3]	68,154	49,871	52,642	45,718	62,539	63,603	59,353	50,176	51,470	48,165	41,447	33,991	37,923	44,153
Other 4-year	63,923	46,776	48,847	43,544	60,200	60,757	58,364	46,822	47,135	46,365	38,775	31,574	33,058	35,120
2-year	51,361	37,583	39,933	34,733	39,454	38,431	40,571	36,349	37,342	35,608	31,818	27,696	25,965	40,373
For-profit	40,374	29,543	30,023	28,942	45,505	44,248	49,693	48,469	53,548	43,389	33,043	29,894	—	27,958
2005–06														
All institutions	76,933	66,172	71,569	58,665	91,208	94,733	81,514	65,714	67,654	62,860	55,106	50,883	45,896	50,425
Public	74,592	64,158	69,191	57,462	87,599	91,080	78,412	65,107	67,077	62,231	55,029	52,297	44,628	50,096
4-year	79,001	67,951	73,353	59,437	91,600	93,976	83,946	66,745	68,475	64,013	56,181	40,044	44,598	47,107
Doctoral[2]	85,447	73,495	79,688	62,509	99,872	101,856	91,960	70,008	71,991	66,659	59,471	39,863	45,222	46,201
Master's[3]	70,273	60,444	63,659	56,157	77,752	78,677	75,547	62,029	62,967	60,706	52,419	39,542	43,502	45,640
Other 4-year	64,764	55,705	58,157	52,490	71,469	73,188	68,141	58,817	59,957	57,061	49,749	42,185	43,951	51,863
2-year	64,415	55,405	56,858	54,082	65,740	67,782	63,544	54,870	55,825	54,004	48,425	57,224	45,427	50,513
Nonprofit	82,782	71,203	77,136	61,985	98,253	101,638	88,144	66,877	68,753	64,074	55,278	41,302	49,777	53,231
4-year	83,033	71,419	77,314	62,212	98,378	101,713	88,379	66,981	68,818	64,226	55,367	41,494	49,786	53,907
Doctoral[2]	100,383	86,342	93,646	72,638	119,187	121,728	109,444	76,945	79,224	73,038	65,038	45,862	51,110	55,289
Master's[3]	68,651	59,048	61,984	55,245	74,334	75,769	71,081	59,962	61,026	58,545	49,804	40,446	45,173	57,505
Other 4-year	66,749	57,413	59,743	54,149	74,655	75,548	72,485	57,536	57,613	57,430	47,629	38,145	45,957	44,713
2-year	45,460	39,101	38,817	39,307	47,174	48,786	45,945	42,433	43,628	41,753	35,437	36,264	38,908	39,399
For-profit	49,388	42,480	42,878	42,027	60,111	59,423	61,417	56,621	55,546	58,393	47,598	35,661	—	41,579
2011–12														
All institutions	77,845	76,570	83,154	68,470	107,091	112,068	95,840	76,175	78,559	73,053	64,009	58,349	53,361	56,922
Public	74,726	73,503	79,550	66,375	101,673	106,653	90,899	74,852	77,270	71,701	63,682	59,941	50,782	55,308
4-year	79,138	77,843	84,443	68,897	106,805	110,441	97,437	76,822	78,958	73,835	65,221	47,205	50,705	55,102
Doctoral[2]	85,437	84,039	91,712	72,589	116,243	119,442	106,503	80,487	82,881	76,942	69,356	45,603	51,612	53,659
Master's[3]	69,576	68,437	71,812	64,514	88,154	89,262	86,034	70,697	71,743	69,388	59,943	45,277	48,926	53,628
Other 4-year	62,150	61,132	63,345	58,713	75,134	78,005	70,642	65,163	66,587	63,339	55,709	55,688	47,615	57,367
2-year	63,610	62,568	63,932	61,433	72,994	74,887	71,246	61,589	62,541	60,812	54,745	66,294	52,902	55,355
Nonprofit	85,220	83,825	91,165	73,838	117,362	121,963	106,047	78,681	80,985	75,634	64,592	48,476	60,323	66,905
4-year	85,342	83,945	91,272	73,951	117,417	122,006	106,124	78,744	81,024	75,720	64,646	48,475	60,336	67,136
Doctoral[2]	99,889	98,254	107,643	83,857	140,363	144,509	128,002	88,938	92,003	84,550	73,718	52,477	61,969	71,779
Master's[3]	68,974	67,845	70,861	64,318	84,844	86,211	82,280	68,405	69,344	67,286	57,032	47,180	54,658	66,251
Other 4-year	67,894	66,782	69,354	63,614	87,737	88,248	86,700	67,097	67,283	66,861	54,943	43,096	54,643	52,858
2-year	49,784	48,969	45,996	50,919	47,496	46,448	48,603	51,787	49,515	52,765	46,598	48,517	28,967	51,805
For-profit	55,318	54,413	55,019	53,738	64,957	64,849	65,150	69,740	70,945	68,560	64,074	43,428	—	42,424
2012–13														
All institutions	77,301	77,301	84,026	69,114	108,310	113,595	96,680	77,089	79,508	73,991	64,632	57,495	53,394	58,254
Public	73,909	73,909	80,072	66,706	101,685	106,945	90,603	75,505	78,038	72,269	64,190	59,120	50,662	57,376
4-year	78,111	78,111	84,822	69,150	107,427	111,224	97,790	77,519	79,750	74,466	65,874	47,701	50,814	54,544
Doctoral[2]	84,316	84,316	92,073	72,999	117,049	120,352	107,171	81,407	83,881	77,837	69,963	46,191	52,141	53,767
Master's[3]	68,037	68,037	71,451	64,116	87,291	88,529	84,983	70,474	71,557	69,141	60,248	45,625	47,691	53,580
Other 4-year	60,575	60,575	62,643	58,337	74,875	77,450	70,912	64,955	66,325	63,277	54,807	55,408	46,542	56,307
2-year	62,781	62,781	64,152	61,652	71,749	73,142	70,496	61,134	62,035	60,423	54,060	64,762	44,505	58,410
Nonprofit	85,448	85,448	92,931	75,424	120,619	125,457	109,033	80,096	82,284	77,281	65,411	48,144	60,874	66,176
4-year	85,546	85,546	93,021	75,513	120,667	125,491	109,102	80,115	82,300	77,302	65,447	48,182	60,874	66,250
Doctoral[2]	99,877	99,877	109,469	85,465	143,814	148,238	131,091	90,498	93,489	86,372	74,218	51,487	62,263	71,302
Master's[3]	68,956	68,956	71,967	65,455	86,657	87,992	84,222	69,624	70,700	68,347	58,181	46,450	56,275	62,380
Other 4-year	67,640	67,640	70,047	64,763	89,013	89,513	88,021	68,072	67,790	68,413	55,575	43,517	57,753	52,970
2-year	48,205	48,205	44,085	51,000	48,111	45,368	50,512	43,650	42,635	44,480	43,117	46,565	—	60,621
For-profit	45,727	45,727	48,650	42,675	73,302	75,475	70,604	77,143	82,509	71,975	65,826	39,289	—	31,824

—Not available.

[1]Constant dollars based on the Consumer Price Index, prepared by the Bureau of Labor Statistics, U.S. Department of Labor, adjusted to an academic-year basis.
[2]Institutions that awarded 20 or more doctor's degrees during the previous academic year.
[3]Institutions that awarded 20 or more master's degrees, but less than 20 doctor's degrees, during the previous academic year.

NOTE: Degree-granting institutions grant associate's or higher degrees and participate in Title IV federal financial aid programs. Some data have been revised from previously published figures. SOURCE: U.S. Department of Education, National Center for Education Statistics, Integrated Postsecondary Education Data System (IPEDS), "Salaries, Tenure, and Fringe Benefits of Full-Time Instructional Faculty Survey" (IPEDS-SA:99), and Winter 2005–06 through Winter 2011–12 and Spring 2013, Human Resources component, Salaries section. (This table was prepared March 2014.)

Average salary of full-time instructional faculty on 9-month contracts in degree-granting postsecondary institutions, by control and level of institution and state or jurisdiction: 2012–13

[In current dollars]

State or jurisdiction	All institutions	Public institutions						Nonprofit institutions						For-profit institutions
		Total	4-year institutions				2-year	Total	4-year institutions				2-year	
			Total	Doctoral[1]	Master's[2]	Other			Total	Doctoral[1]	Master's[2]	Other		
1	2	3	4	5	6	7	8	9	10	11	12	13	14	15
United States	**$77,301**	**$73,909**	**$78,111**	**$84,316**	**$68,037**	**$60,575**	**$62,781**	**$85,448**	**$85,546**	**$99,877**	**$68,956**	**$67,640**	**$48,205**	**$45,727**
Alabama	67,167	69,104	73,882	79,486	60,981	68,071	54,997	57,154	57,154	64,988	50,274	49,795	†	†
Alaska	76,295	77,374	77,440	81,152	75,075	†	69,050	54,063	54,063	†	54,063	†	†	†
Arizona	78,045	78,555	83,691	84,163	†	50,271	69,360	58,993	58,993	†	43,373	71,773	†	70,486
Arkansas	56,415	56,453	61,203	65,460	51,020	58,651	44,170	56,164	56,189	62,710	56,828	51,126	‡	48,168
California	91,862	88,786	94,223	106,300	77,447	73,485	82,505	103,249	103,249	112,503	81,982	89,258	†	†
Colorado	72,613	71,234	76,705	83,645	59,353	63,659	47,339	82,152	82,152	83,972	82,306	62,503	†	31,893
Connecticut	94,524	85,944	91,336	101,798	81,403	†	69,383	103,640	103,640	112,537	89,205	81,456	†	61,939
Delaware	96,781	97,822	101,666	105,928	73,297	†	78,075	86,505	86,505	121,734	64,385	†	†	†
District of Columbia	99,140	82,067	82,067	129,471	77,810	†	†	100,647	100,647	101,396	69,000	†	†	33,150
Florida	71,836	70,180	71,288	80,114	67,057	58,337	52,915	76,805	76,805	89,041	69,086	57,407	†	72,031
Georgia	69,625	67,874	69,973	77,358	58,527	†	53,359	74,959	74,973	91,874	64,862	60,681	‡	†
Hawaii	78,967	79,346	85,115	86,873	†	69,041	66,139	72,539	72,539	†	67,883	83,502	†	†
Idaho	60,762	61,345	64,550	65,087	67,937	49,551	49,198	54,047	54,047	†	51,898	56,036	†	39,951
Illinois	81,749	76,090	79,669	83,428	66,138	‡	69,859	90,298	90,298	105,930	64,910	62,048	†	†
Indiana	73,823	72,943	78,211	84,771	61,204	55,424	43,112	75,596	75,596	89,405	60,768	64,293	†	56,041
Iowa	71,614	77,617	86,911	90,905	70,469	†	54,966	62,330	62,330	68,849	55,444	62,916	†	†
Kansas	63,575	65,981	72,519	77,127	57,633	66,216	51,239	49,104	49,604	†	53,265	43,272	43,524	†
Kentucky	62,386	63,618	68,834	73,634	59,209	†	49,789	57,133	57,133	63,381	51,348	59,274	†	30,111
Louisiana	62,980	59,473	64,755	70,339	55,305	47,701	42,394	78,817	78,817	84,878	57,692	52,714	†	†
Maine	70,349	67,520	71,956	77,728	†	†	60,201	52,527	75,740	75,983	65,544	55,481	86,013	51,930
Maryland	76,229	73,484	77,145	86,128	64,840	†	66,417	86,284	86,284	101,660	65,462	74,397	†	65,606
Massachusetts	100,114	81,226	86,871	96,622	73,804	†	61,033	107,868	107,933	119,662	86,333	83,342	72,631	†
Michigan	81,811	84,387	85,904	88,478	74,620	54,242	77,403	65,402	65,402	79,232	61,156	63,493	†	49,740
Minnesota	71,861	71,506	78,936	95,717	68,281	59,928	59,761	73,034	73,034	76,028	65,302	75,049	†	†
Mississippi	58,709	58,853	63,476	65,740	52,356	†	51,099	57,340	57,340	66,696	58,912	42,475	†	†
Missouri	69,804	65,773	68,967	75,673	59,628	57,484	54,254	76,960	76,960	94,224	59,050	51,496	†	60,512
Montana	57,610	58,933	60,914	63,473	57,195	48,418	44,931	49,055	50,316	†	48,175	51,829	35,678	†
Nebraska	67,957	69,580	74,449	78,662	63,103	†	54,534	63,118	63,274	79,727	54,802	54,105	49,900	†
Nevada	78,888	79,091	80,526	89,020	†	63,724	63,164	62,703	62,703	†	62,703	†	†	†
New Hampshire	85,155	80,729	87,988	96,420	75,569	85,285	52,046	91,566	91,566	119,949	67,416	68,462	†	†
New Jersey	97,292	95,003	103,633	109,927	96,231	†	73,114	102,715	102,715	120,032	77,305	71,835	†	†
New Mexico	63,004	63,004	68,980	74,822	57,939	45,767	48,950	†	†	†	†	†	†	†
New York	89,275	76,415	80,644	98,701	70,054	64,098	68,333	96,962	96,983	108,390	76,817	81,071	77,426	36,394
North Carolina	71,164	67,222	78,149	83,585	68,189	68,477	48,827	81,882	82,121	101,958	56,745	58,840	40,111	87,040
North Dakota	63,228	65,675	67,413	73,864	57,536	52,125	52,128	49,086	49,086	52,188	†	46,726	†	†
Ohio	72,472	75,080	79,083	81,753	54,796	61,699	60,120	69,350	69,393	76,853	62,087	68,987	52,909	15,127
Oklahoma	64,747	64,345	67,698	73,084	60,036	49,493	48,293	66,603	66,603	72,657	56,611	39,580	†	†
Oregon	70,049	69,117	71,093	75,250	55,828	61,552	65,731	73,043	73,043	75,961	63,461	77,315	†	†
Pennsylvania	83,291	79,867	82,817	90,157	78,810	67,254	63,141	86,906	87,336	98,896	70,300	79,438	44,380	53,903
Rhode Island	89,435	72,374	75,990	80,797	67,731	†	61,249	101,310	101,310	123,303	86,115	†	†	†
South Carolina	63,668	65,590	74,226	86,607	65,284	54,533	48,092	57,640	57,777	†	59,777	54,774	49,852	52,308
South Dakota	59,058	60,422	63,240	63,966	64,365	45,440	45,751	52,963	52,963	†	52,736	53,076	†	†
Tennessee	68,335	64,605	70,088	72,142	61,226	†	46,719	75,854	75,854	96,669	55,252	54,249	†	‡
Texas	72,450	70,521	77,644	83,178	63,561	56,632	55,647	81,470	81,551	93,833	65,434	56,048	34,305	‡
Utah	68,886	68,303	70,317	79,913	61,961	55,038	49,735	77,000	78,366	90,785	71,995	†	55,787	‡
Vermont	74,293	75,470	75,470	83,693	59,207	56,990	†	73,213	73,213	†	76,805	52,451	†	†
Virginia	70,365	75,299	80,399	87,402	66,980	67,732	58,644	59,719	59,719	60,066	57,810	59,863	†	35,498
Washington	69,240	68,108	73,585	81,826	67,714	55,280	56,170	73,338	73,364	78,875	61,247	70,157	‡	†
West Virginia	61,063	62,746	65,177	72,478	58,059	53,404	48,150	49,801	49,801	53,751	47,342	48,450	†	27,446
Wisconsin	70,431	72,250	71,073	80,487	58,689	90,577	75,483	64,284	64,284	72,291	59,833	57,743	†	55,687
Wyoming	69,566	69,566	78,955	78,955	†	†	58,606	†	†	†	†	†	†	†
U.S. Service Academies	102,568	102,568	102,568	†	†	102,568	†	†	†	†	†	†	†	†
Other jurisdictions	**56,727**	**63,271**	**63,271**	**49,191**	**69,763**	**52,257**	**42,182**	**26,788**	**26,788**	**31,402**	**29,979**	**17,028**	**†**	**14,815**
American Samoa	29,767	29,767	29,767	†	†	29,767	†	†	†	†	†	†	†	†
Federated States of Micronesia	24,674	24,674	†	†	†	†	24,674	†	†	†	†	†	†	†
Guam	62,641	62,641	66,229	†	66,229	†	53,606	†	†	†	†	†	†	†
Marshall Islands	58,174	58,174	†	†	†	†	58,174	†	†	†	†	†	†	†
Northern Marianas	43,216	43,216	43,216	†	†	43,216	†	†	†	†	†	†	†	†
Palau	†	†	†	†	†	†	†	†	†	†	†	†	†	†
Puerto Rico	59,357	65,265	65,265	49,191	71,629	56,733	†	26,788	26,788	31,402	29,979	17,028	†	14,815
U.S. Virgin Islands	62,810	62,810	62,810	†	62,810	†	†	†	†	†	†	†	†	†

†Not applicable.
‡Reporting standards not met (too few cases).
[1]Institutions that awarded 20 or more doctor's degrees during the previous academic year.
[2]Institutions that awarded 20 or more master's degrees, but less than 20 doctor's degrees, during the previous academic year.

NOTE: Degree-granting institutions grant associate's or higher degrees and participate in Title IV federal financial aid programs. Data include imputations for nonrespondent institutions. SOURCE: U.S. Department of Education, National Center for Education Statistics, Integrated Postsecondary Education Data System (IPEDS), Spring 2013, Human Resources component, Salaries section. (This table was prepared March 2014.)

Average salary of full-time instructional faculty on 9-month contracts in 4-year degree-granting postsecondary institutions, by control and classification of institution, academic rank of faculty, and state or jurisdiction: 2012–13
[In current dollars]

State or jurisdiction	Public doctoral[1]			Public master's[2]			Nonprofit doctoral[1]			Nonprofit master's[2]		
	Professor	Associate professor	Assistant professor	Professor	Associate professor	Assistant professor	Professor	Associate professor	Assistant professor	Professor	Associate professor	Assistant professor
1	2	3	4	5	6	7	8	9	10	11	12	13
United States	**$117,049**	**$81,407**	**$69,963**	**$87,291**	**$70,474**	**$60,248**	**$143,814**	**$90,498**	**$74,218**	**$86,657**	**$69,624**	**$58,181**
Alabama	113,876	79,555	65,152	78,498	65,177	54,809	85,763	67,504	55,956	61,825	52,371	46,982
Alaska	113,682	81,684	67,538	102,753	79,109	66,885	†	†	†	67,416	56,317	47,158
Arizona	117,827	81,762	71,824	†	†	†	†	†	†	‡	63,092	‡
Arkansas	92,227	68,906	62,447	66,216	54,414	49,898	75,296	63,921	58,161	63,746	60,041	51,655
California	133,774	88,431	78,816	93,049	75,770	68,504	149,596	98,747	83,434	99,699	80,086	67,226
Colorado	114,901	84,950	71,627	79,407	63,605	55,334	125,997	81,390	72,872	113,777	72,826	60,594
Connecticut	135,885	92,085	74,559	96,902	78,071	63,153	163,142	89,362	77,511	120,062	86,422	71,493
Delaware	141,691	97,167	82,431	87,419	69,473	66,589	152,547	117,386	97,370	74,865	64,322	54,544
District of Columbia	148,833	115,000	85,788	101,864	76,643	59,525	144,936	94,479	78,388	73,179	65,766	69,162
Florida	109,330	78,003	69,303	96,525	71,929	60,429	122,128	82,423	71,548	89,317	71,907	60,283
Georgia	108,683	76,338	67,156	75,350	63,592	54,504	131,154	83,769	68,201	72,687	58,459	52,466
Hawaii	111,111	84,582	73,217	†	†	†	†	†	†	84,165	72,725	60,071
Idaho	85,346	67,037	58,548	98,034	71,093	56,345	†	†	†	60,845	51,396	42,903
Illinois	119,673	81,910	71,242	91,610	71,453	62,470	156,477	92,054	81,195	82,644	68,790	57,832
Indiana	118,452	82,566	70,584	86,434	67,558	58,110	128,663	81,038	70,103	74,419	62,726	52,337
Iowa	123,740	85,673	74,880	87,708	70,247	61,296	90,172	68,178	56,031	68,305	56,964	49,390
Kansas	107,337	75,046	64,075	73,476	59,756	54,934	†	†	†	61,590	53,547	49,329
Kentucky	104,075	73,671	63,072	76,892	61,893	53,387	79,657	63,076	53,694	61,200	53,445	45,355
Louisiana	96,765	70,808	63,377	73,244	60,511	52,610	123,372	83,352	69,293	67,921	54,802	53,057
Maine	95,457	75,159	61,472	†	†	†	87,793	72,645	64,713	74,108	55,882	49,721
Maryland	119,314	85,563	76,759	85,751	68,222	61,561	147,178	95,041	81,940	83,190	66,756	58,856
Massachusetts	128,755	95,589	79,441	86,867	71,290	62,301	164,211	101,382	89,452	117,703	82,930	65,554
Michigan	121,176	83,719	71,537	93,896	77,065	64,611	108,093	76,237	67,060	72,492	60,091	51,079
Minnesota	126,782	86,677	77,293	82,305	67,834	58,599	99,424	74,892	61,725	76,874	66,000	55,031
Mississippi	92,960	71,314	62,350	65,207	54,057	52,254	83,979	67,390	59,091	76,096	57,718	52,345
Missouri	101,285	73,191	61,754	74,695	60,777	51,822	138,496	84,204	71,681	72,618	60,496	51,845
Montana	76,966	62,566	61,201	71,108	62,439	52,095	†	†	†	55,970	46,893	42,122
Nebraska	103,329	76,248	69,860	77,788	62,930	52,143	106,245	77,367	64,393	64,263	55,070	50,345
Nevada	118,121	84,526	69,809	†	†	†	†	†	†	71,919	65,478	62,542
New Hampshire	116,758	90,711	72,862	89,968	74,047	61,127	150,044	97,228	67,803	84,115	72,258	52,169
New Jersey	149,954	101,586	84,216	119,833	95,161	76,241	168,282	93,263	83,238	95,140	81,864	64,604
New Mexico	98,259	72,718	63,623	71,053	58,592	51,520	†	†	†	†	†	†
New York	131,739	92,390	75,936	90,674	72,218	60,865	154,224	97,771	76,699	97,077	77,139	64,947
North Carolina	121,494	81,350	73,287	89,279	71,163	62,284	153,421	92,067	75,803	67,788	59,256	53,097
North Dakota	99,043	77,325	66,195	76,044	62,291	54,048	68,401	65,732	52,144	†	†	†
Ohio	111,772	80,397	68,950	72,621	62,340	52,832	109,255	74,460	63,394	74,679	63,670	53,150
Oklahoma	102,395	73,003	62,858	74,933	63,715	56,170	93,101	71,891	59,144	67,201	58,674	50,917
Oregon	103,964	78,898	71,168	73,054	58,924	46,957	98,183	74,225	62,005	78,993	65,418	54,925
Pennsylvania	129,129	89,431	69,118	103,099	82,086	65,317	141,050	91,529	78,783	90,130	71,641	60,512
Rhode Island	103,140	77,007	66,609	78,664	67,080	57,452	157,248	101,670	85,880	111,848	84,732	70,990
South Carolina	120,635	85,286	75,220	82,838	66,519	58,958	†	†	†	75,474	58,545	52,740
South Dakota	83,811	67,547	60,150	82,906	67,863	56,816	†	†	†	65,321	52,941	50,966
Tennessee	98,308	73,657	61,672	75,801	66,081	52,703	133,291	87,576	72,982	66,015	54,625	48,470
Texas	121,559	82,550	72,471	84,195	67,767	61,114	128,717	88,657	78,612	83,422	67,440	56,356
Utah	110,647	75,337	64,224	76,289	63,666	55,999	110,754	79,869	68,274	85,472	72,374	59,550
Vermont	115,985	85,441	69,453	71,511	55,534	44,908	†	†	†	103,009	74,285	64,838
Virginia	124,185	83,458	70,256	84,710	67,436	60,128	115,063	83,141	47,527	69,947	59,141	52,165
Washington	107,097	79,686	73,280	84,227	70,255	67,632	106,575	79,604	64,920	77,526	62,238	55,615
West Virginia	92,062	75,746	62,680	70,980	59,930	52,065	69,231	56,008	50,989	56,521	49,352	44,214
Wisconsin	103,642	75,096	69,178	71,018	60,191	56,503	98,890	74,478	62,883	73,834	60,703	53,218
Wyoming	106,226	76,016	67,426	†	†	†	†	†	†	†	†	†
U.S. Service Academies	†	†	†	†	†	†	†	†	†	†	†	†
Other jurisdictions	**65,512**	**†**	**50,566**	**80,156**	**66,908**	**57,702**	**50,061**	**30,556**	**23,343**	**†**	**†**	**†**
American Samoa	†	†	†	†	†	†	†	†	†	†	†	†
Federated States of Micronesia	†	†	†	†	†	†	†	†	†	†	†	†
Guam	†	†	†	89,134	70,677	55,034	†	†	†	†	†	†
Marshall Islands	†	†	†	†	†	†	†	†	†	†	†	†
Northern Marianas	†	†	†	†	†	†	†	†	†	†	†	†
Palau	†	†	†	†	†	†	†	†	†	†	†	†
Puerto Rico	65,512	†	50,566	79,604	65,807	60,216	50,061	30,556	23,343	†	†	†
U.S. Virgin Islands	†	†	†	77,944	66,815	53,062	†	†	†	†	†	†

†Not applicable.
‡Reporting standards not met (too few cases).
[1]Institutions that awarded 20 or more doctor's degrees during the previous academic year.
[2]Institutions that awarded 20 or more master's degrees, but less than 20 doctor's degrees, during the previous academic year.

NOTE: Degree-granting institutions grant associate's or higher degrees and participate in Title IV federal financial aid programs. Data include imputations for nonrespondent institutions.
SOURCE: U.S. Department of Education, National Center for Education Statistics, Integrated Postsecondary Education Data System (IPEDS), Spring 2013, Human Resources component, Salaries section. (This table was prepared March 2014.)

Percentage of full-time instructional faculty with tenure for degree-granting postsecondary institutions with a tenure system, by academic rank, sex, and control and level of institution: Selected years, 1993–94 through 2011–12

Academic year, control and level of institution	Percent of institutions with tenure systems	Percent of full-time instructional faculty with tenure														
		Total			Professor			Associate professor			Assistant professor			Instructor	Lecturer	No academic rank
		Total	Male	Female	Total	Male	Female	Total	Male	Female	Total	Male	Female			
1	2	3	4	5	6	7	8	9	10	11	12	13	14	15	16	17
1993–94																
All institutions	62.6	56.2	62.6	42.7	91.9	92.8	87.7	76.8	77.5	75.1	14.4	13.6	15.5	38.3	10.8	26.0
Public institutions	73.6	58.9	65.4	45.6	92.6	93.6	87.5	80.8	81.6	78.9	17.1	16.1	18.5	45.5	7.2	28.6
4-year	92.6	56.3	63.5	39.3	94.3	94.7	92.0	80.4	81.2	78.4	13.8	13.0	14.8	4.4	5.4	6.1
Doctoral[1]	100.0	54.5	62.1	35.0	94.2	94.7	90.1	81.3	82.1	79.2	7.3	6.7	8.3	2.8	2.1	5.4
Master's[2]	98.3	60.5	67.7	46.1	95.4	95.5	95.0	79.3	80.0	77.7	23.0	23.0	22.9	6.4	11.7	11.0
Other	76.4	51.1	56.3	40.0	88.4	88.8	86.4	76.5	77.3	74.8	22.7	22.8	22.6	4.6	15.0	6.4
2-year	62.1	69.9	75.4	63.0	80.7	83.7	75.5	84.2	86.4	81.5	47.7	51.1	44.6	68.9	39.9	65.7
Nonprofit institutions	62.0	49.5	56.0	35.5	90.3	90.8	88.1	67.6	68.1	66.5	9.0	8.7	9.4	6.1	21.9	18.9
4-year	66.3	49.5	56.0	35.4	90.3	90.8	88.0	67.6	68.1	66.5	9.0	8.7	9.4	5.5	21.6	15.7
Doctoral[1]	90.5	47.6	53.5	31.9	90.5	90.8	88.5	62.5	63.4	60.0	3.7	3.7	3.7	8.9	29.2	15.4
Master's[2]	76.5	51.8	59.2	38.2	90.8	91.1	89.8	71.3	72.2	69.6	13.4	13.6	13.1	2.6	0.7	10.5
Other	58.3	50.4	57.4	37.2	89.4	90.4	85.1	70.6	70.9	70.2	11.9	11.9	11.9	3.9	3.4	20.0
2-year	26.1	47.9	54.5	38.5	88.0	84.3	94.3	63.8	65.1	62.7	12.0	12.3	11.9	20.0	86.7	68.6
For-profit institutions	7.8	33.8	39.0	27.8	95.2	94.1	100.0	—	—	—	‡	‡	‡	32.9	—	—
1999–2000																
All institutions	55.0	53.7	59.6	43.2	92.8	93.1	91.2	76.8	76.9	76.7	11.8	11.0	12.9	34.1	3.4	18.3
Public institutions	72.8	55.9	62.0	45.6	93.9	94.4	91.9	81.0	81.2	80.7	14.1	13.1	15.4	39.8	4.1	21.2
4-year	94.6	53.2	60.3	39.3	94.2	94.6	92.5	80.8	81.0	80.3	10.0	9.5	10.6	3.9	3.0	4.0
Doctoral[1]	100.0	50.4	58.0	34.5	92.9	93.6	89.3	79.9	80.2	79.4	4.7	4.4	5.2	2.1	1.5	1.4
Master's[2]	95.5	59.1	66.0	48.0	96.9	96.9	96.8	82.7	83.0	82.1	18.1	17.8	18.5	6.4	5.9	25.3
Other	86.3	54.7	61.2	43.2	94.9	95.1	94.0	80.7	81.3	79.7	21.8	24.1	18.8	5.8	7.2	49.3
2-year	60.3	67.7	70.6	64.5	91.2	92.2	89.7	83.3	83.6	83.1	53.8	56.0	52.0	60.4	21.2	64.4
Nonprofit institutions	59.0	48.2	54.2	36.8	90.3	90.5	89.7	68.0	67.8	68.4	7.5	6.8	8.2	1.8	1.2	7.4
4-year	63.4	48.1	54.1	36.7	90.3	90.5	89.7	68.0	67.8	68.5	7.4	6.8	8.1	1.6	1.2	4.1
Doctoral[1]	81.2	43.4	49.6	29.6	88.6	88.7	87.6	62.6	62.8	62.2	3.0	2.8	3.2	1.0	1.3	0.5
Master's[2]	72.6	52.3	59.4	41.4	91.2	91.6	90.0	72.0	73.0	70.3	12.1	11.9	12.3	0.9	0.8	22.3
Other	54.9	53.5	59.3	44.0	93.5	93.8	92.8	73.1	71.2	76.0	9.9	9.4	10.5	3.6	1.6	23.5
2-year	14.0	59.7	63.3	53.6	96.0	96.0	96.0	57.1	61.3	54.3	31.6	36.7	28.3	30.2	—	65.8
For-profit institutions	4.0	77.4	77.2	77.6	47.4	50.0	33.3	—	—	—	—	—	—	86.1	—	71.9
2009–10																
All institutions	47.8	48.7	54.5	40.6	90.3	90.7	89.3	74.6	74.5	74.6	7.2	6.9	7.6	28.2	1.4	24.7
Public institutions	71.2	50.6	56.3	42.9	91.6	92.0	90.6	78.3	78.4	78.2	9.1	8.4	9.8	33.7	1.8	30.2
4-year	90.9	47.9	54.6	38.0	92.0	92.2	91.4	78.7	78.6	78.8	5.7	5.4	6.0	2.5	1.2	7.5
Doctoral[1]	99.5	45.7	52.9	34.1	90.2	90.6	88.6	75.6	75.7	75.4	2.4	2.2	2.6	0.9	0.7	1.6
Master's[2]	98.6	53.5	60.0	45.6	97.5	97.5	97.4	86.0	86.2	85.8	11.3	11.5	11.2	3.2	1.8	8.7
Other	72.4	51.2	55.5	46.1	92.2	93.3	90.2	84.6	85.0	84.0	20.5	21.4	19.6	11.8	3.0	58.7
2-year	57.7	64.1	67.2	61.4	88.2	89.6	86.9	74.1	75.2	73.3	45.2	48.3	42.9	58.4	22.6	67.6
Nonprofit institutions	57.1	44.3	50.6	35.2	87.8	88.2	86.6	67.2	67.0	67.6	3.8	3.8	3.7	0.6	0.3	7.1
4-year	59.5	44.3	50.6	35.2	87.8	88.2	86.7	67.2	67.0	67.6	3.8	3.8	3.7	0.5	0.3	7.0
Doctoral[1]	83.8	39.7	46.6	28.4	85.6	86.4	82.7	59.7	60.2	59.0	1.8	1.9	1.7	0.2	0.2	1.0
Master's[2]	65.8	49.8	55.7	42.4	89.7	90.1	88.8	74.0	74.1	73.8	7.2	7.6	6.8	0.7	0.2	20.4
Other	47.4	53.4	59.1	45.8	93.2	92.9	93.8	79.4	78.6	80.5	4.8	5.0	4.5	1.6	1.6	45.7
2-year	12.9	38.5	49.5	31.7	86.7	‡	70.0	59.3	64.7	56.8	20.5	18.5	21.4	8.2	‡	30.0
For-profit institutions	1.5	51.0	58.6	42.1	75.5	74.7	77.8	8.5	3.2	12.5	‡	‡	‡	87.3	‡	‡
2011–12																
All institutions	45.3	48.5	54.2	41.0	89.7	90.1	88.9	74.9	75.0	74.9	6.9	6.4	7.3	27.3	1.3	23.8
Public institutions	71.6	50.7	56.2	43.6	91.1	91.5	90.1	78.6	78.8	78.2	8.8	8.1	9.6	33.1	1.7	29.6
4-year	90.8	48.0	54.5	38.7	91.4	91.6	90.6	78.9	79.0	78.7	5.5	5.2	5.8	2.9	1.1	9.6
Doctoral[1]	99.6	46.0	52.9	35.5	90.0	90.4	88.5	76.2	76.5	75.7	2.5	2.3	2.8	1.1	0.7	1.3
Master's[2]	97.5	55.6	61.9	48.3	97.6	97.6	97.7	88.6	88.9	88.2	13.3	13.3	13.3	1.8	2.4	7.1
Other	70.2	54.2	57.7	50.4	93.2	94.3	91.2	87.8	87.7	87.8	24.3	25.1	23.5	21.3	2.7	63.9
2-year	57.8	64.7	67.3	62.4	88.7	89.9	87.6	75.1	76.2	74.1	44.0	46.2	42.4	58.9	17.2	69.7
Nonprofit institutions	55.6	43.7	49.9	35.1	87.0	87.3	86.3	67.8	67.4	68.3	3.3	3.4	3.3	0.4	0.3	6.7
4-year	58.6	43.7	49.9	35.1	87.0	87.3	86.3	67.8	67.4	68.4	3.3	3.4	3.3	0.4	0.3	6.6
Doctoral[1]	76.4	40.2	46.9	30.3	85.0	85.6	82.9	62.0	62.3	61.7	2.2	2.4	2.0	0.3	0.1	0.7
Master's[2]	59.3	51.0	56.4	44.7	90.9	90.7	91.3	76.7	76.5	76.9	6.7	6.5	7.0	0.7	1.3	32.6
Other	43.1	54.5	60.5	47.1	94.4	94.3	94.5	84.4	83.0	86.2	4.4	4.6	4.2	0.5	0.0	54.9
2-year	8.0	31.4	41.1	25.2	‡	‡	‡	46.3	66.7	42.9	12.3	22.2	7.7	5.1	‡	33.3
For-profit institutions	1.3	31.0	31.4	30.7	72.3	73.8	69.2	30.8	18.9	41.5	1.6	‡	‡	54.4	‡	5.0

—Not available.
‡Reporting standards not met (too few cases).
[1]Institutions that awarded 20 or more doctor's degrees during the previous academic year.
[2]Institutions that awarded 20 or more master's degrees, but less than 20 doctor's degrees, during the previous academic year.
NOTE: The coverage of this table differs from similar tables published in editions of the *Digest* prior to 2003. Previous tenure tabulations included only instructional staff classified as full-time faculty; this table includes all staff with full-time instructional duties, including faculty and other instructional staff. Data for 1993–94 are for institutions of higher education, while later data are for degree-granting institutions. Degree-granting institutions grant associate's or higher degrees

and participate in Title IV federal financial aid programs. The degree-granting classification is very similar to the earlier higher education classification, but it includes more 2-year colleges and excludes a few higher education institutions that did not grant degrees. Beginning in 2009–10, includes institutions with fewer than 15 full-time employees; institutions with fewer than 15 employees did not report staff data prior to 2007–08.
SOURCE: U.S. Department of Education, National Center for Education Statistics, Integrated Postsecondary Education Data System (IPEDS), "Fall Staff Survey" (IPEDS-S:93–99); and Winter 2009–10 and Winter 2011–12, Human Resources component, Fall Staff section. (This table was prepared July 2012.)

Degree-granting postsecondary institutions, by control and level of institution: Selected years, 1949–50 through 2012–13

Year	All institutions			Public			Private			Nonprofit			For-profit		
	Total	4-year	2-year	Total	4-year	2-year	Total	4-year, total	2-year, total	Total	4-year	2-year	Total	4-year	2-year
1	2	3	4	5	6	7	8	9	10	11	12	13	14	15	16
Excluding branch campuses															
1949–50	1,851	1,327	524	641	344	297	1,210	983	227	—	—	—	—	—	—
1959–60	2,004	1,422	582	695	367	328	1,309	1,055	254	—	—	—	—	—	—
1969–70	2,525	1,639	886	1,060	426	634	1,465	1,213	252	—	—	—	—	—	—
1970–71	2,556	1,665	891	1,089	435	654	1,467	1,230	237	—	—	—	—	—	—
1971–72	2,606	1,675	931	1,137	440	697	1,469	1,235	234	—	—	—	—	—	—
1972–73	2,665	1,701	964	1,182	449	733	1,483	1,252	231	—	—	—	—	—	—
1973–74	2,720	1,717	1,003	1,200	440	760	1,520	1,277	243	—	—	—	—	—	—
1974–75	2,747	1,744	1,003	1,214	447	767	1,533	1,297	236	—	—	—	—	—	—
1975–76	2,765	1,767	998	1,219	447	772	1,546	1,320	226	—	—	—	—	—	—
1976–77	2,785	1,783	1,002	1,231	452	779	1,554	1,331	223	—	—	—	—	—	—
1977–78	2,826	1,808	1,018	1,241	454	787	1,585	1,354	231	—	—	—	—	—	—
1978–79	2,954	1,843	1,111	1,308	463	845	1,646	1,380	266	—	—	—	—	—	—
1979–80	2,975	1,863	1,112	1,310	464	846	1,665	1,399	266	—	—	—	—	—	—
1980–81	3,056	1,861	1,195	1,334	465	869	1,722	1,396	326 [1]	—	—	—	—	—	—
1981–82	3,083	1,883	1,200	1,340	471	869	1,743	1,412	331 [1]	—	—	—	—	—	—
1982–83	3,111	1,887	1,224	1,336	472	864	1,775	1,415	360 [1]	—	—	—	—	—	—
1983–84	3,117	1,914	1,203	1,325	474	851	1,792	1,440	352	—	—	—	—	—	—
1984–85	3,146	1,911	1,235	1,329	461	868	1,817	1,450	367	—	—	—	—	—	—
1985–86	3,155	1,915	1,240	1,326	461	865	1,829	1,454	375	—	—	—	—	—	—
Including branch campuses															
1974–75	3,004	1,866	1,138	1,433	537	896	1,571	1,329	242	—	—	—	—	—	—
1975–76	3,026	1,898	1,128	1,442	545	897	1,584	1,353	231	—	—	—	—	—	—
1976–77	3,046	1,913	1,133	1,455	550	905	1,591	1,363	228	1,536	1,348	188	55	15	40
1977–78	3,095	1,938	1,157	1,473	552	921	1,622	1,386	236	—	—	—	—	—	—
1978–79	3,134	1,941	1,193	1,474	550	924	1,660	1,391	269	1,564	1,376	188	96	15	81
1979–80	3,152	1,957	1,195	1,475	549	926	1,677	1,408	269	—	—	—	—	—	—
1980–81	3,231	1,957	1,274	1,497	552	945	1,734	1,405	329 [1]	1,569	1,387	182	165	18	147
1981–82	3,253	1,979	1,274	1,498	558	940	1,755	1,421	334 [1]	—	—	—	—	—	—
1982–83	3,280	1,984	1,296	1,493	560	933	1,787	1,424	363 [1]	—	—	—	—	—	—
1983–84	3,284	2,013	1,271	1,481	565	916	1,803	1,448	355	—	—	—	—	—	—
1984–85	3,331	2,025	1,306	1,501	566	935	1,830	1,459	371	1,616	1,430	186	214	29	185
1985–86	3,340	2,029	1,311	1,498	566	932	1,842	1,463	379	—	—	—	—	—	—
1986–87	3,406	2,070	1,336	1,533	573	960	1,873	1,497	376	1,635	1,462	173	238	35	203
1987–88	3,587	2,135	1,452	1,591	599	992	1,996	1,536	460	1,673	1,487	186	323	49	274
1988–89	3,565	2,129	1,436	1,582	598	984	1,983	1,531	452	1,658	1,478	180	325	53	272
1989–90	3,535	2,127	1,408	1,563	595	968	1,972	1,532	440	1,656	1,479	177	316	53	263
1990–91	3,559	2,141	1,418	1,567	595	972	1,992	1,546	446	1,649	1,482	167	343	64	279
1991–92	3,601	2,157	1,444	1,598	599	999	2,003	1,558	445	1,662	1,486	176	341	72	269
1992–93	3,638	2,169	1,469	1,624	600	1,024	2,014	1,569	445	1,672	1,493	179	342	76	266
1993–94	3,632	2,190	1,442	1,625	604	1,021	2,007	1,586	421	1,687	1,506	181	320	80	240
1994–95	3,688	2,215	1,473	1,641	605	1,036	2,047	1,610	437	1,702	1,510	192	345	100	245
1995–96	3,706	2,244	1,462	1,655	608	1,047	2,051	1,636	415	1,706	1,519	187	345	117	228
1996–97	4,009	2,267	1,742	1,702	614	1,088	2,307	1,653	654	1,693	1,509	184	614	144	470
1997–98	4,064	2,309	1,755	1,707	615	1,092	2,357	1,694	663	1,707	1,528	179	650	166	484
1998–99	4,048	2,335	1,713	1,681	612	1,069	2,367	1,723	644	1,695	1,531	164	672	192	480
1999–2000	4,084	2,363	1,721	1,682	614	1,068	2,402	1,749	653	1,681	1,531	150	721	218	503
2000–01	4,182	2,450	1,732	1,698	622	1,076	2,484	1,828	656	1,695	1,551	144	789	277	512
2001–02	4,197	2,487	1,710	1,713	628	1,085	2,484	1,859	625	1,676	1,541	135	808	318	490
2002–03	4,168	2,466	1,702	1,712	631	1,081	2,456	1,835	621	1,665	1,538	127	791	297	494
2003–04	4,236	2,530	1,706	1,720	634	1,086	2,516	1,896	620	1,664	1,546	118	852	350	502
2004–05	4,216	2,533	1,683	1,700	639	1,061	2,516	1,894	622	1,637	1,525	112	879	369	510
2005–06	4,276	2,582	1,694	1,693	640	1,053	2,583	1,942	641	1,647	1,534	113	936	408	528
2006–07	4,314	2,629	1,685	1,688	643	1,045	2,626	1,986	640	1,640	1,533	107	986	453	533
2007–08	4,352	2,675	1,677	1,685	653	1,032	2,667	2,022	645	1,624	1,532	92	1,043	490	553
2008–09	4,409	2,719	1,690	1,676	652	1,024	2,733	2,067	666	1,629	1,537	92	1,104	530	574
2009–10	4,495	2,774	1,721	1,672	672	1,000	2,823	2,102	721	1,624	1,539	85	1,199	563	636
2010–11	4,599	2,870	1,729	1,656	678	978	2,943	2,192	751	1,630	1,543	87	1,313	649	664
2011–12	4,706	2,968	1,738	1,649	682	967	3,057	2,286	771	1,653	1,553	100	1,404	733	671
2012–13	4,726	3,026	1,700	1,623	689	934	3,103	2,337	766	1,652	1,555	97	1,451	782	669

—Not available.

[1]Large increases are due to the addition of schools accredited by the Accrediting Commission of Career Schools and Colleges of Technology.
NOTE: Data through 1995–96 are for institutions of higher education, while later data are for degree-granting institutions. Degree-granting institutions grant associate's or higher degrees and participate in Title IV federal financial aid programs. Changes in counts of institutions over time are partly affected by increasing or decreasing numbers of institutions submitting separate data for branch campuses.

SOURCE: U.S. Department of Education, National Center for Education Statistics, *Education Directory, Colleges and Universities*, 1949–50 through 1965–66; Higher Education General Information Survey (HEGIS), "Institutional Characteristics of Colleges and Universities" surveys, 1966–67 through 1985–86; Integrated Postsecondary Education Data System (IPEDS), "Institutional Characteristics Survey" (IPEDS-IC:86–99); and IPEDS Fall 2000 through Fall 2012, Institutional Characteristics component. (This table was prepared August 2013.)

Degree-granting postsecondary institutions, by control and level of institution and state or jurisdiction: 2012–13

State or jurisdiction	Total	All public institutions	Public 4-year institutions — Total	Research university, very high[1]	Research university, high[2]	Doctoral/ research university[3]	Master's[4]	Bacca-laureate[5]	Special focus[6]	Public 2-year	All nonprofit institutions	Nonprofit 4-year — Total	Research university, very high[1]	Research university, high[2]	Doctoral/ research university[3]	Master's[4]	Bacca-laureate[5]	Special focus[6]	Nonprofit 2-year	For-profit — Total	For-profit 4-year	For-profit 2-year
1	2	3	4	5	6	7	8	9	10	11	12	13	14	15	16	17	18	19	20	21	22	23
United States	4,726	1,623	689	73	73	28	271	197	47	934	1,652	1,555	34	25	48	364	513	571	97	1,451	782	669
Alabama	77	39	14	2	3	0	8	1	0	25	20	18	0	0	0	1	12	5	2	18	11	7
Alaska	9	5	3	0	0	0	2	1	0	2	2	2	0	0	0	1	1	0	0	2	1	1
Arizona	87	24	3	2	1	0	0	0	0	21	11	11	0	0	0	1	0	10	0	52	36	16
Arkansas	52	33	11	1	0	1	6	3	0	22	14	14	0	0	0	2	9	3	0	5	1	4
California	457	149	35	8	1	0	21	3	2	114	141	135	3	1	10	25	23	73	6	167	87	80
Colorado	93	28	14	2	2	1	4	5	0	14	13	11	0	0	1	3	2	5	2	52	30	22
Connecticut	46	21	9	1	0	0	4	4	0	12	19	19	1	0	0	9	5	4	0	6	5	1
Delaware	12	5	2	1	0	0	0	0	1	3	5	4	0	0	1	0	1	2	1	2	2	0
District of Columbia	20	2	2	0	0	0	0	0	2	0	14	14	1	1	3	0	2	7	0	4	4	0
Florida	239	41	35	4	2	0	4	23	2	6	65	61	1	1	3	13	22	21	4	133	66	67
Georgia	142	61	30	3	0	1	11	14	1	31	35	33	0	2	1	4	18	8	2	46	26	20
Hawaii	21	10	4	1	2	0	0	0	1	6	7	7	0	0	0	2	2	3	0	4	3	1
Idaho	19	8	4	0	2	0	1	1	0	4	4	4	0	0	0	1	2	1	0	7	6	1
Illinois	186	60	12	2	2	1	7	0	0	48	83	80	1	5	4	17	16	37	3	43	26	17
Indiana	85	16	15	2	2	1	6	3	1	1	40	39	0	0	1	9	19	10	1	29	19	10
Iowa	67	19	3	2	1	0	0	0	0	16	34	33	0	0	0	6	24	3	1	14	13	1
Kansas	67	32	8	1	1	0	4	1	1	24	24	24	0	0	0	6	12	6	0	11	6	5
Kentucky	80	24	8	2	0	2	4	0	0	16	27	25	0	0	1	6	13	5	2	29	24	5
Louisiana	72	35	17	1	3	1	5	6	1	18	13	13	1	0	0	3	4	5	0	24	9	15
Maine	32	15	8	0	1	0	4	3	0	7	15	12	0	0	0	3	6	3	3	2	2	0
Maryland	64	29	13	1	1	0	7	1	3	16	23	22	1	0	0	6	12	3	1	12	6	6
Massachusetts	125	30	14	1	1	0	7	2	3	16	84	84	5	5	5	15	24	30	0	11	6	5
Michigan	116	46	15	3	2	0	7	1	2	31	50	47	0	1	1	11	20	14	3	20	14	6
Minnesota	119	43	12	1	2	0	8	0	1	31	36	35	0	0	3	11	12	9	1	40	34	6
Mississippi	42	24	9	2	2	0	4	0	1	15	9	9	0	0	0	3	4	2	0	9	3	6
Missouri	133	27	13	1	2	0	7	3	0	14	56	53	1	0	3	11	24	14	3	50	27	23
Montana	22	17	6	0	1	0	4	0	1	11	2	2	0	0	0	0	1	1	0	3	3	0
Nebraska	43	15	7	1	1	0	3	1	1	8	18	16	0	0	0	5	7	4	2	10	6	4
Nevada	27	7	6	0	3	0	1	2	0	1	3	3	0	0	0	1	0	2	0	17	3	14
New Hampshire	27	12	5	1	1	0	1	2	0	7	13	13	0	0	0	1	3	9	0	2	2	0
New Jersey	70	33	14	1	1	2	7	2	1	19	27	27	1	1	1	10	2	12	0	10	5	5
New Mexico	44	28	9	1	1	1	3	1	2	19	3	3	0	0	0	0	1	2	0	13	2	11
New York	303	78	43	4	4	0	21	12	2	35	178	164	5	5	7	40	27	80	14	47	21	26
North Carolina	149	75	16	2	1	1	7	2	3	59	49	49	1	0	2	7	27	12	0	25	17	8
North Dakota	21	14	9	1	1	0	4	2	1	5	6	6	0	0	0	1	1	4	0	1	1	0
Ohio	225	60	35	8	1	2	19	2	3	25	73	66	2	1	2	20	18	23	7	92	32	60
Oklahoma	66	29	17	1	2	0	8	4	2	12	14	14	0	0	0	4	6	4	0	23	11	12
Oregon	65	26	9	2	1	0	3	2	1	17	24	24	0	0	1	5	7	11	0	15	8	7
Pennsylvania	267	61	45	2	6	3	21	4	9	16	120	106	2	3	2	30	36	33	14	86	12	74
Rhode Island	13	3	2	1	0	0	1	0	0	1	10	10	1	1	0	1	4	3	0	0	0	0
South Carolina	79	33	13	1	1	0	5	4	2	20	24	22	0	0	0	5	14	3	2	22	12	10
South Dakota	25	12	7	0	0	1	4	0	2	5	8	7	0	0	0	2	5	0	1	5	2	3
Tennessee	112	22	9	1	2	0	4	2	0	13	49	45	0	0	2	11	16	16	4	41	24	17
Texas	271	108	45	6	6	7	16	5	5	63	63	55	2	1	2	17	14	19	8	100	43	57
Utah	42	8	7	1	2	0	2	0	2	1	4	3	0	0	0	2	0	1	1	30	24	6

See notes at end of table.

Degree-granting postsecondary institutions, by control and level of institution and state or jurisdiction: 2012–13—Continued

State or jurisdiction	Total	All public institutions	Public 4-year: Total	Research university, very high[1]	Research university, high[2]	Doctoral/research university[3]	Master's[4]	Baccalaureate[5]	Special focus[6]	Public 2-year institutions[1]	All nonprofit institutions	Nonprofit 4-year: Total	Research university, very high[1]	Research university, high[2]	Doctoral/research university[3]	Master's[4]	Baccalaureate[5]	Special focus[6]	Nonprofit 2-year	For-profit: Total	For-profit: 4-year	For-profit: 2-year
1	2	3	4	5	6	7	8	9	10	11	12	13	14	15	16	17	18	19	20	21	22	23
Vermont	24	6	5	0	1	0	1	3	0	1	17	17	0	0	0	4	11	2	0	1	1	0
Virginia	132	40	16	3	3	0	7	2	1	24	38	37	0	0	1	7	20	9	1	54	30	24
Washington	87	43	17	2	0	0	6	7	2	26	24	23	0	0	0	10	5	8	1	20	12	8
West Virginia	43	23	13	1	1	0	3	8	0	10	8	8	0	0	0	0	7	1	0	12	3	9
Wisconsin	91	31	14	1	1	0	10	2	0	17	30	30	0	0	3	8	10	9	0	30	27	3
Wyoming	11	8	1	0	1	0	0	0	0	7	0	0	0	0	0	0	0	0	0	3	2	1
U.S. Service Academies	5	5	5	0	0	0	0	5	0	0	†	†	†	†	†	†	†	†	†	†	†	†
Other jurisdictions	91	26	18	0	1	1	1	12	3	8	47	46	0	0	3	12	19	12	1	18	8	10
American Samoa	1	1	1	0	0	0	0	1	0	0	0	0	0	0	0	0	0	0	0	0	0	0
Federated States of Micronesia	1	1	0	0	0	0	0	0	0	1	0	0	0	0	0	0	0	0	0	0	0	0
Guam	3	2	1	0	0	0	1	0	0	1	1	1	0	0	0	0	0	1	0	0	0	0
Marshall Islands	1	1	0	0	0	0	0	0	0	1	0	0	0	0	0	0	0	0	0	0	0	0
Northern Marianas	1	1	1	0	0	0	0	1	0	0	0	0	0	0	0	0	0	0	0	0	0	0
Palau	1	1	0	0	0	0	0	0	0	1	0	0	0	0	0	0	0	0	0	0	0	0
Puerto Rico	82	18	14	0	1	1	0	9	3	4	46	45	0	0	3	12	19	11	1	18	8	10
U.S. Virgin Islands	1	1	1	0	0	0	0	1	0	0	0	0	0	0	0	0	0	0	0	0	0	0

†Not applicable.

[1]Research universities with a very high level of research activity.

[2]Research universities with a high level of research activity.

[3]Institutions that award at least 20 doctor's degrees per year, but did not have a high level of research activity.

[4]Institutions that award at least 50 master's degrees per year.

[5]Institutions that primarily emphasize undergraduate education.

[6]Four-year institutions that award degrees primarily in single fields of study, such as medicine, business, fine arts, theology, and engineering. Includes some institutions that award degrees primarily in single fields of study, such as medicine, business, fine arts, theology, and engineering. Includes some institutions that have 4-year programs, but have not reported sufficient data to identify program category. Also includes institutions classified as 4-year under the IPEDS system, which had been classified as 2-year in the Carnegie classification system because they primarily award associate's degrees.

NOTE: Branch campuses are counted as separate institutions. Relative levels of research activity for research universities were determined by an analysis of research and development expenditures, science and engineering research staffing, and doctoral degrees conferred, by field. Further information on the research index ranking may be obtained from http://classifications.carnegiefoundation.org/. Degree-granting institutions grant associate's or higher degrees and participate in Title IV federal financial aid programs.

SOURCE: U.S. Department of Education, National Center for Education Statistics, Integrated Postsecondary Education Data System (IPEDS), Fall 2012, Institutional Characteristics component. (This table was prepared August 2013.)

Revenues of public degree-granting postsecondary institutions, by source of revenue and level of institution: 2005–06 through 2011–12

Level of institution and year	Total revenues	Tuition and fees[1]	Grants and contracts Federal	Grants and contracts State	Local and private	Sales and services of auxiliary enterprises[1]	Sales and services of hospitals	Independent operations	Other operating revenues[2]
1	2	3	4	5	6	7	8	9	10

In thousands of current dollars

All levels									
2005–06	$246,164,836	$41,770,600	$30,333,948	$7,207,813	$7,606,076	$18,786,806	$22,100,555	$635,607	$14,483,979
2006–07	268,556,045	44,773,470	30,779,946	7,613,614	8,176,011	20,398,261	22,575,459	688,024	13,765,596
2007–08	273,109,306	48,070,012	25,522,915	7,831,530	8,699,329	20,488,319	25,183,379	1,174,836	14,108,986
2008–09	267,385,180	51,840,367	26,092,100	7,403,141	9,600,416	21,358,319	27,301,883	1,036,660	14,165,654
2009–10	303,329,538	55,930,482	28,397,667	6,904,221	9,620,133	22,173,700	29,236,931	1,343,230	14,814,344
2010–11	323,817,821	60,240,671	29,808,728	7,020,373	10,062,621	23,606,433	31,105,677	1,330,334	15,804,536
2011–12	317,306,882	65,386,643	29,170,906	6,830,610	10,143,900	24,275,773	33,508,840	1,356,396	16,287,670
4-year									
2005–06	202,511,496	34,506,560	25,583,341	5,383,780	7,024,078	16,945,544	22,100,555	635,607	13,753,422
2006–07	221,882,332	37,205,630	26,027,591	5,530,987	7,586,434	18,520,922	22,575,459	688,024	13,057,589
2007–08	223,566,529	40,083,063	23,518,933	5,715,188	8,106,887	18,507,934	25,183,379	1,174,836	13,135,633
2008–09	216,432,317	43,478,018	24,178,064	5,526,583	9,031,844	19,391,219	27,301,883	1,036,660	13,291,611
2009–10	248,104,870	46,943,248	26,272,013	5,301,243	9,062,160	20,099,137	29,236,931	1,343,230	13,894,006
2010–11	265,941,566	51,018,362	27,643,131	5,480,388	9,495,263	21,507,520	31,105,677	1,330,334	14,876,568
2011–12	261,153,808	55,979,010	27,238,924	5,352,808	9,573,172	22,239,682	33,508,840	1,356,396	15,337,305
2-year									
2005–06	43,653,340	7,264,040	4,750,607	1,824,034	581,998	1,841,262	0	0	730,557
2006–07	46,673,713	7,567,840	4,752,356	2,082,627	589,578	1,877,338	0	0	708,007
2007–08	49,542,777	7,986,949	2,003,982	2,116,343	592,442	1,980,385	0	0	973,353
2008–09	50,952,862	8,362,349	1,914,036	1,876,558	568,572	1,967,100	0	0	874,043
2009–10	55,224,668	8,987,234	2,125,654	1,602,978	557,973	2,074,563	0	0	920,338
2010–11	57,876,255	9,222,309	2,165,597	1,539,985	567,358	2,098,913	0	0	927,968
2011–12	56,153,074	9,407,634	1,931,982	1,477,802	570,728	2,036,091	0	0	950,365

Percentage distribution

All levels									
2005–06	100.00	16.97	12.32	2.93	3.09	7.63	8.98	0.26	5.88
2006–07	100.00	16.67	11.46	2.84	3.04	7.60	8.41	0.26	5.13
2007–08	100.00	17.60	9.35	2.87	3.19	7.50	9.22	0.43	5.17
2008–09	100.00	19.39	9.76	2.77	3.59	7.99	10.21	0.39	5.30
2009–10	100.00	18.44	9.36	2.28	3.17	7.31	9.64	0.44	4.88
2010–11	100.00	18.60	9.21	2.17	3.11	7.29	9.61	0.41	4.88
2011–12	100.00	20.61	9.19	2.15	3.20	7.65	10.56	0.43	5.13
4-year									
2005–06	100.00	17.04	12.63	2.66	3.47	8.37	10.91	0.31	6.79
2006–07	100.00	16.77	11.73	2.49	3.42	8.35	10.17	0.31	5.88
2007–08	100.00	17.93	10.52	2.56	3.63	8.28	11.26	0.53	5.88
2008–09	100.00	20.09	11.17	2.55	4.17	8.96	12.61	0.48	6.14
2009–10	100.00	18.92	10.59	2.14	3.65	8.10	11.78	0.54	5.60
2010–11	100.00	19.18	10.39	2.06	3.57	8.09	11.70	0.50	5.59
2011–12	100.00	21.44	10.43	2.05	3.67	8.52	12.83	0.52	5.87
2-year									
2005–06	100.00	16.64	10.88	4.18	1.33	4.22	0.00	0.00	1.67
2006–07	100.00	16.21	10.18	4.46	1.26	4.02	0.00	0.00	1.52
2007–08	100.00	16.12	4.04	4.27	1.20	4.00	0.00	0.00	1.96
2008–09	100.00	16.41	3.76	3.68	1.12	3.86	0.00	0.00	1.72
2009–10	100.00	16.27	3.85	2.90	1.01	3.76	0.00	0.00	1.67
2010–11	100.00	15.93	3.74	2.66	0.98	3.63	0.00	0.00	1.60
2011–12	100.00	16.75	3.44	2.63	1.02	3.63	0.00	0.00	1.69

Revenue per full-time-equivalent student in constant 2012–13 dollars[3]

All levels									
2005–06	$30,478	$5,172	$3,756	$892	$942	$2,326	$2,736	$79	$1,793
2006–07	32,026	5,339	3,671	908	975	2,433	2,692	82	1,642
2007–08	30,644	5,394	2,864	879	976	2,299	2,826	132	1,583
2008–09	28,641	5,553	2,795	793	1,028	2,288	2,924	111	1,517
2009–10	30,119	5,554	2,820	686	955	2,202	2,903	133	1,471
2010–11	30,747	5,720	2,830	667	955	2,241	2,954	126	1,501
2011–12	29,464	6,072	2,709	634	942	2,254	3,112	126	1,512
4-year									
2005–06	41,102	7,003	5,192	1,093	1,426	3,439	4,486	129	2,791
2006–07	43,171	7,239	5,064	1,076	1,476	3,604	4,392	134	2,541
2007–08	40,759	7,308	4,288	1,042	1,478	3,374	4,591	214	2,395
2008–09	37,994	7,632	4,244	970	1,586	3,404	4,793	182	2,333
2009–10	41,045	7,766	4,346	877	1,499	3,325	4,837	222	2,299
2010–11	41,935	8,045	4,359	864	1,497	3,391	4,905	210	2,346
2011–12	39,433	8,453	4,113	808	1,446	3,358	5,060	205	2,316
2-year									
2005–06	13,860	2,306	1,508	579	185	585	0	0	232
2006–07	14,379	2,331	1,464	642	182	578	0	0	218
2007–08	14,455	2,330	585	617	173	578	0	0	284
2008–09	14,001	2,298	526	516	156	541	0	0	240
2009–10	13,716	2,232	528	398	139	515	0	0	229
2010–11	13,813	2,201	517	368	135	501	0	0	221
2011–12	13,542	2,269	466	356	138	491	0	0	229

See notes at end of table.

Revenues of public degree-granting postsecondary institutions, by source of revenue and level of institution: 2005–06 through 2011–12—Continued

Level of institution and year	Nonoperating revenue									Other revenues and additions			
	Appropriations			Nonoperating grants			Gifts	Investment income	Other	Capital appropriations	Capital grants and gifts	Additions to permanent endowments	Other
	Federal	State	Local	Federal	State	Local							
1	11	12	13	14	15	16	17	18	19	20	21	22	23
In thousands of current dollars													
All levels													
2005–06	$1,858,625	$58,720,088	$8,249,690	$2,811,434	$1,177,322	$102,497	$4,975,616	$9,597,624	$2,705,351	$5,421,660	$2,568,688	$1,004,691	$4,046,166
2006–07	1,910,169	63,204,939	8,818,685	2,859,223	1,291,896	129,138	5,589,156	15,588,573	3,950,191	7,332,387	3,509,682	1,039,425	4,562,199
2007–08	1,849,775	68,375,062	9,319,219	10,022,315	1,909,570	177,555	6,070,499	5,278,643	2,251,324	7,578,049	3,090,589	1,133,783	4,973,618
2008–09	2,010,843	65,486,232	9,787,019	12,760,716	2,720,449	265,789	5,893,912	−9,487,915	3,011,240	7,038,658	2,938,605	843,528	5,317,562
2009–10	2,152,228	62,456,235	9,954,504	20,740,102	3,123,358	231,104	5,876,450	10,046,610	5,210,022	6,041,010	3,780,012	869,950	4,427,245
2010–11	1,946,965	63,015,552	10,023,205	24,366,180	3,404,970	228,045	6,286,802	14,185,059	5,623,707	5,640,026	3,744,845	965,007	5,408,083
2011–12	1,835,767	58,789,643	10,214,576	23,205,569	3,559,749	232,167	6,540,837	6,171,056	4,191,861	5,544,504	3,724,320	825,587	5,510,507
4-year													
2005–06	1,720,108	45,591,539	336,424	1,546,322	613,928	33,269	4,713,701	8,927,767	2,330,293	3,680,390	2,250,167	986,771	3,847,930
2006–07	1,786,143	49,216,667	446,923	1,625,932	705,405	71,908	5,332,020	14,616,593	3,365,017	5,064,705	3,161,015	1,016,329	4,281,040
2007–08	1,776,452	53,268,648	453,280	5,177,569	1,201,394	103,824	5,798,732	4,430,479	1,770,108	5,637,968	2,762,277	1,120,806	4,639,141
2008–09	1,934,958	50,863,465	484,689	6,425,434	1,729,985	131,427	5,635,304	−9,958,068	2,601,770	4,987,773	2,554,107	830,264	4,975,326
2009–10	2,006,623	48,721,670	431,615	10,318,977	2,088,155	134,608	5,646,279	9,666,292	4,595,894	4,003,617	3,312,753	853,705	4,172,713
2010–11	1,853,109	48,977,437	507,010	11,849,748	2,320,005	130,451	6,061,073	13,771,423	4,783,422	3,880,567	3,249,730	943,748	5,156,596
2011–12	1,715,489	45,755,610	517,219	11,264,322	2,398,688	130,598	6,274,473	5,994,816	3,491,418	3,884,832	3,357,088	815,973	4,967,146
2-year													
2005–06	138,517	13,128,549	7,913,266	1,265,113	563,394	69,228	261,914	669,858	375,058	1,741,270	318,521	17,920	198,236
2006–07	124,026	13,988,272	8,371,762	1,233,292	586,491	57,230	257,136	971,979	585,175	2,267,682	348,667	23,096	281,159
2007–08	73,324	15,106,414	8,865,938	4,844,746	708,176	73,731	271,766	848,164	481,216	1,940,082	328,312	12,978	334,477
2008–09	75,885	14,622,766	9,302,330	6,335,282	990,464	134,362	258,608	470,153	409,470	2,050,885	384,498	13,263	342,236
2009–10	145,606	13,734,565	9,522,890	10,421,125	1,035,203	96,496	230,170	380,318	614,128	2,037,393	467,258	16,245	254,532
2010–11	93,856	14,038,114	9,516,195	12,516,431	1,084,965	97,594	225,730	413,636	840,284	1,759,459	495,115	21,258	251,487
2011–12	120,279	13,034,033	9,697,357	11,941,246	1,161,061	101,569	266,364	176,240	700,443	1,659,672	367,232	9,614	543,362
Percentage distribution													
All levels													
2005–06	0.76	23.85	3.35	1.14	0.48	0.04	2.02	3.90	1.10	2.20	1.04	0.41	1.64
2006–07	0.71	23.54	3.28	1.06	0.48	0.05	2.08	5.80	1.47	2.73	1.31	0.39	1.70
2007–08	0.68	25.04	3.41	3.67	0.70	0.07	2.22	1.93	0.82	2.77	1.13	0.42	1.82
2008–09	0.75	24.49	3.66	4.77	1.02	0.10	2.20	−3.55	1.13	2.63	1.10	0.32	1.99
2009–10	0.71	20.59	3.28	6.84	1.03	0.08	1.94	3.31	1.72	1.99	1.25	0.29	1.46
2010–11	0.60	19.46	3.10	7.52	1.05	0.07	1.94	4.38	1.74	1.74	1.16	0.30	1.67
2011–12	0.58	18.53	3.22	7.31	1.12	0.07	2.06	1.94	1.32	1.75	1.17	0.26	1.74
4-year													
2005–06	0.85	22.51	0.17	0.76	0.30	0.02	2.33	4.41	1.15	1.82	1.11	0.49	1.90
2006–07	0.80	22.18	0.20	0.73	0.32	0.03	2.40	6.59	1.52	2.28	1.42	0.46	1.93
2007–08	0.79	23.83	0.20	2.32	0.54	0.05	2.59	1.98	0.79	2.52	1.24	0.50	2.08
2008–09	0.89	23.50	0.22	2.97	0.80	0.06	2.60	−4.60	1.20	2.30	1.18	0.38	2.30
2009–10	0.81	19.64	0.17	4.16	0.84	0.05	2.28	3.90	1.85	1.61	1.34	0.34	1.68
2010–11	0.70	18.42	0.19	4.46	0.87	0.05	2.28	5.18	1.80	1.46	1.22	0.35	1.94
2011–12	0.66	17.52	0.20	4.31	0.92	0.05	2.40	2.30	1.34	1.49	1.29	0.31	1.90
2-year													
2005–06	0.32	30.07	18.13	2.90	1.29	0.16	0.60	1.53	0.86	3.99	0.73	0.04	0.45
2006–07	0.27	29.97	17.94	2.64	1.26	0.12	0.55	2.08	1.25	4.86	0.75	0.05	0.60
2007–08	0.15	30.49	17.90	9.78	1.43	0.15	0.55	1.71	0.97	3.92	0.66	0.03	0.68
2008–09	0.15	28.70	18.26	12.43	1.94	0.26	0.51	0.92	0.80	4.03	0.75	0.03	0.67
2009–10	0.26	24.87	17.24	18.87	1.87	0.17	0.42	0.69	1.11	3.69	0.85	0.03	0.46
2010–11	0.16	24.26	16.44	21.63	1.87	0.17	0.39	0.71	1.45	3.04	0.86	0.04	0.43
2011–12	0.21	23.21	17.27	21.27	2.07	0.18	0.47	0.31	1.25	2.96	0.65	0.02	0.97
Revenue per full-time-equivalent student in constant 2012–13 dollars[3]													
All levels													
2005–06	$230	$7,270	$1,021	$348	$146	$13	$616	$1,188	$335	$671	$318	$124	$501
2006–07	228	7,537	1,052	341	154	15	667	1,859	471	874	419	124	544
2007–08	208	7,672	1,046	1,125	214	20	681	592	253	850	347	127	558
2008–09	215	7,015	1,048	1,367	291	28	631	−1,016	323	754	315	90	570
2009–10	214	6,202	988	2,059	310	23	584	998	517	600	375	86	440
2010–11	185	5,983	952	2,314	323	22	597	1,347	534	536	356	92	514
2011–12	170	5,459	948	2,155	331	22	607	573	389	515	346	77	512
4-year													
2005–06	349	9,253	68	314	125	7	957	1,812	473	747	457	200	781
2006–07	348	9,576	87	316	137	14	1,037	2,844	655	985	615	198	833
2007–08	324	9,712	83	944	219	19	1,057	808	323	1,028	504	204	846
2008–09	340	8,929	85	1,128	304	23	989	−1,748	457	876	448	146	873
2009–10	332	8,060	71	1,707	345	22	934	1,599	760	662	548	141	690
2010–11	292	7,723	80	1,869	366	21	956	2,172	754	612	512	149	813
2011–12	259	6,909	78	1,701	362	20	947	905	527	587	507	123	750
2-year													
2005–06	44	4,168	2,512	402	179	22	83	213	119	553	101	6	63
2006–07	38	4,309	2,579	380	181	18	79	299	180	699	107	7	87
2007–08	21	4,408	2,587	1,414	207	22	79	247	140	566	96	4	98
2008–09	21	4,018	2,556	1,741	272	37	71	129	113	564	106	4	94
2009–10	36	3,411	2,365	2,588	257	24	57	94	153	506	116	4	63
2010–11	22	3,350	2,271	2,987	259	23	54	99	201	420	118	5	60
2011–12	29	3,143	2,339	2,880	280	24	64	43	169	400	89	2	131

[1]After deducting discounts and allowances.
[2]Includes sales and services of educational activities.
[3]Constant dollars based on the Consumer Price Index, prepared by the Bureau of Labor Statistics, U.S. Department of Labor, adjusted to a school-year basis.
NOTE: Degree-granting institutions grant associate's or higher degrees and participate in Title IV federal financial aid programs. Includes data for public institutions reporting data according to either the Governmental Accounting Standards Board (GASB) or the Financial Accounting Standards Board (FASB) questionnaire. Detail may not sum to totals because of rounding.
SOURCE: U.S. Department of Education, National Center for Education Statistics, Integrated Postsecondary Education Data System (IPEDS), Spring 2006 through Spring 2013, Finance and Enrollment components. (This table was prepared January 2014.)

Revenues of public degree-granting postsecondary institutions, by source of revenue and state or jurisdiction: 2011–12

[In thousands of current dollars]

State or jurisdiction	Total revenues	Operating revenue							Nonoperating revenue[1]			
		Total	Tuition and fees[2]	Federal grants and contracts	State, local, and private grants and contracts	Sales and services of auxiliary enterprises[2]	Sales and services of hospitals	Independent operations and other[3]	Total	State appropriations	Local appropriations	Other revenues and additions
1	2	3	4	5	6	7	8	9	10	11	12	13
United States......	$317,306,882	$186,960,737	$65,386,643	$29,170,906	$16,974,510	$24,275,773	$33,508,840	$17,644,066	$114,741,226	$58,789,643	$10,214,576	$15,604,918
Alabama..............	6,898,551	4,470,826	1,445,641	638,664	234,802	377,327	1,430,697	343,695	2,266,648	1,332,025	1,277	161,078
Alaska................	984,645	323,106	124,504	63,452	75,364	40,611	0	19,175	494,218	358,441	10,031	167,322
Arizona...............	5,417,482	2,794,932	1,548,148	577,593	174,917	338,428	0	155,846	2,524,426	783,210	749,180	98,124
Arkansas............	3,746,046	2,299,638	441,167	298,138	187,638	246,418	876,544	249,734	1,338,735	755,308	31,131	107,673
California............	43,273,373	25,008,634	6,064,944	3,799,698	2,422,968	1,892,987	6,817,495	4,010,541	15,543,874	7,397,375	2,561,870	2,720,866
Colorado............	5,481,511	4,543,086	1,708,897	949,988	558,591	490,576	478,461	356,573	748,878	30,648	78,374	189,547
Connecticut........	3,112,449	1,705,133	590,081	173,699	98,321	270,590	289,388	283,054	1,117,577	892,046	0	289,739
Delaware............	1,133,613	784,390	423,082	145,096	40,460	128,887	0	46,863	320,566	222,253	0	28,658
District of Columbia......	167,230	56,749	27,050	13,854	12,207	377	0	3,260	84,445	67,362	0	26,036
Florida...............	10,622,365	5,055,543	2,097,380	1,084,379	940,208	771,409	0	162,165	5,205,271	3,037,050	0	361,551
Georgia..............	7,664,812	4,299,845	1,780,346	776,296	529,480	800,241	196,911	216,571	2,979,565	1,847,730	44	385,401
Hawaii................	1,584,602	780,940	238,172	346,662	60,956	87,631	0	47,518	616,659	375,754	0	187,003
Idaho.................	1,282,864	660,724	322,712	120,035	51,578	121,301	0	45,097	581,949	308,986	20,559	40,191
Illinois...............	11,780,728	5,996,283	2,393,531	888,551	394,977	910,618	655,563	753,043	5,582,666	1,815,619	1,015,855	201,779
Indiana...............	6,604,271	4,142,356	2,141,648	609,029	262,448	724,944	0	404,288	2,376,556	1,415,835	9,012	85,359
Iowa..................	5,034,055	3,699,260	843,756	577,340	143,341	470,520	1,319,642	344,661	1,250,437	709,408	114,880	84,357
Kansas...............	3,320,431	1,898,469	758,127	370,136	188,492	307,221	0	274,493	1,323,151	719,033	233,851	98,812
Kentucky............	5,148,333	3,425,174	954,277	438,238	245,000	300,764	1,084,839	402,057	1,623,158	969,989	17,501	100,000
Louisiana............	4,000,467	2,386,961	791,720	333,795	442,797	340,265	287,764	190,621	1,463,053	944,649	0	150,453
Maine................	919,695	493,229	216,316	67,108	68,063	92,353	0	49,385	374,279	255,518	0	52,191
Maryland............	6,381,736	3,731,747	1,548,101	784,837	413,076	649,640	0	336,091	2,242,606	1,411,746	310,463	407,383
Massachusetts..........	4,648,600	2,903,740	1,186,789	407,861	241,733	428,542	0	638,816	1,454,496	1,046,090	0	290,364
Michigan............	13,321,669	9,614,780	3,564,224	1,469,930	418,510	1,072,373	2,601,803	487,939	3,401,418	1,490,701	523,771	305,471
Minnesota...........	5,053,633	2,918,488	1,265,215	513,955	348,166	597,554	0	193,597	1,937,790	1,095,626	0	197,354
Mississippi..........	4,008,102	2,237,835	548,043	384,546	174,346	267,205	704,269	159,426	1,612,497	939,075	59,716	157,771
Missouri.............	4,736,828	3,021,550	1,023,031	265,314	187,060	734,490	656,903	154,752	1,623,104	836,519	146,266	92,174
Montana.............	1,018,626	661,181	279,324	173,977	34,181	86,022	15,484	72,191	325,884	192,386	8,404	31,562
Nebraska............	2,351,516	1,248,587	404,450	245,921	175,016	286,557	25,752	110,892	1,008,319	616,412	127,737	94,609
Nevada..............	1,362,281	694,960	335,187	141,148	65,159	91,760	0	61,706	643,010	466,961	0	24,312
New Hampshire.........	939,405	724,302	371,385	65,790	64,294	198,475	0	24,358	174,129	80,192	0	40,975
New Jersey..........	7,319,457	4,631,023	2,025,314	497,186	410,975	585,610	920,868	191,069	2,531,469	1,495,920	194,452	156,965
New Mexico........	3,203,410	1,822,786	273,385	385,027	157,246	120,755	624,117	262,256	1,301,481	675,069	126,890	79,143
New York............	15,687,238	7,840,647	2,410,166	795,823	1,048,339	927,283	2,459,479	199,557	7,120,420	4,248,791	797,232	726,171
North Carolina............	10,263,991	4,289,664	1,539,459	823,784	309,500	1,427,382	974	188,566	5,330,955	3,387,420	200,980	643,372
North Dakota..............	1,115,052	691,468	275,366	164,278	58,833	113,007	0	79,984	365,624	276,228	2,686	57,960
Ohio..................	12,202,046	8,689,965	3,427,072	791,674	502,995	1,116,246	2,550,550	301,429	3,278,851	1,861,830	158,190	233,230
Oklahoma...........	4,042,219	2,363,087	771,736	269,595	292,237	456,635	67,631	505,254	1,533,106	898,544	50,986	146,025
Oregon...............	5,722,757	4,105,013	1,122,000	675,695	172,101	459,727	1,442,402	233,088	1,493,524	583,336	210,454	124,220
Pennsylvania.......	12,076,791	9,495,751	3,841,626	1,300,138	330,584	984,355	2,412,708	626,339	2,480,199	1,189,943	111,524	100,840
Rhode Island........	780,754	522,339	264,236	87,381	38,536	102,825	0	29,361	209,791	141,208	0	48,624
South Carolina............	4,063,314	2,755,593	1,304,733	416,150	360,754	398,300	0	275,654	1,155,894	465,402	62,126	151,828
South Dakota.......	800,354	512,259	214,192	125,186	43,018	66,209	0	63,654	247,252	159,652	0	40,843
Tennessee..........	4,297,676	2,151,942	992,372	332,362	257,387	299,677	0	270,145	1,903,832	1,002,136	5,655	241,901
Texas................	30,178,634	13,571,633	4,655,347	2,082,244	2,023,194	1,259,078	1,922,484	1,629,287	12,954,728	5,022,641	1,452,266	3,652,272
Utah..................	5,016,569	3,455,190	674,688	433,497	141,904	195,995	1,267,170	741,935	1,107,769	677,217	0	453,610
Vermont.............	760,594	645,422	348,332	127,751	43,807	102,133	0	23,398	105,702	67,894	0	9,835
Virginia..............	9,215,536	6,003,793	2,302,342	850,969	199,854	1,171,606	1,173,193	305,829	2,562,990	1,441,710	5,141	648,753
Washington.........	7,678,762	5,557,323	1,615,340	1,289,869	623,460	522,263	1,097,525	408,867	1,881,491	1,074,462	0	239,948
West Virginia.......	1,922,218	1,128,696	517,199	146,773	185,225	221,689	0	57,811	625,209	429,716	874	168,313
Wisconsin...........	6,404,192	3,558,863	1,294,046	712,773	452,724	482,556	0	616,764	2,393,871	943,010	769,923	451,458
Wyoming............	804,486	281,495	78,962	45,014	62,851	59,262	0	35,405	494,402	333,566	45,274	28,589
U.S. Service Academies...........	1,750,547	304,344	1,480	92,709	4,838	77,093	128,223	0	1,423,303	0	0	22,900
Other jurisdictions.	1,833,704	585,614	122,708	239,686	76,116	14,326	86,819	45,959	1,240,687	891,770	40,258	7,403
American Samoa........	25,002	14,919	4,208	10,036	0	669	0	6	10,083	1,948	0	0
Federated States of Micronesia...........	23,179	6,283	612	2,180	1,206	1,874	0	412	16,896	0	0	0
Guam................	147,097	68,274	15,693	34,233	3,322	2,559	0	12,467	77,719	34,197	14,569	1,104
Marshall Islands	18,067	2,157	534	0	250	1,012	0	362	15,909	2,875	0	0
Northern Marianas.......	19,824	13,279	2,527	9,473	0	1,265	0	16	6,545	3,749	0	0
Palau................	11,310	4,528	3,092	1,081	0	139	0	216	6,781	2,654	0	0
Puerto Rico.........	1,508,112	434,319	81,275	162,460	68,421	3,216	86,819	32,128	1,071,487	846,348	2	2,307
U.S. Virgin Islands........	81,113	41,854	14,768	20,223	2,917	3,593	0	354	35,267	0	25,687	3,992

[1]Includes other categories not separately shown.
[2]After deducting discounts and allowances.
[3]Includes sales and services of educational activities.
NOTE: Degree-granting institutions grant associate's or higher degrees and participate in Title IV federal financial aid programs. Includes data for public institutions reporting data according to either the Governmental Accounting Standards Board (GASB) or the Financial Accounting Standards Board (FASB) questionnaire. Detail may not sum to totals because of rounding.
SOURCE: U.S. Department of Education, National Center for Education Statistics, Integrated Postsecondary Education Data System (IPEDS), Spring 2013, Finance component. (This table was prepared January 2014.)

Endowment funds of the 120 degree-granting postsecondary institutions with the largest endowments, by rank order: Fiscal year 2012

Institution	Rank order, end of FY[1]	Market value of endowment — Beginning of FY (in thousands)	End of FY (in thousands)	Percent change[2]
1	2	3	4	5
United States (all institutions)	†	$420,785,545	$424,587,666	0.9
120 institutions with the largest amounts	†	312,707,855	315,950,083	1.0
Harvard University (MA)	1	32,012,729	30,745,534	-4.0
Yale University (CT)	2	19,174,387	19,264,289	0.5
Princeton University (NJ)	3	17,162,603	17,404,002	1.4
University of Texas System Office	4	14,635,240	17,070,515	16.6
Stanford University (CA)	5	16,502,606	17,035,804	3.2
Massachusetts Institute of Technology	6	9,712,628	10,149,564	4.5
Columbia University in the City of New York (NY)	7	7,789,578	7,654,152	-1.7
University of Michigan, Ann Arbor	8	7,725,307	7,586,547	-1.8
Texas A & M University, College Station	9	6,362,369	7,032,204	10.5
University of Pennsylvania	10	6,582,030	6,754,658	2.6
University of Notre Dame (IN)	11	6,383,344	6,444,599	1.0
University of California System Admin. Central Office	12	5,441,225	6,342,217	16.6
Emory University (GA)	13	5,443,397	5,774,500	6.1
University of Chicago (IL)	14	5,691,013	5,701,419	0.2
Northwestern University (IL)	15	5,474,935	5,574,319	1.8
Duke University (NC)	16	5,747,377	5,555,196	-3.3
Washington University in St. Louis (MO)	17	5,348,871	5,303,196	-0.9
University of Virginia, Main Campus	18	4,707,593	4,734,895	0.6
Rice University (TX)	19	4,498,951	4,448,069	-1.1
Cornell University (NY)	20	3,960,057	3,850,426	-2.8
University of Southern California	21	3,517,173	3,488,933	-0.8
Dartmouth College (NH)	22	3,413,407	3,486,383	2.1
Vanderbilt University (TN)	23	3,375,153	3,360,036	-0.4
University of Texas at Austin	24	2,852,960	2,861,389	0.3
New York University	25	2,724,134	2,800,399	2.8
University of Pittsburgh, Pittsburgh Campus (PA)	26	2,511,816	2,600,314	3.5
Johns Hopkins University (MD)	27	2,598,467	2,593,316	-0.2
Brown University (RI)	28	2,525,662	2,525,091	#
University of Minnesota, Twin Cities	29	2,441,712	2,424,734	-0.7
Ohio State University, Main Campus	30	2,104,611	2,348,193	11.6
University of Washington, Seattle Campus	31	2,248,770	2,206,040	-1.9
University of North Carolina at Chapel Hill	32	2,239,239	2,157,237	-3.7
University of Wisconsin, Madison	33	2,171,258	2,068,495	-4.7
University of Richmond (VA)	34	1,878,169	1,868,910	-0.5
Purdue University, Main Campus (IN)	35	1,944,305	1,861,079	-4.3
California Institute of Technology	36	1,624,331	1,811,497	11.5
Pennsylvania State University, Main Campus	37	1,737,843	1,772,921	2.0
Michigan State University	38	1,758,505	1,760,708	0.1
Williams College (MA)	39	1,755,418	1,728,549	-1.5
Pomona College (CA)	40	1,700,454	1,679,640	-1.2
Amherst College (MA)	41	1,641,511	1,640,666	-0.1
Boston College (MA)	42	1,756,292	1,632,635	-7.0
Georgia Institute of Technology, Main Campus	43	1,619,718	1,608,248	-0.7
Case Western Reserve University (OH)	44	1,703,164	1,600,013	-6.1
University of Rochester (NY)	45	1,622,812	1,581,773	-2.5
George Washington University (DC)	46	1,581,800	1,556,592	-1.6
Swarthmore College (PA)	47	1,508,483	1,498,775	-0.6
Wellesley College (MA)	48	1,523,683	1,468,582	-3.6
Smith College (MA)	49	1,429,527	1,409,755	-1.4
Grinnell College (IA)	50	1,500,220	1,383,856	-7.8
Tufts University (MA)	51	1,403,883	1,351,166	-3.8
University of California, Los Angeles	52	1,110,981	1,317,905	18.6
Washington and Lee University (VA)	53	1,218,132	1,261,553	3.6
University of California, Berkeley	54	945,318	1,218,592	28.9
University of Kansas	55	1,270,511	1,202,585	-5.3
Boston University (MA)	56	1,194,164	1,190,512	-0.3
Southern Methodist University (TX)	57	1,190,709	1,162,415	-2.4
Georgetown University (DC)	58	1,162,239	1,140,486	-1.9
University of Florida	59	1,085,600	1,127,419	3.9
Texas Christian University	60	1,191,900	1,110,868	-6.8
Weill Cornell Medical College (NY)	61	1,099,347	1,096,528	-0.3
University of Delaware	62	1,138,203	1,087,873	-4.4
Lehigh University (PA)	63	1,077,430	1,035,593	-3.9
Soka University of America (CA)	64	1,062,627	1,035,512	-2.6
Wake Forest University (NC)	65	1,058,250	1,025,069	-3.1
University of Illinois at Urbana-Champaign	66	1,006,556	996,226	-1.0
University of Iowa	67	1,044,097	981,104	-6.0
Carnegie Mellon University (PA)	68	1,009,219	979,230	-3.0
Baylor University (TX)	69	1,003,929	964,161	-4.0
Brigham Young University, Provo (UT)	70	920,149	957,010	4.0
University of Kentucky	71	952,248	947,383	-0.5
Tulane University of Louisiana	72	1,004,738	946,176	-5.8
Berea College (KY)	73	978,735	942,618	-3.7
Syracuse University (NY)	74	913,662	940,056	2.9
Yeshiva University (NY)	75	945,790	931,914	-1.5
Trinity University (TX)	76	974,935	915,918	-6.1
Bowdoin College (ME)	77	904,215	902,364	-0.2
Middlebury College (VT)	78	907,668	879,690	-3.1
Princeton Theological Seminary (NJ)	79	913,945	866,930	-5.1
Saint Louis University, Main Campus (MO)	80	880,251	852,842	-3.1
University of Texas Southwestern Medical Center	81	838,838	836,413	-0.3
University of Cincinnati, Main Campus (OH)	82	1,024,525	834,929	-18.5
Berry College (GA)	83	761,534	821,977	7.9
Vassar College (NY)	84	814,130	804,912	-1.1
University of Tulsa (OK)	85	817,324	802,455	-1.8
Juilliard School (NY)	86	814,005	787,698	-3.2
University of Oklahoma, Norman Campus	87	804,886	784,834	-2.5
Indiana University, Bloomington	88	807,627	772,185	-4.4
University of Arkansas	89	788,668	770,550	-2.3
Baylor College of Medicine (TX)	90	797,474	751,378	-5.8
Washington State University	91	722,735	737,428	2.0
University of Louisville (KY)	92	769,337	721,104	-6.3
Oberlin College (OH)	93	738,357	708,238	-4.1
Hamilton College (NY)	94	721,287	693,919	-3.8
Santa Clara University (CA)	95	716,821	688,118	-4.0
Colgate University (NY)	96	700,994	687,474	-1.9
University of Miami (FL)	97	719,852	678,694	-5.7
Brandeis University (MA)	98	703,666	674,522	-4.1
University of Alabama	99	616,925	673,606	9.2
University of Tennessee	100	674,434	665,833	-1.3
Carleton College (MN)	101	653,465	645,654	-1.2
Rutgers University, New Brunswick (NJ)	102	650,570	645,556	-0.8
College of William and Mary (VA)	103	624,726	644,233	3.1
Denison University (OH)	104	671,523	644,201	-4.1
Bryn Mawr College (PA)	105	677,307	641,173	-5.3
Lafayette College (PA)	106	649,588	640,769	-1.4
Cooper Union for the Advancement of Science and Art (NY)	107	609,056	640,536	5.2
North Carolina State University at Raleigh	108	617,632	635,326	2.9
Indiana University, Purdue University, Indianapolis	109	632,004	634,979	0.5
Rochester Institute of Technology (NY)	110	640,762	628,128	-2.0
Macalester College (MN)	111	669,005	625,068	-6.6
University of Missouri, Columbia	112	586,413	624,382	6.5
University of California, San Francisco	113	492,755	623,548	26.5
Wesleyan University (CT)	114	601,478	616,195	2.4
Pepperdine University (CA)	115	622,580	607,953	-2.3
Colby College (ME)	116	611,441	599,557	-1.9
Bucknell University (PA)	117	575,367	599,216	4.1
Icahn School of Medicine at Mount Sinai (NY)	118	607,498	594,968	-2.1
Mount Holyoke College (MA)	119	617,284	594,045	-3.8
College of the Holy Cross (MA)	120	607,713	589,769	-3.0

†Not applicable.
#Rounds to zero.
[1]Institutions ranked by size of endowment at end of 2012 fiscal year.
[2]Change in market value of endowment. Includes growth from gifts and returns on investments, as well as reductions from expenditures and withdrawals.

NOTE: Degree-granting institutions grant associate's or higher degrees and participate in Title IV federal financial aid programs.
SOURCE: U.S. Department of Education, National Center for Education Statistics, Integrated Postsecondary Education Data System (IPEDS), Spring 2013, Finance component. (This table was prepared January 2014.)

Expenditures of public degree-granting postsecondary institutions, by purpose of expenditure and level of institution: 2005–06 through 2011–12

Level of institution and year	Total expenditures	Instruction Total	Instruction Salaries and wages	Research	Public service	Academic support	Student services	Institutional support	Operation and maintenance of plant	Depreciation	Scholarships and fellowships[2]	Auxiliary enterprises	Hospitals	Independent operations	Interest	Other
1	2	3	4	5	6	7	8	9	10	11	12	13	14	15	16	17
								In thousands of current dollars								
All levels																
2005–06	$226,549,889	$62,998,407	$43,202,237	$23,056,406	$9,746,753	$15,299,823	$10,634,906	$18,528,338	$15,117,844	$10,071,291	$8,616,689	$17,314,237	$20,689,224	$744,028	$3,404,166	$10,337,778
2006–07	238,828,801	67,188,249	45,998,524	23,893,564	10,148,312	16,306,542	11,377,541	19,962,037	15,806,925	10,772,442	8,956,265	18,501,797	22,111,404	784,684	3,819,104	9,199,935
2007–08[3]	261,045,829	71,807,253	48,691,508	25,331,167	10,800,588	17,871,280	12,205,110	22,145,030	17,032,966	12,814,049	9,664,173	19,533,181	23,974,721	931,838	4,301,708	12,632,765
2008–09[3]	273,030,301	75,078,714	51,151,501	26,651,018	11,244,501	18,805,325	12,939,434	23,078,908	17,839,601	13,719,465	11,104,773	20,588,239	25,944,900	1,177,848	2,972,642	11,884,935
2009–10[3]	281,368,314	76,292,102	51,812,151	28,077,991	11,506,354	18,878,483	13,137,932	22,685,634	18,052,279	14,306,697	15,435,492	20,457,106	26,674,882	1,236,092	5,061,939	9,565,330
2010–11[3]	296,114,046	79,373,704	53,573,417	29,357,793	11,865,709	19,338,463	13,566,425	23,863,660	18,847,081	15,413,378	17,604,651	21,715,258	27,894,885	1,153,975	5,628,124	10,490,939
2011–12[3]	305,534,191	80,898,639	54,360,626	29,655,988	11,943,858	20,301,350	14,160,344	24,154,135	19,180,861	16,469,939	16,620,812	22,190,775	30,899,227	1,204,016	6,136,311	11,717,934
4-year																
2005–06	186,074,213	47,286,043	32,206,726	23,031,885	9,054,397	12,290,114	6,906,675	12,915,660	11,508,008	8,517,539	5,697,202	15,158,273	20,689,224	744,028	2,856,931	9,418,234
2006–07	196,121,062	50,755,304	34,541,885	23,875,451	9,455,605	13,151,359	7,430,739	14,046,030	12,031,682	9,140,557	6,031,919	16,308,351	22,111,404	784,684	3,129,141	7,868,836
2007–08[3]	215,474,080	54,371,328	36,618,879	25,312,279	10,055,606	14,471,795	8,051,799	15,812,151	13,047,228	10,959,500	6,467,362	17,296,774	23,974,721	931,838	3,523,683	11,198,015
2008–09[3]	225,363,128	57,265,615	38,666,432	26,029,400	10,499,031	15,300,115	8,612,795	16,505,969	13,805,143	11,719,734	7,156,258	18,293,456	25,944,900	1,177,848	2,354,694	10,098,170
2009–10[3]	230,216,045	58,268,076	39,035,682	28,057,280	10,752,578	15,355,204	8,755,313	16,348,654	13,675,766	12,311,881	9,092,603	18,120,806	26,674,882	1,236,092	4,091,219	7,475,682
2010–11[3]	241,754,071	60,607,823	40,407,972	29,336,607	11,099,969	15,720,410	9,112,980	17,294,034	14,260,755	13,184,265	10,103,136	19,321,726	27,894,885	1,153,975	4,502,944	8,160,925
2011–12[3]	251,503,636	62,238,557	41,349,288	29,635,707	11,184,077	16,652,094	9,634,329	17,439,517	14,705,781	14,105,698	9,739,168	19,819,696	30,899,227	1,204,016	4,777,487	9,468,280
2-year																
2005–06	40,475,676	15,702,364	10,995,511	24,520	692,356	3,009,709	3,728,231	5,612,677	3,609,836	1,553,752	2,919,487	2,155,964	0	0	547,234	919,544
2006–07	42,707,739	16,432,945	11,456,639	18,113	692,707	3,155,183	3,946,803	5,916,007	3,775,243	1,631,885	2,924,346	2,193,446	0	0	689,963	1,331,099
2007–08[3]	45,571,749	17,435,926	12,072,630	18,887	744,982	3,399,485	4,153,311	6,332,879	3,985,738	1,854,549	3,196,811	2,236,407	0	0	778,025	1,434,749
2008–09[3]	47,667,173	17,813,099	12,485,070	21,617	745,470	3,505,209	4,326,639	6,572,940	4,034,457	1,999,732	3,948,515	2,294,783	0	0	617,948	1,786,764
2009–10[3]	51,152,269	18,024,027	12,776,469	20,711	753,776	3,523,280	4,382,619	6,336,980	4,376,513	1,994,806	6,342,889	2,336,300	0	0	970,721	2,089,648
2010–11[3]	54,359,975	18,765,881	13,165,446	21,187	766,104	3,618,052	4,453,445	6,569,626	4,586,326	2,229,112	7,501,515	2,393,532	0	0	1,125,180	2,330,014
2011–12[3]	54,030,554	18,660,082	13,011,338	20,281	759,781	3,649,257	4,526,015	6,714,618	4,475,080	2,364,242	6,881,643	2,371,079	0	0	1,358,824	2,249,654
								Percentage distribution								
All levels																
2005–06	100.00	27.80	19.07	10.18	4.30	6.75	4.69	8.18	6.67	4.45	3.80	7.64	9.13	0.33	1.50	4.56
2006–07	100.00	28.13	19.26	10.00	4.25	6.83	4.76	8.36	6.62	4.51	3.75	7.75	9.26	0.33	1.60	3.85
2007–08[3]	100.00	27.51	18.65	9.70	4.14	6.85	4.68	8.48	6.52	4.91	3.70	7.48	9.18	0.36	1.65	4.84
2008–09[3]	100.00	27.50	18.73	9.76	4.12	6.89	4.74	8.45	6.53	5.02	4.07	7.54	9.50	0.43	1.09	4.35
2009–10[3]	100.00	27.11	18.41	9.98	4.09	6.71	4.67	8.06	6.42	5.08	5.49	7.27	9.48	0.44	1.80	3.40
2010–11[3]	100.00	26.81	18.09	9.91	4.01	6.53	4.58	8.06	6.36	5.21	5.95	7.33	9.42	0.39	1.90	3.54
2011–12[3]	100.00	26.48	17.79	9.71	3.91	6.64	4.63	7.91	6.28	5.39	5.44	7.26	10.11	0.39	2.01	3.84
4-year																
2005–06	100.00	25.41	17.31	12.38	4.87	6.60	3.71	6.94	6.18	4.58	3.06	8.15	11.12	0.40	1.54	5.06
2006–07	100.00	25.88	17.61	12.17	4.82	6.71	3.79	7.16	6.13	4.66	3.08	8.32	11.27	0.40	1.60	4.01
2007–08[3]	100.00	25.23	16.99	11.75	4.67	6.72	3.74	7.34	6.06	5.09	3.00	8.03	11.13	0.43	1.64	5.20
2008–09[3]	100.00	25.41	17.16	11.82	4.66	6.79	3.82	7.32	6.13	5.20	3.18	8.12	11.51	0.52	1.04	4.48
2009–10[3]	100.00	25.31	16.96	12.19	4.67	6.67	3.80	7.10	5.94	5.35	3.95	7.87	11.59	0.54	1.78	3.25
2010–11[3]	100.00	25.07	16.71	12.13	4.59	6.50	3.77	7.15	5.90	5.45	4.18	7.99	11.54	0.48	1.86	3.38
2011–12[3]	100.00	24.75	16.44	11.78	4.45	6.62	3.83	6.93	5.85	5.61	3.87	7.88	12.29	0.48	1.90	3.76
2-year																
2005–06	100.00	38.79	27.17	0.06	1.71	7.44	9.21	13.87	8.92	3.84	7.21	5.33	0.00	0.00	1.35	2.27
2006–07	100.00	38.48	26.83	0.04	1.62	7.39	9.24	13.85	8.84	3.82	6.85	5.14	0.00	0.00	1.62	3.12
2007–08[3]	100.00	38.26	26.49	0.04	1.63	7.46	9.11	13.90	8.75	4.07	7.01	4.91	0.00	0.00	1.71	3.15
2008–09[3]	100.00	37.37	26.19	0.05	1.56	7.35	9.08	13.79	8.46	4.20	8.28	4.81	0.00	0.00	1.30	3.75
2009–10[3]	100.00	35.24	24.98	0.04	1.47	6.89	8.57	12.39	8.56	3.90	12.40	4.57	0.00	0.00	1.90	4.09
2010–11[3]	100.00	34.52	24.22	0.04	1.41	6.66	8.19	12.09	8.44	4.10	13.80	4.40	0.00	0.00	2.07	4.29
2011–12[3]	100.00	34.54	24.08	0.04	1.41	6.75	8.38	12.43	8.28	4.38	12.74	4.39	0.00	0.00	2.51	4.16

See notes at end of table.

Expenditures of public degree-granting postsecondary institutions, by purpose of expenditure and level of institution: 2005–06 through 2011–12—Continued

Level of institution and year	Total expenditures	Instruction Total[1]	Instruction Salaries and wages	Research	Public service	Academic support	Student services	Institutional support	Operation and maintenance of plant	Depreciation	Scholarships and fellowships[2]	Auxiliary enterprises	Hospitals	Independent operations	Interest	Other
1	2	3	4	5	6	7	8	9	10	11	12	13	14	15	16	17

Expenditures per full-time-equivalent student in current dollars

Level of institution and year	2	3	4	5	6	7	8	9	10	11	12	13	14	15	16	17
All levels																
2005–06	24,126	6,708	4,601	2,455	1,038	1,629	1,133	1,973	1,610	1,073	918	1,844	2,203	79	363	1,101
2006–07	25,130	7,070	4,840	2,514	1,068	1,716	1,197	2,100	1,663	1,134	942	1,947	2,327	83	402	968
2007–08[3]	26,802	7,373	4,999	2,601	1,109	1,835	1,253	2,274	1,749	1,316	992	2,006	2,462	96	442	1,297
2008–09[3]	27,135	7,462	5,084	2,649	1,118	1,869	1,286	2,294	1,773	1,364	1,104	2,046	2,579	117	295	1,181
2009–10[3]	26,173	7,097	4,820	2,612	1,070	1,756	1,222	2,110	1,679	1,331	1,436	1,903	2,481	115	471	890
2010–11[3]	26,869	7,202	4,861	2,664	1,077	1,755	1,231	2,165	1,710	1,399	1,597	1,970	2,531	105	511	952
2011–12[3]	27,906	7,389	4,965	2,709	1,091	1,854	1,293	2,206	1,752	1,504	1,518	2,027	2,822	110	560	1,070
4-year																
2005–06	32,483	8,255	5,622	4,021	1,581	2,145	1,206	2,255	2,009	1,487	995	2,646	3,612	130	499	1,644
2006–07	33,670	8,714	5,930	4,099	1,623	2,258	1,276	2,411	2,066	1,569	1,036	2,880	3,796	135	537	1,351
2007–08[3]	35,947	9,071	6,109	4,223	1,678	2,414	1,343	2,638	2,177	1,828	1,079	2,886	4,000	155	588	1,868
2008–09[3]	36,707	9,327	6,298	4,337	1,710	2,492	1,403	2,688	2,249	1,909	1,166	2,980	4,226	192	384	1,645
2009–10[3]	35,679	9,030	6,050	4,348	1,666	2,380	1,357	2,534	2,119	1,908	1,409	2,808	4,134	192	634	1,159
2010–11[3]	36,430	9,133	6,089	4,421	1,673	2,369	1,373	2,606	2,149	1,987	1,522	2,912	4,203	174	679	1,230
2011–12[3]	37,354	9,244	6,141	4,402	1,661	2,473	1,431	2,590	2,184	2,095	1,446	2,944	4,589	179	710	1,406
2-year																
2005–06	11,053	4,288	3,003	7	189	822	1,018	1,533	986	424	797	589	0	0	149	251
2006–07	11,609	4,467	3,114	5	188	858	1,073	1,608	1,026	444	795	596	0	0	188	362
2007–08[3]	12,167	4,655	3,223	5	190	908	1,103	1,691	1,064	495	854	597	0	0	208	383
2008–09[3]	12,153	4,542	3,183	6	190	894	1,109	1,676	1,029	510	1,007	585	0	0	158	456
2009–10[3]	11,902	4,194	2,973	6	175	820	1,020	1,474	1,018	464	1,476	544	0	0	226	486
2010–11[3]	12,398	4,280	3,003	5	175	825	1,016	1,498	1,046	508	1,711	546	0	0	257	531
2011–12[3]	12,817	4,426	3,086	5	180	866	1,074	1,593	1,062	561	1,632	562	0	0	322	534

Expenditures per full-time-equivalent student in constant 2012–13 dollars[4]

Level of institution and year	2	3	4	5	6	7	8	9	10	11	12	13	14	15	16	17
All levels																
2005–06	28,050	7,799	5,349	2,855	1,207	1,894	1,317	2,294	1,872	1,247	1,067	2,144	2,562	92	421	1,280
2006–07	28,481	8,012	5,485	2,849	1,210	1,945	1,357	2,380	1,885	1,285	1,068	2,206	2,637	94	455	1,097
2007–08[3]	29,290	8,057	5,463	2,842	1,212	2,005	1,369	2,485	1,911	1,438	1,084	2,192	2,690	105	483	1,417
2008–09[3]	29,246	8,042	5,479	2,855	1,204	2,014	1,386	2,472	1,911	1,470	1,189	2,205	2,779	126	318	1,273
2009–10[3]	27,939	7,575	5,145	2,788	1,143	1,875	1,305	2,253	1,793	1,421	1,533	2,031	2,649	123	503	950
2010–11[3]	28,116	7,537	5,087	2,788	1,127	1,836	1,288	2,266	1,790	1,464	1,672	2,062	2,649	110	534	996
2011–12[3]	28,371	7,512	5,048	2,754	1,109	1,885	1,315	2,243	1,781	1,529	1,543	2,061	2,869	112	570	1,088
4-year																
2005–06	37,766	9,597	6,537	4,675	1,838	2,494	1,402	2,621	2,336	1,729	1,156	3,077	4,199	151	580	1,912
2006–07	38,159	9,875	6,721	4,645	1,840	2,559	1,446	2,733	2,341	1,778	1,174	3,173	4,302	153	609	1,531
2007–08[3]	39,283	9,913	6,676	4,615	1,833	2,638	1,468	2,883	2,379	1,998	1,179	3,153	4,371	170	642	2,042
2008–09[3]	39,562	10,053	6,788	4,675	1,843	2,686	1,512	2,898	2,423	2,057	1,256	3,211	4,555	207	413	1,773
2009–10[3]	38,085	9,639	6,458	4,642	1,779	2,540	1,448	2,705	2,262	2,037	1,504	2,998	4,413	204	677	1,237
2010–11[3]	38,121	9,557	6,372	4,626	1,750	2,479	1,437	2,727	2,249	2,079	1,593	3,047	4,399	182	710	1,287
2011–12[3]	37,976	9,398	6,244	4,475	1,689	2,514	1,455	2,633	2,221	2,130	1,471	2,993	4,666	182	721	1,430
2-year																
2005–06	12,851	4,985	3,491	8	220	956	1,184	1,782	1,146	493	927	685	0	0	174	292
2006–07	13,157	5,062	3,529	6	213	972	1,216	1,823	1,163	503	901	676	0	0	213	410
2007–08[3]	13,296	5,087	3,522	6	217	992	1,212	1,848	1,163	541	933	653	0	0	227	419
2008–09[3]	13,098	4,895	3,431	6	205	963	1,189	1,806	1,109	549	1,085	631	0	0	170	491
2009–10[3]	12,705	4,477	3,173	6	187	875	1,089	1,574	1,087	495	1,575	580	0	0	241	519
2010–11[3]	12,974	4,479	3,142	5	183	863	1,063	1,568	1,095	532	1,790	571	0	0	269	556
2011–12[3]	13,030	4,500	3,138	5	183	880	1,091	1,619	1,079	570	1,660	572	0	0	328	543

[1]Includes other categories not separately shown.
[2]Excludes discounts and allowances.
[3]All expenditures reported by institutions for operation and maintenance of plant category, even in cases where they originally were reported by purpose. Similarly, all expenditures reported by institutions for depreciation have been aggregated in the depreciation category, even in cases where they originally were reported by purpose. In addition, all expenditures reported by institutions for interest have been aggregated in the interest category, even in cases where they originally were reported by purpose.

[4]Constant dollars based on the Consumer Price Index, prepared by the Bureau of Labor Statistics, U.S. Department of Labor, adjusted to a school-year basis.

NOTE: Degree-granting institutions grant associate's or higher degrees and participate in Title IV federal financial aid programs. Includes data for public institutions reporting data according to either the Governmental Accounting Standards Board (GASB) or the Financial Accounting Standards Board (FASB) questionnaire. Detail may not sum to totals because of rounding.

SOURCE: U.S. Department of Education, National Center for Education Statistics, Integrated Postsecondary Education Data System (IPEDS), Spring 2006 through Spring 2013, Finance and Enrollment components. (This table was prepared January 2014.)

Expenditures of public degree-granting postsecondary institutions, by level of institution, purpose of expenditure, and state or jurisdiction: 2008–09 through 2011–12

[In thousands of current dollars]

State or jurisdiction	Total expenditures, 2008–09	Total expenditures, 2009–10	Total expenditures, 2010–11 All institutions	4-year institutions	2-year institutions	2011–12 All institutions Total[1]	Instruction[2]	4-year institutions Total[1]	Instruction[2]	2-year institutions Total[1]	Instruction[2]
1	2	3	4	5	6	7	8	9	10	11	12
United States	$273,030,301	$281,368,314	$296,114,046	$241,754,071	$54,359,975	$305,534,191	$80,898,639	$251,503,636	$62,238,557	$54,030,554	$18,660,082
Alabama	5,964,685	6,324,853	6,649,467	5,839,064	810,403	6,249,322	1,457,529	5,505,628	1,185,672	743,694	271,857
Alaska	750,308	780,028	800,218	779,239	20,978	829,978	217,370	806,882	210,855	23,096	6,515
Arizona	4,523,629	4,721,129	4,968,606	3,612,788	1,355,818	5,126,746	1,494,971	3,711,078	1,042,863	1,415,668	452,107
Arkansas	3,109,431	3,268,738	3,454,422	2,941,157	513,265	3,592,033	727,714	3,079,753	561,865	512,279	165,849
California	39,706,162	39,702,048	42,790,625	31,296,311	11,494,314	45,496,484	10,588,055	34,205,136	7,282,151	11,291,348	3,305,905
Colorado	4,424,140	4,516,268	4,837,724	4,315,611	522,114	5,149,199	1,461,843	4,593,560	1,258,133	555,639	203,709
Connecticut	2,833,427	2,814,866	2,974,554	2,515,522	459,032	2,931,898	805,500	2,476,931	629,957	454,966	175,543
Delaware	937,997	967,381	1,032,228	887,780	144,448	1,128,190	410,987	976,509	343,048	151,681	67,939
District of Columbia	138,348	109,469	152,640	152,640	0	147,034	54,628	147,034	54,628	0	0
Florida	9,220,508	9,721,394	10,413,803	9,810,395	603,408	10,559,827	3,066,934	10,047,373	2,927,676	512,454	139,258
Georgia	6,063,773	6,426,195	7,028,610	5,748,748	1,279,862	7,293,926	1,902,757	6,090,473	1,505,704	1,203,453	397,053
Hawaii	1,531,975	1,406,821	1,523,301	1,290,065	233,236	1,609,315	427,437	1,364,952	323,112	244,363	104,325
Idaho	1,024,541	1,070,934	1,116,296	911,158	205,138	1,216,909	328,272	951,754	269,697	265,155	58,574
Illinois	9,350,383	9,954,173	10,302,240	7,460,195	2,842,045	10,888,678	3,088,692	7,958,821	2,178,967	2,929,857	909,725
Indiana	5,487,959	5,739,211	5,959,191	5,316,900	642,291	6,098,731	2,125,765	5,438,638	1,909,123	660,093	216,643
Iowa	4,193,485	4,169,366	4,332,274	3,464,024	868,250	4,726,859	967,311	3,842,076	634,650	884,783	332,661
Kansas	2,821,376	2,916,446	3,053,391	2,342,731	710,660	3,214,748	940,794	2,490,979	707,310	723,769	233,484
Kentucky	4,513,299	4,723,961	4,889,725	4,193,994	695,731	5,136,705	1,166,682	4,423,207	923,563	713,498	243,119
Louisiana	4,303,137	4,143,613	4,163,519	3,649,282	514,237	4,204,018	1,119,549	3,688,602	930,091	515,416	189,458
Maine	809,983	807,827	837,119	715,786	121,333	844,272	235,727	722,060	186,090	122,212	49,638
Maryland	5,282,745	5,489,313	5,627,221	4,300,679	1,326,541	5,829,195	1,623,747	4,472,795	1,125,279	1,356,400	498,468
Massachusetts	3,731,294	3,941,641	4,224,820	3,443,382	781,438	4,297,014	1,195,062	3,490,312	892,924	806,702	302,138
Michigan	11,928,733	12,411,095	12,793,640	10,841,022	1,952,618	13,384,789	3,345,058	11,447,703	2,675,348	1,937,086	669,710
Minnesota	4,679,338	4,782,817	4,841,837	3,785,610	1,056,227	4,810,022	1,364,177	3,798,676	953,626	1,011,346	410,551
Mississippi	3,445,846	3,591,772	3,717,313	2,809,641	907,672	3,815,187	866,062	2,909,603	564,587	905,584	301,474
Missouri	4,067,585	4,220,808	4,370,406	3,593,302	777,104	4,563,353	1,222,197	3,777,389	943,879	785,964	278,318
Montana	936,000	933,785	961,380	839,058	122,321	980,626	243,570	852,199	212,017	128,427	31,553
Nebraska	1,893,340	2,005,277	2,119,516	1,745,447	374,069	2,176,505	628,518	1,788,005	483,171	388,500	145,347
Nevada	1,417,355	1,423,657	1,452,203	1,382,958	69,245	1,374,536	476,935	1,307,944	450,449	66,592	26,486
New Hampshire	803,946	837,543	916,009	770,735	145,274	894,369	266,551	764,722	220,208	129,647	46,343
New Jersey	6,487,776	6,679,185	6,818,023	5,509,244	1,308,780	7,080,758	1,996,534	5,766,819	1,551,648	1,313,939	444,885
New Mexico	3,033,621	3,094,887	3,195,659	2,584,062	611,597	3,150,710	595,333	2,545,009	397,190	605,701	198,144
New York	14,393,529	14,564,719	15,481,165	12,371,236	3,109,929	16,037,336	4,526,656	12,848,763	3,250,053	3,188,573	1,276,602
North Carolina	8,648,614	9,061,392	9,639,567	7,462,272	2,177,296	9,556,563	3,069,125	7,417,647	2,195,716	2,138,916	873,410
North Dakota	900,709	960,204	993,822	914,830	78,992	1,041,219	351,006	950,491	317,064	90,728	33,942
Ohio	10,690,988	11,191,776	11,618,185	9,997,413	1,620,772	11,808,439	3,139,947	10,182,544	2,562,406	1,625,895	577,541
Oklahoma	3,424,475	3,565,946	3,722,869	3,238,832	484,037	3,859,699	1,088,350	3,377,425	906,703	482,275	181,647
Oregon	4,705,101	4,989,706	5,312,294	4,078,285	1,234,009	5,531,213	1,190,991	4,341,196	802,885	1,190,017	388,106
Pennsylvania	10,424,097	10,880,853	11,287,473	10,099,710	1,187,763	11,823,354	2,993,974	10,615,217	2,568,704	1,208,137	425,271
Rhode Island	639,371	663,552	683,831	571,947	111,884	717,329	193,230	600,406	143,121	116,924	50,109
South Carolina	3,415,654	3,537,943	3,715,311	2,907,953	807,358	3,827,663	1,224,213	3,010,114	940,090	817,549	284,123
South Dakota	626,176	686,412	707,073	628,178	78,895	739,971	213,929	663,378	188,562	76,594	25,367
Tennessee	3,607,113	3,781,861	3,980,862	3,323,326	657,537	4,156,217	1,376,912	3,492,606	1,130,233	663,611	246,679
Texas	24,222,080	25,080,639	26,346,922	21,582,546	4,764,376	26,413,997	6,722,163	21,789,774	5,171,887	4,624,223	1,550,276
Utah	3,797,090	3,940,464	4,248,983	3,945,043	303,940	4,461,853	740,774	4,260,114	661,828	201,739	78,946
Vermont	718,762	761,182	793,941	757,661	36,280	799,662	210,880	762,660	200,699	37,002	10,182
Virginia	7,183,108	7,329,410	7,878,109	6,835,495	1,042,614	8,367,116	2,231,456	7,254,946	1,773,188	1,112,170	458,268
Washington	6,714,962	6,874,560	7,312,805	5,871,046	1,441,759	7,402,548	2,139,459	6,055,036	1,580,896	1,347,512	558,563
West Virginia	1,518,943	1,672,009	1,738,447	1,579,411	159,036	1,813,682	528,639	1,651,111	479,796	162,572	48,842
Wisconsin	5,499,072	5,757,793	5,974,368	4,635,981	1,338,387	5,942,717	1,806,595	4,629,546	1,179,633	1,313,171	626,962
Wyoming	639,509	671,896	706,750	451,090	255,661	752,127	225,402	478,492	136,934	273,635	88,468
U.S. Service Academies	1,844,822	1,699,493	1,653,288	1,653,288	0	1,679,549	512,678	1,679,549	512,678	0	0
Other jurisdictions	1,721,830	1,776,740	1,698,347	1,595,433	102,914	1,727,062	486,963	1,625,469	453,524	101,592	33,439
American Samoa	12,910	13,243	15,942	0	15,942	15,097	6,506	15,097	6,506	0	0
Federated States of Micronesia	22,380	23,128	21,048	0	21,048	23,134	8,692	0	0	23,134	8,692
Guam	106,784	115,262	125,565	93,324	32,242	136,515	31,051	99,800	20,099	36,715	10,952
Marshall Islands	8,503	12,681	17,259	0	17,259	18,381	3,441	0	0	18,381	3,441
Northern Marianas	13,945	14,619	20,214	20,214	0	18,085	8,005	18,085	8,005	0	0
Palau	5,858	5,416	4,856	0	4,856	9,023	3,982	0	0	9,023	3,982
Puerto Rico	1,477,913	1,506,865	1,406,063	1,394,495	11,568	1,418,143	411,183	1,403,804	404,811	14,339	6,372
U.S. Virgin Islands	73,536	85,525	87,400	87,400	0	88,683	14,104	88,683	14,104	0	0

[1]Includes other categories not separately shown.
[2]Excludes expenditures for operations and maintenance, interest, and depreciation, which are included in the total.
NOTE: Degree-granting institutions grant associate's or higher degrees and participate in Title IV federal financial aid programs. Includes data for public institutions reporting data according to either the Governmental Accounting Standards Board (GASB) or the Financial Accounting Standards Board (FASB) questionnaire. All expenditures reported by institutions for operation and maintenance of plant have been aggregated in the operation and maintenance of plant category, even in cases where they originally were reported by purpose. Similarly, all expenditures reported by institutions for depreciation have been aggregated in the depreciation category, even in cases where they originally were reported by purpose. In addition, all expenditures reported by institutions for interest have been aggregated in the interest category, even in cases where they originally were reported by purpose. Detail may not sum to totals because of rounding.
SOURCE: U.S. Department of Education, National Center for Education Statistics, Integrated Postsecondary Education Data System (IPEDS), Spring 2010 through Spring 2013, Finance component. (This table was prepared January 2014.)

Total expenditures of private nonprofit and for-profit degree-granting postsecondary institutions, by state or jurisdiction: Selected years, 1999–2000 through 2011–12

[In thousands of current dollars]

State or jurisdiction	Nonprofit institutions						For-profit institutions					
	1999–2000	2004–05	2008–09	2009–10	2010–11	2011–12	1999–2000	2004–05	2008–09	2009–10	2010–11	2011–12
1	2	3	4	5	6	7	8	9	10	11	12	13
United States ...	$80,613,037	$110,394,127	$141,349,229	$145,141,785	$152,509,741	$159,873,305	$3,846,246	$8,830,792	$16,364,360	$19,973,659	$22,585,686	$23,036,898
Alabama	393,465	459,250	546,535	561,968	583,205	604,992	88,190	60,629	98,444	139,366	244,943	218,687
Alaska	19,042	21,076	17,211	16,249	18,319	17,245	3,559	3,986	9,109	19,302	41,245	53,164
Arizona	143,698	147,825	165,960	176,443	212,911	237,638	278,286	1,095,783	2,722,216	3,412,261	3,623,551	3,419,611
Arkansas	230,860	239,357	287,259	289,868	322,896	341,827	5,828	11,574	26,615	31,263	27,834	29,152
California	7,871,651	10,728,872	13,421,736	13,925,287	14,557,205	15,355,141	666,020	1,243,346	2,047,729	2,552,449	2,952,470	3,016,592
Colorado	376,887	524,349	632,322	627,123	659,716	692,467	154,801	320,550	611,882	661,384	736,387	739,248
Connecticut	2,094,981	2,882,963	3,858,956	3,975,262	4,127,051	4,337,333	18,110	41,931	52,340	59,726	80,628	95,498
Delaware	52,533	87,617	124,757	132,851	141,186	150,054	†	†	†	4,042	4,957	5,191
District of Columbia ..	2,267,409	2,824,081	3,715,850	3,687,042	3,724,430	3,929,951	59,375	127,859	328,919	66,677	77,469	68,746
Florida	2,031,623	3,067,443	4,523,485	4,592,898	5,071,442	5,356,148	315,721	781,280	1,379,974	1,825,704	1,982,163	2,038,395
Georgia	2,635,438	3,442,374	4,340,833	4,497,299	4,796,550	5,346,024	106,794	261,219	509,600	675,496	783,834	811,908
Hawaii	209,135	195,152	214,383	210,680	231,683	251,071	9,422	24,996	37,439	34,299	41,754	46,358
Idaho	118,150	164,694	219,607	228,589	242,764	261,954	5,932	13,073	23,649	32,602	51,944	50,751
Illinois	5,668,566	7,113,842	9,088,501	9,512,165	10,095,051	10,532,731	166,956	620,678	988,986	1,100,032	1,054,104	1,542,922
Indiana	1,343,315	1,796,767	2,185,735	2,251,554	2,360,297	2,502,296	89,932	211,310	433,600	591,600	726,450	730,138
Iowa	740,760	921,320	1,143,991	1,156,393	1,188,889	1,248,348	34,311	146,688	758,054	1,002,405	1,269,406	1,189,547
Kansas	208,729	265,476	357,557	364,286	381,327	414,219	9,156	11,213	35,743	47,645	57,986	58,226
Kentucky	400,513	470,392	589,525	597,495	637,466	683,702	55,010	114,564	187,046	242,672	285,217	288,146
Louisiana	746,629	940,075	1,032,490	1,089,736	1,137,685	1,192,748	31,675	70,241	89,353	111,844	104,007	110,097
Maine	316,114	422,938	530,015	552,463	592,174	619,223	7,137	5,648	11,192	12,409	14,411	13,111
Maryland	2,205,880	3,497,182	4,547,357	4,792,089	5,069,546	5,278,869	5,354	41,717	70,854	115,071	118,794	107,983
Massachusetts	7,591,344	10,799,206	13,916,336	13,862,598	14,533,360	15,252,538	34,893	64,126	103,384	118,526	130,488	127,099
Michigan	995,384	1,327,051	1,563,761	1,638,367	1,680,792	1,751,050	25,340	55,391	100,224	120,070	142,261	151,906
Minnesota	1,004,427	1,297,457	1,626,949	1,622,869	1,664,254	1,729,682	123,571	325,758	784,964	928,396	1,092,542	1,179,028
Mississippi	150,123	178,142	221,582	225,484	234,795	248,970	†	8,369	16,466	21,061	26,002	29,899
Missouri	2,144,299	3,128,635	3,864,444	3,958,548	4,203,742	4,377,146	100,307	196,447	277,715	331,391	426,479	432,200
Montana	69,426	91,446	104,336	116,161	132,829	107,390	†	†	†	†	†	†
Nebraska	387,569	557,724	699,561	709,182	731,588	744,788	12,051	25,524	34,999	42,559	42,926	43,275
Nevada	7,006	9,637	43,433	73,701	85,024	98,835	29,278	104,949	118,434	143,358	156,577	152,954
New Hampshire	589,823	883,914	1,073,128	1,085,570	1,115,169	1,179,386	21,831	41,599	47,523	36,737	47,598	44,532
New Jersey	1,362,090	1,873,156	2,472,048	2,591,234	2,681,051	2,747,352	61,109	85,429	115,467	126,833	137,408	125,946
New Mexico	54,280	54,076	31,149	30,447	31,564	32,930	25,806	35,073	111,888	83,708	104,193	111,639
New York	12,519,671	17,680,799	22,892,724	23,511,385	24,664,171	25,903,697	326,329	624,764	718,608	762,214	876,944	871,255
North Carolina	3,530,337	4,808,306	6,272,149	6,452,783	6,890,504	7,001,839	4,041	38,078	116,192	186,514	242,098	261,901
North Dakota	56,000	88,860	94,477	87,938	93,751	114,109	1,145	7,885	14,835	20,198	18,456	15,292
Ohio	2,211,035	3,017,764	3,551,098	3,582,655	3,732,414	3,803,772	122,531	232,685	437,588	564,498	636,245	658,160
Oklahoma	338,276	392,427	515,934	523,630	550,897	583,898	32,527	72,537	103,780	110,336	129,544	145,509
Oregon	456,683	550,322	706,683	734,883	790,331	832,852	23,175	86,156	118,604	120,490	131,966	134,421
Pennsylvania	7,590,629	9,960,675	12,681,659	13,154,197	13,800,521	14,460,608	306,135	530,515	706,505	842,052	935,748	861,247
Rhode Island	828,715	1,237,106	1,554,627	1,564,624	1,596,480	1,702,209	4,519	10,073	7,084	†	†	†
South Carolina	408,127	563,952	786,592	680,369	717,448	739,911	6,627	18,374	69,377	226,848	273,395	289,770
South Dakota	69,555	99,575	117,711	119,974	125,637	125,509	18,061	23,477	30,354	41,594	47,972	51,505
Tennessee	1,971,564	3,140,336	4,262,494	4,500,016	4,801,285	4,918,450	50,921	142,256	245,140	331,287	346,050	340,537
Texas	2,490,597	3,379,710	4,283,965	4,376,280	4,665,642	4,806,456	172,327	343,221	677,625	803,401	851,581	847,702
Utah	648,035	867,956	962,042	1,012,997	1,061,194	1,177,439	36,348	62,880	115,801	144,226	206,186	211,978
Vermont	347,293	510,623	762,710	717,199	754,383	782,385	24,841	24,914	24,079	17,126	16,242	16,288
Virginia	944,905	1,311,743	1,686,972	1,841,075	1,737,579	1,923,966	65,804	258,642	443,621	614,287	678,326	663,162
Washington	600,315	778,678	964,938	988,571	1,034,761	1,073,689	51,134	104,107	140,546	161,645	178,364	163,426
West Virginia	170,653	181,181	201,699	211,877	222,031	179,112	17,926	28,634	121,720	165,043	214,223	259,876
Wisconsin	999,502	1,410,625	1,889,964	1,929,430	2,024,751	2,119,356	16,333	36,044	102,556	131,140	170,376	172,703
Wyoming	†	†	†	†	†	†	19,766	34,596	36,535	39,869	45,942	40,220
Other jurisdictions	431,216	615,990	727,264	742,820	793,439	855,651	56,116	70,535	116,452	116,452	260,512	258,693
Guam	†	1,535	3,680	2,551	2,215	1,756	†	†	†	†	†	†
Puerto Rico	431,216	614,455	723,583	740,269	791,224	853,895	56,116	70,535	116,452	116,452	260,512	258,693

†Not applicable.
NOTE: Degree-granting institutions grant associate's or higher degrees and participate in Title IV federal financial aid programs. Detail may not sum to totals because of rounding.

SOURCE: U.S. Department of Education, National Center for Education Statistics, Integrated Postsecondary Education Data System (IPEDS), Spring 2001 through Spring 2013, Finance component. (This table was prepared January 2014.)

On-campus crimes, arrests, and referrals for disciplinary action at degree-granting postsecondary institutions, by location of incident, control and level of institution, and type of incident: 2001 through 2011

Control and level of institution and type of incident	2001	2002	2003	2004	2005	2006	2007	2008	2009	2010	2011 Total	2011 In residence hall	2011 At other locations
1	2	3	4	5	6	7	8	9	10	11	12	13	14
All institutions													
Crimes against persons and property	41,596	42,521	43,064	43,555	42,710	44,492	41,829	40,296	34,054	31,919	30,401	14,698	15,703
Murder[1]	17	20	9	15	11	8	44	12	16	15	15	4	11
Negligent manslaughter[2]	2	0	1	0	2	0	3	3	0	1	1	1	0
Sex offenses—forcible[3]	2,201	2,327	2,595	2,667	2,674	2,670	2,694	2,639	2,544	2,919	3,344	2,378	966
Sex offenses—nonforcible[4]	461	261	60	27	42	43	40	35	65	33	45	16	29
Robbery[5]	1,663	1,802	1,625	1,550	1,551	1,547	1,561	1,576	1,409	1,391	1,292	225	1,067
Aggravated assault[6]	2,947	2,804	2,832	2,721	2,656	2,817	2,604	2,495	2,327	2,224	2,211	805	1,406
Burglary[7]	26,904	28,038	28,639	29,480	29,256	31,260	29,488	28,737	23,083	21,190	19,488	10,913	8,575
Motor vehicle theft[8]	6,221	6,181	6,285	6,062	5,531	5,231	4,619	4,104	3,977	3,418	3,373	5	3,368
Arson[9]	1,180	1,088	1,018	1,033	987	916	776	695	633	728	632	351	281
Weapons-, drug-, and liquor-related arrests and referrals													
Arrests[10]	40,348	43,407	44,581	47,939	49,024	50,187	50,558	50,639	50,066	51,423	54,612	27,760	26,852
Illegal weapons possession	1,073	1,142	1,094	1,263	1,316	1,316	1,318	1,190	1,077	1,103	1,028	248	780
Drug law violations	11,854	12,041	12,467	12,775	13,707	13,952	14,135	15,146	15,871	18,510	20,729	11,438	9,291
Liquor law violations	27,421	30,224	31,020	33,901	34,001	34,919	35,105	34,303	33,118	31,810	32,855	16,074	16,781
Referrals for disciplinary action[10]	155,201	167,319	184,915	196,775	202,816	218,040	216,600	217,526	220,987	229,630	250,557	222,912	27,645
Illegal weapons possession	1,277	1,287	1,566	1,799	1,882	1,871	1,658	1,455	1,275	1,308	1,310	869	441
Drug law violations	23,900	26,038	25,753	25,762	25,356	27,251	28,476	32,469	36,344	41,970	52,014	43,367	8,647
Liquor law violations	130,024	139,994	157,596	169,214	175,578	188,918	186,466	183,602	183,368	186,352	197,233	178,676	18,557
Public 4-year													
Crimes against persons and property	18,710	19,563	19,789	19,984	19,582	20,648	19,579	18,695	15,975	15,429	14,679	7,189	7,490
Murder[1]	9	9	5	8	4	5	42	9	8	9	9	3	6
Negligent manslaughter[2]	2	0	1	0	1	0	2	1	0	0	1	1	0
Sex offenses—forcible[3]	1,245	1,278	1,358	1,482	1,398	1,400	1,425	1,317	1,214	1,460	1,630	1,151	479
Sex offenses—nonforcible[4]	207	113	28	16	25	15	23	12	40	15	17	7	10
Robbery[5]	584	659	669	612	696	680	722	750	647	655	616	138	478
Aggravated assault[6]	1,434	1,320	1,381	1,269	1,280	1,338	1,258	1,182	1,134	1,072	1,081	426	655
Burglary[7]	11,520	12,523	12,634	13,026	12,935	14,027	13,371	12,970	10,708	10,170	9,363	5,244	4,119
Motor vehicle theft[8]	3,072	3,092	3,116	2,964	2,667	2,662	2,266	2,027	1,824	1,593	1,610	5	1,605
Arson[9]	637	569	597	607	576	521	470	427	400	455	352	214	138
Weapons-, drug-, and liquor-related arrests and referrals													
Arrests[10]	31,077	33,831	34,657	36,746	38,051	39,900	39,570	40,607	40,780	41,940	45,094	22,910	22,184
Illegal weapons possession	692	745	697	811	878	859	825	759	659	664	631	188	443
Drug law violations	9,125	9,238	9,389	9,620	10,606	10,850	10,693	11,714	12,186	14,318	16,329	9,286	7,043
Liquor law violations	21,260	23,848	24,571	26,315	26,567	28,191	28,052	28,134	27,935	26,958	28,134	13,436	14,698
Referrals for disciplinary action[10]	79,152	84,636	94,365	100,588	100,211	107,289	106,148	104,585	108,756	115,743	129,822	116,244	13,578
Illegal weapons possession	678	675	847	1,001	1,097	972	867	792	669	659	613	448	165
Drug law violations	13,179	13,943	13,811	13,658	13,020	13,798	14,458	16,656	18,260	21,375	27,377	22,809	4,568
Liquor law violations	65,295	70,018	79,707	85,929	86,094	92,519	90,823	87,137	89,827	93,709	101,832	92,987	8,845
Nonprofit 4-year													
Crimes against persons and property	14,844	14,859	15,179	15,523	15,574	16,864	15,452	14,892	11,964	11,128	10,742	6,538	4,204
Murder[1]	5	9	2	4	5	3	2	1	6	5	3	1	2
Negligent manslaughter[2]	0	0	0	0	1	0	1	0	0	0	0	0	0
Sex offenses—forcible[3]	820	914	1,048	1,026	1,088	1,080	1,065	1,083	1,102	1,220	1,406	1,132	274
Sex offenses—nonforcible[4]	113	81	14	5	6	10	8	16	11	8	13	6	7
Robbery[5]	649	735	538	577	500	502	460	437	366	317	325	75	250
Aggravated assault[6]	882	900	773	838	744	834	768	754	661	641	633	291	342
Burglary[7]	10,471	10,561	11,066	11,426	11,657	13,051	11,941	11,551	8,810	8,077	7,444	4,900	2,544
Motor vehicle theft[8]	1,471	1,273	1,385	1,316	1,248	1,077	984	859	834	637	702	0	702
Arson[9]	433	386	353	331	325	307	223	191	174	223	216	133	83
Weapons-, drug-, and liquor-related arrests and referrals													
Arrests[10]	6,329	6,548	6,856	7,722	7,406	6,134	6,732	6,112	5,777	5,417	5,470	3,153	2,317
Illegal weapons possession	167	162	166	184	150	146	178	158	148	137	128	30	98
Drug law violations	1,628	1,723	1,869	1,751	1,691	1,650	1,804	1,883	2,080	2,221	2,370	1,549	821
Liquor law violations	4,534	4,663	4,821	5,787	5,565	4,338	4,750	4,071	3,549	3,059	2,972	1,574	1,398
Referrals for disciplinary action[10]	71,293	77,641	85,184	90,749	96,646	103,484	103,254	105,289	103,457	104,512	110,925	99,218	11,707
Illegal weapons possession	443	424	537	608	590	622	545	457	358	391	433	335	98
Drug law violations	9,688	11,100	10,885	10,903	11,228	12,114	12,685	14,157	15,845	17,814	21,478	18,518	2,960
Liquor law violations	61,162	66,117	73,762	79,238	84,848	90,748	90,024	90,675	87,254	86,307	89,014	80,365	8,649
For-profit 4-year													
Crimes against persons and property	505	592	720	718	829	641	612	574	525	548	502	93	409
Murder[1]	0	0	0	0	0	0	0	0	0	0	1	0	1
Negligent manslaughter[2]	0	0	0	0	0	0	0	0	0	0	0	0	0
Sex offenses—forcible[3]	4	4	8	5	4	12	12	9	9	22	29	13	16
Sex offenses—nonforcible[4]	13	1	2	0	1	0	2	0	1	1	0	0	0
Robbery[5]	64	71	43	46	43	25	31	38	86	70	64	0	64
Aggravated assault[6]	23	45	41	38	59	31	31	63	43	50	47	15	32
Burglary[7]	347	376	542	524	607	489	446	385	299	339	282	65	217
Motor vehicle theft[8]	52	94	80	100	110	78	89	79	85	64	77	0	77
Arson[9]	2	1	4	5	5	6	1	0	2	2	2	0	2
Weapons-, drug-, and liquor-related arrests and referrals													
Arrests[10]	11	17	11	41	28	52	28	40	54	165	204	144	60
Illegal weapons possession	2	3	2	5	2	5	3	8	6	13	13	6	7
Drug law violations	4	9	4	12	16	14	16	14	22	66	62	44	18
Liquor law violations	5	5	5	24	10	33	9	18	26	86	129	94	35
Referrals for disciplinary action[10]	316	399	465	298	529	513	519	566	882	760	987	889	98
Illegal weapons possession	11	25	24	11	42	13	11	13	23	9	22	15	7
Drug law violations	92	133	130	99	128	138	132	159	231	221	352	307	45
Liquor law violations	213	241	311	188	359	362	376	394	628	530	613	567	46

See notes at end of table.

On-campus crimes, arrests, and referrals for disciplinary action at degree-granting postsecondary institutions, by location of incident, control and level of institution, and type of incident: 2001 through 2011—Continued

Control and level of institution and type of incident	Number of incidents										2011		
	2001	2002	2003	2004	2005	2006	2007	2008	2009	2010	Total	In residence hall	At other locations
1	2	3	4	5	6	7	8	9	10	11	12	13	14
Public 2-year													
Crimes against persons and property	6,817	6,860	6,637	6,637	5,981	5,669	5,381	5,464	4,984	4,365	4,098	826	3,272
Murder[1]	2	1	2	3	2	0	0	2	2	1	2	0	2
Negligent manslaughter[2]	0	0	0	0	0	0	0	0	0	1	0	0	0
Sex offenses—forcible[3]	118	118	160	142	175	167	181	210	205	208	261	72	189
Sex offenses—nonforcible[4]	119	61	14	6	10	16	7	12	8	8	15	3	12
Robbery[5]	245	234	230	213	248	284	279	285	251	300	262	12	250
Aggravated assault[6]	545	503	589	497	501	546	462	401	431	415	404	73	331
Burglary[7]	4,132	4,158	3,973	4,068	3,541	3,261	3,202	3,430	2,920	2,371	2,200	662	1,538
Motor vehicle theft[8]	1,552	1,661	1,607	1,620	1,428	1,319	1,174	1,059	1,109	1,018	895	0	895
Arson[9]	104	124	62	88	76	76	76	70	54	43	59	4	55
Weapons-, drug-, and liquor-related arrests and referrals													
Arrests[10]	2,660	2,844	2,950	3,270	3,416	3,993	4,124	3,764	3,335	3,806	3,768	1,527	2,241
Illegal weapons possession	198	221	220	255	278	300	304	258	256	278	251	24	227
Drug law violations	989	996	1,141	1,312	1,326	1,378	1,563	1,490	1,507	1,858	1,919	545	1,374
Liquor law violations	1,473	1,627	1,589	1,703	1,812	2,315	2,257	2,016	1,572	1,670	1,598	958	640
Referrals for disciplinary action[10]	3,529	3,744	4,036	4,371	4,688	5,897	5,987	6,425	7,241	7,945	8,225	6,079	2,146
Illegal weapons possession	127	146	145	167	133	238	218	183	210	241	230	70	160
Drug law violations	761	692	679	858	819	908	1,006	1,302	1,745	2,332	2,587	1,540	1,047
Liquor law violations	2,641	2,906	3,212	3,346	3,736	4,751	4,763	4,940	5,286	5,372	5,408	4,469	939
Nonprofit 2-year													
Crimes against persons and property	248	230	189	166	314	250	258	272	147	120	95	42	53
Murder[1]	1	0	0	0	0	0	0	0	0	0	0	0	0
Negligent manslaughter[2]	0	0	0	0	0	0	0	1	0	0	0	0	0
Sex offenses—forcible[3]	2	7	6	3	8	3	9	16	8	7	11	8	3
Sex offenses—nonforcible[4]	2	2	0	0	0	1	0	0	0	0	0	0	0
Robbery[5]	54	56	64	22	9	7	2	13	9	5	1	0	1
Aggravated assault[6]	23	17	12	17	22	35	52	66	5	9	6	0	6
Burglary[7]	142	123	83	111	266	187	178	160	120	95	72	34	38
Motor vehicle theft[8]	23	21	23	13	7	14	14	9	4	2	5	0	5
Arson[9]	1	4	1	0	2	3	3	7	1	2	0	0	0
Weapons-, drug-, and liquor-related arrests and referrals													
Arrests[10]	108	39	23	48	76	67	59	93	58	49	52	23	29
Illegal weapons possession	1	2	3	2	5	3	4	3	4	6	5	0	5
Drug law violations	21	10	16	16	32	34	27	33	35	18	34	13	21
Liquor law violations	86	27	4	30	39	30	28	57	19	25	13	10	3
Referrals for disciplinary action[10]	624	569	552	447	514	537	519	413	348	377	309	263	46
Illegal weapons possession	2	3	6	5	12	19	10	6	7	4	1	0	1
Drug law violations	91	65	52	58	47	74	73	85	100	105	101	98	3
Liquor law violations	531	501	494	384	455	444	436	322	241	268	207	165	42
For-profit 2-year													
Crimes against persons and property	472	417	550	527	430	420	547	399	459	329	285	10	275
Murder[1]	0	1	0	0	0	0	0	0	0	0	0	0	0
Negligent manslaughter[2]	0	0	0	0	0	0	0	1	0	0	0	0	0
Sex offenses—forcible[3]	12	6	15	9	1	8	2	4	6	2	7	2	5
Sex offenses—nonforcible[4]	7	3	2	0	0	1	0	0	1	1	0	0	0
Robbery[5]	67	47	81	80	55	49	67	53	50	44	24	0	24
Aggravated assault[6]	40	19	36	62	50	33	33	29	53	37	40	0	40
Burglary[7]	292	297	341	325	250	245	350	241	226	138	127	8	119
Motor vehicle theft[8]	51	40	74	49	71	81	92	71	121	104	84	0	84
Arson[9]	3	4	1	2	3	3	3	0	2	3	3	0	3
Weapons-, drug-, and liquor-related arrests and referrals													
Arrests[10]	163	128	84	112	47	41	45	23	62	46	24	3	21
Illegal weapons possession	13	9	6	6	3	3	4	4	4	5	0	0	0
Drug law violations	87	65	48	64	36	26	32	12	41	29	15	1	14
Liquor law violations	63	54	30	42	8	12	9	7	17	12	9	2	7
Referrals for disciplinary action[10]	287	330	313	322	228	320	173	248	303	293	289	219	70
Illegal weapons possession	16	14	7	7	8	7	7	4	8	4	11	1	10
Drug law violations	89	105	196	186	134	219	122	110	163	123	119	95	24
Liquor law violations	182	211	110	129	86	94	44	134	132	166	159	123	36

[1]Excludes suicides, fetal deaths, traffic fatalities, accidental deaths, and justifiable homicide (such as the killing of a felon by a law enforcement officer in the line of duty).

[2]Killing of another person through gross negligence (excludes traffic fatalities).

[3]Any sexual act directed against another person forcibly and/or against that person's will.

[4]Includes only statutory rape or incest.

[5]Taking or attempting to take anything of value using actual or threatened force or violence.

[6]Attack upon a person for the purpose of inflicting severe or aggravated bodily injury.

[7]Unlawful entry of a structure to commit a felony or theft.

[8]Theft or attempted theft of a motor vehicle.

[9]Willful or malicious burning or attempt to burn a dwelling house, public building, motor vehicle, or personal property of another.

[10]If an individual is both arrested and referred to college officials for disciplinary action for a single offense, only the arrest is counted.

NOTE: Degree-granting institutions grant associate's or higher degrees and participate in Title IV federal financial aid programs. Crimes, arrests, and referrals include incidents involving students, staff, and on-campus guests. Excludes off-campus crimes and arrests even if they involve college students or staff.

SOURCE: U.S. Department of Education, Office of Postsecondary Education, Campus Safety and Security Reporting System, 2001 through 2011; and National Center for Education Statistics, Integrated Postsecondary Education Data System (IPEDS), Spring 2002 through Spring 2012, Enrollment component. (This table was prepared November 2013.)

On-campus crimes, arrests, and referrals for disciplinary action per 10,000 full-time-equivalent (FTE) students at degree-granting postsecondary institutions, by whether institution has residence halls, control and level of institution, and type of incident: 2001 through 2011

	Number of incidents per 10,000 full-time-equivalent (FTE) students[1]												
	Total, institutions with and without residence halls										2011		
Control and level of institution and type of incident	2001	2002	2003	2004	2005	2006	2007	2008	2009	2010	Total	Institutions with residence halls	Institutions without residence halls
1	2	3	4	5	6	7	8	9	10	11	12	13	14
All institutions													
Crimes against persons and property	35.619	34.649	34.040	33.580	32.864	33.347	30.568	28.987	22.922	20.782	19.738	26.105	7.625
Murder[2]	0.015	0.016	0.007	0.012	0.008	0.006	0.032	0.009	0.011	0.010	0.010	0.012	0.006
Negligent manslaughter[3]	0.002	0.000	0.001	0.000	0.002	0.000	0.002	0.002	0.002	0.001	0.001	0.001	0.000
Sex offenses—forcible[4]	1.885	1.896	2.051	2.056	2.058	2.001	1.969	1.898	1.712	1.901	2.171	3.099	0.405
Sex offenses—nonforcible[5]	0.395	0.213	0.047	0.021	0.032	0.032	0.029	0.025	0.044	0.021	0.029	0.030	0.028
Robbery[6]	1.424	1.468	1.284	1.195	1.193	1.159	1.141	1.134	0.948	0.906	0.839	0.952	0.624
Aggravated assault[7]	2.524	2.285	2.239	2.098	2.044	2.111	1.903	1.795	1.566	1.448	1.436	1.799	0.744
Burglary[8]	23.038	22.847	22.638	22.728	22.511	23.429	21.549	20.672	15.538	13.797	12.653	17.387	3.646
Motor vehicle theft[9]	5.327	5.037	4.968	4.674	4.256	3.921	3.375	2.952	2.677	2.225	2.190	2.256	2.064
Arson[10]	1.010	0.887	0.805	0.796	0.759	0.687	0.567	0.500	0.426	0.474	0.410	0.570	0.107
Weapons-, drug-, and liquor-related arrests and referrals													
Arrests[11]	34.550	35.371	35.239	36.960	37.722	37.615	36.947	36.428	33.700	33.481	35.457	52.244	3.520
Illegal weapons possession	0.919	0.931	0.865	0.974	1.013	0.986	0.963	0.856	0.725	0.718	0.667	0.824	0.369
Drug law violations	10.151	9.812	9.854	9.849	10.547	10.457	10.330	10.895	10.683	12.052	13.459	19.342	2.265
Liquor law violations	23.481	24.629	24.520	26.137	26.163	26.172	25.654	24.676	22.292	20.711	21.331	32.078	0.886
Referrals for disciplinary action[11]	132.899	136.344	146.165	151.708	156.060	163.421	158.288	156.479	148.751	149.511	162.677	246.400	3.394
Illegal weapons possession	1.093	1.049	1.238	1.387	1.448	1.402	1.212	1.047	0.858	0.852	0.851	1.168	0.247
Drug law violations	20.466	21.218	20.356	19.862	19.511	20.425	20.810	23.357	24.464	27.326	33.771	50.645	1.668
Liquor law violations	111.340	114.077	124.571	130.459	135.101	141.594	136.267	132.076	123.429	121.333	128.056	194.587	1.479
Public 4-year													
Crimes against persons and property	36.191	36.334	35.725	35.522	34.295	35.532	32.837	30.531	24.898	23.426	21.853	23.266	7.973
Murder[2]	0.017	0.017	0.009	0.014	0.007	0.009	0.070	0.015	0.012	0.014	0.013	0.015	0.000
Negligent manslaughter[3]	0.004	0.000	0.002	0.000	0.002	0.000	0.003	0.002	0.000	0.000	0.001	0.002	0.000
Sex offenses—forcible[4]	2.408	2.374	2.452	2.634	2.448	2.409	2.390	2.151	1.892	2.217	2.427	2.633	0.403
Sex offenses—nonforcible[5]	0.400	0.210	0.051	0.028	0.044	0.026	0.039	0.020	0.062	0.023	0.025	0.026	0.016
Robbery[6]	1.130	1.224	1.208	1.088	1.219	1.170	1.211	1.225	1.008	0.994	0.917	0.969	0.403
Aggravated assault[7]	2.774	2.452	2.493	2.256	2.242	2.302	2.110	1.930	1.767	1.628	1.609	1.711	0.612
Burglary[8]	22.283	23.259	22.808	23.154	22.654	24.138	22.425	21.181	16.689	15.441	13.939	14.906	4.446
Motor vehicle theft[9]	5.942	5.743	5.625	5.269	4.671	4.581	3.800	3.310	2.843	2.419	2.397	2.433	2.046
Arson[10]	1.232	1.057	1.078	1.079	1.009	0.897	0.788	0.697	0.623	0.691	0.524	0.572	0.048
Weapons-, drug-, and liquor-related arrests and referrals													
Arrests[11]	60.113	62.833	62.566	65.318	66.641	68.662	66.366	66.315	63.558	63.677	67.132	73.573	3.882
Illegal weapons possession	1.339	1.384	1.258	1.442	1.538	1.478	1.384	1.240	1.027	1.008	0.939	1.017	0.177
Drug law violations	17.651	17.158	16.950	17.100	18.575	18.671	17.934	19.130	18.993	21.739	24.309	26.542	2.384
Liquor law violations	41.123	44.292	44.358	46.776	46.529	48.513	47.048	45.945	43.539	40.930	41.883	46.014	1.321
Referrals for disciplinary action[11]	153.104	157.192	170.355	178.800	175.506	184.628	178.029	170.797	169.504	175.732	193.268	212.708	2.368
Illegal weapons possession	1.311	1.254	1.529	1.779	1.921	1.673	1.454	1.293	1.043	1.041	0.913	0.996	0.097
Drug law violations	25.492	25.896	24.933	24.278	22.803	23.744	24.249	27.201	28.459	32.454	40.756	44.771	1.337
Liquor law violations	126.301	130.043	143.893	152.743	150.782	159.211	152.326	142.303	140.001	142.278	151.598	166.942	0.934
Nonprofit 4-year													
Crimes against persons and property	57.358	55.445	54.891	54.728	54.165	57.681	52.039	49.315	38.658	34.977	33.041	34.948	10.546
Murder[2]	0.019	0.034	0.007	0.014	0.017	0.010	0.007	0.003	0.019	0.016	0.009	0.007	0.039
Negligent manslaughter[3]	0.000	0.000	0.000	0.000	0.003	0.000	0.003	0.000	0.000	0.000	0.000	0.000	0.000
Sex offenses—forcible[4]	3.169	3.410	3.790	3.617	3.784	3.694	3.587	3.586	3.561	3.835	4.325	4.628	0.748
Sex offenses—nonforcible[5]	0.437	0.302	0.051	0.018	0.021	0.034	0.027	0.053	0.036	0.025	0.040	0.033	0.118
Robbery[6]	2.508	2.743	1.946	2.034	1.739	1.717	1.549	1.447	1.183	0.996	1.000	1.024	0.708
Aggravated assault[7]	3.408	3.358	2.795	2.954	2.588	2.853	2.586	2.497	2.136	2.015	1.947	1.999	1.338
Burglary[8]	40.460	39.407	40.017	40.284	40.542	44.639	40.214	38.251	28.467	25.387	22.897	24.301	6.335
Motor vehicle theft[9]	5.684	4.750	5.008	4.640	4.340	3.684	3.314	2.845	2.695	2.002	2.159	2.246	1.141
Arson[10]	1.673	1.440	1.277	1.167	1.130	1.050	0.751	0.632	0.562	0.701	0.664	0.711	0.118
Weapons-, drug-, and liquor-related arrests and referrals													
Arrests[11]	24.456	24.433	24.793	27.225	25.758	20.981	22.672	20.240	18.667	17.026	16.825	17.991	3.069
Illegal weapons possession	0.645	0.604	0.600	0.649	0.522	0.499	0.599	0.523	0.478	0.431	0.394	0.397	0.354
Drug law violations	6.291	6.429	6.759	6.173	5.881	5.644	6.075	6.236	6.721	6.981	7.290	7.721	2.204
Liquor law violations	17.520	17.399	17.434	20.403	19.355	14.838	15.997	13.481	11.467	9.615	9.141	9.873	0.512
Referrals for disciplinary action[11]	275.480	289.709	308.044	319.945	336.127	353.954	347.734	348.663	334.288	328.494	341.188	368.118	23.609
Illegal weapons possession	1.712	1.582	1.942	2.144	2.052	2.127	1.835	1.513	1.157	1.229	1.332	1.425	0.236
Drug law violations	37.435	41.418	39.363	38.440	38.981	41.434	42.720	46.881	51.198	55.992	66.063	71.398	3.148
Liquor law violations	236.333	246.708	266.740	279.362	295.095	310.392	303.179	300.269	281.934	271.274	273.793	295.295	20.225
For-profit 4-year													
Crimes against persons and property	19.109	17.840	17.605	13.650	17.049	9.552	8.095	10.320	7.288	6.596	6.128	10.354	5.138
Murder[2]	0.000	0.000	0.000	0.000	0.000	0.000	0.000	0.000	0.000	0.000	0.012	0.000	0.015
Negligent manslaughter[3]	0.000	0.000	0.000	0.000	0.000	0.000	0.000	0.000	0.000	0.000	0.000	0.000	0.000
Sex offenses—forcible[4]	0.151	0.121	0.196	0.095	0.082	0.179	0.159	0.162	0.125	0.265	0.354	1.544	0.075
Sex offenses—nonforcible[5]	0.492	0.030	0.049	0.000	0.021	0.000	0.026	0.000	0.014	0.012	0.000	0.000	0.000
Robbery[6]	2.422	2.140	1.051	0.875	0.884	0.373	0.410	0.683	1.194	0.842	0.781	0.129	0.934
Aggravated assault[7]	0.870	1.356	1.003	0.722	1.213	0.462	0.410	1.133	0.597	0.602	0.574	1.286	0.407
Burglary[8]	13.130	11.331	13.253	9.962	12.484	7.287	5.899	6.922	4.151	4.080	3.442	6.431	2.742
Motor vehicle theft[9]	1.968	2.833	1.956	1.901	2.262	1.162	1.177	1.420	1.180	0.770	0.940	0.836	0.964
Arson[10]	0.076	0.030	0.098	0.095	0.103	0.089	0.013	0.000	0.028	0.024	0.024	0.129	0.000
Weapons-, drug-, and liquor-related arrests and referrals													
Arrests[11]	0.416	0.512	0.269	0.779	0.576	0.775	0.370	0.719	0.750	1.986	2.490	10.547	0.603
Illegal weapons possession	0.076	0.090	0.049	0.095	0.041	0.075	0.040	0.144	0.083	0.156	0.159	0.643	0.045
Drug law violations	0.151	0.271	0.098	0.228	0.329	0.209	0.212	0.252	0.305	0.794	0.757	3.280	0.166
Liquor law violations	0.189	0.151	0.122	0.456	0.206	0.492	0.119	0.324	0.361	1.035	1.575	6.624	0.392
Referrals for disciplinary action[11]	11.957	12.024	11.370	5.665	10.880	7.645	6.865	10.177	12.244	9.147	12.048	59.361	0.964
Illegal weapons possession	0.416	0.753	0.587	0.209	0.864	0.194	0.145	0.234	0.319	0.108	0.269	1.029	0.090
Drug law violations	3.481	4.008	3.179	1.882	2.632	2.057	1.746	2.859	3.207	2.660	4.297	20.709	0.452
Liquor law violations	8.060	7.263	7.605	3.574	7.383	5.395	4.973	7.084	8.718	6.379	7.483	37.623	0.422

See notes at end of table.

On-campus crimes, arrests, and referrals for disciplinary action per 10,000 full-time-equivalent (FTE) students at degree-granting postsecondary institutions, by whether institution has residence halls, control and level of institution, and type of incident: 2001 through 2011—Continued

Control and level of institution and type of incident	Number of incidents per 10,000 full-time-equivalent (FTE) students[1]											2011	
	Total, institutions with and without residence halls											Institutions with residence halls	Institutions without residence halls
	2001	2002	2003	2004	2005	2006	2007	2008	2009	2010	Total		
1	2	3	4	5	6	7	8	9	10	11	12	13	14
Public 2-year													
Crimes against persons and property	19.867	18.834	18.044	17.903	16.389	15.423	14.388	13.991	11.735	10.042	9.721	17.583	7.804
Murder[2]	0.006	0.003	0.005	0.008	0.005	0.000	0.000	0.005	0.005	0.002	0.005	0.012	0.003
Negligent manslaughter[3]	0.000	0.000	0.000	0.000	0.000	0.000	0.000	0.000	0.000	0.002	0.000	0.000	0.003
Sex offenses—forcible[4]	0.344	0.324	0.435	0.383	0.480	0.454	0.484	0.538	0.483	0.479	0.619	1.234	0.469
Sex offenses—nonforcible[5]	0.347	0.167	0.038	0.016	0.027	0.044	0.019	0.018	0.028	0.018	0.036	0.048	0.032
Robbery[6]	0.714	0.642	0.625	0.575	0.680	0.773	0.746	0.730	0.591	0.690	0.621	0.726	0.596
Aggravated assault[7]	1.588	1.381	1.601	1.341	1.373	1.485	1.235	1.027	1.015	0.955	0.958	1.803	0.752
Burglary[8]	12.042	11.416	10.801	10.974	9.703	8.872	8.561	8.783	6.875	5.454	5.219	12.355	3.479
Motor vehicle theft[9]	4.523	4.560	4.369	4.370	3.913	3.588	3.139	2.712	2.611	2.342	2.123	1.271	2.331
Arson[10]	0.303	0.340	0.169	0.237	0.208	0.207	0.203	0.179	0.127	0.099	0.140	0.133	0.142
Weapons-, drug-, and liquor-related arrests and referrals													
Arrests[11]	7.752	7.808	8.020	8.821	9.360	10.863	11.027	9.638	7.852	8.756	8.938	27.639	4.379
Illegal weapons possession	0.577	0.607	0.598	0.688	0.762	0.816	0.813	0.661	0.603	0.640	0.595	0.956	0.507
Drug law violations	2.882	2.735	3.102	3.539	3.633	3.749	4.179	3.815	3.548	4.274	4.552	11.472	2.865
Liquor law violations	4.293	4.467	4.320	4.594	4.965	6.298	6.035	5.162	3.701	3.842	3.791	15.211	1.006
Referrals for disciplinary action[11]	10.284	10.279	10.973	11.791	12.846	16.043	16.008	16.451	17.049	18.277	19.511	87.844	2.850
Illegal weapons possession	0.370	0.401	0.394	0.450	0.364	0.648	0.583	0.469	0.494	0.554	0.546	1.488	0.316
Drug law violations	2.218	1.900	1.846	2.314	2.244	2.470	2.690	3.334	4.109	5.365	6.137	23.101	2.000
Liquor law violations	7.697	7.978	8.732	9.026	10.237	12.926	12.735	12.649	12.446	12.358	12.829	63.254	0.534
Nonprofit 2-year													
Crimes against persons and property	63.955	58.903	51.594	48.535	91.263	81.948	103.819	99.299	55.894	47.971	28.673	73.101	12.717
Murder[2]	0.258	0.000	0.000	0.000	0.000	0.000	0.000	0.000	0.000	0.000	0.000	0.000	0.000
Negligent manslaughter[3]	0.000	0.000	0.000	0.000	0.000	0.000	0.000	0.365	0.000	0.000	0.000	0.000	0.000
Sex offenses—forcible[4]	0.516	1.793	1.638	0.877	2.325	0.983	3.622	5.841	3.042	2.798	3.320	10.280	0.820
Sex offenses—nonforcible[5]	0.516	0.512	0.000	0.000	0.000	0.328	0.000	0.000	0.000	0.000	0.000	0.000	0.000
Robbery[6]	13.926	14.342	17.471	6.432	2.616	2.295	0.805	4.746	3.422	1.999	0.302	1.142	0.000
Aggravated assault[7]	5.931	4.354	3.276	4.970	6.394	11.473	20.925	24.095	1.901	3.598	1.811	4.569	0.820
Burglary[8]	36.620	31.500	22.658	32.454	77.312	61.297	71.627	58.411	45.627	37.977	21.731	54.826	9.845
Motor vehicle theft[9]	5.931	5.378	6.279	3.801	2.035	4.589	5.634	3.286	1.521	0.800	1.509	2.284	1.231
Arson[10]	0.258	1.024	0.273	0.000	0.581	0.983	1.207	2.555	0.380	0.800	0.000	0.000	0.000
Weapons-, drug-, and liquor-related arrests and referrals													
Arrests[11]	27.852	9.988	6.279	14.034	22.089	21.962	23.741	33.952	22.053	19.588	15.695	51.399	2.872
Illegal weapons possession	0.258	0.512	0.819	0.585	1.453	0.983	1.610	1.095	1.521	2.399	1.509	4.569	0.410
Drug law violations	5.416	2.561	4.368	4.678	9.301	11.145	10.865	12.047	13.308	7.196	10.262	33.124	2.051
Liquor law violations	22.178	6.915	1.092	8.771	11.335	9.834	11.267	20.809	7.224	9.994	3.924	13.706	0.410
Referrals for disciplinary action[11]	160.920	145.722	150.688	130.694	149.393	176.025	208.845	150.774	132.319	150.710	93.263	352.941	0.000
Illegal weapons possession	0.516	0.768	1.638	1.462	3.488	6.228	4.024	2.190	2.662	1.599	0.302	1.142	0.000
Drug law violations	23.468	16.647	14.195	16.958	13.660	24.257	29.375	31.031	38.023	41.975	30.484	115.363	0.000
Liquor law violations	136.937	128.307	134.855	112.274	132.244	145.540	175.446	117.553	91.635	107.136	62.477	236.436	0.000
For-profit 2-year													
Crimes against persons and property	25.385	21.447	24.700	21.845	17.851	18.237	23.658	14.826	13.060	8.477	7.791	16.319	7.511
Murder[2]	0.000	0.051	0.000	0.000	0.000	0.000	0.000	0.000	0.000	0.000	0.000	0.000	0.000
Negligent manslaughter[3]	0.000	0.000	0.000	0.000	0.000	0.000	0.000	0.037	0.000	0.000	0.000	0.000	0.000
Sex offenses—forcible[4]	0.645	0.309	0.674	0.373	0.042	0.347	0.087	0.149	0.171	0.052	0.191	1.718	0.141
Sex offenses—nonforcible[5]	0.376	0.154	0.090	0.000	0.000	0.043	0.000	0.000	0.028	0.026	0.000	0.000	0.000
Robbery[6]	3.603	2.417	3.638	3.316	2.283	2.128	2.898	1.969	1.423	1.134	0.656	0.000	0.678
Aggravated assault[7]	2.151	0.977	1.617	2.570	2.076	1.433	1.427	1.078	1.508	0.953	1.093	0.859	1.101
Burglary[8]	15.704	15.275	15.314	13.472	10.378	10.638	15.138	8.955	6.430	3.556	3.472	12.024	3.191
Motor vehicle theft[9]	2.743	2.057	3.323	2.031	2.947	3.517	3.979	2.638	3.443	2.680	2.296	1.718	2.315
Arson[10]	0.161	0.206	0.045	0.083	0.125	0.130	0.130	0.000	0.057	0.077	0.082	0.000	0.085
Weapons-, drug-, and liquor-related arrests and referrals													
Arrests[11]	8.766	6.583	3.772	4.643	1.951	1.780	1.946	0.855	1.764	1.185	0.656	5.153	0.508
Illegal weapons possession	0.699	0.463	0.269	0.249	0.125	0.130	0.173	0.149	0.114	0.129	0.000	0.000	0.000
Drug law violations	4.679	3.343	2.156	2.653	1.495	1.129	1.384	0.446	1.167	0.747	0.410	3.436	0.311
Liquor law violations	3.388	2.777	1.347	1.741	0.332	0.521	0.389	0.260	0.484	0.309	0.246	1.718	0.198
Referrals for disciplinary action[11]	15.435	16.972	14.057	13.348	9.465	13.895	7.482	9.215	8.621	7.550	7.900	227.605	0.678
Illegal weapons possession	0.861	0.720	0.314	0.290	0.332	0.304	0.303	0.149	0.228	0.103	0.301	4.294	0.169
Drug law violations	4.787	5.400	8.802	7.710	5.563	9.509	5.277	4.087	4.638	3.169	3.253	90.183	0.395
Liquor law violations	9.788	10.852	4.940	5.347	3.570	4.082	1.903	4.979	3.756	4.277	4.347	133.127	0.113

[1]Although crimes, arrests, and referrals include incidents involving students, staff, and campus guests, they are expressed as a ratio to FTE students because comprehensive FTE counts of all these groups are not available.
[2]Excludes suicides, fetal deaths, traffic fatalities, accidental deaths, and justifiable homicide (such as the killing of a felon by a law enforcement officer in the line of duty).
[3]Killing of another person through gross negligence (excludes traffic fatalities).
[4]Any sexual act directed against another person forcibly and/or against that person's will.
[5]Includes only statutory rape or incest.
[6]Taking or attempting to take anything of value using actual or threatened force or violence.
[7]Attack upon a person for the purpose of inflicting severe or aggravated bodily injury.
[8]Unlawful entry of a structure to commit a felony or theft.
[9]Theft or attempted theft of a motor vehicle.

[10]Willful or malicious burning or attempt to burn a dwelling house, public building, motor vehicle, or personal property of another.
[11]If an individual is both arrested and referred to college officials for disciplinary action for a single offense, only the arrest is counted.
NOTE: Degree-granting institutions grant associate's or higher degrees and participate in Title IV federal financial aid programs. Crimes, arrests, and referrals include incidents involving students, staff, and on-campus guests. Excludes off-campus crimes and arrests even if they involve college students or staff. Detail may not sum to totals because of rounding.
SOURCE: U.S. Department of Education, Office of Postsecondary Education, Campus Safety and Security Reporting System, 2001 through 2011; and National Center for Education Statistics, Integrated Postsecondary Education Data System (IPEDS), Spring 2002 through Spring 2012, Enrollment component. (This table was prepared November 2013.)

Average undergraduate tuition and fees and room and board rates charged for full-time students in degree-granting postsecondary institutions, by level and control of institution: 1963–64 through 2012–13

Year and control of institution	Constant 2012–13 dollars[1]												Current dollars											
	Total tuition, fees, room, and board			Tuition and required fees[2]			Dormitory rooms			Board[3]			Total tuition, fees, room, and board			Tuition and required fees[2]			Dormitory rooms			Board[3]		
	All institutions	4-year	2-year	All institutions	4-year	2-year	All institutions	4-year	2-year	All institutions	4-year	2-year	All institutions	4-year	2-year	All institutions	4-year	2-year	All institutions	4-year	2-year	All institutions	4-year	2-year
1	2	3	4	5	6	7	8	9	10	11	12	13	14	15	16	17	18	19	20	21	22	23	24	25
All institutions																								
1963–64	$9,361	$9,647	$5,817	$3,812	$4,145	$1,285	$2,118	$2,090	$1,569	$3,431	$3,413	$2,963	$1,248	$1,286	$775	$508	$553	$171	$282	$279	$209	$457	$455	$395
1964–65	9,503	9,818	6,231	3,926	4,297	1,387	2,190	2,157	1,760	3,388	3,363	3,084	1,283	1,325	841	530	580	187	296	291	238	457	454	416
1965–66	9,598	9,971	6,412	3,977	4,398	1,471	2,252	2,230	1,874	3,369	3,343	3,067	1,324	1,375	884	549	607	203	311	308	258	465	461	423
1966–67	9,685	10,116	6,506	4,034	4,500	1,506	2,309	2,299	1,968	3,342	3,317	3,033	1,378	1,439	926	574	640	214	328	327	280	476	472	431
1967–68	9,627	10,118	6,693	3,997	4,508	1,579	2,327	2,321	2,050	3,304	3,289	3,064	1,415	1,487	984	588	663	232	342	341	301	486	483	450
1968–69	9,461	10,023	6,830	3,868	4,432	1,624	2,337	2,336	2,120	3,256	3,255	3,085	1,459	1,545	1,053	596	683	250	360	360	327	502	502	476
1969–70	9,554	10,255	6,672	3,951	4,624	1,515	2,384	2,400	2,125	3,219	3,231	3,032	1,560	1,674	1,089	645	755	247	389	392	347	526	528	495
1970–71	9,625	10,392	6,525	4,007	4,739	1,453	2,439	2,457	2,152	3,179	3,195	2,980	1,653	1,784	1,120	688	814	249	419	422	369	546	549	501
1971–72	9,729	10,556	6,588	4,069	4,865	1,410	2,501	2,521	2,198	3,158	3,170	2,980	1,730	1,878	1,172	724	865	251	445	448	391	562	564	530
1972–73	9,914	10,975	6,896	4,104	5,136	1,550	2,636	2,661	2,242	3,173	3,178	3,104	1,834	2,031	1,276	759	950	287	488	492	415	587	588	574
1973–74	9,443	10,406	6,740	3,948	4,885	1,630	2,458	2,480	2,132	3,037	3,041	2,978	1,903	2,097	1,358	796	985	328	495	500	430	612	613	600
1974–75	8,858	9,767	6,394	3,615	4,503	1,463	2,359	2,379	2,056	2,884	2,885	2,875	1,983	2,187	1,432	809	1,008	328	528	533	460	646	646	644
1975–76	8,774	9,823	6,146	3,459	4,477	1,240	2,373	2,403	1,977	2,942	2,943	2,929	2,103	2,355	1,473	829	1,073	297	569	576	474	705	706	702
1976–77	8,968	10,157	6,298	3,642	4,803	1,362	2,378	2,408	1,982	2,948	2,947	2,957	2,275	2,577	1,598	924	1,218	346	603	611	503	748	748	750
1977–78	8,905	10,065	6,292	3,636	4,770	1,397	2,383	2,415	1,938	2,885	2,880	2,957	2,411	2,725	1,703	984	1,291	378	645	654	525	781	780	801
1978–79	8,736	9,853	6,174	3,623	4,717	1,388	2,323	2,349	1,942	2,790	2,786	2,844	2,587	2,917	1,828	1,073	1,397	411	688	696	575	826	825	842
1979–80	8,371	9,438	5,899	3,465	4,509	1,344	2,238	2,263	1,871	2,668	2,667	2,683	2,809	3,167	1,979	1,163	1,513	451	751	759	628	895	895	900
1980–81	8,283	9,346	5,956	3,442	4,483	1,405	2,233	2,259	1,882	2,608	2,604	2,670	3,101	3,499	2,230	1,289	1,679	526	836	846	705	976	975	1,000
1981–82	8,578	9,713	6,086	3,581	4,689	1,449	2,335	2,364	1,948	2,662	2,660	2,688	3,489	3,951	2,476	1,457	1,907	590	950	961	793	1,083	1,082	1,094
1982–83	9,138	10,385	6,396	3,832	5,043	1,590	2,507	2,541	2,059	2,798	2,802	2,713	3,877	4,406	2,713	1,626	2,139	675	1,064	1,078	873	1,187	1,189	1,165
1983–84	9,472	10,790	6,488	4,052	5,327	1,660	2,603	2,641	2,082	2,817	2,822	2,746	4,167	4,747	2,854	1,783	2,344	730	1,145	1,162	916	1,239	1,242	1,208
1984–85	9,980	11,288	6,955	4,343	5,616	1,796	2,772	2,804	2,313	2,866	2,867	2,845	4,563	5,160	3,179	1,985	2,567	821	1,267	1,282	1,058	1,310	1,311	1,301
1985–86[4]	10,385	11,702	7,158	4,637	5,920	1,889	2,845	2,880	2,353	2,903	2,902	2,916	4,885	5,504	3,367	2,181	2,784	888	1,338	1,355	1,107	1,365	1,365	1,372
1986–87	10,829	12,405	6,854	4,809	6,327	1,866	2,922	2,967	2,151	3,097	3,110	2,837	5,206	5,964	3,295	2,312	3,042	897	1,405	1,427	1,034	1,489	1,495	1,364
1987–88	10,973	12,527	6,517	4,909	6,393	1,616	2,971	3,028	2,031	3,093	3,106	2,869	5,494	6,272	3,263	2,458	3,201	809	1,488	1,516	1,017	1,549	1,555	1,437
1988–89	11,203	12,839	6,821	5,073	6,628	1,870	3,006	3,071	2,071	3,124	3,139	2,880	5,869	6,725	3,573	2,658	3,472	979	1,575	1,609	1,085	1,636	1,644	1,509
1989–90	11,310	13,140	6,751	5,173	6,924	1,782	2,984	3,051	2,013	3,152	3,164	2,956	6,207	7,212	3,705	2,839	3,800	978	1,638	1,675	1,105	1,730	1,737	1,622
1990–91	11,336	13,132	6,790	5,211	6,926	1,879	3,012	3,078	2,043	3,113	3,128	2,869	6,562	7,602	3,930	3,016	4,009	1,087	1,743	1,782	1,182	1,802	1,811	1,660
1991–92	11,847	13,789	6,850	5,500	7,341	1,991	3,137	3,216	2,026	3,210	3,233	2,833	7,077	8,238	4,092	3,286	4,385	1,189	1,874	1,921	1,210	1,918	1,931	1,692
1992–93	12,097	14,216	6,830	5,709	7,714	2,071	3,147	3,232	2,013	3,241	3,270	2,746	7,452	8,758	4,208	3,517	4,752	1,276	1,939	1,991	1,240	1,996	2,015	1,692
1993–94	12,549	14,709	7,039	6,056	8,100	2,213	3,255	3,340	2,108	3,239	3,270	2,718	7,931	9,296	4,449	3,827	5,119	1,399	2,057	2,111	1,332	2,047	2,067	1,718
1994–95	12,775	14,963	7,127	6,221	8,292	2,288	3,300	3,383	2,147	3,254	3,288	2,691	8,306	9,728	4,633	4,044	5,391	1,488	2,145	2,200	1,396	2,116	2,138	1,750
1995–96	13,178	15,468	7,075	6,496	8,664	2,279	3,390	3,471	2,205	3,292	3,333	2,590	8,800	10,330	4,725	4,338	5,786	1,522	2,264	2,318	1,473	2,199	2,226	1,730
1996–97	13,403	15,783	7,127	6,645	8,908	2,246	3,444	3,526	2,217	3,314	3,349	2,664	9,206	10,841	4,895	4,564	6,118	1,543	2,365	2,422	1,522	2,276	2,301	1,830
1997–98	13,714	16,131	7,427	6,801	9,084	2,424	3,496	3,586	2,285	3,417	3,461	2,717	9,588	11,277	5,192	4,755	6,351	1,695	2,444	2,507	1,598	2,389	2,419	1,900
1998–99	14,167	16,716	7,439	7,048	9,452	2,426	3,596	3,692	2,272	3,523	3,572	2,741	10,076	11,888	5,291	5,013	6,723	1,725	2,557	2,626	1,616	2,506	2,540	1,950
1999–2000	14,254	16,876	7,406	7,136	9,621	2,361	3,671	3,759	2,421	3,447	3,496	2,624	10,430	12,349	5,460	5,222	7,040	1,728	2,686	2,751	1,771	2,523	2,558	1,920
2000–01	14,296	17,075	7,223	7,105	9,740	2,244	3,728	3,822	2,353	3,463	3,512	2,626	10,820	12,922	5,466	5,377	7,372	1,698	2,821	2,893	1,781	2,621	2,658	1,987
2001–02	14,775	17,708	7,424	7,331	10,109	2,337	3,870	3,973	2,399	3,574	3,626	2,688	11,380	13,639	5,718	5,646	7,786	1,800	2,981	3,060	1,848	2,753	2,793	2,070
2002–03	15,262	18,344	7,943	7,625	10,555	2,418	4,039	4,146	2,638	3,598	3,643	2,886	12,014	14,439	6,252	6,002	8,309	1,903	3,179	3,263	2,077	2,832	2,867	2,272
2003–04	16,104	19,276	8,336	8,215	11,225	2,703	4,176	4,287	2,745	3,712	3,765	2,887	12,953	15,505	6,705	6,608	9,029	2,174	3,359	3,448	2,208	2,986	3,028	2,322
2004–05	16,647	19,925	8,563	8,596	11,714	2,822	4,310	4,420	2,841	3,741	3,792	2,901	13,793	16,510	7,095	7,122	9,706	2,338	3,572	3,662	2,354	3,100	3,142	2,404
2005–06	17,014	20,289	8,412	8,838	11,950	2,810	4,430	4,540	2,803	3,746	3,799	2,800	14,634	17,451	7,236	7,601	10,279	2,417	3,810	3,905	2,411	3,222	3,268	2,408
2006–07	17,547	20,934	8,461	9,171	12,385	2,750	4,554	4,665	2,864	3,822	3,881	2,768	15,483	18,471	7,466	8,092	10,931	2,427	4,019	4,116	2,527	3,372	3,424	2,443
2007–08	17,737	21,160	8,346	9,271	12,517	2,753	4,605	4,717	2,880	3,862	3,926	2,713	16,231	19,363	7,637	8,483	11,454	2,519	4,214	4,317	2,635	3,534	3,592	2,483
2008–09	18,421	21,996	8,879	9,584	12,982	2,822	4,792	4,911	2,996	4,045	4,103	3,060	17,092	20,409	8,238	8,893	12,045	2,618	4,446	4,557	2,780	3,754	3,807	2,839
2009–10	18,839	22,515	9,109	9,752	13,205	3,120	4,971	5,108	3,186	4,116	4,202	2,803	17,649	21,093	8,533	9,136	12,370	2,923	4,657	4,785	2,985	3,856	3,937	2,626
2010–11	19,355	23,118	9,323	10,044	13,569	3,238	5,100	5,248	3,220	4,212	4,293	2,864	18,497	22,092	8,909	9,598	12,967	3,095	4,874	5,015	3,077	4,025	4,111	2,737
2011–12	19,741	23,409	9,461	10,349	13,793	3,302	5,180	5,322	3,244	4,213	4,293	2,915	19,418	23,025	9,306	10,180	13,567	3,248	5,095	5,235	3,191	4,144	4,223	2,867
2012–13	20,234	23,872	9,574	10,683	14,101	3,322	5,296	5,433	3,340	4,256	4,338	2,912	20,234	23,872	9,574	10,683	14,101	3,322	5,296	5,433	3,340	4,256	4,338	2,912

See notes at end of table.

Average undergraduate tuition and fees and room and board rates charged for full-time students in degree-granting postsecondary institutions, by level and control of institution: 1963-64 through 2012-13—Continued

Year and control of institution	Constant 2012–13 dollars[1] — Total tuition, fees, room, and board — All institutions	4-year	2-year	Tuition and required fees[2] — All institutions	4-year	2-year	Dormitory rooms — All institutions	4-year	2-year	Board[3] — All institutions	4-year	2-year	Current dollars — Total tuition, fees, room, and board — All institutions	4-year	2-year	Tuition and required fees[2] — All institutions	4-year	2-year	Dormitory rooms — All institutions	4-year	2-year	Board[3] — All institutions	4-year	2-year
1	2	3	4	5	6	7	8	9	10	11	12	13	14	15	16	17	18	19	20	21	22	23	24	25
Public institutions																								
1963–64	6,845	6,966	4,726	1,755	1,825	728	1,874	1,901	1,290	3,216	3,239	2,708	912	929	630	234	243	97	250	253	172	429	432	361
1964–65	6,901	7,045	4,726	1,800	1,895	733	1,934	1,961	1,318	3,167	3,189	2,674	932	951	638	243	256	99	261	265	178	428	431	361
1965–66	7,018	7,219	4,858	1,863	2,015	790	1,991	2,018	1,407	3,163	3,186	2,661	968	996	670	257	278	109	275	278	194	436	439	367
1966–67	7,131	7,372	4,990	1,933	2,125	850	2,047	2,072	1,497	3,152	3,175	2,643	1,015	1,049	710	275	302	121	291	295	213	448	452	376
1967–68	7,180	7,406	5,367	1,925	2,109	980	2,111	2,132	1,653	3,145	3,164	2,735	1,055	1,089	789	283	310	144	310	313	243	462	465	402
1968–69	7,210	7,414	5,728	1,914	2,082	1,103	2,167	2,186	1,803	3,129	3,145	2,822	1,112	1,143	883	295	321	170	334	337	278	482	485	435
1969–70	7,328	7,582	5,824	1,978	2,195	1,090	2,241	2,262	1,886	3,109	3,125	2,848	1,197	1,238	951	323	358	178	366	369	308	508	510	465
1970–71	7,431	7,722	5,812	2,044	2,293	1,089	2,314	2,336	1,968	3,073	3,093	2,755	1,276	1,326	998	351	394	187	397	401	338	528	531	473
1971–72	7,573	7,898	6,033	2,114	2,405	1,079	2,394	2,416	2,058	3,065	3,077	2,895	1,347	1,405	1,073	376	428	192	426	430	366	545	547	515
1972–73	7,849	8,395	6,469	2,200	2,716	1,259	2,547	2,574	2,151	3,102	3,105	3,059	1,452	1,553	1,197	407	503	233	471	476	398	574	575	566
1973–74	7,517	7,920	6,322	2,173	2,548	1,360	2,374	2,399	2,029	2,969	2,972	2,933	1,515	1,596	1,274	438	514	274	479	483	409	598	599	591
1974–75	6,974	7,355	5,981	1,930	2,289	1,237	2,257	2,284	1,894	2,787	2,783	2,850	1,561	1,647	1,339	432	512	277	505	511	424	624	623	638
1975–76	6,937	7,424	5,782	1,806	2,262	1,022	2,267	2,302	1,844	2,864	2,860	2,916	1,663	1,780	1,386	433	542	245	543	552	442	687	686	699
1976–77	7,052	7,628	5,876	1,887	2,430	1,117	2,296	2,333	1,832	2,869	2,864	2,926	1,789	1,935	1,491	479	617	306	582	592	465	728	727	742
1977–78	6,972	7,527	5,872	1,890	2,418	1,132	2,293	2,332	1,795	2,789	2,777	2,945	1,888	2,038	1,590	512	655	306	621	631	486	755	752	797
1978–79	6,733	7,244	5,711	1,833	2,323	1,105	2,212	2,243	1,779	2,688	2,678	2,826	1,994	2,145	1,691	543	688	327	655	664	527	796	793	837
1979–80	6,452	6,936	5,428	1,739	2,198	1,057	2,131	2,161	1,710	2,582	2,577	2,661	2,165	2,327	1,822	583	738	355	715	725	574	867	865	893
1980–81	6,339	6,811	5,414	1,696	2,147	1,045	2,133	2,166	1,714	2,510	2,499	2,655	2,373	2,550	2,027	635	804	391	799	811	642	940	936	994
1981–82	6,546	7,058	5,467	1,755	2,236	1,068	2,236	2,275	1,729	2,555	2,547	2,670	2,663	2,871	2,224	714	909	434	909	925	703	1,039	1,036	1,086
1982–83	6,941	7,534	5,632	1,881	2,431	1,115	2,381	2,429	1,780	2,678	2,674	2,738	2,945	3,196	2,390	798	1,031	473	1,010	1,030	755	1,136	1,134	1,162
1983–84	7,173	7,803	5,759	2,026	2,609	1,200	2,471	2,522	1,820	2,677	2,672	2,739	3,156	3,433	2,534	891	1,148	528	1,087	1,110	801	1,178	1,175	1,205
1984–85	7,455	8,053	6,140	2,123	2,686	1,277	2,616	2,661	2,014	2,715	2,706	2,849	3,408	3,682	2,807	971	1,228	584	1,196	1,217	921	1,241	1,237	1,302
1985–86[4]	7,593	8,203	6,338	2,221	2,801	1,363	2,640	2,685	2,041	2,732	2,717	2,934	3,571	3,859	2,981	1,045	1,318	641	1,242	1,263	960	1,285	1,278	1,380
1986–87	7,914	8,606	6,216	2,301	2,940	1,374	2,706	2,751	2,036	2,908	2,915	2,807	3,805	4,138	2,989	1,106	1,414	660	1,301	1,323	970	1,398	1,401	1,349
1987–88	8,088	8,794	6,122	2,433	3,070	1,410	2,752	2,815	1,883	2,903	2,908	2,830	4,050	4,403	3,066	1,218	1,537	706	1,378	1,410	943	1,454	1,456	1,417
1988–89	8,159	8,931	6,076	2,452	3,143	1,394	2,781	2,855	1,841	2,926	2,933	2,841	4,274	4,678	3,183	1,285	1,646	730	1,457	1,496	965	1,533	1,536	1,488
1989–90	8,206	9,065	6,011	2,471	3,242	1,378	2,757	2,837	1,753	2,978	2,985	2,881	4,504	4,975	3,299	1,356	1,780	756	1,513	1,557	962	1,635	1,638	1,581
1990–91	8,218	9,057	5,990	2,512	3,262	1,424	2,785	2,862	1,813	2,921	2,933	2,753	4,757	5,243	3,467	1,454	1,888	824	1,612	1,657	1,050	1,691	1,698	1,594
1991–92	8,601	9,530	6,064	2,725	3,544	1,567	2,897	2,987	1,798	2,979	2,999	2,699	5,138	5,693	3,623	1,628	2,117	936	1,731	1,785	1,074	1,780	1,792	1,612
1992–93	8,731	9,772	6,166	2,892	3,813	1,664	2,851	2,948	1,795	2,988	3,010	2,707	5,379	6,020	3,799	1,782	2,349	1,025	1,756	1,816	1,106	1,841	1,854	1,668
1993–94	9,010	10,071	6,322	3,073	4,014	1,779	2,963	3,060	1,883	2,974	2,998	2,660	5,694	6,365	3,996	1,942	2,537	1,125	1,873	1,934	1,190	1,880	1,895	1,681
1994–95	9,175	10,260	6,363	3,164	4,123	1,834	3,014	3,111	1,895	2,998	3,025	2,634	5,965	6,670	4,137	2,057	2,681	1,192	1,959	2,023	1,232	1,949	1,967	1,712
1995–96	9,368	10,503	6,314	3,262	4,264	1,856	3,081	3,176	1,941	3,024	3,063	2,517	6,256	7,014	4,217	2,179	2,848	1,239	2,057	2,121	1,297	2,020	2,045	1,681
1996–97	9,507	10,678	6,411	3,307	4,349	1,858	3,127	3,223	1,950	3,073	3,106	2,604	6,530	7,334	4,404	2,271	2,987	1,276	2,148	2,214	1,339	2,111	2,133	1,789
1997–98	9,746	10,976	6,450	3,376	4,448	1,880	3,183	3,291	2,004	3,187	3,237	2,567	6,813	7,673	4,509	2,360	3,110	1,314	2,225	2,301	1,401	2,228	2,263	1,795
1998–99	9,992	11,286	6,474	3,417	4,540	1,865	3,275	3,387	2,039	3,300	3,359	2,570	7,107	8,027	4,604	2,430	3,229	1,327	2,330	2,409	1,450	2,347	2,389	1,828
1999–2000	9,987	11,307	6,464	3,421	4,576	1,842	3,334	3,443	2,117	3,231	3,288	2,506	7,308	8,274	4,730	2,504	3,349	1,348	2,440	2,519	1,549	2,364	2,406	1,834
2000–01	10,024	11,434	6,394	3,385	4,625	1,761	3,394	3,507	2,115	3,244	3,302	2,518	7,586	8,653	4,839	2,562	3,501	1,333	2,569	2,654	1,600	2,455	2,499	1,906
2001–02	10,415	11,940	6,670	3,506	4,850	1,791	3,535	3,657	2,236	3,374	3,433	2,643	8,022	9,196	5,137	2,700	3,735	1,380	2,723	2,816	1,722	2,598	2,645	2,036
2002–03	10,800	12,434	7,116	3,688	5,140	1,884	3,722	3,848	2,482	3,391	3,446	2,750	8,502	9,787	5,601	2,903	4,046	1,483	2,930	3,029	1,954	2,669	2,712	2,164
2003–04	11,496	13,270	7,474	4,126	5,702	2,116	3,861	3,993	2,597	3,509	3,575	2,761	9,247	10,674	6,012	3,319	4,587	1,702	3,106	3,212	2,089	2,822	2,876	2,221
2004–05	11,905	13,790	7,694	4,380	6,067	2,231	3,988	4,126	2,624	3,537	3,597	2,839	9,864	11,426	6,375	3,629	5,027	1,849	3,304	3,418	2,174	2,931	2,981	2,353
2005–06	12,154	14,077	7,547	4,503	6,221	2,250	4,122	4,260	2,617	3,529	3,596	2,681	10,454	12,108	6,492	3,874	5,351	1,935	3,545	3,664	2,251	3,035	3,093	2,306
2006–07	12,522	14,503	7,723	4,649	6,422	2,287	4,258	4,395	2,728	3,616	3,686	2,708	11,049	12,797	6,815	4,102	5,666	2,018	3,757	3,878	2,407	3,191	3,253	2,390
2007–08	12,647	14,675	7,623	4,689	6,495	2,252	4,318	4,461	2,738	3,640	3,720	2,633	11,573	13,429	6,975	4,291	5,943	2,061	3,952	4,082	2,506	3,331	3,404	2,409
2008–09	13,209	15,371	8,156	4,863	6,803	2,302	4,516	4,668	2,871	3,831	3,901	2,984	12,256	14,262	7,568	4,512	6,312	2,136	4,190	4,331	2,664	3,554	3,619	2,769
2009–10	13,667	16,027	8,223	5,071	7,147	2,439	4,696	4,873	3,037	3,900	4,007	2,747	12,804	15,014	7,703	4,751	6,695	2,285	4,399	4,565	2,845	3,653	3,754	2,574
2010–11	14,194	16,657	8,460	5,312	7,467	2,553	4,855	5,048	3,097	4,026	4,142	2,810	13,564	15,918	8,085	5,076	7,136	2,439	4,640	4,824	2,960	3,848	3,958	2,685
2011–12	14,616	17,084	8,715	5,652	7,832	2,696	4,943	5,130	3,141	4,021	4,123	2,878	14,377	16,805	8,572	5,559	7,703	2,652	4,862	5,046	3,090	3,955	4,055	2,831
2012–13	15,022	17,474	8,928	5,899	8,070	2,792	5,062	5,241	3,247	4,061	4,163	2,889	15,022	17,474	8,928	5,899	8,070	2,792	5,062	5,241	3,247	4,061	4,163	2,889

See notes at end of table.

Average undergraduate tuition and fees and room and board rates charged for full-time students in degree-granting postsecondary institutions, by level and control of institution: 1963–64 through 2012–13—Continued

	Constant 2012–13 dollars[1]												Current dollars											
	Total tuition, fees, room, and board			Tuition and required fees[2]			Dormitory rooms			Board[3]			Total tuition, fees, room, and board			Tuition and required fees[2]			Dormitory rooms			Board[3]		
Year and control of institution	All institutions	4-year	2-year	All institutions	4-year	2-year	All institutions	4-year	2-year	All institutions	4-year	2-year	All institutions	4-year	2-year	All institutions	4-year	2-year	All institutions	4-year	2-year	All institutions	4-year	2-year
1	2	3	4	5	6	7	8	9	10	11	12	13	14	15	16	17	18	19	20	21	22	23	24	25
Private nonprofit and for-profit institutions																								
1963–64	13,615	13,575	9,849	7,591	7,582	4,816	2,370	2,346	1,830	3,653	3,647	3,203	1,815	1,810	1,313	1,012	1,011	642	316	313	244	487	486	427
1964–65	14,126	14,194	10,778	8,059	8,125	5,200	2,452	2,448	2,141	3,615	3,621	3,437	1,907	1,916	1,455	1,088	1,097	702	331	330	289	488	489	464
1965–66	14,537	14,588	11,289	8,367	8,428	5,580	2,581	2,567	2,291	3,589	3,593	3,430	2,005	2,012	1,557	1,154	1,162	768	356	354	316	495	496	473
1966–67	14,928	14,961	11,801	8,666	8,724	5,939	2,706	2,682	2,439	3,556	3,555	3,423	2,124	2,129	1,679	1,233	1,241	845	385	382	347	506	506	487
1967–68	15,000	15,126	11,987	8,823	8,960	6,068	2,667	2,655	2,490	3,510	3,511	3,429	2,205	2,223	1,762	1,297	1,317	892	392	390	366	516	516	504
1968–69	15,055	15,283	12,169	8,971	9,192	6,201	2,621	2,624	2,536	3,464	3,467	3,431	2,321	2,356	1,876	1,383	1,417	956	404	405	391	534	534	529
1969–70	15,479	15,671	12,206	9,389	9,566	6,333	2,659	2,667	2,529	3,432	3,438	3,344	2,527	2,559	1,993	1,533	1,562	1,034	434	436	413	560	561	546
1970–71	15,893	16,042	12,248	9,807	9,937	6,459	2,693	2,703	2,528	3,393	3,401	3,261	2,729	2,754	2,103	1,684	1,706	1,109	462	464	434	583	584	560
1971–72	16,317	16,409	12,290	10,222	10,301	6,589	2,730	2,742	2,524	3,355	3,366	3,177	2,902	2,919	2,186	1,820	1,832	1,172	486	488	449	597	599	565
1972–73	16,408	16,706	12,284	10,257	10,529	6,599	2,826	2,846	2,470	3,325	3,331	3,216	3,036	3,091	2,273	1,898	1,948	1,221	523	527	457	615	616	595
1973–74	15,691	15,986	11,958	9,869	10,145	6,465	2,640	2,654	2,397	3,182	3,187	3,096	3,162	3,222	2,410	1,989	2,045	1,303	532	535	483	641	642	624
1974–75	15,135	15,206	11,574	9,457	9,516	6,106	2,582	2,585	2,519	3,096	3,104	2,948	3,388	3,404	2,591	2,117	2,130	1,367	578	579	564	693	695	660
1975–76	15,203	15,305	11,309	9,478	9,558	5,953	2,609	2,622	2,386	3,115	3,124	2,970	3,644	3,669	2,711	2,272	2,291	1,427	625	629	572	747	749	712
1976–77	15,397	15,676	11,711	9,723	9,989	6,275	2,558	2,568	2,394	3,116	3,120	3,041	3,906	3,977	2,971	2,467	2,534	1,592	649	651	607	790	791	772
1977–78	15,360	15,662	11,627	9,691	9,974	6,300	2,579	2,593	2,333	3,090	3,094	2,995	4,158	4,240	3,148	2,624	2,700	1,706	698	702	631	836	838	811
1978–79	15,246	15,568	11,447	9,685	9,990	6,183	2,559	2,570	2,365	3,002	3,007	2,899	4,514	4,609	3,389	2,867	2,958	1,831	758	761	700	889	890	858
1979–80	14,639	14,938	11,179	9,328	9,611	6,144	2,465	2,476	2,284	2,846	2,851	2,751	4,912	5,013	3,751	3,130	3,225	2,062	827	831	766	955	957	923
1980–81	14,609	14,939	11,492	9,342	9,660	6,444	2,451	2,459	2,327	2,816	2,821	2,720	5,470	5,594	4,303	3,498	3,617	2,413	918	921	871	1,054	1,056	1,019
1981–82	15,157	15,561	11,668	9,711	10,112	6,403	2,551	2,553	2,514	2,889	2,896	2,751	6,166	6,330	4,746	3,953	4,113	2,605	1,038	1,039	1,022	1,175	1,178	1,119
1982–83	16,311	16,797	12,644	10,463	10,935	7,090	2,784	2,785	2,775	3,064	3,078	2,779	6,920	7,126	5,364	4,439	4,639	3,008	1,181	1,181	1,177	1,300	1,306	1,179
1983–84	17,067	17,637	12,663	11,025	11,576	7,044	2,904	2,908	2,848	3,137	3,153	2,771	7,508	7,759	5,571	4,851	5,093	3,099	1,278	1,279	1,253	1,380	1,387	1,219
1984–85	17,941	18,485	13,569	11,625	12,153	7,623	3,119	3,119	3,115	3,197	3,213	2,831	8,202	8,451	6,203	5,315	5,556	3,485	1,426	1,426	1,424	1,462	1,469	1,294
1985–86[4]	18,889	19,620	13,845	12,307	13,013	7,657	3,303	3,310	3,189	3,279	3,297	2,849	8,885	9,228	6,512	5,789	6,121	3,602	1,553	1,557	1,500	1,542	1,551	1,340
1986–87	20,125	20,881	13,277	13,136	13,849	7,662	3,449	3,481	2,633	3,540	3,551	2,983	9,676	10,039	6,384	6,316	6,658	3,684	1,658	1,673	1,266	1,702	1,708	1,434
1987–88	20,993	21,288	14,135	13,957	14,212	8,310	3,491	3,515	2,757	3,546	3,561	3,069	10,512	10,659	7,078	6,998	7,116	4,161	1,748	1,760	1,380	1,775	1,783	1,537
1988–89	21,360	21,904	15,209	14,243	14,721	9,196	3,529	3,557	2,940	3,588	3,606	3,072	11,189	11,474	7,967	7,461	7,722	4,817	1,849	1,863	1,540	1,880	1,889	1,609
1989–90	21,898	22,382	15,797	14,844	15,298	9,468	3,504	3,525	3,030	3,549	3,558	3,299	12,018	12,284	8,670	8,147	8,396	5,196	1,923	1,935	1,663	1,948	1,953	1,811
1990–91	22,303	22,868	16,070	15,155	15,691	9,623	3,565	3,589	3,012	3,583	3,588	3,435	12,910	13,237	9,302	8,772	9,083	5,570	2,063	2,077	1,744	2,074	2,077	1,989
1991–92	23,255	23,866	16,124	15,788	16,336	9,632	3,718	3,751	2,994	3,769	3,778	3,498	13,892	14,258	9,632	9,419	9,759	5,754	2,221	2,241	1,788	2,252	2,257	2,090
1992–93	23,754	24,364	16,076	16,138	16,709	9,835	3,811	3,834	3,198	3,805	3,821	3,043	14,634	15,009	9,903	9,942	10,294	6,059	2,348	2,362	1,970	2,344	2,354	1,875
1993–94	24,518	25,164	16,465	16,727	17,329	10,079	3,940	3,966	3,270	3,851	3,869	3,117	15,496	15,904	10,406	10,572	10,952	6,370	2,490	2,506	2,067	2,434	2,445	1,970
1994–95	24,929	25,537	17,182	17,090	17,660	10,635	3,980	4,001	3,435	3,859	3,876	3,111	16,207	16,602	11,170	11,111	11,481	6,914	2,587	2,601	2,233	2,509	2,520	2,023
1995–96	25,768	26,372	17,315	17,766	18,330	10,623	4,100	4,120	3,550	3,903	3,919	3,141	17,208	17,612	11,563	11,864	12,243	7,094	2,738	2,751	2,371	2,606	2,617	2,098
1996–97	26,262	26,850	17,404	18,195	18,754	10,535	4,189	4,206	3,694	3,877	3,890	3,175	18,039	18,442	11,954	12,498	12,881	7,236	2,878	2,889	2,537	2,663	2,672	2,181
1997–98	26,485	27,277	18,482	18,310	19,087	10,677	4,225	4,240	3,822	3,951	3,950	3,983	18,516	19,070	11,953	12,801	13,344	7,464	2,954	2,964	2,672	2,762	2,761	2,785
1998–99	27,232	28,021	18,727	18,881	19,646	11,042	4,323	4,346	3,629	4,029	4,028	4,055	19,368	19,929	13,319	13,428	13,973	7,854	3,075	3,091	2,581	2,865	2,865	2,884
1999–2000	27,623	28,339	19,194	19,269	19,974	11,240	4,422	4,430	4,192	3,932	3,935	3,762	20,213	20,737	14,045	14,100	14,616	8,225	3,236	3,242	3,067	2,877	2,879	2,753
2000–01	28,241	28,879	19,697	19,820	20,441	11,980	4,469	4,482	3,972	3,952	3,955	3,745	21,373	21,856	14,907	15,000	15,470	9,067	3,382	3,392	3,006	2,991	2,993	2,834
2001–02	29,100	29,727	20,547	20,439	21,047	13,088	4,632	4,643	4,046	4,030	4,036	3,419	22,413	22,896	15,825	15,742	16,211	10,076	3,567	3,576	3,116	3,104	3,104	2,633
2002–03	29,652	30,220	22,554	20,813	21,376	13,531	4,767	4,782	4,106	4,072	4,062	4,917	23,340	23,787	17,753	16,383	16,826	10,651	3,752	3,764	3,232	3,206	3,197	3,870
2003–04	30,613	31,167	24,315	21,526	22,083	14,354	4,905	4,914	4,452	4,182	4,170	5,510	24,624	25,070	19,558	17,315	17,763	11,545	3,945	3,952	3,581	3,364	3,354	4,432
2004–05	31,158	31,693	24,497	21,910	22,453	14,630	5,042	5,036	5,401	4,206	4,204	4,465	25,817	26,260	20,297	18,154	18,604	12,122	4,178	4,173	4,475	3,485	3,483	3,700
2005–06	31,284	31,778	24,885	21,930	22,429	14,474	5,116	5,120	4,852	4,238	4,229	5,558	26,908	27,333	21,427	18,862	19,292	12,450	4,400	4,404	4,173	3,645	3,637	4,781
2006–07	32,231	32,774	22,988	22,720	23,253	14,402	5,221	5,228	4,700	4,290	4,293	3,886	28,439	28,919	20,284	20,048	20,517	12,708	4,606	4,613	4,147	3,785	3,788	3,429
2007–08	32,530	33,032	23,698	22,918	23,416	14,345	5,249	5,254	4,890	4,363	4,362	4,452	29,767	30,226	21,685	20,972	21,427	13,126	4,804	4,808	4,484	3,992	3,991	4,074
2008–09	33,199	33,706	24,494	23,248	23,750	14,617	5,416	5,423	4,890	4,536	4,533	4,987	30,804	31,273	22,726	21,570	22,036	13,562	5,025	5,032	4,537	4,209	4,206	4,627
2009–10	33,116	33,612	26,134	22,890	23,386	15,880	5,603	5,603	5,568	4,623	4,623	4,686	31,023	31,488	24,483	21,444	21,908	14,876	5,249	5,249	5,217	4,331	4,331	4,390
2010–11	33,513	34,131	24,979	23,217	23,828	15,139	5,657	5,664	5,157	4,639	4,639	4,683	32,026	32,617	23,871	22,186	22,771	14,467	5,406	5,413	4,928	4,434	4,433	4,475
2011–12	33,608	34,234	24,049	23,230	23,851	14,236	5,718	5,723	5,254	4,660	4,660	4,558	33,058	33,674	23,655	22,850	23,460	14,003	5,624	5,629	5,168	4,584	4,584	4,483
2012–13	34,483	35,074	23,328	23,943	24,525	14,129	5,831	5,837	5,222	4,709	4,712	3,977	34,483	35,074	23,328	23,943	24,525	14,129	5,831	5,837	5,222	4,709	4,712	3,977

See notes at end of table.

Average undergraduate tuition and fees and room and board rates charged for full-time students in degree-granting postsecondary institutions, by level and control of institution: 1963–64 through 2012–13—Continued

Column groups: Columns 2–13 = **Constant 2012-13 dollars[1]**; Columns 14–25 = **Current dollars**. Within each, the four categories are **Total tuition, fees, room, and board** / **Tuition and required fees[2]** / **Dormitory rooms** / **Board[3]**, each broken into All institutions, 4-year, and 2-year.

Year and control of institution	All inst.	4-year	2-year	All inst.	4-year	2-year	All inst.	4-year	2-year	All inst.	4-year	2-year	All inst.	4-year	2-year	All inst.	4-year	2-year	All inst.	4-year	2-year	All inst.	4-year	2-year
1	2	3	4	5	6	7	8	9	10	11	12	13	14	15	16	17	18	19	20	21	22	23	24	25
Nonprofit																								
1999–2000	28,683	29,014	15,973	20,377	20,678	9,419	4,378	4,401	2,890	3,929	3,935	3,663	20,989	21,231	11,688	14,911	15,131	6,893	3,204	3,221	2,115	2,875	2,879	2,680
2000–01	28,982	29,293	15,481	20,607	20,892	9,207	4,423	4,446	2,653	3,952	3,955	3,621	21,934	22,170	11,717	15,596	15,811	6,968	3,347	3,365	2,008	2,991	2,993	2,740
2001–02	29,965	30,195	16,839	21,345	21,557	10,551	4,590	4,602	2,991	4,030	4,036	3,297	23,080	23,257	12,970	16,440	16,604	8,126	3,536	3,544	2,304	3,104	3,109	2,540
2002–03	30,841	31,056	18,347	22,053	22,254	11,315	4,729	4,740	3,362	4,059	4,062	3,670	24,276	24,446	14,442	17,359	17,517	8,907	3,723	3,731	2,646	3,195	3,197	2,889
2003–04	31,932	32,141	19,356	22,911	23,104	11,918	4,857	4,867	3,547	4,164	4,170	3,890	25,685	25,853	15,569	18,429	18,584	9,587	3,907	3,915	2,853	3,349	3,354	3,129
2004–05	32,687	32,894	19,197	23,533	23,718	11,960	4,964	4,972	3,535	4,191	4,204	3,702	27,083	27,255	15,906	19,498	19,652	9,910	4,113	4,119	2,929	3,472	3,483	3,067
2005–06	33,158	33,358	18,984	23,913	24,103	11,996	5,017	5,026	3,507	4,228	4,229	3,481	28,520	28,692	16,329	20,568	20,732	10,318	4,315	4,323	3,017	3,637	3,637	2,994
2006–07	34,186	34,362	20,038	24,753	24,927	12,394	5,137	5,142	4,053	4,296	4,293	3,592	30,165	30,320	17,681	21,841	21,994	10,936	4,532	4,537	3,576	3,791	3,788	3,169
2007–08	34,884	35,025	20,607	25,355	25,494	12,883	5,164	5,169	4,148	4,365	4,362	3,576	31,921	32,050	18,857	23,201	23,328	11,789	4,725	4,730	3,796	3,994	3,991	3,272
2008–09	36,298	36,433	21,847	26,407	26,552	13,583	5,342	5,348	4,191	4,549	4,533	4,073	33,679	33,804	20,271	24,502	24,636	12,603	4,957	4,962	3,889	4,221	4,206	3,779
2009–10	37,295	37,426	22,177	27,127	27,275	13,510	5,523	5,528	4,394	4,646	4,623	4,274	34,939	35,061	20,776	25,413	25,552	12,656	5,174	5,178	4,116	4,353	4,331	4,004
2010–11	37,935	38,053	21,027	27,608	27,755	13,257	5,652	5,659	4,166	4,676	4,639	3,604	36,252	36,364	20,094	26,383	26,523	12,669	5,401	5,408	3,981	4,468	4,433	3,444
2011–12	38,332	38,464	23,307	27,899	28,075	14,312	5,724	5,729	4,352	4,709	4,660	4,643	37,705	37,835	22,925	27,443	27,615	14,077	5,630	5,635	4,281	4,632	4,584	4,567
2012–13	39,173	39,302	22,110	28,569	28,746	13,747	5,839	5,844	4,405	4,766	4,712	3,958	39,173	39,302	22,110	28,569	28,746	13,747	5,839	5,844	4,405	4,766	4,712	3,958
For-profit																								
1999–2000	22,035	22,613	21,501	11,899	11,836	11,979	5,803	6,329	5,346	4,333	4,449	4,177	16,124	16,547	15,734	8,707	8,661	8,766	4,247	4,631	3,912	3,171	3,255	3,056
2000–01	23,371	24,075	22,543	13,467	13,756	13,141	5,955	6,554	5,225	3,949	3,765	4,177	17,688	18,220	17,061	10,192	10,411	9,945	4,507	4,960	3,955	2,988	2,849	3,161
2001–02	24,118	25,671	22,015	14,100	14,371	13,800	6,010	7,006	4,647	4,008	4,293	3,567	18,576	19,772	16,956	10,860	11,069	10,629	4,629	5,396	3,579	3,087	3,307	2,748
2002–03	25,019	25,458	24,651	14,368	14,491	14,138	5,816	6,839	4,484	4,835	4,127	6,029	19,694	20,039	19,404	11,310	11,407	11,129	4,578	5,384	3,530	3,806	3,249	4,746
2003–04	27,129	27,205	27,812	15,265	15,414	14,948	6,330	7,154	4,962	5,534	4,638	7,901	21,822	21,883	22,371	12,278	12,398	12,024	5,092	5,754	3,992	4,451	3,730	6,355
2004–05	27,877	28,260	26,977	15,733	15,928	15,216	6,825	7,076	6,215	5,319	5,256	5,547	23,098	23,415	22,352	13,036	13,197	12,607	5,655	5,863	5,149	4,407	4,355	4,596
2005–06	27,388	27,002	29,845	15,390	15,480	15,066	7,075	7,539	5,553	4,924	3,983	9,226	23,557	23,225	25,670	13,237	13,315	12,959	6,085	6,485	4,776	4,235	3,426	7,935
2006–07	27,205	28,004	24,083	16,181	16,538	14,829	7,032	7,522	5,061	3,993	3,943	4,193	24,005	24,710	21,250	14,277	14,593	13,085	6,205	6,638	4,466	3,523	3,479	3,700
2007–08	27,042	27,411	25,705	15,746	16,004	14,603	7,044	7,410	5,356	4,253	3,998	5,746	24,745	25,083	23,522	14,409	14,644	13,363	6,445	6,781	4,901	3,892	3,658	5,258
2008–09	26,214	26,348	26,587	15,422	15,545	14,793	6,695	6,942	5,280	4,098	3,861	6,514	24,322	24,447	24,669	14,309	14,423	13,725	6,212	6,441	4,899	3,802	3,583	6,044
2009–10	25,433	25,144	27,746	14,659	14,343	16,167	6,669	6,766	6,073	4,104	4,036	5,506	23,826	23,556	25,993	13,733	13,437	15,146	6,248	6,338	5,689	3,845	3,781	5,158
2010–11	24,585	24,393	27,874	14,914	14,819	15,334	5,712	5,733	5,563	3,959	3,840	6,977	23,495	23,310	26,637	14,253	14,162	14,654	5,459	5,479	5,316	3,783	3,669	6,667
2011–12	23,364	23,306	23,989	13,989	13,941	14,225	5,650	5,643	5,721	3,725	3,721	4,042	22,982	22,924	23,596	13,760	13,713	13,992	5,558	5,551	5,628	3,664	3,660	3,976
2012–13	23,158	23,083	23,991	13,766	13,689	14,193	5,738	5,745	5,663	3,653	3,649	4,135	23,158	23,083	23,991	13,766	13,689	14,193	5,738	5,745	5,663	3,653	3,649	4,135

[1] Constant dollars based on the Consumer Price Index, prepared by the Bureau of Labor Statistics, U.S. Department of Labor, adjusted to a school-year basis.

[2] For public institutions, in-state tuition and required fees are used.

[3] Data for 1986–87 and later years reflect a basis of 20 meals per week, while data for earlier years are for meals served 7 days a week (the number of meals per day was not specified). Because of this revision in data collection and tabulation procedures, data are not entirely comparable with figures for previous years. In particular, data on board rates are somewhat higher than in earlier years because they reflect the basis of 20 meals per week rather than meals served 7 days a week. Since many institutions serve fewer than 3 meals each day, the 1986–87 and later data reflect a more accurate accounting of total board costs.

[4] Room and board data are estimated.

NOTE: Data are for the entire academic year and are average charges for full-time students. Tuition and fees were weighted by the number of full-time-equivalent undergraduates, but were not adjusted to reflect student residency. Room and board are based on full-time students. Data through 1995–96 are for institutions of higher education, while later data are for degree-granting institutions.

Degree-granting institutions grant associate's or higher degrees and participate in Title IV federal financial aid programs. The degree-granting classification is very similar to the earlier higher education classification, but it includes more 2-year colleges and excludes a few higher education institutions that did not grant degrees. Because of their low response rate, data for private 2-year colleges must be interpreted with caution. Some data have been revised from previously published figures. Detail may not sum to totals because of rounding.

SOURCE: U.S. Department of Education, National Center for Education Statistics, Projections of Education Statistics to 1986–87; Higher Education General Information Survey (HEGIS), "Institutional Characteristics of Colleges and Universities" surveys, 1969–70 through 1985–86; "Fall Enrollment in Institutions of Higher Education" surveys, 1963 through 1985; Integrated Postsecondary Education Data System (IPEDS), "Fall Enrollment Survey" (IPEDS-EF-86–99) and "Institutional Characteristics Survey" (IPEDS-IC-86–99); IPEDS Spring 2001 through Spring 2013, Enrollment component; and IPEDS Fall 2000 through Fall 2012, Institutional Characteristics component. (This table was prepared March 2014.)

Average undergraduate tuition and fees and room and board rates charged for full-time students in degree-granting postsecondary institutions, by control and level of institution and state or jurisdiction: 2011–12 and 2012–13

[In current dollars]

State or jurisdiction	Public 4-year In-state, 2011–12 Total	Tuition and required fees	Public 4-year In-state, 2012–13 Total	Tuition and required fees	Room	Board	Out-of-state tuition and required fees, 2012–13	Private 4-year 2011–12 Total	Tuition and required fees	Private 4-year 2012–13 Total	Tuition and required fees	Room	Board	Public 2-year In-state, 2011–12	In-state, 2012–13	Out-of-state, 2012–13
1	2	3	4	5	6	7	8	9	10	11	12	13	14	15	16	17
United States	$16,805	$7,703	$17,474	$8,070	$5,241	$4,163	$21,847	$33,674	$23,460	$35,074	$24,525	$5,837	$4,712	$2,652	$2,792	$6,767
Alabama	15,550	7,528	16,546	8,073	4,695	3,777	20,380	21,037	13,041	22,486	13,983	4,378	4,124	3,864	4,048	7,736
Alaska	14,541	5,956	15,415	6,317	5,265	3,833	18,790	28,270	19,211	30,418	21,496	4,123	4,799	3,883	3,972	4,150
Arizona	19,274	9,030	19,064	9,694	5,948	3,421	21,201	20,391	11,865	20,394	11,650	4,979	3,765	1,802	1,842	7,870
Arkansas	13,100	6,377	13,936	6,604	4,113	3,219	15,669	23,939	16,888	25,267	18,004	3,690	3,573	2,435	2,633	4,605
California	20,670	8,830	21,029	8,892	6,474	5,663	30,765	39,177	27,379	40,599	28,345	6,990	5,264	977	1,225	6,267
Colorado	17,161	7,177	18,052	7,656	5,153	5,243	25,470	29,860	19,093	30,907	19,967	6,078	4,861	3,484	3,004	8,882
Connecticut	19,842	9,087	20,655	9,517	5,999	5,139	26,688	46,642	34,208	48,262	35,336	7,229	5,697	3,490	3,596	10,512
Delaware	20,926	10,470	21,940	10,929	6,595	4,416	26,228	23,521	13,182	23,701	12,943	5,135	5,623	3,086	3,242	7,562
District of Columbia	†	7,000	†	7,244	†	†	14,540	47,365	33,774	48,440	35,524	8,557	4,358	†	†	†
Florida	13,622	4,042	14,170	4,377	5,813	3,980	17,050	29,598	19,925	30,123	20,155	5,522	4,446	2,485	2,486	6,889
Georgia	14,828	6,029	15,331	6,325	5,397	3,608	22,393	30,737	20,447	33,177	22,456	5,915	4,807	2,645	2,652	7,554
Hawaii	16,397	7,450	16,987	7,731	4,720	4,536	23,614	24,719	13,408	25,808	14,287	4,969	6,552	2,388	2,484	7,166
Idaho	12,347	5,673	13,476	5,980	3,368	4,128	17,736	13,916	7,118	11,544	6,752	2,356	2,436	2,672	2,915	7,276
Illinois	21,178	11,290	22,222	11,882	5,671	4,668	26,873	35,645	25,091	37,097	26,299	6,274	4,524	3,086	3,192	9,034
Indiana	17,034	7,937	17,758	8,269	4,956	4,533	26,538	34,380	25,259	36,368	26,794	4,901	4,672	3,354	3,455	7,302
Iowa	15,663	7,563	16,358	7,832	4,149	4,376	23,019	22,563	15,819	22,258	15,426	3,017	3,815	3,998	4,099	5,190
Kansas	13,432	6,660	13,901	6,970	3,426	3,505	17,646	27,425	20,023	28,525	20,852	3,635	4,039	2,601	2,621	4,023
Kentucky	15,921	7,942	16,581	8,416	4,150	4,015	19,040	26,450	18,658	28,654	20,639	4,056	3,959	3,268	3,391	11,789
Louisiana	12,596	5,205	14,245	5,817	4,991	3,437	17,405	36,998	27,163	39,088	28,691	5,783	4,614	2,584	2,837	5,781
Maine	18,631	9,294	18,676	9,295	4,450	4,930	24,397	41,456	30,765	42,745	31,558	5,635	5,552	3,409	3,409	6,053
Maryland	17,420	7,801	18,094	8,051	5,680	4,362	20,199	43,406	30,989	44,819	32,580	6,896	5,342	3,356	3,500	8,355
Massachusetts	20,328	10,094	21,094	10,632	6,378	4,084	24,399	48,159	35,586	49,871	36,795	7,457	5,619	4,006	4,186	9,516
Michigan	19,240	10,533	19,865	11,027	4,523	4,315	31,047	25,038	17,043	26,381	18,135	4,076	4,170	2,595	2,736	5,651
Minnesota	17,354	9,908	17,998	10,291	4,175	3,533	16,313	33,864	25,191	35,409	26,499	4,708	4,201	5,195	5,362	6,197
Mississippi	12,831	5,678	13,583	6,147	4,200	3,236	15,055	20,594	14,506	20,881	14,592	3,201	3,089	2,212	2,276	4,284
Missouri	15,665	7,609	16,236	7,815	4,804	3,617	18,885	26,788	18,186	27,615	19,020	4,717	3,878	2,600	2,716	5,384
Montana	13,074	5,995	13,572	6,267	3,463	3,843	20,164	25,590	18,468	27,320	19,737	3,547	4,037	3,120	3,151	8,351
Nebraska	14,577	6,749	15,291	7,023	4,371	3,897	16,702	25,956	18,485	27,212	19,478	4,006	3,727	2,470	2,594	3,415
Nevada	15,141	4,624	15,944	4,953	5,288	5,703	19,156	28,861	15,797	37,710	16,108	7,622	13,980	2,513	2,700	9,345
New Hampshire	23,314	13,339	24,705	14,435	6,098	4,172	24,945	41,411	29,805	42,310	30,202	7,118	4,990	7,194	7,218	15,697
New Jersey	23,151	11,580	23,773	11,955	7,590	4,229	24,447	41,201	29,700	42,831	31,195	6,779	4,857	3,682	3,782	6,591
New Mexico	12,877	5,275	13,225	5,483	4,134	3,608	14,327	24,128	15,417	25,144	16,256	4,727	4,161	1,372	1,399	4,558
New York	17,559	6,183	18,397	6,556	7,446	4,394	15,751	43,605	31,225	45,338	32,438	7,731	5,169	4,143	4,331	7,827
North Carolina	13,692	5,708	14,514	6,223	4,673	3,618	19,733	34,781	25,271	36,194	26,336	5,217	4,640	2,138	2,212	8,171
North Dakota	12,846	6,437	13,210	6,572	2,897	3,741	16,170	16,641	11,582	17,743	12,318	2,422	3,002	3,994	4,048	8,216
Ohio	18,737	8,860	19,453	9,301	5,607	4,545	21,683	34,832	25,568	35,367	25,756	4,884	4,728	3,349	3,480	7,421
Oklahoma	12,662	5,573	13,005	5,882	3,933	3,190	16,543	28,113	19,692	29,230	20,572	4,353	4,305	2,732	2,904	7,101
Oregon	17,601	7,978	18,526	8,294	5,684	4,549	25,067	38,411	28,555	40,655	30,195	5,411	5,049	3,561	3,752	7,689
Pennsylvania	20,978	11,817	21,637	12,184	5,604	3,850	22,891	42,432	31,402	44,407	32,949	6,286	5,173	3,936	4,133	11,009
Rhode Island	20,649	9,936	21,582	10,817	6,715	4,050	26,762	44,511	32,685	46,114	33,940	6,680	5,494	3,676	3,950	10,582
South Carolina	18,073	10,366	18,655	10,691	4,841	3,122	26,042	27,927	20,038	29,165	20,990	4,092	4,084	3,710	3,820	7,910
South Dakota	13,327	6,948	13,858	7,413	2,983	3,462	9,654	25,121	18,035	25,796	18,843	3,260	3,693	4,802	5,066	5,261
Tennessee	14,612	7,005	15,416	7,472	4,337	3,607	22,412	29,941	21,215	31,135	22,046	5,067	4,023	3,380	3,526	13,682
Texas	15,364	7,124	15,940	7,402	4,556	3,983	20,044	33,308	24,051	34,861	25,174	5,363	4,323	1,750	1,815	5,075
Utah	11,297	5,166	12,076	5,375	2,938	3,763	16,631	15,224	7,677	15,330	7,758	3,844	3,728	3,021	3,170	10,012
Vermont	22,504	13,084	23,290	13,524	6,160	3,607	32,650	43,752	33,174	46,255	35,130	5,983	5,142	5,236	5,452	10,804
Virginia	17,963	9,366	18,843	9,866	5,033	3,944	27,079	29,050	20,641	30,483	21,524	4,468	4,491	3,749	3,910	8,592
Washington	17,690	7,789	18,925	8,856	5,319	4,750	26,314	38,443	28,572	40,293	30,133	5,409	4,752	3,713	3,957	6,983
West Virginia	13,476	5,261	14,126	5,599	4,508	4,018	16,582	18,124	10,229	19,120	10,721	3,997	4,402	3,011	3,135	7,798
Wisconsin	14,718	7,864	15,446	8,339	4,166	2,940	20,146	32,830	24,303	34,199	25,500	4,689	4,010	3,874	4,073	6,824
Wyoming	12,022	3,501	12,479	3,642	3,901	4,936	10,962	†	14,177	†	13,562	†	†	2,305	2,420	5,998

†Not applicable.

NOTE: Data are for the entire academic year and are average charges for full-time students. In-state tuition and fees were weighted by the number of full-time-equivalent undergraduates, but were not adjusted to reflect the number of students who were state residents. Out-of-state tuition and fees were weighted by the number of first-time freshmen attending the institution in fall 2012 from out of state. Institutional room and board rates are weighted by the number of full-time students. Degree-granting institutions grant associate's or higher degrees and par-

ticipate in Title IV federal financial aid programs. Some data have been revised from previously published figures. Detail may not sum to totals because of rounding.

SOURCE: U.S. Department of Education, National Center for Education Statistics, Integrated Postsecondary Education Data System (IPEDS), Fall 2011 and Fall 2012, Institutional Characteristics component; and Spring 2012 and Spring 2013, Enrollment component. (This table was prepared December 2013.)

Average undergraduate tuition, fees, room, and board rates for full-time students in degree-granting postsecondary institutions, by percentile, control, and level of institution: Selected years, 2000–01 through 2012–13

[In current dollars]

Control and level of institution, and year	Tuition, fees, room, and board					Tuition and required fees				
	10th percentile	25th percentile	Median (50th percentile)	75th percentile	90th percentile	10th percentile	25th percentile	Median (50th percentile)	75th percentile	90th percentile
1	2	3	4	5	6	7	8	9	10	11
All public institutions[1]										
2000–01	$5,741	$6,880	$8,279	$9,617	$11,384	$612	$1,480	$2,403	$3,444	$4,583
2005–06	7,700	9,623	11,348	13,543	16,264	990	2,070	3,329	5,322	6,972
2009–10	9,433	12,069	14,446	17,146	19,898	1,200	2,492	4,370	6,726	8,726
2010–11	9,889	12,856	15,234	17,860	21,593	1,230	2,628	4,632	7,127	9,420
2011–12	10,730	13,650	16,274	18,801	22,697	1,408	2,907	5,187	7,653	10,164
2012–13	11,283	14,426	17,012	19,481	23,298	1,536	3,048	5,576	8,132	10,514
Public 4-year[1]										
2000–01	6,503	7,347	8,468	9,816	11,611	2,118	2,520	3,314	4,094	5,085
2005–06	8,863	10,219	11,596	13,830	16,443	3,094	3,822	5,084	6,458	8,097
2009–10	11,158	12,793	15,040	17,661	20,253	4,044	4,900	6,458	8,266	9,886
2010–11	11,952	13,604	15,788	18,419	22,191	4,336	5,105	6,780	8,689	11,029
2011–12	12,693	14,478	16,860	19,137	23,024	4,703	5,765	7,175	9,367	12,612
2012–13	13,324	15,102	17,561	19,713	23,686	4,982	6,180	7,554	9,769	12,692
Public 2-year[1]										
2000–01	3,321	3,804	4,627	5,750	6,871	310	724	1,387	1,799	2,460
2005–06	4,380	4,822	6,234	7,567	8,993	691	1,109	1,920	2,589	3,100
2009–10	5,114	6,008	7,048	8,981	10,977	704	1,316	2,380	3,090	3,650
2010–11	5,347	6,327	7,340	9,370	11,312	700	1,412	2,537	3,315	3,840
2011–12	5,770	6,703	7,831	9,674	11,567	960	1,600	2,704	3,542	4,132
2012–13	5,812	6,536	8,291	10,282	12,464	1,183	1,627	2,804	3,717	4,352
Private nonprofit institutions										
2000–01	13,514	17,552	22,493	27,430	32,659	7,800	11,730	15,540	19,600	24,532
2005–06	18,243	23,258	29,497	35,918	41,707	9,981	15,375	21,070	26,265	31,690
2009–10	22,334	28,699	36,550	44,895	50,297	11,696	18,970	25,890	32,816	38,690
2010–11	23,125	29,865	38,063	46,737	52,229	11,794	19,610	26,920	34,250	40,082
2011–12	24,471	31,398	39,540	49,146	54,258	11,986	20,230	28,128	35,992	41,576
2012–13	24,955	32,582	41,412	51,744	56,419	12,048	21,152	29,312	37,830	43,204
Nonprofit 4-year										
2000–01	13,972	17,714	22,554	27,476	32,659	8,450	11,920	15,746	19,730	24,532
2005–06	18,350	23,322	29,598	36,028	41,774	10,300	15,560	21,190	26,500	31,690
2009–10	22,356	28,840	36,665	44,895	50,298	12,240	19,200	26,180	32,910	38,690
2010–11	23,548	29,884	38,129	46,737	52,229	12,220	19,854	27,100	34,417	40,082
2011–12	24,608	31,460	39,596	49,146	54,258	12,338	20,640	28,310	36,130	41,576
2012–13	25,183	32,668	41,476	51,750	56,419	12,464	21,496	29,460	38,000	43,204
Nonprofit 2-year										
2000–01	6,850	6,850	9,995	14,209	20,240	2,430	4,825	7,250	8,266	11,100
2005–06	8,030	15,680	16,830	20,829	28,643	4,218	8,640	9,940	12,270	14,472
2009–10	13,105	18,316	20,369	26,455	40,733	3,530	8,950	12,292	15,177	19,000
2010–11	10,393	19,718	21,186	27,386	30,758	3,840	9,730	12,000	14,640	18,965
2011–12	19,325	20,300	22,303	28,506	32,679	7,036	10,904	14,531	16,131	19,880
2012–13	20,135	22,399	24,480	28,882	30,114	7,124	11,640	14,944	16,162	19,220
Private for-profit institutions										
2000–01	13,396	15,778	19,403	21,400	21,845	6,900	8,202	9,644	12,090	14,600
2005–06	17,278	19,098	25,589	26,499	31,903	7,632	10,011	12,450	14,335	17,740
2009–10	17,789	17,789	21,321	31,433	32,000	9,792	9,792	12,392	15,450	19,950
2010–11	16,097	16,097	17,484	26,175	31,639	10,200	11,520	13,700	16,440	18,209
2011–12	15,827	15,827	15,827	25,518	31,639	9,763	11,415	12,800	15,605	18,048
2012–13	16,115	16,115	16,115	22,612	32,239	9,936	11,202	12,685	16,156	18,650
For-profit 4-year										
2000–01	13,396	15,818	20,417	21,400	21,400	7,206	8,305	9,675	12,800	15,090
2005–06	17,383	19,098	25,589	26,499	31,903	7,632	10,418	12,900	14,450	17,735
2009–10	17,789	17,789	21,321	31,433	32,000	9,792	9,792	11,920	15,071	19,080
2010–11	16,097	16,097	17,484	26,175	31,639	10,200	11,520	14,085	16,500	18,050
2011–12	15,827	15,827	15,827	25,518	31,639	9,648	11,415	12,682	15,660	18,050
2012–13	16,115	16,115	16,115	21,697	32,239	9,936	11,202	12,110	16,156	18,650
For-profit 2-year										
2000–01	15,778	15,778	19,403	21,845	21,845	6,025	7,365	9,644	12,000	14,255
2005–06	13,010	18,281	43,425	43,425	43,425	7,870	9,285	11,550	14,196	19,425
2009–10	22,857	22,857	26,696	26,696	26,696	10,116	11,735	13,548	17,148	21,245
2010–11	23,687	23,687	25,161	25,161	25,161	9,940	12,094	13,599	15,960	20,533
2011–12	24,366	24,366	25,172	25,172	25,172	10,620	12,094	13,500	15,064	17,762
2012–13	23,600	23,600	23,600	25,866	25,866	10,425	12,314	13,240	15,552	18,048

[1]Average undergraduate tuition and fees are based on in-state students only.

NOTE: Data are for the entire academic year and are average charges for full-time students. Student charges were weighted by the number of full-time-equivalent undergraduates, but were not adjusted to reflect student residency. The data have not been adjusted for changes in the purchasing power of the dollar. Degree-granting institutions grant associate's or higher degrees and participate in Title IV federal financial aid programs.

SOURCE: U.S. Department of Education, National Center for Education Statistics, Integrated Postsecondary Education Data System (IPEDS), Fall 2000 through Fall 2012, Institutional Characteristics component; and Spring 2001 through Spring 2013, Enrollment component. (This table was prepared December 2013.)

Average total cost of attendance for first-time, full-time undergraduate students in degree-granting postsecondary institutions, by control and level of institution, living arrangement, and component of student costs: 2009–10 through 2012–13

[In current dollars]

Level of institution, living arrangement, and component of student costs	2009–10				2010–11				2011–12				2012–13			
	All institutions	Public, in-state	Private Nonprofit	Private For-profit	All institutions	Public, in-state	Private Nonprofit	Private For-profit	All institutions	Public, in-state	Private Nonprofit	Private For-profit	All institutions	Public, in-state	Private Nonprofit	Private For-profit
1	2	3	4	5	6	7	8	9	10	11	12	13	14	15	16	17
4-year institutions																
Average total cost, by living arrangement																
On campus	$26,380	$19,312	$38,240	$28,555	$27,435	$20,114	$39,772	$30,130	$28,739	$20,997	$41,418	$30,840	$29,408	$21,683	$42,962	$30,187
Off campus, living with family	19,491	12,103	30,456	18,969	19,940	12,561	31,630	20,226	20,989	13,328	32,939	22,595	21,272	13,648	34,136	21,902
Off campus, not living with family	28,312	20,952	38,753	27,412	29,390	21,665	40,148	29,114	29,736	22,364	41,582	30,121	29,818	22,763	42,516	28,774
Component of student costs																
Tuition and required fees	13,994	6,893	25,702	13,242	14,551	7,249	26,769	14,236	15,359	7,731	27,949	15,643	15,639	8,005	29,115	14,914
Books and supplies	1,055	1,166	1,179	523	1,134	1,194	1,217	799	1,245	1,232	1,238	1,416	1,250	1,243	1,243	1,393
Room, board, and other expenses																
On campus																
Room and board	8,561	8,134	9,071	10,420	8,921	8,502	9,464	9,370	9,271	8,831	9,853	9,533	9,600	9,183	10,181	9,608
Other	2,770	3,118	2,288	4,370	2,829	3,169	2,323	5,726	2,864	3,203	2,378	4,249	2,920	3,253	2,423	4,271
Off campus, living with family																
Other	4,442	4,044	3,575	5,204	4,256	4,118	3,645	5,191	4,385	4,365	3,752	5,537	4,383	4,401	3,778	5,594
Off campus, not living with family																
Room and board	8,584	8,924	8,140	8,472	8,679	9,085	8,391	8,543	8,759	9,263	8,421	8,256	8,485	9,297	8,267	7,584
Other	4,680	3,968	3,732	5,175	5,026	4,137	3,772	5,536	4,372	4,138	3,974	4,807	4,443	4,218	3,891	4,883
2-year institutions																
Average total cost, by living arrangement																
On campus	$14,398	$11,815	$23,553	$29,352	$15,267	$12,398	$24,654	$29,587	$14,383	$12,823	$26,840	$27,713	$14,608	$13,277	$27,478	$28,246
Off campus, living with family	9,822	7,579	17,311	20,477	10,451	7,933	17,334	21,143	9,421	8,150	20,324	19,692	9,385	8,339	19,921	20,086
Off campus, not living with family	17,294	14,873	25,754	28,201	17,934	15,278	25,773	28,805	16,882	15,526	29,301	27,362	16,980	15,896	28,647	27,591
Component of student costs																
Tuition and required fees	4,816	2,640	12,698	14,918	5,230	2,794	12,839	15,373	4,222	2,970	14,335	14,343	4,109	3,080	14,496	14,511
Books and supplies	1,255	1,235	1,229	1,392	1,324	1,292	1,276	1,514	1,314	1,314	1,413	1,301	1,339	1,341	1,373	1,300
Room, board, and other expenses																
On campus																
Room and board	5,518	5,186	7,061	8,979	5,719	5,384	7,460	8,628	5,829	5,552	7,880	8,655	6,093	5,817	8,443	8,753
Other	2,809	2,754	2,565	4,063	2,994	2,928	3,079	4,071	3,018	2,988	3,212	3,414	3,068	3,040	3,167	3,682
Off campus, living with family																
Other	3,751	3,704	3,384	4,167	3,897	3,847	3,219	4,256	3,884	3,866	4,576	4,048	3,937	3,919	4,052	4,274
Off campus, not living with family																
Room and board	7,494	7,344	8,105	7,933	7,539	7,428	8,267	7,836	7,507	7,466	8,270	7,670	7,662	7,645	8,045	7,737
Other	3,729	3,654	3,721	3,958	3,841	3,763	3,391	4,082	3,839	3,776	5,283	4,048	3,870	3,830	4,734	4,043

NOTE: Excludes students who previously attended another postsecondary institution or who began their studies on a part-time basis. Tuition and fees at public institutions are the lower of either in-district or in-state tuition and fees. Data illustrating the average total cost of attendance for all students are weighted by the number of students at the institution receiving Title IV aid. Detail may not sum to totals because of rounding.

SOURCE: U.S. Department of Education, National Center for Education Statistics, Integrated Postsecondary Education Data System (IPEDS), Spring 2010 through Spring 2013, Student Financial Aid component; and Fall 2009 through Fall 2012, Institutional Characteristics component. (This table was prepared November 2013.)

Average graduate tuition and required fees in degree-granting postsecondary institutions, by control of institution and percentile: 1989–90 through 2012–13

Year	Total	Public institutions[1]	Private institutions			Public institutions,[1] by percentile			Nonprofit institutions, by percentile		
			Total	Nonprofit	For-profit	25th percentile	Median (50th percentile)	75th percentile	25th percentile	Median (50th percentile)	75th percentile
1	2	3	4	5	6	7	8	9	10	11	12
					Current dollars						
1989–90	$4,135	$1,999	$7,881	—	—	—	—	—	—	—	—
1990–91	4,488	2,206	8,507	—	—	—	—	—	—	—	—
1991–92	5,116	2,524	9,592	—	—	—	—	—	—	—	—
1992–93	5,475	2,791	10,008	—	—	—	—	—	—	—	—
1993–94	5,973	3,050	10,790	—	—	—	—	—	—	—	—
1994–95	6,247	3,250	11,338	—	—	—	—	—	—	—	—
1995–96	6,741	3,449	12,083	—	—	—	—	—	—	—	—
1996–97	7,111	3,607	12,537	—	—	—	—	—	—	—	—
1997–98	7,246	3,744	12,774	—	—	—	—	—	—	—	—
1998–99	7,685	3,897	13,299	—	—	—	—	—	—	—	—
1999–2000	8,069	4,042	13,821	$14,123	$9,611	$2,640	$3,637	$5,163	$7,998	$12,870	$20,487
2000–01	8,429	4,243	14,420	14,457	13,229	2,931	3,822	5,347	8,276	13,200	21,369
2001–02	8,857	4,496	15,165	15,232	13,414	3,226	4,119	5,596	8,583	14,157	22,054
2002–03	9,226	4,842	14,983	15,676	9,644	3,395	4,452	5,927	8,690	14,140	22,700
2003–04	10,312	5,544	16,209	16,807	12,542	3,795	5,103	7,063	9,072	15,030	25,600
2004–05	11,004	6,080	16,751	17,551	13,133	4,236	5,663	7,616	9,300	16,060	26,140
2005–06	11,621	6,493	17,244	18,171	13,432	4,608	6,209	7,977	9,745	16,222	26,958
2006–07	12,312	6,894	18,108	19,033	14,421	4,909	6,594	8,341	10,346	17,057	29,118
2007–08	13,002	7,415	18,878	19,896	14,713	5,176	6,990	9,288	10,705	17,647	30,247
2008–09	13,647	7,999	19,230	20,485	14,418	5,612	7,376	9,912	11,290	18,270	30,514
2009–10	14,537	8,763	20,368	21,307	14,550	6,084	7,983	10,658	12,285	19,350	31,730
2010–11	14,993	9,247	20,335	21,996	13,506	6,550	8,788	10,933	12,510	19,586	33,215
2011–12	15,787	9,980	21,105	22,872	13,823	7,506	9,445	11,954	12,936	20,625	34,680
2012–13	16,435	10,408	21,955	23,698	14,418	7,706	9,900	12,590	13,030	21,352	36,820
					Constant 2012–13 dollars						
1989–90	$7,534	$3,642	$14,359	—	—	—	—	—	—	—	—
1990–91	7,753	3,811	14,697	—	—	—	—	—	—	—	—
1991–92	8,564	4,225	16,056	—	—	—	—	—	—	—	—
1992–93	8,887	4,530	16,245	—	—	—	—	—	—	—	—
1993–94	9,451	4,826	17,072	—	—	—	—	—	—	—	—
1994–95	9,609	4,999	17,440	—	—	—	—	—	—	—	—
1995–96	10,094	5,165	18,093	—	—	—	—	—	—	—	—
1996–97	10,353	5,251	18,253	—	—	—	—	—	—	—	—
1997–98	10,364	5,355	18,272	—	—	—	—	—	—	—	—
1998–99	10,805	5,479	18,699	—	—	—	—	—	—	—	—
1999–2000	11,027	5,524	18,887	$19,301	$13,134	$3,608	$4,970	$7,056	$10,930	$17,588	$27,997
2000–01	11,138	5,607	19,053	19,102	17,479	3,873	5,050	7,065	10,935	17,441	28,235
2001–02	11,500	5,837	19,689	19,777	17,415	4,188	5,348	7,265	11,144	18,380	28,633
2002–03	11,720	6,151	19,034	19,915	12,252	4,313	5,656	7,530	11,040	17,964	28,838
2003–04	12,820	6,892	20,151	20,895	15,593	4,718	6,344	8,781	11,278	18,685	31,826
2004–05	13,281	7,338	20,217	21,183	15,851	5,112	6,835	9,192	11,224	19,383	31,548
2005–06	13,511	7,549	20,048	21,126	15,616	5,357	7,219	9,274	11,330	18,860	31,342
2006–07	13,953	7,813	20,522	21,571	16,344	5,563	7,473	9,453	11,725	19,331	33,000
2007–08	14,209	8,104	20,630	21,743	16,079	5,656	7,639	10,150	11,699	19,285	33,055
2008–09	14,708	8,621	20,725	22,079	15,539	6,048	7,950	10,683	12,168	19,691	32,887
2009–10	15,518	9,355	21,741	22,743	15,532	6,494	8,521	11,377	13,114	20,655	33,870
2010–11	15,689	9,677	21,279	23,017	14,133	6,854	9,196	11,441	13,091	20,495	34,757
2011–12	16,050	10,146	21,456	23,252	14,053	7,631	9,602	12,153	13,151	20,968	35,257
2012–13	16,435	10,408	21,955	23,698	14,418	7,706	9,900	12,590	13,030	21,352	36,820

—Not available.

[1]Data are based on in-state tuition only.

NOTE: Average graduate student tuition weighted by fall full-time-equivalent graduate enrollment. Data through 1995-96 are for institutions of higher education, while later data are for degree-granting institutions. Degree-granting institutions grant associate's or higher degrees and participate in Title IV federal financial aid programs. The degree-granting classification is very similar to the earlier higher education classification, but it includes more 2-year colleges and excludes a few higher education institutions that did not grant degrees. Some data have been revised from previously published figures.

SOURCE: U.S. Department of Education, National Center for Education Statistics, Integrated Postsecondary Education Data System (IPEDS), "Fall Enrollment Survey" (IPEDS-EF:89–99); "Completions Survey" (IPEDS-C:90–99); "Institutional Characteristics Survey" (IPEDS-IC:89–99); IPEDS Fall 2000 through Fall 2012, Institutional Characteristics component; and IPEDS Spring 2001 through Spring 2013, Enrollment component. (This table was prepared December 2013.)

Percentage of undergraduates receiving financial aid, by type and source of aid and selected student characteristics: 2011–12

[Standard errors appear in parentheses]

Selected student characteristic	Number of undergraduates[1] (in thousands)	Any aid — Total[2]	Any aid — Federal[3]	Any aid — Nonfederal	Grants — Total	Grants — Federal	Grants — Nonfederal	Loans — Total[4]	Loans — Federal[4]	Loans — Nonfederal	Work study — Total[5]
1	2	3	4	5	6	7	8	9	10	11	12
All undergraduates	23,055	70.7 (0.56)	59.4 (0.51)	40.4 (0.44)	59.1 (0.45)	41.5 (0.36)	36.3 (0.42)	41.9 (0.14)	40.3 (0.10)	6.5 (0.14)	5.9 (0.14)
Sex											
Male	9,921	68.4 (0.72)	56.7 (0.73)	39.8 (0.55)	55.1 (0.57)	36.7 (0.55)	35.6 (0.53)	39.0 (0.35)	37.3 (0.35)	6.4 (0.18)	6.0 (0.22)
Female	13,135	72.5 (0.53)	61.5 (0.46)	40.9 (0.47)	62.1 (0.46)	45.1 (0.36)	36.7 (0.45)	44.1 (0.22)	42.6 (0.22)	6.5 (0.17)	5.9 (0.15)
Race/ethnicity											
White	13,345	68.1 (0.59)	55.3 (0.53)	40.0 (0.49)	54.5 (0.47)	33.7 (0.38)	35.9 (0.48)	41.9 (0.34)	40.2 (0.32)	6.8 (0.19)	6.0 (0.17)
Black	3,709	81.0 (0.81)	75.2 (0.87)	36.8 (0.78)	71.4 (0.72)	62.1 (0.80)	32.2 (0.72)	52.3 (0.84)	51.0 (0.82)	6.5 (0.34)	5.1 (0.27)
Hispanic	3,696	72.3 (0.85)	61.9 (0.91)	43.0 (0.89)	64.0 (0.81)	50.1 (0.81)	38.9 (0.90)	35.6 (0.83)	34.2 (0.84)	5.6 (0.27)	5.3 (0.30)
Asian	1,292	60.8 (1.64)	46.3 (1.45)	44.2 (1.46)	53.0 (1.49)	33.4 (1.22)	41.2 (1.36)	28.4 (1.12)	27.0 (1.06)	5.0 (0.49)	9.0 (0.66)
Pacific Islander	119	68.3 (3.58)	56.7 (3.66)	37.4 (3.15)	55.1 (3.32)	39.3 (3.23)	34.9 (3.14)	37.9 (3.28)	37.3 (3.22)	4.6 (1.02)	4.5 ! (1.46)
American Indian/Alaska Native	209	76.3 (3.13)	69.0 (3.23)	40.9 (3.05)	67.6 (3.18)	55.3 (3.10)	37.6 (3.02)	43.0 (3.17)	41.9 (3.12)	5.1 (0.91)	4.7 (1.15)
Two or more races	686	74.8 (1.48)	63.6 (1.43)	46.7 (1.76)	63.9 (1.59)	45.7 (1.45)	41.9 (1.75)	46.1 (1.46)	44.1 (1.40)	8.4 (0.84)	7.2 (0.68)
Age											
15 to 23 years old	12,956	72.1 (0.49)	59.2 (0.41)	48.2 (0.47)	60.9 (0.42)	38.0 (0.29)	44.4 (0.47)	42.8 (0.28)	41.1 (0.25)	7.4 (0.15)	9.0 (0.21)
24 to 29 years old	4,253	70.4 (1.05)	61.9 (1.09)	31.8 (0.76)	59.0 (0.89)	49.1 (0.83)	27.1 (0.70)	41.6 (0.68)	39.9 (0.64)	5.8 (0.30)	2.4 (0.18)
30 years old or over	5,846	67.9 (0.89)	58.2 (0.92)	29.5 (0.64)	55.1 (0.76)	43.7 (0.77)	25.0 (0.60)	40.4 (0.52)	39.1 (0.51)	4.9 (0.25)	1.6 (0.13)
Marital status											
Not married[6]	18,507	71.9 (0.50)	60.6 (0.41)	43.0 (0.46)	60.9 (0.43)	42.2 (0.30)	38.8 (0.44)	43.5 (0.17)	41.9 (0.15)	7.0 (0.14)	7.0 (0.17)
Married	4,087	63.9 (1.21)	52.2 (1.28)	30.0 (0.71)	49.4 (0.92)	35.5 (1.00)	26.0 (0.68)	33.8 (0.75)	32.4 (0.70)	4.3 (0.32)	1.4 (0.14)
Separated	461	82.0 (1.72)	76.6 (1.91)	30.8 (1.62)	74.2 (1.92)	67.1 (2.07)	26.3 (1.72)	50.8 (2.09)	50.0 (2.07)	5.3 (0.88)	1.6 (0.47)
Attendance status[7]											
Full-time, full-year	8,864	84.4 (0.36)	72.8 (0.51)	56.9 (0.46)	72.4 (0.41)	47.4 (0.50)	52.6 (0.45)	56.7 (0.53)	55.5 (0.54)	9.2 (0.22)	11.9 (0.25)
Part-time or part-year	14,192	62.1 (1.05)	51.1 (1.10)	30.1 (0.60)	50.8 (0.87)	37.8 (0.85)	26.1 (0.56)	32.7 (0.48)	30.9 (0.45)	4.8 (0.17)	2.2 (0.12)
Dependency status and family income											
Dependent	11,231	71.6 (0.49)	58.2 (0.40)	49.9 (0.50)	59.6 (0.44)	34.9 (0.30)	46.1 (0.50)	43.4 (0.31)	41.7 (0.29)	7.8 (0.17)	9.8 (0.22)
Less than $20,000	1,775	88.3 (0.68)	83.5 (0.79)	53.2 (1.01)	87.0 (0.67)	82.1 (0.78)	50.8 (1.00)	45.5 (0.84)	44.3 (0.84)	4.9 (0.35)	10.7 (0.56)
$20,000–$39,999	2,011	81.5 (0.88)	74.1 (0.92)	54.7 (0.99)	79.1 (0.92)	70.9 (0.92)	42.8 (1.03)	42.8 (0.80)	41.6 (0.82)	5.6 (0.35)	11.6 (0.54)
$40,000–$59,999	1,389	79.7 (0.89)	70.0 (0.96)	57.5 (1.06)	72.1 (0.97)	54.7 (0.91)	54.3 (1.07)	51.0 (0.96)	49.9 (0.99)	8.5 (0.50)	11.2 (0.53)
$60,000–$79,999	1,535	65.7 (1.06)	49.6 (1.07)	49.0 (0.97)	48.3 (1.00)	14.2 (0.62)	44.3 (1.01)	46.0 (1.02)	43.9 (0.97)	9.8 (0.62)	9.9 (0.59)
$80,000–$99,999	1,339	61.6 (1.29)	45.0 (0.95)	44.5 (1.22)	40.4 (1.17)	2.7 (0.28)	39.6 (1.17)	41.4 (0.89)	41.4 (0.89)	10.2 (0.62)	9.3 (0.65)
$100,000 or more	3,183	59.5 (0.79)	38.7 (0.64)	44.5 (0.74)	40.2 (0.74)	0.7 (0.09)	39.9 (0.74)	38.0 (0.63)	35.9 (0.59)	8.5 (0.34)	7.6 (0.37)
Independent	11,825	69.9 (0.81)	60.6 (0.85)	31.4 (0.55)	58.6 (0.67)	47.7 (0.68)	26.9 (0.52)	40.5 (0.33)	39.0 (0.30)	5.2 (0.20)	2.3 (0.10)
Less than $10,000	3,561	78.6 (0.72)	71.6 (0.74)	35.2 (0.75)	73.5 (0.76)	66.5 (1.12)	30.3 (0.76)	46.7 (0.72)	45.1 (0.73)	5.8 (0.30)	4.4 (0.25)
$10,000–$19,999	2,349	77.0 (1.09)	71.1 (1.05)	32.1 (0.93)	71.2 (1.14)	65.5 (1.20)	27.0 (0.83)	46.9 (0.86)	45.6 (0.87)	5.7 (0.35)	2.3 (0.23)
$20,000–$29,999	1,702	71.4 (1.14)	62.9 (1.41)	30.4 (1.06)	56.6 (1.14)	45.7 (0.98)	25.7 (1.04)	42.3 (0.90)	40.6 (0.91)	5.7 (0.41)	1.8 (0.24)
$30,000–$49,999	1,895	65.5 (1.23)	53.6 (1.36)	30.2 (1.11)	48.7 (1.17)	34.0 (0.98)	25.8 (1.13)	36.8 (0.91)	35.1 (0.92)	5.1 (0.34)	0.8 (0.13)
$50,000 or more	2,318	51.8 (1.73)	37.1 (1.54)	26.6 (0.94)	32.3 (1.08)	13.7 (0.75)	23.2 (0.88)	26.2 (1.25)	25.2 (1.14)	3.7 (0.37)	0.6 (0.12)
Housing status[8]											
School-owned	2,800	85.3 (0.52)	69.6 (0.59)	71.8 (0.63)	74.5 (0.59)	35.5 (0.60)	68.1 (0.64)	63.0 (0.64)	61.4 (0.62)	11.6 (0.39)	23.0 (0.63)
Off-campus, not with parents	10,619	68.1 (0.88)	57.4 (0.87)	34.4 (0.59)	56.1 (0.69)	42.1 (0.67)	30.0 (0.54)	39.1 (0.41)	37.5 (0.39)	5.8 (0.19)	3.1 (0.15)
With parents	7,734	68.3 (0.74)	57.8 (0.69)	36.9 (0.69)	57.7 (0.69)	43.2 (0.65)	33.1 (0.67)	36.5 (0.53)	35.0 (0.53)	5.2 (0.24)	3.6 (0.19)

!Interpret data with caution. The coefficient of variation (CV) for this estimate is between 30 and 50 percent.

[1] Numbers of undergraduates may not equal figures reported in other tables, since these data are based on a sample survey of students who enrolled at any time during the school year. Includes all postsecondary institutions.
[2] Includes students who reported they were awarded aid, but did not specify the source or type of aid.
[3] Includes Department of Veterans Affairs and Department of Defense benefits.
[4] Includes Parent Loans for Undergraduate Students (PLUS).
[5] Details on federal and nonfederal work-study participants are not available.
[6] Includes students who were single, divorced, or widowed.
[7] Full-time, full-year includes students enrolled full time for 9 or more months. Part-time or part-year includes students enrolled part time for 9 or more months and students enrolled less than 9 months either part time or full time.
[8] Excludes students attending more than one institution.

NOTE: Detail may not sum to totals because of rounding and because some students receive multiple types of aid and aid from different sources. Data include undergraduates in degree-granting and non-degree-granting institutions. Data exclude Puerto Rico. Race categories exclude persons of Hispanic ethnicity. In 2012, no students were reported in the "Other" race category.
SOURCE: U.S. Department of Education, National Center for Education Statistics, 2011–12 National Postsecondary Student Aid Study (NPSAS:12). (This table was prepared January 2014.)

Full-time, first-time degree/certificate-seeking undergraduate students enrolled in degree-granting postsecondary institutions, by participation and average amount awarded in financial aid programs, and control and level of institution: 2000–01 through 2011–12

Control and level of institution, and year	Number enrolled	Number receiving financial aid	Percent receiving aid	Percent of enrolled students in student aid programs				Average award for students in aid programs[1]							
								Current dollars				Constant 2012–13 dollars			
				Federal grants	State/local grants	Institutional grants	Student loans[2]	Federal grants	State/local grants	Institutional grants	Student loans[2]	Federal grants	State/local grants	Institutional grants	Student loans[2]
1	2	3	4	5	6	7	8	9	10	11	12	13	14	15	16
All institutions															
2000–01	1,976,600	1,390,527	70.3	31.6	31.2	31.1	40.1	$2,486	$2,039	$4,740	$3,764	$3,285	$2,694	$6,263	$4,974
2001–02	2,050,016	1,481,592	72.3	33.3	32.5	31.5	40.7	2,739	2,057	4,918	3,970	3,556	2,671	6,385	5,154
2002–03	2,135,613	1,553,024	72.7	34.1	30.9	31.5	41.4	2,947	2,189	5,267	4,331	3,744	2,781	6,691	5,502
2003–04	2,178,517	1,610,967	73.9	34.6	31.2	31.9	43.1	2,934	2,226	5,648	4,193	3,647	2,768	7,022	5,213
2004–05	2,260,590	1,689,910	74.8	35.2	31.3	31.7	44.0	2,939	2,343	5,958	4,463	3,547	2,828	7,191	5,386
2005–06	2,309,543	1,731,315	75.0	33.7	30.8	32.7	44.6	2,959	2,441	6,213	4,831	3,440	2,838	7,223	5,617
2006–07	2,427,043	1,766,257	72.8	32.1	30.0	32.2	43.5	3,125	2,526	6,593	5,014	3,542	2,862	7,472	5,683
2007–08	2,532,955	1,914,567	75.6	35.4	30.6	33.6	45.6	3,376	2,580	6,791	6,009	3,690	2,820	7,422	6,567
2008–09	2,675,974	2,089,288	78.1	38.0	30.2	34.1	48.6	3,915	2,705	7,250	6,974	4,220	2,915	7,814	7,517
2009–10	2,857,363	2,323,660	81.3	46.1	28.6	33.2	51.1	4,688	2,766	7,679	7,013	5,005	2,953	8,197	7,486
2010–11	2,654,501	2,184,367	82.3	47.8	30.9	35.7	50.1	4,755	2,844	8,386	6,618	4,976	2,976	8,775	6,926
2011–12	2,571,801	2,140,298	83.2	47.6	30.8	37.9	51.2	4,419	2,910	8,762	6,654	4,493	2,959	8,908	6,765
Public															
2000–01	1,333,236	872,109	65.4	30.0	33.5	22.7	30.7	2,408	1,707	2,275	3,050	3,181	2,255	3,005	4,030
2005–06	1,510,268	1,066,041	70.6	31.1	34.8	25.1	34.2	2,926	2,226	3,162	3,866	3,402	2,588	3,676	4,495
2006–07	1,568,395	1,096,808	69.9	30.9	34.9	25.2	34.2	3,099	2,318	3,316	4,081	3,512	2,627	3,758	4,625
2007–08	1,648,583	1,173,222	71.2	32.6	35.8	25.9	34.7	3,368	2,351	3,530	4,803	3,681	2,569	3,858	5,249
2008–09	1,700,907	1,246,670	73.3	33.7	36.9	26.5	36.3	3,869	2,486	3,755	5,542	4,170	2,679	4,047	5,973
2009–10	1,804,811	1,383,069	76.6	41.1	35.6	26.3	38.6	4,696	2,553	3,897	5,680	5,012	2,725	4,160	6,063
2010–11	1,802,565	1,421,056	78.8	46.0	35.9	27.2	40.2	4,768	2,680	4,157	5,782	4,989	2,805	4,350	6,050
2011–12	1,766,681	1,417,798	80.3	46.7	35.6	29.6	42.5	4,395	2,770	4,429	5,936	4,468	2,816	4,503	6,034
4-year															
2000–01	804,793	573,430	71.3	26.6	36.5	29.6	40.7	2,569	2,068	2,616	3,212	3,395	2,732	3,457	4,244
2005–06	906,948	695,017	76.6	26.6	36.8	34.2	44.4	3,071	2,752	3,573	4,166	3,570	3,200	4,154	4,843
2006–07	949,162	716,323	75.5	26.6	36.7	34.2	43.8	3,365	2,848	3,759	4,433	3,813	3,228	4,260	5,024
2007–08	976,830	753,643	77.2	28.0	37.4	36.2	45.2	3,675	2,963	3,956	5,190	4,016	3,238	4,323	5,672
2008–09	1,007,609	792,028	78.6	28.4	37.9	37.2	46.9	4,157	3,152	4,186	5,972	4,480	3,397	4,511	6,436
2009–10	1,021,259	832,561	81.5	34.4	37.4	38.8	50.0	4,965	3,300	4,339	6,063	5,300	3,522	4,632	6,472
2010–11	1,039,170	858,433	82.6	38.9	38.3	39.6	51.5	4,988	3,474	4,630	6,130	5,220	3,635	4,845	6,415
2011–12	1,059,832	878,851	82.9	39.1	37.1	42.1	52.6	4,466	3,525	4,884	6,348	4,540	3,584	4,965	6,454
2-year															
2000–01	528,443	298,679	56.5	35.2	28.8	12.1	15.3	2,222	1,009	1,004	2,396	2,936	1,334	1,326	3,166
2005–06	603,320	371,024	61.5	38.0	31.9	11.3	19.0	2,774	1,314	1,297	2,812	3,225	1,528	1,508	3,270
2006–07	619,233	380,485	61.4	37.5	32.2	11.6	19.6	2,810	1,393	1,311	2,877	3,184	1,579	1,486	3,261
2007–08	671,753	419,579	62.5	39.1	33.4	10.8	19.4	3,048	1,354	1,458	3,488	3,331	1,480	1,594	3,812
2008–09	693,298	454,642	65.6	41.5	35.4	11.0	21.1	3,584	1,451	1,637	4,152	3,862	1,564	1,764	4,475
2009–10	783,552	550,508	70.3	49.7	33.2	9.9	23.7	4,453	1,460	1,646	4,627	4,753	1,558	1,757	4,939
2010–11	763,395	562,623	73.7	55.6	32.7	10.3	24.8	4,558	1,418	1,681	4,800	4,770	1,484	1,759	5,023
2011–12	706,849	538,947	76.2	58.1	33.4	10.9	27.4	4,324	1,509	1,789	4,747	4,396	1,534	1,819	4,826
Private nonprofit															
2000–01	439,369	363,044	82.6	28.4	31.8	68.1	57.7	2,879	2,998	7,368	4,019	3,804	3,961	9,735	5,311
2005–06	471,069	401,908	85.3	26.5	31.3	73.8	59.8	3,426	3,117	9,932	5,270	3,984	3,624	11,547	6,127
2006–07	477,698	407,247	85.3	26.2	30.5	73.9	59.3	3,704	3,321	10,724	5,544	4,198	3,764	12,154	6,284
2007–08	494,088	424,943	86.0	27.3	30.0	74.4	60.2	3,928	3,386	11,465	6,415	4,293	3,700	12,529	7,010
2008–09	496,638	433,208	87.2	27.4	30.2	76.6	60.6	4,450	3,523	12,699	7,609	4,796	3,797	13,687	8,201
2009–10	501,223	445,309	88.8	33.0	27.8	78.2	62.9	5,067	3,644	13,638	7,440	5,408	3,890	14,558	7,942
2010–11	518,433	463,163	89.3	36.4	27.7	78.2	64.3	5,065	3,544	14,316	7,302	5,300	3,709	14,981	7,641
2011–12	512,814	457,300	89.2	35.0	27.0	79.3	63.5	4,646	3,534	15,064	7,473	4,724	3,593	15,314	7,598

See notes at end of table.

Full-time, first-time degree/certificate-seeking undergraduate students enrolled in degree-granting postsecondary institutions, by participation and average amount awarded in financial aid programs, and control and level of institution: 2000–01 through 2011–12—Continued

Control and level of institution, and year	Number enrolled	Number receiving financial aid	Percent receiving aid	Percent of enrolled students in student aid programs				Average award for students in aid programs[1]							
								Current dollars				Constant 2012–13 dollars			
				Federal grants	State/local grants	Institutional grants	Student loans[2]	Federal grants	State/local grants	Institutional grants	Student loans[2]	Federal grants	State/local grants	Institutional grants	Student loans[2]
1	2	3	4	5	6	7	8	9	10	11	12	13	14	15	16
4-year															
2000–01	419,499	347,638	82.9	27.4	32.2	70.1	58.1	2,930	3,001	7,458	4,000	3,872	3,966	9,854	5,285
2005–06	460,832	393,429	85.4	26.0	31.2	74.6	59.8	3,437	3,121	10,002	5,264	3,996	3,628	11,629	6,120
2006–07	468,969	400,044	85.3	25.8	30.4	74.4	59.4	3,729	3,329	10,797	5,558	4,226	3,773	12,236	6,299
2007–08	484,021	416,405	86.0	26.7	30.0	75.1	60.3	3,960	3,391	11,539	6,435	4,328	3,706	12,610	7,033
2008–09	487,050	424,881	87.2	26.8	30.1	77.4	60.6	4,488	3,523	12,780	7,638	4,837	3,796	13,774	8,232
2009–10	491,136	436,294	88.8	32.3	27.7	79.0	63.0	5,099	3,658	13,733	7,466	5,443	3,905	14,660	7,970
2010–11	504,874	450,906	89.3	35.4	27.7	79.6	64.3	5,098	3,567	14,404	7,314	5,335	3,732	15,073	7,654
2011–12	499,961	445,217	89.1	33.9	27.1	80.5	63.4	4,673	3,551	15,175	7,486	4,751	3,610	15,428	7,610
2-year															
2000–01	19,870	15,406	77.5	49.2	23.9	25.7	49.5	2,269	2,892	2,168	4,509	2,999	3,821	2,864	5,958
2005–06	10,237	8,479	82.8	51.6	36.1	38.5	55.9	3,176	2,974	3,799	5,531	3,693	3,457	4,417	6,430
2006–07	8,729	7,203	82.5	47.6	37.2	44.0	53.5	2,992	2,963	4,122	4,715	3,391	3,358	4,672	5,344
2007–08	10,067	8,538	84.8	53.3	31.6	37.7	54.1	3,161	3,138	4,364	5,323	3,455	3,430	4,769	5,817
2008–09	9,588	8,327	86.8	59.2	32.0	37.5	58.1	3,563	3,550	4,194	6,089	3,840	3,826	4,520	6,562
2009–10	10,087	9,015	89.4	66.9	29.1	41.5	58.6	4,294	3,000	4,798	6,078	4,584	3,202	5,121	6,488
2010–11	13,559	12,257	90.4	73.5	27.4	28.4	65.2	4,470	2,696	5,138	6,844	4,678	2,821	5,377	7,162
2011–12	12,853	12,083	94.0	76.3	24.3	31.8	65.5	4,180	2,830	4,075	7,014	4,250	2,877	4,143	7,130
Private for-profit															
2000–01	203,995	155,374	76.2	49.3	15.2	6.2	63.5	2,312	2,494	1,540	5,517	3,055	3,295	2,034	7,290
2005–06	328,206	263,366	80.2	55.6	11.4	8.8	70.4	2,725	2,796	1,423	6,454	3,168	3,250	1,655	7,503
2006–07	380,950	262,202	68.8	44.8	9.3	8.4	61.7	2,776	2,474	1,545	6,506	3,146	2,803	1,751	7,373
2007–08	390,284	316,402	81.1	57.8	9.5	14.9	72.9	3,066	2,996	1,154	8,010	3,351	3,274	1,261	8,753
2008–09	478,429	409,410	85.6	64.5	6.6	17.2	79.6	3,766	3,167	1,184	8,798	4,058	3,413	1,276	9,482
2009–10	551,329	495,282	89.8	74.5	6.3	15.1	81.3	4,523	3,190	1,171	8,786	4,828	3,405	1,250	9,378
2010–11	333,503	300,148	90.0	75.2	8.9	15.3	82.0	4,479	3,020	1,881	8,003	4,687	3,160	1,968	8,374
2011–12	292,306	265,200	90.7	75.4	8.4	15.2	82.3	4,324	2,993	2,120	7,789	4,396	3,043	2,155	7,918
4-year															
2000–01	81,075	51,739	63.8	36.1	11.9	8.3	57.7	2,295	2,889	1,616	5,749	3,033	3,817	2,135	7,596
2005–06	157,705	116,237	73.7	46.8	8.9	10.9	67.2	2,490	2,945	1,641	7,046	2,895	3,424	1,908	8,192
2006–07	229,746	127,215	55.4	32.5	5.7	8.4	52.0	2,608	2,622	1,878	6,989	2,955	2,972	2,129	7,920
2007–08	210,468	159,991	76.0	51.5	7.2	20.4	68.1	3,030	2,922	1,235	8,790	3,311	3,193	1,350	9,616
2008–09	258,498	221,487	85.7	62.7	5.8	23.5	81.4	3,745	3,139	1,296	9,660	4,036	3,384	1,397	10,411
2009–10	243,429	223,526	91.8	75.3	6.6	23.5	86.1	4,547	2,715	1,311	9,641	4,854	2,898	1,400	10,291
2010–11	113,482	102,643	90.4	73.5	11.3	23.6	82.8	4,736	2,950	2,790	8,484	4,956	3,086	2,919	8,878
2011–12	112,917	102,422	90.7	75.7	10.8	22.3	82.8	4,686	3,000	2,896	8,223	4,764	3,050	2,945	8,360
2-year															
2000–01	122,920	103,635	84.3	58.0	17.3	4.8	67.3	2,319	2,314	1,453	5,387	3,064	3,057	1,919	7,117
2005–06	170,501	147,129	86.3	63.6	13.7	6.8	73.4	2,885	2,706	1,098	5,951	3,354	3,146	1,277	6,919
2006–07	151,204	134,987	89.3	63.4	14.7	8.3	76.4	2,906	2,386	1,029	6,007	3,294	2,704	1,166	6,808
2007–08	179,816	156,411	87.0	65.0	12.3	8.4	77.9	3,100	3,047	924	7,195	3,388	3,330	1,009	7,863
2008–09	219,931	187,923	85.4	66.6	7.6	9.8	77.5	3,788	3,191	869	7,734	4,083	3,439	936	8,335
2009–10	307,900	271,756	88.3	74.0	6.1	8.5	77.5	4,503	3,597	865	8,035	4,807	3,840	923	8,577
2010–11	220,021	197,505	89.8	76.1	7.6	11.0	81.5	4,350	3,074	876	7,751	4,552	3,216	917	8,111
2011–12	179,389	162,778	90.7	75.2	6.9	10.8	82.0	4,094	2,986	1,107	7,513	4,162	3,036	1,126	7,638

[1]Average amounts for students participating in indicated programs.
[2]Includes only loans made directly to students. Does not include Parent Loans for Undergraduate Students (PLUS) and other loans made directly to parents.

NOTE: Degree-granting institutions grant associate's or higher degrees and participate in Title IV federal financial aid programs.
SOURCE: U.S. Department of Education, National Center for Education Statistics, Integrated Postsecondary Education Data System (IPEDS), Spring 2002 through Spring 2013, Student Financial Aid component. (This table was prepared November 2013.)

Average amount of grant and scholarship aid and average net price for first-time, full-time students receiving Title IV aid, and percentage distribution of students, by control and level of institution and income level: 2009–10, 2010–11 and 2011–12

Selected characteristic	2009–10				2010–11				2011–12			
	All institutions	Public	Private Non-profit	Private For-profit	All institutions	Public	Private Non-profit	Private For-profit	All institutions	Public	Private Non-profit	Private For-profit
1	2	3	4	5	6	7	8	9	10	11	12	13
4-year institutions												
Grant and scholarship aid[1]												
All income levels	$9,050	$5,980	$15,560	$4,420	$9,630	$6,420	$16,310	$4,800	$9,740	$6,270	$17,040	$4,990
$0 to $30,000	10,290	9,080	17,460	5,110	10,820	9,500	17,800	5,360	10,750	9,240	18,450	5,410
$30,001 to $48,000	11,170	8,330	18,710	4,530	11,750	8,790	19,390	5,000	11,870	8,560	20,350	5,190
$48,001 to $75,000	9,140	4,910	16,810	2,430	9,700	5,400	17,640	3,150	9,850	5,240	18,560	3,330
$75,001 to $110,000	7,150	2,270	14,650	1,220	7,660	2,470	15,590	1,580	7,980	2,490	16,440	1,990
$110,001 or more	6,300	1,590	11,560	1,020	6,910	1,640	12,440	1,390	7,270	1,680	13,220	2,190
Net price[2]												
All income levels	15,900	11,070	21,780	22,590	16,360	11,570	22,570	22,710	16,910	12,410	23,540	21,330
$0 to $30,000	12,570	7,720	15,970	21,770	12,980	8,190	17,080	22,270	13,340	9,260	17,840	20,680
$30,001 to $48,000	13,110	9,260	17,200	23,590	13,480	9,710	18,120	23,330	14,100	10,900	18,730	22,260
$48,001 to $75,000	16,610	13,290	20,270	26,710	16,890	13,640	21,030	26,230	17,570	14,680	21,650	25,120
$75,001 to $110,000	19,860	16,410	23,900	29,830	20,410	17,100	24,610	28,790	21,000	17,910	25,160	27,690
$110,001 or more	24,080	17,880	30,210	32,910	24,980	18,730	31,050	31,150	25,570	19,500	31,720	30,010
2-year institutions												
Grant and scholarship aid[1]												
All income levels	4,460	4,540	5,180	4,090	4,620	4,680	5,740	4,260	4,480	4,530	5,630	4,110
$0 to $30,000	5,250	5,450	5,540	4,590	5,370	5,510	5,870	4,810	5,240	5,350	5,840	4,680
$30,001 to $48,000	4,380	4,520	5,080	3,670	4,600	4,730	5,680	3,900	4,350	4,510	5,580	3,550
$48,001 to $75,000	2,240	2,250	4,150	1,960	2,470	2,480	5,330	2,100	2,400	2,390	5,360	2,030
$75,001 to $110,000	800	750	3,240	830	890	850	5,060	590	790	740	4,280	560
$110,001 or more	610	600	2,940	470	690	650	5,350	310	550	500	3,940	440
Net price[2]												
All income levels	8,930	6,290	16,270	18,360	9,030	6,550	17,170	18,770	9,160	6,980	17,610	19,300
$0 to $30,000	8,560	5,380	16,500	18,240	8,610	5,690	16,760	18,800	8,640	6,210	17,240	19,130
$30,001 to $48,000	8,720	6,330	16,620	19,070	9,000	6,520	18,090	19,650	9,690	7,050	18,140	20,380
$48,001 to $75,000	10,690	8,810	18,650	21,290	10,750	8,910	19,680	21,850	10,860	9,270	20,400	22,310
$75,001 to $110,000	12,230	10,630	20,760	23,020	12,500	10,780	20,830	24,040	12,570	11,150	21,100	24,250
$110,001 or more	12,760	10,820	20,930	24,620	12,970	11,010	21,900	24,670	12,860	11,350	21,480	25,080
Percentage distribution of students who received any Title IV aid												
4-year institutions												
All income levels	100.0	100.0	100.0	100.0	100.0	100.0	100.0	100.0	100.0	100.0	100.0	100.0
$0 to $30,000	35.0	34.8	25.1	67.6	35.5	35.7	26.0	69.1	36.4	36.7	26.1	73.2
$30,001 to $48,000	15.4	16.3	14.0	14.3	15.5	16.5	14.1	14.2	14.6	15.8	13.3	12.2
$48,001 to $75,000	16.6	17.1	18.0	8.9	16.9	17.7	17.9	8.6	16.3	17.1	17.2	7.7
$75,001 to $110,000	15.6	15.9	18.4	5.2	15.3	15.5	17.8	4.7	15.3	15.4	18.1	4.1
$110,001 or more	17.5	15.8	24.5	4.0	16.8	14.6	24.1	3.4	17.4	15.1	25.3	2.9
2-year institutions												
All income levels	100.0	100.0	100.0	100.0	100.0	100.0	100.0	100.0	100.0	100.0	100.0	100.0
$0 to $30,000	66.4	64.0	68.3	75.2	67.1	65.4	66.9	74.0	67.9	67.0	67.5	72.7
$30,001 to $48,000	15.7	16.4	16.1	13.4	15.4	15.7	17.2	14.2	14.6	14.3	16.0	16.3
$48,001 to $75,000	10.0	10.9	9.0	6.8	10.3	11.1	8.7	7.1	9.9	10.6	9.1	6.6
$75,001 to $110,000	5.2	5.8	4.5	3.0	4.9	5.4	4.7	3.1	5.1	5.5	5.0	2.9
$110,001 or more	2.6	2.9	2.2	1.6	2.3	2.5	2.6	1.6	2.4	2.6	2.4	1.5

[1]Grant and scholarship aid consists of federal Title IV grants, as well as other grant or scholarship aid from the federal government, state or local governments, or institutional sources. Title IV grants include Federal Pell Grants, Federal Supplemental Educational Opportunity Grants (FSEOGs), Academic Competitiveness Grants (ACGs), National Science and Mathematics Access to Retain Talent Grants (National SMART Grants), and Teacher Education Assistance for College and Higher Education (TEACH) Grants. The average amount of grant and scholarship aid by income level was calculated based on all students who received any type of Title IV aid, even those who received zero Title IV aid in the form of grants and received Title IV aid only in the form of work-study aid or loan aid.

[2]Net price is the total cost of attendance minus grant and scholarship aid from the federal government, state or local governments, or institutional sources. However, average net price by income level was calculated based on all students who received any type of Title IV aid, even those who received zero Title IV aid in the form of grants and received Title IV aid only in the form of work-study aid or loan aid.

NOTE: Excludes students who previously attended another postsecondary institution or who began their studies on a part-time basis. Includes only first-time, full-time students who paid the in-state or in-district tuition rate (if they attended public institutions) and who received Title IV aid. Excludes the 18 percent of students who did not receive any Title IV aid. Title IV aid includes grant aid, work-study aid, and loan aid. Data are weighted by the number of students at the institution receiving Title IV aid. Some data have been revised from previously published figures.

SOURCE: U.S. Department of Education, National Center for Education Statistics, Integrated Postsecondary Education Data System (IPEDS), Spring 2013, Student Financial Aid component. (This table was prepared December 2013.)

Amount borrowed, aid status, and sources of aid for full-time, full-year postbaccalaureate students, by level of study and control and level of institution: Selected years, 1992–93 through 2011–12

[Standard errors appear in parentheses]

Level of study, control and level of institution	Cumulative borrowing for undergraduate and graduate education[1] — Percent who borrowed	Average amount for those who borrowed — Current dollars	Average amount for those who borrowed — Constant 2012–13 dollars[4]	Aid status — Nonaided	Source of aid — Any aid[2]	Source of aid — Federal[3]	Source of aid — State	Source of aid — Institutional	Source of aid — Employer
1	2	3	4	5	6	7	8	9	10
1992–93, all institutions	— (†)	— (†)	— (†)	30.7 (1.43)	69.3 (1.43)	44.4 (1.42)	6.9 (0.64)	40.6 (2.02)	5.3 (0.59)
Master's degree	— (†)	— (†)	— (†)	35.5 (2.54)	64.5 (2.54)	33.8 (1.91)	5.8 (0.79)	42.4 (2.97)	8.3 (1.01)
Public	— (†)	— (†)	— (†)	32.8 (2.39)	67.2 (2.39)	33.9 (2.04)	7.8 (1.09)	44.0 (2.68)	7.6 (1.24)
4-year doctoral	— (†)	— (†)	— (†)	32.5 (2.58)	67.5 (2.58)	32.4 (2.24)	6.7 (0.96)	46.3 (3.19)	7.7 (1.27)
Other 4-year	— (†)	— (†)	— (†)	34.6 (4.37)	65.4 (4.37)	42.5 (5.30)	14.4 (4.13)	30.4 (3.67)	6.8 ! (2.66)
Private	— (†)	— (†)	— (†)	39.2 (4.74)	60.8 (4.74)	33.7 (3.62)	3.2 (0.89)	40.2 (6.34)	9.4 (1.88)
4-year doctoral	— (†)	— (†)	— (†)	37.4 (4.70)	62.6 (4.70)	34.2 (4.09)	2.9 ! (1.00)	42.9 (6.75)	8.9 (1.88)
Other 4-year	— (†)	— (†)	— (†)	50.5 (10.60)	49.5 (10.60)	30.5 (7.06)	‡ (†)	22.8 ! (9.39)	‡ (†)
Doctor's degree	— (†)	— (†)	— (†)	30.1 (2.32)	69.9 (2.32)	28.3 (2.14)	5.5 (0.71)	51.6 (2.70)	3.0 (0.79)
Public	— (†)	— (†)	— (†)	29.9 (2.99)	70.1 (2.99)	22.3 (2.26)	6.5 (1.14)	55.5 (3.01)	3.9 (1.00)
Private	— (†)	— (†)	— (†)	30.4 (3.27)	69.6 (3.27)	37.8 (3.54)	‡ (†)	45.5 (3.52)	‡ (†)
First-professional	— (†)	— (†)	— (†)	22.6 (0.96)	77.4 (0.96)	68.2 (1.54)	10.0 (1.33)	37.0 (1.80)	2.3 (0.52)
Public	— (†)	— (†)	— (†)	20.4 (1.02)	79.6 (1.02)	72.4 (1.29)	13.4 (1.75)	37.7 (1.66)	2.3 (0.59)
Private	— (†)	— (†)	— (†)	24.5 (1.65)	75.5 (1.65)	64.3 (2.42)	6.8 (1.19)	36.4 (3.29)	2.3 ! (0.70)
Other graduate	— (†)	— (†)	— (†)	38.2 (6.81)	61.8 (6.81)	42.3 (4.27)	6.7 (1.81)	22.9 (4.02)	6.0 ! (2.97)
1999–2000, all institutions	69.4 (0.74)	$41,720 (859)	$57,010 (1,174)	18.3 (0.66)	81.7 (0.66)	52.6 (0.76)	6.1 (0.59)	49.7 (1.03)	6.0 (0.57)
Master's degree	68.4 (1.10)	31,730 (1,083)	43,360 (1,479)	20.7 (1.15)	79.3 (1.15)	50.5 (1.22)	5.2 (0.66)	45.4 (1.61)	9.1 (1.02)
Public	63.4 (1.58)	27,910 (1,069)	38,140 (1,461)	22.1 (1.52)	77.9 (1.52)	44.6 (1.84)	7.5 (1.13)	50.0 (2.18)	6.9 (1.04)
4-year doctoral	62.7 (1.53)	27,320 (1,220)	37,340 (1,667)	20.0 (1.46)	80.0 (1.46)	43.2 (1.74)	7.1 (1.30)	54.5 (2.06)	7.3 (1.19)
Other 4-year	70.9 (6.04)	31,920 (2,822)	43,620 (3,857)	29.9 (5.08)	70.1 (5.08)	54.7 (6.88)	10.2 ! (3.32)	27.4 (6.85)	5.1 ! (1.79)
Private	74.5 (1.54)	35,650 (1,850)	48,720 (2,528)	18.9 (1.63)	81.1 (1.63)	57.6 (1.85)	2.5 (0.63)	39.9 (2.62)	11.7 (1.87)
4-year doctoral	73.4 (1.75)	38,280 (2,483)	52,310 (3,394)	17.2 (1.94)	82.8 (1.94)	58.3 (2.34)	2.9 ! (0.90)	50.3 (3.23)	8.3 (1.31)
Other[5]	76.8 (3.75)	30,380 (1,946)	41,520 (2,660)	22.5 (2.74)	77.5 (2.74)	56.1 (4.31)	‡ (†)	17.9 (3.91)	18.9 (5.14)
Doctor's degree	56.8 (1.95)	38,940 (3,417)	53,220 (4,669)	12.1 (1.38)	87.9 (1.38)	29.6 (2.80)	2.6 (0.54)	77.3 (1.65)	5.4 (0.63)
Public	54.5 (1.92)	33,600 (1,564)	45,920 (2,138)	11.4 (1.38)	88.6 (1.38)	26.1 (1.86)	3.2 (0.75)	81.0 (1.59)	7.3 (0.88)
Private	60.6 (3.62)	46,530 (7,267)	63,590 (9,931)	13.0 (2.79)	87.0 (2.79)	35.2 (6.25)	‡ (†)	73.0 (3.22)	2.3 (0.55)
First-professional	85.1 (1.14)	60,620 (1,666)	82,840 (2,277)	13.4 (1.17)	86.6 (1.17)	77.2 (1.29)	9.8 (1.63)	41.6 (2.39)	1.7 ! (0.53)
Public	86.9 (1.70)	52,660 (1,963)	71,960 (2,683)	13.7 (1.82)	86.3 (1.82)	78.4 (2.12)	12.7 (2.56)	39.1 (2.84)	1.7 ! (0.87)
Private	83.7 (1.60)	67,450 (3,136)	92,180 (4,285)	13.1 (1.49)	86.9 (1.49)	76.2 (1.83)	7.5 (2.10)	43.7 (3.61)	1.7 ! (0.65)
Other graduate	57.4 (3.88)	27,620 (2,028)	37,750 (2,771)	38.9 (3.64)	61.1 (3.64)	45.4 (3.64)	8.6 (2.41)	25.6 (3.32)	2.8 ! (1.19)
2007–08, all institutions	71.3 (1.04)	$54,980 (992)	$60,080 (1,084)	13.1 (0.80)	86.9 (0.80)	56.5 (1.18)	3.9 (0.29)	43.9 (1.17)	11.6 (0.92)
Master's degree	71.8 (1.76)	43,140 (1,370)	47,140 (1,498)	15.6 (1.33)	84.4 (1.33)	55.4 (1.93)	3.0 (0.43)	35.6 (1.47)	16.3 (1.75)
Public	66.5 (1.77)	37,640 (1,466)	41,130 (1,602)	13.3 (1.27)	86.7 (1.27)	50.5 (1.89)	4.2 (0.85)	52.4 (2.38)	13.5 (1.50)
4-year doctoral	65.1 (1.92)	38,290 (1,636)	41,840 (1,787)	12.0 (1.33)	88.0 (1.33)	49.8 (2.05)	4.3 (0.95)	56.2 (2.60)	14.6 (1.68)
Other 4-year	77.1 (4.81)	33,440 (2,285)	36,540 (2,497)	22.7 (3.92)	77.3 (3.92)	55.6 (5.96)	‡ (†)	23.5 (4.89)	5.1 ! (1.92)
Private	75.5 (2.57)	46,490 (1,969)	50,810 (2,152)	17.2 (1.96)	82.8 (1.96)	58.9 (2.81)	2.2 (0.40)	23.9 (1.58)	18.3 (2.78)
4-year doctoral	71.5 (1.85)	46,370 (1,644)	50,670 (1,797)	19.1 (1.46)	80.9 (1.46)	55.3 (1.51)	2.6 (0.59)	35.9 (2.46)	14.4 (1.17)
Other[5]	80.7 (5.13)	46,630 (3,671)	50,960 (4,011)	14.9 (3.91)	85.1 (3.91)	63.5 (5.95)	1.6 (0.43)	8.4 (1.44)	23.3 (6.22)
Doctor's degree	59.8 (1.73)	55,170 (2,106)	60,290 (2,301)	7.1 (0.87)	92.9 (0.87)	38.4 (2.18)	2.9 (0.41)	70.7 (3.02)	7.9 (0.80)
Public	52.1 (2.16)	44,190 (1,604)	48,290 (1,753)	7.9 (1.48)	92.1 (1.48)	29.6 (1.80)	3.6 (0.65)	81.2 (1.88)	7.9 (0.94)
Private	67.8 (2.41)	64,060 (3,121)	70,010 (3,410)	6.2 (1.08)	93.8 (1.08)	47.7 (3.42)	2.2 ! (0.65)	59.7 (5.01)	8.0 (1.35)
First-professional	85.0 (1.28)	81,140 (1,776)	88,670 (1,941)	11.6 (1.15)	88.4 (1.15)	81.6 (1.37)	7.7 (0.85)	35.5 (1.89)	4.6 (0.75)
Public	84.5 (1.94)	72,750 (2,697)	79,500 (2,948)	11.7 (1.69)	88.3 (1.69)	81.6 (2.14)	10.9 (1.51)	33.7 (2.65)	4.9 (1.43)
Private	85.4 (1.57)	87,760 (2,185)	95,910 (2,388)	11.5 (1.46)	88.5 (1.46)	81.5 (1.67)	5.2 (0.86)	37.0 (2.55)	4.4 (0.71)
Other graduate	62.5 (6.48)	43,700 (3,904)	47,760 (4,267)	30.8 (6.54)	69.2 (6.54)	51.0 (6.62)	‡ (†)	25.4 (5.77)	6.2 ! (2.33)
2011–12, all institutions	73.3 (0.90)	$74,710 (996)	$75,950 (1,013)	13.9 (0.77)	86.1 (0.77)	62.3 (0.93)	2.4 (0.34)	42.2 (1.19)	10.2 (0.48)
Master's degree	73.5 (1.45)	58,590 (1,142)	59,570 (1,161)	17.4 (1.28)	82.6 (1.28)	63.0 (1.44)	1.8 (0.35)	35.1 (1.53)	8.8 (0.70)
Public	71.8 (2.24)	50,200 (1,816)	51,040 (1,846)	16.2 (1.84)	83.8 (1.84)	58.2 (2.41)	3.7 (0.80)	45.6 (2.35)	10.3 (1.17)
4-year doctoral	70.7 (2.41)	50,620 (2,015)	51,460 (2,048)	16.3 (2.03)	83.7 (2.03)	57.0 (2.60)	4.0 (0.89)	47.1 (2.56)	10.8 (1.28)
Other 4-year	82.2 (3.71)	46,900 (2,538)	47,680 (2,581)	15.4 (4.13)	84.6 (4.13)	69.5 (5.18)	‡ (†)	31.2 (3.46)	5.9 (1.68)
Private	74.8 (1.95)	64,510 (1,456)	65,580 (1,480)	18.2 (1.80)	81.8 (1.80)	66.5 (2.13)	0.4 ! (0.19)	27.5 (2.09)	7.8 (0.88)
4-year doctoral	70.1 (2.41)	67,130 (2,165)	68,250 (2,201)	19.6 (2.06)	80.4 (2.06)	59.5 (2.45)	‡ (†)	35.2 (2.96)	7.8 (1.23)
Other[5]	81.8 (3.20)	61,140 (1,816)	62,160 (1,846)	16.1 (3.09)	83.9 (3.09)	77.0 (3.66)	‡ (†)	15.9 (2.70)	7.6 (1.04)
Doctor's degree—research/scholarship	50.5 (1.42)	65,090 (2,343)	66,170 (2,382)	6.6 (0.73)	93.4 (0.73)	27.8 (1.19)	1.5 ! (0.49)	79.8 (1.27)	24.0 (1.25)
Public	47.9 (2.23)	55,500 (2,291)	56,420 (2,330)	5.9 (1.04)	94.1 (1.04)	24.2 (1.41)	2.1 ! (0.78)	87.2 (1.59)	27.0 (1.93)
Private	54.0 (1.86)	76,180 (4,351)	77,450 (4,424)	7.5 (1.07)	92.5 (1.07)	32.3 (2.30)	‡ (†)	70.1 (2.28)	20.1 (1.06)
Doctor's degree—professional practice and other[6]	88.3 (0.90)	110,570 (1,848)	112,410 (1,878)	9.3 (0.88)	90.7 (0.88)	84.4 (1.03)	4.5 (0.96)	35.1 (1.66)	4.4 (0.51)
Public	88.3 (1.00)	102,220 (2,726)	103,920 (2,772)	8.9 (1.09)	91.1 (1.09)	84.4 (1.31)	8.1 (2.27)	40.6 (2.51)	5.4 (0.82)
Private	88.3 (1.28)	116,000 (2,490)	117,930 (2,531)	9.6 (1.22)	90.4 (1.22)	84.4 (1.50)	2.2 (0.53)	31.5 (2.19)	3.7 (0.62)
Other graduate	74.9 (6.28)	57,540 (5,456)	58,500 (5,546)	29.1 (6.46)	70.9 (6.46)	61.4 (7.24)	‡ (†)	16.9 (4.78)	5.5 ! (2.47)

—Not available.

†Not applicable.

!Interpret data with caution. The coefficient of variation (CV) for this estimate is between 30 and 50 percent.

‡Reporting standards not met. Either there are too few cases for a reliable estimate or the coefficient of variation (CV) is 50 percent or greater.

[1]Includes all loans ever taken out for both graduate and undergraduate education. Does not include Parent Loans for Undergraduate Students (PLUS) or loans from families and friends.

[2]Includes students who reported they were awarded aid, but did not specify the source of aid.

[3]Includes Department of Veterans Affairs and Department of Defense benefits.

[4]Constant dollars based on the Consumer Price Index, prepared by the Bureau of Labor Statistics, U.S. Department of Labor, adjusted to a school-year basis.

[5]Includes nonprofit 4-year nondoctoral institutions and for-profit 2-year-and-above institutions.

[6]Professional practice doctor's degrees include most degrees formerly classified as first-professional (such as M.D., D.D.S., and J.D.). "Other" doctor's degrees are those that are neither research/scholarship degrees nor professional practice degrees.

NOTE: Excludes students whose attendance status was not reported. Total includes some students whose level of study or control of institution was unknown. Detail may not sum to totals because of rounding and because some students receive multiple types of aid and aid from different sources. Data for 2007–08 and prior years include Puerto Rico, which is excluded from the 2011–12 data.

SOURCE: U.S. Department of Education, National Center for Education Statistics, 1992–93, 1999–2000, 2007–08, and 2011–12 National Postsecondary Student Aid Study (NPSAS:93, NPSAS:2000, NPSAS:08, and NPSAS:12). (This table was prepared March 2014.)

Weighted average tuition fee for full-time Canadian undergraduate students, by field of study, annual (dollars) (1,2,3,4,5,6)

Field of study grouping	2010/2011	2011/2012	2012/2013	2013/2014	2014/2015
Education	3,850	3,804	4,273	4,394	4,510
Visual and performing arts, and communications technologies	4,748	4,591	5,002	5,138	5,287
Humanities	4,638	4,769	4,941	5,023	5,165
Social and behavioural sciences	4,586	4,656	4,966	5,116	5,262
Law, legal professions and studies	8,657	9,335	9,549	10,039	10,508
Business management and public administration	5,386	5,673	6,097	6,274	6,525
Physical and life sciences and technologies	5,049	5,247	5,335	5,481	5,640
Mathematics, computer and information sciences	5,526	5,781	6,051	6,245	6,471
Engineering	5,992	6,155	6,560	6,871	7,151
Architecture and related technologies	5,179	4,788	5,340	5,495	5,711
Agriculture, natural resources and conservation	4,803	4,961	5,119	5,251	5,407
Dentistry	15,062	16,037	16,678	17,387	18,187
Medicine	10,867	11,313	12,012	12,470	12,959
Nursing	4,662	4,731	4,985	5,140	5,287
Pharmacy	9,014	9,719	10,463	10,691	11,173
Veterinary medicine	5,612	5,889	6,383	6,680	6,926
Other health, parks, recreation and fitness	4,698	4,873	5,232	5,529	5,691

Footnotes:

(1) Data for 2014/2015 are preliminary.

(2) The national and provincial tuition fee averages are weighted with the latest enrolments (2011). If the number of enrolments is unknown for a given program, the program is excluded from the averages. The same student enrolment figures are used for the weighting of both years (2013/2014 and 2014/2015), thereby permitting the comparison of changes in the tuition fees only.

(3) As the distribution of enrolment across the various programs varies from period to period, caution must be exercised when making long-term historical comparisons.

(4) For Quebec, since 1998/1999, and for Nova Scotia, since 2007/2008, the weighted averages take into account the different tuition fees paid by "in province" and "out of province" students.

(5) It is important to note that tuition fee increases are generally regulated by provincial policies. However, some programs may be exempted from these policies resulting in possible increases that exceed provincial limits.

(6) Data in this release do not take into account financial assistance or tax rebates provided to students. Tuition fees and additional compulsory fees represent only a portion of all costs incurred for attending university.

Source:

Statistics Canada. Table 477-0021 - Weighted average tuition fee for full-time Canadian undergraduate students, by field of study, annual (accessed: March 10, 2015)

Weighted average tuition fee for full-time Canadian graduate students, by field of study, annual (dollars) (1,2,3,4,5,6,7)

Field of study grouping	2010/2011	2011/2012	2012/2013	2013/2014	2014/2015
Education	4,981	5,089	5,462	5,536	5,654
Visual and performing arts, and communications technologies	4,834	4,409	4,890	4,700	4,844
Humanities	4,239	4,336	4,522	4,525	4,617
Social and behavioural sciences	4,605	4,556	5,020	5,103	5,236
Law, legal professions and studies	4,487	5,302	5,373	5,834	6,009
Business management and public administration	8,132	7,932	8,547	8,987	9,389
Executive MBA	37,032	36,971	35,448	38,750	39,862
Regular MBA	20,336	22,823	23,049	26,201	27,173
Physical and life sciences and technologies	5,477	5,632	5,913	6,024	6,177
Mathematics, computer and information sciences	5,735	5,716	5,790	6,001	6,145
Engineering	5,522	5,175	6,040	6,168	6,362
Architecture and related technologies	4,834	4,950	5,290	5,483	5,620
Agriculture, natural resources and conservation	4,821	4,769	5,136	5,236	5,370
Dentistry	4,337	4,365	10,753	11,631	12,044
Medicine	n/a	n/a	(U)	(U)	(U)
Nursing	5,090	5,117	5,746	5,844	5,997
Pharmacy	5,411	5,466	5,199	6,456	6,544
Veterinary medicine	3,435	3,173	3,313	3,650	3,727
Other health, parks, recreation and fitness	7,017	7,577	7,858	7,707	7,930

Legend:

n/a Not available

(U) Too unreliable to be published

Footnotes:

(1) Data for 2014/2015 are preliminary.

(2) The national and provincial tuition fee averages are weighted with the latest enrolments (2011). If the number of enrolments is unknown for a given program, the program is excluded from the averages. The same student enrolment figures are used for the weighting of both years (2013/2014 and 2014/2015), thereby permitting the comparison of changes in the tuition fees only.

(3) As the distribution of enrolment across the various programs varies from period to period, caution must be exercised when making long-term historical comparisons.

(4) For Quebec, since 1998/1999, and for Nova Scotia, since 2007/2008, the weighted averages take into account the different tuition fees paid by "in province" and "out of province" students.

(5) It is important to note that tuition fee increases are generally regulated by provincial policies. However, some programs may be exempted from these policies resulting in possible increases that exceed provincial limits.

(6) Data in this release do not take into account financial assistance or tax rebates provided to students. Tuition fees and additional compulsory fees represent only a portion of all costs incurred for attending university.

(7) Starting in 2010/2011, the master of business administration programs have been excluded from the national and provincial weighted averages to eliminate the effect of the high cost of these programs on the overall tuition fee average. Dental, medical and veterinary residency programs offered in teaching hospitals and similar locations that may lead to advanced professional certification have also been

Source:

Statistics Canada. Table 477-0022 - Weighted average tuition fee for full-time Canadian graduate students, by field of study, annual (dollars) (accessed: March 10, 2015)

Weighted average tuition fee for full-time foreign undergraduate students, by field of study, annual (dollars)(1,2,3,4,5)

Field of study grouping	2010/2011	2011/2012	2012/2013	2013/2014	2014/2015
Education	13,219	13,550	14,133	14,998	15,574
Visual and performing arts, and communications technologies	15,587	15,098	16,677	18,237	19,204
Humanities	15,900	16,537	17,282	18,332	19,241
Social and behavioural sciences	15,750	16,296	17,033	17,629	18,521
Law, legal professions and studies	20,487	22,909	21,793	23,254	25,231
Business management and public administration	16,349	17,637	18,185	19,525	20,506
Physical and life sciences and technologies	17,546	18,746	18,778	19,877	20,926
Mathematics, computer and information sciences	18,459	18,854	19,265	20,284	21,416
Engineering	18,526	19,526	20,534	21,861	23,325
Architecture and related technologies	17,247	17,780	17,893	18,733	19,580
Agriculture, natural resources and conservation	16,286	16,439	16,402	17,396	18,106
Dentistry	40,964	42,057	44,162	47,243	49,529
Medicine	35,422	35,502	28,600	(U)	(U)
Nursing	14,283	14,651	15,584	16,221	16,838
Pharmacy	20,795	27,300	29,527	30,728	31,970
Veterinary medicine	48,262	49,538	50,493	51,332	51,937
Other health, parks, recreation and fitness	15,683	16,069	16,882	16,966	17,772

Legend:

(U) Too unreliable to be published

Footnotes:

(1) Data for 2014/2015 are preliminary.

(2) The national and provincial tuition fee averages are weighted with the latest enrolments (2011). If the number of enrolments is unknown for a given program, the program is excluded from the averages. The same student enrolment figures are used for the weighting of both years (2013/2014 and 2014/2015), thereby permitting the comparison of changes in the tuition fees only.

(3) As the distribution of enrolment across the various programs varies from period to period, caution must be exercised when making long-term historical comparisons.

(4) It is important to note that tuition fee increases are generally regulated by provincial policies. However, some programs may be exempted from these policies resulting in possible increases that exceed provincial limits.

(5) Data in this release do not take into account financial assistance or tax rebates provided to students. Tuition fees and additional compulsory fees represent only a portion of all costs incurred for attending university.

Source:

Statistics Canada. Table 477-0023 - Weighted average tuition fee for full-time foreign undergraduate students, by field of study, annual (dollars) (accessed: March 10, 2015)

Weighted average tuition fee for full-time foreign graduate students, by field of study, annual (dollars)(1,2,3,4,5,6)

Field of study grouping	2010/2011	2011/2012	2012/2013	2013/2014	2014/2015
Education	10,467	10,661	12,201	12,802	13,328
Visual and performing arts, and communications technologies	12,449	11,980	11,761	11,840	12,241
Humanities	11,952	12,309	12,189	12,424	12,857
Social and behavioural sciences	11,716	11,853	12,024	12,244	12,676
Law, legal professions and studies	13,872	14,789	14,620	15,396	16,115
Business management and public administration	17,665	17,220	17,537	18,314	18,531
Executive MBA	34,567	34,445	44,159	44,826	46,107
Regular MBA	25,725	28,876	30,537	33,520	34,724
Physical and life sciences and technologies.	11,985	12,152	12,237	12,556	12,947
Mathematics, computer and information sciences	11,749	12,079	11,733	12,099	12,578
Engineering	13,141	13,297	13,806	14,041	14,556
Architecture and related technologies	13,127	13,453	14,534	15,796	16,379
Agriculture, natural resources and conservation	11,215	11,515	11,311	11,370	11,672
Dentistry	12,104	12,370	(U)	19,427	20,129
Medicine	n/a	n/a	(U)	(U)	(U)
Nursing	12,314	12,504	11,212	12,524	13,038
Pharmacy	12,003	12,216	11,966	12,674	12,971
Veterinary medicine	10,969	10,824	8,217	9,268	9,460
Other health, parks, recreation and fitness	12,679	14,069	15,941	15,583	16,079

Legend:

(U) Too unreliable to be published

n/a Not available

Footnotes:

(1) Data for 2014/2015 are preliminary.

(2) The national and provincial tuition fee averages are weighted with the latest enrolments (2011). If the number of enrolments is unknown for a given program, the program is excluded from the averages. The same student enrolment figures are used for the weighting of both years (2013/2014 and 2014/2015), thereby permitting the comparison of changes in the tuition fees only.

(3) As the distribution of enrolment across the various programs varies from period to period, caution must be exercised when making long-term historical comparisons.

(4) It is important to note that tuition fee increases are generally regulated by provincial policies. However, some programs may be exempted from these policies resulting in possible increases that exceed provincial limits.

(5) Data in this release do not take into account financial assistance or tax rebates provided to students. Tuition fees and additional compulsory fees represent only a portion of all costs incurred for attending university.

(6) Starting in 2010/2011, the master of business administration programs have been excluded from the national and provincial weighted averages to eliminate the effect of the high cost of these programs on the overall tuition fee average. Dental, medical and veterinary residency programs offered in teaching hospitals and similar locations that may lead to advanced professional certification have also been excluded.

Source:

Statistics Canada. Table 477-0024 - Weighted average tuition fee for full-time foreign graduate students, by field of study, annual (dollars) (accessed: March 10, 2015)

School board revenues, by direct source of funds, annual (dollars x 1,000)(1,2,3)

School board revenues by direct source of funds	2008	2009	2010	2011	2012
Total revenues	47,872,221	49,724,674	51,644,180	53,617,497	55,279,523
Local taxation sources	12,695,401	12,899,480	13,062,175	13,143,149	13,422,523
Provincial government sources	31,488,794	33,235,682	34,936,172	36,829,019	38,165,260
Federal government sources	289,013	308,786	314,175	309,646	304,803
Student and other school fees	225,802	237,677	243,953	280,325	366,047
Other private sector sources	3,173,211	3,043,049	3,087,705	3,055,358	3,020,890

Footnotes:

(1) Source: Statistics Canada, Culture, Tourism and the Centre for Education Statistics.

(2) Data are or have been converted to a calendar basis, January 1 to December 31.

(3) School boards represent schools which are a part of the elementary and secondary public school system. The revenues and/or expenditures in this table exclude those of other types of publicly run elementary and secondary schools such as federal schools and special needs education schools as well as the elementary and secondary schools which are in the private school system.

Source:

Statistics Canada. Table 478-0010 - School board revenues, by direct source of funds, annual (dollars)
(accessed: March 10, 2015)

School board expenditures, by function and economic classification, annual (dollars x 1,000)(1,2)

Economic classification	2008	2009	2010	2011	2012
Total expenditures by economic classification	47,896,142	50,151,830	51,904,934	53,034,158	54,147,034
Salary and wages expenditures	31,477,180	32,911,465	34,226,301	35,338,155	36,251,844
Fringe benefits expenditures	4,089,749	4,250,886	4,420,034	4,332,646	4,354,706
Supply and services expenditures	3,932,497	4,213,534	4,529,877	4,532,222	4,587,366
Fees and contractual services expenditures	3,274,489	3,328,525	3,034,824	2,911,848	3,528,278
Other operating expenditures	607,771	675,443	1,114,311	1,291,707	654,308
Capital expenditures (non-allocable, outlay and debt charges)	4,514,456	4,771,977	4,579,587	4,627,580	4,770,532

Footnotes:

(1) Source: Statistics Canada, Culture, Tourism and the Centre for Education Statistics.

(2) Data are or have been converted to a calendar basis, January 1 to December 31.

Source:

Statistics Canada. Table 478-0011 - School board expenditures, by function and economic classification, annual (dollars) (accessed: March 10, 2015)

Public and private elementary and secondary education expenditures, annual (dollars x 1,000)(1)

Type of expenditures	2007/2008	2008/2009	2009/2010	2010/2011	2011/2012
Public and private elementary and secondary education expenditures	55,728,261	58,836,775	61,848,463	63,844,950	64,994,576
Public elementary and secondary education expenditures	52,244,764	55,198,663	58,053,927	59,927,089	60,992,262
Public school board and direct government expenditures	50,895,684	53,862,326	56,394,551	58,403,764	59,363,916
Public school board expenditures	45,728,027	47,896,142	50,151,830	51,904,934	53,034,158
Public school board expenditures, net	45,682,353	47,848,425	50,102,441	51,854,141	52,981,937
Public school board expenditures transferred to private schools	-45,674	-47,717	-49,389	-50,793	-52,221
Direct government expenditures on public education	5,213,331	6,013,901	6,292,110	6,549,623	6,381,979
Direct government expenditures on services to public school boards (2)	1,564,891	1,697,780	2,130,280	2,165,802	1,887,809
Direct government expenditures on contributions to public school board teachers' pension funds (2)	2,443,977	3,103,877	3,253,236	3,672,903	3,880,756
Direct government expenditures on public education by the Department of National Defence (3)	177	105	121	1,959	365
Other direct government expenditures on public education (3)	1,204,286	1,212,139	908,473	708,959	613,049
Federal school expenditures	950,622	928,598	1,235,097	1,085,164	1,182,338
Federal school operating expenditures	(T)	(T)	(T)	(T)	(T)
Federal school capital expenditures	(T)	(T)	(T)	(T)	(T)
Special education expenditures on public education	214,264	211,937	220,890	236,880	251,857
Special education expenditures, handicapped outside regular public schools	166,657	163,498	164,240	176,678	182,251
Special education expenditures on provincially licensed correspondence courses	32,741	34,135	31,915	35,103	44,558
Special education expenditures, reform and correctional institutions	4,275	4,330	4,380	4,417	4,465
Special education expenditures on federal penitentiaries	10,591	9,974	20,355	20,682	20,583
Direct provincial government expenditures on administration of public education	184,194	195,802	203,389	201,281	194,151
Private elementary and secondary school expenditures	3,483,497	3,638,112	3,794,536	3,917,861	4,002,314

Symbol legend:

(T) Series is terminated

Footnotes:

(1) Source: Statistics Canada, Tourism and the Centre for Education Statistics.

(2) From 1950 to 1959 there was no separate breakdown available between direct government expenditures on services to public school boards and direct government expenditures on contributions to public school board teachers' pension funds. These were both reported under direct government expenditures on contributions to public school board teachers' pension funds.

(3) From 1950 to 1959, any direct government expenditures on public education by Department of National Defence were reported under other direct government expenditures on public education.

Source:

Statistics Canada. Table 478-0014 - Public and private elementary and secondary education expenditures, annual (dollars)
(accessed: March 10, 2015)

Public and private elementary and secondary education expenditures, by direct source of funds, annual (dollars x 1,000)(1)

Public and private elementary and secondary education expenditures by direct source of funds	2007/2008	2008/2009	2009/2010	2010/2011	2011/2012
All sources	55,728,261	58,836,775	61,848,463	63,844,950	64,994,576
All governments' sources	49,510,198	52,649,183	55,263,098	57,271,016	59,211,670
Federal government sources	1,448,904	1,443,214	1,692,258	1,507,560	1,651,550
Provincial government sources	35,583,659	38,505,438	40,666,052	42,695,922	44,411,495
Local government sources	12,477,635	12,700,531	12,904,788	13,067,534	13,148,625
Student and other school fees	2,186,739	2,262,021	2,366,011	2,452,031	2,533,498
Other private sector sources	4,031,324	3,925,571	4,219,354	4,121,903	3,249,408

Footnotes:

(1) Source: Statistics Canada, Tourism and the Centre for Education Statistics.

Source:

Statistics Canada. Table 478-0015 - Public and private elementary and secondary education expenditures, by direct source of funds, annual (dollars)
(accessed: March 10, 2015)

Labour force survey estimates (LFS), by educational attainment, annual (18)

Labour force characteristics	Educational attainment (11)	2010	2011	2012	2013	2014
Employment rate (rate) (10)	Total, all education levels	61.5	61.7	61.7	61.8	61.4
Employment rate (rate) (10)	0 to 8 years (12)	19.8	19.6	20	19.8	19.1
Employment rate (rate) (10)	Some high school (13)	40.3	40.3	39.5	39.5	39.1
Employment rate (rate) (10)	High school graduate (14)	61.7	61.7	61	60.7	60
Employment rate (rate) (10)	Some postsecondary (15)	60.8	60.4	60.5	59.9	58.8
Employment rate (rate) (10)	Postsecondary certificate or diploma (16)	70.8	70.9	70.5	70.6	70.2
Employment rate (rate) (10)	University degree (17)	75.2	74.7	74.8	74.6	74
Employment rate (rate) (10)	Bachelor's degree	75.3	74.4	74.6	74.6	73.9
Employment rate (rate) (10)	Above bachelor's degree	75.1	75.4	75.1	74.6	74.1

Footnotes:

(10) The employment rate (formerly the employment and population ratio) is the number of persons employed expressed as a percentage of the population 15 years of age and over. The employment rate for a particular group (age, sex, marital status) is the number employed in that group expressed as a percentage of the population for that group. Estimates are percentages, rounded to the nearest tenth.

(11) The following categories refer to the highest level of schooling completed. Questions relating to educational attainment were changed in 1990, to better capture the relationship between educational attainment and labour market outcomes. Because this introduced a break in the education series, this table only contains data from 1990 onwards. Beginning January 1990, data on primary and secondary education reflects the highest grade completed. This provides a more consistent measure for those who accelerate or fail a grade than did years of school. A question on high school graduation has also been added since it is generally believed that persons who have never completed their secondary education have greater difficulty competing in the labour market. With the new questions, any education that could be counted towards a degree, certificate or diploma from an educational institution is taken as postsecondary education. The change allows more persons into the postsecondary education category. For example, trades programs offered through apprenticeship, vocational schools or private trade schools do not always require high school graduation. Such education is now considered as postsecondary while only primary or secondary would have been recognized prior to 1990. Finally, more information is collected on the type of postsecondary education: 1) some postsecondary; 2) trades certificate or diploma from a vocational or apprenticeship training; 3) Non-university certificate or diploma from a community college, CEGEP or school of nursing; 4) University certificate below bachelors degree; 5) Bachelors degree; and 6) University degree or certificate above bachelors degree.

(12) Primary education, grade 8 or lower. In Quebec, secondary II or lower.

(13) Attended but did not complete secondary school. In Quebec, attended at least Secondary III but did not complete Secondary V. In Newfoundland and Labrador, attended at least the first year of secondary but did not complete the fourth year.

(14) Received a high school diploma. In Quebec, completed Secondary V. In Newfoundland and Labrador, completed fourth year of secondary.

(15) Worked toward, but did not complete, a degree, certificate (including a trade certificate) or diploma from an educational institution, including a university, beyond the secondary level. This includes vocational schools, apprenticeship training, community college, Collège d'Enseignement Général et Professionnel (CEGEP), and school of nursing.

(16) Completed a certificate (including a trade certificate) or diploma from an educational institution beyond the secondary level. This includes certificates from vocational schools, apprenticeship training, community college, Collège d'Enseignement Général et Professionnel (CEGEP), and school of nursing. Also included are certificates below a Bachelor's degree obtained at a university.

(17) Attained at least a university bachelor's degree.

(18) The Labour force survey collection of tables, starting with number 282-, is large with many possible cross-tabulations for the 10 provinces and other geographic regions. To ensure respondent's confidentiality, detailed data are suppressed. Data for Canada, Quebec, Ontario, Alberta and British Columbia are suppressed if the estimate is below 1,500, for Newfoundland and Labrador, Nova Scotia, New Brunswick, Manitoba and Saskatchewan, if the estimate is below 500, and for Prince Edward Island, under 200. For suppression levels within census metropolitan areas (CMAs) and economic regions (ERs), use the respective provincial suppression levels above. While suppressing to protect respondent confidentiality has the added effect of blocking-out the lowest-quality LFS data, some remaining non-suppressed data in these very large LFS CANSIM tables may be of insufficient quality to allow for accurate interpretation. Please be warned that the more detailed your LFS CANSIM download, the smaller the sample size upon which your LFS estimates will be based, and the greater the risk of downloading poorer quality data.

Source:

Statistics Canada. Table 282-0004 - Labour force survey estimates (LFS), by educational attainment, sex and age group, annual (persons unless otherwise noted)

(accessed: March 10, 2015)

Glossary of Education Terms

Accountability
measurable proof, usually in the form of student results on various tests, that teachers, schools, divisions and states are teaching students efficiently and well, usually in the form of student success rates on various tests; Virginia's accountability programs is known as the Standards of Learning which includes curriculum standards approved by the Board of Education and required state tests based on the standards.

Accreditation
a process used by the Virginia Department of Education to evaluate the educational performance of public schools in accordance regulations.

Achievement gap
the difference between the performance of subgroups of students, especially those defined by gender, race/ethnicity, disability and socioeconomic status.

ACT
one of the two commonly used tests designed to assess high school students' general educational development and their ability to complete college-level work in four skill areas: English, mathematics, reading, and science reasoning.

Adequate yearly progress (AYP)
a measurement indicating whether a school, division or the state met federally approved academic goals required by the federal Elementary and Secondary Education Act/No Child Left Behind Act (ESEA/NCLB).

Adult/Continuing education
a program of instruction provided by an adult/continuing education instructional organization for adults and youth beyond the age of compulsory school attendance including basic education and English literacy, English for speakers of other languages, civics education, GED testing services, adult secondary education and Individualized Student Alternative Education Plan (ISAEP) programs.

Advanced Placement (AP)
college-level courses available to high school students which may allow a student to earn college credit provided through the College Board.

Alignment
effort to ensure that what teachers teach is in accord with what the curriculum says will be taught and what is assessed on official tests.

Alternative assessment
a method to measure student educational attainment other than the typical multiple-choice test which may include portfolios, constructed response items and other performance-measurement tools.

Alternative education
a school or center organized for alternative programs of instruction.

Assessment
method of measuring the learning and performance of students; examples include achievement tests, minimum competency tests, developmental screening tests, aptitude tests, observation instruments, performance tasks, etc.

At-risk students
students who have a higher than average probability of dropping out or failing school.

Average daily membership (ADM)
the K-12 enrollment figure used to distribute state per pupil funding that includes students with disabilities ages 5-21, and students for whom English is a second language who entered school for the first time after reaching their 12th birthday, and who have not reached their 22nd birthday; preschool and post-graduate students are not included in ADM.

Benchmark
a standard for judging performance.

Block scheduling
a way of organizing the school day into blocks of time longer than the typical 50 minute class period; with the 4X4 block students take four 90-minute classes each day allowing for completion of an entire course in one semester instead of a full year; with an A/B or rotating block students take six to eight classes for an entire year but classes in each subject meet on alternate days for 90 minutes.

Charter school
a school controlled by a local school board that provides free public elementary and/or secondary education to eligible students under a specific charter granted by the state legislature or other appropriate authority, and designated by such authority to be a charter school.

Class period
a segment of time in the school day that is approximately 1/6 of the instructional day.

Cohort
a particular group of people with something in common.

College Board
the organization that administers SAT, AP and other standardized tests to high school students planning on continuing their educations at a post-secondary level.

Combined school
a public school that contains any combination of or all K-12 grade levels that are not considered an elementary, middle or secondary school .

Composite index of local ability to pay
a formula to determine the state and local government shares of K-12 education program costs, which is expressed as a ratio, indicating the local percentage share of the cost of education programs; for example, a locality with a composite

index of 0.3000 would pay 30 percent and the state would pay 70 percent of the costs.

Confined
due to physical, medical or emotional impairments based on certification of need, a student is restricted or limited from attendance at a regular public school during the regular school hours; this does not apply to situations where a student is restricted for discipline or non-medically based situations.

Core curriculum
the body of knowledge that all students are expected to learn in the subjects of English, mathematics, history/social science and science.

Curriculum
a plan or document that a school or school division uses to define what will be taught and the methods that will be used to educate and assess students.

Curriculum alignment
occurs when what is taught includes or exceeds the content defined by the Standards of Learning (SOL).

Data-based decision making (also referred to as "research-based decision making")
organizing, analyzing and interpreting existing sources of information and other data to make decisions.

Direct aid to public education
funding appropriated for the operation of public schools including funding for school employee benefits, Standards of Quality, incentive-based programs, allotment of sales tax and lottery revenues and specific appropriations for programs such as Governor's Schools and adult literacy initiatives.

Disaggregated data
presentation of data broken into subgroups of students instead of the entire student body which allows parents and teachers to measure how each student group is performing; typical subgroups include students who are economically disadvantaged, from different racial or ethnic groups, those who have disabilities or have limited English fluency.

Distance learning
method of instruction in locations other than the classroom or places where teachers present the lessons, which uses various forms of technology to provide educational materials and experiences to students.

Dropouts
students who leave high school before receiving a diploma.

Early childhood education
the education of young children, especially under the age of 5.

Economically disadvantaged
a student who is a member of a household that meets the income eligibility guidelines for free or reduced-price school meals (less than or equal to 185% of Federal Poverty Guidelines).

Elementary & Secondary Education Act (ESEA)
the primary federal law affecting K-12 education; the most recent reauthorization of the law is also known as the No Child Left Behind Act of 2001 (NCLB).

Elementary school
a public school with grades kindergarten through five.

Eligible students
the total number of students of school age enrolled in the school at a grade or course with a Standards of Learning test; does not include students who are allowed an exclusion such as limited English proficient (LEP) students or some students with disabilities.

English as a second language (ESL)
a program of instruction and services for non-English-speaking or limited-English-proficient students to help them learn and succeed in schools.

English-language learners (ELL)
a student whose first language is other than English and who is in a special program for learning English.

Enrollment
the act of complying with state and local requirements for registration or admission of a child for attendance in a school within a local school division; also refers to registration for courses within the student's home school or within related schools or programs.

Even Start
a federally funded program that provides family-centered education projects to help parents become full partners in the education of their children.

First time
the student has not been enrolled in the school at any time during the current school year.

Four core subject/academic areas
English, mathematics, science and history/social science for purposes of SOL testing.

Free and appropriate public education (FAPE)
requirement through the federal Individuals with Disabilities Education Act (IDEA) that education of students with disabilities (between the ages of 3 and 22) must be provided at public expense, under public supervision, at no charge to the parents and based on the child's unique needs and not on the child's disability.

General education
K-12 instruction that meets the commonwealth's Standards of Learning and prepares children for elementary, secondary and postsecondary success.

Gifted
programs that provide advanced educational opportunities including accelerated promotion through grades and classes and an enriched curriculum for students who are endowed with a high degree of mental ability.

Governor's school
a school serving gifted high school students who meet specific admissions criteria for advanced educational opportunities in areas including the arts, government and international studies, mathematics, science, and technology; both academic-year and summer governor's schools are offered.

Graduate
a student who has earned a Board of Education recognized diploma: advanced studies, advanced technical, standard, standard technical, modified standard, special or general achievement.

Head Start
a federally funded child-development program that provides health, educational, nutritional, social and other services to pre-school children from economically disadvantaged families.

Home-based instruction
non-reimbursable educational services provided in the home setting (or other agreed upon setting) in accordance with the student's individual education program who were removed from school for disciplinary or other reasons, but not the result of a medical referral.

Homebound instruction
academic instruction provided to students who are confined at home or in a health-care facility for periods that would prevent normal school attendance based upon certification of need by a licensed physician or licensed clinical psychologist. For a student with a disability, the Individual Education Program (IEP) team must determine the delivery of services, including the number of hours of services.

Home instruction (also referred to as "home schooling")
instruction of a student or students by a parent or parents, guardian or other person having control or charge of such student or students as an alternative to attendance in a public or private school in accordance with the provisions of the Code of Virginia provisions (§22.1-254.1).

Home tutoring
instruction by a tutor or teacher with qualifications prescribed by the Virginia Board of Education, as an alternative to attendance in a public or private school and approved by the division superintendent in accordance with the provisions of the Code of Virginia §22.1-254; often used as an alternative form of home schooling.

Individuals with Disabilities Education Act (IDEA)
federal law guiding the delivery of special education services for students with disabilities which includes the guarantee of "free and appropriate public education" for every school-age child with a disability and allows parental involvement in the educational planning process, encourages access to the general curriculum and delineates how school disciplinary rules and the obligation to provide a free appropriate public education for disabled children mesh.

Individualized education program (IEP)
a written plan created for a student with disabilities by the student's teachers, parents or guardians, the school administrator, and other interested parties. The plan is tailored to the student's specific needs and abilities, and outlines attainable goals.

Individualized education program team (IEP Team)
team charged with developing, reviewing and revising a student's IEP and consisting of the parent(s), the child (if appropriate), a regular education teacher, a special education teacher, an administrator qualified to supervise the provision of services and an individual who can interpret the instructional implications of evaluation results.

Individualized family service plan (IFSP)
a written plan outlining the procedure necessary to transition a child with disabilities to preschool or other appropriate services.

International Baccalaureate (IB)
a program established to provide an internationally recognized; interdisciplinary; pre-collegiate course of study offered through the International Baccalaureate Organization, headquartered in Switzerland, and examination results are accepted by more than 100 countries for university admission.

Licensed clinical psychologist
a psychologist licensed by the Virginia Board of Psychology who must either be in a treatment relationship or establishing a treatment relationship with the student to meet eligibility requirements for requesting homebound services.

Licensed physician
an individual who has been licensed by the Virginia Board of Medicine to practice medicine who can certify medical conditions for requesting homebound services.

Licensed teacher
an individual who has met all the current requirements for a teacher in the Virginia and holds a license from the Virginia State Board of Education, or, if teaching on-line, a license from Virginia or another state.

Limited-English proficient (LEP) -see English-language learners Linear weighted average
a calculation, approximating what most school divisions spend to operate their schools, used to establish the funded cost of many components of the Standards of Quality (SOQ), such as instructional salaries.

Literary fund
established in the Constitution of Virginia (Article VIII, § 8) as a permanent and perpetual school fund that provides low-interest loans to school divisions for capital expenditures, such as construction of new buildings or remodeling of existing buildings.

Locally awarded verified credit
a verified unit of credit awarded by a local school board in accordance with the SOA.

Magnet school/center (also referred to as "specialty school/center")
a public school that focuses on a particular area of study, such as performing arts or science and technology but also offer regular school subjects.

Glossary of Education Terms

Middle school
a public school with grades 6 through 8.

Migrant Education
a program of instruction and services for children who move periodically with their families from one school to another in a different geographical area to secure seasonal employment.

National Assessment of Educational Progress (NAEP) (also referred to as "the Nation's Report Card")
the only nationally representative and continuing assessment of what America's students know and can do in various subject areas including mathematics, reading, science, writing, U.S. history, geography, civics and the arts; the federally funded program (currently contracted to Educational Testing Service in Princeton, N.J.) tests a representative sample of students in grades 4, 8 and 12 and provides information about the achievement of students nationally and state-by-state.

National Blue Ribbon Award
honors public and private K-12 schools that are either academically superior in their states or that demonstrate dramatic gains in student achievement; awarded annually by the U.S. Department of Education through the Blue Ribbon Schools Program.

Nation's Report Card
see "National Assessment of Educational Progress (NAEP)".

No Child Left behind Act of 2001 (NCLB)
see "Elementary & Secondary Education Act".

Norm-referenced tests
standardized tests designed to measure how a student's performance compares with that of other students.

Phonological Awareness Literacy Screening (PALS)
state-provided K-3 screening tool to help reduce the number of children with reading problems by detecting those problems early and providing research-based, small-group intervention.

Pedagogy
the art of teaching.

Planning period
one class period per day (or the equivalent) unencumbered of any teaching or supervisory duties.

Portfolio
a collection of student work chosen to exemplify and document a student's learning progress over time.

Pre-school child care
a school-operated program that provides custodial care of pre-school students enrolled in a school or system before school day starts and/or after a school day ends.

Proficient
test results indicating that the student demonstrated the skills and knowledge outlined in the Standards of Learning (SOL).

Professional/staff development
training for teachers, principals, superintendents, administrative staff, local school board members and Board of Education members designed to enhance student achievement and is required by the Standards of Quality (SOQ).

Psychiatrist
an medical doctor who has been licensed by the Virginia Board of Medicine and trained to practice in the science of treating mental diseases.

Reading First
federal program focuses on putting proven methods of early reading instruction into classrooms to ensure all children learn to read well by the end of third grade.

Recess
a segment of free time during the standard school day in which students are given a break from instruction.

Reconstitution
for a school rated accreditation denied, it is a process to initiate a range of accountability actions to improve pupil performance and to address deficiencies in curriculum and instruction; may include, but is not limited to, restructuring a school's governance, instructional program staff or student population.

Regular school year
the period of time between the opening day of school in the fall and the closing day of school for that school term that is at minimum 180 teaching days or 990 teaching hours.

Remedial program
a program designed to remedy, strengthen and improve the academic achievement of students who demonstrate substandard performance.

Research-based decision making
see "data-based decision making".

Response to intervention (RTI)
a method designed to identify and provide early, effective assistance to children who are having difficulty learning: Tier 1 students need extra help understanding the core curriculum, Tier 2 students consistently showing a discrepancy between their current level of performance and the expected level of performance, and Tier 3 students need even more support.

Restructuring
the implementation of a new organizational pattern or style of leadership and management to bring about renewed, more effective schools. It can mean reorganizing the school day or year and changing conventional practices, such as grouping students by age for an entire school year or giving competitive grades. Or it may refer to changing the roles of teachers and administrators, allocating more decision-making power to teachers, and involving parents in decisions.

Sampling
a way of estimating how a whole group would perform on a test by testing representative members of the group or giving different portions of the test to various subgroups.

SAT
one of the two commonly used tests designed to assess high school students' general educational development and required

for college entrance by many institutions of higher education; administered by The College Board.

School
a publicly funded institution where students are enrolled for all or a majority of the instructional day; those students are reported in fall membership at the institution and the institution, at minimum, meets requirements adopted by the Board of Education.

School age
a child who is age 5 on or before September 30 and has not reached age 20; compulsory attendance school age is 5-18.

Secondary school
a public school with any grades 9 through 12.

Special education (SPED)
a service especially designed and at no cost to the parent/guardian that adapts the curriculum, materials or instruction for students identified as having educational or physical disabilities and tailored to each student's needs and learning style and provided in a general education or special education classroom, home, hospital, separate school or other setting.

Specialty school
see "magnet school/center".

Standardized testing
tests administered and scored under uniform (standardized) conditions. Because most machine-scored, multiple-choice tests are standardized, the term is sometimes used to refer to such tests, but other tests may also be standardized.

Standard school day
a calendar day that averages at least five and one-half instructional hours for students in grades 1-12, excluding breaks for meals and recess, and a minimum of three instructional hours for students in kindergarten.

Standard school year
a school year of at least 180 teaching days or a total of at least 990 teaching hours per year.

Standard unit of credit
earned credit based on a minimum of 140-clock hours of instruction and successful completion of the requirements of the course.

Standards of Accreditation (SOA)
the Board of Education's regulations establishing criteria for approving public schools in Virginia as authorized in the Standards of Quality (SOQ).

Standards of Learning (SOL)
the minimum grade level and subject matter educational objectives, described as the knowledge and skills "necessary for success in school and for preparation for life," that students are expected to meet in Virginia public schools and specified by the Standards of Quality (SOQ).

SOL curriculum frameworks
teacher resource guides for mathematics, science, English and history/social sciences delineating essential knowledge, skills and processes required by the Standards of Learning (SOL).

Standards of Quality (SOQ)
the minimum program that every public school division in Virginia must meet; a major portion of state funding for direct air to public education is based on the SOQ; the standards are established in the Constitution of Virginia, defined in the Code of Virginia and prescribed by the Board of Education, subject to revision only by the General Assembly.

Student
a child age 5 on or before September 30 up to age 18; a child with disabilities age 2-21; a child of limited English proficiency who entered a Virginia school after age 12 but not age 22.

Student periods
means the number of students a teacher instructs per class period multiplied by the number of class periods taught.

Substitute tests
tests approved by the Board of Education as substitutes for SOL end-of-course tests for awarding verified credit for high school; examples include Advanced Placement (AP), International Baccalaureate (IB), SAT II, as well as a number of certifications and licensing examinations in career and technical fields.

Title I
federal funding program authorized by Title I of ESEA/NCLB to support instructional needs of students from low-income families to ensure that all children have a fair and equal opportunity to obtain a high-quality education and reach (at a minimum) proficiency on state academic achievement standards and assessments.

Title 1 school
a school with a high rate of disadvantaged students making it eligible for participation in federal Title I programs.

Title 1 school-wide assistance
Title 1 schools with 40 percent or greater high-poverty, student population may use federal funding to meet the needs of all students at the school.

Title 1 targeted assistance
federal funding is used to meet the needs of the educationally disadvantaged students only and the poverty percentages must be at least 35% or above the district wide average.

Transition plan
plan provided by the licensed physician or licensed clinical psychologist to explain the need for extended homebound instruction which includes the name of the student, justification for the extension of homebound instruction, additional time homebound instruction is anticipated and specific steps planned to return the student to classroom instruction.

Glossary of Education Terms

Verified unit of credit

earned credit based on a standard unit of credit, plus a passing score on the end-of-course SOL test or substitute test approved by the Board of Education.

Vocational

a school or center organized for a program that offers a sequence of courses that are directly related to the preparation of individuals for paid or unpaid employment in current or emerging occupations requiring other than a baccalaureate or advanced diploma

Source: Virginia Department of Education

C

D

E

I

O

Alabama

Alabama Business Education Association, 527
Alabama Commission on Higher Education, 528
Alabama Education Association, 529
Alabama Library Association, 530
Alabama Public Library Service, 531
Alabama State Council on the Arts, 532
Alabama State Department of Education, 3134
Alabama State Education for Homeless Children and Youth, 533
American Educational Studies Association, 3446
Association for Science Teacher Education Annual Meeting, 452, 939
Auburn University at Montgomery Library, 2474
Benjamin & Roberta Russell Educational and Charitable Foundation, 2475
Birmingham Public Library, 2476
Carolina Lawson Ivey Memorial Foundation, 2477
FPMI Communications, 1139
Huntsville Public Library, 2478
Instructional Services, 3136
International Association of Educators for World Peace, 81
JL Bedsole Foundation, 2479
Jefferson State Community College, 3834
Mildred Weedon Blount Educational and Charitable Foundation, 2480
Mitchell Foundation, 2481
Post Secondary Educational Assistance, 1217
Rehabilitation Services, 3138
Student Instructional Services, 3140
Superintendent, 3141
University of South Alabama, 2482

Alaska

Alaska Association of School Librarians, 534
Alaska Commission on Postsecondary Education, 535, 3143
Alaska Department of Education Administrative Services, 3144
Alaska Department of Education & Early Development, 3145
Alaska Department of Education Bilingual & Bicultural Education Conference, 3478
Alaska Library Association, 536
Alaska State Council on the Arts, 537
Alaska State Education for Homeless Children and Youth, 538
Libraries, Archives & Museums, 3146
School Finance & Data Management, 3147
Special Education Service Agency, 1243
Teaching And Learning Support Program, 3148
University of Alaska-Anchorage Library, 2483
Western History Association, 490
Western History Association Annual Meeting, 1065

Arizona

AZLA Conference, 908
Annual Effective Schools Conference, 931
Arizona Commission for Postsecondary Education, 539
Arizona Commission on the Arts, 540
Arizona Department of Education, 2484
Arizona Governor's Committee on Employment of People with Disabilities, 2485
Arizona Library Association, 541
Arizona School Boards Association, 542
Arizona State Education for Homeless Children and Youth, 543
Arizona State Library, Archives, and Public Records, 544
Council of Education Facility Planners-International, 287
Education Services, 2486

Evo-Ora Foundation, 2487
Flinn Foundation, 2488
Grand Canyon University College of Education, 3822
Greenville Foundation, 2520
International Studies Association (ISA), 313
Leona Group, 1173
National School Conference Institute, 1007
Northern Arizona University, 3858
Phoenix Public Library, 2489
Restructuring Curriculum Conference, 3571
STEMtech Conference, 1019
Staff Development Workshops & Training Sessions, 3878
Technology in 21st Century Schools, 1028
Vocational Technological Education, 2492
www.learningpage.com, 3722

Arkansas

Arkansas Arts Council, 545
Arkansas Business Education Association, 546
Arkansas Department of Education, 3150
Arkansas Department of Education: Special Education, 3151
Arkansas Department of Higher Education, 547
Arkansas Education Association, 548
Arkansas Library Association, 549
Arkansas State Education for Homeless Children and Youth, 550
Charles A Frueauff Foundation, 2493
Dawson Education Cooperative, 1106
Dawson Education Service Cooperative, 1107
Dimensions of Early Childhood, 201
Federal Programs, 3152
Northwest Arkansas Community College, 2494
Roy and Christine Sturgis Charitable and Educational Trust, 2495
Southern Early Childhood Annual Convention, 3576
Jones Center For Families, 2496
University of Arkansas at Little Rock, 3891
Walton Family Foundation, 2497
William C & Theodosia Murphy Nolan Foundation, 2498
Winthrop Rockefeller Foundation, 2499

California

Advance Infant Development Program, 1068
Ahmanson Foundation, 2500
Alice Tweed Tuohy Foundation, 2501
American Honda Foundation, 3046
American Institute of Mathematics, 371
Annenberg Foundation, 2950
Apple Education Grants, 3465
Arrillaga Foundation, 2502
Asian American Curriculum Project (AACP), 358
Assessing Student Performance: Exploring the Purpose and Limits of Testing, 3596
Association for Environmental and Outdoor Education (AEOE), 20
Association for Play Therapy, 24
Association for Play Therapy Conference, 938
Association for Refining Cross-Cultured International, 1072
Association of American Educators, 26
Atkinson Foundation, 2503
BankAmerica Foundation, 2504
Bechtel Group Corporate Giving Program, 2505
Bernard Osher Foundation, 2506
Boys-Viva Supermarkets Foundation, 2507
CBEA State Conference, 1057
CCAE/COABE National Conference, 3488
CPM Educational Program, 1078
CSBA Education Conference & Trade Show, 3489
Caldwell Flores Winters, 1079
California Arts Council, 551
California Association for Bilingual Education, 552

California Biomedical Research Association, 454
California Business Education Association, 553
California Classical Association-Northern Section, 554
California Community Foundation, 2508
California Department of Education, 3153
California Department of Education's Educational Resources Catalog, 3154
California Department of Special Education, 3155
California Foundation for Agriculture in the Classroom, 555
California Kindergarten Conference and PreConference Institute, 3490
California Library Association, 556
California Reading Association, 557
California School Library Association, 558
California State Homeless Education, 559
California Student Aid Commission, 560
California Teachers Association, 561
Carnegie Foundation for the Advancement of Teaching, 1081
Carrie Estelle Doheny Foundation, 2509
Center for Civic Education, 36
Center for Critical Thinking and Moral Critique Annual International, 888
Center for Research on the Context of Teaching, 5226
Center on Disabilities Conference, 948
Cisco Educational Archives, 3738
College Bound, 1092
Computer Using Educators, Inc (CUE), 503
Concern-America Volunteers, 284
Conrad N Hilton Foundation, 2808
Consortium on Reading Excellence, 1098
Constitutional Rights Foundation, 43
Council on Islamic Education, 292
Council on Library Technical Assistants (COLT), 365
Creative Learning Systems, 1105
Curriculum & Instructional Leadership Branch, 3156
Dan Murphy Foundation, 2510
Darryl L Sink & Associates, 3805
David & Lucile Packard Foundation, 2511
Disability Rights Education & Defense Fund, 52
Division for Research, 5235
Education, Training and Research Associates, 64
Effective Training Solutions, 1133
Energy Education Group (Educators for the Environment), 455
Epistemological Engineering, 1136
Evelyn & Walter Haas Jr Fund, 2512
Excell Education Centers, 1138
Foundation Center-San Francisco, 2513
Foundation for Critical Thinking, 3819
Foundation for Critical Thinking Annual Conference, 3499
Foundation for Critical Thinking Regional Workshop & Conference, 957
Foundation for Teaching Economics, 481
Foundations Focus, 2514
Francis H Clougherty Charitable Trust, 2515
Freitas Foundation, 2516
Fritz B Burns Foundation, 2517
George Frederick Jewett Foundation, 2518
Geothermal Education Office, 457
Grant & Resource Center of Northern California, 2519
Grantsmanship Center, 3055
HN & Frances C Berger Foundation, 2521
Henry J Kaiser Family Foundation, 2522
Hon Foundation, 2523
Hugh & Hazel Darling Foundation, 2524
IASSIST Annual Conference, 3502
Ingraham Memorial Fund, 2525
International Conference, 896
International Education Exchange Council, 305
James G Boswell Foundation, 2526
James Irvine Foundation, 2527
James S Copley Foundation, 2528
Jobs for California Graduates, 1165
John Jewett & H Chandler Garland Foundation, 2529
Joseph & Edna Josephson Institute, 1168

Canada

Colorado

Connecticut

Delaware

District of Columbia

Florida

Georgia

Hawaii

Kansas

Kentucky

Louisiana

Maine

Maryland

Massachusetts

Michigan

National Coalition of Alternative Community
  Schools, 111, 991
National Heritage Academies, 1205
National Student Assistance Conference, 1009
Office of School Management, 3247
Office of the Superintendent, 3248
Postsecondary Services, 3249
Professional Development Workshops, 3869
Rebus, 1228
Richard & Helen DeVos Foundation, 2768
Rollin M Gerstacker Foundation, 2769
SAP Today, 3772
School Program Quality, 3250
Society for Research in Child Development, 1022,
  5291
Steelcase Foundation, 2770
Student Financial Assistance, 3252
Student Financial Services Bureau, 685
Teacher & Administrative Preparation, 3253
University of Michigan-Dearborn Center for
  Corporate & Professional Development, 3893
Wayne State University, 2771
Whirlpool Foundation, 2772
Worthington Family Foundation, 2597

Minnesota

ATEA Journal, 3660
American Technical Education Association Annual
  Conference, 930
Andersen Foundation, 2773
Bush Foundation, 2774
Cargill Foundation, 2775
Center for Global Education, 3794
Charles & Ellora Alliss Educational Foundation,
  2776
Closing the Gap, 950
Communicating for America, 282
Data & Technology, 3254
Data Management, 3255
Designs for Learning, 1108
Dr. CC & Mabel L Criss Memorial Foundation,
  2805
Duluth Public Library, 2777
Education Funding, 3256
Education Minnesota, 686
Emerging Technology Consultants, 1135
Energy Concepts, 3816
Examiner Corporation, 1137
FR Bigelow Foundation, 2778
Financial Conditions & Aids Payment, 3257
First Bank System Foundation, 2779
Graduate Programs for Professional Educators,
  3821
Hiawatha Education Foundation, 2780
Higher Education Consortium, 1144
Human Resources Office, 3259
IA O'Shaughnessy Foundation, 2781
Innovative Programming Systems, 1150
Insight, 1151
International Listening Association Annual
  Convention, 900
Marbrook Foundation, 2782
Medtronic Foundation, 2783
Minneapolis Foundation, 2784
Minneapolis Public Library, 2785
Minnesota Business Educators, 687
Minnesota Congress of Parents, Teachers &
  Students/Minnesota PTA, 688
Minnesota Department of Children, Families &
  Learning, 3260
Minnesota Department of Education, 3261
Minnesota Leadership Annual Conference, 3523
Minnesota Library Association, 689
Minnesota School Administrators Association, 3524
Minnesota School Boards Association, 690
Minnesota School Boards Association Annual
  Meeting, 3525
National Alliance for Secondary Education and
  Transition, 440
National Association of Geoscience Teachers, 462

National Center on Educational Outcomes, 185
National Computer Systems, 3856
National Orientation Directors Association, 190
Office of Higher Education, 691
Otto Bremer Foundation, 2786
PACER Center, 145
Parent Training Resources, 3628
Residential Schools, 3262
Saint Paul Foundation, 2787
Scholarship America, 3098
State Arts Board, 692
TCF Foundation, 2788
Training & Presentations, 3583

Mississippi

Community Outreach Services, 3263
Educational Consultants of Oxford, 1121
Educational Innovations, 3264
External Relations, 3265
Foundation for the Mid South, 2789
JJ Jones Consultants, 1161
Jackson-Hinds Library System, 2790
Management Information Systems, 3266
Maryland Higher Education Commission, 666
Mississippi Advocate for Education, 694
Mississippi Arts Commission, 695
Mississippi Business Education Association, 696
Mississippi Department of Education, 3267
Mississippi Employment Security Commission,
  3268
Mississippi Institutions of Higher Learning, 697
Mississippi Library Association, 698
Mississippi Library Commission, 699
Mississippi Power Foundation, 2791
National Center for Technology Planning, 513
Office of Accountability, 3269
Phil Hardin Foundation, 2792
Vocational Technical Education, 3270

Missouri

Ameren Corporation Charitable Trust, 2793
Association for Education Finance and Policy, 935
Caleb C & Julia W Dula Educational & Charitable
  Foundation, 2845
Citizens for Educational Freedom, 41
Clearinghouse for Midcontinent Foundations, 2794
College of the Ozarks, 3800
Deputy Commissioner, 3271
Division of Instruction, 3272
Enid & Crosby Kemper Foundation, 2796
Hall Family Foundation, 2797
Instructional Materials Laboratory, 5244
James S McDonnell Foundation, 2798
Kansas City Public Library, 2799
MNEA Fall Conference, 3515
MSBA Annual Conference, 3516
Mary Ranken Jordan & Ettie A Jordan Charitable
  Foundation, 2800
McDonnell Douglas Foundation, 2801
Missouri Arts Council, 701
Missouri Association of Elementary School
  Principals, 702
Missouri Association of Secondary School
  Principals, 703
Missouri Congress of Parents & Teachers/Missouri
  PTA, 704
Missouri Department of Education, 3273
Missouri Department of Higher Education, 705
Missouri LINC, 5251
Missouri Library Association, 706
Missouri Library Association Conference, 1054
Missouri National Education Association, 707
Missouri State Teachers Association, 708
Missouri State Teachers Association Conference,
  3526
Monsanto Fund, 2802

Montana Association of School Librarians (MASL
  ), 713
National Council on Alcoholism & Drug Abuse,
  995
Paideia Group, 3861
Parents as Teachers National Center, 1016, 5281
People to People International, 321
Region 7: Education Department, 3274
Senior Researcher Award, 3473
Special Education Division, 3187, 3275
Supplemental Instruction, Supervisor Workshops,
  3883
Urban & Teacher Education, 3276
Vocational & Adult Education, 3132, 3277
Vocational Rehabilitation, 3149, 3278

Montana

Accreditation & Curriculum Services Department,
  3279
Council for Indian Education, 478
Dillon Foundation, 2664
Division for Early Childhood, 202
Division of Information-Technology Support, 3280
Eastern Montana College Library, 2803
Montana Arts Council, 711
Montana Association of County School
  Superintendents, 712
Montana Association of Elementary School
  Principals Conference, 3527
Montana Department of Education, 3281
Montana High School Association Conference,
  1047
Montana Library Association, 714
Montana School Boards Association, 1198
Montana State Library, 2804
Operations Department, 3282
Parents, Let's Unite for Kids, 146
Western Business and Information Technology
  Educators (WBITE), 715

Nebraska

Administrative Services Office, 3241, 3283
Division of Education Services, 3284
Mountain Plains Business Education Association
  (M-PBEA), 740
Mountain-Plains Business Education Association
  (M-PBEA), 652
National Contact Hotline, 423
Nebraska Arts Council, 717
Nebraska Department of Education, 3285
Nebraska Library Association, 718
Nebraska Library Commission, 719
Nebraska School Boards Association Annual
  Conference, 1048
Nebraska State Business Education Association,
  720
Nebraska State Education Association, 721
Rehabilitation Services Division, 3286
Thomas D Buckley Trust, 2806
W Dale Clark Library, 2807

Nevada

Administrative & Financial Services, 3287
Association for the Study of Higher Education
  Annual Meeting, 942
Cord Foundation, 2809
Donald W Reynolds Foundation, 2810
EL Wiegand Foundation, 2811
Las Vegas-Clark County, 2812
National Conference on Standards and Assessment,
  3540
Nevada Arts Council, 723
Nevada Department of Education, 3289

North Carolina

North Dakota

Ohio

Research for Better Schools, 5285
Research for Better Schools Publications, 3636
Richard King Mellon Foundation, 2964
Rockwell International Corporation Trust, 2965
SIGI PLUS, 5287
Samuel S Fels Fund, 2966
Sarah Scaife Foundation, 2967
Satellites and Education Conference, 1044
Search Associates, 3464
Shore Fund, 2968
Society for Industrial and Applied Mathematics, 382
Stackpole-Hall Foundation, 2969
American Philatelic Society, 370
Total Quality Schools Workshop, 3890
United States Steel Foundation, 2970
Westinghouse Foundation, 3063
William Penn Foundation, 2971

Rhode Island

American Mathematical Society, 924
Career & Technical Education, 3243, 3362
Champlin Foundations, 2972
East Bay Educational Collaborative, 1113
Equity & Access Office, 3363
Higher Education Assistance Authority, 787
Human Resource Development, 3364
Instruction Office, 3365
National Education Association Rhode Island (NEARI), 788
Northeast and Islands Regional Educational Laboratory, 5277
Office of Finance, 3366
Outcomes & Assessment Office, 3367
Providence Public Library, 2973
Resource Development, 3368
Rhode Island Association of School Business Officials, 789
Rhode Island Department of Education, 3369
Rhode Island Educational Media Association, 790
Rhode Island Foundation, 2974
Rhode Island Library Association, 791
School Food Services Administration, 3370
Special Needs Office, 3371
State Council on the Arts, 792
Teacher Education & Certification Office, 3372

South Carolina

Annual Conductor's Institute of South Carolina, 3789
Association for Education in Journalism and Mass Communication Convention, 936
Association of Schools of Journalism and Mass Communication (ASJMC), 336
Budgets & Planning, 3373
Charleston County Library, 2975
Communications Services, 3215, 3374
General Counsel, 3135, 3375
Ingraham Dancu Associates, 1148
Internal Administration, 3376
National Dropout Prevention Center, 5267
National Dropout Prevention Center/Network Conference, 996
Policy & Planning, 3377
Sally Foster Gift Wrap, 3079
Satellite Educational Resources Consortium, 5288
South Carolina Arts Commission, 794
South Carolina Commission on Higher Education, 795
South Carolina Department of Education, 3378
South Carolina Education Association (SCEA), 796
South Carolina Library Association, 797
South Carolina Library Association Conference, 3574
South Carolina State Library, 2976
Support Services, 2491, 3379
Teaching Education, 3702

South Dakota

Finance & Management, 3380
John McLaughlin Company, 1166
Services for Education, 3381
South Dakota Arts Council, 800
South Dakota Community Foundation, 2977
South Dakota Department of Education & Cultural Affairs, 3382
South Dakota Education Association (SDEA), 801
South Dakota Library Association, 802
South Dakota State Historical Society, 3383
South Dakota State Library, 2978
Special Education Office, 3384

Tennessee

Alliance for Technology Access Conference, 494
American Mathematical Association of Two-Year Colleges, 372
Benwood Foundation, 2979
Christy-Houston Foundation, 2980
Country Music Association, 393
Frist Foundation, 2981
Institute of Higher Education, 3828
JR Hyde Foundation, 2982
Lyndhurst Foundation, 2983
Mental Edge, 3713
Modern Red Schoolhouse Institute, 1197
Nashville Public Library, 2984
Oosting & Associates, 1210
Plough Foundation, 2985
RJ Maclellan Charitable Trust, 2986
School Memories Collection, 3081
Special Education, 3194, 3251, 3331, 3331, 3352, 3385
Teaching and Learning, 3386
Tennessee Arts Commission, 804
Tennessee Association of Secondary School Principals (TASSP), 805
Tennessee Department of Education, 3387
Tennessee Higher Education Commission, 806
Tennessee Library Association, 807
Tennessee School Boards Association, 808
Tennessee School Boards Association Conference, 3580
Americana Music Association, 405
Vocational Education, 3142, 3305, 3388, 3388

Texas

Academic Language Therapy Association, 330
Accountability Reporting and Research, 3389
Albert & Ethel Herzstein Charitable Foundation, 2987
American Schools Association of Central America, Columbia-Caribbean and Mexico, 254
Annual State Convention of Association of Texas Professional Educators, 3483
Association for Early Learning Leaders, 194
Burlington Northern Foundation, 2988
Burnett Foundation, 2989
Center for Educational Leadership Trinity University, 3793
Center for Occupational Research & Development, 3797
Center for Play Therapy, 216, 3798
Center for Play Therapy Fall Conference, 3492
Center for Play Therapy Summer Institute, 1053
Chief Counsel, 3355, 3390
Children's Literature Festival, 1058
Choristers Guild's National Festival & Directors' Conference, 949
Clinical Play Therapy Videos: Child-Centered Developmental & Relationship Play Therapy, 3740

Conference for Advancement of Mathematics Teaching, 951
Continuing Education, 3391
Cooper Industries Foundation, 2990
Corpus Christi State University, 2991
Cullen Foundation, 2992
Curriculum Development & Textbooks, 3392
Curriculum, Assessment & Professional Development, 3393
Curriculum, Assessment and Technology, 3394
Dallas Public Library, 2993
Drug Information & Strategy Clearinghouse, 53
Education of Special Populations & Adults, 3395
Educational Technology Design Consultants, 1129
El Paso Community Foundation, 2994
Ellwood Foundation, 2995
Eugene McDermott Foundation, 2996
Ewing Halsell Foundation, 2997
Exxon Education Foundation, 2998
Field Services, 3396
Fondren Foundation, 2999
GTE Foundation, 3051
George Foundation, 3000
Gordon & Mary Cain Foundation, 3001
Haggar Foundation, 3002
Health Occupations Students of America, 224
Hobby Foundation, 3003
Houston Endowment, 3004
Houston Public Library, 3005
Internal Operations, 3397
International Exhibit, 899
International Trombone Festival, 904
Intervention in School and Clinic, 3677
James R Dougherty Jr Foundation, 3006
Journal of Classroom Interaction, 3678
Learning for Life, 3618
Leland Fikes Foundation, 3007
MD Anderson Foundation, 3008
Mary Jo Williams Charitable Trust, 2697
Meadows Foundation, 3009
Military Child Education Coalition, 205
Moody Foundation, 3010
Multicorp, 1202
National Athletic Trainers' Association, 414
National Board for Professional Teaching Standards, 106
National Coalition of Independent Scholars, 112
National Educational Systems (NES), 212
National Policy Board for Educational Administration, 191
National Student Employment Association, 230
Operations & School Support, 3398
Paul & Mary Haas Foundation, 3011
Permanent School Fund, 3399
Perot Foundation, 3012
Psychological Corporation, 193
RW Fair Foundation, 3013
Records Consultants, 1229
Region 6: Education Department, 3400
Royal Barney Hogan Foundation, 2555
Sid W Richardson Foundation, 3014
Southwest Association College and University Housing Officers, 1061
Southwestern Educational Development Laboratory, 5295
Special Interest Group for Computer Science Education, 5296
Storytelling for Educational Enrichment The Magic of Storytelling, 3880
Strake Foundation, 3015
TASA/TASB Convention, 3578
Texas Association of Secondary School Principals (TASSP), 809
Texas Classroom Teachers Association Conference, 1062
Texas Commission on the Arts, 810
Texas Department of Education, 3401
Texas Higher Education Coordinating Board, 811
Texas Homeless Education Office, 812
Texas Library Association (TLA), 813
Texas Library Association Conference, 1063
Texas Middle School Association Conference, 3581
Texas State Teachers Association, 3582

Washington

West Virginia

Wisconsin

Wyoming

Foreign Language

Geography

History

Science

Special Education

Rehabilitation Services, 3138
Roots & Wings Educational Catalog-Australiafor
    Kids, 5139
SAT Services for Students with Disabilities, 6402
Society for Visual Education, 6011
Special Education & Rehabilitation Services, 5160
Special Education Law Report, 4519
Special Education Leadership, 4441
Special Education Report, 4520
Special Education Services, 3139
Special Educator, 4442
Speech Bin, 5161
Synergistic Systems, 5168
V-LINC, 524
Web Feet Guides, 5198
www.specialednews.com, 6082

Technology

AV Guide Newsletter, 4264
Agency for Instructional Technology, 493
Agency for Instructional Technology, 3442
Aid for Education, 3067
American Technical Education Association Annual
    Conference, 930
American Technical Publishers, 4891
American Trade Schools Directory, 4242
Apple Education Grants, 3465
Association for Advancement of Computing in
    Education (AACE), 450
Association for Career and Technical Education,
    496
Association for Educational Communications &
    Technology: Membership Directory, 4243
Association for Educational Communications &
    Technology, 497
Association for Educational Communications &
    Technology Annual Convention, 3484
Association of Science-Technology Centers
    Incorporated Conference, 945

Bayer/NSF Award for Community Innovation, 3466
Center for Educational Technologies, 501
Chronicle Vocational School Manual, 4244
Classroom, 1090
Closing the Gap, 950
Commuter Perspectives, 4286
Computer Learning Foundation, 4942
Computer Literacy Press, 4943
Computer Using Educators, Inc (CUE), 503
Consortium for School Networking, 504
Curriculum Brief, 3668
Directory of Public Vocational-Technical Schools &
    Institutes in the US, 4245
Directory of Vocational-Technical Schools, 4246
EDUCAUSE, 506
Educational Technology Center, 507
Educators Guide to FREE Computer Materials and
    Internet Resources, 3945
Edvantia, 866
Electronic Learning, 4486
Electronic Specialists Inc., 5958
Emerging Technology Consultants, 1135
Four State Regional Technology Conference, 3820
Guide to Vocational and Technical Schools East &
    West, 4248
IASSIST Annual Conference, 3502
Indiana University-Purdue University of
    Indianapolis, IUPUI, 3826
Industrial Teacher Education Directory, 4249
Information Literacy: Essential Skills for the
    Information Age, 4250
Ingenuity Works, 5968
IntelliTools, 5029
International Society for Technology in Education,
    509
International Technology Education Association
    Conference, 903
Internet Resource Directory for Classroom
    Teachers, 4251
Journal of Computers in Math & Science, 4707
K-12 District Technology Coordinators, 4252
Leadership and the New Technologies, 3842
MarcoPolo, 510

Maryland Center for Career and Technology
    Education, 3848
Mathematics & Computer Education, 4710
Michigan Association for Media in Education, 679
Millersville University, 3850
National Association of Media and Technology
    Centers, 511
National Computer Systems, 3856
National Educational Computing Conference, 3546
NetLingo The Internet Dictionary, 5987
New Learning Technologies, 1013
New Learning Technologies Conference, 1014
Pittsburg State University, 3866
Quick-Source, 4254
Robert McNeel & Associates, 3871
STEMtech Conference, 1019
SUNY College at Oswego, 3873
School of Music, 3874
SchoolTech Forum, 3573
Schools Industrial, Technical & Trade Directory,
    4255
Southwestern Oklahoma State University, 3876
Specialized Solutions, 3877
Sunburst Technology, 5166
TESS: The Educational Software Selector, 4256
THE Journal Technology Horizons in Education,
    4523
Tech Directions-Directory of Federal & Federal and
    State Officials Issue, 4257
Technology & Learning Schooltech Exposition &
    Conference, 1026
Technology & Media Division, 518
Technology Student Association, 519
Technology Student Conference, 1027
Technology and Children, 520
Technology and Learning Conference, 1056
Technology in 21st Century Schools, 1028
Technology in Public Schools, 4258
Telemetrics, 521
Tom Snyder Productions, 5181
V-LINC, 52

2015 Title List
Visit www.GreyHouse.com for Product Information, Table of Contents, and Sample Pages.

General Reference
An African Biographical Dictionary
America's College Museums
American Environmental Leaders: From Colonial Times to the Present
Encyclopedia of African-American Writing
Encyclopedia of Constitutional Amendments
Encyclopedia of Gun Control & Gun Rights
An Encyclopedia of Human Rights in the United States
Encyclopedia of Invasions & Conquests
Encyclopedia of Prisoners of War & Internment
Encyclopedia of Religion & Law in America
Encyclopedia of Rural America
Encyclopedia of the Continental Congress
Encyclopedia of the United States Cabinet, 1789-2010
Encyclopedia of War Journalism
Encyclopedia of Warrior Peoples & Fighting Groups
The Environmental Debate: A Documentary History
The Evolution Wars: A Guide to the Debates
From Suffrage to the Senate: America's Political Women
Global Terror & Political Risk Assessment
Media & Communications 1900-2020
Nations of the World
Political Corruption in America
Privacy Rights in the Digital Era
The Religious Right: A Reference Handbook
Speakers of the House of Representatives, 1789-2009
This is Who We Were: 1880-1900
This is Who We Were: A Companion to the 1940 Census
This is Who We Were: In the 1910s
This is Who We Were: In the 1920s
This is Who We Were: In the 1940s
This is Who We Were: In the 1950s
This is Who We Were: In the 1960s
This is Who We Were: In the 1970s
U.S. Land & Natural Resource Policy
The Value of a Dollar 1600-1865: Colonial Era to the Civil War
The Value of a Dollar: 1860-2014
Working Americans 1770-1869 Vol. IX: Revolutionary War to the Civil War
Working Americans 1880-1999 Vol. I: The Working Class
Working Americans 1880-1999 Vol. II: The Middle Class
Working Americans 1880-1999 Vol. III: The Upper Class
Working Americans 1880-1999 Vol. IV: Their Children
Working Americans 1880-2015 Vol. V: Americans At War
Working Americans 1880-2005 Vol. VI: Women at Work
Working Americans 1880-2006 Vol. VII: Social Movements
Working Americans 1880-2007 Vol. VIII: Immigrants
Working Americans 1880-2009 Vol. X: Sports & Recreation
Working Americans 1880-2010 Vol. XI: Inventors & Entrepreneurs
Working Americans 1880-2011 Vol. XII: Our History through Music
Working Americans 1880-2012 Vol. XIII: Education & Educators
World Cultural Leaders of the 20th & 21st Centuries

Education Information
Charter School Movement
Comparative Guide to American Elementary & Secondary Schools
Complete Learning Disabilities Directory
Educators Resource Directory
Special Education: A Reference Book for Policy and Curriculum Development

Health Information
Comparative Guide to American Hospitals
Complete Directory for Pediatric Disorders
Complete Directory for People with Chronic Illness
Complete Directory for People with Disabilities
Complete Mental Health Directory
Diabetes in America: Analysis of an Epidemic
Directory of Drug & Alcohol Residential Rehab Facilities
Directory of Health Care Group Purchasing Organizations
Directory of Hospital Personnel
HMO/PPO Directory
Medical Device Register
Older Americans Information Directory

Business Information
Complete Television, Radio & Cable Industry Directory
Directory of Business Information Resources
Directory of Mail Order Catalogs
Directory of Venture Capital & Private Equity Firms
Environmental Resource Handbook
Food & Beverage Market Place
Grey House Homeland Security Directory
Grey House Performing Arts Directory
Grey House Safety & Security Directory
Grey House Transportation Security Directory
Hudson's Washington News Media Contacts Directory
New York State Directory
Rauch Market Research Guides
Sports Market Place Directory

Statistics & Demographics
American Tally
America's Top-Rated Cities
America's Top-Rated Smaller Cities
America's Top-Rated Small Towns & Cities
Ancestry & Ethnicity in America
The Asian Databook
Comparative Guide to American Suburbs
The Hispanic Databook
Profiles of America
"Profiles of" Series – State Handbooks
Weather America

Financial Ratings Series
TheStreet Ratings' Guide to Bond & Money Market Mutual Funds
TheStreet Ratings' Guide to Common Stocks
TheStreet Ratings' Guide to Exchange-Traded Funds
TheStreet Ratings' Guide to Stock Mutual Funds
TheStreet Ratings' Ultimate Guided Tour of Stock Investing
Weiss Ratings' Consumer Guides
Weiss Ratings' Guide to Banks
Weiss Ratings' Guide to Credit Unions
Weiss Ratings' Guide to Health Insurers
Weiss Ratings' Guide to Life & Annuity Insurers
Weiss Ratings' Guide to Property & Casualty Insurers

Bowker's Books In Print® Titles
American Book Publishing Record® Annual
American Book Publishing Record® Monthly
Books In Print®
Books In Print® Supplement
Books Out Loud™
Bowker's Complete Video Directory™
Children's Books In Print®
El-Hi Textbooks & Serials In Print®
Forthcoming Books®
Large Print Books & Serials™
Law Books & Serials In Print™
Medical & Health Care Books In Print™
Publishers, Distributors & Wholesalers of the US™
Subject Guide to Books In Print®
Subject Guide to Children's Books In Print®

Canadian General Reference
Associations Canada
Canadian Almanac & Directory
Canadian Environmental Resource Guide
Canadian Parliamentary Guide
Canadian Venture Capital & Private Equity Firms
Financial Services Canada
Governments Canada
Health Guide Canada
The History of Canada
Libraries Canada
Major Canadian Cities

2015 Title List

Visit www.SalemPress.com for Product Information, Table of Contents, and Sample Pages.

Science, Careers & Mathematics

Ancient Creatures: Unearthed
Applied Science
Applied Science: Engineering & Mathematics
Applied Science: Science & Medicine
Applied Science: Technology
Biomes and Ecosystems
Careers in Business
Careers in Chemistry
Careers in Communications & Media
Careers in Environment & Conservation
Careers in Healthcare
Careers in Hospitality & Tourism
Careers in Human Services
Careers in Law, Criminal Justice & Emergency Services
Careers in Physics
Careers in Technology Services & Repair
Computer Technology Innovators
Contemporary Biographies in Business
Contemporary Biographies in Chemistry
Contemporary Biographies in Communications & Media
Contemporary Biographies in Environment & Conservation
Contemporary Biographies in Healthcare
Contemporary Biographies in Hospitality & Tourism
Contemporary Biographies in Law & Criminal Justice
Contemporary Biographies in Physics
Earth Science
Earth Science: Earth Materials & Resources
Earth Science: Earth's Surface and History
Earth Science: Physics & Chemistry of the Earth
Earth Science: Weather, Water & Atmosphere
Encyclopedia of Energy
Encyclopedia of Environmental Issues
Encyclopedia of Environmental Issues: Atmosphere and Air Pollution
Encyclopedia of Environmental Issues: Ecology and Ecosystems
Encyclopedia of Environmental Issues: Energy and Energy Use
Encyclopedia of Environmental Issues: Policy and Activism
Encyclopedia of Environmental Issues: Preservation/Wilderness Issues
Encyclopedia of Environmental Issues: Water and Water Pollution
Encyclopedia of Global Resources
Encyclopedia of Global Warming
Encyclopedia of Mathematics & Society
Encyclopedia of Mathematics & Society: Engineering, Tech, Medicine
Encyclopedia of Mathematics & Society: Great Mathematicians
Encyclopedia of Mathematics & Society: Math & Social Sciences
Encyclopedia of Mathematics & Society: Math Development/Concepts
Encyclopedia of Mathematics & Society: Math in Culture & Society
Encyclopedia of Mathematics & Society: Space, Science, Environment
Encyclopedia of the Ancient World
Forensic Science
Geography Basics
Internet Innovators
Inventions and Inventors
Magill's Encyclopedia of Science: Animal Life
Magill's Encyclopedia of Science: Plant life
Notable Natural Disasters
Principles of Chemistry
Science and Scientists
Solar System
Solar System: Great Astronomers
Solar System: Study of the Universe
Solar System: The Inner Planets
Solar System: The Moon and Other Small Bodies
Solar System: The Outer Planets
Solar System: The Sun and Other Stars
World Geography

Literature

American Ethnic Writers
Classics of Science Fiction & Fantasy Literature
Critical Insights: Authors
Critical Insights: New Literary Collection Bundles
Critical Insights: Themes
Critical Insights: Works
Critical Survey of Drama
Critical Survey of Graphic Novels: Heroes & Super Heroes
Critical Survey of Graphic Novels: History, Theme & Technique
Critical Survey of Graphic Novels: Independents/Underground Classics
Critical Survey of Graphic Novels: Manga
Critical Survey of Long Fiction
Critical Survey of Mystery & Detective Fiction
Critical Survey of Mythology and Folklore: Heroes and Heroines
Critical Survey of Mythology and Folklore: Love, Sexuality & Desire
Critical Survey of Mythology and Folklore: World Mythology
Critical Survey of Poetry
Critical Survey of Poetry: American Poets
Critical Survey of Poetry: British, Irish & Commonwealth Poets
Critical Survey of Poetry: Cumulative Index
Critical Survey of Poetry: European Poets
Critical Survey of Poetry: Topical Essays
Critical Survey of Poetry: World Poets
Critical Survey of Shakespeare's Sonnets
Critical Survey of Short Fiction
Critical Survey of Short Fiction: American Writers
Critical Survey of Short Fiction: British, Irish, Commonwealth Writers
Critical Survey of Short Fiction: Cumulative Index
Critical Survey of Short Fiction: European Writers
Critical Survey of Short Fiction: Topical Essays
Critical Survey of Short Fiction: World Writers
Cyclopedia of Literary Characters
Holocaust Literature
Introduction to Literary Context: American Poetry of the 20th Century
Introduction to Literary Context: American Post-Modernist Novels
Introduction to Literary Context: American Short Fiction
Introduction to Literary Context: English Literature
Introduction to Literary Context: Plays
Introduction to Literary Context: World Literature
Magill's Literary Annual 2015
Magill's Survey of American Literature
Magill's Survey of World Literature
Masterplots
Masterplots II: African American Literature
Masterplots II: American Fiction Series
Masterplots II: British & Commonwealth Fiction Series
Masterplots II: Christian Literature
Masterplots II: Drama Series
Masterplots II: Juvenile & Young Adult Literature, Supplement
Masterplots II: Nonfiction Series
Masterplots II: Poetry Series
Masterplots II: Short Story Series
Masterplots II: Women's Literature Series
Notable African American Writers
Notable American Novelists
Notable Playwrights
Notable Poets
Recommended Reading: 500 Classics Reviewed
Short Story Writers

Grey House Publishing | Salem Press | H.W. Wilson | 4919 Route, 22 PO Box 56, Amenia NY 12501-0056

2015 Title List

Visit www.SalemPress.com for Product Information, Table of Contents, and Sample Pages.

History and Social Science

The 2000s in America
50 States
African American History
Agriculture in History
American First Ladies
American Heroes
American Indian Culture
American Indian History
American Indian Tribes
American Presidents
American Villains
America's Historic Sites
Ancient Greece
The Bill of Rights
The Civil Rights Movement
The Cold War
Countries, Peoples & Cultures
Countries, Peoples & Cultures: Central & South America
Countries, Peoples & Cultures: Central, South & Southeast Asia
Countries, Peoples & Cultures: East & South Africa
Countries, Peoples & Cultures: East Asia & the Pacific
Countries, Peoples & Cultures: Eastern Europe
Countries, Peoples & Cultures: Middle East & North Africa
Countries, Peoples & Cultures: North America & the Caribbean
Countries, Peoples & Cultures: West & Central Africa
Countries, Peoples & Cultures: Western Europe
Defining Documents: American Revolution (1754-1805)
Defining Documents: Civil War (1860-1865)
Defining Documents: Emergence of Modern America (1868-1918)
Defining Documents: Exploration & Colonial America (1492-1755)
Defining Documents: Manifest Destiny (1803-1860)
Defining Documents: Post-War 1940s (1945-1949)
Defining Documents: Reconstruction (1865-1880)
Defining Documents: The 1920s
Defining Documents: The 1930s
Defining Documents: The American West (1836-1900)
Defining Documents: The Ancient World (2700 B.C.E.-50 C.E.)
Defining Documents: The Middle Ages (524-1431)
Defining Documents: World War I
Defining Documents: World War II (1939-1946)
The Eighties in America
Encyclopedia of American Immigration
Encyclopedia of Flight
Encyclopedia of the Ancient World
The Fifties in America
The Forties in America
Great Athletes
Great Athletes: Baseball
Great Athletes: Basketball
Great Athletes: Boxing & Soccer
Great Athletes: Cumulative Index
Great Athletes: Football
Great Athletes: Golf & Tennis
Great Athletes: Olympics
Great Athletes: Racing & Individual Sports
Great Events from History: 17th Century
Great Events from History: 18th Century
Great Events from History: 19th Century
Great Events from History: 20th Century (1901-1940)
Great Events from History: 20th Century (1941-1970)
Great Events from History: 20th Century (1971-2000)
Great Events from History: Ancient World
Great Events from History: Cumulative Indexes
Great Events from History: Gay, Lesbian, Bisexual, Transgender Events
Great Events from History: Middle Ages
Great Events from History: Modern Scandals
Great Events from History: Renaissance & Early Modern Era

Great Lives from History: 17th Century
Great Lives from History: 18th Century
Great Lives from History: 19th Century
Great Lives from History: 20th Century
Great Lives from History: African Americans
Great Lives from History: Ancient World
Great Lives from History: Asian & Pacific Islander Americans
Great Lives from History: Cumulative Indexes
Great Lives from History: Incredibly Wealthy
Great Lives from History: Inventors & Inventions
Great Lives from History: Jewish Americans
Great Lives from History: Latinos
Great Lives from History: Middle Ages
Great Lives from History: Notorious Lives
Great Lives from History: Renaissance & Early Modern Era
Great Lives from History: Scientists & Science
Historical Encyclopedia of American Business
Immigration in U.S. History
Magill's Guide to Military History
Milestone Documents in African American History
Milestone Documents in American History
Milestone Documents in World History
Milestone Documents of American Leaders
Milestone Documents of World Religions
Musicians & Composers 20th Century
The Nineties in America
The Seventies in America
The Sixties in America
Survey of American Industry and Careers
The Thirties in America
The Twenties in America
United States at War
U.S.A. in Space
U.S. Court Cases
U.S. Government Leaders
U.S. Laws, Acts, and Treaties
U.S. Legal System
U.S. Supreme Court
Weapons and Warfare
World Conflicts: Asia and the Middle East

Health

Addictions & Substance Abuse
Adolescent Health
Cancer
Complementary & Alternative Medicine
Genetics & Inherited Conditions
Health Issues
Infectious Diseases & Conditions
Magill's Medical Guide
Psychology & Behavioral Health
Psychology Basics

Current Biography
Current Biography Cumulative Index 1946-2013
Current Biography Monthly Magazine
Current Biography Yearbook: 2003
Current Biography Yearbook: 2004
Current Biography Yearbook: 2005
Current Biography Yearbook: 2006
Current Biography Yearbook: 2007
Current Biography Yearbook: 2008
Current Biography Yearbook: 2009
Current Biography Yearbook: 2010
Current Biography Yearbook: 2011
Current Biography Yearbook: 2012
Current Biography Yearbook: 2013
Current Biography Yearbook: 2014
Current Biography Yearbook: 2015

Core Collections
Children's Core Collection
Fiction Core Collection
Middle & Junior High School Core
Public Library Core Collection: Nonfiction
Senior High Core Collection

The Reference Shelf
Aging in America
American Military Presence Overseas
The Arab Spring
The Brain
The Business of Food
Conspiracy Theories
The Digital Age
Dinosaurs
Embracing New Paradigms in Education
Faith & Science
Families: Traditional and New Structures
The Future of U.S. Economic Relations: Mexico, Cuba, and Venezuela
Global Climate Change
Graphic Novels and Comic Books
Immigration in the U.S.
Internet Safety
Marijuana Reform
The News and its Future
The Paranormal
Politics of the Ocean
Reality Television
Representative American Speeches: 2008-2009
Representative American Speeches: 2009-2010
Representative American Speeches: 2010-2011
Representative American Speeches: 2011-2012
Representative American Speeches: 2012-2013
Representative American Speeches: 2013-2014
Representative American Speeches: 2014-2015
Revisiting Gender
Robotics
Russia
Social Networking
Social Services for the Poor
Space Exploration & Development
Sports in America
The Supreme Court
The Transformation of American Cities
U.S. Infrastructure
U.S. National Debate Topic: Surveillance
U.S. National Debate Topic: The Ocean
U.S. National Debate Topic: Transportation Infrastructure
Whistleblowers

Readers' Guide
Abridged Readers' Guide to Periodical Literature
Readers' Guide to Periodical Literature

Indexes
Index to Legal Periodicals & Books
Short Story Index
Book Review Digest

Sears List
Sears List of Subject Headings
Sears: Lista de Encabezamientos de Materia

Facts About Series
Facts About American Immigration
Facts About China
Facts About the 20th Century
Facts About the Presidents
Facts About the World's Languages

Nobel Prize Winners
Nobel Prize Winners: 1901-1986
Nobel Prize Winners: 1987-1991
Nobel Prize Winners: 1992-1996
Nobel Prize Winners: 1997-2001

World Authors
World Authors: 1995-2000
World Authors: 2000-2005

Famous First Facts
Famous First Facts
Famous First Facts About American Politics
Famous First Facts About Sports
Famous First Facts About the Environment
Famous First Facts: International Edition

American Book of Days
The American Book of Days
The International Book of Days

Junior Authors & Illustrators
Tenth Book of Junior Authors & Illustrations

Monographs
The Barnhart Dictionary of Etymology
Celebrate the World
Guide to the Ancient World
Indexing from A to Z
The Poetry Break
Radical Change: Books for Youth in a Digital Age

Wilson Chronology
Wilson Chronology of Asia and the Pacific
Wilson Chronology of Human Rights
Wilson Chronology of Ideas
Wilson Chronology of the Arts
Wilson Chronology of the World's Religions
Wilson Chronology of Women's Achievements